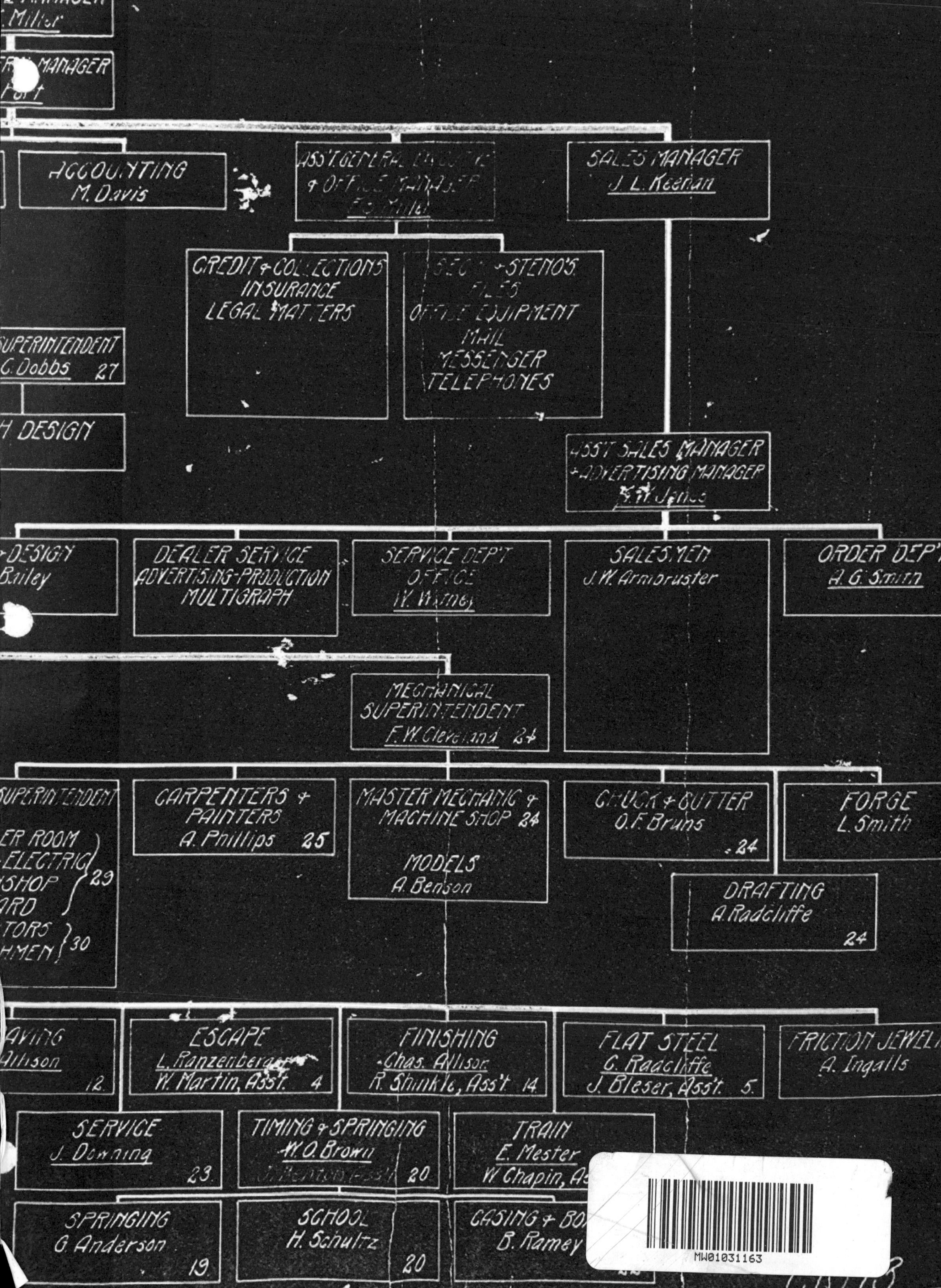
MANAGER
Miller
MANAGER
Port
ACCOUNTING
M. Davis
ASS'T. GENERAL
& OFFICE MANAGER
SALES MANAGER
J. L. Keenan
CREDIT & COLLECTIONS
INSURANCE
LEGAL MATTERS
STENO'S.
OFFICE EQUIPMENT
MAIL
MESSENGER
TELEPHONES
SUPERINTENDENT
C. Dobbs 27
H DESIGN
ASS'T SALES MANAGER
+ ADVERTISING MANAGER
DESIGN
Bailey
DEALER SERVICE
ADVERTISING-PRODUCTION
MULTIGRAPH
SERVICE DEP'T
OFFICE
SALESMEN
J. W. Armbruster
ORDER DEP'T
A. G. Smith
MECHANICAL
SUPERINTENDENT
F. W. Cleveland 24
SUPERINTENDENT
ER ROOM
ELECTRIC
SHOP
ARD
TORS
HMEN
29
30
CARPENTERS &
PAINTERS
A. Phillips 25
MASTER MECHANIC &
MACHINE SHOP 24
MODELS
A. Benson
CHUCK & CUTTER
O. F. Bruns
24
FORGE
L. Smith
DRAFTING
A. Radcliffe
24
AVING
Allison
12.
ESCAPE
L. Ranzenberger
W. Martin, Ass't. 4
FINISHING
Chas. Allison
R. Shinkle, Ass't 14
FLAT STEEL
C. Radcliffe
J. Bleser, Ass't. 5.
FRICTION JEWEL
A. Ingalls
SERVICE
J. Downing
23.
TIMING & SPRINGING
W. O. Brown
20
TRAIN
E. Mester
W. Chapin, As
SPRINGING
G. Anderson
19.
SCHOOL
H. Schultz
20
CASING & BO
B. Ramey

THE VOL 1

ILLINOIS WATCH & ITS HAMILTON YEARS

THE FINALE OF A GREAT AMERICAN WATCH COMPANY

HISTORY OF THE ILLINOIS WATCH COMPANY:

Currents and Crosscurrents in the American Watch Industry

BY
Fredric J. Friedberg

Schiffer Publishing Ltd®

4880 Lower Valley Road • Atglen, PA 19310

DEDICATION

In loving memory of the world's greatest mother, Florence Thompson Friedberg (1917–2013), and with sincere respect, admiration and appreciation, to John L. "Jack" Keenan (1885–1952), the last man standing for the great Illinois Watch Company.

Library of Congress Control Number: 2017933341

Designed by Chris Cornforth, www.chrisworx.com
Cover designs by Fred, Joy, Zach Friedberg and Chris Cornforth

ISBN:978-0-7643-5371-0
Printed in China

Published by Schiffer Publishing, Ltd.
4880 Lower Valley Road
Atglen, PA 19310
Phone: (610) 593-1777; Fax: (610) 593-2002
E-mail: Info@schifferbooks.com
Web: www.schifferbooks.com

For our complete selection of fine books on this and related subjects, please visit our website at www.schifferbooks.com. You may also write for a free catalog.

Schiffer Publishing's titles are available at special discounts for bulk purchases for sales promotions or premiums. Special editions, including personalized covers, corporate imprints, and excerpts, can be created in large quantities for special needs. For more information, contact the publisher.

We are always looking for people to write books on new and related subjects. If you have an idea for a book, please contact us at proposals@schifferbooks.com.

Table of Contents

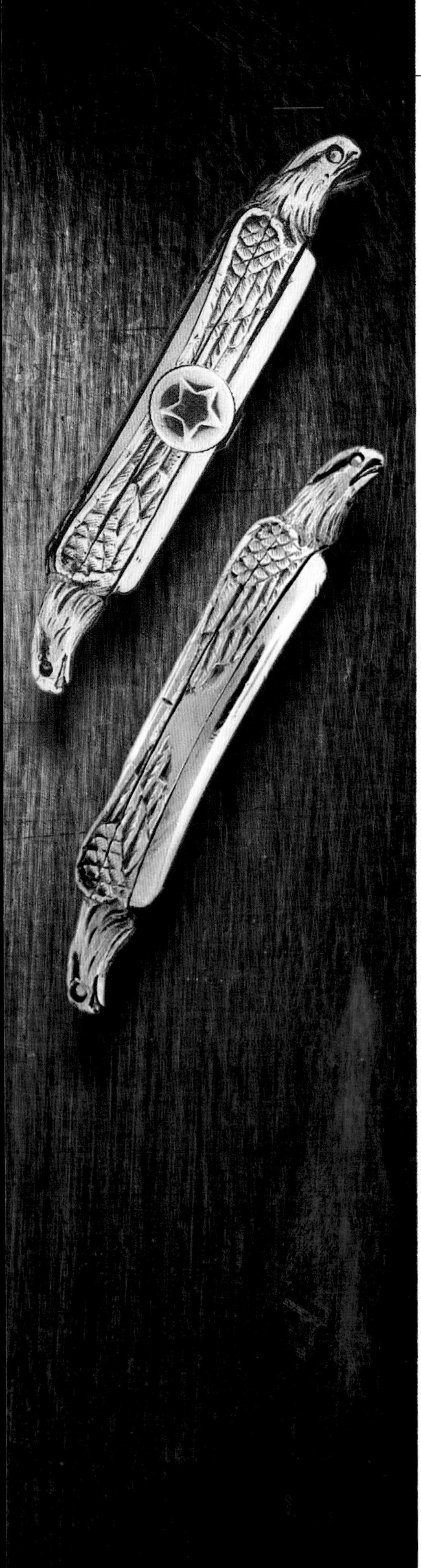

Acknowledgments

When I wrote my first Illinois watch book, *The Illinois Watch: The Life and Times of a Great American Watch Company,* it took all of my free time for an entire three-year period. I did all of the research and writing and relied on two friends to review my work. One did so for technical accuracy and one for proper English usage. The result was, in my view, excellent and the book was extremely well received.

This time, in an effort to produce a high-quality publication in just two years, I enlisted the help of a team of knowledgeable friends. Fortunately, many friends and newly made friends (the latter from the pocket watch and Hamilton contingents) willingly and generously helped me while providing suggestions on background, context and detail. More experts, however, meant additional information and insight, obliterating my idea of finishing the project in two years. With their help, though, the result became so much richer than my original vision.

At the outset, I have to thank my soulmate Joy and great friend Greg Hart for their unbridled support and enthusiasm as I bounced off of them one crazy new idea of mine after another to include in this set of books. Hopefully, the unique approach and additions make this a more collector-friendly reading and research-resource experience, notwithstanding the additional preparation time added by "new" ideas.

To write these volumes, I first sent drafts of each chapter to a group of good friends, all knowledgeable and ardent Illinois watch collectors, for their feedback. Early drafts went to Greg Hart, Ed Kulha and Rick Vess, resulting in "Illinois Summits" where we reviewed and discussed their comments. Then I revised the drafts of the chapters and sent most of them to Bob Ayer, a bright, inquisitive and thorough thinker and researcher, for review and initial editing. Bob and I would have frequent email or telephone dialogue where my theories were further revealed, reviewed and challenged— and, at times, revised, reorganized and additionally researched by Bob. He also added several research items of his own that are noted in the text. Bob's editing greatly helped to smooth and document the story around my research. In addition to being a great writer, Bob is a knowledgeable Elgin, Hamilton and Illinois collector and watch historian. I greatly value his significant input and, even more importantly, his friendship.

After Bob finished with the chapters, I would again revise them and send them off for extensive scrutiny to Bettie Mason, a professional editor who also happens to be an ardent Deco collector. Having extensive experience in editing scholarly books, she has very high standards and is attentive to detail. She was often helped by her multitalented spouse, Jim Mason; their continuous feedback significantly enhanced the quality of the material. Bettie and I would discuss details (or, rather, I would reply to Bettie's seemingly never-ending queries) for months and months. With Bettie's instruction, I reluctantly learned the difference between a hyphen and an N-dash, and between an N-dash and an M-dash; the importance of having levels of headings; and many other mechanical details of editing. Bettie is a benevolent taskmaster whom I respect and value immensely, and many times, Jim Mason was called upon to round out and add to my research, especially in the very technical areas. The improved readability, organization, value and erudition of these books is owed to Bettie Mason, Jim Mason and Bob Ayer. They are the very best!

Additionally, Bettie insisted on strict guidelines for citations. Any historian using this book set should be led in the correct direction owing to Bettie's background and extensive experience in these matters. It meant more work for me, but the results are well worth the effort. Bettie's detailed knowledge, research and great contributions about the ladies' models greatly enhance the value of that chapter and the watch attachment section of the cases chapter; and Jim likewise made similarly significant contributions to the Hamilton-Illinois chapter. She and Jim occasionally added some research nuggets of their own that are noted in the text, as well as enhancing research in additional areas throughout the text. Bettie has a healthy collection of jobbers' catalogs that grew during the length of this project; time and again, they helped fill my research gaps including, in several instances, helping to connect an advertised model with a previously unidentified Illinois watch.

After all of the editorial reviews and revisions, Randy Van Netten "volunteered" to proofread the final drafts of each chapter. His keen eyes found areas needing correction while his historical knowledge base helped the accuracy of the text.

With the first book I relied on a couple of friends for the great bulk of the photography. This time I opened up the opportunity for many collectors to get their "book-worthy" watches featured. So although a great many of the images are from Dr. Wes Betsil in Springfield of my great and long-time pal Farrell Gay's extensive collection and from my super buddy Greg Hart, many images were also supplied by Richard and Linda Daugherty, Don Lavin, Bettie and Jim Mason and Dan Zazove. I also received images from Jon Borden, Mark Cardelucci, Stan Czubernat, Tom Diss, Adam Dubin, Bernard Friedman, Bryan Girouard, Adam Harris, Cary Hurt, Adam Hutira, Jesse Hueg, Ed Kulha, Vic Sundquist, Jerry Treiman, Randy Van Netten, Rick Vess and Alex Villar. My Orange County neighbor Mark Cardelucci, a super photographer, came through in the clutch many times for me and, along with his talented daughter Jessica Nugent, flawlessly imaged many items from my collection.

With this book set, I even crossed two great divides. I reached out first to Hamilton collectors to try to explore the reasons for Hamilton's acquisition of the Illinois Watch Company. Author and Hamilton expert René Rondeau was always very willing and fast to reply to my every question, as were Hamilton-knowledgeable persons Bob Ayer, Randy Van Netten, Rick Vess and others.

For pocket watch information I crossed yet another even greater divide and relied on valuable information received from author and Bunn Special expert Mike Chamelin, and pocket watch collectors Jerry Treiman, Larry Treiman, Fred A.

Hansen, Fred E. Hansen, Terry Hall, Rhett Locke, Ethan Lipsig and others. I was amazed how eager people were to share their valuable information with me.

I thank those friends who shared their special watches so I could write about them and show the many custom features of these precious pieces. Jon Borden, Behrouse Edhaie, Farrell Gay, Greg Hart, Ed Kulha, Bettie Mason, Jim Mason, René Rondeau, Vic Sundquist, Rick Vess and Dan Zazove all allowed me to use and show their special items.

Others helped gather and loan various items of ephemera for me to use. These folks were Conrad Chanzit, Farrell Gay, Adam Harris, Greg Hart, Les McAlister, Ray Porter, Philip Welsh and Liz Zuffi.

I submitted dozens of questions to people who are knowledgeable about the technical details of watch repair. Ed Kulha and Jesse Heug never lost their patience with me and graciously replied to my many repair-related questions. Rob Miller from International Dial generously gave time out of his busy schedule to educate me on dial-making and refinishing. Rob was a great sport and wonderfully candid in his replies; he also reviewed the dial chapter more than once.

Still others helped me try to understand the mid-1950s Hamilton-Illinois wristwatches. For this subject, I received help from Bob Ayer, Tom Diss, Greg Hart, Adam Hutira, Jim Mason, Bruce Shawkey, and others; in addition, René Rondeau and Adam Hutira reviewed and commented on the draft of the Hamilton-Illinois chapter. I relied on Adam and Jim to assure the accuracy of the information concerning the Swiss movements used in these models. Jeffrey Hess provided valuable information on the previously unknown and ultra-rare Hamilton-Illinois solid gold men's wristwatches. Jack Wood helped with the identification of the Pioneer cases used with a couple of these models, and Liz Zuffi helped with the identification of the Huguenin cases used with some others. (She also provided new information regarding an earlier subject, the "Scheufele Clip".)

René, the world's top Hamilton expert, not only generously reviewed and offered his valuable comments on chapters 3, 4 and 5, which focus primarily on Hamilton's motivations and intentions towards Illinois, but also reviewed and provided feedback on the Hamilton-Illinois chapter; and then he graciously reviewed every other chapter in the set. I tremendously value his feedback.

To gain access to the many published articles of L. Michael Fultz, I received help from Kathy Hodgdon and Susan Bowen of *Penworld*.

A very special thanks goes to Sara Dockery and Nancy Dyer for their rapid responses to my many requests for research assistance from the NAWCC Library and Research Center, and to Al Dodson for his help when I visited the library for extensive research. Toby Berger, a dear friend and a Pepperdine University librarian, also helped with my quest for research materials at other libraries.

I value the Springfield research help from Curtis Mann, Curator of the Lincoln Museum in Springfield, and Joanne Weber for her research conducted in Lancaster for these books.

I appreciate the many interesting World War I (and earlier) photographs I received from Adam Harris of soldiers and others wearing the first American wristwatches; Vic Sundquist also provided such images. I also thank Adam Harris for apprising me of the "Scheufele clip" and providing information about early Keystone watch case advertisements, radium dial advertisements and shrapnel guards and related subjects. Adam also shared with me—and freely allowed me to use—his extensive photographic collection of early wristwatch adopters, and more.

I am grateful to the research generosity of Stan Czubernat who provided early Transitional Period wristwatch advertisements. He also enlightened me on the nuances of trench watches and related subjects. Stan also reviewed and commented on all of my detailed descriptions of the Illinois military watches used in this book and granted me permission to use any of his research and material in his Elgin Trench watch book and his new Waltham one.

Thanks to Bill Briska for allowing me to use the material in his excellent book, *Elgin Time*. Thanks to Farrell Gay for allowing me to use the material in his special NAWCC *Bulletin* article on ladies' Illinois. I am continually grateful for Roy Ehrhardt's permission to freely use the material in his Illinois books for my publications. Thanks also to Russ Snyder for permission to use data from his super serial-number Illinois database.

Thanks to Ed Pinter and Michael Sabino of the Wall Street law firm of Ford Marrin Esposito Witmeyer & Gleser, L.L.P., for their help in securing old court house litigation records from National Archive locations throughout the United States. These records disclosed heretofore unknown details of litigation involving the Dubois Watch Case Company (and its Depollier Division, c. 1918) and also the antitrust cases involving Hamilton in the 1940s and 1950s.

I am also grateful to the following individuals and institutions for their help: Patrick Raftery, librarian of the Westchester County Historical Association (Elmsford, NY), for material about the Pioneer Watch Case Co.; Ann Poulos, reference librarian at the Providence Public Library (Providence, RI), for documentation regarding the Baird-North Co.; and Joline Froton, administrative assistant at the Androscoggin Historical Society (Auburn, ME), for information about the history of the jewelry company H. A. Osgood & Son.

My thanks to Patrick Werner of Materials Engineering and Testing Corporation for coordinating the studies of sparkle dial materials.

Others who helped in one way or another are: Charlie Cleves, Dana Gotlieb, Norm Leventin, Len Sequeira and Robert Schussel. I apologize to those I may have inadvertently omitted.

Thanks to our number one son, Josh, for his technical help, especially with the Index and getting good digital frames from the 1923 Illinois silent film.

Thanks to my soulmate Joy and to our number two son, Zach, for his help in creating cool and different book covers.

I am also grateful for all of the technical help I received from media artist Chris Cornforth (*www.chrisworx.com*), who tirelessly worked with me on thousands of images and assisted me in many of the technical areas necessary to produce these massive volumes.

Thus, these Illinois books capture not only what I thought should be covered but also the information and material serious Illinois collectors wanted to see, and—with the great oversight and support of my talented editorial team (first Bob, then Bettie with Jim)—what historians would want to see, hopefully accurately written and properly presented in these five volumes.

I am truly blessed to have been able to rely on the great help of the dear and valued friends noted above.

Last, and perhaps most importantly, I offer tremendous thanks to Linda Daugherty, my loyal assistant of more than twenty-five years, for her hours of "free" time devoted to the numerous drafts of these books. Owing to the sheer volume of material this time, we were assisted with manuscript preparation predominantly by Kelley Brittain (both in California and Missouri), with additional assistance from Gwendolyn Jackson and Carla Polío.

Introduction

As you open these books and consider reading them, you may ask the question: "Why did Fred Friedberg write a second Illinois watch book? Didn't he cover it all in his first book in 2004?" There were actually many good reasons to write a new Illinois book set. Among other things, I wanted: (a) to update the first book; (b) to cover the areas that I did not have the time or space to include previously; (c) to provide information on newly identified or confirmed Illinois wristwatches and related information; (d) to add a full identification guide for the Illinois ladies' wristwatch models; and (e) to document as much information as I could find on the mostly heretofore unknown Hamilton-Illinois Mid-Century Modern wristwatches. In short, I have learned much since 2004 and I felt it only fair that collectors should share in this wealth of knowledge.

From a historical perspective, I wanted to correct some long-standing misconceptions about Illinois during its years under Hamilton control. In my earlier book, *The Illinois Watch: The Life and Times of a Great American Watch Company*, I followed those researchers and authors who had gone before me and blindly accepted that Hamilton acquired Illinois and basically left Illinois unchanged. Then, as the Great Depression dragged on, dire financial straits forced Hamilton to close its Illinois Division. In 2004, I believed this premise to be gospel and did not look further. I was focused primarily on recording, memorializing and relating information on the actual Illinois men's wristwatches themselves.

To correct this fault, the current volumes used the whys of Hamilton's acquisition of Illinois as a starting point, around which the rest of the books were built. It became immediately evident that context would become critical. Hamilton's decisions did not occur in a vacuum. It would be necessary to explain the pre- and post-acquisition economy and its impact on Hamilton, and Hamilton's reaction to events, in order to understand how it treated Illinois. The 1929 stock market crash and the resulting Great Depression had a huge effect on Hamilton's decision-making. So did the death of the longtime Hamilton patriarch and president, Charles F. Miller, in July 1931. It is my hope that when you complete your reading of this entire set of books you will have a clearer understanding of the ever-increasing hardships Illinois endured until its demise as its new corporate parent, faced with life-and-death choices, elected to allow only one watch operation to survive in the face of the most tumultuous economic conditions in the history of the United States.

Also, to understand Hamilton's actions, it was necessary to examine the development of the watch industry in the United States, both before and after Illinois was acquired by Hamilton. Therefore, Volume 1 also delves into the historical background of the American watch industry; its state in the 1920s and the effects of Black Tuesday and the Great Depression on that watch industry in general and on the Hamilton Watch Company and its Illinois Watch Division in particular. This picture developed only after hundreds of hours of research performed at the New York Public Library, the Library of Congress in Washington, D.C., and the NAWCC Museum and Library in Columbia, Pennsylvania, as well numerous discussions and email exchanges with Hamilton and Illinois collectors and experts. It also included weeks reviewing issues of local newspapers in Springfield and Lancaster between 1927 and 1935. Volume 4, describing Hamilton's attempt to resurrect the Illinois name in the mid-1950s, which also required research in the resources mentioned above. All these efforts were made in an attempt to determine why Hamilton handled Illinois in the manner it did.

These volumes also significantly update and supplement information from the previous book as well as add chapters documenting Illinois ladies' models and the Hamilton-Illinois models of the 1950s.

Every effort has been made to minimize the overlap between these volumes and *The Illinois Watch: The Life and Times of a Great American Watch Company*. It is recommended that you use both together to gain a greater appreciation of Illinois.

This set has been organized into five distinct volumes to help the reader understand Illinois in its various aspects.

Volume 1, which includes the first five chapters, places the Illinois Watch Company in the context of the American watch industry.

Chapter 1 deals with the lives, personalities and contributions of key figures who helped build (and shutter) the Illinois Watch Company.

Chapter 2 reports on historic work rules, work conditions and life in the Illinois Watch Factory, including the roles of women in the workforce.

Chapter 3 deals with the development of the American watch industry from its beginnings, including its trials, tribulations and successes in the 1920s, leading up to Hamilton's acquisition of Illinois in 1928. It details all of the likely reasons for the acquisition.

Chapter 4 describes the post-acquisition boom times in the watch industry at the end of the 1920s coupled with the pervasive and intensive fear among manufacturers, jobbers and legitimate retailers about the practices of price-cutters, discounters and easy-credit jewelers.

Chapter 5 reviews in detail the impact of the Great Depression as it hit the watch industry and Hamilton's reaction to it as measured by its quiet but methodical winding down of Illinois, leading ultimately to the demise of that "Great American Watch Company."

Volume 2, consisting of the next three chapters, discusses the major components of the Illinois watch.

Chapter 6 covers updated information on movements and their repair, points out some anomalies in existing movement production databases, explains why Hamilton did not (as had earlier been reported) produce thousands of Illinois wristwatch movements in 1948, describes how an Illinois movement functions (including a unique interview with two watch repairpersons about the nuances of servicing Illinois watches), and provides brief histories of the key private-label Illinois customers.

Chapter 7 covers the transformation of pocket watch dials into wristwatch dials and presents examples of private-label, custom and unusual Illinois dials, along with descriptions on how enamel and metal dials were fabricated. It also examines the refinishing of metal dials via a first-of-its-kind in-depth interview with the leader of the largest dial-refinishing firm in the United States. Debate exists among collectors about the importance of keeping original dials rather than refinishing them. This author firmly believes that dials should not be refinished. For this reason there is also a list of dozens of "Redone Tells" to help a serious collector forensically identify refinished and original dials.

Chapter 8 provides a historical profile of the casemakers utilized by Illinois, and by Hamilton for Hamilton-Illinois wristwatches, along with an updated list of all known Illinois case model numbers. All Illinois models are listed by case shape in this chapter as well as by casemaker. There is also a watch attachment section that focuses on this specialty industry and the watchbands in vogue during the peak years of Illinois wristwatches.

Volumes 3 and 4 focus on the three major lines of Illinois wristwatches: the Illinois men's models, the Illinois ladies' models and the later Hamilton-Illinois watches, which included both men's and ladies' models.

Chapter 9, which occupies all of Volume 3, provides a complete identification guide to all known men's Illinois wristwatch models. Entries include newly identified names and models, recently found advertisements and other information, as well as fascinating and valuable internal corporate documents of Illinois and Hamilton.

Chapters 10 and 11 share Volume 4.

Chapter 10 presents the most comprehensive review of ladies' Illinois wristwatches ever, building on the seminal work of Farrell Gay (with his permission and cooperation) along with relevant advertisements and information.

Chapter 11 documents to the greatest extent possible the Hamilton-Illinois wristwatches introduced and sold by Hamilton from 1953 to 1955 as its moderately priced marketing test case for the use of Swiss-made movements.

Volume 5 provides information for Illinois collectors and collectors-to-be about collecting and suggestions on how to go about doing it.

Chapter 12 covers items of Illinois-related ephemera and other watch-related collectibles not shown in my previous book.

Chapter 13 lists numerous methodologies for collecting a satisfying selection of Illinois wristwatches, along with contemporary strategies to do so by a leading grand-master collector. There's also an extremely interesting and entertaining interview with four knowledgeable watch collectors.

Chapter 14 sets forth a rather lengthy quiz included for your enjoyment to "Test Your Knowledge" of Illinois history and wristwatches, the Hamilton Watch Company, and this book in general.

The earlier book introduced "Fantastic Finds" and "Historical Notes" sidebars, which received enthusiastic reader response. For this reason, I included these again. New features in this book set include interviews with watch repairers, a dial refinisher and serious Illinois collectors. I also gathered brief stories from collectors about "Why I Collect Illinois." These are spread throughout the books. To make these volumes more useful to both experienced and novice collectors, I have added "Tells" (to spot a redone dial), "Technical Tips," "Fraud Alerts" and the information on watch attachments.

I hope I have convinced the reader that significant justification exists to open, read and enjoy these five volumes.

ILLINOIS

CHAPTER 1

Dramatis Personae

The Illinois Watch Company owed its success to various individuals who visualized, organized, financed and produced some of the best watches in the world. They accomplished this feat in Springfield, Illinois, a town best known for its politics. At the dawn of the Civil War, Abraham Lincoln and his rival, Stephen Douglas, used the town as a springboard for their political careers. During the war, Springfield became a hub of military activity. As a consequence, Springfield experienced an 85% increase in population during the decade of the 1860s. By 1870 the population stood at 17,864. The increased commerce, along with the town's largest employer, politics and government, provided conditions ripe for the introduction of high-value manufacturing. It also shaped the careers of some of the movers and shakers of the Illinois Watch Company.

The Catalyst and the Politician

John C. Adams (1834–1909)

Into this fertile environment came John Calhoun Adams. It was the perfect combination. According to Illinois watch expert L. Michael Fultz, Adams was "the most important watch industry entrepreneur of the nineteenth century."[1] Given his accomplishments, this might be considered an understatement. He was the catalyst for widespread watch manufacturing in the United States.

Adams was born in Preble, New York, on October 7, 1834, the son of a wealthy farmer. The Adams family later moved to the fine farmland around Barrington, Illinois. In the 1850s, young Adams traded the life of a farmer for the more urban skill of watchmaker.

The timing for his chosen career could not have been better. Before the 1840s, the ownership of a pocket watch had been the privilege of the well-heeled. Events, though, were about to turn this notion on its head. During the 1850s, the country (in fact, the world) became more conscious of time. In good part, the growth of railroads contributed to this interest.

For Adams, the fifteen-mile distance from his farm to the town of Elgin, Illinois, took the boy on a totally different path. In Elgin he served five years as an apprentice to the English born watchmaker John H. Atkins. He then moved to Janesville, Wisconsin, to work with watchmaker I. E. Spalding. Subsequently, he returned to Elgin to partner with his brother in a company known as G. B. & J. C. Adams, but the partnership lasted only two years. By 1860, Adams had moved to Chicago, where he accepted a position in the watch department of recently formed Hoard & Hoes, silversmiths.[2]

When Adams arrived in Chicago, the town was already serving as a hub for Midwest commerce. With a population exceeding 112,000, it was already the ninth- largest city in the United States. More importantly for a watchmaker, a dozen railroads served the city. Railroads considered it a priority to run on time.

From Hoard & Hoes, Adams moved to the firm of W. H. C. Miller, where he was appointed railroad timekeeper for all lines centered in Chicago. Adams lived in the right place and possessed the right skill. His position and location allowed him to make many industry connections, launching him into his career as "the great starter."

1834
Historical Notes

- Sandpaper is patented by Isaac Fischer, Jr.
- Mt. Vesuvius erupts.
- Cyrus Hall McCormick patents the reaping machine.
- Congress creates "Indian Territory," now Oklahoma.
- The hard-hat diving suit is patented by Leonard Norcross.

TIME SERVICE

Adams was well known in the Midwest as a watchmaker. He gradually developed a business in which he provided "time service" to the railroads with terminals in Chicago. "Time service" was the term employed by the railroads for the system of standards of timekeeping and for the selection, inspection, rating and servicing of timepieces (both watches and clocks) used to regulate train movements and other matters related to safety. Time service also usually involved the transmission of telegraphic time signals so that watches and clocks would be synchronized. It appears that Adams produced forms and procedures for watch inspection and sold a package to the railroads, then recruited local watchmakers to actually inspect the watches. These watchmakers were compensated by the railroad employees because watches had to be cleaned and repaired regularly. Adams operated this business from a base in Chicago for many years.*

*L. Michael Fultz, *InSync* (Feb. 2009), p. 134.

During the Civil War, Adams conceived the idea of starting a watch-manufacturing business. At the time, large-scale watch manufacturing could be found only on the East Coast. Adams visited the Waltham factory in Massachusetts to gauge the interest of some principal members of the Waltham organization in starting watch manufacturing in the West. Finding support there, he then approached Benjamin W. Raymond, who had earlier twice been mayor of Chicago, to find financing for such an effort. With Raymond's financial backing, Adams helped form the National Watch Company in Elgin, a town with which Adams was familiar. In 1867, Elgin produced its first pocket watch. Elgin would eventually grow to become the largest watch manufacturer in the United States.

Benjamin W. Raymond, late middle age

Adams did not invest in the Elgin venture, however. Instead, he served in the role of consultant and advisor, with his expenses paid by Elgin. In honor of his contribution, the company gave him the thirteenth watch assembled (B. W. Raymond, the president of the company, received the first, and other officers and investors received the next eleven). The movement from this watch remained in the Adams family until 2000, when it was acquired by the Elgin Historical Museum in Elgin, where it is on display.

Adams remained a jeweler in Chicago. According to Fultz, Adams continued to earn his living by jobbing or wholesaling watch movements to jewelers. Through his work, he maintained contacts with others in the watch industry.

Adams's role in forming Elgin came to the notice of other Illinois citizens, who recognized the importance of this budding industry. Paul Cornell, a real-estate speculator and lawyer with significant holdings in southern and southeastern areas around Chicago, worked with Adams to form a watch-manufacturing concern in Grand Crossing (now the Hyde Park section of Chicago). Adams, through his contacts in the industry, arranged to obtain the equipment and unfinished movements of the Newark Watch Company of Newark, New Jersey. The venture at Grand Crossing lasted only a few years before being sold to investors in San Francisco, California. However, Cornell named one of its movement calibers in honor of Adams and the role he played in founding the company. In addition, Adams's jewelry concern became the general agent for Cornell.[3]

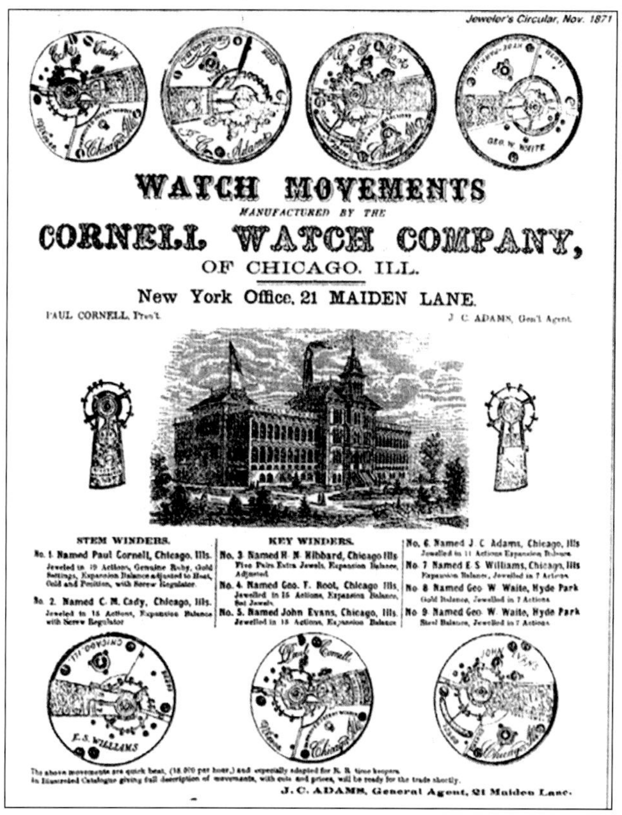

John C. Adams was the general agent for the Cornell Watch Company of Chicago, Illinois, working out of an office at 21 Maiden Lane in New York City.

Noticing the economic stimulus that the watch factory had brought to Elgin, the Springfield, Illinois Board of Trade decided that watch manufacturing would be a boon to that town too. Government had always been the main industry in Springfield. During the Civil War, however, the local economy had come to rely on the military because the Union's second-largest training facility in Illinois, Camp Butler, lay six miles from the city, and this facility also served as a camp for Confederate POW's. But with the conclusion of the war, Springfield's economy returned to relying on government as its main source of commerce.

The Board of Trade called upon Adams's expertise to help organize the watch business, and Adams traveled to Springfield to meet with local business leaders. He encouraged the Springfield Board of Trade and Springfield's leading citizens by pointing out the advantages of watch manufacturing. Chief among those was that the venture would attract highly skilled workers who would be paid good wages. Adams's ideas piqued the interest of John T. Stuart and the financially powerful Bunn family, key community leaders who would soon be drawn into the venture.

For Adams, the formation of this watch company represented a stepping stone in his life's path. Andrew Taylor Call writes of Adams's role: "As the initiator of the formal cause of the enterprise, Adams should be considered the true founder of the Springfield Watch Company."[4] This firm would later be reorganized and renamed the Illinois Watch Company. The backers initially capitalized Springfield at $100,000. As with Elgin, Adams acted as a consultant/facilitator without any equity ownership in the watchmaking business, but the organizers did recognize Adams's contributions by appointing him as one of the firm's directors.

John C. Adams, late middle age

Not until three years later did Adams see his name on a watch company building. In 1874, Adams's reputation motivated the citizens of Lancaster, Pennsylvania, to call upon him to organize a watch-manufacturing company there. Just as it had done in Springfield, the promise of highly skilled, highly trained workmen convinced Lancastrians to push ahead with the organization of the Adams & Perry Watch Manufacturing firm. But Adams did not remain long with this venture, as a dispute over whether the company should manufacture its own movements or buy cheaper movements from Switzerland caused him to disassociate himself from the firm. After several reorganizations, the Lancaster operation spawned the Hamilton Watch Company.

1870
Historical Notes

- Construction begins on the Brooklyn Bridge.
- The U.S. National Weather Service is established by the U.S. Army.
- The U.S. Congress creates the Department of Justice.
- Christmas is declared a federal holiday in the United States.
- The first transcontinental United States rail service begins.
- Mayor William "Boss" Tweed of New York City is accused of robbing the New York Treasury.
- The first New York City subway line opens (pneumatic powered).
- The Cincinnati Red Stockings, the first professional baseball team, is formed.

Adams continued to dabble in watch manufacturing, even as he remained a jeweler and wholesaler. His reputation led others to seek his services. In 1880 the Fredonia Watch Company had been formed by the Howard brothers, who specialized in patent medicine sales but also sold a line of watches. As their private label watch business increased, they created the Independent Watch Company of Fredonia, New York, to make their own watches.

In 1883 the Howard brothers called upon Adams to help them with Fredonia and convinced him to travel to the Fredonia plant. There he examined the machinery and the inventory of completed movements. Inventory included a mind-boggling eight thousand finished movements and about two thousand more partially finished ones. Adams's examination showed that the movements were unsatisfactory, with faulty escapements and poor finish. He suggested that the Howards close the factory temporarily, so that the machinery could be overhauled and new machinery purchased. In addition, he advised them to finish up the remaining partial movements and then sell them at any price. Adams volunteered to sell the movements on their behalf.

The Howards followed this advice, reorganizing the firm as the Fredonia Watch Company, which was recapitalized at $150,000. Adams, for his part, sold the movements for an average of six dollars each, a very good price considering the quality of the movements.

When the firm needed additional capital in order to compete in the pocket watch market of the 1880s, Adams found new backers in Peoria, Illinois. On December 19, 1885, the backers incorporated the Peoria Watch Company with an announced capital of $250,000. The new firm took possession of Fredonia's machinery and moved it to Peoria.

As a wholesaler, Adams worked closely with A. C. Smith's Non-Magnetic Watch Company of Chicago, one of his best customers. Adams sold Peoria movements in quantity to Smith. Later, possibly under the influence of Adams, Smith purchased private-label movements from Illinois and Elgin. As the nineteenth century drew to an end, Adams, a Chicago resident and booster, also became involved with the efforts to organize and promote the display of Swiss watchmaking and clock making at the Columbian Exposition (World's Fair) held in Chicago in 1892 and 1893. Ironically, the World's Fair was held on the site of the old Cornell Watch Company factory at Grand Crossing. After the exposition, Adams retired but, not surprisingly, continued to have an interest in the watch business until his death in 1909.

ADAMS PARK

Adams was honored by the City of Chicago in the naming of Adams Park, located at 7535 South Dobson Avenue. According to the Chicago Park District, the park is "named for John C. Adams, an official of the Cornell Watch Company, which stood across 76th Street from the park around 1900." Adams had an incredibly active career in the watch business. His roles—watch repairer, watch retailer, watch wholesaler, organizer of watch factories and, as always, a promoter of the watch industry—mirror the developments in manufacturing and transportation in the expanding United States of the late nineteenth century.

John T. Stuart (1807–1885)

In selecting a president for the newly organized Springfield Watch Company, the organizers closely followed the Elgin model. Elgin could point to B. W. Raymond, its president, as an element of its success. He had been successful not only as an antebellum politician in Chicago but also as a businessman who operated a woolen mill in Elgin, Illinois.

MAJ. JOHN T. STUART.

John T. Stuart, early in his career

Since Springfield served as the capital of Illinois, its main business was politics. Typical of most state capitals, it also served as a haven for lawyers, both as legislators and as practitioners before the Illinois Supreme Court. According to the Elgin example, the successful corporation president should be a leading citizen and politician. It also would not hurt if the leader of the enterprise could be linked to Springfield's leading citizen, Abraham Lincoln. The organizers selected a person who fit the mold perfectly: John Todd Stuart, who had been a longtime resident of Springfield as well as a practicing attorney and active politician. In 1870 the Board of Directors named Stuart as the Springfield Watch Company's first president.

1832 HISTORICAL NOTES

- The first railroad accident in the United States occurs: Granite Railway, Quincy, Massachusetts. One fatality.
- The Black Hawk War ends as 1,300 Illinois militia defeat Sac and Fox Indians.
- The first streetcar (horse drawn) debuts in New York City. Fare: 12¢.
- John Howe patents a pin-manufacturing machine.

Abraham Lincoln had been a protégé of Stuart's. Like Lincoln, Stuart was born in Kentucky. They first met when they were serving in the Black Hawk War in 1832, Stuart as a major and Lincoln as a captain. Both men served the surrounding Sangamon County in the Illinois House of Representatives in the 1830s. Sometimes they were political allies, sometimes foes, as befit the fluid nature of frontier politics. According to Lincoln historians, Stuart encouraged the young Lincoln's political career as well as his study of law, but as Lincoln outdistanced Stuart in law and politics, Stuart's support transformed into political envy.[5]

In 1832, shortly after the Black Hawk War, Lincoln, as a Whig, lost his first legislative race. Stuart, also a Whig, won his race. Two years later, Democrats approached Lincoln, trying to convince him to run against Stuart. Although both Lincoln and Stuart were Whigs, Stuart approved of Lincoln's negotiations with the Democrats. As a result, Lincoln and John Dawson, another Whig, won easily. Stuart barely finished in the fourth and final spot.[6]

After passing the Illinois bar in 1836, Lincoln moved to Springfield. Stuart became his first law partner. In comparing the two personalities, psychobiographer Edward J. Kemp observed:

> While handsome, debonair Stuart enjoyed numerous friendly connections in Springfield's aristocratic society, his slouchy young partner found life lonely and discouraging. He [Lincoln] had become a social lion (at home) only to find himself neglected in Springfield, where he had expected to be well received after working so effectively in making it the state capital.[7]

BLACK HAWK WAR

The Black Hawk War was a brief conflict fought in 1832 between the United States and Native Americans, headed by Black Hawk, a Sauk leader.* The Black Hawk War is now often remembered as the conflict that gave young Abraham Lincoln brief military service, although he himself engaged in no combat.

Others of historical note who served in this war included Zachary Taylor, afterwards president of the United States; Jefferson Davis, afterwards president of the Confederacy; John T. Stuart, a founder and president of the Illinois Watch Company; William S. Hamilton, son of Alexander Hamilton; and Robert Anderson, the hero of Fort Sumter in the Civil War.

Captain of the company in which Lincoln served was Elijah Iles (1796–1883), one of the first settlers of Springfield, Illinois, and one of its best-known citizens: "a shopkeeper, farmer, politician, landowner and real estate developer . . . [who] died a very wealthy man."†

*Wikipedia, http://en.wikipedia.org/wiki/Black_Hawk_War
†Abraham Lincoln Presidential Library & Museum, http://alplm-cdi.com/chroniclingillinois/items/show/309

LINCOLN ON DOUGLAS

"On one occasion some of Lincoln's friends were talking of the diminutive stature of Stephen A. Douglas, and an argument as to the proper length of a man's legs. During the discussion Lincoln came in, and it was agreed that the question should be referred to him for decision."

"Well," said he, reflectively, "I should think a man's legs ought to be long enough to reach from his body to the ground." *

*Anthony Gross, *The Wit and Wisdom of Abraham Lincoln* (Fall River Press, 1999), p. 65.

With Lincoln running the law offices, Stuart focused increasingly on politics.[8] Stuart especially wished to defeat the cunning and ambitious Stephen A. Douglas for a seat in the United States House of Representatives. In the spring and summer of 1838, Stuart and Douglas stumped from town to town, six days a week, and Lincoln also campaigned hard for his partner. It was a difficult and vicious campaign. Even though the campaign began in friendly fashion, near its end a violent altercation occurred between the two candidates. With the election drawing to a close, both appeared together in Springfield for a debate. As emotions flared, Stuart seized the diminutive Douglas by the neck and carried him around the square. Douglas retaliated by biting Stuart's thumb. Stuart concluded the campaign nursing his half-severed digit.[9]

Where Stuart and Lincoln Had Their Law-Office in 1837.

Site of the John T. Stuart and Abraham Lincoln law practice at No. 4 Hoffman Road (upstairs), Springfield, Illinois, in 1837

The August 1838 election saw Stuart, the Whig, win by a majority of fourteen out of a total of 36,000 votes cast.[10] According to Lincoln legal biographer Albert A. Woldman, because Stuart's interests were elsewhere, "It became Lincoln's duty to prepare the pleadings and briefs in long hand, attend to trial work, and make the entries in the firm account book."[11]

Stuart served in both the Twenty-sixth and Twenty-seventh Congresses (1839 to 1843). In 1843 he became a law partner of Benjamin Edward, with whom he remained affiliated for the rest of his life. His relationship with Lincoln continued, though, as his cousin Mary Todd married Lincoln in 1842.

Stuart continued his political career as a member of the Illinois Senate (1848 to 1852). With the dissolution of the Whigs, he joined the Constitutional Union Party, becoming their gubernatorial candidate in 1860. Unsuccessful in his bid for governor, he switched to the Democratic Party. In 1862 he defeated Republican Leonard Swett for a seat in the Thirty-eighth United States Congress, in what fellow Democrats portrayed as a repudiation of President Lincoln's policies. While declining to debate Swett, Stuart declared: "It is my desire to give the President . . . frank and earnest support."[12]

Stuart defeated Swett by 1,500 votes. Over the next two years, Stuart was a frequent guest at the White House. He served only the one Congressional session, as Shelby Cullom defeated him in 1864.

Since Stuart was a well-known, politically connected citizen of Springfield, the organizers of the Springfield Watch Company hoped that he would lend legitimacy to the budding enterprise, just as Raymond had done for Elgin. These organizers included the following initial members of the Springfield Watch Board of Directors: John Calhoun Adams; John Williams, president of the First National Bank of Springfield; William B. Miller, a local hardware merchant; and John W. Bunn, who, with his brother Jacob, owned a wholesale and retail grocery business. Stuart served as president of the company from 1870 to 1877.

Springfield Watch Company,
State of Illinois.
Shares $100 Each.
THIS IS TO CERTIFY, That ______ is entitled to ______ Shares of ONE HUNDRED DOLLARS EACH of the Capital Stock of The Springfield Watch Company, transferable only on the Books of the Company, in person or by Attorney, upon surrender of this Certificate.
IN WITNESS WHEREOF The President and Secretary of said Company have hereunto subscribed their names, and affixed the Seal of said Company, at Springfield, Illinois, ______ this day of ______ A. D. 187
______ Secretary. ______ President.

An original stock certificate of the Springfield Watch Company

Stuart oversaw Springfield's issuance of stock. Adams, in his prospectus, estimated the first year's costs (including land, building, tools, fixtures and wages) at $82,467. To cover the expense, one thousand shares of stock were authorized to be sold at $100 per share. On March 10, 1870, five-year contracts were signed with Charles E. Mason, Foreman of the Escapement Room, at $3,500 per annum; Daniel G. Currier, Foreman of the Finishing Room, at $3,500; Otis T. Hoyt, Foreman of the Train Room, at $2,500; William F. Dean, Die Maker, at $2,500; and John K. Bigelow, Superintendent, at $5,000. The next day, on March 11, 1870, a lease was signed with Berryman & Rippon for the entire upper floor of their Springfield machine shop at $100 per month. Construction of watch-making machinery began.[13]

Meanwhile, the directors drew up plans for construction of a factory on fourteen acres of land acquired from Henry Converse, on North Grand Avenue, between Ninth and Eleventh Streets.[14] On August 3, 1870, the firm executed a contract with John T. Rhodes to build the factory for $18,025, with completion scheduled for November 1 of that year. By December, machinery and fixtures were being installed in the building. And by May 1871 the Watch Factory produced its first watch parts.[15]

The Illinois Watch Company in the early 1900s

holders' meeting, the directors appointed a committee, consisting of John W. Bunn, W. J. Conkling and Otis Hoyt, to devise some means of relief from this embarrassing situation. Just one week later, on January 10, the committee reported that the Springfield Watch Company should be sold to "any new company which would assume and pay all debts of said company and relieve its stockholders of all liability." In return, the stockholders would release the company of any claims and forego their personal investments; in other words, the Springfield stock would become worthless.[16]

Understanding the desperate nature of their situation, the directors accepted the recommendations and proposed them to the stockholders at a meeting on February 21, 1877. Almost as an afterthought, John T. Stuart made a motion and it "was resolved that the purchaser of the Springfield Watch Company be requested as an act of generosity to present to each stockholder of said company a Springfield watch of value in proportion to the amount of stock held," presumably to ease the pain of their losses. Whether this request was honored is unknown.[17]

Unfortunately, the new Springfield watchmaking enterprise could not duplicate the success of Elgin. The United States economy, which had collapsed after the overheated years of the Civil War, crawled along in a decade-long depression. Adams estimated that the $100,000 would successfully launch the firm. He underestimated the amount of time necessary to produce movements. Even though Elgin organized in 1864, it took until 1867 for it to produce its first watches. For Cornell, the equipment already existed. As would become true also with Adams's venture, Adams and Perry, undercapitalization would cripple the efforts of the Springfield firm to become successful.

Despite its apparent success in the manufacture and sale of watches, Springfield's profit picture remained gloomy. Expenses continued to outdistance income. Company records show that employees and suppliers were forced to accept deferred payment during the years 1872 to 1877. The failure of its attempts to raise additional capital finally forced the company to take remedial action, as creditors lost patience and began to turn to the courts for assistance. In a January 3, 1877, stock-

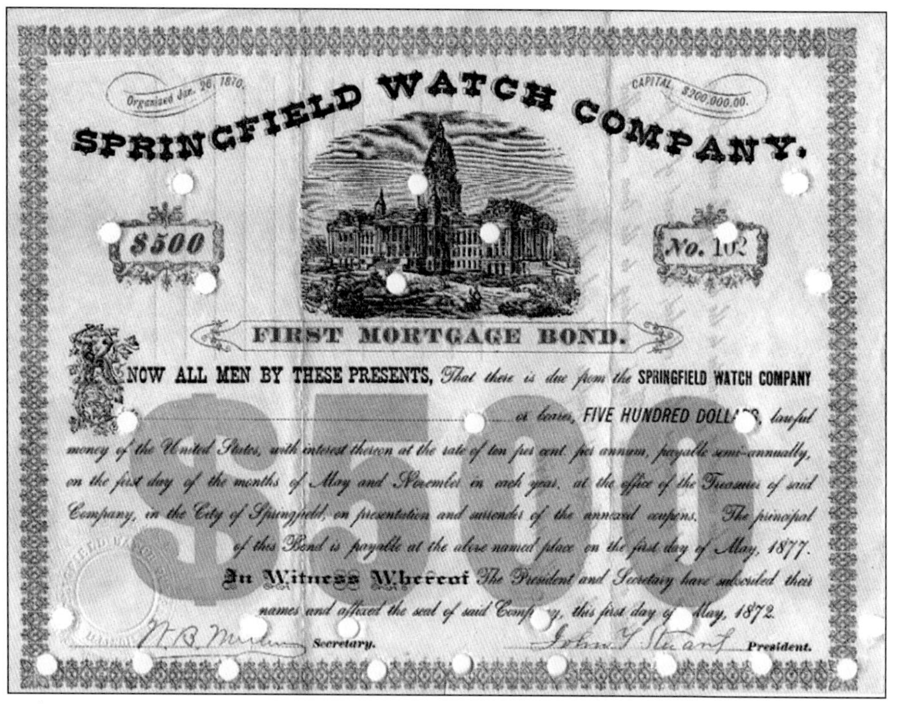

Organized Jan. 26, 1870.

CAPITAL $200,000.00.

SPRINGFIELD WATCH COMPANY.

$500

No. 102

FIRST MORTGAGE BOND.

KNOW ALL MEN BY THESE PRESENTS, That there is due from the SPRINGFIELD WATCH COMPANY .... or bearer, FIVE HUNDRED DOLLARS, lawful money of the United States, with interest thereon at the rate of ten per cent. per annum, payable semi-annually, on the first day of the months of May and November in each year, at the office of the Treasurer of said Company, in the City of Springfield, on presentation and surrender of the annexed coupons. The principal of this Bond is payable at the above named place on the first day of May, 1877.

In Witness Whereof The President and Secretary have subscribed their names and affixed the seal of said Company, this first day of May, 1872.

Secretary.

John T. Stuart President.

A First Mortgage Bond for the Springfield Watch Company, signed by John T. Stuart

THE MANY MOVES OF OTIS HOYT

John C. Adams was not the only person moving from watch company to watch company in the 1800s. Henry G. Abbott relates that "Otis Hoyt left his home in Amesbury to go to work for the Waltham company in 1858. He severed his connection with the company at the time of the war, and served as captain until he was honorably discharged in July, 1864. In the fall of that year he joined forces with Geo. Hunter and several others and went to Elgin, contracting with that company for a term of five years. His health failed him, however, and in 1867 he was compelled to go to California for a change of climate, and from there he returned to Waltham. He soon went to Springfield, Ill., to act as superintendent, and remained in that position until 1871, when he went to Elgin to take charge of the train room, a position which he filled creditably for fourteen years. He died at his residence in Elgin, June 2, 1885, in his forty- eighth year."*

*Henry G. Abbott, *The Watch Factories of America* (Chicago: Hazlitt, 1888), p. 57.

The General and the Financiers

General Erastus Newton Bates (1828–1898)

On March 22, 1877, the Illinois Secretary of State, George N. Harlew, approved a petition to form "A new corporation for the manufacture of watch movements, cases, materials and parts with capitalization of $1,000,000 consisting of 1,000 shares, $100 par, duration 99 years, to be known as the Illinois Springfield Watch Company of Springfield, Illinois." Subsequently, on June 4, 1877, the new company was incorporated with a board of directors consisting of Charles Ridgely, Frank W. Tracy, Erastus Newton Bates, John W. Bunn and Jacob Bunn. Among them, only John W. Bunn survived as a director from the Springfield Watch Company. General E. N. Bates was elected president, and Frank Tracy was elected secretary.[18]

1877
HISTORICAL NOTES

- Crazy Horse fights his last battle with the United States Cavalry.
- Rutherford B. Hayes is inaugurated as the nineteenth president.
- Thomas Edison announces his "talking machine" invention (phonograph).

Like Stuart, "Newton" Bates could be counted as a respected member of the Springfield community. He had been born in 1828 in Massachusetts, a descendant of Pilgrims. When he was about eight years old, his father brought him to Ohio but died soon after, leaving the child in the care of an uncle. Desiring an advanced education, Bates saved money through work as a teacher and manual laborer so that he could attend Williams College in Massachusetts, from which he graduated in 1853.[19]

Erastus N. Bates as a young man. He served as the second president of the Illinois Watch Company.

Bates migrated to New York City to study law but soon found himself on the frontier once again, becoming a lumber merchant in the Minneapolis area. He attended the Minnesota Constitutional Convention in 1856 and became a state senator the next year. Two years later, he moved to Illinois to practice law.

With the beginning of the Civil War, Bates was elected major of the 80th Illinois Volunteer Infantry. During the war, he was captured by Confederate troops and sent to the infamous Libby Prison in Richmond, Virginia. He helped plan the "great escape" from Libby. Unfortunately, the Confederates soon recaptured him. In all, he spent fifteen months as a prisoner of war. Once released, Bates was promoted to lieutenant colonel in 1864. In March 1865 the army honored him with a promotion to brevet (temporary) brigadier general. Forever after, Bates would therefore be known as General Bates, although he held the final permanent rank of colonel when he mustered out in June 1865.

Immediately after the war, he returned to Illinois. In 1866 the citizenry, grateful for his service to the country, elected Bates to the Illinois State Legislature. Two years later he became the Illinois State Treasurer and served in that position until 1873.

A respected war hero and politician, Bates was a natural choice to lend legitimacy to what was now the Illinois Springfield Watch Company. Because stockholders had lost their investments in the earlier watchmaking enterprise, giving the presidency of the new watchmaking enterprise to the former state treasurer helped reassure wary investors that the reorganization put the company on a firmer financial footing.

Bates served for only a very short time as president of Illinois Springfield. He resigned his position in July 1878, after serving only eighteen months. Interestingly, it appears that Bates then became a wholesale grocer, possibly affiliated with the Bunn brothers.

The Watch Company continued operations until near the end of 1878 without a president. By November they had found one. On November 18, 1878, a notice appeared in the Springfield newspapers that the Board of Directors of the Illinois Springfield Watch Company had called a meeting of stockholders to discuss another reorganization. On December 23, 1878, the Directors proposed to transform the corporation into the "Illinois Watch Company." A note in the newspaper, dated December 31, 1878, announced that the name change had been approved. The notice was signed "Jacob Bunn, President." Thus entered Jacob Bunn as the leader of Illinois and began the Bunn dynasty at Illinois, a dynasty that would last for the next forty-eight years.

Jacob Bunn (1814–1897)

The success of the Illinois Watch Company can be attributed to the financial and business acumen of the Bunn brothers. Jacob Bunn had been involved in the watchmaking enterprise since its beginning in 1870 as the Springfield Watch Company. By that time, Bunn had already established himself as a leading confidant, businessman and investor in enterprises. He founded or cofounded more than fourteen businesses. His resume included the following: industrialist, railroad financier, railroad reorganizer, wholesale grocer, commission merchant, newspaper publisher, land developer, coal operator, political advisor, financier, banker and rope manufacturer. To this he now added a new title: president of the newly restructured Illinois Watch Company.

Jacob Bunn, early in his career

Born in Hunterdon County, New Jersey, Jacob Bunn grew up in a wealthy farming family as one of nine children (a tenth died in infancy). In addition to farming, his father, Henry Bunn, engaged in banking. By the time of Henry's death in 1859, he left an estate valued in excess of $34,000 (about $1 million in today's dollars). Both Jacob and his much younger brother John W. wished to trade farming on the East Coast for new opportunities in the West. They settled in Springfield, Illinois.[20]

Jacob began by founding a wholesale grocery business in July 1840, located at Fifth and Adams Streets in Springfield. The grocery business continued to prosper as the Bunn Capitol Company. As a business organization, Bunn Capitol survived the economic panics of 1857, 1873, 1883, 1893, 1907, 1920 and 1929. Bunn Capitol continued successfully in business for over 170 years, until it was acquired by SYSCO Corporation in September 2006. Bunn Capitol's long-term survival remains a tribute both to Jacob Bunn's first Springfield venture and to his business acumen.[21]

In 1851, Jacob married Elizabeth Jane Ferguson, daughter of Benjamin Ferguson and Sarah (Irwin) Ferguson, both natives of Washington County, Pennsylvania. Benjamin Ferguson, a building contractor, participated in the construction of the old Illinois State Capitol in Springfield. Sarah Irwin was the sister of the bankers and merchants Robert and John Irwin. Robert Irwin acted as the personal debt collector for Abraham Lincoln and served as a member of the board of directors of the State Bank of Illinois. By the 1860s, Bunn too had become a banker, in addition to a wholesale grocer.

Association with Lincoln. According to Andrew Call, Jacob Bunn's biographer, Jacob played an important role in Abraham Lincoln's political career. Both Jacob and his brother John W. had become acquainted with Lincoln early in their careers in Springfield. The friendship developed and lasted throughout the remainder of Lincoln's life. The Bunns' involvement could be termed the first instance in United States history in which large-scale business interest supported a candidate for presidency. Jacob became the Republican Party's first corporate supporter. Among other things, the Bunns provided Lincoln with financial support, media promotion and social opportunities in furtherance of his political pursuits.[22]

Railroad enterprises. Like many other entrepreneurs of the period, Jacob Bunn invested in railroads. Not only might railroads themselves be direct sources of income, but by opening up new routes of transportation, the railroads might cause other businesses to thrive. For someone in the wholesale grocery business, improved transportation could be essential for bringing in new goods. The importance of railroads in the brothers' enterprises is shown by both the extent and the period of their investments. Jacob began investing in railroads the year John W. came west to Springfield, long before the watch venture, and the brothers continued long after the watch company was established.

In 1847, Jacob Bunn helped form the Alton and Sangamon Railroad to connect Springfield with the Mississippi River town of Alton, Illinois, just north of St. Louis. Abraham Lincoln and John T. Stuart also helped spearhead this project. Although the initial goal of this railroad was to provide Springfield with a connection to commerce on the Mississippi River, it quickly developed wider ambitions. In 1861, Jacob Bunn served as one of the official reorganizers and incorporators when this became part of the Chicago & Alton Railroad Company. The Alton railroad grew into a major diagonal north-south bridge route connecting Illinois' largest cities with St. Louis and Kansas City.

The Alton is known as being the road on which George Mortimer Pullman developed his sleeping cars in the late 1850s. Abraham Lincoln's body returned to Springfield on the Alton; the train included Pullman's new demonstration car Pioneer, which had just been completed in the Alton shops.[23]

The Alton survived into the twentieth century, mostly under the control of first the Baltimore and Ohio and later the Gulf, Mobile, and Ohio, which eventually became part of the present Illinois Central.

Not all of the Bunn railway projects started so ambitiously; some began as local endeavors. The town of Pana, about forty miles southeast of Springfield, wanted a rail connection to the state capital, and in 1856, Jacob Bunn promoted regional railroading by being an incorporator of the Springfield & Pana Railroad. Then, in 1865, he served as an incorporator of the Pana, Springfield and Northwestern Railroad Company. Pana did become a small rail junction and refueling stop, and the shortline passed through the B&O to the modern CSX Transportation system.

Other ventures. Jacob Bunn made many contributions to the growth of the state of Illinois. In addition to his railroad sponsorship, he was also involved in other enterprises. In 1865, Bunn founded the Chicago Republican Newspaper Company, and in 1869 he served as an incorporator of the Chicago Secure Depository Company, a significant Chicago safety deposit institution. By 1874, Bunn had become a driving force for the construction of a new State Capitol building; he then served as chairman of the commission organized to oversee its construction.

1865 HISTORICAL NOTES

- Congress passes the Thirteenth Amendment, abolishing slavery in America.
- General Robert E. Lee as commander-in-chief of the Confederate armies surrenders.
- President Lincoln is inaugurated for his second term as president.
- President Lincoln is shot by John Wilkes Booth at Ford's Theatre.
- James H. Nason patents the first United States coffee percolator.

Illinois Watch Company. Jacob Bunn's efforts to control and stabilize the new Illinois Watch Company may be counted among his greatest contributions. On December 31, 1878, Bunn officially assumed the office of president. Under his direction, production and employment levels increased consistently, in contrast to the experience of his predecessors.

To help grow the business, Bunn strengthened Illinois' financial condition as well as increasing the size of its labor force and scale of manufacture. In 1882 the number of employees rose to eight hundred. The initial years of the Bunn administration saw Illinois experience solid growth and prosperity, making it a major asset to Springfield's economy. In his twenty years as president, Bunn oversaw a 500% increase in watch production.[24]

The company experimented with new manufacturing materials and movement sizes. In 1879 the Watch Factory (as it was fondly known), manufactured the first nickel watch movement in the United States, and in 1886 it produced the smallest movements made in the country.[25]

Illinois' success depended in part on its ability to cater to numerous and diverse watch markets. The company sought to strengthen its hold on the nascent ladies' watch market by introducing the 6 and 4 size grades, the latter type being the smallest manufactured in the United States. Three years later, in 1889, Illinois entered into competition with the Elgin Watch Company and other similar men's pocket watch manufacturers by introducing its own 16 size watch. Illinois even sought to develop the children's timepiece market, claiming in one advertisement that "every schoolboy needs and desires a watch." It introduced the 14 size grade 120 to meet the needs of youngsters. Although the Illinois Watch Company sought to exploit diverse market segments, its greatest success occurred in the area of railroad pocket watches. Illinois made high-quality timepieces for the railroads, as one of the major players of the timepiece industry.

1879
HISTORICAL NOTES

- Milk was sold in glass bottles for the first time.
- Madison Square Garden in New York City opens.
- F. W. Woolworth opens the first "Five & Dime" store.
- Thomas Edison demonstrates electric light.
- James Ritty patents the first cash register to combat stealing by bartenders in a Dayton, Ohio, saloon.

Events in 1884 caused Bunn to change the market philosophy at Illinois. In that year the American railroads agreed to adopt "standard time" because the transportation industry was increasing its impact on the daily lives of people all over the country. Watches, formerly ornamentation for the rich and ostentatious, became a necessity for the common man. The greater reliability and accuracy resulting from the emphasis on standard time became important for both those operating trains and those affected by them.

Bunn's firm took note and responded to the transformation through the release of their grades 104 and 105 watch movements. The new watches met the railroads' increasing need for accurate timepieces. At the beginning of the final decade of the nineteenth century, Illinois Watch advertisements targeted railroad workers with determination. In 1891 a widely publicized railroad accident, involving the collision of two trains, compelled railroads to establish a national standard for timepiece accuracy. Among watch manufacturers, Illinois became one of the foremost standard-setters.

A Railroad Accident Brought Him His Job as Watch Inspector

FRED L. WILLIAMS, Sr., prominent watchmaker and jeweler, of Atlanta, Georgia, recently completed twenty-five years of service as official watch inspector for trainmen of the Georgia Power Company in Atlanta.

Mr. Williams was appointed official watch inspector for the company on December 2, 1902, following a serious accident the fault of which was traced to a defective watch belonging to a trainman. At that time, every motorman and conductor was ordered to have his watch inspected and regulated twice a year. Since then Mr. Williams estimates that he has regulated 100,000 watches.

At that time, says Mr. Williams, he even found trainmen with watches which had been given as premiums with ten pounds of coffee, and anything which "ticked" was considered good enough to wear! Now no watch may be carried that is not American made or does not have at least seventeen jewels and which is regulated to three positions. All watches are regulated twice a year, and accidents due to defective instruments are now unheard of.

Mr. Williams employs a unique system in his shop to care for the many watches which he must regulate. Several boards, each containing about twenty timekeepers, are employed to hold the watches, and the instruments are passed from board to board as they are regulated. When they reach the final board, they are keeping perfect time, and can then be given out. However, no watch is returned to the owner from the first board or until Mr. Williams is satisfied that it will keep perfect time.

Another "stunt" which Mr. Williams uses is one by which the watches need never be taken off the boards, even at night. Grooves are arranged for the boards in the big safe of the store, and at night they are simply slipped into these.

FRED L. WILLIAMS, Sr.

Mr. Williams says that he is good for another twenty-five years as official watch inspector for the company. He is one of the most popular men on the Georgia Power Company staff and was recently presented with a twenty-year service button by officials of the concern.

In addition to being official watch inspector, Mr. Williams is a successful jeweler, his store at 97 Decatur Street being one of the best known in Atlanta.

Keystone, April 1928

Through Illinois' self-promotion and the promotion by others, the public became aware of Illinois' contributions to reliable watch movements. Illinois timepieces could be found among railroad men throughout the United States, from the Maine Central to the Southern Pacific. *The Illinois State Register* referred to Illinois as the "leading watch manufacturing concern in America." Under Bunn's leadership, the Illinois Watch Company had become world famous.[26]

Bunn's presidency at Illinois coincided with the rise of the American watch industry in general. Illinois ranked third in the United States in production of high-quality watches. At the time, the Swiss regarded American watch design and manufacture so highly that they copied the Americans.

Bank failure and debts. Among his many enterprises, Jacob Bunn established a private bank called the J. Bunn Bank of Springfield, Illinois. The bank rapidly accumulated large capital assets during the 1860s and early 1870s. However, owing to an overextended portfolio of real estate holdings, it was forced into liquidation during the Panic of 1873.

In 1878, when the forced sale of the bank's assets produced only $228,000, Jacob voluntarily assumed personal liability for the remaining portion of the bank's $800,000 indebtedness. Civic pride motivated Bunn to make up the difference; he had no legal obligation to do so. Over a period of thirty-seven years, with the assistance of close family members and associates, he managed to pay off the remaining $572,000.

Upon Jacob's death in 1897, his children honored their father's desire to repay the entire indebtedness by establishing a Memorial Trust. In 1925, the Trust finally completed its task: a distribution that affected approximately five thousand people and, amazingly, included a 5% return.[27]

Notice of Jacob Bunn Sr.'s Death

Died of Old Age in His Office.

Springfield, Ills., Oct. 18. — Jacob Bunn, Sr., president of the Illinois Watch company, was found dead Saturday afternoon in his private office at the factory. James Shaw, superintendent of the factory, had been talking to Bunn fifteen minutes before he was found. After Shaw left him Bunn went into his office to lie down on the sofa to take a rest, and this was the last seen of him before his death. Bunn had complained of not feeling well for two or three days. His death was caused by old age and acute gastritis, he being in his 84th year.

Logansport Pharos-Tribune (Logansport, IN), October 18, 1897; image from *newspapers.com*

John Whitfield Bunn (1831–1920)

In many of his business and political pursuits, John Whitfield Bunn often participated with his older brother. Like Jacob, John W. moved west to Springfield, where he became a corporate leader, financier and industrialist, whose interests stretched from Midwestern railroads, international finance and Republican Party politics to corporate consultation, global manufacturing and participation in various American stock exchanges. The younger Bunn also counted Abraham Lincoln as a close friend, and he benefited from Lincoln's political tutelage.[28] By the time of his death in 1920, John W. Bunn had played a major role in the commercial, civic, political and industrial development and growth in the Midwest, especially in the state of Illinois.

The J. & J. W. Bunn Grocery Company. Jacob convinced his brother, John W., to immigrate to Springfield with glowing descriptions of the opportunities available in the Midwest. Eighteen years junior to Jacob Bunn, John W. left his New Jersey home for Springfield in 1847. Just sixteen years old, the younger Bunn joined Jacob in the wholesale grocery business.

Portrait of John W. Bunn, in middle age

John W. began as an entry-level employee in the wholesale grocery house owned by his brother. He rapidly ascended to increased levels of responsibility. In time, he became a partner, and the firm changed its name to "J. & J. W. Bunn Grocery Company." By 1871 the company generated annual sales of approximately $200,000. By 1880, with only one wholesale grocer left in competition, the annual sales reached $450,000 (today this would equate to over $10,000,000).

Friendship with Lincoln. The move to Springfield had brought John W., like his brother Jacob, in contact with Springfield's first citizen, Abraham Lincoln. Lincoln served as the attorney for the Bunn grocery business in its early years. John W. became a close friend and principal member of Lincoln's political network, serving as treasurer and one of the initial contributors to Lincoln's 1860 presidential campaign.[29]

1847 HISTORICAL NOTES

- Robert Thompson patents the rubber tire.
- The first United States postage stamp goes on sale.
- The donut is created.

Railroad interests. Like his brother Jacob, John W. Bunn was a prolific investor in railroad projects. In 1866, Bunn assisted in the development of an intra-urban transportation infrastructure in Springfield. As part of this, he helped establish and build the Springfield Railway Company. The next year, Bunn became an incorporator of the Belleville City Railway Company of Belleville, Illinois, a line that eventually became part of the Illinois Central.

In 1874 both John W. and Jacob became board members of the Hannibal & Naples Railroad Company, one of the companies that fell under the control of the Wabash Railroad. Later, in 1877, John W. served as founder and president of the Wabash Railway Company of Illinois. By 1880 the Wabash Railroad system possessed approximately 16,000 rail cars. In 1889, Bunn served as one of the five incorporators of the Wabash Eastern Railroad of Illinois. In addition, he participated as a principal founder, consolidator and organizer of the Wabash Railroad Company. By 1902 the Wabash Railroad Company was a major east-west carrier in the Midwest, with corporate assets of nearly $150 million. The Wabash eventually was bought by the Norfolk and Western, part of today's Norfolk Southern.

In 1879, Bunn contributed to the financing and incorporation of the Kansas City Air Line Railway Company, based in Springfield, Illinois, which was intended to serve as a connection with the Chicago and Alton. Eventually this line became part of the Kansas City Southern system. (An "air line" railroad was one that ran in a straight line or bee line.)

Bunn became a member of the board of directors of the Terre Haute & Peoria Railroad Company of Decatur, Illinois, in 1893, as well as a director of the Toledo, Peoria & Western Railroad Company. The Terre Haute & Peoria would later become part of the Pennsylvania Railroad empire. The Toledo, Peoria & Western survived until 1983 before being absorbed by the Santa Fe Railroad.[30]

Over seven hundred railroad companies have been chartered in Illinois, over a hundred in the 1840s and 1850s alone. Few of them survived, but some have left tracks down to the present day as parts of other systems.[31]

Other activities. The wholesale grocery business served as a launching pad for Bunn's numerous commercial and industrial projects and contributed to the development of distinct industrial and civic sectors of Illinois.

Many of these activities were centered in Springfield. From 1857 to 1859, Bunn served as treasurer of the City of Springfield. After it achieved its final reorganization, Bunn served as a founder, director and vice president of the Illinois Watch Company, and his affiliation with Illinois lasted many years. Bunn also served for years as president and director of the Springfield Marine Bank; in 1920 the deposit account held at the bank totaled $5 million. Bunn helped found the Springfield Iron Company in 1871 and served as a director and vice president. This enterprise, which had corporate offices in New York City, Chicago and St. Louis, as well as in Springfield, became one of the largest manufacturers of iron products in the United States. In addition, John W. and his brother Jacob served as incorporators of two separate insurance companies, the American Standard Life Insurance Company and the DuBois Insurance Company, both of Springfield.

Bunn also expanded his activities to include numerous industrial and financial contributions to the economic growth and development of Chicago as well. He was a founder of the shoe and boot manufacturing firm of M. Selz & Company and served as its vice president for several years prior to his death.

John W. Bunn was also important in Illinois state affairs. During the Civil War, from 1861 to 1865, Lincoln appointed Bunn to serve as Pension Agent for the State of Illinois. From 1858 to 1898, Bunn held the position of treasurer of the Illinois State Board of Agriculture. In 1887 his efforts went above and beyond his official role, when he provided $15,000 of his own money to liquidate the debts of the Illinois State Fair Association. He also served as the founding treasurer of the University of Illinois from its inception in 1868 until 1893.

1867

HISTORICAL NOTES

- Bricklayers start working an eight-hour day.
- President Andrew Johnson announces the purchase of Alaska.
- Alfred Nobel patents dynamite.
- The refrigerated railroad car is patented by J. B. Sutherland.

John W. Bunn had become a major industrialist and investor. Not surprisingly, he promoted the interests of the United States as an incorporator and member of the United States Centennial Commission. This group organized and oversaw the United States Centennial International Exhibition of 1876 at Philadelphia, Pennsylvania, which served notice that the United States had become a major manufacturing power.

PHILADELPHIA CENTENNIAL EXPOSITION OF 1876

The first major World's Fair in America, to mark the 100th Anniversary of the signing of the Declaration of Independence, was officially known as the "International Exhibition of Arts, Manufacturers and Products of the Soil and Mine."

The Exposition opened on May 10, 1876, on a 285-acre tract in Fairmount Park overlooking the Schuylkill River. It was immensely popular, drawing nearly nine million visitors at a time when the United States' population was only forty-six million.

The most lasting accomplishment of the Exposition was to introduce America as a new industrial world power. The Exposition closed on November 10, 1876.

Admission to the Centennial Exposition was 50¢, a guidebook cost 25¢, and a glass of soda water was 10¢. The average daily salary of an American worker in 1876
was $1.21.

Some of the consumer products first introduced at the Exposition were:

- Alexander Graham Bell's telephone.
- Remington Typographic Machine (typewriter).
- Heinz Ketchup.
- Kudzu erosion-control plant species.

In the early 1890s, Bunn contributed significantly to both the coordination and the corporate infrastructure of the 1893 World's Columbian Exposition (Chicago World's Fair). He served as a member of the Illinois Board of World's Fair Commissioners.

All his commercial and industrial activities made John W. Bunn a multi-millionaire. His career spanned the years that transformed Illinois from frontier to a major economic center. For his part, Bunn transitioned into a philanthropist with focus on public causes, a role he maintained until his death in 1920.

1893 HISTORICAL NOTES

- The World's Columbian Exposition (World's Fair) opens in Chicago.
- Grover Cleveland is inaugurated as the twenty-fourth United States president.

John W. Bunn.

Special to The New York Times.

CHICAGO, Ill., June 7.—John W. Bunn, a close friend of Abraham Lincoln, died today in Springfield, Ill. Mr. Bunn was 89 years old. He came to Springfield from New Jersey in 1847. He was the owner of the Illinois Watch Company, President of the Marine Bank in Springfield, President of John W. Bunn & Co. and a member of Sein, Schwab & Co. of Chicago.

New York Times, June 8, 1920; image from *newspapers.com*

Three Technological Wizards

Horological Genius: Charles Edward DeLong (1871–1943)

Charles E. DeLong's battles with chronic poor health did not prevent him from making important and varied contributions to horology in general and to the Illinois Watch Company in particular. Paul M. Chamberlain, in *It's About Time*, chronicled DeLong's career. DeLong's varied skills included creative inventor, designer, draftsman and adjuster. Chamberlain characterized him as an expert who could step into any watch manufacturing facility and save hundreds of thousands of dollars from his advice alone.

According to Chamberlain, DeLong "absorbed a desire" for watchmaking at an early age and "by the age of fifteen was doing credible watch repairing" when he began working with a watch-maker in Glens Falls, New York. A year later, in 1887, he joined the jewelry firm of Jones & Podmore in Troy, New York, and the following year he took a job in Albany with M. R. Eliasoff & Brothers, jobbers in watches and jewelry, where he stayed for two years.

In Albany he carried on his own watchmaking work too. He bought on time an American lathe with every available attachment. At noon on Saturdays, DeLong would rent a dray to cart his bench to his lodgings and, from then until Monday morning, would work incessantly on completing watch movements. At the same time, he began studying trigonometry.

DeLong moved west to Peoria, Illinois, in 1894, becoming an instructor in watchmaking at the Bradley Polytechnic Institute. He remained at Bradley for three years. In Peoria he also attended night classes to continue studying mathematics and became as proficient with numbers as he was with his hands.

While at Bradley, he met Fred McIntyre, a fellow student. McIntyre was a jeweler in McAlester, Indian Territory (now Oklahoma), who apparently wished to improve his watchmaking and watch repair skills. As it turned out, the friendship that developed between DeLong and McIntyre would define DeLong's career for the next two decades.[32]

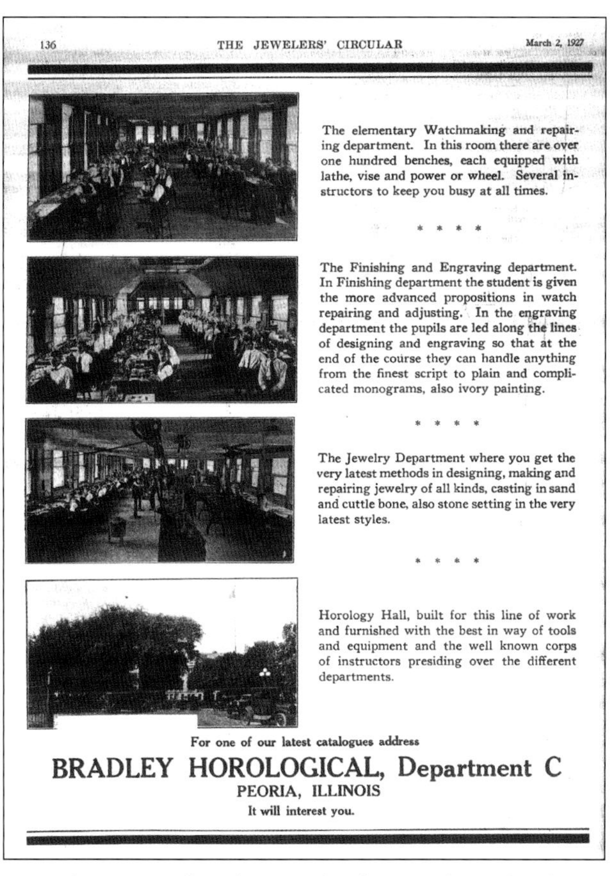
136 THE JEWELERS' CIRCULAR March 2, 1927

The elementary Watchmaking and repairing department. In this room there are over one hundred benches, each equipped with lathe, vise and power or wheel. Several instructors to keep you busy at all times.

* * * *

The Finishing and Engraving department. In Finishing department the student is given the more advanced propositions in watch repairing and adjusting. In the engraving department the pupils are led along the lines of designing and engraving so that at the end of the course they can handle anything from the finest script to plain and complicated monograms, also ivory painting.

* * * *

The Jewelry Department where you get the very latest methods in designing, making and repairing jewelry of all kinds, casting in sand and cuttle bone, also stone setting in the very latest styles.

* * * *

Horology Hall, built for this line of work and furnished with the best in way of tools and equipment and the well known corps of instructors presiding over the different departments.

For one of our latest catalogues address

BRADLEY HOROLOGICAL, Department C
PEORIA, ILLINOIS
It will interest you.

A March 2, 1927 advertisement in The *Jewelers' Circular* for the Bradley Polytechnic Institute

This building with its equipment, and the ground upon which it is built, represents an investment of over $150,000, and is used exclusively for training in Watchwork, Jewelry and Engraving. Not another Horological school in the world can compare with it.

BRADLEY ALWAYS GROWING BIGGER AND BETTER

To the young man who is interested in becoming a first class watchmaker, jeweler and engraver, a tremendous increase in your pay envelope is the result of a complete course in the Horological Department of Bradley Polytechnic Institute, Peoria, Illinois. Does this mean anything to you? If so, get in touch with this department and make arrangements to begin your training immediately. Make these Summer months of immense profit to you. Address a post-card to Bradley Horological, Dept. "K," Peoria, Illinois, asking for a special catalogue pertaining to this particular department. Watchwork, Jewelry and Engraving are taught in this department of Bradley, and you can get all, or you can specialize in any of the lines you wish to take up. School is in session all the year around, no vacations. Work is given by individual instructions, therefore parties can start in at any time it might be convenient for them to do so.

BRADLEY HOROLOGICAL
DEPT. K. PEORIA, ILL.

Keystone, June 1929

Apparently enamored of DeLong's "astounding talents," McIntyre became his greatest promoter. McIntyre told of one occasion when a customer came to DeLong with a broken watch and had to catch a train in an hour. Ascertaining that the center wheel of the movement needed replacing, DeLong was able to cut an eighty-tooth wheel and install it in the watch in time for the customer to catch his train. Another example of DeLong's phenomenal skills: one time McIntyre bet DeLong that DeLong could not spring a watch in half an hour, but DeLong returned the repaired watch to him within eighteen minutes. In other stories, McIntyre recounted how quickly DeLong could make a watch. DeLong himself acknowledged that he could make a movement by hand in fourteen days. He could also design and construct watchmaking tools just as quickly, according to McIntyre.[33]

The accolades for DeLong's work did not come from McIntyre alone. In a 1915 article in the *American Jeweler* about the DeLong escapement, Chamberlain wrote: "It would be all but impossible to enumerate all the devices for watch details, tools and methods for which . . . [DeLong] is responsible. I think I am correct in stating that no one of my rather wide acquaintance would deny him the position *par excellence* in making of tools and watches."[34]

Around the same time that he attended Bradley, McIntyre married Lida Belle Wood, who was from Arkansas. When DeLong moved from Peoria in 1898 to become a jeweler in Hot Springs, he may have been motivated not only by the proximity of McAlester, to which McIntyre had returned, but also by McIntyre's connection with Arkansas.[35] However, the move may also have been prompted by the onset of tuberculosis, which would eventually claim DeLong's life (perhaps he wished to avail himself of the famous Hot Springs therapeutic baths?).

While in Hot Springs, DeLong kept up his friendship with McIntyre. Together they worked on improvements to pocket watch movements. During this time, DeLong also designed and patented a design for a single-trigger rifle mechanism that he subsequently showed and, ultimately, sold to the Remington Arms Company. Finally, in 1901, DeLong moved to McAlester to work side-by-side with McIntyre.[36]

The close friendship between McIntyre and DeLong resulted in plans to further their careers in watchmaking. McIntyre, who had lost his wife and was left to rear his daughter alone, decided to marry again; his new wife was Lola Booth, from a Texas family. So it may have been this Texas connection that led McIntyre to sell his McAlester jewelry store in 1905, and, with DeLong, move to Dallas to establish the Southwest Horological Institute.[37]

In a brochure, the Institute claimed that by that time DeLong had built eight watches himself. The brochure also showed pictures of several other movements made under his supervision.[38]

Ultimately, McIntyre and DeLong wanted to begin their own watch company, using the patents that both had developed for the improved railroad watch. While DeLong busied himself at the Horological Institute, McIntyre searched for capital to establish a watch company. He found backers in Kankakee, Illinois.

Tristate Jewelers' Association

JEWELERS

From Three States Will Convene Here September 10-12.

The annual convention of the Tristate Jewelers' Association will be held in Cincinnati September 10, 11 and 12. More than 1,000 jewelers from Ohio, Indiana and Kentucky are expected to attend the convention, which will be held in the Grand Hotel. In addition to the wholesale and retail merchants of the trade, members of the Kentucky Optical Association will be present at the convention.

The program of business and entertainment, arranged by a committee of local jewelers, contains a number of amusement features and will end with a banquet which the local jobbers will tender the visitors.

Mayor Dempsey will deliver the address of welcome at the opening of the convention. Other speakers will be President Charles D. Rood, of the Hamilton Watch Company; President Duncan, of the Waltham Watch Company; President Bunn, of the Illinois Watch Company; John C. Dueber and A. L. Sackett, of the Dueber-Hampton Watch Company; H. C. Carpenter, of the South Bend Watch Company; S. O. Bigney, of Attleborough, Mass., and others.

The Committee on Entertainment of the local jobbers' association comprises George Gruen, Edgar Fox, Arno Dorst, Herman Promitz and Sig. Strauss. The Reception Committee is composed of Otto C. Lightner, John Bertling, Henry Doepke, M. Moss and Andrew Alich.

Jacob Bunn, Jr., was a featured speaker at the Tristate Jewelers' Association to be held in Cincinnati in September 1907. *Cincinnati Enquirer,* August 29, 1907; image from *newspapers.com*

DeLong's and McIntyre's dream of designing and building watches began to take shape with the development of the charter for the McIntyre Watch Company in the spring of 1908. The promoters filed the charter for McIntyre on August 14, 1908. Initially, the corporation authorized $200,000 in capital stock, with each of the 2,000 shares priced at $100.[39]

The articles of incorporation stated McIntyre's purpose: "To manufacture watches, clocks and chrono-meters and scientific instruments for measuring time or distance." McIntyre met the $200,000 capital requirement creatively. The total cash raised amounted to only $56,000. To make up the rest of the $200,000, he valued the patents belonging to him and DeLong (four granted and five pending) plus three prototype watches at $125,000. Since this still left McIntyre short, he gave the corporation a note for the remaining $19,000. Significantly, McIntyre contributed no cash to the company bearing his name. McIntyre named his close friend DeLong "master maker" for the watch company.

McIntyre took to the road to line up customers among jewelers. His fifteen years' experience as a jeweler probably helped gain an audience with many shop owners, though without products he had little to sell except promises. The seed of the McIntyre Watch Company's failure, however, lay in its undercapitalization. The $56,000 in cash certainly could not pay for the construction and operation of a factory. In June 1909 the board therefore voted to increase the corporation's capitalization to $500,000.

WINE AND DINE

Evidently, as early as 1910 it was not uncommon for Illinois to entertain members of various retail jewelers' associations. Once such example is shown below from the *Belvidere Daily Republican,* Belvidere, Illinois; May 28, 1910.

ASSOCIATION MEETS NEXT AT ROCKFORD.

Jewelers Were Entertained Lavishly at Country Club Dinner.

Fred A. Marean returned last evening from Springfield, where he attended the sessions of the Illinois Retail Jewelers' Association, of which he has been president during the past three years, in fact, since its organization. He preferred that the honor and duties be passed around, and Richard Wieting of Peoria, was chosen president. The next meeting will be held at Rockford.

On the last day of the sessions the Illinois Watch company entertained the visitors at dinner at the handsome Country Club, where they served an elaborate menu, the factory band furnishing a program of music.

Image from *newspapers.com*

Meantime, the McIntyre Watch Company commenced operations in the Foley & Williams plant in Kankakee. At the time, Foley manufactured organs. The new stock offering, which caused McIntyre to lose voting control of the company, brought in a mere $45,500. The company bought machinery with the cash on hand. In an attempt to attract more capital, McIntyre lined up some new investors from Chicago to help fund the increased capitalization, but the investors wanted to see products before investing.

The cash-poor enterprise folded, when Foley & Williams evicted the firm in order to allocate the floor space instead for production of sewing machines. The McIntyre company had produced between six and ten complete watches and possessed about two hundred ébauches in inventory at the time of its closing. Its products and machinery were then packed into freight cars on a nearby siding, where they remained for some time.

THE McINTYRE MASTER WATCH

A well-known example of DeLong's work is the McIntyre Master Watch. This is apparently a sample of the 16-size watch that DeLong and McIntyre intended to manufacture. It has 25 jewels, DeLong's patented motor barrel, and his patented wind indicator. It also has DeLong's "semi-tangential" escapement and his unique method of attaching the dial to the movement with fingers on the perimeter. This watch, signed with the McIntyre Watch Company seal, sold at a Sotheby's auction in 2004 for $51,000.

A second watch, apparently assembled in 1927 by Vance E. LaPorte, who was studying with DeLong in San Diego, was acquired by Tom McIntyre of the NAWCC in 2012. *

*http://mb.nawcc.org/entry.php?59-Bread-Upon-the-Waters

McIntyre continued his friendship with DeLong, even as their paths diverged at this point. After the McIntyre operation closed, DeLong joined the Arthur A. Everts Company in Dallas as a watchmaker. McIntyre joined W. G. Knapp in a partnership to sell jewelry, watches and traveling clocks. By the 1920s, McIntyre was selling auto parts.

Charles DeLong, at middle age

While working with McIntyre, DeLong had developed a new lever escapement. In 1915 he formed the DeLong Escapement Company to manufacture or lease the patent on a royalty basis. Several American manufacturers were interested. DeLong assisted the Hamilton factory in equipping one hundred watches with the new escapement and outfitted two hundred escapements for the Webb C. Ball Company. The Illinois Watch Company placed the escapement in one hundred watches, but decided not to adopt it when problems developed.[40] Later, however, Illinois' A. Lincoln pocket watch movement used part of the escapement design. In 1915, Fred McIntyre convinced Knapp to join him in investing in DeLong's company, but this independent venture soon disappeared.

See Appendix 1.

1915 HISTORICAL NOTES

- Colonel Jacob Ruppert and Colonel Tillinghast Huston purchase the New York Yankees for $460,000.
- Alexander Graham Bell in New York calls Thomas Watson in San Francisco as transcontinental telephone service begins.
- The United States Coast Guard is created from the Living Saving and Revenue Cutter Services.
- The Panama-Pacific International Exposition opens in San Francisco.
- Jess Willard knocks out Jack Johnson in the twenty-sixth round for the heavyweight boxing title.
- The Lusitania is sunk by a German submarine: 1,198 deaths.
- Albert Einstein publishes his "General Theory of Relativity."

The contact with Illinois may have been what led DeLong to move to Springfield to work for them. Because he possessed phenomenal skills and experience, Illinois selected him in 1919 to travel with an interpreter to Switzerland "To acquire first hand such developments in horology as would be advantageous to [the Illinois Watch] company."

According to his passport application, he was to "visit England, France, Italy and Switzerland to purchase watch material for import." While in Europe, he benefited from meetings with eminent horologists, scientists, manufacturers, managers and specialists in the watch industry, as well as observed their manufacturing methods both mechanical and manual.

Illinois found the knowledge gained on this trip to be enormously valuable. DeLong himself gained personal satisfaction by absorbing the practices and ideals of the masters of his beloved art. DeLong's later designs for watches for Illinois bear evidence of the importance of this trip.[41]

SWISS PARTS

It is clear now that DeLong was searching in Europe for parts that could be made at a lower cost than they could be produced by the Illinois Watch Company as there is evidence that Illinois started in the early 1920s to have selected parts manufactured in Switzerland. In fact, one drawing dated September 5, 1922, was found by the author, drawn by DeLong (drawing No. 2053) himself for a "Fourth Wheel" to be produced in Switzerland to Illinois specifications.

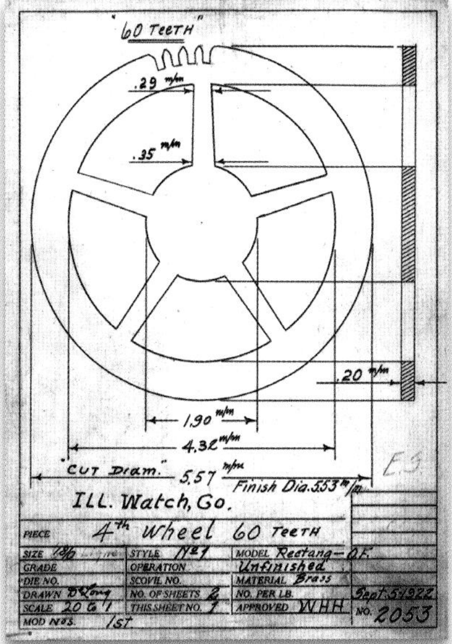

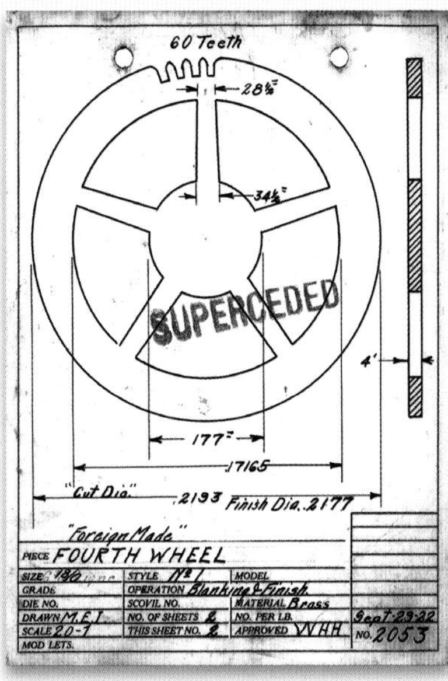

During DeLong's travels in Europe it is likely that he saw the smaller-sized movements that were being produced and sold primarily by the Swiss. Therefore, when he returned to Springfield, he evidently persuaded Illinois to develop its own 18/0 size movement for smaller-sized watches.

As the Swiss were then producing these types of movements with 15 jewels, DeLong could have urged Illinois to one-up the Swiss by developing their first 18/0 size movement in 1923 with 16 rather than 15 jewels, as Illinois did so (see Chapter 6).

DeLong remained the Illinois Watch Factory "general freelancer" into 1922. Besides patents owned directly, DeLong assigned at least two patents to the Illinois Watch Company. The first one is dated November 5, 1918, Number 1,283,476. This patent involves an "improved means for avoiding the objections due to the holding of the mainspring of a watch at the extreme limit of its windings." The second patent, dating from January 21, 1919, Number 1,292,269, "relates to an improved construction of the gearing comprised in the winding mechanism of a stem-winding watch, and particularly to an improved construction of the pinion that is secured to the winding-stem."

1919 HISTORICAL NOTES

- Prohibition is ratified as the Eighteenth Amendment to the Constitution.
- The Fascist Party is formed in Italy by Benito Mussolini.
- The first United States air passenger service starts (New York to Atlantic City).
- Jack Dempsey knocks out Jess Willard in Cuba for the heavyweight championship.
- Babe Ruth is traded by the Boston Red Sox to the New York Yankees.

Temperature Adjusting Facilities Greatly Increased

The continually increasing demand for the higher grades of Illinois watches has made necessary enlarged and improved apparatus for making the temperature adjustments.

Our former facilities enabled us to adjust but 360 movements, but with the new cabinets designed by Messrs. Johnson and DeLong we will be able to adjust 1,000 movements at a time. The low temperature cabinet has already been installed and the high temperature one will be set up in the very near future.

This article about DeLong the "factory freelance" performing another special job for the Watch Factory appeared in the February 1919 *Doings*.

When his health declined, DeLong found it necessary to spend much of each year in a milder climate, first in Arizona and then in California, where he settled in San Diego and later owned a small "Bungalow Court." During his time in California, he assisted watchmakers in performing complex repairs.

While commenting on DeLong's time in California, Chamberlain paid him this compliment: "His talks before the Horological Association of California always attracted a large audience, as DeLong could explain problems nowhere else accessible. None ever asked him for help without receiving it and with it the inspiration to reach out for the highest standards."[42]

In 1933 he moved to the Los Angeles area, where he died in 1942. He is buried at Forest Lawn Cemetery in Glendale.

Engineer and Astronomer: George F. Johnson (1851–1931)

George F. Johnson was born in Lowell, Massachusetts, but later moved with his parents to Rockford, Illinois. There he apprenticed at the Noble & McCormick Machine Shop, and in 1871 he started working for the Rockford Watch Company. Johnson moved to Springfield in 1876 to join the machine department of the Illinois Watch Company but in 1884 left Illinois to become general superintendent of the Aurora Watch Company. After that, Johnson spent some time manufacturing precision instruments in Chicago and later worked for the Dueber-Hampden Watch Company as their General Superintendent.

But Johnson eventually returned to work at Illinois. In 1912, when he was serving as the mechanical superintendent, he recommended that Illinois construct an astronomical observatory on its grounds so that the company could measure its own time. Owing to Johnson's advocacy of the project, the company approved construction of the observatory and placed Johnson in charge of it. The observatory was frequently and proudly featured in Watch Company advertisements and even on its stationery.

Illinois later promoted Johnson to superintendent of the Watch Factory, a position capping a great career in watchmaking.

Johnson received seven patents for his inventions, the last three of which he assigned to Illinois. One of his patents involved a regulator pin which, when rotated, would slide a small metal piece beneath the hairspring in order to keep it in place. (An early Aurora Watch Company trade card mentioned this feature being used in their movements.) One of the patents assigned to Illinois was for a "safety barrel" for a watch.

Johnson's obituary noted that in addition to his expertise in watchmaking, he held diplomas as both doctor of optics and doctor of dentistry. Given his involvement with the observatory, it is not surprising that he was a member of the National Astronomical Society, the Illinois Academy of Sciences and the Astronomical Society of the Pacific. No doubt Johnson's training in optics aided him in providing specifications for the observatory's two telescopes.

George F. Johnson (in his seventies) demonstrating the observatory telescope during the filming of the silent film *How A Watch is Made* in 1923 by the United States Department of the Interior

Observatory postcard, c. 1919

Doings

Vol. 1. January 1919 No. 10

An Evening With Mr. Johnson In The Illinois Watch Company's Astronomical Observatory.

We were very glad for the invitation. Promptly at eight o'clock we assembled at the observatory. Mr. Johnson was there before us and had everything in readiness. Keeping on our heavy coats and wraps we ascended to the dome room on the second floor. This was lighted and we had a splendid opportunity to examine the great equatorial telescope whose searching eye pierces the depths of the heavens. This telescope is a wonderful instrument with a lens eight and a half inches in diameter, set in a tube measuring over twelve feet in length. The whole is mounted on a substantial hollow iron pedestal inside of which there is a clock which automatically keeps the telescope focussed on the star or other celestial objects on which it is set.

When the instrument and its uses was explained to us, Mr. Johnson said he wanted us to see the moon through it. Going to one side of the circular room, he pulled two cords which opened the great dome shutters so that we could look out at the wintry sky. But the moon was not in sight. Suddenly we heard a rumbling noise and all of us were more or less startled as we seemingly felt the entire building turning around from west to east. Mr. Johnson, seeing our surprise, smiled as he pointed to a little lever by means of which he could turn the great dome around from right to left or the reverse until the opening was turned toward the part of the sky he wished to study. In a moment the moon shone in upon us and the telescope was trained upon it. Each in turn gazed in wonder at the silvery ball, seemingly suspended by nothing in the depths of space. Its whole surface was more or less pitted with immense volcanic craters and ring mountains which were clearly visible through this great magnifying lens. The sight of this cold, desolate looking globe made a deep impression upon all of us.

While we were discussing the moon the telescope was trained upon Jupiter, the fiery planet now seen in the eastern sky. Jupiter is surrounded by a remarkable family of satellites which were first seen by Galileo in 1610 and these have the distinction of being the first celestial objects discovered by means of a telescope.

Then one of the ladies asked to see the North Star. The dome was moved again and the telescope pointed to a spot far up in the northern heavens. Judge of our surprise when we found that the Pole Star is not a single, but a double star. We also learned that the present North Star has not always been and will not always continue to be the Pole Star. Thousands of years hence the great star Vega will be the Pole Star of our planet instead of Polaris—the present one. Near Polaris is the Big Dipper and Mr. Johnson suggested that we see if we could make out the double star in the handle of it without the use of the telescope. This he told us was a test of eyesight among the Arabians who named these stars Alcor and Mizar.

Interest in the Big Dipper naturally led some of the party to ask to have a few of the constellations pointed out to them. As these could not be seen in their entirety through the telescope, we went out upon the balcony surrounding the dome. There in the heavens to the south, appeared the belted Orion—possibly the most glorious constellation in the northern sky. As we gazed at it we were reminded that thousands of years ago it was asked of Job if he could bind the sweet influences of the Pleiades or loose the bands of Orion. In the belt of this mighty celestial hero, we saw three stars which point to the brightest star in the heavenly vault. This we were told is Sirius—the Dog Star, the star of ancient lore which, for untold ages, has foretold the annual overflowing of the River Nile with its life giving waters.

Thus we passed a most delightful evening and as we thanked our host and bade him goodnight, we were pleased to be asked to come again.

Doings, January 1919

Watch Parts Prodigy: Fred R. Coats (1866–1951)

American watch companies found success in producing accurate, reliable and reasonably priced timepieces. For the Illinois Watch Company, the success it enjoyed in producing highly regarded watches rested upon the skills of those who produced the precision parts and machinery used in the manufacturing process. In this regard, the work of Fred Coats stands out.

The United States became the world capital of watch production, owing primarily to the expansion of railroads in this country. As the number of trains sharing the same tracks increased, precision timing of train schedules required that each individual responsible for operating the train possess an extremely accurate watch. Otherwise, trains would collide. Just as airplane accidents grab headlines today, so did railroad accidents at the end of the nineteenth century.[43]

The railroads, with the help of jewelers such as John C. Adams and Webb C. Ball, developed precise criteria for railroad timepieces. These mechanical and technological marvels were built to a set of exacting standards. In general, the watch had to be open-faced; with a movement 1 21⁄30 (16 size) to 1 23⁄30 (18 size) in diameter; have a minimum of 17 jeweled bushings at specified pivot points. It was also required to keep time with a gain or loss of no more than 30 seconds a week in any of five positions: face up, face down, stem up, stem left, and stem right. (Later, a sixth position, stem down, was added.) The watch also had to keep its accuracy at a variety of temperatures, ranging from a nearly freezing 34° to a sweltering 100° Fahrenheit. Besides performance criteria, railroads required the watch to have a double roller and a steel escape wheel; set time with a lever; contain a micrometric regulator for adjustment; have the winding stem positioned at 12 o'clock; show its grade on the movement back plate; use plain Arabic numbers printed bold and black on a white dial; and have bold, black hands. In short, the railroad watch had to be a technological marvel at an affordable price. To produce such precise watch movements at a reasonable price, Illinois carefully designed an assembly-line approach.

Standard Time.

Ques.—1. What kind of time does principally all the railroads use in the United States, and how transmitted?

Ans.—Observatory standard time, and is transmitted from the observatory to all designated offices.

Q.—2. How is standard time secured at all points?

A.—By telegraph from the designated offices at a certain hour each day.

Q.—3. Where do employees obtain this time from for each division?

A.—From the clock in the dispatcher's office of each division.

Q.—4. How often should employees compare and regulate their watches?

A.—Daily.

Q.—5. What is the rule generally, with regard to variation of watches?

A.—No excuse will be taken for the variation of watches.

Q.—6. What is the rule with reference to station clocks?

A.—Where station clocks are provided, station agents should see that they show correct time; but trainmen and engineers should not take time from such clocks, unless they are designated as standard.

Q.—7. What is the rule with reference to the watches of conductors and engineers?

A.—Each conductor and engineer should have a reliable watch, which has been examined and certified to on a form provided by a responsible watchmaker.

266

nated officer; this is usually required before he is allowed to take charge of a train or engine.

Q.—8. What is generally required of all conductors and engineers?

A.—Each conductor and engineer is required to compare and regulate his watch by the designated standard clock before starting on each trip, and register his name and the time at which he regulated his watch, on a blank form or in a book provided for that purpose.

Q.—In case a conductor or engineer should be so situated as not to have access to standard time, what should he do in such a case?

A.—Conductors and engineers, whose duties prevent them from having access to standard clock should compare daily with and regulate their watches by those of conductors and engineers who have standard time, and have registered their names as required.

Rules concerning Standard Time (Thomas Annis, *The Railway Employee Book of Ready Reference and General Information*, 1901, pp. 265–66)

Railroad Executives Visit Watch Factory

On June 2nd a distinguished party of railroad officials representing several of the central western railroads visited the Watch Factory. In the party were William C. Finley, president of the Chicago & Northwestern Railroad and his two vice-presidents, Marvin Hughitt, Jr., and A. C. Johnson; J. E. Taussig, president and W. C. Maxwell, vice-president of the Wabash Railroad and General Supt. Pelley, of the Illinois Central.

As a routine matter, railroad executives would visit the Illinois Factory. *DOINGS*, June 1921

Because Illinois pocket watches met and exceeded these standards, they remain highly sought after by collectors today. Reflecting its pride in the precision watch movements, Illinois gave them such names as the "Bunn Special" after the family owning the company; the "Sangamo Special" after the county in which the Watch Factory was located; and the "A. Lincoln" after Springfield's most famous citizen.

Precision equipment was essential to producing Illinois' quality timepieces. From the 1890s to the end of production, Illinois relied on Fred Coats to create these watchmaking tools and parts necessary for its fine watches. Although he was based in Springfield, Fred Coats's talents were known and respected worldwide.

Born in Wyoming County of upper New York State in 1866, Coats moved to Springfield with his family, when he was about seven years old. At the age of twelve or thirteen, he left school to work at the Illinois Watch Factory to supplement the family's income. A local history described him:

> Coats was young and ambitious and found ways to continue his education even after his formal schooling ended. He became an earnest reader of instructive books, perusing with especial zest the literature of mechanics, for which . . . he had a decided taste. . . . From the pages of the Scientific American, which was often found in his hands, he gained many an idea destined in due time to materialize in practical results, and his entire business experience has been concentrated along this line.[44]

1866
HISTORICAL NOTES

- **Jesse James robs his first bank in Liberty, Missouri.**
- **Charles Elmer Hires invents root beer.**
- **Daniel Farragut is appointed as First Admiral of the United States Navy.**
- **U. S. Grant is named First General of the United States Army.**

Coats also learned on the job. He began his career in Illinois' watch train department, rising to assistant foreman within two years. About three years later, still in his teens, Coats went to work for the Aurora Watch Company in Aurora, Illinois, in order to expand his knowledge. After spending two years in Aurora, he moved to the Peoria Watch Company in Peoria, Illinois. As he moved from watch company to watch company, Coats increased his skills. Soon he acquired the knowledge to successfully design parts and movements himself.

He worked at Peoria for two years but returned to Illinois to direct work in the train department, where he had begun working as a boy. Once again, after two years he moved elsewhere, this time to the Columbus Watch Company in Ohio as foreman in the train department.

He finally returned to Springfield, establishing a business for making balance staffs. A little later, in 1895, he built his first factory, on Fifteenth Street.

Only once was he again away from Springfield for any extended period of time. That was when Coats was asked by the Lancashire Watch Company in England to become foreman of its train and jewel department. Because he wished to increase his knowledge about making balance staffs, he took the position temporarily and was away from Springfield for about six months.

In 1899 he built a new building for the Coats Watch Materials Manufactory Company at the corner of Fifteenth and East Washington. The early Springfield history described it:

> It is a two-story building, and the plant is thoroughly equipped, many of the machines now used being of his [Coats's] own designing. The building is also supplied with all the latest types of automatic machines, and a force of seventy workmen is employed. The business has had a rapid but healthy growth, and the output is

> shipped to all parts of the civilized world. He has a large mail-order trade, and the enterprise has become an important one in Springfield and is returning a good profit to the owner.[45]

Fred R. Coats at middle age

A few years later, business was so good that the Coats Watch Materials Manufactory Company outgrew its factory at Fifteenth and Washington, and a new facility was built at East Ash and Yale Boulevard. The original part of that structure, a four-story, square building with a sloping roof, is still in use for another corporation.

Coats Watch Materials Manufactory, 1910

In the 1920s, Coats moved to another new factory (also still standing), at 2220 Yale Boulevard, about two blocks south of the previous factory. Among other items, Coats made balance staffs for Illinois watch movements. At about this same time, it appears that he began making parts or accessories for automobiles, while continuing to manufacture watch equipment. During World War II, the Coats factory devoted much of its efforts to making precision parts for the war effort.

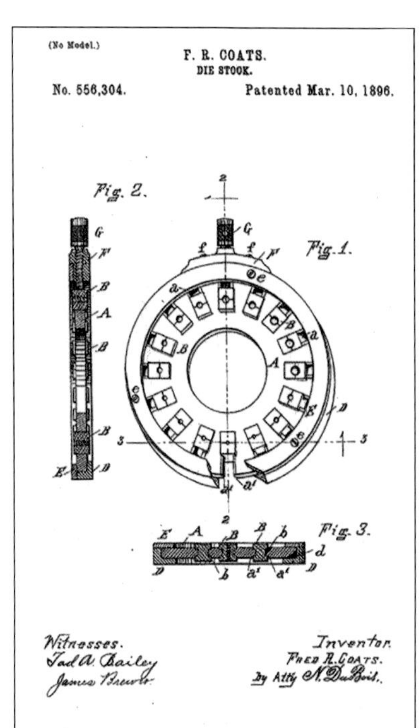

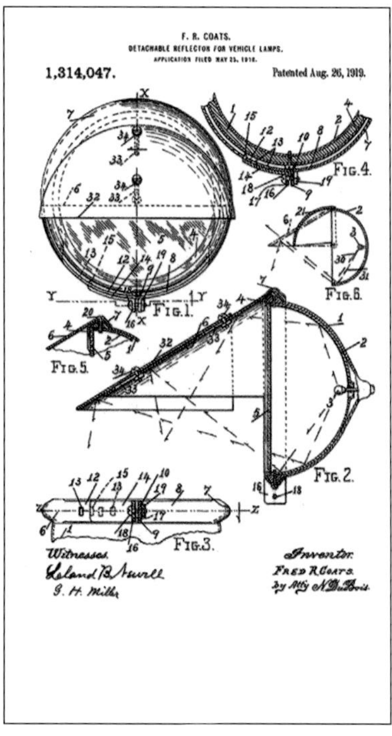

Two automotive-related Coats patents, from 1896 and 1919, respectively

At the height of the war, in 1943, Coats sold his company to the John W. Hobbs Company, then a manufacturer of automotive accessories. After fifty years of running his factories and successfully expanding his business, and nearly sixty-five years of working hard at his craft, Coats had decided it was time, at age seventy-seven, to slow down a bit. A local newspaper carried his explanation of why he decided to retire: "I feel as if I want to take things a little easier. It will give me an opportunity to do many things that I've planned, but which up to this point I haven't been able to do because of the press of the current business."[46]

Coats lived for another eight years in his house of Italian brick at 2181 Yale Boulevard, just across the street from his last factory. He died September 28, 1951, two weeks after his eighty-fifth birthday.

COATS'S NEIGHBORS

In September 2012, Rich and William Locherie, in separate interviews with the author, told about living next door to Coats as children in Springfield. As Coats became older, his day-to-day care and oversight was taken over by the Locherie family, with the brothers' father frequently looking in on him, as he lived alone. In fact, the morning of Coats's death he was found by the elder Locherie in the kitchen of the Coats home.

The Locherie brothers remember Coats as "eccentric" and "a genius." Coats was highly respected for his creative talents throughout Springfield. They mentioned that he was always very formally attired, in a three-piece suit, tie and hat.

The Locherie family ultimately purchased the Coats house. (William Locherie recalled that the Coats estate sold the "beautiful" home to the head of the Hobbs Corporation, who after a while sold it to his parents.) The house was very unusual: constructed to Coats's special specifications and needs, it had all of the bedrooms on one side of the house and the kitchen, dining room and living room facing directly across from the Coats Watch Materials Manufactory. Rich Locherie mentioned that the dining and living rooms were built especially large to provide extra space for entertaining.

The Locherie brothers remembered that Springfield was surprised when Italian-made bricks arrived at the construction site for the Coats home, especially as each brick for the entire house was individually wrapped in paper, a sight never before seen in Springfield.

Sangamo Connections

No study of the Illinois Watch Company would be complete without mentioning the Sangamo Electric Company. Illinois and Sangamo shared common management, facilities, working conditions and rules. Sangamo's success relied upon the financial backing of the Bunn family and the brilliant technical efforts of Robert C. Lanphier.

Lanphier, who cofounded the company, wrote an intimate and personal narrative covering the forty-year period from 1896 to 1936. Much of the following information was gleaned from this interesting book.[47]

Tom Sheridan and Ludwig Gutmann

According to Lanphier, the Sangamo Electric Company began as a direct result of an 1892 lawsuit against the Illinois Watch Company by the Waltham Watch Company. The suit revolved around the design of a pendant watch movement. Such lawsuits occurred frequently in the 1890s.

The Illinois Watch Company's master mechanic, Tom Sheridan, acted as principal expert for the Watch Company during this litigation. As a result of this legal experience, Sheridan quit his Watch Company job to study patent law, and soon became one of the best-known patent lawyers in Chicago. In 1895 his reputation attracted Ludwig Gutmann as a client.

Gutmann, an electrical engineer who had developed some novel ideas relating to electric meters, went to Sheridan to discuss patent applications. Sheridan immediately thought of Illinois Watch as a customer for Gutmann's ideas, since electric meters required a recording train. Sheridan felt that Illinois staff had the skill to produce such a recording train and could provide space and machinery to produce the meters. He also believed that a new product such as an electric meter would give Illinois an economic boost that would be welcome as the company began to recover from the economic depression of 1893.

Bunn Involvement

In early 1896, Sheridan told Jacob Bunn, Jr., then Vice President of Illinois Watch, about Gutmann. After meeting with Gutmann, Bunn described the invention to his father, Jacob Bunn, Sr., and suggested that the Illinois Watch Company consider making Gutmann's electric meters.

1896 HISTORICAL NOTES

- Wilhelm Roentgen announces the discovery of X-rays.
- Gold is discovered in the Klondike region of the Yukon Territory.
- The first modern Olympic Games open in Athens.
- Guglielmo Marconi patents the radio.
- The dial telephone is patented.

The idea did not appeal to the senior Bunn, however, so Bunn Jr. decided to finance Gutmann's ideas on his own in order to determine their viability. He thereupon arranged for Illinois Watch to make the mechanical parts for the models Gutmann wished to build. Gutmann busied himself winding the coils and assembly and testing the models.

Unfortunately, Gutmann found that he had neither the time nor the facilities to work out the necessary improvements to the models. Since no one at the Watch Factory knew enough about electricity to provide technical assistance, Bunn Jr. decided to stop the project. By then he had spent "a couple of hundred dollars" on these models and experiments. He did not feel like throwing away more money on Gutmann's inventions unless he could see some definite progress in the developing the ideas. Gutmann's models were stored in a box in the Illinois drafting department, and there they stayed through the early summer of 1897.

Robert C. Lanphier (1878–1939)

In June 1897, Springfield native Robert C. Lanphier graduated as an electrical engineer from Yale University. He returned to Springfield for a short vacation, intending to continue pursuing his career by joining the student course of the General Electric Company in Schenectady, New York.

Robert C. Lanphier at middle age

At a dinner on the Fourth of July, Lanphier saw Jacob Bunn, Jr., who asked about his electrical studies. Bunn sharedhis experience with Gutmann's electrical meter inventions, noting that Gutmann's models remained in a box at the Watch Factory. He admitted to Lanphier that he did not "know anything about these electrical devices and asked Lanphier whether he "could tell me whether there's anything to this matter." Lanphier went to the Watch Factory the next day to examine the models.

After looking in the box, Lanphier agreed to spend a couple of months to determine if it would be worth pursuing Gutmann's inventions. According to his recollection, Lanphier, "went to the Watch Factory on September 13, 1897, was given a small space in which to work, and was introduced to Otis White, then one of the principal tool makers in the Watch Factory machine shop, and with whom Bunn had arranged to do the fine mechanical work that he [Lanphier] might require in the course of his experiments."

At that time, the Watch Factory had gas lights, using gas made in its own plant. The Watch Factory had no electricity but powered its machinery with one large Corliss engine. Since Lanphier needed electricity to continue his experiments, he moved his work to the Watch Factory's machine shop. After conferring with Gutmann, Bunn authorized new models to be built. From December 1897 to March 1898, Otis White and Lanphier worked on these in the machine shop.

1897
HISTORICAL NOTES

- William McKinley is inaugurated as the twenty-fifth president of the United States.
- Thomas Edison patents his movie camera.

The Founding of Sangamo

In September 1898, Bunn Jr. approved production of the Gutmann meter. He arranged with Illinois Watch for the use of an additional machinist to work alongside White, and in November they rented the old mainspring building of the Watch Factory for their operations. In December 1898, on the cusp of production, Bunn and Gutmann decided to form a company, with Bunn providing the financing and Gutmann the patents. Lanphier's work provided the final ingredient for success.

Mr. Lanphier Goes To Europe

Robert C. Lanphier, General Manager of the Sangamo Electric Company, sailed from New York April 5th on the great Cunard liner, "Aquitania," for a three-months business trip in Europe. He will visit some of the important cities of England, France, Belgium, Holland, Spain, Italy, Denmark and Norway.

In most of these countries Sangamo is well represented at the present time, but where it is not, Mr. Lanphier expects to establish connections with some of the best-known importing houses. We hope that before his return Mr. Lanphier may have an opportunity of personally visiting the war zone in France and Italy and of obtaining some first-hand information as to the great work performed by the American Red Cross, with which he has been so actively associated throughout the entire duration of the war.

From February 1919 issue of *Doings*, reporting on Lanphier's trip to Europe to help expand Sangamo's business

Sangamo Night School

Preliminary arrangements have been made for the organization of three night school classes which will provide instruction in mechanical drawing, elementary electricity and magnetism, and advanced electricity and meter design. The class in mechanical drawing will be taught by Arthur Hahn of the Sangamo Drafting Department and will meet one night each week in the Sangamo Drafting Room from 7:30 to 9:30.

The classes in electricity will meet in the Sangamo Auditorium one night each week. The class in elementary electricity and magnetism will be taught by an experienced teacher in Physics from the City High School.

The class in advanced electricity and meter design will be taught by Mr. R. C. Lanphier and Mr. Fred Holtz.

These classes will be free to employees of the Sangamo Electric Co. and the Illinois Watch Co. and a large enrollment is desired.

Further arrangements will be made as to when these classes will meet.

Employees from the Sangamo Electric Company and the Illinois Watch Company were invited to take free company night school classes in electricity and other subjects. One class was taught by Lanphier. March 1919 issue of *Doings*

Sangamo continued producing electric meters in the Watch Factory's facilities without much change until a series of events altered Sangamo's course. On May 10, 1926, Jacob Bunn Jr., died. (He had probably been president of Sangamo since its inception, although some sources mention his brother Henry as the first one.) Robert Lanphier replaced him as president.[48] In July 1927, Sangamo became a corporation.

1926
HISTORICAL NOTES

- Thomas Edison says Americans prefer silent movies over talkies.
- Gene Tunney beats Jack Dempsey in ten rounds for the heavyweight boxing title.
- Ford announces an eight-hour, five-day work week.
- U.S. Route 66 opens.

The Hamilton-Sangamo Corporation

Hamilton's purchase of Illinois in January 1928 further affected Sangamo's operation as Hamilton management began to oversee the work at the Springfield plant. Illinois' closer association with Hamilton led to Sangamo's purchase of Hamilton's 11-jewel escapements. In September 1928, Hamilton's president, Charles Miller, suggested that Sangamo join Hamilton in entering the electric clock business. As a result, on July 1, 1929, the Hamilton-Sangamo Corporation was founded, owned equally by the two companies. Sangamo continued to manufacture clocks; Hamilton supplied the escapements and the sales experience.

In 1929, Sangamo constructed a giant clock in the shape of an Illinois Beau Brummell wristwatch to be used as a sales promotion tool by the Illinois sales team. Illinois used this clock at trade shows to help attract customers to the Illinois booths. The Great Depression, however, overtook the plans of both Illinois and Sangamo.

A Hamilton strap watch eight feet long was an outstanding hit of the jewelry shows—at both Cincinnati and Chicago. It makes a fine belt for the pigmy elephant in the Cincinnati Zoological gardens where one of the ANRJA meetings was held. Henry W. Von Unruh, President of ANRJA, is helping the elephant face the camera.

A HAMILTON WATCH IN GOOD COMPANY

Some of the ladies attending the recent ANRJA Convention came into the limelight when they were photographed holding this giant Hamilton wrist watch. Left to right they are: Mrs. Ray Grassmuck, Cincinnati; Ruth Adele Dickason, Tyler, Texas; Sue Wagner, Cincinnati; Mrs. L. S. Dickason, Tyler, Texas; Mrs. Frieda Wagner, Mrs. O. B. Wise, Margaret Benish, and Mrs. Clifford Simper, all of Cincinnati.

Shown in this photograph from the October 1934 issue of the *Keystone* is the large Illinois Watch Company advertising display clock manufactured by the Sangamo Electric Company for Illinois Watch. A few years after the acquisition, Hamilton converted this Illinois clock to a Hamilton one and took it to trade shows.

This is how the large display was intended to look before Hamilton converted it to a "Hamilton" model for its trade show use.

Sangamo "Electric" logo

The Depression led to a drop in business at Hamilton-Sangamo. In the spring of 1930, General Time Instrument Corporation (GTI) offered to buy the Hamilton-Sangamo corporation, and the business was sold to GTI Corporation in April 1931. Hamilton and Sangamo retired from the clock business with considerable losses.

The fate of the large Beau Brummell clock symbolized the relationship between Illinois and Hamilton. As Illinois watch sales dwindled, along with Hamilton's interest in the continued viability of Illinois, use of the large clock by Illinois ceased. Hamilton later resurrected the clock, now with the Hamilton name emblazoned on it, and continued using it to promote its own watches. See Chapter 12 for further information.

Another Very Special Bunn
Jacob Bunn, Jr. (1865–1926)

Owing to his father's financial difficulties Jacob Bunn, Jr., the youngest son of Jacob Bunn, was compelled to leave high school at the age of sixteen. On September 13, 1881 he started work at the Illinois Watch Company in its Machine Shop. For the next six years he rotated through most of the company's departments, learning the watch making business from the bottom to the top. He was clearly destined for higher positions. Just over a year after joining the company, he was placed in charge of the Watch Company's display at the Western Mechanic's Fair in Milwaukee, Wisconsin. Then, at the tender age of 21, in January 1887 he was dispatched to New York City to take charge of the Watch Company's New York regional sales office.

In May 1889, Bunn Jr. moved the New York office from its jewelry district location on Maiden Lane to the brand new Corbin building, located at 13 John Street at the corner of Broadway in the financial district of Manhattan.

Corbin Building, 1889. This now landmark building was built in 1888–1889 and was designed by Francis H. Kimball in the Romanesque Revival style. The building was named for Austin Corbin, a president of the Long Island Railroad.

Two years later he sailed for Europe on company business, spending six weeks in London and Paris. This trip helped expand his international knowledge. That same year he was named an Illinois vice president.

From his New York base, Bunn, Jr. also toured different geographic regions in the United States for the Illinois Watch Company, meeting frequently with jobbers and jewelers; learning first hand their issues and needs; and gaining the pulse of the marketplace. After seven years in New York, he returned to Springfield in May, 1894. With his departure, the New York office was closed "for the present" to help Illinois Watch weather the latest national economic meltdown.

In 1897, the 32-year-old Bunn assumed the presidency of the Illinois Watch Company upon the death of his father. By that time, he had already acquired sixteen years of watch making experience and knowledge. No person could have been better prepared and qualified to assume the control of a major watch manufacturing company. At the time of his death, his obituary noted that he had a passion for all the details of his watch business, right down to the typography, design and color of the Illinois catalogs and advertisements.[49]

Having left school before graduating high school, he acquired his knowledge beyond the watch industry by extensive reading, travel and frequent contact with knowledgeable people. Bunn Jr. was known for his "extraordinary mind and almost perfect memory" which enabled him to become "of the best mind and most intelligent of Illinois citizens."[50]

In 1913, at the age of 48, he married Mildred Jeffress of Edwardville, Illinois. She was twenty-two years his junior. Jacob and Mildred had three children: Jacob Jr., Henry III and Alice.[51] In 1930, Jacob Bunn, Jr. and his brother and sister were the principal heirs of the $1.5M estate ($17M in todays' dollars) left by their uncle John W. Bunn in June, 1920, thus immediately making Jacob and his siblings very wealthy.

Bunn, in addition to his twenty-nine years as president of the Watch Company, simultaneously served as president of the Sangamo Electric Company and the Springfield Marine Bank. All of these businesses enjoyed prosperity and growth under his leadership. The Watch Factory, in particular, experienced success and profitability to such an extent that it attracted the acquisition interest of one of its largest competitors following his death.

FEARS RABIES, ENDS HIS LIFE.

Man Bitten by Mad Squirrel Dies to Avoid Hydrophobia.

Springfield, Ill., Sept. 15.—Fred Peterson, 40 years old, ended his life in his room yesterday because he feared he would be a victim of hydrophobia, having been bitten by a rabid squirrel. Peterson swallowed acid while six other victims of the mad animal were preparing to go to Chicago to undergo treatment at the Pasteur Institute. Peterson's body was found this morning by Jacob Bunn, president of the Illinois Watch Company, by whom the decedent was employed as coachman. Peterson was bitten after he had captured the squirrel, and later succeeded in killing the animal. He is a former resident of Chicago.

Jacob Bunn, Jr.'s coachman suffered a tragic end after being bitten by a rabid squirrel. *Hutchinson News* (Hutchinson, KS), September 15, 1908; image from *newspapers.com*

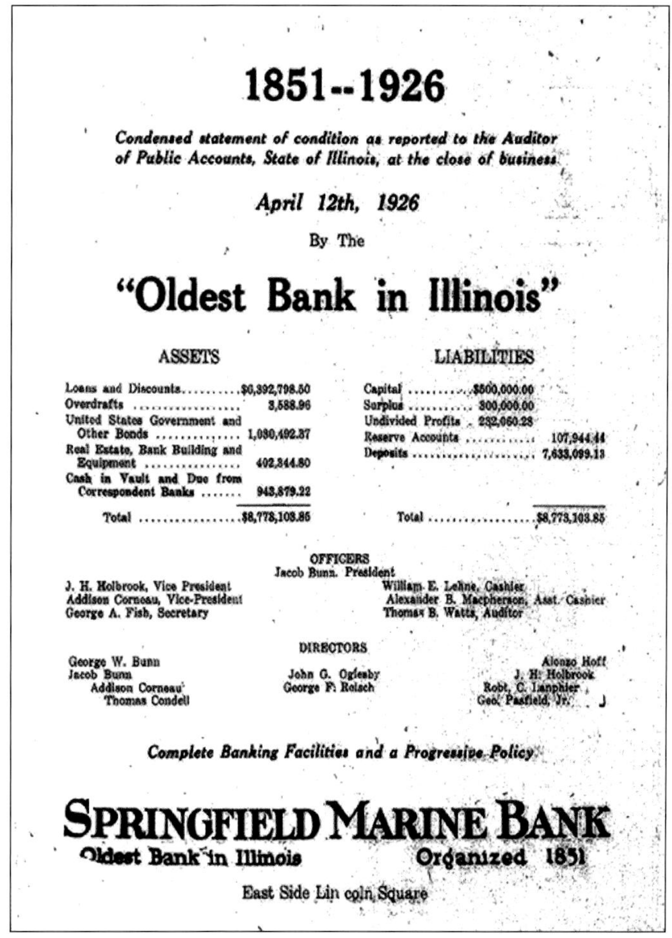

1851--1926

Condensed statement of condition as reported to the Auditor of Public Accounts, State of Illinois, at the close of business

April 12th, 1926

By The

"Oldest Bank in Illinois"

ASSETS		LIABILITIES	
Loans and Discounts	$6,392,798.50	Capital	$500,000.00
Overdrafts	3,588.96	Surplus	300,000.00
United States Government and Other Bonds	1,030,492.37	Undivided Profits	232,060.28
Real Estate, Bank Building and Equipment	402,344.80	Reserve Accounts	107,944.44
Cash in Vault and Due from Correspondent Banks	943,879.22	Deposits	7,633,099.13
Total	$8,773,103.85	Total	$8,773,103.85

OFFICERS

Jacob Bunn, President

J. H. Holbrook, Vice President
Addison Corneau, Vice-President
George A. Fish, Secretary
William E. Lehne, Cashier
Alexander B. Macpherson, Asst. Cashier
Thomas B. Watts, Auditor

DIRECTORS

George W. Bunn
Jacob Bunn
Addison Corneau
Thomas Condell
John G. Oglesby
George F. Reisch
Alonzo Hoff
J. H. Holbrook
Robt. C. Lanphier
Geo. Pasfield, Jr.

Complete Banking Facilities and a Progressive Policy

SPRINGFIELD MARINE BANK

Oldest Bank in Illinois — Organized 1851

East Side Lincoln Square

Illinois State Journal, April 20, 1926

ENGAGEMENT OF COUPLE ANNOUNCED

Mr. Jacob Bunn and Miss Mildred Jeffress to be Wedded.

Illinois State Journal, August 29, 1913

Bunn, like his father Jacob Sr. and Uncle John W. before him, exhibited a talent for founding and guiding new businesses. He was actively engaged in hotels, banks, harness racing tracks and refrigeration companies, in addition to overseeing the Watch Company and the Sangamo Electric Company. He also showed a great sense of civic and moral commitment. By the end of 1925, under his guidance, the Bunn family completed repayment of $800,000 in debt to the five thousand people who had lost money when his father's (Jacob Bunn Sr.'s) bank failed in 1878. In the ensuing thirty-seven-year period, the repayment included 240% in accumulated interest without there being any legal obligation for the family to pay either principle or interest.

Even with all of his many business obligations, Bunn Jr. found time to serve on Republican Party committees; attend social events; play and support baseball (a passion of his); found at least two golf country clubs; and serve on numerous boards . In 1925, true to his benevolent nature, he donated seventy-four acres of land for a Boy Scout camp in Springfield. As the Bunn family biographer Andrew Call stated:

> "After the death of Jacob Bunn, his sons Henry and Jacob Bunn, Jr., perpetuated the civic spirit of the Illinois Watch Company. They ensured that the corporation that they were now managing remained true to its commitment to improve its community and its dedication to aid people in all areas of the United States and abroad. The company continued to exhibit commercially-oriented civic spirit, continued to promote civic improvement through constructive social organizations, and perpetually retained the respect that it had earned from its employees."[52]

Further evidence of this civic spirit was his establishment of the Lincoln Essay Contest in 1924. This program allowed twenty-three thousand American high schools to organize a Lincoln essay contest each year. Bunn never allowed his name to be used in conjunction with the Lincoln Essay Contest and he was very careful that no advertising be associated with the medals. This reflected Jacob Bunn, Jr.'s style, as he consistently performed his civic responsibilities in the "quietest possible manner, never seeking praise for himself.[53] Hamilton halted this program after it acquired Illinois.

Jacob Bunn (seated at left) and his son, Jacob Bunn, Jr., (seated at right) sitting in the principal administrative office of the Illinois Watch Company. (From the Sangamon Valley Collection at the Lincoln Library, Springfield, Illinois)

A very interesting game of base ball will be played at League Park this afternoon at 3:30, when the fourth annual game will take place between the Qui Vives and G. S. D. C.'s. This promises to a very close and hotly contested game, as the losing club will pay all the expenses of a swell dance, to be given in the near future. All the young society ladies will be in attendance, waving the colors of their favorites, which is Qui Vive red, O. S. D. C. blue. Mr. Stuart Brown will act as umpire, and Mr. Peachy Clover as ground superintendent, having full charge of police and water departments, bats, ball, etc. Mr. Jack Nuckols and Mr. Jacob Bunn, jr., will act as captains of their respective sides. In the following contested nines will be recognized some excellent base ball talent:

Qui Vives		O. S. D. C.
Golden	Catcher	Mahoney
Pease	Pitcher	E. Brown
G. Bunn	1st b	Vincent
J. Nuckols, jr.	2d b	Tracy
Ed. Wilkinson	3d b	McCreery
R. Nuckols	L F	F. Dodds
Yates	C F	Wolf
Humphreys	R F	Miller
Ridgely	S S	J. Bunn, jr

Illinois State Register, May 21, 1884. Jacob Bunn, Jr. evidently also played shortstop.

JACOB BUNN IS CRITICALLY ILL AT RESIDENCE

Illinois State Journal, January 3, 1926

Bunn, Jr. caught a slight cold while on a California pleasure trip in September 1925. When he came home, he contracted influenza, adding to his health woes. He was confined to his bed where he was declared to have a "very slim" chance of recovery. His health became progressively worse. On several occasions, reports surfaced that he was not expected to survive, but rallied each time. He finally succumbed on May 10, 1926 at the age of 61. Ironically, back in October, 1918 he served on a state committee to raise funds for the manufacture of a vaccine to prevent influenza developed by a physician at the Mayo Clinic.

Jacob Bunn, Jr., c. 1920s

The *Illinois State Journal*'s extensive and heartfelt obituary, pointed out that his relations with those in his employ, were personal and pleasant. He was approachable, even to the humblest.

> "In all his life. . .he insisted on being himself; a quiet, unassuming, affable, approachable, kindly, honorable man who found pleasure in doing much and in everything he undertook to do; a pleasure enhanced in his enjoyment the less he was praised."[54]

During his tenure as Illinois' president, Bunn, Jr. focused the company on making high grade watches while scrupulously protecting the Illinois watch reputation. "Owing to his high ethical standards he possessed an unusual pride in the quality of his watches. He insisted that the public must be served promptly, cordially, satisfactorily. The humblest customer was as worthy as the largest."[55]

Jacob Bunn, Jr., had a tremendous positive and stable influence on the Watch Company. He championed the production of high quality products and demonstration of ethics in business, as well as openness, fairness and good benefits to his employees. Under his leadership, Illinois transformed from a pocket watch producer to the manufacturer of fashionably popular wristwatches. By the time of his death, he had positioned the company to compete effectively and creatively in the new wristwatch industry.

Hamilton's Miller Dynasty

When the Hamilton Watch Company assumed control of Illinois in January 1928, it named Robert Everts Miller as president and general manager of Illinois. Miller, who had previously served as second vice president in charge of production at Hamilton, was the son of the president of Hamilton, Charles F. Miller.

The Miller family had established roots in Lancaster, Pennsylvania, before the Civil War. Robert's grandfather, Herman Miller, who had emigrated from Württemberg, Germany, began a soap and candle business in Lancaster. Herman died in 1878, but the business continued to be run by the Millers. The firm, known as the Miller Soap Company, specialized in perfumed and specialty soaps.[56]

Charles F. Miller (1861–1931)

Charles Frederick Miller followed in his father's steps. Before the turn of the century, Charles had become the head of the Miller Soap Company. By 1909 he had expanded into the grocery business. Already a well-known businessman in Lancaster, Charles became treasurer of Hamilton in 1909. A year later, he succeeded Charles Rood as Hamilton's president. Because of his background in soap, the workforce nicknamed him "Soapy."

Charles F. Miller became a legend as president of Hamilton. Of Miller's presidency, Don Sauers commented: "[Miller] reigned longer than any other [president]; for 21 peaceful, profitable years—a full generation."[57] His contemporaries saw Charles as "a solid, conservative, paternal person that cared about his people.[58]

Under Charles's leadership, Hamilton's financial position kept improving. In the late 1920s, Miller authorized a Christmas cash bonus for each employee. This so-called wage dividend represented the substantial sum of $93,000, or 5% of Hamilton's annual payroll.[59] The appreciation of Hamilton stock over the years reflected the measure of Miller's success. From 1896 to 1929, Hamilton sold no new common stock, but the total value of the issued stock grew from $500,000 to $6.3 million; an impressive increase of 1,160%.

To further capitalize on Hamilton's financial success, Charles Miller oversaw three acquisitions during his term as president: first, in 1927, the acquisition of the E. Howard Watch Company name and, subsequently, in 1931, the purchase of its goodwill and trademarks; second, the acquisition of the complete Illinois Watch Company operation; and, finally, the absorption of the Sangamo Electric Company.

Of the three, the Illinois acquisition ranked the highest in importance. The Hamilton board of directors authorized the purchase of the Illinois Watch Company, effective January 1, 1928. Hamilton funded this transaction by selling $4.8 million of Hamilton's 6% preferred stock.

1928
Historical Notes

- Amelia Earhardt becomes the first female to fly across the Atlantic.
- Sliced bread is sold for the first time by the Chillicothe Baking Company of Chillicothe, Missouri. It is described as the greatest forward step in the baking industry since bread was wrapped.
- George Eastman shows the first color motion picture.
- Alexander Fleming discovers penicillin.

Robert E. Miller (1891–1974)

On the day Hamilton announced its acquisition of Illinois, Charles Miller sent his son Robert to manage the Illinois operation in Springfield.

Born in Lancaster, Pennsylvania, Robert Everts Miller graduated from Haverford College in 1912 and became the advertising manager at the Hamilton Watch Company in 1915. (This was far from the only instance of nepotism during this Hamilton era.) After serving in the U.S. Army Aviation Signal Corps in 1918 during World War I, he was employed by Hamilton as a vice president until 1928, when he moved to Springfield to become president and general manager of the Illinois Watch Division.

ROBERT EVERTS MILLER —"BOB" "FUZZY"—

Despite a certain tendency toward avoirdupois which has been apparent since his youth, Bob's agility is much in evidence. Witness his leap for liberty from Bickel's classroom window and his wonderful feats of flying; the last time Swarthmore was defeated was when Fuzzy did it with his aeroplane.

And what a ladies' man he is! Fuzzy is one of our "suspected seven," though he does not give evidence of concentration. He maintains (even in the slack season) an average of five feminine notes daily. This extraordinary feat is explained in two ways,—First, Fuzzy has a theory: "There is no use talking nonsense to a girl just because she is a girl." He applies his principle, and—well, he gets results. The other reason is his hair, which, when once cut *à la penitentiary*, defied for six months brushes, tonics, weights, derbies, etc., and upright "showed like a stubble field at harvest home." The girls? Oh, yes, we forgot,—they enjoyed the sensation. Ever since, Bob has been Fuzzy, and so let him remain. It suits him well.

His portly form has so impressed the class that they have elected him Senior President (he is our "justice with fair, round belly!") and made him Business Manager of the Class Record. Too much cannot be said for his efficiency. It is mean work hunting ads.—we speak from the bitterness of experience—and we are only too glad to give honor where honor's due. However, the cares of state do occasionally hang heavy on his shoulders and he has won the class vote of being the biggest gloom (see Statistics).

"For it's simple enough to be grouchy
When nothing is going your way,
But the prize old growl
Is the man who can howl
When everything's going O. K."

But Fuz is most noted for his kinship with "E. I." and his personal edition of the Roman Classics with English translations.

Satirical write-up from the Haverford College yearbook about "Bob" "Fuzzy" "Avoirdupois" Miller in 1912

CALVIN M. KENDIG (1877 -1953)

Calvin M. Kendig, May 1934

Calvin Miles Kendig started to work for the Hamilton Watch Company in 1902. He joined as head bookkeeper and then secured progressively more responsible positions of cost accountant, purchasing agent, assistant treasurer (appointed in March 1920), and secretary to the board of directors (Robert E. Miller held this position in 1922). In 1931 he attained the position of vice president. He then became a vice president of sales, president in 1939 and finally chairman of the board.

Kendig was president of Hamilton from 1939 to 1948. During his tenure, sales increased from $6,491,013 to $15,595,723.

When he and Robert Miller were assigned to run the Illinois Watch Division, although Miller was to serve as the president and general manager of Illinois Watch, Kendig was clearly the more experienced and senior watch executive. In fact, Kendig's annual salary at this time was exactly double that of Miller.

When the National Industrial Recovery Act was passed in 1933, the American Jeweled Watch Manufacturers organized as an entity and Kendig was elected its first president, requiring him to make frequent trips to Washington, D.C.

Calvin Kendig retired as chairman of the board of Hamilton on April 11, 1951, after fifty years of service. Rudolph Kant, then president, also assumed the role of chairman.

Upon his arrival, Robert Miller immediately announced that Hamilton would not interfere with the way Illinois conducted business. Illinois personnel probably took this news with a sense of relief. However, within eight months a massive layoff was announced, and the onset of the Great Depression would force a series of adverse changes for Illinois, ultimately leading to its demise.

The Hamilton announcement had characterized Robert's assignment to Illinois as temporary. For that reason perhaps, Robert accepted his election to the board of directors of the Lancaster YMCA in February 1928. Robert Miller managed Illinois until the end of Springfield production, never returning to Lancaster from his "temporary" assignment.

Charles Miller had also temporarily dispatched another second vice-president, the assistant treasurer Calvin Kendig, to monitor the Illinois operation. Kendig did return to Lancaster and later became a president of the Hamilton Watch Company.

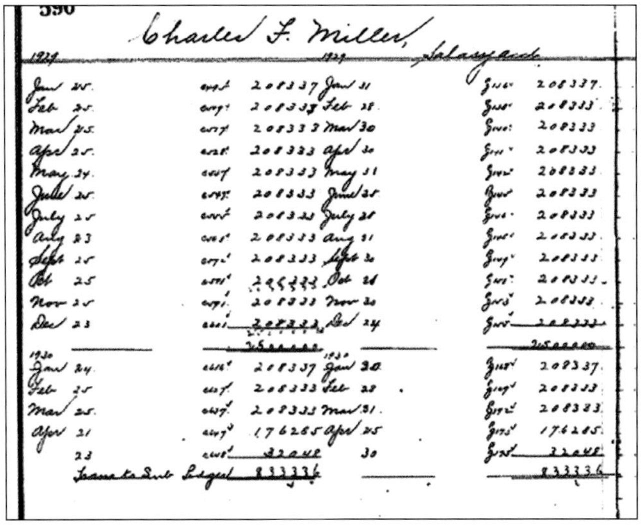

The 1929 Hamilton handwritten General Ledger payroll records for both Millers in 1929

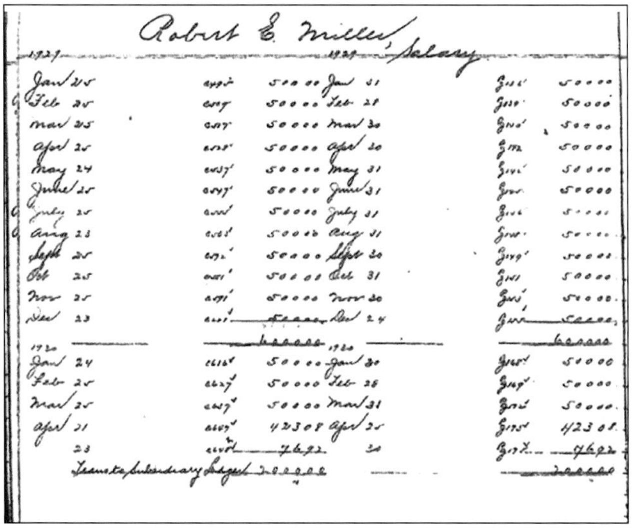

Hamilton's financial records raise questions about Robert's role in the Illinois operation. A review of one of the 1929 Hamilton financial ledgers disclosed that Charles Miller, Hamilton's president, earned a monthly salary of around $2,000 or just over $24,000 per annum. The records show that Kendig earned $12,000 a year. Robert Miller, at the same time, earned only $6,000 per year.

Although in 1933 the Illinois Factory was closed and the machinery moved to Lancaster, Hamilton continued to use the Illinois name and produced watches of that brand on and off until 1955, most of them with Swiss movements (see Chapter 11).

Robert Miller's tenure at Illinois came at a time when Illinois produced its most unique, attractive, and (today) collectible watch models. If we take Miller at his word that Hamilton did not wish to interfere in Illinois' marketing strategy, the impetus behind Illinois' creativity must have been due directly to the efforts of Illinois' own staff. The large numbers and creative and bold styles of wristwatches produced by Illinois did not abate until near the end of production in 1932. Miller's (and Hamilton's) approach to give Illinois staff a free hand in continuing its product plans, strategy and approach not only caused the firm to produce a great variety of interesting models, but also to vastly increase advertising of its watch line. However, most of this advertising was designed to reduce an excessive supply of pocket watch movements and parts (see Chapter 5).

Unfortunately, events overtook Robert Miller and the Illinois Watch Company. The onset of the Great Depression led to a drop in watch sales, decreasing the viability of Illinois as a watch manufacturer under Hamilton. There were other factors as well: Hamilton's president and Robert's father, Charles Miller, died on July 18, 1931.

The Hamilton board of directors did not appreciate the Miller legacy enough to ask Robert Miller to join the board or assume Hamilton's presidency. They left Robert in Springfield. Instead, the board selected Frank C. Beckwith to become Hamilton's new president, succeeding the elder Miller. The board apparently felt Beckwith's experience as first vice president and sales manager to be compelling factors in his selection.

Calvin Kendig, who had accompanied Robert Miller to Springfield, succeeded to the position of first vice president. Kendig ultimately replaced Beckwith as president when the board promoted Beckwith to chairman in 1939.

FRANK C. BECKWITH (1871-1954)

Frank Clarence Beckwith worked for the Joseph Fahys & Company watch case maker for twelve years as its sales manager. He joined Hamilton in 1909, also as sales manager. Beckwith was elected as Hamilton's vice president on February 11, 1920, and in August 1931 was elected president after the death of Charles F. Miller the preceding month.

F. C. Beckwith, May 1934

Beckwith took over the reins of Hamilton when it was about to face the worst economic conditions in its history as the devastating effects of the Great Depression were just starting to impact the entire watch industry severely. As a result, whereas Miller had overseen the acquisition of Illinois, Beckwith, owing to the severe economic conditions, was unfortunately compelled to oversee its demise. Beckwith and Hamilton probably determined by 1931 that the company could not continue to sustain two geographically separate production facilities in the prevailing depressed business conditions (details concerning this decision are in Chapter 5.) Another factor was the "Hamilton Zone Distribution Plan" developed under Beckwith's direction to revamp the sales and marketing methodology of Hamilton to help it survive and prosper in the era of "E.Z. Credit" jewelers and price-cutters.

Beckwith passed away in Lancaster, Pennsylvania, on September 9, 1954, after a long illness.

KEYSTONE—*Jewelry Trade Ne[ws]*

We Hope It's Just Au Revoir, Bob

ROBERT E. MILLER

THE countless trade friends of R. E. "Bob" Miller whose name has long been identified with the Hamilton Watch Co. and more recently with the Illinois Watch will join with "The Keystone" in expressing regret over the announcement that Mr. Miller is leaving the jewelry industry to accept a position as vice-president of the Springfield, Ill., Marine Bank. This is the same bank of which the late Jacob Bunn was formerly president. Mr. Miller assumes his new duties July 1 and in a letter to "The Keystone" states in part: "My regret is that I can't have a last trip around the trade to say 'Goodbye' to a lot of my good friends whom I have enjoyed knowing so well for the past twenty years."

We hope, however, Bob that it is not "Goodbye" but just Au Revoir—and that before many moons we will have you back in the industry of which you were so much a part.

The *Keystone* in July 1933 sadly reported the departure of Robert E. Miller from the Illinois Watch Company.

In July 1933, when Hamilton was in the process of shuttering the watch works in Springfield, Robert Miller resigned to join the Springfield Marine Bank as a vice president in charge of its Trust Department. Miller had been elected a director of this bank while serving as the head of the Illinois Watch Division. (Ironically, the Trust Department at the Springfield Marine Bank had originally been set up by John Whitfield Bunn.[60])

In 1942, Miller left the corporate world for a while, again to join the Army Air Corps, in which he had served during World War I. (Four of his five sons also served in the military during World War II.)

After his years with Hamilton and Illinois, and his positions with the Springfield Marine Bank, Miller was involved with other businesses, retiring in 1961 as president of National Airlines Terminal Corporation, an airport design firm in Ypsilanti, Michigan. (He had also served as a director of the Argus Camera Company.) Thus it is clear that he did achieve success as a businessman, but not through his tenure with the Illinois Watch Company.

(Robert Miller's brother Frederick Stahl Miller [1900–1961] also became a successful businessman. Like his brother, he graduated from Haverford College and later worked for a while in the watch industry. He began his career at Hamilton and then was briefly at Illinois before taking a job with the Armstrong Cork Company. Since Armstrong management served on the Hamilton board and made the iconic celluloid display boxes for Hamilton, that board member probably found the job for Frederick. He moved to the American Smelting and Refining Company in 1941 and continued working there until his death. At the time, he was assistant treasurer and general credit manager of the company.)

Summary

The Illinois Watch Company was founded at a time of great expansion of the American watch industry. Sandwiched between the foundings of Elgin and Rockford, it was representative of manufacturing activity in the Midwest during the era after the Civil War. The Springfield company was long fortunate in the people who took an interest in it, beginning with the horological activist John C. Adams, who played such an important role in the company's founding, just as he had at Elgin and would later do for the predecessors of Hamilton.

Illinois' greatest good fortune, however, was that it attracted the attention of the Bunn family. Typical nineteenth-century entrepreneurs, the Bunns were involved with promoting many enterprises, from their original grocery business to railroads and banking. The Watch Company must have been a particular favorite of theirs, because they were involved with the company from its founding and led it from its reorganization through its next half century as an independent business. How deeply the Bunns were involved is evident from the fact that after its fitful startup, the company eventually became the sole property of the Bunn family.

Under the leadership of the Bunns, Illinois showed not only resilience but flexibility. The company successfully made the transition from manufacturing cheap watches to compete with Waltham and Elgin to concentrating on the high end, where their surviving competition was primarily Hamilton. Illinois was also early to make a transition towards wristwatch manufacturing and making design and style a key to their marketing efforts.

The Bunns were not only outstanding businessmen; they could attract the technological talent needed for the success of their business. Some of the earliest engineering leaders, like Currier, Hoyt, and Mason, came from Elgin, which had previously hired them away from Waltham. And later the Bunns attracted creative technologists like DeLong, Johnson, and Coats, who aided the company in its progression to the top of the watchmaking industry.

What would have happened to Illinois had Jacob Bunn, Jr. not died in 1926 cannot be known, but the sale of Illinois to Hamilton at the end of the next year also never had a chance to evolve unconstrained by external events. In the first year of its ownership, Hamilton seemed to be looking for the right management strategy, only to have Black Tuesday and its aftermath soon change American business in new and unforeseen ways. But that is a story to be examined in later chapters.

CHAPTER 2

A Window into the Illinois Workplace

While contemporary writers celebrated the feats of capitalists and inventors, they tended to ignore the plight of the factory worker. The common wage-earners felt the harshest realities of the decade-long depression of the 1870s. Most workers felt lucky just to hold a job; those at Illinois were luckier than most.

Manufacturers set high standards for their employees. Labor-intensive industries wrung every bit of productivity out of workers. Owners did not do this for greed, but in order to produce manufactured goods at prices the public would and could afford. Significantly, the richest families of the period—the Rockefellers, Vanderbilts, Morgans and DuPonts—did not derive their wealth primarily from manufactured goods, but from transportation, finance or exploitation of raw materials. Most owners of manufacturing plants did not grow exceedingly rich from their investments.

Judging from the history of the Elgin National Watch Company, in Elgin, Illinois, production processes changed in the 1870s to increase productivity. In the early years of the decade, an employee "might have [had] several responsibilities, working on one job for a time, then switching to another."[1] At the time, "many employees were accustomed to socializing on the job." However, task variety and relaxed work ethic "gave way to the efficiencies and disciplines of mass production. 'It is an axiom in manufacturing,' explained [Elgin] Superintendent Hunter, 'that in any line where the volume of business is sufficient, division of labor should be carried to a point where one worker does a single operation, however trivial.'" This led to repetitive, assembly-line operations being performed by each worker.

Manufacturers held factory workers to strict rules to keep productivity high. This can be learned from a description of what was likely to have been the experience of an ordinary factory worker at Elgin in 1879. The factory regimen emphasized punctuality, strict attention to work, and accuracy. In this regard, the Illinois Watch Company was no exception.

Typical Rules for Watch Factory Workers

If you were hired for a new job at a watch factory sometime around 1879, you would have found that management did not draw a strict line between your personal life and your factory career, but dictated that affairs in your life outside the factory also were the company's business. If, for example, evidence had existed that your wages were garnished, either you would not have been hired or you would have been dismissed immediately.[2]

Upon arrival at work, you probably would have been advised by a member of the "industrial relations" department or by your immediate supervisor that the normal expected workday was from 7:00 a.m. to 12:00 noon, and from 1:00 p.m. to 6:00 p.m., Monday through Saturday. In that era, ten-hour workdays were the norm for all workers, regardless of gender or age. Before the beginning of each work day, a bell would ring: first at ten minutes before 7:00 a.m. or 1:00 p.m., with a final warning bell at one minute before the time to commence work.

(Elgin, with a union in place, reduced its workday to nine hours on May 1, 1901, on weekdays and closed at 4:00 p.m. on Saturday instead of at 5:00 p.m.[3] At Illinois, with no union in place, the workers apparently stayed at ten hours per day well into the 1900s, but the Saturday closing moved up to 1:00 p.m.)

The following wholesale jewelers have agreed to close their respective places of business at 1 o'clock p. m. Saturdays from May 4 until Aug. 31: Illinois Watch Company, Elgin National Watch Company, Robbins & Appleton, Joseph Fahy & Co., Brooklyn Watch Case Company, Blauer Watch Case Company, Keystone Watch Case Company, Illinois Watch Case Company, the Weber Company, M. Benjamin, Aikin, Lambert & Co., F. A. Hardy & Co., M. C. Eppenstein & Co., M. A. Mead & Co., F. E. Morse & Son, G. D. Brethauer, H. Muhr's Sons, E. Howard Watch and Clock Company, Courvoisier-Wilcox Manufacturing Company, Western Watch Case Company, Gilbert Clock Company, Ansonia Clock Company, Ingraham Clock Company, Julien Gallet & Co., Lapp & Flershem, Heintz Bros., Henry Oppenheimer & Sons, C. H. Knights & Co., Louis Manheimer, H. F. Hahn & Co., L. Tannenbaum & Co., Metzenberg & Co., Joseph & Greenebaum, A. & L. Feisenthal, Cogswell & Wallis, C. F. Happel & Co., F. M. Sproehnle & Co., A. Hirsch & Co., J. S. Gratz, F. Lewald & Co., Kind, Abt & Co., J. H. Purdy & Co., George E. Marshall, E. W. Burchard & Co., Glickauf & Newhouse, *Jewelers' Review*, B. Grieshaber.

In 1889, the Illinois Watch Company, Elgin, Fahys and Keystone, among others, adjusted their summer hours, agreeing to close at 1:00 p.m. on Saturdays from May 4 until August 31, 1889. *Chicago Daily Tribune*, May 12, 1889; image from *newspapers.com*

As the engines within each department would start promptly at preestablished times, you would be required to be present at your workstation at that time or face a deduction of not less than fifteen minutes from your pay. In fact, as a general practice, the factory door would be locked at five minutes past 7:00 a.m. and 1:00 p.m. each workday. Anyone not arriving before the door was locked was refused admission to their work area until "quarter time," with a commensurate docking of pay.

You would be solely responsible for the tools you used as well as for your work area. You were required to keep both in good order. You would be allowed ten minutes at the close of business on Saturdays to clean your tools and work area; the entire ten minutes had to be devoted to these tasks.

You were not allowed to leave work either at noon or at night, or even make preparations to leave, until the bell sounded. Then there would be stampedes out the front door. (After a while, the Illinois Watch Company decided it had to let women leave first lest they be trampled in the chaotic rush out the door.)

During work hours you were not permitted to have any exchanges with other departments that were not work related. Such discussions had to take place via your foreman or his representative.

Visiting in other departments or in the corridors was strictly prohibited. Your department was expected to be "quiet and orderly" at all times in all sections of the watch factory.

The Illinois Watch Factory, c. 1910s

Reading was not allowed during working hours. Because of the nature of the work, no smoking was permitted in the factory. This non-smoking rule extended even to the grounds of the factory. And nothing was allowed to be thrown out of the watch factory's windows.

You were not permitted to perform any work other than the company's within the watch factory.

If you wanted to be absent from work, you were required to secure permission from the foreman of your department, who in turn had to inform the superintendent of the factory, no matter how short the absence might be.

If employees wanted to leave the factory, they were required to give ten days' advance notice. Employees were not allowed to bring non-employees into any part of the watch factory under any circumstances.

Although some of the rules may seem unduly strict, they were there for good reasons. Many necessarily dealt with issues related to productivity and the smooth running of the company. Others were related to safety issues. Some of these are obvious enough, such as the smoking prohibition. Others are less so. For example, Illinois' decision to let the women leave first to avoid being trampled in the rush may initially have had to do with women's typical attire in the late nineteenth and early twentieth centuries. In the early days of watch factories, women went to work wearing two petticoats, a long sweeping dress that brushed the floor, and high button shoes—a potentially hazardous combination in the rush out the door. (Pictures of factory employees also show that the men wore three-piece suits, ties and hats to work each day.)

The steam-powered belts on the Illinois Watch Factory equipment were very hazardous.

Of course, machinery in industrial operations almost always involves safety issues, even today. In the nineteenth and early twentieth centuries, factories were particularly dangerous places to work, even in relatively light industries like watch manufacture. In a typical shop, dozens of constantly moving belts came down from overhead line shafts to supply power to each machine tool. Workers at watchmaking lathes would find their faces only a few inches from moving belts. Thus, even a momentary distraction might cause a loss of concentration on the task at hand and lead to injury. Perhaps this is what happened in 1889 to Maggie Grady, an employee at the Illinois Watch Factory, who was scalped when her bangs got caught in some hanging shafting.[4] She was probably doing some sort of small parts work and inadvertently let her forehead get too close to the moving belt in her work area.

FASHION occasionally gets a violent setback. For example, Miss Maggie Grady, of Springfield, Ill., rejoiced in a bang of excessive length till Saturday last. Then while she was at work her bang caught in some shafting, and, in less time than the most adept Indian could have done it, she was scalped. Moral: Keep your bang out of your eyes—and out of the shafting.

A not very sensitive and highly offensive report of the tragedy involving Ms. Grady appeared in the *Pittsburgh Dispatch*, February 5, 1889; image from *newspapers.com*

Anti-Sweat Shop Law

As a result of the concern for underage workers and the issue of women's work hours, a new state law was enacted in Illinois in 1893. Companies were prohibited from hiring people under fourteen years of age, and women were not allowed to work more than eight hours per day. Elgin, however, "refused to obey the law, arguing that it was intended to apply only to sweat shops and not to well-lighted, heated and ventilated factories."[5] The Illinois Watch Company also refused to honor this new law. As a result, both Elgin and Illinois were both separately sued by the state. Both companies prevailed in their respective litigation, but "the Illinois Supreme Court later declared the legislation unconstitutional on the grounds that it abridged freedom of contract."[6]

MANUFACTURERS' PROTECTIVE ASSOCIATION

On September 29, 1893, a group of Illinois manufacturers met at the Grand Pacific Hotel in Chicago to organize in opposition to the Sweatshop Law of 1893 that prohibited child labor and mandated an eight-hour workday for women. The manufacturers formed the Illinois Manufacturers' Protective Association "for the purpose of cooperating to test the constitutionality of a recent act of the Legislature of this State limiting the hours of Female Labor." The Manufacturers' Protective Association sponsored a number of test cases that led to the Illinois Supreme Court finding that Section 5 of the Act, which limited women's working week to 48 hours and their day to eight hours, unconstitutional in 1895. The Elgin National Watch Company and Illinois Watch Company litigations were two of the test cases.

Female Workers in the Watch Industry

It is quite surprising that the Illinois Watch Company workforce as early as 1886 was 25% female, decades before Equal Opportunity laws prohibited gender-based discrimination. In that year, Illinois employed 528 total workers; of these, 355 were males and 173 were females, an almost exact 75/25% split. Also, not surprising for that time period, men earned double the daily wage earned by their female counterparts, notwithstanding that they performed exactly the same jobs. Men earned $2.31 per ten-hour day and women less than half that amount: $1.15 per ten-hour day.

And it was not only in wages per se that the women got short shrift. During the 1880s and 1890s, when Illinois was either laying off or discharging many workers because of overproduction, it seems sometimes to have been the women who were targeted. On June 16, 1889, for example, the *Chicago Daily Tribune* noted: "The Illinois Watch Company today discharged 100 more employees, mostly girls," mentioning that the workforce had been "gradually decreased since the first of the year, the reason being an overstocked market and little demand."

Although data about wages are not available from the Illinois Watch Company records for the first decade of the twentieth century, the women's experience there may have been similar to that at upstate Elgin. In 1909, after a woman's training period ended, "she could earn piecework wages, the average [Elgin] woman employee in 1909 could make about $6 to $7 a week, and room and board expenses would be about $4 to $5. No woman could hope to be in charge of one of the departments, but in those days that was to be expected."[7]

The number of female factory workers at Illinois had increased to 42.2% by 1910. According to the federal census completed in Springfield that year, of the total of 919 employees at the Illinois Watch Company, 389 were female and 530 were men. The majority of the women were single, and the majority of the men were married. The average age for the women was 25, and 38 for the men. The female workers were apparently younger than the males because women were pressured to quit work once they got married.

Women performed many job functions at the Illinois Watch Factory. Some of these jobs are illustrated in the accompanying still frames taken from a 1923 silent three-reel film made by the United States Department of the Interior at the Springfield plant.[8]

Women mounted jewels in the movements.

Women made up almost the entire Jeweling Department.

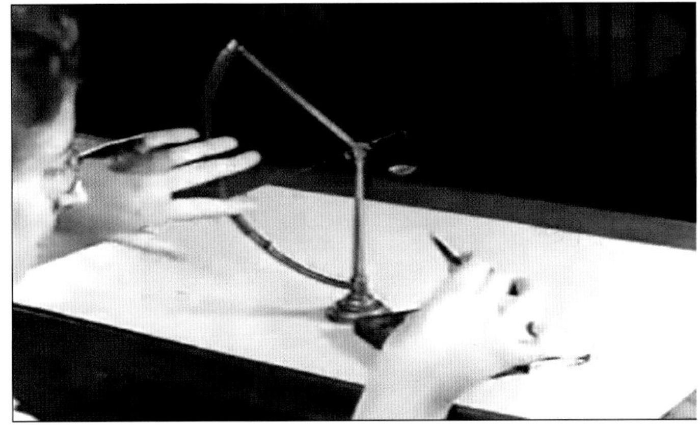

Weighting the balance

Measuring jewels

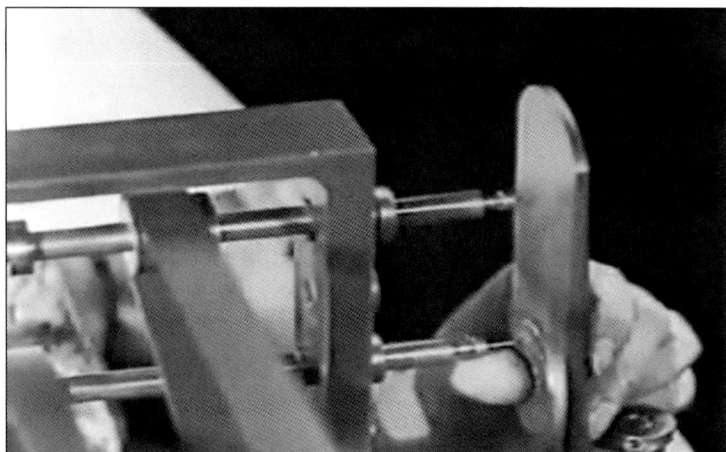

Drilling the main plate

Filling orders in the Materials Department

This 1905 photograph of an Illinois Watch Factory department shows the nearly 50/50 gender split.

The “Girls” of the Illinois Watch Factory

Fortunately, during the last quarter of the twentieth century there was interest in undertaking oral history projects about the experiences of former workers at the Illinois Watch Factory before it was too late to do so. In 1985, Joanna Lynn Harner interviewed a dozen former Illinois Watch Factory employees as part of her research for a master’s thesis in history at the former Sangamon State University, now the University of Illinois Springfield (UIS).[9]

292 **STATISTICS OF LABOR.**

Table XVIII.—Continued.

County and Occupation.	Number in each	Wages.				Working Time.		Payments.			
		Per hour.	Per day.	Per week	Per month.	Hours per day	Weeks per ye'r	Cash or trade.	No. weekly	No. fort-nightly	No. monthly
Sangamon county—Continued.											
Teacher	1				$50 00	8	*a*	Cash.			1
Telegraphers	2				40 00	10	*a*		1		1
Tilemakers	2	*a*				10	*a*		2		
Tinners	3		$3 00			10	*a*	Cash.	3		
Watch-factory workers*	119				35 00	8 10	52	"			119
Scott county	26	*a*				*a*	*a*	Cash.	19		4
Barber	1					12			1		
Butcher	1								1		
Carpenters	3					10			3		
Farmers	3					10					
Laborers	10					10			10		
Liverymen	3					12			3		
Miner	1					10					1
Plasterer	1					10			1		
Railroad-men	3										3
Tazewell county	41	*a*				10	*a*	Cash.	28		13
Cigarmakers	2								2		
Cooper	1								1		
Farmers	5										5
Hostlers	2								2		
Ironworkers	2								2		
Laborers	14								14		
Merchants	3										3
Millers	2										2
Miners	3										3
Painters	4								4		
Woodworkers	3								3		

* *From Pay-Roll of Illinois Watch Company, September, 1886.*

Department.	No. employed.		Average No. days—10 hours.		Average earnings per day—10 hours.		Average month's earnings.		Amount of monthly pay-roll.
	Males	Females	Males	Females	Males	Females	Males	Females	
Totals and Averages	355	173	23.4	23.9	$2 31	$1 15	$54 14	$27 49	$24,165 03
Balance	12	6	25.2	25.8	1 95	1 08	48 94	27 62	752 97
Balance Staff Pivoting	4		24.9		3 55		88 28		353 11
Damaskeening	7		23.7		2 20		52 29		366 04
Dial	18	8	23	25.3	2 99	1 32	68 88	33 30	1,506 24
Engraving	8	2	25.4	26	2 20	1 13	55 71	29 34	504 36
Escapement	20	7	23.2	25.6	2 60	1 39	60 38	35 35	1,455 14
Finishing "A"	38	4	22.8	24.1	2 29	1 18	52 11	28 32	2,093 21
Finishing "C"	41	4	23.9	25.8	2 25	92	53 84	23 68	2,302 09
Gilding	9	7	20.1	22.6	2 49	99	50 17	22 32	607 78
Hairspring	1	3	24.3	24.9	3 00	1 40	72 90	34 94	177 73
Jeweling	26	13	23.8	25.5	1 98	1 02	47 18	26 13	1,566 38
Mainspring	11	2	24.7	23	2 31	1 26	57 27	29 06	688 03
Motion	10	5	24.3	24.5	2 54	1 13	62 04	27 79	759 34
Plate	24	13	23.8	24.6	1 62	93	38 61	22 89	1,225 24
Punch and Hand	4	3	24.7	25	2 22	1 40	54 79	35 07	324 36
Steel Screw	15	39	23.2	23.8	2 32	1 12	53 89	26 66	1,848 47
Stem Wind	16	2	23,6	25.2	2 99	1 25	70 49	31 41	1,190 65
Timing	13	6	20	23.4	2 62	1 11	52 44	25 86	836 78
Train	27	48	23	22.4	2 10	1 23	88 33	27 55	2,627 18
			25.2	26	$2 28	$1 10	$57 67	$24 60	$2,969 93
Carpenters and builders	17		25.8		1 60		41 27		701 51
Machine	29		25.3		2 70		70 74		2,051 43
Material	5	1	23.3	26	1 62	1 10	37 68	28 60	216 99

a Not reported.

1886 payroll statistics for the Illinois Watch Company

Then, in 2001, while I was writing *The Illinois Watch: The Life and Times of a Great American Watch Company,* I found a few other former Illinois employees to interview.[10]

A related oral history project was undertaken by the Illinois Environmental Production Agency [EPA], whose new offices, where it moved in the spring of 1998, were in a building that had earlier been part of the Illinois Watch Factory and the Sangamo Electric Company. Interviews were conducted by EPA staff with their colleagues who had relatives once working at either the Watch Factory or Sangamo.[11]

Harner observed: "Women have always been factory workers. They've always been the first to enter the factories, because they could be paid cheaper wages. As things became more mechanized, that's when they really started moving in, when job skills were less and it was easier to do a job without any skill." At the Watch Factory, women were customarily paid only half what males earned and they were mostly relegated to unskilled jobs. Some women who worked at the Watch Factory told of working in the "timing room," where their job was to keep hundreds of watches wound while they were being tested for accuracy, Harner said.

Since female workers tended to be concentrated in departments that required less training and skill, there was some justification for them to be paid less. This disparity was common in all industries at this time. However, the practice aroused resentment when machines replaced skilled male workers with unskilled women operatives. "If the women were allowed to make the same wages as the men, thus making equal the earning power," reasoned a male employee, "the change from one to the other would only be for incompetence. Then a man with a family to support would stand an equal chance with a woman who in all probability has only herself to support. Men are being replaced by women and girls at every possible opportunity and wages therefore are crowded lower and lower and the wage worker sees himself every day more entirely driven to the wall. In all justice if a woman does the same work that previously required a man to do, pay her the same wages as a man receives when ability to perform this work is equal." [12]

Isabelle Schimenz was approaching age ninety-six when I interviewed her in 2001. In 1921, when she was fifteen, she obtained a work permit to work at the Watch Factory with her two sisters and brother. She told me that all were forced to work when their father, a Springfield fireman, was thrown from a horse-drawn firewagon and killed while racing to a fire. Schimenz's three siblings moved to Lancaster, Pennsylvania, in late 1933 to work at the Hamilton plant when the Illinois Watch Company was in the process of being shut down. Only her brother ultimately returned to Springfield. Isabelle worked in the Watch Factory until 1932, and then transferred to the Sangamo Electric Company, where she worked until she retired in 1968, after forty-seven years of service between the two.

Other women told stories of similar family necessities that compelled them to find jobs at the Watch Factory when they were very young. Selma Stewart, who was interviewed by Harner in 1985, said: "I started work at the Watch Factory when I was just fifteen years old. My father had cancer and my mother was an invalid, so my older sister and I both worked at the Watch Factory to support the family. When I got married they told me that 'we have our rules, we have to let you go.' I didn't think it was right to fire a woman because she was married."

Types of work. At the Watch Factory, women worked in various departments. Frances Bolinger Engel, interviewed in 1985 when she was eighty-seven, worked in the Watch Factory for only a short time, around 1917. "I did pivot work," she said, "little things about the size of the hair on your head. I sat at a big bench, along a lot of open windows. I met my husband [to be] there. I got tired working there so he said, 'let's get married.'" Selma Stewart, mentioned above, was an employee of the company's Balance Department from 1918 to 1926.

Beulah Poulson, age ninety-three when I interviewed her in 2001, had very precise memories about her work at the Watch Factory. She graduated from high school in the spring of 1928 and then went to business school to learn typing, stenography, and other office work. After four months of studying at the business school, she applied for employment at the Watch Factory and was hired to work in the Orders and Shipping Department for $60.00 per month. There she filled orders that were mailed in or were hand-delivered by the salesmen. She "would take their orders, fill out the paperwork and take it to Mr. Marr in the vault," she said. In the vault, which was the size of a room, were stored the finished watches in boxes. She was not allowed in the vault herself, she told me. "Mr. Marr would get the watches and get them shipped."

The finished watches in the vault had been brought there "from the girls in the Strap Room on a dolly, already in their boxes," Poulson said. (I gathered that the girls in the Strap Room had put the watchbands on the watches.) The dolly was brought to the door of the vault, and Mr. Marr would take it from there, as he was the only person allowed in the vault. He was the one who matched the orders to the correct watches. She remarked that during her entire time in the department she never saw a pocket watch.

Larry Eastep, one of the EPA employees interviewed in 1998, said his mother had taken a summer job installing stems in watches at the Watch Factory when she was sixteen. Her family lived nearby, so the job was very convenient for her; she could walk to and from work and go home for lunch.

STEAL 102 WATCHES IN CAPITAL FACTORY

Springfield, June 28.—The Illinois Watch company was the victim Saturday night of the largest single haul of watches ever made by thieves in central Illinois. The value of the goods taken, based on the cost price to the manufactureers, is $2,500. In all, 102 watches and eighty-seven cases were taken.

Despite the security measures in place, thieves still found ways to steal watches from the Watch Factory. *Daily Review* (Decatur, Illinois), June 28, 1915; image from *newspapers.com*

Accommodations and activities. In December 1920, out of concern for its female employees, the Watch Company opened a new dormitory for the "girls from the Watch Factory." The Converse home was acquired by the Watch Company and completely overhauled and refitted to receive the girls, initially accommodating twenty-five of them. (Interestingly, there had been a Converse connection with the Illinois Watch Company since the very beginning; back in 1870, ten acres of land had been donated by Henry Converse for the Watch Factory and four additional acres purchased from him.[13])

The company also sponsored social clubs for its female employees. Among them was the Lincoln Club, which had a glee club and also raised money so as to have parties and other activities. Evidently, many of the planned events of the club were to create matchmaking opportunities for the Watch Factory "girls and men of marriageable age." In 1920 a Leap Year party was organized, to which all the eligible men of marriageable age from the Watch Factory and the Y.M.C.A. were

Photograph of one of the Illinois Watch Company's women's clubs

invited. "Watch Factory girls with or without hope chests . . . were warmly welcomed and given every assistance by the officers and committee members."[14]

The company had also sponsored activities to support the war effort. Starting early in October 1918, a number of "girls" from the Watch Factory began devoting two evenings a week to making surgical dressings for the relief of "our boys overseas." Those evenings they truly showed their devotion, working from 7:00 p.m. to 9:00 p.m. after a ten-hour workday.[15]

Despite the long hours, the young women had opportunities for a social life on the weekends. Beulah Poulson told me that "after work on Saturday the girls would race home, put on their hats and white gloves and go down to the town square to walk around. On Saturday night they would go to Bibble's to dance stag at twenty-five cents per night." And Isabelle Schimenz recalled how "she loved to dance and would go to Moonlight Gardens on Saturday night to dance and drink beer."

Advantages of Working at the Illinois Watch Factory

In detailing her research findings, Harner said: "I was told by a former worker at the plant that, if you were going to work in Springfield, the place to work was at the Watch Factory." There were a number of reasons for such a high opinion of the company. The working conditions were excellent; the plant was clean and well-lit. Moreover, the grounds had beautiful trees and lawns; Harner remarked that from an old picture postcard the factory looked "like a college campus."

The Watch Factory was a friendly place too, Engel remembered. "Everybody was so congenial to one another," she said. "The bosses would speak when they went through. They were never snobbish."

Nor was age an issue. Throughout its history, the Illinois Watch Company had a wide range of ages among its employees. It was not unusual for the Watch Factory to have active employees in their early teens to their late eighties because the company valued knowledge and experience over preconceived beliefs concerning age. In a 1923 advertising brochure, the company proudly proclaimed "that although fifty-three years have passed since the organization of the company, there are at the present time thirty-one employees in active service who started in the year 1880, or before."

The company's Thirty Year Club honored the service of longtime employees; each employee who had been with the company for thirty years was given a diamond pin as an insignia of membership in the club. An Illinois newspaper mentioned that at the 1926 dinner, ninety-four of these employees were present, and three of them had been with the company for over fifty years.[16]

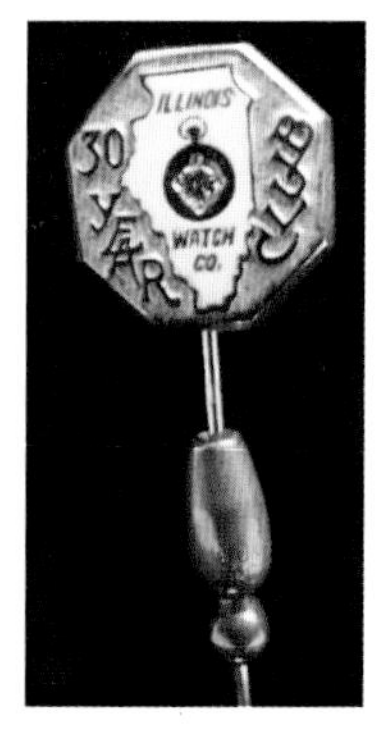

Illinois Watch Company 30 Year Club Pin in 14K gold—could be used as a hat, scarf or tie pin

In many cases, several members of the same family were working at the Watch Factory at the same time. Harner reported that the people she interviewed in 1985 remarked on the "family" atmosphere of the plant. "It was kind of a generational thing," she said, "with children, parents, grandparents and great-grandparents." (In October 1921, *Doings* pointed out that although there were four generations of Wieties, only three were currently at work at the Watch Factory—but the fourth was a newborn!) Engel remarked that her father, aunt and brother all had jobs there. Fred Rader, who worked there from 1928 to 1932, said his sister worked there too.

Photograph of the 30 Year Club at its annual dinner in 1925

ENTERTAINS EMPLOYES

Springfield, Feb. 18—Ninety-four veteran employes of the Illinois Watch company, all members of its 30-year club, were guests of the company this afternoon and evening at a dinner. Three of the employes have been with the company over 50 years. Each employe is given a diamond pin after he has been with the company 30 years as an insignia of membership in the club.

Dinner for the 30 Year Club noted by the *Republican-Northwestern* (Belvidere, IL), February 19, 1926; image from *newspapers.com*

Who's Who In The Watch Factory

There are six men now with the watch company who began work here in 1872. The first on our list is Herman Burkhardt, who has been with us all that time with the exception of ten years from 1893 to 1903 when he was superintendent of delivery at the Springfield postoffice.

Herman Burkhardt

Mr. Burkhardt is very proud of his record and informs us that his father, two sisters, two brothers, wife and four daughters have at one time or another been employees of the Illinois Watch Company.

From a 1919 issue of *Doings*. It was not unusual for entire families and generations of family members to work at the Illinois Watch Factory simultaneously.

Who's Who In The Watch Factory

To have been with the watch factory at its very start and to continue with it until the present is the lot of but one man and he is still actively engaged among us.

Charles DeCamp

It was in 1870 that Mr. Charles De Camp began work in the Machine Shop and now, fifty years later, due to his skill and accurate workmanship, much of our finest work is still entrusted to him.

The likeness of Mr. De Camp is a splendid one and was drawn for "Doings" by Carl Somdal.

Doings, September 1921

This week's issue of The Illinois Issue, the official organ of the Anti-Saloon League of Illinois, makes special mention of the new assignment of superintendents and assistant superintendents in the Illinois districts—Northern, Springfield and Southern. Of the Southern district men, the Issue has the following:

SUPERINTENDENT.

John W. Perry, superintendent of the Southern District, is not a stranger to Southern Illinois. Born in Cairo and living as a boy in Benton, DuQuoin and Olney, he takes up the work of his district knowing much of its territory and conditions. For the past twenty years he has lived in Springfield.

For fourteen years he held a position with the Illinois Watch Company, which he resigned to take up the work of the Anti-Saloon League as assistant district superintendent of the Springfield District. In this position he proved his worth to the cause he served by consistent and intelligent labor, contributing much to the many victories won by the temperance forces of the district in legislative and local option battles.

Mr. Perry is not an unknown quantity aside from anti-saloon work. He has been recognized as one of the prominent laymen of the Illinois Conference. During the past year he has been vice-president of the Lay Association of the Conference. He is considered one of the most practical leaders in Young People's work in the state. For five years he has been corresponding secretary of the Illinois State Epworth League. He goes to the new field as a Christian layman that believes in his religion and in the church being a militant force for God.

In his work in the Springfield District he has made many friends for himself as well as the League in all denominations, and the churches in Southern District will soon learn that he has come down there to do business in a spirit of absolute fairness to all. We bespeak for him in the work in his new field a repetition of the success he has already achieved in the territory he is leaving.

Not all employees stayed their entire careers at the Watch Factory; at least one 14-year veteran left the company to work for the Anti-Saloon League. *Daily Free Press* (Carbondale, IL), July 15, 1911; image from *newspapers.com*

Employees were proud to work for the Illinois Watch Company. It was renowned nationally and internationally for the high quality of its timepieces, and that reflected well on them and their work. Some, like Rader, had learned on the job. He started work at fifteen as an errand boy but decided he didn't want to be doing that the rest of his life, so he "picked up a pair of calipers and started to learn how to 'true' hairsprings." (This is a very tedious job because the tiny hairsprings have to be centered and then leveled.) He progressed well with this job and went on to learn the fine points of truing springs and balances.

Ann Alexander, an EPA employee whose brother Nicholas was a longtime Illinois Watch Factory worker, said she prized a leather billfold that the Watch Factory employees were given, embossed on one side with a drawing of the plant from an aerial perspective and on its face bearing images of Illinois watches.

Steve Colantino, another of the EPA employees interviewed, had two uncles who "polished their skills" working for the Watch Factory before opening their own jewelry stores. "One uncle worked on the production line making Bunn Specials.... The expertise in hairspring work that he gained there eventually enabled him to open his own jewelry/watch store in downtown Springfield." During his fifteen years with the Watch Factory, he played trombone with the company band.

Store Force will Visit Watch Factory

Louis Brandenberger will close his store all day next Friday so that the entire force in the store may make a trip with him to Springfield. Beside visiting the state fair they will visit the factory of the Illinois Watch Company at Springfield and learn how Illinois watches are made. Mr. Brandenberger will be host to his store force during the trip.

The Watch Company was always eager to welcome visitors to its facility. *Alton Evening Telegraph* (Alton, IL), September 19, 1923; image from *newspapers.com*

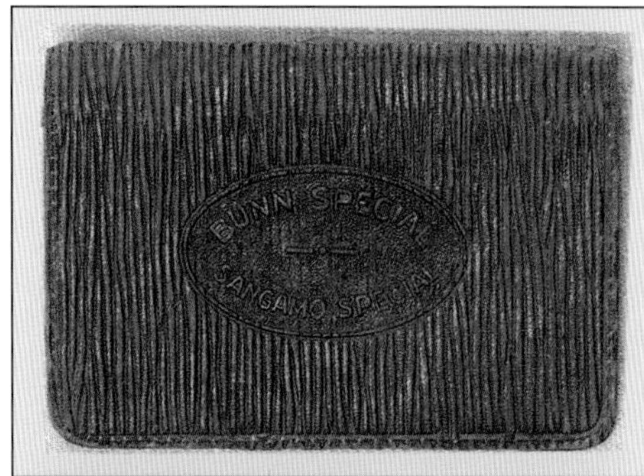

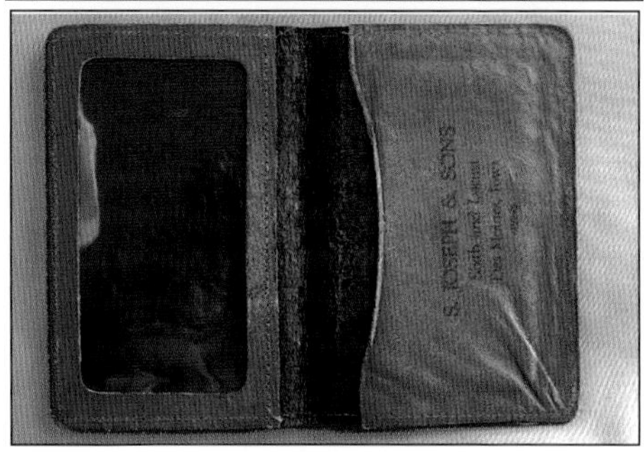

Illinois promotional leather billfold for Railroad Pocket Watch Inspection Card and Holder and a Union Membership Card

The well-known Illinois Watch Factory Band, early 1900s

In the Illinois Watch Factory Rest Room, workers could take a break from work (notice the piano against the far wall).

Watch Company cafeteria, still frame from 1923 silent film

> **1881**
> **HISTORICAL NOTES**
>
> - President James A. Garfield was assassinated.
> - The Tuskegee Institute opens in Alabama.
> - Thomas Edison and Alexander Graham Bell form the Oriental Telephone Company.
> - The American Red Cross names Clara Barton president.

Springfield, Ill., June 20.—Special Telegram.—A ratification meeting was held tonight in the Courthouse Park. The speakers' stand was brilliantly illuminated with electric lights and decorated with flags and bunting. The Illinois Watch Company Band furnished the music. J. O. Humphrey presided and made a short introductory speech. He was followed by James A. Connolly, who has just returned from his duties in Washington. He spoke for over an hour, and dwelt at length on the sound-money question. He spoke of Major McKinley as "our next President" in the highest terms, and predicted a bright future for the country under his administration. Each mention of the great protectionist's name was greeted with tremendous applause. D. T. Littler then made a short but stirring address, and was followed by Joseph M. Grout, A. J. Lester, and G. Murray, candidate for Representative from this county. Then there was a grand display of fireworks, and so the campaign of 1896 was well launched in Sangamon County.

The Illinois Watch Company Band played at a celebration in Springfield during William McKinley's 1986 presidential campaign. *InterOcean* (Chicago, IL), June 21, 1896; image from *newspapers.com*

The Governor's Guards of Springfield passed through the city yesterday on their way home from the late tournament at Grand Rapids, Mich. They number seventy-eight men, and are under the command of Capt. Brinkerhoff. The Illinois Watch Company's band accompanies them on the trip.

In July, 1885 the Watch Factory Band accompanied the 78-man Governor's Guard of Springfield on its trip to a tournament in Grand Rapids, Michigan. *Chicago Daily Tribune*, July 6, 1885; image from *newspapers.com*

Company-Sponsored Activities and Events

The Illinois Watch Factory planned social events for its employees, such as picnics, boat outings and musical interludes at lunch breaks from time to time. And Reservoir Park, now the site of the Lanphier High School and its athletic field, was just across the street from the back of the Watch Factory. With its lagoon and gardens, the park was a popular spot for workers to spend their lunch hours.[17]

The Illinois Watch Factory Band

The famous Illinois Watch Factory Band, organized in 1881, was under the direction of Professor Louis Lehmann, who was brought from Rochester, New York, for that purpose. Until his death in 1923 he continued as director, serving, he said, "both as leader of music as well as mediator between the band and those wishing its services." A monument to him was erected by the citizens of Springfield in gratitude for all he had done for the city in the service of music.[18]

The Illinois Watch Factory Band following a performance, c. 1900

Lehmann's successor in 1924 was Rudolph C. Hartlieb, well known as a composer and arranger.[19] Hartlieb was followed in 1927 by Charles J. Lorch, who had apparently been a protégé of Professor Lehmann's, Lorch, regarded as one of the best cornetists in the country, had been with the Illinois Watch Factory Band for some years.[20]

From Lehmann's time on, the band was much in demand, performing at parades, homecomings, park concerts and other celebrations throughout Illinois.[21] This was the Golden Age of bands in America; open-air performances of music were one of the most popular forms of entertainment, and most municipalities had a bandstand.

The Illinois Watch Factory Band continued under that name until 1933, when it was merged with the Capitol City Band to form the Springfield Municipal Band, which still exists, playing a number of free park concerts each summer and also performing at many military and civic events during the year.[22]

Athletic Teams

The company also sponsored baseball, basketball, bowling, tennis and other sports teams for its employees. One of its baseball players, Jack Weineke, went on to play in the Major Leagues, with the Chicago White Sox. The Watch Factory was represented by teams in various Springfield baseball leagues. The Illinois-Sangamo team won the city championship in 1918, and in 1919 the Illinois Watch Company (IWC) team won the city's Industrial League championship.[23]

Earlier, the Illinois Watch Company, recognizing the country's fascination with the "National Pastime" as an opportunity for good publicity, had presented watches to all the members of the 1912 pennant-winning teams: the New York Giants of the National League and the Boston Red Sox of the American League.[24] Boston went on to win the World Series.

Base Ball

The Red Cross Twilight League has been organized with the following companies represented:

1. Centennials—State House Employes
2. Paris Cleaners
3. Bunnies
4. Modern Woodmen
5. National Zinc Company
6. Weaver Manufacturing Company
7. Illinois Watch Company
8. Sangamo Electric Company

The big game of the season so far was that between the Illinois Watch Company and the Sangamo Electric Company at Lincoln Park diamond, June 10th. The Watch Makers got the Sangamo boys on the run in the first inning with a score of 4 to 0. This lead was maintained and bettered throughout the game; although in the 4th to 7th innings it looked as though the Meter Works team had a chance when they held the Watch Company team to a row of zeros on the score board. Final scores was 11 to 4, but what the Meter Works lacked in ability to roll up scores they made up for in the enthusiasm of their rooters.

Watch Makers vs. Meter Works, June 1917

Watch Factory Bowling League

As in former years, the Bowling League of the Watch Factory has enjoyed a lively season. Six teams have been playing since the season opened in the the fall at the Capitol City Alleys and at present they bowl every Monday night. Keen rivalry exists among the bowlers for a place at the top of the list for team and individual.

Mr. Robert Kiley formerly an employe of the Jewelling Department of the Watch Factory who held the honors as high individual man, joined the Medical Corps recently with Dr. Ottis' Unit and is now located at Camp Ferguson.

A Handi-cap League Ragtime Turnament is being played off at the alleys, having started March 13th and due to close April 7th. Bowlers of the following leagues are represented; Watch Factory, State House, Illinois Traction System, Central Union Telephone Co. So far only a few of the Watch Factory bowlers have bowled, but when they do, the maples sure will be kept busy. Following scores show the line-up of the men and the teams:

Watch Factory League Standing to Date

TEAMS	GAMES	WON	LOST	AVE.
Screw Room No. 2	105	61	44	.581
Motion Room	105	61	44	.581
Screw Room No. 1	95	50	45	.526
Escape Room	95	47	48	.495
Finishing Room	105	46	59	.438
Jewel Setters	95	35	60	.368

Team High Score for five games, Motion Room, 2585

Team High Score for one game, Screw Room No. 1, 591

High Individual Score for five games, A. Swanland, 957.

High Individual Score for one game, F. Metze, 233.

Average for Season to Date

Name	Games	Av.	Name	Games	Av.
Swanland	60	168	Larson	27	151
C. Rebok	59	165	Lavin	80	149
Loften	68	164	Woods	87	149
Bahlow	99	163	Barth	15	146
Peters	95	163	Correthers	20	144
Metze	99	159	Hauer	85	143
G. Kern, Sr.	85	159	F. Boehning	63	141
G. Kern, Jr.	89	157	Londrigan	78	140
Furrow	30	157	Engel	34	140
Randall	61	156	J. Boehning	82	139
Solomon	20	155	Knox	55	131
Moore	67	152	Springfloat	25	129
Brady	85	152	Wattling	10	121
Watkins	60	151			

Clipping from March 1918. The annual bowling scores were very popular. (Notice that a father and son participated in the league.)

Players Get Watches.

The Illinois Watch company at Springfield presented each of the members of the pennant winning team with a valuable watch upon the back of which is engraved the recipient's initials. The watches were said to represent a total value of $1,200.

In September 1912, Illinois presented a watch to each baseball player on the pennant-winning teams. *Daily Review* (Decatur, IL), September 17, 1912; image from *newspapers.com*

Illinois Watch Company Champions of the Industrial Baseball League. Top row, from left; E. Dwyer, Mgr., E. Maurer, H. Alewelt, J. Kilcummings, Capt., P. Burns, E. Wattling, P. Billington and E. N. Bates. Middle row; F. Kroeschner, M. Lascody, L. Ranzenberger and F. English. Bottom row; J. Chestnut, C. Betcher and F. Fernandes.

In 1919 the Illinois Watch Company (IWC) team was the Springfield Industrial Baseball League champion.

Unions

To date, no information has surfaced to indicate that any of the employees of the Illinois Watch Company had ever joined a union. This is surprising as both Elgin and Waltham had employees participating in unions as early as the 1880s, and at some point the Sangamo Electric Company became unionized.

In his history of the city of Elgin, E. C. Alft gives an account of early union activity there:[25]

The first labor union of importance in Elgin was the Noble Order of the Knights of Labor, which rose to prominence in the 1880s. Many of the Knights were watch factory employees, and in 1886, their candidate for the state legislature, Arwin Price, carried the township over his Republican and Democratic opponents. The Order, open to all workers and vague in its aims, dwindled in numbers by the end of the decade. When Henry Demarest Lloyd, the social reformer, addressed an Elgin audience in the spring of 1890, he noted the absence of labor unions in the city.

Nevertheless, at year's end [1890], Local 5504 of the American Federation of Labor was organized. Although [Elgin] management ignored its existence, by late September 1891 the union had more than six hundred members and was encouraging workers at Waltham and other plants to join the movement. [*Author's note:* It is unknown if they were also doing so at the Illinois Watch Company.] At about the same time, a separate union of the company's [Elgin's] machinists was chartered. Employees complained that management officials in Chicago were cold and distant and unacquainted with their problems.

Local 5504 disappeared during the great economic Panic of 1893. However, when prosperity returned in the late 1890s, the union was revived as Local 6091. At the end of the decade there was a labor dispute at the Elgin watch factory that led to a walkout:

In August 1898, the piecework rate among skilled stem-winders [at Elgin] was cut from seventy-seven cents to fifty cents a box. When the male workers protested, they were replaced by women, but twenty-two women joined eighty-nine men in the walkout, the first in Elgin's history. President Samuel Gompers of the American Federation of Labor was involved in the negotiations that led to a settlement. Unrest continued; it was claimed early in 1899 that wages in the plate department were forty per cent lower than in 1892.

Although Elgin's Local 6091 enrolled a majority of the male employees, its bargaining power was weakened by the exclusion of the lady watch makers. Comprising about half the workforce, they were compelled to form an auxiliary of their own. The American Federation of Labor, chiefly interested in representing skilled craftsman, was opposed to the employment of women in factories. It was claimed [chauvinistically] they cheapened wages, were easily manipulated by management and as temporary workers cared little about maintaining hard-won benefits.

Hundreds of women employees, however, had long tenures at the Elgin National Watch Company. . . Many romances were culminated through close relationships at the big factory, and the bride often returned to her bench after the honeymoon. Six women were employed for fifty years or more, and scores worked for more than forty. Despite extended periods of service, the wage discrimination continued. Females were not considered for promotion. None was ever made the head of a department, and it wasn't until 1917 [in the midst of the First World War] that a woman was appointed as jobmaster.

It would be nice to think that the Illinois Watch Company was free of union members because of its great compassion and paternalism towards its workers. Probably another contributing factor was that the company was run in an unusually democratic fashion and often solicited input from the employees before taking certain actions.

Although there were no unions at the Illinois Watch Factory, that did not mean there were never any disagreements that led to strikes. On March 19, 1889, for example, the *Chicago Daily Tribune* noted that "The employees of the steamfitting department of the Illinois Watch Company at Springfield, Ill., last evening struck against a reduction of 12 ½ percent." This was a particularly serious strike; absence of the steamfitters would essentially shut down the plant because it was powered by steam engines as well as heated by steam.

This picture, taken in 1910, shows the near equal mix between male and females in this Illinois Watch department as well as the variances in ages from the very young to more senior employees.

1892
HISTORICAL NOTES

- Ellis Island becomes the reception center for new immigrants to the United States.
- The first basketball game is played in Springfield, Massachusetts.
- A bottle cap with a cork seal is patented by William Painter.
- The first escalator is patented by Jesse W. Reno.
- John Philip Sousa's band makes its first public appearance.
- The Dalton Gang meets its end in a bank robbery shoot-out in Coffeeville, Kansas.

Watch Factory Health Service

The Watch Factory rest room described in our last issue is now completed and is fully prepared to care for all needing medical or minor surgical treatment during working hours. Mrs. J. L. Taylor, a trained nurse of wide experience, is in attendance at all times, while Dr. Amant can be consulted without charge by employees in the rest room between the hours of one and two on Monday, Tuesday, Thursday and Friday afternoons.

Doings, April 1920

All Employes Vaccinated.

Springfield, Ills., Nov. 6.—At the suggestion and expense of their employers, the entire working force of the Illinois Watch company, consisting of 400 men and women, were vaccinated as a precaution against smallpox, which is prevalent in the city.

As early as November 1901, the Illinois Watch Company was vaccinating its employees against smallpox at its own expense. *Daily Review* (Decatur, IL), November 6, 1901; image from *newspapers.com*

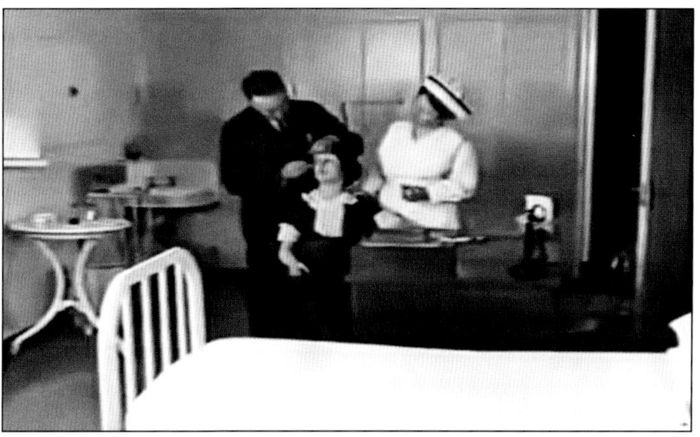

Dr. Amant treating an employee in the Watch Factory infirmary, still frame from 1923 silent film

Employee Care

As has been detailed in *The Illinois Watch: The Life and Times of a Great American Watch Company*, Illinois ran an extremely democratic factory, published a monthly employee newsletter, and introduced conveniences such as a lunch room, rest room and library for its employees. In addition, there was an in-house infirmary staffed by a full-time nurse and a part-time local doctor.[26]

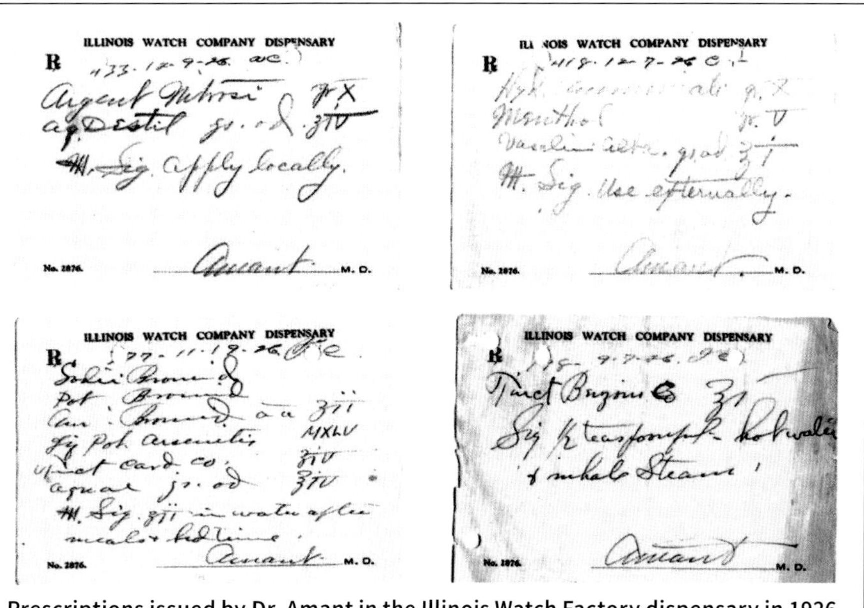

ILLINOIS WATCH COMPANY DISPENSARY

℞

M. D.

ILLINOIS WATCH COMPANY DISPENSARY

℞

M. D.

ILLINOIS WATCH COMPANY DISPENSARY

℞

M. D.

ILLINOIS WATCH COMPANY DISPENSARY

℞

M. D.

Prescriptions issued by Dr. Amant in the Illinois Watch Factory dispensary in 1926

Illinois/Sangamo Relief Association

The Illinois Watch Company was at the forefront of employee benefits for that era. In February 1916 the Illinois Watch Company and the Sangamo Electric Company organized the Illinois/Sangamo Relief Association. Each member of the Association made monthly contributions based on his or her pay rate. Employee members would then receive payments in the event of illness, accidents or other qualifying occurrences.[27]

Suppose You are Sick for the Next 3 Months?

Suppose you meet with a serious accident—suppose you are quarantined at home through sickness in the family?

Where's the money coming from to pay your bills?

You can get benefits equal to ⅔ of your regular wages through the Relief Association: dues vary from ½ cent to 2½ cents per day.

Inducement for joining the Relief Association, posted in *Doings*, February 1916

Each month, in *Doings*, the Relief Association would publish a notice of every penny that was paid out in benefits to any employee during the month. (These were obviously pre-HIPAA patient privacy days.)

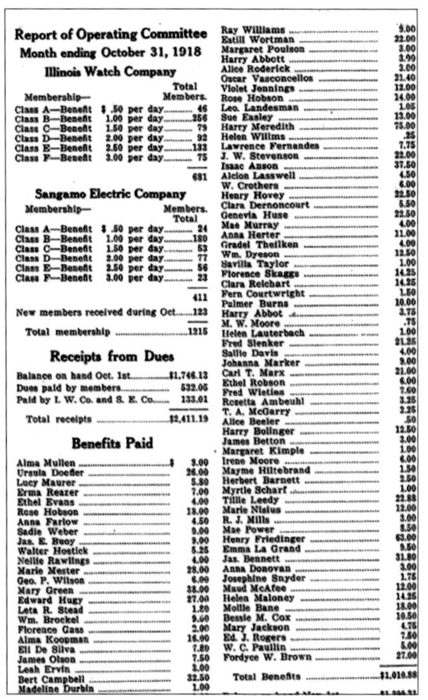

Report of Operating Committee
Month ending October 31, 1918

Illinois Watch Company

Membership—		Total Members.
Class A—Benefit	$ .50 per day	46
Class B—Benefit	1.00 per day	256
Class C—Benefit	1.50 per day	79
Class D—Benefit	2.00 per day	92
Class E—Benefit	2.50 per day	133
Class F—Benefit	3.00 per day	75
		681

Sangamo Electric Company

Membership—		Members. Total
Class A—Benefit	$ .50 per day	24
Class B—Benefit	1.00 per day	180
Class C—Benefit	1.50 per day	53
Class D—Benefit	2.00 per day	77
Class E—Benefit	2.50 per day	56
Class F—Benefit	3.00 per day	23
		411
New members received during Oct.		123
Total membership		1215

Receipts from Dues

Balance on hand Oct. 1st	$1,746.13
Dues paid by members	532.05
Paid by I. W. Co. and S. E. Co.	133.01
Total receipts	$2,411.19

Benefits Paid

Alma Mullen	$ 3.00
Ursula Doefler	26.00
Lucy Maurer	5.80
Erma Reazer	7.00
Ethel Evans	4.00
Rose Hobson	18.00
Anna Farlow	4.50
Sadie Weber	9.00
Jas. E. Buoy	9.00
Walter Hostick	5.25
Nellie Rawlings	4.00
Marie Mester	28.00
Geo. P. Wilson	6.00
Mary Green	33.00
Edward Hugy	27.00
Leta R. Stead	1.20
Wm. Brockel	9.60
Florence Gass	2.00
Alma Koopman	16.00
Eli De Silva	7.80
James Olson	7.50
Leah Ervin	3.00
Bert Campbell	32.50
Madeline Durbin	1.00
Ray Williams	9.00
Estill Wortman	22.00
Margaret Poulson	3.00
Harry Abbott	3.90
Alice Roderick	3.00
Oscar Vasconcellos	21.40
Violet Jennings	12.00
Rose Hobson	14.00
Leo. Landesman	1.05
Sue Easley	13.00
Harry Meredith	75.00
Helen Willms	.25
Lawrence Fernandes	7.75
J. W. Stevenson	22.00
Isaac Anson	37.50
Alcion Lasswell	4.50
W. Crothers	6.00
Henry Hovey	22.50
Clara Dernoncourt	5.50
Genevia Huse	22.50
Mae Murray	4.00
Anna Herter	11.00
Gradel Theilken	4.00
Wm. Dyeson	12.50
Savilla Taylor	1.00
Florence Skaggs	14.25
Clara Reichart	14.25
Fern Courtwright	1.50
Palmer Burns	10.00
Harry Abbot	3.75
M. W. Moore	.75
Helen Lauterbach	1.00
Fred Sienker	21.25
Sallie Davis	4.00
Johanna Marker	9.00
Carl T. Marx	21.00
Ethel Robson	6.00
Fred Wieties	7.60
Rozetta Ambeuhl	3.25
T. A. McGarry	2.25
Alice Beeler	.50
Harry Bolinger	12.50
James Betton	3.00
Margaret Kimple	1.00
Irene Moore	6.00
Mayme Hiltebrand	1.50
Herbert Barnett	2.50
Myrtle Scharf	1.00
Tillie Leedy	22.88
Marie Nisius	12.00
R. J. Mills	3.00
Mae Power	8.50
Henry Friedinger	63.00
Emma La Grand	9.50
Jas. Bennett	31.80
Anna Donovan	3.00
Josephine Snyder	1.75
Maud McAfee	12.00
Helen Maloney	14.25
Mollie Bane	18.00
Bessie M. Cox	10.50
Mary Jackson	4.75
Ed. J. Rogers	7.50
W. C. Paullin	5.00
Fordyce W. Brown	27.00
Total Benefits	$1,010.88

Payments made by the Relief Association as of October 31, 1918

In 1919 an amendment to the Relief Association's By-Laws was published to include a clause that prohibited the payment of benefits for a disability period continuing six days or over, unless certified by a licensed physician.

On July 1, 1920 the By-Laws were amended to provide that "Benefits will not be paid for accidental injuries resulting wholly or partly directly or indirectly from intoxicants or while intoxicated, from or while violating law, or for injuries intentionally self-inflicted, nor for sickness which is caused or increased in whole or in part by sexual immorality, intoxication or the use of intoxicating liquors or narcotics."

A special department managed the program under the direction of Richard Jones, the president of the Relief Association and R. A. Trumbull, its superintendent.

Richard Jones

R. A. Trumbull

Cover of booklet for the Constitution and By-Laws of the Illinois-Sangamo Relief Association, dated August 1, 1923

Benefits of membership.

The Relief Association published monthly examples, some quite gruesome and all very personal, of the benefits of Relief Association membership, such as the following three from the March 1919 issue of *Doings*.

Fred W. Sower employed in the Machine Shop at the Watch Factory had the misfortune, while riding a motorcycle, to collide with a switch engine, causing injuries which necessitated the amputation of his left limb above the ankle. He says "The $2.50 per day benefit that I received for seventy-five days during my disability period was a source of great satisfaction as it enabled me to pay all expenses and to greatly assist in the purchase of my artificial limb. I am certainly glad that I am a member for it always helps at a time of greatest need.

* * *

Following the long sickness and death of Louis Meyerhoff, formerly an employee of the Plate Department of the Watch Factory, his wife, Mrs. Mary A. Meyerhoff, wrote the following note:

"I wish to thank the Illinois-Sangamo Relief Association for the benefits received. I cannot express how much they were appreciated during our time of need."

Sick and death benefits in the above case amounted to $325.00.

* * *

Mrs. Nina Loiseau, mother and beneficiary of Joseph Loiseau formerly an employee of the Train Department of the Watch Factory, states, "The Relief Association has certainly been a friend indeed, during our time of need, caused by the long sick period which resulted in the death of our son.

"We cannot express our full appreciation of the benefits paid and the services rendered by the Association."

Benefits paid in the above case total $387.50.

He Who Grasps Opportunity IS WISE.

Opportunity to provide a liberal income during times of sickness or accident, when your wages stop, is provided by membership in the **Illinois-Sangamo Relief Association.**

BE WISE!

Make Application For Membership TO-DAY.

A 1919 Relief Association promotional item in *Doings* for the Illinois-Sangamo Relief Association

Life Insurance Policies as Reward for Services

As early as October 1918, the Watch Factory provided employees a free $400 life insurance policy after being employed more than six months. The Relief Association advised that "realizing that there are a large number of their employees who do not, at the present time, carry adequate life insurance for the protection of their families in the event of death, the Illinois Watch Company and [the] Sangamo Electric Company have arranged to offer a Traveler's Insurance Policy for each of its employees who have been in their employ for more than six months. The amount of this policy in each case varies with the length of service.

"Undoubtedly, the operation of this insurance plan will bring much satisfaction to both employers and employees for the employees receive a reward for years of service rendered the company and the company, on its part, receives the benefit of the increasing efficiency of old employees."

F. N. Morgan Succumbs To Brief Illness

Well Known Business Man, Musician, Dies at Home

FREDERICK N. MORGAN (1862-1929)

On December 9, 1929, the *Illinois State Journal* announced that Frederick N. Morgan had died after a brief illness. He was born in Minneapolis, Minnesota, in 1862 and moved to Springfield in 1887, joining the Illinois Watch Company as secretary-treasurer. He remained in that capacity for forty years. Morgan was also a well-known organist.

Illinois was a corporate leader in providing strong benefits along with fair and concerned treatment to its loyal employees. As a result, it was one of the few watch entities of that era to remain union free, notwithstanding Samuel Gompers' strong activities in Elgin and Chicago. Illinois' contented workforce produced arguably the best watch movements ever made in the United States, to such a high standard of quality, performance and accuracy that they still function today as they did from the date of their production.

NO UNION

Although Illinois was never unionized, it does not mean its workers were not concerned with the plight of organized labor. In 1917, the Illinois Watch Company employees (as well as those of the Sangamo Electric Company) walked out in sympathy for at least a day on behalf of the striking railway carmen.

GENERAL WALKOUT

(United Press Leased Wire.)

SPRINGFIELD, Ill., Sept. 12.—Unless an agreement is reached this afternoon between striking carmen and the company, sundown will see a tieup of every industry in the city and probable proclamation of martial law by Gov. Lowden.

The state council of defense, in session here today, placed the matter squarely up to the carmen and the company and urged them to reach an agreement before nightfall. The committees of both sides were to meet again this afternoon with the council.

During the day practically every union except the carpenters and the printers walked out in sympathy with the carmen. Ap- the Illinois Watch company and the Sangamon Meter works, which is manufacturing meters for U. S. battleships, refused to go to work pending termination of the car strike.

Three national guard regiments stationed here were preparing today to assume control.

Tacoma Times (Tacoma, WA), September 12, 1917; image from *newspapers.com.*

A Bolt Out of the Blue

These workers, along with other citizens of Springfield, were shocked to learn on New Year's Day 1928 that the revered Bunn families, after almost five decades of active ownership and management of the Illinois Watch Company, had sold all of its assets to Hamilton, one of its chief competitors. Charles F. Miller, the president of Hamilton, immediately assured Springfield that the Illinois Watch Company would remain unchanged; but regrettably, as events unfolded, nothing could have been further from the truth.

Hamilton no doubt had many reasons for the acquisition, some of which it offered in its statement at the time. Others, however, were unstated and became evident only with the passing of time. These will be explored in detail in the next three chapters. But whatever Hamilton's initial goals were, it could hardly have predicted the collapse of the stock market and subsequent Great Depression.

The history of the years following the acquisition is sad reading for admirers of Illinois. But in the brief span of years still left to production in Springfield, the watches were terrific, and they have become a source of enduring pleasure for collectors.

AMILTON WATCH
BUYS IN ILLINOIS

ancaster, Dec. 30. — Confronted
th the necessity of doubling its
tput, the Hamilton Watch Com-
ny, of this city, has purchased
Illinois Watch Company, at
ringfield, Ill., it was announced
re. The transaction involves t
nt, good will and trade nam
Illinois concern. The H
mpany will assume co
1, with Robert
e-president, an
ndig, secretary
management
nt.

January 5, 1928

THE JEWELERS' CIRCULAR

Hamilton Watch Co. in Big Deal

Lancaster Concern Announces the Purchase of the Plant, Good Will and Trade Name of the Illinois Watch Co. of Springfield, Ill.

CHAPTER 3

The Acquisition

This chapter examines the elements that led Hamilton to buy Illinois for $5 million. Ever since that purchase, on January 1, 1928, speculation has grown about the reasons. To clearly understand Hamilton's decision, it must be viewed within the watch market world of the 1920s. In addition, Hamilton's acquisition can only be appreciated by exploring the market as Hamilton saw it in the 1920s, full of potential manufacturing partners and aggressive competitors. Hamilton's interest in Illinois' products and product development, plant location, workforce and capacity must be viewed within this context.

The Wristwatch Market in the 1920s

During the decade and a half from World War I until the advent of the Great Depression, the American watch market experienced a revolutionary transition. At the beginning of this period, American watch manufacturing focused almost entirely on pocket watches. By the onset of the Depression, however, the vast majority of American men purchased watches to wear on their wrists. For established watch manufacturers, this transformation represented both a threat and an opportunity. Each manufacturer responded differently, causing the entire industry to adapt to an entirely new paradigm and the manufacturing landscape to change completely.

America continued to produce great pocket watches in the second decade of the twentieth century, and many consumers saw value in their durability, reliability and accuracy. Although progressively smaller watch movements had been developed from the 1880s until the Great War, most men found only one proper place for their watches: their vest pockets. And ladies favored the wearing of watches as pendants on neck chains or brooches, or as chatelaines on their belts.

For men or women who preferred not to have something hanging (or for men who did not have a vest), the wristlet, a leather pocket-watch holder for the wrist, was the alternative. Unfortunately, the wristlet looked ugly and ungainly. Photographs from the turn of the century indicate that among men it was mostly soldiers who embraced wristlets; women serving as nurses during the war also found them convenient.

World War I Russian soldier wearing a large wristlet

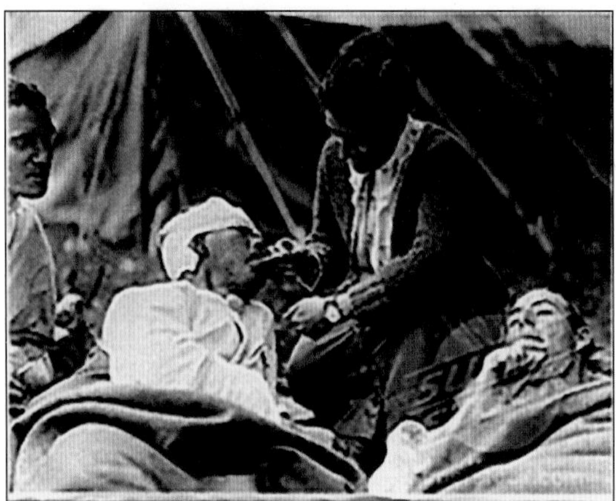
United States Army nurse wearing a wristlet during WWI

Wristwatches for women appeared before those for men. Although women's wristwatches existed from the time of Queen Elizabeth I, the women's wristwatch market remained tiny until around 1910. That lack of interest may have been owing to the large size of most watch movements at the turn of the century. Advertisements from early in the twentieth century seem to suggest that American jewelers wished to discourage men from following this trend by declaring wristwatches to be effeminate—possibly because they feared a lower price point for wristwatches, and thus lower profits.

The Great War changed that. About 1915, Illinois followed other manufacturers by offering smaller 3/0 and 6/0 movements originally intended for ladies' watches. Soldiers prioritized convenience above all else, as they had done in using the wristlet over a decade earlier. But now the existence of smaller movements allowed them to switch from the ungainly wristlet to a more modern strap watch. American soldiers, especially ones from rural areas, probably had never owned a watch before because they could not afford a pocket watch. The lower price of the smaller wristwatch offered them a new opportunity, which they appreciated. These motivations initiated a fifteen-year trend towards general adoption of men's wristwatches.

But sometimes old habits die hard. Manufacturing data from Elgin, Hamilton and Illinois indicate that after the war many Americans still favored pocket watches. As the 1920s moved on, however, purchasers increasingly chose wristwatches instead. There were several reasons for this shift, including more variety of styles available as well as greater acceptance by trendsetters in fashionable society. In the beginning, the design of cases for trench watches, the standard during the war, could only be termed utilitarian in the extreme. Male consumers found wristwatch case choices as limited as those for pocket watches: normally round or cushion-shaped and, occasionally, octagonal. This would change.

The introduction of the smaller-size movements and the rectangular watch movement boosted the trend towards adopting men's wristwatches. A rectangular movement allowed a better fit to the wrist. In 1925, Gruen took maximum advantage of the smaller, convenient shape of its new Quadron movement to begin creating more appealing case designs.[1] The fact that Gruen owned its own watch case company facilitated this change. Soon other case manufacturers offered their watch manufacturer clients more design choices.

Moreover, some movement manufacturers promoted the idea of using a wristwatch for activities such as outdoor sports and leisure time, and emphasized the status gained by owning a wristwatch as well as a pocket watch. They also reminded potential customers that explorers, aviators and other heroes of the day adopted wristwatches for convenience. Bulova and Longines, for example, used Charles Lindbergh's solo flight across the Atlantic in May 1927 to promote their wristwatches.[2] Thus, the epitaph of the pocket watch began to be written. The gradual disappearance of the men's vest, an economy move in the 1930s, was the last straw for the pocket watch.

Hamilton advertisement, c. 1928

Wadsworth pushed the concept of the necessity for a man to have two watches, a pocket watch and a strap one. *Saturday Evening Post*, April 11, 1925.

More than likely, the lower price point for wristwatches also convinced many consumers of the advantage of a smaller, more practical timepiece. Elgin, producer of both low-cost and mid-market movements, appears to have entered the civilian market fairly early in the 1920s with little reservation But manufacturers of high-quality movements, such as Hamilton and Illinois, may have been reluctant to enter the market because of the low price point and profit concerns.

Until 1926, Hamilton had made only a half-hearted attempt to enter the wristwatch market. Illinois' movement production data indicate that it decided to enter the civilian market about the same time. Those manufacturers who wished to survive, though, needed to adapt to the newer, cheaper, more popular timepiece. By the end of the decade, the market moved from priorities of durability, accuracy and reliability to newly adopted ones of convenience and fashion. In the wake of this revolution, heroes, victims and survivors emerged into a whole new world in which Hamilton saw its potential partners and predators.

American Watch Manufacturers

Until after the Civil War, the watch market in the United States relied heavily on imported models. As early as the 1790s, traders were importing Swiss watches through gateways such as Philadelphia and New York. At the time, America's native watch industry relied on small workshops and individual craftsmen. Even when watch imports from Great Britain and France declined, Swiss imports continued. The United States became the major importer of Swiss watches by the middle of the nineteenth century; however, a domestic watch industry soon started to develop.[3]

In the United States, watch manufacturing began in earnest with the founding in 1850 of a firm that would become the Waltham Watch Company. During the next half century, the number of domestic watch manufacturers waxed and waned. According to the United States Manufacturing Census of 1900, the number of operating America watch factories at that time was down to only twelve. A couple were rather small operations. According to Willis I. Milham in his book *Time & Timekeepers*, the largest and arguably the most important American watch manufacturers in the early part of the twentieth century were the following:[4]

- Waltham Watch Company, Waltham, Massachusetts
- E. Howard Watch Works, Waltham, Massachusetts
- Elgin National Watch Company, Elgin, Illinois
- Dueber-Hampden Watch Company, Canton, Ohio
- Hamilton Watch Company, Lancaster, Pennsylvania
- R. H. Ingersoll & Brother, New York, New York
- New York Standard Watch Company, Jersey City, New Jersey
- South Bend Watch Company, South Bend, Indiana
- Gruen Watch Manufacturing Company, Cincinnati, Ohio
- Illinois Watch Company, Springfield, Illinois

These firms are addressed briefly in this chapter and the following one.

The Waltham Watch Co., c. 1850s

American Waltham Watch Company (1850–1957)

In 1850, David Davies, Edward Howard and Aaron Dennison launched a watchmaking business in Roxbury, Massachusetts that eventually became the American Waltham Watch Company. They adopted a business plan to use interchangeable parts and implement mass production techniques in manufacturing inexpensive, quality watches. In 1851 they formed the American Horology Company, changing its name in 1853 to the Boston Watch Company. Finally, in 1854, the firm moved to Waltham, Massachusetts.

By 1857, Appleton Tracy & Co. had bought the company at public auction. Then, in January 1859, Appleton and the Waltham Improvement Company merged to form the American Waltham Watch Company. Waltham continued through the nineteenth century and into the twentieth century as one of the two largest watch movement manufacturers in the United States.

Waltham struggled in the early 1920s because of financial difficulties but consummated its reorganization on February 9, 1923, after almost two years of contentious debate, negotiations and blocking litigation. Its financial problems were related to inflation from the economic boom of 1920, high levels of inventory and the fact that much of its inventory was not marketable.

Historian Vincent P. Carosso indicates that in the mid-1920s, Waltham's finances seemed to be in good shape. In 1925 they were able to pay off a five-year note for $909,000.00. The next year the company had net earnings of $1,291,104.00 after taxes and capital investments. But by 1928 their net earnings were down to $872,303.09 despite an increase of $660,140 in revenue over the previous year.[5]

The decrease in earnings may have reflected the lower profitability of wristwatch manufacturing. According to Carosso, "Wristwatches accounted for 41% of Waltham movement production in 1926. . . . By 1930 the number increased to 76% and by 1935 it had reached 93% of total watch movement production."[6]

In nearly one hundred years of operation, Waltham produced forty million jeweled watches, plus clocks, speedometers, compasses, time fuses for bombs, and other precision instruments before finally going out of business in 1957.

E. Howard Watch Company (1858–1931)

Edward Howard, a veteran of the Waltham experience, started the E. Howard Watch Company in 1858 after the failure of the Boston Watch Company (1853–1857). Howard and his financial partner Charles Rice moved the tools, machinery and "watches in progress" from the defunct Boston Watch Company to their Roxbury factory location in late 1857.

Howard sold out his personal interest in the business and retired in 1882. Twenty years later, the company transferred all rights to the "Edward Howard" brand name to the Keystone Watch Case Company of Philadelphia and ceased operations. Keystone thereafter manufactured watches signed "E. Howard Watch Co." In 1927, Hamilton purchased the Howard name from Keystone, with the idea of marketing watches under the acquired name, and in 1931 acquired the E. Howard Watch Company's goodwill and trademarks from Keystone. Subsequently, Hamilton produced small quantities of watches under this brand name.[7]

Elgin National Watch Company (1864–1968)

As the American Civil War drew to a close, the rise of industry, especially railroads, and increased urbanization led to greater demand for watches in the United States. Entrepreneurs responded, particularly in the Midwest. Between 1864 and 1865 alone, approximately twenty-five watch companies were organized in the United States but most failed fairly quickly. Several were located in Illinois cities: Aurora, Chicago, Elgin, Grand Crossing, Peoria, Rockford, Freeport, Rock Island and Springfield.[8] One of the survivors, the factory in Elgin, spurred development of the "West" as a new center of watchmaking, shifting some of the emphasis away from Massachusetts.

The National Watch Company of Chicago, Illinois, was incorporated on August 27, 1864. During a special stockholders' meeting held in Chicago on May 12, 1874, the name of the company was changed to the Elgin National Watch Company because the movements manufactured by Elgin were universally known as "Elgin watches" or "watch from Elgin."

Elgin's founders looked east to obtain the required technology. Initially, two Waltham employees, Patten S. Bartlett and Ira G. Blake, traveled to Illinois to discuss the matter with John C. Adams. Then Adams made the trip back to Massachusetts to secure the services of key Waltham employees for the new Elgin venture.[9] Thus, Waltham's production techniques found a new home in the Midwest.

In the 1870s, American watch production grew. Waltham and Elgin produced watches at a prodigious pace. The era saw many new entrants in watch manufacturing, although most were short-lived. By 1876 the largest watch manufacturers in the country were Waltham with 900 employees, Elgin with 650 and Springfield (soon to become Illinois) with 300. The increased domestic production led to a direct decrease in Swiss imports. In *Elgin Time*, E. C. Alft and William H. Briska comment that "Imports of Swiss watches plummeted from 366,000 in 1872 to just 75,000 in 1876."[10]

By 1888 the Elgin factory was producing 7,500 movements per week. They employed 2,300 workers, split evenly and progressively between males and females. In 1922 the Elgin factory, now America's largest manufacturing facility producing jeweled watches, covered about twenty-four acres of floor space and employed over 3,000. It manufactured 3,100 watches daily.

Elgin Watch Factory, c. 1920

Elgin's production of almost a million watches a year dwarfed all of its competitors except dollar-watch manufacturer Ingersoll. Elgin also offered watch movements to cover every segment of the market. In 1920, Elgin manufactured 44 different grades of watch movements, 18 of which could be used in wristwatches. Elgin designed the wristwatch movements in three sizes, 3/0, 6/0 and 10/0, each with a cheaper 7- jewel version and a more expensive 15-jewel version.

Because of the company's size, Elgin's strategy served to blanket the market. The 7-jewel versions of its men's watches competed with cheaper 6-jewel Swiss imports. To vie with quality American and Swiss brands, Elgin offered its 15-jewel movement. Many times, the 7- and 15-jewel versions could be found in cases of similar or even identical designs. In its smaller 10/0 movement, targeted at the ladies' market, Elgin also made a 17-jewel variety of the movement.

Following Illinois' introduction of its 18/0 movement in 1923, Elgin introduced its own similarly sized movements in 1925 and 1926 to cover this part of the market in 1925–26. It sandwiched Illinois' 16-jewel ladies' movement between its own 18/0 watch movements with 15 jewels (grade 484) and 17 jewels (grade 483). The timing of the new movements' introductions could not have been considered coincidental by either manufacturer.

With wristwatch sales surging in the late 1920s, Elgin brought out its 7- and 17- jewel 4/0 size movements (grades 485 and 487, respectively) packaged in many different Art Deco style cases. The 7-jewel version aimed squarely at covering the budget-conscious market. The 17-jewel variety, on the other hand, contended directly with the 17-jewel, 3/0 size from Illinois. With its 17-jewel, 6/0 size, grade 489, Elgin competed head-on with Hamilton's and Illinois' offerings in these areas. At the same time, Elgin also produced a cheaper 7-jewel version of its 18/0 size movement for inclusion in low-cost ladies' watches. Elgin seemingly left no market niche uncovered. When Hamilton introduced its 19-jewel, grade 979 watch for high-end models, Elgin soon commenced production of its own 6/0 size, 19-jewel, grade 499. For most wristwatch manufacturers, Elgin remained the primary competition.

Elgin's net earnings in 1927 were $1,819,937.42 from operations after depreciation and taxes; total earnings were $2,071,861.11.

Elgin Stock Certificate, dated June 27, 1927

On March 16, 1928, Elgin reported lower earnings for 1927 than it had recorded in 1926. Nonetheless, DeForest Hulburd, president of Elgin, was sufficiently optimistic to say in his annual report that "1928 should be as good, if not better, than 1927."

"The problem of merchandising watches at the present is more difficult and complicated than it has ever been before," he explained. "We are trying to work out the very best methods in advertising, distribution, and selling and we hope our policies will bear fruit in 1928."[11]

Alft and Briska comment that already in the preceding century "the efforts of Waltham and Elgin indicated clearly that the American watch manufacturing methods had overtaken the Swiss, a point dramatically driven home at the Philadelphia Centennial Exposition in 1876."[12] The Exposition was supported separately by both John C. Adams and John W. Bunn. Both Waltham and Elgin set up exhibits demonstrating their products and machinery; Illinois, still in its formative years, apparently did not. According to Alft and Briska, "Swiss visitors were amazed that the precision of American factory made watches exceeded that of their own handcrafted timepieces. Switzerland still held an edge in making watches with expensive features such as built in calendars, alarms and multiple dials; the public, however, wanted good quality, lower priced American made watches. It was a wake-up call for the Swiss makers, who set about to reorganize their system of manufacturing. It would take them a generation to recover." [13]

Dueber-Hampden Watch Company (1864–1930)

Donald J. Mozart produced a three-wheel watch in 1864; with the assistance of Samuel Rice, he formed the New York Watch Company in 1866 in Providence, Rhode Island, and the next year moved the company to Springfield, Massachusetts. It became the Hampden Watch Company in 1877.[14]

John C. Dueber founded his watch case company in Cincinnati, Ohio, in the 1860s. He soon moved across the Ohio River to facilities in Newport, Kentucky. In 1886 the restrictions imposed on watch case sales by the Watch Trust forced Dueber to purchase the Hampden Watch Company. Two years later, Dueber moved the watch company from Massachusetts and the case company from Kentucky to shared facilities in Canton, Ohio.

In the late 1880s the two companies became two of Canton's largest employers. In 1890 they were producing six hundred watches per day.

A 1931 advertisement in the *American Monthly Review of Reviews* publication

URIOUS CONSPIRACY.

Remarkable Efforts to Rob a Philadelphia Firm of Its Trade Secrets.

The Head of a Kentucky Watch-Case Manufacturing Establishment and Three of His Subordinates Arrested for a Systematic Effort to Wrong a Successful Rival.

John C. Dueber (1841–1907), c. 1890s

The Keystone Watch Case Company in 1882 had John C. Dueber and three of his employees arrested for what we would label today "industrial espionage." The Dueber Watch Case Company had a reputation for making "some of the finest cases . . . in the trade." But the Keystone use of the James Boss patents enabled Keystone to make better cases for less money. Although the patent was of public record, the method of producing the result was a secret. In addition to the Boss patents, Keystone discovered a new way of making a silver watch case "Using one piece of solid silver for each part of the watch-cases instead of making the parts of different pieces of metal, soldered together, as had been the custom. . . . In this way they made a case much finer in appearance and almost absolutely dust and damp proof."

Dueber tried to make his own silver case this way and failed. Facing lost business, he dispatched an employee, Richard Clarke, to Philadelphia to move into a boardinghouse used by Keystone workers. Clarke made friends with these workers and "was very liberal with money" and tried to get hold of Keystone cases in various stages of manufacture to try to learn their processes. The Keystone employees, loyal to their company, reported these advances and Clarke was then followed by the police.

Within days Dueber himself came to Philadelphia with two of his employees. He then invited Keystone workers to dinner and to "partake good cheer." The workers enjoyed the food and drink but reported it to Keystone. Keystone then had the four Dueber men arrested and they were held on bail at $3,000 each.

In affidavits supporting the ensuing litigation, it was clear that unlawful inducements were being made to workers and apprentices of Keystone in an attempt to learn the Keystone trade secrets.

WHY I COLLECT ILLINOIS

Brotherhood of Locomotive Firemen and Enginemen's Magazine
November 1927
Courtesy Catherwood Library
453

The 6-Position 60-Hour Watch

Illinois Watches

ARE BETTER THAN THEY HAVE TO BE

It is typical of the Illinois Watch Company that its watches are better than they have to be. For instance:

The most rigid railroad requirements demand a one-day watch adjusted to five positions.

The Bunn Special and Sangamo Special are adjusted to six positions and are guaranteed to run for 60 hours. Why?

The extra adjustment for position—the most difficult of all—insures the greatest possible accuracy and uniformity in any position.

The 60-hour feature practically eliminates isochronal errors, increases the efficiency of the watch in all six positions and provides an invaluable factor of safety.

Yet even these exclusive improvements cause no advance in price.

Bunn Special, *21 jewels, 10K regular gold filled cases,* $60.00
Sangamo Special, *23 jewels, 14K regular gold filled cases,* $90.00

For the other members of the family, what finer Christmas gift than an Illinois strap watch? The attractive model illustrated here has a 17-jeweled movement in a 14K gold filled case with engraved bezel and curved back. Raised figure luminous dial; hand of green gold with luminous centers, $50.00.

Illinois Watches
ILLINOIS WATCH COMPANY, Springfield, Illinois

Back in the '70s I had become impatient with buying one cheap wristwatch after another that would run for a few days and then stop. I didn't have much money to put into a really good timepiece, so I told my wife, Kathy, that I would like to get an old reliable pocket watch that was made to last. She came home one day with an old 18s 17j Waltham in a silveroid case that she had bought at a farm sale for a few dollars. I got it repaired for not-so-much money and it has been keeping time ever since. Later on we went to another sale and I purchased a 7 jewel key-wind Illinois for $14. I was surprised to find that there had been a watch company in Springfield, and I began to research the topic. Lo-and-behold, there were a number of watch companies all over the state! It seemed like an impossible task at that time, but I decided to try to collect examples of all the watch companies in Illinois: Elgin, Illinois, Rockford, Aurora, Peoria and Cornell. Little by little, over the years, I did just that. I am still missing examples of the McIntyre and Freeport watches, of course, but I am satisfied that I have respectable examples of all the major Illinois watch companies now. I've also been able to find a few private label watches that were made for jewelers around the state, and I think it is an interesting concept to think that I can take a watch to the exact location (same location but an entirely different place) where the watch was sold over 100 years ago and stand there on the sidewalk with the watch still functioning as it did the day it was sold.

"I worked for the railroad for over 40 years, so was especially interested in the reciprocal relationship between the railroad requirements and the evolution of the technology of the railroad watches. I found that the Illinois company always seemed to go a step farther in assuring the quality of the high-grade movements. Where the Hamilton company used a solid gold center wheel, Illinois used an all gold train. Where all the other companies adjusted their movements to five positions, Illinois adjusted theirs to six. Other mainsprings might run for 45 hours, but Illinois developed the sixty-hour movement. And when Hamilton bought the Illinois factory out they recognized that the Illinois name was considered superior in the industry. The first pocket-watches Hamilton adapted when they bought the rights for the new Elinvar alloy were the Illinois Bunn and Sangamo Specials. Hamilton also used the Illinois name on wristwatches after they closed the Springfield Factory down, even when they began using Swiss-made movements. Illinois had this reputation for quality because they always seemed to take pains to keep one step ahead of the technology and insisted on maintaining the highest standard for their railroad grade watches.

"At any rate, when I realized that the Illinois Factory had also made wristwatches for a short time before they sold out to the Hamilton company, and my interest expanded to collecting those as well. It seemed to me that the wristwatches were really scarce until the Internet marketplace opened up all sorts of new possibilities. And when I bought your book my knowledge of and interest in the Illinois wristwatches reached a new threshold! I have been lucky to have a very good watchmaker who does all my work here locally, and I especially enjoy purchasing high-grade watches and bringing them back to life by having them restored. For me the long history of the mechanical watch represents a fascinating evolution of ingenious mechanical and artistic innovation, and it is an astonishing example of sustainable ecological integrity and perpetual ingenuity."

— *Steve Gossard*

The Dueber Watch Case Company and the Hampden Watch Company merged in 1923; Dueber sold the companies to Walter Vrettman in 1925. About this same time, Dueber-Hampden produced two iconic wristwatches: the Man o' Fashion and the Play-Boy. The former was rectangular, the latter square, and each had an engraved bezel. The names of the two models reflect Dueber's attempt to attract younger, fashionable male consumers. The introduction of the Man o' Fashion and the Play-Boy was one of the earliest attempts by any watchmaker to introduce stylish watches to the public.

A Dueber Watch Works aluminum promotional match safe

A very tiny Dueber-Hampden pocket watch promotional item

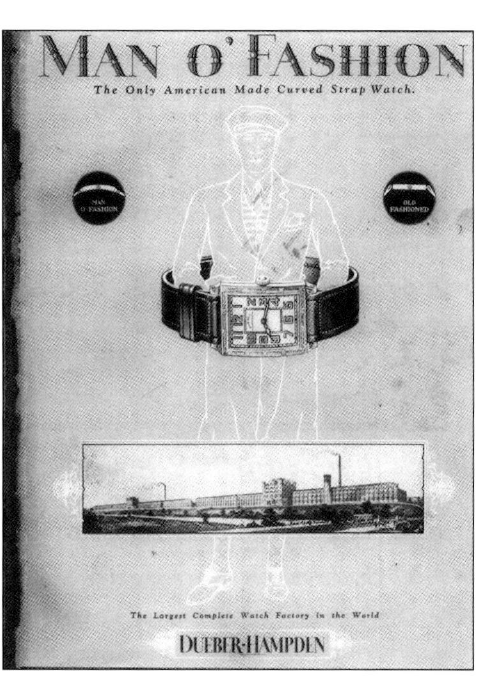

A Dueber-Hampden sales catalog cover featuring the "Man o' Fashion" wristwatch

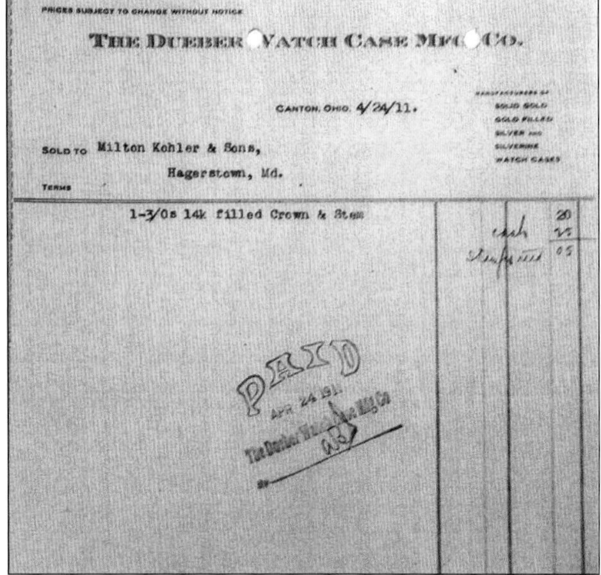

PRICES SUBJECT TO CHANGE WITHOUT NOTICE

THE DUEBER WATCH CASE MFG. CO.

MANUFACTURERS OF SOLID GOLD, GOLD FILLED, SILVER AND SILVERINE WATCH CASES

CANTON, OHIO. 4/24/11.

SOLD TO Milton Kohler & Sons,
Hagerstown, Md.

TERMS

1-3/0s 14k filled Crown & Stem — 20

PAID APR 24 1911

Dueber Watch Case Manufacturing Co. 1911 invoice

THE WATCH TRUST

Beginning in the 1880s, watch manufacturers and casemakers, along with the largest jobbers in the United States, developed a series of "Trusts" to control the sales and prices of watch movements and cases. The manufacturers wanted to ensure that the jobbers would distribute only the products made by the members of the Trust. They also wanted to make certain that only an equal number of cases and movements were sold to jewelers. This froze out independent watch case manufacturers, who did not have a ready source of movements. Dueber solved the problem by buying a movement manufacturer (Hampden). With the passage of Federal antitrust legislation, Dueber decided to sue in Federal court. About the same time, the State of Illinois passed its own antitrust legislation.

The combination of lawsuit and legislation broke the Trust. The Illinois antitrust legislation convinced Elgin, the major manufacturer of movements in the United States, to withdraw from the trust. In addition, Dueber in 1892 won its lawsuit.

At one time the Trust included the Springfield Watch Company, Elgin, Brooklyn Watch Case Company, Waltham, Howard, Blauer Watch Case Company, Hampden Watch Company, Keystone Watch Case Company, Crescent Watch Case Company, Columbus Watch Company, Joseph Fahys and Co., Courvoisier Watch Company, H. Muhr's Sons, and Bates & Bacon. Pursuant to their rules, "No Jobber shall be allowed to sell any American movements without cases. The cases may be of Gold, Gold Filled, Silver, or Base metal, and it is not necessary that they should fit the movements sold with them, but as many cases as movement must be sold in each bill." An additional restriction: "Cases may be sold in excess of, and without movements to any desired extent, but not a movement without a case of some kind accompanying it." John Dueber's main reason for buying the Hampden Watch Company was to be able to offer movements and cases to independent jewelers in equal amounts.

By 1896 most of the trusts fell apart, although periodically they would start again until President Theodore Roosevelt and his "trust busting" campaign put a stop to them. In the early twentieth century, Burlington conducted a several year advertising campaign to beat the trusts (see Chapter 6).

Judging from the number of Man o' Fashions available for purchase secondhand today, it appears that the model enjoyed a solid following. Unfortunately, the new models failed to lift Dueber from its economic doldrums. After falling into receivership in 1927, the companies were sold in 1930 for $325,000 to Armand Hammer on behalf of the Soviet Government and then moved to Russia to form the Amtorg Watch Company. Twenty-eight freight cars loaded with machinery and parts were moved to Russia to establish the first Soviet watch factory. Twenty-one former Dueber-Hampden watchmakers, engravers and various other technicians traveled to Russia for one year to help train the Russian workers in the art of watchmaking as part of the Soviet Union's first Five-Year Plan. Amtorg remains in operation today. (Hammer also purchased the Ansonia Clock Company, which made dollar watches, and moved its equipment to the Soviet Union.)

Americans Will Make Watches in Russia

Soviet Government Buys Equipment of Dueber-Hampden Company and Ansonia Clock Company

***Keystone*, October 1929**

Dueber-Hampden watchmakers leaving for Moscow at the end of 1929

Hamilton Watch Company (1892–1969)

In 1892, on the heels of the dissolution of the original Watch Trust, the Hamilton Watch Company was incorporated. The next year it began production of watches in Lancaster, Pennsylvania, in a watch factory that had existed there since 1874. Hamilton closely followed the trends and regulations set by the nation's railroads. After 1903, Hamilton produced no watches with fewer than 17 jewels. The manufacturing quality of the Hamilton product became renowned throughout the United States.

HAMILTON'S BEGINNINGS

René Rondeau has kindly provided the following valuable information about Hamilton's early history:

"Hamilton filed papers with the State of Pennsylvania on November 18, 1892, to incorporate the Hamilton Watch Company 'for the purpose of the manufacture and sale of watches and watch movements and materials and everything pertaining to watches, from steel, brass, nickel and other metals.' The application was approved officially on December 14, 1892, and Hamilton was 'enrolled in Charter Book No. 39, Page 16' in Harrisburg. The document was next 'Recorded in the office for Recording of Deeds &c, in and for LANCASTER COUNTY, PENNSYLVANIA, in Record Book of Charters Volume 1 Page 529 &c,' on December 16, 1892.

"They spent nearly a year preparing to begin production. The first watches were completed on November 25, 1893, and the first recorded sales were on December 9, 1893. (The original articles of incorporation, as well as the ledgers detailing the first production, are in the NAWCC Library.)"*

*René Rondeau, email to the author, October 5, 2014. He added, "I have #28 in my collection, with the log reference showing it was part of the first day's production as well as first day's sale.

Hamilton movement #28, grade 932, 16 jewels. Just ten were made in the first run. Numbers 21 to 30; only 600 were made in all.

According to Robert I. McCullough, "By 1919, Hamilton's employment had expanded to 750 and its production reached 350 watches per day."[15] In 1922, Hamilton had thirty-two different watch models in sizes from 6/0 to 18 size.

Profitable Watch Selling

A Ten Point Synopsis for the executives of Jewelry Establishments who believe business is conducted on a basis of fair profit which will permit steady development and expansion on the solid foundation of confidence.

In a two-page advertisement in the December 1, 1927 issue of the *Jewelers' Circular*, the Hamilton Watch Company spelled out the ten principles that the Hamilton business had been based on over the previous thirty-five years and, more importantly, the philosophy of its longtime president Charles F. Miller: "business conducted on a basis of profit which will permit steady development and expansion on the solid foundation of confidence." These ten principles, summarized below, clearly show Hamilton's recognition of dependability and accuracy above all else:

1. The watch should be dependable, keeping accurate time.
2. The watch should be "attractively and artistically dialed and cased."
3. The watch should be known as an accurate timekeeper "by the majority of the consuming public."
4. The watch must be priced at a fair price to the consumer.
5. The watch should be kept in stock by the dealer.
6. Watches should not be distributed by sub-jobbers, agencies, brokers, bootleggers or price cutters.
7. Watches should not be sold by a merchant that "seeks to foul a fair name [i.e., Hamilton's] for his own selfish gain."
8. A sale of a Hamilton watch means "not only a real profit [to the seller] in the first sale, but a satisfied customer for other sales."
9. "For the last sixteen years Hamilton have been so well advertised that they became increasingly easy to sell." Hamilton pledged:
10. "A beautiful watch of dependable accuracy" that was "Sold at a fair price with a fair profit," and "Sold through wholesale distributors of our choice, who honor our policies."

***Keystone*, December 1927**

Hamilton's late entry into the wristwatch market forced it to make up ground, as Bryan Girouard and Will Roseman point out:

> Hamilton's successful entrance into the men's wristwatch market had to be done quickly and economically. In April of 1917, Hamilton decided to use two of its existing movements for what it termed the 'Gent's Wrist Watch'—a factory-cased men's wristwatch with either the 17-jewel, grade 983 0- size movement or the 19-jewel, grade 985 0-size movement providing the power.
>
> The 0-size began its life as a factory-cased woman's chatelaine watch in 1908 . . . and . . . was modeled after the Swiss-made Meylan 17-jewel movement. However, the grade 983 and grade 985 0 size movements . . . could be fitted into any standard 0-size case. This allowed Hamilton to eliminate the need for any new case tooling, and subsequently, Hamilton was able to quickly and economically produce a men's wristwatch in a relatively short period of time—just two months. Most importantly, the 983 and 985 were known to be quality movements that could withstand the more rigorous service to which wristwatches were subjected.[16]

However, 0-size movements in wristwatches never caught on. Most manufacturers, including Elgin, Waltham and Illinois, ceased production of this size movement about the time of America's entry into World War I. To most, the size seemed archaic. Since the market did not warm to Hamilton's 0-size wristwatch, few were produced.

Hamilton followed this attempt to enter the men's wristwatch market by promoting a smaller, existing ladies' movement in its men's wristwatches. On November 11, 1922, it announced the availability of a men's 6/0 size watch, using the grade 986 movement originally designed for ladies' watches.[17] But even with the shift to a smaller size, Hamilton's wristwatch sales grew slowly until the late 1920s.

Hamilton's wristwatch line for men finally hit its stride with the introduction of the 6/0 size, 987 grade movement in late 1926. Previously, Hamilton had manufactured a very limited number of men's wristwatches with a seconds register. Beginning with the grade 987, which it had specifically designed for use in a wristwatch, the vast majority of its offerings included the seconds register. In 1928, in order to double its manufacturing capacity, it acquired the Illinois Watch Company. In 1923, railroad watches had accounted for 53% of Hamilton's production; ten years later, in 1933, railroad watches had declined to only 10% of their business. Hamilton continued to trail Elgin and Waltham in wristwatch production, never to catch up.

R. H. Ingersoll & Brother (1892–1922)

When the Ingersoll brothers first went into business, selling low-cost items by mail, both the New Haven Clock Company and the Waterbury Clock Company at Waterbury, Connecticut, were producing cheap watches. Ingersoll contracted for several thousand of these and listed them in its mail-order catalogs for the first time in 1892, pricing them at one dollar. They proved an instant success and the sales increased rapidly. Later, the Waterbury Clock Company contracted with Ingersoll to produce the watches under the Ingersoll name. In 1908, Ingersoll purchased the factory and business of the Trenton Watch Company of Trenton, New Jersey. (Trenton Watch had been founded in 1885.) Thus, by 1908, Ingersoll watches were made in three places: in the factory of the Waterbury Clock Company; in their own factory at Waterbury, Connecticut; and in their acquired factory at Trenton, New Jersey.[18]

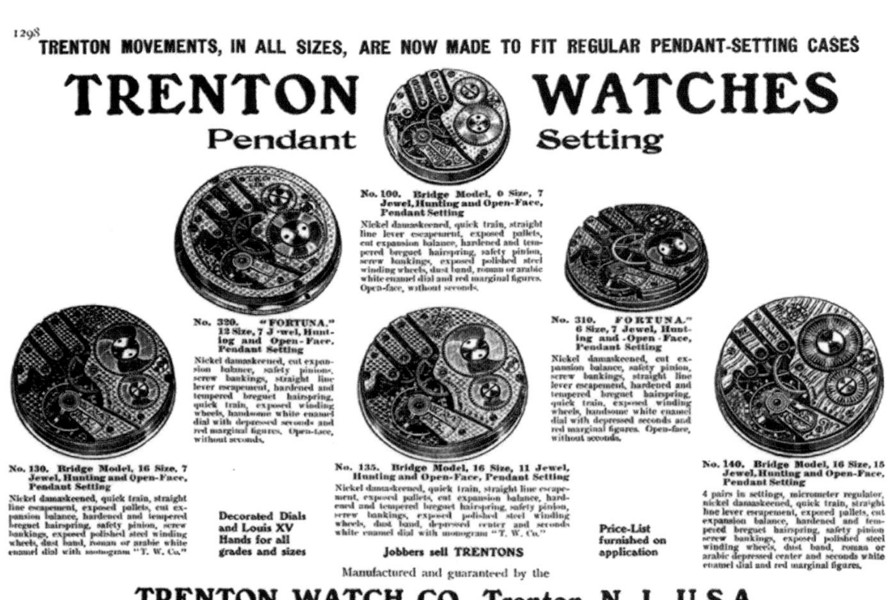

Keystone, August 1905

Many things about Ingersoll watches can be learned by examining print advertisements of the late nineteenth and early twentieth centuries. The addresses listed at the bottom of advertisements indicate that the company's main office was in New York City, at 65 and/or 67 Cortlandt Street and later at 51 and/or 53 Maiden Lane. To judge from the number of advertisements and their variety, the company was quite aggressive in its advertising. The advertisements were often quite clever; for example, a 1900 advertisement entitled "Correct Time for a Dollar!" plays upon biblical text, pointing out that "By Their Works Ye Shall Know Them." Although Ingersoll continued to offer the famous original "Yankee Dollar Watch," the company later had more expensive watches as well. A 1911 Ingersoll-Trenton advertisement for "The best gift of all—a Watch" shows six different levels of watches, including (unjeweled) Ingersolls at $1.00, $1.50, and $2.00 as well as Ingersoll-Trenton models ranging from a 7-jewel one at $5.00 to a 19-jewel one at $25.00.

Milham points out that with the 1922 output at about 20,000 watches a day, Ingersoll "had literally put a watch into every man's pocket."[19] Notwithstanding this robust production, Ingersoll went bankrupt and its assets were purchased by the Waterbury Clock Company in 1922 for $1.5 million. Waterbury Clock sold the London-based arm of Ingersoll, Ltd. to its board of directors in 1930, making it a wholly U.K.-owned company. In 1944 the Waterbury Clock company was renamed United States Time Corporation (now Timex Group U.S.A.), and continued producing Ingersoll watches in the United States through the 1950s.

THE DOLLAR WATCH

"Convinced that there was a large market for their [dollar] watches, Ingersoll . . . ordered a new, specially embossed watch for sale at the 1893 Columbian Exposition in Chicago. . . . They sold about 85,000 of them. . . . By 1895 Ingersoll was ordering half a million watches a year from the Waterbury Clock Company for sale as Ingersolls, and the two companies signed an exclusive agreement. . . . The production of Ingersoll watches became a major part of the Waterbury Clock Company's business and they made tens of millions of watches for Ingersoll over the next 10–15 years."*

*Norman M. Tallen, "The American Dollar Watch—A Watch Everyone Could Afford," NAWCC *Bulletin*, No. 325 (April 2000), p. 166.

An early Ingersoll promotional sign for the United Kingdom with its prices in shillings and pence

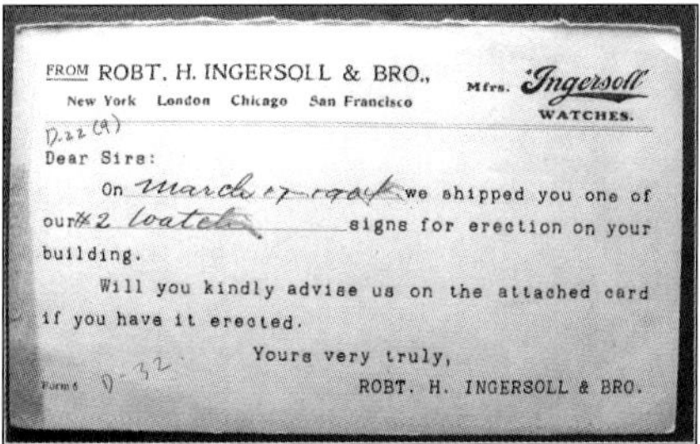

FROM ROBT. H. INGERSOLL & BRO., Mfrs. Ingersoll WATCHES.
New York London Chicago San Francisco

Dear Sirs:

On [illegible] we shipped you one of our #2 watch signs for erection on your building.

Will you kindly advise us on the attached card if you have it erected.

Yours very truly,
ROBT. H. INGERSOLL & BRO.

Form 6

July 20, 1904 postcard

***Recreation Magazine*, December 1898**

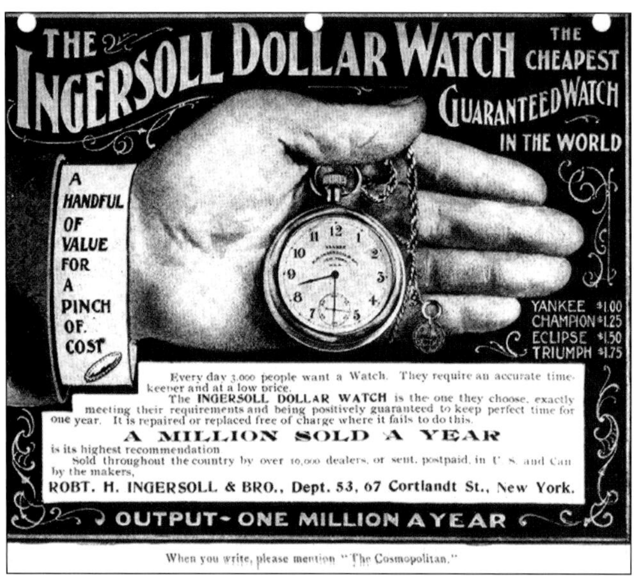

Cosmopolitan, 1900

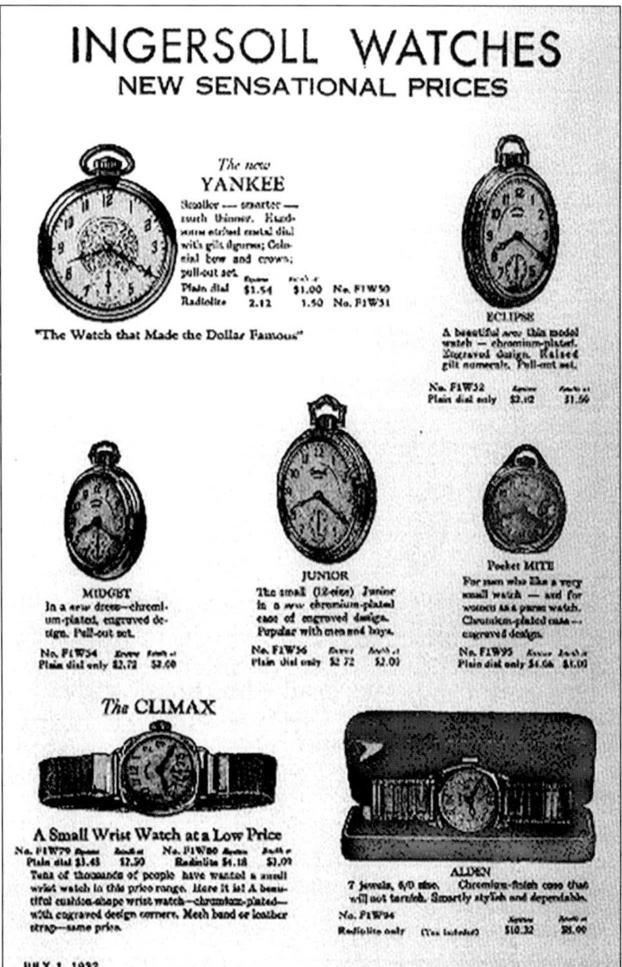

N. Shure catalog, 1932

ROBERT H. INGERSOLL (1859-1928)

Robert H. Ingersoll, c. 1915

When Robert Hawley Ingersoll passed away, his obituary in the September 13, 1928 issue of the Jewelers' *Circular* stated that his name became a "household" word by reason of his "enterprise and innovations, for Mr. Ingersoll was practically the originator of the so-called dollar watch, and his slogan . . . 'The Watch That Made The Dollar Famous' spread from coast to coast, and in fact all over the world."

When Ingersoll started in business, he eventually brought on board his older brother Charles H. Ingersoll. After beginning a rubber stamp business, they then turned to watches in 1892, starting a mail-order business to test-market one thousand pocket watches at one dollar each. To their surprise, the public responded favorably to the idea of dollar watches.

The Ingersolls operated under the premise that their watches must be "practical and timely timekeepers," must sell for a dollar, and have a "sturdy ruggedness that would defy ordinary hand usage."

Charles H. Ingersoll, April 1928

INGERSOLL FOR GOVERNOR

Charles H. Ingersoll announced in September 1934 that he would run for governor of New Jersey as a Single Tax candidate. His campaign slogan was "Plenty for Everybody." He ran as an Independent but, apparently not being as popular as his watches, garnered only a scant 0.049 percent of the popular vote (or 528 total votes).

Ingersoll estimated that, incredibly enough, he and his brother Robert sold more than one hundred million watches and at one time produced as many as twenty thousand a day!

UNITED STATES LEADS IN MANUFACTURE OF TIMEPIECES

In November 1928 it was reported by the United States Government that according to 1925 production numbers, the United States was the largest manufacturer of clocks and watches in the world, followed by Switzerland and Germany, in that order. The production of watches and clocks in the United States was almost equal to the combined production of Switzerland (the closest watch competitor) and Germany (the closest clock competitor).

At this point, the United States was the best market in the world for clocks and watches.

New York Standard Watch Company (1885–1929)

The New York Standard Watch Company was formed in 1885 in Jersey City, New Jersey. (This company is different from the New York Watch Company, which was one of the predecessors of the Hampden Watch Company.) New York Standard was a very early victim of the Great Depression, ceasing operation in 1929 after producing over eight million watches. Although the company made mostly low-grade, low-priced watches, some of the rarer models are quite collectible.[20]

New York Standard was best known for offering a unique, patented straight-line lever "worm gear." This led to its advertising slogan "The watch with a worm in it." Since the company made few of these watches in comparison to its total production, they are somewhat scarce today.

New York Standard advertisement, c. 1903

The escapement with a worm gear drive, patented in 1887 by Robert Clay of Jersey City and William Hanson of Brooklyn, was designed so as to dispense with the usual gear train and thus enable the manufacture of a watch with fewer moving parts.[21] In 1903 the system was sold to the Keystone Watch Case Company.

South Bend Watch Company/ Studebaker Watch Company (1903–1929)

The assets of the bankrupt Columbus Watch Company of Columbus, Ohio, were purchased in 1902 by three Studebaker brothers from South Bend, Indiana—George, J. M. and Clement, Jr. Construction soon began on a factory building in South Bend, and 145 former Columbus Watch employees were hired. The South Bend Watch Company began production in 1903.[22]

SOUTH BEND'S CAKE OF ICE

To proclaim that its watches would withstand temperature extremes, the South Bend Watch Co. was famous for advertisements showing a watch encased in a "cake of ice" with the statement "Every South Bend Watch must stand the ice test."* However, an article in the *South Bend Tribune*, Feb. 16, 1969, mentioned that "one lady who was a file clerk at the factory recalled seeing one letter from a customer stating, 'Your - - - - watch may run in a block of ice, but it won't run in my pants pocket.'" †

*Paul Berg, "The Studebakers and the South Bend Watch Co.," NAWCC *Bulletin*, No. 153, Aug. 1971, pp. 1186–87. He also gives a slightly different version of the letter incident, remarking that the "story circulated through the plant."

†Noted by O. B. Frye in "Jesse Elwood Coleman and the South Bend Story," NAWCC *Bulletin*, No. 252 (Feb. 1988), p. 36. Frye also mentions that the company went to the other temperature extreme in some advertisements, claiming that if properly sealed, the watch would run in boiling water (p. 29).

An outdoor South Bend metal advertising sign

HOW TO FREEZE AN ILLINOIS WATCH IN A CAKE OF ICE

Evidently, some jewelers wanted to display Illinois watches in their store windows with the watches encased in a block of ice (perhaps to compete with the South Bend watch advertisements). Although the Illinois Watch Company was not in favor of this practice, it provided the following advice:

"There is only one way to do this successfully—that is to seal the case so no water or moisture can get into the movement. The cake of ice is then chipped out from the back, making a hole large enough to admit the watch face forward. The chipped ice is then filled in back of the watch, and soon freezes solid.

"No special watch case is required, any Bunn Special case properly sealed with wax, so the water cannot get into the movement, will work. While we do not recommend this class of window display we give the information to those who care to feature such an idea."*

*Typewritten sheet, Hamilton—Ravel Collection, NAWCC [National Association of Watch and Clock Collectors] Library and Research Center, Columbia, Pennsylvania.

A South Bend Watch Company metal movement container

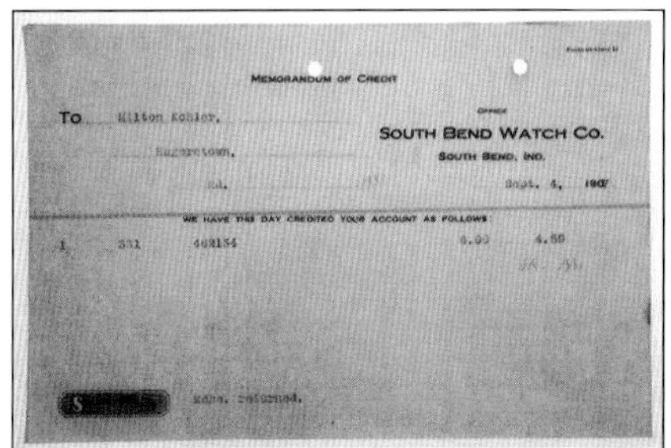
MEMORANDUM OF CREDIT

To

SOUTH BEND WATCH CO.

SOUTH BEND, IND.

WE HAVE THIS DAY CREDITED YOUR ACCOUNT AS FOLLOWS

South Bend Watch Company 1907 invoice

South Bend advertising pin showing the famous image of a South Bend pocket watch encased in a block of ice. On the underside of the pin is printed "Bastian Bros. Co., M'F'R'F of Ribbon Metal and Celluloid Novelties, Rochester, N.Y." Founded in 1895, this company initially operated as a jewelry store. Not long afterward, it was one of the first firms in the city to become a union shop. Today known as the Bastian Company, it continues to be fully unionized.

The history of the South Bend Watch Company can be a bit confusing, as O. B. Frye indicates. "There was no business connection between the watch company and the Studebaker Wagon Company, which later manufactured automobiles. The three brothers who manufactured watches were sons of one of the founders of the wagon company, hence the ongoing confusion between the watch and the car.[23]

To add to the confusion, there were other entities also named Studebaker. Paul Berg points out that "in 1920 the Studebaker Mail Order Co., Chicago, Ill., was formed to become a holding company for the South Bend Watch Co., the Studebaker Watch Co. (incorporated in 1923), and the Studebaker Watch Co., of Canada, Ltd. (incorporated in 1924).[24]

Watches branded South Bend, highly regarded for their fine quality, were sold through dealers. The Studebaker Mail Order Co., which sold various jewelry items, also sold imported wristwatches and Studebaker brand pocket watches. These mail-order watches were offered for sale "direct to the customer with $5 down and $3.50 per month until paid for. A booklet for keeping records of the payments was given to the customer. The buyer only had to get the signature of three businessmen or bonds to establish credit. This was found to be an insecure method of selling and too many accounts were not paid." [25]

When the stock market crashed, the company could not manage its delinquent accounts. As a result, it experienced a quick demise; on November 27, 1929, the plant was closed, never to be reopened. Liquidation of assets began January 31, 1932 and was completed in 1933.[26]

"Thus ended Indiana's only watchmaking company, which in twenty-six years had produced over one million watches and had paid over $20,000,000 in wages," Berg writes. "It, like many other famous American watch firms, learned that the end of the 1920's was the end of the pocket watch era." [27]

Swiss Watch Industry

As described earlier in this chapter, the precipitous decline in Swiss imports to the United States accompanied the rise of the American watch industry. From the end of the nineteenth century until World War I, the American share of Swiss imports remained at around 5%; but by 1929 it had grown to 18.5%.[28] Almost all watches and watch movements imported to the United States were Swiss.

In 1910, Swiss imports represented about 254,000 total movements. In the next decade, growth exploded, especially because American-based watch brands expanded their procurement of Swiss movements to place in American-made cases. The actual number of movements imported from Switzerland reached 2.3 million in 1920, but fell back to 1.2 million by 1930, in line with the general decline of watch production at the end of the 1920s[29]. Before the decline, though, the Swiss enjoyed the same growth in timepiece sales as was experienced in the United States. And this growth did not go unnoticed by American watch manufacturers, some of which started to suffer declining sales in 1929.

Those Who Commit Chablonnage

Besides manufacturers who made and cased their watches in the United States, a second group of United States manufacturers existed: those engaged in chablonnage, the fitting of foreign (almost always Swiss) watch movements into domestically manufactured watch cases. Major brands involved in this practice included Gruen, Bulova, Wittnauer and Benrus. To the Swiss, this practice represented the greatest threat to their continued dominance in the world's watch markets, for they feared a resultant technology transfer at some point in the future. [30]

Of the four major chablonnage participants, one began as a watchmaker and three started their careers as jewelers.

Gruen Watch Company (1874–1958)

The Gruen Watch Company was officially formed in 1894, although the company later traced its history back to 1874, adopting the early career of its founder, Dietrich Gruen, as part of its history. He started the Columbus Watch Manufacturing Company in 1876. With new partners, the company reorganized in 1882 as the Columbus Watch Company. In 1894 it changed its name, yet again, to the New Columbus Watch Company and survived until 1902, when it sold everything to the Studebaker family, who then started the South Bend Watch Company with Columbus's assets.[31]

D. Gruen (1847–1911)

1874
HISTORICAL NOTES

- New York City annexes the Bronx.
- Benjamin Disraeli replaces William Gladstone as English Premier.
- Child Labor Law takes twelve-year-olds out of the workforce.
- William Marcy "Boss" Tweed, of Tammany Hall (New York City) is convicted of defrauding the city of $6M, and is sentenced to twelve years' imprisonment.
- Joseph F. Glidden patents barbed wire.

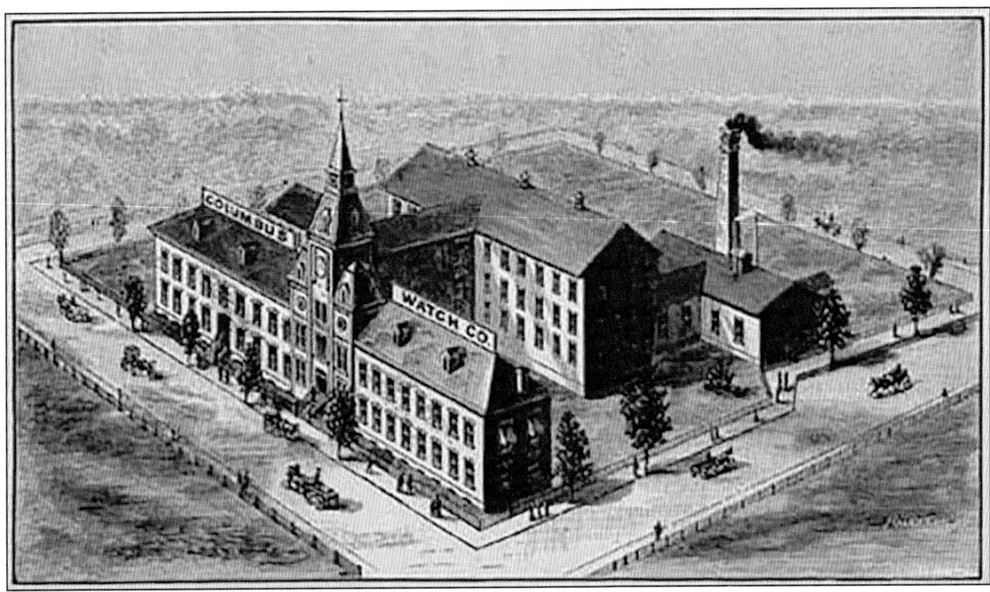

The Columbus Watch Factory in Columbus, Ohio, c. 1880s. It was later to become the South Bend Watch Company.

Subsequently, Fred Gruen, the son of Dietrich Gruen, formed the partnership D. Gruen & Son. When a second son, George, joined the business in 1898, the firm's name was changed to D. Gruen, Sons & Company. In 1898 the company relocated from Columbus to Cincinnati, purchasing the Queen City Watch Case Company and changing its name to the Gruen National Watch Case Company. At first, Gruen purchased movements from Germany, but it later bought movements and dials from Switzerland.

Until 1922 there had been three Gruen companies: D. Gruen, Sons & Company; the Gruen National Watch Case Company of Cincinnati; and the Gruen Watch Manufacturing Company of Biel, Switzerland. In 1922 all three businesses were merged to form the Gruen Watch Company. By the mid-twenties Gruen's total sales exceeded five million dollars; it was said to be the second-largest watch company in America, surpassed in size only by Elgin.

Among Gruen's innovations was the Cartouche, its first movement designed specifically for wristwatches. A 1921 advertisement announcing the Cartouche proclaimed it "the logical wrist watch shape," pointing out that a round movement in an oblong case wasted space and that an oblong movement of the same width provided double the room for parts. The sleek Cartouche models proved very popular, and Gruen eventually came out with more than 500 variants, some of them decorated with colored enamel in striking Art Deco patterns.

Introduced in 1925 was another Gruen innovation, the Quadron movement, which significantly changed the direction of the American men's watch market, doing for it what the Cartouche had done for the ladies' market. The Quadron, so named because it was rectangular, comprised several movement grades. Because of its new shape, the movement could be used in a smaller, thinner, more fashionable case. The introduction of the Quadron began a trend towards smaller men's watches, which fit the wrist more comfortably than earlier ones had done. Later, the Illinois grade 207 movement, announced in 1929, permitted Illinois and, subsequently, Hamilton to enjoy the advantages of a similar rectangular movement.

Paul Schliesser, a Gruen historian, noted that after the Depression started, watch sales in the United States declined; however, most of these were in the lower price range, not the "upscale" watches that Gruen sold. But after 1929, Gruen began to offer many less expensive watches. According to Schliesser, as bad as things were for Gruen, it was actually in a better position relative to others in the United States watch industry. Hardest hit were the companies that failed to move into the wristwatch market, like the E. Howard Company and the South Bend Watch Company.[32]

Bulova (1875–1979)

Joseph Bulova (1851–1936) emigrated from Bohemia in 1872, landing in New York. By 1874 he had founded his own jewelry store, J. Bulova Company, in Maiden Lane. Like most jewelers of his time, Bulova purchased movements and cases separately, then combined them to meet his customer's needs. His business grew, and in 1912 he began manufacturing his own watch movements in Biel, Switzerland, using assembly-line techniques and standardized parts.

As the 1920s dawned, Bulova sensed new trends. Although

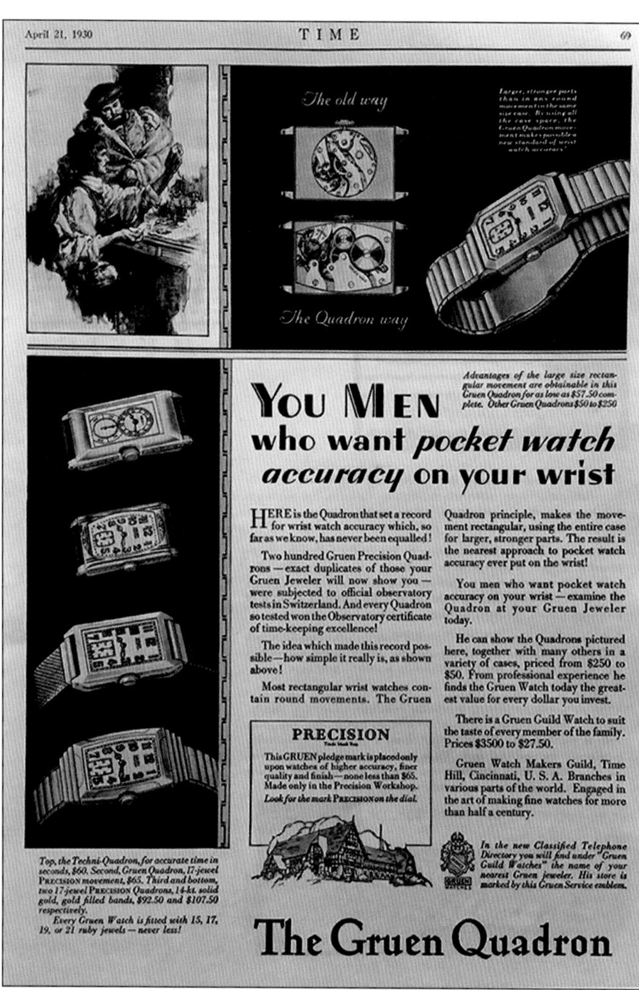

Time, April 21, 1930

Time, October 13, 1930

Bulova stated that in 1919 it offered "the first ever complete line of men's jeweled wristwatches," this assertion cannot be confirmed. There is also confusion about the exact nature of Bulova's offerings, at least partially because its transition from an importer to a manufacturer of a watch brand is not entirely clear in its history. Bulova apparently produced watches branded Hudson Maxim and Rubaiyat, as well as ones under the Lady Maxim name, and the names were for entire lines of watches, not just individual models. The name Rubaiyat was used commercially by Bulova as early as 1916, and a 1922 advertisement for Lady Maxim, though not mentioning Bulova by name, shows the "Goddess of Time," which became one of Bulova's most famous advertising graphics.[33]

Bulova advertisement, 1928. The lovely "Goddess of Time" is one of Bulova's most famous graphics.

In 1920, Bulova moved to 580 Fifth Avenue and set up its own observatory on top of the building to determine universal time. Bulova understood that the evolving market for wristwatches emphasized both convenience and accuracy. In 1923, J. Bulova reincorporated and recapitalized as the Bulova Watch Company. Examples of Bulova branded watches appear about this same time.

Because of its jewelry store roots, Bulova watches emphasized stylish cases with a quality movement at a good price. The combination of fashion and accuracy at a reasonable price proved a winning formula. To this, Bulova added exceptional advertising skills.

Since airplane pilots were rock stars of the 1920s, the marketing-savvy Bulova offered a $1,000 prize to the first pilot to fly nonstop across the Atlantic. This feat had been discussed in aeronautical circles for years; the Orteig Prize of $25,000 for accomplishing it had been announced in 1919 but no one had been able to claim it. Charles Lindbergh accomplished this feat in 1927, and did it flying solo (not a requirement). Accordingly, he was dubbed the "Lone Eagle" by the press. Bulova sent him its $1,000 prize and also a Bulova watch. Thereafter, Bulova continued to promote its connection with Lindbergh through its famous "Lone Eagle" series of wristwatches, severing the connection only when Lindbergh declared his sympathies with the actions of the Third Reich.

Bulova's most important horological innovation was the Accutron watch, which used a resonant tuning fork as a means of regulating the time-keeping function. Appearing in 1960, the Accutron's radical new movement turned the whole watch industry inside-out.

In 1979, Bulova became part of the Loews Corporation. At the beginning of 2008, the Citizen Watch Company purchased Bulova for $250 million.

THE JOSEPH BULOVA SCHOOL OF WATCHMAKING

One of Bulova's most significant horological contributions was the Joseph Bulova School of Watchmaking, founded in 1945 by Arde Bulova, then chairman of the board of the Bulova Watch Company, in honor of his late father.

Joseph (Josef) Bulova, late in life

At the opening of the school, he stated: "For the purpose of aiding war veterans who are physically handicapped, the Bulova School of Watchmaking has been founded to teach the art and trade of watch, clock and instrument making and repairing, including the use of tools, machinery and equipment necessary in carrying on such a trade. Graduates of the school are expected to be placed in positions in jewelry stores throughout the country and thus be assisted in finding a place in life in a useful and happy occupation. This is but a small measure of the gratitude that can be shown to these men for their service to our country in this greatest of all wars."

Although the school was Arde Bulova's idea, there were others involved in its creation. Among them was Stanley Simon, Bulova's director of industrial relations. In an obituary in the *New York Times*,* Margalit Fox notes that he "oversaw the construction of a building specifically tailored to the needs of disabled people" long before the Americans With Disabilities Act. The handsome building was designed with ramps, automatic doors with extra-wide openings (including those of elevators), and non-slip floors.

Fox writes that the first class consisted of "about 20 men from across the country, "who were housed with their families in apartments nearby. For most, as the *New York Times* later wrote, the school 'was their first postwar experience outside hospitals.'

Several students had lost legs. One . . . had lost an arm: he was provided with a special prosthesis, which he helped design that let him hold delicate watch parts without crushing them.

"In 1946, after a year's instruction, the men graduated. They were the first of many hundreds of graduates in the decades that followed, nearly all of whom went on to jobs in watch repair or allied fields like precision toolmaking."

The school, which was tuition-free, was supported entirely by the Bulova Foundation. It lasted for nearly fifty years, finally closing in 1993.

*Margalit Fox, "Stanley Simon, Who Assisted Veterans, Is Dead at 93," *New York Times*, August 16, 2010.

Jewelers Pledge Jobs to Disabled

Seven hundred and fifty-eight jewelers in the country have pledged 1,400 jobs to disabled veterans, it was announced today, as an observanace of "National Employ the Physically Handicapped Week" proclaimed by President Truman.

These jobs were pledged to graduates of the Bulova School of Watchmaking at Woodside. Brooklyn jewelers co-operating are: Eypel Jewelry Stores, 853 Manhattan Ave.; Castle Jewelry Company, 464 Fulton St.; V. Rosenthal & Sons, 188 Havemeyer St.; Vincent's Jewelry Shop, 75 DeKalb Ave., and M. J. Berch, 114 Flatbush Ave.

Queens jewelers offering jobs are Arthur's Jewelry Shop, 131 Rockaway Boulevard, South Ozone Park; Greenwold, 3661 Main St., Flushing; H. L. Gross & Bros., 165-03 Jamaica Ace., Jamaica; A. Rosenstein, 1064 Central Ave., Far Rockaway, and Samuel Zickerman, Woodside.

758 jewelers pledged 1,400 jobs to disabled veterans graduating from The Bulova School of Watchmaking in 1945. *Brooklyn Daily Eagle* (Brooklyn, NY), October 10, 1945; image from *newspapers.com*

Wittnauer (1885–1936)

Swiss-born Albert Wittnauer, a skilled watchmaker, arrived in New York City in 1872 and joined the firm of his brother-in-law J. Eugene Robert, an importer of fine Swiss watches. Two years later, his brother, Louis, also found employment with Robert.[34]

Sensing the need for a watch movement combining well-crafted durability at a competitive price, Albert created his own design in 1880: a movement manufactured in Switzerland specifically for the American market. Five years later,

Robert handed the reins of his business to Albert, and in 1890 officially transferred the firm's title to him as well. Albert then renamed the firm A. Wittnauer & Co., with himself as president. By then, Albert's younger brother Emile also had joined the firm.

A. Wittnauer remained a family firm. When his brother Louis died in 1899, Emile took over as manager of the New York office. Albert himself died at the age of 52 in 1908, leaving Emile to assume the presidency. Their sister, Martha Wittnauer, then became vice president. Emile's death in 1916 led to Martha's becoming a rare female CEO in that era. The Great Depression significantly wounded Wittnauer, forcing Martha to sell the family business in 1936.

As part of their business, the Wittnauers imported and distributed Longines watches. Long after they sold the family business, advertising perpetuated Wittnauer's Longines connection.

National Geographic, May 1928

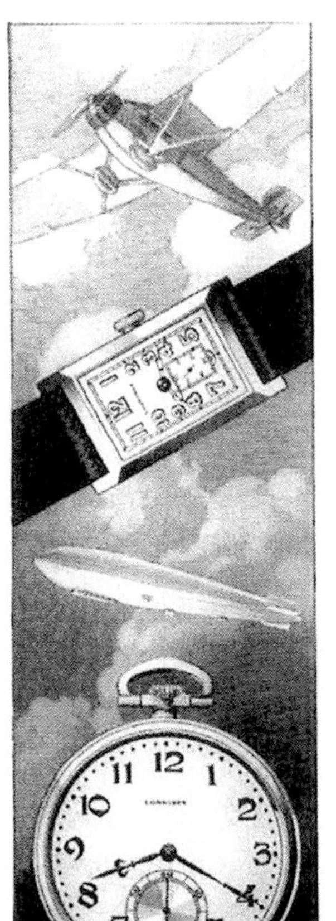

***National Geographic*, December 1929**

During World War I, Wittnauer produced watches and navigational instruments for the early aviation units. The firm became famous for its waterproof, shockproof and anti-magnetic "AllProof Watch" introduced in 1918. In the 1920s, Wittnauer's emphasis continued to be on instrumentation and watches for aviation. In 1932, when Amelia Earhart became not only the first woman to fly alone across the Atlantic but also the first person to accomplish the feat since Lindbergh, her Lockheed Vega-5B was equipped with Wittnauer timepieces.

Benrus (1921–1977)

Sons of Romanian immigrants, the brothers Benjamin, Ralph and Oscar Lazarus (born Lazarowitz) founded the Benrus Watch Company in New York in 1921; the name of the firm is a conflation of Benjamin's first and last names. The Lazarus brothers sensed an opportunity to take advantage of the growing wristwatch market of the 1920s.[35]

Since Benjamin had been employed in the jewelry business before service in the military in World War I, he handled operations when the Benrus company was formed. Oscar, an attorney, helped with administration. Ralph concentrated on sales.

The brothers established their headquarters in New York City. By the late 1920s, they were buying Swiss movements, then making or purchasing American cases and casing the movements at a factory in Waterbury, Connecticut, with some watch assembly completed in New York City. Later they owned a factory in La Chaux-de-Fonds, the center of watchmaking in Switzerland, probably to avoid Swiss restrictions on sales of movements. In the 1920s, Benrus concentrated on middle-quality movements in fashionable cases at reasonable prices.

Time of Transition

Trade relations between Switzerland and the United States had been amicable throughout the nineteenth century. Even after the precipitous decline in Swiss watch purchases in the 1870s, the Swiss share of the United States watch imports held at almost 90%, even though it represented only about 5% of Swiss watch exports.[36] In the twentieth century, however, successively increasing and restrictive tariffs—and finally the Hawley-Smoot Tariff of 1930—soured these relations. The combination of market dislocation, fear of technology transfer, and higher tariffs in America and elsewhere led the Swiss to create cartels to restrict the sales of movements. It was within this fractious, complex and highly unstable watchmaking world at the end of the 1920s that Hamilton made its decision to purchase Illinois.

The 1920s were a time of tremendous transition in the watch industry. This could be seen especially in the men's timepiece market. At the beginning of the decade, the pocket watch reigned supreme. By the end of the decade, however, adoption of new fashion trends made the wristwatch the timepiece of choice.

Major changes could also be found in wristwatch distribution. Jewelers, of course, remained the important retail outlets for watches, as they had through much of the history of the mass-produced watch. Mail-order firms, once a pillar of watch distribution, declined in importance. This appeared to mirror the migration of people from farms to cities. Sears became a brick-and-mortar business in 1925, following in the footsteps of Montgomery Ward. And Babson Bros. Co., which owned the Burlington Watch Company, changed its focus from mail-order items to farm machinery.

At the same time, production records show an almost complete disappearance of private labels. Instead, newspaper advertisements emphasized watch brands. Even as optimism reigned in the late 1920s before the onset of the Depression, wristwatch manufacturers struggled to adjust to the times.

Use of Jobbers and Wholesalers

Through the times of transition, jobbers and wholesalers remained the stalwarts of watch distribution. The Illinois Watch Company, as well as its contemporaries Elgin, Hamilton and Waltham, sold its dials and movements via jobbers, distributors and jewelry wholesalers. Their products were sold by these jobbers, who called upon thousands of independent jewelers spread across the nation. Originally, a jeweler (at a customer's request) married a movement and dial with a case selected by the customer. This practice held true for watch sales during the Transitional Period (when pocket watches were converted to wristwatches) and into the Generic Period (when jewelers and jobbers provided the cases and added the movements and dials from Illinois and other companies into these cases). The Illinois Watch Company and the Hamilton Watch Company never made their own watch cases; however, they increasingly cased the watches in their own factories as the decade wore on.

JOBBER

A jobber is the same as a wholesaler: a person who buys products (e.g., watches) from a manufacturer and sells them directly to retailers (jewelers) rather than to an ultimate customer. The term originally meant a person who works by the piece or at odd jobs. The Illinois Watch Company referred to jobbers, wholesalers and distributors synonymously but most frequently called them all "jobbers."

Jobbers of Illinois Watches

On May 14, 1928, Illinois sold through a group of 105 jobbers located in twenty-one states and the District of Columbia. The 1928 published list of Illinois jobbers is shown here.

JOBBERS
of
ILLINOIS
WATCHES

May 14th, 1928

THE ILLINOIS WATCH
SPRINGFIELD

CALIFORNIA

E. Bastheim Co.
220 W. 5th Street.......Los Angeles
A. I. Hall & Son
150 Post St.......San Francisco
G. G. Voege Co.
700 Metropolitan Bldg.......Los Angeles

COLORADO

The W. W. Hamilton Jewelry Co.
Foster Building.......Denver
The Lehman Jewelry Co., Inc.
Foster Building.......Denver

GEORGIA

Youmans Jewelry Co. (Inc.).......Way Cross

ILLINOIS

C. Becken Co. (Inc.)
180 N. Wabash Ave.......Chicago
Buss, Linthicum, Thorson (Inc.)
35 E. Wacker Drive.......Chicago
J. W. Forsinger Co (Inc.)
31 N State Street.......Chicago
A. Hirsch & Co.
35 E. Wacker Drive.......Chicago
C. H. Knights-Thearle Co.
31 N. State Street.......Chicago
Charles Kolb & Co
7 W. Madison Street.......Chicago
S. Lazarus & Sons
35 E. Wacker Drive.......Chicago
Manheimer Watch Company (Inc.)
31 N. State Street.......Chicago
M. A. Mead & Co. (Inc.)
35 E. Wacker Drive.......Chicago
National Railway Time Service Co. (Inc.)
58 E. Washington Street.......Chicago
The Norris, Alister-Ball-Bridges Co.
58 E. Washington Street.......Chicago

ILLINOIS (Continued)

Rettig, Hess & Madsen (Inc.)
35 E. Wacker Drive.......Chicago
L. H. Schafer & Co. (Inc.)
31 N. State Street.......Chicago
Scott & Barger
29 E. Madison Street.......Chicago
Suite 805
L. Seligman Jewelry Co.
31 N. State Street.......Chicago
Sproehnle (Inc.)
29 E. Madison St.......Chicago
Stein & Ellbogen Co. (Inc.)
31 N. State Street.......Chicago
Otto Young & Co. (Inc.)
29 E. Madison Street.......Chicago
A. S. Wormood
Ferguson Building.......Springfield

INDIANA

Baldwin-Miller Co. (Inc.)
Century Building.......Indianapolis

LOUISIANA

Leonard Krower & Son (Inc.)
623 Canal Street.......New Orleans

MARYLAND

J. Engel & Co.
Baltimore Street and Hopkins Place
.......Baltimore
Max Kohner
104 W. Fayette Street.......Baltimore

MAINE

H. A. Osgood & Son
131 Lisbon Street.......Lewiston

MASSACHUSETTS

I. Alberts' Sons (Inc.)
373 Washington Street......Boston

A. Frisch & Co.
373 Washington Street......Boston

New England Watch and Jewelry Co.
387 Washington St......Boston

M. S. Page & Co.
373 Washington Street......Boston

A. Paul & Co. (Inc.)
373 Washington Street......Boston

D. C. Percival & Co. (Inc.)
373 Washington Street......Boston

E. H. Saxton Co.
387 Washington Street......Boston

MICHIGAN

The E. H. Pudrith Co. (Inc.)
Metropolitan Building......Detroit
33 John R. Street

MINNESOTA

J. M. Bennett Co.
7th St. and 1st Ave., N......Minneapolis

S. H. Clausin & Co. (Inc.)
13-17 S. 6th Street......Minneapolis

Thos. B. Wilson & Co.
100 North 7th Street......Minneapolis

A. L. Haman
Endicott Building......St. Paul

MISSOURI

Edwards-Ludwig-Fuller Jewelry Co. (Inc.)
1113 Walnut Street......Kansas City

C. A. Kiger Co. (Inc.)
Firestone Building......Kansas City

C. B. Norton Jewelry Co. (Inc.)
Gate City Nat'l Bank......Kansas City

Woodstock-Hoefer Watch & Jly. Co. (Inc.)
9th and Walnut Sts......Kansas City

MISSOURI (*Continued*)

Bauman-Massa Jewelry Co. (Inc.)
214 N. 6th Street......St. Louis

Jas. J. Burke Co.
9th & Olive Sts......St. Louis

Eisenstadt Mfg. Co. (Inc.)
Louderman Building......St. Louis
S. W. Cor. Locust & 11th Sts.

NEBRASKA

J. L. Teeters & Co. (Inc.)
123 North 9th Street......Lincoln

Byrne-Duff Jewelry Co. (Inc.)
W. O. W. Building......Omaha

NEW YORK

M. Levitz & Co.
133 N. Pearl Street......Albany

Eliassof Bros. & Co.
100 State St......Albany

King & Eisele Co. (Inc.)
210 Franklin Street......Buffalo

Jas. K. Thompson & Son (Inc.)
Gerrans Building......Buffalo

Van Der Voort Bros. (Inc.)
212 Ellicott Square......Buffalo

Sammet & Lande Corp.
118 Lake St......Elmyra

Aisenstein-Woronock & Sons
22 Eldridge St......New York

Buss, Linthicum, Thorson (Inc.)
20 W. 47th Street......New York

Freudenheim Bros. (Inc.)
170 Broadway......New York

Henry Freund & Bro.
20 W. 47th Street......New York

Henry Ginnel & Co.
15 Maiden Lane......New York

Jonas Koch
20 W. 47th Street......New York

NEW YORK (Continued)

L. Manheimer & Bros. (Inc.)
20 W. 47th Street......New York

I. Ollendorff Co. (Inc.)
20 W. 47th Street......New York

H. N. Schiff
20 W. 47th Street......New York

J. J. Schmukler
133 Canal Street......New York

N. H. White & Co.
21 Maiden Lane......New York

Philip Present Co.
Chamber of Commerce Bldg......Rochester

Morris Rosenbloom & Co.
115 Clinton Ave., S......Rochester

W. P. Hitchcock Co. (Inc.)
319 S. Salina Street......Syracuse

S. A. Liberman & Sons
303 Loew Building......Syracuse

A. H. Pond Co. (Inc.)
214 S. Warren Street......Syracuse

Abelson-Harris Co. (Inc.)
1st Nat'l Bank Bldg......Utica

OHIO

Greenwold-Grift Co.
18 W. 7th Street......Cincinnati

L. Gutmann & Sons
432 Walnut Street......Cincinnati

Hahn-Jacobsen Co. (Inc.)
31 E. 4th Street......Cincinnati

Richter & Phillips Co. (Inc.)
Temple Bar Bldg., N. W. Court and Main Sts.......Cincinnati

A. G. Schwab & Sons
227 E. 6th Street......Cincinnati

OHIO (*Continued*)

M. Schwab Jewelry Co.
411 Race Street......Cincinnati

The Wallenstein-Mayer Co. (Inc.)
31 E. 4th Street......Cincinnati

H. W. Burdick Co. (Inc.)
305 Swetland Building......Cleveland

A. H. Ficken Co. (Inc.)
722 Union Mortgage Bldg......Cleveland

The Scribner & Loehr Co. (Inc.)
1148 Euclid Avenue......Cleveland

The Wagner-Gilger-Cohn Co. (Inc.)
415 Hippodrome Building......Cleveland

W. F. Broer Co. (Inc.)
Dime Bank Building......Toledo

PENNSYLVANIA

The Non-Retailing Co. (Inc.)
36 E. Chestnut Street......Lancaster

H. O. Hurlburt & Sons
813 Chestnut Street......Philadelphia

Louis Sickles
1015 Chestnut Street......Philadelphia

M. Sickles & Sons
900 Chestnut Street......Philadelphia

L. P. White
Sheridan Building......Philadelphia

Biggard & Co.
Room 305-307, Clark Bldg......Pittsburgh

Heeren Bros. Co. (Inc.)
Penn Avenue and 8th Street......Pittsburgh

The W. J. Johnston Co. (Inc.)
Union Bank Building......Pittsburgh

I. Ollendorff Co. (Inc.)
717 Liberty Ave., Clark Bldg......Pittsburgh

Samuel Weinhaus Co. (Inc.)
722 Penn Avenue......Pittsburgh

RHODE ISLAND

The Albert Walker Co.
202 Washington St......Providence

TEXAS

C. L. Norsworthy Co.
1420 Commerce Street......Dallas

Shuttles Bros. & Lewis (Inc.)
Jackson and Browder Streets......Dallas

B. M. Hammond & Co.
111 W. Commerce St......San Antonio

UTAH

Decker Jewelry Co.
Dooly Building......Salt Lake City

WASHINGTON

Mayer Bros. (Inc.)
Mann Bldg.......Seattle

S. H. Clausin & Co. (Inc.)
Hyde Building......Spokane

WASHINGTON, D. C.

E M. Rosenthal Jewelry Co.
1342 G St., N. W......Washington, D. C.

WISCONSIN

Boszhardt-Possin Co. (Inc.)
209 Wisconsin Avenue......Milwaukee

With this sales and marketing approach, the Illinois Watch Company did not have to bear the cost and management of a large direct-sales force. However, Illinois did have on its payroll several employees functioning as regional salespersons; Julius Armbruster and Jack Samuels were two of them. In their geographic regions, they visited local jobbers and wholesalers to obtain orders for Illinois movements and dials. Illinois' regional sales offices were first located at 192 Broadway in New York City and later moved to 21 Maiden Lane, in what was then the jewelry center of New York; at 220 Sutter Street in San Francisco; and in Chicago at 71 Washington Street initially, and later at 104 State Street. During the Deco Period (the late 1920s to the early 1930s) and Moderne Period (the early 1930s) these sales offices would process orders for complete watches cased and shipped directly from the Springfield factory. The Hamilton financial ledgers for Illinois show that by 1929, Illinois had at least fourteen direct sales personnel.

During the Deco and Moderne periods, Illinois had far fewer advertisements for its wristwatches than Elgin or Hamilton had for theirs.

Maiden Lane Jewelry District, New York City, 1932

1934
HISTORICAL NOTES

- The Department of Justice offers a $25,000 reward for John Dillinger, dead or alive.
- TWA and Continental Airlines commence operation.
- Leo Szilard patents the chain-reaction design for the atomic bomb.
- Outside Chicago's Biograph Theatre, "Public Enemy No. 1" John Dillinger is killed by FBI .
- Bank robber "Baby Face" Nelson dies in a shoot-out with the FBI.

JULIUS W. ARMBRUSTER (1871–1964)

Julius W. Armbruster, c. 1932

In the December 1929 issue of the *Illinois Motor Barrel* (a promotional publication of the Illinois Watch Company) there appeared a "retrospect" tribute to Julius W. Armbruster, signed "His Associates of Illinois Watch," that reads: "As we look back over the thirty-nine years which have passed since Julius W. Armbruster first became identified with Illinois Watches . . . we see his hand in all the important advances the company has made. From a small factory, producing fifty watches a day, Julius Armbruster has marked and aided the growth of this organization until now it produces close to one thousand watches each day. . . . We will miss him here in Springfield . . . but we are happy in knowing that he is to manage the affairs of Illinois Watch on the West Coast. Thus . . . we give to Julius Armbruster our thanks for his association and many accomplishments. We wish for him a complete and happy life in his new surroundings." There was even an Illinois pocket watch named after Armbruster.

As the clouds of the Depression grew, Armbruster operated the San Francisco sales office for the Illinois Watch Company before relocating to Los Angeles.

Beulah Poulson, who had been an employee of the company in the late 1920s and early 1930s, remembered that "Mr. Armbruster would bring orders in from California about once a year." He was a "jolly man" and "always handed out candy."* His great-grandchildren still live in Springfield.

*Interview with the author, Springfield, Illinois, December 8, 2001.

J. W. Armbruster Will Move to California

Resigning as sales manager of the Illinois Watch Company, Springfield, Illinois, Julius W. Armbruster, who has been associated with this company for 39 years, will move to the west coast about the first of the year. There he will act as western sales manager for Illinois watches and Hamilton-Sangamo clocks.

J. L. Keenan, at present eastern sales representative of the Illinois Watch Company, will succeed him as sales manager of that company on January 1, 1930.

In explaining this move, Mr. Armbruster said that, after having lived on the road for 39 years, he had long looked forward to a retirement and removal to California.

"Now that this has become possible," he states, "rather than retire at once, I will represent the Illinois Watch Company and the Hamilton-Sangamo Co., in the West for some time. Selling Illinois watches has become more or less of a habit, and I will work around to my final retirement gradually."

October 1929 announcement in the *Keystone* about Armbruster's relocation

Julius W. Armbruster Represents M. A. Mead & Co.

Chicago, Ill.—M. A. Mead & Co., wholesalers of American watches, announce that Julius W. Armbruster will be their Pacific Coast representative. Mr. Armbruster is well known to the trade and was sales manager of the Illinois Watch Company for many years.

Keystone, February 1934. By this time, the Illinois Watch Company was rapidly winding down. M. A. Mead & Co. was an Illinois Jobber based out of Chicago.

Donald Sauers, the hand-picked Hamilton Watch Company historian, points out that in 1893 Hamilton employed only one salesman but by 1924, when the company's first sales convention was held, their number had increased to ten. By 1929 there were sixteen Hamilton salesmen, all of whom attended the sixth annual sales convention.[37] Hamilton also had 105 distributors at this time (matching exactly the number of Illinois jobbers).

According to Sauers, the sales meeting formats changed little over the years, even as late as 1988. The major difference between the meeting that year and the one in 1929 was that Hamilton management presented advertising on the first day of the 1988 meeting and new products on the second. They had reversed these two items on the 1929 agenda.[38]

We wish to announce that the

Hamilton Watch Company
Lancaster, Penna.

has purchased the

Illinois Watch Company
Springfield, Ill.

and will take over the plant and business
January 1, 1928

HAMILTON WATCH COMPANY
Charles F. Miller
President

Keystone, January 1928

Why Did Hamilton Acquire Illinois?

Effective January 1, 1928, Hamilton acquired the Illinois Watch Company. Although documents exist that give Hamilton's reasons for the acquisition, the subsequent saga of Illinois after the acquisition has caused considerable conjecture among Illinois collectors. The rest of this chapter explores both the stated and unstated reasons for Hamilton's purchase of Illinois.

The Stated Reason: Doubling Capacity

With the wristwatch market exploding in the late 1920s, Hamilton decided that it needed to expand capacity via an acquisition in an effort to catch up with its competitors. Its potential targets were extremely limited. It could rule out Elgin and Waltham because they were too large and costly, Gruen because it did not produce its own movements in the United States and the other available companies because they were totally or mostly focused on pocket watches, with rapidly decreasing success and overinflated inventories. This left Illinois, a company with an outstanding history and reputation; a workforce slightly larger than Hamilton's (1,300 versus 1,200); a talented, experienced and contented pool of employees; and a management with strong values similar to its own. Therefore, if Hamilton wanted to expand, the decision to target Illinois was the most logical and reasonable choice.

Hamilton expert René Rondeau has kindly provided me with copies of two very interesting announcements from Hamilton regarding the acquisition; the texts of these follow.

On December 27, 1927, when Hamilton internally shared with its factory foremen the news of the acquisition and the reasons for it, it stated:

"This is an event of major importance in the annals of American watchmaking; it marks the combining under one ownership of two great American watch factories specializing in the manufacture of high grade watches exclusively. The Hamilton Watch Company have found it necessary to increase their capacity. For the past several years they have been unable to supply the demand made upon them and the purchase of the Illinois Watch Company answers their problem in a very definite and immediate way."

Shortly thereafter, a Hamilton press release to the public added: "The plant of the Illinois Watch Company is about the same size as the Hamilton factory. Thirteen hundred employees are on active duty. The acquisition of the plant will practically double Hamilton's capacity for the manufacture of high grade watches and will double the volume of business done by the Hamilton Watch Company."

MANUFACTURERS OF
FINEST QUALITY TIMEPIECES
LANCASTER PA. U. S. A.

CHARLES F. MILLER, PRESIDENT
F. C. BECKWITH, VICE-PRESIDENT
R. E. MILLER, VICE-PRESIDENT
J. W. B. BAUSMAN, TREASURER
C. M. KENDIG, SECRETARY & ASST. TREAS.

December 29th,1927

E.Carlstrom
F.Hauer
G.McCauley
J.Koch
Geo.Ganse
C.Wilson
A.Burkhart
J.W.Rushton
A.Buch
W.I.Everett
P.Lindsay
E.Eshleman
H.Ziplinsky
A.Hammersley
E.Hodgen
W.Welchens
J.Leonard
J.Hergenrother
W.H.Manby
Milton Manby
J.Graf
C.S.Reese
H.L.Shaub
E.Fenstermaker
C.Hostetter
W.Breen
H.Duttenhofer
R.F.Metzger
J.Weise
W.Hoffert
R.Cunningham
W.Martin
W.Broome
J.Willis
H.Coho
Geo.P.Luckey
G.Toney
H.A.Ruthhart
W.R.Atkinson
C.W.Drepperd
H.Lawrence

IMPORTANT MEMORANDUM TO ALL FOREMEN.

We take pleasure in handing you herewith one of the most important announcements ever made by the Hamilton Watch Company. This will be given to the public press today, and you will note will become effective on January 1st, 1928.

There is nothing in this whole matter which in any way effects your relationship with this Company or your work here. The two plants will be operated independent of each other, but co-operating on manufacturing methods where it can be done to advantage. In the same way the sales efforts of the two plants will be co-ordinated where it can be done to good advantage.

The officials of this Company will necessarily be absent from Lancaster for short periods during the next few months until all arrangements are made at the Illinois plant. We have a good organization here at Lancaster in this factory, and we count on their carrying on and functioning as usual, continuing to better the quality of the Hamilton Watch and gradually increasing the production.

Yours very sincerely
Charles F. Miller
President

CFM-AN

Notice dated December 29, 1927, from Charles F. Miller to all Hamilton foremen, about the imminent acquisition

HAMILTON BUYS

ILLINOIS WATCH COMPANY

All the assets, good will, trade name and plant of the Illinois Watch Company of Springfield, Illinois, have been purchased by the Hamilton Watch Company. They will assume charge of the Illinois plant January 1st, 1928.

This is an event of major importance in the annals of American watchmaking; it marks the combining under one ownership of the two great American watch factories specializing in the manufacture of high grade watches exclusively. The Hamilton Watch Company have found it necessary to increase their capacity. For the past several years they have been unable to supply the demand made upon them, and the purchase of the Illinois Watch Company answers their problem in a very definite and immediate way.

The assets of the Illinois company will be acquired by outright purchase.

The Illinois Watch Company, as purchased by Hamilton, is a successful business in full operation. It has, for the past 58 years, been owned and controlled by the Bunn family of Springfield. John W. and Jacob Bunn of Springfield are mentioned in biographies of Abraham Lincoln as having assisted Lincoln, as a rising young lawyer, in the Illinois city.

Robert E. Miller, Vice-President, and Calvin M. Kendig, Secretary of the Hamilton Watch Company will temporarily assume the responsibility of the management of the Illinois plant, January 1, 1928. Most of the present executive force employed by the Illinois company will be retained. It is the intention of the Hamilton company to continue, in a general way, the policies of the Illinois company, maintaining at all times the high standard of quality and excellence that have always been associated with the Illinois product.

The plant of the Illinois Watch Company is about the same size as the Hamilton factory. Thirteen hundred employes are on active duty. The acquisition of the plant will practically double Hamilton's capacity for the manufacture of high grade watches and will double the volume of business done by the Hamilton Watch Company.

The work of co-ordinating production of the two plants and formation of sales policies will go forward after the details attending the transfer are completed. Further announcements will be made, formally, to the Jewelry trade, through the usual channels.

Hamilton's public announcement of the acquisition, January 1, 1928

January 5, 1928 THE JEWELERS' CIRCULAR

Hamilton Watch Co. in Big Deal

Lancaster Concern Announces the Purchase of the Plant, Good Will and Trade Name of the Illinois Watch Co. of Springfield, Ill.

Jewelers' Circular, January 5, 1928

Hamilton had one of its most profitable years in 1928, the year of the Illinois transaction. Hamilton's sales figures for 1929, nearly two years after its Illinois acquisition, totaled $5.8 million with a profit of $1.8 million after taxes for a 31% profit margin.[39] Illinois' contribution to these 1929 sales was at least $2,818,550. Thus Hamilton's own results were barely those from its Illinois Watch Division, and the Illinois sales noted were to only 80 of its jobbers and presumably did not cover sales to its dozens of other jobbers, its direct sales, house accounts, and sales to department stores.

Hamilton's desire to double its capacity never materialized owing to the intervening economic depression that compelled it to announce the "temporary" closing of the Illinois Factory starting in 1932 and transfer of some of the equipment, inventory and some key employees to Lancaster. Ultimately, the Illinois Factory was shut down by July 31, 1933. The healthy profit margins of the 1920s clearly reflect the wisdom and benefit of the Illinois transaction to Hamilton before it experienced the unforeseen adverse impact of the Great Depression.

On January 5, 1928, the *Jewelers' Circular*, using information provided on January 1 by Hamilton in its public announcement about the acquisition, reported that the Hamilton purchase of Illinois "brings together two of the great watch companies of the country, companies whose products have stood ace high in the estimation of the jewelry trade, in railroad circles and wherever accurate timepieces were considered a prime necessity.

For several years past, the Hamilton Watch Co. has been unable to supply the demand for its products and it is stated here generally that the acquiring of the plant of...Illinois...will meet a need so long felt.

Hamilton Watch Company Announces Purchase of Illinois Watch Company

Robert E. Miller, Vice-President, and Calvin M. Kendig, Secretary of the Hamilton Watch Company, Will Take Charge of Illinois Company January 1, 1928—Event One of Major Importance to Jewelry Trade

Keystone, January 1928

In wording taken straight out of Hamilton's press release, the Keystone reported: "The acquisition of the [Illinois] plant will practically double Hamilton's capacity for the manufacture of high grade watches and will double the volume of business done by the Hamilton Watch Co.

HAMILTON WATCH BUYS IN ILLINOIS

Lancaster, Dec. 30. — Confronted with the necessity of doubling its output, the Hamilton Watch Company, of this city, has purchased the Illinois Watch Company, at Springfield, Ill., it was announced here. The transaction involves the plant, good will and trade name of the Illinois concern. The Hamilton company will assume control January 1, with Robert E. Miller, its vice-president, and Calvin M. Kendig, secretary, taking charge of the management of the Springfield plant.

The local Pennsylvania papers were also citing the necessity for Hamilton to double its output. *Harrisburg Telegraph* (Harrisburg, PA), December 30, 1927; image from *newspapers.com*

However, is this truly accurate? Hamilton's production capacity could not, in fact, be doubled if only half of the production would still be for the Hamilton products. Therefore, is it possible that Hamilton had plans and strategic objectives at the outset to close the Illinois brand production at some point and shift total production at both plants to Hamilton products, thus truly doubling Hamilton's production capacity? In fact, Hamilton went so far as to change the plates on Illinois movements to the Hamilton name; but then apparently reversed this decision, possibly to avoid acquisition-related goodwill write-offs. On the other hand, Hamilton's assertion that the purchase would double production may have been simply related to number of units and not to Hamilton's branding of the products.

In an editorial on January 5, 1928, the *Jewelers' Circular* added, "The coming together of two great American watch companies under one management is an event that cannot fail to be of interest to all jewelers, watchmakers and people interested in horological products throughout the world." The editorial noted that "unlike most amalgamations noted in the business world, it is not a bringing together of concerns making different grades of products. The watches of both have stood high in the jewelry trade for their intrinsic merit and both have their strong advocates, friends and boosters." Thus, the industry viewed the transaction as a merger of equals.

The Unstated Reasons

Hamilton's market dilemma. Hamilton enjoyed an unrivaled reputation among American watch manufacturers, a reputation that it jealously guarded. In the early 1900s it produced some of the finest timepieces made in the United States. Railroads, the arbiters of watch quality, held Hamilton in high esteem. Hamilton's own advertisements emphasized accuracy, reliability and durability.

In order to maintain this reputation at a reasonable financial cost, Hamilton produced a well-engineered product, only reluctantly making changes. It took Hamilton the better part of a decade after World War I to produce its first movement intended specifically for a wristwatch. The wristwatch revolution caught Hamilton's management in the dilemma of maintaining its product at a reasonable cost and, at the same time, adjusting to meet the quickly changing market.

With this in mind, it is interesting to review Donald Sauers's observations about Hamilton, because they suggest how a company could reach a condition from which the most expedient escape was a strategic acquisition. According to Sauers's excellent book, *Time for America*, Hamilton management had been:

- *Lulled into complacency.* Hamilton "concentrated on accuracy and durability and had one negative side effect—it lulled the company into complacency regarding other important areas."[40] As a result, Hamilton was repeatedly slow to recognize and adopt new trends.

- *Slow to recognize trends toward wristwatches.* Hamilton failed to recognize the developing shift towards wristwatches, particularly among men. "Many of the soldiers who had served during World War I had seen 'sharp watches' in France and were beginning to demand them. Hamilton, typically wary and conservative, was slow to move. In 1920 wristwatches were only four percent of their output, the remainder being pocket watches. At Waltham that year the level had reached 25%, and at Elgin, in those days more progressive in matters of style, it was 48%—nearly half of the total production."[41] It is difficult to comprehend how Hamilton failed to observe and react faster to this major shift in buyers' preference.

United States soldier wearing a wristwatch during WWI

However, according to Sauers, "inattention to trends had always been a characteristic of Hamilton management." In 1908, as the market for railroad watches was becoming saturated, Waltham and Elgin broadened their lines to include smaller sizes and fancier cases, but Hamilton plodded single-mindedly along, content to be the "Railroad Timekeeper of the World." In that year alone, Hamilton sales slumped one-third, while the total industry declined only 10%.[42]

- *Inattentive to the challenge of Swiss competition.* Sauers comments that "in the middle twenties, just as Hamilton was beginning to wake up and add innovative new wristwatch designs to its line—the 'Art Deco' Piping Rock being a striking example—the company faced a new competitive challenge, this time from overseas. [*Author's note*: Notwithstanding Sauers's comment, the Piping Rock was not introduced until 1928.] The Swiss, becoming more aggressive in the American market and confronted with domestic watches as accurate and dependable as their own, adopted a new strategy. They shifted to a fashion approach, offering high-styled watches

1931 HISTORICAL NOTES

- Congress allows California to build the San Francisco-Oakland Bay Bridge.
- Alka-Seltzer is introduced.
- "The Star Spangled Banner" becomes the National Anthem of the United States.
- The first electric shaver (Schick) goes on sale in the United States.
- Nevada legalizes gambling.
- The Empire State Building opens in New York City.
- Al Capone is indicted on 5,000 counts of prohibition and perjury.
- The *Dick Tracy* comic strip debuts.

in unusual shapes and tiny, jeweled cases—timepieces explicitly designed for increased sales to women. They were the first to sell watches as costume jewelry, and make it smart for women to own two or three. In doing so they more than doubled the market—a market that saw Hamilton's share shrinking so drastically that sales had dropped perilously close to break-even by 1931; a situation due in part to the rapid deepening of the Great Depression." [43]

- *Too attentive to profits.* Sauers further opines that "In 1929 . . . Hamilton enjoyed a 31% return on sales . . . but some critics of the Miller style have questioned whether he might have paid too much attention to profit and not enough to growth. There's no doubt that total revenues would have been higher, market share greater, if the company had spent more time on styling and more money on promotion. Their dealers had been clamoring for such action for years." [44]

- *Inattentive to changes in styling.* Sauers points to another reason for the acquisition when he notes that in September 1929, Frank C. Beckwith, first vice president and sales manager, thought that Hamilton needed "improvements, not in quality of its products, but in their styling and distribution."[45] Illinois' styling, which to that point was clearly more adventuresome and avant-garde, was likely another strong reason for Hamilton to acquire the company.

- *Technology transfer.* In the ensuing years, technology transfer became one of the most valuable aspects of the purchase. At the time of the acquisition, Hamilton possessed only one men's wristwatch movement: the round 6/0 size, grade 987. Acquisition of Illinois allowed Hamilton to enter into and develop markets for other sizes and shapes of wristwatch movements.

- *Hamilton obtained a 3/0 movement with the acquisition.* Elgin and Illinois produced their first 3/0 movements just prior to World War I. The size permitted a comfortable yet readable wristwatch. Hamilton never developed a 3/0 size movement. This omission prevented Hamilton from participating in sales of wristwatches to the United States Army during World War I, whereas sales of 3/0 wristwatches became a big business for Elgin, Illinois and Waltham. In fact, virtually all of Illinois's 3/0 movement production of over 26,000 movements in 1918 was allocated to the government. These same 3/0 wristwatch models were also used in World War II by the United States Army. Hamilton's lack of 3/0 movements also prevented Hamilton distributors and jewelers from utilizing the many 3/0 size generic wristwatch cases from Keystone, Wadsworth, Illinois Watch Case Company, Star and other case manufacturers during the height of the Generic Period.

- *The acquisition also brought Hamilton the design of a 12/0 rectangular movement.* Many

Hamilton collectors believe Hamilton acquired the Illinois Watch Company primarily because Hamilton was struggling to develop its own rectangular watch movement and wanted to move into a different style direction with more contemporary rectangular case designs. Although this reason might seem compelling to some, it should be noted that Hamilton did not request its "Illinois Watch Division" to convert its 12/0, grade 207 movement to Hamilton's 401 movement until May 28, 1929, or seventeen full months after "the acquisition."

Hamilton's 401 Movement

Even though Hamilton did not plan to make long-term use of the 401's, it did find its acquisition of rectangular movement technology to be very useful. The Illinois 207 grade rectangular movement was described by Illinois in its advertisements dated 1929 as being 12/0 size and having 17 ruby and sapphire jewels, raised settings, compensatory balance, double roller escapement, sapphire roller and pallet jewels, polished steel escape wheel, Breguet hairspring, recoil click and black enamel lettering.

Hamilton had been working on its own rectangular movement before its purchase of Illinois. After examining the Illinois 207 information, Hamilton adopted it, but with a small number of changes. Notes prepared in 1948 from Hamilton's internal records by Lowell F. Halligan, who was then its sales and merchandising manager, provide the information. A letter from Hamilton to the"Illinois Plant," dated May 28, 1929, directed that certain changes in specification be made to transform the Illinois 207 grade, 17-jewel, 12/0 movement into the new Hamilton 401 grade, 19-jewel, 12/0 movement. The details, quoted below, are from Halligan's notes about the letter:

1. Shape of bridges according to design #5, submitted by the Illinois Plant.
2. Balance to be 6/0 size Huguenin, quality #2 with bevel arms—8K gold screws.
3. Ratchet and winding wheels to be cupped and polished.
4. Upper Jewel setting to be 8K gold.
5. Center wheel gold.
6. Semi-friction balance jeweling.
7. To be timed ten sec. in 24 hours on the gaining side—compensated to plus or minus 10 sec. in 24 hours between heat and cold.
8. Pattern of damaskeening different than Ill. 17-jewel, 12 size. (Sample to be submitted for approval).
9. Bridges to be marked "Hamilton", "Lancaster, Pa." "Adjusted"—"19-Jewels"—"Grade 401"—Serial number starting with H50,001.
10. To be delivered to the Hamilton [Hamilton] where the dial and case will be furnished.
11. To be Friction Jeweled in the Escape, Fourth, extra Fourth, Third Upper.

Specifications were changed to include Friction Jeweling for the 5,000 Grade 401 watches (first lot ordered) to be made at Illinois.

There were two lots of watches put through the factory— H50,001 to H57,500—total of 7,500 watches.

Watches to be serviced and returned to the Illinois Plant.

In order to provide additional work for Illinois employees, Hamilton stipulated that the 401 would be built at Springfield, Illinois, according to Hamilton's specifications.

As expressed in Hamilton's internal records prepared in 1948 by Lowell F. Halligan, who was then its director of sales research, the idea was to give Hamilton a 12/0 size rectangular movement "quicker than they could otherwise design and build the tools for it and at the same time give the Illinois Watch Factory additional manufacturing in 12/0 size work."

Production records documented by Halligan disclose that Hamilton placed an initial order with its Illinois Watch Division for 5,000 401s on May 28, 1929. A total of 7,500 were produced by Illinois, but no record has been located indicating when the second lot was ordered. Grade 401 began with Hamilton serial number H50,001. When the Hamilton factory in Lancaster received the movements, Hamilton employees dialed, fitted in cases, timed and adjusted the movements.

LOWELL F. HALLIGAN (1900-1968)

Lowell F. Halligan, May 1934

Lowell F. (Feeg) Halligan, a 1922 graduate of Franklin and Marshall College, joined the advertising department of Hamilton in 1925 at the age of twenty-five. About 1928 he was made advertising manager of the Illinois Watch Division. In 1930 he served as the Eastern sales manager of the Hamilton-Sangamo Corporation. Following the sale of the Hamilton-Sangamo Corporation in 1931, Halligan served as sales manager of the Follmer-Cloge Company, but that same year he returned to Lancaster to direct Hamilton's sales research.

During World War II he served as the supervisor of the War Contracts Division at Hamilton. In May 1947 he was promoted to sales and merchandising manager.

In 1949 he was elected assistant secretary of Hamilton. In January 1950, Halligan was named vice-president, sales manager and a director of Hamilton to complete the unexpired term of W. Ross Atkinson, who had resigned because of ill health. Halligan retired in 1959.

Hamilton's Explorer Series

Almost two full years after the acquisition, a letter of December 3, 1930, from Hamilton to its wholesalers announced a new series of watches featuring the 19-jewel, 401 movement: "just in the nick of time for the holiday season that year," Bruce Shawkey comments.[46] Although six models were announced, each named after a famous explorer, only three were actually released in 1930: the Byrd, the Ericsson and the Wilkinson. The Andrews came out in 1931, the Stanley in 1932 and the Livingstone in 1933.

Interestingly, the six watches appear to have been advertised in Hamilton sales catalogs simply as "12-0 Size Strap Watches—Grade 401," albeit with the individual models listed by name. Shawkey, a horology author, points out that they were dubbed the Explorer Series in 1933, in "a stock advertisement that was created by Hamilton's advertising department and mailed to their retailers so that the ad could be placed in their local newspapers or other print media. There was usually space in the ad to include the store's name and address."[47]

In the 1920s people were fascinated with the exploits of explorers and adventurers, much as they later were with the feats of astronauts. Accordingly, Hamilton's idea to name the models of its new, pioneering watch movement after them was a stroke of genius. Although it is not known how Hamilton came to name the watches after those particular six explorers, one might surmise that the company felt that those names would resonate with the public. Richard E. Byrd's polar expeditions had provided much news in the popular press, as had the adventures and discoveries of Roy Chapman Andrews, director of the American Museum of Natural History (thought to have been the inspiration for the character "Indiana Jones" in films of the late twentieth century). Hamilton had already capitalized on the fact that both Byrd and Andrews had used Hamilton watches during their expeditions.[48]

The selection of two of the four other "Explorer" names is less obvious. The medieval Norwegian/Icelandic explorer Leif Ericson might at first glance appear an odd choice, but 1925 had been celebrated as the centennial of the arrival of the first Norwegian settlers in the United States, and Ericson is sometimes credited as being the first European to reach North America. Given the public's continuing fascination with Egyptian archaeology after King Tut's tomb was discovered in 1922, the early nineteenth-century traveler and writer Sir John Gardner Wilkinson, regarded as "the Father of British Egyptology," was an excellent choice. Of course, the familiar story of how Henry M. Stanley searched in Africa for Dr. David Livingstone and greeted him with the words "Dr. Livingstone, I presume?" made the names of that pair indispensable in the series.

New Hamilton Watch Named for Famous Explorer

THE Hamilton Watch Company, Lancaster, Pennsylvania, has announced the introduction of The Andrews, a new 12/0 size rectangular strap watch, with case of strong, simple design, much smaller than other models of the same grade.

The Andrews is available in 14K white and natural yellow gold. Like the other models of the 401 series, it was named for a distinguished explorer; in this case, for Roy Chapman Andrews. One of its practical features is an extra thick lens crystal. It is priced to retail at $100.

Announcement in the *Keystone*, December 1930

FANTASTIC FIND

Randy Van Netten, a friend from Southern California, has this high-flying tale:

"My favorite Hamilton wristwatch is the 'Byrd' model, one of the 'Explorer' 401 movement series from the early 1930s. Admiral Byrd was famous at the time for being the first person to fly an airplane over the North Pole. In fact, Admiral Byrd was awarded an unusual peacetime Congressional Medal of Honor for this achievement, as well as other feats of aviation. Therefore, it is very appropriate that the events in this story occurred in the air."

"In about 1995 (not sure of the year) a NAWCC National Mart was held in Denver. While I was at LAX waiting for my flight, I saw a well-known Los Angeles watch collector and dealer, Irwin Hollander, in the waiting area. We got to talking about our mutual Hamilton passion, and the upcoming Mart, when my eyes, like a laser, focused on the white gold 'Byrd' on Irwin's wrist. I asked if 'it was for sale?' He responded that he had 'promised it to another collector' he was going to meet in Denver, and was committed to sell the watch once the other party had a chance to inspect it. The model was also one of his favorites, but he had a yellow gold version, and he was content to have one 'Byrd.' We spoke a few times at the Mart, where I noticed that he was no longer wearing the watch, so I assumed it was sold. A few days later we both found ourselves airborne in the same plane back to Los Angeles. He came over to my seat and, to my amazement, he was wearing the watch. I asked him if it was 'now available' and he said 'Yes.' We made the deal in the air. The watch is one of the most treasured in my collection!"

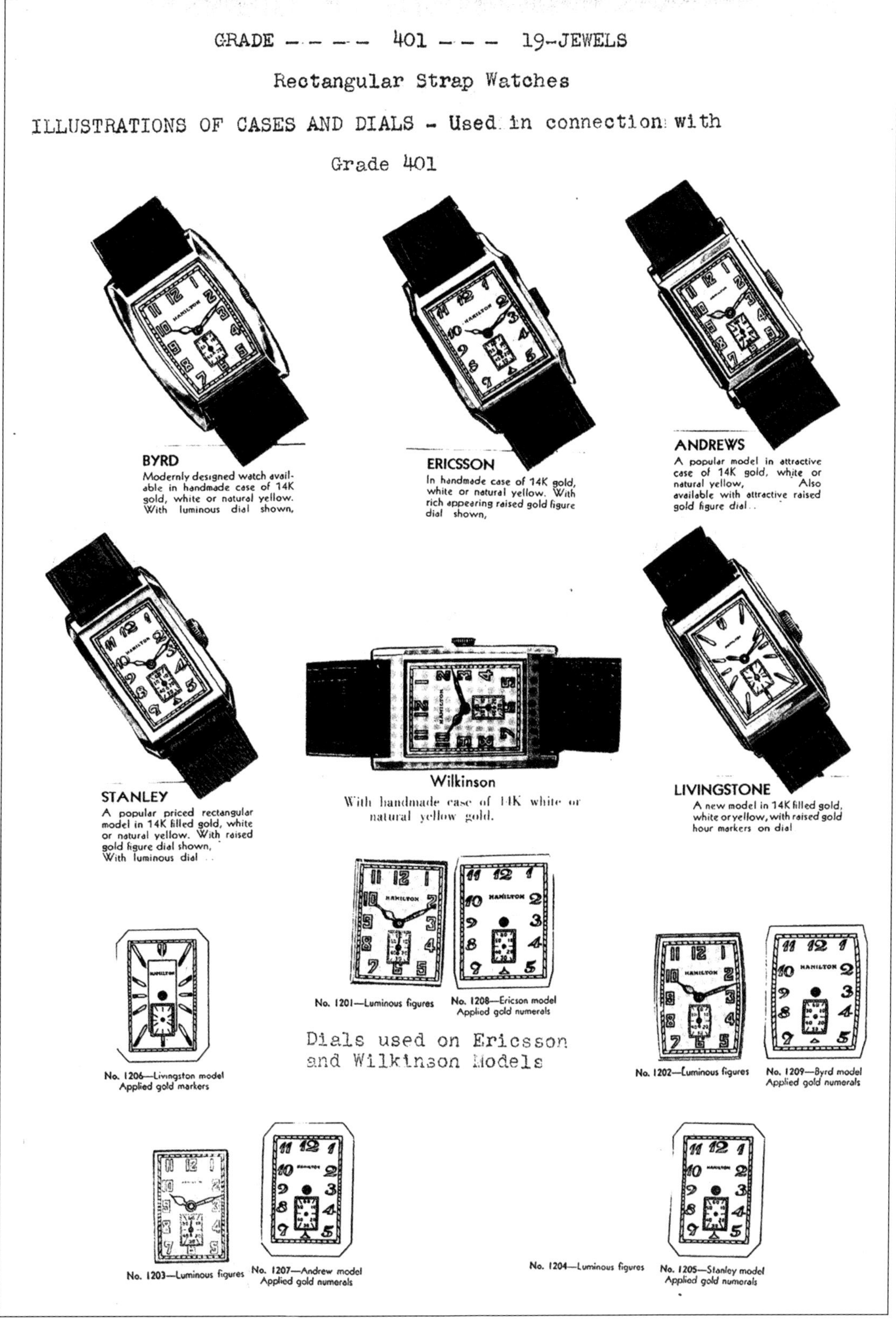

GRADE ----- 401 --- 19-JEWELS

Rectangular Strap Watches

ILLUSTRATIONS OF CASES AND DIALS - Used in connection with Grade 401

BYRD
Modernly designed watch available in handmade case of 14K gold, white or natural yellow. With luminous dial shown,

ERICSSON
In handmade case of 14K gold, white or natural yellow. With rich appearing raised gold figure dial shown,

ANDREWS
A popular model in attractive case of 14K gold, white or natural yellow, Also available with attractive raised gold figure dial..

STANLEY
A popular priced rectangular model in 14K filled gold, white or natural yellow. With raised gold figure dial shown,
With luminous dial ..

Wilkinson
With handmade case of 14K white or natural yellow gold.

LIVINGSTONE
A new model in 14K filled gold, white or yellow, with raised gold hour markers on dial

No. 1206—Livingston model Applied gold markers

No. 1201—Luminous figures

No. 1208—Ericson model Applied gold numerals

Dials used on Ericsson and Wilkinson Models

No. 1202—Luminous figures

No. 1209—Byrd model Applied gold numerals

No. 1203—Luminous figures

No. 1207—Andrew model Applied gold numerals

No. 1204—Luminous figures

No. 1205—Stanley model Applied gold numerals

Illustrations of Explorer cases and dials prepared by Halligan

The Hamilton "Livingstone"

David Livingstone (1813–1873)

The Hamilton "Andrews"

Roy C. Andrews (1884–1960)

The Hamilton "Ericsson"

Leif Ericson (c. 970–1020)

The Hamilton "Stanley"

Henry M. Stanley (1841–1904)

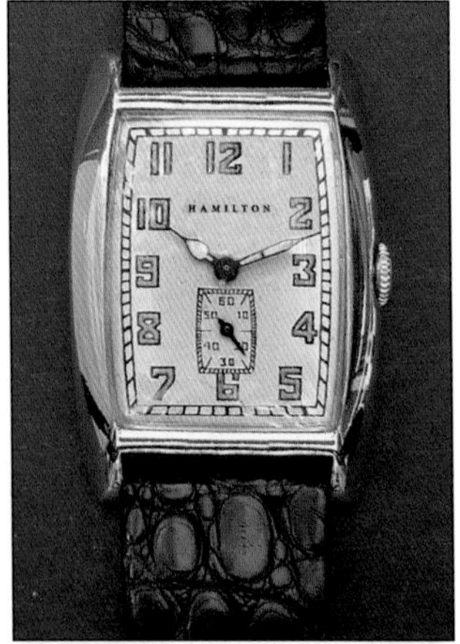

The Hamilton "Byrd"

Admiral Byrd (1888–1957)

According to Halligan's notes on the new series:

For shipment these watches were placed in a velvet and silk lined box of blue leather for the 14K models and leatherette for the gold-filled watches. This box was placed in an outside cardboard box bearing a label with the serial numbers of the movement and case, together with the Grade number and the description of the case and style of dial. Each box carried its own certificate of guaranteed satisfaction bearing serial numbers of movement and case.

Originally, only solid silver dials, with luminous figures were used; later Raised Gold Figures—silver [dial]—on all models except the Livingstone, which carried an Applied-Gold Marker Dial. The Raised Gold Figure Dials carried an additional charge. Black Figure Dials were also furnished when a customer could not be satisfied any other way, by using Hamilton's regular silver dial with the figure filled in with enamel instead of luminous.

Illinois continued to fill its parent company's orders for 401 movements until July 11, 1933. Once the production transfer from Springfield to Lancaster was complete, it was announced within Hamilton via an internal memorandum to its various department heads:

> Since the recent transfer of Illinois production to the Hamilton Division, it has become desirable to transfer the Casing, Jobbing, etc. of the 401 movements that are property of the Hamilton Watch Company to the factory departments which handle similar work on Hamilton watches.
>
> This transfer will be made July 31st, and from this date all matters pertaining to 401 movements belonging to the Hamilton Watch Co., will be taken care of by the regular factory departments.

According to Hamilton factory records, Hamilton cased one 401 movement in 1938 in a "Special (Rockliffe 14K-YG Case)." The Rockliffe, of course, was an Illinois model but could accommodate a 401 movement as easily as a 207 Illinois one because they were virtually identical.

An interesting aspect of the Hamilton production records is that it gives us our first look at what watchmakers such as Hamilton and Illinois paid for their cases. The gold-filled cases had a relatively low cost.

Cost of Explorer Cases

Case Name	Casemaker	Cost to Hamilton
Stanley	Wadsworth	$ 3.95[a]
Livingston	Wadsworth	$ 3.95
Wilkinson	Perrin Watch Case Co.	$ 35.00[b]
Ericsson	Perrin Watch Case Co.	$ 35.00 – $ 38.15[c]
Byrd	Perrin Watch Case Co.	$ 35.00 – $ 38.15[d]
Byrd	Lutringer & Wittmer	$ 35.00 – $ 38.15
Andrews	Wadsworth	$ 10.15 – $ 10.95[e]

a. A special-order 14K gold case cost $13.75 each.

b. Five cases were made in 18K for $40.00 each. A sterling silver case cost $30.00 each and was made by Schwab & Wuischpard.

c. Perrin also made a special 18K case for Tiffany Jewelers for $39.00 each.

d. An 18K gold version of the watch was made by Perrin for Tiffany at $39.00 each.

e. A WG case and a YG case cost the same for Hamilton.

WHY I COLLECT ILLINOIS

"Early Illinois wristwatches are, as a group produced by one company, the most interesting, sophisticated and earliest, Art Deco designs. That, combined with the high grade movements in these fascinating cases make for the ideal watch maker to collect. The other American companies have a few designs each which are interesting, but the large volume of beautifully designed cases in the Illinois line up can't be beat.

"As a Hamilton collector, I am also interested in the watches that are very Hamilton like. That is, the streamlined Moderne designs of the 1930s Illinois watches are also beautiful and pleasurable to wear. The cases made for the 207 movement transition very nicely into the 401 "Explorer" series. They in turn evolved into the very nice 14 size Hamiltons which were made in the 1935 to 1940 period. If Illinois had remained an independent company they well could have produced these watches.

— Randy Van Netten

Halligan also noted that Hamilton produced one Andrews with an engraved bezel in a yellow gold case sold in 1933 and another in green gold with a plain bezel sold in 1933. There were also two engraved white gold-filled Stanleys sold in 1933.

The quantities of the Explorers sold are listed in Halligan's summary, before providing an important insight into the likely even much smaller quantities of Illinois models sold at this time. That helps explain why it is so difficult for Illinois collectors to secure some of the very hard-to-find models so avidly sought.

GRADE ---- 401 ---- 19-JEWELS

Table showing the total number of cases sold
in connection with this grade
Color and quality of cases are listed

	Forward 1930-1934	1935-	1936-	1937-	1938-	1939-	Totals
18K Cases							
Yellow -							
Byrd - Plain	12-	0-	0-	0-	0-	0-	12
Ericsson - Plain	8-	0-	0-	0-	0-	0-	8
Andrews - Plain	3-	0-	0-	0-	0-	0-	3
Special	1-	0-	0-	0-	0-	0-	1
White -							
Ericsson - Engraved and Enamelled	1-	0-	0-	0-	0-	0-	1
14K Cases							
Yellow -							
Wilkinson - Plain	133-	0-	1-	0-	0-	0-	134
Byrd - Plain	283-	2-	0-	0-	0-	0-	285
Ericsson - Plain	155-	0-	0-	0-	0-	0-	155
Andrews - Plain	1,137-	0-	0-	0-	0-	0-	1,137
Andrews - Engraved and Enamelled	1-	0-	0-	0-	0-	0-	1
Special (Rookliffe)	0-	0-	0-	0-	1-	0-	1
White -							
Wilkinson - Plain	146-	2-	0-	0-	0-	0-	148
Byrd - Plain	330-	1-	0-	0-	0-	0-	331
Ericsson - Plain	184-	1-	0-	0-	0-	0-	185
Andrews - Plain	1,124-	4-	1-	0-	0-	0-	1,129
Green -							
Andrews - Plain	1-	0-	0-	0-	0-	0-	1
14K Gold Filled Cases							
White -							
Stanley - Plain	1,268-	0-	0-	0-	0-	0-	1,268
Stanley - Engraved and Enamelled	2-	0-	0-	0-	0-	0-	2
Livingston - Plain	276-	0-	0-	0-	0-	0-	276
Yellow -							
Stanley - Plain	2,311-	0-	1-	0-	0-	0-	2,312
Livingston - Plain	684-	1-	0-	0-	0-	0-	685
Movements only	19-	1-	0-	0-	0-	1-	21
	8,079-	12-	3-	0-	1-	1-	8,096

Totals - - 18K -------	Yellow --	24
	White --	1
14K -------	Yellow --	1,713
	White --	1,793
	Green --	1
14K Gold Filled -	White --	1,546
	Yellow --	2,997
		8,075
Movements only	--	21
		8,096
In stock end of year 1939		10

Total Sales - - Sales Book Record - 8107
Sales-Case Records - 8106

1945 sold
Ericsson - 3
Wilkinson - 4
Andrews - 2

Halligan's summary of Explorer sales

Hamilton sold a mere twenty-one 401 grade uncased movements during this period. That is also a surprisingly low number, since Illinois, as a standard practice, would freely sell its movements uncased to its jobbers and others. Thus there appears to have been a key philosophical difference in the business practices of the two divisions.

On August 9, 1934, a letter from Hamilton was sent to its wholesale distributors notifying them that the entire inventory of grade 401 watches was exhausted. This was not entirely true, however, as Hamilton continued to fill special-order Explorers through 1945.

In 1945, Hamilton produced three Ericssons, four Wilkinsons and two Andrewses, notwithstanding the fact that Hamilton had announced that the supply of 401s had been exhausted in 1934.

A 401 Puzzle

Researching the 401 movements made by Illinois for Hamilton reveals a puzzling conflict. The Hamilton internal records as recorded by Halligan show 7,500 as the total number of 401s produced, pursuant to two orders placed on Illinois. However, if you then total the number of cased Explorers that were sold, using Halligan's numbers, the number comes to 8,106 or 8,107 (Halligan had totals from two different sources). Therefore, if the total number sold is accurate, then the number of 401s claimed to have been produced must be inaccurate. Were some of the models cased with 207 grade Illinois movements, or were another six hundred or so 401s made by Illinois for Hamilton?

As Halligan could find the written order for only the first 5,000 of the 401s ordered by Hamilton, it is possible that the second, unlocated order was for more than 2,500 units. Or perhaps there was even a third order placed on the Illinois Watch Division that Halligan could not find in all of the documentation he had to sort through for his reports.

However, this is really not the apparent or actual solution to the puzzle. Hamilton, as a practice, kept meticulous movement production records, and we know from Halligan and subsequent Hamilton documentation that the 401 movements ranged from serial numbers H50,001 to H57,500. Therefore, Hamilton clearly thought, and recorded, that only 7,500 grade 401s were produced. If so, what movements were in the extra 600+ completed Explorers that were sold?

The answer to the puzzle may be that Halligan added to production when he should have *subtracted* from *sales/shipments*. The page reproduced from his reports shows 8,106 total sales plus inventory of Explorer watches and 401 movements. However, Hamilton had 612 returns of Explorer watches in this period. If they shipped most of these watches back out to other dealers, something like 8100 watches would have been shown as shipped, though only 7,500 were made.

Revised numbers are shown in the tables. The first table shows only 8,105 shipments rather than Halligan's 8,106 because it uses the 9 watches sold in 1945 rather than the 10 still in inventory in 1939. It also reflects a shrinkage of 7, which is less than 1/10 of 1%, a very good figure.

Then, if this is accurate, another question arises: were the 612 returned watches subsequently sold? This is likely, as the inventory numbers were reduced to near zero but for the shrinkage.

A revised table, with correct arithmetic, is provided here. This clarifies and verifies the correct number of 401s produced but still does not address the accuracy of Halligan's summary of the numbers and types of Explorers sold.

401 Movements Produced and Sold 1930–1945

Year	Movements Produced	Watches Sold	Watches Returned
1930	5000	181	24
1931	2500	991	90
1932	0	1793	186
1933	0	3247	111
1934	0	1867	177
1935	0	12	24
1936	0	3	0
1937	0	0	0
1938	0	1	0
1939	0	1	0
1945	0	9	0
Totals	**7500**	**8105**	**612**

Summary accounting for 401 movements

Watches sold	8105
Watches returned	-612
Subtotal	7493
Shrinkage	+7
Total	**7500**

The 401 Cost

If, as some serious Hamilton collectors believe, Hamilton purchased Illinois solely for its rectangular 207 movement, then it was an extremely costly transaction. We now have confirmed that Hamilton ordered a total of only 7,500 modified 207 movements from its Illinois Watch Division to be transformed into Hamilton 401 movements. Therefore, if we divide the 7,500 into the $5 Million cost of the acquisition it comes to an average 401 grade movement cost of $666.66/movement. As the most expensive watches in the Explorer Series sold for $150.00 each, clearly Hamilton did not acquire Illinois solely for its rectangular movement.

The Byrd, Ericsson and Wilkinson models were introduced at $150.00 each in 1930. On March 1, 1932, the prices were reduced to $125.00 as the impact of the Great Depression hit Hamilton. But never wanting to leave money on the table, on June 21, 1932, Hamilton reversed course, increasing the price to $135.00. The Wilkinson was discontinued September 1, 1933; the other two models survived into 1934.

After looking at alternative explanations, Hamilton's stated reason, that it purchased Illinois to acquire increased manufacturing capacity remains the most logical. Unfortunately, with the advent of the Great Depression, Hamilton found it economically unfeasible to operate a totally separate manufacturing facility in Springfield.

Hamilton 12/0 Size Movements after the 401

Although Hamilton ordered only 7,500 of the 401 grade 12/0 size rectangular movements from Illinois, it did go on to produce a total through 1957 of 275,409 movements that were 12/0 size (counting the 401s). These are broken down as follows:

Hamilton 12/0 Size Movement Production Numbers

Movement No.	Jewels	Years	Number Produced
401	19	1930–1934	7,500
752	17	1952–1954	43,059
753	17	1952–1955	94,006
754	19	1952–1955	43,988
770	22	1955–1957	86,856
Total			**275,409**

However, these later Hamilton-produced movements were not based upon the 207 designs (as some collectors believe) but were developed by Hamilton independently.

After discussion with Hamilton expert René Rondeau, I have concluded that Hamilton's 401 clearly used the Illinois 207 as its foundation but the same could not be said for the future Hamilton rectangular grades. In 1928, Hamilton was already working on its own rectangular movement, having realized the importance of that shape.

According to Rondeau, buying Illinois "gave Hamilton a 'jump start' with a ready-made movement to use until the Hamilton rectangular grades 980/982 were fully de-bugged." Once Hamilton had its own 14/0 size, grade 980 ready, it ceased all use of the 401 movement.

Hamilton, along with the rest of the industry, realized the need for a rectangular grade, but according to Rondeau "was slower to get their own design into the market." As a result, Hamilton seized the grade 207 as a handy stopgap to tide it over while finalizing its own rectangular movement.

THE RAVEL COLLECTION

Dr. Robert L. Ravel (1921–2000)

As part of the research for this book, I traveled to the NAWCC Library and Research Center in Columbia, Pennsylvania, and spent one full week reviewing every document housed there relating to Illinois and Hamilton. This material is known as the Ravel Collection.

People in the NAWCC knew Dr. Robert L. Ravel as "an inveterate collector of lots of things horological, especially paper." At his death in 2000 he supposedly had five warehouses full of "stuff." Much, if not all, of the paper came to the NAWCC. According to the NAWCC archivist, Nancy Dyer, "The Swiss had bought Hamilton mostly for its name, reputation, and a few iconic designs; everything else they either sold (if they could find a buyer, and Ravel was a willing one) or pitched. Hamilton was one huge irresistible candy store to Ravel. For example, he bought the whole floor which had been devoted to the production of military timepieces; this included the paper records, all the supply of parts, and the actual machines which had been used in their production (some still to be found in the basement of our school). And he kept most of it until death.

"As far as I know, the paper—Hamilton related and lots of other—was given to the NAWCC Library & Research Center, some as he obtained it, some after he died and his 'warehouses' were cleaned out. Ravel had been more than just the Chairman of the Library Committee. I'm told he worked in the library sorting and cataloging at least one day a week."

The papers in the collection, currently listed under the heading "Hamilton—Ravel Collection," were all in the fifty-plus packing cartons of Ravel papers. These documents remained untouched for over two years. During my visit to the NAWCC in December 2013, they were still being carefully catalogued by a team of library volunteers.

Many of the new items discussed in this book were discovered while reading through this wonderful selection of documents, especially the files from Lowell F. Halligan and Jack L. Keenan and some of the Hamilton-Illinois wristwatch material. Every Hamilton and Illinois collector and historian alike owes a great debt of gratitude to Dr. Ravel.

Hamilton Pocket Watch Movements

Illinois Grade 528 Becoming Hamilton Grade 400

Many Hamilton and Illinois collectors are aware that the Hamilton grade 401, 12/0 size rectangular wristwatch movement was a modified Illinois grade 207, 12/0 size rectangular movement. However, fewer collectors realize that the Hamilton grade 400, 12 size, extra-thin 21-jewel model pocket watch movement was a post-acquisition modified Illinois grade 528, 12 size extra-thin pocket watch movement known and sold at least since 1922 as the "Illini" by the Illinois Watch Company.

The Hamilton grade 400 was described this way: "12-Size Extra Thin Model Pocket Watches – exquisitely slender – with nickel finish bridge movement – gold settings – patent motor barrel – steel escape wheels – double roller escapement – ruby pallets – concave and beveled winding wheel – patent micrometric regulator – compensation balance – Breguet hairspring and patent recoil click. They are pendant set and adjusted to heat, cold and five positions." Hamilton sold this grade only as cased watches.

According to Hamilton documents, the Illini was "very much thinner than its own 12 Size watches and it was in no way interchangeable with any of the Hamilton 12 Size grades."

This was apparently another reason for the Hamilton acquisition of Illinois, as it manufactured no thin model 12 size movement of its own.

Selling Prices
Illinois Watches

May 2nd, 1922

Cover of the May 2, 1922 Illinois Price List

12 Size, *Extremely Thin*, Complete Watches
Open Face Only

ILLINI
12 Size, Extremely Thin
21 jewels, Adjusted 5 Positions

21 extra quality ruby and sapphire jewels; special tempered compensating center arm balance having gold screws including timing screws; adjusted to temperature, five positions and isochronism; Breguet hairspring; double roller escapement; hardened and polished steel escape wheel; patent Illinois superior motor barrel, both pivots of barrel staff operating in sapphire jewels; patent recoil bar and pinion click; concaved and polished winding wheels; perfect pendant setting mechanism of exceptional simplicity entirely in movement; snap bezel; inlaid enamel figured dial.

Fitted in the following cases:

14k Green Gold Plain Bassine - - - - -	$140.00
14k Green Gold Plain Directoire, no cap - -	$150.00
14k Green Gold Engraved Directoire, no cap -	$160.00
14k Green Gold Plain Empire with cap - - -	$155.00
14k Green Gold Engraved Empire with cap - -	$165.00

The May 1922 price listing for the Illinois "Illini" extremely thin 12-size movement

Before initiating production of the grade 400, Hamilton wisely sought first to exhaust the grade 528 movements in Illinois' stock. With the transition to the 400, these movements received subtle changes such as improvements in damaskeening, modified bridges and the name "Hamilton" on the bridges. The Illinois Factory finished and timed the grade 400 movements, then shipped them to Lancaster to be dialed and cased and sold as Hamilton watches. Hamilton called the first grade 400 watches its "Hamilton Diplomat" series. However, in this instance, unlike with the 207 movement, Hamilton directed Illinois to discontinue its use of its grade 528, 12-size model so that it could serve as "an exclusive Hamilton model." This also helps explain why only two hundred "Illini" grade 528 movements were produced by Illinois with 23 jewels.

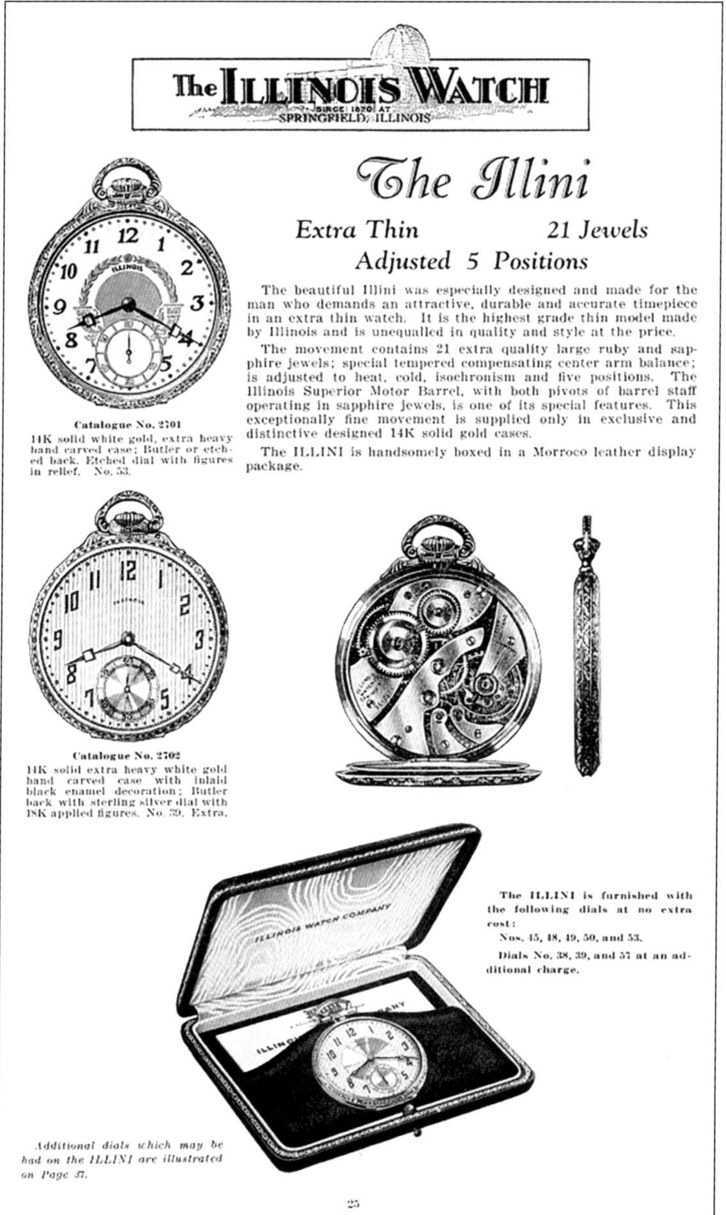

The ILLINOIS WATCH
SINCE 1870 AT SPRINGFIELD, ILLINOIS

The Illini

Extra Thin 21 Jewels
Adjusted 5 Positions

The beautiful Illini was especially designed and made for the man who demands an attractive, durable and accurate timepiece in an extra thin watch. It is the highest grade thin model made by Illinois and is unequalled in quality and style at the price.

The movement contains 21 extra quality large ruby and sapphire jewels; special tempered compensating center arm balance; is adjusted to heat, cold, isochronism and five positions. The Illinois Superior Motor Barrel, with both pivots of barrel staff operating in sapphire jewels, is one of its special features. This exceptionally fine movement is supplied only in exclusive and distinctive designed 14K solid gold cases.

The ILLINI is handsomely boxed in a Morroco leather display package.

Catalogue No. 2701
14K solid white gold, extra heavy hand carved case; Butler or etched back. Etched dial with figures in relief. No. 53.

Catalogue No. 2702
14K solid extra heavy white gold hand carved case with inlaid black enamel decoration; Butler back with sterling silver dial with 18K applied figures. No. 39. Extra.

The ILLINI is furnished with the following dials at no extra cost:
Nos. 45, 48, 49, 50, and 53.
Dials No. 38, 39, and 57 at an additional charge.

Additional dials which may be had on the ILLINI are illustrated on Page 37.

25

Hamilton Illinois Sales Catalog 1928

WHY I COLLECT ILLINOIS

"I always suspected that I was susceptible to the watch collector's virus, but for many years I staved off infection with just a pair of wristwatches; a Patek Philippe and an Audemars Piguet. In 2003, on an unfortunate whim, I bid on an 18K Fritz Piguet pocket watch then being hawked on eBay, and won the auction. The listing did say that the watch was 28mm in diameter, which meant nothing to me at the time. It never occurred to me that I was buying a tiny pocket watch—actually a very nice one that I still have. So, I had to buy a larger pocket watch. That's when the watch collector's virus took off. I started buying both pocket watches and wristwatches, all very nice ones, but in a rather unfocused way. When I discovered Fred's excellent book on Illinois wristwatches, I started collecting those, too, acquiring at least a dozen.

"Now, about 600 watches later, I still have the virus, but my focus has narrowed to high-grade gentlemen's pocket watches in solid gold and platinum cases, and I have sold most of the other kind of watches that I had collected. I particularly focus on Patek Phillipes, Vacheron Constantins, Ekegrens, Ed Koehns, IWCS, Touchons and Meylans among the Swiss makers and Illinois, Waltham, Elgin and Hamilton among the American makers. Why I focus on these brands varies, but all of them made very fine watches, at least in the higher grades that I collect.

"My Illinois pocket watch collection includes (1) one or more examples of every Illini grade, including the very scarce 23 jewel version; (2) four of the very scarce Hallmark PL version of grade 510, plus an Illinois version of that grade; (3) one or more examples of every grade of the 12-size extra thin model, including one in platinum; (4) one of three known examples of the all-aluminum grade 525, and (5) other rarities." —*Ethan Lipsig*

According to Hamilton's production records, the Illinois Factory produced two lots of the grade 400 watches, totaling 2,300 units. When they were received at the Hamilton plant, they were dialed and cased in its Technical Department until such time as it became regular production, when it was to be turned over to the Casing Department. For these 2,300 units, the first production occurred at Illinois on September 19, 1929 (almost twenty-one months post-acquisition) and the last production on February 24, 1932. One lot had Hamilton serial numbers H1001 to 1800, and the other had H2001 to 3500.

Illinois pocket watch expert Jerry Treiman says:

> The 21-jewel grade 528 Illini was the only grade that Illinois produced in their 12-size Extra Thin 2nd model movement, and this model superseded the earlier 13-size grades 538 and 539 (Illini and Illini Extra). This was a high-grade dress watch and it was an ideal addition to the Hamilton product line, as Hamilton did not have another movement this thin. They designated their version as a Grade 400.
>
> There were a number of changes that Hamilton made to make this model their own. First and foremost, they replaced the barrel bridge with a new bridge, properly marked and serial numbered for Hamilton.
>
> The second visible change was the addition of the micrometric regulator on the balance cock. Illinois had used this regulator sporadically on a few of their earlier 13-size Illini, but did not use it consistently until the production of their slightly lower-grade 3rd Series of Extra Thin 12-size watches (c. 1922 to 1928). It was not used on the grade 528 Illini.
>
> The addition of the micrometric regulator required obvious modifications to the balance cock and a groove in the pillar plate to access the regulator screw but, less obviously, also required relocating the balance cock screw. I believe they may have plugged the old hole in the pillar plate and then drilled and tapped a new hole for the screw. They may have made an entirely new balance cock rather than modify the original, but that needs further study.
>
> Other improvements applied by Hamilton to their grade 400 movement included a Côtes de Genève finish to the pillar plate and a lightweight escape wheel, features that Illinois applied only inconsistently on the Illini models. Hamilton also used gold timing screws on the balance wheel instead of the composition screws used by Illinois. (Both used what appear to be platinum meantime screws).
>
> A less significant cosmetic change was the use of a white-finish mainspring barrel on the Hamilton. I do not know if these are just nickel plated or newly made from a white metal. Although the Illinois grade 528 consistently used a brass-finish barrel, some earlier 13-size models were finished with a white-plated brass barrel.
>
> The above changes apply to the first 800 Hamilton movements, which were modified from previous Illinois grade 528 movements. The next 1500 Hamilton grade 400 movements were not modified from already finished stock and were instead made from scratch to new specifications, including a pallet bridge (not illustrated in these photos) instead of a pallet cock.
>
> In summation, it appears that in their Grade 400 movement Hamilton committed to a number of refinements that Illinois was apparently just experimenting with inconsistently during the production of their thin Illini movements.[49]

The Illinois "Illini" grade 528, 12-size, 21-jewel movement

The Hamilton grade 400, 12-size 21-jewel movement

Bob Ayer, after studying the Hamilton pocket watch records and "looking at Illinois in 1927, through Hamilton's eyes," comments:

> It appears that Illinois may have been very attractive for its thin pocket watch movements. In light of Hamilton's obsession with thin pocket watch movements the "Illini" may have been a paramount interest to Hamilton. Several factors point strongly at this: (1) Hamilton completely revamped its own pocket watch line in late 1923 in a move towards thinner movements. It replaced its whole line of 12-size models. Only the 16-size railroad versions seemed to have survived as thicker movements. (2) At that time, Hamilton completely discontinued use of enamel dials in favor of metal dials in the new models to ensure the watches were as thin as possible. (3) The only Illinois pocket watch movement wholly adopted by Hamilton was the "Illini," which became the model 400. (4) Hamilton emphasized its own thin and Illinois "ultra-thin" movements in its joint 1927–1928 catalog. Given Hamilton's predilection towards pocket watches at the time of its 1927 decision to purchase Illinois, the most important technology transfer may have been the "ultra-thin" Illinois movements. Of course, the growing trend toward smaller watches, begun by Gruen, made purchase of the 12/0 technology almost as important.

According to the company's records, Hamilton offered the grade 400 in four 18K solid gold models, all produced by hand. The Carnegie engraved model, the Bok and the Pulitzer were in snap-back cases of white or yellow gold; the Nobel model, supplied in yellow or green gold, had a bascine case, hinged, with an inside cap. All four models had Hamilton's name and case number inside the case back.

The Bok model also came in a platinum case. However, according to Hamilton records, only two were ever sold: one in 1931 and one in 1934.

The Eton model also contained the 400 grade movement but came in a 14K yellow gold-filled case. Frigidaire and General Motors used the Eton for service awards; General Motors owned Frigidaire when these models were released. The Eton was also used for "Tiffany" models, with the name "Tiffany" on the dial in place of "Hamilton."

In a letter of December 3, 1930, Hamilton introduced the "Tycoon Series" models to its wholesalers. The Eton case used for "Special Awards" was not included in the introductory shipment as it was used only for special purposes.

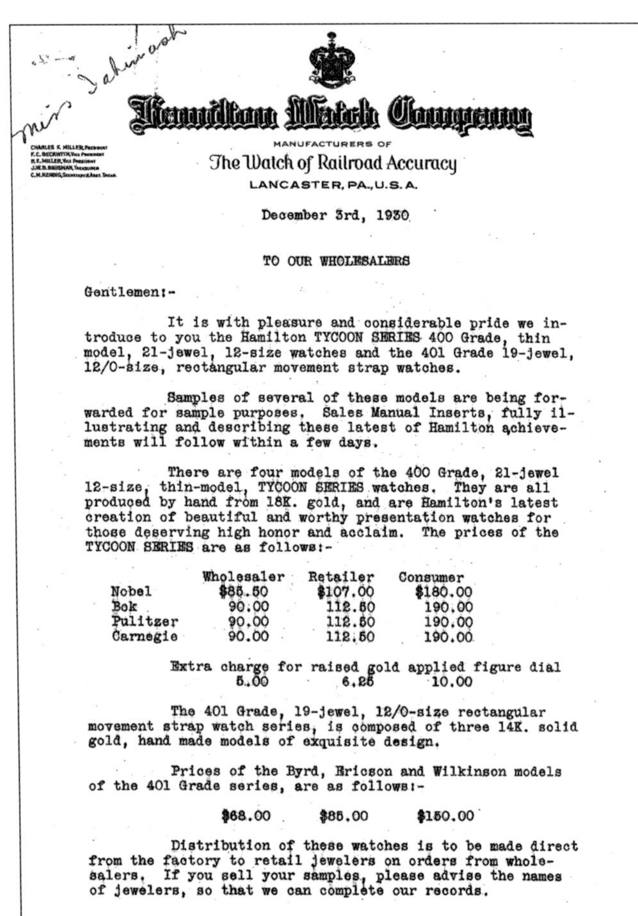

Hamilton Watch Company

CHARLES F. MILLER, PRESIDENT
F.C. BECKWITH, VICE PRESIDENT
R.E. MILLER, VICE PRESIDENT
J.W.B. BAUSMAN, TREASURER
C.H. KENDIG, SECRETARY & ASST. TREAS.

MANUFACTURERS OF
The Watch of Railroad Accuracy
LANCASTER, PA., U.S.A.

December 3rd, 1930

TO OUR WHOLESALERS

Gentlemen:-

It is with pleasure and considerable pride we introduce to you the Hamilton TYCOON SERIES 400 Grade, thin model, 21-jewel, 12-size watches and the 401 Grade 19-jewel, 12/0-size, rectangular movement strap watches.

Samples of several of these models are being forwarded for sample purposes. Sales Manual Inserts, fully illustrating and describing these latest of Hamilton achievements will follow within a few days.

There are four models of the 400 Grade, 21-jewel 12-size, thin-model, TYCOON SERIES watches. They are all produced by hand from 18K. gold, and are Hamilton's latest creation of beautiful and worthy presentation watches for those deserving high honor and acclaim. The prices of the TYCOON SERIES are as follows:-

	Wholesaler	Retailer	Consumer
Nobel	$85.50	$107.00	$180.00
Bok	90.00	112.50	190.00
Pulitzer	90.00	112.50	190.00
Carnegie	90.00	112.50	190.00
Extra charge for raised gold applied figure dial	5.00	6.25	10.00

The 401 Grade, 19-jewel, 12/0-size rectangular movement strap watch series, is composed of three 14K. solid gold, hand made models of exquisite design.

Prices of the Byrd, Ericson and Wilkinson models of the 401 Grade series, are as follows:-

$68.00 $85.00 $150.00

Distribution of these watches is to be made direct from the factory to retail jewelers on orders from wholesalers. If you sell your samples, please advise the names of jewelers, so that we can complete our records.

Hamilton's December 3, 1930 introduction of its Tycoon Series (page 1)

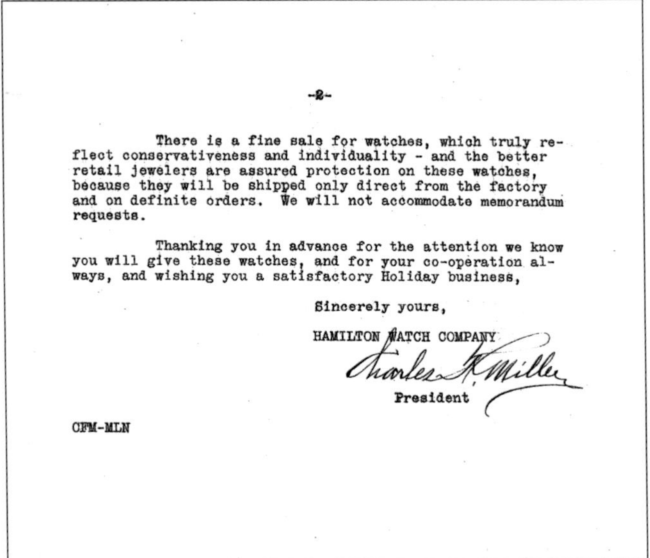

-2-

There is a fine sale for watches, which truly reflect conservativeness and individuality - and the better retail jewelers are assured protection on these watches, because they will be shipped only direct from the factory and on definite orders. We will not accommodate memorandum requests.

Thanking you in advance for the attention we know you will give these watches, and for your co-operation always, and wishing you a satisfactory Holiday business,

Sincerely yours,

HAMILTON WATCH COMPANY

Charles F. Miller

President

CFM-MLN

Hamilton's December 3, 1930 introduction of its Tycoon Series (page 2)

A letter from Illinois to Hamilton, dated March 7, 1930, noted (among other things) that the barrel bridges on the Illinois 528 grade movements had to be changed in order to have the name "Hamilton" appear on the bridge.

Once Hamilton began to close down the Illinois Factory, Lancaster issued an internal memorandum on July 11, 1933, stating: "Since the recent transfer of Illinois production to the Hamilton Division, it has become desirable to transfer the Casing, Jobbing, etc., of the 400 movements that are the property of the Hamilton Watch Co. to the factory departments which handle similar work on Hamilton watches. The transfer will be made July 31, 1933 and from this date all matters pertaining to 400 movements belonging to the Hamilton Watch Co., will be taken care of by the regular factory departments."

On July 15, 1937, Hamilton, via letter, notified the trade that the 400 grade would be discontinued. Thus, Hamilton's use of the 528/400 grade movement also indicates another solid reason for Hamilton's desire to acquire Illinois. The purchase easily allowed Hamilton to acquire technology to produce a very thin pocket watch movement.

WHY I COLLECT ILLINOIS

"I started collecting watches as a young teenager in the 1960s. I was attracted by the intricacy, science and precision of these tiny machines and I collected everything, any brand, any nationality, albeit on a teen's budget. I was especially fascinated by the different escapements and other aspects of the evolution of the modern (19th/20th century) watch.

"So why did I start collecting Illinois watches? I will say right off that I collect many brands. I have had a longstanding interest in the development of the American men's dress watch, and almost all of the American companies made a watch for this market. Although I already had some fine Illinois watches (I love the grade 299 and its various private labels), my interest was really piqued when I discovered an elite group of extra-thin watches that Illinois started to produce around 1918. These were factory-cased in elegant solid gold cases, many with tasteful enamel inlays. I was curious why many of these did not even have the Illinois name of the dial (they are marked "Illinois Watch Co." on the movements though). However, as Illinois always seemed to cater to the retailer, offering private labels and customized finishes, I suspect this was an effort to encourage jewelers to offer an elegant, thin American watch that could compete with the Swiss imports. I have yet to find any catalogs offering these watches (grades 435, 437, 438, 439), and it may just be that the reputation of the jeweler and the elegance of the watches spoke for themselves, supporting the idea that these were made to be marketed by the jewelers.

"The extra-thin movements evolved over the next ten years through several models and grades, but always built on the same basic thin movement and always Factory-Cased in fine and elegant cases. The thin model product line culminated with the grade 528 Illini model. These were obviously intended for a special and discerning market. When Illinois was bought by the Hamilton Watch Company in 1928, Hamilton was very aware that they did not have a watch in their product line that was as thin as this model and they converted the grade 528 as their own Tycoon series (grade 400). It has been a fascinating journey documenting all of the technical and artistic changes during the evolution of this high quality timepiece. There is also the remaining puzzle over why, for the first several years (1918-1921) Illinois did not even advertise their new thin model. It is continuing puzzles like this, and the artistry of the complete cased watches that keep me interested in Illinois watches."

—Jerry Treiman

The 60-Hour Movement

At the time of the acquisition, Hamilton did not have the equivalent of the hugely popular Illinois 60-hour movement, so the desire to acquire this technology also could have spurred Hamilton to purchase Illinois. Evidently, Hamilton was hoping that the Illinois 60-hour mainspring could be replaced with minimal adjustments into a Hamilton 992 movement so as to make it into a 60-hour watch. Unfortunately, the greater width of the Illinois mainspring required a deeper barrel than could be installed comfortably in the 992 movement, and Hamilton discontinued the experiment.

However, a few years later, Hamilton redesigned both the 992 and 950 movements into the 992B and 950B, with new barrels that were the same depth as those Illinois used. The first mainsprings Hamilton made for these new barrels were only slightly longer than their earlier springs and so did not greatly increase run time. Eventually (about 1946), Hamilton introduced their Dynavar mainsprings, and these, with length similar to that of the Illinois ones, would run a watch for 60 hours. Thus, Hamilton finally got the 60-hour movement that would become a pocket watch feature for the company.[50]

Hamilton's Use of and Changes to the Bunn Special

Michael Chamelin shares his notes on the following changes that Hamilton made to the Illinois Bunn Special after the acquisition:[51]

Eleven new Bunn Special case models were introduced and/or used after Hamilton's takeover of the Illinois Watch Company, between 1928 and 1948.

1. Dial hour chapter markers were changed from inward pointing to outward.
2. Dial markings and hour chapter numerals became much more bold, with new "Marked Variants" introduced as well.
3. Dial feet were changed from solid to hollow around late 1928.
4. Hands were switched in color and style from the old purple Illinois style to the then-current blue Hamilton-style hands, sometime around late 1928 or early 1929.
5. The cut-out under the balance wheel on the pillar plate was added in 1929.
6. The marking "Illinois Watch Co." was changed to "Illinois Watch" in 1929.
7. The regulator attachment surrounding the balance jewel setting, which is used to point towards the Slow/Fast adjustment markings, was changed in late 1928. The opening had been near the regulator pins, but Hamilton moved it up adjacent to the Fast/Slow pointing arm of the attachment.
8. Case screws were changed from oval polished to flat polished around 1930.
9. Elinvar balance wheel and non-magnetic hairspring features were added in 1931.
10. The flush-style, gold jewel setting for the balance bridge was changed to a raised rim style around 1932.
11. Friction-set jewels with no screw-down jewel settings were used on the 161B's in the 1940s, much the same as were used on Hamilton's 992B and 950B movements.
12. Dials were changed from double sunk to single sunk around 1946.

Small Movements

Need for an 18/0 Size Movement

Illinois developed and sold its first 18/0 size wristwatch movement in 1923, probably because Charles DeLong, upon his return from Europe, encouraged Illinois to produce one. Illinois called this movement by several grades, including 6¾ (for the number of lignes), 18, 181 and 206, all known versions with 16 jewels. Hamilton, on the other hand, did not produce an 18/0 size movement until considerably later, in 1928 (its 989). From looking at the Hamilton records, Bob Ayer, a dedicated

Hamilton and Illinois collector, notes that Hamilton seems to have had trouble getting its first year's movements out the door. Hamilton apparently acquired cases for the movements in March 1928, but the first production total for 1928 was only 723 movements, of which only 31 were sold.

Thus, it is possible that another reason for the acquisition was to "borrow" the 18/0 size movement skill from Illinois. The fact that Illinois had a five-year head start on Hamilton for 18/0 size movements reinforces Sauers's findings that Hamilton was very slow to adopt new trends. This movement in particular allowed Hamilton to compete in the smaller-sized watches of the burgeoning ladies' wristwatch trend.

1927 HISTORICAL NOTES

- Work begins on Mount Rushmore.
- Josef Stalin takes control of the Communist Party.
- The Holland Tunnel under the Hudson River opens, connecting New York City with New Jersey.
- In Britain, one thousand people a week die from an influenza epidemic.
- *The Jazz Singer* opens.
- The first transatlantic telephone call is made from New York City to London.
- Pan American Airways is formed.

Combined Projects

To accelerate and promote more efficient production post-acquisition, the Hamilton and Illinois Watch Divisions engaged in several joint development projects. For example, in November 1930, individuals from both divisions met to review and determine what parts could be used interchangeably in the divisions' respective 21/0 size movements. Milton F. Manby, the technical superintendent at Hamilton, advised the joint team that "In order to save duplicate die expenses to manufacturing the 21/0S [21/0 size] setting wheel, Hamilton is to furnish Illinois Division with setting wheel blanks."

Interchangeable parts. Various memoranda of the Hamilton Watch Company in November and December 1930 reveal that Hamilton and Illinois were having regular communications to standardize the parts (to the extent possible) between at least their respective 18/0 and 21/0 size movements. Some of these interchangeable parts under study were:

- For the 21/0 size movement:
  Dies for setting wheel
  Click
  Clutch lever
  Setting lever
  Setting cap spring
- For the 18/0 size movement:
  Winding stems
  Winding pinions
  Clutches

The Illinois grade 807B, which introduced interchangeable bridges, may have been a product of this collaboration.

A memorandum, dated November 6, 1930, advises that "The [Hamilton] Technical Department is interested in receiving a detailed list of operations for the method of these parts because they have specified that these particular parts are to be absolutely interchangeable. To make these parts interchangeable, locations of holes and studs as well as the outside shape must be absolutely uniform, one with the other.

At a Hamilton and Illinois interplant factory conference on December 5, 1930, even more details were discussed concerning the following 21/0 size parts:

- Barrel
- Balance staff
- Box jewels
- Center wheel
- Clutch
- Clutch lever, setting lever and setting lever cap
- Hour wheel
- Minute pinion
- Minute wheels
- Pallet
- Pallet arbor
- Ratchet
- Setting wheel
- Winding arbor
- Winding pinion

These various memoranda indicate some of the steps that Hamilton implemented to enable the interchangeability of parts for economies of scale.

Projected 25/0 and 27/0 size movements. In addition to the joint company committees studying the interchangeability of parts from a review of various post-acquisition drawings prepared by the Illinois Watch Division, it is clear that the divisions were also working jointly to develop a 25/0 size movement in 1933 and had even worked on developing a 27/0 one in mid-1932. The 25/0 drawings are shown below.

No design for a 25/0 size nor 27/0 size movement was ever finalized and produced by either division or jointly, but considerable progress was made, as evidenced by the production drawings.

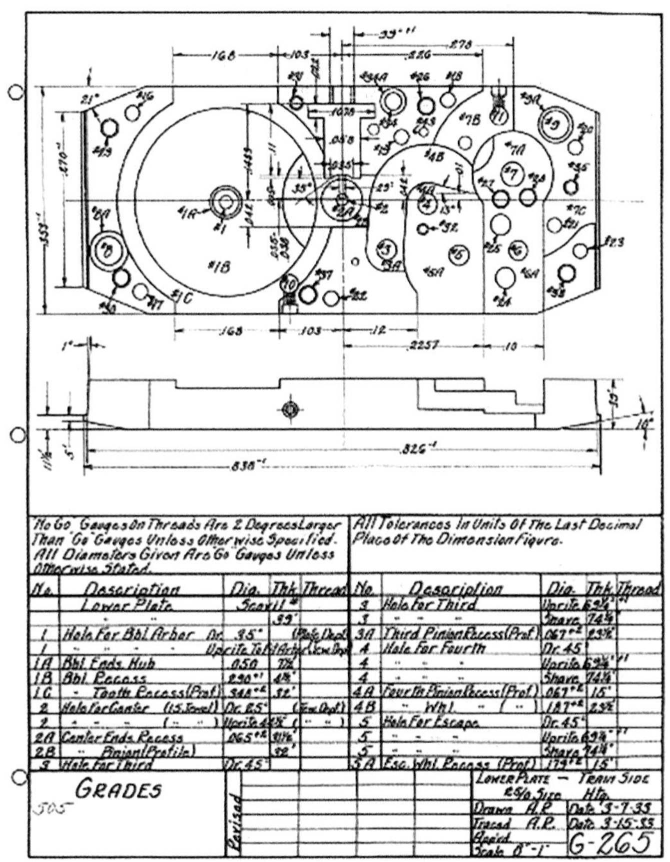

25/0 size lower plate drawing, March 1933

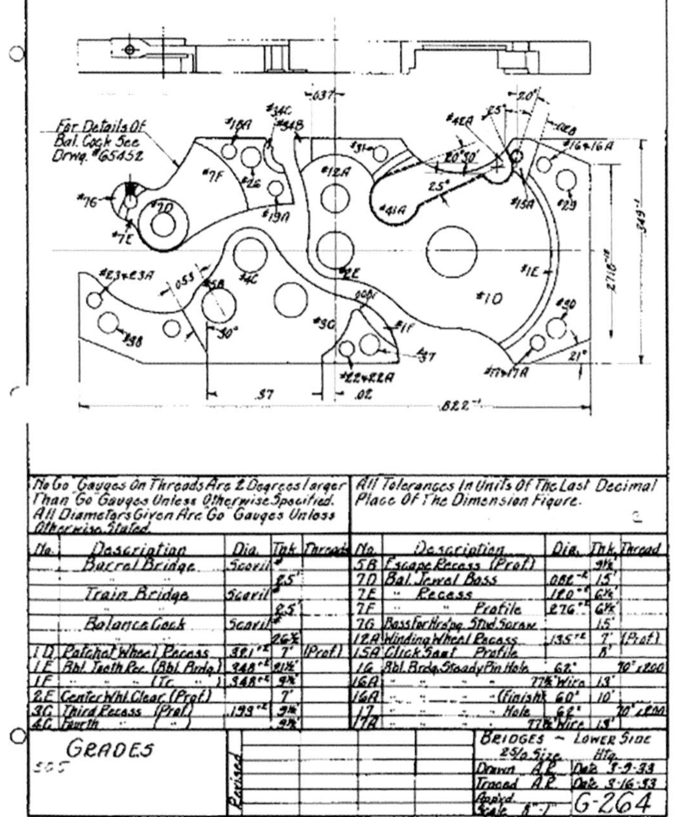

Drawing of a 25/0 size upper plate, March 1933

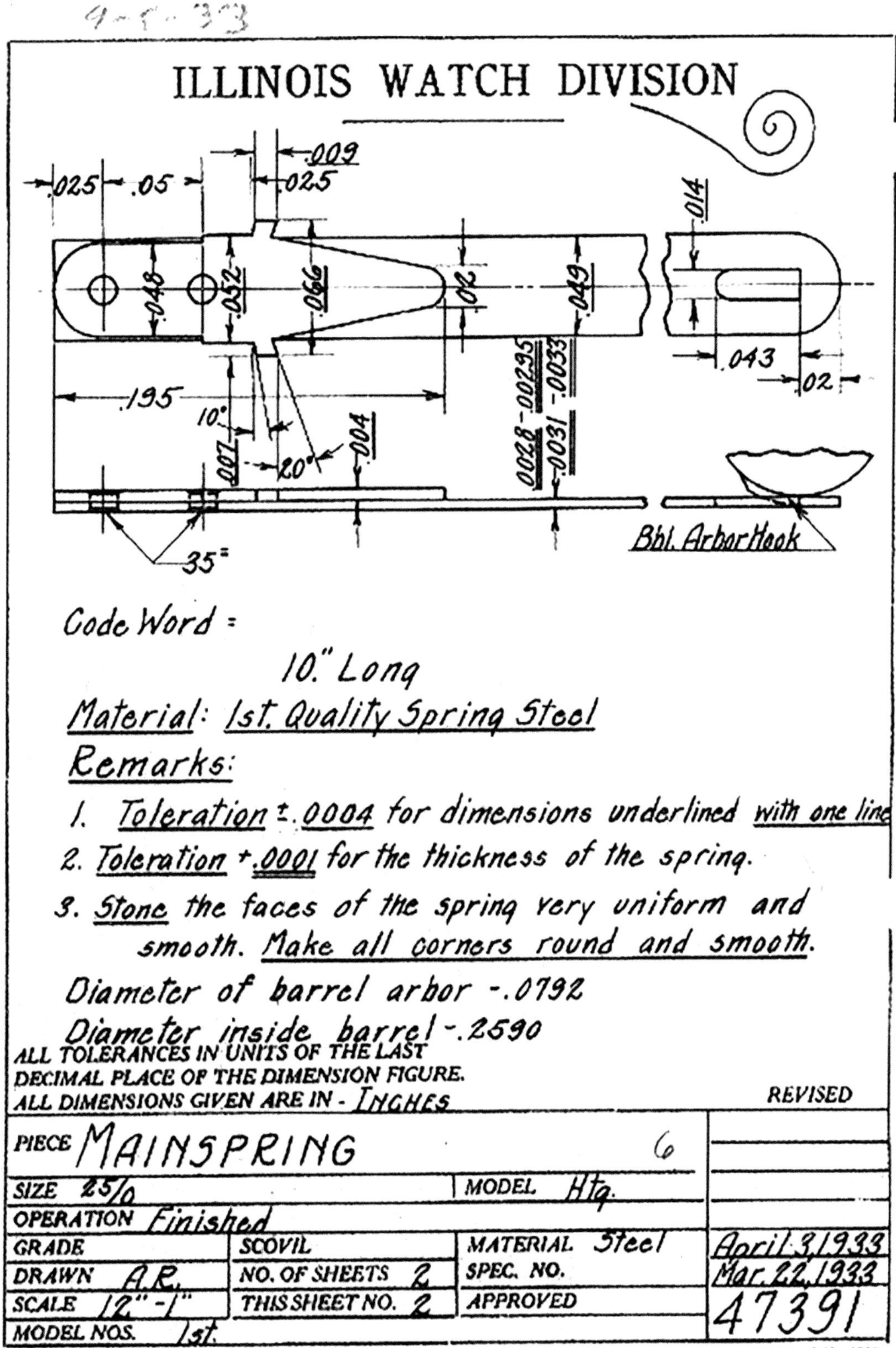
ILLINOIS WATCH DIVISION

Code Word =

10." Long

Material: 1st. Quality Spring Steel

Remarks:

1. Toleration ±.0004 for dimensions underlined with one line

2. Toleration +.0001 for the thickness of the spring.

3. Stone the faces of the spring very uniform and smooth. Make all corners round and smooth.

Diameter of barrel arbor -.0792

Diameter inside barrel -.2590

ALL TOLERANCES IN UNITS OF THE LAST DECIMAL PLACE OF THE DIMENSION FIGURE.

ALL DIMENSIONS GIVEN ARE IN - INCHES

REVISED

PIECE MAINSPRING 6			April 3,1933
SIZE 25/0		MODEL Htg.	Mar. 22, 1933
OPERATION Finished			
GRADE	SCOVIL	MATERIAL Steel	
DRAWN A.R.	NO. OF SHEETS 2	SPEC. NO.	
SCALE 12"-1"	THIS SHEET NO. 2	APPROVED	47391
MODEL NOS. 1st.			

Drawing of a mainspring for a 25/0 size movement, March 1933

PROJECT FOR A MOVEMENT SMALLER THAN 21/0

According to internal records, Hamilton even approached a Swiss company on September 28, 1932, to secure a movement smaller than 21/0 size, Additionally, on September 23, 1932, Hamilton and Illinois officials Halligan, Manby, Keenan, Beckwith, Miller, W. E. Port (Miller and Port were based in the Illinois Watch Division), Atkinson, R. Kant, W. H. Manby, Luckey and M. F. Kransky held a conference and agreed to utilize $1,000 for this study. This would equate to about $16,000 today, still a fairly modest investment.

TRIPLICA' INVESTIGATING ENGINEER

REQUEST for PRELIMINARY INVESTIGATION and REPORT
HAMILTON WATCH CO.---HAMILTON DIVISION

To General Supt's Office Date 9/28/32

Subject: Ladies Wrist Watch Smaller than Grade 995.

Description: (Reason for work and results expected)

In accordance with the decision arrived at in the conference Sept. 23, 1932 at Hamilton Watch Co. attended by Messrs. F. C. Beckwith, R. E. Miller, W. E. Port, J. Keenan, W. R. Atkinson, R. W. Kant, L. F. Halligan, W. H. Manby, G. P. Luckey and M. F. Manby, it is desired to establish a "C" Project on "Ladies Wrist Watch Smaller than Grade 995". The concensus of opinion was that the size and shape will be determined later, but should be smaller than the 21/0 - 995 in width, thickness and length and will be the smallest watch which will be required in future production.

The initial work on this project will cover the study of the design and technical features desired in small size watches to determine the most suitable features for our design.

In order to adequately study watches of this type, such watches as (over)

Date of desired completion Continuous

Department where work can be done Technical
LOCATION

Signed Milton F. Manby Dept. Technical

ORIGINATOR FILLS IN INFORMATION DESIRED ABOVE THE LINE

APPROVED STAFF MEMBER	APPROVED ASST. GEN'L SUPT.		
APPROVED STAFF MEMBER CONCERNED	APPROVED GENERAL SUPT. W. H. Manby		
ASSIGNED TO ENGINEER G. L. Dres	DATE ASSIGNED 9/30/32	DATE TO BE COMPLETED	DATE COMPLETED
PROJECT NO. 3800 INVESTIGATION NO.	NAME Ladies Wrist Watch Smaller than Grade 995.		

APPROPRIATION REQUESTED	APPROPRIATION APPROVED	WORK ORDERS ISSUED
BY W. H. Manby DATE 9/29/32	DATE 9/30/32	BY DATE

FORM 1 (1000-2.13.31)

appear to have new improvements and special design features should be purchased for study from time to time. At the present time it is desired to purchase the Movado 4 lg. rectangular watch recently loaned to us for investigation by Ralph W. Biggs & Co. at a cost of $38.00.

An appropriation for $1000.00 is requested to carry out this work for the first year.

A Look at the Big Picture

In addition to the reasons already discussed, some other justifications for Hamilton's acquisition of Illinois were that:

- *The acquisition not only eliminated a competitor but also provided increased market share and geographical diversification.* The acquisition in 1928 eliminated a competitor at a fair price and increased Hamilton's market share and potential production capacity at a time when Hamilton was far outdistanced by Elgin and Waltham in the production and sale of wristwatches. Moreover, because Illinois, like Hamilton, was by the time of the acquisition making only high-grade watch movements, Hamilton could increase its market share without diluting its brand. Another factor was that the acquisition enabled Hamilton to establish a beachhead in the "West" to compete more efficiently with Elgin and to expand its geographic reach.

- *Illinois was profitable, producing high-quality products as well as possessing a content workforce.* According to the Bunns, 1927 was one of the strongest years in the history of the Illinois Watch Company. Although Illinois, like others, misread the rapid decline in pocket watch demand, it moved rapidly to address its high pocket watch inventory by moving in 1926 to a "short time" production schedule. Thus, this measure and others demonstrated Illinois' ability to adjust to market conditions and continue to thrive. The year 1928 proved to be one of Illinois' most profitable, and 1929 and 1930 were also satisfactory financially. Moreover, the company's workforce was experienced and happy.

- *Illinois had trendsetting deco designs.* Illinois had on its drawing board at the time of the acquisition a very large number of men's and ladies' wristwatches, most with innovative, eye-catching, cutting-edge Art Deco designs then in vogue, starting with the very popular Marquis Strap models. These watches could permit Hamilton to catch the deco design wave with more intensity than it was able to do on its own. When released, these watches significantly supplemented Hamilton's wristwatch lines and its bottom line. In addition to the Illinois Marquis Strap, other wristwatch models for the 1928–1929 time period (for example, the Consul, Ritz, and Chesterfield) clearly evidenced Illinois' uniqueness and its trendsetting abilities.

- *The acquisition provided access to research and development.* Although the Hamilton management placed great value on the reliability and accuracy of its timepieces, Hamilton did not focus its research and development (R&D) investments on advanced product design. As a result, Hamilton could not quickly introduce new and innovative watches in demand in the 1920s. Illinois was attractive because it already had a 3/0 movement, an extremely thin pocket watch movement, a rectangular 12/0 size movement, a successful working 18/0 size movement, a highly sought-after 60-hour pocket watch movement and several other new features. Hamilton had meanwhile either been lagging behind in development or been oblivious to the market need for these innovations. Owing to Hamilton's strong penchant for reliability, accuracy and the bottom line, it repeatedly missed the technology and style curve, and the acquisition of Illinois was an unstated effort to gain technology and style necessary for the future viability of the firm.

1927

HISTORICAL NOTES

- A manual washing machine costs $15.93.
- An electric washing machine costs $79.00.
- A Kodak box Brownie camera costs $2.29.
- A wood-fired kitchen range costs $59.85.

- *The acquisition provided positions for Miller's sons.* Some cynical collectors note that perhaps one reason for the acquisition was to help Charles Miller find positions for his sons Robert and Frederick and establish a Miller dynasty. However, this seems like a very extreme justification for the merger. Although Robert E. Miller later had a successful career, he may have been too inexperienced at the time to manage the Illinois Factory effectively; less than ninety days into the acquisition, William E. Port was put in charge of everyone in Springfield with the exception of Robert E. Miller. His brother Frederick S. Miller, also relocated to Springfield, was probably under much less pressure, as he held the nebulous title of "assistant general executive."

Retrospect

According to E. C. Alft, Elgin amazingly produced half the watches made in America from 1920 through 1928.[52] An Elgin advertisement that appeared in 1928 claimed that there were 14,018 retail jewelers in the United States and that all but twelve of them carried Elgins. The need for Hamilton to increase its production capacity to try to catch up with Waltham and Elgin was the dominant reason—and, in fact, its stated reason—for its desire to acquire Illinois.

The need for increased capacity, the need for a rectangular movement, the need for a very thin pocket watch movement, the need for an 18/0 size movement, the need to catch the contemporary style wave and Illinois' technological advances were undoubtedly the central drivers for the acquisition.

Most of the attention since 1928 has been focused on Hamilton's reasons for the move. But there were also reasons why this was timely on the Illinois side as well. At the time Hamilton acquired the company, Henry Bunn was the president of Illinois, as successor to his brother Jacob Bunn, Jr. Henry was already retired from the family bank, his remaining siblings were of a similar age, and the rest of the family were fully involved in their other business ventures.

On January 5, 1928, only a few days after the public announcement of the sale, the *Jewelers' Circular* published a statement made by Henry Bunn:

> The Hamilton Watch Co. of Lancaster, Pa., has acquired all assets, including good will, of the Illinois Watch Co. The purchaser assumed control of the business Jan. 1, and expects to operate along the same lines that it has been conducted in the past. Most of the present personnel will be retained.
>
> The transaction is considered very favorably by all concerned as it means the combining of the two leading American manufacturers of high grade watches exclusively.
>
> The Illinois Watch Co. has been owned and operated for the last 50 years by members of the Bunn family of Springfield, Ill., and it has enjoyed an enviable success together with a rapid growth. This success and growth was developed under the leadership of its former president, Jacob Bunn, deceased, who was succeeded as president by Henry Bunn.
>
> The sale comes at the close of one of the most successful years in the history of the company. The entire capital stock of the company was owned by two estates of the Bunn family and it is due primarily to this fact that the property has been sold.

Bunn's statement indicates that he expected that the business would continue to be run as it had been and, furthermore, that the merger would work to both companies' advantage, as it would mean no dilution of either brand because both would presumably continue to produce only high-grade watches.

It is significant that Henry Bunn fully credited the success and growth of Illinois to his brother Jacob Bunn, Jr., who had run the company for nearly thirty of its fifty years (from his father's death in 1897 until his own death in 1926). In the current circumstances, Henry probably viewed himself as just a temporary caretaker of the firm. In that capacity, and as a banker, he likely considered that the family was financially overinvested in the watch company and recognized that none of them had the particular expertise to undertake running it.

Thus, it is clear that the Bunns determined after five decades of control that it was the appropriate time to exit the watch industry. Since the acquisition was completed by the end of 1927, Hamilton may very well have started making overtures fairly soon after Jacob Jr.'s death the preceding year. So when Hamilton made a good offer, Henry took it. In light of the unforeseen but nonetheless impending Great Depression, the Bunns' timing could not have been more fortuitous.

From Hamilton's perspective, things may have been different. Within ninety days, a cost accountant was effectively placed in control of Illinois; and less than six months later, in August 1928, a massive layoff was implemented—to the great shock of the Bunns, the workers, their families and the rest of Springfield. Unfortunately, this would just be the start of the adverse treatment Illinois was to endure under its new management.

Henry Bunn (far right) as a young banker in front of the Springfield Marine Bank; from A. T. Call, *Jacob Bunn: Legacy of an Industrial Pioneer*

HENRY BUNN (1858-1934)

Henry Bunn, Member Of Pioneer Sangamon Family, Dies In City

Was Former Cashier Of Marine Bank And Official Of Sangamo Electric, Illinois Watch Firms.

Henry Bunn, son of Jacob Bunn, died at the age of seventy-six in Springfield on December 27 1934, seven years after he helped engineer the sale of the longtime family-run Illinois Watch Company to its East Coast competition, Hamilton. Bunn had served as cashier of the Springfield Marine Bank from 1878 to 1916, when he retired. He also served as president of the Illinois Watch Company and the vice president of Sangamo Electric Company.

Henry, along with his brothers George W. and Jacob, and their sister Alice Bunn in 1925 paid off in full the large $800,000 indebtedness of their father, Jacob, whose bank had gone into voluntary liquidation in 1878. The family took on this responsibility without any legal obligation to do so.

Upon his retirement from the banking business, Henry Bunn divided his time between Washington, New York and Springfield. He never married and was survived by his brother George and sister Alice.

At the start of the Spanish-American War, he organized and was an officer in Troop D, First Illinois Calvary, recruited from residents of Springfield.

ILLINOIS

CHAPTER 4

Price-Cutting Fears Amidst Boom Times

Hamilton's "Plans" for Illinois

Two months after the acquisition, Hamilton published a one-page announcement in the March 1928 issue of the *Keystone* stating, surprisingly, that "we have not as yet been able to formulate any definite policies regarding the Illinois plant or its products." This statement makes it seem as though the acquisition of Illinois was a spur-of-the-moment decision in reaction to the strong growth in the wristwatch market and the rapid market-share gains by Hamilton's chief competition, Elgin and Waltham. However, Hamilton did indicate that it had the following "plans in mind":

- *Hamilton wanted "to materially enhance and strengthen that splendid reputation which Illinois watches have enjoyed during the past fifty-eight years."*

  If so, how would this enable Hamilton to double its own production capacity, their principal stated reason for the acquisition, as it could double Hamilton's capacity only by shifting Illinois' production efforts to Hamilton watches?

- *"The identity of the Illinois watch will be maintained and goodwill fully protected. Manufacture of this watch will be continued as usual at the Springfield Illinois Plant."*

Although the acquisition-related financial records are not available, a sizeable portion of the cost was undoubtedly allocated to goodwill. Therefore, the Illinois brand had to be maintained or Hamilton would have had to face a significant financial write-off of the goodwill.

- *"The Illinois factory will continue to supply materials for watches for all grades so successfully manufactured since 1870."*

This matter also would have been required to avoid a goodwill write-off.

- *"We will endeavor to apply at all times to the management of the Illinois plant and the sale of its products those business principles which have made the Hamilton Watch Company and its products such an outstanding success."*

Yet within eight months, Hamilton "severely" reduced the 1,300-employee workforce of Illinois.

- *"Therefore, you need have no hesitancy in anticipating your needs for Illinois watches and purchasing them at this time. You can purchase Illinois watches with the same assurance of stabilization as is yours when you purchase Hamilton."*

At first, existing business relationships remained basically unharmed by Hamilton's plans; but this would change drastically when the effects of the Great Depression hit at almost the same time as the death of Charles F. Miller, Hamilton's longtime president.

- *"It is natural that changes will be made from time to time as conditions require. But these changes will be evolutionary and constructive. We shall keep in mind always, the good of the Retail Jewelers of America and hope that in turn you will continue to give us that friendly co-operation which we have always enjoyed from you."*

Hamilton was trying to anticipate all the issues and concerns that the retail jewelers might have about the acquisition and allay their fears. Unfortunately, Hamilton could not predict the impending economic disaster that was to strike the American marketplace and render the company unable to make changes that were merely "evolutionary and constructive" at Illinois. For purely internal business reasons, Hamilton in August 1928 cut a huge number of heads at Illinois. However, this occurred over a year before Black Tuesday and the Great Depression's devastating impact caused Hamilton to change its plans for Illinois.

THE KEYSTONE March, 1928

An Important Announcement To all Retail Jewelers—

On December 28, 1927, we made one of the most important announcements in the annals of American watch making, the news of our purchase of the assets of the Illinois Watch Company, of Springfield, Illinois, of which we assumed management on January 2, 1928.

Since that time the jewelry trade has evinced a keen interest in our plans for the Illinois Company. Naturally, we have not as yet been able to formulate any definite policies regarding the Illinois plant or its product. But we do desire at this time to announce to the retail jewelers of America what plans we have in mind. They are as follows:

1. We desire to thank the retail jewelers of America for the hundreds of congratulatory letters sent to us when the first announcement of our purchase of the Illinois Watch plant was made. We assure you that it is our desire to merit the confidence implied in those letters and to materially enhance and strengthen that splendid reputation which Illinois Watches have enjoyed during the past fifty-eight years.
2. The identity of the Illinois Watch will be maintained and good will fully protected. Manufacture of this watch will be continued as usual at the Springfield, Illinois plant.
3. The Illinois factory will continue to supply materials for watches of all grades so successfully manufactured since 1870.
4. We will endeavor to apply at all times to the management of the Illinois plant and the sale of its product those business principles which have made the Hamilton Watch Company and its product such an outstanding success.
5. Therefore, you need have no hesitancy in anticipating your needs for Illinois Watches and purchasing them at this time. You can purchase Illinois Watches with the same assurance of stabilization as is yours when you purchase Hamiltons.
6. It is natural that changes will be made from time to time as conditions require. But these changes will be evolutionary and constructive. We shall keep in mind, always, the good of the Retail Jewelers of America and hope that in turn you will continue to give us that friendly co-operation which we have always enjoyed from you.

Further announcements regarding plans for the development of the Illinois plant will be made from time to time. We shall endeavor to keep you fully informed of every important move.

Sincerely yours,

HAMILTON WATCH COMPANY.

Charles F. Miller PRESIDENT

Keystone, March 1928

New Assistant General Manager

On April 28, 1928, less than ninety days into the acquisition, Robert E. Miller announced that William E. Port of Philadelphia (Hamilton's former cost accountant and factory expert) had been appointed assistant general manager. He was to assume his new duties at once, but had "been in Springfield at frequent intervals during the last sixty days to acquaint himself with conditions of the company."[1]

This move indicates that Charles F. Miller, president of Hamilton, thought that his son Robert E. Miller was not up to the task of effectively managing the Illinois Watch Factory; that Calvin Kendig could not be spared enough from Lancaster to devote the time required at Springfield; and that Port, skilled in cost accounting, would be best suited to manage Illinois, with its excess inventory, in the Hamilton style.

Ultimately, everyone in the Illinois plant, with the exception of Miller himself, would report to Port, as evidenced by a July 1932 organizational chart for Illinois.

WILLIAM E. PORT (1895-1951)

William Edward Port, a Pennsylvania native, served in the United States Army in 1918. By 1929 he was working as a cost accountant in Philadelphia for a "ship corporation."

Thereafter he served as a cost accountant and "factory expert" for Hamilton Watch in Lancaster until he was appointed the assistant general manager of the Illinois Watch Company in 1928. He stayed in Springfield until the plant closed in 1933. In 1944 he apparently became a vice president for Coca-Cola in St. Louis, where he lived until his death.

PORT TO HELP MANAGE LOCAL WATCH PLANT

A Question of Price

Meanwhile, the greatest concern of the jewelry industry, and watch manufacturers in particular, was the rise of a new method of conducting business. As early as 1927, the American jewelry industry expressed worries about "price-cutters" and what it derogatively dubbed "E.Z. Credit jewelers." Watch manufacturers and the trade press condemned these practices as the ruination of the jewelry business as they knew it. Hamilton, in particular, objected strenuously to discounters, price-cutters and those who sold on credit, often sarcastically spelling "credit" with a "k" when referring to them. (The Lancaster firm, among the earliest to attack such entities, spent six years seeking an industry-wide solution, but once that opportunity passed, Hamilton implemented its own plan in 1934 to address this perceived situation.)

Although traditional jewelers and manufacturers were not happy about credit jewelers, the number of credit jewelers steadily increased. In January 1928, the *Jewelers' Circular* noted that in Philadelphia alone eleven credit jewelers used 460 inches of space in a single issue of a Philadelphia newspaper versus 70 inches by traditional jewelry houses. Despite the violent protestations of the jewelry industry, the trend never slowed.

Credit jewelers' advertisements for one weekend day in January 1928, in a Philadelphia newspaper totaled 460 inches.

Keystone, November 1927. The attack on price-cutters and price competition was already relentless well before the Great Depression.

Morris Friedberg, March 1928

National Association of Credit Jewelers

In reaction to the strong attacks on them by politicians, manufacturers, wholesalers, industry advocates and trade publications, the credit jewelers in the United States established the National Association of Credit Jewelers. It was formed in Detroit in April 1927 to bring together in one group the credit jewelers of the United States with the purpose of "getting closer cooperation, a better understanding and to promote cleaner business practices."

Morris Friedberg of Detroit, Michigan, its first president, noted: "It is self-evident that there is a need for an association of credit jewelers, who would join together to correct the radical view of good intentioned folks, who are inclined to see in the credit merchandising policy the downfall of business." Furthermore, there was "a need for a united effort in combating unfair legislation toward installment merchandising by folks who took an antagonistic view toward our class, which view was solely based on the lack of proper understanding."

Friedberg emphasized that "there was a need in our particular field for a association which would set a standard for the installment jewelry business."

Despite strong industry opposition, the association grew each year and its annual conventions had increasingly larger attendance. The organization helped substantially to deflect the vigorous attacks on its members for offering credit and installment sales.

Some credit jewelers tried to defend their credit policy even prior to the formation of the National Association of Credit Jewelers. *Hutchinson News* (Hutchinson, KS), November 26, 1926; image from *newspapers.com*

Price Maintenance Legislation

By early 1928 the jewelry industry and its manufacturers, frustrated with the competition and continued growth of discounters, fully supported Federal Price Maintenance Legislation. Rather than compete with these businesses, they sought their extinction by legislation.

THE PRICE-CUTTER DEFINED

Prior to the stock market crash, the watch and jewelry industries turned their wrath toward their personal villain and all-purpose scapegoat, "The Price-Cutter." In May 1929 the *Keystone* published a reprint of an article defining "The Price-Cutter" as follows:

"The price-cutter is worse than a criminal—he is a fool. He is a commercial maniac.
He not only kills his enemies, but slaughters his friends.

"He not only pulls down the standard of his goods, but he pulls down his competitors and friends.

"He annihilates himself and scuttles the ship in which he, himself, is afloat.

"Nothing is so easy as to cut a price, and nothing is so hard as to get them back once they have been pulled down.

"The man who persistently cuts prices admits his own failure as a salesman.

"He admits that he has been defeated according to the best sales of commercial procedure and honest merchandising.

"He acknowledges his lack of ability.

"He admits his watchword and sole inducement is 'PRICE'.

"He admits he cannot win a fair fight in salesmanship.

"He brands himself as a failure in the business world and a hitter below the belt.

"If the business world was dominated by the price cutter, there would be no business.

"Price-cutting, in fact, is not a business any more than smallpox is health."

It is ironic that today the strongest retailers are the price-cutters that consumers flock to.

Senator Arthur Capper and Representative Clyde Kelly would work continuously for years to try to pass their Capper-Kelly Fair Trade Bill for Price Maintenance Legislation. This proposed bill was to spend seventeen years in committee (Interstate and Foreign Commerce) before it was finally passed by the House of Representatives in 1931. It never passed in the Senate.

Senator Arthur Capper, c. 1931

Representative Clyde Kelly, c. 1931

The bill was ultimately put aside in 1933 for the writing of the National Industrial Recovery Act. After 1933 it was never proposed again at the federal level. The National Recovery Administration (NRA) would encounter its own problems by 1935.

Jewelry industry executives and watchmakers promptly jumped on the Price Maintenance Legislation bandwagon. Charles H. Ingersoll, of dollar-watch fame, remarked in the March 1928 issue of the *Keystone* that "competition will destroy competition . . . price maintenance is the most obvious weapon for the elimination of unfair price competition, as it will prevent the use of well-known products as bait for the exploitation of unfair conditions as to prices in other products."

***Keystone*, March 1928. The jewelry, watch industry and trade press viewed Price Maintenance Legislation as a panacea for their problems.**

DeForest Hulburd, president of Elgin, also supported the legislation, commenting in that same issue of the *Keystone*: "There is no danger of such legislation tending to increase prices. With competition as keen as it is between watch manufacturing concerns, no company is going to set its prices any higher than are absolutely necessary in order to cover the cost of distribution of the product." At this time, Illinois and Elgin and others were routinely exchanging price lists, a practice that would be clearly in violation of antitrust laws today.

Hulburd added, "The principal reason for such a bill is the fact that price-cutting on well-known trade-marked articles is invariably done in order to bring in trade which will purchase other articles of unknown value at prices enjoying excessively large margins of profit."

Charles H. Hulburd, late in life

DeForest Hulburd, c. 1930

DEFOREST HULBURD (1886-1981)

DeForest Hulburd, born in Chicago, graduated from Yale University in 1908. After joining the assembly department of Elgin in 1910, he advanced in the company, in 1913 becoming assistant to the president, Charles H. Hulburd, his father. By 1919 he was a vice-president of the company and on its board of directors. In 1922 he wrote a small booklet entitled "The Box of Wonders in Your Pocket," which provided a basic introduction to the workings of a watch. He later went on to become president of Elgin upon his father's death in 1924, thereafter helping to convert Elgin from a pocket watch company to a wristwatch one.

At the end of 1931, during the heart of the Great Depression, Hulburd resigned to work for the family brokerage firm of Hulburd, Warren and Chandler, although he remained on the Elgin board. He was replaced as president by T. Albert Potter, a 1906 Princeton University graduate, who had spent his entire prior career at Quaker Oats.

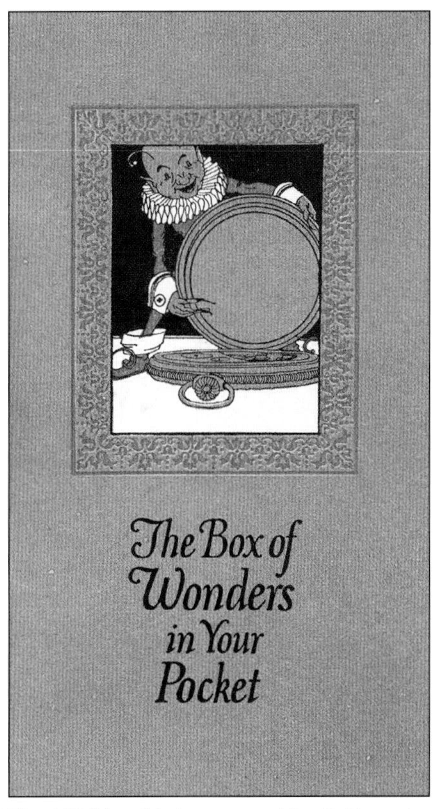

The 1922 booklet prepared by DeForest Hulburd on how a watch works

T. Albert Potter, c. 1931

Thos. A. Potter Elected President of the Elgin National Watch Co.

CHICAGO, Jan. 15.—Thomas Albert Potter was elected, Jan. 8, president of the Elgin National Watch Co., as successor to DeForest Hulburd, who resigned after seven years in the executive position. Mr. Potter was formerly vice-president of the Quaker Oats company with offices in Chicago. He is a graduate of Princeton, is 48 years of age and has been associated with the Quaker Oats Co. since his graduation 25 years ago. Mr. Hulburd, who had succeeded his father to the presidency of the Elgin company in 1924 had entered the firm as a bench worker in 1910, held several positions in various departments until 1914 when he became assistant to the president and five years later vice-president.

Mr. Hulburd retains his position on the board of directors, although resigning to devote further attention to the investment firm, Hulburd, Warren and Chandler, Chicago, of which he is a member.

Jewelers' Circular, February 1932

Competition: The Death of Industry?

On March 20, 1928, the editorial board of the *Jewelers' Circular* continued to preach the evils of price-cutting: "The lack of clear thinking manifest among many of the small merchants of today is exemplified in a letter recently received from one of our subscribers, who objects to the general condemnation of the policy of price-cutting saying 'Why is this not good business? Don't we all know that competition is the life of trade and 'competition' means selling at the lowest possible price?'"

In response, the editors blasted the letter writer: "If ever there was a misapplication of the meaning of the adage it is here exemplified to the *nth* degree. Competition, as our correspondent defines it, is the *death* not the life of any industry. Price-cutting never helped retailer, distributor or manufacturer, and in the long run never helped the ultimate consumer."

It is doubtful that any consumer would support this view today.

Retail Prices

On May 5, 1928, the *Jewelers' Circular* had another of its editorials concerning retail prices, price-cutters and price maintenance. Although it noted that "inquiries coming both from retailers and some manufacturers indicate that many in our trade are under the impression that it is illegal for a manufacturer to designate or suggest a retail price for his product," it clarified by saying that "it is one thing to suggest a price at which an article is to be sold to the consumer and an entirely different thing to take coercive measures to compel a retailer to sell at such a price." (Such a directive would have been unlawful under extant antitrust laws.)

However, the jewelry industry was strongly supporting pending price-maintenance legislation that would enable manufacturers to secure contracts with their customers by which resale prices to the consumer could be legally established on trademarked, standard and nationally advertised articles, such as the products sold by Hamilton, Illinois and their competitors. The editorial warned, "Until we obtain such legislation, the manufacturer who builds up a good will on a standard and branded articles, as well as his customers, are at the mercy of the price cutter who wishes to use this merchandise as bait to induce business."

How ironic it is that what is an accepted practice today was so violently opposed at this time!

A letter to a jeweler from Ross Atkinson, then sales manager at Hamilton, briefly emphasizes Hamilton's position on price maintenance.[2] This letter, dated June 14, 1928, reads, in part:

> "According to the Sherman [Anti-Trust] Laws controlling the restrictions of trade, manufacturers are absolutely not permitted to maintain prices, but they certainly are permitted to suggest prices for which their merchandise is sold to consumers.
>
> "Retail jewelers know the value of standardized prices and when Hamilton watches are sold at less than the suggested prices we always endeavor to explain to the retail jeweler that he cannot profitably sell watches for less than they are marked and render the services so necessary in connection with all watch sales and make a profit.
>
> "Then, too, price cutting controls which are usually the result of a merchant cutting prices on standard merchandise, *merely benefit the public* and do not as a rule create sales, but have a tendency to have the public lose confidence in the dealers as well as the merchandise offered by different dealers at different prices for the same article" (emphasis added). It is amazing that the benefits to the consumer never entered into the Hamilton debate on price-cutting.

Chain Stores

Felix H. Levy, a well-known antitrust lawyer who was counsel for the American National Retail Jewelers Association, often provided legal advice in articles appearing in the *Jewelers' Circular* and the *Keystone* periodicals. In the July 12, 1928 issue of the former, Levy commented, prophetically, that the United States Supreme Court's rulings up to that point gave "encouragement to price-cutters and in the opinion of those who are expert in the subject, it has been the principal basis for the growth of chain stores, and other like establishments, the growth of which is generally followed by the extermination of their smaller, independent rivals."[3]

Later, the Supreme Court provided some relief, declaring that a manufacturer has the right to announce its suggested resale prices and also to announce that it will refuse to make further sales to price-cutters, but only if the manufacturer was acting solely and independently upon its own initiative, and it must not accept any promises or assurances from his customers that they will observe and maintain such suggested prices.

Felix H. Levy, October 1928

FELIX H. LEVY (1869-1953)

Felix Holt Levy, born in San Antonio, Texas, was a well-known attorney with specialized knowledge in price maintenance and antitrust law. He was a former special assistant to the United States Attorney General. With Henry W. Taft, he prosecuted the tobacco trust in the early 1900s, and he was later counsel for the National Wholesale Dry Goods Association as well as the National Wholesale Jewelers' Association.

Dip and Rebound in the Watch Industry

In July 1928, Elgin had 3,500 active, full-time employees.[4] Their president, DeForest Hulburd, attributed the drop in business earlier that year to keen competition between American and foreign manufacturers, which caused a slight falling-off in actual sales demand. Despite a slow start, the year 1928 turned out to be a boom year for most American watch manufacturers. In a full-page announcement in the January 1929 issue of the *Keystone,* Elgin noted: "Our sales in the past three months have been the largest in the history of our Company."

Springfield, Ill., March 23.—The Cook County Business Men's Association, 400 strong, arrived from Chicago on a Wabash special at 7:05 this morning. This imposing delegation came to wage a war until death on the great department stores of Chicago. It was followed about noon by another special train with an additional 200.

The Springfield Business Men's Association and Grocers' Association sent committees to the train this morning, and escorted the visitors to the Leland Hotel. The procession, headed by the Illinois Watch Factory Band, marched through the streets in a drizzling rain. The delegates, wearing yellow badges, filled the Leland Hotel, and headquarters were immediately opened in room No. 4 on the ground floor. The band then went to the other hotels, and escorted to the Leland the delegates which had arrived from other cities.

Shortly after 9 o'clock another procession was formed, and proceeded to the statehouse, passing through the executive grounds. As the delegation approached the executive mansion Governor Tanner appeared on the front porch, and Mrs. Tanner viewed the procession from an upstairs window.

Presented to Governor Tanner.

Moses Salomon greeted the Governor, and briefly explained the mission of the delegation. He said:

"On behalf of this delegation, representing the manufacturing and laboring interests of Illinois, we have come here to ask for a law to abolish department stores. It is a great pleasure for us to pay our respects to the Governor of the state this morning, believing, as we do, you will assist us in the future as you have in the past. Gentlemen, it is my pleasure to introduce Governor Tanner." (Loud applause.)

Some one in the delegation proposed three cheers, which were given enthusiastically. Governor Tanner responded as follows:

"Senator Salomon and fellow citizens of the great City of Chicago and of Illinois: I am more than pleased at this greeting, and compliment. Gentlemen, I thank you. As to the mission you come on, in favor of the department store bill, I wish to say that bill has not yet reached the executive branch of the government. After the Legislative branch has passed upon it, then the executive has the right to exercise his veto. This bill has not reached me, and I can take no action until it does. My sympathies are always with the weak, and if the bill passes both branches of the Legislature I will examine it carefully, and if I believe it is constitutional, I will take great pride in signing the bill." (Applause.)

Three cheers were then given for Mrs. Tanner. The delegation then proceeded to the capitol building.

The Illinois Watch Band performed at a rally to urge the governor of Illinois to sign a law to abolish department stores in 1897; image from *newspapers.com*

To our Retail Jewelers

◆ ◆ ◆

THE end of 1928 has just passed around the corner. Looking backwards we can all see where lots of improvement might have been made in many of our operations. That is experience and places us in a stronger position to do a better and finer work in 1929.

If we have made errors they were of omission rather than commission. Our motives have been clean. Our enthusiasm has been from the heart—and great reward has come to us.

Our sales in the past three months have been the largest in the history of our Company. And for this we sincerely thank you for the important part you played in this successful selling campaign.

The Retail Jeweler, loyal to Elgin Watches and alert to the recognition of constructive Elgin policy has made our Christmas a merry one. We hope that our sincere endeavor has contributed something lasting that will have some part in the making of your Merry Christmas.

ELGIN NATIONAL WATCH COMPANY
U. S. A.

Elgin announcement in the *Keystone,* January 1929

Since Elgin had been in "an unusually prosperous condition" in 1928, with record earnings, the company in January 1929 declared an extra cash dividend of 4%, resulting in a distribution of about $400,000 to its 3,000 stockholders. For the year, Elgin shareholders received a whopping 14% in dividends.[5]

Merger of Three Wholesale Houses

Another sign of the buoyant economy following the strong 1928 financial year was the presence of strong companies seeking to further bolster their market positions. One such move was the A. C. Becken Company's acquisition of two of its longtime rivals, Otto Young & Co. and the C. H. Knights-Thearle Company, on January 25, 1929. All three wholesale/catalog jewelers were based out of Chicago and had operated similar mail-order catalog businesses.

A.C. BECKEN (1855–1932)

Albert C. Becken was born in Buffalo, New York, the son of a tailor. At the age of fourteen he learned to be a barber and continued in that occupation for eight years until failing health compelled him to seek outdoor employment. He sold the barber shop he had established in Driftwood, Pennsylvania, and used the proceeds to fill a bag with watches, chains and razors.

Becken then walked from lumber camp to lumber camp in the area, where he sold these items to former customers of his barber shop. Then he started covering the camps in the northern states via horse and buggy, or by dog sled in the winter. As his business grew, he hired five employees. He sold only the best watches and arranged with local watch repairers in the lumbering towns to adjust or repair the ones he sold.

In 1887, Becken relocated to St. Paul, Minnesota, opening a wholesale watch house, and in 1890 moved his business to Chicago, where he bought the jewelry catalog firm of Morse, Mitchell and Williams, changing the name to the A. C. Becken Company. The Becken Catalog dates from 1892. His business grew rapidly into one of the foremost in the country.

November, 1929 — *The KEYSTONE* — Page 13

What the Becken Catalog *Brings You*

96 *pages of* Watches	Leading American and Imported makes. A wide selection of all that is new in watches.
56 *pages of* Diamonds	Our own importation. Unusual values in all shapes and sizes. Loose or mounted. Fashion's newest creations in platinum or gold mountings.
254 *pages of* Jewelry	Costume jewelry in great variety. Semi-Precious jewels in rings, necklaces and men's jewelry. A comprehensive selection from leading makers.
277 *pages of* Silverware	Sterling and plated ware from leading manufacturers. Nationally advertised Pewter. Silver for every occasion.
96 *pages of* Clocks	Imported and Domestic clocks to meet every purpose. Stately hall clocks, chimes and novelties at wide range of prices.
168 *pages of* Novelties	A complete gift department. Compacts, mesh bags, bridge sets, smoker's articles, leather and imported novelties.
29 *pages of* Electrical	Coffee sets and other table electrical pieces in Silverplate, Chromium and Nickel.
70 *pages of* Miscellaneous	A section devoted to umbrellas, luggage, cameras, binoculars and many other items for the jewelry store.

One thousand forty-six pages of merchandise to meet your every requirement.

We issue a separate catalog for your Repair and Optical Departments. *Total Catalog pages 1458.*

A. C. Becken Company
35 East Wacker Drive
CHICAGO

Page 12 — *The KEYSTONE* — November, 1929

For Your Convenience

Our 1930 Catalog
IS ISSUED IN TWO VOLUMES

A Counter Sales Book

• This thousand forty-six page catalog with its De Luxe Library Binding possesses that air of superfine quality which quietly, unobtrusively conveys to the mind of your prospect the idea that here is shown merchandise of quality and style entirely out of the ordinary.

• The customer is reconciled to your price long before he knows what it is—it is therefore an ideal Counter Sales Book. Its completeness in every department makes it your logical catalog for stock replenishment.

A Tool, Material and Optical Book

• Four hundred twelve pages of everything needed for your repair and optical departments.

A. C. Becken Company
35 East Wacker Drive . . Chicago, Ill.

Keystone, November 1929. It was not unusual for the A. C. Becken company to have two- and even three-page advertisements in its glory days.

ANNOUNCING
THE CONSOLIDATION
of
The C.H. Knights-Thearle Co.
and
Otto Young & Co.
with
The A. C. Becken Company

— signifying the dawn of a new character of service to the retail jeweler.

For the time being, the three organizations will be operated separately except that their resources and purchasing power will be pooled and their management centralized

A.C. Becken, Jr., will head the consolidation as President and Chairman of the Board

A.C.Becken Company - 35 E.Wacker Drive
Otto Young & Co., - 29 E.Madison Street
C.H.Knights-Thearle Co - 31 N.State Street
CHICAGO

Announcement of the jobber mergers, *Keystone*, January 1929

A. C. Becken, Jr., August 1928

It was Becken's goal to enhance its buying power by consolidating the three operations. The merger brought together three of the largest, oldest and best-known jobbers in the industry, with an invested capital exceeding $1.25 million. All had experienced great individual success. Unfortunately, Becken bit off more than it could comfortably digest. When the effects of the Depression hit, Becken was forced into receivership in 1932.

Illinois Reduction in Force

Illinois had also experienced "satisfactory" results in 1928 in a "splendid way," according to Robert E. Miller. However, Illinois had to endure "severe" workforce reductions to achieve these results. On August 21, 1928, Miller, the General Manager of the Illinois Watch Division, announced first to the superintendent and foremen of the Watch Factory that the temporary slowing of operations was required to reduce inventory and keep the work in process to a lower amount (notwithstanding that he was later to pronounce the results for the year "satisfactory").

All Illinois foremen were instructed to review each worker under them and to "reduce the number of workers to the minimum required for present operations." Miller commented that "despite the reduction in working force which we have found necessary to make . . . we are generally optimistic over the future of the operations of the plant and the future for this business."

He added that the "urgency of this situation required that this rather drastic step be taken. We have only taken it after studying the situation for a period of over seven months, and only adopted the plan when business did not pick up sufficiently to warrant the organization of our full force."

Judging from production numbers, pocket watch demand was down but wristwatches were enjoying robust growth at this time. Therefore, the layoff was probably owing to excess pocket watch movements and parts in inventory and rapidly diminishing pocket watch sales. Miller explained, "We have large inventories of parts accumulated over a period of years, and accumulated because of a change of watch styles." Thus the drastic drop in pocket watch sales left Hamilton with excessive inventory levels for Illinois pocket watch parts and movements. To reduce the inventories, Hamilton was committed to making every effort, including increasing the Illinois sales force and sales expenses.

Many of the American watchmakers were caught off guard by the surge in wristwatch sales after 1926, but not Elgin, whose movement production, for example, swung from about 31.9% for wristwatches in 1926 to 88.8% in 1928.[6] Illinois, however, had apparently continued to emphasize pocket watch movements and thus suffered from surplus inventory when demand dropped. As a result, Miller noted, for the last two years Illinois had been "working on a short time basis" (evidently, reduced work hours) and with the reduced workforce hoped to get back to a more satisfactory economic arrangement with a "nearer" full-time operation. To help promote business there was to be a "very large investment in advertising and sales promotion work to bring the name 'Illinois Watch' before the public's mind."

The fact that Illinois had been on a reduced work schedule and had a high level of inventory should have been very apparent to Hamilton through the acquisition's due diligence process. That Hamilton, a very conservatively managed entity, chose to follow through with the acquisition must have meant that the purchase price reflected these concerns, and that even before consummation of the acquisition it was likely already contemplating a reduction in force and inventory unless pocket watch sales improved quickly.

TRADE SHOW 1928

Black-tie banquet at the Third Annual Jewelry and Allied Trade Show, August 1928

Both Hamilton and Illinois attended this trade show in Chicago, but Hamilton did not opt to combine their booths. This was consistent with its marketing approach at that time, which was to continue to operate and display Illinois as a separate business. Hamilton seemed intent on not blurring the strong individual trade names of Hamilton and Illinois.

The Illinois display booth at the Third Annual Jewelry and Allied Trade Show, August 1928

At this trade show Illinois was represented by J. W. Armbruster, sales manager; W. J. Barns, advertising manager; W. E. Port, assistant general manager; and Howard E. Atkinson and Jack Samuels (salesmen).

Four months after the huge layoff in August, Miller of Illinois stated on December 22, 1928, that he had hoped "reductions in force would be postponed indefinitely." He explained: "We knew that the reduction in force was a remedy for much of our difficult conditions here and our judgment in this matter has been confirmed by the splendid progress of the business since the early part of September." Illinois' growth of sales in the last quarter of 1928 mirrored Elgin's experience.

But he added this comment: "The sales of watches this fall has been gratifying and yet we have not substantially reduced the very large inventory of parts and finished watches." Wristwatch sales were booming but pocket watch orders were in steep decline. Miller thought that this problem would continue and take "a couple of years at least to work out of." Thus, he was setting the stage for continuing to have a reduced workforce, although about two hundred employees were reinstated a year later, in January 1930.

Looking forward to 1929, Miller felt that it would bring "a new year of fine business profits, and to a year of fuller and steadier employment for those employees at present here at the plant." However, even though the Illinois workforce was to grow again, the level would not be sustained because the stock market was to crash nine months later, leading ultimately to the Great Depression.

Louis Manheimer & Bros., Inc., an Illinois jobber, in a full-page advertisement in the January 1929 issue of the *Keystone*, touted its record year.

Hamilton Positions Illinois

Today, conflicting statements about Hamilton's motivation for purchasing Illinois create confusion and raise questions about Hamilton's true intentions. At the time of the acquisition, Hamilton proclaimed its intention to double its capacity. But only two months after the acquisition, it sought to reassure retailers that it would operate Illinois as a separate entity with a separate identity. At all trade shows both attended, Hamilton and Illinois maintained separate booths; but at other shows, Hamilton did not allow Illinois to participate at all. Never did the two firms appear jointly. Moreover, Hamilton and Illinois advertising campaigns remained entirely separate. These actions beg the question about how Hamilton intended to relate to its new Illinois Watch Division.

Hamilton-Illinois 1928–1929 Sales Catalog

Hamilton did issue a "joint" sales catalog with Illinois dated 1928–1929. Interestingly, this catalog indicates that Hamilton intended it to be used by its Export Sales Division. The absence of a domestic version of the catalog suggests that Hamilton may have wanted to keep its domestic sales separate but combine international sales for efficiency. In fact, the Illinois export department was the first Illinois operation folded into Hamilton.

Dating of catalogs. In later years Hamilton and Illinois often dated catalogs over a range of two years, normally the first year being the year of publication. It appears from the models listed in the 1928–1929 catalog that Hamilton prepared the joint catalog sometime in the late summer or early fall of 1928. For instance, the catalog shows Hamilton's newest top-of-the-line wristwatch offerings: the Piping Rock, the Hastings and the Meadowbrook. Hamilton announced the addition of the Meadowbrook to its product line in October 1928. At the same time, though, it shows a picture of an Illinois Model 18, 16-jewel, 18/0 size movement, manufactured about 1923, while touting the 17-jewel model.

Hamilton featured its initial Chevy Chase ladies' model prominently in the catalog. The Chevy Chase, with its brand-new 989 grade movement, was Hamilton's initial launch into the 18/0 size ladies' market. According to Halligan's records, Hamilton did not announce the Chevy Chase to jewelers until February 1929. The early mention of the Chevy Chase in the catalog could have been to counterbalance the fact that it listed Illinois' 18/0 size models in the catalog—watches with a movement that had existed in Illinois' product line for years. Whatever the reasons for all the inconsistencies, it seems most likely that Hamilton prepared the catalog sometime in the latter part of 1928.

The list of Illinois offerings also supports a date in the second half of 1928. The catalog shows many generic case designs for Illinois, but only two of Illinois' named designs: the Marquis Strap and the Major. The Marquis Strap appeared in advertisements as early as April 1928 and the Major at least by June 18, 1928. National magazine advertisements for other new models such as the Beau Brummell,

Mate, Consul and Tuxedo did not appear until later in the year. Possibly, because Hamilton published the catalog, the Illinois information could have been dated, or there was little or no consultation with Illinois. The 1923 date of manufacture of the 18/0 size movement pictured in the catalog would support this conjecture. Also, interestingly, the catalog maintained the previous Illinois practice of offering only luminous wristwatch dials. But this would soon change as the Illinois line gained attractive alternatives.

***Keystone*, July 1928. Another Major wristwatch advertisement was dated June 28, 1928.**

Pocket watches. Most notably, and strangely enough, Hamilton was heavily promoting the pocket watches of the two companies. Given the almost complete disappearance of the pocket watch market over the previous year, this appears in hindsight to be a curious choice. Although plummeting pocket watch sales should have given management some indication that this market would practically cease to exist, conservative Hamilton may have been banking on the wristwatch phenomenon being simply a fad. In any event, the higher price point of pocket watches, and the probable profit from them, may have convinced Hamilton to cling to the hope of a pocket watch renaissance.

Many Hamilton pocket watch models in the catalog were described as being "thin"; for many of the Illinois ones, however, the descriptive term was "ultra-thin." The emphasis on extra thinness may have become a sore point with Hamilton, leading to its later absorption of the Illinois "Illini" model into Hamilton's own product line. Indeed, access to the ultra-thin Illinois "Illini" grade 528 movement could have been a driving force for the acquisition, as Hamilton was no doubt becoming aware of the value of a stylish ultra-thin pocket watch.

Complete Strap Watches

3/0 SIZE

The complete strap watches shown on this page are fitted with 3/0 size No. 24 Bridge model 17 Jewel movements with luminous dials.

Cased and timed at the factory.

Each watch is delivered in an attractive display package.

Illustration and specifications of movement on Page 35.

The Major — Plain or Engraved

14K white gold filled, plain	Cat. No. 2801
14K white gold filled, engraved	Cat. No. 2802
14K green gold filled, plain	Cat. No. 2803
14K green gold filled, engraved	Cat. No. 2804

The Cushion — Plain Only

14K white gold filled	Cat. No. 2805
14K green gold filled	Cat. No. 2806
10K yellow gold filled	Cat. No. 2807
Sterling silver	Cat. No. 2808

The Cushion Form — Plain or Engraved

14K white gold filled, plain	Cat. No. 2809
14K green gold filled, plain	Cat. No. 2810
14K white gold filled, engraved	Cat. No. 2811
14K green gold filled, engraved	Cat. No. 2812

31

The Illinois wristwatch models shown in the 1928–1929 joint Hamilton and Illinois sales catalog

6-0 Size Complete Strap Watches

The Marquis
STRAP

17 and 19 jewels, 6/0 size movement. 14K white or green gold filled cases with plain or engraved bezels. Curved case which conforms to the arc of the wrist.

	No. 905, 17 Jewels With Luminous Dial Catalog No.	No. 907, 19 Jewels With Luminous Dial Catalog No.
14K gold filled, white, plain bezel	2901	2902
14K gold filled, white, engraved bezel	2903	2904
14K gold filled, green, plain bezel	2905	2906
14K gold filled, green, engraved bezel	2907	2908

The Square
STRAP
Plain or engraved

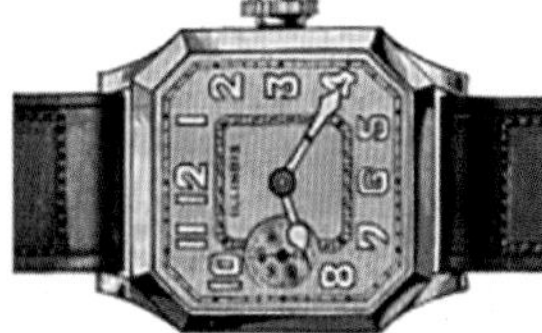

Fitted with 15, 17 or 19 jewe' 6/0 size movement, luminous dial.

	No. 903, 15 Jewels With Luminous Dial Catalog No.	No. 905, 17 Jewels With Luminous Dial Catlog No.	No. 907, 19 Jewels With Luminous Dial Catalog No.
14K solid gold, white, engraved	2909	2910	2911
14K solid gold, white, plain	2912	2913	2914
14K solid gold, green, engraved	2915	2916	2917
14K solid gold, green, plain	2918	2919	2920
14K gold filled, white, engraved	2921	2922	2923
14K gold filled, white, plain	2924	2925	2926
14K gold filled, green, engraved	2927	2928	2929
14K gold filled, green, plain	2930	2931	2932

The Cushion Form
STRAP
Plain or engraved

Fitted with 15, 17 or 19 jewel 6/0 size movement, luminous dial.

	No. 903, 15 Jewels With Luminous Dial Catalog No.	No. 905, 17 Jewels With Luminous Dial Catalog No.	No. 907, 19 Jewels With Luminous Dial Catalog No.
14K gold filled, white, plain	2933	2934	2935
14K gold filled, white, engraved	2936	2937	2938
14K gold filled, green, plain	2939	2940	2941
14K gold filled, green, engraved	2942	2943	2944

The Cushion
STRAP
Plain case only

Fitted with 15, 17 or 19 jewel 6/0 size movement, luminous dial.

	No. 903, 15 Jewels With Luminous Dial Catalog No.	No. 905, 17 Jewels With Luminous Dial Catalog No.	No. 907, 19 Jewels With Luminous Dial Catalog No.
14K gold filled, white, plain	2945	2946	2947
14K gold filled, green, plain	2948	2949	2950

6/0 size movements used in these watches are illustrated and described on Page 35

Delivered in Attractive Display Package

32

The Illinois wristwatch models shown in the 1928–1929 joint Hamilton and Illinois sales catalog

Wristwatch lines. For its own lines of men's and women's wristwatches, Hamilton concentrated heavily on the 6/0 size, grade 987 movement. Although Hamilton showed the 18/0 size, grade 989 Chevy Chase model in the catalog, it had no product available until the following year. On the other hand, its Illinois line offered a variety of wristwatch models in 3/0, 6/0 and 18/0 size. According to the price list accompanying the catalog, it appears that the smaller the movement, the higher the price. If the Cushion Form Plain gold-filled models are used as a yardstick, the sales catalog priced the Illinois 3/0 size version at about 75% of the Illinois 6/0 size version. Apparently, the market valued the smaller size more highly. As the Illinois line developed later, it would produce more and more smaller models, especially in the 1930s.

The catalog offers many more pages of men's watches than of ladies' models. In fact, ladies' watches appear almost as an afterthought. Hamilton, slow to react to trends, may have had an archaic view of women's purchasing power; or perhaps it felt that ladies would not buy watches for themselves. Nonetheless, contemporary magazine advertisements, including those for Illinois, regularly featured a mixture of men's and women's watches on about equal footing.

Most importantly, the catalog defined Hamilton's view of its relationship with Illinois. In a memorandum written about three and a half years later, on April 1, 1932, Robert Miller stated as one of Illinois "definded" [*sic*] policies: "To bring Illinois Watches into what we have termed "the middle price range to the consumer." In 1928 the Illinois line differed from its Hamilton counterpart by offering 6/0 size movements with 15, 17 and 19 jewels, while Hamilton included 17-jewel, 6/0 size movements only in certain defined models and a 19-jewel version in other specific high-end models. Illinois offered the consumer different jewel counts in the same watch case model; to the consumer this meant different levels of quality and price points. Although Illinois' and Hamilton's 17-jewel Cushion Form models commanded the same suggested retail price, Illinois offered its 15-jewel version in the same case for 10% less and its 19-jewel version for 10% more. Hamilton, though, priced its 17-jewel Square Cut Corner at 10% more than Illinois for the equivalent jewel count. Interestingly, when one compares the price to the retailer with the suggested retail price, it is clear that jewelers could make a bigger profit selling similar Illinois models.

The real difference in products and pricing could be found in the named models. Hamilton's three named models in the catalog—the Piping Rock, the Meadowbrook and the Hastings—came in solid gold, but only the Hastings was also offered in gold-filled. On the other hand, for the two named models listed for Illinois, the Major and the Marquis Strap, the consumer had no option but to purchase the watches in gold-filled cases. Hamilton thus delineated between brands by positioning itself at the higher end of the middle range and Illinois as the more affordable alternative.

In a memorandum on April 1, 1932, defining Illinois policies and goals since the acquisition, Miller stated that one goal had been "to afford a variety of size and style appeal in Illinois Watches for men and women, in the sprit [*sic*] of the modern tempo." Illinois' new offerings, which it began advertising in April 1928, showed a stylishness that not only caught the public's attention at the time but also continues to appeal to collectors today.

WHY I COLLECT ILLINOIS

Illinois watches first caught my attention by the placement of the second hand by the "9." I had been collecting watches for about two years at the time and hadn't seen any other vintage watches that had the placement of the second hand in this location. Once I started to investigate, I was completely taken by the variety of dials, movements, bezels and cases and spent the next 7 years focusing on Illinois watches. While I have moved on and broadened my collection to include numerous other manufacturers, I still consider my Illinois watches among my favorites. *—Andy Federbusch*

The Major and the Marquis Strap most certainly made a statement about Illinois' place in the market. The unusual rounded lines of the cases, especially when enhanced by deco-style engraved cases and striking exploding-numeral dials, outshone competition, particularly Elgin's. The percentage growth in Illinois wristwatch production in 1928 and 1929, compared with Elgin's shrinking numbers, testified to the popularity of the new Illinois designs. By the end of the year, Illinois added the Beau Brummell, Mate, Consul and Tuxedo models, plus four new ladies' models, giving Illinois an even more attractive product line.

"Satisfactory" Results for Illinois

In prior years, the Illinois Factory was normally closed the entire week of the Christmas holidays. However, since 1928 was closing as a "satisfactory" year for Illinois, Hamilton announced that the usual holiday/vacation at the Springfield Plant would be reduced to four days because the new owners anticipated marked improvement in business in 1929. There were also indications that the workforce would be increased. (And it did, for a short period a year later.) Hamilton also announced that "new lines of watches are being brought out and it feels very much encouraged over the prospects of good business during 1929." These new lines were some of the most daring and innovative watches ever offered for sale.

Both 1928 and 1929 were very strong years for Illinois, proving Hamilton's wisdom in acquiring a company so well prepared to take advantage of the burgeoning wristwatch market. In 1928, Illinois introduced at least ten new men's wristwatch models and at least eight new ladies' ones. In 1929 it would release even more: at least fifteen new men's and at least twenty-one new ladies'.

Why So Few Illinois Models in Solid Gold?

Collectors have long wondered why so few Illinois men's models are available in solid gold cases. Immediately after the acquisition Illinois introduced two of them, the Tuxedo and Consul, but subsequently only four more, the Baronet, Rockliffe, Schmukler (No. 250) and Varsity (No. 650). Analysis of sales catalogs and Hamilton correspondence leads to the conclusion that the small number of solid gold Illinois wristwatch models is a reflection of Hamilton's determination to be the high-end marketplace leader of its two watch divisions. As Robert Miller stated, the intention was for Illinois to be in "the middle price range."

Hamilton men's solid gold watches with special names seem not to have appeared until 1928 (the Piping Rock, Meadowbrook and Hastings). Still more arrived the next year (the Langley, Pinehurst, Spur, Coronado and Glendale). It is possible that the Pinehurst and Glendale were calculated to challenge the Illinois Consul and Tuxedo head-on, and the striking Spur meant to compete with the avant-garde Jolly Roger and other imaginative Illinois designs that were available only in gold-filled cases.

Once Illinois was under Hamilton control, it may have been that of the Factory-Cased solid gold men's models only the Tuxedo, Consul, Baronet and Rockliffe were intended for full-scale production and release. The Schmukler and the Varsity and Special Cushions in solid gold were probably models requested by individual jobbers or jewelers. (See Chapter 9 for discussion of these models, including the names for No. 250 and No. 650.)

To date, only one advertisement for a Schmukler has been found (but with no specific model name given), and none for the Varsity. Although the Schmukler and Varsity have case model numbers, Illinois either issued only very few of these or else changed its plans, perhaps because of orders from Lancaster not to release any more solid gold models lest they compete with Hamilton's own.

As an exchange of letters included in the next chapter will show, Hamilton was discouraging the production of more solid gold Illinois wristwatches. A review of the 1934 and 1935 Hamilton dealer catalogs makes it abundantly clear why. Listed in the 1934 catalog are the following models in 14K solid gold: the Ericsson, Byrd, Andrews, Oakmont, Langley, Flintridge, Piping Rock and Glenn Curtiss. The 1935 catalog has the platinum Rutledge and the 18K Richmond, plus the following 14K models: Sherwood/Seneca, Custer, Lowell, Ardmore, Wayne and Donovan.

Stylistically, Illinois' Schmukler and Rockliffe in particular would have been in competition with a number of the Hamilton models that had similar case shapes. And other Illinois designs, if they had been rendered in solid gold, would have clearly outshone most of the Hamilton ones. Thus it appears likely that Hamilton pressured Illinois from the very beginning, perhaps even as early as whatever negotiations were taking place in 1927, not to release its stellar Art Deco designs in solid gold and challenge Hamilton in the high-end market.

Advertising and Related Market-Stratifying Measures

Hamilton's plan to have Illinois fill the mid to low market price tiers was further reflected in Illinois' disappearance from advertising in upscale, prestigious publications such as the *National Geographic*. Hamilton itself advertised more frequently in *National Geographic;* Hamilton advertisements appeared at least every other month in 1929, but Illinois not once. Illinois was relegated to advertise in "popular press" magazines like the - *Post* and Hamilton retained the high end (and the *National Geographic*) to itself.

As time went on, Illinois was stripped by Hamilton of its option to offer sparkle finish dials for cost savings. See the Dial chapter. It earlier had to cease its practice of Factory-Casing diamond-set ladies' models for its jobbers. All these measures instituted by Hamilton were to further distinguish (degrade) Illinois' price tier from that of Hamilton.

A Seemingly Strong Start for 1929

For the watch industry, the new year began as though all expected a continuation of the good results from 1928. In January 1929, Hamilton attacked "E.Z. Credit" jewelers and price-cutters with an unusual full-page advertisement in the Keystone that emphasized Hamiltonian determination not to reduce its prices. It boldly stated: "The public will be educated to high standards in watches. They will buy watches by deliberate choice and not on a basis of price or economic pressure."

What wishful thinking! Once the impact of the Great Depression was felt, Hamilton was forced to eat these words. By April 1932 it was reluctantly announcing its own "new low priced watches," willing even to take a "loss" to move its inventory. And in April 1934, Hamilton would again be introducing "lower priced watches," along with unveiling its revolutionary "New Zone Distribution Plan."

January, 1929 | *The KEYSTONE* | Page 45

This Year......

AMERICAN WATCHES

The public will be educated to high standards in watches.

They will buy watches by deliberate choice and not on a basis of price or economic pressure.

They realize the importance of the character of the watch manufacturer and when making a selection will turn to the American made watch for dependability and service.

The retail jeweler will profit by carrying a good assortment of American watches during the year 1929.

THE HAMILTON WATCH IS AN AMERICAN WATCH

Keystone, January 1929

Elsewhere in the jewelry and watch industry, other manufacturers were similarly beguiled by their 1928 results and fully expecting the same success in 1929. John W. Sherwood, president of the Solidarity Watch Case Company, commented in February 1929: "We are most encouraged at the turn business is now taking and have every reason to feel that 1929 will be a good year for the fine watchcase trade." Regrettably, in October 1931 the well-respected Solidarity Watch Case Company became a victim of the Great Depression and was forced to liquidate. Many other American casemakers would also fall by the wayside as the Depression lingered.

Bulova Results

Like others in the industry, the Bulova Watch Company had enjoyed a very successful 1928; it had profits of $1,201,004, following profits of $696,784 in 1927 and $291,066 in 1926. Accordingly, Bulova in February 1929 completed a Convertible Preferred Stock offering to help prepare for more anticipated growth, which heretofore had been handled by reinvestment of its earnings.[7]

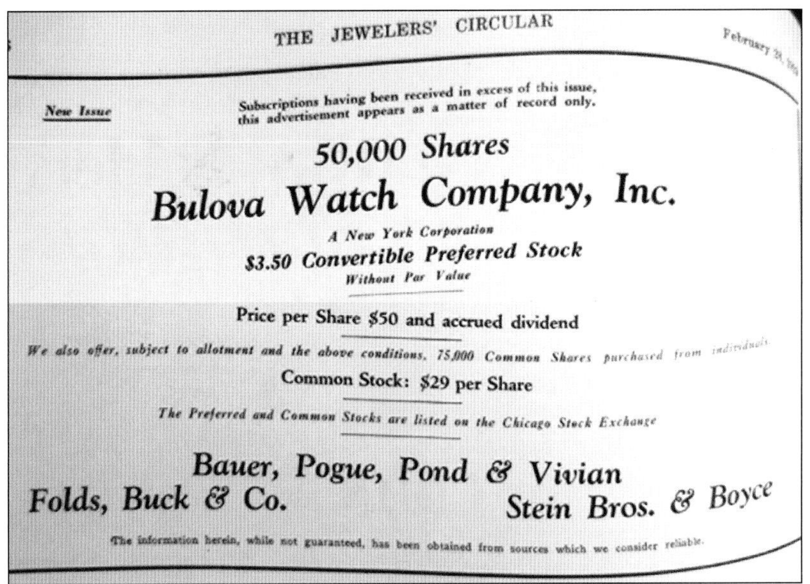

Bulova's convertible preferred stock offering in February 1929 was promoted in the *Jewelers' Circular*.

This special financing was based on Bulova's positive view of the future of the watch industry. At this time, Bulova employed 2,000 workers: not only in New York City and in Providence, Rhode Island, but also at Bienne, Switzerland.

A Great Opportunity?

After strong results for Illinois and Hamilton in 1928, Miller of Hamilton stated in February 1929: "There never was a time when the enterprising jeweler could push his business with more assurance of success than the present. In the watch line he can build up a business in American watches with a positive guarantee of quality which, together with fair profits, make up the foundation for permanent business."

But others in the industry were less optimistic. Elgin reduced production and cut work hours by eliminating Saturday work as early as April 1929. And, of course, Illinois had cut its workforce severely in August 1928 after reducing work hours two years earlier.

Watch Merger Rumors Denied

Apparently, jewelers and other close to the watch industry knew of the economic issues faced by manufacturers. In March 1929 there were persistent industry reports that Elgin was merging with the Gruen Watch Company. On March 11, 1929, Hulburd, president of Elgin, definitively denied the rumors of a merger of Elgin with the Wadsworth Watch Case Company, the Gruen Watch Company and the Keystone Watch Case Company, saying:

"There are several obvious reasons why such a merger would not be of interest to . . . Elgin . . . but it would suffice to say that we have the largest watch factory in the world . . . and do not feel it would strengthen our position to include . . . Gruen . . . which simply imports its movements from Switzerland and cases them at Time Hill. It is true we purchase goods from all the old line high grade watch case companies but we never seriously considered absorption of, or combination with, any one of them."[8]

Evidently, because the newspapers in Cincinnati were reporting this alleged merger, Hulburd was compelled to speak; and in doing so, he took a clear and direct slap at Gruen. The disdain American watch manufacturers had for American firms that assembled foreign parts into watches would intensify greatly once the effects of the Great Depression hit.

Report of Watch Merger Unfounded

President Hulburd of the Elgin National Watch Co. Emphatically Denies Rumor That His Company Will Merge or Combine with the Gruen Watch Co. or Any of the Case Manufacturers

Jewelers' Circular, March 14, 1929

Gruen, on the other hand, merely sent a succinct telegram on March 12 to the *Jewelers' Circular:* "Various merger rumors are unfounded as far as we are concerned."

Gruen Watch Co. Denies Rumors of Merger

CINCINNATI, OHIO, March 12.—A telegram to THE JEWELERS' CIRCULAR from the Gruen Watch Co. sent today read as follows:

"Various merger rumors are unfounded as far as we are concerned."

Gruen's March 1929 denial of the merger rumors

International Issues

The jewelry industry had failed in 1928 to gain passage of legislation related to prices. But in 1929 the industry started to get traction towards tariffs on imports.

Seeing this coming, in July 1929 the Swiss government filed a formal protest with the United States Government, complaining that proposed new duty rates on movements were prohibitive and urging that the watch schedules be completely revised. The Swiss maintained that duty rates were already too high and that the proposed increases were "enormous"—so much so that they would "threaten to stop almost completely" Swiss imports to the United States.

They added: "The prosperity and very appreciable profits of the American watch industry are the best evidence . . . that the protection sought . . . is already fully assured under the present tariff act."[9]

Hawley-Smoot Tariff Act

Hawley (left), Smoot (right), April 1929

The Tariff Act of 1930, known as the Hawley-Smoot Tariff for its sponsors, Senator Reed Smoot and Representative Willis C. Hawley, had its roots in Herbert Hoover's campaign promise to farmers to increase tariffs on agricultural products. Once Hoover became president, he asked the Republican-controlled Congress to pass a bill to increase rates on agricultural products and to decrease rates on industrial goods. But as the legislation made its way through Congress, industrial interests, which included watch manufacturers, added to the bill. This resulted in large duty increases on imported watch movements.*

* http://en.wikipedia.org/wiki/Smoot%E2%80%93Hawley_Tariff_Act

Elgin and Waltham, America's largest and second-largest watch manufacturers, believed that it was critical to stop the competition of cheaper imported timepieces. Accordingly, both companies lobbied for significantly higher duties on imported watches, and soon Congress added them.

Watch Duties under the 1930 Hawley-Smoot Tariff Act[10]

Class	Ligne	Jewels	NetCost USA	1922 Tariff	New Tariff (1930)
731	10½	6	$ 1.41	$ .75	$ 3.75
751	10½	15	$ 2.24	$ 2.00	$ 4.35
737	6¾	6	$ 1.68	$ 0.75	$ 4.25
757	6¾	15	$ 2.41	$ 2.00	$ 5.85
159	5½	15	$ 7.06	$ 2.00	$ 7.10
258	6½	15	$ 5.20	$ 2.00	$ 7.10
879	5½	?	$ 8.33	$ 3.50	$ 8.50

As can be seen from the table, the tariff focused especially on cheaper 6-jewel watches, which saw a 500% increase in customs duties. The implementation of these harsh tariffs spelled the end of the 6-jewel wristwatch market and severely harmed the other sizes because their tariffs also rose significantly.

In 1930, as the measure approached final approval, 15,000 workers marched in Biel, Switzerland, in protest. Bulova, Gruen and Omega all had factories in the Biel area.[11] The Swiss workers rightly considered that the new tariff act would significantly discourage Swiss watch imports and force those buying Swiss movements for casing in the United States to move a greater portion of their watch-assembly operations there.

After President Hoover signed the Hawley-Smoot Act into law on June 17, 1930, Swiss exports to the United States declined by almost 48%. In retaliation, the Swiss boycotted American products. The Swiss Federal Post Office Department implemented a policy against buying American-made automobiles; the Swiss Federal Railways and Swiss Banks halted any purchases from American firms.[12]

Further Developments in Springfield

Results of "Severe" Illinois Reductions

On August 21, 1928, when Miller announced that the reduction of employees was "severe," no percentages were provided. But on January 23, 1929, he delivered a speech to the Springfield Lion's Club reporting that "the local plant now completes daily an average of 650 watches, each of which takes nine months to manufacture." [*Author's note:* At 650 watches per day, there would have been about 156,000 watches produced in 1928.]

Then he said: "Nearly 1,000 persons are employed at the local division with additions to that number probably in the near future." Now, for the first time, we can ascertain the scale of the bloodbath that occurred in August 1928. Illinois had 1,300 employees on January 1, 1928, the date of the acquisition. If, on January 23, 1929, Illinois had around 1,000 employees, that means that 23% of the Illinois workforce lost their jobs in August 1928—almost one-fourth of Illinois' loyal employees. As for any "probable" additions in the future, the workforce did grow to near 1,200 again by January 1930 (following the record 1929 Illinois results). However, it is clear that from the outset Hamilton was prepared to take aggressive steps to reduce costs at its Illinois Watch Division.

1928 HISTORICAL NOTES

- The home pregnancy test is first introduced in France.
- The Iron Lung is invented.
- Japan breaks off relations with China.
- D. H. Lawrence's novel *Lady Chatterley's Lover* is banned in the United States and England.

Formation of Hamilton-Sangamo Corporation

In April 1929, Hamilton announced that it would increase its capitalization from $5,000,000 to $10,000,000. This move was to position Hamilton to fund its planned acquisition agreement with the Sangamo Electric Company of Springfield to market electric clocks. In June 1929, Hamilton and the Sangamo Electric Company of Springfield, Illinois, announced the formation of the Hamilton-Sangamo Corporation. Miller and Kendig of the Illinois Watch Division were named to the board of directors of the new company. Miller was also appointed a vice president and Kendig treasurer of the clock company.

This relationship between Hamilton and Sangamo would prove to be short-lived, however. Hamilton would develop major initiatives but was quick to abandon them if events started to turn negative. It retreated from the deal by 1931 when it began to confront the adverse impacts of the Depression on its business. The arrangement with Sangamo had of course been conceived and implemented prior to the devastating impact of the Great Depression on the American watch manufacturing industry.

Hamilton-Sangamo Corporation Formed to Market Electric Clock

The Hamilton-Sangamo Corporation is the name of the new company which will market Hamilton-Sangamo clocks, a joint product of the Hamilton Watch Company, Lancaster, Pennsylvania, and the Sangamo Electric Company of Springfield, Illinois.

The Hamilton-Sangamo Corporation was formed as a means of unifying the efforts of these well-known concerns in promoting sales of the clock line, and a definite advertising and sales promotion program combining their joint experience is now in the process of formation.

According to a recent announcement, national advertising will carry the Hamilton-Sangamo story to millions of American homes, while the marketing and sales promotion experience of the Hamilton Watch Company will be put immediately behind the clocks. New additions to the already popular Sangamo line are being planned.

For the present, all correspondence should be addressed to the Hamilton-Sangamo Corporation at Springfield, Illinois. However, just as soon as arrangements permit, the new corporation will be quartered in the factory and offices of the Hamilton Company, in Lancaster, Pennsylvania. A western sales office will be maintained at Springfield, and it is expected that considerable distribution will be made from that point. Distribution will be confined to jewelry stores.

Keystone, May 1929

Railroad time

for the home

...in 45 styles of electric clocks

Think of it—railroad time for your home in a clock of captivating beauty!

Maybe you prefer an historic period model—or a masterpiece in bronze or marble—or a colorful creation in rich leather,—or a smart, graceful model in mahogany or walnut. And you can have it in a Sangamo . . . at prices from $25 to $400.

Unlike many electric clocks Sangamo is not dependent upon the electric current for its accuracy. A tiny motor—guaranteed for life—keeps the mainspring wound to the same tension at all times. The maintenance of this uniform spring tension in Sangamo produces accuracy undreamed of in old key-wind clocks.

Sangamo has no complicated electrical parts—no batteries. Current fluctuations do not affect it. In fact, it will run for many hours with the current off. It requires no leveling—no key winding.

In construction as well as in its time-keeping qualities, Sangamo can be compared only with the finest railroad watches. It has the finest of escapements—Illinois-Hamilton—with jewels for all important bearings. It has the precision cut gears and stainless steel staffs and pinions with mirror-like finish that you find in high grade watches.

At The Better Jewelry Stores

See this modern timepiece at your local jewelry store—in 45 fascinating styles and color designs. "Telling Time," an interesting book showing many famous old clocks as well as new styles, will be mailed free upon request.

Sangamo Electric Company, Springfield, Ill.

Manufacturers also of Sangamo Electric Meters—5,000,000 in service—Sangamo Radio Condensers and Transformers

Foreign Factories:

Canada: Sangamo Electric Co. of Canada, Ltd., Toronto
England: British Sangamo Co., Ltd., Ponders End, Middlesex, Eng.

SANGAMO

ELECTRIC CLOCK

Models priced at

$25 to $400

A very deco Sangamo advertisement from *National Geographic*, May 1929

New Distribution Policy. Perhaps a precursor to the Hamilton New Distribution Plan of May 1, 1934, was the "new distributive policy" announced as early as October 1929 by Hamilton-Sangamo. According to the new policy, a certain territory was to be set aside for each of the nineteen wholesalers that furnished and serviced Hamilton-Sangamo clocks. However, the Chicago and New York territories were to be handled by Hamilton-Sangamo directly.

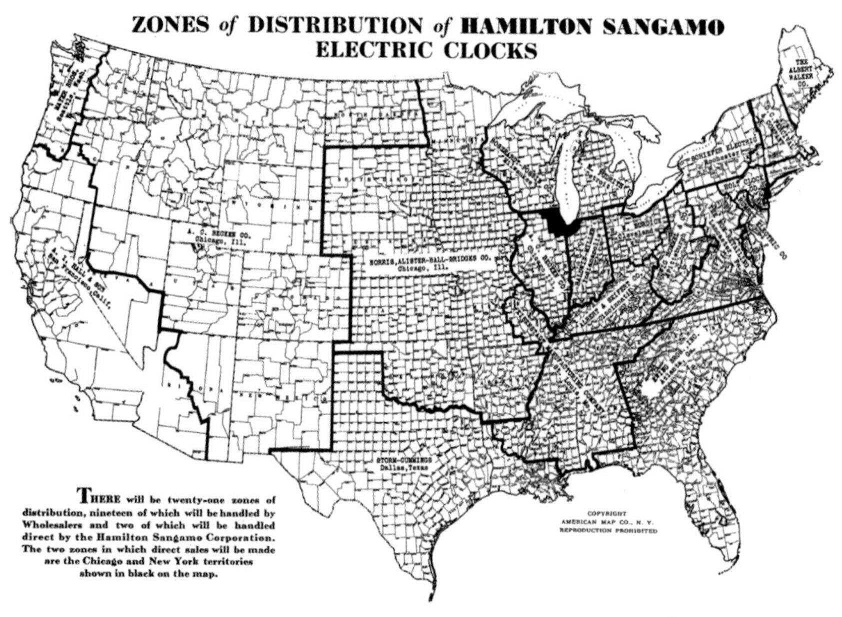

Hamilton-Sangamo Distributor map, October 1929

LOCAL BANQUET

On June 1, 1929, eighteen months after the acquisition, Charles F. Miller, president of Hamilton, held a dinner for thirty-seven department heads and foremen of the Illinois Watch Division.

C. F. MILLER, HEAD OF HAMILTON WATCH CO., GIVES LOCAL BANQUET

Charles F. Miller, president of the Hamilton Watch company, ga[illegible] a dinner to thirty-seven depar[illegible]n heads and foremen of the I[illegible]ois Watch division last evening at 6:30 o'clock at the Sangamo club.

Mr. Miller gave an outline of business conditions and spoke of the brilliant prospects of the Illinois division during the past fourteen months while in the midst of the reconstruction period.

R. E. Miller, general manager of the Springfield plant, acted as toastmaster. Addresses also were given by C. W. Drepperd, vice-president of the Hamilton Sangamo Electric Clock corporation and a number of others.

Those present were:

R. E. Miller, W. E. Port, J. B. Jones, J. W. Armbruster, John Smurr, William Withey, W. J. Barnes, Robert R. Scott, August Maurer, Arthur Smith, Herman Noll, Calvin Allison, J. H. Linthwaite, Frank Cleveland, Paul Taft, Louis De Souza, O. C. Pottorff, I. F. Wielles, Louis Scharf, George Winn, Frank Metze, Ernest Mester, Louis Ranzenberger, Joseph De Silva, Fred Jones, R. F. Fulkerson, Otto F. Bredemeyer, Louis F. Acker, Charles L. Allison, Walter H. Chapin, William H. Hibbs, H. C. Dobbs, Charles Radcliffe, Benjamin Ramey, J. H. Schumacher and Walter Brown.

Illinois State Journal, June 2, 1929

Increased Demand for Illinois Watches

Illinois continued to have booming business midway through 1929; as a consequence, Miller of Illinois had to shorten summer vacations. In 1928 all departments had been closed for summer vacation for three weeks. But in 1929 six departments would only have one week of vacation and the rest of the Watch Factory only two weeks off.

On June 9, 1929, Miller stated: "The demand for Illinois watches has been constantly increasing and there has been a large amount of overtime work in the factory this year. A good demand is expected in the fall months and stock is being built up to take care of that demand."

This indeed was the sweet spot for Illinois. Its many new deco designs for men's and ladies' wristwatches were apparently being well received by jobbers, jewelers and consumers alike. Although demand was still down and continuing to decline for pocket watch sales, the opposite was true for the dazzling array of stylish new Illinois wristwatch offerings.

With wristwatch sales sizzling at Illinois, a charter was issued by the Secretary of the State of Illinois to the Illinois Watch Company on June 10, 1929, with a capital stock of $50,000. The object was "to manufacture and sell watches, parts thereof, and time and speed and distance recording and measuring devices." The incorporators were R. E. Miller, J. Barclay Jones and W. Port.

For some reason, Hamilton chose to reincorporate its Illinois Watch Division. This move may have been for tax reasons, as business for Illinois was accelerating at this time. Not only had two hundred employees been rehired since the massive August 1928 layoff, but the Springfield Factory was also working overtime to fill orders and would shortly announce curtailed vacations to stock up for the approaching holidays.

An article in the *Illinois State Journal* on September 16, 1929, indicated that the number of Illinois employees was 1,100. So the workforce was up by 200 workers from the number remaining after the huge layoff in August 1928, but it was still 200 below the number of employees at the time of the acquisition.

The Illinois display booth at the Fourth Annual Jewelry and Allied Trade Show, August 1929, held at the Sherman Hotel in downtown Chicago. Illinois again exhibited its watches separately from Hamilton. (Notice the two large Illinois display clocks in the shape of a Beau Royale wristwatch model; the "Big Watch" was formally introduced to the Illinois jobbers and jewelers in 1929.)

Julius W. Armbruster Resigns

Longtime Illinois employee Julius Armbruster resigned his post as sales manager and after thirty-nine years in Springfield moved to California. Where he was to serve as the Western Sales Manager for both the Illinois Watch Company and for the Hamilton-Sangamo Clock Company.

J. W. Armbruster Resigns As Sales Manager of Illinois Watch Co.

SPRINGFIELD, ILL., Oct. 3.—J. W. Armbruster, for 39 years associated with the Illinois Watch Co., is moving from this city to the West Coast about the first of the year. He will become western sales manager for the Illinois watch and for Hamilton-Sangamo clocks.

As sales manager of the Illinois Watch Co., Julius Armbruster is one of the best known figures in the jewelry trade. He became associated with this firm in 1891, and has a wide personal acquaintance among jewelers from coast to coast. Mr. Armbruster's voluntary decision to resign as sales manager of the Illinois watch, and to take up the representation of that company on the Pacific Coast, arises from purely personal reasons.

Announcement of Armbruster's resignation as sales manager, October 3, 1929

Jack L. Keenan to Become Sales Manager of Illinois

At the end of October 1929, the *Jewelers' Circular* reported: "Jack L. Keenan, well known in watch circles . . . left New York . . . by automobile for Springfield, Ill., where on Dec. 1 he will assume the duties of sales manager of the Illinois Watch Company. Mr. Keenan succeeds J. W. Armbruster.

"Since July, 1926, Mr. Keenan has represented the Illinois concern and maintained an office in New York. He covered the territory East of Pittsburgh, Cleveland and Hamilton, Canada. After Dec. 1 he will reside permanently in Springfield.

"Before becoming associated with the Illinois Watch Co., Mr. Keenan was manager of the New York office of the Keystone Watch Case Co., and previous to that time managed the Howard Watch Works at Waltham, Mass. Preceding these connections, Mr. Keenan was in charge of the Boston office of the Crescent Watch Case Co."

Keenan would turn out to be the major player for Illinois and its jobbers in the post-acquisition Illinois Watch Division, especially with respect to communications—not only with its longtime jobbers and jewelers but also within Hamilton.

John L. Keenan, November 1929

JOHN L. KEENAN (1885-1952)

A native of Massachusetts (born in Dedham), Jack Keenan spent his early years in the jewelry and watch industry in that state. He ran the Boston office of the Crescent Watch Case Company and later managed the Howard Watch Works in Waltham.

At some point he took a position as manager of the New York office of the Keystone Watch Case Company. Beginning in 1926, he represented the Illinois Watch Company and kept an office in New York, though still maintaining a residence in Waltham.

It had apparently been while he was working at the Howard company in Waltham that he met his first wife, a clerk there. A son, Richard, was born in 1923. By 1930, however, his wife had died. (He married again much later, in 1943.)

He seems to have been deeply attached to his home in Waltham, for he kept it even after he assumed the position of Sales Manager for Illinois and moved to Springfield and a residence there. After Illinois' merger with Hamilton, he moved to Lancaster and lived there as a boarder but continued to keep the house in Waltham.

In the mid-1930s he was still working for Hamilton, representing the company at trade shows (such the 1936 Nebraska Retail Jewelers Association convention, where he gave a presentation). By 1941 he had become Hamilton's District Sales Manager in Chicago, and by 1948 he was living at 40 East Oak there. He died in 1952 (likely in Chicago), but was interred in Waltham.

During his tenure with Illinois, Jack Keenan's dedication to his job and loyalty to the Illinois brand, its products, jobbers, and employees was exemplary. With diplomacy, respect, integrity and dignity, Keenan tried to bridge the gap between the Hamilton plans for Illinois and their implementation. It is through his surviving correspondence that it has been possible to reconstruct much of Illinois' later history that appears in these books.

False Hopes at Year's End

Misreadings by Industry Publications

On November 21, 1929, less than one month after Black Tuesday, the *Jewelers' Circular* boldly stated: "Within the last few weeks the business world of the country has been tried in the balance and has not been found wanting. Our business structure has proved to be on a solid and permanent foundation—even more so than most of us believed. The psychological panic that followed the recent break in the stock market, in former years might have wrecked or, at least, retarded the business structure of the country for many months to come but, today, it has passed with but a ripple, here and there, in the sea of progressive business. The men and women of the country have learned, to their delight, that irrespective of the flights of the stock market by artificial inflation and deflation, the business of the country has been built on a solid economic foundation and that this structure can withstand without injury the tempest, cyclones or upheavals in the world of speculation."

This premature and naïve proclamation of victory over the "break" in the stock market would prove to be something the *Jewelers' Circular* would learn to regret.

1929 HISTORICAL NOTES

- The United States and Canada sign an agreement to protect Niagara Falls.
- The population of the United States reaches 120 million.
- Vatican City gains independence from Italy.
- 7-Up is invented.
- The first car radio is made by Motorola.
- The *Tarzan* and *Popeye* comic strips appear.
- President Hoover authorizes the building of Boulder Dam (Hoover Dam).
- Dow Jones hits a record peak of 381.17.
- Women are finally considered "persons" under Canadian law.
- October 29, 1929, "Black Tuesday," is the day of the stock market crash contributing to the Great Depression.
- Admiral Richard E. Byrd makes the first South Pole flight.

Continuing its positive spin on the economy, the *Jewelers' Circular* in December 1929 proclaimed that buyers were again crowding Fifth Avenue and noted that "it does interest the people of the country as a sign, a symbol—a manifestation that the psychological panic which followed the crash in the stock market is disappearing from the minds of the ordinary buyers, and what is happening on Fifth Avenue in New York will happen on main streets of the principal towns and villages of the country." This misreading of events and lack of a deep understanding of the ramifications of the market crash would once again, unfortunately, permit the *Jewelers' Circular* and the *Keystone* to unwittingly mislead their readers. Eventually, the fate of both publications would also be seriously affected by their inability to interpret the economic signals accurately.

The editorial in the December 1929 issue of the *Keystone* (in much the same vein as the one in its chief competitor, the *Jewelers' Circular*) told its readers that the stock market crash was nothing for them to be concerned about, saying that the "Big Crash" was "not the calamity some would have us believe it is." Unfortunately, however, its readers, relying on these false positives, continued to stock their shelves with jewelry and watch items that would prove difficult to sell as the effects of the Depression effects took hold. As a result, many of these business would not survive.

Owing to the Great Depression, the total domestic consumption of watches dropped from 5,088,434 in 1929 to 854,241 in 1932, then to 821,240 in 1933.[13]

Wall Street Crash *Not* Viewed With Alarm

***Keystone*, December 1929**

Hamilton's Wage Dividends

Unfazed by the recent stock market catastrophe, Miller of Hamilton on December 19, 1929, announced a year-end wage dividend of $97,000 to its 1,250 employees in Lancaster. The wage dividend (or bonus) was equivalent to approximately 4% of each employee's annual salary for 1929. Interestingly, the Hamilton workforce had grown since the Illinois acquisition, unlike the company's other Watch Division, based in Springfield.

In addition, a special stock bonus was given to 250 employees whose names were on the Hamilton "Service Honor Roll," which included employees who had worked for the company for fifteen or more years.

In looking forward to the coming year, Charles F. Miller said that "the business outlook for 1930 is fully as favorable as was the outlook a year ago." Thus, less than one month into the collapse of the stock market, Hamilton still forecast a rosy 1930 and provided generous bonuses to its employees. The effects of the market crash on the watch industry were not to be strongly felt for almost another year and a half.

Mislabeled Stock Offering

In December 1929 local Springfield newspapers reported that nearly $80,000 worth of stock in the Illinois Watch Company was made available for purchase by its employees. Actually, this was an error: the stock was for the Hamilton Watch Company, not Illinois. In less than two days, all of the stock was purchased.

It was also reported that many of the employees who purchased the stock were among those who lost heavily in the North Side State Bank failure in Springfield three years earlier. An Illinois Watch Company official pointed out the prompt purchase of all of the stock available as proof that those who suffered losses were well on their way to a recovery from that financial calamity. Evidently, nearly three hundred Watch Company employees had lost money in the bank failure. The quick sellout of this special stock offering, soon after the stock market collapse, demonstrated that neither the company nor its employees' enthusiasm for the Illinois Watch business had dimmed. Unfortunately, they were shortly going to be hurt again financially, since the Illinois Watch Company would face being closed by Hamilton. The purchasers of the stock later sued Hamilton for repayment of these shares in accordance with its terms of sale.

Satisfied and Confident Retailers

The *Jewelers' Circular*, already leading the industry bandwagon by trumpeting that all was back to normal, reported on January 9, 1930: "Surveys made by *Jeweler's Archive* correspondents among retail jewelers in many of the large cities through the country indicate that most retailers enjoyed good business over the holiday period and many all through the year. Further[,] the trade is encouraged by this unexpected spurt of business and jewelers all over the United States are looking optimistically on the business situation for 1930. Without exception, those interviewed predicted good trade for the next twelve months and feel confident that as the new year gets fully under way business will be greatly improved, public confidence will have been restored and this country will be enjoying greater prosperity."

RECEIVER FOR BANK ON NORTH SIDE IS NAMED

On March 3, 1927, the North Side State Bank, located at 719 North Grand Avenue in Springfield, was suddenly closed by the state auditor of public accounts pending an examination of its books and an adjustment of its assets and liabilities. The bank was then placed into receivership and a receiver was appointed. A Grand Jury in June 1927 returned thirty-three indictments charging the principals of the bank with conspiracy and receiving deposits after the bank was known to be insolvent.

The president of the bank, Roy A. McKown, was convicted by a jury in circuit court and sentenced to serve a term of one to three years in a penitentiary and to pay a fine of $180.00.

Many Illinois Watch Company employees had lost most of their savings kept at the North Side Bank.

Ironically, this forecast (at least for watch manufacturers) proved accurate for the most part, as most of the large watch companies were still to enjoy a robust 1930. Accordingly, many businesses continued lining their shelves with merchandise.

Substantial 1929 Net Earnings for Elgin

In January 1930, Elgin president, Hulburd, announced that the company would report net earnings about equal to those of 1928 ($1,846,067). He further indicated that as in the year before, an extra dividend could be declared at 4%.

Hulburd denied the rumors that "substantial reductions in the plant force" were planned and "expressed hope that, by summer, the daily output would be increased to 4,500 movements daily." Already by April 27, 1929, however, Elgin had reduced its output to 3,500 movements per day, down from 4,000; it also eliminated half-day employment on Saturday. And by December 1929 its workforce was down to 3,400 after a high of 4,379 in 1927.[14] Thus, Elgin was reacting to market conditions well before its competitors and before the adverse effects of the stock market crash were generally felt.

***Keystone*, January 1930. This cartoon depicts the stock market crash as an isolated event, harmful to market speculators but not to businesses that were "hitting along on all six as usual."**

Recovery on the Way?

Stalwart in its misconceptions, the *Jewelers' Circular* was already preaching recovery on January 30, 1930, stating: "BUSINESS, having emerged from a temporary condition of financial shell-shock, has reached the perfectly natural state of convalescence which always precedes recovery." This theme—that recovery is here or just around the corner—innocently glossed over an otherwise disastrous situation that was definitely not "a temporary condition."

Record-Breaking Year for Illinois

In January 1930, Miller of Illinois reported that nearly 1,200 employees of the Illinois Watch Company would share in a $30,000 cash bonus payable on January 18, 1930, on the basis of 2% of annual wages during the year. In announcing the bonus distribution, Miller reviewed the year and made an optimistic forecast regarding 1930, as his father had done. He further noted that October 1929 was the best single month in the history of the company and added that the year as a whole was sound. So, notwithstanding its inventory woes, Illinois was a solid profit-maker for Hamilton. The new Illinois offerings that were flowing out of the Illinois Watch Factory were being very favorably received.

As was mentioned earlier, Illinois experienced sales of $2,818,550 for 1929, but this total was only to 80 of its over 100 jobbers. It is unknown what the total sales were—including all jobbers, direct sales, house accounts and department store sales. In 1929, Illinois employed at least seven salesmen and one sales manager to help promote its watches to jobbers and jewelers. This was up at least one salesperson from 1928. And by 1930 the number had grown to eight salesmen and one sales manager.

In addition to the strong financial performance of Illinois following the acquisition, it was returning a high preferred dividend to its parent each month. According to the Hamilton financial ledgers for 1929, Illinois was paying Hamilton a monthly preferred dividend in the amount of $71,476.50. (This dividend was probably paid in 1928, 1929 and 1930, before the ill effects of the stock market crash hit the watch industry.) This annual payment of $857,718.00 would have gone a long way toward providing Hamilton with a healthy return on its investment in Illinois. Unfortunately, this robust return was greatly impacted, if not completely vitiated, starting in 1931.

1930 HISTORICAL NOTES

- Average house cost was $7,145.00.
- Average income per year was $1,970.00.
- A gallon of gasoline was 10¢.
- Average cost of a new car was $640.00.

Considering what ultimately happened to the company, it is sadly ironic that after being acquired, Illinois produced sound results for Hamilton—first in 1928, then again in 1929 and even in 1930. Illinois forecasted continued growth and profits for 1931, as did Hamilton. When the Depression took hold, however, Hamilton eventually concluded that it had to plan for its own survival. And that meant placing economic clamps on Illinois.

Summary

Even before the sudden collapse of the world economy, Hamilton, like the other great American watch manufacturers, viewed with increasing anxiety the changes in American markets that were becoming evident. New kinds of marketing that focused on price rather than quality, as well as the rise of consumer credit, seemed threats to companies like Hamilton and Illinois that had aimed at premium markets. Thus, when new competition arose from Swiss makers and from domestic companies that assembled and cased Swiss components, the old-line watchmakers were already jittery.

After the acquisition, Hamilton seemed at first to be enjoying the popularity of Illinois' products. But when the effects of the crash began to sink in across the broader economy, Hamilton came close to panic. Determined to save its original core business and not willing to subject itself to the severe contraction that Elgin and Waltham imposed on themselves, Hamilton chose instead to forego whatever good it had initially intended to achieve through the acquisition and impose most of the contraction on Illinois.

For Illinois, this was the beginning of the end.

CHAPTER 5

Ravages of the Great Depression

For over two years after the acquisition, Hamilton and Illinois had profitable business results despite the crash of the stock market on Black Tuesday, October 29, 1929. Both companies continued to forecast, and indeed experienced, favorable growth and profitability for 1931. Although Illinois probably had a greatly reduced workforce starting sometime in 1930, it was not until mid-1931 that the aftermath of the stock market crash started to hit the bottom line of Hamilton, Illinois and other domestic watchmakers severely. Then, a number of factors influenced Hamilton as it struggled to chart the course for its own survival—and eventually the demise of its Illinois Watch Division.

Overall, 1929 had proved to be a boom year for American watch manufacturers. However, starting with the stock market crash on October 29, the watch industry would have to react to two major developments: not only the aftermath of the crash but also the rapid and continuing decline in the demand for pocket watches. Already flooded with pocket watch parts and movements, and then hammered by the Great Depression, some of the manufacturers started to reduce work hours and employees, even shutting down production entirely for extended periods of time.

To understand how and why Hamilton and Illinois responded to the catastrophic downturn in the watch industry, it is helpful to look at the responses of some other major players.

Patterns in the Watch Industry, 1930–1931

Reductions at Elgin

Charles W. Moore notes in *Timing a Century*, his history of the Waltham Watch Company, that the total domestic consumption of watches dropped from 5,088,434 in 1929 to 854,241 in 1932, then to 821,240 in 1933.[1] Elgin responded quickly to the shift in market trends and demands. Although it shared in the boom year of 1929, with profits at a lofty $1,972,971, it sensed economic problems ahead, and by December 1929, its workforce was reduced to 3,400 after a high of 4,379 in 1927.[2]

Soon there were more layoffs—massive ones. By March 1930, Elgin had cut its workforce to 1,100 employees. Beginning as early as October 1, 1930, all departments were reduced to a three-day work week. Elgin's 1930 financial results were in the red, with a loss of $70,543. The downturn continued into 1931, resulting in Elgin's shutting down from May 27 to July 6.[3]

Elgin again shut down operations in September 1931, for a full week. In October, with the impact of the Depression settling in on the balance sheets of the American watch industry, Elgin, which had already reduced its work week, announced further austerity measures by moving to a five-day, 20-hour work week at its plant in place of the three-day, 24-hour work week that had been in effect since the summer. The Elgin general manager of Manufacturing said that plant officials had adopted this schedule in the belief it would permit operating economies. Each workday was from 8:00 a.m. to noon. This move effectively cut their production capability in half, when Elgin up to this point had been one of the best-performing watchmakers and the American market share leader. The Elgin plant closed again for a month from December 18, 1931, until January 18, 1932, after which the work was cut back to four days.[4]

Caution at Waltham

Moore points out that Waltham did not share in the feverish industrial activity that had characterized the boom year of 1929. Steady work was provided for its 2,300 employees, who averaged 50¢ per hour in wages. Sales in 1929 increased by 6% over 1928, but earnings dropped a disappointing 8% from 1928.[5]

Waltham's production schedule picked up in the spring of 1930. As 1930 began, its headcount stood at 2,392; it began to increase in early February and reached a peak in May. However, stock prices collapsed again in June, and Waltham closed its factory, ostensibly for its annual two-week holiday. However, when it reopened three weeks later, only 1,599 workers were recalled.[6]

After Waltham had gone through a painful, contentious and litigious reorganization in 1923, the company was determined to take quick, substantive action if threatened with adverse economic conditions. Going forward, Waltham tried never to carry more than twenty-one days of inventory.

1930
HISTORICAL NOTES

- President Hoover signs the 1930 Smoot-Hawley Tariff Bill.
- British unemployment hits one million.
- United States' unemployment hits 8.7%.
- The United States suffers its worst-ever drought, leading to the Dust Bowl years.
- The Chrysler Building in New York City is completed.
- Pluto, the ninth planet, is discovered (but was later reclassified as a "dwarf planet").

THE NEW *JEWELERS' CIRCULAR*

The slowdown of the economy by August 28, 1930 struck even the ever-optimistic *Jewelers' Circular,* although the editors still tried to put a positive spin on it. No doubt because of declining advertising revenue and subscribers, it announced that effective October 1930, it would go from a weekly to a monthly publication.

Some businesses, such as the Star Watch Case Company, had long had a full-page color advertisement in virtually every issue of the *Jewelers' Circular.* However, in 1930 some of the regular advertisers went from a full page or more in 1929 to a small one-inch by two-inch advertisement. Other advertisements disappeared entirely. As a result, the size of the monthly edition was smaller than the former weekly versions.

As the effects of the Great Depression wore on, the *Jewelers' Circular* and the *Keystone* would be compelled to merge.

TWO WATCHES FOR EVERY MAN

The November 1930 issue of the *Jewelers' Circular* reported on an interesting resolution that had recently been passed by the American National Retail Jewelers' Association at its annual convention, which read:

> "We recommend that men wear a wrist watch for great convenience and a pocket watch for accuracy; two watches for better satisfaction.
>
> "This should be impressed on every watch salesman of the country and if necessary, printed and framed for use in every jewelry store. The slogan 'two watches for better satisfaction' is one around which good business may and should be built.
>
> "The sentiment should be brought home to the customer in advertising and display as well as in sales talks. Properly done it should create no resistance on the part of the customer for the possession of two kinds of watches will bring real satisfaction to every wearer as well as increased business to the jeweler.
>
> "Let the watch salesman realize that every wearer of a wrist watch should be a prospect for a pocket watch and *vice versa*. Let him first be 'sold' himself on the merit of the ideas and it is then easy to sell the customer."

Obviously, jewelers were also suffering from excess pocket watch inventory and were trying to continue the promotion of pocket watches to empty their shelves and display cases.

Gruen Reactions

In May 1931, the Gruen Watch Company reported that its increased advertising helped to give it a "nice profit" during the fiscal year ending March 31, 1931, according to the report of its treasurer, George J. Gruen. The company reported earnings of $1.42 a share after preferred dividends against $2.56 a share the previous year (down $1.14 per share). The profits were $299,247, compared with $441,452 for fiscal year 1930. These profits seem rather paltry, but when compared to its largest competitor, Elgin, they were actually quite good, as Elgin was in the red for these years with significant losses exceeding one million dollars in 1931 alone.[7]

George J. Gruen, (1877–1952) Treasurer of Gruen

Although Gruen maintained profitability in its 1931 fiscal year, the profits were modest and down significantly from its 1930 profits.

American watch manufacturers now had to be concerned about their ability to remain in the black in the down economy.

On October 12, 1931, Gruen reported: "Whether it is because of the approaching holiday season or just another step in the return to normalcy cannot be determined, but the fact remains that the Gruen Watch Co. is experiencing a decided increase in business. Fred Gruen, president of the firm, announced today that shop men are working three nights a week in addition to the day shift to take care of the increasing number of orders.

"The plant worked in full operation all during September and had to put in two extra nights a week on top of the regular run, but the overtime work was increased recently to take care of the business. Gruen also declared that shipments from Time Hill ... during August and September, were greater than those in the same period of 1930."[8] However, notwithstanding this brief uptick in business, Gruen was shortly again lamenting the weak state of the watch industry.

It is likely, however, that Gruen was working on a reduced-hours basis prior to September 1931. As we know, Illinois had been on a reduced-hours schedule (that they called "short time") since July 1926 owing to its overabundance of pocket watch parts and movements in inventory.

Casemakers Suffering

The watch manufacturers were not alone in implementing a reduced work week. Other watch concerns, such as the case manufacturers, had also been reducing work hours and employees.

Solidarity Watch Case Liquidation. By October 1931, two years after Black Tuesday, the effects of the Great Depression started to rattle the American watch industry. That month Solidarity, an Illinois and Hamilton case supplier, announced its voluntary liquidation and filed a Certificate of Liquidation with the Secretary of State of New York.[9] A number of other case manufacturers would follow suit.

Solidarity, established in 1885, was one of the country's oldest watch casemakers. Based in New York City, it specialized in the manufacture of solid gold watch cases as well as raised figure dials made under a patented process.

Solidarity's president, the greatly respected John W. Sherwood, had been ill at his home since early May 1931 and died in 1932.

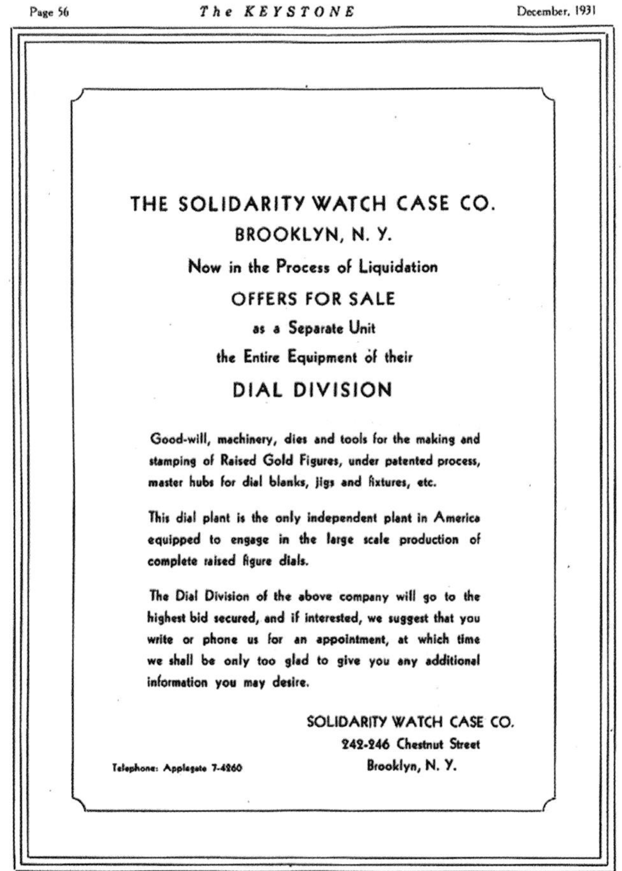
Page 56 *The KEYSTONE* December, 1931

THE SOLIDARITY WATCH CASE CO.
BROOKLYN, N. Y.
Now in the Process of Liquidation
OFFERS FOR SALE
as a Separate Unit
the Entire Equipment of their
DIAL DIVISION

Good-will, machinery, dies and tools for the making and stamping of Raised Gold Figures, under patented process, master hubs for dial blanks, jigs and fixtures, etc.

This dial plant is the only independent plant in America equipped to engage in the large scale production of complete raised figure dials.

The Dial Division of the above company will go to the highest bid secured, and if interested, we suggest that you write or phone us for an appointment, at which time we shall be only too glad to give you any additional information you may desire.

SOLIDARITY WATCH CASE CO.
242-246 Chestnut Street
Brooklyn, N. Y.

Telephone: Applegate 7-4260

Keystone, December 1931

Illinois Watch Case Company Situation. Although the Illinois Watch Case Company of Elgin, Illinois, reported in October 1931 that its increased volume of business was responsible for placing the majority of the factory personnel on a full-time basis, the statement meant that only a bit more than half of its employees of approximately five hundred were back to full-time work. Their president, L. A. Eppenstein, stated at the time that "indications are that business improvements in this line is on the upgrade."[10] This remark turned out to be premature.

Reductions in workforces and work hours were common at this time for the watch industry. For most companies, it was not until the last quarter of 1933 and the year 1934 that business started reflecting normalcy.

Keystone, October 1931

Hamilton's Tactics with Illinois

Hamilton, quite fiscally aware, had long been paying very careful attention to the economic impact of developments in the industry. As a result, Hamilton was not only reducing the employee's work hours, inventory and product releases of its Illinois Watch Division but also implementing major restructuring of it.

Aggressively moving to lower Illinois prices, Hamilton may very early on have mapped out a worst-case scenario that would methodically proceed towards closing Illinois, because that is exactly what later occurred.

Keystone, August 1931

Consolidated Research Department

Hamilton's first overt sign of retrenchment had been in June 1930, when Charles F. Miller, president of the company, sent a memorandum to all foremen, announcing the establishment of a centralized research department. Then his son, Robert E. Miller, general manager of the Illinois Watch Division, parroted his dad and provided the same information to all Illinois foremen in Springfield.

The messages pointed out that "There used to be a time when research work could be done in different departments of the factory, but it seemed far more economical to work out all of the problems that came up in the development and production of the product in one department, and that department is now called the Research Department."

The Research Department, although established in Lancaster, was for the benefit of all three divisions of Hamilton: Hamilton Watch, Illinois Watch and the Hamilton-Sangamo Corporation. The Research Department was to be headed by George P. Luckey of Hamilton.

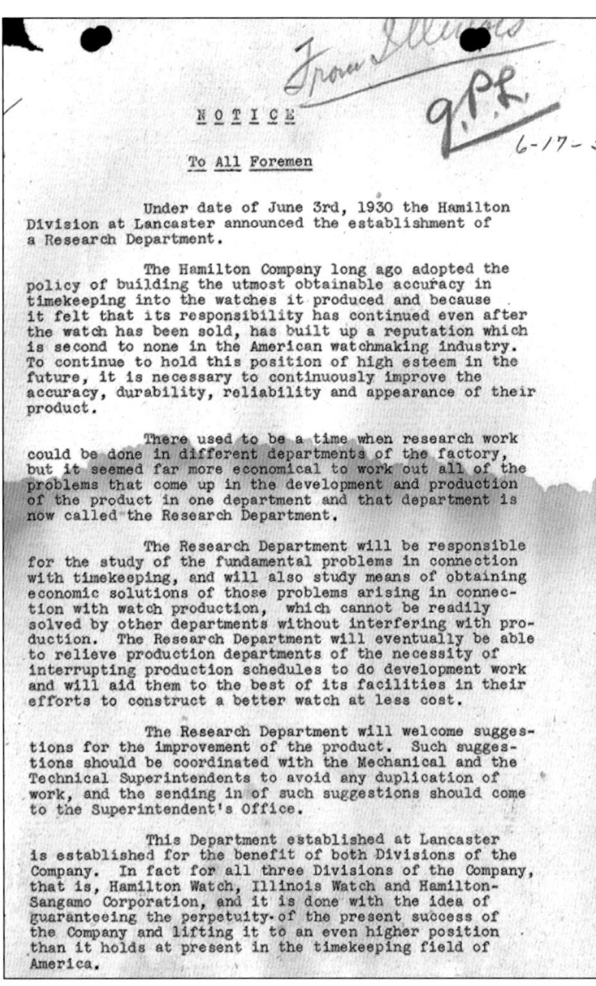

NOTICE

6-17-30

To All Foremen

Under date of June 3rd, 1930 the Hamilton Division at Lancaster announced the establishment of a Research Department.

The Hamilton Company long ago adopted the policy of building the utmost obtainable accuracy in timekeeping into the watches it produced and because it felt that its responsibility has continued even after the watch has been sold, has built up a reputation which is second to none in the American watchmaking industry. To continue to hold this position of high esteem in the future, it is necessary to continuously improve the accuracy, durability, reliability and appearance of their product.

There used to be a time when research work could be done in different departments of the factory, but it seemed far more economical to work out all of the problems that come up in the development and production of the product in one department and that department is now called the Research Department.

The Research Department will be responsible for the study of the fundamental problems in connection with timekeeping, and will also study means of obtaining economic solutions of those problems arising in connection with watch production, which cannot be readily solved by other departments without interfering with production. The Research Department will eventually be able to relieve production departments of the necessity of interrupting production schedules to do development work and will aid them to the best of its facilities in their efforts to construct a better watch at less cost.

The Research Department will welcome suggestions for the improvement of the product. Such suggestions should be coordinated with the Mechanical and the Technical Superintendents to avoid any duplication of work, and the sending in of such suggestions should come to the Superintendent's Office.

This Department established at Lancaster is established for the benefit of both Divisions of the Company. In fact for all three Divisions of the Company, that is, Hamilton Watch, Illinois Watch and Hamilton-Sangamo Corporation, and it is done with the idea of guaranteeing the perpetuity of the present success of the Company and lifting it to an even higher position than it holds at present in the timekeeping field of America.

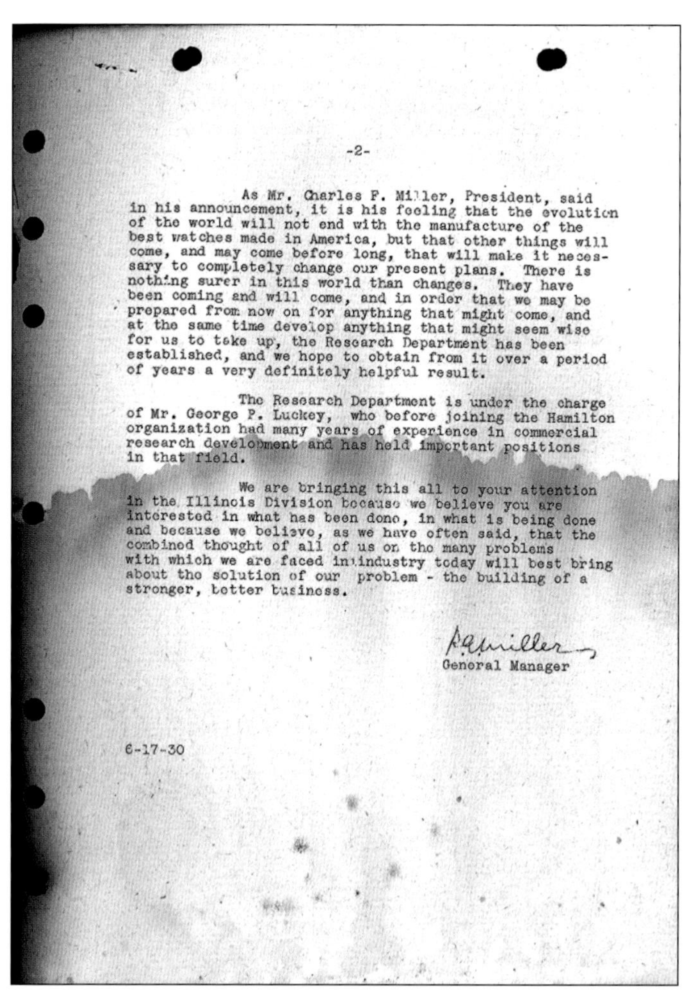

-2-

As Mr. Charles F. Miller, President, said in his announcement, it is his feeling that the evolution of the world will not end with the manufacture of the best watches made in America, but that other things will come, and may come before long, that will make it necessary to completely change our present plans. There is nothing surer in this world than changes. They have been coming and will come, and in order that we may be prepared from now on for anything that might come, and at the same time develop anything that might seem wise for us to take up, the Research Department has been established, and we hope to obtain from it over a period of years a very definitely helpful result.

The Research Department is under the charge of Mr. George P. Luckey, who before joining the Hamilton organization had many years of experience in commercial research development and has held important positions in that field.

We are bringing this all to your attention in the Illinois Division because we believe you are interested in what has been done, in what is being done and because we believe, as we have often said, that the combined thought of all of us on the many problems with which we are faced in industry today will best bring about the solution of our problem - the building of a stronger, better business.

R.E. Miller
General Manager

6-17-30

R. E. Miller's memorandum, dated June 17, 1930, about the closing of the Illinois Research Department

This move made good business sense and was economically sound, because the effects of the stock market crash were beginning to be felt. It allowed Hamilton to consolidate research and development operations as well as reduce headcount and related resources.

However, the inability of Illinois to innovate following the research move to Lancaster would prove to be devastating. The units' sales for 1931 through 1934 reflect this impact on Hamilton's sales.

TABLE I

PERCENT OF FREE SERVICE TO PREVIOUS YEAR'S SALES

	SALES	RETURNS	PERCENT	
1931	97,428			
32	67,113	3,962	4.07%	
33	65,031	2,710	4.03	
34	113,213	2,825	4.35	
35	173,408	4,987	4.40	
36	252,151	8,064	4.65	
37	310,269	15,020	5.95	
38	217,790	16,339	5.27	
39	257,059	19,125	8.78	
1940	314,028	18,188	7.07	
41	380,044	12,707	4.04	
42	259,300	7,779	3.05	
43	172,999	2,972	1.15	Not
44	187,119	703	.47	Representative
45	148,713	421	.23	War
46	302,638	2,514	1.69	Years
47	483,820	5,875	1.94	
48	615,606	9,431	1.95	
49	605,532	11,795	1.92	
1950	590,802	13,053	2.15	
51	497,433	16,531	2.80	
52	406,529	17,286	3.50	
53	444,933	13,007	3.20	
54		10,505	2.36	

Hamilton product performance study November 18, 1954, by W.R. Slaugh, Head Watchmaker

Wage Dividend for Hamilton Employees

Notwithstanding the Depression, Hamilton still enjoyed a profitable 1930 and distributed a $93,000 wage dividend to its employees. In 1931, however, it barely broke even, and that would prove to be its last profitable year until 1934. Illinois was profitable in 1930 but started to decline in 1931.

The *Keystone* editorial staff in November 1930 was optimistically and inaccurately signaling its readers that the worst of the Depression had passed. The editorials of the *Keystone* and the *Jewelers' Circular* for years during the Great Depression tried to put a sanguine view on the

GEORGE P. LUCKEY (1891-1981)

George P. Luckey, May 1934

George Paul Luckey joined Hamilton on January 1, 1927, as manager of the Tachometer Division. Thereafter, he rose in the Hamilton organization. On June 3, 1930, he was appointed director of research and assistant superintendent, reporting to William H. Manby, the longtime general superintendent. In 1933 he was made factory manager.

In his first year in that position, according to Don Sauers, "Luckey developed and put into use the Time Microscope. This instrument revolutionized the timing of watches by reducing to a few minutes the days and weeks it had taken previously to adjust newly assembled watches to constant time."* The time microscope thus made obsolete older, costlier and less efficient factory methods for timing newly assembled watches.

As a manager, however, "his style irritated almost everyone," Sauers reports. When asked how Luckey and Manby got along, a former worker said, "It wasn't easy getting along with Mr. Luckey at any time."

Sauers writes: "A former executive stated flatly 'I liked him personally, but George just couldn't get along with people very well.' Others described him as "simply an unhappy man."

Luckey's personality issues notwithstanding, Sauers says that "Luckey's tighter standards and stricter procedures . . . resulted in a 30% reduction in the man-hours it took to make a watch."

On February 28, 1952, George P. Luckey was elected president and board chairman of Hamilton. He retired two years later.

*All quotations here are from Sauers' *Time for America: Hamilton Watch, 1892–1992* (Lititz, PA: Sutter House, 1992), pp. 92–94.

economy and the imminent return to brighter days. This cartoon shows another premature attempt to mark the demise of the jewelry industry's severe economic malaise.

The *Jewelers' Circular* continued its overly positive and misleading opinion of the economy. In November 1930, its cartoon indicated "The Skys are Clearing" and "normal business" had returned.

F.T.C. BLOW TO PRICE MAINTENANCE

The *Jewelers' Circular* reported in August 1931 that the Federal Trade Commission (F.T.C.) had sent its final report to Congress on the Capper-Kelly Bill, stating that it could see no present need for resale price legislation.

The F.T.C. wisely noted it would be difficult to provide government regulations on price maintenance that would bring relief to the makers of trademarked goods without doing injustice to consumers and, at the same time, meet the tests of practical administration.

Beckwith's New Position

Hamilton's longtime president, Charles F. Miller, died on July 18, 1931. In August, Frank C. Beckwith was elected to replace him. Miller's death, sinking 1931 results and fears for 1932 performance were to focus careful attention on Hamilton's ability to sustain two geographically separate facilities in a devastatingly down market. In its October 1931 issue, the *Jewelers' Circular* reported:

> "In acknowledging congratulations on his new position, Mr. Beckwirth said recently: "I am mindful of the great honor conferred upon me, but am not unmindful of the great responsibility as well." And when asked for a message to the watch trade on the fall business, he modestly asked to be excused, saying, "I am reminded of what Grace, the president of the Bethlehem Steel Co., said the other day. 'Let's stop prophesying and go to a Cathedral and pray.'"

Beckwith's fear for Hamilton as 1932 approached was palpable, and its Illinois Watch Division in particular was to continue to feel its impact. Nevertheless, on November 20, 1931, the company surprisingly obtained rights to the name "Howard," formerly the trademark of the E. Howard Watch Company. Also in 1931, but more true to form, Hamilton unloaded the Hamilton-Sangamo Corporation on General Time Instruments, a corporation owned jointly by the Western Clock Company and Seth Thomas Clock Company.

Hamilton-Sangamo Corporation Sold To Clock Concern

At the same time that industry consolidation was taking place, with stronger companies absorbing weaker ones, in December 1930 the Seth Thomas Clock Co. of New York and the Western Clock Co. of La Salle, Illinois, announced a proposed merger. The two companies were among the largest in the clock business, although making different types of clocks.

These combined companies went on to be merged with the General Time Equipment Instruments Co., Inc. of La Salle, Illinois. In May 1931, General Time then took over the Hamilton-Sangamo Corporation of Lancaster, Pennsylvania.

Illinois Jobbers in 1931

In 1930, Illinois had apparently offered jewelers (through its jobbers) an "Earned Discount on Extra Business." If a jeweler made a one-time purchase of $20,000 during the year, they would earn an extra discount of 15 percent; but few expected such volume purchases to occur in 1931.[11]

DISCOUNTS

1930

EARNED DISCOUNT ON EXTRA BUSINESS

In the same manner as other manufacturers, we have advised you and our distributors, that there is a methdd whereby a jeweler definitely merchandising American watches - particularly Illinois manufactured - can in our opinion, earn, providing the distributor wishes to afford it, an extra discount up to the amount of 15%.

This extra discount to be earned on the idea of a qauntity order basis, delivery at one time to the retail jeweler, sufficiently large to indicate a consumption and use of American watches in volume during the year, of around $20,000. sales value.

This matter has been very freely discussed during the past two years, and it seemed to be rather well understood because of certain types of contract accounts being established, which based upon a volume business, did offer the opportunity of earning the extra 10% discount.

At no time do we instruct any of our distributors that they must afford discounts other than the 6% cash. However, there are times when so-called house accounts of real strong users of watches, do carry on this situation, of providing an earned discount for loyalty and quantity business given at one time which overcomes the expense of selling efforts and office detail.

You are quite right in your feeling that if the extra discount was a promiscuous affair to any account wherein commissions to salesmen and overhead expenses were involved, the firm offering this extra discount generally fails to carry on.

Taken from JLK's letter to N.A.B.B.Co.

Keenan's 15% discount letter

A list of current Illinois jobbers, dated March 10, 1931, comprised 125 total jobbers: 113 based in the United States, ten in Canada and one each in Mexico and the Philippines. This expanded list reflected Hamilton's desire to secure more firms to try to reduce Illinois inventory while Hamilton itself was contemplating severely limiting the number of its watch distributors.

Wholesale Distributors OF GENUINE ILLINOIS WATCH MATERIAL

MARCH 10, 1931

The ILLINOIS WATCH
Springfield, Illinois

ALABAMA
Alexander Fish .... Birmingham
1019 Watts Bldg.
F. T. Skelton, Inc. .... Birmingham
1921½ N 2nd Ave.

CALIFORNIA
E. W. Reynolds Co. .... Los Angeles
3rd Floor Metropolitan Bldg.
R. & L. Myers .... San Francisco
717 Market St.
Nordman & Aurich .... San Francisco
150 Post St.
Williams & Petersen .... San Francisco
150 Post St.

COLORADO
Cosley Jewelry Co. .... Denver
301 University Bldg.
Lehman Jewelry Co. .... Denver
420 University Bldg.
United Manufacturing Jewelers .... Denver
201 Quincy Bldg.

CONNECTICUT
M. S. Levenson .... Hartford
42 Asylum St.

DISTRICT OF COLUMBIA
Blustein & Blackman, Inc. .... Washington
904 G St., N. W.
Kur Jewelry Co. .... Washington
417 7th St., N. W.

DELAWARE
B. Kleitz & Brother Co. .... Wilmington
6th & Market Sts.

GEORGIA
Ewing Brothers .... Atlanta
5 Plaza Way
Jewelers Supply Co. .... Atlanta
84 Peachtree St.

ILLINOIS
Benj. Allen & Co. .... Chicago
10 S. Wabash Ave.
A. C. Becken Co. .... Chicago
35 E. Wacker Drive
Braude & Sons .... Chicago
Heyworth Bldg.
C. & E. Marshall Co. .... Chicago
1445 W. Jackson Blvd.
Henry Paulson & Co. .... Chicago
37 S. Wabash Ave.
Swartchild & Co. .... Chicago
Heyworth Bldg.
Victoria Watch Co. .... Chicago
35 E. Wacker Drive

INDIANA
Hoffman & Co. .... Indianapolis
765 Century Bldg.
Indiana Jlrs. Supply Co. .... Indianapolis
316 State Life Bldg.

KENTUCKY
Geo. Katzman Co. .... Louisville
3rd & Walnut Sts.

MAINE
The Skillin Co. .... Portland
235½ Middle St.

MARYLAND

Max Kohner........................Baltimore
104 W. Fayette St.

John A. Tschantre........................Baltimore
28 E. Baltimore St.

MASSACHUSETTS

I. Alberts Sons, Inc........................Boston
373 Washington St.

Harkins & Murphy........................Boston
373 Washington St.

Haselton-Goodman Co........................Boston
373 Washington St.

Hub Material Co........................Boston
373 Washington St.

J. M. Kirby Co........................Boston
373 Washington St.

Charles May & Son Co........................Boston
373 Washington St.

H. J. McGrath Co........................Boston
373 Washington St.

Harry Parritz & Bro........................Boston
387 Washington St.

D. C. Percival & Co........................Boston
373 Washington St.

MICHIGAN

Michigan Jewelers Supply Co........................Detroit
512 Metropolitan Bldg.

Henry Staats........................Detroit
1011 Metropolitan Bldg.

MINNESOTA

Duluth Jewelers' Supply Co........................Duluth
Armstead Bldg.

J. M. Bennett Co........................Minneapolis
Jewelers Exchange Bldg.

S. H. Clausin & Co........................Minneapolis
13-17 S. 6th St.

Duluth Jewelers Supply Co........................Minneapolis
100 N. 7th St.

MINNESOTA (Continued)

C. M. Thomsen Co........................Minneapolis
100 N. Seventh St.

W. O. N. Jewelers Supply........................Owatonna
105 Main St.

Esslinger & Co........................St. Paul
510 Ryan Building

MISSOURI

Clark Tool & Material Co........................Kansas City
1210 Federal Reserve Bank Bldg.

Meyer Jewelry Co........................Kansas City
Boley Bldg.

Bauman-Massa Jewelry Co........................St. Louis
Republic Bldg.

Ilch & Radecke........................St. Louis
632-634 Arcade Bldg.

W. F. Kemper Co........................St. Louis
307-8 Equitable Bldg.

NEBRASKA

The Bergman Co........................Omaha
409 So. 15th St.

NORTH CAROLINA

C. M. Waldorf........................Wilmington
508 Southern Bldg.

NEW JERSEY

New Jersey Jewelers Supply Co........................Newark
95-97 Bank St.

H. Prostick........................Paterson
93 Van Houten St.

NEW YORK

Albany Jewelers Supply Co........................Albany
17 Steuben St.

Eliassof Brothers & Co........................Albany
100 State St.

King & Eisele Co........................Buffalo
Franklin & Huron Sts.

NEW YORK (Continued)

Queen City Material Co........................Buffalo
Brisbane Bldg.

F. J. Boesse & Co........................New York
68 Nassau St.

Buhl, Peer & Keefe........................New York
37-39 Maiden Lane

Conover & Quayle........................New York
2 Maiden Lane

Henry Diamond........................New York
90 Canal Street

George J. Doehrmann........................New York
15 Maiden Lane

H. S. Kramer........................New York
176 Fulton St.

Lieberman Brothers........................New York
64-66 Nassau St.

John A. Poltock & Co........................New York
15 Maiden Lane

Phillip Sloves & Sons, Inc........................New York
35 Maiden Lane

S. Stanley Solomon........................New York
21 Maiden Lane

Glazer Jewelry Co........................Rochester
149 Main St., E.

Morris Rosenbloom & Co........................Rochester
115 Clinton Ave., S.

W. P. Hitchcock Co........................Syracuse
301 S. Salina St.

A. H. Pond Co........................Syracuse
214-216 S. Warren St.

Gould & Gould........................Watertown
101 Charlebois Bldg.

OHIO

The Akron Jewelers Supply........................Akron
606 United Bldg.

Lindner & Co........................Cincinnati
18 W. Seventh St.

OHIO (Continued)

The E. & J. Swigart Co........................Cincinnati
32 W. 6th St.

Chas. Swigart........................Cincinnati
403 Strand Bldg.

Colman Bros........................Cleveland
400 Schofield Bldg.

The Merit Company........................Cleveland
1010 Euclid Ave.

Earl Sculler........................Columbus
401-3 Citizens Bank Bldg.

Wm. S. McCaw Co........................Toledo
315 Superior St.

OREGON

Bernard Italie Co........................Portland
P. O. Box 761

Butterfield Brothers........................Portland
Mohawk Bldg.

PENNSYLVANIA

Bert Meyers........................Allentown
312 Colonial Theatre Bldg.

H. S. Meiskey Co........................Lancaster
Duke & Chestnut Sts.

Saul L. Solomon........................Lancaster
444 N. Queen St.

Jos. Bechtel & Co........................Philadelphia
729 Sansom St.

S. Goldin & Co........................Philadelphia
124½ S. 8th St.

Kramer Bros........................Philadelphia
725 Sansom St.

Rothman & Meyer........................Philadelphia
134 S. 8th St.

M. Sickles & Sons........................Philadelphia
900 Chestnut St.

Williams & Waples........................Philadelphia
727 Sansom St.

A. Zlotnick & Co........................Philadelphia
708 Sansom St.

PENNSYLVANIA (Continued)

Martin Gluck & Son........................Pittsburgh
718 Penn Ave.

Heeren Bros........................Pittsburgh
Penn Ave. & Eighth St.

J. M. Kurtz Co........................Pittsburgh
214 Bessemer Bldg.

Landaw Bros........................Pittsburgh
628 Penn Ave.

A. J. Wagner........................Scranton
420 Coal Exchange Bldg.

Watchmakers Supply House....Wilkes Barre
Simon Long Bldg.

RHODE ISLAND

Geo. H. Taylor & Co........................Providence
204 Westminster St.

TENNESSEE

S. Fargotstein & Sons........................Memphis
822-24 Exchange Bldg.

A. Graves & Steuwer Co........................Memphis
147 Madison Ave.

Young-Neal Co........................Nashville
215 6th Ave. North

TEXAS

H. H. Hawley Co........................Dallas
P. O. Box 1298

John H. Clary Co........................El Paso
Mills Bldg.

B. M. Hammond & Co........................San Antonio
111 W. Commerce St.

UTAH

Primrose Jewelers Supplies....Salt Lake City
215 Clift Bldg.

VIRGINIA

Fishers Supply House........................Roanoke
23½ West Church Ave.

Herr & Kline........................Norfolk
231-35 Granby St.

WASHINGTON

L. A. Clark Co........................Seattle
1404 2nd Ave.

Mayer Brothers........................Seattle
P. O. Box 1914

WISCONSIN

Wm. F. Gollberg Co........................Milwaukee
209 Wisconsin Ave.

CANADA

ALBERTA

McGeachie & Holdsworth........................Calgary
308 8th Ave., W.

MANITOBA

McGeachie & Holdsworth........................Winnipeg
504 Canada Bldg.

NOVA SCOTIA

Arthur W. Thomas........................Halifax
P. O. Box 393

ONTARIO

E. & A. Gunther Co., Ltd........................Brantford
Murray and Bruce Sts.

The Levy Bros. Co........................Hamilton
58-60 King St., E.

Ash Bros........................Toronto
56 King St., E.

Lacy & Co........................Toronto
45 Richmond St., E.

Rixon, Lacy & McCarroll........................Toronto
103 Church St., Cor. Richmond St.

QUEBEC

H. R. Millard........................Montreal
222 St. James St.

A. Wittnauer Co........................Montreal
Guardian Building

MEXICO

H. Steele & Company........................Mexico City, D. F.
5 De Mayo Numero No. 20, Apartado No. 2584

PHILIPPINE ISLANDS

MANILA

H. E. Heacock Co........................Manila
127-131 Escolta

By November 1931 the jobbers that Illinois customarily dealt with were also clearly suffering from the effects of the Great Depression. Therefore, in a letter dated November 10, 1931, Illinois advised them that they could now be eligible for Illinois' minimum discount of 3% for a reduced value of $5,000 in annual purchases; this was a 50% reduction from its normal $10,000 discount threshold.

Illinois claimed in this communication that "during the past few weeks there has been a decided pickup in the demand from our Greater Value ribbon and strap watches in the $32.50, $35.00 and $37.50 range, to say nothing of the 'over demand' on the 21/0 size American Beauty Series." These were mostly offerings of ladies' models. Certainly, with these lower-priced offerings, it would be even more difficult in any event for the jobbers to hit the minimum volume discount level.

~~LETTER TO 3%~~ "DISCOUNT" ~~JOBBERS~~
Letter to jobbers when not earned
November 10th, 1931.

Dear Mr.

For several years now it has been necessary to advise those few customers of ours whose volume of purchases during the year became reduced below a minimum that the ~~3%~~ cash discount was not being earned and could not be applied to their accounts until yearly volume was reached.

You can readily appreciate the fact that the cost of affording service and providing you with assistance in the handling of our franchise; truly represents an expense and a loss in the small amount billed to you this year.

We have no desire to discontinue franchise and therefore advise you in advance that because of situation in general business volume, we have this year set a minimum of $5,000 volume on an accont that could be serviced to advantage for the year; this compares with $10,000 minimum used in 1929.

Your account for the year through October 25th shows purchases in the amount of $3,980; to reach our minimum requirement further purchases in November and December of $1,020 is necessary.

There has been during past fewweeks a decided pickup in the demand for our Greater Value ribbon and strap watches in $32.50, $35.00 and $37.50 range, to say nothing of the over demand on the 21/0 size American Beauty Series.

In bringing this matter to your attention now it seems reasonable that you can easily reach the volume of $5,000 for this year, therefore earn the 3% discount and enjoy taking 3% cash disoont in 1932.

Should this $5,000 volume not be reached this year and you wish to retain our franchise the watches you buy in 1932 would be billed at cost price, net, until volume set for that year is reached.

We are confident you can and will meet the goal required during these next two months.

Very truly yours,

THE ILLINOIS WATCH

JLK:ET

Sales Manager.

Keenan's discount letter

ONE WATCH FOR PERSONAL USE

As a special concession to jewelers that purchased Illinois watches, each jeweler was entitled to receive one watch at 25% off the jeweler's list price. According to the letter below, the jeweler was able to purchase a brand-new Andover model for a set price of $20.63. In 1934, Illinois, under Hamilton's direction, was to introduce an Illinois Sangamon men's wristwatch model with a list price at the record low price of $25.00.

PERSONAL USE

January 26, 1932.

PERSONAL
Mr. Bergman,
Bergman Company, Inc.,
409 So. 15th Street,
Omaha, Nebraska.

Dear Sir:

We were very pleased to learn through our representative Mr. J. Paul Branyen, that you are interested in the purchase of one of our Andover, 12/0 size, 17 jewel, strap watches in natural gold filled for your own use.

As a special concession to proprietors of jewelry stores we supply one watch for personal use on the basis of one-fourth off jewelers list price and we shall be glad to extend this courtesy to you.

Under this arrangement, one of the Andover watches, such as you desire, would cost you $20.63 net.

However, all transactions of this kind are on a cash basis, so when sending us your order kindly enclose your check for the correct amount and shipment of the watch will be made to you promptly.

We wish to compliment you upon the selection of the Andover for your own personal wear, and we feel confident that you will be well pleased with the attractiveness of this model, as well as the service which you receive from it.

Assuring you of our appreciation of your interest in Illinois watches, we are

Very sincerely yours,

THE ILLINOIS WATCH

AGS:ALD

By

Jewelers were allowed a special discount for one watch for personal use.

PROFIT SEEKING

During the Great Depression, the jewelry industry sought initiatives to stimulate store traffic revenue and profits by any reasonable means. One such initiative was to promote the sale of scarf pins. Another was a campaign to promote "National Watch Cleaning and Jewelry Repair Week."

The *Jewelers' Circular* was fully supporting National Watch Cleaning Week and published many articles to promote it; February 1932.

Watch Repair Week Proves Successful

1457 Stores Take Part in Nation-wide Event

NEW YORK CITY—An analysis of reports on National Watch Cleaning and Jewelry Repair Week held the week of Feb. 24 under auspices of the American National Retail Jewelers' Association shows that 1457 jewelers participated.

Every state in the Union, the District of Columbia, Canada and Hawaii had participants in the campaign and, in all, 853 cities and towns were represented. In New York 183 jewelers displayed the posters provided by the A. N. R. J. A.; in Pennsylvania 140, Illinois 89, Ohio 88, California 84, Massachusetts 73, and Wisconsin 64. Those participating in other states ranged in number from one to fifty.

"Considering that this was the first time that such a movement was undertaken by our industry, the results are gratifying," said Secretary Charles T. Evans, of the A. N. R. J. A. "We received requests for posters from retailers who heretofore have not participated in trade events, indicating that the promotion of watch cleaning and jewelry repair work has a widespread appeal.

"Unquestionably the results of this first attempt to educate the public through the retail stores to take better care of their watches and to have their jewelry repaired hold forth promise of far greater returns from similar movements in the future."

Observation of the progress of this campaign disclosed unmistakably that retail jewelers are aware that the future of their trade depends in no small part upon the efficiency and popularity of their repair departments.

Keystone, April 1932

REPAIR DEPARTMENT PROFITS

1932

Why Not Start This Ball Rolling Now?

(Left) *Jewelers' Circular*, January 1932; editorial cartoon supporting repair business

Sell Scarf Pins—Make Him Move Along!

Keystone, April 1932

Illinois Stamped Hamilton

It is possible that as the severe economic conditions hit, Hamilton contemplated and started to execute a production strategy in 1931 to eliminate the Illinois trade name as it planned the methodical shutdown of its Illinois Watch Division. The Hamilton internal records include an enlightening list of "Illinois Finished Movements."

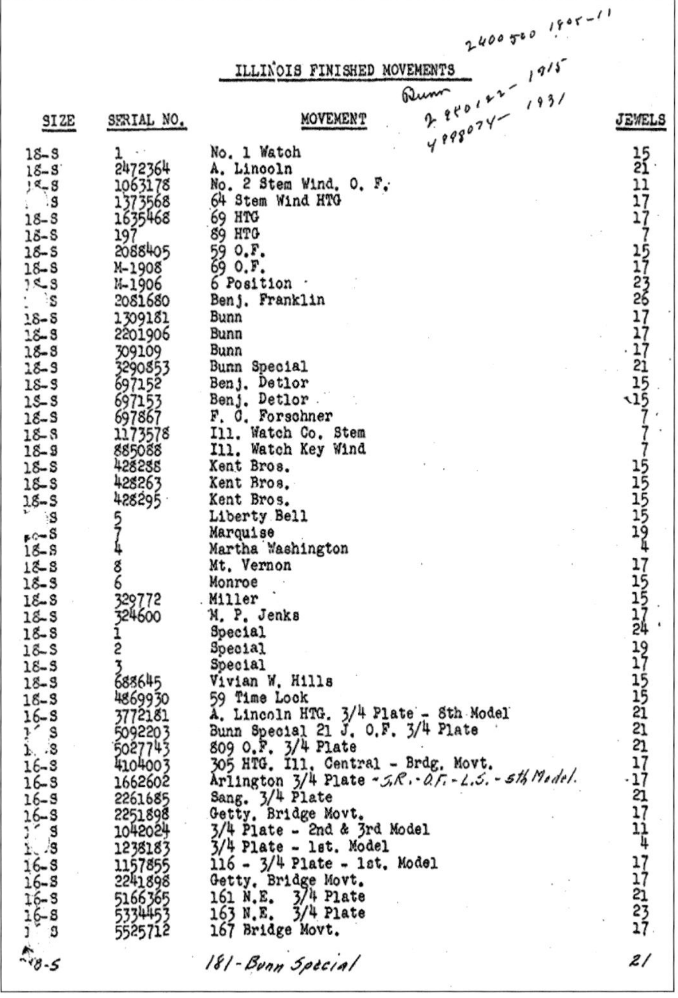

2400500 1905-11

ILLINOIS FINISHED MOVEMENTS

Bunn 2880122 – 1915
4998074 – 1931

SIZE	SERIAL NO.	MOVEMENT	JEWELS
18-S	1	No. 1 Watch	15
18-S	2472364	A. Lincoln	21
[illegible]-S	1063178	No. 2 Stem Wind. O. F.	11
[illegible]-S	1373568	64 Stem Wind HTG	17
18-S	1635468	69 HTG	17
18-S	197	89 HTG	7
18-S	2088405	59 O.F.	15
18-S	M-1908	69 O.F.	17
[illegible]-S	M-1906	6 Position	23
[illegible]-S	2081680	Benj. Franklin	26
18-S	1309181	Bunn	17
18-S	2201906	Bunn	17
18-S	309109	Bunn	17
18-S	3290853	Bunn Special	21
18-S	697152	Benj. Detlor	15
18-S	697153	Benj. Detlor	15
18-S	697867	F. C. Forschner	7
18-S	1173578	Ill. Watch Co. Stem	7
18-S	885088	Ill. Watch Key Wind	7
18-S	428288	Kent Bros.	15
18-S	428263	Kent Bros.	15
18-S	428295	Kent Bros.	15
[illegible]-S	5	Liberty Bell	15
[illegible]-S	7	Marquise	19
18-S	4	Martha Washington	4
18-S	8	Mt. Vernon	17
18-S	6	Monroe	15
18-S	329772	Miller	15
18-S	324600	M. P. Jenks	17
18-S	1	Special	24
18-S	2	Special	19
18-S	3	Special	17
18-S	688645	Vivian W. Hills	15
18-S	4869930	59 Time Lock	15
16-S	3772181	A. Lincoln HTG. 3/4 Plate - 8th Model	21
[illegible]-S	5092203	Bunn Special 21 J. O.F. 3/4 Plate	21
[illegible]-S	5027743	809 O.F. 3/4 Plate	21
16-S	4104003	305 HTG. Ill. Central - Brdg. Movt.	17
16-S	1662602	Arlington 3/4 Plate - S.R. - O.F. - L.S. - 5th Model.	17
16-S	2261685	Sang. 3/4 Plate	21
16-S	2251898	Getty. Bridge Movt.	17
[illegible]-S	1042024	3/4 Plate - 2nd & 3rd Model	11
[illegible]-S	1238183	3/4 Plate - 1st. Model	4
16-S	1157855	116 - 3/4 Plate - 1st. Model	17
16-S	2241898	Getty. Bridge Movt.	17
16-S	5166365	161 N.E. 3/4 Plate	21
16-S	5334453	163 N.E. 3/4 Plate	23
[illegible]-S	5525712	167 Bridge Movt.	17
[illegible]8-S		181 - Bunn Special	21

- 2 -

SIZE	SERIAL NO.	MOVEMENT	JEWELS
[illegible]-S	5497874	161-A 3/4 Plate	21
[illegible]-S	5448678	163-A 3/4 Plate	23
16-S	3704575	307 O.F. Bridge Movt. 7th Model	19
16-S	5417549	165 Ham. Ill. Bridge Movt. Grade 167	15
16-S	3705504	307 HTG Bridge Movt. 7th Model	19
16-S	3937445	707 O.F. Bridge Movt. 9th Model	19
[illegible]-S	5129569	706 O.F. Bridge Movt.	17
[illegible]-S	3800686	810 Ball Watch 3/4 Plate	23
16-S	4166853	Sang. Spec. Bridge Movt.	23
16-S	3915614	707 HTG Bridge Movt.	19
16-S	4557705	609 O.F. 3/4 Plate	21
16-S	4726167	Bunn 3/4 Plate	19
[illegible]-S	5180397	Bunn Spec. O.F. 3/4 Plate	23
[illegible]-S	5075391	305 O.F. Bridge Movt.	17
16-S	5269027	107 Burl. Bridge Move.	21
16-S	3900007	108 Burl. HTG Bridge Movt.	21
16-S	2998765	Benj. Franklin 3/4 Plate	25
16-S	5456332	Bunn Special Grade 163A 60 Hr. Elinvar	23
16-S	5417032	Illinois-Hamilton (Stamped "Hamilton") 167L	17
16-S	5511220	Bunn Special Grade 161A 60 Hr. Elinvar	21
16-S	5094030	Bunn Special 60 Hr.	21
14-S	1026011	123 3/4 Plate	15
14-S	1003003	120 3/4 Plate	7
14-S	1022993	993 120 Key Wind Full Plate	7
14-S	1028022	125 3/4 Plate	17
14-S	1022432	120 Full Plate	7
[illegible]-S	1020041	126 3/4 Plate	22
[illegible]4-S	1010187	3/4 Plate	11
12-S	4827726	Ill. Autocrat Grade 427 Thin Movt.	17
12-S	5469721	127 Illinois-Hamilton (Stamped "Hamilton")	17
12 T-S	3869193	Illini Bridge Movt.	21
12 T-S	4677225	527 A. Lincoln 3/4 Plate	19
12 T-S	4905458	525 Marg. Auto. 3/4 Plate	17
12-S	4979311	127 Bridge Movt.	17
12-S	1933411	219 O.F. Bridge Movt.	11
12-S	4511041	405 O.F. Bridge Movt.	17
12-S	1685763	273 Bridge Movt.	17
12-S	5278287	279 O.F. 3/4 Plate	21
12-S	2410259	Bridge Movt.	11
[illegible]-S	4056573	407 HTG. 3/4 Plate	19
[illegible]-S	B407371	417 O.F. Ball 3/4 Plate	19
12-S	4478152	A. Lincoln O.F. Bridge Movt.	21
12-S	5005810	275 O.F. Burl. Bridge Movt.	21
12-S	2960378	404 O.F. Bridge Movt.	17
12-S	3911079	275 HTG. Burl. Bridge Movt.	21
[illegible]-S	4395062	Sterling 3/4 Plate	21
[illegible]-S	3221916	Santa Fe Special 3/4 Plate	21
12-S	1780701	273 Bridge Movt.	17
12-S	4757802	Autocrat Bridge Movt.	17
12-S	3742319	470 O.F. Bridge Movt.	23
12-S	3225865	Bridge Movt.	15
[illegible]-S	3820317	405 HTG. Ill. Central Bridge Movt.	17

\- 3 -

SIZE	SERIAL NO.	MOVEMENT	JEWELS
[illegible]-S	3031573	255 Ill. Stewart Bridge Movt.	17
[illegible]S	4478962	A. Lincoln HTG Bridge Movt.	21
12-S	4951825	415 O.F. Bridge Movt.	17
12-S	4395435	410 Bridge Movt.	23
12-S	3959541	509 Bridge Movt.	19
12/14-S	4111911	Ariston Semi Bridge	17
12/14-S	2386748	Ariston Semi Bridge	21
[illegible]14-S	2406153	Ariston Semi Bridge	21
8-S	520611	154 Stem Wind 3/4 Plate	17
8-S	104805	151 Stem Wind 3/4 Plate	11
8-S	100322	Key Wind	7
6-S	1158895	143 Stem Wind 3/4 Plate	15
6-S	1167942	149 Stem Wind 3/4 Plate	15
[illegible]	1488184	3/4 Plate	17
6-S	924537	Full Plate	7
6-S	1671978	166 Stem Wind 3/4 Plate	17
4-S	714342	3/4 Plate	16
0/0-S	1825432	33 3/4 Plate	11
3/0-S	2994587	23 HTG Bridge Movt.	15
3/0-S	5194337	24 HTG. Bridge Movt.	17
3/0-S	5536799	207 Illinois-Hamilton (Stamped "Hamilton")	17
6/0-S		Illinois Movement 607	17
6/0-S		Illinois Movement 607	17
6/0-S	5427420	Illinois Movement 607	17
6/0-S		Illinois Movement 607	17
6/0-S	5408813	Illinois Movement 607	17
[illegible]-S	5435046	Illinois Movement 607	17
[illegible]0-S	5514855	Illinois-Hamilton (stamped "Hamilton")	17
6/0-S	5642187	Illinois Grade 605	15
6/0-S	4917700	903 O.F. Bridge Movt.	15
6/0-S	4241165	909 O.F. Bridge Movt.	21
6/0-S	4832878	907 O.F. Bridge Movt.	19
6/0-S	5051702	905 O.F. Bridge Movt.	17
6/0-S	5475148	605 Bridge Movt.	15
6/0-S	5541645	607 Bridge Movt.	17
6/0-S	5463066	607 Jump Hour	17
6/0-S	93147	605E	16
6/0-S	3286370	1st Model 3/4 Pl., O.F., P.S.	15
12/0-S	5453577	207	17
[illegible]/0-S	5384197	Illinois Grade 207 17J	17
[illegible]0-S	5486600	Illinois Movement 807A	17
18/0-S	5630035	Illinois Grade 805	15
18/0-S	5530432	807A Illinois-Hamilton (Stamped "Hamilton")	17
18/0-S	5014517	807 3/4 Plate	17
18/0-S	5517954	807A 3/4 Plate	17
[illegible]/0-S	4870181	806	16
[illegible]0-S	4484249	206	16
18/0-S	5644541	805E	15
18/0-S	5674447	805	15
21/0-S	5624011	Illinois 107	17
21/0-S	5665038	Illinois Grade 107	17
[illegible]/0-S	5670906	107 3/4/ Plate	17

\- 4 -

SIZE	SERIAL NO.	MOVEMENT	JEWELS
[illegible]0-S	5690414	105 3/4 Plate	15
[illegible]-S		Illinois Unfinished Model	
		"Incabloc" Shock Absorbing Device	
	57081	Ill. Sang. Escape	11
		Mosler Time Lock (Less escapement) (Illinois)	
		Mosler Time Lock (Complete) (Illinois)	

1900	1,000,000
1910	3,000,000
1930	5,100,000
1940	5,650,000

This undated list, possibly prepared by Lowell Halligan in the early 1940s, mentions 16-size, 12-size, 3/0 size, 6/0 size and 18/0 size Illinois movements with specific serial numbers and the notation "Illinois-Hamilton (Stamped 'Hamilton')." For example: "18/0-s, 5530432, 807A "Illinois-Hamilton (Stamped 'Hamilton')." Thus, post-acquisition Illinois movements in these sizes were produced in the Illinois Factory and stamped "Hamilton U.S.A." instead of "Illinois Watch Company." We know of the existence of one of these 6/0 size movements because René Rondeau discovered an Illinois grade 607, 17-jewel, 6/0 size movement in an Illinois New Yorker case with "Hamilton U.S.A." signed on its plate in place of Illinois.[12] Although no other 6/0 size movement so signed has been located to date, the movement with the "stamped Hamilton" notation from the list of Illinois Finished Movements List has a different serial number from the one 6/0 movement that has surfaced. We also now know that three 3/0 size as well as three 16-size Illinois movements have been found stamped "Hamilton U.S.A." on their plates.

The data collected to date concerning these special and very rare movements are shown here.

16-size movements:

- The list of Illinois Finished Movements identifies movement number 5,417,032, produced in 1931, as stamped "Hamilton."
- Illinois production records disclose that the above movement was part of a run in 1931 of 1,000 grade 167, 16-size movements with serial numbers ranging from 5,417,001 to 5,418,000.
- Therefore, the movement noted in the Hamilton records was the 32nd produced in that production run.
- We do not know if only one or all 1,000 in this production run were stamped "Hamilton."

12-size movements:

- The list of Illinois Finished Movements identifies movement number 5,469,721, produced in 1931, as stamped "Hamilton."
- The list of Illinois Finished Movements discloses that the above movement was part of a run in 1931 of 2,000, grade 127, 12-size movements with serial numbers from 5,468,001 to 5,470,000.
- Therefore, the movements noted in the Hamilton records was the 1,721st produced in that production run.
- We do not know if only one or all 2,000 in this product run were stamped "Hamilton."

3/0 size movements:

- The list of Illinois Finished Movements identifies movement number 5,536,799, produced in 1932, as stamped "Hamilton."
- Illinois production records disclose the above movement was part of a run in 1932 of 2,000 grade 307, 3/0 size, 17-jewel movements with serial numbers ranging from 5,536,001 to 5,538,000.
- Therefore, the movement noted in the Hamilton records was the 799th produced in that production run.
- Three grade 307, size 3/0 movements have been found stamped "Hamilton" —two of which have serial numbers 5,536,772 and 5,537,098 respectively.
- We do not know if only three or all 2,000 in this production run were stamped "Hamilton."

A 6/0 size, 607 grade Illinois movement stamped "Hamilton"

6/0 size movements:

- The list of Illinois Finished Movements identifies movement number 5,514,855, produced in 1932, as stamped "Hamilton."
- Illinois production records disclose the above movement was part of a run in 1932 of 2,000 grade 607, 6/0 size, 17-jewel movements with serial numbers ranging from 5,514,001 to 5,516,000.

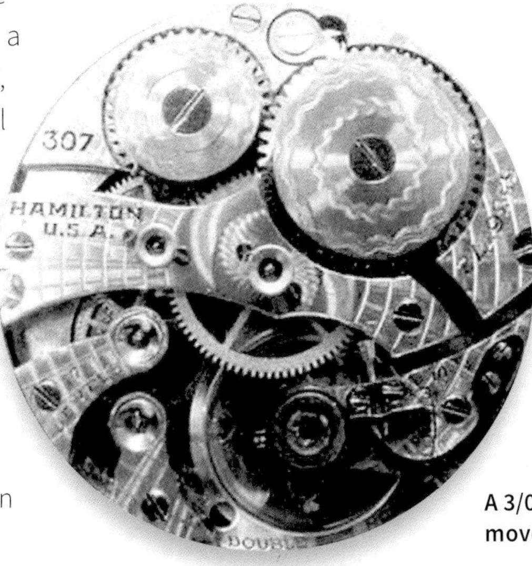

A 3/0 size, 307 grade, 17-jewel Illinois movement stamped "Hamilton"

- Therefore, the movement noted in the Hamilton records was the 855th produced in that production run.
- We know of the existence of one such 6/0 movement stamped "Hamilton." This known 6/0 size movement has serial number 5,514,697, or the 697th movement produced in that production run.
- We do not know if only one or all 2,000 in this production run were stamped "Hamilton."

18/0 size movements:

- The list of Illinois Finished Movements identifies movement number 5,530,432, produced in 1931, as stamped "Hamilton."
- Illinois production records disclose that the above movement was part of a run in 1931 of 3,000, grade 807A, 18/0 size, 17-jewel movements with serial numbers ranging from 5,528,001 to 5,531,000.
- Therefore, the movement noted in the Hamilton records was the 2,432nd produced in that production run.
- We do not know if one or all 3,000 in this production run were stamped "Hamilton."

These new findings indicate it is possible that Hamilton had the entire production runs listed above stamped "Hamilton." It is quite likely that when the effects of the Depression started to hit, Hamilton wanted to start branding in 1931 these products in the Hamilton name and discontinue the use of the Illinois name. But if all of these were so stamped, why have only seven of these specially stamped movements been located to date? One can only speculate. Perhaps they were stamped Hamilton, but then Hamilton decided not to use them and replaced that portion of the movement plate with one rightfully stamped "Illinois." If so, it is possible that a few were missed and ultimately found their way to the open market.

If all of these movements (totaling 10,000) were stamped "Hamilton," we would have expected more than seven of them to have surfaced by now. Therefore, maybe all movements in the production runs noted above were not stamped "Hamilton," or if they were, Hamilton decided not to use them and replaced the plates as noted. It is a certainty that they were not scrapped.

If these were small runs of movements all stamped "Hamilton," it could explain why only seven are known to exist. Also, all signed movements found have serial numbers that occur within production runs, and it would have been unlikely for Illinois to disrupt its production line at an odd place and insert a Hamilton-signed plate. If Illinois had wanted to do this for Hamilton, we would expect the movement number to be either the first in the production series or the last one, but not in between.

It is most likely that Hamilton had decided to stop marketing these watches as Illinois and to change all Illinois movements and dials to be Hamilton ones. If so, Hamilton had contemplated abandoning Illinois sales and converting all of the Illinois watches to Hamiltons as early as 1931, when the economy started to falter badly. But then Hamilton had a change of heart, probably recognizing the potential, costly good-will write-off it would have encountered. One last possibility is that the movements were used for European sales; but again, if so, why have so few been sighted?

1931
HISTORICAL NOTES

- United States unemployment doubles to 16.3% (eight million people).
- The Empire State Building in New York City is completed.
- Japan invades Manchuria in China.
- Nevada legalizes gambling.
- Prices of consumer goods drop an estimated 17% from 1930.

Pocket Watch Inventory Reduction

To further reduce inventory, Hamilton was resorting to any measure to exhaust the Illinois pocket watch stock. Michael Chamelin, an authority on Bunn Specials, writes: "During the Great Depression of the early 1930s, we know due to very slow sales, that Hamilton decided to reduce the inventory of remaining 'Pre Elinvar' [Illinois] watches for wholesale prices or even less! Around this time period as well, some [Bunn Special] movement inventory was even placed in NON Bunn Special cases by the factory and offered for sale in this more 'humble' fashion."[13]

Hamilton's Reaction to 1931

In the February 1932 issue of the *Jewelers' Circular,* Beckwith described the effects of the preceding year:

> We have all passed through perhaps one of the most trying years in our experience—a year that has tried men's souls. The time will come when we shall look back upon 1930 and 1931 as history, and be stronger for having conquered.
>
> We have watched a tall tree swaying in a storm until it seemed about to be blown down, but often we find instead that it has sent its roots deeper and wider and thus secured a firmer grip by reason of what it had to undergo. So it has been with us in the past year.
>
> Let us be optimistic in a true sense, facing facts courageously, keeping our vision clear and holding faith in each other. I am sure we have much to be thankful for and that the star of Hope still shines in its ascendancy.

Hamilton was about to suffer in 1932 and 1933 the only two years of losses in its history to this point. These losses greatly influenced its views toward and plans for its Illinois Watch Division.

Watch Industry Issues in 1932

On January 6, 1932, the *Illinois State Journal* published a message from Robert E. Miller to Illinois Watch employees. Echoing the theme already stated by Beckwith about the wicked 1931 period, Miller said, in part:

> We are glad that 1931 is now a closed chapter in the book of experiences. We have been confronted during the past two years with not only a depression in our own industry, but a nation-wide and an international economic depression. We cannot hope for a return of normal satisfactory business until the factors which create this international economic situation are bettered, and until the world politically, socially and economically is on a more even keel.
>
> In the meantime, and during the trying period through which we are passing, it behooves us to put our house in order from a manufacturing and internal standpoint. This we have been doing during the past year, and are continuing to do as rapidly and as safely as possible . . .
>
> . . . the management pledges itself to do everything within its power to provide the maximum employment for the greatest number in 1932, consistent with the condition of the business and the shrinkage of volume and profit in the watch and jewelry business throughout the country.
>
> It is a well-known fact that depressions in the past were followed by higher levels of prosperity, and we may hope that this period will not be an exception to this rule. Then possibly we will look back on 1931 as history and will feel that we are stronger for having been through it. [Author's note: These were almost exactly the words used by his boss Beckwith.]
>
> We have found great encouragement in the message from the new president of our company, Mr. Beckwith, when he said 'Let us be optimistic in a true sense, facing facts courageously, keeping our vision clear, and holding faith in each other...

Unfortunately, the year 1932 turned out to be a rough one for Illinois, Hamilton and everyone else in the watch industry.

Closeouts at Elgin

Elgin reported in February 1932: "We have now completed our program of closing out discontinued models of Elgin watches at reduced prices and there are no more available. A few still remaining in some of the wholesaler's stocks should not now interfere with . . . regular purchases of Elgin watches and movements."[14] It is not clear whether this closeout related just to pocket watches or whether it applied to wristwatches as well. However, it is likely that there were discontinued wristwatch models and Elgin wished to clear them out of its stock.

Cuts at Waltham

Although Waltham acted expeditiously to cut heads in 1930, "its reduction of wages was long delayed," Moore points out. "The volume of orders dwindled, and the schedule of operations at Waltham was curtailed more and more to keep pace with the falling demand. Finally, in the first weeks of 1932, the payroll was reduced to a mere handful of workers. In the week of January 30 there were only 311 employees remaining; the plant was practically closed." On February 8, 1932, Waltham announced a drastic cut of 30% in wages. As its orders dwindled, it "curtailed more and more operations to keep pace with falling demand."[15]

Waltham's plan to cut workers, wages and prices made it possible to keep its plant open. The losses in 1932 were half of its 1931 loss and total hours of employment increased 8% above 1931 levels, but total wages fell 24%. Production was allowed to rise from "a virtual standstill in the early months of 1932 to a rate that was better than the national average."[16]

Although there is no documentation that Illinois had reduced wages, it is very likely that Hamilton, following the Waltham example, was reducing wages in Springfield. Hamilton had no hesitation in implementing strong austerity measures at its Illinois Watch Division.

Depression in the Swiss Watch Industry

The period from 1931 through 1933 would prove to be devastating for most watchmakers, domestic and global. As early as March 29, 1930, the association of Swiss Gold Watch Case Manufacturers had already introduced a 35-hour work week in all factories because of a decrease in orders. In April 1932, it was reported in the industry press that the Geneva watch industry in 1931 had the lowest results in its history. The number of people out of work was so great that the Canton of Geneva granted watch industry employees out-of-work unemployment benefits distributed over the whole year, at the rate of three days of each week.[17]

Swiss watch movement exports to the United States for the fourth quarter of 1931 totaled $19,880 compared to $74,776 in 1930.[18] This was a drop of 73.5%.

Overcapacity

Moore reported that Waltham was in a "sharp struggle" for a share of the 1932 watch market. The capacity of the American watch industry was far too great for the demand, resulting in "cutthroat competition." The capacity of the domestic industry was estimated at 3,700,000 movements; actual production in 1928 was 1,741,495 movements; and in 1932, it was down to 434,441. This represented a contraction of 75% over five years.[19]

Furthermore, overcapacity also existed in Switzerland—so much so that the Swiss Government prohibited "the opening of new enterprises in the watchmaking industry, or enlargement, transformation, or transfer of existing properties without the authorization of the Department of Public Economy."[20]

According to Moore, "competition from Swiss imports was kept partially in check by the Smoot-Hawley Tariff Act of 1930 but the Swiss manufacturers continued to get the lion's share of the United States market."[21]

In 1926, pocket watch production was 60% of Waltham's sales. By 1932, wristwatch production was at 80% and pocket watches were down to 20% of total production.[22] Hamilton lagged woefully behind this trend line.[23]

President Roosevelt eventually relented to Swiss government pressure and the tariff was rolled back by 34% on jeweled watch movements. This further exacerbated the problems of America watch producers.[24]

Assembling Imported Parts

For a while, the high tariffs held in check the assembling of foreign parts into watches in the United States. But when the tariffs were reduced, such watch assemblers were able to grow and compete strongly against American watch producers. Thus, in 1932, American watch manufacturers faced:

- Overcapacity in the United States market;
- Organized Swiss competition;
- Cheap foreign labor;
- Weak tariff protection;
- Rampant smuggling;

WATCH SMUGGLING

The United States wristwatch industry was harmed not only by overcapacity and cutthroat competition but also by watch smuggling and the assembling of foreign watch parts in American factories.

Smuggling increased rapidly after the passage of the Smoot-Hawley Tariff Act, becoming a thriving industry of its own. And even lower priced watch items entered the American marketplace when seized items were sold for drastically lowered prices at public auctions.

Federal Agents Seize Large Shipment of Watch Movements

WORKING under Alvin McK. Sylvester, Assistant U. S. District Attorney, federal agents at New York City on Oct. 25 seized a large shipment of smuggled watch movements, valued at about $100,000, and arrested Richard Beishuns and Henry Sacks.

This is the second large seizure made recently under the direction of Mr. Sylvester who prosecuted and convicted the members of two watch smuggling rings a few years ago. Beishuns was a member of one of those rings and was sent to Atlanta prison for a year and a day.

The movements were brought to the United States from Amsterdam enclosed in bales of rabbit furs which are admitted duty free. Through information from abroad, the federal agents were on the lookout but did not make the seizure until the bales of fur were claimed and delivery made to Sacks and Beishuns.

Keystone, November 1932

Smuggled Watch Movements to Be Sold at Utica, N. Y., April 17

UTICA, N. Y., March 21—A large number of Swiss watches, 2052 in all, of an appraised value of $10,294, will be sold by the United States Marshal at room 307 of the Federal bldg., in this city, Wednesday, April 19, at 2 p. m. These watches were seized from Sol Seidman and Samuel Simon at Rouses Point, N. Y., Dec. 8 last, and forfeited under Section 497 of the Tariff Act on the ground that they were smuggled.

United States Marshal William N. Cromie is naturally anxious that the property realize as much as possible and is endeavoring to get bids from members of the jewelry trade who will pay a proper price for the merchandise.

Under the statute, all smuggled merchandise seized and forfeited must be sold at public auction but as sometimes the prices realized have been even less than the duty on the articles, these sales have caused distinct protest from the jewelers, inasmuch as they have permitted articles to come back into the trade at prices that no legitimate concern can compete with. The marshal sales have not been widely attended by legitimate dealers and often the goods have gone back into the hands of smugglers or of price cutters to the detriment of the industry.

Marshal Cromie is, therefore, endeavoring to interest the jewelers to come to this sale both for the sake of the revenue to the government and in the interests of their own industry.

This article, dated April 17, 1933, further emphasizes the point made by American watch manufacturers that the public auction of smuggled parts at drastic price reductions further exacerbated the plight of domestic watchmakers.

Waltham Official Estimates That 200,000 Swiss Movements Are Smuggled Into U. S. Annually

In a statement to the *Associated Press* on Feb. 9, I. E. Boucher, general manager of the Waltham Watch Co., Waltham, Mass., said that in his opinion the 92,000 illegally imported Swiss watch movements which have been seized by customs officials during a four-year period represent but one-tenth of the total number of movements being smuggled into this country.

The value of the confiscated movements he placed at $366,915, which represented, he said, a loss of 1,800,000 hours of employment to American labor.

"Through auctions," the press dispatch states, "the Federal government received $95,528 from the sale of 60,456 seized movements, but, if the confiscated material had come into the country legally, duty of about $240,000 would have been collected."

A February 1933 article shows the continued Waltham concern about the smuggling of Swiss movements into the United States.

- Public auctioning of smuggled items at greatly reduced prices;
- Domestic assembly of Swiss parts; and
- Aggressive selling tactics by importers of watches.

As a result, Waltham, Hamilton and Illinois (among others) were compelled at this time to reduce their prices to fight for market share.

INGERSOLL LOWERS PRICES

Elgin, Hamilton, Illinois and Waltham were not alone in trying to recover business by lowering prices. Prices on the entire Ingersoll line of watches, already at an industry low, were reduced in May 1932 by the Waterbury Clock Company to "speedily and surely bring back prosperity."

Ingersoll's famous "Yankee" watch was brought back to its original dollar price and its "Climax" watch was set at a new low of $2.50.

But even Ingersoll would face receivership in the near future, notwithstanding its price-reduction efforts.

Uphill Battle

Although by 1932 the full force of the Great Depression had already been hitting the watch and jewelry industry with a vengeance, it took quite a while for the editors of the *Jewelers' Circular* to finally realize that the year was an "Uphill battle for everybody." Of course, they used their editorial proclamation to secure more advertising revenue, as their May 1932 "Advertorial" indicates.

100 THE JEWELERS' CIRCULAR May, 1932

It's an Uphill Battle

This year, 1932, is an uphill battle for everybody. It is a fight for business that plays no favorites. Dealers are fighting for every dollar's worth of business they get. Manufacturers and wholesalers are fighting—and while every man is fighting for himself—he is fighting for the industry.

Advertising is going to create more business. To do a good advertising job, two things are necessary—a good line of merchandise and an unalterable confidence in one's mechandising ability.

The wise genius who penned the lines—"Good Goods well bought are more than half sold" was undoubtedly talking about the Jewelry Industry; for the jeweler is the selector of merchandise for his community—he is the determining factor in the profitable distribution of Jewelry and Allied Lines.

It is acknowledged that he controls 80% of the sales in his store. In other words, eight out of ten consumers who walk out of the jewelry store with purchases have bought that which the jeweler has recommended.

It is of prime importance, therefore, no matter what other distribution plans are in mind, that an advertising message be directed consistently and in a dominating way to the retail jeweler through an impartial, unbiased, all-inclusive source—his business paper.

The logical medium for such regular message is THE JEWELERS' CIRCULAR, because of its tremendously improved editorial content and its stable editorial policy, its paid Circulation Leadership and Greater Reader Interest.

THE JEWELERS' CIRCULAR with the largest paid circulation of all Jewelry publications, A. B. C., continues its 63 years of Leadership as the recognized authority of the Jewelry Industry.

Jewelers' Circular, May 1932

Hamilton's Responses in 1932

Combined Material Sales

As a further cost reduction and restructuring measure, Beckwith announced on February 14, 1932, that the material sales departments of the Hamilton and Illinois Watch Divisions would be combined into one and managed out of Lancaster by Harry Ruthhart. This was a prudent but telling move by Beckwith that the winding down of the Illinois Watch Division was in process.

Reduced Illinois Hours

The impact of the Depression on the normal operations of the Illinois Watch Division is reflected in a draft memorandum written by its sales manager, Jack L. Keenan, on March 7, 1932. Keenan stated, dramatically:

> Every conceivable means have been exercised so that the one thousand families here in Springfield, Illinois who depend upon the income devised by some member of that family in our plant, can be clothed and fed.
>
> Continuing lack of sales made it necessary to reduce working time. Now after two years we have found it to be entirely proper to place in the market at this off season period a quantity of watches—the manufacture of which was discontinued last year.

HARRY A. RUTHHART (1881-1968)

Harry Ruthhart, August 1951

On August 31, 1951, Harry Albert Ruthhart, material sales manager of Hamilton, retired after fifty-four years of service. He started at Hamilton in 1897 as an errand boy at the age of fifteen in the motion department. He later became assistant foreman of this department and continued in that capacity until August 1, 1926, when he was named to head the material sales department. In 1928, when Hamilton purchased Illinois, Ruthhart was given the responsibility of supervising Illinois' material sales until Hamilton closed the Illinois Factory and the material stocks were incorporated with the inventory at the Lancaster plant.

Ruthhart served under every Hamilton president to the point of his retirement.

Hamilton Watch Company

MANUFACTURERS OF

The Watch of Railroad Accuracy

LANCASTER, PA., U.S.A.

OFFICE OF THE PRESIDENT

February 16, 1932.

Mr. Ruthhart's activities in connection with material sales have been handicapped for some time by his additional duties as Manager of our Service Department. In order to permit Mr. Ruthhart actively to promote material sales both for our Hamilton and Illinois Divisions, it has been decided to relieve him of Service Department responsibilities as rapidly as the separation of activities can be effected.

Effective this date, Mr. Pollard will assume the duties of Manager of the Service Department, and Mr. Ruthhart will be in full charge of material sales for both Hamilton and Illinois Watch Divisions.

Bruce C. Beckwith

President

Announcement of Harry Ruthhart becoming head of both Illinois and Hamilton Material Sales, February 16, 1932

> This amount is less than one-fourth of our usual yearly volume. By moving this inventory, we make it possible to give employment to our faithful workers this Spring.

Thus, Illinois, suffering severely from the Great Depression, and with its parent Hamilton in the throes of the worst financial year in its history, was compelled not only to reduce employee hours, almost four years after Hamilton had instituted a draconian 23% reduction in the Illinois workforce, but also to rerelease products whose manufacture had already been discontinued in Springfield. These moves, however, resulted in continued but reduced hours for the employees and the potential for reduced but continued sales.

Whereas Elgin was dropping prices to move discontinued models, Illinois was reintroducing ones that had previously been discontinued. It is doubtful that Hamilton was of the view that this would lead to resurgent sales. At best, it was a holding pattern to see whether market conditions would improve, as well as a means to further reduce inventory. Regrettably, sales would never recover for Illinois because when the market finally began to improve, Illinois had been stripped of its ability to fulfill orders.

From Keenan's draft of March 7, 1932, it is known for the first time that the Illinois Factory suffered from "continued lack of sales" for the two previous years. Because of the struggling economy, already in the midst of the Great Depression, there was a huge negative impact on Illinois sales, its ability to keep its plant operating at full capacity and its ability to offer new watch models. This is also another explanation as to why there are so few Illinois wristwatches available for collectors today. Illinois was producing less than 25% of its usual annual volume of watches in the 1931–1932 time period and beyond. Indeed, very few completed watches were produced from 1930 through mid-1933, while Illinois was methodically being shuttered by Hamilton. And we now know that even fewer Illinois watches were being offered and sold between 1933 and 1935.

Chamelin notes that "the once mighty Illinois Watch Company with so many pocket watch models to choose from, had very little to be excited about in 1932. There were only four 16 size pocket watches listed [in its sales catalog]; a little over a half a dozen wrist watches to pick from and less than half a dozen of the small 12 size pocket watches."[25]

WAR AGAINST DEPRESSION

In an March 1932 announcement in the *Jewelers' Circular,* Illinois joined the War Against Depression campaign to support the efforts of the American Legion, the American Federation of Labor and the Association of National Advertisers to help American employment by asking merchants to buy American made products, stating that "American people do not want to purchase foreign made watches." At the same time, other countries, such as England, Germany and France, were urging their businesses to buy only British-, German- or French-made domestic products, respectively.

112 THE JEWELERS' CIRCULAR March, 1932

RECONSTRUCTION

***by* UNITED ACTION:**

The American Legion, American Federation of Labor, and the Association of National Advertisers, are sponsoring *War Against Depression Campaign* by *United Action for Employment.* The Illinois Watch is a party to this great movement.

American merchandise must be sold to increase American employment. England's slogan is "Buy British Goods in Great Britain." France, Germany, and other foreign countries are sponsoring similar campaigns.

What is America to do? What part will the Jewelry industry play?

We are doing our part to help American Employment. The greatest value is represented in American merchandise. American people do not want to purchase foreign made watches.

Your best merchandising plan is to fill your windows with American-made merchandise. Tell the people you are a party to this action for employment. Win the admiration of your community and the great organizations that are sponsoring the movement.

***The* ILLINOIS WATCH**

Springfield, Illinois

March 1933 Reconstruction advertisement in the *Jewelers' Circular*

Hamilton's "Slightly" Downward Pricing

In response to the extended down market, Hamilton announced "To the Retail Jewelers of America," in a full-page advertisement in the March 1932 issue of the *Jewelers' Circular*, that a "slightly downward pricing of Hamilton watches to wholesalers, retailers and consumers went into effect on March 1, 1932. This is the Hamilton Watch Company's answer to the demand of a new economic era for orderly adjustment."

Hamilton added it that it had "protected its market for the past two years at considerable sacrifice of sales volume. It has made this contribution to you that prices might be stabilized and to insure you a profit on your Hamilton watch sales. The company has consistently avoided drastic price reductions that would obsolete large portions of your stock of Hamilton watches." With respect to the new lower prices, Hamilton pointed out that it was "taking a loss on that point of its inventory made under higher production costs."

Page 66 The KEYSTONE March, 1932

You Can Depend On HAMILTON!

To the Retail Jewelers of America:

- A slightly downward pricing of Hamilton watches to wholesalers, retailers and consumers, will go into effect on March 1, 1932. This is the Hamilton Watch Company's answer to the demand of a new economic era for orderly adjustment. Manufacturing economies made possible by changed conditions have been adopted without sacrifice of Hamilton quality, which always comes first.
- Hamilton has protected its market for the past two years at considerable sacrifice of sales volume. It has made this contribution to you that prices might be stabilized and to insure you a profit on your Hamilton watch sales. The company has consistently avoided drastic price reductions that would obsolete large portions of your stock of Hamilton watches.
- Hamilton intends to insure with its March 1st repricing, that stabilization which is lacking today on many other products throughout the industry. The Hamilton Watch Company is taking a loss on that part of its inventory made under higher production costs. There is still a fair profit for you from the Hamilton watches now in your stock even at the new consumer prices. There is a slightly greater profit for you in the repriced Hamilton line which you can now purchase with assurance.
- The Hamilton Watch Company is determined to prove to the jewelry industry that a time-honored, prestige and quality product like its watches can survive this, another of America's recurrent economic crises without loss of face, value and acceptance.
- We are confident this will be welcome news to the entire jewelry industry. You can be assured that Hamilton policies will remain constant. We are determined, as always, to keep Hamilton, America's finest high-grade timepiece. We have every confidence in the future of the retail jewelry structure of America. You, in turn, can depend on Hamilton just as you always have.
- Write to your wholesaler for the new Hamilton retail price list and further details.

HAMILTON WATCH COMPANY

***Keystone*, March 1932**

A. C. BECKEN GIVING A DEED OF TRUST

Bad industry-related financial events continued to multiply into 1932. In March the A. C. Becken Co., one of the largest wholesale jewelers and diamond importers in the United States, executed a Deed of Trust. The trustee took possession on March 16 as Becken was unable to raise funds for operating expenses and maturing liabilities.

On January 25, 1929, in far more buoyant times, Becken had consummated its acquisition of two of its largest competitors. But these mergers, like the Hamilton ones for Illinois and then Sangamo, were to turn what was considered prudent business strategies into failed ones owing to the intervening economic collapse.

A very reluctant Hamilton, always ultraprotective of its bottom line and brand value, was finally compelled to announce lower prices in an attempt to start rebounding from its economic doldrums. Other watch entities, such as Waltham and Elgin, had started reducing prices much earlier. Hamilton was using, and would continue to use, its "Illinois brand" as its principal low-price offering in an attempt to protect the image and prestige of the "Hamilton brand" name for as long as possible.

Illinois April 1932 Price List

It is noteworthy that of the men's models in the Price List for Illinois Greater Value Watches, dated April 1, 1932, only the Andover and Metropolitan were actual completely new releases. The rest were reissues from prior years, some with different dials or with metal bracelets instead of leather straps.

RETAIL JEWELERS

PRICE LIST

ILLINOIS

Greater Value

WATCHES

APRIL 1, 1932

KEYSTONE LIST
CONSUMER

RETAIL JEWELERS

ILLINOIS
Greater Value
WATCHES

PRICE LIST—APRIL 1, 1932

LADIES WATCHES

GRADE 805, 18/0 SIZE, 15 JEWELS	Consumer	Keystone List
Sylvia	$32.50	$40.00
Rita	35.00	40.00
Florentine	37.50	40.00
Elissa	37.50	40.00
Glenna (14K filled attachment)	42.50	44.00
Barbara (Silk cord attachment)	42.50	41.60
Lakewood (14K gold)	47.50	47.50
Princess (14K gold)	50.00	50.00
Greta (14K gold)	50.00	50.00
GRADE 807, 18/0 SIZE, 17 JEWELS		
Argyle (14K gold)	60.00	67.00
GRADE 107, 21/0 SIZE, 17 JEWELS		
Coquette	52.50	55.00
Charmette	52.50	55.00
Minuette	52.50	55.00
Annette (14K filled attachment)	60.00	60.00
Alouette (14K gold)	65.00	68.50

RAILROAD WATCHES

GRADE 161A, 21 JEWELS, SIX POSITIONS		
Bunn Special Elinvar, 14K filled	65.00	72.00
Bunn Special Elinvar, 10K filled	60.00	65.00
Engraved case extra	2.00	1.50
GRADE 163A, 23 JEWELS, SIX POSITIONS		
Bunn Special Elinvar, 14K filled	75.00	81.50
Bunn Special Elinvar, 10K filled	70.00	74.50
Engraved case extra	2.00	1.50

Above Railroad Watches available in case styles 107, 108, 206, 29. See illustrations, New Spring 1932 Catalogue.

MEN'S WATCHES

GRADE 605, 6/0 SIZE, 15 JEWELS	Consumer	Keystone List
Beau Geste	$35.00	$40.00
Arlington	37.50	42.00
Commodore	37.50	42.00
Yorktown	37.50	42.00
Metropolitan	40.00	42.00
Bostonian (14K filled attachment)	47.50	46.50
GRADE 607, 6/0 SIZE, 17 JEWELS		
Ritz	42.50	48.40
Blackstone	42.50	48.40
Derby	42.50	48[illegible]
GRADE 207, 12/0 SIZE, RECTANGULAR, 17 JEWELS		
Larchmont	52.50	55.00
Andover	52.50	55.00
Finalist	55.00	55.00
Futura	55.00	55.00
Hudson (A.N.D.)	60.00	60.00
Kenilworth	60.00	63.20
Vernon (14K filled attachment)	60.00	60.00
Rockliffe (14K gold A.N.D.)	75.00	80.00
GRADE 427, 17 JEWELS, 12 SIZE THIN POCKET WATCH		
Springfield (14K gold A.N.D.)	75.00	78.00

UNCASED WATCHES

Grade 167, 16 Size, 17 J., L.S. or P.S.	24.00	25.20
Grade 127, 12 Size, 17 J., Open Face	25.00	25.80
*Grade 605, 6/0 Size, 15 J., cased at Factory	......	....
*Grade 805, 18/0 Size, 15 J., cased at Factory	......	....
*Grade 107, 21/0 Size, 17 J., cased at Factory	......	....

* *Casing at Factory.*

Illinois Price List, April 1932

New Low-Priced Illinois

Complementing its parent's pricing moves, Illinois was heavily emphasizing its new low-priced models. In a June 1932 advertisement, Illinois introduced two sterling silver ladies' models: the Lady Mary and Queen Anne, at $29.75 and $32.50, respectively. They were advertised in bold letters as "A NEW LOW PRICED QUALITY PRODUCT."

More low-priced offerings were to follow for Illinois at the direction of Hamilton. Among the men's watches would be 10K gold-filled models with only 15-jewel movements and even one in a very inexpensive base metal case.

Page 4 *The KEYSTONE* June 1932

ANOTHER GREAT ACHIEVEMENT

Sterling Points the Way to Increased Profits

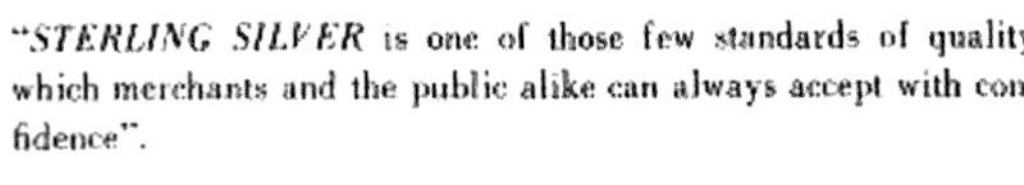

"*STERLING SILVER* is one of those few standards of quality which merchants and the public alike can always accept with confidence".

Now THE GREAT AMERICAN WATCH WITH STERLING SILVER CASES

Giving you a quality watch in precious metal tarnish-resisting case to compete with watches of lower jewel content and cases of nondescript metals—chromium, nickel and what-not.

LADY MARY

QUEEN ANNE

A NEW LOW PRICED QUALITY PRODUCT

Write to us or to your distributor for details

CASES BY WADSWORTH WATCH CASE COMPANY

ILLINOIS WATCH

Springfield, Illinois

Keystone, June 1932

1932 HISTORICAL NOTES

- Thirteen million Americans are unemployed—more than 24.5% of the population.
- Franklin Delano Roosevelt wins a landslide presidential election.
- New York City Radio City Music Hall opens.
- Charles Lindbergh's son is kidnapped.
- The parking meter is invented.

Hamilton Downsized

In June 1932, via a carefully worded internal company memorandum, Hamilton quietly announced further restructuring efforts within itself to help adjust to declining sales. Although no similar documentation could be found concerning Illinois, it is apparent that Illinois was leading the efforts in this area, since its workforce was less than one-third of what it had been in 1928.

The general superintendent of Hamilton, William H. Manby, announced on June 21, 1932, that "present business conditions make it essential to operate a reduced organization at the maximum efficiency," pointing out that "this necessitates saving not only in direct labor but also indirect labor expenses."

As a result, the following departments within Hamilton were reorganized:

- The Balance and Flat Steel Departments were combined.
- Damaskeening and Gilding were combined.
- The old-style Jewel Setting Unit was to be transferred from the Jeweling Department to the Manufacturing Jewel Setting Department.
- The Finishing Department and the 6/0 Finishing Department were to be reorganized into a Timing and Casing Department.

Although this is the only documentation of possible reductions at Hamilton that have been located to date, it is also likely that during this difficult period certain positions were eliminated as these departments were combined and reorganized.

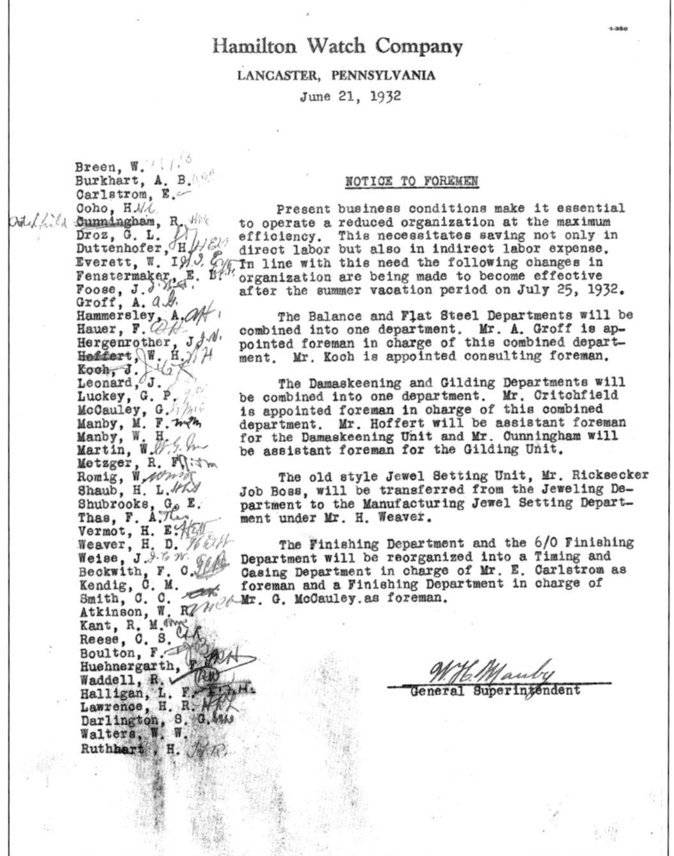

Hamilton Watch Company

LANCASTER, PENNSYLVANIA

June 21, 1932

Breen, W.
Burkhart, A. B.
Carlstrom, E.
Coho, H.
~~Cunningham~~, R.
Droz, G. L.
Duttenhofer, H.
Everett, W. I.
Fenstermaker, E. B.
Foose, J.
Groff, A.
Hammersley, A.
Hauer, F.
Hergenrother, J.
~~Hoffert~~, W. H.
~~Koch, J.~~
Leonard, J.
Luckey, G. P.
McCauley, G.
Manby, M. F.
Manby, W. H.
Martin, W.
Metzger, R. F.
Romig, W.
Shaub, H. L.
Shubrooks, G. E.
Thas, F. A.
Vermot, H. E.
Weaver, H. D.
Weise, J.
Beckwith, F. C.
Kendig, C. M.
Smith, C. C.
Atkinson, W. R.
Kant, R. M.
Reese, C. S.
Boulton, F.
Huehnergarth, F.
Waddell, R.
Halligan, L. F.
Lawrence, H. R.
Darlington, S. G.
Walters, W. W.
Ruthhart, H.

NOTICE TO FOREMEN

Present business conditions make it essential to operate a reduced organization at the maximum efficiency. This necessitates saving not only in direct labor but also in indirect labor expense. In line with this need the following changes in organization are being made to become effective after the summer vacation period on July 25, 1932.

The Balance and Flat Steel Departments will be combined into one department. Mr. A. Groff is appointed foreman in charge of this combined department. Mr. Koch is appointed consulting foreman.

The Damaskeening and Gilding Departments will be combined into one department. Mr. Critchfield is appointed foreman in charge of this combined department. Mr. Hoffert will be assistant foreman for the Damaskeening Unit and Mr. Cunningham will be assistant foreman for the Gilding Unit.

The old style Jewel Setting Unit, Mr. Ricksecker Job Boss, will be transferred from the Jeweling Department to the Manufacturing Jewel Setting Department under Mr. H. Weaver.

The Finishing Department and the 6/0 Finishing Department will be reorganized into a Timing and Casing Department in charge of Mr. E. Carlstrom as foreman and a Finishing Department in charge of Mr. G. McCauley as foreman.

W. H. Manby
General Superintendent

Manby's consolidation memorandum

"Be Not Over-Distressed"?

The advertisement Hamilton placed in the June 1932 issue of the *Locomotive Firemen and Enginemen's Magazine* targeted new graduates, telling them that they should be "eternally thankful" that they were graduating when "jobs are few and dollars tight," and that they should "be not over-distressed" but "rather relieved." Unfortunately for Illinois, Hamilton would not practice such advice on itself; Hamilton was clearly "over-distressed" about how it must deal with its Illinois Watch Division.

Locomotive Firemen and Enginmen's Magazine, June 1932

BE THANKFUL THEY ARE GRADUATING IN A TOUGH YEAR!

A group of men who had finished school in the panic year of 1907 met at a class reunion in the boom year 1929. They were all men whose names make front-page news.

One thought kept recurring in their conversation. They were eternally thankful that they HAD graduated in a year when jobs were few and dollars were tight. They pitied the fellows who had missed the moulding lessons of their early struggles by graduating into a too soft and ready world!

So be not over-distressed. Be rather relieved that the 1932 graduate hits life exactly when he does.

And then give him—or her—this solid bit of encouragement. Give a HAMILTON.

The prices of Hamiltons have been reduced to meet 1932 requirements. It is one bit of honest value in these years when so few things seem to stay put. And there are cold, hard business men who even claim that the unerring accuracy of a Hamilton will lend something of its regularity to the mind and habits of its wearer!

Hamilton's *Locomotive Firemen and Enginemen's Magazine* advertisement, June 1932

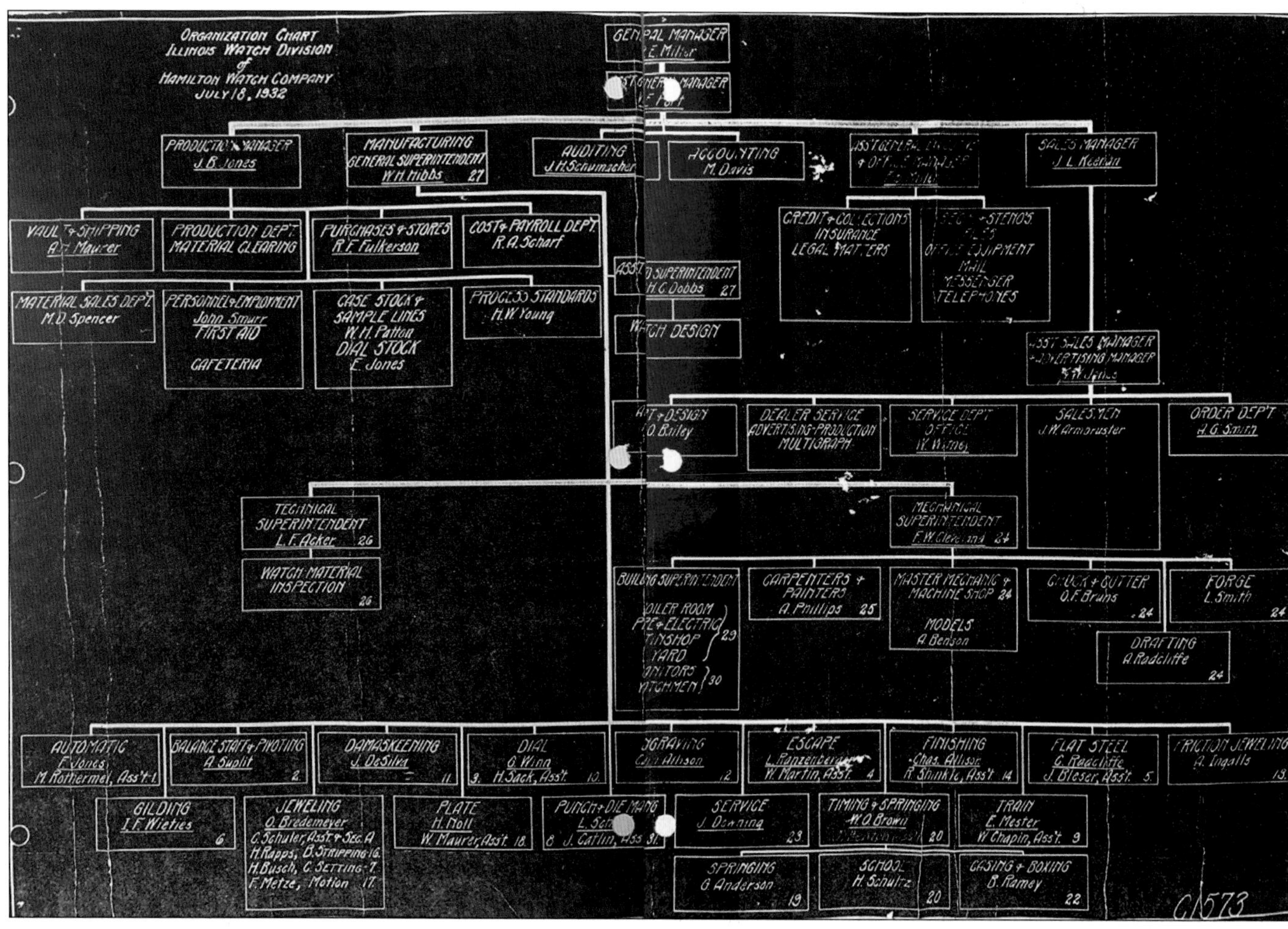

1932 Illinois Organization Chart

The Illinois Watch Division organizational chart dated July 18, 1932, is instructive for two important reasons. It shows, surprisingly, that only one person reported to Miller, the Illinois Watch Division general manager. Instead, all of the key positions of the Illinois Division reported to the assistant general manager, Port, who had been appointed to this position in April 1928, within ninety days of the acquisition. This is unusual for an American company, as normally the heads of finance, sales, manufacturing, legal and industrial relations would report directly to the general manager. Perhaps Miller did not have a big role to play at Illinois after all and got his directions for the most part from Lancaster and/or Port. The chart shows that at this time the Illinois Watch Division had at least fifty-two departments under Port.

In addition, it shows that by July 18, 1932, Illinois was employing only one person in direct sales: longtime sales manager Julius W. Armbruster, who had relocated to California in October 1929 to devote much of his time to the sale of Hamilton-Sangamo clocks. In contrast, Illinois in 1928 had employed at least fourteen Illinois direct salesmen (not counting J. Armbruster), to judge from the names gleaned from the handwritten Illinois financial ledgers: A. C. Smith, J. L. Keenan, J. C. Samuels, W. D. Cox, Edward Reauley, M. R. Coats, Frank A. Johnson, James Graham, B. F. Towne, Mr. Henry, F. Plaisted, C. F. Buck, H. Atkins and Mr. Burnett.

By June 1929, however, it would appear that Illinois had in its employ only six full-time direct salesmen reporting to Armbruster: Coats, Burr W. Freer, Johnson, Keenan, Reauley and Samuels. It is clear that Hamilton must have known that the sales of Illinois would continue to decline after such a drastic reduction in its sales personnel, the key interface with its distributor/jobber network. This burden would ultimately fall exclusively on the shoulders of Keenan, who would succeed Armbruster.

RECEIVER APPOINTED FOR THE WATERBURY CLOCK COMPANY

With business failures starting to accumulate in the watch and jewelry industry, the Waterbury Clock Company, on August 20, 1932, was the latest enterprise to appoint a receiver. The attempt was "to keep the debtors at bay until hopefully business could be restructured and sustained." If Waterbury had not taken this step, it would have had "to close down at once." The receiver was to be eliminated "as soon as business picks up."

At the time, the Waterbury Clock Company was one of the most prominent businesses in the industry, with an impressive $4 million capitalization. Its factory took up an entire square block. In addition, it owned a case factory and the former New England Watch Company's factory. But no company was immune from the lingering economic meltdown.

Further Retrenchment by Hamilton

Reduction of Capital. In August 1932, Hamilton reported that it planned to reduce its common stock from $5,000,000 to $1,000,000 and would transfer the difference of $4,000,000 to its capital surplus account. After the proposed change, the company would have 50,000 shares of preferred stock at a par value of $100 and 500,000 shares of no par common with a stated value of $1,000,000.

Hamilton, always fiscally conservative and obviously fearing further impact of the economy on its business, was retrenching in many ways and in many areas, hoping to improve the company's balance sheet in order to survive the hard times. It was introducing very few new models in 1932. At the same time, it was forcing the Illinois Watch Division not only to reduce its workers, hours and costs to eliminate inventory but also to limit production and its new offerings—measures so severe that they would assure a slow death for Illinois.

Compact Illinois Depression Lines

Owing to the impact of the Great Depression, Illinois in 1932 offered by its own admission a "compact line" of watches. This was announced in August 1932, and the models were limited to the following:

Ladies'	Men's
Beverly	Chesterfield
Florette	Gallahad
Irene	Pimlico
Juliette	Wentworth
Lynette	
Rosette	
Suzette	

With the exception of the Beverly, all of the ladies' models in the August 1932 announcement were likely new, as were two of the four men's models (the Chesterfield and Wentworth).

Then, on September 13, 1932, the sales department of Illinois notified its jobbers that it was adding the following watches to its line since the publication of its April 1932 price list:

Ladies'	Men's
Arlene	Pimlico
Florette	
Irene	
Lynette	
Rosette	
Suzette	

But in reality, none of these were completely new models.

The list of these additional ladies' models included statements about the status of certain other models: "The Janette sample will be forwarded about October 10th—there will be no samples of Babette (Solid Gold)" and "The Beverly sample to be found about October 10th."

The one men's model on the list, the Pimlico, was accompanied by the statement "The Potomac sample will follow about October 25th."

In addition, the jobbers were told that their dummy samples of the following were to be returned:

Ladies'	Men's
Argyle	Arlington
Charmette	Beau Geste
Coquette	Blackstone
Florentine	Bostonian
Glenna	Hudson
Lakewood	Larchmont
Rita	Metropolitan
	Yorktown

In the list of men's models to be returned were annotations regarding the reasons: the Beau Geste "for the fitting of a new dial" and the Larchmont "for replacing straps with 14K filled band." Regarding the change from strap to band for the Larchmont was this statement: "This model case will be shown only as a Vernon in the future."

The Illinois watches listed in the September 10, 1932 Price List were:

Ladies'	Men's
Arlene	Beau Geste
Babette	Chesterfield
Beverly	Gallahad
Coquette	Pimlico
Florette	Potomac
Irene	Rockliffe
Janette	Wentworth
Juliette	Vernon
Lady Mary	
Lynette	
Suzette	
Rosette	
Queen Anne	
Suzette	

But, of these models, only the ladies' Babette, Lady Mary, Muzette and Queen Anne may have been new models to the 1932 line and the Potomac for the mens'.

This "new" list of models was compact, and their production numbers were less than 25% of Illinois's standard volume, which was already typically very low. This explains why so few of these Illinois models are available to collectors today, absent dedicated and consistent hunting. It is possible when former Illinois Factory employee Beulah Paulsen said during her 2001 interview with me that "a lot of New Yorkers were produced, around five hundred," this could have been indeed an accurate statement, as evidence now points to production runs of low hundreds and fewer for most Illinois men's wristwatch models.

Hamilton itself offered only three new men's wristwatch models in 1932 and four new ones in 1933. They all had 987/979 movements, so it would not have been a supply issue; Hamilton had enough movements, but perhaps not the cash to purchase additional cases. Only one new Hamilton pocket watch was introduced in 1932–1933. This was the Adams, introduced in late 1933. As for Hamilton women's watches, seven new models were introduced in 1932 and five more in 1933.

According to Chamelin, Illinois introduced no new pocket watches and features from 1931 onward, with the exception of the Elinvar hairspring, and very few wristwatches.

On September 20, 1932, the *Illinois State Journal* reported that four hundred Illinois employees returned to work the day before, following what must have been a very extended summer plant shutdown. Not all departments would be at full schedule, as Illinois announced that "the working schedule will vary between departments." Thus, Illinois, like Elgin and Waltham, was for all intents and purposes at a virtual standstill, since it would be difficult to assemble watches with this greatly reduced staff.

Dummy Samples

Illinois historically sold through a network of 105 or more jobbers, wholesalers and distributors located throughout the United States as well as in Canada, Mexico and the Philippines. Illinois rarely sold directly to consumers; in fact, at some point direct sales to other than established retail jewelers was evidently restricted by the Federal Trade Commission.

April 15, 1930.

Mr. Thomas G. Sadler, Jr.,
Sadler Brothers,
South Attleboro, Mass.

Dear Sir:

We have your letter of April 10th, with check enclosed amounting to $20.45 to cover the cost to you of one of our Jolly Roger model strap watches at the dealers price, and are sorry that we are obliged to return your check herewith.

In compliance with being signatory, upon Trade Practice rulings of Federal Trade Commission, we are greatly in sympathy with merchandising through established retail jewelers.

We kindly ask, therefore, that you obtain the Illinois watch selected in the regular manner through a jeweler in the Attleboro's and we feel sure that you will understand our reason for making this request.

Should your jeweler not have the particular Illinois watch on hand that you desire, we will be very glad to make shipment of one immediately to him, for you, as soon as we have his request to do so.

Thanking you for your interest in products of our manufacture, we are

Very truly yours,

ILLINOIS WATCH

By-

AGS:ALD

AN FTC RULING AFFECTING ILLINOIS

Apparently, an FTC Trade Practice ruling required the Illinois Watch Company in 1930 to sell its watches directly to only "established retail jewelers." Because of this ruling, Illinois refused to sell a Jolly Roger men's wristwatch model to the Sadler Brothers firm in Attleboro, Massachusetts, at the "dealer price of $20.45" as it was "not an established retail jeweler."

According to Attleboro industry history, the firm of Sadler and Stanley was formed in 1863 and later became Sadler Brothers, Inc., at South Attleboro, where it produced celluloid goods and novelties. Thomas G. Sadler was treasurer and Thomas G. Sadler, Jr., the putative purchaser, was the clerk of the corporation.

Letter from Illinois to Sadler Brothers regarding FTC ruling

To help the jobbers sell Illinois watches, they were routinely supplied with at least two sales tools by the Illinois Sales Department: a catalog or brochure of that year's new releases or seasonal offerings plus "dummy samples" of the new models. These dummy samples are believed to have consisted of the actual cases of the watches being offered for sale, along with their dials, hands and crystals. The missing item was the movement, the most valuable part of the watch but not necessarily required to close a deal, as the sales personnel were also equipped with see-through glass and metal movement containers that could demonstrate the beauty of the damaskeening and the workings of the movements.

Illinois movement display containers

The dial and hands were attached to a dummy movement to hold them in place for demonstration purposes. Thus, the dummy sample was the pivotal sales aid for the distributor's "travelers," their sales personnel who would go to the jewelers within their sales territories.

Case Shortages

The normal method of selling Illinois watches via the use of dummy samples was totally disrupted during September and October of 1932. Correspondence from the Illinois Sales Department (Keenan) to the various jobbers shows a complicated juggling act that had to be performed because the Illinois wristwatch case inventory was insufficient. Hamilton, secretly planning to close the Illinois Division, was applying great pressure on Illinois to eliminate or minimize inventory, and the result was that Illinois did not have enough cases to fulfill orders or to be used in the dummy samples for the "travelers" employed by its jobbers. This was a significant blow to Illinois, since not having dummy samples affected the ability of the jobber travelers to sell Illinois watches, and in many instances prevented them from doing so.

Because its wristwatch case inventory was so low, Illinois began asking its jobbers to return the dummy samples. A letter in September 1932, for example, demanded the immediate return of samples for the Bostonian, Arlington, Yorktown, Hudson, Blackstone, Metropolitan, Rita, Glenna, Florentine, Argyle, Charmette, Coquette and Lakewood wristwatch models. This was shortly followed by a letter on October 28 pleading for the prompt return of other dummy samples (for the Irene, Wentworth, Gallahad and Chesterfield models).

It was becoming intensely challenging for the Illinois Sales Department to try to secure sales, keep its distributors happy and their travelers supplied with dummy samples, and also to heed orders from Lancaster to reduce all inventory to the lowest levels possible, while simultaneously trying to process and ship watches—or, in other words, consummate sales. Illinois obviously needed these cases returned to be able to complete watches in its factory to fulfill sales orders. What would later be called "just-in-time inventory" practices had arrived in Springfield because of desperation. These problems were to be further exacerbated after the Illinois Factory was closed and the ability to assemble needed wristwatch movements to fulfill sales moved to subcritical levels in 1933 and 1934.

"After the Storm"

Keystone, September 1932

Even in September 1932, the *Keystone* still didn't get it right; the storm was by no means over.

DON'T SELL JUNK

In his address before the American National Retail Jewelers' Association (A.N.R.J.A). Convention in October 1932, T. Albert Potter, president of Elgin, warned of the potential fallout from selling low-cost, foreign-made watches.

"I do not know anything that the jeweler is doing today which, if he continues, will kill his business faster and kill the retail jewelry industry faster than the selling of *junk*.

"I believe I can say without hesitancy that there has been a lot of junk sold in the form of watches, and I think I can further say that there have not been any American watches or goods sold under this caption.

"Danger lies in undermining the confidence of the public in our retail jewelers. The reason the retail jewelry trade has existed is due to the fact that you have built up in the past prestige and confidence in the public so that they will come to you and not to a grocery store to buy a watch. Take this confidence away from the public and what excuse is there for them to come to a retail jewelry store to buy jewelry, diamonds and watches? None.

"If you put in their minds that they can buy poor quality watches in your store, as well as any place else, they are going to lose faith in you and will be content to buy their goods through any distributing channel, whether or not the distributor knows anything about watches."

Attempts to Reduce Stock During the Depression

The Illinois Watch Company was not the only entity attempting to reduce its inventory in 1932; its jobbers were also looking to offload watches. On March 3, 1932, Illinois advised L. Manheimer and Brothers, Inc., of Chicago and New York City, a long-standing jobber for Illinois, that it could not accept for credit the return of thirty-two Illinois watches. This problem became compounded as jobbers and jewelers with excess or unwanted inventory were not in a position to order new watches.

WATCHES NOT TO BE TAKEN BACK

March 3rd, 1932.

L. Manheimer and Bros. Inc.
20 West 47th Street,
New York City.

Attention: Mr. J. C. Goodman.

Gentlemen:

Our Delivery Department brought to my attention your memorandum No. E-8591, covering thirty-two watches returned for credit.

Regret very much Joe, to say that it is not in the works for us to take back into our stock these watches.

True when I was in New York I went over with John the various items that we could re-case and make into the current watches that are in our standard line for 1932.

In keeping with our action toward our other distributors in similar cases, it is necessary for us to return these thirty-two watches to you for your stock.

Very truly yours,

THE ILLINOIS WATCH

JLK-ald

Sales Manager.

Keenan refusing to take back watches from jobber

THE WHOLESALERS' PLEA

In a June 1932 article in the *Manheimer Watchman*, Arthur Manheimer, president of L. Manheimer and Brothers, of Chicago, pleads for a little consideration of the wholesalers' selling problems:

"Everybody wants the wholesaler to buy—even during a period of depression— and when he does, he's a good fellow and very popular with the manufacturers. He is also popular with the retailer because the latter likes the idea of being able to call on the wholesaler for some watch and jewelry item that is unusual, and be sure that the wholesaler has it in stock. The difficulty arises when the wholesaler wants to sell. No two of his friends can agree on how or to whom he should sell. The retailer, of course, is urging him not to sell to the department store, the mail order house or the sub-jobber. The mail order house and sub-jobbers are urging him not to sell too cheap to the retailer so their reduced catalog price will look better. The manufacturers give the wholesaler much unsolicited advice as to whom he should sell and how. If the wholesaler were to listen to all these people and try to please them all, he would not sell to anyone.

". . . We are, however, getting more scientific methods in the field of economics, and it is not at all improbable that this difficult problem will be solved within the next few years. In the meantime, I think I speak for all progressive wholesalers when I say we are doing our level best to please you all."

In fact, however, it took jobbers, jewelers and watchmakers years to reduce their pocket watch inventory, some never succeeding.

Mixed Messages

Finally, after three years, the president of the *Jewelers' Circular,* Everit B. Terhune, admitted the extent of the economic calamity, saying, "I AM AN AMERICAN. Just one of a great number of ordinary, hard-working, fairly conscientious citizens who have grinned, groaned and pawed their way through three years of hard pickings.

"The Depression has affected me directly and indirectly, perpendicularly and horizontally, positively and negatively, specifically and generally, within and without."

Thus, in November 1932, the *Jewelers' Circular* was compelled to cry uncle. It could no longer put a rose-colored spin on the ongoing, unrelenting devastating effects of the Great Depression.

November, 1932 THE JEWELERS' CIRCULAR 75

★

I AM AN American

I AM AN AMERICAN.

Just one of a great number of ordinary, hard-working, fairly conscientious citizens who have grinned, groaned and growled their way through three years of hard pickings.

The depression has affected me directly and indirectly, perpendicularly and horizontally, positively and negatively, specifically and generally, within and without.

I have been bombarded, deluged, overwhelmed with charts, statistics, graphs and opinions from economic card readers, congenital star observers and neurotic crystal gazers in 48 different states and 99 different languages.

I have been Babsoned, Ayred, Gibsoned and Brookmired until I am well-nigh cuckoo, groggy, cock-eyed and flambolluxed.

My mind has been open, receptive and flexible to every new thought, principle, philosophy and panacea for human ills and ailments.

And now, to cap the climax, I have had it projected into my feverish brain that it's a grand and glorious condition to be poor again; that there's a real thrill in discovering how much you can get along without and how little you can get along with; how much more interesting and odoriferous a 10¢ movie on Third Avenue is than the perfumed cinema palace (94¢) on Broadway; how proud I should be to display that 1927 tailor's label in the inside pocket of my old grey suit; how good a job Pietro Bambino can do in re-soling my old shoes for $1.25.

But, brother—and here's where I come out of the ether—I want to tell you it's all plain damn boloney, bunkum, balderdash, or what have you.

So, on behalf of this great army of fellow-sufferers, I am organizing a club that I know you will all want to join. It will be known as the I-Need-A Club. You know what I mean, brother—I-Need-A new hat, I-Need-A new pair of shoes, I-Need-A new alarm clock, I-Need-A new this, and I-Need-A new that.

You and I and all the rest of us are accustomed to a high standard of living and we will never be satisfied with anything less than just that; and our rational dissatisfaction is the very motive power that is going to drive us on to prosperity again.

In my own case, in order to replenish the old darned sock, I intend to carry out the following program:

I am determined to do a better job—I shall make my business render a greater service—I shall shout my wares from the house-tops so that they will still be heard in the din of competition. I shall endeavor to be a useful cog in the economic wheel—I shall, to the best of my ability, help the other fellow get on his feet again—I shall punch the schnozzle of the pessimist and the slanderer of good times—I shall once again dare to look and march forward.

And for all of this I shall expect—and get—a better reward for my efforts. Then I can go places and do things.

All of which I insist upon

BECAUSE I AM AN AMERICAN!

Everit B. Terhune

PRESIDENT, THE JEWELERS PUBLISHING CORPORATION

Editorial in the *Jewelers' Circular*, November 1932

WHAT ARE YOU GOING TO DO ABOUT IT?

—Why do rivers flow by the *big* towns?

—Which came first, the chicken or the egg?

—It *is* difficult at times, I'll admit, to differentiate between cause and effect; but when it comes to the relationship of lessened purchasing power and unprofitable prices for merchandise, I have a fixed idea.

—It is my opinion that reduced purchasing power has not caused cut prices; but rather that cut prices have greatly damaged purchasing power.

—Unbridled competition is the most destructive factor in the present-day economic situation. The slashing of prices to meet competition, often imaginary, brings about lower wages, and lower wages invariably lead to unemployment.

—Therefore I believe that the problem of prices and profits rests entirely in the hands of manufacturers and retailers who, after all, are the ones who fix prices and should know how to figure profits.

—As soon as manufacturers and retailers decide that they will *not* sell goods at a loss, but will insist on at least a living margin of profit, just so soon will wages rise, unemployment decrease, and normal times return.

—And it's all within the control of the producer and distributor.

—The public always pays the price.

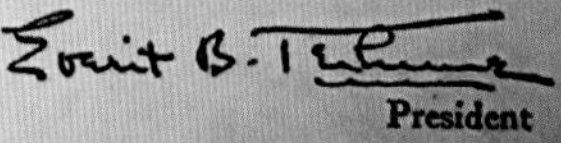

President

80 THE JEWELERS' CIRCULAR for December, 1932

Jewelers' Circular, December 1932. Notwithstanding his editorial the month before, Terhune was still blaming the Depression on "unbridled competition."

Illinois Sales Brochure

At some point toward the end of 1932, Keenan encouraged the Illinois distributors to start buying again because there had been "a change for the better the last few weeks," and he issued an unusual sales brochure.

A DEPRESSION BABY
Now STALWART at 62

1870

We were just an infant in arms, so to speak, in 1873 when there was ushered into the world a depression with five years of nation-wide misery and bread lines.

These years gave strength to us. Then came the anxious days of '84, '93, 1921. Nothing new. The same causes for each. The inevitable recovery afterwards.

For nearly three years now we have lived through another depression. We are strengthened by it in many ways. Until recently there was little

1932

in the general outlook to point to more than a slight recovery. There has been a change for the better the last few weeks. You have seen this favorable change in your immediate surroundings. Perhaps not startling—but decided improvement. People soon will be as eager to buy as they recently were afraid. Mr. Jeweler—"Fillup" those empty shelves. Carry stocks that will impress your trade. Buy now when prices are still at low levels.

For the future we have only confidence. Share it with us.

J. L. KEENAN, *Sales Mgr.*
ILLINOIS WATCH
Springfield, Illinois

Please enter our order for the following watches and bill through our selected distributor:

(Name Distributor) ______

☐ *We are also interested in special merchandising feature that you might suggest.

*Check in square if interested and give name of distributor.

1932 Illinois Sales Brochure

CEASE WEARING WRISTWATCHES?

In January 1933, the *Jewelers' Circular* reported: "Popular as the wrist watch continues to be with men in various walks of life, there are some vocations in which it apparently will not supplant the pocket watch either now or in the future. Among these are the railways services, whose employees still wear the pocket watch under orders of the company officials.

"Referring to a recent Associated Press dispatch to the effect that the United Electric Railways Co. of Providence had ordered 750 bus and street car operators to cease wearing wrist watches, Alonzo R. Williams, vice-president and general manager of the company, said that the order did affect but four of the employees and not 750, as all but these four were using pocket watches.

"We have long had a rule in our 'rule book' requiring employees to carry standard pocket watches and to check them each morning with our clocks. The reason we do not permit wrist watches to be used is because they are not always absolutely reliable. Even some of those priced as high as $750 cannot compare with the timekeeping qualities of some good pocket watches. This we have found by experience and we are sticking to pocket watches as a result. What we in the transportation field require is correctness of time rather than style, appearance or convenience.

"It is conditions such as cited by Mr. Williams on which jewelers can rely for a steady demand for pocket watches for many years to come."

However, this was not to be the case. Sales of pocket watches in the United States had been in free fall for years.

BIG DROP FOR WATCH CASE MANUFACTURERS

In December 1932 the figures on the watch case industry showed the biggest drop of any product of the jewelry trade between 1929 and 1931. According to the Census Bureau, in "a preliminary tabulation of data collected in the Census of Manufacturers taken in 1932, the value of watchcases made in the United States in 1931 . . . amounted to $3,166,271 . . . a decrease of 72.5 per cent as compared with $11,503,586 reported for 1929, the last preceding census year."

A picture from September 1932 shows the inventory of the King & Eisele jewelry store in Buffalo, New York, being auctioned off to the public by the Maynard Levy professional liquidation firm. (King & Eisele had been an Illinois jobber.) Scenes such as this one were unfortunately commonplace during this time period.

MAYNARD LEVY
404 South Wells St.
Second Floor

Satisfactory Results

in an auction sale are assured if conducted by a man who uses only ethical business methods and has a thorough knowledge of merchandise.

Many years of successful selling of jewelry store merchandise in many of the best stores of the country gives me this knowledge and experience as hundreds of leading merchants will testify.

Just completed my third sale for W. J. FRANK CO., 61 years established in Akron, Ohio. Other recent sales are KING & EISELE CO., well known wholesale house of Buffalo, N. Y.; W. C. DEAN, Oklahoma City, Okla.; and J. M. McEMPEE & SONS, Muskogee, Okla. Write to these and I will furnish many other nationally known references if desired.

If you want to reduce stock, raise ready cash, or close out your stock, write or wire

MAYNARD LEVY
CHICAGO

Jewelers' Circular, October 1932. The Levy firm, as well as several of its competitors, advertised in every issue of the *Jewelers' Circular* and the *Keystone* during the Depression years.

Hamilton Results

That Hamilton sales in 1929, two full years after the Illinois acquisition, were $5.8 million, with a profit of $1.8 million after taxes, suggests the wisdom of the acquisition. This was, of course, prior to the effects of the soon-to-strike Depression. In 1932, five full years after the acquisition and in the teeth of the Great Depression, sales hit a low of $1.6 million, with a loss of just under $1.0 million. Sales began to recover in the fourth quarter of 1933, but it was still a second consecutive loss year for Hamilton.

Elgin Results

The Elgin plant closed again for a month from December 18, 1931, until January 18, 1932, after which the work was cut back to four days. In January 1933, Elgin was down to about 480 employees; this was less than 15% of what its workforce had been in 1929.[26] To reflect a decline of more than $5 million in Elgin's earned surplus, stated capital was lowered from $10 million to $6 million by a reduction in par value of the 400,000 shares of stock from $25 to $15 per share. The Great Depression was continuing to take huge bites out of the American watch industry.

Potter of Elgin described 1932 as follows: "Never in the history of the watch industry have conditions been so demoralizing as they have been during the year just past. There has been a large quantity of distressed merchandise sold by American manufacturers as well as foreign distributors. While imports have materially declined, such watches as were imported have been sold at unusually low prices. Throughout the country all makes of watches have been sold below the cost of present day reproduction."[27] In other words, watch manufacturers were forced to sell their inventory of watches at a loss.

Fred G. Gruen, October 1931

But Gruen, who had become gun-shy, made a more cautious statement: "I do not like to make any more predictions but I do positively believe that the tendency is now upward. Lots of concerns are ... start[ing] out from 'scratch' with the idea of making profits from now on." He commented that "all inventories are low [at jewelers] and there is no doubt we are headed for gradual improvement which will accelerate as time goes on."

Gruen had clearly toned down his rhetoric and become conservative in his views after seeing the 1932 fiscal results for Gruen in particular and the America watch and jewelry industry in general.

Gruen Results

Eugene T. Fuller, a Gruen expert, notes that "like all watch companies, Gruen had ups and downs. The Depression of the thirties was especially harrowing—they were faced with a drastic reduced market for quality watches and this problem was compounded by a drastically increased tariff on imported watch movements. The rate in 1913 was 30 per cent *ad volorem*, and in 1932 it was increased to 45 per cent" [under the Smoot-Hawley Tariff Act].[28]

In May 1933, Fred G. Gruen, president of Gruen, was still trying to present a favorable outlook on business prospects. The *Keystone* commented that Gruen was "another trade leader who has faith in the future and the ultimate success of the New Deal."

National Industrial Recovery Act

President Franklin D. Roosevelt's main remedy for the Great Depression, the National Industrial Recovery Act, went into effect on June 16, 1933. As a result, the National Recovery Administration (NRA) became the primary New Deal agency. The goal was to eliminate "cut-throat competition: by bringing industry, labor and government together to create codes of fair practices and set prices."

The codes were intended not only to reduce "destructive competition" and price-cutting but also to help workers by setting minimum wages and maximum weekly hours as well as minimum prices at which products could be sold. The NRA, symbolized by the Blue Eagle, was popular with workers. Businesses that supported the NRA put the symbol in their shop windows and on their packages and advertisements.

NRA Blue Eagle Poster

Jewelers' Circular, June 1933 editorial cartoon about the NRA panacea

Hamilton's advertisement announcing price increases, showing the use of the NRA Eagle, *Jewelers' Circular*, September 1933

The 1934 Illinois Sales Catalog cover page shows the use of the NRA Eagle.

Likewise Hamilton and Illinois featured the Blue Eagle in their advertisements after the enactment of the law in 1933.

The September 1933 advertisement affirmed Hamilton's allegiance to the principles of the NRA, proclaiming that "recovery is on its way." However, it also stated that "prices are going up." So Hamilton, true to its fiscal conservatism, quickly reversed its price cuts granted that April for its grades 987 and 989, effective September 15, and, chomping at the bit, also noted that further increases "in the near future seem probable."

Though participation in the NRA was "voluntary," businesses that did not display the eagle were often boycotted, making it seem mandatory for survival. The NRA was based on the premise that the Great Depression was caused by market instability and that government intervention was necessary to balance the interests of farmers, business and labor. However, in 1935, the United States Supreme Court unanimously declared the NRA unconstitutional, ruling that it infringed on the separation of powers under the United States Constitution.

NRA Codes Declared Invalid

As this issue goes to press, the National Industrial Recovery Act has been practically invalidated by the decision of the Supreme Court of the United States in the Schechter poultry case. By a unanimous decision, the court held the National Industrial Recovery Act to be unconstitutional and in effect this made void about 750 codes which the NRA has been enforcing on the different industries.

The Supreme Court held that the code making provisions of the NRA constituted invalid delegation of power by Congress of its authority to legislate to persons wholly disconnected with the legislative functions of the government. The dictum of the court in this case was that the exercising of Congressional powers over Congressmen was definitely restricted to interstate commerce or to such activities as had a probable direct connection with interstate commerce. No economic emergency, said the court, could justify the breaking down of the limitations that had been placed on Federal authority as prescribed by the Constitution. These powers were reserved to the states.

The immediate effect of the decision denied the right of Congress or its agents to fix wages or hours in intrastate activities and practically puts the code authorities and the industrial organizations that formulated the wages and trade practices without any legal jurisdiction whatsoever.

Immediately after the decision, May 27, suspension of all NRA enforcement was announced by Donald Richberg, Chairman of the National Industrial Recovery Board, who appended in the announcement an appeal to all employers to maintain the standards of labor and fair practice achieved under the code system.

An Attractive Design

The design for the clip-brooch reproduced here strongly suggests the flying insignia of the ever romantic Air Corps. Beautifully executed in a combination of baguette, penta-

gon and round diamonds set in platinum, this piece will arouse the imagination of the most exacting buyer.

The modernistic trend is present but not to the degree that it will outrage the taste of the jeweler's more conservative clientele.

The design is the work of Macey Stein, designer for Katz & Ogush, New York.

***Jewelers' Circular*, June 1935**

Even before the Supreme Court ruling, the NRA was discovering it could not enforce its rules. Black markets sprouted up. Only the most strenuous police methods could assure enforcement. So, even before the Supreme Court ruling, the NRA was doomed to failure.

Moore notes that the passage of the NRA in 1933 crushed the ability of watch enterprises to maintain low wages and prices. The NRA Code for the watch industry in 1933 provided for minimum wages of 35¢ per hour, or $14 for a 40-hour week. A 48-hour week was permitted in the "rush season," but the average for the year could not exceed 40 hours per week. The minimum wage for "learners" was 80% of the minimum for workers. "Office boys and runners" were paid the same wage as learners. Learners had to be paid workers' wages after three months of training or be discharged.[28]

As a result, on August 7, 1933, Waltham had to raise wages 20% or more. For most workers, this meant their minimum weekly pay was $14, but the NRA Code mandated additional increases, eventually resulting in a 28% overall pay raise. By the end of 1934, Waltham had 2,500 employees working a full 40-hour week. Waltham had a yearly "loss of $315,350, owing almost entirely to the fact that the percentage increase in wages was double the increase in sales."[29]

For Hamilton, the NRA regulations provided another reason to bring its Illinois Watch Division to an end, as Hamilton did not want to pay higher wages to its Springfield workers, not even to assemble the dummy Illinois samples necessary for sales efforts.

The lack of cases with which to supply samples for Illinois jobbers was already hampering sales toward the end of 1932, and the situation became even more problematic during the course of 1933. It was further exacerbated by Hamilton's decision, announced by its president Beckwith on April 20, 1933, that Hamilton was consolidating the operations of the Hamilton and Illinois Watch Divisions in Lancaster. Therefore, for the rest of 1933, Illinois efforts would be "confined to completing Illinois items at Lancaster."

The NRA Code, meant as a salvation for United States industry, seemed to work effectively at its outset, but its requirements for minimum wage rates were clearly detrimental to Illinois under the management of Hamilton. Because it was a careful steward of its businesses compared to Elgin and Waltham, Hamilton seems to have suffered the least, financially, during the tumultuous times brought about by the Depression. Accordingly, it is understandable why Hamilton took this approach to Illinois production, especially as the fate of Illinois under Hamilton had already been sealed.

SMALLER ADVERTISEMENTS FOR A.C. BECKEN

Before the Great Depression, A. C. Becken would sometimes have two and three full-page advertisements in the weekly trade publications. By 1933 its monthly advertisement was reduced to a scant 1 x 2 inches and read simply:

> **A. C. BECKEN CO.**
> **Wholesale Jewelers**
> P.O. Box 1
> 35 E. Wacker Drive, Chicago

INGERSOLL-WATERBURY WAGE INCREASE

As the economy started to stabilize and companies looked forward to the benefits of the National Industrial Recovery Act, some companies started increasing wages after a prolonged wage freeze and wage reductions. For example, the Ingersoll-Waterbury Company announced on June 12, 1933, an increase of 5% in the wages and salaries of all employees. Its president noted, "The increase is a reward to our people for the loyalty they have shown through the last few years of economic depression." He further stated: "Production at the Waterbury plant is increasing by leaps and bounds at the present time and management took advantage of its first opportunity to advance the earnings of its employees."

Hamilton and Illinois in 1933

With the awful results of 1932 fresh in everyone's mind, the Illinois jobbers were wondering what was going to happen to the company. On January 24, 1933, Miller of Illinois wrote to the company's distributors "in reply to inquiries . . . asking "What is THE ILLINOIS WATCH going to do in 1933?"

> Certain of our Distributors have suggested that a part of their terms and discounts problem will be solved if we will provide a good assortment of uncased movements for wholesalers' casing. Certain others have suggested that our cased at the factory lines should continue.
>
> We take pleasure in supporting both suggestions by:
>
> (a) Furnishing a good assortment of uncased movements at popular price levels.

(b) Furnishing a well assorted compact line of cased watches in popular styles.

We request that movements bearing our trade mark be cased in cases of sufficiently good quality to allow the movements to function properly.

We are enclosing our new price list which becomes effective January 26th, 1933.

Thus, during the Depression, Illinois was trying to satisfy the needs of its distributors while not further adversely impacting the company's business results; very conservatively, it was offering only "compact lines" of Illinois watches. However, was Miller being disingenuous? By mid-April of 1933, only a few months after Miller's letter to the distributors, Beckwith of Hamilton was announcing the closure of the Springfield Watch Factory. Hamilton did arrange for a few key employees to relocate from Springfield to Lancaster as well as particular equipment needed to help finish certain works-in-progress.

"Temporary" Closing

On April 20, 1933, perhaps without candor, Beckwith announced the "temporary" closing of the Illinois Factory in Springfield. It was also disclosed for the first time in the trade press that operations at the Illinois Watch Factory had been suspended by Hamilton on April 1.

Illinois Watch Co.'s Headquarters Temporarily at Lancaster, Pa.

Chicago, April 20.—Manufacturing operations at the Illinois watch factory, Springfield, Ill., were suspended on April 1. After May 1, all the normal functions—production, merchandising, distribution, servicing and material sales—of the Illinois Division of the Hamilton Watch Co., will be continued from Lancaster. J. K. Keenan will continue to direct distribution and sales of Illinois watches.

This consolidation of activities of executives, craftsmen and technicians of the two divisions under one roof, according to a statement from Frank C. Beckwith, president of the Hamilton Watch Co., is a temporary and economic expediency to avoid excessive production which the present day market cannot absorb.

Assurance is given that the Illinois watch line will continue as an active and progressive product. Its relations with its wholesale and retail dealers will not be affected in any way by this change.

Until announcement of the reestablishing of Illinois Watch headquarters at Springfield, all correspondence pertaining thereto, should be addressed to Lancaster, Pa.

Article in the *Jewelers' Circular*, April 20, 1933

Notwithstanding Beckwith's announcement, very few of his words turned out to be true. By the end of July 1933, the Springfield operation was completely shuttered and never to be reopened for normal operation again.

With Beckwith's April 1933 announcement, the sales efforts for Illinois shifted to Lancaster, as was reflected in the newly printed Illinois stationery.

The Illinois Watch
LANCASTER, PENNA.

New Illinois envelope, April 1933

Before Beckwith's announcement on April 16, 1933, that "Springfield will be temporarily shut down," Port (not Miller) in Springfield had announced on April 3, 1933, that "there is not enough sales to justify the manufacture of watches in both plants [Lancaster and Springfield] and as a result . . . the [Springfield] plant will be forced to shut down for some time." Port's announcement was reported the next day in the *Illinois State Journal*.

THE ILLINOIS WATCH
A GREAT AMERICAN WATCH SINCE 1870
LANCASTER · PENNSYLVANIA · U · S · A

New Illinois letterhead, April 1933

Watch Factory To Close Soon For Indefinite Period

All Work Will Be Done At Lancaster, Pa., Plant.

The Illinois Watch factory will be shut down for an indefinite period sometime this month, employes of the place were notified yesterday by William E. Port, assistant general manager. All work of the Hamilton Watch company, owners of the local plant, will be carried out at the Lancaster, Pa., plant of the company, officials announced.

Between three and four hundred persons have been employed part time at the local plant during the last three years. The peak of employment at the local plant was reached in 1929 when more than 1,300 persons were employed full time.

There is not enough sales to justify the manufacture of watches in both plants, Port said last night, and as a result of this, the local plant will be forced to shut down for some time.

Only a small stock of finished watches is on hand at the local plant and this will be removed to Lancaster to serve wholesalers and retailers.

While the plant will be shut down, the company plans to keep it up in good order and be ready for immediate reopening should business warrant it, Port said.

Since 1870 the local plant has been in operation with the exception of two years from 1893 to 1895. It reopened at that time and has been operating ever since.

Illinois State Journal, April 4, 1933, p. 12

Interestingly, this newspaper account states for the first time that "between three and four hundred persons have been employees part time at the [Springfield] plant during the last three years." If the statement means that only this number of workers were employed, the Illinois Watch Company had thus been operating at nearly shutdown levels for the three years prior to April 3, 1933. Perhaps there was a small workforce in place to complete wristwatch movements as orders for them were received.

It is clear now that Illinois wristwatch production was at its best in 1928, 1929, 1930 and part of 1931. It is astounding that Illinois was able to design, assemble, market and sell such a tremendously vast variety of models, movements, jewel counts, cases and dials in such large possible configurations and combinations during this very short period of time.

Port's April 1933 announcement, in mentioning that "only a small stock of finished watches is on hand . . . and this will be moved to Lancaster to serve wholesalers and retailers," helps explain why the few watches introduced from 1931 onward are so challenging for collectors to locate today.

Low-Priced Hamiltons

In April 1933, Hamilton introduced and advertised its new low-priced offering "for Today's Market." The advertisement was for its $42.50 Grant, with an economical 10K gold-filled case.

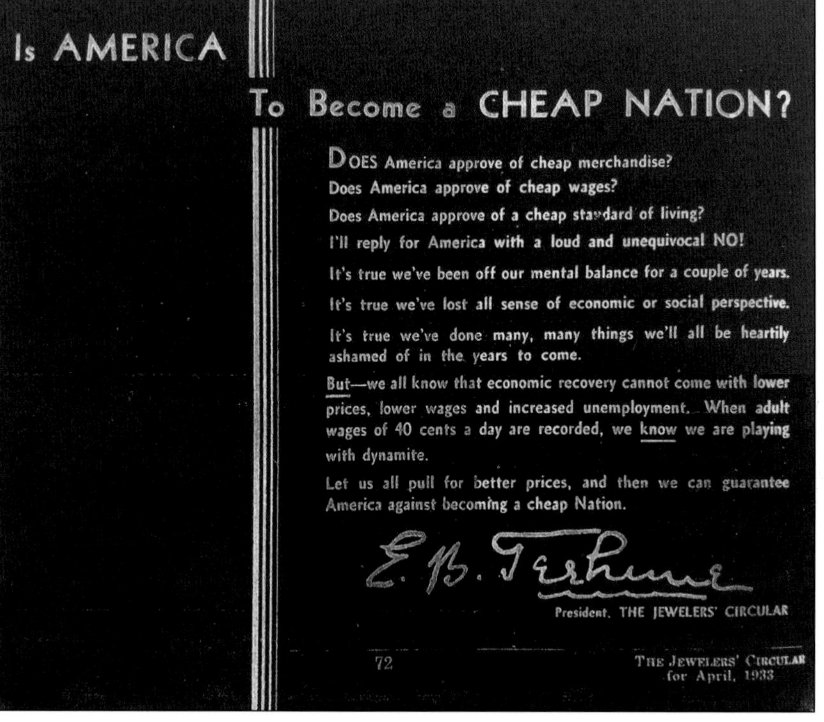

Not surprisingly, the president of the *Jewelers' Circular* at this same time was still distressed at the possibility of lower prices. *Jewelers' Circular*, April 1933

$42.50 *That is the consumer price for this new 17 jewel 6/0 size Hamilton strap watch. It's the GRANT—available in 10K filled yellow gold—fitted with a handsome new luminous dial. It is also available with a raised gold figure dial, consumer price,* **$45.00**

This is one of the most significant announcements Hamilton has made in years. It marks the beginning of a new deal for the retail jewelers of America.

Think of it! A 17 jewel accurate, dependable Hamilton strap watch at $42.50. This is not an old or discontinued number. It is a brand new April 1933 model and styled to the tempo of today. It is the one watch your customers have been waiting for. And it should, by all means, be a featured item in every jeweler's stock of fine watches.

Here's another announcement of importance: Downward price revisions on two Hamilton grades—987 and 989—are now in effect. The 14K filled gold 987's are available to the consumer with either black figure or luminous dial at $47.50 or with raised gold figure dial at $50.00. The grade 989 14K filled gold ribbon watches now retail at $45.00.

Never could your customer get so much accuracy for so little money. Never were there so many Hamiltons in the lower price range. The aggressive retail jeweler cannot fail to see Hamilton's increased importance as a profit making item. *Hamilton has what it takes to get sales in 1933!* When you rebuild your stock for Spring and Summer selling, include a representative line of Hamilton watches at the new prices.

Hamilton

The Watch of Railroad Accuracy

Keystone, April 1933

Hamilton proclaimed: "This is one of the most significant announcements Hamilton has made in years. It marks the beginning of a new deal for the retail jewelers of America." (Those in Springfield would have countered that a far more significant announcement had already occurred with the suspension of its watch operations there.)

"This is not an old or discontinued number," Hamilton said. "It is a brand new April 1933 model and styled to the tempo of today." Furthermore, the advertisement announced that Hamilton was reducing its prices for its Hamilton grade 987 and 989 models. "Never could your customer get so much accessory for so little money," Hamilton told the jewelers. "Never were there so many Hamiltons in the lower price range."

Thus, Hamilton, a strong holdout on reducing prices, finally waved the white flag and introduced new low-priced products under its own brand name. And the next month, Hamilton promoted additional "new lower prices."

W. H. HIBBS, 62, IS FOUND DEAD IN HIS GARAGE

Carbon Monoxide Gas Is Fatal To Former Watch Plant Superintendent.

Illinois State Journal, May 15, 1933

BECKWITH FALLOUT

A tragic and almost immediate fallout of the Beckwith announcement to shut the Illinois Watch Factory on a "temporary" basis was the suicide of the superintendent of the Illinois Factory by carbon monoxide poisoning.

William H. Hibbs was apparently extremely despondent over the closure of the Springfield operation.

The local *Illinois State Journal* reported that "all of the employees {had been} thrown out of work." It was small solace to Hibbs that Hamilton had offered him a position in Lancaster.

Keystone, May 1933

Hamilton also introduced models priced even lower for its Illinois Watch Division.

PRICE IS NEVER TOO HIGH

When Compared

WITH SOMETHING WORTH WHILE

When the Question Arises
"The Price is Too High"
It is Answered by—
"Compared with What?"

QUALITY, REPUTATION OF

ILLINOIS WATCHES

Gives You Courage of Your Convictions. You Can Sell This Great American Watch

TODAY, TOMORROW AND FOR YEARS TO COME

ILLINOIS WATCH

The Great American Watch

Springfield, Illinois

SPECIAL MATERIAL OFFER—Write Material Department, Illinois Watch, Springfield, Illinois for information concerning thirty-day offer saving you fifty per cent on necessary material.

Keystone, April 1933

One year later Hamilton would release a "New Deal" to better control the distribution of its products, but with far greater fanfare and impact.

It is interesting that the gold-filled Grant watch case was made by Solidarity, because Solidarity went out of business in October 1931, as was mentioned earlier. Therefore, Hamilton either purchased the cases prior to the Solidarity closure, acquired case stock that existed at the time of the Solidarity liquidation or purchased cases from someone who had obtained the rights to the case design. In any event, Hamilton likely obtained the cases at a distressed price for the introduction of its first low-priced offering.

Illinois Watch Distributors

There were about eighty Illinois Watch Distributors as of April 7, 1933; noted in pencil on the list are the buyers at each company. On the fifth page are listed the department stores that Illinois sold to directly as "house accounts" and not via jobbers. During this period Hamilton and Illinois each had jobbers ranging in number from eighty to just under one hundred.

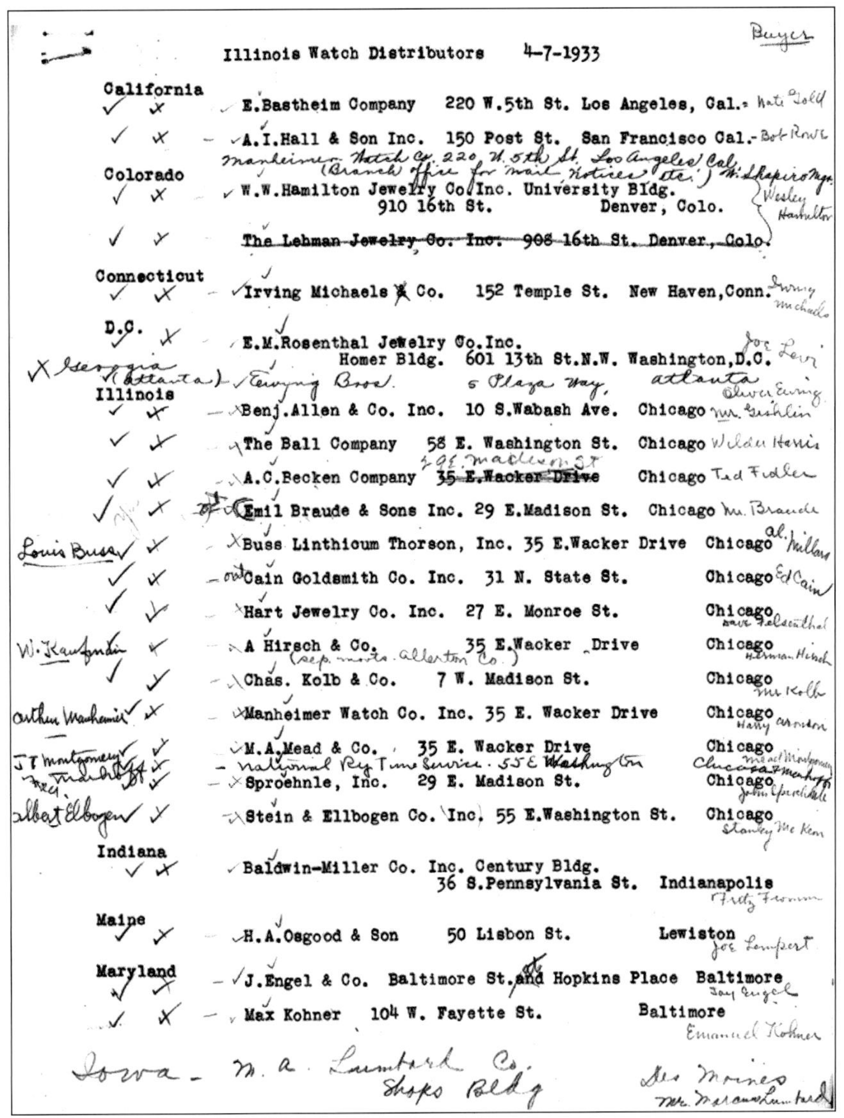

Illinois Watch Distributors 4-7-1933

Buyer

California
E.Bastheim Company 220 W.5th St. Los Angeles, Cal.
A.I.Hall & Son Inc. 150 Post St. San Francisco Cal.

Colorado
W.W.Hamilton Jewelry Co.Inc. University Bldg. 910 16th St. Denver, Colo.
~~The Lehman Jewelry Co. Inc. 908 16th St. Denver, Colo.~~

Connecticut
Irving Michaels & Co. 152 Temple St. New Haven, Conn.

D.C.
E.M.Rosenthal Jewelry Co.Inc. Homer Bldg. 601 13th St.N.W. Washington, D.C.

Illinois
Benj.Allen & Co. Inc. 10 S.Wabash Ave. Chicago
The Ball Company 58 E. Washington St. Chicago
A.C.Becken Company ~~35 E.Wacker Drive~~ Chicago
Emil Braude & Sons Inc. 29 E.Madison St. Chicago
Buss Linthicum Thorson, Inc. 35 E.Wacker Drive Chicago
Cain Goldsmith Co. Inc. 31 N. State St. Chicago
Hart Jewelry Co. Inc. 27 E. Monroe St. Chicago
A Hirsch & Co. 35 E.Wacker Drive Chicago
Chas. Kolb & Co. 7 W. Madison St. Chicago
Manheimer Watch Co. Inc. 35 E. Wacker Drive Chicago
M.A.Mead & Co. 35 E. Wacker Drive Chicago
Sproehnle, Inc. 29 E. Madison St. Chicago
Stein & Ellbogen Co. Inc. 55 E.Washington St. Chicago

Indiana
Baldwin-Miller Co. Inc. Century Bldg. 36 S.Pennsylvania St. Indianapolis

Maine
H.A.Osgood & Son 50 Lisbon St. Lewiston

Maryland
J.Engel & Co. Baltimore St.and Hopkins Place Baltimore
Max Kohner 104 W. Fayette St. Baltimore

Iowa - M. A. Lumbard Co. Shops Bldg Des Moines

Illinois Watch Distributors, April 7, 1933

-2-

Massachusetts

I. Alberts Sons Inc. 709-711 Jewelers' Bldg Boston, Mass

A. Frisch & Co. 373 Washington St. Boston, Mass

M.S.Page & Co. Inc. 373 Washington St. Boston, Mass.

D.C.Percival & Co.Inc. 373 Washington St. Boston, Mass.

E.H.Saxton Co.Inc. 387 Washington St. Boston, Mass

Michigan

E.H.Pudrith Co.Inc. Metropolitan Bldg. 33 John R St. Detroit

Minnesota

S.H.Clausin & Co. Inc. 13-17 S.6th St. Minneapolis

Thos.B.Wilson & Co. Inc. ~~100 N. 7th St.~~ Minneapolis

Missouri

Edwards-Ludwig-Fuller Jewelry Co. 1113 Walnut St. Kansas City, Mo.

C.A.Kiger Co. Inc. Federal Reserve Bank Bldg. 10th & Grand Ave. Kansas City, Mo.

Woodstock-Hoefer Watch & Jewelry Co. Inc 9th & Walnut Sts., Kansas City, Mo.

Bauman-Massa Jewelry Co. Inc. 720 Olive St. St.Louis

Jas.J.Burke Co. Inc. 9th & Olive Sts. St.Louis

Eisenstadt Manufacturing Co. Inc. Louderman Bldg. Locust & 11th Sts., St.Louis

Nebraska

Byrne-Duff Jewelry Co. Inc. 204 W O W Bldg. 14th & Farnum Sts. Omaha, Nebr.

New York

Eliassof Bros. & Co.	100 State St.	Albany
M.Levitz & Co.	133 N. Pearl St.	Albany
~~King & Eisele Co. Inc.~~	~~210 Franklin St.~~	Buffalo
Aisenstein Woronock & Sons Inc.	580 Fifth Ave.	New York
American Watch Distributors	15 Maiden Lane	New York
Buds Linthicum Thorson Inc.	20 West 47th St.	New York
Freudenheim Bros. Inc.	170 Broadway	New York
~~Henry Freund & Bro.~~	~~20 West 47th St.~~	New York
Henry Ginnel & Co.	15 Maiden Lane	New York
A.L.Brown	15 Maiden Lane	New York

Illinois Watch Distributors, April 7, 1933 (Cont'd)

-3-

New York

L.Manheimer & Bros. Inc.	20 West 47th St.	New York
I.Ollendorf Co. Inc.	20 West 47th St	New York
J.J.Schmukler	133 Canal St.	New York
N.H.White & Co.	21 Maiden Lane	New York
~~American Watch Distributors~~	~~207 Commerce Bldg.~~	~~Rochester~~
Morris Rosenbloom & Co. Inc.	115 Clinton Ave. S.	Rochester
A.H.Pond Co. Inc.	214 S.Warren St.	Syracuse

Ohio

Frohman & Co.	~~31 E. 4th St.~~	Cincinnati
A.G.Schwab & Sons	227 E. 6th St.	Cincinnati
~~M.Schwab Jewelry Co. Inc.~~	411 Race St.	~~Cincinnati~~
Wallenstein-Mayer Co. Inc.	31 E.4th St.	Cincinnati, O
~~H.W.Burdick Co. Inc.~~	~~305 Swetland Bldg. 1010 Euclid Ave.~~	Cleveland
A.H.Ficken Co. Inc.	722 Union Mortgage Bldg. 850 Euclid Ave.	Cleveland

Oregon

Butterfield Bros.	Mohawk Bldg. 3rd & Morrison St.	Portland

Pennsylvania

Non Retailing Company	36 E.Chestnut St.	Lancaster
H.O.Hurlburt & Sons	817 Chestnut St.	Philadelphia
Louis Sickles	1015 Chestnut St.	Philadelphia
M. Sickles & Son	900 Chestnut St.	Philadelphia
Biggard & Co. Inc.	Room 305 Clark Bldg 717 Liberty Ave	Pittsburgh
~~W.J. Johnston Co.~~	~~Union Bank Bldg.~~ 4th Ave. & Wood St.	Pittsburgh
I Ollendorf Co. Inc.	717 Liberty Ave.	Pittsburgh
Samuel Weinhaus Co. Inc.	722 Penn Ave.	Pittsburgh

Rhode Island

The Albert Walker Co.	202 Washington St.	Providence

Illinois Watch Distributors, April 7, 1933 (Cont'd)

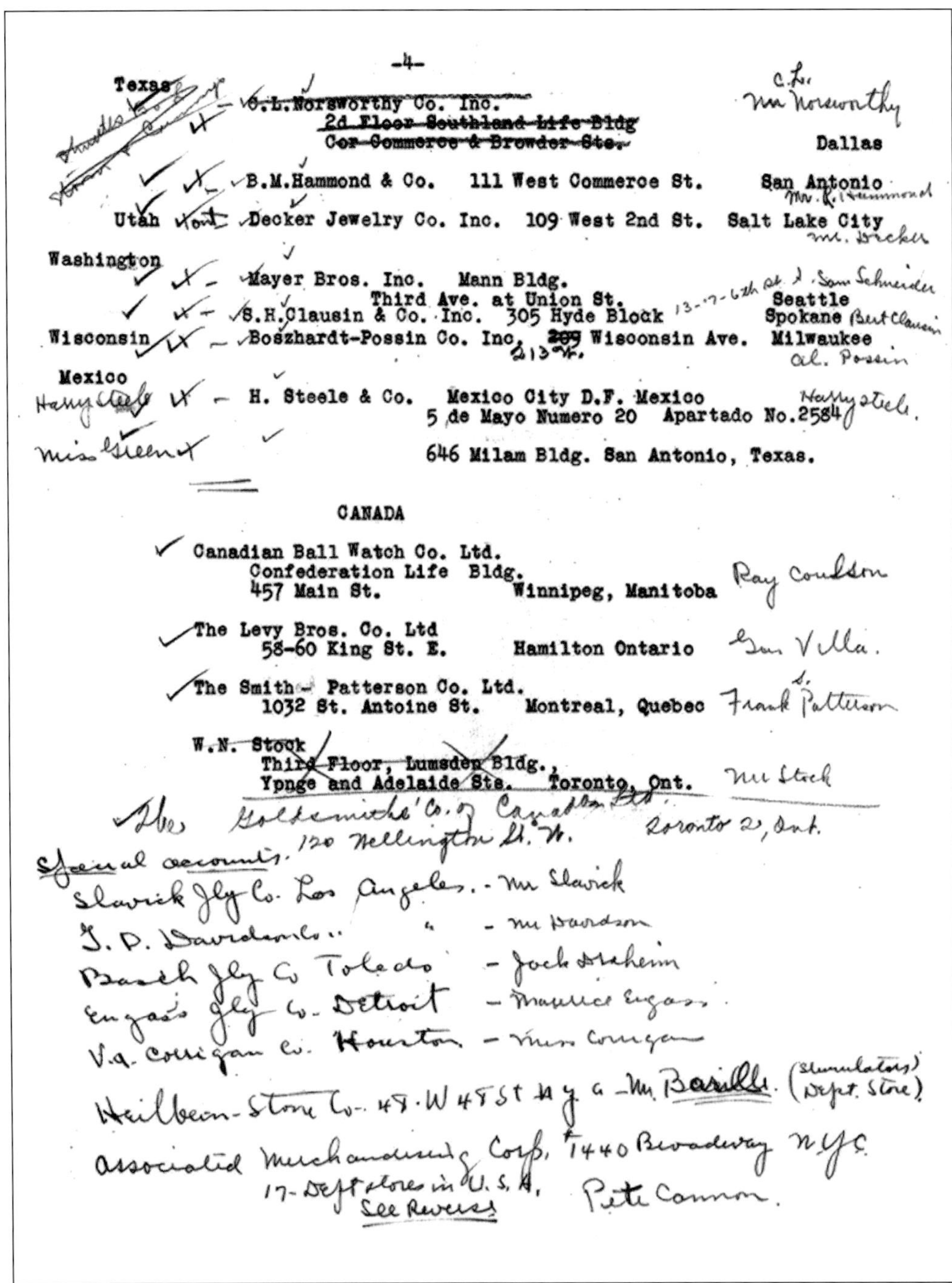

-4-

Texas — ~~O.L. Norsworthy Co. Inc. 2d Floor Southland Life Bldg Cor Commerce & Browder Sts.~~ Dallas — C.L. Mr Norsworthy

B.M.Hammond & Co. 111 West Commerce St. San Antonio — Mr. R. Hammond

Utah — Decker Jewelry Co. Inc. 109 West 2nd St. Salt Lake City — Mr. Decker

Washington — Mayer Bros. Inc. Mann Bldg. Third Ave. at Union St. Seattle — Sam Schneider

S.H.Clausin & Co. Inc. 305 Hyde Block Spokane — Bert Clausin

Wisconsin — Boszhardt-Possin Co. Inc. ~~209~~ 213 W. Wisconsin Ave. Milwaukee — Al. Possin

Mexico — H. Steele & Co. Mexico City D.F. Mexico 5 de Mayo Numero 20 Apartado No.2584 — Harry Steele

Miss Green — 646 Milam Bldg. San Antonio, Texas.

CANADA

Canadian Ball Watch Co. Ltd. Confederation Life Bldg. 457 Main St. Winnipeg, Manitoba — Ray Coulson

The Levy Bros. Co. Ltd 58-60 King St. E. Hamilton Ontario — Geo. Villa.

The Smith - Patterson Co. Ltd. 1032 St. Antoine St. Montreal, Quebec — Frank S. Patterson

~~W.N. Stock Third Floor, Lumsden Bldg., Ynge and Adelaide Sts. Toronto, Ont.~~ — Mr Stock

The Goldsmiths' Co. of Canada Ltd. 120 Wellington St. W. Toronto 2, Ont.

Special accounts.

Slavick Jly Co. Los Angeles. - Mr Slavick

J. D. Davidson Co. " - Mr Davidson

Basch Jly Co Toledo - Jack Alaheim

Engass Jly Co. Detroit - Maurice Engass

V.A. Corrigan Co. Houston - Mrs Corrigan

Heilbron-Stone Co. 48 W 48 St N.Y. C. - Mr Baruelle (stimulators) (Dept. Store)

Associated Merchandising Corp. 1440 Broadway N.Y.C. 17 - Dept stores in U.S.A. Pete Cannon

See Reverse

Illinois Watch Distributors, April 7, 1933 (Cont'd)

List of Dept. stores in Associated Merchandising Group -

	Store Name	Place	Buyer
1	Abraham and Strauss	Brooklyn	Jones
2	Ayres	Indianapolis	
3	Bloomingdale	New York City	Parsee
4	Bullocks	Los Angeles, Cal.	Mc McClanahan
5	Capwell	Oakland, Cal.	
6	Dayton	Minneapolis	Dewey
7	Emporium	San Francisco	
8	Filene	Boston	(Miss) Uhland
9	Forman	Rochester	
10	Horne	Pittsburgh	
11	Hudson	Detroit	Moffett
12	Hutzler	Baltimore	Miss Kaufman
13	Lazarus	Columbus O.	
	Pike-Kumler	Dayton O.	
	Shillito	Cincinnati	
	Stix Baer Fuller	St Louis	
	Strawbridge & Clothier	Phila	Miss Fox
	Taylor	Cleveland	Cummings
	R. H. White Co	Boston	

Orders secured from stores but billed thru Associated Merchandising Corp
1440 Broadway
New York City -
Mr. O. Cannon Mgr.

Illinois House Accounts , April 7, 1933

Joint Watch Distributors

By May 26, 1933, Hamilton and Illinois shared approximately one hundred distributors.

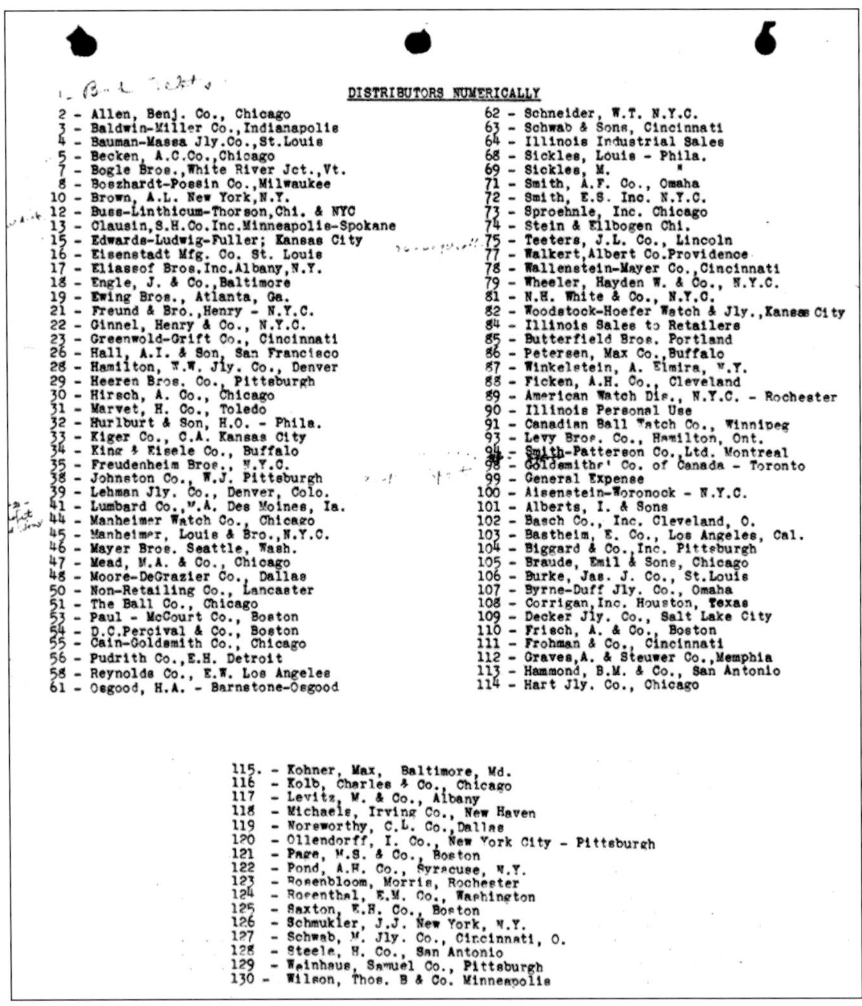

DISTRIBUTORS NUMERICALLY

2 - Allen, Benj. Co., Chicago
3 - Baldwin-Miller Co., Indianapolis
4 - Bauman-Massa Jly.Co., St.Louis
5 - Becken, A.C.Co., Chicago
7 - Bogle Bros., White River Jct., Vt.
8 - Boszhardt-Possin Co., Milwaukee
10 - Brown, A.L. New York, N.Y.
12 - Buss-Linthicum-Thorson, Chi. & NYC
13 - Clausin, S.H.Co.Inc. Minneapolis-Spokane
15 - Edwards-Ludwig-Fuller; Kansas City
16 - Eisenstadt Mfg. Co. St. Louis
17 - Eliassof Bros. Inc. Albany, N.Y.
18 - Engle, J. & Co., Baltimore
19 - Ewing Bros., Atlanta, Ga.
21 - Freund & Bro., Henry - N.Y.C.
22 - Ginnel, Henry & Co., N.Y.C.
23 - Greenwold-Grift Co., Cincinnati
26 - Hall, A.I. & Son, San Francisco
28 - Hamilton, W.W. Jly. Co., Denver
29 - Heeren Bros. Co., Pittsburgh
30 - Hirsch, A. Co., Chicago
31 - Marvet, H. Co., Toledo
32 - Hurlburt & Son, H.O. - Phila.
33 - Kiger Co., C.A. Kansas City
34 - King & Eisele Co., Buffalo
35 - Freudenheim Bros., N.Y.C.
38 - Johnston Co., W.J. Pittsburgh
39 - Lehman Jly. Co., Denver, Colo.
41 - Lumbard Co., W.A. Des Moines, Ia.
44 - Manheimer Watch Co., Chicago
45 - Manheimer, Louis & Bro., N.Y.C.
46 - Mayer Bros. Seattle, Wash.
47 - Mead, M.A. & Co., Chicago
48 - Moore-DeGrazier Co., Dallas
50 - Non-Retailing Co., Lancaster
51 - The Ball Co., Chicago
53 - Paul - McCourt Co., Boston
54 - D.C.Percival & Co., Boston
55 - Cain-Goldsmith Co., Chicago
56 - Pudrith Co., E.H. Detroit
58 - Reynolds Co., E.W. Los Angeles
61 - Osgood, H.A. - Barnstone-Osgood
62 - Schneider, W.T. N.Y.C.
63 - Schwab & Sons, Cincinnati
64 - Illinois Industrial Sales
68 - Sickles, Louis - Phila.
69 - Sickles, M. "
71 - Smith, A.F. Co., Omaha
72 - Smith, E.S. Inc. N.Y.C.
73 - Sproehnle, Inc. Chicago
74 - Stein & Ellbogen Chi.
75 - Teeters, J.L. Co., Lincoln
77 - Walkert, Albert Co. Providence
78 - Wallenstein-Mayer Co., Cincinnati
79 - Wheeler, Hayden W. & Co., N.Y.C.
81 - N.H. White & Co., N.Y.C.
82 - Woodstock-Hoefer Watch & Jly., Kansas City
84 - Illinois Sales to Retailers
85 - Butterfield Bros. Portland
86 - Petersen, Max Co., Buffalo
87 - Winkelstein, A. Elmira, N.Y.
88 - Ficken, A.H. Co., Cleveland
89 - American Watch Dis., N.Y.C. - Rochester
90 - Illinois Personal Use
91 - Canadian Ball Watch Co., Winnipeg
93 - Levy Bros. Co., Hamilton, Ont.
94 - Smith-Patterson Co., Ltd. Montreal
98 - Goldsmiths' Co. of Canada - Toronto
99 - General Expense
100 - Aisenstein-Woronock - N.Y.C.
101 - Alberts, I. & Sons
102 - Basch Co., Inc. Cleveland, O.
103 - Bastheim, E. Co., Los Angeles, Cal.
104 - Biggard & Co., Inc. Pittsburgh
105 - Braude, Emil & Sons, Chicago
106 - Burke, Jas. J. Co., St.Louis
107 - Byrne-Duff Jly. Co., Omaha
108 - Corrigan, Inc. Houston, Texas
109 - Decker Jly. Co., Salt Lake City
110 - Frisch, A. & Co., Boston
111 - Frohman & Co., Cincinnati
112 - Graves, A. & Steuwer Co., Memphis
113 - Hammond, B.M. & Co., San Antonio
114 - Hart Jly. Co., Chicago

115. - Kohner, Max, Baltimore, Md.
116 - Kolb, Charles & Co., Chicago
117 - Levitz, M. & Co., Albany
118 - Michaels, Irving Co., New Haven
119 - Noreworthy, C.L. Co., Dallas
120 - Ollendorff, I. Co., New York City - Pittsburgh
121 - Page, M.S. & Co., Boston
122 - Pond, A.H. Co., Syracuse, N.Y.
123 - Rosenbloom, Morris, Rochester
124 - Rosenthal, E.M. Co., Washington
125 - Saxton, E.H. Co., Boston
126 - Schmukler, J.J. New York, N.Y.
127 - Schwab, M. Jly. Co., Cincinnati, O.
128 - Steele, H. Co., San Antonio
129 - Weinhaus, Samuel Co., Pittsburgh
130 - Wilson, Thos. B & Co. Minneapolis

Hamilton Sued by Former Illinois Employees

Not only did Hamilton "suspend operations" in Springfield, resulting in the loss of jobs (except for the very few employees assuming positions in Lancaster), but also demonstrated a lack of good faith by breaching its repurchase guarantee to the Illinois employees who had purchased Hamilton stock in 1929. This repugnant behavior resulted in two lawsuits filed by former Illinois employees in district court in April 1933.

SUIT AGAINST LOCAL WATCH FIRM IS FILED

The *Illinois State Journal* reported on April 20 and April 22, 1933, that first thirty-three former employees, and then an additional twenty-two employees, filed two separate lawsuits against the Hamilton Watch Company. Both suits requested the court to order Hamilton to repurchase stock which the employees held in the corporation.

Both suits ironically alleged that on October 29, 1929 (Black Tuesday), Hamilton offered to sell employees shares of Hamilton Watch Company stock at $95.00 per share, with payments being permitted in installments; and, furthermore, that Hamilton's offer included a promise to repurchase the stock whenever the employees chose during the period of making payments. The employees claimed that they elected to have Hamilton repurchase the stock and Hamilton refused to do so.

The second suit additionally alleged that Hamilton violated the Illinois State Securities Act by selling the stock without filing with the Secretary of State a statement of the company's assets and liabilities.

WATCH FIRM IS AGAIN NAMED IN LAW SUIT

The second suit maintained that on March 1, 1930, Hamilton listed its stock on the "New York curb exchange" at $50 a share and thirty days later split the stock offering two shares for one with a list price of $25 per share. On October 29, 1929, Hamilton sold the complaining employees' shares at $95 per share, the lawsuit said, thus extracting twice the value from the employees.

Both cases were heard in district court within several months of their filing, and Hamilton was ordered by the judge to pay the guaranteed repurchase amount promptly. It is regrettable that the former and presumably then unemployed Illinois employees had to resort to the courts to require Hamilton to honor its legal obligations.

Illinois Inventory Liquidation

The May 1933 issue of the *Keystone* reported that the Illinois Watch Company had announced a special thirty-day offer under which Illinois watch materials might be obtained at a savings of 50%. This drastic move was without precedent. The parts offered were for 3/0, 6/0, 12/0, 18/0 and 21/0 size movements. Clearly, Hamilton viewed the parts inventory of these key movements for Illinois wristwatches as excessive and not needed to complete anticipated watch sales.

This, of course, was another step in Hamilton's plan to liquidate as much inventory as possible at Springfield before closing the Illinois Factory. But at this time the focus was on wristwatch parts—surprising, as this material would have been largely produced under Hamilton's ownership and tight managerial control.

Practices such as these were eventually to be vigorously protested by Keenan, the Illinois Sales Manager. Then located in Lancaster, he was starting to realize that it would be extremely difficult if not impossible for Illinois to rebound from such drastic inventory reduction measures. Regrettably, Keenan would turn out to be correct.

Illinois Closed

Once Hamilton shuttered the Illinois Factory on July 31, 1933, it became apparent that it was planning the cessation of Illinois sales. One indication is that the Hamilton dial drawings of 1933 and beyond for Illinois show only two new case designs and only two exclusive cases from Illinois' usual casemakers. Furthermore, the other "new" Illinois dials being worked on by Hamilton were solely variations of existing Illinois models, such as the Futura, Baronet and Blackstone. In addition, the line of Illinois dials being worked up by Hamilton was for the replacement market and most of them had silver finish, no butler centers, and painted black numerals; it is likely that not many were actually produced, as it is very rare to find them today.

Hamilton was making Illinois product decisions almost exclusively on the basis of maximizing its ability to reduce its stock of Illinois movements and parts. In the Illinois dial diagrams drawn by Hamilton in Lancaster, the only mentions of a 1934 sales catalog are on drawings dated between September 25 and November 27, 1933. Some of the new Hamilton drawings were for dials on Illinois watches in the 1934 Hamilton/Illinois sales catalog such as the Antoinette, Chatham, Rockingham, Sangamon, Standish and Urbana wristwatch models. All of these, with the exception of the Chatham and Standish, used 18/0 size movements without subsidiary seconds to help exhaust the stock of these "ladies'" movements constructed under Hamilton management.

Transfers from Springfield

The shutdown of the Illinois Factory was set for July 31, 1933, and the names of a few fortunate Illinois employees who were invited to move and were willing to relocate to Lancaster started to be announced in Lancaster in June and July 1933. Among these transfers were:

- *L. F. Acker.* Formerly a Technical Superintendent of the Illinois Watch Division, he joined Hamilton as "Assembly Consultant." Acker was to report directly to the Hamilton General Superintendent's Office and was to consult on "all matters pertaining to the design, assembly and assembly methods, etc."

- *W. D. Brown.* Formerly a foreman in charge of Timing and Springing at the Illinois Watch Division, he was appointed "Job Boss" in the Hamilton Timing and Casing Department.

- *H. C. Dobbs.* Formerly the assistant to the Superintendent of the Illinois Watch Division, he was appointed the Hamilton foreman "in charge of drafting watch parts and process drawings and the coordination of the process and methods used in the production of watch patents." Dobbs was also to be available for "consultation on any questions arising in connection with Illinois drawings and processes." Dobbs was still in Lancaster in September 1937, since he signed the hand drawing set forth at right.

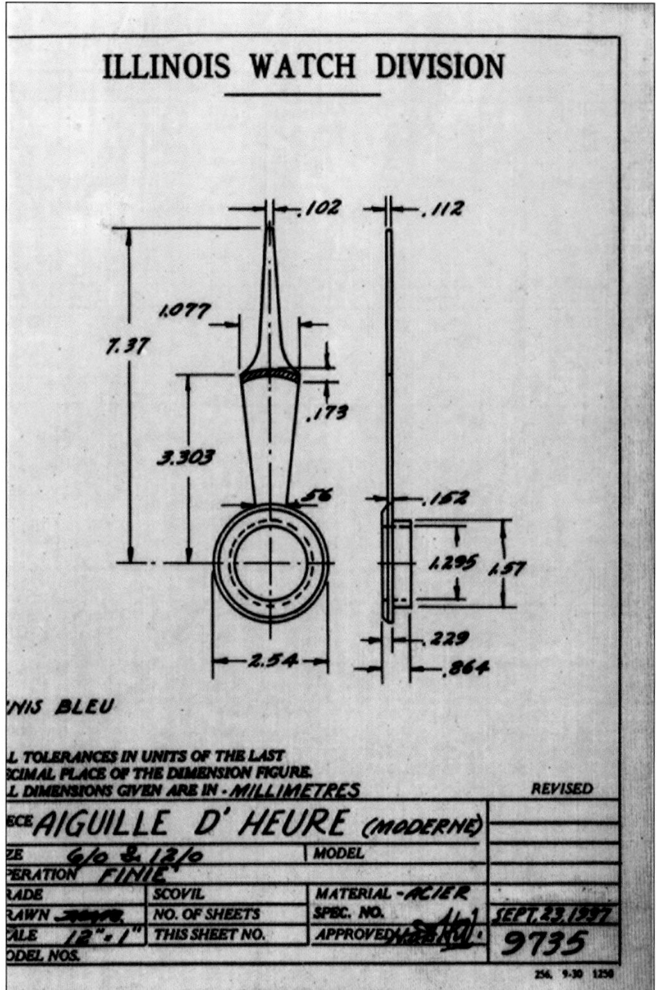

Drawing approved by H. C. Dobbs on September 23, 1937, in Lancaster

- *J. B. Jones.* Formerly Production Manager of the Illinois Watch Division, he was appointed Hamilton "production manager." Jones was to be in charge of the Personnel and Employment; Production Planning and Rate Setting and Time Study departments of Hamilton.

- *James Downing.* Formerly foreman in charge of the Illinois Watch Division Service Department, he was appointed foreman of the Hamilton Escape Department.

- *Ernest Mester.* Formerly foreman in charge of the Illinois Train Department, he was appointed Assistant Foreman of the Hamilton Train Department.

Hamilton apparently tried to encourage certain of the experienced Illinois managers and foremen to transfer to Hamilton. Of course, there had to have been an available open position and an employee willing to relocate with his family from Springfield to Lancaster.

When the reduction of work hours, then the reduction of employees, and even the 50% parts cost reduction still failed to eradicate the Illinois movement and parts inventory, Hamilton adopted other methods.

Illinois 1933 Sales Results

A glimpse of Illinois sales results is provided by the records Keenan kept for the first quarter of 1933. These anemic sales are not surprising in light of the Hamilton restrictions imposed on Illinois from 1931 through 1933 (and earlier as well). The first-quarter records reflect sales totaling only $61,000 for Illinois. However, the total results for 80 jobbers listed came to $548,316 for 1933, and this total did not include sales to its other unlisted distributors or sales to house accounts, direct sales, and sales to department stores. Needless to say, Hamilton's handling of Illinois in the strong headwinds of the Great Depression could not have produced anything other than these paltry results.

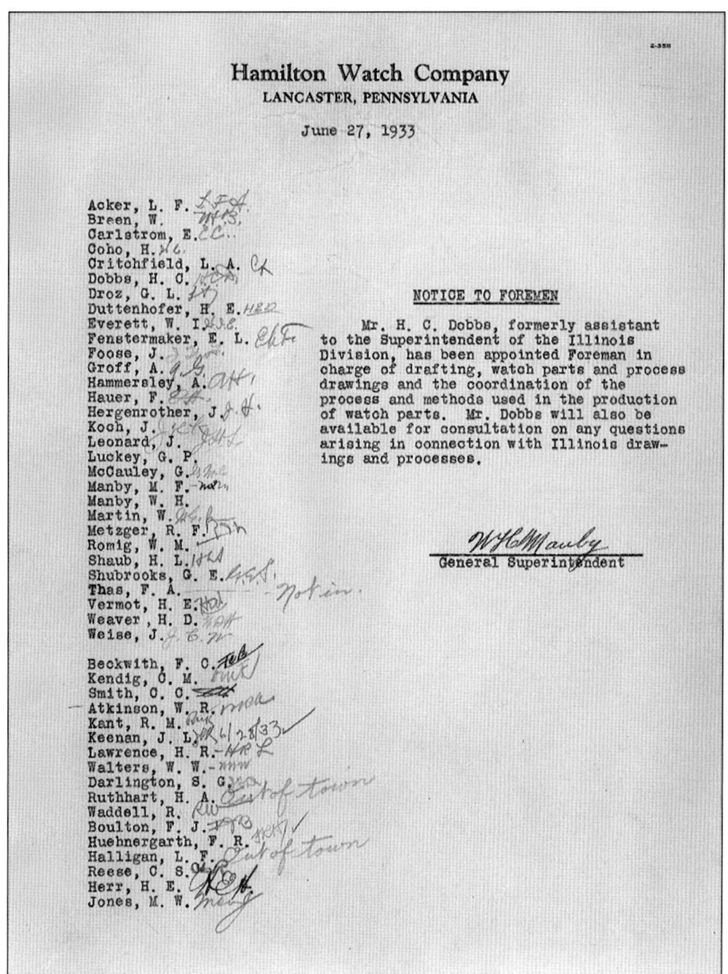

Hamilton Watch Company
LANCASTER, PENNSYLVANIA

June 27, 1933

Acker, L. F.
Breen, W.
Carlstrom, E.
Coho, H.
Critchfield, L. A.
Dobbs, H. C.
Droz, G. L.
Duttenhofer, H. E.
Everett, W. I.
Fenstermaker, E. L.
Foose, J.
Groff, A.
Hammersley, A.
Hauer, F.
Hergenrother, J.
Koch, J.
Leonard, J.
Luckey, G. P.
McCauley, G.
Manby, M. F.
Manby, W. H.
Martin, W.
Metzger, R. F.
Romig, W. M.
Shaub, H. L.
Shubrooks, G. E.
Thas, F. A. — Not in.
Vermot, H. E.
Weaver, H. D.
Weise, J.

Beckwith, F. C.
Kendig, C. M.
Smith, C. C.
Atkinson, W. R.
Kant, R. M.
Keenan, J. L. 6/28/33
Lawrence, H. R.
Walters, W. W.
Darlington, S. G.
Ruthhart, H. A. Out of town
Waddell, R.
Boulton, F. J.
Huehnergarth, F. R.
Halligan, L. F. Out of town
Reese, C. S.
Herr, H. E.
Jones, M. W.

NOTICE TO FOREMEN

Mr. H. C. Dobbs, formerly assistant to the Superintendent of the Illinois Division, has been appointed Foreman in charge of drafting, watch parts and process drawings and the coordination of the process and methods used in the production of watch parts. Mr. Dobbs will also be available for consultation on any questions arising in connection with Illinois drawings and processes.

W.H. Manby
General Superintendent

W.H. Manby's internal memorandum to Hamilton foremen and executives, announcing the transfer and assignment of H.C. Dobbs from Springfield to Lancaster, dated June 27, 1933

Monthly Volume Sheets

WATCH JOBBERS SALES & NUMBER OF WATCHES

THE ILLINOIS WATCH

	April	March 1933	Total 1933	Total
Aisenstein-Woronock & Sons.	—	929.65	956.65	956.65
I. Alberts' Sons, Inc.	31.50	75.00	951.77	920.27
Benj. Allen & Co.	—	46.90	34.74	34.74
American Watch Distributors	2032.30	88.50	145.80	2178.10
Baldwin-Miller Co.	—	81.00	35.18	35.18
The Ball Company	410.60	760.20	357.34	767.94
Barnstone-Osgood & Co.	194.00			194.00
E. Bastheim Co.	3163.70	1400.00	1933.15	5096.85
Bauman-Massa Jly. Co.	20.00	127.50	267.50	287.50
A. C. Becken Co.	237.00	310.80	360.40	123.40
Biggard & Co.	130.50			130.50
Boszhardt-Possin Co.	—	180.00	151.15	151.15
A. ... & Brown	6.75			6.75
H. W. Burdick Co.	—	252.00	252.00	252.00
J. J. Burke Co.	—		19.50	19.50
Buss, Linthicum, Thorson, Inc.	6526.55	545.90	176.43	6350.12
Butterfield Bros.	—	62.00	88.23	88.23
Byrne-Duff Jly. Co.	1829.25		18.65	1847.90
Cain-Goldsmith Co.	—		143.69	143.69
S. H. Clausin & Co.	1888.85	30.00	30.00	1858.85
Decker Jly. Co.			17.55	17.55
Edwards-Ludwig-Fuller Jly. Co.	32.05	108.00	108.00	75.95
Eisenstadt Mfg. Co.	38.30	24.20	10.00	48.30
Eliassof Bros. & Co.	—	81.90	64.35	64.35
J. Engel & Co.	45.35	35.50	282.00	236.65
A. H. Ficken Co.	1291.00	26.00	26.00	1265.00
K. Frisch Co.	145.00	544.75	544.75	689.75
Frohman & Co.	—	121.00	108.00	108.00
Henry Ginnel & Co.	76.50	105.00	697.90	774.40
Freudenheim Bros.	—		54.00	54.00

-3-

		March 1933	Total 1933	
H. Steele & Co.	1139.40	1139.40	2638.80	3778.20
Stein & Ellbogen Co.	833.60	29.10	252.10	1085.70
The Wallenstein-Mayer Co.	—	20.00	124.00	124.00
N. H. White & Co.	—	75.00	64.27	64.27
Thos. B. Wilson Co.	—		220.00	220.00
Samuel Weinhaus Co.	800.70			800.70
	43,544.59	11149.45	17473.57	61000.61
				17.55
				61018.16

The personal accounts kept by Keenan of 1933 first-quarter Illinois sales

Master List of Case Control

The "Master List of Case Control," dated June 5, 1933, shows the status of Illinois watches available that could be sold to distributors. Incredibly, only one men's model was available without any limitation, and only three others were available even in limited supply. All the other men's models had been discontinued. In light of Hamilton's stranglehold on Illinois, the 1933 projected sales results should therefore not be a surprise.

The following models were discontinued entirely by June 5, 1933 (or were available with limitations).

Master List, Case Control Sheet (retyped for legibility)

21/0 Size - Discontinued	21/0 Size - Available	6/0 Size - Discontinued	6/0 Size - Available
Babette, 14K, W	Louette, W or Y	Ensign	Potomac, W or Y
Alouette	Juliette, W or Y	Marquis	Derby, Y only
Muzette	Rosette, W only	Cadet	
Suzette	Minuette, W only	Blackstone	
Lynette, W only	Florette, W or Y	Graystone	
	Charmette, Y only	Haddon Hall	
	Annette, W or Y	Commodore	
	Janette, W or Y	Belmont	
		LaSalle	
		Bostonian	
18/0 Size – Discontinued	**18/0 Size – Available**	Derby	
Lenox, 14K, W	Beverly	Arlington	
Lakewood	Roslyn	Latonia	
Narragansett, 14K	Queen Anne	Pimlico	
Glencoe	Lady Mary	Metropolitan	
Arlene, 14K, W		Puritan	
Greta		Townsman	
Argyle		**12/0 Size – Discontinued**	**12/0 Size – Available**
Vardon		Futura	Larchmont, Y only
Edgewater		Finalist	Andover, Y only
Glenna		Chesterfield	
Joan		Trophy	
Hollywood		Wentworth	
Rita		Frontenac	
Latonia		Commander	
Vanity Fair		Gallahad	
Debutante		Kenilworth	
		Ardsley	
		Larchmont, W	
		Andover, W	
		Exeter	
		Rockliffe	

Thus, in June 1933 the only men's Illinois wristwatch available for sale without limitation of case color was the Potomac; in limited supply were the Andover, Derby and Larchmont models, in yellow gold-filled only. Of the ladies' models, nine were available without limitations and three with limitations.

Hamilton Inventory Reduction Initiatives for Illinois

From early to mid-1933 through 1934, after the Illinois Factory had been effectively shuttered and supposedly some of its equipment, some works-in-process and some employees relocated to Lancaster, Hamilton instituted further steps to try to reduce or exhaust the Illinois inventory. Some of the measures ordered by Hamilton were questionable, unless Hamilton had no plans to restart Illinois production.

Illinois Discounted Parts

Hamilton's campaign to liquidate the Illinois parts inventory, which started in March 1933, continued with "the Illinois Watch Co . . . . [notifying the one thousand plus] owners of Illinois watch material cabinets of a special 30-day offer with a saving of 50 per cent to the retail jeweler."

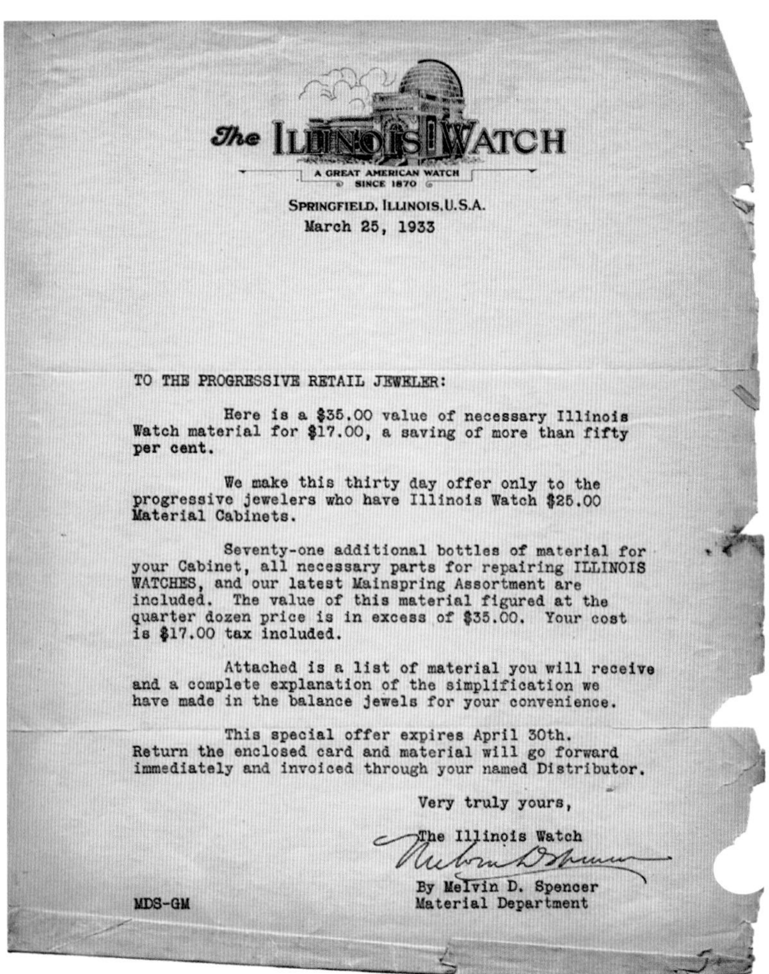

The ILLINOIS WATCH

A GREAT AMERICAN WATCH

SINCE 1870

SPRINGFIELD, ILLINOIS, U.S.A.

March 25, 1933

TO THE PROGRESSIVE RETAIL JEWELER:

Here is a $35.00 value of necessary Illinois Watch material for $17.00, a saving of more than fifty per cent.

We make this thirty day offer only to the progressive jewelers who have Illinois Watch $25.00 Material Cabinets.

Seventy-one additional bottles of material for your Cabinet, all necessary parts for repairing ILLINOIS WATCHES, and our latest Mainspring Assortment are included. The value of this material figured at the quarter dozen price is in excess of $35.00. Your cost is $17.00 tax included.

Attached is a list of material you will receive and a complete explanation of the simplification we have made in the balance jewels for your convenience.

This special offer expires April 30th. Return the enclosed card and material will go forward immediately and invoiced through your named Distributor.

Very truly yours,

The Illinois Watch

By Melvin D. Spencer
Material Department

MDS-GM

Illinois Material Department letter, dated March 25, 1933

Special Offer on Illinois Watch Materials

THE Illinois Watch Co., Springfield, Ill., has announced a special 30-day offer under which Illinois watch materials may be obtained at a saving of 50%. This offer is made with the idea of enabling watchmakers to bring their Illinois material cabinets up-to-date to take care of the new materials which have been added during the recent years. Seventy-one bottles of material are included in this offer and watchmakers who are interested should write direct to the Illinois Watch Material Department.

It is said that 24 different jewels are now all that are needed for Illinois watches. They replace 110 jewels. One-half whole sizes are now available. In addition to this, material has been added for the 3/0 size double roller, 6/0 size hunting and 12/0, 18/0 and 21/0 size watches.

Keystone, May 1933

Redesigned Dials

In 1933, five years after the Illinois acquisition, Hamilton started to redesign dials for specific existing Illinois models, such as the Baronet, Blackstone and Futura, as was mentioned earlier. More surprising is that it started designing Illinois dials for specific cases manufactured and/or offered for sale by the Star Watch Case Company, the Manheimer Watch Company, the jewelry and diamond firm of Aisenstein–Woronock & Sons, Inc. and the Keystone Watch Case Company. In fact, Hamilton was designing dials for specific numbered cases offered by Star; the Star case numbers were indicated directly on the dial drawings.

I have dubbed these watches "Conneric" models because they are not Generic Period watches and they are not "Contract" cases; instead, they are a different kind of watch that is a hybrid between a Generic Period and Contract case model. Some of the resulting Conneric watch models are shown in Chapter 9 so the reader can match the dial drawing to the Star case. To date, no sales catalog or sales material has been found to indicate the cases that match the case numbers indicated on the Hamilton dial drawings. However, I believe it is highly likely that the Connerics were cased in Lancaster. (See Chapter 9 for examples of these models).

Illinois 6/0 and 18/0 Size Movements Used in Conneric Case Models

Watches sold during the Generic Period came with movements and dials mainly from either Illinois, Elgin or Waltham, in cases supplied by independent casemakers directly to the over fourteen thousand independent jewelers that existed in the United States during the Generic Period. Therefore, one was likely to find the same case being offered with at least three different dial/movement variations, for each of the main American watch manufacturers during this period. (Examples of Generic Period Illinois men's and ladies' wristwatches are shown in Chapters 9 and 10.)

Even after the Generic Period, generic watch cases continued to be offered for sale well into the 1930s on a "contract basis" to jewelers located throughout the United States. A jeweler or customer could then select which dial and movement from either Illinois, Elgin or Waltham he or she wished to house in a particular case. Thus, a contract case is basically the same as a generic one except for being sold independently of the dial and movement and being cased after the Generic Period.

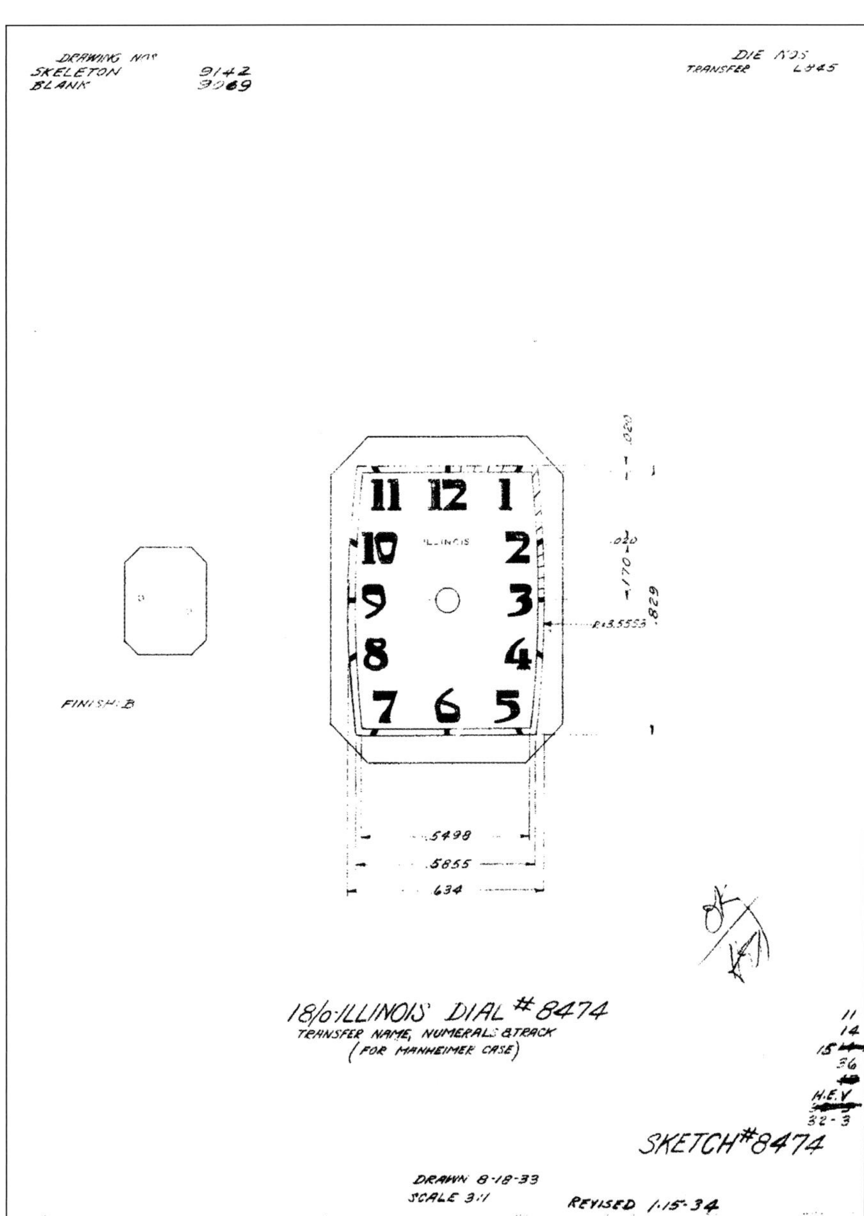

Hamilton drawing, dated August 18, 1933, for an Illinois dial to be used in a Manheimer case

DRAWING NOS.
SKELETON 9142
BLANK 9072
BLANK WITH FEET 9156
TRIMMING 9229

DIE NOS.
TRANSFER L884

NOTE:-
FOR DIMENSIONS OF TRACK & NUMERALS
SEE SKETCH # 8732

FINISH "B"

18/0 ILLINOIS DIAL #8738
TRANSFER TRACK, NAME & NUMERALS
(AISENSTIEN & WORONOCK)

SCALE 5:1
DATE 6-15-34
DRAWN

DRAWING #8738

Hamilton drawing, dated June 15, 1934, for an Illinois dial to go in an Aisenstein–Woronock case

Keystone, October 1933. Conneric is on the right.

Several of the Conneric models are shown in Star advertisements during this time period.

THE KEYSTONE, Vol. 62, No. 1; issued Monthly by the Keystone Publishing Co., Business Offices: 19th & Federal Sts., Camden, N. J., and Mt. Airy P. O., Philadelphia, Pa. Subscription price in U. S. A. $2.00 a year, Canada $3.50; Foreign $3.80. Entered as Second-class matter June 1, 1912, at the Post Office at Camden, N. J., under act of March 3, 1879.

A Star advertisement in the *Keystone*, 1933: “Attractive cases. Illus. at left is an 18/0s Elgin ladies’ ribbon case, while right illustrates case for Waltham or Illinois wrist watch.”

By examining the dial drawings along with some of the actual watches in Chapter 9 and here, one gets a good sense of these Conneric models. For decades, collectors thought that these watches were mere "contract" watches of little importance and value. But it is now clear that these Conneric models (or more accurately, later generation Generic watches) were planned and issued by Hamilton for at least three Illinois jobbers that had cases made specifically for them and possibly more we are not currently aware of. Hamilton also produced at least six Conneric dials for specific Star cases and at least four Conneric dials for four Keystone cases. (See the **Conneric** listing in Chapter 9.)

Star Case Model Numbers

The Star Watch Case Company case numbers appearing on the 1933–1934 Hamilton dial drawings for Illinois watches are: 1099, 1117, 1266, 1227, 1291 and 1292. As was indicated, we have been unable to identify these six Star cases.

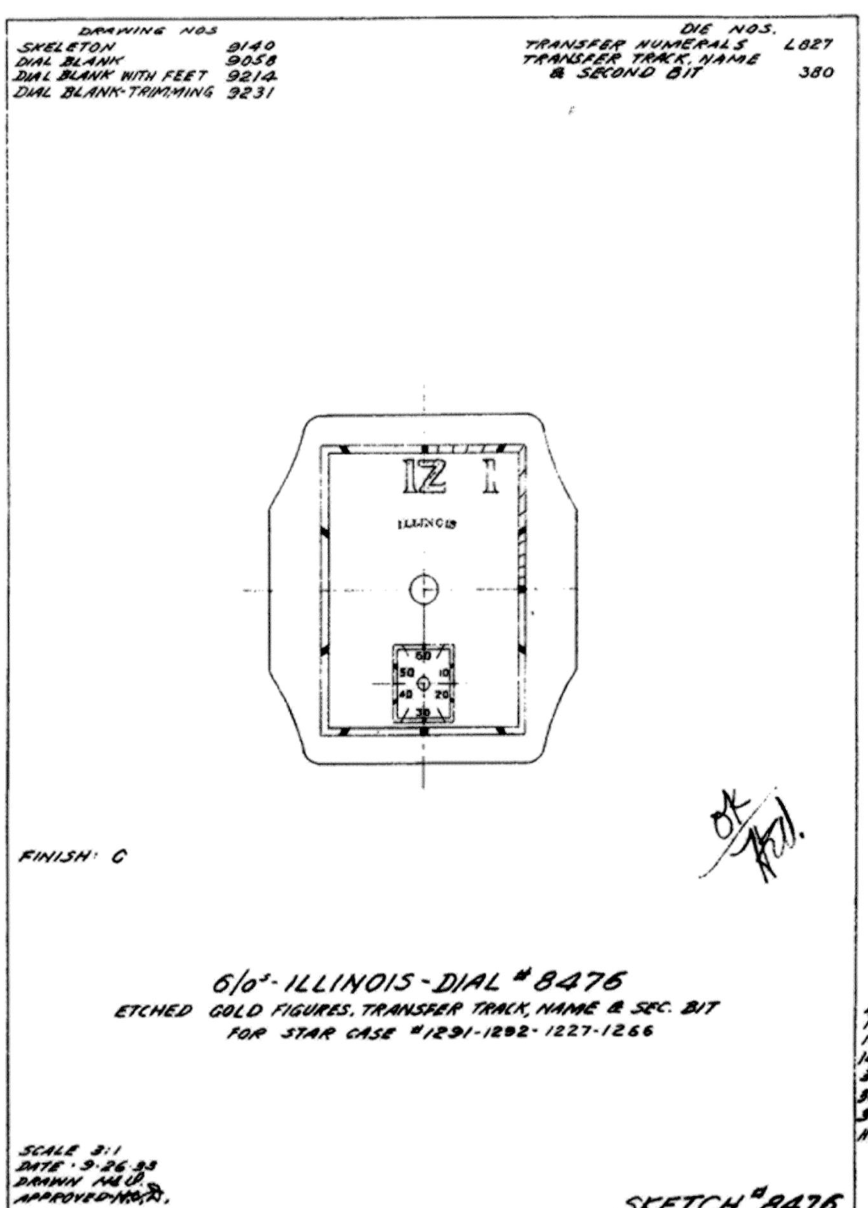

Hamilton drawing, dated September 26, 1933, for an Illinois dial for a Star-cased Conneric model

Conneric, white gold

There were at least three ladies' Illinois models in Star cases that were factory cased by Hamilton in Lancaster about 1933; the Juliette, Muzette and Suzette, all of which are discussed in Chapter 10 (Examples of the dials used and the Illinois men's Connerics introduced in 1933 and after are shown in Chapter 9).

Keystone Case Model Numbers

The Hamilton drawings also had dial drawings for use in Keystone cases numbered 649, 716, 738 and 741, but no cases with these models have been found to date.

Men's and Unisex Models with 18/0 Movements

In 1934, Illinois (via Hamilton) started to issue new wristwatch models in cases that would accommodate the excess inventory of 18/0 size ladies' movements, without subsidiary seconds, for models that were first advertised by Illinois as men's watches, then for both sexes or, in effect, "unisex" wristwatches. The Sangamon and Urbana were issued in 1934 with these 18/0 size movements. These models, plus the Rockliffe 18/0 (issued at the end of 1934 or in early 1935), the Tuxedo (issued in 1929) and the Biltmore 18/0 were the only Illinois men's wristwatches offered for sale without a subsidiary seconds option. However, unlike the others, the Biltmore 18/0 model was first advertised as a ladies' model, then offered to both sexes. The Tuxedo, on the other hand, was advertised as a men's watch before being advertised for both sexes. The 3/0 Caprice (issued in 1931), a purse or desk watch, was offered to both women and men at the outset; it was like the abovementioned wristwatches in having no subsidiary seconds.

Rockliffe 18/0 Model

To further reduce the 18/0 size movement inventory, Hamilton in 1934 modified the Illinois Rockliffe solid gold 12/0 size case to accommodate an 18/0 size Illinois movement. Thus, Hamilton could offer for sale in the 1935 timeframe a Rockliffe 18/0 model without subsidiary seconds, because the 18/0 size movement, intended primarily for ladies' wristwatch models, had no subsidiary seconds. This modification allowed the further reduction of Hamilton's inventory of Illinois movements. Hamilton designed specific new "Illinois" dials for the Rockliffe 18/0. This was, tragically, the last true Illinois wristwatch ever introduced for sale. Some of the Hamilton-designed Rockliffe 18/0 dials are shown here and the actual watches are shown in Chapter 9.

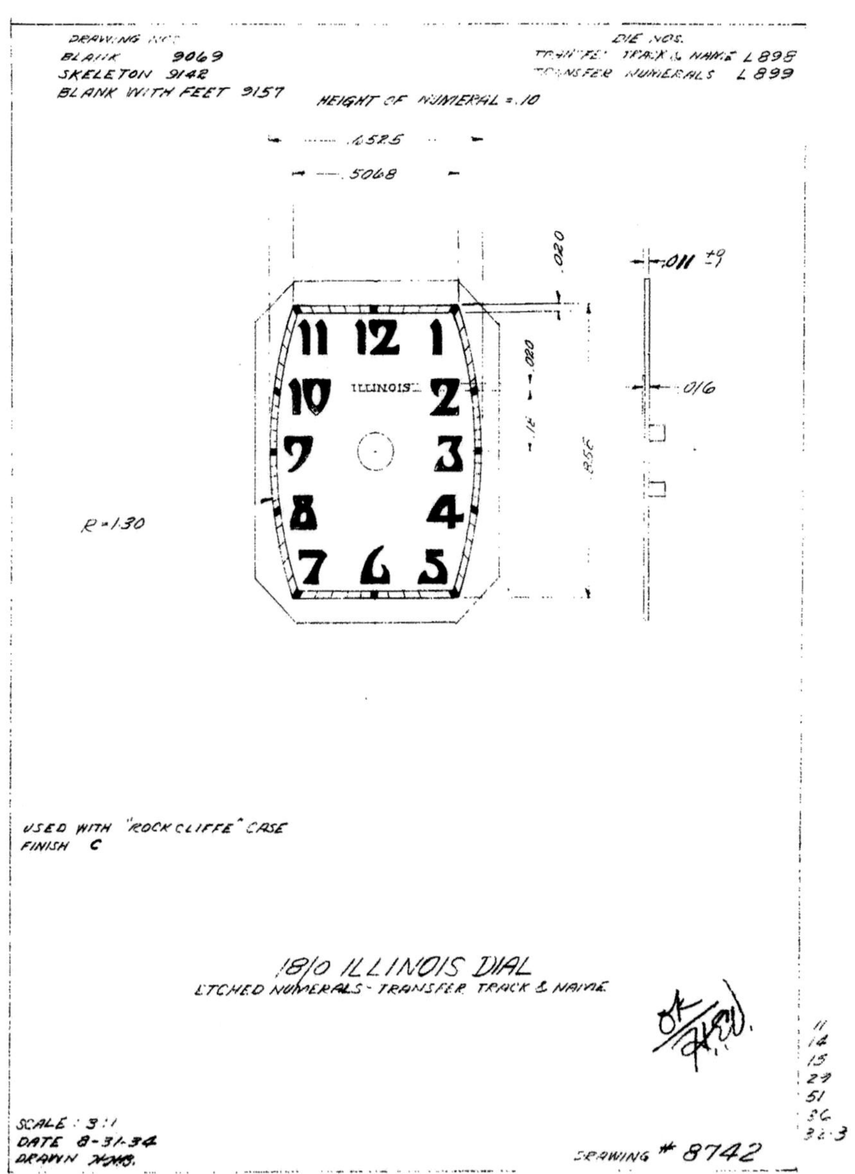

Hamilton drawing, dated August 31, 1934, for Illinois Rockliffe 18/0 (numerals)

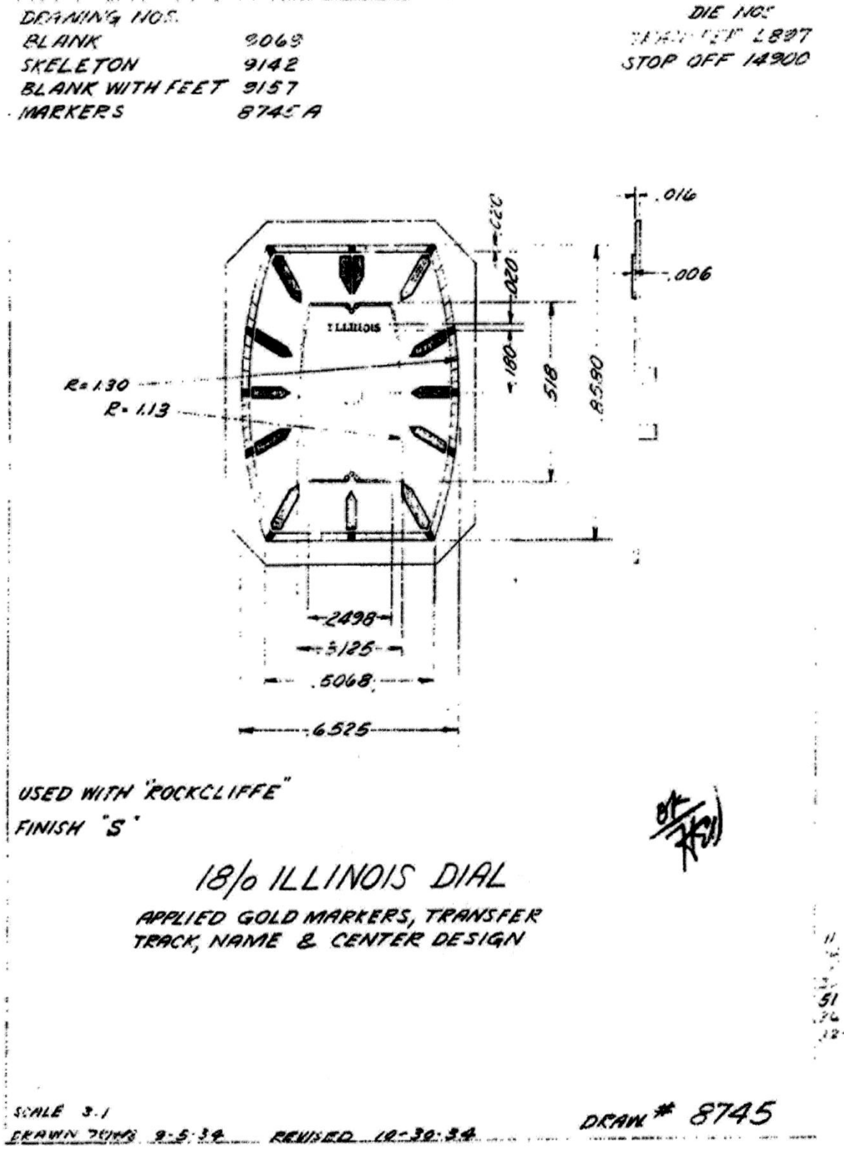

Hamilton drawing dated October 30, 1934 for Illinois Rockliffe 18/0 (markers)

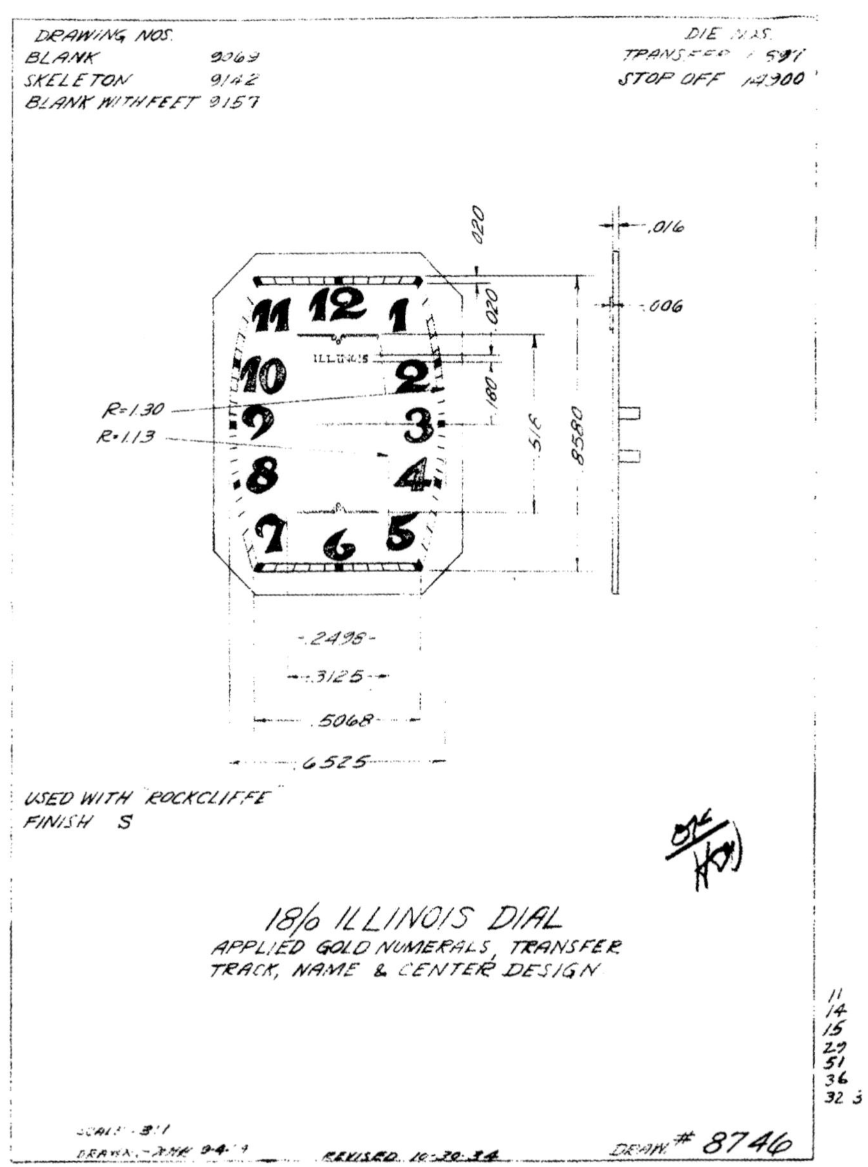

Hamilton drawing dated October 30, 1934, for Illinois Rockliffe 18/0 (numerals)

A ROCKLIFFE 18/0 MYSTERY

It is generally assumed that Hamilton issued the solid gold Illinois Rockliffe 18/0 model with an 18/0 size movement to help deplete its inventory of these movements, but the question then arises: Why put this small ("ladies'") movement into a solid gold case? At least one knowledgeable Hamilton and Illinois collector, Rick Vess, speculates that "perhaps the solid gold case was easier to modify to accommodate the 18/0 size movement." Vess further opines that the "filled gold cases likely required a case supplier to perform the modification, while Hamilton could likely perform the solid gold work in-house." This savings would have appealed to Hamilton.

Perhaps Hamilton had excess Rockliffe cases to liquidate as well, and we know of at least one instance where Hamilton fitted its Illinois-produced 401 movement into an Illinois Rockliffe model.

This could have been an inventory reduction practice of Hamilton, Vess further offers, as "some 1920s-type Hamilton Cushions, albeit in odd-numbered and marked cases, were released for some strange reason in never advertised 10K gold-filled cases. (Only the 14K solid and 14K gold-filled cases were advertised, and also far outnumber the 10K gold-filled cases). Additionally, they all seemed to utilize long-out-of-production 986 and 986A ladies' pendant movements (some with subsidiary seconds at 9.)"

However, the Rockliffe 18/0 mystery may have more to do with the reduction of 18/0 size movement inventory, as it is unlikely that there was an excess of Rockliffe cases in inventory. Also, Hamilton may have wanted a higher-end solid gold watch to appeal to post-Depression consumers.

Further Hamilton Economizing

In yet another economy move in 1934, Hamilton took the 14K gold-filled Illinois ladies' Florette model released in 1931 and rereleased it as an Antoinette in a 10K gold-filled case. The marketing ploy was apparently unsuccessful as only two Antoinette models are known to exist and one of them was customized with diamonds. (See listing for **Antoinette** in Chapter 10.) This release, too, also was motivated by Hamilton's strong desire to exhaust 21/0 size Illinois movement inventory.

This cost savings practice by Hamilton apparently first showed up in the 1933 Illinois sales catalog; the 6/0 size Potomac was merely listed as being in "natural filled gold" (not mentioning 10K gold-filled) and the 18/0 size Beverly 852 and the 21/0 size Janette in 10K gold-filled.

The Hamilton switch to lower-quality cases also appeared with the Illinois Lynette model, listed with a 14K white gold-filled case in the 1933 catalog, but degraded to 10K gold-filled in the 1934 catalog.

Illinois was not singled out in this cost savings practice as Hamilton was doing this itself in its own line of watches starting in 1934; that year they released the Grant and Lee models in 10K gold-filled and the Grant also in sterling silver. In 1935 they added still more 10K gold-filled models: Dixon, Drake, Mason, Scott and Turner.

INGERSOLL-WATERBURY WORKING TO CAPACITY

In speaking about conditions at the Ingersoll-Waterbury Co.'s plant in November 1933, with the economy slowly returning to normalcy, C. H. Granger, vice-president, said:

"Our plant is working to capacity at the present time to fill demands. Employees have been increased from a low of 1250 in April, working one or two days a week, to over 2500 at the present time, working the full 45 hours allowed under the Code for the Clock Manufacturers Association."

1933 HISTORICAL NOTES

- This is the worst year of the Great Depression; unemployment hits 25.2%.
- Prohibition is repealed.
- Work starts on the Golden Gate Bridge.
- Vacuum cleaners cost $17.75.
- A loaf of bread costs 7¢.
- Campbell's Vegetable Soup costs 10¢.
- The average house rental is $18.00 per month.

BULOVA NOT TO TAKE WATCH PLANT

Illinois State Journal, October 31, 1933

Bulova Rumors

On October 31, 1933, the *Illinois State Journal* put to rest a rumor that the Bulova Watch Company had purchased the closed Illinois Watch Factory. Bulova had apparently looked at buying the Springfield plant but elected instead to locate its new production facility in Waltham, Massachusetts. This revelation was a huge disappointment to the Springfield community and the former Illinois workers.

Bulova Watch Co. to Open Plant in Waltham

WALTHAM, MASS., July 25.—Announcement was made this morning that the Bulova Watch Co. is to establish a plant in Waltham with operations to start in the immediate future. This follows investigations made by officials of the company and is a positive indication of Waltham being the home of many skilled operatives, especially those engaged in watch making and the producing of precision instruments. The following telegram received by the Chamber of Commerce this morning gives the story.

"This is to officially advise you that we have consummated arrangements for the manufacture of Bulova watches in the Old Howard Watch Co. plant. We will probably start operation on or about Aug. 15, and in accordance with request made in the President's speech last night, we are putting in effect immediately, the proposed code of our industry of a forty hour week and a minimum wage of 35c. per hour. This code is going into effect today in all manufacturing subsidiaries of the Bulova Watch Company."

Signed,
Bulova Watch Company
Joseph Bulova, President.

In arranging for the coming of this new company to Waltham, work has been started in preparing the space in the former E. Howard Watch Co. plant on Charles St. for the installation of machinery and the equipment necessary to evolve the nationally known watch to be assembled in this Waltham plant. It is expected that machinery will arrive within the next few days and that complete operations will be inaugurated not later than Aug. 15.

Jewelers' Circular, August 1933

Illinois in Desperate Straits: Cancelled Chatham Order

On December 21, 1933, Keenan was compelled to cancel an order for a yellow gold-filled Chatham because the Lancaster factory could not assemble 6/0 and 18/0 size Elinvar movements "in anywhere near the quantity originally planned" So, before the end of December 1933, Illinois was already not able to provide completed watches for sale, notwithstanding that the Chatham was one of the few new models offered in the 1934 Illinois Sales Catalog. This also serves to emphasize why the Illinois 1934 models such as the Chatham and Standish are so very scarce today.

December 21,1933

H.M.Jacobson,
917 F Street, N.W.
Washington, D.C.

Dear Sir:

Referring to your unfilled order of November 11th our Back Order No. 458 covering---

1- #605R Chatham Natural

to be billed thru I. Ollendorff Co. of New York - because of failure on the part of our factory to finish the 6/0-size and 18/0-size Elinvar movements in anywhere near the quantity originally planned, we find it necessary to cancel the above order.

We thank you for your patience with us this Fall and feel that you realize thoroughly what manufacturers have been through, trying to produce goods for this rush that came so late in the year. We really could not handle it because earlier in the year there was no indication that we ought to indulge in the pastime of making inventory to go on the shelves.

Very truly yours,

ILLINOIS WATCH DIVISION

Sales Manager

JLK-MMS

CC to I. Ollendorff Co., New York, N.Y.

Keenan's December 21, 1933 letter about the Chatham

Extremely Low Supplies

A little later, on January 8, 1934, Keenan explained to a jobber that "at the present time we are in a position to handle a few orders for the Urbana and Sangamon sports type of strap watches, also the Rockingham, Standish and Chatham . . . [but] we could not offer to supply large quantities because of the fact production of these movements is very light and will not pick up for some time to come." This hoped-for production increase never occurred. Therefore, even at the beginning of 1934, Illinois was in for a struggle to fulfill any orders for any of the wristwatches listed in its latest 1934 sales catalog. And this, regrettably, would be the last Illinois Sales Catalog.

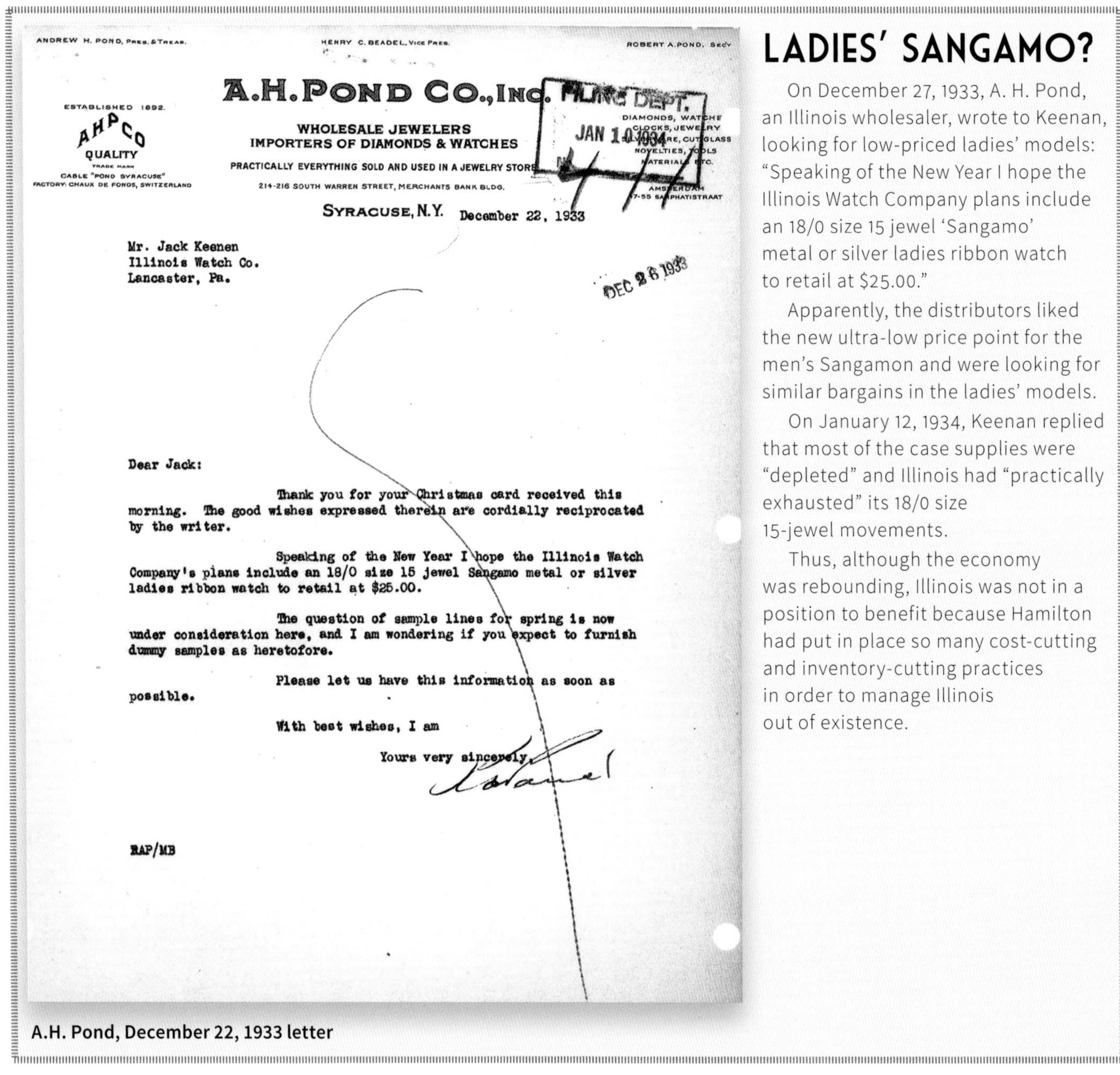

ANDREW H. POND, PRES. & TREAS. HENRY C. BEADEL, VICE PRES. ROBERT A. POND, SEC'Y

A.H.POND CO., INC.

ESTABLISHED 1892.

AHPCO QUALITY

CABLE "POND SYRACUSE"
FACTORY: CHAUX DE FONDS, SWITZERLAND

WHOLESALE JEWELERS
IMPORTERS OF DIAMONDS & WATCHES

PRACTICALLY EVERYTHING SOLD AND USED IN A JEWELRY STORE

214-216 SOUTH WARREN STREET, MERCHANTS BANK BLDG.

DIAMONDS, WATCHES, CLOCKS, JEWELRY, SILVERWARE, CUT GLASS, NOVELTIES, TOOLS, MATERIALS, ETC.

AMSTERDAM 57-55 SARPHATISTRAAT

FILING DEPT. JAN 10 1934

SYRACUSE, N.Y. December 22, 1933

Mr. Jack Keenen
Illinois Watch Co.
Lancaster, Pa.

DEC 26 1933

Dear Jack:

Thank you for your Christmas card received this morning. The good wishes expressed therein are cordially reciprocated by the writer.

Speaking of the New Year I hope the Illinois Watch Company's plans include an 18/0 size 15 jewel Sangamo metal or silver ladies ribbon watch to retail at $25.00.

The question of sample lines for spring is now under consideration here, and I am wondering if you expect to furnish dummy samples as heretofore.

Please let us have this information as soon as possible.

With best wishes, I am

Yours very sincerely,

RAP/MB

A.H. Pond, December 22, 1933 letter

LADIES' SANGAMO?

On December 27, 1933, A. H. Pond, an Illinois wholesaler, wrote to Keenan, looking for low-priced ladies' models: "Speaking of the New Year I hope the Illinois Watch Company plans include an 18/0 size 15 jewel 'Sangamo' metal or silver ladies ribbon watch to retail at $25.00."

Apparently, the distributors liked the new ultra-low price point for the men's Sangamon and were looking for similar bargains in the ladies' models.

On January 12, 1934, Keenan replied that most of the case supplies were "depleted" and Illinois had "practically exhausted" its 18/0 size 15-jewel movements.

Thus, although the economy was rebounding, Illinois was not in a position to benefit because Hamilton had put in place so many cost-cutting and inventory-cutting practices in order to manage Illinois out of existence.

Supply Exhausted

The supply availability for Illinois and the beleaguered Keenan continued to worsen. On January 12, 1934, Keenan told a jobber that "we have exhausted our complete supply of the 17 jewel, 6/0-size and 12/0-size movements that are discontinued and were being cleaned up." In fact, no further watches equipped with either of these movements were ever issued by Illinois.

Keenan further noted that "we are extremely short of grade #105 which is the 21/0-size 15 jewel movements, making up the complete watches, under the names of Lynnette, Janette, Marlette and Antoinette."

January 12, 1934

James J. Burke Co.
St. Louis, Mo.

Attention Mr. Carl J. Teschner

Gentlemen:

We have your letter of the 10th and would advise that we have exhausted our complete supply of the 17jewel 6/0-size and 12/0-size movements that are discontinued and were being cleaned up.

We have nothing left of any description, either in ladies watches or men's watches or for that matter, pocket watches that are what you term 'close-out items'.

The demand for our various items was extremely strong in December and exhausted our planned upon stock of cases, particularly in the natural color.

Because of this shortage of cases, also the fact that by the time we have new cases made up, sufficient in quantity for sample lines, the Spring will be very well advanced and our plan to have new case items, makes us decide that we will not have standard sample lines this Spring.

Just now we are extremely short of grade #105 which is the 21/0-size 15 jewel movements, making up the complete watches, under the names of Lynette, Janette, Marionette and Antoinette.

Other than that we are able to make fairly good deliveries against the balance of our line, as shown in the 1934 catalog.

The writer is planning to be in Chicago and the Middle West possibly in the next week or ten days and looks forward to a visit with you in St. Louis at that time.

Very truly yours,
ILLINOIS WATCH DIVISION

JLK-MMS

Sales Manager

Keenan's January 12, 1934 letter

No Sales Positions

In 1934 Keenan utilized a form letter to reply to those interested in a sales position at Illinois, stating almost oxymoronically: "As you are aware, and as the enclosed catalog indicates, we still have a very comprehensive but limited line of Illinois watches for sale in 1934." Of course, by 1934 business had not turned around for Illinois. It would have been impossible to expect otherwise in light of the fate Hamilton had determined for Illinois once the effects of the Great Depression started to impact Hamilton itself.

The form reply to sales applicants confirms that Keenan was now the only salesperson left employed by the Illinois Watch Division, for he says, "Surely, until things turn around for the better, we are leaning entirely on the selling efforts of our wholesale dealers and their salesmen." However, because these dealers had already been stripped of their dummy samples and were provided with only "a limited line" of items for sale, even the possibility of further Illinois sales would have required Herculean efforts. Hamilton had much earlier planned the demise of Illinois, and it was not long until that would occur. It is sad to trace, step-by-step, the death of a great American watch company.

To start the year, Beckwith had issued a letter on January 16, 1934, to all of the "Illinois Wholesale Distributors," reemphasizing the consolidation efforts and the need to complete Illinois watches. Beckwith noted that "they completed in Lancaster such Illinois matters as were far enough along in process so that they could be delivered last Fall. Only the necessary tools and equipment for this production were transferred."

Hamilton's desired focus in 1934 was on transferring additional tools and machinery, "together with equipment and parts in process," from Springfield to Lancaster. Oddly enough, Beckwith added that Hamilton has "to analyze inventory thoroughly—before it can determine Illinois complete production plans for the year." That Hamilton at this point did not know the Illinois inventory inside-out is beyond belief. No doubt the various inventory reduction plans for Illinois previously implemented had vitiated Illinois' ability to have sufficient parts, cases available, or workers to allow even meager Illinois movement production and sales of complete watches.

The equipment to be transferred was only what was required to finish work in process from Springfield that was being moved to Lancaster to be completed, such as movements that were in production. However, since Hamilton was subsequently unable to assemble Illinois movements

January 16, 1934

TO ILLINOIS WHOLESALE DISTRIBUTORS

Gentlemen:

On April 6th we informed you that we were consolidating operations of our Hamilton and Illinois Divisions.

During the remainder of 1933 our efforts were confined, for the most part, to completing at Lancaster such Illinois matters as were far enough along in process so that they could be delivered last Fall. Only the necessary tools and equipment for this production were transferred.

Now for 1934 we find that additional machinery together with equipment and parts in process must be transferred. Considering this and the need to analyze our inventory thoroughly it will be some little time before we are able to outline complete Illinois production plans for the year.

At the earliest possible moment we will notify you of these plans and in the meantime Mr. Keenan will either be able to see you or communicate with you.

Yours very sincerely,

HAMILTON WATCH COMPANY

President

Frank C. Beckwith
AH

Beckwith's letter of January 16, 1934

in Lancaster, the required equipment was likely not moved from Springfield after all.

One day after Beckwith's letter to all the Illinois distributors, Keenan wrote to S. H. Clausin and Co. on January 17, 1934, advising that:

- "We truly are endeavoring in every Way possible to provide for Illinois Watches for the trade this year.
- "Yesterday, Mr. Beckwith, our President, sent out a letter to all our wholesalers asking them to give us a little breathing room space so that we can have more time to analyze our inventory position together with manufacturing possibilities before seeing definitely what can be the continuing line of Illinois watches.
- "At the present time we are able to take care of orders in any quantity for our various railroad watches.
- "In a limited way we can take care of requests for the 21/0 size 17 jewel ladies watches in the Babette, Débette, Mariette and Marlette styles in white only.
- "On the 21/0 size 15 jewel watches in the Lynette, Janette, Marionette and Antoinette case model there is a shortage in the delivery of these movements out of the Factory.
- "In regard to the 18/0 size and 6/0 size strap watches—we will take care of your orders as listed and could handle limited requests for these, but cannot promise good deliveries."

Remarkably, this shortage was "out of the Factory" in Springfield that had been closed at the end of July 1933. Former Illinois employees were still periodically being sent into the shuttered Illinois Factory to try to assemble certain needed movements. By January 17, 1934, however, even fewer models were available, as indicated in Keenan's letters to S. H. Clausin & Co., Inc., and Freudenheim Brothers, Inc.

January 17,1934

Freudenheim Brothers, Inc.
2 Maiden Lane,
New York, N.Y.

Attention Mr. Milton Freudenheim

Gentlemen:

Have your letter of the 13th and surely do look forward to being able to visit with you in New York quite shortly and be able to discuss definitely the ability of our Company to deliver Illinois movements.

While I was in New York last week it was entirely on a different subject and I did not have an opportunity of visiting with all of our customers; in fact did not plan to do so at the time I went to New York.

You have now received a letter from Mr. Beckwith asking for a breathing spell wherein we will be able to analyse definitely the Illinois inventory of parts and make plans regarding production on watches.

Just now it is impossible to make any definite promises covering delivery. We are extremely short of movements in the 18/0-size; 6/0-size and 21/0-size 15 jewel grades.

In fact, in the 21/0-size 15 jewel grade used to make up the complete Lynette, Janette, Marionette and Antoinette, our supply of movements is exhausted and we will not be able to even furnish the complete watches shown in our catalog, until late in February or the first of March.

On the other styles shown in our catalog we can give fairly reasonable deliveries but cannot at this time release any separate movements in any grade for jobber casing.

Very truly yours,

ILLINOIS WATCH DIVISION

JLK-MMS

Sales Manager

One of Keenan's January 17, 1934 letters

January 17, 1934

S. H. Clausin & Co., Inc.
Minneapolis, Minn.

Attention Mr. R. F. Reed

Gentlemen:

We have your letter of the 15th and thank you greatly for your additional order #12101 covering Illinois Watches.

We truly are endeavoring in every way possible to provide for Illinois Watches for the trade this year.

Yesterday, Mr. Beckwith, our President, sent out a letter to all of our wholesalers asking them to give us a little breathing space so that we can have more time to analyze our inventory position together with manufacturing possibilities before seeing definitely what can be the continuing line of Illinois Watches.

At the present time we are able to take care of orders in any quantity for our various railroad model watches.

In a limited way we can take care of requests for the Midland and Medallion Pocket Watches; also for the 21/0-size 17 jewel ladies watches in the Babette, Debette, Mariette and Marlette styles in white only.

We could supply a few of these in natural but not very many because the Case Companies are still behind in the delivery of cases and do not promise these natural cases until late in February or around the first of March.

On the 21/0-size 15 jewel watches in the Lynette, Janette, Marionette and Antoinette case models there is a shortage in the delivery of these movements out of the factory and our factory manager does not promise relief for about 60 days.

The demand for our watches in December far

#2- S. H. Clausin & Co. 1/17/34

exceeded our plans and reduced our inventory to this serious condition.

In regard to the 18/0-size and 6/0-size strap watches - we will take care of your orders as listed and could handle limited requests for these, but cannot promise good deliveries at least 60 days or maybe some time in April.

It occurs to the writer that you possibly did not receive, or have an opportunity to read our letter of December 8th in regard to Trade Practices and particularly terms. We attach you herewith a copy of that letter and you will note in it why we are unable to date, in advance, any invoices covering delivery of watches in any current month.

Very truly yours,

ILLINOIS WATCH DIVISION

Sales Manager

JLK-MMS

Another January 17, 1934 Keenan letter

Thus, by January 17, 1934, Illinois was out of 6/0, 12/0 and 18/0 size movements as well as 21/0 size 15-jewel ones.

"Error to Let It Die"

Any distributor receiving Beckwith's message should have seriously questioned the viability of the Illinois watch brand. Keenan, who moved to Lancaster as the sole sales manager and company sales representative of Illinois, was during this time struggling under a constant barrage of questions from the distributors seeking answers to the plans for Illinois watches. From the very end of 1933 through the middle of 1934, he responded with grace, diplomacy and sincerity to this constant siege of letters.

To a query from Bauman-Massa Jewelry Co., "Looking for sample lines" (September 26, 1933), Keenan replied, "all cases available for samples have been exhausted" (October 1933).

The Bull Company also wrote, "Looking for sample line" (October 3, 1933). Keenan replied, by return mail, that as there were not enough available cases to furnish dummy samples, it was "impossible to set aside the additional labor required to assemble sample lines."

On October 4, 1933, Keenan used the NRA to explain to a jobber why dummy samples could not be provided: "We do hope that by the first of the year this pressure and labor requirement under NRA Code will be more flexible and we can then see that your men are properly equipped to do a good job selling Illinois Watches." As has been noted, Hamilton did not want to pay its workers the new required higher wage rates to have the Illinois dummy samples assembled.

The queries continued through the year.

- S. H. Clausin wrote, "Want to know what sample lines will be available" (December 27, 1933), also asking "how about sample lines this year? In a good position to use a quantity of Illinois watches."
- On December 29, 1933, Baldwin-Miller Co. observed, significantly, "Unable to get sample line last Fall on new models, it seriously curtailed our sales efforts—looking for sample line for February, 1934."
- Bauman-Massa queried again on December 30, 1933: "We ... write you today ... to see if you could give up some information regarding sample lines and lines for the coming season, as we are now making up our watch lines for Spring." That letter contained this remarkable postscript: "I was told the other day that Hibbs was back in Springfield and a few more of the boys are commencing to wander back there. Sincerely hope that it means the re-opening of the old Illinois Watch Factory as an individual unit instead of a branch of the Hamilton Watch Company in Lancaster, as I know you would much rather function that way "

In fact, some former Illinois employees had gone back to Springfield to desperately try to assemble some needed Illinois movements for Hamilton in Lancaster.

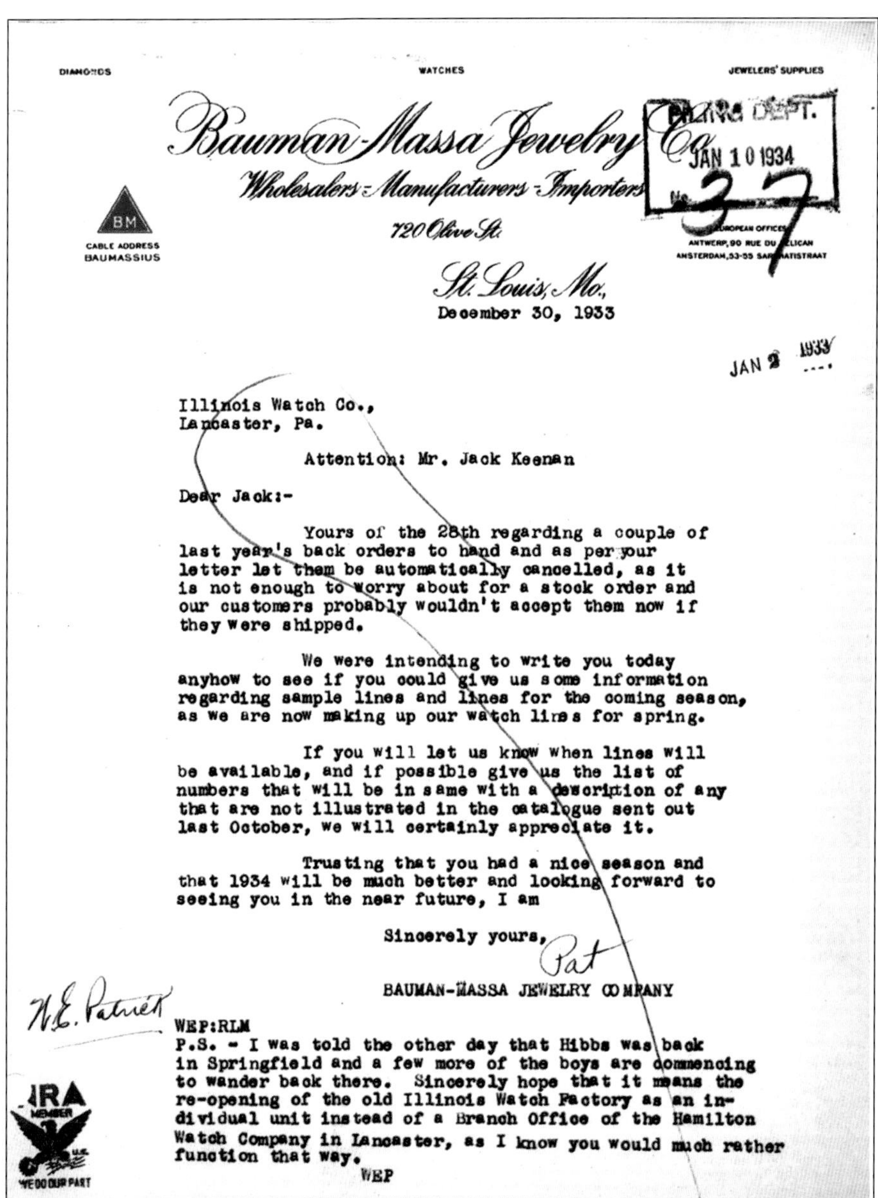

DIAMONDS WATCHES JEWELERS' SUPPLIES

Bauman-Massa Jewelry Co.
Wholesalers - Manufacturers - Importers
720 Olive St.
CABLE ADDRESS BAUMASSIUS
St. Louis, Mo.

December 30, 1933

JAN 10 1934
No. 37
JAN 2 1934

Illinois Watch Co.,
Lancaster, Pa.

Attention: Mr. Jack Keenan

Dear Jack:-

Yours of the 28th regarding a couple of last year's back orders to hand and as per your letter let them be automatically cancelled, as it is not enough to worry about for a stock order and our customers probably wouldn't accept them now if they were shipped.

We were intending to write you today anyhow to see if you could give us some information regarding sample lines and lines for the coming season, as we are now making up our watch lines for spring.

If you will let us know when lines will be available, and if possible give us the list of numbers that will be in same with a description of any that are not illustrated in the catalogue sent out last October, we will certainly appreciate it.

Trusting that you had a nice season and that 1934 will be much better and looking forward to seeing you in the near future, I am

Sincerely yours,
Pat
BAUMAN-MASSA JEWELRY COMPANY

W. E. Patrick

WEP:RLM
P.S. - I was told the other day that Hibbs was back in Springfield and a few more of the boys are commencing to wander back there. Sincerely hope that it means the re-opening of the old Illinois Watch Factory as an individual unit instead of a Branch Office of the Hamilton Watch Company in Lancaster, as I know you would much rather function that way.
WEP

NRA MEMBER WE DO OUR PART

December 30, 1933 jobber letter with an amazing "P.S."

On January 8, 1934, Keenan wrote another jobber: "The definite program of Illinois Watches will be depending a great deal upon this inventory and our ability to work in production plans as well as new costs under the various NRA Codes." Surely, if there had been as many movements produced in 1932 as some historians have claimed, the movement inventory should not have been a problem at this time for Illinois. (See Chapter 6, Movements.)

But the new year brought only more queries, with samples as a continuing theme. Butterfield Bros. wrote on January 6, 1934, "Looking for sample lines." Manheimer wrote that during the last part of the past year, they were unable to "show pictures instead of merchandise to try to secure sales" (January 9, 1934). Shortly thereafter, A. I. Hall observed, similarly, that during the last part of the previous year, they were unable to "show a representative stock of Illinois watches due to uncertainty of the release of new models" (January 13, 1934). Manheimer wrote again on January 15 that the jobbers "need material for salesmen going out to their territories, with no dummy samples ... so that we can both get the most amount of business for your line." A. G. Schwab & Sons, Inc., pleaded on January 15 that they need "Illinois samples for our travelers."

The situation was getting desperate, and the jobbers became more insistent. S. H. Clausin asked quite directly on January 17: "What products can be delivered in 1934?" The jobbers were not unaware of what might be happening. A. I. Hall & Son said as much on January 23, pointing out that they needed "sample lines" to do "a good selling job on the same basis as the Hamilton lines." This letter would indicate that sample lines or dummy samples still existed for the Hamilton brand.

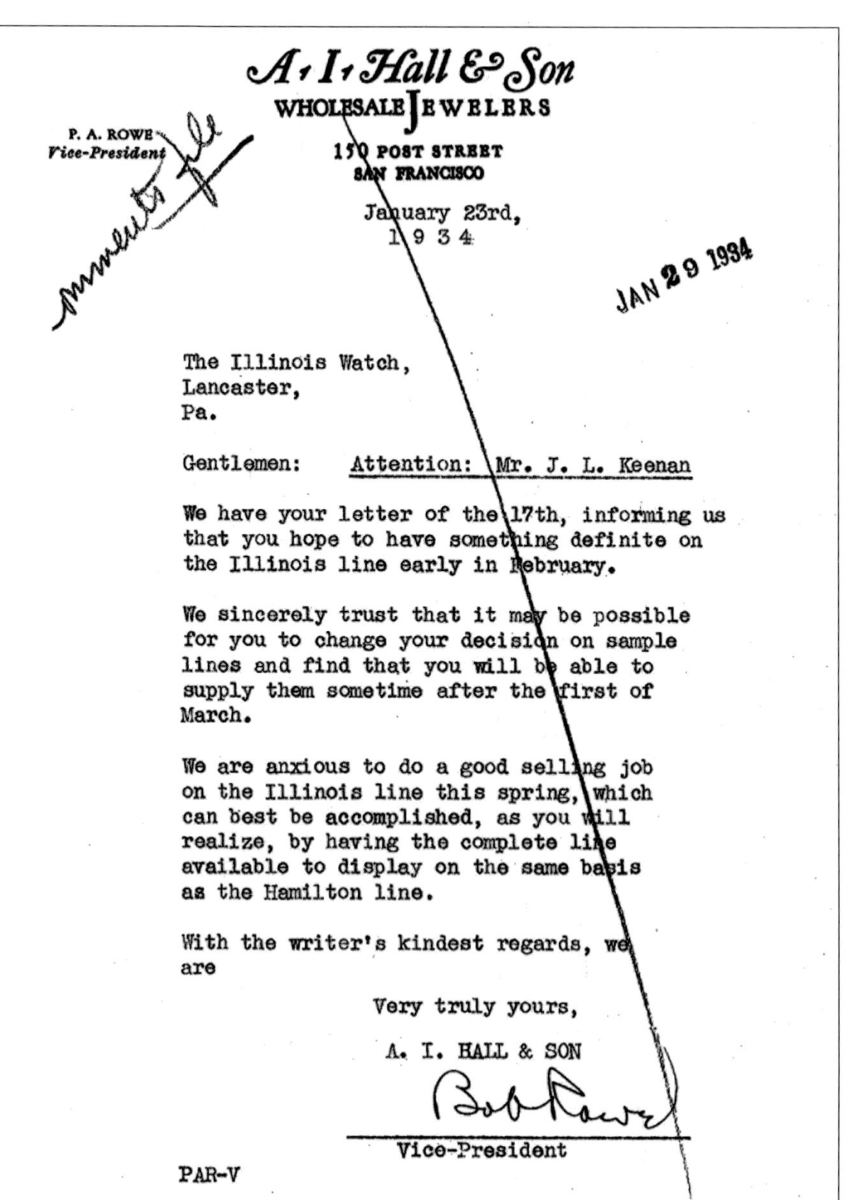

A. I. Hall & Son
WHOLESALE JEWELERS
150 POST STREET
SAN FRANCISCO

P. A. ROWE
Vice-President

January 23rd,
1 9 3 4

JAN 29 1934

The Illinois Watch,
Lancaster,
Pa.

Gentlemen: Attention: Mr. J. L. Keenan

We have your letter of the 17th, informing us that you hope to have something definite on the Illinois line early in February.

We sincerely trust that it may be possible for you to change your decision on sample lines and find that you will be able to supply them sometime after the first of March.

We are anxious to do a good selling job on the Illinois line this spring, which can best be accomplished, as you will realize, by having the complete line available to display on the same basis as the Hamilton line.

With the writer's kindest regards, we are

Very truly yours,

A. I. HALL & SON

Bob Rowe

Vice-President

PAR-V

A.I. Hall & Sons letter noting, in January 1934, that Hamilton was still issuing dummy samples for its line

Keenan could only reply as he did on January 8, 1934, to E. Bastheim Company: "We ran very close in our plans on cases so that we have no excess quantity of cases to make up sample lines ... We are also taking a very definite inventory of Illinois watch parts and assemblys [*sic*] with the idea of having a definite program that we can offer to the trade sometime around the middle of February."

On January 12, 1934, Keenan could tell Manheimer only that "Beckwith of Hamilton is evaluating this situation and will issue an announcement soon."

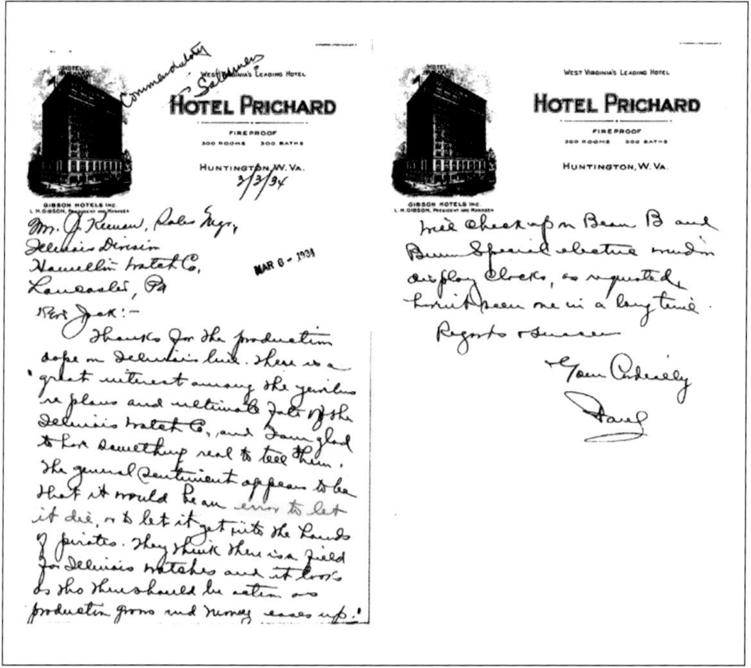

Commendatory
to Salesmen

WEST VIRGINIA'S LEADING HOTEL
HOTEL PRICHARD
FIREPROOF
300 ROOMS 300 BATHS
HUNTINGTON, W. VA.
3/3/34

GIBSON HOTELS INC.
L. H. GIBSON, PRESIDENT AND MANAGER

Mr. J. Keenan, Sales Mgr.,
Illinois Division
Hamilton Watch Co.,
Lancaster, Pa

MAR 6 - 1934

Dear Jack:—

Thanks for the production dope on Illinois line. There is a great interest among the jewelers in plans and ultimate fate of the Illinois Watch Co., and I am glad to have something real to tell them. The general sentiment appears to be that it would be an error to let it die, or to let it get into the hands of pirates. They think there is a field for Illinois watches and it looks to [illegible] there should be action as production grows and money eases up!

WEST VIRGINIA'S LEADING HOTEL
HOTEL PRICHARD
FIREPROOF
300 ROOMS 300 BATHS
HUNTINGTON, W. VA.

GIBSON HOTELS INC.
L. H. GIBSON, PRESIDENT AND MANAGER

Will check up on Beam B and Beam Special electric [illegible] display clocks, as requested, haven't seen one in a long time.

Regards & success

Yours Cordially

Paul

"Error to let it die." West Virginia distributor, March 3, 1934. (Highlight added)

The jobbers' frustration with ongoing shortage of Illinois watches and samples shows clearly in the letter from "Paul," who must have known Keenan well: "It would be an error to let it die."

On March 9, 1934, Keenan sent a memorandum to the Hamilton executives indicating the completed watches that could be sold, if finished movements were available. Although portions of his document are difficult to read, it basically states:

- Grade 161: Had enough to last through August.
- Grade 163: Enough in stock for one year's sales.
- Grade 167: "All are sold."
- Grade 427: "All will be sold."
- Grade 605: "389 in present stock are all sold," "2000 have been sent in from Springfield" and the Hamilton "Production Department promises deliveries to start in August." [It is doubtful many of these were completed.]
- Grade 207: "The remaining lot of 176 are sold ... Can sell 5000 more of these at return of $10.00 each net if we can commence deliveries by October." [No further grade 207s were ever produced after 1932.]
- Grade 805E: "All sold. We have orders for 470 complete watches and must wait for deliveries out of the 4,300 which have been sent in from Springfield. Again you will note this item of 470 complete watches which are unfilled mail orders covering watches in our catalogue and we, of course, can use as much before August as factory can deliver." [Very few of these were completed in Lancaster.]
- Grade 107: "There are only 256 remaining to be finished, these are sold and will be delivered this month. We have unfilled order for 725 additional—there are 3510 that have been sent in from Springfield. Some of these are ready for friction jewel and perhaps Production Department can get them through promptly." [Very few of these were to be completed.]

- Grade 105: "All available have been sold and delivered. We have orders for 1259 complete watches for which we have cases and, therefore, these… should receive preference on production. In fact, Production Department has promised to get behind the first lot of 600 pieces that were *rushed in* from Springfield." [Very few of these were to be completed.]

Remarkably enough, orders were still coming in from the ever loyal Illinois jobbers, even as Hamilton was steadily forcing an end t o Illinois availability.

Towards the end of the year, A. I. Hall was asking why certain models "cannot be delivered in 1934, as they are in the 1934 catalog?" (November 17). So even the very limited offerings in the 1934 Illinois Sales Catalog were not available for delivery.

Another jobber, Albert Walker Co., on October 16, 1933 remarked, "Orders for new Elinvar watches are waiting for the dummy line so we could order 214 watches." They did end up ordering 214 watches for their sales force.

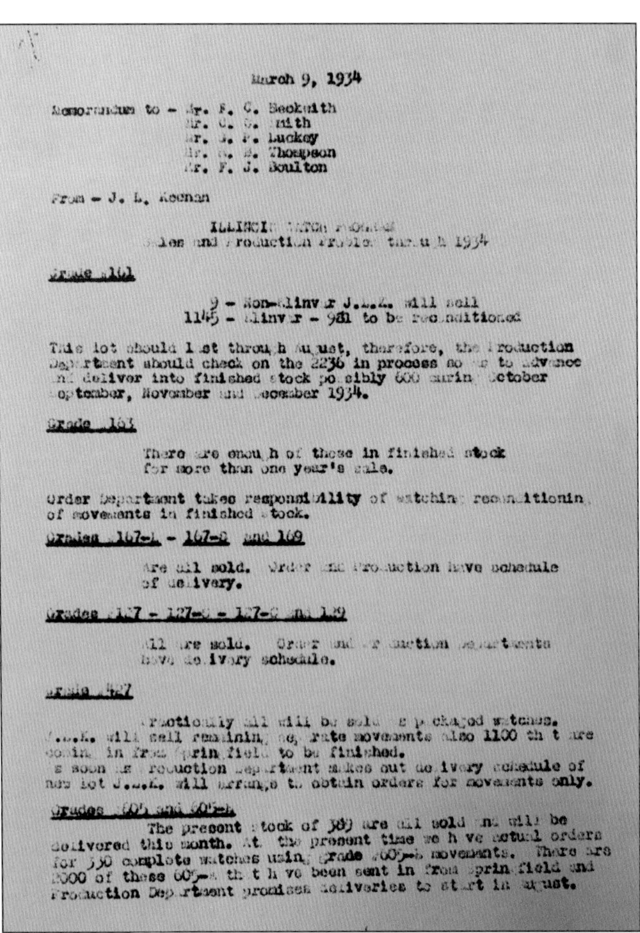

March 9, 1934

Memorandum to - Mr. F. C. Beckwith
Mr. C. S. Smith
Mr. J. F. Luckey
Mr. [illegible] Thompson
Mr. F. J. Boulton

From - J. L. Keenan

ILLINOIS [illegible]
Sales and Production Problem through 1934

Grade [illegible]161

9 - Non-Elinvar J.L.K. will sell
1145 - Elinvar - 981 to be reconditioned

This lot should last through August, therefore, the Production Department should check on the 2236 in process so as to advance and deliver into finished stock possibly 600 during October September, November and December 1934.

Grade [illegible]163

There are enough of these in finished stock for more than one year's sale.

Order Department takes responsibility of watching reconditioning of movements in finished stock.

Grades [illegible]167-[illegible] - 167-[illegible] and 169

Are all sold. Order and Production have schedule of delivery.

Grades [illegible]127 - 127-[illegible] - 127-[illegible] and 129

All are sold. Order and Production Departments have delivery schedule.

Grade [illegible]427

Practically all will be sold as packaged watches. J.L.K. will sell remaining separate movements also 1100 that are coming in from Springfield to be finished.
As soon as Production Department makes out delivery schedule of new lot J.L.K. will arrange to obtain orders for movements only.

Grades [illegible]605 and 605-E

The present stock of 389 are all sold and will be delivered this month. At the present time we have actual orders for 330 complete watches using Grade #605-E movements. There are 2000 of these 605-E that have been sent in from Springfield and Production Department promises deliveries to start in August.

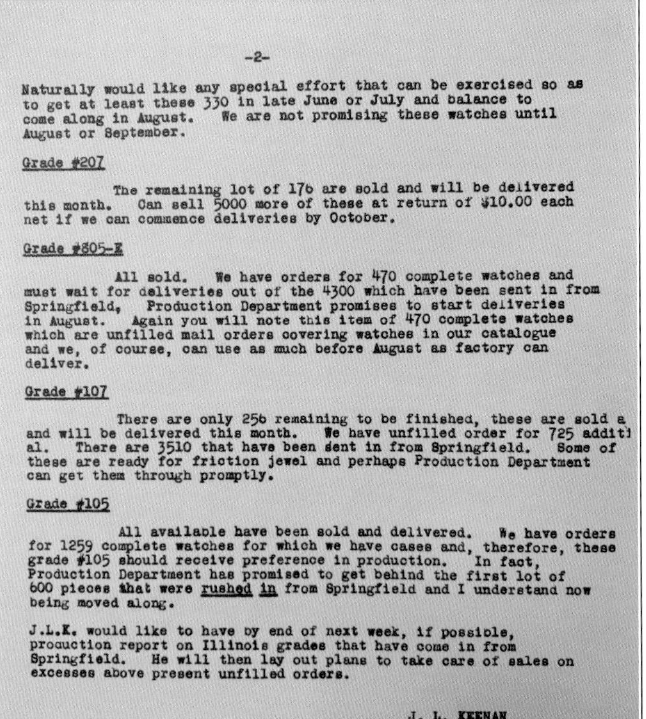

-2-

Naturally would like any special effort that can be exercised so as to get at least these 330 in late June or July and balance to come along in August. We are not promising these watches until August or September.

Grade #207

The remaining lot of 176 are sold and will be delivered this month. Can sell 5000 more of these at return of $10.00 each net if we can commence deliveries by October.

Grade #805-E

All sold. We have orders for 470 complete watches and must wait for deliveries out of the 4300 which have been sent in from Springfield, Production Department promises to start deliveries in August. Again you will note this item of 470 complete watches which are unfilled mail orders covering watches in our catalogue and we, of course, can use as much before August as factory can deliver.

Grade #107

There are only 256 remaining to be finished, these are sold a and will be delivered this month. We have unfilled order for 725 additi al. There are 3510 that have been sent in from Springfield. Some of these are ready for friction jewel and perhaps Production Department can get them through promptly.

Grade #105

All available have been sold and delivered. We have orders for 1259 complete watches for which we have cases and, therefore, these grade #105 should receive preference in production. In fact, Production Department has promised to get behind the first lot of 600 pieces that were rushed in from Springfield and I understand now being moved along.

J.L.K. would like to have by end of next week, if possible, production report on Illinois grades that have come in from Springfield. He will then lay out plans to take care of sales on excesses above present unfilled orders.

J. L. KEENAN

Keenan's memorandum to the Hamilton executives, March 9, 1934

Finally, Hamilton's continuous efforts into 1934 to liquidate the Illinois parts inventory incurred the wrath of the sales head of Illinois. Keenan, at his wits' end, wrote a blistering memorandum to his Lancaster counterparts, objecting to these practices.

In addition, Keenan wrote an internal memorandum on March 26, 1934, to his then boss, W. Ross Atkinson, Hamilton's director of sales: "I have always stood with you that Hamilton Inventory could best be handled by not cleaning house in the Waltham—'Clean any we have off the shelves' program, at any and all times, or the Elgin 'We are overstocked and are correcting other management errors' and, of course the old bromide our executives used 'Hamilton is in the hands of bankers and must raise a million dollars' and so dumped Illinois."

That Keenan was very upset is further evidenced by his statement "The fact that you did keep faith with dealers and Hamilton Watches were not sacrificed is, I believe one of the reasons your new Zone Program is being accepted. [*Author's note:* He wrote this on March 26, 1934, notwithstanding the "Zone Program" was not publicly announced by Hamilton until May 1, 1934, so Hamilton must have released it in advance to certain of its distributors that were to be retained]. Now, what I am shooting at, is need to have our executives and board understand that you stood steadfast against foolish liquidation so that when market changed to an upward trend you could capitalize." Keenan continued along this vein, pointing out how Waltham could not take advantage of low-priced parts in stock but had to start over, building watches more expensively from scratch.

From Keenan's memo, it appears clear that Hamilton took care of its distributors and customers but sacrificed those of Illinois as it threw Illinois under the bus: "Hamilton Watches were not sacrificed." Nor did Hamilton apply to itself the draconian measures it implemented with Illinois. Thus, as a shrewd business strategy, Hamilton devised ways to utilize existing Illinois inventory until the inventory could be depleted, as they had no plans to produce Illinois watches or to maintain the Illinois brand other than as a means to further exhaust inventory.

Another fascinating feature of this memorandum is Keenan's apparent discussion of wages and prices with "Potter," then the president of Elgin—subjects that are clearly illegal under current antitrust laws.

The most amazing discovery in Keenan's memorandum is not his outrage about Hamilton's liquidation plans for Illinois inventory, but the possibility that before March 1934 he might not have been aware of Hamilton's plans to discontinue the sale of Illinois products. Looking back, even with our limited perspective on this history, we can see that were several clear signs of Hamilton's plan. The fact that this may have been intentionally kept from Keenan is understandable, since he was still needed by Hamilton as an interface with Illinois sales representatives, distributors and customers to actively promote Illinois for Hamilton for as long as Hamilton deemed necessary. Yet it is surprising that Keenan might not have yet read the writing on the wall.

March 26, 1934

Memorandum to - Mr. W. R. Atkinson

From - J. L. Keenan

HAMILTON INVENTORY LIQUIDATION POSITION

Just another of my effusions but I have always stood with you that Hamilton Inventory could best be handled by not cleaning house in the Waltham - "Clean any we have off the shelves" program, at any and all times, or the Elgin "We are overstocked and are correcting other management errors" and, of course the old bromide our executives used "Hamilton is in the hands of bankers and must raise a million dollars" so dumped Illinois.

The fact that you did keep faith with dealers and Hamilton Watches were not sacrificed is, I believe one of the reasons your new Zone Program is being accepted. Now, what I am shooting at, is need to have our executives and board understand that you stood steadfast against foolish liquidation so that when market changed to an upward trend you could capitalize.

This came to my mind yesterday evening while talking with Potter. He was putting the "Bee" on price range and I led him afield. First he said "Waltham is having labor trouble. I understand the factory people voted for A.F. of L." Not knowing anything about it I said, "Just feel it is the unfortunate position of administration that is causing this. I feel generally watch workers are satisfied and happy with their own shop committees".

He expressed the feeling that A.F. of L. would succeed. Anyway was of opinion he would raise factory rates 10%. My reply was that I knew nothing now as to rates as we had no workers in Springfield and was not at all familiar with Lancaster. Then he said "You fellows must not have reduced your rates if you can continue to put your line out at low prices." I ducked this by saying our price range, if anything, at present is equal to or higher than 1929. He came back and said his factory rates now would be equal to 1929 rates and he was going to raise prices on some of his goods to dealers. Also he understood Bulova was increasing.

What I think, Ross, is that both he and Waltham are now finding out the foolishness of having dumped inventory at extreme prices. Their present replacement cost is out of proportion to market and if they can keep you from cashing in on your steadfast market work of last three years they will.

The plan you have regarding #979 - #987 - #989 and eventually #912 - #918 is completely sound. The executives and directors must be kept <u>constantly</u> on your side; that is, if they had sacrificed prestige and inventory value two years ago it would have cost them more by far than the present writing down of in-process inventory on these models which puts Hamilton in the current active market price range and under your zone plan have an opportunity to click this Fall. It will be two or three years before conditions permit \$50 - \$60 weekly payrolls and, therefore, strong market on these price units.

-2-

My experience has proven that average weekly industrial workers' incomes establish the average unit price willingly paid for suits, radios, watches, etc. Our Hamilton line this year must carry plenty of good items under \$50.00 to consumer and don't give up readily on any \$35.00 to \$40.00 possibilities.

Waltham and Elgin both have to make their current goods, because they cleaned shelves at sacrifice. You can have your inning now, by following your plan and make it tough for them by balancing your in-process inventory and be in a good competitive position in 1935.

Standard costs are good, actual costs are comparative but must not now interfere with your chance to continue to keep faith with the dealer. You waited for the time to put goods into the market, last Fall helped and I feel you should not be taken off your plan this Fall, merely because Elgin has to raise their prices. We are going after "Retail jeweler sales" and believe me they need as many Hamiltons as we can get to them this Fall at around \$40.00 to keep them enthused.

J. L. KEENAN

(Written from notes sent in from road.)

Keenan's memorandum to Atkinson, March 26, 1934

The dealers, perhaps sensing Keenan's frustration, had already made their feelings known at higher levels. On January 29, 1934, J. J. Schmukler & Son wrote directly to the president of Hamilton about the increasing popularity of Illinois watches and their desire to sell solid gold 12/0 size watches. They had already gone so far as to contact a case manufacturer to assure themselves of a supply of cases. This model we now believe was the No. 250 (Schmukler). See Chapter 9.

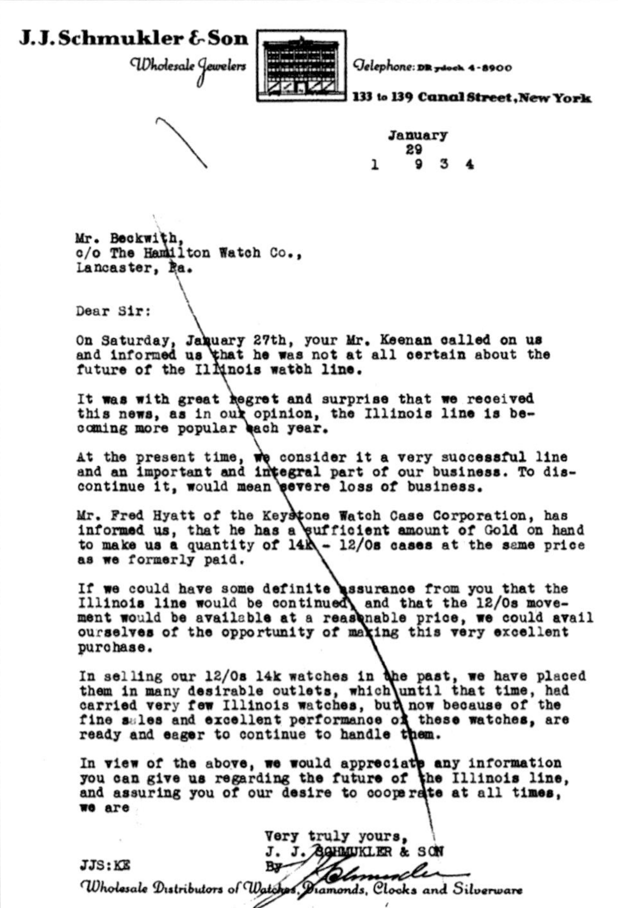
J. J. Schmukler & Son
Wholesale Jewelers
Telephone: DRydock 4-8900
133 to 139 Canal Street, New York

January 29 1934

Mr. Beckwith,
c/o The Hamilton Watch Co.,
Lancaster, Pa.

Dear Sir:

On Saturday, January 27th, your Mr. Keenan called on us and informed us that he was not at all certain about the future of the Illinois watch line.

It was with great regret and surprise that we received this news, as in our opinion, the Illinois line is becoming more popular each year.

At the present time, we consider it a very successful line and an important and integral part of our business. To discontinue it, would mean severe loss of business.

Mr. Fred Hyatt of the Keystone Watch Case Corporation, has informed us, that he has a sufficient amount of Gold on hand to make us a quantity of 14K - 12/0s cases at the same price as we formerly paid.

If we could have some definite assurance from you that the Illinois line would be continued, and that the 12/0s movement would be available at a reasonable price, we could avail ourselves of the opportunity of making this very excellent purchase.

In selling our 12/0s 14k watches in the past, we have placed them in many desirable outlets, which until that time, had carried very few Illinois watches, but now because of the fine sales and excellent performance of these watches, are ready and eager to continue to handle them.

In view of the above, we would appreciate any information you can give us regarding the future of the Illinois line, and assuring you of our desire to cooperate at all times, we are

Very truly yours,
J. J. SCHMUKLER & SON
By

JJS:KE

Wholesale Distributors of Watches, Diamonds, Clocks and Silverware

A dealer's letter expressing a desire for Illinois solid gold models. This request, I believe is for the No. 250/Schmukler solid gold model.

Beckwith's reply is polite but cool and brief. He is still analyzing the Illinois inventory, but there is little evidence that he will give the jobber what he desires. The 207 grade was last made in 1932 and Beckwith had no intention to make any more. So his reply lacks candor. Again, in March, Beckwith rejected Keenan's request to make 5,000 more 12/0 size 207 grade Illinois movements.

January 30, 1934

Mr. J. J. Schmukler,
133 Canal Street,
New York, N. Y.

Dear Mr. Schmukler:

I acknowledge receipt of yours of the 29th and wish to thank you for your letter and the consideration that you have always given the Illinois Watch; also for the appraisal of its present and future possibilities.

Mr. Keenan has returned and told me that he had gone over the matter with you, and I can only add that as soon as our plans are matured we certainly will be very pleased, indeed, to acquaint you with same. At the present time we are going into our inventory of parts, etc., which is quite a job I can assure you.

In the meantime, believe us

Very sincerely yours,

HAMILTON WATCH COMPANY

President

Frank C. Beckwith
AN

Beckwith's reply regarding solid gold Illinois watches

Hamilton Developments

Major News: New Business Plan

In April 1934, with Illinois nearing its end, Hamilton announced in the trade media, in full-page advertisements, that it would unveil a revolutionary new business plan on May 1 to counter unacceptable practices of "E-Z-Kredit" jewelers, price-cutters and related evil discounters in the retail jewelry market.

from **THE HAMILTON WATCH COMPANY**

WILL BE ANNOUNCED MAY 1ST

The manufacturer, the wholesaler, the retailer—like Athos, Porthos and Aramis in Dumas' novel, The Three Musketeers, they will pull together—"all for one and one for all"—under the new Hamilton plan.

BUSINESS lives and thrives on *fair profits*. There must be fair profits for the manufacturer, for the wholesaler, for the retailer. To protect these profits, all three—the manufacturer, the wholesaler, the retailer—must pull together. Like the Three Musketeers in Dumas' famous novel, they must be "all for one and one for all."

The Hamilton Watch Company will announce a new plan May 1st which will make possible closer cooperation between the Hamilton Watch Company, the Hamilton wholesaler, and the Hamilton retailer than has ever existed before. *In supporting the efforts of the honest retailer to secure reasonable profits, this plan will be of the utmost significance to every jeweler in America.*

Watch for further news of the Hamilton New Deal—May 1st.

NRA MEMBER U.S. WE DO OUR PART

HAMILTON WATCH COMPANY, LANCASTER, PENNA.

The Watch of Railroad Accuracy

HAMILTON

April, 1934 Page 9

***Keystone*, April 1934**

After two consecutive years of losses, Hamilton had a salvation plan, established largely by Beckwith "with the energetic support of ... Atkinson, his dapper sales manager," to salvage the Hamilton brand and to position itself to be able to survive in the more price-competitive and cost-cutting marketing environment of the Great Depression. Supposedly, the Hamilton New Zone Distribution Plan would rapidly propel its sales and profits. It is clear that Hamilton had no plans to include Illinois in its New Plan except for perhaps some extremely low-end, uninspiring offerings—some starting as low as $25.00 per watch—as fodder for price cutters, and these watches would not bear the more "valuable" Hamilton brand name.

NEGLECT OF ILLINOIS IN A HISTORY OF HAMILTON

In Don Sauers's excellent history of the Hamilton Watch Company, *Time for America*, the Illinois Watch Company is listed only once in its index; and out of a total of 315 pages of text there are exactly six sentences and a grand total of 99 words that refer to the Illinois Watch Company in any capacity. This lack of coverage is at a minimum symbolic of the lack of importance that Illinois had in the overall history of Hamilton as chronicled by its hand-picked historian.

W. ROSS ATKINSON (1888-1950)

W. Ross Atkinson c. 1934

William Ross Atkinson was born in Harrisburg, Pennsylvania. Early on, the diminutive Atkinson (5 feet, 4 inches tall) was a foreman in a shop making and bending pipes. Since his father was a turner and a tinsmith, there is a strong possibility that he worked for his father. Later he changed professions and become a watchmaker in a jewelry store.

After joining Hamilton in 1921, Atkinson was made assistant sales manager in 1922. He was promoted to sales manager in 1927 and held that post until 1937, when he became director of all sales activities and was elected vice president in charge of sales. In April 1947 he was elected a company director. Atkinson resigned from those positions in November 1949 because of ill health.

As the industry shifted from producing a commodity (the generic wristwatch) to creating value (proprietary models with names and unique designs), Atkinson seems to have taken a lead at Hamilton. His jewelry store experience and work as a watchmaker would have opened some doors there. By 1928 he had become part of the team determining Hamilton's product line. Sauers notes that Atkinson "discussed the company's merchandising activities and experiences" at the 1929 sales convention.*

Atkinson and Lowell were also the key people within Hamilton who developed the Hamilton New Zone Distribution Plan introduced on May 1, 1934. At that point, Atkinson had been with Hamilton for twelve years and had been its director of sales for the last ten years. He was given "the authority to handle all matters pertaining to the new plan of controlled distributors."†

*Donald J. Sauers, *Time for America: Hamilton Watch, 1892–1992* (Lititz, PA: Sutter House, 1992), p. 71.

†*Hamilton Watchmen,* May 1934.

Beckwith's Report to Hamilton Employees

On April 19, 1934, Beckwith reported on the state of the Hamilton company, disclosing the losses in 1932 and 1933 but emphasizing that all money owed to the banks had been paid in full. He said he thought the worst of the Depression was past and hoped to offer "increasingly greater employment." However, he pointed out that "while the number of watches sold since the first of the year shows an increase over the same months in 1933, this number is but one third that of the same period during 1929 and 1930." From what he said, it appears likely that Hamilton also reduced its workforce during the Depression and was "converting the inventories and accounts receivable into cash and not from earned income" during that difficult period.

TO OUR EMPLOYEES

April 19, 1934

The management of the Hamilton Watch Company desires to keep its employees informed at all times of the condition of this business in which we are all vitally interested.

In the Company's Annual Statement for 1931, under liabilities, there is an item, "Notes Payable, banks $2,000,000". During 1932 this was reduced to $917,000; and by December 1933 it was reduced to $400,000. We are now happy to announce that this money owing to the banks has been paid in full.

The Statement of 1932 showed that the Company lost $987,642.70, and in 1933, $148,560.12.

By way of explanation, you will understand that these payments to the banks were made possible by converting the inventories and accounts receivable into cash and not from earned income.

We believe the worst of the depression is past. We are very grateful that since the first of the year we have been able to give increasingly greater employment. Our inventories must be built up in anticipation of better business even though the present conditions and orders received at this time do not justify increased production.

While the number of watches sold since the first of the year shows an increase over the same months in 1933, this number is but one third that of the same period during 1929 and 1930.

Your company is doing everything in its power to increase the sale of Hamilton watches and thus be able, insofar as possible, to insure its employees continuous and increased employment. On May first a new selling plan for Hamilton watches goes into effect which we believe will, in the course of time, increase our sales. It is our very definite belief that if we all work together in manufacturing the highest grades watches as economically as possible—then, insofar as we can accomplish this end, we will all prosper. You may rest assured that as business conditions improve and your company gets on an earning basis, its employees will receive first consideration.

President

Beckwith's written announcement to all Hamilton employees, April 19, 1934

Keenan in Chicago

In an internal memorandum dated April 30, 1934, from Keenan to several Hamilton personnel, he reported that "practically all of the equipment in J.L.K's office will be sent to Chicago," but noted, "From time to time J.L.K., of course, will be in Lancaster."

Once Keenan left for Chicago, there was zero Illinois sales presence in Lancaster—or effectively anywhere else, for that matter. But this was fine with Hamilton, as it had no further traditional sales plans for Illinois other than those that would permit the continued liquidation of any Illinois inventory (doubtless to avoid its financial write-off). Moreover, this move further reinforced Hamilton's exclusion of Illinois from its new Distribution Plan.

Keenan Is Feted By Hamilton Watch

LANCSSTER, PA.—Jack L. Keenan recently named director of sales in the middlewest for the Hamilton Watch Co. was the guest at a testimonial dinner held in Hotel Brunswick recently. Mr. Keenan will be located in Chicago.

W. Ross Atkinson, director of sales of the Hamilton Watch Co., was toastmaster. Among the speakers was F. C. Beckwith, president of the company.

Jewelers' Circular, April 1934

New Zone Distribution Plan Launched

In May 1934, Hamilton officially launched with tremendous fanfare its "New Zone Distribution Plan" not long after it had named Keenan director of sales in the "middlewest" for the Hamilton Watch Company. Thus, with Keenan's relocation, the last Illinois advocate in Lancaster was gone from Hamilton, though it turned out that Keenan was from time to time, (even from Chicago) trying to support the sales of Illinois watches down into 1935 and the Illinois Whitman model as late as 1946 (see Chapter 9).

On May 1, 1934, Hamilton issued more than twelve full-color pages of announcements and advertisements in the *Keystone* and the *Jewelers' Circular* describing their new plan of zone distribution. Basically, the Hamilton Plan reduced the number of its distributors from 105 to thirty-nine; and those thirty-nine were then assigned to twenty-one modified, exclusive geographical zones.

The HAMILTON WATCHMEN

ALL FOR ONE
ONE FOR ALL

Devoted to the welfare of regular retail jewelers —also to Hamilton's designated zone distributors and to the Hamilton Watch Company.

The public must be served and served well. Business has become a public trust. Intelligent co-operation produces best service to the consumer.

VOL. 1—No. 1 PUBLISHED BY THE HAMILTON WATCH COMPANY, LANCASTER, PENNA., MAY 1934.

BIG NEWS FROM HAMILTON

NEW PLAN ZONE DISTRIBUTION

(SEE FOLLOWING PAGES FOR FULL DETAILS)

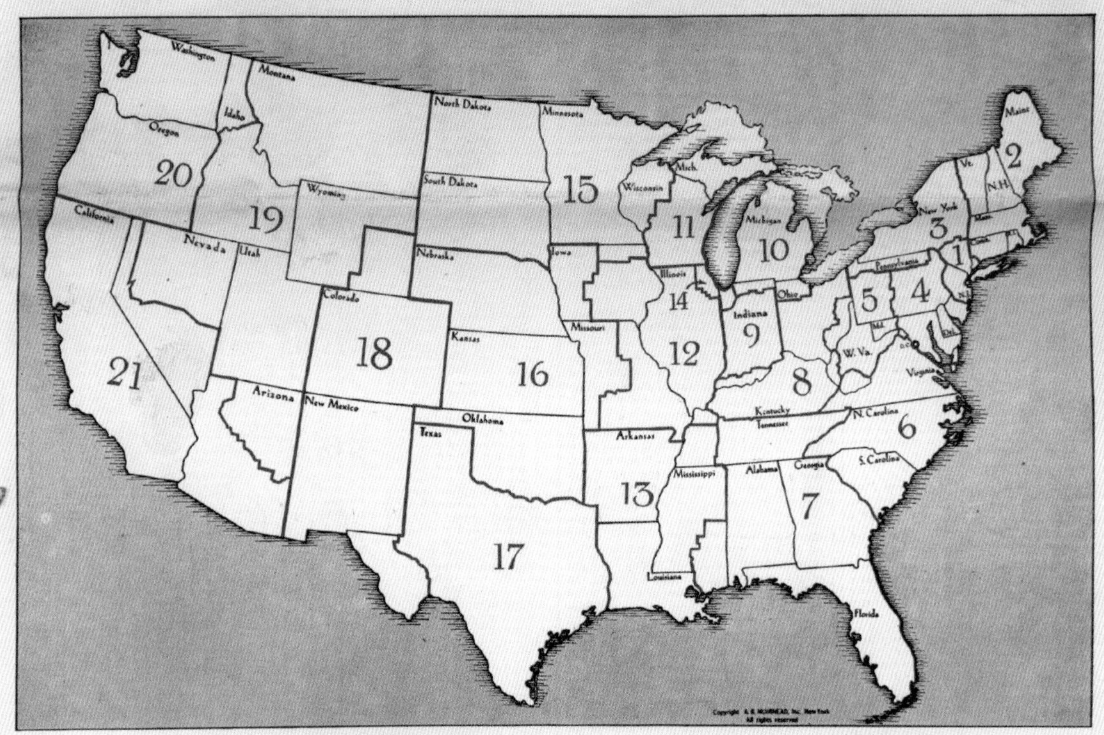

New List of Designated Hamilton Distributors By Zones

ZONE 1

Distributors of Hamilton Watches in Zone 1:

ALPHEUS L. BROWN
New York, N. Y.

BUSS-LINTHICUM-THORSON, INC.
New York, N. Y. Chicago, Ill.

FREUDENHEIM BROS., INC.
New York, N. Y.

HENRY GINNEL & CO.
New York, N. Y.

LOUIS MANHEIMER & BROS., INC.
New York, N. Y.

N. H. WHITE & CO., INC.
New York, N. Y.

The territory included in Zone 1 is as follows: Metropolitan New York City and Long Island; and the following Counties in New York: Dutchess, Orange, Putnam, Rockland, Sullivan, Ulster and Westchester.

The following Counties in New Jersey: Bergen, Essex, Hudson, Hunterdon, Mercer, Middlesex, Monmouth, Morris, Passaic, Somerset, Sussex, Union and Warren.

Fairfield County, Connecticut.

ZONE 2

Distributors of Hamilton Watches in Zone 2:

I. ALBERTS SONS, INC.
Boston, Mass.

LOUIS MANHEIMER & BROS., INC.
New York, N. Y.

D. C. PERCIVAL & CO., INC.
Boston, Mass.

THE ALBERT WALKER CO.
Providence, R. I.

The territory included in Zone 2 is as follows: The entire States of Maine, Massachusetts, New Hampshire, Rhode Island, Vermont and all of Connecticut except Fairfield County.

(Continued on last page)

Keystone, May 1934

2 THE HAMILTON WATCHMEN May 1934

NEW PLAN FOR BETTER BUSINESS

CLOSER COOPERATION BETWEEN RETAIL JEWELER, WHOLESALER & HAMILTON WATCH COMPANY

CONTROLLED DISTRIBUTION IS NEW HAMILTON POLICY

W. ROSS ATKINSON, DIRECTOR OF SALES, HAMILTON WATCH CO.

To the Hamilton Sales Manager, Ross Atkinson, has been given the authority to handle all matters pertaining to the new plan of controlled distribution.

Mr. Atkinson has been with the Hamilton Company 12 years and has been Director of sales 10 years. He is well known throughout the jewelry trade and may be depended upon to always be a staunch advocate of the new plan and a believer in "All for one and one for all."

SAYS MR. ATKINSON:

"Hamilton's new Modified Zone Plan of distribution is not an overnight inspiration. It is the outcome of a comprehensive investigation covering a period of three years, during which we thoroughly analyzed Hamilton's position in the market and the situation of the retail and wholesale jeweler. This survey clearly indicated the need for a policy which would provide protection for legitimate channels of distribution, and which would effect merchandising control.

"We are just as firmly convinced as ever that the retail jeweler is the only suitable outlet for a quality product such as the Hamilton Wat h, and we are fully cognizant of the handicaps under which the retailer has been operating in recent years. Consequently, our new policy of restricted and controlled distribution has been adopted to eliminate harmful and destructive competitive practices and to confine the sale of Hamilton Watches to ethical retail outlets, thus insuring a fair profit to dealers and an honest value to consumers.

"The inauguration of the plan involves many changes in our distributing organization, as well as the sacrifice of a considerable volume of business. However, I believe that in restricting the sale of our product to the legitimate retail jeweler and in giving him the protection he has sought, our new plan will get the whole-hearted support of the trade which it merits, and which it must have to be successful."

Aim of New System is Elimination of Trade Evils and the Protection of Fair Profits for Retail Jeweler and Wholesale Distributor

LANCASTER, PA., May 1st—An important and far-reaching decision has been made by the directors and officers of the Hamilton Watch Company. In line with modern business and the New Deal in general, the Hamilton Company has adopted a plan of modified zone distribution for Hamilton watches which it is expected will mean more satisfactory business relations between the company, its wholesale distributors and the thousands of retail jewelers all over the United States.

The Hamilton Company recognizes the fact that its growth and success have resulted from the loyalty and support of retail jewelers. The company has always produced watches of accuracy and of fine appearance in order to give the public reliable time service. But without the cooperation and endorsement of the retail jeweler, the business could not have reached the success it has enjoyed.

Of late years this happy and mutually profitable relation has been dimmed by business evils which have grown up in the trade to a point where they seriously interfere with the success of the company and of the retailer. The company wants to remove these barriers.

It is because of the realization that business lives and thrives on fair profits that the company has made the vital decision to revise its method of distribution. There must be fair profits for the manufacturer, for the wholesaler and for the retailer. Hamilton's new plan proposes an accord between the manufacturer, wholesaler and retailer on a basis that will allow all to pull together. To symbolize this common interest and to serve as a reminder of its significance, we have chosen the famous characters of Dumas' novel "The Three Musketeers" whose close association led them to adopt the slogan "All for One and One for All." Like these characters, the wholesaler and the retailer are urged to join with the Hamilton Watch Company on the strong basis of "All for One and One for All."

As shown on the map of the United States on the first page of this issue of the Watchmen, care has been exercised in the division of the zones so that every retail jeweler, no matter where located, will be given prompt service from Hamilton distributors near at hand.

Wholesalers' discounts will be uniform. Thus each wholesaler will be on an equal footing. Constant contact between the designated wholesalers and the sales and production departments of the Hamilton Watch Company, will result, it is hoped, in a better distribution of Hamilton Watches than has ever been attained. On the basis of the new plan, the designated wholesaler will be able to provide improved service to the retail jewelers. Because the relations between wholesaler and retailer will be on a service basis, there will be more reason to discuss ways and means of securing more business. Increased interest in the sales of Hamilton Watches will be justified.

The Hamilton Company stakes its future on the continued support of the legitimate retail jeweler. It asks for the retailer's whole-hearted confidence in the new plan and promises to be faithful to its part of the trust.

Every retailer and each distributor is urged to remember that the main objective of Hamilton's new plan is better service to the public. The public is the court of last resort.

For many years the Hamilton Watch Company has devoted a percentage of its total sales to national advertising. The purpose of this advertising was to inform the public of the merits of the Hamilton Watch. Hamilton advertising has never been guilty of extravagant claims. The main point stressed in all Hamilton advertising has been the accuracy which the Hamilton Company has always built into its watches. There is no change in that policy. Hamilton advertising will continue to be truthful and fair. Hamilton accuracy will continue to be the theme.

For 1934 there has been prepared what we believe to be some of the most effective Hamilton advertising we have ever published. Featuring the graduation selling season, you will notice advertisements for the national magazines are reproduced in this issue of The Hamilton Watchmen. Please read them. Note what is said about the Hamilton watch and make these words your own when you discuss the Hamilton with customers in front of your counter.

Will Hamilton's new plan of modified zone distribution succeed? The answer is "yes," if we may be assured of your cooperation. Everything hinges on that. There will be difficulties, disappointments, mistakes. Please have faith and if necessary have patience. If we all trust each other and work together success will be the reward. It is worth working for. The plan, as adopted is the result of long study and nation-wide field investigation. At this date it has been more enthusiastically received by the trade than we had expected. We are encouraged to believe that the cooperation we ask for will be forthcoming. Remember—"One for All and All for One."

The Three Musketeers

What have these three characters to do with the watch business? Why mention these three old time swashbucklers in this busy and eventful year of 1934.

Well, Mr. Jeweler get out your copy of Dumas' famous novel and read up on what these boys did way back yonder in those old days. All through that fascinating novel you will notice that the three musketeers were loyal to each other. Not only did they say "All for one and one for all"—but they meant it and they acted accordingly.

That's why we call your attention to the three musketeers in this modern age of 1934. We show this picture as a symbol of another three part situation which is important to you. The interest of the Hamilton Watch Company and the retail jeweler and the wholesale distributor are one and the same thing. If these three act on the basis of "All for one and one for all," the Hamilton modified zone distribution plan will succeed. As a result the retail watch business, the wholesale watch business and the watch making business will be on a sounder basis.

Furthermore, it is worth remembering that Hamilton's new plan is in accordance with the N.R.A. ideals. So you can serve your own interests and keep in step with Federal government plans for business recovery by cooperating with Hamilton's new plan of controlled distribution.

"All for one and one for all"—it's a grand slogan, and let's all stick by it.

The Hamilton Watchmen, May 1934

GREETS THE NEW HAMILTON PLAN OF CONTROLLED DISTRIBUTION

THE HAMILTON NEW DEAL, announced one month ago, has met with country-wide cooperation from retail and wholesale jewelers. This enthusiastic "OK" has come *in spite of* the fact that under this plan wholesalers are geographically restricted, and that many old relationships between retailers and wholesalers are changed.

This is significant indeed in proving that the jewelers of America appreciate the very real need for steps which will protect fair profits for the retailer, the wholesaler and the manufacturer. The hearty endorsement of Hamilton's new plan of Controlled Distribution is evidence enough that its benefits far outweigh the sacrifices and adjustments necessary to put it into operation.

In the future, as in the past, Hamilton will depend on legitimate retail jewelers. We are confident indeed that the future of Hamilton is in safe hands. We sincerely thank you for your cooperation.

(The following two pages of this section show a map of the United States with Hamilton's 21 zones outlined, and the new list of designated Hamilton distributors by zones.)

Under Hamilton's new plan of Controlled Distribution, the retailer, the wholesaler and the manufacturer are—like the Three Musketeers—"all for one and one for all."

HAMILTON. *The Watch of Railroad* ACCURACY

Keystone, May 1934

HAMILTON..*The Watch of Railroad* ACCURACY

TO INSURE the success of our new plan of modified zone distribution—and thus to eliminate unbusinesslike practices which have grown up in the sale of watches—we, the Hamilton Watch Company, will do our part to the very best of our ability.

All of our thirty-nine distributors pledged themselves to do their part after our plan was explained to each of them in person.

This company has grown and prospered because of the support of retail jewelers.

Already we have been assured by many retail jewelers that they will enthusiastically support this new plan.

Retail jewelers occupy respected positions in their communities. They render a very real and desired service to their customers. It is in such establishments that Hamilton Watches belong—and that is where we want the public to find them.

We know we can count on your cooperation. We know that once you understand all the details of our plan you will realize that its benefits are mutual and equitable—for you, for our distributors, and for ourselves.

We are anticipating that you will give our designated distributors your wholehearted cooperation. If you do not understand all about the plan, ask your Hamilton distributor or write to us.

Let us all work together toward better and happier business conditions. Again, I repeat, we are counting on you.

Sincerely yours,

Frank C. Beckwith

President

HAMILTON WATCH COMPANY

Lancaster, Pennsylvania

Keystone, May 1934

According to an article in Fortune magazine quoted by Sauers, "Hamilton's larger wholesalers had been 'high-spotting' the market in the early '30s', concentrating on the biggest accounts where selling costs were lowest and growing richest," and the smaller wholesalers had to fight for what was left. "The little fellows sought to make up in quantity of retail outlets what they lacked in quality. Hamilton watches were on sale with the Borax in barber shops and coal company commissaries."

Sauers explains: "Many of the larger wholesalers were among the first to go. Atkinson liked to work with the lean and hungry operators who would work hard to promote the Hamilton line. In exchange for their loyalty and dedication, they were assigned clearly defined, well-protected territories. It was part of the master plan: wholesalers were allocated territories on the basis that preserved the elements of free and open competition, but that restricted them to the area they were geographically best located to serve."[30]

Hamilton undoubtedly had cash-flow problems in 1934, although that did not stop it from promoting its new zone plan very extensively. Mentioned earlier were the many advertisements in the spring of 1934, and efforts continued into the fall.

THE HAMILTON PLAN MEANS BUSINESS!

Business for the Designated Wholesale Distributor—MORE business because the Plan has already freed him from the devastating, profit-sapping, unfair trade practices which for years have dogged his every move. He knows that the Hamilton Plan is a *fact*—that it *works*. He knows that it is not a mere promise of future reform, but actual performance already in action. He knows that real business machinery has been newly created to make the Plan work. He is cooperating fully with the Hamilton Watch Co. and with the legitimate retail jewelers in the Zone where he distributes Hamilton Watches. He is in a position to give every regular jeweler in his Zone adequate service on Hamilton's entire line—*and he is now doing it.*

Business for Retail Jewelers—MORE business—hundreds are now getting *much* more business in Hamilton sales. Jewelers, encouraged by the new Plan, are enthusiastically cashing in on the strong public preference for Hamilton Watches created by Hamilton's persistent National Advertising, which for forty years has regularly presented to the American public incontrovertible evidence, convincing facts, interesting figures and technical data showing the accuracy of the Hamilton. The theme of Hamilton's powerful National Advertising has *never* changed. Always the story in Hamilton's advertising is Accuracy—Accuracy—Accuracy. The retail jeweler, now freed by the Hamilton Plan from the unfair trade practices which have irritated him and hindered sales, can from this time on, wholeheartedly and with full confidence in the Plan, back the Hamilton Watch and profit by the business to which he is entitled. The public has learned to closely associate "Accuracy" and "Hamilton." "The Watch of Railroad Accuracy" is also the watch of public preference. If you doubt this, put it to the test in your own community. Remember—forty years of Accuracy in the watch—forty years of Accuracy in the advertising. Result—Hamiltons are easy to sell.

And NOW—the Hamilton Plan, which states without compromise that Hamilton Watches will be distributed *only* through a limited number of wholesalers and *only* through desirable retailers. And best and most important of all, the Public will get honest, trustworthy service in its watch buying—service the legitimate jeweler knows how to render.

Yes, this plan—The HAMILTON PLAN—means Business. If you fail to get your share, whose fault will it be?

[THE LINE OF HAMILTONS IS COMPLETE—AND NEWLY PRICED DOWNWARD]

RETAIL JEWELERS CHEER FOR HAMILTON PLAN

Many state retail jewelers' associations at recent annual meetings have passed resolutions endorsing the Hamilton Plan. Among these states are New York, New Jersey, Delaware, Minnesota, Washington, North Carolina, Maryland, Wisconsin, California. In addition hundreds of individual jewelers have praised the Plan in letters to the Hamilton Watch Company. From this steadily growing tide of high approval it seems to be evident that the Plan is greeted and cheered as the best thing that has happened in the jewelry trade in years and years—and years!

The Hamilton Watch Company *alone* has put this plan into operation. It is the HAMILTON Plan. It is in effect exclusively for the sale and distribution of HAMILTON Watches. It is not a bandwagon on which anybody can climb and shout "Me Too." It is a HAMILTON idea—backed by HAMILTON and HAMILTON Wholesale Distributors for the benefit of HAMILTON Retail Jewelers—"All For One—One For All."

EXHIBITS

Hamilton Watches will be shown at A.N.R.J.A. Convention, Netherland Plaza, Cincinnati, week of September 10th, and at Convention of N.A.C.J., Hotel Sherman, Chicago, September 24th to 28th.

HAMILTON WATCH COMPANY, LANCASTER, PENNSYLVANIA

HAMILTON *The Watch of Railroad* **ACCURACY**

September, 1934 Page 9

Keystone, September 1934

Positive results were almost instantaneous. During 1935, under the new "Plan," sales rose 70%, to $7.5 million. Hamilton, its wholesalers and its retailers were all pleased. However, it is unclear how much of this success could be attributed to the new Hamilton Plan and how much to the pent-up demand of the marketplace after the Great Depression bottomed out. Waltham's experience seems to suggest that the latter was the case.

Confidential Price List

The partial Confidential Illinois Price List, issued on May 1, 1934, was apparently sent to about 144 people and companies. Quite remarkably, this "confidential information" was also sent to the general manager of the Waltham Watch Company and the sales manager of the Elgin National Watch Company. Such a move would be a clear antitrust violation today.

Also of note is that the address given for Miller on this mailing was the Springfield Marine Bank, Springfield, Illinois, as Miller left the Watch Company at the end of July 1933. Miller was then vice president of the Bunns' bank.

LIST OF PEOPLE TO WHOM CONFIDENTIAL
ILLINOIS PRICE LISTS ARE SENT
OR DELIVERED
also a copy latest Catalogues or Folders as published

1. F. C. Beckwith, Pres. #5
2. W. R. Atkinson #6
3. J.L.Keenan - Desk #7
4. J.L. Keenan - Sample Line #8
5. J.L.Keenan - Bible #9
6. J.L.Keenan - Eastern Book #10
7. J.L.Keenan - Central Book #11
8. J.L.Keenan - Western Book #12
9. Mr. C.M. Kendig #13
10. C.C. Smith #14
11. R.M.Kant #15
12. F. J. Boulton #1— #2
13. F. Huehnergarth #16 #122
14. L. Halligan #17 — Barrington Associates - Mr Lathrop
15. Miss M. Sabinash— 253
16. Billing Clerk - Delma Afflebach #18
17. Invoice Checker - Mrs. Shank #19
18. R. Waddell #20
19. Mr. H. Lawrence #21
20. Mr. R. Gunder (3 copies if printed here) -193-194
Marine Bank #141

22. Mrs. Mayme Davis
23. Ed. Miller
24. M. W. Jones
25. Melvin Spencer
26. Harry Ruthhart
27. John Hall - N.Y.C. - Rec'd
28. Burr W. Freer
29. J. R. Philp
118. C. S. Gause
117. Paul Seibel
116. R. L. Barger Rec'd
108. Mr. I. E. Boucher, Gen.Mgr.
Waltham Watch Co.
Waltham, Mass.
119. Mr. Howard Schaeffer, Sales Manager
Elgin National Watch Co.
35 E. Wacker Drive
Chicago, Ill.
109. Mr. W. F. Drexmit Rec'd.
C/o Keystone Watch Case Corp.
35 E. Wacker Drive
Chicago, Ill.
113. Mr. F. E. Hyatt, V-P.
Keystone Watch Case Corp.
Riverside, N. J.
115. Mr. J.W.Armbruster
800 S. Beverly Glen Blvd.,
Los Angeles, Cal.
114. Mr. R. E. Miller, Vice-Pres.
Springfield Marine Bank
Springfield, Ill.

Then to Owner, Manager or Watch Dept. Mgr.
of each Active Illinois wholesale account.
Include---
H. Steele Co., Both San Antonio - Mr. Fox 78 Miss Green
Mexico City - Mr. Steele- 77
~~W. N. Stock, Toronto~~
128 Smith-Patterson Co., Montreal Frank S Patterson
130 Levy Bros., Hamilton – Miss Gorge
129 Canadian Ball Co., Winnipeg Mr P.C. Corilson
133 Enggass Jly. Co., Detroit - Mr.Maurice Enggass
213 Monroe ave.
134 Basch Co. Co., Toledo - Mr. Sylvan Basch
340 Summit St.
135 Sante Fe Watch Co
Topeka Kans. Mr A. C Thomas
131 Goldsmith - Montreal
~~155 Samuel J Basil Nyc~~

Confidential price list recipients, May 1, 1934

In May 1934, F. C. Dumaine, then president of Waltham, announced at the annual meeting of the stockholders that the workforce of the company had increased, explaining:

> A year ago it appeared very much as if a drastic curtailment in operations would be imperative. However, a radical reduction in prices enabled the sales department to dispose of the stock, justifying running the factory and providing considerable work for a substantial number, at that time much desired. Lowered prices and small production were not conducive for profits for owners, and I sincerely regret coming before you with an account not warranting dividends, as disappointing to me as to you.
>
> Although a code for watch factories has not yet been executed, the work week has been reduced, two advances in wages volunteered and the working force increased from 1300, the low point, to nearly 2300 at present. Should we be fortunate enough to maintain the present force, much of the free cash appearing in the balance sheet will be required, for, as you know, it takes about 12 months from the time you start processing a watch until you receive payment for it.[31]

Since Waltham, which was not to introduce its own new distribution plan for several more years, was also experiencing a resurgence in business in May 1934, perhaps it was more the general turnaround in the watch industry than the introduction of the Hamilton Plan of Zone Distribution that resulted in improved performance in Lancaster.

The 1934 Illinois Sales Catalog

With the Hamilton Plan in place for itself, Hamilton had implemented a new and still lower-end product direction for Illinois. Most of the men's Illinois models released from this point forward were 10K gold-filled ones with 15 jewels, and one was even in base metal—all at record-low end price points for Illinois men's wristwatches.

Hamilton had some Illinois parts in inventory, but it expected the cases to be purchased with excess cash, not by draining the Hamilton coffers. The Illinois accounts, inventory and records were kept separately from Hamilton's.

Use ILLINOIS

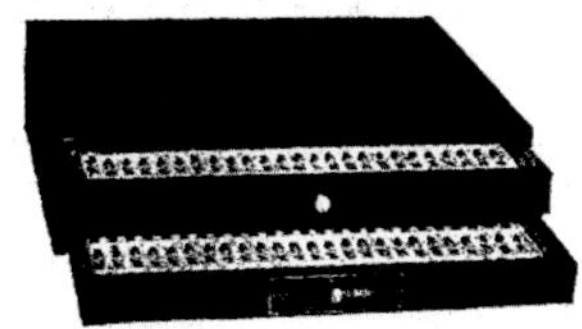

GENUINE MATERIAL

ILLINOIS Watch owners have the right to expect the use of **genuine** Illinois parts in their Illinois watches. Failure to do this may result in loss of the customer's good-will and that loss is far greater than a slightly higher profit made through using imitation parts.

Every watch repair department needs the convenient two-drawer material cabinet illustrated above. Furnished in mahogany, it is 13¼" wide, 9¼" deep, and 3⅜" high. It contains 200 vials—15 of which are empty to provide space for adding new material. The assortment is made up of material ranging from 18 size down to 21/o size. Its actual retail value, based on the dozen price, is **$37.00.** Complete with hinged index charts and extra set for general use, **$27.50.** All refills come sealed from the factory. Order direct or through your Illinois material wholesaler.

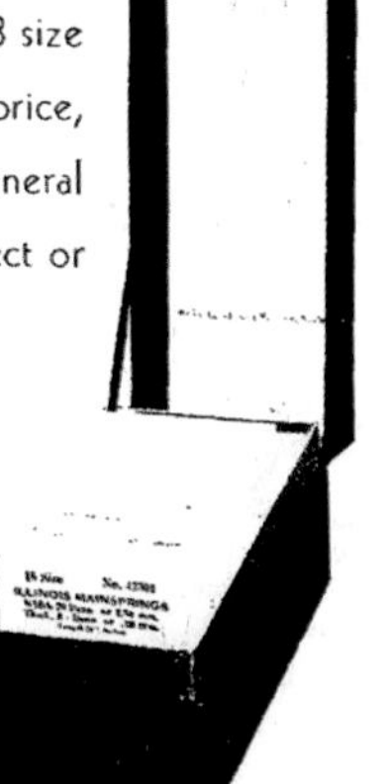

Mainspring Assortment

The Illinois genuine mainspring assortment (shown right) contains springs of 36 different sizes and strength. Each is packed and sealed in the standard Illinois Glassine envelope. Furnished complete with charts and information. Actual value, **$13.00.** Your cost, **$8.00.** Order direct or through your Illinois material wholesaler.

ILLINOIS WATCHES

Material Department

LANCASTER, PENNSYLVANIA, U.S.A.

Page 4 of the 1934 Illinois sales catalog

The 1934 Illinois Sales Catalog was issued primarily to move the excess 18/0 and 21/0 size movements in inventory and, to a lesser extent, the 6/0 size, 15-jewel ones. Hamilton did not wish to show the Potomac as being the only available Illinois Men's model, so it was converted to the "Rockingham" with a new Hamilton-designed butler center dial and an Elinvar hairspring. A few other inexpensive models were added to show some semblance of an Illinois product line.

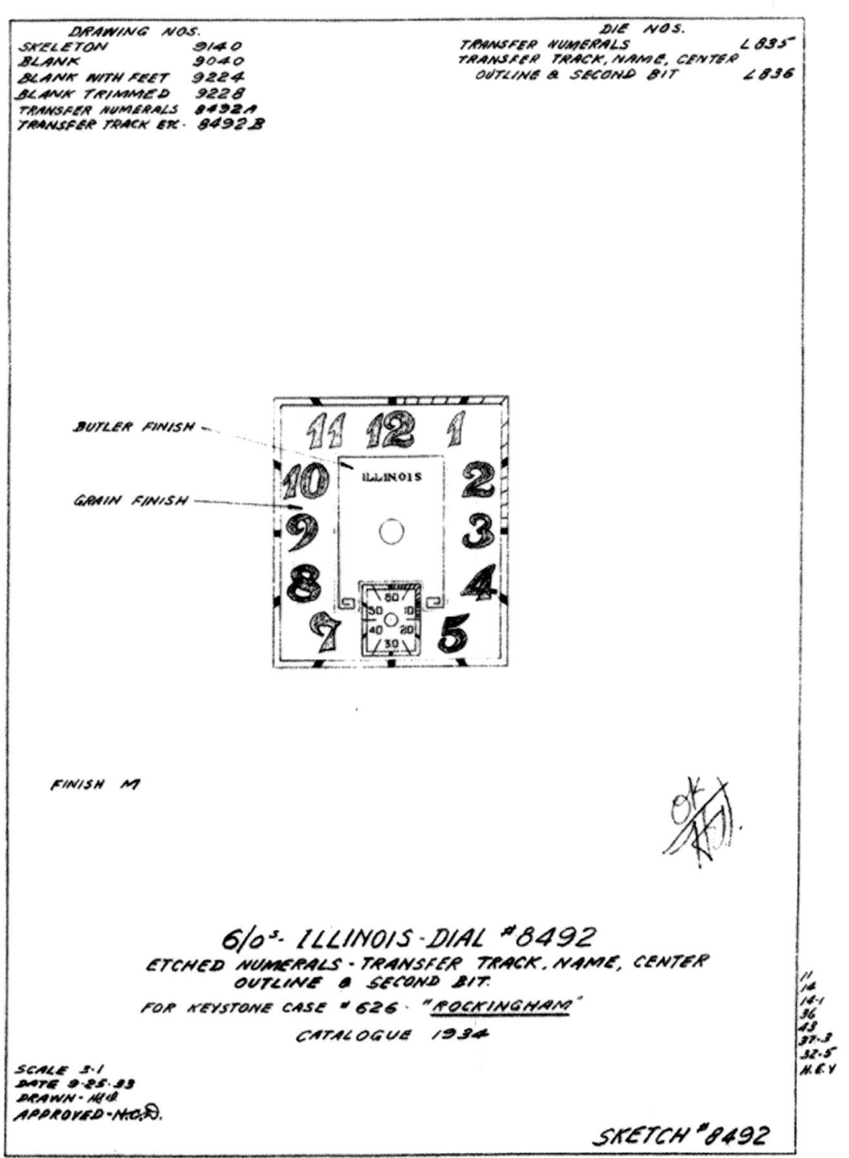

Hamilton drawing for the “New” Illinois Rockingham model, dated September 25, 1933

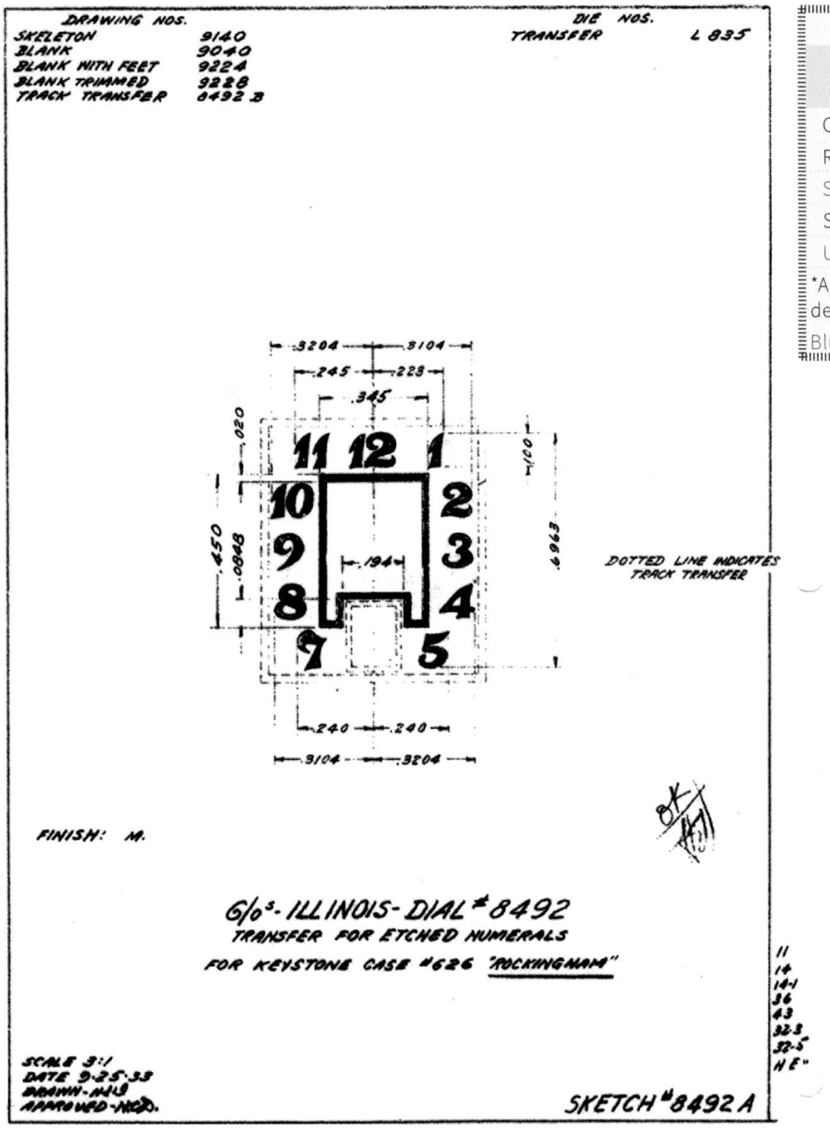

Hamilton drawing for the "New" Illinois Rockingham model, dated September 25, 1933

1934 Illinois Men's Models

Model	Karats	Price	Release Date
Chatham	10K YGF or WGF	$35.00	1934
Rockingham*	10K YGF or WGF	$40.00	1934
Sangamon	Base Metal	$25.00	1934
Standish	10K YGF or WGF	$35.00	1934
Urbana	10K YGF	$32.50	1934

*Actually a rereleased Potomac with a different, Hamilton-designed dial

Blue = Unisex

Presumably, Hamilton wanted to arm its distributors with these inexpensive Illinois models so as to be better able to compete against the "E-Z-Kredit" and cost-cutting competitors. Although it was not yet ready to throw its Hamilton brand into the bargain-basement market segment, Hamilton was reluctantly forced to commence sales of its own line of new lower-priced model watches, but prices for them were still above the record-low Illinois price points.

The other men's watches on the 1934 Price List were the Chatham, Sangamon, Standish and Urbana. The Sangamon, in a base metal case, had a bargain-basement price of $25.00; the other models, including the Rockingham in 10K gold-filled, ranged in price from $25.00 to $40.00. Because of the Depression, they were in "the lower price range" in order to appeal to Depression-scarred buyers.

The ladies' models were the Babette, Débette, Mariette, Marlette in 21/0 size, 17 jewels, and the Antoinette, Janette, Lynette and Marionette in 21/0 size, 15 jewels. All of these movements came equipped with Elinvar hairsprings.

MAY 1934 — THE HAMILTON WATCHMEN — 11

NEW HAMILTON MODELS TO SELL AT LOWER PRICES

Wide Selection Available Between $37.50 & $52.50

With this issue of The Hamilton Watchmen comes the new 1934 catalog showing the finest line of modern watches Hamilton has ever offered. In this attractive book is the real reason why you will be able to sell *more* Hamilton watches after May 1st, 1934. Complete information — illustrations, descriptions and new prices—everything is there.

Study this new catalog carefully before placing it behind your counter for instant reference. Note how Hamilton's price-range has been broadened to include many models in the lower price brackets. Some of the new models will sell as low as $37.50 —an all-time minimum for Hamilton strap watches. Retailers will recognize this move as being distinctly to their advantage because it immediately opens an immense new market for high grade Hamilton watches.

In producing models to sell at the new low prices, the Hamilton standard of accuracy has not been reduced. In fact, new equipment and improved scientific methods now in use in the Hamilton plant, all tend to produce a better product and to increase, if possible, the degree of accuracy for which the Hamilton watch has always been famous.

Orders for all watches shown in the catalog are receivable at once—although only a limited quantity of the new lower price models will be available the first of May. However, production is being increased rapidly and it is expected that by the middle of the month a sufficient quantity will be ready so that orders can be filled immediately upon their receipt.

Below we briefly list the principal revisions in the line since the last Hamilton catalog was released. Read them carefully and visualize the tremendous opportunity offered by this splendid new selection of Hamilton watches.

WRIST WATCHES

Grade 989, 18/0 size, has three new ribbon models in 10K filled gold, priced at $40.00. The previous minimum for this grade was $42.50 in sterling silver case. 14K filled gold models now sell at $45.00—with attractive filled gold bracelets, $47.50. Prices on the solid gold models remain unchanged.

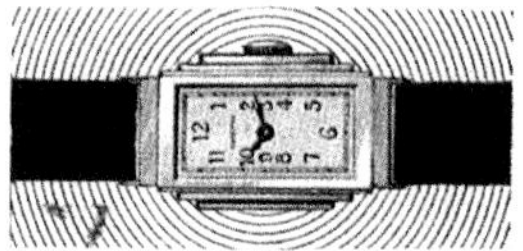

GAIL. A new modern watch available in 10K filled gold only. Consumer price, $40.00. Two other models are available at this same price.

The very small grade 995 offers several new modern models, as well as new filled gold chains and attachments for those already in the line. One model particularly —the ALCOTT—has special significance as Hamilton's first small round watch with a dial that is surprisingly easy to read. 14K filled gold ribbon models in this grade retail at $50.00, cord models at $52.50. Filled gold bracelets increase the price $2.50. Prices on the solid gold models remain unchanged—although the solid gold cord watches are regularly fitted with cords equipped with filled gold attachments at $5.00 reduction.

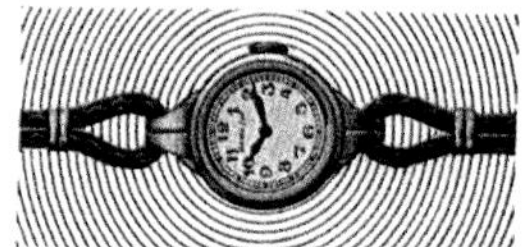

ALCOTT. A new watch that sets a new mode. One of several important additions to the popular grade 995. Consumer price, $52.50.

STRAP WATCHES

Two major changes have been made in the strap watch groups: The 6/0 size, 17 jewel, grade 987 movement is available only in a new line of 10K filled gold cases priced to the consumer at $37.50 with luminous dial, or $40.00 with raised gold figure dial.

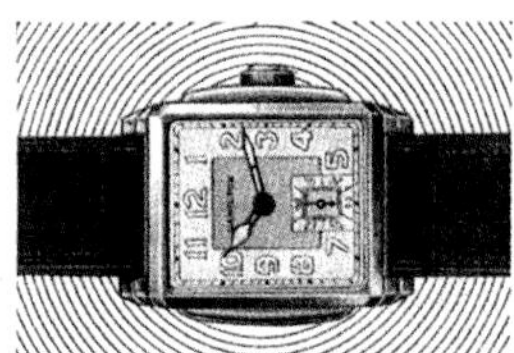

DIXON. One of three new 17 jewel models in 10K filled gold only. Consumer prices: With luminous dial, $37.50. With R. G. F. dial, $40.00.

Grade 979, 19 jewel movement may now be obtained in 14K filled or solid gold cases. The five filled gold models (which previously carried the 17 jewel 987 movement) retail from $50.00 to $55.00—depending on the case and dial.

POCKET WATCHES

Two new 12 size watches without inside caps, considerably reduce the pocket watch minimum. The WARREN, 10K filled gold, is $42.50 with the 17 jewel 912 movement, $57.50 with the 19 jewel grade 918. The CARTER, in 14K filled gold, is $45.00 with the 17 jewel movement and $60.00 with the 19 jewel. These watches should do much to stimulate demand for high grade pocket models.

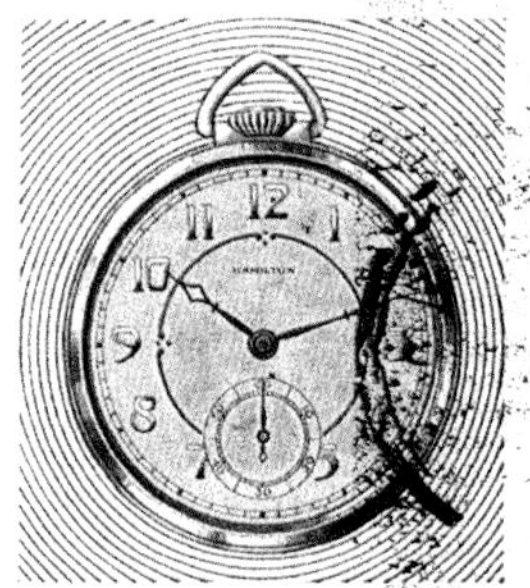

CARTER. A new 12 size in 14K filled gold without inside cap. Consumer prices: 17 jewels, $45.00. 19 jewels, $60.00.

Hamilton's Attractive New Catalog Deserves a Prominent Place on Your Counter—Ready for Instant Reference.

NEW CATALOG SHOWS CONSUMER PRICES ONLY; JEWELER COST ON SEPARATE PRICE LIST

In addition to giving a comprehensive picture of the new 1934 Hamilton line, Hamilton's new catalog has another decided asset—beauty. Notice how attractively the watches are set off by the rich blue background. It isn't hard to visualize such a catalog in a place of prominence on your watch counter—ready to answer any consumer questions which may come up. The catalog was designed with this thought in mind—its silver cover is durable as well as beautiful and it literally invites consumer inspection. Use it as you would a reference book to add weight to your arguments.

And notice, too, that you can show it to your customers, because it contains consumer prices only. The retail price list is enclosed on a separate sheet of convenient size for filing.

You Are Invited

PLEASE REMEMBER THAT THE HAMILTON WATCH FACTORY AT LANCASTER, IS ON THE LINCOLN HIGHWAY.

WHEN YOU ARE ON THAT AUTOMOBILE TOUR, TAKE A LITTLE TIME TO VISIT THE FACTORY AND SEE FOR YOURSELF HOW ACCURACY IS BUILT INTO AMERICA'S FINEST WATCH.

ANY RETAIL JEWELER WHO VISITS THE HAMILTON FACTORY WILL SEE MUCH OF INTEREST AND WILL SECURE MUCH ADDED INFORMATION WHICH HE WILL FIND OF VALUE IN DISCUSSING WATCHES WITH HIS CUSTOMERS.

An Important Announcement

Please note that the Hamilton mark-up to the Retail Jeweler has been substantially increased so that the reduction of discount to 2% does not change your actual profit on Hamilton Watches.

May 1934 issue of the *Hamilton Watchmen*, announcing the new lower-priced Hamilton models

Hamilton Style vs. Illinois Style

During the Deco and Moderne eras, Illinois was in the forefront of the popular styles of the period. Its case and dial designs were cutting-edge: daring and eye-catching. Coupled with its innovative case designs and shapes were some of the most attractive avant-garde dials ever produced.

Hamilton, on the other hand, based its entire business model on high reliability and accuracy at a middle price point. To create reliability at moderate cost meant standardizing designs and creating efficient work processes. The whims of fashion pushed wristwatch case design far more than pocket watch design. Therefore Hamilton, in the 1920s, determined that the part needing reliability and accuracy, the movement, would be standardized, while the case and dial would reflect the fashion changes— actually a simple but sensible business model. If one notes how many wristwatch designs carried variations of the Hamilton 987 movement and their postwar 753/754/770 movements, one begins to appreciate how much Hamilton watch management valued this business model and adhered to it.

Since the major cost in making a watch is in engineering and assembling the movement, the Hamilton model kept labor costs low. In the 1950s, when labor costs exceeded the level at which Hamilton could economically make a watch and sell it for a decent profit, the company gradually moved the manufacture of movements to Switzerland, which then had lower labor costs. (Switzerland, of course, was known for its highly skilled workforce.) But Hamilton did not make this move until after first resurrecting the Illinois name with its Hamilton-Illinois line to test the market while protecting its Hamilton brand name. Hamilton's idea was high reliability at moderate cost. (Rolex employs the same model today, with very profitable results. Their designs are not cutting-edge, but the movements are extremely reliable and accurate.)

Convergence of Design

Other evidence of Hamilton's intention to stop the sale of Illinois watches is the convergence of design that appeared in 1934 between Hamilton and Illinois. The Illinois Rockingham and Chatham models, introduced early that year, were similar in style to the Hamilton Dixon and Scott models, the dials for which were on the Hamilton drawing board on March 16, 1934, and March 29, 1934, respectively. In addition, the striking similarity of the Hamilton-issued Illinois Standish model and the Hamilton Grant model bears witness to the merging of Illinois design by Hamilton into the Hamilton design theme. In fact, some other models, such as the fairly plain Illinois Varsity, Chatham and Standish, are more like Hamilton designs than traditional Illinois ones.

STANDISH, GRANT AND ELGIN MODEL E-3 SIMILARITIES

The cases of the Illinois Standish, Hamilton Grant and the Elgin Model E-3 are similar but not identical. Hamilton offered the Grant with applied gold numerals or luminous dials; Illinois offered the Standish with etched numerals and flush gold numerals. The four different dial styles could have been an effort by Hamilton to try to differentiate the Grant and Standish further.

Another interesting fact is that Hamilton used cases from three different case makers for the Standish and Grant. The Illinois Standish with case Model No. 651 was made by Keystone; the sterling silver Hamilton Grant was made by Wadsworth and the yellow gold-filled Hamilton Grant case was made by Solidarity. It could be that Hamilton was spreading its business out among its different case suppliers to help keep them viable during the Great Depression. Solidarity normally produced solid gold cases for Hamilton, and the yellow gold-filled Grant was the last Solidarity case ever made for Hamilton. Hamilton may have drawn upon the Elgin Model E-3 case design (from 1928) to save design costs and efforts during the difficult economic times.

1934 HISTORICAL NOTES

- Unemployment in the United States decreases to 22%.
- Bonnie and Clyde are killed by the FBI.
- The *Queen Mary* luxury ocean liner is launched in Scotland.
- Donald Duck appears for the first time in *The Little Wise Hen.*

ILLINOIS ☆ WATCHES

★ ★ ★ As AMERICAN as their name ★ ★ ★

NEW DEAL *Elinvar* STRAP WATCHES AT MODERATE PRICES

6/0 Size—15 Jewels

These finely made new models for men are up-to-the-minute in every respect. They are built to withstand hard usage. Styled for tomorrow as well as today, they meet the current demand for a truly accurate strap watch in the lower price range. Available in 10K filled gold cases only.

STANDISH

Splendid new strap model in 10K filled gold; white or natural. 15 jewels. Flush gold figure dial. Consumer, **$35.00.**

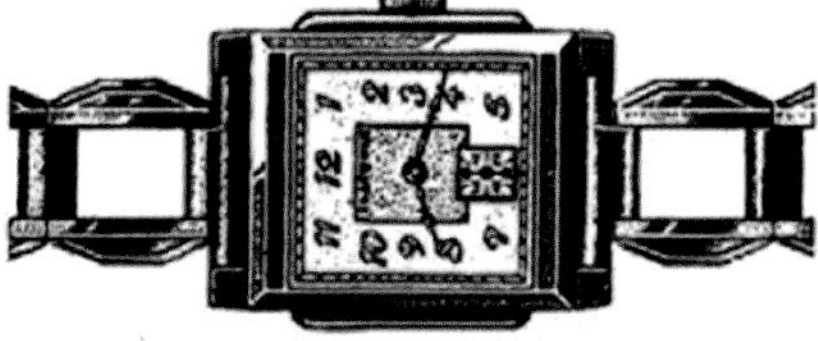

ROCKINGHAM

Very practical and dependable watch with easily read raised gold figure, two-tone dial. 10K filled gold; white or natural, with bracelet to match in style and quality. 15 jewels. Consumer, **$40.00.**

CHATHAM

For sports or business wear. 10K filled gold; white or natural, raised gold figure dial. 15 jewels. Consumer, **$35.00.**

Elinvar makes a watch more resistant to common dangers which disrupt an ordinary timepiece. Magnetism cannot permanently harm an Elinvar watch.

Top of page 3 of the 1934 Illinois sales catalog

Hamilton had taken advantage of design commonalities earlier with its Explorer series, using a modified Illinois 207 movement for its 401 movement. In terms of cases, the Hamilton Byrd is a heavier version of an Illinois Rockliffe and the Hamilton Ericsson is a steroid-enhanced version of its weaker-looking cousin, the Illinois Andover. For its Explorer series, Hamilton was thus wisely building on, modifying and, in some instances, improving the designs it acquired from Illinois. (Examples of some more of the Illinois and Hamilton look-alikes are shown in Chapter 9.)

"Our True Situation"

On June 26, 1934, Keenan sent along with the 1934 Illinois Sales Catalog an incredibly telling internal memorandum to all Hamilton salesmen describing, among other things, the "*true situation* in regard to possible deliveries" (emphasis added). Keenan stated:

- The salesmen could "give good selling effort on Bunn Special Elinvar series of watches. Then, next, there is the Medallion stainless steel $27.50 pocket watch and the Midland gold filled selling at $40.00."
  - "On the 6/0-size Standish, Chatham and Rockingham models we cannot encourage you to do any selling or pushing effort on these items," Keenan said, because "we are now experiencing a break in production" affecting those watches "for the next 60 or 90 days."
- "In reference to the 18/0 size sport watches, Sangamon and Urbana, we are getting some of the movements through regularly, and, therefore, can take care of reasonable orders ... that you can obtain possibly during the next two months." Hamilton requested some of the former Illinois workers to go into the Springfield Factory to attempt to assemble the needed 6/0 and 18/0 size movements, especially as Keenan was discouraging orders for the 15-jewel, 21/0 size movements for the Lynette, Janette, Marionette and Antoinette models. For these small ladies' watches, he said, "the situation here is an absolute lack of movements. In December our sales were way beyond expectations and every available movement was milked out of the [Hamilton] Timing and Finishing Rooms and early in January [1934] our supply became absolutely exhausted as to movements." These comments confirm that Hamilton did not move further works-in-process or equipment to Lancaster, despite Beckwith's statement on January 16, 1934 that such was the intention (and that Hamilton had to "analyze [the Illinois] inventory thoroughly").
- With respect to 21/0 size, 15-jewel models, Keenan added that "we have a reasonable supply of these cases and the factory is pushing along 600 of these movements on the *Jewel-Stripping Job at Springfield* (emphasis added) so that they ought to get in here to Lancaster for final Timing and Finishing by the end of February." Therefore, it was clear that at least in the first quarter of 1934 former Illinois workers were, amazingly, being sent back into the closed Illinois Factory to try to assemble movements to satisfy sales needs. Apparently, Hamilton's efforts to kill Illinois were meeting jobber, jeweler and consumer resistance, as there was still keen interest in the Illinois brand.
- Keenan explained further: "Basically we are doing the preliminary work on plates, bridges and even uprighting at Springfield on our various

items and the major assemblies, timing, dialing and casing is done here in Lancaster."

- He added, "There is no reason to permit the trade to feel that the brand named Illinois Watch is an orphan or a thing of the past." However, as things turned out, Illinois would release only one more Illinois orphan, the 18/0 size modified Rockliffe 18/0 in 1935, a last-gasp effort by Hamilton to improve its balance sheet by further eliminating inventory.

- Keenan pointed out, "You, as well as all retailers definitely know that in 1933 not only the Illinois Watch but other watches were having a tough time, and our Corporation did the only thing that could have been done, that is, conserved their cash position by spending money only to keep one plant operating rather than losing plenty of money by keeping two plants operating." Keenan was perhaps too close to the situation; from a more distant perspective it could be argued that Hamilton was contemplating the shutdown of its Illinois Watch Division from the early 1930s and made no determined effort to preserve both manufacturing operations.

- In closing, the ever-optimistic Keenan said, "There is every hope that general business will continue to pick up as it is doing now and, therefore, greater production efforts can be instituted by appropriation on not only the Hamilton line by Illinois and in the meantime we must ask our Trade, wholesale and retail to bear with the Hamilton Corporation in trying to straighten out this situation." It was clear that the Hamilton factory was up and running, but it was purely aspirational that the same situation would apply to Keenan's Illinois Watch Company.

January 26, 1934

MEMORANDUM - To All Hamilton Salesmen

From - J. L. Keenan

ILLINOIS DELIVERIES

Tried to tell you the situation on Illinois and herewith I am enclosing our 1934 catalog also a copy of a letter sent out by Mr. Beckwith on January 16th to all Illinois Jobbers, and a copy of a letter written to Mr. Montgomery of M.A.Mead & Company, Chicago explaining to him our true situation in regard to possible deliveries.

Naturally, we feel that you can give a good selling effort to the Bunn Special Elinvar series of watches. Then, next, there is the Medallion stainless steel $27.50 pocket watch and the Midland gold filled selling at $40.00.

On the 6/0-size Standish, Chatham and Rockingham models we cannot encourage you to do any selling or pushing effort on these items. The best story here is to say that our factory, because of general conditions early in 1933 did not put enough of these watches into process and we are now experiencing a break in production that affects these 6/0-size watches for the next 60 or 90 days.

In reference to the 18/0-size sport watches, Sangamon and Urbana, we are getting some of these movements through regularly, and, therefore, can take care of reasonable orders on either the Sangamon or Urbana that you can obtain possibly during the next two months, and by that time we hope to be able to give you even a better promise on 18/0 as well as 6/0.

In reference to the Ladies 21/0-size watches - we can handle all the orders you can send in on the 17 jewel grades in Babette, Debette, Mariette and Mariette white. However, on the natural we can handle a few on the Babette and Mariette; also can handle good quantities on the Debette but very few on the Mariette, in Natural.

In reference to the 15 jewel 21/0-size Lynette, Janette, Marionette and Antoinette the situation here is an absolute lack of movements. In December our sales were away beyond expectations and every available movement was milked out of the Timing and Finishing Rooms and early in January our supply became absolutely exhausted as to movements.

However, we have a reasonable supply of these cases and the factory is pushing along 600 of these movements on the Jewel-Stripping Job at Springfield so that they ought to get in here to Lancaster for final Timing and Finishing by the end of February and we will be in a position to take care of 15 jewel 21/0-size ladies watch orders early in March, or at least during March.

Keenan's memorandum of January 26, 1934, detailing the "True Situation" to all Hamilton salesmen (page 1)

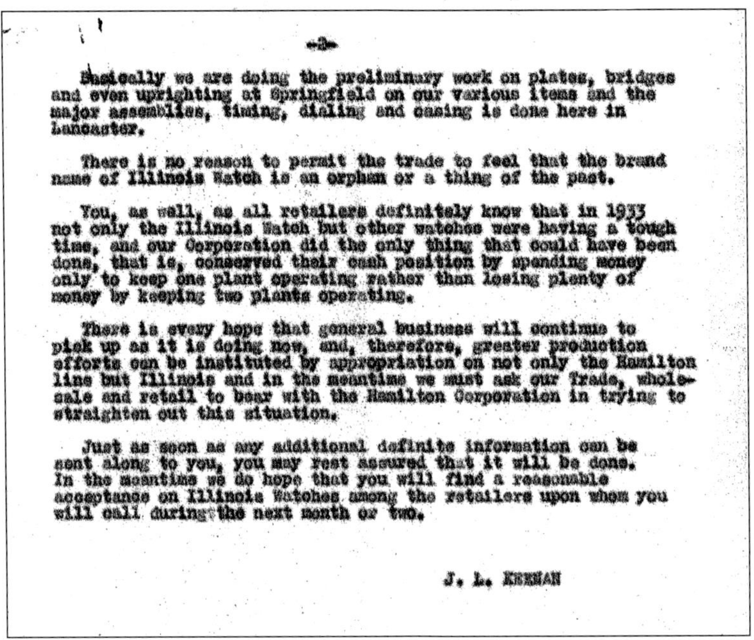

-2-

Basically we are doing the preliminary work on plates, bridges and even uprighting at Springfield on our various items and the major assemblies, timing, dialing and casing is done here in Lancaster.

There is no reason to permit the trade to feel that the brand name of Illinois Watch is an orphan or a thing of the past.

You, as well, as all retailers definitely know that in 1933 not only the Illinois Watch but other watches were having a tough time, and our Corporation did the only thing that could have been done, that is, conserved their cash position by spending money only to keep one plant operating rather than losing plenty of money by keeping two plants operating.

There is every hope that general business will continue to pick up as it is doing now, and, therefore, greater production efforts can be instituted by appropriation on not only the Hamilton line but Illinois and in the meantime we must ask our Trade, wholesale and retail to bear with the Hamilton Corporation in trying to straighten out this situation.

Just as soon as any additional definite information can be sent along to you, you may rest assured that it will be done. In the meantime we do hope that you will find a reasonable acceptance on Illinois Watches among the retailers upon whom you will call during the next month or two.

J. L. KEENAN

Keenan's memorandum of January 26, 1934, detailing the "True Situation" to all Hamilton salesmen (page 2)

Orders Not Accepted

Finally, after being under a constant assault of questions from loyal distributors for almost two years, Keenan was compelled to write a very difficult memorandum on June 15, 1934, to "All Illinois Wholesalers" stating, dutifully and sadly: "With deepest regret it is necessary to advise you that because of factory production conditions, it is impossible to accept any more orders for Illinois watches for delivery this year."

The pronouncement applied to "all items of separate movements and complete watches" from the 1934 Illinois Sales Catalog, with the exception of 23-jewel and 21-jewel Bunn Specials and the thin pocket watch models named "Midland" and "Medallion." Keenan further explained that no catalogues would be prepared for those pocket watch models. In fact, disappointingly, the 1934 Illinois Sales Catalog was to be the last ever published for Illinois watches.

This was effectively the death knell for the Illinois Watch Company. Nonetheless, Keenan had still not given up, and he ended his letter "With every hope that general business will develop this Fall so that our next advice to you regarding Illinois deliveries can and will be more encouraging." But that was not to be. It had likely never been the "Hamilton Plan for Illinois."

June 15, 1934

TO ALL ILLINOIS WHOLESALERS

Gentlemen:

With deeprest regret it is necessary to advise you that because of factory production conditions, it is impossible to accept any more orders for Illinois Watches for delivery this year.

This applies to all items of separate movements and complete watches illustrated in our present catalogue - copies of which you have - except the 23 jewels and 21 jewels Bunn Special, also the thin model pocket watches, Midland and Medallion.

The pocket watches will be available in limited quantities through the remainder of the year. The Bunn Specials (except for the next 60 days on style #107 Natural Case) will continue to be available this year and next.

We will not have any catalogue plates for wholesale catalogue purposes. Cuts of the Bunn Special Watches or pocket watches can be had if it is desired to show them in your Catalogue.

Because of this limited production condition it is also not practicable to make up sample lines. Such watches as you now have on order will be delivered between now and the late Fall. Schedule of expectancy on these deliveries will be about as follows:

21/0-size 17 jewels - July - August - September
21/0-size 15 jewels - July - August - September
18/0-size 15 jewels - October - November
6/0-size 15 jewels - August - September

Should you not wish to have us hold open your orders on 18/0 and 6/0-size watches, we would be pleased to have you advise us as we truly are oversold and therefore need to adjust orders.

The writer has visited many of the Illinois wholesalers and hopes before long to have seen all, explaining the situation.

With every hope that general business will develop this Fall so that our next advice to you regarding Illinois deliveries can and will be more encouraging, we are

Very truly yours,

ILLINOIS WATCH DIVISION

J. L. Keenan

JLK-[illegible]

Sales Manager

Keenan's June 15, 1934, letter stating no more orders would be accepted

An internal memorandum In September 1934 from Keenan to Hamilton personnel emphasizes the lack of Illinois offerings available. This communication also shows that Keenan, though then based in Chicago, was still the only person within Hamilton assigned the responsibility of marketing and selling Illinois watches.

September

MEMORANDUM – to Mr. F. J. Boulton
F. Muehnergarth
R. M. Kant
M. W. Jones
N. H. Sabinash
J.L.K. Sample Kit

From – J.L.Keenan

ILLINOIS PRICES

As our fiscal October month starts Tuesday the 26th, will be necessary to work in accordance with price list that th becomes effective.

On all orders received for 21/0-size old model case o associate the order with the new watches as listed in the 1934 Substitute or write the customer, calling attention to the chan use the October 1st price list for billing.

In other words, if request is received for a Minuette really means that we should supply the Marlette. There are sev similar instances of change in style and, of course, reduction price. Under no circumstances should we charge customer the o prices.

In 18/0-size we have only two 'Moderne' wrist watche Therefore, should we receive an individual request while we hav cases in stock, our prices, because of the fact that they are d continued, will be as follows——

#805 in Gold Case $13.50 Net
805 in Filled " 12.50 "
805 in Silver " 11.50 "

In regard to the 15 jewel 6/0-size invidivual request might receive for discontinued styles, fill them at prices acco to the October 1st price list. A Pimlico would now be the Ro or Potomac would be the Chatham, etc.

Regarding discontinued movements used for individual requests, they will be priced as follows——

Grade #169 at $6.00 net
167 " 6.75 "
121 " 9.00 "
127 " 7.50 "

In other words, if request is received for a Minuette really means that we should supply the Marlette. There are sev similar instances of change in style and, of course, reduction price. Under no circumstances should we charge customer the o prices.

In 18/0-size we have only two 'Moderne' wrist watche Therefore. should we receive an individual request while we hav

-2-

continued number and we will send the one at the net price.

As soon as you get low on an item it is satisfactory to refuse orders and, of course, we must not accept orders fro any customer, other than individual orders, for more than five or ten pieces of a specially sold item. In fact, it is my preference that you refuse more orders for these discontinued items than you accept. However, cannot make the rule blanket as there are some individual requests that we should honor and judgement is as good as mine.

J.L.KEENAN

Keenan's memorandum, dated September 1934, explaining the lack of available Illinois wristwatches

Price List Exhausted

By September 17, 1934, Keenan noted again from Chicago, this time in a handwritten internal memorandum, that even the printed Price List for 1934 Illinois Watches had been exhausted and requested that a "couple hundred" be printed. So Keenan had found Illinois sales and marketing efforts to be without dummy samples, most cases, most movements, no direct sales personnel, no sales manager, no Illinois presence in Lancaster—and now without even an inexpensive printed paper price list.

Hamilton Watch Company (Original)
INTER - DEPARTMENTAL
MEMORANDUM

To Mr. Boulton / Miss Sobmach Dept. Date 9/17/34

From J. L. Keenan Dept.

Illinois Price Lists

Please refer to the yellow Illinois retail price lists, showing consumer & Keystone price list.

These are sent out at request of retailers or wholesalers when Illinois price list is wanted. also when catalogue is mailed to a retailer one should be attached.

As our supply is exhausted a couple hundred more should be printed. If we have a lot would ask Stanley Rhinehart to imprint in Red and over print as per sample.

Signed JLK 9/17/34

If an answer is indicated in above Memo, let us have your reply as soon as possible. Always write and date reply. Avoid verbal communications whenever possible.

Kindly send me 25 - after collected in Red.

Keenan's handwritten memorandum of September 17, 1934, seeking more 1934 Illinois Price Lists

CASH DISCOUNT 10

PRICE LIST—1934

ILLINOIS *Greater Value* WATCHES

EFFECTIVE ~~OCT.~~ Sept 1, 193~~3~~4

		Consumer List	Keystone List
BAGUETTE STYLE			
21/0 Size Grade No. 107, 17 Jewels, Elinvar			
Babette	14K Solid gold, white or natural, Filled Clasp	$50.00	$50.00
Debette	14K Filled gold, white or natural, Bracelet	47.50	46.00
Mariette	14K Filled gold, white or natural, Ribbon	42.50	42.50
Marlette	14K Filled gold, white or natural, Ribbon	42.50	42.50
21/0 Size Grade No. 105, 15 Jewels, Elinvar			
Lynette	10K Filled gold, white or natural, Bracelet	$40.00	$40.70
Janette	10K Filled gold, white or natural, Bracelet	40.00	40.70
Marionette	14K Filled gold, white only, Cord	35.00	40.00
Antoinette	10K Filled gold, white or natural, Ribbon	32.50	38.00
MODERNE WRIST WATCHES			
18/0 Size Grade No. 805, 15 Jewels, Elinvar			
Urbana	10K Filled gold, Natural only, Strap	$32.50	$35.00
Sangamon	Sangamo Metal—White only, Strap	25.00	30.60
MEN'S WRIST WATCHES			
6/0 Size, Grade No. 605, 15 Jewels, Elinvar			
Rockingham	10K Filled gold, white or natural, Bracelet	$40.00	$40.00
Standish	10K Filled gold, white or natural, Strap	35.00	36.60
Chatham	10K Filled gold, white or natural, Strap	35.00	36.60
POCKET WATCHES			
Thin Model, Grade No. 427, 17 Jewels Adjusted. Non-Elinvar			
Midland	10K Filled gold, white or natural, A. N. Dial	$40.00	$40.00
Medallion	Sangamo Metal, White only.	27.50	30.60
RAILROAD WATCHES			
16 Size, Grade 161-A, 21 Jewels, 60 Hour, Elinvar			
Bunn Special	10K Filled gold, Natural	$60.00	~~$65.00~~ $63.40
Bunn Special	14K Filled gold, White or Combination	65.00	~~66.00~~ 73.90
16 Size, Grade 163-A, 23 Jewels, 60 Hour, Elinvar			
Bunn Special	10K Filled gold, Natural	$70.00	$70.00
Bunn Special	14K Filled gold, White or Combination	75.00	70.00

1-10023 ILLINOIS WATCH — LANCASTER, PA.

The exhausted 1934 Illinois Price List as modified by Keenan on September 17, 1934

Stanley Rinehart

F. J. Boulton 9/19/34

Please print up 200 pricelists like the enclosed sample—making note of corrections and additions to same.

The End of the Road for Illinois

In 1935, when Hamilton issued a modified Rockliffe case that could house an 18/0 size Illinois movement without subsidiary seconds, it was only in an attempt to exhaust a supply of 18/0 movements.

To further milk Illinois before its demise, Hamilton rereleased certain Bunn Special pocket watches to the market in February 1935 by letter and advertisements, but these watches were issued in 10K gold-filled cases to keep their price points low. To stimulate interest, the movements were equipped with the Elinvar hairspring. It was Hamilton's contention that with "railroad business on the upturn, railroad men are buying again."

This may have been true, but was probably disingenuous; it is perhaps more likely that Hamilton was only interested in liquidating its inventory of Bunn Special movements and parts. (According to Chamelin, the Bunn Special cases offered for sale in 1935 and in 1936 were not signed "Bunn Special" so that Hamilton could use the case for any of its or Illinois' railroad pocket watch movements.)[32]

The ILLINOIS WATCH
A GREAT AMERICAN WATCH
SINCE 1870
LANCASTER.PENNSYLVANIA.U.S.A.

February 1, 1935

To Illinois Watch Distributors

ILLINOIS marches on!

A new ILLINOIS BUNN SPECIAL ELINVAR Railroad model is now available ... a watch true to the ILLINOIS tradition of accuracy, in a sturdy modern case, styled for tomorrow as well as today!

Already an advertising campaign is under way! The twenty-one leading railroad publications will carry the news to more than a million railroad men in March. Consumer demand is sure to be stimulated ... sales are in the making!

Will you be ready?

To get your share of this ready-made business - place your order for the new railroad model #118 now! It is available in 10K filled natural yellow gold only, 21 or 23 jewels, at the following prices:

Bunn Special	Retail	Consumer
21 Jewels - 60 Hour	$31.95	$60.00
23 Jewels - 60 Hour	35.00	70.00

With Railroad business on the upturn, railroad men are buying again. Be prepared to supply dealer orders.

These Elinvar Bunn Special watches are the only Illinois grades now available. All other models in all sizes have been discontinued and their construction ceased last year.

We are unable to accept orders for any size or models in Illinois other than these Bunn Specials.

In your next Bulletin to your salesmen and office force please see that you are fully posted covering this new model cased, Bunn Special Elinvar as well as give them information concerning our inability to handle orders on any other models.

Very truly yours,

J. L. Keenan

Keenan February 1, 1935 letter offering "A new ILLINOIS BUNN SPECIAL ELINVAR"

Thus, the history of the Illinois Watch Company was coming to a very quiet ending at the same time Hamilton was successfully re-inventing itself with its "Hamilton Zone Distribution Plan." One wonders whether any consideration was ever given to including its Illinois Watch Division in the new Plan. Regrettably, I suspect not.

Losses during the Depression Years

According to Sauers, "Hamilton hit bottom the year after Charles F. Miller passed away . . . the company lost $998,000 on sales of $1.6 million [in 1932] after barely breaking even in the 1931. The entire watchmaking industry was suffering." (Waltham suffered losses in 1931, 1932, 1933 and 1934; Elgin did so in 1930, 1931, 1932 and 1933.) Sauers maintains that Hamilton lost money only in 1932, but this is not accurate. Beckwith, in his message to employees on April 19, 1934, noted that Hamilton lost $987,642.70 in 1932 and $148,560.12 in 1933. Although this error is not significant in Hamilton's overall history, it was extremely important in Hamilton's decision-making process concerning the life expectancy of its Illinois Watch Division. [33]

Elgin's Profit and Loss*

Year	Profit/(Loss)
1927	2,071,861
1928	1,971,067
1929	1,972,971
1930	(70,543)
1931	1,057,558
1932	1,193,782
1933	263,372
1934	736,358
1935	1,071,656

*Briska, p. 108

Decrease in Watch Case Manufacturing

THERE was a distinct decrease of over 51 per cent in the value of the watch cases made in the United States in 1933, as against those made in 1931, according to the preliminary statistics made available last month by the Director of the Census in the Biennial Census of Manufacturers for 1933, but taken in 1934.

The number of establishments dropped in those years from 31 to 20, a drop of 30 per cent. The costs of materials, fuels, etc., dropped from $1,361,195 to $760,343, a drop of 41.1 per cent, and the total products dropped from $4,219,133 to $2,657,402, a drop of 37 per cent.

As far as the watches alone were concerned, the drop in value was from $3,348,917 to $1,636,950, a drop of 51.1 per cent.

DECREASE IN WATCH CASE MANUFACTURERS

Although the market was finally improving in 1934, the devastating effects of the Great Depression were still there. The watch case manufacturers in the United States had declined by 30% from 1931 to 1933, going from thirty-one firms to twenty. During that same period, there was a 51% decrease in the value of watch cases made in the United States.

***Jewelers' Circular*, October 1934**

Hamilton was always a financially savvy and tightly run, strongly profit-centric company. Therefore, its loss years, coupled with those of its Illinois Watch Division, must have been tremendously unpalatable to the Hamilton executives and board of directors. Its sales in 1933 were less than half of those for 1929. Thus, something had to give, and the only choice for Hamilton seemed to be Illinois.

In an article on the Hamilton Watch Company, Robert L. McCollough points out that the Depression years following the financial crash of 1929 took their toll on all American businesses. The jewelry trade, dealing in luxury merchandise, was particularly hard hit. Abuses born of desperation threatened the very existence of Hamilton, along with many others. Hamilton's method of distributing its product had always been through a selected list of wholesalers selling to the retail jewelers of America. But, McCollough observes, "as the market shrunk, sub-jobbing, discount, industrial catalog houses and parasitic cut-price retailers of doubtful reputation infested the erstwhile ethical jewelry business like a plague."[34]

COMPETITION

Hamilton expressed its own view of competition in a short blurb in the May 1934 issue of the *Hamilton Watchmen:*

"There are two kinds of competition. One is the honest, open fair sort which is the life of trade. The other is the secret, deceptive underhand, unfair kind which hurts business and destroys public confidence."

"The new zone distribution plan of the Hamilton Watch Company is designed to assist and support the retailer who believes in fair and honest competition and to discourage the cheater and chiseler whose influence is destructive and discouraging."

According to McCollough, “Something had to be done if the company was to be saved from the graveyard in which some sixty other American watch enterprises had been interred since Colonial days.”[35] Hamilton evidently agreed and survived, while delivering Illinois to the graveyard.

Domestic Movement Consumption

According to the United States Tariff Commission, apparent consumption of movements were:

Year	Apparent Consumption of Movements	Imports/ Number of Movements
1929	5,088,434	3,400,313
1930	3,610,707	2,300,029
1931	1,416,917	815,208
1932	854,241	421,781
1933	821,240	432,005
1934	1,266,666	610,183

Death in a Time of Renewal

Profits for Elgin and Hamilton

In 1934, since Elgin was paying an average of seven cents per hour more than Waltham, the latter, to avoid future labor trouble, surprised its workers with a 10% wage increase. Moore points out that “this brought the average rate of Waltham to approximately fifty cents per hour, which was the wage level before the depression.”[36] Both Elgin and Waltham were unionized at this point; Illinois and Hamilton were not.

In 1935, Elgin announced 1934 profits of $736,358 and a workforce growing to 1,900 employees by September.[37] Hamilton had a 1934 profit of $289,461.

The Elgin financial statement was its first fiscal report to show a profit since 1929. In 1933 it had suffered losses of $263,372. Its president, Potter, remarked that “business in 1935 had run well ahead of volume for the same period of 1934.”[38]

For Hamilton, Beckwith reported “a marked improvement” in the financial condition of the company in 1934 after the first two years of losses in its history. The recovery, he said, began during the last four months of 1933 and during 1934, causing an increase in employment and production. Unfortunately, by this time Hamilton had all but pulled the plug on Illinois.

Illinois had sales for 1934 of at least $271,406 from eighty of its jobbers. This total does not include its other two dozen jobbers, direct sales, house accounts, or its sales to department stores.

In March 1935, Elgin began paying dividends again, and by the end of the year its workforce had grown to 2,200.[39]

On November 19, 1935, Hamilton moved a group of pinion-cutting machines from Springfield to Lancaster. It was announced that Hamilton was looking for a chance to dispose of the Illinois Factory, which had been closed down for several years.

SWISS INCREASES

The Swiss watch industry was also back in good health in 1934. In May 1935 it was reported that the United States had substantially increased its purchases of Swiss watches and watch movements in 1934.

The total value of watch exports to the American market during 1934 amounted to 12.6 million francs versus 7.3 million francs in 1933—an increase of more than 70%.

From Jewelers’ Circular, June 1935

Illinois Sales Results

Sales in 1935. The Illinois sales results for the first eleven months of 1935 totaled just over $126,000. However, as in 1934, this total included only sales to eighty of its jobbers—no direct sales, house accounts, or department store sales. This amount, although low, is actually remarkably high considering the adverse selling conditions that Illinois faced and only one new watch model, in the form of a modified Rockliffe 18/0. That any sales were consummated is quite surprising.

Partial Sales Totals. The known Illinois sales to eighty of its jobbers for years 1926, 1929, 1933, 1934, and 1935 are set forth below. Evidently, Keenan was comparing these sales—to the same eighty or so jobbers it was selling to in 1935— to other years, notwithstanding that in 1926, 1929, and 1933 the company was actually using a greater number of distributors.

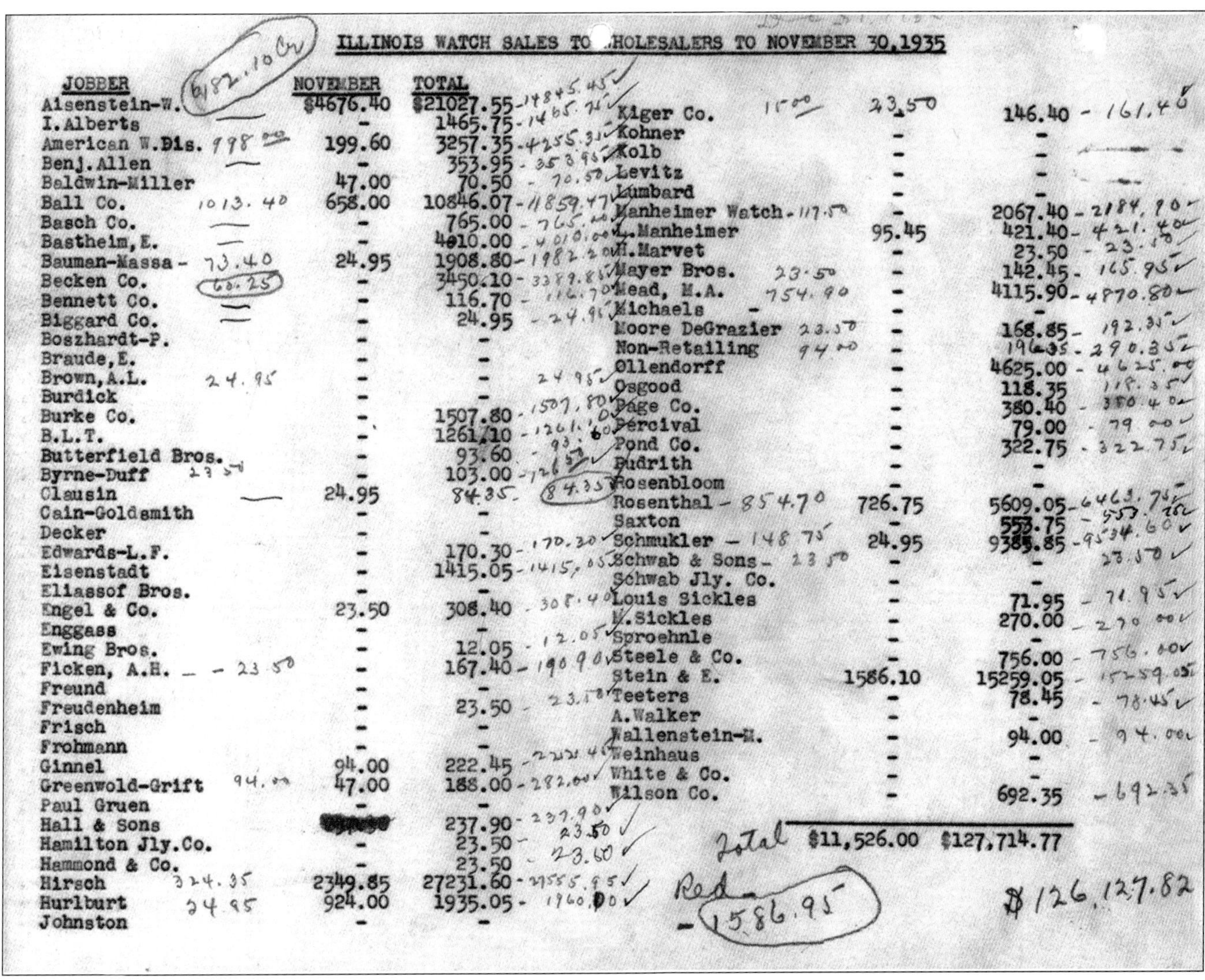

ILLINOIS WATCH SALES TO WHOLESALERS TO NOVEMBER 30,1935

JOBBER	NOVEMBER	TOTAL
Aisenstein-W.	$4676.40	$21027.55
I.Alberts	-	1465.75
American W.Dis.	199.60	3257.35
Benj.Allen	-	353.95
Baldwin-Miller	47.00	70.50
Ball Co.	658.00	10846.07
Basch Co.	-	765.00
Bastheim,E.	-	4010.00
Bauman-Massa	24.95	1908.80
Becken Co.	-	3450.10
Bennett Co.	-	116.70
Biggard Co.	-	24.95
Boszhardt-P.	-	-
Braude,E.	-	-
Brown,A.L.	-	-
Burdick	-	-
Burke Co.	-	1507.80
B.L.T.	-	1261.10
Butterfield Bros.	-	93.60
Byrne-Duff	-	103.00
Clausin	24.95	84.35
Cain-Goldsmith	-	-
Decker	-	-
Edwards-L.F.	-	170.30
Eisenstadt	-	1415.05
Eliassof Bros.	-	-
Engel & Co.	23.50	308.40
Enggass	-	-
Ewing Bros.	-	12.05
Ficken, A.H.	-	167.40
Freund	-	-
Freudenheim	-	23.50
Frisch	-	-
Frohmann	-	-
Ginnel	94.00	222.45
Greenwold-Grift	47.00	188.00
Paul Gruen	-	-
Hall & Sons	[illegible]	237.90
Hamilton Jly.Co.	-	23.50
Hammond & Co.	-	23.50
Hirsch	2349.85	27231.60
Hurlburt	924.00	1935.05
Johnston	-	-
Kiger Co.	-	146.40
Kohner	-	-
Kolb	-	-
Levitz	-	-
Lumbard	-	-
Manheimer Watch	-	2067.40
L.Manheimer	95.45	421.40
H.Marvet	-	23.50
Mayer Bros.	-	142.45
Mead, M.A.	-	4115.90
Michaels	-	-
Moore DeGrazier	-	168.85
Non-Retailing	-	196.35
Ollendorff	-	4625.00
Osgood	-	118.35
Page Co.	-	380.40
Percival	-	79.00
Pond Co.	-	322.75
Pudrith	-	-
Rosenbloom	-	-
Rosenthal	726.75	5609.05
Saxton	-	553.75
Schmukler	24.95	9385.85
Schwab & Sons	-	-
Schwab Jly. Co.	-	-
Louis Sickles	-	71.95
M.Sickles	-	270.00
Sproehnle	-	-
Steele & Co.	-	756.00
Stein & E.	1586.10	15259.05
Teeters	-	78.45
A.Walker	-	-
Wallenstein-M.	-	94.00
Weinhaus	-	-
White & Co.	-	-
Wilson Co.	-	692.35
Total	$11,526.00	$127,714.77

Red – 1586.95

$126,127.82

Illinois Sales Results, Year-To-Date, November 1935

Keenan's notations on sales results for eighty of the Illinois jobbers for the time periods, noted on his chart, shows surprisingly robust numbers considering all of the destructive measures that Hamilton imposed on Illinois.

Illinois Sales to Eighty of its Jobbers

Year	Totals
1926	$1,914,711.00
1929	2,818,550.00
1933	548,316.00
1934	271,406.00
1935	126,351.15

January 4, 1934

JOBBER	1933	1934	1929	1926	1935
1. I. Alberts	86,240	16030	58,590	48,601	1465
2. Hirsch Co.	52,679	23,750	94,680	36,013	27555
3. Ollendorff	51,736	9707	83,263	124,860	4625
4. Manheimer & Bro.	24,778	4072	91,884	50,051	421
Manheimer Watch	16,697	12028	70,416	38,934	2185
5. Schmukler	25,144	11275	28,255	11,064	9534
6. E. Bastheim	23,488	2375	68,330	41,080	4010
7. M.A.Mead & Co.	20,709	19363	138,060	145,704	4870
8. Ginnel & Co.	19,484	3297	37,115	8,253	222
9. American Watch Dis.	19,024	4460	6,275	8,996	4255
10. Mayer Bros.	16,453	443	31,419	10,706	166
11. The Ball Co.	12,967	9904	340,576	243,579	11859
12. Saxton Company	12,615	5260	22,503	4,749	552
13. Frisch Co.	12,412	7087	40,354	18,732	—
14. Steele & Co.	10,325	7295	26,407	22,514	756
15. Stein & Ellbogen	10,236	17649	40,412	67,241	15259
16. H.O.Hurlburt	9,895	3501	56,796	26,308	1960
17. Ficken Company	9,796	1645	36,571	20,367	191
18. Hall & Sons	9,606	640	49,182	-	238
19. Becken Co.	9,400	10,558	86,010	64,698	3390
20. Buss-Linthicum-T.	8,550	10728	204,874	160,877	1261
21. Aisenstein-Woronock	7,751	18615	17,528	14,159	14845
22. Rosenthal	7,056	5921	79,879	92,044	6464
23. Byrne-Duff	5,349	2038	8,492	5,485	126
24. Clausin	5,310	2626	24,119	17,300	(84.35)
25. Pond Co.	4,783	4444	20,915	8,195	322
26. Burke Co.	4,564	4993	20,934	-	1508
27. Wallenstein-Mayer	4,098	1640	14,957	26,291	94
28. Percival	3,869	9276	42,435	31,774	79
29. Weinhaus Co.	3,776	3900	17,533	17,852	—
30. Non-Retailing Co.	3,768	3309	10,485	15,287	290
31. Butterfield Bros.	3,732	1479	-	-	93
32. A.Walker Co.	3,365	170	9,418	4,598	—
33. Biggard Co.	3,284	5632	47,540	17,304	25
34. Page Company	2,643	1490	41,061	22,570	380
35. Greenwold-Grift	2,625	128	4,404	17,024	282
36. Engel & Co.	2,479	600	14,469	10,523	308
37. Osgood	1,992	3358	-	-	118
38. Benj. Allen	1,939	1736	28,389	-	354
39. Eliassof Bros.	1,359	1032	27,155	-	—
40. Frohman & Co.	1,294	526	28,364	-	—
41. Ewing Bros.	1,177	89			72
42. M.Kohner	1,176	845	19,708	8,495	—
43. Bauman-Massa	1,013	3103	24,299	21,759	1982
44. Eisenstadt	966	3344	105,773	14,650	1415
45. Kolb	956	274	7,508	2,137	—
46. Freudenheim	778	487	34,532	15,666	23.50
47. L. Sickles	712	53	31,989	26,549	270.
48. Hamilton Jly. Co.	652	48	7,569	4,204	23
49. Kiger Co.	573	648	17,783	14,394	161
50. A.L. Brown	526	—	-	-	25

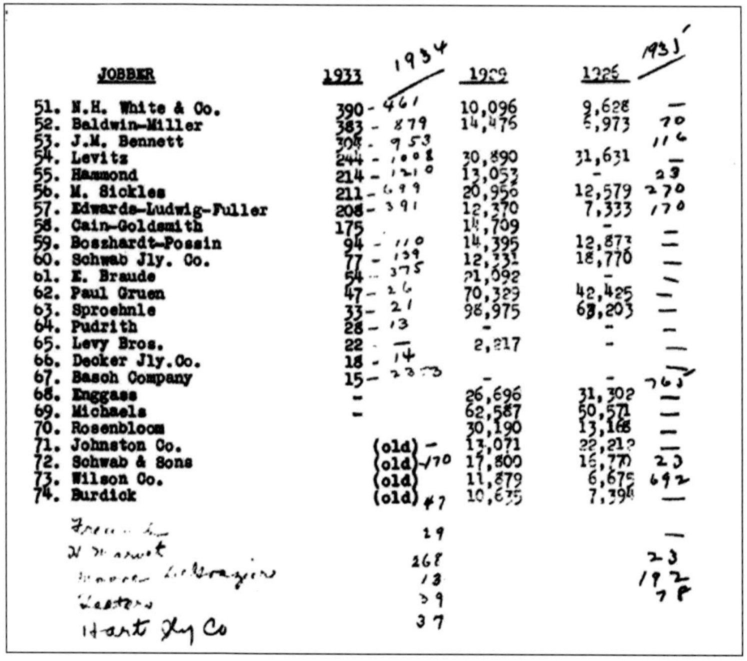

JOBBER	1933	1934	1929	1926	1935
51. N.H. White & Co.	390	461	10,096	9,628	—
52. Baldwin-Miller	383	879	14,476	5,973	70
53. J.M. Bennett	308	953			116
54. Levitz	244	1008	30,890	31,631	—
55. Hammond	214	1210	13,053	-	23
56. M. Sickles	211	699	20,956	12,579	270
57. Edwards-Ludwig-Fuller	208	391	12,370	7,333	170
58. Cain-Goldsmith	175		14,709	-	
59. Boszhardt-Possin	94	110	14,395	12,873	—
60. Schwab Jly. Co.	77	139	12,331	18,770	—
61. E. Braude	54	375	21,092	-	—
62. Paul Gruen	47	26	70,329	42,425	—
63. Sproehnle	33	21	98,975	68,203	—
64. Pudrith	28	13	-	-	—
65. Levy Bros.	22	—	2,217	-	—
66. Decker Jly.Co.	18	14			—
67. Basch Company	15	2373	-	-	763
68. Enggass	-		26,696	31,302	—
69. Michaels	-		62,587	50,571	—
70. Rosenbloom			30,190	13,168	—
71. Johnston Co.	(old)	—	13,071	22,212	—
72. Schwab & Sons	(old)	170	17,800	16,770	23
73. Wilson Co.	(old)		11,879	6,675	692
74. Burdick	(old)	47	10,675	7,394	—
[illegible]		29			—
[illegible]		268			23
[illegible]		13			192
[illegible]		39			78
Hart Jly Co		37			

Keenan's partial sales totals for various years

MERGER OF THE *JEWELERS' CIRCULAR* AND THE *KEYSTONE*

Yet another casualty of the Great Depression was announced in January 1935. Because of declining numbers of subscriptions and thus declining revenue, two jewelry industry publications, the *Jewelers' Circular* and the *Keystone,* both once robust weeklies, were now merging to become one monthly publication. It is perversely ironic that both of these once strong publications that failed to read correctly and anticipate the impact of the 1929 stock market crash would themselves have to transform totally together to continue in operation.

Cartoon from the first issue of the *Jewelers' Circular–Keystone*, January 1935

A
BIGGER, BROADER, BETTER

TWO great publications . . . the Keystone and The Jewelers' Circular . . . in this issue merge their aims and purposes to furnish a broader service to a great industry. For more than fifty years both papers have trod parallel paths, working toward the same ideals and dedicating their efforts to the service of the retail jeweler.

Today those paths have become one. The vast experience of both papers in business journalism . . . their wide contacts and great facilities, are welded into one vital force for the promotion of the jewelry industry . . . a force that provides a vigorous, timely impetus to merchandising at the very beginning of a new business era.

74 The Jewelers' Circular—Keystone for January, 1935

Jewelers' Circular–Keystone, January 1935

BUSINESS MAGAZINE

Another National Step Forward in The Jewelry Trade

THE splendid new publication formed by the union of The Keystone and The Jewelers' Circular performs two great services for the jewelry trade. For Readers . . . last minute, authoritative information on effective business methods and profitable merchandise, gleaned from a wealth of national and world sources. For advertisers . . . complete penetration of retail jewelry markets and active contact with a "Sterling Fine" circulation, reaching 925/1000 of the industry's purchasing power.

The Jewelers' Circular-Keystone is geared for a 1935 of increased activity and usefulness. The tremendous body of merchants and manufacturers who form its reading public will be supplied with accurate facts, clearly and tersely presented in the manner that 118 years of jewelry publishing experience has taught is most valuable. Spontaneous expressions of approval and good will have already reached us from friends in the trade . . . but the final endorsement lies in YOUR employment of the outstanding facilities and opportunities now available to you.

THE JEWELERS PUBLISHING CORP.
239 WEST 39th STREET NEW YORK CITY

The Jewelers' Circular—Keystone for January, 1935 75

Jewelers' Circular–Keystone, January 1935

Illinois Parts

Hamilton, not wanting to leave any money on the table, would issue formal price lists for remaining Illinois parts in 1938, 1947 and again in 1953, in final efforts to try to exhaust its inventory of Illinois parts.

Revised List Effective February 15, 1938

SUPERSEDES ALL PREVIOUS PRICE LISTS

ILLINOIS WATCH MATERIAL PRICE LIST — RETAIL

SUBJECT TO 2% DISCOUNT ONLY

MATERIAL	Each	¼ Doz.	½ Doz.	1 Doz.
ARBORS, Barrel	$ .75	$1.80	$3.50	
" Clutch	.50	1.05	2.00	
" Pallet	.60	1.25	2.35	
" Winding (Not Threaded)	.65	1.45	2.75	
" Winding (Threaded)	.35	.70	1.25	
BALANCES, Gold screws	2.60	6.00		
" Brass screws	1.50	3.50		
BALANCE AND STAFF, Gold screws	3.30			
" " " Brass screws	2.20			
BALANCE, Staff, Roller, Hairspring, Gold screws	5.45			
" Staff, Roller, Hairspring, Brass screws (12/0 and larger)	4.35			
" Staff, Roller, Hairspring, Brass screws (18/0 and smaller)	5.80			
BANDS Dust	.35	.70	1.25	
BARS, Slide	.35	.70	1.25	
" Swing	.35	.70	1.25	
" Swing with pinion	.75	1.80		
BARRELS, Regular	.75	1.80		
" Motor — (Not sold without staff)				
" Regular and arbor	1.50	3.50		
" Jeweled and arbor	3.90	9.10		
" Motor and staff	2.50	5.75		
BEARINGS, Motor Barrel Staff Upper	.55	1.15		
" Winding Arbor	.35	.70	1.25	$2.25
BRIDGES, Winding	.55	1.15		
" Winding with pinion	1.10	2.70		
CAPS, Click Spring	.40	.85		
" Hairspring Stud	.40	.85		
" Minute Wheel	.40	.85		
" Minute Wheel and Lock Lever Spring combined	.50	1.05		
" Ratchet Wheel	.50	1.05		
" Setting Wheel	.40	.85		
" Motor Barrel Ratchet Wheel with Jewel	1.95	4.65		
CLICKS	.35	.70	1.25	2.25
" No. 1044	1.10	2.70		
CLUTCHES, Winding and Setting	.65	1.45	2.75	
COLLETS, Hairspring	.30	.55	1.00	
CUPS, Barrel Arbor	.55	1.15		
DIALS, Metal, Plain	1.25	3.15	6.25	
" Etched	1.95	4.85		
" Applied Gold Numerals (Wrist)	4.00			
" Applied Gold Numerals (Pocket)	8.50			
DIES	4.35	10.20		
FORKS	.75	1.80		
HANDS, Hour and Minute, 12/0 size and larger	.25	.45	.80	1.50
" Hour and Minute, 18/0 size and smaller	.30	.55	1.00	1.75
HANDS, Second all		.25	.30	.35
HUBS, Motor Barrel Ratchet	1.05	2.40		
" Motor Barrel Snailed	1.05	2.40		
" Winding Wheel	.45	.90		
INDEX, Regulator	.55	1.15		
JEWELS, Balance, Escape and Pallet for cone pivots	.40	1.00	1.80	3.50
" Balance, Unset	.30	.55		
" Endstone, Gold Setting	.70	1.60		
" Endstone, Gold Figure 8 setting	.85	1.95		
" Endstone, Dome setting	.85	1.95		
" Endstone, Composition setting	.35	.70	1.25	2.25
" Endstone, Unset	.25	.45	.80	1.50
" Barrel Arbor, Gold setting	1.75	4.05		
" Motor Barrel Staff, Gold setting	1.75	4.05		
" Motor Barrel Staff, Composition setting	1.10	2.70		
" Center, Gold setting	1.50	3.50		
" Center, Composition setting	1.10	2.70		
" Center, Unset	1.00	2.25		
" Train and Pallet, Gold setting, Straight Pivots	.95	2.25		
" Train and Pallet, Composition setting, Straight pivots	.75	1.80		
" Train and Pallet, Unset	.65	1.45		
" Pallet Stones, Sapphire and Ruby	.60	1.25		
" Pallet Stones, Garnet	.45	.90	1.70	3.30
" Roller (Jewel Pins) Sapphire and Ruby	.40	.85	1.60	3.00
" Roller (Jewel Pins) Garnet	.20	.25	.40	.70
LET DOWNS	.50	1.05		
LEVERS, Clutch, Locking, Setting	.50	1.05	2.00	3.80

MATERIAL	Each	¼ Doz.	½ Doz.	1 Doz.
NUTS, Regulator Adjusting screw	$ .40	$ .85	$1.60	$3.00
PALLETS, with stones (No Fork)	1.60			
" and Fork (1 piece) with stones	1.60			
" and Fork (2 piece) with stones and arbor	3.10			
" and Fork (1 piece) with stones and arbor	2.25			
PINIONS, Bevel or winding	.60	1.25	2.35	
" Cannon	.55	1.15	2.25	
" Center (without staff)	.55	1.15	2.25	
" Center and Staff (1 piece)	.75	1.80		
" Escape, Third, Fourth, Fifth, or Extra	.65	1.45		
PINS, All	.30	.55	1.00	
PLATES, Setting	.40	.85		
REGULATORS	.65	1.45	2.75	
ROLLERS, Combination without pin	.50	1.05	1.90	
" Impulse without pin	.35	.70	1.25	
" Impulse, with Balance, but without pin (No. 1816)	2.60	6.00		
" Guard	.45	.90	1.70	
" Combination, with jewel pin	.95	2.15		
" Impulse, with jewel pin	.85	1.95		
" Impulse and Balance and Pin (No. 1817)	3.30	7.70		
" (Impulse and Guard) Staff & Pin (No. 1454)	.85	1.95		
SCREWS, Balance, Gold All	.20	.30	.60	1.00
" Micrometer Regulator Adjusting	.25	.45	.80	1.50
" Gold plated		.25	.40	.70
" All others		.25	.35	.50
SLEEVES, Winding Arbor	.50	1.05	2.00	3.85
SPRINGS, **Flat Steel** — Click, Clutch, Lifting, Locking Lever, Setting Lever, Inter-winding Wheel, Yoke	.30	.55	1.00	1.80
" **Wire** — Click, Clutch, Locking Lever, Fifth Pinion, Setting Lever, Yoke	.25	.35	.65	1.00
" Hair Colleted (12/0 and larger)	.75	1.80		
" Hair Colleted (18/0 and smaller)	1.10	2.70		
" Lock Lever and Minute Wheel Cap combined	.50	1.05		
" Main, 60 Hour	.40	.85	1.60	3.00
" Main, All others	.30	.70	1.30	2.50
" Regulator only (No. 2042, No. 886)	.65	1.45		
" Regulator, with adjusting screws	.85	1.95		
STAFFS, Balance with oil grooves (No. *1506, No. 1684)	.45	1.10	2.10	4.00
" Balance (No. 1442, Style No. 1)	.45	1.10	2.10	4.00
" Balance, All others	.35	.85	1.60	3.00
" Motor Barrel	.65	1.50		
" Center (no pinion)	.65	1.50		
" Center and Pinion (1 piece)	.85	1.95		
STRAPS, Regulator with adjusting screw	.55	1.15		
STUDS, Hairspring	.30	.55	1.00	1.80
TAPS, Crown and Screw	.40	.85	1.60	
WASHERS, Main Winding Wheel Hub	.30	.55	1.00	
WHEELS, Center, Third and Fourth, Gold	.85	1.95		
" Center, Third and Fourth, Brass	.45	.90		
" Center, Gold and Staff (no pinion)	1.65	3.80		
" Center, Brass and Staff (no pinion)	1.10	2.70		
" Center, Gold, Staff and Pinion (1 piece)	2.05	4.90		
" Center, Brass, Staff and Pinion (1 piece)	1.65	3.80		
" Center, Gold, Staff, Pinion & Cannon Pinion	2.70	6.30		
" Center Brass, Staff, Pinion & Cannon Pinion	2.20	5.20		
" Clutch	.35	.70		
" Escape, Steel	.75	1.80		
" Escape, Steel (No. 1835)	2.50	5.75		
" Escape, Brass	.55	1.15		
" Escape, Steel and Pinion	1.50	3.50		
" Escape, Steel and Pinion (No. 1882)	3.70	8.55		
" Escape, Brass and Pinion	1.30	2.95		
" Fourth and Third, Gold with pinion	1.75	4.05		
" Fourth and Third, Brass with pinion	1.30	2.95		
" Hour and Pipe	.40	.75	1.35	
" Intersetting and Interwinding	.40	.75	1.35	
" Minute and Pinion	.40	.75	1.35	
" Ratchet (Unexposed)	.40	.75	1.35	
" Ratchet, Motor Barrel	1.50	3.50		
" Ratchet (Exposed) Concaved	1.10	2.70		
" Ratchet (Exposed) Not concaved	.90	2.15		
" Regulator Index	.40	.75		
" Setting	.40	.75	1.35	
" Winding, Crown	1.10	2.70		
" Winding, Flat	.85	1.95		
" Winding, Base	.40	.75		
YOKES	.65	1.45		
" with Interwinding wheel	.95	2.25		
MATERIAL CABINET, containing 200 bottles	25.00			
MAINSPRING ASSORTMENT, containing 4 dozen	8.00			

*No. 1506 Balance Staffs will be furnished without oil grooves if so specified on order at the "all other" staff prices.

Above prices apply where specified quantities of one factory number are ordered. Mainsprings may be assorted as to strength, balance staffs as to pivot diameter, jewels as to hole size.

10% additional discount on all items purchased in gross lots.

ILLINOIS WATCH MATERIAL DEPARTMENT
Lancaster, Penna.

IT PAYS TO USE GENUINE ILLINOIS WATCH MATERIAL

1—10041 (Over)

Illinois Material Price List, February 15, 1938

Revised List Effective September 15, 1947 **SUPERSEDES ALL PREVIOUS PRICE LISTS**

JEWELER AND WATCHMAKER PRICE LIST OF GENUINE ILLINOIS WATCH MATERIAL

	Each	¼ Doz.	½ Doz.	1 Doz.
ARBORS, Barrel	$ .75	$1.80	$3.50	
" Clutch	.50	1.05	2.00	
" Pallet	.60	1.25	2.35	
" Winding (Not threaded)	.90	2.15		
" Winding (Threaded)	.35	.70	1.25	
BALANCES, Gold screws	2.60	6.00		
" Brass screws	1.50	3.50		
BALANCE AND STAFF, Gold screws	3.30			
" " " Brass screws	2.20			
BALANCE, Staff, Roller, Hairspring, Gold screws	5.45			
" Staff, Roller, Hairspring, Brass screws (12/0 and larger)	4.35			
" Staff, Roller, Hairspring, Brass screws (18/0 and smaller)	5.80			
BARS, Slide	.35	.70	1.25	
" Swing	.35	.70	1.25	
" Swing with pinion	.75	1.80		
BARRELS, Regular	.75	1.80		
" Motor—(Not sold without staff)	1.50	3.50		
" Regular and arbor	3.90	9.10		
" Motor and staff	2.50	5.75		
BEARINGS, Motor Barrel Staff Upper	.55	1.15		
" Winding Arbor	.35	.70	1.25	$2.25
BRIDGES, Winding	.55	1.15		
" Winding with pinion	1.10	2.70		
CAPS, Click Spring	.40	.85		
" Hairspring Stud	.40	.85		
" Minute Wheel	.40	.85		
" Minute Wheel and Lock Lever Spring combined	.50	1.05		
" Ratchet Wheel	.50	1.05		
" Setting Wheel	.40	.85		
" Motor Barrel Ratchet Wheel with Jewel	1.95	4.65		
CLICKS	.35	.70	1.25	
" No. 1044	1.10	2.70		
CLUTCHES, Winding and Setting	.65	1.45	2.75	
COLLETS, Hairspring	.30	.55	1.00	
CUPS, Barrel Arbor	.55	1.15		
DIALS, Metal, Plain	1.50	3.75		
" Etched	3.00			
" Applied Gold Numerals (Wrist)	4.00			
" Applied Gold Numerals (Pocket)	5.35			
FORKS	.75	1.80		
HANDS, Hour and Minute	.45	1.00	1.60	3.00
" Second all		.45	.85	1.50
HUBS, Motor Barrel Ratchet	1.05	2.40		
" Motor Barrel Snailed	1.05	2.40		
" Winding Wheel	.45	.90		
INDEX, Regulator	.55	1.15		
JEWELS, Balance, Escape and Pallet for cone pivots	.50	1.35	2.40	4.50
" Balance, Unset	.40	.85		
" Endstone, Gold setting	.70	1.60		
" Endstone, Gold Figure 8 setting	.85	1.95		
" Endstone, Dome setting	.85	1.95		
" Endstone, Composition setting	.40	.85	1.50	2.80
" Endstone, Unset	.25	.45	.80	1.50
" Barrel Arbor, Gold setting	1.75	4.05		
" Motor Barrel Staff, Gold setting	1.75	4.05		
" Motor Barrel Staff, Composition setting	1.10	2.70		
" Center, Gold setting	1.50	3.50		
" Center, Composition setting	1.10	2.70		
" Center, Unset	1.00	2.25		
" Train and Pallet, Gold setting, Straight Pivots	.95	2.25		
" Train and Pallet, Composition setting, Straight Pivots	.75	1.80		
" Train and Pallet, Unset	.65	1.45		
" Pallet Stones, Sapphire and Ruby	.65	1.45		
" Pallet Stones, Garnet	.45	.90	1.70	
" Roller (Jewel Pins) Sapphire and Ruby	.45	.90	1.70	
LET DOWNS	.50	1.05		

	Each	¼ Doz.	½ Doz.	1 Doz.
LEVERS, Clutch, Locking, Setting	$ .50	$ 1.05	$ 2.00	$ 3.80
NUTS, Regulator Adjusting Screw	.40	.85	1.60	3.00
PALLETS and Forks	2.50			
" and Forks and Arbors	3.00			
PINIONS, Bevel or Winding	.75	1.70		
" Cannon	.75	1.70		
" Center (without staff)	.75	1.70		
" Center and Staff (1 piece)	1.00	2.25		
" Escape, Third, Fourth, Fifth, Extra	.75	1.70		
PINS, All	.30	.55	1.00	
PLATES, Setting	.40	.85		
REGULATORS	.75	1.80	3.50	
ROLLERS, Impulse, with Balance, but without pin (No. 1816)	2.60	6.00		
" Guard	.45	.90	1.70	
" Combination, with jewel pin	1.30	2.95		
" Impulse, with jewel pin	1.10	2.55		
" Impulse and Balance and Pin (No. 1817)	3.30	7.70		
SCREWS, Balance, Gold All	.25	.35	.60	1.10
" Micrometer Regulator Adjusting	.35	.60	1.10	
" Gold plated	.25	.35	.60	1.10
" All others	.20	.30	.50	.90
SLEEVES, Winding Arbor	.50	1.05	2.00	3.85
SPRINGS, Flat Steel—Click, Clutch, Lifting, Locking Lever, Setting Lever, Interwinding Wheel Yoke	.30	.55	1.00	1.80
" Wire—Click, Clutch, Locking Lever, Fifth Pinion, Setting Lever, Yoke	.25	.35	.65	1.00
" Hair Colleted (12/0 and larger)	1.00	2.50		
" Hair Colleted (18/0 and smaller)	1.25	3.25		
" Lock Lever and Minute Wheel Cap combined	.50	1.05		
" Main, 60 Hour	.45	1.10	2.10	4.00
" Main, All others	.40	1.00	1.80	3.50
" Regulator only (No. 2042, No. 886)	.75	1.70		
" Regulator, with adjusting screws	1.00	2.50		
STAFFS, Balance	.50	1.35	2.40	4.50
" Motor Barrel	.75	1.70		
" Center (no pinion)	.75	1.70		
" Center and Pinion (1 piece)	1.10			
STRAPS, Regulator with adjusting screw	.55	1.15		
STUDS, Hairspring	.30	.55	1.00	1.80
TAPS, Crown and Screw	.40	.85	1,60	
WASHERS, Main Winding Wheel Hub	.30	.55	1.00	
WHEELS, Center, Gold, Staff and Pinion	2.05	4.90		
" Center, Brass, Staff and Pinion	1.65	3.80		
" Clutch	.35	.70		
" Escape, Steel	1.10	2.75		
" Escape, Brass	.70	1.60		
" Escape, Steel and Pinion	1.85			
" Escape, Brass and Pinion	1.30			
" Fourth and Third, Gold with pinion	1.75	4.05		
" Fourth and Third, Brass with pinion	1.30	2.95		
" Hour and Pipe	.40	1.00	1.80	
" Intersetting and Interwinding	.40	1.00	1.80	
" Minute and Pinion	.40	1.00	1.80	
" Ratchet (Unexposed)	.40	.80	1.35	
" Ratchet, Motor Barrel	1.50	3.75		
" Ratchet (Exposed)	1.30			
" Regulator Index	.40	.80	1.35	
" Setting	.40	.80	1.35	
" Winding, Crown	1.30			
" Winding, Flat	.85	1.95		
" Winding, Base	.40	.80	1.35	
YOKES	.65	1.45		
" with Interwinding wheel	.95	2.25		
MAINSPRING ASSORTMENT, containing 4 dozen	12.00			

Above prices apply where specified quantities of one factory number are ordered. Mainsprings may be assorted as to strength, balance staffs as to pivot diameter, jewels as to hole size. Items purchased in gross lots, consisting of not less than one dozen of a number are subject to an additional 10% discount. Items purchased in one-quarter gross lots, consisting of not less than one dozen of a number are subject to an additional 5% discount.

ILLINOIS WATCH MATERIAL DEPARTMENT
Lancaster, Pa.

3-10041A

ALL PRICES SUBJECT TO CHANGE WITHOUT NOTICE

IT PAYS TO USE GENUINE ILLINOIS WATCH MATERIAL

Material Price List, September 15, 1947

Effective July 26, 1953

SUGGESTED JEWELER AND WATCHMAKER PRICE LIST OF GENUINE ILLINOIS WATCH MATERIAL

This price list applies to parts for Illinois watch movements manufactured in Springfield, Illinois and Lancaster, Pennsylvania. Your Authorized Hamilton Materials Wholesaler will supply parts prices for imported Illinois movements.

	Each	For ¼ Dz.	For ½ Dz.	For 1 Dz.
ARBORS, Barrel	$1.00	$ 2.40		
" Clutch	.50	1.05		
" Pallet	.80	1.95		
" Winding	1.00	2.25		
" " Threaded	.55	1.00	$ 1.80	$ 3.40
BALANCES, With Screws	2.95			
BALANCE COMPLETE, 16S Non-Magnetic	7.50			
" " All Others	6.50			
BAR, Slide and Swing	.35	.70		
" Swing with Pinion	.75	1.80		
BARREL AND CAP	1.40			
" " " With Arbor Fitted	2.50			
BEARINGS, Motor Barrel Staff, Upper	.55	1.15		
" Winding Arbor	.35	.70		
BRIDGES, Winding	.55	1.15		
" Winding with Pinion	1.10	2.70		
CAPS, Motor Barrel Ratchet Wheel with Jewel	1.95	4.65		
" All Others	.65	1.65		
CLICKS	.80	2.00		
" No. 1044	1.20			
CLUTCHES	.80	2.00		
COLLETS	.50	1.20		
CUPS, Barrel Arbor	.55	1.15		
DIALS, Metal Plain	1.50	3.75		
" Etched	3.00			
" Applied Gold Numerals (Wrist)	4.00			
" Applied Gold Numeral (Pocket)	5.25			
FORKS	.45	1.00		
HANDS, Hour and Minute (Pr.)	.50	1.05	1.90	
" H&M, Luminous or Double Hour (Pr.)	.70	1.90		
" Second, All	.25	.60	1.10	
HUBS, Motor Barrel Ratchet or Snailed	1.05	2.40		
" Winding Wheel	.55	1.30		
INDEXES	.70			
JEWELS, Balance, Escape or Pallet, Olive Hole	.55	1.45	2.60	4.90
" Endstone, Gold Setting	.80	1.65		
" Endstone, Gold Figure 8 or Dome Setting	.85	1.95		
" Endstone, Composition Setting	.45	1.00		
" Barrel, Gold Setting	2.25			
" Barrel, Composition Setting	1.50			
" Center, Gold Setting	1.65			
" Center, Composition Setting	1.10			
" Center, Unset	1.00			
" Plate, Gold Setting	1.25			
" Plate, Composition Setting	.85			
" Plate, Unset	.65	1.45		
" Pallet Stones	.45	.90		
" Roller	.50	1.05		
LET DOWNS	.50	1.50		

	Each	For ¼ Dz.	For ½ Dz.	For 1 Dz.
LEVERS, Clutch, Locking, Setting	.75	1.75		
NUTS, Regulator Adjusting Screw	.40	.85		
PALLETS AND FORKS	2.80			
PALLETS, FORKS AND ARBORS	3.50			
PINIONS, Cannon or Winding	.85	1.80		
" Escape or Fifth	1.05	2.25		
PINS, All	.30	.55		
PLATES, Setting	.30	.85		
REGULATORS	1.05	2.85		
ROLLERS With Jewel	.90	2.00		
" Small Double	.75	1.60		
" Combination with Jewel	1.50			
SCREWS, Regulator	.35	.65		
" All Others	.35	.55		
SLEEVE, Winding Arbor	.50	1.05		
SPRINGS, Flat Steel—Click, Clutch, Lifting, Lock Lever, Setting Lever, Interwinding Wheel, Yoke	.45	.85	$ 1.30	
" Wire—Click, Clutch, Locking Lever, Fifth Pinion, Setting Lever, Yoke	.30	.45	.55	
" Hair, Steel	1.20	3.10		
" Hair, Elinvar Extra	1.55	4.00		
" Lock Lever and Setting Wheel Cap Combined	.50	1.05		
" Main, 80-Hour	.50	1.15	2.10	$ 4.00
" All Others	.45	1.10	2.00	3.85
" Regulator (No. 2042 or No. 886)	.75	1.70		
" Regulator with Screw	1.55			
STAFF, Balance	.55	1.50	2.65	4.95
STRAPS, Regulator with Adjusting Screws	.70	1.40		
STUDS, Hairspring	.40	.80	1.10	
WASHERS, Main Winding Wheel Hub	.30	.55	1.00	
WHEELS, Center Staff and Pinion, Gilt	1.80			
" Center Staff and Pinion, Gold	2.50			
" Clutch	.35	.70		
" Escape	1.10			
" Escape and Pinion	2.15			
" Fourth and Third with Pinion—Gilt	1.50			
" Fourth and Third with Pinion—Gold	2.25			
" Hour, Minute, Setting, Intersetting and Interwinding	.40	1.00		
" Ratchet	.70			
" Ratchet, Exposed	1.50			
" Regulator Index	.40	.80		
" Winding	1.30			
YOKES	.80			
" With Interwinding Wheel	.95	2.35		

Above prices apply where specified quantities of one factory number are ordered. Mainsprings may be assorted as to strength, balance staffs as to pivot diameter, jewels as to hole size. Items purchased in gross lots, consisting of not less than one dozen of a number are subject to an additional 10% discount. Items purchased in one-quarter gross lots, consisting of not less than one dozen of a number are subject to an additional 5% discount.

ILLINOIS WATCH MATERIAL DEPARTMENT
Lancaster, Pa.

6-10041A

ALL PRICES SUBJECT TO CHANGE WITHOUT NOTICE

IT PAYS TO USE GENUINE ILLINOIS WATCH MATERIAL

Illinois Material Price List, 1953

Later-released replacement parts. In 1936 Hamilton issued an Illinois Material Catalog showing white dials and black painted numerals for most Illinois wristwatch models. These later-released Lancaster replacement dials were apparently produced only when an order for one or more was received by Hamilton, as very few of these dials are seen today. (See Chapter 7 for illustrations of these later-released Lancaster replacement market dials.

The Burning Question Revisited

Now that we have reviewed the history of the Illinois Watch Company before and after the acquisition as best as it can currently be reconstructed, it is useful to revisit the reasons why Hamilton sought to acquire Illinois.

At the time, Hamilton was far behind Elgin and Waltham in the wristwatch market. Accordingly, Hamilton's stated public reason for the acquisition was to double what was then its production capacity. But how could Hamilton have doubled the capacity for Hamilton watches if the Illinois Factory remained producing Illinois watches? Also, if Hamilton wanted to double its capacity, why not merely add an extra 8-hour Lancaster work shift? Perhaps it would have taken too long for Hamilton to hire and train the necessary workers fast enough without falling farther behind its stronger wristwatch competitors. But it certainly would have been cheaper than spending $5 million for Illinois.

So there were obviously additional reasons for Hamilton's interest in Illinois. As we have learned, Illinois was more advanced technologically than its new corporate parent in several key areas. Illinois had products and features released or near completion that Hamilton lacked or its own development lagged behind. Therefore, it is very possible that Hamilton may have purchased Illinois to help catch up and leapfrog the industry technologically.

It is also possible that even at the beginning Hamilton never intended to have Illinois continue making its own branded watches but instead planned to convert production to Hamilton movements to truly double its production. But then something very dramatic occurred. Illinois starting going gangbusters in the market with its daring, innovative Art Deco and Moderne wristwatches. Its monthly and yearly sales results hit record highs in 1928, 1929 and most of 1930. The variety of its offerings was astonishing; in a span of barely three years, Illinois had the capability to offer almost 10,000 different Factory-Cased wristwatches if one takes into consideration every possible case, dial, movement and jewel permutation and combination that could be offered.

So while Hamilton may have planned to discontinue the Illinois brand early on, it was thwarted from doing so by the great success of the Illinois product offerings in the 1928 to 1930 timeframe, especially as the Illinois line contained the breadth and depth that the Hamilton line so lacked.

In June 1930, however, Hamilton abolished both the Illinois Research Department and the Materials Department, establishing instead centralized departments in Lancaster. Although the consolidation made sound business sense superficially, Illinois had always had great technological strength, and the elimination of its independent research department had a strong negative impact on the company's ability to continue to innovate and differentiate itself in the marketplace. In fact, Hamilton attempted to convert all Illinois movements to Hamilton ones by stamping the Hamilton name on the movements in place of the Illinois name. And other than the addition of the Elinvar hairspring, there was apparently no significant new feature added for any Illinois wristwatch or pocket watch after 1931.

It was in 1931 that the effects of the Great Depression hit the watch and jewelry industry with a vengeance. At about the same time occurred the death of Hamilton's patriarch Charles F. Miller died after heading the company for twenty-one years. The panicked reaction of its new president, Beckwith, and the Hamilton Board was to protect Hamilton during the economic calamity by planning quickly for the methodical, sub-rosa winding down of the Illinois Watch Company.

The plan that Hamilton implemented ultimately impacted Illinois adversely in three key areas: design, production and sales. Without an ability to perform adequately in these areas, the Illinois Watch Company would eventually be unable to function at all.

- **Design.** Not only was there convergence of design and style between Hamilton and Illinois, but Hamilton even stopped Illinois from entering into exclusive case supply contracts with its normal case suppliers. Moreover, Hamilton permitted Illinois casemakers to offer lower-value cases, in rolled gold plate, for some of the very same case models offered by Illinois. Hamilton also forced Illinois to offer a very inexpensive base metal men's model, its first and only one. In addition, it had been clear from the beginning that Hamilton wanted the high-end market for itself and was unwilling to share it with Illinois. Accordingly, it discouraged Illinois from producing men's wristwatch models either in solid gold or with enamel decoration, and for that reason there are few of those to be found today.

- **Production.** Hamilton greatly reduced the number of Illinois workers, cutting heads to less than a third of what they were at the date of the acquisition. Hamilton extended the normal Illinois plant shutdown periods, and it is likely that wages of the workers that remained employed were cut severely.

After Hamilton consolidated Illinois' operations with Hamilton's in Lancaster, conditions finally reached a point in 1934 that virtually no Illinois movements could be assembled there. Out of desperation, former Illinois employees had to be sent back to Springfield into the shuttered Illinois Factory to try to assemble movements or to get them to the point they could be easily completed in Lancaster. Hamilton also reduced case supplies so severely that Illinois was basically compelled to fill orders watch by watch, and in many instances it could not assemble the watches needed. By 1934 the same situation existed for Illinois dials as well.

- **Sales.** Hamilton reduced Illinois inventory to subcritical levels and sold off the Illinois parts inventory at half price. Hamilton not only eliminated the Illinois direct sale force but also made it impossible for Illinois to provide dummy samples for its jobbers.

Hamilton resorted mainly to simply reissuing previously released Illinois men's models instead of providing new models; for instance, existing models were given new names when metal bracelets were substituted for leather straps or different dials were supplied. By the end of 1932, Hamilton was restricting what it allowed Illinois to issue as new men's models: 15-jewel movements or 18/0 size ladies' movements without subsidiary seconds, housed in inexpensive cases (most 10K gold-filled but one base metal). Furthermore, the models that were released were at less than 25% of their former production quantities. Nonetheless, even the small numbers of models set to be released in 1934 were already unavailable to consummate sales to any reasonable extent at the end of 1933.

Hamilton used the Illinois name for low-end watches to help combat the E-Z-Credit jewelers and price-cutters while offering better watches, with the Hamilton name, via its new Zone Distribution Plan. But Hamilton made no effort to salvage the Illinois line by making it part of the distribution plan.

While Hamilton was developing plans to greatly reduce its number of jobbers, the opposite was occurring with Illinois at the end, since Hamilton was looking for any possible venue to try to unload another Illinois part or watch. Hamilton's new Zone Distribution Plan, later claimed to be its salvation, was only a survival plan—and for it alone, not Illinois as well. Indeed, the Zone Distribution Plan was all too successful for Hamilton, in just a few years landing the company in a lawsuit that would result in an antitrust indictment. (For details, see Appendix 2.)

What If . . . ?

The unanswered question is whether Illinois would have survived the Great Depression had it not been acquired by Hamilton in 1928. We know that by 1926 Illinois had amassed a large inventory of pocket watch parts and movements that compelled it to reduce its work hours for about a year and a half before it was acquired by Hamilton. However, the greatly respected Bunn family of Springfield had an impressive track record in successfully managing Illinois through the economic crises of 1873, 1883, 1893, 1907 and 1920, so it was likely that the company would have survived if the Bunns had been able to continue running it.

The Illinois management, although loyal to its employees, was willing to make tough decisions to help its balance sheet, as is documented not only by its very early move to go on a "short time" basis in 1926 to reduce costs but also by its prescience in shifting its focus to wristwatch parts and movements. Notwithstanding its excess pocket watch inventory, the company was well equipped to produce and issue a large and stylistically varied selection of wristwatches that were popular with consumers.

In order to survive the tough economic times of the Great Depression, Illinois would surely have adopted the tactics of Elgin and Waltham—reducing hours and employees' wages as well as having layoffs and closing the plant for set intervals. (In fact, these are exactly the measures that Illinois itself had taken when it was faced with problems of overproduction in the previous century.) But Illinois would certainly not have instituted such severe controls as those Hamilton implemented, that cut off Illinois' prospects for maintaining, increasing or renewing its business. For example, it is doubtful that Illinois would have foolishly choked off the opportunity for sales by not supplying dummy samples to its jobbers; neither would it have reduced the inventory of wristwatch cases and movements to the point that it could not fulfill orders.

Even in the throes of the Great Depression, its loyal, longtime jobbers were clamoring for new Illinois models and dummy samples to continue the sale of Illinois watches. If Illinois had been able to remain independent, it surely would have found the means to weather the storm, just as Elgin, Waltham and Hamilton did. It had the requisite management acumen and persistence as well as the worker loyalty to do so.

A Return to Reality

Although it is interesting to speculate "what if," such is the realm of fantasy. Unfortunately, reality intrudes, and the fact is that circumstances worked against the survival of the Illinois Watch Company. We should not think badly of the Bunns for selling the company. Jacob Jr., who had run the company for much of its existence and done it exceedingly well, had been involved intimately in the day-to-day life of the Watch Factory since the time he was a boy, working his way up from a lowly position and learning every step of the watch manufacturing process as he progressed. When his father died in 1897, Jacob Jr. had thus been the logical successor as head of the company.

However, it appears that when Jacob Jr. died in 1926, after a long illness, there was no one in the family prepared to take his place. Of his three siblings— Henry, George and Alice— two were successful businessmen, but their expertise was not in watch manufacturing. Neither were his three children, Jacob, Henry and Mildred— positioned to run the company. Thus when Hamilton, a well-established company of high-quality watches, provided assurances that Illinois would continue to operate as it always had, the family accepted Hamilton's offer. But, as we have learned, there were signs early on that Hamilton would not keep its word.

The Great Depression finally sealed Illinois' fate. Beckwith, at the helm of Hamilton, opted out of keeping two geographically distinct plants in operation during difficult times. The course he charted for Hamilton was for its survival; sadly for Illinois, he charted its ultimate end: the Finale of a Great American Watch Company.

In the later 1930s, several curious twists and turns provide a certain symmetry to the story. Beckwith, the architect of Illinois' demise, asked to be relieved of his active leadership as president of Hamilton, though he was retained as chairman of the board. On April 11, 1937, a new president was elected: Calvin Kendig, the executive sent to Springfield along with Robert Miller on January 1, 1928, to oversee the Illinois acquisition.

Then, when Hamilton sold the land, buildings and equipment of the Illinois Watch Company in June 1937, the buyer was the Sangamo Electric Company, and the statement about the purchase was made by Robert Lanphier, the Bunns' old friend who had succeeded Jacob Jr. as president of Sangamo in 1926.

With that sale Hamilton ended the sixty-seven–year presence of the Illinois Watch Company in Springfield. Although we mourn what was lost and what might have been, we rejoice in what is left: the many wonderful watches, which continue to amaze and delight.

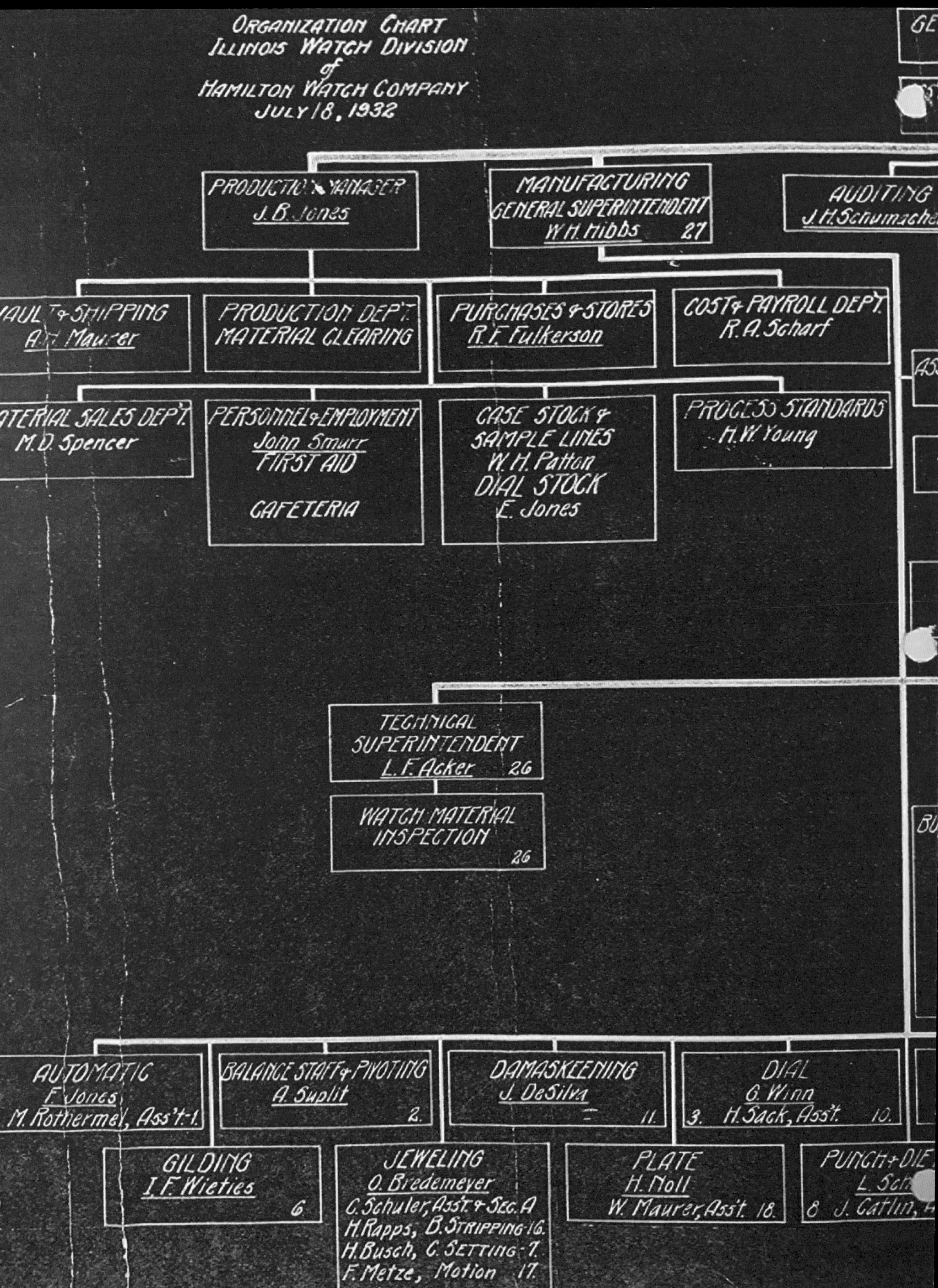
ORGANIZATION CHART
ILLINOIS WATCH DIVISION
of
HAMILTON WATCH COMPANY
JULY 18, 1932
PRODUCTION MANAGER
J. B. Jones
MANUFACTURING
GENERAL SUPERINTENDENT
W. H. Hibbs 27
AUDITING
J. H. Schumacher
VAULT & SHIPPING
A. H. Maurer
PRODUCTION DEP'T.
MATERIAL CLEARING
PURCHASES & STORES
R. F. Fulkerson
COST & PAYROLL DEP'T.
R. A. Scharf
MATERIAL SALES DEP'T.
M. D. Spencer
PERSONNEL & EMPLOYMENT
John Smurr
FIRST AID
CAFETERIA
CASE STOCK &
SAMPLE LINES
W. H. Patton
DIAL STOCK
E. Jones
PROCESS STANDARDS
H. W. Young
TECHNICAL
SUPERINTENDENT
L. F. Acker 26
WATCH MATERIAL
INSPECTION
26
AUTOMATIC
F. Jones
M. Rothermel, Ass't-1.
BALANCE STAFF & PIVOTING
A. Suplit
2.
DAMASKEENING
J. DeSilva
11.
DIAL
G. Winn
3. H. Sack, Ass't. 10.
GILDING
I. F. Wieties
6.
JEWELING
O. Bredemeyer
C. Schuler, Ass't. & Sec. A
H. Rapps, B. Stripping 16.
H. Busch, C. Setting - 7.
F. Metze, Motion 17.
PLATE
H. Noll
W. Maurer, Ass't. 18.
PUNCH & DIE
8 J. Catlin,

5564846
601
MOTOR BARREL
ILLINOIS WATCH
SPRINGFIELD
21 JEWELS

THE VOL 2

ILLINOIS WATCH & ITS HAMILTON YEARS

THE FINALE OF A GREAT AMERICAN WATCH COMPANY

The Illinois Watch

BY
Fredric J. Friedberg

4880 Lower Valley Road • Atglen, PA 19310

Library of Congress Control Number: 2017933341

Designed by Chris Cornforth, www.chrisworx.com
Cover designs by Fred, Joy, Zach Friedberg and Chris Cornforth

ISBN:978-0-7643-5371-0
Printed in China
Published by Schiffer Publishing, Ltd.
4880 Lower Valley Road
Atglen, PA 19310
Phone: (610) 593-1777; Fax: (610) 593-2002
E-mail: Info@schifferbooks.com
Web: www.schifferbooks.com

CHAPTER 6

Movements and Their Repair

For the men and women of the Illinois Watch Company, the watch movement was the most important part of a timepiece. All of their focus, skills and talent went into producing some of the finest movements ever manufactured in the United States. The fact that these movements still perform their intended purpose almost one hundred years later stands as testimony to the care, pride and dedication invested in their design and production.

Movement Basics

Basically, a watch movement consists of a power source connected by gears to a device regulating the speed at which the gears turn. The rotation of the gears moves the hour, minute and second hands above the dial of the watch to indicate the time. The genius of this machine, though, lies in the engineering and production details.

1. The **winding and setting mechanism** includes the watch stem, several gears, the mainspring and mainspring barrel. The mainspring, a 12.5- to 13-inch strip of spring steel, serves as the power reservoir in an Illinois watch. Winding the crown tightens the mainspring. A stop or click keeps the mainspring from unwinding. This built-up tension establishes a reservoir of power, similar to that in a windup toy. The mainspring is encased in a brass cylinder called the barrel.

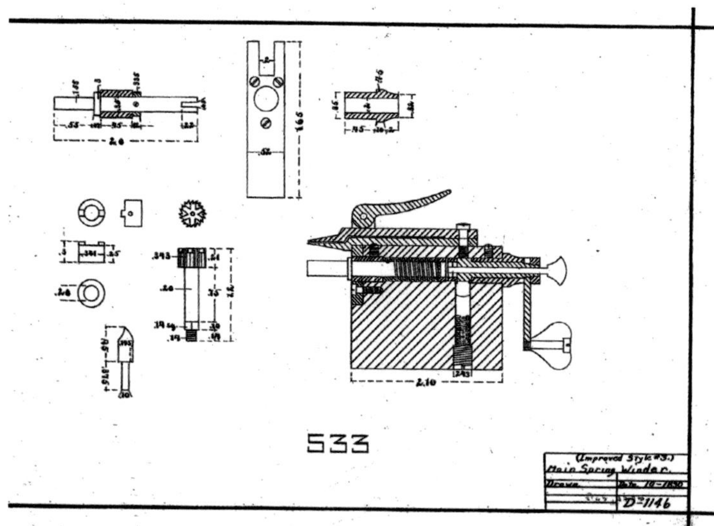

Drawing for an Illinois mainspring winder, October 1890

2. The **gear train** transmits power from the mainspring to the escapement mechanism. Along the way, it moves the hands of the watch. Watch manufacturers refer to the big gears as wheels and to the smaller gears as pinions. A wheel and a pinion are mounted together on a shaft called an arbor which turns in jeweled bearings. The ratios of the teeth on the wheels to those on the pinions with which they are engaged are such that the rapid motion of the escapement is slowed down to a single revolution of the center wheel in an hour. The teeth on the mainspring barrel drive the pinion of the center wheel. An extension of the center arbor through the plate drives the cannon pinion and the motion work that moves the hands. In Illinois watches with subsidiary seconds (except for those with 207 grade movements), an extension of the fourth-wheel arbor through the plate and dial carries the second hand.

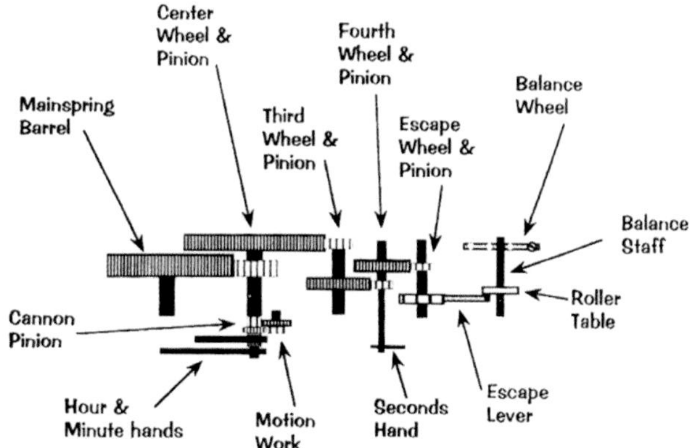

A highly simplified watch train, viewed on edge and dial down to illustrate its wheels and pinions

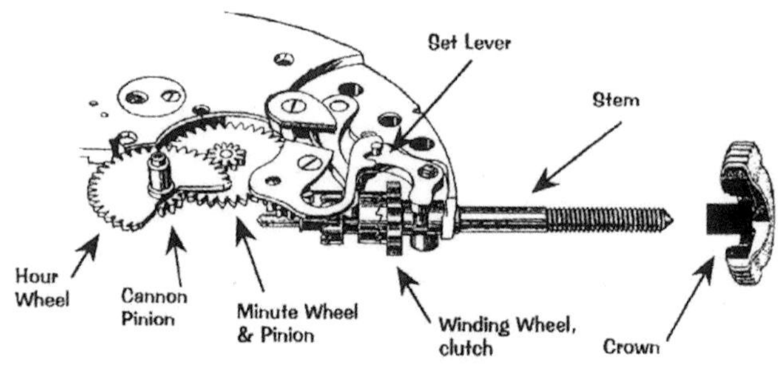

A cutaway drawing of a typical wristwatch movement, viewed from its dial side

3. The **balance wheel and escapement mechanism**, the heart of the watch, is made up of the escape wheel, the anchor-shaped pallet fork, and the balance wheel and roller, which share an arbor with the hairspring. The oscillation of the balance wheel controls the rate at

which the teeth of the escape wheel are allowed to pass the pallets on the lever; as each tooth escapes past a pallet, it also supplies a small impulse to keep the balance moving.

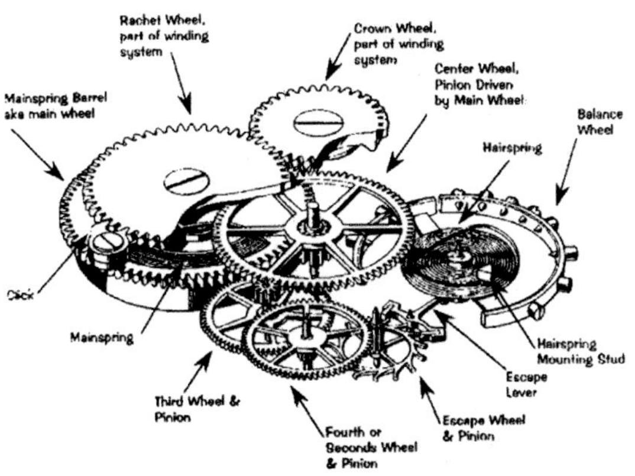

A typical wristwatch movement, seen from the back, with its plates removed

4. **Jewels** act as almost frictionless bearings for the pivots on the ends of the arbors. The number and placement of the jewels reveals much about the movement design. Most watchmakers believe that a quality watch must have a minimum of 15 jewels.

5. The **plate and bridges** provide the skeletal structure and support for the springs, wheels and balance. The plate, known as a pillar or base plate, lies adjacent to the dial and serves as the bearing base for the watch movement structure. Illinois watchmakers divided the upper plate of small movements into two bridges, the barrel bridge and the train bridge, and a small finger bridge or cock to hold the balance. Breaking the upper plate into bridges simplified assembly and maintenance of the movement.

WATCH JEWELS

A watch consists of wheels, a spring and a balance mounted on pivots. In order to permit these pivots to move with the least amount of friction and ensure the greatest durability, watchmakers devised a bushing, originally made from natural jewels, such as rubies, sapphires and diamonds. The introduction of jeweling reduced the amount of wear on the contact points in the movement. Initially, the use of natural substances confined use of jewels to only the most expensive watch movements. Even the better American movement manufacturers did not adopt jeweling until the middle of the nineteenth century.

Nineteenth-century watchmakers commonly believed that a high-quality watch could be designed with 15 jewels. The jewels were of four configurations: hole jewels, cap jewels, pallet jewels and a roller jewel. This allowed jewels to be placed in all frequently moving parts and pivots, including an impulse jewel (on the roller table of the balance), two pallet jewels, four balance staff jewels (a hole jewel and a cap jewel on each end of the pivot), two on the pallet fork, two on the escape wheel, two on each of the third and fourth wheels. Until almost the middle of the twentieth century, high-quality Swiss manufacturers, such as Rolex and Omega, produced excellent 15-jewel movements. The European market was content with 15-jewel watches. In the United States, this was not the case.

Beginning in the 1890s, the Hampden Watch Company of Canton, Ohio, heavily advertised the concept that quality watches should have more than 15 jewels. They promoted their 17-jewel movements, which allowed the center wheel to be jeweled at both ends, ignoring the fact that the center wheel pivots did not wear substantially because they rotated only once an hour. Although this was more a promotional play than a mechanical necessity, Hampden's efforts instilled in the American mind that more jewels made for a better watch. Railroads' emphasis on jeweling, when adopting their approval standards, reinforced this belief. The invention of artificially made jewels at the turn of the twentieth century made additional jeweling more of a labor cost than a materials cost. Watch movements began appearing with 19, 21, 23 and even 25 jewels.

American watch manufacturers wishing to emphasize the quality of their movements increased the number of jewels. They found the public willing to pay more for a higher-jeweled movement. The increased cost of adding the jewels (mere pennies) returned additional dollars in profits.

Illinois took great care to design and engineer superior watch movements. To help a non-technical public understand this, Illinois played to the American belief that more jewels meant a higher-quality movement. For instance, it offered practically the same 6/0 size movement with 15 jewels, 17 jewels, 19 jewels and 21 jewels. *—Bob Ayer*

JEWELING PATTERNS IN ILLINOIS WRISTWATCH MOVEMENTS

The pattern of jeweling in Illinois' 3/0 movements was the one conventionally used by American manufacturers: cap and hole jewels on each end of the balance staff, a roller jewel, two pallet jewels, and paired hole jewels on the pivots of the arbors for the lever, escape wheel, fourth, third, and center wheels.

With the early 6/0 movements used in the Transitional Period, Illinois used different jeweling patterns, closer to European designs. The 15-jewel 904 and 908 and the 17-jewel 904 and 905 movements had cap jewels on both pivots of the escape wheel, and omitted the jewels on the unseen lower pivots of the fourth and third wheels. The later 15-jewel 605 and 605A movements had the more conventional pattern of paired jewels except on the center arbor. The 17-jewel 607 and 607A movements were like the 3/0 movements, with paired jewels all the way to the center. In the 19-jewel 907 movement and the 21-jewel 601 and 909 movements, cap jewels reappeared on the escape pivots. The 21-jewel movements added two jewels on the motor-barrel pivots.

The 17-jewel Illinois 12/0 207 movement was conventional in its jeweling pattern. To convert the 207 into the 19-jewel 401 movement for Hamilton, Illinois added two jewels to the fifth-pinion arbor that drove the second hand.

The 18/0 and 21/0 movements used conventional 15- and 17-jewel patterns. However, Illinois also made some 16-jewel 18/0 movements that had only an upper jewel on the center arbor pivot. *—Jim Mason*

ILLINOIS FILM VIEWED BY CLUB

"Did you ever stop to think that the balance wheel of your watch traveled 5,000 miles every day?

"Did you know that one oiling of your watch would keep it in good shape for about 18 months, and that the entire amount of oil necessary to put the time piece in good shape as far as lubrication is concerned is a drop the size of the head of a pin?

"Did you know that even after 18 months pass by and you don't give the "machinery" an oiling, your faithful old watch will probably go on ticking for eight or ten years—but the minute bearings will be wearing all the time and you will have to pay for it in the way of a jeweler's bill sooner or later?

"These were some of the things that the members of the Exchange Club learned last evening, when D. Leslie White, through the courtesy of the Illinois Watch Company, showed a three reel film illustrating every phase in the manufacture of a watch. The films were of exceptional interest and Mr. White was given a vote of thanks for an entertaining as well as instructive evening."*

**Portsmouth Daily Times* (Portsmouth, Ohio), January 17, 1923.

Manufacturing an Illinois Watch

An Illinois watch movement contained an average of 175 different parts, some so small that their details can be seen only with powerful magnification. Many of these parts underwent from fifty to seventy distinct manufacturing processes.[1] Each process was usually performed by a machine especially designed for this particular work. Many of these operations appeared in a 1923 three-reel silent film produced by the United States Department of the Interior in cooperation with the Illinois Watch Factory.[2]

Parts Manufacture

The Illinois Watch Company divided its operation into two main areas: parts manufacture and parts assembly. Building an Illinois movement entailed over fifteen hundred manufacturing operations. The critical operations were:

1. **Plates and bridges.** Manufacture of the skeletal structure or ébauche required more than two hundred separate operations. In the plate itself nearly forty holes were drilled, threaded, and beveled. Many of these holes had to be placed with several thousandths of an inch tolerance. In addition, many recesses, each with a prescribed outline and depth, had to be precisely milled.

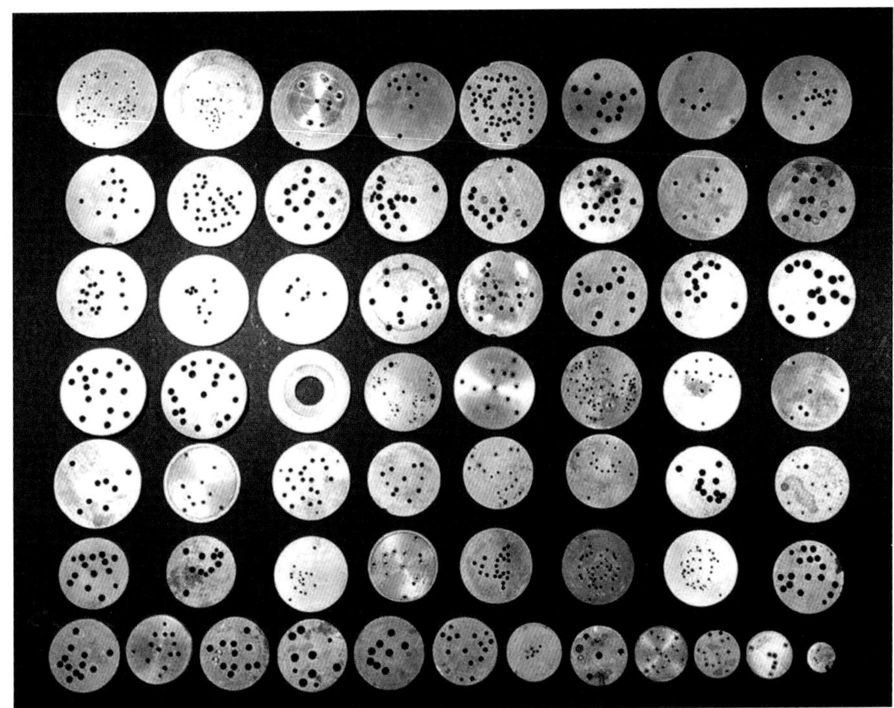

An almost complete set of Illinois Master Plates

2. **Wheels.** The main wheels were punched out of a strip of brass and polished so that they were absolutely flat. The teeth in the wheel had to be cut so that their contours would mesh exactly with those of their mating pinions. The balance wheel had to meet balance and weight specifications exactly.

Punching the balance wheels in the Illinois Factory, still frame from the 1923 silent film

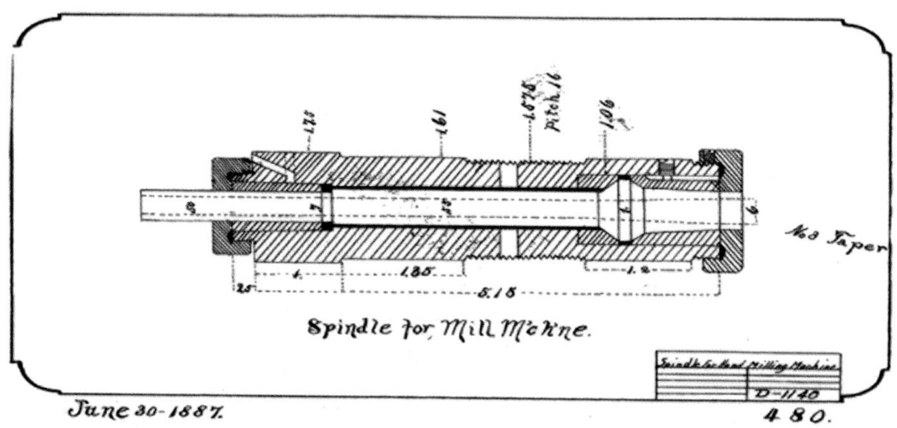

Illinois drawing for spindle for hand milling machine, June 1887

3. **Jewels and hairsprings.** The manufacture of these specialty items required large volume for economy.

A watch jewel, usually a ruby, started as a rough pebble. This pebble was placed on a base, over which had been laid a piece of blotting paper only 2/1,000 inch thick. The base had first been covered with liquid shellac, and because the paper was perforated, the shellac squeezed out through the holes and fastened the pebble in place. It was then sawed through, from above, by disks of phosphor bronze that had been rolled in diamond dust. The ruby was cut into pieces only about 1/50 inch thick. And the machine which cut them operated with such precision that the disks stopped when they cut down through the stone and halfway through the paper under it that is only 2/1,000 inch thick. The slices of ruby were then cut up into circles about the size of a pinhead and a hole was drilled through the center of each. The pivots of the wheel arbors turned in these pierced rubies. The balance pivots also rested on end jewels that were about the size of a pinhead. Sometimes diamonds rather than rubies were used for the balance end stones.

The spring steel alloy for **hairsprings** was rolled in a mill, then swaged into a long, thin, narrow strip. The strip was then pulled through a series of dies until it reached the thinness required for the spring. The spring was then coiled to the right size and attached to the collet for the balance arbor at its inner end and to the stud to for the balance jack at the outer end.

The Illinois Machine Shop, still frame from the 1923 silent film

4. **Pinions.** Automatic machines cut pieces from bar stock and turned them into final shape. The teeth of the pinion gears were cut by machines. The pivot points of the arbors were ground and polished to provide a smooth bearing surface and a precise fit into the jewels. To ensure high quality, workers checked every pinion to assure that the diameter fell within a tolerance of 2/1000 of an inch.

5. **Balance assembly**. The heart of a watch, the balance assembly, required the most precise manufacturing techniques used in the Watch Factory. The assembly consisted of several components: the wheel itself, the hairspring that controlled its motion, the roller assembly that connected the balance to the lever, and the balance staff or arbor on which the parts were mounted. Different departments in the Illinois Factory were responsible for the parts of the assembly.

WHY I COLLECT ILLINOIS

Anyone familiar with mechanical watches knows that it is positively mesmerizing to remove the back and watch the balance wheel oscillating as it sends its lifegiving power through the gear train much as a heart pumps blood through a body. The fact that this marvel of micromechanics performs its assigned function 432,000 times per day with an accuracy rate of 99.99% is incredible. In the case of Illinois wristwatches, we must remember that all of this was accomplished some 90 years ago, long before computers or even electronic calculators. These watches were designed by engineers using drawing boards, mechanical drawing instruments, and slide rules, and were produced on manually controlled machines that most industrial operations relegated to the scrap heap or to museums decades ago. How many items in your house today operate reliably with 99.99% accuracy?

We live in a time when most things are disposable. Cell phones are routinely tossed aside or placed on eBay for a few bucks after a few years, cars are considered old at 7 to 10 years, and in many locations even houses are frequently torn down after 20 to 30 years in order to build "something better". How different it is to own something as timeless and beautiful as an Illinois watch!

What is it about the Art Deco styling so wonderfully characteristic of Illinois wristwatches? I'm an engineer, not a philosopher or psychologist. Art Deco styling simply has a visceral appeal I find hard to explain. The beauty of the dials, the wonderful chasing of the cases, and the damaskeening of the movement plates all speak to an age where people built products with pride of workmanship simply not present today. While many companies adopted this style, I think Illinois did it best. Illinois was a bit smaller than their rivals Hamilton and Elgin, but also pioneered quite a number of innovations in the industry.

To me, vintage mechanical watches represent engineering with elegance, and Illinois did it best.

—*Rick Liebson*

The balance wheel itself had several components. The rim of the wheel was in two semicircular pieces, each of which was made of laminated strips of steel and brass. The rim pieces were each attached at one end to the crossbar of the wheel, the other ends being free to move in and out, according to temperature, to compensate for variations in hairspring strength. Dynamic balancing to adjust a balance and do fine regulation of time is done with tiny screws inserted into holes in the rim.

The balance arbor or staff is one of the most fragile parts in a watch, and the one requiring the most precision in manufacture. Because so little power is available to drive the balance, the pivots must be exceptionally smooth. But they are also tiny and easily bent or broken if a watch is dropped or jarred. Makers have attempted to cushion the pivots from Breguet's "pare-chute" of 1790 (still in use after more than two centuries) through the more modern devices like the Incabloc. Illinois never used cushioned pivots, though there is evidence they were considering the Incabloc (see the discussion later in this chapter).

(Under ideal circumstances, broken pivots should be repaired by restaffing the balance assembly. Unfortunately, replacement pivots for Illinois are difficult to find, and repair can sometimes be accomplished by transplanting a whole balance assembly, with its matching hairspring, from another movement.)

6. **Cleaning.** The important final manufacturing operation was cleaning, after which the parts were protected from dust and contact with human hands.

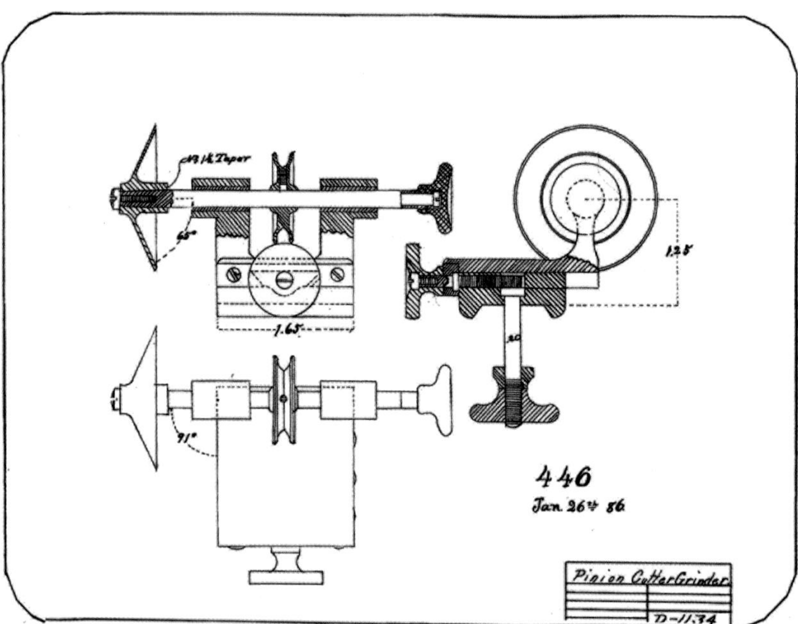

Drawing of an Illinois pinion cutter grinder, January 26, 1886

Inspection

Requirements for precision in parts manufacture made frequent inspection essential. The parts-making stages determined much of the accuracy of the finished watch. Illinois workers sampled parts quality by using a special magnifying projector together with a template to check pieces from automatic screw, gear-cutting, or milling machines. Machine operators themselves used gauges, dials, micrometers, and magnifiers to test for quality during manufacture. A final inspection was made of all important parts after cleaning or upon receipt from a supplier. This final inspection usually included 100% visual inspection plus sampling of dimension measurements and template comparison on a magnifier.

Do You Know

how a good watch is made?

We have been fortunate in securing from the Illinois Watch Company of Springfield, Illinois, one of the most novel and complete exhibits ever shown in Indianapolis.

This exhibit shows a watch from the rough state to the finished product, also a number of watches running without hairsprings, 500,000 jewels in settings, loose wheels, pinions, hairsprings, pallets, arbors, dials, etc., etc. On one large frame the shape of a watch are 450 running movements, including the famous Bunn Specials and Sangomos, which are favorites among railroad men, who must have accurate timepieces.

This large exhibit is in our window and we want you to see it, as it is the first time such a thing has been seen in Indianapolis, and we know that it will interest you.

J. H. Reed, Jeweler

38 West Washington Street

An announcement about an Illinois watch exhibit loaned out by the Watch Company to local jewelers to be displayed in their windows, *Indianapolis Star*, October 7, 1908; image from *newspapers.com*

Tools and Dies

The precision required in parts manufacture necessitated exacting accuracy in tool setups, machine tools, and dies. For example, more than one hundred jigs and dies were needed for stamping, holding, and punch-marking the plate and bridges for a single grade of watch. These small dies, which often require location of the points within +/-2/1,000th of an inch, were laid out on special machines with the aid of optical magnifying and centering apparatus.

Assembly

The assembly of a watch movement required great skill. Illinois used an assembly-line approach permitting the use of less experienced workers for installing the winding and setting mechanism and the main wheels, and the concentration of more skilled workers on installing the escapement and balance wheels and making final adjustments.

MOVEMENT-CARRYING TRAYS

Michael C. Harold, in an excellent article in the NAWCC *Bulletin* (Supplement Number 14, Spring 1984), mentioned that "When parts were sufficiently complete to be serial numbered with their mating pieces, the numbered set moved through the building in a compartmented traveling tray. As it neared a finished state, the movement could then be assembled and housed in a serial numbered box, in which it was ultimately shipped from the factory."

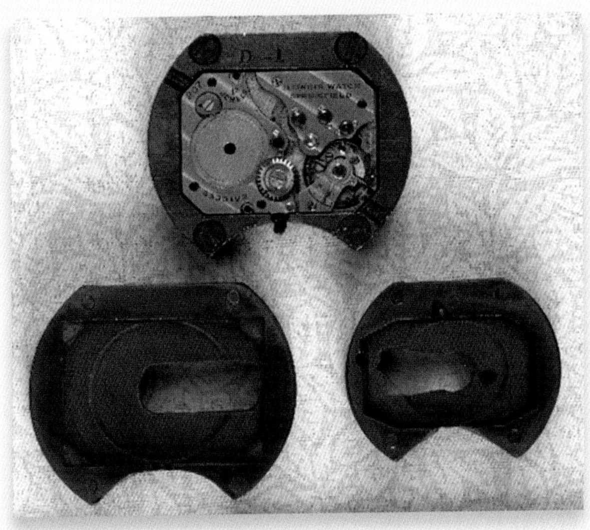

Illinois traveling trays

Adjustment and Installation

The critical operations in watch assembly were the adjustment and installation of the escapement–balance wheel mechanism and its subsequent regulation. When the balance wheel subassembly was ready, it was put into the movement along with the anchor fork. This operation required the highest skill in watchmaking, for a number of very fine adjustments had to be made—for example, shifting jewels to eliminate binding or to ensure exactly correct contact between anchor fork and escapement wheel, and final positioning of the regulating lever which permitted minute adjustments in the length of the hairspring, which in turn controlled the oscillating frequency of the balance wheel and thus the accuracy of the watch.

Decoration of Movements

Before the watch manufacturers started casing their watches at the factory, one of their selling points was the beauty of the finishing on the movements. Although decoration of the movement did nothing for its performance, its quality at least suggested that the maker had expended similar care on finishing of mechanical parts, and makers cited it in their advertising. One of the interesting aspects of collecting Illinois watches, particularly for those who collect early pocket watches, is appreciating the interesting and varied types of artwork with which the maker embellished the back and even the interior of its movements.

Illinois' earliest pocket watch movements used brass plates with a thin wash of gilt for protection and decoration. In the 1880s, however, Illinois switched from gilt plates to nickel-plated ones, and with the move, they also began to decorate the plates by a process called "damaskeening." The name was probably meant to suggest another quite different method of decorating metal, often called Damascene work. Unlike that ancient process, which involved exposing patterns in folded, laminated, and fire-welded steel, damaskeening was a surface treatment.

First introduced in America by the United States Watch Co., of Marion, New Jersey, around 1869, damaskeening is the technique of embellishing watch movement plates by using small polishing laps of ivory or boxwood with an abrasive paste to produce designs in the plates. Damaskeening was an important selling point when a customer visited a jewelry store to purchase a watch movement and select a case for it. Eye appeal was a big selling feature for the movement, and Illinois yielded to no other maker in the quality of its decoration.

A 2002 article by Greg Frauenhoff, Tom McIntyre and Dr. Russell W. Snyder in the NAWCC *Bulletin*[3] mentions that Illinois first engraved designs on movements with its grades 104 and 105 pocket watches, starting in 1883. Illinois also engraved its movements with text throughout its production, but on the early movements the lettering was particularly decorative. The company name was engraved on a swooping, banner-like baseline and the engraving filled with gold coloring. "An examination of watch production in chronological order reveals that two subsequent runs of Grade 64 watches in 1884–85 featured gold-filled engraving (524,601–524,700 and 524,700–525,000). Illinois watches did not again feature gold-filled engraving on watch movements until around 1890."[4]

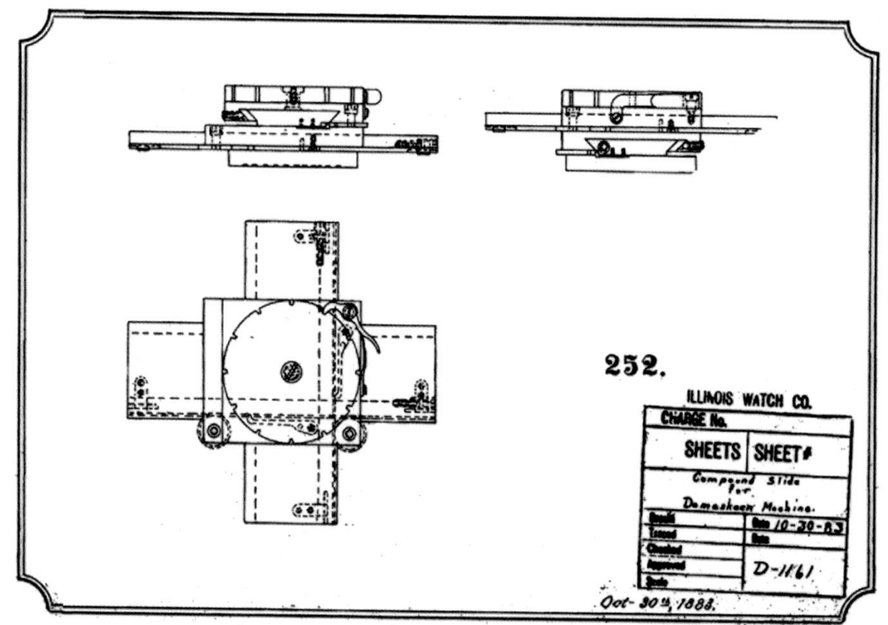

Illinois drawing of a compound slide for an Illinois Factory damaskeen machine, October 30, 1883

This engraving with and without gold-fill continued throughout the production history of Illinois.

Illinois employed various engraving techniques for its movements, such as the use of a mechanical engraver that worked like a reducing pantagraph; the designs would have been traced from large-scale patterns machined or carved in wood. Engraving with and without gold filling or other coloring continued throughout the production history of Illinois.

An Illinois worker on a damaskeening machine, still shot from the 1923 silent frame

Final Testing

Final testing of the completed movement included extended time, position and temperature tests. Illinois performed extended time tests over several days in various positions and under various temperature conditions.

The Illinois Timing Department, still frame from the 1923 silent film

Cases, Dials and Hands

The manufacture of cases, dials and hands required a substantial number of operations, many of which called for costly equipment. Normally, watch manufacturers such as Illinois purchased these products from outside sources. Illinois obtained its cases from artisans and craftsmen as well as from case manufacturing companies.

Illinois Watch Movements

Over its years in operation, the Illinois Watch Company made watch movements that could be used in wristwatches in 0 size, 3/0 size, 6/0 size, 12/0 size, 18/0 size and 21/0 size. Illinois intended none of the 0 size nor the initial models of 3/0 and 6/0 size movements for wristwatches. On the other hand, Illinois designed all of the 12/0, 18/0 and 21/0 sizes specifically for wristwatches. The 0-size and the early 3/0 and 6/0 movements were used in pocket and pendant watches. They were also used in wristwatches, mostly in the early Transitional Period.

WATCH MOVEMENT SIZES: A PRIMER

The Illinois Watch Company produced movements in various sizes: 18, 16, 14, 12, 10, 6, 4, 0, 3/0, 6/0, 12/0, 18/0 and 21/0, strange designations in a world dominated by inches and millimeters. The American watch industry grew up with this unique way to describe the size of their movements. The sizes referred to the Lancashire Gauge, a measurement used by Lancashire watchmakers. The use of this obscure measurement system serves as a reminder of the English origins of the American watch industry; French and Swiss watchmakers used the ancient French measurement of the ligne instead. Today, most use millimeters to describe size.

Originally, watch manufacturers produced and shipped only watch movements, which local jewelers matched with watch cases selected by their customers. This historical separation remained until the end of watch production in the United States. Later, watch manufacturers cased their own movements, but continued to buy cases from outside watch case companies. This curious separation forced the watch manufacturers and the case manufacturers to agree on standard size descriptions for watch movements and watch cases. Soon all the watch manufacturers used the same size designations for their products.

Watchmakers measured the size of their round movements by the diameter of the front plate of the movement, with 0 representing 1-5/30 inch and each size designation above 0 representing 1/30 inch. Therefore a 10 size movement would be 1 + 15/30 or 1-1/2 inches wide.

In the latter part of the nineteenth century, watch movements grew smaller and smaller for both men's and women's watches. Illinois originally produced only 18-size movements (nominally 1-23/30 inch at the front plate). In about 1884, however, Illinois started producing smaller 8-size movements (nominally 1-13/30 inch at the front plate). Waltham and Elgin produced even smaller 0-size movements, beginning around 1890. Ostensibly, the manufacturers produced these smaller sizes to appeal to the growing women's market.

Once watch manufacturers produced watches smaller than 0-size, the watch size designation system threatened to come apart. In 1902, Waltham produced its first sub–0-sized movement. Initially, it switched to Lignes, designating the size as 10 Ligne. Elgin used 00 and 000. Finally, manufacturers settled on designating movements smaller than 0-size by placing a /0 under the number of 30ths smaller than 0. Therefore a 6/0 size watch movement is smaller than a 3/0 size movement.

The advent of rectangular and oval wristwatch movements forced wristwatch manufacturers to be creative once again. These movements did not have a circumference to measure. Therefore, watchmakers invented another rule: non-round movements shall be measured at their narrowest point.

To make things just a little more confusing, manufacturers measured a bit differently. In one Illinois catalog, after a table of watch sizes, the authors appended the following explanation, "We call attention to the fact that our 18-size does not conform to this standard but corresponds to the 19-size given in the table." In another instance, Hamilton produced its first 6/0 movement, the 988, but the movement had to be specially cased, because it did not measure the same as other manufacturers' 6/0 movements.

—Bob Ayer

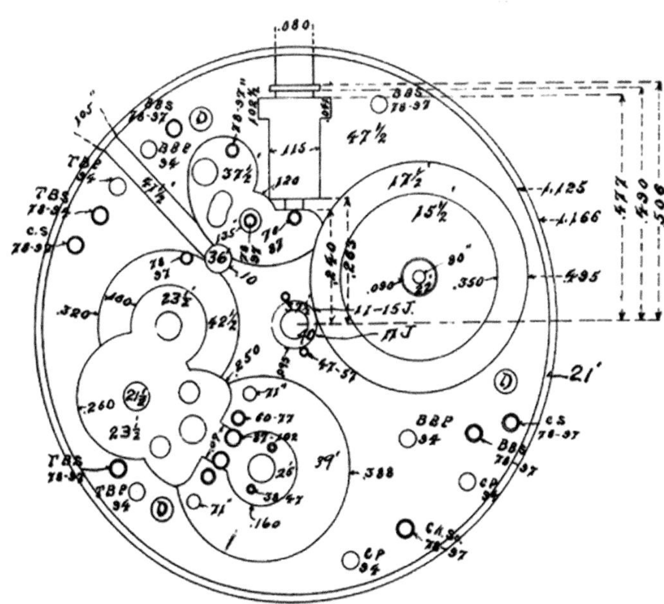

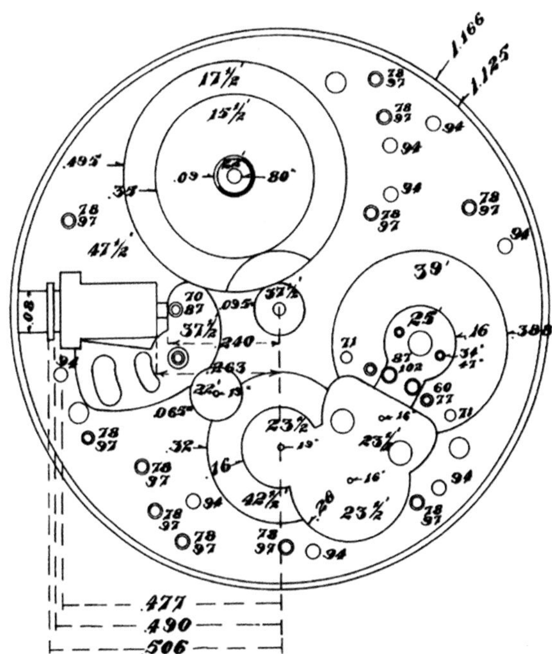

Illinois 0-size movement drawings

The following table gives a complete list of Illinois movements 0-size and smaller which could be used in wristwatches.

Illinois Wristwatch Movements

Size	Grade	Jewels	Size	Grade	Jewels
0	33	11	6/0	605	15
0	35	11	6/0	605A	15
0	35	15	6/0	607	17
0	35	16	6/0	607A	17
0	37	17	6/0	609	19
0	37	17	6/0	903	15
0	38	11	6/0	904	17
0	38	15	6/0	905	17
0	38	17	6/0	907	19
0	39	17	6/0	909	21
0	39	19	12/0	207	17
0	57	17	18/0	181	16
0	201	11	18/0	181	17
0	203	15	18/0	206	16
0	204	17	18/0	206	17
0	205	*	18/0	206ml	17
3/0	21	11	18/0	805	15
3/0	23	15	18/0	805A	15
3/0	24	12	18/0	805A	17
3/0	24	17	18/0	807	16
3/0	25	*	18/0	807	17
3/0	30	*	18/0	807A	17
3/0	32	11	18/0	807B	17
3/0	34	15	18/0	807	18
3/0	36	17	18/0	6¾	*
3/0	307	17	21/0	105	15
6/0	585	15	21/0	107	17
6/0	601	21			

*Jewel Count Unknown

Illinois originally used all of the 18/0 and the 21/0 size movements in its ladies' wristwatches. Hamilton, on the other hand, used the Illinois 18/0 movement in four of Illinois' late-model (1934) men's wristwatches.

At least eighteen Factory-Cased men's Illinois wristwatches came with 3/0 size movements. At least thirty-one came with 6/0 size movements. At least twenty-seven came with 12/0 size movements, and five of the men's wristwatches came with 18/0 size movements. There were no men's size 21/0 wristwatches. For the ladies' models there were at least seventy models that came with 18/0 size movements and eighteen models that came with 21/0 size movements. This does not include the Illinois ladies' Diamond-Set models that were called Mary Todds by the Illinois jobbers.

A wide variety of Military and Transitional watch cases contained 0-size and 3/0 movements. Jewelers and jobbers cased most of these watches in round or cushion-shaped cases. A very few were placed in Admiral Evans octagonal cases; these are highly prized by collectors.

In the Generic Period, men's wristwatch cases (those with standard geometrically shaped cases used by all watch manufacturers) came with 3/0 and 6/0 size movements. Many were cased by jewelers and jobbers. At least seven different Generic Period case shapes (Atlantic, Maxine, Round, Square, Tonneau, Cushion Cushion and Cushion Round) housed the 3/0 movement. Smaller cases in many of these same shapes held 6/0 movements. The 6/0 could also be found in Southampton, Square Cut Corner and Canby shaped cases.

MOVEMENTS BETWEEN 1926 AND 1931

According to a letter from the Illinois Watch Material Sales Department to Wholesalers, dated February 26, 1931, "the following new watches were placed on the market since 1926".

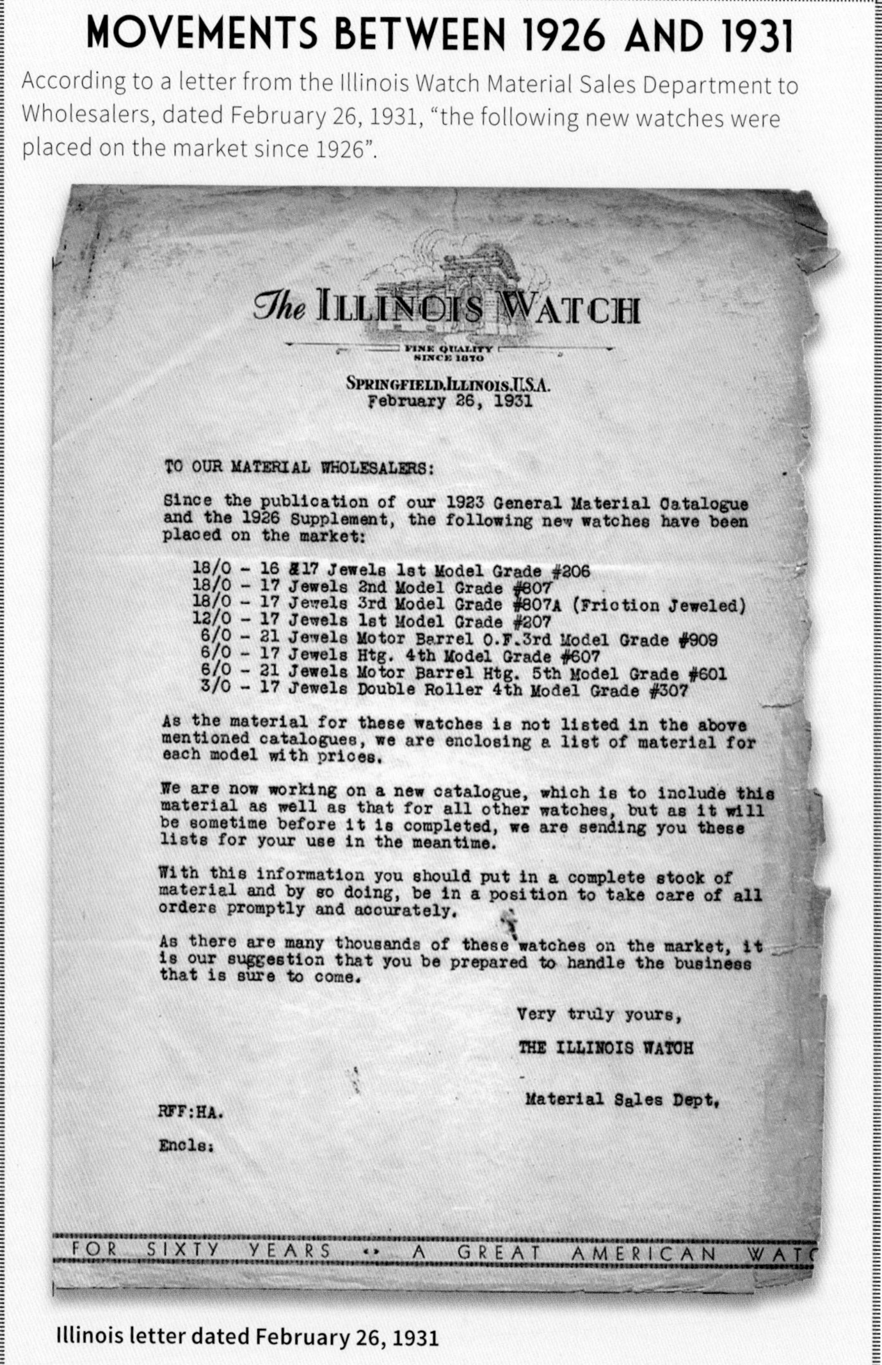

The ILLINOIS WATCH

FINE QUALITY SINCE 1870

SPRINGFIELD, ILLINOIS, U.S.A.
February 26, 1931

TO OUR MATERIAL WHOLESALERS:

Since the publication of our 1923 General Material Catalogue and the 1926 Supplement, the following new watches have been placed on the market:

18/0 - 16 &17 Jewels 1st Model Grade #206
18/0 - 17 Jewels 2nd Model Grade #807
18/0 - 17 Jewels 3rd Model Grade #807A (Friction Jeweled)
12/0 - 17 Jewels 1st Model Grade #207
6/0 - 21 Jewels Motor Barrel O.F.3rd Model Grade #909
6/0 - 17 Jewels Htg. 4th Model Grade #607
6/0 - 21 Jewels Motor Barrel Htg. 5th Model Grade #601
3/0 - 17 Jewels Double Roller 4th Model Grade #307

As the material for these watches is not listed in the above mentioned catalogues, we are enclosing a list of material for each model with prices.

We are now working on a new catalogue, which is to include this material as well as that for all other watches, but as it will be sometime before it is completed, we are sending you these lists for your use in the meantime.

With this information you should put in a complete stock of material and by so doing, be in a position to take care of all orders promptly and accurately.

As there are many thousands of these watches on the market, it is our suggestion that you be prepared to handle the business that is sure to come.

Very truly yours,

THE ILLINOIS WATCH

Material Sales Dept,

RFF:HA.

Encls;

FOR SIXTY YEARS •• A GREAT AMERICAN WAT

Illinois letter dated February 26, 1931

Movements Between 1915 and 1932

From 1915 to 1932, Illinois produced at least 583,000 3/0, 6/0 and 12/0 size movements, plus almost 25,000 0-size ones. Of these, over 152,100 movements in 3/0 and 6/0 sizes, and all of the 0 size, were made from 1915 to 1922. Although almost all of these were not intended for wristwatches, they could be used in that way. In total, 43,000 watches were made with 12/0 size movements, 128,100 with 18/0 size and around 23,600 with 21/0 size.

Normally, Illinois produced its movements in both the open face and hunting case configurations. For the open face configuration, the movement was designed so that the winding crown and the second hand stood directly opposite each other. This configuration had been used for pocket watches for over one hundred years and worked well for pendant watches. Installing such movements in wristwatches with crowns customarily placed at the 3 o'clock location caused the seconds register to be placed at the 9 o'clock position.

A hunting case pocket watch had a cover over the dial, ostensibly to protect the watch while the wearer was hunting in the woods. In such watches, watchmakers placed the winding crowns with the cover latch and directly opposite the case cover hinges. The winder and the seconds hand were situated 90° apart. Many small women's pendant watches in the early 1900s also had hunting cases. When used in wristwatches, movements in the hunting configuration placed the seconds register in the more traditional 6 o'clock position on the wristwatch. Illinois produced movements of the same grade in both configurations to cover the widest audience. To the end of its days, Illinois referred to the configurations as open face and hunting.

In the Beginning

In the last part of the nineteenth century, Illinois cemented its reputation for producing high-quality pocket watches. In the 1880s it experimented with smaller ladies' models in 4 and 6 size. In approximately 1890, Elgin and Waltham produced even smaller movements in 0 size.

Illinois did not offer a 0-size movement until 1905, probably initiating production of the smaller movement at the behest of its large department store customers. Ladies liked the small watches because of their versatility; they could be worn as pendants from necklaces or brooches as well as chatelaines from belts.

Illinois made the 0 size with various numbers of jewels: the 11-jewel, grade 33; the 15-jewel, grade 35; and the 17-jewel, grade 37. In the next decade, Illinois produced small numbers of these watches, plus a few 17-jewel, grade 38 and grade 39, the latter made with a different configuration for the train bridge, probably for large Private Label customers.

The smaller size of this movement allowed it to be used for a wristwatch, though there is no documentation that any of these movements initially appeared in wristwatches. In its documentation, Illinois designated these 0-size movements as 0-size Model 1 (open face, seconds at 9) and Model 2 (hunting face, seconds at 6).

A Change in Design

After a few years, Illinois improved its 0-size movement by engineering its Model 1911, which became the basis for the second generation of 0-size watches, known internally as the Model 3 (open face) and Model 4 (hunting face). Illinois introduced these movements to the public in late 1915 or early 1916 as its 11-jewel, grade 201; its 15-jewel, grade 203; and its 17-jewel, grade 204.

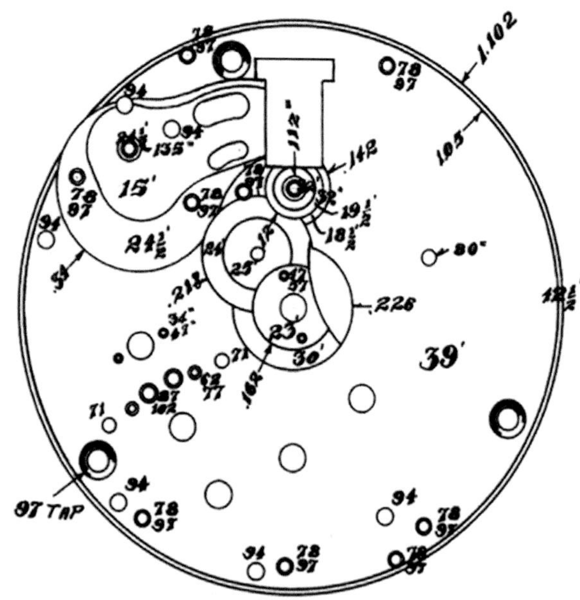

3/0s Bridge Model 1911. O.F.
Dial Side 17 Jew.

Illinois 3/0 movement drawings

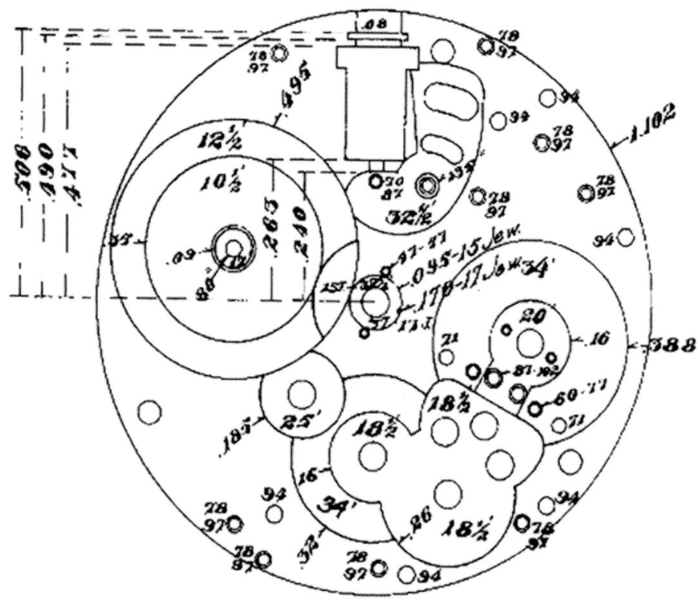

3/0s Bridge Model 1911. O.F.
Train Side 17 Jew.

Cleverly, Illinois produced a 3/0 size movement by eliminating a flange around the pillar plate, but using the same mainspring barrel, wheels, balance and bridges as were in the 0-size model. Illinois conveniently numbered the 3/0 grades by keeping only the first and last digits of the 0-size movement grades, producing grades 21, 23 and 24. Illinois' introduction of this new design proved both ingenious and fortuitous.

By the time Illinois commenced production of the 200-series movements, the market for 0-size watches had practically disappeared. Elgin and Waltham produced their last 0-size watch movements around 1917. Only Hamilton would soldier on into the 1920s, trying to squeeze as many sales as possible out of its 983 and its reworked 981 brethren as 0-size men's wristwatches The public apparently saw the 0 size as too small for a pocket watch and too large for a wristwatch, preferring their wristwatches with smaller 3/0 movements. The 21, 23 and 24 grade Illinois 3/0 movements would enjoy years of production as wristwatch movements.

Popularity of smaller-size watch movements skyrocketed with the arrival of World War I. Jobbers and jewelers cased Illinois 0-size and 3/0 movements as wristwatches to sell to soldiers clamoring for a timepiece that could be conveniently strapped to the wrist. Soldiers' needs forever changed the future course of Illinois' offerings. From this point, Illinois started on its path to becoming a wristwatch manufacturer.

3/0 Size Movements

In 1931 some jobber catalogs described the Illinois 3/0, grade 307, in the following terms: "The 17 jewel 3/0 size Illinois watch will bear the closest examination. Note the sturdiness of its construction—the 17 Ruby and Sapphire jewels; the compensating balance with its timing screws; the steel escape wheel and the Breguet hairspring; the micrometric screw regulator. Here is a splendid watch which responds to the need for accurate time under severe tests." The 1930 Illinois Factory Catalog added to this description "rayed center wheel; safety screw center pinion; safety recoil click; rayed bracket and winding wheels; damaskeened in a circular striped pattern, black enamel lettering." It retailed for $25.00.

1930
HISTORICAL NOTES

- *Mickey Mouse* and *Blondie* comic strips first appear.
- The first radio broadcast of The *Lone Ranger* occurs.
- The first traffic lights are installed in Manhattan.
- Hostess Twinkies are invented by bakery executive James Dewar.
- Synthetic rubber is first produced.
- The 1,046-foot-tall Chrysler Building, an Art Deco icon, opens in New York City.
- The United States' tobacco industry produces 123 billion cigarettes in 1930.

From 1915 to 1932, the Illinois 3/0 movement changed very little. Through the decade of the 1920s, it remained the same. With the grade change from 24 to 307, Illinois merely modernized the regulator mechanism and provided a double roller escapement. The rest of the movement, even the damaskeening on the bridges, stayed unchanged.

Almost 232,000 3/0 size movements were produced in the Watch Factory in Springfield, Illinois, in 11-, 15- and 17-jewel configurations. Of these, approximately 154,080 were expressly intended for wristwatches, although all of the 3/0s could be used that way.

The 3/0 size movement production quantities are broken down by grade and jewel count as follows:

3/0 Size, 11 Jewel Movement Production Quantities

Year	Grade	Quantity
1915	21	4,860
1915	32	100
1916	21	10,200
1916	32	660
1917	21	4,700
1917	32	380
1918	21	2,320
1918	32	350
1919	21	0
1919	32	50
Total 21:		**22,080**
Total 32:		**1,540**
Total 11-jewel:		**23,620**

3/0 Size, 12 Jewel Movement Production Quantities

Year	Grade	Quantity
1915	24	100
1916	24	100
1917	24	300
1918	24	300
Total 12-jewel:		**800**

Avon 3/0 size, grade 21, 12-jewel private-label Illinois movement

3/0 Size, 15 Jewel Movements Production Quantities

Year	Grade	Quantity
1915	23	910
1915	34	140
1916	23	7,200
1916	34	400
1917	23	3,000
1917	34	180
1918	23	13,420
1918	34	500
1919	23	5,400
1919	34	200
1920	23	4,000
1920	34	0
Total 23:		**33,930**
Total 34:		**1,420**
Total 15-jewel:		**35,350**

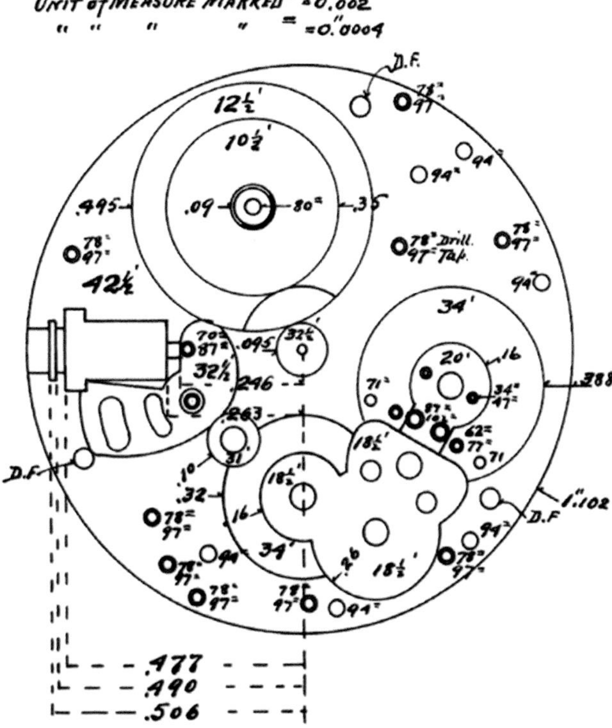

Illinois 3/0 size, 15-jewel hunting movement drawing

3/0 size, grade 24, 17-jewel Illinois movement

3/0 Size, 17-Jewel Movements Production Quantities		
Year	Grade	Quantity
1915	24	1,050
1915	36	1,200
1916	24	3,250
1916	36	1,500
1917	24	1,400
1917	36	1,910
1918	24	4,920
1918	36	1,830
1919	24	0
1919	36	1,000
1920	24	0
1920	36	0
1921	24	0
1922	36	450
1922	24	0
1923	24	0
1924	24	0
1925	24	0
1926	24	3,000
1927	24	12,230
1928	24	25,000
1929	24	54,000
1930	24	6,000
1930	307	30,000
1931	307	0
1932	307	18,100
~~1948~~*/ 1932–1933	307	4,700
Total 24:		**110,850**
Total 36:		**7,890**
Total 307:		**52,800**
Total 17-jewel:		**171,540**

*These movements were most likely produced in Springfield in 1932 (or earlier), not in 1948 in Lancaster. The 1948 date could possibly stem from the fact that Hamilton from 1947 to 1948 removed many of the 809 standard Illinois Bunn Special movements grade 161A, without balances and hairsprings from the still leftover Springfield inventory. These movements were then fitted with Hamilton 992B balances and hairsprings with the standard Bunn Special balance staff. The 1948 Hamilton records likely noted the last date shipped, not the manufactured date. There is no evidence that Hamilton produced any Illinois wristwatch size movements in 1948.

3/0 Size, Unknown-Jewel Movement Production Quantities*		
Year	**Grade**	**Quantity**
1915	30	70
1918	25	600
Total 30:		**70**
Total 25:		**600**

*These are likely private-label watches.

Total 3/0 Size Movement Production Quantities	
Jewels	**Quantity**
11	23,620
12	800
15	35,350
17	171,540
Unknown	670
Total 3/0:	**231,980**

As can be seen from the tables, Illinois almost completely stopped producing 3/0 size wristwatch movements shortly after the end of World War I. When the firm decided to reenter wristwatch production in 1926, it resurrected the 17-jewel variation, known as the grade 24. Initially, Illinois produced its 3/0 watches in both the hunting and open face configurations. When production restarted, Illinois realized that all the movements would be cased as wristwatches. With the exception of a 2,000-unit run in 1926, Illinois produced all the subsequent movements in the hunting configuration. For this reason, almost all Illinois 3/0 wristwatches have the seconds register in the 6 o'clock position.

Illinois designed 0 and 3/0 size watch movements with a standard progression of jeweling. For the 11-jewel grade 21, Illinois provided an impulse jewel, two pallet jewels, two balance staff hole jewels, two balance staff cap jewels, two jewels for the pallet fork and two hole jewels for the escape wheel. The 15-jewel model added two jewels to each end of the third and fourth wheels. The 17-jewel version added jewels to the center wheel. The jewel locations and types were standard for American wristwatch movements.

Horology expert Bill Meggers says that the 15-jewel movements "were called 'full-jeweled' by the trade and almost invariably the eight extra jewels are arranged in four pairs, positioned on each end of the third, fourth, escape and pallet arbors, leaving only the center and barrel arbors unjeweled. The 17 jewel version is probably the best known jewel configuration."[5] Illinois employed this jeweling progression for all of its movements, except the 900 grade 6/0 movements.

3/0 Size Illinois Factory-Cased Wristwatch Models	
Model Name	**Notes**
Akron/ Aluminum Prototype	Only three known to exist
Convertible	Introduced in 1910
Greyhound	Only three known to exist
Guardian	Rotor subsidiary seconds
Guardsman	Rotor subsidiary seconds
Hercules	Identity unknown
Jolly Roger	
Major	
Mate	
Motor Coach	Only three known to exist
Off-Duty	
Seneca	
Skyway	
Sportsman	For exclusive sale by the Seaver & Williams Co.
Speedway	
Speedway 178	
Viking	
Red = Ladies' model	

3/0 Size Illinois Wristwatch Models Not Factory-Cased

Model Name	Notes
Ace	Also came in 6/0 size
Admiral Benson	
Admiral Evans	Also came in 0 size
Ariston	
Armored Case	Also came in 0 size
Atlantic	Also came in 6/0 size
Atlantic Enamel	
Aviator	
Blackhawk	
Brandt Park	
Burlington	
Chevalier	
D-D Utility	
Depollier Water/Dust Proof	
Devon	Some 6/0 size Devons were Factory-Cased
General Funston	
Gift Series	
Guardsman Military	Only two known to exist
Integrated Guard	
Masonic Dial	Only one known to exist
Maxine	
Off-Set Crowns	Also came in 0 size
Ongard	
Ongard Off-Set	
Osgood	
Police Special	Only three known to exist
Riley	
Santa Fe Tank	One has never been seen
Senator	
Special	
Square Cut Corner Large	
Telephone Dial	Also came in 6/0 size
Transitional Watches	Also came in 0 size and 6/0 size
United States Army	
Washington Watch Company	
Wayne	
Whippet	Also came in 6/0 size

3/0 SIZE MOVEMENT THICKNESS

Although there are two different thicknesses for Illinois 3/0 size movements, this has not been noted to present a problem except in two instances: the thicker 3/0 size movement does not fit into the Depollier Water/Dust Proof case or into the Speedway 178 or Guardian cases.

3/0 Size Parts List

The Illinois Materials Department Price List for its 3/0 size movement, dated February 20, 1931, 4th Model, is shown here.

#307

THE ILLINOIS WATCH
3/0 Material - 4th Model
(Grade Number Stamped on Barrel Bridge)
February 20, 1931.

Factory Number	Name & Description	Price Dozen
941	Arbor, Barrel - Style #1 - Grade #3	$ 6.00
995	Arbor, Pallet - Style #1 - Grade #3	4.00
758	Arbor, Winding - Style #1 - Grade #3	6.00
915	Balance and Staff - Style #1 - Grade #2	21.00
2298	Balance Complete - Style #1 - Grade #2	35.00
956	Balance - Style #1 - Grade #2	16.00
939	Barrel - Style #1 - Grade #3	5.00
1307	Barrel and Arbor - Style #1 - Grade #3	12.50
1396	Bar, Slide - Style #1 - Grade #3	2.50
934	Cap, Setting and Minute Wheel - Style #2 - Grade #3	2.50
974	Click - Style #1 - Grade #3	2.50
1239	Clutch - Style #1 - Grade #3	4.50
986	Collet, Hairspring - Style #1 - Grade #3	1.00
927	Hub, Winding Wheel - Pattern #5	2.00
1325	Jewel, Balance Upper - Style #2 - Olive Hole Sapphire - Brass - Semi-Friction Diameter .083 - Not Shouldered	4.00
1112	Jewel, Balance Lower - Style #2 - Olive Hole Sapphire - Brass - Semi-Friction Diameter .083 - Not Shouldered	4.00
1171	Jewel, Balance Upper Endstone - Style #3 Sapphire - Oreide - Semi-Friction Diameter .083 - Shouldered .002	2.00
1113	Jewel, Balance Lower Endstone - Style #2 Sapphire - Brass - Semi-Friction Diameter .083 - Shouldered .010	2.00
1382	Jewel, Center Upper - Style #1 Pale Ruby - Oreide - Screwed In - Raised Setting	9.00
1383	Jewel, Center Lower - Style #2 Pale Ruby - Oreide - Screwed In - Jeweled Inside	7.50
1394	Jewel, Escape Upper - Style #1 Pale Ruby - Oreide - Shouldered .006 - Rubbed In	6.00
1329	Jewel, Escape Lower - Style #2 Pale Ruby - Oreide - Rubbed In - Shouldered .006	6.00
1399	Jewel, Fourth Upper - Style #1 Pale Ruby - Oreide - Rubbed In	6.00
1333	Jewel, Fourth Lower - Style #2 Pale Ruby - Oreide - Rubbed In - Shouldered .006	6.00
1354	Jewel, Pallet Upper - Style #1 Pale Ruby - Brass - Rubbed In	6.00
1337	Jewel, Pallet Lower - Style #2 Pale Ruby - Brass - Rubbed In - Shouldered .006	6.00
1339	Jewel, Third Upper - Style #2 - Shouldered .006 Pale Ruby - Oreide - Screwed In - Raised Setting	6.00
1341	Jewel, Third Lower - Style #2 Pale Ruby - Oreide - Rubbed In - Shouldered .006	6.00

-2-

No.	Item	Price	
[illegible]	Jewel, Pallet Stone - Style #1 - Sapphire (Always state Right or Left when ordering)	6.00	
1321	Jewel, Roller - Style #2 - Sapphire	3.00	
928	Lever, Clutch - Style #1 - Grade #3	2.50	
943	Lever, Locking - Style #1 - Grade #3	2.00	
997	Pallet and Fork with Stones - Style #1 Sapphire - Double Roller	11.50	1.15
998	Pallet, Fork and Arbor with Stones - Style #1 Sapphire - Double Roller	22.00	2.[illegible]
929	Pinion, Winding - Style #1 - Grade #3	3.50	[illegible]
976	Pinion, Cannon - Style #1 - Grade #3	4.00	[illegible]
958	Pinion, Center - Style #1 - Grade #1	5.00	[illegible]
952	Pinion, Escape - Style #1 - Grade #3	4.50	[illegible]
949	Pinion, Fourth - Style #1 - Grade #3	4.00	[illegible]
1291	Pinion, Third - Style #1 - Grade #3	4.00	[illegible]
596	Pin, Winding Arbor Push	1.50	[illegible]
841	Regulator - Style #3 - Grade #3	5.00	[illegible]
2041	Roller, Double Impulse with Guard and Pin	5.00	.55
1345	Screw, Balance - Brass	.35	
1345	Screw, Balance - Gold	1.00	
1346	Screw, Balance Meantime - Nickel	.35	
1065	Screw, Banking	.35	
1105	Screw, Barrel and Train Bridge - Flat Head	.45	
1105	Screw, Barrel and Train Bridge - Cornered Head	.50	
1299	Screw, Setting and Minute Wheel Cap - Flat Head	.35	
1108	Screw, Case - Flat Head - Dia. Head .072	.50	
1294	Screw, Click - Flat Head	.35	
1107	Screw, Balance Cock - Flat Head	.45	
1107	Screw, Balance Cock - Cornered Head	.50	
1371	Screw, Pallet Bridge - Flat Head	.35	
1109	Screw, Dialfoot - Flat Head	.35	
1372	Screw, Jewel, Center Upper - Flat Head	.35	
1372	Screw, Jewel, Center Upper - Cornered Head	.40	
2036	Screw, Jewel, Center Lower - Flat Head	.35	
1372	Screw, Jewel, Third Upper - Flat Head	.35	
1372	Screw, Jewel, Third Upper - Cornered Head	.40	
1302	Screw, Lever, Clutch - Flat Head	.35	
1295	Screw, Lever, Locking - Flat Head	.35	
1373	Screw, Regulator Micrometer - Flat Head - Long	1.00	
1373	Screw, Regulator Micrometer - Beveled Head - Long	1.00	
891	Screw, Regulator Spring - Flat Head - Short	.35	
891	Screw, Regulator Adjusting Screw Strap - Flat Head	.35	
1398	Screw, Stud, Hairspring - Flat Head	.35	
1103	Screw, Wheel, Ratchet - Flat Head	.35	
1103	Screw, Wheel, Ratchet - Cornered Head	.40	
1295	Screw, Winding Wheel Hub - Flat Head	.35	
1295	Screw, Winding Wheel Hub - Cornered Head	.40	
629	Spring, Click - Style #1 - Grade #3	1.00	[illegible]
870	Spring, Lever, Clutch - Style #1 - Grade #3	1.00	[illegible]
1156	Spring, Hair	6.00	[illegible]
981	Spring, Main - Width 1.70 M/M - Strength .125 M/M Tee Brace	2.50	[illegible]
886	Spring, Regulator - Style #1 - Grade #3	5.00	[illegible]
989	Staff, Balance - Style #1 - Grade #1	3.00	

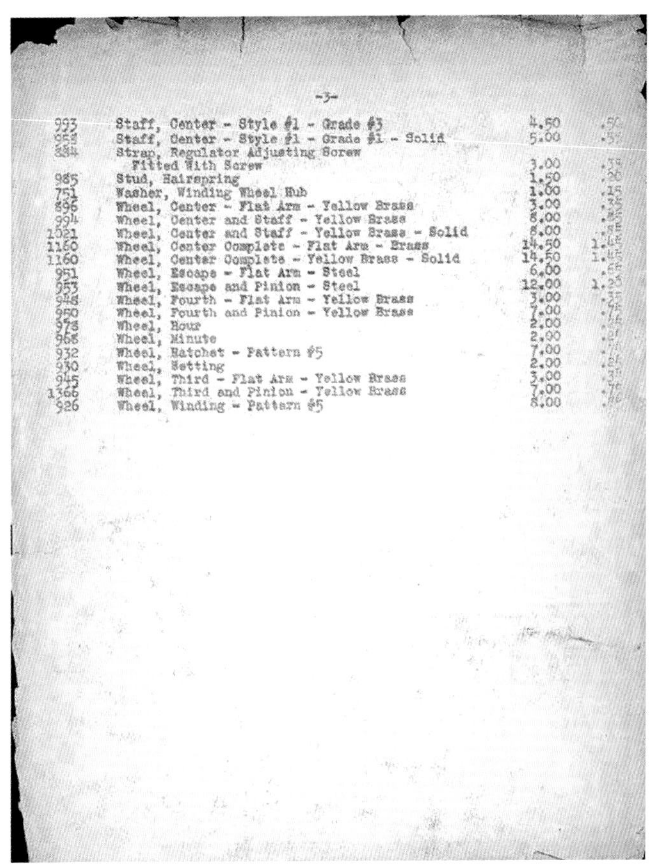

-3-

No.	Item	Price	
993	Staff, Center - Style #1 - Grade #3	4.50	.50
958	Staff, Center - Style #1 - Grade #1 - Solid	5.00	[illegible]
884	Strap, Regulator Adjusting Screw Fitted With Screw	3.00	[illegible]
985	Stud, Hairspring	1.50	.20
751	Washer, Winding Wheel Hub	1.00	.15
896	Wheel, Center - Flat Arm - Yellow Brass	3.00	.35
994	Wheel, Center and Staff - Yellow Brass	8.00	[illegible]
1021	Wheel, Center and Staff - Yellow Brass - Solid	8.00	[illegible]
1160	Wheel, Center Complete - Flat Arm - Brass	14.50	1.45
1160	Wheel, Center Complete - Yellow Brass - Solid	14.50	1.45
951	Wheel, Escape - Flat Arm - Steel	6.00	.65
953	Wheel, Escape and Pinion - Steel	12.00	1.25
948	Wheel, Fourth - Flat Arm - Yellow Brass	3.00	.35
950	Wheel, Fourth and Pinion - Yellow Brass	7.00	.75
973	Wheel, Hour	2.00	[illegible]
968	Wheel, Minute	2.00	[illegible]
932	Wheel, Ratchet - Pattern #5	7.00	[illegible]
930	Wheel, Setting	2.00	.25
945	Wheel, Third - Flat Arm - Yellow Brass	3.00	.35
1366	Wheel, Third and Pinion - Yellow Brass	7.00	.75
926	Wheel, Winding - Pattern #5	8.00	[illegible]

6/0 Size Movements

The Illinois 6/0 size movement came with 15, 17, 19 or 21 jewels and in grades 903, 904, 905, 907, 909, 601, 605, 607 and 609. There were also 6/0 size movements marked 605A and 607A; Illinois used the letter "A" in these variants to denote the change to friction jeweling.

Illinois introduced its first 6/0 movements in 1915, at the same time it developed the 3/0 21, 23 and 24 grades. Illinois designated the first 6/0 movements as grades 903 (15 jewels) and 907 (19 jewels). Although the 3/0 utilized the same design as Illinois contemporary 0-size movements, the 6/0 design differed in several ways from its 0-size or 3/0 counterparts. For one thing, Illinois jeweled the early 6/0 differently from the other small movements. While the jeweling on the 3/0 could be termed standard American practice, the 6/0 jeweling bore some resemblance to European designs. The escapement in the 15- and 17-jewel models received cap jewels on both the base plate and the train bridge. On the other hand, Illinois installed hole jewels for the third and fourth wheels only on the bridge side.

In addition, the first 6/0 movements (903s known as Model 1) received a differently designed barrel bridge and train bridge. The fact that several of the early production runs carried Marshall Field's "Ariston" private label may explain both the unusual jeweling and unique bridge design. Unfortunately, no explanatory documentation exists. Soon after, though, Illinois produced the Model 2, with both train bridge and barrel bridge more closely matching the 3/0 design. But the unique jeweling remained until superseded in the late 1920s by the 6/0 movements of the 600 grades.

In describing the grade 907, the 1930 Illinois Sales Catalog noted that the 19-jewel, 6/0 size movement had "19 ruby and sapphire jewels in settings; compensating balance with timing screws; steel escape wheel; double roller escapement; Breguet hairspring; concaved and polished racket and winding wheels; recoil click; escape pinion, cap jeweled."

Although Illinois produced the 3/0 movements in both the open-face and hunting configurations, it initially manufactured the 6/0 movements only in the open-face design, at least until the introduction of the 601 grade in 1928. This may have reflected Illinois' original intention to use them for small ladies' pendant watches. For wristwatches, of course, the open-face configuration placed the seconds register at 9 o-clock, creating the iconic Illinois watch configuration so loved by collectors.

Illinois Superior Motor Barrel (21 Jewels)

The Illinois Watch Company made two 6/0 21-jewel "Superior Motor Barrel" movements for wristwatches.[6] These remain the crowning achievement of Illinois wristwatch movement design. Illinois borrowed the Superior Motor Barrel concept from its 21-jewel movements for 16-size and 12-size pocket watches.

Illinois apparently first designed the 21-jewel grade 601 in an attempt to produce a high-value movement specifically for installation in wristwatches. For this reason, Illinois used a hunting configuration, leading to the seconds register in the 6 o'clock position.

Illinois' marketing of the grade 601 showed an understanding of the pricing issues involving wristwatches. Understandably, manufacturers pegged most wristwatches at price points below those of contemporary pocket watches. The 21-jewel movement, which included a jeweled motor barrel, sold for a $25 premium over similar models with lesser movements. This allowed Illinois to price some watches at $100.00 (or about $1,350.00 in today's dollars). This placed wristwatches on a similar plane with their pocket watch contemporaries. The fact that Illinois later produced a grade 909, 21-jewel motor barrel movement with a seconds register at 9, indicates that Illinois believed its top-of-the-line design to be quite profitable.

There were at least 5,000 grade 601s made and about 2,930 grade 909s. Because these are now considered to be the best-made Illinois wristwatch movements, they are very collectible. Accordingly, one could add a significant extra value to a watch. The following Illinois wristwatch models are the only models with known advertisements or catalog descriptions offering them for sale with a 21-jewel movement: Baronet, Beau Brummell, Beau Brummell/Viking, Beau Monde, Consul, Fifth Avenue, Kingston, Manhattan, New Yorker and Santa Fe Tank (possibly).

Illinois followed the innovative 601 grade with the 15-jewel, grade 605 and 17-jewel, grade 607 variations with a standard mainspring barrel. Unlike the earlier Illinois 6/0 movements, all of these were jeweled similarly to the 3/0 ones.

Production numbers show the 17-jewel variation to be more popular than the 15-jewel model, as the total quantity of 17-jewel movements produced is nearly double that of 15-jewel ones.

6/0 Size Movement Production Quantities

From 1915 to 1932, Illinois produced about 305,000 6/0 size movements. The production quantities of the 6/0 size movements are broken down by grade and jewels as follows:

6/0 Size, 15-Jewel Movements Production Quantities

Year	Grade	Quantity
1915	903	1,300
1916	903	5,300
1917	903	7,550
1918	903	7,870
1919	903	10,600
1920	903	10,400
1921	903	6,000
1922	903	17,000
1923	903	22,000
1924	903	4,000
1925	903	3,000
1926	903	13,000
1927	903	20,000
1928	903	16,600
1929	903	24,100
~~1948~~* / 1932–1933	605	15,900
~~1948~~* / 1932–1933	605A	800
Total 903:		**168,720**
Total 605/605A:		**16,700**
Total 15-jewel:		**185,420**

*These movements were most likely produced in Springfield in 1932 or earlier, not in 1948 in Lancaster.

6/0 Size, 17-Jewel Movements Production Quantities

Year	Grade	Quantity
1916	904	1,000
1917	904	1,900
1918	904	1,600
1918	904	2,400
1920	904	2,100
1928	905	28,400
1929	905	13,000
1930	905	3,000
1930	607	6,000
1931	607	16,000
1932	607	13,800
1932	607A	10,000
~~1948*~~/ 1932–1933*	607A	1,600
Total 904:		**9,000**
Total 905:		**44,400**
Total 607:		**35,800**
Total 607A:		**11,600**
Total 607/607A:		**47,400**
Total 17-jewel:		**100,800**

*These movements were most likely produced in Springfield in 1932 or earlier, not in 1948 in Lancaster.

6/0 size, grade 903, 15-jewel Illinois movement

6/0 size, grade 904, 17-jewel Illinois movement

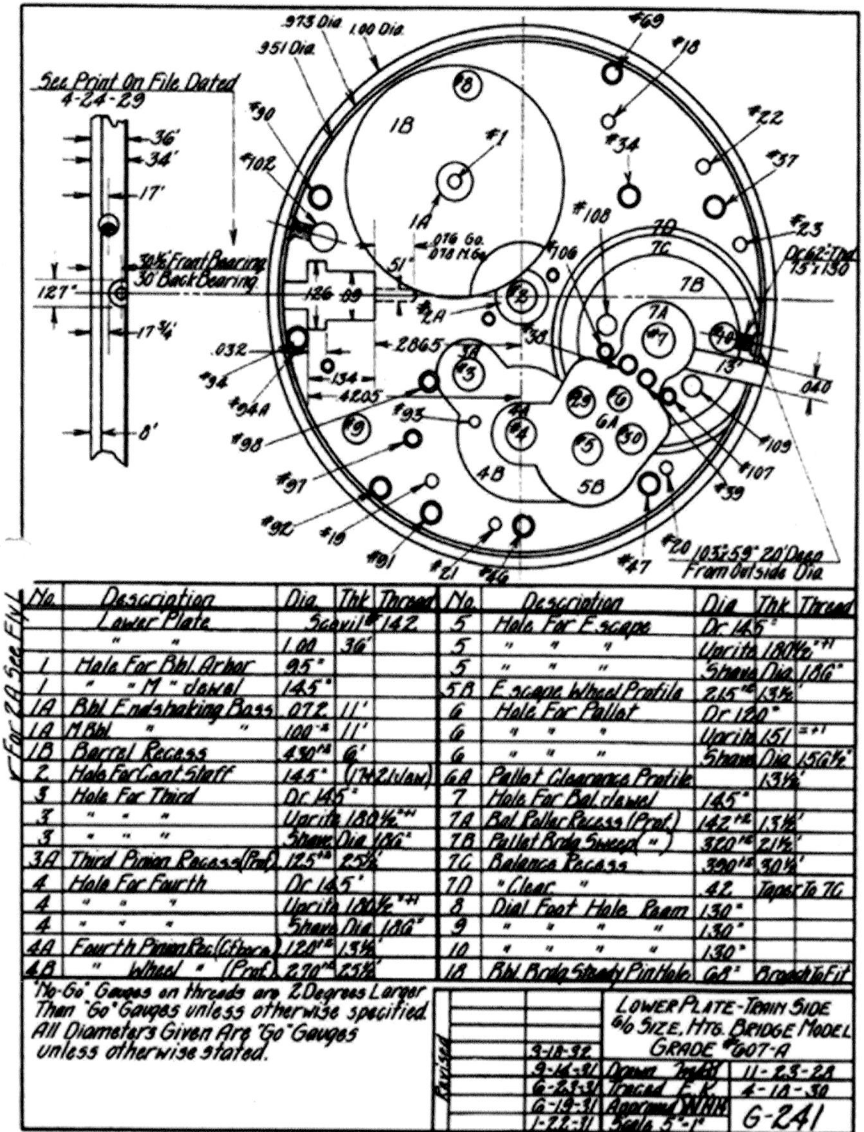

No.	Description	Dia	Thk	Thread
	Lower Plate	Scovil	#142	
	" "	1.00	36'	
1	Hole For Bbl. Arbor	95"		
1	" " "M" Jewel	145"		
1A	Bbl Endshaking Boss	.072	11'	
1A	M Bbl " "	100	11'	
1B	Barrel Recess	430	6'	
2	Hole For Cent Staff	145"	(17 & 21 Jew)	
3	Hole For Third	Dr 145"		
3	" " "	Uprite	180½	
3	" " "	Shave Dia	186"	
3A	Third Pinion Recess (Prof)	125	25½'	
4	Hole For Fourth	Dr 145"		
4	" " "	Uprite	180½	
4	" " "	Shave Dia	186"	
4A	Fourth Pinion Rec (Ctbore)	120	13½'	
4B	" Wheel " (Prof)	270	25½'	

No.	Description	Dia	Thk	Thread
5	Hole For Escape	Dr 145"		
5	" " "	Uprite	180½	
5	" " "	Shave Dia	186"	
5B	Escape Wheel Profile	215	13½'	
6	Hole For Pallet	Dr 120"		
6	" " "	Uprite	151	
6	" " "	Shave Dia	156½"	
6A	Pallet Clearance Profile		13½'	
7	Hole For Bal. Jewel	145"		
7A	Bal Roller Recess (Prof)	142	13½'	
7B	Pallet Brdg Sweep (")	320	21½'	
7C	Balance Recess	390	30½'	
7D	" Clear "	.42	Taper To 7C	
8	Dial Foot Hole Ream	130"		
9	" " " "	130"		
10	" " " "	130"		
18	Bbl Brdg Steady Pin Hole	68"	Broach To Fit	

"No-Go" Gauges on threads are 2 Degrees Larger Than "Go" Gauges unless otherwise specified. All Diameters Given Are "Go" Gauges unless otherwise stated.

LOWER PLATE-TRAIN SIDE
6/0 SIZE, HTG. BRIDGE MODEL
GRADE #607-A
Drawn 11-23-28
Traced E.K. 4-10-30
Approved
Scale 5"-1"
G-241
Revised 9-18-32, 9-16-31, 6-23-31, 6-19-31, 1-22-31

No	Description	Dia	Thk	Thread
19	Bbl Brdg. Steady Pin Hole	68"	Broach To Fit	
20	Train " " " "	68"	"	" "
21	" " " " "	68"	"	" "
22	Bal Cock " " "	68"	"	" "
23	" " " " "	68"	"	" "
29	Peep Hole	145"		
30	" "	145"		
34	Bbl Brdg. Screw Hole	72"	85"	x130
37	Bal. Cock " "	72"	85"	x130
38	Banking " "	85"	99"	x170
39	" " "	85"	99"	x170
46	Train Brdg " "	72"	85"	x130
47	" " " "	72"	85"	x130
69	Case " "	72"	85"	x130
90	Bbl Brdg " "	72"	85"	x130
91	" " " "	72"	85"	x130
92	Case " "	72"	85"	x130
93	Cent Hole For Cl Lev. Spr Ct	62"		
94	Locking Lever Screw	78"	Broach 86"	
94A	" " Scr. Ctbore	117"	3' Deep	
97	Setting Wheel Cap Screw	62"	75"	x130
98	" " " "	62"	75"	x130
102	Dial Foot Hole Ream	130"		
106	Pallet Brdg Screw Hole	55"	70"	x140
107	" " " "	55"	70"	x140
108	" " Steady Pin Hole	92"	Broach To Fit	
109	" " " " "	92"	"	" "
2A	Center Pin Rec. (15 Jew.)	.120	31½'	

Lower plate of Illinois 6/0 size, grade 607 drawing

6/0 SIZE MOVEMENT, GRADE 905

The No. 905, 17-Jewel, 6/0 size Bridge Model, Open Face, Pendant Setting movement is described by Illinois as follows: "17 ruby and sapphire jewels in settings; compensating balance with timing screws; steel escape wheel; double roller escapement; Breguet hairspring, recoil click; escape pinion cap jeweled and rayed winding wheels."

6/0 Size, 19-Jewel Movements Production Quantities		
Year	**Grade**	**Quantity**
1915	907	600
1916	907	850
1917	907	200
1918	907	1,550
1919	907	200
1920	907	500
1921	907	0
1922	907	0
1923	907	1,000
1924	907	0
1925	907	0
1926	907	2,000
1927	907	3,000
1928	907	4,000
1929	907	5,000
1930	907	1,000
Total 19-jewel:		**19,900**

6/0 SIZE MOVEMENT, GRADE 907

The 1929 Illinois Sales Catalog described the 6/0 size, No. 907, 19 Jewels, Bridge Model, Open Face and Pendant Setting movement as follows: "19 ruby and sapphire jewels in settings, compensating balance with timing screws; steel escape wheel, double roller escapement; Breguet hairspring, concaved and polished ratchet and winding wheels; recoil click; escape pinion cap jeweled. " It retailed for $35.00.

The description of the 6/0 size, 905 grade, 17-jewel and 903 grade, 15-jewel movement was the same except for the number of jewels. The 903 retailed for $25.00 and the 905 for $30.00.

The following Men's Illinois wristwatch models came also with 19-jewel movements: Beau Brummell, Beau Brummell/Viking (official name unknown), Cadet, Consul, Manhattan, Marquis Strap and New Yorker.

6/0 size, grade 907, 19-jewel Illinois movement

6/0 Size, 21-Jewel Movements Production Quantities		
Year	**Grade**	**Quantity**
1923	909	30
1924	909	0
1925	909	0
1926	909	0
1927	909	0
1928	909	0
1929	909	2,900
1930	909	1,000
1931	601	1,000
1932	601	4,000
Total 909:		**3,930**
Total 601:		**5,000**
Total 21-jewel:		**8,930**

6/0 size, grade 909, 21-jewel Illinois movement

6/0 size, grade 601, 21-jewel Illinois movement

6/0 SIZE MOVEMENT: 601 VS. 909

Many collectors think that the 6/0 size, 21-jewel, grade 601 movement is identical to the 6/0 size, 21-jewel, 909 grade movement. Although their finger bridges are the same, the position of the motor barrel mainspring is different. The 909 is an open-face type (seconds at 9), while the 601 is hunting style (with seconds at 6). That is the big difference between the 600 series and the 900 series. Since most Consuls did not have a seconds register, it did not matter. All the 900 series (903, 904, 905, 907, 909) had seconds at 9 or opposite the winder, while all 600 series had seconds at 6, 90° from the winder.

Total 6/0 Size Movement Production Quantities

Jewels	Quantity
15	185,420
17	90,800
19	19,900
21	8,930
Total 6/0:	**305,050**

6/0 Size Movement Parts List

The Illinois Materials Department Price List for the 6/0 Movement, dated February 18, 1931, 4th Model, Grade 607 is shown here.

[illegible]
6/0 Material - 4th Model
Sold as Grade #607
February 18, 1931
(Grade Number Stamped on Barrel Bridge)

Factory Number	Name & Description	Price Dozen
722	Arbor, Barrel - Style #1 - Grade #3	$ 6.00
1441	Arbor, Pallet - Style #3 - Grade #3 - Friction	4.00
1441	Arbor, Pallet - Style #4 - Grade #3 - Friction	4.00
1445	Arbor, Winding - Style #5 - Grade #3	3.50
811	Balance and Staff - Style #1 - Grade #1	21.00
2295	Balance Complete - Style #1	35.00
1433	Balance - Style #1 - Grade #2 - Bimetallic	16.00
899	Barrel - Style #1 - Grade #3	5.00
920	Barrel and Arbor - Style #1 - Grade #3	9.50
962	Cap, Setting and Minute Wheel - Style #1 - Grade #3	3.00
1920	Click,- Style #1 - Grade #3	5.00
1444	Clutch - Style #1 - Grade #3	4.50
1475	Collet, Hairspring - Style #1 - Grade #3	1.00
	Hands - SEE LATEST DIAL AND HAND SUPPLEMENT	
1917	Hub, Wheel, inding - Style #2 - Grade #3 - .034 Thick	2.00
1714	Jewel, Balance Upper - Olive Hole - Style #2 Sapphire - Brass - Semi-Friction	4.00
1715	Jewel, Balance Lower - Olive Hole - Style #3 Sapphire - Brass - Semi-Friction	4.00
1716	Jewel, Balance Upper Endstone - Style #2 Sapphire - Oreide - Semi-Friction	2.00
1717	Jewel, Balance Lower Endstone - Style #3 Sapphire - Brass - Semi-Friction	2.00
1701	Jewel, Center Upper - Style #1 Pale Ruby - Oreide - Screwed In - Raised Setting	9.00
1702	Jewel, Center Lower - Style #1 . Pale Ruby - Brass - Screwed In	7.50
1451	Jewel, Escape Upper - Style #1 Pale Ruby - Oreide - Screwed In	6.00
1452	Jewel, Escape Lower - Style #2 Pale Ruby - Oreide - Rubbed In	6.00
[illegible]	Jewel, Fourth Upper - Style #1 Pale Ruby - Oreide - Screwed In	6.00
[illegible]	Jewel, Fourth Upper - Style #1 Pale Ruby - Oreide - Friction	6.00
[illegible]	Jewel, Fourth Lower - Style #1 Pale Ruby - Oreide - Screwed In	6.00
[illegible]	Jewel, Fourth Lower - Style #2 Pale Ruby - Oreide - Rubbed In	6.00
[illegible]	Jewel, Pallet Upper - Style #2 Pale Ruby - Brass - Rubbed In	6.00
[illegible]	Jewel, Pallet Lower - Style #2 Pale Ruby - Brass - Rubbed In	6.00
[illegible]	Jewel, Third Upper - Style #1 Pale Ruby - Oreide - Screwed In - Raised Setting	6.00
[illegible]	Jewel, Third Lower - Style #1 Pale Ruby - Oreide - Rubbed In	6.00
[illegible]	Jewel, Pallet Stone - Style #2 - Sapphire ([illegible] state Right or Left when ordering)	5.00

-2-

No.	Part	Price
1720	Jewel, Roller - Style #2 - Sapphire	3.00
897	Lever, Clutch - Style #1 - Grade #3	2.50
827	Lever, Locking - Style #1 - Grade #3	2.00
1494	Pallet and Fork with Stones - Style #3 Sapphire - Double Roller	11.50
1494	Pallet and Fork with Stones - Style #4 Sapphire - Double Roller	11.50
1248	Pallet, Fork and Arbor with Stones - Style #3 Sapphire - Double Roller	22.00
1248	Pallet, Fork and Arbor with Stones - Style #4 Sapphire - Double Roller	22.00
723	Pinion, Winding - Style #1 - Grade #3	3.50
1436	Pinion, Cannon - Style #1 - Grade #3	4.00
1435	Pinion, Center - Style #1 - Grade #1	5.00
1449	Pinion, Escape - Style #1 - Grade #3	4.50
1439	Pinion, Fourth - Style #1 - Grade #3	4.00
1437	Pinion, Third - Style #1 - Grade #3	4.00
1721	Regulator - Style #1 - Grade #3	5.00
2003	Roller, Impulse and Guard and Pin - Style #1	5.00
1899	Screw, Balance - Brass	.35
1899	Screw, Balance - Gold	1.00
1900	Screw, Balance Meantime - Nickel	.35
1576	Screw, Banking	.35
1453	Screw, Barrel and Train Bridge - Flat Head	.45
1453	Screw, Barrel and Train Bridge - Cornered Head	.50
1908	Screw, Setting and Minute Wheel Cap - Flat Head	.35
1456	Screw, Case - Flat Head	.50
660	Screw, Click - Cornered Head	.40
1455	Screw, Balance Cock - Flat Head	.45
1455	Screw, Balance Cock - Cornered Head	.50
2045	Screw, Pallet Cock - Flat Head	.35
1485	Screw, Dialfoot - Flat Head	.35
1372	Screw, Jewel, Center Upper - Flat Head	.35
1372	Screw, Jewel, Center Upper - Cornered Head	.40
2161	Screw, Jewel, Center Lower - Flat Head	.35
1372	Screw, Jewel, Escape Upper - Flat Head	.35
1372	Screw, Jewel, Escape Upper - Cornered Head	.40
1372	Screw, Jewel, Fourth Upper - Flat Head	.35
1372	Screw, Jewel, Fourth Upper - Cornered Head	.40
1372	Screw, Jewel, Third Upper - Flat Head	.35
1372	Screw, Jewel, Third Upper - Cornered Head	.40
1470	Screw, Lever, Locking - Flat Head	.40
1935	Screw, Locking Lever Stop - Flat Head	.40
2072	Screw, Stud, Hairspring - Flat Head	.35
1479	Screw, Wheel, Ratchet - Cornered Head	.40
1974	Screw, Wheel, Winding Hub - Cornered Head	.40
936	Spring, Click - Style #1 - Grade #3	1.00
[illegible]	Spring, Clutch Lever - Style #1 - Grade #3	1.00
[illegible]	Spring, Hair	6.00
1095	Spring, Main - Width 1.41 M/M - Strength .11 M/M	2.50
1012	Staff, Balance - Style #1 - Grade #1	3.00
1436	Staff, Center - Style #1 - Grade #1	5.00
[illegible]	Stud, Hairspring - Style #1 - Grade #1	1.50
1919	Washer, Winding Wheel Hub	1.00

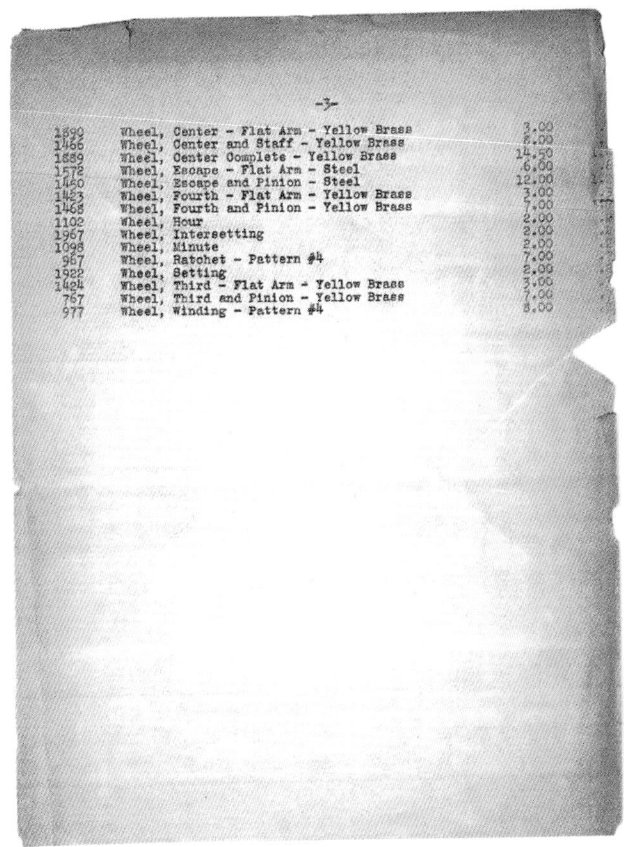

-3-

No.	Part	Price
1890	Wheel, Center - Flat Arm - Yellow Brass	3.00
1466	Wheel, Center and Staff - Yellow Brass	8.00
1889	Wheel, Center Complete - Yellow Brass	14.50
1572	Wheel, Escape - Flat Arm - Steel	6.00
1450	Wheel, Escape and Pinion - Steel	12.00
1423	Wheel, Fourth - Flat Arm - Yellow Brass	3.00
1468	Wheel, Fourth and Pinion - Yellow Brass	7.00
1102	Wheel, Hour	2.00
1967	Wheel, Intersetting	2.00
1098	Wheel, Minute	2.00
967	Wheel, Ratchet - Pattern #4	7.00
1922	Wheel, Setting	2.00
1424	Wheel, Third - Flat Arm - Yellow Brass	3.00
767	Wheel, Third and Pinion - Yellow Brass	7.00
977	Wheel, Winding - Pattern #4	8.00

WHY I COLLECT ILLINOIS

First and foremost, I like Illinois and the other high-grade grade American watches. The reason is really very simple. The American watch companies built better watches than any other country. The American watch industry produced huge numbers of high-grade watches. And for lower prices. The styling was the best of the era.

The Swiss watch industry was vexed by the conquering Americans. I like to show my fellow watch collectors how the finish on the plates of Illinois and Hamilton movements was superior to even the much vaunted Patek Philippe. Compare the Illinois shaped movement to an Aegler/Rolex/Gruen shaped movement. The Illinois featured a large, rugged balance wheel with massive mainspring, shaped in a way as to avoid any movement in the case without case screws. And this movement design led to the greatest shaped movement ever, the Hamilton 980 family. Many had screwed-in jewel settings and super fine regulation.

Our engineers and factory workers were the envy of the world. American watches were exported to the rest of the world much as Buick, Dodge or Hudson cars were shipped overseas. American-made products were considered the finest available. At one time the United States was the largest car exporter in the world. The above three car companies shipped 10% of their production overseas.

The watches of this era, and especially Illinois, represented everything good that this experiment in democracy called the United States represented. Unbridled optimism with real ingenuity. A brilliantly engineered product at a price that most folks could afford. Stylish without the freakish details. That is why I collect these brilliant American watches.

– Adam Ross

6/0 Size Illinois Factory-Cased Wristwatch Models

Model Name	Notes
Arlington	
Arliss	Identity unknown
Baronet	
Barrymore	Identity unknown
Beau Brummell	
Beau Brummell/Viking	Official name unknown
Beau Geste	
Beau Monde	
Beau Royale	
Belmont	
Ben Hur	Identity unknown
Biltmore 6/0	
Blackstone	
Bostonian	
Brunswick	Identity unknown
Bryce	
Cadet	
Canby	White gold-filled and green gold-filled models by Keystone Watch Case Company and solid gold Devon by the Solidarity Watch Case Company cased by Illinois in Springfield
Caprice	
Carlton	Identity unknown
Cavalier	
Charter Oak	Identity unknown
Chatham	Cased by Hamilton in Lancaster
Chevalier	
Chieftain	
Commodore	
Consul	
Convertible	
Derby	
Devon	White gold-filled and green gold-filled models by Keystone Watch Case Company and solid gold Devon by the Solidarity Watch Case Company cased by Illinois in Springfield
Ensign	
Falcon	Identity unknown
Fifth Avenue	
Graduate	Identity unknown
Greystone	
Haddon Hall	
Hawthorne	
Harvard	Identity unknown
Jackson	Identity unknown
Kingston	
LaSalle	
Lord Calvert	Identity unknown
Lowell	Identity unknown
Manhattan	
Marquis Strap	
Metropolitan	
Mohican	Identity unknown
Monticello	Identity unknown
New Yorker	
New Yorker Enamel	
Ollendorff I	
Paul Revere	
Penn Charter	Identity unknown
Piccadilly	
Pimlico	
Potomac	
Puritan	
Richmond	
Ritz	
Rockingham	
Rye 6/0	Identity unknown
Sherwood	
Southampton	
Square	White gold-filled and green gold-filled models by Keystone Watch Case Company and solid gold Devon by the Solidarity Watch Case Company cased by Illinois in Springfield
Square Cut Corner	White gold-filled and green gold-filled models by Keystone Watch Case Company and solid gold Devon by the Solidarity Watch Case Company cased by Illinois in Springfield
Standish	Cased by Hamilton in Lancaster
Statesman	Identity unknown
Suburban	Identity unknown
Townsman	
Yorktown	
Valedictorian	
Winchester	Identity unknown
Yankee Clipper	May have been only in 3/0 size

Blue = Unisex Red = Ladies

6/0 Size Illinois Factory-Cased Watch Models with Subsidiary Seconds at 9	
Model Name	**Notes**
Beau Brummell	Also came with subsidiary seconds at 6
Beau Brummell/Viking	Also came with subsidiary seconds at 6
Beau Royale	Also came with subsidiary seconds at 6
Cadet	Also came with subsidiary seconds at 6 and with no subsidiary seconds; at least three original Marquis Strap came with subsidiary seconds at 6
Canby	Only came with subsidiary seconds at 9
Chieftain	Only came with subsidiary seconds at 9
Consul	Only one known to exist; also came with subsidiary seconds at 6 and with no subsidiary seconds
Devon	Also came with subsidiary seconds at 6
Ensign	Also came with subsidiary seconds at 6
Fifth Avenue	Also came with subsidiary seconds at 6
Kingston	Also came with subsidiary seconds at 6
Manhattan	Also came with subsidiary seconds at 6
Marquis Strap	At least three original Marquis Strap came with subsidiary seconds at 6; also came with no subsidiary seconds
New Yorker	Also came with subsidiary seconds at 6
New Yorker Enamel	Also came with subsidiary seconds at 6
Piccadilly	Only came with subsidiary seconds at 9
Square	Only came with subsidiary seconds at 9
Square Cut Corner	Only came with subsidiary seconds at 9
Standish	Also came with subsidiary seconds at 6
Whippet	Also came with subsidiary seconds at 6

12/0 Size Movements

About the time of its purchase by Hamilton, Illinois began designing a 17-jewel 12/0 rectangular watch movement. This became Illinois' grade 207. The specifications for the 207 were: "12/0 size, 17 ruby and sapphire jewels; raised setting compensatory balance; double roller escapement; sapphire roller and pallet jewels; polished steel escape wheel; Breguet hairspring; recoil click; black enamel lettering." In mid-1929, Illinois finished the design work. Even though Illinois introduced and advertised the 207 in 1929, manufacturing records show that the first movements likely shipped in 1930.

In its promotional material, the Illinois Watch Company referred to the 207 as "America's first free training rectangular watch with second hand. The exceptional design and construction permits the use of larger, stronger working parts—thus assuring its owner the very best in strap watch performance."

Describing the "craftsmanship" of the 12/0, the Illinois Watch Company claimed that "the Illinois 12/0 is a triumph of watchmaking and is a worthy tribute to the engineering skill of Illinois technicians. The construction of this rectangular watch permits the use of very large and sturdy moving parts which makes it possible to attain exceptional accuracy in a strap watch. Extreme thinness affords smart case designs."

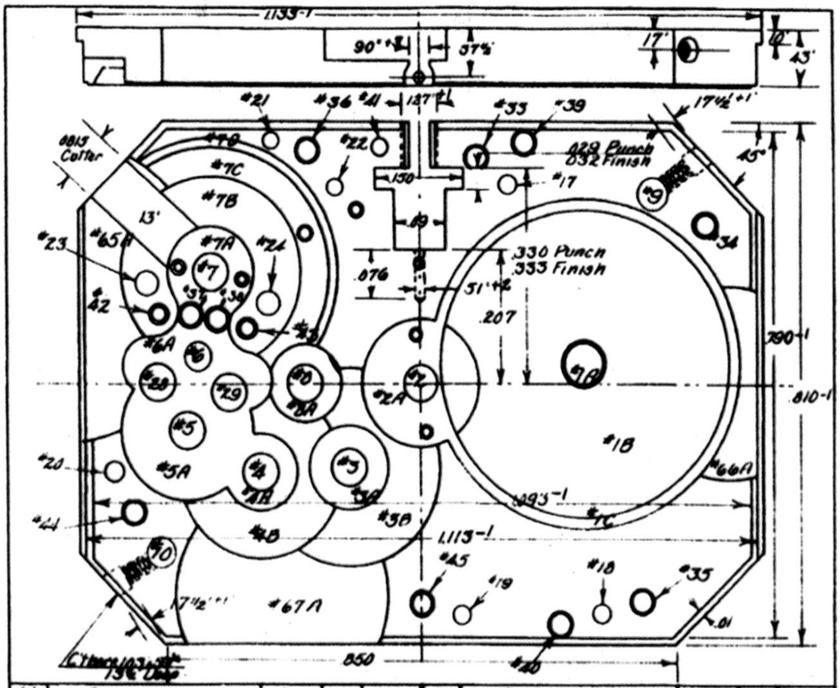

No	Description	Dia	Thk	Thread	No	Description	Dia	Thk	Thread
	Lower Plate	Scovil		#214	5	Hole for Escape	145'		
	" "		44		5A	Escape Whl. Rec. (Profile)	215+2	12'	
1A	Barrel Endshaking Hub	.072	12'		6	Hole for Pallet	112'		
1B	" Recess	476+2	7'		6A	Pallet Profile		12'	
1C	" Teeth "	.516+2	32'		7	Hole for Balance Staff	145'		
2	Hole for Center	145'			7A	Bal. Roller Rec. (Profile)	.142+2	12'	
2A	Center Pinion Recess	200+2	32'		7B	Pallet Bridge Sweep	299+2	22'	
3	Hole for Third	145'			7C	Balance Recess	390+2	30'	
3A	Third Pinion Recess	130+2	15'		7D	" "	420+2	Taper to 7C	
3B	" Wheel "	310+2	36'		8	Hole for Extra Pinion	145'		
4	Hole for Fourth	145'			8A	Extra Pinion Recess	120+2	14'	
4A	Fourth Pinion Rec. (Profile)	120+2	12'		9	Dial Foot Hole	Ream	130'	H
4B	" Wheel "	270+2	24'		10	" " "	"	130'	H

"NoGo" Gauges on threads are 2 Degrees larger than "Go" Gauges unless otherwise specified.
All Diameters Given are "Go" Gauges unless otherwise stated.

Lower Plate - Train Side
12/0 Size - Htg.

Drawn	3/7/28	
Traced	4/21/28	
Approved		G211
Scale 6:1		

No	Description	Dia	Thk	Thread
17	Barrel Bridge Steady Pin Hole	68'	Broach to fit	
18	" " " " "	68'	"	" "
19	Train " " " "	68'	"	" "
20	" " " " "	68'	"	" "
21	Balance Cock " " "	65'	"	" "
22	" " " " "	65'	"	" "
23	Pallet Bridge " " "	92'	"	" "
24	" " " " "	92'	"	" "
28	Peep Hole	145'		
29	" "	145'		
33	Bbl Brdg Screw Hole	72'		85x130
34	" " " "	72'		85x130
35	" " " "	72'		85x130
36	Bal Cock " "	72'		85x130
37	Banking " "	84'		99x170
38	" " "	84'		99x170
39	Case " "	72'		85x130
40	" " "	72'		85x130
41	Locking Lever " "	Dr 60'	Broach to 67+	
42	Pallet Bridge " "	55'		70x140
43	" " " "	55'		70x140
44	Train " " "	72'		85x130
45	" " " "	72'		85x130
65A	Balance Peep Hole Rec.	474+2	23'	
66A	Barrel " " "	300+2	36'	
67A	Train " "	350+2	36'	

Lower plate of 12/0 size, grade 207 Illinois movement drawing

The shape allowed Illinois designers to have more freedom in watch case design and permitted Illinois to join the trend towards smaller men's watches. The first rectangular watches offered with the grade 207 movement were the Medalist/Wembley, Trophy, Futura/Paul Revere, Finalist, Hudson/Ardsley, Kenilworth/Gallahad and Rockliffe. The first released 207 grade movement was housed in a Medalist case and the second in a Futura.

12/0 Size Movement Parts List

The material parts list, dated September 5, 1929, for the Illinois 12/0 size, 1st Model, Grade 207 movement, is shown here.

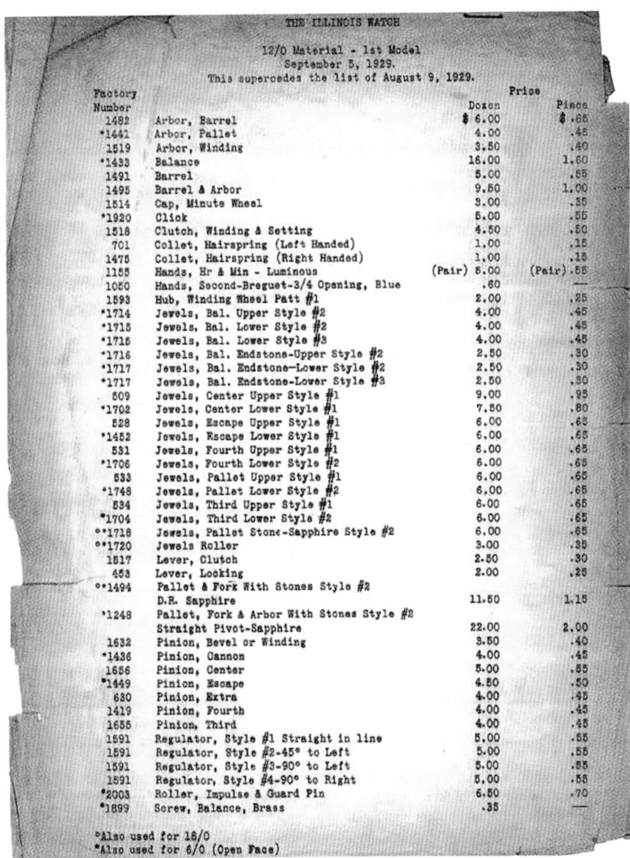

THE ILLINOIS WATCH

12/0 Material - 1st Model
September 5, 1929.
This supercedes the list of August 9, 1929.

Factory Number		Price Dozen	Price Piece
1482	Arbor, Barrel	$ 6.00	$ .65
*1441	Arbor, Pallet	4.00	.45
1519	Arbor, Winding	3.50	.40
*1433	Balance	16.00	1.60
1491	Barrel	5.00	.55
1495	Barrel & Arbor	9.50	1.00
1514	Cap, Minute Wheel	3.00	.35
*1920	Click	5.00	.55
1518	Clutch, Winding & Setting	4.50	.50
701	Collet, Hairspring (Left Handed)	1.00	.15
1475	Collet, Hairspring (Right Handed)	1.00	.15
1155	Hands, Hr & Min - Luminous	(Pair) 5.00	(Pair) .55
1050	Hands, Second-Breguet-3/4 Opening, Blue	.60	—
1593	Hub, Winding Wheel Patt #1	2.00	.25
*1714	Jewels, Bal. Upper Style #2	4.00	.45
*1715	Jewels, Bal. Lower Style #2	4.00	.45
*1715	Jewels, Bal. Lower Style #3	4.00	.45
*1716	Jewels, Bal. Endstone-Upper Style #2	2.50	.30
*1717	Jewels, Bal. Endstone-Lower Style #2	2.50	.30
*1717	Jewels, Bal. Endstone-Lower Style #3	2.50	.30
509	Jewels, Center Upper Style #1	9.00	.95
*1702	Jewels, Center Lower Style #1	7.50	.80
528	Jewels, Escape Upper Style #1	6.00	.65
*1452	Jewels, Escape Lower Style #1	6.00	.65
531	Jewels, Fourth Upper Style #1	6.00	.65
*1706	Jewels, Fourth Lower Style #2	6.00	.65
533	Jewels, Pallet Upper Style #1	6.00	.65
*1748	Jewels, Pallet Lower Style #2	6.00	.65
534	Jewels, Third Upper Style #1	6.00	.65
*1704	Jewels, Third Lower Style #2	6.00	.65
°*1718	Jewels, Pallet Stone-Sapphire Style #2	6.00	.65
°*1720	Jewels Roller	3.00	.35
1517	Lever, Clutch	2.50	.30
453	Lever, Locking	2.00	.25
°*1494	Pallet & Fork With Stones Style #2 D.R. Sapphire	11.50	1.15
*1248	Pallet, Fork & Arbor With Stones Style #2 Straight Pivot-Sapphire	22.00	2.00
1632	Pinion, Bevel or Winding	3.50	.40
*1436	Pinion, Cannon	4.00	.45
1656	Pinion, Center	5.00	.55
*1449	Pinion, Escape	4.50	.50
630	Pinion, Extra	4.00	.45
1419	Pinion, Fourth	4.00	.45
1655	Pinion, Third	4.00	.45
1591	Regulator, Style #1 Straight in line	5.00	.55
1591	Regulator, Style #2-45° to Left	5.00	.55
1591	Regulator, Style #3-90° to Left	5.00	.55
1591	Regulator, Style #4-90° to Right	5.00	.55
*2003	Roller, Impulse & Guard Pin	6.50	.70
*1899	Screw, Balance, Brass	.35	—

°Also used for 18/0
*Also used for 6/0 (Open Face)

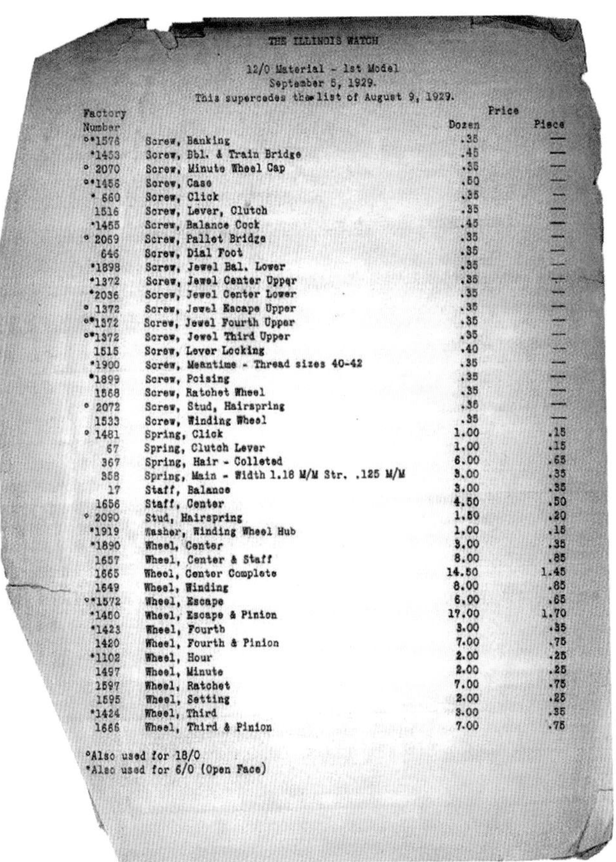

THE ILLINOIS WATCH

12/0 Material - 1st Model
September 5, 1929.
This supercedes the list of August 9, 1929.

Factory Number		Price Dozen	Price Piece
°*1576	Screw, Banking	.35	—
*1453	Screw, Bbl. & Train Bridge	.45	—
° 2070	Screw, Minute Wheel Cap	.35	—
°*1456	Screw, Case	.50	—
* 660	Screw, Click	.35	—
1516	Screw, Lever, Clutch	.35	—
*1455	Screw, Balance Cock	.45	—
° 2069	Screw, Pallet Bridge	.35	—
646	Screw, Dial Foot	.35	—
*1898	Screw, Jewel Bal. Lower	.35	—
*1372	Screw, Jewel Center Uppqr	.35	—
*2036	Screw, Jewel Center Lower	.35	—
° 1372	Screw, Jewel Escape Upper	.35	—
°*1372	Screw, Jewel Fourth Upper	.35	—
°*1372	Screw, Jewel Third Upper	.35	—
1515	Screw, Lever Locking	.40	—
*1900	Screw, Meantime - Thread sizes 40-42	.35	—
*1899	Screw, Poising	.35	—
1568	Screw, Ratchet Wheel	.35	—
° 2072	Screw, Stud, Hairspring	.35	—
1533	Screw, Winding Wheel	.35	—
° 1481	Spring, Click	1.00	.15
67	Spring, Clutch Lever	1.00	.15
367	Spring, Hair - Colleted	6.00	.65
358	Spring, Main - Width 1.18 M/M Str. .125 M/M	3.00	.35
17	Staff, Balance	3.00	.35
1656	Staff, Center	4.50	.50
° 2090	Stud, Hairspring	1.50	.20
*1919	Washer, Winding Wheel Hub	1.00	.15
*1890	Wheel, Center	3.00	.35
1657	Wheel, Center & Staff	8.00	.85
1665	Wheel, Center Complete	14.50	1.45
1649	Wheel, Winding	8.00	.85
°*1572	Wheel, Escape	6.00	.65
*1450	Wheel, Escape & Pinion	17.00	1.70
*1423	Wheel, Fourth	3.00	.35
1420	Wheel, Fourth & Pinion	7.00	.75
*1102	Wheel, Hour	2.00	.25
1497	Wheel, Minute	2.00	.25
1597	Wheel, Ratchet	7.00	.75
1595	Wheel, Setting	2.00	.25
*1424	Wheel, Third	3.00	.35
1666	Wheel, Third & Pinion	7.00	.75

°Also used for 18/0
*Also used for 6/0 (Open Face)

12/0 Size Movement Production Quantities

The price for the 207 grade movement ranged from $5.00 to $20.00 when new. Illinois produced only one model of the 207. The production quantities of the 207 movements are shown here.

12/0 Size, 17-Jewel Movement Production Quantities		
Year	Grade	Quantity
1930	207	16,000
1931	207	21,000
1932	207	6,000
Total 12/0:		**43,000**

Two Illinois 12/0 size, grade 207 movements; note their two different damaskeening patterns.

12/0 Size Illinois Factory-Cased Wristwatch Models	
Model Name	**Notes**
Andover	
Ardsley	
Chesterfield	
Chesterfield Stepped Bezel	Official name unknown
Exeter	
Finalist	
Finalist Deco	Official name unknown
Frontenac	
Futura	
Gallahad	
Hudson	
John Alden	Identity unknown
Kenilworth	
Kensington	
Larchmont	
Medalist	
No. 250/Schmukler	(see Chapter 9)
Paul Revere	
Richmond 12/0	
Rockliffe	
Rye 12/0	Identity unknown
Trophy	See Chapter 9
Vernon	
Wembley	
Wentworth	
Westchester	

HAMILTON GRADE 401 MOVEMENTS

When it purchased the Illinois Watch Company in 1928, Hamilton did not yet manufacture its own rectangular movement. To expand their styling offerings and to save time until they could produce their own 980 rectangular movement, Hamilton requested that Illinois modify the Illinois 207 grade rectangular movement for Hamilton's use. It had Illinois add two jewels plus some other minor features and relabeled it a Hamilton 401 grade movement. The 401 "had raised gold jewel settings, a double roller escapement and sapphire roller and pallet jewels. Grade 401 movements started with serial number H50,001 (7,500 were ultimately made). Illinois originally manufactured the movements at its Factory according to Hamilton specifications. They were stamped with the Hamilton name and Lancaster, Pennsylvania address." (For more information on the 401 grade Hamilton movement, see Chapter 3.)

18/0 Size Movements

In 1922, Illinois finished the design of its 16-jewel, 18/0 size rectangular watch movement. Illinois intended this movement specifically for ladies' small rectangular wristwatches, to capitalize on their growing popularity at the time. The movement went by several grades designations in Illinois records: 6¾ (for the size in lignes), 18 and 181. These appear to be just different appellations for the original movement.

With the introduction of the grade 206, Illinois increased the number of jewels to 17 by adding a whole jewel to the base plate at the center wheel. In the middle of grade 206 production, Illinois improved the barrel wheel click. This same movement became the grade 807, with no observable change. The change to friction jeweling caused Illinois to change the grade designation again to 807A. Illinois named its final version the 807B to accommodate another modification, very likely a change in the bridge to permit interchangeability with 805 bridges.

Specifications for the 18/0 size movement were: "size eighteen-0 or six and three-fourths ligne, 17 ruby and sapphire jewels, safety recoiling, click, double roller escapement, tempered and hardened compensatory balance, steel escape wheel, concaved and polished winding wheels." With the exception of the Biltmore 18/0, Sangamon, Tuxedo, Urbana and the late-model Rockliffe 18/0 (1935) with no subsidiary seconds, this movement was used exclusively in ladies' Illinois wristwatches. There are also 18/0 size rectangular movements that can be found with 15, 16, or 17 jewels. The existence of 18-jewel 18/0 size Illinois movements has been rumored but not confirmed; none have been found listed in the Illinois Factory production records.

18/0 SIZE MOVEMENTS

Although Gruen had used Swiss-made 18/0 (6¾ lignes) movements at least as early as 1921, Illinois' introduction of its 16-jewel 18/0 in 1923 may make it the earliest American manufacturer of that size of movement. Elgin released its first 18/0, the 7-jewel 483, in 1925, and a year later came out with a 15-jewel one. Before that, Elgin's smallest movement was a 16/0. Hamilton did not release an 18/0 size movement until 1928, and it apparently was a problematic release as only 723 of these grade 989 movements were produced and only 31 were sold.

18/0 Size Movement Parts Price List

A material parts price list for the 18/0 issues by the Illinois Material Department, dated February 14, 1931, 18/0 movement, 1st Model, Grade #206 is shown here.

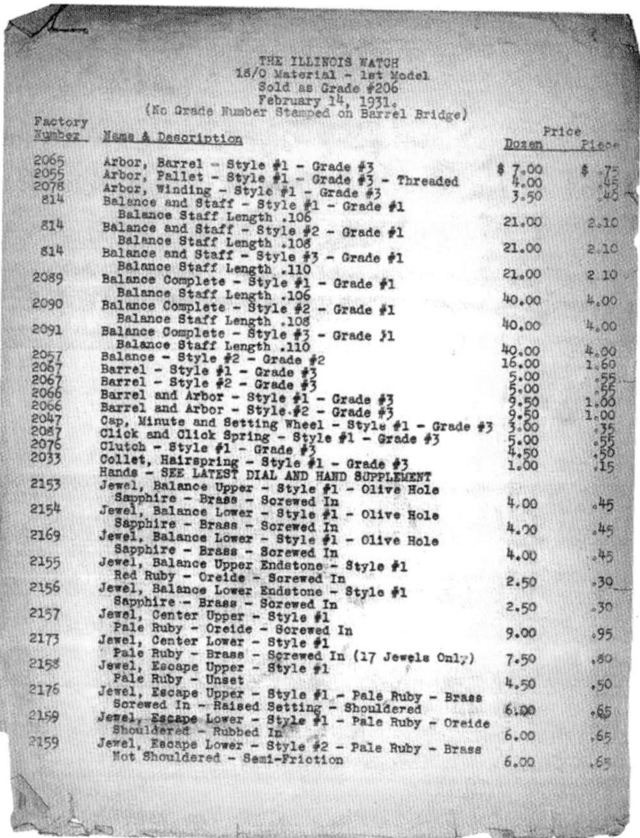

THE ILLINOIS WATCH
18/0 Material - 1st Model
Sold as Grade #206
February 14, 1931.
(No Grade Number Stamped on Barrel Bridge)

Factory Number	Name & Description	Price Dozen	Price Piece
2065	Arbor, Barrel - Style #1 - Grade #3	$ 7.00	$ .75
2055	Arbor, Pallet - Style #1 - Grade #3 - Threaded	4.00	.45
2078	Arbor, Winding - Style #1 - Grade #3	3.50	.40
814	Balance and Staff - Style #1 - Grade #1 Balance Staff Length .106	21.00	2.10
814	Balance and Staff - Style #2 - Grade #1 Balance Staff Length .108	21.00	2.10
814	Balance and Staff - Style #3 - Grade #1 Balance Staff Length .110	21.00	2.10
2089	Balance Complete - Style #1 - Grade #1 Balance Staff Length .106	40.00	4.00
2090	Balance Complete - Style #2 - Grade #1 Balance Staff Length .108	40.00	4.00
2091	Balance Complete - Style #3 - Grade #1 Balance Staff Length .110	40.00	4.00
2057	Balance - Style #2 - Grade #2	16.00	1.60
2067	Barrel - Style #1 - Grade #3	5.00	.55
2067	Barrel - Style #2 - Grade #3	5.00	.55
2066	Barrel and Arbor - Style #1 - Grade #3	9.50	1.00
2066	Barrel and Arbor - Style #2 - Grade #3	9.50	1.00
2047	Cap, Minute and Setting Wheel - Style #1 - Grade #3	3.00	.35
2087	Click and Click Spring - Style #1 - Grade #3	5.00	.55
2076	Clutch - Style #1 - Grade #3	4.50	.50
2033	Collet, Hairspring - Style #1 - Grade #3	1.00	.15
	Hands - SEE LATEST DIAL AND HAND SUPPLEMENT		
2153	Jewel, Balance Upper - Style #1 - Olive Hole Sapphire - Brass - Screwed In	4.00	.45
2154	Jewel, Balance Lower - Style #1 - Olive Hole Sapphire - Brass - Screwed In	4.00	.45
2169	Jewel, Balance Lower - Style #1 - Olive Hole Sapphire - Brass - Screwed In	4.00	.45
2155	Jewel, Balance Upper Endstone - Style #1 Red Ruby - Oreide - Screwed In	2.50	.30
2156	Jewel, Balance Lower Endstone - Style #1 Sapphire - Brass - Screwed In	2.50	.30
2157	Jewel, Center Upper - Style #1 Pale Ruby - Oreide - Screwed In	9.00	.95
2173	Jewel, Center Lower - Style #1 Pale Ruby - Brass - Screwed In (17 Jewels Only)	7.50	.80
2158	Jewel, Escape Upper - Style #1 Pale Ruby - Unset	4.50	.50
2176	Jewel, Escape Upper - Style #1 - Pale Ruby - Brass Screwed In - Raised Setting - Shouldered	6.00	.65
2159	Jewel, Escape Lower - Style #1 - Pale Ruby - Oreide Shouldered - Rubbed In	6.00	.65
2159	Jewel, Escape Lower - Style #2 - Pale Ruby - Brass Not Shouldered - Semi-Friction	6.00	.65

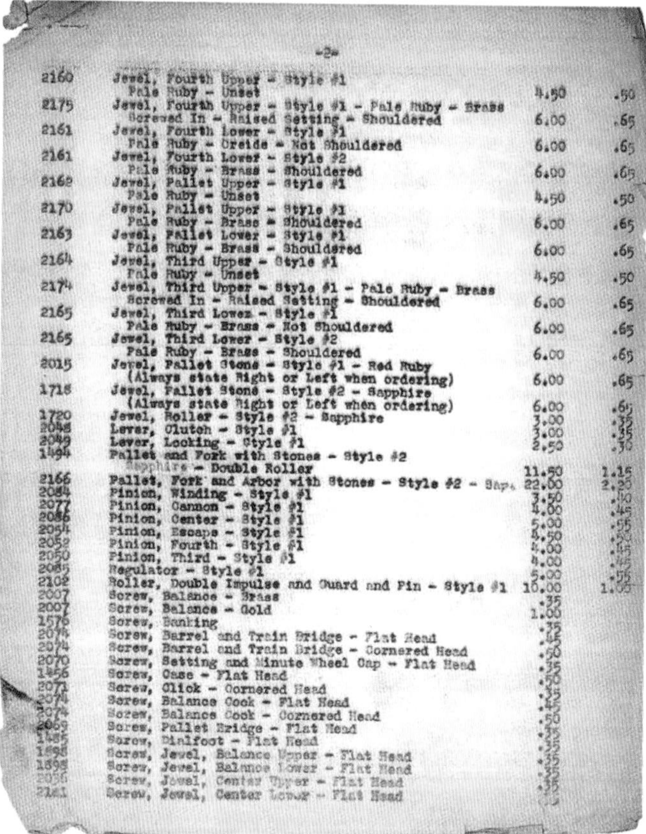

-2-

Factory Number	Name & Description	Price Dozen	Price Piece
2160	Jewel, Fourth Upper - Style #1 Pale Ruby - Unset	4.50	.50
2175	Jewel, Fourth Upper - Style #1 - Pale Ruby - Brass Screwed In - Raised Setting - Shouldered	6.00	.65
2161	Jewel, Fourth Lower - Style #1 Pale Ruby - Oreide - Not Shouldered	6.00	.65
2161	Jewel, Fourth Lower - Style #2 Pale Ruby - Brass - Shouldered	6.00	.65
2162	Jewel, Pallet Upper - Style #1 Pale Ruby - Unset	4.50	.50
2170	Jewel, Pallet Upper - Style #1 Pale Ruby - Brass - Shouldered	6.00	.65
2163	Jewel, Pallet Lower - Style #1 Pale Ruby - Brass - Shouldered	6.00	.65
2164	Jewel, Third Upper - Style #1 Pale Ruby - Unset	4.50	.50
2174	Jewel, Third Upper - Style #1 - Pale Ruby - Brass Screwed In - Raised Setting - Shouldered	6.00	.65
2165	Jewel, Third Lower - Style #1 Pale Ruby - Brass - Not Shouldered	6.00	.65
2165	Jewel, Third Lower - Style #2 Pale Ruby - Brass - Shouldered	6.00	.65
2015	Jewel, Pallet Stone - Style #1 - Red Ruby (Always state Right or Left when ordering)	6.00	.65
1718	Jewel, Pallet Stone - Style #2 - Sapphire (Always state Right or Left when ordering)	6.00	.65
1720	Jewel, Roller - Style #2 - Sapphire	3.00	.35
2048	Lever, Clutch - Style #1	3.00	.35
2049	Lever, Locking - Style #1	2.50	.30
1494	Pallet and Fork with Stones - Style #2 Sapphire - Double Roller	11.50	1.15
2166	Pallet, Fork and Arbor with Stones - Style #2 - Sap.	22.00	2.20
2084	Pinion, Winding - Style #1	3.50	.40
2077	Pinion, Cannon - Style #1	4.00	.45
2086	Pinion, Center - Style #1	5.00	.55
2054	Pinion, Escape - Style #1	4.50	.50
2052	Pinion, Fourth - Style #1	4.00	.45
2050	Pinion, Third - Style #1	4.00	.45
2085	Regulator - Style #1	5.00	.55
2102	Roller, Double Impulse and Guard and Pin - Style #1	10.00	1.00
2007	Screw, Balance - Brass	.35	
2007	Screw, Balance - Gold	1.00	
1576	Screw, Banking	.35	
2074	Screw, Barrel and Train Bridge - Flat Head	.45	
2074	Screw, Barrel and Train Bridge - Cornered Head	.50	
2070	Screw, Setting and Minute Wheel Cap - Flat Head	.35	
1456	Screw, Case - Flat Head	.50	
2071	Screw, Click - Cornered Head	.35	
2074	Screw, Balance Cock - Flat Head	.45	
2074	Screw, Balance Cock - Cornered Head	.50	
2069	Screw, Pallet Bridge - Flat Head	.35	
1485	Screw, Dialfoot - Flat Head	.35	
1698	Screw, Jewel, Balance Upper - Flat Head	.35	
1698	Screw, Jewel, Balance Lower - Flat Head	.35	
2056	Screw, Jewel, Center Upper - Flat Head	.35	
2161	Screw, Jewel, Center Lower - Flat Head	.35	

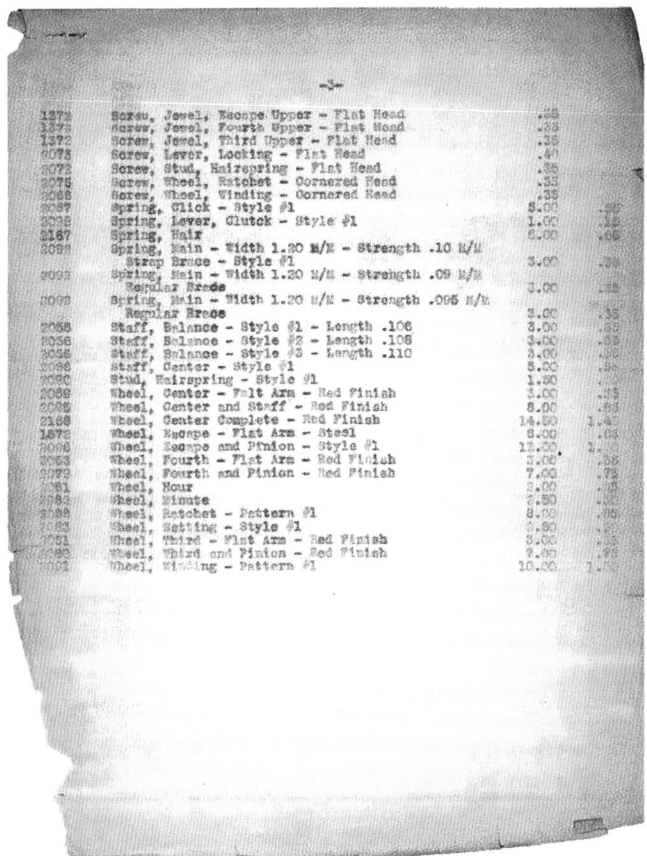

-3-

1372	Screw, Jewel, Escape Upper - Flat Head	.35	
[illegible]	Screw, Jewel, Fourth Upper - Flat Head	.35	
1372	Screw, Jewel, Third Upper - Flat Head	.35	
2075	Screw, Lever, Locking - Flat Head	.40	
2072	Screw, Stud, Hairspring - Flat Head	.35	
2075	Screw, Wheel, Ratchet - Cornered Head	.35	
2068	Screw, Wheel, Winding - Cornered Head	.35	
2087	Spring, Click - Style #1	5.00	[illegible]
2098	Spring, Lever, Clutck - Style #1	1.00	.15
2167	Spring, Hair	6.00	.65
2093	Spring, Main - Width 1.20 M/M - Strength .10 M/M Strap Brace - Style #1	3.00	[illegible]
2093	Spring, Main - Width 1.20 M/M - Strength .09 M/M Regular Brace	3.00	[illegible]
2092	Spring, Main - Width 1.20 M/M - Strength .095 M/M Regular Brace	3.00	.35
2056	Staff, Balance - Style #1 - Length .106	3.00	.35
2056	Staff, Balance - Style #2 - Length .108	3.00	.35
2056	Staff, Balance - Style #3 - Length .110	3.00	[illegible]
2086	Staff, Center - Style #1	5.00	[illegible]
2090	Stud, Hairspring - Style #1	1.50	[illegible]
2089	Wheel, Center - Flat Arm - Red Finish	3.00	[illegible]
2085	Wheel, Center and Staff - Red Finish	8.00	[illegible]
2168	Wheel, Center Complete - Red Finish	14.50	1.45
1572	Wheel, Escape - Flat Arm - Steel	8.00	[illegible]
[illegible]	Wheel, Escape and Pinion - Style #1	12.00	[illegible]
2053	Wheel, Fourth - Flat Arm - Red Finish	3.00	[illegible]
2079	Wheel, Fourth and Pinion - Red Finish	7.00	.75
2081	Wheel, Hour	2.00	[illegible]
2083	Wheel, Minute	2.50	[illegible]
2088	Wheel, Ratchet - Pattern #1	8.00	[illegible]
[illegible]	Wheel, Setting - Style #1	[illegible]	[illegible]
2051	Wheel, Third - Flat Arm - Red Finish	3.00	[illegible]
[illegible]	Wheel, Third and Pinion - Red Finish	7.00	[illegible]
[illegible]	Wheel, Winding - Pattern #1	10.00	[illegible]

The 18/0 size movement production quantities are broken down by grade and jewel count as follows:

18/0 Size, Unknown-Jewel Movements Production Quantities

Year	Grade	Quantity
1923	6¾	30
Total 6¾		**30**

18/0 Size, 15-Jewel Movements Production Quantities

Year	Grade	Quantity
~~1948~~/ 1932–1933	805 805A	29,700
Total 805/805A		**29,700**

18/0 size, grade 805, 15-jewel Illinois movement

18/0 Size, 16-Jewel Grade 181 Movement Production Quantities

Year	Grade	Quantity
1923	181	1,000
1924	181	0
1925	181	3,000
1926	181	1,000
1927	181	500
Total 181:		**5,500**

18/0 size, grade 181, 16-jewel Illinois movement, front and back

18/0 Size, 17-Jewel Grade 181 Movement Production Quantities		
Year	Grade	Quantity
1927	181	500
Total 181:		**500**

18/0 SIZE MOVEMENT

The 1929 Illinois Sales Catalog describes the 18/0 size movement as follows: "Size Eighteen-0 or six and three-fourths ligne. 17 ruby and sapphire jewels, safety recoiling click, double roller escapement, tempered and hardened compensating balance, steel escape wheel, concaved polished winding wheels."

18/0 Size, 17-Jewel Grade 206 Movement Production Quantities		
Year	Grade	Quantity
1927	206	3,000
1928	206	5,000
1929	206	4,000
1929	206	1,000
1930	206	1,900
Total 206:		**14,900**

18/0 Size, 17-Jewel Grade 807 Movement Production Quantities		
Year	Grade	Quantity
1930	807 807A	14,100
1931	807 807A	22,000
1932	807A 807B	32,000
~~1948/~~ 1932– 1933	807B	3,100
Total 807:		**71,200**

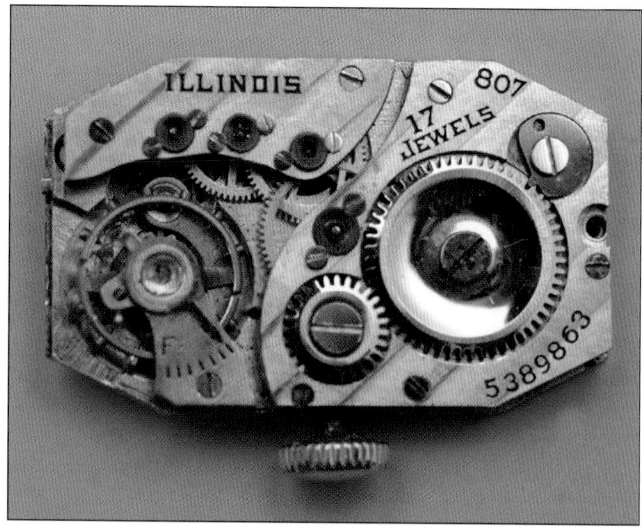

18/0 size, grade 807, 17-jewel Illinois movement

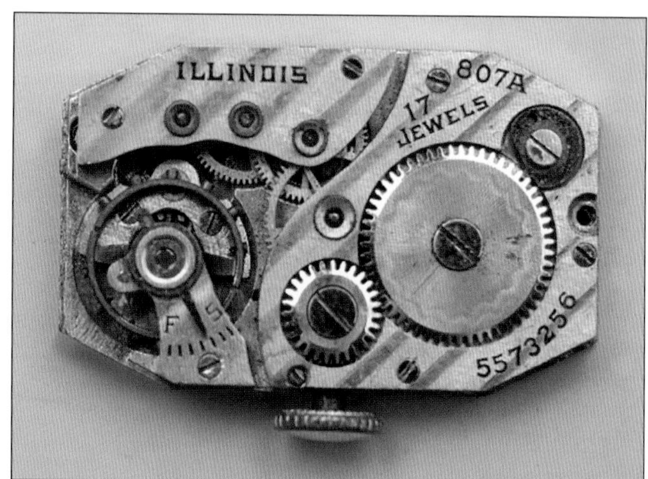

18/0 size, grade 807A, 17-jewel Illinois movement

18/0 size, grade 807B, 17-jewel Illinois movement

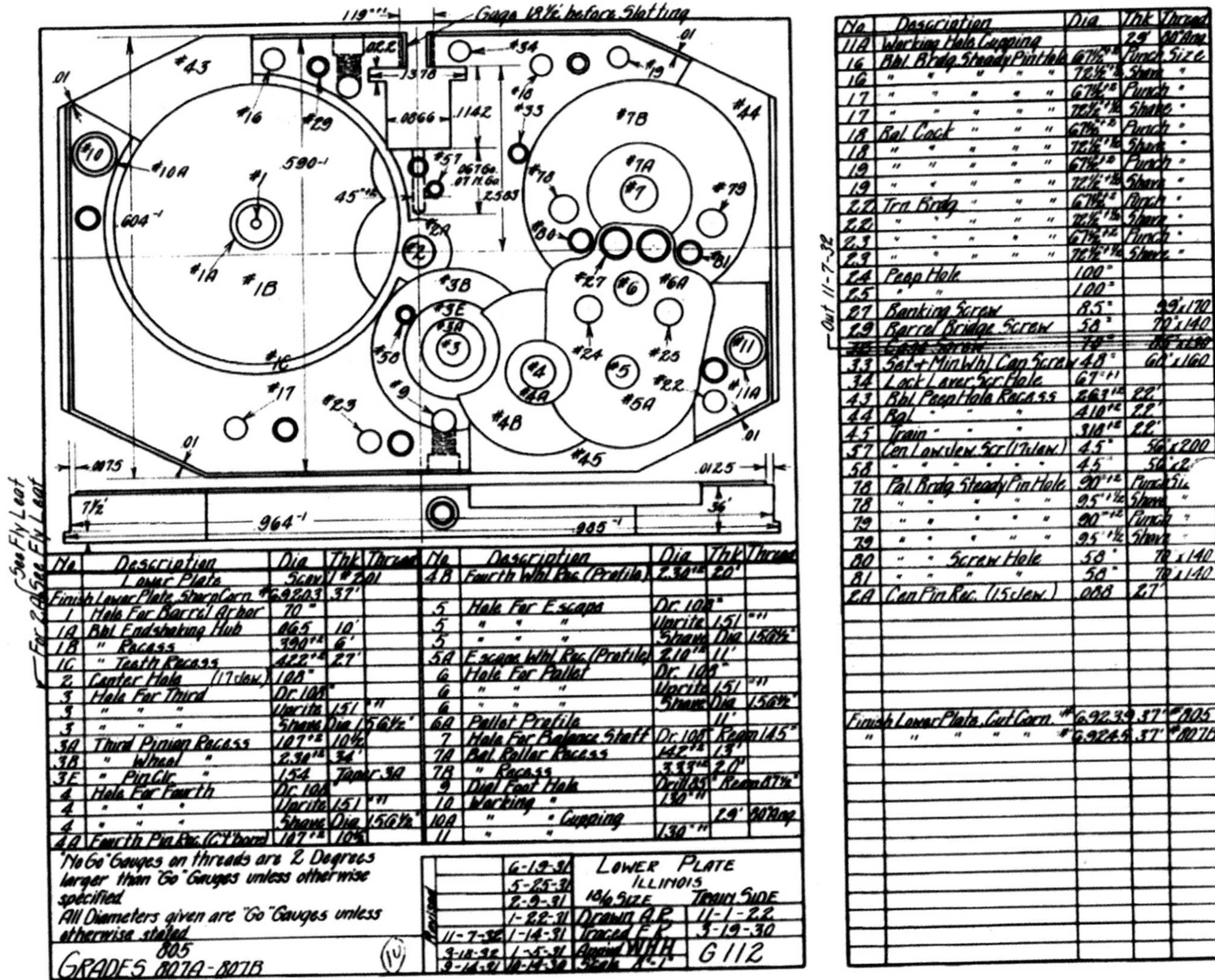

18/0 size Illinois lower plate drawing

Total 18/0 Size Movement Production Quantities

Jewels	Quantity
15	29,700
16	5,500
17	128,100
18	*
Unknown	30
Total 18/0:	**163,330**

*Only rumored to exist.

MOVEMENT GRADE MARKINGS

At this point it is not known why on some Illinois movements the grade number is stamped on the back of the movement and on others it is not. This is a matter that requires further study.

Elgin did not stamp its grades on its movements. Hamilton did, starting in the 1920s. The number of jewels available on an Illinois movement was far greater than Elgin (normally 7 or 15 jewels) or Hamilton (normally 17 or 19 jewels.

The 18/0 Size Family of Movements

18/0 Size Illinois Factory-Cased Wristwatch Models

Argyle	Daytona 154	Irene	Princess
Arlene	Daytona 155	Joan	Priscilla*
Avalon	Daytona 155A	Lady Mary	Queen Anne
Barbara	Debutante	Lakewood	Redonda 153
Bar Harbor 156	Del Monte 155	Lenox	Redonda 154
Bar Harbor 158	Del Monte 157	Long Beach	Rita
Berkeley 153	Diamond-Set Bezels	Marilyn	Rockliffe 18/0**
Berkeley 154A	Edgewater 155	Mary Todd	Roslyn
Berkeley 154B	Edgewater 175	Mary Todd 203	Sangamon
Berkshire	Edgewater 208	Mary Todd 204	Saratoga Leaf
Beverly 185	Edgewater 222	Mary Todd GG	Saratoga Notched Leaf
Beverly 852	Elissa	Mayflower*	Sylvia
Biloxi	Fairfax	Miami 155	Tuxedo
Biltmore 18/0	Fairport	Miami 157	Urbana**
Brighton	Florentine	Narragansett	Vanity Fair
Claudette	Glencoe	Newport 174	Vardon
Co-ed*	Glenna	Newport 223	Victoria
Constance	Gloria	No. 241	Vogue
Coronado	Graduate*	Ollendorff II	
Countess	Greta	Patricia	
Daytona 153	Hollywood	Pearl*	

*Identity unknown
**Cased by Hamilton in Lancaster.

Red = Ladies' models
Blue = Unisex models
Black = Men's models

EFFECTIVE OCTOBER 26, 1931 SUPERSEDES ALL PREVIOUS PRICE LISTS

ILLINOIS WATCH MATERIAL PRICE LIST—JOBBERS

SUBJECT ONLY TO 3% DISCOUNT IF PAID 15TH OF MONTH FOLLOWING PURCHASE

MATERIAL	Each	¼ Doz.	1 Doz.	6 Doz.	12 Doz
ARBORS, Barrel	.42	.91	3.00		
" Clutch	.28	.55	1.80		
" Pallet Cone Pivot	.49	1.07	3.60	20.55	
" Pallet Straight Pivot	.35	.75	2.40	13.70	
" Winding	.42	.91	3.00	17.10	
BALANCES, Gold Screws	1.68	3.58	12.60		
" Brass Screws	.98	2.08	7.20		
BALANCE & STAFF, Gold Screws	1.95	4.20			
" " " Brass Screws	1.30	2.85			
BALANCE, STAFF, Roller, Hairspring Gold Screws	3.25	6.93			
" STAFF, Roller, Hairspring, Brass Screws 12/0 and larger	2.60	5.58			
" STAFF, Roller, Hairspring, Brass Screws 18/0 and smaller	3.45	7.38			
BANDS, Dust	.21	.39	1 20		
BARS, Slide	.21	.39	1.20		
" Swing	.21	.39	1.20		
" Swing with Pinion	.49	1.07	3.60		
BARRELS, Regular	.42	.91	3.00		
" Motor (Not sold without Staff)					
" Regular & Arbor	.91	1.92			
" Jeweled & Arbor	2.28	4.95			
" Motor & Staff	1.50	3.15			
BEARINGS, Motor Barrel Staff Upper	.33	.69			
" Winding Arbor	.21	.39	1.20		
BRIDGES, Winding	.32	.65	2.10		
" Winding with Pinion	.56	1.24	4.20		
CAPS, Click Spring	.21	.39	1.20		
" Hairspring Stud	.21	.39	1.20		
" Minute Wheel	.21	.39	1.20		
" Minute Wheel & Locking Lever Spring combined	.32	.65	2.10		
" Ratchet Wheel	.32	.65	2.10		
" Setting Wheel	.21	.39	1.20		
" Motor Barrel Ratchet Wheel with Jewel	1.17	2.55			
CLICKS,	.28	.55	1.80	10.30	
" No. 1044	.72	1.47			
CLUTCHES, Winding & Setting	.39	.85	2.70	15.40	
COLLETS, Hairspring		.20	.60	3.45	
CUPS, Barrel Arbor	.35	.75	2.40		
DIALS—(See Latest Dial & Hand Catalog)					
DIALS, Enamel .... Retail $17.50 Doz.	1.14	2.63	10.50		
" " " 20.00 "	1.30	3.00	12.00		
" " " 22.50 "	1.46	3.38	13.50		
" " " 25.00 "		4.06	15.00		
" " " 27.50 "	1.79	4.13	16.50		
DIALS, Metal .... Retail 12.50 Doz.	.81	2.03	7.50		
" " " 15.00 "	.98	2.25	9.00		
" " " 17.50 "	1.14	2.63	10.50		
" " " 25.00 "	1.50	3.75	15.00		
" " " 30.00 "	1.95	4.50	18.00		
" " " 35.00 "	2.28	5.25	21.00		
" " " 100.00 "	6.00	15.00	60.00		
DIALS, Second Bits, Rotor, Retail 4.50 Doz.	.29	.68	2.70		
DIES	2.80	6.05			
FORKS	.49	1.07	3.60		
HANDS, Hour, Minute & Second—(See latest Dial & Hand Catalog)					
HANDS, Hr. & Min., Retail 1.50 Doz. Prs.		.25	.95	5.45	10.20
" " " " " 1.75 " "		.29	1.10	6.35	12.00
" " " " " 4.00 " "		.65	2.40	13.80	25.80
HANDS, Seconds ..... Retail .35 Doz.			.23	1.30	2.50
" " " .50 "			.33	1.85	3.60
HUBS, Motor Barrel Ratchet	.60	1.33	4.50		
" Motor Barrel Snailed	.60	1.33	4.50		
" Winding Wheel	.28	.55	1.80		
INDEXES, Regulator	.33	.69			
JEWELS, Balance, Escape & Pallet for Cone Pivots		.68	2.40	13.80	25.80
" Balance Unset	.28	.55	1.80		
" Endstone Gold Setting	.42	.91	3.00		
" Endstone Gold Fig. 8 Setting	.56	1.24	4.20		
" Endstone Dome Setting	.56	1.24	4.20		
" Endstone Composition Setting		.39	1.20	6.85	13.00
" Endstone Unset	.20	.29	.90		
" Barrel Arbor Gold Setting	1.12	2.41	8.40		
" Motor Barrel Staff Gold Setting	1.12	2.41	8.40		
" Motor Barrel Staff Composition Setting	.77	1.59	5.40		
" Center Gold Setting	.98	2.08	7.20		
" Center Composition Setting	.77	1.59	5.40		
" Center Unset	.63	1.43	4.80		
" Train & Pallet Straight Pivot Gold Setting	.60	1.33	4.50		
" Train & Pallet Straight Pivot Composition Setting	.49	1.07	3.60		
" Train & Pallet Unset	.42	.91	3.00		
" Pallet Stone Sapphire & Ruby	.42	.91	3.00	17.10	
" Pallet Stone Garnet	.28	.55	1.80	10.30	
" Roller (Jewel Pins) Sapphire & Ruby	.28	.55	1.80	10.30	
" Roller (Jewel Pins) Garnet		.20	.42	2.40	
LET DOWNS	.28	.55	1.80		
LEVERS, Clutch	.28	.55	1.80	10.30	
" Locking	.28	.55	1.80	10.30	
" Setting	.28	.55	1.80	10.30	

MATERIAL	Each	¼ Doz.	1 Doz.	6 Doz.	12 Doz.
NUTS, Regulator Adjusting Screw	.21	.39	1.20		
PALLET, with Stones (No Fork)	1.26	2.76	9.60		
" & FORK (1 piece) with Stones	1.26	2.76	9.60		
" & FORK (2 piece) with Stones & Arbor	2.31	5.04	18.00		
" & FORK (1 piece) with Stones & Arbor Cone Pivot	1.76	3.78			
" & FORK (1 piece) with Stones & Arbor Straight Pivot	1.56	3.30			
PINIONS, Bevel or Winding	.35	.75	2.40		
" Cannon	.35	.75	2.40		
" Center (without Staff)	.35	.75	2.40		
" Center & Staff (1 piece)	.49	1.07	3.60		
" Escape, Fourth, Third, Fifth or Extra	.42	.91	3.00		
PINS, Hairspring, Collet & Stud		.20	.60	3.45	
" Winding Arbor Push		.29	.90	5.15	
" Setting		.29	.90	5.15	
PLATES, Setting	.21	.39	1.20		
REGULATORS	.42	.91	3.00		
ROLLERS, Combination without Pin	.32	.65	2.10		
" Impulse without Pin	.25	.49	1.50		
" Impulse With Balance But without Pin No. 1816	1.68	3.58	12.60		
" Guard	.28	.55	1.80		
" Combination with Jewel Pin	.60	1.33	4.50		
" Impulse with Jewel Pin	.53	1.14	3.90		
" Impulse & Balance & Pin No. 1817	1.95	4.20			
" (Impulse & Guard) Staff & Pin No. 1454	.56	1.24	4 20		
SCREWS, Balance Gold All		.20	.60	3.30	6.00
" Micrometer Regulator Adjusting	.20	.29	.90		
" Gold Plated			.42		
" All Other			.30	1.65	3.00
SLEEVES, Winding Arbor	.32	.65	2.10		
SPRINGS, Flat Steel—Click, Clutch, Lifting Locking Lever, Setting Lever, Interwinding Wheel, Yoke	.20	.29	.90	5.15	9.75
" Wire—Click, Clutch, Locking Lever, Fifth Pinion, Setting Lever, Yoke		.20	.42	2.40	4.60
" Hair colleted (12/0 and larger)	.49	1.07	3.60	20.55	
" Hair colleted (18/0 and smaller)	.77	1.59	5.40	30.80	
" Locking Lever & Minute Wheel Cap Combination	.32	.65	2.10		
" Main, Motor Barrel			1.95	11 10	21.60
" Main, All Others			1.60	9.30	18.00
" Regulator Only Nos. 2042, 886	.42	.91	3.00		
" Regulator with Adjusting Screws	.53	1.14	3.90		
STAFFS, Balance No. 1506 & 1684 with Oil Grooves		.68	2.40	14.10	27.35
" Balance (No. 1442, Style No. 1)		.65	2 20	12.90	
" Balance All Others		.55	1.90	11.10	21.60
" Motor Barrel	.42	.91	3.00		
" Center (no Pinion)	.39	.85	2.70		
" Center & Pinion (1 piece)	.49	1.07	3.60		
STRAPS, Regulator with Adjusting Screws	.35	.75	2.40		
STUDS, Hairspring	.20	.29	.90		
TAPS, Crown	.21	.39	1.20		
" Screw	.21	.39	1.20		
WASHERS, Main Winding Wheel Hub		.20	.60		
WHEELS, Center, Third & Fourth Gold	.56	1.24-	4.20		
" Center, Third & Fourth Brass	.28	.55	1.80		
" Center Gold & Staff (no Pinion)	1.05	2.24	7.80		
" Center Brass & Staff (no Pinion)	.77	1.59	5.40		
" Center Gold, Staff & Pinion (1 piece)	1.33	2.93	10.20		
" Center Brass, Staff & Pinion (1 piece)	1.05	2.24	7.80		
" Center Gold, Staff, Pinion & Cannon Pinion	1.75	3.74	13.20		
" Center Brass, Staff, Pinion & Cannon Pinion	1.40	3.00	10.80		
" Clutch	.21	.39	1.20		
" Escape Steel	.49	1.07	3.60		
" Escape Steel No. 1894	1.61	3.41	12.00		
" Escape Brass	.35	.75	2.40		
" Escape Steel & Pinion	.98	2.08	7.20		
" Escape Steel (No. 1894) & Pinion	2.31	5.04	18.00		
" Escape Brass & Pinion	.84	1.76	6.00		
" Fourth & Third Gold with Pinion	1.12	2.41	8.40		
" Fourth & Third Brass with Pinion	.84	1.76	6.00		
" Hour & Pipe	.21	.39	1.20		
" Intersetting	.21	.39	1.20		
" Interwinding	.21	.39	1.20		
" Minute & Pinions	.21	.39	1.20		
" Ratchet (Unexposed)	.21	.39	1.20		
" Ratchet Motor Barrel	.98	2.08	7.20		
" Ratchet (Exposed) Concaved	.77	1.59	5.40		
" Ratchet (Exposed) not Concaved	.53	1.14	3.90		
" Regulator Index	.21	.39	1.20		
" Setting	.21	.39	1.20		
" Winding Crown	.77	1.59	5.40		
" Winding Flat	.53	1.14	3.90		
" Winding Base	.21	.39	1.20		
YOKES	.42	.91	3.00		
" With Interwinding Wheel	.60	1.33	4.50		
MATERIAL CABINETS Retail $25.00	16.75				

Above prices apply where specified quantities of one factory number are ordered. No charge for matching.

5% additional discount on all items purchased in 10 gross lots.
10% additional discount on all items purchased in 25 gross lots.

ILLINOIS WATCH MATERIAL DEPARTMENT
Springfield, Illinois, U.S.A.

Illinois Material Price List, October 1931

21/0 Size Movements

Near the end of the Illinois Watch Factory's existence, it made a very small rectangular 21/0 size movement with 15 and 17 jewels for use in tiny baguette or semi-baguette ladies' wristwatches that were the height of fashion at the time. These movements were marked grade 105 for the 15-jewel version and grade 107 for the 17-jewel one. On October 26, 1931, the Illinois Materials Department sent a price list of 21/0 movements, 1st Model, Grade Number 107 parts to its customers. It is shown here.

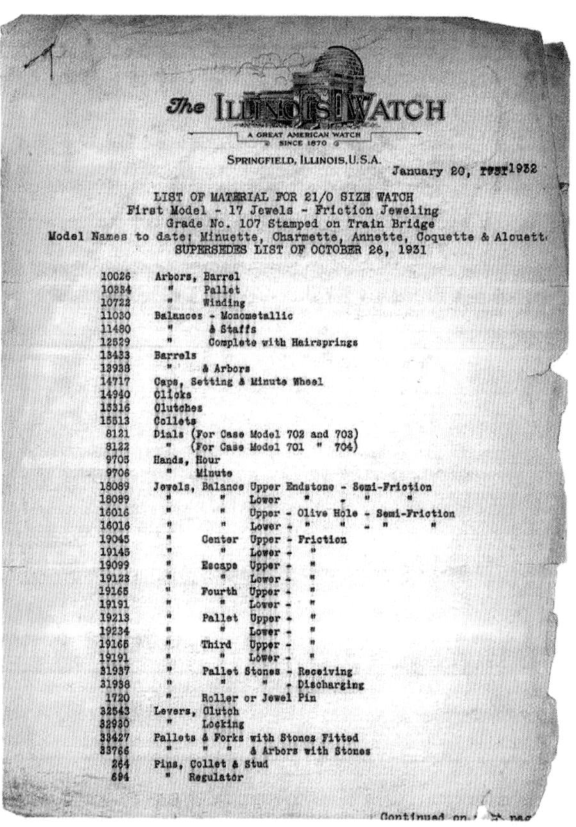

The ILLINOIS WATCH
A GREAT AMERICAN WATCH
SINCE 1870
SPRINGFIELD, ILLINOIS, U.S.A.

January 20, ~~1931~~1932

LIST OF MATERIAL FOR 21/0 SIZE WATCH
First Model - 17 Jewels - Friction Jeweling
Grade No. 107 Stamped on Train Bridge
Model Names to date: Minuette, Charmette, Annette, Coquette & Alouett
SUPERSEDES LIST OF OCTOBER 26, 1931

10026 Arbors, Barrel
10334 " Pallet
10722 " Winding
11030 Balances - Monometallic
11480 " & Staffs
12529 " Complete with Hairsprings
13433 Barrels
13938 " & Arbors
14717 Caps, Setting & Minute Wheel
14940 Clicks
15316 Clutches
15513 Collets
8121 Dials (For Case Model 702 and 703)
8122 " (For Case Model 701 " 704)
9705 Hands, Hour
9706 " Minute
18089 Jewels, Balance Upper Endstone - Semi-Friction
18089 " " Lower " - " "
16016 " " Upper - Olive Hole - Semi-Friction
16016 " " Lower - " " - " "
19045 " Center Upper - Friction
19145 " " Lower - "
19099 " Escape Upper - "
19123 " " Lower - "
19165 " Fourth Upper - "
19191 " " Lower - "
19213 " Pallet Upper - "
19234 " " Lower - "
19165 " Third Upper - "
19191 " " Lower - "
31937 " Pallet Stones - Receiving
31938 " " " - Discharging
1720 " Roller or Jewel Pin
32543 Levers, Clutch
32930 " Locking
33427 Pallets & Forks with Stones Fitted
33766 " " " & Arbors with Stones
264 Pins, Collet & Stud
694 " Regulator

Continued on …

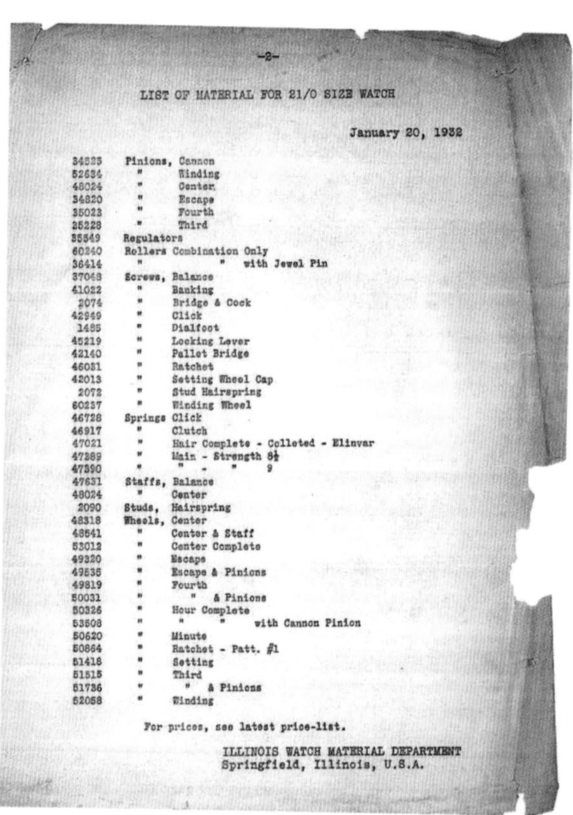

-2-

LIST OF MATERIAL FOR 21/0 SIZE WATCH

January 20, 1932

34525 Pinions, Cannon
52634 " Winding
48024 " Center
34820 " Escape
35023 " Fourth
25228 " Third
35549 Regulators
60240 Rollers Combination Only
36414 " " with Jewel Pin
37048 Screws, Balance
41022 " Banking
2074 " Bridge & Cock
42949 " Click
1485 " Dialfoot
45219 " Locking Lever
42140 " Pallet Bridge
46031 " Ratchet
42013 " Setting Wheel Cap
2072 " Stud Hairspring
60237 " Winding Wheel
46728 Springs Click
46917 " Clutch
47021 " Hair Complete - Colleted - Elinvar
47389 " Main - Strength 8½
47390 " " - " 9
47631 Staffs, Balance
48024 " Center
2090 Studs, Hairspring
48318 Wheels, Center
48541 " Center & Staff
53012 " Center Complete
49320 " Escape
49535 " Escape & Pinions
49819 " Fourth
50031 " " & Pinions
50326 " Hour Complete
53508 " " " with Cannon Pinion
50620 " Minute
50864 " Ratchet - Patt. #1
51418 " Setting
51515 " Third
51736 " " & Pinions
52058 " Winding

For prices, see latest price-list.

ILLINOIS WATCH MATERIAL DEPARTMENT
Springfield, Illinois, U.S.A.

21/0 Size Movement Production Quantities

The production quantities for the 21/0 size movement are broken down as follows:

21/0 Size Movement Production Quantities			
Year	Grade	Jewels	Quantity
~~1948*~~ 1932–1933	105	15	9,800
~~1948*~~ 1932–1933	107	17	13,800
Total 21/0:			**23,600**

*These movements were most likely produced in Springfield in 1932 or earlier, not 1948 in Lancaster.

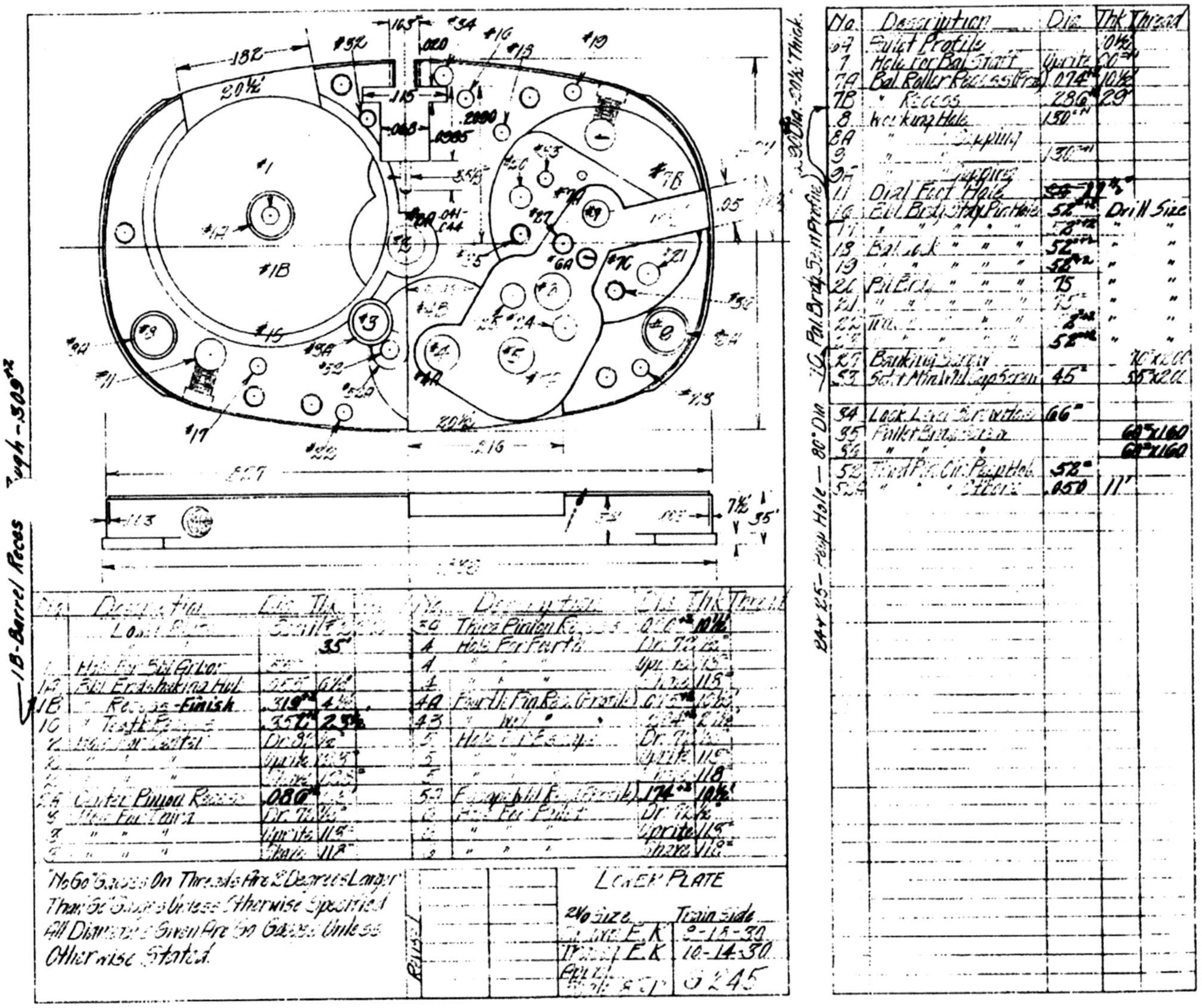

21/0 size Illinois lower plate (poor quality)

21/0 size, grade 105, 15-jewel Illinois movement

21/0 Size Illinois Factory-Cased Wristwatches (All Ladies' Models)

Alouette	Débette	Lynette	Rhea*
Annette	Debutante	Mariette	Rose*
Antoinette	Florette	Marionette	Rosette
Babette (I and II)	Janette	Marlette	Ruth*
Charmette	Juliette	Minuette	Suzette
Coquette	Louette	Muzette	

*Identity unknown

See Appendix 3 for tables of all Illinois movements intended for wristwatches by date, production quantities and serial numbers.

EXISTING ILLINOIS MOVEMENT PRODUCTION DATABASES

Although the Meggers and Ehrhardt book, *American Pocket Watches, Volume 2: Illinois Watch Co.,* and Dr. Russell Snyder's electronic database of Illinois movement production both indicate that Hamilton produced Illinois movements in 1948, this is not likely the case. A review of Chapter 5 of this book will demonstrate that Illinois production capability had ceased to exist long before 1948. Moreover, very few, if any, employees familiar with Illinois movements were still working for Hamilton in 1948. Hamilton had introduced several special Illinois inventory reduction programs in the 1933–1934 time-frame and beyond. These efforts were to such an extent that even in 1933 and 1934, after the Illinois plant had been shuttered by Hamilton, Hamilton sent former Illinois employees back into the closed plant in Springfield in an attempt to gather up enough parts to try to assemble 6/0 size and 21/0 size, 15-jewel movements to enable Hamilton to record some more sales of Illinois watches.

By 1948 there were few workers with the necessary experience available to construct complete movements, only limited parts on hand and certainly no consumer demand for models last offered for sale fourteen years earlier. Thus, it is likely that these movements were not made in 1948 but in 1932 or earlier. Perhaps the Hamilton records reflected sales in 1948 of some of these movements, but not their date of manufacture.

Interesting Movement Projects

16-Jewel, 6/0 Size Movement

According to the list of "Illinois Finished Movements" prepared by Hamilton around 1940, Illinois produced a 6/0 size, 16-jewel, 605E grade movement with the serial number 93147. This entry is odd for a number of reasons. First of all, Illinois is not known to have produced any identified 6/0 size, 16-jewel movements. Furthermore, this entry contains an incorrect serial number; it is likely that the serial number 93147 should instead have read 5,693,147. If so, it fits perfectly within the last batch of 6/0 size movements completed by the Illinois Watch Factory in 1932.

The "E" after 605 means this movement contained an Elinvar hairspring. In its production run of serial numbers 5,692,501 through 5,694,500, all are recorded as 15-jewel, 605 grade, 6/0 size movements with Elinvar hairsprings. Therefore, we do not know if only movement number 5,693,147 or all two thousand movements from this run were made with 16 jewels. However, if all two thousand were, it is quite likely that some would have been sighted by now.

As was explained earlier, Illinois did have a history of occasionally making 16-jewel movements. Illinois produced a 16-jewel, 4-size pocket watch and a 16-jewel, 18/0 size movement, grade 181.

Jump-Hour Movement

The list of "Illinois Finished Movements" contains a 6/0 size, 17-jewel, grade 607 movement, serial number 5,463,066, with the notation that it was a " Jump Hour. " This 1931 production run had two thousand movements numbered 5,462,001 to 5,464,000. As this volume was set to go the printer, an Illinois Jump Hour Prototype surfaced, with movement number 5,463,066. It was in a 14K yellow gold and sterling silver deco-styled case, somewhat similar to a Baronet.

This is the only one known to exist and was owned by the last president of Hamilton before the company was sold. It is shown below.

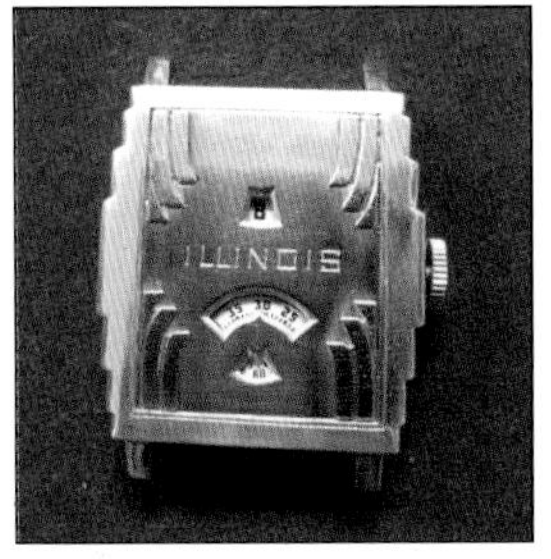

Jump Hour Prototype, yellow gold and sterling silver

Jump Hour Prototype, movement and dials

Incabloc Project

Another revelation from the list of "Illinois Finished Movements" is a note that Illinois in the 1930s had been assigned a project to produce a 25/0 size "Incabloc Shock Absorbing device." This is fascinating news, as the Incabloc system of mounting balance jewels was invented in 1934 but did not take hold in the United States until after World War II. This project was marked "unfinished" by Hamilton, and no Illinois Incabloc movement was ever produced. No other records concerning this unfinished project have been located to date. This information was recorded in the 1940s by Hamilton's Halligan. He likely labeled this an "Incabloc" Project, but as the Illinois project pre-dates the invention by Incabloc, it was probably a quest to develop internally a shock-proof movement. (See Chapter 11.) See Appendix 4 for a partial list of Illinois intellectual property.

Elinvar Watches

Although Hamilton first introduced Elinvar hairsprings in its 992 grade pocket watches in 1931, it did not install them in wristwatches until 1934. In the 1934 Illinois Sales Catalog, it was noted that "The Illinois Watch takes pleasure in being the first to announce a complete line of American watches equipped with Elinvar hairsprings and monometallic balance wheel!"

Elinvar is a nickel-steel alloy having the following major properties:

- It remains comparatively unaffected by temperature changes.
- It is rustless.
- It cannot be permanently magnetized.

For the Buyer

NEW GOODS, NEW LINES AND SEASONABLE OFFERINGS

Elinvar Hairsprings for Hamilton and Illinois Watches

AFTER long experimentation, the Hamilton Watch Company of Lancaster, Pennsylvania, and the Illinois Watch Company, Springfield, Illinois, have adopted Elinvar to their products. This is a nickel steel alloy developed by Dr. Ch. Ed. Guillaume of France over a period of twenty years. The use of Elinvar for watch hairsprings offers a possibility of eliminating the error due to temperature—one of the most serious problems in all watch construction.

An announcement by Milton F. Manby, technical superintendent of the Hamilton Watch Company, states in part:

"As a result of this experimental work, it is now possible to produce watches of railroad grade in which not only automatic temperature compensation is achieved with the use of an Elinvar hairspring and a solid-rim, mono-metallic balance wheel, but many other advantages as well.

"The Elinvar hairspring will not rust and the development of rust spots, (the cause of one of the greatest difficulties in obtaining accurate time over a long period of time) is eliminated. It has also been possible to construct the new movement with its mono-metallic balance wheel and Elinvar hairspring in such a way that it is only slightly affected by magnetism. Even when all the steel parts in the watch are permanently magnetized to their highest degree, the watch will not only run and keep time but its rate is only slightly different from that of the same watch when none of the steel parts is magnetized.

"Only a person who has experienced the extremely erratic timing qualities of an ordinary watch, slightly magnetized, can really appreciate the remarkable forward step which has been made in producing a watch free from this trouble.

"The error in compensation in the bi-metallic balance existed in watches until recently when the research work of Dr. Guillaume, who is director of the International Bureau of Weights and Measures, developed a special nickel steel alloy, which could be used in place of the steel in the rim of a bi-metallic balance wheel and thus eliminate the error. Guillaume bi-metallic balance wheels being very costly to manufacture have only been used in the very highest grade watches and chronometers.

"More recently, however, further brilliant research by Dr. Guillaume made it possible to go back to the hairspring itself and remove the original source of error—that is, the change in elasticity of the hairspring with temperature. This alloy, developed by Dr. Guillaume and improved by him over a period of twenty years, has been called ELINVAR and it is the product which has been adapted to Hamilton and Illinois products."

Keystone, September 1931

HAMILTON INTRODUCES ELINVAR

According to Hamilton, its new research department in 1931 introduced the first revolutionary change in fine watchmaking in four hundred years: it obtained the sole American rights for the use and sale of Elinvar, a new steel alloy invented by Dr. Charles Eduard Guillaume, for which he won the Nobel Award in Physics.

This new and superior nickel-steel alloy, replacing the steel formerly used in hairsprings, greatly reduced timekeeping inaccuracies caused by rust, magnetism and temperature changes. The name *Elinvar* is a contraction of the words "elasticity" and "invariable."

Charles Eduard Guillaume

ELINVAR

For Watches.
Claims use since May 9, 1930.

Ser. 301,105. HAMILTON WATCH Co., Lancaster, Pa. Filed May 23, 1930.

Elinvar trademark registration notice filed May 23, 1930

ELINVAR UPGRADE

In 1931, after Illinois introduced the Elinvar hairspring in certain pocket watch models, its jobbers and many dealers wanted to know if they could get their existing pocket watch stock "reconstructed." (To translate into today's language: that would mean asking if the old stock could be retrofitted or upgraded to contain the revolutionary Elinvar hairspring.) There is a series of correspondence concerning this issue in the Illinois Sales Department files. As a solution, Illinois generously quoted a price of $10.00 per watch to have the watch returned to the Illinois Factory for it to be "reconstructed." Illinois suggested that jewelers charge their customers $15.00 for an Elinvar "reconstruct".

Hamilton-Illinois Movements

For information on the movements utilized in the Hamilton-Illinois wristwatch line from 1953 to 1955, see Chapter 11.

Private-Label and Special-Label Movements

Illinois produced thousands of watch movements either individually branded or co-branded with a name created by a wholesaler or retailer. Collectors call these private-label watches. Some of the private-label watches might be: (a) watches that are actually private-label ones but have no other labeling to indicate what they are; (b) watches that have both dial and movement co-branded; (c) watches that have both Illinois and the private label on the dial but only Illinois on the movement; (d) watches with only the private label on the dial but both the private label and Illinois on the movement; (e) watches with only the private label on the dial and only Illinois on the movement and (f) watches with only Illinois on the dial and only the private label on the movement.

The Illinois Watch Company holds the distinction of having made a greater variety of private-label watches than any other American watch manufacturer. Illinois probably encouraged the practice to a greater extent than the others. The compilation contained in Appendix 5 (with initial data gathered by Meggers and Ehrhardt and since heavily supplemented by the author) represents, in their view, over one thousand major entries. Based on what they knew about the way these watches were sold, their conservative estimate was that perhaps only "25%" of the total number of Illinois private labels are represented on this list. I simplified their list to the name of the private-label customer, its location and approximate date. I have since added names to this list as I have found them.

Illinois made most private-label movements for pocket watches but produced a lesser number specifically intended for wristwatches. Illinois was said to be the most accommodating watch manufacturer in offering special branding. Eventually, this practice wound down as the novelty wore off; another factor was that the Railroad Time Service rules became stricter, outlawing watches privately labeled that otherwise would have been approved for railroad service.

According to Meggers and Ehrhardt, the first Illinois private-label movements appeared in 1872. They think that most of the Illinois private labels are rare because usually only from six to ten individual movements were generally produced in a run.[7]

From 1915 to 1932, Illinois made private-label and special-label smaller-size movements. Presumably, many of these were intended for wristwatches. Some of these special-label movements are very rare. The tables below list some of the private-label names and quantities of movements Illinois produced:

The Master				
Year	**Size**	**Grade**	**Jewels**	**Quantity**
1929	6/0	907	19	50
1930	3/0	27	17	500
1930	3/0	307	17	500
1932	3/0	307	17	1,000
Total 1929–1932:				**2,050**

3/0 size, 17-jewel Illinois private-label The Master movement

"s.a.w." Special Aluminum Watch*				
Year	Size	Grade	Jewels	Quantity
1932	3/0	307	17	200
Total 1932:				**200**

*This was a prototype movement made out of aluminum to be contained in an all-aluminum wristwatch case. Five of these movements and three Akron wristwatches are known to exist. For information about this model, see the **Akron** listing in Chapter 9.

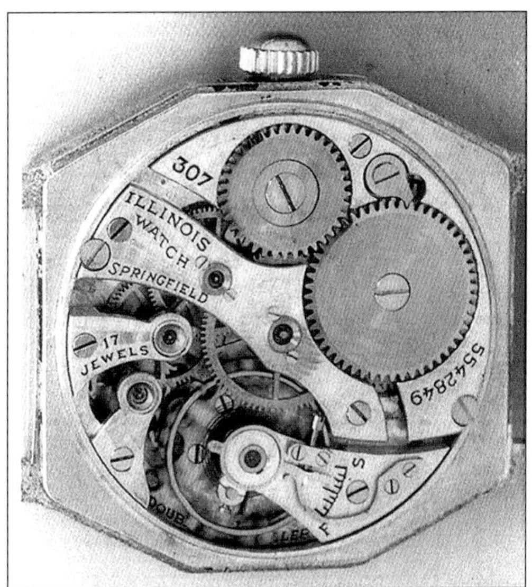

Akron, 3/0 size, 17-jewel, "s.a.w." Illinois movement

Time King				
Year	Size	Grade	Jewels	Quantity
1929	3/0	24	17	2,000
Total 1929:				**2,000**

3/0 size, grade 24, 17-jewel Illinois private-label Time King movement

Aristocrat				
Year	Size	Grade	Jewels	Quantity
1928	3/0	24	17	300
1928	6/0	905	17	1,000
1928	6/0	903	15	100
1929	6/0	905	17	400
Total 1928–1929:				**1,800**

The Aristocrat was a private label for the Kay Jewelry Co.

6/0 size, grade 905, 17-jewel Illinois private-label Aristocrat movement

Sterling				
Year	Size	Grade	Jewels	Quantity
1928	6/0	903	15	900
1928	6/0	905	17	300
Total 1928:				1,200

6/0 size, grade 903, 15-jewel Illinois private-label Sterling movement

Reading Times (Reading, PA), April 14, 1917; image from *newspapers.com*. The Illinois Sterling was apparently a private-label watch for the Kay Jewelry Co.

Washington Herald (Washington, DC), April 4, 1921; image from *newspapers.com*

Illinois Central				
Year	Size	Grade	Jewels	Quantity
1928	6/0	903	15	250
1928	6/0	905	17	50
1928	6/0	907	19	100
1928	3/0	24	17	200
1929	6/0	907	19	150
Total 1928–1929:				**750**

Ser. 285,260. Engass Jewelry Co., Detroit, Mich. Filed June 8, 1929.

ILLINOIS
CENTRAL

For Watches.
Claims use since March 15, 1914.

Trademark registration notice for the private-label "Illinois Central," June 8, 1929, by the Enggass Jewelry Co. in Detroit, Michigan

Illinois Central movement

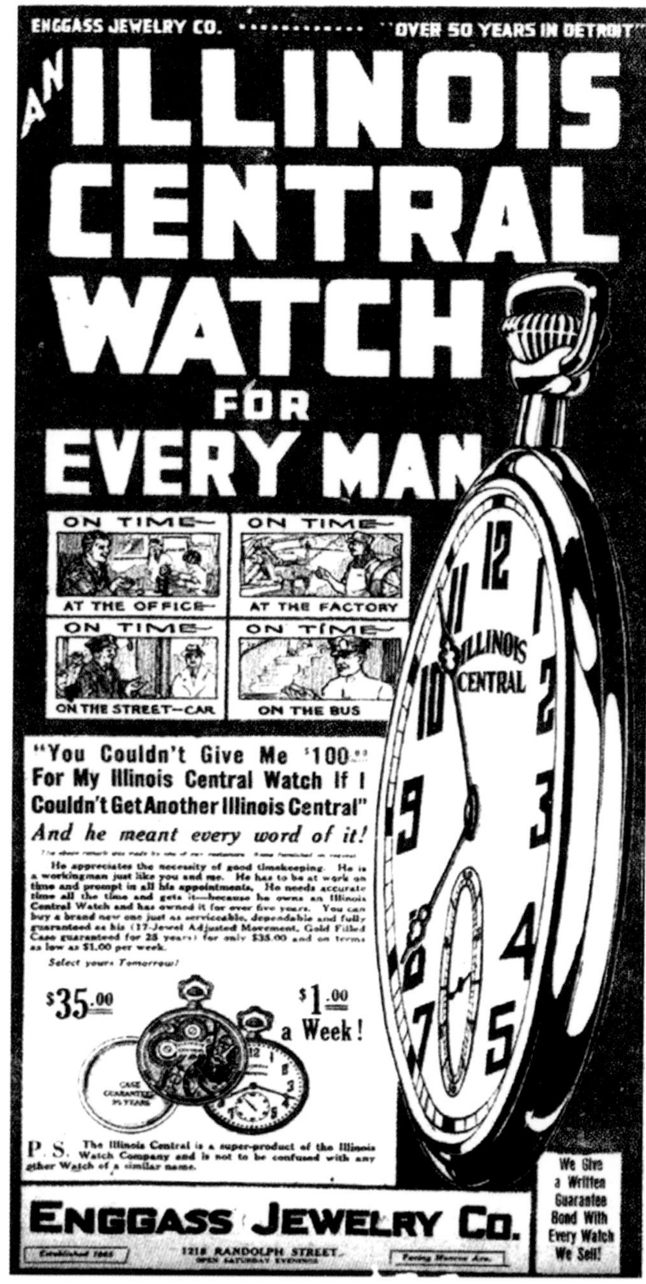

Enggass Jewelry Co. advertisement, *Detroit Times*, May 11, 1923

Many of the Illinois dials and/or movements that have special names on them are thought to be private labels—that is, trade names owned by certain jewelers for their exclusive use. (Aristocrat and Sterling, for example, seem to have been private labels for the Kay Jewelry Company.)

MOVEMENT DATABASES AND DATES

To obtain the approximate date of any Illinois movement, it is best to consult the Meggers and Ehrhardt list in their book *American Pocket Watches, Volume 2: Illinois Watch Co.,* p. 326 (included as Appendix 10 of *The Illinois Watch: The Life and Times of a Great American Watch Company*) or Dr. Russell Snyder's electronic Illinois movement database. However, the collector should bear in mind that the original handwritten Illinois Factory-recorded production documents used by Dr. Snyder only contain dates for the first 500,000 movements produced, and the complete original database housed at the NAWCC has no dates on it. It is likely that different departments within the Illinois Factory had different sets of hand written records. Therefore, the dates appearing in the noted databases may be up to a year or two off for the following reasons and are most accurate for the first 500,000 movements.

There are apparent anomalies with both of these databases. For example, for the years 1915, 1916, 1917, 1918, 1919, 1920, 1921 and 1922, the total annual production quantity is represented at or very near to 184,000 movements per year. These annual totals cannot be accurate, as it is impossible to believe that as the business grew and contracted, the same total number of movements was produced each of those years.

Also, for the years 1925, 1926, 1927, 1928 and 1929, the total production amounts for each year are represented to be at or near 150,000 units per year. Again, such totals defy the laws of business and common sense. However, these databases, long relied upon by collectors, are still valuable because they provide a very good ballpark estimate of the movement date of manufacture

Swiss-Made Parts

From the early 1920s following Charles DeLong's trip to Europe, Illinois would from time to time send drawings of parts to be made in Switzerland, presumably to save costs. Some examples of these drawings and parts are shown here.

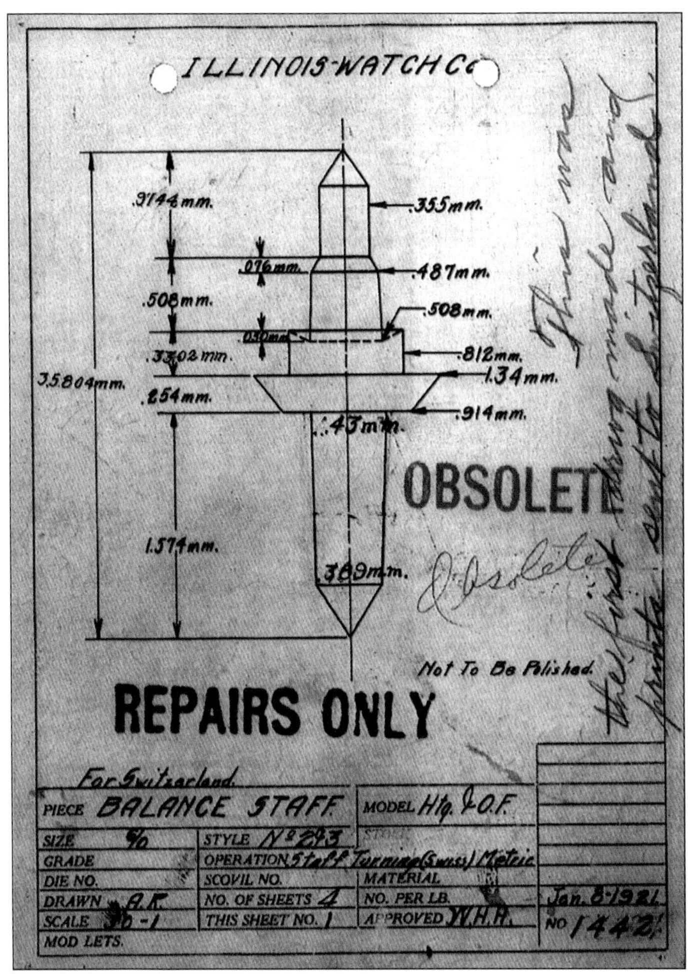

Illinois drawing for a balance staff, revised January 8, 1921. Notice the handwritten notation that this was the first drawing made and the print was sent to Switzerland.

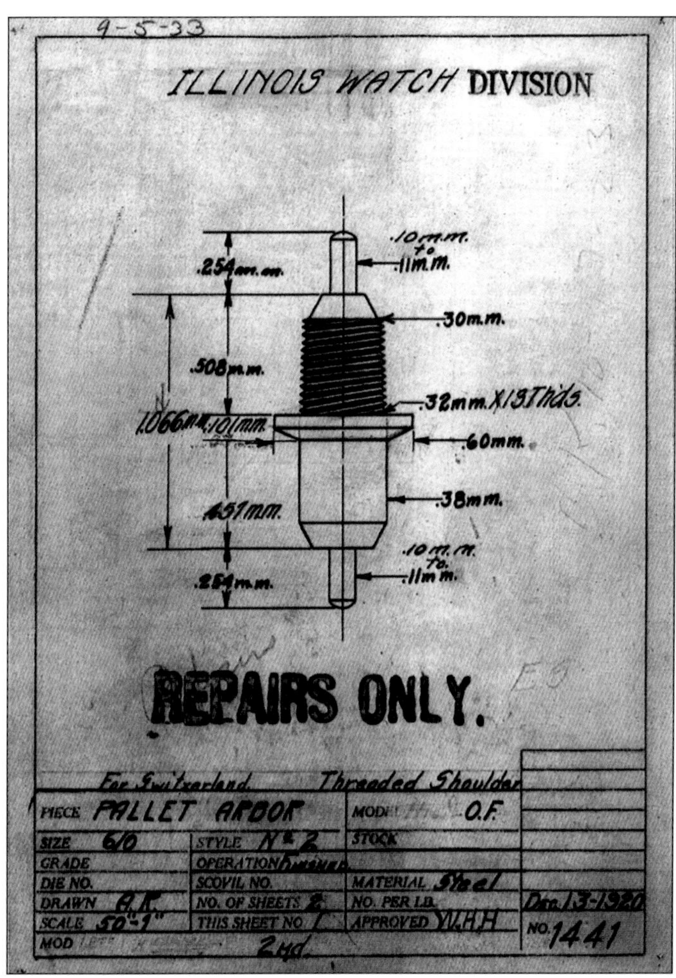

A pallet arbor ordered from Switzerland in 1926

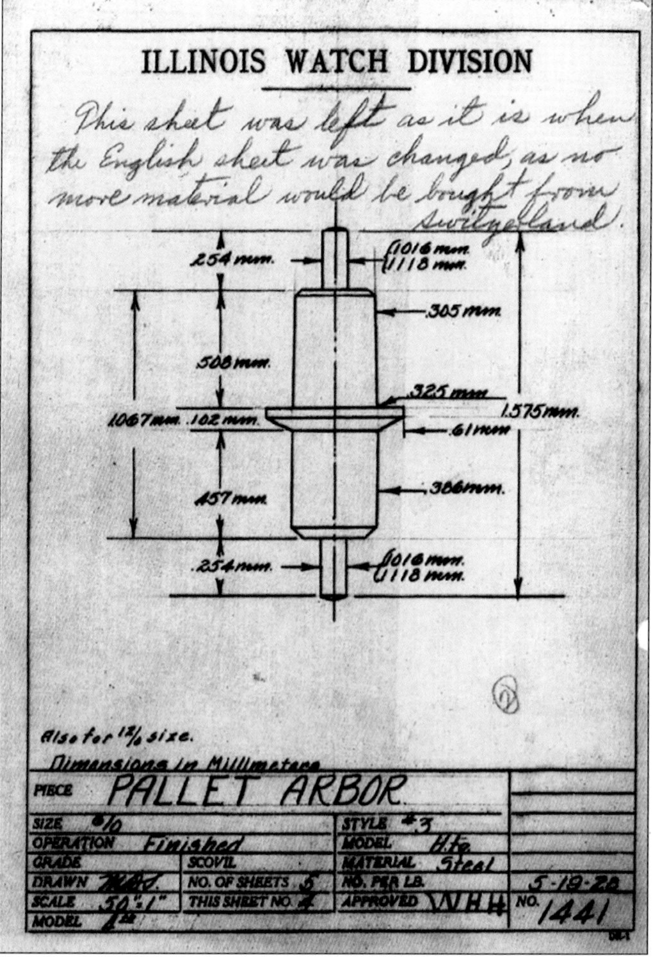

A pallet arbor previously ordered from Switzerland. Notice the handwritten notation that on May 14, 1928, no more material was to be bought from Switzerland. (But this proved not to be the case.)

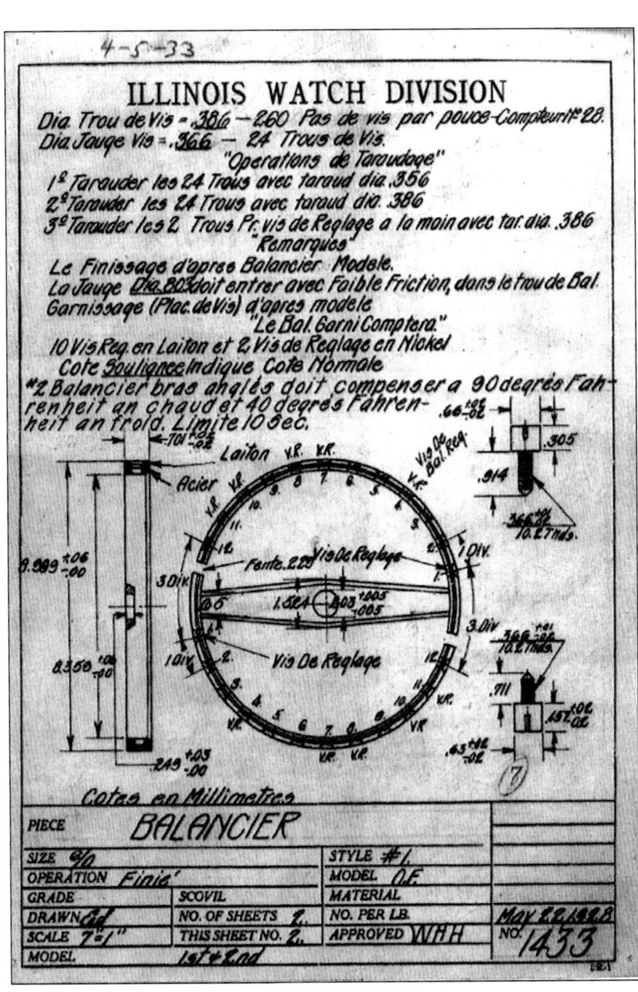

A drawing, May 22, 1928, of a 6/0 size balance to be fabricated in Switzerland

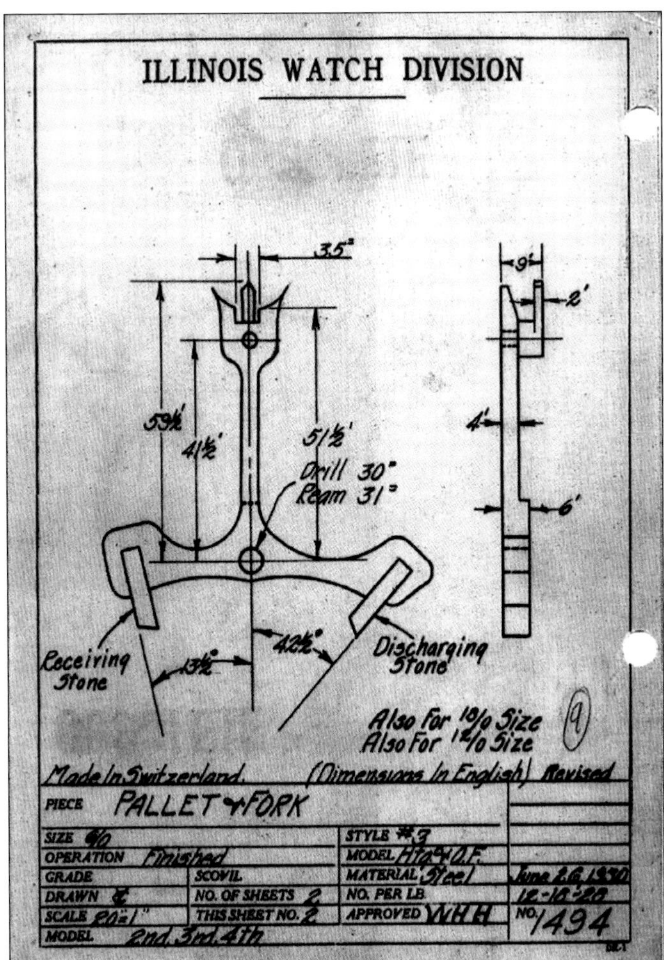

A drawing, revised June 26, 1930, of a 6/0 size pallet and fork to be fabricated in Switzerland

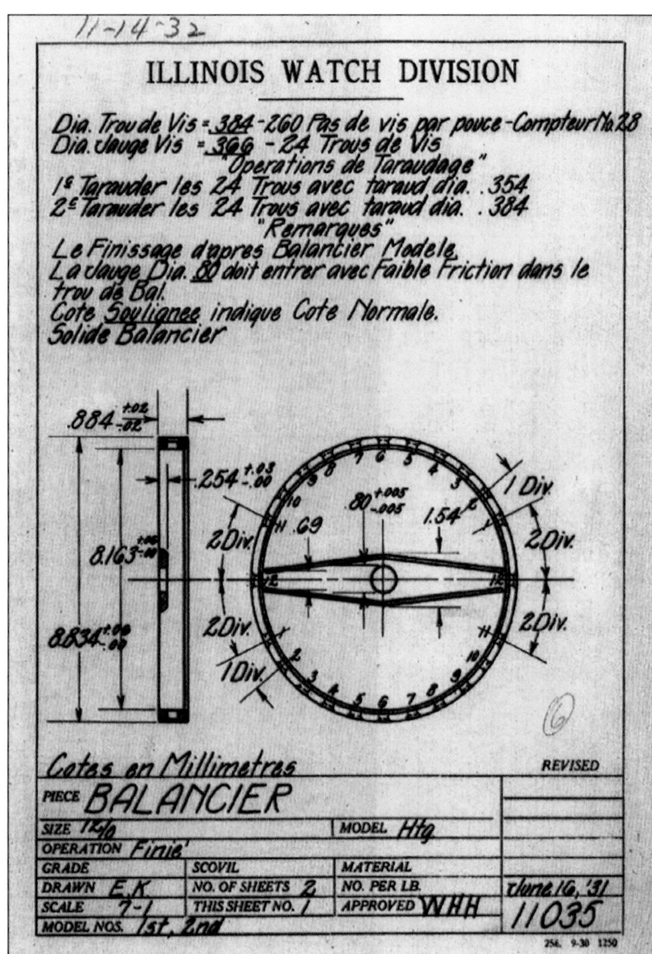

A drawing, June 16, 1931, of a 12/0 size balance to be fabricated in Switzerland

Original Dials for Private-Label Watches

Interestingly, Meggers and Ehrhardt note: "Not all private-label watches have private-label dials; in fact, quite the contrary. Usually, the cost of placing the private label on the movement was minimal to non-existent but the special dial marking was always charged for. Consequently, many private-label–marked watches have Factory or unmarked dials. This fact coupled with the fact that dials are easily changed makes it difficult to establish which watches should have private -label dials unless examples of such are known."[8]

Original Cases for Private-Label Watches

Many of the private-label watches were originally cased in specially marked cases. This most often applied to the high-production private labels. Thus, Santa Fe Watch Co. watches were always originally cased in cases marked Santa Fe Watch Co. and Burlington Watch Co. watches in Burlington Watch Co. cases, etc.

Unique Bridgework on the Back of the Movement

For Burlington, Montgomery Ward and many other large customers, Illinois customized the bridgework on the back of the movement. Where Illinois mostly used a cutaway train bridge, private-label movements carried a more solid bridge. The reasons for this difference remain obscure, but the change in bridgework did serve to differentiate between the Illinois product and its private-label brethren.

Partial List of Illinois Private-Label Watches

A partial list of known private-label Illinois movements and dials, arranged alphabetically, is contained in Appendix 5.

The largest purchasers of Illinois private-label watches were the Burlington Watch Company, Santa Fe Watch Company, Montgomery Ward and Company, Baird-North Company, Sears, Roebuck and Company, and Marshall Field and Company. These firms are briefly described below. It should be noted that their Illinois watches were not Factory-Cased; the companies either cased the watches themselves or outsourced the work.

WHY I COLLECT ILLINOIS

I started collecting Illinois watches for a variety of reasons. The bug bit me and I have never looked back.

For a 12-size collector, there are probably a 1,000 different brand names. I became a specialist (in some of the contract names) and have had very little competition. Some of the names have a special allure for me, such as Ben Franklin, Precis, and Abe Lincoln and Interstate Chronometer. Then there are brands such as the Washington Watch Company, Burlington Special, 19j 12 size Ball and Ariston (Marshall Field's) whose ébauche are different from the standard Illinois layouts. Very little is still known about some of these.

The cases and dials of some Illinois are works of art, like the Illini Grade 538 which sold for $220 (with a hand-engraved dial) in 1922. Unlike collectors of Railroad watches, I pay a lot of attention to the aesthetics of a watch. There are Illinois watches with cases and dials that are magnificent and to kill for that are still very affordable (A Lincoln, Marquis Autocrat thin model and the thin model grades 435–438).

Even though the *Illinois Watch Company Encyclopedia and Price Guide* by Meggers and Ehrhardt is fairly extensive, I own grades that are not listed there. How many people can say they discovered one of a kind or previously unknown grades, etc.? Due to the number of brands, there are still many discoveries to be made. For example, I have the only intact 23j grade 299 hunter (an Ariston) and the movement of a 17j Ariston Hunter (grade 506) with a 14-size dial and 12-size movement. Sure wish I could find the case that went with it. I even have a 23j Ariston with a certificate of rating similar to Railroad watches.

—Robert Schussel

At the request of the private label buyer if it was large enough, Illinois would modify the plates on their private-label movements to distinguish them visually from the Illinois movements and movements of their private-label competitors.

The Rowe
JEWELRY SHOP
WEDDING RINGS
WEDDING GIFTS

SPECIAL REDUCTION SALE

Our special sale of silverware, both in sterling and plate, cut glass and all goods suitable for wedding gifts, will be continued until further notice.

We can also furnish you with the F. W. Rowe special watch, manufactured by the Springfield Illinois Watch Company, in all sizes and grades of cases.

We are prepared to do all kinds of repairing promptly and carefully.

Est. of F. W. ROWE, 175 S. Broad St.

Trenton Evening News, May 29, 1911; image from *newspapers.com*. The Rowe Jewelry Shop of Trenton, NJ, was a private-label customer of Illinois Watch in 1911.

Burlington Watch Company

The Burlington Watch Company, of Chicago, sold watches by mail directly to consumers. It began operation in 1906 and sold Illinois watches until the mid-1920s, purchasing its private-label movements and dials from the Illinois Watch Company and then casing the watches in signed Burlington cases.

Burlington Watch Co. private-label Illinois movement

For about ten years, Burlington concentrated on selling 19-jewel watches, many of which (such as the "Burlington Special") were marketed in contemporary publications. Offering the watches at only $2.50 a month, Burlington's advertisements compared its low prices to those of jewelers, stressing that the "Watch Trust" caused the high prices found elsewhere. Some of the Burlington advertisements against the trusts from 1910 are shown here.

Color cover of the eighty-page 1911 "Trust Busting" Burlington brochure

How the Watch Trust Gained its Power

It seems almost unbelievable that a handful of men should be able to set prices as high as $60 and $75 on the better grades of watches, and *absolutely cut out competition while holding the prices at these enormous figures.*

Yet that is exactly what has happened, and by a very "easy" trust method. It came gradually and let us tell you how.

Forty years ago the individual watch factories in America amounted to but little. Switzerland sent over three-fourths of the watches sold every year. But the superior skill of the American mechanic gradually won out. The American factories doubled, trebled, quadrupled their output; Swiss watches were largely crowded out by American competition.

Then gradually the American factories established their superior quality abroad. Superiority combined with lower prices enabled Americans to export watches and sell them in Europe right next door to Swiss competition.

That began about fifteen years ago, at the time trusts were crystallizing in America like frosted snow on a window pane.

Magnates Agree to "Co-operate"

Then the men at the head of the various watch factories and watch case factories began to get their heads together. They saw their opportunity in a wonderfully growing business. They were rich men, very rich men, with the keenest abilities, and they knew just how to do things without violating the law. These heads of the watch factories, while recognizing that they must sell cheap abroad, had magnificent tariff barriers to protect them against competition at home So they appeared to work in harmony without "too much" competition among themselves, getting long profits for each factory and forcing the trade into line.

How we Hit the Trusts with Our Offer

THIS watch now sold direct at *rock-bottom* price—the same price exactly as *any* wholesale jeweler would have to pay.

A watch, factory-fitted, factory-tested, sent direct from us to the public on our approval plan. Sent prepaid, not one cent to pay until *after* the watch has been inspected by you and found thoroughly satisfactory. And that means satisfactory to you, you to judge.

(And in order to spread the direct offer quickly over the largest possible area, we even allow terms of $2.50 per month during this offer—these easy terms at the same rock-bottom price as for cash).

We Do Not Care

what this fight costs us—we do not care how many profits we must sacrifice—We *will* put our superior Burlington watch before the consumer and let *him* decide upon the merits of this as against any trust product.

The quickest, the surest way is our *rock-bottom* offer *direct* to the public.

Thus we *paralyze* trust method competition.

While *you* get the benefit.

So Let Us Explain

Secrets which the public ought to know—FACTS about the watch industry.

Some *spicy* inner information must come out, even though our best friends among retail and wholesale jewelers take offense.

It is your *right* to know.

Our giant competitors may demur and protest against our methods of talking so frankly about the "trade secrets;" *they* of course do *not* want you to know. But *we* recognize that the more the consumer, the ultimate buyer, knows about watches, the methods of fixing prices, the marketing of watches, etc., the better it is for the manufacturers of *quality* products.

The next time *you*, Mr. Consumer, want to buy a watch, you will know more about watches. You will understand the "how" of fixing prices, and you will *see why* in the United States Congress and before the United States Department of Justice at Washington, D. C., the trust methods of boosting watch prices have been attacked.

1910 Burlington advertisements, emphasizing their "Trust Busting" methods

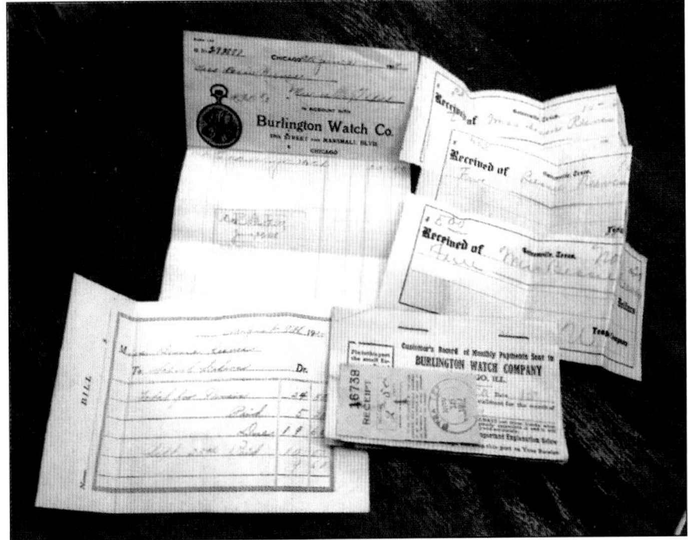

Burlington Watch Co. documents from 1917 to 1920

FIGHTING the Trust!!

The Smashing Anti-Trust Fight Now On!

Trust Prices Eclipsed at Last

An absolutely *first-class* **high-grade** watch at a price within the reach of the people—The Burlington Special Anti-Trust Watch.

The World's Masterpiece of watch manufacture—the Burlington Special—now sold direct to the public at its *rock-bottom, anti-trust* price (and besides without middlemen's profits.)

We do not care what it costs—we *will* uphold our independent line, and so we are making the most sweeping, baffling offer ever made on watches.

Some trusts are legal and some are not. **We do not say that the watch trust is illegal;** but we do say that the **methods** of the giant factories in making "contracts" with dealers **to uphold double prices** on watches is very **unfair**—unfair to **us** and unfair to **you.** Hence our **direct** offer on the Burlington at the **very same** price the **Wholesale** Jeweler must pay.

This is *your* opportunity—**NOW**—while this great Anti-trust offer lasts—get the best watch made anywhere at one-third the price of other high-grade watches. Furthermore, in order to fight the trust most effectually, we even allow terms of **$2.50 a month** on our finest watch—easiest possible payments at the rock-bottom price, the identical price the **Wholesale** jeweler must pay.

Watch Book on request

Now do not miss this opportunity. At least we want you to know about WATCHES and WATCH PRICES. Write Today.

BE POSTED

Send a postal or letter, or simply mail coupon without sending a letter, and get the free book.

BURLINGTON WATCH CO.
Dept. 7233
19th and Marshall Blvd.
CHICAGO

Burlington Watch Co., Dept. 7233. 19th and Marshall Blvd., CHICAGO

Please send me *without obligation* and prepaid your free book on watches and copy of your $1,000.00 challenge—with full explanations of your cash or $2.50 a month offer on the Burlington Watch.

Name ....

Address ....

No letter necessary. Coupon will do.

American Carpenter & Builder, 1910

Technical World, 1910

$1,000.00 Burlington Challenge

We Challenge the Waltham and Elgin factories to a test to prove their watches are equal in quality to the Burlington of the same grade.

We Challenge these factories to deposit $1,000.00 against our $1,000.00 for this competitive test.

We Challenge and defy these factories to prove themselves <u>not superior</u>, <u>but only equal</u> to the factory producing the Burlington.

And in case of a tie the Burlington shall be the loser.

Burlington for several years offered its "$1000 challenge"; here is one from 1911.

We Want a Test

After the Waltham Watch Co. came out with their cleverly phrased challenge, we *answered* that challenge.

The Waltham challenge was so phrased as not to include American competitors; they challenged only the Swiss watches which everybody knows to be inferior.

So we challenged the Waltham (and the Elgin too).

But these factories have not come forward for the test.

HERE IS THE
Waltham Challenge
To Foreign Watches ONLY

WALTHAM WATCHES

The best watches are made by Americans at American wages, with American tools. To prove it we are prepared to offer fifty Waltham watches to be run against fifty watches of any foreign make in a competitive test of timekeeping---the one hundred watches to be placed for this purpose in the hands of some competent and disinterested authority and the WHOLE NUMBER to become the property of the winner.
WALTHAM WATCH CO.
Waltham, Mass.

HERE IS THE
Burlington Challenge
The Challenge to the Waltham and Elgin Companies---The Challenge to the World

OUR $1,000.00 CHALLENGE

To The Giant Watch Factories

We challenge the Elgin and Waltham to a test to prove their watches equal in quality to the Burlington Watches of the same grade. We have deposited $1,000.00 in the Colonial Trust and Savings Bank, of Chicago, and our competitors may deposit an equal sum against this, the loser to forfeit his $1,000.00.

The Swiss factories have not accepted the Waltham challenge. Why not? Because *they knew they would lose.*

Neither the Elgin nor the Waltham have accepted the Burlington Challenge.

Can you suggest better evidence to prove the superiority of the Burlington Watch?

The Burlington Special

BURLINGTON DIRECT GUARANTEE ON BOTH MOVEMENT AND CASE
ANTIQUE BOW OF SOLID GOLD
STEM WIND
FRENCH PATTERN BAR
DOUBLE SUNK DIAL
INTERCHANGEABILITY OF ALL PARTS
19 JEWELS IMPORTED
LEVER SET
REGULATED AUTOMATICALLY TO TEMPERATURE
HAND HAMMERED IMPORTED MAIN SPRING
TUNGSTEN STEEL PINIONS
REGULATED TO STANDARD POSITION
HAND ENGRAVED CASE SOLID GOLD HINGES

Adjusted to the Second

This diagram shows some of the fine points of the Burlington Special.

For full description of the Tungsten Steel, the Superior Mainspring, Micrometer Regulator, and other features, see our catalogue.

But the diagram may give you a faint idea of the exquisite workmanship, the superb quality and finish of the material which will strike your eye when you get this watch (prepaid on approval) and open the back to look at the movement.

Remember---This is our highest grade product, and the factory making the Burlington produces none but high grade watches. To make the best watches requires a factory in which none but high grade watches are made. No rush piece work, no careless workmen.

It takes years of training to make every workman in a factory realize that "*almost right*" is *not good enough.*

Burlington, in its c. 1920s advertising brochure, announced its own Burlington Challenge to Elgin and Waltham to prove that their watches are equal in quality to Burlington's.

In this period, though, the issue was actually free trade rather than the earlier "Watch Trust" matter. Burlington positioned itself as the "trust-busting" company at a time when President Theodore Roosevelt and others were railing against the excess costs imposed by large corporations restraining trade. Watch companies were again trying to implement pricing restrictions, but this time the participants did not trumpet their participation. In order to work around antitrust proscriptions, those involved enforced fair trade practices instead, prohibiting retailers from discounting their watches.

As far as can be ascertained, the Illinois Watch Company did not take part in the fair trade reincarnation of the Watch Trust. This allowed them to sell to Burlington and other Private Labels, which promoted their products as "Trust Busting." However, Burlington's positioning itself as a trust-busting firm was somewhat disingenuous, because much of Henry Babson's (the head of Burlington) income came from being the national distributor for Victor Talking Machines, and that amounted to a trust itself.

In February 1917, Burlington discontinued selling 19-jewel watches and introduced an Illinois-supplied 21-jewel, model 5, Sangamo-grade movement, adjusted to temperature and positions (the number of positions was not indicated). These watches were advertised as "Railroad Time Service" watches in the *Railroad Conductor, the Locomotive Firemen and Engineering Magazine* and related contemporary publications.

1917
HISTORICAL NOTES

- The United States pays Denmark $25M for the Virgin Islands.
- The first jazz recording is made ("Darktown Strutter's Ball").
- The United States ship *Housatonic* is sunk by a German submarine.
- The United States declares war on Germany and enters World War I.
- Jeannette Rankin becomes the first female member of Congress.
- The United States Supreme Court upholds an eight-hour workday for railroad employees.
- The Raggedy Ann doll is invented.
- World War I draft lottery is held.
- First-class mail now costs 3 cents per ounce.
- New York allows women to vote.

In the late teens Burlington started offering men's wristwatches, triple-signed: cases, movements and dials. Burlington advertised them in 1918 as a "Real Man's Wrist Watch." It is still fairly easy today to find Burlington-signed movements in various sizes. In the mid-1920s, Burlington offered for sale its 16-size, 21-jewel Burlington "Bull Dog" pocket watch in the North American Watch Company's heavy-duty railroad case, also signed "Burlington."

UNITED STATES NAVY

Burlington touted its sales of 6,003 watches to the United States Navy in national advertisements.

POPULAR MECHANICS ADVERTISING SECTION 13

6,003 Burlingtons in the U. S. Navy—

A WATCH has to be made of sturdy stuff in order to "make good" on a man-of-war. The constant vibration, the extreme heat in the boiler rooms, the cold salt air and the change of climate from the Arctic to the Tropical are the most severe tests on a watch. If a watch will stand up and give active service aboard a man-of-war, it'll stand up anywhere.

6003 Burlingtons have been sold to the men aboard the U. S. battleships. Practically every vessel in the U. S. Navy has a Burlington aboard. Some have over 100 Burlingtons. The victory of the Burlington in the U. S. Navy is testimony to Burlington superiority.

21-Jewel Burlington $2.50 A Month

And yet you may get a 21-jewel Burlington for only $2.50 a month. Truly it is the master watch, 21 ruby and sapphire jewels, adjusted to the second, temperature, isochronism and positions. Fitted at the factory in a gold strata case, warranted for 25 years. All the newest cases are yours to choose from. You pay only the ***rock-bottom-direct-price***—positively the exact price that the wholesale dealer would have to pay.

See It First! You don't pay a cent to anybody until you see the watch. We ship the watch to you ***on approval***. You are the sole judge. No obligation to buy merely because you get the watch on approval.

Write for Booklet!

Put your name and address in the coupon or on a letter or post card now and get your Burlington Watch book free and prepaid. You will know a lot more about watch buying when you read it. Too, you will see handsome illustrations in full color of all the newest cases from which you have to choose. The booklet is free. Merely send your name and address on the coupon.

Burlington Watch Company,
19th St. & Marshall Blvd., Dept. 1196, Chicago, Ill.

Burlington Watch Co., Dept. 1196
19th Street & Marshall Blvd., Chicago, Ill.

Please send me (without obligations and prepaid) your free book on watches with full explanation of your cash or $2.50 a month offer on the Burlington Watch.

Name ....

Address ....

Popular Mechanics, January 1919

Burlington sold Illinois watches until the late 1920s. The cessation of Babson's Burlington line occurred about the time that Hamilton bought Illinois.

BURLINGTON WATCH COMPANY

In 1906, Henry Babson used a successful career as a phonograph salesman for the Victor Talking Machine Company to capitalize his own company, Babson Brothers, in Chicago. Although Henry spearheaded the firm, his brothers Fred, Gus (aka Nick) and Sanford actively participated in the company. Initially, the firm sold phonographs by mail order from 149–150 Michigan Avenue, Chicago. In order to make ownership easier, Babson sold the high-cost phonographs for low monthly payments. Soon it used the same formula for high-cost items by mail, including watches, tailor-made clothing and agricultural machines, for low monthly payments.

Sanford soon left the company and Gus focused on selling the clothing. Henry, as president, and Fred, as secretary, established a related company to sell quality pocket watches for low monthly payments. To emphasize a close connection with railroad men, the most important market for high-quality (and high-profit) watches, Babson Brothers borrowed the brand name from a nearby rail line, the Chicago, Burlington and Quincy ("The Burlington Route"). The concept of the Burlington watch was born. The brand name attempted to capitalize on America's fascination with its railroads. Further cementing the connection, initial advertisements listed Burlington's address as Millard Station, though it was probably only a mail drop. However, Chicago residents would have recognized this as one of the urban train stations on the Burlington rail line.

Babson Brothers and Burlington maintained a common address at 2845 West 19th Street, Chicago. In order to separate the mail-order business from the retail operation, Babson used the more general address of 19th Street and Marshall Boulevard in its Burlington advertisements.

BABSON BROTHERS' OTHER VENTURES

Henry called upon another brother, George Babson, to head up a Canadian branch of Babson Brothers in Winnipeg. George, a graduate of McGill University in Montreal, had been working in the phonograph end of the business in New York. In an attempt to imitate its American success, Babson introduced Burlington watches in Canada, using H. Moser & Cie. movements in place of the Illinois movements. The Canadian Pacific, for one, accepted the Burlington as an approved watch.

Watches represented only a small part of Babson's business. In these years, Babson Brothers offered a wide array of products through its mail order catalog. Babsons sold everything from electric wall furnaces, using the name "Bulldog," to musical instruments. With the advent of radio, the market for phonographs diminished. In the end, it was Fred's passion for dairy cattle that finally determined the direction of the company.

In the early days of the firm, it offered Belgian-made Mellote Cream Separators for sale, having an exclusive distributorship in the United States. By 1916, Babson began manufacturing what it named the Pine Tree Milking Machine. Then, in 1922, Herbert McCornack, a Babson employee, invented a new milking machine that would tug and pull in a motion, imitating a calf taking milk. Farmers found the machine easy to use and easy to clean. From the time Babson introduced the machine in 1923, it sold well over a million of what it dubbed "The Surge Bucket Milker."

A metal advertising sign for the Surge Milker

After the 1920s, Babson focused more and more attention on selling farm machinery, especially automatic milking apparatus of successively improved designs. In 1999, a German-company, GEA Group AG, purchased Babson Brothers and merged it with a German dairy company to become GEA Farm Technologies.

HENRY BABSON (1875-1970)

Born in Nebraska, Babson moved to Chicago, worked at the World's Columbian Exposition and became associated with fellow Nebraskan Leon Douglass, an inventor of phonograph technology. Soon Babson joined the Victor Talking Machine Company selling phonographs internationally. Since Douglass held the position of vice president at Victor, it is not surprising that Babson soon received a major United States franchise from Victor, selling to retailers, as well as operating a burgeoning mail-order business.

About 1907 he engaged the services of famed architect Louis Sullivan to design his country estate in Riverside, Illinois. The Babson House remains his physical legacy.

Always a lover of fine horses, Babson had discovered his love for Arabian horses at the Columbian Exposition. Around 1930, Babson left the operation of Babson Brothers to others in order to follow his twin passions: breeding Arabian horses and racing sailboats.

The cover of the Babson Brothers Edison Phonograph Sales Brochure, c. 1907

The Babson Brothers produced an impressive 24-page brochure promoting the sale of Edison phonographs in the 1906–1907 time period. The cover of that brochure is pictured here.

BURLINGTON GUARANTEE

To keep up with its competitors, the Burlington Watch Company issued an extremely strong guarantee with each of its watches. The watch was "warranted to be absolutely perfect in the construction and material used in both the case and movement, and should this watch at any time fail to perform its duty properly through the fault of original defective material or workmanship REGARDLESS OF THE NUMBER OF YEARS that have expired since its purchase, it will be replaced by a watch of the same grade or repaired by us without a cent of expense to the purchaser." Thus, a lifetime warranty.

MOVEMENT No. 868747 — OUR DIRECT — CASE No. 1376833

BURLINGTON GUARANTEE

THIS IS TO CERTIFY THAT THE

BURLINGTON SPECIAL WATCH

shipped this day to Mr. James Russell is warranted to be absolutely perfect in the construction and material used in both the case and movement, and should this watch at any time fail to perform its duty properly through the fault of original defective material or workmanship REGARDLESS OF THE NUMBER OF YEARS that have expired since its purchase, it will be replaced by a watch of the same grade, or repaired by us without a cent of expense to the purchaser

We Also Guarantee that the price at which this watch is offered by us direct is positively and absolutely rock bottom. We guarantee that this is the lowest price at which the BURLINGTON SPECIAL is ever sold. We guarantee that it is the lowest price to any wholesaler also the lowest export price, in fact, the lowest price at which this watch is sold in any quantities anywhere

Chicago, Illinois, OCT 9 - 1911

BURLINGTON WATCH CO.

Per E. G. Tuerk

CORPORATE SEAL

A 1911 Burlington Guarantee

Santa Fe Watch Company

The Santa Fe Watch Company, of Topeka, Kansas, started in 1913 and functioned as a mail-order business. Santa Fe ordered private-label movements and dials from the Illinois Watch Company, which signed them "Santa Fe." Its most famous watch was the 21-jewel, 16-size, Santa Fe Special grade 561 pocket watch. Most of these movements were sold in pocket watch cases also signed Santa Fe; the Illinois Watch Case Company made many of them.

Santa Fe watches were sold exclusively via mail order, in much the same way that Burlington watches were sold. Santa Fe advertised extensively in industry periodicals such as *Railroad Trainsman, AT&SF Employee, STL & SF Employee, MK & T Employee, Bo LFE, Popular Mechanics* and *Carmen's Journal.* The advertisements were sizeable, ranging from one-fourth page to a full page and usually emphasizing railroad themes.

There were one thousand 21-jewel Santa Fe Special grade 561 movements produced, all adjusted to temperature, isochronism and five positions. The watches were sold on time (a 1920 advertisement in *Popular Mechanics* puns "Be 'On Time'"), but the actual watch price was not indicated in the advertisements.

Although no connection has been found between the Burlington and Santa Fe operations, they shared a number of common characteristics. Besides borrowing the name of a nearby railroad, each bought watches from Illinois and sold them under its own private-label name. Each sold watches by mail, allowing customers to pay on time. Each advertised widely and guaranteed its product, using very similar promotion and positioning themes. Moreover, each also sold Victor Talking Machine products as part of its business. Santa Fe, as did Burlington, started selling certain wristwatches in the mid to late 1920s to counteract the decline of pocket watch sales. In 1927, Santa Fe advertised a ladies' wristwatch and a men's Illinois Tank model. By April 1930, Santa Fe was advertising the Illinois Marquis Strap model. (See Chapter 9.)

Santa Fe private-label Illinois movement

Important Features of the Santa Fe Special

The Santa Fe Watch Company noted important features of its famous Santa Fe Special watch in one of its advertisements.

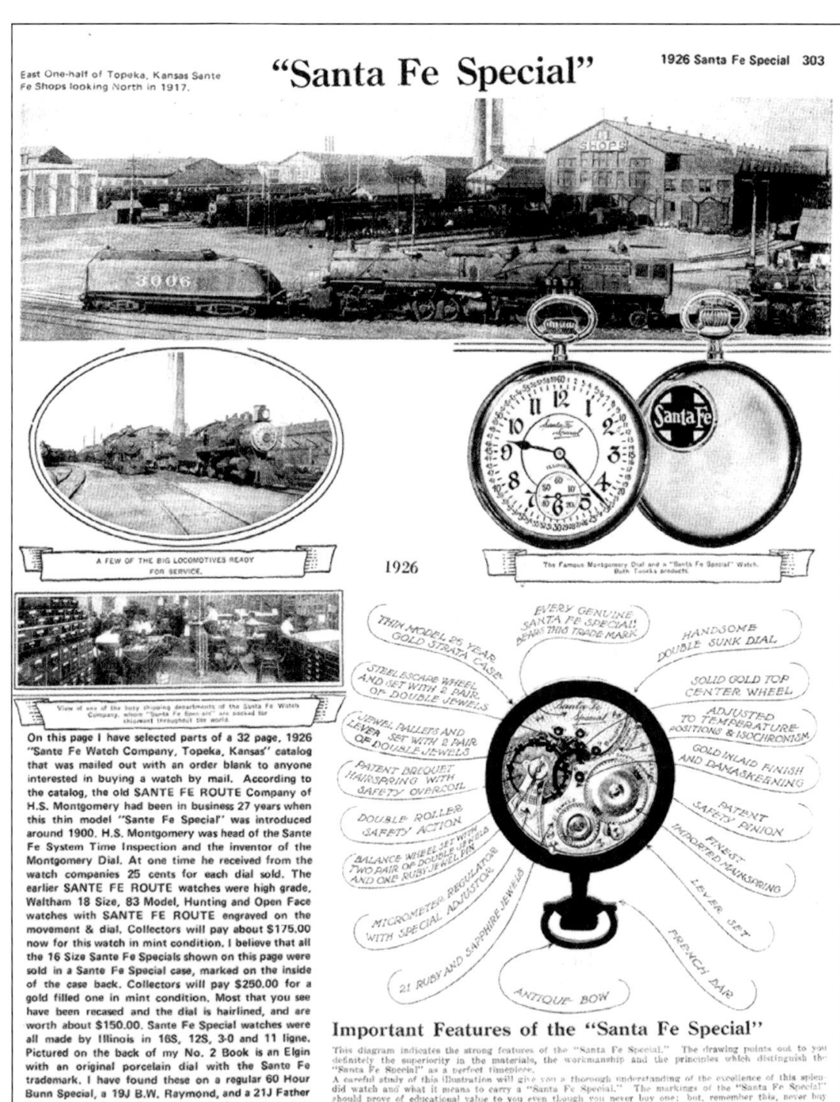

East One-half of Topeka, Kansas Sante Fe Shops looking North in 1917.

"Santa Fe Special"

1926 Santa Fe Special 303

A FEW OF THE BIG LOCOMOTIVES READY FOR SERVICE.

1926

The Famous Montgomery Dial and a "Santa Fe Special" Watch. Both Topeka products.

View of one of the busy shipping departments of the Santa Fe Watch Company, where "Santa Fe Specials" are packed for shipment throughout the world.

On this page I have selected parts of a 32 page, 1926 "Sante Fe Watch Company, Topeka, Kansas" catalog that was mailed out with an order blank to anyone interested in buying a watch by mail. According to the catalog, the old SANTE FE ROUTE Company of H.S. Montgomery had been in business 27 years when this thin model "Sante Fe Special" was introduced around 1900. H.S. Montgomery was head of the Sante Fe System Time Inspection and the inventor of the Montgomery Dial. At one time he received from the watch companies 25 cents for each dial sold. The earlier SANTE FE ROUTE watches were high grade, Waltham 18 Size, 83 Model, Hunting and Open Face watches with SANTE FE ROUTE engraved on the movement & dial. Collectors will pay about $175.00 now for this watch in mint condition. I believe that all the 16 Size Sante Fe Specials shown on this page were sold in a Sante Fe Special case, marked on the inside of the case back. Collectors will pay $250.00 for a gold filled one in mint condition. Most that you see have been recased and the dial is hairlined, and are worth about $150.00. Sante Fe Special watches were all made by Illinois in 16S, 12S, 3-0 and 11 ligne. Pictured on the back of my No. 2 Book is an Elgin with an original porcelain dial with the Sante Fe trademark. I have found these on a regular 60 Hour Bunn Special, a 19J B.W. Raymond, and a 21J Father Time with no Sante Fe markings on the movement or case. These are later watches and are fine collector pieces and now bring about $250.00–when you can find one.

Important Features of the "Santa Fe Special"

This diagram indicates the strong features of the "Santa Fe Special." The drawing points out to you definitely the superiority in the materials, the workmanship and the principles which distinguish the "Santa Fe Special" as a perfect timepiece.

A careful study of this illustration will give you a thorough understanding of the excellence of this splendid watch and what it means to carry a "Santa Fe Special." The markings of the "Santa Fe Special" should prove of educational value to you even though you never buy one; but, remember this, never buy a watch without such markings are plainly engraved on the movement plate, as the law strictly provides that only the true facts regarding the movement be engraved thereon.

1926 Santa Fe advertisement

Santa Fe advertisement, c. 1926

The Santa Fe Watch Company issued an "Iron-Clad Guarantee" with the sale of every Bunn Special: "'The Bunn Special' is fully guaranteed in every respect; warranted to be absolutely perfect in construction, material and workmanship. Should it fail to perform its duty through any fault of original material or workmanship, it will be repaired or a new watch given in place of the defective movement, all without any charge to you."

Santa Fe advertisement, c. 1926

Montgomery Ward and Company

The Washington Watch Company was a private label of Montgomery Ward, a large department store and mail-order catalog operation, now defunct. Illinois produced these movements under contract with Montgomery Ward and stamped the movements and dials "Washington Watch Company." Montgomery Ward would then place their private-label movements and dials in cases of its choice and offer them for sale in its many stores throughout the United States or via its large mail-order catalog, which was updated yearly.

Montgomery Ward and Company issued the following guarantee with its Washington watches: "Our guarantee on higher grades of Washington watches is the most liberal we have ever known. It does not balk at anything, but agrees to keep your watch in order for three years NO MATTER WHAT HAPPENS TO IT. If the watch requires cleaning and re-oiling, we do the work free. If it is dropped and damaged we repair it free and don't ask any questions, also we pay the express charges BOTH WAYS. A printed guarantee to this effect goes with every "Lafayette," "Army and Navy" and "Senate" watch... The lower price Washington watches are guaranteed for one year. This does not mean that they will only last for a year, indeed every Washington watch made will last an ordinary lifetime with proper usage." Talk about a "bumper-to-bumper" warranty!

Montgomery Ward & Co., Kansas City, Mo. Catalogue No. 78

Specially Guaranteed Washington Watches Best for the Money

Prices Complete in Cases are Given on This and Following Pages

If you want to own a distinctively American watch, built on honor and not to sell cheap, buy a Washington. You can show it in any part of the World and truthfully say "This is the best American watch made" and consequently the best watch in the world.

Washington watches are not new experiments. We have sold them for many years with unvarying satisfaction to the users. We control the factory output of Washington watches and we use our control to keep the quality high and the price low. The descriptions of Washington watches in our catalogue are positively accurate and truthful. When we say that a Washington watch is adjusted to position, we mean just what we say.

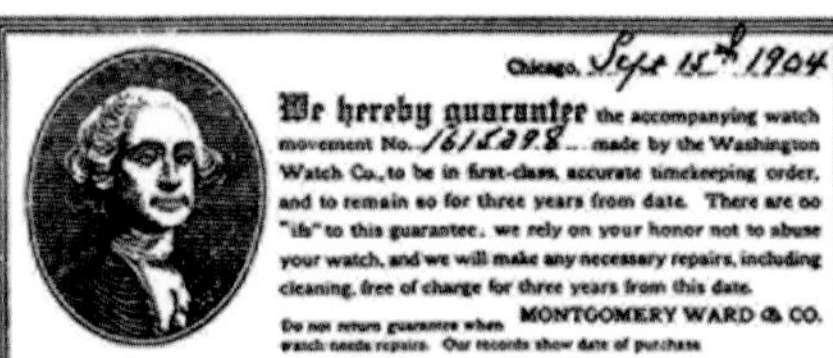
Chicago, Sept 15th 1904

We hereby guarantee the accompanying watch movement No. 1615298 made by the Washington Watch Co., to be in first-class, accurate timekeeping order, and to remain so for three years from date. There are no "ifs" to this guarantee, we rely on your honor not to abuse your watch, and we will make any necessary repairs, including cleaning, free of charge for three years from this date.

MONTGOMERY WARD & CO.

Do not return guarantee when watch needs repairs. Our records show date of purchase

You will find each position adjusted Washington movement stamped accordingly, and if you care to test the watch by running it for 24 hours each in different positions, face up, face down, stem up, stem down, etc., you will find only the slightest variation in each position.

The majority of watches advertised as adjusted to temperature and position have only the ordinary temperature adjustment, and if tested will show a great variation in different positions. The manufacturer does not sell such a watch as "position adjusted," but simply as "adjusted to heat and cold" and the position adjustment exists only in the advertiser's mind.

Washington Watch guarantee

Washington Watch Co., private-label 11-jewel Illinois movement

AARON MONTGOMERY WARD (1843-1913)

A. M. Ward, c. 1890

Aaron Montgomery Ward is credited for starting the American mail-order industry in 1872 in Chicago. None of Ward's friends or business associates joined in his enthusiasm for his revolutionary idea. Although his idea was generally considered lunacy and his first inventory was destroyed by the Great Chicago Fire, he persevered. In 1872, with two employees and a total capital of $1,600, he formed Montgomery Ward and Company. His first mail-order catalog contained 163 products. Though frequently reviled by other retailers, his catalog became known as the "Wish Book" and was a favorite in households all across America. Other retailers such as Sears, Roebuck & Company copied his catalog with their own.

Montgomery Ward died wealthy. His wife bequeathed a large portion of their estate to Northwestern University and other educational institutions.*

*Wikipedia

Plymouth Watch Company private-label Illinois movement

Sears, Roebuck and Company

The Plymouth Watch Company was a private label of Sears, Roebuck and Company, the giant mail-order catalog business and national department store chain. The Plymouth Watch Company was a brand name owned by Sears and sold exclusively by it; its watch dials and movements, made by Illinois, were signed "Plymouth Watch Co. U.S.A."

RICHARD W. SEARS (1863-1914)

R. W. Sears, c. 1900

Sears was founded by Richard Warren Sears and Alvah Curtis Roebuck in 1893 as a mail-order catalog business. In 1925 it began opening retail department stores. Sears was bought by Kmart in 2005.

Richard W. Sears was a railroad station agent in North Redwood, Minnesota, when a large shipment of watches arrived but were refused by a local jeweler. Thereupon Sears bought them, then sold them to other railroad station agents at a large profit. As a result, he ordered more watches for resale and started a business selling watches through mail-order catalogs. The following year, when he moved to Chicago, he met Roebuck, who then joined him in business. In 1893 their company name became Sears, Roebuck and Company.

Interstate Chronometer was another private-label watch made by Illinois for Sears, Roebuck and Company. They were made in 15 and 17 jewels in 0 size; 17 and 21 jewels in 12 size; 17 and 23 jewels in 16 size and 18 size.

Sears sold them as complete-cased watches, usually in a Dueber gold-filled case. The movements and dials were signed "Interstate Chronometer."

Marshall Field & Company

Ariston U.S.A. was a private-label for the Chicago-based Marshall Field & Company department store. The movement and dial, made by Illinois but cased by Marshall Field's, usually came in an Ariston-signed watch case. The Ariston movements were said to be finished to a higher standard than the equivalent Illinois movement. The Aristons are viewed by collectors as "beautiful and elegant watches."

Some of the movements were signed "Ariston Jr." or "Ariste" and others were signed "Ariston Rated." Ariste-branded movements appear among the very first 6/0 size, grade 903 movements produced by Illinois. Marshall Field's issued a special guarantee with the Ariston Rated watch, the text of which is shown here.

THE ARISTON RATED WATCH GUARANTEE

Ariste private-label Illinois movement

"The purchase of a watch should be considered as an investment.

"When a man buys an Ariston Rated watch he buys a lifelong companion—he makes an investment that will net him good service as long as he lives.

"The Ariston Rated watch is one of the few watches that may be relied upon by scientists, technical men, railroad officials and business men alike.

"The essentials of faultless construction, perfect finish and style correctness are embodied in these watches.

"They are built to meet the requirements of railroad and other exacting service.

"They are adjusted to various positions and temperatures, in their cases, before leaving the factory—are timed and tested for a long period before being shipped.

"The rating of these watches is a positive assurance to the purchaser that he is getting what he desires—a perfect time piece—for the rating is a record of the daily running of the watch in the various positions and temperatures it would naturally be subject to in practical use.

"A factory rating card accompanies each Ariston Rated watch and shows exactly the time the watch has kept during its various tests.

"If the daily running and timing shows undue variation in the different positions and temperatures the movement is readjusted—even rebuilt to overcome the slightest defect in its time keeping qualities.

"The rating card is then an insurance that the watch will keep perfect time, for it is an actual record of what it had done and will do.

"We consider the Ariston Rated watch one of the best and most reliable watches on the market, and guarantee it to keep perfect time and give absolute satisfaction."

MARSHALL FIELD (1834-1906)

M. Field, c. 1890

Marshall Field was born on a Massachusetts farm in 1834. When he was nineteen, he moved to Chicago and found employment in a dry-goods store. After the owner retired, he and another employee, Levi Leiter, took over the business. Later he and Leiter opened their own department store. After a disagreement with Leiter, Field bought him out, changing the name of the store to his own.

Marshall Field's went on to become one of the greatest department stores in the world. Field's motto was "Give the lady what she wants." With an emphasis on customer service, the store offered liberal credit and accepted returned merchandise without question. Among its innovations were the first bridal registry and the first in-store restaurant.

Marshall Field & Company was acquired in 1990 by the department store division of Dayton-Hudson (now Target Corporation) and then bought by Macy's in 2005. Marshall Field's flagship store is now known as Macy's at State Street.

The handsome twelve-story granite building, declared a National Historic Landmark as well as a Chicago Landmark, is listed on the National Register of Historic Places. Famous for its interior, which boasts a beautiful mosaic Tiffany favrile glass ceiling containing over 1.6 million pieces designed by Louis Comfort Tiffany and hand-blown by Tiffany's workshop. It took fifty men a year and a half to complete the dome over a five-story atrium. The building is also known for its huge outdoor clocks.

In the history of Chicago, the name of Marshall Field is prominent in other contexts, as well. He was the first major benefactor of the Columbian Museum of Chicago, which had been founded in 1893 as part of the World's Columbian Exposition. In 1905 it was renamed the Field Museum of Natural History in his honor and to better reflect its focus on the natural sciences.

R. H. Macy & Co.

1858, Rowland Hussey Macy founded a small dry-goods store at the corner of 14th Street and 6th Avenue in New York City. By 1877, R. H. Macy & Co. had become a large department store, utilizing space in neighboring buildings to accommodate an ever-increasing number of departments.

Continuing to grow, Macy's needed to find another location, settling on Herald Square on Broadway and 34th Street, where it moved in 1902. After an expansion to more than one million square feet of retail space in 1924, Macy's claimed the title of "World's Largest Store."

Among Macy's offerings over the years were watches, including its Illinois private-label Herald Square movement, named after the location of Macy's flagship store. (Illinois also made the Hallmark private-label watch for Macy's.) Advertisements for private-label watches often made extravagant claims, and Macy's promotion of the Herald Square was no exception, as can been seen from the advertisement shown here.

MACY'S REPUTATION FOR RELIABILITY RESULTS FROM 51 YEARS OF HONEST DEALING

MACY'S RELIABLE HERALD SQUARE WATCH MOVEMENT

Herald Square private-label Illinois movement

"Probably you have often heard of the famous Herald Square Watch Movements, for they are carried by men and women in all parts of the United States, and by American tourists the world over.

"You may not, however, be familiar with the history of the famous Herald Square Watch Movements which were originated and designed by R. H. MACY & CO. nearly eight years ago.

"We became convinced that it was possible to offer American men and women a higher grade, more reliable timepiece for less money, than they had ever been able to purchase it for in the United States.

"The usual MACY method under such conditions was followed. We investigated every point of merit to be found in the various makes of watches offered to the public, and determined to produce a superior Watch Movement and to sell it to our customers on the basis of the actual production cost, plus the extremely small margin of profit which the MACY organization ever ask.

"The now world-renowned Herald Square Watch Movement was the result of our long efforts and has during the past few years won popularity solely upon its merits as a high grade, accurate and economical timepiece, honestly made and honestly sold.

"We specified the standard of excellence that should be maintained and can today say that the 21 Jewel Herald Square Movement is the best timepiece made in America."

Source: William "Bill" Meggers and Roy Ehrhardt, *American Pocket Watches, Vol. 2: Illinois Watch Co.* (Heart of America Press, 1985), p. 299.

The "Herald Square" Watch.

The "Herald Square" Watch is for men—the movements are made and adjusted expressly for us by one of the leading manufacturers in America. Eleven, fifteen, seventeen and twenty-one jewels—warranted to keep time accurately.

Size 16—14 K. Gold Hunting* Case, $25.68 and $31.22.
Size 16—14 K. Gold Open Face, $24.46 and $45.43.
Size 16—Gold-filled Hunting Case, guaranteed for twenty-five years, $ [illegible].92; some in Open Face, $12.92.
Size 16—Solid Silver Hunting Case, $9.68; Open Face, $9.41.
Gun Metal, Open Face, $9.68.

Evening World (New York City), April 29, 1903; image from *newspapers.com*

Hallmark was a private-label Illinois for R. H. Macy & Co.

ROWLAND H. MACY (1822-1877)

R. H. Macy, c. 1870

Rowland Hussey Macy, founder of the world-famous department-store chain, was born in 1822 on Nantucket Island in Massachusetts. He was the fourth of six children in a Quaker family.

In his teens, while he was working as a sailor on a whaling ship, he had a red star tattooed on his hand. A red star was later to become part of the logo for the Macy stores.

Macy began his business career with a succession of dry-goods stores between 1843 and 1851. Although none of these businesses was a success, Macy was able to learn from his failures. Moving to New York City, he established a new dry-goods business there. This became R. H. Macy & Co, one of the greatest success stories in business history.

Originally sole owner of his firm, Macy in 1875 took on two partners in 1875: Robert M. Valentine, a nephew; and Abiel T. LaForge, husband of one of Macy's cousins.

In 1877, Macy died in Paris of Bright's disease.*

**Source:* http://en.wikipedia.org/wiki/Rowland_Hussey_Macy

Baird-North Company

Baird-North Company, gold-and silversmiths, sold watches by mail under the Lexington name. Unlike Burlington and Santa Fe, though, Baird-North targeted the well-heeled market, selling well-crafted jewelry, eye-catching fountain pens and well-made watches, along with other high-quality items. Illinois produced some grade 205, 17-jewel, 0-size watch movements for Lexington-brand ladies' pendant watches. Baird-North also offered Illinois pocket watches for men, some private label (including grades 273 and 404) and, later, Bunn Specials and Sangamo Specials.

Lexington private-label Illinois movement for Baird-North

Not to be outdone by the aggressive guarantees of its competitors Santa Fe and Burlington, Baird-North offered a "positively and unconditionally guaranteed" watch to its mail-order customers. Although it also offered "Waltham, Elgin, Illinois, Hamilton, and New England watches," Baird-North "especially recommend[ed] the Lexington." Of course, the Lexington was merely a private-label Illinois watch made for Baird-North.

Founded in 1895, Baird-North continued in Providence, Rhode Island, as an independent company until about 1929 when it merged with the Boston firm Jason Weiler & Sons, becoming Jason Weiler–Baird North, located in Boston. Jason Weiler & Sons had been jewelry manufacturers in the wholesale and retail business since 1870 and also diamond importers since 1876.

Baird-North, like Santa Fe, Burlington and other private-label customers of Illinois, cased and timed its watches itself. It claimed that "every watch before leaving our establishment is thoroughly cleaned, oiled, inspected, and adjusted by our expert watchmaker. This is necessary in order to remove the gummy oil, dust, and lint which accumulates in a movement before it is put into a case."

WILLIAM HUSSEY (1857-1908)

Born in Maine, William Hussey moved to Salem, Massachusetts in 1893. Although he was the son of a farmer and granite quarry owner, William decided to try his hand at the jewelry business. Soon his firm became well known as goldsmiths and silversmiths. In 1895 he founded Baird-North, which in the next twenty-five years grew to be the largest mail-order jewelry firm in the United States. Baird-North moved to Providence, Rhode Island, in 1907 in order to benefit from that city's position as a center of jewelry manufacturing. However, within weeks of the move, William died.

After William's death, his son George took control of the business and moved to expand sales. Mostly known for ladies' jewelry, silverware and quality fountain pens, Baird-North also offered quality watches, some under its private Lexington label.

The BAIRD-NORTH Establishment is one of the favorite show places of Providence, whidh is the textile and jewelry center of the world. The building occupies an entire block on Broad Street, about two miles from the center of the city.

Postcard of the Baird-North facility in 1921

GEORGE HUSSEY (1884-1918)

George Hussey was born in Augusta, Maine. When he was about nine, his father moved the family to Salem, Massachusetts, and soon established a mail-order jewelry firm. George finished high school in Salem and attended Dartmouth College. He also studied at the Waltham School of Horology. George soon joined his father's firm and worked in its various departments to familiarize himself with the business.

In 1907 he moved with Baird-North to Providence. Weeks later, after his father died, George, at age twenty-three, took over Baird-North. Contemporary sources credited his efforts for the expansion of Baird-North into the largest mail-order jewelry firm in the country, which additionally made it the fourth-largest mail-order firm in the United States.

Cover of the 1931 Jason Weiler–Baird North catalog

Cover of the 1923 Baird-North catalog

Jewelers' Circular, February 1922

Almost 100 years later, Illinois watches continue to run at the same high degree of accuracy and reliability—with proper care and maintenance— as explained in the Repairperson Interviews that follow.

Repairperson Interviews

To help learn about some of the idiosyncrasies and special features, techniques and practical advice concerning working on vintage Illinois watch movements, the following interviews were conducted by me (FJF) with Ed Kulha (EK), a hobbyist/repairperson, and Jesse Hueg, a professional "Master Watchmaker" (JH) in Albany, New York.

Ed Kulha has a degree in mechanical engineering, which certainly has something to do with his interest in and fascination with vintage wristwatches. It started after seeing an ad in *GQ* magazine showing a vintage Rolex Bubbleback. Initially, it was purely buying and collecting—Bulova, Gruen, Elgin, etc. His favorite quickly became Hamilton and, surprisingly, Illinois was just not his thing! Not until joining the NAWCC and thereby gaining access to my "Anything Illinois" mailings did he eventually purchase some Illinois watches and catch the bug. Since then, he has spent many years collecting Illinois, though never has he neglected collecting *any* interesting vintage watch of another brand as well.

Moving to New Hampshire in 1991, Kulha met Fred Jamros, owner of a jewelry and watch repair shop in North Chelmsford, Massachusetts. Seeing Kuhla's interest in learning, Jamros, a graduate of the Waltham School of Horology, offered to teach him everything he knew about watch repair. Vintage watch repair and restoration then became Kulha's passion, while pursuing his "real" career as an executive in support equipment for the semiconductor industry.

Jesse Hueg, after completing the two-year program at the Joseph Bulova School of Watchmaking, went on to a three-year apprenticeship. He then received factory training by Rolex, Jaeger Le Coultre, Tag Heuer and Ebel (to name a few). Hueg now performs precision repairs for all brands of watches from his Albany repair center.

WATCH REPAIRING

The profession of watch repairing was promoted as a good opportunity for gainful employment as early as 1917 in various *Popular Mechanics* advertisements. Later, the Bradley Polytechnic Institute in Peoria, Illinois, would be the most prominent school for watchmakers.

LEARN WATCHMAKING

Big Demand For Trained Men

Great shortage of watchmakers, watch and clock repair men! Grasp this amazing opportunity. Steady employment in any section of the country. Uncrowded money-making field. We help you get big-pay job. Or you can own your own repair shop—easy to start—we show you how—fine income right from the beginning. NOW is the time to start—employers are writing us for trained men. Greatest opportunity of your life!

WE TEACH YOU QUICKLY

Takes but a few months to learn. Day or night school, no books; all personal instruction. Our profit-sharing plan helps you earn tuition. Work your way through school. We help you get part-time job.

FREE BOOK Write today for interesting book on watchmaking. It shows you the tremendous growth of the watch and clockmaking industry, the need for expert watchmakers and the wonderful money making prospects for men who are trained by our competent instructors **Write Today.** NO OBLIGATION.

NATIONAL SCHOOL OF WATCHMAKING
1340 South Michigan Avenue Dept. 13 Chicago, Ill.

Popular Mechanics, October 1917

LEARN WATCH REPAIRING

You can learn by our modern and original system of instruction every part of the **Watch Repairing Trade** at home as good or better than at a shop. You can earn money while learning and secure a well paying position or start in business after completing our course of instruction. Good watch repairers are always in demand and earn from $20 to $35 per week. For particulars apply to the **Wisconsin School of Watchmaking, Stroh Bldg., Milwaukee, Wis.**

Popular Mechanics, December 1917

1. FJF: What is the best way to acquire parts for repairs?

EK: Relative to American wristwatches, Illinois is somewhat unique in that the Illinois wristwatch was relatively short-lived as compared to other American brands such as Hamilton, Elgin, Waltham, etc. As such, parts were never as plentiful as many other brands. Illinois wristwatches started with Transitional Period watches, wristwatches made from men's and more often ladies' pocket watch and pendant movements in the 1910s and 1920s. In the mid-1920s, Illinois primarily transitioned to wristwatch-specific movements, moving away from using the small pocket watch and pendant movements. Having a few dependable parts supply houses to work with is a must. Having a selection of old movements is also a must and can save lots of time searching with outside sources.

JH: If new parts are not available, purchasing old movements can be very helpful in securing needed items. Just remember that these movements are on the market and not working for a reason, so do not assume that they will have all the parts you may need. If purchasing a movement for salvage, ask if it is running before deciding on a price.

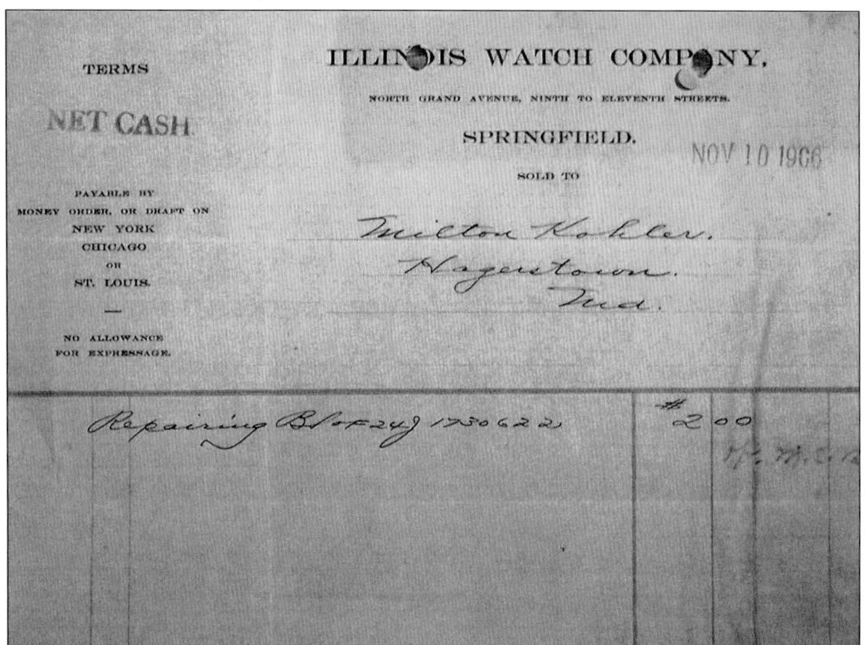
TERMS

NET CASH

PAYABLE BY
MONEY ORDER, OR DRAFT ON
NEW YORK
CHICAGO
OR
ST. LOUIS.

NO ALLOWANCE
FOR EXPRESSAGE.

ILLINOIS WATCH COMPANY.

NORTH GRAND AVENUE, NINTH TO ELEVENTH STREETS.

SPRINGFIELD.

NOV 10 1906

SOLD TO

Milton Kohler,
Hagerstown.
Ind.

Repairing B of 24J 1730622 — $2.00

1906 Illinois repair invoice for an 18-size, 24-jewel Pennsylvania Special movement

2. FJF: Can you still find New Old Stock (NOS) parts?

EK: In my experience repairing wristwatches for over twenty-four years, I honestly have never seen a NOS Illinois-labeled wristwatch part other than mainsprings, crystals and a few dials. The mainsprings, being spring steel, often have some level of oxidation noticeable which should be carefully cleaned off prior to use. Other commonly needed parts such as balance staffs, wheels and gears, I have only acquired through a few of my favorite parts houses as "used" parts. Of course, it never hurts to have a stash of a variety of used Illinois movements available for parts salvage. Over the years, watch cases, especially the solid gold ones, have been victims of meltdown value and left many lone movements to exist without a case, if they were not thrown away altogether. There has been a resurgence of this reality in recent times owing to the record-setting gold prices.

JH: Many, but not all, commonly used parts such as balance staffs and mainsprings are still being manufactured as replacements, but parts such as train wheels and other major NOS components are difficult to find at best. Your watchmakers' connections to material houses will be helpful in securing hard to find parts. The collector can be helpful by doing some research on his/her own, thereby freeing the watchmaker to concentrate on repairs.

3. **FJF: Can parts from other manufacturers be substituted for Illinois parts?**

EK: Other than mainsprings and crystals, parts for Illinois movements are unique to the Illinois brand, as far as I know. Some parts are interchangeable amongst different model Illinois pocket and wristwatch movements, but not with other brands. There are some original varieties of Illinois hands that do not appear to be common to other brands. In particular, I have found the luminous Illinois hands to have a unique style to Illinois. Finding "generic" luminous hands to perfectly match the original-style hands sold on Illinois has proven impossible for me. As such, many Illinois watches with replacement luminous hands simply do not have that "exact" look that was original to the Illinois watch.

JH: This is very limited, as Illinois was the sole manufacturer of their movements. I have found some limited interchangeability with mainsprings.

Page 112 The KEYSTONE July, 1921

Why sell the best watches and use imitation materials in repairing them?

Your reputation is as much at stake in the one transaction as in the other.

Why not be genuine all through?

Genuine materials are standard in size and quality. They are interchangeable, and when you replace a damaged part with new material from the factory the watch is of the same high quality as before.

This is not the case when imitation materials are used. They are not standard and the quality is open to question. Besides, they cause you more trouble and annoyance than you save in the difference in cost.

Why not increase your satisfaction and get better prices for your watch work by using the genuine materials when repairing *Illinois-Springfield Watches?*

Your material jobber can supply you with these whenever needed, or if you prefer, you can send your orders direct to the factory, where they will be given prompt attention.

A net price list will be sent upon request

ILLINOIS WATCH COMPANY
SPRINGFIELD, ILLINOIS

Keystone, July 1921. Illinois always promoted the use of genuine parts.

4. FJF: What parts are most likely to fail and why?

EK: Unlike other American-made vintage wristwatches, Illinois watches were only made of higher jewel count movements. Metal-to-metal bearing surfaces and associated wear was virtually nonexistent in the drive train, as most bearing surfaces were jeweled. If a vintage Illinois watch has been taken care of over the years, it is likely even now that the watch just needs a full dismantle, cleaning of all the parts, reassembly with new oil in the bearing surfaces, etc. Sometimes the winding/setting clutch and/or the winding pinion will need to be replaced. Remember, there was a time that a man or woman likely had one watch; as such, that watch was wound and worn daily. With the winding train being exercised daily for many years, the metal-to-metal contact surfaces were prone to wear. Eventually, such wear will lead to a sloppy stem-to-movement fit allowing slippage and grinding of wind-set components; the same goes for the clutch and winding pinion.

TRAIN

From the mainspring, the power travels through a series of four wheels, called the train, to the balance wheel. Three of the wheels are brass, with toothed edges. The teeth must be absolutely exact in size; in many watches, they measure only two thousandths of an inch in diameter, midway between their base and their center point.

Equally important to cleaning the movement is cleaning of the case and the crystal, as dust and dirt does tend to migrate into the watch. Actually, atmospheric changes can help induce transfer of such contaminants. This is the reason watch cases, crowns and crystal eventually moved towards more and more sophisticated levels of gasketing. A new mainspring is always a good idea because, by design, each time a mainspring winds down, there is metal-to-metal friction along the entire length of the spring. The watches were prone to being magnetized if placed alongside a picture-tube type TV, speaker or other magnetic source. Demagnetizing is a simple operation with the right equipment, one not too strong to alter the delicate nature of the hairspring. A likely part to fail as a result of abnormal abuse from shock due to impact or a drop is the balance staff. Jewels can break as a result, too. Illinois watches were in the era prior to Incabloc, a shock-absorber mechanism built right into the upper and lower jewels of the balance wheel.

JH: Balance staffs tend to break due to extreme shock, and mainsprings fail due to age and forced overwinding.

Mainspring boxes

ILLINOIS WATCH MAINSPRING CHART
Springfield, Illinois, October 26th, 1931

New Number	Size	Old Number	Millimeter Thickness	Millimeter Width	Dennison Thickness	Dennison Width	Length Inches	Style Brace	Cabinet Compartment No.	Remarks
47301	18	53	.20	2.93	3½	20	21½	T		
47302	18	53	.21	2.93	3	20	21½	T		
47303	18	53	.22	2.93	2	20	21½	T	193	
47309	16	1759	.15½	3.00	6¾	21	27	M. Bbl.		All 60 Hour
47314	16	573	.18	2.70	5	18	20½	Double		Small Barrel .744" Tooth Diameter
47315	16	573	.18½	2.70	4½	18	20½	Double		
47316	16	573	.19	2.70	4	18	20½	Double	196	
47317	16	573	.20	2.70	3½	18	20½	Double	197	
47321	16	1770	.18	2.70	5	18	22½	Double	199	Large Barrel .762" Tooth Diameter
47322	16	1770	.18½	2.70	4½	18	22½	Double	198	
47326	16	1954	.17	2.70	6	18	22½	M. Bbl.	200	For All Bunn Special M. Bbl. Watches Except 60 Hour
47327	16	1954	.17½	2.70	5½	18	22½	M. Bbl.	200	
47330	16 Extra Thin	1952	.17	2.70	6	18	22½	M. Bbl.		Sangamo Special
47331	16 Extra Thin	1952	.17½	2.70	5½	18	22½	M. Bbl.		
47333	16	124	.20	2.90	3½	20	20½	T	195	Thick Barrel .150"
47334	14 & 16	365	.21	2.50	3	16	20	T	194	Thin Barrel .138"
47336	12 & 13 Extra Thin	1845	.16	1.34	6½	5	18½	M. Bbl.	204	Motor Barrel
47337	12 & 13 Extra Thin	1845	.17	1.34	6	5	18½	M. Bbl.		
47338	12 & 13 Extra Thin	1845	.18	1.34	5	5	18½	M. Bbl.		
47343	12	1236	.17	1.99	6	11	18½	Double	202	
47344	12	1236	.18	1.99	5	11	18½	Double	201	
47349	12	1953	.15	1.99	7	11	18½	M. Bbl.	203	Motor Barrel
47350	12	1953	.16	1.99	6½	11	18½	M. Bbl.		
47353	4 & 6	171	.16	1.77	6½	9	14	T	205	
47354	4 & 6	171	.17	1.77	6	9	14	T		
47355	8	311	.18	1.77	5	9	17	T		
47357	O & 3/0	981	.12½	1.70	9¼	8	13	T		
47358	O & 3/0	981	.13	1.70	9	8	13	T		
47359	O & 3/0	981	.13½	1.70	8½	8	13	T	206	
47363	6/0 O.F.	1422	.12½	1.18	9¼	3	10½	Double	207	Open Face
47364	6/0 O.F.	1422	.13	1.18	9	3	10½	Double		
47365	6/0 O.F.	1422	.14	1.18	8	3	10½	Double	208	
47370	6/0 Htg.	1095	.11	1.41	10	5	12½	Double		Hunting
47371	6/0 Htg.	1095	.11½	1.41	9¾	5	12½	Double		
47376	12/0	358	.12	1.18	9½	3	14½	Double		
47377	12/0	358	.12½	1.18	9¼	3	14½	Double		
47380	18/0	2092	.10	1.20	11	3	12	Tongue		Hook in Barrel
47383	18/0	2092	.09	1.20	12	3	10	Double		
47384	18/0	2092	.09½	1.20	11½	3	10	Double		
47389	21/0	....	.08½	1.02	12½	1	8 3/10	Double		
47390	21/0	....	.09	1.02	12	1	8 3/10	Double		

Please order by the new numbers to insure prompt and accurate filling of your orders. For instance "6 dozen No. 47301"
Each spring packed in glassine envelope and sealed at the factory. These envelopes show the above dimensions.

Illinois mainspring chart, October 26, 1931

Illinois mainspring box

Mainspring box

5. **FJF: What is the most difficult fix on an Illinois movement? And the easiest?**

EK: If a part is broken and a replacement cannot be found, a suitable part must be made from scratch, which can be quite a task, requiring an expert, full-service watch craftsman or precision machinist and associated metal cutting/forming tools and machinery. As for repairs of watches along with their original parts, replacing balance staffs can be sometimes be challenging for hobbyists, along with setting up/adjusting the pallet jewels and their interface with the escape wheel. Replacing broken jewels is precision work too, being careful not to damage the seat upon removal of the broken jewel and to not break the new jewel upon press-fit insertion.

JH: The most difficult repair is undoing a previous repair that has been poorly done.

FTC COMPLAINT

On June 20, 1930, the Federal Trade Commission filed a complaint against Bulova for unfair competition in the stamping of its watches as to jewels and adjustments.

The complaint charged that certain watches made and sold by Bulova were stamped 17, 19, 21 and other numbered jewels when, in fact, all of the jewels of these watches did not serve a mechanical purpose as a functional bearing.

Another charge pertained to the practice of some of the watches being marked "adjusted" or "adj" in a way to imply that the watches had been adjusted to heat, cold, isochronism, and position when, in fact, the watches had not been adjusted to all of these conditions.

Bulova initially strongly rejected these charges but, on July 25, 1932, agreed "to cease and desist" from these practices.

6. FJF: How do you remove a 3/0 movement from its case?

EK: 3/0 size movements are basically small pocket watch movements that were small enough to use in a wristwatch as well. Once the technology got more modern in the mid-1920s, it became possible to make more desirable watch case designs via use of rectangular movements and smaller designs with smaller movements. 3/0 size movements were typically installed in three-piece watch cases; that is, a front bezel, a body and a back. Typically the bezel and back were snap on. Removing the 3/0 movement from the case is accomplished as follows:

Remove the front bezel. Protecting the dial with a thin piece of paper or plastic, use a hand puller to carefully remove the hour, minute and second hand (if the watch has one). Remove the hands before you remove the case back to avoid pushing on the balance and breaking the staff while removing the hands. Then remove the back of the case, leaving the movement still mounted in the center section of the case. Again, be very careful not to push on the watch movement internals, especially the balance wheel. Remove the two movement mounting screws at the rear of the movement that secure it to the case. Pull out the watch crown to the "set time" mode. This withdraws the stem, which on a 3/0 size movement is part of the watch case, not the movement. This will lend to easier removal of the movement. Preferably with clean latex gloves, gently push the movement from the back side to enable the movement to be removed from the front side of the case. You should push the back side of the movement from the side of the dial opposite the stem, which is at 3 o'clock; that allows you to angle the watch out of the case away from the stem still partially inserted into the movement. Once the movement is removed, the dial can be carefully removed via loosening the two or three tiny case screws in the movement sides.

JH: With a forklift and a hammer— Just checking if you're still paying attention—

First you must know if your watch has a screwed-on or friction-fit bezel! If the watch is rectangular or cushion shaped, then you can safely assume that it is friction fit and will snap on and off. If it is round, get some advice before attempting the removal. First remove the two casing screws; these will be at the outer edge of the movement making contact with the inner edge of the case. Once these are out, remove the bezel with a thin, sharp blade by first anchoring it in the groove between the bezel and the case and then applying a slight prying motion. If the bezel does not come off easily, you can move down the case and repeat the procedure. Once the bezel has been removed, gently guide the movement out of the case through the opening of the bezel. Then pressure should be first put on the side opposite the stem. To reinstall the movement, repeat the procedure in reverse, paying careful attention to the alignment of the stem into the square on the movement's 3 o'clock side. The stem should slide into this square, and then the movement can be pushed gently into place.

FJF: Please note that Skyway, Greyhound, Motor Coach and Off-Duty models have screw-on bezels and case backs; the same goes for the sterling silver Telephone Dial cases.

Jewelers' Circular, **February 27, 1930. One wonders what the "new improved models" were.**

7. FJF: Are there usually stem issues with Illinois watches?

EK: With the 6/0 size movements and others that have the winding stem integral to the movement, not the watch case, the stem can be rusted and/or broken off over time. It is fairly easy to replace a broken stem, though not trivial for a rookie repair person by any means. Depending on where the stem breaks, it may be necessary to nearly dismantle the entire movement to get the broken piece out. Once a replacement stem is found, it likely will be necessary to cut the stem to the proper length, a trial-and-error process, little by little, to get the right length that provides the right look and fit of the winding crown to the case, so that the crown is close to the case with no visible gap whilst still allowing proper function of the wind and set modes of the stem.

Another common problem is wear on the movement in the area of the main body of the movement that acts as a guide to the stem. Over many years of winding, that section of the case is prone to wear owing to metal-to-metal contact from winding the watch on a daily basis. As previously stated, there was a time when a person may have had just one watch, wearing it daily, winding it day after day, year after year. Today, vintage watch collectors may own dozens or even hundreds (yes, believe it or not!) of watches, so this type of symptom will not be much of a factor anymore due to lack of usage. Such wear will cause slop in the stem fit within the movement and upsets the fit of the wind/set clutch and the clutch wheel, causing a grinding sound and poor winding and setting functionality. Some brands (Gruen, for instance) even made replacement stems with an oversized shaft to close that gap from wear and negate the "slop" it causes in the wind/set operation of the watch. With 3/0 size movements, the small pocket watch type movements used in wristwatches, the stem is part of the case, not the actual movement. As such, the stem has attributes associated with the case design as well as its interconnectivity attributes with the movement. A missing stem from this type of wristwatch is much more challenging to replace as a result.

JH: Most Illinois watches employ a "negative setting" mechanism, which means that the watch will go into the setting position when the movement is removed from the case. This means that the stem and case sleeve must be properly adjusted after changing either the stem or the crown. I wouldn't call this a problem, but it can be a concern if the repairer is unfamiliar with the system. If the watch is left in the setting position, the extra parts that are engaged will add drag and eventually stop the watch. If the setting mechanism is slow to return, a quick polish of the underside of the setting parting and a lightening of the shipper spring will return the watch to smooth working order.

TECHNICAL TIP WINDING AND SETTING

As no Illinois watch "strikes," there is no issue if the hands are moved forward or backward.

Your watches should be wound regularly. The best time to do so is in the morning as you are more likely to do so at the same time each day, and a spring that is fully wound is less sensitive to bumps and jarring.

Also, never wind or try to set your watch while you are wearing it on your wrist as this will cause wear in the movement hole where the stem enters the case (metal on metal). It also puts stress on the stem and could cause it to bend or break.

8. FJF: How should an enamel dial be handled during watch repairs?

EK: I want to make a point about the enamel dials used on the 3/0 size movements such as the Telephone Dial. These enamel dials are very delicate and should be handled with the utmost of care. They are very prone to cracks, mainly from handling and mishandling. When removing such a dial, carefully loosen the three dial screws within the side of the movement. Removing the screws entirely is not necessary and will certainly lessen the likelihood of losing these tiny screws. Even with the screws loosened it may be necessary to gently pry the dial away from the movement. Maybe better terminology would be to "gently coax" the dial away from the movement. Please be aware that any stress transferred to the delicate enamel may produce a crack. Pushing the dial back onto the movement requires the same level of care too. Once the dial is set into its final position, flat on the movement without any gaps, tighten the screws a little at a time, ever so carefully, so as not to overtighten. Overtightening will apply a movement to the dial foot and surely damage the enamel in the area of the mounting feet. I have seen more enamel dials damaged in the area of the feet than I care to talk about.

JH: Yes, very carefully for metal and enamel dials! In many cases the top coat of a dial has been damaged, leaving the original paint exposed to the elements, making them fragile. That said, collectors who want to handle dials and movements should use some form of protection, such as finger cots, latex gloves or a simple plastic bag, to keep finger oils and moisture away from these delicate items. It is best to treat enamel dials as a thin piece of glass, so avoid any twisting, uneven pressure or anything that could possibly scratch them.

TECHNICAL TIP ENAMEL DIALS

The enamel used on dials is a form of glass, which can be very delicate and susceptible to chipping and developing hairline fractures.

An important matter for the watchmaker, especially when removing the dial: once the screws are loosened, one might try to "pry" off the dial by inserting a tool such as a screwdriver between the movement and dial. If the screws are loosened fully, this might be acceptable, but extreme care must still be taken.

Even the storage of an unmounted dial is critical. Be careful. When mounting the dial back on the case, make sure the foot screws are fully loosened to allow the dial feet to slip easily into place. If there is any resistance from the dial screws, the tendency is to push on the dial. It can crack! Also, this attracts fingerprints.

Once the dial is mounted, it is extremely important to ever so gently tighten the screws until they just make contact with the feet. Over-tightening will surely bend the soft feet, causing a movement at the plane of the dial, cracking the enamel on the dial face in that area. Most often cracks are noticed at the 11, 4 and 8 positions right where the mounting screws and dial feet are located.

WAR ON "60¢ WATCH REPAIRING"

In September 1932, the Greater Detroit Watchmakers (in cooperation with "the better type of jewelry stores") were waging "a determined war" on an era of "60 cent watch repairing."

They complained that hole-in-the-wall places of business on street floors carried huge signs reading "Any kind of watch repair, 60 cents." Sandwich men plied the streets with similar announcements for all sorts of shops on upper floors.

Many countermeasures were being taken to combat the low price threat to the jewelry store service business and presumed profit makers.

Watchmakers claimed: "It is impossible for anyone to repair all watches, regardless of condition, at a standard, set price. To attempt to do so is to cheapen materials and workmanship to the lowest possible level so that a good watch becomes no better than the cheapest."

Suggested Minimum Watch and Clock Repair Prices

THE following suggested *minimum* repair prices have been compiled by THE KEYSTONE from jewelers in all parts of the country, large cities and small towns alike. The list is presented in the full knowledge that it is impossible to present anything of this sort which might apply to all jewelers alike. Prices suggested, however, do represent a fair average for the country at large and, in our opinion, jewelers who are doing work for less than the figures stated are doing both themselves and their trade an injustice.

In compiling these figures, no attempt has been made to compensate for advancing prices which, in many industries have been the order of the day for sometime past. Thus, more than ever, the prices quoted should be regarded as a minimum and not, by any manner of means, a maximum.

Many of the finer stores—and even many of the small ones which pride themselves on the excellence of their workmanship—are accustomed to charging from 50% to 100% more, and their work is well worth it to the discriminating customer who well enough realize that there is more than one way of cleaning or repairing a watch.

WATCH REPAIRS

Barrels	2.50
Cleaning, 7 J.	2.00
Cleaning, 15 J.	2.50 to 3.00 up
Cleaning, 17 J., under R'y grades	2.50 to 3.50 up
Cleaning, R'y grades, 5 position watches	3.50 to 4.00 up
Cleaning, cheap horsetimers	2.50 to 3.00 up
Cleaning, repeaters, chronographs, etc.	8.50 to 15.00 up
Clicks	1.25
Demagnetizing	.50
Dials fitted, plain	2.50
Dials fitted, double sunk	4.00
Hairsprings, flat	2.25
Hairsprings, breguet, common grades	2.75
Hairsprings, R'y grades	3.75
Hairsprings, readjusting	1.25
Hands, each	.25
Hands, radium, each	.50
Jewels, balance hole, 7 J.	1.25
Jewels, balance hole, 15 and 17 jeweled	1.50
Jewels, Balance R'y grades	2.00
Jewels, Cap 7 J.	1.50
Jewels, Cap 15 and 17 J.	1.50
Jewels, Cap R'y grades	2.00
Jewels, center	2.50
Jewels, plate, ordinary grades	1.50
Jewels, plate, R'y grades	2.25
Jewels, Pallett, per pair, ordinary grades	1.50
Jewels, Pallett, per pair, R'y grades	2.50
Jewels, Roller, 17 J. and R'y grades	1.50
Jewels, Roller, 7 and 15 J.	1.50
Mainsprings, 7, 15 and 17 J.	1.75
Mainsprings, R'y grades	2.50
Mainsprings, Chronographs	3.50
Mainsprings, Horsetimers	2.50
Pallet Arbor, ordinary grades	2.00
Pallet Arbor, R'y grades	2.50
Pinions, center	2.50
Pinions, cannon	2.25
Plate and Case screws, each	.30
Poising balance	1.25
Ratchets	1.25
Regulators	1.00 to 3.00 up
Roller table, single	1.50
Roller table, double	2.50
Staff, center, ordinary grades	2.25
Staff, center, R'y grades	3.00
Staff, balance, 7 J.	2.50
Staff, balance, 15 and 17 J.	2.50
Staff, balance, R'y grades	3.50
Timing screws, each	.75
Wheels, 3rd, 4th and 'scape	2.00
Wheels, steel, 'scape	3.00
Wheels, center complete	3.00
Wheels, hour and minute	1.25
Wheels, stem wind	1.25
Yoke Springs	1.50

BRACELET WATCHES

Cleaning, 10 ligne or larger	3.00
Cleaning, 9 ligne	3.25
Cleaning, under 9 ligne	3.50
Mainsprings, 10 ligne or larger	1.50
Mainsprings, 9 ligne or smaller	2.25

CASE REPAIRS

Bezels, 10K	3.00
Bezels, gold filled	2.00
Bezels, silver	2.00
Bows, 10K	2.00
Bows, 14K	2.50
Bows, best filled	1.00
Bows, filled or silver	.75
Bows, silver chat	.60
Bows, nickel	.40
Crowns, gold	2.00
Crowns, gold filled or silver	1.00
Crowns, nickel	.75
Joints, gold, each	1.50
Joints, filled, each	1.50
Joints, silver, each	1.50
New catch piece	1.50
Pendant, new ears, gold, each	1.50
Pendant, new ears, gold filled or silver, each	.75
Pendant, new sleeve	1.25
Pendant, screw	.40
Springs, Lifting Composition	1.50
Springs, Lifting Steel	1.50
Springs, lock, steel	1.75
Watch glass, Geneva	.50
Watch glass, mi-concave	.50
Watch glass, extra thick, flat	.60
Watch glass, lentille	.65
Winding stem	1.50

CLOCK REPAIRS

Cleaning, common nickel	1.00
Cleaning, repeater alarm	1.50
Cleaning, kitchen mantel	2.00
Cleaning, fine American	3.50 to 7.50 up
Cleaning, French	4.00 to 7.50 up
Springs, kitchen mantel	1.50
Springs, repeat alarms	1.25
Springs, common nickel	1.25
Springs, French clocks	2.50
Cleaning hall time clocks	5.00
Cleaning mantel tubular chime	8.00
Cleaning hanging tubular chime	8.00
Cleaning hall chime, single tube	8.00
Cleaning hall chime, three or more tubes	10.00
New cord, hall clocks, each	1.75
Pendulum rods fitted	1.75

(Suggested trade shop discount is 33 1/3% from this list)

SALESMEN: DON'T KICK IF THE BOSS KICKS—If he finds it worth while to correct you, he'll probably find it well worth while to keep you. If he's the right kind of a boss, he wouldn't waste his time cutting specks out of a rotten apple.

. . . Harold Franklin

Keystone, October 1933

Reduced Watch Repair Prices

THE NATIONAL WATCH REPAIRING CO., 727 Sansom street, Philadelphia, is offering reduced trade watch repair prices designed to enable jewelers to beat the watch repair racketeers who are operating in many cities. High quality work is promised. A special price list may be had upon request.

The April 1933 "For The Buyer" column in the *Keystone* (above) noted reduced repair prices to counter "watch repair racketeers."

9. FJF: What are the major repair differences between Illinois movements and Hamilton movements?

EK: Parts, parts, parts!!! In my experience, there are more Hamilton parts available than Illinois parts. I might add that technology was a bit more advanced in the Hamilton movements as they were the next era with some improvements.

JH: Hamilton movements are somewhat simpler than their Illinois counterparts, having fewer parts and fewer variations within calibers.

10. FJF: How should a wristwatch be wound?

EK: It should be wound in one direction until you hit a hard stop. This reduces the metal-on-metal interface of the stem outer diameter and the movement inside diameter by 50%, so it is a good idea to wind that way. Winding the ratchet back and forth is okay too, but again this doubles the motion and susceptibility to wear. However, for guys like us who have so many watches that we wear, it's not too much of a factor, I guess, considering the amount of time we actually wear each watch. Back in the day when you likely owned one watch and wore it daily, it was a big factor. Maybe even more importantly, you should never wind the watch when it is on your wrist, as that puts added stress and wear at that same location. Some companies even produced "oversize" replacement stems to compensate for that wear on the movement that would occur over the years. Gruen was one, and I recently found a NOS oversize stem with the Hamilton brand on it.

JH: A watch only "winds" in one direction, generally clockwise. Turning the crown in the other direction simply ratchets the mechanism. If you are confident that the watch has been recently serviced, ratcheting it backwards will not harm it.

Science Knows Just One Law and That is the Law of Infinite Patience and Care—and "Winding Time" Tells Whether or Not the Watchmaker Has Learned This Lesson

Winding the Watches

Too Much Importance Cannot Be Placed Upon This Daily Task Which So Frequently Shows Up the Worst as Well as the Best Features of the Watchmakers' Work

Keystone, October 1933

11. FJF: When buying a donor movement, what should the buyer look for?

EK: (a) Is the movement complete or missing parts? If incomplete, it still has value as a parts donor.
(b) Are there any signs of rust or light oxidation?
(c) As a bonus, sometimes a movement has a nice dial and hands.
(d) Are the balance staff and hairspring good? These are very important.

JH: First, open the watch!! If the watch is in a case, you can check the winding and setting functions normally. If the movement is loose, it may be necessary to borrow a "bench key" or buy and carry a stem with a crown attached with you as part of your "shopping tools"; i.e., case knife, loupe, winding stem with crown, coin-size plastic bags and heavy brass tweezers.

If the watch is running, is it running in all positions?

See if you can get the watch to stop by rotating the watch and observing the action of the balance wheel. Also, see if the watch winds and sets.

If the watch is not running:

(a) Ask the seller if the balance is broken; if they don't know, ask them to check (snapping the watch in a quick rotation should cause the balance wheel to move.)

(b) Is there visible rust?

(c) Does the watch wind and come to the end of the mainspring? (If not, the spring may be broken.)

(d) Does the watch set in both directions?

(e) Is the movement badly scratched or otherwise appear to have been badly mishandled?

February 20th, 1930.

Gentlemen:

We have your letter of February 18th, with which you bring to our attention two invoices for 5¢ each, covering cartons furnished through our Service Department.

We can understand wherein an instance of this type could be and is, without a doubt, disturbing, - but there are certain definite methods of procedure in our material and service departments, that have to be carried out.

Our program in such matters of service is, wherein the request is definitely one indicating a replacement of any - thing, rather than an adjustment of an unsatisfactory condition that may have arisen, - there is a charge attached.

By this, we mean that if the request by our customer at the time a service work is sent in, - is definitely that indicating necessity of doing whatever is requested without charge, our service or material department can very quickly decide that from the information our customer sends in.

If there is no indication of any need of a gratis or considerate action, the regular established charge for work involved is made.

By carrying out this particular method, we do have as you have written in to us, certain letters which readily bring the matter to a head, and we are able to make an adjustment.

It does not seem practicable to have a blanket coverage method wherein all service or articles that might be required are sent out without the correct charge attached. We do feel that by asking our customers when making requests of us for service of this calibre, if they will give us the angle that brought up the need of asking for the service, we can then more readily work out the problem with our customer, to the satisfaction of all involved.

These two invoices will be returned to you by our Accounting Department with the necessary credit invoices to offset the original charge.

Thank you very much for having brought the matter to our attention, and giving us this opportunity of explaining how we are endeavoring to give our customers the quality service they deserve.

Very truly yours,

ILLINOIS WATCH

J.L.Keenan - og

Sales Manager.

A 1930 letter agreeing to withdraw two service invoices that totaled 10 cents, or 5 cents each

12. FJF: Is it better to switch the entire movement out, or replace one part—i.e., a balance staff—from the donor movement to the existing movement?

EK: It depends on what is wrong with the primary movement. For example, if there is any rust, it is best to replace it. If no rust, it may be easier to replace the entire balance wheel if repairing a broken staff in the primary movement.

JH: These movements are of a finite supply, so I recommend repairing them first. Loose parts often become unidentifiable. Also, unless you are proficient in the handling of small watch parts, you may lose or break the intact part you are trying to use.

THE BALANCE

The balance is the heart of the watch. The adjustment of the balance wheel, and of the hairspring which is inside of it, is what makes a watch "keep time." Most service issues related to a vintage Illinois watch are related to its balance. In fact, many appear on eBay and other sales sites with this part missing because lazy repair people just swap out the whole balance without trying to repair it properly.

13. FJF: What parts cannot be switched from one movement to another, owing to wear patterns, for example?

EK: Balance bridges on some movements are serial number coded to match the main movement. Even though it is a matched set, they can be interchanged, though some adjustment may be required to allow the right "play" in the balance staff/wheel. Other parts should have no limitations on interchangeability as long as they are compatible. There are reference books that indicate what parts are compatible between movements. As I have stated before, it is typical with Illinois wristwatches to be forced to use used parts when needing a part for a watch. New parts are typically not available. As such, the used part must not be worn to the point where it will not work well. Two common parts that need replacing when doing a repair are the winding/setting clutch and the winding pinion. Sometimes it is by trial and error to find a used part that works well.

JH: This is a very involved question since there are many variations within each Illinois caliber.

14. FJF: Can any parts be interchanged between 3/0 and 6/0 size Illinois movements?

EK: Probably not other than screws maybe, but I don't have a definite answer at this moment. The reference books mentioned will list such parts.

JH: For the most part, no.

15. FJF: Can parts of the different grade 6/0 size Illinois movements be interchanged?

EK: Likely some; check the reference books.

JH: This is a very involved question! The short answer is no!

16. FJF: Can parts from an Illinois 207 and a Hamilton 401 movement be interchanged?

EK: It is my understanding that there is some interchangeability of parts, though likely there is not an "official" cross-reference chart from one of these companies. Looking at the movements, you can see they do appear nearly identical, which makes sense owing to the acquisition of Illinois by Hamilton.

JH: Most of the pivot sizes are different between the two movements, so careful inspection is a must before attempting any interchange.

FJF: Please see Chapter 3 for the mainly superficial differences between these two movements.

ILLINOIS WATCH COMPANY,
SPRINGFIELD.
Sept 17 1897.
Your movement No. 1271530 / 6829 received today, for repair, shall have our prompt attention, and will be returned as soon as possible.

Yours respectfully,
ILLINOIS WATCH COMPANY.

Illinois Factory postcard repair receipt dated September 17, 1897

17. FJF: What parts wear the most in a movement?

EK: The non-jeweled bearing surfaces. This includes the type of shaft that fits in a hole, such as a seconds pinion (4th wheel). Or where the winding stem rotates is clam-shelled between the two case halves where the stem enters the movement. The hole opens up, and this causes a major issue where the watch stem is sloppy in the hole and causes grinding/skipping when winding and setting the watch due to the stem being able to wobble and misalign the winding pinion with the crown/main wheel. The mainspring rubs against itself and gets worn, and causing drag and changing the power it can transmit to the watch due to drag. The winding/setting clutch and/or the winding pinion wears and causes winding and setting issues.

JH: The mainspring is the most often changed part, as it spends its time confined to the small diameter of the barrel even when not in use. The second would have to be the center wheel, as it is greatly affected by the power and torque of the mainspring. The third is the balance staff, due to the frequency of its rotation. Proper maintenance and lubrication can minimize the wear on these parts.

FROM SERVICE DEPT.

December 10th, 1931.

Mr. H. B. Thurston,
705 W. Lake Street,
Minneapolis, Minn.

Dear Mr. Thurston:

Our Service Department has brought to my attention for consideration your letter of December 5th.

The attitude of the Service Department in the matter is correct in that any watch subjected to a strong magnetic field becomes magnetized unless constructed so as they do not absorb magnetism.

On the face of it the only thing our Service Department could do would be de-magnetize this watch, re-ráte and return to you.

However, as a commercial situation and because you have recently shown every courtesy to our representative in your territory, Mr. Branyen, the writer is authorizing our Service Department to furnish in exchange without charge a new Bunn Special Elinvar movement of this grade.

This action in no way is a criterion but because we wish to have yourself and Mr. Olson entirely pleased with the performance of Illinois watches.

Very truly yours,

THE ILLINOIS WATCH

JLK:ET

By

Illinois letter dated December 10, 1931, concerning magnetism

MAINSPRING

The mainspring of a watch is subject to break at any moment. Even electrical and atmospheric conditions could affect it. In the past, watch repairers sometimes had an increase in mainspring replacements during thunderstorm season.

Original mainsprings may break within a week or last for years.

18. FJF: Are mainsprings readily available for all Illinois watch movements?

EK: They are getting harder and harder to find. As such, prices are going up. And many times the ones found, even NOS ones, have oxidation and rust.

JH: Many are available but many variations are not. Mainspring variations were often available to accommodate higher jewel counts within base models. The higher the jewel count, the weaker the mainspring needed to drive the movement.

19. FJF: What parts are readily available and what parts are hard to find?

EK: Some parts are still relatively easy to find because the years when cases were melted down for the gold content lent to many movements being stockpiled for parts. But this situation will change over the years, naturally. NOS parts are virtually nonexistent, and so you must search for good-quality used parts. There are still many parts houses out there, and the Internet helps the search.

JH: Unfortunately, many of these parts require some research to acquire. I always buy with the future in mind.

HE ILLINOIS WATCH GRADE AND MODEL NUMBER CHART

	Size	Jewels	Model	Grade	Size	Jewels	Model	Grade	Size	Jewels	Model
167	16	17	7th	127	12	17	3rd	805	18/0	15	4th
L167	16	17	9th	121	12	21	1st	807	18/0	17	2nd
169	16	19	7th	307	3/0	17	Improved 4th	807A	18/0	17	3rd
L169	16	19	9th	605	6/0	15	6th	807B	18/0	17	4th
161	16	21	14th Bunn Spec.	607	6/0	17	4th	105	21/0	15	1st
161A	16	21	15th Bunn Spec.	607A	6/0	17	6th	107	21/0	17	1st
163	16	23	14th Bunn Spec.	601	6/0	21	5th				
163A	16	23	15th Bunn Spec.	207	12/0	17	1st				

Size	Model	Plate Design	Setting	Hunting or Open Face	Type of Barrel	Started with Serial Number	REMARKS
18	1st	Full	Key	Hunting	Regular	1	Coarse Train
	2nd	"	Lever	"	"	38,901	Quick Train
	3rd	"	"	"	"	46,201	Quick Train, 5th Pinion Type
	4th	"	Pendant	Open Face	"	1,050,001	Fast Train
	5th	"	Lever	Hunting	"	1,256,101	Fast Train, R. R. Grade
	6th	"	"	Open Face	"	1,144,401	" " " "
16	1st	Full	Lever	Hunting	Regular	1,030,001	Thick Model
	2nd	"	Pendant	Open Face	"	1,037,001	" "
	3rd	"	Lever	" "	"	1,038,001	" "
	4th	¾ Plate	"	Hunting	"	1,300,001	Getty Model
	5th	" "	"	Open Face	"	1,300,601	" "
	6th	¾ Pl. & Brdg.	Pendant	Hunting	"	2,160,111	Mostly D. R. & Improved R. R. Model
	7th	" " "	"	Open Face	"	2,160,011	" " " " "
	8th	" " "	Lever	Hunting	"	2,523,101	" " " " "
	9th	" " "	"	Open Face	"	2,522,001	" " " " "
	10th	Cent. Brdg.	"	" "	Motor	3,178,901	Also 17s, Ex. Thin R. R. Grade, 48
	11th	¾ Plate	"	" "	"	4,001,001	R. R. Grade, 48 hr.
	12th	" "	"	Hunting	"	4,002,001	" " " "
	13th	Cent. Brdg.	"	Open Face	"	4,166,801	Also 17s, R. R. Grade, 60 hr.
	14th	¾ Plate	"	" "	"	4,492,501	R. R. Grade, 60 hr.
	15th	" "	"	" "	"	5,448,301	" " " " Elinvar Hairspri
14	1st	Full	Lever	Hunting	Regular	1,009,501	Thick Model
	2nd	"	Pendant	Open Face	"	1,000,001	" "
	3rd	"	Lever	" "	"	1,001,001	" "
12	1st	¾ Plate	Pendant	Open Face	Regular	1,685,001	¾ Plate
	2nd	" "	"	Hunting	"	1,748,751	" "
	3rd	Cent. Brdg.	"	Open Face	"	2,337,011	Center Bridge
	4th	" "	"	Hunting	"	2,337,001	" "
	5th	" "	"	Open Face	Motor	3,742,201	Motor Barrel
	6th	" "	"	Hunting	"	4,395,301	" "
12T	1st	True Cent. Brdg.	Pendant	Open Face	Motor	3,700,001	1 Tooth Click. Also 13s
	2nd	" " "	"	" "	"	3,869,301	5 " "
	3rd	¾ Plate	"	" "	"	3,869,201	2 " "
8	1st	Full	Key & Lever	Hunting	Regular	100,001	Plate not recessed
	2nd	"	Lever	"	"	100,101	Plate is recessed
6	1st	¾ Plate	Lever	Hunting	Regular	552,001	
4	1st	¾ Plate	Lever	Hunting	Regular	551,501	
0	1st	¾ Plate	Pendant	Open Face	Regular	1,815,901	
	2nd	" "	"	Hunting	"	1,749,801	
	3rd	Cent. Brdg.	"	Open Face	"	2,644,001	
	4th	" "	"	Hunting	"	2,637,001	
3/0	3rd	Cent. Brdg.	Pendant	Open Face	Regular	2,816,201	
	4th	" "	"	Hunting	"	2,793,901	
	Improved 4th	" "	"	"	"	5,319,001	Improved Regulator Adj. & Doul
6/0	1st	¾ Plate	Pendant	Open Face	Regular	2,689,101	Split Winding Wheel Hub
	2nd	Cent. Brdg.	"	" "	"	3,501,001	
	3rd	" "	"	" "	Motor	5,239,001	Motor Barrel
	4th	" "	"	Hunting	Regular	5,364,001	
	5th	" "	"	"	Motor	5,009,001	Motor Barrel
	6th	" "	"	"	Regular	5,551,001	riction Jeweling
12/0	1st	¾ Plate	Pendant	Hunting	Regular	5,308,001	
18/0	1st	¾ Plate	Pendant	Hunting	Regular	4,241,141	
	2nd	" "	"	"	"	5,148,001	Improved Click
	3rd	" "	"	"	"	5,345,001	Friction Jeweling
	4th	" "	"	"	"	5,604,601	Interchangeable Bridges
21/0	1st	¾ Plate	Pendant	Hunting	Regular	5,624,001	

o identify the Grade or Model Number of Watch, first look for Grade Number stamped on top side of bridges. If Grade Number does not ar. look for Model Number sta late. The above chart gives the necessary information to enable you to locate art in (over)

The Illinois Watch Grade and Model Number Chart, December 1932

20. FJF: Which movement is the most difficult to work on?

EK: These are basic "tell time" watches and do not have any complications in their movements to drive calendars, days of the week, chronograph and stopwatch functions, etc. As such, there's not much difference in level of difficulty.

JH: None of the Illinois movements are difficult to work on providing they have been treated well during their previous repairs.

21. FJF: Which movement is the easiest to work on?

EK: Ones that have been properly taken care of over the years.

JH: The ones that have never been repaired before. Other than that, Illinois movements are very straightforward but do require a knowledge of the negative setting mechanism.

22. FJF: Which is your favorite Illinois movement?

EK: The 207.

JH: The 307 and the 607 ones.

23. FJF: Which is your least favorite Illinois movement?

EK: The ones with the negative set mechanism. I love to work on these movements, but I am not a fan of the primitive stem/set mechanism, which is actually part of the case.

JH: That is a very difficult question to answer. Illinois never made a bad movement. The company used a very straightforward yet elegant approach to movement making, which is why so many of them survive to this day.

24. FJF: How about cases? Do you ultrasound cases to clean them?

EK: Sometimes I use an ultrasonic cleaner to clean cases, yes. More often I use just dish soap and a soft toothbrush.

JH: Yes, but as minimally as necessary. Most of the modern polishing compounds are very clean to work with and do not require long periods in the ultrasonic device.

25. FJF: What case repairs can you make, and what repairs do you farm out to a jeweler?

EK: I sometimes correct a bent lug, though it is a risk to break it right off the case as they are typically soldered on. Most repairs go to a jeweler.

JH: I can make most case repairs, but the ones that require intricate soldering are best sent to a goldsmith.

26. FJF: Do you think it is best to restore case lug attachment pins so that original female spring bars can be used, or is it best to drill out the damaged pins so that standard male spring bars can be used?

EK: Restore as originally designed is preferable.

JH: They need to be replaced or repaired. I would never advise drilling a case unless all other remedies have been exhausted. I have only done it once or twice in twenty years.

FJF: Please have the male lugs restored properly as it is an easy and inexpensive fix.

"Illinois Watches Are Not Advertised to Death, But They Make A Remarkable Showing and Back You to the Limit"

—writes an eastern jeweler who was very much impressed by the following interesting experience

"Some three or more years ago I sold one of your better grade watches to a customer feeling that I could give him as good value for each dollar of the price as in any watch made in the world and the watch has backed me to the limit. At the time he had never heard of a watch by the name Illinois and left the matter entirely to my knowledge of watches.

"This morning he comes into the store with an interesting anecdote which I feel you ought to know. In the course of his business he is on Pullmans a great part of the time and, as he says, many of the great questions of the day are settled on such cars by those who have plenty of time to sit around and discuss them. After a group of five had settled automobiles, politics and a number of other matters the subject of watches arose. More or less discussion was had relative to the merits of various makes, but when the census of watches was actually taken in the group of five men three of them were carrying your make and all were perfectly satisfied with their timepieces.

"As your watch is not made in the biggest shop in the land and is not advertised to death, I think that this showing is remarkable and worthy of your attention."

There is no secret about the remarkable showing made by Illinois Watches. They *satisfy,* and for years *satisfied customers* have been their best advertisements.

Such advertising will mean much to your store.

ILLINOIS WATCH COMPANY
Springfield

Jewelers' Circular, promoting Illinois Watch quality, January 1922

WHY I COLLECT ILLINOIS

1. American-Made. Most people forget that the United States was once the premier country for the production of reliable, durable watch movements. Just as it produced some of the finest automobiles in the world, it produced some of the finest watches. Illinois, as a brand, celebrates this historic strength of United States industry and engineering. Together with Hamilton, Elgin, Waltham and (early-on) Hampden, United States-produced watches that reflected our manufacturing strength. On the other hand, other major wristwatch manufacturers, such as Bulova and Gruen, used mostly Swiss-made movements. Although they are "American" brands, they are not United States produced watch movements. Ingraham and Ingersoll (the "dollar watch" manufacturers) also produced many American-made watches, but these are far less collectible today.

2. Quality Movements. Elgin produced movements with quality all over the map. If we use number of jewels as a measure of quality (roughly equates the level of engineering and design effort invested and the perceived value at the time), Elgin produced 7-jewel watches, as well as watches with a much higher number of jewels. As for Waltham, the firm, during the wristwatch era, was always in financial trouble. They skimped on design and engineering. As to quality, Waltham wristwatches are hit or miss. Only Hamilton and Illinois movements consistently offered well-designed and well-engineered wristwatches. Of these two, only Illinois produced a 21-jewel model during "the day." I always consider my two-tone, 21-jewel Consul the best watch money could buy.

3. Durable and Repairable. Illinois movements are so well engineered that ninety years later they can be repaired. Ingersoll and Ingraham wristwatches, which were very cheaply made are difficult, if not impossible to repair. Waltham watches can be a challenge to repair, depending on the movement. Elgins and Hamiltons are the only other brands for which parts are not completely impossible to find.

Cases

Illinois cases are "flash." During the 1920s, they reflected the era well with its emphasis on Deco styling and distinctiveness. Even today, Illinois watches are eye-catching because they capture an era. The Illinois transition from Deco to Moderne in the 1930s again mirrored the transition to a more utilitarian and less ostentatious age. For those interested in placing history on the wrist, Illinois are among the best reflections of their times.

Dials

Like the cases of Illinois watches, the dials also show the aesthetic tendencies of the time. From the exploding dials of a Major to the flush gold numerals of a Rockcliffe and from the sparkle-finish dials to the drop-shadow numeral dials, Illinois dials present well. Combined with the cases, Illinois dials make for an attractive package.

Backstory

A watch is only as valuable as its backstory. With books available describing the different models and the history of manufacture and the manufacturer, Illinois allows the wearer to understand the story behind the little machine on his or her wrist: when it was produced; the idea behind the watch (its original positioning); the variation with each case/model design; and the current rarity of the watch. Thanks to you Fred, there is more documentation on Illinois than any other watch manufacturer.

Collectibility

1. Illinois produced wristwatches for only a few years, during the first great period of wristwatch design in the United States. The watches reflect the strength of case design and movement engineering during this period.

2. It is actually possible to collect a majority of the watches without having to mortgage or move out of the house. As opposed to almost eleven hundred different Hamilton models offered, there are less than one hundred Illinois models. In addition, just collecting the Hamilton models offered in the year 1930 can be as expensive as buying a luxury car. On the other hand, most Illinois are moderately priced. Only if you are intent on collecting every variation could the cost get out of hand.

For the watch collector truly interested in having an attractive, quality watch reflective of the time, there really is no equal to Illinois.

—Bob Ayer

27. FJF: Can a collector safely make any repairs, such as tightening so a case back fits better, or straightening lugs?

EK: I tend to do this, very carefully, but would not recommend a collector do so.

JH: I generally do not recommend this on any watch that the collector is not prepared to ruin. I remember telling a collector, "If you are going to cry, then don't try." The relationship you have with your watchmaker should include the occasional minor adjustment for an avid collector. (I recommend the use of baked goods as a lubricant in these situations).

28. FJF: As for dials, do you have a cleaning method you can recommend?

EK: I have had some excellent successes on some silver-based dials with liquid silver dip, but I would not recommend this to somebody to try unless the dial is not important to you because you can also ruin it rather than make it look nicer.

JH: The use of Rodico, a putty-like cleaner designed exclusively for watches, can be used for many light cleanups. I strongly recommend testing it on a scrap dial first to see how it works and how much pressure to apply. I use a cropped sable hair brush to remove particulate matter.

FJF: Check with your friends as there are many custom concoctions out there that work effectively (some of which are discussed in *The Illinois Watch: The Life and Times of a Great American Watch Company).*

29. FJF: Crystals—do you use a different cement for glass vs. plastic crystals?

EK: I do not, though I have often wanted to try the cement that is cured by ultraviolet light (black light)

JH: Yes. I use ultraviolet cement with the proper curing lamp for all glass crystals. Plastic crystals are best installed with the cement designed for their use. The problem is not simply adhesion, but ease of removal without damage.

30. FJF: Are Illinois original crystals difficult to find?

EK: Many are available in plastic but harder to find in glass. I typically prefer glass and get them made special.

JH: There are many crystal-cutting services that will do an excellent job when an original is not available.

FJF: There is a person on eBay that routinely sells original NOS glass Illinois wristwatch crystals.

Jewelers' Circular, February 23, 1928

31. FJF: Do you make your own crystals?

EK: Even plastic and glass crystals designed and labeled for the exact watch model typically need to be fitted to the case. With plastic it is quite tedious requiring trial and error sanding and if you go too far it will not fit right or look terrible with large gaps, etc. It is even more tedious with glass; you have to be careful not to chip it, and it requires wet-sanding on a special turntable. Fitting crystals is a lot more work than a collector realizes.

JH: I do not make my own crystals (although I do alter them for a custom fit).

TECHNICAL TIP CRYSTALS

If you break a crystal or if it is loose, replace it as quickly as possible, as the dust which gets on the dial will find its way to the movement.

32. FJF: Why is my watch repair person always so late in doing my work?

EK: When a watch is received for repair, the initial inspections include some basic observations. If the mainspring is fully wound to a hard stop and the balance staff is good, it is likely the watch needs a basic service. That requires a complete dismantling of the watch and cleaning of all the parts either in an ultrasonic cleaning machine or the old "three-jar" machine, always with the proper solutions for cleaning and rinsing. If after such a service the watch still does not run, the analysis to find out the culprit can be time-consuming and involves a lot of trial and error. If parts are needed, Illinois parts, unlike the more common and mass-produced Bulova, Elgin, etc., can be difficult to locate. Parts availability can add to delays as parts are getting harder and harder to find. Tricky symptoms can be puzzling and result in numerous efforts to troubleshoot problems, adding to the delays.

JH: Finding parts is always an issue when working on older watches. Many times parts that are ordered are then back-ordered with little or no notice, leaving us with unexpected delays. The other problem that adds to repair times is previous repairs done incorrectly. An example that comes to mind is of a watch that needed a new balance staff. The correct staff was ordered and received. After installing the new staff, I then noticed that both the upper and lower balance jewels did not fit the new staff, which I knew to be the correct one for the watch. After three additional hours of examination and comparison with other movements and staffs, I found that the original broken staff was not correct for the watch and that the jewels had been changed to accommodate the previous repair. This forced me to spend the better part of a day undoing this mistake and finding and installing the additional correct parts.

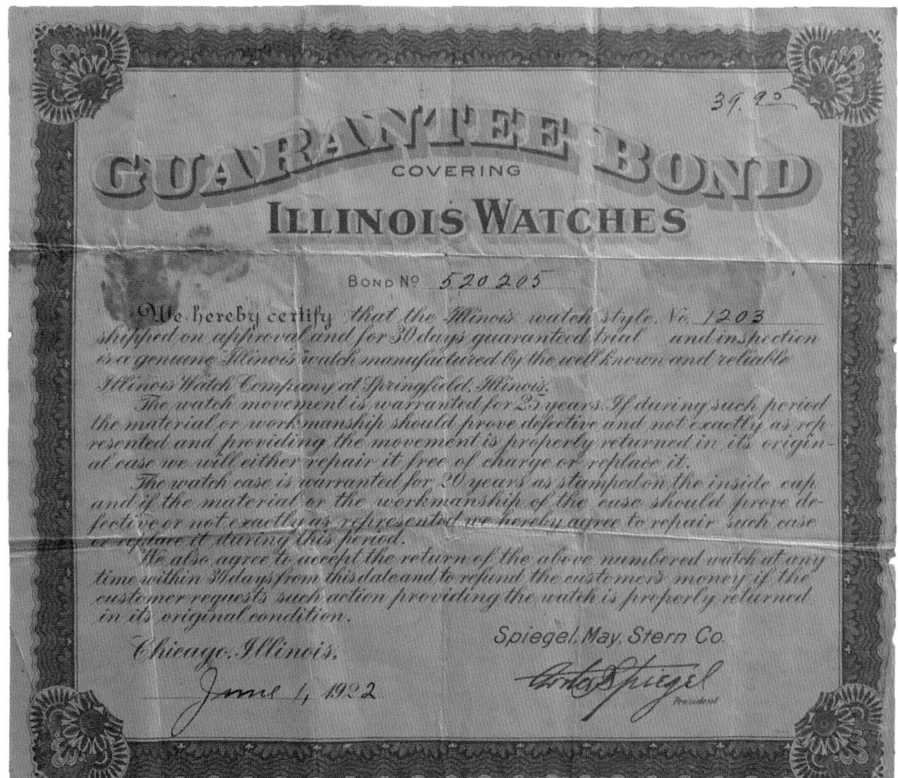

39.90

GUARANTEE BOND
COVERING
ILLINOIS WATCHES

BOND NO 520205

We hereby certify that the Illinois watch style No. 1203 shipped on approval and for 30 days guaranteed trial and inspection is a genuine Illinois watch manufactured by the well known and reliable Illinois Watch Company at Springfield, Illinois.

The watch movement is warranted for 25 years. If during such period the material or workmanship should prove defective and not exactly as represented and providing the movement is properly returned in its original case we will either repair it free of charge or replace it.

The watch case is warranted for 20 years as stamped on the inside cap and if the material or the workmanship of the case should prove defective or not exactly as represented we hereby agree to repair such case or replace it during this period.

We also agree to accept the return of the above numbered watch at any time within 30 days from this date and to refund the customer's money if the customer requests such action providing the watch is properly returned in its original condition.

Chicago, Illinois. Spiegel, May, Stern Co.

June 1, 1922

President

Spiegel, May, Stern Co., Illinois Watch 25-year watch guarantee bond, 1922

Over the years these timepieces could have passed through the hands of many different watchmakers who each used his own "unique" method of doing a repair. Sometimes the repair was done as a "quick fix" to get the watch working again, with no thought as to the longevity of the watch. We need to remember that most of these beloved timepieces were worn daily and hence repaired for decades with no thought to their long-term collectibility or the interest they would receive from future generations.

FJF: Sorry, men, but I felt compelled to ask that question!

"ILLINOIS WATCHES; - REASON FOR BEING"

Our story to the distributors' salesmen and to the retail jeweler, is about as follows:

Illinois Watches are custom finished constructed. Not mechanically assembled and are of the double roller, steel escapement type, with a minimum quality jeweling complement of 15 precious jewels. Our thought in establishing ourselves in this particular position is not merely arbitrary, but based upon the fact that when the Government originally instructed railroads to have their General Time Inspectors establish grades of watches that could be accepted for service, complement of 15 precious jewels was taken as a minimum.

Taking this Government grading as a definite stage which would automatically separate the machine-made, low jeweled or metal bushing, mechanically assembled watch; - and establish the accurately developed interchangeable custom-matched material; custom-finished and custom-assembled watch, it gives us a position that can be definitely advertised, merchandised, and accepted by the consumer as the reason of our quality. Our people work on nothing but custom-made watches. We concentrate on one or at the most, two grades in a size, thus obtaining reduced cost thru quantity production of few styles.

In 1933 an added feature, the "Elinvar" Hairspring became standard equipment. This provides a rust-proof anti-magnetic watch.

Illinois has constantly "stuck to its knitting" in this matter of making of watches along these lines of custom finishing, having truly used more of the essential quality hand-finishing, hand assembling, or what is better - custom-assembling ideas, than many others. Using its one brand name for compact price range line.

This, therefore, readily makes a merchandising story somewhat along these lines, that the machine-made mechanically assembled watch, with bearings of metal, or seven to eleven, low grade jewels; also the low quality fifteen jeweled watch stepped up from seven jewels; fitted in metal or gold plated cases are in a certain quality and price category, - say, $5.00 up to $15.00. Thus, a 15 or 17 jewel Government specification custom-finished line of watches, in various desired sizes of the mode, in price range from $18.00 up to $75.00; - depending somewhat upon the type of dial, also Sterling Silver, 14K Federal Standard Gold Filled or Solid Gold quality cases for price stages; has a definite position, and Illinois is shooting at it.

Our casing endeavors would naturally be in a bulk proposition, and, therefore, in a reduced cost range from cases that might be hand-made or somewhat more heavily decorated, this assisting us to afford attractive consumer price values.

We would further succeed in getting our price range, by affording retailers low profit items and long profit items, using gold filled metal attachments for wrist watches, and 6/0 or 12/0 size watches to get differentials for men - 18/0, 21/0, and 26/0 sizes for women.

Then we can apply the dramatic automobile merchandising idea of the bulk production four and six cylinder cars equal to 7 and 11 jeweled low price watches and the custom motored 6 and 8 cylinder cars to 15 and 17

-2-

jeweled custom-made watches which is our line.

Then comes into the story, - the hand-made case; quality watch which possibly might be the heavy 8 cylinder or 16 cylinder car. Each of these automobiles are and therefore any watch, we feel, can be definitely sold to the retail jewelers, and by him to the consumer with an idea of giving in the price range, - the best dollar value. Thus our Greater Value line of American Watches develops.

Timed, cased and packaged at the factory.

J.L.K.

John L. Keenan's 1933 memorandum to Illinois salesmen and jewelers on Illinois' "reason for being"

33. FJF: Is there a special way to handle non-enamel Illinois dials?

EK: It is best to not touch the face of the dial as fingerprints can be a bit difficult to remove, especially on glossy black dials. Fingers can also leave an oily residue on the dial. The green Rodico putty stick sold by parts houses is great for removing fingerprints from dials. "Dirty" dials can be cleaned "sometimes," depending on the type of dial. But always with great care and avoid the desire to rub! And there is always the option to have a dial professionally refinished, though most true collectors would rather leave even the ugliest original dial intact rather than have it redone. Also, you should not force the dial onto the movement—possibly the feet are misaligned with the holes in the movement and forcing can deform the dial.

JH: Yes, very carefully! In many instances, the top coat of the dial has been damaged, leaving the original paint exposed to the elements, making it fragile. That said, collectors who want to handle dials and movements should use some form of protection such as finger cots, latex gloves or a simple plastic bag to keep finger oils and moisture away from these delicate items.

34. FJF: Is it more difficult to service a smaller-sized Illinois movement than a larger-sized one; e.g., an 18/0 size movement versus a 3/0 size movement?

EK: With Illinois, I would say "not really," as even the ladies' movements are really not that small. But some ladies' movements made by Hamilton, Bulova, Gruen, etc., are quite tiny and as such are harder to reassemble and work on.

JH: It can be, depending on the skill, age and patience of your watchmaker. I have found the quality of Illinois movements to be consistent throughout the sizes, making them a pleasure to work with.

35. FJF: Is it easy to detect a redone Illinois dial from an excellent redone dial?

EK: A Factory dial looks different than a refinished dial—that "Factory quality" goes unmatched. Illinois dials had silver content and as such tended to be prone to tarnishing. So an old dial with a perfect face likely will look old with a nice patina. Redone dials are more shiny on their reverse sides, whereas an original dial will show tarnish and age. I have yet to see any dial refinisher replicate the Illinois "sparkle" dial that gives off an unique and very attractive look. One of the premier dial refinishers in the industry told me he has tried and tried but cannot produce the same or even similar results. The "sparkle" was a unique and highly specialized additive that remains a challenge to reproduce.

JH: It's not always easy, as some of these dials were redone with factory templates and with the company's permission. The majority of redials, though, have inconsistencies in the print. The factories used very expensive hand-engraved templates, leaving no room for mistakes such as the overrun on a letter or inconsistent paint distribution.

36. FJF: How accurate can a collector expect a vintage Illinois to run today?

EK: In my opinion, I am content with a vintage Illinois watch to run accurate within 4 minutes in a 24-hour period. These watches are 90+ years old; there has been wear and tear on many of the parts and bearing surfaces. It is not practical to restore such a watch to its original new "right out of the factory" condition, in my opinion.

JH: That really depends on the condition of the movement. A movement that has had dozens of repairs over its lifetime will probably not be as accurate as one that has been in a sock drawer since the Eisenhower administration. I think an average plus or minus 1 to 2 minutes a day or less is a reasonable expectation. I have also seen many Illinois movements that run as well as modern watches, so again, conditions will be a factor.

WHY I COLLECT ILLINOIS

A few of the reasons I collect Illinois are that the family of Illinois collectors are among the most passionate and helpful in the world. Although you can count on almost every quality Illinois watch that shows up for public purchase being purchased by someone within a tight group of Illinois collectors, there is always someone that will tell you if you're about to purchase a quality Illinois watch. The Illinois enthusiasts are like a family and it makes the brand acquisition very attractive and it is easy to find like-minded collectors.

I also find it incredibly easy to appreciate the Illinois Watch Company's amazing quality. Regardless of the state of the economy, Illinois continued to produce extremely high-quality timepieces with no tolerance for failure. I find it fascinating that you can wind up a ninety-year-old watch and have it keep time +/- 2 seconds per day!

Lastly, I am driven to the Illinois brand because of the great depth of their offerings. With so many customization options you can have five of the same watch and they'll all be vastly different. Everything from sunburst and pinstripe dials, to two-toned cases, to deeply carved engraving make the Illinois brand one of the most unique that the world has ever seen. I find it extremely difficult to not appreciate all of their watches, even as I am nearly obsessed with symmetry, I can find thoughtful balance and control in every design. Illinois' production designs are so revolutionary that many watches designed today appear to be inspired by the Illinois Watch Company that hasn't existed in its original form for greater than a half century!

— *Jeff Bair*

37. FJF: What are the most common ways an Illinois watch owner can damage his watch?

EK: Wearing it often and rarely servicing it. Even though I use the synthetic oils today that are not subject to breakdown of the lubricity, these watches should be serviced every couple of years at least. Exposure to moisture will cause corrosion. Exposure to magnetic sources such as stereo speakers, picture-tube TV sets, etc., can magnetize the watch and cause it to run erratically and typically very fast. Shock from dropping a watch on a hard surface will surely break the balance staff. These watches should not really be worn for golfing, chopping wood or any activity that could expose the watch to a shock from impact.

JH: The two most common ways are dropping it on a hard surface and exposing it to moisture. Another would be breaking the mainspring by forcing it. Also, winding your watch while wearing it puts undue pressure on the stem and main plates of the watch and should be avoided. A very common mistake by watch owners.

TECHNICAL TIP CASE BACK

Never open your case back when you are outdoors or where the air is full of dust. When closing the case back, do not press on the center of the case—press on its edges.

38. FJF: Are there any proper usage rules you can recommend to an owner of an Illinois watch?

EK: Watches are meant to be wound all the way to the "hard stop" and then left alone for at least twenty-four hours, at which time you can wind it again all the way to the hard stop. It is best for the watch to allow the mainspring to wind down (on these non–self-winding watches) completely rather than constantly winding the watch during the day while you are wearing it.

JH: As a rule, I stand with my hand over something such as a table or bureau when putting my watch on and I put my watch in my pocket at the first sign of rain. When it comes to winding your watch, simply wind it until the crown stops and pushes back. Most experienced collectors know not to wear a vintage watch during activities such as gardening, golfing and manual labor, but the new collector may want to use the "when in doubt, take it off" doctrine to avoid unnecessary repairs.

39. FJF: How often should an Illinois be serviced?

EK: My suggestion is every two years, though for collectors with dozens if not hundreds of watches that is not all that practical or affordable!

JH: That would depend on the wearing habits of the owner. A watch worn daily should be serviced frequently, every three to five years. Pieces worn weekly or biweekly can go five to seven years between services. These intervals are based on the use of modern synthetic lubricants now used by the watchmaker. Older natural oils tend to coagulate quickly, requiring more frequent servicing.

WHAT YOUR WATCH DOES FOR ITS KEEP

"The center wheel, carrying the hands, revolves 24 times a day. The balance wheel makes nearly half a million swings in 24 hours. Actually in a pocket size watch the rim of the balance wheel travels 23 miles every day, a long and tiring march to do year in and year out with seldom a stop. More often than not it does it without a drop of oil; in fact it only takes a spot of oil to lubricate the entire movement for 12 months and even this all too frequently gets dried out by the changes in temperature due to normal wear.

"It is not advisable for the owner to oil a watch. He will certainly put too much on, mostly on the wrong places and in such a way that the oil he puts on will draw away from the bearing the oil the watchmaker uses. All watches should be cleaned and oiled at least once a year. Very small watches should have attention even more frequently because the smaller the movement the more minute is the supply of oil which it can contain.

"A watch works 168 hours or 10,080 minutes, or 604,800 seconds a week. This means 8,736 hours or 524,160 minutes or 31,449,600 seconds a year. A balance wheel makes five beats a second or over 150,000,000 beats a year.*

**Jewelers' Circular*, December 1932

40. FJF: How and where should one store his vintage Illinois watches?

EK: In a room temperature environment not exposed to large swings in temperature. Dry conditions are best, as opposed to humid.

JH: The standard cool and dry practice applies. If you are going to use plastic storage, make sure to add a deoxidizer or desiccant in with the watch and change these as often as your local weather conditions dictate.

41. FJF: What does it mean if a repairperson is a "Certified Master Watchmaker"?

EK: It means the individual received professional training, like from the Waltham School of Watch Repair or some equivalent.

JH: It means that they have gone through a level of testing by the American Watchmakers-Clockmakers Institute (AWCI).

42. FJF: What is a "CMW21"?

EK: It's a specific training criteria, though I am not familiar with the specifics.

JH: It means that they have gone through a new level of testing by the American Watchmakers and Clockmakers Institute. The current testing focuses on modern watches.

43. FJF: Do you have to pay a higher service fee to a CMW?

EK: I would imagine so, as these schools are very expensive to attend. As such, the graduates are a special breed, have paid for that education and tend to charge accordingly.

JH: Not necessarily. Most prices are determined by region and workflow. There is no standard premium charged by the holders of a certification.

ILLINOIS ENTERTAINS HOROLOGY GRADUATES

Among the news items in the May 1932 issue of the *Jewelers' Circular* was this one: "The Illinois Watch Co. entertained the graduating class of School of Horology, Bradley Polytechnic Institute, on Monday, April 11. Thirty-four members of the 1932 graduating class under the guidance of George J. Wild, Dean, inspected the factory manufacturing methods which were thoroughly explained by J. Barclay Jones, production manager. After a noonday repast in the cafeteria, Lou Acker, technical superintendent, explained the use of Elinvar as now adopted in Illinois movements. Mr. Dobbs, assistant factory superintendent, addressed the group on the technique of friction jeweling. The young men were sped on their way with the hearty good wishes of Jack Keenan, sales manager."

44. FJF: If I wear my watch once a month or less, how often should I get my watch serviced?

EK: Traditional oils break down and lose their lubricity in time. I use very expensive synthetic oils for all of the bearing parts and as such prolong the time intervals between services. With traditional oils and the occasional wearing of the watch, I would recommend every four years; with synthetic oils you can nearly double that time period.

JH: With vintage watches the amount of protection the case provides will have an effect on the service intervals. For example, most Illinois cases at best are dust proof, so the wearing environment will have an effect. Rain or any type of moisture will decrease the time between services. All that said, when modern synthetic lubricants are used, most watches will run well for six to eight years between routine services. The use of desiccants in storage can help as well.

45. **FJF: Does running a watch that hadn't been serviced in a long time really destroy the internal parts?**

EK: Yes, it can. Dried gummy oil likely will not even allow the watch to run. But dried oil and lack of lubricity will certainly tend to wear at bearing surfaces much faster than a well lubricated watch.

JH: It can; the combination of sticky oil and dirt can create a compound that will score polished pivots.

WATCH OIL

When the Illinois watches were made, the oil for lubricating them came from a cavity in the jawbone of the blackfish. Most of these fish were caught off the coast of Cape Cod. To be tested, the oil was taken to Vermont, where the temperature can drop below zero. The best grade of oil remained practically unchanged at those very low temperatures. One drop of this oil was used to lubricate a watch. Today there are synthetic oils that work much better and can keep a watch properly lubricated for years.

1932 LUBRICATING OILS

A brief article in the November 1932 *Jewelers' Circular,* warns of the dangers of acid in watch lubricating oils.

An expert in the manufacturing of lubricating oils warns watchmakers and jewelers of the danger of the slightest trace of acid in the lubricant they use. "Watch oils," said he, "must be neutral, for the presence of acid means blackened and corroded pivots and tends to produce gumming. Even the best qualities in oil are nullified if it contains a trace of acid.

"The watchmaker must be very careful that he himself is not responsible for the introduction of acid. Oil may leave the factory absolutely neutral, but if an unclean tool is used to take the drop of oil from the bottle to the oil cup some substance may have adhered to the tool which, when introduced in the oil, will set up an acid formation."

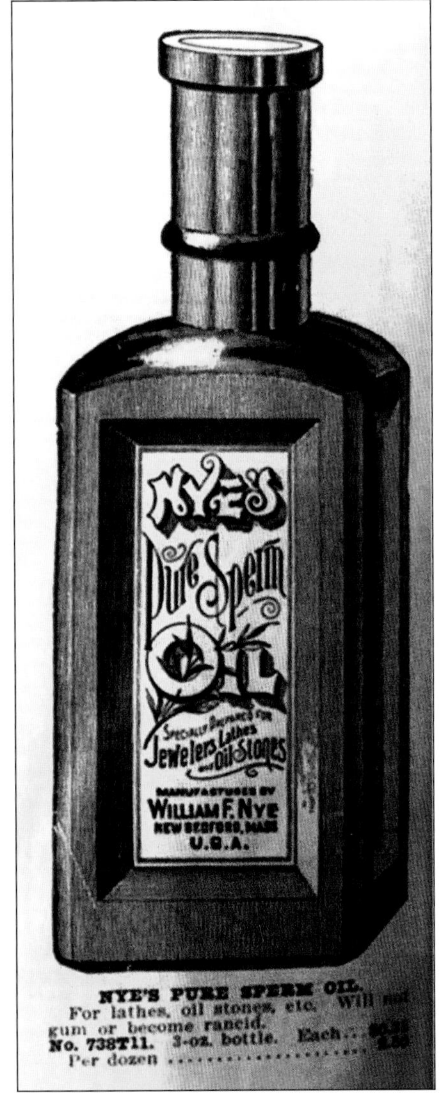

Advertisement in A. C. Becken catalog, 1931. Watchmakers were using pure sperm whale oil into the 1930s.

Revised List Effective June 21, 1932
Prices include Federal Excise Tax

SUPERSEDES ALL PREVIOUS PRICE LISTS

ILLINOIS WATCH MATERIAL PRICE LIST—RETAIL

SUBJECT TO 6% DISCOUNT FOR CASH IN TEN DAYS

MATERIAL	Each	¼ Doz.	1 Doz.
ARBORS, Barrel	$.65	$1.50	$5.50
“ Clutch	.45	.95	3.30
“ Pallet Cone pivot	.75	1.80	6.60
“ Pallet Straight pivot	.55	1.25	4.40
“ Winding (Not Threaded)	.65	1.50	5.50
“ Winding (Threaded)	.35	.65	2.20
BALANCES, Gold screws	2.60	6.00	
“ Brass screws	1.50	3.50	
BALANCE & STAFF Gold screws	3.30		
“ “ Brass screws	2.20		
BALANCE, Staff, Roller, Hairspring Gold screws	5.45		
“ Staff, Roller, Hairspring Brass screws (12/0 and larger)	4.35		
“ Staff, Roller, Hairspring Brass screws (18/0 and smaller)	5.80		
BANDS, Dust	.35	.65	2.20
BARS, Slide	.35	.65	2.20
“ Swing	.35	.65	2.20
“ Swing with Pinion	.75	1.80	
BARRELS, Regular	.65	1.50	
“ Motor—(Not sold without staff)			
“ Regular & Arbor	1.50	3.50	
“ Jeweled & Arbor	3.90	9.10	
“ Motor & Staff	2.50	5.75	
BEARINGS, Motor Barrel Staff Upper	.55	1.25	
“ Winding Arbor	.35	.65	2.20
BRIDGES, Winding	.50	1.05	
“ Winding with Pinion	.85	2.05	
CAPS, Click Spring	.35	.65	
“ Hairspring Stud	.35	.65	
“ Minute Wheel	.35	.65	
“ Minute Wheel & Lock Lever Spring comb.	.50	1.05	
“ Ratchet Wheel	.50	1.05	
“ Setting Wheel	.35	.65	
“ Motor Barrel Ratchet Wheel with Jewel	1.95	4.65	
CLICKS	.45	.95	3.30
“ No. 1044	1.10	2.70	
CLUTCHES, Winding & Setting	.60	1.40	4.95
COLLETS, Hairspring	.20	.30	1.00
CUPS, Barrel Arbor	.55	1.25	
DIALS, Enamel Single Sunk	1.75	4.40	17.50
“ “ Single Sunk Montgomery	2.15	5.40	21.50
“ “ Double Sunk	2.75	6.90	27.50
“ “ Double Sunk Montgomery & 24 hour	3.15	7.90	31.50
“ Metal Plain	1.25	3.15	12.50
“ “ Sparkle	1.60	4.00	16.00
“ “ Etched & Plain Rotor	1.95	4.85	19.25
“ “ Luminous	2.20	5.50	22.00
“ “ Luminous Rotor	3.50	8.75	35.00
“ “ Applied Gold Numeral (wrist)	6.00		
“ “ Applied Gold Numeral (pocket)	8.50		
“ Rotor Second Bit	.50	1.25	4.95
DIES	4.35	10.20	
FORKS	.75	1.80	
HANDS, Hour & Minute 12/0 Size and larger	.25	.40	1.50
“ “ “ “ 18/0 Size and smaller	.30	.45	1.75
“ “ “ “ Luminous	.45	.85	3.30
HANDS, Second all	.....	.20	.35
HUBS, Motor Barrel Ratchet	.95	2.25	
“ Motor Barrel Snailed	.95	2.25	
“ Winding Wheel	.45	.95	
INDEX, Regulator	.55	1.05	
JEWELS, Balance, Escape & Pallet for cone pivots	.50	1.10	4.00
“ Balance Unset	.45	.95	3.30
“ Endstone Gold setting	.65	1.50	5.50
“ Endstone Gold Fig. 8 setting	.85	2.05	
“ Endstone Dome setting	.85	2.05	
“ Endstone Composition setting	.35	.65	2.20
“ Endstone Unset	.25	.45	1.50
“ Barrel Arbor Gold setting	1.75	4.05	
“ Motor Barrel Staff Gold setting	1.75	4.05	
“ Motor Barrel Staff Composition setting	1.10	2.70	
“ Center Gold setting	1.50	3.50	
“ Center Composition setting	1.10	2.70	
“ Center Unset	1.00	2.40	
“ Train & Pallet Gold setting Str. Pivots	.95	2.25	
“ Train & Pallet Comp. setting Str. Pivots	.75	1.80	
“ Train & Pallet Unset	.65	1.50	
“ Pallet Stones Sapphire and Ruby	.60	1.40	
“ Pallet Stones Garnet	.45	.95	3.30
“ Roller (Jewel Pins) Sapphire & Ruby	.40	.85	2.75
“ Roller (Jewel Pins) Garnet	.20	.25	.70
LET DOWNS	.45	.95	
LEVERS, Clutch, Locking, Setting	.45	.95	3.30
NUTS, Regulator Adjusting screw	.35	.65	2.20

MATERIAL	Each	¼ Doz.	1 Doz.
PALLETS, with stones (No Fork)	1.95	4.65	
“ & Fork (1 piece) with stones	1.95	4.65	
“ & Fork (2 piece) with stones & arbor	3.70	8.55	
“ & Fork (1 piece) with stones & arbor cone pivot	2.95	6.85	
“ & Fork (1 piece) with stones & arbor straight pivot	2.70	6.30	
PINIONS, Bevel or winding	.55	1.25	4.40
“ Cannon	.55	1.25	4.40
“ Center (without staff)	.55	1.25	4.40
“ Center & Staff (1 piece)	.75	1.80	
“ Escape, 3rd, 4th, 5th, or Extra	.65	1.50	
PINS, Hairspring Collet & Stud	.20	.30	1.00
“ Winding Arbor Push	.25	.45	1.50
“ Setting	.25	.45	1.50
PLATES, Setting	.35	.65	
REGULATORS	.65	1.50	5.50
ROLLERS, Combination without pin	.50	1.05	3.85
“ Impulse without pin	.35	.80	2.75
“ Impulse With Balance But without pin (No. 1816)	2.60	6.00	
“ Guard	.45	.95	3.30
“ Combination with jewel pin	.95	2.25	8.25
“ Impulse with jewel pin	.80	1.95	7.15
“ Impulse & Balance & Pin (No. 1817)	3.30	7.70	
“ (Impulse & Guard) Staff & Pin (No. 1454)	.85	2.05	
SCREWS, Balance, Gold All	.20	.30	1.00
“ Micrometer Regulator Adjusting	.25	.45	1.50
“ Gold plated		.25	.70
“ All other		.20	.45
SLEEVES, Winding Arbor	.50	1.05	3.85
SPRINGS, **Flat Steel**—Click, Clutch, Lifting, Locking Lever, Setting Lever, Inter-winding Wheel, Yoke	.25	.45	1.50
“ **Wire**—Click, Clutch, Locking Lever, Fifth Pinion, Setting Lever, Yoke	.20	.25	.70
“ Hair Colleted (12/0 and Larger)	.75	1.80	
“ Hair Colleted (18/0 and Smaller)	1.10	2.70	
“ Lock Lever & Minute Wheel Cap Comb.	.50	1.05	
“ Main Motor Barrel & 21/0 size	.40	.90	3.15
“ Main, All others	.35	.75	2.50
“ Regulator Only (No. 2042, No. 886)	.65	1.50	5.50
“ Regulator with adjusting screws	.80	1.95	7.15
STAFFS, Balance with oil grooves (No. *1506, No. 1684)	.50	1.10	4.00
“ Balance (No. 1442, Style No. 1)	.50	1.10	4.00
“ Balance all others	.40	.90	3.15
“ Motor Barrel	.65	1.50	
“ Center (no pinion)	.60	1.40	
“ Center & Pinion (1 piece)	.75	1.80	
STRAPS, Regulator with adjusting screw	.55	1.25	
STUDS, Hairspring	.25	.45	1.50
TAPS, Crown & Screw	.35	.65	2.20
WASHERS, Main Winding Wheel Hub	.20	.30	1.00
WHEELS, Center, 3rd & 4th Gold	.85	2.05	
“ Center, 3rd & 4th Brass	.45	.95	
“ Center Gold, & Staff (no pinion)	1.65	3.80	
“ Center Brass, & Staff (no pinion)	1.10	2.70	
“ Center Gold, Staff & Pinion (1 piece)	2.05	4.90	
“ Center Brass, Staff & Pinion (1 piece)	1.65	3.80	
“ Center Gold, Staff, Pinion & Cannon Pinion	2.70	6.30	
“ Center Brass, Staff, Pinion & Cannon Pinion	2.20	5.20	
“ Clutch	.35	.65	
“ Escape Steel	.75	1.80	
“ Escape Steel (No. 1835)	2.50	5.75	
“ Escape Brass	.55	1.25	
“ Escape Steel & Pinion	1.50	3.50	
“ Escape Steel & Pinion (No. 1882)	3.70	8.55	
“ Escape Brass & Pinion	1.30	2.95	
“ Fourth & Third Gold with Pinion	1.75	4.05	
“ Fourth & Third Brass with Pinion	1.30	2.95	
“ Hour & Pipe	.35	.65	2.20
“ Intersetting & Interwinding	.35	.65	2.20
“ Minute & Pinion	.35	.65	2.20
“ Ratchet (Unexposed)	.35	.65	2.20
“ Ratchet Motor Barrel	1.50	3.50	
“ Ratchet (Exposed) concaved	1.10	2.70	
“ Ratchet (Exposed) not concaved	.80	1.95	
“ Regulator Index	.35	.65	
“ Setting	.35	.65	2.20
“ Winding Crown	1.10	2.70	
“ Winding Flat	.80	1.95	
“ Winding Base	.35	.65	
YOKES	.65	1.50	
“ with Interwinding Wheel	.95	2.25	
MATERIAL CABINET, containing 185 bottles of active Illinois Material	27.50		

* No. 1506 Balance Staffs will be furnished without oil grooves if so specified on order at the "all other" staff prices.

Above prices apply where specified quantities of one factory number are ordered. Mainsprings may be assorted as to strength, balance staffs as to pivot diameter, jewels as to hole size.

10% additional discount on all items purchased in gross lots.

No charge for matching.

ILLINOIS WATCH MATERIAL DEPARTMENT
Springfield, Illinois, U.S.A.

IT PAYS TO USE GENUINE ILLINOIS WATCH MATERIAL

(Over)

Illinois Material Price List, June 21, 1932

ILLINOIS WATCH

Genuine Material Cabinet

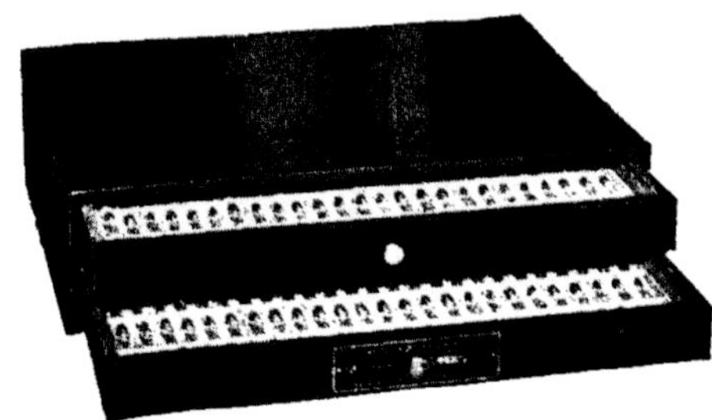

THIS convenient two-drawer cabinet is beautifully finished in dark mahogany and is just 13¼ inches wide, 9¼ inches deep and 3⅜ inches high. It contains 200 vials—15 of which are empty, providing space for material to be added from time to time.

The assortment is made up of material ranging in size from 18 to 18/0. Its actual retail value, based on the dozen price, is $37.00.

Complete with hinged index charts. Also extra set of charts for general use.

$27.50 Tax Included

"All refills come sealed from the factory."

THE ILLINOIS WATCH COMPANY
Springfield, Illinois

CABINETS CAN BE OBTAINED FROM ANY OF OUR MATERIAL JOBBERS OR DIRECT FROM OUR FACTORY.

THE ILLINOIS WATCH

Genuine Mainspring Assortment

OUR LATEST ASSORTMENT is ready to serve you. It consists of 36 different sizes and strengths. An assortment of mainsprings for the majority of all ILLINOIS WATCHES now in service.

Each spring is packed and sealed in the Standard ILLINOIS Glassine Envelope.

When your stock of a certain number is exhausted just re-order from your jobber and file them in their proper place.

The three dozen mainsprings are priced at less than the dozen price for this quantity. Their actual value is in excess of $13.00. Complete with charts and information.

$8.00 Tax Included

Can Be Obtained from Your Material Jobber or from

THE ILLINOIS WATCH
MATERIAL DEPARTMENT
SPRINGFIELD, ILL., U. S. A.

Illinois Sales Brochure, c. 1934

THE ILLINOIS WATCH - SPRINGFIELD ILLINOIS
RETAIL PRICES OF REFILL MATERIAL FOR $25.00 AND $50.00 MATERIAL
CABINETS ACCORDING TO NEW RETAIL PRICE LIST OF OCTOBER 26TH 1931

	½ DOZ.	1 DOZ.	6 DOZ.
HOUR & MINUTE HANDS			
BOTTLES 1-2-3-4-5-6-7-8-10-11-12-14-15-17-19	.38	1.50	9.00
BOTTLES 181-182	.44	1.75	10.50
BOTTLES 9-13-16-18	1.00	4.00	24.00
SECOND HANDS			
BOTTLES 20-21-22-23-24-26-28		.35	2.10
BOTTLES 25-27-185		.50	3.00
JEWELS BALANCE.			
UPPER-BOTTLES 29 TO 46 INCLUSIVE. 187 TO 192 INCLUSIVE	1.05	3.80	21.70
LOWER-BOTTLES 47 TO 71 INCLUSIVE. 195 TO 202 INCLUSIVE	1.05	3.80	21.70
SCREWS - BRIDGE.			
BOTTLES 72 TO 80 INCLUSIVE & 205	.20	.45	2.60
SCREWS - CASE.			
BOTTLES 81-82-83-85-86-88-89	.20	.45	2.60
BOTTLES 84-87	.25	.70	
SCREWS - JEWEL.			
BOTTLES 90 TO 95 INCLUSIVE	.20	.45	2.60
SCREWS - DIALFOOT.			
BOTTLES 96 TO 101 INCLUSIVE	.20	.45	2.60
SPRINGS - CLICK.			
BOTTLES 102-103 105 TO 109 INCLUSIVE & 207	.25	.70	
BOTTLE 104	.45	1.50	
SPRINGS - CLUTCH LEVER.			
BOTTLES 110 TO 115 INCLUSIVE & 209-210-211	.25	.70	
STAFFS - BALANCE.			
BOTTLES 116-117-120-121-122 125 TO 132 INCLUSIVE 144-145-146-150-151 154 TO 161 INCLUSIVE 165 TO 177 INCL.	.85	3.00	17.10
BOTTLES 136-137-138-142-143	1.05	3.80	21.70
BOTTLES 162-163-164	1.00	3.50	
PINIONS - WINDING.			
BOTTLES 213-214-215-216	1.15	4.00	
MAINSPRINGS - REGULAR.			
COMPARTMENTS 193-194-195-196-197-198-199-201-202-205 206-207-208	.75	2.50	14.25
MAINSPRINGS - MOTOR BARREL.			
COMPARTMENTS 200-203-204-209	.85	3.00	17.10

MAINSPRINGS & BOTTLES 41 & 42 ARE IN THE $50.00 CABINET ONLY.
BOTTLES IN $50.00 CABINET NUMBER 1 TO 167 INCLUSIVE.

When ordering mainsprings for Cabinet order must read "Compartment" and not "Refill" since some of the compartment numbers in the $50.00 Cabinet also apply to refill material in the $25.00 cabinet. December 8, 1931

Illinois Refill Material for Cabinets price list, October 26, 1932

46. FJF: Do all movements with the same jewel count keep time about as well, or are other features more important?

EK: Jewels allow for reduced wear and lubricated bearing surfaces. In general, the higher the jewel count, the better—but mainly for longevity. This is a difficult question to answer because there are so many other facets to consider in the design of a movement that are factors in its accuracy.

JH: Jewel counts are more of a sign of quality and movement longevity than accuracy. The timekeeping ability of any watch is affected more by the quality of the escapement than by the jewel count of the going train (the gear train). A fully jeweled going train of 17 jewels or more allows for the even flow of power from the mainspring as well as greatly reduced wear throughout. Most Illinois vintage wristwatches are capable of accuracy to within a minute or less a day even after many decades of us, provided they have been restored to good working order.

47. FJF: How can I verify that my crown is original or a replacement?

EK: Really, it is by size and look, which can be verified by old ads, reference books, etc. As you stated in *The Illinois Watch: The Life and Times of a Great American Watch Company*, very few Illinois crowns have survived the test of time.

JH: It's very difficult. There was a fluidity between the case manufacturers back then so interchangeability was easy and therefore inevitable. The main concern now is period correctness. The characteristics of vintage crowns are easily learned by the study of well-known and well-restored pieces that can be found in reference books and advertisements of the period. The choice of a replacement crown should involve the following considerations: case size (is the diameter correct?), case contour (does the roundness or squareness of the crown match the design of the case?), finish and color and finally, functionality (is it easy to use?).

48. FJF: Can enamel dials with hairlines be repaired?

EK: Yes, though the experts that do it right command top dollar and it can cost from $400 to over $1,000, depending on the extent of the damage.

JH: Yes, but you can try cleaning them first so that the dirt in the crack is removed and then lines become very difficult to see.

FJF: There are extremely talented enamel experts trained to perform museum-quality repairs, but they are very difficult to find—and when found, they command sky-high prices.

49. FJF: Can I repair gold-filled that has worn on case corners?

EK: Yes, though again, this is tricky and requires the right talent, tools and expertise. Gold-filled is actually thin solid gold sheet, pressure pressed, sandwiching a base metal such as nickel or silver within. Wear-through spots on the gold allow exposure to the base metal. Two metals layered are difficult to work on since each metal has different properties, such as melting temperature.

JH: Yes, but I recommend this be done by an experienced jeweler that is familiar with vintage watch case repairs. This work can generally be done only once, and correcting botched repairs is very difficult if not impossible.

50. FJF: In your view, do Illinois 6/0 and 3/0 size movements have a weakness in their winding stem/watch mechanism?

EK: Not sure what you mean by "weakness." The 3/0 movement has the stem encapsulated as part of the case, not the movement. This was a carryover from pocket watch designs. It is somewhat primitive and its wind/set action is not all that smooth. The springs in the watch movement for the wind/set have a tendency to break over time, in my experience, and they are a bit difficult to work on. The 6/0 is more traditional and more "modern" and as such much smoother and more "friendly" for a horologist like me to work on.

JH: Not when they are properly maintained.

FJF: If all else fails, give the following undated prayer to your watchmaker!

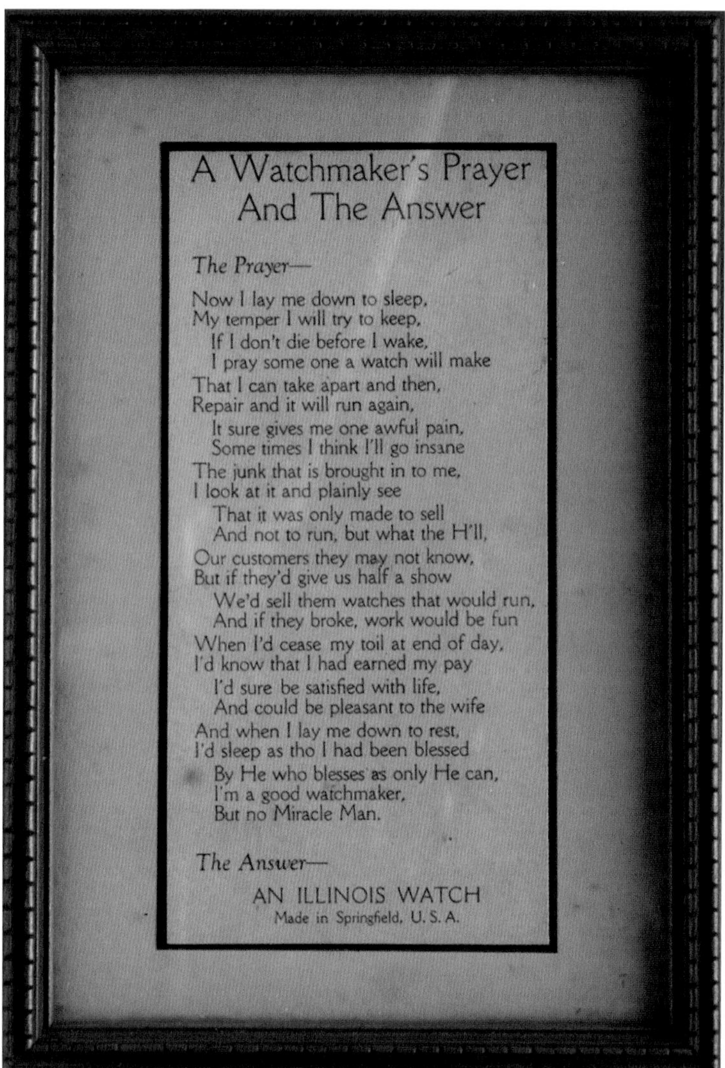

A Watchmaker's Prayer
And The Answer

The Prayer—

Now I lay me down to sleep,
My temper I will try to keep,
If I don't die before I wake,
I pray some one a watch will make
That I can take apart and then,
Repair and it will run again,
It sure gives me one awful pain,
Some times I think I'll go insane
The junk that is brought in to me,
I look at it and plainly see
That it was only made to sell
And not to run, but what the H'll,
Our customers they may not know,
But if they'd give us half a show
We'd sell them watches that would run,
And if they broke, work would be fun
When I'd cease my toil at end of day,
I'd know that I had earned my pay
I'd sure be satisfied with life,
And could be pleasant to the wife
And when I lay me down to rest,
I'd sleep as tho I had been blessed
By He who blesses as only He can,
I'm a good watchmaker,
But no Miracle Man.

The Answer—

AN ILLINOIS WATCH
Made in Springfield, U. S. A.

"A Watchmaker's Prayer"

51. FJF: Is there anything special a collector should know about fitting a strap band on an Illinois watch?

EK: Nothing looks worse than a poorly fitted watchband; that is, do not squeeze an 18mm band between 16mm wide lugs or put a 16mm band on a watch that requires an 18mm band. Bands do come in short, regular and long, so it's best to choose one that works well with your watch and wrist size.

Some Illinois case designs interfere with the leather band, but this can be minimized by choosing the thinnest spring bar you can find. Spring bars do come in different diameters or thicknesses. They also come curved, and this sometimes can help avoid band-to-case interference on round watches and even some rectangular tank styles. Choosing the right length is important too as you do want the spring bar to have lots of spring tension between the watch lugs so that your precious watch does not fall off your wrist and break–or worse yet, get lost!

Personally I wish there were "High-Grade" spring bars made and offered for a few more dollars. Here we are relying on a spring bar that costs less than five cents to secure our precious vintage watch to our wrist! Some military straps still secured the watch even if one of the spring bars broke or loosened because the strap was a single piece.

JH: The strap should completely fill the space between the lugs. Also, many modern straps are too thick for simple snap-back watches, causing the case to "torque" and pop open.

52. FJF: Is there anything a collector should be aware of concerning spring bars?

EK: Condition, corrosion, etc.; these get exposed to moisture, acids from the skin and eventually get tired and break. It's a good idea to inspect the spring bars on occasion by physically removing them from the watch and from the band. Choosing the correct type and size for the watch and band is important. You should also have a matched set on each side.

JH: If the lugs have holes, then a shouldered spring bar is not necessary. If there are no holes in the lug, then you must use a shouldered spring bar.

53. FJF: What is the difference between a male and female spring bar?

EK: Vintage wristwatches primarily have lugs with through holes or dead-ended holes, and both types require the use of male spring bars to secure a band to the watch. Some brands such as Illinois and Hamilton had a few models that had male lugs. These require female spring bars. This offers challenges in the modern era as modern female spring bars are not all that easy to find; worse yet, they typically do not have a large enough inside diameter (ID) to accommodate the outer diameter (OD) of vintage wristwatch male lugs. Vintage female spring bars came in at least two types, one with an internal spring and one with an external spring. Typically, both sides were the same size and had an ID large enough to accommodate male lugs found on Illinois watches. In my experience, modern female spring bars have too small an ID and some styles have one side that is smaller than the other side! Often you will find a Jolly Roger or other male lug vintage watch with the lugs drilled out and converted to accept male spring bars. I suspect this is because of the great difficulties we experience trying to find female spring bars in this era of time. Even with the correct female spring bars, installation of the leather band is quite tedious; and if you're not careful, you can really scar the ends of your beautiful watchband, as you have to deform it by squeezing its width to fit over the male lugs of the watch. Even after doing so, you must carefully inspect the lugs to make sure they are engaging with the spring bars and secured with the ID of the spring bar. If you're not careful, the male lug may not be inside the spring bar at all and your watch is only held on your wrist by the male lugs and its contact with the leather strap. This is dangerous, as the watch will eventually fall off!

JH: Go ask your mother.

FEMALE SPRING BARS

The following Illinois Factory-Cased men's wristwatches came with female spring bars: Futura, Jolly Roger, Piccadilly and Wentworth.

54. FJF: Is it easy to obtain spring bars?

EK: Yes, male ones can be purchased from any watch supply house. They are very inexpensive and typically made in China. Female ones are harder to find; and even if found, they often do not have a large enough hole, in my experience. Finding a bag of vintage ones would be a treasure!

JH: Agree.

Female spring bar for male lugs on an Illinois Jolly Roger

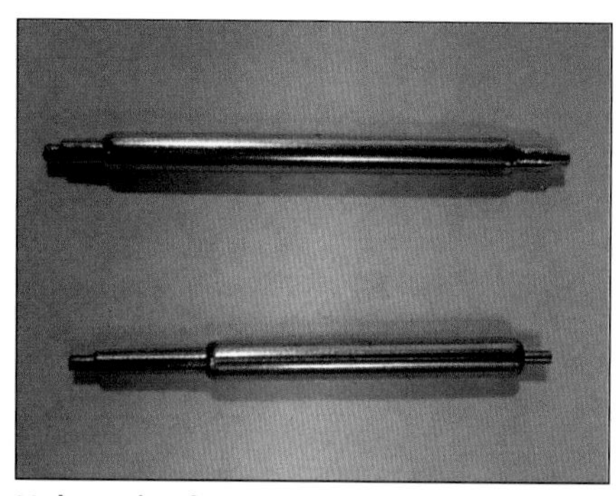

Male spring bars

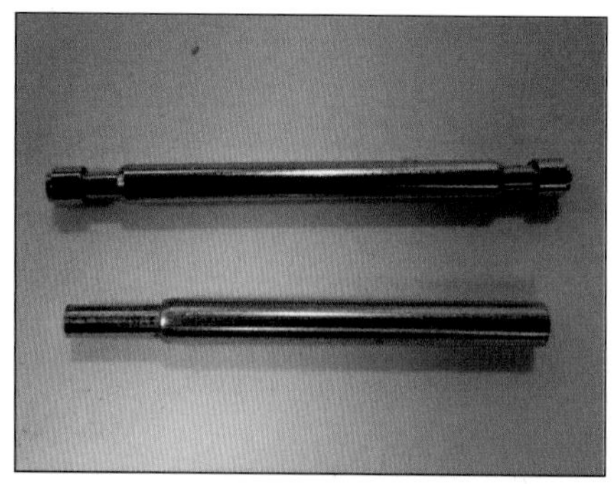

Other female spring bars

CARE OF YOUR WATCH*

"All men neglect time, all regret its loss."—Voltaire

We take the statement literally as referring to the delicate timepiece. A dependable watch is often neglected.

An ILLINOIS WATCH is a great American achievement. It is composed of approximately 175 different pieces. The balance has 18,000 beats or vibrations per hour, or 157,680,000 in one year. It travels about 9 ¾ miles, depending on the size of the watch, every twenty-four hours, or 3,588 ½ miles in one year.

It is important to have your watch overhauled periodically. The tiny mechanism needs this attention, as do the automobile and locomotive. The watch should be taken apart, cleaned and freshly oiled.

Have your watch repaired by an experienced watchmaker. Men's pocket watches should be overhauled every eighteen months, men's strap watches every twelve months, and ladies' small watches every eight months.

*Illinois undated brochure

CHAPTER 7

DIALS AND HANDS

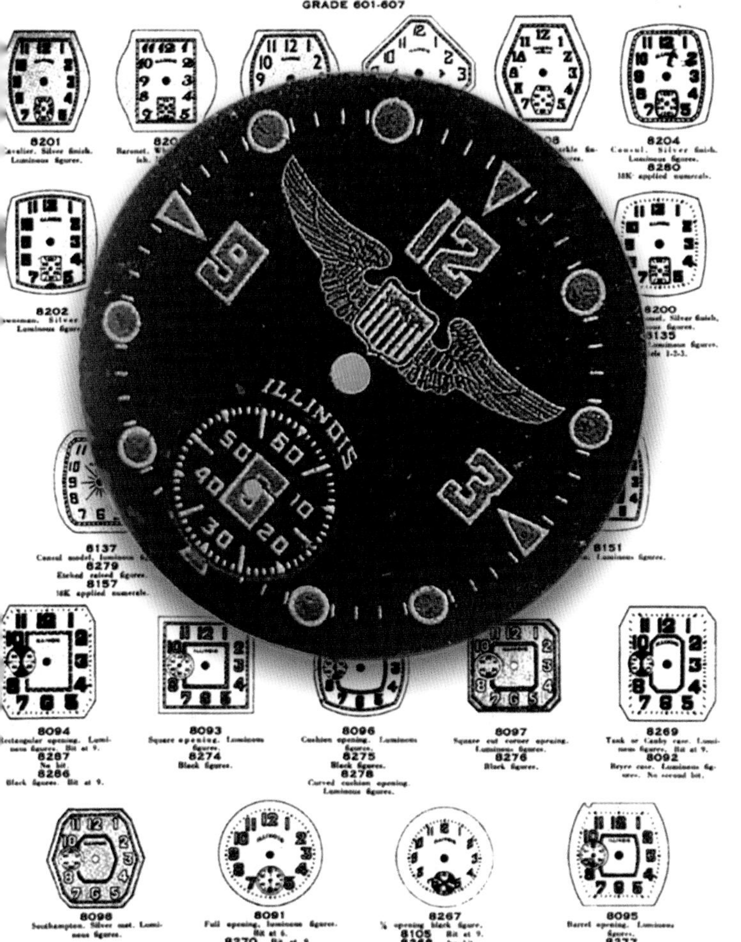

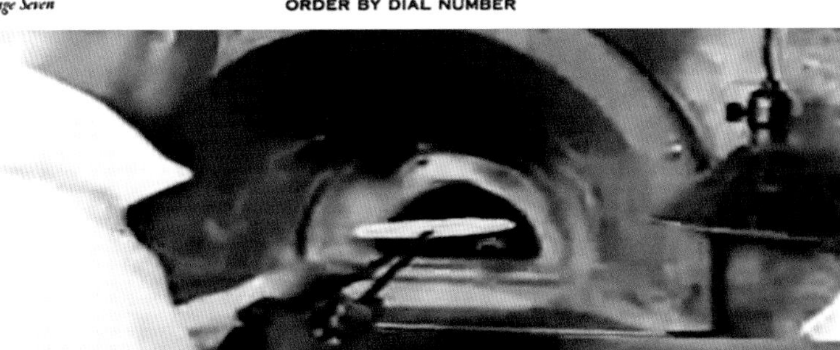

The Illinois wristwatch line featured some of the most attractive dials ever seen on watches of the era. The combination of design features presented a compelling complement to the cases designed for Illinois models. The dial designs still strongly attract collectors today, just as they drew customers many decades ago. They have survived the design test of time.

Only four published Illinois dial catalogs are known to be extant: the 1923 *Illinois Material* catalog (a hardcover volume), the 1927 and 1930 Illinois Dial and Hand Circulars, and the 1936 Illinois Materials Catalog issued by Hamilton.

Illinois wristwatch dials combined a number of unusually creative features. Many of these attractive design elements originated in the pocket watch dials offered by Illinois and others. From among these design elements, Illinois and the dial manufacturers with whom it contracted chose features for the wristwatch dials. The 1923 *Illinois Material* catalog and the 1927 Illinois Dial and Hand Circular show many handsome special features introduced by Illinois for its pocket watch dials from which it wisely borrowed various ideas for its wristwatch line.

In the early 1900s, casemakers offered customers few alternative shapes for pocket watches. For the most part, the case would be round. As the century progressed, a few options appeared, such as Hamilton's pear-shaped Van Buren, the octagonal Illinois Trustee and the cushion-shaped Illinois Marquis-Autocrat models, but most customers bought round cases with either a plain or engraved bezel. This lack of case options shifted much of the artistic design to the large dial itself, where artisans used various techniques to make dials more appealing. Many of these elements found their way to wristwatch dial design. The following descriptions of the design elements that were chosen or foregone provide an understanding of the direction envisioned by Illinois stylists for the Illinois wristwatch line.

Illinois sales catalog, c. 1926

It should be noted that Illinois wristwatch dials of the 1920s used a metal base, although Illinois continued to sell enamel pocket watch dials at least through 1927, as its dial catalog of that year indicates. By the mid-1920s, Illinois had chosen to use a couple of sterling silver dials for its pocket watches but used almost exclusively silvered brass for its wristwatch dials. (A few years later it also offered a few sterling silver dials for wristwatches, but only for its very finest models.) After adding the design elements on top of the metal, dial makers added a preservative lacquer coating. Most of the patina as well as the dial blemishes seen on Illinois watches today can be traced to the aging of this protective coating.

Dial Materials and Coatings

Sterling Silver

Illinois chose sterling silver dials for its top-of-the-line watches. For its most expensive pocket watches, such as the Barrister and Cambridge models in its 1925 catalog, Illinois featured pocket watch dials made of solid silver by the Solidarity Watch Case Company. One of these is shown below.

Sterling silver pinstripe dial (Barrister model)

Back of Barrister dial

Illinois also offered a pocket watch with a "sterling silver dial, a polished center band, pearled minute track, and 18K applied gold numerals." As with its pocket watches, Illinois reserved the sterling silver option for its finest men's and ladies' wristwatches. At least two versions of the Illinois Consul dial used a sterling silver base. The versions of the well-known sunburst pattern dial featured inlaid enamel in most instances, and inlaid enamel required a sterling silver dial. The iconic pinstripe Consul dial was also made of sterling silver. In addition, Illinois offered at least one sterling silver dial for its high-end ladies' watches, such as the Mary Todd 203 and Coronado models. For the most part, though, Illinois did not embrace sterling silver for its wristwatch dials. The choice to limit sterling silver dials reflected the firm's conscious positioning of its wristwatches, most likely under strong direction from its parent Hamilton.

Metallic-Coated Dials

Illinois used brass coated with precious metal for the vast majority of its watch line, both for its pocket watch and its wristwatch products. With Illinois, the use of silver, gold and green metallic coatings for dials originated with its pocket watches. These were offered at times with three choices of finish—silver, yellow gold or green gold. On the other hand, Illinois chose a silver finish for almost all of its wristwatch dials.

- *Silver finishes.* Illinois used several different types of silver finishes for both pocket watch and wristwatch dials. These are discussed in sections below on inscriptions and polishing.

- *Gilt finishes.* Illinois' gilded pocket watch dials could be ordered with either a yellow gold or green gold finish. For a couple of wristwatch models, Illinois offered a gold finish; the Ensign model was advertised with one of these, and it is quite striking. In addition, the firm included a two-tone gold dial option by combining a gold dial with a contrasting butler center finished in a deeper gold tone for a dramatic two-tone effect. Illinois made this option available for Beau Brummells, Beau Brummell/Vikings, Beau Royales, Manhattans and various New Yorkers, including the New Yorker Enamel yellow gold-filled model, where it is most prevalent. Collectors find these alternative dials quite attractive, especially prizing the double gold-toned (two-toned) dials.

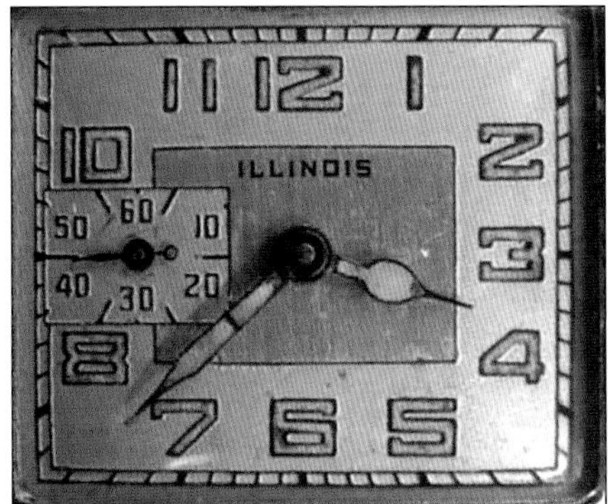

Two-tone gold dial, blue radium numerals (New Yorker dial)

Two-tone gold dial, blue radium numerals (Beau Royale dial)

Although Illinois' line of pocket watch dials included some with green gold finish and background for its pocket watches, the firm did not in general seem to have offered either option for its wristwatches, probably because green gold was going out of fashion. (In the 1925 Illinois catalog, there are two 6/0 size watches offered in green gold, with matching dials, but both are Generic ladies' watches.) By the late 1920s, yellow gold had replaced green gold as a customer favorite.

- *Sparkle finish.* Of all Illinois watch dials, sparkle finish ones remain among the most popular and alluring. As is mentioned in the interview toward the end of this chapter, dial refinishers today do not know the exact process for reproducing the sparkle effect, but do believe it to be caused by tiny granules of silver mixed into the coating on the dial. It is exciting that recent laboratory studies, commissioned for these books, have revealed new details about the dials (see "The Sparkle Dial Puzzle," a section later in this chapter).

The use of the sparkle finish originated with Illinois pocket watch dials. As early as the 1927 Dial and Hand Circular, a dial was noted as being "For Solid Gold Thin A. Lincoln only. Etched Dial, White Sparkle Finish Background." And that dial may possibly have appeared even earlier: a 1925 Illinois Factory advertisement shows what appears to be exactly the same dial for the Pioneer model, one of the solid gold A. Lincoln thin watches. The dial was described as follows: "Two-color, green and white gilded new process etched dial with ancient Roman figures in relief." Perhaps the "new process" was what was later called sparkle finish?

PIONEER MODEL
No. L1. 14k solid green or white gold. Full chased center and bezels. Attractive etched, lined or Butler back. Queen case. Two-color, green and white gilded new process etched dial with ancient Roman figures in relief.
$120.00

Illinois Sales Brochure, 1925

At any rate, by the late 1920s both Illinois pocket watches and wristwatches were being offered with white sparkle finish background dials.

White sparkle finish (Finalist dial)

***American Magazine*, November 1928; Illinois A. Lincoln advertisement**

Apparently, to save costs, Illinois stopped the sales of its watches with sparkle finishes in 1932 (probably at the direction of Hamilton). This economy measure brought to an end one of the quintessential Illinois design features. By the end of 1932, no further sparkle-finish dials were produced by Illinois.

Inscriptions

In order to provide further design variety, dial stylists called for inscribing their dials. Among the types of inscriptions used were the following: engine-turning, moiré, and pinstriping. Each of these is described in the sections that follow.

Engine-Turned Centers and Backgrounds

The term "engine-turned" refers to geometric patterns inscribed in the dial metal. A skilled craftsman produced this effect using an abrasive tool. When he desired swirl patterns, he would affix the tool to a drill press. These patterns were most likely created by the use of a rose engine, a kind of lathe that belongs to the same family as the tool used for geometric damaskeening. For damaskeening, the craftsman used a spinning piece of wood or ivory to polish a pattern onto the surface. But for engine-turned dials, he used a graver that cut into the metal. This tool is similar to a geometric lathe that cuts printing blocks that have the complicated patterns used on paper currency. Illinois frequently used this process on the center of its pocket watch dials.

Illinois also offered pocket watch dials with engine-turned backgrounds. Such engine-turning could produce a stunning effect, as can be seen on the pocket watch dials shown below. However, Illinois never adopted simple engine-turning for its wristwatch dials. Instead, it adopted the slightly more complex moiré technique for at least two Generic Period models in its ladies' wristwatch line.

Engine-turned center and butler center subsidiary seconds bit

Engine-turned center subsidiary seconds bit and butler center

Engine-turned entire background

Moiré Dials

Combining two different engine turned patterns in metal created the moiré effect. The engine that cut these dials did not just cut lines of uniform depth; it could move the tool up and down so it could make humps, such as a floral wreath or other patterns on a dial. This technique can produce interesting effects—shimmering and iridescent, looking almost like mother-of-pearl.

Illinois used moiré for several pocket watch dials. In addition, certain early Illinois ladies' wristwatches produced during the Generic Period incorporated fascinating moiré-center dials similar in style to what was used by Illinois at times on its pocket watch dials. The dials on these smaller ladies' Illinois watches have fine enough rules that they border on crude diffraction gratings; they produce colored fringes, contributing to the moiré effect.

Illinois used moiré to a much greater extent in its pocket watch dials. Some featured white or green gold special moiré centers and borders, such as the ones shown here.

Green gold special moiré center

Fancy moiré center, with butler subsidiary seconds and the start of the use of exploding numerals

Pinstripe Dials

Illinois featured inscribed dials using parallel lines cut into the dial. To produce such pinstripe patterns, a press dragged the inscribing tool through the metal to cut parallel lines. This design feature was originated for pocket watch dials. For wristwatch dials, as previously mentioned, Illinois offered this option only for some of its top-of-the-line models.

Pinstripe dials for pocket watches were popular with the public in the 1920s. Illinois' Barrister model, shown earlier, featured such an option.

The only men's wristwatch dial with pinstriping that Illinois offered was for its flagship Consul model. This dial, of sterling silver, was made for Illinois by the Flückiger Company in Switzerland. Its style of pinstriping was similar to that on the dial for the Barrister. The Consul's dial had a muted silver finish rather than the bright-lined effect of the Barrister, but dials for the contemporary Hamilton Square and Cushion Form wristwatch models featured the attractive bright- lined design.

The back of these dials are stamped "ZJ" (for the initials of the founder of the dial company, Zélim Jacot) and "Argent" (French for "silver"), along with a Swiss stamp. The Illinois pinstripe Consul dial is stamped exactly the same as the Hamilton Cushion dial and are both pictured at right, identifying all of these dials as originating with the Flückiger dial firm of Switzerland.

Illinois Consul pinstripe Flückiger dial

Back of Illinois Consul pinstripe Flückiger dial

Hamilton Cushion pinstripe-center Flückiger dial

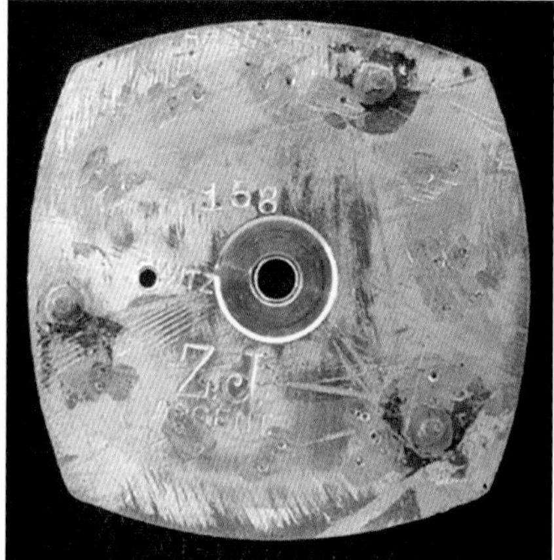
Back of Hamilton Cushion pinstripe-center Flückiger dial

Illinois custom pinstripe-center dial (Canby dial)

Illinois also offered a sterling silver pinstripe Flückiger dial for its finest ladies' wristwatch models, such as the Mary Todd 203, Mary Todd 204 and Coronado. This beautiful dial featured a pinstriped background and was further ornamented with a delicate floral motif at the edge of the pinstriping at the top and bottom. This dial, too was stamped "ZJ" and "Argent."

ZÉLIM JACOT AND THE FLÜCKIGERS

Z. Jacot, c. 1860

Zélim Jacot was born in Boudeviliers, Switzerland, in 1842. In 1860, he established a workshop in his name for making watch dials, which moved to several different locales before finally settling in Saint-Imier in 1884. The company's enamel dials were made by hand until 1895.

The business became known as ZJ Flückiger & Cie after Jacot took on Fritz Flückiger (1866–1908) as a partner. Fritz was the brother of Lise Anna Flückiger, whom Jacot married in 1885. (His first wife had been Julie Adèle Huguenin, whom he had married in 1866.)

After Jacot's death in 1904, the company was run by his brother-in-law and business partner. It was during this time that some semiautomatic machinery was introduced for polishing and other processes.

When Flückiger died, his wife took the reins of the company, assisted by their two sons. After 1909 the firm was thus called Flückiger et Fils SA. By the end of 1914, the company had begun to expand its manufacturing, particularly with regard to metal watch dials, including silver ones as well as dials for compasses.

The two brothers, André (1892–1979) and Fernand (1890–1932), took over running the company in 1923, the former handling business matters, the latter dealing with technical issues. After Fernand, an aviation enthusiast, was killed in an accident in 1932, André headed the company by himself. In 1941, he was succeeded by his son Pierre, and in 1974 by his grandson Pierre-André.

In 2004, Patek Philippe bought Flückiger et Fils SA, creating a new company named Cadrans Flückiger SA, which has continued to make watch dials.

Sources (in French): Anne Beuchat-Bessire and Catherine Krüttli, "Jacot, Zélim," in *Dictionnaire Historique de la Suisse* (http://www.hls-dhs-dss.ch/textes/f/F41258.php), and Emma Chatelain, "Flueckiger et Fils SA," in Dictionnaire du Jura (http://www.diju.ch/f/notices/detail/6494). Both apparently rely on M. Crélerot and L. Loze, *Centenaire de la fabrique de cadrans ZJ Flückiger & Cie,* 1960.

Ladies' Illinois sterling silver dial (Mary Todd 203, Mary Todd 204, Coronado et al.)

Bright-lined centers. Illinois enhanced the pinstripe effect on its pocket watch pinstripe dials by using a bright silver finish. (This effect was not used on Illinois pinstripe wristwatch dials, though it was on Hamilton's. See the discussion above.) Illinois designers created the effect by polishing the silver to shine like the mirrored surface of a tea service. Some pocket watch dials combined the highly polished silver with pinstripe engraving to produce what Illinois called the bright-line effect. Some Illinois pocket watch dials came with bright-cut, engine-turned, lined and silver finish, as shown here.

Silver finish, all-over bright-lined, engine-turned pattern

Engraving

Engraving involved a greater invasion of the metal surface than inscribing. To create engraved dials, craftsmen used a special engraving tool to create magnificent patterns in the dial metal, many with a floral or beaux arts flavor.

Illinois offered pocket watch dials with engraved centers. Occasionally an Illinois wristwatch collector can also find a standard Illinois dial with a custom engraved center. These engraved centers have been seen mostly, if not exclusively, on various Generic Period wristwatches such as the Canby, Square, Cushion, Devon, and Whippet models. It is not known if these custom features were added by the Illinois Watch Company or by jewelers as so few are known to exist.

Engraved center dial (Whippet dial)

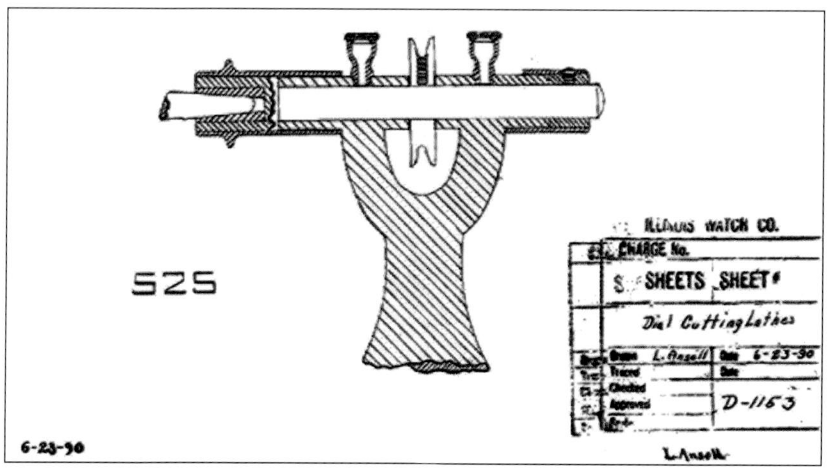

Drawing for an Illinois dial-cutting lathe, June 23, 1890

Some pocket watch dials had engraved green gold centers. There are a few custom wristwatch dials with engraved yellow gold centers, and at least one has been found with a custom engraved green gold center.

Green gold engraved center, wreath and silver butler finish subsidiary seconds

Engraved green gold center (Square dial)

Polishing

Almost all of the Illinois wristwatch dials incorporated a brass core coated with silver. Once the core was coated with silver, Illinois' dial manufacturers used various silver polishes and buffing techniques on the dials to produce bright, butler and matte finishes. A similar procedure was followed with the gold-finish dials. This chapter and the dials shown in this book demonstrate the great number of silver-finished Illinois wristwatch dials.

Butler Finish Background

Historically, goldsmiths and silversmiths incorporated specialized polishing techniques to produce varied effects in silver. They called a soft or satin finish a butler finish. Predictably, the use of butler finish spread to metal watch dials. Some Illinois pocket watches dials included butler finish backgrounds. The butler finish gave the dial a soft, satin-like appearance. In 1927 and earlier, Illinois used silver butler finishes on its dials for Generic Period models. After 1927 it limited the use of the butler finish technique on its wristwatch dials to the center of the dial or the subsidiary seconds.

Butler Center Dials

A butler finish center section for gold-or silver-coated dials gave them a two-toned appearance. The highly polished centers or subsidiary seconds bits of these dials, in either silver or gold, were produced by the use of cutting wheels (according to Robert Miller, president of International Dial Company). It is not known whether Illinois was the first to use this polishing technique, but it certainly mastered its use. Today the silver butler centers are more common, because the silver ones were used in white gold or white gold-filled wristwatch cases, which survived better over the years than the yellow cases that utilized the gold butler centers.

Silver Butler Finish

Unless an Illinois dial catalog stated "All over silver butler finish," the description "silver butler finish" or "silver butler center" could refer either to the center of the dial itself or to its subsidiary seconds bit. A fair number of wristwatch dials had either butler centers or silver butler center seconds bits.

Butler center subsidiary seconds bit (Square dial)

Silver Finish with Butler Center

Both Illinois pocket watch and wristwatch dials occasionally came with silver finish and butler centers, and some wristwatches came with gold butler centers.

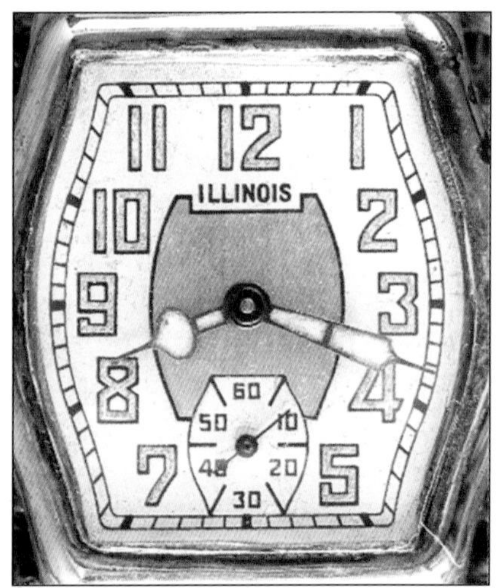

Silver butler center (Mate dial)

Silver Butler Center Subsidiary Seconds Dials

In the past, Illinois collectors deemed certain Illinois dials to be factory original if they had bright silver butler center subsidiary circles, as seen in the Square Cut Corner, Square, and Skyway dials. However, both NOS Locke and Skyway dials exist that have either bright silver center subsidiary seconds or without bright silver subsidiary seconds circles. Whereas almost all Illinois dials with silver butler center subsidiary seconds can be considered original, dials cannot automatically be deemed original if they have non-silvered subsidiary second circles. The collector intent on determining originality is advised to continue to judge based upon careful study, a trained eye, a powerful loupe and healthy skepticism.

Silver Matte Finish

Whereas butler finish dials exhibit a satin finish or silver white finish, silver matte dials have a flatter, almost gray look. From time to time, Illinois offered both Illinois pocket and wristwatches with silver matte finishes, although very few were offered on wristwatches.

Bright Silver Background

Some Illinois pocket watches came with bright silver backgrounds. No Illinois wristwatch dials had a bright silver background, although the vast majority of Illinois wristwatch dials had a silver finish.

Silver butler finish, fancy moiré center

Numerals

Luminous Numerals

Although Illinois used luminous (radium) numeral dials on some of its pocket watch dials, it used them much more frequently on its wristwatch dials. In fact, in its 1927 dial catalog, Illinois offered only luminous figures for its men's wristwatch dials.

Inlaid Enamel Numerals

With Illinois, inlaid enamel was applied only to silver dials. The technique could not be used with metal-coated dials. In any event, Illinois never used inlaid enamel for numerals on its wristwatch dials. On the other hand, several Illinois pocket watch dials came with inlaid enamel numerals. Pocket watch dials at times came with inlaid enamel and second bits; the Illinois wristwatch dials never did for the reason described above.

Non-Luminous Dials

Perhaps owing to the radium dial tragedy (discussed later in this chapter), there are at least two Illinois Finalist dials that are signed "non-luminous" on its very top, where it would be covered by the bezel of the watch.

Non-luminous signed dial (Finalist dial)

Black Numerals

Many Illinois pocket watches sported black numerals, as did many of the Illinois wristwatches. There were several different styles of fonts.

Extra-Heavy Arabic Numerals

This bold numeral option was featured on pocket watches and a few wristwatch dials, such as the Off-Duty and several Depollier models.

Off-Duty dial

The option to have extra-heavy Gothic Arabic numerals was available only for pocket watch dials.

Raised Gold-Finished Numerals

Illinois featured raised gold-finished numerals on some of the pocket watch dials. Although the Illinois wristwatch dials did not have this feature, several came with raised etched gold figures. Dial makers etched dials by protecting the raised portions of the watch with a waxy substance while washing the rest of the dial with a corrosive or acidic material.

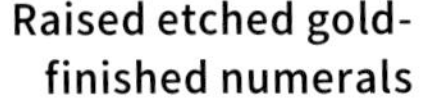

Raised etched gold-finished numerals

Silver Finish, Etched Raised Numerals

Illinois offered both pocket watch and wristwatch dials in this configuration. However, it offered it in combination with a raised wreath only on pocket watch dials.

Etched-raised gold numerals (Blackstone dial)

SOLIDARITY DIALS

The Solidarity Watch Case Company had a patented process to make applied figures for dials; it probably made some of these dials for Illinois.

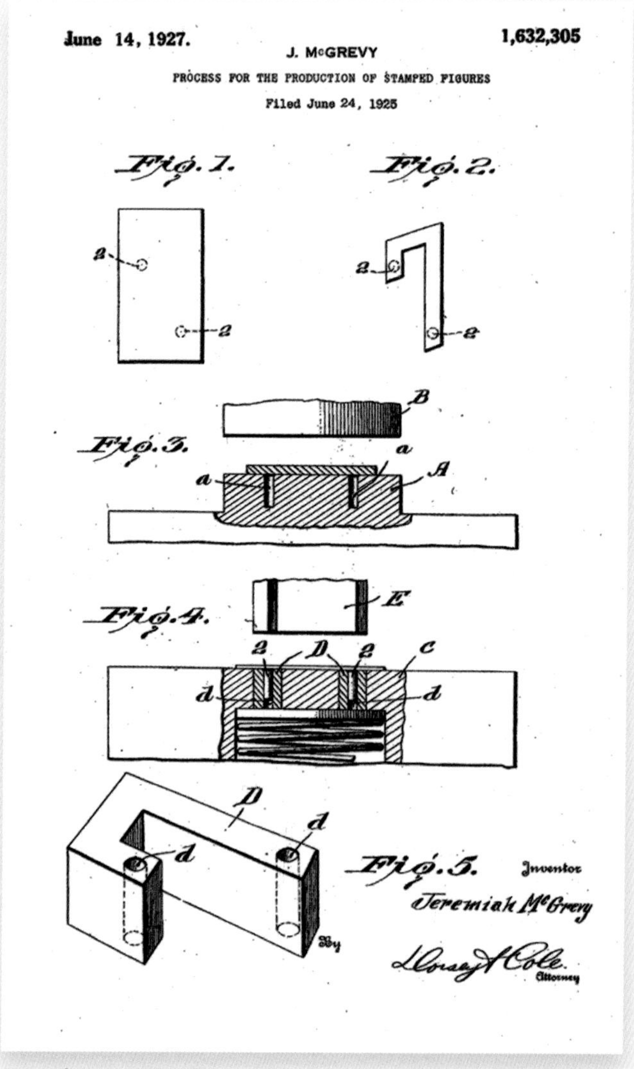

June 14, 1927. J. McGREVY 1,632,305

PROCESS FOR THE PRODUCTION OF STAMPED FIGURES

Filed June 24, 1925

Fig. 1. Fig. 2. Fig. 3. Fig. 4. Fig. 5.

Inventor
Jeremiah McGrevy
By
Lorsey Cole
Attorney

Issued June 4, 1927

Applied Gold Numerals

Toward the end of the Roaring Twenties, applied gold numerals became fashionable. Because the numerals had some thickness and lay on the surface of the dial, they created an attractive three-dimensional effect. This option became very popular with consumers, who viewed it as an improvement over the once-ubiquitous luminous numbers painted on the dial.

The attractiveness and popularity of this option allowed watch manufacturers to charge a premium for it, adding several dollars to the cost of a watch. For Illinois, applied gold numerals appeared most frequently on its most expensive wristwatches. Since dial makers used 18K gold for their applied gold numerals and dial workers placed them on the dial by hand, the material used and the labor involved justified adding a premium to the cost of the dial.

18K applied gold numerals (Rockliffe dial)

18K applied gold numeral (Hudson dial)

No Illinois wristwatch dial was offered with applied 18K green gold raised figures. However, several pocket watch dials were.

Flush Gold Numerals

Initially, two options existed for gold numerals. The first, known as flush gold numerals, did not have a three-dimensional quality and looked more like gold leaf. With the advent of raised gold numerals, this option virtually disappeared into obscurity. The Illinois ladies' Babette II model, released in 1934, sported flush gold numerals and an occasional men's dial could be acquired so configured.

Enamel Bezel Numerals

Placing the numbers in an enamel ring on the watch case, rather than on the dial, became popular in the late 1920s and early 1930s. Some designs included figures painted directly on the bezel, but most had a dark enamel bezel (blue or black) with numbers done in a contrasting enamel or, more commonly, using the bare metal itself. Illinois' Chevalier and Osgood/Brandt Rock and Hamilton's Coronado are three of the best examples.

Numeral Styles

Exploding numerals

The exaggerated numeral feature that appeared on some Illinois pocket watch dials, such as the Trustee model, would ultimately evolve into a more extreme form on Illinois wristwatch dials, becoming one of Illinois' signature features: exploding numerals. The numbers, placed radially at angles and on their backs, looked as if they "exploded" from the center of the dial. Although the design style did not originate with Illinois, Illinois greatly enhanced it. Exploding numeral dials are much in demand from today's collectors. In fact, this feature has been liberally copied by watchmakers of today.

Exaggerated numerals (Trustee dial)

Exploding numerals (Major dial)

Black Painted Numerals

Many Illinois pocket and wristwatch dials came with silver finish and black painted figures.

Drop Shadow Numerals

The use of drop shadow numerals was limited to certain wristwatches only.

Drop shadow numerals (Derby dial)

Drop shadow numerals (Kenilworth dial)

Wreaths

Illinois offered many of its pocket watch dials with wreaths, usually appearing as an interconnected design in the shape of a square, rectangle or cross around the center of the watch. In the pocket watch era, wreaths could be found on pocket watch dials from most manufacturers. With the advent of the wristwatch, however, most other watch manufacturers dropped the wreath motif. Illinois, however, persevered in offering wreath designs on dials. The wreath thus became one of Illinois' signature dial features. For wristwatches, the wreath always utilized the interlocking Greek-key pattern.

Some of the pocket watch dials that Illinois offered with Greek-key wreaths on them had the wreaths engraved in the center of the dial. On some pocket watches, Illinois offered engraved wreaths in green gold.

Green gold engraved center and wreath

For wristwatches, Illinois simplified production of the wreath by printing it on the dial, rather than engraving it. Usually, but not always, the wristwatch wreath would conform to the shape of the bezel opening.

Wreath (Marquis Strap dial)

Some original Illinois dials intended mainly for certain Generic Period cases have an attractive added feature, a cross-pattern wreath in the center of the dial.

Cross-pattern wreath (Locke dial)

Rotor Seconds

Dials with silver finish and rotor subsidiary seconds were available on some Illinois pocket watch and wristwatch models. Among the Illinois wristwatch models with rotor subsidiary seconds was the Guardsman, shown here.

NOS rotor subsidiary seconds dial (Guardsman dial)

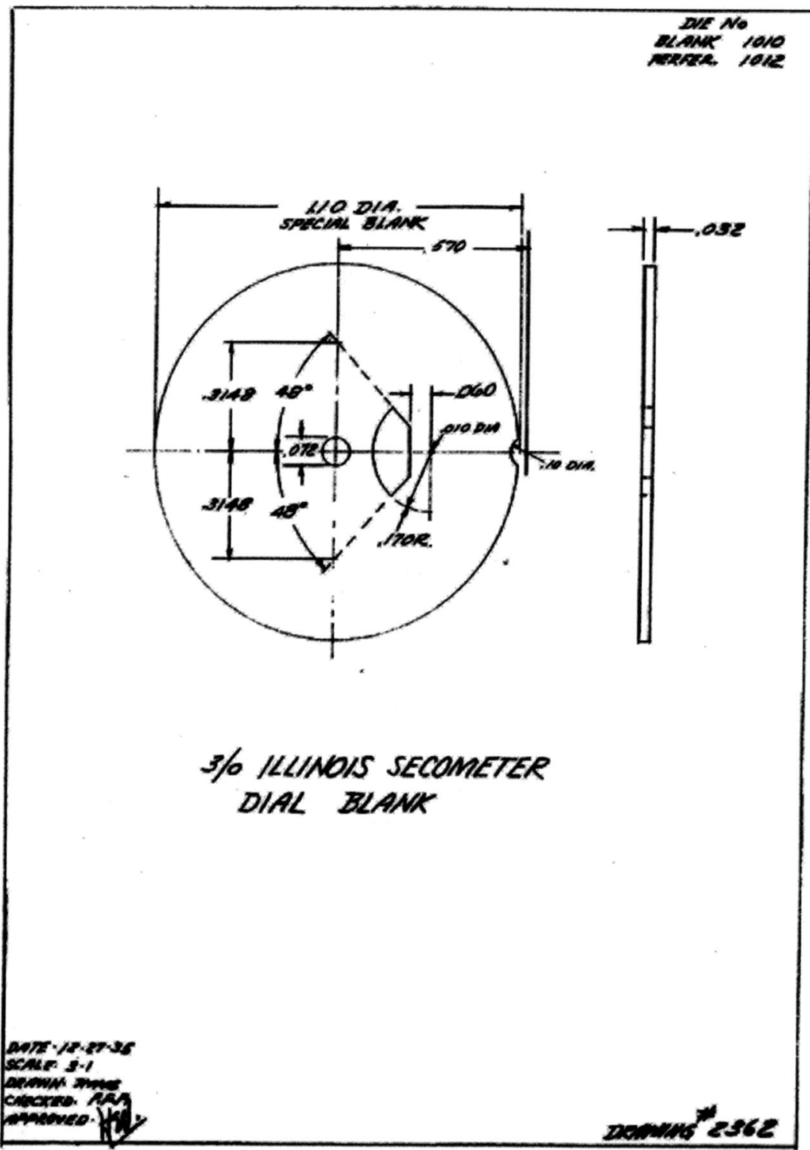

Illinois Guardsman dial blank drawing by Hamilton, December 27, 1935

PRICES On EXPORTS

March 5, 1930.

My dear Jack:

Many thanks for your letter of February 26th, and am very glad to note that you will make up rotor second dials on #127 129, 121 as well as #307 without extra charge in lots of ten.

We are writing Heacock & Cheeck today as well as one or two other outlets along these lines.

For your information would advise that the price which we quote on these movements to the export jobbers is as follows:-

#127 - $10.35. #129 - $13.50. #121 - $16.35. #307 - $11.95.

These prices are subject to a cash discount of 6% which brings the net return to the Illinois Co. the same as if the 3% cash discount was allowed. We are raising it to 6% in order that both Hamilton and Illinois Watches may be invoiced - subject to the same cash discount, thus making it unnecessary to make two separate invoices showing two separate cash discounts and complicating matters with these foreigners whom it is advisable to make things just as simple and easy to understand as is possible.

There is one point that I would like to mention at this time in connection with prices and that is the #127. You probably recall that the Illinois made up a quantity of #415's which was a special 12-size 17j having a brass escape wheel, etc. which we priced at $9.55 subject to a cash discount of 6%-making a net return to the Company of $8.99.

We have sent a quantity of these #415 movements to Japan and as advised Mr. R.E.Miller in my letter of September 4th, it would place us in an embarrassing position to immediately revise this price when shifting over to #127's and discontinuing the #415's, and Mr. Miller has agreed to allow the price of $9.55 to stand for export on the #127.

However, as there are only a few points that we will furnish the movement only, in fact KHattori & Co. are about the only concern that we have contacted with and quoted prices of $9.55 on this movement, the writer believes that he can confine it to this one account. However, when quoting any other firm we will use the price basis of $10.35 on the #127 as a movement alone or fitted in a customer's case.

I would suggest that you go ahead andput thru a lot of #129's to take care of the requisitions which you now have and I am writing Heacock & Cheek today advising that I wan an order for seven more of these to take care of the lot of ten that we are putting thru at the present time.

Very truly yours,

(Signed) Fred

FJBoulton/EBR

Letter concerning Illinois rotor dial models to be exported. F. J. Boulton was a Hamilton manager in Lancaster, and "Jack" was J. L. Keenan, the Illinois sales manager.

Although Illinois dial designers often referred visually to pocket watch features for wristwatches, they did not use the whole library of pocket watch dial design elements. Some examples of elements *not* used are noted here.

- *White sparkle finish, butler center, etched figures.* Illinois offered this combination among its pocket watch dial alternatives, but no wristwatch dial sported this combination.
- *Bright-lined center*
- *Bright silver background*
- *Engine-turned center and seconds bit*
- *Applied raised steel figures*
- *Enamel numerals.* Some Illinois pocket watch dials were offered with the choice of blue or black enamel numerals. No Illinois wristwatch was offered with enamel numerals; however, there are some custom wristwatch dials that have unusual blue radium numerals.

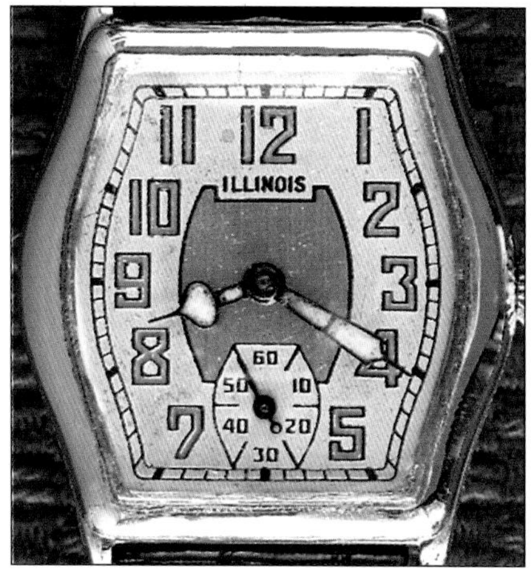

Blue radium numerals (Mate dial)

- *Montgomery style.* This type of dial was available only for pocket watches.

Montgomery-style numeral dial

- *24-hour dial.* Twenty-four hour dials show numerals 1 through 12 around the circumference of the dial, and the numbers 13 through 24 appear above the first twelve numbers. Customers found such dials useful for military service, where a 24-hour clock was used. Illinois offered a pocket watch dial option for a 24-hour dial, but did not offer a similar feature for any wristwatch dial.
- *Silver or gold wood-grain finish*
- *Bright-cut sun-ray pattern.* This pattern of dial was offered on the Illinois Autocrat pocket watch model but never on a wristwatch dial.

Features Found Only on Wristwatch Dials

- *Sunburst dials.* Illinois produced only one sunburst dial. It was for the high-end Consul model, and the color of the sunburst could be black, silver or gold.

Sunburst dial, close-up (Consul dial)

Mr. Lee Henry,
Gibson Hotel,
Cincinnati, O.

Dear Pat:

On your order No.18 sent in for watches to be shipped to Wallenstein-Mayer Company, you make note that we advised by letter the railroads upon which Montgomery dials are accepted when fitted upon railroad watches.

We are not sure whether you wanted us to write Wallenstein-Mayer or if you wishes this information yourself. As you are to be in Cincinnati, and if it was Wallenstein-Mayer that wanted the information, you can pass it along. Do so in a verbal manner.

The Montgomery dial is a dial, as you will note from the attached illustration, made up with the minute margin figures from one to sixty arranged in an upright position around the outer edge of dial, each of the five minute figures in red and the others in black. Also, the hour figure six in the center of the second bit.

This dial is patented by Mr. R. D. Montgomery who is General Time Inspector of the Atchison, Topeka and Santa Fe Railway System. As General Time Inspector of that System he requires that all watches taken into service be equipped with Montgomery dials. To insure the watches being constructed properly and equipped with the correct type of dial. All new watches purchased by any employee of the Santa Fe System must have the watches certified by the General Time Inspector at Topeka, Kansas and certificate issued.

This is the only system that has this definite ruling. On the M.K.T. Railway system of which Mr. Montgomery is also Time Inspector, the Montgomery dial is a standard equipment.

There may be a few other connecting lines to these two systems that use the Montgomery dial, but on all other large systems throughout the United States, the plain heavy Arabic figure dial is the dial that is accepted.

Most of the other General Time Inspectors, as you will notice from the attached copy of a General notice, state very definitely that no watches equipped with fancy dials will be accepted, for service. If the information as given is not all that you and your customer wanted, get the specific questions and we will gladly answer them.

Very truly yours,

ILLINOIS WATCH

JLK:ALD — Sales Manager

March 1930 Illinois letter about Montgomery dials from Jack Keenan

- *Dials signed "17 Jewels."* For an added marketing feature, Illinois would from time to time sign some of its dials "17 Jewels" it is mostly seen on some of its 12/0 size dials and occasionally on a Ritz dial. This is somewhat surprising as it probably would have been more advantageous for Illinois to do so on its models with 19 or 21 jewel movements. It appears that Hamilton signed the number of jewels on its dials intended for export, so perhaps it directed Illinois to do this at times as well.

Dial signed "17 Jewels" (Ritz dial)

"Lift At 12"

Some 12/0 size Illinois dial have printed on the bottom of the dial an instruction to "Lift at 12" when removing the dial and movement from the case.

"Lift at 12" and drop shadow numerals (Kenilworth dial)

Shared Dial Features

As this chapter has shown, Illinois pocket watch dials and wristwatch dials shared some features. As the vast majority of pocket watch dials were round, their design basically had to account for only their round shape. Therefore, to distinguish the pocket watch, many different dial designs and techniques were employed. Whereas wristwatches varied more as to case and dial shapes and designs, with pocket watches the variation of the design was frequently in the dial itself. Designers chose design elements to accommodate the opportunities and limitations of each.

By 1927, during the close of the Generic Period, Illinois Watch Company wristwatches featured at least one dozen distinct dial shapes for its men's and women's models.

With wristwatches, the shape of the wreath mirrored the bezel opening in most but not all instances. For pocket watches, the wreath was almost universally round. On the other hand, by 1927 the Illinois wristwatch dials already had three different shaped wreaths. This permitted more design possibilities. Many dial design elements, except perhaps the exploding numerals, sunburst dials and drop shadow numerals, existed on Illinois pocket watches before migrating to Illinois wristwatch dials.

Illinois Wristwatch Dial Features

The following lists categorize the various design features used on Illinois wristwatches, by model. Men's are in black type, ladies' in red type and unisex models in blue type.

18K Applied Gold Numerals		
Ardsley	Baronet	Hudson
Beau Geste	Cavalier	Rockliffe
Beau Monde	Consul	

Flush Gold Numerals		
Antionette	Chatham	Rockingham

Silver Finish, Raised Etched-Gold Numerals		
Andover	Chatham	Rockliffe
Argyle	Consul	Rockliffe 18/0
Avalon	Manhattan	Standish
Baronet	Mary Todd	Tuxedo
Beau Geste	New Yorker	Urbana
Beau Monde	Piccadilly	Vardon
Berkshire	Potomac	
Blackstone	Rockingham	

Square Cut Corner Large NOS dial

Black Figures		
Ace	Consul	Medalist
Andover	Countess	New Yorker
Antoinette	Cushion	Newport
Ardsley	Devon	Off-Duty
Argyle	Débette	Paul Revere
Arlington	Derby	Piccadilly
Atlantic	Edgewater	Pimlico
Avalon	Ensign	Potomac
Babette	Fairport	Princess
Baronet	Finalist	Puritan
Beau Brummell	Finalist Deco	Rectangular
Beau Brummell/ Viking	Frontenac	Redonda
Beau Geste	Futura	Rita
Beau Monde	Glencoe	Ritz
Beau Royale	Gloria	Southampton
Belmont	Haddon Hall	Special
Berkshire	Hawthorne	Speedway
Beverly	Hollywood	Speedway 178
Biltmore 6/0	Janette	Square
Blackstone	Jolly Roger	Standish
Bostonian	Kenilworth	Suzette
Brighton	Kingston	Tank
Bryce	Larchmont	Townsman
Canby	Large Square Cut Corner	Trophy
Caprice	LaSalle	Urbana
Cavalier	Lynette	Vanity Fair
Charmette	Major	Vardon
Chevalier	Manhattan	Viking
Chieftain	Marquis Strap	Wentworth
Claudette	Marlette	Whippet
Commodore	Mate	Yorktown

Butler Centers		
Ace	Kingston	Potomac
Berkeley 153	Long Beach	Rockingham
Bryce	Major	Saratoga – Notched Leaf
Chieftain	Manhattan	Saratoga Leaf
Coronado	Marquis Strap	Southampton
Cushion	Mary Todd	Square Cut Corner
Daytona 153	Medalist	Speedway
Daytona 155	Miami 157	Speedway 178
Del Monte 157	Narragansett	Tank
Devon	New Yorker	Whippet
Ensign	New Yorker Enamel	
Jolly Roger	Newport 223	

Butler Center Subsidiary Seconds		
Ace	New Yorker	Special
Atlantic	New Yorker Enamel	Square
Bryce	Octagon	Square Cut Corner
Canby	Off-Duty	Square Cut Corner Large
Cushion	Police Special	Tank
Devon	Rectangular	Tonneau
Manhattan	Skyway	Whippet
Marquis Strap	Southampton	

Embossed Centers and/or Numerals		
Berkeley 154	Mary Todd GG	Redonda
Diamond-Set	Mary Todd 204	Redonda 154
Mary Todd	Newport 223	

Engraved Centers	
Bryce	Square
Canby	Whippet
Rectangular	

Extra Heavy Arabic Numerals	
D-D Utility	
Depollier Dustproof/ Waterproof	Off-Duty Special
Mary Todd	

Fancy Moiré Centers	
Octagon	Tonneau

Gold Finish	
Beau Brummell	Kingston
Beau Royale	Manhattan
Beau Brummell/Viking	New Yorker
Ensign	New Yorker Enamel

Silver Matte Finish	
Mary Todd	Southampton
Puritan	Townsman
Skyway	

Exploding Numerals		
Edgewater 208	Major	Speedway 178
Edgewater 222	Newport 174	
Jolly Roger	Speedway	

Luminous Numerals		
Ace	Finalist Deco	Seneca
Akron / Aluminum Prototype	Frontenac	Skyway
	Futura	Southampton
Atlantic	Greyhound	Special
Beau Brummell	Greystone	Speedway
Beau Brummell/Viking	Guardian	Speedway 178
Beau Geste	Guardsman	Sportsman
Beau Monde	Haddon Hall	Square
Beau Royale	Jolly Roger	Square Cut Corner
Biltmore 18/0	Kingston	Square Cut Corner/Large
Blackhawk	Major	Tank
Blackstone	Manhattan	Townsman
Bryce	Marquis Strap	Trophy
Canby	Mate	Tuxedo
Cavalier	Medalist	United States Army
Chieftain	Motor Coach	Viking
Consul	New Yorker	Wentworth
Cushion	New Yorker Enamel	Whippet
Devon	Paul Revere	
Ensign	Piccadilly	
Finalist	Rectangular	

Silver Finish						
Ace	Beverly 185	Derby	Hudson	Muzette	Saratoga Leaf	Vogue
Alouette	Beverly 852	Devon	Irene	Narragansett	Saratoga Notched Leaf	Wentworth
Andover	Biloxi	Diamond Sets	Janette	New Yorker		Whippet
Annette	Biltmore 18/0	Edgewater	Joan	Newport	Sherwood	Yorktown
Antoinette	Blackstone	Edgewater 155	Jolly Roger	Newport 174	Skyway	
Ardsley	Brighton	Edgewater 175	Juliette	Newport 223	Southampton	
Argyle	Bryce	Edgewater 208	Kingston	No. 241	Special	
Arlene	Canby	Edgewater 222	Larchmont	Octagon	Speedway	
Arlington	Cavalier	Elissa	Lady Mary	Off-Duty	Speedway 178	
Atlantic	Charmette	Ensign	Lakewood	Osgood	Square	
Avalon	Chatham	Fairfax	LaSalle	Patricia	Square Cut Corner	
Babette	Chevalier	Fairport	Latonia	Paul Revere	Square Cut Corner Large	
Bar Harbor 156	Chieftain	Finalist	Lenox	Piccadilly		
Bar Harbor 158	Claudette	Finalist Deco	Long Beach	Pimlico	Sportsman	
Barbara	Commodore	Florentine	Lynette	Princess	Standish	
Beau Brummell	Consul	Florette	Major	Potomac	Suzette	
Beau Brummell/ Viking	Coronado	Frontenac	Manhattan	Queen Anne	Sylvia	
Beau Geste	Coquette	Futura	Mariette	Rectangular	Tank	
Beau Monde	Countess	Glenna 186	Marilyn	Redonda	Tonneau	
Beau Royale	Cushion	Glenna 239	Marionette	Rita	Townsman	
Belmont	Daytona 153	Glencoe	Marlette	Ritz	Trophy	
Berkeley 153	Daytona 154	Gloria	Marquis Strap	Rockingham	Tuxedo	
Berkeley 154A	Daytona 155	Greta	Mary Todd	Rockliffe	Urbana	
Berkeley 154B	Daytona 155A	Guardsman	Mary Todd 203	Rockliffe 18/0	Vanity Fair	
Berkshire	Daytona 155B	Hawthorne	Mate	Rosette	Vardon	
Beverly	Débette	Hollywood	Medalist	Roslyn	Viking	

Silver Finish, Rotor Subsidiary Seconds	
Akron/ Aluminum Protype	Guardsman
Aluminum Prototype	Guardsman Military
Blackhawk	Seneca
Guardian	Sterling

White Sparkle Finish		
Andover	Commander	Latonia
Arlington	Commodore	Locke
Ardsley	Daytona	Metropolitan
Avalon	Derby	Miami 155
Babette II	Edgewater	Newport
Baronet	Exeter	No. 250/ Schmukler
Beau Geste	Fairport	Paul Revere
Beau Monde	Finalist	Pimlico
Belmont	Finalist Deco	Redonda
Berkshire	Futura	Richmond
Biltmore 6/0	Gallahad	Ritz
Blackstone	Glencoe	Rockcliffe
Bostonian	Greystone	Roslyn
Brighton	Haddon Hall	Valedictorian
Caprice	Hawthorne	Vanity Fair
Chesterfield	Hudson	Vernon
Chesterfield Stepped Bezel	Kenilworth	Wentworth
Claudette	Larchmont	
	LaSalle	

Wreaths		
Ace	Devon	Southampton
Atlantic	Fairport	Speedway
Atlantic Enamel	Jolly Roger	Speedway 178
Avalon	Major	Standish
Berkshire	Marquis Strap	Tank
Biltmore 18/0	Rectangular	Tuxedo
Brighton	Riley	Vanity Fair
Bryce	Square	Whippet
Canby	Square Cut Corner	
Cushion	Square Cut Corner Large	

The Tragic Story of Radium Numeral Dials

In the early twentieth century, the hazards of dealing with radium were not known, and dial painters were initially assured that their work was safe. Typically it was young girls, aged eleven to mid-twenties, who were involved in painting luminous dials. They were taught to "lip-point" their paint brushes, putting the little brush between their lips to get a good point on it in order to paint dials more accurately. But in doing this, they were ingesting radium as well as paint. They suffered the horrible consequences.

One of the largest employers of these dial painters was the Radium Dial Company, of Ottawa, Illinois. When news broke about the national scandal involving the hazards of painting radium dials, these "radium girls" became known as "The Ottawa Society of the Living Dead."[1]

Fortunately, the Illinois Watch Company did not employ radium dial painters, and the vast majority of the wristwatch dials used by Illinois were produced after 1925, when the practice of lip-pointing brushes had already been banned in the United States.

Litigation seeking recompense for the horrific ill-effects and deaths suffered by these dial painters was vigorously contested by the dial-painting companies. Although the plaintiffs generally prevailed in the litigations, victories were never easy and the battles were long. The cases won were largely pyrrhic victories as the damage awards were usually for only a few hundred dollars.

Radium Paint Inventor Dies, Victim of His Own Discovery

In the December 1928 issue of the *Keystone* was this note: "Dr. Sabin Von Sochocky, inventor of luminous radium paint, died November 14 in East Orange, New Jersey, the victim of his own invention. He was a consulting expert for the United States Radium Corporation and had been ill for more than a year. Eleven blood transfusions were resorted to in the effort to overcome the radioactive substance found in his body. His colleague in research work, Dr. Edward Lehman, died of radium poisoning in 1925."

Investigate Use of Radium in Watch and Clock Industries

The *Keystone*, reporting in its January 1929 issue about a recent conference in Washington regarding the use of radium in the clock and watch industry and other lines of work, noted: "Labor, generally, is opposed to the use of radium, it was indicated by Ethelbert Stewart, chief of the bureau of labor statistics of the Department of Labor. Mr. Stewart declared that . . . the elimination of brushes in painting the dials might be of some help although he asserted the problem of safeguarding workers' lives can not be solved as long as they are exposed to radium rays. . . ."

But another perspective was also reported, "American watch companies would gladly discontinue the production of luminous watches if the competition of the foreign product could be prevented, it was declared by T. S. Springer, representing the Elgin Watch Company. . . . However, he added, so long as watches with luminous dials may be imported from abroad, it is essential that the domestic manufacturers produce a similar article to meet the competition."

Plan Examination for Every Radium Dial Painter

In April 1929, the *Keystone* noted: "Physical and electroscopic examination of every radium dial painter in the United States, with a view to determining the health hazards involved in the use of this substance for illuminating watch and clock dials, will be undertaken during the course of an investigation to be made by officials of the Public Health Service."

A group of five health officials was to conduct the study. The results were to be used to develop recommendations for state laws to regulate the use of radium so as to minimize danger to workers.

Seek Protection for Workers Exposed to Radium

In the August 1929 issue of the *Keystone* was this announcement:

"Protection for workers using radium compounds will be sought at a conference of federal and state health officials to be held upon conclusion of an investigation into the dangers of exposure to radium now being conducted by the United States Public Health Service."

It was noted that radium painting of watch and clock dials had already proved fatal to twenty-one workers. The plan was to examine several hundred workers who were exposed to radium rays.

112 THE JEWELERS' CIRCULAR-WEEKLY January 9, 1918.

Radium Luminous Compound
"LUMA"

We can help you to a bigger share of the luminous dial business. The proper technic in applying is almost as essential to good luminescence as the quality of the compound. We furnish "LUMA" and our experts apply it to dials of every description.

RADIUM DIAL COMPANY
Forbes and Meyran Aves., Pittsburgh, Pa.
New York Office—1612 Astor Trust Bldg.

Luminous Watches

Any watch that has good hand clearance can be made luminous by our factory. Radium Dials should have a reputation for quality behind them. Let us tell you how we can illuminate yours.

We are the pioneers in America for self-luminous (Radium) compounds and the many uses for them.

Military Wrists Pocket Watches
Dials Hands Repairs

Radium Luminous Material Shines in the Dark

TEST YOUR DIALS AT NIGHT

Radium Luminous Material Corporation
Fifty-five Liberty Street NEW YORK CITY

138 THE JEWELERS' CIRCULAR-WEEKLY August 29, 1917.

Mining Carnotite in the Paradox Valley

Come to the Ingersoll booth at the convention and get a sample of carnotite from which radium and Ingersoll Radiolite are Made. If you're not at the convention, sample will be mailed on request

We are distributing one hundred pounds of carnotite to our friends in the trade so that you can see the ore which is responsible for the glow on the Ingersoll Radiolite watches. It takes a ton of this ore to make a small fraction of a gram of radium.

Ingersoll Radiolite contains real radium and will shine in the dark for years entirely through its own power. It is the radium striking against the other twelve minerals of which Radiolite is made that causes the glow.

We back our statement that Radiolite does contain Radium with our entire resources and our twenty-five years in business. Write or ask at the booth about the black paper test, and be sure and get the book "Radiolite, A Discovery for Watches." All without charge. Address the New York branch at 315 Fourth Avenue.

ROBT. H. INGERSOLL & BRO., New York, Boston, Chicago, San Francisco

Shown are various 1917–1918 advertisements capitalizing on the demand for military-like radium dials with luminous numerals during World War I. Note that Ingersoll was distributing carnotite samples at trade shows.

Defends Use of Radium on Watch and Clock Dials

During the controversy in the United States over the use of radium on dials, Hugo Buchser of Geneva, representing various Swiss manufacturers, wrote to the *Keystone*. In his letter, published in the March 1930 issue, he stated that after inspection of Swiss facilities "there had been no known case of illness or harmful exposure due to the effects of radium."

Buchser added that "every new workman has his attention drawn to the fact that it is extremely dangerous to lick the brushes used for the luminous paint and he must carefully wash his hands before leaving the room. As long as the workers observe these simple rules there is not the slightest risk of infection."

He commented that all the dial painters "looked very healthy. In fact, the very small quantity of radio-active sales in luminous materials as a health stimulant acting in a similar fashion to the radio-active springs." Buchser did not cite any scientific support for his views.

RADIUM SULPHUR SPRINGS
NATURAL RADIO-ACTIVE MINERAL WATER
It Sparkles and Foams Like Champagne

Hot Baths and Treatments cure Rheumatism, Sciatica, Neuritis, Paralysis, Locomotor Ataxia, Poor Circulation, Heart, Stomach, Liver, Kidney, Diabetes, Bright's, Blood and Nervous Diseases, Female Troubles. Doctor's advice free. Water delivered. Send for Booklet.

Melrose Ave. Cars Direct to Springs, Los Angeles

SANITARIUMS AND MINERAL BATHS

Radium Sulphur Springs COLEGROVE, LOS ANGELES

TAKE BATHS IN LIQUID SUNSHINE
DRINK THE MOST CURATIVE MINERAL WATER IN CALIFORNIA.

It is radio-active, germicidal and purifies your blood by destroying disease germs, thereby revivifying, rejuvenating and increasing your Vital Force and circulation

THE RADIUM SULPHUR HOT BATHS

Quickly relieve and cure Rheumatism, Alcoholism, Stomach Troubles, Constipation, Chronic Colds, Liver, Kidney, Blood and Skin Troubles, Poor Circulation, Bright's Disease, Sciatica, Neuralgia, Paralysis, Locomotor Ataxia, Nervous Prostration, diseases of the spine and nervous system, Female Troubles. The Beauty Baths for Skin clear the complexion, make the skin velvety, eyes bright, hair glossy, stops hair falling, grows new hair.

IT SPARKLES AND FOAMS LIKE CHAMPAGNE.

Wonderful cures are no doubt due to germicidal and radio-active gaseous emanation from Radium Rays, deep in the mineralized earth, whence this water comes. Chronic and seemingly hopeless cases cured. Medical advice free. Send for booklet. Water by bottle or case. Take "Melrose Avenue" cars via Broadway, direct to Springs; 5c fare.

Radium cure advertisements, c. 1920s

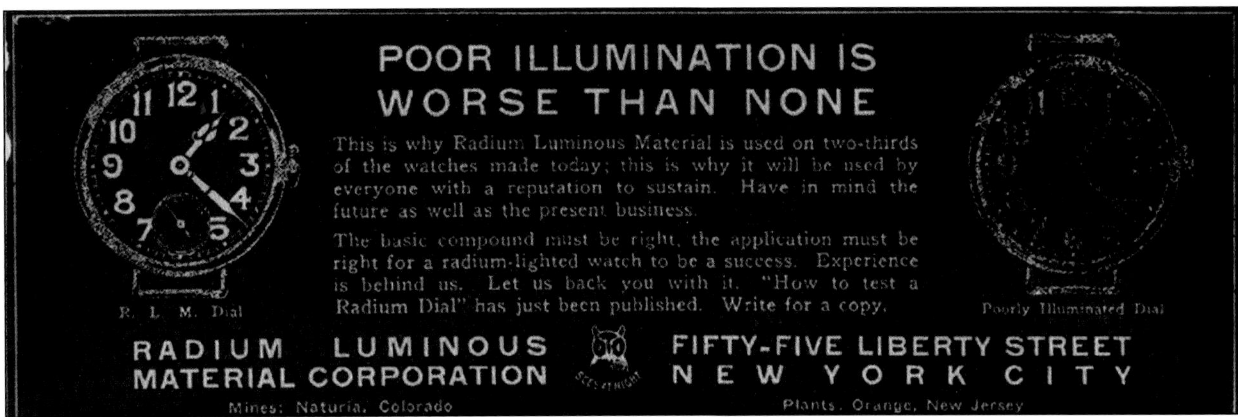

Jewelers' Circular-Weekly, February 27, 1918; advertisement for radium dials

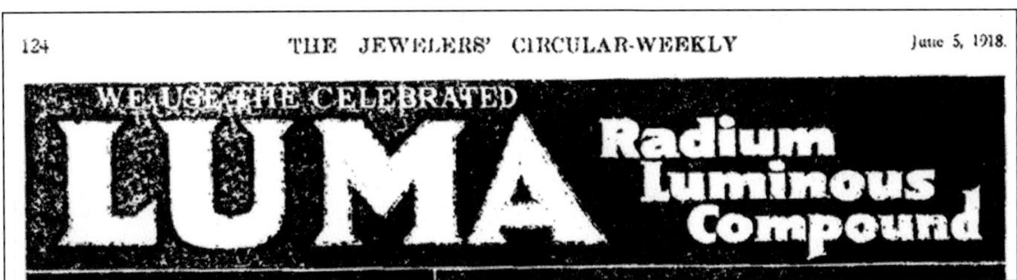

Jewelers' Circular-Weekly, June 5, 1918

LAST RADIUM GIRL DIES AT 107

The *New York Times* reported on March 13, 2014 that Mae Keane, the last known Radium Girl, had died. At the age of eighteen, Mary O'Donnell (nicknamed Mae) started to work as a radium dial painter in 1924 for the Waterbury Clock Company in Waterbury, Connecticut. There she was taught to lip-point her brush. She did not like the "gritty" texture of the radium paint in her mouth.

Fortunately for her, as it turned out, she was not very good at her job and was let go after a few months. Within twenty years she had lost all of her teeth, and she later had colon and breast cancer, but if she had remained working at Waterbury, she would likely have died young.

Lip-pointing was banned starting in 1925 by new federal regulations. Decades later, when bodies of some of the Radium Girls were exhumed, their bones were still radioactive.

Office of the Waterbury Clock Company in Waterbury, CT, c. 1920s

LUMINOSITY GUARANTEED FOR THE LIFE OF THE WATCH

In February 1918, Ingersoll advertised that their Radiolite Day-and-Night watches had "Luminosity guaranteed for the life of the watch." If they had only known!

Saturday Evening Post, February 23, 1918

TECHNICAL TIP

HALF-LIFE OF RADIUM

David Boettcher points out the half-life of radium is about 1,600 years, so over the 100 or so years since a watch dial was painted with luminous paint, the radium activity will have decayed about 4%, about 1% for every 25 years. This means that paint that was made with radium 100 years ago will still be 96% as radioactive today as the day it was made. Radium and its fission decay products (such as radon gas) have the potential to cause various health risks, and therefore watches with radium paint should be handled carefully and in ways to minimize the risks. The danger is not so much from radiation received from the watch when wearing or being near it, but more from inhalation or ingestion of paint particles or contaminated dust.*

*vintagewatchstraps.com

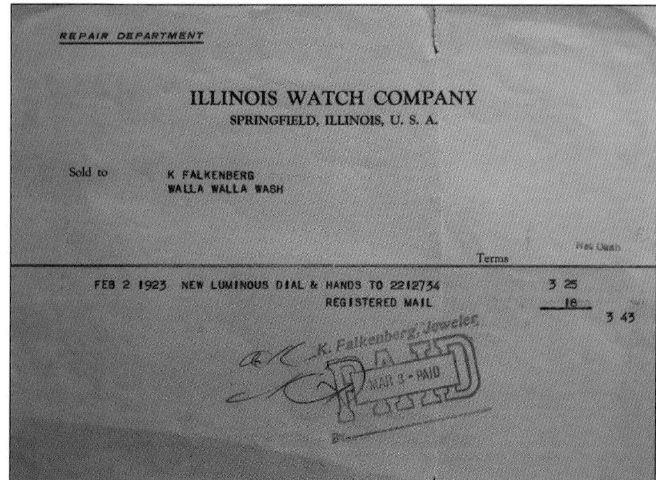

REPAIR DEPARTMENT

ILLINOIS WATCH COMPANY
SPRINGFIELD, ILLINOIS, U. S. A.

Sold to K FALKENBERG
WALLA WALLA WASH

Terms Net Cash

FEB 2 1923 NEW LUMINOUS DIAL & HANDS TO 2212734 3 25
REGISTERED MAIL 18
3 43

K. Falkenberg, Jeweler
MAR 3 - PAID

Illinois dial and hands invoice, dated February 2, 1923

Dial painters at the Ottawa Radium Dial Company, 1924. *Deadly Glow*, Ross Mullner, PhD, MPH.

> ## TECHNICAL TIP
> ### TESTING LUMINOUS PAINT FOR RADIOACTIVITY
>
> Boettcher further notes that if you think your watch has luminous paint on the hands and numerals, the first easy test is to keep it in the dark overnight and examine it while still in the dark. Then expose it to sunlight and take it into a dark room. If it was dark after being kept in the dark overnight, and then charged up in the sunlight and glows brightly in the dark, it has a modern "light charged" luminous compound and is quite safe. Although zinc sulphide will charge up in sunlight and then glow in the dark, old radiation-damaged zinc sulphide exhibits very little response to sunlight, and its characteristics are very different from those of modern luminous paint. If the zinc sulphide doesn't glow in the dark due to radium radioactivity, but does glow when charged up by sunlight, then logic says there isn't any radium present.
>
> However, if the paint remains dark at all times, then it may have radium paint. If it does glow faintly in the dark but doesn't charge up in sunlight, then it almost certainly has radium paint.*
>
> *vintagewatchstraps.com

Illinois Radium Vial Found

In April 2015, Adam Harris, a guest curator at the National Watch & Clock Museum, Library and Research Center (NAWCC), came across two vials of radium dial paint powder (zinc sulfide) while he was examining some items in secure storage at the museum. One was marked "Hamilton" and one "Illinois." This still highly active material appeared light lime green in color; in pitch-black conditions it glowed bright green from the effects of the radium excitation.

In terms of its life cycle, the radium in these vials is still in its infancy; in almost one hundred years it has degraded by a little over four percent.

Harris later reported that when apprised of the discovery, the curator of the museum immediately contacted the Pennsylvania Department of Environmental Protection (DEP). Following their advice, the museum purchased a Geiger counter and acquired a thick lead storage box. The two vials are currently stored in that.[2]

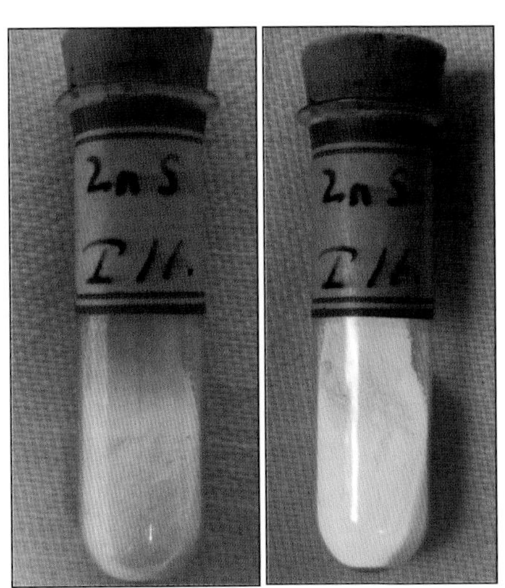

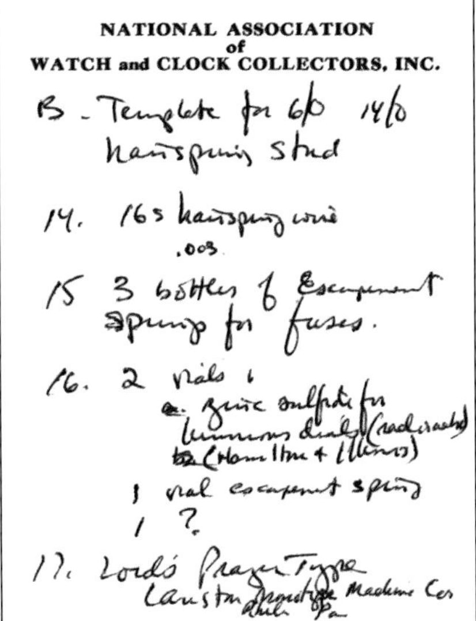
NATIONAL ASSOCIATION of WATCH and CLOCK COLLECTORS, INC.

13. Template for 6/0 14/0 hairspring stud

14. 16s hairspring wire .003

15 3 bottles of Escapement springs for fuses.

16. 2 vials
a. zinc sulfide for luminous dials (radioactive) (Hamilton + Illinois)
1 vial escapement spring
1 ?

17. Lord's Prayer Type ... Machine Co

Left: **Vial directly out of closed storage box, only fluorescent light in room.** *Right*: **Vial with light off, glowing in darkness.** *Far Right*: **NAWCC inventory record for the vials. Photographs courtesy of the National Watch & Clock Museum, Library and Research Center (NAWCC), Columbia, PA**

COUNTERFEIT DIALS

In May 1935, the Elgin, Hamilton, Illinois and Waltham watch companies secured an injunction in Federal District Court in Birmingham, Alabama, against the Benson Gold Refining Company for infringement of the trademark names of Elgin, Hamilton, Illinois and Waltham, for selling spurious, bogus or counterfeit dials containing their trademark names. This was not an uncommon offense in the 1930s.

Watch Companies Get Injunction and Damages Against Alabama Concerns Which Used Counterfeit Dials

BIRMINGHAM, ALA., May 4—There is considerable interest in the jewelry and watch industries in the decisions just rendered in the matter of suits brought in the Federal Southern District Court in Birmingham, by the Elgin National Watch Co., the Hamilton Watch Co., the Illinois Watch Co., and the Waltham Watch Co., against Robert L. Benson, doing business as Benson Gold Refining Co.; B. T. Clifton, and Benson-Porter Co., Inc., of Birmingham, Ala. The suits allege infringement of trademark names of the above mentioned watch companies, for selling spurious, bogus or counterfeit dials, these containing American watch company's trademark names.

The decrees handed down by the U. S. District Judge, Honorable W. I. Grubb, is in favor of the complainant watch companies and grants perpetual injunctions against said defendants, forever enjoining and restraining them in buying, selling, and handling spurious, bogus and counterfeit dials, bearing said American watch company's trademark names.

The Court also awarded complainant watch companies punitive damages and taxed the defendants with Court cost proceedings.

Jewelers' Circular, May 1933

1935 HISTORICAL NOTES

- The first canned beer, Krueger Ale, is sold by the Krueger Brewing Company.
- The first radio broadcast of *Fibber McGee and Molly* airs.
- Babe Ruth announces his retirement from baseball.

Dial Patina

Aging and, in some cases, deterioration of the dial lacquer cause the dial to achieve a unique patina. If you cannot find a NOS dial for your watch, an interesting and attractive alternative is to find a dial with aged patina on it. Some, in fact, think that an original dial with aged patina adds more character to the watch than even a NOS one. Of course, if the patina results from deterioration, failure to correct the problem may further damage the watch dial.

FRAUD ALERT

There are unethical dealers and watchmakers who place Illinois dials on top of coffee or beer cans and place a lit cigar or other tobacco product in a cut- out at the bottom of the can. The smoke evidently ages either a refinished dial or an original one. This patina looks nice, I understand, but easily wipes off if touched. Be on the alert for this fraud.

WHY I COLLECT ILLINOIS

"I collect Illinois watches for many reasons. The unique beauty of the dials and cases in multiple combinations makes each piece seem like a work of art. Every time I wear one of the Illinois pieces, I find myself admiring the elegance of the watch, almost forgetting the functional reason for wearing it. All of the Illinois that I own reflect a bygone era that was simple yet creative and beautiful. I think most Illinois wristwatches have a flair and presence so special to the Illinois brand."

—Rick Broern

Black Dials

Illinois manufactured very few black-dialed wristwatches. Of these few, collectors most value the black dial option offered for the Skyway (there was also a white Skyway dial which is slightly less popular). Other original black dials are found on the Illinois United States Army Watch and occasionally on Military and Transitional Period watches. (The U.S. Army Watch in the Men's Identification Chapter was issued with an original black dial with green radium numerals in the late 1910s.) All other Illinois black dials should be suspect until they can be confirmed as original.

Major dial

Black dial (D-D Utility dial)

Black dial (Skyway dial)

Police Special dial

Custom Dials

Among the attributes of the Illinois Watch Company was its willingness to produce custom dials at the request of its customers. In fact, the 1923 *Illinois Material* catalog states on page 24: "Enamel dials, regular quality, will be supplied with letters of a name in place of regular figures." Sometimes the production run for a custom dial totaled just one. Few if any of its competitors were as accommodating.

As a result, it is possible to find very rare and unusual dials with special features such as letters in lieu of numerals, subsidiary seconds at 9 instead of at 6 when the latter was the norm for a specific model, a star on the dial, Masonic symbols, names spelled out around the dial or names hand-painted in cursive on the dial. The cursive-signed dials with hand-painted names are so uniform from one dial to another they were likely painted on at the Watch Factory as special orders. Examples of these fascinating custom dials follow.

Masonic dial

Jolly Roger dial

Masonic dial

Trophy custom dial

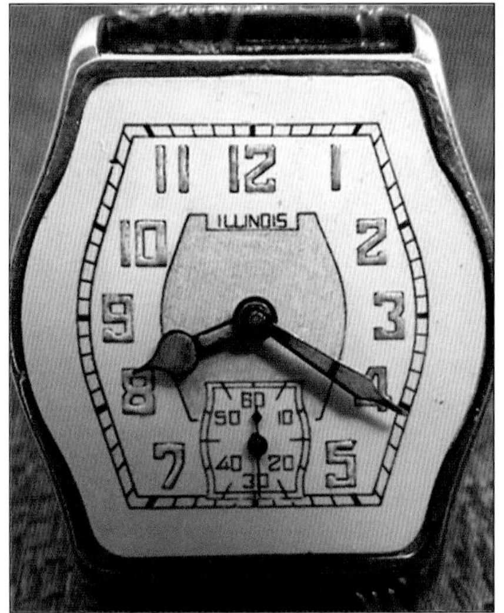

Mate (blue center) dial

Rockliffe dial

Square dial

Custom dial

Viking dial

Guardian dial

Futura dial

Beau Royale dial

Beau Royale dial

Beau Royale dial

Finalist Deco dial

Square Cut Corner dial

Andover dial

Custom fraternity emblem dial (Delta Tau Delta)

Custom dial with picture of the Illinois Watch Factory

Medalist dial

Medalist dial

Hess & Culberston

Private-Label Dials

Illinois produced thousands of private-label movements for jewelers, jobbers, third-party watch companies, and major catalog and department stores, mainly for use in pocket watches. Some of these private-label dials, though, appeared on wristwatches. At times Illinois would also supply custom dials so the movements and dials would be signed the same; such as those supplied to the Burlington and Washington Watch Companies (the latter having been a private label of Montgomery Ward). Some watches could legitimately have custom-signed dials with otherwise standard Illinois movements.

Although there were undoubtedly more private-label movements than private-label dials, it is still possible to find these special movements with matching dials. Examples of private-label dials are shown here.

Illinois Elite

Hyman Berg & Co., Chicago

Illinois Sterling was a private label for the Kay Jewelry Co.

W. L. Turner

Herbert L. Moor

O. W. Bailey, Calais, Maine

Lady Perry

Washington Watch Co. was a private label for Montgomery Ward & Co.

G. D. Davidson, Jersey City

Illinois Central was a private label for the Enggass Jewelry Store, Detroit, MI.

Jos. M. Parker, Jr., Philadelphia

Illinois Sterling

Illinois Central was a private label for the Enggass Jewelry Co., Detroit, MI.

Illinois Captain, along with the Lieutenant, General and Colonel, were private-labels for the Landis Watch Co., Chicago, IL.

F. J. Williams, Adams, NY

Illinois Master

Illinois Sportsman was a priivate label for the Seaver-Williams Co., Boston, MA.

Illinois Victor

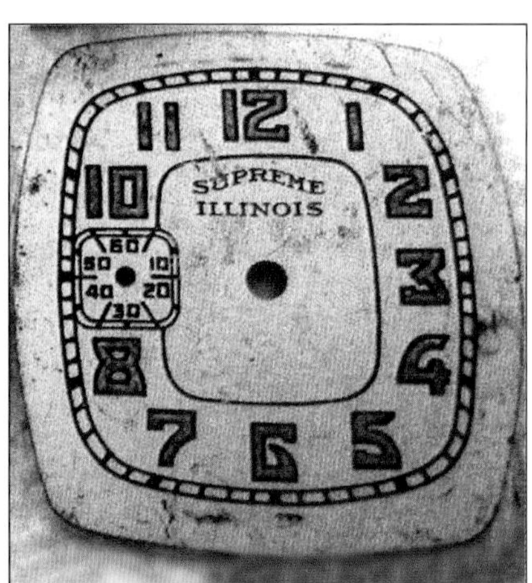

Supreme Illinois

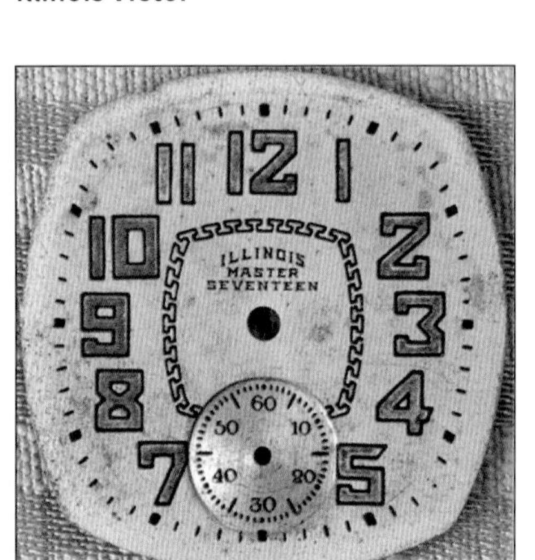

Illinois Master Seventeen

Illinois Aristocrat was a private label for the Kay Jewelry Co.

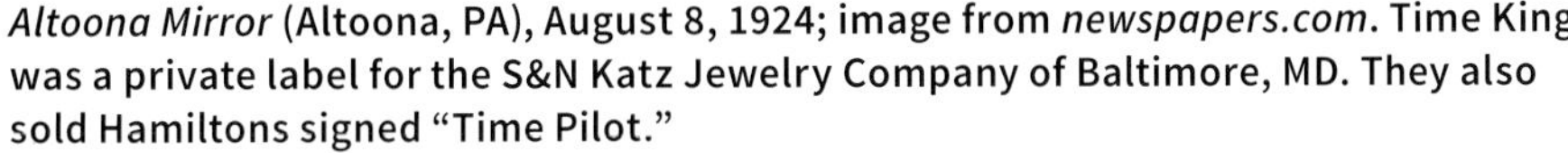
Altoona Mirror (Altoona, PA), August 8, 1924; image from *newspapers.com*. Time King was a private label for the S&N Katz Jewelry Company of Baltimore, MD. They also sold Hamiltons signed "Time Pilot."

Time King

Illinois Time King

Illinois Masterbilt

Burlington Special was a private label for the Burlington Watch Co.

Illinois Penn Special

Illinois Sterling

Hallmark was a private label for the R. H. Macy Co.

M. M. Bovard & Son private label

J. S. James, Inc. private label

Rowe Bros. private label

Jacob Ramser private label

Dial Blanks

Illinois prepared dial blank drawings in 1931 and 1933 to send to dial fabricators in both the United States and Switzerland. Examples of these drawings are shown here.

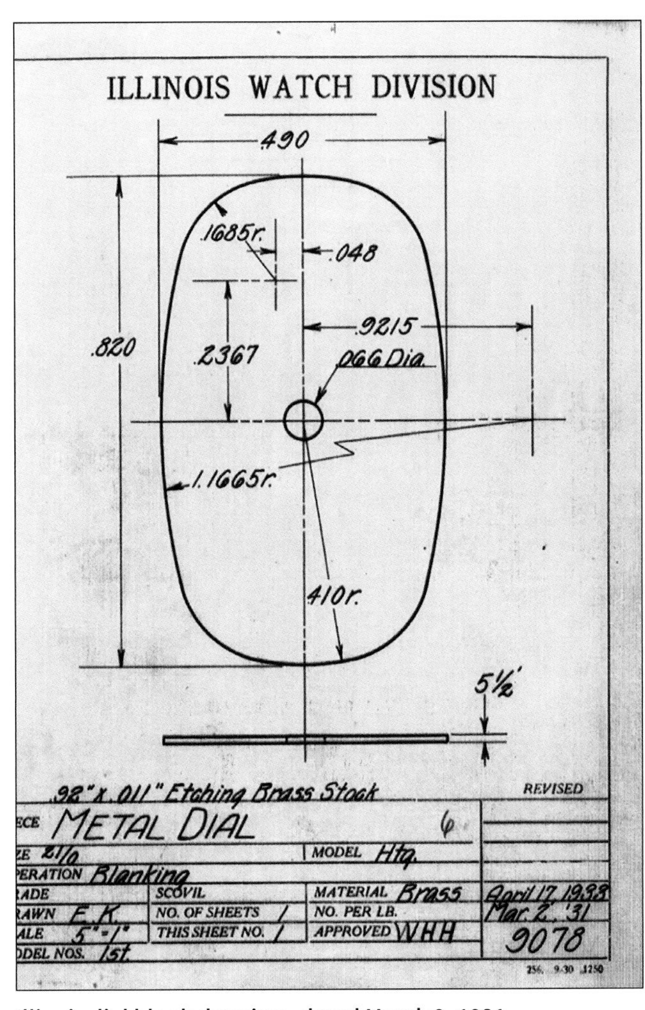

Illinois dial blank drawing, dated March 2, 1931

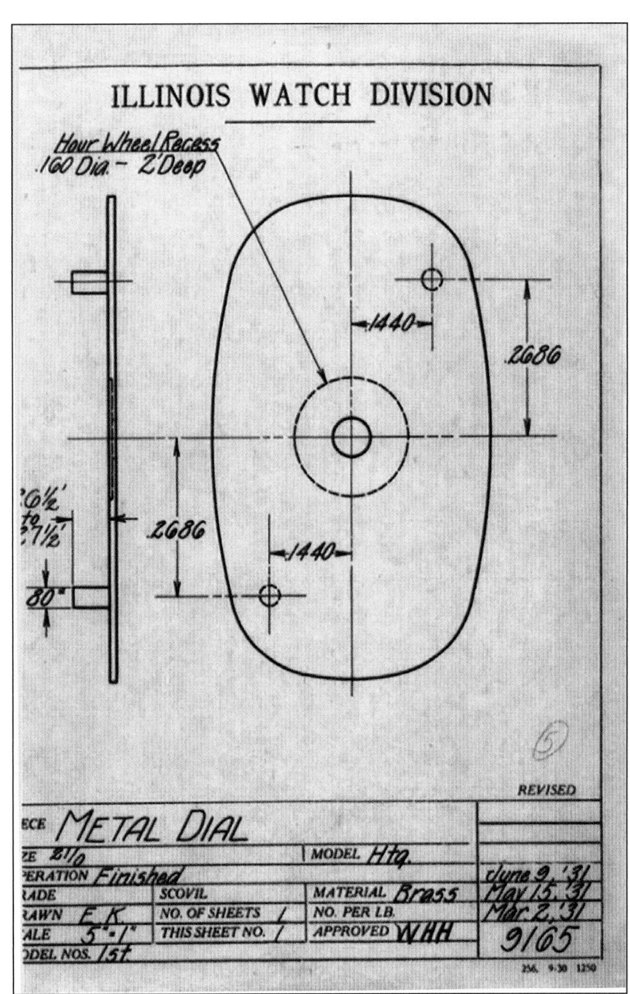

Illinois dial blank drawing, side and back of previous dial, dated March 2, 1931

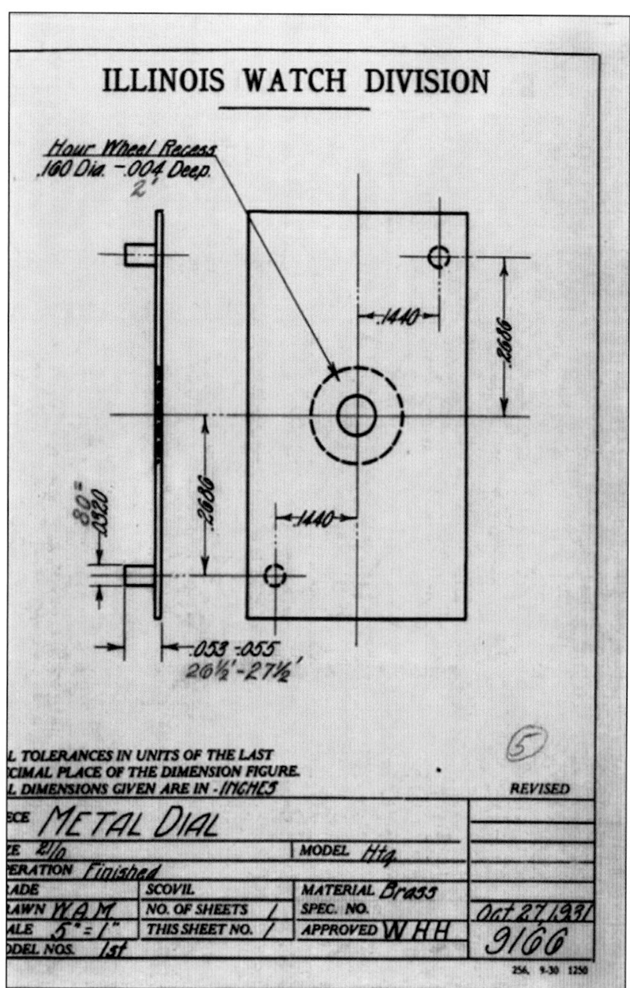

Illinois dial blank drawing, dated October 27, 1931

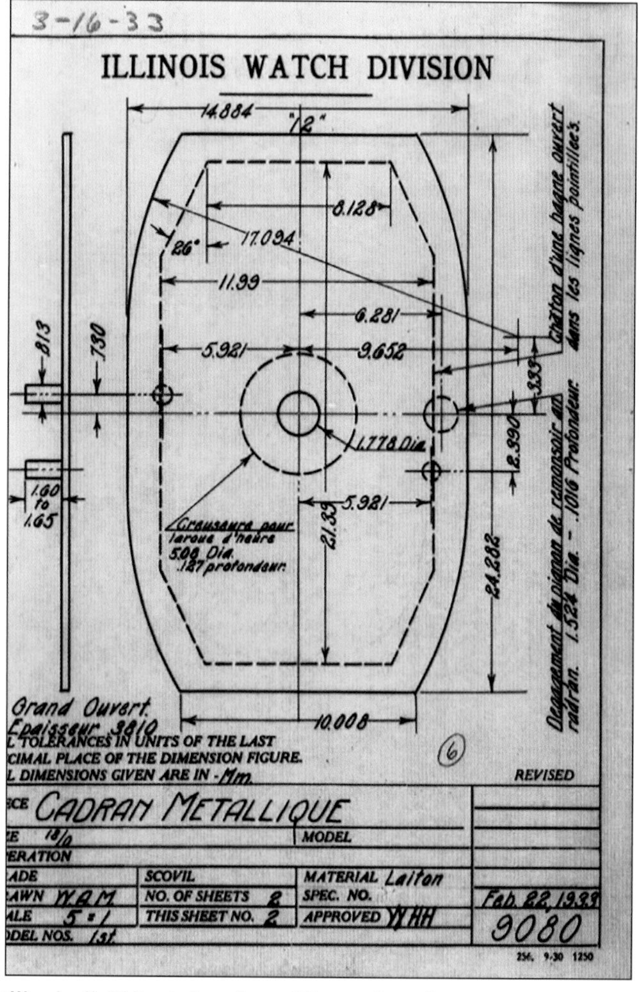

Illinois dial blank drawing with metric units, dated February 22, 1933

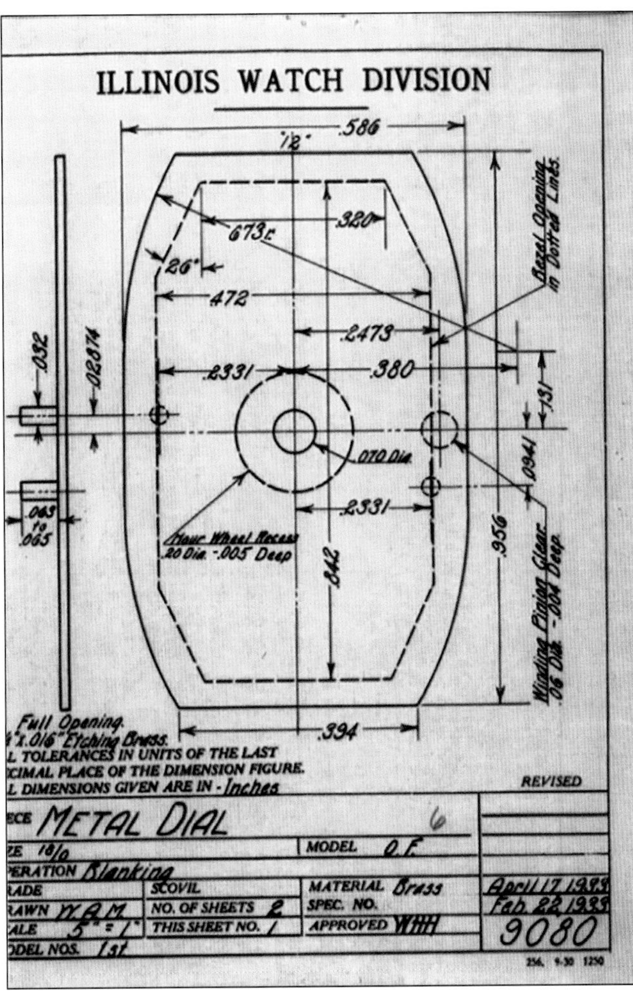

Illinois dial blank drawing revised to English units, dated February 22, 1933

Master Dial Printing Plates

Illinois wristwatch dials were produced using pantograph machines, which could copy a figure to a desired scale. A pantograph uses proportional parallelograms to reduce (or enlarge) a template. A greatly enlarged version of a dial (a master dial plate) is traced by the operator's stylus, and an engraving point cuts the much smaller cliché that will be used for printing. Two examples of these master dial printing plates used to make the clichés are shown here.

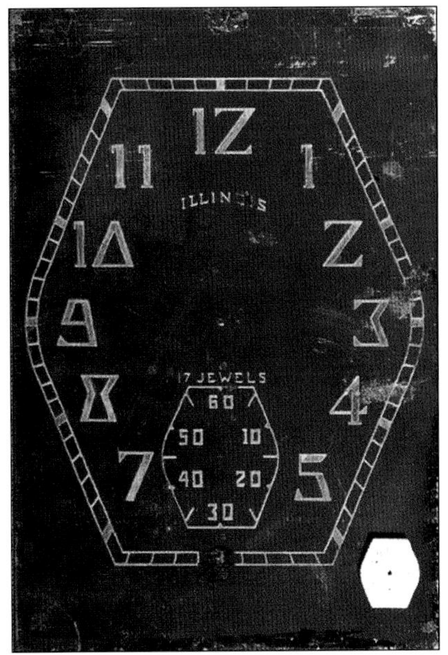

An Illinois Ritz master dial plate is 700% larger than the actual dial.

An Illinois Piccadilly master dial plate is 760% larger than the actual dial.

These two master plates can be instructive to demonstrate what some of the features are that would normally be present on an original Illinois dial:

- The outer minute track conforms precisely to the case bezel opening for the Illinois case model.
- The subsidiary bits match the shape of the dials (although this is not always the case).
- None of the numerals touch the minute track.
- None of the numerals touch the subsidiary seconds bit.
- None of the lettering or numerals touch any line on the dial (although this is not always the case).
- The minute track runs directly into the five-minute markers on the minute track.
- All numerals are uniform and line up straight and accurately from their opposing numerals.
- None of the painting on the numerals touches any other area of the numeral.
- The signing of "Illinois" is clean and crisp, without any excess paint or letters touching one another.
- The subsidiary seconds bits have markers in place.
- The subsidiary seconds bits have numerals in place.
- The signed "Illinois" is precisely centered below the numeral 12 and above the 6.

These are some of the "Tells" for how an original dial should look. "Tells" for redone dials are discussed later in this chapter.

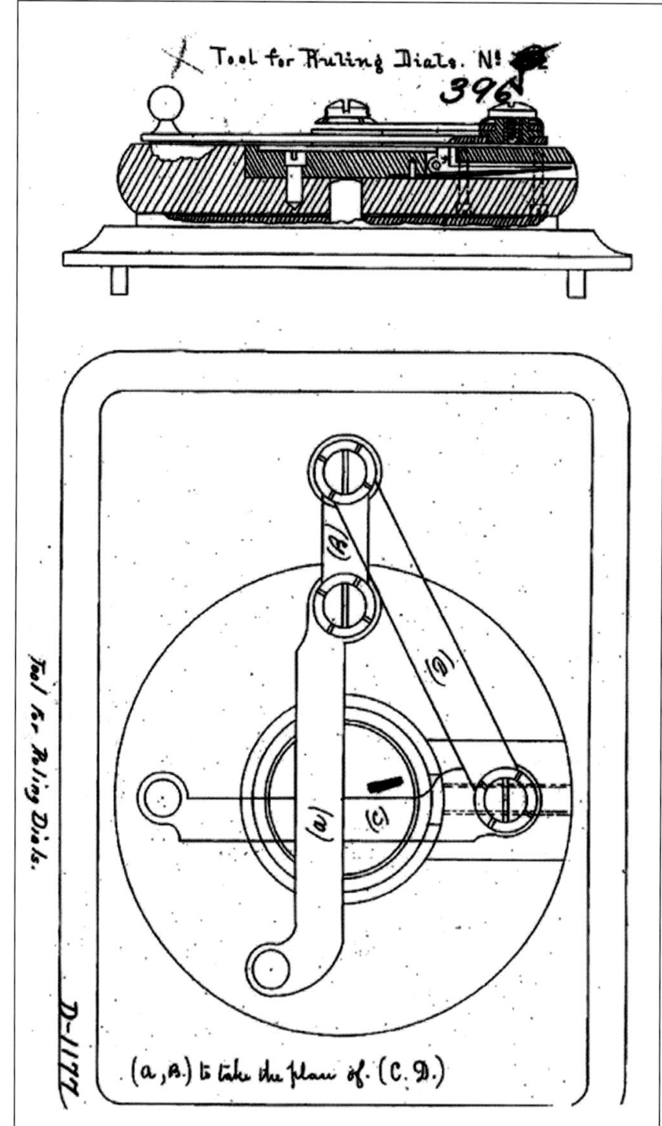

Early Illinois tool for ruling dials, c. 1890

New Old Stock (NOS) Dials

It is still possible with proper due diligence to find NOS Illinois wristwatch dials. Some examples of these dials are shown here.

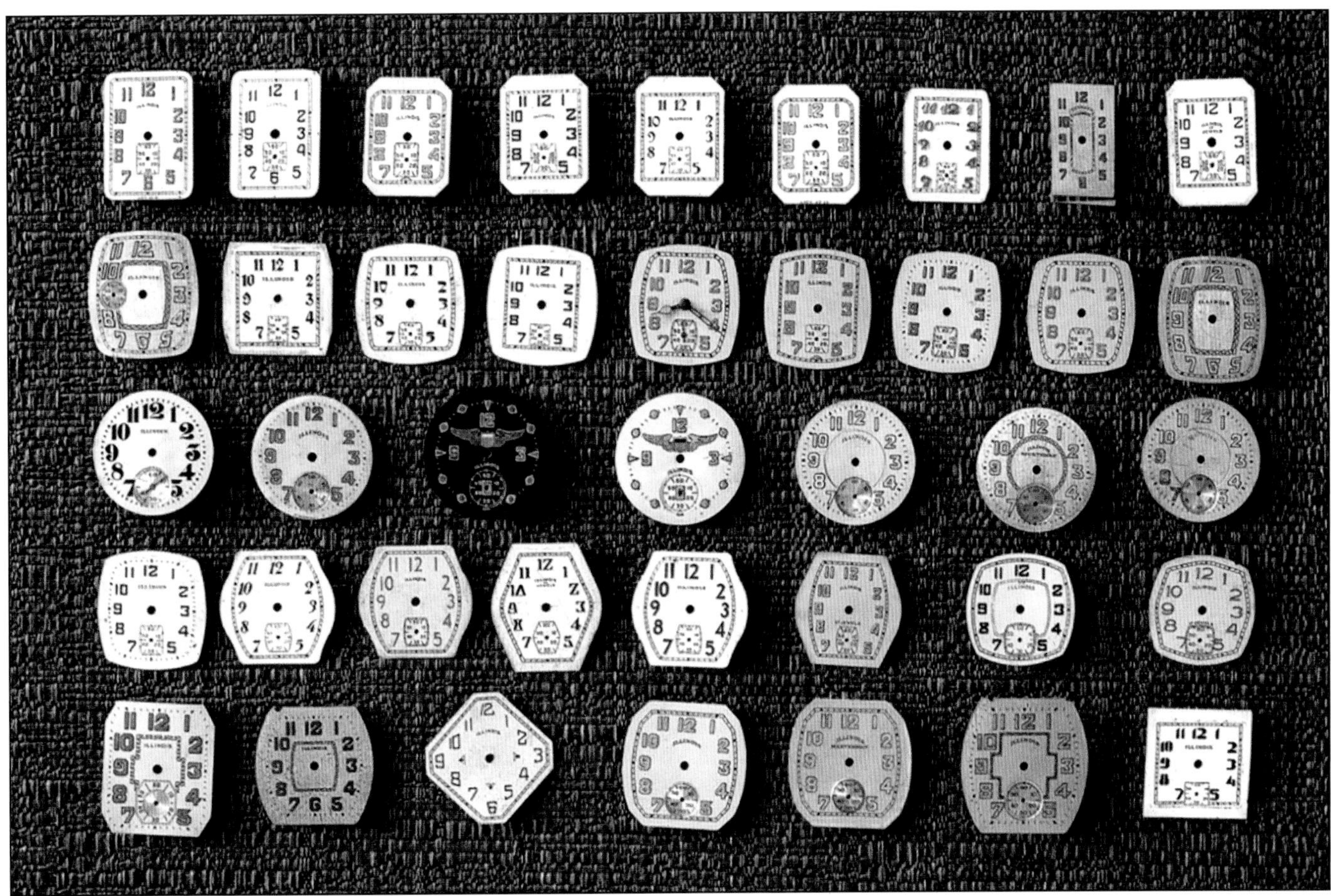

Chart Key for Men's NOS Dials (left to right):

Row 1: Trophy, Hudson, Futura, Finalist, Finalist, Futura, Baronet, Biltmore 18/0, Chesterfield

Row 2: Marquis Strap, Potomac, Derby, Arlington, Consul, Townsman, Beau Brummell, Consul, Marquis Strap

Row 3: Off-Duty, Special/Military, Skyway, Skyway, Special, Military, Special

Row 4: Beau Royale, Beau Monde, Beau Monde, Ritz, Beau Monde, Cavalier, Devon, Blackstone

Row 5: Locke, Whippet, Caprice, Atlantic, Atlantic, Whippet, Commodore

Blue = Unisex

Dial and Hand Catalogs

From time to time Illinois would release a Material Catalog that would contain dials and hands. Some of these catalog pages are shown here.

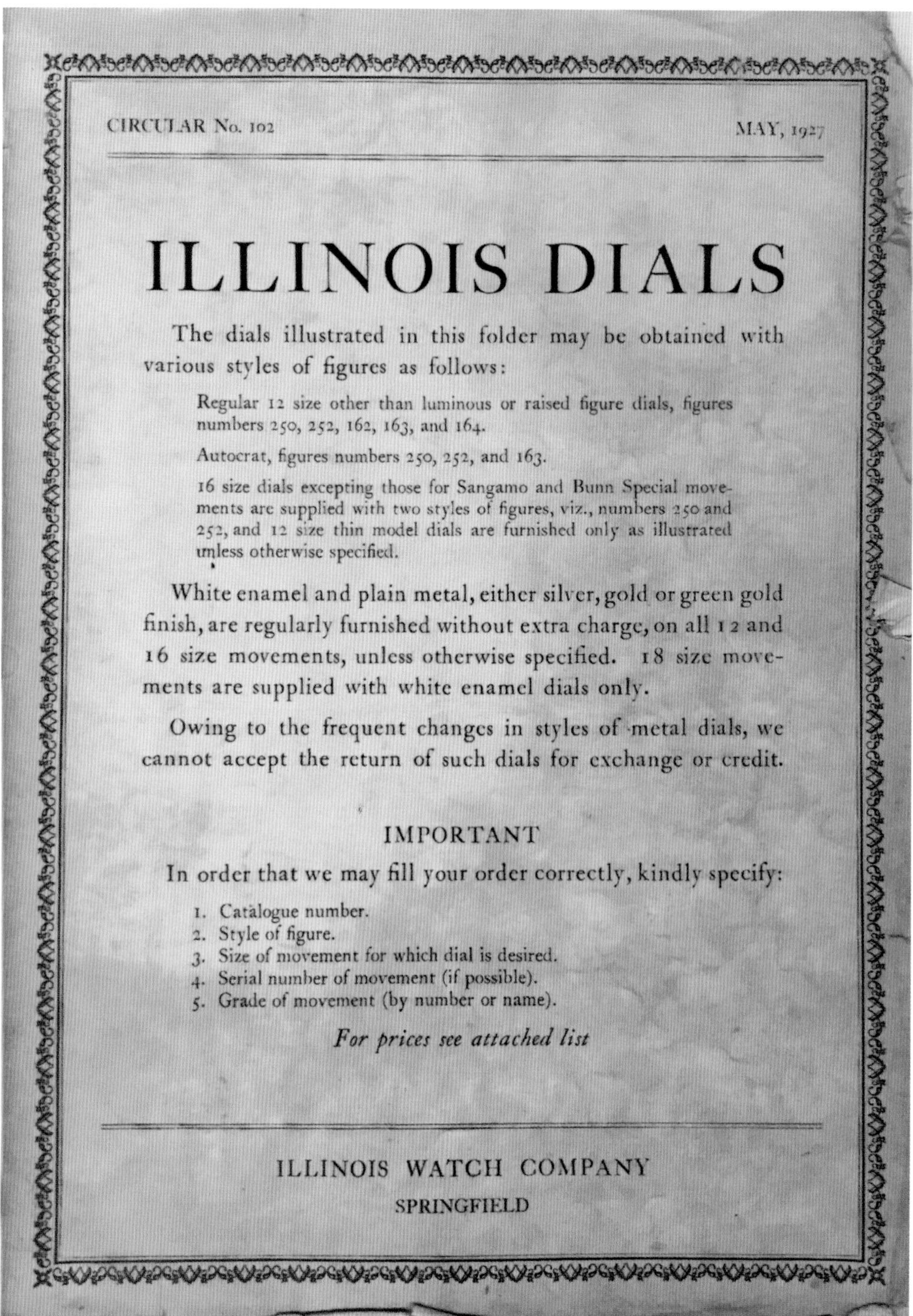

CIRCULAR No. 102 MAY, 1927

ILLINOIS DIALS

The dials illustrated in this folder may be obtained with various styles of figures as follows:

Regular 12 size other than luminous or raised figure dials, figures numbers 250, 252, 162, 163, and 164.

Autocrat, figures numbers 250, 252, and 163.

16 size dials excepting those for Sangamo and Bunn Special movements are supplied with two styles of figures, viz., numbers 250 and 252, and 12 size thin model dials are furnished only as illustrated unless otherwise specified.

White enamel and plain metal, either silver, gold or green gold finish, are regularly furnished without extra charge, on all 12 and 16 size movements, unless otherwise specified. 18 size movements are supplied with white enamel dials only.

Owing to the frequent changes in styles of metal dials, we cannot accept the return of such dials for exchange or credit.

IMPORTANT

In order that we may fill your order correctly, kindly specify:

1. Catalogue number.
2. Style of figure.
3. Size of movement for which dial is desired.
4. Serial number of movement (if possible).
5. Grade of movement (by number or name).

For prices see attached list

ILLINOIS WATCH COMPANY

SPRINGFIELD

Cover page of the Illinois Watch and Hand Circular, No. 102, May 1927

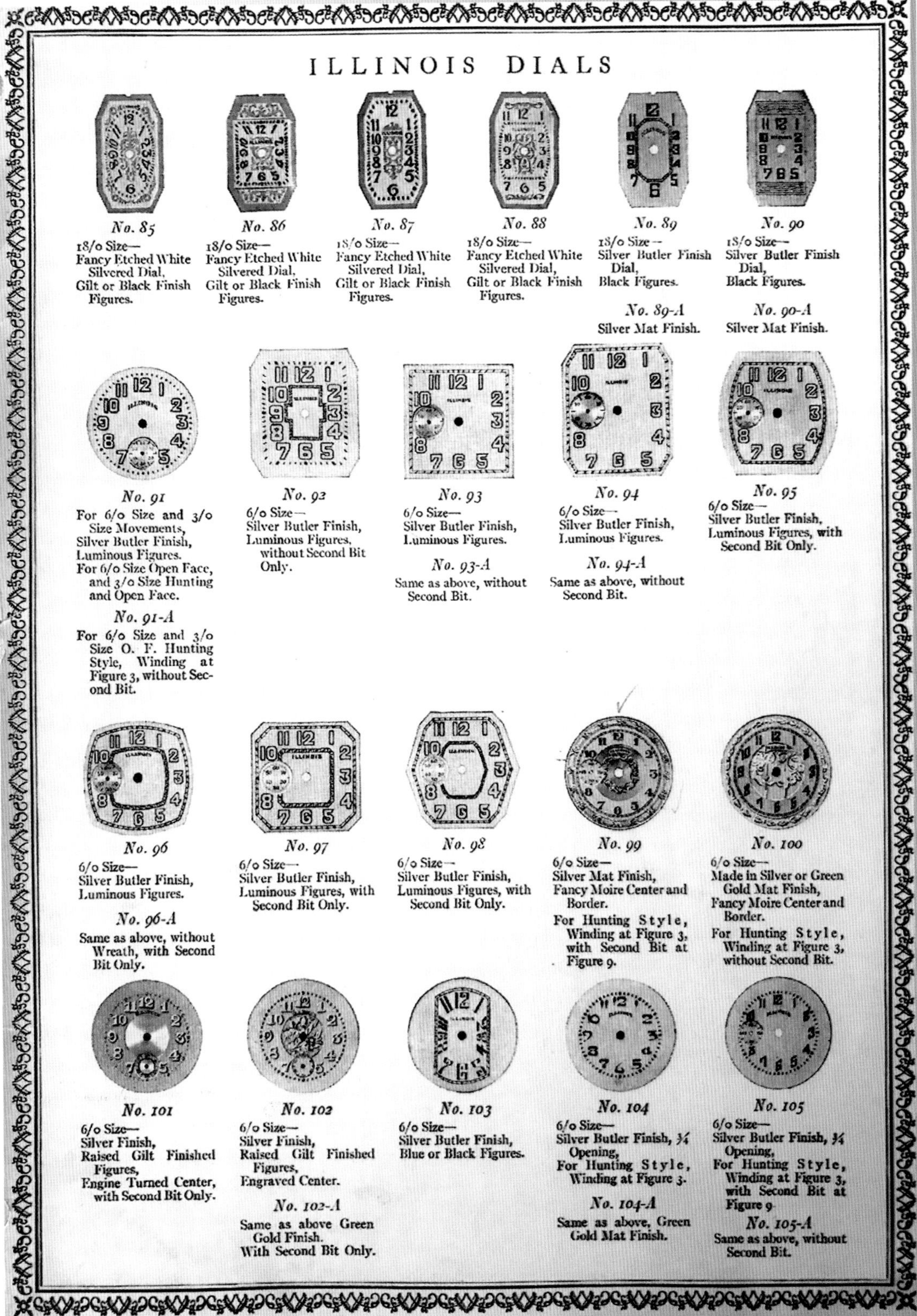

ILLINOIS DIALS

No. 85
18/0 Size—
Fancy Etched White Silvered Dial,
Gilt or Black Finish Figures.

No. 86
18/0 Size—
Fancy Etched White Silvered Dial,
Gilt or Black Finish Figures.

No. 87
18/0 Size—
Fancy Etched White Silvered Dial,
Gilt or Black Finish Figures.

No. 88
18/0 Size—
Fancy Etched White Silvered Dial,
Gilt or Black Finish Figures.

No. 89
18/0 Size—
Silver Butler Finish Dial,
Black Figures.

No. 89-A
Silver Mat Finish.

No. 90
18/0 Size—
Silver Butler Finish Dial,
Black Figures.

No. 90-A
Silver Mat Finish.

No. 91
For 6/0 Size and 3/0 Size Movements,
Silver Butler Finish,
Luminous Figures.
For 6/0 Size Open Face, and 3/0 Size Hunting and Open Face.

No. 91-A
For 6/0 Size and 3/0 Size O. F. Hunting Style, Winding at Figure 3, without Second Bit.

No. 92
6/0 Size—
Silver Butler Finish,
Luminous Figures, without Second Bit Only.

No. 93
6/0 Size—
Silver Butler Finish,
Luminous Figures.

No. 93-A
Same as above, without Second Bit.

No. 94
6/0 Size—
Silver Butler Finish,
Luminous Figures.

No. 94-A
Same as above, without Second Bit.

No. 95
6/0 Size—
Silver Butler Finish,
Luminous Figures, with Second Bit Only.

No. 96
6/0 Size—
Silver Butler Finish,
Luminous Figures.

No. 96-A
Same as above, without Wreath, with Second Bit Only.

No. 97
6/0 Size—
Silver Butler Finish,
Luminous Figures, with Second Bit Only.

No. 98
6/0 Size—
Silver Butler Finish,
Luminous Figures, with Second Bit Only.

No. 99
6/0 Size—
Silver Mat Finish,
Fancy Moire Center and Border.
For Hunting Style, Winding at Figure 3, with Second Bit at Figure 9.

No. 100
6/0 Size—
Made in Silver or Green Gold Mat Finish,
Fancy Moire Center and Border.
For Hunting Style, Winding at Figure 3, without Second Bit.

No. 101
6/0 Size—
Silver Finish,
Raised Gilt Finished Figures,
Engine Turned Center, with Second Bit Only.

No. 102
6/0 Size—
Silver Finish,
Raised Gilt Finished Figures,
Engraved Center.

No. 102-A
Same as above Green Gold Finish.
With Second Bit Only.

No. 103
6/0 Size—
Silver Butler Finish,
Blue or Black Figures.

No. 104
6/0 Size—
Silver Butler Finish, ¾ Opening,
For Hunting Style, Winding at Figure 3.

No. 104-A
Same as above, Green Gold Mat Finish.

No. 105
6/0 Size—
Silver Butler Finish, ¾ Opening,
For Hunting Style, Winding at Figure 3, with Second Bit at Figure 9.

No. 105-A
Same as above, without Second Bit.

Wristwatch dials featured in the Illinois Watch and Hand Circular, No. 102, May 1927

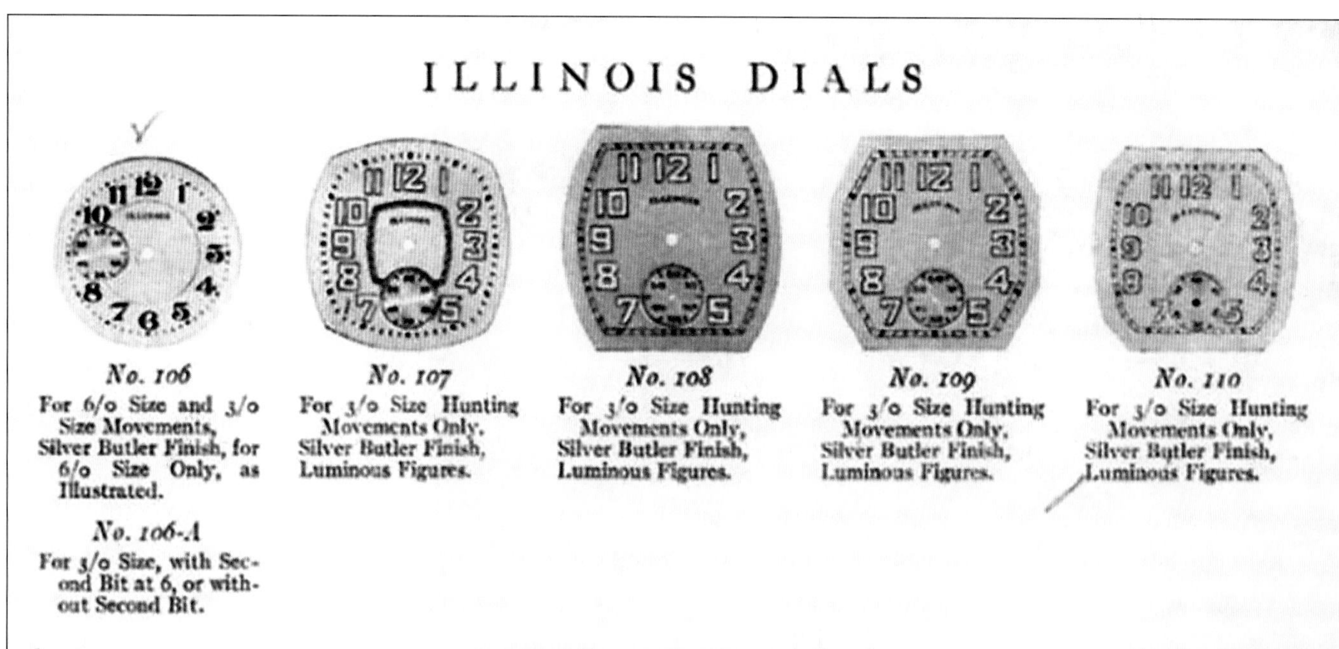

ILLINOIS DIALS

No. 106
For 6/o Size and 3/o Size Movements, Silver Butler Finish, for 6/o Size Only, as Illustrated.

No. 106-A
For 3/o Size, with Second Bit at 6, or without Second Bit.

No. 107
For 3/o Size Hunting Movements Only, Silver Butler Finish, Luminous Figures.

No. 108
For 3/o Size Hunting Movements Only, Silver Butler Finish, Luminous Figures.

No. 109
For 3/o Size Hunting Movements Only, Silver Butler Finish, Luminous Figures.

No. 110
For 3/o Size Hunting Movements Only, Silver Butler Finish, Luminous Figures.

Wristwatch dials featured in the Illinois Watch and Hand Circular, No. 102, May 1927

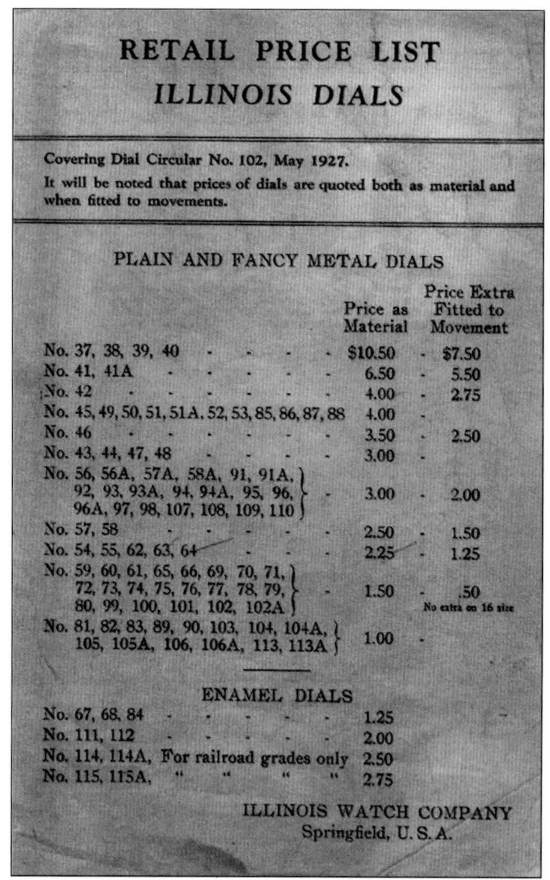

RETAIL PRICE LIST
ILLINOIS DIALS

Covering Dial Circular No. 102, May 1927.
It will be noted that prices of dials are quoted both as material and when fitted to movements.

PLAIN AND FANCY METAL DIALS

	Price as Material	Price Extra Fitted to Movement
No. 37, 38, 39, 40	$10.50	$7.50
No. 41, 41A	6.50	5.50
No. 42	4.00	2.75
No. 45, 49, 50, 51, 51A, 52, 53, 85, 86, 87, 88	4.00	
No. 46	3.50	2.50
No. 43, 44, 47, 48	3.00	
No. 56, 56A, 57A, 58A, 91, 91A, 92, 93, 93A, 94, 94A, 95, 96, 96A, 97, 98, 107, 108, 109, 110	3.00	2.00
No. 57, 58	2.50	1.50
No. 54, 55, 62, 63, 64	2.25	1.25
No. 59, 60, 61, 65, 66, 69, 70, 71, 72, 73, 74, 75, 76, 77, 78, 79, 80, 99, 100, 101, 102, 102A	1.50	.50 No extra on 16 size
No. 81, 82, 83, 89, 90, 103, 104, 104A, 105, 105A, 106, 106A, 113, 113A	1.00	

ENAMEL DIALS

	Price
No. 67, 68, 84	1.25
No. 111, 112	2.00
No. 114, 114A, For railroad grades only	2.50
No. 115, 115A, " " " "	2.75

ILLINOIS WATCH COMPANY
Springfield, U. S. A.

Illinois Retail Price List for dials, May 1927

ILLINOIS WATCH DIALS

12 SIZE THIN

MODELS 1, 2 AND 3

8172
Silver finish, fancy centers, embossed figures.

8218
Silver finish, etched wreath and figures.

8160
Sterling silver, polished center band, pearled minute track, 18K applied numerals.

8159
Silver finish, black lined figures. Trustee model.

8158
Silver finish, Butler center, etched raised wreath and figures. Oxford model.

8126
Silver finish, etched raised wreath and figures. Cushion model.

12/0 SIZE DIALS

8198
Kenilworth model. White sparkle finish, black figures.

8197
Rockliffe model. White sparkle finish, 18K applied numerals.

8168
Frontenac-Trophy. Silver finish. Luminous figures.

8196
Ardsley model. White sparkle finish. Black figures.

8167
Futura model. Silver finish. Luminous figures.

8164
Medalist model. Silver finish, Butler center, Luminous figures.

8165
Finalist model. Silver finish. Luminous figures.
8308
Sparkle finish, black figures.

ORDER BY DIAL NUMBER

Page Six

Wristwatch dials from the 1930 Illinois Dial and Hand Catalog

ILLINOIS WATCH DIALS

6-0 SIZE DIALS

GRADE 601-607

8201 Cavalier. Silver finish. Luminous figures.

8209 Baronet. White sparkle finish. 18K applied numerals.

8206 Beau Monde. Silver finish, etched raised figures.
8324 18K applied numerals.

8205 Caprice. White sparkle finish. Black figures.

8208 Ritz. White sparkle finish. Black figures.

8204 Consul. Silver finish. Luminous figures.
8280 18K applied numerals.

8202 Townsman. Silver finish. Luminous figures.

8281 Blackstone. Silver finish. Etched raised figures.

8203 New Yorker. Manhattan. Silver finish. Luminous fig.
8207 Etched raised figures.
8152 Bit at 9. Luminous figures. Models 1-2-3.

8199 Ensign. Silver finish, Butler center, luminous figures.
8136 Bit at 9. Luminous figures. Models 1-2-3.

8200 Beau Brummel. Silver finish, luminous figures.
8135 Bit at 9. Luminous figures. Models 1-2-3.

6/0 SIZE DIALS FOR MODELS 1-2-3 ONLY

SILVER FINISH

8137 Consul model, luminous figures.
8279 Etched raised figures.
8157 18K applied numerals.

8134 Marquis Strap. Butler center, luminous figures.

8153 Piccadilly. Etched raised figures. Luminous dots.

8151 Chieftain. Luminous figures.

8094 Rectangular opening. Luminous figures. Bit at 9.
8287 No bit.
8286 Black figures. Bit at 9.

8093 Square opening. Luminous figures.
8274 Black figures.

8096 Cushion opening. Luminous figures.
8275 Black figures.
8278 Curved cushion opening. Luminous figures.

8097 Square cut corner opening. Luminous figures.
8276 Black figures.

8269 Tank or Canby case. Luminous figures. Bit at 9.
8092 Bryce case. Luminous figures. No second bit.

8098 Southampton. Silver mat. Luminous figures.

8091 Full opening, luminous figures. Bit at 6.
8270 Bit at 9.
8266 No bit.
8210 Black figures. Bit at 6.

8267 ½ opening black figure.
8105 Bit at 9.
8268 No bit.

8095 Barrel opening. Luminous figures.
8277 Black figures.

Page Seven

ORDER BY DIAL NUMBER

Watch dials from the 1930 Illinois Dial and Hand Catalog

ILLINOIS WATCH DIALS

18/0 SIZE DIALS

8154
Full opening. Sterling silver. Inlaid figures.

8174
Full opening. White sparkle finish. Black figures.

8089
Full opening. Silver finish. Etched raised figures.

8191
Full rectangular, for Berkshire and Avalon models.

8155
Full opening. White sparkle finish. Black figures.

8147
Six sided opening. White sparkle finish. Black figures.

8169
Square opening. Silver finish. Black figures.

8170
Edgewater opening. White sparkle finish.

8171
Diamond set case opening. Silver finish.

8148
Biltmore model. Silver finish. Luminous figures.

8141
Tuxedo model. Silver finish. Luminous figures.

8193
Etched raised figures.

8192
Berkshire and Avalon models. Silver finish. Black figures.

8195
Vardon and Argyle models. Silver finish. Etched raised figures.

8090
Fairport, Brighton, and Vanity Fair. White sparkle finish. Black figures.

8282
Glencoe model. White sparkle finish. Black figures.

3/0 SIZE AND 0 SIZE DIALS

SILVER FINISH

8260
3/0 Size. Luminous figures.

8261
Black figures.

8013
0 Size. Luminous.

8014
0 Size. Black figures.

8142
Luminous figures.

8107
Luminous figures.

8289
Black figures.

8214
Luminous figures.

8292
Black figures.

8109
Luminous figures.

8291
Black figures.

8110
Luminous figures.

8290
Black figures.

8108
Luminous figures.

8288
Black figures.

8265
For enamel bezel cases.

8212
For enamel bezel cases.

8133
Mate model. Luminous figures.

8132
Major, Speedway, Jolly Roger. Luminous figures.

8343
Skyway model. Silver mat. Luminous.

8215
Guardsman. Rotor second. Luminous figures.

8213
Rotor-Second bit only.

8173
Viking model. Luminous figures.

ORDER BY DIAL NUMBER

Page Eight

Wristwatch dials from the 1930 Illinois Dial and Hand Catalog

PRICE LIST

EFFECTIVE DECEMBER 26, 1930

NOTE: The Dozen price will apply to orders for three or more dials of one number. Orders for less than three dials of one number will be invoiced at individual price which is one-tenth of dozen price.

ILLINOIS WATCH DIALS

Dial No.	Price Per Dozen	Dial No.	Price Per Dozen	Dial No.	Price Per Dozen	Dial No.	Price Per Dozen
8013	$ 30.00	8146	$ 17.50	8195	$ 17.50	8260	$ 30.00
8014	12.50	8147	15.00	8196	15.00	8261	12.50
8045	25.00	8148	30.00	8197	100.00	8265	12.50
8051	17.50	8149	17.50	8198	15.00	8266	30.00
8052	17.50	8151	30.00	8199	30.00	8267	12.50
8053	40.00	8152	30.00	8200	30.00	8268	12.50
8068	12.50	8153	30.00	8201	30.00	8269	30.00
8081	12.50	8154	30.00	8202	30.00	8270	30.00
8089	17.50	8155	15.00	8203	30.00	8274	12.50
8090	15.00	8157	100.00	8204	30.00	8275	12.50
8091	30.00	8158	17.50	8205	15.00	8276	12.50
8092	30.00	8159	15.00	8206	17.50	8277	12.50
8093	30.00	8160	100.00	8207	17.50	8278	30.00
8094	30.00	8161	17.50	8208	15.00	8279	17.50
8095	30.00	8162	25.00	8209	100.00	8280	100.00
8096	30.00	8163	27.50	8210	12.50	8281	17.50
8097	30.00	8164	30.00	8212	12.50	8282	15.00
8098	30.00	8165	30.00	8213	4.50	8286	12.50
8105	12.50	8167	30.00	8214	30.00	8287	30.00
8107	30.00	8168	30.00	8215	35.00	8288	12.50
8108	30.00	8169	12.50	8218	17.50	8289	12.50
8109	30.00	8170	15.00	8220	12.50	8290	12.50
8110	30.00	8171	12.50	8222	12.50	8291	12.50
8113	12.50	8172	17.50	8223	12.50	8292	12.50
8116	17.50	8173	30.00	8224	12.50	8294	12.50
8126	17.50	8174	15.00	8225	12.50	8295	12.50
8132	30.00	8175	17.50	8226	25.00	8296	12.50
8133	30.00	8176	15.00	8227	20.00	8300	17.50
8134	30.00	8177	17.50	8228	27.50	8303	25.00
8135	30.00	8178	17.50	8229	20.00	8304	27.50
8136	30.00	8183	17.50	8230	12.50	8305	4.50
8137	30.00	8184	20.00	8236	12.50	8308	15.00
8141	30.00	8185	17.50	8237	12.50	8324	100.00
8142	30.00	8191	17.50	8245	22.50	8335	15.00
8144	25.00	8192	12.50	8247	12.50	8336	12.50
8145	27.50	8193	17.50	8250	17.50	8343	30.00

ILLINOIS WATCH HANDS

No order filled for less than one-quarter dozen pairs of hour and minute hands of one number
No order filled for less than one dozen second hands of one number

Hours and Minutes	Price Per Doz. Pairs	Hours and Minutes	Price Per Doz. Pairs	Hours and Minutes	Price Per Doz. Pairs	Second Hands	Price Per Dozen
9505—04	$1.50	9551—48	4.00	9625—26	1.50	9902	$ .35
9507—08	1.50	9555—56	4.00	9629—30	1.50	9903	.35
9509—10	1.50	9559—60	1.50	9631—32	1.50	9908	.35
9525—26	1.50	9569—70	1.50	9633—34	1.50	9909	.35
9527—28	1.50	9575—76	1.50	9639—40	1.50	9910	.35
9529—30	1.50	9581—82	1.50	9657—58	4.00	9911	.35
9531—32	1.50	9591—92	4.00	9659—60	4.00	9912	.50
9533—34	1.50	9605—06	1.50	9661—62	1.50	9915	.35
9535—36	1.50	9607—08	1.50	9665—66	4.00	9927	.50
9539—40	1.50	9611—12	4.00	9669—70	1.75	9932	.35
9539—42	1.50	9615—16	4.00	9675—76	4.00	9933	.35
9543—44	1.50	9617—18	4.00	9677—78	4.00	9937	.35
						9939	.50

Page Ten

Price List from the Illinois Dial and Hand Catalog, December 26, 1930

ILLINOIS WATCH

DIAL AND HAND CATALOGUE

THE following pages illustrate dials and hands available for Illinois Watches. These parts are of the highest quality materials and workmanship.

Please follow instructions for ordering these parts, so that you may receive prompt and accurate service. Price List for hands and dials appears on page 10.

DIALS: Order by number. The illustrations show general style of dials. Detailed description is given under each number for your convenience.

To determine correct dial for particular movement turn to page 9 and consult chart for location of dial feet. Place dial face down with the figure 12 coinciding with same figure on the chart and match for feet position and diameter. If in doubt, forward old dial or serial number of movement with order.

On orders for Luminous Dials we will send hands unless advised to the contrary. This is to insure a correct match for color.

HANDS: Order by number. When ordering pairs, give numbers assigned to hour and minute hands respectively. Illustrations of hands in this catalogue are exact size.

If you desire to duplicate dials or hands not shown in this catalogue, submit samples and they will be matched as nearly as possible from stocks on hand.

ILLINOIS WATCH
MATERIAL DEPARTMENT

ILLINOIS WATCH HANDS

SECOND HANDS

NUMBERS	Size	DESCRIPTION	COLOR	EXACT SIZE
9902	18	Heavy Spade	Blue	
9910	17&16	Extra Heavy Spade	Blue	
9909	16	Extra Heavy Spade	Wine	
9908	16	Heavy Spade Long	Wine	
9903	16	Heavy Spade	Blue	
9912	16	Breguet	Blue	
9911	16	Ball End	Blue	
9927	12	Open Diamond	Blue	
9915	12	Spade	Blue	
9932	3/0	Spade	Blue	
9933	3/0	Spade	Wine	
9937	6/0	Spade	Blue	
9939	6/0	¾ Breguet	Blue	

Page One

Hands from the Illinois Watch Dial and Hand Catalog, December 26, 1930

ILLINOIS WATCH HANDS

HOUR AND MINUTE HANDS

NUMBERS Hour	NUMBERS Minute	Size	DESCRIPTION	COLOR
9505	9504	18	Light Spade—Key Wind	Blue
9509	9510	18	Extra Heavy Spade	Blue
9507	9508	18	Heavy Spade	Blue
9525	9526	17	Heavy Diamond	Blue
9543	9544	16	Extra Heavy Whip	Blue
9527	9528	16	Light Spade	Blue
9551	9548	16	Double Time—Reversible	Red&Blue
9531	9532	16	Heavy Spade	Blue
9555	9556	16	Luminous	Green
9529	9530	16	Heavy Spade	Wine
9535	9536	16	Extra Heavy Spade	Wine
9533	9534	16	Extra Heavy Spade	Blue
9539	9542	16	Breguet	Blue
9539	9540	16	Breguet Long Minute	Blue
9581	9582	12	Open Diamond	Blue
9575	9576	12	Cubistes	Blue
9559	9560	12	Heavy Spade	Blue
9569	9570	12	Breguet	Blue
9591	9592	12	Luminous	Green
9605	9606	3/0&0	Light Spade	Wine
9607	9608	3/0&0	Heavy Spade	Blue
9625	9626	3/0	¾ Breguet	Blue
9611	9612	3/0&0	Luminous	Green
9615	9616	3/0	Luminous	Green
9617	9618	3/0	Luminous	Green
9629	9630	6/0	Light Spade	Blue
9631	9632	6/0	Breguet	Blue
9633	9634	6/0	¾ Breguet	Blue
9639	9640	6/0	Moderne	Blue
9657	9658	6/0	Luminous	Green
9659	9660	6/0	Luminous	Green
9661	9662	12/0	Moderne	Blue
9665	9666	12/0	Luminous	Green
9669	9670	18/0	Open Diamond	Blue
9675	9676	18/0	Luminous	Green
9677	9678	18/0	Luminous	Green

Page Two

Hands from the Illinois Watch Dial and Hand Catalog, December 26, 1930

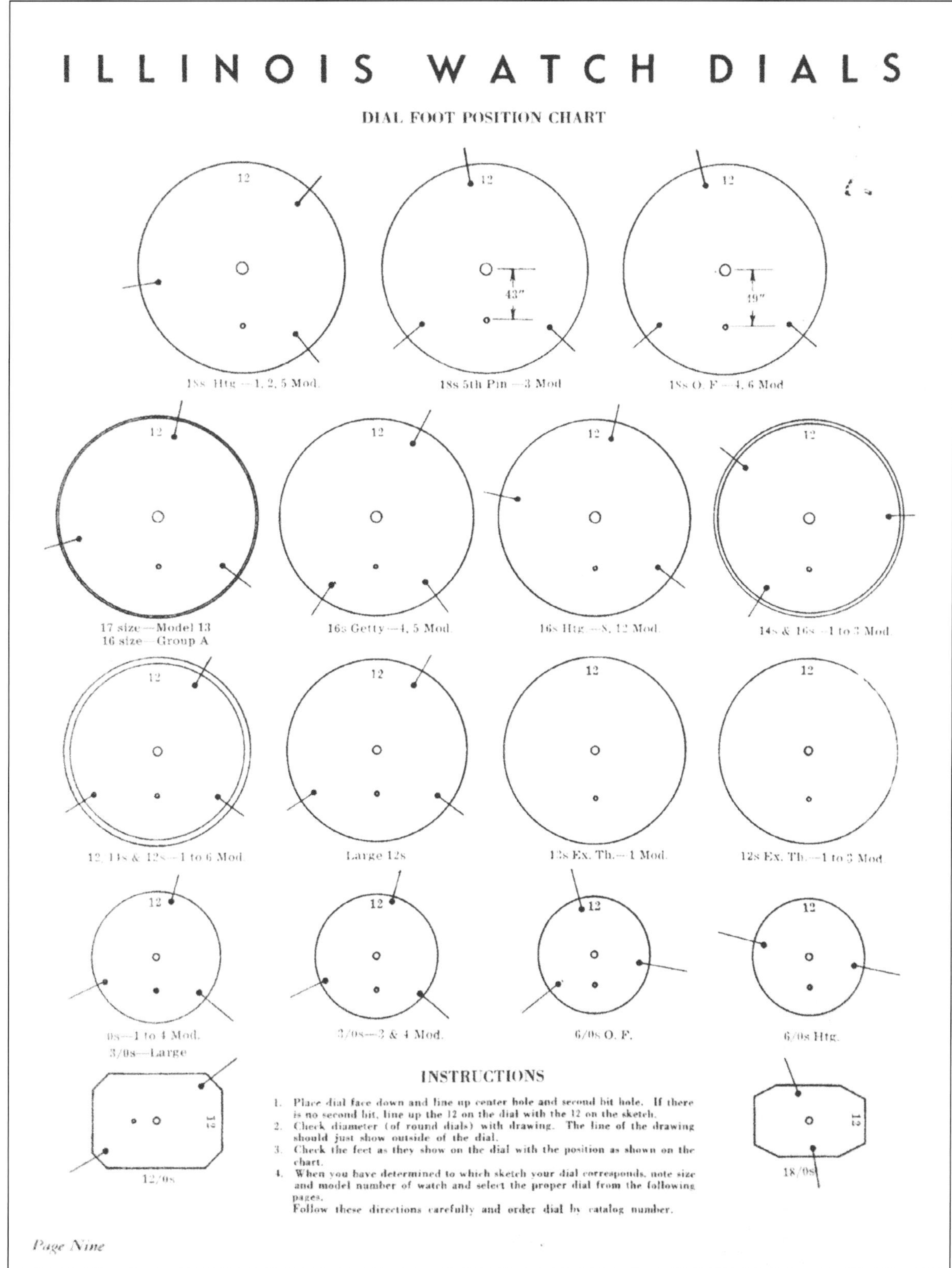

ILLINOIS WATCH DIALS

DIAL FOOT POSITION CHART

INSTRUCTIONS

1. Place dial face down and line up center hole and second bit hole. If there is no second bit, line up the 12 on the dial with the 12 on the sketch.
2. Check diameter (of round dials) with drawing. The line of the drawing should just show outside of the dial.
3. Check the feet as they show on the dial with the position as shown on the chart.
4. When you have determined to which sketch your dial corresponds, note size and model number of watch and select the proper dial from the following pages.

Follow these directions carefully and order dial by catalog number.

Page Nine

Dial foot position chart from the Illinois Watch and Dial and Hand catalog, December 26, 1930

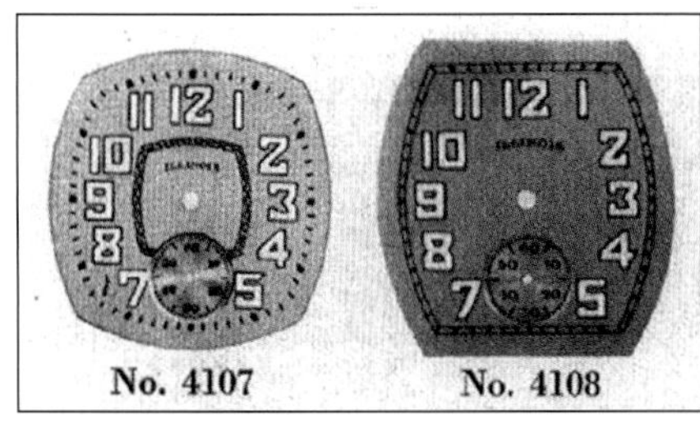

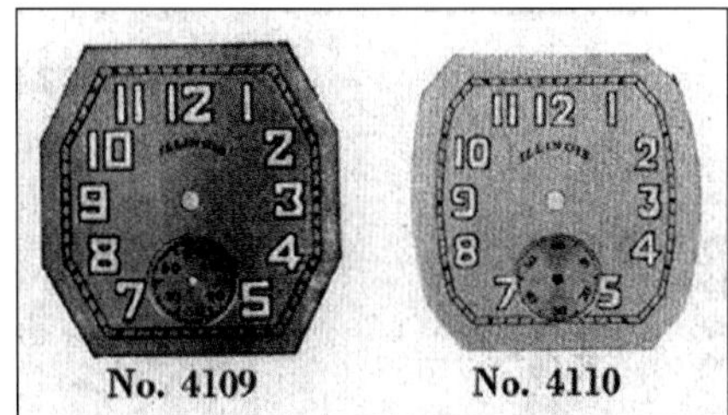

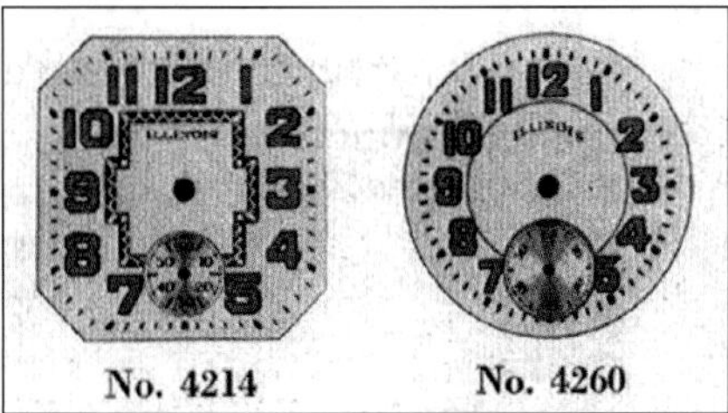

Wristwatch dials from the Illinois Sales Catalog, 1930–1931

Undated Illinois Watch Assortment #100 Price List

Apparently, Illinois issued the dial price list shown to the right sometime between the publication of the May 1927 Dial Circular No. 102 and the December 26, 1930 Dial and Hand Catalog. This price list has Generic Period watch dials as well as dials for proprietary Illinois-designed models such as the Biltmore 18/0, Tuxedo, Medalist, Marquis Strap, New Yorker, Chieftain and Ensign. Interestingly, the "Stock No" for these dials in some instances matches the watch model's case Model Number but in no instance do the stock numbers for wristwatch models match the dial numbers in the three known published dial catalogs.

Some of the numbers (e.g., numbers 5317-A and 5302) appear to be standard Illinois dial numbers, but since the 8000 series dial numbers first appeared in the 1930 catalog, there are likely some missing catalogs between May 1927 and December 1930, as well as between December 1930 and 1936, the date of the last Illinois dial catalog.

ILLINOIS WATCH DIAL ASSORTMENT #100

Quantity	Size	Stock No	Description	Style	Retail Price
5	18/0	89	Etched Raised figures	Full opening	1.50
5	18/0	174	Baked black enamel fig.	Full opening	1.50
5	18/0	169	Baked black enamel fig.	Square opening	1.50
5	18/0	147	Baked black enamel fig.	6 sided opening	1.50
1	18/0	148	Lum figures	Biltmore case	3.00
1	18/0	141	" "	Tuxedo case	3.00
2	12/0	164	" "	Medalist case	3.00
2	6/0	134	" " O.F.	Marquis strap	3.00
2	6/0	135	" " O.F.	Beau Brummel	3.00
2	6/0	152	" " O.F.	New Yorker	3.00
2	6/0	151	" " O.F.	Chieftain	3.00
1	6/0	153	Etched raised fig.-Lum O.F.	Piccadilly	3.00
2	6/0	136	Lum figures O.F.	Ensign	3.00
2	6/0	94	" " O.F.	Rectangular open	3.00
2	6/0	95	" " O.F.	Barrel openings	3.00
2	6/0	93	" " O.F.	Square opening	3.00
2	6/0	97	" " O.F.	Square cut corner	3.00
2	6/0	91	" " Convertible	Round Bit at 6	3.00
2	6/0	91-B	" " O.F.	Round Bit at 9	3.00
1	6/0	98	" " O.F.	Southampton	3.00
1	6/0	92	" " O.F.	Tank	3.00
2	6/0	96	" " O.F.	Cushion cushion	3.00
3	6/0	105	Black enamel fig. Convertible	Round no second	1.00
3	6/0	105-A	Black enamel figures O.F.	Round bit at 9	1.00
2	3/0	91	Lum figures	Round opening	3.00
2	3/0	110	Lum figures	Fahys Atlantic	3.00
2	3/0	108	Lum figures	Barrel opening	3.00
2	3/0	109	Lum figures	Rectangular Tank	3.00
2	3/0	107	Lum figures	Cushion cushion	3.00
1	3/0	97-A	Lum figures	Square cut corner	3.00
1	3/0	142	Lum figures	Rectr. opening	3.00
2	3/0	132	Lum figures	Major case	3.00
3	3/0	106-A	Black enamel fig.	Round opening	1.00
3	3/0	5311	Enamel dials-black fig. S.S.	Round opening	1.25
3	0	5317-A	Enamel dials-lum fig. S.S.	Round opening	3.00
3	0	5311-A	Enamel dials-black fig. S.S.	Round opening	1.25
10	12	116	Etched Raised figures	Round opening	1.50
10	12	146	Etched Raised figures	R-und opening	1.50
10	12	149	Etched Raised figures	Round opening	1.50
5	12	82	Silver black figures	Round opening	1.00
5	12	81	Butler center black fig.	Round opening	1.00
6	12	5302	Enamel dial black fig. S.S.	Round opening	1.25
10	L12	-----	Assorted engine turned	Autocrat case	1.00
10	L12	175	Etched raised figures	Autocrat case	1.50
3	12thin	176	Etched dial	Round opening	1.50
1	12thin	52	Etched Roman figures	Round opening	4.00
3	12thin	126	Etched raised figures	Cushion opening	1.50
3	12thin	158	Etched raised figures	Oxford case	1.50
3	12thin	57-A	Raised figuresB. C.	Round opening	3.00
10	16	162	D.S.O.F. Bunn 23 Jewel Enamel	R.R. GRADE	2.50
3	16	163	D.S.O.F. Bunn 23 Jewel Enamel	R.R. GRADE	2.75
8	16	144	D.S.O.F. Ill. Enamel	R.R. GRADE	2.50
3	16	145	D.S.O.F. Ill. Enamel	R.R. GRADE	2.75
8	16	183	S.S.O.F. Ill. Enamel	R.R. GRADE	1.75
8	16	177	S.S.O.F. Ill. Enamel	R.R. GRADE	1.75
5	16	178	Etched raised figures	Round opening	1.50
5	16	118	Engine turned centers	Round opening	1.00
2	16	179	Butler center dials	Round opening	1.00
3	16	180	D.S. Htg Enamel dials	Round opening	2.50
3	16	181	D.S L.S. Enamel dials	Round opening	2.50
3	17	5280	D.S.O.F. Enamel dials	Sangamo Special	2.50
1	17	5279	D.S.O.F. En. dials. Mtg.	Sangamo Special	2.75
		[illegible]	S.S.O.F. En. dials. H.A.	Round opening	1.25

Dial Price List from between 1927 and 1930

Illinois Drawings for Hands

Illinois from time to time prepared drawings for hands to be fabricated domestically and in Switzerland. In this era, there were companies specializing in hand production just as there were companies concentrating only on manufacturing cases or dials.

Some examples of Illinois drawings from 1931 through 1933 for hands are shown here.

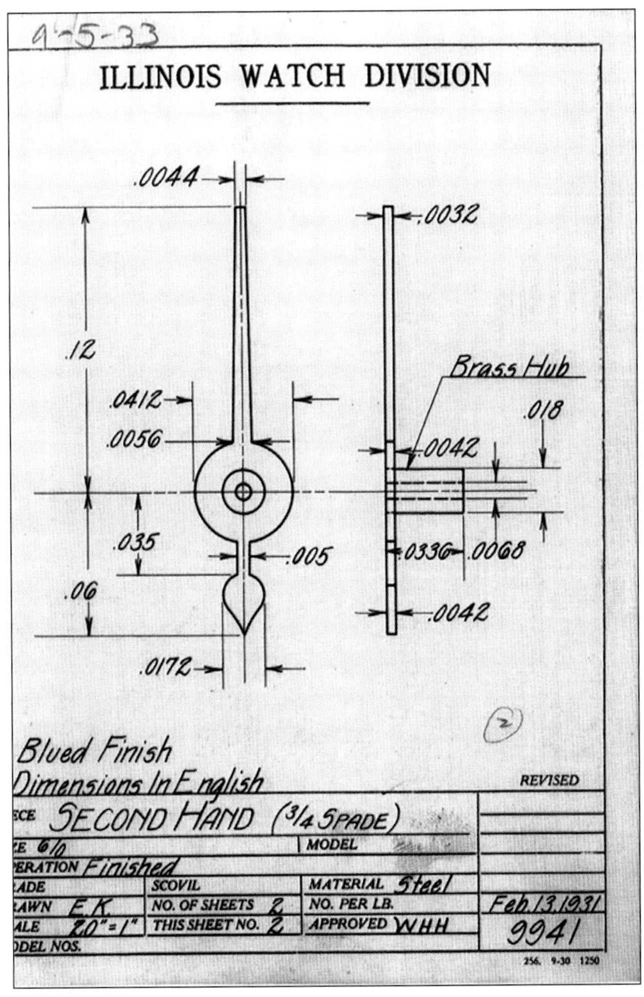

Illinois hand drawing dated February 13, 1931

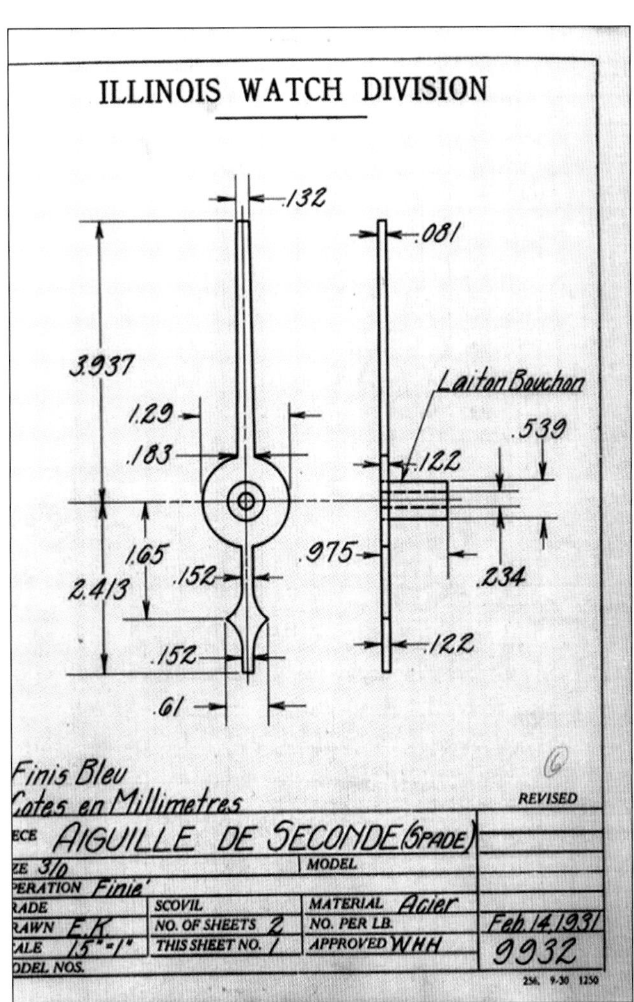

Illinois hand drawing in French, dated February 13, 1931, was to be manufactured in Switzerland.

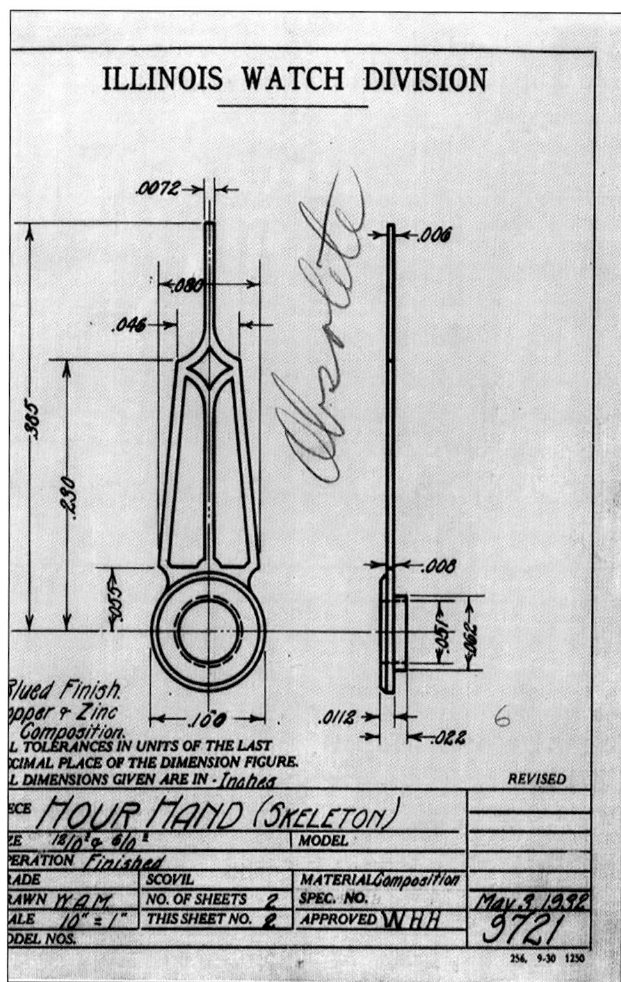

Illinois hand drawing dated May 3, 1932

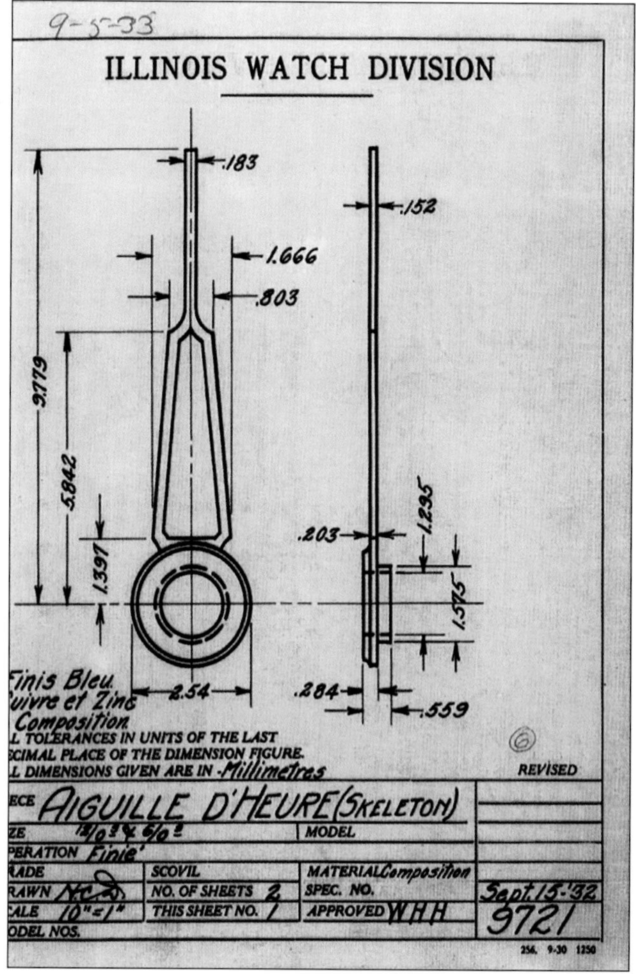

Illinois hand drawing dated September 15, 1932

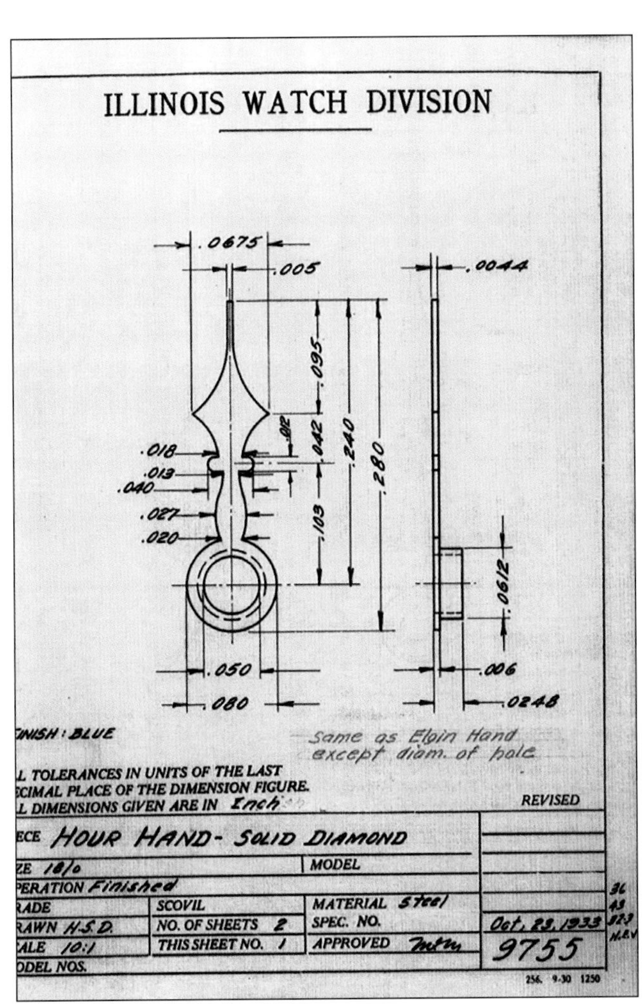

Illinois hand drawing dated October 23, 1933

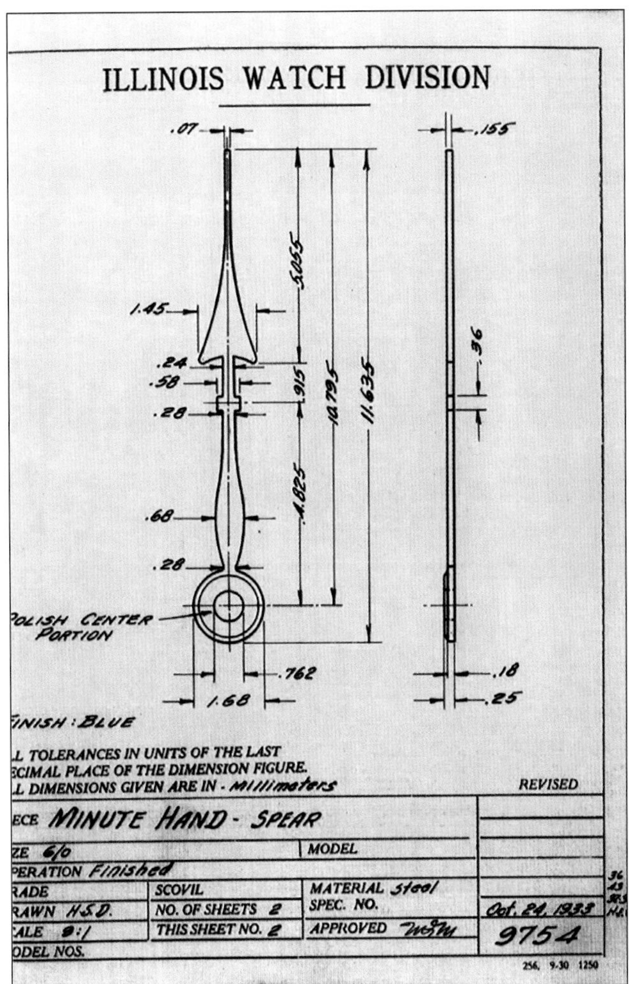

Illinois hand drawing dated October 24, 1933

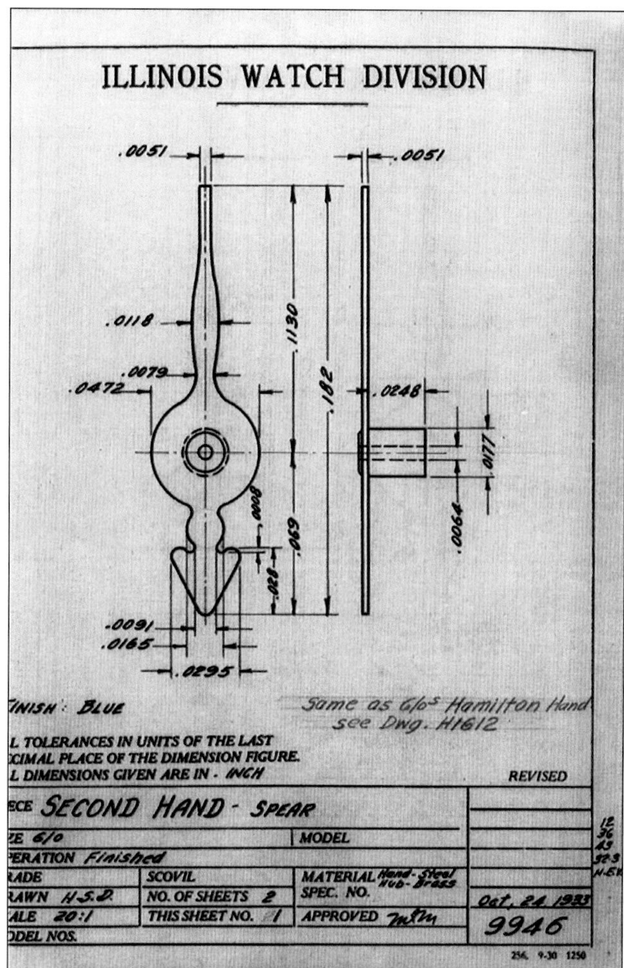

Illinois hand drawing dated October 24, 1933

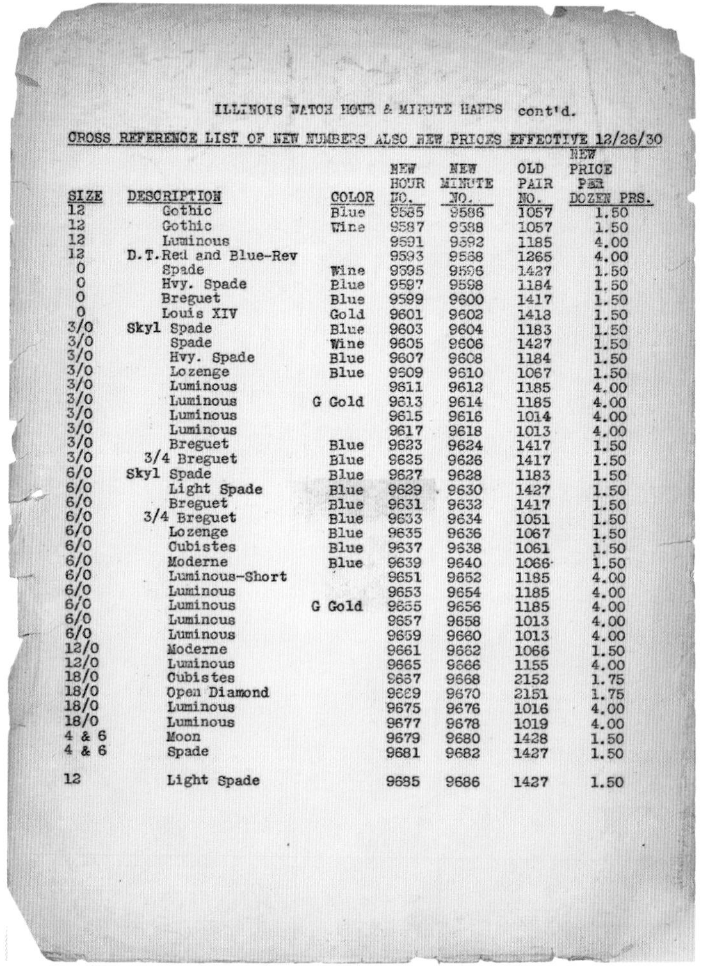

ILLINOIS WATCH HOUR & MINUTE HANDS cont'd.

CROSS REFERENCE LIST OF NEW NUMBERS ALSO NEW PRICES EFFECTIVE 12/26/30

SIZE	DESCRIPTION	COLOR	NEW HOUR NO.	NEW MINUTE NO.	OLD PAIR NO.	NEW PRICE PER DOZEN PRS.
12	Gothic	Blue	9585	9586	1057	1.50
12	Gothic	Wine	9587	9588	1057	1.50
12	Luminous		9591	9592	1185	4.00
12	D.T. Red and Blue-Rev		9593	9568	1265	4.00
0	Spade	Wine	9595	9596	1427	1.50
0	Hvy. Spade	Blue	9597	9598	1184	1.50
0	Breguet	Blue	9599	9600	1417	1.50
0	Louis XIV	Gold	9601	9602	1418	1.50
3/0	Skyl Spade	Blue	9603	9604	1183	1.50
3/0	Spade	Wine	9605	9606	1427	1.50
3/0	Hvy. Spade	Blue	9607	9608	1184	1.50
3/0	Lozenge	Blue	9609	9610	1067	1.50
3/0	Luminous		9611	9612	1185	4.00
3/0	Luminous	G Gold	9613	9614	1185	4.00
3/0	Luminous		9615	9616	1014	4.00
3/0	Luminous		9617	9618	1013	4.00
3/0	Breguet	Blue	9623	9624	1417	1.50
3/0	3/4 Breguet	Blue	9625	9626	1417	1.50
6/0	Skyl Spade	Blue	9627	9628	1183	1.50
6/0	Light Spade	Blue	9629	9630	1427	1.50
6/0	Breguet	Blue	9631	9632	1417	1.50
6/0	3/4 Breguet	Blue	9633	9634	1051	1.50
6/0	Lozenge	Blue	9635	9636	1067	1.50
6/0	Cubistes	Blue	9637	9638	1061	1.50
6/0	Moderne	Blue	9639	9640	1066	1.50
6/0	Luminous-Short		9651	9652	1185	4.00
6/0	Luminous		9653	9654	1185	4.00
6/0	Luminous	G Gold	9655	9656	1185	4.00
6/0	Luminous		9657	9658	1013	4.00
6/0	Luminous		9659	9660	1013	4.00
12/0	Moderne		9661	9662	1066	1.50
12/0	Luminous		9665	9666	1155	4.00
18/0	Cubistes		9667	9668	2152	1.75
18/0	Open Diamond		9669	9670	2151	1.75
18/0	Luminous		9675	9676	1016	4.00
18/0	Luminous		9677	9678	1019	4.00
4 & 6	Moon		9679	9680	1428	1.50
4 & 6	Spade		9681	9682	1427	1.50
12	Light Spade		9685	9686	1427	1.50

Partial Illinois Hour and Minute Hand Price List, dated December 26, 1930

Illinois Dials by Hamilton

After the Springfield Factory closed, Hamilton's Dial Design Department started in 1933 to design dials for Illinois models. Some of these were for existing Illinois models (such as the Tuxedo, Kenilworth and Baronet); some were for variations to existing dials (such as a Blackstone dial with subsidiary seconds at 9); some were for new Illinois models (such as the Chatham, Rockingham, Sangamon, Standish and Urbana models); and, finally, some were for new Conneric models. Connerics were watches that used Hamilton factory-designed Illinois dials for specific Generic and Contract cases made by the Star Watch Case Company, the Manheimer Watch Company or the Aisenstein and Woronock Company. (See the **Conneric** listing of Chapter 9.) Examples of these dials are shown here.

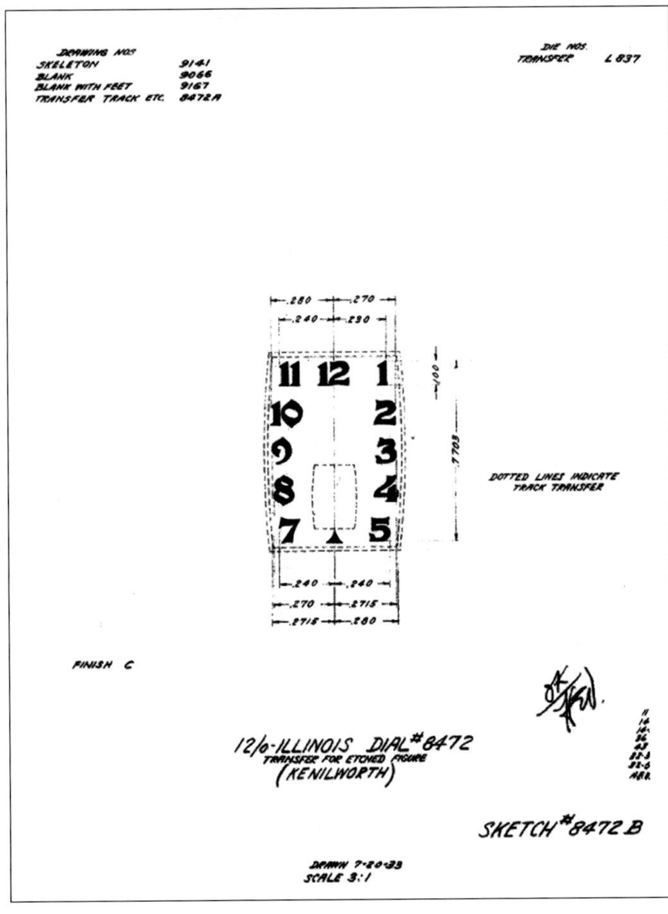

A later Hamilton drawing of a Kenilworth Illinois dial, dated July 20, 1933, presumably for a replacement dial. This dial was apparently not released.

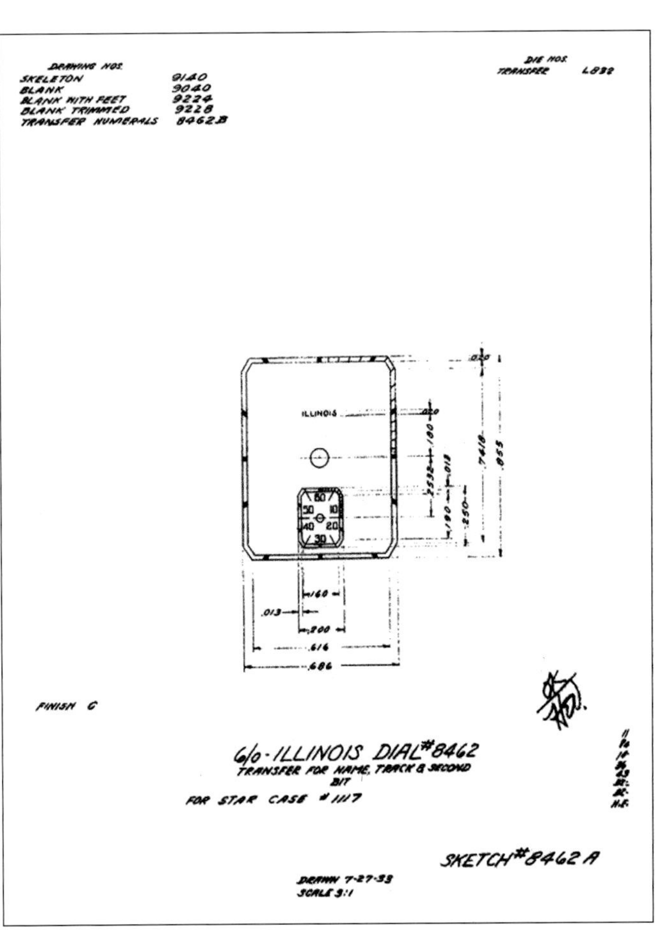

Hamilton drawing of an Illinois Conneric dial, dated July 27, 1933, for Star Watch Case Company case #1117

Later-Released Lancaster Replacement Dials

In 1936, Hamilton issued an Illinois Material Catalog. Included in it were a very comprehensive selection of Illinois wristwatch dials for its men's and ladies' models. For the most part, these dials were silver finish with black-painted numerals (although the ones I have seen looked like the dials were painted white), all for the replacement market. As these dials are seldom seen today, it is very likely that during the Depression era, Hamilton produced an Illinois dial only if it had an order for one. (This subject is also covered in Chapter 5.)

The dials shown are from the 1936 Illinois Material Catalog.

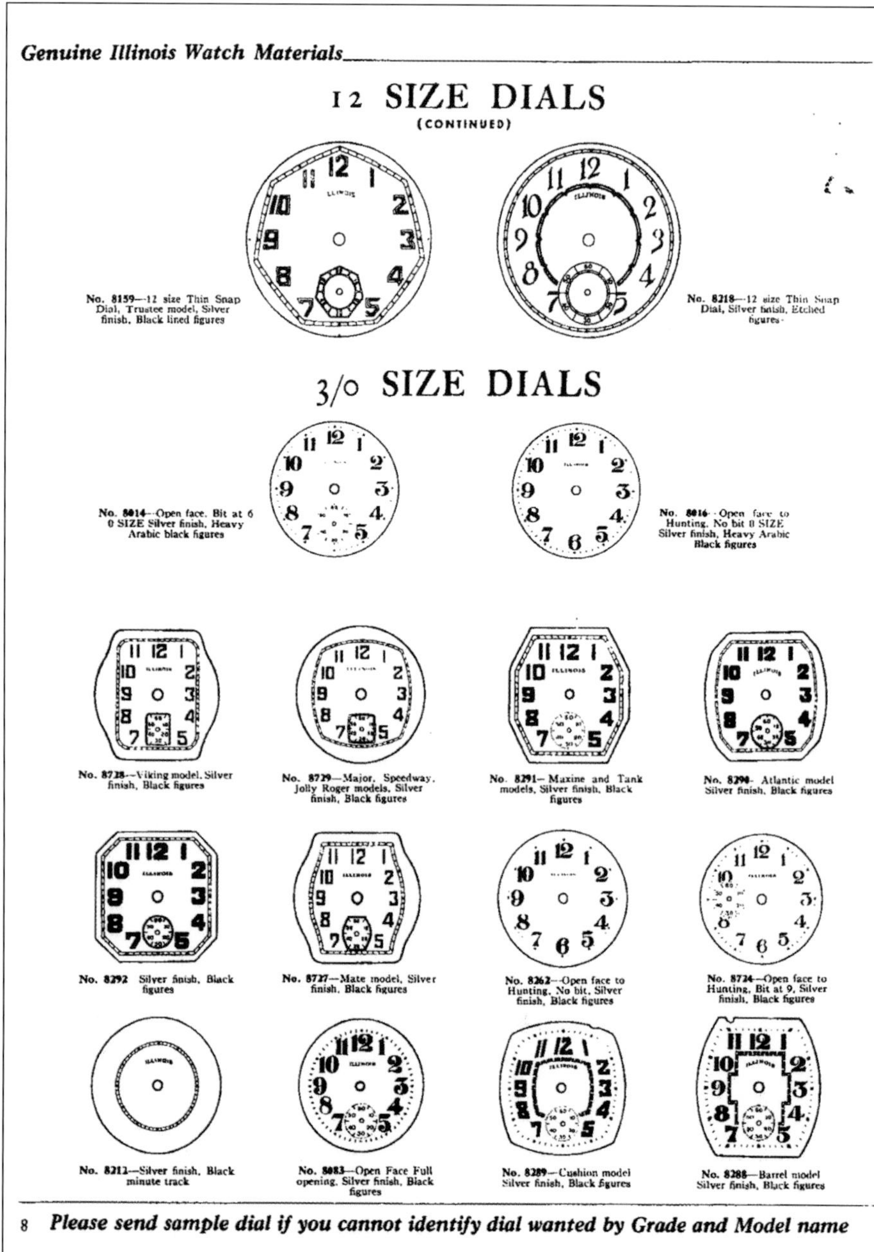

Genuine Illinois Watch Materials

12 SIZE DIALS

(CONTINUED)

No. 8159—12 size Thin Snap Dial, Trustee model, Silver finish, Black lined figures

No. 8218—12 size Thin Snap Dial, Silver finish, Etched figures

3/0 SIZE DIALS

No. 8014—Open face, Bit at 6 0 SIZE Silver finish, Heavy Arabic black figures

No. 8016—Open face to Hunting, No bit 0 SIZE Silver finish, Heavy Arabic Black figures

No. 8728—Viking model, Silver finish, Black figures

No. 8729—Major, Speedway, Jolly Roger models, Silver finish, Black figures

No. 8291—Maxine and Tank models, Silver finish, Black figures

No. 8290—Atlantic model Silver finish, Black figures

No. 8292 Silver finish, Black figures

No. 8727—Mate model, Silver finish, Black figures

No. 8262—Open face to Hunting, No bit, Silver finish, Black figures

No. 8724—Open face to Hunting, Bit at 9, Silver finish, Black figures

No. 8212—Silver finish, Black minute track

No. 8083—Open Face Full opening, Silver finish, Black figures

No. 8289—Cushion model Silver finish, Black figures

No. 8288—Barrel model Silver finish, Black figures

8 ***Please send sample dial if you cannot identify dial wanted by Grade and Model name***

1936 Illinois Materials Catalog

Jolly Roger later-released Lancaster replacement dial

Genuine Illinois Watch Materials

12/0 SIZE DIALS

No. 8419—Etched figures
No. 8066—Black figures
Andover model, Silver finish

No. 8733—Medalist model
Silver finish, Black figures

No. 8456—Futura model
Silver finish, Black figures

No. 8055—Larchmont model
Silver finish, Black figures

No. 8751—Frontenac, Trophy models, Silver finish, Black figures

No. 8238—Finalist, Wentworth models, Silver finish, Black figures

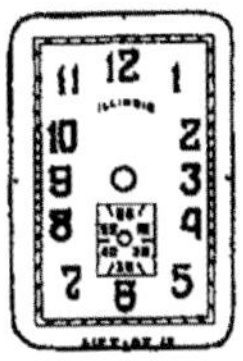

No. 8196—Ardsley model
Silver finish, Black figures

No. 8416—Rockcliffe model
Silver finish, Etched figures

18/0 SIZE DIALS

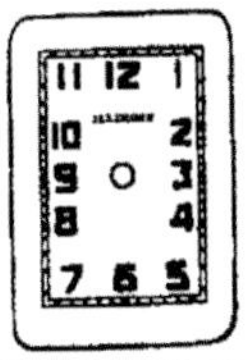

No. 8494—Urbana model, Silver finish, Etched figures

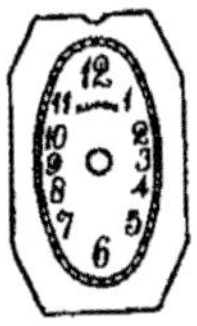

No. 8090—Fairport, Brighton, Vanity Fair models, Silver finish Black figures

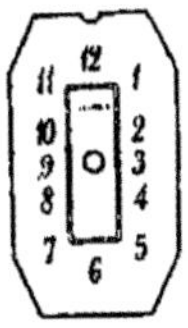

No. 8414—Silver finish, Black figures

No. 8171—Diamond set case opening, Silver finish, Black figures

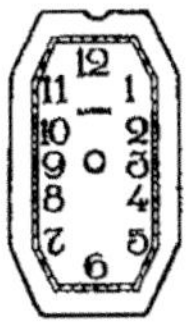

No. 8174—Newport model, Silver finish, Black figures

No. 8394—Beverly model, Silver finish Black figures

No. 8147—Redonda model, Silver finish Black figures

No. 8344—Hollywood model, Silver finish, Black figures

No. 8364—Edgewater model, Silver finish, Black figures

No. 8169—Silver finish, Black figures

No. 8346—Gloria, Vardon, Argyle models, Silver finish, Black figures

21/0 SIZE DIALS

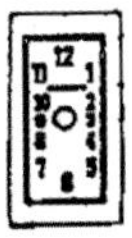

No. 8374—Suzette model, Silver finish, Black figures

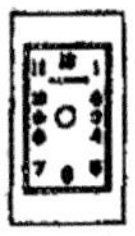

No. 8385—Janette model, Silver finish, Black figures

No. 8372—Lynette model, Silver finish, Black figures

No. 8122—Babette, Marlette, Debette models, Silver finish, Black figures

No. 8732—Charmette, Antonette models, Silver finish, Black figures

 Please send sample dial if you cannot identify dial wanted by Grade and Model name

1936 Illinois Materials Catalog

Genuine Illinois Watch Materials

6/0 SIZE DIALS

No. 8703—Open face Silver finish, Black figures

No. 8267—Open face Silver finish, Black figures

No. 8210—Open face Silver finish, Black figures

No. 8268—Open face to Hunting, Silver finish Black figures

No. 8272—Open face Piccadilly model Silver finish, Black figures

No. 8120—Hunting Beau Geste model Silver finish, Black figures

No. 8277—Open face Barrel model, Silver finish, Black figures

No. 8254—Open face Marquis model, Silver finish, Black figures

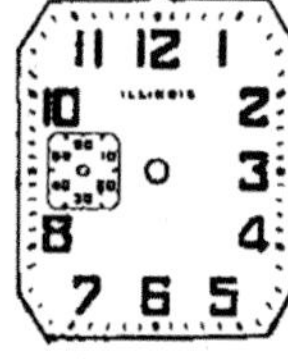
No. 8286—Open face Silver finish, Black figures

No. 8701—Open face Silver finish, Black figures

No. 8708—Open face Consul model, Silver finish, Black figures

No. 8702—Open face Southampton model Silver finish, Black figures

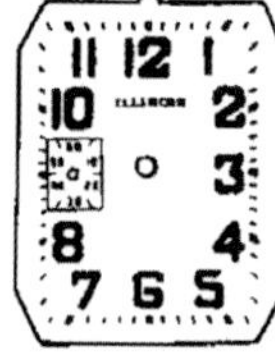
No. 8711—Open face Tank and Canby models, Silver finish Black figures

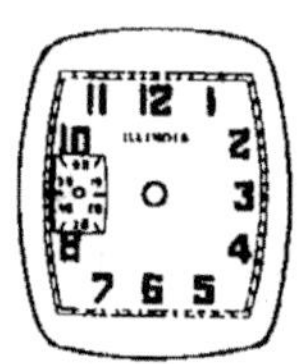
No. 8709—Open face Chieftain model Silver finish, Black figures

No. 8725—Hunting Baronet model, Silver finish, Black figures

No. 8389—Hunting Potomac model, Silver finish, Black figures

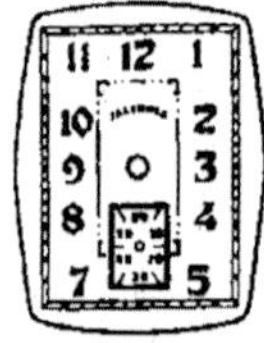
No. 8499—Hunting Chatham model Silver finish, Etched figures

No. 8073—Hunting Arlington model Silver finish, Black figures

No. 8050—Hunting Derby model, Silver finish, Black figures

No. 8737—Hunting Cavalier model, Silver finish, Black figures

No. 8205—Hunting to Open face, Caprice model. Silver finish Black figures

No. 8492—Hunting Rockingham model Silver finish, Etched figures

No. 8736—Hunting Townsman model Silver finish, Black figures

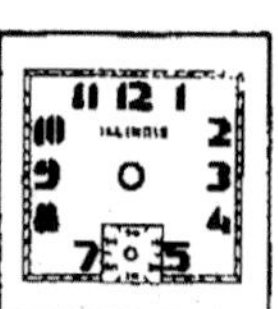
No. 8077—Hunting Commodore model Silver finish, Black figures

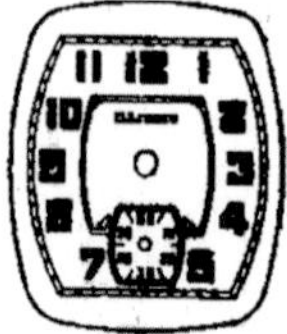
No. 8495—Hunting Standish model Silver finish Etched figures

No. 8208—Hunting Ritz model Silver finish, Black figures

No. 8731—Hunting Consul model Silver finish Black figures

No. 8101—Open face, Bit at 9
No. 8065—Hunting Bit at 6
Ensign model Silver finish Black figures

No. 8275—Open face, Bit at 9
No. 8458—Hunting Bit at 6
Blackstone and Cushion models Silver finish Black figures

No. 8710—Open face, Bit at 9
No. 8072—Hunting Bit at 6
New Yorker, Yorktown and Manhattan models Silver finish Black figures

No. 8730—Open face, Bit at 9
No. 8064—Hunting Bit at 6
Beau Brummel, Beau Royale models, Silver finish, Black figures

It Pays to Use Genuine Illinois Watch Materials

9

1936 Illinois Materials Catalog

After-Market Dials

There are many after-market dials available but they are not very appealing. Most, for some reason, are for tonneau-shaped cases. Examples of these dials are shown here.

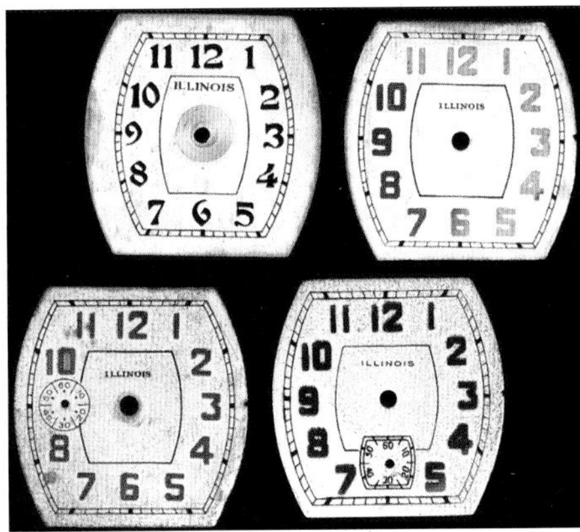

Illinois Replacement Hands by Hamilton

The replacement Illinois hands offered for sale by Hamilton in 1936 are shown here.

Genuine Illinois Watch Materials

ILLINOIS WATCH HANDS

On this page are illustrated the standard hands available for Illinois watches from 18 size to 21/0 size. Illustrations show exact size of the hands. Please order by catalog number to receive prompt and accurate service. If you desire to duplicate hands not shown in this supplement, please submit samples and they will be matched as nearly as possible from stocks on hand.

It is always advisable when one hand is damaged and needs replacing, to order a complete new set of hands so they will fit properly and be uniform in both style and color.

HOUR AND MINUTE HANDS

Catalog Number		Size	Description		
Hours	Minutes				
9509	9510	18	Extra Heavy Spade	Blue	
9533	9534	16	Extra Heavy Spade	Blue	
9719	9720	12	Solid Diamond	Blue	
9737	9738	3/0–0	Moderne	Blue	
9733	9734	6/0	Moderne	Blue	
9735	9736	12/0	Moderne	Blue	
9699	9700	18/0	Railway	Blue	
9705	9706	21/0	Railway	Blue	

SECOND HANDS

Catalog Number	Size	Description		
9945	18	Ball end	Blue	
9911	16	Ball end	Blue	
9915	12	Solid Diamond	Blue	
9932	3/0–0	Spade	Blue	
9937	6/0–12/0	Spade	Blue	

It Pays to Use Genuine Illinois Watch Materials 11

1936 Illinois Materials Catalog

Illinois Dial Manufacturing

At its inception, the Illinois Watch Company purchased its dials from the New York Watch Company, based in Springfield, Massachusetts. A few years later in 1873, Illinois established its own small dial department that expanded to meet the increased demand for Illinois watches in subsequent years. There is no evidence that Illinois produced its own dials for wristwatches. In general, Illinois wristwatch dials were designed internally and their designs were sent to dial manufacturing firms for fabrication. In many instances, the wristwatch dials were as distinctive and daring as the cases and frequently contained design features exclusive to Illinois's innovation and style, as was discussed earlier. In the 1933–1934 time period, Hamilton was designing dials in Lancaster for new models of Illinois watches as well as for previously released ones.

The Sparkle Dial Puzzle

Among collectors, some of the most popular Illinois dials have been the ones with a sparkle effect. Although these have usually all been called "sparkle dials," close examination makes clear that Illinois used at least two different sparkle techniques for dials on its wristwatches.[3] It is possible they were from two different dial makers (most likely Swiss).

One of the techniques, utilized on the Caprice dial, results in a flat, white surface, but embedded in thick white binder of some sort are jagged and irregularly shaped, sparkly silver pieces, which are widely spaced. The silver flakes are often jagged and twisted; they look like the chips produced as scrap from machining metal. On the Caprice these particles look like they are depressed into the surface of the white base of the dial, and the white ground around the silver particles occupies most of the area of the dial. Although the white base material is full of clumps, like cottage cheese, and there are small voids between the clumps, the surface is quite flat, as though it has been ground or scraped to a level. A close-up magnified image of a Caprice dial is shown here.

Macro photograph of a Caprice dial, at about two times magnification

Detail of Caprice dial shot with oblique illumination

The second sparkle-finish technique is shown on the dial of a Larchmont. This dial is entirely different; its surface is covered with tiny granules of silver. At low magnifications, the particles look almost like the glass beads used on reflective highway signs. The effect of the particles is like that of the coating on signs: from whatever angle the viewer observes a dial, there will always be some surfaces in position to reflect light. Unlike the Caprice dial, where there is a lot of binder around the sparkles, on the other Illinois sparkle-finish dials the whole surface is covered with silver granules and no binder is evident. The granules are not uniform in shape or size; the whole surface is covered with these granules, without flat space between them. These particles are markedly smaller than the sparkles on the Caprice. This Larchmont dial is also an example of a drop-shadow dial, and the second material outlining the black of the numerals is quite obvious.

Macro photograph of a Larchmont dial, at about four times magnification

Detail of Larchmont dial shot with oblique illumination

In an attempt to determine how the sparkle finish was produced, the same two dials, a Caprice and a Larchmont, were sent to a metallurgical testing laboratory for examination. The dials were first subjected to photomicrographs up to 40 times magnification, and the silver particles were measured. The photomicrographs are shown below, with the actual sizes of the typical silver particles indicated. The particles on the Caprice dial, mostly larger than 0.002 inches, are several times the size of the particles on the Larchmont, which are all smaller than 0.001 inch.

Caprice photomicrographic particle measurements at 40× magnification. Particles are about 0.002 inches or larger.

Larchmont photomicrographic particle measurements at 40× magnification. Grains are less than 0.001 inch.

After making the photomicrographs, the laboratory examined the same dials with a scanning electron microscope (SEM). The SEM images are not truly photographs; the SEM responds to shapes, textures, materials, and sizes, not colors (there is no light involved). The SEM has a secondary capability of X-ray fluorescence spectroscopy, which reveals some of the elemental composition of the dials. While this analysis shows what elements are present, it does not indicate how they are combined chemically or physically: all it discovers is what is present in some form, at least for materials that can be activated by X-rays. (Not all elements respond. Hydrogen, in particular, is transparent to X-rays, so this system does not detect it, and so hydrocarbon products such as paints are not accurately represented in the analysis.)

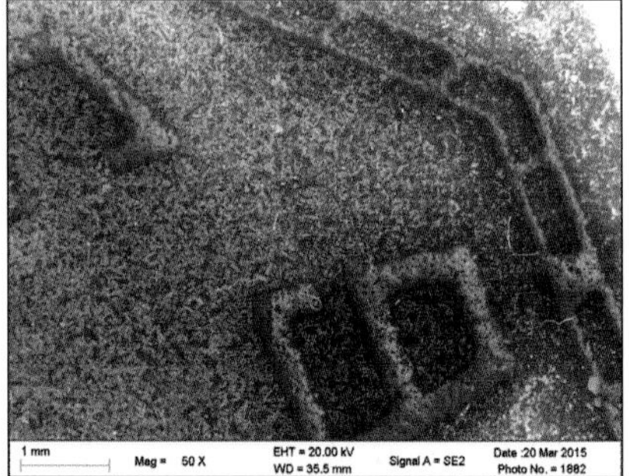

Caprice dial 50×

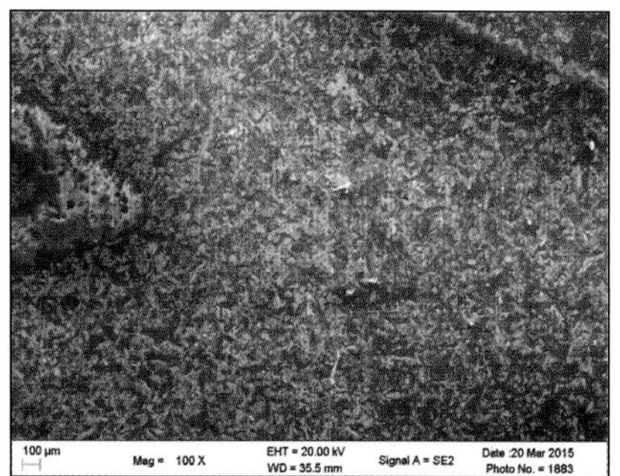

Caprice dial, part of numeral "5", 100×

Caprice dial 250×

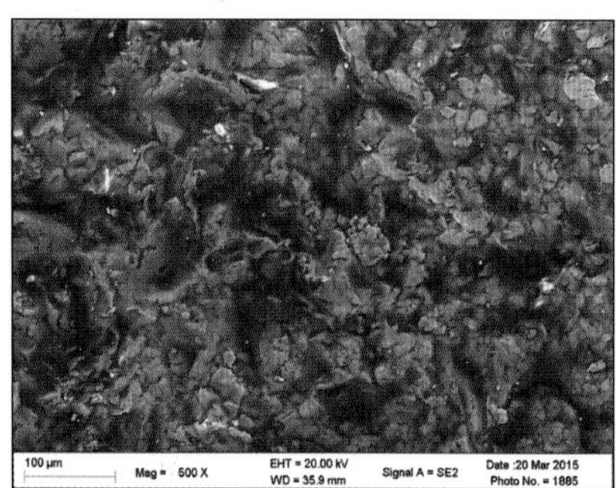

Caprice dial 500×

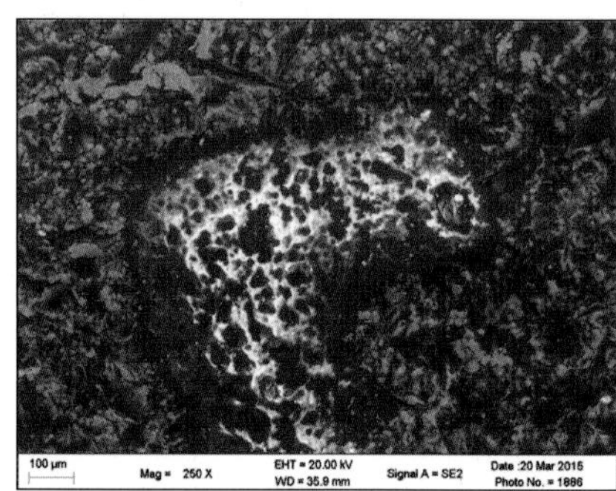

Caprice dial, part of numeral "6", 250×

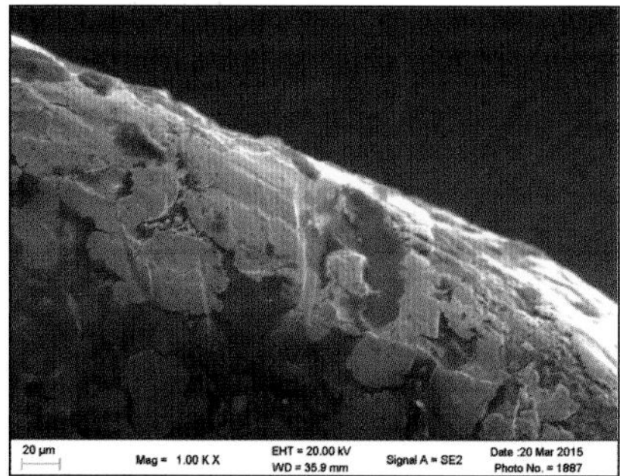

Caprice dial blank edge 1000×

The first four pictures zoom in on the lower right-hand part of the Caprice dial. How the white background material is full of clumps, with voids between them becomes increasingly evident at higher magnifications. The silver fragments are less evident in the SEM images than they are in the color photomicrographs. The printing on the dial clearly stands on top of the white base, and what appears to have just a matte finish in the photographs turns out to have a complex texture, with a lot of particles (probably carbon) embedded in another material. The thickness of the printing, which appears in the photographs to be directly on the base material, is exaggerated in the SEM images. On the Caprice dial, the base coating extends to the edge of the dial blank, and the combination of clumps and voids is evident there.

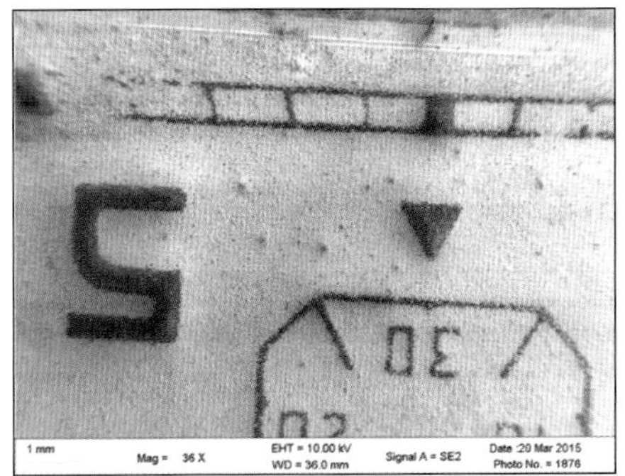

Larchmont dial (upside down) 36×

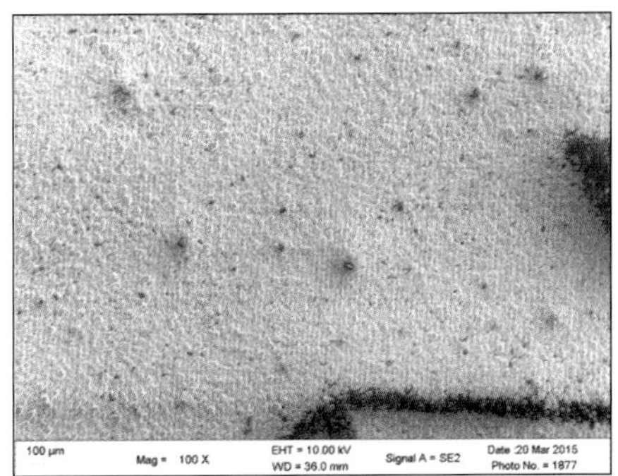

Larchmont dial 100×

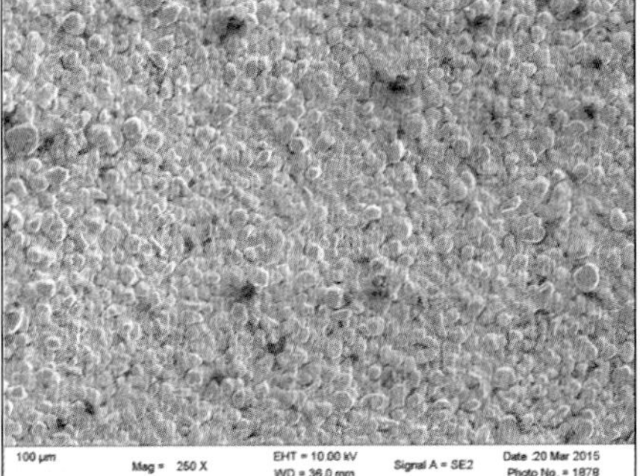

Larchmont dial 250×

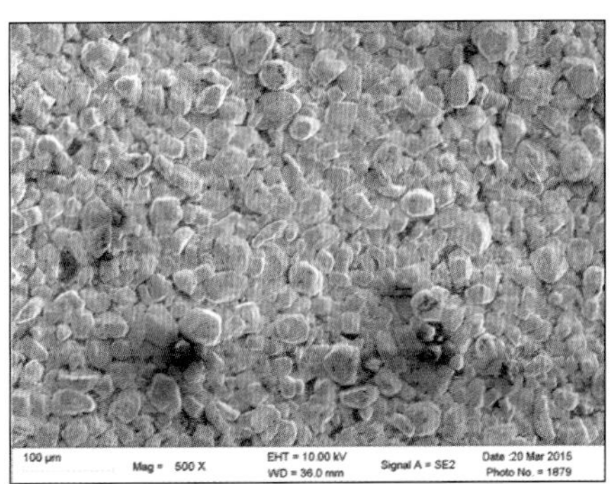

Larchmont dial 500×

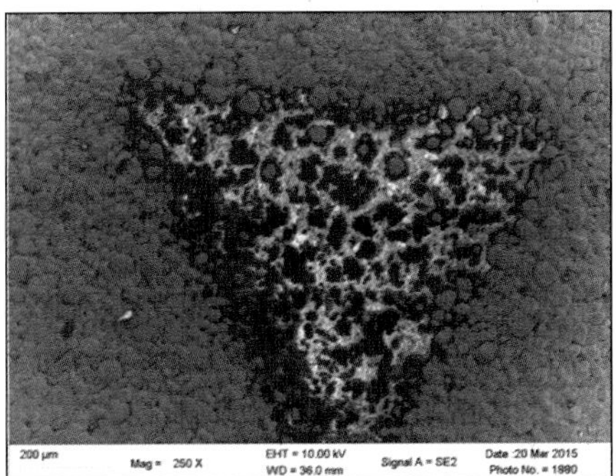

Larchmont dial "6" marker (upside down) 250×

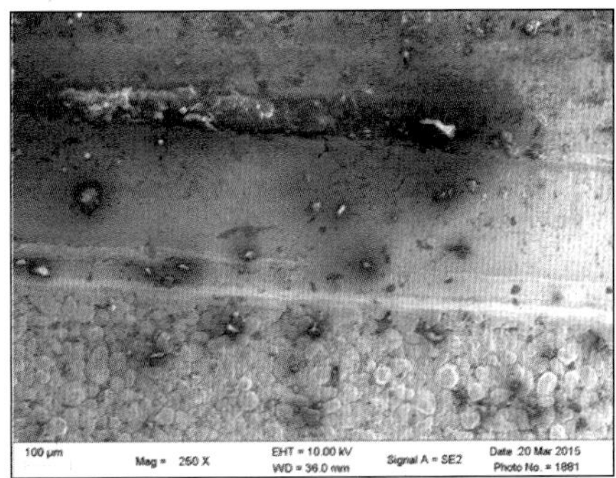

Larchmont dial base, outside sparkle area 250×

The first four SEM scans of the Larchmont dial zoom in on the lower portion of the dial, gradually revealing the shapes of the particles on the dial. (That the printed parts of the dial show up in black is incidental; these are not photographs. There are also some bits of contamination on the surface of the dial that also show up as black.) Even at 36 magnification, it is clear that the surface is not smooth. At 100, the granular surface is becoming more evident, and at 500, the irregular sizes and shapes of the grains are quite evident. It is also clear that the grains are piled up on top of each other, several layers deep, completely covering the dial blank. At high magnification, the triangular marker at the "6" position on the dial shows that it too has a rough surface. Again, the thickness of the printing is exaggerated by the SEM process. The last image, taken near the edge of the dial, shows that the grainy surface is cut off sharply, leaving just the base of the dial (there is some extraneous contamination outside the sparkle area). Whether this means the perimeter of the dial was masked during the application of the silver grains or it was ground down to the blank afterwards is not certain.

The SEM is also capable of doing analysis of some of the elemental composition of the surface, though it does not capture all materials, nor does it show precisely where they appear on the dial or how they are related to each other mechanically or chemically.

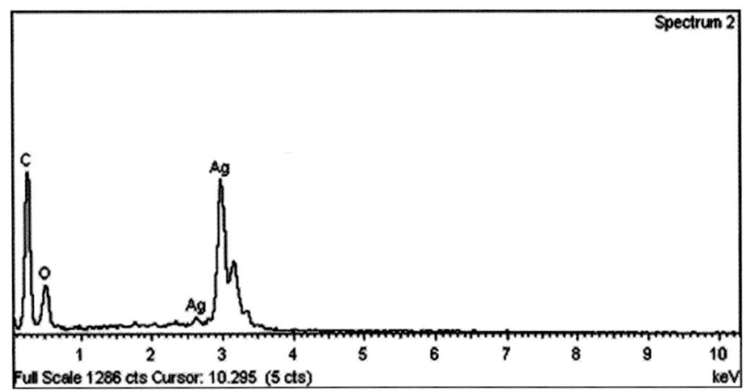

Caprice dial X-ray fluorescence spectrum of white background

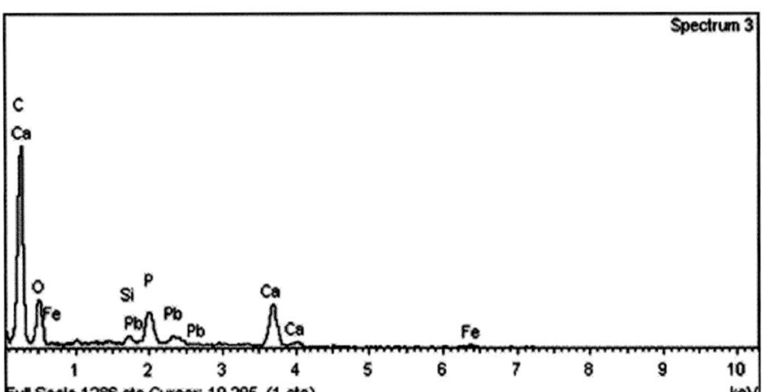

Caprice dial X-ray fluorescence of print area

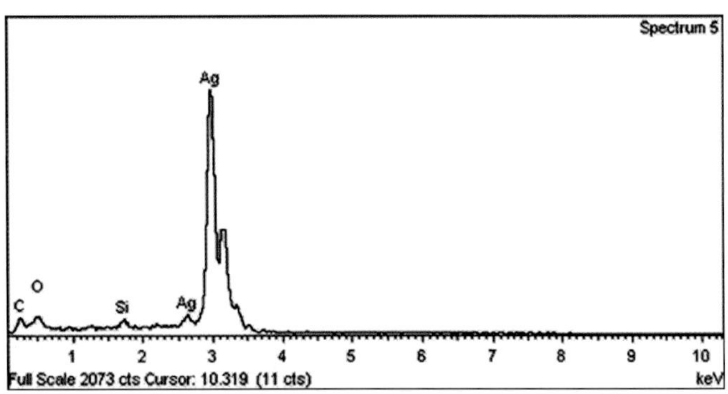

Larchmont dial X-ray fluorescence spectrum of sparkle area

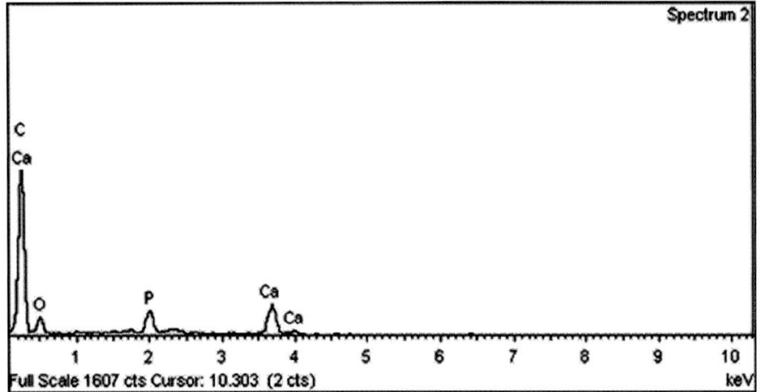

Larchmont dial X-ray fluorescence of print area

The strong signal for silver (Ag) for the background areas both dials confirms what had long been thought: that the sparkle comes from silver particles. (A similar spectrum from the backs of the dials also confirms that the dial blanks are either silver or silver-coated.) There is also a signal for carbon (C), which might be from the print on the dial or from contamination, such as oil that has wandered from the watch movement. It is not clear why the dials return signals for oxygen (O) or why the Larchmont dial shows the presence of silicon (Si).

The spectrograms of the print areas show much stronger signals for carbon and calcium (Ca). The carbon is almost certainly the coloring agent in the paint. The reason for calcium is not obvious. The Caprice dial also shows the presence of numerous other materials, including lead (Pb) and iron (Fe), whose role is unknown.

Although this analysis of sparkle dials confirms some things suspected before, such as that the sparkle comes from silver particle, it also reveals other things not previously discussed, such as the fact that there are two different manufacturing processes. But it does not discover other things, particularly what those processes were.

The process used for the Caprice dials would probably be easiest to recreate: silver chips are scattered through an opaque, chalky binder, which is then smoothed in preparation for printing. However, there may be less demand for this process than for the other because it appears to apply to only one model, and the dials of the Caprice, being protected by both case and crystal, are frequently in good condition.

The process for the sparkle dials used on other models still has unsolved elements. Knowing that the coating is silver particles suggests why tarnish-removing solutions are frequently helpful in partial restoration of dials. The tests also show the general size of the particles and that there is hardly anything on the surface of the dial but the silver grains. That leaves unresolved how the grains are held on the dial.

If there is some sort of cement or binder, it is not evident in either the magnified images or the spectrograms. One possibility is that the dial surface is built up by sintering, a process applied to metal powders that are heated enough to cause grains to fuse together without actually melting. It may not be possible to reconstruct the exact original process, but the new data might give a starting point for experimentation. In any event, owing most likely to their cost, Hamilton stopped the production of any more Illinois sparkle-finish dials in 1932.

Enamel Dial-Making

The process of making enamel dials was technically complex, so Illinois initially outsourced this operation. The enamel dials had a copper disk with brazed-on feet and was coated on both sides with a paste of fine white enamel powder. The enamel was fused in a furnace, then smoothed and polished. After being fired a second time in the furnace, it was transferred to dial painters. The dial painters, with black enamel paint, put on the Illinois name, numerals, minute divisions and chapter rings. These were hand-applied with camel hair brushes. These features were later transferred onto the dials by the use of rubber printing blocks. The enamel lettering was then fused in a furnace. The enamel for both sides of the dial prevented it from distorting during its three trips in and out of the furnace. To accommodate a subsidiary seconds bit, the enamel had to be ground away on both sides and the copper disk etched with acid. Once the hole was polished, a separate seconds dial was soldered in place.

TECHNICAL TIP

Although it has uniformly been contended that it is not possible to refinish or redo an enamel dial, that is no longer the case. Some enamel experts who do restoration work for museums can effectively restore a damaged enamel dial. However, since this process is long and generally very expensive, it should involve a dial worthy of the investment. In addition, you have to find such a artisan who is interested in taking on such a project. The before-and-after images of a very rare Illinois enamel-exploding numeral dial show how much can be done to improve such a dial that has damage.

Before restoration

After restoration

MAKING ENAMEL DIALS

An article by Gerrit Nijssen in the April 2007 issue of the NAWCC *Bulletin* includes a description of the basic steps for making an enamel dial in the early 1900s.* That section of his article is quoted below:

"Copper was cast and rolled into sheets 0.015-0.040 thin (determined by the size of the movement). The dial blanks were then punched out of the sheet and the sharp edges were smoothed. The majority of the blanks had a slightly rolled edge. The slightly dished surface guaranteed a more uniform enamel thickness.

"The next step was to attach the dial feet. Initially, they were brazed, then spin welded (ca. 1895). Later they were electrically welded. It should be noted that the brazing temperature was only about 40° higher than the flowing temperature of the first enamel layer.

"Soft and hard enamel was determined by the firing temperature of the enamel, which ranges from around 1,200°F to 2,000°F.

"Soft enamel dials were made with a coarser enamel and were less expensive to produce, but they did not have the quality finish and sheen of the hard enamel/glass dials. They were mainly used for industrial products such as telephone dials and water and gas meters on stoves. The hard enamels and 'underglazed' dials have a higher hardness and sheen and were used on high-grade watches and other 'fine' products. . . .

"After the dial feet were attached, a layer of scrap enamel (which has the highest melting point of any of the enamels), or frit, was applied to the back of the dial. When the frit was fused to the copper, it would warp the dial toward the blank enamel side, making the face side of the dial concave. This happened because the expansion of copper is about twice that of enamel.

"The next step was to apply layers of white enamel on the face of the dial blank.

"At this point there were variations in the manufacturing process with regard to when the holes for the fourth wheel pinion and the center were drilled. Each white layer was 'stoned' with Scotch stone and/or emery before the next white layer was applied. These layers counteracted the warp of the dial back. The trick was to balance the amount of warping from both sides and to end up with a relatively flat or slightly convex dial face. . . .

"If the dial was to have a sunk subsidiary-seconds dial, at this point of the process was placed on a lathe, the seconds bit hole was partially cut from both sides with emery or another hard substance, and the remaining copper base was removed with acid.

"It should be noted that over the years processes were developed that did not require the use of acid.

"The dial edge, center hole, and seconds hole were then polished.

"The next step was to chamfer the face and in some cases the back of the dial. Depending on the quality of the dial, it could then receive a final polish. . . .

"If a flat dial was desired, the fired dial was at this point sandwiched between heated steel blocks (steel block/sheet of mica/dial/sheet of mica/steel block) and allowed to cool slowly. Because of this cooling process additional stress was created between the copper and the enamel layers, making the dial more susceptible to hairline cracks.

"Depending on the type of dial and decorations several layers were applied to the face of the dial. If different colors were used, the dial was fired several times, with each consecutive enamel layer having a lower melting temperature than the previous layer to prevent a meltdown. Silver and gold leaf appliqués were applied just under the last glass layer.

"When this last glass layer was in liquid form, the appliqués floated to the surface.

"The second's bit was made with a similar process.

"The numbers and decorations were initially hand-painted on the dial. To bring the labor cost down, decals, silk-screening, and other processes were introduced. The decal transfer process was favored by the dial industry, but it had two drawbacks: (1) the registration and the contact between the decal and the 'white' (a 'white' is a polished blank white enamel dial) was not dependable and (2) the generation of black debris when the paper was burned during the firing of the dial required retouching of the dial or increased the rejection rate. The goal was to reduce the manual labor, improve rejection rates, and simultaneously circumvent patent rights."

*"The O'Hara Story: Part 1: Watch Dials," NAWCC *Bulletin*, No. 367 (April 2007), pp. 182-83.

Enamel Dials Being Made in the Illinois Watch Factory Still Frames from the 1923 Silent Film

Preparing enamel dials for firing in the Illinois Factory by automatically sifting a uniform thickness of enamel powder

Inserting enamel dials to be fired

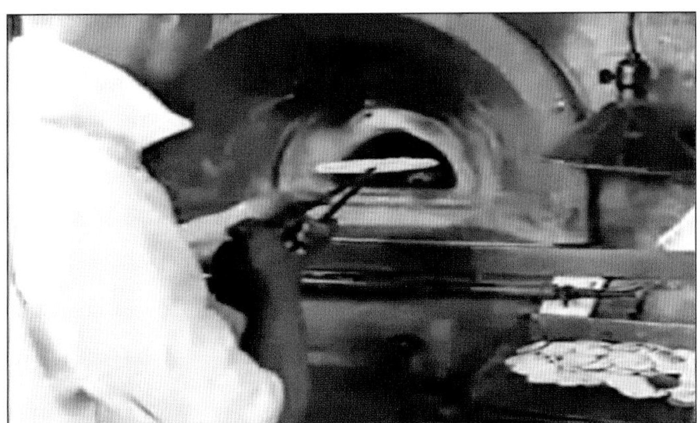
Removing dials from the furnace

Stamping the numbers and Illinois lettering on the dials

Stoning the dial for its next layer

Attaching the seconds bit

Illinois manufactured its own enamel dials; examples of a wide assortment of these dials are shown here.

A collection of mostly NOS enamel Illinois dials, along with some gently used ones

Exploding Enamel Dials

The Illinois Factory produced at least six very rare and collectible enamel dials with exploding numerals. One is shown here.

Rare enamel exploding numeral dial

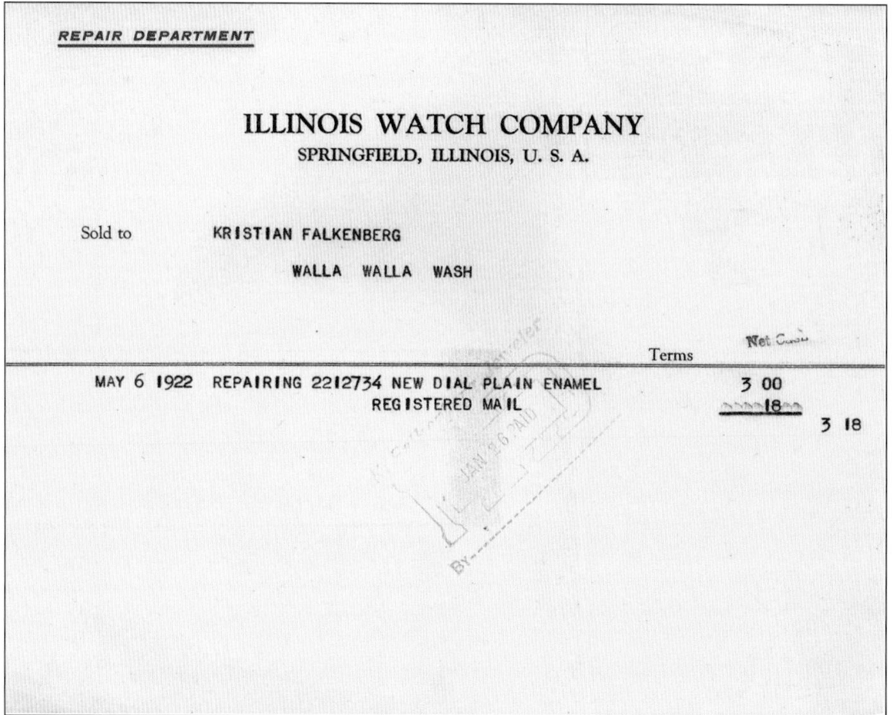

REPAIR DEPARTMENT

ILLINOIS WATCH COMPANY
SPRINGFIELD, ILLINOIS, U. S. A.

Sold to KRISTIAN FALKENBERG
WALLA WALLA WASH

Terms Net Cash

MAY 6 1922 REPAIRING 2212734 NEW DIAL PLAIN ENAMEL 3 00
REGISTERED MAIL 18
3 18

Illinois invoice, dated May 6, 1922, for repairing an enamel dial

Metal Dial Fabrication and Dial Refinishing: An Interview

Although there is much information about how an enamel dial is made, there is very little about the specific steps required to produce a metal dial or to refinish one. However, the owner of International Dial, Robert Miller (RM), kindly agreed to an interview with the author (FJF) to describe the process of fabricating a metal dial most likely used by Illinois as well as to respond to many questions concerning original dial making in the time of Illinois wristwatch production and refinishing dials today. International Dial (ID), the industry leader in watch dial restoration/refinishing, handles almost any dial refinishing job. ID has been led by Robert Miller since 1989. The Q&A follows.

1. **FJF: How does metal dial production begin?**

   RM: Watch dial manufacturing begins with the dial design. The dial design takes into account the dial thickness, size, dial material, movement specifications, case design/shape and how all the components of the watch will fit together. Once the Illinois dial design department finalized its design, its toolmakers would begin making the tools, jigs and dies required to manufacture the dial.

2. **FJF: What are the next steps?**

   RM: Dial manufacturing consists of many steps. These steps may occur in different order for different dials; however, the end result will be getting a dial blank the correct size (shape and thickness) with dial feet attached in the correct positions with respect to the movement and any needed holes in the dial in the correct position so that the hands can be attached properly and accurately.

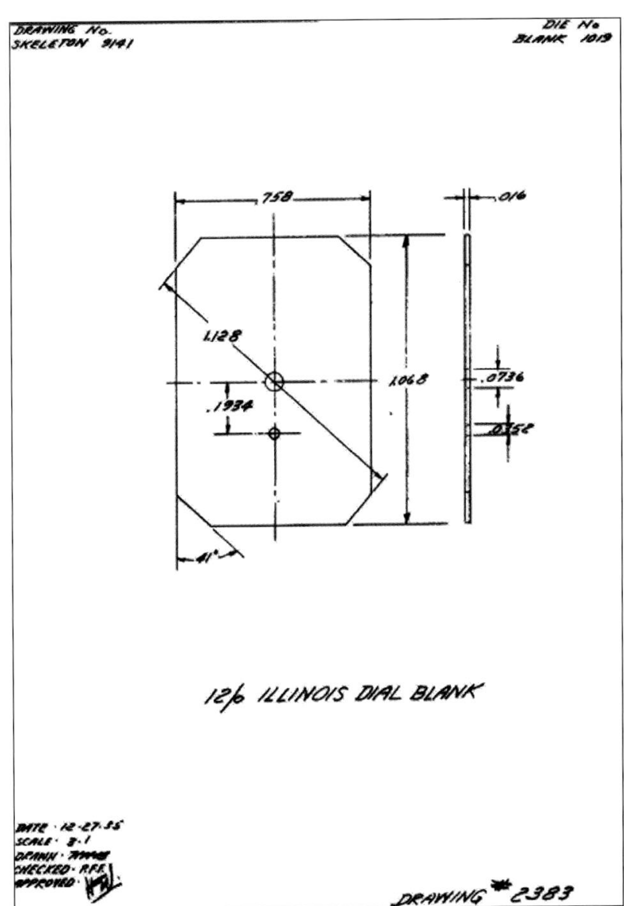

Hamilton drawing of an Illinois 12/0 size dial blank, dated December 27, 1935, for a later-released Lancaster replacement dial

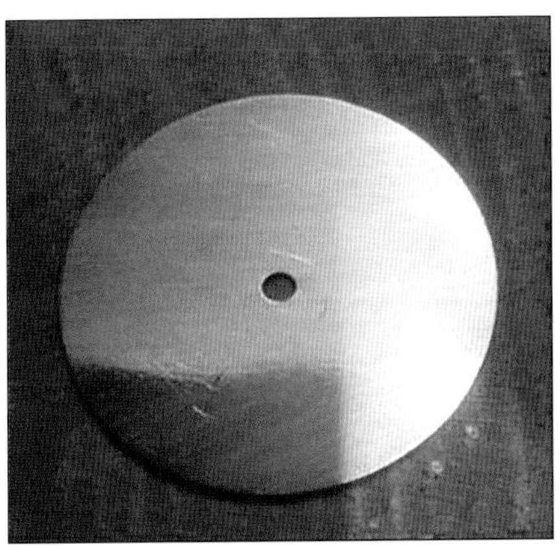

A dial blank in silver before its feet are attached

3. FJF: When is the dial trimmed and its feet added?

RM: In some instances, the dial shape is blanked out first, then the center hole punched. The dial is then placed into a jig so that the dial feet can be attached in the correct locations, using the center hole as a reference point. In other cases, the dial feet can first be attached to a rough blank. This blank is placed in a jig using the attached feet to locate the dial properly. Once in the jig, the dial will be "trimmed" using a die to conform the dial to its final shape. Then the holes for the hands will be punched again, using the dial feet to locate the dial properly in a jig.

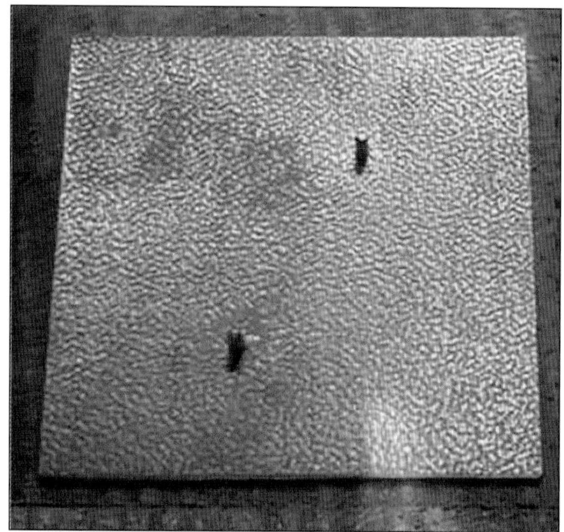

This dial blank starts with a rough blank; then the feet are attached. This blank needs trimming and then its hand holes punched.

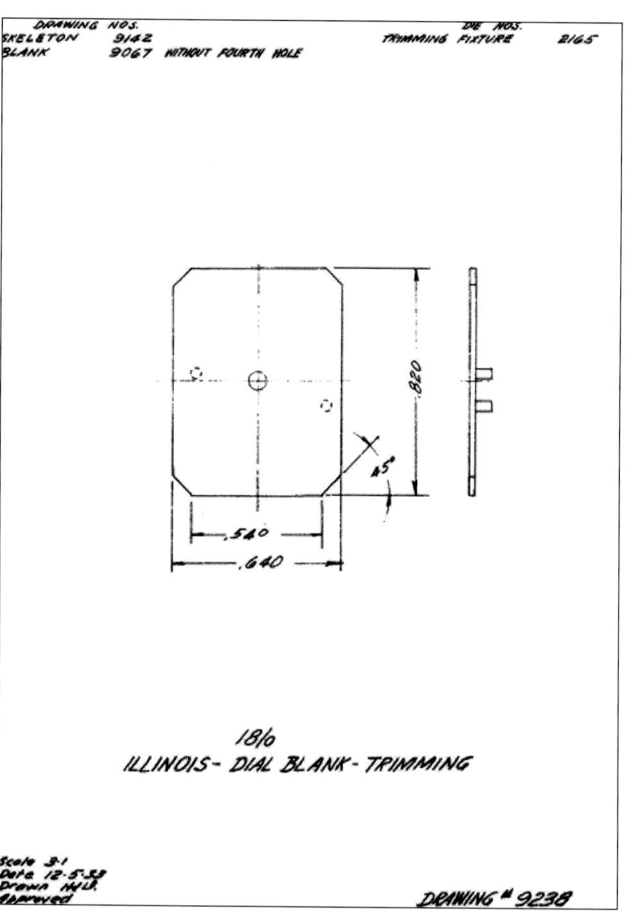

Hamilton drawing of a 18/0 size Illinois dial blank for dial trimming, dated December 5, 1933

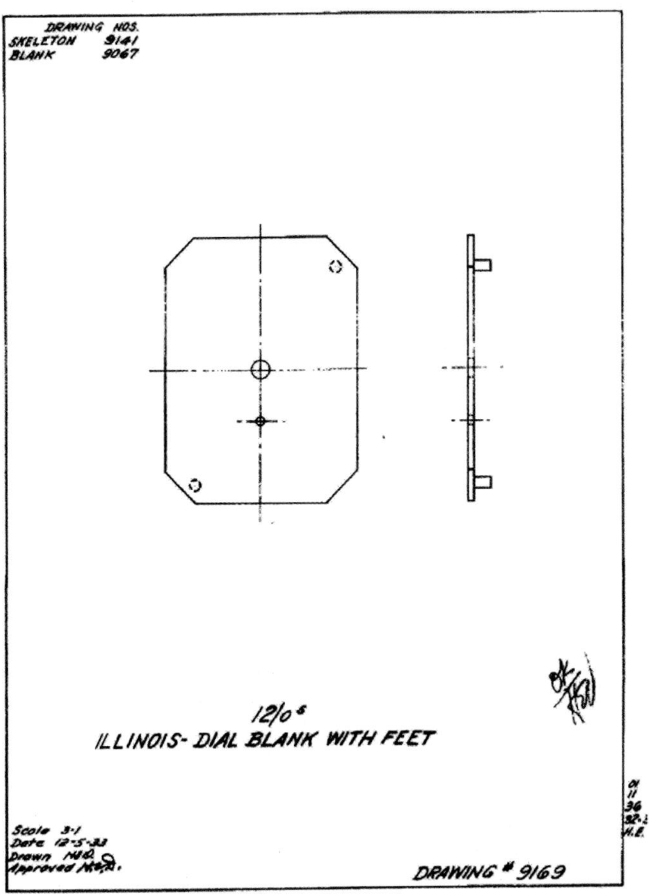

Hamilton drawing of a 12/0 size Illinois dial blank with feet, dated December 5, 1933

4. FJF: Does it make a difference if the dial has applied gold numerals versus printed numerals?

RM: If the dial has applied gold markers or numerals, the dial will go to a drilling station. Again using a jig to insure proper alignment, the dial will be drilled with the appropriate holes which will accept the applied markers.

This dial blank was first stamped with an embossing die, then the feet were attached, then the dial was trimmed. Note that this is the back side of the dial and the hand hole has yet to be punched.

5. FJF When is the dial finish applied?

RM: Once the dial blank is finished with respect to its shape, size, holes and has its feet properly attached, the dial blank is ready to have its "finish" applied. Dial finishes can be almost any treatment to the surface of the dial that will make the dial match the design parameters assigned by Illinois. The dial finish could be paint, plastic, enamel, glass, wood, etc. In most cases (in the early days of wristwatches), Illinois dials were treated with some form of plating, primarily silver. In fact, Illinois utilized a proprietary silver finish and sparkle finish containing actual silver flakes/particles.

Most dials from the 1920s, 1930s and through the 1960s are silver or white. No dials with a "painted" surface were utilized by Illinois and its competitors. Painted surfaces did not come into regular use until the 1970s, primarily because paint just did not hold up as well.

6. FJF: So then was the silvered finish the most common finish in the late 1920s–1930s?

RM: Yes, "silvered" was the prevalent dial finish at that time, although the silvering could be done in different ways to produce different effects.

7. FJF: How is the silver dial finishing done?

RM: Dial finishing can be done in several ways. The most common way is to "silver" the dial. As most dial blanks are made of brass, it is a simple task to prepare the surface for plating. Illinois, as did others, used their own methods and formulations but the practice is essentially the same, except Illinois employed some specialized techniques. The dial surface must be prepared for its final appearance as to texture and surface appearance. Since the silver plating will not hide any imperfection in the dial surface, any imperfection must be removed. *Note:* The paint and the silvering may be only a few microns thick.

Aged original Ritz dial with sparkle finish and painted figures

8. FJF: What does plating entail?

RM: The plating process may involve plating the dial with copper first, but most times the plating will go directly onto the brass blank. Once the dial is silvered the dial must be washed, cleaned and a clear coat of lacquer applied. Now the dial is ready for printing.

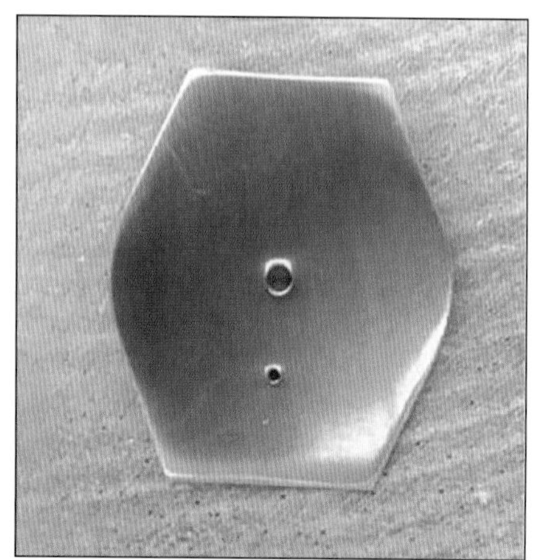
Same Ritz dial, stripped of its original finish. At this point the dial is at the same stage where refinishing or finishing for an original dial begins.

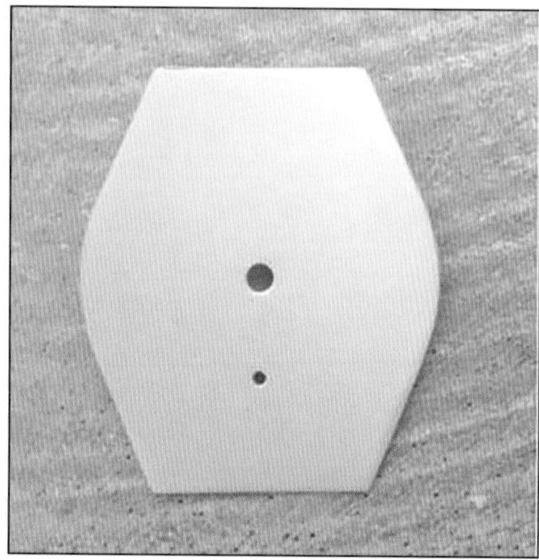
Same Ritz dial with a new white/silver finish and clear coat

9. FJF: Is this the same basic process to produce an original dial before the refinishing process commences?

RM: Yes, the original dial and a refinished one are prepped the same up until the refinishing process.

10. FJF: Then how does a refinished dial differ from what you described?

RM: In dial refinishing we try to get the dial to the same point in the manufacturing process from which we can go forward in the same manner as it was first produced. Basically, it does not differ at all if the refinisher uses the same technique as the original manufacturer. In the case of dials with printed, luminous or applied gold numerals, we can sand off the old finish and move forward from the smooth brass blank using the same steps as when the dial was manufactured.

Once the dial has been silvered, a clear coat of lacquer must be applied. The clear coat is needed to prevent the dial from oxidizing. The main reason that a watch dial needs restoration is that the original protective coating has deteriorated, allowing oxygen and moisture to begin oxidizing the silver surface of the dial. This oxidation discolors the surface, often making the dial unreadable. Although there are several ways to remove the oxidation, many of these methods also remove the printing, basically destroying the dial. Note that if you can remove the oxidation it means there is no longer any clear coat on the dial and the dial will tarnish again in a very short time.

Workshop Notes

Conducted by JOHN J. BOWMAN (*Technical Editor*, THE KEYSTONE)

Subscribers wishing inquiries answered in this department must send name and address—not for publication, but as an evidence of good faith. No attention will be paid to anonymous communications

Refinishing Watch Dials

Please let me know how to refinish metal dials of bracelet watches. I refer especially to the dull finish on them which peels off occasionally.—W. H.

The first thing to determine, in any case of a metal dial which is discolored, is whether the numerals are of hard or soft enamel. Hard enamel is really glass melted into numerals engraved or otherwise hollowed-out in the metal of the dial. These hard enameled dials may be recognized usually by the fact that the enameled figures are flush with the surface of the dial—no higher. Soft enamel figures stand up above the surface of the dial. These are just painted or printed on the metal—not "set in"; and the material of them is not glass, but is easily dissolved off of the dial. These cheaper soft-enameled dials cannot be replated economically; if not too badly discolored, they may be dipped in cyanide of potassium solution, as used for cleaning watches and silverware, rinsed, and allowed to dry by evaporation, which may be hastened if desired by *dabbing* with clean linen rags—but not in any case by rubbing, as this is likely to smear softened enamel over the dial. The enamel being dissolvable, the above dipping must be done as quickly as possible, to avoid removing the numerals. If the discoloration is very deep, a good job of restoration can hardly be done on these cheaper dials, and the dial should be replaced with a new one, which will cost less than both replating and repainting numerals would. If the dial has hard-enameled figures on it, no matter how badly stained or tarnished it is, it may in the first place be vigorously cleaned with cyanide with no fear of injuring the figures; and if this is found to be insufficient to restore the appearance like new, the dial may be replated right over the numerals, which will remain unaffected by any of the solutions used for plating.

Keystone, February 1933

11. FJF: When can you print on the dial?

RM: Once the clear coat dries, the dial is ready for printing. Printing is done using a pad printer. This is a very common technique and pad printing is still used today (although very automated).

12. FJF: What is pad printing?

RM: In pad printing, first the printing die (cliché) is made. The die plate holds the ink that will be transferred to the dial. The dial will be placed in a jig that will hold the dial in the proper location. The die plate is inked. The pad comes down, picks up the ink and it is transferred to the dial.

13. FJF: So, in other words . . .

RM: Yes, the desired cliché is set up and pad printed. Ink is applied to the cliché. A rubber pad then comes down and picks up the ink. The dial then slides under the pad. The pad comes down and transfers the ink to the dial.

Please note that in manufacturing, the use of alignment jigs allows for multiple dials to be printed one after another very quickly. In refinishing, as only one dial type is done at a time, each dial requires a different die plate and a different setup. This is very time-consuming.

14. FJF: Can you explain what a "cliché" is?

RM: A cliché is an object that holds the ink for a pad printing machine. The cliché is a positive image of the desired print recessed into some type of material.

An actual ID cliché for a Devon dial

A dial refinisher's cliché plate for several Illinois dials, among others

15. FJF: How is a cliché created?

RM: Clichés can be made in a number of ways. They can be molded, laser-engraved, hand-engraved, machine-engraved or photo-etched. Any manner of getting a recess into the material will work. The main reason for the different methods would be the required detail of the print. Coffee mugs and baseball hats do not require the detail or precision of a watch dial.

16. FJF: Do you have original clichés from the various watch manufacturers?

RM: Yes. We do have some of the original clichés from several manufacturers, including Bulova, Hamilton and Illinois. We have others also; however, their use is limited. We have also been making our own clichés since the company started.

17. FJF: How many clichés do you have?

RM: Approximately 40,000 different clichés. We do also have some duplicates, and we have some from other dial refinishers that we have purchased as they have closed. These purchased clichés we have found do not print with the quality of detail we require, so we seldom use them. All told I would guess the total is around 75,000 clichés.

18. FJF: What material is the cliché made of?

RM: Almost anything. I have some very old ones made of glass, steel, tool steel and aluminum. I've seen plastic, vinyl and resin. The main factor again is the desired detail and anticipated length of service. Our plates are made of special steel, hardened and polished to a mirror finish. Each plate cost approximately $200.00 before it is engraved. Expensive, but they last several lifetimes. Last week ID used plate No. 2, which was made in the 1930s.

19. FJF: What happens if a cliché is damaged, lost or wears out?

RM: We simply make a new one. I retain the masters from all the clichés we have made. One problem we have now is maintaining the extensive catalog of clichés as it is almost a full-time job. We are constantly making new dies as well as remaking old ones.

20. FJF: Is there a difference between a die, a plate and a cliché?

RM: Essentially no; a die is a pattern, a plate can hold more than one cliché, a cliché is one image on a plate. We use them interchangeably in our shop. Some of our plates have fifteen clichés, some have only one.

21. FJF: How does the cliché hold the ink to allow the dial to be printed?

RM: The image is below the surface. When ink is applied to the surface, a squeegee is used to remove the excess.

22. FJF: Is it expensive to make a cliché?

RM: Not in material. The main factor is time as they are done by hand. Most clichés take at least four hours to make.

23. FJF: How is a cliché made?

RM: The way we make our clichés is the same way it has been done for one hundred years. Our method is very old, and I am sure more modern techniques are available. We still do it this old way because that is how I learned; and since it duplicates the original technique, I think it better duplicates the original dial.

Newer dials made with newer techniques may make us change, but since we see very few of these dials we have no plans to change at this time.

24. FJF: Who creates the master dial plates?

RM: I create the masters for the clichés made at ID.

25. FJF: How were the Illinois master plates created and how are they utilized?

RM: This is supposition on my part. Once the art work is finalized, the master would be made using a pantograph engraving machine. Once the master is made it would be used on a different engraving machine to make the actual cliché. Today masters are not made. Almost all clichés would be made digitally, using a photo-etching technique of some kind.

26. FJF: How is the master plate engraved?

RM: That would be up the person making them; ID's are made by hand.

27. FJF: How is the master plate shrunk down to make the cliché?

RM: We use a pantograph engraving machine that was hand built by the original owner of ID. It is a unique machine; I've never seen another one like it. The machine is very precise and can make incredible detail. New methods are finally getting more detail than I can match. I am sure digital high-resolution photo engraving is being used on modern items.

28. FJF: Can you explain why it seems that refinishers cannot recreate the butler silvered subsidiary seconds used on some original Illinois dials?

RM: We could, provided we had the proper tooling and the required time, as it is labor intensive. The subsidiary seconds would have been cut into the dial last in the manufacturing process, and before the dial was printed. Once the blank was stamped out, the feet would have been welded in place. Then the dial would be trimmed to its final shape, and holes punched for the center and subsidiary hands. Next, the dial would be finished. At this stage the dial would have been all one color. An end mill would then be used to cut the recess for the subsidiary bit, cutting through the finish and exposing the brass base metal. The profile of the cutter would also cut in the "ring" detail. This brass area would be plated silver. The dial would then be lacquered and then printed. In refinishing we can mask off this area after the dial is stripped of the old finish and plate it silver after the finish is applied. We cannot recut the subsidiary bit as the dial would get too thin and we could actually cut all the way through the dial. So, we could do it, but it is a long a complicated process, adding significantly to the dial's cost.

29. FJF: Could you polish a redone subsidiary seconds to make it look silvered?

RM: Yes.

30. FJF: Do you know how Illinois produced its unique butler centers?

RM: Yes; however, I do not know that they are unique, as several companies used the butler type finish in creating two-tone dials. Although I do not know the exact formulation for the silver used to create the Illinois butler finish, we do have the formulae used by Bulova, Elgin and Hamilton. Because the Hamilton Company purchased Illinois prior to ID starting business, it may very well be that Hamilton adopted the same formula used on Illinois dials for its own.

31. FJF: Do you know how Illinois produced its unique sparkle finish on its dials?

RM: No. We have tried to duplicate this finish and we have come close, but the exact finish is difficult to duplicate. We believe it has to do with the grain size of the silver powder being applied to the dial, and I believe with further experimentation we could figure out the exact process. However, since the application of this finish is so limited, we don't feel that the time and expense of experimenting further is justified.

The sparkle-finish effect is still noticeable on this original Caprice dial.

Note: Illinois employed a very special technique, unique to it, on the surface of many of its dials, involving silver particles that uniquely caused the dial to sparkle like the sun shining on freshly fallen snow or like light shining through Japanese rice paper. New research on sparkle dials, done since this interview took place, is discussed earlier in the chapter—*FJF*

32. FJF: Why can't dial refinishers reproduce the Illinois sparkle finish effect?

RM: Without knowing the exact formula for the silver powder applied to the dial and the exact technique used to apply the silver, it is pretty much left to experimentation. This is time-consuming and expensive.

33. FJF: Do you believe that if time and money were not issues that you could, by extensive experimentation, replicate the great Illinois sparkle-finish dial technique?

RM: Yes.

Note: The author is on record as disliking redone dials to the point of preferring poor originals to excellent redone ones; however, this is a highly subjective subject. In the spirit of fairness, examples of before-and-after refinished dials from ID are shown on the next two pages. The partial steps to refinish an Illinois Rockcliffe and a New Yorker follow in numerical sequence.

Partial Dial Refinishing Steps (Illinois Rockliffe dial)

Applied numeral Illinois Rockliffe dial before refinishing. This dial is actually a redone dial with the incorrect subsidiary track.

Same Rockliffe dial with the applied gold numerals polished

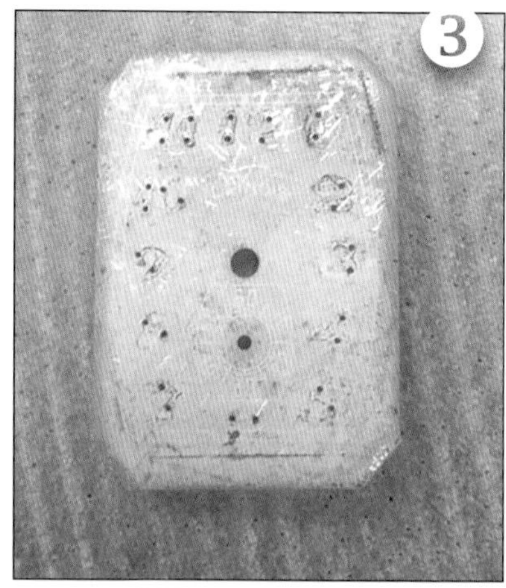

Same Rockliffe dial with gold applied numerals removed

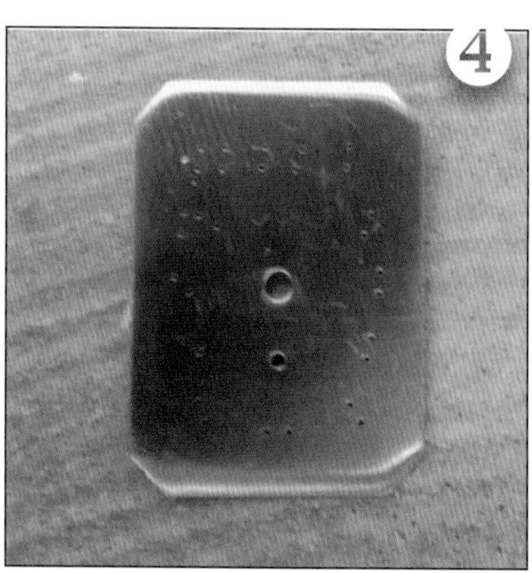

Same Rockliffe dial stripped and sanded smooth. At this point the dial is at a stage equal to when it was first manufactured; so going forward, the refinisher can attempt to duplicate the original manufacturing process, applying the same finish and printing.

Applied numeral dial for an Illinois Rockliffe, expertly refinished by ID. *Note*: It now has the correct subsidiary second track.

Partial Dial Refinishing Steps (Illinois New Yorker dial)

Two-tone original New Yorker dial to be refinished

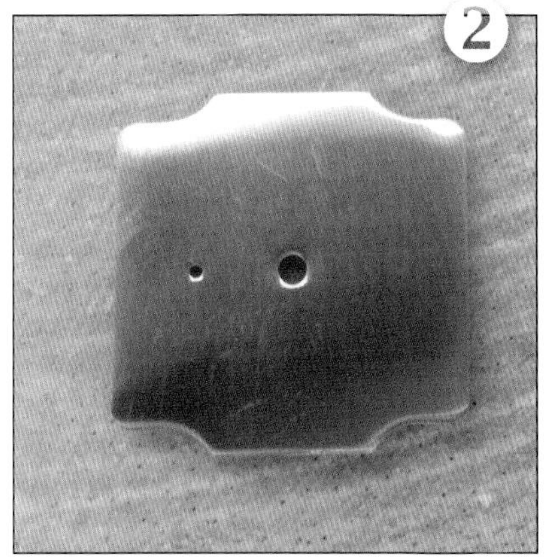

Same New Yorker dial stripped down to bare brass and prepped for new silver base finish

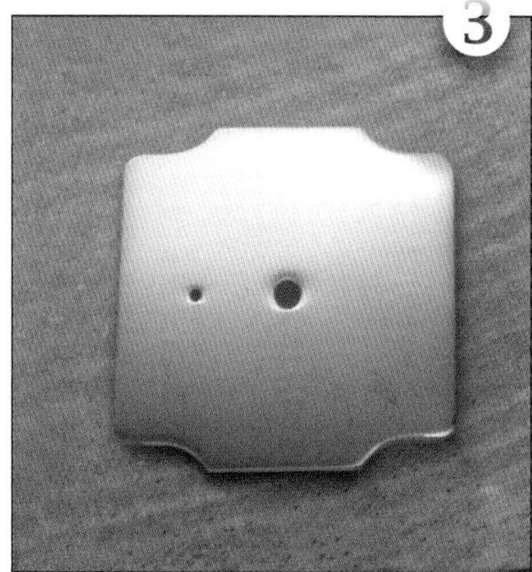

Same New Yorker dial, blank with new silver finish

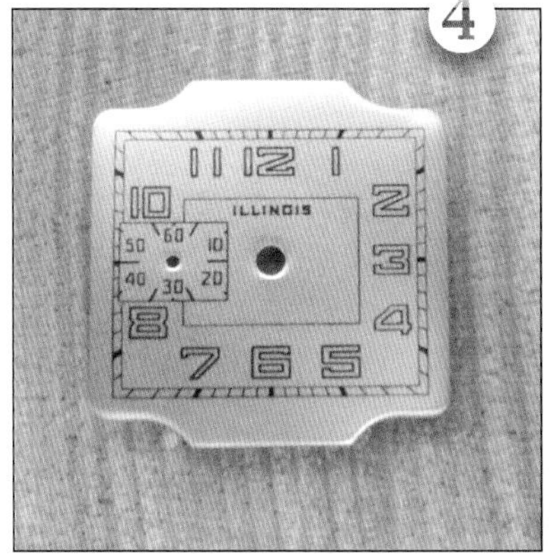

At this point, the print will be used to apply a mask to that part of the dial that is to remain this color.

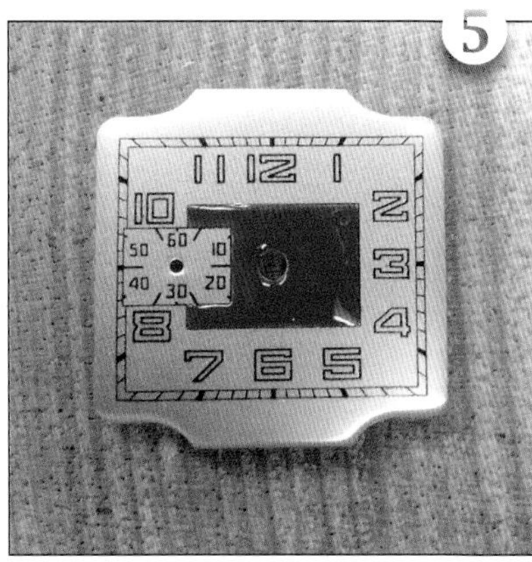

Dial with mask applied. Mask is tinted orange so it will show up in this image.

New white finish applied to outside area. Silver finish remains under mask.

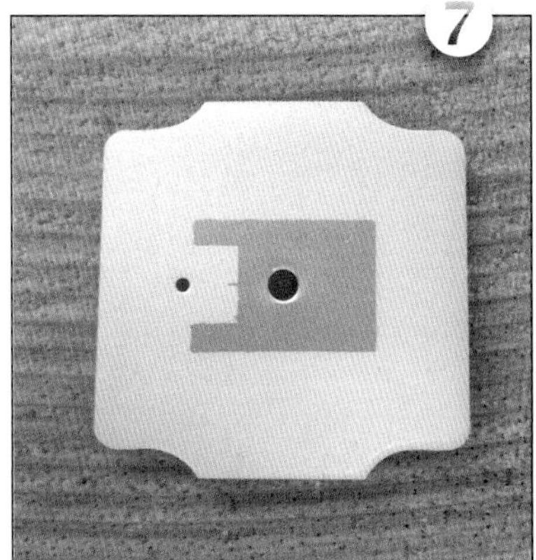

Dial with second color applied and mask removed. The dial has also been clear-coated and is ready for printing.

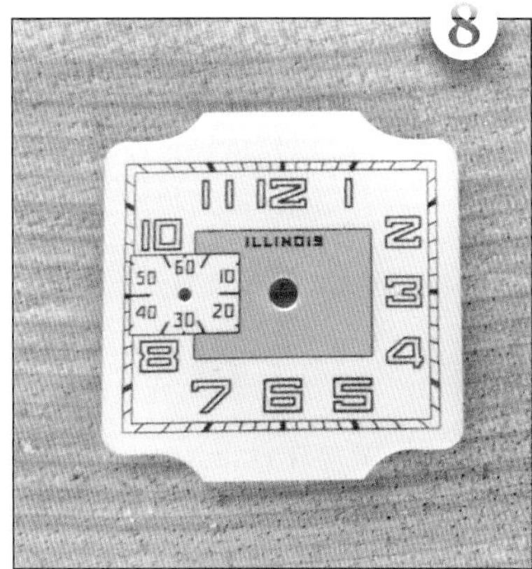

Dial printed. Luminous figures still need to be filled in.

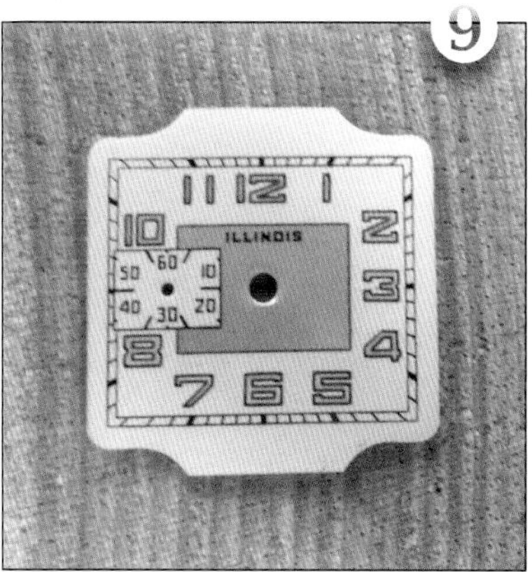

Dial for an Illinois New Yorker, expertly refinished by ID and with luminous applied

34. FJF: Are unscrupulous persons using laser technology to attempt to recreate Illinois dials and pass them off as originals?

RM: Not that I am aware of.

35. FJF: Can enamel dials be refinished by your company?

RM: No.

36. FJF: Can your firm repair hairlines on enamel dials?

RM: No.

37. FJF: Can a refinisher repair chips on enamel dials?

RM: No.

38. FJF: What do you use in place of radium for luminous numerals today?

RM: Luminova powder mixed with a binder.

39. FJF: How do you apply the luminous to the numerals on your refinished dials?

RM: Luminous powder is mixed with a binder to the correct consistency. It is then applied by hand just as it was done 100 years ago, with a steady hand and a fine brush.

40. FJF: Does the luminous you use glow in the dark?

RM: Of course.

41. FJF: Do you get requests to customize Illinois dials?

RM: Yes. Most of the time this is limited to changing the color or color combination in the background of the dial. We can also add different color pigments to the luminous powder to achieve the desired color the customer wants. Rarely do we get a request to change the print, but that is also something we can do.

42. FJF: Do you get requests to personalize Illinois dials?

RM: Yes, but rarely. A few customers have asked to have their own names added to the dial.

43. FJF: Do you need a dial plate of some sort to refinish an Illinois dial?

RM: We only refinish dials sent in by customers, if that is what you mean. We sometimes need a movement top plate in order to reattach dial feet but the movement plate is not needed for refinishing.

44. FJF: Is it easier to refinish Hamilton dials than Illinois ones?

RM: In some cases. Each dial is different and as we try to reproduce the manufacturing process during refinishing, it is difficult to generalize, but as a general rule, applied dials are easier to refinish than embossed dials (although it takes longer). Printed dials and luminous dials are the easiest; two-tones would be the most difficult.

45. FJF: How did Illinois produce its drop-shadow numerals?

RM: The drop-shadow effect is in the printing plate—nothing very special about it.

46. FJF: How did Illinois produce its dials that had green radium around black painted numerals on its dials?

RM: We believe the radium would have been mixed with a binder and printed on the dial using a printing plate specifically designed to work with that material.

A close-up of an original Metropolitan sparkle dial with drop-shadow numerals

A Kenilworth dial with drop shadow numerals

An example of a sparkle-finish dial on a Mary Todd Diamond-Set model

47. FJF: Is there a special way to clean a refinished dial?

RM: Not that I am aware of. Refinished dials should not need to be cleaned. Our dials have a clear coat applied to the background before printing or luminous is added. Any type of solvent could break down the clear coat and expose the background to the atmosphere. That same solvent may destroy the printing.

Workshop Notes

Conducted by JOHN J. BOWMAN (*Technical Editor, THE KEYSTONE*)

Subscribers wishing inquiries answered in this department must send name and address—not for publication, but as an evidence of good faith. No attention will be paid to anonymous communications

Cleaning Watch Dials

Can you tell us how to refinish watch dials without destroying the figures?—T. J. C.

Dials of metal in which the numerals are of hard enamel fired into engraving may be refinished safely without any chance of destroying the numerals. However, the cheaper dials with painted numerals which may be ascertained by the raised appearance of the latter can be cleaned only superficially because the paint will dissolve under any of the liquids used for removing tarnish from metals. If enameled, dip the dial in cyanide solution, brush with a soft watch brush moistened with water and bi-carbonate of soda. Rinse in water and dry in sawdust. This generally restores the fine frosted appearance of a good dial. If not, replating will be necessary.

On painted dials about all that can be done is to dip it quickly into cyanide, rinse and dry in air. If still stained, a new dial is about the only remedy. It will cost less than repainting the numerals on the old one.

Q&A from the Workshop Notes section of the February 1932 issue of the *Keystone*. Yes, that is "cyanide" that is being recommended!

48. FJF: Your dial refinishing seems very extensive and time-consuming. How can you price your refinishing services so low?

RM: We work on volume and try to do things in the most efficient manner. Although dials are printed one at a time, we do try to refinish dials in groups.

49. FJF: How do you determine how much to charge to refinish a dial?

RM: Price is based on time, difficulty, and the amount of extra work each dial requires.

50. FJF: What factors or features increase its costs?

RM: Each dial is priced according to how much work is done on the dial. Two-tones are more because they need to be refinished twice. Applied dials are more because the figures have to be polished, removed and reattached to the dial. Luminous dials are more because the luminous numbers must be painted in by hand.

51. FJF: Do refinishing techniques differ between dial-refinishing companies?

RM: Absolutely.

52. FJF: Can you replicate the two-tone gold process that was utilized on certain Illinois original dials?

RM: I am sure I can, but again I do not know now the exact formulation of the gold plating solutions that would be used.

53. FJF: How many steps are required to refinish an Illinois metal dial?

RM: From check-in to check-out, seven steps for a plain white or silver-finished dial with printed numbers; ten steps for a two-tone dial; eleven steps for a luminous dial; ten steps for an applied dial.

54. FJF: Why do refinishers scratch a four-digit code on the back of each refinished dial?

RM: No paperwork follows the dial into the shop. All of the dials received go into the shop in one group; as the finishes are removed, it is the code numbers that allow the staff to check the work order. Some days we might receive fifty Hamilton dials, many of the same model; it is the code number that differentiates the dial.

Redone and Fraudulent Dial "Tells"

For collectibility and value, the best possible original dial is the way to go. However, as it is getting difficult to find good original dials and more dials are getting redone, it is important to be able to spot a fraudulent dial and to be able to tell a redone dial from an original one.

You get a good sense of the difference between an original Illinois dial and a redone dial after observing enough of them. Even if you don't handle many of these dials, there are certain "Tells" or features that certain "redone" dials may exhibit that may give them away as having been redone. Examples of dials with "tells" follow. It will also help to study the dials in the identification chapters of this book as well as the NOS dials in this chapter to get a sense of the proper look of an original Illinois dial.

Tell #1

A good place to look at to determine if an Illinois dial is redone is its subsidiary seconds track. This track on an Illinois was always enclosed. Therefore, if the subsidiary second bit is not enclosed, it is likely redone.

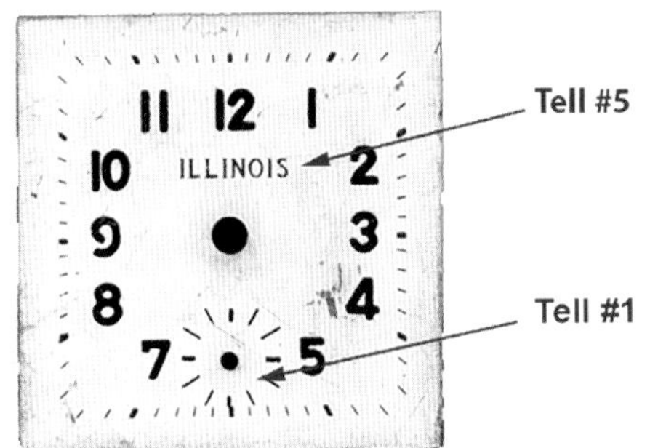

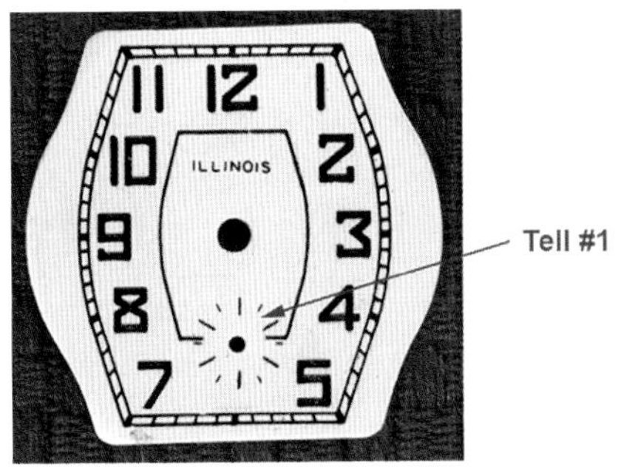

Tell #2

An original Illinois subsidiary seconds track always had at least some lines/divisions and numbers marking the second marks. Therefore, if a dial lacks these division markers or numbers, or there is an obvious open area in the subsidiary ring, the dial is likely redone.

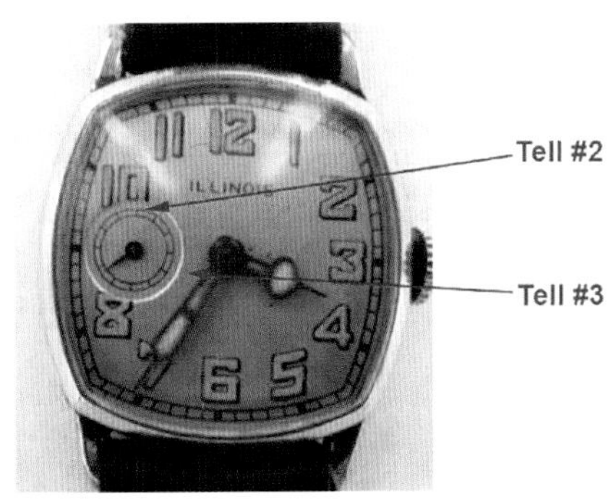

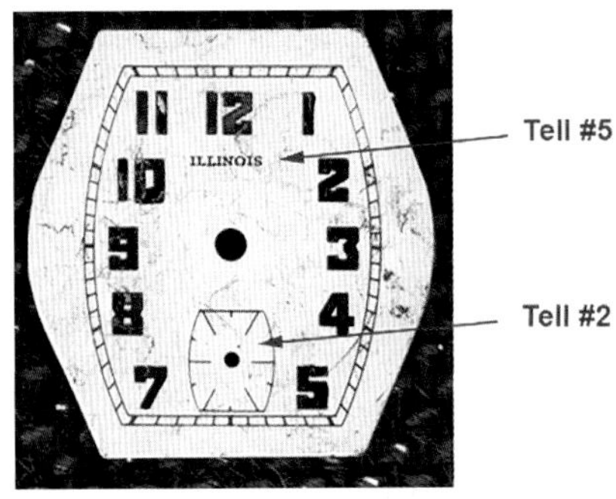

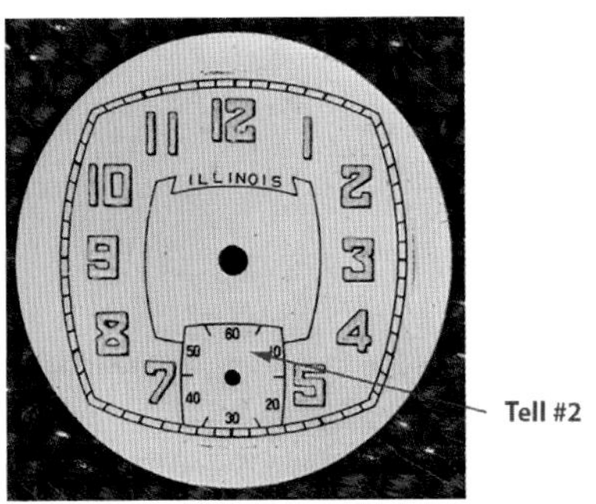

Tell #3

The subsidiary seconds bit on an original Illinois dial should fill the entire recess or circle for it. If it does not, the dial is likely redone. In addition, the subsidiary seconds markers were almost always enclosed on an Illinois dial. If the dial lacks this feature, it may be redone.

Tell #4

An original Illinois dial with radium numerals always had distinct aged/faded radium in the numerals. If you see enough of these, you know what this looks like. Therefore, if a dial has unusually colored radium numerals or brightly colored numerals, or excess radium that goes beyond the usual black numeral outlines, the dial is likely redone.

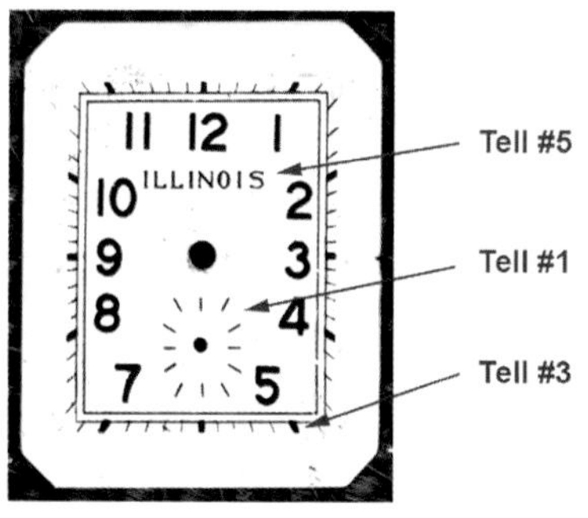

Tell #5

Another subtle tell for an original Illinois dial is the placement of the "Illinois" on the dial. To judge the correct placement, please study the dials in this book, especially the NOS dials in this chapter. Frequently, with a refinished dial, the signed "Illinois" is done incorrectly: too close to the numerals; too large, too small or too blocky in appearance; too black; or with the letters of different sizes, run together or not centered properly under the numeral 12 and above the 6. Some examples of redone dials are shown here to help you distinguish an original Illinois dial from a redone dial.

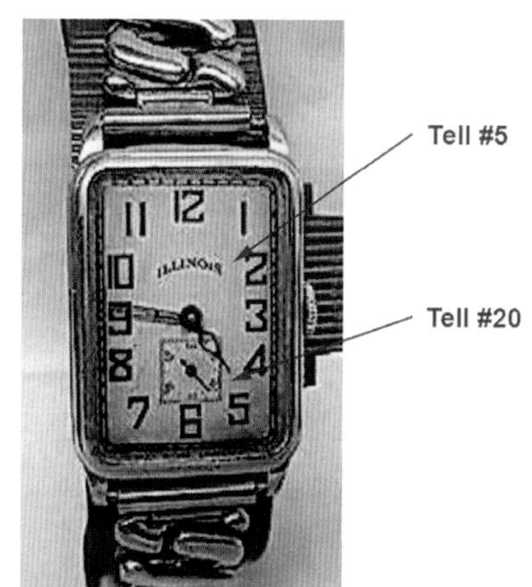

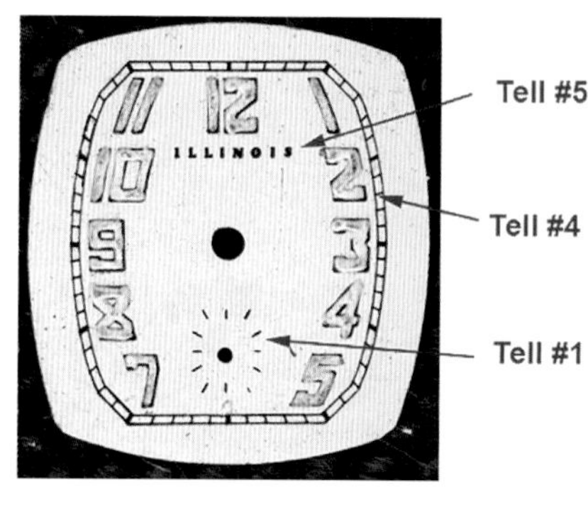

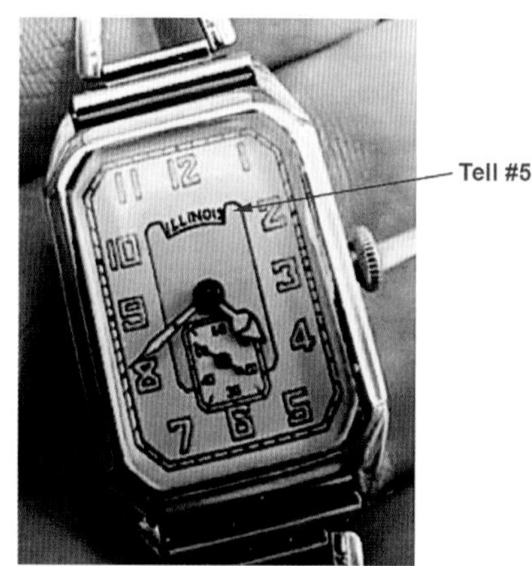

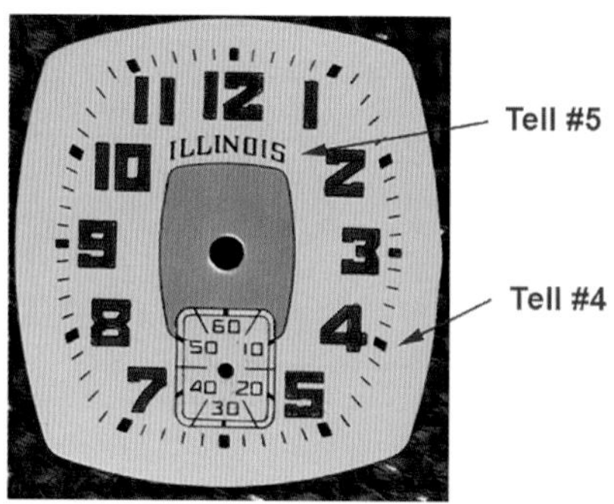

Tell #6

The numerals and lettering on an original Illinois dial do not touch or cross any line on the dial or encroach into the center of the dial. Therefore, if a dial has numerals that touch the subsidiary seconds track or minute track, or are shaky and uneven, it is likely a redone dial.

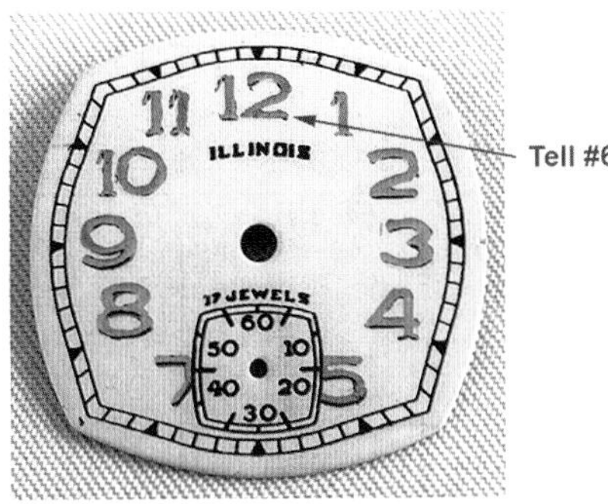

Tell #7

Several Illinois dials possess butler centers that are the result of proprietary Illinois polishing techniques, resulting in a distinctive and highly polished center of the dial. Therefore, if a dial has a weak, uneven or unattractive butler center that is not highly polished, is the wrong shape or is not silvered, it could be a redone dial. Also, if a dial has a butler center and a butler subsidiary seconds bit, it is usually redone.

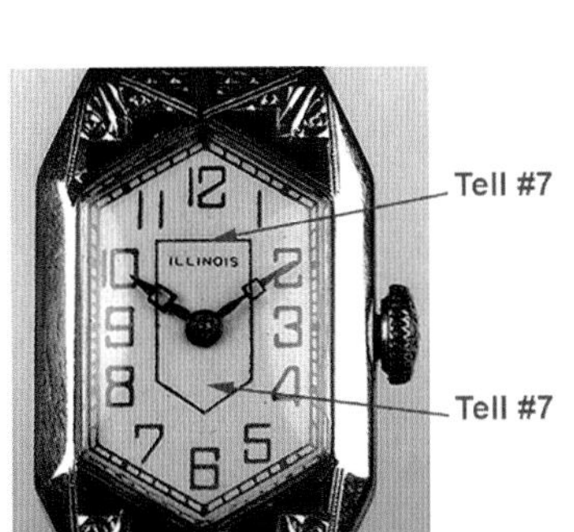

Tell #8

Also with respect to butler centers: on an original dial the center color never bleeds over the outer edge of the butler center or onto or over the Grecian wreath. If a dial has center color that is on the other side of its black border or into the subsidiary seconds track, it is a redone dial. And if the butler center is too long or too narrow, or encroaching onto the subsidiary seconds, it is a redone dial.

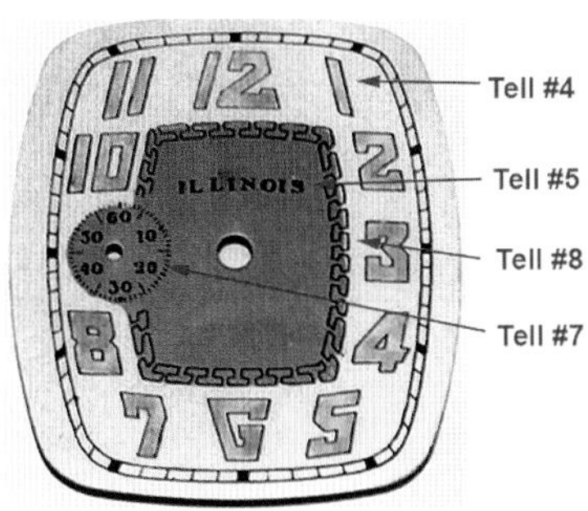

An otherwise nearly perfect refinished dial except for the butler center overrun. But this dial is so good that perhaps it was originally produced this way.

Tell #9

On an original Illinois dial with applied gold numerals, the numbers are affixed to the dial straight and do not encroach into the minute track. Therefore, if a dial has one or more of its applied gold numerals crooked or out of alignment, it is probably a redone dial.

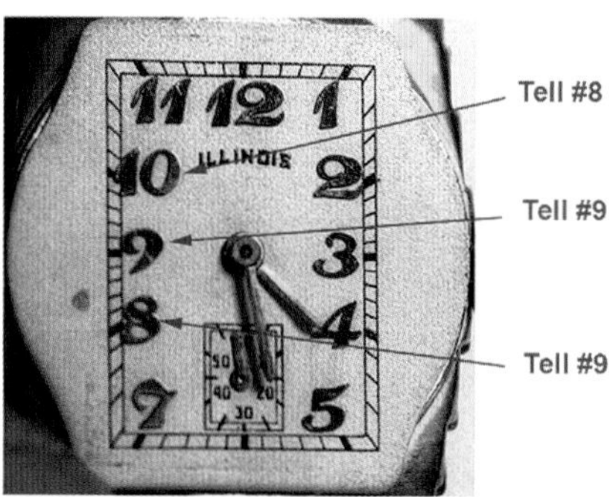

Tell #10

An original Illinois dial has a minute track that always conforms exactly to the shape of the bezel. If a dial has a minute track that does not conform exactly to the shape of the inside of the bezel of the watch, it is a redone dial. This is a common flaw with redone dials and is easy to spot, so you should be certain to check this out. Also, with just a few exceptions, almost all Illinois dials have their minute tracks enclosed, so a dial with open minute markers may be a redone dial.

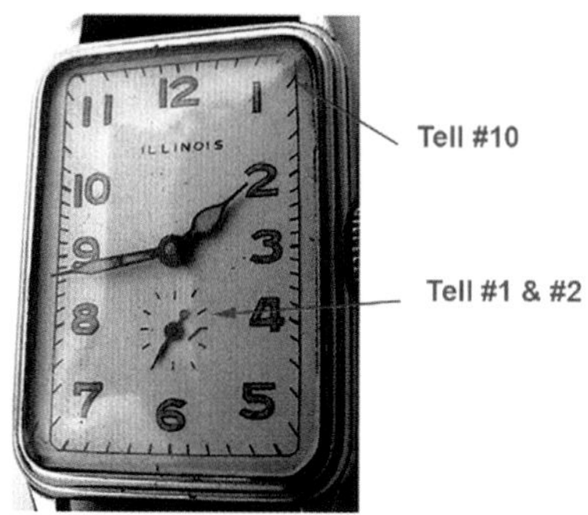

Tell #11

Another area of the dial to focus on is its corners. Usually, if a case has a squared bezel opening, its dial will be squared off on its corners. If the bezel opening corners are rounded or curved, then its dial should mirror that. If the corners on a dial are square and they should be rounded, it could be a redone dial (*Note:* The New Yorker model, however, is the exception to the rule; its dial corners are squared off rather than being slightly rounded like its bezel opening.)

Tell #12

A few Illinois dials have subsidiary seconds shapes that mirror the shape of the watch case. For example, the Illinois Ritz dial is tonneau-shaped and its subsidiary seconds shape is also tonneau-shaped. The Piccadilly dial is oval, as it its subsidiary seconds shape. On an Ensign, the subsidiary seconds ring is tonneau-shaped, so if it is round on a dial you are looking at, it is a redone dial. In short, if the shape of the subsidiary seconds area on a dial for one these models does not mirror the case shape, it may be a redone dial.

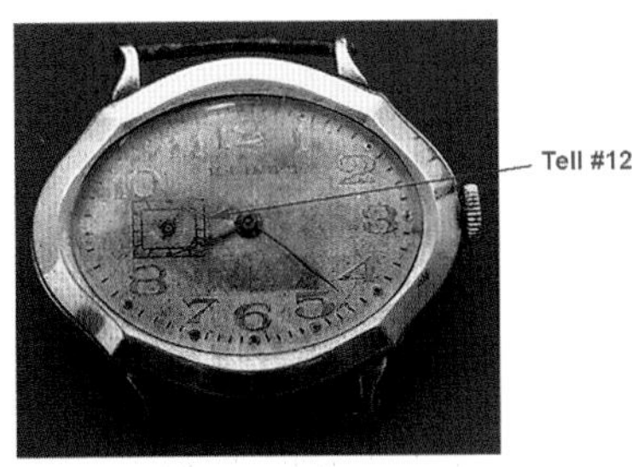

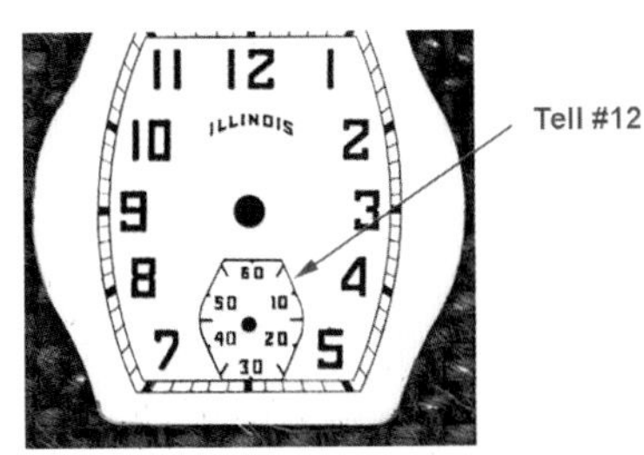

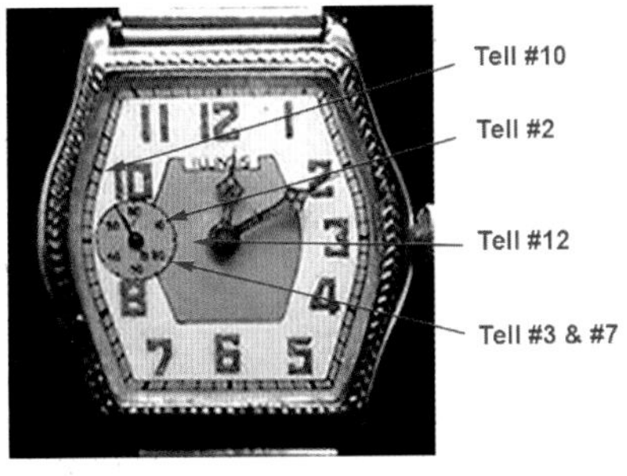

Tell #13

On some Illinois original 12/0 size dials there is printed on the bottom of the dial, below the minute track, the instruction "Lift at 12." Therefore, if a 12/0 size dial lacks this notification, it may be a redone dial; however, not all originals were so marked.

Tell #14

Certain Illinois dials are supposed to have specific types of numerals. Therefore, if a dial ordinarily has gold applied numerals but has black painted numerals instead, the dial could be redone. Similarly, if a dial is supposed to have painted numerals yet it has radium numerals, it could be a redone dial. And if the numerals are too small or too large or the wrong color, it could be a redone dial.

Tell #15

Illinois used enlarged engraved master dial plates to make dials using a pantograph machine. Therefore, it was virtually impossible for the dial to have misaligned type, print running over lines, print ending short of its destination point, uneven or overrun print lines. Therefore, if a dial does exhibit such flaws, it is almost certainly a redone dial.

Tell #16

Most Illinois dials have a silver matte, silver finish or sparkle finish. The sparkle finish was a proprietary Illinois technique that involved actual silver particles being used on the dial surface. No refinishing company has ever mastered this technique. Therefore, if your dial lacks this silver and/or sparkle effect, it could be a redone dial. For example, if your dial is merely colored butler-like silver all over (without a sparkle finish) or has a silver dial and a silver subsidiary second circle, or center and butler subsidiary seconds, two-tone silver, this is an indication it is redone.

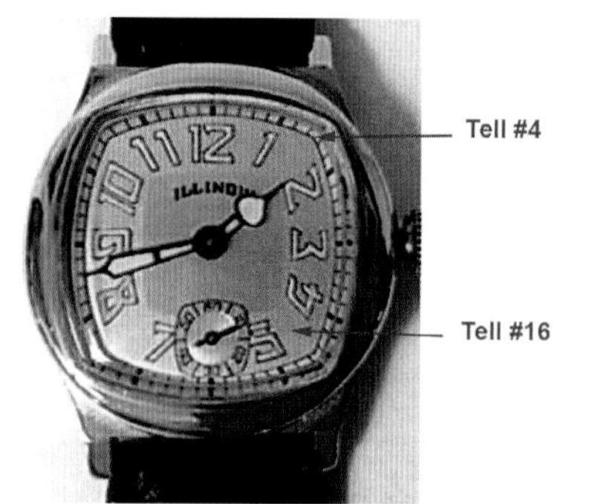

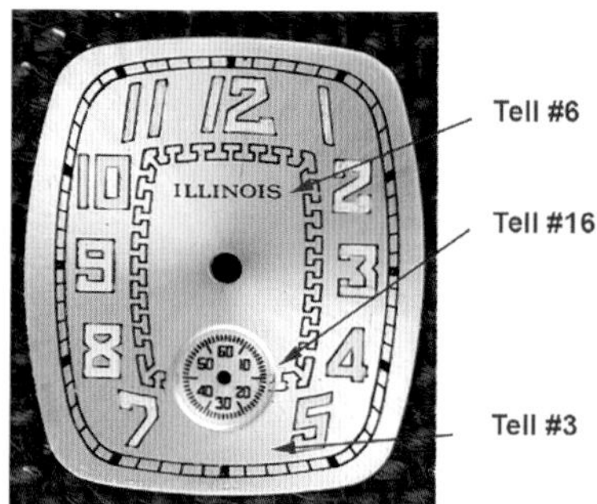

Tell #17

Illinois dials had either a silver matte, silver or sparkle finish. Therefore, if a dial has a high-gloss look and it is not an enamel dial, it is likely a redone dial. (Please note that enamel dials are rarely correct except for a very few special Illinois models.)

Tell #18

Recently, some dials have appeared that are fraudulent. These are purported to be original Skyway or Telephone Dials, but they are actually newly fabricated dials being passed off as originals. Therefore, before purchasing one of these dials, be sure to confirm that it is an original Illinois dial. (See the **Skyway** and **Telephone Dial** descriptions in Chapter 9.) If in doubt, please email the author at fred@illinoiswatches.com for verification. These fraudulent dials are usually metal dials painted white to effectively look like enamel for the Telephone Dial or painted black to pass for a Skyway one, but they may even involve the use of a decal. Be highly suspicious if a supposed enamel dial does not have any hairline cracks on it.

Tell #19

Original Illinois dials frequently contained butler center subsidiary seconds configurations. Most redone dials do not replicate this feature. Not all Illinois dials have silvered subsidiary seconds, but if the dial does not, examine it extra carefully to assure it is not redone.

There are exceptions, so be careful; for example, original Off-Duty and/or Locke dials could come with either a butler center subsidiary seconds ring or a painted one. Study the dials in this book and elsewhere to get a sense for what is correct.

Tell #20

For an Illinois dial, the size of its subsidiary seconds ring is important. Frequently, a redone dial exhibits a subsidiary seconds ring that is too small, too large, the wrong shape or partially covers a numeral when it should not. Again, it is best to get a familiarity with what is correct so it will be easier to spot what is incorrect and redone.

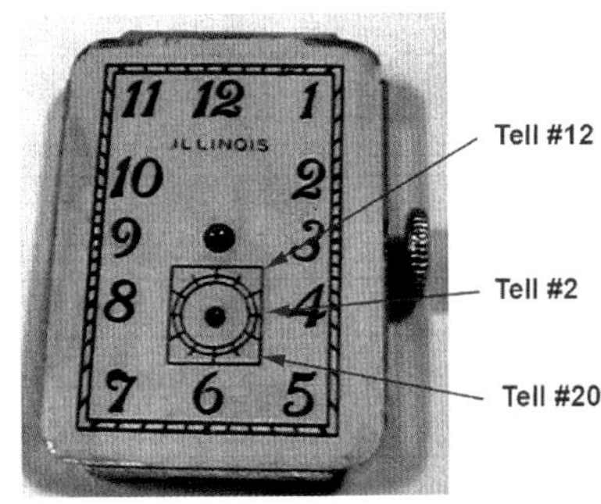

Tell #21

The placement of the subsidiary seconds configuration on an original Illinois dial is also important. Sometimes it is placed above the 6; sometimes it covers part of the 6; sometimes it replaces the 6 entirely. Also, some sixes are replaced on original dials with markers shaped like half-moons. The Futura and Townsman dials are examples of this feature. Again, it is best to get familiar with what is correct so it will be easier to spot what is incorrect and redone.

Tell #22

Another obvious tell is if the original dial has subsidiary seconds and the redone dial does not. Once again, learn what the watch in question should have so you are not disappointed by a redone dial.

Tell #23

With new technology come, unfortunately, new methods for defrauding buyers. There is at least one watch dealer who has used some sort of color laser technology to customize and/or redo Illinois dials. In *The Illinois Watch: The Life and Times of a Great American Watch Company,* under the "Major" model description, there was a hand-painted custom original dial with palm trees on it.[4] Now, someone with a laser printer is placing palm trees and similar scenes on watch dials and is selling them as genuine Illinois dials. Beware of this scam!

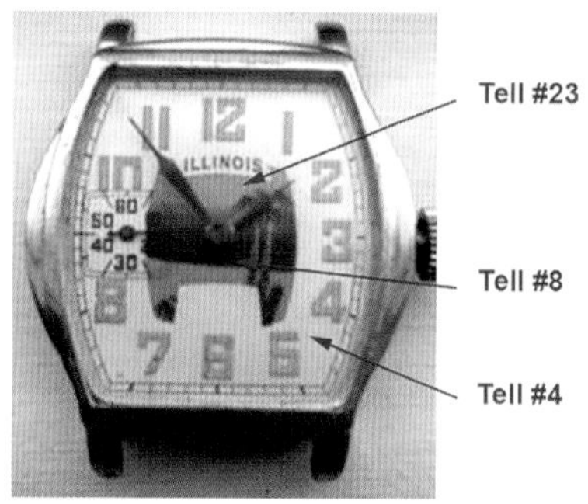

Dial with computer-generated palm tree scene being falsely represented as an original Illinois dial

The original palm tree dial

Tell #24

The use of decals or stickers is another method now used to make phony Illinois dials. As Elgin trench watch expert Stan Czubernat points out, "Dial stickers or overlays have been around for nearly one hundred years. Originally, they were used to convert civilian type dials into military type dials with Radium-lum; then they would simply swap out the spade hands for Radium-lumed skeleton hands."[5] Now this technique is being used to make fraudulent Telephone Dials and probably others.

Below are some images of the very first dial stickers or overlays.

FRAUD ALERT

Be on the lookout for the new practice of printing dials or parts of dials on plastic laminate or paper stickers and placing the sticker on a dial so it appears to be a NOS dial or a dial with a unique feature. It is alleged that with the use of such stickers, people have tried to pass off metal dials as original Illinois enamel Telephone Dials. These fakes can be tough to spot, so be sure to study a dial (particularly the subsidiary seconds track) if it looks too good to be true.

A dial sticker overlay

Admiral Evans with a radium vintage overlay sticker

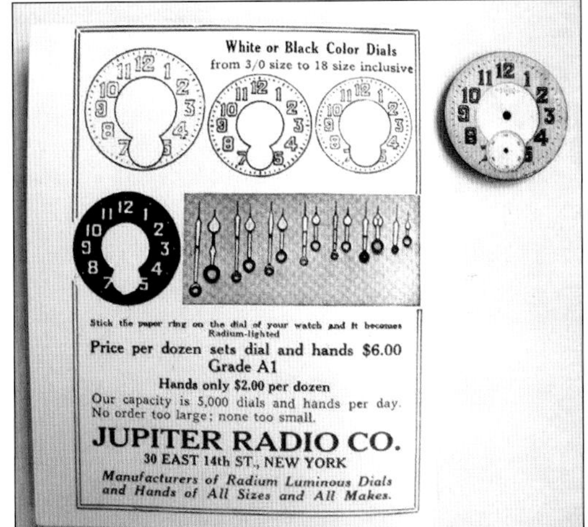

Dial stickers and luminous hands for sale, c. 1917, with dial to which sticker has been applied

This is an Illinois Montgomery dial with a computer-generated laser sticker on it. The seller of this model offered to sell it with or without "the picture," which would be removed if unwanted!

Tell #25

A method of detecting if an applied gold numeral dial is redone is to examine its reverse side. If the numbers are etched through the back side of the dial, it is likely a redone dial.

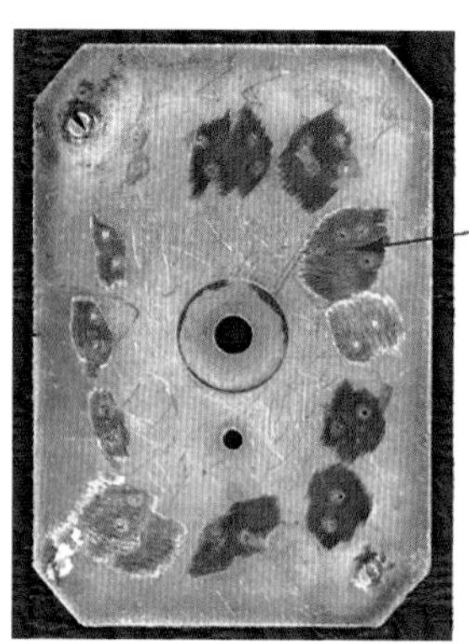

Tell #26

Many original Illinois dials have black date stamps on their backs. Therefore, if you have a dial with such a date stamp, it is probably an original one. However, be aware that the absence of a date stamp does not necessarily mean the dial is redone. Moreover, since some refinished dials may retain the date stamp, you need to study the face of the dial carefully. Generally, if a dial has been refinished but retains the date stamp on the back of the dial, the surface of the back is white or looks cleaned (and the date stamp sometimes looks faded). This signals a redone dial.

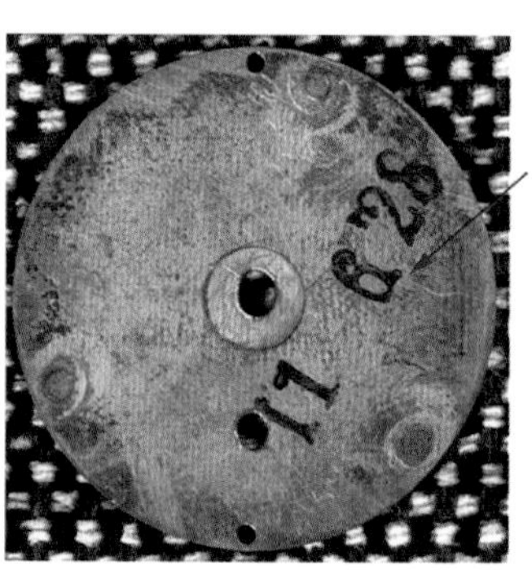

Tell #27

Another potential tell is that on a redone dial sometimes the minute track inside the case bezel does not run continuously into the division markers. On an original dial the minute track runs directly into the markers; on a redone dial, it sometime stops just short of them. Be on the lookout for this nuance.

Tell #28

Some redone dials have the subsidiary seconds section drop below the outer edge of the minute track on the dial. Illinois original dials rarely did that; therefore, if a dial does, it is likely a redone dial.

Tell #29

Illinois usually did not leave an open plain circle in the middle of its subsidiary seconds section unless the center section was silvered. Therefore, if a dial has a blank circle around the subsidiary seconds hand, it is likely a redone dial.

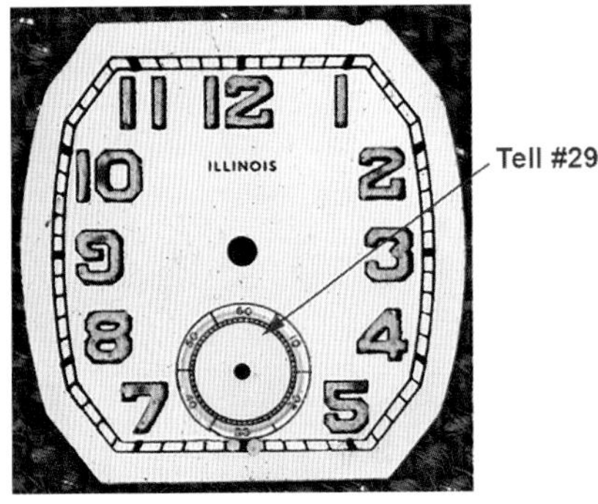

Tell #30

Illinois never signed its name below the subsidiary second circle. A dial signed that way is a fraudulent or a redone one.

Tell #31

Black-dialed watches are very popular among Illinois collectors, but only a scant few models had original black dials (e.g., Kitchener, Skyway, United States Army Watch). Yet black dials appear periodically that collectors want to believe are original. If a black dial is too shiny, it is probably redone. If its radium is too bright or is an odd color, it is probably redone. If the luminous is gold or white, it is likely a redone dial. If the lettering on the dial runs together in places, it is a redone. All black dials should be deemed suspect until they are carefully verified by an expert.

Tell #32

In the past, a strong tell for Illinois rotor subsidiary seconds dials was that dial refinishers never included the black outline around the rotor cutout on the dial. Now, perhaps owing to my first Illinois Watch book, some knowledgeable refinishers are adding the black outline. For that reason, more scrutiny now has to be given to these dials. Of course, a dial should not have both a rotor opening and a subsidiary seconds bit).

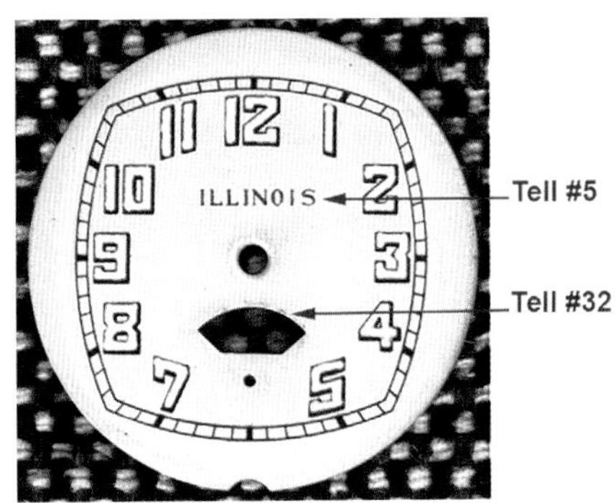

Tell #33

Today people skilled on computers are capable of making watch dials out of layered photo stock paper. They can even replicate double-sunk pocket watch dials. These computer-generated dials come without dial feet and require "glue dots" where the feet should be to secure them in place. There is at least one person selling these online; but he is totally upfront about their being purely new replacement dials. The potential area of concern, however, is if a purchaser buys one of these replacement dials, puts it on a watch and then sells the watch as all-original. Therefore, you have to be on the lookout for such dials. The owner of the website advised me that his equipment does not have the required tolerances to make wristwatch dials; but that does not mean that others may not attempt to do so in the future.

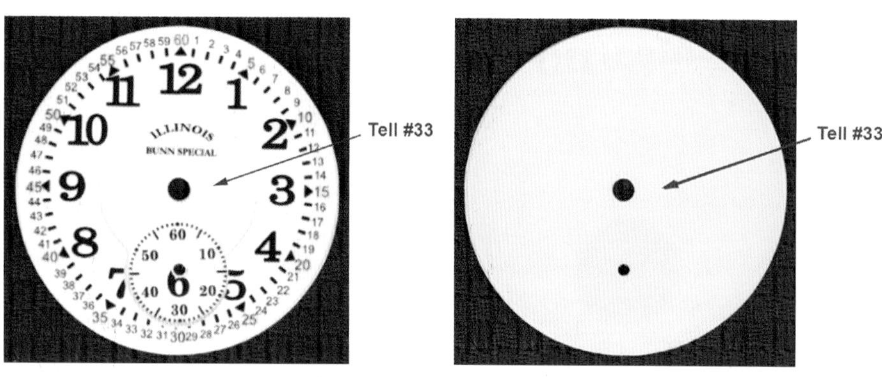

Computer generated replacement dials made of photo stock

The owner of the website selling these "new old dials" described how they are made: "Our dials are made by hand using computer-drawn images patterned after genuine porcelain. . . . We start with a genuine dial to use as a template or model. We then hand draw a computer image of the dial. This image is then printed on heavy photo stock one layer at a time. The layers are then cut out, punched, dressed and assembled to produce single and double sunk dials. This process produces a very beautiful and durable dial that is very close to the thickness of an original dial. The dials have blank backs—that is, no feet. They must be held in place by double-sided . . .'glue dots.' Glue dots, sometimes called dial dots, are gelatin-like adhesive disks about 3/16" in diameter and very sticky. They can be placed over or near the foot holes on the watch frame and will hold the dial firmly in place."

Tell #34

Several original Illinois dials have subsidiary seconds chapters that are slightly recessed. This feature is almost never replicated on a redone dial. So if, for example, you are offered a Skyway dial with a surface that is completely flat, it is probably a redone dial.

Tell #35

An original dial has one distinct shape for its subsidiary seconds area; it could be round or tonneau or another shape. But it cannot be a combination of two shapes. If you have a dial like that, it is redone.

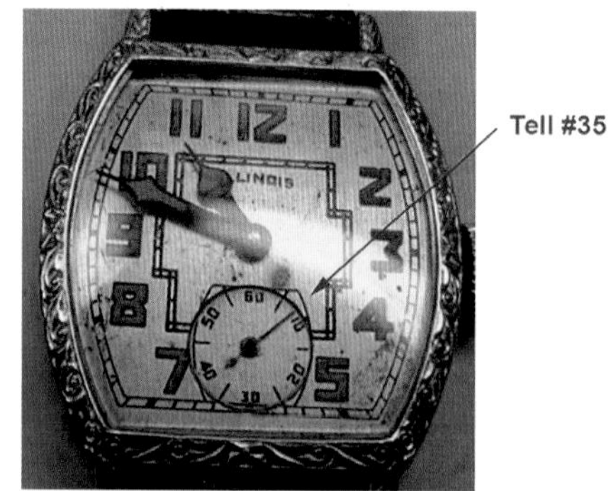

Tell #36

The Illinois original wristwatch dials acquired many design features that migrated from pocket watch dials. One such feature is what Illinois called "wreaths" or "Grecian wreaths" on its pocket watch dials. These wreaths also appear in modified form on many of the Illinois original wristwatch dials. The Marquis Strap, Tank and Canby dials are examples of these modified or "contemporized" wreaths. The wreaths had special designs; therefore, if you have a dial with an unusual or weak-looking wreath; it is likely redone.

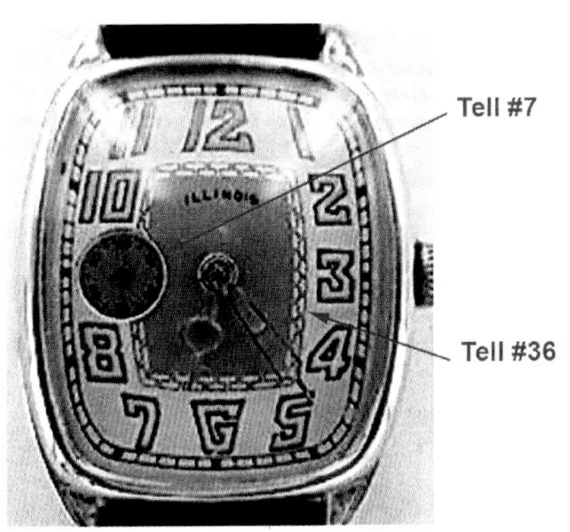

WHY I COLLECT ILLINOIS

Many years ago when still very much a novice watch collector, I had an Art Deco Goering wristwatch in a gold-filled case with fancy hinged lugs and a beautiful bezel ringed by enamel numbers. It was a great watch, but I had no one to repair it, inside or out. I hung onto it anyway. I even wore it around sometimes, in its non-operative state.

One Sunday, while at a local flea market, I walked over to a dealer in old watches and clocks I always saw on the local circuit: a nice older Middle-Eastern gentleman, softer-spoken with none of the hard sell. He didn't judge—Elgin, Cartier, Bulova, Buren . . . I always looked into the corners of his flat cases, where he kept the unrestored, damaged, or incomplete watches. There in the bottom left corner of his first case rested a very strange sight, what from a distance of a few feet looked like an egg. A flattened egg. Behind the sun-reflecting glass lid and a faded plastic crystal was the outline of an apparently very detailed dial in this white, unpolished egg-shaped case. This was definitely not like the usual parade of military watches, glittery Gruens, scientific chronographs, and dollar watches. I asked to see this strange old watch, and without boasting or trying to sell me on it at all, my friend handed me the first Illinois Marquis I'd ever seen. Asking what it was, he took out a blade and carefully removed the bezel, and handed to me what immediately looked like an entire Hollywood Art Deco theatre ceiling and stage squeezed into a little egg-shaped case. A dial with wildly exaggerated green Egyptian-style numbers, zigzag inner-tracking, two-tones, and with a second hand floating up at the nine o'clock position . . . and these giant balloon hands!... absolutely outrageous! I thought this kind of detail was only reserved for fancy cars, and even they didn't fit this much character per square inch!

I asked how much; I don't remember, but it was less than $100. I thought and thought and thought and thought. And he asked about the watch I had on, that Goering. I took it off and let him see it, rather embarrassed to be wearing a non-working watch, but . . . He much admired it. He told me, were I interested, he'd be willing to trade. I knew enamel watches were valuable: Coronados, Piping Rocks, and the like . . . High-priced watches I'd never own. I thought . . . and thought . . . and thought . . . and I actually said, "Well, let me think about it." He said that in the meantime, he'd get this Illinois one working. I didn't care so much about that . . . and I left! I left it there!

At dinner that week with an aunt who dealt in fancy Tiffany-level antiques, I was advised with regard to the trade idea to "be careful; you don't know how valuable something is until you give it away." I never changed my mind, though, about wanting that Illinois. And I spent the next five days hoping he'd be at the next weekly flea market on Sunday . . . that he hadn't sold it, that he hadn't dropped it, or scratched the dial, or lost it . . . or changed his mind . . .

Sunday morning came; I went straight to his spot. Belying my far greater enthusiasm, I said "Hi" and . . . "Sure, why not!" and made the trade. I could not take my eyes off that watch for hours and days afterward. It was as though I'd stepped back into Times Square on New Year's Eve, 1928. He managed to get it running, not great, but running, and I have never had it serviced since. No new crystal, no polish, no fancy lizard band. Just a safe place in line with a little family of other Marquis Straps, each with its own personality and history.

—Anonymous

Tell #37

If your dial has its subsidiary seconds hole filled in, it is a redone dial. The dial pictured below had its seconds post hole filled in to make a Consul dial with no subsidiary seconds.

Tell #38

Perhaps the most conclusive method to determine if a dial has been refinished is to look at its reverse side. If the back of the dial is very shiny and/or has a four-digit code scratched into it, there is an almost 100% certainty that it is a redone dial. This is easy to do if you are evaluating a separate dial. However, very few sellers will be willing to remove a dial from a movement in a cased watch, much less let you do it. If you are curious about the dial on one of your own watches and wish to study it, that is a different matter, of course. Just make sure you do not damage anything in the process of removing the dial.

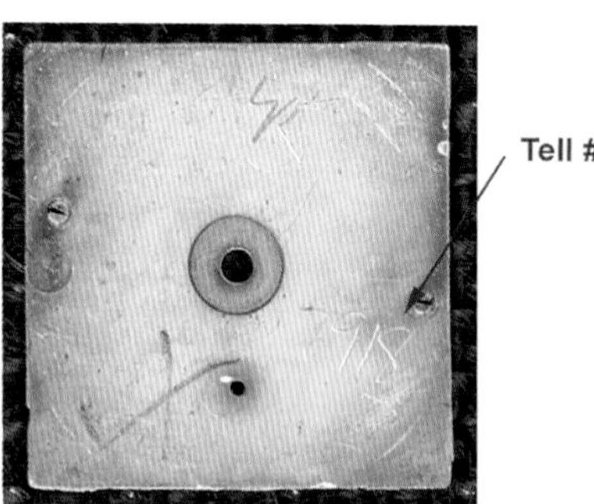

THE "JDLR" RULE

Knowledgeable collectors follow the JDLR Rule. If it "Just Doesn't Look Right," be careful! If it appears something is just not right, determine what it is before you make a purchase. Hopefully, these "Tells" will be of help to you.

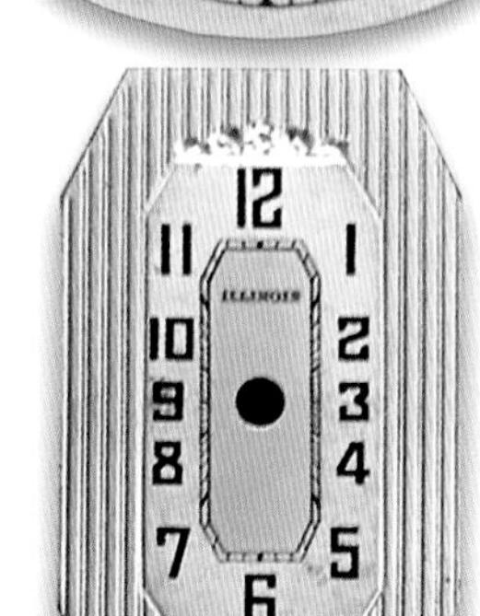

Three NOS dials, from top to bottom, Blackstone; Mary Todd/Coronado; Motor Coach

POLICE
SPECIAL
ILLINOIS
ILLINOIS
STERLING
ILLINOIS

CHAPTER 8

Casemakers, Case Model Numbers and Watch Attachments

As its title suggests, this chapter comprises three main parts. The first is an overview of the histories of companies from which Illinois and its successor Hamilton purchased cases for Illinois models. The second part, which deals with the case model numbers that Illinois assigned to its men's and ladies' wristwatches, categorizes the cases according to metal content, shape and other attributes. (A special feature of this section is a detailed analysis of data regarding one of Illinois' most famous men's models, the Consul.) The last part of the chapter provides a general survey of the watch attachments industry, with brief histories of some important manufacturers of watchbands.

Illinois Wristwatch Case Producers

The watch case was born along with the mechanical watch: from the earliest beginnings, some means was needed to protect the delicate mechanism. Making watch cases began in America even before watchmaking; colonial silversmiths and goldsmiths made cases for movements imported from England and Europe. The industrial mass production of watch cases in America arose along with the introduction of the factory-made watch movement in the 1850s and 60s, so that by the time Illinois started selling watches, the buyer had a variety of sources for cases.

Like most American watch movement manufacturers, the Illinois Watch Company did not make any of its own watch cases. Historically, jobbers and jewelers bought watch cases at the wholesale or retail level to case their watches. When watch manufacturers began to case watches in their own factories during World War I, they continued to use outside casemakers rather than produce the cases themselves. This manufacturing separation lasted until the end of United States' domestic watch production in the 1970s.

For its Factory-Cased men's wristwatches, the Illinois Watch Company utilized six main casemakers: the Keystone Watch Case Company, the Wadsworth Watch Case Company, the Solidarity Watch Case Company, the Fahys Watch Case Company, J. Milhening Inc. and the Pioneer Watch Case Company. However, Illinois housed by far the largest number of its men's models in Keystone and Wadsworth cases. Star produced only one men's watch model; that case was supplied by a jobber to Illinois. Pioneer and J. Milhening produced a scant two and four models, respectively. Solidarity made only eight models: four in solid 14K gold and four in gold-filled. For the ladies' Factory-Cased models, Illinois utilized cases by Keystone, Wadsworth and Star. (The Star cases were acquired and issued by Hamilton.) One model was cased by Fahys.

Earlier, during the Transitional and Generic time periods, cases by many of these same makers were used for Illinois watches that were not Factory-Cased. Only a few were Factory-Cased during these periods; instead, they were mostly cased by jobbers and jewelers who offered Elgins or Walthams as well as Illinois in many case models. Illinois watches were also sometimes housed in cases made by the Illinois Watch Case Company, Dubois Watch Case Co., and the North American Watch Company.

Later, during 1933 and 1934, Hamilton placed Conneric model Illinois watches in cases made by the Manheimer Watch Company, Star and Keystone. (For discussion of the contract-generic watches I call "Connerics," see Chapters 5 and 9.)

During Hamilton's resurrection of the Illinois label from 1953 to 1955, Hamilton chose Schwab and Wuischpard and Star to make most of the cases, but used Pioneer for a couple of models and Huguenin Frères for six others. (The casemakers for the Hamilton-Illinois watches are also discussed in Chapter 11.)

All of these casemakers will be discussed briefly later in this chapter with the exception of Huguenin, which is covered in Chapter 11.

Case Designs

No definitive information exists about who designed the cases for Illinois watches. In general, among manufacturers, case design often involved an iterative process between designers for case manufacturers and for the watch case companies. The larger watch manufacturers probably assigned a top executive to procure specially designed cases from the casemakers, case designers, and independent artists and craftsmen. It is likely there was an agreement to purchase these cases on an exclusive basis in order to have first right of refusal on new designs. Virtually none of the cases used for wristwatches cased in the Illinois Factory appear with any other manufacturers' movements and dials until the 1934 time frame, when Hamilton cased the Illinois watches in Lancaster (see Chapter 5).

In retrospect, it would seem that casemakers reserved their boldest, most stylish and most distinctive designs for the innovative and stylistically advanced Illinois Watch Company. This may have reflected Illinois' view about where it wanted to position itself in the market. Based on his interviews with former Wadsworth Watch Case Company employees in Cincinnati, Ohio, Charlie Cleves, an expert on Wadsworth, concluded that the watch companies frequently presented "flat drawings" of a case design to casemakers, who would then make a three-dimensional model of the case. And Illinois did have a design department at least as late as July 1932.

WHY I COLLECT ILLINOIS

"I collect Illinois watches because they best combine superior mechanical engineering with innovative styling that captures the 'irrational exuberance' of the era when America transitioned from being a somewhat insular state to a global leader." —*Conrad Chanzit*

The Keystone Watch Case Company

In 1853, Randolf and Reese Peters founded the Keystone Watch Case Company in Philadelphia, Pennsylvania. They employed James Boss, who on May 3, 1854, received a revolutionary patent for watch cases made with two gold outer sheets sandwiched around base metal. The industry named this process "gold-filled." Boss became a partner in the firm. Keystone unconditionally guaranteed that the gold on the cases would not wear through to the base metal for twenty-one years.

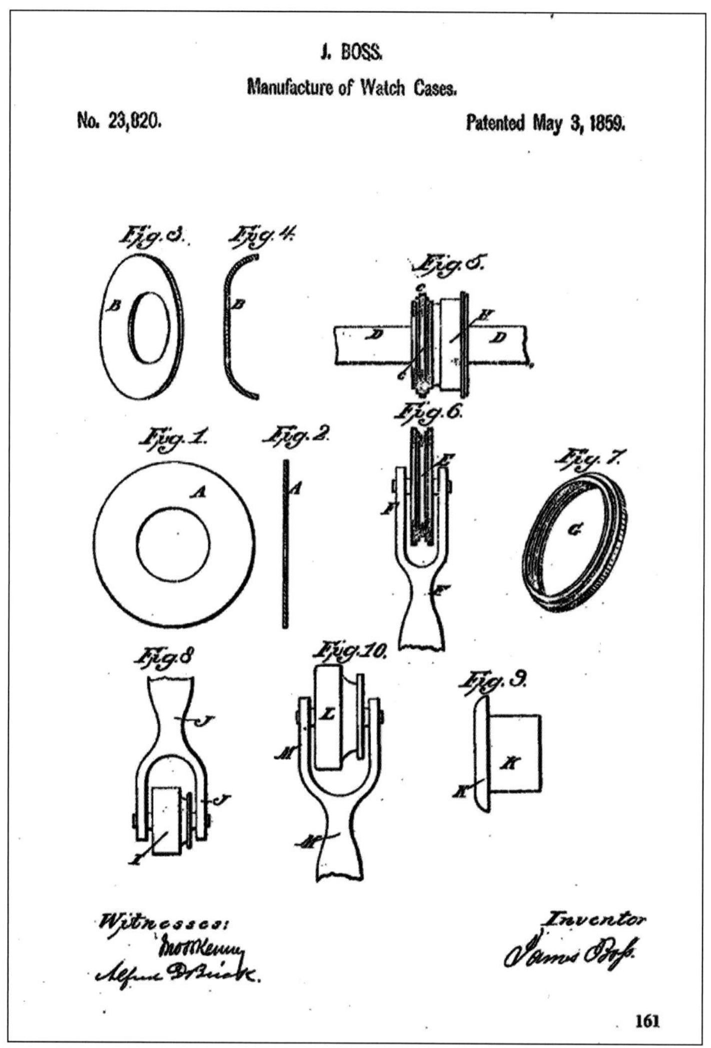

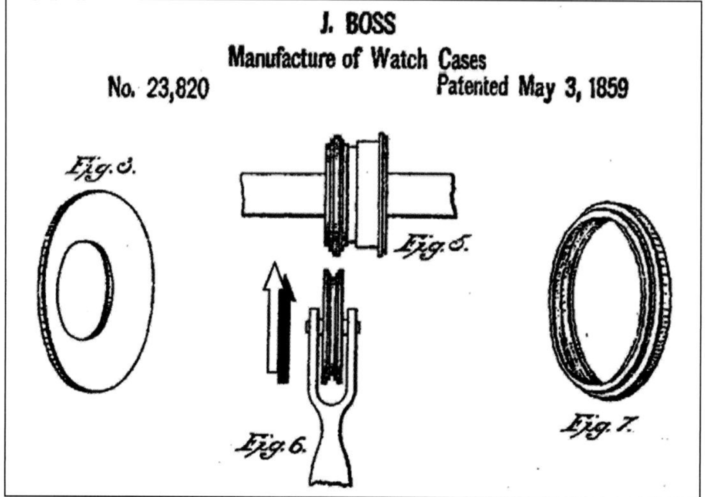

Patent of James Boss for the "Improvement in the Manufacture of Watch-Cases"

United States Patent Office.

JAMES BOSS, OF PHILADELPHIA, PENNSYLVANIA.

IMPROVEMENT IN THE MANUFACTURE OF WATCH-CASES.

Specification forming part of Letters Patent No. **23,820**, dated May 3, 1859.

To all whom it may concern:

Be it known that I, James Boss, of Philadelphia, in the county of Philadelphia, in the State of Pennsylvania, have invented a new and Improved Mode of Constructing Watch-Cases; and I do hereby declare that the following is a full and exact description thereof, reference being had to the accompanying drawings, and to the letters of reference marked thereon.

The nature of my invention consists in the application of the well-known operation of spinning up sheet metal for the purpose of manufacturing watch-cases by the employment of a mandrel and spinning-wheels, instead of the usual laborious and costly method of turning them out of the solid material.

By this invention in the introduction of mandrel and spinning-wheels for spinning up sheet metal in the manufacturing of watch-cases, I am enabled to produce a planished plated sheet-metal watch-case more durable and beautiful and comparatively less expensive than the manufacture of galvanized and turned watch-cases heretofore made.

Before my invention the galvanized watch-cases were first turned into form by the means of cutting-tools and afterward galvanized. This process was expensive, and both the body of the case and the galvanizing were not as solid nor as durable as the watch-case of my manufacture. I spin up the case into form with the plating previously fixed to the body of the case, the body and plating having been first rolled out solidly into the sheets of proper thickness, from which the metal is cut of a proper size. By thus spinning up of the plated metal a case is formed with a planished close texture, which is more durable and less expensive in proportion to its utility than the old manufacture of galvanized and turned watch-cases.

The manner of conducting the plating of the metal is as follows: I take a bar of any kind of composition metal—say one-half inch thick—and then placing plates of gold, silver, or any kind of metal whatsoever on one or both sides of the bar to be plated upon and fastened by the means of sweating or soldering by applying it to a certain temperature of heat, after which it is then rolled out to a proper thickness suitable for the spinning up or making of the case. The labor in spinning up of this sheet metal into a case by my invention is so little that the plating is never removed a particle, showing the most economical process in plating known in the manufacture of watch-cases.

There is another important feature in this process of plating by my invention, which is that the plating adheres much better to the metal and is not liable to rub off of the case by attrition from constant use, which is invariably the fault of all watch-cases plated or galvanized by the present method of turning them out or finishing them up from the solid stuff.

To enable others skilled in the manufacturing watch-cases to make and use my invention, I will proceed to describe its construction, &c., reference being had by letters to the drawings forming part of this specification.

In Figure 1, A shows the sheet-plate. In Fig. 2, A shows the same in section. In Fig. 3, B shows in perspective the same turned up. In Fig. 4, B shows same in section. In Fig. 5, D shows the mandrel on which the centers and bezels of case are formed; C, center form; H, bezel form. In Fig. 6, E shows the spinning-wheel for center, and F the handle. In Fig. 7, G shows in perspective the center of case finished. In Fig. 8, I shows the spinning-wheel for bezel, and J the handle. In Fig. 9, K shows the lathe-chuck for backs of case. In Fig. 10, L shows the spinning-wheel for backs, and M the handle.

In the several views similar letters represent like parts.

From sheet metal of the proper thickness is cut the ring A, which is turned up by a common tool into the form shown at B. It is then slipped over the mandrel D onto the form C. The spinning-wheel E, pivoted in the stock F, is now brought to bear upon the mandrel, the ring B being interposed, and by a few revolutions of the lathe-wheel it is caused to assume the desired form, as seen in the sketch at G, which is the center of watch-case finished.

The backs and bezels of cases are to be made in the same manner as above described. The mandrel on which the bezel is spun is in one with that of the mandrel forming center

162

of case, as seen in drawings, letters H I, the spinning-wheel of bezel being of course compatible with the shape to be formed.

Be it here understood that by my invention of the mandrel and spinning-wheels for spinning up sheet metal for the purpose of manufacturing watch-cases it is more particularly applied to plated cases—that is, those made of plated sheet metal, substantially as above described. Be it also understood that each section of these cases made by my invention is formed entirely of one solid piece of sheet metal, forming a complete watch-case, without the use of solder or any kind of metal to connect them together, except the bearing for the movement in the center, as is the case of all watch-cases turned from the solid material.

I do not claim as new the process of plating metal as herein described, for I am aware that has been done before; but

What I claim, and desire to secure by Letters Patent, is—

1. Spinning up of watch-cases by the employment of a mandrel and spinning-wheels constructed to operate in the manner substantially as set forth.

2. Spun plated sheet-metal watch-case constructed as herein specified.

In testimony whereof I have hereunto set my hand and seal this the 7th day of April, A. D. 1859.

JAMES BOSS. [L. S.]

Witnesses:

Jno. B. Kenney,
Alfred D. Brick.

1859 patent of James Boss, showing spinning of a case center from a single sheet of stock with no solder joint, as described in the NAWCC *Bulletin*. The stock is next formed into a steep-sided cup, then placed over the rotating mandrel. It is then squatted onto the mandrel by the shaped form wheel to form a case center. There are also tools for spinning covers and bezels with integral lips. The process is aimed at gold-filled stock, available only in sheets, but can be used on any sheet material. Operating skill determines final part diameter, and human strength determines the maximum thickness at which the material can be worked.

In 1871, Boss sold his patent to John Stuckert of Philadelphia. Four years later Hagstoz & Thorpe bought Stuckert's business along with the rights to the Boss patent. In 1885, Hagstoz & Thorpe was renamed the Keystone Watch Case Company. At that time it had 1,050 workers and a production rate of 1,500 pocket watch cases per day.

Keystone J. Boss case back for an Urbana

Charles N. Thorpe, first president of Keystone Watch Case Co., c. 1870s

In *American Watch Casemakers*, Warren Niebling notes that "The Keystone Watch Case Co. produced a variety of cases: the well-known nickel case, trade named 'silveroid,' the J. Boss gold-filled case as well as solid gold and coin and sterling silver." As Niebling points out, the name "J. Boss" appears only on gold-filled watch cases, not on those made of solid gold.[1]

In 1904, Keystone merged with the Philadelphia Watch Case Company, the Crescent Watch Case Company and the Bates and Bacon Watch Case Company. They maintained the Keystone Watch Case name. Up to the 1920s, Keystone made mostly pocket watch cases, but then began the shift to wristwatches as the 1920s progressed.

CRESCENT WATCH CASE COMPANY

The Crescent Watch Case Company started in Chicago, Illinois, in 1882, as the Chicago Watch Case Company, manufacturing mostly 10K gold cases. After a few years, it relocated to Brooklyn, New York, and was renamed the Crescent Watch Case Company. In 1891 it moved to Newark, New Jersey, and a new plant was constructed, where silver and nickel cases were produced. At some point Crescent acquired the Bay State Watch Case Company plus several other watch case companies that produced mostly silver cases.

In 1904, Crescent merged with the Philadelphia Watch Case Company, the Bates and Bacon Watch Case Company and the Keystone Watch Case Company.

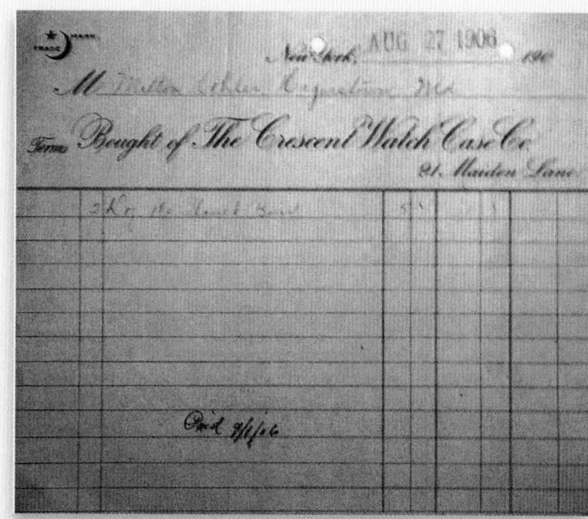
New York, AUG 27 1906

Bought of The Crescent Watch Case Co.

21 Maiden Lane

Crescent Watch Case Co., 1906 invoice

PHILADELPHIA WATCH CASE COMPANY

The Philadelphia Watch Case Company started as the Leichty & Le Bouba Watch Case Company in Philadelphia, Pennsylvania. Theophilus Zurbrugg bought the Leichty & Le Bouba Company in 1884. Around 1888, Zurbrugg changed the company name to the Philadelphia Watch Case Company. Philadelphia trademarks included one with a crown and another with an arm and hammer. The company moved in 1902 to Riverside, New Jersey, and then, in 1904, to Philadelphia. As noted above, that same year the Crescent Watch Case Company, the Bates and Bacon Watch Case Company and Keystone merged, keeping the Keystone Watch Case Company name.

Philadelphia Watch Case Co., c. 1910

It also seems that the T. Zurbrugg Company had moved to Riverside in 1898 and bought the J. Muhr & Brother Watch Case Company. The T. Zurbrugg Company was apparently absorbed by the Philadelphia Watch Case Company in 1899.

In 1901 the Philadelphia firm purchased the United States Watch Company at Waltham, a little more than a year after New York Standard Watch Company was bought by Keystone and T. Zurbrugg. Around this time the Zurbrugg, New York Standard and Philadelphia companies shared an office on Maiden Lane in New York City.

"Victory" was a Philadelphia case grade that was initially gold-filled, guaranteed for ten years, and in later years used for rolled-gold plated cases.

Philadelphia inside case back for a Whippet case

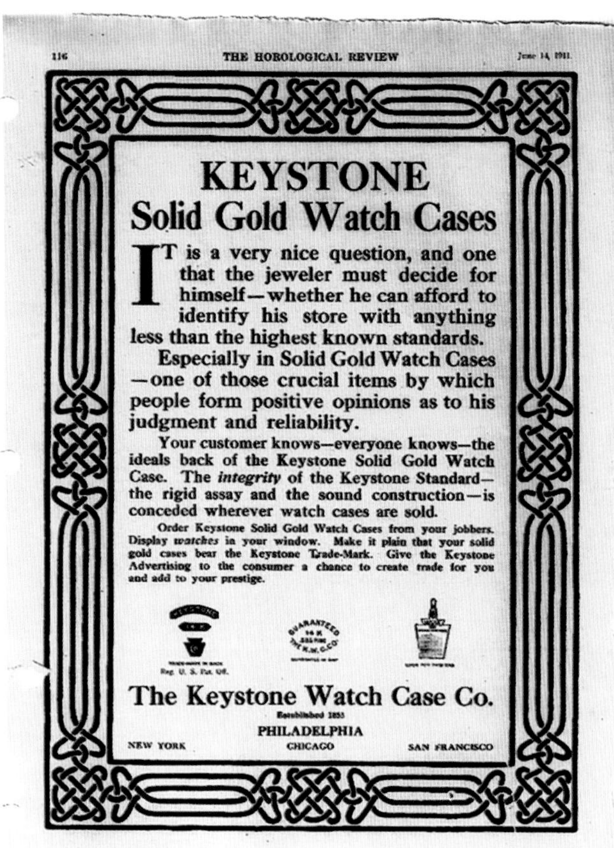

Horological Review, June 14, 1911

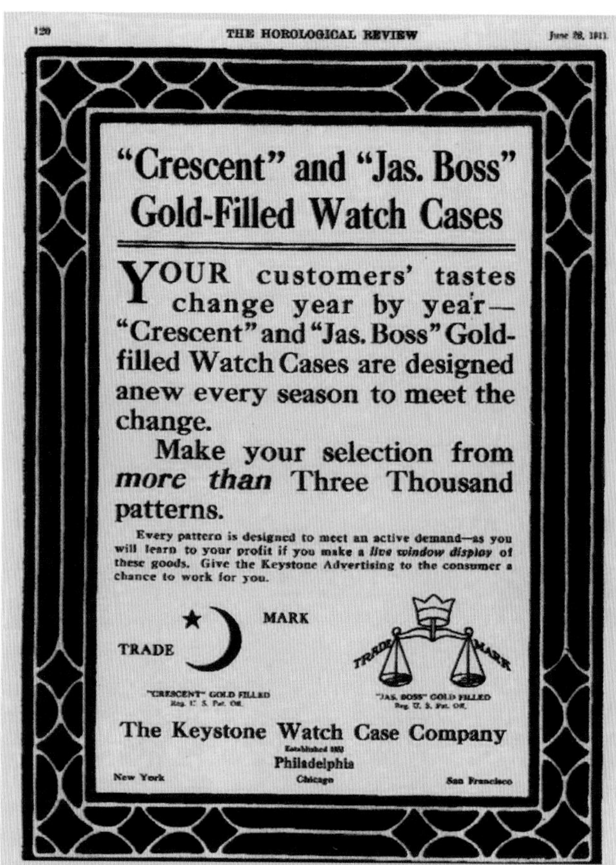

Horological Review, June 28, 1911

Keystone advertisement for its early military wristwatches, including two with off-set crowns; *Keystone*, September 1918

Several examples of promotional watch case openers from Keystone (and other companies) plus an old metal Illinois sign

Keystone wood shipping container, viewed from the top

Keystone Boss wood shipping container

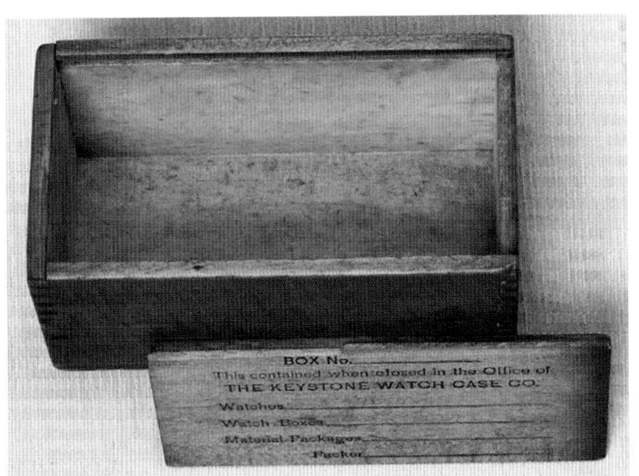

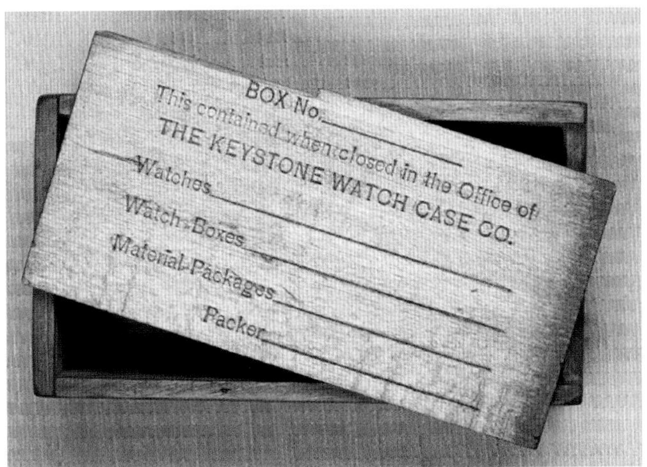

Wood box for the shipment of "Silveroid" Keystone cases

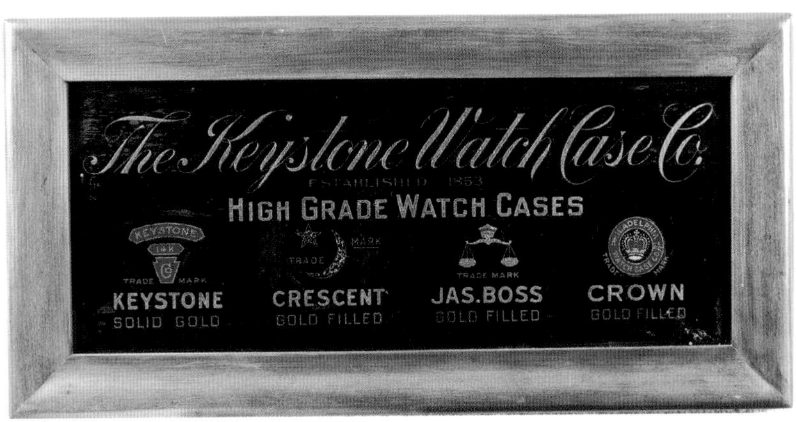

This is a Keystone Watch Case Company promotional mirror for use by jewelry stores. It shows some of the main trade names and trademarks used by Keystone.

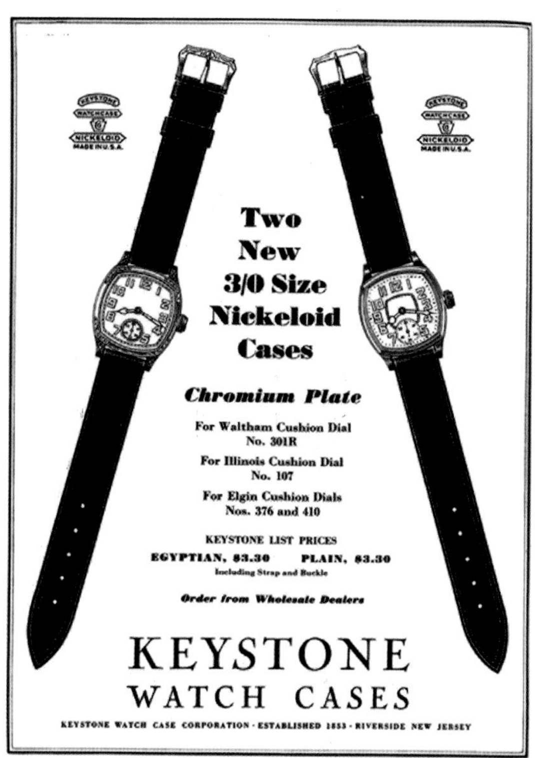

Keystone, May 1930; Keystone advertisement for cushion chromium-plated cases for Elgin, Illinois, and Waltham watches. Note Dial No. 107 for the Illinois Cushion Dial.

An actual Keystone chromium case fitted with an Illinois movement and dial (No. 107)

Keystone promotional pin

SEND ALL REMITTANCES TO PHILADELPHIA

TERMS NET

INVOICE FROM

No. ________

THE KEYSTONE WATCH CASE CO.

PHILADELPHIA

CHARGE ACCOUNT OF

Mather Bros. Co.,

113 Washington St.,

New Castle, Pa.

(Crescent Acct.)

DATE April 16, 1910. OUR NO.

	Job	.52
	Duplicate	

Invoice from the Keystone Watch Case Co. to Mather Bros. Co. of New Castle, PA, April 16, 1910

Owing to a great shortage of metal during World War II, Keystone production moved to compasses and flight navigational instruments. In 1949, Keystone started making cases for the U.S. Time Corporation. By 1956 the watch casemaker was closed.

Keystone made at least thirty-five different Factory-Cased men's wristwatch models for the Illinois Watch Company, four were solid gold. Keystone produced at least forty-five different Factory-Cased ladies' wristwatch models for Illinois; fifteen were solid gold. They are listed later in this chapter.

Keystone inside case back for a Square Cut Corner

KEYSTONE DESIGNS

In his interviews with me, Warren Niebling stated that Keystone had an employee named Mr. Altorfer who designed cases from 1880 to the 1920s.* After his hand-designed paper models were approved, they were turned over to the engraving department. In 1920, Keystone began to utilize a "master machine" that could house one case design that then could be used to cut 25 cases at a time. Prior to that, wristwatch cases were made by hand and some by stamping. Although the Illinois watches were almost all stamped, a few seem to have been made by hand by cutting parts and soldering them together.

After another company took over the Keystone building, Niebling was allowed to remove any Keystone material that he wanted. He recalled being in one room 20 x 20 feet, with a height of 15 feet, filled entirely with watch crystals. This supply suggests that the casemakers must have fitted the cases with crystals prior to shipment to the watch manufacturers. In addition to many crystals, Niebling removed fifty to one hundred original Keystone patents, trademarks, important papers and secret formulae for polishing and finishing cases, among other things.

*Warren Niebling, interviews by the author, June 5, 12 and 17, 2001.

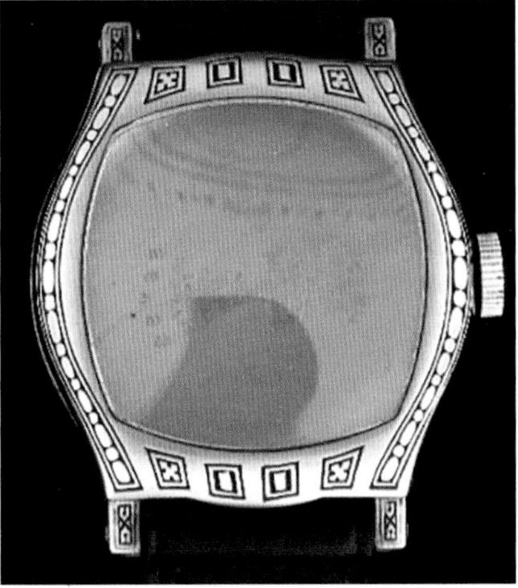

Speedway 178 case, Keystone NOS, unpolished

The Wadsworth Watch Case Company

In 1857 twelve-year-old Harry Arthur Wadsworth immigrated with his family from England to the United States. The son of a jeweler and watchmaker, he became an apprentice at the Cummings Watch Case Company in New York. He then worked in the case factory of the American Waltham Watch Company. As a young adult, Wadsworth first worked at the watch case firm of Duhme & Company in Cincinnati and then at the Dueber Watch Case Manufacturing Company of Newport, Kentucky. About the time that Dueber moved to Canton, Ohio, to merge its facilities with the Hampden Watch Company in 1889, Wadsworth and J. H. Stegman formed H. A. Wadsworth & Company. In 1892 they incorporated as the Wadsworth Watch Case Company.

Wadsworth served as president of the company from its inception until his death in 1934 at age eighty-eight. His eldest son, Arthur W. Wadsworth, who had served as vice president and secretary, ultimately became president. Arthur devoted at least part of his time to case design, as evidenced by several design patents issued in his name, including some for Illinois model cases.

Harry A. Wadsworth

In 1900 the Wadsworth factory moved to Dayton, Kentucky. Initially, Wadsworth sold only to wholesalers and jobbers, but after moving to Dayton it sold cases directly to watchmakers such as Elgin, Hamilton, Illinois and Waltham. In 1953, Elgin purchased Wadsworth, making the firm a division of the Elgin National Watch Company. Arthur W. Wadsworth remained president of the division. Owing to loss of sales to foreign imports, its factory closed in 1958. At that time an auction was held to sell its property and fixtures. Unfortunately, no one bid for its production records and they were destroyed—a tragic loss for horological history.

The Wadsworth Watch Case Co., c. 1920s

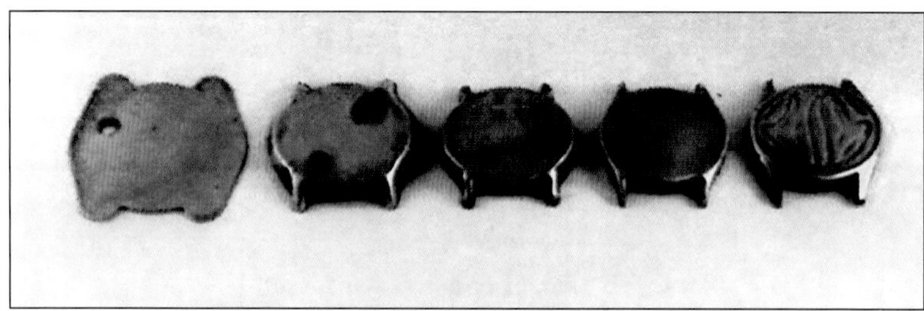

Wadsworth Case Production Stages

The images shown demonstrate some of the case production stages performed by the Wadsworth Watch Case Company. The caes were fabricated on a progressive die basis, with the first die cutting out the model shape in the flat. The second die cut makes it three-dimensional (3-D). The third die enhances the 3-D. The fourth die creates the front of the case detail. The fifth die stamps the seat for the crystal and the last die (which is only shown for the ladies' model) would cut out the crystal opening. After this was done, the final step would be to solder four small rectangular pieces of 14K gold on the back of each of the lugs to cover the raw edge where the brass center is exposed. If the lugs were wider than this and there was a hollow spot in each lug then a brass plug would be made to fill the lug solid before the gold cap was added.*

***Charlie Cleves**

A Wadsworth Watch Case Company sign for use on the counter of jewelry stores that carried Wadsworth cases

Wadsworth glass advertising slide

Illinois Trophy inside case back

New Yorker NOS case, unpolished

Wadsworth made cases for at least twenty-nine Factory-Cased men's models for Illinois (only one was in solid gold) and at least thirty Factory-Cased ladies' models; at least one dozen were solid gold (not counting Diamond-Set models). They are listed later in this chapter.

RENEWED

MARKS SYMBOLS ART. of MF

UNITED STATES PATENT OFFICE.

THE WADSWORTH WATCH CASE COMPANY, OF DAYTON, KENTUCKY.

TRADE-MARK FOR WATCHCASES.

97,006. Registered May 19, 1914.

Application filed June 16, 1913. Serial No. 71,143.

STATEMENT.

To all whom it may concern:

Be it known that THE WADSWORTH WATCH CASE COMPANY, a corporation duly organized under the laws of the State of Kentucky, and located in the city of Dayton, county of Campbell, and State of Kentucky, and doing business at the corner of Fifth and Clay streets, Dayton, Kentucky, has adopted and used the trade-mark shown in the accompanying drawing, for watchcases, in Class No. 27, Horological instruments.

The trade-mark has been continuously used in the business of said corporation, since June 1st, 1890.

The trade-mark is applied or affixed to the goods, or to the packages containing the same, by stamping, or by placing thereon a printed label on which the trade-mark is shown.

THE WADSWORTH WATCH CASE COMPANY,
By H. A. WADSWORTH,
Pres.

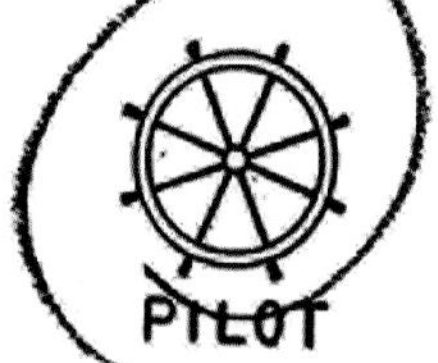

DECLARATION.

State of Kentucky county of Campbell ss:

H. A. WADSWORTH, being duly sworn, deposes and says that he is the president of the corporation, the applicant named in the foregoing statement; that he believes the foregoing statement is true; that he believes said corporation to be the owner of the mark sought to be registered; that no other person, firm, corporation, or association, to the best of his knowledge and belief, has the right to use said mark in the United States, either in the identical form or in any such near resemblance thereto as might be calculated to deceive; that said mark is used by said corporation in commerce among the several States of the United States; that the description and drawing presented truly represent the mark sought to be registered; that the specimens show the mark as actually used upon the goods; and that the mark has been in actual use as a trade-mark of the applicant for ten years next preceding February 20, 1905, and that, to the best of his knowledge and belief, such use has been exclusive.

H. A. WADSWORTH.

Subscribed and sworn to before me, a notary public, this 11th day of June, 1913.

[L. S.] JOSEPH D. HENGELBROK,
Notary Public.

109

A Wadsworth 1914 Trademark Registration

Robbers Get $50,000 Watch Factory Loot

CINCINNATI, Sept. 30.—(AP)—Four robbers entered the Wadsworth Watch Case Manufacturing company building here last night, handcuffed two night watchmen, cracked two safes and escaped with golf bullion and watch cases estimated to be worth between $50,000 and $60,000.

The robbery was discovered this morning when a day watchman went to the plant and found the two night watchmen blindfolded and handcuffed together.

Montana Standard (Butte, MT), October 1, 1928; image from *newspapers.com.* Because of their supplies of valuable case metals, major watch case factories such as Wadsworth were magnets for robbers. There had been a spectacular heist at the IWCCo the year before.

Page 96 | *The KEYSTONE* | July, 1930

Completing the circle of quality

... *a Wadsworth Band!*

A PERSON takes pride in his watch. And if it happens to be a wrist watch, he doesn't want his pride to stop where the band begins. The band is an integral part of the ensemble—and he wants to be proud of that, too!

Any fine watch and a Wadsworth Band makes an endless circle of quality. The colors, the style, and the workmanship are the same. For Wadsworth Bands are made of precious metal—by the same skilled craftsmen who make Wadsworth Cases for the world's leading watch manufacturers.

Ask your wholesaler to show you these smart, nationally advertised bands. We're sure you'll agree that this is the band a fine watch deserves. The Wadsworth Watch Case Company, Dayton, Kentucky. Offices: New York, 20 W. 47th Street; San Francisco, 150 Post Street; Chicago, 35 E. Wacker Drive.

The new Wadsworth Model B (upper left)—a flexible mesh band for men. Easily adjusted! Extremely comfortable! Not affected by perspiration. Locking device always remains in exact center of the wrist. Priced to the consumer at $10.

The "Lady Wadsworth" band for women, (upper right) like the "Lord Wadsworth" for men, is made in white or green gold filled. Advertised prices to consumer—$10 to $12.50.

The Wadsworth "Model A" bracelet (lower left) has links fastened together with pin bars, and is easily fitted without special tools. Priced to the consumer at $6.50.

On the Air!

Every Wednesday evening, the powerful Blue Network Stations of the National Broadcasting Company listed below carry the Wadsworth message—your message—to a vast audience of radio listeners. Listen in!—and let us have your comments and suggestions.

City	Station	Time
Chicago	WLS	CDT—8:00 PM
Boston	WBZA	EDT—9:00 PM
Springfield	WBZ	EDT—9:00 PM
Detroit	WJR	EST—8:00 PM
Kansas City	WREN	CST—7:00 PM
St. Louis	KWK	CST—7:00 PM
New York	WJZ	EDT—9:00 PM
Rochester	WHAM	EDT—9:00 PM
Cincinnati	WCKY	EST—8:00 PM
Pittsburgh	KDKA	EDT—9:00 PM

CDT—Central Daylight Time
EDT—Eastern Daylight Time
EST—Eastern Standard Time
CST—Central Standard Time

Wadsworth Watch Case Company advertisement featuring all-Illinois models, *Keystone*, July 1930

Wadsworth Sales Conferences. The Wadsworth Watch Case Company held annual sales conferences in the assembly room of its factory in Dayton, Kentucky. The report from the March 1929 issue of the *Jewelers' Circular,* shown here, describes such a meeting.

Wadsworth Watch Case Company Holds Sales Conference

The annual sales conference of the Wadsworth Watch Case Company was conducted in the assembly room of its factory, in charge of Forrest J. Alvin, merchandizing manager. The company's engineers and its entire sales personnel attended the meeting, and were guests of the company at the annual dinner.

Round-table discussions were conducted by various department heads. D. T. Wadsworth, vice-president and chief engineer, discussed the new products of the company; L. G. Kuhlman, general manager and treasurer, discussed last year's business and outlined plans for 1929. A. W. Wheeler, purchasing agent and officer in charge of the order department, talked on the proper methods of handling orders; R. Crosby, credit manager, discussed credit and its relation to the business; R. Clark, assistant factory manager, told of co-operation between the factory and sales organizations, and William Miller, traffic manager, urged prompt shipments as one means of boosting sales.

Joseph Pohlman, president of the company, was toastmaster at the annual dinner, when various officials made short addresses.

Jewelers' Circular, March 1929

Joseph Fahys, c. 1918

Joseph Fahys & Co.

In 2001, John H. Wilterding, Jr. wrote a fascinating article about Joseph Fahys & Co. for the NAWCC *Bulletin,* detailing the rich history of the company.[2] In 1848, Joseph Fahys and his mother immigrated to America from France and settled in Hoboken, New Jersey. Fahys apprenticed for five years with watch casemaker Ulysse Savoye and then worked as a journeyman. In 1856 he married Maria L'Homedeu Payne, of Sag Harbor, Long Island, New York. The Fahys would later reside at 540 Park Avenue, New York City, and summer at Sag Harbor.

In 1857, Fahys opened his own watch case shop at 75 Nassau Street in New York City but in 1861 re-located to 16 Maiden Lane, in the city's jewelry hub. Together with Jacob and Joseph Fortenback, Fahys created plans for a "modern" watchcase factory in Carlstadt, New Jersey. Fahys subsequently became sole owner of the newly named Fortenback Watch Case Factory.

Fahys joined other investors in purchasing the Montauk Steam Cotton Mill in Sag Harbor in 1874. A fire in October 1879 destroyed the cotton mill and left Sag Harbor without any major industry. In an effort to revitalize Sag Harbor's economy, Fahys met with the Sag Harbor Business Aid Committee and offered to make Sag Harbor the future site of a new watch case factory. The new facility opened on October 21, 1881, and Fahys moved the watch case machinery from Carlstadt the 100 miles east. Machinery tests were completed by the end of December, and in January 1882 production began.

In 1880 Fahys' son-in-law, Henry Francis Cook, became a partner and took over general supervision of manufacturing. Fahys finally incorporated the firm as the Fahys Watch Case Co. in 1881 when Cook became a partner. The firm in New York City, located in the Fahys Building at 54 Maiden Lane, remained Joseph Fahys & Co. In 1887, Fahys' son, George E. Fahys, headed the financial and sales divisions.

Henry F. Cook, vice president and treasurer, c. 1919

George E. Fahys, president, c. 1919

By the end of 1890, twelve hundred Fahys pocket watch cases were made daily. Wilterding points out that this translated into $6,000 worth of gold smelted daily, and the annual "sweepings" of gold amounted to $80,000 per year. Fahys preferred marketing gold-filled cases, however. In fact, Fahys extolled the benefits of gold-filled cases ("Made like a Sandwich") over solid gold cases in the early 1890s.

To diversify, Fahys absorbed the Alvin Manufacturing Company of New Jersey, a noted maker of sterling silver products. In the early twentieth century it was the largest manufacturer of silverware in the United States.

Fahys formed the Brooklyn Watch Case Company of Brooklyn, New York in 1865 to produce solid gold watch cases, a product not manufactured at either Carlstadt or Sag Harbor. (Decades later, the Brooklyn Watch Case Company would produce a version of Illinois' Southampton men's wristwatch.)

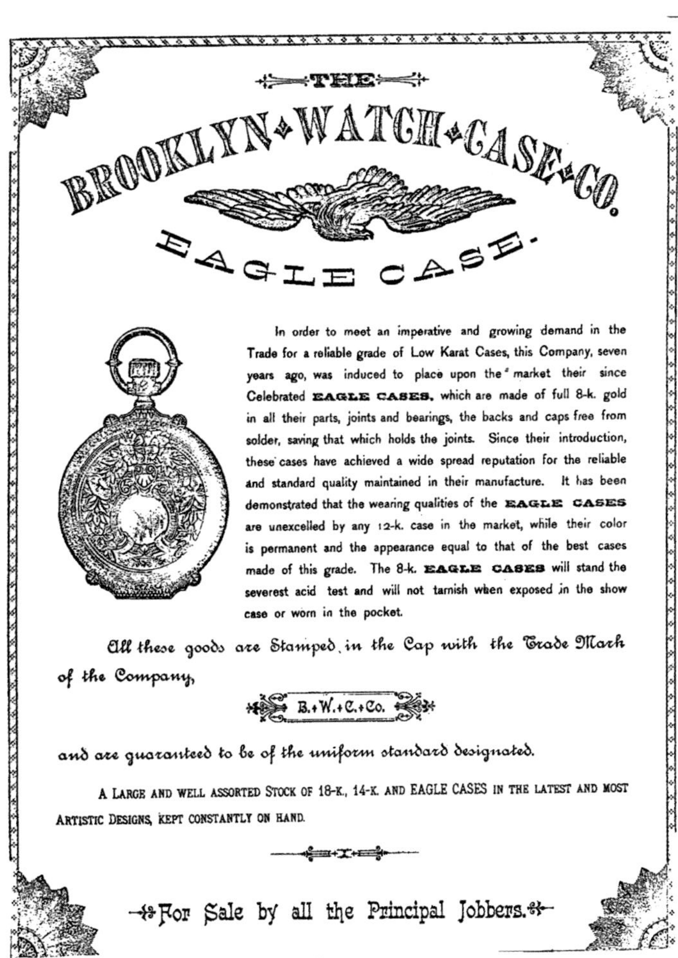

Early advertisement for the Brooklyn Watch Case Company, c. 1890s

Fahys

Cases

for Men's Wrist Watches

Made in Two Shapes

Cushion Shape—Made in O Size

20-Year Montauk or Sterling Silver cases

Round Shape—Made in 3/O and O Size

THE cases are our 20-year Montauk, or Sterling silver, and we make them in both cushion and round shapes. Placed in such stout leather wrist straps as are shown above, they look thoroughly masculine. We supply the cases only.

JOSEPH FAHYS & CO.

Established 1857

BOSTON NEW YORK

Fahys advertisement for its military cases, c. 1918

Fahys inside case back for an Illinois Viking

Initially, the factory workforce was composed mainly of key Carlstadt employees, together with locally recruited workers. To house the employees, Fahys constructed fifty new houses in Sag Harbor. Many Jewish men (most of them German) and their families arrived directly from Ellis Island between 1886 and 1888. According to a local history, "Recruiters from the factory went directly to Ellis Island where the people got off the boat from Europe and offered the immigrants jobs. Whole families would transfer to the steamer going directly to Sag Harbor without ever setting foot in New York."[3]

Brooklyn Watch Case Co. Conqueror grade inside case back for an Illinois Southampton

Fahys Watch Case factory in Sag Harbor, c. 1890

The Fahys Watch Case Company placed a two-page "advertorial" entitled "A Plant with a Personality" in the 50th Anniversary Edition of the *Jewelers' Circular Weekly*. The author of this piece, in describing his visit to the Fahys plant in Sag Harbor, noted: "The fact that there are many fathers and sons who have worked throughout their lifetime for the Joseph Fahys Company speaks volumes for the fine factory conditions and generous policy of the company. It is a clean, many-windowed factory in a clean, seaside town. Its employees say that it is a pleasure to work there."

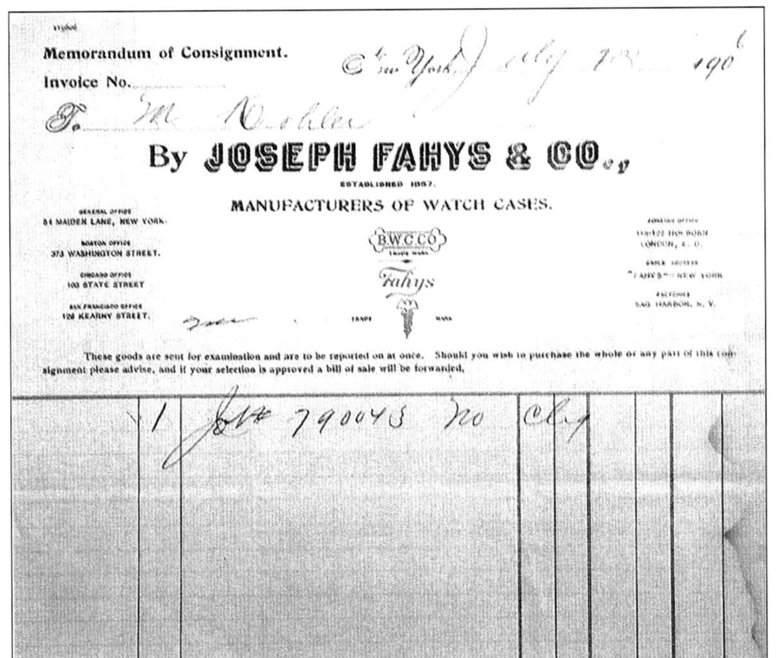

Memorandum of Consignment.

Invoice No.

By JOSEPH FAHYS & CO.,

ESTABLISHED 1857.

MANUFACTURERS OF WATCH CASES.

GENERAL OFFICE
54 MAIDEN LANE, NEW YORK.

BOSTON OFFICE
373 WASHINGTON STREET.

CHICAGO OFFICE
103 STATE STREET

SAN FRANCISCO OFFICE
120 KEARNY STREET.

B.W.C.CO.
TRADE MARK

Fahys

TRADE MARK

SAG HARBOR, N. Y.

These goods are sent for examination and are to be reported on at once. Should you wish to purchase the whole or any part of this consignment please advise, and if your selection is approved a bill of sale will be forwarded.

Fahys 1906 invoice

NOS Fahys case for a Marquis Strap

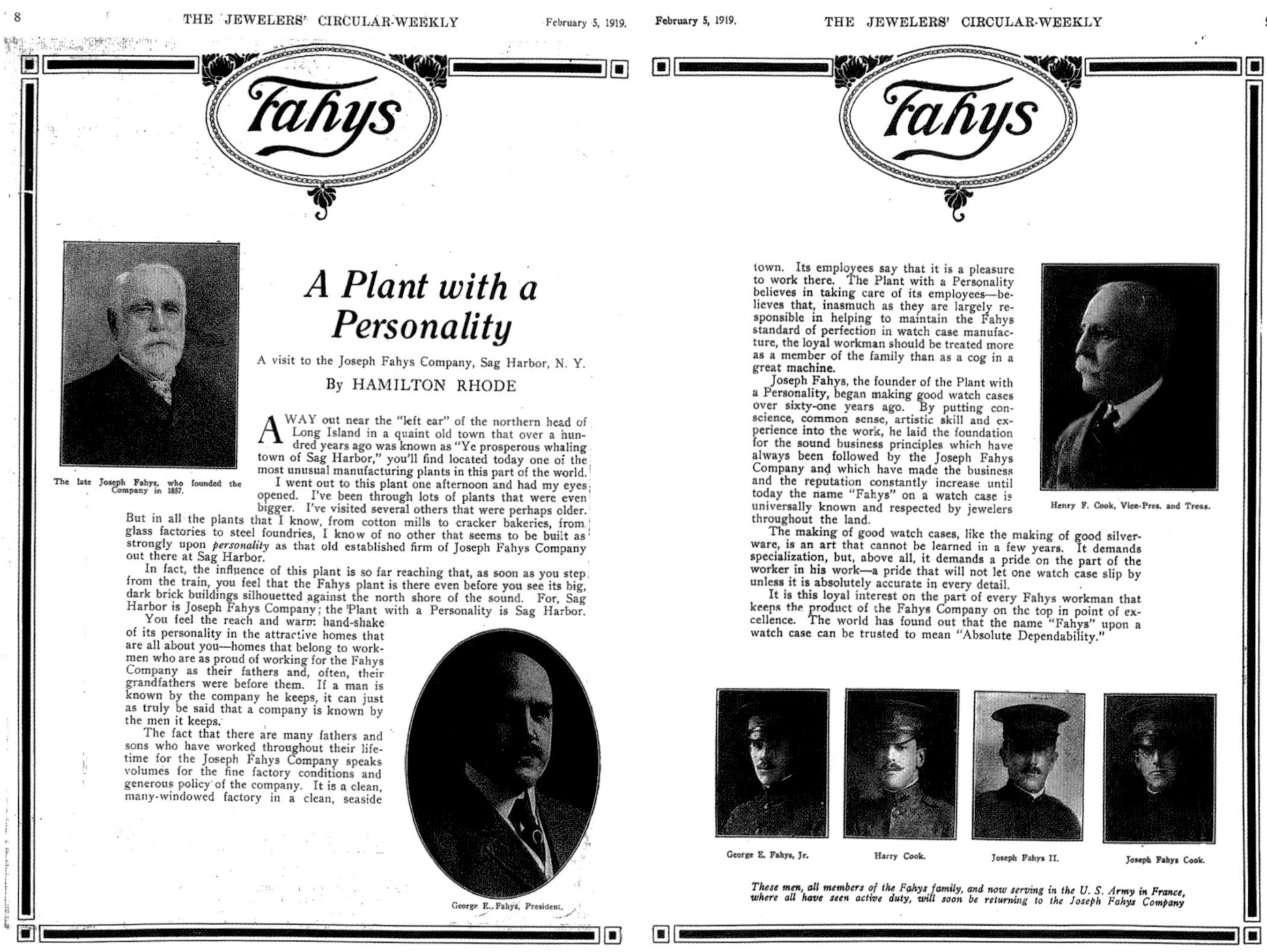

8 THE JEWELERS' CIRCULAR-WEEKLY February 5, 1919.

February 5, 1919. THE JEWELERS' CIRCULAR-WEEKLY 9

Fahys

A Plant with a Personality

A visit to the Joseph Fahys Company, Sag Harbor, N. Y.

By HAMILTON RHODE

The late Joseph Fahys, who founded the Company in 1857.

AWAY out near the "left ear" of the northern head of Long Island in a quaint old town that over a hundred years ago was known as "Ye prosperous whaling town of Sag Harbor," you'll find located today one of the most unusual manufacturing plants in this part of the world.

I went out to this plant one afternoon and had my eyes opened. I've been through lots of plants that were even bigger. I've visited several others that were perhaps older. But in all the plants that I know, from cotton mills to cracker bakeries, from glass factories to steel foundries, I know of no other that seems to be built as strongly upon *personality* as that old established firm of Joseph Fahys Company out there at Sag Harbor.

In fact, the influence of this plant is so far reaching that, as soon as you step from the train, you feel that the Fahys plant is there even before you see its big, dark brick buildings silhouetted against the north shore of the sound. For, Sag Harbor is Joseph Fahys Company; the Plant with a Personality is Sag Harbor.

You feel the reach and warm hand-shake of its personality in the attractive homes that are all about you—homes that belong to workmen who are as proud of working for the Fahys Company as their fathers and, often, their grandfathers were before them. If a man is known by the company he keeps, it can just as truly be said that a company is known by the men it keeps.

The fact that there are many fathers and sons who have worked throughout their lifetime for the Joseph Fahys Company speaks volumes for the fine factory conditions and generous policy of the company. It is a clean, many-windowed factory in a clean, seaside town. Its employees say that it is a pleasure to work there. The Plant with a Personality believes in taking care of its employees—believes that, inasmuch as they are largely responsible in helping to maintain the Fahys standard of perfection in watch case manufacture, the loyal workman should be treated more as a member of the family than as a cog in a great machine.

George E. Fahys, President.

Joseph Fahys, the founder of the Plant with a Personality, began making good watch cases over sixty-one years ago. By putting conscience, common sense, artistic skill and experience into the work, he laid the foundation for the sound business principles which have always been followed by the Joseph Fahys Company and which have made the business and the reputation constantly increase until today the name "Fahys" on a watch case is universally known and respected by jewelers throughout the land.

Henry F. Cook, Vice-Pres. and Treas.

The making of good watch cases, like the making of good silverware, is an art that cannot be learned in a few years. It demands specialization, but, above all, it demands a pride on the part of the worker in his work—a pride that will not let one watch case slip by unless it is absolutely accurate in every detail.

It is this loyal interest on the part of every Fahys workman that keeps the product of the Fahys Company on the top in point of excellence. The world has found out that the name "Fahys" upon a watch case can be trusted to mean "Absolute Dependability."

George E. Fahys, Jr. | Harry Cook. | Joseph Fahys II. | Joseph Fahys Cook.

These men, all members of the Fahys family, and now serving in the U. S. Army in France, where all have seen active duty, will soon be returning to the Joseph Fahys Company

Fahys "advertorial," ***Jewelers' Circular-Weekly,*** **February 5, 1919**

Joseph Fahys died at Sag Harbor on December 11, 1915. He was eulogized as a gentleman and friend to everyone.

In 1927 the officers of Fahys & Company were: Henry F. Cook, chairman of the board; George E. Fahys, president; J. Fahys Cook, vice president; E. Ernest Fahys, Jr., vice president; Harry Cook, vice president; and Joseph Fahys, secretary. In the late 1920s, Fahys employed approximately one thousand workers in total at all its sites. It also had sales offices at 20 West 47th Street in New York City and in Chicago at 35 East Wacker Drive.

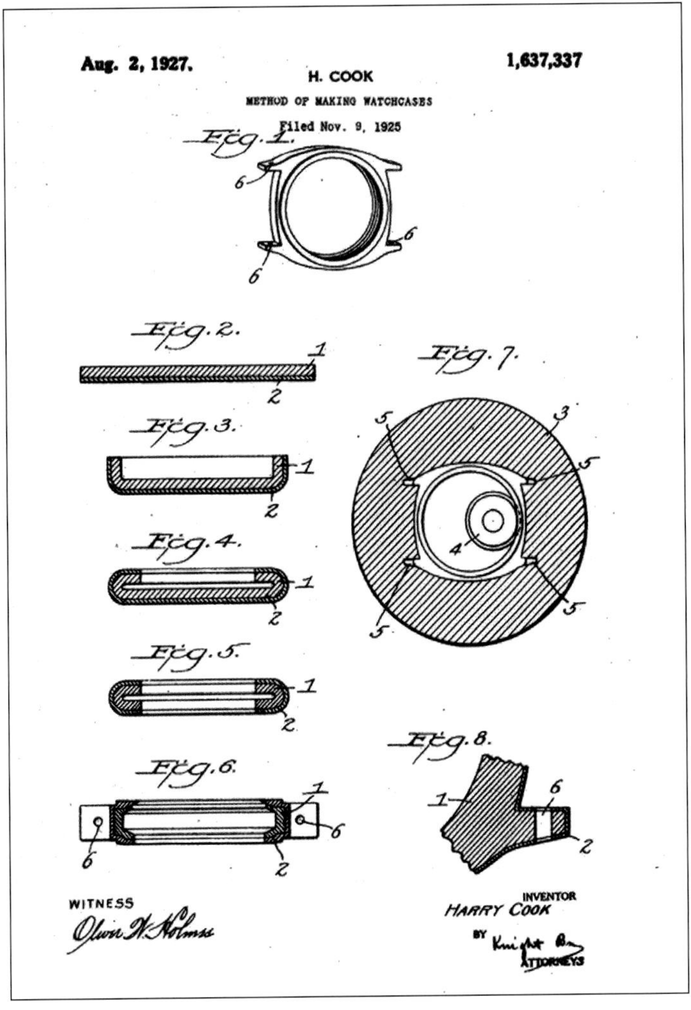

1927 Fahys patent

The factory shut down in 1928 after a nasty dispute developed among Joseph Fahys' heirs. None of the heirs wanted to invest in the company and upgrade equipment needed to compete with foreign demand, most notably from Bulova.

By 1931, after fifty years of watch case production, Fahys closed because of the Great Depression. In 1937 the Bulova Watch Company took a ten-year lease on the building and later purchased it. Bulova operated the factory until after World War II.

Fahys made at least fourteen different men's Factory-Cased watch models for the Illinois Watch Company (all using gold-filled cases); the models are listed later in this chapter. They made only one Factory-Cased ladies' wristwatch model for Illinois. They also made sterling silver cases that are some of the most aesthetically pleasing Illinois Transitional Period military wristwatches (see Chapter 9 for examples).

Fahys inside case back for a Medalist

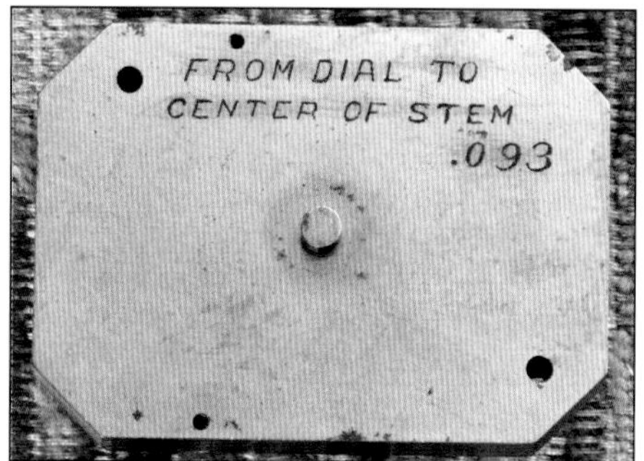

Top of 12/0 size Illinois movement die mock-up sent to casemakers to check fit of movements in their cases (from its top)

Bottom of Movement die (from its bottom)

Side of Movement die (from its side)

The Solidarity Watch Case Company

The Solidarity Watch Case Company was another of the many watch case companies established in the New York area in the late 1800s. The company started business in 1885 with a staff of eight men and for a long time made only solid gold watch cases. In four years its workforce grew to ninety-four.

> **1898**
> **HISTORICAL NOTES**
> - The United States annexes Hawaii.
> - Will Kellogg invents corn flakes.
> - Scientists Pierre and Marie Curie discover radium.

John W. Sherwood, the longtime and greatly respected president of Solidarity, was born in Rockport, Maine, on April 27, 1862. He entered the jewelry business in 1880 in Manchester, New Hampshire, with the Dunlop & Baker Company. In 1884 he moved to New York City, where he entered the jewelry business with Henry C. Haskell at 12 John Street. The next year, Sherwood became the eastern agent for the Dueber Watch Case Company and worked for Dueber for seven years.

In 1892, Sherwood started a watch jobbing business. Then, in 1904, he joined the Solidarity Watch Case Company. He was named president of Solidarity in 1912 and held that position until his death twenty years later. Sherwood's picture frequently appeared on the pages of the *Jewelers' Circular* and the *Keystone* as he was very active in the Maiden Lane Historical Society and was its president for many years. He served on the National Jewelers' Board, was past president of the Brotherhood of Traveling Jewelers, past president of the 24-Karat Club, honorary member of the Boston Jewelers' Club and had life membership in the Masonic fraternity.

The October 1931 issue of the *Jewelers' Circular* reported that the Solidarity Watch Case Company was to be discontinued. At the time of Sherwood's death, on January 24, 1932, Solidarity was still in the process of liquidation.

Prior to its closure, Solidarity made at least six different Factory-Cased men's watch models for the Illinois Watch Company. Four were solid gold: the Consul, Cushion Devon (Cushion Engraved), Square Cut Corner and Tuxedo. Solidarity also made a rare gold-filled Derby and the Special Cushion Solidarity model. The Derby is the only Factory-Cased Illinois wristwatch that had two separate casemakers, Solidarity and Wadsworth.

SOLIDARITY WATCH CASE CO. LISTED FOR SALE

An Unusual Opportunity" was the heading for a listing among the "Business Opportunities" in the *Brooklyn Daily Eagle* on Sunday, September 13, 1931.

The listing read: "Nationally known company, est. 1883, manufacturer of solid gold watch cases; also raised figure dials, wishes to sell as going concern, 2-story and basement brick building, in excellent condition, 10,000 sq. ft. floor space. For full particulars apply to Solidarity Watch Case Co., 242–246 Chestnut St., Brooklyn, N.Y.

John W. Sherwood later in life

Maiden Lane Historical Society Meets

The annual meeting of the **Maiden Lane Historical Society** was held on Thursday **afternoon, March 28, in the Jewelers' 24-Karat Club rooms, 15 Maiden Lane. Officers were elected** as follows: **John W. Sherwood, president; Alpheus L. Brown,** G. **Ernest Fahys, Dr. George F. Kunz, Henry Abbott and Harry** C. **Larter, vice-presidents; Leo Wormser, treasurer, and Jos.** D. **Little, secretary. Various matters pertaining to the preservation of historic spots in the Maiden Lane district were discussed.**

Article from the *Jewelers' Circular*, April 1929

TRADE-MARK.

No. 69,293. REGISTERED JUNE 2, 1908.

SOLIDARITY WATCH CASE COMPANY.

WATCHCASES.

APPLICATION FILED FEB. 13, 1908.

UNITED STATES PATENT OFFICE.

SOLIDARITY WATCH CASE COMPANY, OF BROOKLYN, NEW YORK.

TRADE-MARK FOR WATCHCASES.

No. 69,293. Statement and Declaration. Registered June 2, 1908.

Application filed February 13, 1908. Serial No. 32,749.

STATEMENT.

To all whom it may concern:

Be it known that SOLIDARITY WATCH CASE COMPANY, a corporation created under and existing by virtue of the laws of the State of New York, and located and doing business at 242 Chestnut street, in the city of Brooklyn, county of Kings, and State of New York, has adopted for its use the trade-mark shown in the accompanying drawing.

The trade mark has been continuously used in business by said corporation since about October, 1885.

The particular description of goods to which the trade mark is appropriated is watch cases, comprised in Class 27, Horological instruments.

The trade mark is usually displayed by impressing same directly upon the goods and by printing or otherwise affixing same on packages containing the goods.

SOLIDARITY WATCH CASE COMPANY.
LOUIS J. MONTAGNON,
Sec'y & Treas.

DECLARATION.

State of New York, county of New York.

LOUIS J. MONTAGNON being duly sworn, deposes and says he is the secretary and treasurer of the corporation, the applicant named in the foregoing statement; that he believes that the foregoing statement is true; that he believes said corporation to be the owner of the trade-mark sought to be registered, that no other person, firm, corporation, or association, to the best of his knowledge and belief, has the right to use said trade-mark, either in the identical form, or in any such near resemblance thereto, as might be calculated to deceive; that the said trade-mark is used by the applicant in commerce among the several States of the United States, that the drawing presented truly represents the trade-mark sought to be registered and that the specimens (or facsimiles) show the trade-mark as actually used upon the goods.

LOUIS J. MONTAGNON.

Subscribed and sworn to before me, this 31st day of January 1908.

[L. S.] HUGO MOCK,
Commissioner of Deeds for the City of New York.

Solidarity's 1908 United States Trade-Mark Registration. The Solidarity Watch Case Company frequently used this registered trademark, but there was also a trademark using a stylized globe overlaid with an "S" within a triangle. Yet another mark was used in the Tuxedo case back.

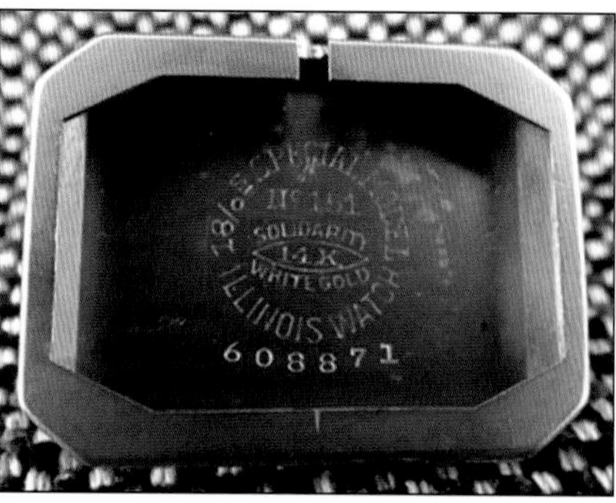

Solidarity inside case back for a Tuxedo

TYCOON SERIES

The Nobel pocket watch, introduced by Hamilton in late 1930, with a modified "Illini" extra-thin Illinois movement called a Hamilton grade 400, was part of the "Tycoon Series" and was housed in a Solidarity-signed case. It was marketed by Hamilton from 1930 to 1937.

Halligan's notes mention that on December 3, 1930, a letter to Hamilton's wholesalers introduced the new series; and that on July 15, 1937, a letter announced that the grade 400 was being discontinued. The "Tycoon Series" appeared in Hamilton sales catalogs for only five years, 1932 through 1936.

The J. Milhening Watch Case Company

In 1870, Joseph Milhening founded J. Milhening & Co. in Chicago, Illinois, to manufacture diamond mountings and other fine jewelry. A native of Scotland, Milhening had apprenticed as a jeweler in New Britain, Connecticut, before moving to Chicago. His business survived the Great Fire of 1871 and flourished in the latter years of the nineteenth century, importing diamonds in addition to producing platinum and gold jewelry and wristwatch cases. After several moves around the city, Milhening finally located his sales office at 27 East Monroe Street and maintained a factory on Ravenswood Avenue. He also had a New York sales office at 542 Fifth Avenue.

In 1893, seventeen-year-old Frank Milhening, Joseph's son, joined the business. After his father's retirement in the 1910s, Frank continued to grow the business. In 1929, Milhening reportedly built a "large and handsomely equipped factory" at 4626 Ravenwood Avenue.

Frank Milhening as a young man

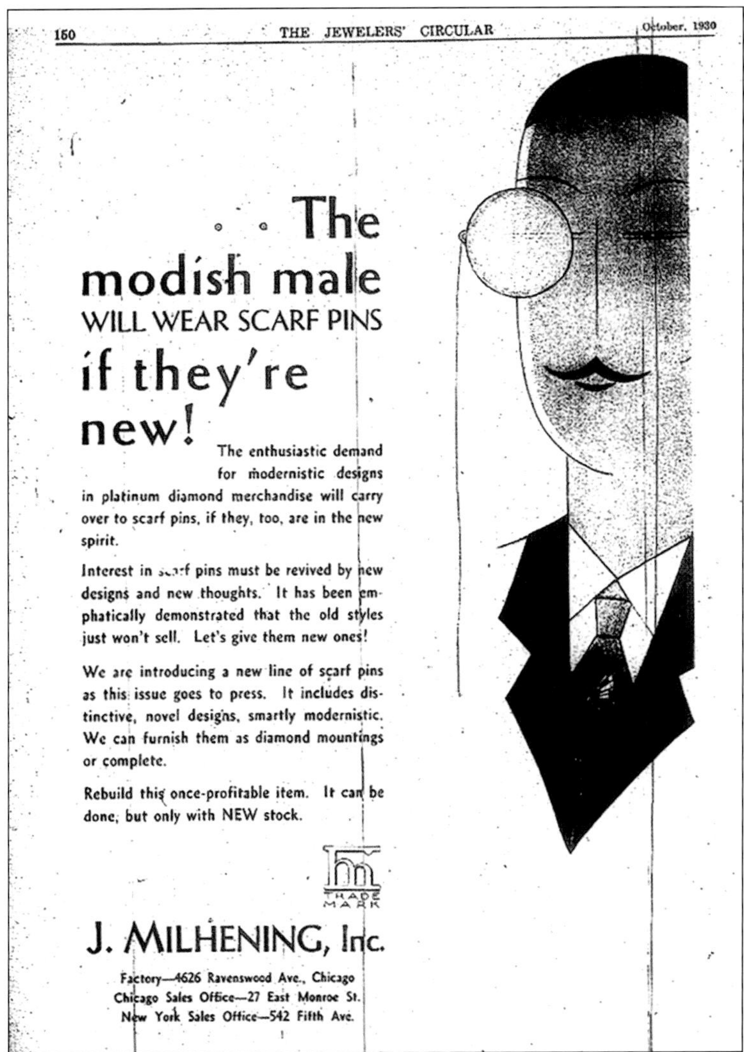

J. Milhening, Inc. advertisement for scarf pins. ***Jewelers' Circular*, October 1930**

THE STRANGE ADVENTURE OF A TRUNK

Odd News From Big Cities

Stories of Strange Happenings in the Metropolitan Towns

Thought He Was Robbed of Jewels

NEAR LOSS OF TRUNK FULL OF JEWELS

New York, Nov. 18.—Frank Milhening, a member of a Chicago jewelry firm, spent several anxious hours tonight until he found his trunk, containing $35,000 worth of jewels, which disappeared from in front of the Herald Square hotel tonight, where he had placed it in a taxicab. A porter, who had been cautioned to watch the trunk, was responsible for the loss. He left the trunk with the taxicab chaffeur and the latter, when a man and woman appeared as passengers a few minutes later, took them for the owners of the trunk and drove away. Three hours later the taxicab returned with the trunk and valuables safe.

In November 1909, Frank Milhening had been on a business trip to his company's New York office. Leaving his hotel to catch a train, he asked a porter to call a cab, put his trunk in it, and stay there and watch it until he came back and got in the cab. Unfortunately, the porter did not do as instructed. A few minutes later, when a man and woman got in the cab as passengers, the driver thought that the trunk was theirs, and off he went.

Only when he delivered his passengers to their destination did the cabdriver discover that the trunk did not belong to them. So back he went to the hotel where he had started. In the meantime, several hours had passed and Milhening had become greatly distressed, fearing that the trunk had been stolen—the contents included jewels worth $35,000! But when the cabdriver arrived with the trunk, Milhening found, to his great relief, that everything in the trunk was undisturbed.

Sources: "Odd News," *Portville Review* (Portville, NY), January 14, 1910; image from fultonhistory.com. "Near Loss," *Topeka Daily Capital* (Topeka, KS), November 19, 1909; image from *newspapers.com.*

Milhening continued importing diamonds and making fine platinum jewelry in addition to wristwatch cases. Between 1916 and 1935, Frank Milhening filed a number of patents for jewelry items, including rings and scarf pins.

Over the years, J. Milhening made fancy diamond-set ladies' wristwatch cases for Girard-Perregaux and other well-known watchmakers. The Elgin "Lady and Tiger" wristwatch case stands as one of its most enduring achievements (the design of the enameling has been attributed to the atelier of Lucien Lelong).

Milhening produced only two men's wristwatch cases for Illinois, the Arlington/Hawthorne and the Andover/Exeter, and no ladies' models.

J. Milhening inside case back for an Andover in 10K yellow gold-filled

J. Milhening inside case back for an Arlington

"YELLOW" GOLD VERSUS "NATURAL" GOLD

In its April 1931 issue, the *Jewelers' Circular* raised the question of the use of the term "yellow gold" versus "natural gold":

"From reports in all sections, it is apparent that there is steady increasing popularity of articles made in yellow gold though its progress is slow. There is as yet no strong call for general lines of mountings that will supersede those of white gold and platinum . . . But the call for some jewelry in gold colors is distinctly apparent and if it develops on broader lines it will prove popular with a large number of the jewelers themselves.

"With this has come a question of nomenclature. Some dealers refer to this merchandise with a special name for the gold finish used; others speak generally of "yellow" gold, still others refer to these lines as "natural" gold. Many manufacturers seem to prefer the word "natural" gold in designating the gold products of a hue that is familiar to the past generation as this includes the bright yellow of virgin gold and the normal colors of 10, 14 and 18 karat alloys.

"The question is a small one, but is deemed important in advertising and sales promotion literature. What does the retail jeweler prefer to use—"yellow," "natural," or any other term? Our columns are open to those who care to express an opinion on this subject."

The Illinois Watch Company (in its advertisements and catalogs) consistently referred to yellow gold or yellow gold-filled as "natural" gold.

STYLE is the greatest driving force in business today. To be "in style" is one of the most powerful incentives to make people spend money!

So it stands to reason . . . the best way for the jeweler to create business for *his store* is to offer "new styles" his customers can't buy in *other stores*!

Today, you have that opportunity!

For months, the trend toward Natural Gold has been gathering force. Fashion authorities sponsored it. The better stores both here and abroad are showing it. Leading watch manufacturers are featuring it regularly in their national advertising. And more customers every day are requesting it!

Natural Gold has reached the proportion of a new and popular *style*. And it should be welcomed with open arms by every jeweler in America. For it presents the greatest opportunity in years to re-establish jewelry store standards.

Think of these advantages:

It is a fine precious metal that can't be easily imitated in cheap base metals.

It is the kind of merchandise that belongs *in a fine jewelry store.*

It will lift you above competition from cheap stores selling imitations of your fine merchandise.

It gives you a fair margin of profit.

It makes it necessary for people who want to be "in style" to patronize the jewelry store.

If you want better business this summer . . . if you are one of the thousands of jewelers who want to help bring jewelry buyers back to the JEWELRY store . . . follow the trend toward—NATURAL GOLD!

The Wadsworth Watch Case Company, Incorporated, Dayton, Kentucky. Offices: 20 W. 47th Street, New York; 150 Post Street, San Francisco; 35 E. Wacker Drive, Chicago.

Ask your wholesaler to show you the newest WADSWORTH Belt Buckles and Watch Bands in Natural Gold. Smart, style merchandise that will stimulate your summer sales!

Wadsworth

WORKERS IN PRECIOUS METALS

Keystone, June 1932

The Pioneer Watch Case Company

Brothers Herbert and Harry Kolberg owned the Pioneer Watch Case Company. Immigrants from Eastern Europe, they had come to the United States in 1900 as children. A decade later, both were salesmen in the jewelry industry. While being employed as salesmen by the jewelry manufacturing firm of E. A. Slade, they formed their own company, H. I. & H. Kolberg to act as agents for jewelry manufacturers.

The Kolbergs became agents for the Charles H. Mason Jewelry Co., a jewelry manufacturer in Providence, Rhode Island. By 1925 they had adopted the name Pioneer Watch Case Company for their watch case products, with Mason as their partner in Providence. Pioneer maintained its New York City offices at 48 West 48th Street, while manufacturing cases in Providence at 150 Chestnut Street, in the heart of the city's jewelry manufacturing district.

Pioneer Watch Case Co.

Manufacturers of

Gold Filled Watch Cases

of the Better Kind

extend to their many friends and acquaintances in the trade their

Sincerest Greetings

for A Merry Christmas and A Prosperous New Year

To better serve our increasing trade we have moved to larger quarters at

15 MAIDEN LANE

Telephone Cortland 5283

New York

Make 1926 A "Pioneer" Year

Christmas and New Year's Greetings from the Pioneer Watch Case Co., *Jewelers' Circular.* December 30. 1925

Pioneer salesman's display case (closed)

Pioneer salesman's display case (for wristwatch cases), 8" x 8"

Page 162 *The KEYSTONE* September, 1927

Pioneer Cases Have Quality

Workmanship Beyond Question

For Complete Satisfaction and Pleased Customers Demand PIONEER CASES

PIONEER chooses to establish—and to hold what it has established—(your good will) by continuing to furnish Quality, Service, and a REAL SQUARE DEAL.

At no time do we intend to produce a Case that we feel would not do justice to the PIONEER NAME, and send it out as a fit representative of our organization. Irrespective of other manufacturers' manner of conducting their business, PIONEER will always represent the symbol of QUALITY and FAIR DEALING.

"PIONEER" WILL CONTINUE TO "PIONEER"—RETAIN WHAT IT HAS "PIONEERED" AND "PIONEER" FURTHER.

Ask Your Wholesaler

Pioneer Watch Case Company

48 West 48th Street, New York

FACTORY—150 CHESTNUT STREET, PROVIDENCE, R. I.

Keystone, September 1927

UNITED STATES PATENT OFFICE

Pioneer Watch Case Co., New York, N. Y.

Act of February 20, 1905

Application July 5, 1935, Serial No. 367,000

STATEMENT

To the Commissioner of Patents:

Pioneer Watch Case Co., a corporation duly organized and existing under and by virtue of the laws of the State of New York and located and doing business at 305 East 46th Street, in the city, county, and State of New York, has adopted and used the trade-mark shown in the accompanying drawing, for WATCH CASES, in Class 27, Horological instruments, and presents herewith five specimens of the trade-mark as actually used by the applicant upon the goods and requests that the same be registered in the United States Patent Office in accordance with the act of February 20, 1905, and hereby appoints William S. Gluck, registry No. 11,191, of 521 Fifth Avenue, New York, its attorney to prosecute this application for registration, to make alterations and amendments therein to enter opposition in its name against the registration of the same or any similar trade-mark in favor of other applicants and to reply to any opposition or petition for cancellation which may be filed against the registration of this trade-mark, to transact all business in the Patent Office connected therewith and the certificate to be granted thereupon, to sign its name to the drawing, and to receive the certificate of registration when issued.

The trade-mark has been used in said business of Pioneer Watch Case Co. since January 1, 1935.

The trade-mark is applied directly to the goods by stamping or imprinting the trade-mark thereon and by applying to the goods, or the package in which the goods are shipped a label upon which the trade-mark appears.

PIONEER WATCH CASE CO.,
By HERBERT I. KOLBERG,
President.

Pioneer's 1935 United States Trademark Registration

During the 1920s, Pioneer made various gold-filled watch cases for the ladies' market. In the early 1930s, the firm manufactured two men's wristwatch models for Illinois. The models bear identical designs. The casemaker, however, made them from two different unusual materials. Pioneer produced the standard Illinois Factory-Cased Seneca model (formerly known as the Blackhawk) in low-end base metal plated with chrome, while fashioning the other model, the Akron, in aluminum, as a prototype. (See Chapter 9 for discussion of these two models.)

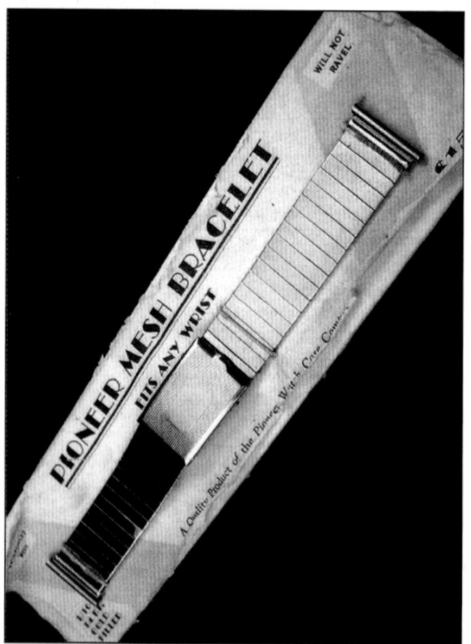

Pioneer also made metal bracelets, *Keystone*, April 1929

Pioneer advertisement, *Keystone*, July 1929

Around 1931 the Kolbergs split with Mason, and a few years later they decided to move the Pioneer plant to 305 East 48th Street in New York City. When the firm was incorporated in April of 1935, Herbert Kolberg was made president. In 1938 the plant moved to Mount Vernon, New York.[4]

PIONEER ROBBED

On February 4, 1935, the Pioneer Watch Case Company, then located at 305 East 48th Street, New York City, was robbed of gold plate and finished merchandise valued at $13,000. One hopes that none of the ultra-rare Akron Illinois cases were stolen!

Keystone, April 1929

In the mid-1930s, Herbert Kolberg began to seek patents for watch case models that he designed, and he continued to submit patent applications up until the time of his death in 1941. After Herbert's death, his son, Abner, assumed the presidency, but his brother Harry continued to help run the company as secretary and treasurer.[5]

Pioneer Watch Case Company Grew From Small Partnership

"The history of the Pioneer Watch Case Company, Inc., is only 11 years in length, but it encompasses a story of steady growth which has seen the firm advance from a small partnership employing nine workers at Providence, R.I., to a large modern factory in Mount Vernon housing 280 employees and conducting a million dollar a year business.

The firm was started in Providence in 1931 by the late Herbert I. Kolberg, who was assisted by his brother Harry. Several years later business had reached such proportions that the partners decided to shift to New York, setting up their plant at 305 East 46th Street.

"Herbert then lived in Mount Vernon, and the city and its industrial resources appealed so strongly to him that in 1938 the plant was moved here after the firm constructed its own factory, a modern fully-equipped plant at Hartford Avenue and Lyons Place, just off Third Street.

"Business gains increased after that as the new facilities of the factory helped step up production, and this year the firm confidently expects to run its income over the $1,000,000 mark.

"Herbert Kolberg was made president of the firm when it was incorporated in April of 1935. After he died Feb. 1, 1942, at the age of fifty-four, his place as president was taken by his son, Abner, who had joined the firm after being graduated from New York University and who had served as secretary up until his father's death. Harry Kolberg became treasurer and secretary of the corporation.

"The firm specializes in the manufacture of watch cases for nationally known watches and also for Swiss imports. It maintains a showroom at the International Building, Rockefeller Center, New York City. At present the plant also is engaged in some defense work."*

**Daily Argus* (Mount Vernon, NY), April 1, 1942. Article courtesy of the Westchester County Historical Society, Elmsford, NY.

Although the firm was most closely associated with Gruen, it also produced cases for Rolex. Evidently, Rolex commissioned Pioneer to produce watch cases during World War II. Pioneer manufactured the "Rolex Skyrocket" watch case and/or the Rolex Aviator cases for Canadian aviators headed overseas during the war; these models were marketed for fighter pilots. Rolex did not sign many of these cases, because allegedly it retained Pioneer to produce the cases in Canada to circumvent import duties.

Pioneer operated for about ten years after World War II but filed for bankruptcy on July 20, 1955.[6] Harry Kolberg, the remaining founder, died in 1963.

LEGAL NOTICES

UNITED STATES DISTRICT COURT—SOUTHERN DISTRICT OF NEW YORK
In the Matter of PIONEER WATCH CASE CO., INC. of Hartford & Lyons Place, Mt. Vernon, New York, Debtor No. 91128.

NOTICE IS HEREBY GIVEN that on the 20th day of July, 1955 the above named debtor filed its petition to effect an arrangement with its creditors under the provisions of Chapter XI of the Act of Congress relating to Bankruptcy and that a meeting of its creditors will be held before the undersigned Referee, at his Courtroom, 20 South Broadway, Yonkers, New York on the 23rd day of September, 1955 at 10:30 A. M. at which time creditors may attend, prove claims, file written acceptances of the proposed plan of arrangements and nominate a trustee. The debtor shall be examined and witnesses heard on any relevant matter. All applications for fees, costs and disbursements must be filed with the Referee on or before September 30, 1955.

NOTICE IS ALSO HEREBY GIVEN that the application to confirm the arrangement shall be filed with the Court on or before October 5, 1955. October 7, 1955 at 11:00 A. M. is fixed as the time for hearing on the confirmation and of such objections as may be made to the confirmation and as to whether the Debtor shall be adjudged bankrupt and bankruptcy proceeded with or the proceeding dismissed on any of the grounds specified in Section 376 of the Bankruptcy Act.

Accompanying this notice is a copy of the proposed plan of arrangement and a summary of the scheduled assets and liabilities.

Dated: Yonkers, New York,
September 7, 1955
ARTHUR J. DORAN
Referee in Bankruptcy
(9—-9)

Pioneer Watch Case Co. bankruptcy notice. *Daily Argus* (Mount Vernon, NY), 1955. Clipping courtesy of the Westchester County Historical Society, Elmsford, NY

Jacques Depollier and Son

In 1887, Jacques Depollier, along with L. Duval and J. Dubois, formed the Dubois Watch Case Company in Brooklyn, New York. In 1904, Dubois bought the firm of Andrew K. Shiebler and Son, another company known for making high-grade watch cases. When Depollier's son Charles joined his father in business, a new company was formed: Jacques Depollier and Son. Depollier also operated as the sales and merchandise division of the Dubois Watch Case Company.

In the late 1910s, Depollier had a special contractual relationship with the Waltham Watch Company and usually featured Waltham movements and dials in its many watch case advertisements. In these advertisements, Depollier frequently stated that the company was the "Manufacturer of High Class Specialties for Waltham Watches." According to Charles Moore in *Timing a Century,* Depollier's exclusive relationship for selling Waltham movements in Depollier patented cases ended in 1923;[7] however, Illinois expert L. Michael Fultz maintained that Depollier did not always follow this exclusive arrangement.[8]

Jacques Depollier, c. 1914

WHO OWNED WHOM?

Until now it was thought that Jacques Depollier and Son formed, owned and controlled the Dubois Watch Case Company. However, testimony was given in a 1919 patent infringement litigation by a member of the Dubois accounting staff that clarified this matter as follows.*

Plaintiff lawyers' questions to Clarence A. Walter:

Q24 I notice that these billheads and memoranda bear the name Jaques Depollier & Sons; what relation has that concern to the Du Bois Watch Case Company? A Jaques Depollier & Son is the sales division of the Du Bois Watch Case Company. The Du Bois Watch Case Company manufactures but Jaques Depollier & Son disposes of the merchandise, sells it.

Q25 Does the Du Bois Watch Case Company sell cases at retail? A No.

Q26 Does it sell complete watches? A No.

Q27 In what name are the watch cases and watches sold at retail? A Jaques Depollier & Sons.

Thus, surprisingly, Dubois owned and controlled Depollier not the reverse as commonly thought.

**Golden vs. Depollier,* June 1919 transcript.

DEPOLLIER'S ATELIERS

In a February 5, 1919 advertisement in the *Jewelers' Circular,* Jacques Depollier & Son touted its company as a group of "artists and craftsmen, leaders in all branches of the watch-case maker's, watchmaker's and jewelers Art of the old and modern schools."

Ateliers is the plural form of the French word meaning a workshop or studio, especially of an artist, artisan or designer.

The advertisement pointed out that the Depollier had the following departments:

Art Studio	Engraving
Designing	Chasing
Modeling	Engine Turning
Hand case-making	Enameling

18 THE JEWELERS' CIRCULAR-WEEKLY February 5, 1919.

The Home of Jacques Depollier & Son Dubois Watch Case Company

Exclusive Casings for Waltham Colonial "A" Waltham Opera Watches 7½ Ligne Waltham 10 Ligne

Patented Wrist Watches
Registered Trade Marks

The "D-D" UTILITY WATCH
The "D-D" KHAKI WATCH
Depollier MOISTURE WRISTY WATCH DUSTPROOF
Depollier THERMO WRIST WATCH
Depollier WATERPROOF and DUSTPROOF Watch
Miladi Militaire

All above have Unbreakable Non-Inflammable Glass with Double Clinched Bezel

Ladies Convertible
Disappearing Eye
"No Fuss" Clasp
Platinum Gold
Silver Nickel

Manufacturers of High Grade Watch Cases
Platinum for Solid Gold
American and Complicated Swiss Movements
High Grade Specialties for Waltham Watches

Depollier's Ateliers

represent without a doubt the only watch case manufacturing institution either in the United States or abroad that has assembled under one roof, a trained corps of the foremost artists and craftsmen, leaders in all branches of the watch-case maker's, watchmaker's and jeweler's Art of the old and modern schools.

These Artisans, furnished as they are with the best tools and requisites, have made it their lifelong study to produce only results which will bear the closest scrutiny from the standpoint of artistic merit and utility.

Departments: Art Studio, Designing, Modeling, Hand Case-making, High Grade Watch Repairing, Engraving, Chasing, Engine Turning, Enameling and Crystal Grinding *Regular and Odd Shapes.*

Double Clinched Bezel for Unbreakable Glass, Expansion Bracelet, "No-Fuss" Clasp for Silk and leather straps on Wrist Watches. Lapidary, Calibre Stone Cutting. Platinum Jewelry Department and Fancy Chain Makers.

The actual experience of *Depolliers Ateliers* covers more than Fifty Years both in Switzerland and America.

Ateliers
316 Herkimer Street
Brooklyn, N.Y.

Salesrooms
Fifteen Maiden Lane
New York City

A February 5, 1919 Depollier advertisement with an image of the production facility and a list of some of its trade names, along with other information

Charles Depollier took over the active management of the companies after the death of his father on August 16, 1914, from injuries suffered in a car accident. Jacques was seventy years old at the time. Subsequently, Charles designed some of the innovative watch cases offered by Depollier.

Charles Leon Depollier was born in Switzerland shortly before his parents immigrated to the United States. Well known for his waterproof watch patents, he is credited with perfecting the innovative Depollier Waterproof and Dustproof watch model. Depollier had several patents issued for his waterproof designs and also patented other watch-related items. Filing as Charles L. Depollier of the Dubois Watch Case Company in Brooklyn, New York, he applied for patents for various wristwatch cases, bracelets, straps and fasteners. The U.S. Patent Office granted many of these patents, and subsequently the designs were put into production.

Depollier was perhaps the first American watchmaker to sell complete watches and was one of the few casemakers to do so. Since the company advertised directly to consumers, its sales were not exclusively through jobbers.

Waterproof Patents. World War I spurred Depollier's research into water resistance and waterproof technology for wristwatches. Fultz pointed out that work toward this goal continued after the armistice.[9] The designs necessary for a waterproof watch reached fruition in 1918 and 1919. The company combined these ideas into the **Depollier Waterproof and Dustproof Watch** (see Chapter 9).

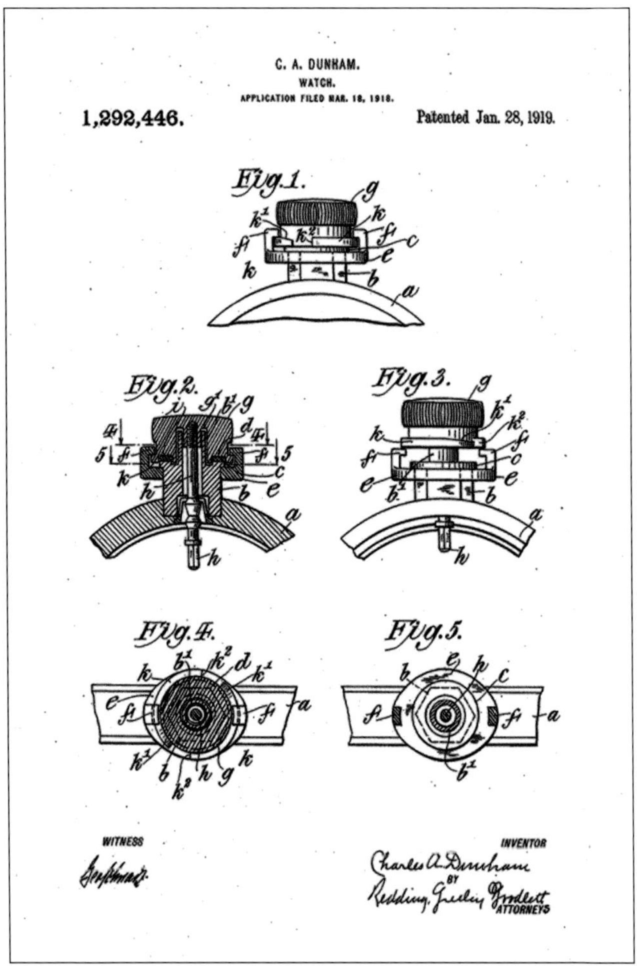

Dunham Crown Patent, U.S. Patent No. 1,292,446, January 28, 1919

Owing to the Depollier's close relationship with Waltham, the Depollier Waterproof and Dustproof watch was initially marketed with Waltham's 3/0 size 15-jewel movement. The watch sported a porcelain dial, luminous Arabic numerals and luminous hands. However, Depollier later sold his waterproof cases to various jobbers, some of whom inserted Illinois movements and dials.

According to Fultz, the Illinois Watch Company purchased some of the Depollier waterproof cases for testing, and perhaps sold some of the Depollier waterproof cases to the United States military.[10] One Depollier advertisement claims, "This Depollier Waterproof watch case is the same as adopted by the United States Army since the War." Factory-Cased Illinois/Depollier waterproof watches do exist, with "U.S.A." engraved on the gold discs on the case back.

1918
HISTORICAL NOTES

- The first case of Spanish Flu occurs, starting a devastating worldwide pandemic.
- Congress authorizes time zones and Daylight Savings Time.
- The Supreme Court rules child labor laws unconstitutional.
- Samuel Riddle buys Man O' War for $5,000.
- Sergeant Alvin York single-handedly kills 25 and captures 135 German soldiers.
- Germany surrenders, ending World War I.

Depollier inside case back for an Illinois "D-D" Utility watch

American Watch Casemakers *	
Name	**Year Founded**
American Watch Case Co.	1893
Bates & Bacon	1884
Bay State Watch Case Co.	1889
Bell Watch Case Co.	1890
Brooklyn Watch Case Co.	1865
Camm Watch Case Co.	1890
Courvoisier-Wilcox Mfg. Co.	1875
Crescent Watch Case Co.	1882
Dennison Watch Case Co.	1874
Dubois Watch Case Co.	1887
Dueber Watch Case Mfg. Co.	1860
Elgin Giant Watch Case Co.	1910
Essex Watch Case Co.	1884
Giles Bros. & Co.	1860
Gruen Watch Case Co.	1902
Gruen National Watch Case Co.	1902
H. Muhr's Sons	1880
Illinois Watch Case Co.	1886
Jeannot & Schiebler	1880
Joseph Fahys & Co.	1857
Keystone Watch Case Co.	1853
Ladd Watch Case Co.	1865
Newark Watch Case Material Co.	1874
North American Watch Co.	1902
Northwestern Watch Case Co.	1880
Pennsylvania Watch Case Co.	1908
Philadelphia Watch Case Co.	1884
Queen City Watch Case Mfg. Co.	1896
Roy Watch Case Co.	1885
Solidarity Watch Case Co.	1885
Star Watch Case Co.	1897
Wadsworth Watch Case Co.	1892

*http://mb.nawcc.org/showwiki.php?title=Category:Watch_case_makers

The Illinois Watch Case Company

Brothers Max and Sol Eppenstein founded the Illinois Watch Case Company (IWCCo) in 1886 as an outgrowth of the Chicago jewelry firm of M. C. Eppenstein & Co. Max served as president while Sol held the position of vice president. In 1890, Max agreed to move his company to Elgin in exchange for land and a building on Dundee Avenue, both provided by the city. In return, the firm agreed to employ at least one hundred employees its first year, fifty more the second year, and an additional fifty the third year.

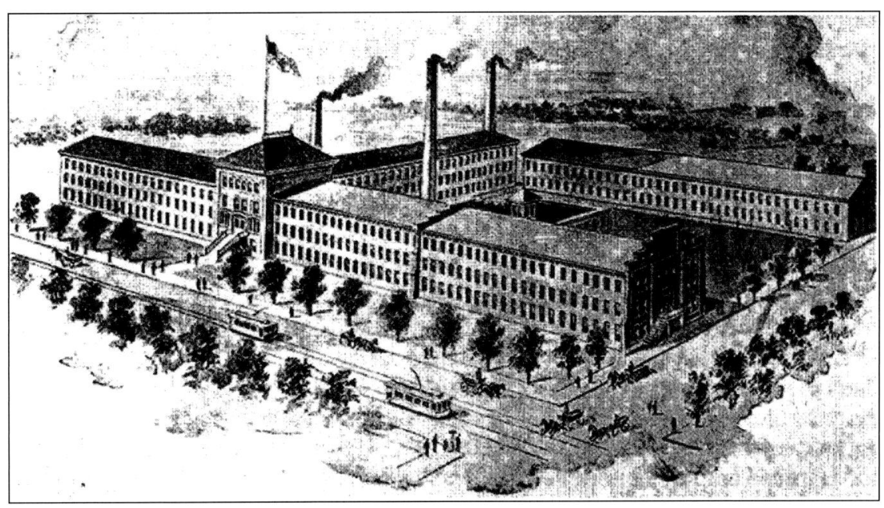

The Illinois Watch Case Company in 1901

THE ILLINOIS WATCH CASE CO.

The business of the Illinois Watch Case Company was founded in 1886 by M. C. Eppenstein, native of Kolmar, Germany, who at the age of eighteen went to Australia and began to handle jewelry. In 1870 he came to this country and entered the wholesale jewelry business in Chicago. In 1886 he began the manufacture of watch cases. Associated with him was his brother, Sol C. Eppenstein. They established their plant in Elgin, Illinois, and the company within a short time expanded into one of the leading watch case manufacturers in the country. The Elgin American Manufacturing Company was organized about 1912 as a subsidiary concern manufacturing novelties, and this also grew into one of the leading concerns in that branch.

M. C. Eppenstein died in 1921, and his son, Louis A. Eppenstein, is the present head of the Illinois Watch Case Company and the Elgin American Manufacturing Company. His career with the company dates back many years, having started in the shipping department and worked his way through the various departments to secure a first-hand knowledge of the business.

Keystone, June 1932

The Eppensteins intended to change the firm's name to the Elgin Watch Case Company. In response, the Elgin National Watch Company quickly moved to form a corporation with the same name, owing to their concern about possible industry confusion. Then Eppenstein countered by organizing the National Watch Case Company of Elgin.

The Elgin National Watch Company tried to prevent the Illinois Watch Case Company from using the name "Elgin," claiming ownership as a legitimate trademark. Many lawsuits and years later, the legal dispute ended up before the United States Supreme Court. In 1901 the Supreme Court, reversed an 1898 United States Circuit Court decision, ruling that the name "Elgin" cannot be trademarked as it was a geographical description and existed before the Elgin National Watch Company.

Apr 6, 1898. THE JEWELERS' CIRCULAR Courtesy NAWCC Library 21

Important.

Trade Mark Decision of Especial Interest to the Watch Trade.

In a suit brought by the Elgin National Watch Company to restrain the Illinois Watch Case Company from using the word "Elgin" upon watch cases made and sold by the latter, Judge Showalter, of the United States Circuit Court for the Northern District of Illinois, in a decision rendered March 31st, 1898, decided that the said word "Elgin" is a legitimate trade mark and that its use in connection with watches belongs to and is the exclusive property of the Elgin National Watch Company. Under this decision, any infringement of our rights will subject the infringers to prompt prosecution in the United States Courts.

Elgin National Watch Co.

Notice published on April 6, 1898, in the *Jewelers' Circular* by the Elgin National Watch Company concerning its victory in the United States Circuit Court decision. This was subsequently reversed by the United States Supreme Court in 1901.

Meanwhile, the Illinois Watch Case Company prospered. Within a year of its arrival in Elgin, it employed about two hundred fifty workers and produced about nine hundred pocket watch cases daily. It doubled its plant capacity before the decade was over.

Around the beginning of the twentieth century, Jacob Franks, Sol's brother-in-law, joined IWCCo. In a reorganization, he became president, while Max served as general manager. Franks apparently brought additional capital to the enterprise. In 1901, Franks and the Eppensteins purchased the financially strapped Rockford Watch Company of Rockford, Illinois. IWCCo sold Rockford pocket watches through its Chicago sales offices. The Rockford venture finally closed its doors in 1915, having produced close to half a million watches while under IWCCo control.

An Illinois Watch Case Co. signed movement. IWCCo at times sold its cases with its own signed movements and dials on them. The movement and dial were made by the Illinois Watch Company (see Appendix 5)

Illinois Man Shoots George B. Jennings in New York City.

New York, Feb. [illegible]. George B. Jennings, president of the Jennings Adjustable Shade company, was shot and killed Thursday in his office in Brooklyn by Frank McNamara, superintendent of one of the departments of the Illinois Watch company's factory at Elgin, Ill. According to two of Jenning's clerks, who were in the office, Jennings and McNamara were engaged in a heated argument, the subject of which is unknown, when McNamara thrust a revolver against Jennings and fired, the bullet passing through the heart. McNamara threw away the revolver and ran into the street, pursued by two clerks, who captured him and turned him over to the police. McNamara refused to say why he shot Jennings.

The Daily Telegram (Eau Claire, WI), February 19, 1904; image from *newspapers.com*. Several violent actions were associated with individuals connected to the IWCCo. This article reports that one of the company's superintendents had shot and killed a man in Brooklyn, NY. (Newspapers often confused the IWCCo with the Illinois Watch Company, and it sometimes takes a mention of the location for the reader to tell which one it was.)

LEOPOLD-LOEB CRIME

Jacob Franks, a principal in the Illinois Watch Case Company at one time, is tied tragically to the "Crime of the Century," as it was his son Bobby who at the age of fourteen was kidnapped and killed in 1924 by Leopold and Loeb in their attempt to commit a "perfect crime."

"Bobby" Franks with his father Jacob, sometime after 1920

MACHINE GUN BANDITS GET $100,000 LOOT

Four Automobile Loads of Gangsters With Yeggdom's Latest Weapon Attack Elgin Watch Company Plant.

PARTY OF FIFTEEN MEN USES EXCEPTIONAL STRATEGY

One Squad Works on Safe, Another Guards Approaches, and Third Keeps Watchmen on Regular Rounds.

GOLD, TAKEN IN ELGIN ROBBERY FOUND IN CREEK

Gleam of Metal Seen by Boy Leads to Finding Some of Loot

Chicago, May 25— (AP) —A "gold rush" was in progress today at Schaumburg, where in a creek a boy found gold identified as part of the $50,000 loot taken by robbers from the Illinois Watch Case Company at Elgin.

A large section of the population of Schaumburg and curiosity seekers today sought to help detectives "prospect" in the creek where Roy Nebl, 19, first saw the metal.

On the night of April 8, 1927, a gang of fifteen bandits, in four automobiles, overpowered five night watchmen and broke into the vaults of the Illinois Watch Case Company and looted what was said to be about $100,000 in sheet and gold brick from the company, located in Elgin, Illinois. Reports were in newspapers all over the U.S., including the one here from the *Dunkirk Evening Observer* (Dunkirk, NY), April 9, 1927; image from *newspapers.com.* Later reports revealed that this bold robbery had been an inside job, and that the loss estimate was actually $50,000. The robbers must have found part of the loot from the IWCCo too hot to handle. About six weeks later, a boy found some of the gold partially buried in a creekbed. *Dixon Evening Telegraph* (Dixon, IL), May 25, 1927; image from *newspapers.com.*

With the onset of World War I, the demand for wristwatches skyrocketed. The Illinois Watch Case Company met this need with both round and cushion-shaped watch cases in gold, gold-filled, silver and nickel. During the Great War, the Illinois Watch Company produced Factory-Cased watches in IWCCo cases for the United States Army. The army even used some of these watches at the beginning of World War II. The army watches represented the only time that the Illinois Factory-Cased its watches in IWCCo cases.

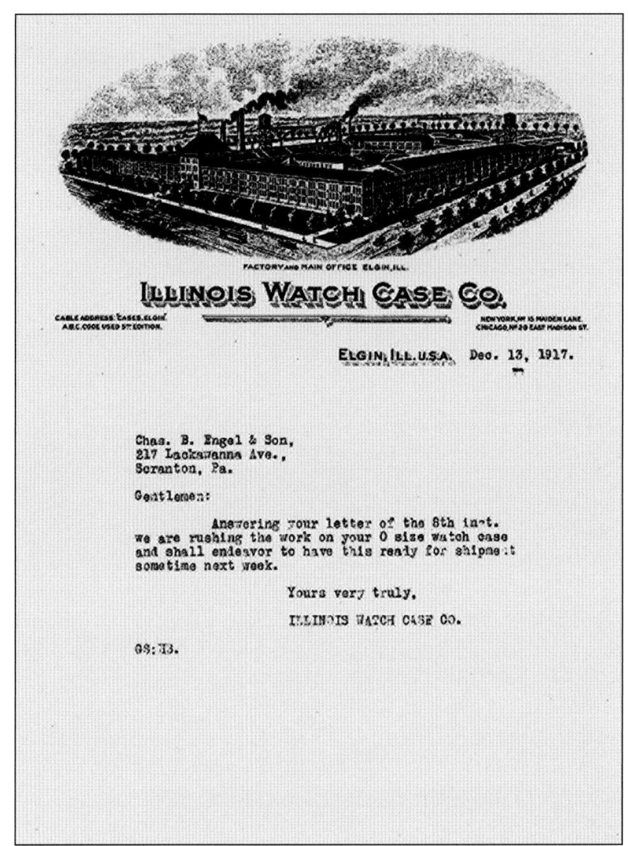

FACTORY AND MAIN OFFICE ELGIN, ILL.

ILLINOIS WATCH CASE CO.

CABLE ADDRESS: "CASES, ELGIN" A.B.C. CODE USED 5TH EDITION.

NEW YORK, Nº 15 MAIDEN LANE. CHICAGO, Nº 29 EAST MADISON ST.

ELGIN, ILL. U.S.A. Dec. 13, 1917.

Chas. B. Engel & Son,
217 Lackawanna Ave.,
Scranton, Pa.

Gentlemen:

Answering your letter of the 8th inst. we are rushing the work on your 0 size watch case and shall endeavor to have this ready for shipment sometime next week.

Yours very truly,

ILLINOIS WATCH CASE CO.

GS:HB.

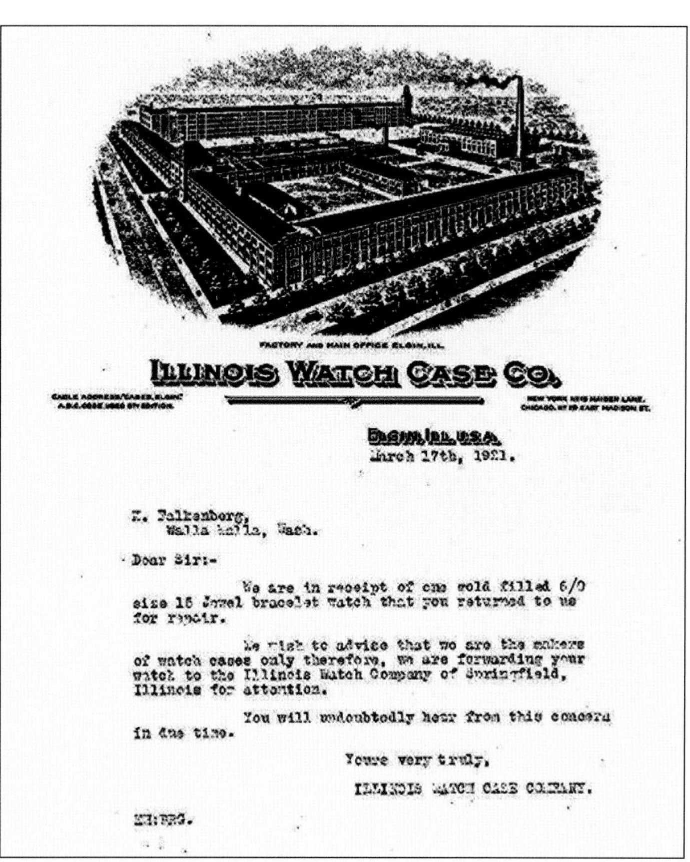

FACTORY AND MAIN OFFICE ELGIN, ILL.

ILLINOIS WATCH CASE CO.

ELGIN, ILL. U.S.A.
March 17th, 1921.

H. Falkenberg,
Walla Walla, Wash.

Dear Sir:-

We are in receipt of one gold filled 6/0 size 15 Jewel bracelet watch that you returned to us for repair.

We wish to advice that we are the makers of watch cases only therefore, we are forwarding your watch to the Illinois Watch Company of Springfield, Illinois for attention.

You will undoubtedly hear from this concern in due time.

Yours very truly,

ILLINOIS WATCH CASE COMPANY.

Two Illinois Watch Case Co. letters, from 1917 and 1921, respectively.

IWCCo Factory, 1928 postcard

Complimentary watch case opener from IWCCo

82 THE JEWELERS' CIRCULAR July 12, 1928

MASTERPIECES of Gold and Silver

will be on display at our Booth at the Third Annual Jewelry [and Allied Trades] Show

Chicago, August 6th–10th.

Visit our Factories at Elgin, Illinois

A cordial invitation is extended to all.

Illinois Watch Case Company
Elgin American Manufacturing Co.

NEW YORK · CHICAGO · CINCINNATI · SAN FRANCISCO · TORONTO · LONDON

Jewelers' Circular, July 12, 1928

Admiral Evans, in an IWWCo case

When Max Eppenstein passed away in 1921, his brother Sol succeeded him as president. Sol remained president through the decade of the 1920s. In 1931, Louis A. Eppenstein, Max's son, took over the firm from Sol. At that point, Louis had worked in the company for thirty-four years.

L. A. Eppenstein Heads Illinois Watch Case Company

An agreement for the transfer of complete control of the Illinois Watch Case Company, Elgin, Illinois, to the M. C. Eppenstein estate, was concluded on February 26. The M. C. Eppenstein estate through its administrator, L. A. Eppenstein, vice-president of the company and son of the late founder, thus acquires the interests of President S. C. Eppenstein and A. J. Franks.

Under the new regime L. A. Eppenstein will become president and treasurer and Eugene Edelstein, now general manager, will become vice-president. H. H. Loomer will continue as secretary and Edward Howard as general superintendent. S. C. Eppenstein who was head of the company for the past eleven years will retire and, as yet, has made no announcement of his plans for the future.

The business of the Illinois Watch Case Company and its subsidiary, the Elgin American Manufacturing Company, will be continued as in the past. Watch cases and novelties will be manufactured and a gradual increase in production is planned. In normal times the Illinois Watch Case Company employs upward of 1500 men and women.

L. A. Eppenstein who now becomes president, is son of the late M. C. Eppenstein and nephew of S. C. Eppenstein. His career with the company dates back thirty-four years when, as a youth, he entered the shipping department.

Eugene Edelstein, the new vice-president, has been with the company for forty-five years, beginning at the age of fifteen with the late M C. Eppenstein when the concern was operating in Chicago as a wholesale jewelry business and watch case manufacturer.

Mr. Loomer has a record of thirty-four years with the company, while Mr. Howard has seen forty years of service.

The Illinois Watch Case Company was founded by M. C. Eppenstein in Chicago in 1885. The industry was located in Elgin in 1888 and branched out from the manufacture of watch cases several years ago to the making of novelties of many types, this phase of the business being conducted by the Elgin American Manufacturing Company, a subsidiary.

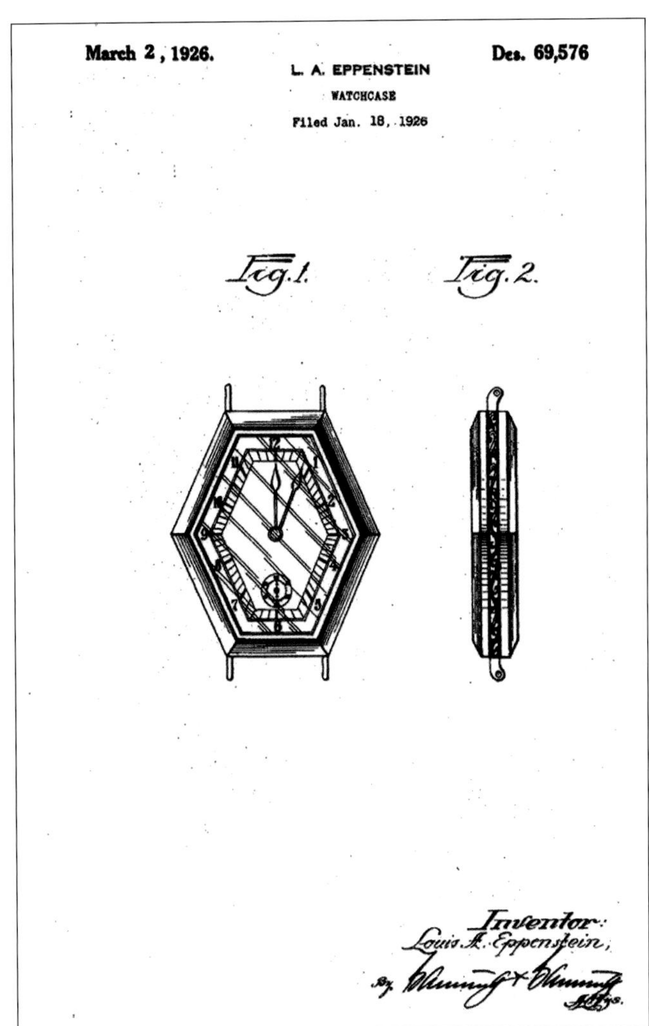

L. A. Eppenstein patent for IWCCo

Announcement about L. A. Eppenstein taking over the casemaking company started by his father, Max; *Keystone*, April 1931

The IWCCo maintained a close relationship with the Elgin National Watch Company throughout its existence. Between the company itself and its subsidiaries, IWCCo produced jewelry, lockets and cigarette lighters, as well as the well-known "Elgin American" Art Deco style ladies' compacts in a variety of shapes and styles. In World War II, the company won an Army-Navy Excellence award for its production of mortar shells and war-related materials. The company closed its doors in approximately 1963, a victim of foreign competition.

IWCCo inside case back for an Illinois Military model

IWCCo Tivoli inside back of an Illinois Locke

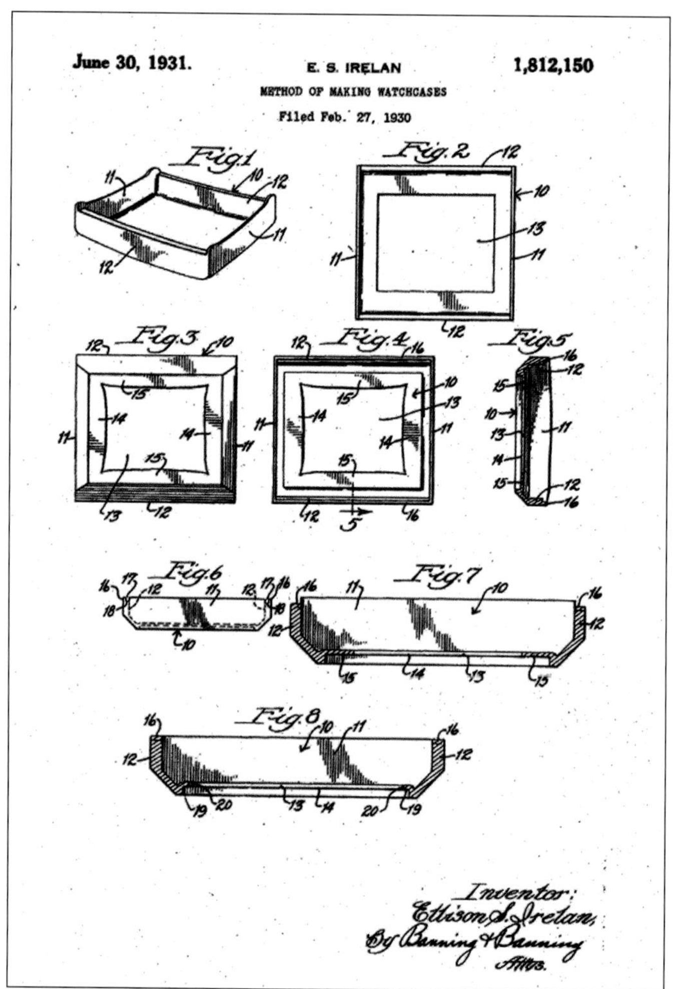

IWCCo watch case making patent

ILLINOIS WATCH CASE COMPANY TRADE NAMES

Some of the well-known registered trade names used by the Illinois Watch Case Company were:

- Elgin Giant
- Elgin Pride
- Tivoli
- Spartan
- Elgin Commander
- Elgin America
- Elgin
- USA

The Elgin Giant, Tivoli and Spartan names can be found on Illinois Generic Period men's wristwatch cases.

The Star Watch Case Company

In 1898, Otto A. Starke and Fred Hermann founded the Illinois Watch Case Company in Elgin, Illinois. Alfred W. Church joined in 1902 as a third partner. Confusing as it may seem, the founders originally called the company by the same name as the watch case company founded by the Eppensteins. Initially, the firm made pocket watch cases for the Elgin National Watch Company.

In a few years the firm relocated to Ludington, Michigan, changing its name to the Star Watch Case Company and incorporating on February 7, 1905, with assets of $257,243.83. Officers included Otto A. Starke, president; Fred Hermann, vice president; Warren Antoine Cartier, secretary; and Alfred W. Church, treasurer. The company had chosen to move to Ludington because of the incentives offered by the city of Ludington, which included providing land for the factory without charge, though with the stipulation that the company's payroll must reach $500,000 within ten years. The payroll surpassed the stipulated figure in less than six years, and at the ten-year mark was approaching $1 million.[11]

Star opened its national sales offices in New York City at 37 Maiden Lane and in the Heyworth Building in Chicago. It adopted a new trademark: a star with a two-headed eagle.[12]

The Ludington plant opened in 1906 and the company's operations in Elgin closed down. Star moved one hundred employees and their families as well as machines and inventory to Ludington. The rest of the assets in Elgin were liquidated.[13]

Franz Baumgartner, front row (with mustache), was the key engraver at the Star plant in 1906.

Stamping presses in the Star plant, c. 1900s

Early Star Watch Case factory, c. 1906

Final Star Watch Case factory, c. 1940s

By 1913, Star employed about 150 employees, making it Ludington's largest employer. Star's factory and administrative office on South Rath Avenue stood three stories tall, and over time it expanded to over 70,000 square feet. Star made watch cases for Elgin, Gruen, Hamilton, Longines, Manistee, Omega and Pulsar, among others.[14]

Until World War I, Star made only pocket watch cases. Star produced its first wristwatch cases during World War I.

Star advertisement for its military cases, *Jewelers' Circular*, January 30, 1918

In the late 1920s, as cases became more complex, Star employed 475 employees. At first, its cases were solid gold or gold-filled, but Star also made lesser quality cases of rolled gold, gold plate, sterling silver, and nickel silver and brass. Later, it made chrome-plated ones.[15]

In 1927, Starke's son, Otto A. Starke, Jr., joined the company as junior vice president. (As a mechanical engineering student at Cornell University, he had been elected to Tau Beta Pi, the honorary engineering society in 1926 as a junior, so the position with Star was presumably his first job after graduation.[16]) When the elder Starke died in 1929, the younger Starke, at the age of twenty-four, became the president and treasurer. Under his leadership, Star successfully rode out the Depression by concentrating on less expensive cases. The firm's prosperity would last for another forty years.[17]

Otto A. Starke, 1929

Star inside case back for an Illinois Ace model

Surprisingly, pocket watch cases remained 90% of Star's production up to 1938.[18] Star seemed to have had a different business model than most other casemakers, and didn't change it when other casemakers changed.

In the 1930s, when most case manufacturers supplied their products directly to watch manufacturers, Star sold primarily through jewelers. All casemakers had done that before World War I; Star continued to do so. For this reason, Star consistently advertised in jewelers' trade papers. After the advent of factory-cased wristwatches, Star continued its old sales methods. For pocket watches (and soon all watches), jewelers derived some income from replacing old watch cases. Jewelers could offer Star cases when the original cases wore out or when the owner desired a more expensive or (more commonly) a less expensive case. For this reason, Star appeared to be a prudent alternative for the financially strapped public, and the recasing business process helped get Star and the jewelers through the Depression.

Upon the entry of the United States into World War II, Star converted a portion of its factory to make brass compass cases, small weapons and submarine parts. Star also manufactured components of military navigational aids during the war. One such component was the top-secret Norden bombsight, used for dropping bombs accurately from airplanes.[19]

During the war, the company also earned a reputation for making quality stainless steel cases for military watches and compasses. Star received several large military contracts, producing the cases for the Bulova A-17A and 3818B hacking aviation watches as well as for the rare Hamilton "Grade II" watch. These watches are considered among the finest quality United States military watches ever made. Employment peaked at 550 during the war. Unfortunately, the war years were also a period of low profits because of high corporate taxes designed to eliminate war profiteering. This, and the inability of the company to invest in new machinery, led to severe financial problems after the war.

HAMILTON CASEMAKERS

Hamilton used Star infrequently before World War II in men's watches. Its first use of Star for men's watches was the 1936 Taylor model. The only other pre-war one was the 1937 Talbot model. Hamilton used Fahys initially and then Wadsworth for most early watches. For its more notable designs (such as the Meadowbrook, Piping Rock, Coronado, Glendale, Spur), it used Schwab & Wuischpard after 1928. For high-end gold, Hamilton also used Solidarity and Perrin.

In 1948, at the urging of the Elgin National Watch Co., Star merged with another casemaker, Schwaibold and Northman Co., of New York. However, the name of the company remained the Star Watch Case Company. During the post-war years, Star also made watch cases for Elgin, Gruen, Hamilton, Longines-Wittnauer and Waltham.[20]

In the 1960s the fortunes of the Star Watch Case Company followed those of the rest of America's watch industry. Competition from the Swiss and Japanese with their newer, more efficient manufacturing factories, led to decreased sales and a bleak future. Still, Star continued to produce very high-quality cases through the 1970s, including the cases for the first Pulsar digital watch and the innovative Hewlett-Packard calculator watch.

In 1972, after forty-three years as president of Star Watch Case Co., O. A. Starke, Jr. sold the company to Edgar A. Schwaibold. The new owner acquired all shares of the company and became its president and treasurer.[21]

In 1978, Omega contracted with Star to make the cases for the legendary Speedmaster Professional, one of which was worn by astronaut Eugene A. Cernan on a trip to the moon. (This watch is commonly referred to as the "Moonwatch.") Omega chose Star, in part, to comply with a NASA procurement rule that 50% of the parts used in any watch for the space program be made in the United States. But Omega must have been pleased with the quality, because it also contracted with Star to produce gold-filled cases for dress watches.[22]

In 1979, Precision Watch Case Co., a subsidiary of the Swiss watchmaking conglomerate SSIH, purchased Star. Three years later, Precision shut down production at the Ludington facility. Operations ceased on April 30, 1982.[23]

The last cases produced by Star were apparently used for the very first Hamilton reissue, when they launched a limited edition remake of the Boulton model in a yellow gold-filled case with a mechanical movement.

STAR CASE GRADES*

Case grade materials included:

- Star, gold-filled, guaranteed for 20 years as late as November 1906; 25 years by April 1909
- Defiance, gold-filled, guaranteed for 10 years
- Majestic, gold-filled, guaranteed for 5 years
- Stellar, 10K rolled gold plate
- Scepter, gold-filled or rolled gold plate
- Excellence, silver

*http://mb.nawcc.org/showwiki.php?title=Star_Watch_Case_Co.

Illinois Generic watches can be found in Star's Stellar and Scepter cases. The term "Scepter" came to be generically known to mean gold-filled.

GOLD "DUST"

"When the Star Watch Case Company factory closed after 75 years, it was believed that there might be a substantial accumulation of gold [dust] embedded in and between the boards of the wood floors. The floorboards, which covered the concrete subfloor, were taken up and burned to separate and reclaim the gold. It was said that $80,000 worth of gold was salvaged from the ashes."*

*Jack Linahan, "Star Watch Case Company 1897–1982," NAWCC *Bulletin*, No. 360 (February 2006), p. 7.

A list of Star's registered trade names

STAR GOLD

According to Star Watch Case Company historian Jack Linahan, "The material of choice for watch cases has always been gold, either solid or filled. Star ordered its gold in 24 karat bars from dealers who shipped the gold to Ludington. The bars were stored in a local bank until needed at the factory.

"Once the gold was brought to the factory, the bars were stamped with the Star trademark. Then they were placed in Star's vault until the alloy was added to reduce the quality to 10, 14 or 18 karats. They always had about $200,000 worth of gold on hand.

"An employee once managed to steal some of the gold bars. He took them to Chicago and tried to sell them to a pawn shop. The pawn shop owner took one look at the trademark on the bars and called the police. The thief, of course, went to jail."*

*Jack Linahan, "Star Watch Case Company 1897–1982," NAWCC *Bulletin*, No. 360 (February 2006), p 6.

TIME GUARANTEES ON WATCH CASES

In February 1930 a contingent of watch case manufacturers met with the Federal Trade Commission in New York City where they developed resolutions to agree on the official minimum standard time guarantees for cases (e.g., 20- and 10-year guarantees). Some of the key industry persons in attendance were:

O. A. Starke – Star Watch Case Company

H. M. Stegman – Wadsworth Watch Case Company

Louis Eppenstein – Illinois Watch Case Company

J. Fahys Cook – Joseph Fahys & Co.

Fred E. Hyatt – Keystone Watch Case Company

Herbert Kolberg – Pioneer Watch Case Company

All of these companies supplied cases to the Illinois Watch Company at one time or another.

Fred E. Hyatt, vice president of the Keystone Watch Case Company, c. 1930

The North American Watch Company

The North American Watch Company (or "NAWCo," as it was called) manufactured watch cases in the former factory of the Bell Watch Case Company of Mansfield, Ohio. NAWCo's trademark featured an outline of the continent of North America.

Like Depollier, NAWCo also served as a dealer in watch cases and completed watches. (The movements were made by other companies.) According to a 1902 advertisement in the *Jewelers' Circular*, the company incorporated and commenced operations in 1902. NAWCo stayed in business as late as 1925, when it was still advertising in *The Railway Conductor*, the journal of the *Order of Railway Conductors*.

Mail order retailers favored the NAWCo "Heavy Duty" case. For example, O. F. Bale used it to house Bunn Specials; Burlington Watch Company selected the "Heavy Duty" for its "Bull Dog" watches; and the South Bend/Studebaker Watch Companies cased their "Royal Order" in the "Heavy Duty." At least two Illinois men's wristwatch models came in NAWCo cases; the **Ongard** and the **Ongard Off-Set** (see Chapter 9).

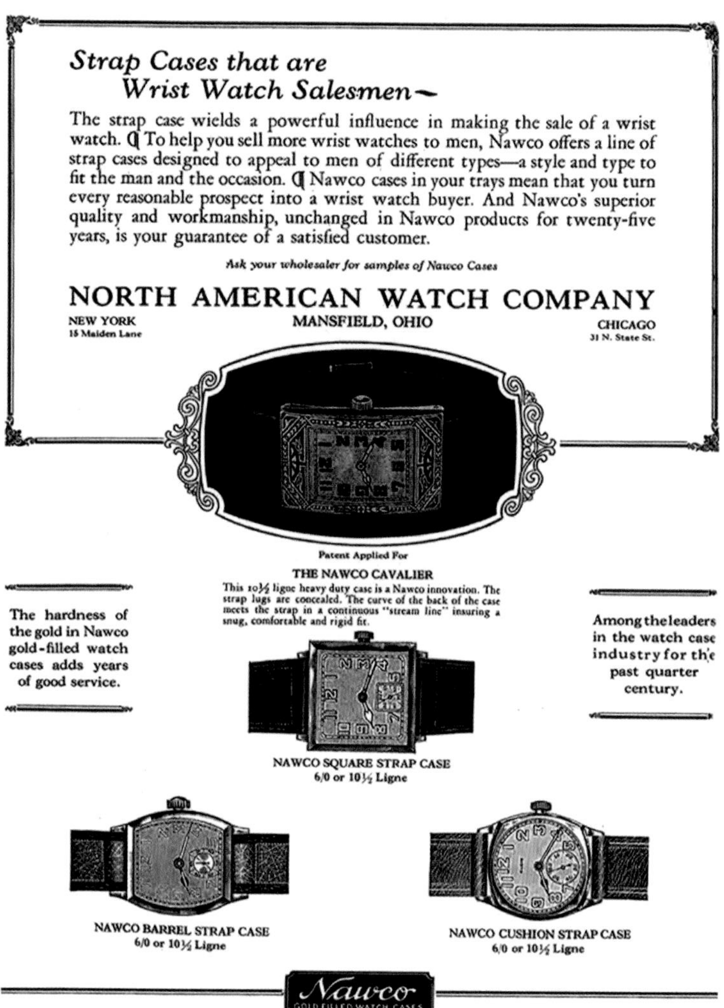

Keystone, October 1927

Jewelers' Circular-Weekly, February 1919

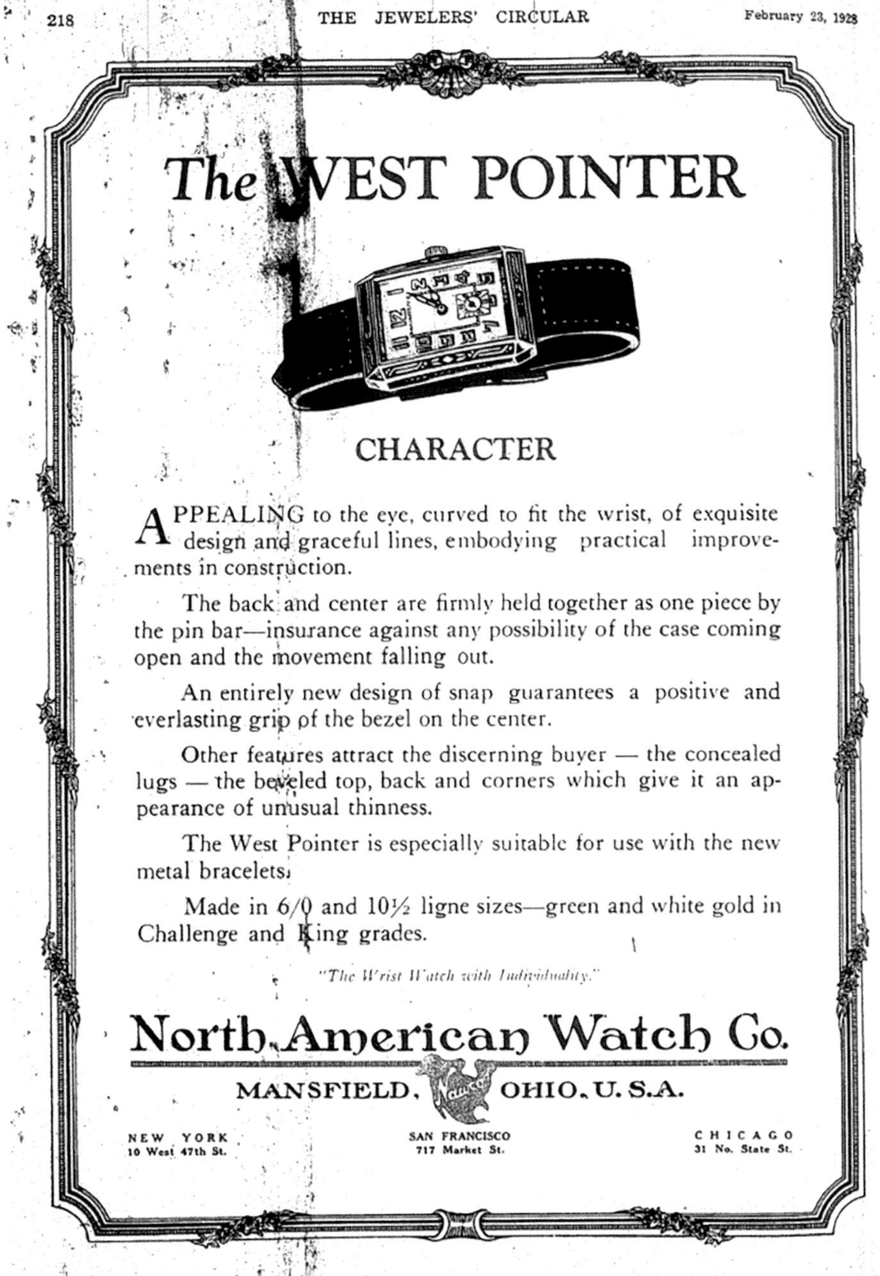

218 THE JEWELERS' CIRCULAR February 23, 1928

The West Pointer

CHARACTER

APPEALING to the eye, curved to fit the wrist, of exquisite design and graceful lines, embodying practical improvements in construction.

The back and center are firmly held together as one piece by the pin bar—insurance against any possibility of the case coming open and the movement falling out.

An entirely new design of snap guarantees a positive and everlasting grip of the bezel on the center.

Other features attract the discerning buyer — the concealed lugs — the beveled top, back and corners which give it an appearance of unusual thinness.

The West Pointer is especially suitable for use with the new metal bracelets.

Made in 6/0 and 10½ ligne sizes—green and white gold in Challenge and King grades.

"The Wrist Watch with Individuality."

North American Watch Co.

MANSFIELD, OHIO, U.S.A.

NEW YORK 10 West 47th St. | SAN FRANCISCO 717 Market St. | CHICAGO 31 No. State St.

Jewelers' Circular, February 23, 1928

The NAWCo Ongard wristwatches, with their distinctive spiral cutout, were the most unusual of the Armored-Cased/Cut Bezel watches offered for sale.

A North American Watch Company inside case back, signed "Ongard" and showing the company's trademark

Manheimer Watch Company

Born in Kentucky in 1853, Louis Manheimer clerked at the Indianapolis watch, clock and jewelry firm of J. H. Colclazer while still in his teens. His brother, Joseph, born a year earlier in Indiana, kept books for their uncles' clothing store, Dessar Brothers & Company, also in Indianapolis. In 1875 the brothers joined to form the wholesale jewelry firm of Louis Manheimer & Brothers. The Manheimers remained in Indianapolis for the next decade before moving their business to Chicago. Among other items, they offered pocket watch cases to house the growing number of watches being sold by jewelers.

The Manheimers also bought watches in bulk from such manufacturers as Hamilton, Waltham and Illinois, which they then combined with their own cases for wholesale to jewelers. They branded their Hamilton watches "Thor" (which is not to be confused with Hamilton's mid-twentieth-century shield-shape "Thor" man's wristwatch). The operation expanded to New York City, maintaining offices at both 31 North State Street in Chicago and 35 Maiden Lane in New York.

On January 2, 1923, they split on geographic lines into two separate corporations. The Chicago entity was called Louis Manheimer & Son Co., with the following officers: Louis Manheimer, president; J. H. Manheimer, vice-president; and E. A. Manheimer, secretary. The New York corporation was called Louis Manheimer and Brothers with the following officers: William S. Manheimer, president; Bertram H. Manheimer, vice-president; and Joseph C. Goodman, secretary. In that same year, Joseph passed away; Louis died a year later.

A notice in the December 22, 1927 issue of the *Jewelers' Circular* announced that the Louis Manheimer & Son Co. would change its name to the Manheimer Watch Company. The Manheimer Watch Company, a wholesaler of American watches, was incorporated under the laws of Illinois on December 17, 1927.

We take pleasure in announcing
that after January 1, 1928

Louis Manheimer & Son Co.
will be succeeded by
Manheimer Watch Company

THE personnel of the organization will remain the same as heretofore, with the exception that Mr. Julian H. Manheimer, President of the company, will retire and will not be connected with the new company. The officers of the new corporation will be as follows:

President	EDWARD A. MANHEIMER
First Vice President	ARTHUR E. MANHEIMER
Second Vice President	WILLIAM SHAPIRO
Treasurer	ARTHUR E. MANHEIMER
Secretary	HELEN A. CROWLEY

WE FEEL confident that the pleasant business relationships which it has been our privilege to enjoy for more than fifty years will continue. Such changes in policy as are in contemplation are all designed to enable us to render more prompt, efficient and complete service to our customers. We desire to express our appreciation for the consideration shown us in the past, and to assure all in the trade of our full and hearty cooperation in the future.

LOUIS MANHEIMER & SON CO.

MANHEIMER WATCH COMPANY
Wholesalers of American Watches Since 1875
THIRTY ONE NORTH STATE STREET · CHICAGO
Successors

Announcement of the change of name of Louis Manheimer & Son Co. to the Manheimer Watch Company, *Keystone*, January 1928

THE MANHEIMER WATCH CO.

1884 saw the coming into Chicago of the Manheimer Watch Co., still a large factor in its field. The business was started in 1875 in Indianapolis, Ind., by Louis Manheimer, who had a window display, a small show case, and a work-bench in a clothing store. He sold watches and jewelry at retail, mostly to the clothing store's customers. The jewelry did not sell as well as the watches, so Mr. Manheimer packed it up and disposed of it. The watch business was continued and later, when he moved into larger quarters in the Occidental Hotel, he added clocks. His store was remarkable. More than three hundred clocks lined the walls, all kept wound up and set to the second, and all striking and chiming at once. Mr. Manheimer got into wholesaling, and as this business grew he gave up the retail end and moved into the wholesale district on South Meriden street, where he added silverware, tools and materials. His business became far-flung, and in 1884 he moved to Chicago as a more convenient wholesaling center. His brother Edward A. Manheimer joined him at this time. They closed out the clocks, silverware and materials and by 1890 the company became an exclusively American watch house.

Keystone, June 1932

The Manheimer Watch Company ordered cases from the Star Watch Case Company to house Illinois pocket watch movements and dials. They may have also done so with late model Illinois Connerics. (Manheimer had long been on the official list of Illinois distributors, and both the New York firm, Louis Manheimer & Brothers, and the Chicago one, the Manheimer Watch Company, were on the 1933 list.)

REGISTERED TRADE NAMES

Some of the registered trade names of Manheimer were:

- The Pear-agon
- Opera
- Monoplane
- Hampden

Arthur E. Manheimer Heads Manheimer Watch Company

At the annual meeting of the Manheimer Watch Company, 31 North State street, Chicago, Illinois, Arthur E. Manheimer was elected president of the company succeeding Edward A. Manheimer who retired from the presidency to become treasurer. After active service in the business for more than forty years, the latter has decided to take things easier and allow the younger generation to carry on with the work.

Other officers of the company are: William Shapiro, first vice-president; W. B. Felsenthal, second vice-president; Sol G. Cogan, executive vice-president; and Harry Aronson, secretary. Miss Helen A. Crowley, who has been secretary of the company for the past five years, tendered her resignation.

Announcement of Arthur E. Manheimer becoming president of the Manheimer Watch Company, *Keystone*, March 1930

Jewelers' Circular, September 1935

When the Dueber-Hampden Company was sold to the Soviet Government in 1930, the sale did not include its trade names (see Chapter 3). Accordingly, the Manheimer Watch Company was able to obtain the registration rights to the "Hampden" name.

Little information exists on the subsequent history of the Manheimer Watch Company. However, in a transcript of the *Lowenthal v. Commissioners of Internal Revenue* case, court records described why the Hampden name was rescued by Manheimer:

> Manheimer Watch Company was incorporated under the laws of Illinois on December 17, 1927. During the period here material [late 1930s to early 1940s] it was engaged in distributing American manufactured watches under franchises from the Hamilton, Elgin and Waltham watch companies. The Company had succeeded to a business of similar nature established in 1875 by the Manheimer family. The Company was well established and had an outstanding reputation.
>
> In 1939 the Waltham line accounted for approximately $350,000 of the Company's total business. In the spring of that year Waltham changed its method of distribution in a manner which led the officers of the Company to believe that it would lose 80 to 85 percent of its Waltham business. To offset this, the Company organized the Hampden Watch Company, an Illinois corporation, as a wholly-owned subsidiary, on May 6, 1939.

Manheimer used Hampden Watch to import Swiss watch movements and sell them to customers that Manheimer had expected to lose as a result of the change in Waltham's distribution policy. Eventually, Hampden was separated from Manheimer so that Manheimer would not lose its franchise as a distributor for Waltham. Evidently, Manheimer feared that Waltham would purge many of its distributors as Hamilton had done in 1934.

Arthur Manheimer took over the Hampden Watch Company in 1940 and ran it separately for seventeen years.

In the "Windy City" there had been four hold-ups of jewelry salesmen in the last two weeks (six in the last two months), and the wave of robberies had gotten the attention of not just the police but also the F.B.I. "G-Men."

The victims of the most recent hold-up were Aisenstein-Woronock salesman Jack Hoffman and his assistant William Verbeck. (Aisenstein-Woronock was one of the Illinois Watch Company's longtime distributors in New York City.) The two men were on their way along a busy Chicago street to call on customers, and Verbeck was carrying two briefcases filled with diamonds and watches.

Two gunmen jumped them from a parked car where a third man was waiting. One of them pointed a revolver at Hoffman while the other grabbed the two briefcases from Verbeck. Then they leaped back in the car and took off through heavy traffic.

An official of the Chicago Jewelers' Association commented that since the same tactics had been used in all the robberies, they were likely the work of the same group.

G-MEN HUNT GEM THIEVES

Daylight Holdup on Busy Chicago Street Nets Loot Worth $17,500

CHICAGO (AP) The "G men", relentless trackers of law breakers, swung into the investigation of a recent wave of Chicago jewel robberies Friday.

Sources: Details from *Herald Statesman* (Yonkers, NY), September 20, 1935; *New York Times*, September 21, 1935; *Reading Times* (Reading, PA), September 21, 1935; and *Decatur Herald* (Decatur, IL), September 21, 1935 (image of headline from *newspapers.com).*

Schwab & Wuischpard

Two pairs of brothers, Alphonse and Louis Wuischpard and Max and Robert Schwab, formed Schwab & Wuischpard (S&W) in 1925. S&W located its offices in New York City across from what would one day be the sight of the United Nations Building, but later relocated to Woodside (Queens), New York. The Schwabs sold out to the Wuischpards around 1930.

S&W cemented its reputation in the watch industry with a rapid succession of famous designs for the Hamilton Watch Company: the Piping Rock, the Meadowbrook, the Coronado, the Glendale and the Spur. The first three designs became quite popular with watch customers, and all have become valuable to collectors. S&W became Hamilton's go-to company for its iconic designs, including the best-selling Boulton. (See Chapter 11 for some examples of Schwab & Wuischpard cases.)

S&W also designed and manufactured watch cases for Elgin, Girard-Perregaux, Longines, Patek Philippe and Rolex as well as for other watch importers. During World War II it switched to making compasses and inclinometers for the war effort.

Jean M. Wuischpard was the vice president and director of manufacturing for S&W from 1936 to 1963. He designed for Hamilton from 1963 to 1968 and also was a senior stylist designer for Pulsar Time Computer. He died on April 30, 2006.

When Hamilton introduced the "Watch of the Future," the world's first electric watch, it sought out the celebrated automobile designer Richard Arbib to create unique watch cases. Hamilton then turned to S&W to make these designs a reality. These designs included the famous Ventura and Pacer models. A survey of these designs is contained in René Rondeau's book *The Watch of the Future, The Story of the Hamilton Electric Watch.*[24] In 1963, when S&W closed its doors, Hamilton turned to Star, one of the last surviving watch casemakers, to continue producing its cases.

Case Model Numbers

No Case Model Numbers

Illinois stamped model numbers inside the case backs of most of its men's and ladies' watches. Some models, such as the Baronet, Daytona, Major, Mary Todd, and Rockliffe can be found with or without model numbers. However, cases without model numbers appear to be rarer. Although the unnumbered cases could merely be early production runs, collectors have developed a number of other theories about the inconsistency. Some believe that the unnumbered cases represent either sample, prototype or first-released cases. Others think that the unstamped cases allowed the casemaker to offer the case model to other watch manufacturers until such time as one of them requested an exclusive arrangement on that particular case model. This latter theory is unlikely. (See the **Baronet** listing in Chapter 9 for examples of multiple case model numbers.)

Production Quantities

No information exists about the number of each watch model produced by Illinois. On the other hand, there is fairly good information concerning the number of each size and grade of movement made by Illinois. Movements were interchangeable among different watch models, and extra movements were made for sales, repairs and replacements. In fact, Illinois would freely sell uncased movements (unlike Hamilton, for example). The case serial numbers stamped inside the case back by the casemaker have thus far provided little help.

In an interview, Warren Niebling, the expert on American watch casemakers, told me that the casemaker records were "horrible."[25] He could find no information concerning what production quantities of cases went to the Illinois Watch Company—or any other watchmaker, for that matter. He could locate no production numbers for any of the companies that produced watch cases for Illinois. He also said that the serial numbers for cases were of no value either, since they served merely to get the case parts through the case factory in an orderly sequence. In short, Niebling found "no rhyme or reason to the serial numbers used on the cases." adding that "the casemaker records were far worse than those of the watch manufacturers."[26]

However, since my interview with Niebling, some bright wristwatch collectors have discovered the code used to date certain Gruen cases made by Wadsworth, and some Illinois pocket watch collectors and author Michael Chamelin have discovered the date code used on Bunn Special pocket watch cases made by Wadsworth. So there may be hope that with further study, dates and production quantities of certain casemakers will be unlocked.

At least one recent attempt has been made to make sense out of this disorder for one particular Illinois wristwatch model. Illinois Consul and deco enthusiast Rick Vess, with modest help from me, assembled the data set forth in the accompanying spreadsheet. The data are based on reviewing sales listings on auction sites and contacting collectors who owned a total of sixty-one Consuls. (The list is Vess's work; I merely used my Illinois contacts to help gather the data.)

Consul Case, Movement and Dial Examples in Order of Case Numbers (part 1)

Possible Date	Case No.	Case Type	Bezel	Lugs	Center Spacer	Subsidiary Seconds	Mvmt	No. Jewels	Dial & Notes	Movement No.	Presentation Dates
1928	598268	White	Engraved	Engraved	Nickel	No	970	19	Silver sunburst, aged	5193946	
1928	598316	White	Engraved	Engraved			907	19		4984050	
1928	598628	Two-Tone	Engraved	Engraved	Nickel	No	907	19	Silver sunburst	5125857	July 22, 1929
1928	598632	Two-Tone	Engraved	Engraved	Nickel	No	907	19	Silver sunburst	5109089	
1928	598648	Two-Tone	Engraved	Engraved	Nickel	No	907	19	Standard plain black enamel	4832605*	
1928	598647	Green	Engraved	Engraved	Nickel	No	907	19		5193800	
1928	598652	Green	Engraved	Engraved	Nickel	No	907	19	Silver sunburst	5193216	
1928	598672	Green	Engraved	Engraved	Nickel	No	907	19	Black sunburst	5193149	
1928	598682	Green	Engraved	Engraved	Nickel	No	907	19	Silver sunburst	5193054	
1929	604129	White	Engraved	Engraved	Nickel	No	907	19	Undertaker Consul, custom name*	5204386	December 25, 1929
1929	604148	White	Engraved	Engraved	Nickel	No	907	19	Silver sunburst	5204633	
1929	604199	White	Engraved	Engraved	Nickel	No	907	19	Pinstripe, ZJ	5193919	
1929	604268	White	Engraved	Engraved	Nickel	No	909	21	Silver star (redone)	5239008*	
1929	624286	White	Plain	Plain			907	19	????	5303343	
1929	604292	White	Engraved	Engraved	Nickel	No	907	19	Silver sunburst	5193535	1929 Presentation
1929	604312	White	Engraved	Engraved				19		5193694	
1929	604490	White	Plain	Plain	Nickel	No	907	19	Yellow gold sunburst	5204352	
1929	604534	White	Plain	Plain	Nickel	No	907	19	Standard plain black enamel	5204292	
1929	607558	Two-Tone	Engraved	Engraved	14K	No	909	21	Original sunburst	5239865	None
1929	607560	Two-Tone	Engraved	Engraved	14K	No	909	21	Pinstripe, ZJ	5266860	
1929	507567	Two-Tone	Engraved	Engraved	14K	No	909*	21	Sunburst	5239990	
1929	607579	Two-Tone	Engraved	Engraved	14K	No	909	21	Pinstripe, ZJ	5266855	
1929	607586	Two-Tone	Engraved	Engraved	14K	No	909	21	Pinstripe, ZJ	5239297	
1929	607612	White	Engraved	Engraved	14K	No	909	21	Silver sunburst, redone dial	5239900	
1929	607661	White	Engraved	Engraved	14K	No	909	21	Silver sunburst	5239074	
1929	607701	White	Engraved	Engraved	14K	No	909*	21	Sunburst	5266698	
1929	607720	White	Engraved	Engraved	14K	No	909*	21	Pinstripe, ZJ	5239638	
1929	607724	White	Engraved	Engraved	14K	No	909*	21	Sunburst	5230112	None
1929	607739	White	Engraved	Engraved	14K	No	909	21	Pinstripe, ZJ	5266741	
1929	607756	White	Engraved	Engraved	14K	No	909	21	Yellow gold sunburst	5239228	
1929	607797	White	Engraved	Engraved	14K	No	909	21	Silver sunburst, black enamel refilled	5239128	
1929	607788	White	Engraved	Engraved	14K	No	909	21	Pinstripe, ZJ	5239002	

Consul Case, Movement and Dial Examples in Order of Case Numbers (part 2)

Possible Date	Case No.	Case Type	Bezel	Lugs	Center Spacer	Subsi-diary Seconds	Mvmt	No. Jewels	Dial & Notes	Movement No.	Presentation Dates
1929	607823	White	Engraved	Engraved	14K	No	909	21	Silver sunburst	5239666	
1929	607862	White	Engraved	Engraved	14K	No	909	21	Plain	5239116	
1929	607893	White	Engraved	Engraved	14K	No	909	21	Silver sunburst	5239643	
1929	608018	White	Engraved	Engraved	14K	No	907	21	Redone sunburst dial	5299750	
1929	608039	White	Engraved	Engraved	14K	No	907	21	Silver sunburst	5299098	December 31, 1930 (GM)
1929	608082	White	Engraved	Engraved	14K	No	909	21	Silver sunburst	5239117	
1929	608169	White	Engraved	Engraved	14K	No	909	21	Sunburst	5266833	
1929	608182	White	Engraved	Engraved	14K	No	907	19	Plain	5303783	
1929-1930	608323	White	Engraved	Engraved	14K	No	909	21	Silver sunburst	5239666	
1929-1930	608344	White	Engraved	Engraved	14K	Yes	607	17	Standard sub-6	5462279*	
1929-1930	608411	White	Plain	Plain	14K	No	909	21	Black sunburst/foil	5239750	
1929-1930	608461	White	Engraved	Engraved	14K	No	907	19	Black sunburst	5239152	
1929-1930	608462	White	Engraved	Engraved	14K	No	909	21	Pinstripe dial	5239652	
1929-1930	608472	White	Engraved	Engraved	14K	Yes, at 9	909	17	Unusual Sub-9 starburst**	5265312	
1929	608489	White	Engraved	Engraved	14K	Yes, at 9	909	21	Convict Consul, Sub-9, pinstripe, ZJ*	5266145	June 30, 1929
1930-1931	611305	White	Engraved	Engraved	14K	No	909	19	Silver sunburst	5304661	
1930-1931	613261	White	Engraved	Engraved	14K	Yes	601	21	Standard sub-6	5564959*	
1930-1931	613420	White	Engraved	Engraved	14K	No	905	21	Silver sunburst	5136999*	
1930-1931	613440	White	Engraved	Engraved	14K	Yes	607	21	Standard sub-6	5450127	
1930-1931	613456	White	Engraved	Engraved	14K	No	601	21	Pinstripe, ZJ	5239208	
1930-1931	613587	White	Plain	Plain	14K			21	Sunburst	5316085	
1931-1933	619116	White	Engraved	Engraved	14K	Yes	607	17	Standard sub-6	5394593	
1931-1933	619237	White	Engraved	Engraved	14K	Yes	607	17	Standard sub-6	5462279	
1931-1933	619253	White	Engraved	Engraved	14K	Yes	601*	21	Standard sub	5524389	
1931-1933	619320	White	Engraved	Engraved	14K	Yes	601	21	Sub 6/wrong dial	5488650	
1931-1933	619337	White	Engraved	Engraved	14K	No	607	17	Black sunburst (redone aged dial)	5395703	
1931	619478	White	Engraved	Engraved	14K	Yes	907	19	Standard sub-6	5204269*	Engraved 12-12-31
1931-1933	619504	White	Engraved	Engraved	14K	Yes	601	21	Standard sub-6 (newly redone)	5545434	

*See Appendix 6 for details on the "Convict Consul" and "Undertaker Consul" ** Likely a redone dial

Advertised Consul Pricing

Date	Advertisements	Description/Illustration	Price	
1928	Illinois booklet	19 jewels in solid gold case	$75.00	
June 1929	*Liberty* magazine	Pinstripe dial		
Dec. 1929	The *American Magazine*			
1929	Factory catalog	14K solid gold white pl or eng, TT eng, 21 jewels, lum dial	$90.00/$103.50	14K applied #s, $10 extra
1929	Factory catalog	14K solid gold white pl or eng, TT eng, 19 jewels, lum dial	$75.00/ $86.00	14K applied #s, $10 extra
1930	Factory catalog	21 jewels in white gold w/solid gold numerals	$137.40	
1930	Factory catalog	19 jewels in white gold w/ lum dial	$103.20	
1930	May & Malone catalog, "Council" [*sic*]	21 jewels in white gold eng w/solid gold numerals, starburst dial, no subs	$137.40	
1930	May & Malone catalog. "Council" [sic]	19 jewels in white gold eng w/ lum numerals, starburst dial, no subs	$103.20	
1930-1931	A. I. Hall catalog	17 jewels in white gold eng, kind of numerals not indicated, plain dial, sub 6	$65.00	
1931	A.C. Becken cataolg	Sub 6		
1931	May & Malone catalog	17 jewels w/starburst dial	$88.80	
1931	L.& C. Mayers catalog	17 jewels in 6/0 size		

A review of the data discloses some basic findings that reinforce views that I expressed in *The Illinois Watch: The Life and Times of a Great American Watch Company.* The information further confirms the rarity of the green gold engraved bezel Consul, the plain bezel white gold one and the two-tone versions. To date, only five green gold Consuls have been located, only six white gold Consuls with plain bezels and under a dozen two-tone Consuls, whereas there were forty white gold Consuls recorded with engraved bezels (still, a remarkably low number).

The information also reinforces previously expressed views concerning dial rarity. The recorded data show only nine pinstripe dials and only one custom pinstripe dial with subsidiary seconds at 9, only seven original (and two redone) dials with subsidiary seconds at 6 and one redone Consul with subsidiary seconds at 9 and a sunburst dial.

Unfortunately, the information gives no clue about how many Consuls Illinois produced. We do know that the two-tone and green-gold versions of the Consul were listed on the September 1, 1929 Illinois Price List. See Chapter 12.

With respect to Consul dials, the spreadsheet supports the idea that purchasers chose the sunburst pattern dial most often. Clearly, the pinstripe dials were very rare as was the version of the Consul with subsidiary seconds at 6. It also supports the theory that the Consul with subsidiary seconds at 6 came later in the production cycle, with mostly 17- jewel, 607 grade movements.

Another detail covered in the Consul database has to do with the spacer that held the watch movement in place. From the data he has gathered, Vess believes that Illinois offered its first Consuls with inexpensive nickel spacers, then later switched to solid 14K gold ones. The latter appear to be more common.

Vess also points out that an L. & C. Mayers jobber catalog from the early 1930s lists 17-jewel Consuls selling for a lower price than 14K gold-filled, 12/0 size models. Perhaps by then the Consul looked old and out-of-style compared to the modern rectangular watches and movements. An Illinois advertisement in a 1930–31 A. I. Hall catalog suggests as much: the 17-jewel Consul is described as "conservative in design," while the other solid gold watch listed on the same page, a 21-jewel Baronet, is described as "reflecting the modern design in case construction." Two of the gold-filled 6/0s on that page are described much like the Baronet: the Cavalier ("Thoroughly modern in design") and the Ritz ("The modern flair, embodied in watch design").

Perhaps the jobbers just wanted to get rid of older case models, such as the Consul, because they had become slow sellers. Alternative theories exist, but no definitive information.

Consul center section "spacers" to hold the movement: solid gold on the left, nickel on the right

THE ILLINOIS WATCH

21 Jewel Strap Watches of Character

6-0 Size » » 21 Jewels

The BARONET
21 Jewels
The finest strap watch value—reflecting the modern design in case construction. The Baronet is a watch of artistic merit. The dial is sterling silver with 18K applied numerals. 14K solid white and natural gold.
Suggested consumer price, $100.

The BEAU MONDE
21 Jewels
Designed to fit the wrist perfectly. Flowing curves and individual engraving pattern greatly increase the acceptance of this new watch. The Beau Monde is 14K white and natural filled gold.
Suggested consumer price, $75.

The NEW YORKER
21 Jewels
The most popular 21 Jewel strap watch. Simplicity in design and richness in appearance places it in a class of its own in the fine watch field. 14K white or natural filled gold. Plain or engraved cases.
Suggested consumer price, $75.

6-0 Size » » 17 Jewel Strap Watches

The BLACKSTONE
Here is a fine strap watch at a new low price. 14K white or natural filled gold.
Suggested consumer price, $42.50

The CAVALIER
Thoroughly modern in design and of handsome appearance. 14K white or natural filled gold.
Suggested consumer price, $45.

The TOWNSMAN
The unusual case combination of this white and natural gold watch produce a most pleasing harmony. 14K white filled gold with natural gold center.
Suggested consumer price, $47.50.

The CONSUL
A solid gold strapwatch, conservative in design with handsomely carved bezel. 14K solid white gold.
Suggested consumer price, $65.

The RITZ
The modern flair, embodied in watch design. 14K white filled gold with natural gold center.
Suggested consumer price, $42.50

The ENSIGN
The Ensign has long been a popular Illinois style. 14K white filled gold plain or engraved or natural engraved cases.
Suggested consumer price, $45.

The MANHATTAN

The NEW YORKER

The Manhattan is a most harmonious combination of watch and flexible metal band, beautifully presented in 14K white natural filled gold.
Suggested consumer price, 21 jewels, $85.
Suggested consumer price, 17 jewels, $55.

The New Yorker. The modern smartness of this square cut watch will appeal to all men. 14K white or natural filled gold, plain or engraved cases. *Suggested consumer price, $50.*

The BEAU BRUMMELL
This watch is a tremendously popular design with young men. 14K white or natural filled gold, plain or engraved cases.
Suggested consumer price, $50.

A GREAT AMERICAN WATCH SINCE 1870

CONSUMER AND KEYSTONE LIST PRICES PAGE TWELVE

page four

Illinois sales catalog 1930-31

It is unfortunate that no clearer conclusions can be drawn from this survey of Consuls. It does, at a minimum, confirm that these Illinois models are rare.

In Chapter 3 there is information about the production numbers of certain Hamilton wristwatch models that provides a useful insight regarding the low production numbers for Illinois.

List of Case Model Numbers

As mentioned above, Illinois inscribed model numbers inside the case of many of the men's and ladies' Illinois watches produced at Springfield. The table here shows a list of known numbers. With Illinois, one quickly discovers that no rule is iron-clad regarding the use of these case numbers. An example is the Major, which comes in cases marked Number 170 and Number 171 and sometimes have no numbers at all. Nevertheless, all are authentic.

Major without a case Model Number

Another example is the Baronet, some of which come with unnumbered cases while others are marked Number 220 or Number 625.

Factory-Cased Illinois Case Numbers, Model Names and Casemakers (pt 1)

Case Model Number	Model Name	Casemaker
151 (Special Model)	Tuxedo	Solidarity
152 (Special Model)	Consul	Solidarity
153	Berkeley	Wadsworth
153	Daytona	Wadsworth
153	Long Beach	Wadsworth
153	Redonda	Wadsworth
153	Saratoga Notched Leaf	Wadsworth
154	Berkeley[1]	Wadsworth
154	Daytona	Wadsworth
154	Redonda	Wadsworth
155	Daytona	Wadsworth
155A	Daytona	Wadsworth
155B	Daytona	Wadsworth
155	Del Monte	Wadsworth
155	Edgewater	Wadsworth
155	Joan	Wadsworth
155	Miami	Wadsworth
156	Bar Harbor	Wadsworth
157	Del Monte	Wadsworth
157	Miami[1]	Wadsworth
158	Bar Harbor	Wadsworth
161	Biltmore 18/0	Wadsworth
162	Fifth Avenue	Wadsworth
162	New Yorker	Wadsworth
152	Manhattan	Wadsworth
162	Richmond 6/0	Wadsworth
162	Yorktown	Wadsworth
162	New Yorker, Enamel	Wadsworth
163 (Special Model)	Chieftain	Fahys
164	Piccadilly	Keystone
168	Narragansett	Keystone
168	Countess	Keystone
168	Princess	Keystone
169	Coronado	Keystone
170	Guardsman	Keystone
170	Major[1]	Keystone
171	Major[1]	Keystone
171	Guardian	Keystone
171	Guardsman	Keystone

Factory-Cased Illinois Case Numbers, Model Names and Casemakers (pt 2)

Case Model Number	Model Name	Casemaker
174	Newport[1]	Keystone
175	Edgewater[1]	Keystone
176	Jolly Roger	Keystone
178	Speedway	Keystone
178	Speedway 178	Keystone
185	Beverly	Keystone
186	Biloxi	Keystone
186	Glenna	Keystone
193 (Special Model)	Medalist	Fahys
193 (Special Model)	Wembley	Fahys
195 (Special Model)	Viking	Fahys
196	Chesterfield	Wadsworth
196	Chesterfield Stepped Bezel	Wadsworth
196	Finalist	Wadsworth
196	Finalist Deco	Wadsworth
197	Futura	Keystone
197	Paul Revere	Keystone
197	Wentworth	Keystone
198	Metropolitan	Keystone
198	Puritan	Keystone
198	Townsman	Keystone
199	Berkshire	Keystone
200	Fairport	Keystone
201	Brighton	Keystone
202	Frontenac	Wadsworth
202	Kensington	Wadsworth
202	Trophy	Wadsworth
202	Westchester	Wadsworth
203	Mary Todd 203	Keystone
204	Mary Todd 204	Keystone
205	Avalon	Keystone
208	Edgewater	Keystone
209 (Special Model)	Cavalier	Fahys
210	Ritz	Wadsworth
210	Valedictorian	Wadsworth
211	Skyway	Wadsworth
211	Off-Duty	Wadsworth
211	Greyhound	Wadsworth
211	Motor Coach	Wadsworth
212	Beau Geste	Keystone
212	Beau Monde	Keystone
213	Caprice	Keystone
214	Larchmont	Keystone
214	Vernon	Keystone
214	Richmond 12/0	Keystone

Factory-Cased Illinois Case Numbers, Model Names and Casemakers (pt 3)

Case Model Number	Model Name	Casemaker
215	Andover	J. Milhening
215	Exeter	J. Milhening
216	Rockliffe	Keystone
216	Rockliffe 18/0[1]	Keystone
217	Gallahad	Keystone
217	Kenilworth	Keystone
218	Hudson	Wadsworth
218	Ardsley	Wadsworth
219	Blackstone	Wadsworth
219	Greystone	Wadsworth
219	Haddon Hall	Wadsworth
220	Baronet[1]	Keystone
222	Edgewater	Keystone
223	Newport	Keystone
224	Lenox	Keystone
238	Glencoe	Keystone
238	Lakewood	Keystone
239	Glenna	Keystone
239	Roslyn	Keystone
240	Vardon	Wadsworth
241	No. 251	Keystone
242	Claudette	Wadsworth
242	Vogue	Wadsworth
250	No. 250/Schmukler	Keystone
616	Commodore	Keystone
616	Belmont	Keystone
616	Bostonian	Keystone
616	Biltmore 6/0	Keystone
616	LaSalle	Keystone
617	Derby	Wadsworth
617	Pimlico	Wadsworth
617	Derby[2]	Solidarity
618	Arlington	J. Milhening
618	Hawthorne	J. Milhening
625	Baronet[1]	Keystone
626	Potomac	Keystone
626	Rockingham	Keystone
650	Sherwood[3]	Keystone
651	Standish[3]	Keystone
652	Chatham[3]	Keystone
701	Minuette[3]	Keystone
701	Rosette	Keystone
702	Coquette[3]	Keystone
703	Annette	Keystone
703	Antoinette	Keystone
703	Charmette[3]	Keystone

Factory-Cased Illinois Case Numbers, Model Names and Casemakers (pt 4)

Case Model Number	Model Name	Casemaker
703	Florette[3]	Keystone
704	Alouette[3]	Keystone
704	Babette	Keystone
706	Juliette[1]	Star
707	Muzette	Star
707	Suzette[1]	Star
710	Lynette[3]	Keystone**
711	Janette[3]	Keystone**
711	Glenna	Keystone
714	Babette II	Star
807-5	Greta	Wadsworth
807-5	Argyle	Wadsworth
807-5	Arlene	Wadsworth
807-5	Lady Mary	Wadsworth
807-5	Queen Anne	Wadsworth
807-6	Debutante	Wadsworth
807-6	Suzette	Wadsworth
807-6	Vanity Fair	Wadsworth
828	Gloria	Wadsworth
829	Barbara	Wadsworth
829	Constance	Wadsworth
830	Elissa	Keystone
830	Irene	Keystone
803	Sylvia	Keystone
830	Marilyn	Keystone
831	Hollywood	Keystone
831	Rita	Keystone
833	Patricia	Keystone
834	Fairfax	Keystone
834	Florentine	Keystone
852	Beverly	Keystone
875	Sangamon[3]	Keystone
876	Urbana[3]	Keystone
Special Model	Marquis Strap	Fahys
Special Model	Cadet	Fahys
Special Model B	Ensign	Fahys
Special Model B	Kingston	Fahys
Special Model C	Beau Royale	Fahys
Special Model C	Beau Brummell	Fahys
Special Model C	Beau Brummell/ Viking	Fahys
Special Model H	Mate	Fahys
Special Model H	Yankee Clipper 3/0	Fahys
Special Model 151	Tuxedo	Solidarity
Special Model 152	Consul	Solidarity
Special Model 163	Chieftain	Fahys
Special Model 193	Medalist	Fahys

Factory-Cased Illinois Case Numbers, Model Names and Casemakers (pt 5)

Case Model Number	Model Name	Casemaker
Special Model 193	Wembley	Fahys
Special Model 195	Viking	Fahys
Special Model 209	Cavalier	Fahys
No Case Number	Canby, WGF, GGF	Keystone
No Case Number	Devon, WGF, GGF	Keystone
No Case Number	Devon, Cushion, Engraved Solid Gold, WG, GG	Solidarity
No Case Number	Diamond-Set Models	Wadsworth
No Case Number	Devon, Round, WGF, GGF	Keystone
No Case Number	Major	Keystone
No Case Number	Mary Todd	Keystone
No Case Number	Notched Lug	Wadsworth
No Case Number	Rectangular, WGF, GGF	Keystone
No Case Number	Rockliffe, 18/0[3]	Keystone
No Case Number	Saratoga Leaf	Wadsworth
No Case Number	Special Wadsworth Models (18K)	Wadsworth
No Case Number	Sportsman	Star
No Case Number	Square Cut Corner, WGF, GGF[4]	Keystone
No Case Number	Square Cut Corner, Gold-Filled/Solid Gold, WG, GG[4]	Solidarity
No Case Number	United States Army	Illinois Watch Case Co.
No Case Number	Whippet, WGF, GGF[4]	Keystone
Unknown Case No.	Débette	Unknown
Unknown Case No.	Louette	Unknown
Unknown Case No.	Mariette	Unknown
Unknown Case No.	Marionette	Unknown
Unknown Case No.	Marlette	Unknown
Unknown Case No.	Victoria	Unknown

[1] Sometimes comes in unnumbered cases; for the Berkeley 154, Miami 157, and Suzette, this applies only to the rare solid gold specimens.

[2] The Derby had two different casemakers, Wadsworth and Solidarity.

[3] Cased by the Hamilton Watch Company in Lancaster, Pennsylvania.

[4] The solid gold Square Cut Corner and Whippet models were cased at the Illinois Watch Factory in Solidarity cases. The white gold-filled and green gold-filled Square Cut Corner models were cased at the Watch Factory in Keystone cases.

Red = Ladies'
Black = Men's
Blue = Unisex

Factory-Cased Illinois Wristwatch Models Still Unidentified

Admiral	Harvard	Pearl
Arliss	Hercules	Penn Charter
Barrymore	Jackson	Rhea
Ben Hur	John Alden	Rose
Brunswick	Louette*	Ruth
Carlton	Lord Calvert	Rye 6/0
Charter Oak	Lowell	Rye (12/0)
Co-Ed	Mayflower	Statesmen
Falcon	Mohican	Suburban
Graduate	Monticello	Winchester
Graduate	Motor Coach	

*The Louette may or may not exist. Although its name is on one official Illinois list and one from Hamilton, both lists have some errors; and therefore Louette may be a typographical error for the Alouette model.
Red = Ladies'   Black = Men's

THE new vogue in precious metals—NATURAL GOLD!

In 1930, Wadsworth foresaw this style trend and introduced Natural Gold watch cases through national advertising. Since then, fashion articles have featured gold in its natural color, more and more. Your customers, unable to keep gold in coin, take new pride in displaying it on their watch cases.

When you order watches with the names of leading movement makers on the dials, ask specially for those in cases of WADSWORTH NATURAL GOLD.

The Wadsworth Watch Case Company, Incorporated, Dayton, Ky. Offices 20 W. 47th Street, New York; 150 Post Street, San Francisco; 35 E. Wacker Drive, Chicago.

Wadsworth WORKERS IN PRECIOUS METALS

Page 12   *The Keystone*

Keystone, October 1934

LIST OF NAMES OF CASED ILLINOIS WATCHES BY SIZES

16 Size, Reg.	12 Size, Reg.	12/14 Size	12 Size, Thin	3/0 Size	6/0 Size	12/0 Size	18/0 Size	21/0 Size
Dispatcher	Ben Milam	Autocrat	Acorn	Akron	Admiral	Andover	Argyle	Alouette
	Davy Crockett	Shriner's Special	Barrister	Greyhound	Arlington	Ardsley	Arlene	Babette
	Dorian		Bourse	Guardian	Arliss	Chesterfield	Avalon	Charmette
	Trimount		Cambridge	Guardsman	Baronet	Finalist	Barbara	Coquette
			Capitol	Hercules	Barrymore	Frontenac	Bar Harbor	Florette
			Chicagoan	Jolly Roger	Beau Brummel	Futura	Berkeley	Janette
			Cushion	Major	Beau Geste	Gallahad	Berkshire	Juliette
			Dean	Mate	Beau Monde	Hudson	Beverly	Louette
			Dictator	Motor Coach	Beau Royale	John Alden	Biloxi	Lynette
			Director	Off Duty	Belmont	Kenilworth	Biltmore	Minuette
			Eton	Seneca	Ben Hur	Kensington	Brighton	Muzette
			Midland	Skyway	Biltmore	Larchmont	Claudette	Rhea
			Oxford	Speedway	Blackstone	Medalist	Co-ed	Rose
			Paramount	Sportsman	Bostonian	*Richmond	Constance	Rosette
			Pioneer	Viking	Brunswick	Rockliffe	Coronado	Ruth
			Rialto		Cadet	*Rye	Countess	Suzette
			Springfield		Caprice	Trophy	Daytona	
			Statesman		Carlton	Vernon	Debutante	
			Trustee		Cavalier	Wembley	Del Monte	
					Charter Oak	Wentworth	Edgewater	
					Chevalier	Westchester	Elissa	
					Chieftain		Fairfax	
					Commodore		Fairport	
					Consul		Florentine	
					Derby		Glencoe	
					Ensign		Glenna	
					Falcon		Gloria	
					Fifth Avenue		Graduate	
					Graduate		Greta	
					Greystone		Hollywood	
					Haddon Hall		Irene	
					Harvard		Joan	
					Hawthorne		Lady Mary	
					Jackson		Lakewood	
					Kingston		Latonia	
					LaSalle		Lenox	
					Lord Calvert		Long Beach	
					Lowell		Marilyn	
					Manhattan		Mary Todd	
					Marquis-Strap		Mayflower	
					Mohican		Miami	
					Monticello		Narragansett	
					New Yorker		Newport	
					Paul Revere		Patricia	
					Penn Charter		Pearl	
					Piccadilly		Princess	
					Pimlico		Priscilla	
					Potomac		Queen Anne	
					Puritan		Redonda	
					*Richmond		Rita	
					Ritz		Roslyn	
					*Rye		Saratoga	
					Statesman		Sylvia	
					Suburban		Tuxedo	
					Townsman		Vanity Fair	
					Valedictorian		Vardon	
					Winchester		Victoria	
					Yankee Clipper		Vogue	
					Yorktown			

*Please specify size of watch

Where the name is not stamped on bridges this chart will make it easier for identification

ILLINOIS WATCH MATERIAL DEPARTMENT

Springfield, Illinois, U.S

December [illegible]1, 193[illegible]

(over)

List of Names of Cased Illinois Watches by Sizes, dated December 31, 1932

List of Names of Cased Illinois Watches by Sizes

The Illinois Watch Material Department published a "List of Names of Cased Illinois Watches by Sizes" dated December 31, 1932. This represents the official tally of all wristwatches cased in the Factory by Illinois to that date. The importance of this list is further underscored by the observation that it contains the model names of all Factory-Cased Illinois wristwatches, *including thirty-four in the 3/0, 6/0, 12/0, 18/0 and 21/0 sizes that remain unidentified.* It is possible that some of the 3/0 and 6/0 size names may be for pocket or pendant watches (or a variation of a known watch with an attached metal bracelet resulting in a new name), but none of the unknown names could be matched to any known pocket watch or pendant names or advertisements.

The Hamilton Master List–Case Control Sheet

On June 5, 1933 Hamilton prepared a "Master List" of available Illinois wristwatch cases; however, some items in the list are clearly wrong. For the men's models these are the Marquis (as it is not another name for an Ensign) and the Derby (not also called an Arlington).

For the ladies' models, the following are not correct: the Vardon is not the same model as an Arlene, Greta and Argyle; the Beverly and Roslyn models are not the same; the Narragansett is not the same model as the Lakewood and Glencoe; the Edgewater is not the same model as the Glenna and Joan; and the Lenox and Lakewood are not the same models. Hamilton may have been confused because several of the above models share the same dials.

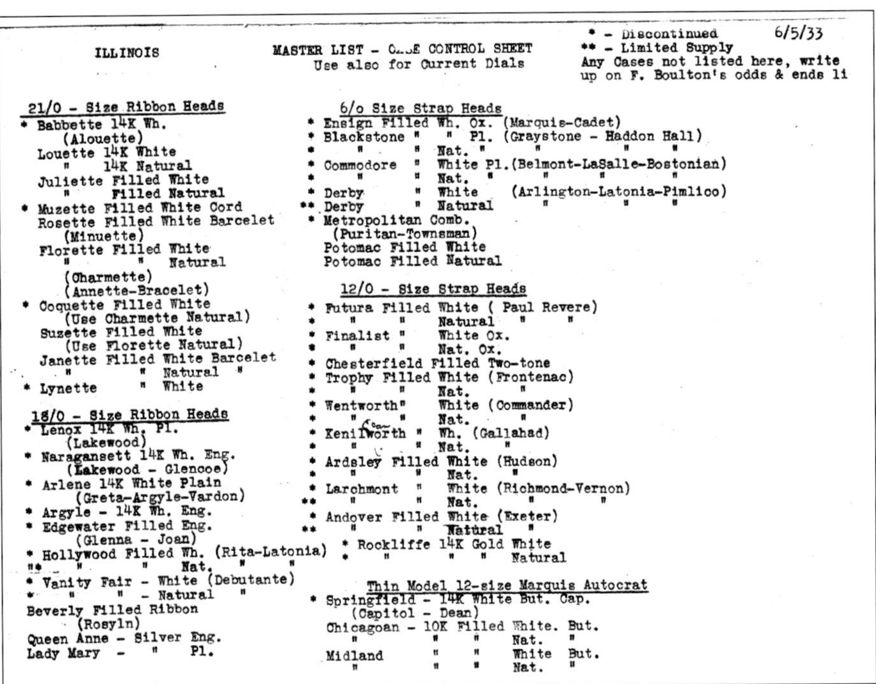

ILLINOIS

MASTER LIST - CASE CONTROL SHEET
Use also for Current Dials

* - Discontinued 6/5/33
** - Limited Supply
Any Cases not listed here, write up on F. Boulton's odds & ends li

21/0 - Size Ribbon Heads
* Babbette 14K Wh.
(Alouette)
Louette 14K White
" 14K Natural
Juliette Filled White
" Filled Natural
* Muzette Filled White Cord
Rosette Filled White Barcelet
(Minuette)
Florette Filled White
" " Natural
(Charmette)
(Annette-Bracelet)
* Coquette Filled White
(Use Charmette Natural)
Suzette Filled White
(Use Florette Natural)
Janette Filled White Barcelet
" " Natural "
* Lynette " White

18/0 - Size Ribbon Heads
* Lenox 14K Wh. Pl.
(Lakewood)
* Naragansett 14K Wh. Eng.
(Lakewood - Glencoe)
* Arlene 14K White Plain
(Greta-Argyle-Vardon)
* Argyle - 14K Wh. Eng.
* Edgewater Filled Eng.
(Glenna - Joan)
* Hollywood Filled Wh. (Rita-Latonia)
** " " Nat. " "
* Vanity Fair - White (Debutante)
* " " - Natural "
Beverly Filled Ribbon
(Rosyln)
Queen Anne - Silver Eng.
Lady Mary - " Pl.

6/o Size Strap Heads
* Ensign Filled Wh. Ox. (Marquis-Cadet)
* Blackstone " " Pl. (Graystone - Haddon Hall)
* " " Nat. " " " "
* Commodore " White Pl. (Belmont-LaSalle-Bostonian)
* " " Nat. " " " "
* Derby " White (Arlington-Latonia-Pimlico)
** Derby " Natural " " "
* Metropolitan Comb.
(Puritan-Townsman)
Potomac Filled White
Potomac Filled Natural

12/0 - Size Strap Heads
* Futura Filled White (Paul Revere)
* " " Natural " "
* Finalist " White Ox.
* " " Nat. Ox.
* Chesterfield Filled Two-tone
* Trophy Filled White (Frontenac)
* " " Nat. "
* Wentworth" White (Commander)
* " " Nat. "
* Kenilworth " Wh. (Gallahad)
* " " Nat. "
* Ardsley Filled White (Hudson)
* " " Nat. "
* Larchmont " White (Richmond-Vernon)
** " " Nat. " "
* Andover Filled White (Exeter)
** " " Natural "
* Rockliffe 14K Gold White
* " " " Natural

Thin Model 12-size Marquis Autocrat
* Springfield - 14K White But. Cap.
(Capitol - Dean)
Chicagoan - 10K Filled White. But.
" " " Nat. "
Midland " " White But.
" " " Nat. "

The Hamilton Master List–Case Control Sheet, dated June 5, 1933—sheds some light on the unidentified models but also adds some degree of confusion of its own.

1932
HISTORICAL NOTES

- The United States railway unions accept a 10% wage reduction.
- Al Capone is sent to prison after conviction for income tax evasion.
- Charles Lindbergh, Jr. is kidnapped in New Jersey.
- President Hoover suggests a five-day work week.
- Amelia Earhardt makes the first female transcontinental non-stop flight.
- Franklin D. Roosevelt is elected the 32nd President of the United States.
- Radio City Music Hall opens in New York City.

Case Inscriptions and Monograms

Some Illinois jobbers actively encouraged the use of inscriptions on case backs. May and Malone note in their 1929 catalog: "Many people find that a watch purchased for a gift is not complete without a suitable monogram or inscription to give it a personal touch as well as to identify it in case of loss." They can also have important historical significance and help establish providence and human interest, as I pointed out in my NAWCC *Bulletin* article contained in Appendix 6.

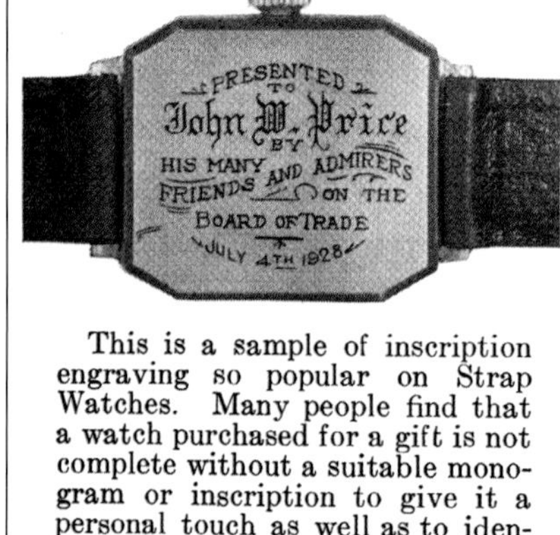

This is a sample of inscription engraving so popular on Strap Watches. Many people find that a watch purchased for a gift is not complete without a suitable monogram or inscription to give it a personal touch as well as to identify it in case of loss. See Page 391 for styles and prices.

May and Malone catalog, 1929

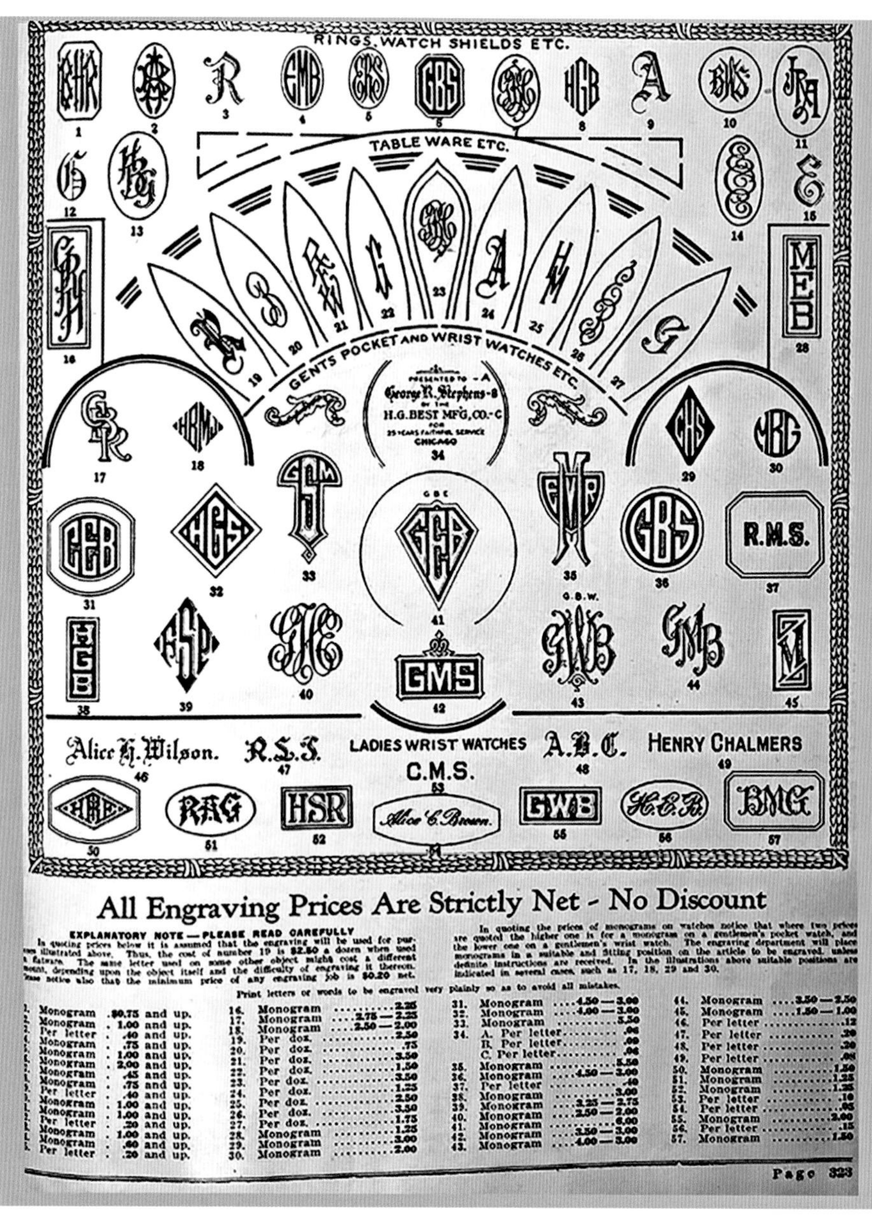

All Engraving Prices Are Strictly Net - No Discount

EXPLANATORY NOTE — PLEASE READ CAREFULLY

In quoting prices below it is assumed that the engraving will be used for pur- ...es illustrated above. Thus, the cost of number 19 is $2.50 a dozen when used ...a flatware. The same letter used on some other object might cost a different ...ount, depending upon the object itself and the difficulty of engraving it thereon. ...ease notice also that the minimum price of any engraving job is $0.20 net.

In quoting the prices of monograms on watches notice that where two prices are quoted the higher one is for a monogram on a gentlemen's pocket watch, and the lower one on a gentlemen's wrist watch. The engraving department will place monograms in a suitable and fitting position on the article to be engraved, unless definite instructions are received. In the illustrations above suitable positions are indicated in several cases, such as 17, 18, 29 and 30.

Print letters or words to be engraved very plainly so as to avoid all mistakes.

1.	Monogram	$0.75 and up.
2.	Monogram	1.00 and up.
3.	Per letter	.40 and up.
4.	Monogram	.75 and up.
5.	Monogram	1.00 and up.
6.	Monogram	2.00 and up.
7.	Monogram	.45 and up.
8.	Monogram	.75 and up.
9.	Per letter	.40 and up.
10.	Monogram	1.00 and up.
11.	Monogram	1.00 and up.
12.	Per letter	.20 and up.
13.	Monogram	1.00 and up.
14.	Monogram	.60 and up.
15.	Per letter	.20 and up.
16.	Monogram	2.25
17.	Monogram	2.75—2.25
18.	Monogram	2.50—2.00
19.	Per doz.	2.50
20.	Per doz.	.75
21.	Per doz.	3.50
22.	Per doz.	1.50
23.	Per doz.	3.50
24.	Per doz.	1.25
25.	Per doz.	2.50
26.	Per doz.	3.50
27.	Per doz.	1.75
28.	Monogram	1.25
29.	Monogram	3.00
30.	Monogram	2.00
31.	Monogram	4.50—3.00
32.	Monogram	4.00—3.00
33.	Monogram	3.50
34.	A. Per letter	.06
	B. Per letter	.09
	C. Per letter	.06
35.	Monogram	5.50
36.	Monogram	4.50—3.00
37.	Per letter	.40
38.	Monogram	3.00
39.	Monogram	3.25—2.75
40.	Monogram	2.50—2.00
41.	Monogram	6.00
42.	Monogram	3.50—3.00
43.	Monogram	4.00—3.00
44.	Monogram	3.50—2.50
45.	Monogram	1.50—1.00
46.	Per letter	.12
47.	Per letter	.20
48.	Per letter	.20
49.	Per letter	.08
50.	Monogram	1.50
51.	Monogram	1.25
52.	Monogram	1.25
53.	Per letter	.10
54.	Per letter	.05
55.	Monogram	2.00
56.	Per letter	.15
57.	Monogram	1.50

Page 323

May and Malone catalog, 1929

Townsman monogram

Jolly Roger monogram

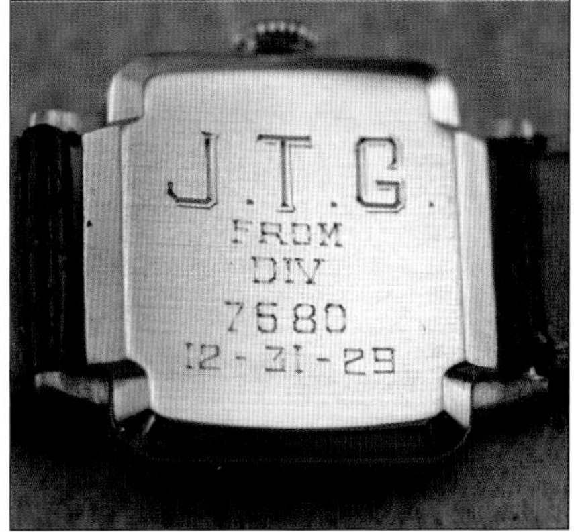

New Yorker inscription

General Motors Consul presentation watch

Special inscription, case back; see inside of case back on right

Special inscription, inside case back

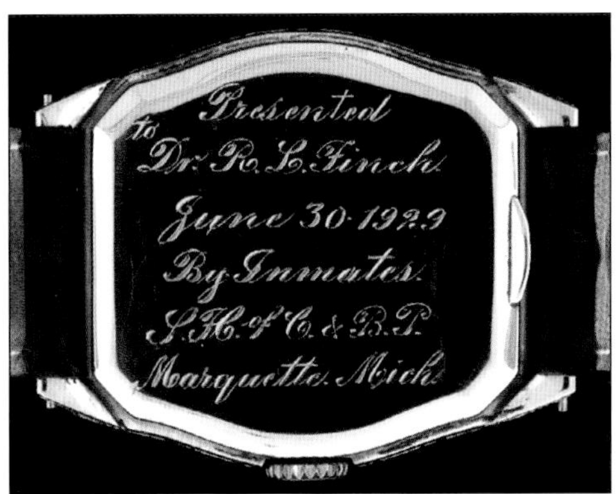

Convict Consul inscription

Undertaker Consul inscription

Newly Identified Models

Since the publication of *The Illinois Watch: The Life and Times of a Great American Watch Company*, eleven more of the previously unidentified models have been identified. These are listed below.

Newly Identified Illinois Wristwatch Models		
Akron/ Aluminum Prototype	Kensington	Saratoga
Belmont[1]	LaSalle[6]	Seneca
Cadet[2]	Latonia[7]	Sherwood
Commander[3]	Motor Coach	Sportsman
Countess	Paul Revere[8]	Varsity
Exeter[4]	Puritan[9]	Vogue
Haddon Hall[5]	Richmond 6/0	Yankee Clipper

[1] Appears to be another name for a Commodore
[2] Appears to be another name for a Marquis Strap
[3] Appears to be another name for a Wentworth
[4] Appears to be another name for an Andover
[5] Appears to be another name for a Blackstone
[6] Appears to be another name for a Commodore
[7] Appears to be another name for a Derby
[8] Appears to be another name for a Futura
[9] Appears to be another name for a Townsman

Red = Ladies'
Black = Men's

Factory-Cased Watches for Which Authentic Names are Unknown*		
Beau Brummell/Viking	No. 241	Square Cut Corner
Chesterfield Stepped Bezel	No. 250/Schmukler	Square Cut Corner, Large
Finalist Deco	Richmond 12/0	
New Yorker Enamel	Square	

* The names in this list have been used to identify certain models by price guide authors, collectors and/or this author. Unfortunately, at this time we do not know their authentic factory names.

Red = Ladies'
Black = Men's

Cases of Mistaken Identity

In continuing to pursue solutions to the Illinois puzzle, we are finding it is clear that collectors have been laboring with some cases of mistaken identity. For example, we now feel that the wristwatch models listed in the following table are more correctly named as indicated. (For an explanation of these assumptions, see the description for each of these watches in Chapter 9.)

Formerly Known As	Currently Known As
Aluminum Prototype	Akron
Art Deco	Finalist Deco[1]
Aviator	Locke
Beau Brummell	Beau Royale (if it has 15 jewels)
Beau Royale	Beau Brummell (if it has 17 or 19 jewels)
Bennett	Square Cut Corner
Black Enamel Cushion	Chevalier
Blackhawk	Seneca also
Large Bennett	Square Cut Corner Large
Burlington Cushion	Aviator
Canby	Canby Rectangular
Chesterfield Plain Bezel	Finalist Plain Bezel[1]
Cut Bezel	Armored Case
Daytona Leaf	Saratoga Leaf
Daytona Notched Leaf	Saratoga Notched Leaf
Guardian	Is not a Guardsman (it is likely a Guardian dial in a Speedway 178 case)
Manhattan	New Yorker (if it does not have an original metal band)
Manhattan	Fifth Avenue if it has 21 jewels in a white gold-filled engraved case and an original metal band
Manhattan	Richmond 6/0 if it has 17 jewels in a yellow gold-filled engraved case and an original metal band
Maxine	Ace/Wayne or Maxine
New Yorker	Manhattan if it has an original metal band regardless of jewel count or subsidiary second location
No.178	Speedway 178[1]
No. 250/Schmukler	No. 650
No. 650	Varsity
Prince	Atlantic
Rectangular	also Canby
Ronald	Ace/Wayne or Maxine
Round Enamel Bezel	Osgood[1]
Sangamo	Sangamon
Special	Sportsman (with Sportsman signed dial)
Stephen	Square
Tank	Tank/Bryce[2]

1. These are also fabricated names, but they are better supported by documentation.
2. This name was taken from an advertisement by the Illinois Watch Case Company, and an Illinois material catalog.

Red = Ladies' Black = Men's

Case Shapes For Men's Models

Rectangular		
Andover	Frontenac	Richmond 12/0
Ardsley	Futura	Rockliffe
Baronet	Gallahad	Rockliffe 18/0
Biltmore 18/0	Hudson	Sangamon
Bryce	Illinois Whitman	Schmukler
Canby	Kenilworth	Tank
Chatham	Larchmont	Trophy
Chesterfield	Manhattan	Tuxedo
Chesterfield Stepped Bezel	Medalist	Urbana
Commander	New Yorker	Vernon
Exeter	New Yorker Enamel	Wembley
Fifth Avenue	No. 250	Wentworth
Finalist	Paul Revere	Westchester
Finalist Deco	Rectangular	Yorktown

Round		
Armored Cases*	Integrated Guard	Ongard
Brandt Park	Integrated Guard Off-Set	Ongard Offset
D-D Utility	Motor Coach	Osgood
Depollier Dust/ Water Proof	Off-Duty	Police Special
Greyhound	Off-Set Crowns	Skyway
Guardsman Military	Off-Set Crowns	Telephone Dial
*Also came in a Cushion case		

Cut Corner		
Atlantic	Consul	Square Cut Corner
Atlantic Enamel	Rectangular	Square Cut Corner Large
Canby	Riley	

Decagonal		
Decagon	Decagon Jr.	Southampton

Tonneau		
Akron / Aluminum Prototype	Beau Royale	Kingston
	Blackhawk	Marquis Strap
Barrel	Cadet	Mate
Beau Brummell	Cavalier	Seneca
Beau Brummell/ Viking	Chieftain	Standish
Beau Geste	Consul	Tonneau
Beau Monde	Ensign	Whippet

Square		
Arlington	Derby	Potomac
Belmont	Hawthorne	Rockingham
Biltmore 6/0	LaSalle	Square
Bostonian	Latonia	Sterling
Burlington	Metropolitan	Varsity
Commodore	Pimlico	

Octagonal		
Ace	Maxine	Southampton
Admiral Evans	Riley	Wayne

Tank	
Arlington	Hawthorne
Bryce	Tank

Unusual		
Caprice	Ritz	Viking
Metropolitan	Townsman	
Puritan	Valedictorian	

Oval
Piccadilly

Cushion		
Ariston	Eagle	Integrated Guard Off-Set
Armored Case*	Greystone	Jolly Roger
Aviator	Guardian	Major
Blackstone	Guardsman	Special;
Burlington	Haddon Hall	Speedway
Chevalier	Integrated Guard	Speedway 178
Chrysanthemum		Sportsman
*Also came in a round case.		

Exclusivity

It seems apparent that when Illinois selected a model from a casemaker it entered into an exclusive contractual supply relationship with that casemaker. Hamilton halted this practice in the 1933–1934 time frame.

The only known instances of the same Illinois case models being used by another manufacturer are for the Biltmore and Urbana models. Gruen and Longines each sold a wristwatch using the "Biltmore" case, and Waltham sold a wristwatch case identical to the Illinois Urbana except for its case color. Keystone supplied the Urbana cases, while Wadsworth produced the Biltmore cases. Elgin sold an Urbana in a yellow rolled gold-plated case by Keystone under its Philadelphia "Victory" brand. (See Chapter 9 for the details concerning those models.)

OXIDIZED VS. ENAMELED

Casemakers occasionally used enameling or oxidation to enhance their designs. These processes are different, and Illinois, as well as other watch manufacturers, was careful to distinguish between the two in descriptions of cases. Enamel, properly called "vitreous enamel," is a glass material, applied as a powder (or powder suspended in a fluid base) to a substrate like metal and then fired until it becomes solid glass. Oxidation is instead a chemical process that causes a change in some component in the metal alloy that darkens it.

A common oxidizing agent is "liver of sulfur," which is most often a sulfide or sulfate of potassium. Such agents are applied to engraved cases and wiped off the surface but allowed to stay in the cuts until they react. The goal of oxidation is not to serve as decoration in and of itself, but simply to increase contrast and make the engraved design more visible.

However, because the changed layer is very thin, the area darkened by oxidation tends to fade over time. Some modern restorers use black enamel paint on engraved cases to refresh the oxidized contrast that has faded, but this should not be confused with true vitreous enamel, and it is misleading to speak of "replacing enamel" on cases that were originally oxidized, not enameled.

— Jim Mason

Men's Illinois Factory-Cased Wristwatches In Keystone Cases

Baronet	Larchmont	Sangamon
Beau Geste	Major	Speedway
Beau Monde	Metropolitan	Speedway 178
Canby*	No. 250/Schmukler	Square Cut Corner**
Chatham	Paul Revere	Standish
Chevalier	Piccadilly	Townsman
Devon*	Potomac	Urbana
Futura	Puritan	Varsity
Gallahad	Rectangular*	Vernon
Guardian	Richmond 12/0	Wentworth
Guardsman	Rockliffe	
Jolly Roger	Rockliffe 18/0	
Kenilworth	Rockingham	

* These models were Factory-Cased in Springfield in white gold-filled or green gold-filled Keystone cases with subsidiary seconds at 9.

**This model was Factory-Cased in Springfield in a white gold or green gold case by Solidarity as well as in a white gold-filled or green gold-filled Keystone case, both versions with subsidiary seconds at 9.

Ladies' Illinois Wristwatches Factory-Cased in Keystone Cases		
Alouette	Edgewater 208	Marlette
Annette	Edgewater 222	Marilyn
Antoinette	Elissa	Mary Todd
Avalon	Fairfax	Mary Todd 203
Babette	Fairport	Mary Todd 204
Berkshire	Florentine	Minuette
Beverly 185	Florette	Narragansett
Beverly 852	Glencoe	Newport 174
Biloxi	Glenna 186	Newport 223
Brighton	Glenna 239	No. 241
Charmette	Hollywood	Patricia
Coquette	Irene	Princess
Coronado	Janette	Rita
Countess	Lakewood	Rosette
Edgewater 175	Lenox	Roslyn
Edgewater 155	Lynette	Sylvia

Men's Illinois Wristwatches Factory-Cased in Wadsworth Cases		
Ardsley	Greyhound	Notched Lug
Biltmore 18/0	Greystone	Off-Duty
Blackstone	Haddon Hall	Richmond 6/0
Chesterfield	Hudson	Ritz
Chesterfield Stepped Bezel	Illinois Whitman	Skyway
Derby	Kensington	Trophy
Fifth Avenue	Manhattan	Valedictorian
Finalist	Motor Coach	Westchester
Finalist Deco	New Yorker	Yorktown
Frontenac	New Yorker Enamel	

Ladies' Illinois Wristwatches Factory-Cased in Wadsworth Cases		
Argyle	Daytona 155A	Miami 155
Arlene	Daytona 155B	Miami 157
Barbara	Debutante	Redonda 153
Bar Harbor 156	Del Monte 155	Redonda 154
Bar Harbor 158	Del Monte 157	Saratoga Leaf
Berkeley 153	Diamond-Set	Saratoga Notched Leaf
Berkeley 154	Edgewater 155	Queen Anne
Berkeley 154A	Gloria	Vanity Fair
Claudette	Greta	Vardon
Constance	Joan	Vogue
Daytona 153	Lady Mary	Wadsworth Special Models
Daytona 154	Long Beach	
Daytona 155	Lynette	

Men's and Ladies' Illinois Wristwatches Factory-Cased in Fahys Cases		
Beau Brummell	Chieftain	Mate
Beau Royale	Ensign	Medalist
Beau Brummell/ Viking	Fahys Special Model	Viking
Cadet	Kingston	Wembley
Cavalier	Marquis Strap	Yankee Clipper
Red = Ladies	Black = Men's	

Men's Illinois Wristwatches in Pioneer Cases		
Akron./ Aluminum Prototype*	Blackhawk	Seneca*
*Factory-Cased in Springfield		

Men's Illinois Wristwatches Factory-Cased in J. Milhening Cases	
Andover	Exeter
Arlington	Hawthorne

Men's Illinois Wristwatches Factory-Cased in Solidarity Cases		
Consul	Pimlico	Tuxedo
Derby	Special Cushion (Solidarity)	Whippet*
Devon*	Square Cut Corner**	

*If in white gold or green gold, Solidarity case with an engraved bezel
**If in white gold or green gold, Solidarity case

Men's Illinois Wristwatch Cases by the Illinois Watch Case Company		
Ace	Cushion Form	Off-Set Crown
Admiral Benson	Cut Bezel	Rectangular
Admiral Evans	Devon	Riley
Armored Case	General Funston	Southampton
Atlantic	General Joffre	Special
Atlantic Large	Generics	Tank
Aviator	Integrated Guard Kitchener	Transitional
Bryce	Locke	United States Army Watch*
Canby	Maxine	Wayne
Cushion	Military	
*Factory-Cased in Springfield		

Men's and Ladies' Illinois Wristwatch Cases by the Star Watch Case Company		
Babette II	Marionette	Square Cut Corner
Bryce	Muzette	Square Cut Corner Large
Canby	Rectangular	Sterling
Connerics	Sportsman	Suzette
Juliette	Square	
Red = Ladies' Black = Men's		

Men's Illinois Wristwatch Cases by NAWCo	
Ongard	Ongard Off-Set

Men's Illinois Wristwatch Cases by Depollier/Dubois		
Bullet Dial	Depollier Water/Dust Proof	"D-D" Utility Watch

Men's Illinois Wristwatch Cases by Osco	
Brandt Rock	Osgood

Men's Illinois Wristwatch Cases by Two or More Casemakers		
Ace	Cut Bezel	Rectangular
Admiral Evans	Cushion	Riley
Admiral Evans Off-Set	Cushion Form	Special
Armored Case	Decagon	Southampton
Ariston	Decagon Jr.	Square
Atlantic	Devon	Square Cut Corner
Atlantic Large	General Joffre	Standish
Aviator	Generic	Sterling
Bryce	Guardsman Military	Telephone Dial
Canby	Integrated Guard	Tank
Chevalier	Kitchener	Tonneau
Decagon	Latonia	Transitionals
Decagon, Jr.	Locke	Washington Watch Co.
Decagon Jr. Off-Set	Maxine	Wayne
Derby	Military	Whippet
Conneric	Off-Set Crowns	
Contract	Pimlico	

Hamilton-Illinois Men's and Ladies' Wristwatch Cases by Huguenin		
Automatic Model B	DatomaticModel	Signamatic Model A
Career Girl Model A	Nautilus Model A	Signamatic Model B
Red = Ladies' Black = Men's		

Ladies' Hamilton-Illinois Wristwatch Cases by Major Watch Case Company*		
No. 5312	No. 5557	Unnumbered Two-Tone
*All in diamond-set 14K gold cases		

Hamilton-Illinois Men's and Ladies' Wristwatch Cases by Pioneer	
Debonair K	Lady Gay E
Red = Ladies' Black = Men's	

Hamilton-Illinois Men's and Ladies' Wristwatch Cases by Schwab & Wuischpard		
Automatic Model A	Debonair Model B	Kimberly Model C
Automatic Model D	Debonair Model C	Lady Gay Model C
Career Girl Model B	Debonair Model E	Lady Gay Model D
Coquette Model A	Debonair Model F	Lady Gay Model G
Coquette Model B	Debonair Model L	Lady Gay Model H
Coquette Model C	Golden Treasure Model A	Lady Gay Model K
Coquette Model D	Golden Treasure Model B	Topper Model A
Coquette Model E	Kimberly Model A	Topper Model B
Debonair Model A	Kimberly Model B	
Red = Ladies' Black = Men's		

Hamilton-Illinois Men's and Ladies' Wristwatch Cases by Star Watch Case Company		
Debonair Model D	Debonair Model J	Lady Gay Model B
Debonair Model G	Lady Gay Model A	Lady Gay Model F
Red = Ladies' Black = Men's		

Hamilton-Illinois Men's Wristwatch by Unidentified Casemaker
Golden Male "A" * Golden Male "B" *
Golden Male "C" *
Golden Male "D" *
*14K gold

The American Watch Attachment Industry

For centuries, most watches dangled from chains around necks or nestled in pockets. When watches moved to the wrist, they presented a whole new set of challenges and opportunities.

An elegant solution for women soon appeared: the bracelet watch. (See Chapter 10 for the early history of this type of wristwatch.) Many bracelet watches indeed seemed at first glance to be no more than bracelets, since the face of the watch often had an elaborately decorated cover. For convenience in telling the time, however, the wearer needed to be able to see the face immediately. Thus open-face pocket watches became adapted for use in wristwatches.

The convertible watch (basically an open-face small pocket watch) could be worn not only as a pendant on a chain or brooch but also as a bracelet with an expansion-link attachment. Soon, non-convertible versions also became available, sometimes with various kinds of bracelets from which to choose.[26] Both types of watches were becoming popular in England by the early 1890s, but it took a little longer for them to catch on in the United States. By early in the twentieth century, they were being offered by various domestic watch manufacturers, including Illinois. The first Illinois wristwatch was introduced in 1912: a convertible model issued under the "Ariste" label for Marshall Field's. By 1915, Illinois Factory advertisements were showing two ladies' wristwatches: a convertible, now with Illinois' own name on it, as well as a non-convertible bracelet watch.

In the meantime, another type of watch attachment had been introduced: the Scheufele Clip, introduced in Europe in 1912. This device, a patented metal housing that accommodated a pocket watch so it could be clipped in place and worn on a wrist, was used primarily by ladies, and in Europe (see Chapter 10 for further discussion of it). Although the Scheufele clip permitted conventional pocket watches to be worn on the wrist, it never became as popular with women as the bracelet option of the new convertible watch, and men tended to avoid it because it was too bracelet-like and thus feminine in appearance.

More widely used by men was the wristlet, a large leather wrist strap with a pouch in the middle into which the wearer could place a pocket watch. At least initially, wristlets appealed primarily to soldiers. In fact, the first proof of wristlet use appears in an 1888 photograph taken of British colonial soldiers during the Hazara Expedition in Pakistan, though the military use of wristwatches may have begun earlier. The first known legal evidence of the wristlet is the British-issued patent to the Garstin Company in 1893 for a "Watch Wristlet." A photograph of Teddy Roosevelt's Rough Riders in 1898, during the Spanish-American War, shows one of the soldiers wearing a wristlet; this is the first indication of wristlet use by a United States soldier. During the Second Boer War (1899) and immediately thereafter, the wristlet was the wrist attachment of choice for soldiers, as pictures attest.

So the wristlet, ugly and ungainly though it was, enjoyed at least a limited following. Surprisingly enough, this type of attachment remained available quite a long time, continuing to be offered in jobbers' catalogs well into the 1930s; the 1934 A. C. Becken catalog, for example, had a listing for wristlets, which it called "Cup Watch Bracelets."

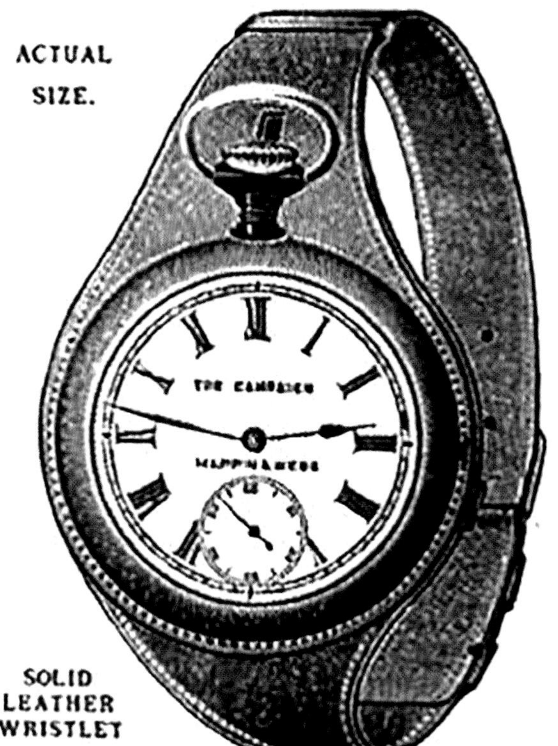

Wristlet advertisement, *Illustrated Sporting and Dramatic News*, September 7, 1901

Borgzinner Brothers, Ltd, advertisement for wristlets, *Watchmaker, Jeweler and Silversmith*, 1901

The wristlet may have been unattractive and somewhat uncomfortable to wear, but its widespread use indicated acknowledgement that wearing a timepiece on the wrist was an increased convenience. Moreover, the wristlet was important for showing how useful leather could be as an attachment material. Just before World War I, jewelers began affixing metal loops (or lugs, as they were called) to the ends of pocket watches. Watch manufacturers followed suit, producing military wristwatches with a similar design. During this period, leather straps with buckles became the attachments of choice, and many companies rapidly emerged to meet this demand. Among these early suppliers of leather watchbands were the F. Speidel Company, Jacques Kreisler & Company, and A. Hirsch & Company.

Image courtesy of the National Watch and Clock Museum Library & Research Center (NAWCC), Columbia, PA. It is from one of their exhibits.

A Boer War soldier sporting a wristwatch, c. 1899

Boer War soldiers wearing early wristwatches, c. 1899

Women operating stock boards at the Waldorf-Astoria Hotel in New York City during World War I. The Waldorf was the first to employ women in its various departments in order to release men for war work. One is wearing high button shoes and a wristwatch. ***Source:*** **National Archives at College Park, https://research.archives.gov/id/533759**

Although the first men's wristwatches used leather straps, the first watchbands for ladies' watches with fixed lugs used ribbons, which were inserted through the lugs; with beautifully decorated sliding metal clasps to allow adjustments. Manufacturers of men's wristwatches initially equipped them with fixed lugs but soon offered lugs with holes in them so that spring bars could be inserted. This allowed bands to be replaced more easily.

The first leather watch bands were constructed primarily out of plain pigskin and calfskin. Later there were more choices offered to meet fashion trends. Among these possibilities were two-tone leather; Morocco suede; and black, brown or tan pigskin. Further options included a choice of smooth or grained leather; straight or tapered ends; braided inlay; and availability with or without a buckle.

The watch chain industry took notice of the trend toward wristwatches. Experienced in metal work, they began offering metal watchbands. Although watch manufacturers' catalogs of the period indicate that most models featured leather bands, enterprising jewelers could offer the buyer a metallic band instead, both increasing his profit and enhancing the appearance of the watch. In the late 1920s and early 1930s, bracelets, most made of flexible metal, were offered for sale and quickly became very popular.

Because wristwatches were becoming more popular than pocket watches, many makers of pocket watch chains found themselves going into a death spiral. Accordingly, they seized the opportunity to convert their machines and processes, easily and quickly, to metal bracelet fabrication. It is for this reason that almost all of the first manufacturers of metal watch attachments were originally pocket watch chain companies, many based in the well-known jewelry manufacturing areas of Massachusetts and Rhode Island.

Then, in rapid order, there were many watch attachment innovations: methods of adjustment to wrist size, improvements in means of fastening the metal bracelet to the watch, and enhancements to snaps, buckles or catches for putting the watch on or taking it off the wrist. There were many refinements in expandable links, folding buckles in design and finish—plus an intense battle to combat the evil, corrosive effect of perspiration on the bands themselves.

A new metal bracelet industry emerged to meet the need for millions of these bands each year. Many wristwatch wearers needed simply to replace metal bands damaged by perspiration; others wished to take advantage of the latest innovations in design.

Watch manufacturers, recognizing this trend, started offering metal "bracelet" options for their wristwatch models. In the early 1930s, Illinois acknowledged the increased importance of the watchband when it changed model names simply because of a different attachment.

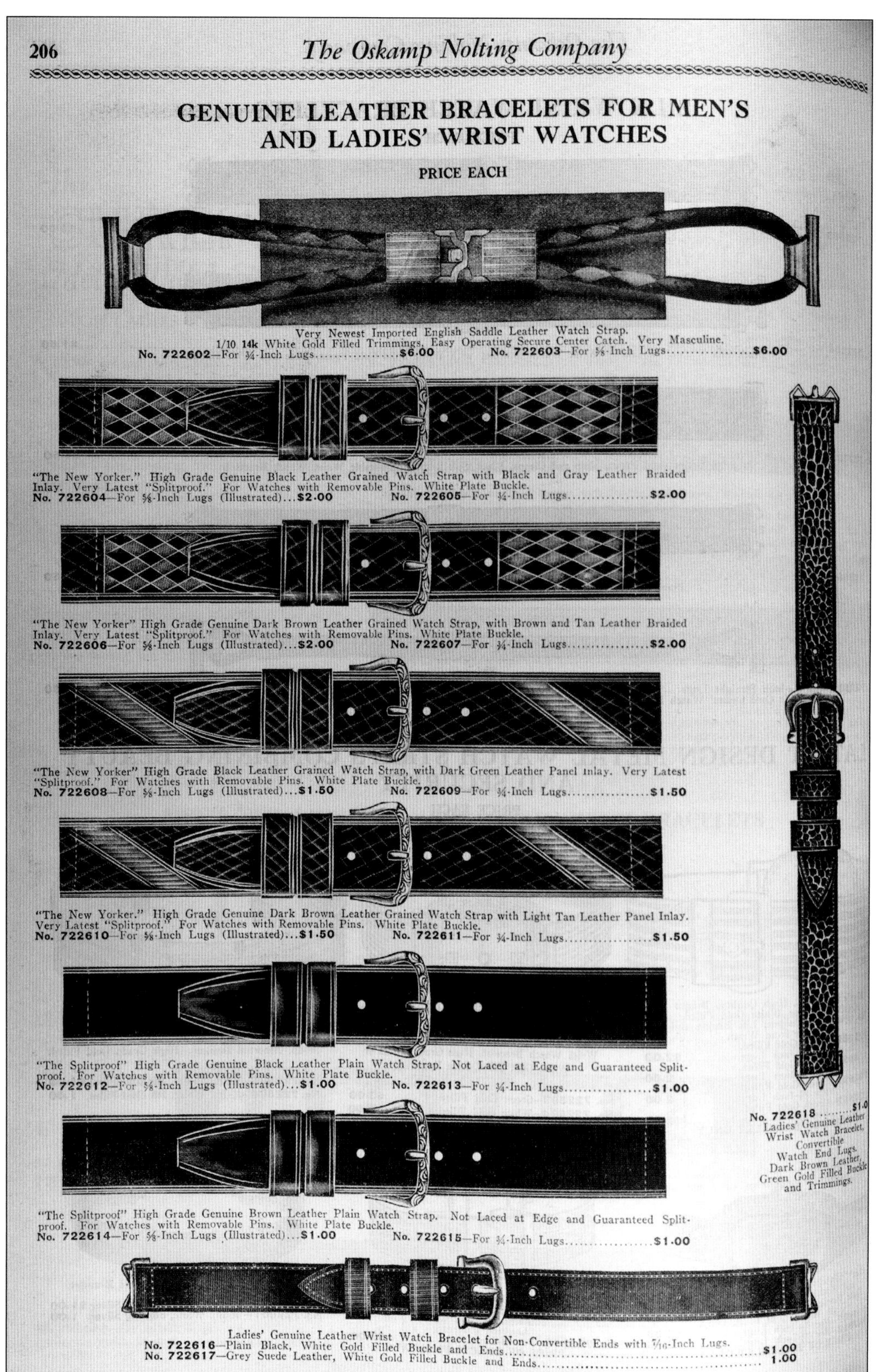

206 *The Oskamp Nolting Company*

GENUINE LEATHER BRACELETS FOR MEN'S AND LADIES' WRIST WATCHES

PRICE EACH

Very Newest Imported English Saddle Leather Watch Strap.
1/10 14k White Gold Filled Trimmings. Easy Operating Secure Center Catch. Very Masculine.
No. 722602—For ¾-Inch Lugs..................$6.00 No. 722603—For ⅝-Inch Lugs..................$6.00

"The New Yorker." High Grade Genuine Black Leather Grained Watch Strap with Black and Gray Leather Braided Inlay. Very Latest "Splitproof." For Watches with Removable Pins. White Plate Buckle.
No. 722604—For ⅝-Inch Lugs (Illustrated)...$2.00 No. 722605—For ¾-Inch Lugs.................$2.00

"The New Yorker" High Grade Genuine Dark Brown Leather Grained Watch Strap, with Brown and Tan Leather Braided Inlay. Very Latest "Splitproof." For Watches with Removable Pins. White Plate Buckle.
No. 722606—For ⅝-Inch Lugs (Illustrated)...$2.00 No. 722607—For ¾-Inch Lugs.................$2.00

"The New Yorker" High Grade Black Leather Grained Watch Strap, with Dark Green Leather Panel Inlay. Very Latest "Splitproof." For Watches with Removable Pins. White Plate Buckle.
No. 722608—For ⅝-Inch Lugs (Illustrated)...$1.50 No. 722609—For ¾-Inch Lugs.................$1.50

"The New Yorker." High Grade Genuine Dark Brown Leather Grained Watch Strap with Light Tan Leather Panel Inlay. Very Latest "Splitproof." For Watches with Removable Pins. White Plate Buckle.
No. 722610—For ⅝-Inch Lugs (Illustrated)...$1.50 No. 722611—For ¾-Inch Lugs.................$1.50

"The Splitproof" High Grade Genuine Black Leather Plain Watch Strap. Not Laced at Edge and Guaranteed Splitproof. For Watches with Removable Pins. White Plate Buckle.
No. 722612—For ⅝-Inch Lugs (Illustrated)...$1.00 No. 722613—For ¾-Inch Lugs.................$1.00

"The Splitproof" High Grade Genuine Brown Leather Plain Watch Strap. Not Laced at Edge and Guaranteed Splitproof. For Watches with Removable Pins. White Plate Buckle.
No. 722614—For ⅝-Inch Lugs (Illustrated)...$1.00 No. 722615—For ¾-Inch Lugs.................$1.00

No. 722618 ....$1.0
Ladies' Genuine Leather Wrist Watch Bracelet, Convertible Watch End Lugs. Dark Brown Leather, Green Gold Filled Buckle and Trimmings.

Ladies' Genuine Leather Wrist Watch Bracelet for Non-Convertible Ends with 5/16-Inch Lugs.
No. 722616—Plain Black, White Gold Filled Buckle and Ends..........$1.00
No. 722617—Grey Suede Leather, White Gold Filled Buckle and Ends..........1.00

Leather watchbands, Oskamp Nolting catalog, 1932

In order to keep introducing "new" models, especially during the Great Depression, Illinois would at times simply put a metal bracelet rather than a leather strap on an existing model and change its name. There are many examples of this Illinois phenomenon: for example, a Ritz provided with a metal band became a Valedictorian, and in like manner a Trophy became a Kensington.

To a very limited extent, Hamilton did the same thing with one or more of its own models. Halligan's notes show that Hamilton gave its Greenwich model (1931) a leather cord band instead of a conventional strap and named the "new" model the Greenwood. Introduced on June 1, 1933, the Greenwood appeared in Hamilton's September 1933 price list.

Hamilton was evidently trying to get plenty of mileage out of the Greenwich case. The Greenwich was introduced with a leather strap, but the next year, 1932, Hamilton offered three options: a leather strap, a metal band, or a hybrid band of leather and metal, described as an "open link leather strap," which was Hadley's very popular "Piccadilly" model.

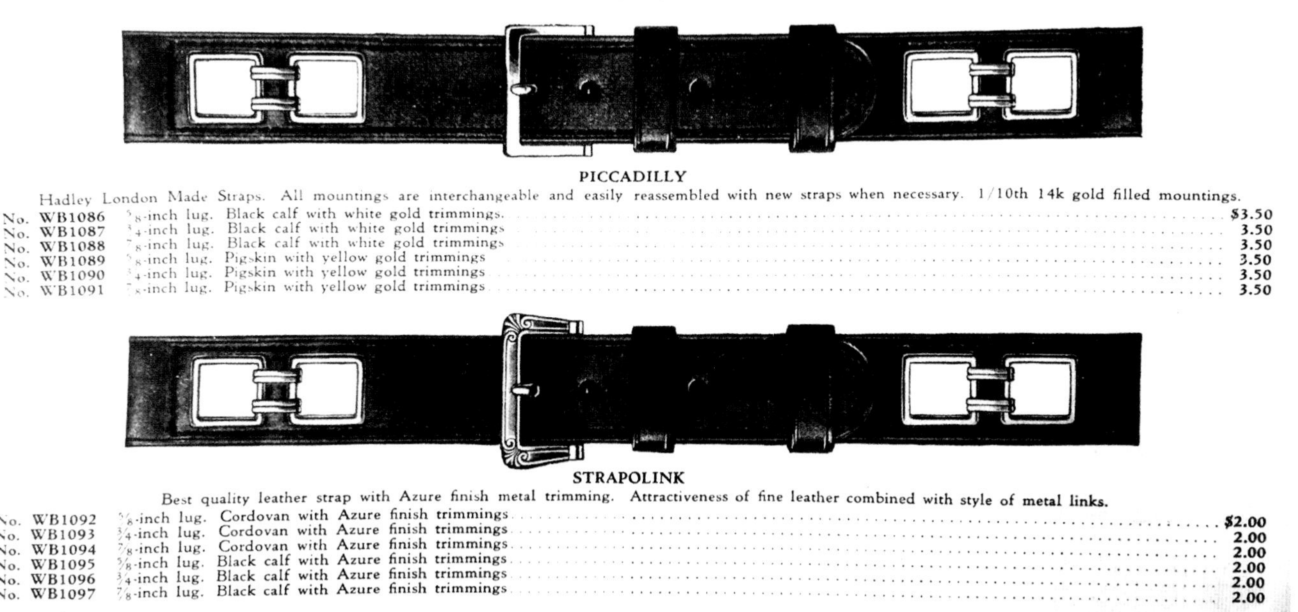

LATEST CREATIONS BY HADLEY

Already acclaimed as establishing the ultra in style. Finest quality leather straps with interchangeable gold filled trimmings.

PICCADILLY

Hadley London Made Straps. All mountings are interchangeable and easily reassembled with new straps when necessary. 1/10th 14k gold filled mountings.

No. WB1086	5/8-inch lug.	Black calf with white gold trimmings	$3.50
No. WB1087	3/4-inch lug.	Black calf with white gold trimmings	3.50
No. WB1088	7/8-inch lug.	Black calf with white gold trimmings	3.50
No. WB1089	5/8-inch lug.	Pigskin with yellow gold trimmings	3.50
No. WB1090	3/4-inch lug.	Pigskin with yellow gold trimmings	3.50
No. WB1091	7/8-inch lug.	Pigskin with yellow gold trimmings	3.50

STRAPOLINK

Best quality leather strap with Azure finish metal trimming. Attractiveness of fine leather combined with style of metal links.

No. WB1092	5/8-inch lug.	Cordovan with Azure finish trimmings	$2.00
No. WB1093	3/4-inch lug.	Cordovan with Azure finish trimmings	2.00
No. WB1094	7/8-inch lug.	Cordovan with Azure finish trimmings	2.00
No. WB1095	5/8-inch lug.	Black calf with Azure finish trimmings	2.00
No. WB1096	3/4-inch lug.	Black calf with Azure finish trimmings	2.00
No. WB1097	7/8-inch lug.	Black calf with Azure finish trimmings	2.00

Hadley's hybrid leather and metal bands, A. C. Becken catalog, 1932

There is little known about the specific metal watchband fabricators used by Illinois. However, we definitely know that it did offer some of its models equipped with metal bracelets fabricated by the Hadley Company and the R. F. Simmons Company. Some jobbers' advertisements have been found noting that some of the Illinois models offered with metal bands were equipped with Hadley and Simmons bracelets, and other jobbers' catalogs show Illinois models with unidentified metal bands that exactly match ones advertised in catalogs as Hadleys.

Because watchbands could be switched so easily, often the purchaser left the store with a watch looking somewhat different from what was in the catalog. To familiarize the collector with the various period attachment options available from jewelers, some of the major wristwatch bracelet companies active in the 1920s to early 1930s are described below.[27] Many of the principals in the watch attachment industry in the 1920s and 1930s invented and patented their own unique product features.

Although some of the companies manufacturing watch attachments were located in New York City or its environs, most were concentrated in Attleboro, Massachusetts, and Providence, Rhode Island.[28]

J. F. Sturdy's Sons Company

According to Orra L. Stone's *History of Massachusetts Industries,* John F. Sturdy and his brother James H. originally had a die forging and jewelry making business in Providence, Rhode Island, but in 1849 relocated in Attleboro, Massachusetts. After inventing a method of producing what became known as rolled gold plate, they took on a partner, Herbert M. Draper, and established Draper, Sturdy & Company. Stone points out that this firm "introduced into Attleboro the manufacture of rolled gold plated stock and jewelry. They were philanthropists in a way as they disclosed their production secrets to other local manufacturers."[29]

The firm became known as J. F. Sturdy & Sons in 1865, when John's sons Frederick, Herbert, and Frank became associated with it.[30] The company utilized the rolled gold plate process for the manufacture of watch chains. From time to time it introduced other specialty items, such as pencils, knives and lockets.

Sturdy introduced its first watch bracelet in 1915: a seven-link expanding, flexible bracelet with end hooks of new design. This met with success and was followed by a narrower nine-link model of the same type with still more advanced concepts in end-hook construction. These two bracelets remained popular until going out of style around 1923. Soon afterwards, Sturdy resumed its leading position by creating the block type of expanding flexible bracelet with separable links originally called "Flexpand" and afterwards, with improvements, called "Sturdymaid." These were followed by another metal bracelet known as "Sturdystrap," equipped with a new idea in buckle construction.[31]

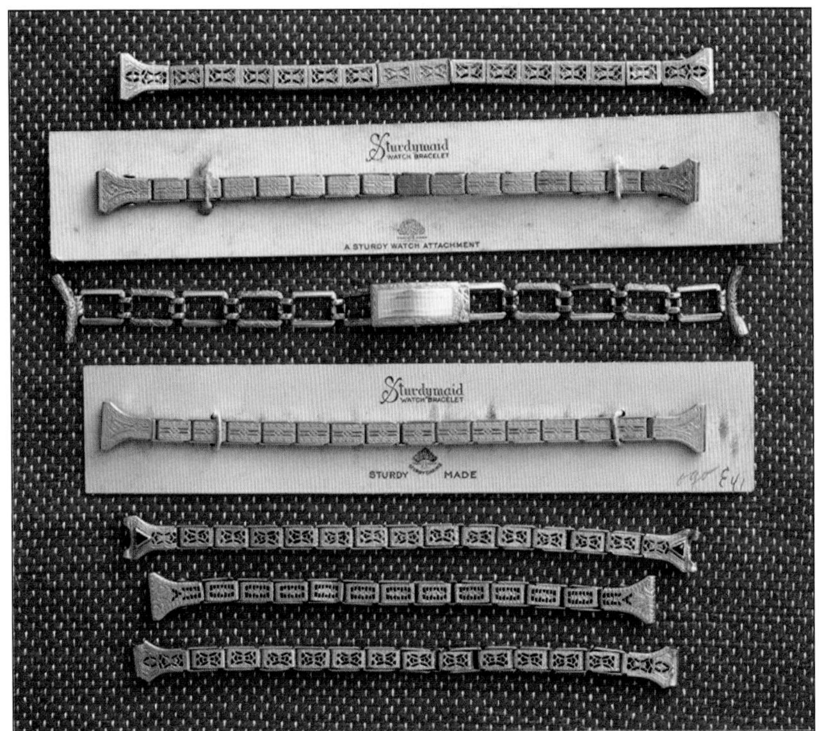

A group of Sturdy ladies' watchbands. The two on their original sales cards (Sturdymaids, one white gold-filled and the other yellow) are probably Sturdy's most popular ladies' model.

Two Sturdystraps, one attached to an Illinois ladies' Miami 157 model

In 1918, Sturdy produced a solid gold "US" clasp for a military khaki strap, as shown here.

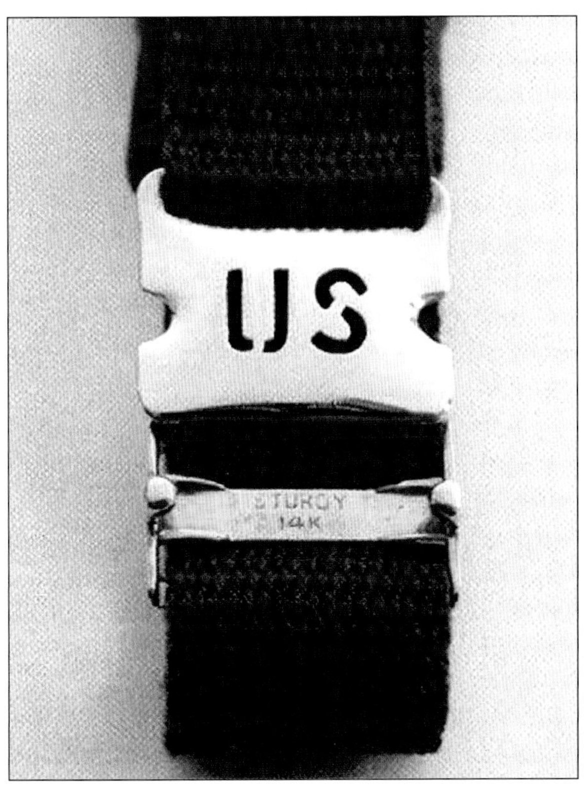

Sturdy solid gold 1918 Military U.S. Clasp (front); only one is known to exist.

J. F. Sturdy's U.S. khaki straps, advertisement, *Jewelers' Circular-Weekly*, September 4, 1918

June, 1918 THE KEYSTONE Page 9

THE NEW STURDY—MAN'S BRACELET

A Real Khaki Strap

(PATENT PENDING)

7540

Men in uniform and out acknowledge the usefulness and convenience of the wrist watch. They will demand khaki straps with their watches, because they give service and are comfortable.

The STURDY Strap will perform a practical purpose. Our Fasteners make it strong, safe, easy to adjust and mannish in appearance. Our Khaki Webbing is very closely woven and finely finished, and is far superior in strength and appearance to any webbing now in use.

7530 U. S.

Look for the name STURDY stamped on the inside of every fastener.

Made in two widths, ½ inch and ⅝ inch, with sterling silver, nickel silver, 12k 1/10 gold filled and 14k gold fasteners.

Also furnished in Navy blue webbing.

ORDER THRU YOUR JOBBER

7530

MADE BY

J. F. STURDY'S SONS COMPANY

ATTLEBORO FALLS, MASS.

J. F. Sturdy's Son's Company advertisement, *Keystone*, June 1918

In 1932, Sturdy specialties in watch attachments included the "Sturdybilt" for men with a ratchet "Wonfold" buckle and a new idea called "concealed expansion," whereby the expanding of the bracelet did not change its appearance. A new specialty in ladies' bracelets was the "Link Sturdymaid," which incorporated an innovation in ratchet buckle construction that made the operation of the ratchet optional with the wearer. That bracelet had expanding separable links and interchangeable end-hooks and was produced in gold-filled and in gold-filled with a Nuwite finish. Sturdy used non-corrosive Allegheny metal in several of its bracelets to combat sweat.[32]

Sturdy trademark

Sturdy men's watch bracelet of Allegheny metal

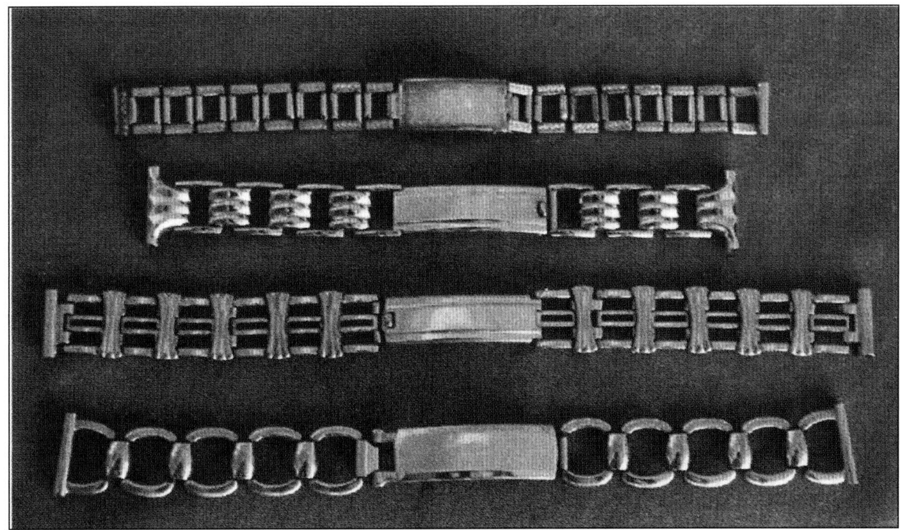

A selection of vintage men's metal bands. The top one is an A & Z "Sturdyfold," second and third from the top are by J. Bruner, and the bottom one is a Gemex.

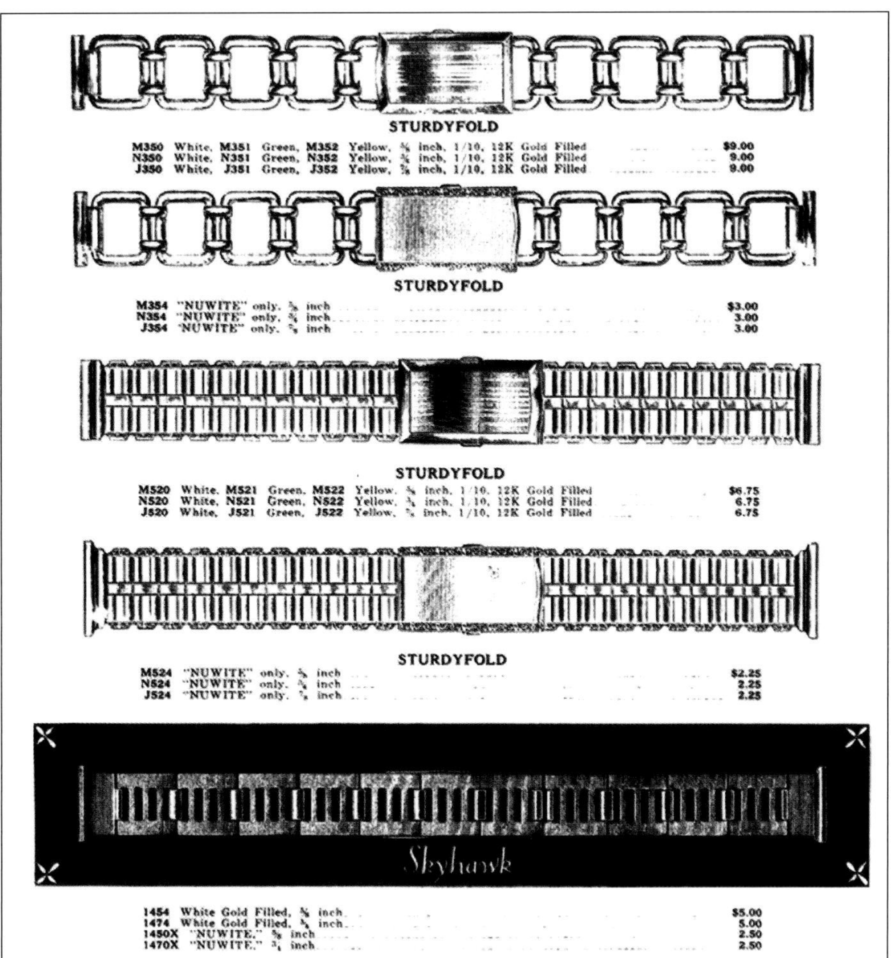

Sturdyfold bands by J. F. Sturdy's Sons, S. H. Clausin catalog, 1931

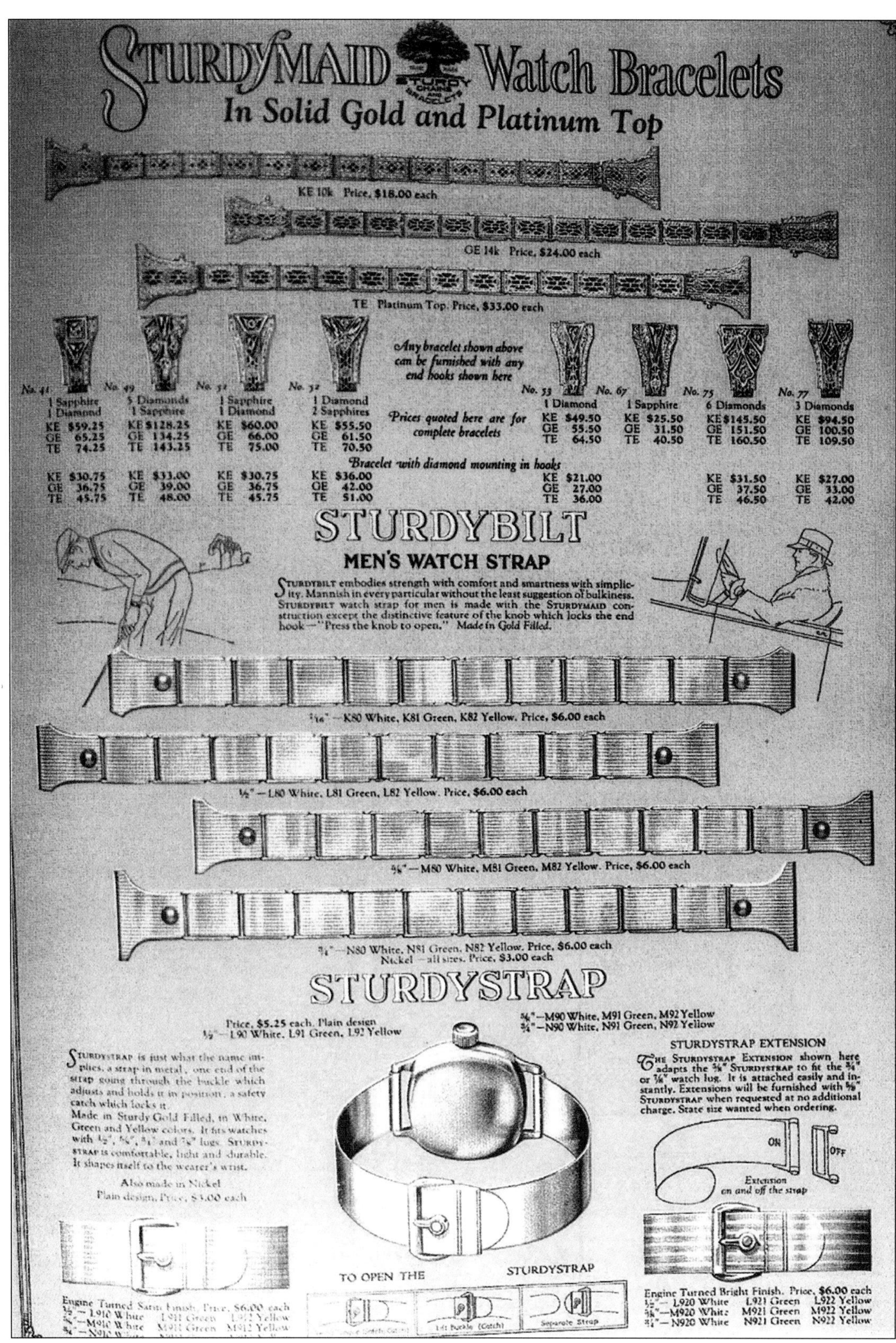

J. F. Sturdy's Sons watchbands, A. C. Becken catalog, 1928

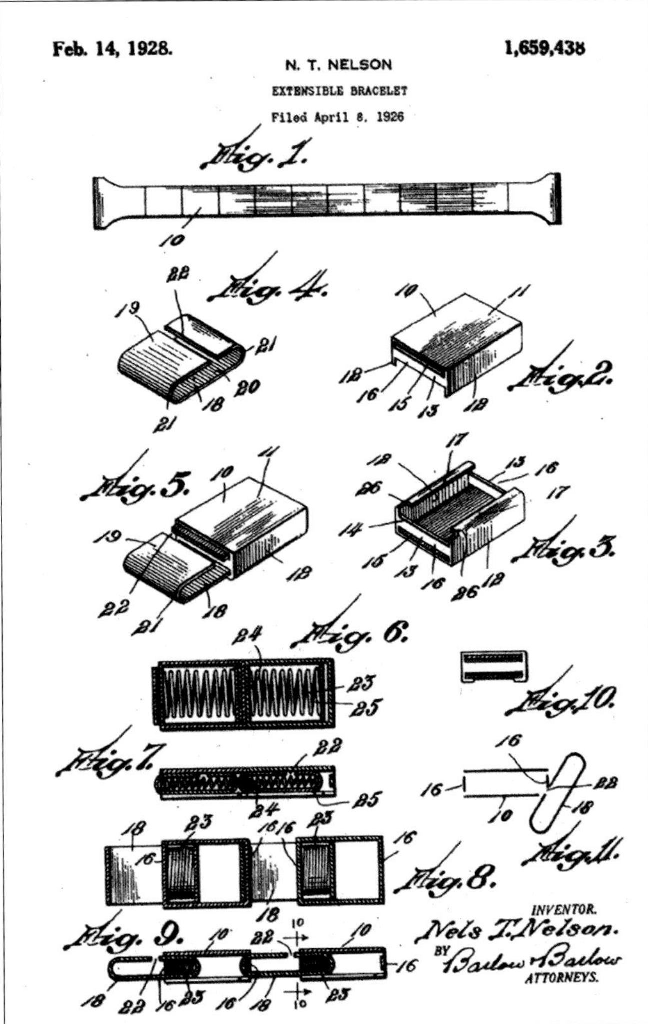

Patent assigned to Sturdy

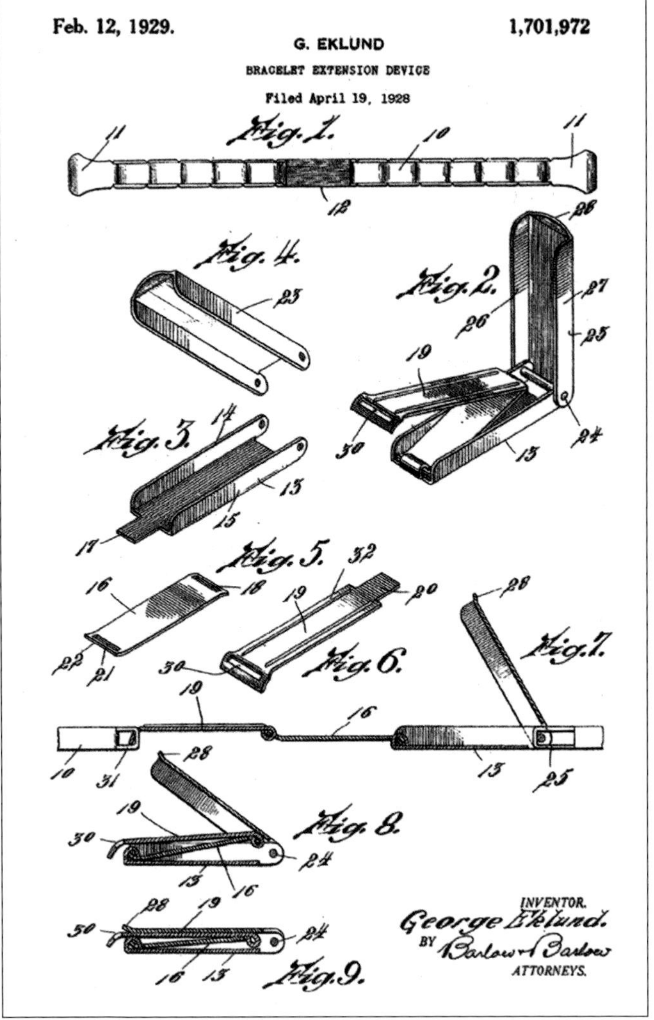

Patent assigned to Sturdy

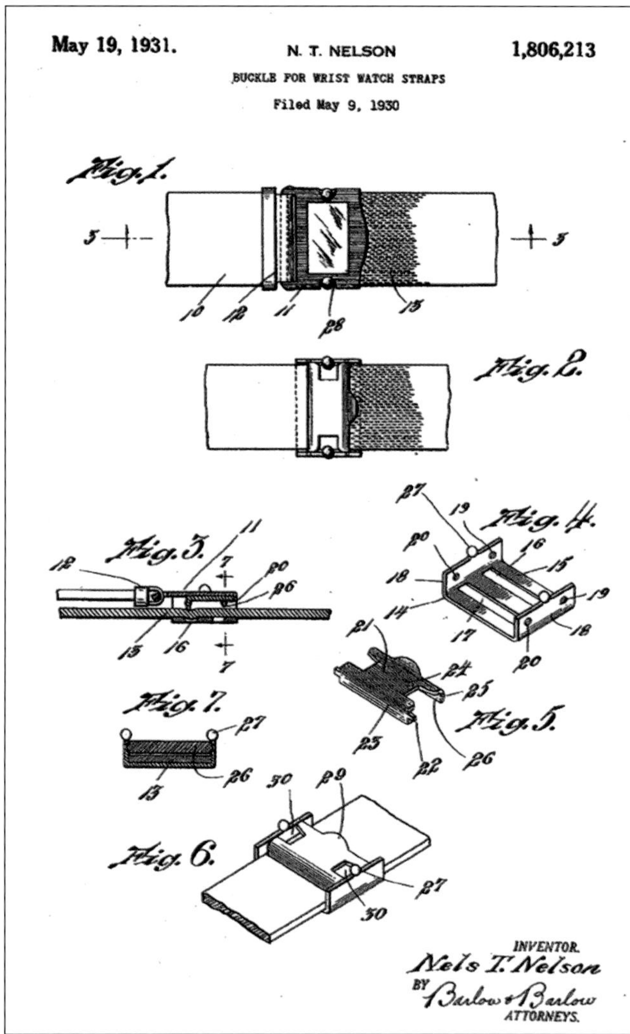

Patent assigned to Sturdy

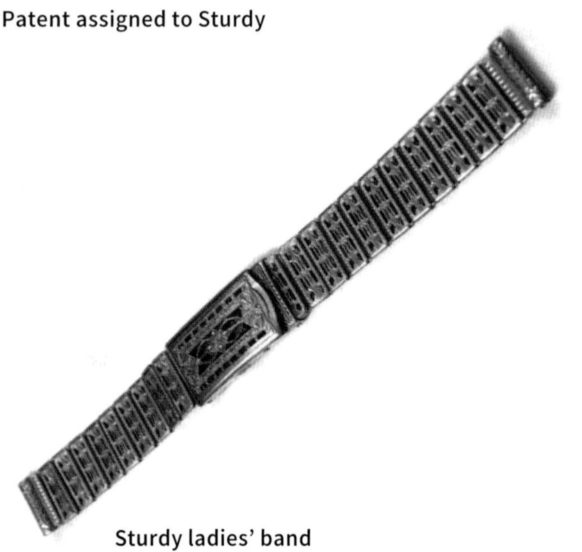

Sturdy ladies' band

Speidel Company

Friedrich Speidel founded the Speidel Company in 1867, when he started making gold and silver chains in the basement of his home in Pforzheim, Germany. The company constructed its first factory in 1896, using machinery to make chains that had previously been made by hand.

Later, Speidel sent his three sons—Albert, Edwin and Eugene—to America to establish a branch of the family's chain manufacturing business. In 1904, the F. Speidel Co. was established in Providence, Rhode Island. Another Speidel enterprise, the Automatic Gold Chain Co., was begun in 1912. During the 1920s, Speidel added costume jewelry and watchbands to its line, selling its bands primarily to wholesalers.[33]

During World War I, the Speidels suffered catastrophic loss. Anti-German sentiment was widespread in the United States, particularly after the U.S. entered the war, and people with Germanic names suffered accordingly. Among these were the Speidels and their partners, Wilhelm and Walter Forstner. Using powers granted under the Trading with the Enemy Act of 1917, seized their assets and sold them in a public auction.[34] The buyers, which had bid jointly, were the J. F. Sturdy's Sons Co. and the Leach & Garner Co., of Attleboro, Massachusetts. Thus the Speidel and Forstner property went to competitors located in an area that was one of Providence's chief rivals in jewelry manufacturing.

The Speidels were resilient, however, and were back in business within a few years. In 1922, the *Jewelers' Circular* mentioned in its August 30 issue that Eugene and Frederick Speidel were the new owners of the Providence Findings Co., and on September 13 noted that the Speidel Chain Co. had "commenced business." Both business were located at the same address, 71 Willard Avenue. And the Forstners too were able to reestablish themselves.

Alien Enemy Property Sale

J. F. Sturdy's Sons' Co. and Leach & Garner Co. Jointly Bid in Property of F. Speidel Co. in Auction at Providence, R. I., by Alien Property Custodian

In Providence, Rhode Island, on the night of April 29, 1918, U.S. Government agents conducted a spectacular raid of plants in which the Speidels and their partners, Wilhelm and Walter Forstner, were controlling interests. The May 1918 issue of the *Insurance Monitor* reported that the plants searched were W. Forstner Co, chain manufacturers; F. Speidel Co., chain manufacturers; Automatic Gold Chain Co.; S. & W. Machine Co.; General Manufacturing & Exporting Co.; Paul Stierle Co.; and W. A. H. Wells Co.

The Forstner brothers and some of their employees seem to have been singled out for punishment. Declared dangerous enemy aliens, they were arrested and then held at a Rhode Island state prison before being sent to Fort Oglethorpe for detention.

On December 7. 1918, the property seized was sold at auction by the Alien Property Custodian. Included were not only the plants themselves, but also patents and trademarks.

But the Forstners, like the Speidels, were able to recover. The November 1920 issue of the *Metal Industry* noted that the Universal Chain Co., Inc., of Providence, had "capitalized at $25.000. . .and been granted a charter under the laws of Rhode Island. . . . The concern will manufacture jewelry and jewelers' findings. . . . The president is Wilhelm Forstner, of this city, who has another and larger manufacturing facility at Irvington, N.J., under the name of the Forstner Chain Company."

Forstner's plant in New Jersey became a well-known manufacturer of jewelry. Among its offerings were metal watchbands. Wilhelm Forstner (who had later anglicized his given name to William) retired in 1955 as president of the Forstner Chain Corporation, and a group of its executives formed a new corporation, Forstner, Inc., to continue the business (*New York Times*, August 2, 1955).

General Chain Company

General Chain Company, incorporated in 1918, immediately replaced the F. Speidel Co. after Speidel's assets were seized by the U.S. Government and sold in a public auction to J. F. Sturdy's Sons and the Leach & Garner Co. Sturdy, the principal owner of General Chain, then began manufacturing chains in Providence with the resources it had acquired from Speidel. (Leach & Garner was in a closely related business, the manufacture of findings.) The brands of General Chain's four main lines of pocket watch chains were Sovereign, Record, SP and Aurora—all trademarks that had belonged to Speidel.[35]

General Chain continued to operate from its factory in Providence, Rhode Island, adding regional sales offices in New York City, Chicago and San Francisco. The company touted the fact that it enjoyed a national and worldwide reputation. For wristwatches, it made the very popular "Genco," a box-link expanding bracelet.

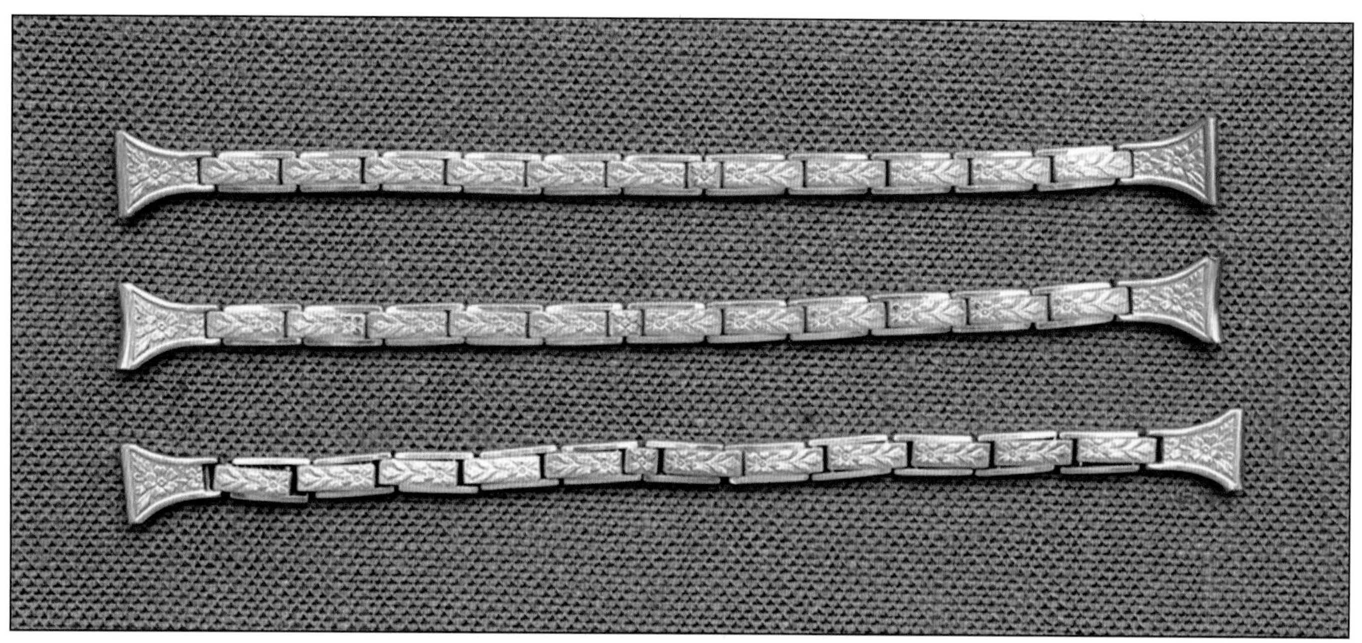

Genco watch bracelets in a popular pattern. ***Top to bottom:*** **yellow gold-filled, straight ends; yellow gold-filled, curved ends; white gold-filled straight ends**

As styles changed, General Chain modernized its product line with new watch attachments. It made both men's and women's watch bracelets in open link patterns, with an adjustable foldover center.[36]

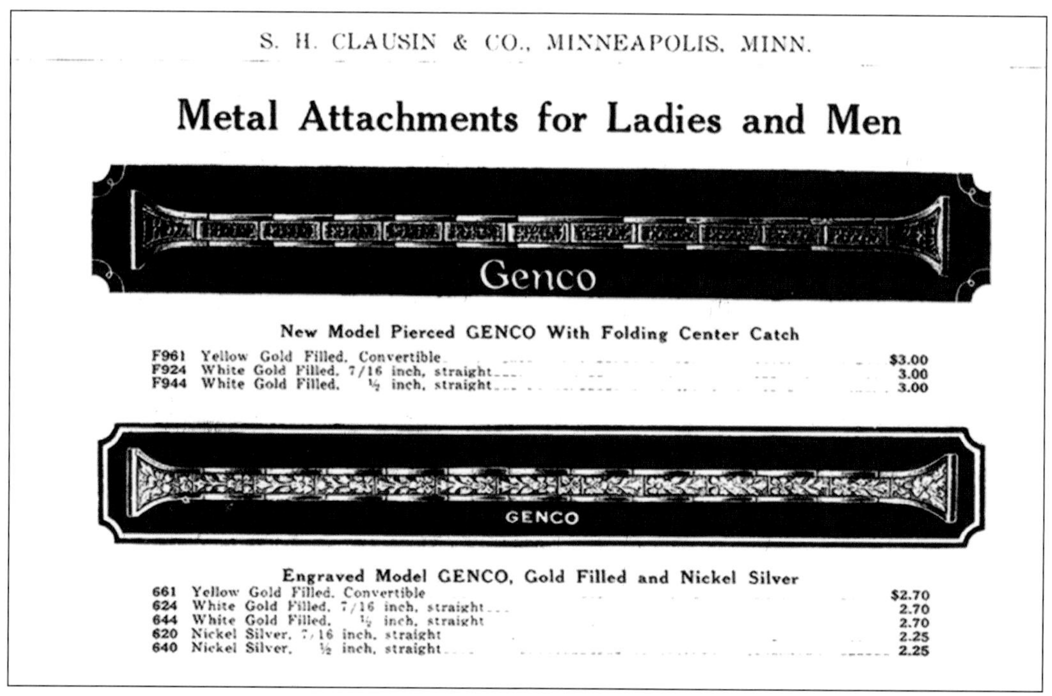

S. H. CLAUSIN & CO., MINNEAPOLIS, MINN.

Metal Attachments for Ladies and Men

New Model Pierced GENCO With Folding Center Catch

F961	Yellow Gold Filled. Convertible	$3.00
F924	White Gold Filled. 7/16 inch, straight	3.00
F944	White Gold Filled. ½ inch, straight	3.00

Engraved Model GENCO, Gold Filled and Nickel Silver

661	Yellow Gold Filled. Convertible	$2.70
624	White Gold Filled. 7/16 inch, straight	2.70
644	White Gold Filled. ½ inch, straight	2.70
620	Nickel Silver. 7/16 inch, straight	2.25
640	Nickel Silver. ½ inch, straight	2.25

Genco watchbands by General Chain Company, S. H. Clausin catalog, 1931

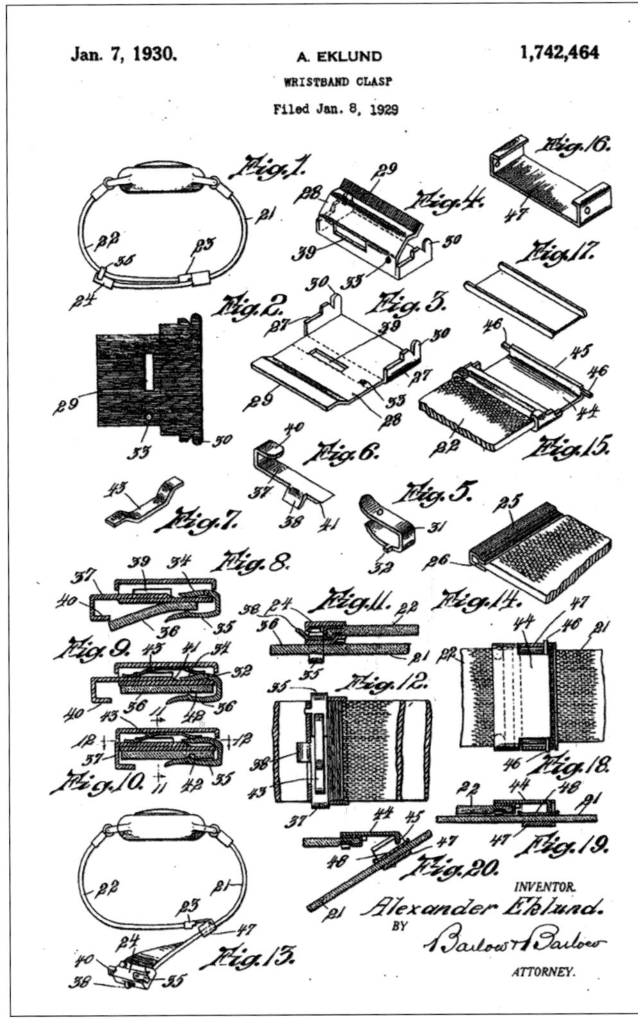

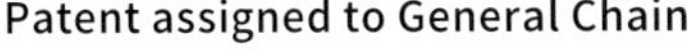
Patent assigned to General Chain

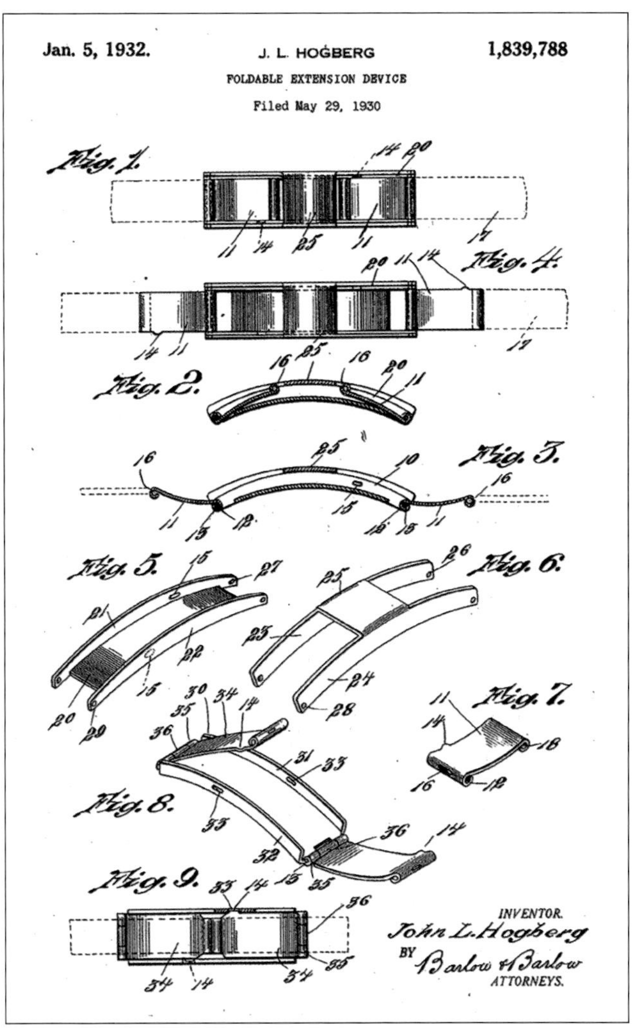

Patent assigned to General Chain

A. Hirsch Company

The history of the A. Hirsch Company can be traced to 1765 in Klagenfurt, Austria. Since then, the company's main business has been processing leather. It has been responsible for a number of innovations, such as the invention of the "remborde" technique, by which the upper material and the lining of a watch strap are bonded together seamlessly; the development of water-resistant leather; and a system for hindering leather allergies.[37]

R. F. Simmons Company

Founded in 1873 in Attleboro, Massachusetts, Simmons in the beginning primarily produced chains for men's pocket watches, but it also made some ladies' jewelry, including bracelets. In 1913 it pioneered the use of expansion bracelet attachments for watches. The very next year it invented and patented the separable-link expansion bracelets that were to be the basis of the entire initial watch bracelet industry. Simmons later introduced open-link watch bracelet bands for use by both men and women.[38]

Simmons men's strap bracelet, in 18K yellow gold-filled

Simmons had also continued making bracelets as well, developing an ingenious clasp, which it patented, for its sterling silver filigree bracelets; these were ornamented with glass stones of colors resembling gems such as emeralds, sapphires, and amethysts. The filigree watch bracelets that Simmons developed for women are similar in style to those bracelets.

Two Simmons watch bracelets and one of its famous sterling filigree bracelets (*left*)

On or about May, 1933, Simmons purchased all the rights to the Betsy Ross bracelet line from Harvey Clap & Company. These bangle bracelets, in Victorian Revival Style, are very popular with jewelry collectors of today, as are the sterling silver filigree ones.

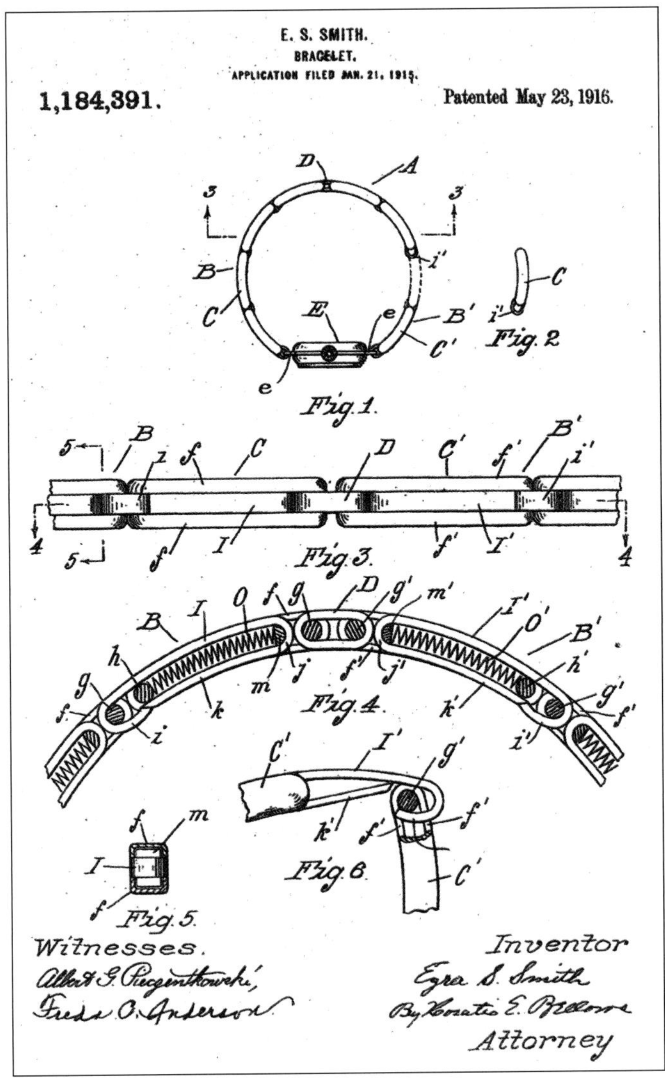

Patent assigned to R. F. Simmons

Dec. 1, 1925.
L. J. VETTER
CATCH
Filed Jan. 26, 1925
1,563,881
Inventor:
Louis J. Vetter,
by Roberts, Roberts & Cushman
attys.

Patent assigned to R. F. Simmons

The Hadley Company

The Hadley Company was founded by Art Hadley (1885–1941). Born in South Africa to British parents, he moved with them to Providence, Rhode Island, when he was about three years old. He graduated from the Technical High School in Providence and worked initially as a toolmaker.[39]

According to the October 1932 issue of the *Keystone*, "The manufacture of wristwatch attachments by the Hadley Company dates back to 1912, where, in a little shop in Providence, the production of metal watch bracelets was started by Art Hadley, who conceived the idea from a display in a jeweler's window in Paris."[40] Subsequently, Hadley converted his operations exclusively to the creation of wristwatch bands, as the company's letterhead breezily points out:

Makers of Watch Attachments, That's all
"Because we make so many"

A. H. Hadley, c. 1920s

Hadley developed many features of construction and design that became well known. These include the first solderless expansion bracelet, the Duofold two-piece folding center, the Trifold three-piece folding center, the Ratchet adjustable center and adjustable end hooks for men's bracelets. In addition, Hadley's adaptation of a patented construction used for the center catch of women's expansion bracelets made it possible to have interchangeable end hooks for those bracelets.[41]

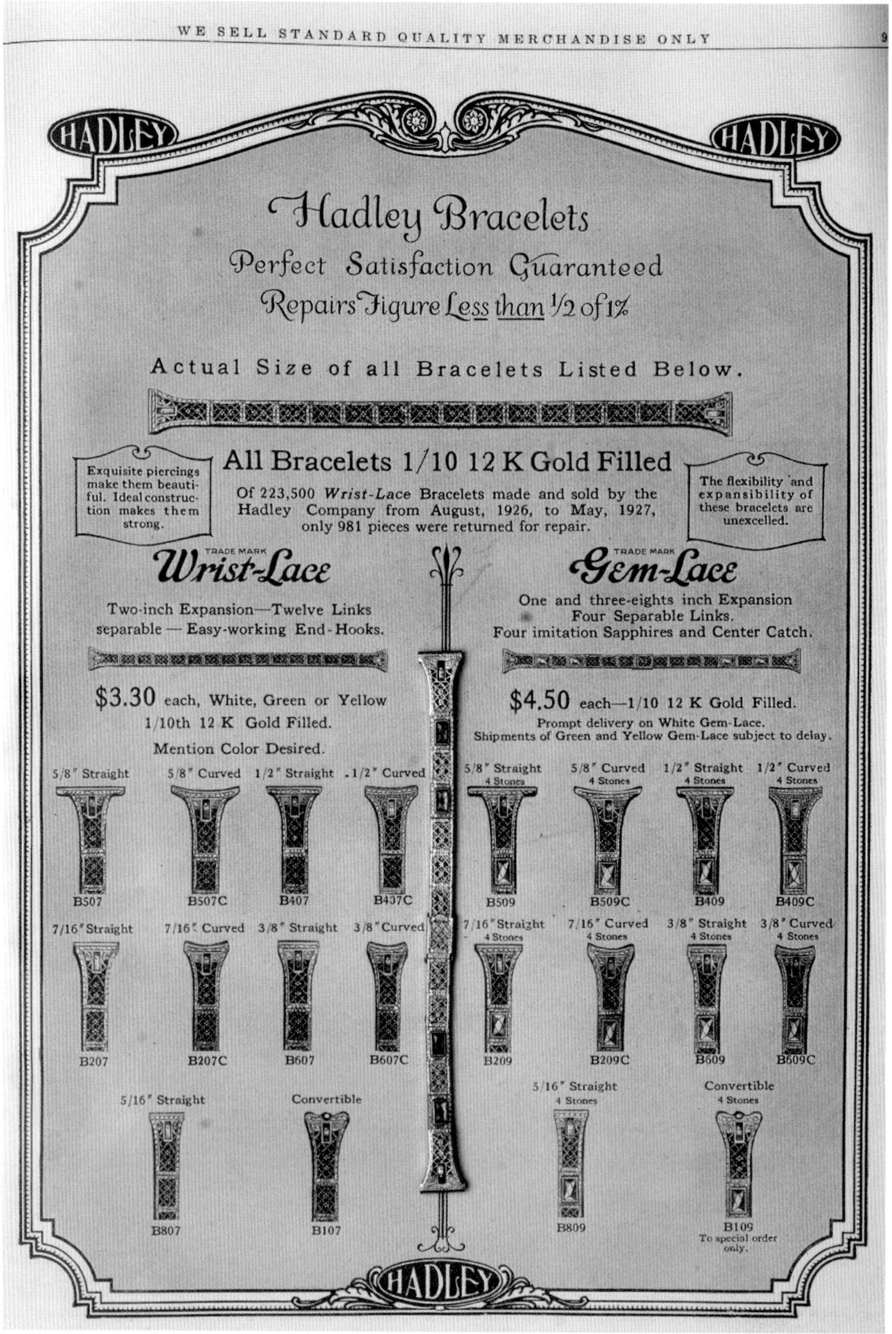

WE SELL STANDARD QUALITY MERCHANDISE ONLY 9

HADLEY HADLEY

Hadley Bracelets

Perfect Satisfaction Guaranteed

Repairs Figure Less than 1/2 of 1%

Actual Size of all Bracelets Listed Below.

All Bracelets 1/10 12 K Gold Filled

Exquisite piercings make them beautiful. Ideal construction makes them strong.

Of 223,500 *Wrist-Lace* Bracelets made and sold by the Hadley Company from August, 1926, to May, 1927, only 981 pieces were returned for repair.

The flexibility and expansibility of these bracelets are unexcelled.

TRADE MARK *Wrist-Lace*

Two-inch Expansion—Twelve Links separable — Easy-working End-Hooks.

$3.30 each, White, Green or Yellow 1/10th 12 K Gold Filled.

Mention Color Desired.

5/8″ Straight B507 · 5/8″ Curved B507C · 1/2″ Straight B407 · 1/2″ Curved B407C

7/16″ Straight B207 · 7/16″ Curved B207C · 3/8″ Straight B607 · 3/8″ Curved B607C

5/16″ Straight B807 · Convertible B107

TRADE MARK *Gem-Lace*

One and three-eights inch Expansion Four Separable Links. Four imitation Sapphires and Center Catch.

$4.50 each—1/10 12 K Gold Filled.

Prompt delivery on White Gem-Lace. Shipments of Green and Yellow Gem-Lace subject to delay.

5/8″ Straight 4 Stones B509 · 5/8″ Curved 4 Stones B509C · 1/2″ Straight 4 Stones B409 · 1/2″ Curved 4 Stones B409C

7/16″ Straight 4 Stones B209 · 7/16″ Curved 4 Stones B209C · 3/8″ Straight 4 Stones B609 · 3/8″ Curved 4 Stones B609C

5/16″ Straight 4 Stones B809 · Convertible 4 Stones B109 To special order only.

HADLEY

Hadley "Gem-Lace" watch bracelet superimposed on 1928 A. C. Becken catalog page

Hadley trademark

Because all-metal watch bracelets had been found to be subject to the corrosive effects of perspiration, the Hadley Company sought to develop an alloy that would not corrode. After much study and experimentation, the company came out with "Hadleyite," which was claimed to be unconditionally guaranteed against corrosion under any conditions of wear. (Purportedly, over one million Hadleyite bracelets were sold without a single complaint about corrosion.)[42]

Very early on, the Hadley Company adopted a policy of restrictive distribution, selecting certain "reputable" wholesalers to be the sole distributors of its products.[43]

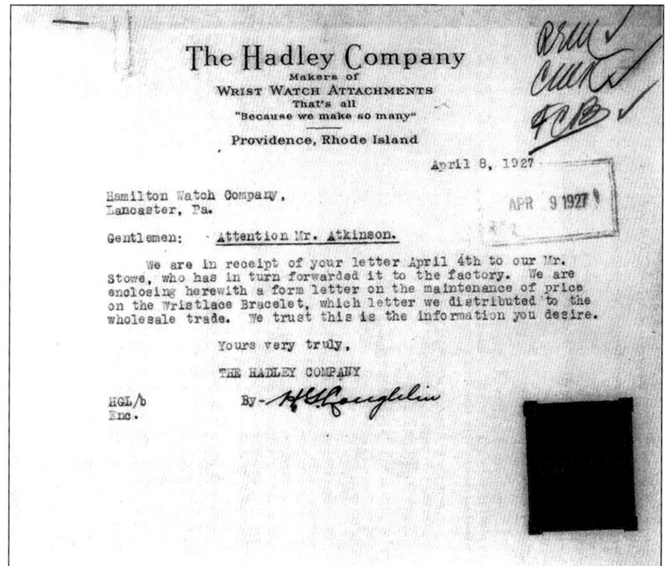

The Hadley Company
Makers of
WRIST WATCH ATTACHMENTS
That's all
"Because we make so many"

Providence, Rhode Island

April 8, 1927

APR 9 1927

Hamilton Watch Company,
Lancaster, Pa.

Gentlemen: Attention Mr. Atkinson.

We are in receipt of your letter April 4th to our Mr. Stowe, who has in turn forwarded it to the factory. We are enclosing herewith a form letter on the maintenance of price on the Wristlace Bracelet, which letter we distributed to the wholesale trade. We trust this is the information you desire.

Yours very truly,

THE HADLEY COMPANY

By-

HGL/b
Enc.

Letter of April 8, 1927, from the Hadley Company to the Hamilton Watch Company

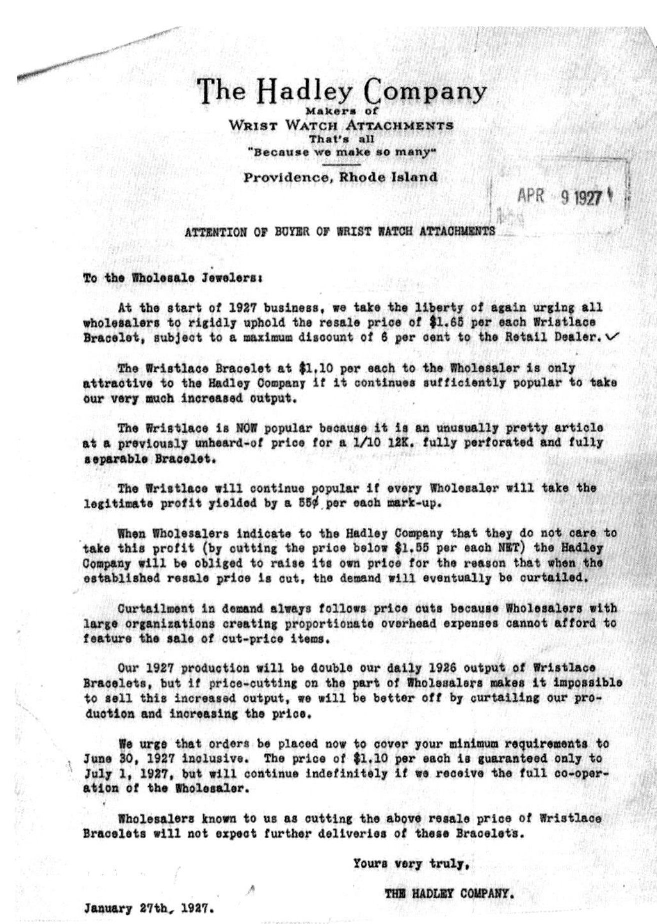

The Hadley Company
Makers of
WRIST WATCH ATTACHMENTS
That's all
"Because we make so many"

Providence, Rhode Island

APR 9 1927

ATTENTION OF BUYER OF WRIST WATCH ATTACHMENTS

To the Wholesale Jewelers:

At the start of 1927 business, we take the liberty of again urging all wholesalers to rigidly uphold the resale price of $1.65 per each Wristlace Bracelet, subject to a maximum discount of 6 per cent to the Retail Dealer.

The Wristlace Bracelet at $1.10 per each to the Wholesaler is only attractive to the Hadley Company if it continues sufficiently popular to take our very much increased output.

The Wristlace is NOW popular because it is an unusually pretty article at a previously unheard-of price for a 1/10 12K. fully perforated and fully separable Bracelet.

The Wristlace will continue popular if every Wholesaler will take the legitimate profit yielded by a 55¢ per each mark-up.

When Wholesalers indicate to the Hadley Company that they do not care to take this profit (by cutting the price below $1.55 per each NET) the Hadley Company will be obliged to raise its own price for the reason that when the established resale price is cut, the demand will eventually be curtailed.

Curtailment in demand always follows price cuts because Wholesalers with large organizations creating proportionate overhead expenses cannot afford to feature the sale of cut-price items.

Our 1927 production will be double our daily 1926 output of Wristlace Bracelets, but if price-cutting on the part of Wholesalers makes it impossible to sell this increased output, we will be better off by curtailing our production and increasing the price.

We urge that orders be placed now to cover your minimum requirements to June 30, 1927 inclusive. The price of $1.10 per each is guaranteed only to July 1, 1927, but will continue indefinitely if we receive the full co-operation of the Wholesaler.

Wholesalers known to us as cutting the above resale price of Wristlace Bracelets will not expect further deliveries of these Bracelets.

Yours very truly,

THE HADLEY COMPANY.

January 27th, 1927.

Letter of April 9, 1927, from the Hadley Company to its wholesale jewelers, urging them "to rigidly uphold the resale price" of its wristwatch attachments

EVERYTHING NEEDED BY JEWELERS 97

HADLEY Gold Filled Watch Attachments for Men HADLEY

Patent Pending

NARSES—1/10 14 Karat Gold Filled—White, Green or Yellow
Each in a beautiful Display Box. Links are removable. Adjustable without tools

5/8 inch No. 8322 $12.00 Each (List) 3/4 inch No. 8324 $12.00 Each (List) 7/8 inch No. 8326 $12.00 Each (List)

Patent No. 1,756,769

MASTERFOLD—1/10 14 Karat Gold Filled—White, Green or Yellow
Unsurpassed for Strength and Durability. Every link soldered and flexible

5/8 inch No. 7662 $12.00 Each (List) 3/4 inch No. 7664 $12.00 Each (List) 7/8 inch No. 7666 $12.00 Each (List)

Patent Pending

HADLEFOLD—1/10 14 Karat Gold Filled—White, Green or Yellow
Invisible folding clasp. New removable ends. Easy adjustment

5/8 inch No. 7152 $8.00 Each (List) 3/4 inch No. 7154 $8.00 Each (List) 7/8 inch No. 7156 $8.00 Each (List)

Patent Pending

MARQUIS—1/10 14 Karat Gold Filled—White, Green orYellow
Engraved effect of attractive design. Same construction as Hadlefold

5/8 inch No. 7142 $8.00 Each (List) 3/4 inch No. 7144 $8.00 Each (List) 7/8 inch No. 7146 $8.00 Each (List)

Patent Pending

CONNAUGHT—1/10 14 Karat Gold Filled—White, Green or Yellow
Adjusts like a ribbon. Not a Folding Attachment. Finest soldered edge mesh

5/8 inch No. 7452 $12.00 Each (List) 3/4 inch No. 7454 $12.00 Each (List) 7/8 inch No. 7456 $12.00 Each (List)

Patent No. 1,756,769

CORNWALL—1/10 14 Karat Gold Filled—White, Green or Yellow
Finest soldered edge mesh. Engine turned folding and adjustable clasp

5/8 inch No. 7192 $9.00 Each (List) 3/4 inch No. 7194 $9.00 Each (List) 7/8 inch No. 7196 $9.00 Each (List)

Patent No. 1,760,384

CORINTHIAN—1/20 12 Karat Gold Filled—White, Green or Yellow
Strong removable ends. Metal bound mesh. New invisible folding clasp

5/8 inch No. 7472 $6.00 Each (List) 3/4 inch No. 7474 $6.00 Each (List) 7/8 inch No. 7476 $6.00 Each (List)
5/8 inch Curved Ends No. 7477 $6.00 Each (List) 3/4 inch Curved Ends No. 7478 $6.00 Each (List)

Patent No. 1,760,384

NUFOLD—1/20 12 Karat Gold Filled—White, Green or Yellow
Mesh has reinforced edge. New ends and invisible folding clasp

5/8 inch No. 7132 $5.00 Each (List) 3/4 inch No. 7134 $5.00 Each (List) 7/8 inch No. 7136 $5.00 Each (List)
5/8 inch Curved No. 7137 $5.00 Each (List) 3/4 inch Curved No. 7138 $5.00 Each (List)

1

PRICES ARE SUBJECT TO CHANGE WITHOUT NOTICE

1931 S. H. Clausin catalog offering Hadley bands

98 S. H. CLAUSIN & CO., MINNEAPOLIS, MINN.

HADLEY

Azure Finished Watch Attachments

(Chrome Plated)

HADLEY

Patent Pending

BONDMAN—Nickel, Chrome Plated New Flat Folding Center — Matches the Links.
Furnished extra long. Links are removable. Adjustable without tools

5/8 inch No. 8382 $2.50 Each (List) 3/4 inch No. 8384 $2.50 Each (List) 7/8 inch No. 8386 $2.50 Each (List)

Patent Nos. 1,751,475 1,756,769

VALIANT—Nickel, Chrome Plated
A mannish attachment. Unsurpassed for strength and practicability

5/8 inch No. 8152 $3.00 Each (List) 3/4 inch No. 8154 $3.00 Each (List) 7/8 inch No. 8156 $3.00 Each (List)

Patent Pending

AZUREFOLD—Nickel, Chrome Plated
Exceptionally strong link construction. New invisible folding clasp. New removable hook

5/8 inch No. 7172 $2.00 Each (List) 3/4 inch No. 7174 $2.00 Each (List) 7/8 inch No. 7176 $2.00 Each (List)

WARRIOR—Nickel, Chrome Plated—**Engraved Design**—Same construction as Azurefold.

5/8 inch No. 7162 $2.00 Each (List) 3/4 inch No. 7164 $2.00 Each (List) 7/8 inch No. 7166 $2.00 Each (List)

Patent Pending

RAINIER—Nickel, Chrome Plated
A new attachment that adjusts like a ribbon. Soldered edge mesh

5/8 inch No. 7462 $4.50 Each (List) 3/4 inch No. 7464 $4.50 Each (List) 7/8 inch No. 7466 $4.50 Each (List)

Patent Pending

BONDMAID—Nickel, Chrome Plated
Furnished extra long. Links are removable. Adjustable without tools

Straight Ends		List Price	Straight Ends		List Price	Curved Ends		List Price	Curved Ends		List Price
5/8 inch	No. 8447	$2.50 Each	7/16 inch	No. 8443	$2.50 Each	5/8 inch	No. 8448	$2.50 Each	7/16 inch	No. 8444	$2.50 Each
1/2 inch	No. 8445	$2.50 Each	3/8 inch	No. 8441	$2.50 Each	1/2 inch	No. 8446	$2.50 Each	3/8 inch	No. 8442	$2.50 Each
			5/16 inch	No. 8449	$2.50 Each						

Patent Nos. 1,751,475

VALKYRIE—Nickel, Chrome Plated
A distinctive attachment. Flexible and strong

Straight Ends		List Price	Straight Ends		List Price	Curved Ends		List Price	Curved Ends		List Price
5/8 inch	No. 7377	$3.00 Each	7/16 inch	No. 7373	$3.00 Each	5/8 inch	No. 7378	$3.00 Each	7/16 inch	No. 7374	$3.00 Each
1/2 inch	No. 7375	$3.00 Each	3/8 inch	No. 7371	$3.00 Each	1/2 inch	No. 7376	$3.00 Each	3/8 inch	No. 7372	$3.00 Each

Patent Pending

SOUBRETTE—Nickel, Chrome Plated
Easy and novel method of adjusting length. Engraved effect harmonizes with most cases

Straight Ends		List Price	Straight Ends		List Price	Curved Ends		List Price	Curved Ends		List Price
5/8 inch	No. 8297	$2.00 Each	7/16 inch	No. 8293	$2.00 Each	5/8 inch	No. 8298	$2.00 Each	7/16 inch	No. 8294	$2.00 Each
1/2 inch	No. 8295	$2.00 Each	3/8 inch	No. 8291	$2.00 Each	1/2 inch	No. 8296	$2.00 Each	3/8 inch	No. 8292	$2.00 Each

ORLEANS—Nickel, Chrome Plated
Same construction as Soubrette with plain ribbed links. Simple length adjustment

Straight Ends		List Price	Straight Ends		List Price	Curved Ends		List Price	Curved Ends		List Price
5/8 inch	No. 8277	$2.00 Each	7/16 inch	No. 8273	$2.00 Each	5/8 inch	No. 8278	$2.00 Each	7/16 inch	No. 8274	$2.00 Each
1/2 inch	No. 8275	$2.00 Each	3/8 inch	No. 8271	$2.00 Each	1/2 inch	No. 8276	$2.00 Each	3/8 inch	No. 8272	$2.00 Each

Patent Pending

LA PETITE—Nickel, Chrome Plated
Adjusts like a ribbon. Fine soldered edge mesh

Straight Ends		List Price	Straight Ends		List Price	Curved Ends		List Price	Curved Ends		List Price
5/8 inch	No. 755	$3.60 Each	7/16 inch	No. 752	$3.60 Each	5/8 inch	No. 775	$3.60 Each	7/16 inch	No. 772	$3.60 Each
1/2 inch	No. 754	$3.60 Each	3/8 inch	No. 756	$3.60 Each	1/2 inch	No. 774	$3.60 Each	3/8 inch	No. 776	$3.60 Each

PRICES ARE SUBJECT TO CHANGE WITHOUT NOTICE

1931 S. H. Clausin catalog offering Hadley bands

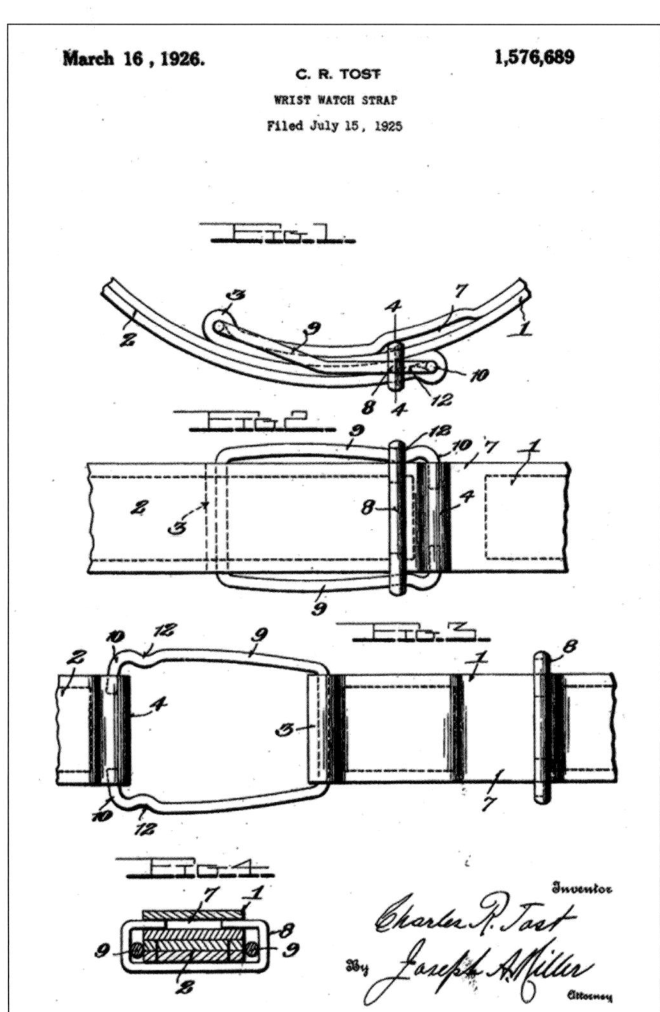

Patent assigned to Hadley

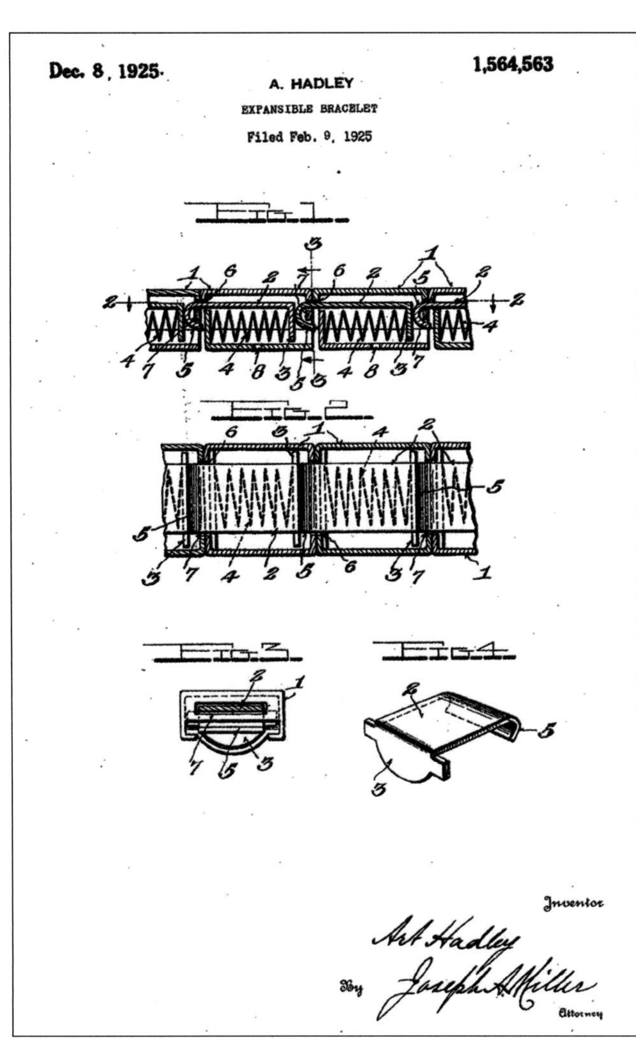

Hadley patent by Art Hadley as inventor

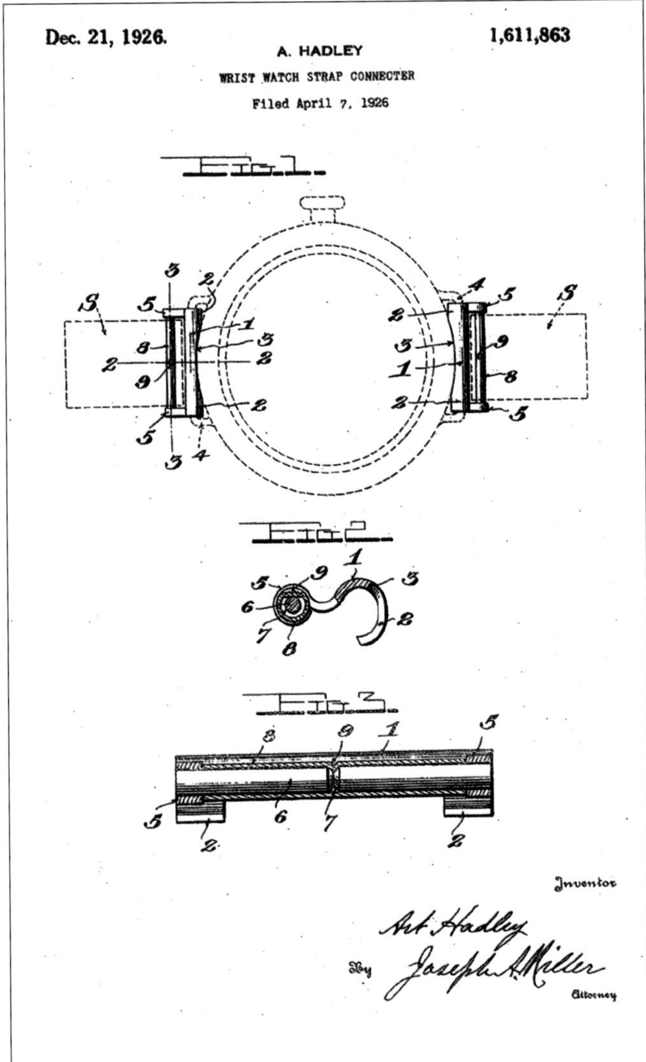

Hadley patent by Art Hadley as inventor

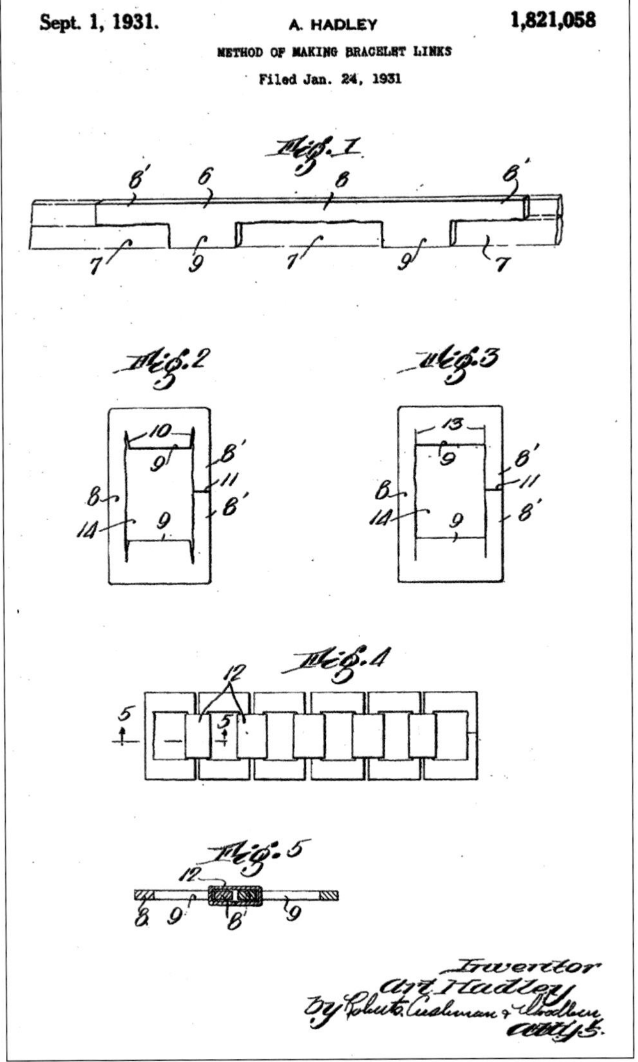

Hadley patent by Art Hadley as inventor

Kreisler Manufacturing Corporation

In 1914, Jacques Kreisler, a Hungarian immigrant, in partnership with Marcus Stern, started Stern-Kreisler Jewelry Company in New York City. By 1920, the firm had changed its name to Jacques Kreisler & Co., and two of Stern's sons, Tobias and Edward, were involved in its operations. In 1928, Jacques Kreisler and Tobias Stern formed the Kreisler Manufacturing Corporation; by then there was a Kreisler branch office in Chicago.[44]

Kreisler began as a maker of fine jewelry in precious metals, which it sold to jewelry and department stores. The company's listing in a 1931 trade directory describes it as "manufacturers of diamond-platinum and sport watches; 14 and 18K gold, platinum and diamond-platinum watch bands; gold, platinum and diamond jewelry." [45]

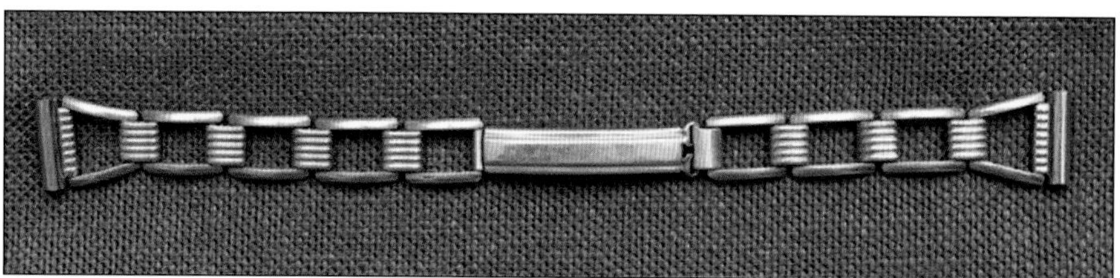

Kreisler men's watch bracelet

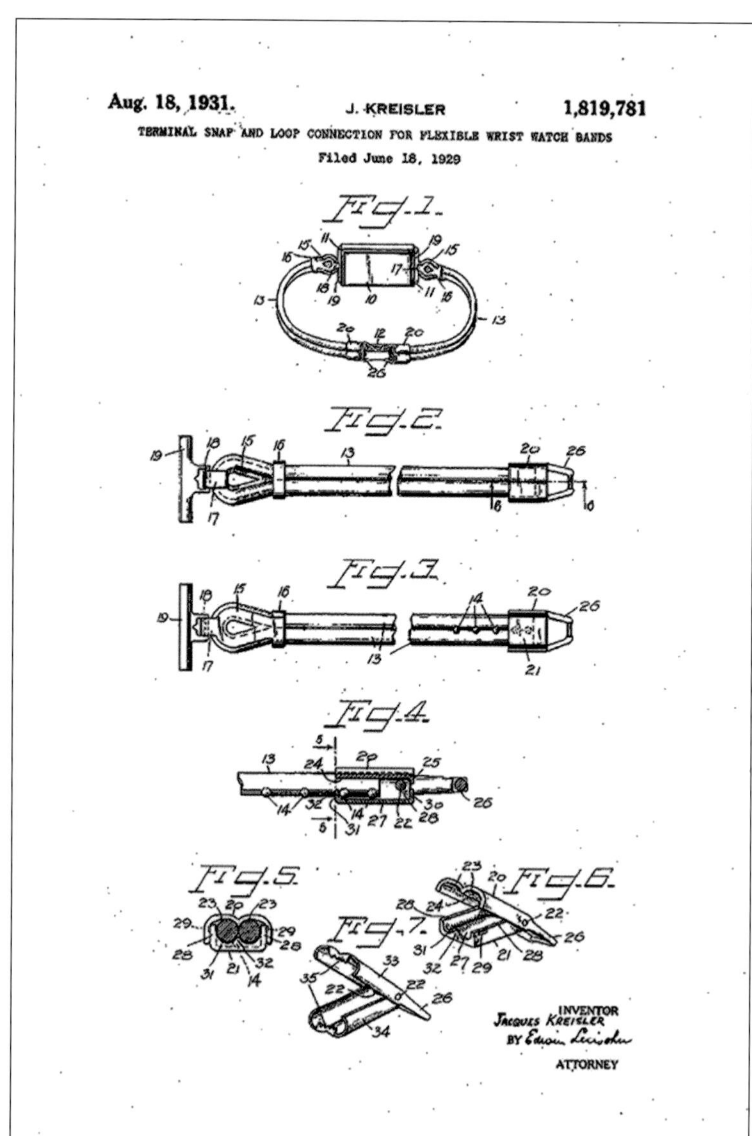

Kreisler patent by Jacques Kreisler as inventor

Edward L. Stern & Brother, Inc.

Edward L. Stern and Brother, Inc. was a spin-off from Jacques Kreisler & Co., which had been producing high-end solid gold and platinum watch bracelets for years. Because these were greatly admired for both their design and their craftsmanship, there became a demand for gold-filled ones of "the same inspired design and careful craftsmanship typical of all Kreisler supervised jewelry." and the Stern company filled this niche. Stern also introduced a new endurable metal called Duro-Brite. The company distributed its products directly to retailers.[46]

Kestenman Brothers Manufacturing Company

Established in 1916 in Providence, Rhode Island, the Kestenman Brothers Manufacturing Company specialized in the manufacture of high-quality wristwatch straps and achieved "many notable improvements in design, quality and mechanical structure." Kestenman stressed "styles to harmonize with the watches in vogue, quality to withstand the strenuous wear a watch strap is subjected to; and construction to afford utmost comfort to the wearer."[47]

There were four Kestenman brothers: Abraham, Charles, Louis and Max (from oldest to youngest). Charles, who had a number of patents, was no doubt the one chiefly responsible for the company's improvements to watchband designs. Abraham held a patent for a lingerie clasp. He and Charles also had a company that manufactured other jewelry items; the August 30, 1922 issue of the *Jewelers' Circular* noted that Abraham Kestenman and Charles Kestenman had "started in business at 74 Clifford St. as the Costmo Mfg. Co., manufacturing a general line of jewelry.")

The Kestenman trademark was "Kestenmade."

KESTENMADE

Kestenmade trademark

Kestenmade men's watch bracelet

Now Here To Guard Your Lady Customer's Watch

SENTINEL

"GUARDS YOUR WATCH"

—FOR LADIES

PATENTS PENDING

This very newest addition to our lines is made in 14K. gold filled, white, green and yellow. Pierced design.

Embodying every quality of the "Sentinel" men's watch bracelet, plus many additional important features. Beautifully pierced design adds to its great attractiveness.

The Ladies' "Sentinel" is an expansion watch bracelet with individuality, which, as with the men's bracelet, is easily distinguished from the rest, by its mechanical superiority and design.

· · *Retailers* · ·

You who carry the men's "Sentinel" are advised to order a stock of the ladies' pattern to complete your line of these most popular bracelets. If you do not as yet carry the "Sentinel", you should, for your own sake, inspect this product and compare it with any other watch bracelet on the market. There are many reasons why these accessories have run ahead of the field. You surely should know the reasons.

The "SENTINEL" for men—More Popular Than Ever

Sold Exclusively Thru the Wholesale Trade

KB **KESTENMAN BROS. MFG. CO.** 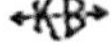

150 Chestnut Street, Providence, R. I.

Kestenman advertisement for "Sentinel" metal expansion bands, *Keystone*, September 1927

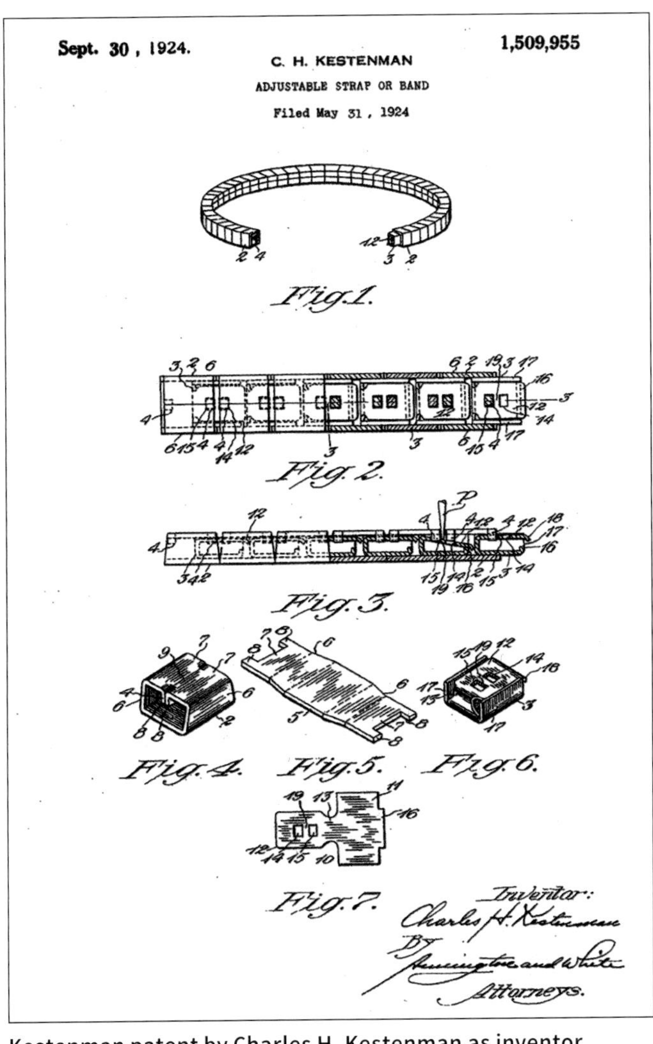

Kestenman patent by Charles H. Kestenman as inventor

Armbrust Chain Company

In 1923 the Armbrust Chain Company of Providence, Rhode Island, obtained its charter of incorporation; the incorporators were Gottlob Armbrust, Heinrich Jaegle and Frederick W. Bopp.[48]

As a manufacturer of watch attachments, Armbrust focused on offering "a well-fitting bracelet, one which would stay on the wrist snugly and comfortably under all conditions."[49] Accordingly, it developed a spring expansion that it incorporated in the buckle.

In introducing its "Aviator" Curblink bracelet, Armbrust pioneered the manufacture of open-link watch attachments.

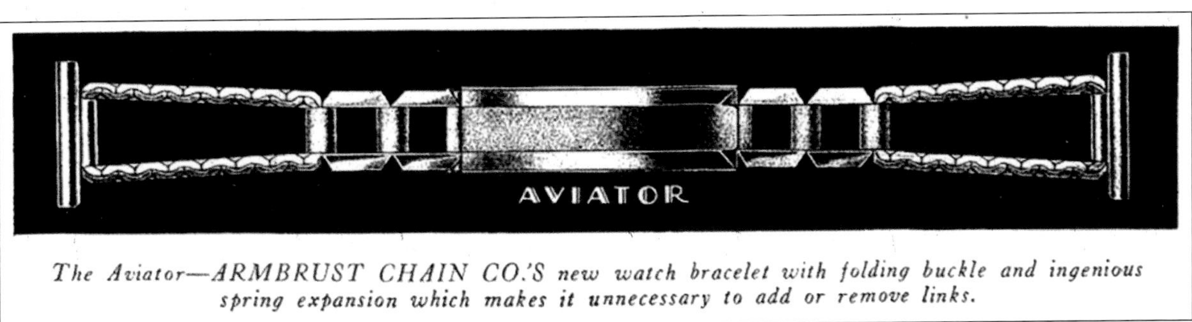

The Aviator—ARMBRUST CHAIN CO.'S new watch bracelet with folding buckle and ingenious spring expansion which makes it unnecessary to add or remove links.

Announcement of the new Aviator metal bracelet by Armbrust Chain Co. in "For the Buyer" column. *Keystone*, October 1932. Armbrust also offered a ladies' version.

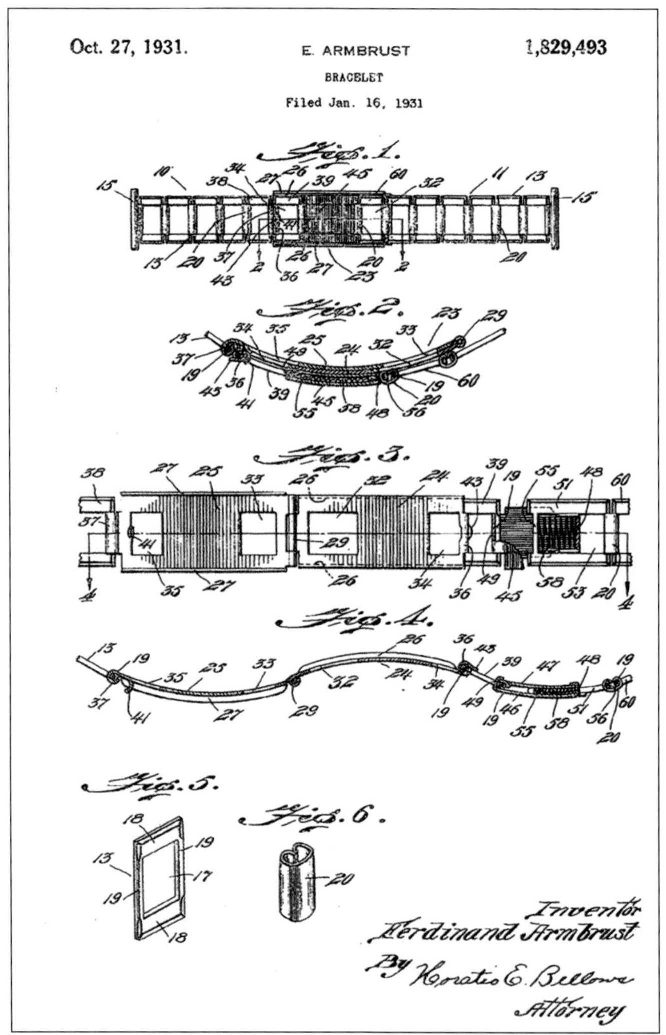

Armbrust patent by Ferdinand Armbrust as inventor

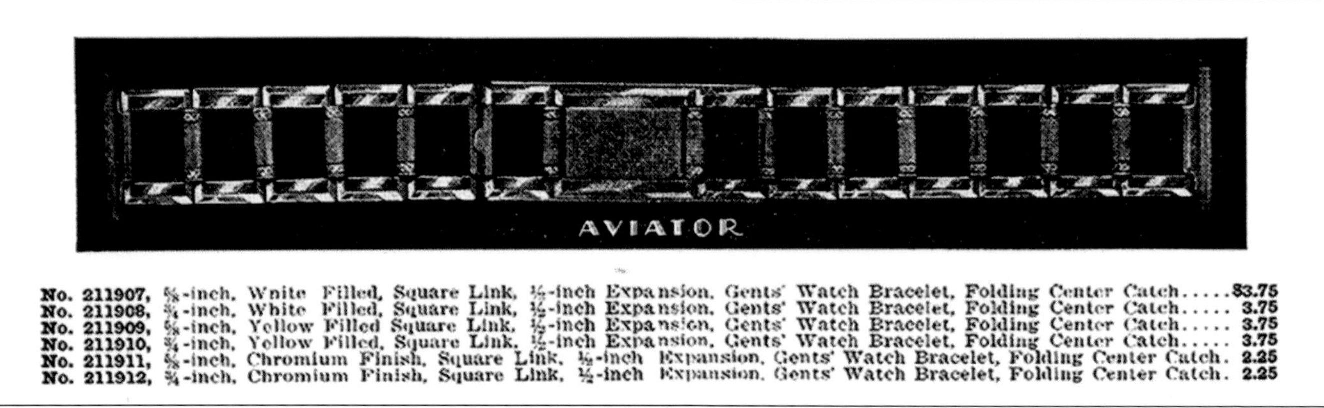

No. 211907, ⅝-inch, White Filled, Square Link, ½-inch Expansion, Gents' Watch Bracelet, Folding Center Catch.....$3.75
No. 211908, ¾-inch, White Filled, Square Link, ½-inch Expansion, Gents' Watch Bracelet, Folding Center Catch..... 3.75
No. 211909, ⅝-inch, Yellow Filled Square Link, ½-inch Expansion, Gents' Watch Bracelet, Folding Center Catch..... 3.75
No. 211910, ¾-inch, Yellow Filled, Square Link, ½-inch Expansion, Gents' Watch Bracelet, Folding Center Catch..... 3.75
No. 211911, ⅝-inch, Chromium Finish, Square Link, ½-inch Expansion, Gents' Watch Bracelet, Folding Center Catch. 2.25
No. 211912, ¾-inch, Chromium Finish, Square Link, ½-inch Expansion, Gents' Watch Bracelet, Folding Center Catch. 2.25

Another Armbrust "Aviator" model, Wallenstein Mayer catalog, 1932. This style closely resembles the patent drawing shown here.

E. B. Richards Company

The E. B. Richards Company, based in Attleboro, Massachusetts, was organized in the spring of 1930, absorbing what had been Smith & Crosby, a firm founded in 1872 by William H. Smith and Alfred H. Crosby.[50]

Although E. B. Richards offered a complete line of its own stylish bracelets, it continued to offer many popular patterns from the S&C line, a special feature of which was the lock and slide adjustable center buckle; this allowed unusual extension and also allowed the bracelet to be adjusted without removing it from the wrist.[51]

Among the most popular of these watch bracelets were the "Peggy Lou" and "Betty Lou" models for ladies, and the Chesterfield model for men.

"Peggy Lou" watch bracelets, a line that E. B. Richards inherited from Smith & Crosby

A & Z Chain Company

The A & Z Chain Company, founded in 1905 in Providence by Carl Anshen and Saul Zeitlin, began with the manufacture of watch chains. In 1915 it introduced its first all-metal watch bracelet, which had spring-expansion links and an end hook known as the "Snap-Lock Catch," a feature that was considered a great innovation in its day.

Continuing to increase its offerings, the company produced one of the best-known watchbands of that period, the "Superfold," which was followed rapidly by other models. Probably the most popular style up to that time was the company's "Superlink," an open-link style band. An improvement eventually made to increase the serviceability and convenience of that model resulted in the "Synchroslide," a patented buckle with many exclusive patented features.

The A & Z practice was to sell directly only to a select list of retail jewelers. Its large salesforce maintained contact with practically all leading American retail jewelry establishments.[52]

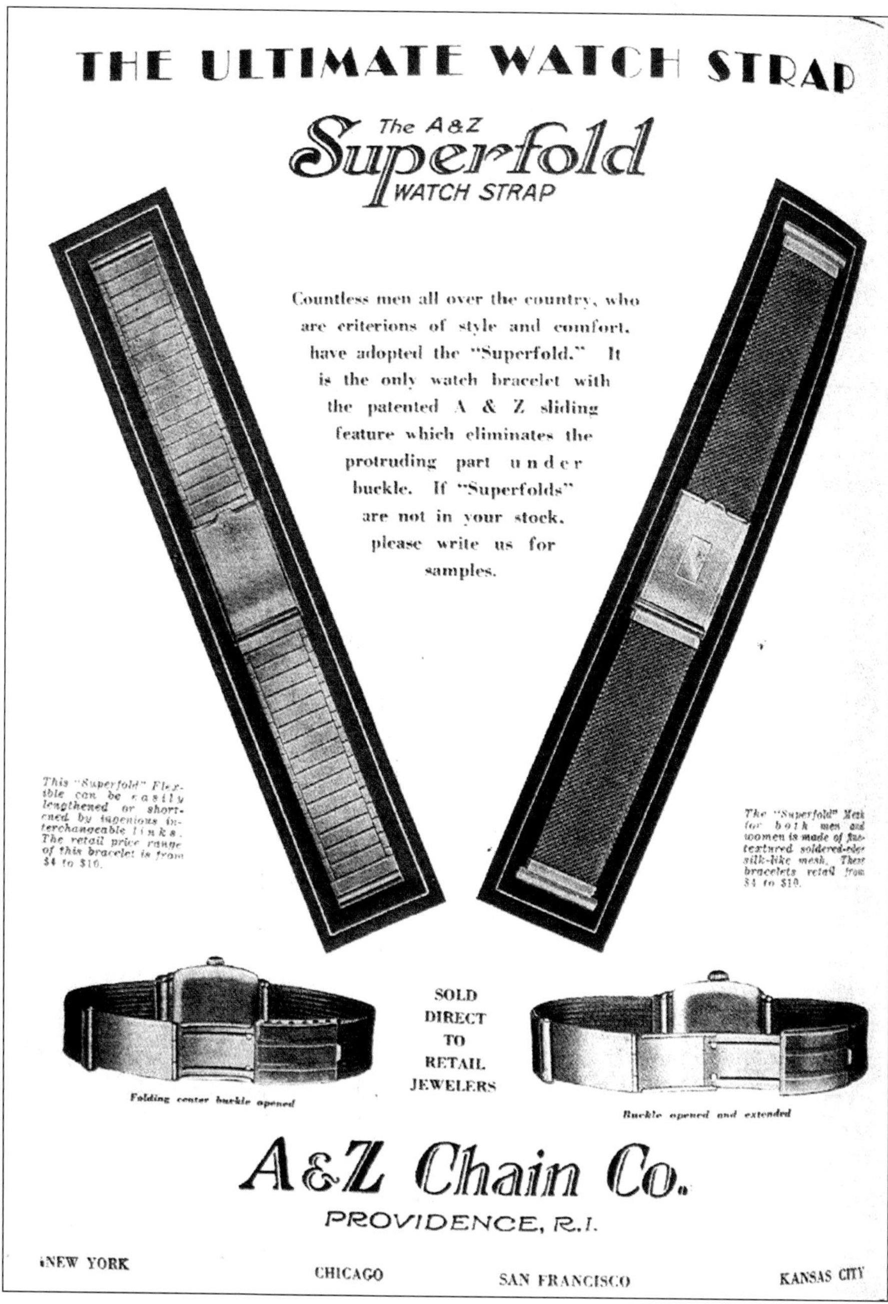

Jewelers' Circular, August 15, 1929

The M.S. Company

The M.S. Company, of Attleboro, Massachusetts, started in business "making raw chain of every quality and description for the manufacturing trade, to which they later added chain-findings, like swivels and spring rings, bars and toggles."

The wristwatch bracelet was "an item well suited to a chain manufacturer's equipment, so with the introduction of the wrist watch, it was a natural step to manufacture wrist watch bracelets," for which the company trademarked the name 'Viking".[53]

The M.S. Company still exists, continuing to focus on manufacturing chain. According to its website (www.mscompany.net), it produces "jewelry chain, chain findings and finished jewelry." The company notes that it sells only to wholesalers and manufacturers.

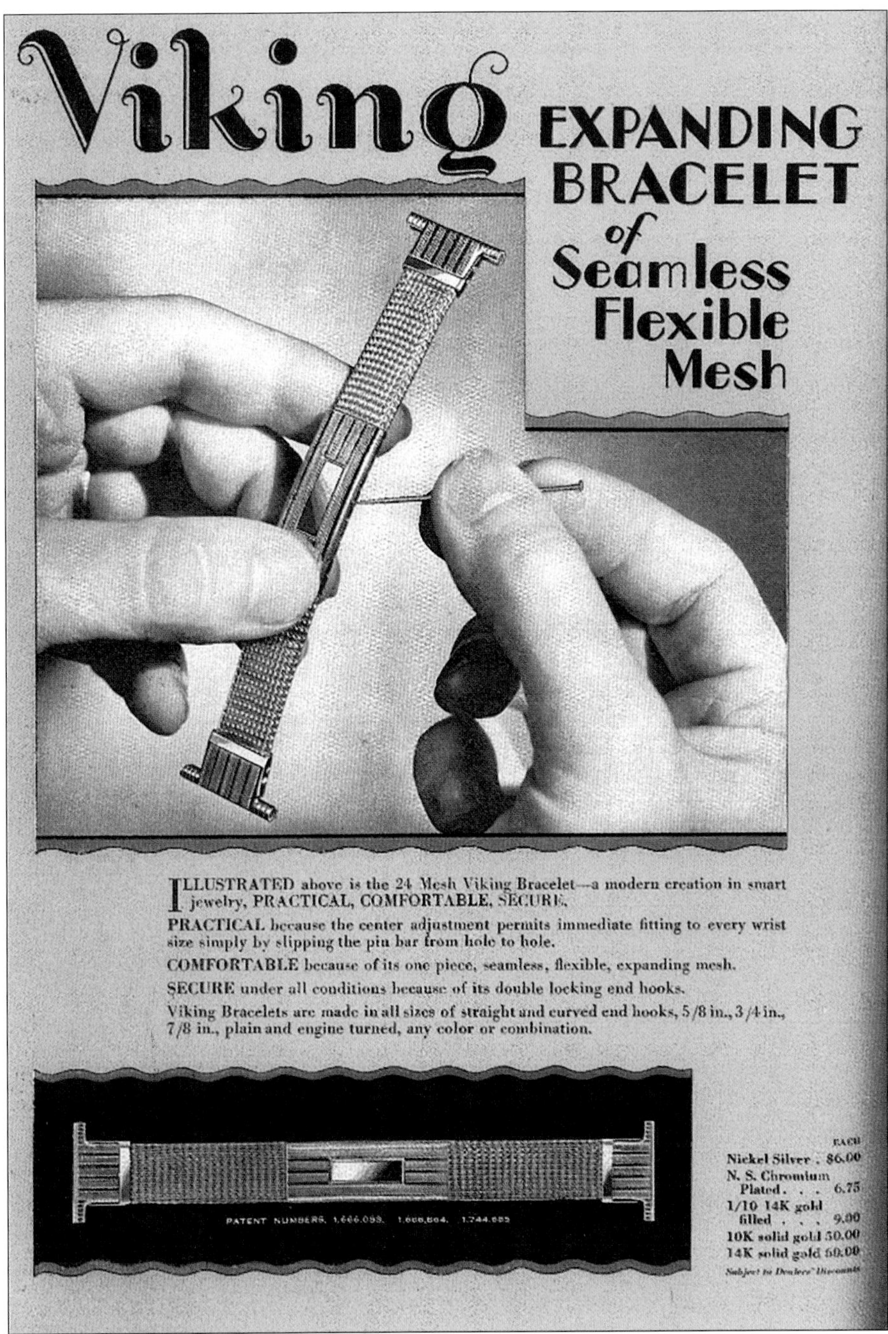

Full-page color advertisement for the Viking expanding metal watch bracelet of seamless flexible mesh from the S. H. Clausin catalog, 1931

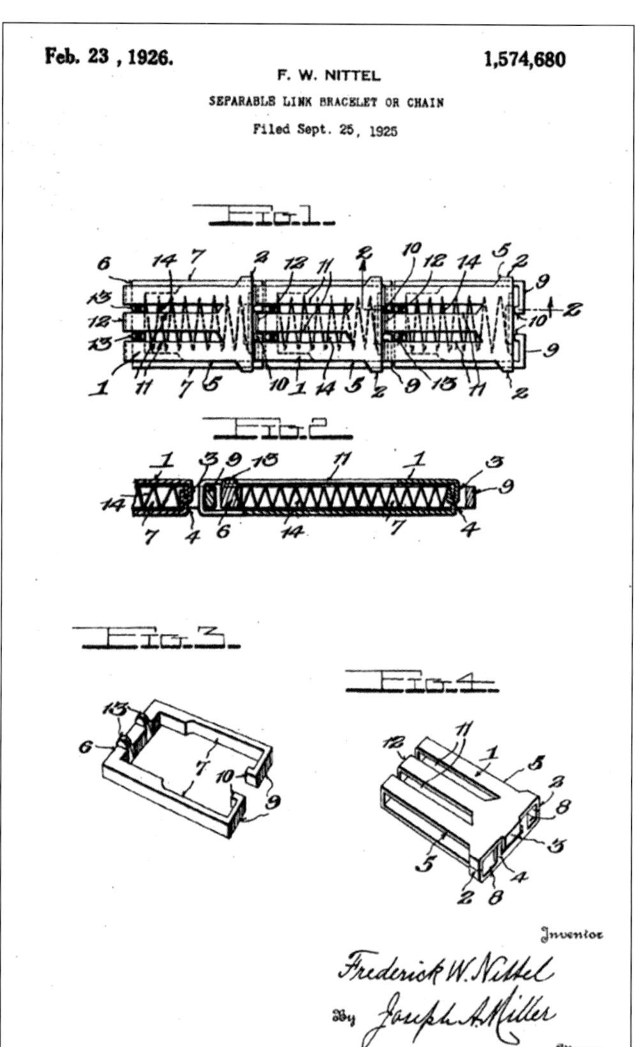

Patent assigned to the M.S. Company

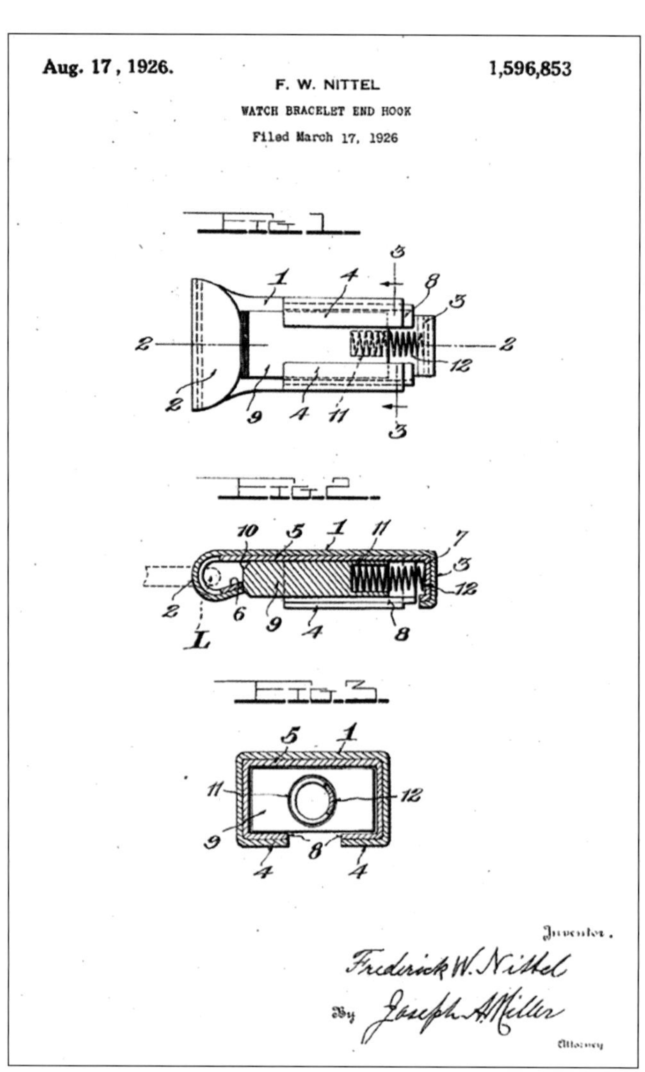

Patent assigned to the M.S. Company

S. Bruner, Inc.

"Contrary to the usual history of the watch bracelet manufacturers, most of which were originally in the business of making watch chains, S. Bruner, Inc., based in New York City, started as a manufacturer of watch cases," the *Keystone* pointed out in its October 1932 issue. "Demand for a quality bracelet, designed and constructed to match its watch cases led S. Bruner, Inc., to engage in bracelet manufacture. The concern succeeded in producing a line that has met every quality demand and is sold as a complete unit with their watches by many of the best known watch manufacturers and importers."[54]

Ten years earlier, in the September 13, 1922 issue of the *Jewelers' Circular* there had been this item: "The 10th floor of the building at 154 W. 14th St. was leased last week to Simon Bruner, manufacturing jeweler, this city. The new quarters occupy about 18,000 square feet of floor space. The lease is for a term of 10 years." At that point, Bruner must have already been in business for quite a while; one of his patents dates back to 1916.

Illinois ladies' Generic Period watch in 14K white gold hinged case by S. Bruner

S. Bruner watchcase back, beautifully engraved

"S. Bruner" signed inside the case back

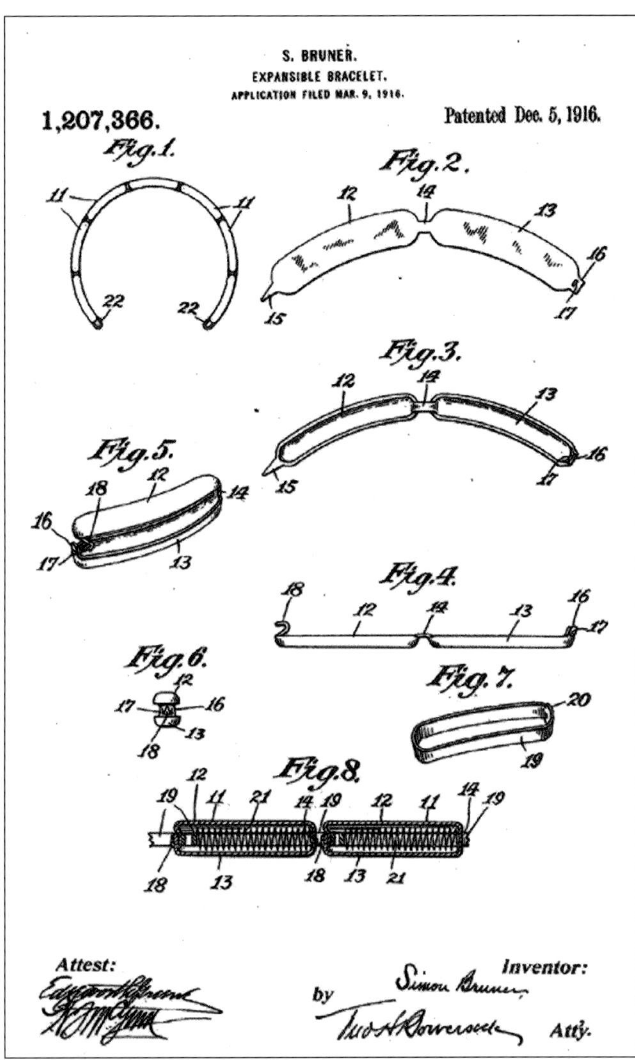

Bruner patent by Simon Bruner as inventor

Louis Stern Company

The Louis Stern Company of Providence, Rhode Island, established about 1871, was one of the recognized leaders in the bracelet industry. Its products were very popular, especially its flexible spring ladies' bracelet. Stern developed the first center catch used on bracelets, the success of which reportedly kept its factory busy day and night. Another notable development for the company was the "Syncro-Matic" fold-over center catch, permitting size adjustment while the bracelet was on the wrist.[55]

"Lustern" (a brand name constructed from the name of the company) and "Wristacrat" were two Louis Stern lines of watch bracelets.

Louis Stern, April 4, 1929 advertisement in the *Jewelers' Circular*

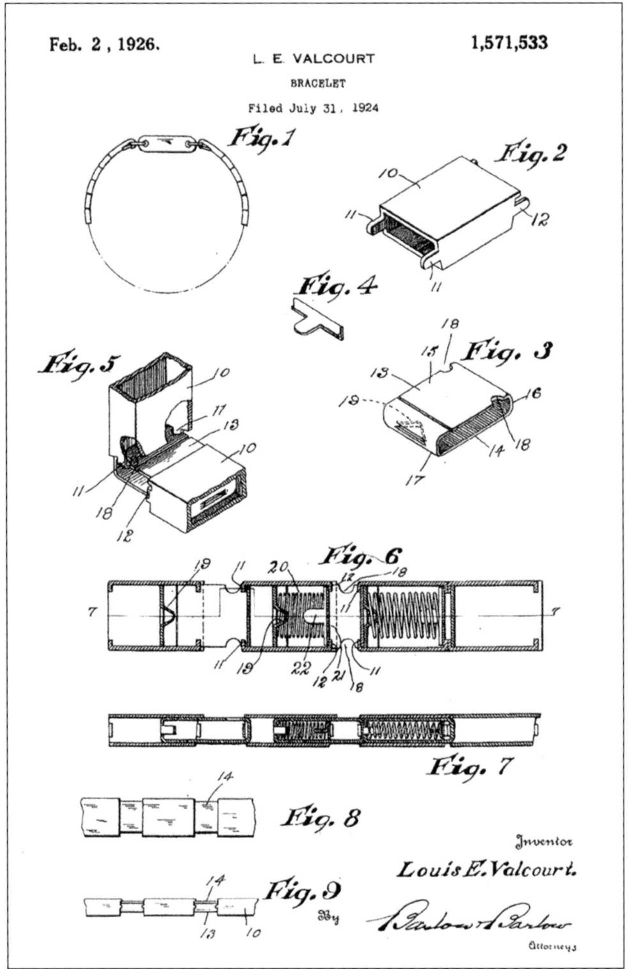

Patent assigned to Louis Stern Company

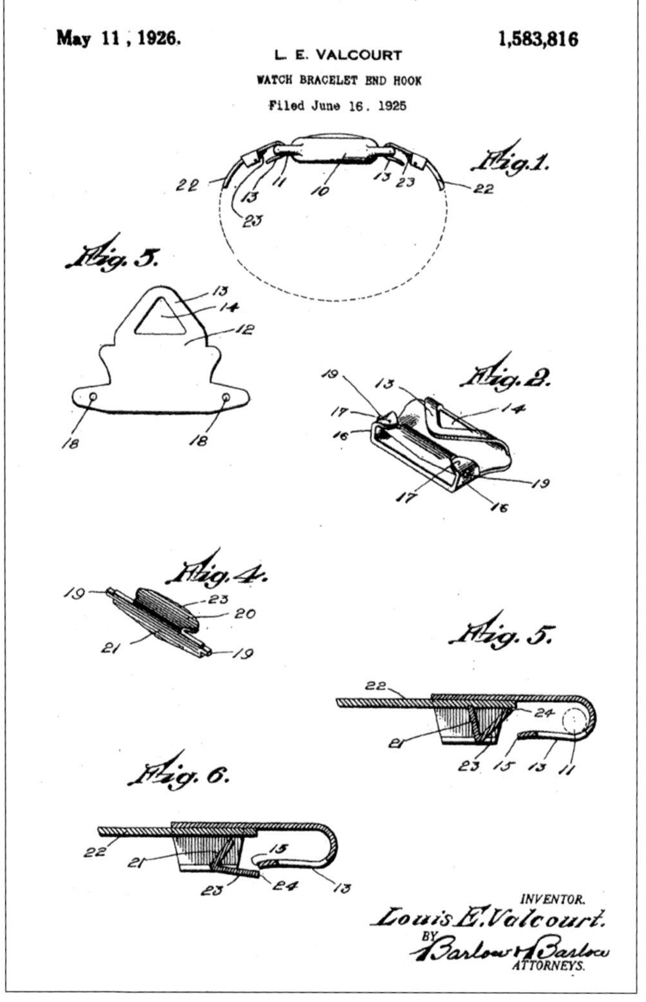

Patent assigned to Louis Stern Company

Harvey Clap & Company

Harvey Clap & Company, located in Attleboro, Massachusetts, originally manufactured a large line of watch chains and then produced one of the first spring-expanding watch bracelets. That was the forerunner of the widely popular and well known "Anne Louise" pierced, block-spring bracelet and later the equally popular "Anne Elaine" model. Both of these bracelets were equipped with a folding center, and all links could be removed by hand, permitting speedy and simple adjustment.[56] Even today some ladies' wristwatches can be found with these bands still intact.

Harvey Clap's "Anne Louise" flexible metal expansion bands, *Keystone*, September 1927

"Anne Louise" watch bracelet by Harvey Clap, on its original sales card

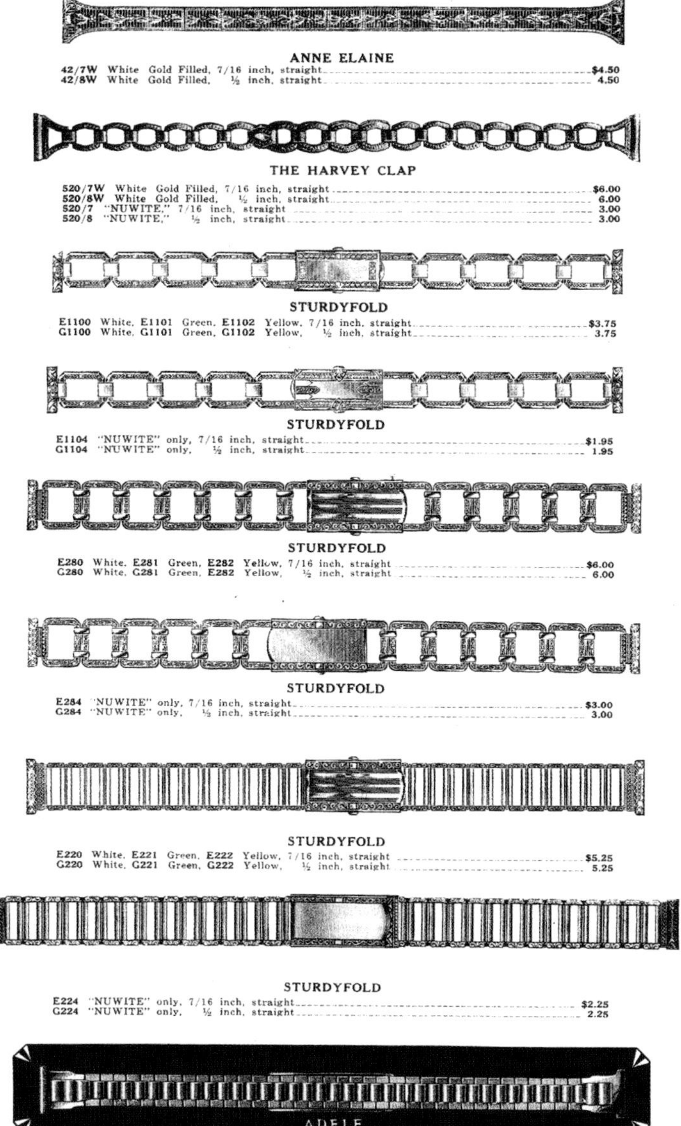

Folding Attachments for Ladies

ANNE ELAINE

42/7W White Gold Filled, 7/16 inch, straight $4.50
42/8W White Gold Filled, ½ inch, straight 4.50

THE HARVEY CLAP

520/7W White Gold Filled, 7/16 inch, straight $6.00
520/8W White Gold Filled, ½ inch, straight 6.00
520/7 "NUWITE," 7/16 inch, straight 3.00
520/8 "NUWITE," ½ inch, straight 3.00

STURDYFOLD

E1100 White, E1101 Green, E1102 Yellow, 7/16 inch, straight $3.75
G1100 White, G1101 Green, G1102 Yellow, ½ inch, straight 3.75

STURDYFOLD

E1104 "NUWITE" only, 7/16 inch, straight $1.95
G1104 "NUWITE" only, ½ inch, straight 1.95

STURDYFOLD

E280 White, E281 Green, E282 Yellow, 7/16 inch, straight $6.00
G280 White, G281 Green, E282 Yellow, ½ inch, straight 6.00

STURDYFOLD

E284 "NUWITE" only, 7/16 inch, straight $3.00
G284 "NUWITE" only, ½ inch, straight 3.00

STURDYFOLD

E220 White, E221 Green, E222 Yellow, 7/16 inch, straight $5.25
G220 White, G221 Green, G222 Yellow, ½ inch, straight 5.25

STURDYFOLD

E224 "NUWITE" only, 7/16 inch, straight $2.25
G224 "NUWITE" only, ½ inch, straight 2.25

ADELE

1024 White Gold Filled, 7/16 inch, straight $4.50
1044 White Gold Filled, ½ inch, straight 4.50

PRICES ARE SUBJECT TO CHANGE WITHOUT NOTICE

Metal bracelets by Harvey Clap and Sturdy, S. H. Clausin catalog, 1931

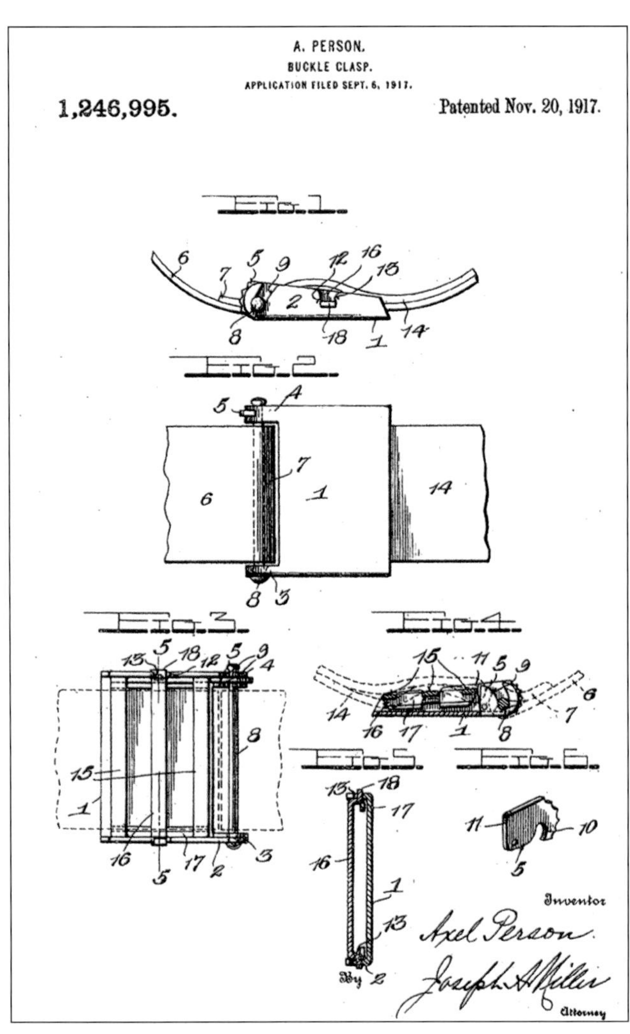

Patent assigned to Harvey Clap & Company

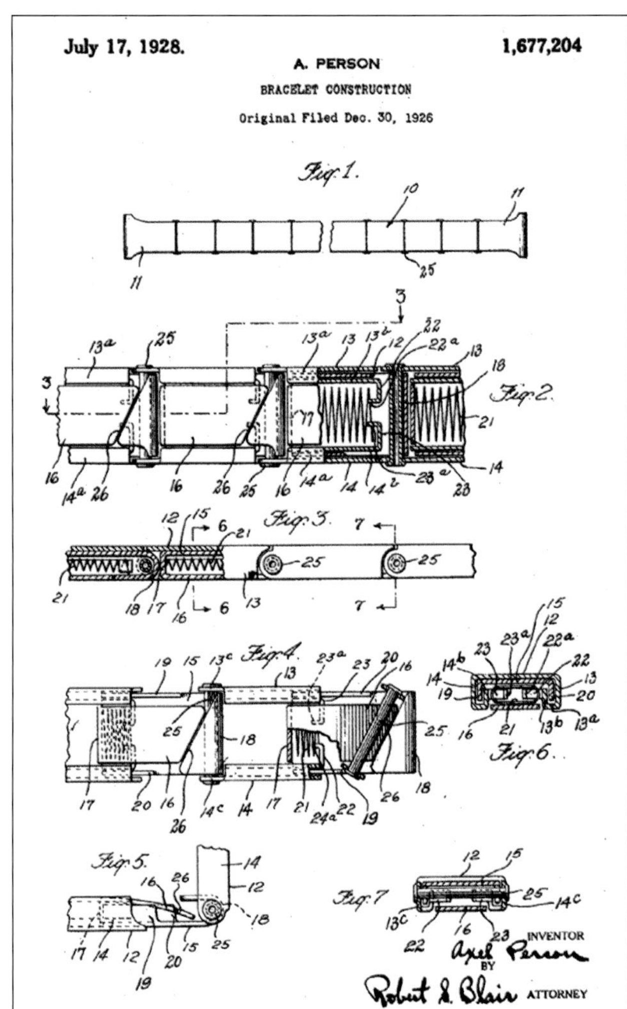

Patent assigned to Harvey Clap & Company

Levy & Anderson

From its beginning, Levy & Anderson specialized in medium-priced and popular-priced watch bracelets. The company's objective was "not only to make products to retail at slightly under average prices, but also to offer bracelets of a higher quality which could still be sold at a reasonable but profitable figure." With this policy, Levy & Anderson developed a large and extensive line that retailed from 75 cents to $5.00 per band, that still retained all the desirable features of more expensive bands, Yet suffered no reduction of quality and workmanship.

The Levy & Anderson factory was based in Providence, Rhode Island, with branch sales offices in New York, Chicago and San Francisco. Distribution was strictly through wholesalers.[57]

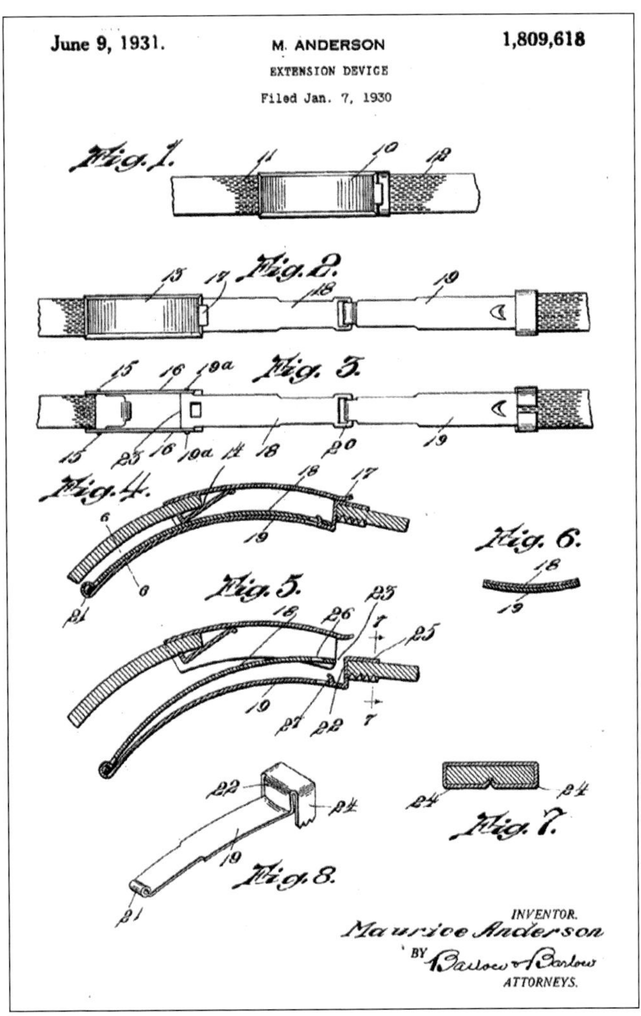

Levy & Anderson patent by Maurice Anderson as inventor

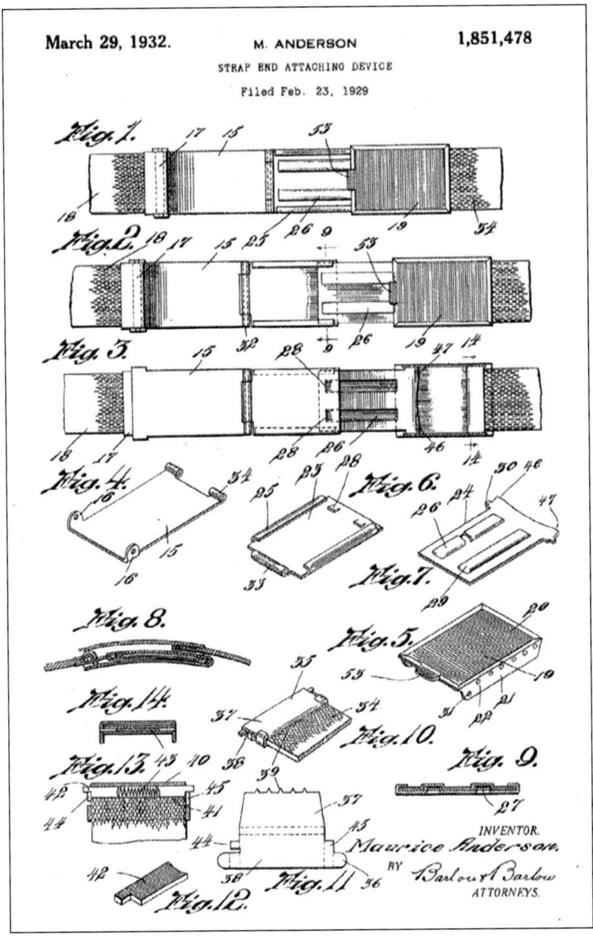

Levy & Anderson patent by Maurice Anderson as inventor

The Gruen Watch Company

Fred Gruen, president of Gruen, even found the time to invent and file patents, including some involving watchbands.

Mentioned in the October 1932 issue of the *Keystone* was that "the Gruen Watch Company, Time Hill, Cincinnati, [had] recently introduced a line of wrist watch straps under the trade marked name of 'Sweat Proof.' These straps are offered in many attractive styles, the sweat proof black leather which constitutes the band being topped with genuine pigskin, lizard, brown, tan and other finishes and being equipped with a strong, practical buckle or folding catch." [58]

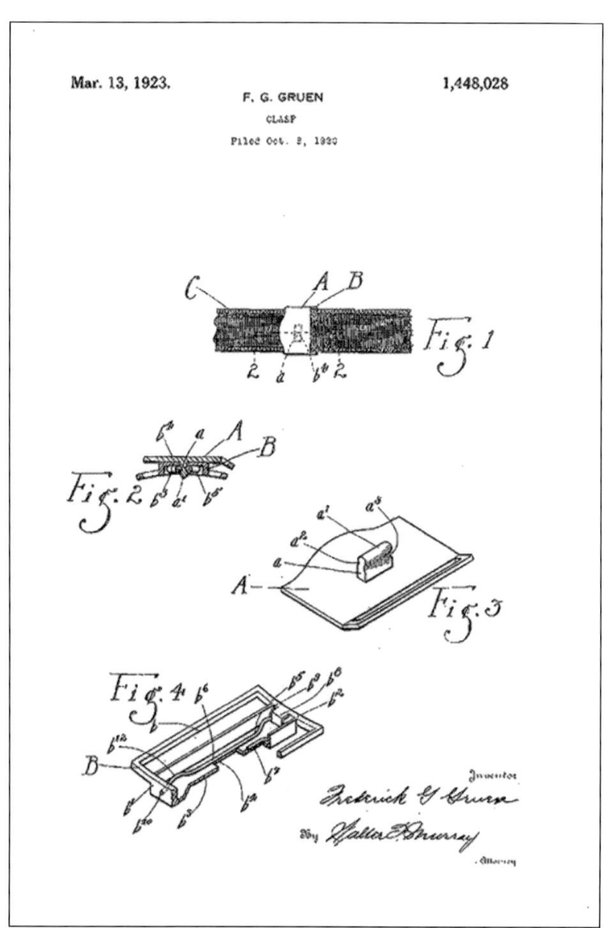

Gruen patent by Frederick G. Gruen as inventor

Bliss Brothers Company

The E. A. Bliss Company started business in 1878 in Attleboro, Massachusetts, later becoming the Bliss Brothers Company and ultimately the Napier Company. Bliss manufactured high-quality jewelry items, cameos, rings, lockets, compacts and pocket watch fobs. The company relocated to Meriden, Connecticut, in 1890.

In the 1920s, Bliss began fabricating metal expansion bracelets under the "Surefit" trade name. In April 1929, Bliss introduced several models of its "Surefit" metal watch strap with "Surefold," an improved three-fold buckle permitting the removal of both watch and strap over the hand without detaching the strap from the watch.[59]

Bliss advertised directly to consumers in national periodicals such as the *Saturday Evening Post, Life, Photo Play* and the *New Yorker.*

Bliss Brothers trademark

FOUR great magazines will carry *repeated* messages about SUREFIT Metal Watch Straps to more than FOUR MILLION people this fall. This powerful advertising constitutes a force to build more SUREFIT business for you. In 1926 three and one half times as many people bought SUREFIT Metal Watch Straps as in 1924. 1927 holds further sales increases for retail jewelers who display these fast-selling metal watch straps prominently and who overlook no opportunities to recommend them to customers. If you do not stock SUREFIT or if your stock is incomplete, get in touch with your jobber at once.

There is no other watch strap made like SUREFIT

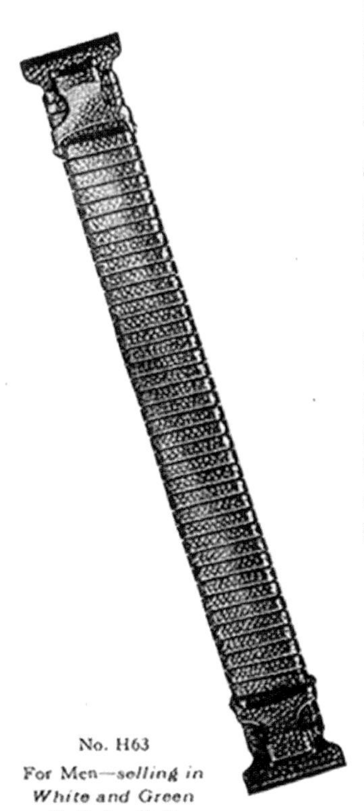

No. H63
For Men—*selling in White and Green G. F. for $5.50*

SUREFIT
TRADE MARK
Metal Watch Straps

No. 196
For Ladies—*selling White, Green or English G. F. for $4.50*

BLISS BROTHERS COMPANY
ATTLEBORO ∴ ∴ MASSACHUSETTS

Made under exclusive patents of September 24, 1918 and July 22, 1919

Every Wrist Watch Wearer is a SUREFIT Prospect-Sell Him!

"Surefit" metal watch straps by Bliss Brothers, *Keystone*, September 1927

Bliss Brothers "Surefit" bands, A. C. Becken catalog, 1928

"Surefit" ladies' bands by Bliss Brothers, A. C. Becken catalog, 1928. A watchband is superimposed on the page.

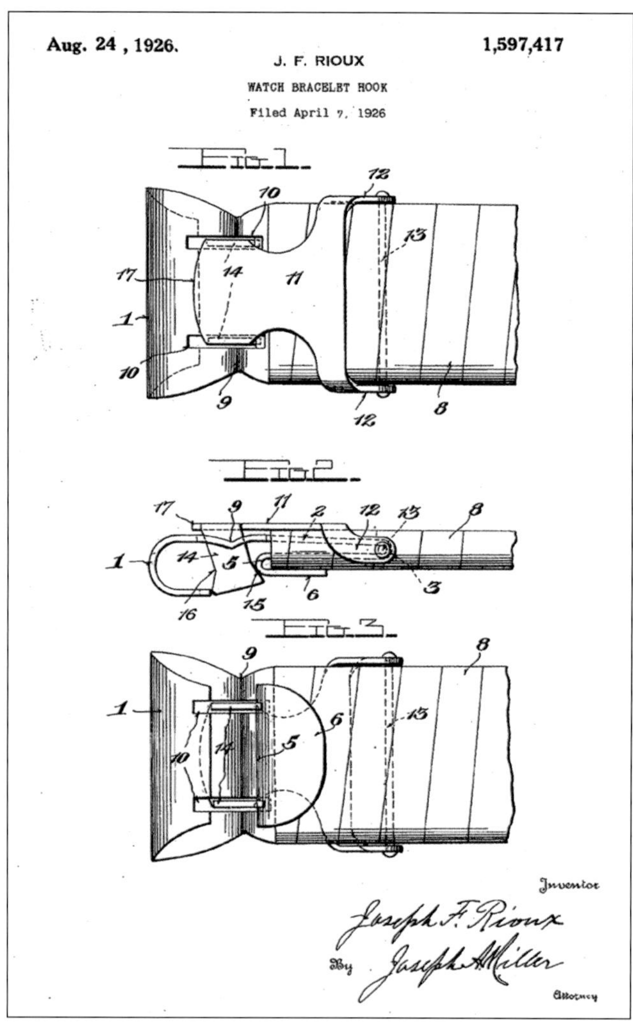

Patent assigned to Bliss Brothers Company

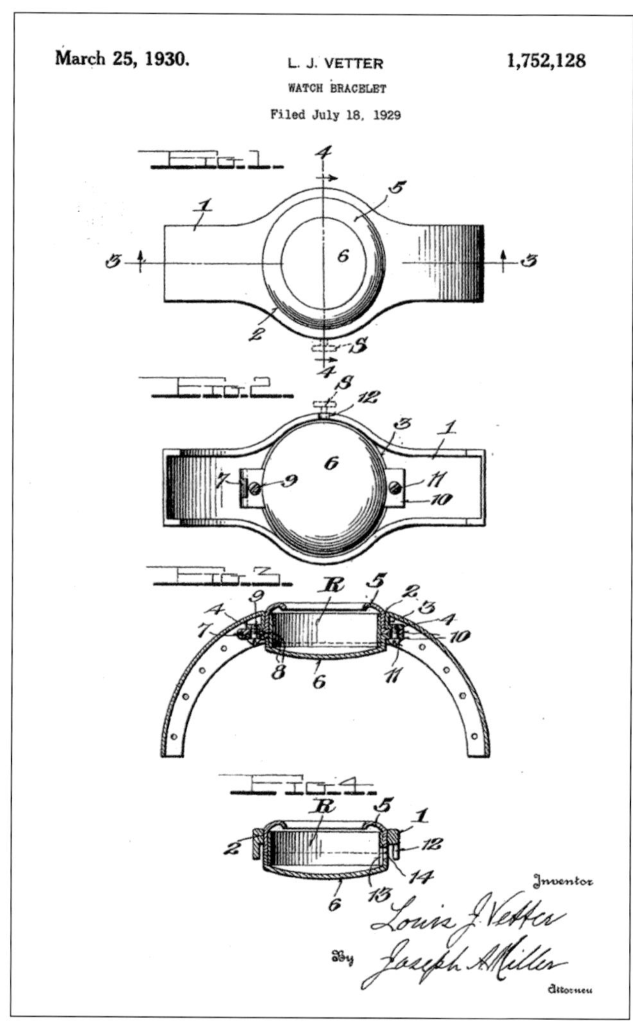

Patent assigned to Bliss Brothers Company

Manheimer Watch Company

The Manheimer Watch Company of Chicago, a longtime Illinois Watch Company jobber, offered its own cases and even straps. The April 1929 issue of the *Keystone* announced in its "For the Buyer" department that "after ten months of experimenting and development work," the company had introduced the Manheimer Lug-less Strap Watch. The watch was manufactured in five models in 10/0, 6/0 and 3/0 sizes.

The announcement continued: "This watch is featured by the fact that lugs and spring bars are entirely eliminated. The strap or band slides into the top and bottom edges of the case, giving the appearance of the strap penetrating the case. . . . To remove the strap from the watch it is only necessary to remove the back of bezel, and when this is snapped on, the strap is automatically locked into place."

94 THE JEWELERS' CIRCULAR September 6, 1928

AT LAST!!!

A Wrist Watch Without Lugs or Spring Bars

The Manheimer *Lug-less* Strap Watch

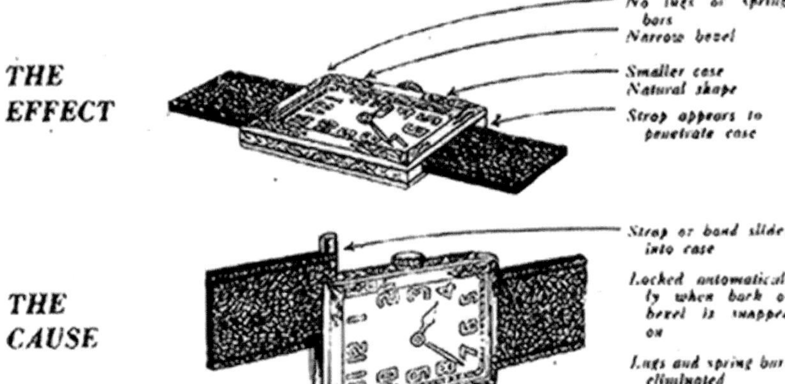

THE ADVANTAGES

1. Greatly improved appearance. Only watch and strap or band visible. No unsightly projections.
2. Strap or band removed or inserted in less than one-third the time required for lug models. Nuisance of handling spring bars eliminated.
3. Smaller watches without smaller movements. Center of the case utilized.
4. Relieves wear on strap or band.

TRADE COMMENTS

(By leading designers and manufacturers—quoted.)

"The wrist watch of the future."

"The greatest improvement ever made in strap watches."

"A knock-out."

Sold complete and boxed, in 14K gold-filled cases fitted with Elgin, Waltham or Illinois movements. Choice of English straps or trifold leather or mesh bands. 10/0, 6/0 or 3/0 sizes now available in several attractive models.

United States and foreign patents pending by

MANHEIMER WATCH COMPANY

Wholesalers of American Watches Since 1875

THIRTY ONE NORTH STATE STREET · CHICAGO

TELEPHONES CENTRAL 1044

Eastern Distributors: LOUIS MANHEIMER & BROS., 20 West 47th St., New York City

Jewelers' Circular, September 6, 1928, Manheimer lug-less strap watch

For the Buyer

New Goods, New Lines and Seasonable Offerings

Lug-less Strap Watches Make Their Bow to the Trade

AFTER ten months of experimenting and development work, the Manheimer Watch Company, of Chicago, announced the fact that the Manheimer Lug-less Strap Watch is now being manufactured in five models and definitely placed on the market.

This watch is featured by the fact that lugs and spring bars are entirely eliminated. The strap or band slides into the top and bottom edges of the case, giving the appearance of the strap penetrating the case. The case is smaller and of natural shape, and the bezel is narrow. To remove the strap from the watch, it is only necessary to remove the back or bezel, and when this is snapped on, the strap is automatically locked into place.

The five models now being marketed are in 10–0, 6–0 and 3–0 sizes.

Arthur E. Manheimer, inventor and patentee of the lug-less watch, announces that some of the largest watch manufacturers in the country are contemplating manufacturing wrist watches under his patent, and are now having models submitted. Their manufacture is restricted by specific provisions in the patents and contracts to 14-karat gold filled or solid gold cases. No cheaper quality cases are permitted under the patents.

The lug-less wrist watch was first conceived by Mr. Manheimer three months after he first became identified with the watch business.

Keystone, April 1929

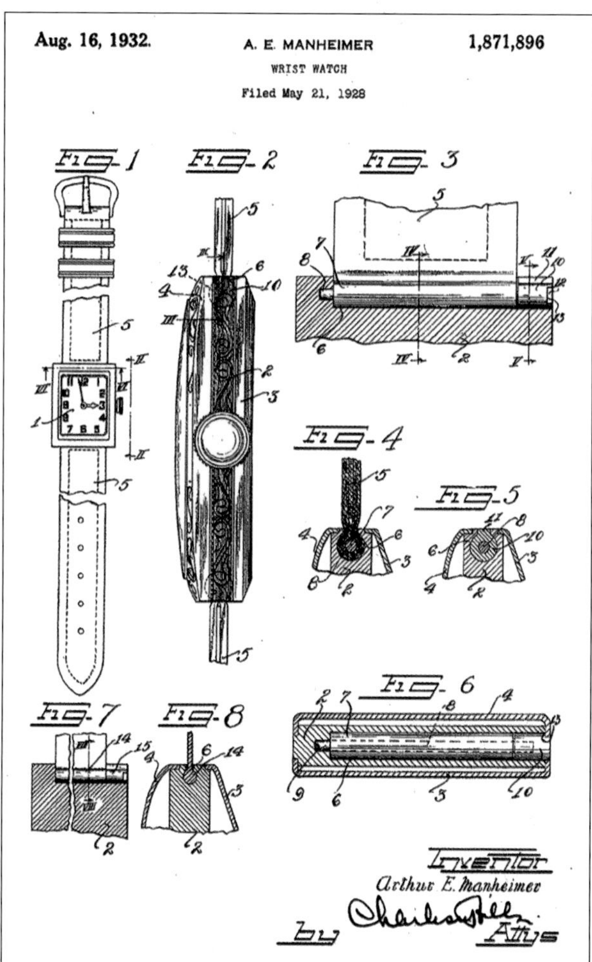

Manheimer patent by Arthur E. Manheimer as inventor

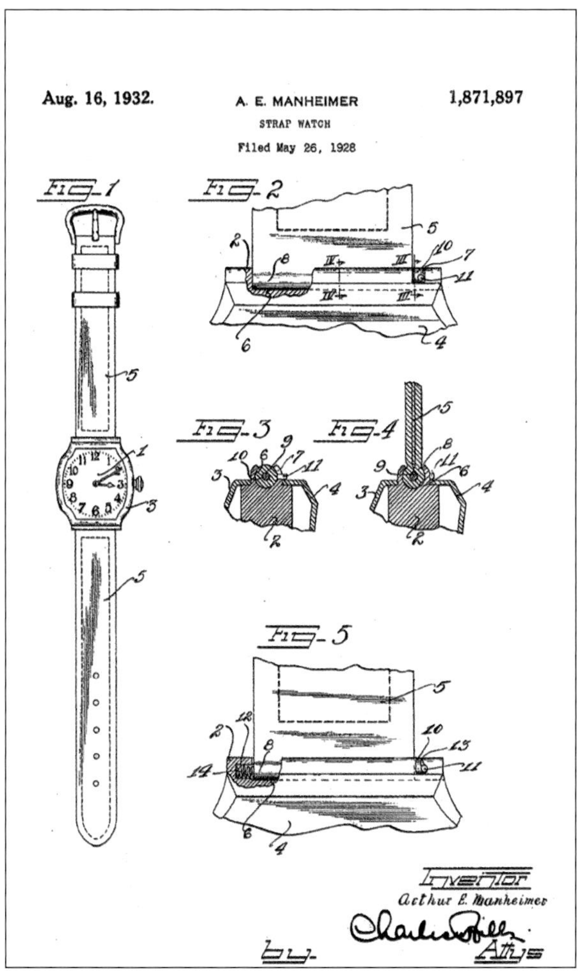

Manheimer patent by Arthur E. Manheimer as inventor

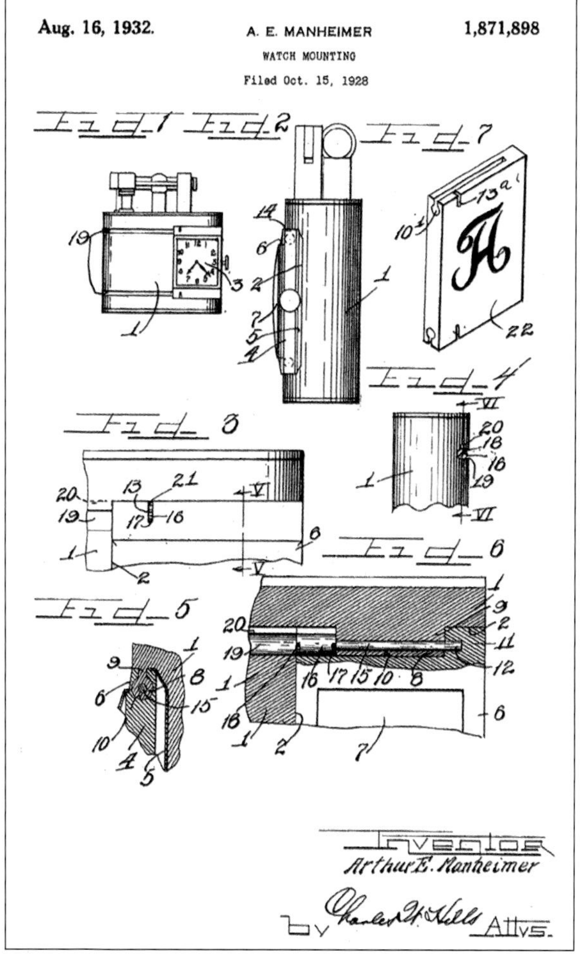

Manheimer patent by Arthur E. Manheimer as inventor

Rosenheim Co., Inc.

Rosenheim Co., Inc. opened in 1930 as the Great Depression was beginning. It started as the "Tiny Jewel Box," a one hundred square foot store on G Street N.W. in Washington, D.C. It is now operated by the third generation of Rosenheims. It sold watch attachments to jobbers in its early days of operation. Among its brands were Flexebar, Flexeweave and Flexed'or.

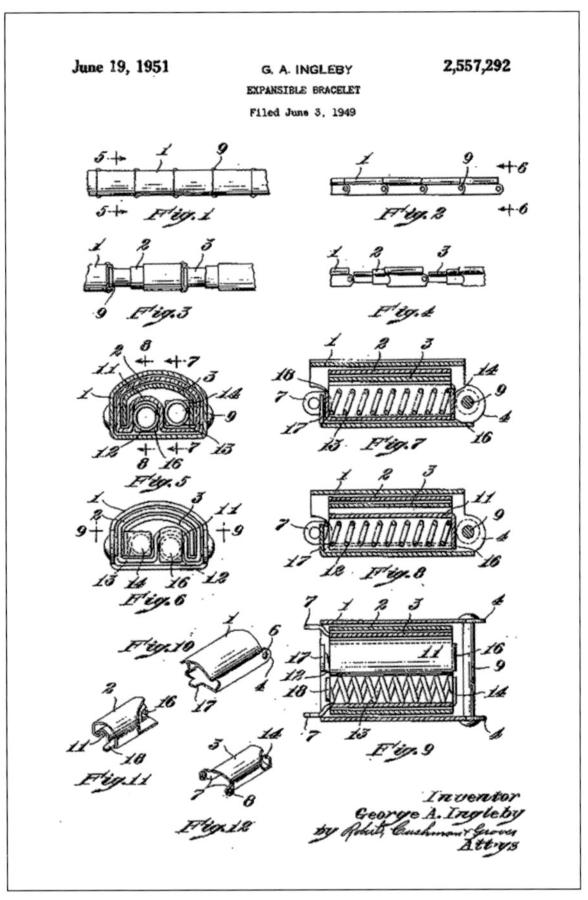

Patent assigned to Rosenheim Co., Inc.

The Tiny Jewel Box

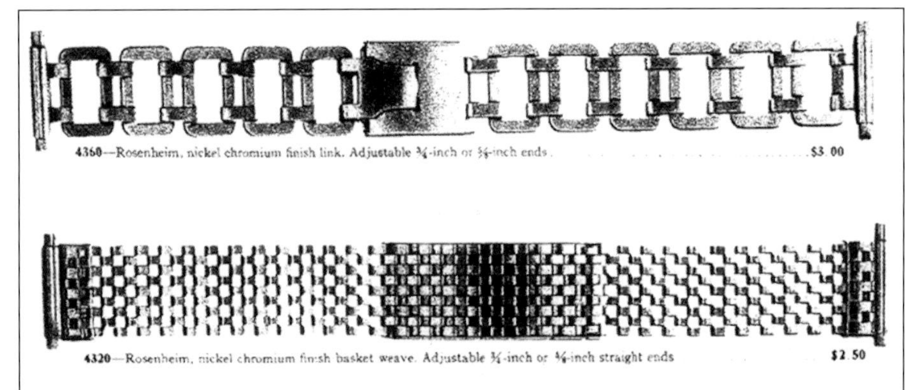
4360—Rosenheim, nickel chromium finish link. Adjustable ¾-inch or ⅝-inch ends $3.00

4320—Rosenheim, nickel chromium finish basket weave. Adjustable ¾-inch or ⅝-inch straight ends $2.50

Rosenheim bands, A. I. Hall catalog, 1930–31

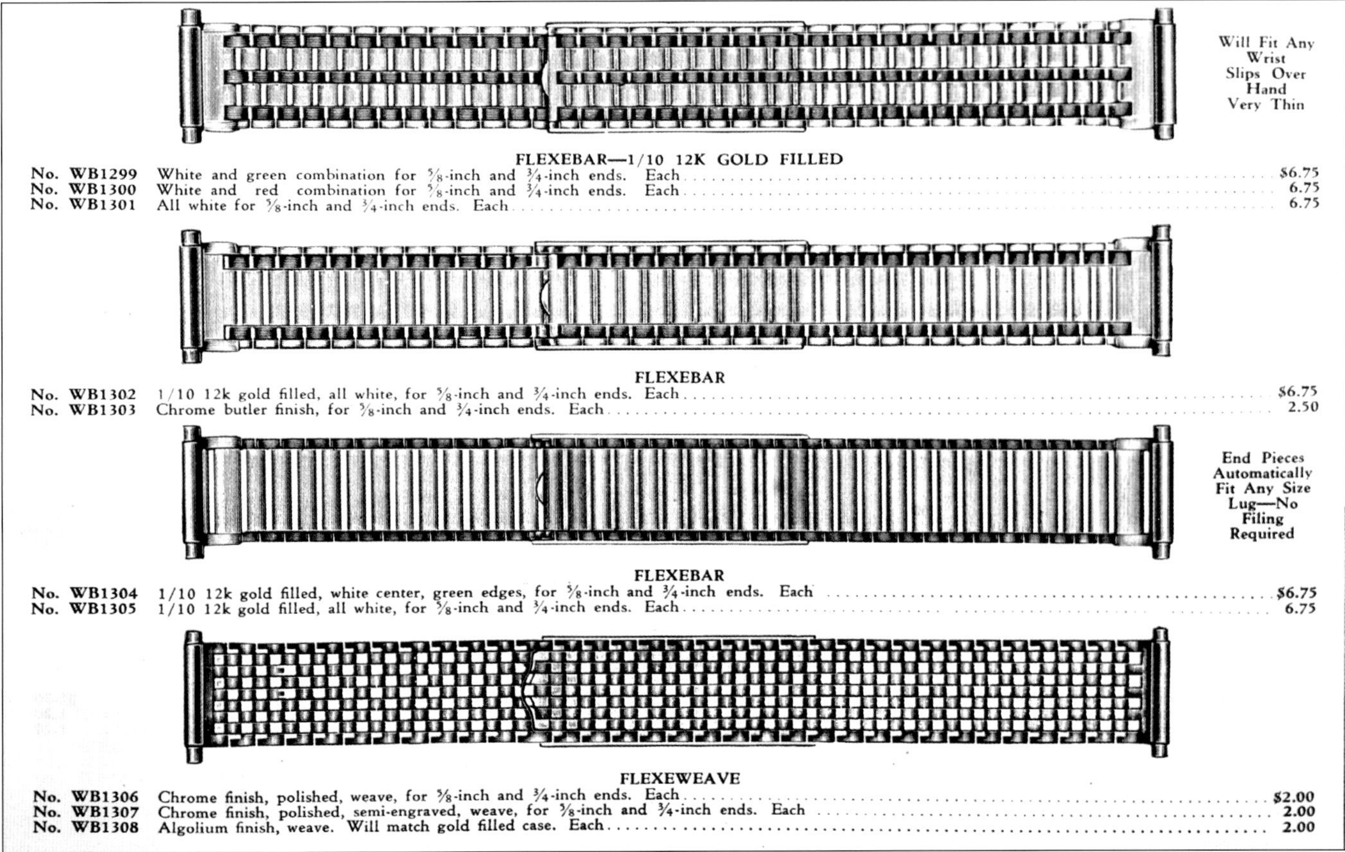

Will Fit Any Wrist Slips Over Hand Very Thin

FLEXEBAR—1/10 12K GOLD FILLED

No. **WB1299** White and green combination for 5/8-inch and 3/4-inch ends. Each $6.75
No. **WB1300** White and red combination for 5/8-inch and 3/4-inch ends. Each 6.75
No. **WB1301** All white for 5/8-inch and 3/4-inch ends. Each 6.75

FLEXEBAR

No. **WB1302** 1/10 12k gold filled, all white, for 5/8-inch and 3/4-inch ends. Each $6.75
No. **WB1303** Chrome butler finish, for 5/8-inch and 3/4-inch ends. Each 2.50

End Pieces Automatically Fit Any Size Lug—No Filing Required

FLEXEBAR

No. **WB1304** 1/10 12k gold filled, white center, green edges, for 5/8-inch and 3/4-inch ends. Each $6.75
No. **WB1305** 1/10 12k gold filled, all white, for 5/8-inch and 3/4-inch ends. Each 6.75

FLEXEWEAVE

No. **WB1306** Chrome finish, polished, weave, for 5/8-inch and 3/4-inch ends. Each $2.00
No. **WB1307** Chrome finish, polished, semi-engraved, weave, for 5/8-inch and 3/4-inch ends. Each 2.00
No. **WB1308** Algolium finish, weave. Will match gold filled case. Each 2.00

"Flexebar" and "Flexeweave" watchbands by Rosenheim, A. C. Becken catalog, 1932

Bates & Bacon

The Bates & Bacon company, of Attleboro, Massachusetts, began in 1857 as Skinner, Viall & Company but in 1858 became Bates, Capron & Williams. Bates sold his interests in that company and in 1860 began a business under his own name. In 1867 he took George M. Bacon as a partner in the firm, which thereafter was known as Bates & Bacon. It produced bracelets in rolled gold plate as well as other jewelry items. In 1882, the company also began producing watch cases also. Apparently, it was the first jewelry manufacturer in Attleboro to go into that line.[60]

With the arrival of wristwatches, Bates & Bacon added metal watchbands to its offerings, a logical move for a company that had long produced bracelets. The company's "Claspet" line of watchbands became particularly well known.

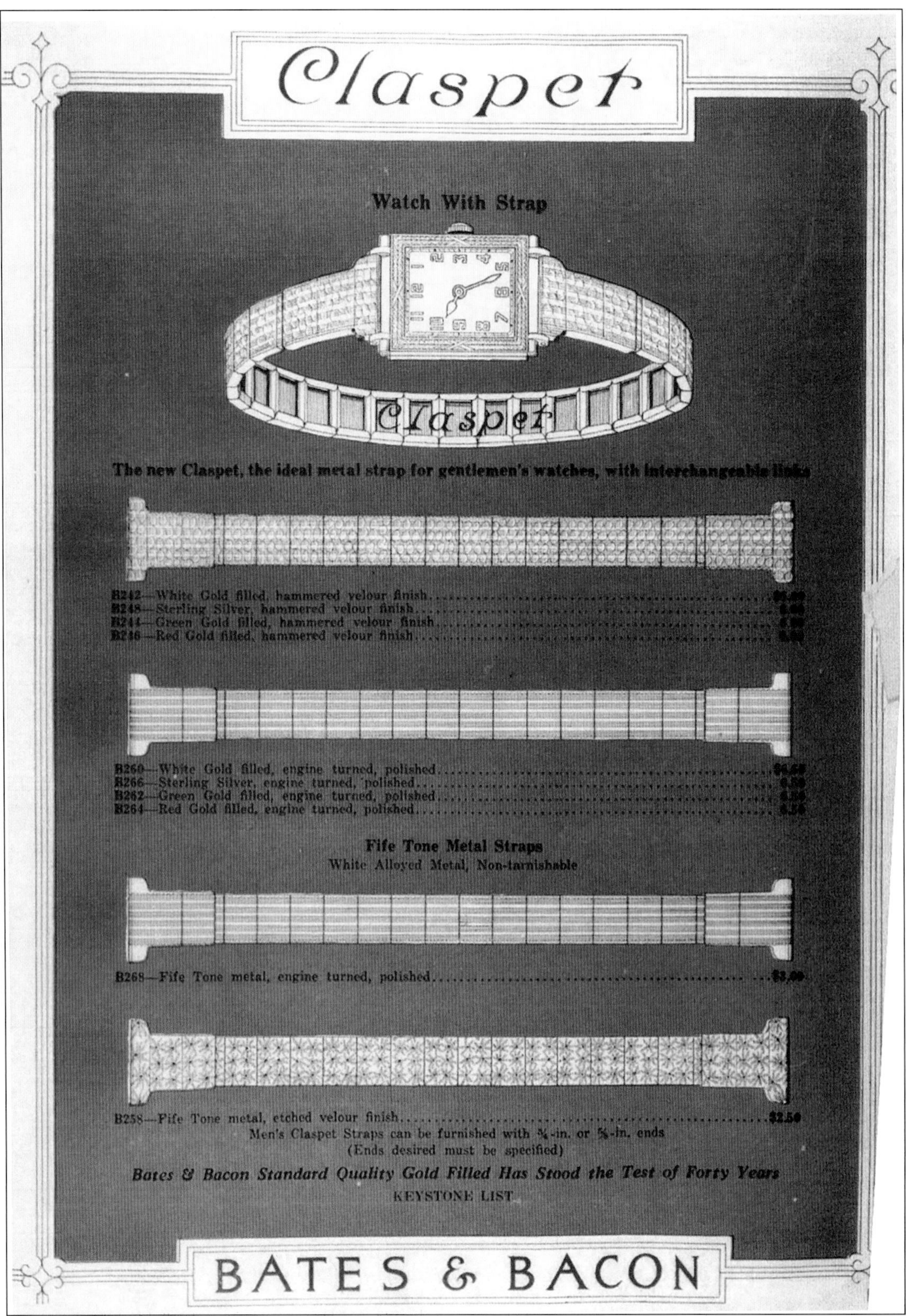

"Claspet" bands by Bates and Bacon, May & Malone catalog, 1928

Bugbee & Niles

The Bugbee & Niles Company, of North Attleboro, Massachusetts, originated in 1859 under the partnership of Smith & Ginnodo; it then became C. E. Smith & Company. Later it became the Bugbee & Niles Company, under the partnership of Samuel H. Bugbee and Gardner H. Niles.

The company had been a manufacturer of high-grade gold jewelry for many years before adding watch accessories to its product line. Among those accessories: "all that is latest and most fashionable in wrist-watch bracelets." Bugbee & Niles is said to have originated "the fourfold balanced mesh type, the expanded block type, exclusive buckle types with ribbon or leather, on all of which it [held] basic patents."

In addition to its main office in North Attleboro, Bugbee & Niles had a branch in New York. The company enjoyed a worldwide reputation.[61]

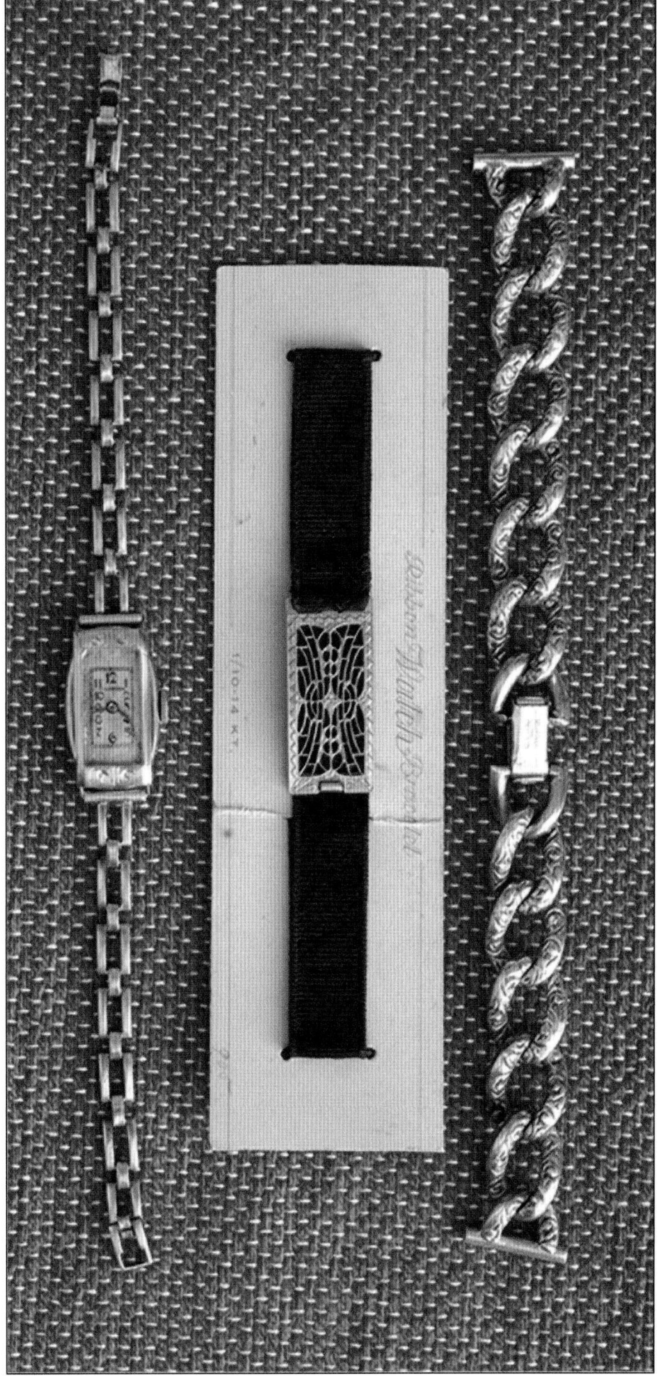

Bugbee and Niles watch bracelets. Left to right: ladies' sterling silver with white gold overlay, attached to an Illinois ladies' "Coquette" model; ladies' silk ribbon band with white gold-filled "spiderweb" clasp, on its original sales card; men's sterling silver with white gold overlay

An original Bugbee & Niles strap buckle, date stamped July 16, 1918

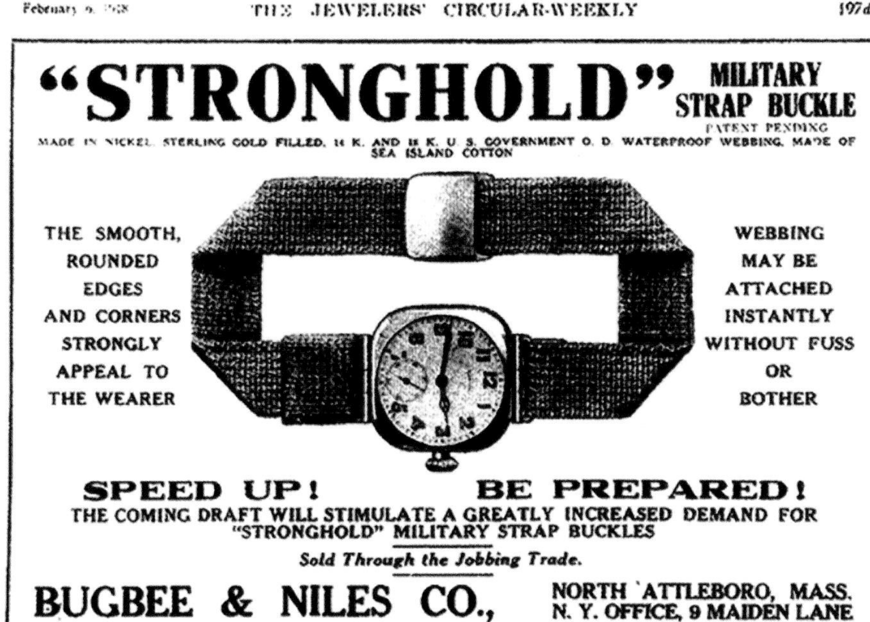

Bugbee & Niles advertisement, February 6, 1918

Patent assigned to Bugbee and Niles

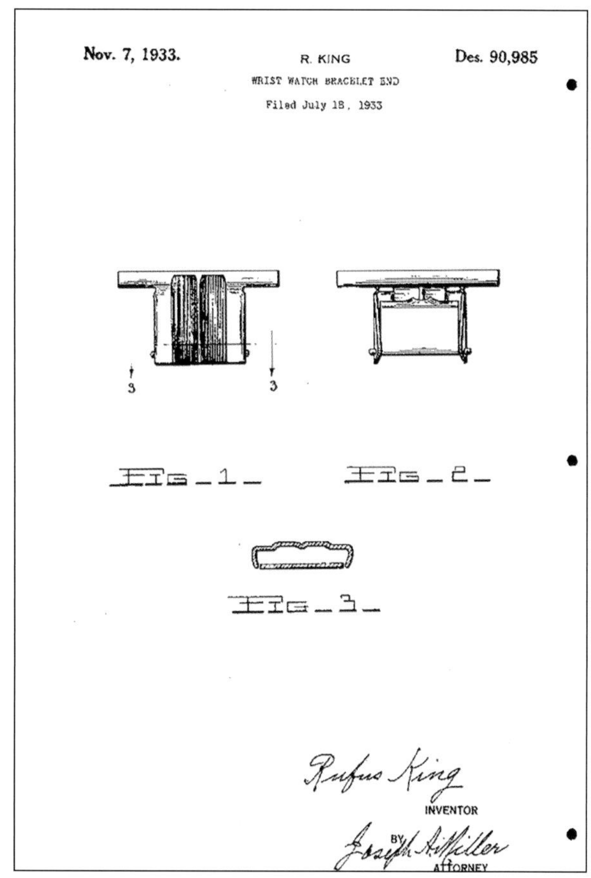

Patent assigned to Bugbee & Niles

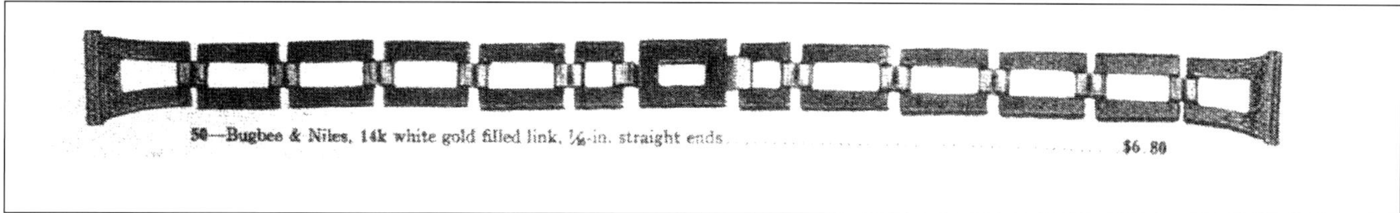

Bugbee & Niles band, A. I. Hall catalog, 1930–31

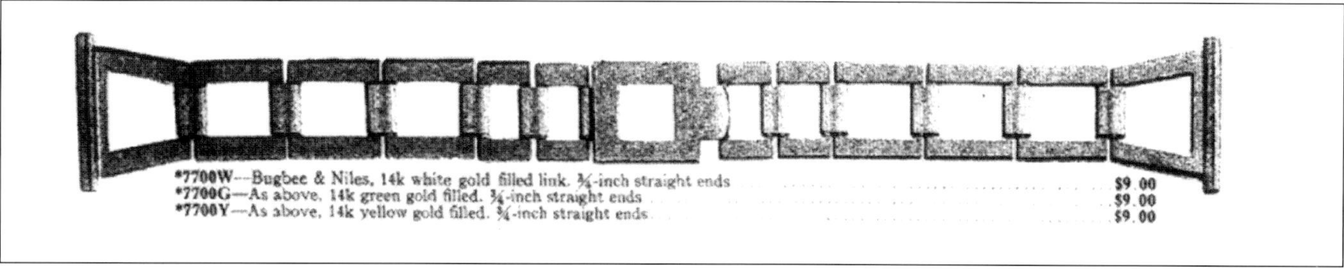

Bugbee & Niles band, A. I. Hall catalog, 1930–31

Mandalian Manufacturing Company

Sahatiel Mandalian (1869–1949), born in Turkey, came to the United States in 1889 and settled in North Attleboro, Massachusetts. The Mandalian company began in 1903 as Casper & Mandalian, then became Mandalian & Hawkins in 1906 when Eugene A. Hawkins replaced Casper, and ultimately became the Mandalian Manufacturing Company in 1915 after Mandalian purchased Hawkins's interest.[62]

The Mandalian company is best known for its exquisite enamel mesh Deco purses for women, which remain in great demand among collectors today. These were made using fish-scale mesh manufactured on a machine that Mandalian invented. Production of this mesh involved a patented process to achieve a unique pearlized finish that Mandalian trademarked as "Lustro Pearl." A Mandalian specialty was its "Baby Mesh," whose "smaller links allowed for a more supple flow of the material."[63]

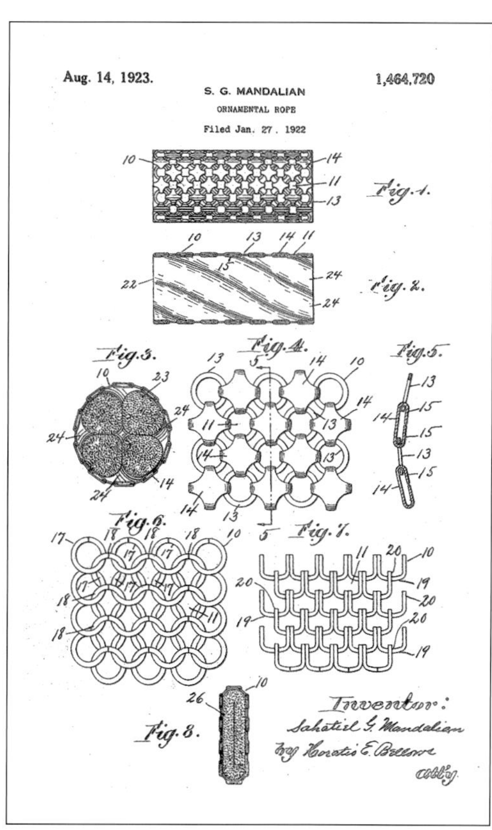

Mandalian patent for ornamental rope, showing how a product using small armor mesh links was made

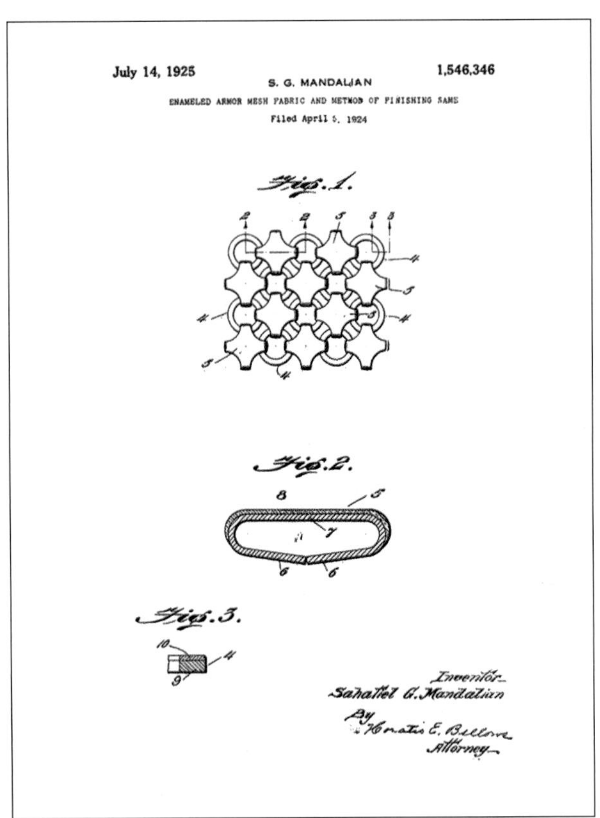

Mandalian patent for a method of finishing enameled armor mesh fabric

Four Mandalian mesh purses

In addition to its famous purses, Mandalian produced colored mesh watchbands for women. In 1929 the company ran a series of advertisements in color for its mesh bands, showing them on the Illinois ladies' Daytona model. These watchbands are rarely if ever found today, possibly because enameled mesh on a watchband would have been extremely prone to damage and watchbands of this type might have been thrown away once the enameling was spoiled.

A Mandalian-like mesh watchband, little enamel remaining

One end of the Mandalian-like band, showing a bit of enamel

The Mandalian Manufacturing Company lasted until 1944, when it was sold to the Whiting & Davis Company.[64]

March, 1929 The KEYSTONE Page 73

Lustro-Pearl Watch Bracelet *by* MANDALIAN

(Patent Pending)

COLOR

sways the mode—in jewelry as well as apparel. Here is the very latest expression of color in new and original watch bracelets by Mandalian. They are soft and pliable—light in weight —exceedingly smooth—easily adjustable—with a baked-on exclusive lustro-pearl finish—expressing many different colors and combinations.

These colorful bracelets complete the smart ensemble. This is their claim to popularity.

Lustro-Pearl Bracelets are priced to retail profitably at $5.00. Your wholesaler will be glad to show them.

The MANDALIAN MFG. CO.

Manufacturing Jewelers

NORTH ATTLEBORO MASSACHUSETTS

MANDALIAN

Makers of the famous lustro-pearl mesh bag

Mandalian advertisement, *Keystone,* March 1929, featuring an Illinois Daytona model

May, 1929 The KEYSTONE Page 65

Lustro-Pearl Watch Bracelets *by* MANDALIAN
(Patent Pending)

IN EVERY MODISH COLOR

These newest of watch bracelets are meeting with widespread approval. They are finished in exclusive Lustro-Pearl Enamels in a myriad of modish colors. They are fashioned by a patented process from hundreds of tiny pieces of enmeshed metal, and are silky-smooth, flexible, light as a feather. Fitted with standard end-sizes, they are easily attached.

The market is ready-made for such a remarkable bracelet, retailing as it does for the popular price of $3.00.

Mandalian Lustro-Pearl Watch Bracelets and Mesh Bags are sold only through wholesalers. If your wholesaler cannot show you Mandalian products let us know, and we will send you the names of many who can.

The MANDALIAN MFG. CO.

Manufacturing Jewelers
NORTH ATTLEBORO
MASSACHUSETTS

MANDALIAN

Makers of the famous lustro-pearl mesh bag

Mandalian advertisement, *Keystone*, May 1929, featuring an Illinois Daytona model

Mandalian advertisement, *Keystone*, May 1929, featuring an Illinois Daytona model

Dubois Watch Case Company

The Dubois Watch Case Company owned Jacques Depollier and Son in Brooklyn, New York. In addition to producing fascinating World War I wristwatch cases (also through its Dubois brand), they patented and manufactured many special metal watch attachments. Perhaps their most famous was its 1914 United States patent, No. 1,113,885, involving an "expansible securing device for watch bracelets," as shown here.

C. L. DEPOLLIER & E. C. DUNCUFF.
EXPANSIBLE SECURING DEVICE FOR WATCH BRACELETS.
APPLICATION FILED FEB. 10, 1914.
1,113,885. Patented Oct. 13, 1914.

C. L. Depollier & E. C. Duncuff patent assigned to Dubois Watch Case Company, October 13, 1914

This watch attachment clasp was invented by Charles L. Depollier, the son of Jacques Depollier, and Edward Cruzell Duncuff, a salesman. They also collaborated on other watch-related patents, also assigned to Dubois.

Evidently, Dubois felt so strongly about the Depollier and Duncuff invention that it vigorously protested its alleged infringement, going so far as to file an infringement lawsuit against one purported infringer and published a "Notice to the Trade" in a full-page announcement in the *Keystone Weekly* on September 21, 1915.

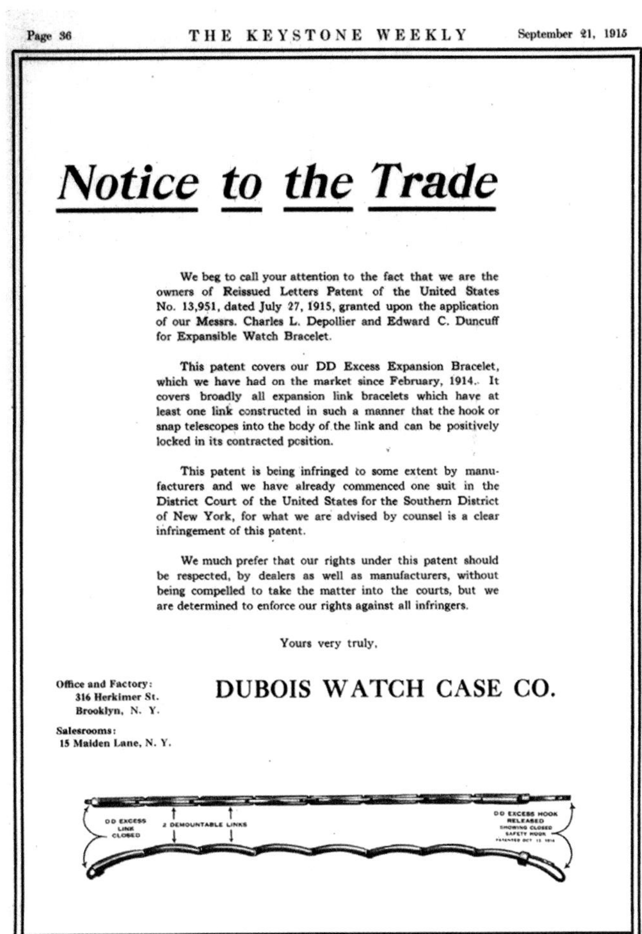

Page 36 THE KEYSTONE WEEKLY September 21, 1915

Notice to the Trade

We beg to call your attention to the fact that we are the owners of Reissued Letters Patent of the United States No. 13,951, dated July 27, 1915, granted upon the application of our Messrs. Charles L. Depollier and Edward C. Duncuff for Expansible Watch Bracelet.

This patent covers our DD Excess Expansion Bracelet, which we have had on the market since February, 1914. It covers broadly all expansion link bracelets which have at least one link constructed in such a manner that the hook or snap telescopes into the body of the link and can be positively locked in its contracted position.

This patent is being infringed to some extent by manufacturers and we have already commenced one suit in the District Court of the United States for the Southern District of New York, for what we are advised by counsel is a clear infringement of this patent.

We much prefer that our rights under this patent should be respected, by dealers as well as manufacturers, without being compelled to take the matter into the courts, but we are determined to enforce our rights against all infringers.

Yours very truly,

DUBOIS WATCH CASE CO.

Office and Factory:
316 Herkimer St.
Brooklyn, N. Y.

Salesrooms:
15 Maiden Lane, N. Y.

Keystone Weekly, September 21, 1915

The one lawsuit was obviously meant as a shot across the bow of the watch attachment industry to preclude their use of this proprietary right. Depollier was also to claim exclusive rights to the name "Khaki" for watches, but it is unknown if any case was ever filed by the company.

It is also possible that the "D-D" on the D-D Utility watch stands for "Depollier and Duncuff" and not "Depollier and Dubois." But this is not likely because the D-D Utility watch case was invented by E. C. Fitch and assigned to Depollier.

DUBOIS WATCH CASE COMPANY VS. BUGBEE & NILES COMPANY, INC.

It turns out that the one suit was filed by Dubois to enforce its "DD Excess Expansion Bracelet" patent on August 31, 1915 was against the Bugbee & Niles Company ("B & N"). The Bill of Complaint, signed by Charles L. Depollier, president of Dubois, alleged that B & N infringed the patent jointly invented by Charles L. Depollier and Edward C. Duncuff for "certain new and useful improvements in 'Expansible Securing Devices for Watch Bracelets.' The litigation concerned U.S. Patent No. 1,113,885. Dubois further claimed that B & N was making and selling expansible watch bracelets embodying the improvements shown in the patent without a license to do so. Dubois sought the profits and gains B & N realized from its unlawful actions and to enjoin B & N from selling such watch bracelets.

Although B & N vigorously defended these allegations for one year, the court found B & N had infringed the Dubois patent. B & N promptly took a license with Dubois and Dubois dropped its claim for damages for past infringement on September 30, 1916 via a Decree and Consent.

It is likely that other watch attachment makers (yet to license this technology) rapidly entered into licensing agreements with Dubois to be able to continue to manufacture and sell similar expansible watch attachments or face the threat of litigation from Dubois.*

**Dubois Watch Case Company vs. Bugbee & Niles Company, Inc.*, U.S. District Court, Southern District of New York, September 1, 1915

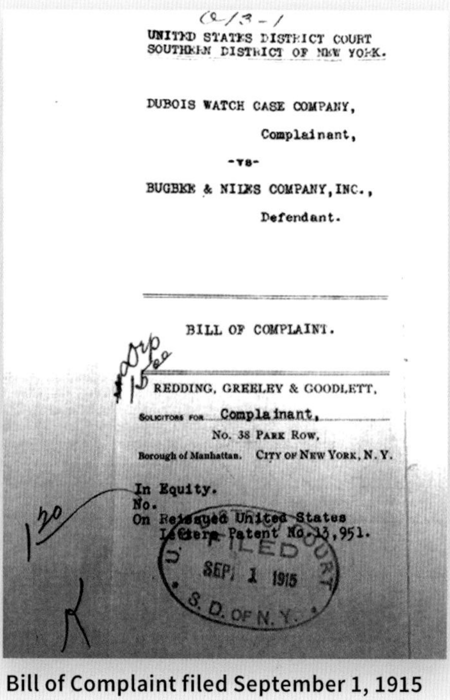

E/13-1

UNITED STATES DISTRICT COURT
SOUTHERN DISTRICT OF NEW YORK.

DUBOIS WATCH CASE COMPANY,
Complainant,
-vs-
BUGBEE & NILES COMPANY, INC.,
Defendant.

BILL OF COMPLAINT.

REDDING, GREELEY & GOODLETT,
SOLICITORS FOR Complainant,
No. 38 PARK ROW,
Borough of Manhattan. CITY OF NEW YORK, N. Y.

In Equity.
No.
On Reissued United States Letters Patent No. 13,951.

U.S. DISTRICT COURT FILED SEP 1 1915 S. D. OF N. Y.

Bill of Complaint filed September 1, 1915

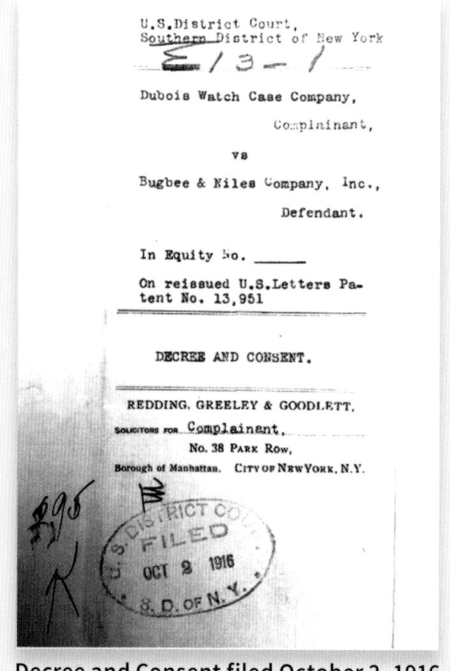

U.S. District Court,
Southern District of New York
E/13-1

Dubois Watch Case Company,
Complainant,
vs
Bugbee & Niles Company, Inc.,
Defendant.

In Equity No. ______

On reissued U.S. Letters Patent No. 13,951

DECREE AND CONSENT.

REDDING, GREELEY & GOODLETT,
SOLICITORS FOR Complainant,
No. 38 PARK ROW,
Borough of Manhattan. CITY OF NEW YORK, N.Y.

U.S. DISTRICT COURT FILED OCT 2 1916 S. D. OF N. Y.

Decree and Consent filed October 2, 1916

Other Watchband Manufacturers

A number of the prominent watch case companies were also producing their own watch attachments. Two of these were Wadsworth and the Illinois Watch Case Company (both described earlier in this chapter).

Wadsworth's attractive metal strap bracelets were widely advertised in magazines. Men's models included the Ben Hur and the Olympian; for the ladies there were the Athena, Diana and Amazon. Some of the models were available in solid 14K gold as well as gold-filled. One disadvantage to Wadsworth's strap bracelets was that the ends had to be fitted onto the lugs of a watch by a jeweler. Another was that it then had to be slipped over the wrist and its expansion mechanism adjusted. (Sturdy's strap bracelets, in contrast, had endpieces that simply clipped onto the lugs, so they could be easily detached and used on more than one watch. The sliding "buckle" adjustment was also easy to use.)

64 *The Literary Digest for November 17, 1928*

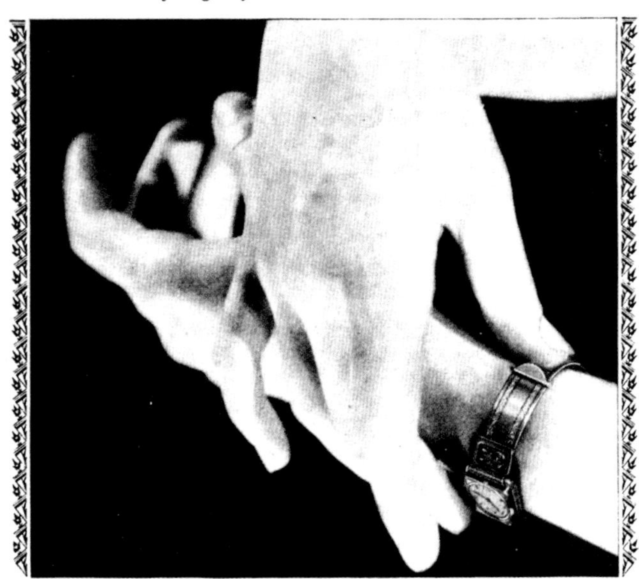

Your watch deserves it!

The new Lady Wadsworth Band—one of many styles for women. Links expand to slip over the hand, contract to fit the wrist. Wadsworth Quality Gold Filled, $5 to $8.25

THAT wrist watch of yours—how carefully you chose it! For materials, workmanship, style.

Surely it deserves a band that completes its beauty and usefulness—a Wadsworth Watch Band.

Made in white or green gold filled, or in solid gold, it matches the watch itself. Like a fine watch, too, its beauty is lasting, its style up to the minute!

Clean, bright, sanitary. Safe and economical—no danger of losing your watch, no replacements. And Wadsworth Bands are so constructed that when properly adjusted by your jeweler they assure utmost comfort on the wrist.

The Wadsworth mark stamped inside is the same which for more than thirty-five years has been a recognized assurance of style, quality, and fine workmanship in watch cases.

Your jeweler has the Wadsworth Bands pictured here, and many other models in both flexible and link designs. He can fit one in a moment to any modern wrist watch. Ask him to show you a style which will exactly harmonize with the watch you're now wearing!

THE WADSWORTH WATCH CASE CO.
Dayton, Kentucky, Opposite Cincinnati, O.
Case makers for the leading watch movements

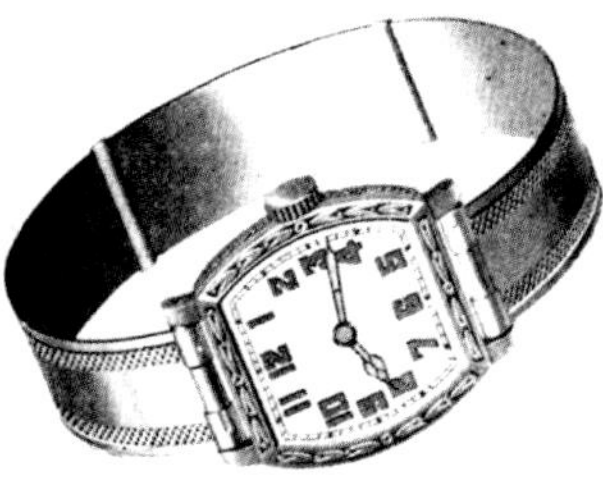

The Olympian model, for men. Expands to slip over the hand, readily adjusted, secured by a snap lock. 14-kt. solid gold: plain, $28; decorated, $30. Gold filled: plain, $7.50; decorated, $8.50. Many other distinctive designs for men

Wadsworth

WORKERS IN PRECIOUS METALS

***Literary Digest,* November 17, 1928. Pictured are the Lady Wadsworth filigree watchband and the men's Olympian strap bracelet.**

Literary Digest, June. 1, 1929. The ladies' wristwatch on the left at the bottom of the page is the rare Illinois Daytona 155B, sporting Wadsworth's "Athena" strap bracelet.

Three Wadsworth metal bracelets. *Top to bottom:* Olympian, Athena and Amazon (opened at the middle, unlike the other two)

The "Lord Wadsworth" model, with its flexible metal links and convenient clasp, was very popular. Elgin and Waltham chose this watchband to go on some of their watches, and the integral band for the Illinois Frontenac model and the Hamilton Clinton was apparently an ingenious variant of the "Lord Wadsworth" (see the listing for the **Frontenac** in Chapter 9).

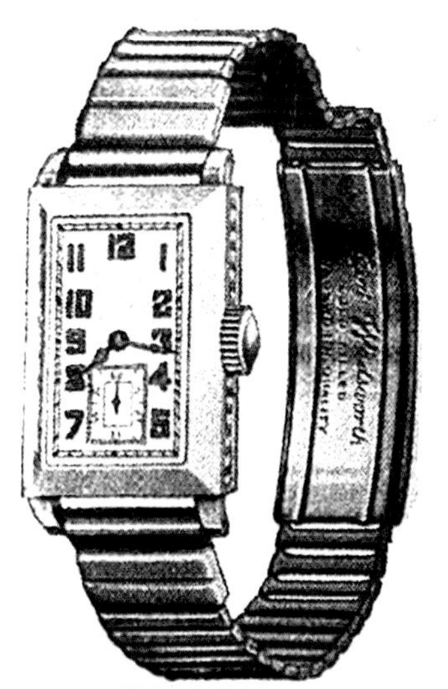

WADSWORTH WATCH BANDS

The "Lord Wadsworth" Truly the Greatest Achievement in a Metal Watch Band. Its Style is Keenly Distinctive. A Flexible Band of Slender Links Fastened with a Small V Shaped Buckle. Adjustable Arm Size. Buckle Opens to Remove Watch. Fits All Sizes of Lugs.

W4493-14Kt. Gold Filled **$13.60**
Specify Green or White Gold

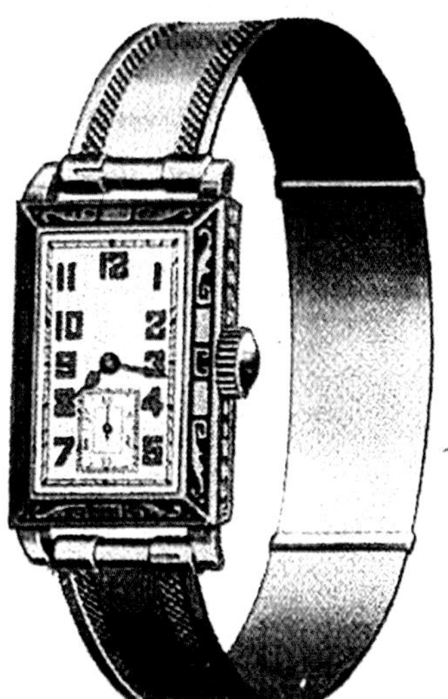

WADSWORTH WATCH BANDS

A Fine Dignified Looking Band. Decorated Borders. Adjusts in the Center; conforms to the Wrist and Fastens in the Back;—Secured By a Safety Lock. Bright Finish. Fits All Sizes of Lugs.

W4494-14Kt. Solid Gold **$40.70**
W4495-14Kt. Gold Filled **11.70**
Specify White Gold or Green

Wadsworth bands, L. & C. Mayers Catalog, 1929; "Lord Wadsworth" *(top)*, "Olympian" *(bottom)*

Illinois Watch Case Company "Adonis," L. & C. Mayers catalog, 1929

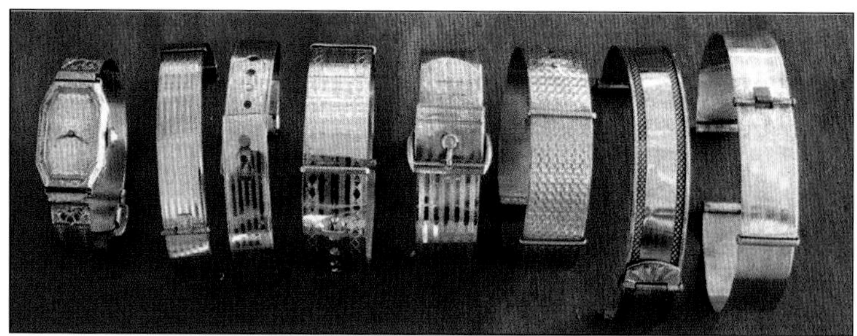

Left to right: Sturdy; Wadsworth (Athena); Wadsworth (Amazon); IWCCo (Jupiter); Sturdy; IWWCo (Adonis); Wadsworth (Olympian) and Wadsworth

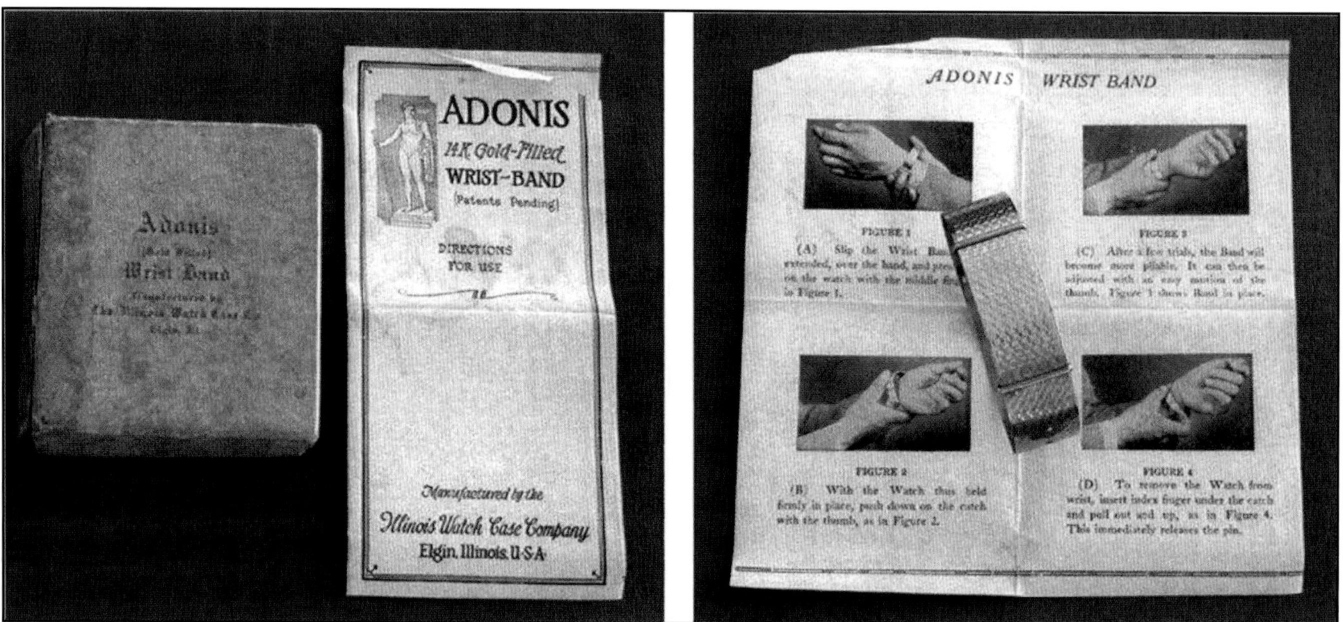

An Adonis band with its original box and paperwork

Many other companies also supplied bands to jewelers during the late 1920s and early 1930s. Among these were Pontiac, Fuller, Martin-Copeland, Gemex, Town & County, Pro-Tecto, Bon-Ton, Trafalgar, Duchess, Just-Rite and Holdfast. A few advertisements for some of these companies follow.

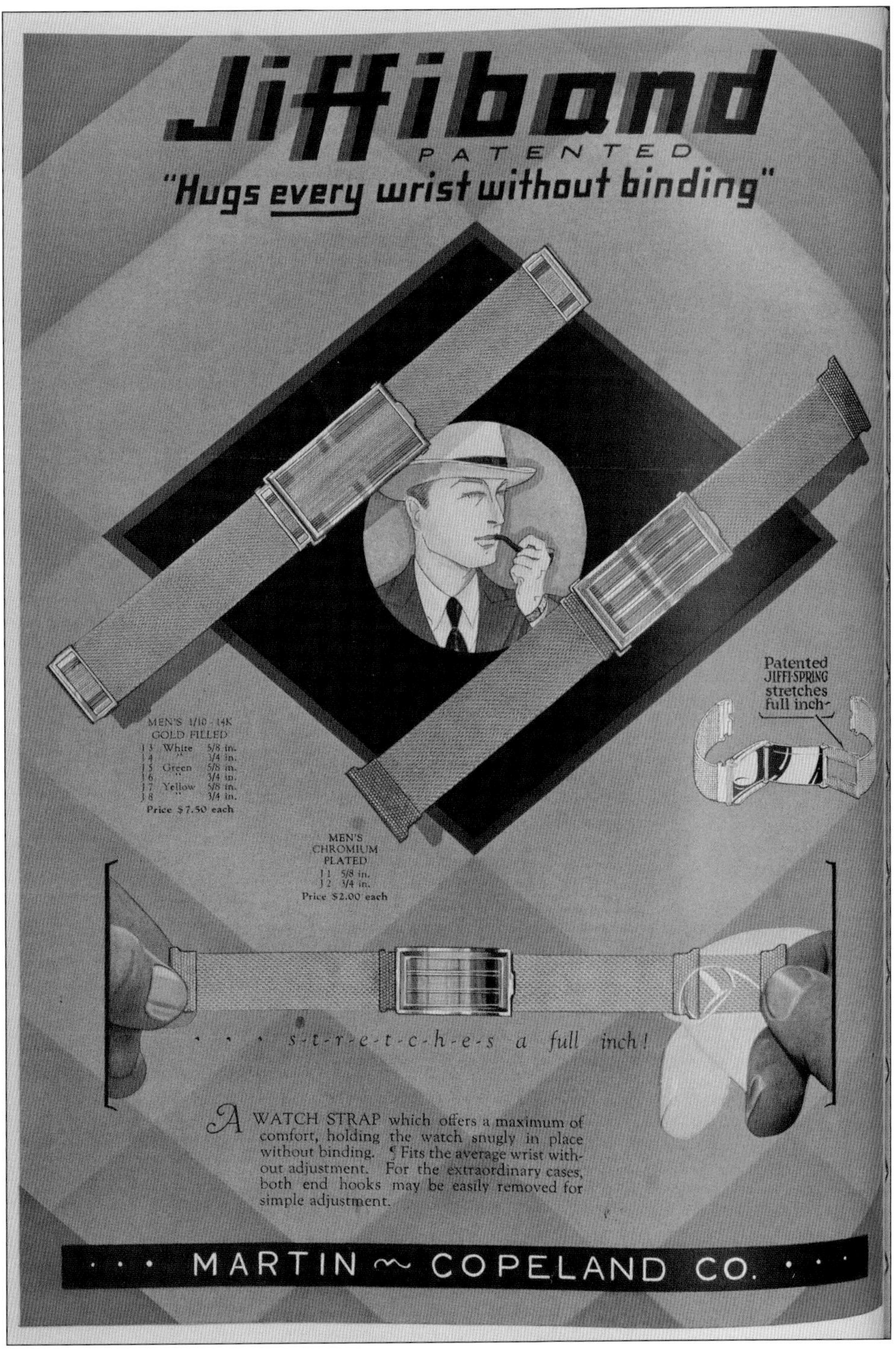

Jiffibands by Martin Copeland offered in the L. & C. Mayers catalog, 1930

Jiffibands by Martin Copeland offered in the L. & C. Mayers catalog, 1930

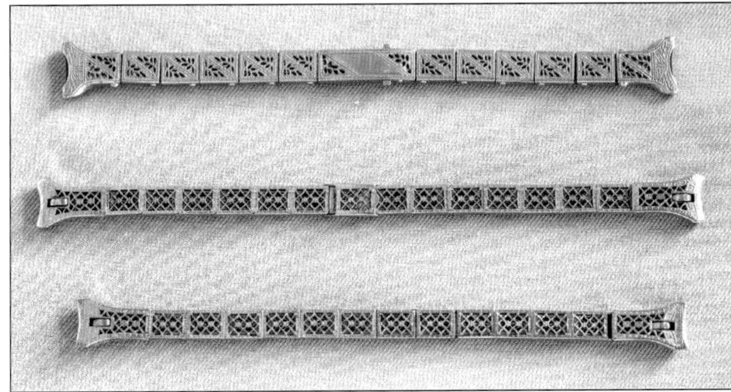

A group of filigree ladies' bracelets. The top one is marked "Carmeta," the middle one is unknown and the bottom one is stamped "Wrist Lace."

Fuller's Legion bands offered in the Otto Young catalog, 1929

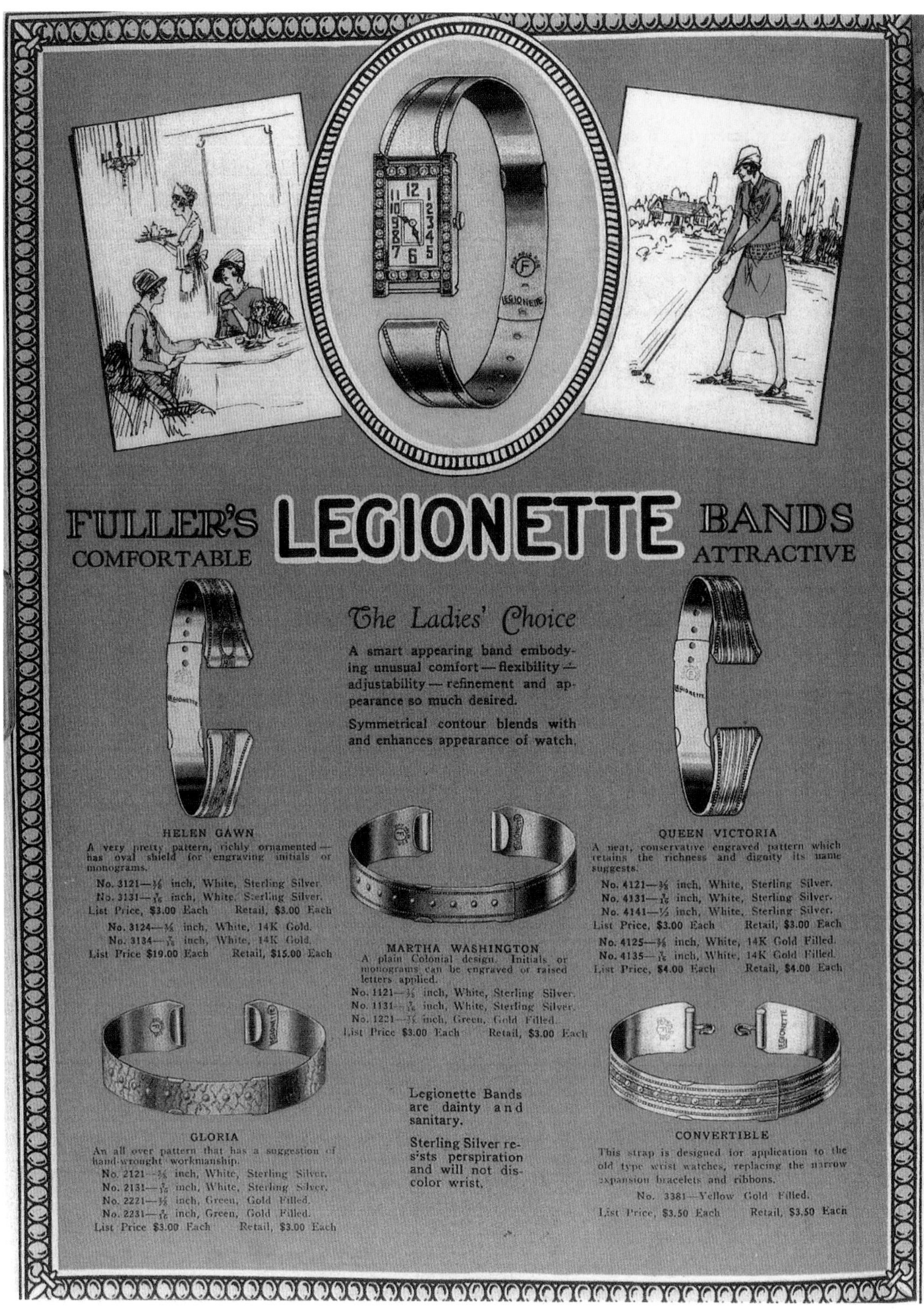

Fuller's Legionette bands offered in the Otto Young catalog, 1929

Advice to Jewelers

To help promote the sale of metal bracelets, the *Keystone* in October 1932 offered the following advice to jewelers:

" ...Do not sell a man's watch with a leather strap without also offering an attractive metal bracelet that harmonizes with the case...

"Sweat has made business for you ... Millions of people have just gone through a summer sweating and ruining leather straps and metal bands that are either made of or plated with metal which perspiration acids will attack. Some of them will not buy new bracelets during the 'sweat season' but when cooler weather comes then the new bands are in demand and that is the time to sell bracelets that you can guarantee against injury by perspiration...

"Don't repair a watch band. When a band comes in broken, or damaged by perspiration, try to avoid repairing it in the one case or replating it in the other. Neither is good salesmanship. Try to sell a new band...

"Take advantage of manufacturers' dealer helps. Many manufacturers of watch bracelets are prepared to furnish you with effective dealer helps in the shape of window and counter display cards, stands, booklets, circulars and electrotypes for newspaper advertising...

"Look over your watch repair rack. Make it a habit to examine the watches that are hanging on your repair rack periodically and notice those that would be improved by new bracelets. Have a special round red tag ... and fasten it on to every such watch as a reminder ... to try for a new bracelet sale when the customer comes in to pay for the repair job ...

"Have a special display case for watch attachments. Anything well displayed is half sold. Many stores lose hundreds of opportunities to sell new watch bracelets because they keep them hidden in drawers and boxes ... It is worth while to use a case or glass top counter for a regular display of watch attachments...

"Do some advertising. Devote some of your newspaper space regularly to advertising of watch attachments. If you have a mailing list, cover it periodically with circulars calling attention to your stock ...

"Wear it yourself. Above all things—be sure that you are wearing a fine watch bracelet on your own wrist and be equally sure that every employee of your organization is also wearing a good quality, good looking, up-to-date watch bracelet that harmonizes with the case of the watch and that will make a good impression on customers ..."

Summary

The evolution of watch attachments reflected an evolving market in convenience and fashion. Metal bracelets enjoyed a heyday in the late 1920s and early 1930s, involving a variety of design unrivaled since. Although leather bands did not evolve as much in fashion and design, they have remained the mainstay of the watch attachment industry. Today, leather remains the attachment of choice for daily wear, but the many styles of metal bands offer a fascinating area for collectors to explore.

ILLINOIS

12
9
3
ILLINOIS
60
50
10
40
20
30

ILLINOIS
17
JEWELS

THE ILLINOIS WATCH & ITS HAMILTON YEARS — VOL 3

THE ILLINOIS WATCH & ITS HAMILTON YEARS

THE FINALE OF A GREAT AMERICAN WATCH COMPANY

The Identification Guides: Illinois Men's Wristwatches

By
Fredric J. Friedberg

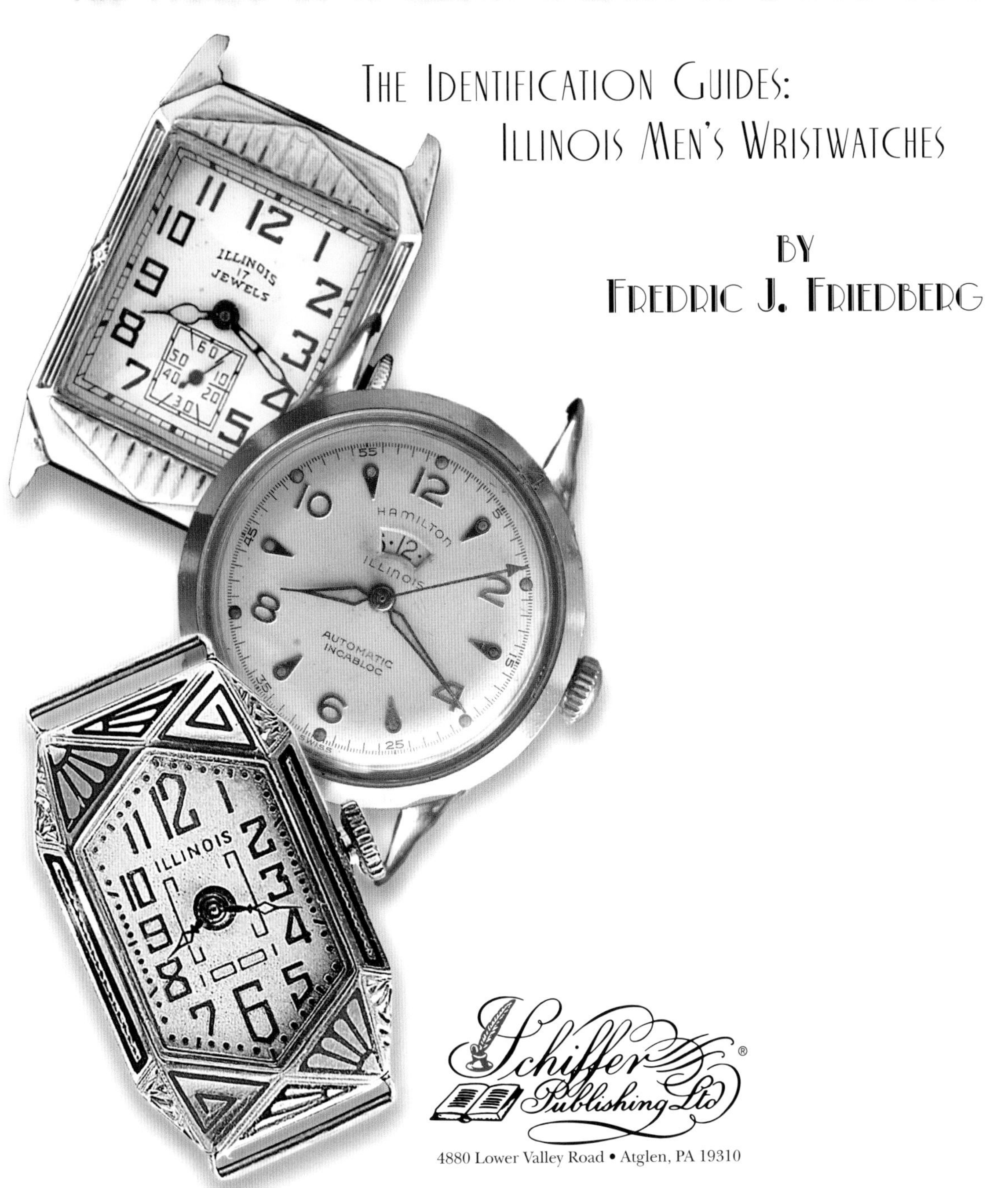

Schiffer Publishing Ltd®
4880 Lower Valley Road • Atglen, PA 19310

Library of Congress Control Number: 2017933341

Designed by Chris Cornforth, www.chrisworx.com
Cover designs by Fred, Joy, Zach Friedberg and Chris Cornforth

ISBN:978-0-7643-5371-0
Printed in China
Published by Schiffer Publishing, Ltd.
4880 Lower Valley Road
Atglen, PA 19310
Phone: (610) 593-1777; Fax: (610) 593-2002
E-mail: Info@schifferbooks.com
Web: www.schifferbooks.com

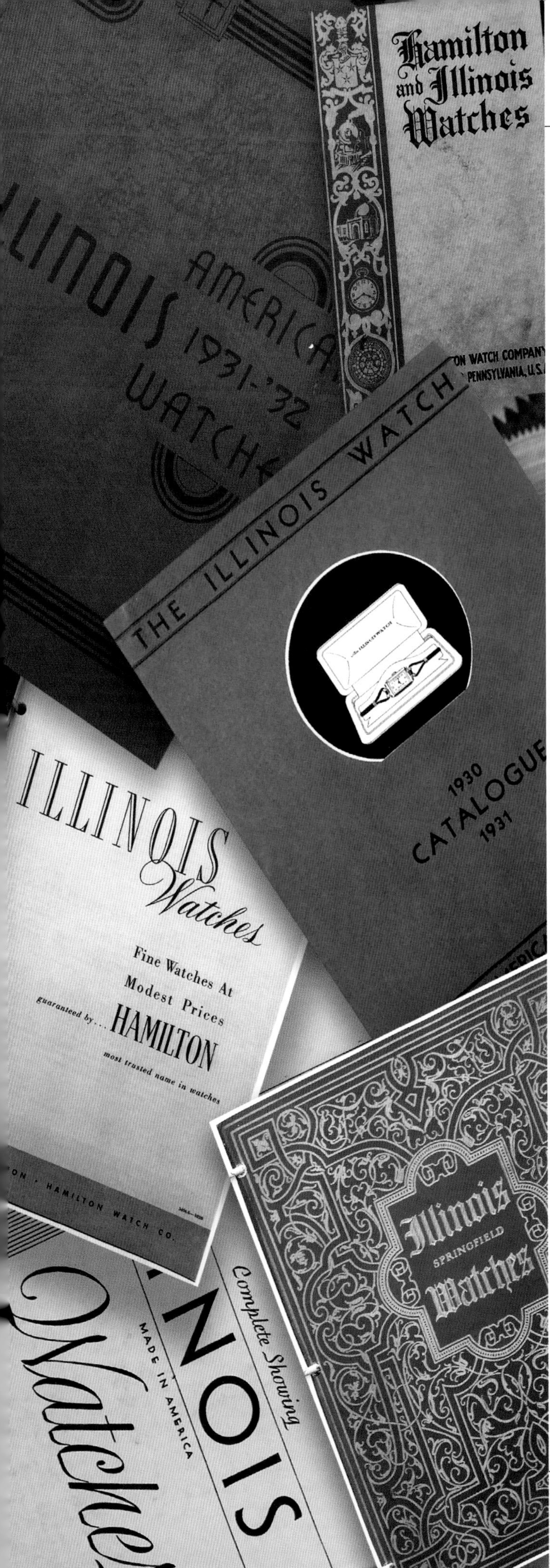

VOLUMES 3 AND 4: THE IDENTIFICATION GUIDES

INTRODUCTION TO THE GUIDES

Volumes 3 and 4 provide identification guides to the three major lines of Illinois wristwatches. This volume contains the first guide, Chapter 9, which identifies all recognized men's Illinois models. The second and third guides appear in Volume 4. The second guide, in Chapter 10, addresses watches marketed primarily to ladies. The third guide is in Chapter 11, which covers Illinois models offered when Hamilton resurrected the "Illinois" name for a short period in the mid-1950s.

Each entry includes pictures, specifications and marketing themes, and the text discusses items of interest concerning each model. At the beginning of each entry is a list providing key details for each model, including the time period for the case styling, information about case and dial configurations plus other data. An assessment of the model's rarity, collectibility and case durability is also provided—important information for those who desire to build an Illinois wristwatch collection.

Because a number of the models include variants that were given different names, each of those names is also listed, together with a cross-reference to the primary model.

Each of the three identification guides uses a similar format, and thus the key provided below applies to all three.

In addition to the all-important key, this short introduction includes details about the sources by which the various Illinois models have been identified, a table listing the models by year of probable first appearance, lists of recently identified models and those still unknown, as well as other information of interest to the collector.

Name: Listed are all the names by which this model has been called in an Illinois publication of any kind, in advertisements by casemakers or jobbers/jewelers' catalogs, or by collectors' routine usage.

Time Periods: Helps establish the wristwatch design environment in which each model appeared:

1. Transitional: Pre-World War I to the early 1920s
2. Generic: Early 1920s to early 1930s
3. Deco: Late 1920s to early 1930s
4. Moderne: Early 1930s
5. Post-Moderne: mid-1930s
6. Mid-Century Modern: mid-1950s

Case Color: The following abbreviations are used:

A = Aluminum
BM = Base Metal
C = Chrome-plated base metal (usually nickel)
GG = Green Gold (solid)
GGF = Green Gold-Filled
N = Nickel
PGF = Pink Gold-Filled
RG = Rose Gold (solid)
RGF = Rose Gold-Filled
RGP = Rolled Gold Plate
SS = Sterling Silver
SSB = Stainless Steel Back*
So = Silverode
StS = Stainless Steel*
TT = Two-tone (White Gold-filled Bezel and Back, Green Gold-filled or Yellow Gold-filled Center)
TTG = Two-tone (White Gold-filled Center, Green Gold-filled or Yellow Gold-filled Bezel and Back)
TTGG = Two-tone (White Gold Bezel and Back Yellow Gold or Green Gold center) (Solid)
WG = White Gold (solid)
WGF = White Gold-filled
YG = Yellow Gold (solid)
YGF = Yellow Gold-filled

"ART DECO" WRISTWATCHES

In his "Art Deco" article in the December 2005 NAWCC *Bulletin*, noted wristwatch authority Bruce Shawkey defines what "Art Deco" meant for wristwatches.

"Basically, Art Deco uses straight, angled and zigzag geometric lines (and sometimes circles) often combined with one another and/or 'stacked' in concentric forms. Watchcases designed in the Art Deco style, therefore, not only have height and width, but depth—depth beyond what is necessary to hold the actual movements. The combination of straight, angled, and circular shapes often leaves 'blank' areas on the cases where the case designer is able to show his ingenuity. These areas are often filled in with artistic patterns and shapes—either in paint or enamel—showing Far and Middle Eastern design, Greek and Roman themes, and even Egyptian and Mayan influence. Thus, Art Deco is a modernization and conglomeration of many artistic styles and themes from the past."

*There are no known legitimate Illinois Watch Company Factory-Cased models that came with a stainless back. Some Sterling models have stainless steel backs, but no Sterling model was Factory-Cased. A few specimens of three models (Chatham, Larchmont and Standish) have also been found in rolled gold plate cases, but without case Model Numbers. There are even some models in chromium-plated base metal cases that are valid Illinois watches—the Blackhawk, Sterling, Chevalier (enamel bezel) and Osgood/Brandt Rock (enamel bezel). None of these models is known to have been Factory-Cased; instead, they were likely cased by jobbers or jewelers.

The Hamilton-Illinois watch line featured many models with stainless steel case backs; these were cased by Hamilton in Lancaster. In addition, several Hamilton-Illinois models came in all-stainless cases and were cased in Switzerland.

Karat Material: Whether the case was gold-filled or solid gold and its karat count; or whether it was sterling, base metal, chromium-plated, aluminum, or another material.

Bezel: Description of the bezel design: whether it was engraved (Completely or partially), plain or smooth, enameled (completely or partially), molded or grooved.

- P = Plain/Smooth Bezel
- E = Engraved Bezel (completely or partially)
- M = Molded Bezel (deeply sculpted)
- EE = Enameled Bezel (completely or partially)
- G = Grooved Bezel (partially)
- B = Brushed

Sides: Plain or engraved.

Case Back: Flat or curved (men's models); plain or engraved (ladies' models).

Lugs: Whether the tops of the lugs are engraved or plain, or if they came both ways, or had covered lugs.

Lug Size: Inside measurement.

Springbar: Male, female or integrated spring bars; or fixed lugs, swivel lugs or attached swivel lugs. If swivel whether their arms are straight or angled.

Lug Sizes

Inches	Millimeters
5/16	8mm
25/64	10mm
7/16	11mm
15/32	12mm
35/64	14mm
5/8	16mm
45/64	18mm
3/4	19mm

Integrated springbars

Casemaker: The watch case manufacturer.
Case Pieces: Number of case parts, or if the case is hinged.
Case Model No.: Most Factory-Cased Illinois wristwatches had case Model Numbers engraved in the inside of the case back. The Hamilton-Illinois models usually had their case model numbers engraved on their case backs.
Crown: Recessed into the case or standard.

NO CASE MODEL NUMBERS

Many Factory-Cased Illinois wristwatch came in a case with a Model Number stamped inside the case back. A few models, such as the Baronet, Major and Rockliffe came with more than one Model Number. Sometimes, however, the cases for these models had no case Model Number stamped inside the case back. These are seen less frequently than the cases with the Model Numbers. A logical theory for the unnumbered cases could be that these were either sample or first-released cases, before the Illinois Watch Company fully committed to adding the watch model to its exclusive line of watches. Another possibility is that a model with no case Model Number might have been provided by a different casemaker.

Thus, perhaps, the unstamped cases were to allow the casemaker to offer the case model to other watch manufacturers until such time as the Illinois Watch Company requested an exclusive arrangement regarding that particular case model. But this theory is unlikely because no competitor used cases similar to the Major or Rockliffe models, for example.

Dimensions: Approximate watch size from the tip of the top of the lug to the tip of the bottom lug and from the outer side of the case to the outer opposite case side, not including the crown.
Durability: How the case held up to wear.

◷ Poor
◷◷ Fair
◷◷◷ Good
◷◷◷◷ Excellent

ILLINOIS CASE WEAR

Most of the Illinois wristwatches were supplied in gold-filled cases. As explained in Chapter 5, Hamilton did not want Illinois to compete in the high-priced watch market. The gold-filled cases did not hold up as well as solid gold ones, and yellow or green gold-filled ones fared worse than white gold-filled cases. The front of the cases were subject to wear because of rubbing from the cuffs of shirts, and the case backs were subject to perspiration and interaction with the owners' skin. Because of these factors, an Illinois wristwatch case found with little or no visible case wear is very special.

Movement Grade: The movement grades that existed for the size of movement from the date of the model's likely introduction date. Sometimes a movement dated after the model's introduction date may be found in the watch. Although such a watch may be authentic, it would not be as it was released from the Watch Factory.

Movement Size: The size of the movement: e.g., 12-size, 6-size, 0-size, 3/0, 6/0, 12/0, 18/0, 21/0.

Grade: The Factory-designated grade of the movement.

Jewels: The number of jewels contained in the movement that is normally found in this model.

Seconds At: The position on the watch dial, where the subsidiary seconds register (if any), is located; e.g., 6, 9 or None.

Dial No: Dial number (if known) from an Illinois Material or jobber catalog.

Dial Opening: The shape of the dial; e.g., round, square, tonneau, rectangular, etc. Dials of some ladies' models are difficult to classify, as they are not quite square but do not appear conventionally rectangular, so they are called "short rectangular."

Numerals: Whether the dial numerals were painted, luminous, embossed, etched, etched raised or applied gold numerals; flush gold numerals or markers; or other.

Hands: Whether the hands were steel, brass or luminous.

Cased in Factory: Whether the watch was cased in the Illinois Factory (those cased by Hamilton in Lancaster, Pennsylvania are noted).

Collectibility: Whether, in the author's opinion, a serious Illinois collector should have an example in his or her collection:

🕒 Important
🕒🕒 More Important
🕒🕒🕒 Very Important
🕒🕒🕒🕒 Essential

Rarity:	Rating
🕒🕒🕒🕒🕒🕒🕒	Custom or special order model; possibly one-of-a- kind example
🕒🕒🕒🕒🕒🕒	Nearly Impossible to Find
🕒🕒🕒🕒🕒	Extremely Difficult to Find
🕒🕒🕒🕒	Very Difficult to Find
🕒🕒🕒	Fairly Difficult to Find
🕒🕒	Mildly Difficult to Find
🕒	Easy to Find

Advertisement: If the watch was found in any magazine or newspaper advertisement, a "Yes" is noted. Many of the advertisements are shown in this chapter and others. (Catalog listings are not considered to be in the same category as advertisements; obviously, almost all of the Illinois models appeared at one time or another in Illinois Factory sales catalogs and also in the catalogs of companies that sold Illinois watches. Information about both types of catalogs is included later in this section.)

Marketing Theme: Catch phrases or slogans utilized to market the specific watch models.

Retail Price New: The price of the watch when it was first sold.

Values: For current values, please contact me directly at **fred@illinoiswatches.com** or **fredric777@gmail.com**. Also, check values at **illinoiswatches.com.**

Unique Case Design: Marked "Yes" if the case was a proprietary/unique design believed utilized only by the Illinois Watch Company.

Unique Dial Design: Marked "Yes" if the dial was a proprietary/unique design believed used only by the Illinois Watch Company.

"ILLINOIS SUMMITS"

On Sunday, June 23, 2013, three of the most knowledgeable Illinois collectors met at the Renaissance Hotel at Times Square in New York City to start reviewing the descriptions of men's models in this chapter. This review continued via telephone meetings on Sunday, November 17, 2013, and Sunday, November 24, 2013, and periodically thereafter until these books were sent to the publisher.

Mysteries Still Unsolved

At the time this book set was sent to the publisher, there were still names of models from the list of Factory-Cased Illinois wristwatches that remain unidentified.

The Remaining Unknowns By Size

3/0 Size	6/0 Size	12/0 Size	18/0 Size	21/0 Size
Hercules	Admiral	John Alden	Co-Ed	Louette**
	Arliss	Rye	Graduate*	Rhea
	Barrymore		Latonia*	Rose
	Ben Hur		Mayflower	Ruth
	Brunswick		Pearl	
	Carlton		Priscilla	
	Charter Oak			
	Falcon			
	Graduate			
	Harvard			
	Jackson			
	Lord Calvert			
	Lowell			
	Mohican			
	Monticello			
	Penn Charter			
	Rye			
	Statesman			
	Suburban			
	Winchester			

Black = Men's Red = Ladies'

*Since all we know about these models is that they had 18/0 movements, it is unclear whether they were actually ladies' models or, instead, might have been unisex ones (perhaps variants of the Biltmore 18/0?). For the Latonia in particular, it seems unlikely that it was a ladies' model, as there are no examples of Illinois using exactly the same name for a ladies' model and a men's (there is a Latonia 6/0 that was likely named for a racetrack).

**It is possible that "Louette" was a typographical error for "Alouette," though it is also possible that it might be a new name attached to the same model, since the Louette was shown on the June 5, 1933 list as being available in both white gold and yellow, whereas the Alouette had come only in white gold.

Former Unknowns Identified since 2004

3/0 Size	6/0 Size	12/0 Size	18/0 Size	21/0 Size
Akron	Belmont*	Exeter*	Countess	Babette II
Greyhound	Cadet*	Kensington	Lenox	
Motor Coach	Commander*		Saratoga	
Seneca	Haddon Hall*		Sherwood	
	LaSalle*		Vogue	
	Latonia 6/0*			
	Paul Revere*			
	Richmond 6/0			
	Varsity			
	Yankee Clipper			

Black = Men's
Red = Ladies'

*Since each of these model names appears on a June 5, 1933 internal Hamilton document in conjunction with a known primary model, all of these models appear to be variants of the primary models. As yet, however, we have not been able to locate them in any catalogs or magazine advertisements.

Models Not Shown on the December 31, 1932 List*

Men's	Ladies'
Chatham	Antoinette
Rockingham	Débette
Rockliffe 18/0	Mariette
Sangamon	Marionette
Standish	Marlette
Urbana	Sherwood
Varsity	

Black – Men's
Red = Ladies'
Blue = Unisex

* A number of wristwatch models were introduced after the December 31, 1932 "List of Names of Cased Illinois Watches by Sizes" was compiled and therefore do not appear on that list. With three exceptions, all of these were introduced in the 1934 Illinois Sales Catalog. The exceptions are the Rockliffe 18/0, which was introduced in 1935 via jobbers' catalogs, and the Sherwood and Varsity.

Probable Introduction Dates by Model

Introduction Date: For establishing the most probable introduction date of a given model, the primary source is whatever Illinois-issued sales or material catalog (or sales brochure) first shows the complete watch or its dial; the date of the publication will give a good indication of when the watch was released. Other reliable sources are jobbers' catalogs, many of which use advertisements straight from the most recent Illinois sales catalog. The dates when the movement improvements were manufactured are not used, as this method is not foolproof. Movements could have been made prior to or after the release of the case design or replaced with another movement during a repair. Moreover, certain 0, 3/0 and 6/0 movements were initially manufactured for pocket watches and/or pendant watches and were not utilized in wristwatch cases until years after their production dates. The probable model introduction date table that follows utilizes all known Illinois–issued official sales and material catalogs, sales brochures and price lists by date.

Illinois Wristwatch Models
Listed in Extant Illinois Sales and Materials Catalogs, Brochures and Price Lists by Date

MODEL NAME	Sales Catalog 1926	Sales Catalog 1927	Sales Brochure 1928	Sales* Catalog 1928-29	Price List 9/1/29	Sales Catalog 1929-30	Price List 1930	Dial & Hand Catalog 1930	Sales Catalog 1930-31	Sales Brochure 1931	Sales Catalog 1931-32	Price List 4/1/32	Sales Catalog 1932	Hamilton-Illinois Sales Catalog 1932-33	Sales Catalog 1933	Sales Catalog 1934	Sales Brochure May 1934
Ace		X						X	X								
Alouette												X	X				
Andover												X	X	X	X		
Annette												X	X				
Antoinette																X	X
Ardsley								X	X								
Argyle								X	X		X	X	X				
Arlene														X	X		
Arlington										X	X	X	X				
Atlantic (Fahys)		X						X	X								
Avalon								X	X								
Babette														X	X	X	X
Bar Harbor					X	X			X								
Barbara												X	X				
Baronet								X	X		X						
Beau Brummell			X		X	X		X	X								
Beau Geste												X	X	X	X		
Beau Monde								X	X		X						
Beau Royale										X	X						
Berkeley					X	X			X								
Berkshire								X	X								
Beverly					X	X								X	X		
Biloxi					X	X			X								
Biltmore								X	X								
Blackstone								X	X	X	X	X	X				
Bostonian										X	X	X	X				
Brighton								X	X								
Bryce		X															
Canby	X	X						X									
Caprice								X	X		X						
Cavalier								X	X		X						
Charmette										X	X		X				
Chatham																X	X
Chesterfield														X	X		

Illinois Wristwatch Models
Listed in Extant Illinois Sales and Materials Catalogs, Brochures and Price Lists by Date (Continued)

MODEL NAME	Sales Catalog 1926	Sales Catalog 1927	Sales Brochure 1928	Sales* Catalog 1928-29	Price List 9/1/29	Sales Catalog 1929-30	Price List 1930	Dial & Hand Catalog 1930	Sales Catalog 1930-31	Sales Brochure 1931	Sales Catalog 1931-32	Price List 4/1/32	Sales Catalog 1932	Hamilton-Illinois Sales Catalog 1932-33	Sales Catalog 1933	Sales Catalog 1934	Sales Brochure May 1934
Chevalier								X									
Chieftain					X	X	X	X	X								
Claudette										X	X						
Commodore											X	X	X				
Constance											X						
Consul			X		X	X		X	X								
Coquette										X	X	X	X				
Coronado					X	X			X								
Cushion - Cushion	X	X						X	X								
Cushion - Round	X	X		X													
Cushion Form (Cushion)		X		X					X								
Daytona					X	X											
Débette																X	X
Debutante										X	X						
Del Monte					X	X			X								
Derby											X	X	X				
Edgewater			X		X	X		X	X								
Elissa												X	X				
Ensign					X	X		X	X		X						
Fairport								X	X								
Finalist							X	X	X		X	X	X				
Florentine										X	X	X	X				
Florette														X	X		
Frontenac								X	X								
Futura					X	X	X	X	X		X	X	X				
Galahad														X	X		
Glencoe								X	X		X						
Glenna										X	X	X	X				
Gloria											X						
Greta												X	X				
Guardsman								X	X								
Hollywood											X						
Hudson										X	X	X	X				
Irene														X	X		
Janette														X	X	X	X
Joan										X	X						
Jolly Roger					X	X	X	X	X								
Juliette														X	X		
Kenilworth								X	X		X	X	X				
Lady Mary														X	X		
Lakewood												X	X				
Larchmont											X	X	X				
Large Square Cut Corner								X	X								
Lenox									X								
Locke								X									
Long Beach			X	X		X	X										
Lynette														X	X	X	X
Major			X	X	X	X		X									
Manhattan									X								
Mariette																X	X

Illinois Wristwatch Models
Listed in Extant Illinois Sales and Materials Catalogs, Brochures and Price Lists by Date (Continued)

MODEL NAME	Sales Catalog 1926	Sales Catalog 1927	Sales Brochure 1928	Sales* Catalog 1928-29	Price List 9/1/29	Sales Catalog 1929-30	Price List 1930	Dial & Hand Catalog 1930	Sales Catalog 1930-31	Sales Brochure 1931	Sales Catalog 1931-32	Price List 4/1/32	Sales Catalog 1932	Hamilton-Illinois Sales Catalog 1932-33	Sales Catalog 1933	Sales Catalog 1934	Sales Brochure May 1934
Marilyn										X	X						
Marionette																X	X
Marlette																X	X
Marquis - Strap			X	X	X	X		X									
Mary Todd	X	X	X		X	X			X		X						
Mate			X		X	X		X	X								
Medalist					X	X		X	X								
Metropolitan												X	X				
Miami			X		X	X			X								
Minuette										X	X						
Motor Coach									X								
Muzette														X	X		
Narragansett						X	X			X							
New Yorker						X			X	X		X					
Newport						X	X			X							
Octagon	X																
Off-Duty												X					
Osgood									X								
Patricia												X					
Piccadilly						X	X		X	X							
Pimlico														X	X		
Potomac														X	X		
Princess											X	X	X				
Queen Anne														X	X		
Rectangular		X															
Redonda			X		X	X			X								
Rita												X	X				
Ritz								X	X		X	X	X				
Rockliffe								X	X		X	X	X	X	X		
Rockingham																X	X
Rosette														X	X		
Roslyn									X								
Sangamon																X	X
Saratoga									X								
Skyway							X	X	X								
Southampton		X						X									
Special								X	X								
Speedway					X	X		X									
Speedway 178									X								
Square		X						X									
Square Cut Corner	X			X													
Standish																X	X
Suzette														X	X		
Sylvia												X	X				
Tank		X						X									
Tonneau	X																
Townsman								X	X		X						
Trophy								X	X		X						
Tuxedo			X		X	X		X	X								
Urbana																X	X
Vanity Fair								X	X								
Vardon								X	X		X						
Vernon											X	X	X	X	X		

Illinois Wristwatch Models
Listed in Extant Illinois Sales and Materials Catalogs, Brochures and Price Lists by Date (Continued)

MODEL NAME	Sales Catalog 1926	Sales Catalog 1927	Sales Brochure 1928	Sales* Catalog 1928-29	Price List 9/1/29	Sales Catalog 1929-30	Price List 1930	Dial & Hand Catalog 1930	Sales Catalog 1930-31	Sales Brochure 1931	Sales Catalog 1931-32	Price List 4/1/32	Sales Catalog 1932	Hamilton-Illinois Sales Catalog 1932-33	Sales Catalog 1933	Sales Catalog 1934	Sales Brochure May 1934
Viking					X			X	X								
Wembley											X						
Wentworth														X	X		
Westchester											X						
Whippet		X						X	X								
Yorktown												X	X				

Black = Men's
Red = Ladies'
Blue = Unisex
*During the 1928–1929 time frame, Illinois produced at least two small sales brochures for use by jewelers. No models or approximate dates on those brochures are different from the ones noted in this chart

Other Catalogs as Sources

In addition to appearing in Illinois Factory catalogs, Illinois wristwatches were shown in the catalogs of companies to which Illinois sent its own catalogs and other advertising material. Some of these Illinois customers were large-scale jobbers (e.g., A. C. Becken, Benj. Allen, Wallenstein Mayer), others were large department stores with jewelry departments (e.g., Carson Pirie Scott) and still others were independent jewelry companies (e.g., Geo. T. Brodnax). The following catalogs of various years were consulted.

Name of Firm	Location
Aisenstein-Woronock & Sons	New York, NY
Benj. Allen & Co.	Chicago, IL
Baird-North Co.	Providence, RI
Ball Company (Ball Blue Book)	Chicago, IL
A. C. Becken Co.	Chicago, IL
Bennett Brothers (House of Bennett)	Chicago, IL
Geo. T. Brodnax, Inc.	Memphis, TN
Carson Pirie Scott & Co.	Chicago, IL
S. H. Clausin & Co.	Minneapolis, MN; Spokane, WA
Edwards-Ludwig-Fuller Jewelry Co. (ELF Red Book]	Kansas City, MO
J. Engel & Co.	Baltimore, MD
Marshall Field & Company	Chicago, IL
Fort Dearborn Watch & Clock Co.	Chicago, IL
A. I. Hall & Son	San Francisco, CA
Holsman Company (Holsman's Jewelry Drummer)	Chicago, IL
C. H. Knights-Thearle Co.	Chicago, IL
H. M Manheim & Co.	New York, NY
May & Malone, Inc.	Chicago, IL
L. & C. Mayers Co.	New York, NY
Liberty Diamond & Watch Co.	Chicago, IL
C. & E. Marshall Co.	Chicago, IL
Moore & Evans	Chicago, IL
Henry Paulson & Co. (Paulson's Material & Supplies)	Chicago, IL
John Plain Company	Chicago, IL
E. L. Rice & Co.	Detroit, MI
Richter & Phillips Co.	Cincinnati, OH
Rohde-Spencer Co. (Criterion)	Chicago, IL
A. G. Schwab & Sons	Cincinnati, OH
Sears, Roebuck & Co.	Chicago, IL
N. Shure Co. Shure Winner	Chicago, IL
Swartchild & Company	Chicago, IL
J. E. Von Wald	Baraboo, WI
Wallenstein Mayer Co.	Cincinnati, OH
Montgomery Ward & Co.	Chicago, IL
Jason Weiler & Sons	Boston, MA
Jason Weiler–Baird-North	Boston, MA
Otto Young & Co.	Chicago, IL

"Keystone" Lists

During research for this book we encountered numerous Illinois Factory price lists with Consumer Prices in one column and a "Keystone" price in another column. "Keystone" was originally a reference to a trade publication entitled the *Keystone*. This publication strongly advocated that retail jewelers sell at "the Keystone price," which was calculated at 200% of the jewelers' cost. Later, in an attempt to maintain retail pricing, manufacturers introduced controlled discounting by quoting both a suggested retail price for which the goods would be sold and a "Keystone Price" upon which the typical 50% discount would be calculated. (Jobbers' catalogs often use the words "Suggested consumer price" for the former and "List" for the latter.)

Most Probable Introduction Dates of Factory-Cased Models (part 1)

Men's	Ladies'	Men's	Ladies'	Men's	Ladies'
1910		New Yorker Enamel	Daytona 155	Rockliffe	
	Convertible	Piccadilly	Daytona 155A	Skyway	
1918		Speedway	Daytona 155B	Special	
United States Army Watch		Speedway 178	Del Monte 155	Townsman	
1925		Viking	Edgewater 155	Trophy	
Square*			Long Beach	Yankee Clipper	
Square Cut Corner*			Mary Todd 203		
1926			Mary Todd 204	***1931***	
Whippet*	Mary Todd		Mary Todd GG	Akron (Aluminum Prototype)	Charmette
1927			Miami 155	Arlington	Claudette
Sportsman			Narragansett	Beau Royale	Constance
1928			Newport 174	Belmont***	Coquette
Beau Brummell	Berkeley 154		Redonda 153	Blackhawk	Debutante
Beau Brummell/Viking	Berkeley 154A	***1930***		Bostonian	Florentine
Beau Royale	Del Monte 157	Ardsley	Argyle	Commodore	Glenna 186
Chevalier	Edgewater 175	Baronet	Avalon	Derby	Glenna 239
Consul	Miami 157	Beau Monde	Bar Harbor 158	Fifth Avenue	Gloria
Gift Series	Miami 157A	Biltmore 18/0	Berkshire	Greystone***	Hollywood
Locke	Redonda 154	Blackstone	Brighton	Hudson	Joan
Major		Caprice	Edgewater 208	Kensington	Marilyn
Marquis Strap		Cavalier	Edgewater 222	Kingston	Minuette
Mate		Finalist	Fairport	LaSalle***	Patricia
Square Cut Corner Large		Finalist Deco	Glencoe	Larchmont	Vanity Fair
Tuxedo		Frontenac	Lenox	No. 250 (Schmukler)	
1929		Greyhound	Newport 223	Puritan***	
Cadet***	Bar Harbor 156	Guardian	No. 241	Richmond 6/0	
Chieftain	Berkeley 153	Guardsman	Roslyn	Seneca	
Ensign	Beverly 185	Kenilworth	Saratoga Leaf	Vernon	
Futura	Biloxi	Manhattan	Saratoga Notched		
Jolly Roger	Coronado	Motor Coach	Vanity Fair	Valedictorian	
Medalist	Daytona 153	Paul Revere***	Vardon	Wembley	
New Yorker	Daytona 154	Ritz		Westchester	

Most Probable Introduction Dates of Factory-Cased Models (part 2)

Men's	Ladies'
1932	
Andover	Alouette
Beau Geste	Annette
Biltmore 6/0	Barbara
Chesterfield	Elissa
Chesterfield Stepped Bezel	Fairfax
Gallahad	Greta
Haddon Hall***	Lady Mary
Hawthorne	Lakewood
Metropolitan	Princess
Off-Duty	Queen Anne
Pimlico	Rita
Potomac	Sylvia
Richmond 12/0	Vogue
Senator	
Wentworth	
Yorktown	
1933	
Commander***	Arlene
Exeter***	Babette I
Latonia 6/0***	Beverly 852
Varsity (No. 650) ***	Countess
	Florette
	Irene
	Janette
	Juliette
	Lynette
	Muzette
	Rosette
	Sherwood***
	Suzette
1934	
Chatham	Antoinette
Rockingham	Babette II
Sangamon	Débette
Standish	Mariette
Urbana	Marionette
	Marlette
1935	
Rockliffe 18/0	
1942	
Illinois Langford**	
Illinois Pierre**	
Illinois Whitman	

Black = Men's Red = Ladies' Blue = Unisex

*Some models
**May not exist; see text in Men's Identification Guide for explanation.
***For these models, the year of introduction is an educated guess, since these are not listed in Illinois Factory catalogs or jobbers' catalogs that we have located, but the names appear on Hamilton or Illinois internal documents; or, in three cases (Greystone, Sherwood and Varsity), cards that would have been included with the boxed watches have been found. For ones that are variants of known models, we follow what seems to have been Illinois' general pattern of issuing variants and estimate the introduction date as one year after that of the primary model.

Themes of Model Names

An intriguing unknown is why the various Illinois men's and ladies' Factory-Cased wristwatch models were assigned their particular names. (For certain models, however, there are some plausible theories, and these are mentioned in their listings in the Identification Guides.) Possible categories of themes for names of Illinois Men's and Ladies' Factory-Cased wristwatches might be as shown below. *Please note:* There is a certain amount of repetition, as some names can logically be included in more than one category.

Actors

Arliss
Barrymore

Beaches

Avalon
Bar Harbor
Brighton
Coronado
Daytona
Edgewater
Fairport
Lakewood
Long Beach
Manhattan
Miami
Narragansett
Newport
Redonda

Hotels

Arlington
Avalon
Blackstone
Coronado
Hawthorne
Newport
Piccadilly
Ritz
Manhattan
Monticello
Piccadilly
Pimlico
Richmond (twice)
Ritz
Rye (twice)
Vernon
Westchester
Yorktown

Illinois

Arlington
Chatham
Hawthorne
Kenilworth
Sangamon
Urbana

Massachusetts/New England

Bostonian
Charter Oak
John Alden
Lowell
Paul Revere
Puritan
Rockingham
Standish
Vernon

New York

Arlington
Brunswick
Chatham
Fifth Avenue
Hawthorne
Hudson
Kensington
Kingston
Larchmont

Academic

Andover
Exeter
Harvard
Penn Charter
Valedictorian
Wentworth

Urban

Metropolitan
Townsman

United Kingdom

Andover
Ardsley
Avalon
Blackstone
Brighton

Brunswick
Chatham
Chesterfield
Derby
Exeter
Greystone
Hawthorne
Kenilworth
Kensington
Kingston
Larchmont
Newport
Piccadilly
Pimlico
Rockingham
Rye
Wembley
Wentworth
Westchester
Yorktown

Military

Cadet
Guardian
Guardsman
Major
Off-Duty

Native American

Blackhawk
Chieftain
Mohican
Potomac
Seneca

Nautical

Admiral
Commodore
Ensign
Jolly Roger
Mate
Viking
Yankee Clipper

Racing

Arlington
Bar Harbor
Belmont
Beverly
Blackhawk
Brighton
Daytona
Derby
Exeter
Hawthorne
Hollywood
LaSalle
Latonia
Miami
Pimlico
Rockingham
Saratoga Leaf
Saratoga Notched Leaf
Speedway (twice)
Vernon

Royalty/Government/Personage

Baronet
Ben Hur
Blackstone
Cavalier
Chesterfield
Consul
Countess
Frontenac
Greystone
Haddon Hall
Hercules
Lord Calvert
Marquis Strap
Paul Revere
Princess
Standish
Statesman
Winchester

Sporting Events

Finalist
Finalist Deco
Medalist
Speedway (twice)
Sportsman
Trophy

Transportation

Greyhound
Motor Coach
Skyway

Style

Beau Brummell
Beau Brummell/Viking
Beau Geste
Beau Monde
Beau Royale
Derby
Tuxedo

Black = Men's
Red = Ladies'
Blue = Unisex

Chapter 9

Men's Identification Guide

Chapter 9 identifies all recognized men's Illinois wristwatch models and provides an entry for each in alphabetical order. For models that may have been given more than one name, entries are provided for all of them, with a cross-reference to the primary model where you will find full information.

At the beginning of each full entry is a list of the principal details to consider regarding that particular model. For interpreting the list, please refer to the key provided in "Introduction to the Guides," which precedes this chapter. Since Illinois had a rich selection of men's models, there are many ways to approach beginning a collection. (See Chapter 13 for some suggestions.)

The Most Sought-After Men's Illinois Models

For Illinois collectors, the most popular and sought-after wristwatches are the following:

The Most Sought-After Men's Illinois Watches	
Name	**Ranking**
Ritz	1
Skyway	2
Piccadilly	3
Chesterfield	4
Consul	5
Jolly Roger	6
Baronet	7
Metropolitan	8
Chieftain	9
Admiral Evans	10

The Rarest Men's Illinois Models

As of this printing, the rarest Illinois wristwatches, on the basis of empirical observations by collectors, are the ones listed below. If any reader is aware of any other verifiable rare specimens, please notify me and these numbers will be adjusted accordingly:

The Rarest Men's Illinois Watches	
Model	**Known Examples**
Finalist, WGF	0*
Finalist Deco, YGF, Plain	0*
Frontenac, YGF	0*
Tuxedo, GG, Plain	0*
Admiral Evans, RG	1
Admiral Evans, Jr.	1
Andover, Engraved Bezel	1
Ardsley, no seconds	1
Atlantic Jr., Black Enamel	1
Beau Brummell/Viking TT	1
Beau Monde, Braille/Hinged Bezel	1
Biltmore 18/0, GGF	1
Blackstone, TT	1
Caprice, Engine-turned Outer Case	1
Caprice, 14K WG	1
Chesterfield - TT, Bezel YGF Back	1
Chevalier, YG	1
Consul, Pinstripe Dial, Seconds at 9	1
Eagle	1
Finalist Deco, YG	1
Guardsman, RGF, Engraved	1
Marquis Strap, TT, Plain Bezel	1
Medalist, Special Engraved Bezel	1
Notched Lug, SS	1
Ongard Off-Set	1
Piccadilly, WGF, Fully Engraved Bezel	1

The Rarest Men's Illinois Watches (Continued)	
Model	**Known Examples**
Piccadilly, Two-tone	1**
Ritz, No Seconds	1
Special Cushion Fahys SS	1
Special Cushion Solidarity WG	1
Special Cushion Solidarity GG	1
Square, Black Enamel, WGF	1
Square Cut Corner Large, Braille, Hinged Bezel	1
Square Cut Corner, TT	1
Admiral Evans, YGF	2
Andover, 14K GF	2
Armored Case, Off-Set Crown	2
Beau Brummell, GGF, Plain Bezel	2
Chatham, WGF	2
Decagon	2
Decagon, Jr.	2
Greyhound	2
Medalist, Special Plain Bezel	2
Ongard	2
Piccadilly, WGF, Partially Engraved	2
Square, Black Enamel, YGF	2
Standish, WGF	2
Square WG	2
Akron	3
Frontenac, WGF	3
Marquis Strap, Seconds at 6	3
Medalist, YGF	3
Motor Coach	3
Osgood, Black Enamel	3
Osgood/Brandt Rock, Blue Enamel	3
Southampton, Black Enamel	3
Chevalier, Blue Enamel	4
Notched Lug, YG	4
Admiral Evans, Off-Set Crown	5
Consul, GG, Engraved	5
Larchmont, RGP	5
Tuxedo, WG, Plain Bezel	6
*Offered for sale by Illinois but never seen	**Yet to be confirmed

Other Rare Illinois		
Only 7 to 15 of these models are known to exist		
No. 250 (Schmukler)	Illinois Whitman	New Yorker, Enamel, YGF
Atlantic Black Enamel, GGF	Marquis Strap, No Seconds	Standish, YGF
Chatham YGF	Marquis Strap, TTG/E	
Chesterfield Stepped Bezel	New Yorker, Enamel, WGF	

The Rarest Men's Dials	
Dial	**Known Examples**
Consul, Seconds at 9 and Pinstripe	1
Ritz, No Subs	1
Off Duty, Black Dial	2
Trophy, Oval Dial	2
Greyhound	3
Marquis Strap, Seconds at 6	3
Police Special	4
Chevalier, Enamel Dial	5
Major, Exploding Enamel Dial	6

Illinois Men's Wristwatches Models with 9:00 Subsidiary Seconds

Some of the most attractive and alluring Illinois men's watches are the models with subsidiary seconds at 9. These are:

Models with Subsidiary Seconds at 9		
Beau Brummell*	Cushion*	Southampton
Beau Royale*	Ensign*	Square
Bryce***	Kingston	Square Cut Corner
Cadet**	Marquis Strap**	Standish*
Canby	New Yorker*	Tank ***
Chieftain	Piccadilly	Whippet*
Consul***	Rectangular	

* Also came with subsidiary seconds at 6.
** Also has rare model with no subsidiary seconds and ultra-rare model with subsidiary seconds at 6.
*** Came with subsidiary seconds at 6, 9 or with None

No Subsidiary Seconds

The following Illinois wristwatch models came without subsidiary seconds. (In addition, none of the ladies' Illinois wristwatches except the Tonneau and Octagon Transitional models came with subsidiary seconds.)

Models Without Subsidiary Seconds		
Biltmore 18/0	Marquis Strap**	Sangamon
Cadet**	Ritz**	Tuxedo
Caprice*	Rockliffe 18/0	Urbana
Consul**		

* Came with a second post at the 3, but never had a second hand.

** Also came with subsidiary seconds at 6 or 9.

Illinois Didn't

The Illinois Watch Company did not make any of the following:

- A doctor's wristwatch
- A chronograph
- A rolled-gold plate wristwatch*
- A wristwatch with a stainless steel back**
- An alarm wristwatch
- A self-winding wristwatch***
- A character watch
- An electric watch
- A diamond-dial watch
- A platinum wristwatch
- An 18K gold men's wristwatch
- A driver's watch
- An asymmetrical watch

* There are at least two Chatham and Standish models with a rolled-gold plated case perhaps not originally intended for an Illinois, and a few rolled-gold plated Larchmonts have been found. These were all cased in Keystone Philadelphia "Victory" brand cases.

** Hamilton used stainless backs on many of the Hamilton-Illinois models, and some Sterling models came in non-factory cases with stainless steel backs.

*** Some of the Hamilton-Illinois models were self-winding automatic watches.

Caveat Emptor: What to Avoid When Buying an Illinois Wristwatch

- Do not buy an alleged Illinois wristwatch with a stainless steel back unless it is a Sangamon, which is all steel, or a Sterling model; or, if it is a Hamilton-Illinois model.
- Do not buy an Illinois wristwatch in which the minutes track on the dial does not completely conform to the shape of the bezel. It is most likely a redone dial or is placed in the wrong case. (See Chapters 7 and 8.)
- Do not confuse the Illinois Watch Case Company (IWCCo) with the Illinois Watch Company. An IWCCo case does not make it an Illinois wristwatch. They were two entirely different companies.
- Do not buy an Illinois two-tone watch if the case numbers do not match. The last four digits of the serial number inside the case back should match the four numbers stamped on the center section of the case and the four Roman numerals scratched inside the back of the bezel.
- Tastes are subjective. However, avoid buying a watch with a redone dial even if you can only get a poor original dial. For the best value, an all-original watch is always preferable.
- Avoid buying watches with extensive case repairs. However, with a rare watch, if that is the only way you can obtain one, this is acceptable.
- Do not buy a watch which has been replated. They usually look shiny and gaudy; the replating process significantly diminishes the watch's value. Although many collectors (as with vintage cars) routinely have their cases filled, repaired and replated, most serious Illinois collectors and dealers would prefer not to own one unless it is a very rare example.
- Do not buy a model because it is alleged to be green. Illinois made only a few models that have been confirmed to have green gold cases. Green gold or green gold-filled cases always command a higher price and are usually rarer, so some overzealous sellers (and buyers) often see green when they should see yellow.

WATCH BRACELET ALERT!

After Hamilton took over the marketing of Illinois watches, models began to proliferate at a greater rate than actual new designs. To create a "new" model, an existing one might be given a metal bracelet rather than a leather strap. For example, the New Yorker, issued in 1929 with a leather strap, was transformed into a Manhattan with a metal bracelet. Sometimes a pair of such models were even issued the same year, one with a leather strap and one with a metal band: e.g., the Commodore/Bostonian and the Larchmont/Vernon.

To be identified as one of these models with metal bracelets, a specimen must have a bracelet of exactly the same make and design as what was shown in the original Illinois catalog picture. (Some major jobbers also used illustrations that were issued from Illinois, and these too can be relied on.) It isn't a question of having "a" metal bracelet; it must be "the" correct one.

Since Illinois most often used Hadley bracelets, finding a Hadley mark may be an indicator, but Hadley had an enormous line of bracelets and it may be difficult to determine which was exactly the one that was advertised with the particular Illinois model. Illinois also sometimes used bracelets of other makers.

Original bracelets, at this great distance from the original issue, are often worn and too frail for practical use. It is not sufficient that the bracelet on an Illinois watch look period-correct: it must be a match, and recognizing one takes careful study of the old catalogs.

In most cases, the original metal bracelet has long since been replaced with a leather strap, and in those cases it is virtually impossible to ascertain what model the watch was intended to be.

RUMORED TO EXIST

A serious wristwatch collector, who for very sound and personal reasons no longer attends watch shows or openly discusses his collection, has in the past told collectors that he possesses the following Illinois watches:

- Solid gold Ritz
- Solid gold Guardsman
- Solid gold two-tone Andover
- Platinum Factory-Cased Rockliffe-like Illinois, with three steps on its sides.

This collector, who refuses to be identified and refuses even to show these models for examination, keeps these alleged models under tight security along with the rest of his collection.

Please note: During my preparation of *The Illinois Watch: The Life and Times of a Great American Watch Company,* this collector also refused to confirm or deny these models. When approached by a third party on my behalf for this book set, he again refused, unfortunately.

Models Not Known to Be Factory-Cased Contained in this Chapter		
Admiral Benson	"D-D" Utility Watch	Notched Lug
Admiral Benson, Jr.	Decagon	Ollendorff I
Armored Case	Decagon, Jr.	Ollendorff II
Aviator	Depollier Waterproof/Dustproof	Osgood
Blackhawk	General Funston	Senator
Brandt Rock	General Joffre	Special Cushions
Chrysanthemum	Gift Series	United States Army
Connerics	Integrated Guard	

Men's Models in Solid Gold		
Ace[1]	Consul	Rockliffe
Admiral Evans	Devon[3]	Rockliffe 18/0
Baronet	Eagle	Special Cushions[5]
Caprice[1]	No. 250 (Schmukler)	Square
Chrysanthemum	Notched Lug[4]	Tuxedo
Canby[2]		Varsity (No. 650)

[1]There is one known in solid gold.
[2]Certain Canbys were solid gold.
[3]Solidarity made a white or green gold Cushion-Cushion engraved model that was Factory-Cased.
[4]Also came in sterling silver.
[5]Made by Fahys or Solidarity.

Men's Models in Sterling Silver		
Admiral Benson	Cut Bezel	Ongard
Admiral Benson, Jr.	"D-D" Utility Watch	Ongard Offset
Admiral Evans	General Funston	Police Special
Admiral Evans, Jr.	General Joffre	Special Cushion Fahys
Ariston	Guardsman Military	Telephone Dial
Armored Case	Integrated Guard	Washington Watch Co.
Aviator	Notched Lug	
Burlington	Offset Crowns	

Men's Models in 10K Gold-Filled		
Andover	Illinois Whitman	Standish
Chatham	Potomac	Urbana
Exeter	Rockingham	

Men's Models in Base Metal Cases		
Blackhawk	Osgood	Senator
Brandt Rock	Sangamon	Seneca

Men's Models in 14K Gold-Filled Cases		
Ardsley	Gallahad	Paul Revere
Arlington	Greyhound	Piccadilly
Atlantic	Greystone	Pimlico
Atlantic Enamel	Guardian	Puritan
Beau Brummell	Guardsman	Rectangular
Beau Brummell/Viking	Haddon Hall	Richmond 12/0
Beau Geste	Hawthorne	Riley
Beau Monde	Hudson	Ritz
Beau Royale	Jolly Roger	Skyway
Belmont	Kenilworth	Speedway
Biltmore 18/0	Kingston	Speedway 178
Biltmore 6/0	Larchmont	Sportsman
Blackstone	LaSalle	Townsman
Cadet	Major	Trophy
Chesterfield	Manhattan	Valedictorian
Chesterfield Stepped Bezel	Marquis Strap	Vernon
Chieftain	Mate	Viking
Derby	Maxine	Wayne
Ensign	Medalist	Wembley
Fifth Avenue	Motor Coach	Wentworth
Finalist	New Yorker	Westchester
Futura	New Yorker Enamel	Yankee Clipper
	Off-Duty	Yorktown

Men's Identification Guide		
Models Listed		
Ace	Depollier	Ongard
Admiral Benson	Depollier Waterproof/Dustproof	Ongard Off-Set
Admiral Benson, Jr.	Derby	Osgood
Admiral Evans	Devon	Paul Revere
Admiral Evans Off-Set	Eagle	Piccadilly
Akron (Aluminum Prototype)	Ensign	Pimlico
Andover	Exeter	Police Special
Ardsley	Fifth Avenue	Potomac
Ariston	Finalist	Puritan
Arlington	Finalist Deco	Riley
Armored Case	Frontenac	Rectangular
Atlantic	Futura	Richmond 6/0
Atlantic Enamel	Gallahad	Richmond 12/0
Atlantic Large	General Funston	Ritz
Atlantic, Jr.	General Joffre	Rockliffe
Aviator	Generic	Rockliffe 18/0
Baronet	Gift Series	Sangamon
Beau Brummell	Greyhound	Senator
Beau Brummell/Viking	Greystone	Seneca
Beau Geste	Guardian	Skyway
Beau Monde	Guardsman	Southampton
Beau Royale	Guardsman Military	Special
Belmont	Haddon Hall	Special Cushion
Biltmore	Hawthorne	Special Cushion Fahys
Biltmore 6/0	Hudson	Special Cushion Solidarity
Biltmore 18/0	Illinois Langford	Speedway
Blackhawk	Illinois Pierre	Speedway 178
Blackstone	Illinois Whitman	Sportsman
Bostonian	Jolly Roger	Square
Brandt Rock	Kenilworth	Square Cut Corner
Bryce	Kensington	Square Cut Corner Large
Bullet Dial	Kingston	Standish
Burlington	Kitchener Military	Sterling
Cadet	Larchmont	Tank
Canby	LaSalle	Telephone Dial
Caprice	Latonia	Tonneau
Cavalier	Locke	Townsman
Chatham	Manhattan	Transitional Watches
Chesterfield	Major	Trophy
Chesterfield Stepped Bezel	Marquis Strap	Tuxedo
Chevalier	Masonic Dial	United States Army
Chieftain	Mate	Urbana
Chrysanthemum	Maxine	Valedictorian
Commander	Medalist	Varsity (No. 650)
Commodore	Metropolitan	Vernon
Conneric	Military	Viking
Consul	Military Crown at 12	Washington Watch Company
Contract	Motor Coach	Wayne
Cushion	New Yorker	Wembley
Cushion Form	New Yorker Enamel	Wentworth
Cut Bezel	No. 250 (Schmukler)	Westchester
"D-D" Khaki	Notched Lug	Whippet
"D-D" Utility	Off-Duty	Yankee Clipper
Decagon	Off-Set Crowns	Yorktown
Decagon, Jr.	Ollendorff I	
	Ollendorff II	
Black = Men's	Blue = Unisex	

Ace / Maxine / Wayne

Official Name = Ace (derived from early jobbers' advertisements)
Secondary Name(s) = Maxine, Wayne (derived from IWCCo advertisements)
Formerly Known As = Ronald (named after the friend of an early American price guide author); Pilot
Time Period = Generic
Case Variations/Rarity = 🕒 WGF/P
🕒🕒 WGF/E
🕒🕒🕒 BM/P
🕒🕒🕒🕒 YGF/P
🕒🕒🕒🕒🕒🕒 GGF/P, YG/E
Case Durability = 🕒🕒
Material = 14K GF, 14K YG, BM
Bezel = Plain, Engraved
Sides = Plain, Engraved
Lugs = Plain, Engraved
Lug Size = 16mm
Springbar = Male
Casemakers = Elgin, Star, IWCCo, Others
Case Closure = 3-Part Snap-On Bezel and Back
Case Number = None
Case Shape = Octagon
Case Back = Flat
Dimensions = 39 x 30mm
Movement Size = 3/0
Movement Grades/Jewels = 21/11, 24/17, Others
Seconds at = 6, 9
Dial Numbers = 109, 144, 4109, 8109, 8291
Dials = Silver Finish, Butler Center
Dial Opening = Octagon
Dial Variations/Rarity = 🕒🕒 Silver Finish/Luminous Numerals
🕒🕒🕒 Silver Finish/Cross Pattern
🕒🕒🕒🕒 Silver Finish/Butler Center
🕒🕒🕒🕒🕒🕒🕒 Seconds at 9
Numerals = Painted, Luminous
Hands = Luminous
Cased in Factory = No
Unique Case Design = No
Unique Dial Design = Yes
Introduction Date = 1927
Retail Price New = $ 42.50
Collectibility = 🕒🕒🕒
Advertisements = Yes
This watch style was advertised in early jobbers' catalogs and advertisements. IWCCo advertised this Generic Period case model periodically in the *Jewelers' Circular* and the *Keystone*. As a Generic Period watch, it was advertised for use with Elgin, Waltham or Illinois movements and dials.
Marketing Theme = "Style can be seen at a glance, but quality is the hidden value ...."

Ace, white gold-filled with private label dial

Ace, yellow gold

Ace, white gold-filled, subs at 9; only one known to exist

Keystone, October 1928. An Ace (identified here as a Wayne) is featured on the right.

cross-like wreath design (shown below) in the center of the dial that improves the appearance as well as increases the value of this watch.

There is only one (and thus very rare) known Ace watch that has subsidiary seconds at 9.

Ace, white gold-filled with a private-label dial and cross-like wreath

The Illinois Material Catalogs referred to the Ace dial as a "Maxine" owing to its shape. In the first American wristwatch price guide, the authors called this watch, unidentified at the time, the "Ronald" after the son of one of their friends. This is a fairly common watch in white gold-filled, but is extremely difficult to find in yellow or green gold-filled. Only two green gold-filled ones are known to exist (one was very worn). Only one in solid yellow gold has been reported; it has an engraved bezel and is in a case made by Star.

The Ace is a good starter watch for a new Illinois collector as they are readily available in white gold-filled cases, usually at a very reasonable price. The watch occasionally comes with a highly collectible

Advertisement from Wittman Jewelers, showing the Ace. *Reading Times* (Reading, PA), January 31, 1930; image from *newspapers.com*

Strap Watches Are Winning Converts Every Day

GIFTS THAT LAST | GIFTS THAT LAST

Sturdy and Mannish. *Convenient* *Accurate and Reliable*

Featuring Gents' "3/0" Size Elgin, Waltham and Illinois Strap Watches

Silver and Luminous Dials. *14k White or Green Gold Filled Cases.* *Complete with Strap and Buckle.*

Ideal as Birthday, Christmas or Graduation Gifts

NOTE: The Waltham Watches on this page can be furnished with SILVER DIAL and RAISED METAL FIGURES instead of luminous dial for $5.40. Less than the prices quoted.

3/0 SIZE CUSHION SHAPE
14K WHITE OR GREEN GOLD FILLED
Luminous Dial and Hands

14k White or Green Gold Filled Case. The popular cushion shape. Round glass. Luminous Dial and Hands. Complete with strap and buckle. Choice of 7 and 15-jewel Elgin or Waltham and 17-Jewel Illinois Movements, as quoted. An ideal style and size, attractively priced in this important selling.

No. 7250 7-Jewel Elgin Movement. Complete........**$38.30**
No. 7251 7-Jewel Waltham Movement. Complete........**$38.30**
No. 7252 15-Jewel Elgin Movement. Complete........**$46.80**
No. 7253 15-Jewel Waltham Movement. Complete........**$46.80**
No. 7254 17-Jewel Illinois Movement. Complete........**$49.45**

Be sure to state whether White or Green Gold Filled Case is wanted when ordering.

3/0 SIZE CUSHION SHAPE
(Commodore Model)
Etched Oxidized Bezel
14K WHITE OR GREEN GOLD FILLED
Luminous Dial and Hands

14k White or Green Gold Filled Case. Square Cut Corner Design. Plain Bezel. Luminous Dial and Hands. Complete with strap and buckle. Choice of 7 and 15-Jewel Elgin or Waltham and 17-Jewel Illinois Movements, as quoted. A real mannish and sturdy watch and very popular among the men.

No. 7255 7-Jewel Elgin Movement. Complete......**$40.00**
No. 7256 7-Jewel Waltham Movement. Complete......**$40.00**
No. 7257 15-Jewel Elgin Movement. Complete......**$48.50**
No. 7258 15-Jewel Waltham Movement. Complete......**$48.50**
No. 7259 17-Jewel Illinois Movement. Complete......**$51.15**

Be sure to state whether White or Green Gold Filled Case is wanted when ordering.

3/0 SIZE SQUARE CUT CORNER SHAPE
Etched Oxidized Bezel
14K WHITE OR GREEN GOLD FILLED
Luminous Dial and Hands

14k White or Green Gold Filled Case. Square Cut Corner Design. Etched oxidized bezel. Luminous Dial and Hands. Complete with strap and buckle. Choice of 7 and 15-Jewel Elgin or Waltham and 17-Jewel Illinois Movements, as quoted. Very serviceable and dependable in every respect.

No. 7260 7-Jewel Elgin Movement. Complete......**$41.00**
No. 7261 7-Jewel Waltham Movement. Complete......**$41.00**
No. 7262 15-Jewel Elgin Movement. Complete......**$49.60**
No. 7263 15-Jewel Waltham Movement. Complete......**$49.60**
No. 7264 17-Jewel Illinois Movement. Complete......**$52.20**

Be sure to state whether White or Green Gold Filled Case is wanted when ordering.

3/0 SIZE BARREL SHAPE
14K White or Green Gold Filled; Luminous Dial and Hands

14k Gold Filled, with choice of White or Green finish. Barrel design case, plain polished, luminous dial and hands, complete with strap and buckle. It is a popular design and is fitted with choice of 7 and 15-Jewel Elgin or Waltham and 17-Jewel Illinois Movements, as quoted.

No. 7265 7-Jewel Elgin Movement. Complete......**$39.40**
No. 7266 7-Jewel Waltham Movement. Complete......**$39.40**
No. 7267 15-Jewel Elgin Movement. Complete......**$47.40**
No. 7268 15-Jewel Waltham Movement. Complete......**$47.40**
No. 7269 17-Jewel Illinois Movement. Complete......**$50.55**

Be sure to state whether White or Green Gold Filled Case is wanted when ordering.

3/0 SIZE BARREL SHAPE
14K White or Green Gold Filled; Luminous Dial and Hands

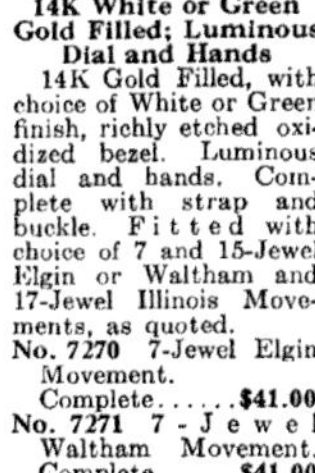

14K Gold Filled, with choice of White or Green finish, richly etched oxidized bezel. Luminous dial and hands. Complete with strap and buckle. Fitted with choice of 7 and 15-Jewel Elgin or Waltham and 17-Jewel Illinois Movements, as quoted.

No. 7270 7-Jewel Elgin Movement. Complete......**$41.00**
No. 7271 7-Jewel Waltham Movement. Complete......**$41.00**
No. 7272 15-Jewel Elgin Movement. Complete......**$49.60**
No. 7273 15-Jewel Waltham Movement. Complete......**$49.60**
No. 7274 17-Jewel Illinois Movement. Complete......**$52.20**

Be sure to state whether White or Green Gold Filled Case is wanted when ordering.

3/0 SIZE RECTANGULAR SHAPE
14K White or Green Gold Filled; Luminous Dial and Hands

14k White or Green Gold Filled Case. Plain rectangular design. Luminous dial and hands. Complete with strap and buckle. Fitted with choice of 7 and 15-Jewel Elgin or Waltham and 17-Jewel Illinois Movements, as quoted. Priced very low in this selling.

No. 7275 7-Jewel Elgin Movement. Complete......**$39.40**
No. 7276 7-Jewel Waltham Movement. Complete......**$39.40**
No. 7277 15-Jewel Elgin Movement. Complete......**$47.40**
No. 7278 15-Jewel Waltham Movement. Complete......**$47.40**
No. 7279 17-Jewel Illinois Movement. Complete......**$50.55**

Be sure to state whether White or Green Gold Filled Case is wanted when ordering.

3/0 SIZE RECTANGULAR SHAPE
14K White or Green Gold Filled; Luminous Dial and Hands

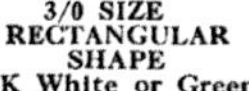

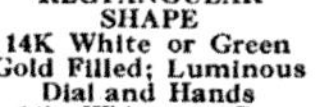

14k White or Green Gold Filled Case. Artistically etched oxidized bezel. Luminous dial and hands. Complete with strap and buckle. Fitted with choice of 7 and 15-Jewel Elgin or Waltham and 17-Jewel Illinois Movements, as quoted. A very popular and attractive design.

No. 7280 7-Jewel Elgin Movement. Complete......**$41.00**
No. 7281 7-Jewel Waltham Movement. Complete......**$41.00**
No. 7282 15-Jewel Elgin Movement. Complete......**$49.60**
No. 7283 15-Jewel Waltham Movement. Complete......**$49.60**
No. 7284 17-Jewel Illinois Movement. Complete......**$52.20**

Be sure to state whether White or Green Gold Filled Case is wanted when ordering.

3/0 SIZE CUSHION SHAPE
14K White or Green Gold Filled; Luminous Dial and Hands

14k White or Green Gold Filled Case. Plain design. Formed Glass. Luminous dial and hands. Complete with strap and buckle. Fitted with choice of 7 and 15-Jewel Elgin or Waltham and 17-Jewel Illinois Movements, as quoted. An Ideal Birthday, Christmas, or Anniversary Gift.

No. 7285 7-Jewel Elgin Movement. Complete......**$39.40**
No. 7286 7-Jewel Waltham Movement. Complete......**$39.40**
No. 7287 15-Jewel Elgin Movement. Complete......**$47.40**
No. 7288 15-Jewel Waltham Movement. Complete......**$47.40**
No. 7289 17-Jewel Illinois Movement. Complete......**$50.55**

Be sure to state whether White or Green Gold Filled Case is wanted when ordering.

3/0 SIZE CUSHION SHAPE
14K White or Green Gold Filled; Luminous Dial and Hands

14k White or Green Gold Filled Case, attractive etched oxidized bezel. Formed Glass. Luminous Dial and hands. Complete with strap and buckle. Fitted with choice of 7 and 15-Jewel Elgin or Waltham and 17-Jewel Illinois Movements, as quoted. Excellent construction and careful finish.

No. 7290 7-Jewel Elgin Movement. Complete......**$41.00**
No. 7291 7-Jewel Waltham Movement. Complete......**$41.00**
No. 7292 15-Jewel Elgin Movement. Complete......**$49.60**
No. 7293 15-Jewel Waltham Movement. Complete......**$49.60**
No. 7294 17-Jewel Illinois Movement. Complete......**$52.20**

Be sure to state whether White or Green Gold Filled Case is wanted when ordering.

Fort Dearborn Gift Book and General catalog, 1929. Note the plain bezel and the engraved bezel Aces among these Generic offerings.

ADMIRAL BENSON

Admiral Benson, gunmetal finish, straight swivel lugs

Admiral Benson, sterling silver, straight swivel lugs

Admiral Benson, sterling silver, straight swivel lugs

Official Name = Admiral Benson (derived from IWCCo advertisements)
Secondary Name(s) = Cushion Military
Formerly Known As = Transitional
Time Period = Transitional
Material = SS, Gunmetal Finish, 14K YGF
Case Variations/Rarity = 🕒🕒 SS 3/0 Size (fixed lugs)
🕒🕒🕒🕒🕒 SS "0" Size, SS/Swivel Lugs
🕒🕒🕒🕒🕒🕒 14K YGF, SS 12 Size, Gunmetal Finish
🕒🕒🕒🕒🕒🕒🕒 SS 6/0 Size
Case Durability = 🕒🕒 YGF
🕒🕒🕒🕒 SS
Bezel = Plain
Sides = Plain
Lugs = Plain
Lug Size = 14mm, 16mm
Springbar = Fixed Lugs, Swivel Lugs, 1917 version Straight Swivel Lugs; 1918 version Angled Swivel Lugs
Casemakers = IWCCo
Case Closure = 3-Part Snap-On Bezel and Back
Case Number = None
Case Shape = Cushion
Case Back = Flat
Dimensions = Various
Movement Sizes = 0, 3/0, 6/0, 12 size
Movement Grades/Jewels = 21/11, 24/17, 32/11, 36/17, 38/17, 204/17, 903/15, 904/17
Seconds at = 6
Dial Numbers = None
Dials = Enamel, Silver Finish
Dial Opening = Round
Dial Variations/Rarity = 🕒🕒 Enamel, Silver Finish
🕒🕒🕒🕒🕒🕒 Enamel 6/0
Numerals = Painted
Hands = Steel, Luminous
Cased in Factory = No
Unique Case Design = No
Unique Dial Design = No
Introduction Date = 1917
Retail Price New = Unknown
Collectibility = 🕒🕒🕒🕒
Advertisements = Yes
Marketing Theme = "Wrist Watches for Uncle Sam's Boys"

The true name of the Admiral Benson was determined by the discovery of the 1917 advertisement in the *Jewelers' Circular* (shown below) found by Stan Czubernat, the Elgin trench watch expert.

Notice the "Springfield Movements" notation, probably to avoid confusion between IWCCo and the Illinois Watch Company. *Jewelers' Circular*, September 5, 1917

For the longest time, the Admiral Benson model was only known as a Transitional Cushion Military watch. Until the 1917 IWCCo advertisement was discovered, we never knew that this watch had a model name. In 3/0 size and in sterling silver, this is a fairly common watch, but less so in 0 size. If the 3/0 size has swivel lugs, it is rare as only a few are known to exist. It is also rare in yellow gold-filled, and it is difficult to find a yellow one without significant case wear. If it contained a Burlington dial and movement, this same model in 0 or 3/0 size with fixed lugs was called an Aviator. A true Admiral Benson or Aviator should be in an IWCCo case, according to Czubernat.

In addition to the Admiral Benson cushion wristwatch in 0 size and 3/0 size, there is at least one very rare Admiral Benson, Jr. model in a 6/0 size sterling silver case. The case is made by the IWCCo. The "JS" stamped on the inside of the case back indicates that it is a 6/0 size case for a Waltham "Jewel Series" movement.

The 12-size version of this model does exist, according to Czubernat, but only one has been seen to date.

This is the case for an Admiral Benson, Jr. The "J.S." stamped inside the case signifies that it was for Waltham "Jewel Series" movements, which were 6/0 size.

Admiral Benson, sterling silver, no subs

Admiral Benson, case back

Admiral Benson, c. 1917

ADMIRAL WILLIAM S. BENSON (1855-1932)

Born in Macon, Georgia, September 25, 1855, William Shepherd Benson graduated from the United States Naval Academy in 1877. He commanded several cruisers and battleships, as well as serving as Commandant of the Philadelphia Navy Yard. He was appointed the first Chief of Naval Operations in 1915. Admiral Benson served in this position until his retirement in 1919. He died in Washington, D.C., on May 20, 1932.*

**Dictionary of American Naval Fighting Ships*, http://www.hazegray.org/danfs/

Admiral Evans / Admiral Evans Off-Set

Admiral Evans, sterling silver, angled swivel lugs

Admiral Evans, yellow gold-filled, straight swivel lugs

Admiral Evans, sterling silver, off-set crown

Official Name = Admiral Evans (derived from IWCCo advertisements)
Secondary Name(s) = None
Formerly Known As = None
Time Period = Transitional
Case Variations/Rarity = ◷◷◷ SS/P
◷◷◷◷◷ YGF/P, YG/P, YGF/P 6/0
◷◷◷◷◷◷◷◷ RG/P
◷◷◷◷◷◷◷◷ YGF Off-Set
Case Durability = ◷◷ YGF
◷◷◷◷ SS, RG
Material = SS, 14K YG, 14K RG, 14K YGF
Bezel = Plain
Sides = Plain
Lugs = Plain
Lug Size = 14mm
Springbar = Fixed Lugs, Swivel Lugs (straight or angled)
Casemakers = IWCCo, Solidarity, Star, Wadsworth
Case Closure = 3-Part Snap-On Bezel and Back
Case Number = None
Case Shape = Octagon
Case Back = Flat
Dimensions = 43 x 31mm
Movement Sizes = 12s, 0, 3/0, 6/0
Movement Grades/Jewels = 38/17, 21/11, 24/17, 32/11, 36/17, 204/17, 903/15, 904/17
Seconds at = 6
Dial Numbers = 8190, 8210
Dials = Enamel, Silver Finish
Dial Opening = Round
Dial Variations/Rarity = ◷◷ Silver Finish, Luminous Numerals
◷◷◷ Silver Finish, Bold Black Numerals
◷◷◷◷ Enamel, Black Numerals
◷◷◷◷◷ Enamel, Blue Numerals
Numerals = Painted, Luminous
Hands = Steel
Cased in Factory = No
Unique Case Design = No
Unique Dial Design = No
Introduction Date = 1917
Retail Price New = Unknown
Collectibility = ◷◷◷◷
Advertisements = Yes
The Admiral Evans was advertised in September 1918 by IWCCo. No advertisement has been found for an Admiral Evans with an off-set crown or a case that is in rose gold. As late as September 13, 1928, Solidarity advertised a solid yellow gold Admiral Evans in the *Jewelers' Circular*.
Marketing Theme = "Wrist Watches for Uncle Sam's Boys"

September, 1918 THE KEYSTONE Page 49

Wrist Watches for Uncle Sam's Boys

ARMY—AVIATION—NAVY

New Added Feature:
COMPASS OR PHOTOGRAPH

Equipment on Strap Supplied with Any Model

Solid Gold Gold Filled
Sterling Silver

ALL SHAPES, including Round, Square, Octagon and Cushion Shape

All Sizes to Fit

Elgin, Waltham, Illinois and All Standard American and Swiss Movements

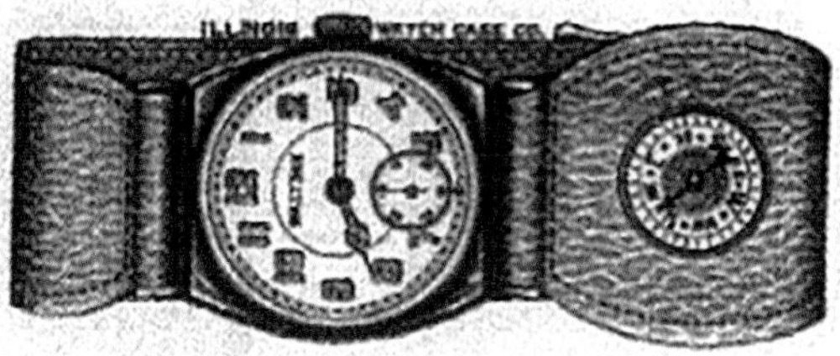

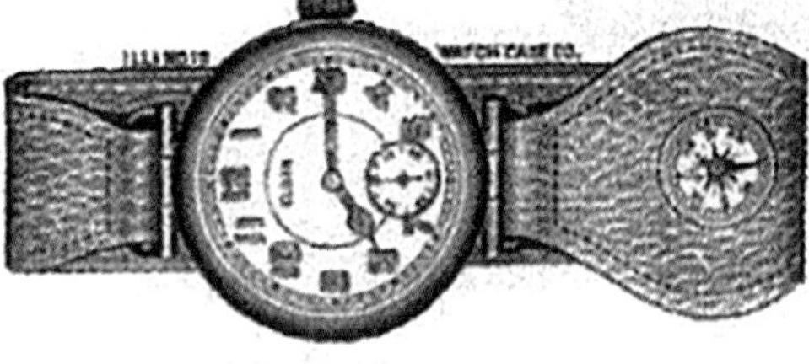

Gold Filled
fitted with Heavy Navy Straps and **Gold Filled Buckles.**

Sterling Silver
fitted with Heavy Navy Straps and **Sterling Silver Buckles.**

Sizes include 12s, 0s, 3.0s and Jewel Series

ASK YOUR JOBBER
to show you our
LADIES' WRIST WATCH CASES
AND
GENERAL LINE OF WATCH CASES OF ALL KINDS

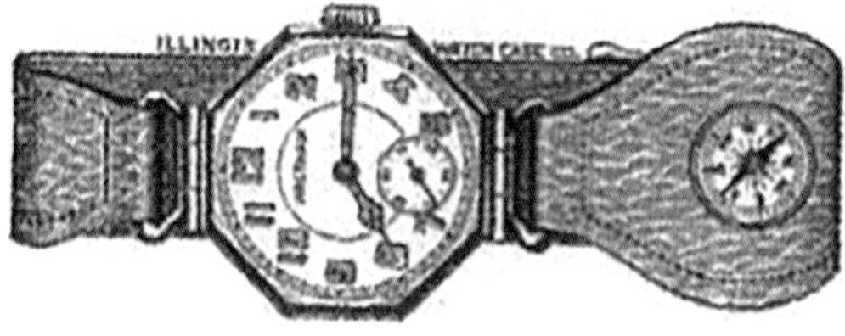

Illinois Watch Case Co.

FACTORY AT ELGIN, ILLINOIS

15 Maiden Lane NEW YORK | 704 Market Street SAN FRANCISCO | 904 Heyworth Building CHICAGO

Keystone, September 1918

The Admiral Evans, along with the Telephone Dial model, are two of the most sought-after Illinois watches of the Transitional Period. The Admiral Evans models with swivel lugs are more valuable and collectible than the ones with fixed lugs. The Admiral Evans with an off-set crown is extremely rare; only about ten are known to exist. There is also a 6/0 size version of the Admiral Evans, Jr. Normally, their cases were made by Star and Wadsworth in 14K yellow gold-filled.

As with many Illinois watch models, the dial can make the watch. This is true with the Admiral Evans as well, especially if you can find enamel dials with bold black or blue numerals. A good metal dial with bold, black numerals can also make an attractive Admiral Evans.

To date, there has been only one solid rose gold Admiral Evans found; it has swivel lugs and is in an IWCCo case. One yellow gold-filled Admiral Evans with an off-set crown has been found in an IWCCo case. Only one 12s Admiral Evans has been located; it is in a yellow gold-filled IWCCo case containing an Elgin movement and dial.

Admiral Evans, sterling silver with straight swivel lugs and black dial

IWCCo inside case back for an Illinois Admiral Evans model in yellow gold-filled

ADMIRAL ROBLEY D. EVANS (1846-1912)

Admiral Evans, c. 1900

Robley Dunglison Evans served in the United States Navy from the American Civil War to the first decade of the 20th Century, attaining the rank of Rear Admiral. He graduated from the United States Naval Academy in 1864.

During the Confederate attacks on Fort Fisher, North Carolina, he exhibited great gallantry under fire. On January 15, 1865, he led a party of United States Marines through heavy fire to charge the Confederate defenses. Evans continued to fight even after his fourth wound, drawing his pistol and threatening to kill any man who attempted to amputate his leg in surgery when he was evacuated.

He went on to hold numerous important sea commands. In 1907–1908 he commanded the Great White Fleet on the first leg of its worldwide cruise from the Atlantic Ocean through the Straits of Magellan to the Pacific Ocean. He retired from the Navy upon reaching the mandatory retirement age of 62 on August 18, 1908.*

*http://www.spanamwar.com/evans.htm

Akron, aluminum, a prototype model

AKRON

Official Name = Akron (derived from the airship USS *Akron*, made of duraluminum; and the Illinois List of Factory-Cased Watches)
Secondary Name(s) = Aluminum Prototype (derived from collectors' usage before its true name was determined)
Formerly Known As = None
Time Period = Moderne
Material = A
Case Variation/Rarity = ◷◷◷◷◷◷ A/P
Case Durability = ◷◷◷
Bezel = Plain
Sides = Plain
Lugs = Plain
Lug Size = 16mm
Springbar = Male
Casemaker = Pioneer
Case Closure = 3-Part Snap-On Bezel and Back
Case Number = None
Case Shape = Tonneau
Case Back = Flat
Dimensions = 35 x 27mm
Movement Size = 3/0
Movement Grades/Jewels = 307/17
Seconds at = Rotor at 6
Dial Number = Unknown
Dial = Silver Finish
Dial Opening = Tonneau
Dial Variations/Rarity = ◷◷◷ Silver Finish, Black Numerals
◷◷◷◷ Silver Finish, Luminous Numerals
Numerals = Luminous
Hands = Luminous
Cased in Factory = Yes
Unique Case Design = No
Unique Dial Design = Yes
Introduction Date = 1931
Retail Price New = Unknown
Collectibility = ◷◷◷◷
Advertisements = No. There is no known advertisement for this model.
Marketing Themes = Unknown

Akron NOS dial

The Illinois Watch Company pioneered the use of aluminum in watch movements and watch cases. These efforts resulted in the Akron prototype wristwatch. No information exists about Illinois' attempts to distribute this model. To date, only three complete Akrons have been found and only five aluminum wristwatch movements have been located. According to manufacturing records, Illinois produced a total of two hundred aluminum 17-jewel, 3/0 size movements.

Pioneer fabricated the duraluminum watch case and watchband for this model. Owing to the small number of aluminum movements made by Illinois, collectors believe that Illinois manufactured the Akron for testing and evaluation. Illinois offered the exact same shaped case made out of chrome as the Seneca. (See the **Seneca/Blackhawk** listing.)

ALUMINUM WATCH

After the discovery of aluminum the firms making it sought various markets for it. They approached watchmakers but it was not until the 1800s when J. P. Stevens made some early watches with a pallet fork made of aluminum/copper alloy to reduce mass that it was first used.

"The Philadelphia Watch Case Company made a series of production cases for pocket watches using an alloy that contained aluminum. In the 1880s the Rockford Watch Company made a few 18 size experimental movements with aluminum plates. Still, it took until about 1900 for a production aluminum watch—both case and movement of the metal—to be made.

"As early as 1900, the A. C. Becken's Catalog advertised an all-aluminum case and movement pocket watch made by the Kelly Watch Company in Chicago, Illinois. It sold for $2.20 . . . "*

A. C. Becken catalog, 1900

*L. Michael Fultz, "Aluminum: Light-weight or Watch Heavyweight?", *InSync* Magazine, October 2006.

DURALUMIN

Duralumin, now known as "duraluminum," is an alloy that combines copper, manganese, and magnesium into a strong aluminum compound.

German metallurgist Alfred Wilm at Dürener Metallwerke Aktien Gesellschaft developed duraluminum.

In 1903, Wilm discovered that after heating an aluminum alloy containing 4% copper, the substance would slowly harden when left for several days at room temperature. Further improvements led to the introduction of duralumin in 1909.

Designers first used this alloy in rigid airship frames, eventually including all those of the "Great Airship" era of the 1920s and 1930s: the German passenger Zeppelins LZ 127 *Graf Zeppelin*, LZ 129 *Hindenburg*, LZ 130 *Graf Zeppelin II* and U.S. Navy airships USS *Los Angeles* (ZR-3, ex-LZ126), USS *Akron* (ZRS-4) and USS *Macon* (ZRS-5). With this new rip-resistant mixture, the use of duraluminum quickly spread through the aircraft industry in the early 1930s, because it was well suited to the new monocoque construction techniques.*

Someone at Illinois or at the Pioneer Watch Case Company came up with the innovative idea of linking a wristwatch with the emerging high-tech world of dirigibles, Zeppelins and metal-sheathed fixed-wing aircraft. The aerospace industry of that era used duraluminum much like they use titanium alloy or carbon fiber today. In a similar fashion, many of the watchmakers of today now use "space age" materials with which to encase their mechanisms.

*http://www.britannica.com/technology/duralumin

Illinois' interest in aluminum watches began a decade prior to the Great Depression. In 1920, the Illinois Watch Company made aluminum 12-size, 17-jewel, motor barrel movements and contracted with Wadsworth to make matching aluminum cases. The movements carry the serial numbers 3,869,251 to 3,869,300. The cases are not numbered. These fifty watches do not seem to have been released to the public but rather held for testing and experimentation. Even so, only three of these aluminum watches survive now in watch collections.

In 1931, three years after Hamilton purchased the Illinois Watch Company, Illinois manufactured a group of two hundred aluminum 3/0 size, 17-jewel, 307 grade, double-roller movements. To these, the list appends a cryptic designation "s.a.w." which would seem to stand for "special aluminum watch." These movements were placed in aluminum cases with matching aluminum bracelets made by the Pioneer Watch Case Co. The cases are stamped "Illinois Watch Co. Duraluminum Springfield, Ill. Pioneer Watch Case Co."

Even though Illinois produced four times as many of the 3/0 size wristwatch movements as it did 12-size ones for pocket watches, the wristwatches seem to have had a much worse survival rate—only three examples of the entire wristwatch are known to exist.

A very similar watch with a nickel 17-jewel movement and chrome case marked "Pioneer Chrome" was offered for sale, as is described in the **Seneca** listing. Although only three Akrons have been located, the Seneca/Blackhawk model is much easier to find.

A 3/0 size aluminum movement with serial number 5,542,802.

Akron inside case back

SENATOR ROSCOE C. McCULLOCH

According to the owner of this aluminum pocket watch movement, he "bought [the] watch from the grandson of the original owner" and that "the original owner was Roscoe Conkling McCulloch, a U.S. Congressman from Ohio (1912–1918) and later U.S. Senator from 1928–30. Between 1918 and 1928, he was an attorney representing the American National Retail Jewelers Association. In recognition of his service to that group, the Illinois Watch Company gave him the aluminum watch in 1921."

One of three aluminum Illinois pocket watch movements known to exist. This is Serial No. 3,869,277.

Akron duraluminum inside watch band

Duralumin USS Akron watch fob

FANTASTIC FIND

Being the consummate collector of all things Illinois, I am always gathering spare parts, cases and movements for the collection. One day, I see a pile of parts for sale on eBay and like so many before, I grab it for peanuts. I send the package directly to my watchmaker Jesse and it sits in his drawer for months along with my other piles of spare parts.

On one of my visits, I decide to help him out and sort the hundreds of bits and pieces. I see a bag full of stuff and as I am sorting, I pick up a case and movement that just doesn't feel right. . . . It is way too light. Figuring that the movement inside is only a partial, I pop off the case back and what I see next makes my jaw hit the ground. Having seen an aluminum movement before, I knew what it was immediately.

I checked the serial number and sure enough, it looks like the real deal. I was so excited I had to call Fred. . . (Ring, Ring) Fred, being the man he is, answers the phone and says, "Hey, I was just sitting down for Passover dinner." Unable to contain myself, I said, "Fred I am so sorry to call, but I just found a perfect Aluminum movement in a bag of parts!!!"

As his family is sitting down for dinner (I am sure) I am reading off the serial number to confirm. . . . I can hardly contain myself as Fred and I realize that this is truly one of the most Fantastic Finds of my life! A Passover I will never forget!

—Greg Hart

Andover, white gold-filled

Andover, yellow gold-filled

Andover / Exeter

Official Name = Andover (derived from Illinois advertisements and Illinois Sales and Material catalogs)
Secondary Name(s) = Exeter (derived from a Hamilton internal document)
Formerly Known As = None
Time Period = Moderne
Case Variations/Rarity = 🕐🕐 YGF/P
🕐🕐🕐 WGF/P
🕐🕐🕐🕐🕐🕐🕐🕐 YGF/E
Case Durability = 🕐🕐 YGF/P
🕐🕐🕐 WGF/P
Material = 10K GF, 14K GF
Bezel = Plain, Engraved
Sides = Plain
Lugs = Plain
Lug Size = 16mm
Springbar = Male
Casemaker = J. Milhening
Case Closure = 2-Part Snap-On Back
Case Number = 215
Case Shape = Rectangular
Case Back = Flat
Dimensions = 38 x 24mm
Movement Size = 12/0
Movement Grade/Jewels = 207/17
Seconds at = 6
Dial Numbers = 8066, 8419
Dials = Silver Finish, Sparkle Finish
Dial Opening = Rectangular

Dial Variations/Rarity = 🕒🕒 Silver Finish, Black Numerals
🕒🕒🕒🕒 Silver Finish, Etched Numerals;
Sparkle Finish, Black Numerals
Numerals = Painted, Etched
Hands = Steel
Cased in Factory = Yes
Unique Case Design = Yes
Unique Dial Design = No
Introduction Date = 1932
Retail Price New = $52.50
Collectibility = 🕒🕒🕒🕒
Advertisements = No. As yet, no magazine advertisement has been located.
Marketing Themes = "A case of character and distinction for sports wear"
"Graceful flowing lines"

The Andover appeared on an April 1, 1932 Illinois price list and was among the models shown in the 1933 Illinois Greater Value Watches sales catalog, where it was featured as one of Illinois' "Wrist Watches of Character for Men."

A recently discovered Hamilton internal record discloses that the Andover may have also been called an "Exeter"; perhaps the Exeter model came equipped with a metal band or a different dial variation.

The Andover is subject to severe case wear on the sides of the bezel, and, as a result, it is difficult to find one without wear. This model is more difficult to locate in white gold-filled than yellow gold-filled. Although the Andover was advertised as being in 14K gold-filled, only two yellow gold-filled have been sighted and three in white gold-filled; the other specimens are in 10K gold-filled cases.

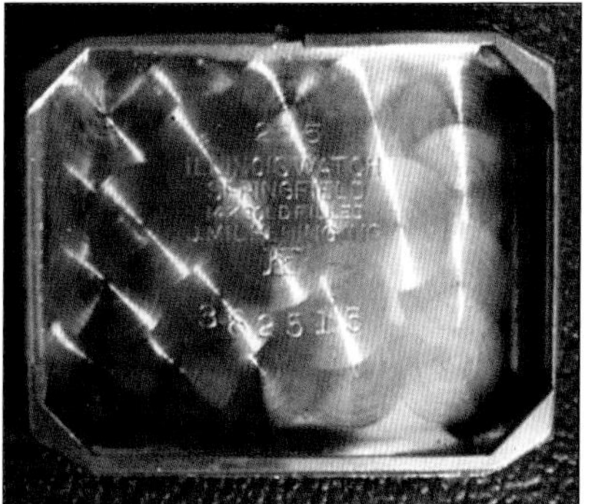

The inside case back of a rare 14K yellow gold-filled Andover

The Andover is one of the small number of Illinois men's wristwatches made in 10K gold-filled. The other 10K gold-filled Illinois models were offered in 1934 by Hamilton as bargain Depression offerings.

The Andover case is subtly designed; the sides of the case are curved inward below and above the dial, tapering down to its lugs. This simple model has more style to it than some of its rectangular contemporary competitors.

In 2008 a very rare 14K yellow gold-filled Andover was found with sides of the bezel engraved, a small modification that greatly enhanced this model's visual appeal.

Andover engraved bezel (with a redone dial)

The Andover was one of only two case models that the J. Milhening Company made for Illinois; the other was the Arlington/Hawthorne model. In addition, the Andover is the only example of an Illinois model that came with two different karat cases—14K gold-filled and 10K gold-filled—made by the same casemaker. It is possible that it was first offered in 14K gold-filled, then changed to 10K gold-filled to price it lower. Both versions are signed the same except for the karat count.

The Andover came with three different dial variations: one with sparkle finish and black numerals, one with silver finish and black numerals, and one with a silver finish and etched gold numerals.

Look-Alike

The Hamilton Ericsson (as discussed earlier in this book) is a steroid-enhanced version of the Andover, or (perhaps more accurately) the Andover is a slimmed-down version of the Ericsson). The Ericsson released in 1930 came in 14K and 18K white or yellow gold.

In the 1934 film "Berkeley Square", its star, Leslie Howard, wore an Illinois Andover wristwatch. Unfortunately, it is not visible on this publicity poster.

Ericsson

Ardsley

See listing for **Hudson**

ARISTON

Ariston, sterling silver

Official Name = Ariston (derived from Marshall Field & Company advertisements)
Secondary Name(s) = None
Formerly Known As = None
Time Period = Transitional
Case Variations/Rarity = ◷ SS/P Cushion
◷◷ SS/P Round
Case Durability = ◷◷◷◷
Material = SS
Bezel = Plain
Sides = Plain
Lugs = Plain
Lug Size = 16mm
Springbar = Fixed Lugs
Casemakers = Fahys, Others
Case Closure = 3-Part Snap-On Bezel and Back
Case Number = None
Case Shape = Cushion, Round
Case Back = Flat
Dimensions = 28 x 28mm, Others
Movement Size = 3/0
Movement Grades/Jewels = 37/17, 21/11, 24/17, 32/11, 36/17
Seconds at = 6
Dial Number = None
Dial = Enamel
Dial Opening = Round
Dial Variations/Rarity = ◷◷◷◷◷ Enamel, Painted Numerals
Numerals = Painted
Hands = Steel
Cased in Factory = No
Unique Case Design = No
Unique Dial Design = No
Introduction Date = 1916
Retail Price New = Unknown
Collectibility = ◷◷
Advertisements = Yes
Marketing Themes = "When a man buys an Ariston rated watch he buys a life long companion."
"The purchase of a watch should be considered an investment."

The Ariston was a private-label watch made by the Illinois Watch Company for the exclusive use of the Marshall Field department store in Chicago.

Illinois made hundreds of private-label movements, most of them for pocket watches. (A partial list of them is contained in Appendix 5.) Several of the private-label brands are featured in this Identification Guide. Under the **Burlington** listing of this chapter there are specific Burlington-signed movements, dials and cases.

Illinois produced one thousand Ariston-signed, 3/0 size movements in 1916; most, if not all, were intended for use in pendant watch cases. Burlington advertised in 1918 a sterling silver cushion watch shaped exactly like the Ariston model but with a Burlington-signed enamel dial and called it an "Aviator" in its advertisement.

For information on Ariston, Burlington, and other private labels, see Chapter 6.

Arlington, white gold-filled

Arlington, yellow gold-filled

ARLINGTON / HAWTHORNE

Official Names = Arlington and Hawthorne (derived from Illinois Sales and Material Catalogs, magazine advertisements and jobbers' catalogs)
Secondary Name(s) = None
Formerly Known As = None
Time Period = Moderne
Case Variations/Rarity = ◷◷ YGF/P
◷◷◷ WGF/P
Case Durability = ◷ YGF/P
◷◷ WGF/P
Material = 14K GF
Bezel = Plain
Sides = Plain
Lugs = Plain
Lug Size = 16mm
Springbar = Male
Casemaker = J. Milhening
Case Closure = 2-Part Snap-On Back
Case Number = 618
Case Shape = Rectangular
Case Back = Flat
Dimensions = 37 x 27mm
Movement Size = 6/0
Movement Grades/Jewels= 605/15, 605A/17 (Arlington), 607/17 (Hawthorne)
Seconds at = 6
Dial Number = 8073

Dials = Silver Finish, Sparkle Finish
Dial Opening = Rectangular
Dial Variations/Rarity = ⏲⏲⏲ Silver Finish, Black Numerals; Sparkle Finish, Luminous Numerals
Numerals = Painted, Luminous
Hands = Steel, Luminous
Cased in Factory = Yes
Unique Case Design = No
Unique Dial Design = No
Introduction Date = 1931 (Arlington), 1932 (Hawthorne)
Retail Price New = $37.50
Collectibility = ⏲⏲⏲⏲
Advertisements = Yes
Marketing Theme = "Has the appearance of a much more expensive watch" (Arlington)
"Very up-to-date model" (Hawthorne)

The Arlington/Hawthorne was one of the few tank-shaped wristwatch cases sold by Illinois. It has a very thick and strong-looking bezel that, unfortunately, is still prone to bezel wear. Its case, either white or yellow gold-filled, is one of two models made by J. Milhening for Illinois (the other model is the Andover/Exeter).

This watch, with a crisp, excellent dial in either silver or sparkle finish, makes for a very striking watch which as yet is much underappreciated by the collector world.

The Arlington, equipped with a 15-jewel movement, appeared in the 1931–32 Illinois Sales Catalog. It was also included in an Illinois advertisement in the December 12, 1931 issue of the *Saturday Evening Post.*

A. C. Becken 1932 catalog

The Hawthorne, however, is something of a puzzle. First of all, though introduced a year *after* the Arlington, it was equipped with a 17-jewel movement rather than a 15-jewel one. This is the exact opposite of Illinois' usual pattern when making a small change in an existing model and relisting it as a "new" model with a different name. Moreover, although given a higher-grade movement, the Hawthorne had exactly the same retail price as the Arlington: a Depression-era bargain price of $37.50.

Another strange detail is that a model named Hawthorne does not appear in any Illinois Sales Catalog or Materials Catalog that we have located. And although we have found this model listed in two jobbers' catalogs (as shown), the listing is not part of an Illinois Factory-issued advertising page.

Both the Arlington and the Hawthorne appear on the Illinois Watch Company Materials Department's List of Cased Illinois Watches by Size, dated December 1, 1932, but only the Arlington is included in the June 6, 1933 Master List—Case Control Sheet. A dial for the Arlington is included in the 1936 Hamilton-issued Illinois Materials Catalog, but without a mention of its sibling.

It is interesting that both Arlington and Hawthorne were the names of horse racing tracks in Illinois. Jacob Bunn, Jr. was an investor in several harness tracks (perhaps prompting these names). In addition, Hawthorne was the area of Springfield where the Bunns lived.

Hawthorne listing in N. Shure 1933 catalog

Arlington original price card

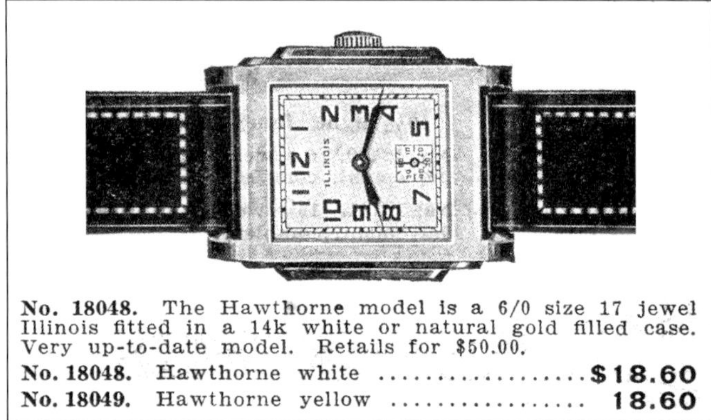

Holsman's Jewelry Drummer 1932–33 catalog, showing wholesale price

Armored Case / Integrated Guard / Cut Bezel

Armored Case, cushion (unpolished sterling silver)

Armored case, round (unpolished sterling silver)

Official Name = Armored Case (derived from a September 26, 1917 Fahys advertisement in the *Jewelers' Circular*)

Secondary Name(s) = Cut Bezel (derived from collectors' usage), Integrated Guard (derived from collectors usage)

Formerly Known As = Shrapnel Guard

Time Period = Transitional

Case Variations/Rarity = 🕒🕒 N, So
🕒🕒🕒 SS/Round
🕒🕒🕒🕒 SS/Cushion
🕒🕒🕒🕒🕒 Non-Std Cut-Out
🕒🕒🕒🕒🕒🕒 YGF/Round; RGF/Round; SS/Off-Set Crown

Case Durability = 🕒🕒🕒🕒

Material = SS, GF, N, So

Bezel = Plain

Sides = Plain

Lugs = Plain

Lug Size = 16mm, 18mm

Springbar = Fixed Lugs, Swivel Lugs

Casemakers = Fahys, IWCCo

Case Closure = 3-Part Snap-On Bezel and Back Case (Cushion), 4-Part in Round

Case Number = None

Case Shape = Round, Cushion

Case Back = Flat

Dimensions = 40 x 33mm in Round, 40 x 32mm in Cushion

Movement Sizes = 0, 3/0

Movement Grades/Jewels = 37/17, 38/17, 39/17, 24/17, 36/17

Seconds at = 6

Dial Number = 106A

Dials = Silver Finish, Enamel

Dial Opening = Round

Dial Variations/Rarity = 🕒 Silver Finish, Luminous Numerals
🕒🕒 Enamel, Painted Numerals

Numerals = Painted, Luminous

Hands = Steel

Cased in Factory = No

Unique Case Design = No

Unique Dial Design = No

Introduction Date = 1917

Retail Price New = Unknown

Collectibility = 🕒🕒🕒🕒

Advertisements = Yes
The Armored Case was advertised by Fahys in the September 26, 1917 issue of the *Jewelers' Circular.*

Marketing Themes = "An Armored Case for The Soldier"
"A brand new idea that makes the wrist watch doubly practical"

A FAHYS FIRST

The Armored Case, released by Joseph Fahys & Co., was the first case to integrate the "crystal guard" or "watch protector," as it was called then (not "shrapnel guard") directly into the case as part of it. This guard would snap directly onto an outer ring around the bezel or, if the case was semi-hermetic, screw into place.

The four pieces of a round Armored Case

The Armored Case is a highly popular military Transitional Period wristwatch, introduced towards the end of 1917 as the Great War was winding down. According to its advertisement, the round case version came only in 3/0 size, whereas the Cushion version came in either 3/0 or 0 size cases. (However, Czubernat advises that the advertisement is not entirely correct; both cases are available in 0 and 3/0 size).

When the advertisement was issued by Fahys, only the round case was available for sale in 3/0 size. The cut-out bezel served as a crystal guard or shrapnel protective guard. According to its promotion, the case was "made in Sterling Silver only, in the round and cushion styles, and is sold only with Khaki strap as illustrated, in individual boxes." Fahys advertised this model as an "Armored Protected Front, Watch Case."

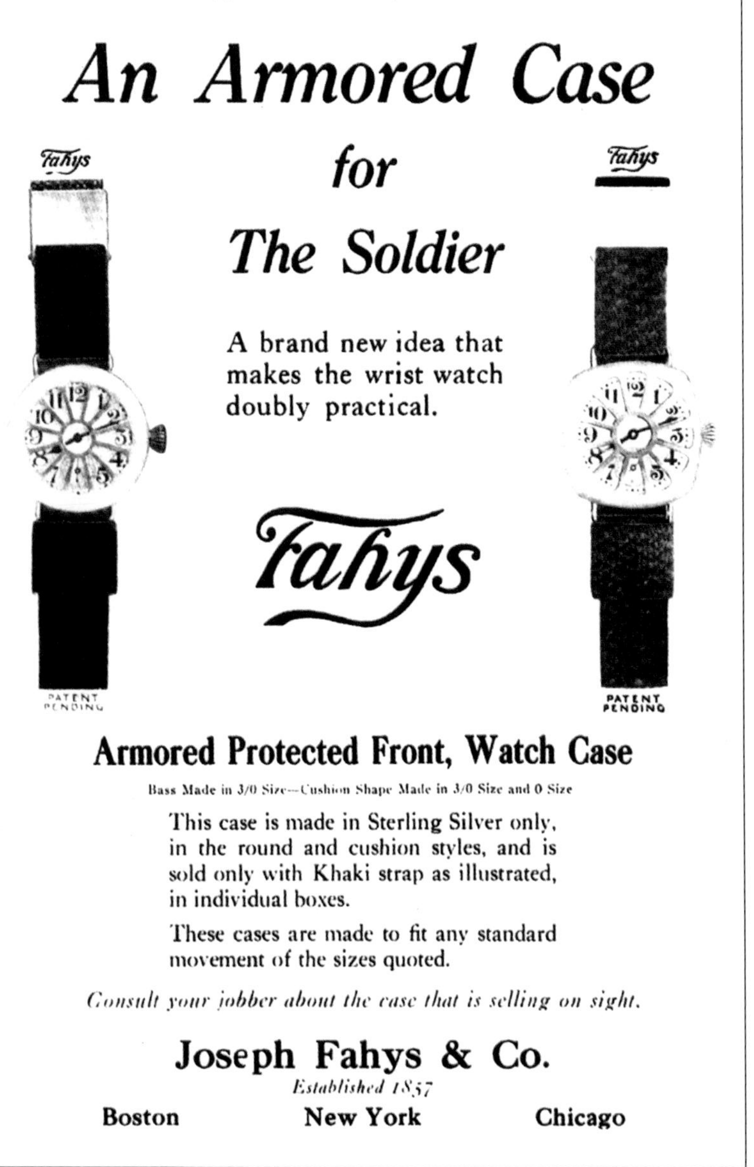

Jewelers' Circular, **September 26, 1917**

The majority of these models are found in round sterling silver cases. Fahys sold these watches only in sterling and silverode cases. These models are much rarer in 0 size.

The cut-out portion came in several variations; the cut-out with the double bars across the middle is the rarest and more desirable configuration to collect. The Armored Case is easier to find in a round case configuration than the cushion shape. The Armored Case was offered for sale with Elgin, Waltham or Illinois movements and dials, but the Illinois watches command higher prices today. To date, only three Armored Cases with off-set crowns have been located. These are considered quite rare and valuable.

In addition to the various Armored Case watches shown in advertisements, a yellow gold-filled round Armored Case cased by the IWCCo, with attached swivel lugs, has been found; this is the first specimen of its sort to be seen. Another rarity is a round Integrated Guard Case in rose gold-filled that has been located—the only one to date that has surfaced, made by IWCCo in a semi-hermetic "threaded" case.

FRAUD ALERT

Currently, there is at least one disreputable watch seller that is skillful enough to fabricate an Armored Case wristwatch using sterling silverware. He melts down silverware and turns it into Armored Cases. At times, he shapes it into very unusual cut-outs that are not shown in any old advertisement. It is possible that the inside case backs do not have the usual markings that such a case would ordinarily have. The best protection from this fraud is to buy an Armored Case from a reputable dealer or friend.

Please note: The perpetrator of this fraud has sold his work on eBay, so be vigilant.

A rare 10K yellow gold-filled Integrated Guard watch with swivel lugs

Armored Case, sterling silver cut-out with double bar

A United States World War I soldier wearing a Transitional Period military wristwatch with an attached shrapnel guard

UNITED STATES PATENT OFFICE.

GILBRETH BROWN, OF PROVIDENCE, RHODE ISLAND, ASSIGNOR TO THE E. A. POTTER CO., OF PROVIDENCE, RHODE ISLAND, A CORPORATION OF RHODE ISLAND.

DESIGN FOR A WATCHCASE-PROTECTOR.

51,298. Specification for Design. **Patented Sept. 25, 1917.**

Application filed July 30, 1917. Serial No. 183,632. Term of patent 3½ years.

To all whom it may concern:

Be it known that I, GILBRETH BROWN, a citizen of the United States, residing at the city of Providence, county of Providence, State of Rhode Island, have invented a new, original, and ornamental Design for a Watchcase-Protector, of which the following is a specification, reference being had to the accompanying drawing, forming part thereof.

Figure 1, is a plan view of a watchcase protector and Fig. 2 is an edge view illustrating my new design.

I claim:

The ornamental design for a watch case protector as shown.

GILBRETH BROWN.

Copies of this patent may be obtained for five cents each, by addressing the "Commissioner of Patents, Washington, D. C."

"US" shrapnel guard patent

US shrapnel guard, a rare shrapnel guard with "US" on its face. Its patent is shown on the left.

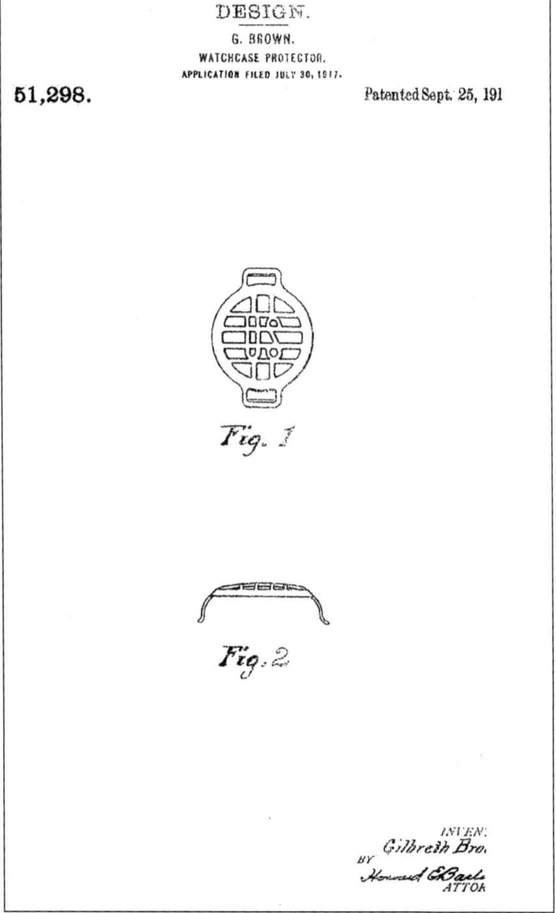

DESIGN.
G. BROWN.
WATCHCASE PROTECTOR.
APPLICATION FILED JULY 30, 1917.

51,298. Patented Sept. 25, 191

Fig. 1

Fig. 2

INVEN:
Gilbreth Bro.
BY
Howard E. Barlow
ATTOR

"US" shrapnel guard patent

Atlantic / Riley / Atlantic Large

Official Name = Atlantic (derived from Fahys and IWCCo 1926 advertisements)
Secondary Name(s) = Riley (derived from IWCCo advertisements)
Formerly Known As = Prince (derived from early price guides)
Time Period = Generic
Case Variations/Rarity = ◷ WGF/P, WGF/E
◷◷ GGF/P, GGF/E
◷◷◷ BM/P, BM/E
◷◷◷◷ TT/Large
◷◷◷◷◷ BM/EE
Material = 14K GF, BM
Bezel = Plain, Engraved, EE
Sides = Plain, Engraved
Lugs = Plain/Engraved
Lug Size = 16mm
Springbar = Male
Casemakers = Fahys, IWCCo, Wadsworth, Others
Case Closure = 3-Part Snap-On Bezel and Back
Case Number = None
Case Shape = Tonneau
Case Back = Curved
Dimensions = 38 x 31mm
Movement Size = 3/0
Movement Grades/Jewels = 21/11, 24/17
Seconds at = 6
Dial Numbers = 110, 4110, 8110, 8290
Dials = Silver Finish, Butler Center
Dial Opening = Tonneau
Dial Variations/Rarity = ◷◷ Silver Finish, Luminous Numerals
◷◷◷◷ Silver Finish, Center Cross
Numerals = Painted, Luminous
Hands = Luminous
Cased in Factory = No
Unique Case Design = No
Unique Dial Design = No
Introduction Date = 1926
Retail Price New = Unknown
Collectibility = ◷◷◷
Advertisements = Yes
The Atlantic case was advertised by Fahys in the *Jewelers' Circular* on April 13, 1926. The case was also advertised by the IWCCo in the *Jewelers' Circular* dated October 4, 1928.
Marketing Themes = "A big successful seller based on outstanding merit"
"Style can be seen at a glance, but quality is the hidden value."

Atlantic, white gold-filled

Atlantic, white gold-filled

Atlantic Large, two-tone

Fahys filed its case patent for the Atlantic on June 24, 1925, and the patent was issued on November 17, 1925.

The Fahys cases for the Atlantic came in white or green 14K gold-filled. The Atlantic cases were prone to noticeable wear on case corners, as well as along the outside edges of the case backs. The Atlantic is more difficult to find in green gold-filled cases. There is a two-tone version of this watch with a larger center section that sticks out from the sides of the bezel and case back, making this variant very interesting. This model is called an Atlantic Large.

It is still possible to find NOS dials for this model with butler center subsidiary second rings. This model also came with private-label signed movements and dials. Examples of these private-label names are: Master, Masterbilt, Captain and Illinois Central. These private-label models command higher prices and are more collectible. (This model, in its basic configuration, is fairly easy to obtain.)

Atlantic, white gold-filled, private-label dial

Atlantic, green gold-filled private label dial

3/0 size 14k white or green gold filled case, engraved bezel, Atlantic shape, fitted with the following luminous dialed movements:

R10256½	15J	Elgin	**Each $52.00**
R10257½	15J	Waltham	**Each 52.00**
R10258½	17J	Illinois	**Each 55.00**

Generic Atlantic, 1927 Carson Pirie Scott catalog

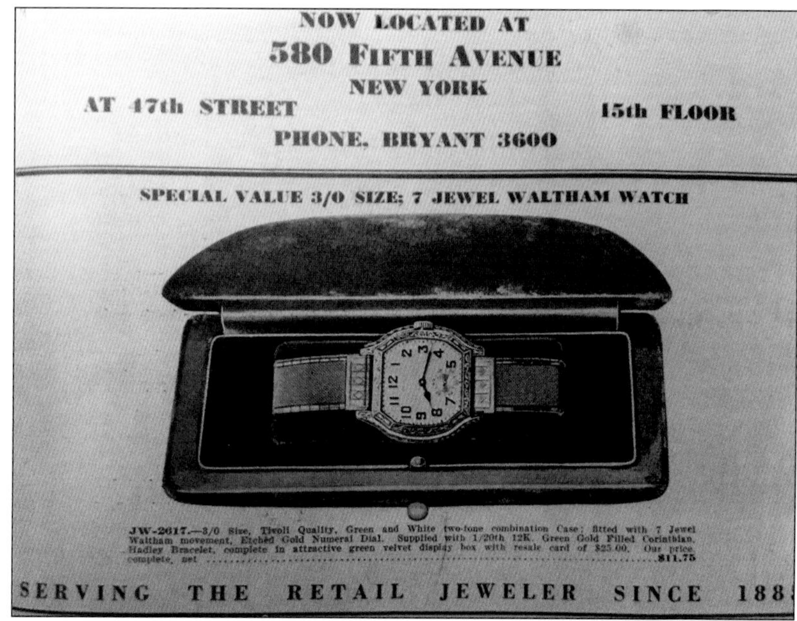

Aisenstein-Woronock, an Illinois jobber, advertised an Atlantic Large with a Waltham dial and movement in 1926.

ATLANTIC ENAMEL / ATLANTIC ENAMEL, JR.

Official Name = Atlantic Enamel (derived from April and November 1926 Joseph Fahys & Co. advertisements in the *Jewelers' Circular*)
Secondary Name(s) = None
Formerly Known As = Prince (derived from early price guides)
Time Period = Generic
Case Variations/Rarity = 🕒🕒🕒🕒 WGF/EE
🕒🕒🕒🕒🕒 GGF/EE
🕒🕒🕒🕒🕒🕒 WGF/EE (JR)
Case Durability = 🕒🕒🕒
Material = 14K GF
Bezel = Engraved, Black Enamel
Sides = Plain
Lugs = Plain
Lug Size = 16mm
Springbar = Male
Casemaker = Fahys
Case Closure = 3-Part Snap-On Bezel and Back
Case Number = None
Case Shape = Tonneau
Case Back = Curved
Dimensions = 38 x 31mm
Movement Sizes = 3/0, 6/0
Movement Grades/Jewels = 21/11, 24/17
Seconds at = 6
Dial Numbers = 8110, 8290
Dial = Silver Finish
Dial Opening = Tonneau
Dial Variations/Rarity = 🕒 Silver Finish, Luminous Numerals
🕒🕒🕒 Silver Finish, Center Cross
Numerals = Painted, Luminous
Hands = Luminous
Cased in Factory = No
Unique Case Design = No
Unique Dial Design = No
Introduction Date = 1926
Retail Price New = Unknown
Collectibility = 🕒🕒🕒
Advertisements = Yes
The Atlantic Enamel was advertised by Fahys in both the *Jewelers' Circular* and the *Keystone* in September 1927.
Marketing Theme = "The Atlantic Case is a Big Successful Seller Based on Outstanding Merit."

Atlantic Enamel, white gold-filled

Atlantic Enamel, green gold-filled

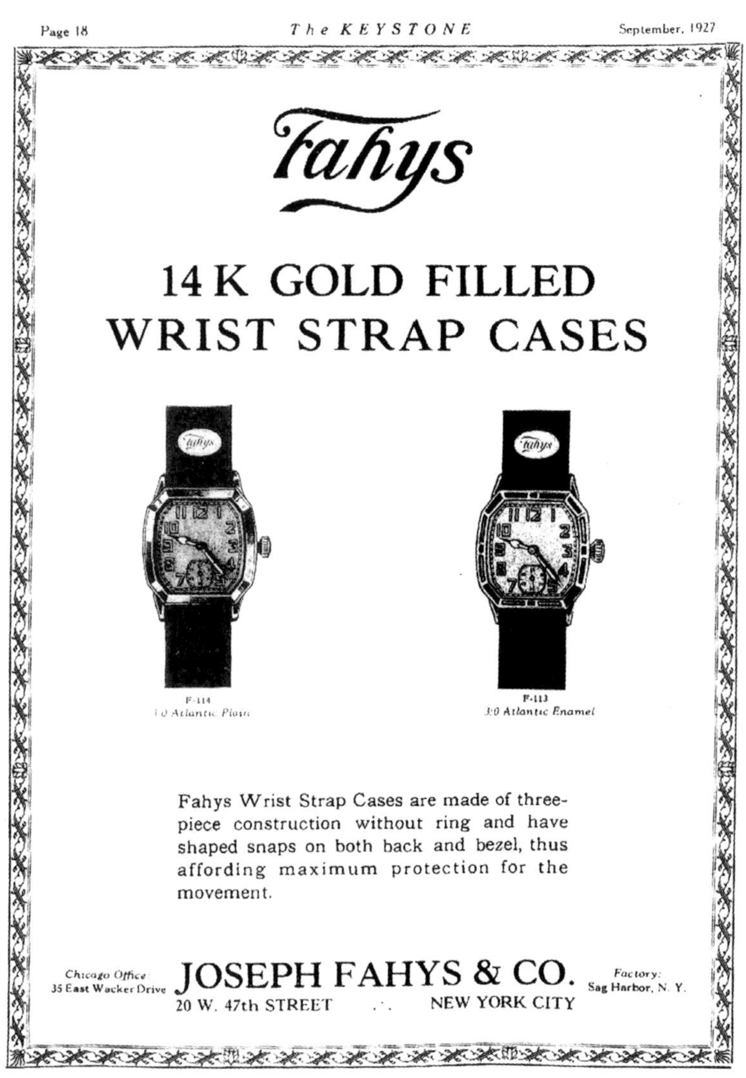

***Keystone*, September 1927**

Atlantic Enamel, Jr., white gold-filled

Atlantic Enamel, special enamel design

Fahys stated that "Fahys Wrist Strap Cases are made of three-piece construction without ring and have shaped snaps on both back and bezel, thus affording maximum protection for the movement."

The Atlantic Enamel came only in white gold-filled or green gold-filled cases. The green gold-filled model is more difficult to locate.

The Atlantic Enamel, Jr. is a very rare version of this model in 6/0 size; only four of these attractive versions have been spotted to date. The Atlantic Enamel, Jr. was advertised by Elgin in the December 15, 1927 issue of the *Jewelers' Circular*. The advertisement noted: "This strap watch may be had in a variety of 14-karat gold-filled cases—plain, engraved or enameled."

The Atlantic dial is listed in the Illinois Materials Catalog, but the Atlantic model, as a Generic watch, is not contained in the List of Factory Cased Illinois Watches. The Atlantic Enamel is a more appealing and enhanced version of the far more common Atlantic model.

Aviator

Burlington, sterling silver

Aviator, yellow gold-filled

Official Name = Aviator (derived from a February 1918 advertisement in *Outing* magazine)
Secondary Name(s) = Burlington
Formerly Known As = Military
Time Period = Transitional
Case Variations/Rarity = 🕒🕒 SS/P
🕒🕒🕒🕒 YGF
Case Durability = 🕒🕒🕒 YGF
🕒🕒🕒🕒 SS
Material = SS, 14K YGF
Bezel = Plain
Sides = Plain
Lugs = Plain
Lug Size = 16mm
Springbar = Fixed Lugs
Casemaker = NAWCo, IWCCo, Fahys, Others
Case Closure = 3-part Snap-On Bezel and Back
Case Number = None
Case Shape = Cushion
Case Back = Flat
Dimensions = 28 x 28mm
Movement Size = 3/0
Movement Grades/Jewels = 21/11, 24/17, 32/11, 36/17
Seconds at = 6
Dial Numbers = None
Dials = Enamel, Silver Finish
Dial Opening = Round
Dial Variations/Rarity = 🕒🕒 Enamel, Painted Numerals; Silver Finish, Painted Numerals
Numerals = Painted, Luminous
Hands = Steel, Luminous
Cased in Factory = No
Unique Case Design = No
Unique Dial Design = No
Introduction Date = 1918
Retail Price New = Unknown
Collectibility = 🕒🕒🕒
Advertisements = Yes
The Aviator was advertised in *Popular Mechanics* in 1917 and the February 1918 issue of *Outing* magazine.
Marketing Themes = "A Real Man's Wrist Watch"
"Built for Aviators"

The 1917 advertisement proclaimed: "The day of the wrist watch is here! A wrist watch is part of every officer's equipment in the European armies. Practically every officer in the U.S. army wears one. *It has been proven the most convenient watch in the world.*"

The advertisement claimed that this model "was built for aviators and is adjusted to keep time to the second anywhere. 17 jewels—finest nickel movement. Square design. Clear, distinct military dial. Extra heavy hands. Buckles with sturdy pig skin strap that cannot slip."

In the 1918 advertisement the Aviator was touted as being fitted with a radium dial, "the same as is used on the very best scientific instruments."

Aviator's Wrist Watch

Just out! The new Burlington Wrist Watch is ready for distribution for the first time.

The day of the wrist watch is here! A wrist watch is part of every officer's equipment in the European armies. Practically every officer in the U. S. army wears one. *It has been proven the most convenient watch in the world.*

And here is the Aviator's model. This New Burlington was built for aviators and is adjusted to keep time to the second anywhere. 17 jewels—finest nickel movement. Square design. Clear, distinct, military dial. Extra heavy hands. Buckles with sturdy pig skin strap that cannot slip. Designed especially for aviators and is the favorite of aviators everywhere.

See It First

You don't pay a cent to anybody until you see the watch. We will send you this master watch without a cent down. If you decide to buy it—you pay *only* the rock-bottom price—the same price that even the wholesale jeweler must pay. Strap it on your wrist and then realize the satisfaction and convenience of a *man's* wrist watch.

Only $2.50 a Month

Just think of it! $2.50 a month—less than ten cents a day will pay, at the rock-bottom price, for the master watch. This perfect time-piece will be sent direct to you, without a cent deposit so that you can see and examine it for yourself. When you hold it in your hand you will realize what a gigantic value it is—and you will know how the Burlington has brought the highest watch value within the reach of all.

Send the Coupon for FREE Watch Book

Get the Burlington Watch Book by sending this coupon now. You will know a lot more about watch buying when you read it. You will know why a man who has become accustomed to the convenience of a wrist watch would never go without one again. Read what makes a watch movement perfect. Send the coupon today for book and our special offer. Mail it now.

Burlington Watch Co. 19th and Marshall Boulevard, Dept. 7955, Chicago, Ill.

BURLINGTON WATCH COMPANY,
Dept. 7955, 19th and Marshall Blvd.,
Chicago, Illinois.

Please send me (without obligation and prepaid) your free book on watches with full explanation of your cash or $2.50 a month offer on the Burlington Watch.

Name ....

Flying, May 1917

A 1918 magazine advertisement for Burlington

The same issue of *Outing* featured a brief editorial about the Aviator entitled "A Masculine Watch," which included an illustration of the watch (with its band installed incorrectly).

The Aviator could be ordered directly by mail from the Burlington Watch Company, based in Chicago. Burlington was the Illinois Watch Company's largest private-label customer. Other major Illinois private label customers for the Illinois Watch Company included Montgomery Ward, Marshall Field, Santa Fe Watch Company, Sears and Roebuck, and the R. H. Macy Company.

Burlington almost always cased its Illinois "Burlington"-signed movements and dials in its own Burlington-signed cases. The Burlington wristwatches were usually triple-signed. Some of the Burlington cases were made for it by the North American Watch Company. The Aviator is usually found in a sterling silver cushion-shaped case, but some yellow gold-filled cases are occasionally seen. An Aviator has never been found in a yellow solid gold case, although the editorial noted above stated that it was available "in either gold or silver." Certainly, advertisements by casemakers that supplied Burlington with cases for the Aviator show that some of them, such as IWCCo, were making similar military cases in 14K gold.

This model is also called an Admiral Benson when equipped with an Illinois movement and dial.

Aviator, with Burlington signed movement

Aviator, inside Burlington case back

Baronet, white gold

Baronet, yellow gold

Baronet

Official Name = Baronet (derived from Illinois advertisements and Illinois Sales and Material Catalogs)
Secondary Name(s) = None
Formerly Known As = None
Time Period = Moderne
Case Variations/Rarity = ◷◷◷ YG/P
◷◷◷◷ WG/P
Case Durability = ◷◷◷◷
Material = 14K WG, YG
Bezel = Plain
Sides = Plain, Engraved
Lugs = Plain
Lug Sizes = 16mm, 19mm
Springbar = Male
Casemaker = Keystone
Case Closure = 3-Part Snap-On Bezel and Back; 2-Part Snap-On Back
Case Numbers = 220, 625, No Number
Case Shape = Rectangular
Case Back = Flat
Dimensions = 34 x 27mm
Movement Size = 6/0
Movement Grades/Jewels = 605/15, 607/17, 601/21
Seconds at = 6
Dial Numbers = 8209, 8725*, 8743*, 8748* (*Designed by Hamilton)
Dials = Silver Finish, Sparkle Finish, Sterling Silver
Dial Opening = Rectangular
Dial Variations/Rarity = ◷◷ Sparkle Finish, Applied Gold Numerals
◷◷◷ Silver Finish, Black Numerals; Silver Finish, Etched Numerals; Sterling Silver, Applied Gold Numerals
◷◷◷◷ Sparkle Finish, Black Numerals
◷◷◷◷◷◷◷◷ Sterling Silver, Etched Gold Markers
Numerals = Painted, Etched, Applied Gold Numerals (18K), Gold Markers
Hands = Steel
Cased in Factory = Yes
Unique Case Design = No
Unique Dial Design = No
Introduction Date = 1930
Retail Price New = $60.00 (15J); $75.00 (17J); $100.00 (21J)
Collectibility = ◷◷◷◷
Advertisements = Yes
Marketing Themes = "Finest strap watch value"
"A watch of artistic merit"
"The finest strap watch a man may own"

Illinois advertisement announcing its Baronet model, *Keystone*, October 1930

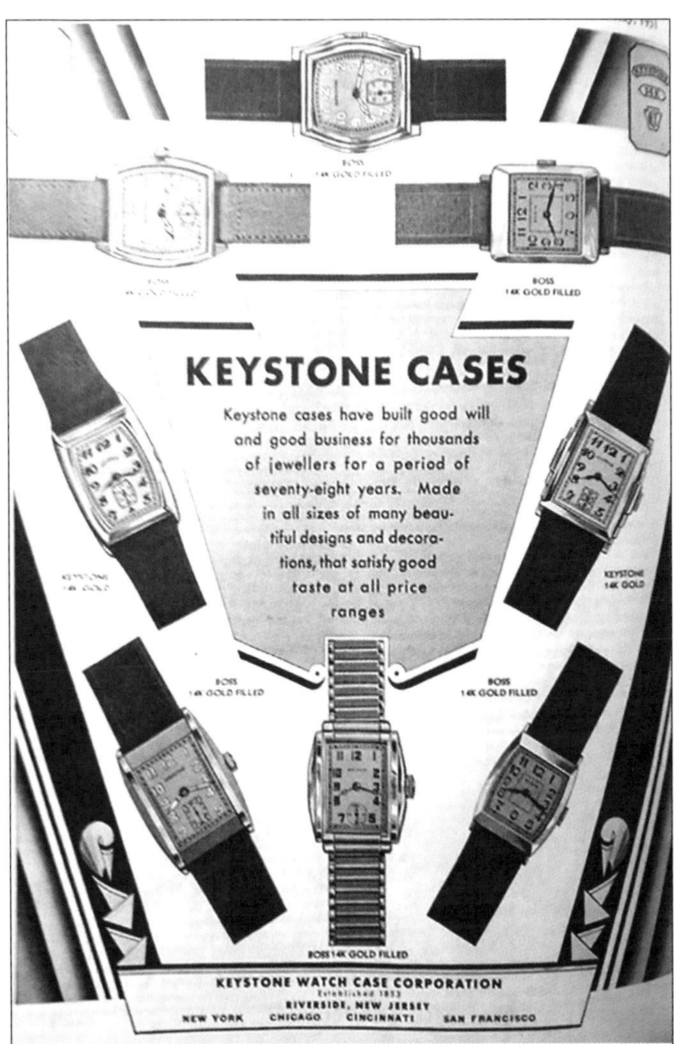

Keystone advertisement showing the solid gold Rockliffe and Baronet, May 1930

The Baronet was one of the very few solid gold men's wristwatches offered for sale by Illinois. The Baronet came with two different case Model Numbers (220 and 625) as well as one version without a model number. There are certain Baronet cases that have an extra ridge on the bezel, which gives even more definition to the case. Some models' original cases came with large, thick, domed "Rock Crystals." The Baronet was one of nine Illinois models offered with the prestigious 21-jewel, motor barrel, 6/0 size movement. The Baronet is more difficult to find in white gold than yellow gold. This model is one of the most popular and highly sought-after Illinois men's wristwatches.

Interestingly, most yellow gold models came with two-part cases and most of the white gold versions came in three- part ones. All cases were made by Keystone. The watches in case Model No. 220 are usually three-piece cases and white gold, while those in case Model No. 625 usually have two-piece cases and are yellow gold. The white gold cases usually have 19mm lugs and the yellow gold ones usually have 16mm lugs. Furthermore, the yellow gold cases with case numbers have no straight lines engraved on their case sides but the yellow gold cases with no case Model Numbers do have engraved sides.

Baronet with case Model No. 220

Baronet with case Model No. 625

Baronet no case Model Number

Advertisements for the Baronet appeared in jobbers' catalogs and in national magazines as well as in Illinois Sales Catalogs. In the 1930–31 Illinois catalog, where it was introduced, it was advertised with a 21-jewel movement and had a retail price of $100.00. The following year it was also offered with a 17-jewel movement and priced at $75.00 retail. By 1934, Hamilton was busy liquidating Illinois inventory; for its last appearance, the Baronet was issued in 1935 with a 15-jewel movement and retailed for only $60.00, as noted in the L. & C. Mayers 1935 catalog.

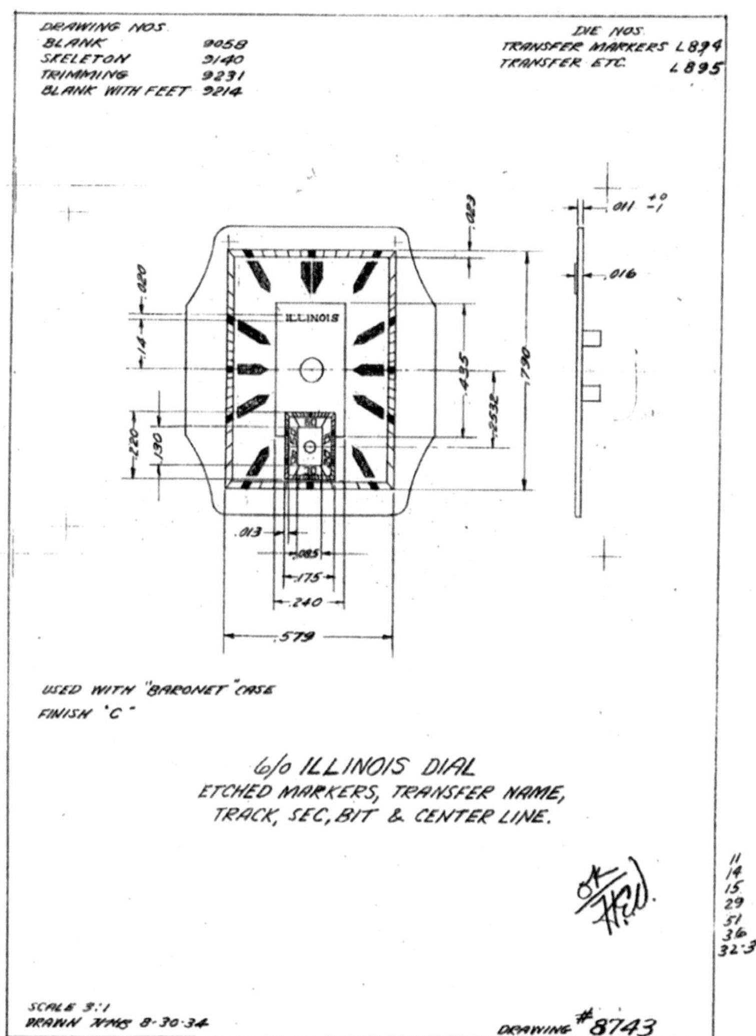

Hamilton drawing of an Illinois Baronet dial, dated August 30, 1934, showing etched gold markers. One Baronet has been found with this dial. It is shown on the next page.

The Hamilton watch drawings for dial numbers 8725, 8743, and 8748 were intended for the rerelease of the Illinois Baronet in 1935. Some of these dials appear in 1935 or later jobbers' catalogues.

Look-Alikes

The Baronet and the Hamilton Putnam are somewhat similar in appearance. The Baronet was issued in 1930 and the Putnam in 1932. The Baronet is solid gold and was available in white gold or yellow gold. The Putnam was available in 14K white or yellow gold-filled cases. The Baronet case was made by Keystone and the Putnam case by Wadsworth.

The Hamilton-designed Baronet dial with gold markers

The BARONET
21 Jewels

The finest strap watch value—reflecting the modern design in case construction. The Baronet is a watch of artistic merit. The dial is sterling silver with 18K applied numerals. 14K solid white and natural gold.
Suggested consumer price, $100.

A. I. Hall catalog, 1930–31

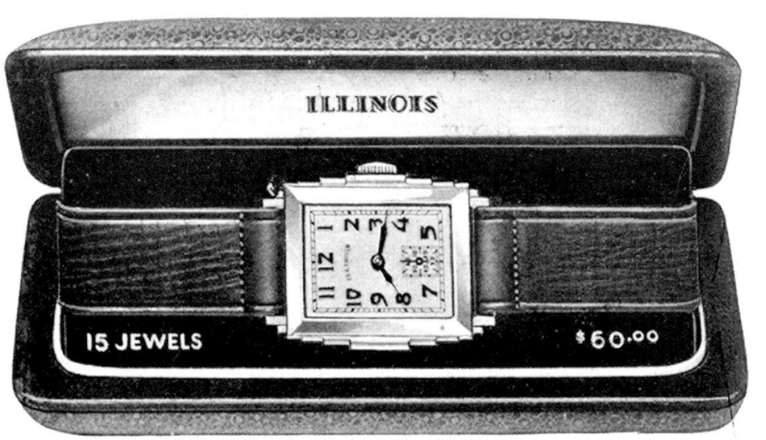

THE BARONET—BY ILLINOIS

DW1298 Illinois Baronet; 14 kt. Solid Yellow Gold, 15 Jewels.................... **$62.50**
DW1299 Illinois Baronet; 14 kt. Solid White Gold, 15 Jewels.................... **62.50**

Retails for $60.00

A plain dignified style by Keystone. 14 kt. solid gold, substantial weight, bright finish, step effect. Fitted with the famous Illinois 6/0 size 15 jewel movement. Stylish dial, embossed gilt numerals. Detachable fine leather straps, buckles same quality as cases. Cased, timed and regulated at the factory. Attractive presentation box.

L. & C. Mayers catalog, 1935

Illinois Baronet

Hamilton Putnam

Illinois Baronet case back

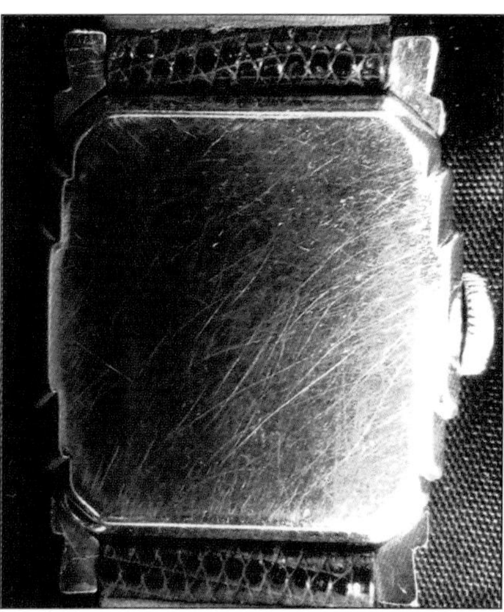

Hamilton Putnam case back

Baronet dial with etched gold numerals

End of outer card box for a Baronet model with 15 jewels and yellow markers

FANTASTIC FIND

An anonymous collector from California points out that “The Illinois solid gold Baronet is one of the more coveted watches in the Illinois series. The seller on an auction site offered a dark photograph of a watch without a watchband, but by the distinct outline and the raised gold numerals it appeared to be an Illinois Baronet or a close facsimile. The seller also forgot to describe the material composition of the watch case, making it difficult to determine if this might have just been a Baronet in a look-alike case. The watch was sitting at $50.00 with just minutes to go. Suddenly the price moved, but not far. Apparently someone else had the same suspicions as I. I decided to take a shot at it at $300.00 and found that I had won the watch for $286.00. Of course, as soon as I received the watch in the mail, I opened the case to determine whether this was actually a solid gold Baronet case and check its case Model Number. Imagine my surprise and joy when I found out that I had actually won this Baronet on the site for $286.00.”

Beau Brummell / Beau Royale

Beau Brummell, white gold-filled

Beau Brummell, two-tone gold-filled

Official Names = Beau Brummell and Beau Royale (if it has 17 or more jewels, Beau Brummell; Beau Royale if it has 15 jewels) (derived from Illinois advertisements, including but not limited to the November 10, 1928 issue of the *Saturday Evening Post* and the September 7, 1929 issue of *Collier's*)
Secondary Name(s) = None
Formerly Known As = Collectors earlier called the model with the Southwestern Indian motif the Beau Brummell and the model with the ropelike engraving around the bezel the Beau Royale.
Time Period = Deco
Case Variations/Rarity = ◷◷ WGF/E
◷◷◷ YGF/E
◷◷◷◷ GGF/E
◷◷◷◷◷ WGF/P, TT/E
◷◷◷◷◷◷ YGF/P, GGF/P
Case Durability = ◷◷◷
Material = 14K GF
Bezel = Plain, Engraved
Sides = Plain, Engraved
Lugs = Plain
Lug Size = 16mm
Springbar = Male
Casemaker = Fahys
Case Closure = 3-Part Snap-On Bezel and Back
Case Number = Special Model C
Case Shape = Tonneau
Case Back = Curved
Dimensions = 38 x 28mm
Movement Size = 6/0
Movement Grades/Jewels = 605/15, 903/15, 607/17, 905/17, 909/21
Seconds at = 6, 9
Dial Numbers = 8064, 8135, 8200, 8730
Dials = Silver Finish, Butler Center, Two-Tone
Dial Opening = Tonneau
Dial Variations/Rarity = ◷◷ Silver Finish, Luminous Numerals
◷◷◷ Silver Finish, Silver Butler Center;
◷◷◷◷ Silver Finish, Gold Butler Center
◷◷◷◷◷ Silver Finish, Black Numerals; Silver Finish, Gold Butler Center, Two-Tone Gold
◷◷◷◷◷◷◷ Silver Finish, Luminous Blue Numerals
Numerals = Painted, Luminous
Hands = Steel, Luminous
Cased in Factory = Yes

Beau Royale, green gold-filled, two-toned dial

Unique Case Design = Yes
Unique Dial Design = Yes
Introduction Date = 1928
Retail Price New = $35.00 (15J); $50.00 (17J); $60.00 (19J); $69.50 (21J)
Collectibility = 🕓🕓🕓🕓
Advertisements = Yes
Marketing Themes = "A tremendously popular design with young men"
"The greatest watch value for the consumer"
(Beau Royale)

The Beau Royale, which had a 15-jewel movement, was introduced in the 1931–32 Illinois Sales catalog on a page featuring 6/0 size watches with a "new low price range," priced at $35.00 retail, it was described as "the greatest watch value for the consumer."

These models appeared in a good number of Illinois' advertisements in most of the major national magazine publications of the era, such as the *Saturday Evening Post* and *Collier's*.

The 1929–1930 Illinois Factory Catalog had this listing for the Beau Brummell: "14K gold filled cases, curved back and bezel, supplied in plain or engraved white, natural, green or combination green center with white bezel and back, with 17 or 19 jewel movement and full figure luminous dial."

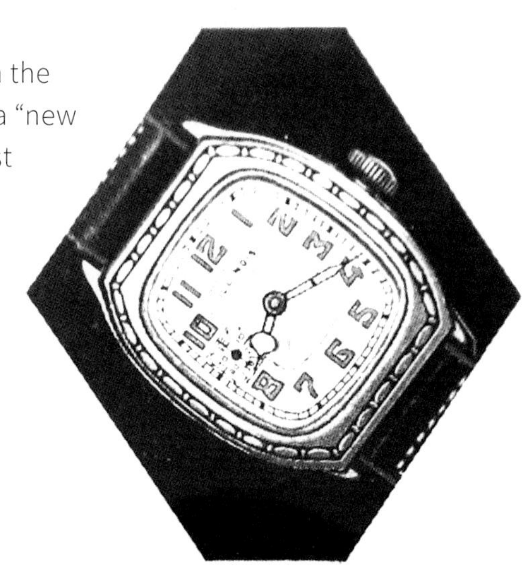

The Beau Brummell is style plus! Tailored to the wrist, the eye and the heart. It is one of those watches that improve with the wearing, creating new pride of possession each day. Illinois tradition underwrites its fine 17-jewel movement in beautiful 14k gold-filled case. $50.

Beau Brummell, one of the watches featured in a 1928 Illinois advertisement ("The Joy of Living")

Beau Brummell, green gold-filled, two-tone gold dial

Beau Brummell, green gold-filled, plain bezel

Beau Royale, two-tone, gold-filled

Illinois at times spelled Beau Brummell with one "L" but usually used two. This is a beautiful model if it can be found without its all-too-frequent corner bezel wear. The plain bezel white gold-filled model is difficult to find, and the green gold-filled plain bezel is nearly impossible to find (to date, only two have been sighted).

For this model, jewel count determined the name of the watch. With 15 jewels it was known as a Beau Royale, whether the bezel was plain or engraved, or whether the dial had subsidiary seconds at 6 or 9. Any model with above 15 jewels was called by Illinois a Beau Brummell, regardless of whether its bezel was plain or engraved, or whether subsidiary seconds were at 6 or 9. Both models are also difficult to find in two-tone cases.

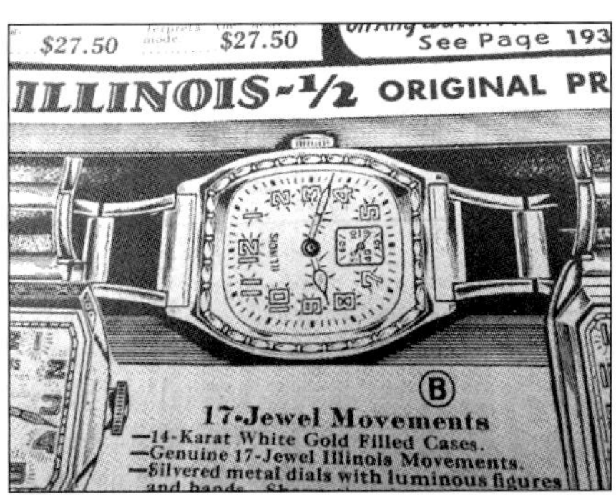

Montgomery Ward 1932–1933 catalog listing for a Depression-induced half-price Beau Brummell. Notice how the radium numerals are depicted.

Beau Brummell bezel close-up

The Beau Brummell wristwatch shown below has blue radium numerals on its dial. This version of the Beau Brummell was offered by John Garland in its wholesale catalog in 1930. It came in its blue Garland box with all of its paperwork. The Garland paperwork makes it clear that the watch was not being sold directly by Illinois, and the blue display box it came in was routinely marketed by Garland in its annual sales catalogs to jewelers.

A Beau Brummell with blue luminous numerals, offered in the John Garland Blue Book Catalog, with its own Garland Blue Book display box and paperwork.

Beau Brummell

Is Now On Display

We are now displaying the new Illinois Beau Brummell and we can readily recommend this dependable, sturdy strap model. Illinois watches are exclusively high grade and are entirely satisfactory. They not only carry our guarantee but the guarantee of the makers, The Illinois Watch of Springfield, Illinois. It is part of our store policy to sell only high quality merchandise that we can guarantee and the Beau Brummell is an excellent example of the policy maintained by us.

Beau Brummell paperwork

The BEAU BRUMMELL

A 17 jeweled watch made of the finest materials obtainable

Guaranteed by

THE ILLINOIS WATCH

SPRINGFIELD

Movement has been carefully rerated and timed in 14K Gold Filled Case

$50.00

Original price card for Beau Brummell sold by John Garland

The BEAU BRUMMELL

This watch is a tremendously popular design with young men. 14K white or natural filled gold, plain or engraved cases.

Suggested consumer price, $50.

A. I. Hall catalog, 1930–31

Look-Alikes

The Illinois Beau Brummell with a plain bezel is similar to a Hamilton Langley. The Beau Brummell was available in a 14K yellow gold-filled, white gold-filled, green gold-filled, or two-tone case, made by Fahys. The Langley is 14K, white or yellow gold in a three-part hinged case made by Solidarity. Around 1933, the Langley cases were made by Schwab & Wuischpard (S&W) in a two-part case version and came in 14K white or yellow gold. Five 18K cases were made for Tiffany & Company. The Beau Brummell was issued in 1928 and the Langley in 1929.

Illinois Beau Brummell, white gold-filled, plain bezel

Hamilton Langley

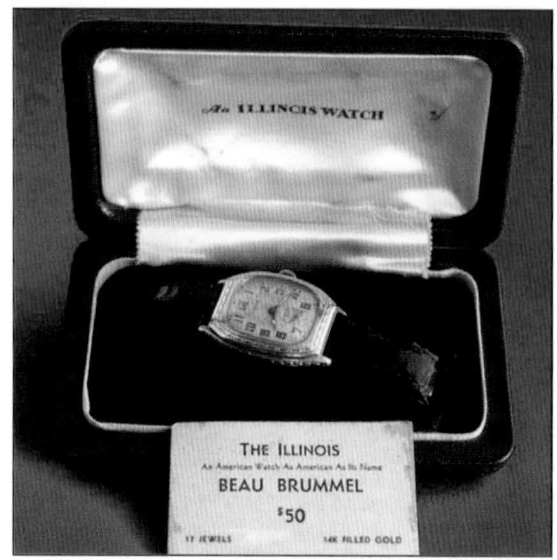

Beau Brummell with its original display box and price card

Holsman's Jewelry Drummer catalog 1932-33 with Depression-era wholesale prices

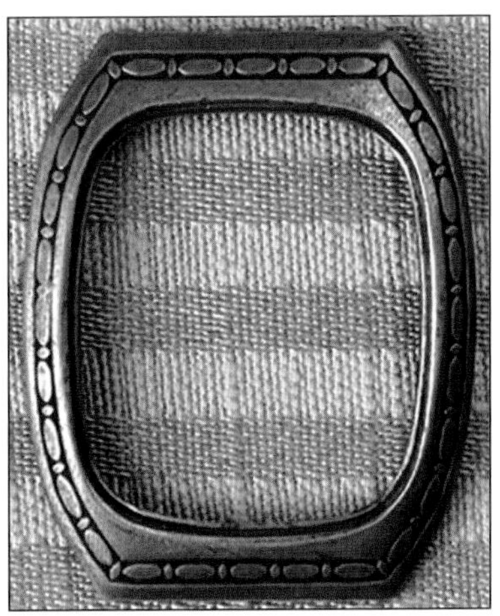

Beau Royale NOS bezel unpolished

WHY I COLLECT ILLINOIS

"I really don't collect Illinois wristwatches—I just like them due to their unusual shapes (Piccadilly, Locke, Jolly Roger, etc.), 'different' placement of the subsidiary second hand (New Yorker/Manhattan, Marquis, Chieftain, Beau Brummell and others). Many have three-part cases, and that adds to the uniqueness and collectibility of Illinois wristwatches. The quality of the mechanics of Illinois wristwatches is also above average." —*Marty Saeman*

Beau Brummell/Viking

Official Name = Beau Brummell/Viking (derived from collectors seeking to distinguish this model from the Beau Brummell/Beau Royale and the Viking models)
Secondary Name(s) = Beau Brummell (derived from a jobber's catalog)
Formerly Known As = None
Time Period = Deco
Case Variations/Rarity = ◷◷◷◷ WGF/M
◷◷◷◷◷ GGF/M
◷◷◷◷◷◷◷ WGF/GGF/TT/M
Case Durability = ◷◷
Material = 14K GF
Bezel = Molded
Sides = Plain
Lugs = Plain
Lug Size = 16mm
Springbar = Male
Casemaker = Fahys
Case Closure = 3-Part Snap-On Bezel and Back
Case Number = Special Model C
Case Shape = Tonneau
Case Back = Curved
Dimensions = 38 x 28mm
Movement Size = 6/0
Movement Grades/Jewels = 605/15, 903/15, 607/17, 905/17, 907/19, 909/21
Seconds at = 6, 9
Dial Numbers = 8064, 8135, 8200, 8730

Beau Brummell/Viking, white gold-filled

Beau Brummell/Viking, green gold-filled

Dials = Silver Finish, Butler Center, Two-Tone Gold
Dial Opening = Tonneau
Dial Variations/Rarity = 🕒🕒 Silver Finish, Luminous Numerals; Silver Finish, Silver Butler Center
🕒🕒🕒🕒 Silver Finish, Gold Butler Center
🕒🕒🕒🕒🕒 Silver Finish, Black Numerals; Silver Finish, Gold Butler Center, Two Tone Gold Dial
Numerals = Painted, Luminous
Hands = Steel, Luminous
Cased in Factory = Yes
Unique Case Design = Yes
Unique Dial Design = Yes
Introduction Date = 1928
Retail Price New = $70.80 (WGF/M); $70.80 (GGF/M)
Collectibility = 🕒🕒🕒🕒
Advertisements = Yes
Marketing Theme = "The best value in America"

ILLINOIS BEAU BRUMMEL
17 Jewel, Small 6/0 Size

The famous Illinois Beau Brummel in a very attractive case. Has accurate 17 jewel, 6/0 size, adjusted Illinois movement, fitted to the comfortably curved case that fits the wrist. Has silvered dial, luminous hands and numerals. Comes in your choice of Green or White 14K Gold Filled case. Please specify color when ordering.
5G21094 Specify color. PRICE................**$70.80**

John Plain catalog, 1930

This model was listed in the 1930 John Plain catalog as a Beau Brummell, but collectors over the years have come to call this model a Beau Brummell/Viking to distinguish it from the Beau Brummell/Beau Royale and the Viking models. Its molded bezel is similar to but not identical to its Viking cousin.

The John Plain catalog described the watch as follows: "The famous Illinois Beau Brummell in a very attractive case. Has accurate 17 jewel, 6/0 size, adjusted Illinois movement, fitted to the comfortably curved case that fits the wrist. Has silvered dial, luminous hands and numerals. Comes in your choice of Green or White, 14K Gold Filled case. . . . Price: $70.80." This advertisement also stated: "You will rarely see the Illinois Watch advertised. Yet in spite of this, the Illinois Watch Company manufactures more high-grade movements than any watch factory in the United States. This means that Illinois watches have won first place through sheer merit. Jewelers everywhere recommend them as the best value in America."

The dramatic and unusual bezel of this model is prone to severe case wear. This highly collectible model is difficult to find in white gold-filled/molded and much more difficult to find in green gold-filled/molded. Only one in a two-tone case is known to exist.

Beau Brummell/Viking, close-up of bezel

Both the Beau Brummell/Viking and the Viking (see later entry) sported similar molded designs in the bezel. The Viking, however, has the larger 3/0 size movement rather than the 6/0 size contained in the Beau Brummell/Viking model. It is a special watch of special value when the green gold-filled model can be found with the very special two-tone gold dial. To date, only one advertisement has been found for the Beau Brummell/Viking, and this model was called a "Beau Brummell" in the John Plain advertisement on the preceding page.

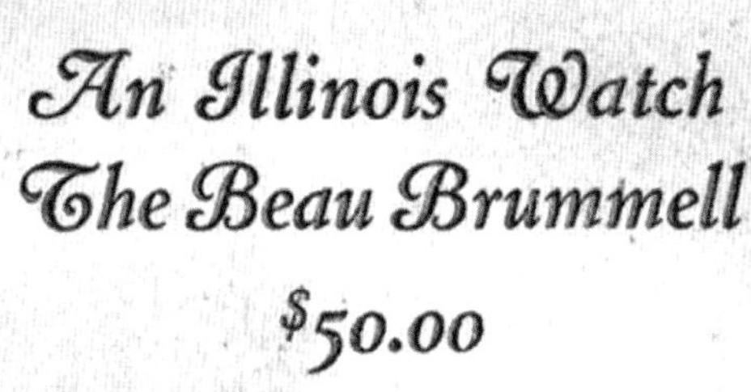

An Illinois Watch
The Beau Brummell
$50.00
17 Jewel Movement   14K Gold Filled Case

Beau Brummell original price card

Beau Brummell/Viking, two-tone white and green gold-filled. Only one is known to exist.

Beau Monde / Beau Geste

Beau Monde, white gold-filled, applied gold numerals

Official Names = Beau Monde and Beau Geste (This model is called a Beau Monde if it has a 17-jewel or 21-jewel movement and a Beau Geste if it has a 15-jewel movement; derived from Illinois advertisements and Illinois Sales and Material Catalogs)
Secondary Name(s) = None
Formerly Known As = None
Time Period = Deco
Case Variations/Rarity = 🕒🕒🕒 WGF/E
🕒🕒🕒🕒 YGF/E
🕒🕒🕒🕒🕒🕒🕒 WGF/Braille Hinged Bezel
Case Durability = 🕒🕒🕒🕒
Material = 14K GF
Bezel = Engraved
Sides = Engraved
Lugs = Plain

Beau Monde, yellow gold-filled, luminous numerals

Beau Monde, yellow gold-filled, painted numerals

Lug Size = 16mm
Springbar = Male
Casemaker = Keystone
Case Closure = 3-part Snap-On Bezel and Back; 2 Part, Hinged Bezel and Snap-On Back
Case Number = 212
Case Shape = Tonneau
Case Back = Curved
Dimensions = 37 x 27mm
Movement Size = 6/0
Movement Grades/Jewels = 605/15, 607/17, 601/21
Seconds at = 6
Dial Numbers = 8120, 8128, 8206, 8324
Dials = Silver Finish, Sparkle Finish
Dial Opening = Tonneau
Dial Variations/Rarity = 🕒🕒 Silver Finish, Luminous Numerals
🕒🕒🕒🕒 Sparkle Finish, Luminous Numerals; Silver Finish, Applied Gold Numerals
🕒🕒🕒🕒🕒🕒 Silver Finish, Black Numerals; Silver Finish, Etched Numerals
Numerals = Painted, Luminous, Etched, Applied Gold Numerals (18K)
Hands = Steel, Luminous
Cased in Factory = Yes
Unique Case Design = Yes
Unique Dial Design = Yes
Introduction Date = 1930 (Beau Monde), 1932 (Beau Geste)
Retail Price New = $35.00 (15J); $50.00 (17J); $75.00 (21J)
Collectibility = 🕒🕒🕒🕒
Advertisements = Yes
Marketing Themes = "21 jewels raises this watch above the average."
"Neatly engraved case"
"Curved to fit wrist snugly"
"Designed to fit the wrist perfectly"

The Beau Monde and Beau Geste appeared in various Illinois catalogs and jobbers' catalogs in the 1930–1933 time period. The Beau Monde, introduced with a 21-jewel movement in the 1930–31 Illinois Sales Catalog, was at the time one of the company's more expensive models, with a retail price of $75.00. That catalog described the Beau Monde as "Designed to fit the wrist perfectly. Flowing curves and identical engraving patterns greatly increase the acceptance of this new watch."

A later catalog advised that the Beau Geste was "15 jewels, 6/0 size, 14K filled white or natural oxidized gold."

The cases for these watches were extremely durable in either white gold-filled or yellow gold-filled. Unfortunately, this cannot be said for many Illinois wristwatch cases. The 21-jewel Beau Monde commanded a $40.00 premium over its lower-priced 15-jewel Beau Geste brother. These models, along with the Beau Brummell/Beau Royale, Beau Brummell/Viking and Marquis Strap models were some of the Illinois men's wristwatches with curved case backs to conform to the wrist.

The Beau Monde was one of nine Illinois men's wristwatches that were offered with the top-of-the-line Illinois 21-jewel, motor-barrel, 6/0 size movement. The other Illinois watches that came with 21 jewels were the Baronet, Beau Brummell, Beau Brummell/Viking, Consul, Kingston, Fifth Avenue, Manhattan, and New Yorker.

Close-up of the Beau Geste bezel

A very recent discovery is that the Beau Monde was also offered with a 17-jewel movement. A specimen was found in its original display case, with its original price card (shown below).

17-jewel Beau Monde with its original price card indicating 17 jewels

The one hinged-bezel Beau Monde is now thought to have been intended for use as a Braille watch. This is a very rare and valuable model.

Beau Monde Braille watch

End of the Beau Monde outer cardboard box

Beau Geste

See listing for **Beau Monde**

Beau Royale

See listing for **Beau Brummell**

Belmont

See listing for **Commodore**

Biltmore 18/0, white gold-filled

Biltmore 18/0, two-tone gold-filled

Biltmore 18/0 / Biltmore

Official Name = Biltmore 18/0 (derived from the List of Factory Cased Illinois Watches dated December 31, 1932)
Secondary Name(s) = Biltmore (derived from advertisements such as the April 1930 issue of the *American Magazine)*
Formerly Known As = None
Time Period = Moderne
Case Variations/Rarity = 🕒🕒🕒 WGF/P
🕒🕒🕒🕒 WGF/GGF/TT/P
🕒🕒🕒🕒🕒🕒🕒 GGF/P
Case Durability = 🕒🕒🕒
Material = 14K GF
Bezel = Plain
Sides = Plain, Engraved
Lugs = Plain
Lug Size = 16mm
Springbar = Male
Casemaker = Wadsworth
Case Closure = 2-Part Snap-On Back
Case Number = 161
Case Shape = Rectangular
Case Back = Curved
Dimensions = 34 x 20mm
Movement Size = 18/0
Movement Grades/Jewels = 805/15, 807/17, 807A/17
Seconds at = None
Dial Number = 8148
Dial = Silver Finish
Dial Opening = Rectangular
Dial Variations/Rarity = 🕒🕒🕒🕒 Silver Finish, Luminous Numerals
🕒🕒🕒🕒🕒 Silver Finish, Black Numerals; Silver Finish, Painted Deco Numerals
Numerals = Painted, Luminous
Hands = Steel, Luminous
Cased in Factory = Yes
Unique Case Design = No
Unique Dial Design = No
Introduction Date = 1930
Retail Price New = $50.00
Collectibility = 🕒🕒🕒🕒
Advertisements = Yes
The Biltmore 18/0 was first advertised and sold as a ladies' wristwatch but shortly thereafter was marketed by Illinois for both sexes. It was featured in the April 1930 issue of the *American Magazine*.
Marketing Theme = "Ladies' sport watch of simple design

The Biltmore 18/0 could be one of the first examples of unisex advertisements and products for sale in the United States. In the cultural context of the 1930s, Illinois' decision to market a product to both sexes was a bold move. Illinois similarly marketed the Sangamon, Tuxedo, Caprice and Urbana watches as unisex models.

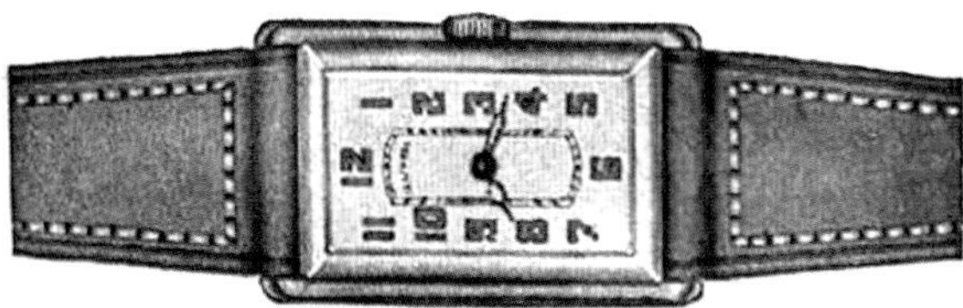

The BILTMORE
This ladies' sport watch is of simple design and is for the woman of varied activities.
14K white or green filled gold.
Suggested consumer price, $50.

Illinois 1930 Sales Catalog. Note that the Biltmore was first introduced as a ladies' sports watch

Louis Sickles Service Satisfies

New For 1930

New Biltmore
Illinois Sport Strap, $50

•••

New Raleigh
Hamilton Strap, $57

•••

New Elgin
Pocket Watch, $80

•••

New Hadley
"Arbor Lace" Ready for Delivery

•••

Moral
"Fresh Merchandise Means Increased Sales"
The Best in Watches—American Made

HADLEY ATTACHMENTS

Louis Sickles
WHOLESALE WATCH SERVICE
1015 CHESTNUT STREET
Philadelphia, Pa.

Louis Sickles advertisement introducing the Biltmore. *Keystone*, February 1930

This model is called a Biltmore 18/0 to distinguish it from the Biltmore 6/0 models. (The Biltmore 6/0 was also apparently called a Commodore, Belmont, LaSalle, or Bostonian by Illinois.) The Biltmore 18/0 model is not easy to locate and is fairly difficult to find in two-tone. Only one is known to exist in all green gold-filled; it is especially striking in green.

The Biltmore 18/0 is larger than most of the Illinois wristwatches that utilize the 18/0 size movement. This model is very sleek looking, especially with its recessed crown. It joins the Rockliffe, Consul, Gallahad, Kenilworth, Tuxedo and No. 250/Schmukler Illinois models as the only Illinois models with recessed crowns.

Biltmore 18/0, green gold-filled; only one known to exist

Wadsworth made exactly the same case for the Gruen Watch Company but without a case model number, and for Longines with an attractive engraved bezel. The inside case back is configured differently to accommodate the different movement shapes and sizes between Illinois, Gruen and Longines. The Gruen dial differs from the Illinois dial variations, but all three have a classic deco look. For some reason not yet known, Wadsworth was able to sell this case, with slight variations, to Gruen and Longines for their watch lines.

On the left is the Longines version of the "Illinois Biltmore" that has the same Wadsworth 14K gold-filled case. The engraved bezel greatly enhances the aesthetic appeal of the Longines version.

WADSWORTH HITS A TRIFECTA

The Wadsworth Watch Case Company hit a trifecta with its Biltmore-styled case, as they successfully marketed the same case to Gruen, Illinois and Longines. The respective inside case backs had to be modified to accommodate the different movement shapes and sizes from one company to another.

Examples of the Illinois Biltmore 18/0 with two different dial types and the Gruen version on the right. Notice the private-label Herbert-signed dial on the middle watch.

Owing to its 18/0 size movement, the Biltmore 18/0 lacks subsidiary seconds. It is only one of nine men's Illinois wristwatch models that have no subsidiary seconds. The other models are the Caprice, Consul, Marquis Strap, Ritz, Rockliffe 18/0, Sangamon, Tuxedo and Urbana.

FANTASTIC FIND

Always on the lookout for Illinois wristwatches, my husband and I have occasionally had good luck on eBay because sellers haven't provided good pictures or accurate descriptions. One day he came across an Illinois listed as a men's watch that wasn't identified as to model, and the pictures weren't very clear. But after scrutinizing them and then consulting our "Bible," *The Illinois Watch: The Life and Times of a Great American Watch Company*, by Fredric J. Friedberg, he determined that it was a "Biltmore," a model that is not easy to find, so he put in a bid. We ended up getting it for a very low price!

He and I had a friendly argument about whether it would turn out to be the white gold-filled version or the even rarer two-tone green-and-white gold-filled (the pictures were too dark to tell). When the watch arrived, I was delighted to see what I'd won; it was the two-tone! The seller mentioned that it had come from a North Carolina estate—interesting since Asheville, N.C., is the location of the Vanderbilts' famous "Biltmore" estate. (Maybe that's why the original owner selected that model?)

A few months later, as I surfed eBay late at night, I came across another unidentified but unmistakable "Biltmore," this one listed as a ladies' watch. (As Fred points out, that model was initially sold as a ladies' sport watch but was later advertised for both sexes.) What I'd found was almost certainly the white gold-filled version. Since it had just been listed as a "Buy It Now" for a very low price, I pushed the button very quickly!

When it arrived, the watch indeed proved to be WGF, and the Wadsworth case was in beautiful shape. The movement was running well, too. The dial was very interesting: "Illinois" above the center and "Herbert" below. It looked to be original; the style of the numerals was identical to what I'd seen on some other Illinois models. I was assuming that Herbert was the name of the jewelry company that sold the watch and this was a private-label dial, but until recently I'd been able to find no leads. (Sadly, all too many of the independent jewelry companies of yesteryear have long since gone out of business.) But I've at last found a candidate: W. L. Herbert, of Ruston, Louisiana, who had a jewelry store that was active during the Illinois years.

Since I'm fond of vintage wristwatches, I enjoy looking at Bryan Girouard's beautiful Web site (ArtDecoWristwatches.com) now and then. I kept finding myself drawn to a lovely Gruen he'd identified as the Cartouche 344 model. Such elegant simplicity, I thought, and a two-tone green-and-white gold-filled case. Then it occurred to me: "That case design looks awfully familiar. Could it possibly be . . .?"

In Bryan's photographs, even the pattern of the detailing around the outside of the bezel was perfectly clear—and it looked just like what was on my two-tone Illinois "Biltmore"! Just to make sure, I asked him whether the case was by Wadsworth. Yes! The price was more than reasonable, and the watch looked like a superb specimen, so I knew I had to have it!

When the Gruen arrived, my husband and I got out its Illinois counterpart and looked at them together. Externally, the cases are identical, and the inside of the back of each shows that it is a Wadsworth. But it's not simply a generic case; the Gruen is inscribed "Gruen" as well as "Wadsworth" inside the case back, and the shape of the case back cutout is different in order to accommodate the Gruen movement.

I'd never come across an "Illinois Gruen" before. Surprises like that are part of the fun of watch collecting—you're always learning something new!

—Bettie Mason

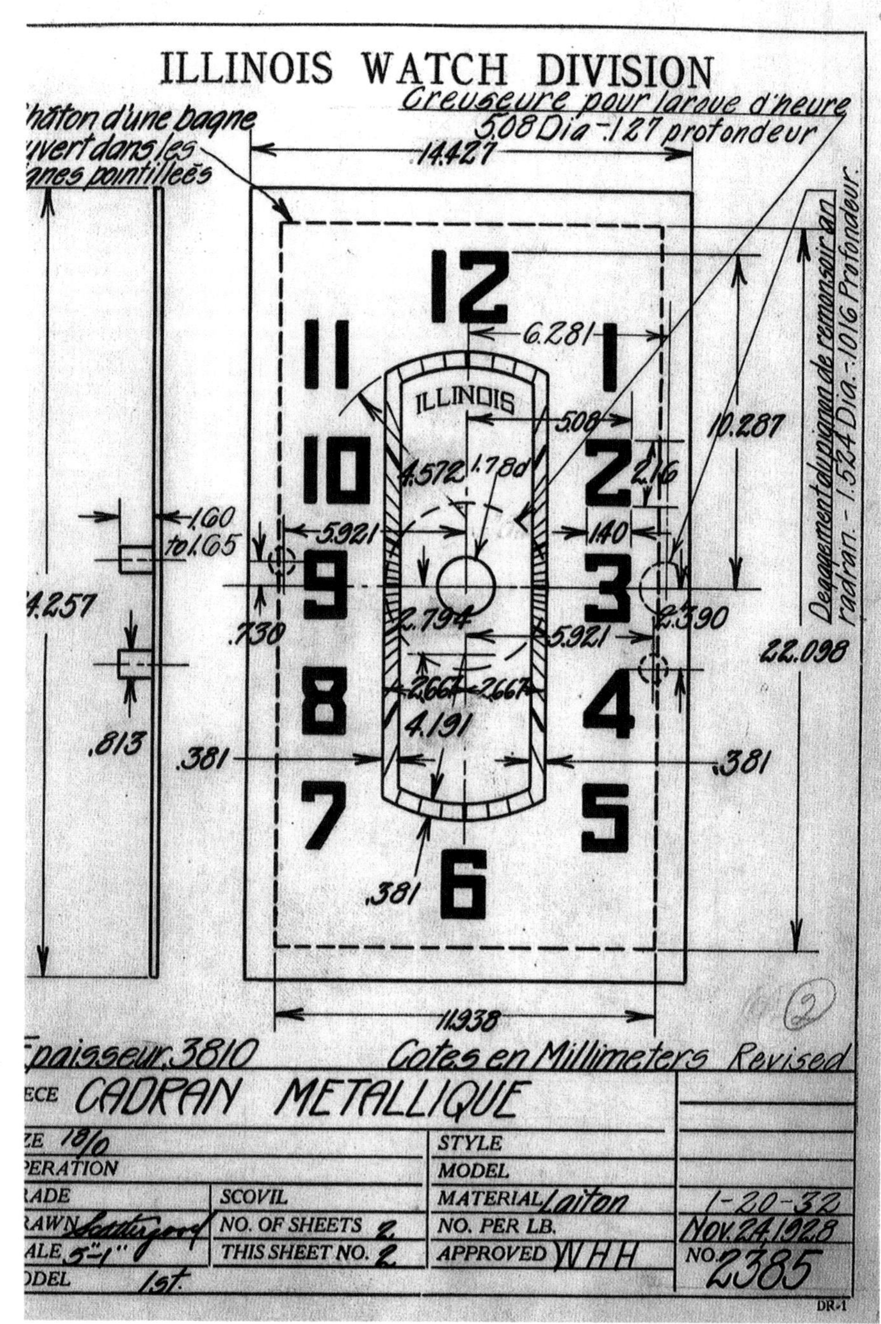

Blueprint of the Biltmore dial to be fabricated in Switzerland

Biltmore 6/0

See listing for **Commodore**

Blackhawk

See listing for **Seneca**

Blackstone / Greystone / Haddon Hall

Official Name = Blackstone (derived from Illinois advertisements and Illinois Sales and Material Catalogs)
Secondary Name(s) = Greystone (derived from an original Illinois price card); Haddon Hall (derived from an internal Hamilton record)
Formerly Known As = None
Time Period = Moderne
Case Variations/Rarity = 🕒 YGF/P
🕒🕒 WGF/P
🕒🕒🕒🕒🕒🕒🕒 TT/P
Case Durability/Rarity = 🕒🕒🕒
Material = 14K GF
Bezel = Plain
Sides = Engraved
Lugs = Plain
Lug Size = 16mm
Springbar = Male
Casemaker = Wadsworth
Case Closure = 3-Part Snap-On Bezel and Back
Case Number = 219
Case Shape = Octagonal
Case Back = Flat
Dimensions = 34 x 27mm
Movement Size = 6/0
Movement Grade/Jewels = 607/17
Seconds at = 6
Dial Numbers = 8281, 8451 (Hamilton drawing, Seconds at 9), and 8458 (Black Enamel Numerals)
Dials = Silver Finish, Sparkle Finish
Dial Opening = Octagonal
Dial Variations/Rarity = 🕒🕒 Silver Finish, Etched Numerals
🕒🕒🕒 Silver Finish, Luminous Numerals
🕒🕒🕒🕒🕒 Sparkle Finish, Black Numerals
Numerals = Painted, Luminous, Etched
Hands = Steel, Luminous
Cased in Factory = Yes
Unique Case Design = Yes
Unique Dial Design = Yes
Introduction Date = 1930
Retail Price New = $42.50; Greystone, $50.00
Collectibility = 🕒🕒🕒🕒

Blackstone, white gold-filled

Blackstone, yellow gold-filled (with incorrect hands)

Advertisements = Yes
The Blackstone model appeared in Illinois Sales Catalogs and various national publications, such as the *Saturday Evening Post.*

Marketing Theme = "Perfect for the small wrist"
"A fine strap watch at a new low price"

The 1930–31 Illinois Sales Catalog announced, "Here is a fine strap watch at a new low price." And the 1931–32 catalog pronounced the Blackstone "Perfect for the small wrist."

There is a variation of the Blackstone called a Greystone that has black enamel numerals instead of etched ones. It should be noted that the minute track of the Blackstone dial comes to points at its corners, but frequently the Blackstone can be found with an incorrect cushion-shaped dial that has a minute track rounded at its corners.

The white gold-filled case is more durable than the yellow gold-filled one and can usually be found in excellent condition. Because the Blackstone/Greystone came with a 17-jewel movement, it should not contain a 15-, 19- or 21-jewel movement. This model is underappreciated, so it can be obtained at a very reasonable price.

In November 1933, Hamilton was designing a Blackstone dial with subsidiary seconds at 9, but it is unknown if they ever released such a dial.

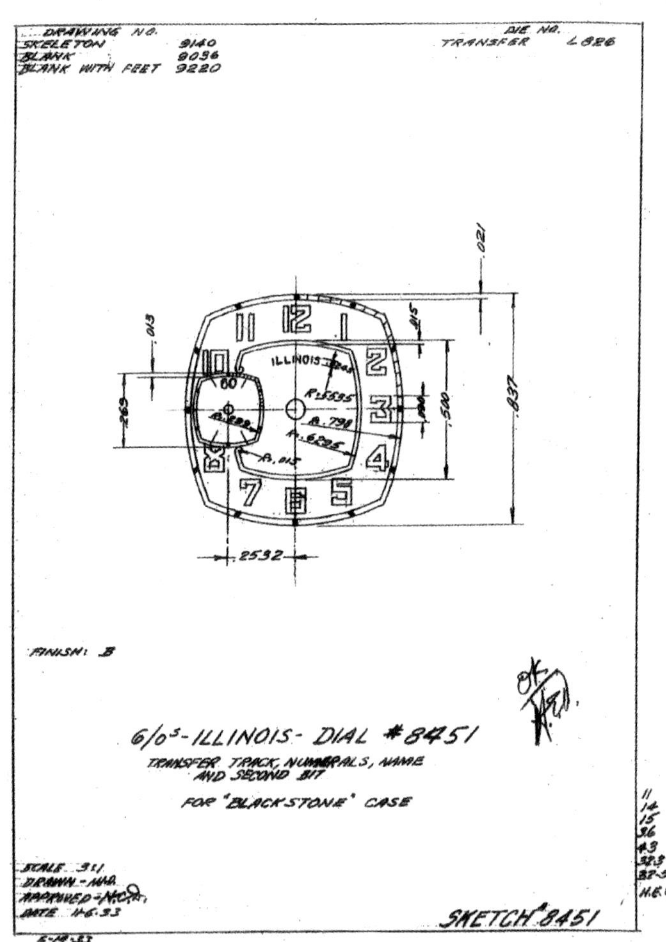

Hamilton drawing of a Blackstone with subsidiary seconds at 9. One such dial has been found.

There also exists a Hamilton-designed dial for the replacement market that has a white painted dial with black painted numerals. Presently, we do not know what distinguished the Haddon Hall model from the Blackstone and Greystone models. Perhaps it was to house the dial with subsidiary seconds at 9 or one with black enamel numerals, or perhaps to equip the watch with a metal bracelet. The existence of a very rare, one-of-a-kind two-tone Blackstone with matching case numbers has been confirmed, and it is pictured below.

Blackstone two-tone; only one known to exist

Greystone, white gold-filled; only one known to exist

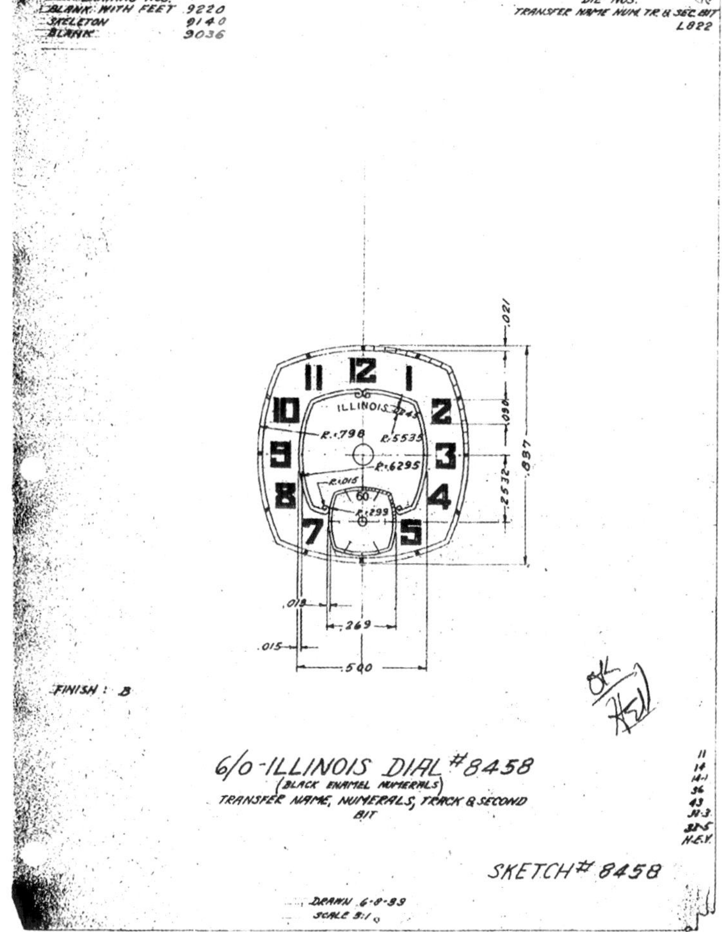

Greystone original price card

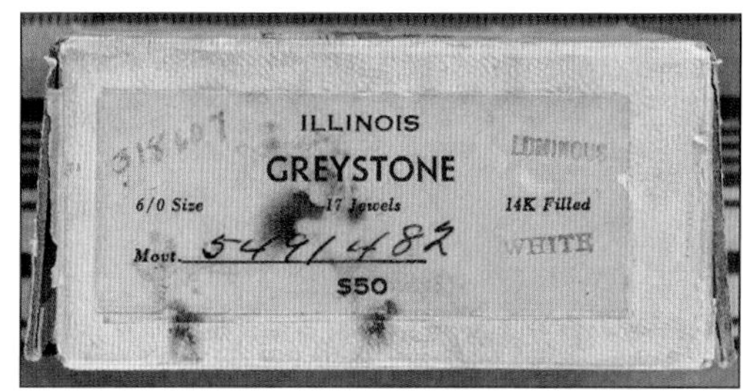

Greystone, end of its outer cardboard box

Hamilton drawing of an Illinois Greystone dial dated June 8, 1933

BOSTONIAN

See listing for **Commodore**

BRANDT ROCK

See listing for **Osgood**

BRYCE

See listing for **Tank**

Bullet Dial sterling silver; only one known to exist

BULLET DIAL

Official Name = Unknown
Secondary Name(s) = Bullet Dial (derived from collectors' usage)
Formerly Known As = Military
Time Period = Transitional
Case Variations/Rarity = 🕒🕒🕒🕒🕒 SS
Case Durability = 🕒🕒🕒🕒 SS
Material = SS
Bezel = Plain
Sides = Plain
Lugs = Plain
Lug Size = 16mm
Springbar = Fixed Lugs
Casemaker = Depollier
Case Closure = 3-Part Snap-On Bezel and Back
Case Number = None
Case Shape = Cushion
Case Back = Curved
Dimensions = 40 x 32mm
Movement Sizes = 3/0
Movement Grades/Jewels = 24/17, 36/17, 37/17, 38/17, 39/17
Seconds at = 6
Dial Number = None
Dials = Silver Finish
Dial Opening = Round
Dial Variations/Rarity = 🕒🕒🕒🕒🕒🕒🕒 Silver Finish, Painted Bullet Markers
Numerals = Painted
Hands = Steel
Cased in Factory = No
Unique Case Design = No
Unique Dial Design = No
Introduction Date = 1917
Retail Price New = Unknown
Collectibility = 🕒🕒🕒🕒
Advertisements = No
Marketing Themes = Unknown

This Bullet Dial model is the only such model known to exist for Illinois. However, Elgin used a similar watch dial.

The Bullet Dial is found in an extra-thick Depollier sterling silver case with an extra ridge around its bezel. The watch shown also has an original "Khaki"-signed Depollier crown. This model is extremely popular with military collectors and others; and, for that reason, it is very valuable.

Bullet Dial side view with its signed "Khaki" crown

Burlington

Official Name = Burlington (was one of hundreds of private label watches made by the Illinois Watch Company and the most prevalent)
Secondary Name(s) = Aviator (if in a sterling silver cushion case)
Formerly Known As = None
Time Period = Transitional
Case Variations/Rarity = 🕒🕒 SS/Round
🕒🕒🕒 SS/Cushion
🕒🕒🕒🕒🕒 SS/Square Off-Set
🕒🕒🕒🕒🕒🕒 WG/P, Cushion; GGF/P, Cushion; WGF/P, Square
🕒🕒🕒🕒🕒🕒🕒 GG/P, Square; WG/P, Tonneau; GG/P, Tonneau; GG/P, Tonneau; GGF/E, Square
Case Durability = 🕒🕒 WGF, GGF
🕒🕒🕒🕒 SS, WG
Material = SS, 14K GF
Bezel = Plain, Engraved
Sides = Plain, Engraved
Lugs = Plain
Lug Size = Various
Springbar = Fixed Lugs

Burlington, sterling silver

Casemaker = Burlington
Case Closure = Various
Case Number = None
Case Shape = Round, Cushion, Square, Tonneau
Case Back = Flat
Dimensions = Various
Movement Sizes = 0, 3/0, 6/0
Movement Grades/Jewels = Various
Seconds at = 6, 9
Dial Number = None
Dials = Enamel, Silver Finish
Dial Opening = Round, Cushion, Square, Tonneau
Dial Variations/Rarity = ◷◷ Enamel, Painted Numerals
◷◷◷ Silver Finish, Luminous Numerals
Numerals = Painted, Luminous
Hands = Steel, Luminous
Cased in Factory = No
Unique Case Design = No
Unique Dial Design = No
Introduction Date = 1917
Retail Price New = Unknown
Collectibility = ◷◷◷◷
Advertisements = Yes
The Burlington Watch Company advertised frequently in various publications, such as *Popular Mechanics*. Around 1927, Burlington also produced a multi-page color 31-page catalog that featured several different wristwatch models.
Marketing Themes = "A real man's wristwatch"
"Quality, quality and still more quality"

In its military wristwatch advertisements, Burlington referred to its Aviator model as "A real man's wristwatch" with a "Luminous Radium Dial." Burlington offered its watches for sale with a $2.50 per week payment plan. Burlington sold by mail order directly to the consumer.

Burlington, sterling silver

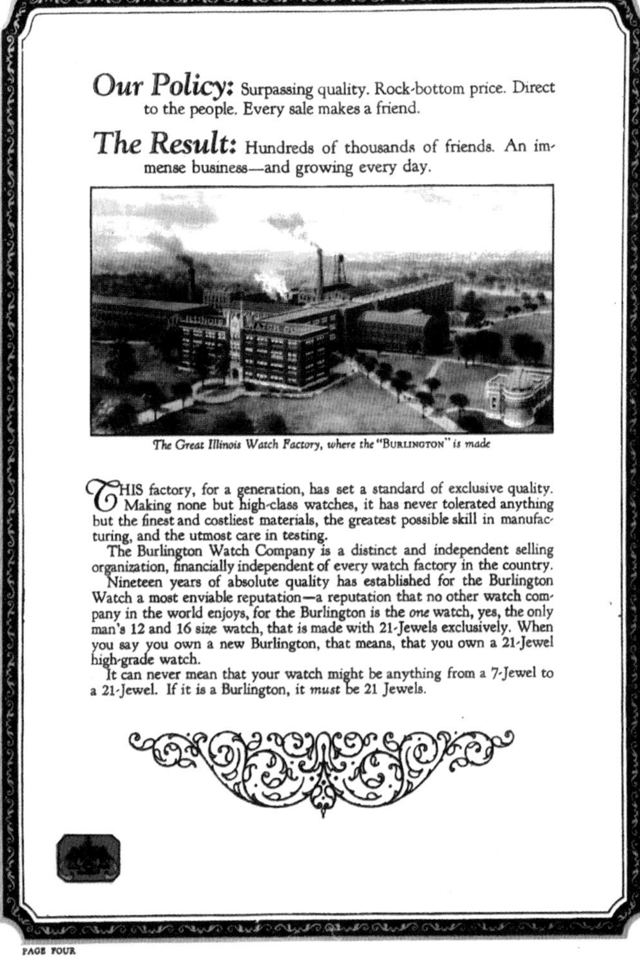

Our Policy: Surpassing quality. Rock-bottom price. Direct to the people. Every sale makes a friend.

The Result: Hundreds of thousands of friends. An immense business—and growing every day.

The Great Illinois Watch Factory, where the "BURLINGTON" is made

THIS factory, for a generation, has set a standard of exclusive quality. Making none but high-class watches, it has never tolerated anything but the finest and costliest materials, the greatest possible skill in manufacturing, and the utmost care in testing.

The Burlington Watch Company is a distinct and independent selling organization, financially independent of every watch factory in the country.

Nineteen years of absolute quality has established for the Burlington Watch a most enviable reputation—a reputation that no other watch company in the world enjoys, for the Burlington is the *one* watch, yes, the only man's 12 and 16 size watch, that is made with 21-Jewels exclusively. When you say you own a new Burlington, that means, that you own a 21-Jewel high-grade watch.

It can never mean that your watch might be anything from a 7-Jewel to a 21-Jewel. If it is a Burlington, it *must* be 21 Jewels.

PAGE FOUR

Burlington Sales Policy, c. 1927, from its 31-page sales brochure

Our Quality Policy:

THE BURLINGTON is not a price watch—it is a watch of wonderful quality at a remarkably low price. Every man's Burlington 16 and 12 size has 21 jewels—nothing else is worthy of Burlington quality. Every man's Burlington case is guaranteed to wear 25 years. It is covered both inside and outside with sheets of 14-karat solid gold. You must never think of the word "Burlington" in connection with the Burlington watch without also thinking of the words "quality, QUALITY and STILL MORE QUALITY."

The ladies' Burlington, on account of its size, has 17 jewels instead of 21. It is very small, but the quality is so high that it will give better service than most ladies' watches that are a great deal larger in size. In order that the case of this lady's watch may equal the quality of the movement, we are casing them only in 14-karat and 18-karat solid gold.

The Burlington Man's Strap Watch on account of its size also has 17 jewels instead of 21 and is fitted in a 14-Karat Gold Strata case guaranteed to wear for 25 years.

Our Price Policy:

Our Price Policy is just as radical as our Quality Policy. We are selling direct to the consumer at the lowest rock-bottom price. Your Jeweler cannot buy a Burlington one penny cheaper than you can.

COMPARE "BURLINGTON" PRICES

The shrewd buyer first determines quality, next comes price. The Burlington's quality has long since been established beyond question. Now let us investigate price value. Go to your local jeweler and ask him his price on a 21-jewel watch with a 14-karat gold strata case. Next take the mail order catalogs and compare our prices with those of watches very much inferior. The more questions you ask and comparisons you make, the better. If, after making these comparisons, you are the least bit skeptical, just write and say you would like to have us send you a Burlington on approval so you can thoroughly examine it and better determine its wonderful value.

BURLINGTON WATCH COMPANY
19TH STREET AND CALIFORNIA AVENUE · *Chicago*

PAGE FIVE

Burlington's quality and pricing policies from page 4 of its color sales brochure

The Illinois Watch Company produced thousands of private-label movements and dials for its customers. The Burlington Watch Company, an arm of the giant mail-order firm of Babson Brothers, used thousands of Illinois movements, making it Illinois' best private-label customer.

Burlington sold many Transitional Period military watch models. Some models had subsidiary seconds at 9. Burlington also produced several Generic Period wristwatch models such as a Square, Cushion and Whippet, with Burlington-signed dials, movements and cases. Many of its cases were made by NAWCo. The catalog page of Burlington's men's wristwatch offerings c. 1927 is featured on the next page.

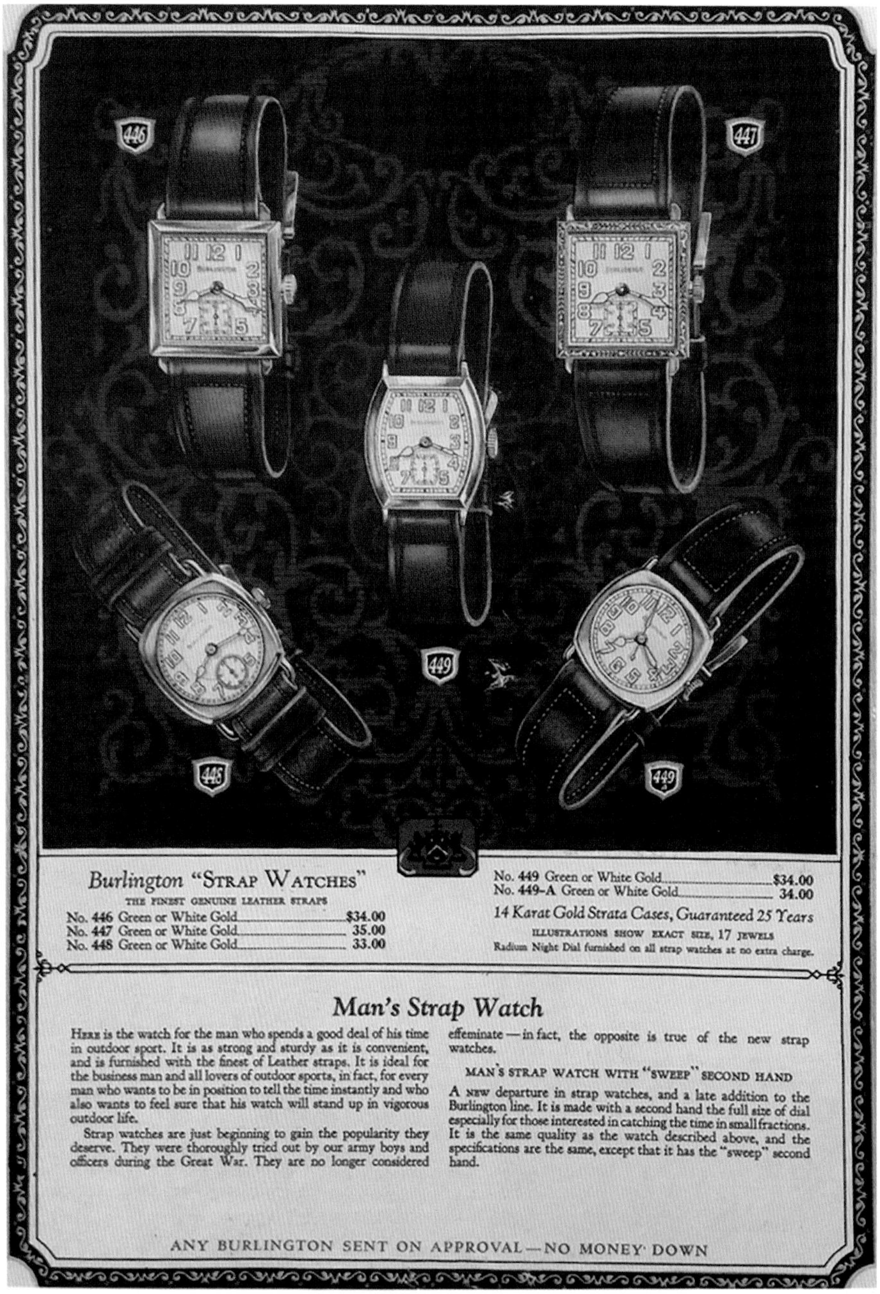

Burlington "STRAP WATCHES"

THE FINEST GENUINE LEATHER STRAPS

No. 446 Green or White Gold $34.00
No. 447 Green or White Gold 35.00
No. 448 Green or White Gold 33.00
No. 449 Green or White Gold $34.00
No. 449-A Green or White Gold 34.00

14 Karat Gold Strata Cases, Guaranteed 25 Years

ILLUSTRATIONS SHOW EXACT SIZE, 17 JEWELS

Radium Night Dial furnished on all strap watches at no extra charge.

Man's Strap Watch

HERE is the watch for the man who spends a good deal of his time in outdoor sport. It is as strong and sturdy as it is convenient, and is furnished with the finest of Leather straps. It is ideal for the business man and all lovers of outdoor sports, in fact, for every man who wants to be in position to tell the time instantly and who also wants to feel sure that his watch will stand up in vigorous outdoor life.

Strap watches are just beginning to gain the popularity they deserve. They were thoroughly tried out by our army boys and officers during the Great War. They are no longer considered effeminate — in fact, the opposite is true of the new strap watches.

MAN'S STRAP WATCH WITH "SWEEP" SECOND HAND

A NEW departure in strap watches, and a late addition to the Burlington line. It is made with a second hand the full size of dial especially for those interested in catching the time in small fractions. It is the same quality as the watch described above, and the specifications are the same, except that it has the "sweep" second hand.

ANY BURLINGTON SENT ON APPROVAL—NO MONEY DOWN

Men's watches featured in Burlington's 31-page color sales catalog

Burlington Square, white gold-filled; only one known to exist

Burlington Square, inside case back

Burlington Square, green gold-filled; only one known to exist

Besides using Illinois movements, Burlington purchased Swiss watch movements. (Burlington's Canadian affiliate used H. Moser movements in many of its watches.) The cushion model shown on the prior page with the sweep seconds likely contains a Swiss movement, as Burlington advertised in the same catalog its ladies' nurses' watch with sweep seconds as containing a Swiss movement.

In 1917 and 1918, Burlington advertised an Aviator model military wristwatch in a sterling silver cushion case with a Burlington-signed enamel dial and movement (see listing for **Aviator**).

See Chapter 6 for more information on the Burlington Watch Company.

Cadet

See listing for **Marquis Strap**

Canby / Rectangular

Official Name = Canby (derived from Illinois Material Catalogs)
Secondary Name(s) = Rectangular (derived from the Illinois Dial Catalogs)
Formerly Known As = None
Time Period = Generic
Case Variations/Rarity = 🕒 WGF/P, WGF/E, BM/P, BM/E
🕒🕒 YGF/P, YGF/E
🕒🕒🕒 GGF/P, GGF/E
🕒🕒🕒🕒 WG/P, WG/E, YG/P, YG/E
🕒🕒🕒🕒🕒 GG/P, GG/E
🕒🕒🕒🕒🕒🕒🕒 YGF/E/Diamond, SS
Case Durability = 🕒🕒🕒
Material = 14K GF, 14K WG, 14K YG, 14K GG, BM, SS
Bezel = Plain, Engraved, Diamonds
Sides = Plain, Engraved
Lugs = Plain
Lug Size = 16mm
Springbar = Male, Attached
Casemakers = Elgin, Star, Keystone, Others
Case Closure = 3-Part Snap-On Bezel and Back; 2-Part Snap-On Bezel; 1-Part Hinged Bezel and Hinged Back
Case Number = None
Case Shape = Rectangular
Case Back = Flat
Dimensions = 38 x 27mm
Movement Size = 6/0
Movement Grades/Jewels = 903/15, 905/17, 907/19
Seconds at = 9
Dial Numbers = 8092, 8094, 8269, 8286, 8287
Dial = Silver Finish
Dial Opening = Rectangular

Canby, white gold-filled

Canby, yellow gold-filled

Dial Variations/Rarity = ◷ Silver Finish, Luminous Numerals
◷◷◷◷ Silver Finish, Luminous Numerals, Butler Center
◷◷◷◷◷ Silver Finish, Black Numerals
◷◷◷◷◷◷◷◷ Silver Finish, Luminous Numerals, Butler Center, Pinstripe
Numerals = Painted, Luminous
Hands = Luminous
Cased in Factory = Yes/No
Unique Case Design = No
Unique Dial Design = Yes
Introduction Date = 1925
Retail Price New = Unknown
Collectibility = ◷◷◷◷
Advertisements = Yes
Marketing Theme = “Made for timekeeping purposes — not merely as ornaments”

The Canby, introduced in 1925, was one of the first men’s wristwatches advertised by the Illinois Watch Company. The Canby model case was advertised by Star in 1925 and by Keystone in 1926.

Illinois generally sold the movement and dial for the Canby uncased. However, certain of the Canbys were Factory-Cased by Illinois, most likely in both plain and engraved Keystone cases in 14K white gold-filled or green gold-filled. Illinois noted in other advertisements for the movements: “Attractive cases may be selected from stock at your retail jeweler.”

The Canby is one of the most popular and readily available of the Generic Period watches. Its subsidiary seconds at 9 feature makes it very attractive to new as well as seasoned Illinois collectors.

The Canby can be acquired in gold-filled cases at reasonable prices today. The models in solid gold cases are highly sought-after and usually demand a premium price. The hinged cases are rarer and are generally considered more collectible than the standard three-piece cases. The Canby with a diamond bezel may be a one-of-a-kind special-order model. There is also an ultra-rare and valuable sterling silver Canby in a case by Wadsworth. Only one of these cases has been sighted to date. It also has a unique butler center, pinstriped dial.

Canbys are also sometimes seen with private-label dials and movements marked Illinois Central or Sterling, but these tend to be hard to find. (The latter seems to have been a private label of the Kay Jewelry Company.) By using a private-label dial and movement with a generic case, a jeweler could produce what would be an “exclusive” model.

Wadsworth inside case back for a sterling silver Illinois Canby model; only one known to exist

Solidarity white gold Canby inside case back

Canby yellow gold-filled, diamond bezel; only one is known to exist

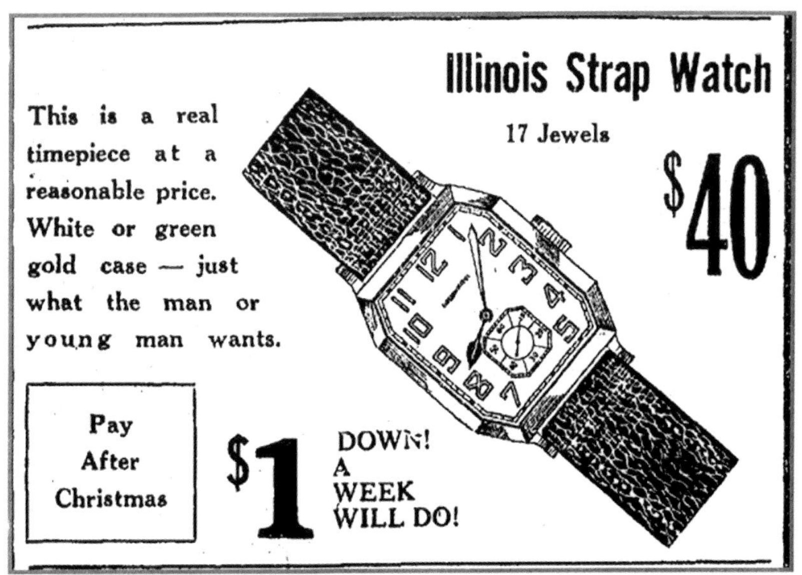

Advertisement for an Illinois "Canby" by Meyerding, Inc., which advertised itself as a "Dignified Credit Jeweler." *Hutchinson News* (Hutchinson, KS), November 26, 1926; image from *newspapers.com*

Caprice

Official Name = Caprice (derived from Illinois advertisements and Illinois Sales and Material Catalogs)

Secondary Name(s) = None

Formerly Known As = None

Time Period = Deco

Case Variations/Rarity = 🕒🕒 WGF/P

🕒🕒🕒🕒🕒🕒 WGF/Snakeskin green, WGF/Snakeskin brown; WGF/Ostrich Skin

🕒🕒🕒🕒🕒🕒🕒 WGF/Engine turned

🕒🕒🕒🕒🕒🕒🕒 WG

Case Durability = 🕒🕒🕒🕒

Material = 14K GF, WG

Bezel = Plain

Sides = Plain

Lugs = N/A

Lug Size = N/A

Springbar = N/A

Casemaker = Keystone

Caprice, brown snakeskin

Caprice, green snakeskin

Case Closure = 4-Part Outer Case Push Button, Snap-On Bezel and Back
Case Number = 213
Case Shape = Square (when closed); Diamond (when opened)
Case Back = Flat (when opened); Curved (when closed)
Crown = Standard
Dimensions = 34 x 34mm (when closed)
Movement Size = 6/0
Movement Grades/Jewels = 607/17
Seconds at = None
Dial Number = 8205
Dial = Sparkle Finish
Dial Opening = Diamond
Dial Variations/Rarity = ◷◷ Sparkle Finish, Painted Numerals
Numerals = Painted
Hands = Steel
Cased in Factory = Yes
Unique Case Design = Yes
Unique Dial Design = Yes
Introduction Date = 1930
Retail Price New = $50.00
Advertisements = Yes
Marketing Themes = "Just the watch for the handbag, pocket or desk" "Smartness—beauty and incomparable accuracy"

This remarkable watch was the first unisex watch ever offered by Illinois, and it may well be the first unisex watch offering in America. "Just the watch for the handbag, pocket or desk," the 1930–31 Illinois Sales Catalog pointed out. Moreover, the Caprice was versatile: "a watch for all occasions—business, dress or sport—for men and women."

The Caprice was advertised in the May 1930 issue of the *Keystone* as well as in jobbers' catalogs.

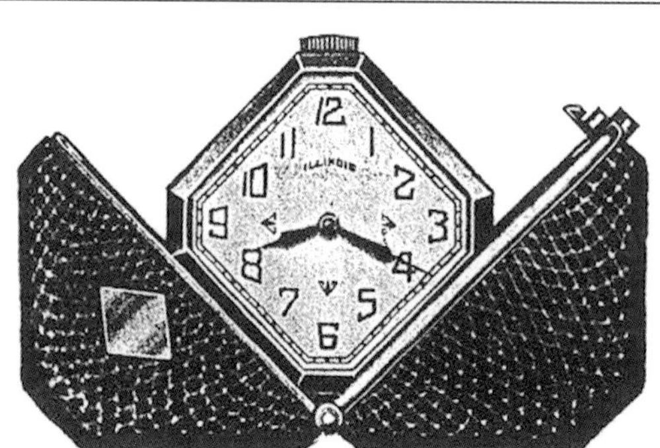

The CAPRICE

Smartness — beauty and incomparable accuracy are truly defined in the Illinois Caprice. It is "a watch for all occasions"—business, dress or sport—for men and women. Caprice is a 6/0 size 17 jewel timekeeper. Offered in individual coverings of natural ostrich, jade green and natural watersnake. The inner case is 14K filled white gold.

Suggested consumer price, $50.

A. C. Becken catalog, 1931

Page 96 The KEYSTONE May, 1930

CAPRICE

The Watch of Fashion

By ILLINOIS

The FRONTENAC
$65

Caprice!—A departure from the usual in watches—an answer to the desire for a watch for all occasions. Men and women will carry it for business—dress or sport, in handbag or pocket. Surpassing in workmanship and style "Caprice" is an accurate, 17 jeweled timekeeper—containing the same fine qualities that has made Illinois such a great watch during the past sixty years.

Order this watch from your wholesaler now. It opens a definite, new field of watch sales for you. "Caprice" is far above the novelty watch class and will be bought by men and women everywhere for its practical worth as a watch of beauty and accuracy.

You may order Caprice in jade green or natural water snake and natural ostrich. The inner case is in 14K filled white gold. The price is $50.

The SARATOGA
$55

The ILLINOIS WATCH

SPRINGFIELD, ILLINOIS

Affiliated in Resources and Engineering

The HAMILTON WATCH The ILLINOIS WATCH The HAMILTON-SANGAMO Electric Clock

Keystone, May 1930

The Caprice was offered with a choice of coverings: green or brown snakeskin, or brown ostrich. It is very difficult to find a Caprice with its outer snakeskin covering intact; ostrich seems more durable. But even with the skin off, the Caprice is very attractive with its plain white gold-filled outer case. (It is possible to have snakeskin or another material reattached to the outside case surface. However, I have never seen it redone effectively.) There is one known special-order solid white gold Caprice with its brown snakeskin intact and a case doubly signed 14K gold, inside its case back and inside its outer case.

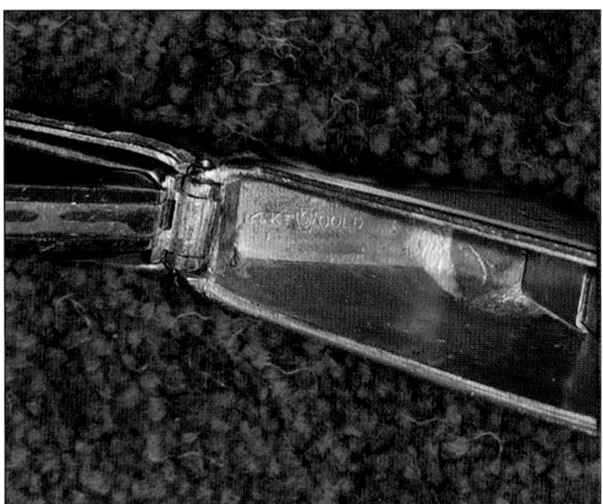

Caprice, signed 14K solid gold inside its outer case and inside its caseback. Only one known to exist.

Caprice without its snake skin

The Caprice sparkle finish dial is usually in excellent shape because it is, in effect, double-cased (i.e., the dial is behind a snap-on bezel with a crystal that is enclosed in an outer case). Although the dial has a small post at the three o'clock position that could accommodate a small subsidiary seconds hand, it should not have a second hand. This is actually a hole for the fourth-wheel arbor to poke through. A decoration was added to the dial to disguise the presence of the hole. This is like the hole on the rotor-seconds Illinois dials on the Guardian/Guardsman models, which also have a hole that is usually disguised in the printing of the six; this enabled Illinois to use these movements without going to the time and expense to convert them to a short fourth-wheel arbor. This technique was utilized by Hamilton on some pocket watches, such as the Farragut model.

The left side of the outer front cover of the Caprice has a small, raised diamond shape that echoes the diamond-shaped cased enclosure. Sometimes initials are found engraved on the dial, but usually not. When the outer case is closed, its shape mirrors the inner case that you see with the outer case open. This is a very sleek and clever design.

Caprice, brown ostrich, seen from front of closed case

When the outer case of the Caprice is closed, there is a small button on top of the case that, when depressed, opens the outer case. When open, the case can stand upright on a flat surface such as a desk or table top. The Caprice sometimes can be found with a hook at its bottom so that a chain can be attached and the watch worn around one's neck, much like a pendant watch.

The Caprice was sold packaged in a special wood display box, with a formed insert in the shape of the open watch case. There exists at least one custom Caprice with an interesting engine-turned design outer case.

There also exists at least one Caprice without its outer case that has been converted to a wristwatch with a very dramatic effect.

A Caprice converted to a wristwatch

A custom ordered Caprice with engine-turned outer case, in its original wood display box

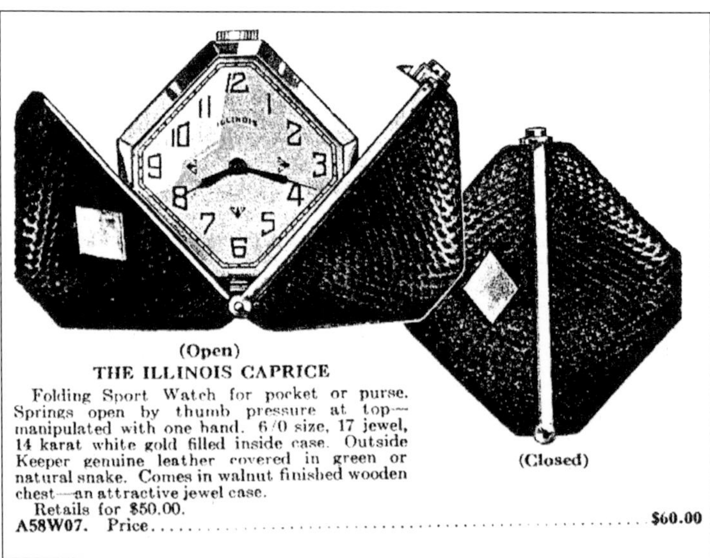
(Open)
THE ILLINOIS CAPRICE
Folding Sport Watch for pocket or purse. Springs open by thumb pressure at top—manipulated with one hand. 6/0 size, 17 jewel, 14 karat white gold filled inside case. Outside Keeper genuine leather covered in green or natural snake. Comes in walnut finished wooden chest—an attractive jewel case.
Retails for $50.00.
A58W07. Price.......... $60.00
(Closed)

May & Malone catalog, 1931

Caprice with brown ostrich skin, in its wood display box

BAD DEAL

One very confused jeweler in May 1931 insisted that Illinois swap his Caprice for an Illinois ladies' Edgewater. Not a wise deal.

May 8th, 1931.

Mr. D. G. Gallett,
309 South Main St.,
Aberdeen, South Dakota.

Dear Sir:

We have your letter of April 28th, and also, acknowledge receipt of the Caprice model watch you returned, requesting that we exchange it for an Edgewater model, 18/0 size ladies wrist watch.

Our plan of distribution is the selling of Illinois watches through a selected number of wholesalers nationally located, who act as warehouses for our product and are equipped to serve retail jewelers in their respective territories.

It is unusual for us to handle transactions of this kind with the jeweler but because of your good efforts and the interest you have in the sale of Illinois watches we are making an exception in this instance. The Edgewater model ladies watch, is being shipped to you in place of the Caprice and we are handling the charge and credit through your jobber S. H. Clausin & Company.

Please, however, do not consider this as a criterion for future action.

You, we believe, will clearly understand the responsibility that must be accepted by the jeweler in relation to his purchases.

Very truly yours,

THE ILLINOIS WATCH

AGS:ALD

By-

May 18, 1931 Illinois letter; HRC: NAWCC

Cavalier, white gold-filled

Cavalier, yellow gold-filled

CAVALIER

Official Name = Cavalier (derived from Illinois advertisements and Illinois Sales and Material Catalogs)
Secondary Name(s) = None
Formerly Known As = None
Time Period = Deco
Case Variations/Rarity = 🕒🕒🕒 WGF/P
🕒🕒🕒🕒 YGF/P
Case Durability = 🕒🕒🕒
Material = 14K GF
Bezel = Molded
Sides = Plain
Lugs = Plain
Lug Size = 16mm
Springbar = Male
Casemaker = Fahys
Case Closure = 3-Part Snap-On Bezel and back
Case Number = Special Model 209
Case Shape = Tonneau
Case Back = Flat
Dimensions = 36 x 28mm
Movement Size = 6/0
Movement Grades/Jewel = 607/17
Seconds at = 6
Dial Number = 8201, 8737
Dial = Silver Finish
Dial Opening = Tonneau
Dial Variations/Rarity = 🕒🕒 Silver Finish, Luminous Numerals
🕒🕒🕒🕒🕒 Silver Finish, Black Numerals
Numerals = Painted, Luminous
Hands = Luminous
Cased in Factory = Yes
Unique Case Design = Yes
Unique Dial Design = No
Introduction Date = 1930
Retail Price New = $45.00
Collectibility = 🕒🕒🕒🕒
Advertisements = Yes
Marketing Themes = "Thoroughly modern in design and of handsome appearance"
"A strap watch of handsome design"
"Modern as tomorrow"

Although the Cavalier appears at first glance to be rather plain, it actually has a fascinatingly complex design. Like the earlier Mate and Ensign models, it has a case whose outlines are a double ogive curve. The curves are further emphasized by the molded bezel, which present the curves at two levels. The lugs, standing out from the sides of the case, further emphasize the graceful tapering of the curves.

The CAVALIER
A strap watch of handsome design—in 14K filled white or natural gold. 17 jewels, black enamel figure dial...... $40

J. Engel catalog, 1932

The Cavalier was shown in the 1930-31 and 1931-32 Illinois Sales Catalogs and was advertised in such periodicals at the *American Magazine* and the *Saturday Evening Post*. In its advertising copywriting, Illinois frequently emphasized the modernity of the Cavalier ("Modern as tomorrow" and "Thoroughly modern in design"), very appropriate for the forward-looking design of this interesting watch.

The Cavalier is much harder to find in white gold-filled than in yellow. However, the yellow gold-filled case is severely prone to case wear, making it difficult to locate one in excellent condition.

Despite the nice design features of its very special Deco-looking case, the Cavalier has thus far been underappreciated. As a result, it is easy to acquire one at a reasonable price.

The CAVALIER

Thoroughly modern in design and of handsome appearance. 14K white or natural filled gold.

Suggested consumer price, $45.

A. I. Hall catalog, 1931

Cavalier inside case back

Look-Alikes

The Cavalier and the Hamilton Whitney are similar in shape and style. The Cavalier was introduced in 1930 and the Whitney in 1932. Both watches were offered in a choice of white or yellow gold-filled cases. The Cavalier's case was made by Fahys and the Whitney's by Keystone.

Hamilton Whitney, yellow gold-filled

Chatham, white gold-filled

Chatham

Official Name = Chatham (derived from Illinois Advertisements and Sales Catalogs)
Secondary Name(s) = None
Formerly Known As = None
Time Period = Moderne
Case Variations/Rarity = ◷◷◷◷◷ YGF/P
◷◷◷◷◷◷ WGF/P, RGP/P
Case Durability = ◷◷ YGF, RGP
◷◷◷ WGF
Material = 10K GF, 10K RGP
Bezel = Plain
Sides = Plain
Lugs = Plain
Lug Size = 16mm
Springbar = Male
Casemakers = Keystone, Philadelphia "Victory" Brand
Case Closure = 2-Part Snap-On Back
Case Number = 652, No Number
Case Shape = Rectangular
Case Back = Flat
Dimensions = 35 x 24mm
Movement Size = 6/0
Movement Grades/Jewel = 605/15, 605A/15
Seconds at = 6
Dial Number = 8499

Dial = Silver Finish
Dial Opening = Rectangular
Dial Variations/Rarity = 🕒🕒🕒🕒🕒🕒 Silver Finish, Etched Raised Gold Numerals, Broken Line Center Box
🕒🕒🕒🕒🕒🕒🕒 Silver Finish, Flush Numerals, No Center Box
Numerals = Flush, Etched
Hands = Steel
Cased in Factory = Yes (cased by Hamilton in Lancaster)
Unique Case Design = No
Unique Dial Design = Yes
Introduction Date = 1934
Retail Price New = $35.00
Collectibility = 🕒🕒🕒🕒
Advertisements = Yes
Marketing Themes = "For sports or business wear"
"Up to the minute in every respect"
"Styled for tomorrow as well as today"

Chatham, yellow gold-filled

The Chatham was featured in the 1934 Illinois Sales Catalog, the last sales catalog ever issued by Illinois. This model was one of the bargain-priced Depression offerings by the Illinois Watch Division of Hamilton. It featured an inexpensive 10K gold-filled case with a 15-jewel movement. The 1934 A. C. Becken catalog, following the Illinois advertising copy, described the Chatham as a watch "For sports or business wear."

The 1934 Illinois Sales Catalog described the Standish, Rockingham and Chatham this way: "These finely made new models for men are up-to-the-minute in every respect. They are built to withstand hard usage. Styled for tomorrow as well as today, they meet the current demand for a truly accurate strap watch in the lower price range. Available in 10K filled gold cases only." Although the advertisement stated otherwise, these models were not able to withstand hard usage as the cases were subject to extreme wear. Their movements, however, were equipped with Elinvar hairsprings.

The Chatham was one of the most inexpensive and one of the last Illinois watches ever offered for sale. Released under Hamilton, after the Illinois Factory had been closed, this watch was aimed at the "bargain shopper." Its 10K gold-filled case and 15-jewel movement attest to Hamilton's desire to keep the price low.

The dial has an interesting design feature with a dotted line pattern on the rectangular box in the center of the dial. The etched and raised Deco-styled numerals are also attractive. This dial, designed by Hamilton, is very difficult to find. There was also a dial without the dotted line box (see advertisement later in this listing).

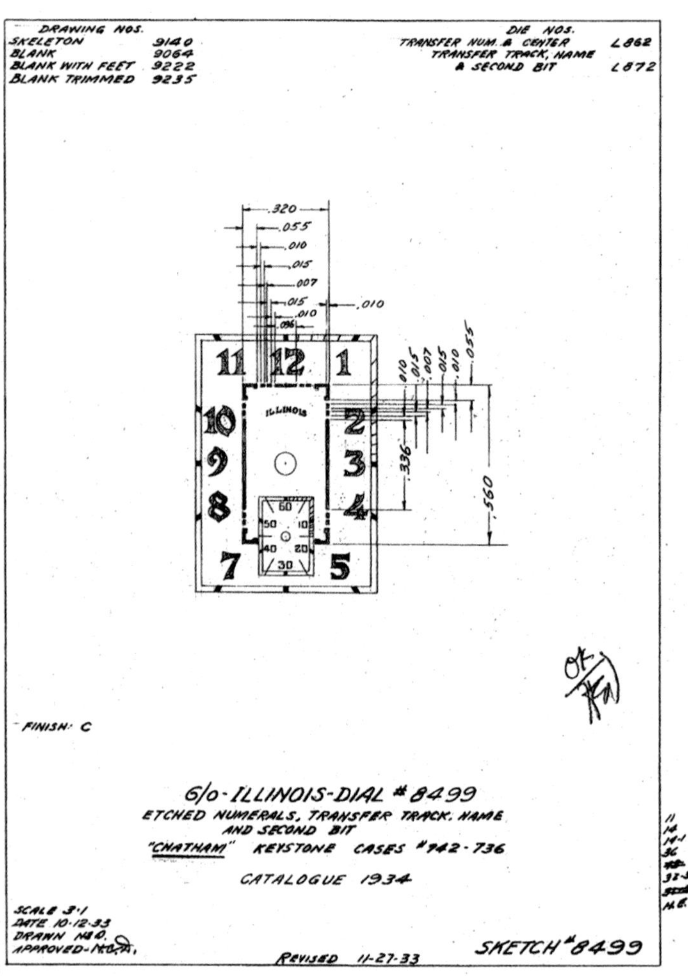

Hamilton drawing of an Illinois Chatham dial, dated November 27, 1933

DIAL SCARCITY

The Chatham, Sangamon, Standish and Urbana were all released around 1934; as such, they were four of the last five men's Illinois wristwatches offered for sale. At this time, the Illinois Factory had been closed for over a year and Hamilton was having difficulty assembling enough Illinois movements to fill orders for even these models. As a result, very few of these watches were released. Today it is almost impossible to find good original dials for these models because so very few were probably produced. Most likely, Hamilton would authorize the making of a dial only if it had an order for one of these models in hand.

More Standish dials can be found than dials for the other three models because its dial is also used also on an Illinois Whippet 6/0 size. Dials for the Chatham, Sangamon and Urbana models, on the other hand, were unique.

Chatham dial

The Chatham case Model No. 652 was produced by Keystone. Keystone also made the Standish case, also in 10K gold-filled, with case Model No. 651. The sequentially numbered Chatham and Standish were produced for Hamilton to use as part of its Depression-era low-price Illinois offerings to the market.

The Chatham was still being offered for sale by the A. C. Becken Company as late as 1937 in "white only." This is ironic, as only two white gold-filled Chathams have been located to date. The Chatham was released during the period Hamilton maintained extremely tight control over what remained of its Illinois Watch Division. The Chatham is a very rare model; only two have ever been found in white gold-filled cases and under ten or so are known to exist in yellow gold-filled cases. The fairly plain design of this model is more similar in style to a Hamilton model than to a typical Illinois watch. One motivation for the release of this watch was to help exhaust Hamilton's inventory of 6/0 size Illinois movement parts. By the actual time of the release, Hamilton was limited by its poor ability to assemble the parts into movements. For this reason, it is extremely difficult to find Chathams today.

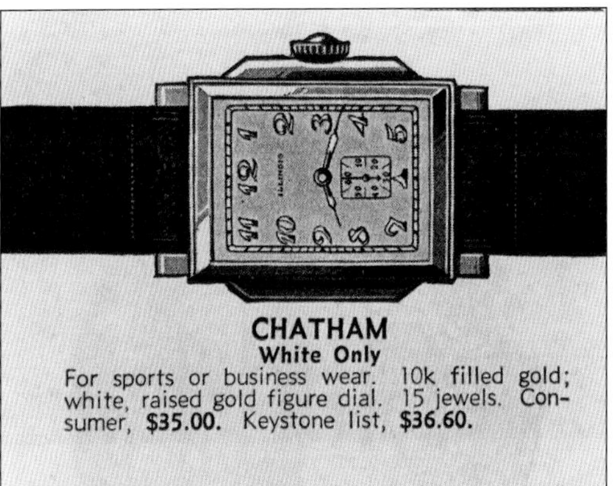

A. C. Becken 1937 catalog, showing Chatham in "white only." Notice there is no dotted-line box dial.

There are at least four Chathams without case Model Numbers: three in a 10K rolled gold plate Philadelphia "Victory" case and one in a 10K gold-filled Keystone case.

VICTORY WATCH CASE

A "Victory" watch case was described as being made of rolled gold plate with a ten-year warranty. The "Victory" trademark was formerly owned by H. Muhr's Sons Watch Case Company. When the Philadelphia Watch Case Company bought Muhr in 1898, the trademark was included in the purchase. Both Philadelphia Watch Case and H. Muhr's Sons ended up being owned by Keystone. Therefore, Keystone used only its own name on the 10K gold-filled Chatham case version for Illinois and the Keystone Philadelphia Victory brand on the even lower end rolled gold plate version of the Chatham. Heretofore, there was never an Illinois offered for sale in a 10K rolled gold plate case other than a very rare Larchmont model.

Keystone inside case back for an Illinois Chatham case Model No. 652

Philadelphia inside case back for an Illinois Chatham in 10K yellow rolled gold plate

The likely explanation for the Philadelphia Victory rolled gold plate Chatham is the failure of Hamilton to enter into exclusive supply contracts for material variations for the Chatham case with Keystone. As a result, Keystone was apparently free to offer a lesser material version of exactly the same case to jobbers and jewelers directly. This was also the same situation for the Standish model, and perhaps even for the late Larchmont model offerings. We now know that, during this timeframe, Hamilton did not allow Illinois to obtain exclusive agreements for its new models; as a result, for example, Elgin, Waltham and Gruen came out with variations of the Urbana case, and Gruen and Longines of the Biltmore 18/0 case.

To date, only three Chatham cases have been found in a Philadelphia Victory rolled gold plate case; it is possible that this case was intended for a non-Illinois movement and dial, but it is certainly appropriate for an Illinois movement and dial to reside in this case. The Chatham, the Standish and the Rockingham were all released for sale in 1934, equipped with an Elinvar hairspring.

The Chatham is perhaps named for Chatham, Illinois, a city adjacent to Springfield.

WHY I COLLECT ILLINOIS

"The Illinois watch is a timepiece that transcends timekeeping into a celebration of the Art Deco era. One would be hard pressed to find any American watch company that has captured the feel of the 1920s and 1930s like the Illinois Watch Company. The design of these timepieces reflects the monuments of that unique period between the wars. When I see the Chrysler Building, I think of the Illinois Ritz with its two-tone case and Egyptian numbers. Then there is the Illinois Chatham with its stepped case design, reminiscent of the Golden Gate Bridge. When you combine this with excellent mechanical movements and the premier engineering of the period, you will achieve a desirable timepiece.

"I knew a watch collector who had amassed a series of American watches. In the display of all of these watches he did not have one Illinois watch. I asked why there was no Illinois watch represented and was told "without an Illinois, my collection is not yet complete.'" *—Len Sequeira*

FANTASTIC FIND

Longtime friend Larry Holzman from Illinois tells me, "In the early 1990s, I advertised in the NAWCC Mart looking to buy men's Hamilton and Illinois wristwatches. In January 1994, I received a phone call from a gentleman who said he had both a Hamilton and an Illinois that I could be interested in. Since he lived relatively close to me, we agreed to meet at the next NAWCC local chapter's meeting. I cannot remember anything about the Hamilton wristwatches I acquired from him, but the Illinois was very plain looking and I did not recognize the model when he showed it to me. He asked for $200.00, and since it was in very nice condition I agreed to that price, still not knowing exactly what I was buying.

"When I arrived home (this was before the days of your *Illinois Watch* book) I pulled out my Illinois Watch Company reference material and identified the watch as a Chatham. The case was 10K yellow gold-filled and the 15-jewel, grade 605, 6/0 size movement. A few months later during a conversation with you (FJF), I mentioned that I had recently acquired a Chatham. You were very skeptical and indicated that you were not sure if you 'knew of anyone that had a 'Chatham.' I was quite surprised, to say the least. I seem to recall sending you a photo of my Chatham just to confirm what it was. About twelve years later I sold this Chatham on eBay for $1,500.00 to an avid Illinois collector."

FANTASTIC FIND

Debra Ciaburri from the Nutmeg State reports: "I purchased your book many years ago for my husband as a gift. Years later we were enjoying the book and identifying our watches in our collection and to my surprise realized that we have a rare Illinois Chatham. The case is signed Model No. 652 Keystone Watch Case Company, 10K gold-filled. It looks like a greenish-yellow gold-filled case. All these years I thought of contacting you to verify that what we have was truly a Chatham. But, for one reason or another I never got around to it.

"Back in 2012, when we received the November/December issue of the NAWCC Watch & Clock *Bulletin*, I was reading your 'Fantastic Finds' article and came across the story of the 'Chatham? Chatham? What Chatham?'. I realized then, after wondering all these years, that ours is indeed an Illinois Chatham. Everything looks right, and it does have the original dial and grade 605 15-jewel movement. Ours could have been number two, as I confirmed in 2004 when I purchased your book. At that time you stated in the book that there were two white gold-filled and one yellow Chatham that had been identified so far.

"We purchased this watch in a lot of four watches at a well-known watch and clock auction house in New Hampshire (Jones and Horan) in 2000. We paid one hundred dollars for the lot. Two were gold-filled Elgins and two Illinois. The other Illinois was a plain white gold-filled cushion style. At the time we were thrilled winning the lot. In a room full of watch collectors to our surprise they did not get a lot of interest. We were just starting to collect Illinois watches at that time and thought because they were somewhat plain nobody really wanted them. It is getting harder and harder to be able to buy nice original examples. But when we do, it makes all the looking and chasing worth it."

Chesterfield

Official Name = Chesterfield (derived from Illinois Sales Catalogs)
Secondary Name(s) = None
Formerly Known As = None
Time Period = Moderne
Case Variations/Rarity = 🕒🕒🕒🕒🕒 TT/WGF/YGF Bezel
🕒🕒🕒🕒🕒🕒🕒 TT/WGF/YGF Bezel, YGF back
Case Durability = 🕒🕒🕒
Material = 14K GF
Bezel = Engraved
Sides = Engraved
Lugs = Plain
Lug Size = 16mm
Springbar = Male
Casemaker = Wadsworth
Case Closure = 2-Part Snap-On Back
Case Number = 196
Case Shape = Rectangular
Case Back = Curved
Dimensions = 37 x 22mm
Movement Size = 12/0
Movement Grade/Jewels = 207/17
Seconds at = 6
Dial Numbers = 8108, 8165, 8238, 8308

Chesterfield two-tone, gold-filled

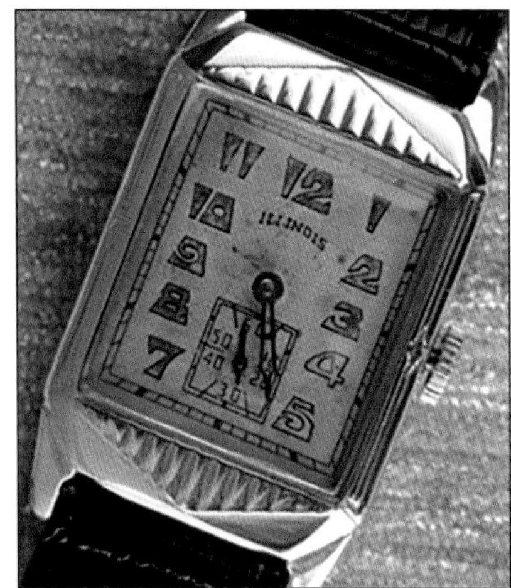

Chesterfield two-tone, gold-filled, Moderne dial

Dials = Silver Finish, Sparkle Finish
Dial Opening = Rectangular
Dial Variations/Rarity = ◷◷◷ Silver Finish, Luminous Numerals
◷◷◷◷ Sparkle Finish, Painted Numerals; Sparkle Finish, Luminous Numerals
◷◷◷◷◷ Silver Finish, Black Numerals
◷◷◷◷◷◷ Silver Finish, Deco Numerals
Numerals = Painted, Luminous
Hands = Steel, Luminous
Cased in Factory = Yes
Unique Case Design = Yes
Unique Dial Design = No
Introduction Date = 1932
Retail Price New = $55.00
Collectibility = ◷◷◷◷
Advertisements = Yes
Marketing Theme = "A clever design"
"Cleverly designed case"

The Chesterfield appears in the 1933 Illinois Sales Catalog as one of the "Pioneers of Greater Values." It is possible that this model is a variation of the Finalist Deco or Finalist as they all share the case Model No. 196. The Chesterfield is only one of two Illinois men's wristwatches that have two-tone white gold-filled and yellow gold-filled bezels. The other model is the Metropolitan. However, the Metropolitan has only a few racing stripes of yellow gold-filled, while the Chesterfield has two pyramids full of yellow gold-fill on the top and bottom of its bezel.

The Chesterfield, an example of the great, bold designs offered by the Illinois Watch Company, is a highly popular and sought-after Deco/Moderne-inspired watch. The design of the Chesterfield is similar in theme to the Ritz with its use of sharp edges, angles, steps and two-tone of yellow and white gold-filled.

A perhaps one-of-a-kind version of the Chesterfield has been found. It has the standard two-tone bezel, but a yellow gold-filled case back in place of the standard white gold-filled case back. The watch is completely legitimate as its case numbers match (illustrated in the images below). In addition, it was inspected and tested by a master watch repairer for authenticity. This, in effect, is a double two-tone watch, making it extremely rare and very valuable. This variation was probably a special Illinois factory order.

The inside bezel of the double two-tone Chesterfield has case numbers matching those on its inside case back.

The yellow gold-filled case back of the ultra-rare double two-tone Chesterfield

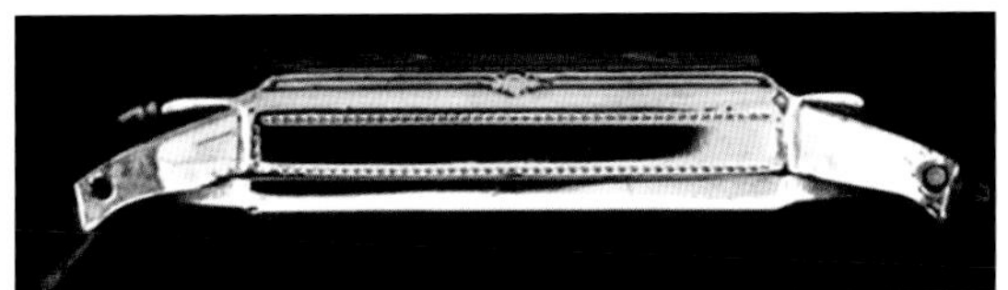

Side of the double two-tone Chesterfield

FANTASTIC FIND

"I don't know why I randomly decided to check out e-Bay today . . . I always have dreams of looking, hoping that something incredible will simply pop up with a cheap "Buy It Now." Anyway, I see a new item pop up labeled "Finalist Deco." Well, well, well, that Finalist Deco turns out to be a Chesterfield and guess what, with a Buy It Now for $450. The funny part is the seller included an option to "Make an Offer!" Now in the world of eBay, the first person who hits the Buy It Now gets the prize. I thought for half a second to make an offer, but realized that this watch would be gone in seconds if I messed around. Bam! The Buy It Now button was pushed, and a beautiful Chesterfield, one of the most desirable Illinois known, was had. The Chesterfield is a rare, two-toned watch that has a beautiful yellow gold-filled pyramid shape on the bezel at 12 and 6 . . . a truly gorgeous Art Deco marvel.

A super day on the bay!" —*Greg Hart*

Chesterfield Stepped Bezel

Official Name = Unknown
Secondary Name(s) = Chesterfield Stepped Bezel (derived from collectors usage reflecting the stepped design of its bezel)
Formerly Known As = None
Time Period = Moderne
Case Variations/Rarity = 🕒🕒🕒🕒🕒🕒 WGF/E
Case Durability = 🕒🕒
Material = 14K GF
Bezel = Engraved (lightly)
Sides = Engraved
Lugs = Plain
Lug Size = 16mm
Springbar = Male
Casemaker = Wadsworth
Case Closure = 2-Part Snap-On Back
Case Number = 196
Case Shape = Rectangular
Case Back = Curved
Dimensions = 37 x 22mm
Movement Size = 12/0
Movement Grade/Jewels= 207/17

Chesterfield Stepped Bezel, white gold-filled

Seconds at = 6
Dial Numbers = 8108, 8165, 8238, 8308
Dials = Silver Finish, Sparkle Finish
Dial Opening = Rectangular
Dial Variations = 🕒🕒🕒 Silver Finish, Luminous Numerals
🕒🕒🕒🕒 Sparkle Finish, Painted Numerals; Sparkle Finish, Luminous Numerals
🕒🕒🕒🕒🕒 Silver Finish, Black Numerals
Numerals = Painted, Luminous
Hands = Luminous
Cased in Factory = Yes
Unique Case Design = Yes
Unique Dial Design = Yes
Introduction Date = 1932
Retail Price New = Unknown
Collectibility = 🕒🕒🕒🕒
Advertisements = No
Marketing Theme = Unknown

It remains a mystery why this rare member of the Illinois Chesterfield family does not appear in any known Illinois advertisement or Illinois Sales Catalog. This model has the same case Model No. 196 as the Chesterfield, Finalist and the Finalist Deco. Although it is in the Chesterfield family, its official name is unknown. This model is very rare; fewer than one dozen have been located.

Its design can be distinguished from the two-tone Chesterfield. While the Chesterfield sports a gold pyramid at the top and bottom of its white gold-filled bezel, the stepped bezel displays a stepped pyramid in the top and bottom of the bezel, with delicate engraved lines on the inside of the steps. The design of this Deco/Moderne watch is very subtle and striking at the same time.

The name of this watch may be one of the unidentified names on the List of Factory Cased Illinois Watches. Candidates for its name are John Alden or Rye, the two remaining unidentified 12/0 size watches on this list.

It is possible that the Stepped Bezel may have contained yellow at one time, as several examples found have a yellow cast in the pyramid. If so, then there were two types of two-tone Chesterfields. The corners of the bezel were prone to wear on the Chesterfield Stepped Bezel. However, it is so rare and collectible that there are eager buyers for them in any condition. The Chesterfield Stepped Bezel is one of the most sought-after Illinois watches.

Chevalier

Official Name = Chevalier (derived from the December 1928 advertisement in the *Keystone* for Rosenberg Brothers Jewelers on Canal Street in New York City)
Secondary Name(s) = None
Formerly Known As = Black Enamel Cushion (so called by collectors until the above-noted advertisement was discovered)
Time Period = Deco
Case Variations/Rarity = 🕒🕒🕒🕒 C/E (Black)
🕒🕒🕒🕒🕒🕒 C/E (Blue)
🕒🕒🕒🕒🕒🕒🕒 YG/E (Black)
Case Durability = 🕒
Material = C, 14K YG
Bezel = Black Enamel, Blue Enamel
Sides = Engraved
Lugs = Plain
Lug Size = 16mm
Springbar = Male
Casemakers = Keystone, Unknown (unsigned)
Case Closure = 3-Part Snap-On Bezel and Back
Case Number = None
Case Shape = Cushion
Case Back = Flat
Dimensions = 37 x 31mm
Movement Size = 3/0
Movement Grades/Jewels = 24/17
Seconds at = 6
Dial Number = 8265
Dials = Enamel, Silver Finish
Dial Opening = Cushion
Dial Variations/Rarity = 🕒🕒🕒 Silver Finish
🕒🕒🕒🕒🕒🕒 Enamel
Numerals = Form shaped enamel numerical bezel
Hands = Steel
Cased in Factory = Yes
Unique Case Design = No
Unique Dial Design = No
Introduction Date = 1928
Retail Price New = $25.00
Collectibility = 🕒🕒🕒🕒
Advertisements = Yes
Marketing Themes = "Presenting tomorrow's style sensation today"
"Styled in the modern manner"
"Guaranteed for life against wear"

Chevalier, chrome, black enamel; enamel dial

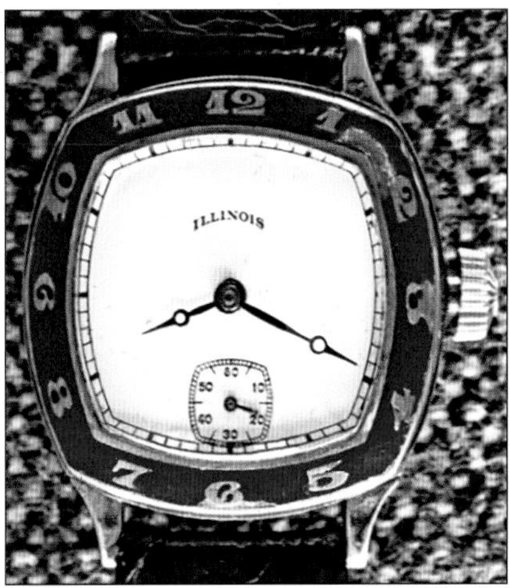

Chevalier, chrome, blue enamel

The Chevalier was advertised by the Rosenberg Brothers Jewelers of New York City in the November 22, 1928 issue of the *Jewelers' Circular* and in the December 1928 issue of the *Keystone*. The advertisement touts the Chevalier's "Salient Features" as:

- "Special Keystone chromium plated case, with exclusive buckle.
- The hour numerals appearing on the form shaped bezel are surrounded by a field of genuine hard-baked enamel.
- Guaranteed for life against wear."

The advertisement claims: "Guaranteed for life against wear." However, unfortunately, the chromium-plated case back is highly porous and is extremely susceptible to bad pitting and wear, notwithstanding the strong claim to the contrary in the advertisement. But one should not be discouraged, as the case back can be easily and inexpensively repaired.

The 1928 advertisement further claims that this is the first time this watch is being shown, "embodying the rapidly increasing vogue of a form shaped enamel numerical bezel." The advertisement further asserts that the case was executed by "one of the foremost ranking casemakers of today, the Keystone Watch Case Co."

December, 1928 *The KEYSTONE* Page 51

The NEW *Waltham* CHEVALIER

(Cased and Timed at the Waltham Factory)

Presenting tomorrow's style sensation—today

Styled in the modern manner

STEALING a march on the advance style of the coming year, we are showing for the first time a Waltham Strap Watch embodying the rapidly increasing vogue of a form shaped enameled numerical bezel, to sell at the popular retail price of $25. This figure assures you VOLUME sales. The case was created by the Waltham Watch Co. and executed for them by one of the foremost ranking case makers of today, The Keystone Watch Case Co. We have arranged with the Waltham Watch Co. for the exclusive distribution of this new model. This is for your protection in merchandising.

WALTHAM CHEVALIER

SALIENT FEATURES OF THE NEW WALTHAM CHEVALIER

Special Keystone Chromium plated case, with exclusive buckle.

The hour numerals appearing on the form shaped bezel are surrounded by a field of genuine hard-baked enamel. Guaranteed for life against wear.

Fitted with specially prepared Waltham CHEVALIER seven jewel movement with gold etched minute track and second markings.

Straps of unusual leather design; . . . Nile Green presentation box with special silver Modernistic design.

A popular price for appearance and rich beauty that is to be found only in much higher-priced watches.

Cased, timed, regulated and guaranteed by the Waltham Watch Company.

RETAIL PRICE **$25.00**

YOUR PRICE **$13.75**

less 6%

Terms, 10th of the following month. Initial Distribution on or about December 1st.

SOLE DISTRIBUTORS

Rosenberg Bros.

Dept M

121 Canal Street

NEW YORK

Keystone, December 1928

The Chevalier-type watch was not unique to Keystone, Waltham or Illinois. Other casemakers offered very similar (if not identical) enameled bezel cases, and other watch manufacturers, such as Elgin and some Swiss firms, also offered this type of model. To be considered a legitimate Illinois version, it must come housed in a Keystone-signed case or in an unsigned case. The rarest by far are the Illinois Chevaliers that came with enamel dials. To date, only six of these beautiful dials have been identified. The metal dials for this model are listed in the December 26, 1930 Illinois Watch Dial and Hand Catalogue, where the listing specifies dial "8265 for enamel bezel cases." This dial is not contained in the 1936 Illinois Materials Catalog. The bezel came in black or blue, but the black is by far the more prevalent.

Under the Osgood entry in this chapter, there is a round enamel bezel version of the Chevalier. It is believed that the Chevalier was cased in the Illinois Watch Factory, as the "Chevalier" is on the List of Factory Cased Illinois Watches. However, the Chevalier is listed under the 6/0 size watches, not 3/0 size, so it may have been listed under the wrong column and should have been with the 3/0 size watches.

One extremely rare, perhaps one-of-a-kind Chevalier has been found in a solid yellow gold case by Keystone with an enamel dial. There is also a Waltham version of this model in a solid yellow gold case with a blue enamel bezel in a case made by the Dennison Watch Case Company.

Chevalier, yellow gold case

Chieftain, white gold-filled

Chieftain, yellow gold-filled, wrong hands

Chieftain

Official Name = Chieftain (derived from Illinois advertisement and Illinois Sales and Material Catalogs).
Secondary Name(s) = None
Formerly Known As = None
Time Period = Deco
Case Variations/Rarity = 🕒🕒 WGF/E
🕒🕒🕒🕒🕒 YGF/E
Case Durability = 🕒 YGF
🕒🕒 WGF
Material = 14K GF
Bezel = Engraved
Sides = Engraved
Lugs = Covered
Lug Size = 16mm
Springbar = Male
Casemaker = Fahys
Case Closure = 3-Part Snap-On Bezel and Back
Case Number = 163
Case Shape = Tonneau
Case Back = Flat
Dimensions = 33 x 28mm
Movement Size = 6/0
Movement Grade/Jewels= 905/15
Seconds at = 9
Dial Number = 8709
Dials = Silver Finish, Butler Center
Dial Opening = Tonneau
Dial Variations/Rarity = 🕒🕒🕒 Silver Finish Luminous Numerals; Silver Finish, Silver Butler Center
🕒🕒🕒🕒🕒 Silver Finish, Black Numerals; Silver Finish, Gold Butler Center
Numerals = Painted, Luminous
Hands = Luminous
Cased in Factory = Yes
Unique Case Design = Yes
Unique Dial Design = Yes
Introduction Date = 1929
Retail Price New = $40.00
Collectibility = 🕒🕒🕒🕒
Advertisements = Yes
Marketing Themes = "Patterned after the signs and symbols of America's first people"
"Unusually designed case"

The 1929–30 Illinois Sales Catalog referred to the Chieftain's "unusually designed case." The American Indian bezel motif further prompted Illinois, in its 1930–31 catalog, to elaborate on the description: "The engraving design of the Chieftain has been patterned after the signs and symbols of America's first people, giving the watch background an attractive design."

The Chieftain appeared in several national publications, such as *Collier's* magazine (June 1, 1929) and the *American Magazine* (August 1929), as well as in various jobbers' catalogs.

The Illinois Chieftain, *15 jewels, 14k gold-filled, $40.*

American Magazine, August 1929

The Chieftain is one of the most sought-after Illinois models. The powerful, deco-inspired Southwestern motif of the bezel makes this an unusual, striking and popular model. Unfortunately, the Chieftain is prone to severe case wear on the top and bottom of its bezel. The yellow gold-filled version was even more susceptible to wear than the white gold-filled one; as a result, it is extremely difficult to find a yellow one in excellent condition. The Chieftain's 15-jewel movement helped to keep its sales price low.

The white gold-filled watches came with a silver butler center dial, and the yellow gold-filled models came with an unusual gold butler center dial. It is the only Illinois model offered with covered lugs. As one of the larger Illinois models, it is suitable for collectors with large wrists.

Chieftain and Ensign advertisement, *Iola Register* (Iola, KS), May 11, 1929; image from *newspapers.com*

Chieftain silver butler center dial

FRAUD ALERT

In September 2014, a vintage watch dealer discovered that an alleged two-tone Chieftain being offered to him had a center section of the case that had been replated white. Its bezel and case back were yellow gold-filled, but even the lugs had still visible wear underneath the plating. Be extra-careful if offered a watch in two-tone that is not known to exist in two-tone.

Look-Alikes

The Illinois Chieftain is very similar to the Hamilton Barrel B model. The Chieftain came in a 14K yellow or white gold-filled case by Fahys. The Barrel B was 14K gold-filled or 14K white or green gold in a case also made by Fahys. The Chieftain was issued in 1929, as was the Barrel B. Both are subject to heavy wear.

Chieftain inside case back

Hamilton Barrel B

WHY I COLLECT ILLINOIS

"My reasons for collecting Illinois watches go back to my interest in Art Deco things—architecture, art, textiles, watches, and many others. For example, one of my prized favorites is the Chieftain. Still looks good after all the years."

—Steve Scarborough

WHY I COLLECT ILLINOIS

"Oddly enough, I was at first not attracted to the Illinois brand! My first attraction to vintage watches was a Rolex I saw in *GQ* in 1985. I went from Rolex dealer to Rolex dealer, magazine in hand, asking 'Where can I buy one like this?' One dealer finally explained that was a vintage Rolex, not new and not available from dealers. I researched some vintage watch dealers and bought my first vintage watch, a Rolex Viceroy on Madison Ave and boy I paid dearly for it! I still have it today. Initially I focused on collecting Bulova and Gruen. Then I discovered Hamilton, fell in love with the look. Being a mechanical engineer, I became fascinated by the mechanical movements. Then living in New Hampshire, I ran into a Massachusetts watch repair shop and met a wonderful old chap, Fred Jamros, then in his seventies, who offered to teach me the fine skill of vintage mechanical watch repair. He was a graduate of the Waltham Watch School. The lessons would occur at 6:00 a.m. every Sunday morning in his shop about 40 minutes from my home in New Hampshire. Yes, it was early but what an opportunity! I went every Sunday for well over a year.

The Hamilton look and ultimately working on Hamiltons became my passion, collecting and repairing. Pre-Internet, off I went each weekend, early mornings again, but now searching local flea markets and antique shows initially in New Hampshire, then later in Pennsylvania, having relocated there. Now I was living in Bucks County, within an hour from Hamilton country, Lancaster, Pennsylvania. Wow, did my Hamilton interests and collection explode! Also I became a member of the NAWCC and routinely attended the Chapter 1 MART, which was incredible for 'Fantastic Finds' back then! Naturally I ran into Illinois watches in my weekend hunts, but the unique, almost Victorian look was just not my thing. Not yet anyway! Being part of the NAWCC, and reading the *Bulletin* every other month, there were ads by collectors and fellow hobbyists selling watches via paper lists obtainable by sending a Self-Addressed Stamped Envelope (SASE). I sent many SASEs out, including one to Mr. Fred Friedberg, who was advertising his Illinois watches for sale via wonderful color photocopied lists of Illinois wristwatches he laid out on the copier. Imagine color photocopies, how awesome was that! Fred was 'cutting edge'; everybody else had black and white.

Well, the person that made the turn for me was Fred with his lists, and the watch that attracted me like no other Illinois or other watch at the time was the Illinois Chieftain due to its American Indian–like motif! But the attraction of such designs broke the barrier for me, and I was hooked on the brand I now realized was like no other: Illinois! Why I was so blind prior I cannot answer as I do not know! So the factors for my collecting are the uniquely fascinating case designs, representing the era these watches came out! Being the first wristwatches after the pockets, the sub-seconds at nine was so different and cool! And not to forget the movements, also a unique look of their own, and craftsmanship and pride seen in every one. I love the time spent on the damaskeening of some of the movements! Thank you, Fred, and thank you, Illinois!"

—Ed Kulha

Chrysanthemum, yellow gold

Chrysanthemum, yellow gold

Chrysanthemum

Official Name = Chrysanthemum (derived from the research of the late L. Michael Fultz, Illinois expert and frequent author on vintage watches)
Secondary Name(s) = Telephone Dial (derived from collectors' usage)
Formerly Known As = None
Time Period = Deco
Case Variations/Rarity = 🕒🕒🕒🕒🕒🕒 YG/E
🕒🕒🕒🕒🕒🕒🕒 WG/E
Case Durability = 🕒🕒🕒🕒
Material = 14K WG, 14K YG
Bezel = Engraved
Sides = Engraved
Lugs = Engraved
Lug Size = 16mm
Springbar = Male
Casemaker = Solidarity
Case Closure = 3-Part Snap On-Bezel and Back
Case Number = None
Case Shape = Cushion
Case Back = Flat
Dimensions = 33 x 28mm
Movement Size = 6/0
Movement Grades/Jewels = 904/17, 905/17
Seconds at = 9
Dial Number = None
Dial = Enamel
Dial Opening = Round
Dial Variations/Rarity = 🕒🕒🕒🕒🕒🕒🕒 Enamel, Luminous Numerals
Numerals = Luminous
Hands = Steel
Cased in Factory = No
Unique Case Design = Yes
Unique Dial Design = Yes
Introduction Date = 1926
Retail Price New = Unknown
Collectibility = 🕒🕒🕒🕒
Advertisements = No
Marketing Theme = Unknown

The dial design of the Chrysanthemum was inspired by the invention and release of the rotary dial telephone.

The aforementioned Fultz evidently discovered the name of this very rare and perhaps one-of-a-kind special-order dial and watch. This is the only original Telephone Dial in 6/0 size known to exist. In addition, it is the only original Telephone Dial known to exist with subsidiary seconds at 9. The dial was most likely a custom order request to the Illinois Watch Factory. The factory was well known for accommodating such requests.

This uniquely-designed yellow gold case has what are apparently chrysanthemum flowers engraved on each corner of its bezel. There is at least one similar case in white gold known to exist, but without the Telephone Dial. In *The Illinois Watch: The Life and Times of A Great American Watch Company*, this watch was mistakenly noted to be in yellow gold-filled, but it is solid yellow gold.

Chrysanthemum inside case back

Commander

See listing for **Wentworth**

Commodore / Bostonian / Biltmore Belmont / LaSalle

Commodore, white gold-filled

Official Names = Commodore and Bostonian (derived from Illinois advertisements and Illinois Sales and Material Catalogs)
Secondary Name(s) = Biltmore 6/0 (derived from Illinois advertisements, Illinois Sales and Material Catalogs and jobbers catalogs). Belmont and LaSalle (pursuant to internal Hamilton records).
Formerly Known As = None
Time Period = Moderne
Case Variations/Rarity = 🕒🕒 YGF/P
🕒🕒🕒 WGF/P
Case Durability = 🕒🕒🕒
Material = 14K GF
Bezel = Plain
Sides = Plain
Lugs = Plain
Lug Size = 16mm
Springbar = Male
Casemaker = Keystone
Case Closure = 3-Part Snap-On Bezel and Back
Case Number = 616
Case Shape = Rectangular
Case Back = Flat
Dimensions = 34 x 27mm
Movement Size = 6/0

Commodore, yellow gold-filled

Movement Grade/Jewels = 607/17
Seconds at = 6
Dial Number = 8077
Dial = Silver Finish
Dial Opening = Rectangular
Dial Variations/Rarity = 🕐🕐 Silver Finish, Black Numerals
🕐🕐🕐🕐 Sparkle Finish, Black Numerals
🕐🕐🕐🕐🕐🕐 Sparkle Finish, Luminous Numerals
Numerals = Painted
Hands = Steel
Cased in Factory = Yes
Unique Case Design = No
Unique Dial Design = Yes
Introduction Date = 1931 (Commodore); 1931 (Bostonian); 1932 (Biltmore 6/0)
Retail Price New = $37.50; $47.50 (with bracelet); $60.00 Biltmore 6/0 (with Bracelet)
Collectibility = 🕐🕐🕐🕐
Advertisements = Yes
Marketing Themes = "Will appeal to men of medium stature"
"Extremely masculine in appearance"
"Conservatively plain"

"Modern in design and an exceptional value" was the description given the Commodore in the Illinois 1931–32 Sales Catalog. It was advertised in the *Saturday Evening Post* in December 1931 as well as in several jobbers' catalogs.

If the Commodore came equipped with a metal bracelet, it was called a Bostonian. In the Illinois Factory pages in the 1932 A. C. Becken, the listing for the Bostonian read: "A striking combination of 14K filled case and perfectly matched bracelet."

A recent discovery has been made about the Biltmore 6/0. Illinois turned the Commodore into a Biltmore by upping the movement from 15 jewels to 17 jewels (just as we have discovered it did when making the Arlington into a Hawthorne). A Biltmore is pictured in the 1932–33 Holsman's Jewelry Drummer catalog, where it is listed only in white gold-filled and shown with a leather strap. The 1933 Chicago World's Fair edition of the Shure Winner Catalog No. 120 depicts the same watch, though offered in yellow gold-filled as well as white, equipped with a metal bracelet and called a Biltmore De Luxe (presumably because of the attachment). Both catalogs list the watch as having a 6/0 size 17-jewel movement. (There is also an 18/0 size Illinois wristwatch named Biltmore, but it has no similarity to either the Biltmore 6/0 or the Commodore, Bostonian, LaSalle or Latonia models.)

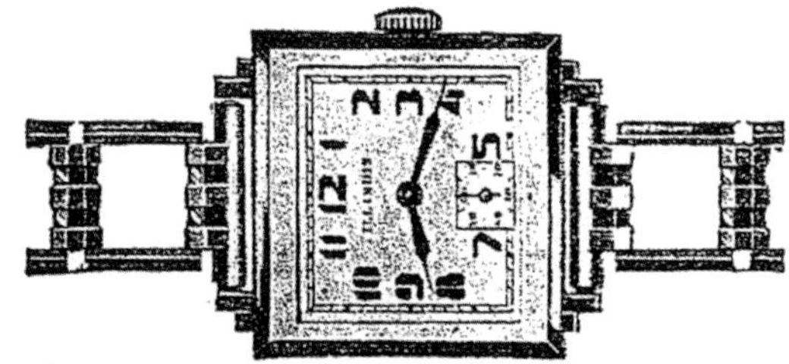

Illinois Biltmore De Luxe, 6/0 size, 17 jewel, 14K white or natural yellow gold filled case, metal band to match. Black figure dial.
No. 22W42. White Gold. Each............... **20.50**
No. 22W43. Yellow Gold. Each............... **20.50**
(Retail price 60.00)

Shure Winner catalog, 1933

Bostonian with its original metal band

The Commodore is an attractive Deco/Moderne-style watch that is greatly underappreciated. It is still available at very reasonable prices today. The sparkle dial version of this model is especially eye-catching. Both the white and yellow gold-filled cases are subject to modest corner bezel wear. The white gold-filled case holds up better than the yellow one; however, the case is more difficult to locate in white than yellow.

The Illinois Watch Company had a pocket watch named the Commodore after Commodore Perry.

COMMODORE PERRY (1794-1858)

Matthew Calbraith Perry, a commodore of the U.S. Navy, commanded U.S. naval forces during the Mexican-American War (1846–48). He is probably most famous for the leading role he played in the opening of Japan to the West, culminating in the Convention of Kanagawa in 1854.

Portrait of Commodore Matthew C. Perry, Commander of the United States Expedition to Japan, in *The Illustrated London News*, May 7, 1853

A recently discovered internal Hamilton document indicates that this model was apparently also called a Belmont and LaSalle. Both of these names are on the "List of Names of Cased Illinois Watches by Sizes." We do not know what distinguished these named models from the Commodore, Bostonian or Biltmore 6/0. It is also possible that Hamilton may have listed these names in the wrong place on its list. Perhaps one of these models' names signified that the model had a sparkle finish dial with luminous numerals, as one might infer from the recently discovered NOS dial shown below.

No. 18045. The Biltmore is a 6/0 size 17 jewel Illinois fitted in a **14k** gold filled white or natural gold case. A very handsome mannish looking watch. Special dial. Retails for **$50.00.**

No. 18045. Biltmore white.......................**$18.60**
No. 18046. Biltmore white.......................18.60

Holsman's Jewelry Drummer 1932–33 catalog, with Depression-era wholesale price. Note that the Biltmore 6/0 is listed only in white gold-filled and shown with a leather strap.

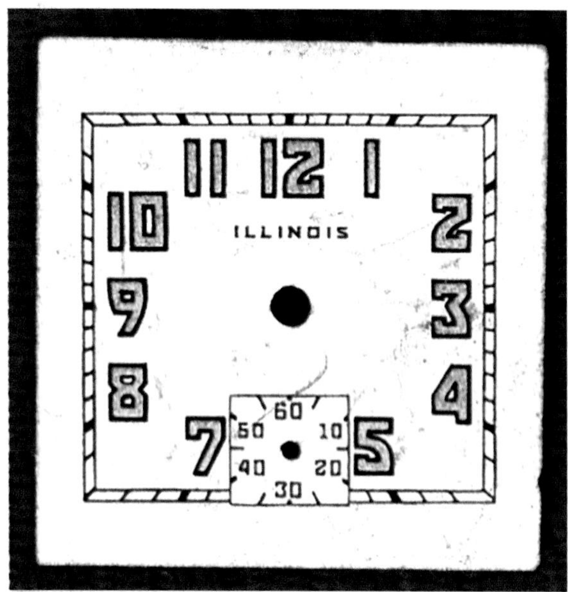

NOS Commodore dial, sparkle finish, luminous numerals

Commodore inside case back

Conneric Watches / Generic / Contract

Official Name = Connerics (Derived from a combination of Generic and Contract Case Models in the Post-Generic and Post-Deco Time Periods)
Secondary Name(s) = Generic, Contract
Formerly Known As = Contract
Time Period = Post-Moderne
Case Variations/Rarity = 🕐 10K, WGF, 10K, YGF, Others
🕐🕐🕐🕐 14K YG
🕐🕐🕐🕐🕐 14K WG
Case Durability = 🕐🕐 WGF, YGF
🕐🕐🕐🕐 WG, YG
Material = 14K WG, 14K YG, 10K WGF, 10 YGF
Bezel = Plain, Engraved
Sides = Plain, Engraved
Lugs = Plain, Engraved
Lug Size = 16mm
Springbar = Male
Casemakers = Star, Keystone, Manheimer, Others
Case Closures = 2-Part Snap-On Bezel and Back; 3-Part Snap-On Bezel and Back
Case Numbers = 1099, 1117, 1266, 1227, 1291, 1292
Case Shapes = Rectangular, Square, Tonneau, Others
Case Backs = Flat
Dimensions = Various
Movement Sizes = 6/0, 18/0
Movement Grades/Jewels = 605/15, 607/17, 805/15, 805A/15, 807/17
Seconds at = 6, None
Dial Numbers = 8475, 8476, 8462, 8463 8489
Dial = Silver Finish
Dial Openings = Square, Rectangular, Tonneau
Dial Variations = 🕐🕐🕐🕐 Silver Finish, Etched Numerals; Sparkle Finish, Applied Gold Numerals
Numerals = Etched, Applied Gold Numerals
Hands = Steel
Cased in Factory = No
Unique Case Design = No
Unique Dial Design = No
Introduction Date = 1933–1935
Retail Price New = Unknown
Collectibility = 🕐🕐🕐
Advertisements = Yes
Marketing Theme = Various

Conneric, white gold-filled

Conneric, yellow gold-filled

The Star Watch Case Company frequently advertised many of the cases for these models for use with Elgin, Illinois and Waltham movements and dials. Some examples are shown here. First is a solid gold Conneric model, in its presentation box, from the May & Malone 1934 catalog. Below it are photographs of two gold-filled Conneric models.

Conneric, white gold-filled

Conneric, yellow gold-filled

A Generic Period watch is one from the early 1920s to the early 1930s that contained a movement and dial from either Elgin, Waltham or Illinois that could be placed in a watch case supplied by a jeweler or jobber. Thus, identical cases could be offered for sale with the watches distinguished only by their dials and movements. This practice characterized the Generic Period. A "Contract Case" was a case supplied by watch casemakers to anyone after the Generic Period that could contain movements and dials from various watch manufacturers. The Generic and Contract watches were seldom cased and sold by the watch manufacturing companies.

However, during the research for this book it was discovered that in 1933 and 1934, Hamilton began designing dials for Illinois to help deplete inventory of Illinois 6/0 and 18/0 size parts and movements. Hamilton did so by specifying the cases that these dials were being designed for. For example, Hamilton was designing dials for Star Watch Case Company cases (case numbers 1099, 1117, 1227, 1266, 1291, and 1292) and also for cases from distributors Aisenstein-Woronock, the Manheimer Watch Company, and for Keystone (case numbers 649, 736, 741 and 742). Hamilton may also have supplied at least one such dial and 18/0 size movement for an Ollendorff case, but this dial has not been found among the identified Hamilton Conneric dials. (See the listing for **Ollendorff** later in this chapter.)

Thus, these models, when complete, were not Generic watches as they were after that time period, and were not Contract watches as Hamilton knew the cases that were housing their Illinois-designed dials and movements. Since they were neither Generic nor Contract, they are considered now a hybrid of a Contract and Generic watch or a "Conneric" watch. It is highly likely that these cases were purchased by certain Illinois jobbers (e.g., Manheimer and Aisenstein-Woronock) and used to house the Illinois movements and dials supplied by Hamilton. We know from the drawings shown in Chapter 5 that Hamilton was designing dials for Aisenstein-Woronock and Manheimer.

Hamilton also provided other movements and dials of this nature for Post-Moderne cases then manufactured by Star and Keystone. The same Post-Moderne Star and Keystone cases were also sold to Waltham and Elgin. Owing to Hamilton's desire to exhaust Illinois' inventory, Illinois had thus gone full circle; at Illinois' end of life, Hamilton was offering Illinois dials and movements for these Conneric models which were, in effect, later generation "Generic" models. The Connerics were not likely cased and timed in the Hamilton factory in Lancaster, but by jobbers and others.

Examples of Conneric Hamilton dial drawings for Illinois Conneric models are shown here.

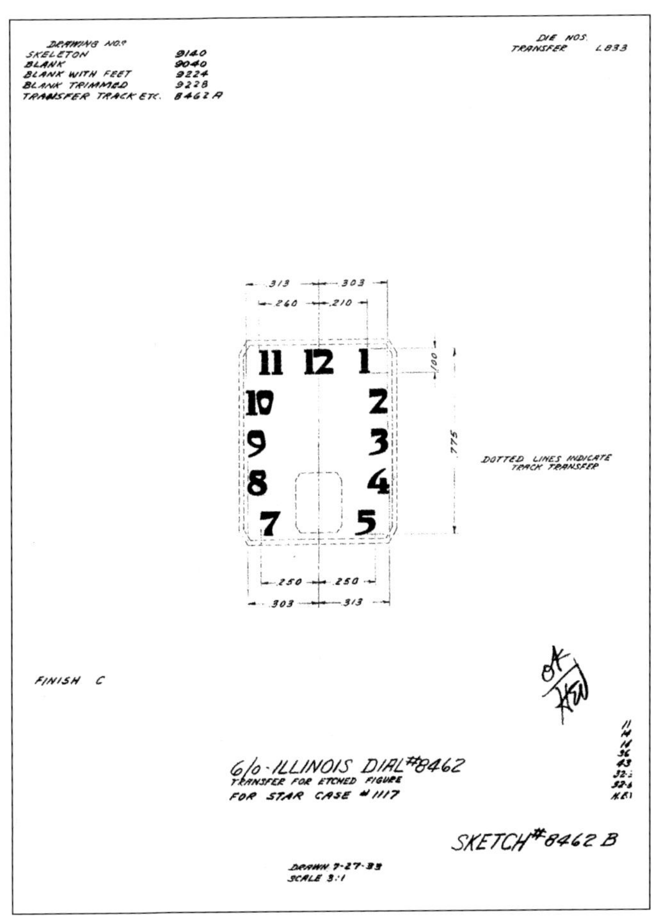

An Illinois dial for a Conneric model in Star case #1117

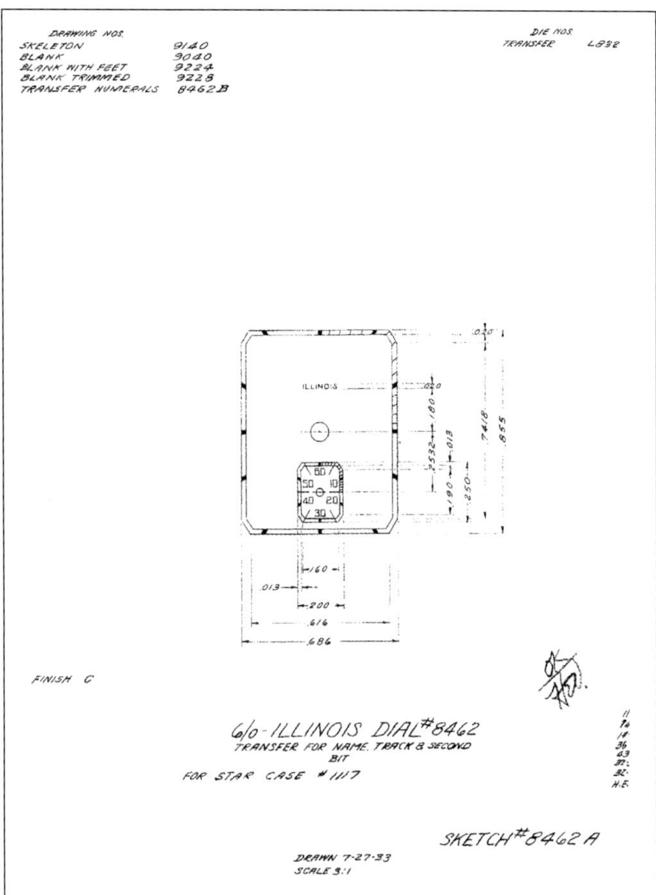

An Illinois dial for a Conneric model in Star case #1117

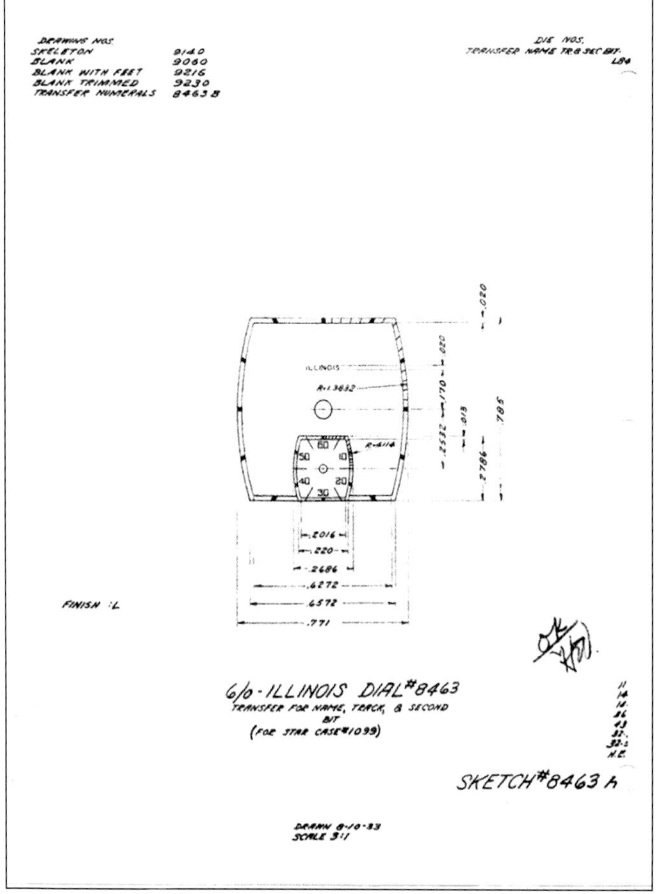

An Illinois dial for a Conneric model in Star case #1099

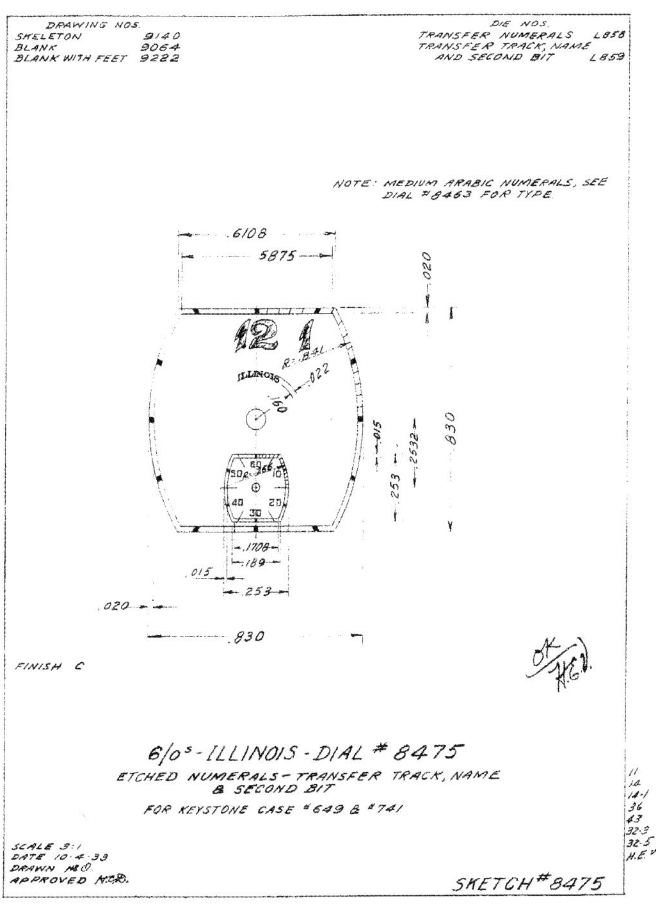

An Illinois dial for Conneric models in Keystone cases #649 and #741; no examples of these Keystone Conneric cases have been found to date.

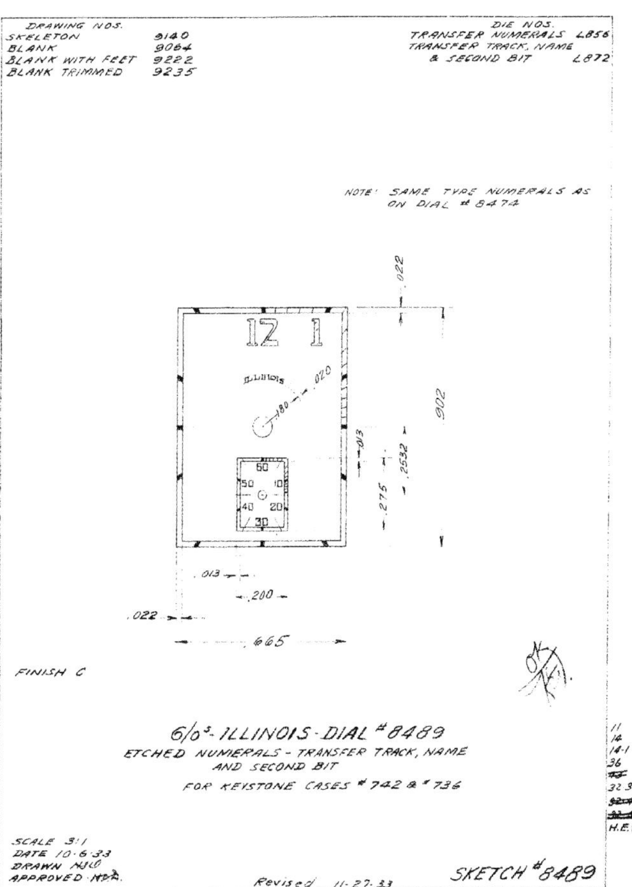

Although the two above Hamilton drawings for Illinois dials in Keystone cases were prepared, no example of any of the Keystone Conneric cases has been found to date.

Conneric, yellow gold-filled case

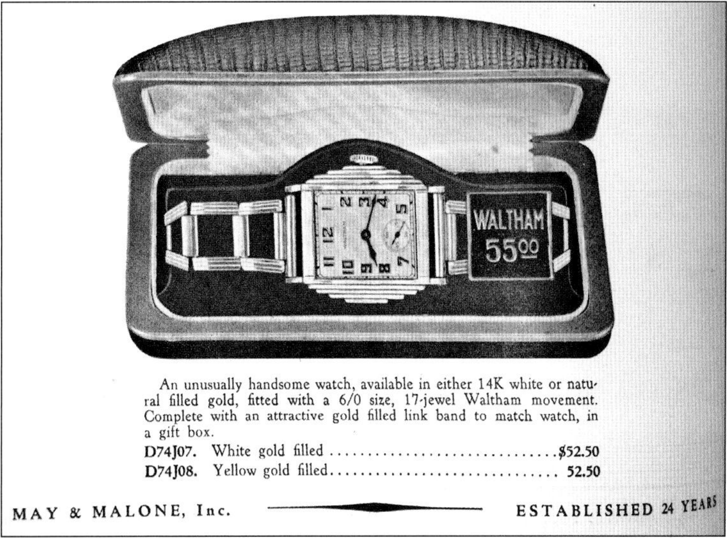

An unusually handsome watch, available in either 14K white or natural filled gold, fitted with a 6/0 size, 17-jewel Waltham movement. Complete with an attractive gold filled link band to match watch, in a gift box.

D74J07. White gold filled $52.50
D74J08. Yellow gold filled 52.50

MAY & MALONE, Inc. ESTABLISHED 24 YEARS

May & Malone catalog, 1935

Consul, white gold

Consul two-tone, white and green gold

Consul

Official Name = Consul (derived from Illinois advertisements and Illinois Sales and Material Catalogs)
Secondary Name(s) = None
Formerly Known As = None
Time Period = Deco
Case Variations/Rarity = 🕒🕒🕒 WG/E
🕒🕒🕒🕒🕒 WG/P, TT/E
🕒🕒🕒🕒🕒🕒 GG/E
Case Durability = 🕒🕒🕒🕒
Material = 14K WG, 14K GG, 14K WG/GG
Bezel = Plain, Engraved
Sides = Engraved
Lugs = Plain, Engraved
Lug Size = 16mm
Springbar = Male
Casemaker = Solidarity
Case Closure = 3-Part Snap-On Bezel and Back
Case Number = Special Model 152
Case Shape = Tonneau
Case Back = Curved
Dimensions = 37 x 29mm
Movement Size = 6/0
Movement Grades/Jewels = 601/21, 607/17, 905/17, 907/19, 909/21
Seconds at = 6, 9 or None
Dial Numbers = 8137, 8157, 8204, 8279, 8280, 8705
Dials = Silver Finish, Sunburst, Pinstripe
Dial Opening = Tonneau
Dial Variations/Rarity = 🕒🕒🕒 Silver Finish, Luminous Numerals
🕒🕒🕒🕒 Silver Finish, Luminous Numerals, Sunburst Black; Silver Finish, No Subs
🕒🕒🕒🕒🕒 Silver Finish, Black Numerals, Silver Finish, Luminous Numerals, Sunburst Silver; Silver Finish, Luminous Numerals, Sunburst Gold; Silver Finish, Pinstripe; Silver Finish, Gold Applied Numerals
🕒🕒🕒🕒🕒🕒 Silver Finish, Seconds at 6
🕒🕒🕒🕒🕒🕒🕒 Silver Finish, Pinstripe, Seconds at 9
Numerals = Painted, Luminous, Applied Gold Numerals (14K and 18K)
Hands = Steel
Cased in Factory = Yes
Unique Case Design = Yes
Unique Dial Design = Yes
Introduction Date = 1928

Retail Price New = $88.80 (17J), 1931 Becken catalog; $75.00 (19J); $90.00 (21J); $10.00 Extra for Applied Gold Numerals
Collectibility = ⏲⏲⏲⏲
Advertisements = Yes
Marketing Themes = "Conservative in design"
"A Watch of Dignity"

Consul, white gold

The Consul was well advertised by the Illinois Watch Company in national periodicals, such as *Liberty* and the *American Magazine,* and in its special brochure, "A Book of Watches," published in 1928. It was also featured in a number of jobbers' catalogs, such as those of A. C. Becken and Wallenstein Mayer. "A Book of Watches" stated: "The Consul takes it's [*sic*] place in the Illinois line as a watch for the man of affairs. A fine 19 jeweled Illinois 6/0 movement, fitted in a beautiful 14K solid gold case is a combination that makes this model a watch of dignity. $75." The 1930 Factory Sales Catalog listing for the model read: "The Consul. 14K solid gold case, furnished in white with engraved bezel, white all plain, and green center with white back and engraved white bezel. 21 Jewel, Luminous dial. Consumer price, $90.00. 19 Jewel, Luminous dial. Consumer price, $75.00. Silver dial, 14K applied figures, $10.00 extra." This was by far the most expensively priced Illinois men's wristwatch. Notably absent from the case options in that 1930 listing was 14K solid green gold. Until two discoveries made just as this book was about to go to press, no mention of this option had been encountered in any Illinois Factory price lists, magazine advertisements or jobbers' catalogs. The first discovery was an Illinois Factory retail price list dated September 1, 1929, which included these entries: "CONSUL, 21 jewels, 14K white, green or comb. solid gold case, luminous dial. $90.00. CONSUL, 19 jewels, 14K white, green or comb. solid gold case, luminous dial.$75.00. Consul supplied with silver dial with 14K gold applied figures, extra. $10.00."The other discovery was a page in the 1930 Wallenstein Mayer catalog showing two pairs of Consuls, one pair with 21 jewels ($90.00), the other with 19 jewels ($75.00). One watch in each pair was white gold, and one green. All had engraved cases and sunburst dials with luminous figures and hands. (There was no mention of the optional dial for $10.00 extra.)

The solid gold Consul is a striking watch which came in many configurations, including white gold with an engraved or plain bezel, two-tone engraved bezel case and a solid green gold engraved one. Among the dial options is an unusual and beautiful sunburst dial—the enamel sunbursts could have black, gold, or silver lines radiating out from the center of the dial. These sunbursts required a sterling silver dial.

Perhaps this 1930 passage in an Illinois advertising brochure explains the reason behind the Consul sunburst dial: "Capturing the elusive shadow and making it the phantom finger of time was a gracious gesture of beauty. Everyone thrills to the romance of an old-fashioned sundial. Even after its authority was usurped by improved methods of telling time, sun-time was the standard until finer calculations proved the greater accuracy of the stars."

There are also plain dials with no subsidiary seconds and a quite rare pinstripe dial. In addition, there is an exceptionally rare pinstripe dial with subsidiary seconds at 9.

In total, there are fewer than ten two-tone cases, fewer than five solid green gold cases, fewer than seven with plain bezels, about seven dials with subsidiary seconds at 6, and fewer than ten dials with pinstripe dials. Most often the pinstripe dial came in the plain bezel white gold model of the Consul. The dial with the subsidiary seconds at 6 is listed in the Illinois Materials Catalog. The pinstripe dials were sterling silver and made by the Flückiger Company, of Switzerland (see Chapter 7).

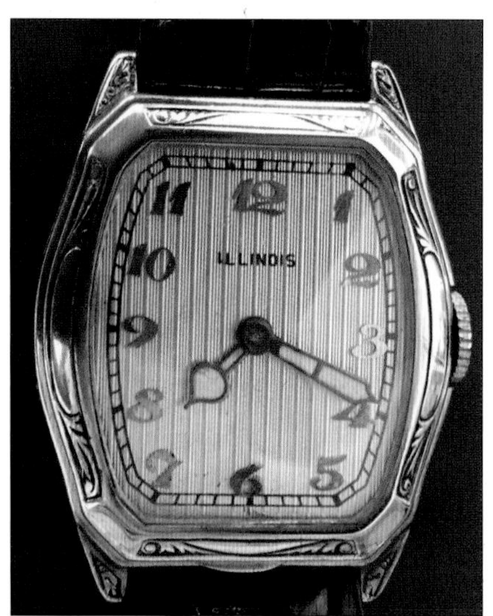

Consul with pinstripe dial

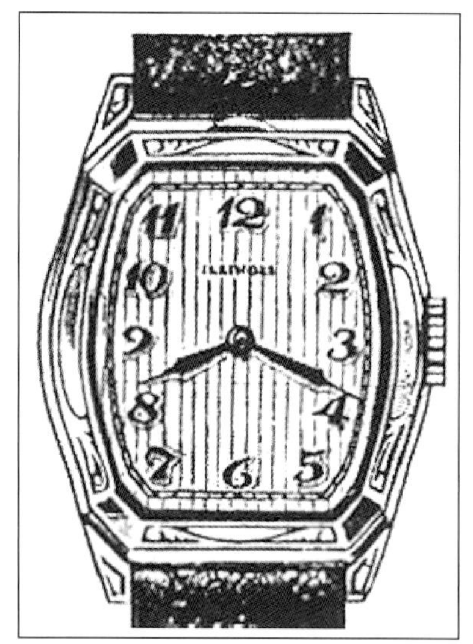

A. G. Schwab catalog, 1930

There was a time when collectors did not know whether a Consul came legitimately with subsidiary seconds at 6. However, in fact, the 1931 Becken catalog actually shows a Consul with subsidiary seconds at 6, as does the A. G. Schwab & Sons 1930 catalog. Many of the Consuls came equipped with the top-of-the-line 21-jewel Illinois, 6/0 size, Superior Motor Barrel movement.

Consul, white gold, seconds at 6

A. G. Schwab catalog, 1930

Consul, green gold

Consul, two-tone case and matching two-tone solid gold band

The Consul with a plain bezel is rare, as is the two-tone model, but the green gold Consul is even rarer, as fewer than five have been identified to date. There is one two-tone Consul with a matching two-tone white gold/green solid gold metal bracelet that is awesome. There are also at least two extremely rare special-order Consuls. One has a rare pinstripe dial with subsidiary seconds at 9; another has a person's name spelled out around the dial in applied gold letters in lieu of numbers. All of these are extremely collectible and valuable.

Convict Consul, white gold; custom pinstripe dial, subsidiary seconds at 9

Undertaker's Consul, white gold; custom dial with name spelled out

See Appendix 6 for an article I wrote for the March/April 2012 issue of the NAWCC *Watch and Clock Bulletin* on the Consul with the pinstripe dial, subsidiary seconds at 9 (the so-called Convict Consul) and the Consul with the name spelled out around the dial (the so-called Undertaker's Consul). The Consul model has also served as the basis of a research survey conducted by Rick Vess with some very minor help from me. (The findings of this study are set forth in Chapter 8.) The Consul model is now considered the flagship Illinois men's watch.

FANTASTIC FIND

Rick Vess, an ardent Michigan-based Art Deco watch collector, notes that he "came across on eBay an Illinois 'Consul' model wristwatch that "was TOTALLY rusted and seemingly ruined solid White Gold 'Consul' that popped up midday about 4 or 5 years ago. I shared fast emails with the seller and I got it for a little more than melt value: $400. (I think he thought it was almost worthless otherwise!) Sadly, I do not have a 'before' photo, but visualize a block of rust inside a nice solid gold wristwatch case. The movement gave my repair guy fits—that was the one he searched for parts to repair (after it soaked for months in oil, I think). It took over a year to get it running properly. Amazingly, the dial was a yellow gold (or perhaps brass) Sunburst, but I did not know it until long after it arrived because the yellow numbers were totally covered with crusty yuck and it was stuck to the rust-brown movement. International Dial redid the dial nicely."

Some Consuls came with 14K center spacer pieces to hold the movement. Others came with nickel center spacers, although the gold spacers are more prevalent. (See Chapter 8.)

Consul side view

Consul inside case back

Consul in its original display case

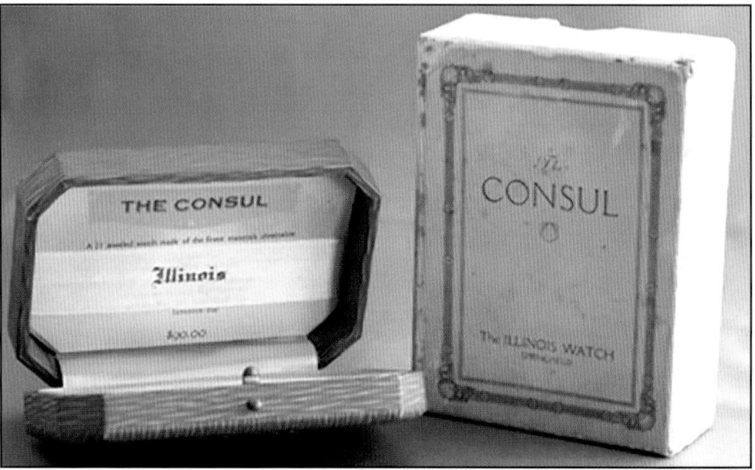

Consul outer cardboard box and display case

Convertible

See listing in **Chapter 10**. Although the Convertible is a ladies' model, it is included in the listings here as well because of the model's historic importance as the very first Illinois wristwatch. At least one specimen of the Convertible should be included in any serious Illinois collection.

Cushion

See listing for **Devon**

Cut Bezel

See listing for **Armored Cases**

"D-D" Utility Watch / Military Crown at 12 / "D-D" Khaki

Official Name = The "D-D" Utility Watch (derived from a February 5, 1919 advertisement in the *Jewelers' Circular-Weekly* by Jacques Depollier & Son)
Secondary Name(s) = Military Crown at 12 (derived from collectors' usage), "D-D" Khaki Watch (derived from Depollier advertisements)
Formerly Known As = None
Time Period = Transitional
Case Variations/Rarity = 🕒🕒🕒🕒 Sterling Silver
🕒🕒🕒🕒🕒🕒 WG
Case Durability = 🕒🕒🕒🕒
Material = SS, WG
Bezel = Plain
Sides = Plain
Lugs = Plain
Lug Size = 14mm
Springbar = Swivel Lugs, Straight
Casemaker = Dubois Watch Case Company (signed Depollier)
Case Closure = 3-Part Snap-On Bezel and Back, Screw-On Bezel and Back
Case Number = None
Case Shape = Round
Case Back = Flat
Dimensions = 48 x 31.5mm (swivel lugs); 36 x 31mm (straight lugs)
Movement Size = 3/0

"D-D" Utility, sterling silver

"D-D" Utility, sterling silver

Movement Grades/Jewels= 24/17, 36/17
Seconds at = 6
Dial Number = None
Dials = Painted, Enamel
Dial Opening = Round
Dial Variations/Rarity = ◷◷ Silver Finish, Luminous Numerals
◷◷◷ Silver Finish, Painted Numerals; Enamel, Painted Numerals
Numerals = Painted, Luminous
Hands = Luminous
Cased in Factory = Yes
Unique Case Design = No
Unique Dial Design = No
Introduction Date = 1915
Retail Price New = Unknown
Collectibility = ◷◷◷◷
Advertisements = Yes
Marketing Themes = "A modern watch for active men"
"ONE WATCH FOR ALL OCCASIONS."

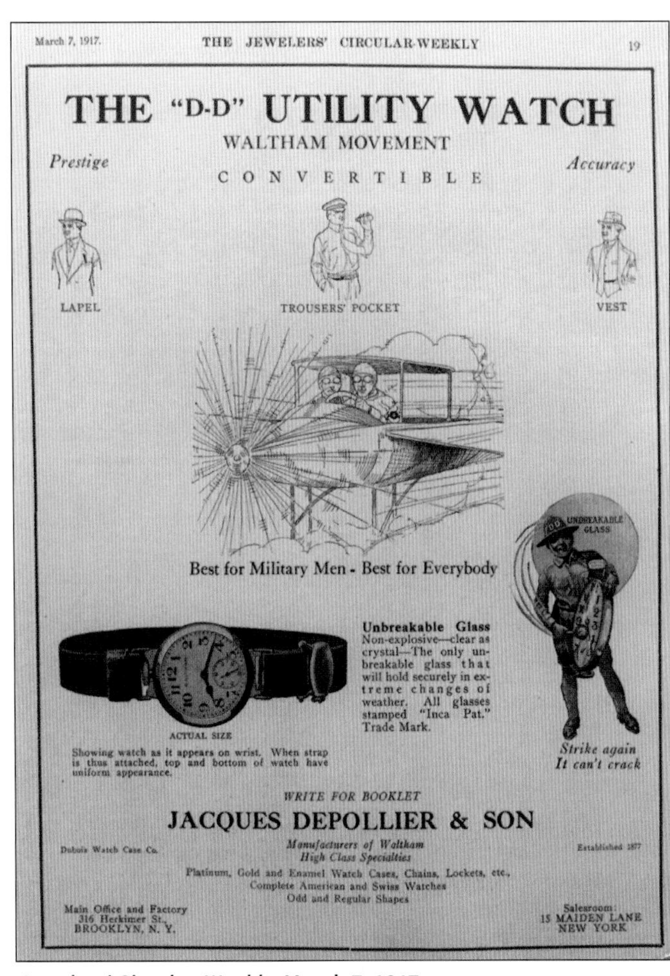

Jewelers' Circular-Weekly, March 7, 1917

The "D-D" Utility Watch was advertised in a number of publications, including the *Keystone,* the *Jewelers' Circular,* and the *Jewelers' Circular-Weekly,* among others.

On February 5, 1919, the "D-D" Utility Watch was advertised in the 50th Anniversary Edition of the *Jewelers' Circular-Weekly.* In its advertisement, the Depollier Watch Case Company described this model as "A modern watch for active men [and] ONE WATCH FOR ALL OCCASIONS." At the top of the page, four drawings illustrated the watch's versatility: it could be worn on one's vest, wrist, chain or lapel. There was also a clever border of smaller drawings showing men in various activities—skating, flying, rowing, hunting, running, riding a motorcycle, working as a doctor, fishing, golfing and traveling—while wearing this watch model.

The text reads: "With the increased popularity of the wrist watch which has resulted from the war, civilians are now in the majority of wearers. The civilian-soldiers created by the new state military training which drills the young men while still in school and business also demand a watch that they can make the best use of. The 'D-D' Utility

Watch which is convertible to other ways of wearing embodies patented features of especial value to these men and other civilians. It can be worn in the vest pocket, from the lapel with waldemar chain, and on the wrist. Its convenience in different ways of wearing has made it one of the popular watches."

The 1919 advertisement also notes that the "D-D" is "Made in Solid Gold, Solid Silver; with non-flammable, Unbreakable Glass and Luminous Dial. All features of the "D-D" Utility Watch are fully protected by patents and patents applied for in the United States and Foreign Countries." The name "'D-D' Utility Watch" was a registered trademark of Jacques Depollier & Son. Depollier also had a registered trademark for the "'D-D' Utility Watch" that featured a green cloth shard strap with a sterling silver or white gold clasp.

***Jewelers' Circular-Weekly*, Feb. 5, 1919**

The Depollier advertisements usually featured this model with a Waltham movement and dial but it could just as easily accommodate Elgin and Illinois 3/0 size movements and dials. The watch came with a luminous or non-luminous dial. When found, this model is usually in a sterling silver case. It is believed by some that the "D-D" stands for "Depollier/Duncuff" because Charles L. Depollier and Edward C. Duncuff filed many patents together and separately on behalf of Jacques Depollier & Son and the Dubois Watch Case Company. Most likely, though, "D-D" stands for Depollier/Dubois, as these two related firms closely partnered on the production and sales of many watch cases during the Transitional Period. One of their patents is shown on the next page. To date, no "D-D" has been located in a solid white gold case.

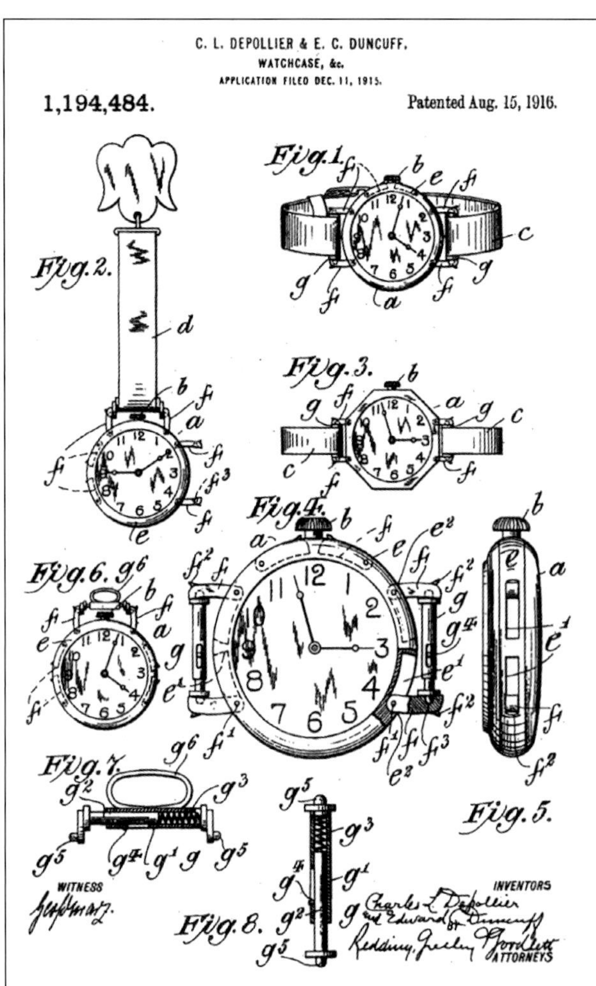

Depollier & Duncuff 1916 patent

The case was made by the Dubois Watch Company and sold through Jacques Depollier & Son, acting as its sales arm. Dubois had two facilities: the main office and factory was at 316 Herkimer Street, Brooklyn, New York, with a salesroom at 15 Maiden Lane, virtually next door to the Illinois Watch Company's New York City's sales location. Although Depollier advertised itself as "Manufacturers of High Class Specialties for Waltham Watches," the "D-D" model was a Transitional Period watch, and thus could have easily been found with an Illinois or Elgin movement and dial, as was mentioned earlier.

E. C. Fitch was the inventor of this watch case. The patent for the 12 o'clock crown wristwatch was first filed on January 18, 1912, a surprisingly early date. This is before men's wristwatches gained popularity in the United States.

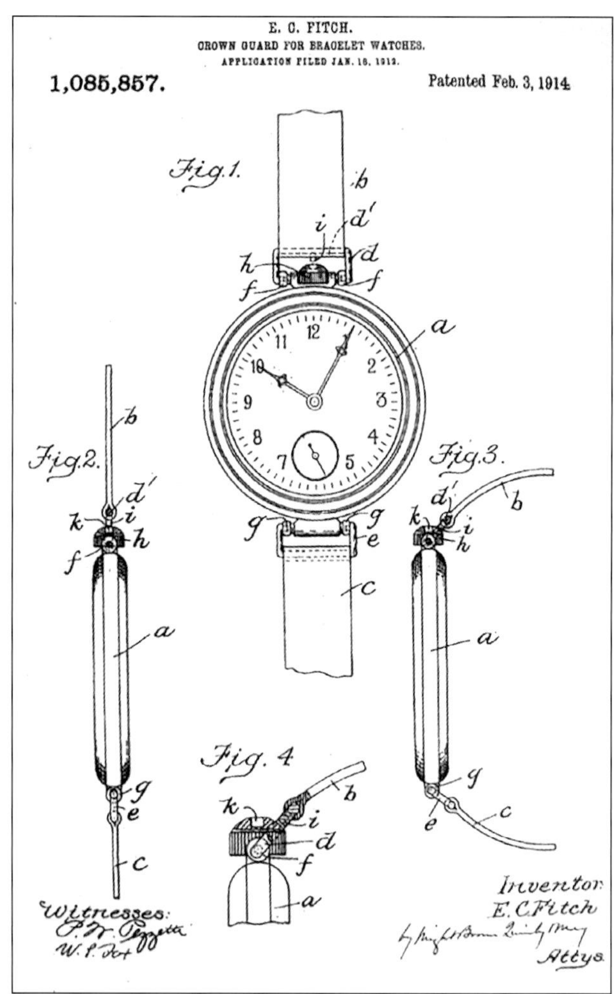

Patent for the "D-D" Utility Watch, dated February 3, 1914

The crystal for this watch was double-thick glass to help make it shatter-resistant. These watches were painted black for wartime use, as specified by the United States Army in 1917.

"D-D" Utility watch. Note some of its original black paint is still intact.

"Khaki" signed crown

"D-D"S

Stan Czubernat notes, "There was more than one "D-D" Depollier case; there are at least seven; some were:

- The "D-D" Utility Watch (1915);
- The "D-D" Khaki Watch (1917); and
- The "D-D" Field and Marine Watch, (aka The Depollier Waterproof Watch 1918, version #1)

"The "D-D" Field and Marine Watch had a coin edge bezel & case back and a threaded bezel and case back. This watch case design was scrapped shortly after it came out in very late 1918 as Depollier's claims of it being waterproof proved untrue. In late 1918 Depollier planned a ten piece advertising and marketing campaign for the "D-D" Field and Marine Watch but only advertisement number one ever hit the trade publications. The other nine (if prepared) were never released."*

*Czubernat, email correspondence with the author, September 26, 2014.

"KHAKI"

Depollier first used the tradename "Khaki" with wristwatches, as its "D-D" Khaki Watch and some of its other models came equipped with canvas straps in khaki color. Canvas straps proved to be very popular. As a result, the use of this name and description started to be used by other watchmakers for similar trench watches. Depollier, in advertisements and elsewhere, threatened to commence legal action over the alleged infringement of this tradename, but apparently never moved forward with any such actions.

October 24, 1917. THE JEWELERS' CIRCULAR-WEEKLY 19

"KHAKI"

A Registered Trade Mark for Watches

Certificate of Registration 118,958, U. S. Pat. Off.

Announcement

About March 23, 1917, we adopted and began to use extensively the word "KHAKI" as a trade mark for watches, especially adapted for field use as wrist watches.

The name caught on with the trade at once and we began and have since continued to receive orders in great numbers for our "KHAKI" watches.

The fitness of the name appealed not only to our trade but to certain manufacturers who would like to take advantage of our popularizing of the name, and one or two, regardless of our rights, have recently commenced to offer goods under the same name. Soon after our adoption of the name, we applied for registration of the same as a trade mark in the United States Patent Office. This application was allowed in due course, the mark was duly published in the Official Gazette, no opposition to our registration was offered, and on October 16, 1917, the certificate of registration was duly issued.

Being now in a position to defend our rights in the Federal Courts we will forthwith take action against those who persist in the unlawful use of the mark.

We therefore now caution the trade against purchasing or offering for sale under the name "KHAKI," watches not supplied through us, whether with or without wrist straps, and against substituting other makes of watches in the boxes in which our regular "KHAKI" watches are supplied.

We have made the name "KHAKI" a valuable asset of our business and we shall enforce our rights against all who infringe them.

DUBOIS WATCH CASE CO.
JACQUES DEPOLLIER & SON.

Strike again! It can't crack!

THE "D-D" KHAKI WATCH

Prestige **WALTHAM MOVEMENT** *Accuracy*

Dubois Watch Case Co.
Main Office and Factory
316 Herkimer St.
BROOKLYN, N. Y.

JACQUES DEPOLLIER & SON

Manufacturers of High Class Specialties for Waltham Watches

Established 1877
Salesroom:
15 MAIDEN LANE
NEW YORK

"Khaki" trademark announcement, *Jewelers' Circular,* October 24, 1917

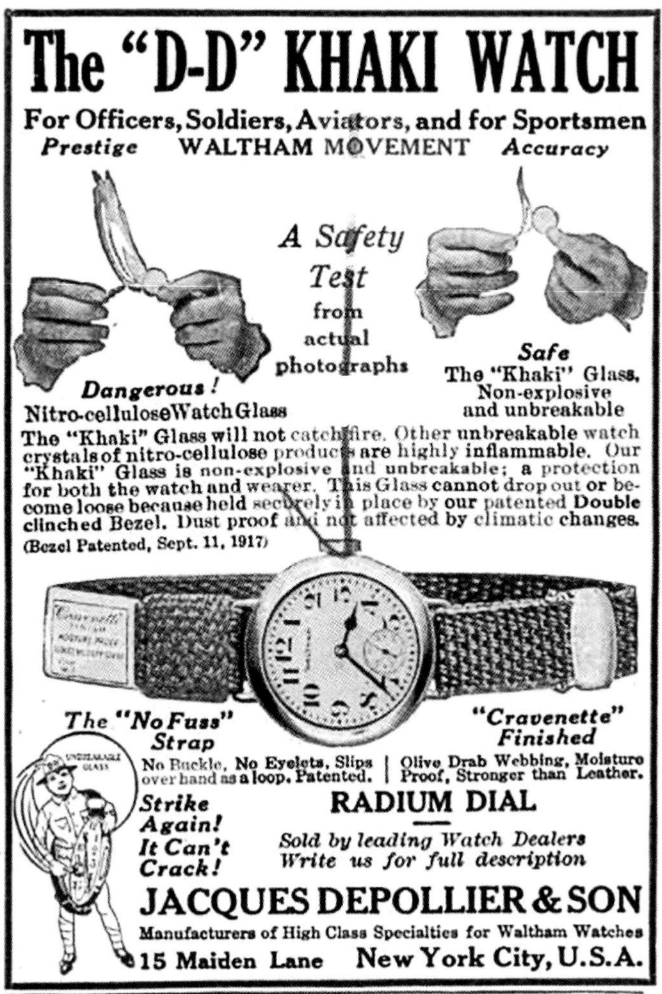

Popular Mechanics, December 1917

WHY I COLLECT ILLINOIS

When asked why I collect Illinois wristwatches, my reply is usually enthusiastic and simple. Illinois wristwatches represent a unique piece of American history that exemplifies both the engineering and artistic skills of early 1900 watchmakers. Furthermore, the beauty and different designs of these wristwatches represents to me an era of creative thought that is rarely seen in today's world. I have been collecting Illinois watches for nearly two decades and have yet to lose that internal enthusiasm that originally led me to collect them in the first place. Like many collectors, I find the hunt represents one of the key driving forces behind my passion. Over the years, however, this passion has also led me to slowly increase my subject knowledge on the watches, enabling me to better understand the unique beauty and mechanical quality of each piece. More importantly, my years of searching have allowed me to meet some of the best people in my life who share the same passion for this great American company and its watches. I can honestly say that these collectors have increased my desire to continue my lifelong effort to complete my collection and share it with others. In essence, collecting Illinois wristwatches allows me to learn about a unique piece of my country's past, as well as to learn about the people who made these unique pieces of art.

As a military officer, I have developed a special connection to these watches, as it was the soldiers in WWI who originally strapped their pocket watches on their arms, creating the wristwatch we know today. In fact, these very soldiers who wore their wristwatches home after the war helped change social perceptions in America from one of distaste of the wristwatch to a desire to have a watch that represented the personality of the person wearing the timepiece. To this day, I personally hold a connection to the previous generations of soldiers who paved the way for watch companies, like Illinois, to introduce the various unique designs that have stood the test of time. Interest originally drove me to collect Illinois wristwatches. Personal desire enabled me to continue collecting these timepieces over the years. Now, passion drives me to complete my collection in order to share this unique piece of history with the next generation.

—Victor H. Sundquist, III

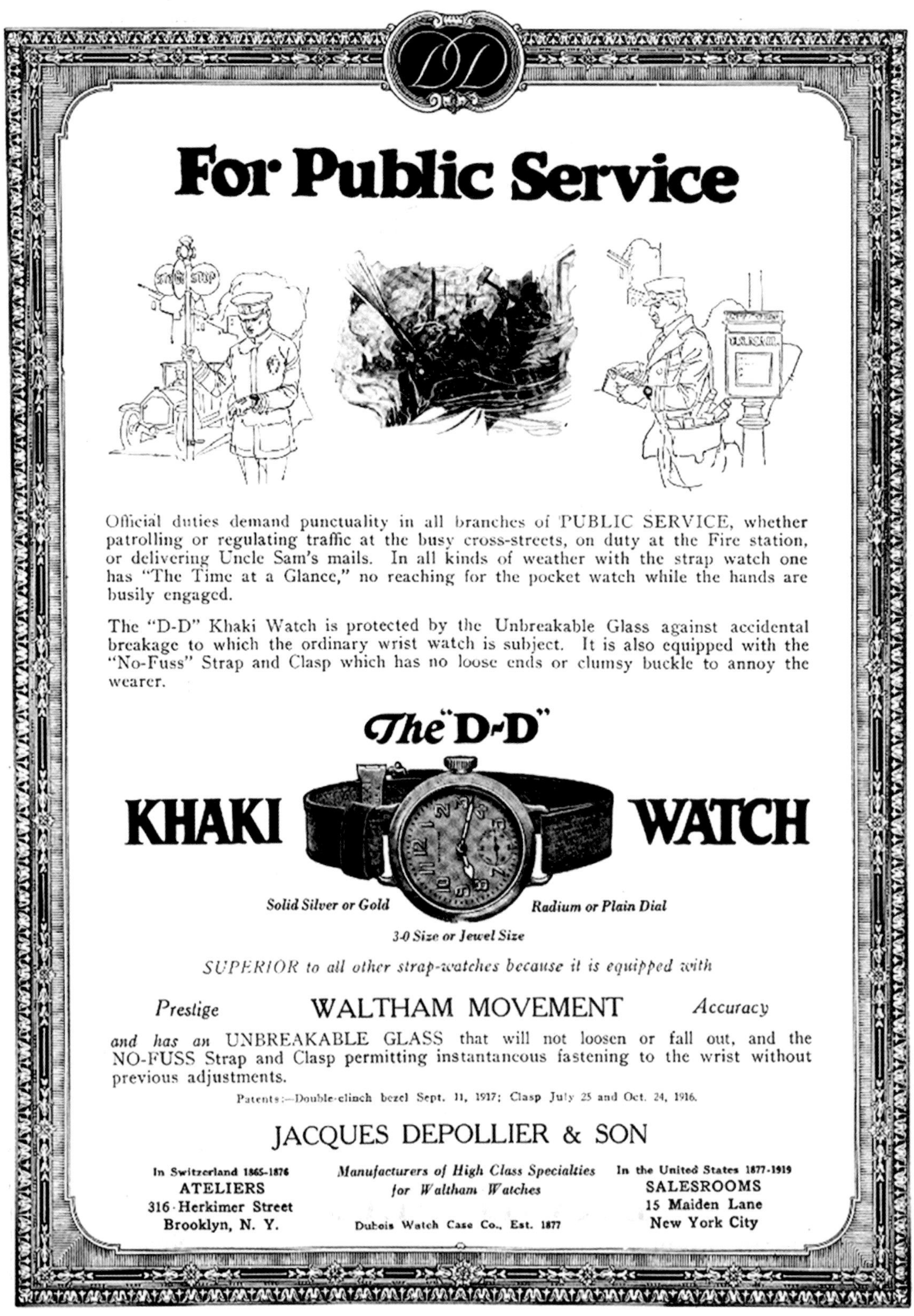

Jewelers' Circular, July 9, 1914

May 31, 1916. THE JEWELERS' CIRCULAR-WEEKLY 19

Three-in-One for waistcoat, lapel or wrist

Made in
PLATINUM
SOLID GOLD
SOLID SILVER
Gold Filled
NICKEL

with leather and silk straps. Also can be worn with a chain.

No Sliding Clasp.
Self-Adjustable.

DEPOLLIER PATENT
MAY 11, 1915.

Other Patents Applied For.

NO FUSS

No Buckle.
No Eyelets.
No Slides.
No Hook.
No Strap Ends.
No trouble due to stretching of leather or silk.
No contortions required to apply to wrist.
No removing of watch necessary to cleanse hand.
No accidental dropping of watch from the arm in either applying or removing.
No slipping after once secured to the wrist.

ONE HAND APPLICATION.

Fits any size wrist and over garment or glove.

JACQUES DEPOLLIER & SON

SOLE DISTRIBUTORS

DUBOIS WATCH CASE CO. — Manufacturers of Waltham High Class Specialties — EST. 1887

PLATINUM, GOLD AND ENAMEL WATCH CASES
COMPLETE AMERICAN AND SWISS WATCHES
ODD AND REGULAR SHAPES

Main office and factory
316 HERKIMER ST.
BROOKLYN, N. Y.

Salesroom
15 MAIDEN LANE
NEW YORK

Jewelers' Circular-Weekly, May 31, 1916

Decagon / Decagon Jr. / Decagon Jr. Off-Set

Decagon, yellow gold

Official Name = Decagon (derived from a June 1919 Wadsworth advertisement in the *Saturday Evening Post*)

Secondary Name(s) = Decagon, Jr.

Formerly Known As = Admiral Evans, Jr.

Time Period = Transitional

Case Variations/Rarity = 🕒🕒🕒🕒🕒 14K YGF, 6/0, SS, 6/0
🕒🕒🕒🕒🕒🕒 14K YGF, 3/0
🕒🕒🕒🕒🕒🕒 YG, 3/0
🕒 YGF

Case Durability = 🕒🕒🕒🕒 SS

Material = 14K YGF, SS, YG

Bezel = Plain

Sides = Plain

Lugs = Plain

Lug Size = 16mm

Springbar = Fixed Lugs

Casemaker = Wadsworth, Star

Case Closure = 3-Part Snap-On Bezel and Back

Case Number = None

Case Shape = Decagon

Case Back = Flat

Dimensions = 36 x 32mm (3/0)

Movement Sizes = 3/0, 6/0

Movement Grades/Jewels = 24/17, 36/17, 903/15, 904/17

Seconds at = 6

Dial Numbers = Painted

Dials = Enamel, Silver Finish

Dial Opening = Round

Dial Variations/Rarity = 🕒 Silver Finish
🕒🕒 Enamel 3/0
🕒🕒🕒🕒🕒🕒 Enamel 6/0

Numerals = Painted

Hands = Steel

Cased in Factory = No

Unique Case Design = No

Unique Dial Design = No

Introduction Date = 1919

Retail Price New = Unknown

Collectibility = 🕒🕒🕒

Advertisements = Yes

Marketing Theme = "Especially suitable for outdoor activities—golfing, tennis, motoring and the like"

Decagon, yellow gold-filled

Decagon, Jr. Off-Set, sterling silver

The Decagon, as shown in a Wadsworth advertisement, *Saturday Evening Post*, June 14, 1919

The Decagon was advertised by Wadsworth in the June 14, 1919 issue of the *Saturday Evening Post.* There are three Decagon models known to exist. Although the Decagon is deemed to be from the Transitional Period, this particular watch was always a wristwatch—it was not converted from a pocket watch. According to Czubernat, the 6/0 size Decagon models (now called Decagon, Jr.) could possibly be a ladies' model. It has been found a few times in sterling silver cases. The 3/0 size Illinois model is very rare and valuable, as only two are known to exist. Only three of the Illinois Decagon, Jr. models have been spotted to date in yellow gold-filled, and two very rare Decagon Jr. models with off-set crowns in sterling silver have been located; however, it is nearly impossible to locate 6/0 size enamel Illinois dials. There are at least two examples of the 3/0 size Decagon in yellow gold.

Decagon, yellow gold-filled case by Star in 3/0 size

Decagon 3/0, yellow gold-filled case back by Star

DEPOLLIER WATERPROOF/DUSTPROOF

Depollier Waterproof/Dustproof

Official Name = Depollier Waterproof and Dustproof (derived from Depollier advertisements such as in the October 1, 1919 issue of the *Jewelers' Circular*)
Secondary Name(s) = Depollier (derived from collectors' usage that refers to this model simply as a Depollier, not specifying type)
Formerly Known As = None
Time Period = Transitional
Case Variations/Rarity = ◷◷◷◷◷ Nickel/Painted
◷◷◷◷◷◷◷ Sterling Silver
Case Durability = ◷◷◷◷
Material = Nickel, SS
Bezel = Plain
Sides = Plain
Lugs = Plain
Lug Size = 16mm
Springbar = Fixed Lugs
Casemaker = Depollier
Case Closure = 3-Part Screw-On Bezel and Back
Case Number = None
Case Shape = Round
Case Back = Flat
Dimensions = 44 x 36mm
Movement Size = 3/0
Movement Grades/Jewels = 24/17, 36/17
Seconds at = 6
Dial Number = 8343
Dials = Painted, Enamel
Dial Opening = Round
Dial Variations/Rarity = ◷ Silver Finish, Painted Numerals; Silver Finish, Luminous Numerals
◷◷◷ Enamel, Painted Numerals
◷◷◷◷ Silver Finish, Off-Duty Numerals
Numerals = Painted, Luminous
Hands = Steel
Cased in Factory = Yes/No
Unique Case Design = Yes
Unique Dial Design = No
Introduction Date = 1919 (released the day before the Treaty of Versailles was signed on June 28, 1919)
Retail Price New = $4.00 (case only)
Collectibility = ◷◷◷◷
Advertisements = Yes
Marketing Themes = "New world's altitude record 34,610 feet."
"For soldiers, sailors, aviators…"

There are several advertisements for the Depollier Waterproof and Dustproof wristwatches in various 1918 and 1919 publications such as *Outing*, the *Jewelers' Circular, Aerial Age Weekly,* and *Flying*.

The advertisements often depict troops walking in water, with one arm raising a gun above the water and the other arm below the water with a Depollier Waterproof and Dustproof Watch strapped onto the wrist. Some advertisements state simply that "For many years there has been a demand for a waterproof watch, that is, a watch that would absolutely prevent the access of water to the inner works of the watch, even though it might be completely submerged in water." Advertisements claim that this is a watch for "soldiers, sailors, aviators and others engaged in the open." Some advertisements tout its ability to work accurately at an altitude of 34,610 feet, "Over six miles above the earth, and from summer heat to 44° below zero and back to normal again without the variation of a second."

On December 4, 1918, the Dubois Watch Case Company signed a contract with the United States War Department to produce the Depollier Waterproof and Dustproof Watch for the Signal Corps of the United States Army. This model has become one of the most sought-after of all the military Transitional Period Illinois wristwatches. It was one of the first waterproof and dustproof watches (if not the first). Although Depollier had an exclusive arrangement with Waltham for years, models can be found today with Illinois movements and dials in them. This case utilizes a special crown which locks in place when screwed down. When released, the crown pops up so it can be wound; fully extended, it can be turned to set the watch. The crown used by Depollier on this model was the subject of a patent infringement lawsuit brought in 1919 against Depollier and Dubois (discussed in Chapter 8).

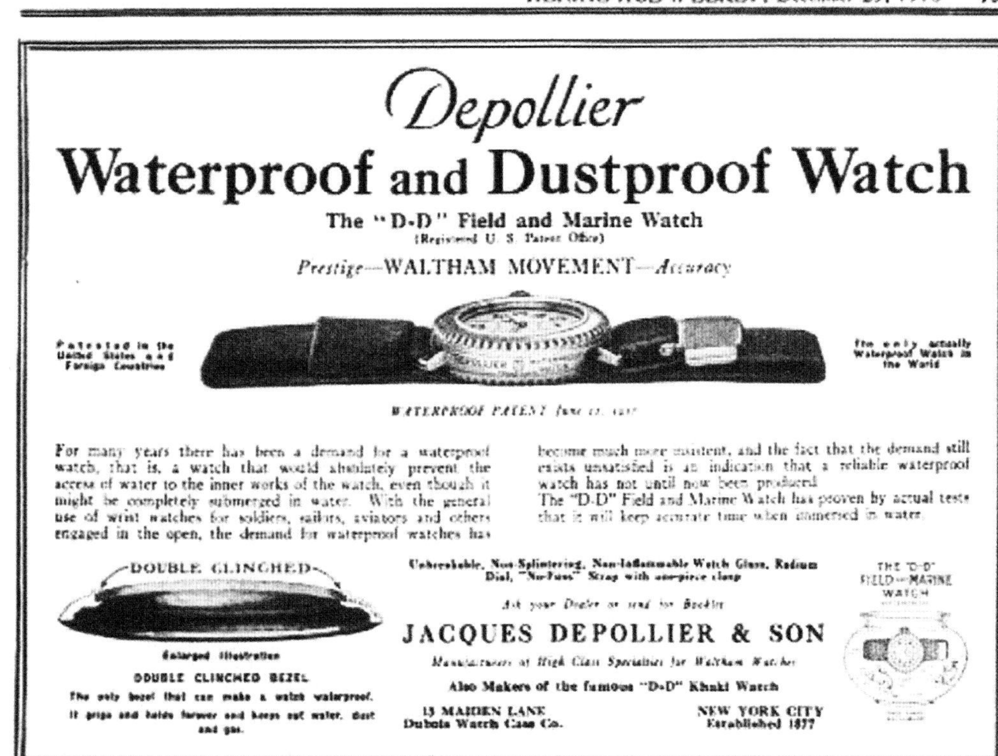
AERIAL AGE WEEKLY, December 23, 1918 787

Depollier

Waterproof and Dustproof Watch

The "D-D" Field and Marine Watch

(Registered U. S. Patent Office)

Prestige—WALTHAM MOVEMENT—Accuracy

Patented in the United States and Foreign Countries

The only actually Waterproof Watch in the World

WATERPROOF PATENT June 12, 1917

For many years there has been a demand for a waterproof watch, that is, a watch that would absolutely prevent the access of water to the inner works of the watch, even though it might be completely submerged in water. With the general use of wrist watches for soldiers, sailors, aviators and others engaged in the open, the demand for waterproof watches has become much more insistent, and the fact that the demand still exists unsatisfied is an indication that a reliable waterproof watch has not until now been produced.

The "D-D" Field and Marine Watch has proven by actual tests that it will keep accurate time when immersed in water.

DOUBLE CLINCHED

Enlarged Illustration

DOUBLE CLINCHED BEZEL

The only bezel that can make a watch waterproof. It grips and holds forever and keeps out water, dust and gas.

Unbreakable, Non-Splintering, Non-Inflammable Watch Glass, Radium Dial, "No-Fuss" Strap with one-piece clasp

Ask your Dealer or send for Booklet

JACQUES DEPOLLIER & SON

Manufacturers of High Class Specialties for Waltham Watches

Also Makers of the famous "D-D" Khaki Watch

13 MAIDEN LANE
Dubois Watch Case Co.

NEW YORK CITY
Established 1877

Aerial Age Weekly, **December 23, 1918**

GOLDEN VS. DEPOLLIER

The examination of Charles L. Depollier in this 1918 patent litigation revealed the following details of the contractual specification for the famous Depollier Waterproof/Dustproof model.

Some of the modifications ultimately made involved the crown construction (see Chapter 8). Its finish turned out to be painted black, not oxidized. It is not known if an asbestos heat disk was utilize. The "U.S.A." was stamped on the disk but not all the models had "U.S.A." stamped on it, and the disk was not made of silver but of solid white gold.*

**Golden v. Depollier,* United States District Court, Southern District of New York, March 8, 1918, pp. 15–16.

C H A R L E S L. D E P O L L I E R, a witness called in behalf of the Plaintiff, being duly sworn, testifies as follows:

DIRECT EXAMINATION BY MR. ANDERSON:

Q1 Mr. Depollier, you have produced here a copy of a contract with the War Department dated December 4, 1918, a contract for watches. Is that a contract still in existence between the Du Bois Watch Case Company and the Government? A Yes.

Q2 That contract calls for 10,000 cases, wrist watches, waterproof; as per following specifications:

1. To be similar in construction to sample submitted with the exception as follows:

(a) Case to be of nickel, oxidized finish, with silver disk on back.

(b) All notches to be omitted except two for engaging key designed to open the case.

(c) Asbestos heat disk to be supplied, set in depression in the back of case to prevent drying out of oil on the works due to heat from the body.

(d) Letter "U.S.A' to be stamped on the case.

Depollier

(e) Cases to be serially numbered from 1 to 10,000 inclusive, on outside of silver disk,

at $4.00 each, 40,000.00

Less 2% 10 days from date of receipt of voucher in the office of the Disbursing Officer, Signal Corps 800.00

$39,200.00"

Now that refers to a sample, Mr. Depollier. Was that sample constructed like the drawing Plaintiff's Exhibit 3? A It was.

Q3 Those watches have not been delivered? A They have not.

Q4 But the contract is still in force? A Yes.

Q5 You are obligated to deliver 10,000 of those watches according to the sample? A Not according to the sample; modifications were made since and have been made since.

October 2, 1918. THE JEWELERS' CIRCULAR-WEEKLY 19

JACQUES DEPOLLIER & SON

Complete Solid Gold Watches in All Sizes

MANUFACTURERS OF SOLID GOLD WATCH CASES

14K-18K YELLOW
14K-18K RED
14K-18K GREEN
14K-18K WHITE

FOR ALL SIZES WALTHAM WATCHES

PATENTED SPECIALTIES

1. Double Clinched Bezel for Non-Explosive Unbreakable Glass: preventing loosening of glass; making waterproof and dustproof.
2. "No Fuss" Clasp.
3. Disappearing Eye.

EXCLUSIVE MILITARY WATCHES

1. Famous "D-D" Khaki Watch.
2. The "D-D" Moistureproof Watch.
3. The "D-D" Utility Watch.
4. "*Miladi Militaire*" Watch.
5. Depollier Waterproof and Dustproof Watch.

Patented in the United States and Foreign Countries.

We Sell

Waltham Watches

Exclusively

Jacques Depollier & Son

Manufacturers of High Class Specialties for Waltham Watches

Main Office and Factory:
116 Herkimer St., Brooklyn, N. Y.
Salesroom:
15 Maiden Lane, New York

Dubois Watch Case Co.
Est.. 1877

DEPOLLIER

Waterproof and Dustproof Watch

WATERPROOF TESTS

Inspection and Examination

Our Waterproof Watches are thoroughly tested. The case alone is first tested in water under pressure to prove that it is waterproof and dustproof. The complete watch is then immersed and kept under observation for several days.

The Depollier Waterproof Watch is not sealed by any such means as Paraffine, Cement, or Rubber, all of which deteriorate in a short time. It is made waterproof and dustproof by patented devices which retain their efficiency indefinitely.

Patented in the United States and Foreign Countries.

THE "D-D" FIELD AND MARINE WATCH

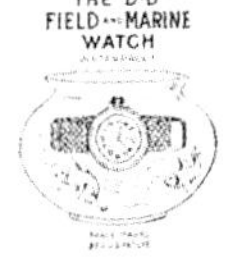

THIS IS THE LAST OF A SERIES OF TEN ADVERTISEMENTS

***Jewelers' Circular-Weekly*, October 2, 1918**

The screw case construction was a predecessor of the Rolex Oyster concept as well as the lock-down auto-disengaging crown system. The stem in the crown is subject to rusting and can be quite troublesome for most watchmakers to repair. Even in a new old stock (NOS) case, the stem is likely to be rusted in place. A less significant issue with this case is that the black anodized paint is subject to extreme wear. This may discourage some collectors. However, this wear is not a major drawback nor is a case with all its black paint off; when completely or even partially exposed, the nickel base metal is very attractive and perfectly acceptable. There is a special spanner wrench that was supplied by Depollier to remove the case front and back.

This model also came with a difficult-to-find 14K solid gold disk on the case back that was usually engraved "U.S.A." with a serial number. The disk on the case back was provided as a heat sink for the mechanism to protect its oils from congealing in extreme cold. According to the Signal Corps' contract, this disk was to be an "asbestos heat disk to prevent drying out of oil on the work due to heat from the body." It is unknown if asbestos was ever used. When found in place, the disks have been solid gold. The one below was the 148th produced for the contract for 10,000 cases.

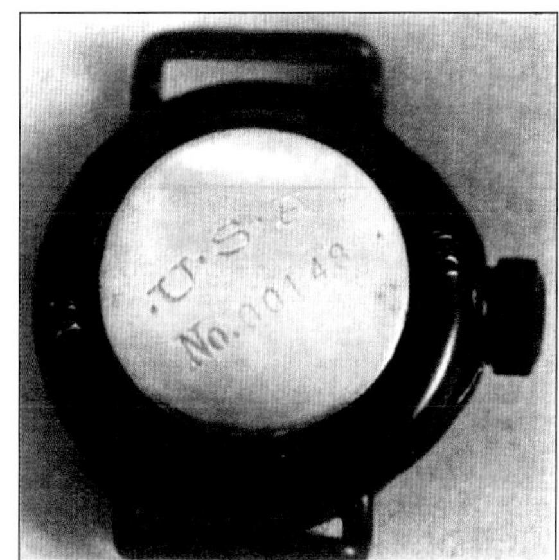

Solid gold heat sink disk on case back

Some collectors place Skyway dials, either in white or in black, in this case, as this watch is especially attractive (although not original) when so equipped. (See Chapter 8 for more information on Jacques Depollier and Sons.)

Depollier spanner wrench

Depollier with a Skyway dial

Longtime Illinois enthusiast L. Michael Fultz believed that Illinois cased and tested some of these models in its factory for sale to the United States government, but the contract that Depollier had with the United States Signal Corps called only for it to supply cases. Apparently, only the first dozen sterling cases were fully assembled, and then hand-carried by Charles L. Depollier to Washington, D.C., for testing and evaluation.

DEPOLLIER WATERPROOF WATCHES—THREE GENERATIONS

The Depollier Waterproof/Dustproof watch was Dubois' third marketing attempt at this waterproof model. The first generation design was called the "Depollier Field and Marine Watch" and was released on August, 10, 1918. This design did not use the spanner wrench to remove its bezel and caseback. The second and third generations used the spanner wrench. The first two did not use a screw-down crown; only the last one featured in this listing used that type of crown.

The second generation version was called the "Depollier Thermo Wrist Watch." It was made in sterling silver and solid gold. This model did not work as a waterproof watch and few were sold.

The third generation was the "Depollier Waterproof/Dustproof Watch," painted black, with a successful screw-down waterproof crown.

July 17, 1918. THE JEWELERS' CIRCULAR-WEEKLY 19

DEMONSTRATION

FOR ALL INTERESTED—SALESROOM 15 MAIDEN LANE

DEPOLLIER WATERPROOF WATCH

Prestige **WALTHAM MOVEMENT** *Accuracy*

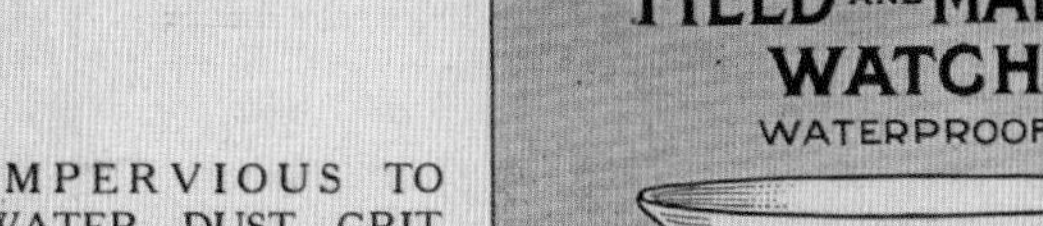

IMPERVIOUS TO WATER, DUST, GRIT AND ALL EXTERNAL ELEMENTS.

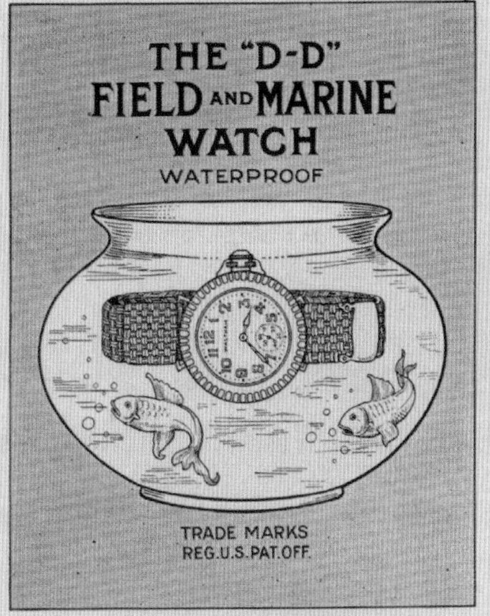

For the duration of the war the sale of this watch is confined exclusively to men in the Army and Navy, due to the shortage in high grade movements. It will not be sold to civilians.

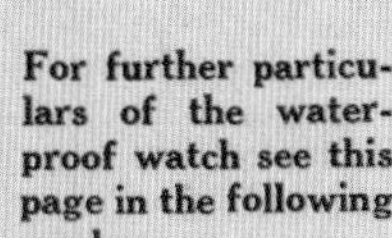

For further particulars of the waterproof watch see this page in the following weeks.

INSPECTION AND EXAMINATION

Our Waterproof Watches are thoroughly tested. The case alone is first tested in water under pressure to prove that it is waterproof and dustproof. The complete watch is then immersed and kept under observation for several days.

The Depollier Waterproof Watch is not sealed by any such means as Parafine, Cement, or Rubber, all of which deteriorate in a short time. It is made waterproof and dustproof by patented devices which retain their efficiency indefinitely.

Patented in the United States and foreign countries

Also makers of the famous "D-D" KHAKI WATCH

JACQUES DEPOLLIER & SON

Dubois Watch Case Co. **Established 1877**

Manufacturers of
High Class Specialties for Waltham Watches

Main Office and Factory:
316 HERKIMER ST., BROOKLYN, N. Y.

Salesroom:
15 MAIDEN LANE, NEW YORK

Jewelers' Circular-Weekly, July 17, 1918

July 31, 1918. THE JEWELERS' CIRCULAR-WEEKLY 19

HEADQUARTERS FOR WALTHAM

Complete Solid Gold Watches in All Sizes

MANUFACTURERS OF SOLID GOLD WATCH CASES

14K-18K YELLOW
14K-18K RED
14K-18K GREEN
14K-18K WHITE

FOR ALL SIZES WALTHAM WATCHES

PATENTED SPECIALTIES

1. Double Clinched Bezel for Non-Explosive Unbreakable Glass: preventing loosening of glass: making waterproof and dustproof.
2. "No Fuss" Clasp.
3. Disappearing Eye.

EXCLUSIVE MILITARY WATCHES

1. Famous "D-D" Khaki Watch.
2. The "D-D" Moistureproof Watch.
3. The "D-D" Utility Watch.
4. "*Miladi Militaire*" Watch.
5. Depollier Waterproof and Dustproof Watch.

Patented in the United States and Foreign Countries.

We Sell

Waltham Watches

Exclusively

Jacques Depollier & Son

Manufacturers of High Class Specialties for Waltham Watches

Main Office and Factory:
314 Herkimer St., Brooklyn, N. Y.

Salesroom:
15 Maiden Lane, New York

Dubois Watch Case Co.
Est., 1877

DEPOLLIER

Waterproof WATCH *Dustproof*

Prestige WALTHAM MOVEMENT *Accuracy*

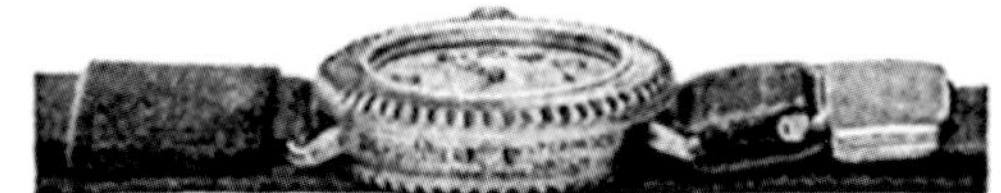

THIS IS THE FIRST OF A SERIES OF TEN ADVERTISEMENTS

Jewelers' Circular-Weekly, July 31, 1918

Jewelers' Circular, October 1, 1919

Derby, white gold-filled

Derby, yellow gold-filled

Derby / Pimlico / Latonia

Official Name = Derby (derived from Illinois advertisements and Illinois Sales and Material Catalogs)
Secondary Name(s) = Pimlico (derived from Illinois advertisements and Illinois Sales Catalogs); Latonia (from an internal Hamilton document)
Formerly Known As = None
Time Period = Moderne
Case Variations/Rarity = 🕒🕒 YGF/P, Wadsworth
🕒🕒🕒 WGF/P, Wadsworth
🕒🕒🕒🕒🕒🕒 WGF/P, Solidarity, YGF/P, Solidarity
Case Durability = 🕒🕒
Material = 14K GF
Bezel = Plain
Sides = Plain
Lugs = Plain
Lug Size = 16mm
Springbar = Male
Casemakers = Wadsworth, Solidarity
Case Closure = 3-Part Snap-On Bezel and Back
Case Number = 617
Case Shape = Rectangular
Case Back = Flat
Dimensions = 33 x 27mm
Movement Size = 6/0
Movement Grades/Jewels = 607/17 (Derby), 605/15 (Pimlico)
Seconds at = 6
Dial Number = 8050
Dials = Silver Finish, Sparkle Finish
Dial Opening = Rectangular
Dial Variations/Rarity = 🕒🕒 Silver Finish, Black Numerals
🕒🕒🕒 Sparkle Finish, Painted Numerals
🕒🕒🕒🕒 Sparkle Finish, Luminous Numerals
Numerals = Painted, Luminous
Hands = Steel
Cased in Factory = Yes
Unique Case Design = No
Unique Dial Design = Yes
Introduction Date = 1931 (Derby), 1932 (Pimlico)
Retail Price New = $42.50
Collectibility = 🕒🕒🕒🕒
Advertisements = Yes
Marketing Themes = "Smart, good looking watch"
"One of the snappiest models"
"Thoroughly masculine in design"
"Attractive Illinois model"

The DERBY
Thoroughly masculine in design. 14K filled white or natural gold.
17 jewels.................................... $42.50

A. C. Beckcn catalog, 1932

PIMLICO
Smart, good-looking watch of 15 jewels. The case and band are of same quality, 14 Karat natural or white filled gold. (6/0 size.)
$42.50

Benj. Allen catalog, 1933

The Derby was advertised in Illinois advertisements and appeared in the 1931–32 Illinois Sales Catalogs; the Pimlico was featured in the Illinois 1933 Sales Catalog. Each appeared in various jobbers' catalogs. The Derby came with a leather strap. When Illinois changed the attachment to a metal bracelet, the name of the model was changed to Pimlico. The Derby came equipped with a 17-jewel movement, but the Pimlico's was only 15 jewels. Even though the Pimlico came with a metal bracelet, which usually increased the price of an Illinois model, the cost could remain the same as the Derbys because of the lower-grade movement in the Pimlico.

Another variation of the Derby may be called a Latonia. Since Latonia is a racetrack in Kentucky, such an appellation would follow the Derby and Pimlico racing themes. The white gold-filled Derby is harder to locate than the yellow gold-filled one. This model is not as common as once thought.

The yellow case of the Derby is fairly prone to case wear; the white case is less prone but still usually has some modest wear. This model represents the only time that Illinois purchased stock from two casemakers, Wadsworth and Solidarity. Both versions displayed the same case Model No. 617. The Solidarity version is significantly harder to find; to date, fewer than four Derby cases by Solidarity have been located. Solidarity cases have been found in both white gold-filled and yellow gold-filled.

FANTASTIC FIND

Longtime watch buddy Gary Ockey from the 'City by the Bay' has described this interesting "Fantastic Find": "It was the early 1980s and I was up in Washington State on vacation. As always, I would scour the antique and jewelry stores for vintage wristwatches—my passion at the time. I went into a little antique/junk store called 'Granny's Attic.' I asked 'Granny' if she had any old, wind-up wristwatches. She said, 'No, but I have a couple of old pocket watches.' I said, 'I'm not particularly interested in pocket watches and don't know much about them, but I'll take a look anyway'. She showed me a large silver cased pocket watch and a smaller, yellow gold colored pocket watch. I opened up each watch case and looked at the movements. The larger one was a Waltham with a damaged dial. The smaller watch had 'Illinois' on the dial and the movement read 'Bunn Special 21 Jewels.' I asked Granny what she wanted for the watches. She said 'seven' for the Waltham and 'two-fifty' for the Illinois.

"I didn't know exactly what the watches were worth, but knew enough to examine and ask further about the 'Bunn Special.' I wound the watch and it started running. I was able to check that it would set when I pulled out the lever. The case was gold-filled with no obvious wear or damage. I asked Granny if she could 'do any better on the price for the Illinois?' She told me that she 'would not take anything less than the two dollars and fifty cents' she had quoted. I almost had a coronary, but was able to get out $2.50 and pay Granny her asking price for the Illinois 16S, 21 jewel 'Bunn Special.' After that, I tried to remember to never take anything for granted and to always ask questions when buying a vintage watch."

Derby inside case back by Wadsworth

Derby inside case back by Solidarity

Even though the Derby and the Metropolitan share the same dial face, the dials are not meant to be interchangeable, owing to the different shapes of their respective dial plates. (See the **Metropolitan** listing in this chapter.) One rare and highly attractive Derby/Metropolitan dial has a sparkle finish coupled with dark luminous numerals in green outlined in black. This is an awesome dial, much valued by collectors. In a white gold-filled case without case wear and with an excellent sparkle finish dial, the Derby makes for a very handsome wristwatch.

End of outer cardboard box for a Derby

Devon / Cushion / Cushion Form / Sante Fe Cushion

Official Name = Devon (derived from a Sears & Roebuck sales catalog)
Secondary Name(s) = Cushion (derived from collectors' usage referring to its case shape); Cushion Form (derived from the 1928–1929 Hamilton-Illinois Sales Catalog); Santa Fe Cushion (from *Popular Mechanics* advertisements in 1929)
Formerly Known As = None
Time Period = Generic
Case Variations/Rarity = ◷ WGF/P, WGF/E
◷◷ YGF/P, YGF/E
◷◷◷ GGF/P, GGF/E
◷◷◷◷ TT/P, TT/E, WG/P, WG/E, YG/P, YG/E
◷◷◷◷◷ GG/P, YG/EE
Case Durability = ◷◷◷◷
Material = 10K WGF, 10K YGF, 10K GGF, 14K WGF, 14K YGF, 14K WG, 14K YG, 14K GG
Bezel = Plain, Engraved, Enamel
Sides = Plain, Engraved
Lugs = Plain, Engraved
Lug Size = 16mm
Springbar = Male
Casemakers = Solidarity, Keystone, Others
Case Closure = 3 Part Snap-On Bezel and Back
Case Number = None
Case Shape = Cushion
Case Back = Flat
Dimensions = Various
Movement Sizes = 24/17, 307/17, 903/15 905/17
Movement Grades/Jewels = Various
Seconds at = 6, 9
Dial Numbers = 8096, 8107, 8275, 8278, 8289
Dials = Silver Finish, Painted
Dial Opening = Cushion
Dial Variations/Rarity = ◷ Silver Finish/Seconds at 9; Silver Finish, Seconds at 6; Painted, Seconds at 9; Painted, Seconds at 6; Silver Finish, Painted Numerals; Silver Finish, Luminous Numerals
◷◷◷ Painted, Painted Numerals
◷◷◷◷◷ Silver Finish, Exploding Numerals
◷◷◷◷◷◷ Silver Finish, Etched Exploding Numerals
Numerals = Painted, Luminous
Hands = Luminous
Cased in Factory = Yes/No
Unique Case Design = No

Devon, white gold-filled

Cushion, yellow gold-filled, private-label dial

Santa Fe Cushion, yellow gold-filled

Unique Dial Design = No
Introduction Date = 1926
Retail Price New = $42.50 WGF, (15J); $47.50 WGF/E, (17J); $52.50 WGF/E, (19 J); $47.50 WG/P, $49.50 WG/E.
Collectibility = ◷◷◷◷
Advertisements = Yes
Marketing Themes = Various

Since the publication of *The Illinois Watch: The Life and Times of a Great American Watch Company*, documents have come to light that identify the model name for this Cushion wristwatch. The Sears Roebuck 1929 catalog calls this model the "Devon." Therefore, until further documentation is uncovered, it seems appropriate to call the Illinois Cushion wristwatch a "Devon" as well. However, in the Hamilton-Illinois 1928–1929 joint sales catalog, the Cushion model with a cushion-shaped dial was called the "Cushion Form" model.

The Devon was one of the first Illinois wristwatches advertised by Keystone and appeared in the November 26, 1926 issue of the *Jewelers' Circular*. The 6/0 size Generic cases for the Square Cut Corner, Rectangular, and Whippet models were also featured in this advertisement for Elgin, Waltham and Illinois models.

At least six different dial versions for this model are contained in several Illinois Material Catalogs. One dial that is quite striking has etched exploding numerals. This dial could have been for the exclusive use of the Santa Fe Watch Company. The Devon, a Generic Period model, is featured in dozens of jobbers' catalogs, starting in 1926. As a Generic Period watch, its case could have also contained Elgins or Walthams. In gold-filled, this model is quite common and can be acquired at very reasonable prices (solid gold ones are rarer and more expensive).

A large number of case and dial configurations exist for this model. The Devon can be found with 3/0 or 6/0 size movements and jewel counts of 15, 17 or 19. As a general rule, green gold cases are more desirable and collectible than the yellow gold ones, and the yellow ones are more valuable and collectible than the white ones. Interestingly, most Devons came with subsidiary seconds at 9. Watches with seconds at 6 are actually more difficult to find for this model, but not as desired by collectors. The gold-filled Devon is one of the most readily available and reasonably priced Illinois wristwatches, whether in 3/0 or 6/0 size. The most desirable Devons, with engraved bezels, subsidiary seconds at 9 and in solid gold cases, can still be located as well.

The Factory-Cased models for the Devon family of watches were most likely cased in Solidarity or Keystone cases, as indicated by various Illinois advertisements and Sales Catalogs. Illinois records indicate that the Devon described as a Cushion Engraved was Factory-Cased by Illinois in solid white gold or green gold Solidarity cases. This is confirmed by a 1928 Illinois Watch Factory advertisement.

There is a rare Devon that has an inside dustcover for its case. It is shown on the next page.

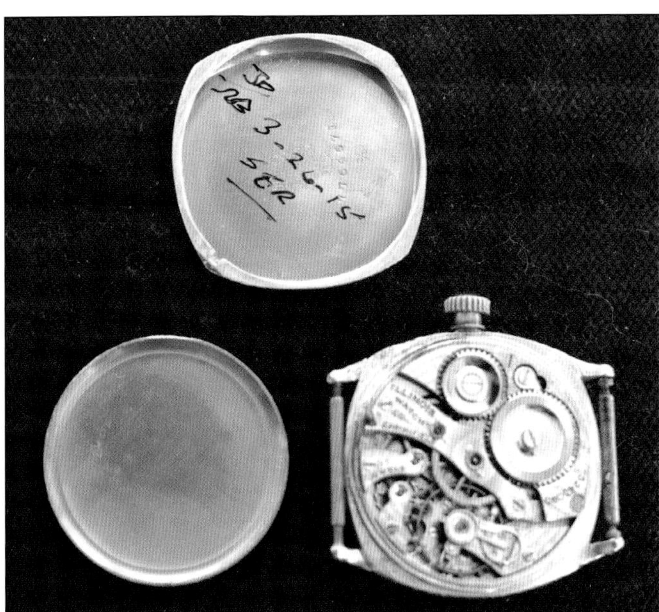

Devon with its inner dustcover off

Factory-Cased solid gold Solidarity versions came with a strap buckle also in solid matching gold. Factory-Cased Devons were also assembled in plain Keystone cases with subsidiary seconds at 9, as well as in white gold-filled or green gold-filled cases. It is best to find Devon cases marked with an "I" inside the case back. This "I" mark meant that the case was specifically made for use by the Illinois Watch Company.

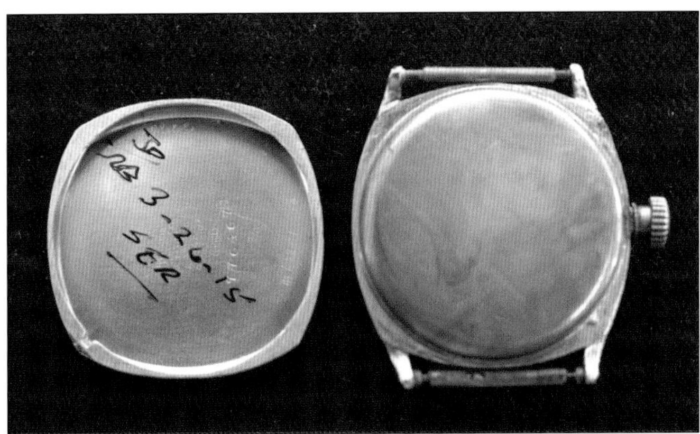

Devon dustcover in place

Solidarity 14K yellow gold Devon inside case back

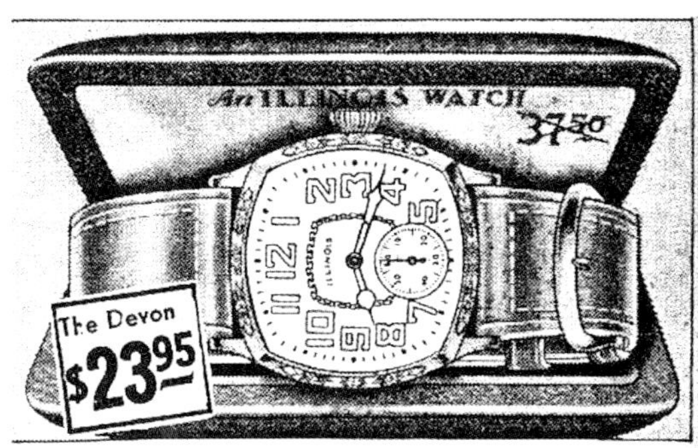

Sears, Roebuck catalog, 1929

In the 1928 A. C. Becken catalog, under the listing "Waltham and Illinois Gents' Strap Watches," there are two Illinois Devons illustrated, both in 14K white gold or green gold cases by Solidarity, with plain or engraved bezels.

CUSHIONED ENGRAVED

6/os 14k Solid white or green gold 15-jewel Waltham or Illinois movements. Leather straps with 14k gold buckle to match.

14k White Gold.		
No. **2138**	15-jewel Waltham	**$71.50**
No. **2139**	15-jewel Illinois	**67.00**
14k Green Gold.		
No. **2140**	15-jewel Waltham	**71.50**
No. **2141**	15-jewel Illinois	**67.00**

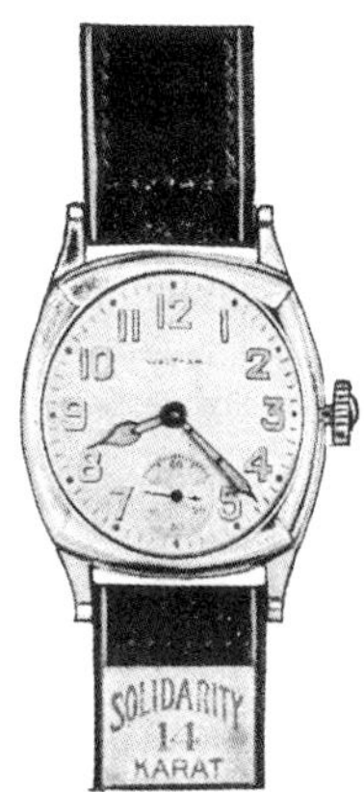

CUSHION PLAIN

6/os 14k Solid white or green gold 15-jewel Waltham or Illinois movements. Leather straps with 14k gold buckle to match.

14k White Gold.		
No. **2142**	15-jewel Waltham	**$68.20**
No. **2143**	15-jewel Illinois	**63.70**
14k Green Gold.		
No. **2144**	15-jewel Waltham	**68.20**
No. **2145**	15-jewel Illinois	**63.70**

Solidarity solid gold Illinois Cushion models, A. C. Becken catalog, 1928

Devons are known to exist in solid green gold, 6/0 size, with inlaid black enamel on their engraved bezels. This case is, of course, highly collectible.

The Santa Fe Watch Company and the R. H. Macy & Co. offered a Devon model for sale that contained an awesome deco dial as shown here.

Special! My 1929 Offer to You

I Will Save You Money

Read my 1929 Offer to You

My sole aim, during the year 1929, shall be to place as many standard, dependable Watches as I can in the hands of men throughout the land REGARDLESS OF PRICE OR PROFIT. To do this I have cut the price to ABSOLUTELY ROCK BOTTOM. I know that if I can distribute 5,000 "Santa Fe Specials" this year on this NO-PROFIT PLAN, that every Watch will be a salesman and sell at least one more. I am making this STARTLING AND UNHEARD OF OFFER to those who will tell their friends of this remarkable Watch value, if they find the Watches all and more than I claim for them.

President, Santa Fe Watch Co.

Save ⅓ to ½ of Your Money

Most Liberal Offer Ever Made

Our "Direct-to-you" low wholesale terms and EXTRA SPECIAL DISTRIBUTION PLAN is fully explained in the New Santa Fe Special booklet just off the press. The "Santa Fe Special Plan" means a BIG SAVING of money and you get the BEST watch value on the market today. Watch sent to you to see without one penny down. These Watches are NOW in the service on practically every Railroad in the United States and in every branch of the Army and Naval service. Thousands of them are distributed all over the world.

Write for FREE Watch Book Today

shows newest watch case designs in 4 colors. READ the so-called SECRETS of watch making. READ how you can save from ONE THIRD to ONE HALF of your money—Buy "Direct." The wise man will act quickly if he wants a watch.

EASY PAYMENTS TO SUIT YOU—Don't delay—Fill out and mail the coupon below for the FREE Watch Book.

SANTA FE WATCH COMPANY

36 THOMAS BUILDING TOPEKA, KANSAS

SANTA FE WATCH COMPANY,
36 Thomas Building, Topeka, Kansas.

Please send me the New Watch Book with the understanding that this request does not obligate me in any way.

Name..........

Address..........

State..........

Popular Mechanics, 1929

Santa Fe Cushion dial

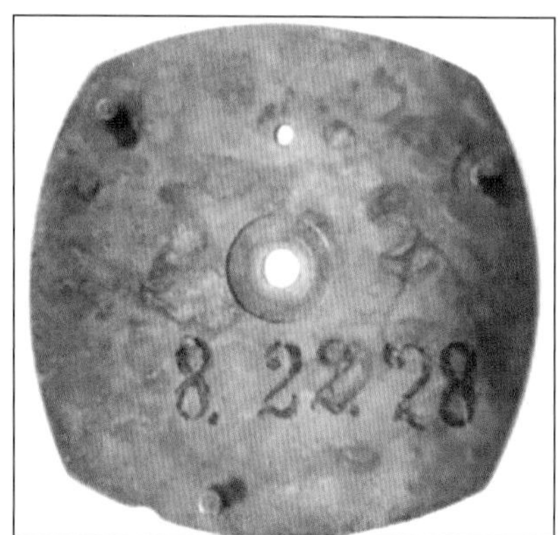

Santa Fe Cushion dial back

Illinois also supplied a similar private-label dial for R. H. Macy & Co.

Eagle

Eagle, green gold

Official Name = Unknown
Secondary Name(s) = Eagle (derived from the eagles engraved on the lugs of this model)
Formerly Known As = None
Time Period = Deco
Case Variations/Rarity = 🕒🕒🕒🕒🕒🕒🕒 GG/E
Case Durability = 🕒🕒🕒🕒
Material = 15K GG
Bezel = Engraved
Sides = Engraved
Lugs = Engraved
Lug Size = 16mm
Springbar = Male
Casemaker = Unknown
Case Closure = 3 Part Snap-On Bezel and Back
Case Number = None
Case Shape = Round
Case Back = Flat
Dimensions = 36 x 28mm
Movement Size = 6/0
Movement Grade/Jewels = 903/15
Seconds at = None
Dial Number = None
Dial = Painted Metal
Dial Opening = Round
Dial Variations/Rarity = 🕒🕒🕒🕒🕒 Painted, Luminous Numerals
Numerals = Luminous
Hands = Luminous
Cased in Factory = No
Unique Case Design = Yes
Unique Dial Design = No
Introduction Date = 1928
Retail Price New = Unknown
Collectibility = 🕒🕒🕒🕒
Advertisements = No
Marketing Theme = None known, but the theme of the "Eagle and the Stars" is highly patriotic and very American in inspiration.

Mystery surrounds "The Eagle." It ranks among the most distinctive and attractive wristwatches ever designed. Although the star and eagle design point to an unabashedly American patriotic motif, the 15K gold case composition reflects more European practice. Throughout the history of American wristwatch design, few examples exist of stars appearing on wristwatch bezels. In fact, it appears to be an almost uniquely Illinois trait. Stars can be found not only on the Eagle case, but also on the Skyway/Off-Duty/Greyhound/Motor Coach model case as well as one Whippet case variant.

The Eagle derives its name from the beautifully rendered eagle lugs. The lugs represent one example of the attention to detail, as each eagle's eye has been placed at the hole for the springbar. Detail can also be seen in the star added to the center of the solid gold crown. Overall, the Illinois Eagle can be considered the height of artistry in watch case design.

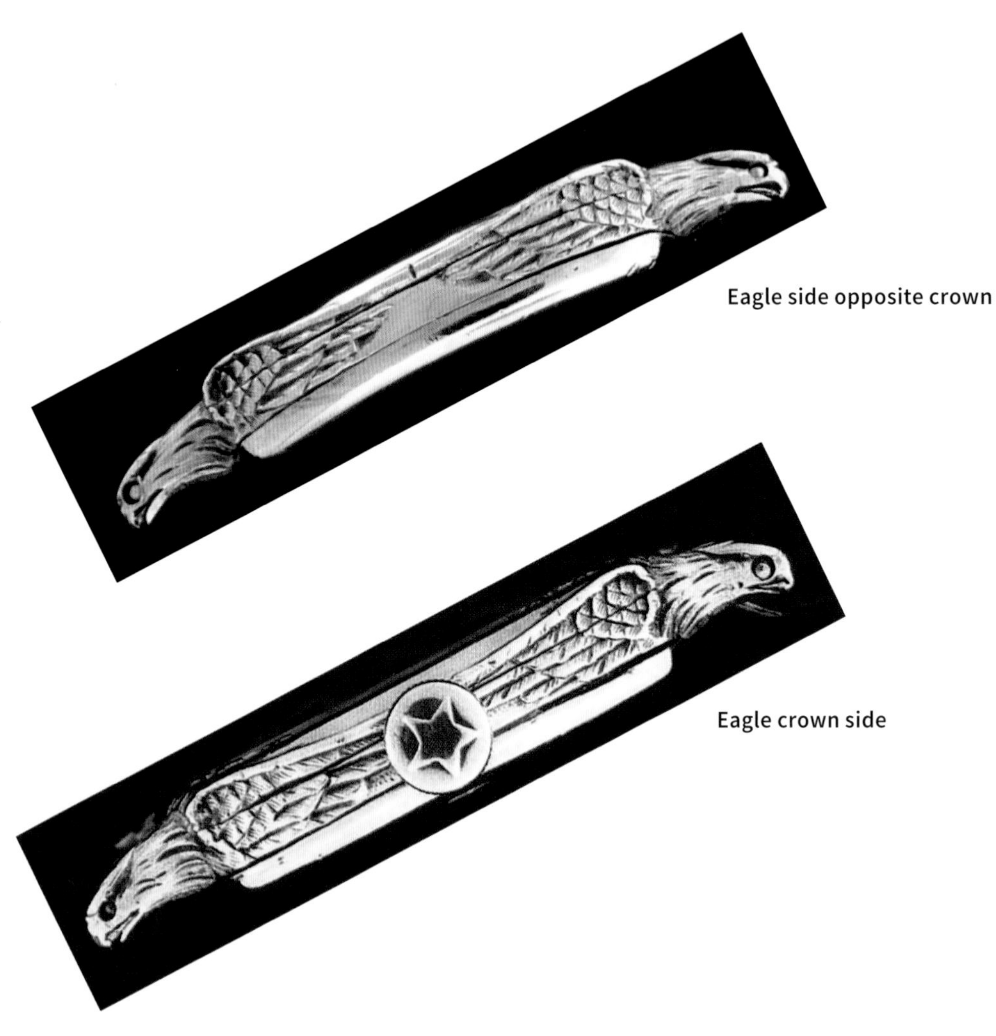

Eagle side opposite crown

Eagle crown side

Ensign / Yankee Clipper / Kingston

Ensign, green gold-filled

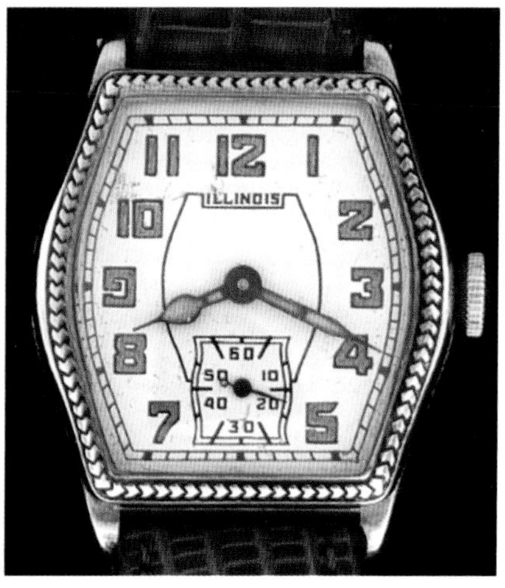

Ensign, white gold-filled

Official Name = Ensign (derived from the Illinois advertisements and Illinois Sales and Material Catalogs)
Secondary Name(s) = Kingston (derived from a 1933 Shure Winner catalog and internal Hamilton Watch Company documentation); Yankee Clipper, possibly if it came with a metal bracelet
Formerly Known As = None
Time Period = Deco
Case Variations/Rarity = ◷ WGF/E
◷◷◷ WGF/P, YGFEG, GGF/E
◷◷◷◷ GGF/P
◷◷◷◷◷ TT/E
Case Durability = ◷◷◷
Material = 14K GF
Bezel = Plain, Engraved
Sides = Engraved
Lugs = Plain
Lug Size = 16mm
Springbar = Male
Casemaker = Fahys
Case Closure = 3-Part Snap-On Bezel and Back
Case Number = Special Model B
Case Shape = Tonneau
Case Back = Flat
Dimensions = 34 x 28mm
Movement Size = 6/0
Movement Grades/Jewels = 601/21, 605/17, 607/19 903/15, 905/17, 907/19
Seconds at = 6, 9
Dial Numbers = 8065, 8101, 8136, 8199
Dial = Silver Finish, Butler Center
Dial Opening = Tonneau
Dial Variations/Rarity = ◷◷ Silver Finish, Luminous Numerals; Silver Finish, Seconds at 6
◷◷◷ Silver Finish, Butler Center; Silver Finish, Seconds at 9; Silver Finish, Butler Center, Seconds at 6; Silver Finish, Butler Center, Seconds at 9;
◷◷◷◷◷ Silver Finish, Etched Numerals; Silver Finish, Black Numerals
Numerals = Painted, Luminous, Etched
Hands = Luminous
Cased in Factory = Yes
Unique Case Design = Yes
Unique Dial Design = Yes
Introduction Date = 1929 (Ensign); 1931 (Kingston)
Retail Price New = $40.00 in 15J; $45.00 (17J)
Collectibility = ◷◷◷◷
Advertisements = Yes
Marketing Themes = "Has long been a popular Illinois style"
"Popular priced strap-watch"
"Smartly decorated case"

American Magazine, April 1929

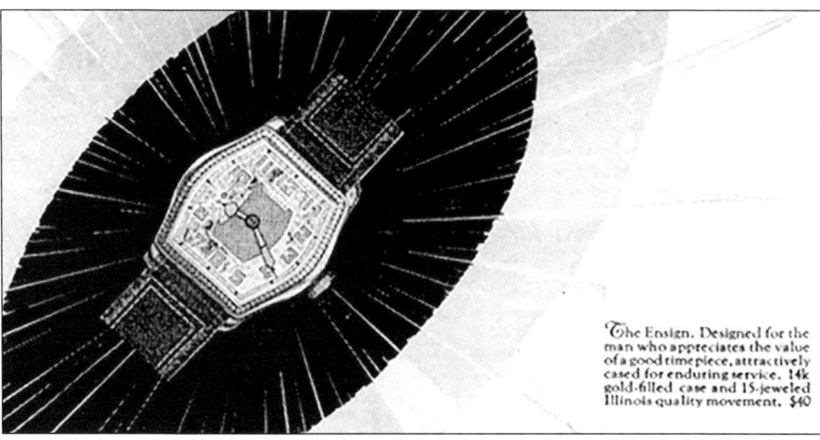

American Magazine, February 1929

The Ensign, one of Illinois' most enduringly popular models, appeared in many Illinois advertisements and Illinois Sales Catalogs between 1929 and 1932, and was listed in many jobbers' catalogs, some as late as 1933.

In 1930 an advertisement stated that the Ensign was "Designed for the man who appreciates the value of a good timepiece, attractively cased for enduring service." That same year, the L. & C. Mayers catalog drew attention to the "Stylish case, neatly engraved," and the May & Malone catalog pronounced the model "winning." The 1931–32 Illinois Sales Catalog called the Ensign a "Popular priced strap-watch."

The 6/0 Ensign is a smaller-size version of the 3/0 Illinois Mate wristwatch. The Mate has subsidiary seconds only at 6, whereas the Ensign came with subsidiary seconds at either 6 or 9. The Ensign also could be found with a silver-finish dial with etched raised gold numerals, a dial that is seldom seen today.

The 1933 Chicago World's Fair Edition of the Shure Winner Catalog No. 120 listed an Ensign with subsidiary seconds at 6 with a 17 or 21 jewel movement and called it a "Kingston." The Kingston name is on the List of Factory Cased Illinois Watches.

Ensign, two-tone green and white gold-filled

Ensign, white gold-filled

The Shure Winner Catalog (1933) referred to the 21-jewel and 17-jewel versions of this model as the Kingston, while the Holsman Company's Jewelry Drummer catalog (1932–33) called its 21-jewel and 17-jewel an Ensign. Collectors know of no reason for the difference in names for the same model watch.

The Ensign is considered a fairly common Illinois model, and it can be acquired at very reasonable prices. This model, in every configuration, is prone to significant corner bezel wear. The Ensign was one of the nautical-themed watches issued by Illinois; some of the others were the Admiral (a 6/0 size model as yet unidentified), Commodore, Jolly Roger, Mate, Yankee Clipper and Viking.

As the Yankee Clipper was listed under the 6/0 size watches for Factory-Cased Illinois watches, it is quite likely that Illinois called the Ensign a Yankee Clipper when equipped with a metal bracelet. One original price card for a Yankee Clipper has been found.

Advertisement from a 1931 Geo. T. Brodnax catalog, showing an engraved Ensign with subsidiary seconds at 6 and a metal mesh band. This is the only Factory-Cased Illinois known to have been marketed with a mesh band.

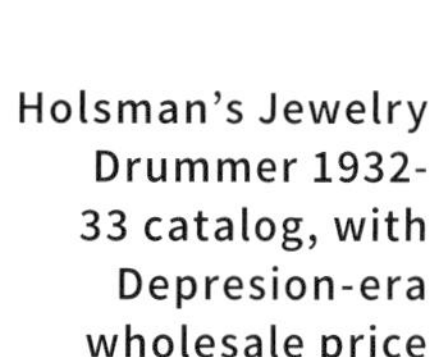

Holsman's Jewelry Drummer 1932-33 catalog, with Depresion-era wholesale price

End of outer cardboard box for an Ensign model

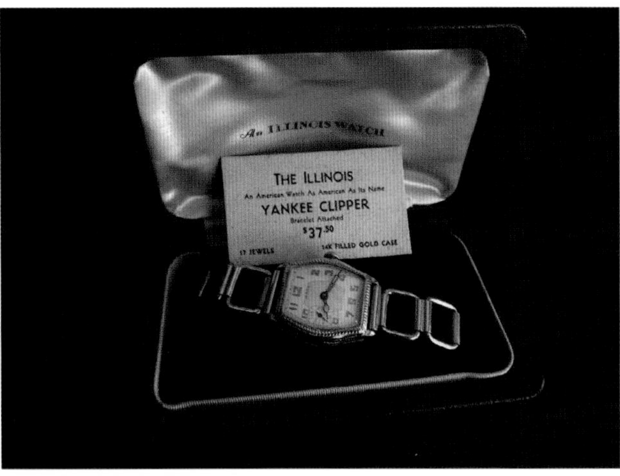

Possible Yankee Clipper with original price card, metal bracelet by Hadley is period correct, but it is unknown if the Yankee Clipper came with this band.

EXETER

See listing for **Andover**

FIFTH AVENUE

See listing for **New Yorker**

Finalist, yellow gold-filled

FINALIST

Official Name = Finalist (derived from the Illinois advertisements and Illinois Sales and Material Catalogs)
Secondary Name(s) = None
Formerly Known As = None
Time Period = Moderne
Case Variations/Rarity = ◷◷◷ YGF/E
◷◷◷◷ WGF/P
◷◷◷◷◷◷◷ WGF/E*
*Although advertised, this model has never been seen.
Case Durability = ◷◷◷
Material = 14K GF
Bezel = Plain, Engraved
Sides = Engraved
Lugs = Plain
Lug Size = 16mm
Springbar = Male
Casemaker = Wadsworth
Case Closure = 2-part Snap-On Bezel and Back
Case Number = 196
Case Shape = Rectangular
Case Back = Curved
Dimensions = 37 x 22mm
Movement Size = 12/0

Movement Grade/Jewels= 207/17
Seconds at = 6
Dial Numbers = 8104, 8165, 8238, 8308
Dial = Silver Finish, Sparkle Finish
Dial Opening = Rectangular
Dial Variations/Rarity = ◷◷ Silver Finish, Luminous Numerals
◷◷◷◷ Sparkle Finish, Painted Numerals
◷◷◷◷◷ Silver Finish, Black Numerals; Sparkle Finish, Luminous Numerals
Numerals = Painted, Luminous
Hands = Luminous
Cased in Factory = Yes
Unique Case Design = Yes
Unique Dial Design = Yes
Introduction Date = 1930
Retail Price New = $55.00
Collectibility = ◷◷◷◷
Advertisements = Yes
Marketing Themes = "A striking case design—quite different from the usual"
"A striking engraved case design"

The Finalist was listed by Illinois in several of its Sales Catalogs and also appears in various jobbers' catalogs. The Finalist was among the 12/0 size models that Illinois listed in its 1930–31 Sales Catalog as "America's Finest Rectangular Watches." It was touted as having "a striking case design—quite different from the usual—white or natural, oxidized or white plain." The Finalist also appeared in a Wadsworth advertisement, although its model name was not shown. Today, this attractive model is very popular with collectors.

The Finalist, Finalist Deco, Chesterfield and Chesterfield Stepped Bezel all share the same dials and case Model No. 196. (The Wentworth and Commander models also used these same dials.) The Finalist bezel displays a rectangular engraving at the top and bottom of its bezel, while the Finalist Deco's bezel has a triangular engraving at its top and bottom. Although today collectors differentiate the Finalist and the Finalist Deco because of their different bezel engravings, Illinois referred to both as Finalist models.

The Finalist is subject to minor corner bezel wear. This model can be found with its black oxidation intact; if not, it can easily be retouched with some carefully applied black enamel paint.

The Finalist was advertised as coming in a "white" oxidized case as well as a "natural" one (the engraving pattern was oxidized to make the pattern stand out); however, not one of the white ones has yet been found. For years collectors thought the plain bezel Finalist was a plain-bezel Chesterfield, but the 1930–31 Illinois Sales Catalog listing, quoted above, makes it quite clear that Finalist came in "white plain" cases too. Therefore, the plain bezel model is a Finalist (or perhaps even a Finalist Deco) but not a Chesterfield. And since both the Finalist and Finalist Deco models are advertised as having white gold-filled plain models, they may be identical watches.

The FINALIST

A striking case design—quite different from the usual—white or natural, oxidized or white plain.

Suggested consumer price, $55.

A. I. Hall catalog, 1930–31

Finalist outer cardboard box

The Finalist

The Finalist is a 12/0 size **Rectangular Strap Watch. 17 Jewel Illinois fitted in a 14 kt. Gold Filled case. Strikingly engraved design. Luminous dial. Retails for $55.00.**

D129.. Finalist White.
Our special net price.......... **$21.60**

D130. Finalist Yellow.
Our special net price.......... **$21.60**

Holsman's Jewelry Drummer 1932–33 catalog, Depression-era wholesale price. This model has never been seen in white gold-filled.

WHY I COLLECT ILLINOIS

"In 1993, I was new to vintage watch collecting, and a watchmaker friend of mine showed me a Hamilton 982M wristwatch movement. It was beautifully made, and he told me 'Hamilton made fantastic quality watches—you should collect these.' So I began collecting Hamilton wristwatches. As I started to read more about Hamilton, I learned they had purchased the Illinois Watch Company and that a few Hamilton watches used Illinois movements, so I researched Illinois. I learned they made some really great watch designs—some of the most interesting of the late 1920s and early 1930s. About the same time, another watch dealer friend started buying Illinois, and showed me some of the wonderful watches he was finding. At this point in time, even many experienced watch dealers didn't understand Illinois, and they could be bought inexpensively. I remember one dealer selling me a perfect Illinois Finalist (aka 'Art Deco') for $45.00. I also collect Art Deco items, and had picked up a few ladies Deco enameled wristwatches. When I discovered Illinois, I found they had made some beautiful enameled ladies' (and a few men's) wristwatches. It seemed nobody wanted *ladies'* wristwatches, and I was able to buy them very inexpensively. How times have changed!" *—Chris Odgers*

Finalist Deco

Finalist Deco, white gold-filled

Finalist Deco, yellow gold-filled

Official Name = Unknown
Secondary Name(s) = Finalist Deco (early price guides called this watch the "Art Deco" which was changed by collectors' usage to "Finalist Deco" to distinguish it from the "Finalist;" Illinois advertisements called it a "Finalist")
Formerly Known As = Art Deco
Time Period = Moderne
Case Variations/Rarity = ◷ WGF/E
◷◷◷◷ YGF/E
◷◷◷◷◷ WGF/P
◷◷◷◷◷◷◷ YGF/P*, YG/E**
* Although advertised, this model has never been seen.
** Only one is known to exist
Case Durability = ◷◷◷
Material = 14K GF, 14K YG
Bezel = Plain, Engraved
Sides = Engraved
Lugs = Plain
Lug Size = 16mm
Springbar = Male
Casemaker = Wadsworth
Case Closure = 2-Part Snap-On Bezel and Back
Case Number = 196
Case Shape = Rectangular
Case Back = Curved
Dimensions = 37 x 22mm
Movement Size = 12/0
Movement Grade/Jewels= 207/17
Seconds at = 6
Dial Numbers = 8108, 8165, 8238, 8308
Dials = Silver Finish, Sparkle Finish
Dial Opening = Rectangular
Dial Variations/Rarity = ◷◷ Silver Finish, Luminous Numerals
◷◷◷◷ Sparkle Finish, Painted Numerals
◷◷◷◷◷ Silver Finish, Black Numerals; Sparkle Finish, Luminous Numerals
Numerals = Painted, Luminous
Hands = Luminous
Cased in Factory = Yes
Unique Case Design = Yes
Unique Dial Design = Yes
Introduction Date = 1930

Retail Price New = $55.00
Collectibility = ◷◷◷◷
Advertisements = Yes
Marketing Themes = "You cannot afford to pass up the opportunity to merchandise ILLINOIS watches"
"Characteristic Illinois workmanship"

The Finalist Deco was introduced in 1930 as a "full Rectangular Illinois Watch." The sales brochure containing this model from Illinois advised jewelers that "you cannot afford to pass up the opportunity to merchandise ILLINOIS watches. They are smart—chic, if you please—and dependable. Characteristic excellent ILLINOIS workmanship has so constructed this watch to permit a larger barrel, resulting in longer run. The even rate, freedom of performance, and more compact casing, give this watch its popularity."

THE ILLINOIS "FINALIST" 17 JEWELS ADJUSTED

Here is very fine quality Illinois watch that is completely cased, timed and boxed at the Illinois factory. It comes in your choice of white or yellow 14K gold filled case with a gold filled bracelet to match. The case is nicely engraved in a modern design. The movement is a 17 jewel adjusted movement and the hands and dial are luminous. Our price is greatly reduced.

2R23209	White. PRICE	$59.50
2R23210	Yellow. PRICE	59.50

John Plain catalog, 1933

For years (owing to inaccurate popular price guides) this model was mistakenly called an "Art Deco." However, advertisements and brochures from 1930 disclosed that Illinois called this model a "Finalist." To distinguish the two Finalist models, the model with the rectangular bezel engraving is now called the "Finalist" and this model, with the triangular bezel engraving, is called the "Finalist Deco." As both the Finalist and Finalist Deco share the same case model number and dials, they are probably technically both Finalists, but to avoid confusion, each has been given a separate name by collectors.

The 1930–31 Illinois Sales Catalog shows an image of the Finalist rather than the Finalist Deco as the company's "Finalist" model, and so do some contemporary jobbers' catalogs, such as the 1931 A. C. Becken and the 1930–31 A. I. Hall (which simply use the Illinois catalog page). However, for its graduation-theme magazine advertisement of May 1930 headed "The gift that keeps on giving," Illinois did use an image of the Finalist Deco. The watch is shown there with a leather strap. Later, an image of what we call the Finalist Deco also appears in a John Plain catalog (1933), but there it is sporting a matching bracelet.

Finalist Deco, white gold-filled, Moderne dial

Finalist Deco inside case back, custom solid gold model

The Finalist Deco is much more common in white gold-filled than yellow gold-filled. The advertisements for the Finalist Deco list a yellow gold-filled plain-bezel version; however, one has never been located. The plain-bezel white gold-filled Finalist Deco is difficult to find and, although rare, is not overly popular with collectors. Still, it is considered a must-have for a serious Illinois collector. To date, only one solid yellow gold Finalist Deco has been found and may thus have been a custom order.

All of the Finalist Deco models in gold-filled are susceptible to minor corner bezel wear but nonetheless remain popular with collectors.

Finalist Deco and/or Finalist, white gold-filled plain

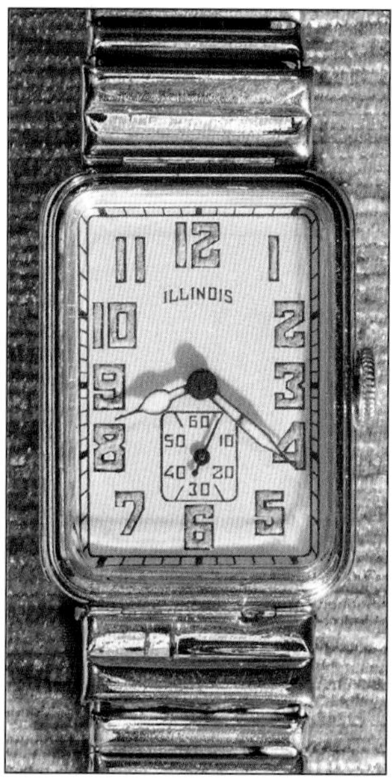

Frontenac, white gold-filled

Frontenac

Official Name = Frontenac (derived from Illinois advertisements and jobbers' catalogs)
Secondary Name(s) = None
Formerly Known As = None
Time Period = Moderne
Case Variations/Rarity = 🕓🕓🕓🕓🕓🕓 WGF/P
🕓🕓🕓🕓🕓🕓🕓YGF/P*
*Although advertised, this model has never been seen.
Case Durability = 🕓🕓**
**As so few of this model have been seen, it is likely that the bands did not hold up and the watches were discarded. For this reason, the durability for this model has been rated "fair."
Material = 14K GF
Bezel = Plain
Sides = Plain
Lugs = N/A
Lug Size = 16mm
Springbar = Integrated Band with Case
Casemaker = Wadsworth
Case Closure = 3-Part Snap-On Bezel and Back
Case Number = 202
Case Shape = Rectangular
Case Back = Flat
Dimensions = 39 x 30mm
Movement Size = 12/0
Movement Grade/Jewels = 207/17
Seconds at = 6
Dial Numbers = 8168, 8751
Dial = Silver Finish
Dial Opening = Rectangular
Dial Variations/Rarity = 🕓🕓 Silver Finish, Luminous Numerals
🕓🕓🕓🕓🕓 Silver Finish, Black Numerals
Numerals = Painted, Luminous
Hands = Luminous
Cased in Factory = Yes
Unique Case Design = Yes
Unique Dial Design = No
Introduction Date = 1930
Retail Price New = $65.00
Collectibility = 🕓🕓🕓
Advertisements = Yes
Marketing Themes = "Masculine smartness"
"Time must be right and style comes into the case."

2 THE LITERARY DIGEST

Illinois Watches

cases by Wadsworth

Shown on this page is a representative group of watches with movements by Illinois and cases by Wadsworth. Wadsworth Cases are sold to the makers of good watches only. Therefore, one way to be sure of getting a good watch is to ask your jeweler to show you the name Wadsworth in the case.

The Wadsworth Watch Case Company

Dayton, Ky., Opposite Cincinnati, Ohio

Case makers for the leading watch movements

Frontenac advertisement by Wadsworth, *Literary Digest*, 1930

The Frontenac was featured as one of the "Rectangular Strap Watches of Distinction" in the 1930–31 Illinois Sales Catalog, which states: "Masculine smartness is typified in this new watch. The beautiful flexible band is part of the case and satisfies that demand for a perfectly matched watch and bracelet combination. The Frontenac is offered in 14K white or natural filled gold."

There are at least two Illinois magazine advertisements for this model, plus one from Wadsworth. The Frontenac was also featured in several jobbers' catalogs. In addition, it was shown in an article about innovative new watches in the October 1930 issue of the *Jewelers' Circular.*

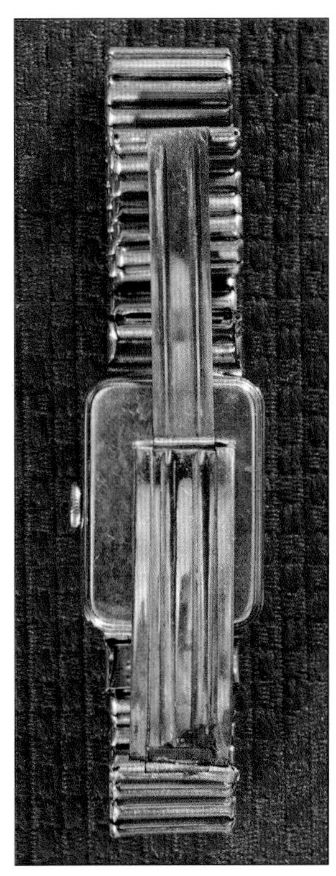

Frontenac integrated band

Frontenac integrated band

Louis Sickles Service Satisfies

Your Customers Demand Quality at a Reasonable Price

FOR GRADUATION SALES ADD THESE NEW MODELS TO YOUR STOCK

6½ L. 15J. Consumer, $50
Waltham Toneau

This beautiful series of the newest watches of American manufacture combine beauty and time-keeping accuracy with greater profits for you.

The new $50.00 Waltham Wrist Watch with G. Fld. case, 15 J. movement is the smallest American Watch made. List price, $57.30.

Hamilton No. 992, No. 7 is the latest addition to this famous railroad watch series. List price, $72.90.

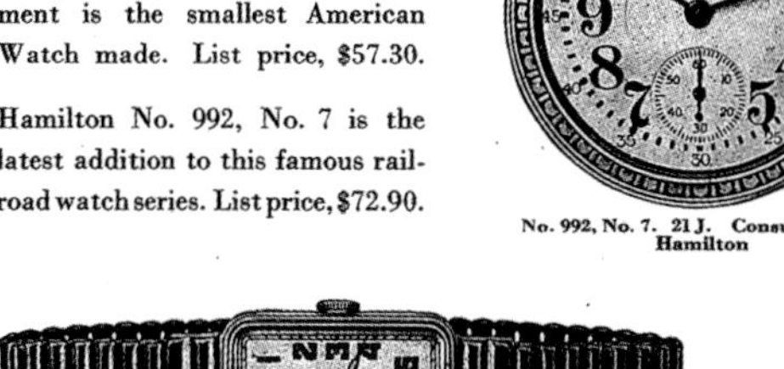

No. 992, No. 7. 21 J. Consumer, $65
Hamilton

Avigo Elgin No. 461, has been designed for air-minded Americans and is exceedingly accurate. List price, $44.40.

The Frontenac Illinois is the latest combination of the 17J. 12/0 rectangular watch with band. An exceedingly smart watch. List price, $72.40.

Nydia and Bondmaid—new ladies' attachments are but two of the latest additions to the fine Hadley Line.

FRONTENAC—Illinois 17 J Consumer, $65

AVIGO—No. 461, Elgin 17 J. Consumer, $40

NYDIA—G. F. in Box. Consumer, $8.00 · BONDMAID—Chrome Plated—Carded. Consumer, $3.00

AMERICAN WATCHES AND HADLEY ATTACHMENTS ADEQUATELY FILL YOUR NEEDS

LOUIS SICKLES

Wholesale Watch Service

1015 Chestnut Street » » Philadelphia, Pa.

Keystone, **May 1930 advertisement from Louis Sickles, an Illinois jobber. Although it is advertising Hadley attachments, the Frontenac's is a Wadsworth!**

The Frontenac was the only Illinois watch originally offered with an integrated metal bracelet. The use of an integrated band by Illinois could possibly be a design first for a major watch manufacturer. Conceptually, a watch with an integrated band seems to be related to the earlier Manheimer "Lug-less Strap Watch" innovation (see the discussion and illustrations in Chapter 8).

The Frontenac case itself is the rather plain Trophy/Westchester/Kensington model, whose bezel is decorated only with understated banding of ridges. The integrated metal band, however, transforms it into something very unusual and stylish. To date, only three intact Frontenacs with original bands have been found; a fourth has its band broken off at both ends. All four are white gold-filled. Although this model was also advertised in yellow gold-filled, one has never been located. The metal bracelet (also made by Wadsworth) had an adjustable clasp so it could be adjusted to the wearer's wrist.

Frontenac integrated Wadsworth band

Frontenac with its band broken off

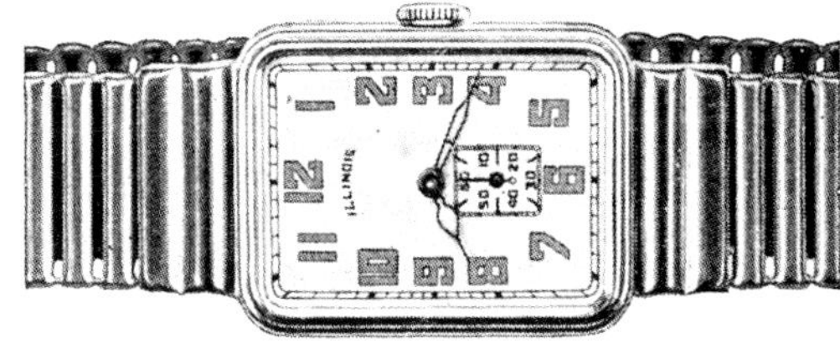

The FRONTENAC

Masculine smartness is typified in this new watch. The beautiful flexible band is a part of the case and satisfies that demand for a perfectly matched watch and bracelet combination. The Frontenac is offered in 14K white or natural filled gold.

Suggested consumer price, $65

A. I. Hall catalog, 1931

In 1932, two years after the Frontenac was introduced, Hamilton came out with its Clinton model, also in white or yellow gold-filled, which used the same integral watchband as the Frontenac. (There was also a version of the Clinton called the Greely, which had lugs and was equipped with a leather strap.)

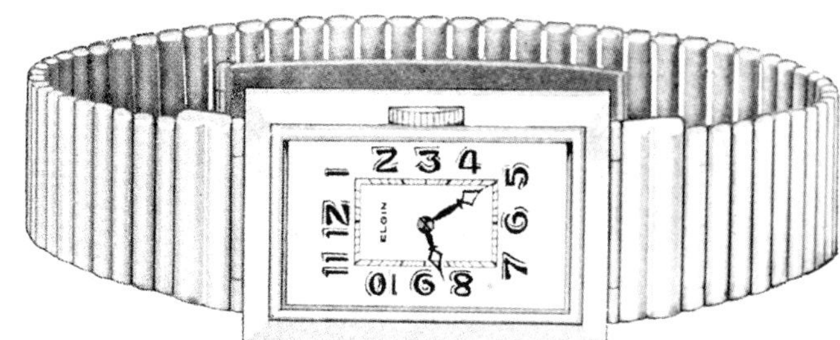

841 (White)—A rectangular Elgin that is distinctly different in design. Has a 17 jewel 18/0 size movement fitted in a 14karat gold filled case. Has new style Wadsworth gold filled band to match.
Consumer Price ***$65.00***
1041—Same model as above with yellow gold filled case and band.
Consumer Price ***$65.00***

Elgin with Wadsworth integral bracelet, A. I. Hall 1930–31 catalog

A pair of Hamilton Clintons, with the Lord Wadsworth integral bracelet

It is interesting that Wadsworth's ingenious bracelet attachment, called the Lord Wadsworth, was also used on Elgin and Waltham lugless models too. Elgin employed it on its Presentation 841 (white) and 1041 (yellow), both gold-filled watches, c. 1930–31; Waltham also used it on a gold-filled watch (yellow or white) that it began marketing as a "Gents' or Ladies' Sport Model" as early as the 1930 Fort Dearborn catalog (in white gold-filled only). The Elgin and Waltham cases themselves were plain rectangular ones, much less individual in design than either the Illinois Frontenac or the Hamilton Clinton.

No. 4027 . . . $89.40

$65.00 WALTHAM SERIES
Pictured at left
Gents' or Ladies' Sport Model
7¼ Ligne
14K White Gold Filled Case
15-Jewel WALTHAM Precision Movement
Lord Wadsworth Bracelet Attached

This watch will make a striking appeal to the Gent who wishes a distinctive Dress Watch or to the Lady who desires a SPORT WATCH. It is of finest workmanship and finish and should appeal to those seeking a watch of an exclusive design. 14K White Gold Filled Case with Lord Wadsworth Bracelet attached to watch. Fitted complete with 15-Jewel WALTHAM Precision Movement, and encased in an exquisite presentation box. Plain Dial.
No. 4027 Each $89.40

Waltham with Wadsworth integral bracelet, Fort Dearborn 1930 catalog

Futura / Paul Revere

Official Name = Futura (derived from Illinois advertisements and Illinois Sales and Material Catalogs)
Secondary Name(s) = Paul Revere (derived from an internal Hamilton document).
Formerly Known As = None
Time Period = Moderne
Case Variations/Rarity = 🕒🕒 WGF/P
🕒🕒🕒 YGF/P
Case Durability = 🕒🕒
Material = 14K GF
Bezel = Plain
Sides = Plain
Lugs = Plain
Lug Size = 16mm
Springbar = Female
Casemaker = Keystone
Case Closure = 3-Part Snap-On Bezel and Back
Case Number = 197
Case Shape = Rectangular
Case Back = Flat
Dimensions = 36 x 23mm
Movement Size = 12/0
Movement Grade/Jewels = 207/17
Seconds at = 6
Dial Numbers = 8167, 8456
Dials = Silver Finish, Sparkle Finish
Dial Opening = Rectangular
Dial Variations/Rarity = 🕒🕒 Silver Finish, Luminous Numerals
🕒🕒🕒🕒 Sparkle Finish, Luminous Numerals
🕒🕒🕒🕒🕒 Silver Finish, Black Numerals; Silver Finish, Applied Gold Numerals
🕒🕒🕒🕒🕒🕒 Sparkle Finish, Applied Gold Numerals;
Sparkle Finish, Raised Gold Numerals
Numerals = Painted, Luminous
Hands = Luminous, Steel
Cased in Factory = Yes
Unique Case Design = Yes
Unique Dial Design = Yes
Introduction Date = 1929
Retail Price New = $60.00
Collectibility = 🕒🕒🕒🕒
Advertisements = Yes
Marketing Themes = "Beautifully unusual case lines"
"Further evidence of Illinois craftsmanship"
"Smooth flowing modern case lines"

Futura, white gold-filled

Futura, yellow gold-filled

Illinois referred to the Futura as "Further evidence of Illinois craftsmanship in the 12/0 size watch field." The 1930–31 Sales Catalog commented on its "beautifully unusual case lines," and the 1931–32 Sales Catalog accurately described the Futura as having "Smooth flowing modern case lines." This model was aptly named. With its futuristic design, it is as advanced today as it was when introduced in 1929.

Interestingly, the Futura first appeared *with* but not *in* the 1929–1930 Illinois Sales Catalog; since it was a last-minute addition, it was on a separate page. Magazine advertisements for it began appearing at the end of 1929, in time for the holiday trade, and it was listed in later Illinois Sales Catalogs as well as jobbers' catalogs.

The dial has an unusual half-moon design feature in place of the numeral 6. The rounded corners of the dial elegantly conform to the bezel opening of the case. There is a rare Futura sparkle finish dial with gold applied numerals that is difficult to acquire. The Futura was unfortunately prone to bezel wear on its top and bottom, particularly on the yellow gold-filled case.

Rare Futura dial with raised gold numerals

Possible Paul Revere

Although the Hamilton internal documentation shows that Hamilton referred to the Futura model as the Paul Revere, the Paul Revere is under the 6/0 size watches on the List of Factory Cased Watches. Therefore, either the Factory List or the Hamilton documentation is in error or the Paul Revere could have been a Futura equipped with a metal bracelet or perhaps had a sparkle dial with applied gold numerals.

R. F. Simmons & Co. metal bracelet for the possible Paul Revere

Collectors sometimes confuse the Futura with the Illinois Wentworth model, as they are somewhat similar. The Futura model, however, has an extra ridge on its bezel. In addition, its case is rounded inside the bezel corners, while the Wentworth's is square. Although the Futura and the Wentworth have different bezels, they share the same case Model No. 197, and their case backs and center case sections are interchangeable. This was a design economy employed by Illinois.

Futura inside case back

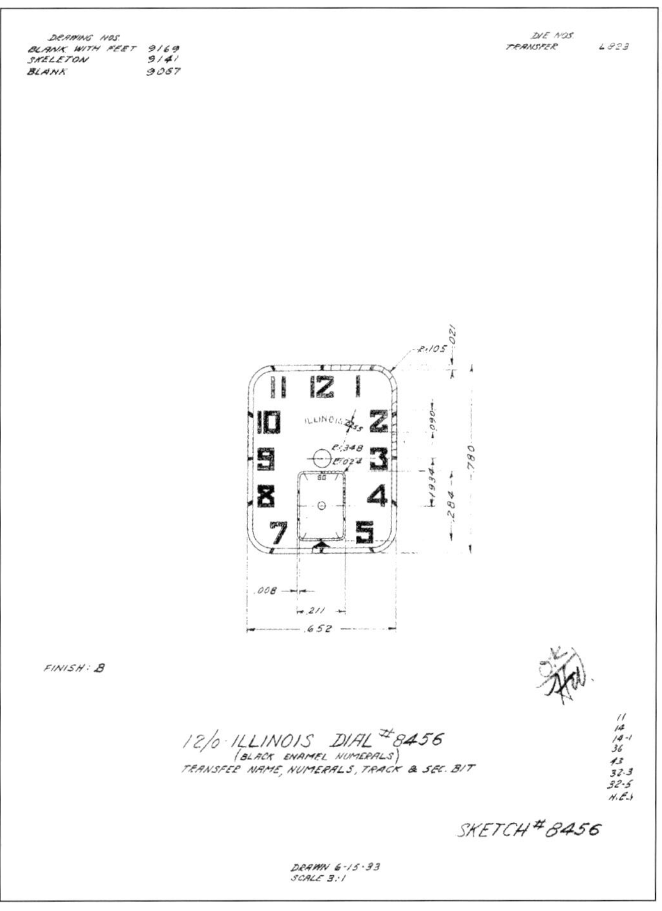

Lancaster drawing of a later-released Futura dial with black enamel numerals

WHY I COLLECT ILLINOIS

I had been an occasional collector through the 1990s and the early part of the last decade—a Rolex here, a Vacheron there—when I came across Gene Stone's *The Watch*, which focuses primarily on European watches but had an intriguing section on Hamilton. After looking at many of the watches featured in that book, I started collecting Hamiltons, especially the art deco Piping Rock, Coronado and Spur models. I bought Don Sauers's *Time for America* (about the Hamilton watch) and then Faber and Unger's *American Wristwatches*, whose section on "The Decorative Period" included two pages of color photographs of Illinois watches. I loved what I saw and, realizing Hamilton had acquired Illinois, I started collecting a few Illinois watches. I then called Gene Stone, whom I know, and asked him why he hadn't mentioned Illinois in his book, and he said he hadn't known of the brand when he wrote it. That stunned me, but it didn't dissuade me. It did prompt me to look elsewhere, and soon after, I came across your book. It expanded on Faber & Unger, and it probably had more to do with my deciding to focus on Illinois than anything else. The combination of great photography, history and detail gave me confidence as a collector. I tend to focus on watches with Arabic numerals whose dials and movements have held up over the decades. The range of watches Illinois produced is stunning, from the somewhat ornate Piccadilly and Jolly Roger models to the simpler Futura. Until now, I have never been a collector of anything. No stamps. No rocks. No cars. Nothing. But the Illinois line gives great pleasure, in part because it isn't well known (I don't think I have ever seen anyone else wearing something I own), and in part because the watches are so clean and elegant. — *Anonymous*

FANTASTIC FIND

Good friend and Hamilton and Illinois collector Randy Van Netten reports: "In the pre-internet 1980s very nice wristwatches could be found regularly at local Southern California flea markets. Some of my earliest finds, and my best contacts with dealers and collectors, were at such markets. I regularly went to two Southern California flea markets in particular: The Rose Bowl in Pasadena on the second Sunday of the month and Long Beach Veterans Stadium on the third Sunday of the month.

For the uninitiated, an "antique" flea market contains mostly material for sale from thirty to fifty years old and some items that are older. There are usually a mixture of regular, professional dealers and casual sellers. The regular dealers have impressive displays, with valuable items, like wristwatches, inside glass cases. The casual sellers have varying degrees of sophistication in their displays, ranging from glass cases to a blanket spread out on the ground with a few items on display. It was from one of the blanket dealers that the watch in this story is about.

The Long Beach market opens to the public at 8:00 a.m., but an 'early bird pass' can be bought which lets you in between 6:00 and 8:00 a.m., while the dealers are setting up. Since I was in competition with dealers, pickers and other collectors, I usually arrived during the early bird period. One such Sunday I entered in the pre-dawn hours and saw a dealer lay a wristwatch on her blanket. I immediately snapped it up. It was so dark I had trouble seeing the watch, but I did see it was an Illinois 'Futura', a model with the desirable 207 rectangular movement. I could not tell if it was yellow or white gold-filled. I can't recall the exact price quoted, but my usual routine was to offer about 75% of the asking price and haggle a bit. I had a $50 maximum in those days, so I acquired the watch for some amount under $50. After sunrise I examined the watch and found it had a flawless case and a running movement. I was very proud of this find as I shared it with other collectors that day.

I still attend the flea markets, but the majority of merchandise now seems to be collectibles from the 60s through 80s, so I do not find as many gems in my target collecting era as I used to. But, who knows? The occasional treasure can still be found in your hometown flea market!

See listing for in **Kenilworth**

General Funston

General Funston, sterling silver

Official Name = General Funston (derived from a 1917 IWCCo advertisement)
Secondary Name(s) = Telephone Dial (derived from collectors' usage if it has a Telephone Dial)
Formerly Known As = Military
Time Period = Transitional
Case Variations/Rarity = 🕒🕒🕒🕒🕒 SS/P, YGF
🕒🕒🕒🕒🕒🕒🕒 SS/P/OFF-SET
Case Durability = 🕒🕒🕒🕒
Material = SS, N, 10K YGF
Bezel = Plain
Sides = Plain
Lugs = Plain
Lug Size = 14mm
Springbar = Swivel Lugs, Angled or Straight
Casemaker = IWCCo
Case Closure = 3-Part Screw-On Bezel and Back
Case Number = None
Case Shape = Round
Case Back = Flat
Dimensions = 50 x 34mm (0 size); 45 x 34mm (3/0 size)
Movement Sizes = 0, 3/0
Movement Grades/Jewels = 21/11, 24/17, 32/11, 201/11, 36/17, 204/17
Seconds at = 6
Dial Numbers = Painted/Luminous
Dial = Enamel
Dial Opening = Round
Dial Variations/Rarity = 🕒🕒🕒 Enamel
🕒🕒🕒🕒🕒 Enamel Telephone Dial
Numerals = Painted, Luminous
Hands = Steel
Cased in Factory = No
Unique Case Design = No
Unique Dial Design = Yes (Telephone)
Introduction Date = 1917
Retail Price New = Unknown
Collectibility = 🕒🕒🕒🕒
Advertisements = Yes
Marketing Themes = "Our latest creations"
"Further evidence of Illinois craftsmanship"
"Wrist watches for Uncle Sam's Boys"

Until recently, collectors did not know the correct model name for this military Transitional Period watch. With the discovery of a 1917 IWCCo advertisement, we now know that this round sterling silver case with swivel lugs is called a General Funston. If the case came equipped with an Illinois Watch Company movement and an Illinois Telephone dial, today's collectors would call it a Telephone Dial watch. (See the **Telephone Dial** listing in this chapter.)

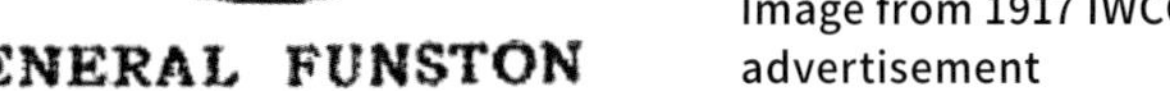

Image from 1917 IWCCo advertisement

General Funston, angled swivel lugs

The General Funston came in both 0 size and 3/0 size cases. IWCCo advertised this model, along with the Admiral Benson, Admiral Evans and the General Joffre case models. All of these models, along with the Telephone Dial, are described in this chapter. The General Funston came with either straight or flared swivel lugs. To date, there has been one ultra-rare General Funston with an off-set crown located; it housed an Elgin movement and dial, according to Czubernat.

GENERAL FREDERICK FUNSTON (1865-1917)

General Funston, c. 1900

"In 1901 scarcely an American lived who was unfamiliar with the name of Frederick Funston, the hero of the Philippine insurrection. Through a daring ruse this Kansan captured the rebel leader and broke the back of the uprising.

"Funston's adult life was one of almost unbelievable adventure. In the early 1890s he participated in scientific expeditions in the Dakota Badlands, Death Valley, and in Alaska along the Klondike and Yukon Rivers. In 1896 he joined the forces of Cubans who were fighting for independence from Spain. He was immediately made a captain of artillery. Two years later, when he was sent home because of malaria, he was a lieutenant colonel.

"Hardly had Funston returned home before the Spanish American War broke out and Kansas was called upon for troops. Funston was appointed colonel of the 20th Kansas Infantry, which was soon sent to the Philippine Islands. On February 4, 1899, the insurrection broke out. Because of his leadership, Funston was awarded the Congressional Medal of Honor and promoted to the rank of Brigadier General Volunteers.

". . . Funston returned to the Philippines in late December, 1899 He personally led the small cadre of American soldiers and Macabebe [native] scouts in the capture of the famed Filipino insurrectionist, Emilio Aguinaldo. Criticized by some for unethically posing as a spy to bring about the capture, Funston was nevertheless awarded a commission as a Brigadier General, Regular Army, June, 1901. At the time, Funston was 35 years old and the youngest general in the army. He was also awarded the Congressional Medal of Honor.

"In 1906 he did much to keep law and order in San Francisco and to provide relief to sufferers of the great earthquake. In 1914 he was in command of American troops on the Texas border during the difficulties with Pancho Villa. Future general, John J. Pershing, was one of his subordinates. On November 17, 1914, Funston was made a Major General.

"A heart attack took the life of the 51-year-old general on February 19, 1917."*

*Kansas Historical Society, "Frederick Funston": http://www.kshs.org/kansapedia/frederick-funston/12060

On April 4, 1902, Admiral Robley D. Evans went out of his way to laud General Funston.

ADMIRAL EVANS LAUDS FUNSTON

Says General Holds His Position Because of His Ability.

Special Dispatch to The Call.

KANSAS CITY, Mo., April 3.—Admiral Robley D. Evans was in Kansas City today en route to San Francisco, whence he will sail shortly for the China station, where he has been assigned to a command. He was accompanied by his wife and daughter.

Admiral Evans said of General Funston:

You can't throw down a man like Funston because of what he says. He enjoys his position because of what he has done. He is not a general of the United States army for what he said, but for what he did, not on one occasion or on two occasions, but on several emergencies, and that's what generals are for. It does not matter where a man got his ability in war. It may be in his blood. It may come through rough, hard experience. It may be acquired at the academies at Annapolis or West Point. But wherever or however a man got it, if he displays that he has the power to command, he finds recognition, and that is Funston's style. He is a fighting man and he won his general's star by fighting. Regardless of what he says, the fact remains that he has made good, that he made good before he got his general's star and that is the best basis for promotion in the army or the navy.

San Francisco Call, Vol. 87, # 125, April 4, 1902

General Joffre, sterling silver

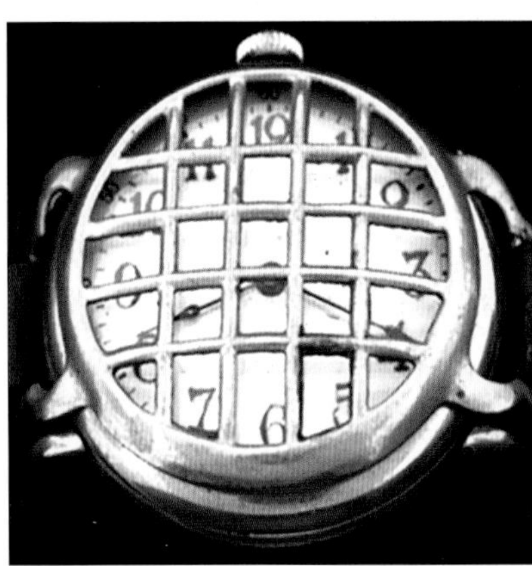

General Joffre, nickel with a mesh shrapnel guard

General Joffre

Official Name = General Joffre (derived from a 1917 IWCCo advertisement)
Secondary Name(s) = Military
Formerly Known As = None
Time Period = Transitional
Case Variations/Rarity = ◷◷◷◷◷◷ So, SS
◷◷◷◷◷◷◷ YGF
Case Durability = ◷◷◷◷
Material = SS, N, 10K YGF
Bezel = Plain
Sides = Plain
Lugs = Plain
Lug Size = 14mm
Springbar = Fixed Lugs, Swivel Lugs
Casemaker = IWCCo, Philadelphia, Bates & Bacon
Case Closure = 3-Part Snap-On Bezel and Back and Semi-Hermetic Cases
Case Number = None
Case Shape = Round
Case Back = Flat
Dimensions = 37mm for Snap-On/39mm for Semi-Hermetic Cases; 52 x 37mm
Movement Size = 6
Movement Grades/Jewels = Various
Seconds at = 6
Dial Number = None
Dials = Enamel, Silver Finish
Dial Opening = Round
Dial Variations/Rarity = ◷◷◷◷ Enamel
◷◷◷◷◷ Silver Finish
Numerals = Painted
Hands = Steel
Cased in Factory = No
Unique Case Design = No
Unique Dial Design = No
Introduction Date = 1917
Retail Price New = Unknown
Collectibility = ◷◷◷◷
Advertisements = Yes
Marketing Theme = "Wrist Watches for Uncle Sam's Boys"

General Joffre case back

Until recently, collectors did not know the true model name of this military Transitional Period watch. With the discovery of a 1917 IWCCo advertisement, we now know that IWCCo called this round 6-size case a General Joffre.

Image from 1917 IWCCo advertisement

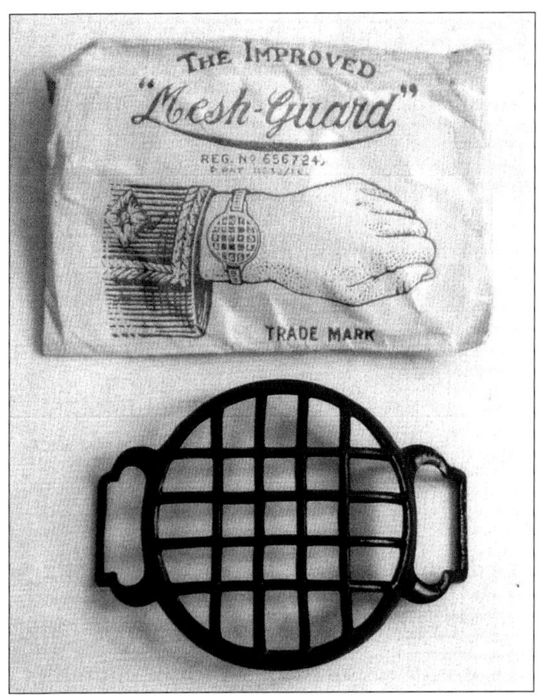

Mesh guard for a size 6 General Joffre with original package

Czubernat notes with respect to the very rare General Joffre model that it is "one of the most desirable (and expensive) American Trench Watches. . . These watches are prized both for their beauty and their unusually large size. Most American Trench Watches of the Great War were much smaller; they were a size 3/0 or 0s. These two sizes ranged from 33mm up to 34mm going across without counting the crown. A giant 6s trench watch measures 37mm up to 40mm across, making it highly sought after by collectors. . . . The Illinois 6s trench watch cases were made of solid nickel, sterling silver, or 10K yellow gold-filled. Out of all of these cases I would have to say that the rarest one by far is the Illinois case that is semi-hermetic with swivel lugs, [because] these are VERY hard to obtain."[1]

Czubernat and I confirm that we only know of about fifteen General Joffre models. Six are Elgin and nine are Illinois models. The known Illinois variations are: four in a nickel case with swivel lugs, like the advertisement; two in a nickel case with fixed lugs; three in silverore and two in sterling silver.

General Joffre, late 1920s

GENERAL JOSEPH JOFFRE (1852–1931)

Marshal Joseph Jacques Césaire Joffre was a French general during World War I. He is most well-known for regrouping the retreating allied armies to defeat the Germans at the strategically decisive First Battle of the Marne in 1914. His popularity led to his nickname of Papa Joffre.

Joffre retired in 1919 and was made a member of the Académie française. He died on January 3, 1931, in Paris. His memoirs, in two volumes, were published posthumously in 1932.*

* http://www.firstworldwar.com/bio/joffre.htm

IDENTIFIES WATCH FOUND ON VERDUN BATTLEFIELD

As an identification tag a soldier's watch, picked up on the battlefield of Verdun, has proved as good as the regulation tags furnished by the United State sramy. But it was not checked up as quickly.

Charles E. Seng, a jeweler, 306 East Market street, received a request yesterday from a jobber asking him if he could name the owner of a watch he had sold, which two American soldiers had picked up after a battle at Verdun. On looking up his records Mr. Seng found that he sold the watch last February to Jesse Holbrook, of Glenwood, Ky. It was one of a lot purchased by him October, 1917, from a consignment sold the jobber by the Illinois Watch Company. The soldiers who found the watch wrote to the makers, the Illinois Watch Company, they wrote to a jobber and the jobber wrote to Mr. Seng. Whether Holbrook was killed or wounded or merely lost the watch in some dealings with the enemy is not known.

Identification of watch found on a WWI battlefield in France, *Hartford Republican* (Hartford, KY), February 28, 1919; image from *newspapers.com*

LLINOIS WATCH AS MILITARY DOGTAG

The newspaper clipping shown here recounts the tale of an Illinois watch lost on a battlefield, then later found and the owner identified through a very orderly chain of communications. Because of its serial numbers, the watch served in effect as an identification tag!

An American soldier serving in France during World War I lost his watch on a battlefield. Other American soldiers found it, contacted the Illinois Watch Company, which contacted the jobber, who sold it to the jeweler, whose records showed he had sold it to one Jesse Holbrook, of Glenwood, Kentucky.

Unfortunately, we are left hanging with questions unanswered: What happened to Holbrook? Did he survive the war, and were he and his watch ever reunited?

Note: The newspaper surely recognized that this was an appealing story, but it apparently didn't check the facts. Perhaps the information about the location where the watch was found was simply relayed wrong at some point in the chain of communication. It is quite unlikely, however, that the battlefield in question was at Verdun, because the Battle of Verdun was in 1916 and the United States didn't enter the war until April 1917; moreover, the Illinois watch wasn't even sold to the jeweler until October 1917, and Holbrook would have had to have purchased it sometime after that.

Generic Watches

Official Name = Generic Watches (derived from the time period from the early 1920s to early 1930s)
Secondary Name(s) = None
Formerly Known As = None
Time Period = Generic
Case Variations/Rarity = Various
Case Durability = Various
Material = Various
Bezel = Plain, Engraved
Sides = Plain, Engraved
Lugs = Plain, Engraved
Lug Size = 14mm, 16mm, 18mm
Springbar = Male
Casemakers = Keystone, Star, Fahys, Wadsworth, IWCCo, Others
Case Closure = 3-Part Snap-On Bezel and Back
Case Number = None
Case Shape = Various
Case Back = Flat, Curved
Dimensions = Various
Movement Sizes = 3/0, 6/0
Movement Grades/Jewels = 24/17, 307/17, 605/15, 607/17
Seconds at = 6, 9, None
Dial Numbers = 92, 93, 93A, 94, 95, 96, 96A, 97, 98, 99, 107, 108, 109, 110, 4107, 4108, 4109, 4110, 4214, 8092, 8093, 8095, 8096, 8098, 8097, 8107, 8108, 8109, 8110, 8142, 8155, 8268, 8275, 8286, 8287, 8290, 8701, 8703, 8711, 8278, 8277, 8289, 8291, 9292.
Dials = Various
Dial Openings = Various
Dial Variations/Rarity = Various
Numerals = Various
Hands = Steel, Luminous
Cased in Factory = No
Unique Case Design = No
Unique Dial Design = No
Introduction Date = 1923 to 1932
Retail Price New = $11.70 to $26.50
Collectibility = ◷◷
Advertisements = Yes
Marketing Theme = "A revelation in 3/0 watches"

Generic, white gold-filled, private-label dial

Generic Keystone Victory Pony Model

During the Generic Period (from the early 1920s to the early 1930s), many watches with Illinois movements and dials were cased in a wide array of cases made by various watch case manufacturers such as the Star, Fahys, IWCCo, Keystone and Wadsworth companies, among others, that at that time could also house Elgin or Waltham movements and dials. A number of the early Generic watch models were Factory-Cased by the Illinois Watch Company, including certain Canby, Devon, Rectangular, Square, Square Cut Corner, and Whippet models.

Examples of Generic Period Watches in this Chapter		
Ace	Locke	Special
Atlantic	Rectangular*	Square*
Bryce	Riley	Square Cut Corner*
Canby*	Santa Fe Cushion	Tank
Cushion*	Santa Fe Tank	Wayne
Cushion Form*	Southampton*	Whippet
Devon*		

*Some of these models were cased in the Illinois Watch Factory. See their individual listings in this chapter for more information.

VICTORY PONY SERIES

In 1928 Keystone advertised a selection of rolled gold plate Victory cases for use with Elgin, Illinois and Waltham 3/0 size movements. They first called these models the "Victory Pony Series" and then changed "Pony" to "Polo".

Keystone, September 1928 Generic models

Generic Keystone Victory Pony model

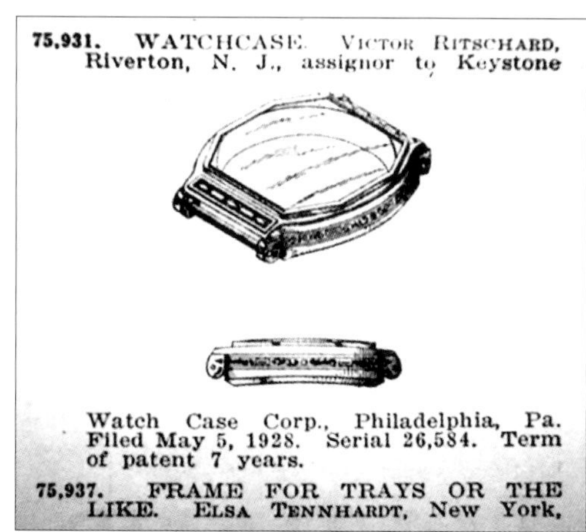

75,931. WATCHCASE. VICTOR RITSCHARD, Riverton, N. J., assignor to Keystone Watch Case Corp., Philadelphia, Pa. Filed May 5, 1928. Serial 26,584. Term of patent 7 years.

75,937. FRAME FOR TRAYS OR THE LIKE. ELSA TENNHARDT, New York,

Patent dated May 5, 1925 for a Keystone Generic Victory Pony model watch case

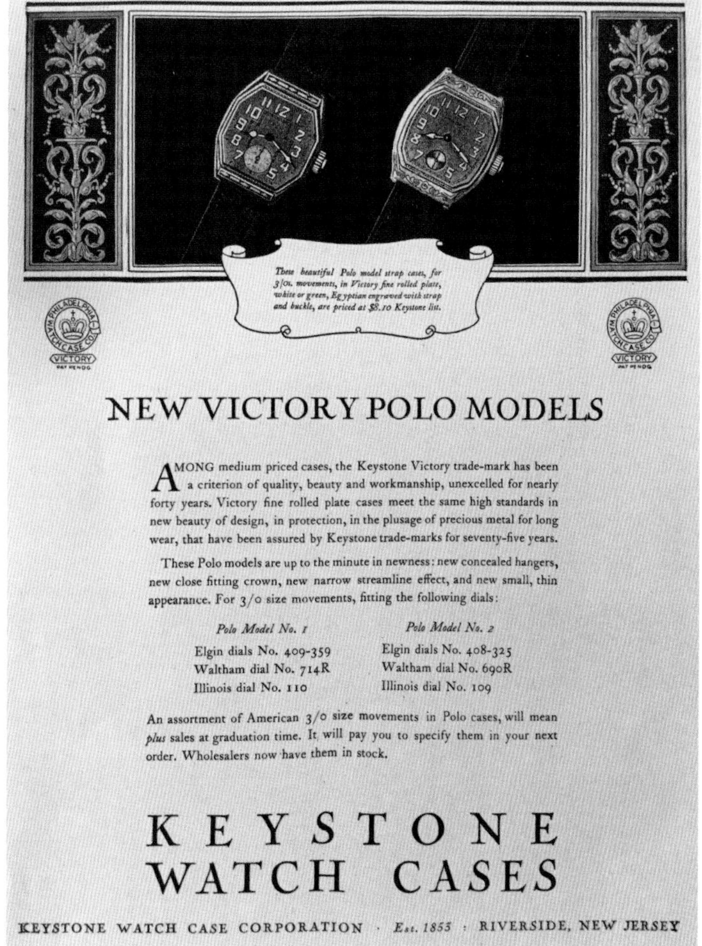

Keystone, May 1928

ROYALTY SERIES

Waltham used the Pony Series for its own product releases but called them its "Royalty Series," and each dial was signed Waltham "Royalty Series," as shown below. These used the same Keystone Victory rolled gold plate cases as shown here.

***Keystone*, September 1929. Note that some of these are from the Keystone Victory "Pony Series."**

GIFT SERIES

Illinois Square Cut Corner Gift Series, white gold-filled

Gift Series advertisement

Illinois Square Cut Corner Gift Series, white gold-filled

Official Name = Gift Series (derived from 1928–1929 Richter & Phillips Co. advertisements)

Secondary Name(s) = None

Formerly Known As = None

Time Period = Generic

Case Variations/Rarity = ◷◷◷◷◷◷ WGF/E Tonneau
◷◷◷◷◷◷ WGF/E Square Cut Corner Large

Case Durability = ◷◷◷

Material = 14K WGF

Bezel = Plain

Sides = Plain

Lugs = Plain

Lug Size = 16mm

Springbar = Male

Casemaker = Star

Case Closure = 3-part Snap-On bezel and back

Case Number = None

Case Shape = Tonneau, Square Cut Corner Large

Case Back = Flat

Dimensions = 28 x 35mm (6/0)

Movement Sizes = 3/0, 6/0

Movement Grades/Jewels = 307/17, 903/15, 905/17

Seconds at = 9

Dial Numbers = Luminous

Dial = Silver Finish

Dial Opening = Tonneau

Dial Variations/Rarity = ◷◷◷◷◷◷ Silver Finish

Numerals = Luminous

Hands = Luminous

Cased in Factory = Yes

Unique Case Design = No

Unique Dial Design = No

Introduction Date = 1928

Retail Price New = Unknown

Collectibility = ◷◷◷◷

Advertisements = Yes

Marketing Theme = "Latest Designs in Wrist Watches"

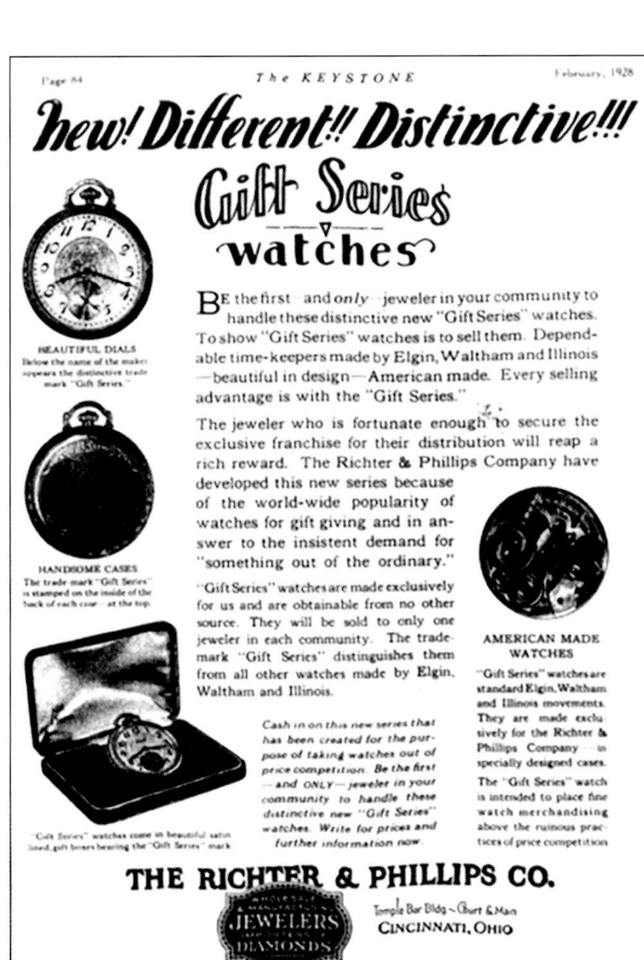

Page 84 The KEYSTONE February, 1928

New! Different!! Distinctive!!!

Gift Series watches

BE the first—and *only*—jeweler in your community to handle these distinctive new "Gift Series" watches. To show "Gift Series" watches is to sell them. Dependable time-keepers made by Elgin, Waltham and Illinois—beautiful in design—American made. Every selling advantage is with the "Gift Series."

The jeweler who is fortunate enough to secure the exclusive franchise for their distribution will reap a rich reward. The Richter & Phillips Company have developed this new series because of the world-wide popularity of watches for gift giving and in answer to the insistent demand for "something out of the ordinary."

"Gift Series" watches are made exclusively for us and are obtainable from no other source. They will be sold to only one jeweler in each community. The trade-mark "Gift Series" distinguishes them from all other watches made by Elgin, Waltham and Illinois.

Cash in on this new series that has been created for the purpose of taking watches out of price competition. Be the first—and ONLY—jeweler in your community to handle these distinctive new "Gift Series" watches. Write for prices and further information now.

BEAUTIFUL DIALS
Below the name of the maker appears the distinctive trade mark "Gift Series."

HANDSOME CASES
The trade mark "Gift Series" is stamped on the inside of the back of each case—at the top.

"Gift Series" watches come in beautiful satin lined, gift boxes bearing the "Gift Series" mark.

AMERICAN MADE WATCHES
"Gift Series" watches are standard Elgin, Waltham and Illinois movements. They are made exclusively for the Richter & Phillips Company—in specially designed cases.

The "Gift Series" watch is intended to place fine watch merchandising above the ruinous practices of price competition.

THE RICHTER & PHILLIPS CO.
WHOLESALE & MANUFACTURING JEWELERS IMPORTERS OF DIAMONDS
Temple Bar Bldg.—Court & Main
CINCINNATI, OHIO

Keystone, February 1928

Illinois Square Cut Corner Large Gift Series, case back inside

March, 1928 THE KEYSTONE Page 87

Gift Series watches

Offer You The Opportunity To Make Your Full Profit

THE "Gift Series" was created to discourage ruinous price cutting and give the dealer his full profit. To that end, the "Gift Series" will be sold to only one jeweler in each community. The one who is selected to distribute this line in his territory will enjoy a ***marked advantage.*** He will absolutely ***control the sale,*** thereby eliminating unfair practices in price cutting.

While they are the product of Elgin, Waltham and Illinois, these watches are made ***exclusively*** for The Richter & Phillips Company and are distinct from all others produced by these three popular American makers. Each watch bears the "Gift Series" mark on dial, movement and case and comes in a handsome gift box, also bearing the "Gift Series" mark.

Latest Designs in Wrist Watches Included

The "Gift Series" line includes not only a wide assortment of new and unique case designs in pocket watches, but also exceptionally attractive wrist watches in sizes 6/0 to 3/0. In both pocket watches and wrist watches, there is a sufficiently wide range to meet every practical need. From every angle, the "Gift Series" is the ideal medium to put high-grade watch selling on a profitable basis. The dealer who secures the exclusive "Gift Series" franchise will have absolute protection. No other dealer can have the same line.

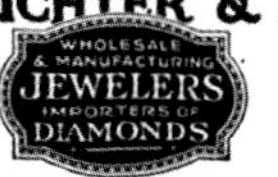

Dealers everywhere are showing great interest in this new line. Hundreds have lost no time in securing the exclusive sale franchise. By prompt action, you, too, can put your watch sales on a profitable basis—unless, some more aggressive competitor has already been granted the "Gift Series" privilege.

Write today for complete information

THE RICHTER & PHILLIPS CO.
WHOLESALE & MANUFACTURING JEWELERS IMPORTERS OF DIAMONDS
Temple Bar Bldg.—Court & Main
CINCINNATI, OHIO

Keystone, March 1928

The Richter & Phillips Co. of Cincinnati, Ohio, a jobber for Elgin, Waltham, Hamilton and Illinois, introduced the concept of the "Gift Series" in 1928. The plan (which it advertised extensively in 1928) called for providing exclusive sales territories for jewelers in certain cities and surrounding areas for watches that were tripled-signed "Illinois" and "Gift Series" on their dials, movements and cases. Richter & Phillips offered this "exclusive" line with movements and dials from Elgin, Illinois or Waltham.

Although these models were advertised extensively in 1928–1929 by Richter & Phillips, they are quite rare today, and only about three wristwatches with Illinois dials and movements have been seen. So it is likely this concept did not catch on.

According to Richter & Phillips, the "'Gift Series' is created to discourage ruinous price cutting and give the dealer his full profit. To that end, the 'Gift Series' will be sold to only one jeweler in each community. The one who is selected to distribute this line in his territory will enjoy a *marked advantage*. He will absolutely *control the sale*, thereby eliminating unfair practices in price cutting.

"While they are the product of Elgin, Waltham and Illinois, these watches are made exclusively for The Richter & Phillips Company and are distinct from all others produced by these three popular American makers. Each watch bears the 'Gift Series' mark on dial, movement and case." Rather than coming in the particular watch manufacturer's own box, these watches came from Richter & Phillips in special presentation boxes that had the words "Gift Series" on the inside top lining of the box.

In any event, Richter & Phillips had bigger issues to contend with, because in 1928 they were terminated as a distributor by Hamilton. Richter & Phillips claimed that Hamilton dropped them because they were a "price cutter" and asserted Hamilton's action violated the antitrust laws. Richter & Phillips also accused Hamilton of attempting to obtain a monopoly by acquiring the Illinois Watch Company. Note that Hamilton was not a participant in the Gift Series.

The case, heard in United States District Court, was thrown out of court on a directed verdict by the judge after Richter & Phillips presented its case; thus Hamilton never had to defend its termination of Richter & Phillips.

Court Upholds Hamilton Sales Policy

Suit Resulting from Dropping of Richter & Phillips Company from Hamilton Watch Company's List of Distributors Brings Verdict in Favor of Latter

Keystone, May 1929

May 9, 1929 THE JEWELERS' CIRCULAR

Hamilton Watch Co. Wins Test Case

Action Brought by Richter & Phillips Co. Alleging Violation of Anti-Trust Law Comes to Sudden End When Court Orders Decision for Defendant

Jewelers' Circular, May 9, 1929

By December 1929, Richter & Phillips had filed for receivership and protection from its creditors, and by March 1930 it had reorganized.

Cincinnati

(From The Keystone Special Correspondent)

Receiver Appointed for Richter & Phillips Company

Richter & Phillips Co. in Course of Reorganization

A new company, bearing the same name, is preparing to take over the liabilities of the Richter & Phillips Co., wholesale jewelers in the Temple Bar Building, Cincinnati, Ohio, and liquidate them on the basis of 65 cents on the dollar.

Formation of the new company to replace the old one which has been in receivership since last Fall, will mean a lifting of the receivership and a complete reorganization of the concern. New capital has been interested, it is announced.

Authority for the formation of the new company was given by Judge Stanley Struble in Common Pleas Court, at the request of C. Edward Richter, receiver of the company and a member of the old firm. He is slated for the presidency of the new company.

The liquidation plan has the authority of 95 per cent of the general creditors, it is said. The new company will have an initial cash capital of $100,000.

Keystone, December 1929

Perhaps because of the success of the litigation against Richter & Phillips, Hamilton felt confident of the legality of its New Hamilton Plan of Zone Distribution introduced in May 1934. Hamilton's plan resulted in the successful termination of sixty-six Hamilton distributors.

Greyhound / Motor Coach

Official Name = Greyhound and Motor Coach (derived from the List of Factory Cased Illinois Watches coupled with empirical evidence)
Secondary Name(s) = None
Formerly Known As = Skyway (until the Greyhound and Motor Coach models were properly identified, collectors considered this watch to be a Skyway)
Time Period = Deco
Case Variations/Rarity = ◷◷◷ WGF/M
Case Durability = ◷◷◷
Material = 14K WGF
Bezel = Molded
Sides = Plain
Lugs = Plain
Lug Size = 16mm
Springbar = Male
Casemakers = Wadsworth
Case Closure = 3-Part Screw-On Bezel and Back
Case Number = 211

Greyhound, white gold-filled

Case Shape = Round
Case Back = Flat
Dimensions = 38 x 32mm
Movement Size = 3/0
Movement Grades/Jewels = 24/17, 307/17
Seconds at = 6
Dial Number = None
Dial = Enamel
Dial Opening = Round
Dial Variations /Rarity = 🕒🕒🕒🕒🕒 Enamel signed Greyhound
Numerals = Luminous
Hands = Luminous
Cased in Factory = Yes
Unique Case Design = Yes
Unique Dial Design = Yes
Introduction Date = 1930
Retail Price New = $45.00
Collectibility = 🕒🕒🕒🕒
Advertisements = None
Marketing Theme = Unknown

The Greyhound, Motor Coach, Skyway and the Off-Duty share the same case model (Model No. 211), but each sports a very different dial. Illinois never listed the Greyhound in its Sales Catalog nor did it appear in any Illinois advertisement; however, its name is listed under the 3/0 size watches on the List of Factory Cased Illinois Watches. No jobber's catalog ever included it.

As a result, for years collectors did not know the real name of this mystery watch. To date, only three Greyhound models and three Motor Coach models are known to exist, perhaps indicating that these were special-order items. The Skyway is rarer than an Off-Duty, and the Greyhound and Motor Coach Models are significantly scarcer than the Skyway.

The Greyhound and Motor Coach enamel dials really pop when contained in the star bezel case, case Model No. 211. This case has a screw-on bezel and back. Unfortunately, it is subject to wear on the tops of the lugs.

FANTASTIC FIND

So to get the really good stuff, you really have to look outside of the box. I search so many places for watches, it is hard to describe. I am constantly on the lookout and try to go to places the average collector wouldn't even think of... With this said, today was one of those random days and it turned out to be the stuff of watch dreams. I have heard of the mysterious Illinois Greyhound from reading your book and I see a strange photo on a strange site. There in front of my eyes is a Skyway case with an enamel dial and the words Illinois Greyhound. I think to myself, this can't be real, so I look at the photos and my mind starts to get fuzzy with excitement. The seller says this is from an estate and it looks to be in fantastic condition with a totally intact dial. I am so nervous with anticipation that I can't buy this watch fast enough. . . The price was incredible and I had to pinch myself as I was paying. There have to be only a few of these in the world and I am so excited to have actually found one to show to the world someday. *—Greg Hart*

Motor Coach, white gold-filled

Late-Breaking News: The Motor Coach Identified!

Another Illinois mystery has now been solved: the identity of a heretofore puzzling wristwatch model named the Motor Coach! Unfortunately, this exciting news came in too late to provide the model a separate listing in this book, since that would have caused serious editorial problems and delayed publication. However, we felt that we should include this important information, and we do so here because it not only sheds light on the Greyhound as well, but also provides a case study in horological research. What follows here is Bettie Mason's account of how the identification of the Motor Coach came about:

Watch Detective Tracks Clues

Among the surviving documents from the Illinois Watch Company is an official "List of Names of Cased Illinois Watches by Size," dated December 1, 1932. One of Fred's goals in writing his new book set was the identification of models on this list that were as yet unknown. As the books show, there are now quite a few of these that have been determined, though some still remain.

Since I have a large collection of major jobbers' catalogs and others from that era, I'd been more than happy to look for Illinois models, and on occasion had hit pay dirt with identifications. Yet the Motor Coach kept eluding me. Though I looked through Illinois watches in catalog after catalog, I found no picture of the Motor Coach anywhere, and only one mention of it. But this one turned out to be an important clue! It was on the Consumer and Keystone Price List in the Illinois Watch Company's own pages of advertisements included in the A. C. Becken 1931 catalog.

On this list the group of men's wristwatches with Grade 307, 17-jewel movements comprised seven models: Mate, Jolly Roger, Speedway, Viking, Guardsman, Skyway and Motor Coach. I found it odd that all six of the others were pictured together on another Illinois page in the catalog, but not the Motor Coach. Another oddity about that page was that although the page had the heading "Sturdy 3-0 Size, 17 Jewel Strap Watches," the seventh watch in the display was the Chieftain, with a caption for it beginning "6/0 size—15 jewels"! And except for the caption text itself, there was nothing pertaining to that model on the page. It was as if the Illinois advertising department had made a last-minute and illogical substitution of models.

Southland Greyhound advertisement, *El Paso Evening Post* (El Paso, TX), November 7, 1930; image from *newspapers.com*

In addition, I noticed that on the Consumer and Keystone list three of the 3/0 size models (Guardsman, Skyway and Motor Coach) had higher prices than the other four. This was another clue: it said to me that there was something special about those three models. For the Guardsman and Skyway, we know what the special attributes were: rotor dial for the former (as noted on the catalog list) and both an emblematic dial and star-embossed case for the latter.

Advertisement for Pickwick-Greyhound Lines, *San Bernadino County Sun* (San Bernadino, CA), May 28, 1930; image from *newspapers.com*

So what was/were the special attribute(s) of the Motor Coach? It wouldn't be a rotor dial, because none was listed for it. Nor was it likely to have some sort of appropriate transportation-theme emblematic dial, since as far as I know, none has ever turned up. (At that point, I was thinking that the Motor Coach might be like the Skyway in that respect.)

When I asked my husband, a fellow Illinois collector, what he thought a Motor Coach would look like, he immediately said "round, like a tire." At that point it had already started looking as if at least one reason for the higher price of the Motor Coach was likely the starry case. But what type of dial?

Later, things started coming into focus about yet another issue that had come up: the possible relationship of the Motor Coach and the Greyhound. (After all, "motor coach" was an early name for bus.) Perhaps the Motor Coach might have had a plain porcelain dial, with just the name Illinois on it, and the Greyhound dial was made by simply adding that name to the basic Illinois-signed dial?

For a model that Illinois provided to major jobbers (like Becken) with large and geographically diverse distribution lists, a generic name like Motor Coach would have been the way to go for the initial model rather than the very brand-specific Greyhound (and that's indeed the pattern followed with the generic names Skyway and Off-Duty). Moreover, the Greyhound is not listed anywhere in any catalog that has yet been found.

It's obvious that Illinois under Hamilton was phasing out their wristwatches with 3/0 movements. Although there had been the group of seven on the Illinois Consumer and Keystone Price List in 1931 jobbers' catalogs, no group of 3/0 Illinois models was present in the corresponding list in the 1932 catalogs. In the 1932 list, the 307 movement was included only under "Uncased Watches"; and in complete watches it appeared only in the newly introduced "Off-Duty Strap Watch," listed under the heading "Railroad Watches" rather than under "Men's Wrist Watches."

Then I realized what was going on: marketing strategies at work! As we've found in so many other instances, a "new" Illinois model in the Hamilton years was very often an existing model that had been tweaked somehow. So this might be why an image of the Motor Coach would not have appeared in the 1931 catalogs along with the other six 3/0 models, one of which was the Skyway, even though the Motor Coach was on the Consumer and Keystone Price List. The answer is likely that Illinois didn't want the unmistakable image of that striking case on the same page twice lest it detract from the "newness" of the Skyway.

It was in 1932 that the starry case made its last appearance, again solo and with yet another new dial, but this time marketed simply to railroaders.

Then, how does the Motor Coach fit into the scheme of things? Thus far we haven't found the Illinois catalog or flyer that introduced it, and I feel that there must have been one, since that fits the pattern of models appearing in the Consumer and Keystone lists. In a catalog of a given year, the official Illinois price list showed both the newly introduced wristwatch models and ones introduced earlier that were still available.

In the years we're concerned with, the catalogs that the Illinois Watch Company sent to jobbers and jewelers for use in their own catalogs had split-year designations, indicating fall of one year through spring of the next. (Most jobbers used just the latter year in dating their catalogs, though a few didn't.) The Motor Coach is not present in the Illinois 1929–1930 catalog and thus not in the 1930 jobbers' catalogs either, as I have found.

In terms of publication deadlines, the Motor Coach was apparently produced too late to include it in the Illinois 1929–1930 catalog, and it wasn't pictured in the one for 1930–1931 (for the reasons I suggest above). However, Illinois sometimes issued an additional seasonal catalog, so perhaps the Motor Coach was in one of these. (Maybe a Spring 1930 issue, which has yet to be found?)

I think it's clear that the Motor Coach would have been the first of the models in the molded-star case. Since the trend in fashion was toward smaller watches, the Illinois marketing plan may have been to use up their 3/0 movements in three new models, each in that striking case but each with a different dial and introduced a year apart (1930, 1931 and 1932), and each with a transportation theme. Another scenario is also plausible: the starry case may have been designed specifically for the Motor Coach, but perhaps the model proved less popular than anticipated, and thus the Skyway and Off-Duty dials were designed after the fact to go with the excess cases.

As for the relationship of the Motor Coach and the Greyhound, it's interesting that the bus company officially became the Greyhound Corporation in 1930, as I learned from the company's website celebrating the 100th anniversary of its beginnings in Hibbing, Minnesota, in 1916: "After years of names like Hibbing Transportation, Mesaba Transportation, Northland Transportation and Motor Transit, they needed one that really captured people's imaginations, one that would stick. They decided to borrow from 'Ride the Greyhounds,' a marketing phrase used eight years earlier for Eckstrom's Safety Motor Coach Company (which became part of Motor Transit in 1926). Motor Transit Corporation holding company formally changed its name to the Greyhound Corporation and moved its head office to Chicago, Illinois." Perhaps the special Greyhound dial was produced to align with this event? The 1930 date would fit this hypothesis.

A continuing mystery is the genesis of the Greyhound watches. Who ordered them, and how many were made? Might they have been a special order from a jeweler in or near Hibbing, Minnesota, or one in Chicago? Were the watches sold to the general public? Or might they have been ordered by the Greyhound Corporation as special watches to be presented to the company's executives?

No matter how the Greyhound originated, it is clear that it was Factory-Cased, since it as well as the Skyway and Off-Duty are on the official Illinois list from December 1, 1932. However, the fact that there is no trace of the model in any Illinois catalogs suggests that the Greyhound had too small a run to have been widely available. So we have yet another Illinois mystery to pursue!

Will Motor Coach Replace Street Car? Railway Head Not Sure But More Lines Motorized Each Year

Daily Times (Davenport, IA), February 14, 1928; image from *newspapers.com*

Advertisement for Greyhound Lines, *Saturday Evening Post*, 1931; image from *newspapers.com*

GREYSTONE

See listing for **Blackstone**

Guardian, white gold-filled

Guardian

Official Name = Guardian (derived from the List of Factory Cased Illinois Watches and empirical evidence)

Secondary Name(s) = None

Formerly Known As = "No Name"/"No. 178" (derived from Illinois watch expert L. Michael Fultz's usage before more official evidence surfaced concerning this model)

Time Period = Deco

Case Variations/Rarity = ◷◷◷◷ WGF/E

Case Durability = ◷◷◷

Material = 14K GF

Bezel = Engraved

Sides = Plain, Engraved

Lugs = Engraved

Lug Size = 16mm

Springbar = Male

Casemaker = Keystone

Case Closure = 3-Part Snap-On Bezel and Back

Case Number = 178

Case Shape = Round

Case Back = Flat

Dimensions = 36 x 31mm

Movement Size = 3/0

Movement Grades/Jewels = 24/17, 307/17

Seconds at = Rotor at 6

Dial Number = None

Dial = Silver Finish

Dial Opening = Tonneau

Dial Variations/Rarity = ◷◷◷◷◷ Silver Finish, Luminous Numerals/signed "Guardian"

Numerals = Luminous

Hands = Luminous

Cased in Factory = Yes

Unique Case Design = Yes

Unique Dial Design = Yes

Introduction Date = 1930

Retail Price New = Unknown

Collectibility = ◷◷◷◷

Advertisements = No

Marketing Theme = Unknown

There is no known advertisement or catalog featuring the Guardian. This model has been designated the Guardian because the dial has been found about ten different times in the Model No. 178 case with a rotor subsidiary seconds dial signed "Illinois Guardian." The Guardian's name is on the List of Factory Cased Illinois Watches under the 3/0 size models. The Guardsman model is also listed under the 3/0 size watches on the List of Factory Cased Watches. Therefore, it is clear that the Guardian is a separate and distinct model from the Guardsman.

The Speedway 178, Speedway and Guardian all shared the Model No. 178 case. This case, without the Guardian dial, was advertised as a Speedway. The case pattern featured here is called the Speedway 178 to distinguish it from the standard Speedway, which has a different engraving design. Of the three models, only the Guardian had the dial with rotor seconds. The Guardian, the Speedway and the Speedway 178 only came in one case color: white gold-filled. This case is subject to some corner bezel wear. A case in excellent condition, with the black oxidation still present to set off the engraving, makes for an extremely attractive watch. (If the oxidized areas have faded with time, a little black enamel paint can be applied carefully to them to restore the contrast.)

Guardsman

Official Name = Guardsman (derived from Illinois advertisements and Illinois Sales and Material Catalogs)
Secondary Name(s) = None
Formerly Known As = None
Time Period = Deco
Case Variations/Rarity = 🕒🕒 WGF/E
🕒🕒🕒🕒 WGF/P, GGF/P, GGF/E
🕒🕒🕒🕒🕒 TT/E
🕒🕒🕒🕒🕒🕒🕒 PGF/E
Case Durability = 🕒 PGF
🕒🕒🕒 WGF, GGF
Material = 14K GF
Bezel = Plain, Engraved
Sides = Plain
Lugs = Plain, Engraved
Lug Size = 16mm
Springbar = Male
Casemaker = Keystone
Case Closure = 3-part Snap-On Bezel and Back
Case Number = 171, 172, No Number
Case Shape = Round
Case Back = Flat
Dimensions = 36 x 31mm
Movement Size = 3/0

Guardsman, white gold-filled

Guardsman, yellow gold-filled

Guardsman, green gold-filled

Movement Grades/Jewels = 24/17, 307/17
Seconds at = Rotor at 6
Dial Numbers = 8213, 8215
Dial = Silver Finish
Dial Opening = Tonneau
Dial Variations/Rarity = ◷◷◷ Silver Finish, Luminous Numerals
◷◷◷◷◷ Silver Finish, Black Numerals
Numerals = Painted, Luminous
Hands = Luminous
Cased in Factory = Yes
Unique Case Design = Yes
Unique Dial Design = Yes
Introduction Date = 1930
Retail Price New = $45.00
Collectibility = ◷◷◷◷
Advertisements = Yes
Marketing Theme = "An unusual idea in men's wrist watches"

The Guardsman was included in an Illinois advertisement in the December 6, 1930 issue of the *Saturday Evening Post*. With the heading "Good Tiding of Greater Values," it focused on the holiday trade, pointing out that "Good jewelers are showing the complete line of Illinois watches. Priced mostly from $37.50 to $60.00—setting a new standard."

The same cases used for the Illinois Major are also used for the Guardsman model. The rotor subsidiary seconds is the key feature for the Guardsman. The Guardsman, as well as the Major, came in cases with three different case Model Numbers: 171, 172 or No Number. It is generally thought that the unnumbered cases were either the earliest Watch Factory runs for a case and/or before Illinois signed an exclusive arrangement with the casemaker for the case design. This model is most common in white gold-filled engraved cases, rarer in white gold-filled plain, and more difficult to find in green gold-filled plain or engraved or in two-tone cases. To date, only one ultra-rare pink gold-filled Guardsman case has been found. This was probably a custom ordered watch. It is the only confirmed pink gold-filled Illinois wristwatch (although some collectors are of the belief that certain Urbanas are also pink in color).

Guardsman, pink gold-filled, only one known to exist

Guardsman, two-tone, gold-filled

Illinois offered at least five different models with rotor subsidiary seconds: the two Military-cased Guardsmans, the Sterling model with a rectangular-shaped dial, the Akron and the Seneca/Blackhawk. The original rotor subsidiary seconds dials have a black line outline around the cutout window for the subsidiary seconds. Redone dials do not usually have this feature. Illinois referred to its digital disc feature on these models as rotor subsidiary seconds, whereas Hamilton referred to this feature as a "secometer" dial. The reason for this distinction is that Hamilton licensed the use of the "secometer" tradename; Illinois did not. See the **Caprice** listing for an explanation of the hole on most of the Illinois rotor seconds dials hidden in the printing of numeral 6.

Guardsman original price card

FANTASTIC FIND

Bill Thomas of Minnesota reports: "About 20 years ago I was going antiquing in southern Minnesota (usually in larger towns along U.S. highways) and I ventured into a small antiques store in Faribault, Minnesota. As I had been on the prowl for watches for quite a while up to then, I always looked at the glass showcases first. At the rear of the store in a small locked case was an Illinois 'Guardsman' in a two-tone green and white gold filled case, in very nice condition except that the stem and crown were missing. It had a price tag marked '$25.00 AS IS.' Well, I didn't dicker, just told the person in charge to bring the watch up front and I'd continue browsing. Later that evening I had a new stem and crown fitted to the watch and it took right off and kept good time. I sold it a week later to a local vintage watch dealer for $250.00."

WHY I COLLECT ILLINOIS

"I became interested in Illinois wristwatches when I first spied one at my first watch show back in 1995. This watch was unlike any I had seen before. Its art deco reliefs and odd shapes stood in stark contrast to the 'Submariner Look' popular in the 1990s. I later learned that this watch was the Guardsman and through my research I found that it was not even the most daring Illinois design. These were the early days of the Internet, so information on Illinois wristwatches was not easy to come by. Fortunately, I came across a small ad in the back of a watch magazine placed by Fred Friedberg. Fred's knowledge of Illinois wristwatches and guidance were instrumental in the creation of my small collection. I enjoyed receiving his occasional newsletters with black & white, and later color photos of watches he had for sale. I'd close my office door and spend the next hour or so determining which of these Illinois lovelies I couldn't live without. The watches came in all shapes and sizes, with unusual enameling, one-of-a-kind dials, and a variety of case color combinations. And, of course, there were always opportunities to find little gems at the watch shows. I even beat Fred out for a mint condition Piccadilly at the New Orleans NAWCC national meeting. I think he's forgiven me for that."

—Jeff Friedman

Guardsman Military, sterling silver

Guardsman Military, sterling silver

Guardsman Military

Official Name = Unknown
Secondary Name(s) = Guardsman Military (derived from combining the Military Transitional Period case with the Guardsman-type rotor subsidiary seconds dial)
Formerly Known As = None
Time Period = Transitional
Case Variations/Rarity = ◷◷◷◷◷◷ SS/Round, SS/Cushion, YGF
Case Durability = ◷◷◷◷
Material = SS
Bezel = Plain
Sides = Plain
Lugs = Plain
Lug Size = 16mm
Springbar = Fixed, Swivel (Straight)
Casemakers = Fahys, Others
Case Closure = 3-Part Snap-On Bezel and Back
Case Number = None
Case Shape = Round, Cushion
Case Back = Flat
Dimensions = Various
Movement Size = 0
Movement Grade/Jewels = 204/17
Seconds at = Rotor at 6
Dial Numbers = None
Dial = Silver Finish
Dial Opening = Round
Dial Variations/Rarity = ◷◷◷◷◷◷ Silver Finish, Painted Numerals
Numerals = Painted
Hands = Steel
Cased in Factory = No
Unique Case Design = No
Unique Dial Design = Yes
Introduction Date = Unknown
Retail Price New = Unknown
Collectibility = ◷◷◷◷
Advertisements = None
Marketing Theme = Unknown

Collectors call this model a "Guardsman Military" because it consists of a military Transitional Period watch case with a rotor subsidiary seconds bit. Only three Military Guardsman watches have been located to date. Two of them are also unusual in that they have 0 size movements, whereas all the rotor second models—the Guardsman, Guardian, Sterling, Akron and Seneca/Blackhawk—have 3/0 size movements with rotor subsidiary seconds. A second version of the Military shown here has a yellow gold-filled case and most likely has a redone dial (which looks great, except for the spelling of "Illinois").

Guardsman Military, yellow gold-filled. Note how "Illinois" is spelled.

Haddon Hall

See listing for **Blackstone**

Hawthorne

See listing for **Arlington**

Hudson / Ardsley

Official Names = Ardsley and Hudson (derived from Illinois advertisements and Illinois Sales and Material Catalogs)
Secondary Name(s) = None
Formerly Known As = None
Time Period = Moderne
Case Variations/Rarity = 🕑 YGF/P
🕑🕑 WGF/P
Case Durability = 🕑🕑🕑
Material = 14K WGF, YGF
Bezel = Plain
Sides = Engraved
Lugs = Plain
Lug Size = 16mm
Springbar = Male
Casemaker = Wadsworth
Case Closure = 2-Part Snap-On Bezel and Back

Hudson, white gold-filled

Hudson, yellow gold-filled

Case Number = 218
Case Shape = Rectangular
Case Back = Curved
Dimensions = 37 x 23mm
Movement Size = 12/0
Movement Grade/Jewels = 207/17
Seconds at = 6
Dial Number = 8196
Dial = Silver Finish, Sparkle Finish
Dial Opening = Rectangular
Dial Variations/Rarity = ◷◷◷ Silver Finish, Applied Gold Numerals; Sparkle Finish, Painted Numerals
◷◷◷◷ Silver Finish, Black Numerals
◷◷◷◷◷ Sparkle Finish, Applied Gold Numerals
Numerals = Painted (Ardsley), Applied 18K Gold Numerals (Hudson)
Hands = Steel
Cased in Factory = Yes
Unique Case Design = No
Unique Dial Design = Yes
Introduction Date = 1930 (Ardsley), 1931 (Hudson)
Retail Price New = $60.00
Collectibility = ◷◷◷◷
Advertisements = Yes
Marketing Themes = "Individuality and character"
"Curved to fit the wrist perfectly"

These two models are rather plain watches that are quite similar to several of their Hamilton cousins. The Ardsley, the earlier of the two, came with a silver finish or sparkle finish dial with black painted numerals. The later model, which had a dial with applied gold numerals, was called a Hudson; it is all the more Hamilton-like in appearance because of its applied gold numerals. The Ardsley's dial makes that model more distinctive.

The Ardsley appeared in the 1930–31 Illinois Sales Catalog, which noted: "Individuality and character mark the appearance of this new curved strap watch." This model was also advertised in the August 1930 issue of the *American Magazine.* The Hudson, shown the next year in the 1931–32 Illinois Sales Catalog, was said to be "Curved to fit any wrist perfectly."

The Ardsley and the Hudson, as well as the Marquis Strap and several other Illinois models were advertised as being curved to fit the wrist. They may have inspired the Model No. 250/Schmukler, or vice versa, as the Hudson/Ardsley and Kenilworth/Gallahad seemed to have merged to form the No. 250/Schmukler model. However, the No. 250/Schmukler and Kenilworth/Gallahad models possess a far more attractive design than the fairly plain Hudson/Ardsley.

The case of the Ardsley/Hudson was subject to corner bezel wear.

Ardsley, white gold-filled

Because of the bland design, this model is often available at very reasonable prices.

There exists at least one Ardsley without subsidiary seconds. This may have been a custom order. The dial from this variation is shown here and features a Watch Factory original Ardsley dial that was apparently refinished a long time ago.

Ardsley original dial without subsidiary seconds

Illinois Whitman / llinois LangFord / Illinois Pierre

Official Name = Illinois Whitman (derived from internal Hamilton records)
Secondary Name(s) = None
Formerly Known As = None
Time Period = Moderne
Case Variations/Rarity = 🕒🕒🕒🕒🕒 YGF/P
Case Durability = 🕒🕒🕒
Material = 10K GF
Bezel = Plain
Sides = Plain
Lugs = Plain
Lug Size = 16mm
Springbar = Male
Casemaker = Wadsworth
Case Closure = 2-Part Snap-On Bezel and Back
Case Number = None
Case Shape = Rectangular
Case Back = Flat
Dimensions = 38 x 24mm
Movement Size = 14/0

Illinois Whitman, yellow gold-filled

Movement Grades/Jewels = W980 (by Hamilton signed Illinois)
Seconds at = 6
Dial Number = None
Dial = Silver Finish
Dial Opening = Rectangular
Dial Variations/Rarity = 🕒🕒🕒🕒🕒 Silver Finish, Applied Gold Numerals
Numerals = Applied Gold Numerals
Hands = Steel
Cased in Factory = Yes, by Hamilton in Lancaster
Unique Case Design = No (same case as Hamilton Whitman)
Unique Dial Design = No
Introduction Date = 1942 and/or 1946
Retail Price New = Unknown
Collectibility = 🕒🕒🕒🕒
Advertisement = No
Marketing Theme = Unknown

The Illinois Whitman, Illinois Langford and Illinois Pierre are an entirely separate and distinct category of models from the mid-1950s reintroduction of the Illinois brand name as Hamilton's low-cost watch. (See Chapter 11.) Instead, Hamilton released these models to continue to preserve the Illinois trademark in 1942 or 1946.

According to Hamilton internal records, Hamilton produced a total of 1,041 of W980 movements. This explains why so few are seen today. I have seen only six of these over the last fifteen years. According to Halligan's handwritten notes in the 1940s, at least 976 of these were sold.

Hamilton made 980 grade movements signed Hamilton, Illinois, and E. Howard. These movements are rarely seen. One is pictured to the right. This model used a Hamilton 980 movement modified by signing the bridge to read "W980" and "Illinois Watch Company, Lancaster, Pennsylvania."

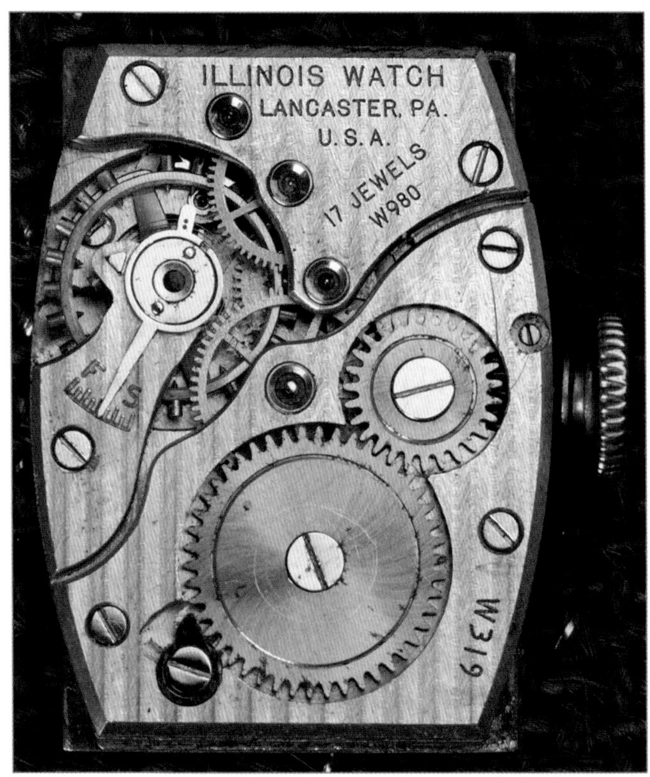

W980 movement signed Illinois

The standard production Hamilton Grade 980 movement was modified via a "conversion kit" to an "Illinois" or E. Howard signed movement by changing only the signed bridge on the back of the movement. Some Hamilton experts claim that Hamilton never released any 980 models signed "Illinois" to retailers and that it changed back all of the Illinois-signed plates to Hamilton ones before they were released for sale. However, these movements signed Illinois do exist, as shown on the preceding page.

Hamilton conversion kit to an Illinois W980 (*left*) and a Howard H980 (*right*)

A recently discovered handwritten internal Hamilton memorandum from Lowell Halligan to Fred Boulton, dated August 18, 1942, indicates that Hamilton was also planning to place forty-four of the W980-signed Illinois movements into Hamilton Langford cases and six into Hamilton Pierre cases. Fifty-one H980s signed Howard were to be placed in Pierre cases. Halligan noted that Jack Keenan and former Illinois salesmen John Hall and Burr Freer were to place these directly with retail jewelers at a wholesale cost of $29.50 and a suggested retail price of $71.50. These movements were so modified "to protect our [Hamilton's] legal rights to the trade names," according to Halligan. This handwritten memorandum is shown here.

8/18/42 Memo from Mr Halligan
to Mr F.J.B.

We have a total of 51-14K Howard
strap watches, to be sold to protect
our legal rights to the trade
names.

A quantity of 44 of the Illinois
strap watches are cased in Langford
cases (12 52) + 6 Ill. are cased
in Pierre cases (12.29)

The entire quantity of 51 Howard
watches are cased in Pierre cases

John Hall, Jack Keenan, & Burr Freer
will place these watches with retail
jewelers, whom we will bill direct
at a cost of $29.50 on our
regular terms.

In invoicing these watches to
retail jewelers, will you deliver an
extra copy to Mr. [illegible] Mr. Heilman.

Price to Consumer 65.00 + 10% tax 71.50

Halligan records, HRC: NAWCC

These models will now be known as the Illinois Langford and the Illinois Pierre. However, to date, neither of these models has been sighted, so it is possible that they were never issued.

There is further confusion because Halligan noted that on July 3, 1942, Hamilton released its Whitman model in a Wadsworth case that cost $3.20/case. He then continued on the next page that on July 20, 1946, saying this case "was used as Illinois." Thus, we do not know if the W980s were first used in 1942 or 1946 or both. Halligan, in a separate handwritten notation, noted that the "Illinois" was issued on July 20, 1946 in a Whitman case by Wadsworth costing $3.69/case. This notation also includes the tally of the Illinois Whitmans that were sold.

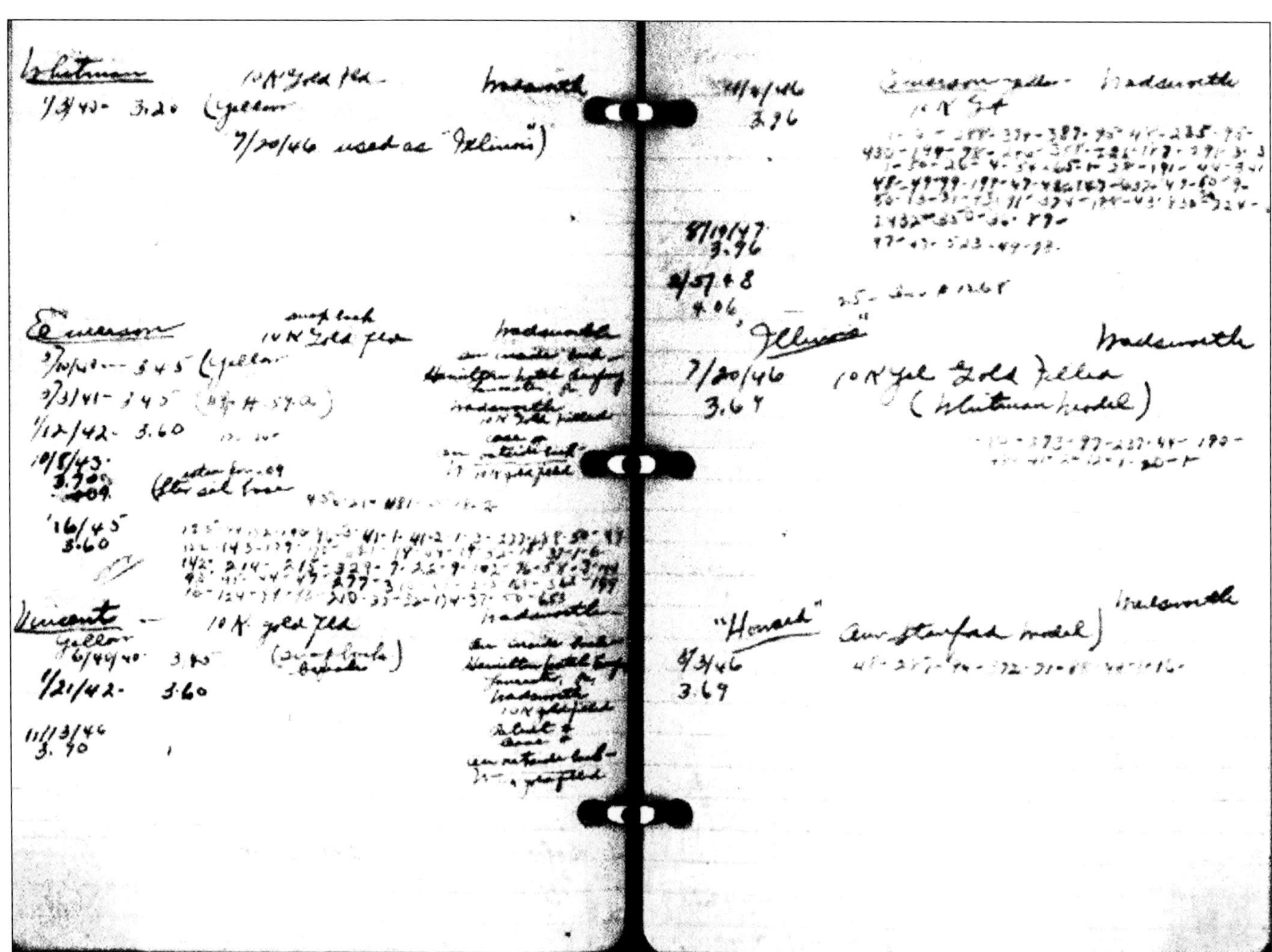

Whitman 10K Gold Fld. Wadsworth
7/3/42 3.20 (yellow
7/20/46 used as "Illinois")

Emerson 10K Gold Fld. Wadsworth

Vincent 10K gold Fld. Wadsworth
6/4/40 3.45
1/21/42 3.60
11/13/46 3.90

"Illinois" Wadsworth
7/20/46 3.69 10K yel Gold filled (Whitman model)

"Howard" Wadsworth
4/3/46 3.69

Halligan records: HRC: NAWCC

If we add the total sold noted above, it equals 976. If we add the fifty to be issued in Langford and Pierre cases, the total reaches 1,036, five movements away from the total of 1,041 produced from 1942 to 1947, as shown here.

14/0 - SIZE MOVEMENTS

GRADE	JEWELS	TYPE		SETTING		PRODUCED		QUANTITY	REMARKS
		O.F.	Htg.	Pend.	Lev.	From	To		
980	17		X	X		1934	1951	668,471	
980A	17		X	X		1935	1951	5,001	See 1
980B	17		X	X		1937	1951	8,799	See 3
W980	17		X	X		1942	1947	1,041	Ill. Watch, See 2
H980	17		X	X		1939	1954	637	Howard Watch, See 2
982	19		X	X		1935	1951	677,580	
982M	19		X	X		1940	1952	203,381	Gold Medallion
								1,564,910	Total

1. About 2000 produced as 980's in 1935, 980A started with # 13601.
2. Same as grade 980A except some minor changes in train and brand name.
3. No product for 1944-45-46; production re-started in 1947; completed 9-21-48.

HRC: NAWCC

It may never be known if Hamilton issued the W980 movement signed Illinois in Langford and Pierre cases. My guess is that they did not. It is also possible that Halligan's dates are wrong and the Illinois Whitman was released in 1942, or that none were issued in 1942 or 1946 or ever—and that all were issued in 1946. Although the stated goal was to preserve and extend the Illinois trade name, Hamilton could have done that by merely selling one Illinois Whitman in interstate commerce.

On the typewritten Hamilton historical list of "Names of Watches Used in the Hamilton Watch Line," the Illinois Whitman was noted as simply "Illinois"— evidently not even worthy of a model name. The same is reflected in Halligan's recorded history above.

See listing for **Armored Case**

Jolly Roger, white gold-filled

Jolly Roger, green gold-filled

JOLLY ROGER

Official Name = Jolly Roger (derived from Illinois advertisements and Illinois Sales and Material Catalogs)
Secondary Name(s) = None
Formerly Known As = None
Time Period = Deco
Case Variations/Rarity = 🕒🕒🕒 WGF/E
🕒🕒🕒🕒🕒 WGF/P
🕒🕒🕒🕒🕒🕒 GGF/P, GGF/E
Case Durability = 🕒🕒 GGF
🕒🕒🕒 WGF
Material = 14K GF
Bezel = Plain, Engraved
Sides = Plain
Lugs = Plain
Lug Size = 16mm
Springbar = Female
Casemaker = Keystone
Case Closure = 3-Part Snap-On Bezel and Back
Case Number = 176
Case Shape = Cushion
Case Back = Flat
Dimensions = 38 x 34mm
Movement Size = 3/0
Movement Grades/Jewels = 24/17, 307/17
Seconds at = 6
Dial Numbers = 8132, 8729
Dial = Silver Finish, Butler Center
Dial Opening = Cushion
Dial Variations/Rarity = 🕒🕒🕒 Silver Finish, Luminous Numerals; Silver Finish, Butler Center
🕒🕒🕒🕒 Silver Finish, Exploding Straight Numerals
🕒🕒🕒🕒🕒 Silver Finish, Black Numerals; Silver Finish, Exploding Round Numerals
Numerals = Painted, Luminous
Hands = Luminous
Cased in Factory = Yes
Unique Case Design = Yes
Unique Dial Design = Yes
Introduction Date = 1929
Retail Price New = $42.50
Collectibility = 🕒🕒🕒
Advertisements = Yes
Marketing Theme = "Gay, unconventional design"

One of the most popular Illinois wristwatches with collectors, the Jolly Roger exhibits unconventional styling with its flared, engraved corners. The 1931 A. C. Becken catalog (using the 1930–31 Illinois Sales Catalog's copywriting) described it as "A sturdy strapwatch of gay, unconventional design—with an appeal to the adventurous spirit." Although originally available in both white and green gold-filled cases, collectors find the green gold version almost impossible to locate.

The exploding dials used on the Jolly Roger are incredibly popular and command very high prices on their own. Some of the exploding dials have numerals with straight edges and others with rounded numerals. Both are very striking and much sought after. The rounded numeral dials are the rarer of the two.

The Jolly Roger is very rare in green gold-filled. To date, fewer than one dozen green gold-filled engraved bezel Jolly Rogers have been sighted. The engraving on the bezel of the Jolly Roger was called in its advertisements "White, skip engraving" or "Green, skip engraving." With some Illinois cases it is difficult to determine if the case is yellow gold-filled or green gold-filled, but not with the Jolly Roger, as its greenish color is clearly discernible.

Jolly Roger, white gold-filled

Jolly Roger, green gold-filled

Jolly Roger, green gold-filled

Jolly Roger, white gold-filled

Jolly Roger, white gold-filled with a rare, later-released Lancaster dial

It is possible that a plain bezel Jolly Roger was called a "Hillcrest" by the Gensler-Lee jewelry company and given a dial signed "Meritime" (a house brand of that company), but one has never been seen and Hillcrest is not on the List of Factory-Cased Illinois Watches.

$27.75

"Hillcrest"
15-Jewel Meritime
White or Green Gold

NOTHING DOWN

MAN'S guaranteed 15 jewel MERITIME strap watch in a 14k White or Green Gold filled case in a new fancy design. Radium dial, leather straps and very good-looking. Special at $27.75 on terms of NO MONEY DOWN—$1.00 a week. Sold with a written guarantee and no interest!

A Gensler-Lee advertisement for a Jolly Roger–like wristwatch. *Oakland Tribune* (Oakland, CA), May 25, 1928; image from *newspapers.com*

TECHNICAL TIP

Please advise your repairperson not to install the rare enamel exploding dial found on the Major Speedway and Speedway 178 on a Jolly Roger case. The internal bezel thickness of the Jolly Roger is apparently thicker than the ones on those other 3-case models. The dial will fit on the movement but will get crushed once the bezel is put into place. —*Ed Kulha*

TECHNICAL TIP

Jolly Roger lugs are often found "drilled-out," such that the watch can then accept the more common male spring bars. This modification lessens the value and changes the originality. There are expert jewelers familiar with and capable of converting drilled-out lugs back to male lugs or repairing the male lugs to accommodate female spring bars.

FANTASTIC FIND

Bill Thomas of Minnesota reports: "I just have to give you this 'Fantastic Find'—it happened today [June 30, 2012]. After starting out at a big flea market, I went into a secondhand store in the western Minnesota town of Hutchinson and I noticed in a showcase a rather sorry-looking wristwatch head with a darkened discolored dial that I first thought might be a 6/0 size Waltham but then noticed the distinctly Illinois style of radium hands. When I got the clerk to open the showcase, I inspected the watch and could just make out the 'Illinois' name on its dial. The white gold-filled case was fancy but its bezel was unengraved. Then it struck me that this was a 'Jolly Roger'—I didn't know that they came in plain bezel cases until I got home and consulted your book. Examining the watch on my bench, I saw the case was marked Model 173, Keystone Watch Case Co., etc. That confirmed it. The movement 3/0 size, grade 307 is in good shape with a good staff, no rust, winds and sets; just a broken mainspring to be replaced, and it needs a cleaning. The case shows moderate high-point wear. But for the price of $5.00 + tax I paid for the watch I will gladly pay what it takes to restore the watch!"

FOR CRAFTSMANSHIP AND STYLE

ILLINOIS

THE MARY TODD

There is unusual refinement displayed in the case of the Mary Todd through the use of jet black enamel, inlaid in 14K solid white gold. The movement is 17 jewels. Illinois quality.

Retail, $75 *List, $86*

DAYTONA

The engraving of 14K solid gold in a delicate design offers in the Daytona an unusual appeal to milady, who prefers simplicity in adornment. Fitted with a 17 jeweled movement.

Retail, $65 *List, $74*

JOLLY ROGER

A pronounced preference for watches of dependable service places the Illinois "Jolly Roger" foremost in strap watch designs. A 3/0 size 17 jeweled Illinois, fitted in a pleasing case of 14K gold filled.

Retail, $42.50 *List, $43.50*

THE DIRECTOR

A new Illinois "A Lincoln" furnished in 14K solid gold with raised gold figured dial. A watch that will increase pocket style sales.

Retail, $110 *List, $135*

THE OXFORD

Another splendid watch added to the line of Illinois Marquis-Autocrats. Furnished in 14K gold filled case and fitted with a 17 jeweled movement.

Retail, $50 *List, $56*

PICCADILLY

Expressing a new thought in watch designs—the Illinois Piccadilly has found unusual acceptance with a public eager for a watch of pleasing design and enduring performance. Fitted with 17 jewel movement and encased with 14K filled gold.

Retail, $45 *List, $50*

W. J. JOHNSTON CO. ∴ Union Bank Building ∴ PITTSBURGH, PA.

Keystone, June 1929

Kenilworth, white gold-filled

Kenilworth, yellow gold-filled

Kenilworth / Gallahad

Official Name = Kenilworth and Gallahad (derived from Illinois advertisements and Illinois Sales and Material Catalogs)
Secondary Name(s) = None
Formerly Known As = None
Time Period = Moderne
Case Variations/Rarity = ◷◷◷◷ WGF/P, YGF/P
Case Durability = ◷◷
Material = 14K GF
Bezel = Plain
Sides = Plain
Lugs = Plain
Lug Size = 18mm
Springbar = Male
Casemaker = Keystone
Case Closure = 2-part Snap-On Bezel and Back
Case Number = 217
Case Shape = Rectangular
Case Back = Curved
Dimensions = 35 x 25mm
Movement Size = 12/0
Movement Grade/Jewels = 207/17
Seconds at = 6
Dial Numbers = 8198
Dial = Silver Finish, Sparkle Finish
Dial Opening = Rectangular
Dial Variations/Rarity = ◷◷◷ Silver Finish, Luminous Numerals
◷◷◷◷ Sparkle Finish, Luminous Numerals; Sparkle Finish, Painted Numerals
◷◷◷◷◷ Silver Finish, Black Numerals; Silver Finish, Painted Drop-Shadow; Sparkle Finish, Painted Drop-Shadow Numerals; Sparkle Finish, Egyptian Numerals
Numerals = Painted, Luminous
Hands = Steel, Luminous
Cased in Factory = Yes
Unique Case Design = Yes
Unique Dial Design = Yes
Introduction Date = 1930 (Kenilworth); 1932 (Gallahad)
Retail Price New = $60.00 (Kenilworth); $55.00 (Gallahad)
Collectibility = ◷◷◷◷
Advertisements = None found as yet
Marketing Themes = "A thin curved strapwatch that will fit any wrist perfectly"
"Correctly styled"

The Kenilworth appeared in the 1930–31 Illinois Sales Catalog, where it was described as follows: "A thin curved strapwatch that will fit any wrist perfectly. It is correctly styled and will appeal strongly to the man who is particular in his selection of personal furnishings." The L. & C. Mayers 1931 catalog offered its own version of Illinois' advertising copy: "A thin, smartly curved watch with curved back that fits any wrist. Perfectly plain, correctly styled."

Like the Marquis Strap, Hudson, Ardsley and Rockliffe, this model had a curved back to fit the wrist better. The Kenilworth could come equipped with an awesome drop-shadow numeral dial. The drop-shadow numeral version of this dial is highly coveted by collectors as it adds much pizzazz and value to the watch.

The Kenilworth was listed again in the 1931–32 Illinois Sales Catalog, and, with a change of dial, it became a "new" model, the Gallahad, in the 1933 catalog. (Yes, that's how Illinois spelled the name, even though the model was presumably named for King Arthur's knight Sir Galahad.) The Gallahad dial version also came with a rare Egyptian-looking numeral dial. Over the years, the dials of the Kenilworth, Gallahad and No. 250/Schmukler have been used interchangeably.

The Kenilworth/Gallahad looks similar to the solid gold Illinois Rockliffe, Rockliffe 18/0, and No. 250/Schmukler models. Dials used for this model also fit perfectly into the No. 250/Schmukler case.

This much underappreciated watch is highly attractive on the wrist and very special with a sparkle finish dial, with or without the drop-shadow numerals.

See Chapter 7 for a Hamilton drawing of Kenilworth dial with bold etched numerals that apparently was not released.

Kensington

See listing for **Trophy**

Kingston

See listing for **Ensign**

Kitchener, yellow gold-filled

Kitchener Military Watch

Official Name = Kitchener Military (derived from 1917 advertisements by the Militaire Watch Company in the *Army and Navy Register* and *Popular Mechanics*)
Secondary Name = Military
Formerly Known As = None
Time Period = Transitional
Case Variations/Rarity = ◷◷◷ Nickel, YGF
◷◷◷◷◷◷ Gunmetal Finish
Case Durability = ◷◷◷ YGF
◷◷◷◷ N
Material = N, Gunmetal (finish), 14K GF
Bezel = Plain
Sides = Plain
Lug Size = 14 mm
Springbar = Fixed Lugs
Casemakers = Philadelphia, IWCCo, Others
Case Closure = 3-Part Snap-On Bezel and Back
Case Number = None
Case Shape = Round
Case Back = Flat
Dimensions = 40 x 33mm
Movement Size = 0, 3/0
Movement Grades/Jewels = 21/11, 24/17, 32/11, 36/11, 201/11, 204/17
Seconds at = 6
Dial Numbers = Painted, Luminous
Dial = Enamel
Dial Opening = Round
Dial Variations/Rarity = ◷ Enamel; Silver Finish
◷◷◷◷◷◷◷ Black Dial ("Night Dial")
Numerals = Painted, Luminous
Hands = Steel, Luminous
Cased in Factory = No
Unique Case Design = No
Unique Dial Design = No
Introduction Date = 1917
Retail Price New = $11.75 (11J and Standard Dial); $16.00 (17J, Standard Dial); $14.00 (11J, Radium Dial); $18.25 (17J, Radium Dial); and 50¢ extra (Gunmetal Finish)
Collectibility = ◷◷◷◷
Advertisements = Yes
Marketing Themes = "The watch made famous on the world's great battlefields"
"The famous Kitchener Military Watch"

The Kitchener Military watch was advertised at least twice as shown here in the *Army and Navy Register* magazine in 1917, and in the October 1917 issue of *Popular Mechanics*.

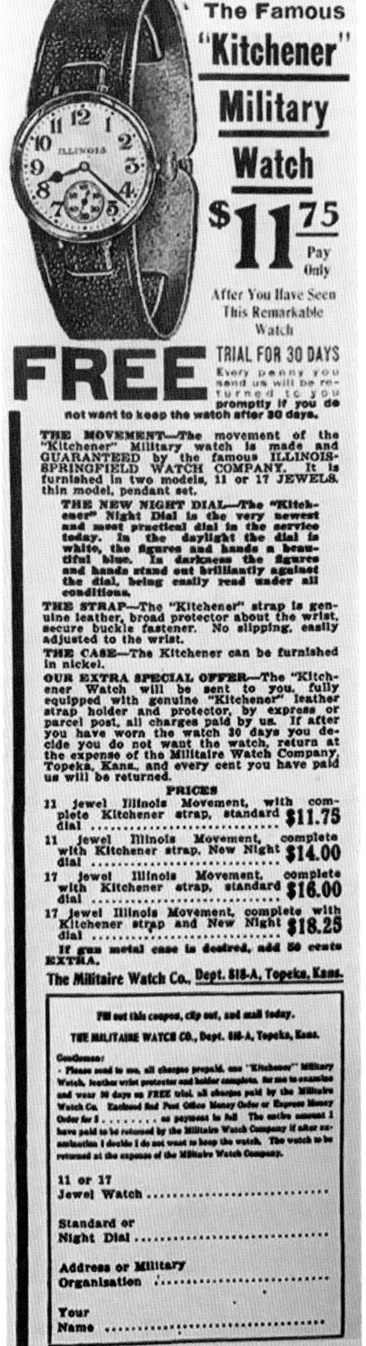

1917 *Army and Navy Register* advertisement

1917 *Army and Navy Register* advertisement

The Militaire Watch Company called the Kitchener "the watch sensation of the day—the newest, the most practical watch for all men of the Army and Navy." The model was offered with either a nickel or gunmetal finish and either a genuine leather strap protection or a shrapnel guard known as a "protector."

This is one of the few Transitional Period model watches for which we know the true name. Now we know the names for the following Transitional models: Admiral Evans, Admiral Benson, General Joffre and Admiral Funston. Previously, we had no idea that these models had proper identifiers.

This model was evidently named after its special Kitchener brand leather band, and the Kitchener band was named after Field Marshal Horatio Herbert Kitchener, 1st Earl Kitchener, overall leader of the British military effort in World War I.

H. H. Kitchener c. 1910

HORATIO KITCHENER, 1ST EARL KITCHENER (1850-1916)

Field Marshal Horatio Herbert Kitchener, 1st Earl Kitchener, won fame in 1898 for winning the Battle of Omdurman and securing control of the Sudan. He was Chief of Staff in the Second Boer War. He later became the British Commander-in-Chief (1902–1909). In 1914, at the start of World War I, Lord Kitchener became Secretary of State for War and a British Cabinet Minister. One of the few to foresee a long war, he organized the largest volunteer army that Britain, and indeed the world, had seen. His commanding image appeared on recruiting posters demanding "Your Country Needs You!"

Kitchener was killed in 1916 when the warship taking him to negotiations in Russia was sunk by a German mine.*

*http://www.britannica.com/EBchecked/topic/319651/Horatio-Herbert-Kitchener-1st-Earl-Kitchener

Lord Kitchener recruiting poster, c. 1914

For years, collectors viewed this as just one of many types of trench watches—a rather plain Transitional Period model. Further research into period advertisements, however, revealed its true name, as well as additional information about the watch. Advertisements mention several special features, such as the fact that it often came in a nickel case with a gunmetal finish option for 50¢ more. Kitcheners were available with a standard dial or a "night dial" with radium numerals and with a leather band apparently sold exclusively for the Kitchener Military Watch.

This is only the second known Illinois model that was offered with a gunmetal finish. The gunmetal option makes sense, as it would not be reflective on the battlefield. Eventually, in September 1917, the United States Army issued specifications requiring that military watches and dials be painted black. This was also the first Illinois wristwatch offered with a black dial, called a "Night Dial." It is likely that this model came in both 0 and 3/0 size cases.

Popular Mechanics, October 1917. Note the "night dial."

The mail-order advertisements promised "A Special Offer" for a protector and a special guarantee that the buyer could return the watch, for any reason, after thirty days and receive a full refund. Payment had to be made by Post Office Money Order or Express Money Order. Its movement, in either 11 or 17 jewels, was "guaranteed by the famous Illinois-Springfield Watch Company."

To date, no further information can be found about the Militaire Watch Company with its Post Office Box location in Topeka, Kansas, but literally thousands of such watch companies sprang up during the Great War.

J. Selinger Jewelry Store display window full of military watch bands and military watches in 1918. Note the sign showing Kitchener military bands for 10¢ each. Julius Selinger was a jeweler located at 820 F Street NW in Washington, DC.

LASALLE

See listing for **Commodore**

Larchmont / Vernon / Richmond 12/0

Larchmont, white gold-filled

Larchmont, yellow gold-filled

Official Names = Larchmont and Vernon (derived from Illinois advertisements and Illinois Sales and Material Catalogs)
Secondary Name = Richmond 12/0 (derived from jobbers' catalogs)
Formerly Known As = None
Time Period = Moderne
Case Variations/Rarity = ◷◷◷ YGF/P
◷◷◷◷ WGF/P
◷◷◷◷◷◷ RGF/P (10K Rose), RGF/P (14K Rose)
Case Durability = ◷◷◷
Material = 14K GF, 14K RGF, 10K RGF, 10K RGP
Bezel = Plain
Sides = Plain
Lugs = Plain
Lug Size = 16mm
Springbar = Male
Casemaker = Keystone
Case Closure = 2-Part Snap-On Bezel and Back
Case Number = 214
Case Shape = Rectangular
Case Back = Flat
Dimensions = 37 x 23mm
Movement Size = 12/0
Movement Grade/Jewels = 207/17
Seconds at = 6
Dial Number = 8055
Dial = Silver Finish, Sparkle Finish
Dial Opening = Rectangular
Dial Variations/Rarity = ◷◷ Silver Finish, Luminous Numerals
◷◷◷◷◷ Silver Finish, Black Numerals; Sparkle Finish, Painted Numerals; Sparkle Finish, Luminous Numerals
Numerals = Painted, Luminous
Hands = Steel, Luminous
Cased in Factory = Yes
Unique Case Design = No
Unique Dial Design = No
Introduction Date = 1931 (Larchmont); 1931 (Vernon); 1932 (Richmond 12/0)
Retail Price New = $52.50 (Larchmont); $60.00 (Vernon); $60.00 (Richmond 12/0)
Collectibility = ◷◷◷◷
Advertisements = Yes
Marketing Themes = "Handsome creation with original appointments and refinements that will appeal to every man"
"Case appears exceedingly small".
"Fashionably neat"

The Larchmont appeared in an advertisement in the December 1931 issue of the *Saturday Evening Post* and was shown in the 1931–32 Illinois Sales Catalog. The Vernon was described in that same Illinois catalog, with this caption: "The Larchmont model used with harmonious 14K filled gold band for those who desire this combination."

Keystone made the Larchmont cases. The white gold-filled cases are much less prone to wear than the yellow gold-filled variety. There have been a few very rare Larchmonts discovered in 10K rose rolled gold-plate cases, although no advertisements exist for Illinois watches with rose gold- plate cases. Keystone also made these cases, but under its "Victory" brand, which it used on rolled gold plate products. The gold plate version does not have a case model number.

Inside case back of 10K rose rolled gold-plate Larchmont in Keystone "Victory" brand case

The 1933 Chicago World's Fair Edition of the Shure Winner Catalog No. 120 called a Larchmont with a metal bracelet a "Richmond." Illinois models typically changed names when equipped with a metal band instead of a leather strap. This is the only known advertisement that refers to a Richmond. The bracelet shown with it appears to be exactly the same one that Illinois shows with the Vernon.

On the List of Illinois Factory Cased Watches the Richmond name appears both under 6/0 and 12/0 sizes; thus, this 12/0 size Larchmont with a metal band is called a "Richmond 12/0" to distinguish it from the "Richmond 6/0." However, to further confuse things, a Larchmont with a metal bracelet was also called a "Vernon" in another catalog. The metal band on the Vernon was offered at a $7.50 premium.

VERNON.
No. 42W2. 17 jewels....................**$62.30**
Consumer $60.00
Available in 14 karat white or natural filled gold, same quality band.

Jobber's catalog, c. 1931

Illinois Richmond De Luxe, 12/0 size, 17 jewel, 14K white or natural yellow gold filled case. Black figure dial. Metal band to match.
No. 22W44. White Gold. Each................ **24.85**
No. 22W45. Yellow Gold. Each.............. **24.85**
(Retail price 70.00)

Illinois Richmond 12/0

The original price card for a Richmond 12/0 model

End of a cardboard outer box for a Richmond 12/0

See listing for **Derby**

Locke

Locke, white gold-filled

Locke, yellow gold-filled

Official Name = Locke (derived from IWCCo advertisements dated October 1928 in the *Jewelers' Circular* and the *Keystone*)
Secondary Name = None
Formerly Known As = Aviator (derived from early price guides)
Time Period = Generic
Case Variations/Rarity = ◷◷ WGF/P, WGF/E, YGF/P, YGF/P, Chrome
◷◷◷◷◷◷ WG/P, YG/P, YG/E
◷◷◷◷◷◷◷◷ WG/E
Case Durability = ◷◷◷
Material = 14K GF, 14 WG, 14K YG
Bezel = Plain, Engraved (partially)
Sides = Plain, Engraved
Lugs = Plain, Engraved
Lug Size = 16mm
Springbar = Male
Casemakers = Elgin, IWCCo., Star, Others
Case Closure = 3-Part Snap-On Bezel and Back
Case Number = None
Case Shape = Rectangular
Case Back = Flat
Dimensions = 31 x 38mm
Movement Size = 3/0
Movement Grades/Jewels = 24/17, 903/15, 905/17
Seconds at = 6, 9, None
Dial Numbers = 92, 8142
Dial = Silver Finish
Dial Opening = Rectangular
Dial Variations/Rarity = ◷◷◷◷ Silver Finish, Black Numerals;
◷◷◷◷◷ Sparkle Finish, Luminous Numerals, Center Cross
Numerals = Painted, Luminous
Hands = Luminous
Cased in Factory = No
Unique Case Design = No
Unique Dial Design = No
Introduction Date = 1928
Retail Price New = Unknown
Collectibility = ◷◷◷◷
Advertisements = Yes
Marketing Themes = "Style can be seen at a glance, but quality is the hidden value."
"A 3/0 size watch, which looks smaller"

The Locke was inadvertently omitted from *The Illinois Watch: The Life and Times of a Great American Watch Company*. As this model is a Generic Period watch, an Elgin or Waltham movement can also be found in a similar case. The Locke is larger than the average Illinois wristwatch, so it appeals to large-wristed vintage collectors.

IWCCo advertised the Locke in the *Keystone* in April 1928 and in the *Jewelers' Circular* on October 4, 1928.

This model was advertised by IWCCo as being available in solid gold, but only one solid white gold example has been found to this point. Early price guides referred to this model as an "Aviator," but no supporting documentation could be found to confirm that name, although the advertisement shown here depicts the image of a flyer, with airplanes in the background. The Locke can be found with subsidiary seconds at 6, 9 or with none at all.

Page 98 *The KEYSTONE* April, 1928

The Man's Size Watch

[a 3/0 size watch, which looks smaller]

In Solid Gold or Gold Filled, these handsome cases are built for hard wear. There are also many other styles, built to fit American made movements,-by a factory whose name has long stood for Quality and Precision

Illinois Watch Case Company

Factory and Main Office at Elgin, Illinois, U.S.A

New York 20 West 47th St. | Chicago 35 E Wacker Drive | San Francisco 704 Market St. | Toronto 17 King St. E. | London 65 Holborn Viaduct

Keystone, April 1928

Locke inside case back by Star

Locke inside case back by IWCCo

Major

Major, white gold-filled

Major, green gold-filled

Major, green gold-filled

Official Name = Major (derived from Illinois advertisements and Illinois Sales and Material Catalogs)
Secondary Name = None
Formerly Known As = None
Time Period = Deco
Case Variations/Rarity = ◷◷ WGF/E
◷◷◷◷ GGF/E
◷◷◷◷◷ WGF/P, GGF/P, TT/E
Case Durability = ◷◷◷◷ WGF
◷◷◷ GGF
Material = 14K GF
Bezel = Plain, Engraved (fully/partially)
Sides = Plain, Engraved
Lugs = Plain, Engraved
Lug Size = 16mm
Springbar = Male
Casemaker = Keystone
Case Closure = 3-Part Snap On Bezel and Back
Case Numbers = 171, 172, No Number
Case Shape = Round
Case Back = Flat
Dimensions = 36 x 31mm
Movement Size = 3/0
Movement Grades/Jewels = 24/17, 307/17
Seconds at = 6
Dial Numbers = 8132, 8729
Dials = Silver Finish, Butler Center, Enamel
Dial Opening = Cushion
Dial Variations/Rarity = ◷◷ Silver Finish, Luminous Numerals
◷◷◷ Silver Finish, Butler Center*
◷◷◷◷ Silver Finish, Exploding Straight Numerals
◷◷◷◷◷ Silver Finish, Black Numerals; Silver Finish, Exploding Rounded Numerals
◷◷◷◷◷◷ Enamel, Exploding Numerals
*Some dials have butler centers with exploding numeral dials
Numerals = Painted, Luminous
Hands = Luminous
Cased in Factory = Yes
Unique Case Design = Yes
Unique Dial Design = Yes
Introduction Date = 1928
Retail Price New = $42.50
Collectibility = ◷◷◷◷
Advertisements = Yes
Marketing Theme = "High grade dependable strap watch"
"Rugged in construction"

Illinois presented the Major in its 1928 booklet entitled "A Book of Watches" and first advertised the Major in the June 28, 1928 issue of the *Jewelers' Circular.* Over the years, the Major was one of the most advertised Illinois wristwatches, appearing in various magazines and newspapers as well as in jobbers' catalogs.

The Major did not appear in regular jobbers' catalogs until the next year, so it is interesting that a catalog for the Carson Pirie Scott department store in Chicago, dated October 1928, shows the Major (and also the Marquis Strap), though not identified by name.

R1866 3/0 size, 14k white or green gold, curved back case, plain or engraved bezel, square shape, 17 jewel Illinois movement luminous dial.
Each $56.00

Carson Pirie Scott catalog, October 1928, showing unidentified Major

Illinois, "A Book of Watches," 1928

In "A Book off Watches," Illinois noted that the Major was "built to withstand the severe shock and strains of work or play." Ruggedness was an attribute of the Major that was emphasized, such as in the 1929 "Criterion" wholesale catalog of the Rhode-Spencer Co., which comments: "Has very sturdy lugs. A watch for the man who likes rugged things with good lines."

No. 4497 "THE MAJOR" MAN'S ILLINOIS STRAP WATCH. 3/0s, new Cushion shape, Genuine 14K Gold Filled stock, in White or Green Gold, and may be had in Plain or Engraved. Has very sturdy lugs. A watch for the man who likes rugged things with good lines. Fitted with a 17J. Illinois movement of very fine quality. Fancy Center dial with Second, Luminous figures and hands, with a fine quality strap. Each in gift box, with Resale Ticket. Each **21.75**

Rhode-Spencer "Criterion" catalog, 1929. The price shown is wholesale.

The 1929–30 Illinois Sales Catalog pointed out that the Major contained "A fine 17 jewel Illinois movement with a patent regulator and full-luminous-figure dial fitted in 14K white or green, plain or engraved or combination gold-filled cases."

MAJOR

In the multi-page Illinois Factory advertisement in the 1929 Otto Young catalog, the Major was featured as "The Great American Strap Watch. The Major is a high grade, dependable, durable strap watch, as sturdy in construction as the average 12 size pocket model. Its small compact case is exceptionally attractive. It is furnished in either white or green 14K gold filled. You have your choice of four different case designs, which are as follows: white engraved oxidized; green engraved oxidized; white plain and green plain. The movement is fitted with a two-toned luminous figure polished center dial."

Illinois offered this model in white and green gold-filled, but never in yellow gold-filled. The Major case is one of the more durable Illinois cases, so it is possible to find them today in excellent condition. This model has indeed proved to be "rugged in construction," as the Illinois advertising claimed.

There are three versions of the bezel used on the Major (and Guardsman): unengraved, engraved on all four sides with a pattern like ears of wheat, and engraved with a series of small flowers on all four sides but with the two horizontal sides broken in the middle by a small engraved box and the top and bottom by an unengraved rectangular area. This third bezel design occasionally is seen rotated ninety degrees (even in some catalog illustrations), so that the unengraved areas are vertical, at the sides. However, there is usually a small locator bump on the midcase, with a corresponding notch inside the bezel, to indicate the correct orientation, with the unengraved areas at the top and bottom.

17 Jewels

The Illinois Major

3/0 Size No. 24

The Great American Strap Watch

The Major is a high grade, dependable, durable strap watch, as sturdy in construction as the average 12 size pocket model. Its small compact case is exceptionally attractive. It is furnished in either white or green 14K gold filled. You have your choice of four different case designs, which are as follows: white engraved oxidized; green engraved oxidized; white plain and green plain. The movement is fitted with a two-toned luminous figure polished center dial.

ENGRAVED CASE
Retail $42.50 List $43.50

SPECIFICATIONS
17 ruby and sapphire jewels; 3/0 size; Steel escape wheel; Patent regulator.

PLAIN CASE
Retail $42.50 List $43.50

Otto Young catalog, 1929

Major, white gold-filled

Major, green gold-filled

Major, green gold-filled

Major, white gold-filled

Major, white gold-filled

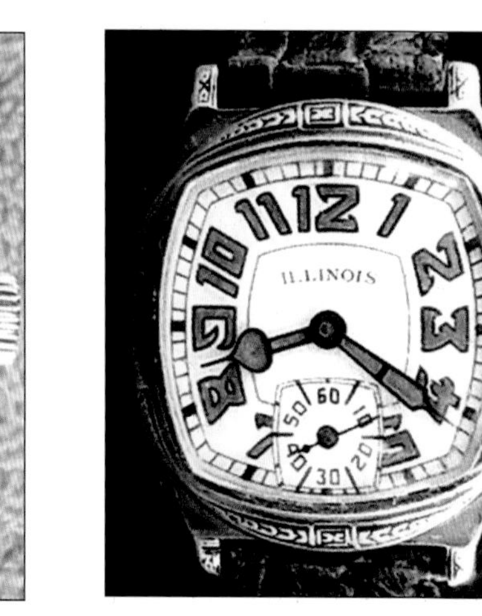

Major, two-tone, enamel dial

The Major is particularly prized by collectors when it is equipped with the rare and iconic Illinois exploding numeral dial. Illinois offered both a rounded-numeral and a sharp-edged numeral variation of this dial, but the rounded-numeral version is seen less often. This same dial fits the cases of the Jolly Roger, Speedway and Speedway 178 models as well as the Major. A very rare enamel version of the exploding dial looks awesome in the Major, Speedway and Speedway 178. To date, fewer than six of the enamel variant have been found. *Please note:* Owing to the inside configuration of the Jolly Roger case, the enamel exploding numeral dial will not fit this model.

Although Illinois' production records by model have never been located, empirical evidence indicates that Illinois produced the Major, Marquis Strap and New Yorker models in greater quantities than any other Illinois men's models.

For most of its models, Illinois had case numbers stamped inside the case back. For the Major, three different case model number variations exist: 171, 172 and No Number. I presume that Illinois first released this case without a case Model Number, but then had Keystone add case model numbers once it entered into an exclusive supply contract with the casemaker.

Major inside case back. Model No. 171

Major inside case back, no Model No.

FANTASTIC FIND

An anonymous Michigan collector says, "I love the Fantastic Finds articles in the NAWCC *Bulletin!* Here is my contribution.

"As well as repairing watches, I also buy and sell antiques and collectibles. I always set up a booth at the Allegan Antique Show in Allegan, Michigan (first Sunday of the month, April through September) and sell some antiques, watches, and advertise my watch repair services. My wife and I have been doing the shows off and on since 2002, and it's always a great place to buy, also. This past weekend was the last show of the season, and I was browsing for items of interest when I found a dirty toolbox in a dealer's booth filled with junky-looking miscellaneous watches, parts, and closed tins filled with parts and parts watches. I found what looked to be a decent-looking antique Art Deco style Illinois wristwatch in a closed parts tin with several other nondescript wristwatches. At first I thought the case back was missing, but after a thorough search of the tin, I found it. It seemed odd to me that the case back and bezel were one color, and the frame was another. I inquired of the price, and was told $5 for the tin. I also bought a 7-jewel Art Deco style Waltham wristwatch for $5.

"When I got home, I looked and found the serial numbers of the case back and frame matched. I did a quick Google search and found mention of another two-tone Illinois wristwatch case. Long story short— the watch I found is an Illinois 'Major' with a 17-jewel, grade 307 movement. These watches came in white gold-filled, green gold-filled, or two-tone cases. The two-tone cases are the hardest to find. The watch I found has a white gold-filled bezel and case back, and a green gold-filled frame. It is complete minus the minute and seconds hand. It should clean up nicely. It always pays to do a thorough search!"

FANTASTIC FIND

In August 2012, I found my first two-tone Illinois wristwatch, a Major with engraved bezel. I wrote to Fred and he agreed to include it in his Fantastic Finds article in the NAWCC *Bulletin*. I love searching eBay for good deals, and happened upon a lot of watches with this title: 'Antique Set of Three Wristwatch Cases Repair or Parts.' The auction was actually for three wristwatches: a ladies' Bulova, a ladies' Glamor, and an Illinois. There were only four pictures and it was not even possible to read the 'Illinois' marking on the dial (mostly because the crystal was so discolored), but I was sure the watch was a two-tone Major with engraved lugs and bezel, and I was right. The dial is a little discolored, but the movement is in excellent condition. The three watches cost me $18.97, delivered. — *Anonymous*

ILLINOIS STRAP WATCH "The Gaurdsman" a new model, 17 jeweled in 14-K green or white gold filled case. A famous watch that will give years and years of perfect time-keeping satisfaction. Priced **$45.00**
$1.50 a Week

A Major misadvertised as a "Gaurdsman" by the Philip H. Caplan Jewelry Store in the *Evening News* (Harrisburg, PA), May 9, 1930; image from *newspapers.com*

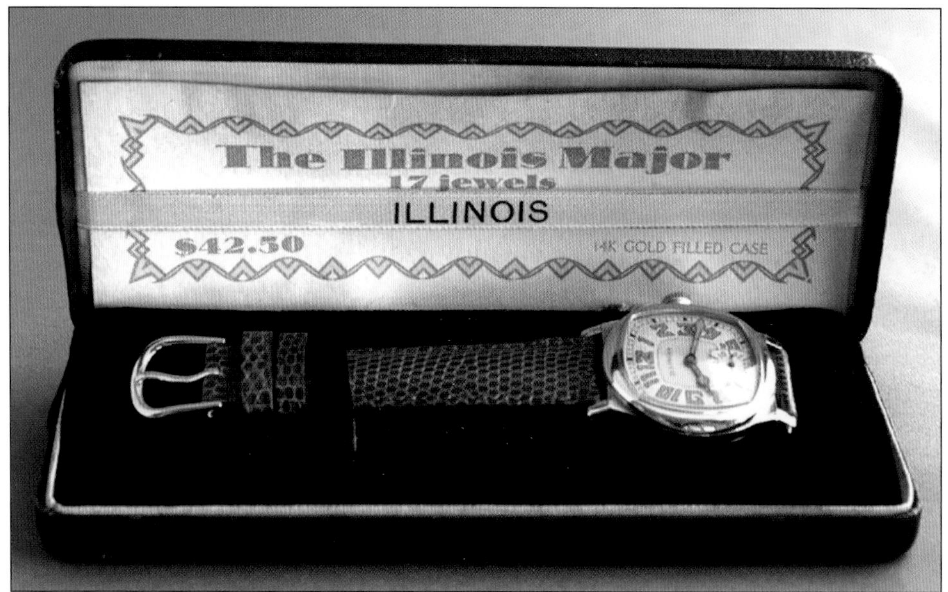

Major in its original display box with its original paperwork

See listing for **New Yorker**

Marquis Strap / Cadet

Official Name = Marquis Strap (derived from advertisements and Illinois Sales and Material Catalogs)
Secondary Name = Cadet (derived from internal Hamilton documentation)
Formerly Known As = None
Time Period = Deco
Case Variations/Rarity = 🕒🕒 WGF/E
🕒🕒🕒🕒 WGF/P, YGF/E
🕒🕒🕒🕒🕒 YGF/P, GGF/P, GGF/E, TT/E
🕒🕒🕒🕒🕒🕒 TTG/E, TT/P
Case Durability = 🕒🕒🕒🕒
Material = 14K GF
Bezel = Plain, Engraved
Sides = Plain
Lugs = Engraved
Lug Size = 16mm
Springbar = Male
Casemaker = Fahys
Case Closure = 3-Part Snap-On Bezel and Back
Case Number = Special Model
Case Shape = Tonneau
Case Back = Curved
Dimensions = 39 x 29mm
Movement Size = 6/0
Movement Grades/Jewels = 903/15, 904/17, 905/17, 907/19
Seconds at = 6, 9, None
Dial Numbers = 8134, 8254
Dials = Silver Finish, Butler Center
Dial Opening = Tonneau
Dial Variations/Rarity = 🕒🕒 Silver Finish, Luminous Numerals, Seconds at 9
🕒🕒🕒 Silver Finish, Luminous Numerals; Silver Finish, Luminous Numerals, Butler Center
🕒🕒🕒🕒🕒 Silver Finish, Black Numerals
🕒🕒🕒🕒🕒🕒 Silver Finish, Luminous Numerals, Seconds at 6; Silver Finish, Luminous Numerals, No Subs
Numerals = Painted, Luminous
Hands = Luminous
Cased in Factory = Yes
Unique Case Design = Yes
Unique Dial Design = Yes
Introduction Date = 1928
Retail Price New = $50.00 (17J); $60.00 (19J)
Collectibility = 🕒🕒🕒🕒
Advertisements = Yes
Marketing Themes = "One of the most popular strap watches made"
"Unusually attractive"

Marquis Strap, green gold-filled

Marquis Strap, two-tone gold-filled

Marquis Strap, yellow gold-filled

Illinois advertised the Marquis Strap wristwatch more often than any other Illinois men's wristwatch model. The Marquis Strap was the first wristwatch advertised following the acquisition of the Illinois Watch Company by Hamilton. It was also advertised by the Santa Fe Watch Co. at least as early as November 1927. This model was called "The Marquis Strap" to distinguish it from the Illinois pocket watch that was also named "Marquis" (The Marquis-Autocrat).

The new Marquis-Strap. Unusually attractive 14k gold-filled case, curved to the arc of the wrist, fitted with 17-jeweled movement of very high quality. $50.00

American Magazine, June 1928 Illinois advertisement

American Magazine, November 1928 Illinois advertisement

Advertisements noted that the case was "curved to the arc of the wrist" or "distinctly curved to fit the wrist." It was also described as "one of the most popular strap models made" and as being "unusually attractive."

THE MARQUIS STRAP

The Illinois Factory advertisement shown in the 1929 Otto Young catalog describes the Marquis Strap as follows: "This beautiful, new and distinctive strap model possesses an individuality characteristic of the popular Marquis-Autotocrat pocket watch. It is supplied in either 14K white or green gold filled case, with plain or engraved bezel. The entire case is curved to fit snug and conform to the arc of the wrist which assures the wearer the highest degree of comfort. The Marquis Strap is representative of the progress in artistic merit which has been maintained for years by ILLINOIS."

Illinois produced the Marquis Strap in a large number of case and dial configurations. At least nine different case configurations, three different subsidiary second varieties (at 6, 9 and none) and six different dial styles have been identified. Today the white gold-filled case variation can be found more easily than yellow gold-filled and green gold-filled versions. Illinois even produced the Marquis Strap in an unusual two-tone variation with a white center and green gold bezel and back, whereas Illinois offered all its other two-tone watches with white bezels and backs and yellow or green gold centers. At least three rare Marquis Straps with subsidiary seconds at 6 have been located. One two-tone case version with a plain bezel has been located.

The wide variety of Marquis Strap types indicates its great popularity in the late 1920s. This model remains very popular today because its stylized deco numerals, attractive case shape and engraving reflect the height of Art Deco wristwatch design.

17 and 19 Jewels — ***The Marquis-Strap*** — *905 and 907 6/0 Size*

THIS beautiful, new and distinctive strap model, possesses an individuality characteristic of the popular Marquis-Autocrat pocket watch. It is supplied in either 14K white or green gold filled case, with plain or engraved bezel. The entire case is curved to fit snug and conform to the arc of the wrist which assures the wearer the highest degree of comfort. The Marquis-Strap is representative of the progress in artistic merit which has been maintained for years by ILLINOIS.

ENGRAVED MARQUIS-STRAP
905, 17 J., Retail $50.00 List $58.00
907, 19 J., Retail $55.00 List $63.50

SPECIFICATIONS

17 and 19 jewel, 6/0 size movement. 14K white or green gold filled cases with plain or engraved bezels. Curved case which conforms to the arc of the wrist.

PLAIN MARQUIS-STRAP
905, 17 J., Retail $50.00 List $58.00
907, 19 J., Retail $55.00 List $63.50

Otto Young catalog, 1929

Marquis Strap, yellow gold-filled

Marquis Strap, white gold-filled

Marquis Strap, green gold-filled

Marquis Strap, two-tone

Marquis Strap, two-tone, gold-filled

Marquis Strap, green gold-filled

Marquis Strap, white gold-filled

According to a recently discovered internal Hamilton document dated June 5, 1933, the "Cadet" appears to be another name for the Marquis Strap. Cadet is listed under the 6/0 size watches on the "List of Names of Cased Illinois Watches by Sizes," dated December 31, 1932. It is possible the Cadet came with a metal bracelet.

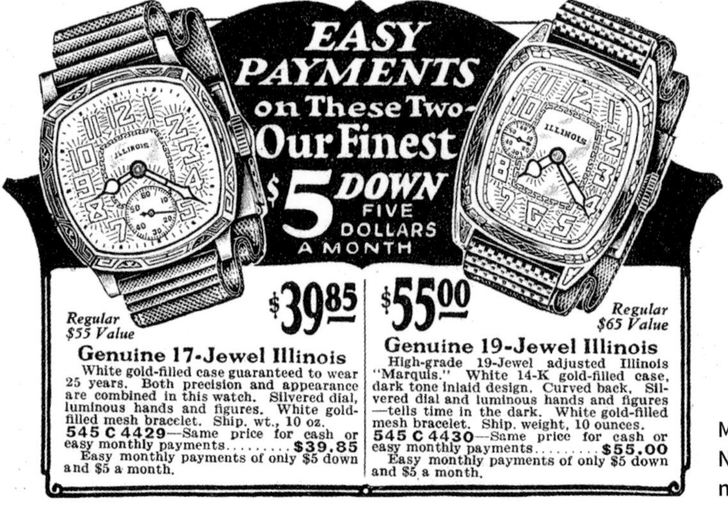

Montgomery Ward catalog, 1934. Notice how the glowing radium numerals and hands are depicted.

THE ILLINOIS
An American Watch As American As Its Name
MARQUIS
$55
17 JEWELS 14K FILLED GOLD

Marquis Strap original price card

WHY I COLLECT ILLINOIS

"I began to have an interest in vintage wristwatches long ago after inheriting my grandfather's Hamilton Brock—a 30 year gift from General Motors. It had been sitting broken in a box for years. At the time, I found an old watchmaker and jeweler who brought it back to life while also teaching me quite a bit about wristwatches. I soon learned that most people who collect American made watches seemed to admire Hamilton—as it was, arguably, the flagship American watch company. From this, I evolved to an appreciation for their earlier Art Deco–inspired models. The first vintage wristwatch I purchased was a WGF engraved Hamilton Oval from about 1928, followed by a Tonneau, a Square, and a few other early Geometric-named wristwatches. From there, Art Deco Illinois models were a pretty simple next step—especially once I learned that Hamilton had acquired Illinois, perhaps their leading competitor when it came to case design and movement quality, just as both companies were at their peak in 1927–29. This was when both companies were making the watches that I like the most.

"When it comes to collecting, I tend to prefer things that everyone else doesn't have. Illinois wristwatches clearly fit this too! As a fan of art and design, I like how most Factory-Cased Illinois wristwatches are the perfect combination of form and function— trend-setting Art Deco cases along with top-of-the-line 17 to 21 jewel American movements inside. The first time I saw a 3/0 size Illinois 307 grade movement, I was struck by the stylized damaskeening on it and many of their other movements. Once I discovered Illinois, it was not long before I became friends with Fred Friedberg and purchased my first Illinois—a WGF engraved white Marquis. This was about a year or two before his flagship book came out. Once I saw an Illinois Consul for the first time, I was hooked! Since then I have bought many Illinois wristwatches including more than a dozen Consuls and Marquis'. The Consul, Marquis, and Jolly Roger remain my favorite Illinois wristwatches . . . and the Hamilton Oval and Tonneau remain my favorite Hamilton wristwatches. (Though, I must admit, the Consul will always be my favorite!)"

—*Rick Vess*

Masonic Dial, sterling silver

MASONIC DIAL

Official Name = Masonic Dial (derived from the Masonic dial contained in this watch)
Secondary Name = None
Formerly Known As = None
Time Period = Transitional
Case Variations/Rarity = ◷◷ SS/P
Case Durability = ◷◷◷◷
Material = SS
Bezel = Plain
Sides = Plain
Lugs = Plain
Lug Size = 16mm
Springbar = Fixed
Casemaker = Fahys
Case Closure = 3-Part Snap-On Bezel and Back
Case Number = None
Case Shape = Cushion
Case Back = Flat
Dimensions = 27 x 27mm
Movement Size = 3/0
Movement Grades/Jewels = 24/17, 36/17
Seconds at = 6
Dial Number = None
Dial = Silver Finish
Dial Opening = Round
Dial Variations/Rarity = ◷◷◷◷◷◷◷ Silver Finish
Numerals = Painted
Hands = Steel
Cased in Factory = No
Unique Case Design = No
Unique Dial Design = Yes
Introduction Date = c. 1920
Retail Price New = Unknown
Collectibility = ◷◷◷◷
Advertisements = No
Marketing Theme = Unknown (a special-order dial)

The Masonic dial is a good example of Illinois efforts to produce specialized dials in very low quantities to meet customer needs. Masonic dials are found more commonly on Illinois pocket watches, but the example shown above contains the rare round version of the Masonic Dial for a 3/0 size watch. A unique square 6/0 size Illinois Square Masonic dial exists with an unsigned dial; the 6/0 version locates the seconds at the 9 position. As with the Illinois "Police Special" dial, the Masonic could have been placed in any 3/0 size case.

Mate

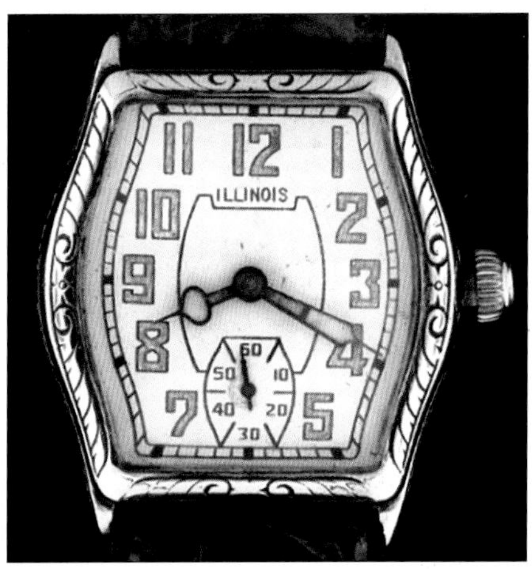

Mate, white gold-filled

Mate, green gold-filled

Official Name = Mate (derived from Illinois advertisements and Illinois Sales and Material Catalogs)
Secondary Name = None
Formerly Known As = None
Time Period = Deco
Case Variations/Rarity = 🕒 WGF/E
🕒🕒 YGF/E
🕒🕒🕒 WGF/P
🕒🕒🕒🕒 YGF/P, GGF/E, TT/E
🕒🕒🕒🕒🕒 GGF/P
Case Durability = 🕒🕒🕒
Material = 14K GF
Bezel = Plain, Engraved
Sides = Engraved
Lugs = Plain
Lug Size = 18mm
Springbar = Male
Casemaker = Fahys
Case Closure = 3-Part Snap-On Bezel and Back
Case Number = Special Model H
Case Shape = Tonneau
Case Back = Curved
Dimensions = 37 x 31mm
Movement Size = 3/0
Movement Grades/Jewels = 24/17, 307/17
Seconds at = 6
Dial Numbers = 8133, 8729
Dials = Silver Finish, Butler Center
Dial Opening = Tonneau
Dial Variations/Rarity = 🕒🕒 Silver Finish, Luminous Numerals
🕒🕒🕒🕒 Silver Finish, Butler Center, Luminous Numerals
🕒🕒🕒🕒🕒 Silver Finish, Black Numerals
Numerals = Painted, Luminous
Hands = Luminous
Cased in Factory = Yes
Unique Case Design = Yes
Unique Dial Design = Yes
Introduction Date = 1928
Retail Price New = $42.50
Collectibility = 🕒🕒🕒🕒
Advertisements = Yes
Marketing Themes = "A reliable companion for a man in business"
"For the man of action"
"Sturdy, rugged and dependable"

The Mate was apparently introduced in the 1928 Illinois sales brochure entitled "A Book of Watches." It was a very popular model, appearing thereafter in Illinois Sales Catalogs and various Illinois magazine and newspaper advertisements.

Illinois described the Mate this way: "Sturdy, rugged, dependable by nature, the Illinois Mate is a reliable companion to the man in business who thoroughly realizes the value of his time." It was also accorded the aesthetic advantages of being "rich in design and far advanced in style."

As with its other 3/0 size wristwatch models of the time, Illinois often noted the presence of a "patent regulator" (micrometric regulator) in the Mate's movement. This feature was mandatory in railroad-grade pocket watches and often appeared in other pockets watches, but it was very uncommon in wristwatches of this period.

The MATE

A watch for the man of action who demands accuracy under all conditions. The Mate is a compact watch of unusual design which affords it extra protection. 14K white or green filled gold; plain or engraved cases.

Suggested consumer price, $42.50.

A. I. Hall catalog, 1930–31

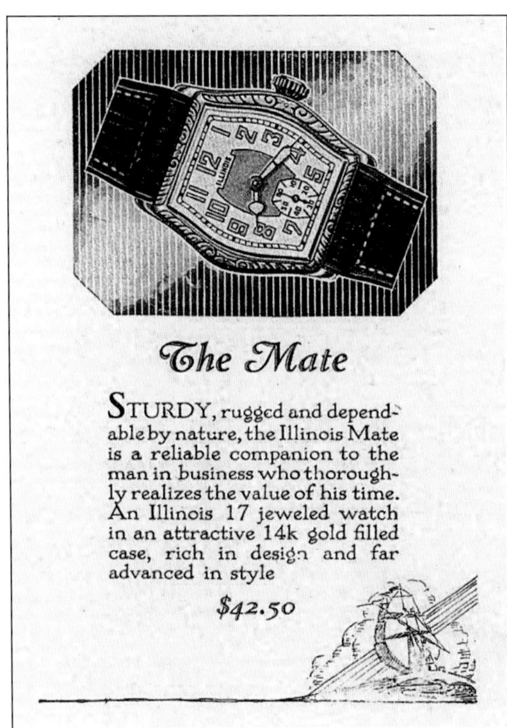

Illinois, "A Book of Watches," 1928

THE MATE

Sturdy, rugged and dependable. The Illinois Mate is a reliable companion to the man in business who thoroughly realizes the value of time. An Illinois 17-jeweled watch in an attractive 14K gold filled case. 3/0 Size, Luminous dial.

68W11. White engraved oxidized.......................................**$52.20**
68W12. White plain front and back, green center............................**52.20**

May & Malone catalog, 1930

The Mate looks like a larger version of an Illinois Ensign. It came with subsidiary seconds at 6, whereas the Ensign could have subsidiary seconds at 6 or 9. Collectors most commonly find the Mate in a white gold-filled engraved case, less often in a white gold-filled plain bezel case, and seldom in yellow or green gold-filled plain bezel cases or in two-tone cases. The Mate, with a plain bezel, was advertised in the November 10, 1928 issue of the *Saturday Evening Post*.

The Mate is subject to corner bezel wear in all case colors. In an excellent engraved case, a Mate makes a beautiful Deco-era watch. Illinois produced most Mate dials with butler centers, in silver for white cases and in yellow for yellow or green cases.

Mate, yellow gold-filled

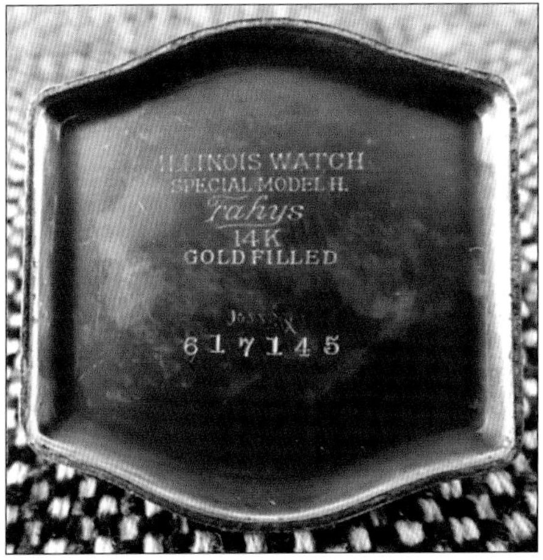

Mate inside case back

A few rare, probably custom-ordered Mate dials have been found with blue radium numerals. This color makes for a remarkably striking wristwatch. There is a Beau Brummell model watch that also has a dial containing blue radium numerals. In fact, the Hamilton Greeley model was offered with blue radium numerals.

Mate, white gold-filled, blue radium numerals

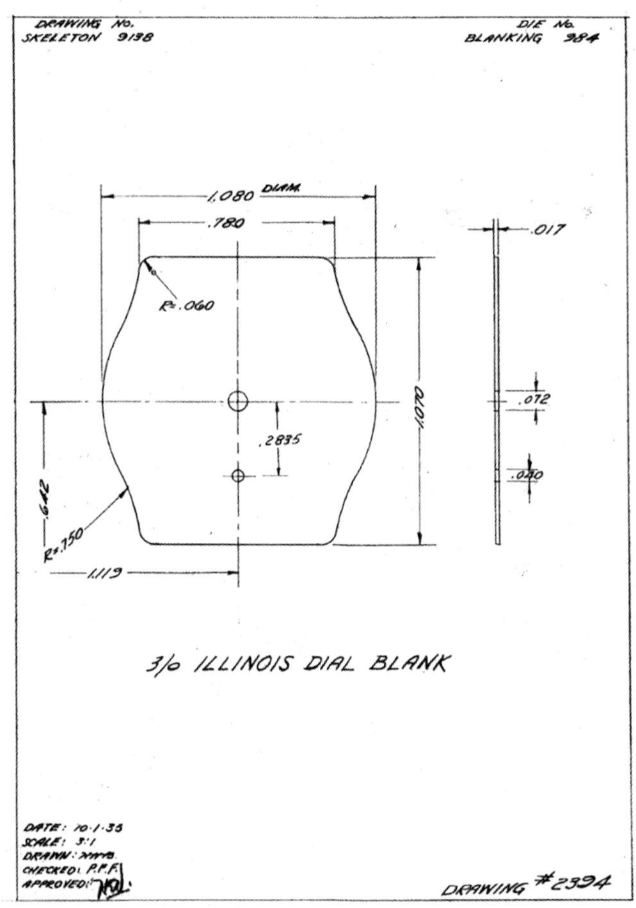

Hamilton drawing of an Illinois Mate dial blank, dated October 1, 1935

WHY I COLLECT ILLINOIS

I may have been fated to become a watch collector a long time ago, though I wasn't aware of it at the time. One of my father's colleagues (and eventually one of my graduate school professors) gave me a vintage Omega for a high-school graduation present. That was my first serious watch; it served me as primary timekeeper through college and into graduate school. My next watch was a Bulova '23' that I inherited from my father's brother. I wore it as my dress watch through the rest of graduate school and into my working days. Eventually I also inherited my father's Hamilton "Dixon" and "Emerson" and my mother's Elgin 'William Osler' (with its boxes and papers) as well. Those five watches are still the basis of my collection.

But watch collecting would have to wait a while. I went to work in a tech industry, and for many years my watch of choice would be a wristwatch calculator, the more functions, the better. (Need trigonometric functions or logarithms? I can do that! Lots of buttons to push!)

Many years later, one of my colleagues took to collecting railroad watches. He was frequently at our house because he and my wife performed early music together. One night he brought a few watches along, and she got interested, eventually buying some ladies' pocket watches from him. I had him take my old Omega to the watchmaker who was his mentor for servicing. Meanwhile, my wife had started buying a few more watches online. Eventually we went to see the watchmaker and took him my parents' watches for servicing. We looked at some of his pocket watches, and, urged on by my wife, I wound up walking out of the shop with a Hamilton 992B and an Illinois 60-hour "Sangamo Special."

I knew very little about Illinois, but I recognized the 'Sangamo' name from electronic components made by an Illinois spin-off, Sangamo Electric. I'd used Sangamo capacitors in various projects. We both started studying watches more and buying more, including not a few Illinois pocket watches.

I wasn't buying wristwatches, other than an occasional Hamilton bargain (my target price, $35). But one day I noticed an Illinois wristwatch with an odd-shaped case and a micrometric regulator. I'd seen plenty of those on pocket watches but never one on a wristwatch before. I was intrigued and wound up buying my first Illinois 'Mate.' Already beginning to be hooked, I picked up a few more Illinois watches, including a 'Canby' and a 'New Yorker.'

We were visiting the watchmaker frequently by then, as he'd started teaching me as well. One day he showed us Fred Friedberg's book on Illinois wristwatches. My wife noticed I was interested and gave me a copy for Christmas that year. We both started studying it heavily.

One night, scanning auctions, I noticed a solid-gold Illinois watch. It wasn't spectacular looking, but I eventually recognized it as a 'No. 650.' I followed the auction for several days, and then I decided to 'poke' it to see whether the bid would go up. It didn't; I was suddenly the high bidder on a rare Illinois. I fretted about this as the last day of the auction came and I was still on top. I was sure someone would come in at the last minute and outbid me. As the time wound down, I was shouting, 'Come on, snipers, save me from myself!' But no sniper came, and suddenly I found myself buying my first exotic Illinois. After we got over the shock, we readjusted our goals and accepted that we'd entered the Illinois club. The seller put me in contact with a serious Illinois collector who had advised him, and for the first time we had another Illinois wristwatch collector to talk to.

Maybe having a 'serious' watch pushed us over the edge into Illinois collecting. I still prowl for bargains. But I'm now also always on the lookout for parts movements and spare dials. Studying watches works on you in strange ways. You start to think, after you've bought a green 'Marquis' and then a white one, maybe a two-tone would be nice, even if that dial in the picture is all wrong. Dials can be found, eventually. And a 'serious' watch tends to get its way about other things; not only did the 'No. 650' want a new balance staff and a better dial, it eventually decided it wanted a 'No. 250' for a companion.

I still collect a Hamilton now and then, and an occasional Elgin, though most from later periods. But I don't think their watches from the period of Illinois' greatest productivity are nearly as creative in design. Could there be anything better than a 'Ritz'? (Yes, a 'Ritz' in its original boxes.)

I'm lucky my wife is also an Illinois collector, though she mostly concentrates on ladies' watches. (A 'Cushion' and a 'Wentworth' did just migrate into one of her folders, so I guess I'll need to find another 'Wentworth.') At least she understands the disease. Another collector has brought us into contact with a lot of interesting people on the watch forums. So, we keep looking together. There's always another one out there! —*Jim Mason*

See listing for **Ace**

Medalist, yellow gold-filled

Wembley, white gold-filled

Medalist / Wembley

Official Names = Medalist and Wembley (derived from Illinois advertisements and Illinois Sales and Material Catalogs)
Secondary Name = None
Formerly Known As = None
Time Period = Moderne
Case Variations/Rarity = ◷◷ WGF/P
◷◷◷◷◷◷ YGF/P
◷◷◷◷◷◷◷ WGF/Custom Bezel, WGF/E
Case Durability = ◷ YGF
◷◷ WGF
Material = 14K GF
Bezel = Plain
Sides = Plain
Lugs = Plain
Lug Size = 16mm
Springbar = Male
Casemaker = Fahys
Case Closure = 3-part Snap-On Bezel and Back
Case Number = 193
Case Shape = Rectangular
Case Back = Curved
Dimensions = 37 x 24mm
Movement Size = 12/0
Movement Grade/Jewels = 207/17
Seconds at = 6
Dial Numbers = 8164, 8733
Dial = Silver Finish, Butler Center
Dial Opening = Rectangular
Dial Variations/Rarity = ◷◷ Silver Finish, Luminous Numerals
◷◷◷ Silver Finish, Butler Center, Luminous Numerals
◷◷◷◷◷◷ Silver Finish, Black Numerals; Silver Finish, Etched Raised Numerals
Numerals = Painted, Luminous
Hands = Luminous, Steel
Cased in Factory = Yes
Unique Case Design = Yes
Unique Dial Design = No
Introduction Date = 1929 (Medalist); 1931 (Wembley)
Retail Price New = $60.00
Collectibility = ◷◷◷◷
Advertisements = Yes
Marketing Themes = "Beautiful in its simplicity"
"Has long been a favorite"
"A handsome combination watch and matched bracelet" (Wembley)

Illinois released its first Illinois 207 grade movement in a Medalist case and featured that model in the 1929–30 Illinois Factory Catalog, where it was described as follows: "The curved back, which fits the wearer's wrist snugly, is a very desirable feature of the Medalist made possible by the thinness of the movement. The second hand, another feature of this new watch which goes to make it such a remarkable small timepiece, is further evidence that in the Medalist, Illinois has set a new standard in the manufacture of a fine 12/0 size watch.

More of its attributes are singled out for attention: "The case of the Illinois Medalist is beautiful in its simplicity. A distinctly modern note is struck in the plain bezel, and in the attractively cut border in relief whose polished surface contrasts with the dull white gold finish of the case..." [Of course, they meant white gold-filled finish.]

The Medalist model was advertised by Illinois in the November 2, 1929 issue of *Collier's* and in 1930 appeared in various jobbers' catalogs, including those of A. C. Becken and A. G. Schwab. The L. & C. Mayers 1931 catalog described the Medalist as "Always a favorite of watch buyers who demand style and accuracy. Plain design, curved back to fit the wrist."

The New Illinois 12/0 Size Rectangular Movement Sets The Pace In American Watch Design.

In this new 12/0 size rectangular 17 jewel men's strap watch, the Medalist, Illinois again sets the pace in American watch design.

The Illinois 12/0 is a triumph of watchmaking, and is a worthy tribute to the engineering skill of Illinois technicians. The construction of this rectangular movement permits the use of very large and sturdy moving parts for a watch of this small size. To both the jeweler and the consumer this is a vital feature, for it is now possible to secure a really fine men's strap watch in the popular 12/0 size without sacrificing durability and accuracy.

Its extreme thinness is another virtue of the new rectangular movement. Here again is a distinct achievement of the technical skill of Illinois engineers. The curved back, which fits the wearer's wrist snugly, is a very desirable feature of the Medalist made possible by the thinness of the movement. The second hand, another feature of this new watch which goes to make it such a remarkable small timepiece, is further evidence that in the Medalist, Illinois has set a new standard in the manufacture of a fine 12/0 size watch.

The MEDALIST

Consumer price, $60.00

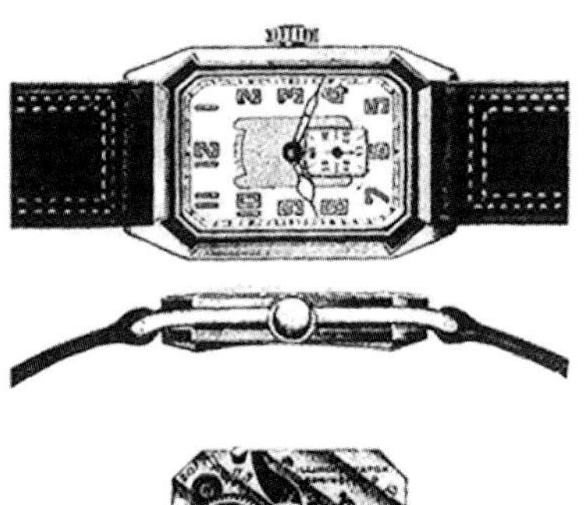

SPECIFICATIONS

12/0 size, 17 ruby and sapphire jewels, raised settings; compensating balance, double roller escapement; sapphire roller and pallet jewels; polished steel escape wheel; Breguet hairspring; recoil click; black enamel lettering.

The case of the Illinois Medalist is beautiful in its simplicity. A distinctly modern note is struck in the plain bezel, and in the attractively cut border in relief whose polished surface contrasts with the dull white gold finish of the case.

Sixty years of expert Illinois craftmanship have contributed to the production of this small rectangular movement, which has the accuracy and dependability of every Illinois watch. It is a marvel of precision and durability - - a fine rectangular 12/0 that will stand real wrist watch usage.

The Medalist in 14K filled white gold case, with full luminous figure dial. Consumer price $60.00

Prices quoted are consumer prices. For cost to dealer see current Illinois Price List.

A. G. Schwab & Sons catalog, 1930

When the watch was equipped with a dial with etched raised gold numerals, Illinois called this model a "Wembley." Collectors used to consider the Medalist/Wembley a common watch, especially in white gold-filled. In recent years, however, examples of the Medalist have become increasingly difficult to find. Only four yellow gold-filled versions of the Medalist are known to exist. Both the white gold-filled and yellow gold-filled cases are prone to severe corner bezel and case back wear, so the added challenge is to find one in good condition.

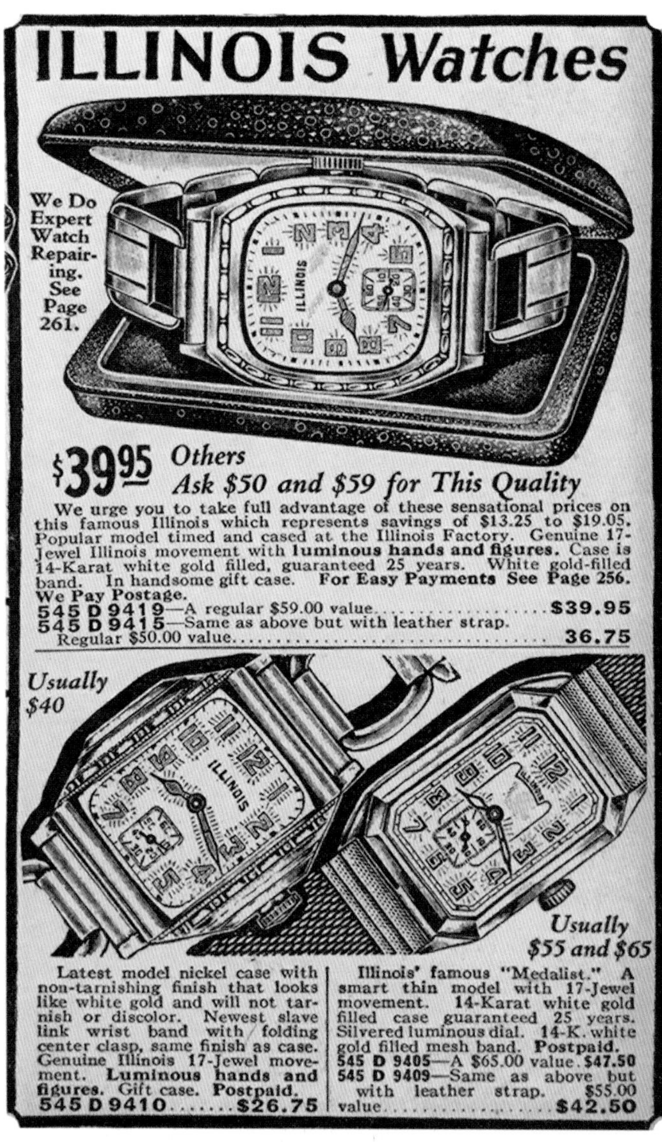

Montgomery Ward catalog, 1932–1933, shows a half-price Medalist (right). Note that the watch on the left may be a Senator model.

Medalist with an Adonis metal watch attachment. (See "Attachments" section of Chapter 8.)

Fahys produced most of the Medalist cases. However, two examples of this model exist in cases made by Wadsworth: one has a continuous edge around the bezel instead of the normal cut border, while the other has a remarkable engraved bezel. One Medalist includes a custom dial with the 12 o'clock at the 3 position, and another custom dial substitutes Roman numerals for Arabic ones. (See Chapter 7.)

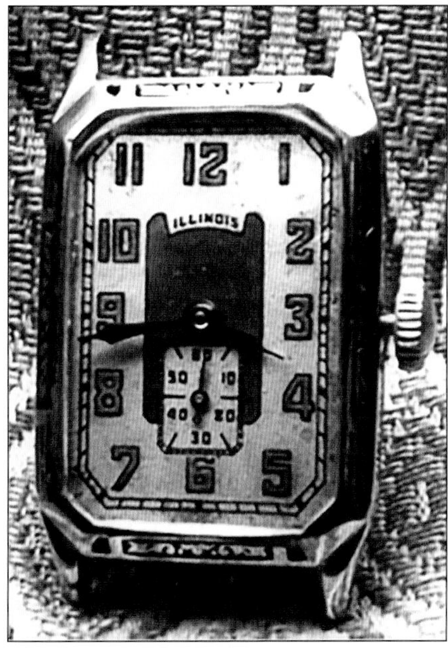

A rare, perhaps sample Medalist case by Wadsworth with an engraved bezel

Bezel for the Medalist prototype case by Wadsworth

Medalist inside case back

Medalist, yellow gold-filled prototype case

Metropolitan two-tone, gold-filled

METROPOLITAN

Official Name = Metropolitan (derived from the 1932 Illinois Sales Catalog)
Secondary Name = None
Formerly Known As = None
Time Period = Moderne
Case Variations/Rarity = 🕐🕐🕐🕐🕐 TT/TT Bezel
Case Durability = 🕐🕐🕐
Material = 14K GF
Bezel = Plain (with Grooves)
Sides = Engraved
Lugs = Plain
Lug Size = 16mm
Springbar = Male
Casemaker = Keystone
Case Closure = 3-Part Snap-On Bezel and Back
Case Number = 198
Case Shape = Cushion
Case Back = Flat
Dimensions = 35 x 29mm
Movement Size = 6/0
Movement Grades/Jewels = 903/15, 605/15
Seconds at = 6
Dial Number = 8050
Dials = Silver Finish, Sparkle Finish
Dial Opening = Tonneau
Dial Variations/Rarity = 🕐🕐 Silver Finish, Luminous Numerals
🕐🕐🕐🕐 Sparkle Finish, Luminous Numerals
🕐🕐🕐🕐🕐 Silver Finish, Black Numerals; Sparkle Finish, Luminous Drop-Shadow Numerals
Numerals = Painted, Luminous
Hands = Steel
Cased in Factory = Yes
Unique Case Design = Yes
Unique Dial Design = Yes
Introduction Date = 1932
Retail Price New = $40.00
Collectibility = 🕐🕐🕐🕐
Advertisements = No
Marketing Theme = Unknown

The Metropolitan model is very rare and quite popular with collectors. The Metropolitan and the Chesterfield are the only two Illinois men's wristwatches produced solely with two-tone bezels. The Metropolitan displays two sets of three stylish grooves on the top and bottom of its bezel, and these grooves are filled with yellow gold. The center of the case is yellow gold-filled. Because it has both a two-tone bezel and a yellow gold-filled center, the Metropolitan is, in effect, a double two-tone watch.

Interestingly, the center section and case back of the Metropolitan are identical to the center section and case back of the Illinois Townsman/Puritan model. Therefore, they can be interchanged; but the bezels cannot be.

The Metropolitan apparently appeared only in the Spring 1932 Illinois Sales Catalog and in an April 1, 1932 Illinois Price List. Strangely enough, we have not found it shown in any jobbers' catalogs or magazine advertisements that we have thus far located.

METROPOLITAN—15 jewels, 6/0 size, 14k filled two-tone white and natural gold **$40.00**

Illinois Sales Catalog, Spring 1932

The Metropolitan and the Derby share the same dial face, but the dial shapes are not identical owing to the different configurations of their respective dial plates. Both models appear on the same page in the Spring 1932 Illinois Sales Catalog, sporting the same dial. (The Derby had already been presented in the 1931–32 catalog.)

The Derby dial plate has cut corners, and the Metropolitan dial plate has rounded corners. Nonetheless, collectors have been known to try to put a Derby dial into a Metropolitan case. The pictures below show how a Derby dial has been forced into a Metropolitan case in one instance, while the proper dial has been installed in the other. (Thanks to Ed Kulha for this discovery and for the photos and accompanying commentary.)

Cut corner dial has considerable interference with ridge of Metropolitan case center section. The rounded dial conforms precisely to the Metropolitan case center section.

Rounded dial (top) and cut-corner dial (bottom) give the same appearance with the Metropolitan's bezel on.

The shared dial design and interchangeable case parts of the Metropolitan and the Derby were undoubtedly Depression-inspired engineering economies. The interchangeable case parts of the Metropolitan and Townsman/Puritan are another such economy. In addition, Hamilton management at that time encouraged the use of interchangeable movement parts wherever possible, even between its Illinois and Hamilton divisions.

From the evidence it would appear that the Metropolitan was perhaps conceived as an ultra-economy effort, making use of "spare parts," as it were: back and midcase from the Townsman, dial from the Derby and just a new bezel. Moreover, it was granted only a 15-jewel movement. What is puzzling is why the Metropolitan was not included in the 1933 catalog and widely distributed. The brilliant design of its bezel made it stand out—there was nothing like it.

The Metropolitan's unique case design makes it a highly desirable model, especially when it equipped with a sparkle finish dial with drop-shadow numerals. The one drawback to this model is that the bezel corners are prone to some case wear, although it is still possible to find the case in superb condition.

Military Crown at 12

See listing for **"D-D" Utility**

New Yorker / Manhattan / Yorktown / Fifth Avenue / Richmond 6/0

Official Names = New Yorker, Manhattan and Yorktown (derived from Illinois advertisements and Illinois Sales and Material Catalogs)
Secondary Names = Fifth Avenue (derived from Illinois internal documentation and L. & C. Mayers 1933 catalog) Richmond 6/0 (derived from Oskamp Nolting 1932 catalog)
Formerly Known As = None
Time Period = Deco
Case Variations/Rarity = 🕒🕒 WGF/P, WGF/E, YGF/P
🕒🕒🕒🕒 YGF/E
Case Durability = 🕒🕒🕒
Material = 14K GF
Bezel = Plain, Engraved
Sides = Engraved
Lugs = Plain
Lug Size = 16mm
Springbar = Male
Casemaker = Wadsworth
Case Closure = 3-Part Snap-On Bezel and Back
Case Number = 162, No Number
Case Shape = Rectangular
Case Back = Flat
Dimensions = 34 x 28mm
Movement Size = 6/0
Movement Grades/Jewels = 905/17, 909/21, 601/21, 607/17, 605/15 (Yorktown only)
Seconds at = 6, 9
Dial Numbers = 8072, 8152, 8203, 8207, 8710
Dials = Silver Finish, Butler Center
Dial Opening = Rectangular
Dial Variations/Rarity = 🕒🕒 Silver Finish, Luminous Numerals
🕒🕒🕒 Silver Finish, Butler Center
🕒🕒🕒🕒🕒 Silver Finish, Black Numerals; Silver Finish, Two-Tone Gold, Butler Center, Luminous Numerals
🕒🕒🕒🕒🕒🕒🕒 Etched Raised Numerals
Numerals = Painted, Luminous
Hands = Luminous
Cased in Factory = Yes
Unique Case Design = Yes
Unique Dial Design = Yes

New Yorker, white gold-filled

New Yorker, yellow gold-filled

Yorktown, white gold-filled

Introduction Date = 1929 (New Yorker); 1930 (Manhattan); 1931 (Fifth Avenue); 1931 (Richmond 6/0); 1932 Yorktown)
Retail Price New = $50.00 (17J), $75.00 (21J)
Collectibility = 🕓🕓🕓🕓
Advertisements = Yes
Marketing Themes = "The most popular 21 jewel strap watch"
"Simplicity in design and richness in appearance"
"An increasingly popular Illinois strap watch"
"Smartly modern"
"A most harmonious watch and flexible metal band"

"THE NEW YORKER—America's Best Selling Strap Watch" was the claim made by the Illinois Watch Company in December 1929. Illinois admitted that "We do not have sales statistics on all of the strap watches sold in the United States, but we DO have the figures on the ILLINOIS NEW YORKER—as a result we unhesitatingly entitle it 'America's Best Selling Strap Watch.'"

Thus begins the announcement in the December 1929 issue of the company's publication called the *Illinois Watch Motor Barrel.*

To help jewelers capitalize on the tremendous popularity of the New Yorker, Illinois offered them "four attractive advertising mats" for the counters of their display cases. The advertising accompanying the announcement was presented in four panels, each bearing an image of the New Yorker and each with text focusing on a different attribute of the model. These panels represented the "four attractive mats."

The ILLINOIS WATCH *Motor Barrel*

The *New Yorker*-America's Best Selling Strap Watch

WE do not have sales statistics on all of the strap watches sold in the United States, but we DO have the figures on the ILLINOIS *New Yorker*—and as a result we unhesitatingly entitle it "America's Best Selling Strap Watch."

To help you capitalize on the tremendous popularity of the *New Yorker*, we offer you these four attractive mats—free. Order any or all of them on the coupon on Page Seven.

The New Yorker by ILLINOIS

Stop in! Let us show you the New Yorker—the Illinois strap watch which has become so popular within the last few months.

Smartly modern, and with its accurate 17 jewel movement the New Yorker merits the recognition it has received.

Priced Fifty Dollars

DEALER'S NAME HERE

Mat No. 2904

The New Yorker by ILLINOIS

A masculine strap watch for men who prefer the newer designs. With its fine Illinois 17 jewel movement the New Yorker is a genuine timekeeper.

We offer this strap watch in a variety of case designs, and at terms that will be convenient for you.

Priced Fifty Dollars

DEALER'S NAME HERE

Mat No. 2906

The New Yorker by ILLINOIS

There is a New Yorker to suit every man's strap watch taste.

We offer this popular Illinois model in white or natural gold—with plain or engraved case. And, you are assured of a fine time keeper in the New Yorker as it contains the famous Illinois 17 jewel movement.

Priced Fifty Dollars

DEALER'S NAME HERE

Mat No. 2907

The New Yorker by ILLINOIS

In accord with the modern trend this 17 jewel Illinois strap watch is also an accurate timekeeper

We invite your inspection of the New Yorker—see its variety of case designs. Let us explain our convenient payment plan to you.

Priced Fifty Dollars

DEALER'S NAME HERE

Mat No. 2905

Page FIVE

Full-page announcement in the *Illinois Watch Motor Barrel*, December 1929

"Stop in!" one message urged. "Let us show you the New Yorker—the Illinois strap watch which has become so popular within the last few months. Smartly modern, and with its accurate 17 jewel movement, the New Yorker merits the recognition it has received."

Another proclaimed: "A masculine strap watch for men who prefer the newer designs. With its fine Illinois 17 jewel movement, the New Yorker is a genuine timekeeper. We offer this strap watch in a variety of case designs and at terms that will be convenient for you.

Yet another pointed out: "There is a New Yorker to suit every man's strap watch tastes. We offer this popular Illinois model in white or natural gold—with plain or engraved case. And, you are assured of a fine time keeper in the New Yorker as it contains the famous Illinois 17 jewel movement.

And a message to wrap things up: "In accord with the modern trend, the 17 jewel Illinois strap watch is also an accurate timekeeper. We invite your inspection of the New Yorker—see its variety of case designs. Let us explain our convenient payment plan to you. Price $50.00."

The New Yorker was introduced in the 1929–30 Illinois Sales Catalog. Illinois featured that model in national magazines such as the *Saturday Evening Post*, *Collier's* and others, and jewelers sometimes featured it in their newspaper advertisements.

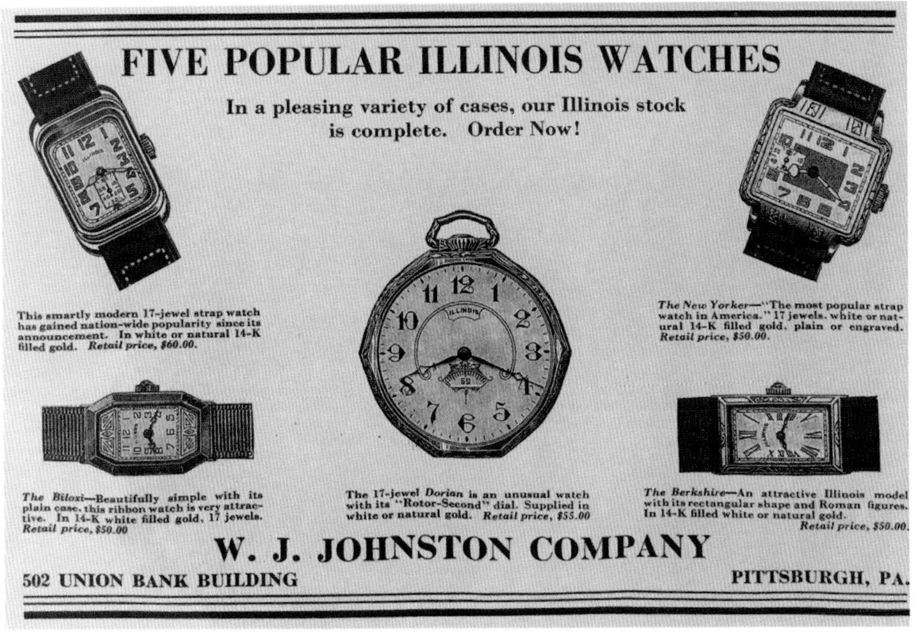

W. J. Johnston Company advertisement in the *Keystone*, January 1930

Issuing the New Yorker with a metal band, the 1930–31 Illinois Sales Catalog announced the "new" model: "The Manhattan is a most harmonious combination of watch and flexible metal band, beautifully presented in 14K white or natural filled gold. Suggested consumer price, 21 jewels, $85.00. Suggested consumer price, 17 jewels, $55.00." The 1931 L. & C. Mayers catalog praised the Manhattan "A smart style, neatly engraved bezel, plain back. Stylish flexible attachment, center catch adjustable to wrist size."

The New Yorker and its variants are a favorite of Illinois collectors and non-Illinois collectors alike. A truly unique design, it conformed nicely to the wrist. Its 9 o'clock subsidiary second configuration with an engraved deco case and butler center dial makes for a highly attractive look. No wonder the New Yorker remains popular nearly ninety years after its introduction.

The cases are subject to wear on the inside corners of the bezel and on the corners of the case back. It came with a 6/0 size movement in either 17 or 21 jewels.

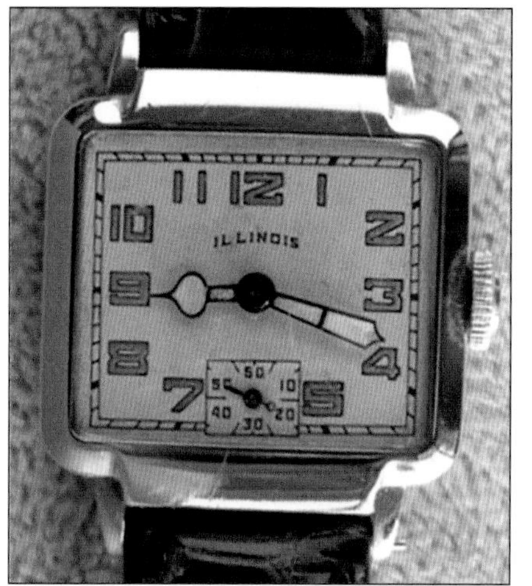

New Yorker, white gold-filled

In its advertisements, the Illinois Watch Company frequently referred to the Manhattan as a New Yorker and vice versa. For years collectors thought that the confusion existed within the Illinois Marketing Department. Collectors called the watch a New Yorker if it had subsidiary seconds at 9 and a Manhattan if the subsidiary seconds existed at 6. Based on further research, however, it is now clear that a New Yorker and Manhattan are identical, whether seconds are at 6 or 9; the only distinguishing feature was the band. If it had an original metal flexible expansion band Illinois called it a Manhattan; otherwise, they identified it as a New Yorker.

New Yorker, yellow gold-filled

Manhattan, with its original Hadley metal attachment

Manhattan, showing more of original Hadley metal attachment

New Yorker side view. Note that the large glass crystal prevents wear on the inside corners of the bezel.

If the watch had a white gold-filled plain or engraved bezel case, a 21-jewel movement and a leather strap, it was also called a "Fifth Avenue." The Fifth Avenue is on the List of Factory Cased Illinois Watches.

THE FIFTH AVENUE—BY ILLINOIS

BW1658 14 Kt. White Gold Filled (plain as shown): 21 Jewels.................................. $60.00
BW1659 14 Kt. White Gold Filled (neatly engraved): 21 Jewels................................. 60.00

Retail Price $75.00

The most popular 21 jewel strap watch made in America. This thin model Wadsworth case, simple in design and rich in appearance places it in a class of its own in the field of fine watches. 14 Kt. White Gold Filled, satin finish throughout. Fitted with the famous 6/0 size Illinois 21 jewel thin model movement. Full radium dial and hands. Detachable fine leather strap; buckle same quality as case. Handsome presentation box.

L. & C. Mayers catalog, 1933

The names Fifth Avenue, Manhattan, New Yorker, and Yorktown all express a link to New York City, New York. Although these models were originally sold as men's watches, today they have high collector and retail appeal to both sexes and are easily worn by either. In 1929, Illinois advertised the New Yorker as its best-selling strap watch. Perhaps that is why the company produced so many variations of it.

If the model came in a yellow gold-filled engraved case with a gold-filled bracelet to match and had a 17-jewel movement and an etched gold numeral dial with subsidiary seconds at 6, Illinois apparently called it a Richmond 6/0. (It, too, has a New York City connection, as Staten Island is in Richmond County.)

ILLINOIS

No. 12739.. $55.00
RICHMOND—6/0 Size, 17-Jewel Movement. Etched Gold Numerals. 14k Yellow Gold Filled Case. Gold Filled Bracelet to Match.

Oskamp Nolting catalog, 1932

The Yorktown, New Yorker, New Yorker Enamel, Manhattan, and Fifth Avenue all shared case Model Number 162. The Yorktown, however, can be distinguished from its three cousins as it came only with a silver finish dial with bold black painted numerals and with subsidiary seconds at 6. The New Yorker and Manhattan dials could have subsidiary seconds at 6 or 9.

The Yorktown model appeared in only one advertisement, the Spring 1932 Illinois Sales Catalog (also the only known advertisement for the ultra-rare Metropolitan model). This variant made the last Illinois Factory catalog appearance of what had been one of the company's most popular watch designs. Unlike the New Yorker and its other variants, the Yorktown was a bargain model, equipped with just a 15-jewel movement and priced at a mere $37.50. None of the other variants had been offered with a movement of fewer than 17 jewels, and there had been a choice of plain or engraved cases. The one advertisement for the Yorktown showed only a plain case and did not mention that an engraved one was offered, but at least there was still a choice of white gold-filled or yellow.

The Yorktown looks most striking in a white gold-filled case with an excellent original white dial and black painted numerals. In general, white dials with black numerals were cased in white Illinois cases. Hamilton advertised a wide variety of white Illinois dials with black numerals for the replacement market. However, because Hamilton produced these aftermarket Lancaster dials only on an as-needed basis, collectors have difficulty locating them now.

YORKTOWN—15 jewels, 6/0 size, 14k filled white or natural gold.....$37.50

Illinois Sales Catalog, Spring 1932

THE ILLINOIS

An American Watch As American As Its Name

YORKTOWN

$37.50

15 JEWELS

14K FILLED GOLD

Yorktown original price card

Some collectors believe that the Manhattan, New Yorker and possibly Yorktown came in green gold-filled cases. However, no documentation, including any advertisement or Illinois Factory Catalog, supports that claim.

Several yellow gold-filled New Yorkers have been found without a case model number. They are signed only "Wadsworth," and "Illinois" is not mentioned. There are no case numbers stamped on these variants. These could be sample cases before Illinois secured its exclusive design from the case manufacturer or before Illinois signed an exclusive contract for the rights to this model. One of the cases contains a patent number, so perhaps Illinois did not sign a contract for the New Yorker case until the Wadsworth patent was issued.

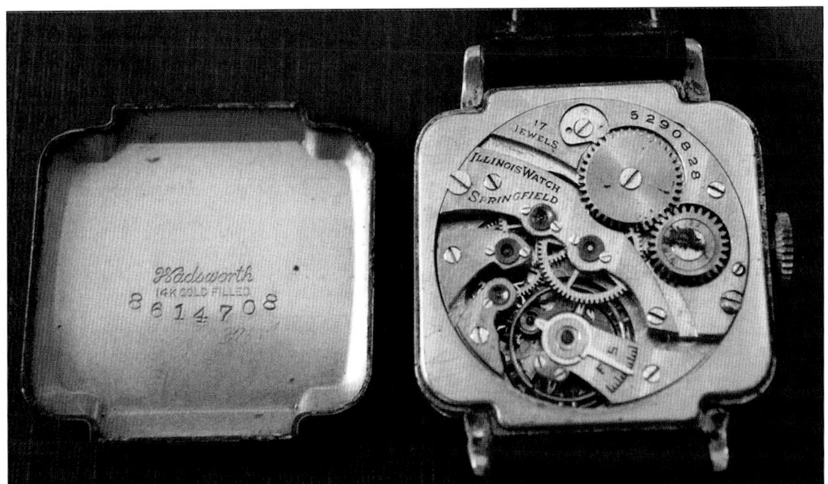

New Yorker inside case back and center section. Note there is no case Model No., no "Illinois" signed name and no serial numbers on the center section of the case.

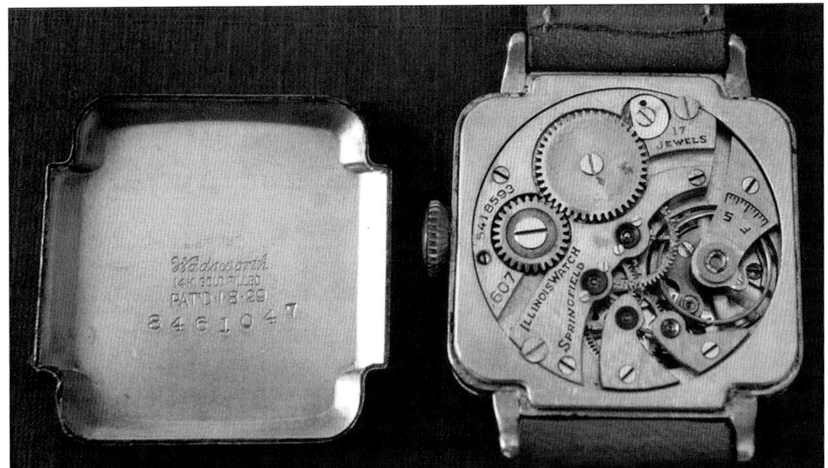

New Yorker inside case back and center section. Note there is no case Model No., no "Illinois" signed name and no serial numbers on the center section of the case. However, its patent date, January 8, 1929, is present.

The New Yorker dial is an exception to the rule that rounded cornered cases have outer minutes registers with rounded corners; New Yorker dials have slightly rounded corners but minutes registers with square corners. No New Yorker model has been seen with etched, raised numerals using Dial No. 8207. It is shown below.

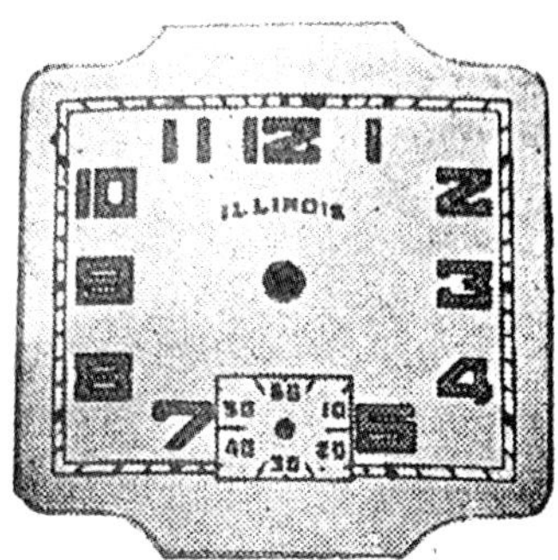

6/0 SIZE. SILVER FINISH

No. 8203
New Yorker. Manhattan.
Luminous figures.

No. 8207
Etched raised figures.

No. 8152
Bit at 9.
Luminous figures.
Models 1-2-3

C. & E. Marshall catalog, 1933

New Yorker inside case back

End of the outer cardboard box for a New Yorker

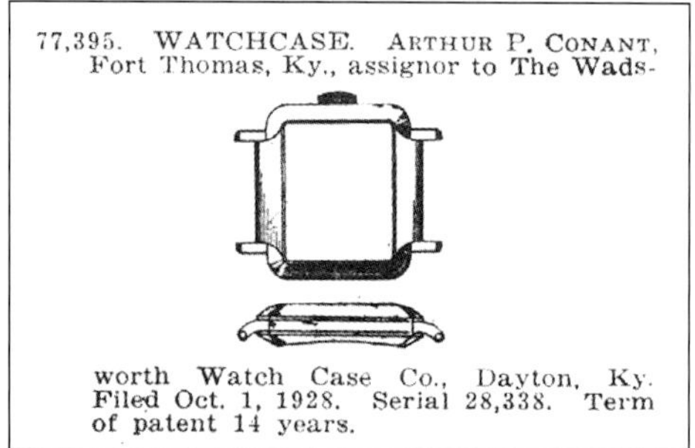
77,395. WATCHCASE. Arthur P. Conant, Fort Thomas, Ky., assignor to The Wadsworth Watch Case Co., Dayton, Ky. Filed Oct. 1, 1928. Serial 28,338. Term of patent 14 years.

Wadsworth case patent

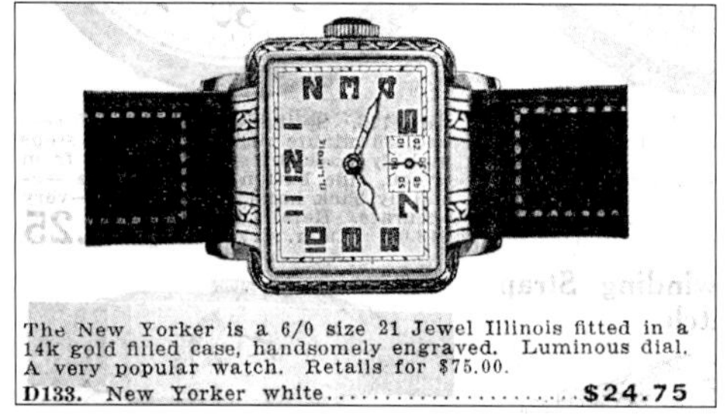
The New Yorker is a 6/0 size 21 Jewel Illinois fitted in a 14k gold filled case, handsomely engraved. Luminous dial. A very popular watch. Retails for $75.00.
D133. New Yorker white........................$24.75

The 1932–33 Holsman's Jewelry Drummer catalog offered the New Yorker at a Depression price of $24.75 (wholesale).

WHY I COLLECT ILLINOIS

I collect Illinois watches for several reasons, here are some that come to mind:

1. The designs are as varied as they are beautiful. In an era dominated by simple round or simple geometric designs, Illinois watches broke the mold with daring styles such as the Telephone Dial, the Chieftain, the Ritz, and of course the Piccadilly. The folks at the Illinois Watch Company obviously took risks with such designs, which were often ahead of their time. Collecting most (all would be almost impossible) is the foundation of a challenging hobby that you can wear on your wrist.
2. Many designs have several variations, such as different colored cases, engravings, dial style and numbering, etc. You could easily build a collection around a particular model, such as the New Yorker, and collect dozens of variations, some common, and some very rare. There are many models that share this characteristic, including custom features such as personalized dials.
3. There are many interesting watches at low as well as higher price points. Models such as the Ace, Square, and the Cushion case are quite striking and can be had for very reasonable prices.
4. Illinois watches are a technology time capsule—the "iPod" of their times, so to speak. Most Illinois wristwatches were made in a very short time period. Studying their designs allows one to gain a better understanding of what was considered popular style in the 1920s and early 1930s. It's also amazing that a tiny mechanical device made almost one hundred years ago still operates so well today. *—Nick Melillo*

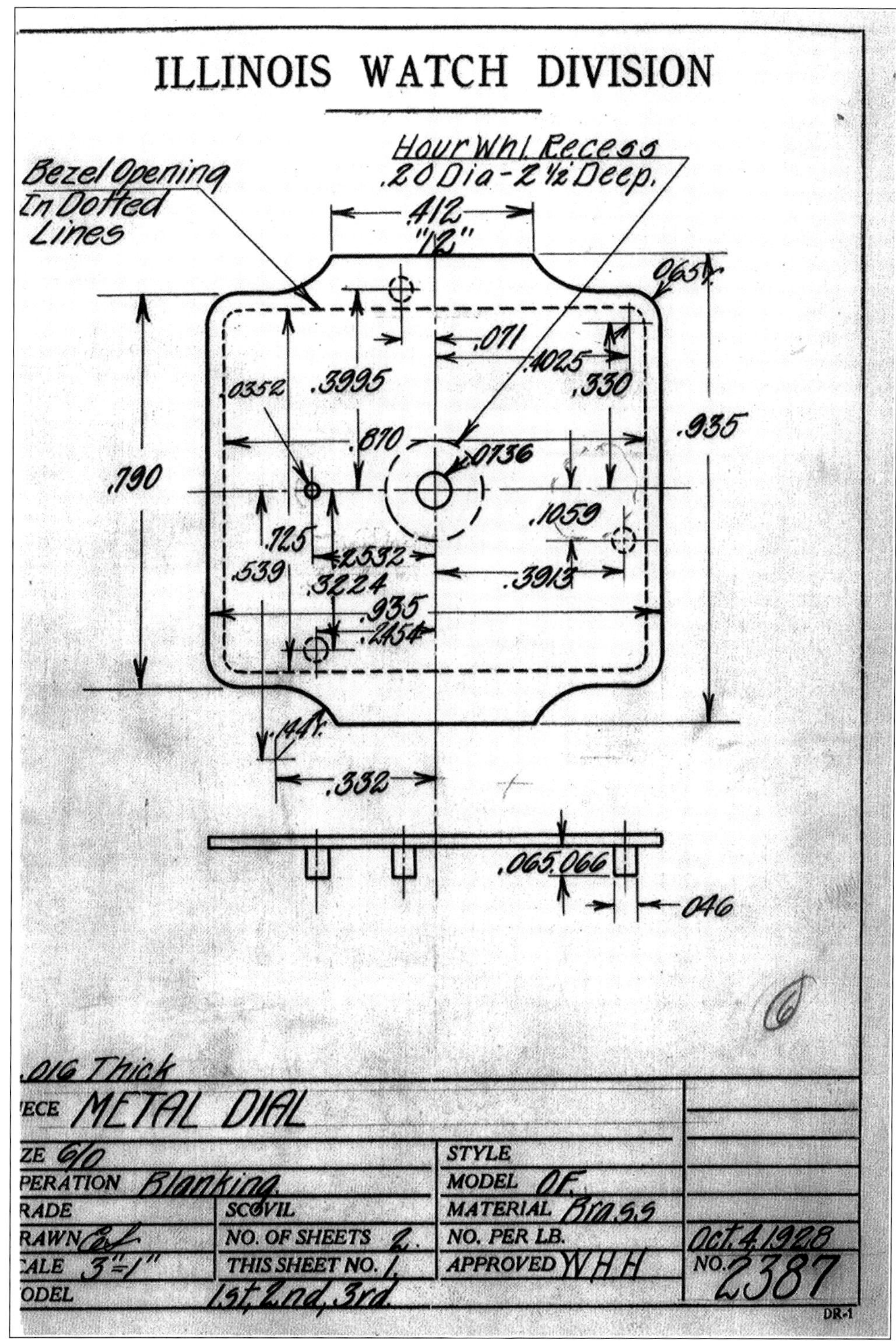

Blueprint dial blank drawing of a New Yorker dial, dated Oct. 4, 1928

New Yorker Enamel, white gold-filled

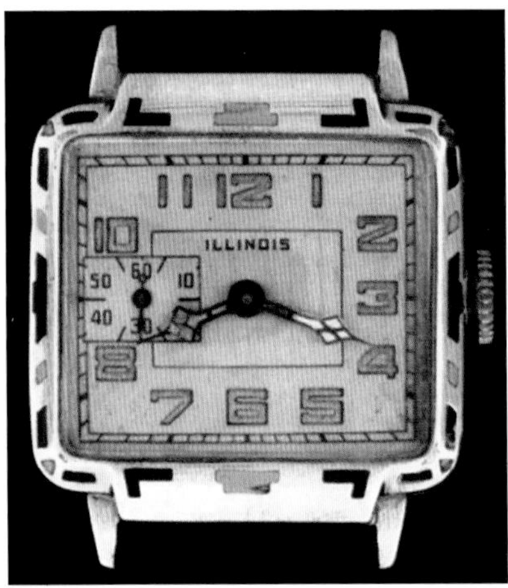

New Yorker Enamel, yellow gold-filled

New Yorker Enamel / New Yorker

Official Name = Unknown
Secondary Name = New Yorker Enamel (derived from collector usage to distinguish this model from other Illinois New Yorker models)
Formerly Known As = None
Time Period = Deco
Case Variations/Rarity = 🕒🕒🕒🕒🕒🕒 WGF/Black Enamel, YGF/Green and Black Enamel
Case Durability = 🕒🕒🕒
Material = 14K GF
Bezel = Enamel
Sides = Engraved
Lugs = Plain
Lug Size = 16mm
Springbar = Male
Casemaker = Wadsworth
Case Closure = 3-Part Snap-On Bezel and Back
Case Number = 162
Case Shape = Rectangular
Case Back = Flat
Dimensions = 34 x 28mm
Movement Size = 6/0
Movement Grades/Jewels = 905/17, 909/21
Seconds at = 6
Dial Numbers = 8072, 8152, 8710
Dials = Silver Finish, Butler Center
Dial Opening = Rectangular
Dial Variations/Rarity = 🕒🕒 Silver Finish, Luminous Numerals
🕒🕒🕒 Silver Finish, Butler Center
🕒🕒🕒🕒🕒 Silver Finish, Black Numerals; Silver Finish, Two-Tone Gold, Butler Center, Luminous Numerals
Numerals = Painted, Luminous
Hands = Luminous
Cased in Factory = Yes
Unique Case Design = Yes
Unique Dial Design = Yes
Introduction Date = 1929
Retail Price New = Unknown
Collectibility = 🕒🕒🕒🕒
Advertisements = No
Marketing Theme = Unknown

This rare model never appeared in any Illinois advertisement or sales catalog, nor did it appear in any known jobbers' catalogs. It is possible that these were special-order watches. The New Yorker Enamel in the white gold-filled case is slightly less popular than the one in the yellow gold-filled case, even though the white one is rarer. Both versions are immensely popular and are much sought after. The yellow gold-filled New Yorker Enamel with a two-tone gold dial and gold butler center is incredibly striking and commands the highest price.

All New Yorker Enamel models came only with subsidiary seconds at 9. The white gold-filled model is sometimes referred to as the "Locks" model, because the design of the black enamel around the bezel resembles locks. The yellow gold-filled model is sometimes referred to as the "Southwestern" model, because the green and black inlaid enamel motif is Southwestern in style.[2] Both versions of the New Yorker Enamel with excellent dials are some of the most spectacular and unique Illinois men's wristwatches. These watches represent Illinois' bold and daring styling at its best.

WHY I COLLECT ILLINOIS

I often ask myself how I got interested in collecting Illinois wristwatches. I started collecting clocks and favored the Vienna regulator types. After a few years, the lady of the house said, "No more. This house looks like a clock shop.

I became a member of the NAWCC in 1995 and became interested in wristwatches. The *Bulletins* were great reading. The April 1996 *Bulletin* with the Illinois New Yorker, with a green and black enamel bezel, on the cover caught my attention. After reading Phil Harnage's extensive article on Illinois watches, I was hooked. I attended the NAWCC National Mart that was held in Atlanta in 1996 and purchased a gold Illinois Rockliffe which is still in my collection. Phil Harnage said that the more you look, the more you find. After twenty years of searching, I have almost a complete collection of Illinois watches. I have upgraded each watch several times. I attend at least five NAWCC Marts every year to look for rare Illinois watches and to sell my extras.

I am aware that one day I will have to let my collection go, but not yet. Collecting is too much fun, and, who knows, there may be a rare one right around the corner.

—*Gene Livingston*

Notched Lug, yellow gold

Notched Lug, sterling silver

Notched Lug

Official Name = Unknown
Secondary Name = Notched Lug (derived from Illinois wristwatch collectors' usage)
Formerly Known As = None
Time Period = Transitional
Case Variations/Rarity = ◷◷◷◷◷◷ YG/P
◷◷◷◷◷◷ SS/P
Case Durability = ◷◷◷◷
Material = 14K YG, SS
Bezel = Plain
Sides = Plain
Lugs = Plain
Lug Size = 16mm
Springbar = Male
Casemaker = Wadsworth
Case Closure = 3-Part Snap-On Bezel and Back
Case Number = None
Case Shape = Cushion
Case Back = Flat
Dimensions = 32 x 27mm
Movement Size = 6/0
Movement Grades/Jewels = 903/15, 905/17, 907/19
Seconds at = 6
Dial Numbers = None
Dial = Silver Finish
Dial Opening = Round
Dial Variations/Rarity = ◷◷◷◷◷ Silver Finish, Luminous Numerals
Numerals = Luminous
Hands = Luminous
Cased in Factory = No
Unique Case Design = No
Unique Dial Design = No
Introduction Date = 1923
Retail Price New = Unknown
Collectibility = ◷◷◷◷
Advertisements = Yes
Marketing Theme = "Made for timekeeping purposes—not merely as ornaments"

Surprisingly, the Notched Lug was one of the first four men's wristwatches advertised by the Illinois Watch Company in 1923, along with the Generic Period Canby, Square, and Devon.

The 1923 Illinois advertising brochure read, in part, "Illinois Wrist Watch Movements are high-grade and made for timekeeping purposes—not merely as ornaments. Attractive cases may be selected from stock at your retail jeweler." The advertisement also stated that "Every Illinois watch is fully guaranteed to be perfect in construction and to be a satisfactory timekeeper."

The Notched Lug watch is very rare and highly collectible for several reasons:

- It is solid gold or sterling silver;
- It has an off-set crown that cuts partially and interestingly directly into its top right lug;
- It was the first solid gold men's wristwatch offered for sale by Illinois and only three of these rare models have been sighted to date; and
- Only two in sterling silver are known to exist.

A sixth 6/0 size Notched Lug has been found, this one in a solid gold case with a Waltham dial and movement in it. The Illinois Notched Lugs, shown above, have an "I" for "Illinois" stamped inside the case back. Although some Transitional or Generic cases have a "W" for "Waltham" stamped inside their case backs, this one has the letters "JS." This is an abbreviation for "Jewel Series," some of Waltham's better-grade movements, which include the "Ruby" and "Sapphire" grades.[3] Since this 6/0 size case is Waltham-specific, it is possible that most Illinois 6/0 movements would not fit in it. (Even if they did, the resulting watch would not be correct.)

In the Notched Lug 1923 advertisement, a gentleman in a dress hat, suit and bow tie is shown behind the wheel of an automobile with a wristwatch on his left wrist.

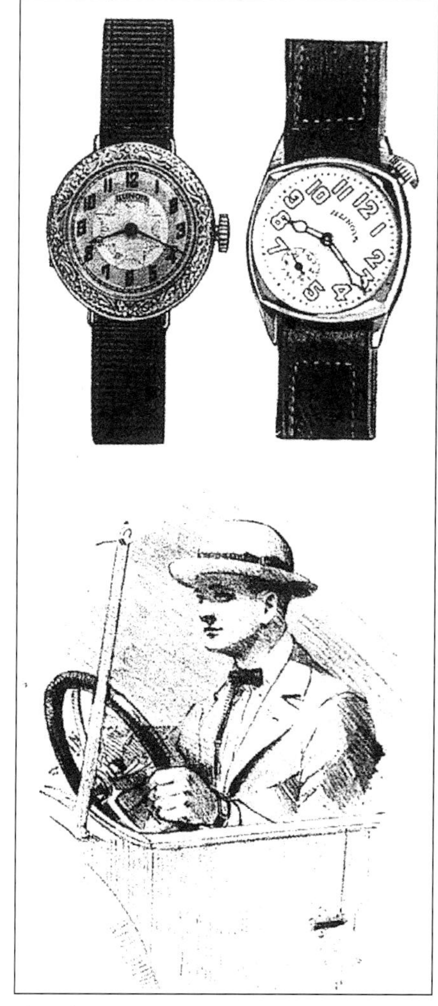

Illinois sales brochure, 1923

Illinois noted in its advertisement that the movements were "Only delivered fitted in cases supplied by jobbers"; therefore, the Notched Lug was not a Factory-Cased model. The advertisement further noted that the "Illustrations simply indicate some of the different styles of cases, made by various manufacturers, for these movements."

No. 250, yellow gold

No. 250, yellow gold

No. 250 / Schmukler

Official Name = Unknown
Secondary Name = No. 250 (derived from its case Model Number usage by Illinois collectors); Schmukler (named after the Illinois jobber J. J. Schmukler & Son that apparently custom ordered this model)
Formerly Known As = None
Time Period = Moderne
Case Variations/Rarity = 🕒🕒🕒🕒🕒🕒 YG/P
Case Durability = 🕒🕒🕒🕒
Material = 14K YG
Bezel = Plain
Sides = Plain
Lugs = Plain
Lug Size = 16mm
Springbar = Male
Casemaker = Keystone
Case Closure = 2-Part Snap-On Bezel and Back
Case Number = 250
Case Shape = Rectangular
Case Back = Flat
Dimensions = 38 x 25mm
Movement Size = 12/0
Movement Grade/Jewels = 207/17
Seconds at = 6
Dial Number = 8198 (same dial was used on a Kenilworth)
Dials = Silver Finish, Sparkle Finish
Dial Opening = Rectangular
Dial Variations/Rarity = 🕒🕒🕒 Silver Finish, Luminous Numerals
🕒🕒🕒🕒 Sparkle Finish, Luminous Numerals; Sparkle Finish, Painted Numerals
🕒🕒🕒🕒🕒 Silver Finish, Black Numerals; Silver Finish, Painted Drop-Shadow; Sparkle Finish, Painted Drop-Shadow
🕒🕒🕒🕒🕒🕒🕒 Silver Finish, Etched Numerals
Numerals = Painted
Hands = Steel
Cased in Factory = Yes
Unique Case Design = No
Unique Dial Design = Yes
Introduction Date = Unknown
Retail Price New = Unknown
Collectibility = 🕒🕒🕒🕒
Advertisements = Yes
Marketing Theme = Unknown

After the manuscript for this book was submitted to the publisher, I discovered that this watch was most likely a special order one for the J. J. Schmukler & Son Company of Canal Street in New York City. This model will therefore be called a "Schmukler." It was too late to remove the references to the "No. 250" in this book. Schmukler evidently supplied the completed watch to Montgomery Ward.

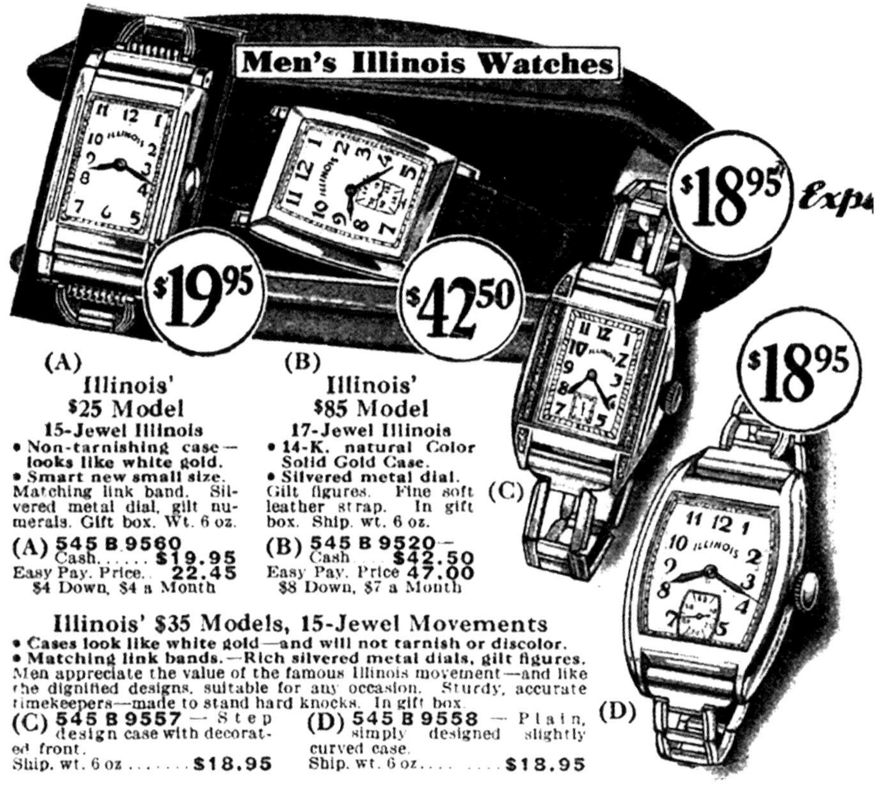

Montgomery Ward 1934 catalog, with Sangamon (top, left), and No. 250 next to it

The Schmukler was a special-order model for J. J. Schmukler & Son, an Illinois jobber from New York City; as so few exist, perhaps very few were produced. Schmukler wanted to have more of these models made. Keystone agreed to make more 14K yellow gold cases for Schmukler. On January 29,1934 Schmukler wrote to Beckwith at Hamilton requesting to have more 12/0 size Illlinois movements produced for the solid gold cases. (See Chapter 5.) Beckwith declined. Thus far, the only known advertisement for this rare model is in a 1934 Montgomery Ward catalog.

No. 250 inside case back

The Schmukler is best described as a hybrid of a Hudson/Ardsley and a Kenilworth/Gallahad. Seen from directly above, the Schmukler resembles a thinner version of a Kenilworth/Gallahad. From the sides, the differences are far more dramatic: the Schmukler resembles a Hudson/Ardsley without the engraved sides and is not nearly as curved as a Kenilworth/Gallahad. The Schmukler came with the same 12/0 size, 207 grade, 17-jewel movement as the Hudson, Ardsley, Kenilworth and Gallahad.

The Schmukler shares the same dial as the Kenilworth and Gallahad models. A dial that has drop-shadow numerals greatly enhances the appearance and value of these models. Only two Schmukler dials have been located with etched gold numerals.

Off-Duty, white gold-filled

OFF-DUTY

Official Name = Off-Duty (derived from Illinois advertisements, price lists, and an Illinois Sales Catalog)
Secondary Name = None
Formerly Known As = None
Time Period = Deco
Case Variations/Rarity = 🕒🕒🕒🕒🕒 WGF/M
Case Durability = 🕒🕒🕒
Material = 14K GF
Bezel = Molded
Sides = Plain
Lugs = Plain
Lug Size = 16mm
Springbar = Male
Casemaker = Wadsworth
Case Closure = 3-Part Screw-On Bezel and Back
Case Number = 211
Case Shape = Round
Case Back = Flat
Dimensions = 38 x 32mm
Movement Size = 3/0
Movement Grades/Jewels = 24/17, 307/17
Seconds at = 6
Dial Number = 8083
Dial = Silver Finish
Dial Opening = Round
Dial Variations/Rarity = 🕒🕒 Silver Finish, Painted Numerals
🕒🕒🕒🕒🕒 Silver Finish, Painted Numerals, Butler Center Subs
🕒🕒🕒🕒🕒🕒 Silver Finish, Painted Numerals, Red Number 12
🕒🕒🕒🕒🕒🕒 Black Finish, Painted Numerals
Numerals = Painted
Hands = Steel
Cased in Factory = Yes
Unique Case Design = Yes
Unique Dial Design = Yes
Introduction Date = 1932
Retail Price New = $40.00
Collectibility = 🕒🕒🕒🕒
Advertisements = No
Marketing Theme = “Rugged, dependable strap watch”

Off-Duty Strap Watch

Rugged, dependable strap watch—screw back and bezel. Heavy crystal ground and fitted in deep reflector dust and moisture proof case. 17 jewels, compensating balance; steel escape wheel and breguet hairspring; micrometric screw regulator. Available in 14 karat white gold filled case **$40**

J. Engel catalog, 1932

The Off-Duty model appeared in the 1931–32 Illinois Sales Catalog and in one small Illinois sales brochure, as well as in several jobbers' catalogs that used the advertisement Illinois had provided.

In its advertising copy Illinois described the "Off-Duty" as a "Rugged, dependable strap watch—screw back and bezel. Heavy crystal ground and filled in deep reflector dust and moisture proof case." Illinois promoted this watch to men who already owned pocket watches, as Illinois stated: "Many Railroad Men have expressed a desire for a convenient strap watch to wear in conjunction with the Bunn Special Railroad Watch." However, Illinois did feel compelled to issue a disclaimer that "The strap watch will not pass railroad requirements." The appearance of the Off-Duty dial was designed to appeal to a Railroad Man but the watch was only to be used "in conjunction" with a "Railroad Approved" Illinois Bunn Special pocket watch.

Illinois was attempting to strike a delicate balance with its customers. At this time, Illinois, along with other manufacturers, was experiencing a precipitous decline in sales of pocket watches. It did not want to offend railroads, which maintained strict standards for timepieces, but did wish to expand sales to the railroad workers by encouraging them to make the move to a rugged strap watch, with the look of a pocket watch, for their off-hours use.

The Off-Duty is one of the most sought-after Illinois wristwatches. It uses the same case as the Greyhound, Motor Coach and Skyway models. The Off-Duty is a very striking watch when equipped with a bold and crisp Off-Duty dial or one with a butler center subsidiary seconds bit. If equipped with an Off-Duty dial with a red numeral 12, the combination looks off-the-charts gorgeous. As yet, only two Off-Duty dials with a red numeral 12 have been spotted and only two Off-Duty black dials found.

Off-Duty, white gold-filled

Off-Duty, black dial, only two known to exist

The Off-Duty, Skyway, Motor Coach and Greyhound models are the only Factory-Cased Illinois watches with screw-on bezels and case backs. All four models used the same case Model No. 211, which has stars on its bezel and back.

This model was prone to significant case wear on the tops of the lugs, although the rest of the case holds up well. The Off-Duty, Skyway, Motor Coach and Greyhound came in white only.

TECHNICAL TIP

The Case Model 211 has a screw-on bezel and case back. Watch repairers and collectors have punctured holes in the case back and/or fouled the threads by mistakenly trying to pry it off with a case knife instead of merely screwing it off.

WHY I COLLECT ILLINOIS

I suppose I collect Illinois watches for the same reasons I got into collecting anything in the first place—it's my nature. All my life I've been a collector of things. As a boy I collected baseball cards, Star Wars toys, you name it, if there were more than one available, I probably collected it.

As I got older, my fascination with history grew and so I started collecting things with historical value—coins and such. By the time I reached my twenties I was a graphic designer and so my interests narrowed to collecting historical items that were well designed, had character, and were small. I had always had an interest in wristwatch design, but it wasn't 'til around 10 years ago that a friend of mine showed me his first vintage Hamilton watch. I didn't know the story behind it or where it came from, but I knew I wanted one of my own.

After doing some research and learning a bit about the history of wristwatches, I decided the company that had the most interest to me was the Illinois Watch Company. In my opinion they had the most beautiful designs and best movements of any watch company from that period. Their relatively short life in the wristwatch industry also made them a perfect candidate for a collection—a place to start and a place to finish. To get all of the Illinois watches was an attainable dream. They had the most eccentric case designs, and even the dials appealed to me. Watches like the Skyway or Off-Duty and the Jolly Roger had a certain masculine look that many from other companies lacked, and then there were watches like the New Yorker or Ritz that had such a unique look compared to the competition. I was hooked, and so started my collection of Illinois watches. It was the creative way they designed their watches that made me the collector I am today.

—Ty Albert Rulli

Off-Set Crowns / Military

Official Name = Off-Set Crowns (derived from usage by Illinois and military watch collectors)

Secondary Name = Military (almost all Off-Set Crown models are also Military watches)

Formerly Known As = None

Time Period = Transitional

Case Variations/Rarity = 🕒🕒🕒 N, So
🕒🕒🕒🕒 SS
🕒🕒🕒🕒🕒🕒 YGF, YG

Case Durability = 🕒🕒🕒 YGF
🕒🕒🕒🕒 N, So, YG

Material = SS, 14K YG, 14K YGF, N, So

Bezel = Plain

Sides = Plain

Lugs = Plain

Lug Size = 16mm

Springbar = Fixed Lugs

Casemakers = Fahys, IWCCo., Keystone, NAWCo., Others

Case Closure = 3-Part Snap-On Bezel and Back

Case Number = None

Case Shape = Round, Cushion

Case Back = Flat

Dimensions = 30 x 30mm

Movement Size = 0, 3/0

Movement Grades/Jewels = 24/17, 36/17, 37/17, 38/17, 39/17, 204/17

Seconds at = 6

Dial Numbers = None

Dial = Silver Finish, Enamel

Dial Opening = Round

Dial Variations/Rarity = 🕒🕒 Silver Finish, Painted Numerals; Silver Finish, Luminous Numerals
🕒🕒🕒 Enamel

Numerals = Painted, Luminous

Hands = Steel

Cased in Factory = No

Unique Case Design = No

Unique Dial Design = No

Introduction Date = 1915

Retail Price New = Unknown

Collectibility = 🕒🕒🕒🕒

Advertisements = Yes

Marketing Themes = Various

Off-Set Crown, sterling silver

Off-Set Crown, sterling silver

Off-Set Crown, yellow gold-filled

Cut Bezel Off-Set, sterling silver

There are various advertisements by Fahys, Keystone and the NAWCo for Off-Set Crown cases. The advertisements featured Off-Set Crown models along with other Military Transitional cases offered for sale contemporaneously.

Collectors find Off-Set Crown models most frequently in inexpensive nickel cases and various silverore-type cases, but less often in sterling silver, yellow gold-filled or solid gold.

Only two Off-Set Crowns are known to exist in an Ongard case manufactured by the NAWCo. One of these two, however, is missing its cut-out integrated guard. (See listing for **Ongard**.)

There are three solid yellow gold Illinois Notched Lug models with Off-Set Crowns that cut directly into a lug and two in sterling silver. Most of the round Off-Set Crowns have the crowns at the 1:00 o'clock position; fewer have the crown at the 1:30 o'clock position. The solid gold Notched Lug watch was one of the first wristwatches advertised by the Illinois Watch Company in 1923. (See listing for **Notched Lug**.)

There are Off-Set Crowns with the crown at the 12:00 o'clock position with sterling silver cases. These are now known as "D-D" Utility Watches. (See listing for **"D-D" Utility** Watch.) Cut Bezel wrist-watches with round cases and off-set crowns are extremely rare; there are only two known examples.

Square Off-Set, sterling silver

American soldiers with a gunner crew. Look closely: one is wearing an Off-Set crown at 1:30.

Ollendorff / Ollendorff II

Official Name = Unknown
Secondary Name = Ollendorff I and Ollendorff II (derived from Ollendorff Watch Company watches)
Formerly Known As = Contract
Time Period = Deco (WGF), Post-Moderne (YGF)
Case Variations/Rarity = 🕓🕓🕓🕓🕓🕓 WGF/E
🕓🕓🕓🕓🕓🕓 YGF
Case Durability = 🕓🕓🕓 YGF
🕓🕓🕓🕓 WGF
Material = 14K WGF, 14 YGF
Bezel = Engraved (WGF), Plain (YGF)
Sides = Engraved (WGF), Plain (YGF)
Lugs = Plain
Lug Size = 16mm
Springbar = Male
Casemaker = Star
Case Closure = 3-Part Snap-On Bezels and Back (WGF), 2-Part Snap-On Bezel and Back (YGF)
Case Number = None
Case Shape = Tonneau
Case Back = Flat
Dimensions = 35 x 27mm (WGF)
Movement Size = 6/0 (WGF), 18/0 (YGF)
Movement Grades/Jewels = 905/17 (WGF), 206/17 (YGF)
Seconds at = 9
Dial Number = None
Dial = Silver Finish
Dial Opening = Tonneau
Dial Variations/Rarity = 🕓🕓🕓🕓🕓🕓 Silver Finish, Luminous Numerals (WGF)
🕓🕓🕓🕓🕓🕓 Etched Gold Numerals (YGF)
Numerals = Luminous
Hands = Luminous (WGF), Steel (YGF)
Cased in Factory = No
Unique Case Design = Yes (WGF), No (YGF)
Unique Dial Design = No
Introduction Date = Unknown
Retail Price New = Unknown
Collectibility = 🕓🕓🕓🕓
Advertisements = No
Marketing Themes = Unknown

Ollendorff I, white gold-filled

Ollendorff II, yellow gold-filled

These models were likely exclusive offerings by the Ollendorff Watch Company, a longtime watch manufacturer and Illinois jobber. Ollendorff probably purchased the cases for these watches directly from the Star Watch Case Company (both cases are signed "Ollendorff" and one is also signed Star). Then they ordered Illinois movements and dials from the Illinois Watch Company, and Ollendorff cased and timed these models itself. The Ollendorff II may qualify as a Conneric model as that term is defined under the Conneric listing of this chapter, since it had its own signed case but its dial was not found among the Hamilton Conneric dial drawings shown in this book.

Ollendorff I, side view

Ollendorff I, inside case back

Over the years I have seen only three of these completed watches in white gold-filled and two in yellow gold-filled, so they were probably not sold in large quantities. The Ollendorff I model above is a pared-down version of a Ritz—not as attractive, but still far from plain. The Ollendorff II (with an 18/0 size movement) was from the 1933–34 Post-Moderne time frame.

Ollendorff II, inside case back

OLLENDORFF

The I. Ollendorff Company was founded by Isador Ollendorff in 1868. It was located in New York City, where it manufactured clocks, movements, watches and watch and clock cases. By 1930 its product lines expanded to include watch and clock parts and clock dials.

According to United States Patent & Trademark Office records, the company operated as the I. Ollendorff Company from 1868 to 1922; by 1927 through 1931 the company was known as the I. Ollendorff Company, Inc.; and by 1946 through 1954 it changed its name to Ollendorff Watch Company, Inc. For a brief time in 1950, the company was identified as I. Ollendorff Watch Company, Inc.

Ollendorff, a longtime Illinois jobber, also carried Elgin, Hamilton and Waltham watches.

"Gotham" and the "Gotha-matic" were watch brands of the Ollendorff Watch Company that were sold into the 1950s. Ollendorff finally closed its doors in the early 1960s.

October, 1928 *The KEYSTONE* Page 60

One of the oldest watch houses in the country

Specialists in watches by

ELGIN
WALTHAM
ILLINOIS
HOWARD

20 West 47th Street
New York City

717 Liberty Avenue
Pittsburgh

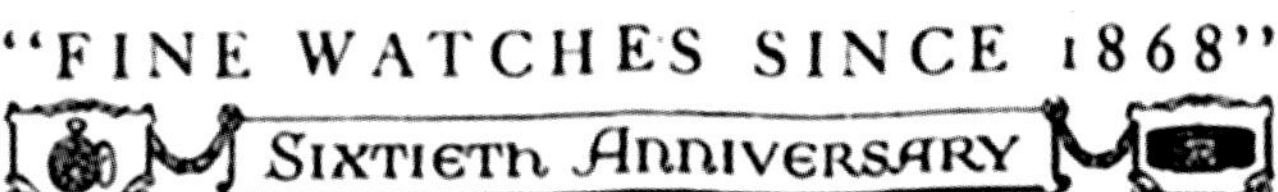

Keystone, October 1928

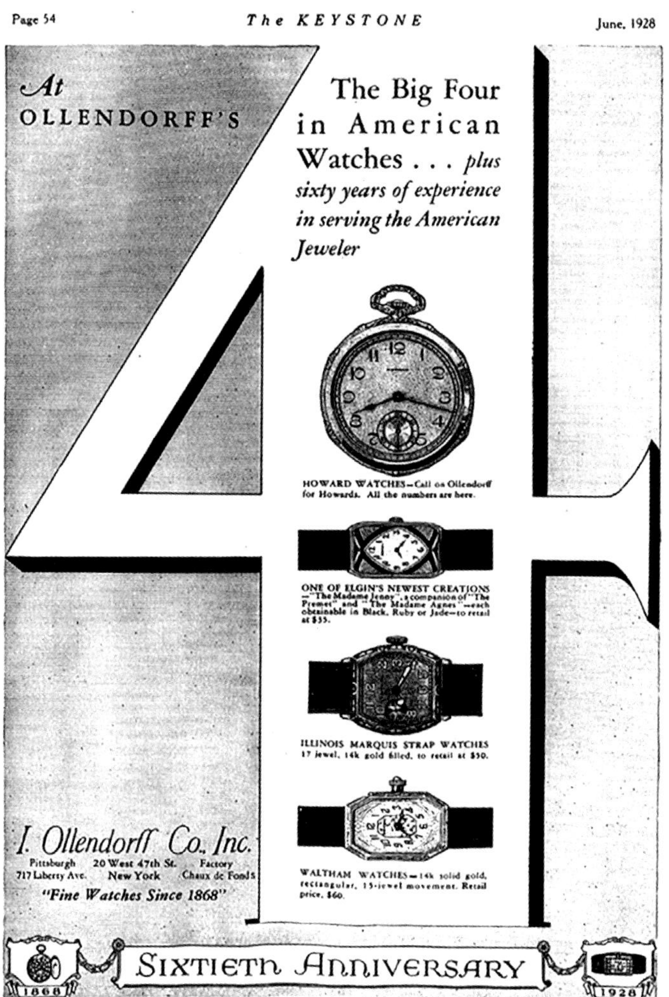

Keystone, June 1928

Saturday Evening Post, November 1929

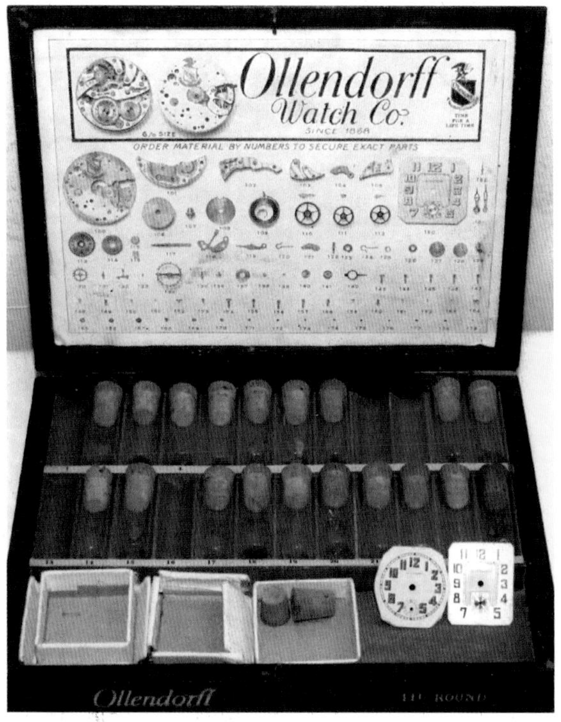

Ollendorff watch parts case

Ongard / Ongard Off-Set

Official Name = Ongard (derived from advertisements for the Ongard by NAWCo in the July 31, 1918 issue of the *Jewelers' Circular-Weekly*)
Secondary Name = Integrated Guard, Integrated Guard Off-Set, Cut Bezel, Cut Bezel Off-Set (derived from collectors' usage)
Formerly Known As = None
Time Period = Transitional
Case Variations/Rarity = 🕒🕒🕒🕒🕒🕒 SS/P
YGF/P, WGF/P, SS/Off Set
Case Durability = 🕒🕒🕒🕒
Material = SS, 14K YGF, 14K WGF
Bezel = Cut Bezel
Sides = Plain
Lugs = Plain
Lug Size = 16mm
Springbar = Fixed
Casemaker = NAWCo
Case Closure = 4-Part Snap-On Bezels and Back
Case Number = None
Case Shape = Round
Case Back = Flat
Dimensions = 38 x 33.5mm
Movement Size = 0
Movement Grades/Jewels = 24/17, Others
Seconds at = 6
Dial Number = None
Dial = Silver Finish
Dial Opening = Round
Dial Variations/Rarity = 🕒 Silver Finish, Luminous Numerals
🕒🕒 Silver Finish, Painted Numerals
Numerals = Luminous
Hands = Steel
Cased in Factory = No
Unique Case Design = Yes
Unique Dial Design = No
Introduction Date = 1918
Retail Price New = Unknown
Collectibility = 🕒🕒🕒🕒
Advertisements = Yes
Marketing Themes = "The Last Word in a Military Watch Case"
"Built for Service"

Ongard, sterling silver

Ongard Off-Set, sterling silver

The

ONGARD

The Last Word in a Military Watch Case
Built for Service

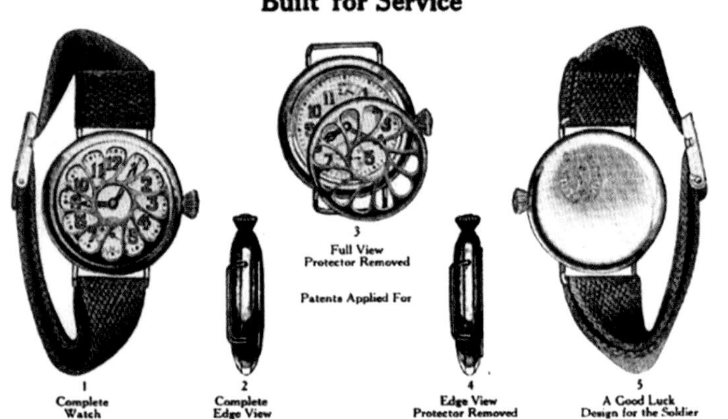

No. 1—Distinctly a man's Wrist Watch and guarded for hard usage. The hands are clearly visible in every position.

No. 2—The guard is as secure as a part of the case. This is the thinnest protector front Watch Case made.

No. 3—A quick change back to the standard with all the good qualities of a case without a protector. The protector simply snaps on over the glass.

No. 4—The **ONGARD** is quickly and easily removed for cleaning the crystal.

No. 5—The Good Luck design is furnished without extra charge.

Made in 3 0s Sterling Silver, 15-, 20- and 25-Year Gold Filled and Silver Filled.

Prices and samples furnished on request. Invoiced through jobbers only

North American Watch Company, Mansfield, O.

Makers of the NAWCO 15-Year Line

15 Maiden Lane, New York **31 N. State Street, Chicago**

The Ongard was apparently first advertised on July 31, 1918 by NAWCo in the *Jewelers' Circular-Weekly.*

Ongard Off-Set inside case back in sterling silver

This watch is very rare, as only two complete Ongard Off-Sets and two that are not Off-Sets are known to exist. One Ongard Off-Set is missing its integrated guard, but it can still function effectively without the guard in place, because of the design of its four-piece case. The watch could be worn with or without its guard in place. The cut-out crystal guard on the Ongard snapped onto the front of the case, The swirl design of its cut-out is quite distinctive and different from the typical Armored Cases described elsewhere in this chapter. NAWCo sometimes engraved a horseshoe on the case back as "A good luck design for the soldier."

Osgood / Brandt Rock

Osgood, base metal, black enamel

Osgood, base metal, blue enamel

Official Name = Unknown
Secondary Name = Osgood (derived from an H. A. Osgood & Son advertisement in the March 1929 *Keystone*), Brandt Rock (derived from a 1930 Jason Weiler–Baird-North catalog)
Formerly Known As = Round Enamel Bezel (before the Osgood advertisement was found, collectors called this model simply the "Round Enamel Bezel")
Time Period = Deco
Case Variations/Rarity = ◷◷◷◷◷◷ BM/ Black EE, BM/Blue EE
Case Durability = ◷◷
Material = BM
Bezel = BM/EE
Sides = Engraved
Lugs = Plain
Lug Size = 16mm
Springbar = Male
Casemaker = OSCO
Case Closure = 3-Part Snap-On Bezel and Back
Case Number = None
Case Shape = Cushion
Case Back = Curved
Dimensions = 35 x 28mm
Movement Size = 3/0
Movement Grades/Jewels = 24/17
Seconds at = None
Dial Number = 8212
Dial = Silver Finish
Dial Opening = Round
Dial Variations/Rarity = ◷◷◷◷◷◷ Silver Finish, No Numerals
Numerals = Enamel Numerals
Hands = Steel
Cased in Factory = Possibly (see text below)
Unique Case Design = No
Unique Dial Design = No
Introduction Date = 1929
Retail Price New = Osgood, Unknown; Brandt Rock, $30.00
Collectibility = ◷◷◷◷
Advertisements = Yes
Marketing Themes = "It's Thin."
"An exclusive model"

H. A. Osgood & Son, a jobber, advertised this striking enamel-bezel model in the March 1929 issue of the *Keystone*. The advertisement listed this watch as "an exclusive model" manufactured solely for the H. A. Osgood & Son. The thinness of the OSCO-produced case was advertised as "A feature found only on high-priced watches."

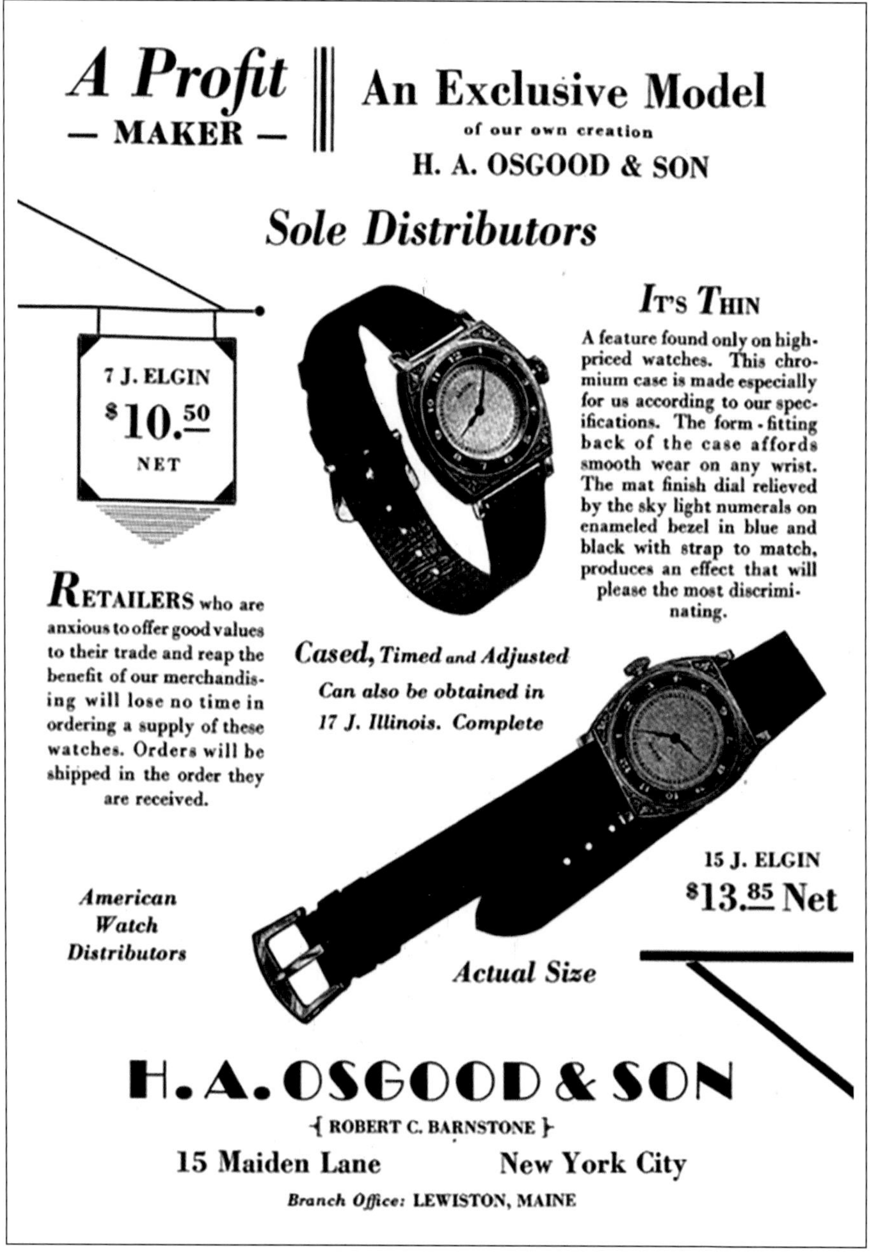

Keystone, March 1929

Only seven Illinois Osgood models have been found: four with black bezels and three with blue bezels. The H. A. Osgood firm was on the official 1928 List of Illinois Jobbers, with a Lewiston, Maine, address for its branch office and a Maiden Lane address for its main office. Therefore, it would have been easy for Osgood to obtain movements and dials to market the "Osgood" round enamel model out of its New York City headquarters. (The main office had earlier been in Maine and the branch in New York City.)

H. A. OSGOOD & SON

The jeweler Henry A. Osgood (1818–1905), worked in South Berwick, Maine, 1845 to 1857, before moving to Lewiston, Maine, in 1858 and establishing his business there the next year. His son, Charles H. Osgood (b. 1849) joined his father's firm after completing his education, and by the age of twenty-one was a partner in the business.

The Osgoods' business thrived. By 1892–93 they expanded, erecting an elegant building at 131 Lisbon Street. An advertisement in an 1898–99 directory lists the business as "H. A. Osgood & Son, Diamonds, Watches, Jewelry, Silverware and Optical Goods." The Osgood Building was described as being "of brick, four stories and finished basements. The front is of white enamel brick, imported from Leeds, England, at a cost of two hundred dollars per thousand. All the trimmings are gilded with pure gold leaf. It is the finest building of its size in Maine. The architects are J. L. Coburn & Sons."

After his father died, the business continued under Charles Osgood's leadership until he retired, around 1920, and sold both the business and the building to Robert C. Barnstone, another jeweler in Lewiston. Charles H. Osgood apparently died in 1921 or 1922.

An article in the July 22, 1922 issue of the *Jewelers' Circular,* entitled "Modern Horological Schools: The New England Jeweler's Institute," mentions that "Through the generosity of the late Col. Charles H. Osgood, whose life was spent in bettering the position of the retail jeweler, an adjoining piece of property was given the institute, and provides an excellent residence for members of the faculty."

Sources: Biographical material about the Osgoods is from *Representative Men of Maine,* compiled by Henry Chase (Portland, ME: Lakeside Press, 1893), http://www.onlinebiographies.info/me/rmm/osgood-ch.htm. Information about the Osgood Building is courtesy of the Angroscoggin Historical Society, Auburn, ME, which has a collection of directories from Lewiston.

The Osgood company claimed this enamel-bezel model as of our "own creation," further stating that this "thin chromium case is made especially for us according to our specifications. The form-fitting back of the case affords smooth wear on any wrist. The mat finish dial relieved by sky light numerals on enameled bezel in blue and black with strap to match, produces an effect that will please the most discriminating." The advertisement advised: "RETAILERS who are anxious to offer good value to their trade and reap the benefits of our merchandising will lose no time in ordering a supply of these watches." (Unfortunately, the base metal/chromium case has proved subject to severe wear and pitting on its case back.)

In the advertisement, the watch is listed at $10.50 when equipped with a 7-jewel Elgin movement, or $13.85 with a 15-jewel Elgin movement. (This was the *wholesale* price, as the advertisement text is pitched to retailers acquiring stock.) In the center of the advertisement are the words "Cased, Timed and Adjusted." On the line below is this: "Can also be obtained in 17 J. Illinois. Complete." No price is shown, but it was doubtless more than what was asked for the 15-jewel Elgin.

The big question is whether the Illinois "Osgood" was a Factory-Cased model or not. The words and their positioning in the advertisement are ambiguous. Perhaps "Cased, Timed and Adjusted" meant that this was done by Osgood itself, regardless of whether the movement installed in the special case was the 7-jewel or 15-jewel Elgin being shown or, instead, the 17-jewel Illinois option. However, the placement of the word "complete" in conjunction with the Illinois option suggests that it may apply *only* to the Illinois, and Illinois' usage of that term has been found to mean that a given model was Factory-Cased. So it seems plausible that the Illinois "Osgood" might have been Factory-Cased, but I do not know for sure.

The 1930 Illinois Materials Catalog offered two dials, No. 8265 and No. 8212, that were specified as being "For enamel bezel cases." The former, for a cushion-shaped dial opening, was presumably for the Chevalier and the latter, for a round dial opening, for the Osgood. (In the catalog, no specific model name was attached to either dial number.) As the Chevalier case was equipped occasionally with an awesome enamel dial, it is possible that an enamel dial exists for the Osgood as well, but one has never been seen.

Attempts to find the name and location of "OSCO," the case manufacturer, have come up empty. As this is a poor-quality case, it is possible that one of the well-known casemakers produced this case but signed it differently so the low quality would not reflect badly on its regular product line. According to Stan Czubernat, this practice was quite common. Apparently, some American casemakers produced not only their high-quality cases, which were marked with their names, but also some lower-end product lines with alternate names. In some instances, they did not even inscribe a maker's mark on these low-end cases. I believe that "OSCO" may possibly be just an encoded version of the H. A. Osgood Company's name.

Osgood inside case back

A startling recent discovery is that the Illinois wristwatch formerly known as the Round Enamel Bezel has not just one identity, but two. A Jason Weiler–Baird-North (JWBN) catalog of 1930, apparently the first one issued after the merger of these two longtime mail-order firms in 1929, shows a wristwatch with a design exactly like the one advertised by H. A. Osgood & Son, but called a Brandt Rock. The advertisement is on the back cover of the catalog, in full color.

The catalog has this caption for the watch: "Here's the smartest model of the day, 'The Brandt Rock,' with Mesh Bracelet, an entirely new style in a Permanent White Finish Case with the numerals finished in the hard French Blue Enamel circle on the case. With fine 7-jewel Elgin or Waltham Movement . . . $17.50. With 15-jewel Elgin or Waltham Movement ... $22.50. With 17-jewel Illinois Movement ... $30.00."

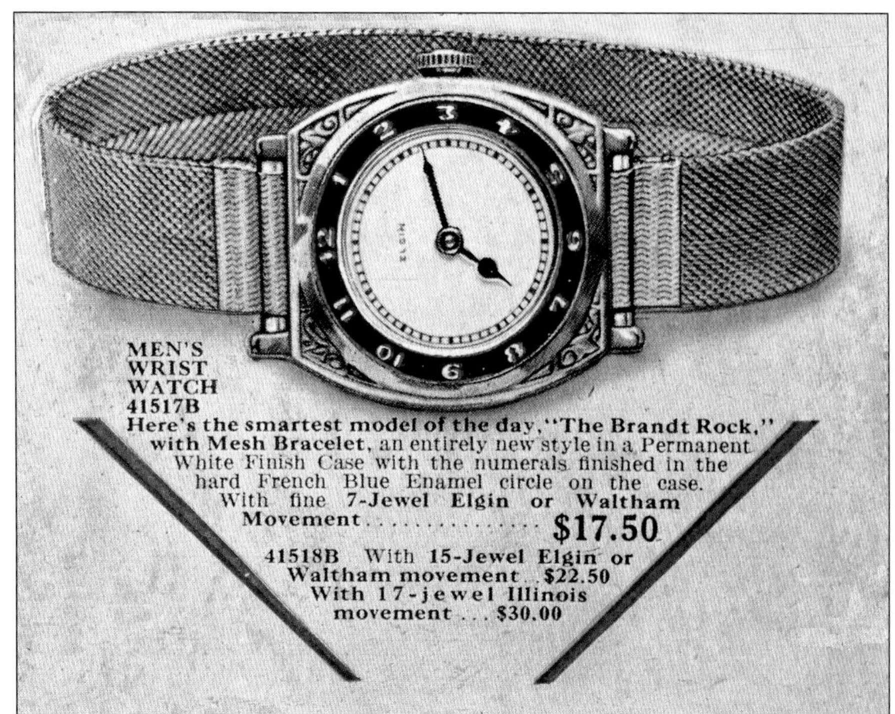

"Brandt Rock" in Jason Weiler–Baird-North catalog, 1930

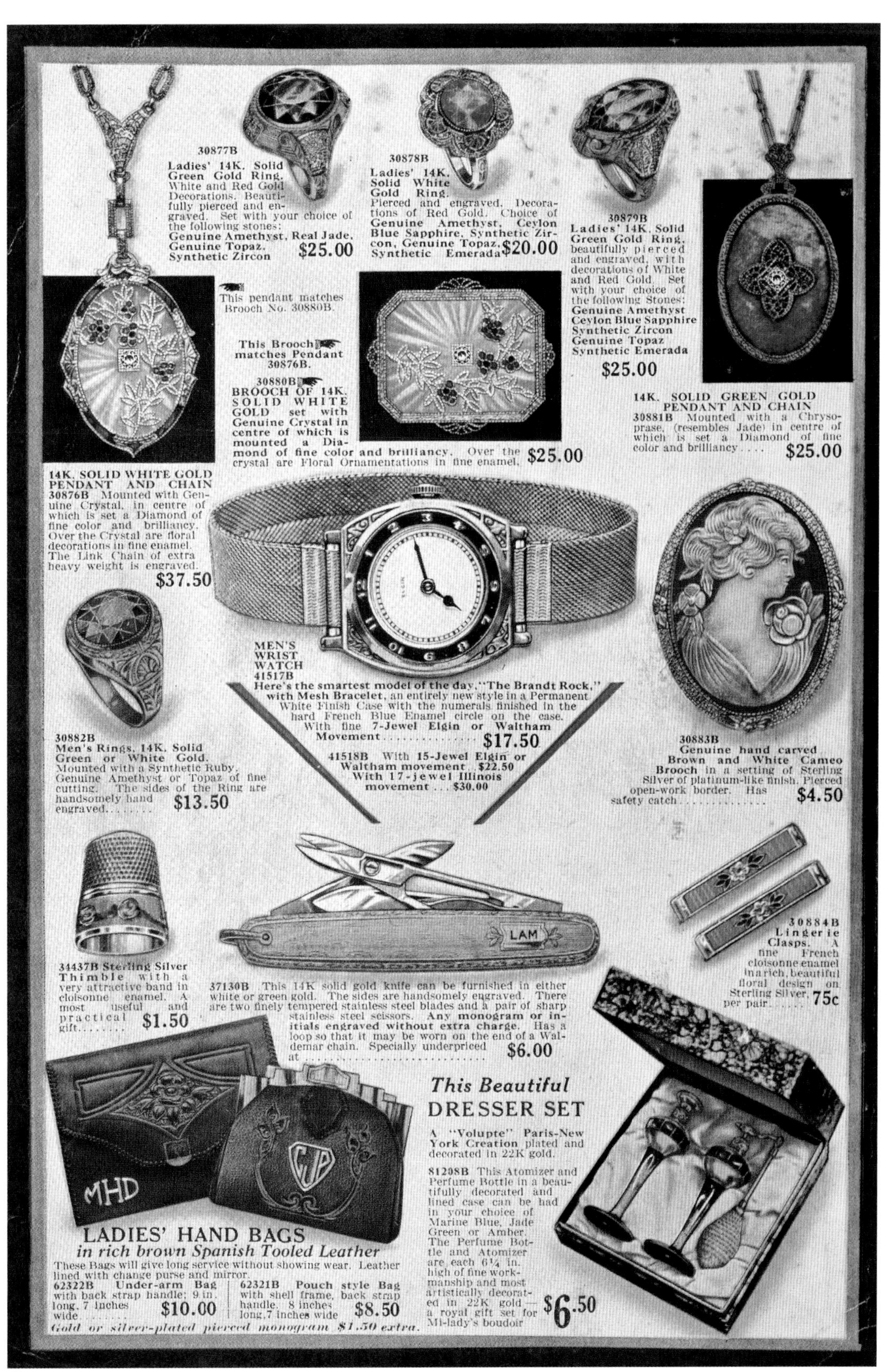

JWBN 1930 catalog, back cover

There are a few details that differ between this listing and that in the Osgood advertisement. The Osgood watch came equipped with a strap; the Brandt Rock had a mesh bracelet. Also, the Osgood was available with either black or blue enamel, but the Brandt Rock was offered only in blue.

Both companies offered 7-jewel and 15-jewel Elgin movements and 17-jewel Illinois as options; however, only JWBN offered Waltham movements (in a choice of 7-jewel or 15-jewel). In terms of prices, JWBN would at first glance to seem higher: $17.50 for the 7-jewel Elgin option, as opposed to Osgood's $10.50, and $22.50 for the 15-jewel Elgin instead of Osgood's $13.85. But a careful examination of the text of the two advertisements reveals the reason for the difference in prices: Osgood's is clearly wholesale (as mentioned above) while JWBN is retail (the catalog stated that it sold "by mail direct from factory to family").

If the watch offered by the H. A. Osgood company was, as the advertisement claimed, "An Exclusive Model of our own creation," with a case "made especially for us according to our specifications," how do we account for the presence of the Brandt Rock in the JWBN catalog?

There are some possible explanations. One might be to take the "Exclusive Model" claim loosely; in a sense, the Brandt Rock is a different model by virtue of being equipped with a mesh band. However, that does not account for the case. A more likely explanation is that H. A. Osgood decided a bit later to end, or at least modify, its claim of exclusiveness for the watch. Perhaps Osgood did not allow others in the New York area to market the watch, but permitted the Boston-based firm JWBN to do so if the watch was modified in some way so as to appear to be a new model—hence the mesh bracelet.

But why and how might the Osgood company have come to such a decision? Perhaps it found that the watch was not moving as fast as had been expected in New York and some other sales venue was needed. If so, whose idea might it have been to make an arrangement with JWBN? It appears that Robert C. Barnstone might have been the link.

Barnstone, whose name is listed below the name of H. A. Osgood & Son in the March 1929 advertisement in the *Keystone* (shown earlier), was president of the company and had owned it for nearly a decade, as an announcement from Boston in the February 11, 1920 issue of the *Jewelers' Circular* shows: "One of the largest real estate transactions in the business section in Lewiston, Me., was consummated Feb. 2 when Robert C. Barnstone, a jeweler, well known in Boston, and his brother, purchased the Osgood building at 127–131 Lisbon St. The structure was owned by Col. Charles H. Osgood, who conducted for many years a wholesale and retail business there under the name H. A. Osgood & Son. Mr. Barnstone will continue the business in this location as well as his own at 50 Lisbon St."

That Barnstone was "well known in Boston" suggests that he had numerous contacts there in the jewelry industry, and a likely one was the well-established mail-order firm Jason Weiler & Sons, which later, after acquiring Baird-North, became Jason Weiler–Baird-North. (Baird-North, located in Providence, Rhode Island, had been a private-label customer of Illinois.)

First inside page of JWBN catalog, 1930

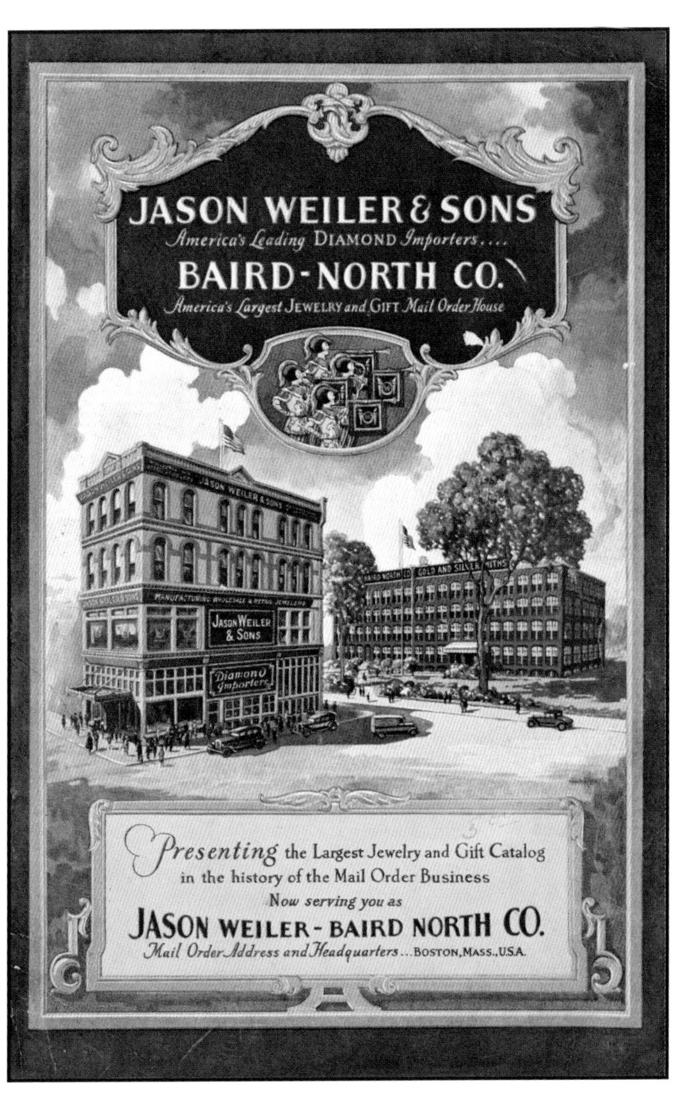

Front cover of JWBN catalog, 1930, "Presenting the Largest Jewelry and Gift Catalog in the history of the Mail Order Business"

Initially, the presence of the H. A. Osgood company in New York City was simply via an agent, as a New York item in the May 17, 1922, issue of the *Jewelers' Circular* indicates: "It was announced last week that Abe Oppenheimer has just completed arrangements to represent H. A. Osgood & Son, Lewiston, Me." The address given was 3 Maiden Lane. By 1926, however, Barnstone seems to have decided to have a more extensive operation in New York and had moved. A Lewiston business directory of that year shows "H. A. Osgood & Son (R. C. Barnstone), 50–52 Lisbon St., Lewiston, and 15 Maiden Lane, New York." [4]

The 1929 *Keystone* advertisement shows that the main business of H. A. Osgood & Son was by then at that Maiden Lane address and the company's presence in Lewiston was only a branch—located at what had earlier been Barnstone's store, not at the Osgood Building.

In trade publications, the last mention we have found of H. A. Osgood & Son's presence in New York is a note, entitled "R. B. Barton Resigns from H. A. Osgood & Son," from the April 1931 issue of the *Keystone:* "Robert B. Barton resigned his position as vice-president of H. A. Osgood & Son, New York wholesale house, on April 1, according to an announcement by Robert C. Barnstone, president of the concern. Mr. Barton was formerly sales manager for the Elgin National Watch Company."

Since the listings in the Lewiston directories remain the same until 1932, but the 1933 directory does not have the company listed, perhaps H. A. Osgood & Son had gone out of business, another victim of the Great Depression.

FANTASTIC FIND

Being the consummate Illinois hunter, I am always thinking about those elusive finds that I hope will pop up one day. Well, today was that day. Years ago I saw that Farrell Gay had a blue enamel Osgood (back then we knew it only as a Round Enamel Bezel). I dreamed of finding one someday, and every once in a while I would do my regular wish-list search around the web. Well, after a very long day at work I decided to do a quick search before going home and put in "blue enamel watch." Why I did this, I have no idea. What pops up but a beautiful Blue Enamel Osgood for $350. I was so excited I couldn't press the "Buy It Now" button and pay for it fast enough! I literally had one finger on the computer and the other on the phone to call Fred. I almost forgot to finalize the payment I was so excited telling him about the "Fantastic Find." An OsGREAT Day! —*Greg Hart*

See listing for **Futura**

PICCADILLY

Official Name = Piccadilly (derived from Illinois advertisements and Illinois Sales and Material Catalogs)
Secondary Name = None
Formerly Known As = None
Time Period = Deco
Case Variations/Rarity = 🕒🕒🕒 WGF/P
🕒🕒🕒🕒 GGF/P
🕒🕒🕒🕒🕒🕒 WGF/E
🕒🕒🕒🕒🕒🕒🕒🕒 TT*
*Yet to be confirmed
Case Durability = 🕒🕒 GGF
🕒🕒🕒 WGF
Material = 14K GF
Bezel = Plain, Engraved
Sides = Plain
Lugs = Plain
Lug Size = 16mm
Springbar = Female
Casemaker = Keystone
Case Closure = 3-Part Snap-On Bezel and Back
Case Number = 164
Case Shape = Oval
Case Back = Flat
Dimensions = 30 x 35mm
Movement Size = 6/0
Movement Grades/Jewels = 905/17
Seconds at = 9
Dial Numbers = 8153, 8272
Dial = Silver Finish
Dial Opening = Oval
Dial Variations/Rarity = 🕒🕒🕒 Silver Finished, Raised Numerals
🕒🕒🕒🕒🕒 Silver Finish, Black Numerals; Silver Finish, Luminous Numerals
Numerals = Painted, Luminous, Raised Luminous Dots
Hands = Steel, Luminous
Cased in Factory = Yes
Unique Case Design = Yes
Unique Dial Design = Yes
Introduction Date = 1929
Retail Price New = $45.00
Collectibility = 🕒🕒🕒🕒
Advertisements = Yes
Marketing Theme = "An original design"

Piccadilly, white gold-filled

Piccadilly, green gold-filled

The Piccadilly appeared in the 1929–30 Illinois Sales Catalog and in several advertisements. The first one appeared in the May 18, 1929 issue of *Collier's*. Illinois correctly promoted the Piccadilly as "an original design." Illinois may well have been the first American watch manufacturer to introduce a bold oval wristwatch with a daring transverse orientation on the wrist.

Because of its design, the Piccadilly is generally considered to be Illinois' signature piece among the Illinois men's wristwatches (though the solid gold Consul is considered the Illinois flagship model). At one time, the Piccadilly was the most sought-after Illinois watch, but that may no longer be the case. The Piccadilly is relatively difficult to find in white and more difficult to locate in green. The green cases are fairly susceptible to bezel wear, making it difficult to find one in excellent condition.

There currently exist three super-rare custom-ordered white gold-filled Piccadillys with engraved cases. One has a completely engraved case and two have partially engraved cases. This engraving greatly adds to the beauty and value of this model. Interestingly, the custom engraving pattern differs on all three engraved models. There is also rumored to be a two-tone Piccadilly; however, its existence has not been confirmed.

Piccadilly, white gold-filled

Piccadilly, white gold-filled

THE NEW ILLINOIS PICCADILLY, *17 jewels, 14k gold-filled case, raised figure dial with luminous dots, $45. Other men's strap watches from $40 to $75.*

American Magazine, June 1929

Piccadilly inside case back

Piccadilly NOS dial

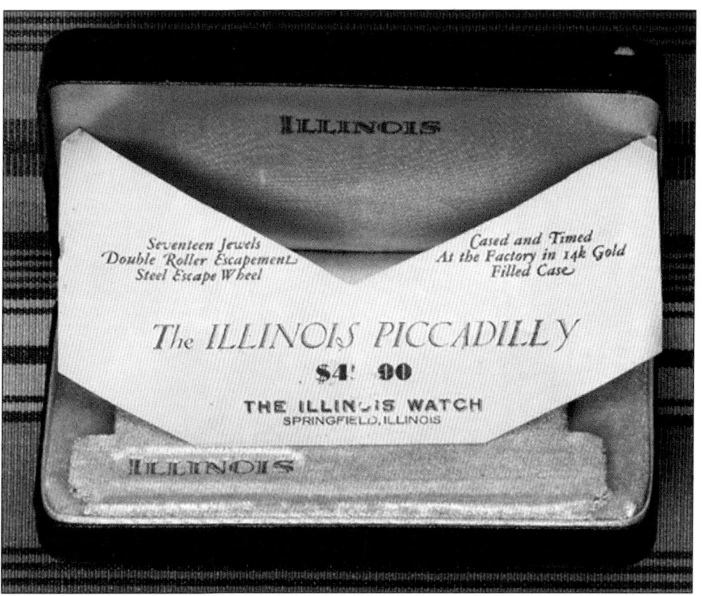

Piccadilly display case and paperwork

THE ILLINOIS

An American Watch As American As Its Name

PICCADILLY

$45

15 JEWELS 14K FILLED GOLD

Piccadilly original price card

End of Piccadilly's outer cardboard box

WHY I COLLECT ILLINOIS

I get a distinct pleasure, amidst this high-tech age, in being obliged to wind a watch to keep it going. There's something "right" about the obligation, the intervention. A few years ago, my uncle gave me my grandfather's vintage Swiss wristwatch and I had it repaired at a small shop in Los Angeles. When I came by to pick it up one afternoon, the owner showed me an Illinois "Piccadilly" that someone had brought in the week before. I had grown up in Illinois and was amazed that an Illinois watchmaker had offered such a flamboyant design in the late 1920s. This sparked my interest in the company, with led to Fred's surprising book—surprising because it turned out, of course, that the Illinois Watch Company had dozens of inspired designs. I find these wristwatches in general to be under-appreciated jewels. The tiny mechanics are so brilliant, yet from an earlier age. Combining this with the surprisingly high artistry emerging from downstate Illinois tantalized me, and I've become an avid collector of this marvelous intersection of art and history ever since. *—Bernard Friedman*

Page 144 *The KEYSTONE* May, 1929

The New HAMILTONS

Modern, Yet Keeping their Sense of Dignity

THE SPUR
With a definite flair for the modern. Available in 14K yellow or white gold, 19-jewel, $125.00. List, $147.80.

THE HASTINGS
A strap watch of simple lines and satisfying accuracy. 17-jewel, 14K filled yellow or white gold, $55.00. List, $67.50.

THE RITTENHOUSE
Engraved 14K filled green or white gold. Grade 918 $70.00; list, $78.80. Grade 902 $95.00; list, $115.20. Grade 922 $120.00; list, $145.50. Dial shown No. 23, extra charge $12.00. List, $15.00.

THE CHEVY CHASE-DESIGN D
A smart 18-0size ladies' wrist watch for the woman who insists upon accuracy. 14K engraved white gold with enamel design, $80.00. List, $94.60.

THE CHEVY CHASE-DESIGN B
A full engraved and extremely handsome pattern with silver dial No. B3. 14K white gold, $75.00. List, $88.50.

The Illinois

Latest Designs in a Great American Watch

The cushion Marquis-Autocrat is pleasing in its unconventional case and is sure to win the favor of your pocket watch trade. The usual care of Illinois craftsmen is built into its 17 jewel movement. The case is 14-karat white filled gold and the dial is raised Roman figures.
List.......$63.00 Retail.......$55.00

Radiating the spirit of modernism, the Piccadilly disregards all set customs of the past for conventional design in strap watch cases. The bezel is plain, yet rich in its simplicity, and further enhanced by a dial of etched gold figures and luminous hands of gold outline. The movement is a 6/0 size 17 jewel.
List........................... $50.00
Retail......................... 45.00

For the men in your community who desire the dignity of a pocket watch, the A. Lincoln will be found indispensable for your sales program. It is furnished in 19-jewels, and 14-karat solid gold case. The new process etched dial has ancient Roman figures in relief.
List......$120.00 Retail......$100.00

The Consul may now be had in 21 jewels and a dial silver lined with solid gold applied figures.
19-J. lum. dial, List. $86.00 Retail. $75.00
21-J. lum. dial, List. $103.50 Ret.. $90.00
Gold fig. dial, List. $114.50 Ret.. $100.00

GREENWOLD-GRIFT CO.
Wholesale Jewelers
18 West Seventh Street
CINCINNATI, OHIO

The Chieftain is a new 6/0 size watch sure to win the favor of your trade, because of its rugged construction and the unusual appeal of the case design. Furnished in 15 jewels.
List.......$30.00 Retail.......$45.00

Keystone, May 1929. Note that the Consul is called a Chieftain and the Chieftain a Consul.

FANTASTIC FIND

An anonymous collector writes that out of the blue a person contacted him via email a year ago. "The person indicated that he knew that I collected Illinois watches and he had an 'unusual' watch that he thought that I 'might want.' I asked him to describe it, and the seller wrote that 'I only have knowledge about Hamilton Electric watches so I will send you images of it.'

"Two days later a few images came via email. I looked at them and realized immediately that I was being shown a white gold-filled (WGF) 'Piccadilly,' the signature piece of a Illinois wristwatch collection. I was very excited and very interested in this WGF 'Piccadilly' watch as I was eager to add this rare watch to my collection.

"Not wanting to express my strong interest, I merely told the seller, 'Yes, I am interested in the watch at the right price.' I added, 'Please let me know what you want for it.'

"Two days later the prospective seller wrote back that he would 'take $160 for it.'

"I was in shock as well as quandary as WGF 'Piccadilly's' usually sell (depending upon their condition) in the range of $1,600.00 to $1,850.00, whereas $160.00 was a great bargain. However, the seller did not include a decimal point in his email; if the seller intended to type '$1,600' and mistakenly typed '$160' it might not be worth pursuing the watch.

"I could not decide what to do as I did not want to risk losing the watch if its price was truly '$160.' After pondering this situation overnight I wrote the seller and cleverly (I thought) asked: 'How much would the total be with shipping?'

"I then tossed and turned for three more nights thinking that I had blown this great bargain by not agreeing immediately to the $1,600.00 price.

"Finally, after the fourth day, the seller wrote and merely stated that "'The watch would be $163.50 with shipping.'

"With tremendous relief (after thankfully seeing a properly located decimal point), with pleasure I wrote back, 'Should I PayPal you or send a check?'

"PayPal was fine."

— *Anonymous*

See listing for **Derby**

Police Special, sterling silver

Police Special

Official Name = Unknown
Secondary Name = Police Special (derived from the custom dial on this model)
Formerly Known As = None
Time Period = Transitional
Case Variations/Rarity = ⏲⏲⏲⏲⏲⏲ SS/P/Swivel Lugs
Material = SS
Bezel = Plain
Sides = Plain
Lugs = Plain
Lug Size = 16mm
Springbar = Swivel Lugs
Casemaker = Fahys
Case Closure = 3-Part Snap-On Bezel and Back
Case Number = None
Case Shape = Round
Case Back = Flat
Dimensions = 31 x 31mm
Movement Size = 3/0
Movement Grades/Jewels = 24/17, 36/17
Seconds at = 6
Dial Numbers = None
Dial = Silver Finish
Dial Opening = Round
Dial Variations/Rarity = ⏲⏲⏲⏲⏲⏲ Silver Finish, Luminous Numerals, Butler Center Subs
Numerals = Luminous
Hands = Luminous
Cased in Factory = No
Unique Case Design = No
Unique Dial Design = Yes
Introduction Date = 1920
Retail Price New = Unknown
Collectibility = ⏲⏲⏲⏲
Advertisements = No
Marketing Theme = Unknown

This model is known as the Police Special because of its dial, apparently a custom special-order one for a police department. The dial never appeared in any Illinois Sales or Material Catalogs.

The Police Special is the most sought-after Illinois custom dial. It has great appeal to law enforcement personnel in particular. To date, only four Police Specials have ever been seen. The Police Special dial depicts an old-style policemen's bonnet and nightstick. The style of the "Illinois" trade name printed around the top of the butler center subsidiary seconds register looks similar to that used on the Skyway dial. There exists one custom Major dial that also displays a hand-painted policemen's bonnet and night stick on it, but the presentation is not as dramatic as that of the Police Special. (See Chapter 7.) The Police Special came in a General Funston case.

SHOT HIS OWN WATCH

The February 1931 issue of the *Jewelers' Circular* reported the following tale:

"Lynn, Mass, Jan. 2 – John I. Noble, jeweler, of 247 Western Avenue, heard a noise downstairs on Dec. 29 in the middle of the night. He sleeps over the store. He grabbed his gun from under his pillow. He took the receiver off the telephone beside his bed, a signal to central that something was wrong.

"When he got downstairs he saw a man helping himself from the jewelry case. He opened fire. The robber ran.

"A few minutes later the motor police patrol picked him up as he ran along the street. Out of his vest pocket they took a watch, one from the jeweler's stock. The case was bent and broken, for it had stopped a bullet from Noble's gun.

"The thief was bound over to the grand jury . . ."

(Maybe he stole a Police Special?)

Potomac, white gold-filled

Potomac, yellow gold-filled

Potomac / Rockingham

Official Names = Potomac and Rockingham (derived from Illinois advertisements and Illinois Sales and Material Catalogs)
Secondary Name = None
Formerly Known As = None
Time Period = Moderne
Case Variations/Rarity = ◷◷◷ YGF/P
◷◷◷◷ WGF/P
Case Durability = ◷◷◷◷
Material = 10K YGF (Potomac), 10K YGF or WGF (Rockingham)
Bezel = Plain
Sides = Engraved
Lugs = Plain
Lug Size = 16mm
Springbar = Male
Casemaker = Keystone
Case Closure = 2-Part Snap-On Back
Case Number = 626
Case Shape = Rectangular
Case Back = Flat
Dimensions = 36 x 26mm
Movement Size = 6/0
Movement Grades/Jewels = 605/15, 605A/15
Seconds at = 6
Dial Numbers = 8389, 8492
Dials = Silver Finish, Butler Center
Dial Opening = Rectangular
Dial Variations/Rarity = ◷◷◷◷ Silver Finish, Etched Numerals; Silver Finish, Flush Gold Numerals
◷◷◷◷◷ Silver Finish, Black Numerals; Silver Finish, Butler Center, Etched Numerals; Silver Finish, Etched Numerals, Close to Dial Center
Numerals = Painted, Etched, Flush Gold
Hands = Steel
Cased in Factory = Yes, Potomac by Illinois in Springfield and Rockingham by Hamilton in Lancaster
Unique Case Design = Yes
Unique Dial Design = Yes
Introduction Date = 1932 (Potomac), 1934 (Rockingham)
Retail Price New = $35.00 (Potomac), $40.00 (Rockingham)
Collectibility = ◷◷◷◷
Advertisements = Yes

Marketing Themes = "Leader in value"
"New value in 15 jewel watch"
"Very practical and dependable"
"With bracelet to match in style and quality" (Rockingham)

Rockingham, white gold-filled

At the height of the Depression, Hamilton chose to market a line of bargain-priced Illinois 10K gold-filled, 15-jewel models in an obvious attempt to appeal to the cost- conscious consumer. The Potomac model was cased and timed in the Illinois Watch Factory. The Rockingham, however, was cased and timed in Hamilton's Lancaster factory, and its movement was equipped with the new Elinvar hairspring,

The Potomac appeared in the 1933 Illinois Sales Catalog (where it was listed as being in "natural filled gold," without the gold content indicated). The Rockingham, which appeared in the 1934 Illinois Sales Catalog, was offered in white gold-filled as well as yellow and equipped with a matching metal bracelet. It also had a new dial designed by Hamilton in Lancaster to distinguish this "new" model still further from the Potomac.

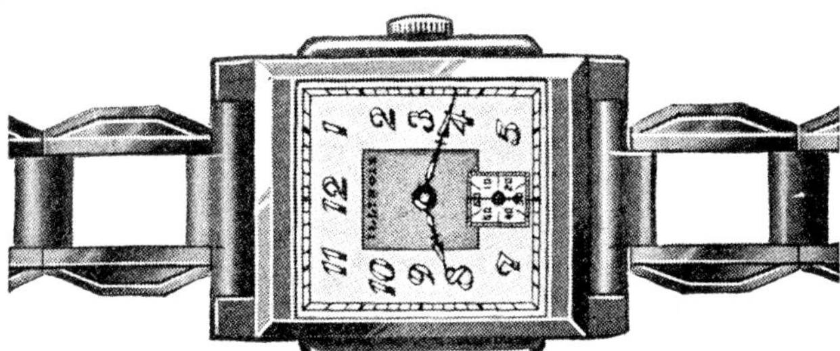

ROCKINGHAM

Very practical and dependable watch with easily read raised gold figure, two-tone dial. 10k filled white gold with bracelet to match in style and quality. 15 jewels. Consumer, **$40.00.** Keystone list, **$40.00.**

A. C. Becken catalog, 1934

In reality, the Rockingham was basically just a reissued Potomac with a Hamilton-designed dial and issued with a metal bracelet instead of a leather strap. This was a familiar pattern for Illinois during the Hamilton years, as we have seen. (The metal bracelet increased the price of the Rockingham to $40.00; the Potomac was $35.00.)

The Potomac/Rockingham models look like slimmed-down Arlington/Hawthorne or beefed-up Commodore/Bostonian models.

Possibly owing to the reformulation of the gold layer from 14K to 10K, these cases, particularly in yellow, were subject to case wear. Hamilton encountered the same problem at the same time with both its 14K and 10K gold filled cases. The casemakers tried to reformulate to reduce product cost, and this did not go well at first.

Although the Potomac and Rockingham share the same case, each model offered different dial options. The Potomac dial (No. 8389) had a silver finish and black painted numerals. As an alternate, consumers could purchase a Potomac dial with etched numerals. There is also a rarer version dial that has silver finish with etched gold numerals that are grouped closer to the center of the dial.

The Rockingham dial (No. 8492) featured a silver finish with etched gold numerals. The Rockingham also could be purchased with an optional butler center dial including a decorative center outline.

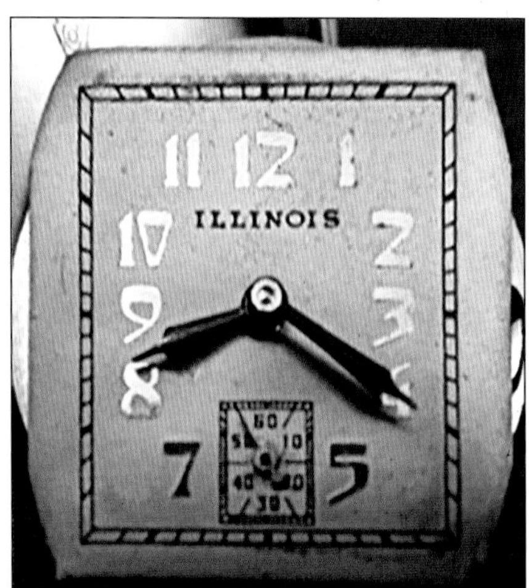

Potomac dial close-up

There is a rare solid yellow gold Illinois watch called the Varsity, with a design very similar to the Potomac/Rockingham. At one time, collectors thought the Varsity was simply a Potomac in solid gold, but now it is clear that their cases are distinguishable. The Potomac/Rockingham is housed in case Model No. 626, whereas the Varsity is in case Model No. 650.

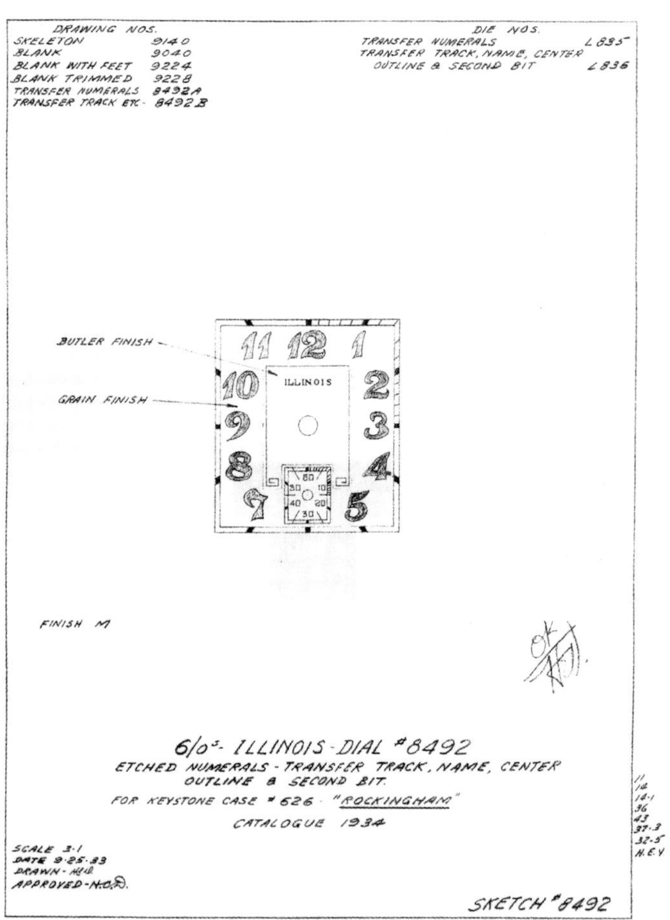

Hamilton drawing for Rockingham dial, dated September 25, 1933

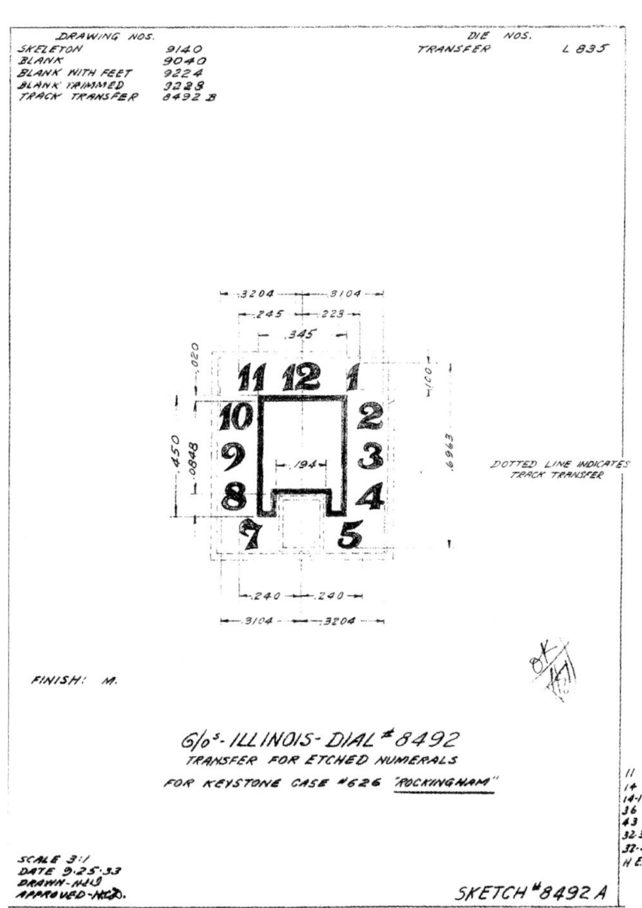

Hamilton drawing for Rockingham dial, dated September 25, 1933

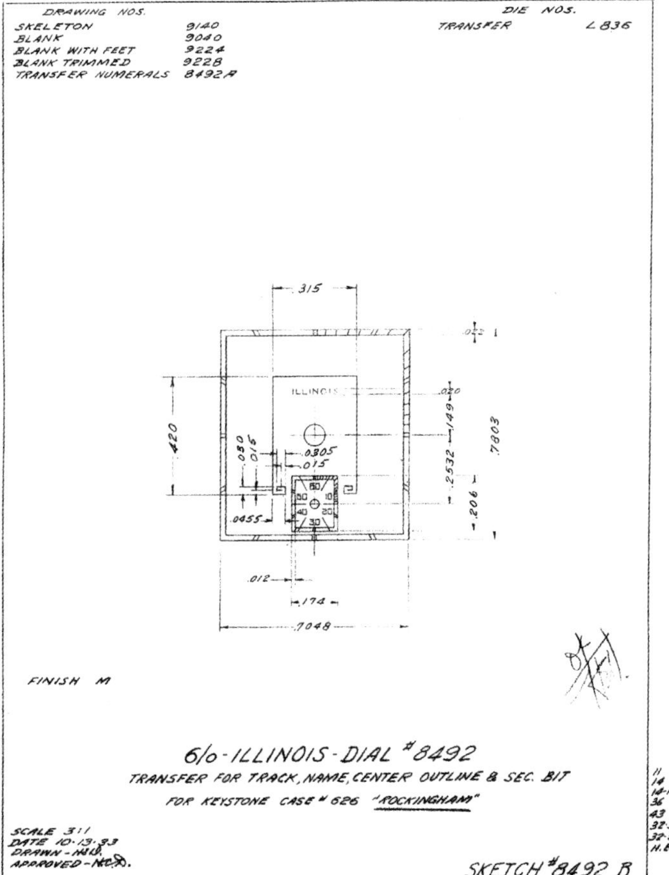

Hamilton drawing for Rockingham dial, dated October 13, 1933

Puritan

See listing for **Townsman**

Rectangular

See listing for **Canby**

Richmond 6/0

See listing for **New Yorker**

Richmond 12/0

See listing for **Larchmont**

Riley

See listing for **Atlantic**

Page 34 The KEYSTONE December, 1932

Keystone, December 1932. A Potomac is in the center of the page.

Ritz / Valedictorian

Ritz two-tone, gold-filled

Official Names = Ritz and Valedictorian (derived from Illinois advertisement and Illinois Sales and Material Catalogs)
Secondary Name = None
Formerly Known As = None
Time Period = Deco
Case Variations/Rarity = 🕒🕒🕒🕒 TT/P
Case Durability = 🕒🕒
Material = 14K GF
Bezel = Plain
Sides = Plain
Lugs = Plain
Lug Size = 16mm
Springbar = Male
Casemaker = Wadsworth
Case Closure = 3-Part Snap-On Bezel and Back
Case Number = 210
Case Shape = Tonneau
Case Back = Curved
Dimensions = 36 x 27mm
Movement Size = 6/0
Movement Grade/Jewels = 905/17
Seconds at = 6, None
Dial Numbers = 8209
Dials = Silver Finish, Sparkle Finish
Dial Opening = Tonneau
Dial Variations/Rarity = 🕒🕒🕒 Silver Finish, Painted Egyptian Numerals
🕒🕒🕒🕒 Sparkle Finish, Painted Egyptian Numerals
🕒🕒🕒🕒🕒🕒 Silver Finish, Luminous Arabic Numerals
🕒🕒🕒🕒🕒🕒🕒 Sparkle Finish, Egyptian Numerals, No Subs
Numerals = Painted, Luminous
Hands = Steel
Cased in Factory = Yes
Unique Case Design = Yes
Unique Dial Design = Yes
Introduction Date = 1930
Retail Price New = $42.50
Collectibility = 🕒🕒🕒🕒
Advertisements = Yes
Marketing Themes = "An unusual effect"
"The modern flair, embodied in watch design"
"An extremely popular, youthful design"

Collectors consider the Ritz to be among the finest Illinois men's wristwatch designs. With an innovative and distinctive tier-stepped yellow center section set against a white gold-filled tonneau-shaped bezel, it displays one of the most distinctive Deco designs of any watch of the era. The 1930–31 Illinois Sales Catalog, where it first appeared, described it as "The modern flair, embodied in watch design."

Illinois advertised its Ritz model in various national magazines such as the *American Magazine* and the *Saturday Evening Post*, and of course it appeared in jobbers' catalogs. The 1931 L. & C. Mayers catalog aptly and succinctly stated that the Ritz had "An unusual effect."

The Ritz and its unique design was said to be inspired by the discovery of King Tut's tomb in the 1920s. Some models came with spectacular white sparkle-finish dials with bold, black painted shadow Egyptian-inspired numerals.

There is also a Ritz dial with regular Arabic numerals. Although it is rarer, it does not look as nice on the watch, nor is it usually as valuable as the Egyptian numeral version. Shown below is one (perhaps a one-of-a-kind) Arabic numeral version, with numbers that are an unusual brown color (or have aged that way). One Ritz specimen without subsidiary seconds is known to exist.

The bezel is subject to light corner wear. The steps on the center section are subject to being worn down, so when shopping for this model, look for an example with crisp edges on its center section.

The Ritz was called a "Valedictorian" if it came equipped with a metal bracelet.

Ritz with regular Arabic numerals

Ritz with unusual Arabic numerals, only one known to exist

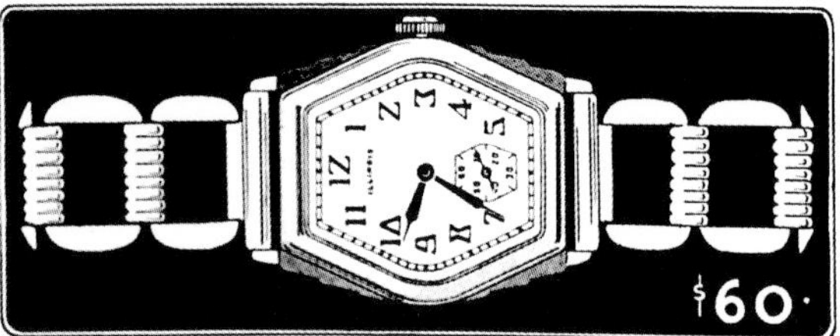

Illinois Valedictorian, 6/0 size, 17 Jewel, etched figures, 14K two tone gold filled case white bizil and back with yellow center. Complete with a new style gold filled open link band. Each in a display box with $60.00 resale price card.

No. 22W14. Each.......................... $45.20

N. Shure catalog, 1933

No. 18047. The Ritz model is a 6/0 size 17 jewel Illinois fitted in a 14k gold filled white case with natural gold center special dial to harmonize with case. Retails for $50.00.

No. 18047. Ritz white.......................... **$18.60**

Holsman's Jewelry Drummer 1932–33 catalog offered the Ritz at a Depression price of $18.60 (wholesale).

The Ritz case design patent by Wadsworth was filed on August 28, 1928. Like the Chesterfield, Metropolitan, Puritan, and Townsman, this model came only in two-tone white and yellow gold-filled. If a collector wanted to own one quintessential Illinois wristwatch representative of the Deco Period, the Ritz would be it.

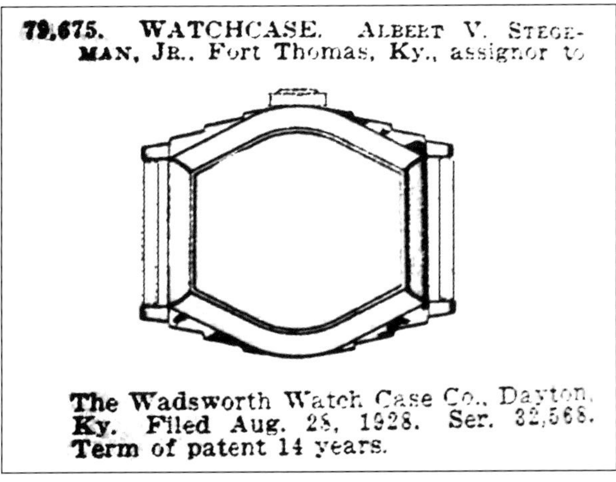

79,675. WATCHCASE. Albert V. Stegeman, Jr., Fort Thomas, Ky., assignor to The Wadsworth Watch Case Co., Dayton, Ky. Filed Aug. 28, 1928. Ser. 32,568. Term of patent 14 years.

A patent by Wadsworth for the Ritz watch case, dated August 28, 1928

Illinois Ritz front

Reverse Look-Alikes

The Ritz and the Hamilton Clinton do not resemble each other from the front, but from the back it is a different story. There they are almost identical. The Ritz and Clinton cases were made by Wadsworth. The Ritz was released in 1930 and the Clinton in 1931. The Ritz was 14K yellow and white gold-filled and the Clinton was 14K white gold-filled or yellow gold-filled.

Hamilton Clinton front

Illinois Ritz back

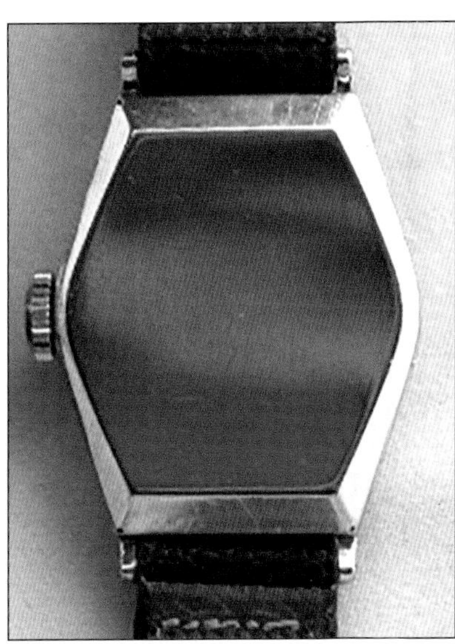

Hamilton Clinton back

RUMOR

There is a rumor that there is a solid gold Ritz. However, this watch has yet to be verified.

Rockingham

See listing for **Potomac**

Rockliffe, white gold, etched numerals

Rockliffe 18/0, white gold

Rockliffe / Rockliffe 18/0

Official Name = Rockliffe (derived from Illinois advertisements and Illinois Sales and Material Catalogs)
Secondary Name = None
Formerly Known As = None
Time Period = Moderne
Case Variations/Rarity = 🕒🕒🕒 YG/P (12/0 Size)
🕒🕒🕒🕒 WG/P (12/0 Size), YG/P (18/0 Size)
🕒🕒🕒🕒 WG/P (18/0 Size)
🕒🕒🕒🕒🕒🕒🕒 WG/B (18/0 Size)
Case Durability = 🕒🕒🕒🕒
Material = 14K WG, 14K YG
Bezel = Plain, Brushed
Sides = Plain
Lugs = Plain
Lug Size = 19mm
Springbar = Male
Casemaker = Keystone
Case Closure = 2-Part Snap-On back
Case Numbers = 216, No Number
Case Shape = Rectangular
Case Back = Curved
Dimensions = 38 x 26mm
Movement Sizes = 12/0, 18/0
Movement Grades/Jewels = 207/17, 805/15
Seconds at = 6, None
Dial Numbers = 8197, 8416, 8742*, 8744*, 8746*
*Designed and issued by Hamilton at Lancaster.
Dials = Silver Finish, Sparkle Finish
Dial Opening = Tonneau
Dial Variations/Rarity = 🕒🕒 Silver Finish, Applied Gold Numerals, with Seconds; Silver Finish, Applied Gold Numerals, No Seconds
🕒🕒🕒🕒 Silver Finish, Etched Numerals, with Seconds; Silver Finish, Etched Numerals, No Seconds
🕒🕒🕒🕒🕒🕒 Silver Finish, Applied Gold Markers, No Subs
Numerals = Applied Gold Numerals (14K), Raised Gold Markers, Etched
Hands = Steel

Cased in Factory = Yes (12/0 and seconds, cased by Illinois in Springfield; and 18/0, no seconds, cased by Hamilton in Lancaster)
Unique Case Design = Yes
Unique Dial Design = Yes
Introduction Date = 1930 with seconds; 1935 without seconds
Retail Price New = $75.00
Advertisements = Yes
Marketing Themes = "A watch of distinction"
"Finest men's rectangular watch we offer"
"Unusually attractive in appearance"
"Gracefully snugs the wrist"

Rockliffe, yellow gold, applied gold numerals

The Rockliffe was called by Illinois an "acceptable watch of class and distinction."

Collectors find it more difficult to locate the Rockliffe in white gold than in yellow gold. The 1930 Rockliffe used an Illinois 12/0 size, 207 grade, 17-jewel movement with subsidiary seconds. The 1935 Rockliffe 18/0 used an 18/0 size, 805 grade, 15-jewel movement without subsidiary seconds. Hamilton modified the inside of the Rockliffe 18/0 case to accommodate the smaller 18/0 size movement. Illinois cased and timed the 1930 Rockliffe at its Springfield Factory. Hamilton cased and timed the 1935 Rockliffe 18/0 in Lancaster.

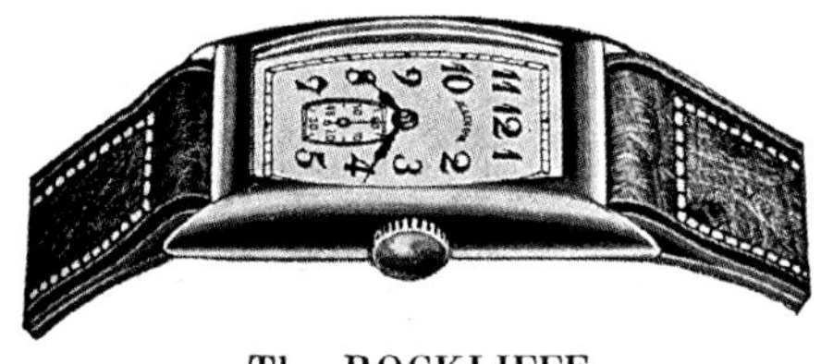

The ROCKLIFFE

The 14K solid gold Rockliffe is the finest men's rectangular watch we offer. It is curved to fit the wrist correctly. The beautiful 18K applied numeral dial blends perfectly with the character of the case. The Rockliffe may be ordered in natural or white gold.

Suggested consumer price, $75.

A. I. Hall catalog, 1931

The original 12/0 size Rockliffe was shown in the 1930–31 Illinois Sales Catalog, which called it "the finest rectangular watch we offer." It was also advertised in the March 28, 1931, issue of the *Saturday Evening Post*. The Rockliffe 18/0 offered in the 1935 L. & C. Mayers catalog was described as "a watch of distinction."

L. & C. Mayers also advertised the Rockliffe 18/0 in 1935 with a "plain English finish." We believe this meant the watch had a brushed bezel and caseback. In 1937, another L. & C. Mayers advertisement featured a "bright finish" for the case.

It is possible that by 1935, L. & C. Mayers had purchased Hamilton's remaining stock of Rockliffe models and was attempting various methods of marketing them, including modifying some cases with a brush finish. (Only one such Rockliffe 18/0 has been seen. The dials were also modified, as the catalog descriptions indicate; in 1935, the Rockliffe's "stylish dial" had "embossed gilt numerals," but in 1937 there were "sterling silver dials, raised 14K gold numerals" for this model."

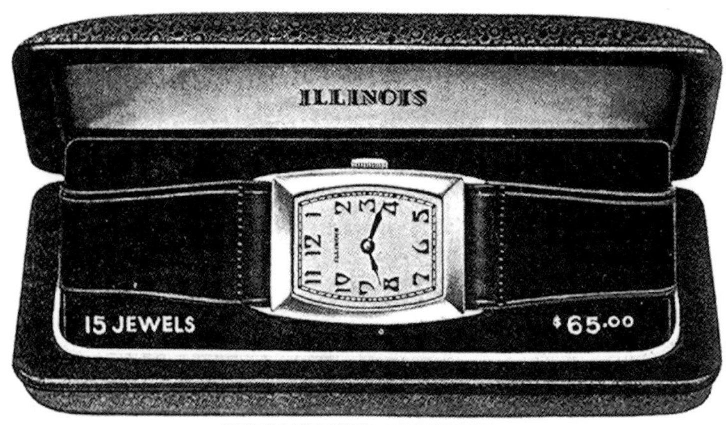

THE ROCKLIFFE—BY ILLINOIS

DW1296 Illinois Rockliffe, 14 kt. Solid Yellow Gold, 15 Jewels.................................. **$68.00**
DW1297 Illinois Rockliffe, 14 kt. Solid White Gold, 15 Jewels.................................. **68.00**

Retails for $65.00

The watch of distinction. An outstandingly attractive, thin model 14 kt. solid gold case by Keystone. Substantial weight, plain English finish, curved back. Fitted with the famous Illinois 6/0 size 15 jewel movement; stylish dial, embossed gilt numerals; crown set flush. Detachable fine quality leather straps, buckles same color as cases. Cased, timed and regulated at the factory. Attractive presentation box.

Rockliffe 18/0 in L. & C. Mayers 1935 catalog. "Plain English Finish" meant it had a brushed finish, likely added by Mayers.

FW1820 Illinois Rockcliffe, 14 Kt. Solid Yellow Gold, 15 Jewels.. **$73.00**
FW1820A Illinois Rockcliffe, 14 Kt. Solid White Gold, 15 Jewels... **73.00**

Suggested Retail Price $65.00

Illinois watches are made, timed and regulated at the Hamilton Watch Co.'s factory, Lancaster, Pa. Stylish thin model, 14 kt. solid gold cases, substantial weight, bright finish curved back. Illinois famous 15 jewel 6/0 size movement. Sterling silver dials, raised 14 kt. gold numerals. Detachable fine leather strap and buckle. Fine gift box.

Rockliffe 18/0 in L. & C. Mayers 1937 catalog. "Bright finish" probably meant a plain finish ordinarily found on plain bezel Illinois models.

Hamilton was apparently attempting to liquidate its inventory of Illinois 18/0 size parts and movements. The Rockliffe 18/0 is more difficult to find than the original Illinois version, but both versions are rarer in white gold than yellow gold. The Rockliffe looks like a slimmed down Hamilton "Byrd" model—or, rather, the Byrd is a steroid-enhanced version of the Rockliffe.

Rockliffe 18/0 inside case back modified by Hamilton

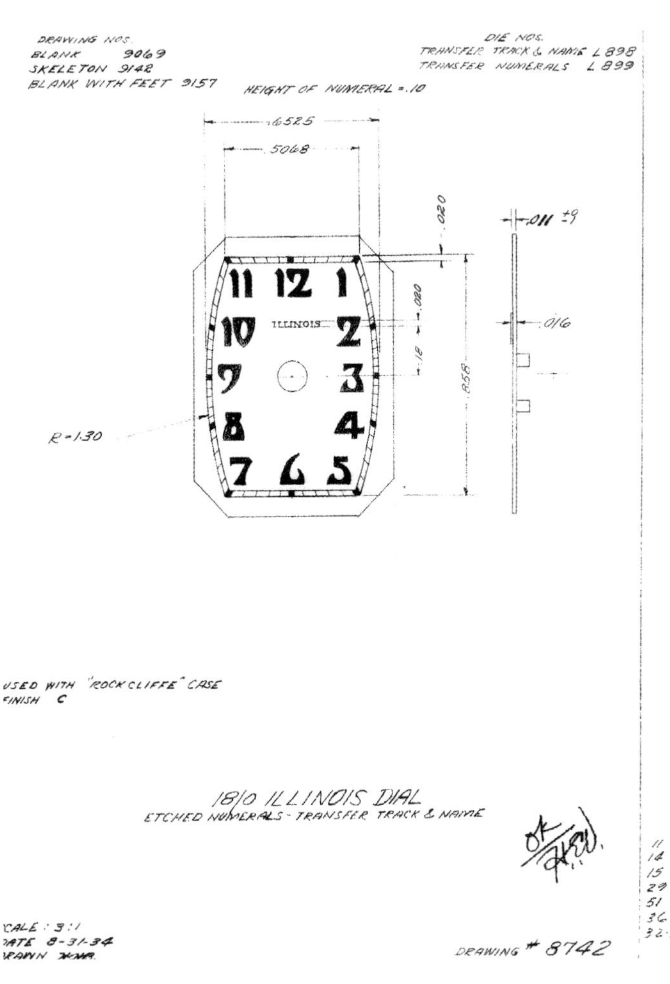

Hamilton drawing for Rockliffe 18/0 dial

In 1934, Hamilton designed new dials with no subsidiary seconds for the Rockliffe 18/0; one of these dials is particularly Hamilton-like in style, with raised gold pointed markers in place of numerals. A drawing and a photograph of that version are illustrated below.

Illinois dial designed by Hamilton for Rockliffe 18/0

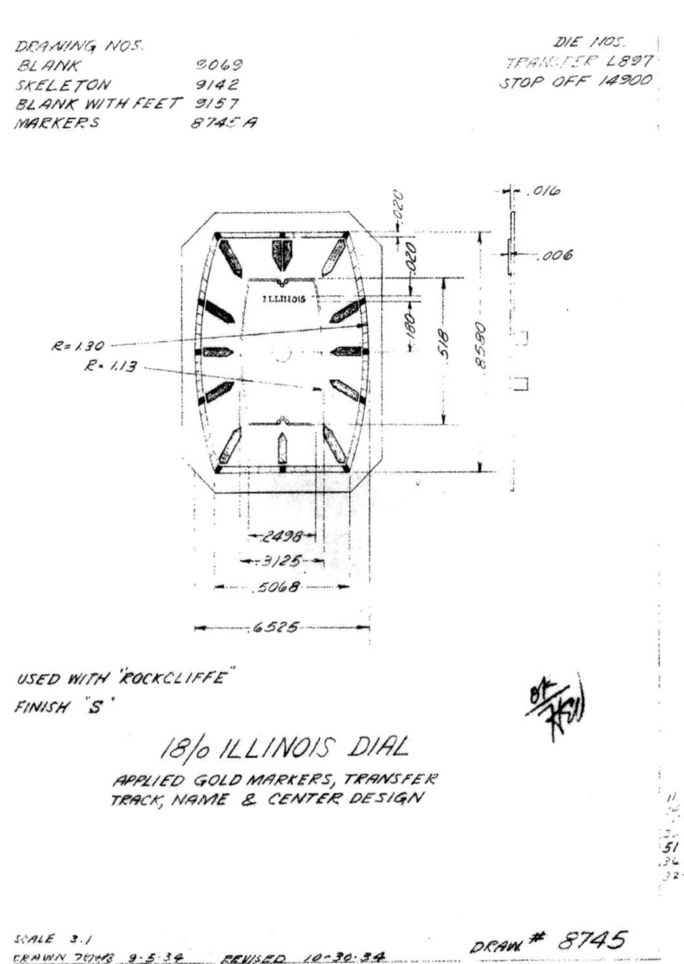

Hamilton drawing for Rockliffe 18/0 marker dial

Another Rockliffe dial designed by Hamilton has a large silver center section. This dial, No. 8746, was actually produced by Hamilton with the dial drawing carrying the date of October 30, 1934. Both the drawing and a photograph of the actual dial are shown here.

Rockliffe 18/0 dial No. 8746

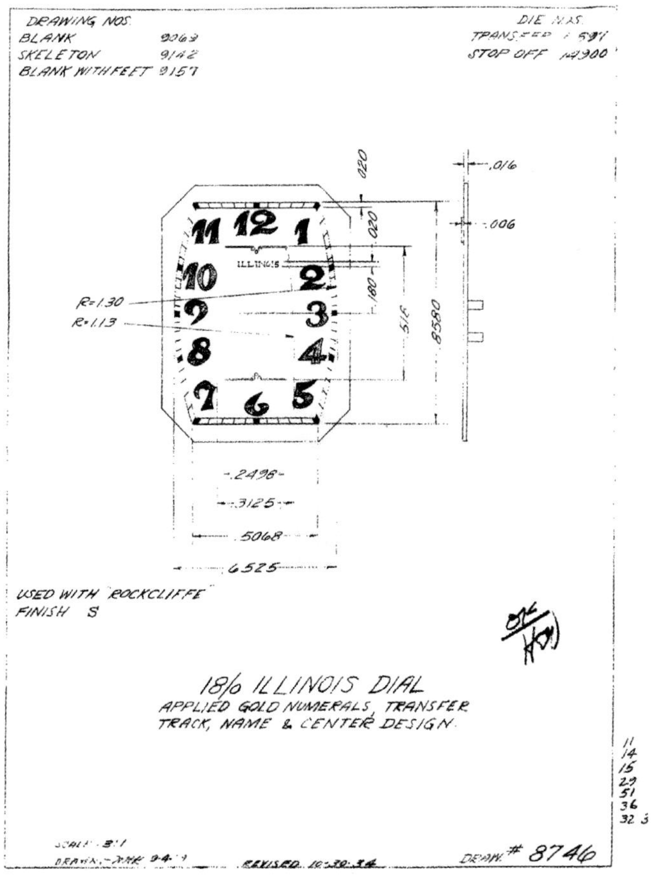

Rockliffe 18/0 dial drawing No. 8746

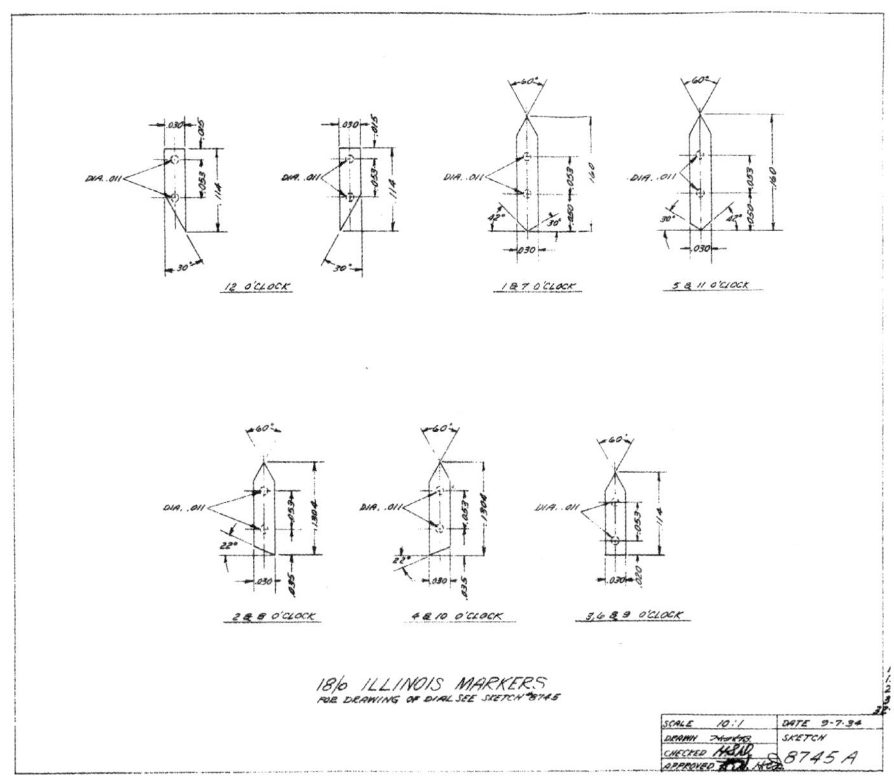

Hamilton drawing for Rockliffe 18/0 markers, dated September 7, 1934

Illinois marker dial designed by Hamilton for Rockliffe 18/0

Look-Alikes

As stated above, the Illinois Rockliffe is similar to the Hamilton Byrd model. The Rockliffe came in 14K solid yellow or white gold in a case made by Keystone. The Byrd was released in December 1930 and came in a 14K white or yellow gold case made by Perrin.

Rockliffe, yellow gold

Hamilton Byrd, white gold

Sangamon

Sangamon, base metal

Official Name = Sangamon (derived from Illinois advertisements and an Illinois Sales Catalog)
Secondary Name = None
Formerly Known As = Sangamo (derived from collectors' usage until the correct name was discovered)
Time Period = Moderne
Case Variations/Rarity = 🕒🕒🕒🕒🕒 BM/Sangamo Steel
Case Durability = 🕒🕒🕒🕒
Material = BM
Bezel = Molded
Sides = Plain
Lugs = Plain
Lug Size = 16mm
Springbar = Male
Casemaker = Keystone
Case Closure = 2-Part Snap-On Back
Case Number = 875
Case Shape = Rectangular
Case Back = Flat
Dimensions = 39 x 22mm
Movement Size = 18/0
Movement Grades/Jewels = 805/15, 805A/15
Seconds at = None
Dial Numbers = 8493 (by Hamilton)
Dial = Silver Finish
Dial Opening = Rectangular
Dial Variations/Rarity = 🕒🕒🕒🕒🕒 Silver Finish, Etched Numerals
Numerals = Etched
Hands = Steel
Cased in Factory = Yes (by Hamilton in Lancaster)
Unique Case Design = No
Unique Dial Design = No
Introduction Date = 1934
Retail Price New = $25.00
Collectibility = 🕒🕒🕒🕒
Advertisements = No
Marketing Themes = "Modish new sport leather strap model"
"Sturdily constructed"
"Practically indestructible"

The Sangamon appeared in the 1934 Illinois Sales Catalog, which was to be the last one ever issued by Illinois. For decades, Illinois collectors called this model a "Sangamo" until that catalog was discovered. The Sangamon was named for the location of the Illinois Watch Company in Sangamon County, Illinois.

Remarkably, Illinois advertised both the Sangamon and the Urbana as unisex watches. Illinois' advertising copywriting, repeated in various jobbers' catalogs, presented those two models as "Moderne Wrist Watches" and described them as follows: "Solidly constructed 18/0 size timepieces for men or women. 15 Jewels only. Elinvar equipped. These models meet the demand for a stylish wristwatch with clearly visible dial."

In 1934, Hamilton marketed the Sangamon to the Depression-ravaged buyer as part of its line of bargain-priced watches. Hamilton's low-priced group of Illinois wristwatches included the Standish, Chatham, Rockingham and Urbana in addition to the Sangamon. With the exception of the base-metal Sangamon, these watches were offered in low-end 10K gold-filled cases. All used Illinois' 15-jewel movements, cased and timed in the Hamilton factory in Lancaster. Hamilton equipped all of these models with the Hamilton Elinvar hairspring prior to introducing this innovation in its own small watch movements. The Sangamon's $25.00 retail price was the lowest price ever offered by either Illinois or Hamilton for a men's wristwatch.

Hamilton released these models to enable it to offer low-priced models for sale without degrading or damaging the Hamilton brand name. These offerings also allowed Hamilton to deplete its inventory of 6/0 and 18/0 size Illinois movements.

Although small, the Sangamon is larger than the Tuxedo model, as well as all of the Illinois ladies' wristwatch models with which it shared the 18/0 size movement. Its sleek design clearly represents the transition from the Deco to the Moderne time period.

The Sangamon is very similar to the Urbana. Like the Urbana, the Sangamon lacks subsidiary seconds, allowing it to utilize the leftover Illinois 18/0 size "Ladies'" movements. The Urbana has grooves on the top and bottom of its bezel and the Sangamon does not. They have different case Model Numbers and are made out of different case materials. Illinois offered the Sangamon only in white base metal and the Urbana only in yellow gold-filled. Both are difficult to locate but the Sangamon model is more easily found than the Urbana.

Dials, on the other hand, can be difficult to locate for most of the bargain series watches: the Chatham, Sangamon and Urbana. Because they were the last Illinois models offered, Hamilton severely restricted the supplies and inventory of Illinois material. In order to close down the Illinois product line, it produced the bare minimum number of dials needed for these models, most likely only on an as-needed basis.

Although some collectors have long thought that the same dial was issued on both the Sangamon and the Urbana, that is not the case, despite the fact that either dial will fit either model. A careful examination of the 1934 Illinois Sales Catalog illustrations for the two models shows that the numerals are somewhat different: the dial with the smaller, more deco-style numbers is for the Sangamon and the dial with the plainer, more robust numerals is for the Urbana. The Urbana uses dial No. 8494, as shown in the 1936 Illinois Materials Catalog issued by Hamilton. The Sangamon uses dial No. 8493; this dial is not listed in the 1936 materials catalog, but there is a Hamilton drawing for it, dated October 17, 1933.

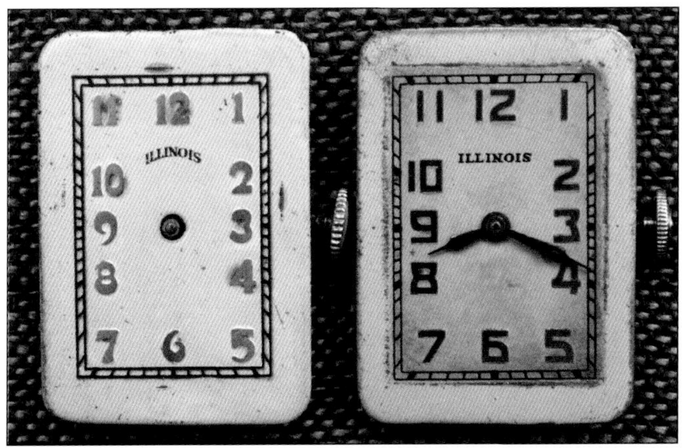

Left, Sangamon dial, No. 8493. Right, Urbana dial, No. 8494. Both dials have etched gold numerals, but of different styles.

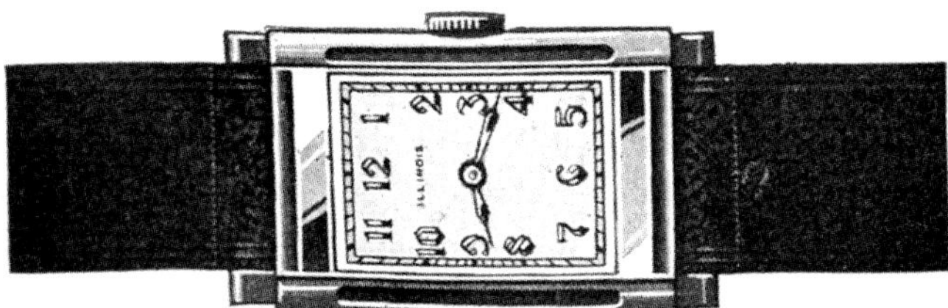

SANGAMON. Modish new sport leather strap model. In white **only,** with case of Sangamo metal—which is practically indestructible. Raised figure dial. 18/o size. 15 jewels. Consumer, **$25.00.** Keystone list, **$30.60.**

A. C. Becken catalog, 1934

It is interesting that at this point in Illinois' history, Hamilton issued two otherwise interchangeable dials for these two low-priced new models. Perhaps the deco-style numerals were chosen for the Sangamon to give a touch of stylish "edge" to what was a very plain model. And since the Urbana's bezel had a row of decorative grooves at the top and bottom of its bezel, the plainer numerals for it may have been chosen so as not to take away from that design feature.[5]

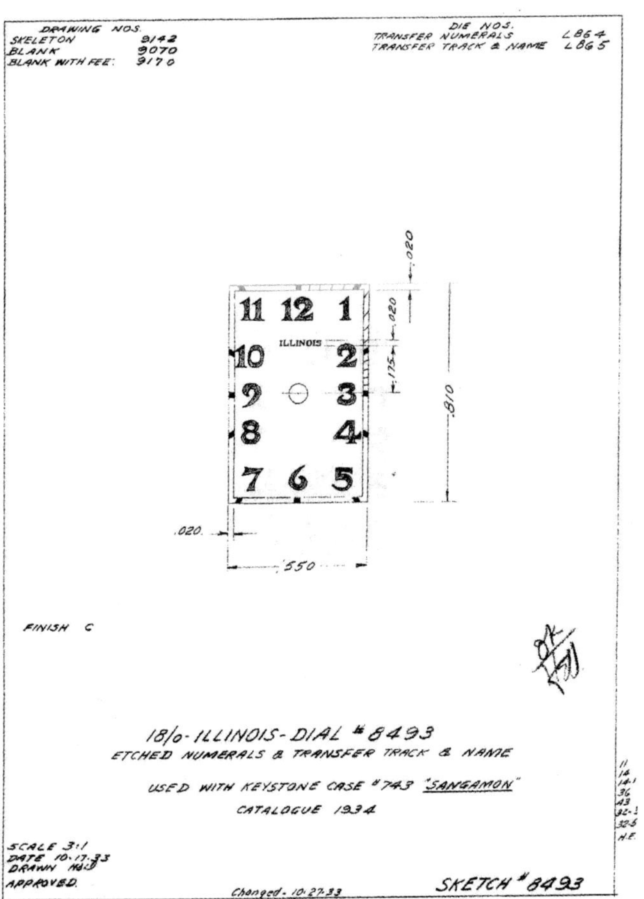

Hamilton drawing of a Sangamon dial, dated October 17, 1933. It is labeled as being for the Sangamon; however, the case number noted is not for a Sangamon case.

Interestingly, Waltham also released a wristwatch in a case identical to the Sangamon. Keystone manufactured both cases, so it is clear that neither company had an exclusive contract for this case with Keystone.

Waltham "Sangamon," base metal

On December 22, 1933, A. H. Pond, an Illinois distributor, wrote Illinois seeking "an 18/0 size 15 jewel Sangamo metal or silver ladies ribbon watch to retail at $25.00." This price point evidently appealed to Illinois' jobbers.

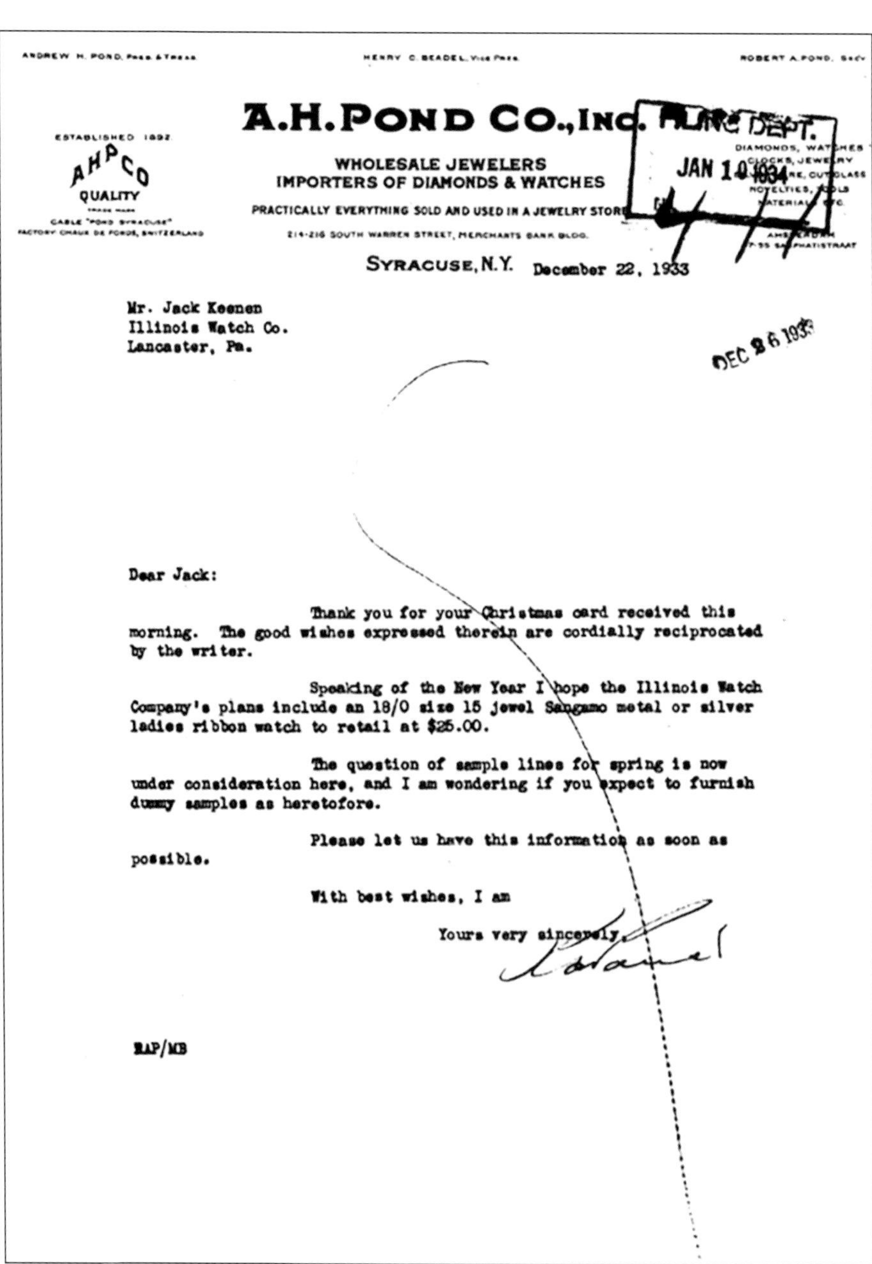

ANDREW H. POND, PRES. & TREAS. HENRY C. BEADEL, VICE PRES. ROBERT A. POND, SEC'Y

ESTABLISHED 1892
AHPCO QUALITY
TRADE MARK
CABLE "POND SYRACUSE"
FACTORY CHAUX DE FONDS, SWITZERLAND

A.H. POND CO., INC.

WHOLESALE JEWELERS
IMPORTERS OF DIAMONDS & WATCHES
PRACTICALLY EVERYTHING SOLD AND USED IN A JEWELRY STORE
214-216 SOUTH WARREN STREET, MERCHANTS BANK BLDG.

DIAMONDS, WATCHES, CLOCKS, JEWELRY, ...WARE, CUT GLASS, NOVELTIES, TOOLS, MATERIAL, ETC.
AMSTERDAM
...55 SARPHATISTRAAT

...DEPT. JAN 10 1934

SYRACUSE, N.Y. December 22, 1933

Mr. Jack Keenen
Illinois Watch Co.
Lancaster, Pa.

DEC 26 1933

Dear Jack:

Thank you for your Christmas card received this morning. The good wishes expressed therein are cordially reciprocated by the writer.

Speaking of the New Year I hope the Illinois Watch Company's plans include an 18/0 size 15 jewel Sangamo metal or silver ladies ribbon watch to retail at $25.00.

The question of sample lines for spring is now under consideration here, and I am wondering if you expect to furnish dummy samples as heretofore.

Please let us have this information as soon as possible.

With best wishes, I am

Yours very sincerely,

RAP/MB

Letter from A. H. Pond, a jobber, dated December 22, 1933

Sangamon case back

Sangamon inside case back

Waltham "Sangamon" inside case back

Santa Fe Tank

Sante Fe Tank

Official Name = Santa Fe Tank (derived from Santa Fe advertisements in *Popular Mechanics*, November 1927)
Secondary Name = Bryce (derived from Illinois Material Catalogs)
Formerly Known As = Contract
Time Period = Generic
Case Variation/Rarity = Unknown
Case Durability = Unknown
Material = Unknown
Bezel = Engraved
Sides = Unknown
Lugs = Plain
Lug Size = Unknown
Springbar = Unknown
Casemaker = Unknown
Case Closure = Unknown
Case Number = None
Case Shape = Rectangular
Case Back = Flat
Dimensions = 40 x 27mm
Movement Size = 6/0
Movement Grade/Jewels = 903/15, 904/17
Seconds at = 6
Dial Numbers = 8269, 8292, 8711
Dial = Silver Finish
Dial Opening = Rectangular
Dial Variations/Rarity = 🕒🕒🕒🕒🕒🕒🕒🕒 Silver Finish, Luminous Numerals, Signed "Santa Fe"
Numerals = Luminous
Hands = Luminous
Cased in Factory = No
Unique Case Design = No
Unique Dial Design = No
Introduction Date = 1927
Retail Price New = Unknown
Collectibility = 🕒🕒🕒🕒
Advertisements = Yes
Marketing Theme = "New case designs."

Collectors have always thought that the Santa Fe Watch Company sold only pocket watches with private-label movements and dials supplied by the Illinois Watch Company. However, it has been discovered that the company advertised a wristwatch model in the November 1927 issue of *Popular Mechanics*. With the discovery of this advertisement, it is clear that Santa Fe, like Burlington, shifted to the sale of private-label strap watches in the face of declining pocket watch sales. (For discussion of Santa Fe, see Chapter 6.)

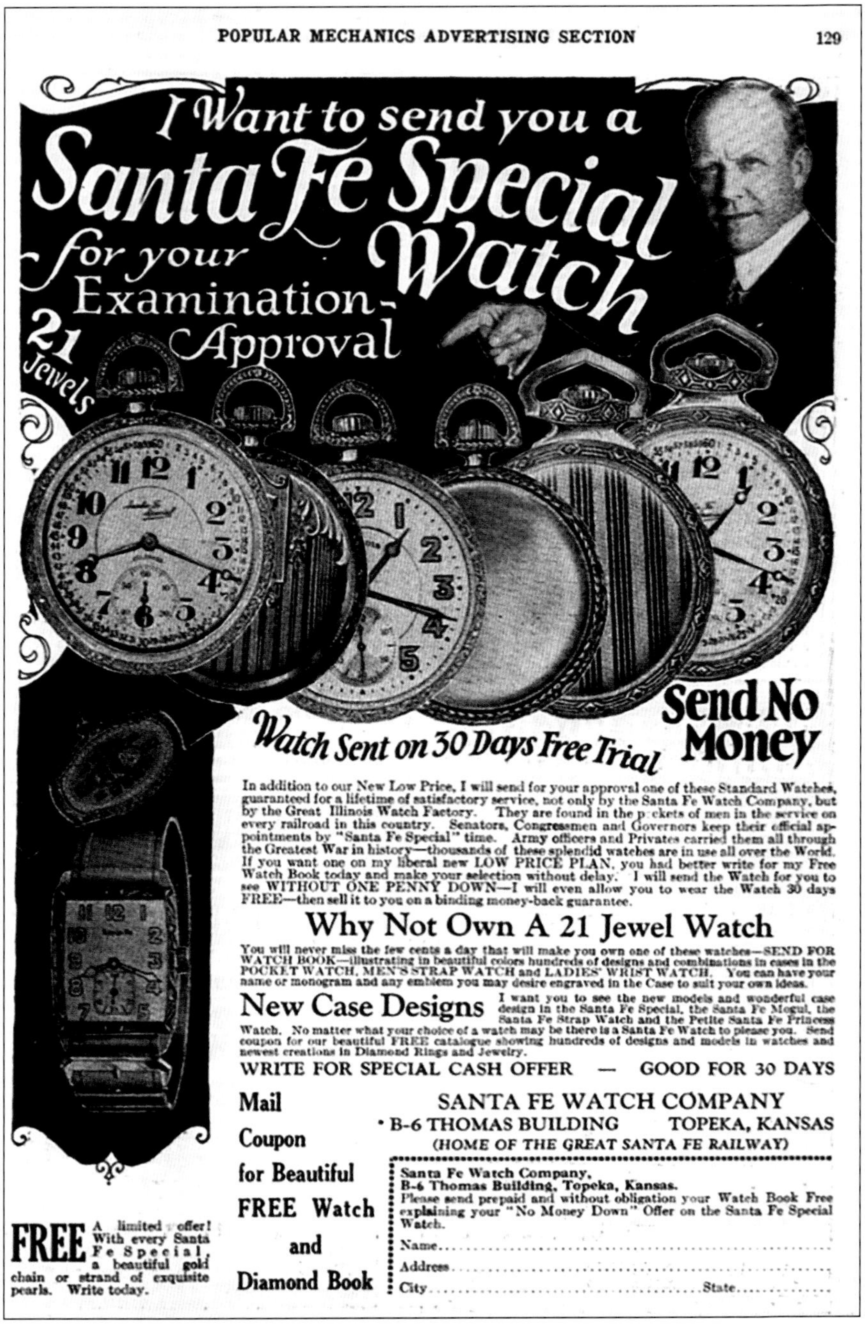

POPULAR MECHANICS ADVERTISING SECTION
129
I Want to send you a
Santa Fe Special Watch
for your Examination-Approval
21 Jewels
Send No Money
Watch Sent on 30 Days Free Trial
In addition to our New Low Price, I will send for your approval one of these Standard Watches, guaranteed for a lifetime of satisfactory service, not only by the Santa Fe Watch Company, but by the Great Illinois Watch Factory. They are found in the pockets of men in the service on every railroad in this country. Senators, Congressmen and Governors keep their official appointments by "Santa Fe Special" time. Army officers and Privates carried them all through the Greatest War in history—thousands of these splendid watches are in use all over the World. If you want one on my liberal new LOW PRICE PLAN, you had better write for my Free Watch Book today and make your selection without delay. I will send the Watch for you to see WITHOUT ONE PENNY DOWN—I will even allow you to wear the Watch 30 days FREE—then sell it to you on a binding money-back guarantee.
Why Not Own A 21 Jewel Watch
You will never miss the few cents a day that will make you own one of these watches—SEND FOR WATCH BOOK—illustrating in beautiful colors hundreds of designs and combinations in cases in the POCKET WATCH, MEN'S STRAP WATCH and LADIES' WRIST WATCH. You can have your name or monogram and any emblem you may desire engraved in the Case to suit your own ideas.
New Case Designs
I want you to see the new models and wonderful case design in the Santa Fe Special, the Santa Fe Mogul, the Santa Fe Strap Watch and the Petite Santa Fe Princess Watch. No matter what your choice of a watch may be there is a Santa Fe Watch to please you. Send coupon for our beautiful FREE catalogue showing hundreds of designs and models in watches and newest creations in Diamond Rings and Jewelry.
WRITE FOR SPECIAL CASH OFFER — GOOD FOR 30 DAYS
SANTA FE WATCH COMPANY
B-6 THOMAS BUILDING TOPEKA, KANSAS
(HOME OF THE GREAT SANTA FE RAILWAY)
Mail Coupon for Beautiful FREE Watch and Diamond Book
Santa Fe Watch Company,
B-6 Thomas Building, Topeka, Kansas.
Please send prepaid and without obligation your Watch Book Free explaining your "No Money Down" Offer on the Santa Fe Special Watch.
Name.
Address
City State
FREE A limited offer! With every Santa Fe Special, a beautiful gold chain or strand of exquisite pearls. Write today.

Popular Mechanics, November 1927

Possibly the movement of this wristwatch, like its dial, was signed Santa Fe; however, no such movement, dial, or watch has been sighted to date. It is probable, however, that the case was by Star, since the pattern of the case engraving for the Santa Fe Tank in this advertisement appears to be identical to that found on a Star case in a catalog. (See **Tank** listing.)

It should be noted that (at least by the end of 1927) Santa Fe started offering Illinois Marquis Strap wristwatch models for sale.

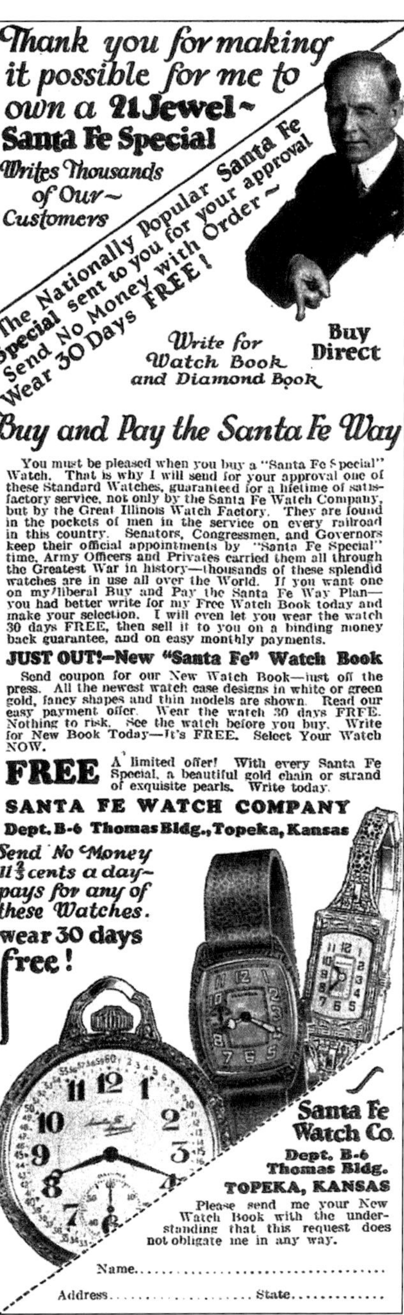

Thank you for making it possible for me to own a 21 Jewel ~ Santa Fe Special
Writes Thousands of Our ~ Customers
The Nationally Popular Santa Fe Special sent to you for your approval
Send No Money with Order ~
Wear 30 Days FREE!
Write for Watch Book and Diamond Book
Buy Direct
Buy and Pay the Santa Fe Way
You must be pleased when you buy a "Santa Fe Special" Watch. That is why I will send for your approval one of these Standard Watches, guaranteed for a lifetime of satisfactory service, not only by the Santa Fe Watch Company, but by the Great Illinois Watch Factory. They are found in the pockets of men in the service on every railroad in this country. Senators, Congressmen, and Governors keep their official appointments by "Santa Fe Special" time. Army Officers and Privates carried them all through the Greatest War in history—thousands of these splendid watches are in use all over the World. If you want one on my liberal Buy and Pay the Santa Fe Way Plan—you had better write for my Free Watch Book today and make your selection. I will even let you wear the watch 30 days FREE, then sell it to you on a binding money back guarantee, and on easy monthly payments.
JUST OUT!—New "Santa Fe" Watch Book
Send coupon for our New Watch Book—just off the press. All the newest watch case designs in white or green gold, fancy shapes and thin models are shown. Read our easy payment offer. Wear the watch 30 days FREE. Nothing to risk. See the watch before you buy. Write for New Book Today—It's FREE. Select Your Watch NOW.
FREE A limited offer! With every Santa Fe Special, a beautiful gold chain or strand of exquisite pearls. Write today.
SANTA FE WATCH COMPANY
Dept. B-6 Thomas Bldg., Topeka, Kansas
Send No Money 11⅔ cents a day—pays for any of these Watches.
wear 30 days free!
Santa Fe Watch Co.
Dept. B-6 Thomas Bldg.
TOPEKA, KANSAS
Please send me your New Watch Book with the understanding that this request does not obligate me in any way.
Name.
Address State

Popular Mechanics, November 1927

Senator, base metal

Senator

Official Name = Senator (derived from the 1932 Jason Weiler–Baird-North catalog)
Secondary Name(s) = None
Formerly Known As = Generic
Time Period = Moderne
Case Variations/Rarity = 🕒🕒🕒 WGF
Case Durability = 🕒🕒🕒🕒
Material = BM, chrome plated
Bezel = Engraved (partially)
Sides = Engraved
Lug Size = Unknown
Lugs = Plain
Springbar = Male
Casemaker = IWCCo
Case Closure = 3-Part Snap-On Bezel and Back
Case Number = None
Case Shape = Square Cut Corner with Flared Sides
Case Back = Unknown
Dimensions = Unknown
Movement Size = 3/0
Movement Grades/Jewels = 307/17
Seconds at = 6
Dial Number = Unknown
Dial = Silver Finish
Dial Opening = Square Cut Corner
Dial Variations/Rarity = 🕒🕒🕒🕒 Silver Finish, Black Numerals
🕒🕒🕒🕒🕒 Silver Finish, Luminous Numerals
Numerals = Luminous
Hands = Luminous
Cased in Factory = No
Unique Case Design = No
Unique Dial Design = No
Introduction Date = 1932
Retail Price New = $24.50
Collectibility = 🕒🕒🕒
Advertisements = Yes
Marketing Themes = "12 Points of Perfection"

Jason Weiler–Baird-North (JWBN), a huge jobber and mail-order firm headquartered in Boston, Massachusetts, offered an Illinois watch that they called the "Senator."[6] (They also promoted the Illinois "Seneca" model, which is the next listing in this chapter.) Although they referred to this watch as an Illinois and described it as a model "nationally advertised" by Illinois, no further documentation currently exists that confirms this model was a Factory-Cased Illinois. Possibly JWBN supplied the cases for this model to Illinois to be timed and cased; however, it is more likely that JWBN cased it themselves.

The case material for the Senator is not indicated in its advertisement. However, an advertisement for a case of this exact design but holding a Waltham movement has been found in the 1931 Carson Pirie Scott catalog. The case for the watch shown there is described as being "3/0 size nickel chrome plated, fancy shaped." The catalog image shows the watch with a leather strap on which appear the words "Illinois Watch Case Co.," identifying the casemaker.

3/0 size nickel chrome plated, fancy shaped strap case, with genuine leather strap and chrome plated buckle. Can be had with the following movements.
R3775 7 jewel Waltham, etched dial. Each, $25.00

Carson Pirie Scott catalog, 1931

The wording in this advertisement is almost exactly the same as used in JWBN's earlier advertisement for the Seneca model:

> Here is an opportunity that comes but once in a lifetime to the watch buyer! On account of the great volume of our world-wide business we have been able to secure the famous nationally advertised Illinois watch "Senator" for men and young men at a big price concession! Measure this watch by any standard you desire. Make any comparisons you wish. If you will do so we are confident that you will prove to your own satisfaction that this is a watch value unmatchable. This smart model is the latest vogue of the day, just the right size, weight and thickness for style, comfort and utility. The high grade 17-jewel movement with Luminous numerals and Luminous hands is warranted a perfect time keeper both by the Illinois Watch Company and ourselves. Note the illustration of the right indicating the 12 points of perfection. Each watch is furnished with a white wrist bracelet or band as illustrated—the complete ensemble in an attractive gift box. You save $15.00 on this high grade timekeeper. Instead of $39.50 our price direct to you is $24.50.

Wristwatches of this general type were very popular in the early 1920s, and many different styles were available. Today, cases can sometimes be found in NOS condition for as little as $10.00. Shown below is an example of an actual watch that appears to contain the same movement, dial and hands as the Senator shown in the JWBN catalog. The case, however, is quite different.

Illinois offering in Generic base metal case

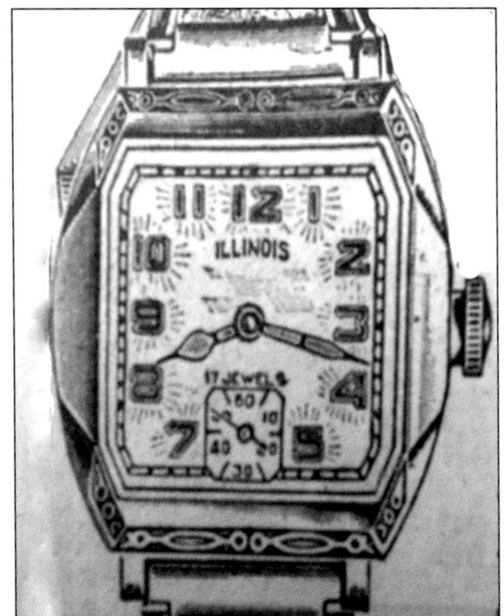

Illinois Generic model offering in Montgomery Ward catalog, 1932–33, is somewhat similar to the Senator model.

Senator NOS case

Jason Weiler–Baird-North catalog, 1932

The one and apparently only difference between the JWBN advertisements for the Senator and the Seneca is their respective display boxes. The display box for the Seneca has printed "An American Watch as American as Its Name" under the "Illinois," as do other Illinois display boxes of the period, but this phrase is missing in the display box for the "Senator." Perhaps this omission indicates that this model is not truly a Factory-Cased Illinois model but instead a custom offering assembled, cased and timed by the Jason Weiler–Baird-North Company. Until further information is uncovered, collectors should classify this model as a custom Illinois watch sold exclusively through Jason Weiler–Baird-North.

Seneca / Blackhawk

Seneca, chrome

Official Name = Seneca (derived from a 1931 Jason Weiler–Baird-North catalog)
Secondary Name(s) = Blackhawk (derived from Gensler-Lee 1931 newspaper advertisements and a *Liberty* magazine advertisement dated November 28, 1931)
Formerly Known As = None
Time Period = Moderne
Material = C
Case Variations/Rarity = 🕒🕒🕒🕒 C/P
🕒🕒🕒🕒🕒🕒🕒🕒 YGF
Case Durability = 🕒🕒 C
🕒🕒🕒 YGF
Bezel = Plain
Sides = Plain
Lug Size = 16mm
Lugs = Plain
Springbar = Male
Casemaker = Pioneer
Case Closure = 3-Part Snap-On Bezel and Back
Case Number = None
Case Shape = Tonneau
Dimensions = 35 x 27 mm
Case Back = Flat
Movement Size = 3/0
Movement Grades/Jewels = 307/17
Seconds at = Rotor at 6, Seconds at 6
Dial Number = Unknown
Dial = Silver Finish
Dial Opening = Tonneau
Dial Variations/Rarity = 🕒🕒🕒🕒 Silver Finish, Black Numerals
🕒🕒🕒🕒🕒 Silver Finish, Luminous Numerals
🕒🕒🕒🕒🕒🕒🕒🕒 Silver Finish, Luminous Numerals, Seconds at 6
Numerals = Painted, Luminous
Hands = Luminous
Cased in Factory = No
Unique Case Design = No
Unique Dial Design = Yes
Introduction Date = 1931
Retail Price New = $29.75 (Seneca); $37.50 (Blackhawk)
Collectibility = 🕒🕒🕒🕒
Advertisements = Yes

Marketing Themes = "New rotor dial"
"Matchless timekeeper"
"Absolutely accurate under severest tests"
"Fully guaranteed in writing"
"12 Points of Perfection"
"Latest vogue of the day. . ."

The Seneca appeared in 1931 in the Jason Weiler–Baird-North Co. catalog (JWBN). In the early 1930s, JWBN was a huge jobber and mail-order firm headquartered in Boston. (Baird-North, which had been a longtime Illinois jobber and private-label customer located in Providence, RI, had been merged with Jason Weiler in 1929.) On the West Coast, the Gensler-Lee jewelry store chain advertised the same model as the Blackhawk. It was advertised in the November 28, 1931 issue of *Liberty* Magazine as well as several newspaper advertisements in that year and the next.

The JWBN catalog had this to say about the Seneca:

> Here is an opportunity that comes but once in a lifetime to the watch buyer! On account of the great volume of our world-wide business we have been able to secure the famous nationally advertised Illinois watch "The Seneca" for men and young men at a big price concession! Measure this watch by any standard you desire. Make any comparisons you wish. If you will do so we are confident that you will prove to your own satisfaction that this is a watch value unmatchable. This smart model is the latest vogue of the day, just the right size, weight and thickness for style, comfort and utility. The high grade 17-jewel movement with Black numerals and Luminous hands is warranted a perfect time keeper both by the Illinois Watch Company and ourselves. Note the illustration on the right indicating the 12 points of perfection. Each watch is furnished with a white wrist bracelet or band as illustrated—the complete ensemble in an attractive gift box. You save $10.00 on this high grade timekeeper. Instead of $39.75 our price direct to you is $29.75.

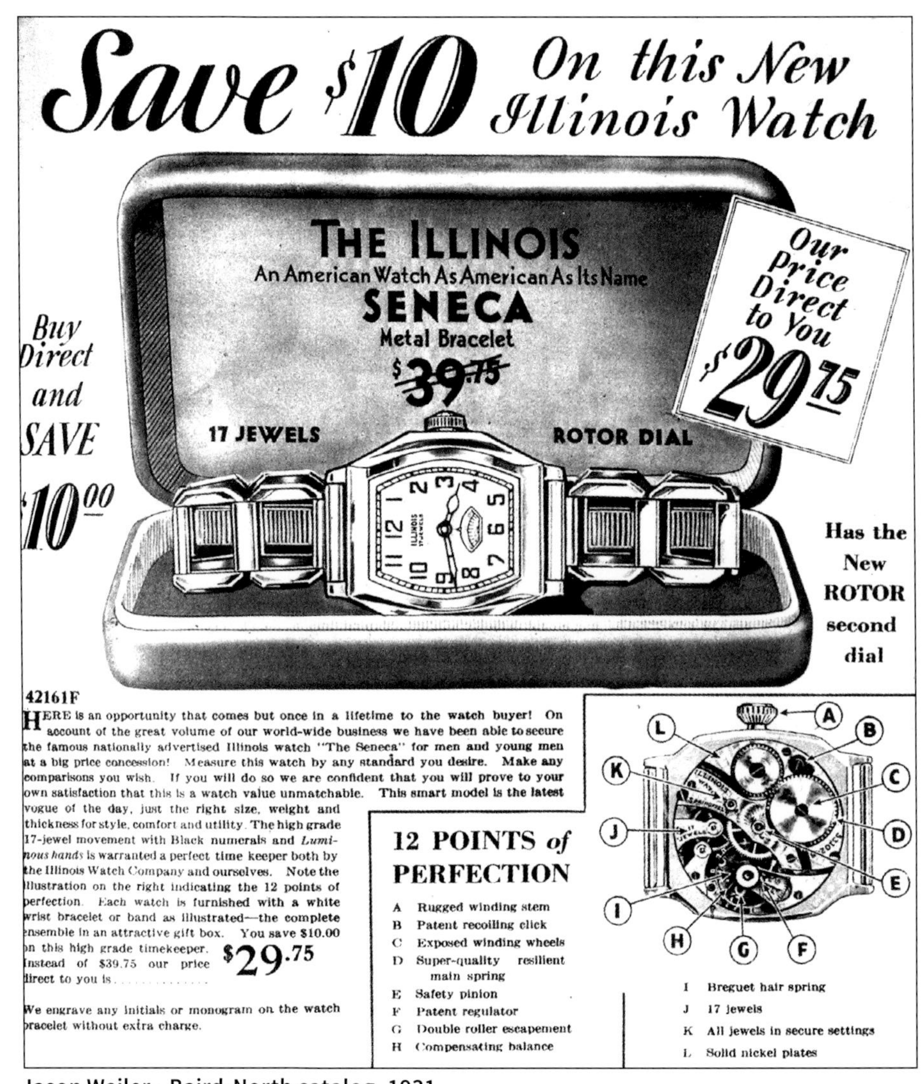

Jason Weiler—Baird-North catalog, 1931

Illinois lists the Seneca model in its published list of Factory-Cased models. Therefore, most likely Illinois first offered the watch exclusively through Jason Weiler–Baird-North. Then, for some reason, Gensler-Lee, a chain of jewelry stores based on the West Coast, started selling exactly the same model as the "Blackhawk." Gensler-Lee probably cased and timed its version, as well as conceiving the Blackhawk name, since the Blackhawk does not appear on the list of Illinois Factory-Cased models.

Gensler-Lee described its Blackhawk model as follows:

> You will want this new Illinois watch for its good looks, but you will find even greater satisfaction in its performance. Precision features, never before offered at so low a price, account for perfect timekeeping! Note these exclusive features: 17 Ruby and Sapphire Jewels, patented micrometric screw regulator, double roller escapement, gold center wheel, Breguet hairspring, Illinois shockproof movement—really the finest 17-jewel watch possible to build! Accurate under the most severe tests! Fully guaranteed in writing. Special feature is the Rotor Second Dial; instead of a second hand, the entire second dial rotates. New white metal case, luminous radium dial and hands, Hollywood metal band. A most exceptional value at $37.50, on special low terms of NO MONEY DOWN, $1.00 a week. Same price cash or credit. No interest or extras!

Modesto News-Herald (Modesto, CA), March 17, 1931; image from *newspapers.com*

In 1932, however, advertisements show that Gensler had raised the rate to $1.25 a week, though the price of the watch remained $37.50.

The origin of the name "Blackhawk" for Gensler-Lee's watch is unknown; however, it may possibly have been named for the San Francisco Blackhawks, a local hockey team active during that era.

Seneca inside case back

Although the chrome Seneca/Blackhawk model can be found fairly easily, locating one with a case in good condition and with a good dial presents a real challenge. As with most chrome-plated watches, their case backs are subject to severe pitting.

The L. & C. Mayers catalog in 1931 advertised an Illinois in a Blackhawk chrome case with a non-rotor subsidiary seconds bit for $21.00. As yet, a specimen of this variant has not been seen.

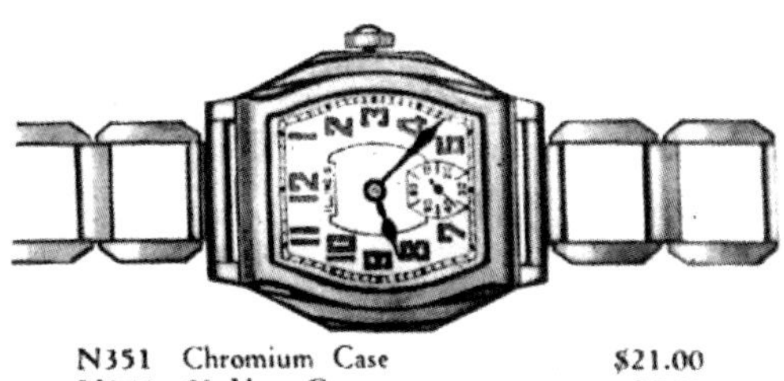

L. & C. Mayers catalog, 1931

Pioneer case back

Pioneer inside case back

To date, all Senecas and Blackhawks have been found in chrome cases. Even though the Gensler-Lee advertisement described its Blackhawk model as being in white metal, it may have been inaccurate about the case composition. Interestingly, the advertisement for the Seneca made no mention of its case material. A further complication: Waltham also sold watches in exactly the same chrome case. Moreover, at least one Pioneer case in yellow gold-filled has been found that is almost identical to the Seneca/Blackhawk case, but this watch did not have rotor seconds. Its case is shown here.

Pioneer front

Illinois 17JEWEL "BLACKHAWK"

ROTOR DIAL!

$1.00 A WEEK

NO MONEY DOWN!

YOU will want this new Illinois watch for its good looks, but you will find even greater satisfaction in its performance. Precision features, never before offered at so low a price, account for perfect timekeeping! Note these exclusive features: 17 Ruby and Sapphire Jewels, patented micrometric screw regulator, double roller escapement, gold center wheel, Breguet hairspring, Illinois Shockproof movement—really the finest 17-jewel watch possible to build! Accurate under the most severe tests! Fully guaranteed in writing. Special feature is the new Rotor Second Dial; instead of a second hand, the entire second dial rotates. New white metal case, luminous radium dial and hands, Hollywood metal band. A most exceptional value at $37.50, on special low terms of NO MONEY DOWN, $1.00 a week. Same price cash or credit. No interest or extras! Call at our store, or mail coupon TODAY for free inspection!

GENSLER-LEE

907 TENTH STREET, MODESTO

31 Years of Service. 16 Stores in America

Modesto News-Herald (Modesto, CA), July 31, 1931; image from *newspapers.com*

GENSLER-LEE

G. J. Gensler, 1929; *Bakersfield Californian*, April 22, 1932; image from *newspapers.com*

The story of Gensler-Lee reflects the rise to prominence of jeweler Goodman Julius Gensler. Gensler's father, Julius, a Prussian Jew, emigrated to the United States about 1864, becoming a tailor in his adopted city of San Francisco. Julius married another Prussian expatriate. They had six children. Goodman "Goody" Gensler, born in San Francisco on October 21, 1880, became a violin prodigy at an early age. About 1899, as a teenager, he began working for watchmaker Isaac Hassan. After a few years, he moved to the Alexandra Jewelry Company. By 1910 he was a partner in the jewelry firm of Gensler & Hahn.

During the next decade, he continued his career as a jeweler, finally joining forces with his brother Edward to form the firm of Edward E. Gensler Jewelry. After World War I, Goody partnered with Ralph C. Lee (March 27, 1876–April 19, 1963) from Sherman, Texas, to form Gensler-Lee Jewelers. In 1920, Goody sold his share of Edward E. Gensler Jewelry to his brother (Edward) and embarked on an expansion program with Lee.

At Gensler-Lee, Gensler held the position of president, while Lee served as secretary. Other accounts in San Francisco city records show Gensler as board chairman and Lee as president; their executive office was apparently at 278 Post Street in San Francisco. By 1930, Gensler-Lee operated sixteen stores, including ten or eleven in California, as well as locations in Denver, Chicago, Boston, Philadelphia and New York City. The firm became known as experts in blue-white diamonds. They claimed to sell more diamonds than any other jeweler in the West. When Gensler died in 1963, the firm had twenty-five stores. The firm lasted until September 1990.

Lee, who lived in San Mateo, California, remains a mystery. Lee may have provided the money, while Gensler provided the knowledge.

In Sacramento they were located at 730 K Street. In Denver, their store was located on 16th Avenue.

The Gensler-Lee Jewelry Store on 818 Market Street, San Francisco, in the 1930s

The Gensler-Lee Jewelry Store on 16th Avenue in Denver, 1934

Gensler-Lee Company Plans to Open Branch in Fresno

Providing a petition to ease the premises is given judicial sanction, the Gensler-Lee Jewelry Company, chain jewelry store operators with headquarters in San Francisco, will open a branch at 920 Fulton street, Fresno, California, on March 1st. The lease in question is for five years with monthly rentals ranging from $200 for the first year to $250 for the final year.

The Gensler-Lee Jewelry Company now operates ten stores in the following cities: San Francisco, Oakland, Richmond, Sacramento, Bakersfield, Santa Barbara and Los Angeles, California; Denver, Colorado; Chicago, Illinois and New York City.

Keystone, March 1930

The Gensler-Lee Jewelry Store on 730 K Street, Sacramento, California in the 1940s

Skyway, white gold-filled

Skyway, white gold-filled

Skyway

Official Name = Skyway (derived from Illinois advertisements and Illinois Sales and Material Catalogs)
Secondary Name = Greyhound (derived from the List of Factory Cased Illinois Watches)
Off-Duty (derived from Illinois advertisements, Illinois Dial and Material Catalogs and jobbers' catalogs)
Formerly Known As = None
Time Period = Deco
Case Variations/Rarity = ◷◷◷◷◷ WGF/M
Case Durability = ◷◷◷
Material = 14K GF
Bezel = Molded
Sides = Plain
Lugs = Plain
Lug Size = 16mm
Springbar = Male
Casemaker = Wadsworth
Case Closure = 3-Part Screw-On Bezel and Back
Case Number = 211
Case Shape = Round
Case Back = Flat
Dimensions = 38 x 32mm
Movement Size = 3/0
Movement Grades/Jewels = 24/17, 307/17
Seconds at = 6
Dial Number = 8343
Dial = Silver Finish
Dial Opening = Round
Dial Variations/Rarity = ◷◷◷ Skyway White
◷◷◷◷◷ Skyway Black
◷◷◷◷◷◷◷ Skyway White, Silver Center Sub Seconds
Numerals = Luminous
Hands = Steel
Cased in Factory = Yes
Unique Case Design = Yes
Unique Dial Design = Yes
Introduction Date = 1930 (Skyway), 1932 (Off-Duty)
Retail Price New = $45.00
Collectibility = ◷◷◷◷
Advertisements = Yes
Marketing Theme = "For Air-Minded America"

The 1930–31 Illinois Sales Catalog described the Skyway model (featured there with a black dial) as "For Air-Minded America. Designed to meet the particular requirements of aviation, this strapwatch is proving popular throughout the nation. In its makeup you will find no compromise with ordinary watch construction. Equipped with standard aeronautical dial, dust-proof case with screw back and bezel. 14K white gold filled case; extra strength crystal." Strangely, the advertisement made no mention of the unique stars design on the front and back of the watch case.

The SKYWAY

For Air-Minded America. Designed to meet the particular requirements of aviation, this strapwatch is proving popular throughout the nation. In its makeup you will find no compromise with ordinary watch construction. Equipped with standard aeronautical dial, dust-proof case with screw back and bezel, 14K white gold filled case; extra strength crystal.

Suggested consumer price, $45.

A. C. Becken catalog, 1931

The Skyway is one of the most sought-after Illinois wristwatches. Collectors prefer the black dial to the white one, but each is stunning. The Skyway has strong crossover appeal to military watch collectors and aviators. The case and dial represent Illinois at its innovative best, with the stars on the case (front and back), the winged dial and the unusual sub-second track with a luminous numeral 6 in its center combining for a compelling design. The dial features only four numerals in total, strategically placed on the inside of the dial along with bold luminous dots and bullet hour markers. Illinois claimed this watch to be "dust-proof" owing to its screw-on case back and bezel.

Four different Illinois models shared the same case Model No. 211: the Greyhound, Motor Coach, Off-Duty and Skyway. The Skyway appeared in the 1930–31 Illinois Sales Catalog and the Off-Duty in the 1931–32 one. The Skyway also appeared in an advertisement for Louis Sickles, a Philadelphia jobber, in the April 1930 issue of the *Keystone*.

FANTASTIC FIND

My longtime pal Farrell Gay reports, "One of my 'Fantastic Finds' was still early on in my collecting years, probably around 1991–1992. You and I had known each other by that time and I was becoming more familiar with what was collectible in Illinois wristwatches by then. I had a watchmaker who worked on my Illinois pieces, and he had a friend who would come up with occasional Illinois wristwatches of all sorts and conditions. I was still 'a little green around the gills,' but familiar enough to know most of the pieces and I would buy one now and then if it was decent, and they would keep bringing others around. The two of them bowled together on Tuesday nights and would call me if they had come up with anything to sell and I would go meet them. One night they called and I went to meet them and they showed me a watch that was in excellent condition with an original dial. They were asking $100.00 for it. I had the impression they thought they were making a killing on it and I was an easy mark. I gave them the $100.00 and told them to keep hunting for others Illinois, and left with my new near-mint Illinois 'Skyway' wristwatch (with a black dial) and went happily on my way home with my reverse killing."

The dial also has the wings connected to a grill emblem that gives the impression of "Stars and Stripes." A few Skyway dials feature a silvered subsidiary seconds circle in lieu of the standard painted ones. This gives the already spectacular dial added pop. The Skyway dial appeared only in the 1930 Illinois Material Catalog.

Many more Skyways exist than Off-Duty models, probably owing to the fact that collectors often try to convert the Off-Duty models to Skyways, because Skyways tend to be more popular, attractive, collectible and valuable. Additionally, the greater number of Skyways available can be attributed to an early 1990s discovery of approximately one hundred NOS Skyways dials, reportedly found in the basement of a former Illinois employee's home in Springfield. For a short while the dials flooded the market, appearing in various military sterling silver cushion and round cases.

Skyway dial with butler center subs

FANTASTIC FIND

I started collecting watches in 1989 and I quickly gravitated to the beautiful Art Deco designs of Illinois wristwatches. As all collectors know, you go through stages of desire. At first everything is great and you are buying virtually anything you can find using the guidebook as your compass. I remember not being able to sleep the night before a NAWCC Mart as I was so excited to see thousands of watches in one place, since that was the only way to see a number of them in those pre-Internet days. You then start getting picky, looking for better examples and some of the rarer pieces. The final stage is where you pick your grails and you do anything to find them. In Illinois, the one watch I really wanted was the Skyway. I had only seen a picture but this watch with the stars on the bezel and back case and the winged dial was an obsession.

I happened to be in Chicago for the Regional Mart and I first visited Mike Fultz at his shop and finally saw one from his collection. It was magnificent and solidified my thinking that I had to get one. I went to the show and was browsing when I saw a gentleman trying to work a deal with one of the dealers. He had a bunch of older stuff, seemingly junk, and the dealer did a quick look and said he wasn't interested. Out of the corner of my eye, I happened to notice that one of the watches had a very unusual bezel and when I got closer, I noticed the unmistakable stars on the outer bezel. The interesting thing was that it had a very plain dial, obviously the Off-Duty model and most likely why nobody had noticed this gem. I quickly asked him what he wanted for it and he said $150. I paid him and rejoiced in my good fortune.

Now to find the dial. I went to another dealer at the show who I knew had a dial operation and asked him if he could help me find an original Skyway dial. To my astonishment, he asked me whether I wanted black or white as he happened to have both! I couldn't decide so I wound up buying both for $300. Eventually I settled on the black dial, selling the silver one for $200; so for a total investment of $250, I finally had my Skyway. Seeing how they are now north of $3000, this was one of my best finds ever. *—Jeff Jewett*

FANTASTIC FIND

An avid Illinois collector from Florida, notes that "The Daytona, Florida NAWCC Regional Mart was moved to Kissimmee, Florida, for the 2010 Mart due to construction at the Daytona location space. The Mart was well attended and sales were above average. After about three hours, I was able to secure my cases and look for deals in Illinois watches. After a search, I was about to give up when I found a dealer with two interesting 0-size Illinois wristwatches. One had a great standard 'Skyway' dial. The second watch had a white porcelain military dial with wings across the top and the name Illinois across the bottom. The dial had a 9 o'clock second bit with black Arabic numbers with a red 12. The dial had stars around the outer track. I negotiated a fair price and had my 'Fantastic Find' for the show." [*Author's note*: This unfortunately was a fraudulent dial.]

FANTASTIC FIND

My very good friend Greg Hart notes that "Several months ago it was brought to my attention through a very good friend (you) that an extremely rare porcelain Illinois 'Skyway' wristwatch dial with a sub 9 and a Red 12 not only existed, but was spotted in the wild. Now to an Illinois collector, this would be a 'Trifecta Grail!' The combination of these three traits (porcelain, sub seconds at 9 and a red number 12) in ONE dial would be too much to even dream about, let alone own!

So . . . on a trip today, I happened to be strolling down midtown Manhattan with a watch buddy of mine, hitting the usual vintage spots when lo and behold . . . my jaw DROPS at what I see in the window! Could this possibly be 'my grail' just sitting there staring at me with the Red 12 and 'Skyway' wings? I gingerly ask the salesman if I could possibly see the watch and he says, 'Oh, certainly.' As I hold the beauty in my hand, I ask, 'Can you tell me a little bit about where you got it and what it is?' and he says, 'Oh, this is a perfect original example of a very rare watch, my friend' (now we are best buddies!). 'For you (the price said $2,000), 50% off today: $1,000!' my new friend announces. 'I got it at a trade show.' So now I am thinking, how can I get this guy to actually take the dial off and show me the back of it?

Using good old 'streets-smarts,' I go with my gut and figure this guy is a total phony and this dial is too good to be true. . . . But what if it was real and I lose out on a find of a lifetime? Rolling the dice, I say, "Hey, if this dial has a special marking on it, I will pay quite a lot for it. Without those marks, I am out the door.' Mr. Salesman quips, 'What marks should it have, my friend?' 'A date,' I say, 'and don't ask me which one because I will know the right one when I see it.' Now his watchmaker is standing behind him, furious at me for even asking to have him take off the dial of this 'incredible watch.' 'This watch is completely original, top to bottom, trust me!' says the watchmaker. (Now at this point in my life, when someone says 'Trust me' I know I am in for a good one.) 'Then you should have no problem taking off the dial real quick for me then!' I fight back. Furious, the watchmaker goes to his bench and pops off the dial, and hands it to the salesman, who after careful scrutiny hands it to me.

My hunch was right. Not only was this dial too good to be true, it was not even porcelain . . . a painted metal dial with a clear coat on it—convincing enough in front, but a total disaster in back; shiny new brass in color with feet hastily slapped on. [*Author's note*: Usually a sure giveaway for a redone dial.] This dial looked like it was made yesterday in China instead of one hundred years ago in Springfield! I grabbed a few quick photos front and back with a bit of inner joy. Needless to say, I couldn't wait to send them to you right away to tell you that this mythical dial did exist and was a complete FRAUD! Unfortunately, I am sure the unscrupulous seller will simply pop it right back into the watch and some poor buyer will get taken for a ride for BIG bucks on the same scandalous sales pitch!

FRAUD ALERT

An alert collector reports that he saw on sale in a New York City watch store an enamel Skyway-like dial with subsidiary seconds at 9 with a red number 12. Upon careful examination of the back of the dial, it was easy to determine that it was a fake dial. A couple of these dials were also reportedly sold at an NAWCC Regional.

Fake Skyway dial. This dial is painted metal, not enamel.

More than one year later, I tracked down the person selling these dials plus the black Skyway dials with subsidiary seconds at 9. He proudly said that he had them made in Hong Kong, along with fake Illinois Telephone Dials with subsidiary seconds at 9 and Illinois dials with palm trees in their centers.

Fake Skyway dial. Notice where the numeral 9 is.

Case Model 211 family. *Left to right:* Skyway white dial, Skyway black dial, Off-Duty black dial, Off-Duty white dial, Off-Duty red 12, Off-Duty custom dial, Motor Coach, Greyhound

TECHNICAL TIP

The Skyway case has a screw-on bezel and case back. Unaware repairpersons and collectors have punctured holes in the case back and/or fouled the threads by mistakenly trying to pry it off with a case knife instead of merely screwing it off.

The highly unusual Illinois case feature makes surviving examples all the more valuable and scarce. Think how many were destroyed!

Skyway inside case back

Southhampton

Official Name = Southampton (derived from Joseph Fahys and Company October 27, 1926 advertisement in the *Jewelers' Circular* and Illinois Materials Catalog)
Secondary Name = None
Formerly Known As = None
Time Period = Generic
Case Variations/Rarity = ◷◷◷◷◷ WGF/P, WGF/E
◷◷◷◷◷◷ GGF/P, GGF/E
◷◷◷◷◷◷◷ WGF/EE, BM
Case Durability = ◷◷◷
Material = 14K GF, BM
Bezel = Plain, Engraved, Enamel
Sides = Plain
Lugs = Plain
Lug Size = 16mm
Springbar = Male
Casemaker = Fahys, Brooklyn Watch Case Company
Case Closure = 3-Part Snap-On Bezel and Back
Case Number = None
Case Shape = Decagon
Case Back = Flat
Dimensions = 36 x 29mm
Movement Size = 6/0
Movement Grades/Jewels = 903/15, 607/17, 904/17
Seconds at = 9
Dial Numbers = 8098, 8702
Dials = Silver Finish, Silver Matte, Butler Center
Dial Opening = Decagon
Dial Variations/Rarity = ◷◷◷◷◷◷ Silver Finish, Luminous Numerals; Silver Matte, Luminous Numerals
◷◷◷◷◷◷ Silver Finish, Luminous Numerals, Butler Center
Numerals = Luminous
Hands = Luminous
Cased in Factory = No
Unique Case Design = No
Unique Dial Design = Yes
Introduction Date = 1926
Retail Price New = Unknown
Collectibility = ◷◷◷◷
Advertisements = Yes
Marketing Theme = "A new and exclusive shape"

Southampton, white gold-filled

Southampton, green gold-filled

Southampton, white gold-filled with black enamel; one of only two known to exist.

Fahys advertised the Southampton case, along with a generic Atlantic model case, in the October 27, 1926 issue of the *Jewelers' Circular*. The Fahys advertisement, which touted the Southampton's unusual shape for the 6/0 size case, listed it in green or white 14K gold-filled quality with a plain, engraved or enamel bezel. The 1930 Illinois Dial and Hand Catalog also shows the Southampton dial. (It also appears later in the Hamilton-issued 1936 Illinois Material Catalog.)

Although a Generic Period model, the Southampton is far from common. The white gold-filled case is more frequently found than the green gold-filled version. The enamel bezel case is extremely rare; only two are known to exist. They are both in white gold-filled engraved bezel cases with black enamel. Illinois is known to have cased a few particular Generic Period models at its Watch Factory, but the Southampton is not one of them.

In their catalogs, jobbers advertised this shaped case for movements and dials by Waltham and Elgin as well as for Illinois. One Illinois jobber, Richter & Phillips, promoted the Illinois Southampton along with an Illinois pocket watch as a "Union Set" in its 1928 catalog: "Every man should have a Union Set, consisting of a Pocket Watch and a Wrist Watch. The Union Set is as necessary to complete attire as the coat and trousers are to a suit of clothing. Sell your Trade the complete Outfit. Every man needs a set of this kind at all times and for all occasions."

THE RICHTER AND PHILLIPS COMPANY

Union Set

Created and Distributed Exclusively by
THE RICHTER & PHILLIPS CO.

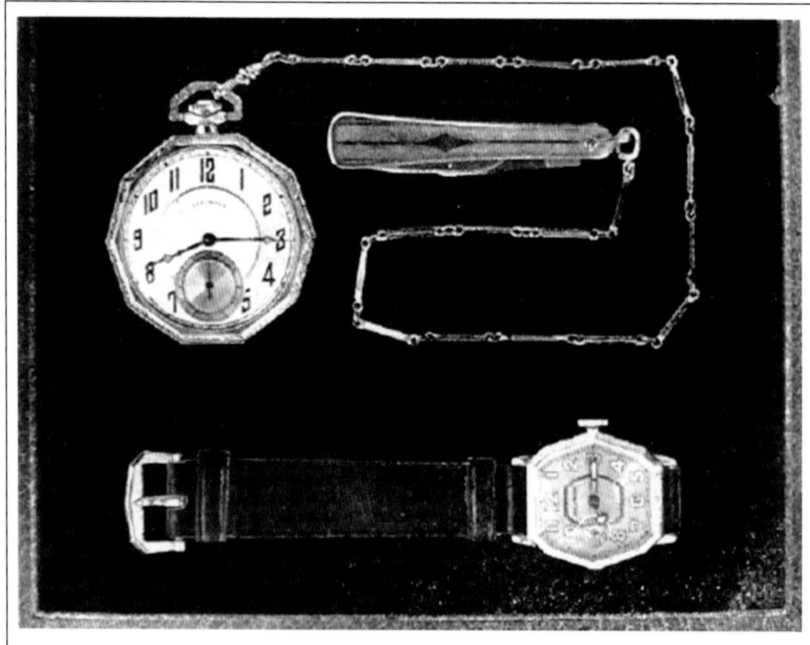

No. P401—A combination of a very high grade 19-jewel adjusted Illinois pocket watch, fancy shaped, engraved 14k white gold filled case, with attractive high grade white gold filled knife and chain, combined with a 19-jewel Illinois Strap Watch, luminous dial, in a 14k white gold filled case to match—a complete **Union Set**.
Price **$128.80**

Donnelly's National Jewelry catalog, 1927–1928

All of the Illinois Southamptons have subsidiary seconds at 9, whereas Elgin's version of this Generic Period model has subsidiary seconds at 6. A true Illinois-cased Southampton should have a capital "I" stamped inside the case back for "Illinois" or "E/I" for Elgin/Illinois, or no letter mark at all. If the case carries only an "E" stamped inside the case back, the case was specifically designated for an Elgin, not an Illinois. The Southampton case in and of itself in any variation is difficult to find, but their dials are even more scarce. Most watches found have poorly redone dials. It is extremely difficult to locate original Southampton dials in any condition.

Southampton, white gold-filled

There are at least three Southampton cases made of base metal; they are much better looking than they sound. They were made by the Brooklyn Watch Case Company, a Fahys subsidiary.

This very interesting ten-sided model, coupled with its 9 o'clock subsidiary seconds, makes for a fascinating watch that appeals to a very broad section of non-Illinois collectors as well as to die-hard Illinois fans. The Southampton dials in most demand are the ones with butler centers or silver center subsidiary seconds.

There are also some rare private-label Southampton dials signed "Illinois Central," with movements also signed "Illinois Central." These were models made exclusively for the use of the Enggass Jewelry Company in Detroit. (See Chapter 6.) Needless to say, this private label enhances these watches' value and collectibility.

Southampton Illinois Central private label

Southampton in base metal BWCC case

As shown below, J. Fahys filed the patent application for the Southampton case design on November 2, 1926, six days after the case was first advertised to the public.

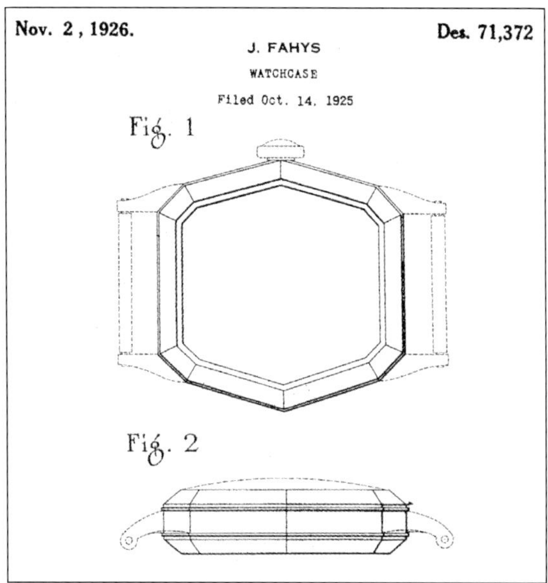

Special, yellow gold-filled, private-label dial

Special

Official Name = Special (derived from a 1930 Illinois Factory advertisement for “Men’s Illinois Strap Watches”)
Secondary Name = Sportsman (if the dial is signed “Sportsman”; see the **Sportsman** listing)
Formerly Known As = Cushion (collectors formerly referred to this model as merely a Cushion watch)
Time Period = Deco
Case Variations/Rarity = ◷◷ WGF/P 0, 3/0, 6/0 Size
◷◷◷ GGF/P 0, 3/0, 6/0 Size; N/E 3/0 Size
◷◷◷◷ YGF/P 0, 3/0, 6/0 Size
◷◷◷◷◷◷ YG/P 3/0 Size
◷◷◷◷◷◷◷ SS 6/0 Size
Case Durability = ◷◷◷
Material = 14K GF, SS, N
Bezel = Plain
Sides = Plain/Engraved
Lugs = Plain

Lug Size = 16mm
Springbar = Male
Casemakers = Various
Case Closure = 3-Part Snap-On Bezel and Back
Case Number = None
Case Shape = Cushion
Case Back = Flat
Dimensions = Various
Movement Sizes = 0, 3/0, 6/0
Movement Grades/Jewels = Various
Seconds at = 6, 9, None
Dial Numbers = 8013, 8014, 8210, 8260, 8261, 8262, 8270
Dial = Silver Finish, Enamel, Silver Finish and Butler Sub Center
Dial Opening = Round
Dial Variations/Rarity = 🕒🕒 Silver Finish, Painted Numerals
🕒🕒🕒 Silver Finish, Luminous Numerals
Numerals = Painted, Luminous
Hands = Steel, Luminous
Cased in Factory = Yes (as a Sportsman model only)/No
Unique Case Design = No
Unique Dial Design = No
Introduction Date = 1930
Retail Price New = $16.75
Collectibility = 🕒🕒🕒🕒
Advertisements = Yes (as a Sportsman model only)/No
Marketing Themes = "A triumph!"
"Free trial!"
"Shock proof"

Jobbers such as Aisenstein-Woronock & Sons advertised this model from time to time.

7W-1083. 3/0 Size, Green or White, Scepter or Napoleon Quality, Cushion Shaped Case; fitted with 17 Jewel Illinois movement, full radium dial and hands, fine leather strap and Gold Filled buckle. This is the lowest priced 17 Jewel American-made Strap Watch on the market in this quality. Our price, each net............. **$16.75**

Aisenstein-Woronock & Sons catalog, 1930

In the 1930 May & Malone catalog, the Special appeared along with the Ensign, Consul, Jolly Roger, Mate, and Tuxedo models—lofty company for this very common and fairly lackluster watch (particularly since the one being advertised was in merely a nickel chromium case).

ILLINOIS SPECIAL
3/0 size, 17 jewels, full luminous dial. Case is engraved nickel chromium.
68W16...$39.80

May & Malone catalog, 1930

Olsen & Ebann jewelry store advertisement suggesting that the buyer acquire a strap watch as well as a pocket watch. Both watches shown are Illinois; the wristwatch is a Special. *Decatur Daily Review* (Decatur, IL), November 5, 1926; image from *newspapers.com*

The Special is a very common model, plain and relatively unappealing. It gains added collectibility if it comes with a custom dial and/or movement. For example, Seaver-Williams Company of Boston, Massachusetts ordered the private-label Illinois Sportsman, which is a Special, for its exclusive distribution through mail-order sales (see the **Sportsman** listing).

Sometimes the Special dial can be found with other custom collectible private labels, such as Captain, Master, Masterbilt, Sterling, etc. (See Chapter 6.)

This model is much harder to find in 0 size than in 6/0. Some 6/0 size versions of the Special are more attractive than the usual ones. There are a few sterling silver 6/0 size Special watches, and they make a very handsome watch, but it has become very difficult to locate nice original Illinois 6/0 size round dials.

There have been several solid yellow gold 3/0 size Specials located. They are quite rare; one is shown here.

Special, yellow gold, with an aftermarket dial (See Chapter 8 for the inscriptions on its caseback and inside its caseback.)

Special Cushions

Official Names = Unknown
Secondary Name(s) = Special Cushion Solidarity (derived by its casemaker name and case shape); Special Cushion Fahys (derived by its casemaker name and case shape)
Formerly Known As = None
Time Period = Generic
Case Variations/Rarity = ◷◷◷◷◷◷◷ WG/E, GG/E, SS
Case Durability = ◷◷◷◷
Material = WG, GG, SS
Bezel = Engraved (partially)
Sides = Plain
Lugs = Plain, Engraved
Lug Size = 16mm
Springbar = Male, Fixed
Casemaker = Solidarity, Fahys
Case Closure = 3-Part Snap-On Bezel and Back
Case Number = None
Case Shape = Cushion
Case Back = Flat
Dimensions = 27 x 33mm
Movement Size = 6/0
Movement Grade /Jewels = 607/17

Special Cushion by Solidarity, white gold

Special Cushion by Solidarity, green gold

Seconds at = 9
Dial Number = None
Dials = Enamel, Silver Finish
Dial Opening = Cushion
Dial Variations/Rarity = 🕒🕒🕒🕒🕒 Enamel
🕒🕒🕒🕒🕒🕒 Silver Finish, Luminous Numerals
Numerals = Luminous
Hands = Luminous
Cased in Factory = No
Unique Case Design = Yes
Unique Dial Design = No
Introduction Date = Unknown
Retail Price New = Unknown
Collectibility = 🕒🕒🕒🕒
Advertisements = No
Marketing Theme = Unknown

Special Cushion by Fahys, sterling silver

So far, collectors have located only one sterling silver Special Cushion Fahys case with the partial engraving on two of its bezel corners. The white gold Special Cushion Solidarity version and the green gold version both possess the same partial engraving on their bezels and are signed "I" for Illinois on their inside case backs. To date, these three models are all unique.

Illinois Special Cushion Solidarity inside case back

Illinois Special Cushion Fahys inside case back

SPECIAL CUSHIONS

It is possible that the solid gold Special Cushions were special watches made by Fahys and Solidarity to sell to Illinois, then sold to Tiffany and Company. Waltham sold sterling silver watches in Depollier Special Cushion cases for Tiffany and Company's exclusive use, according to Czubernat.

SPEEDWAY

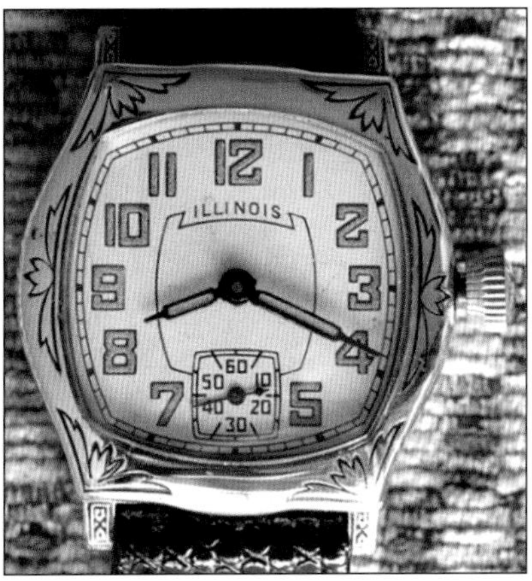

Speedway, white gold-filled

Official Name = Speedway (derived from Illinois advertisements and Illinois Sales and Material Catalogs)
Secondary Name = None
Formerly Known As = None
Time Period = Deco
Case Variations/Rarity = 🕒🕒🕒🕒🕒 WGF/E
Case Durability = 🕒🕒
Material = 14K GF
Bezel = Engraved
Sides = Engraved
Lugs = Engraved
Lug Size = 16mm
Springbar = Male
Casemaker = Keystone
Case Closure = 3-Part Snap-On Bezel and Back
Case Number = 178
Case Shape = Cushion
Case Back = Flat
Dimensions = 36 x 31mm
Movement Size = 3/0
Movement Grades/Jewels = 24/17, 307/17
Seconds at = 6
Dial Numbers = 8132, 8729
Dials = Silver Finish, Butler Center, Enamel
Dial Opening = Cushion
Dial Variations/Rarity = 🕒🕒 Silver Finish, Luminous Numerals
🕒🕒🕒🕒 Silver Finish, Luminous Numerals, Butler Center
🕒🕒🕒🕒🕒 Silver Finish, Black Numerals; Silver Finish, Exploding Numerals; Silver Finish, Exploding Numerals, Butler Center
🕒🕒🕒🕒🕒🕒 Enamel, Exploding Numerals
Numerals = Painted, Luminous
Hands = Luminous
Cased in Factory = Yes
Unique Case Design = Yes
Unique Dial Design = Yes
Introduction Date = 1929
Retail Price New = $42.50
Collectibility = 🕒🕒🕒🕒
Advertisements = Yes

Speedway, white gold-filled

Marketing Themes = "Uncanny accuracy"
"Great endurance"
"A thoroughbred Illinois Watch of craftsmanship"

The Speedway, inspired by and named after the Indianapolis Motor Speedway, is one of the few Illinois wristwatches for which we can determine the origin of its name. Its advertising copy in the 1929–30 Illinois Sales Catalog read: "During this grueling grind of the Indianapolis race the Speedway strapped to the wrist of the drivers ticked off the seconds with uncanny accuracy. Ample evidence of the great endurance of the 17 jeweled movement." Ten of the leading drivers were equipped with an Illinois Speedway for that 1929 race.[7] (The historian at the Brickyard Museum unfortunately had no knowledge of this matter.)

Collectors consider the Speedway model one of the most distinctive Illinois wristwatches. It is highly popular because of its deco design, featuring stylized leaf engraving on its bezel, and thus has become difficult to locate. It is especially hard to find one without some corner bezel wear. The Speedway is one of five Illinois wristwatches that were offered only in white gold-filled cases.

THE SPEEDWAY

W1833 .... $52.30
3-0 size, 14 Kt. white gold filled, oxidized finish. 17 Jewel movement. Detachable leather strap.

Consumer price $42.50

L. & C. Mayers catalog, 1930

Strangely enough, the Speedway does not seem to have appeared in any of Illinois' own magazine advertisements, though it was well advertised in jobbers' catalogs supplied with Illinois Sales Catalogs. The H. W. Burdick Co. of Cleveland advertised it in the August 1929 issue of the *Keystone*.

Illinois produced a second Illinois model also cased in case Model No. 178 but with a different bezel design. Collectors call it the Speedway 178 (see its separate listing). The exploding dials for the Speedway are highly coveted and very difficult to find. The Speedway dials are interchangeable with the Illinois Speedway 178, Major and Jolly Roger.

Enamel exploding dials were also available for these models and look quite spectacular. To date, however, only six enamel exploding dials for these models have been found.

TECHNICAL TIP

The internal dimension of the bezel of the Speedway model has a different thickness than the Speedway 178 bezel. As a result, some of the Guardian dials and movements with rotor seconds may not fit interchangeably. There is also a difference in movement thickness between some 3/0 size movements. — *Ed Kulha*

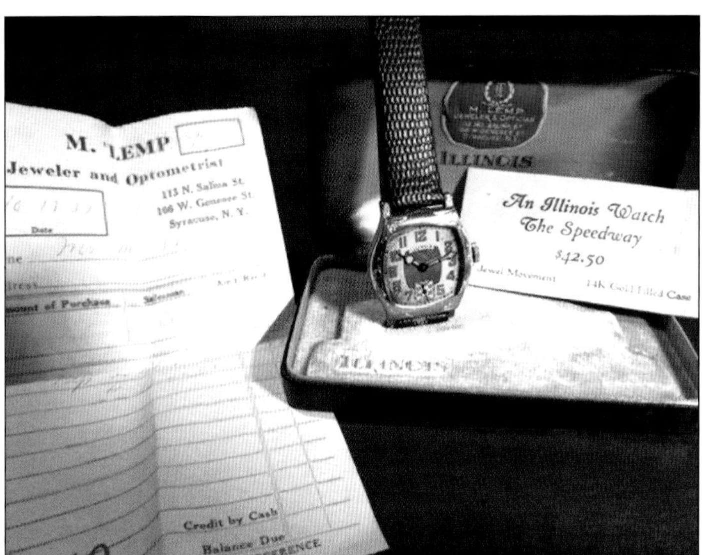

Speedway with its original price card, display box and receipt, dated October 17, 1933, from M. Lemp, Jeweler and Optician, Syracuse, NY

When You're "Flagged"

PUBLIC'S wants these days are like the 20th Century Limited . . . here and gone in a flash. A strong advertisement, the dictates of a Paris or London fashion critic, or the appeal of a new creation, will cause a sudden and lively demand for certain lines.

This profitable business will pass you up like a "flier" unless you're ready (with the wanted lines) the instant it is "flagged." Ride in on these selling waves by taking advantage of our 1 to 24 hour service.

If it's nationally advertised — fast selling and profitable to you, The H. W. Burdick Company carries it. The very next time you're needing watches, clocks, flatware and jewelry, prove the distinct advantage of our 1 to 24 hour service within 200 miles of Cleveland.

The H. W. Burdick Co.
1010 Euclid Avenue, Cleveland, Ohio
A MILLION AT WHOLESALE BUT NOT A CENT AT RETAIL

The "Speedway"

Here's a winner! A new wrist watch by Illinois that gives every indication of leading sales in the wrist watch field. It's 3/0 size—17 jewel, having a patent screw regulator. The case is by Keystone and fashioned in 14k in white oxidized; the dial is butler center with luminous figures. Keystone price $42.50. We'll give immediate delivery. Mail your order.

H. W. Burdick advertisement. *Keystone*, August 1929. Owing to the Great Depression, Burdick went out of business in 1933.

Speedway 178

Speedway 178, white gold-filled

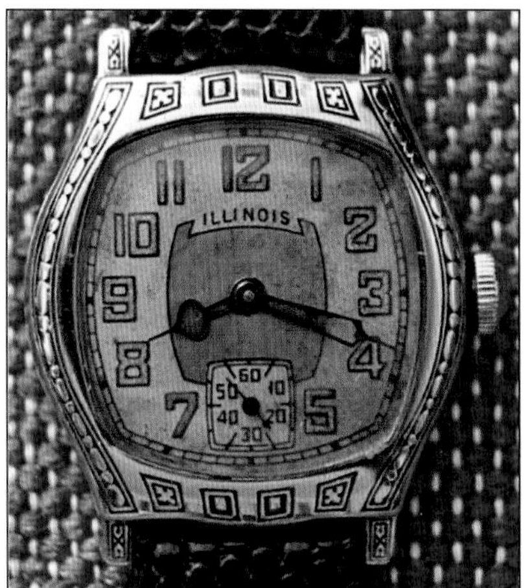

Speedway 178, white gold-filled

Official Name = Speedway (Illinois called both the Speedway and Speedway 178 Speedways; in order to better distinguish the two, this model is called the Speedway 178)
Secondary Name = Speedway 178
Formerly Known As = "No Name" and "No. 178" (derived from M. Fultz's old Illinois price lists)
Time Period = Deco
Case Variation/Rarity = 🕒🕒🕒🕒🕒 WGF/E
Case Durability = 🕒🕒
Material = 14K GF
Bezel = Engraved
Sides = Engraved
Lugs = Engraved
Lug Size = 16mm
Springbar = Male
Casemaker = Keystone
Case Closure = 3-Part Snap-On Bezel and Back
Case Number = 178
Case Shape = Cushion
Case Back = Flat
Dimensions = 30 x 31mm
Movement Size = 3/0
Movement Grades/Jewels = 24/17, 307/17
Seconds at = 6
Dial Numbers = 8132, 8729
Dials = Silver Finish, Butler Center, Enamel
Dial Opening = Cushion
Dial Variations/Rarity = 🕒🕒 Silver Finish, Luminous Numerals
🕒🕒🕒🕒 Silver Finish, Luminous Numerals, Butler Center
🕒🕒🕒🕒🕒 Silver Finish, Black Numerals; Silver Finish, Exploding Numerals; Silver Finish, Exploding Numerals, Butler Center
🕒🕒🕒🕒🕒🕒 Enamel, Exploding Numerals
Numerals = Painted, Luminous
Hands = Luminous
Cased in Factory = Yes
Unique Case Design = Yes
Unique Dial Design = Yes
Introduction Date = 1929
Retail Price New = $42.50
Collectibility = 🕒🕒🕒🕒
Advertisements = No
Marketing Themes = "A thoroughbred Illinois Watch"
"Dressy, dependable and sturdy"

In the past, collectors referred to this model as the "No Name" or "No. 178" (for its case Model Number) as no one knew its true name. Research determined the Speedway 178 to be another version of the Speedway. They share the same case Model No. and dials but can be distinguished by their very different, unique bezel engravings. Some think that the engraving on the Speedway 178 case symbolizes the Indianapolis checkered raceway victory flags. The Speedway 178 can be found only in white gold-filled cases.

The 1930–31 Illinois Sales Catalog called the Speedway 178 "A thoroughbred Illinois Watch of craftsmanship. It is a dressy, dependable and sturdy timepiece. This is the watch that withstood the strain of the 1929 Indianapolis race, strapped to the wrists of ten of the leading drivers." Although this Speedway 178 was advertised in Illinois' own catalogs and those of its jobbers, Illinois seems not to have given it any magazine advertising—a very strange decision, since it is a striking model with an unusual story.

The Speedway 178, like the Speedway, came only in white gold-filled. Both models are prone to case wear on the top and bottom of their bezels.

The Speedway 178 shares the same dials with the Speedway, Major and Jolly Roger Illinois models. As with those three models, an original exploding dial on the Speedway 178 greatly enhances the watch.

The ultra-rare exploding enamel dial provides an even more exceptional look for the Speedway 178, but as yet only six of the exploding enamel dials have surfaced.

The SPEEDWAY

A thoroughbred Illinois Watch of craftsmanship. It is a dressy, dependable and sturdy timepiece. This is the watch that withstood the strain of the 1929 Indianapolis race, strapped to the wrists of ten of the leading drivers. 14K white filled gold.

Suggested consumer price, $42.50.

A. I. Hall catalog, 1930–31

Speedway 178 with an enamel exploding dial

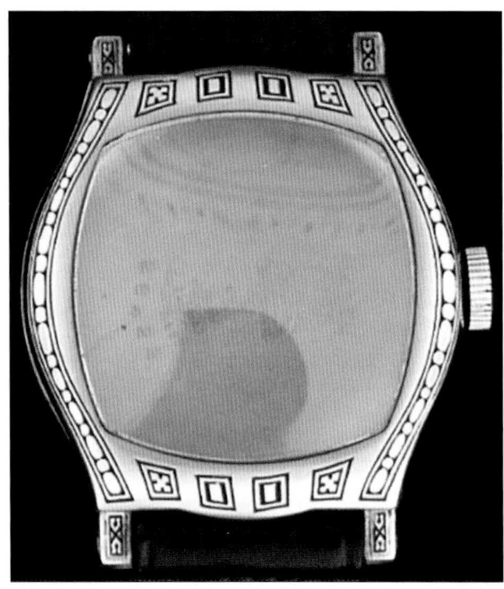

Speedway 178 NOS case

Speedway 178 NOS case side

Sportsman, white gold-filled

SPORTSMAN / CUSHION / SPECIAL

Official Name = Sportsman (derived from Illinois Watch Company letter dated June 21, 1927 and advertisements in *Popular Mechanics* issues dated November 1927 and April 1928)
Secondary Names = Special, Cushion
Formerly Known As = Generic, Cushion
Time Period = Generic
Case Variations/Rarity = ◷◷◷ WGF/P
◷◷◷◷ GGF/P
Case Durability = ◷◷ GGF/P
◷◷◷ WGF/P
Material = 14K WGF, 14K GGF
Bezel = Plain
Sides = Engraved
Lugs = Plain
Lug Size = 16mm
Springbar = Male
Casemaker = Star (Stellar)
Case Closure = 3-Part Snap-On Bezel and Back
Case Number = None
Case Shape = Cushion
Case Back = Flat
Dimensions = 37 x 32mm

Sportsman, green gold-filled

Movement Size = 3/0
Movement Grades/ Jewels = 24/17, 307/17
Seconds at = 6
Dial Number = None
Dial = Silver Finish
Dial Opening = Round
Dial Variations/Rarity = ◷ Painted Metal, Luminous Numerals
Numerals = Luminous
Hands = Luminous
Cased in Factory = Yes
Unique Case Design = No
Unique Dial Design = Yes
Introduction Date = 1927
Retail Price New = $33.95
Collectibility = ◷◷◷◷
Advertisements = Yes
The Sportsman was advertised in the November issue of *Popular Mechanics* in 1927 and in the April issue in 1928.
Marketing Themes = "SHOCK-PROOF"
"WATER PROOF"
"MOISTURE PROOF"
"Free Trial!"
"A Triumph!"

The Sportsman, which is named on the List of Factory-Cased Illinois Watches, was long thought to be a private-label dial furnished to various jobbers and wholesalers by the Illinois Watch Company. However, we now know that the Seaver-Williams Company of Boston, Massachusetts, owned the exclusive rights to the "Sportsman" name. In fact, Seaver-Williams supplied the 3/0 size Star cases to Illinois, which then cased and timed the 3/0 movement.

These details were learned from a recently discovered letter from Illinois responding to an inquiry from a person wishing to purchase a movement from Illinois with the special dial labeled "Illinois Sportsman." Illinois politely replied that it could not accommodate this request because Seaver-Williams had exclusive rights to that name, also noting that Seaver-Williams supplied the cases, which Illinois then fitted with movements and dials.

In its advertising the Seaver-Williams Company claimed this watch to be "shock-proof." However, as Illinois pointed out in reply to the inquiry mentioned above, "The Seaver-Williams Co., in defining the term Shock-Proof, state that each watch before leaving their office is tested by subjecting it to the jars and shocks it would ordinarily receive on the wrist of the average individual in daily use. They do not claim that the watch can be dropped from a tall building or be run over by a steam roller and still run."

SHOCK PROOF WATCHES

June 21st, 1927.

Mr. W. J. Perdue,
Orrick, Mo.

Dear Sir:

We are pleased to acknowledge receipt of your favor of June 17th, with reference to the Illinois Sportsman strap watch of our manufacture. This is one of our standard #24 Hunting movements which we fit with special dials imprinted with the name Illinois Sportsman in cases at the factory furnished by the Seaver-Williams Company, Boston, Mass.

It would not be possible for us to supply you with one of these movements fitted with this special dials, as we understand this firm have the right to the exclusive use of the name Sportsman in the United States. However, we are sure you could easily obtain a movement of this grade with regular Illinois dial, fitted in a case very similar to the one illustrated from any of our regular distributors as per the enclosed list.

In regard to the term "Shock-Proof", we wish to explain that this is not a patented feature found only in our watches, but we believe that all high grade watches made by American Factories have this quality. The Seaver-Williams Co., in defining the term Shock-Proof, state that each watch before leaving their office is tested by subjecting it to the jars and shocks it would ordinarily receive on the wrist of the average individual in daily use. They do not claim that their watch can be dropped from a tall building or be run over by a steam roller and still run.

There are thousands of persons throughout the country wearing strap watches that are jarred and shocked many times a day, for instance the motion with their arms, they run for cars, they play golf and tennis, and the watches still run. Our watches are made to stand the abuse which they receive during daily service and strenuous sports. We believe, that the 3/0 size watch we manufacture represents a good value and we know that thousands of individuals who have purchased them are more than pleased.

Very truly yours,

THE ILLINOIS WATCH

By-

AGS:MH

Illinois letter dated June 21, 1927, concerning the Sportsman model

Seaver-Williams sold exclusively through mail-order channels and also enjoyed a thriving import/export business.[8] Its magazine and newspaper items offered for sale seem to have been sports and military oriented. Thus a wristwatch named the Sportsman fit in well with their other offerings.

An advertisement for the Sportsman watch in the November 1927 issue of *Popular Mechanics* was headed "**SHOCK-PROOF 2-in 1 Strap Watch**" and included a picture with the watch with six special features identified and arrows pointing to them: "Dustproof Moisture Proof Case, 17 Jewel Shockproof Movement, Radium Dial, Slender [Case] Hugs the Wrist, Grooved Stem [for] Easy Grip, Second Hand for Timing Purposes."

The watch was described as follows:

> **A TRIUMPH!**
>
> **Illinois 'Sportsman'—the 2-in-1 strap watch: for SPORTS-wear, for DRESS-wear!** Has remarkable SHOCK-PROOF movement. RESILIO WHEELS, plates, escapement, secret process tempered. Genuine Ruby Jewels—not 7 or 15—but **17 Jewels** for Precision! Created by ILLINOIS WATCH CO., Springfield, Illinois. The U.S. Government during the World War, requested their entire output of Military Watches because they proved best. BUSINESS MEN, Professional Men, Executives, Sportsmen, are ASTOUNDED at its splendid performance under action! Terrific

drives down the fairway, smashes on the tennis court, vigorous lines of work, motoring, office use, intense heat or cold, do not effect its time-keeping! It's SHOCK-PROOF. WEATHER-PROOF! DUST-PROOF! MOISTURE-PROOF! Green or white case. Handsome Cushion Shape. RADIUM dial GLOWS time BRIGHTLY in darkness. Men are PROUD to display it. List price $50. Our price for LIMITED TIME to advertise our **Direct-to-User Values** . . . $33.95."

On top of all of that, Seaver-Williams offered a different payment plan: "We ask for NO money in advance. NOTHING on Delivery. See, try, test, ENJOY "Sportsman' for 10 days **ABSOLUTELY FREE!** If pleased you may pay on Budget Plan: **$6.00 MONTHLY.**"

Another Seaver-Williams advertisement featuring this model appeared in the April 1928 issue of the same magazine. This time the company was emphasizing that "**The GOVERNMENT Picked This Watch**" for military issue. The same image was used, and arrows again pointed to the same features labeled the same way, but with one exception: the movement was now labeled "17 Jewel Military Movement" to go with the new heading. The text too was adjusted slightly, with "Aviators" included in the list of those "astounded" at the performance of the watch.

The text continued with the same type of exaggerated claims as in the earlier advertisement, claiming the movement was "WEATHERPROOF" and "SECRET PROCESS TEMPERED" (whatever that means). It did, however, accurately add that it "Has radium dial—GLOWS time brightly in darkness."

Popular Mechanics, April 1928

Square, white gold-filled

Square, white gold-filled, black enamel

Square, green gold-filled

Square / Burlington Square

Official Name = Square (derived from Illinois Sales and Dial Catalogs)
Secondary Name = None
Formerly Known As = Stephen (derived from the name of one of the sons of one of the first contributors to the American wristwatch price guides)
Time Period = Generic
Case Variations/Rarity = 🕓 WGF/P
🕓🕓 WGF/E; YGF/P; YGF/E
🕓🕓🕓 GGF/P
🕓🕓🕓🕓 GGF/E
🕓🕓🕓🕓🕓🕓 WGF/EE
🕓🕓🕓🕓🕓🕓 WG/E
Case Durability = 🕓🕓🕓🕓
Material = 14K GF, 14K WG
Bezel = Plain, Engraved (Fully/Partially)
Sides = Plain, Engraved
Lugs = Plain, Engraved
Lug Size = 18mm
Springbar = Male
Casemakers = Star, Tivoli, Stellar, Fahys, Others
Case Closure = 3-Part Snap-On Bezel and Back; 3-Part Hinged Bezel and Back
Case Number = None
Case Shape = Square
Case Back = Flat
Dimensions = 35 x 27mm
Movement Size = 6/0
Movement Grades/Jewels = 903/15, 905/17, 907/19
Seconds at = 9
Dial Numbers = 93, 93A ,8093, 8274, 8707, 9083
Dials = Silver Finish, Butler Center
Dial Opening = Square
Dial Variations/Rarity = 🕓🕓 Silver Finish, Luminous Numerals
🕓🕓🕓🕓 Silver Finish, Butler Center, Elaborate Deco Numerals
🕓🕓🕓🕓🕓 Silver Finish, Elaborate Deco Numerals
🕓🕓🕓🕓🕓🕓 Silver Finish, Moiré Center
🕓🕓🕓🕓🕓🕓🕓 Silver Finish, Embossed Center
Numerals = Painted, Luminous
Hands = Luminous

Cased in Factory = Yes/No
Unique Case Design = No
Unique Dial Design = Yes
Introduction Date = 1925
Retail Price New = Unknown
Advertisements = No
Marketing Theme = "Not merely as ornaments"

The Square appears as early as 1925 in Illinois Factory advertisements for its watch movements. The Burlington Watch Company also included Squares in its early full-color, multi-page advertising brochure, c. 1927. (See the **Burlington** listing.)

Under the heading "Wrist Watch Movements," the 1925 Illinois Factory advertisement says: "Illinois Wrist Watch Movements are high-grade and made for timekeeping purposes—not merely as ornaments. Attractive cases may be selected from stock at your retail jeweler." Four wristwatches are pictured: the Canby and Square men's models and the Octagon and Tonneau ladies' models. (For the latter two, see Chapter 10.) The men's models include one with no subsidiary seconds and one with subsidiary seconds at 9. The advertisement describes the movements as "6-0 Size or Eleven Ligne." These movements were No. 907, 19 jewels, at \$40.00, and No 903, 15 jewels, at \$29.00. These prices were for the movements only. The advertisement describes the movements as follows:

> 19 and 15 ruby and sapphire jewels; compensating balance with timing screws; double roller escapement; Breguet hairspring; safety screw center pinion; polished winding wheels, recoil click; silvered or gilt metal dials; full or three-quarter opening.
>
> The 19 jewel movement has a steel escape wheel.
>
> **Only delivered fitted in cases supplied by jobbers**
>
> Illustrations simply indicate some of the different styles of cases, made by various manufacturers, for these movements.
>
> **Made in open face only. May be fitted with hunting dials as illustrated with or without second hand.**

Illinois tried hard to tout the features of its movements so that these early watches would be considered serious timekeepers, not merely decorative ornaments or jewelry.

The Square is a very common Generic Period wristwatch. Squares also came with Elgin or Waltham movements and dials. The Illinois distinguished itself from its contemporary competitors by the use of the 9 o'clock subsidiary seconds, making it a more interesting piece. Contrary to the general rule with Illinois cases, more Squares can be found today with plain bezel cases than with engraved ones.

The engraved cases are more attractive than the plain bezel ones, and the engraved bezel models with black enamel accents are quite spectacular. They transform a very common Generic model into a real eye-catcher. Unfortunately, the Square version with enamel bezel is exceedingly rare, as only two have been found to date. The case of the Square Enamel is by Fahys and was used by Elgin as well as Illinois. Inside the case backs of the specimens that have been found is "6/0" for the size and either an "I" for the Illinois or an "E" for the Elgins.

The Burlington Watch Company sold a Square that was triple signed "Burlington": on its dial, movement and inside its case back. As of today, only two Burlington Square wristwatches have been found. One is in a white gold-filled case with a plain bezel, and one is in a green gold-filled case with an engraved bezel. (See the **Burlington** listing.)

Illinois, in its advertisements and the Illinois Dial Catalog, shows the Square with square subsidiary second rings, but no such dial has been located; the subsidiary seconds chapter have always been round. Star featured the Square in a 1926 advertisement. To date, only two solid gold Squares have been found: each is in a white gold Star case with an engraved bezel.

Square, white gold-filled, NOS dial

Square, white gold-filled

Square Cut Corner, white gold-filled

Square Cut Corner

Official Name = Square Cut Corner (derived from Illinois Sales and Material Catalogs)
Secondary Name = None
Formerly Known As = Bennett (derived from the name of a son of one of the consultants for Illinois watches in one of the first American watch price guides)
Time Period = Generic
Case Variation/Rarity = 🕓🕓 WGF/P, YGF/P, GGF/P
🕓🕓🕓 WGF/E, YGF/E
🕓🕓🕓🕓 GGF/E
🕓🕓🕓🕓🕓 WG/E, GG/P, GG/E
🕓🕓🕓🕓🕓🕓 WG/P, YG/P
🕓🕓🕓🕓🕓🕓🕓🕓 TT/WGF/YGF
Case Durability = 🕓🕓🕓🕓
Material = 14K GF, WG, GG
Bezel = Plain, Engraved
Sides = Engraved
Lugs = Plain, Engraved
Lug Size = 16mm
Springbar = Male
Casemakers = Keystone, Star, Emerson, Others
Case Closure = 3-Part Snap-On Bezel and Back

Case Number = None
Case Shape = Square Cut Corner
Case Back = Flat
Dimensions = 33 x 27mm
Movement Size = 6/0
Movement Grades/Jewels = 903/15, 905/17, 907/19
Seconds at = 9
Dial Numbers = 97, 8097, 8276
Dials = Silver Finish, Butler Center
Dial Opening = Square Cut Corner
Dial Variation/Rarity = 🕒 Silver Finish, Luminous Numerals;
Silver Finish, Painted Numerals
🕒🕒🕒 Silver Finish, Painted Numerals, Butler Center
Numerals = Painted, Luminous
Hands = Luminous
Cased in Factory = Yes/No
Unique Case Design = No
Unique Dial Design = Yes
Introduction Date = 1925
Retail Price New = \$45.00 (15J); \$50.00 (17J); \$55.00 (19J)
Collectibility = 🕒🕒🕒🕒
Advertisements = Yes
Marketing Themes = "A new Keystone creation"
"A necessary article of man's apparel"

Square Cut Corner, yellow gold-filled

Among Generic cases, the Square Cut Corner shape was particularly popular. In the September 16, 1925 issue of the *Jewelers' Circular*, the S. Weissman Co., a New York City jeweler, had an advertisement proclaiming that "Nothing has gained so in favor as Strap Watches. Golf, Boating and Motoring have made Strap Watches a necessary article of Man's Apparel." The image chosen to illustrate the point was a Square Cut Corner case by the Emerson Watch Case Co.[9] Although the dial does not show the name of Illinois (or any other watch company, for that matter), it is possible that some of Illinois' jobbers may have occasionally used Emerson cases to house Illinois movements.

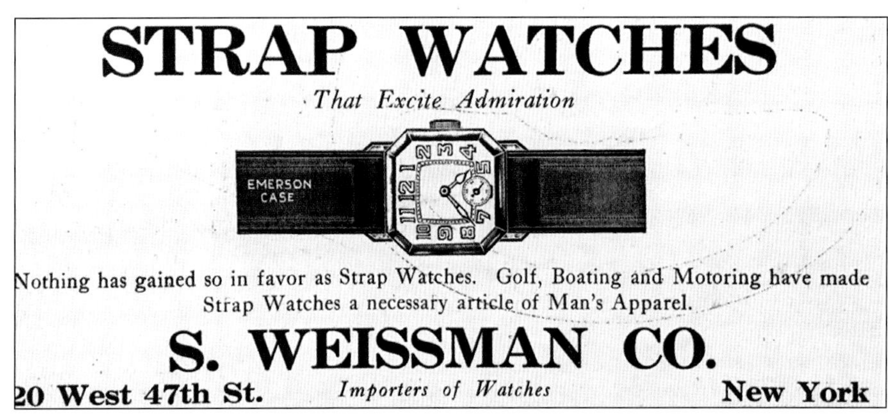

Jewelers' Circular, September 16, 1925

Keystone advertised the "Cut Corner" case as "A new Keystone creation" with an "Egyptian engraved bezel" in the *Jewelers' Circular* on July 28, 1926. Star also frequently advertised this case in the *Jewelers' Circular* and in the *Keystone* in the 1926–27 time frame.

3/0 size 14k white or green gold filled case, engraved bezel, square cut corner shape, fitted with the following luminous dialed movements:

R10256	15J	Elgin	Each $52.00
R10257	15J	Waltham	Each 52.00
R10258	17J	Illinois	Each 55.00

Generic Square Cut Corner listed in the Carson Pirie Scott catalog, 1927

supplied "with strap and buckle," and each watch was "boxed at the factory in an attractive leatherette covered, silk and plush lined display case." Illinois also noted, "Our price and description card is inserted in the lid of each box."

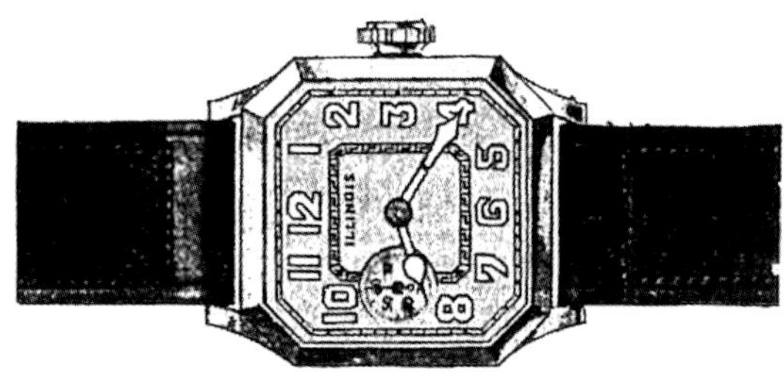

In 14K gold filled, white square shape, luminous dial, 15 jewel.

W10160. .... $55.50

W10161. Same in 19 jewel.............................. 70.00

In 14K gold filled, green square shape, luminous dial, 15 jewel.

W10162. .... $55.50

W10163. Same as in 19 jewel.......................... 70.00

May & Malone catalog, 1928

The Illinois Factory advertising insert appearing in several 1928 jobbers' catalogs (A. C. Becken and Edwards-Ludwig-Fuller, among others) included a page featuring "Complete Strap Watches," with this statement: "These watches are supplied with luminous dials and are cased and timed in the factory." Among the models listed were "square cut corner, plain" and "square cut corner, engraved oxidized," offered in either green or white gold-filled cases. In addition, there were two solid 14K gold offerings, Model "No.15, square cut corner, engraved, oxidized" and Model "No. 16, square cut corner, plain." The gold-filled watches as well as the solid gold ones were

This model was first called a "Bennett" because it was unidentified and a price-guide author gave it the name of a friend's son. The Square Cut Corner is generally easy to find, especially in a white gold-filled case, and is a good starter watch for a new collector as its price is generally very affordable. This model sports the ever-popular Illinois design feature of 9 o'clock subsidiary seconds. The Square Cut Corner is attractive in an engraved white, yellow or green case with a butler center dial. The gold-filled cases, however, are subject to corner case wear, front and back. The solid gold cases, usually made by Keystone, hold up much better and are naturally more valuable and collectible. There is one confirmed two-tone model in a Keystone case.

Square Cut Corner, two-tone, gold-filled

Square Cut Corner, yellow gold-filled

A 1930 Illinois Factory advertisement that included the Square Cut Corner offered further confirmation that at least some of that model were Factory-Cased. Shown in that advertisement along with the Square Cut Corner were four other Generic Period models that were noted as being sold "fitted and timed." These were: the "Cushion Plain" (Devon Plain); "Cushion Cushion" (Devon); "Canby" (Rectangular); and "Whippet." The Square Cut Corner was offered by Illinois with either 15, 17 or 19 jewel movements. Each two jewels cost the consumer approximately $5.00 or $2.50/jewel in 1930, offered by Illinois with either 15, 17 or 19 jewel movements. Each two extra jewels beyond 15 jewels cost the consumer approximately $5.00 in 1928.

Various jobbers continued to promote the Square Cut Corner, such as Aisenstein-Woronock & Sons in their 1931 catalog.

Complete Strap Watches

THE complete strap watches illustrated on this page are furnished in either No. 907, 19 jewel, No. 905, 17 jewel or No. 903, 15 jewel. Illinois 6/0 size movements are built of the finest materials and are constructed with a view of producing the best possible timekeepers. These watches are supplied with luminous dials and are cased and timed in the factory.

Illinois

Each watch is boxed at the factory in an attractive leatherette covered, silk and plush lined display case. Our price and description card is inserted in the lid of each box.

We will continue to supply the 6/0 size movements fitted in 14K gold filled and solid gold cases furnished us by our wholesalers.

The following styles are furnished in white or green 14K gold filled cases with strap and buckle complete:

Cushion, plain round crystal.
Square cut corner, plain.
Square cut corner, engraved oxidized.
Cushion cushion, plain.
Cushion cushion, engraved oxidized.
Rectangular, plain.
Rectangular, engraved oxidized.

Models No. 15, square cut corner, engraved oxidized, and No. 16, square cut corner, plain, are supplied with luminous dials, fitted and timed in 14K solid gold cases with strap and buckle, complete in display boxes. *Prices furnished upon request.*

Illinois Factory advertisement, 1928

WHY I COLLECT ILLINOIS

My interest in vintage wristwatches started in the 1980s when a co-worker and friend, George, came to work in clothes tailored in the style from the 1940s. He wanted his accessories to match, so he wore a vintage watch. I remembered seeing this type of watch worn by my Uncle Alfred and now wanted one of my own. I asked George where I might find a similar watch and what the cost might be. He told me to go to a store in the Greenwich Village area of New York City that sold vintage jewelry and watches. The Village was not far from where we worked in Manhattan and I soon found my first vintage watch. It was a gold-filled 1940s Bulova that cost me $95.

Collecting vintage watches was not my intention until I purchased an Illinois watch in the 1990s. I had not seen an Illinois watch before and was amazed by the beauty of its design and workmanship needed to create this watch. It was a Square Cut Corner model in white gold-filled. The bezel was engraved and the face had luminous numbers. The most interesting feature of the watch was the subsidiary seconds at 9 o'clock. Curious to know what other models might have been produced by the Illinois Watch Company, I bought a reference book. There I saw other watches in the Art Deco style that I would soon be looking for.

Today that Illinois watch is part of the core group in my collection from the Art Deco period. The Art Deco era is part of our history and can still be seen in the city, whether I am in sight of the Chrysler Building or looking at the watch on my wrist.

—*Gerald Deieso*

Square Cut Corner NOS Star case

Square Cut Corner Large / Gift Series

Square Cut Corner Large, white gold-filled

Official Name = Square Cut Corner Large (so named to distinguish it from the standard-sized Illinois Square Cut Corner model)
Secondary Name = Gift Series (derived from Richter-Phillips advertisements)
Formerly Known As = Large Bennett (this case design was originally named the "Bennett" after the son of a price guide author's friend)
Time Period = Generic
Case Variations/Rarity = 🕒🕒🕒🕒 WGF/E
🕒🕒🕒🕒🕒🕒🕒 WGF/E/Hinged Bezel
🕒🕒🕒🕒🕒🕒🕒 YGF/P
Case Durability = 🕒🕒🕒🕒
Material = 14K GF
Bezel = Plain, Engraved
Sides = Engraved
Lugs = Plain
Lug Size = 18mm
Springbar = Male
Casemaker = Star
Case Closure = 3-Part Snap-On Bezel and Back; 2-Part Hinged Bezel
Case Number = None
Case Shape = Square Cut Corner
Case Back = Flat
Dimensions = 30.4 x 38mm
Movement Size = 3/0
Movement Grades/Jewels = 24/17, 307/17
Seconds at = 6
Dial Numbers = 8214, 8292
Dial = Silver Finish
Dial Opening = Square Cut Corner
Dial Variations/Rarity = 🕒🕒🕒🕒 Silver Finish, Luminous Numerals
🕒🕒🕒🕒🕒 Silver Finish, Painted Numerals
Numerals = Painted, Luminous
Hands = Luminous
Cased in Factory = Yes
Unique Case Design = No
Unique Dial Design = No
Introduction Date = 1928
Retail Price New = Unknown
Collectibility = 🕒🕒🕒🕒
Advertisements = Yes
Marketing Theme = Unknown

The shape and engraving detail of the Square Cut Corner Large reflect the Square Cut Corner, except that the case has been designed to take the larger 3/0 movement. This model, however, has subsidiary seconds at 6 o'clock, not 9 o'clock as the standard Square Cut Corner does. Although the dial for the Square Cut Corner Large appears in the 1930 and 1936 Illinois Material Catalogs, this model does not appear in any of Illinois' own advertisements. This model is fairly rare, as only a small number have been discovered to date.

The Square Cut Corner Large is deemed to be a legitimate Illinois wristwatch, although its true name from the List of Factory Cased Illinois Watches has yet to be determined. This model is hard to find in white gold-filled and has yet to be located in a yellow gold-filled case. A one-of-a-kind version with a hinged bezel exists. It is very possible that the hinged bezel allowed the Square Cut Corner Large to function as a Braille watch. It is nearly impossible to find these models in solid gold.

Square Cut Corner Large Braille watch

Original dials can be found with painted subsidiary seconds or butler center second bits.

The Richter & Phillips Company offered the Square Cut Corner Large as part of its Gift Series wristwatch collection. (See the **Gift Series** listing.)

Burnett Bros. Jewelry Store advertisement for a Square Cut Corner Large, but biased in favor of Hamilton; *Oregon Statesman* (Salem, OR), December 14, 1928; image from *newspapers.com*

Standish

Official Name = Standish (derived from Illinois advertisements and Illinois Sales Catalogs)
Secondary Name = None
Formerly Known As = None
Time Period = Moderne
Case Variations/Rarity = 🕒🕒🕒🕒🕒 YGF/P
🕒🕒🕒🕒🕒🕒 WGF/P, RGP/P, RGF/P
Case Durability = 🕒🕒 RGP, RGF
🕒🕒🕒 YGF
🕒🕒🕒🕒 WGF
Material = 10K GF
Bezel = Plain
Sides = Plain
Lugs = Plain
Lug Size = 16mm
Springbar = Male
Casemakers = Keystone, Regal
Case Closure = 2-Part Snap-On back
Case Number = 651
Case Shape = Tonneau
Case Back = Curved
Dimensions = 31 x 24mm
Movement Size = 6/0
Movement Grades/Jewels = 903/15, 605/15, 605A/15
Seconds at = 6, 9
Dial Numbers = 8495 (by Hamilton)
Dial = Silver Finish
Dial Opening = Tonneau
Dial Variations/Rarity = 🕒🕒 Silver Finish, Luminous Numerals
🕒🕒🕒🕒 Silver Finish, Flush Gold Numerals; Silver Finish, Etched Numerals
Numerals = Luminous, Etched, Flushed Gold Numerals
Hands = Steel, Luminous
Cased in Factory = Yes (by Hamilton in Lancaster)
Unique Case Design = No
Unique Dial Design = Yes
Introduction Date = 1934
Retail Price New = $35.00
Collectibility = 🕒🕒🕒🕒
Advertisements = No
Marketing Themes = "Splendid new strap watch"
"As modern as the minute"

Standish, white gold-filled

Standish, yellow gold-filled

The Foreword to the 1934 Illinois Sales Catalog, in which the Standish was introduced, stated: "Illinois, since 1870, has made good watches. The 1934 line is better. It's as modern as the minute—incorporating all of the horological advances which have occurred in the past sixty years. Now—as always—you can't go wrong with Illinois watches . . . pioneers of progress."

Illinois pitched the Standish in its catalogs as a "Splendid new strap model in 10K filled gold, white or natural. 15 Jewels. Flush gold figure dial."

Standish, yellow gold-filled, etched numeral dial.

Notwithstanding the advertising copy, Hamilton included the Standish as part of its 1934 low-priced Illinois bargain offerings. Its 10K gold-filled case and 15-jewel movement attest to its positioning as a low-cost watch. Today, however, this model is a very rare one in either case color. Only two white gold-filled Standish models are known to exist: one is in a Keystone case; the other is in a Regal case with an interesting design change on its bezel.

Fewer than ten Standish models have been located in yellow gold-filled cases to date. No more than three have been sighted in unsigned rose gold-filled cases.

The dial could be found with subsidiary seconds at 6 or 9, exploding or Arabic numerals, and etched or flush gold numerals. Hamilton designed dial number 8495 in-house as the dial for the Standish; the drawing is shown below.

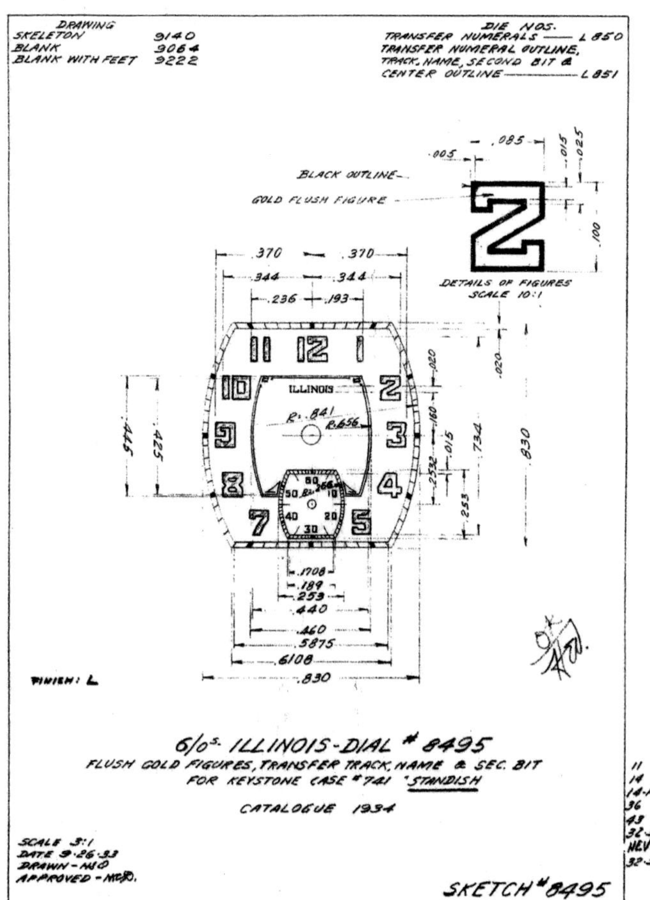

Hamilton drawing for Standish dial

Standish inside case back

Standish NOS dial, etched gold numerals

The white gold-filled and yellow gold-filled cases are found in Model No. 651 Keystone cases. The Regal case in white gold-filled has no case Model Number. There are also a few rare rose gold-plate cases with no Model Number manufactured by Philadelphia. Hamilton's own Grant model, which was very similar in design, came in both a sterling silver case made by Wadsworth and in 10K and 14K yellow gold-filled cases made by Wadsworth and Solidarity. (The similar but earlier Elgin E-3 model had come in Wadsworth solid gold and gold-filled cases.)

The Standish came equipped with an Elvinar hairspring as did all the other Illinois wristwatch models introduced in 1934.

The Standish is not on the List of Factory Cased Illinois Watches as it postdated the December 31, 1932 list.

Look-Alikes

As mentioned above, the Illinois Standish and the Hamilton Grant model have very similar designs. The Standish, introduced in 1934, came in a 10K yellow or white gold-filled case made by Keystone. The Grant as initially released in 1933 came in a 14K white or yellow gold-filled cases made by Solidarity. But in 1934 it was issued in a lesser-quality 10K yellow gold-filled case, though again by Solidarity, and its "white" sibling was in a sterling silver case by Wadsworth.

ELINVAR

In its 1934 catalog announcing its complete line of watches equipped with Elinvar hairsprings, Illinois made this statement: "Elinvar is a nickel-steel alloy having the following major properties: 1. It is rustless. 2. It cannot be permanently magnetized. 3. It remains comparatively unaffected by temperature changes. When used as a hairspring it automatically eliminates the most common causes of watch irregularities."

The term "Elinvar" is a construct made by combining parts of the words "elasticity" and "invariable." (See Chapter 6.)

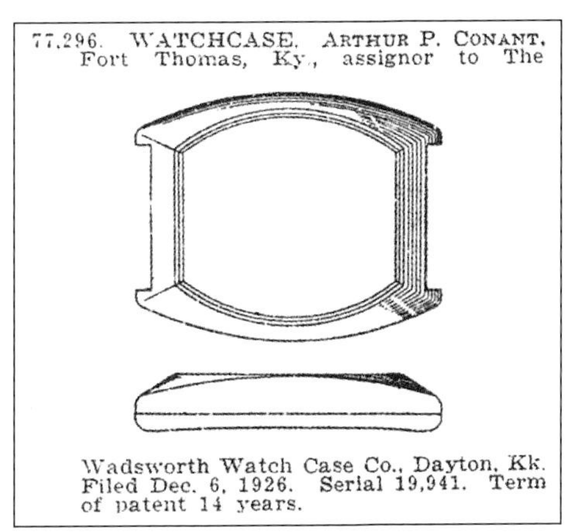
77,296. WATCHCASE. Arthur P. Conant, Fort Thomas, Ky., assignor to The Wadsworth Watch Case Co., Dayton, Kk. Filed Dec. 6, 1926. Serial 19,941. Term of patent 14 years.

Standish case design patent filed by Wadsworth on December 6, 1926

Hamilton Grant with a wood grain dial

Sterling, chrome

Sterling, chrome

Sterling, chrome

Sterling

Official Name = Sterling (so called by collectors because its movement and dial are signed "Sterling" under the Illinois)
Secondary Name = None
Formerly Known As = None
Time Period = Deco
Case Variations/Rarity = 🕒🕒🕒🕒 BM/P, C
🕒🕒🕒🕒🕒 WGF/P, YGF/SSB
🕒🕒🕒🕒🕒🕒 YGF/E/SSB
Case Durability = 🕒🕒🕒🕒
Material = 14K GF, BM, C
Bezel = Plain, Engraved
Sides = Engraved
Lugs = Plain
Lug Size = 16mm
Springbar = Male
Casemakers = Star, Others
Case Closure = 3-Part Snap-On Bezel and Back
Case Number = None
Case Shape = Rectangular (sometimes Tonneau)
Case Back = Flat
Dimensions = 35 x 38mm, Others
Movement Size = 3/0
MovementGrades /Jewels= 24/17
Seconds at = Rotor at 6
Dial Number = None
Dial = Silver Finish
Dial Opening = Rectangular (sometimes Tonneau)
Dial Variations /Rarity = 🕒🕒🕒🕒🕒 Silver Finish, Luminous Numerals
Numerals = Luminous
Hands = Luminous
Cased in Factory = No
Unique Case Design = No
Unique Dial Design = Yes
Introduction Date = 1930
Retail Price New = Unknown
Collectibility = 🕒🕒🕒🕒
Advertisements = No
Marketing Theme = Unknown

This model is called Sterling because its dial is often signed "Sterling" under the Illinois. The Sterling is one of the few Illinois models with rotor subsidiary seconds; other models are the Akron, Blackhawk, Guardian, Guardsman, Military Guardsman and Seneca. Collectors highly prize all of the rotor subsidiary seconds Illinois models. The Sterling's case and dial are usually rectangular, but a Tonneau-shaped case and dial are occasionally seen. The only rotor subsidiary seconds dial listed in an Illinois Materials Catalog, however, is the Guardsman/Guardian one. The Guardsman and Guardian models came in numbered cases; the Sterling did not.

No advertisement of this model has been found, nor does it appear in any Illinois or jobbers' catalogs. However, since it has been discovered that the Kay Jewelry Company had "Sterling" private-label Illinois movements and dials, it seems quite plausible that the Illinois Sterling wristwatch was also a Kay's model.[10] (The collector should note that there are Generic Period models such as the Canby that have been found with not only dials but also movements marked Sterling, and these too were presumably for Kay's. However, these Illinois watches retain their Generic Period names; they are not considered Sterling models.)

The Sterling is usually found in inexpensive base metal/chrome cases that are generally easy to acquire. Two Sterlings have been found with yellow gold-filled bezels and stainless steel case backs. Although the dial was clearly made by the Illinois Factory, the Sterling came only in contract cases most likely manufactured during the Deco Period. It most frequently came in Star cases. Such Star cases can be easily found inexpensively even today in NOS condition. Even in a common, low-grade case, its combination with the elegant rotor subsidiary second dial makes it an attractive watch that is difficult to find and fun to own.

FANTASTIC FIND

Greg Hart reports that he was "on another one of my treks through the swamps of eBay and I came across a barrel-shaped case with an Illinois dial on it. The case was in extremely rough shape with a yellowed crystal. The seller of course put it up as an 'Old watch for parts' and it was going for next to nothing. I grabbed it. The hands were covering the name on the dial in the image and I could barely make out what appeared to be another word under the name Illinois on the dial: S******g. Could it be a signed 'Sterling' dial? Well, it was cheap, so why not see?

"Anyway, the package comes and I pop the bezel to reveal a beautiful Illinois dial with sub seconds at 9 signed 'Sterling.' Just to see what was under the hood, I decide to pop the back. Well, what do you know, a beautiful movement signed 'Sterling' on it as well. Wow! I had never seen one!

"Sometimes there are diamonds in the rough—you just have to look."

Tank, white gold-filled

Tank, green gold-filled

TANK / BRYCE

Official Name =	Tank and Bryce (derived from Illinois Material Catalogs)
Secondary Name =	None
Formerly Known As =	Contract
Time Period =	Generic
Case Variations /Rarity =	◷◷◷ WGF/P, WGF/E ◷◷◷◷ YGF/P, YGF/E, GGF/P, GGF/E
Case Durability =	◷◷ GGF ◷◷◷◷ WGF
Material =	14K GF
Bezel =	Plain, Engraved
Sides =	Engraved
Lugs =	Plain/Engraved
Lug Size =	16mm
Springbar =	Male
Casemakers =	Elgin, IWCCo
Case Closure =	3-Part Snap-On Bezel and Back; 2-Part Snap-On back; 2-Part Hinged Back
Case Number =	None
Case Shape =	Rectangular
Case Back =	Flat
Dimensions =	40 x 27mm
Movement Size =	6/0
Movement Grades / Jewels =	903/15, 905/17
Seconds at =	9, None
Dial Numbers =	8092, 8269, 8292, 8711
Dial =	Silver Finish
Dial Opening =	Rectangular
Dial Variations/Rarity =	◷◷◷ Silver Finish, Luminous Numerals; Silver Finish, No Subsidiary Seconds ◷◷◷◷◷ Silver Finish, Painted Numerals; Silver Finish, Butler Center Seconds
Numerals =	Painted, Luminous
Hands =	Luminous
Cased in Factory =	No
Unique Case Design =	No
Unique Dial Design =	No
Introduction Date =	1923
Retail Price New =	$52.00
Collectibility =	◷◷◷◷
Advertisements =	Yes
Marketing Theme =	Unknown

For years, collectors believed that the Illinois Tank model was an example of a contract watch. However, appearance of its dials in at least two Illinois Material Catalogs refutes that thinking. For collectors with large wrists, this model fits perfectly. Several Generic Period cases work with the Tank dial.

An Illinois Tank model offered in either a green or white gold-filled case was shown in a catalog from May & Malone in 1928.

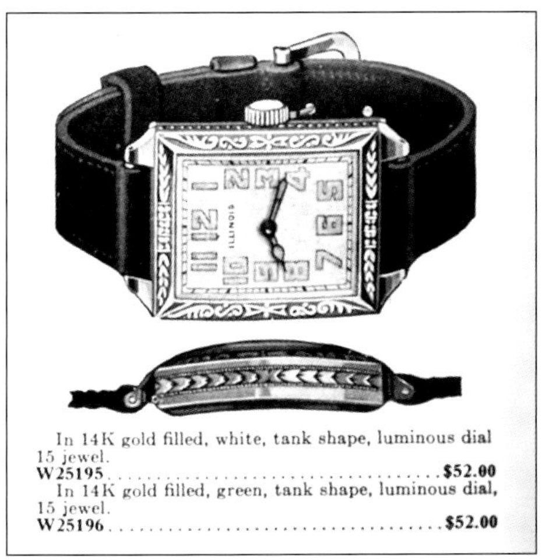

May & Malone catalog, 1928

Some tanks have hinged cases, but most do not. Some have bezels that are strict rectangles and others are slightly curved toward the top and bottom. Although there were plain Tank cases available, most cases seem to have bezels displaying very deep and dramatic engravings.

Most Tanks have subsidiary seconds at 9 or 6; however, the Bryce model came without subsidiary seconds.

In the 1925 to 1927 time period, the Santa Fe Watch Company offered the Tank model for sale with a signed Santa Fe dial with subsidiary seconds at 6. It is not known if the movement was also signed Santa Fe, since an example of this model has never been seen. (See the **Santa Fe Tank** listing.)

A Generic engraved Tank case that is shown with a Waltham in it in the 1928 A. C. Becken catalog looks just like the cases of the Illinois Tanks shown in the photographs at the top of this listing. The 6/0 size case by IWCCo has an engraving pattern on it that appears to be identical to what is on those watches. Moreover, it also appears to be a match for the case shown for the Santa Fe Tank in its advertisement.

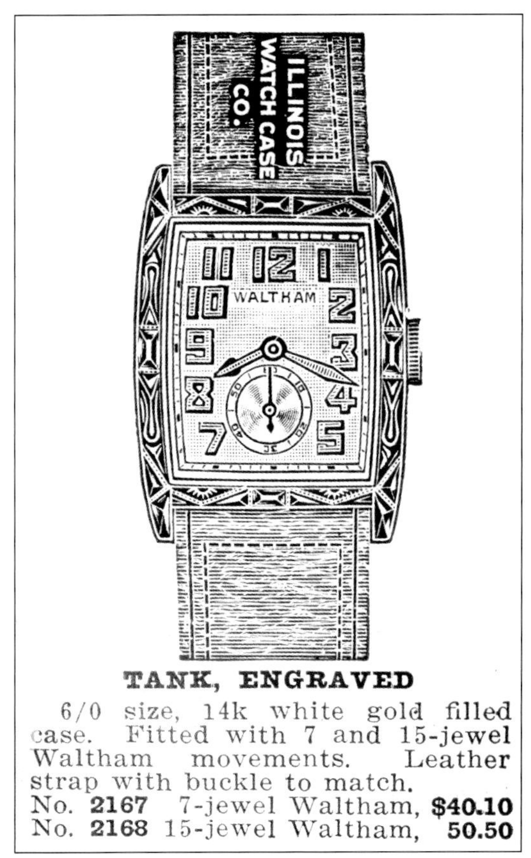

A. C. Becken catalog, 1928

Telephone Dial, sterling silver

Telephone Dial with its radium mostly intact

TELEPHONE DIAL

Official Name = Telephone Dial (derived from collectors' usage for the dial that was inspired by issuance of the first rotary telephone in the United States)
Secondary Name = General Funston (derived from IWCCo Advertisement for this case)
Formerly Known As = None
Time Period = Transitional
Case Variations/Rarity = ◷◷◷◷ SS/P
Case Durability = ◷◷◷◷
Material = SS
Bezel = Plain
Sides = Plain
Lugs = Plain
Lug Size = 14mm, 16mm
Springbar = Swivel Lugs
Casemakers = Fahys, Elgin, and Others
Case Closure = 3-Part Snap-On Bezel and Back/screw-on Bezel and Back
Case Number = 5316
Case Shape = Round
Case Back = Flat
Dimensions = Various
Movement Size = 3/0
Movement Grades/Jewels = 24/17, 36/17
Seconds at = 6
Dial Number = 5316 – 308-D
Dial = Enamel
Dial Opening = Round
Dial Variations/Rarity = ◷◷◷◷ Enamel, Painted Numerals (Luminous Missing)
◷◷◷◷◷◷ Enamel, Luminous Numerals (Luminous Intact)
Numerals = Painted, Luminous
Hands = Steel/Luminous
Cased in Factory = No
Unique Case Design = No
Unique Dial Design = Yes
Introduction Date = 1919
Retail Price New = Unknown/$1.25 for one dial.
Collectibility = ◷◷◷◷
Advertisements = No
Marketing Theme = Unknown

The Telephone Dial model was inspired by the introduction of the rotary telephone. The dial was shown in the December 1923 Illinois Materials Catalog, but no other references to this model have been found.

No. 5316–308-D

3/0 Size Luminous
S. S. Only

Illinois Materials Catalog, 1923

As one of the most popular Illinois wristwatches, the Telephone Dial model is always in great demand. When released from the Illinois Factory, the dials had radium inside the numbers, but over the years most of that radium has flaked off or disappeared from other causes. The dial itself was offered for sale in 1923 for $1.25 per dial. The Telephone Dial was listed in the 1923 Illinois Materials Catalog, but it was not in either the 1930 or 1936 Illinois Material Catalog.

Although the Telephone Dial was probably intended for a pocket watch, it is now found almost exclusively in a round sterling silver General Funston wristwatch case with attached swivel lugs. Occasionally this dial is found in cushion cases of various case metals and military-type cases in nickel and silverore. There is a one-of-a-kind 6/0 size Telephone Dial with subsidiary seconds at 9 in a yellow gold case. (See the **Chrysanthemum** listing.)

This proprietary Illinois dial, being enamel, often experiences some hairline cracks. The dial often cracks just under the numeral 4. It is speculated that this was caused in the Watch Factory by the dial-makers' tongs consistently being placed at that spot to remove the dials from the oven. Over-tightening the dial feet can also cause stress cracks in the dial by the numeral 4 and elsewhere. In addition, cracks could have occurred from the improper removal of enamel dials by watch repairers. In other words, the factory knew how to install them, but those in the field often did not know how to remove and properly handle them.

Almon Brown Strowger
1839–1902

ROTARY DIAL

The first patent for a rotary dial was filed by an undertaker, Almon Brown Strowger, on December 21, 1891, and it was awarded to him on November 29, 1892 as United States Patent No. 486,909. He also invented the automatic telephone dialing system after becoming annoyed with his phone service.

TECHNICAL TIP

The Telephone case usually has a screw-on bezel and case back. Unaware repairpersons and collectors have sometimes damaged the case back and/or fouled the threads by mistakenly trying to pry it off with a case knife instead of merely screwing it off.

Tonneau

See listing for **Whippet**

FRAUD ALERT

As in the case with the fraudulent Skyway dial with a red 12, fake Telephone Dials have also been sighted; the giveaway on the Telephone Dial is the font used in the subsidiary seconds track. Another tell is the placement of the name Illinois on the dial. These models are not enamel dials; they are metal dials painted white to appear like enamel. Some also have subsidiary seconds at 9. A fraudulent Telephone Dial watch sold in October 2013 on eBay for $510.00 to an unaware purchaser.

This fraudulent Telephone Dial was represented to be enamel but is painted metal. Its subsidiary seconds track is too large, the circle around the six is not round, and the dot under the six is out of alignment.

Townsman, two-tone gold-filled

Townsman / Puritan

Official Name = Townsman (derived from Illinois advertisements and Illinois Sales and Material Catalogs)
Secondary Name = Puritan (pursuant to an internal Hamilton document)
Formerly Known As = None
Time Period = Moderne
Case Variations/Rarity = 🕒🕒🕒🕒 TT/WGF/YGF
Case Durability = 🕒🕒🕒🕒
Material = 14K GF
Bezel = Engraved (partially)
Sides = Engraved
Lugs = Plain
Lug Size = 16mm
Springbar = Male
Casemaker = Keystone
Case Closure = 3-Part Snap-On Bezel and Back
Case Number = 198
Case Shape = Cushion
Case Back = Flat
Dimensions = 34 x 28mm
Movement Size = 6/0
Movement Grades/Jewels = 607/17
Seconds at = 6
Dial Numbers = 8202, 8736
Dial = Silver Finish
Dial Opening = Tonneau
Dial Variations/Rarity = 🕒🕒🕒🕒 Silver Finish, Luminous Numerals
🕒🕒🕒🕒🕒 Silver Finish, Black Numerals

Numerals = Painted, Luminous
Hands = Luminous
Cased in Factory = Yes
Unique Case Design = Yes
Unique Dial Design = Yes
Introduction Date = 1930
Retail Price New = $47.50
Collectibility = ◷◷◷◷
Advertisements = Yes
Marketing Theme = "Unusual case combination"

The Townsman was listed in the 1932 Illinois Sales Catalog and was also advertised in the May 10, 1932 issue of *Collier's*. The Illinois catalog stated merely: "The Townsman, in an engraved case of combination 14K filled white and natural gold. 17 jewels . . . $47.50."

A. C. Becken catalog, 1932

A. I. Hall catalog, 1931

The Townsman/Puritan came only in a two-tone case configuration. The Illinois Chesterfield, Ritz and Metropolitan models also came solely with two-tone cases. The bezel of the Townsman has only engraved sides.

Although unusual for an Illinois design, this case exudes a very Moderne look and feel. The Townsman is not quite rectangular and not quite Tonneau-shaped, but instead quite elegantly in between. The slightly rounded top and bottom of its case add to its great design feel. In place of the number 6, the dial design substitutes a half-moon, with a shape conforming to the top and bottom of the bezel. (The Futura model also uses the half-moon design element.)

The Townsman's sides display a distinctive rope-like engraving that strongly stands out. (The Metropolitan shares the same center section and case back with the Townsman.) Strangely enough, the Townsman's incredible moderne design as yet remains largely underappreciated by collectors. The Hamilton 1931 model "Square B Engraved" includes design features vaguely similar to the Townsman but not nearly as dramatic or stylish, while the 1928 Hamilton "Tonneau Engraved" possesses a similar shape, but not as nice a design expression.

According to a recently discovered Hamilton internal document dated June 5, 1933, the Puritan seems to be an alternative name for the Townsman model. The Puritan name is listed under the 6/0 size watches on the "List of Names of Cased Illinois Watches by Sizes" dated December 31, 1932.

Townsman inside case back

WHY I COLLECT ILLINOIS

I'm still trying to come to grips with how I became a collector. My wife (girlfriend at the time) bought me an 18-size Illinois pocket watch many years ago, and I remembered someone telling me a brief history of the Illinois Watch Company. Two simple events, and I was hooked.

I bought my first vintage American watch back in 1994—a 14K Waltham Barrel. While I was looking at the dealer's watches, I kept coming back to three Illinois he had, all of them generics. I bought the Waltham only.

After a few weeks, I realized I "needed" a few to be able to switch around and avoid the wear and tear of everyday use. I went back to the same dealer, and worked out a package deal: three watches—an Ace, a Locke and a Square Cut Corner with subs at 9. They just spoke to me.

The Internet started to boom, which allowed me to broaden my search radius. Prior to that, it had been more about hanging out in old jewelry stores asking questions. I think those folks got tired of me after a few visits. Eventually (twenty watches later), I became friends with the same dealer I bought my first pieces from. After about six months, he sensed I was bored with the stuff in his shop and hinted that he had some other Illinois in his collection. I got a bit excited (bad poker face) and ended up buying twelve of the thirteen watches he had in his collection. These included a NOS Townsman, a New Yorker, and a mint Beau Monde. It was the first time I had ever seen any of these in person.

From there, it was back to the Internet, joining the NAWCC, and eventually turning over my paychecks to some dude in California named Fred Friedberg. By 2002, I had purchased over 400 Illinois, traded out many, upgraded some, and sold a few. I still get the bug, but mostly love the hunt, and would rather trade/sell stuff to others looking to build their own collections.

In short, that's how I got my start. More importantly, though, is what's kept me in it all these years (besides the thrill of the hunt, of course), which is having met some great, like-minded people who share my passion for quality American-made products of yore and, in particular, the watches and history of the Illinois Watch Company. —*Guy Malaby*

Transitional Watches

Transitional Cushion, unpolished sterling

Transitional Military Cushion Large, yellow gold-filled

Official Name = Transitional Watches (derived from the time period from Pre-World War I to the early 1920s)
Secondary Name = Military, Trench
Formerly Known As = None
Time Period = Transitional
Case Variation/Rarity = Various
Material = SS, N, So, YGF, Others
Bezel = Plain
Sides = Plain
Lugs = Plain
Lug Size = 14mm, 16mm
Springbar = Fixed
Casemakers = Elgin, Fahys, IWCCo, Solidarity, Others
Case Closure = 3-Part Snap-On Bezel and Back; Screw-On Bezel and Back
Case Number = None
Case Shapes = Round, Cushion
Case Backs = Flat
Dimensions = Various
Movement Sizes = 0, 3/0, 6/0
Movement Grades/Jewels = Various
Seconds at = 6
Dial Numbers = Painted, Luminous
Dial = Silver Finish, Enamel
Dial Opening = Round
Dial Variations/Rarity = Various
Hands = Steel, Luminous
Cased in Factory = No
Unique Case Design = No
Unique Dial Design = No
Introduction Date = Various
Retail Price New = Unknown
Advertisements = Yes
Marketing Themes = Various

Several Illinois jobbers showed Transitional Military wristwatches in their catalogs, and the Illinois Watch Case Company (IWCCo) also advertised them.

During the period from the last years of World War I to the early 1920s, many military and military-inspired wristwatches appeared. A number had been converted from pocket watches to wristwatches by the attachment of wire lugs. Others resulted from the movement and dials being removed from pocket watches and pendant watches and placed into wristwatch cases. Most are fairly easy to acquire, and fun to own and wear.

Transitional Watches with specific names that are listed in detail in this chapter are the Admiral Evans, Ariston, Armored Case, General Funston, Admiral Benson, General Joffre, Burlington, Depolliers, Masonic, Police Special, Telephone Dial, and Washington Watch Company. Examples of other Transitional watches are shown below. (Ladies' Transitional watches are discussed in Chapter 10.)

Transitional, yellow gold-filled

Transitional, sterling silver

Transitional, round sterling silver

Transitional, sterling silver

Transitional, sterling silver

Transitional Depollier, yellow gold case. 14K yellow gold "US" clasp is the only one known to exist.

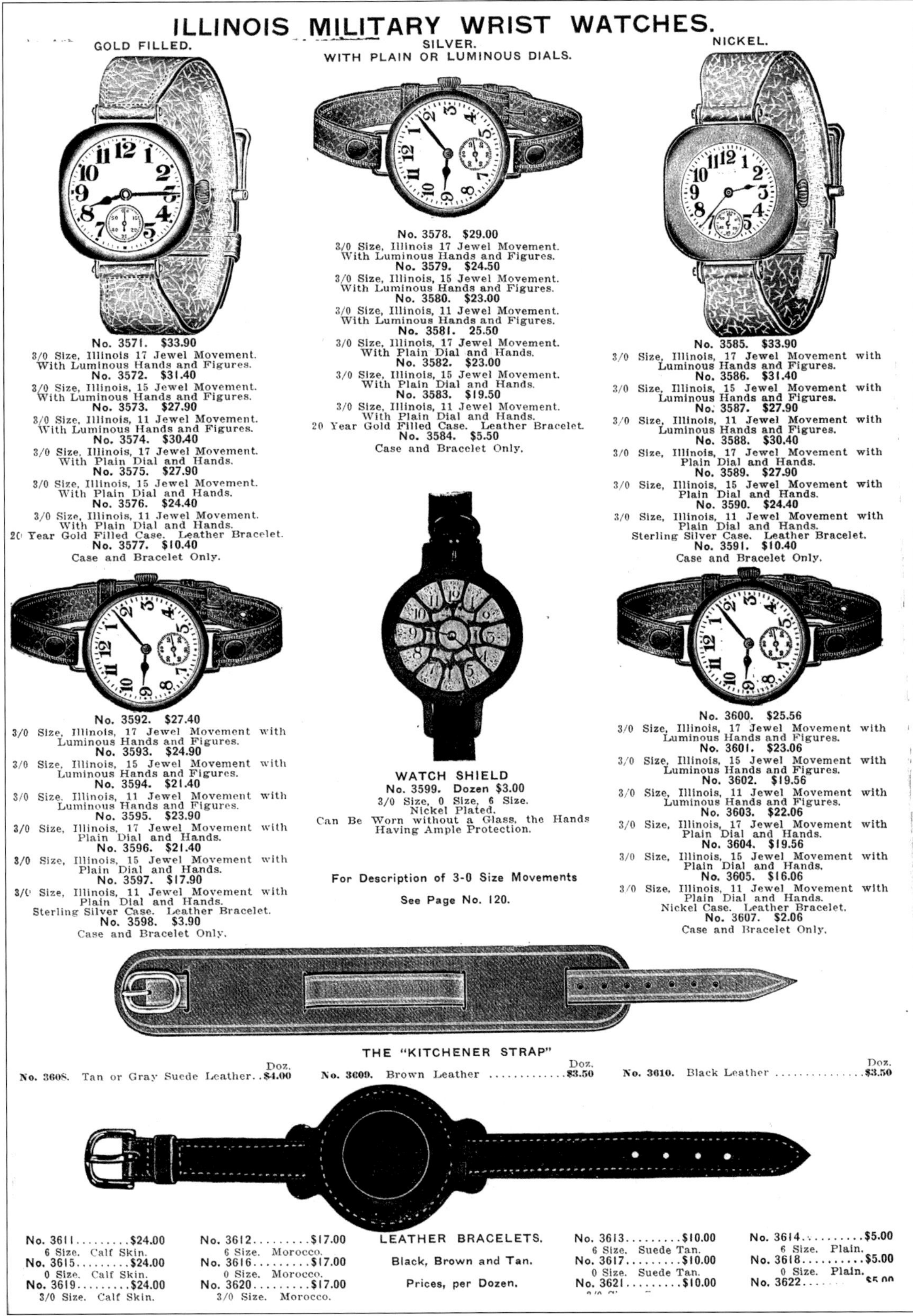

ILLINOIS MILITARY WRIST WATCHES.

GOLD FILLED.

No. 3571. $33.90
3/0 Size, Illinois 17 Jewel Movement. With Luminous Hands and Figures.
No. 3572. $31.40
3/0 Size, Illinois, 15 Jewel Movement. With Luminous Hands and Figures.
No. 3573. $27.90
3/0 Size, Illinois, 11 Jewel Movement. With Luminous Hands and Figures.
No. 3574. $30.40
3/0 Size, Illinois, 17 Jewel Movement. With Plain Dial and Hands.
No. 3575. $27.90
3/0 Size, Illinois, 15 Jewel Movement. With Plain Dial and Hands.
No. 3576. $24.40
3/0 Size, Illinois, 11 Jewel Movement. With Plain Dial and Hands.
20 Year Gold Filled Case. Leather Bracelet.
No. 3577. $10.40
Case and Bracelet Only.

SILVER.
WITH PLAIN OR LUMINOUS DIALS.

No. 3578. $29.00
3/0 Size, Illinois 17 Jewel Movement. With Luminous Hands and Figures.
No. 3579. $24.50
3/0 Size, Illinois, 15 Jewel Movement. With Luminous Hands and Figures.
No. 3580. $23.00
3/0 Size, Illinois, 11 Jewel Movement. With Luminous Hands and Figures.
No. 3581. 25.50
3/0 Size, Illinois, 17 Jewel Movement. With Plain Dial and Hands.
No. 3582. $23.00
3/0 Size, Illinois, 15 Jewel Movement. With Plain Dial and Hands.
No. 3583. $19.50
3/0 Size, Illinois, 11 Jewel Movement. With Plain Dial and Hands.
20 Year Gold Filled Case. Leather Bracelet.
No. 3584. $5.50
Case and Bracelet Only.

NICKEL.

No. 3585. $33.90
3/0 Size, Illinois, 17 Jewel Movement with Luminous Hands and Figures.
No. 3586. $31.40
3/0 Size, Illinois, 15 Jewel Movement with Luminous Hands and Figures.
No. 3587. $27.90
3/0 Size, Illinois, 11 Jewel Movement with Luminous Hands and Figures.
No. 3588. $30.40
3/0 Size, Illinois, 17 Jewel Movement with Plain Dial and Hands.
No. 3589. $27.90
3/0 Size, Illinois, 15 Jewel Movement with Plain Dial and Hands.
No. 3590. $24.40
3/0 Size, Illinois, 11 Jewel Movement with Plain Dial and Hands.
Sterling Silver Case. Leather Bracelet.
No. 3591. $10.40
Case and Bracelet Only.

No. 3592. $27.40
3/0 Size, Illinois, 17 Jewel Movement with Luminous Hands and Figures.
No. 3593. $24.90
3/0 Size, Illinois, 15 Jewel Movement with Luminous Hands and Figures.
No. 3594. $21.40
3/0 Size, Illinois, 11 Jewel Movement with Luminous Hands and Figures.
No. 3595. $23.90
3/0 Size, Illinois, 17 Jewel Movement with Plain Dial and Hands.
No. 3596. $21.40
3/0 Size, Illinois, 15 Jewel Movement with Plain Dial and Hands.
No. 3597. $17.90
3/0 Size, Illinois, 11 Jewel Movement with Plain Dial and Hands.
Sterling Silver Case. Leather Bracelet.
No. 3598. $3.90
Case and Bracelet Only.

WATCH SHIELD
No. 3599. Dozen $3.00
3/0 Size, 0 Size, 6 Size.
Nickel Plated.
Can Be Worn without a Glass, the Hands Having Ample Protection.

For Description of 3-0 Size Movements
See Page No. 120.

No. 3600. $25.56
3/0 Size, Illinois, 17 Jewel Movement with Luminous Hands and Figures.
No. 3601. $23.06
3/0 Size, Illinois, 15 Jewel Movement with Luminous Hands and Figures.
No. 3602. $19.56
3/0 Size, Illinois, 11 Jewel Movement with Luminous Hands and Figures.
No. 3603. $22.06
3/0 Size, Illinois, 17 Jewel Movement with Plain Dial and Hands.
No. 3604. $19.56
3/0 Size, Illinois, 15 Jewel Movement with Plain Dial and Hands.
No. 3605. $16.06
3/0 Size, Illinois, 11 Jewel Movement with Plain Dial and Hands.
Nickel Case. Leather Bracelet.
No. 3607. $2.06
Case and Bracelet Only.

THE "KITCHENER STRAP"

No. 3608. Tan or Gray Suede Leather. . Doz. $4.00
No. 3609. Brown Leather .... Doz. $3.50
No. 3610. Black Leather .... Doz. $3.50

LEATHER BRACELETS.
Black, Brown and Tan.
Prices, per Dozen.

No. 3611.........$24.00
6 Size. Calf Skin.
No. 3615.........$24.00
0 Size. Calf Skin.
No. 3619.........$24.00
3/0 Size. Calf Skin.

No. 3612.........$17.00
6 Size. Morocco.
No. 3616.........$17.00
0 Size. Morocco.
No. 3620.........$17.00
3/0 Size. Morocco.

No. 3613.........$10.00
6 Size. Suede Tan.
No. 3617.........$10.00
0 Size. Suede Tan.
No. 3621.........$10.00

No. 3614..........$5.00
6 Size. Plain.
No. 3618..........$5.00
0 Size. Plain.
No. 3622....... $5.00

Otto Young catalog, 1921

Trophy / Westchester / Kensington

Trophy, white gold-filled

Trophy, yellow gold-filled

Official Names = Trophy and Westchester (derived from Illinois advertisements and Illinois Sales and Material Catalogs); Kensington (derived from 1932 Oskamp Nolting catalog)
Secondary Name = None
Formerly Known As = None
Time Period = Moderne
Case Variations/Rarity = ◷◷ WGF/P
◷◷◷ YGF/P
Case Durability = ◷◷◷ WGF
◷◷◷ YGF
Material = 14K GF
Bezel = Plain
Sides = Plain
Lugs = Plain
Lug Size = 16mm
Springbar = Male
Casemaker = Wadsworth
Case Closure = 2-Part Snap-On Bezel and Back
Case Number = 202
Case Shape = Rectangular
Case Back = Flat
Dimensions = 38 x 22mm
Movement Size = 12/0
Movement Grade/Jewels = 207/17
Seconds at = 6
Dial Number = 8751
Dial = Silver Finish
Dial Opening = Rectangular
Dial Variations/Rarity = ◷◷ Silver Finish, Luminous Numerals
◷◷◷◷◷ Silver Finish, Black Numerals
Numerals = Painted, Luminous
Hands = Luminous
Cased in Factory = Yes
Unique Case Design = No
Unique Dial Design = No
Introduction Date = 1930
Retail Price New = $55.00 (Trophy), $60.00 (Westchester), $62.00 (Kensington)
Collectibility = ◷◷◷◷
Advertisements = Yes
Marketing Themes = "Neat in design and extremely modern"
"In accord with modern design"
"Modern style of extremely simple design"
"Handsome combination watch and matched bracelet"

The Trophy, listed in the 1930–31 Illinois Sales Catalog, was introduced as follows: "In accord with modern style this strapwatch is of extremely simple design. It does appeal to the man who appreciates simplicity and true worth." It was also advertised in 1930 in the *American Magazine* and in *Collier's*.

The TROPHY

In accord with modern style this strapwatch is of extremely simple design. It does appeal to the man who appreciates simplicity and true worth. In 14K white or natural filled gold.

Suggested consumer price, $55.

A. I. Hall catalog, 1930–31

Simplicity was the latest trend in fashion of the times, and the sleek lines of the Trophy had great appeal. Its bezel was embellished only by its ridged border, a nice touch that looked ahead to Streamline Moderne designs.

Although Illinois called this model by various names—Trophy, Westchester, Kensington, and Frontenac—all these models shared the same case Model No. 202. The Trophy came with a leather strap. The Westchester and Kensington came equipped with metal bracelets. The metal bracelet on the Westchester, which was by Hadley, made this model cost $5.00 more than the Trophy. Illinois called the same watch a Kensington if it was yellow gold-filled and came equipped with a metal bracelet of another design (but likely also by Hadley), as shown below.

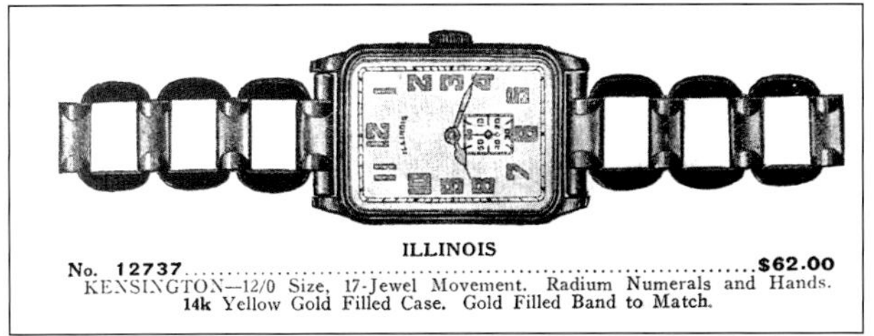

Oskamp Nolting catalog, 1932

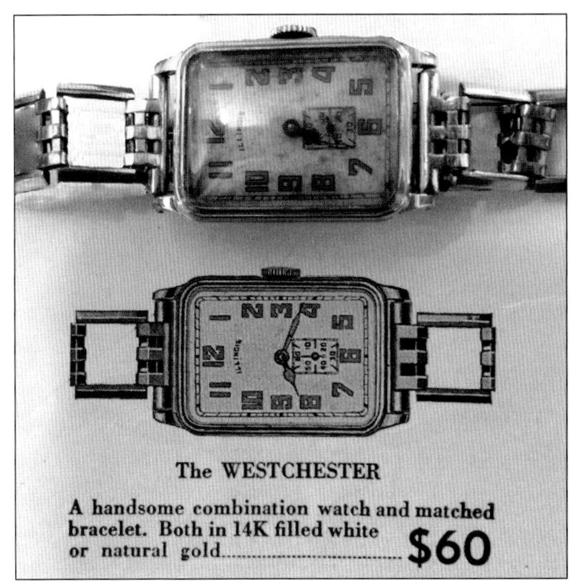

A. C. Becken catalog, 1932. An actual Westchester, complete with its original bracelet, is superimposed.

The Frontenac came with an innovative integrated metal bracelet in place of lugs. Its band was built directly into the top and bottom of its case. (See the **Frontenac** listing.)

The Trophy, with its leather strap, is a very plain-looking watch, and its simplicity was emphasized in Illinois' advertisements, as was noted earlier. The bracelets of the Westchester and Kensington gave it a different look.

The white gold-filled Trophy model can be found more easily than the yellow one, but both are fairly common and generally available. One custom dial for the Trophy that greatly adds to its design and beauty as a strap watch displays an ornate oval shape with interesting corner design features. However, only two of these custom dials have been found thus far.

Trophy with custom dial

Trophy inside case back

Tuxedo, white gold

Tuxedo

Official Name = Tuxedo (derived from Illinois advertisements and Illinois Sales and Material Catalogs)
Secondary Name = None
Formerly Known As = None
Time Period = Moderne
Case Variations/Rarity = 🕒🕒🕒🕒 WG/E
🕒🕒🕒🕒🕒 TT/E
🕒🕒🕒🕒🕒🕒🕒 GG/P*
*Although advertised, this model has never been seen.
Case Durability = 🕒🕒🕒
Material = 14K GF, WG, GG
Bezel = Plain, Engraved
Sides = Engraved
Lugs = Plain, Engraved
Lug Size = 14mm, 16mm
Springbar = Male
Casemaker = Solidarity
Case Closure = 2-Part Snap-On Back
Case Number = Special Model No. 151
Case Shape = Rectangular
Case Back = Curved
Dimensions = 36 x 23mm
Movement Size = 18/0
Movement Grade/Jewels = 206/17
Seconds at = None

Dial Numbers = 8141, 8193
Dial = Silver Finish
Dial Opening = Rectangular
Dial Variations/Rarity = ◷◷◷◷◷ Silver Finish, Luminous Numerals; Silver Finish, Etched Numerals; Sterling Silver, Applied Gold Numerals
◷◷◷◷◷◷ Moderne Dial, Luminous Numerals
Numerals = Luminous, Etched, Applied Gold (18K)
Hands = Luminous
Cased in Factory = Yes
Unique Case Design = Yes
Unique Dial Design = Yes
Introduction Date = 1928
Retail Price New = $85.00 (Applied Gold Numerals), $75.00 (Luminous Dial)
Collectibility = ◷◷◷◷
Advertisements = Yes
Marketing Themes = "Quite popular with both sexes"
"Distinctive strap watch"
"Extremely smart and attractive"

Tuxedo, two-tone gold

The Tuxedo was introduced in 1928 in the small Illinois sales booklet entitled "A Book of Watches." It appeared in the Illinois advertisement in the October 5, 1929, issue of *Collier's* magazine.

In advertising the Tuxedo in its 1929–30 Sales Catalog, Illinois noted: "This 18/0 size strap watch is a most desirable addition to the Illinois line. It is extremely smart and attractive, and meets the demand of modern life for a 'watch for every occasion.' As a ladies' watch for sport or business wear, the Tuxedo proves quite adaptable. On the other hand, this very handsome model can quite appropriately be regarded as a man's strap watch for formal wear. The Tuxedo has wide appeal among both men and women, and is quite popular with both sexes. This dressy sport watch is available in a case of 14K solid gold, plain white, engraved white oxidized, or white with green center."

RECTANGULAR STRAP WATCHES

18/0 Size *17 Jewels*

This 18/0 size strap watch is a most desirable addition to the Illinois line. It is extremely smart and attractive, and meets the demand of modern life for a "watch for every occasion". As a ladies' watch for sport or business wear, the Tuxedo proves quite adaptable. On the other hand, this very handsome model can quite appropriately be regarded as a man's strap watch for formal wear.

SPECIFICATIONS
Size Eighteen-0 or six and three-fourths ligne, 17 ruby and sapphire jewels, safety recoiling click, double roller escapement, tempered and hardened compensating balance, steel escape wheel, concaved and polished winding wheels.

The Tuxedo has a wide appeal among both men and women, and is quite popular with both sexes. This dressy sport watch is available in a case of 14K solid gold, plain white, engraved white oxidized, or white with green center.

Sterling silver dial with applied 14K gold figures. Consumer price $85.00

Full luminous figure dial, black outline figures. Consumer price $75.00

A. G. Schwab catalog, 1930

The Tuxedo model is one of the few solid gold models offered for sale by Illinois. Perhaps owing to its small size, this model has been greatly underappreciated by collectors. Illinois originally marketed it as a young man's watch before promoting its use by both sexes. In this regard, Illinois was a trendsetter for offering unisex watches.

Unlike its corporate parent Hamilton, Illinois made bold and brave decisions regarding design and market placement in an attempt to persuade "real men" to own a wristwatch in addition to their pocket watches. Illinois also advertised and promoted some wristwatch models (the Biltmore 18/0, Sangamon, Tuxedo and Urbana) as well as the Caprice "purse" or "desk watch" for use by both sexes. Its unisex marketing efforts may have been unique in the watch industry.

There are only five known white gold Tuxedos with plain bezels, making it quite a rare variant. Illinois listed a green gold plain bezel model in an Illinois Sales Catalog, but one has never been seen. It has been noted that most Tuxedos have 14mm lugs, but some came with 16mm lugs.

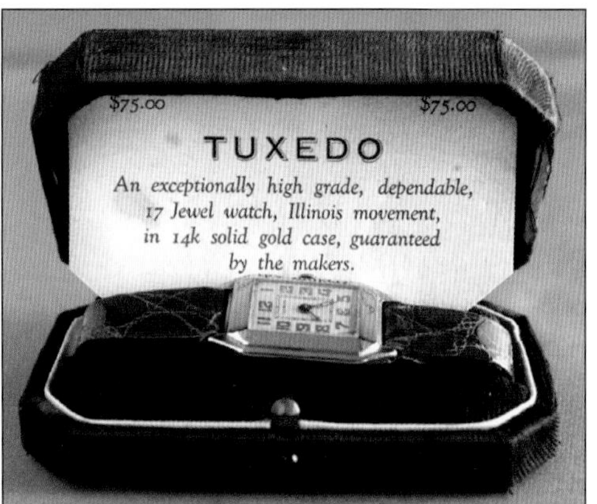

Tuxedo in its original display box

Tuxedo inside case back

Tuxedo, white gold, Moderne dial

RUMOR

There is rumored to be a three-tone Tuxedo (a tricolor case), but such a case has yet to be confirmed.

FANTASTIC FIND

One of those "extra early to rise" mornings I perused eBay and saw a somewhat fuzzy photo of what appeared to be a plain bezel Tuxedo. I contacted my Illinois counterparts, Fred, Greg, and Rick, to confirm my suspicions. Amazing as it was, I secured the purchase of this rare beauty for $400.00.

—*Ed Kulha*

The Tuxedo

BENEATH the beautiful outward appearance of this distinctive strap watch is one of those excellent 17 jeweled rectangular movements, made by the Illinois Watch. The thin rectangular case is fashioned from 14k solid gold.

$75

Illinois, "A Book of Watches," 1928

United States Army

United States Army, black paint intact

United States Army, paint worn off

Official Name = United States Army Watch (derived from the War Department's Technical Manual 9-575; see text below)
Secondary Name = None
Formerly Known As = Military
Time Period = Transitional
Case Variations/Rarity = 🕒🕒🕒🕒 N/P
Case Durability = 🕒🕒🕒🕒
Material = N
Bezel = Plain
Sides = Plain
Lugs = Plain
Lug Size = 16mm
Springbar = Fixed
Casemaker = IWCCo
Case Closure = 3-Part Snap-On Bezel and Back
Case Number = None
Case Shape = Round
Case Back = Flat
Dimensions = 40 x 31.5mm
Movement Size = 3/0
Movement Grades/ Jewels = 24/17, 36/17
Seconds at = 6
Dial Numbers = None
Dial = Painted
Dial Opening = Round
Dial Variations/Rarity = 🕒🕒🕒🕒🕒 Painted Black, Luminous Numerals
Numerals = Luminous
Hands = Luminous
Cased in Factory = No
Unique Case Design = No
Unique Dial Design = No
Introduction Date = 1918
Retail Price New = Unknown
Collectibility = 🕒🕒🕒🕒
Advertisements = None
Marketing Theme = None

In *The Illinois Watch Company: The Life and Times of A Great American Watch Company*, it was stated that there were only two confirmed original black-dial Illinois, the black dial Skyway and the 3/0 round military black dial. However, we did not know then what case it was intended for, other than it could fit into any 3/0 size Transitional Period case.

We now know that this Illinois military black dial was intended for United States Army use in a nickel semi-hermetically sealed case. This discovery was made from an illustration in what at first glance might seem a very unlikely source chronologically: U.S. Army specifications dating from 1942, during World War II. The Army illustrated this model in the United States Army War Department's Technical Manual (TM) 9-575, Auxiliary Fire-Control Instruments (Field Glasses, Eyeglasses, Telescopes, and Watches), dated May 4, 1942. On page 21, Figure 21, the United States Army watch is illustrated.

Regarding that watch, one of "15 or more jewels," TM 9-475 has this to say: "This wrist watch (fig. 21) is authorized for war issue only to all services except that meteorological control and observation stations receive this watch in times of peace also…The watch is a small open-face timepiece fitted with a wristlet for fastening to the wrist. It is stem-wound and stem-set and is dust and moisture proof. The dial is round and black. Hour numerals and the hour and minute hands are luminous coated; second graduations, numerals, hands, and minute graduations are white. The case has a durable finish and the wristlets may be of russet leather or olive drab webbing."

United States Army watch without its bezel on

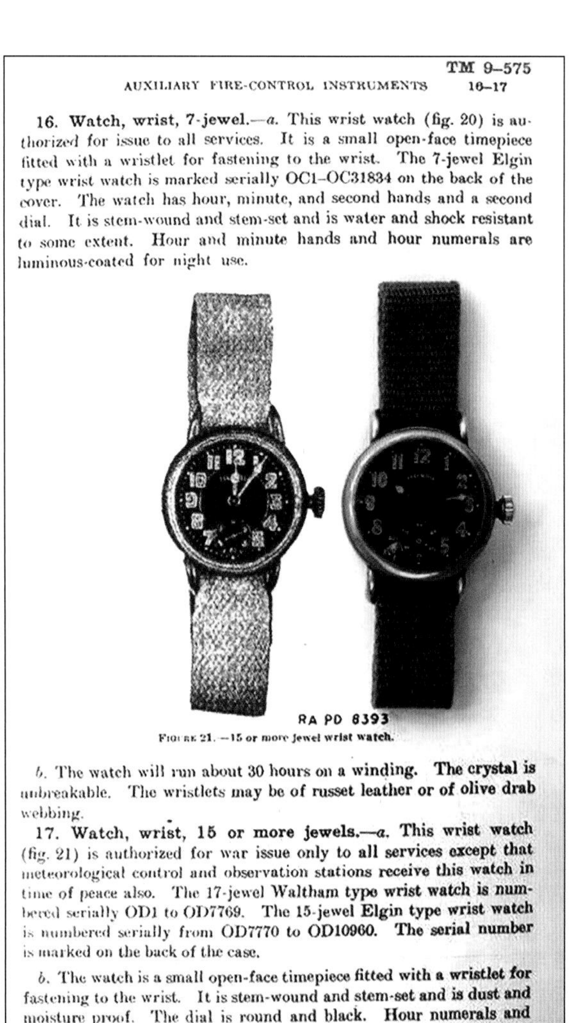

TM 9–575

AUXILIARY FIRE-CONTROL INSTRUMENTS 16–17

16. **Watch, wrist, 7-jewel.**—*a.* This wrist watch (fig. 20) is authorized for issue to all services. It is a small open-face timepiece fitted with a wristlet for fastening to the wrist. The 7-jewel Elgin type wrist watch is marked serially OC1–OC31834 on the back of the cover. The watch has hour, minute, and second hands and a second dial. It is stem-wound and stem-set and is water and shock resistant to some extent. Hour and minute hands and hour numerals are luminous-coated for night use.

RA PD 8393

FIGURE 21.—15 or more jewel wrist watch.

b. The watch will run about 30 hours on a winding. The crystal is unbreakable. The wristlets may be of russet leather or of olive drab webbing.

17. **Watch, wrist, 15 or more jewels.**—*a.* This wrist watch (fig. 21) is authorized for war issue only to all services except that meteorological control and observation stations receive this watch in time of peace also. The 17-jewel Waltham type wrist watch is numbered serially OD1 to OD7769. The 15-jewel Elgin type wrist watch is numbered serially from OD7770 to OD10960. The serial number is marked on the back of the case.

b. The watch is a small open-face timepiece fitted with a wristlet for fastening to the wrist. It is stem-wound and stem-set and is dust and moisture proof. The dial is round and black. Hour numerals and the hour and minute hands are luminous-coated; second graduations, numerals, hands, and minute graduations are white.

c. The case has a durable finish and the wristlets may be of russet leather or olive drab webbing.

Illinois model superimposed on page of Technical Manual

In the 1942 document, Waltham and Elgin watches were also illustrated with black dials and in exactly the same IWCCo case as the Illinois model. The Elgin watch had 7 jewels or 15 jewels and the Waltham had 17 jewels, the latter the same as the Illinois shown in Figure 21 as a "15 or more jewel wrist watch." (Hamilton was excluded from this particular procurement effort, having never produced a 3/0 size movement.)

To account for the presence of the image of the Illinois military watch from 1918 in a government document from 1942, it is plausible to assume that some Illinois might still have remained from a supply procured in 1918. However, it is also quite possible that this was a convenient half-tone cut used simply to indicate the type of watch that was being specified rather than to indicate availability of Illinois military watches in particular. Either way, the image provides the solution for what had earlier been a puzzle.

Illinois manufactured the movements for its U.S. Army watch in 1918. In fact, the United States Government purchases exhausted the Illinois Watch Company's entire output of 3/0 size movements in 1918, compelling Illinois to post a full-page notice to the trade in the October 2, 1918 issue of the *Jewelers' Circular-Weekly*, stated: "As the government has taken over our entire production of 3/0 size movements we will be unable to supply any more of these movements to the trade until further notice."

THE JEWELERS' CIRCULAR-WEEKLY

As the government has taken over our entire production of 3/0 size movements we will be unable to supply any more of these movements to the trade until further notice.

Illinois Watch Company
Springfield

Jewelers' Circular-Weekly, October 2, 1918

U.S. Army white dial

In 1918 the Illinois Watch Factory produced the following quantities of 3/0 size movements: 2,770 with 11 jewels; 11,620 with 15 jewels; and 4,850 with 17 jewels. This military model was most likely used during World War I by the cavalry and infantry branches of the United States Army. Some very rare cases display the United States Government serial number engraved on their case backs; only about a half dozen of these have been spotted to date. These are, of course, far more collectible and valuable than ones without the ordnance marking. There is also a super-rare variant that has "US Army" stamped on its case back.

U.S. Army gun metal finish; very rare

“US Army” signed caseback, very rare

U.S. Army caseback with no signage

September 26, 1917. THE HOROLOGICAL REVIEW 117

Wrist Watches Purchased for the Army

Chief Signal Officer Supplies Official Specifications for Movements, Cases, and Straps of Wrist Time Pieces Which Government Buys for Soldiers.

WASHINGTON, D. C., Sept. 20.—The Chief Signal Officer of the army has provided your correspondent with the following specifications and drawings of the wrist watch as it is ordered for use by the United States army. It is apparent from the stocks exhibited for sale by many retailers that there is considerable difference between the watches generally sold to soldiers and those the government buys.

The said rules and specifications apply specifically to wrist watches bought by the Government for the United States Army. The question arose as to whether such specifications apply to watches purchased by individual members of the army or presented to the soldiers by their friends. In other words, whether the specifications of the Government in regard to buying watches were, in effect, regulations as to the watches that should be worn.

This question was taken up by THE JEWELER'S CIRCULAR correspondent with officials of the War Department by whom he was informed that the specifications in question apply to *purchases made by the Government* and that there were no restrictions on private purchases made by individual members of the military forces.

This is in line with the ruling of the Adjutant-General's office, published in another column, in regard to tokens carried by soldiers.

The wrist watch specifications adopted Nov. 3, 1914, and revised as of October 24, 1916. The existing specifications and design for strap follows:

GENERAL SPECIFICATION, No. 579-D.
(Oct. 24, 1916.)

WRIST WATCH.

1. *Preliminary.*—This specification describes the general requirements for a wrist watch and wristlet for use by the United States army.

2. *Drawing.*—The following drawing forms a part of this specification:

Strap for wrist watch........1035

3. *Inspection.*—When the order under this specification is complete, the contractor shall notify the Chief Signal Officer of the army, who will cause an inspection to be made. The contractor shall remedy all defects pointed out by the inspector, and will be held accountable for any imperfections which the inspector may overlook.

The watches shall be regulated, and shall be wound and set so that the inspector may readily compare the regulation.

4. *Workmanship and material.*—Workmanship and material throughout shall be first class, and the completed article must be neat in finish and general appearance.

5. *Description of movement.*—(*a*) The movement to be of nickel, standard American manufacture, open face, with lever escapement, compensation balance, Breguet hair spring, nickel damaskeened frames, with not less than seven jewels; diameter of the movement or dial not to be over 1 5/32 inches. It shall be stem winding and stem setting, and shall indicate seconds.

(*b*) *Dial.*—The dial is to be white enamel, and shall have all figures marked in black or blue. A small round spot of radium (luminous) material of sufficient size to be easily seen shall be placed under each set of figures.

(*c*) *Figures.*—Hour figures to be upright Arabic numerals, not less than 1/10 inch in height, and seconds dial orbit shall have each 10-second division indicated in Arabic numerals.

(*d*) *Hands.*—The hands to be of blued steel and of a size and style not confusing to the eye, and shall be coated with a radium (luminous) material.

(*e*) *Case.*—The case shall be of oxidized nickel, with dull, black finish. The case shall be jointed and have inside cap, and the stem shall be practically dust proof. Both the cap and the back of case shall snap well into place, making a good, close joint all around, and shall be easily opened without undue prying.

(*f*) *Crystal.*—The crystal shall be of best quality, clear glass, about 0.06 inch thick, and shall be properly seated in the bezel.

6. *Wristlet.*—A wristlet shall be furnished with each watch. This wristlet shall be made of single-ply genuine pigskin, and shall be of the dimensions and made up as shown upon drawing, paragraph 2(*a*). The cup shall hold the watch tightly, and shall have a snug fitting opening to allow the ring and stem of watch to protrude.

7. *Sample.*—Each bidder shall submit with his proposal, charges prepaid, a sample watch and wristlet of the type he proposes to furnish. The type of movement, case, and quality and workmanship of the wristlet will be considered in awarding the contract.

The sample furnished by the successful bidder will be held for the guidance of the inspector until the final delivery of the order is made.

8. *Guarantee.*—In furnishing watches under this specification, the contractor guarantees for one year after delivery to make repairs to all watches when such repairs are made necessary by defects in material or workmanship, without charge to the Signal Corps.

9. *Packing.*—Great care must be taken in packing material purchased under this specification. Not more than 50 watches shall be packed in one box. Several boxes containing 50 watches each may, however, be inclosed in a larger and stronger box. All boxes shall be marked prominently in red, "KEEP DRY," and shall indicate on the outside the order number, number and kind of instruments contained therein. Articles purchased for export shipment shall be packed with extra care, and a reasonable compensation will be allowed the contractor to cover the expense incident thereto. The contractor will be held accountable for any damage during transportation which could have been avoided by careful packing.

GEORGE P. SCRIVEN,
Brigadier General, Chief Signal Officer of the Army.
Office of the Chief Signal Officer of the Army.

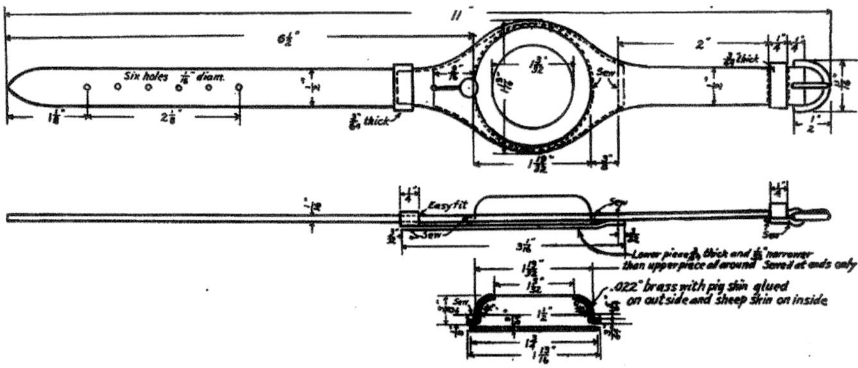

SPECIFICATION OF STRAP FOR WRIST WATCH.

Made of pig skin, tan color. Upper piece, 1/16" thick; lower, 3/64". Upper thread, silk; lower, flax. Buckle brass, black oxidized.

Specifications for wristwatches to be purchased for U.S. Army use in 1917

Officer's Kit for the Front.

Luminous wrist watch with unbreakable glass.
Revolver.
Field glasses.
Periscope.
Compass and Service Protractor.
Army Book 153, with pencils.
Man's mess tin and good pocket flask.
Water bottle.
Wire cutters.
Map case (waterproof).

From *Knowledge for War: Every Officer's Handbook for the Front* (1916)

In 1917, the United Stated entered World War I, and the military purchased motorcycles and wristwatches for the war effort. Motorcycles had already been used by the military in the Pancho Villa Expedition, but WWI was the first time they had been adapted for combat. Harley-Davidson provided about 15,000 machines to the United States military forces during WWI.

U.S. ARMY WATCH

On October 24, 1916, the United States Army issued revised specifications for wristwatches. The revised specifications required that all wristwatch cases be painted black, including the watch crown and buckle. Then, in the middle of 1918, another revision required the dial also to be black. On many of the military watches we find today from World War I, most of its black paint has been worn away. However, traces of this paint can frequently be found in the grooves of the case (it if has a screw-on bezel and case back) or in other locations.

Shown below is the inside of a bezel from a United States Army watch. The black paint still present indicates that originally the bezel was all black.

Urbana, yellow gold-filled

Urbana

Official Name = Urbana (derived from Illinois advertisements and Illinois Sales and Material Catalogs)
Secondary Name = None
Formerly Known As = None
Time Period = Moderne
Case Variations/Rarity = ◷◷◷◷◷ YGF/E
Case Durability = ◷◷
Material = 10K GF
Bezel = Engraved (partially)
Sides = Plain
Lugs = Plain
Lug Size = 16mm
Springbar = Male
Casemaker = Keystone
Case Closure = 2-Part Snap-On back
Case Number = 876
Case Shape = Rectangular
Case Back = Flat
Dimensions = 39 x 22mm
Movement Size = 18/0
Movement Grades/Jewels = 206/17, 807/17, 807A/17, 807B/17
Seconds at = None
Dial Number = 8494
Dial = Silver Finish
Dial Opening = Rectangular
Dial Variations/Rarity = ◷◷◷◷◷ Silver Finish, Etched Numerals
Numerals = Embossed
Hands = Steel
Cased in Factory = No (by Hamilton in Lancaster)
Unique Case Design = No
Unique Dial Design = No
Production Date = 1934
Retail Price New = $32.50
Collectibility = ◷◷◷◷
Advertisements = No
Marketing Themes = "Plain, modern design"
"Particularly adapted to the use of leather cord attachment"

The Urbana appeared in the 1934 Illinois Sales Catalog, where it was listed as follows: "Plain, modern design in brightly polished 10K filled gold; natural only with leather strap; this watch particularly adapted to the use of leather cord attachment." It also appeared various 1934 jobbers' catalogs, such as May & Malone and A. C. Becken, which, as usual, picked up the Illinois advertising copy (and in some cases the entire Illinois catalog page).

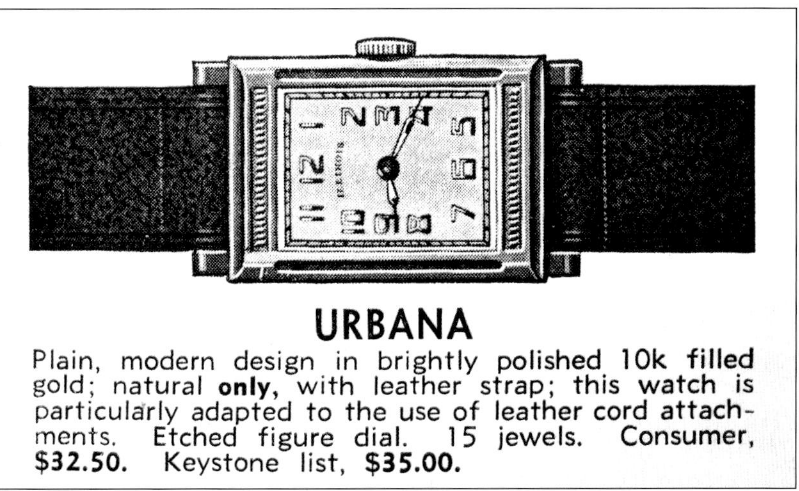

A. C. Becken catalog, 1934

It is interesting that the advertising copy remarks that the Urbana came with just a leather strap but then immediately adds that it was "particularly adapted to the use of leather cord attachment." This type of watchband had gained great favor in the early 1930s, and the copywriter was perhaps thinking of something like Hadley's popular "Polo" model, pictured below.

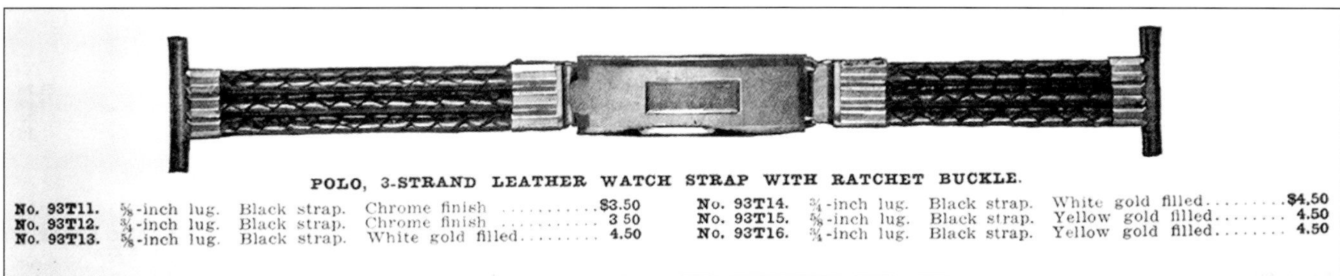

POLO, 3-STRAND LEATHER WATCH STRAP WITH RATCHET BUCKLE.

No. 93T11.	5/8-inch lug.	Black strap.	Chrome finish	$3.50
No. 93T12.	3/4-inch lug.	Black strap.	Chrome finish	3 50
No. 93T13.	5/8-inch lug.	Black strap.	White gold filled	4.50
No. 93T14.	3/4-inch lug.	Black strap.	White gold filled	$4.50
No. 93T15.	5/8-inch lug.	Black strap.	Yellow gold filled	4.50
No. 93T16.	3/4-inch lug.	Black strap.	Yellow gold filled	4.50

Hadley's "Polo," shown in A. C. Becken catalog. 1934

Given the Urbana's design feature of ridging along the top and bottom of the bezel, such a watchband would have been a harmonious and stylish choice. Then why was the Urbana equipped with a strap instead of one of these? The likely answer is that the Urbana, like the Sangamon, was an economy model, and Hamilton did not wish to have the extra expense of providing a special Hadley attachment.

Hamilton offered the Urbana as one of its bargain-priced offerings initiated to appeal to the Depression-shocked consumer. The Urbana is one of only a few Illinois models offered in a 10K gold-filled case, as well as the only Illinois watch offered solely in a yellow gold-filled case. Since Waltham offered a version of the Urbana in a white gold-filled case, Hamilton apparently did not contract with Keystone for exclusive use of the design. However, it appears that Illinois sold only the yellow version and Waltham only the white one.

Waltham white gold-filled version of the Illinois Urbana

Elgin "Urbana" inside case back in 10K rolled gold plate

Elgin "Urbana"

In addition to the white gold-filled version of the Urbana, a Keystone Victory case variant exists in a yellow rolled gold-plate case without a case Model Number. Illinois purchased most Keystone cases as exclusive designs with case Model Numbers engraved on the case back. However, not being bound by an exclusive contract for the Urbana design, Keystone was free to offer a cheaper rolled gold-plate version to its other customers. Elgin also offered an "Urbana" watch in a Keystone Victory 10K rolled-gold plate case.

The Urbana is a narrow, attractive rectangular watch, only slightly larger than the Tuxedo model. The Urbana and the Sangamon, paired in the 1934 Illinois Sales Catalog as "Modern Wrist Watches" and described as "Sturdily constructed 18/0 size timepieces for men or women," are two of five watches offered by Illinois for use by both sexes (the other three were the Biltmore 18/0, Tuxedo and Caprice).

The Urbana's sleek contemporary design clearly and convincingly marks the transition in design by Illinois from the Deco Period to the Moderne Period. The Urbana and Sangamon share a nearly identical design outline, differing only in bezel details. The Urbana has engraving or ridges on the top and bottom of its bezel. The Sangamon has a plain, unengraved bezel. The Sangamon came only in white steel and the Urbana only in yellow gold-filled.

The Urbana and Sangamon also have different case Model Numbers. Both are relatively scarce, with the Urbana being the rarer of the two. Both were equipped with an Elinvar hairspring—another indicator that Hamilton cased and timed these models in Lancaster. The $32.50 retail price for the Urbana represented a bargain for a 17-jewel watch, but the $25.00 Sangamon set the record for the lowest Illinois men's wristwatch price ever. Both watches provided Hamilton with low-price offerings in a Depression-ravaged marketplace without sacrificing the Hamilton brand name.

We now know that the Arlington, Chatham, Hawthorne, Potomac, Sangamon, Sterling and Urbana were probably named after cities or counties in Illinois.

Urbana dial with special etched numerals

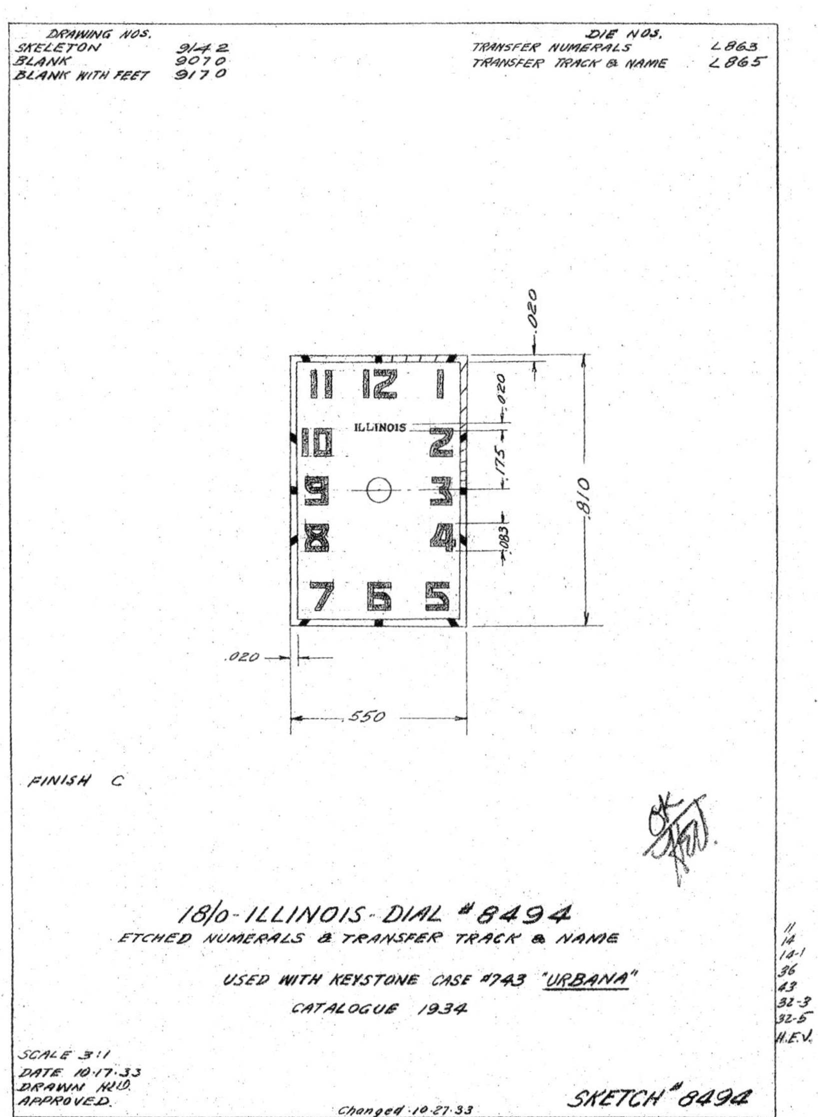

Hamilton drawing of an Illinois Urbana dial, dated October 17, 1933. The case number noted, however, is not for an Urbana.

See listing for **Ritz**

Varsity, yellow gold, black numerals

Varsity, yellow gold, etched gold numerals

VARSITY

Official Name = Varsity (derived from original Illinois price card)
Secondary Name = None
Formerly Known As = No. 650 (derived from collectors' usage of this model's case Model Number until its proper name was discovered)
Time Period = Moderne
Case Variations/Rarity = 🕐🕐🕐🕐🕐 YG/P
Case Durability = 🕐🕐
Material = 14K YG
Bezel = Plain
Sides = Engraved
Lugs = Plain
Lug Size = 16mm
Springbar = Male
Casemaker = Keystone
Case Closure = 2-Part Snap-On back
Case Number = 650
Case Shape = Rectangular
Case Back = Flat
Dimensions = 36 x 26mm
Movement Size = 6/0
Movement Grade/ Jewels = 605/15, 605A/15
Seconds at = 6
Dial Numbers = 8389, 8492
Dial = Silver Finish
Dial Opening = Rectangular
Dial Variations/Rarity = 🕐🕐🕐🕐 Silver Finish, Etched Numerals; Silver Finish, Flush Gold Numerals
🕐🕐🕐🕐🕐 Silver Finish, Black Numerals; Silver Finish, Butler Center, Etched Numerals; Silver Finish, Etched Numerals, Close to Dial Center
Numerals = Painted, Etched
Hands = Steel
Cased in Factory = Yes
Unique Case Design = Yes
Unique Dial Design = Yes
Introduction Date = 1932
Retail Price New = $65.00
Collectibility = 🕐🕐🕐🕐
Advertisements = No
Marketing Theme = Unknown

The Varsity is a watch of some mystery among Illinois collectors. It did not appear in any Illinois Sales Catalog, and there is no known advertisement for it. Men's models in 14K solid gold are rare among Illinois' production, and one with no catalog entries is particularly puzzling. Like the No. 250, whose name is yet to be confirmed, this model was long known only by its case Model Number, No. 650. That the watch was solid gold but had only a 15-jewel movement was also a subject of curiosity.

For years, collectors mistook the Varsity for a solid gold version of the Potomac/Rockingham model. However, a very careful examination of the bezel of each model discloses a subtle difference. The Varsity case has a smooth slope down from the bezel to the ends of the lugs, whereas the Potomac/ Rockingham model has an obvious joint.

It can now be understood that the Varsity and Potomac share the same bezel and lugs designs, except for the material. However, when the lugs were soldered to the bezel of the Varsity, additional gold solder was apparently added on top of the lugs to provide a smooth transition from the bezel. On the Potomac, the lugs were simply soldered to the sides of the bezel.

Varsity (*bottom*), Potomac/Rockingham (*top*)

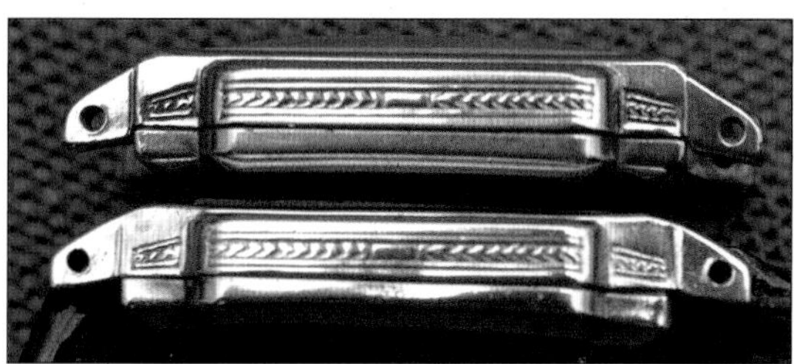

Potomac/Rockingham (*top*), Varsity (*bottom*). Their sides are identical.

The Varsity is not as rare as once thought but it is still difficult to find as fewer than fifteen are known to exist. The Varsity uses the same dials as the Potomac model; however, the case Model Numbers are different for the Varsity (No. 650) and the Potomac (No. 626).

The name Varsity comes from price cards such as those Illinois characteristically put in its watch boxes. There are so very few 14K Illinois wristwatch models that finding a card indicating one of these with a 15-jewel movement might eventually have led to the No. 650 by the process of elimination, but in this case it was much easier because the Varsity card came in an Illinois display case with a No. 650 in it!

Not long before the Varsity card and watch were found, another card for an unknown Illinois model named Sherwood had been found with information that the case for it was 14K and the movement was 15 jewels. Accordingly, for a while it was thought that Sherwood might be the name of the No. 650, but the later discovery of an outer box for a Sherwood put that theory to rest. The information on the box shows that the Sherwood was an 18/0 size watch; the No. 650 is 6/0 size. (For more about the **Sherwood**, see the listing for it in Chapter 10.)

We do not know precisely when the Varsity was issued or whether it was commissioned by some particular customer. However, since the Potomac was introduced in late 1932, it is likely that the Varsity appeared sometime during 1933.

Original Varsity price card

Although the card indicates that the Varsity came with a metal bracelet, none of the known specimens of this model has been found with its original attachment. Metal bracelets of that era did not hold up well, as they were prone to damage from perspiration and thus were often discarded.

As to why this watch was produced, there may never be a definite answer. Nonetheless, the history of Hamilton's pattern in closing down the Illinois operations may provide some clues. As can be seen in Chapter 5, the jobbers with whom Illinois worked were continuing to request solid 14K watches. However, during this time period, in the depths of the Great Depression, Hamilton was attempting to cut costs by moving from 14K gold-filled cases to 10K ones in its Illinois line (and for some models in its own line as well). In this same time period Hamilton was also marketing Illinois watches with only 15-jewel movements in order to liquidate its inventory of those Illinois movements.

Varsity inside case back

Varsity case back

It may well have been that because some longtime customer was so insistent, Hamilton let Illinois ask Keystone to produce a limited number of 14K solid gold cases based on an existing model but also to do something to disguise the similarity between the original and modified cases. Adding a fillet of gold on top of the lugs may have served this purpose. Even though it is solid gold, in a sense this is still a cost-cutting bargain case; the weight of gold is less than that of a case like the Consul, and Varsity cases have been observed to wear through. If the Varsity was a special order for a certain customer, that could explain not only why the model did not appear in Illinois' sales catalogs but also why it is relatively rare.

FANTASTIC FIND

Gene Livingston, a longtime friend and Illinois and Le Coultre collector reports that "at the 2009 Daytona NAWCC Regional Mart, while construction was in progress for the new Mart space, I was set up at a table at the center of the room to sell my extra watches, mostly Swiss and a few of my extra Illinois and Hamiltons. In the afternoon, when the traffic slowed, there was time to look at the other sellers' offerings. After about 20 minutes of looking, I spotted an Illinois wristwatch that appeared to be a yellow gold-filled 'Potomac.' Its price was $375. I asked to see the watch and removed the back and noted 'Model 650, 14K solid gold.' I placed the watch in my pocket, paid the $375 and happily made my way back to my table. I thought to myself, 'Life is good.'"

Vernon

See listing for **Larchmont**

Viking

Official Name = Viking (derived from Illinois Sales and Material Catalogs and jobbers' catalogs)
Secondary Name = None
Formerly Known As = None
Time Period = Deco
Case Variations/Rarity = ◷◷◷◷ WGF/M
◷◷◷◷◷ YGF/M
Case Durability = ◷
Material = 14K GF
Bezel = Molded
Sides = Plain
Lugs = Plain
Lug Size = 16mm
Springbar = Male
Casemaker = Fahys
Case Closure = 3-Part Snap-On Bezel and Back
Case Number = 195
Case Shape = Rectangular
Case Back = Flat
Dimensions = 38 x 30mm
Movement Size = 3/0
Movement Grades/Jewels = 24/17, 307/17
Seconds at = 6
Dial Numbers = 8173, 8728
Dial = Silver Finish
Dial Opening = Rectangular
Dial Variations/Rarity = ◷◷◷ Silver Finish, Luminous Numerals
◷◷◷◷◷ Silver Finish, Black Numerals
Numerals = Painted, Luminous
Hands = Luminous
Cased in Factory = Yes
Unique Case Design = Yes
Unique Dial Design = No
Introduction Date = 1929
Retail Price New = $42.50
Collectibility = ◷◷◷◷
Advertisements = No
Marketing Themes = "Very distinctive in appearance"
"Cased so exceptionally small that it appears more the size of a 6/0 watch"

Viking, white gold-filled

Viking, yellow gold-filled

The Viking was introduced in the 1929–30 Sales Catalog on a page with the heading "Six New Illinois Watches Announced Since Foregoing Pages Were Compiled." (The other new models were the Futura wristwatch and four pocket watches: the Dean, the Rialto, the Bourse and the Model 181 Bunn Special.) The catalog described the Viking as "A new Illinois 3/0 size strap watch, very distinctive in appearance. Furnished in 14K white or yellow gold-filled, with the sturdy, accurate 17 jewel Illinois movement, and a full luminous dial." This model appeared in jobbers' catalogs, but no magazine advertisements for it have been found.

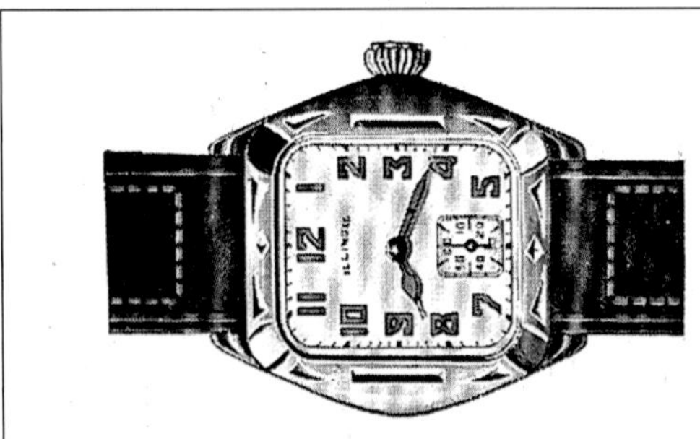

A. I. Hall catalog, 1930–31

Because the Viking is one of the largest Illinois wristwatches, it holds special appeal for large-wristed collectors. The molded bezel of the Viking is deeply sculpted. It is subject to severe case wear, more so on the yellow case than the white one. (There is also a 6/0 Illinois model with a similar but not identical style of bezel, known by collectors as a Beau Brummell/Viking because it looks like a Beau Brummell but with a Viking bezel; its official name is not known.) The 1930–31 Illinois Sales Catalog described the Viking as "An attractive Illinois strapwatch—cased so exceptionally small that it appears more the size of a 6/0 watch." This is remarkably misleading, as the 3/0 Viking is a massive watch, especially for an Illinois.

No two-tone versions of the Viking exist.

Viking inside case back

A Viking in its display box with its original price card. Since Illinois advertised the Viking specifically as a strap watch, the original owner of this one likely decided to swap the leather band for a fashionable new metal bracelet. (See "Attachments" section of Chapter 8.)

A FANTASTIC FIND

James Kubicki from Illinois writes: "I will give you my story. Things started out with a trip to the grocery store with my wife, Rose, and daughter, Carleigh, in nearby Carpentersville, just north of Elgin (yes, that Elgin). Just adjacent to the Woodman's grocery store is the Goodwill store. Rose and Carleigh hate waiting around while I sift through what is for sale. We split up—the girls going to the grocery store while I take my time to peruse the Goodwill store. I always like to stop in there and maybe find something interesting. After going through all the housewares and picking up a really nice old iron and a vintage mortar and pestle, I ventured toward the front of the store for checkout.

"Near the checkout are the two cases that are supposed to have the more 'valuable items' and are locked up. Most of the time there isn't much of anything of interest. If there is a watch—any watch—I have to have a look. There was one watch on the top shelf, about 5 ½ feet up, poorly displayed, lying on its back. In other words, only the side of the watch could be viewed. I found a clerk and had the case opened up so I could have a closer look. Upon seeing the 'Illinois' name, I thought it would be worth considering. Keep in mind my only knowledge of the Illinois Watch Company is the fact that Hamilton bought them out. I knew a Hamilton was a good watch (I do possess a Hamilton 'Barton').

"When I saw the price of $75.00 for the Illinois watch, I wasn't sure I should buy it. I know what you're thinking. Please keep in mind I am not knowledgeable about this maker and thought more about what my wife would say after I purchased another watch. I even attempted to haggle—no dice. I decided to purchase it just for the styling and overall great condition. The watch appeared to be completely original (even the band), with a nearly perfect dial, which we all know is VERY important. I purchased it and met my wife at the grocery store, getting the expected reaction. My wife just doesn't understand the watch thing. I started collecting watches for my admiration of the mechanical intricacies and craftsmanship. Upon returning home, I went online to find out more about my purchase. After seeing the asking prices (retail), I was dumbfounded. Pure, dumb luck. Not only am I happy that I got a deal, this Illinois Viking model watch will be well taken care of."

Washington Watch Company

Official Name = Washington Watch Company (derived from Washington Watch Company advertisements and Montgomery Ward & Co. Sales Catalogs)
Secondary Name = None
Formerly Known As = None
Time Period = Transitional
Case Variations/Rarity = 🕒🕒 SS/Round
🕒🕒🕒🕒 SS/Cushion
Case Durability = 🕒🕒🕒🕒
Material = SS
Bezel = Plain
Sides = Plain
Lugs = Plain
Lug Size = 14mm, 16mm
Springbar = Fixed Lugs
Casemakers = Fahys, Others
Case Closure = 3-Part Snap-On Bezel and Back
Case Number = None

Washington Watch Company, sterling silver

Washington Watch Company, sterling silver

Case Shape = Round, Cushion
Case Back = Flat
Dimensions = Various
Movement Sizes = 0, 3/0
Movement Grades/Jewels = 24/17, 34/17, 36/17, 37/17, 38/17
Seconds at = 6
Dial Numbers = None
Dial = Enamel
Dial Opening = Round
Dial Variations/Rarity = 🕒🕒🕒🕒🕒 Enamel
Numerals = Painted
Hands = Steel
Cased in Factory = No
Unique Case Design = No
Unique Dial Design = No
Introduction Date = 1913
Retail Price New = Unknown
Collectibility = 🕒🕒🕒
Advertisements = No
Marketing Themes = Various

The Washington Watch Company was a house brand of Montgomery Ward & Co. (See Chapter 6 for more information on the Washington Watch Company.) Illinois manufactured hundreds of private-label watches for jewelers, jobbers, large catalog houses and department stores. Watches by the Washington Watch Co. were advertised in the Montgomery Ward mail-order sales catalog.

The Washington Watch Company intended most if not all of its movements and dials for men's and ladies' pocket watches. During the Transitional Period, however, many of these movements and dials migrated into military-type Transitional Period wristwatch cases as wristwatches became socially acceptable.

Other private-label brands are covered in this chapter. A well-rounded Illinois wristwatch collection should include a few private-label ones.

See listing for **Ace**

Wentworth / Commander

Official Name = Wentworth (derived from the Illinois Sales Catalog "Pioneers of Progress" in 1933)
Secondary Name = Commander (pursuant to internal Hamilton records)
Formerly Known As = None
Time Period = Moderne
Case Variations/Rarity = ◷◷◷◷◷ YGF/P
◷◷◷◷◷ WGF/P
Case Durability = ◷◷ YGF
◷◷◷ WGF
Material = 14K GF
Bezel = Plain
Sides = Engraved
Lugs = Plain
Lug Size = 16mm
Springbar = Female
Casemaker = Keystone
Case Closure = 3-Part Snap-On Bezel and Back
Case Number = 197
Case Shape = Rectangular
Case Back = Flat
Dimensions = 36 x 23mm
Movement Size = 12/0
Movement Grade/Jewels = 207/17
Seconds at = 6
Dial Number = 8238
Dials = Silver Finish, Sparkle Finish
Dial Opening = Rectangular
Dial Variations/Rarity = ◷◷◷ Silver Finish, Luminous Numerals
◷◷◷◷◷ Silver Finish, Painted Numerals; Sparkle Finish, Luminous Numerals
Numerals = Painted, Luminous
Hands = Painted
Cased in Factory = Yes
Unique Case Design = Yes
Unique Dial Design = Yes
Introduction Date = 1933
Retail Price New = $50.00
Collectibility = ◷◷◷◷
Advertisements = No
Marketing Themes = "Conservative streamline effect"
"Will appeal to men"
"Distinguished case"

Wentworth, white gold-filled

Wentworth, yellow gold-filled

The Wentworth was introduced in the 1933 Illinois Sales Catalog. Entitled "Illinois Greater Value Watches" to appeal to consumers then in the depths of the Great Depression, the catalog featured the slogan "Pioneers of Extra Values" at the top of pages throughout.

In its catalog caption, Illinois touted the Wentworth's "distinguished case," a description reiterated by such jobbers as Benj. Allen. Advertisements also commented that the case design "will appeal to men" and mentioned its "conservative streamline effect"—very fitting for a Moderne Period watch.

Benj. Allen catalog, 1933

An internal Hamilton document dated June 5, 1933, called this watch a Commander. Possibly, the Commander came equipped with a metal bracelet. The Wentworth/ Commander shares the same case Model Numbers as its close cousin, the Futura. The center section and case back are interchangeable between the Wentworth and the Futura.

The Wentworth resembles the Futura but without the ridge on its bezel. Both models feature a sleek and elegant Moderne design. The Wentworth dial opening is square at its corners, whereas the Futura dial opening has rounded corners.

Futura, white gold-filled

Wentworth, white gold-filled

The Wentworth is much rarer than the Futura and a white gold-filled Wentworth is much more difficult to find than a yellow one. Both white and yellow cases are prone to case wear on the top and bottom of their bezels, but the wear is worse on the yellow cases.

The Wentworth shares the same dials as the Finalist Deco, Finalist and Chesterfield. With a crisp, clean white sparkle dial, the Wentworth has a beautiful streamlined look.

Wembley

See listing for **Medalist**

Westchester

See listing for **Trophy**

Whippet / Tonneau Gift Series

Whippet, white gold-filled

Whippet, two-tone gold-filled

Official Name = Whippet (derived from jobbers' advertisements and catalogs)
Secondary Name = Tonneau (derived from a 1930 Illinois Factory advertisement) Gift Series (derived from Richter & Phillips advertisements)
Formerly Known As = Barrel/Tonneau (derived from its case shape before its official name was discovered)
Time Period = Generic
Case Variations/Rarity = 🕐 WGF/P, WGF/E, YGF/P, YGF/E, GGF/P, GGF/E
🕐🕐🕐🕐🕐 YG/P, YG/P, GG/P, GG/E, TT/GF
🕐🕐🕐🕐🕐🕐 WG, TT/E
Case Durability = 🕐🕐🕐🕐
Material = 14K GF, 14K YG
Bezel = Plain, Engraved
Sides = Plain, Engraved
Lugs = Plain, Engraved
Lug Size = 16mm
Springbar = Male
Casemakers = Keystone, Wadsworth, Others
Case Closure = 3-Part Snap-On Bezel and Back, 2-Part Hinged Bezel and Back
Case Number = None
Case Shape = Tonneau
Case Back = Flat
Dimensions = 3/0 (40 x 28mm), 6/0 (35 x 28mm)
Movement Sizes = 3/0, 6/0
Movement Grades/Jewels = 903/15, 905/17, 907/17. 605/15, 607/17, 907/19
Seconds at = 6, 9
Dial Numbers = 8095, 8108, 8277, 8288
Dial = Silver Finish
Dial Opening = Tonneau
Dial Variations/Rarity = 🕐🕐 Silver Finish, Luminous Numerals
🕐🕐🕐🕐 Silver Finish, Luminous Numerals, Butler Center
🕐🕐🕐🕐🕐 Silver Finish, Black Numerals; Silver Finish, Painted Numerals, Etched Center; Silver Finish, Etched Numerals; Silver Finish, Cross Pattern
Numerals = Etched, Luminous
Hands = Steel, Luminous
Cased in Factory = Yes/No
Unique Case Design = No
Unique Dial Design = Yes
Introduction Date = 1926

Retail Price New = $45.00 (15J), $50.00 (17J), $55.00 (19J)
Collectibility = 🕓🕓🕓🕓
Advertisements = Yes
Marketing Theme = "A very popular model of fine timekeeping qualities."

Barrel-shaped cases were great favorites during the Generic Period, and the Illinois Whippet's case is one of that type. An image of the Whippet was included in a case advertisement by Keystone for its J. Boss line in the November 26, 1926 issue of the *Jewelers' Circular*. An Illinois advertisement in the May 1928 issue of the *American Magazine* calls the Whippet "A very popular model of fine timekeeping qualities. 17 jeweled movement in 14K gold-filled case with an engraved bezel and curved back." The Whippet also appears in several other Illinois Factory advertisements, including one in 1930 that refers to it as a "Tonneau" strap watch.

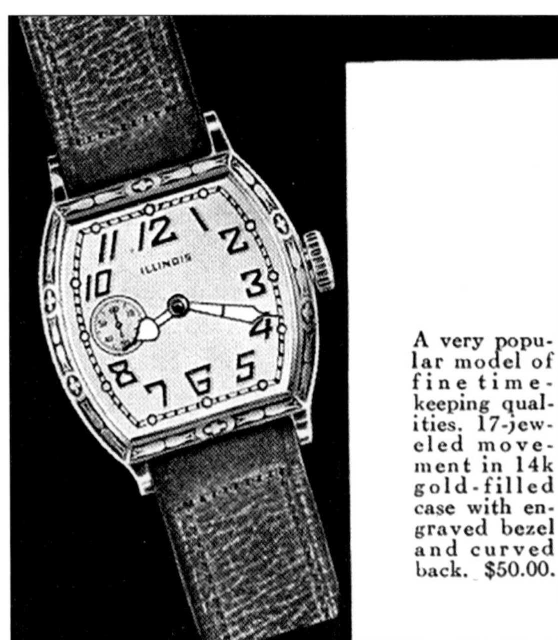

***American Magazine*, May 1928**

The Illinois Whippet case looks similar to many comparable Elgin and Waltham barrel watches. Surprisingly, though, Illinois "cased and timed" some Whippets in its watch factory. The Factory-Cased version came in a white or green gold-filled Keystone J. Boss case with an engraved bezel and subsidiary seconds at 9. A 1930 Illinois Factory advertisement notes that this "Tonneau" came in "6/0 size, with luminous dial, fitted and timed in Boss white or green, 14K gold-filled cases with strap and buckle complete in display boxes." These were the Whippets in Keystone cases with engraved bezels.

It is understandable why Keystone's J. Boss three-piece cases were selected for Illinois' gold-filled Whippets. In the 1926 advertisement for its J. Boss line mentioned above, Keystone pointed out that such case construction had several advantages: "It provides a sturdier case, better able to protect the movement against blows. It permits perfect fitting. It excludes dust and moisture."

The Illinois Whippet stands out from its Elgin and Waltham competition by its quintessential Illinois 9 o'clock subsidiary seconds and interesting dial designs. (It should be noted that a few of Elgin's barrel case watches also have subsidiary seconds at 9.) There are some beautiful Illinois Whippet dials with silver butler centers, bold green luminous numerals and subsidiary seconds at 9 o'clock. Other dials have silver finishes, bold black numerals, silvered subsidiary seconds and a cross pattern on the center of the dial. Dials can also have etched centers in interesting patterns with silvered subsidiary seconds at 9 o'clock. (The Standish dial, with its etched numerals, also fits in the 6/0 size Whippet case and makes for a fantastic look.)

Whippets are hard to find in solid yellow gold and green gold cases. No solid white gold Whippet case has been found. Two-tone Whippet cases are rare and thus highly collectible. There is also at least one two-tone white and yellow gold-filled Whippet with an engraved bezel that is partially enameled. Another rarity is a white gold Whippet in a plain bezel case; the case is signed "R.W.C. Co." Yet another is a two-tone Whippet with a larger center section. Finally, there is a perhaps one-of-a-kind two-tone Whippet in white and yellow gold-filled with stars on the center section of its case. (The only other Illinois wristwatches with stars on their cases are the Eagle, Greyhound, Motor Coach, Off-Duty and Skyway models.)

Whippet, two-tone white and yellow gold-filled, with stars on its bezel

Whippet, green gold-filled

"ILLINOIS" MAN'S STRAP WATCH. 6/0 size Barrel shape, with sturdy lugs—fancy chased bezel, polished back. Fine quality Lever movement with luminous dial and hands with second. Fitted with high-grade sewed leather strap. Each in gift case.
No. 3940 17J. Each **29.00**
No. 3941 19J. Each **31.75**

Rohde-Spencer catalog, 1929

The Whippet was also a Gift Series wristwatch offered for sale by the Richter & Phillips Company. (See the listing for **Gift Series**.)

Yankee Clipper

See listing for **Ensign**

Yorktown

See listing for **New Yorker**

ILLINOIS

ILLINOIS

ILLINOIS

THE VOL 4

ILLINOIS WATCH & ITS HAMILTON YEARS

THE FINALE OF A GREAT AMERICAN WATCH COMPANY

The Identification Guides

Illinois Ladies' Wristwatches

Hamilton-Illinois Wristwatches

BY

Fredric J. Friedberg

Schiffer Publishing Ltd

4880 Lower Valley Road • Atglen, PA 19310

Library of Congress Control Number: 2017933341

Designed by Chris Cornforth, www.chrisworx.com
Cover designs by Fred, Joy, Zach Friedberg and Chris Cornforth

ISBN:978-0-7643-5371-0
Printed in China
Published by Schiffer Publishing, Ltd.
4880 Lower Valley Road
Atglen, PA 19310
Phone: (610) 593-1777; Fax: (610) 593-2002
E-mail: Info@schifferbooks.com
Web: www.schifferbooks.com

CHAPTER 10

Illinois Ladies' Wristwatches: History and Identification Guide

The Illinois Watch Company is best known for its varied and high-grade pocket watches; it is less well known for its wristwatches (although they represent some of the most creative, bold and stunningly Art Deco and Moderne watches ever produced), and almost overlooked entirely are the great variety of Illinois ladies' wristwatches. When my book *The Illinois Watch: The Life and Times of a Great American Watch Company* was published in 2004, I stated that research on the Illinois ladies' wristwatches was still a "works-in-progress."[1] Since then, with the dedicated research efforts of ardent Illinois collector and Illinois ladies' wristwatch expert Farrell Gay, he and I have endeavored to document the Illinois ladies' landscape more fully in this book.[2]

The World's First Ladies' Wristwatch

Before the Illinois ladies' models in particular are addressed, it should be noted that signs of the first ladies' wristwatches appeared in the mid-1500s. Dominique Fléchon writes:[3]

> In his letter to the Duke of Ferrara dated July 19th, 1488, Jacopo Trotti, ambassador at the court of the Sforzas, wrote that Ludovic Sforza had ordered three silk costumes, each adorned with a watch. . . . Less than a century later, in 1571 or 1572, the Earl of Leicester, favourite and Equerry of Elizabeth I, presented the queen with a round watch inlaid with diamonds and suspended from an armlet.[4] For historians, this is the ancestor of the wristwatch. In his *Histoire de Port Royal*, Gazier notes that Pascal (1623–1662) wore his watch on his wrist. In May 1927, *L'Horloger* published a vintage engraving showing four horses drawing a chassis on wheels. One of the riders clearly has a watch attached to his sleeve. . . .
>
> The 1772 *Almanach du Dauphin* makes reference to the bracelet-watches and ring-watches of a Parisian watchmaker on Rue de Buci. An entry in the ledgers of Jacquet-Droz et Leschot in Geneva for 1790 describes 'a watch that can be set into a bracelet.' While both private and museum collections include numerous ring-watches from various eras, the oldest-known surviving bracelet-watches date from the very early nineteenth century, when fashion dictated shorter sleeves for women.
>
> In 1811, Nitot, jeweler of Napoleon I, delivered to the princess Augusta of Bavaria, wife of Eugène de Beauharnais, two bracelets set with emeralds and pearls. In one Nitot incorporated a watch and in the other a calendar showing the date and month, both with visible dials. On June 8th, 1810, Caroline Murat, Queen of Naples, placed an order with Abraham Louis Breguet for an oblong repeater watch with an off-centre hour ring and thermometer. It was mounted on a bracelet of hair interwoven with gold threads.

Abraham-Louis Breguet, approaching middle age

ABRAHAM-LOUIS BREGUET (1747-1823)

Abraham-Louis Breguet, considered the most celebrated of all French clock and watch makers, was born in Neuchâtel, Switzerland, on January 10, 1747. When his father died in 1758, his mother remarried Joseph Tattet, who came from a family of watchmakers. Tattet had a showroom in Paris, and in 1762 Abraham-Louis was sent there to serve as an apprentice to an unknown master as a watchmaker. After he finished his apprenticeship, he set up a business at 39 Quai de l'Horloge in Paris.

As a watchmaker, Breguet was extremely innovative. He invented different escapements including the famous and acclaimed tourbillion, automatic winding mechanisms, and the overcoil (an improvement to the balance spring with a raised outer coil). Within ten years he had commissions from the aristocratic families of France and even the French queen, Marie-Antoinette.

When Marie-Antoinette grew fascinated by Breguet's self-winding pocket watch, Louis XVI bought several of his watches. One of her male admirers (or lovers), likely Count Hans Axel von Fersen, commissioned a pocket watch for her from Breguet that was to contain every watch function known to exist at that time, including a clock, perpetual calendar, minute repeater, chime, thermometer, chronograph, power reserve, and pare-chute (a shock absorber for the balance pivot). This design was a massive undertaking, and Marie-Antoinette never lived to see it, as it was not completed until 1827, by Breguet's son, thirty-four years after she had been executed. (A recent book by John Biggs, *Marie Antoinette's Watch: Adultery, Larceny & Perpetual Motion*, deals with the strange history of this famous timepiece.)

Breguet did not man his workshops with unskilled apprentices, as was the norm. Instead, he hired the most skilled craftsmen he could to make watches of his design. In the early 1800s, Breguet took his son on as a business partner after having sent him to London to study with the great English chronometer maker John Arnold, who, in turn, sent his son to spend time with Breguet.

Continuing to grow, the business was carried on by Breguet's son after Breguet's death in 1823, and it still exists today.

Source: https://en.wikipedia.org/wiki/Abraham-Louis_Breguet

Illinois' First Wristwatch: A Ladies' Model

The first documented evidence of a wristwatch offering by the Illinois Watch Company is in a 1910 advertisement for a lady's "Convertible," a watch so named to indicate its versatility: it could be worn as wristwatch with a detachable, expandable metal band or a ribbon one; used as a pocket watch with the band removed; worn as a pendant on a chain around the neck; or hooked onto a watch pin and pinned to a blouse or dress.[5] This wristwatch was aimed exclusively at the ladies' market. The particular Convertible in the advertisement shown here, a private-label product for the Marshall Field Department Store in Chicago, was signed "Ariston USA" on its dial. Illinois made hundreds of private-label watches, mostly for pocket watches (see Chapter 6).

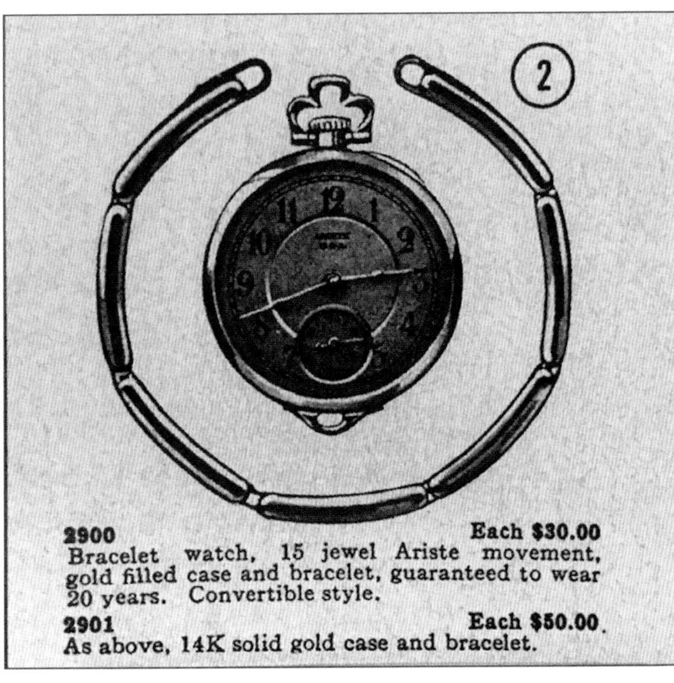

Ariston Convertible, 1910

Illinois Watch Eras

The introduction and design of the Illinois ladies' wristwatches tracked basically the same eras as those for the men's: the Transitional, Generic, Deco and Moderne Periods. The ladies' wristwatches offered by the Illinois Watch Company ranged from the rather plain convertible models of the Transitional Period, to the ultra-feminine watches with elaborately engraved bezels of the Generic Period, to the rectangular and highly stylized ones of the Deco Period, to some larger, more nearly man-sized (if not really quite "man-sized") wristwatches of the Moderne Period. (During the Moderne Period, Illinois also offered some of the tiny ladies' watches then in vogue, the semi-baguette and baguette models.) But of all the time periods, the deco models remain the most popular, sought-after and collectible today.

Transitional Period: Pre–World War I to the Early 1920s

Men's wristwatches during the Transitional Period were at first just modified or reconfigured pocket watches. It was easy for jewelers to solder fixed lugs on standard-issue pocket watches and attach a band to them. Thus, pocket watches were "transitioned" to wristwatches.

Since women usually adopt new styles and fashion trends more quickly than men, wristwatches became popular with women and marketable to them far before men accepted them. Whereas women starting wearing wristwatches as early as 1907 in the United States, men did not commence wearing them in earnest until after World War I. Initially, men considered wristwatches effeminate. But because wristwatches were used by men during the war, albeit owing to military necessity, they started becoming acceptable in the years thereafter.

The ladies' Illinois of this era, even upon casual observation, readily display their pocket watch ancestry. With the addition of clips, hooks, clasps, bands, lugs and other creative attachments, former pocket watches were converted to more stylish wristwatches. The very first Illinois ladies' wristwatch, the Ariston "Convertible," pictured earlier, was one of that sort. Yellow gold, either gold-filled or solid gold, was overwhelmingly the metal of choice for ladies' transitional watches.

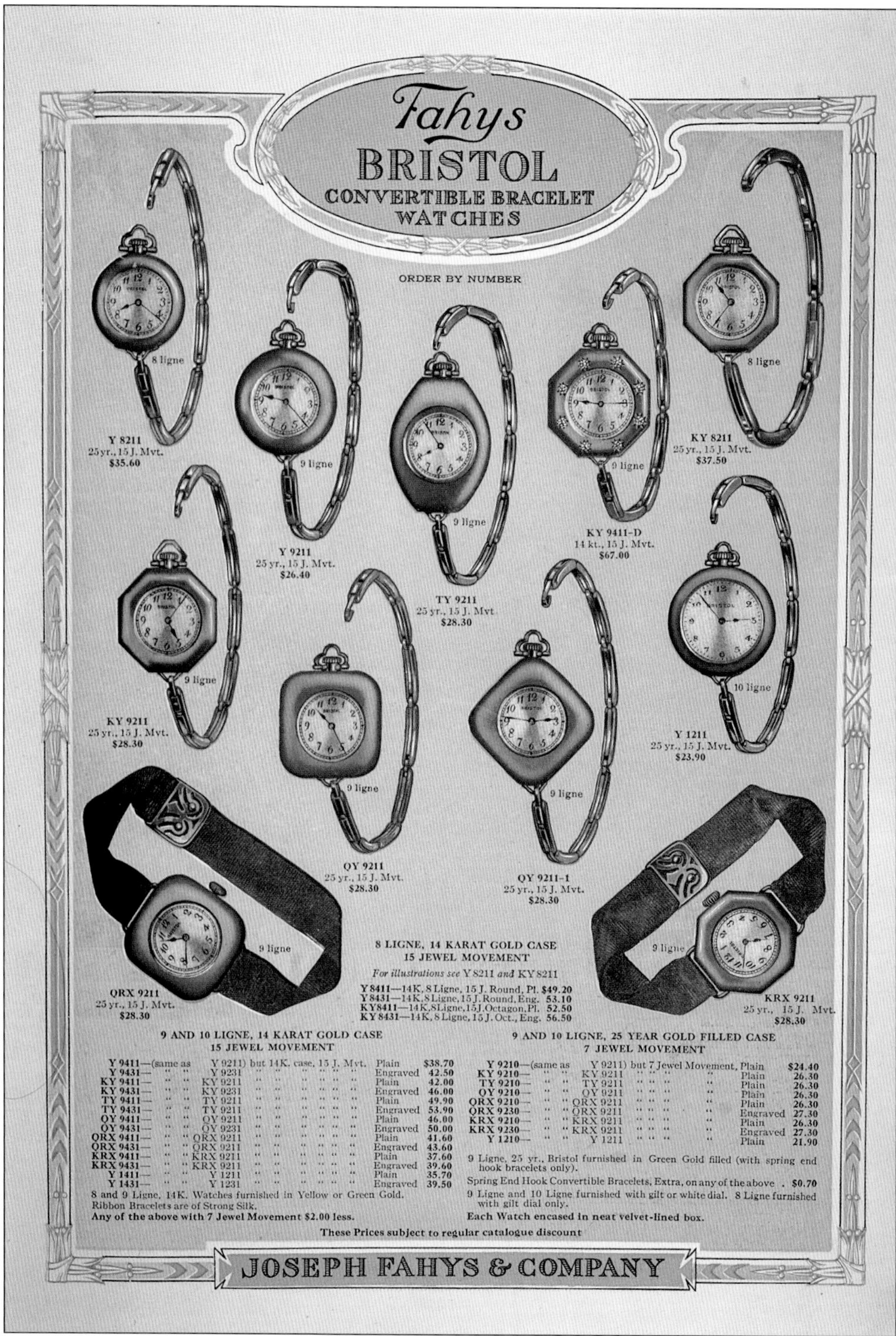

Some convertibles shown in the 1917 A. C. Becken catalog

Scheufele Watch Clip. The Scheufele family of Pforzheim, Germany, for over one-hundred years owned a jewelry and watch manufacturing company. Its founder, Karl Scheufele, in 1912 invented an ingenious clip that could be used to affix to the wrist a ladies' pocket watch or pendant watch. Scheufele's clip, basically a bracelet equipped in its center with an open construction to hold a watch securely,[6] was awarded a United States Patent in 1914.

As a result, Karl Scheufele's watch clip was a big success and his business thrived. Fashionable ladies were particularly enamored of the device, which made it so convenient for them to jump on the fashion bandwagon and convert their timepieces into newfangled wristwatches. This clever invention brought prosperity to the Scheufele family.[7]

Precious clips were made from solid gold in Karl Scheufele's workshop, and ones in lesser metals were made under license by several of his colleagues in Pforzheim; gold-plated watch clips, for example, were produced by Kollmar & Jourdan. Others were made by Friedrich Speidel, as Liz Zuffi discovered while researching a wristlet clip that she had acquired; the hallmark on the inside of the clip matches the mark shown in a Speidel advertisement. (More information about the Speidel family is included in the "Attachments" section of Chapter 8.)

Underside of Speidel's Scheufele clip, holding a small pocket watch

Side view of the watch in the clip

The Scheufele clip by itself

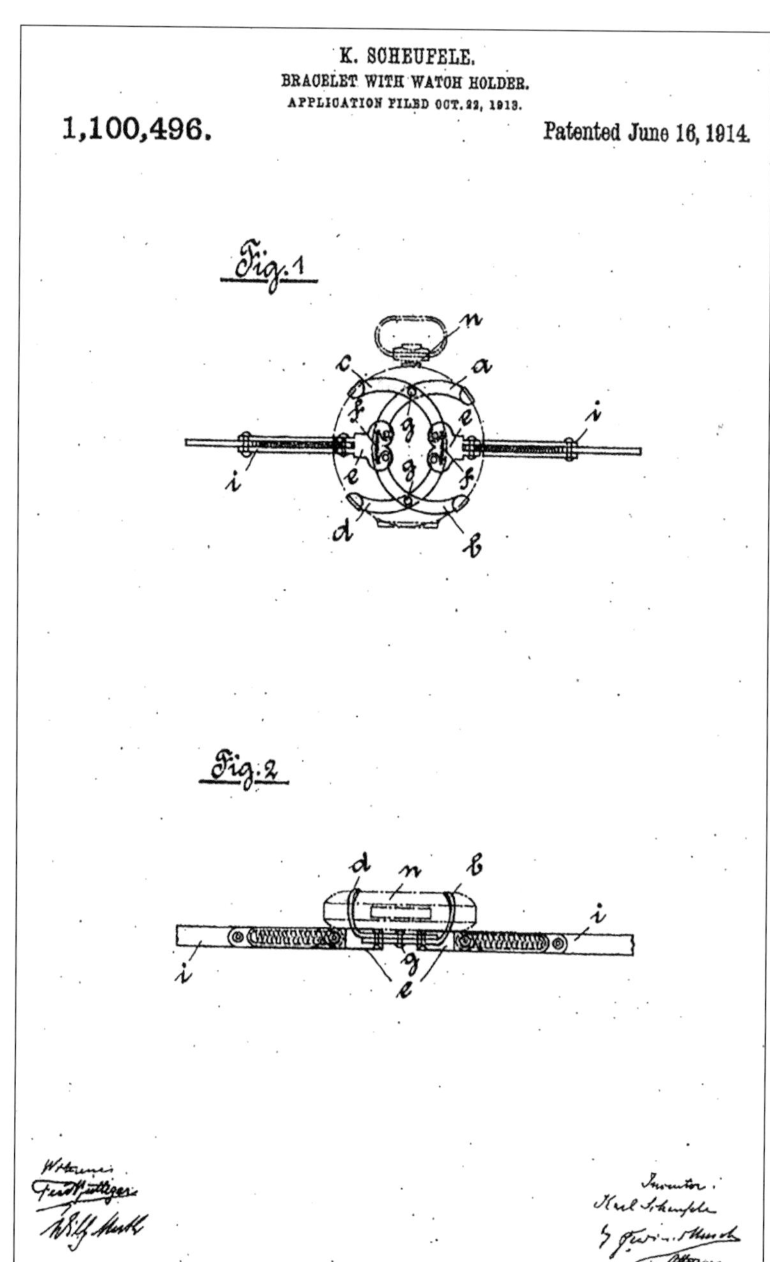

K. SCHEUFELE.
BRACELET WITH WATCH HOLDER.
APPLICATION FILED OCT. 22, 1913.

1,100,496. Patented June 16, 1914.

Patent for the Scheufele Clip, June 16, 1914

UNITED STATES PATENT OFFICE.

KARL SCHEUFELE, OF PFORZHEIM, GERMANY.

BRACELET WITH WATCH-HOLDER.

1,100,496. Specification of Letters Patent. Patented June 16, 1914.

Application filed October 22, 1913. Serial No. 796,646.

To all whom it may concern:

Be it known that I, Karl Scheufele, a subject of the Grand Duke of Baden, residing at Pforzheim, in the Grand Duchy of Baden, German Empire, have invented certain new and useful Improvements in Bracelets with Watch-Holders, of which the following is a specification.

This invention relates to a bracelet with a device for holding a watch so that, although being securely held, it can be easily removed. This watch-holder consists of two pairs of levers linked together so that they securely clamp in the watch.

In the accompanying drawings the invention is shown by way of example.

Figure 1 shows the holding device in a plan view. Fig. 2 is a front elevation of the same.

The holding device consists of four curved levers *a*, *b*, *c* and *d* arranged so that two pairs of levers *a*—*b* and *c*—*d* are formed. The inner ends of the levers *a*—*b* and the inner ends of the levers *c*—*d* are pivotally mounted in two brackets *e* to which the ends of the bracelet *i* are fixed. Springs *f* located in said brackets maintain said levers in position. The levers *a*—*c* and *b*—*d* are connected by means of pivot pins *g*. The ends of the levers are bent upward and form claws which hold the watch *n*.

The device operates as follows:—To put the watch into the holder *r* the ends *i* of the bracelet to which the brackets *e*—*e* are fixed, are moved the one toward the other whereby the claw-shaped ends of the lever pairs *a*—*c* and *b*—*d* respectively are moved away from each other putting the pressure springs *f* under compression. As soon as the parts *i* of the bracelet are released the levers are made to turn around the pivots *g* through the action of the springs *f* whereby the watch *u* is securely gripped by the claw-shaped ends of said levers. Particularly if the bracelet is of the extensible type the claw-shaped lever ends are continuously pressed against the rim of the watch through the expansion of the bracelet so that the watch is always securely maintained.

I claim:—

A bracelet with watch-holder comprising in combination with a bracelet two brackets fixed in said bracelet, four curved levers pivotally fixed with their inner ends in said brackets and pivotally connected at about the middle of their arms which cross each other in two oppositely extending pairs, claws at the outer ends of the levers and springs located in said brackets and attached to the inner ends of said levers for pressing said levers against the rim of a watch to be held, substantially as described and illustrated.

In witness whereof I have hereunto set my hand in the presence of two witnesses.

KARL SCHEUFELE.

Witnesses:

Karl Friedrich Gehring,

Paul Heinram.

Copies of this patent may be obtained for five cents each, by addressing the "Commissioner of Patents, Washington, D. C."

Patent for the Scheufele Clip, June 16, 1914

T-32 S. KIND & SONS—LARGE SELECTION OF BRACELET WATCHES—PHILADELPHIA

Silver and Gun Metal Bracelet Watches.

Illustrations are actual size, although the entire length of bracelet is not shown. These bracelet watches are all supplied with expansion links, and most of our bracelets have a security catch at back. This enables the bracelet to be unhooked so that it may be removed from the arm without the necessity of stretching the bracelet to slip over the hand. These clasps are so arranged that even if they become unhooked when bracelet is worn it will not fall off.

2336 Sterling silver, light blue enamel, jeweled Swiss lever movement, white dial $18 00

2337 Sterling silver, plain case, jeweled Swiss lever movement, silver dial 15 00

2338 Sterling silver, plain case, jeweled Swiss lever movement, white dial 12 00
Same watch, gun metal 12 00

2339 Sterling silver or gun metal, plain case, jeweled Swiss lever movement, white dial 21 00

2340 Sterling silver or gun metal, nurse's bracelet watch, plain case, has large sweep second hand for taking pulse or other observations, jeweled Swiss lever movement $12 00

2341 Bracelet watch holder, to convert your watch into a perfect bracelet watch or back again instantly. The holder shown permits the turning of the watch after it is clasped to have the figure 12 on a line with the bracelet.
Solid 14kt gold 27 00
" 10kt " 21 00
Gold filled or sterling silver 6 00

Wrist Watches and Watch Holders.

Illustrations show several desirable styles of leather strap wrist watches. We pack them in suitable cases.

2342 Watch holder with expansion bracelet to convert your watch into a perfect bracelet watch.
Solid 14kt gold $15 00
" 10kt " 12 00
Gold filled 4 00
Sterling silver 3 75

2343 Watch holder with leather bracelet straps.
Solid 14kt gold 15 00
" 10kt " 12 00
Gold filled 3 75
Sterling silver 2 50

All leather strap bracelets are furnished with metal buckles at prices quoted. With gold, silver and filled buckles at additional cost as follows:
14kt, $2.00; 10kt, $1.50; filled, 50 cents; silver ... $0 50

2344 Leather wrist watch for gentlemen, nickel or gun metal case, jeweled Swiss movement 5 00

2345 Leather wrist watch for ladies, sterling silver case, jeweled Swiss movement 8 00
With gun metal case 7 50

2346 Nurse's or doctor's watch, leather bracelet, large second-hand for use in taking pulse and other observations. Sterling silver or gun metal case, jeweled Swiss movement 9 00

S. Kind & Sons catalog, 1916

Generic Period: Early 1920s to Early 1930s

Just as happened with the men's wristwatches of this Generic Period, the ladies' wristwatches were cased and assembled by thousands of jewelers and jobbers located throughout the United States. The major American watch companies of this era, such as Illinois, Elgin and Waltham, manufactured the movements and some of the dials and sold them to jewelers and jobbers that then married them with cases and bands and sold them directly to the consumer. This period is called the Generic Period because it is characterized by a genre: the very similarly styled if not identical cases that various casemakers made and offered for sale to jewelers and jobbers.

During the Generic Period most of the cases used for Illinois ladies' wristwatches were manufactured by the Fahys, Star, Philadelphia and Wadsworth case companies. (Brief histories of these companies can be found in Chapter 8.) Most American watch manufacturing enterprises of this time promoted similarly cased watches, differentiated only by their movements, dials and promotional materials. From at least the perspective of Illinois watches, it was rare to see an offering from this time in other than a white gold-filled or white solid gold case. As a result, the yellow and green gold-filled and the yellow and green solid gold ones are far more desirable and collectible today.

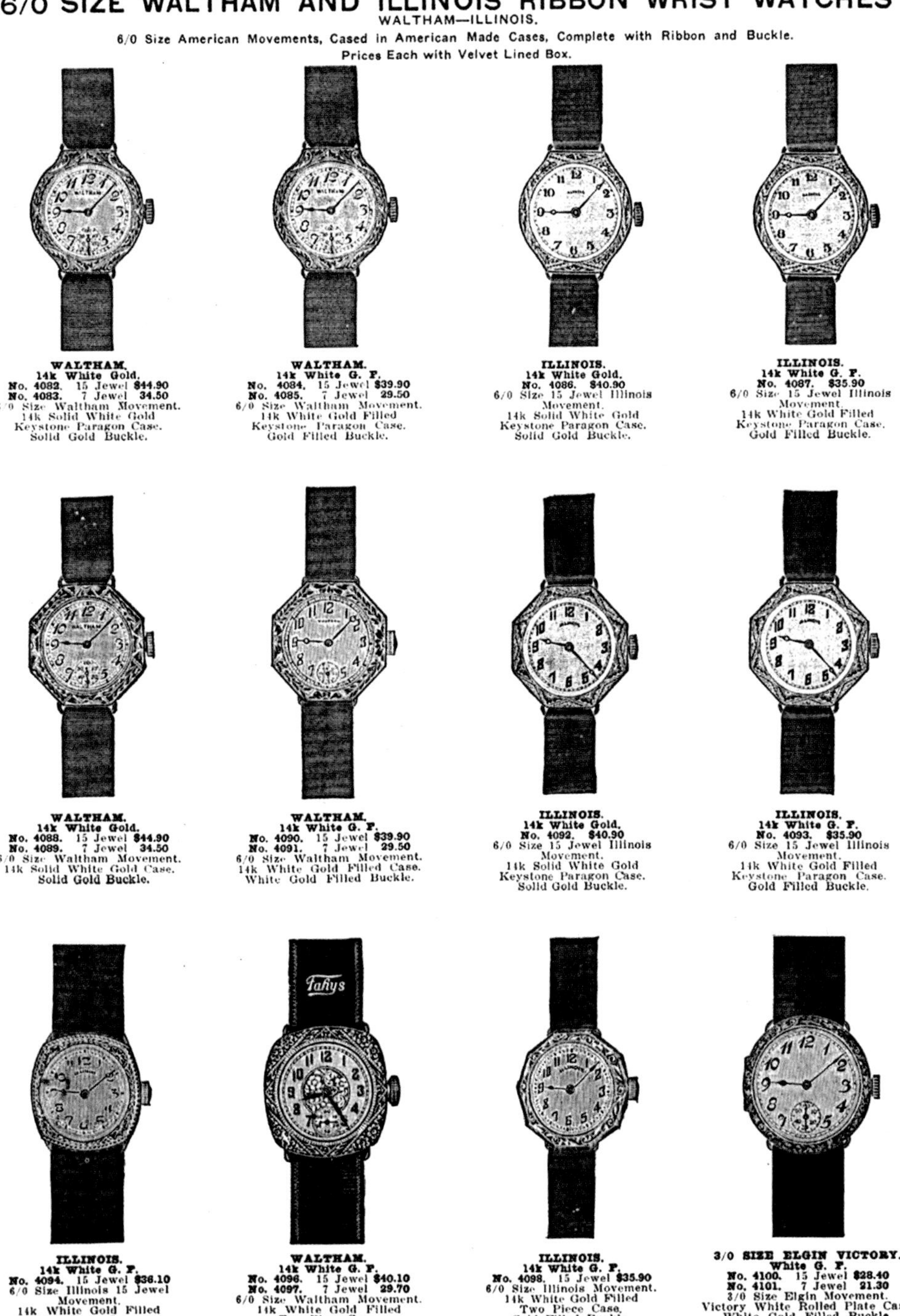

6/0 SIZE WALTHAM AND ILLINOIS RIBBON WRIST WATCHES

WALTHAM—ILLINOIS.

6/0 Size American Movements, Cased in American Made Cases, Complete with Ribbon and Buckle.
Prices Each with Velvet Lined Box.

WALTHAM.
14k White Gold.
No. 4082. 15 Jewel $44.90
No. 4083. 7 Jewel 34.50
6/0 Size Waltham Movement.
14k Solid White Gold
Keystone Paragon Case.
Solid Gold Buckle.

WALTHAM.
14k White G. F.
No. 4084. 15 Jewel $39.90
No. 4085. 7 Jewel 29.50
6/0 Size Waltham Movement.
14k White Gold Filled
Keystone Paragon Case.
Gold Filled Buckle.

ILLINOIS.
14k White Gold.
No. 4086. $40.90
6/0 Size 15 Jewel Illinois
Movement.
14k Solid White Gold
Keystone Paragon Case.
Solid Gold Buckle.

ILLINOIS.
14k White G. F.
No. 4087. $35.90
6/0 Size 15 Jewel Illinois
Movement.
14k White Gold Filled
Keystone Paragon Case.
Gold Filled Buckle.

WALTHAM.
14k White Gold.
No. 4088. 15 Jewel $44.90
No. 4089. 7 Jewel 34.50
6/0 Size Waltham Movement.
14k Solid White Gold Case.
Solid Gold Buckle.

WALTHAM.
14k White G. F.
No. 4090. 15 Jewel $39.90
No. 4091. 7 Jewel 29.50
6/0 Size Waltham Movement.
14k White Gold Filled Case.
White Gold Filled Buckle.

ILLINOIS.
14k White Gold.
No. 4092. $40.90
6/0 Size 15 Jewel Illinois
Movement.
14k Solid White Gold
Keystone Paragon Case.
Solid Gold Buckle.

ILLINOIS.
14k White G. F.
No. 4093. $35.90
6/0 Size 15 Jewel Illinois
Movement.
14k White Gold Filled
Keystone Paragon Case.
Gold Filled Buckle.

ILLINOIS.
14k White G. F.
No. 4094. 15 Jewel $36.10
6/0 Size Illinois 15 Jewel
Movement.
14k White Gold Filled
Two Piece Case.
Gold Filled Buckle.

WALTHAM.
14k White G. F.
No. 4096. 15 Jewel $40.10
No. 4097. 7 Jewel 29.70
6/0 Size Waltham Movement.
14k White Gold Filled
Two Piece Case.
Gold Filled Buckle.

ILLINOIS.
14k White G. F.
No. 4098. 15 Jewel $35.90
6/0 Size Illinois Movement.
14k White Gold Filled
Two Piece Case.
Gold Filled Buckle.

3/0 SIZE ELGIN VICTORY.
White G. F.
No. 4100. 15 Jewel $28.40
No. 4101. 7 Jewel 21.30
3/0 Size Elgin Movement.
Victory White Rolled Plate Case.
White Gold Filled Buckle.

7

Generic Models in the Otto Young catalog, 1928

Deco Period: Late 1920s to Early 1930s

Some of the most distinctive deco-inspired wristwatch designs were offered in the United States by the Illinois Watch Company, and the ladies' selections were just as cutting-edge fashionable as the men's. Their striking, innovative designs are Art Deco at its best.

Deco elements permeated all aspects of design in that era, appearing not only in jewelry and watches but in other accessories as well—purses, compacts, cigarette cases and lighters, for example.

An Art Deco compact by Evans, c. 1930. In the first half of the twentieth century, and especially during the 1920s and 1930s, almost every woman had one or more decorative compacts as accessories. Since these were intended to be very visible, carried by their chains or finger rings rather than being tucked away in a purse, they often had very eye-catching designs.

An iconic Art Deco design on an enameled Karess compact, c. 1928, made by the Scovill Manufacturing Company. Karess was a line of compacts offered by the Woodworth perfume and cosmetics company.

EVANS

E1550—White finish, engine turned design with French enamel decoration, fitted with mirror, loose powder container and rouge, French enamel lipstick handle. $3.00 ea.

E1551—White finish, thin watch case model, engine turned design with French enamel decoration and contrasting border, fitted with mirror, loose powder container. $1.50 ea.

E1552—White finish, thin model, engine turned brocade design in modernistic pattern, with hand painted French enamel decoration, flexible handle, fitted with mirror, loose powder container and rouge. $3.75 ea.

E1553—White finish, thin model, French enamel front, contrasting colors, flexible handle, fitted with large mirror, loose powder container and rouge ......$5.52 ea.

E1554—White finish, thin knife edge watch case model. French enamel cover with genuine Marcasite set decoration fitted with mirror, loose powder container and rouge........................$6.40 ea.

E1555—White finish, thin model, French enamel front with decorative placque, fitted with large mirror, loose powder container and rouge, French enamel lipstick handle........................$5.25 ea.

E1556—White finish, thin model, French enamel front, contrasting colors, fitted with mirror, loose powder container and rouge, finger ring and chain........$4.50 ea.

E1557—White finish, thin knife edge model, French enamel cover, with decorative placque, fitted with mirror, loose powder container and rouge, French enamel lipstick handle .... $6.75 ea.

E1558—White finish, thin model French enamel front in modernistic design, fitted with mirror, loose powder container and rouge, flexiule handle............$5.25 ea.

—Green gold finish, thin model genuine Viennese enamel front and back with genuine hand engraved Viennese enamel cover, fitted with mirror, loose powder container and rouge............$12.75 ea.

E1560—White finish, thin knife edge model, French enamel front and back with French enamel cover in contrasting colors, finger ring and chain............$9.00 ea.

E1561—Green gold finish, thin knife edge model, genuine Viennese enamel front and back with genuine hand engraved Viennese enamel cover, fitted with mirror, loose powder container and rouge..$15.00 ea.

Illustrations four-fifth size.

The LINE with the STERLING TOUCH

Evans vanity cases shown in the 1930 L. & C. Mayers catalog. Vanities were like compacts in having mirrors and containing powder and/or rouge, but they were larger, sometimes with additional features such as cigarette and coin holders built in. The Evans Case Company, one of America's leading manufacturers of compacts, was located in North Attleboro, Massachusetts, long a major center for jewelry manufacture.

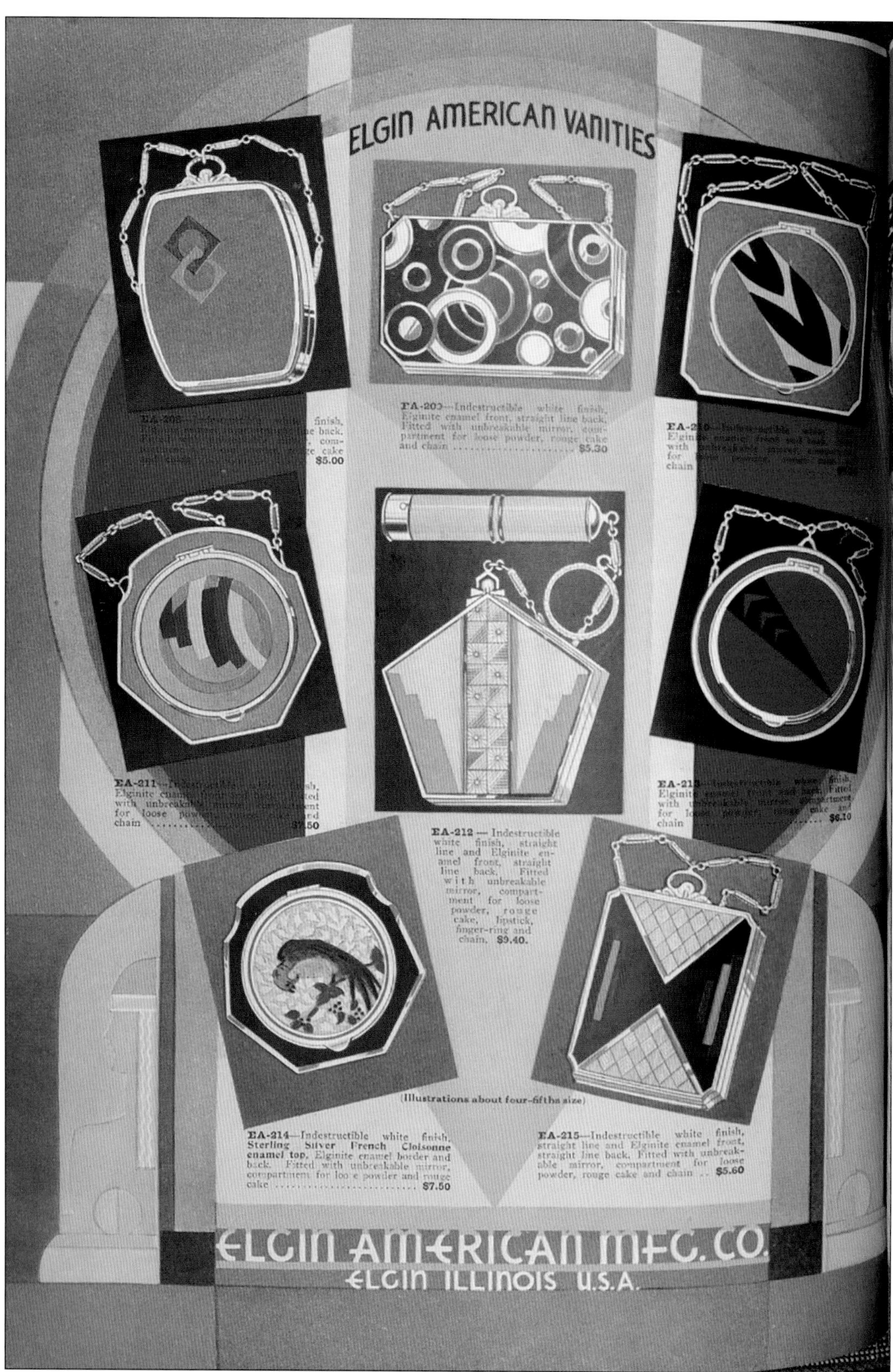

Elgin American (EAM) vanities shown in the 1931 Oskamp Nolting catalog. Elgin American, a leading manufacturer of compacts and vanities, was an enterprise of the Illinois Watch Case Company. Although the company was located in Elgin, Illinois, it had no relation to the Elgin National Watch Company of that city.

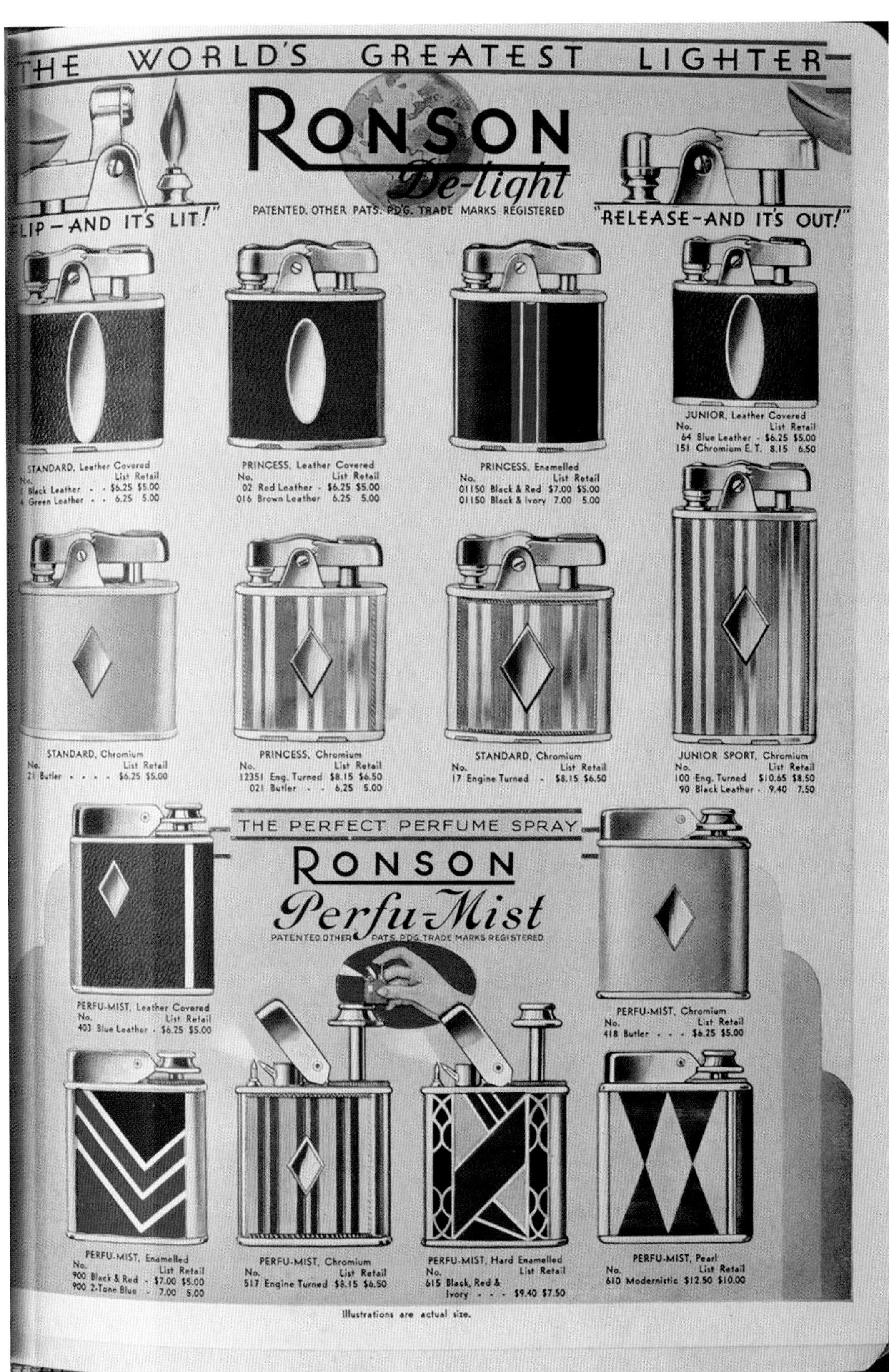

Ronson Art Deco lighters, L. & C. Mayers catalog, 1930

In the Deco Period, metals of silvery color were preferred. Accordingly, the Illinois Watch Company at first offered most of its ladies' wristwatch models only in solid white gold or white gold-filled cases. Beginning about 1930, however, it did offer some models in a choice of white or yellow gold or gold-filled.

During the Deco Period, most of the cases utilized by the Illinois Watch Company for its ladies' wristwatches were provided by the Keystone and Wadsworth firms. The models with enameled designs on their bezels are particular favorites among collectors.

The deco designs of ladies' Illinois wristwatches are as timeless and appealing today as they were when first issued. Because they have thus far remained a "hidden gem," they can still sometimes be obtained at very reasonable prices.

Moderne Period: Early 1930s

The Moderne Period, often viewed as an evolution of Art Deco, is characterized by streamlined forms with a minimum of decoration. The Illinois ladies' watch models of the early 1930s reflect this trend.

In 1928, immediately prior to the Moderne Period, the Illinois Watch Company had already consummated the sale of its company to the Hamilton Watch Company (discussed in detail in Chapters 3, 4 and 5). As a result, there were Moderne models offered for sale and issued by the Hamilton Watch Company under the Illinois trade name. Since this was the time of the Great Depression, the emphasis was on simplicity of style, good quality at affordable prices.

Ladies' Watchband Styles

The watchbands that came with transitional watches were usually expansion bracelets, mostly ones with longish, narrow links.

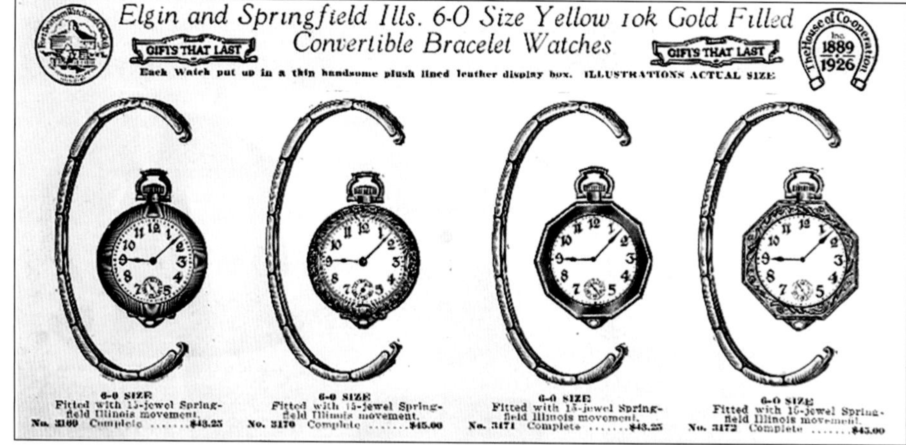

"Springfield Illinois" 6/0 size convertible bracelet watches in the 1926 Fort Dearborn catalog. Notice the decagon (*3rd from left*) and engraved octagon (*4th from left*).

Some of the bracelets featured plain, polished links, but others had links with engraved patterns. Such bracelets were attached to the watches by means of endpieces with hooks that fastened at one end to the bow of the watch and at the other to the small metal loop at the bottom of the watch case.

The ladies' transitional watches offered by Illinois and other manufacturers often came in special boxes whose linings had an indentation of the correct size for holding the watch and also a narrow indentation, either curved or straight, for holding the metal band. The Illinois Ariston "Convertible," mentioned earlier, came in such a box.

Ribbon watch bracelets were also popular for transitional watches. These, too, had special metal endpieces with hooks for attaching them to the watch; they also had decorative metal clasps for adjusting the bracelet on the wrist. Most common were bracelets of plain black silk grosgrain ribbons, but ladies could also procure commercially made bracelets of colorfully patterned silk ribbons.

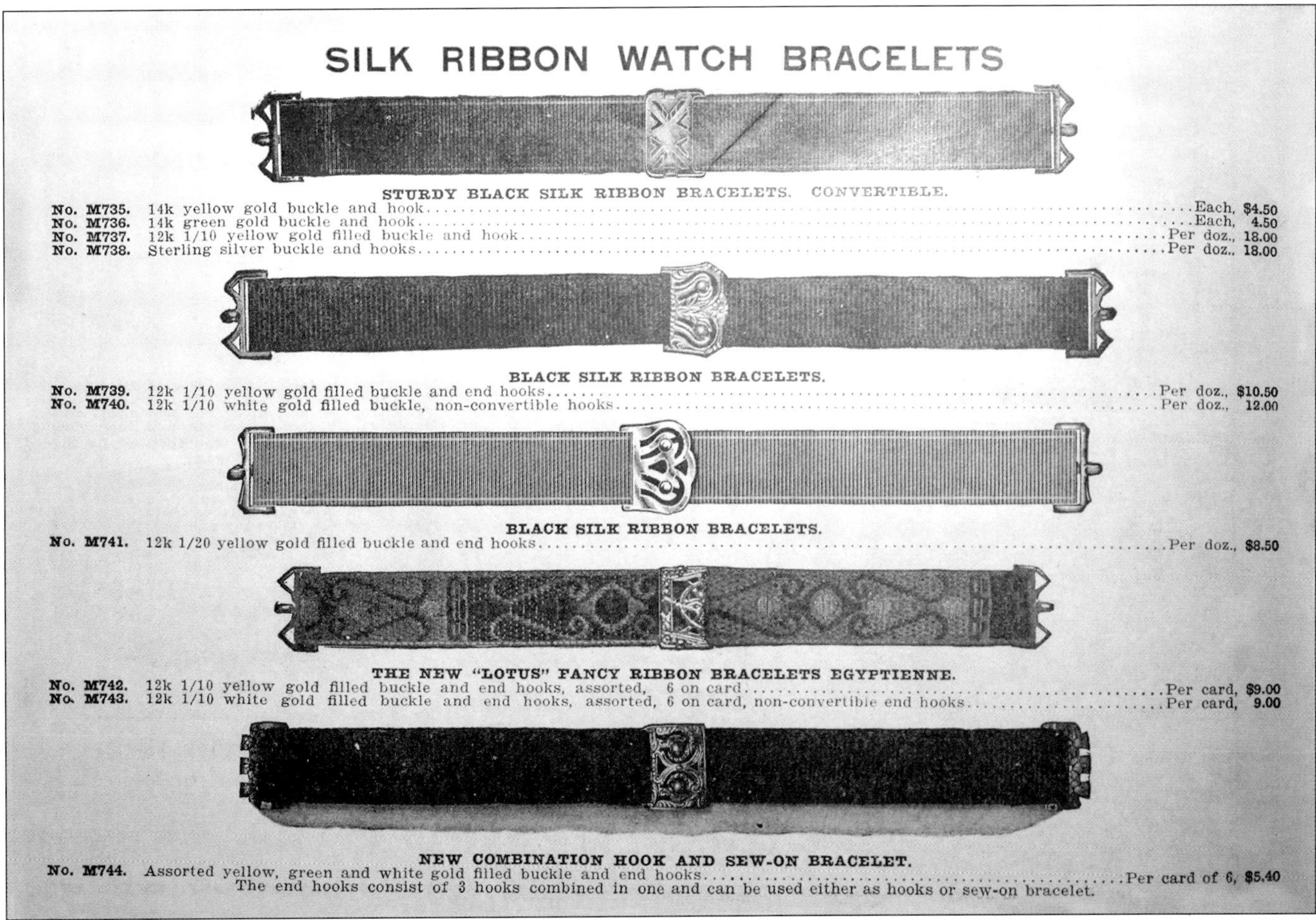

SILK RIBBON WATCH BRACELETS

STURDY BLACK SILK RIBBON BRACELETS. CONVERTIBLE.

No. M735. 14k yellow gold buckle and hook.................Each, $4.50
No. M736. 14k green gold buckle and hook.................Each, 4.50
No. M737. 12k 1/10 yellow gold filled buckle and hook.................Per doz., 18.00
No. M738. Sterling silver buckle and hooks.................Per doz., 18.00

BLACK SILK RIBBON BRACELETS.

No. M739. 12k 1/10 yellow gold filled buckle and end hooks.................Per doz., $10.50
No. M740. 12k 1/10 white gold filled buckle, non-convertible hooks.................Per doz., 12.00

BLACK SILK RIBBON BRACELETS.

No. M741. 12k 1/20 yellow gold filled buckle and end hooks.................Per doz., $8.50

THE NEW "LOTUS" FANCY RIBBON BRACELETS EGYPTIENNE.

No. M742. 12k 1/10 yellow gold filled buckle and end hooks, assorted, 6 on card.................Per card, $9.00
No. M743. 12k 1/10 white gold filled buckle and end hooks, assorted, 6 on card, non-convertible end hooks.................Per card, 9.00

NEW COMBINATION HOOK AND SEW-ON BRACELET.

No. M744. Assorted yellow, green and white gold filled buckle and end hooks.................Per card of 6, $5.40
The end hooks consist of 3 hooks combined in one and can be used either as hooks or sew-on bracelet.

A 1929 Otto Young catalog listing of silk ribbon watch bracelets. The special "Lotus" pattern "Egyptienne" ribbon is an example of 1920s Egyptomania.

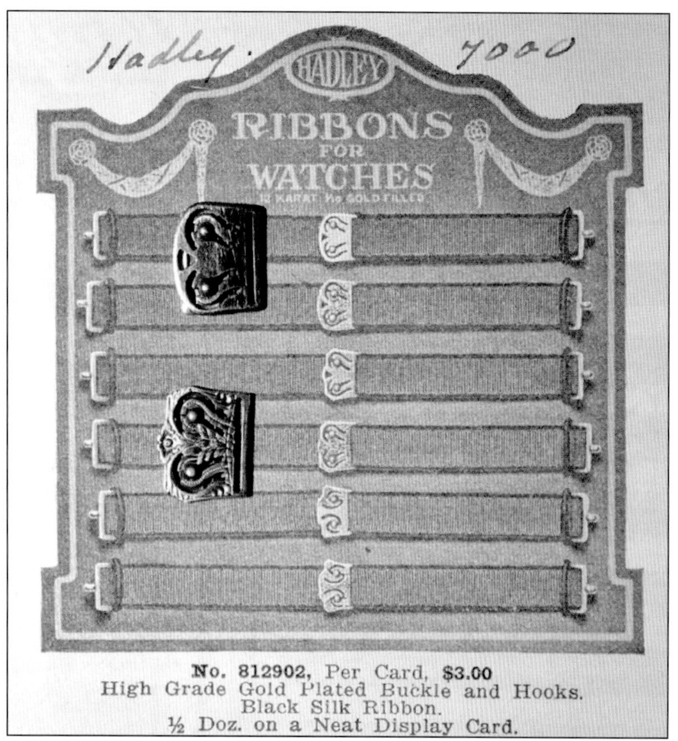

Wallenstein Mayer 1928 catalog advertisement showing cards of Hadley ribbon watchbands for convertible watches. Superimposed are two of the actual clasps illustrated.

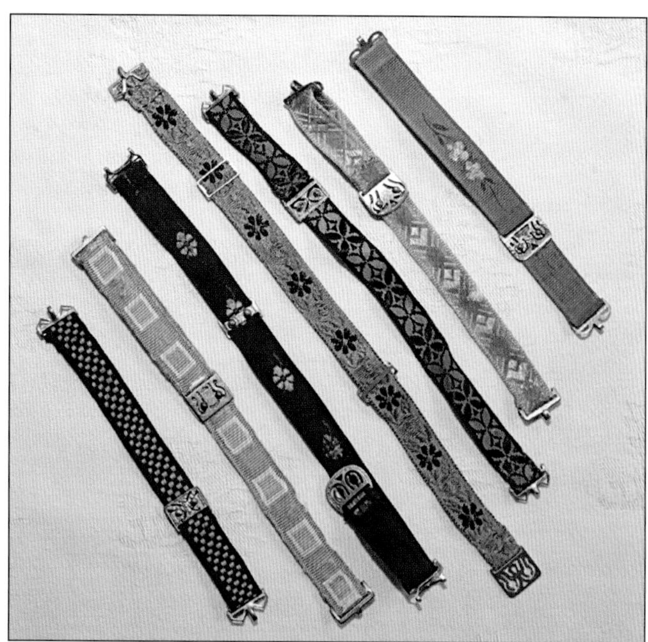

Group of patterned ribbon watchbands. Except for the black one with blue embroidered flowers, all of these have endpieces for transitional watches. The endpieces on the black one are a type that will fit over wire lugs.

Vintage black ribbon watchbands for transitional watches are seen fairly frequently on eBay (often still attached to the watches), and sometimes patterned ones are available. On rare occasions, an original display card with an assortment of these still attached can be found. Ladies could also make their own ribbon watch bracelets, buying ribbon of their choice and then sewing the metal attachments into place.

Since most of the ladies' transitional watches were yellow gold (either gold-filled or solid gold), it is not surprising that the metal bracelets as well as the findings (endpieces and clasps) for the ribbon bands were mostly yellow gold, as well.

By the mid-1920s and later, interest in transitional convertible watches had waned, and the focus was on another type of ladies' wristwatches: ones with wire lugs. Nonetheless, old-style bands continued to be offered in many jobbers' and jewelers' catalogs into the late 1920s and early 1930s, because many ladies still had their transitional watches. A few catalogs even offered a leather wristlet-type device for holding a small pocket watch.

CUP WATCH BRACELETS.

No. 94T10. 3/0 size. Fine Morocco leather, black. Each
No. 94T11. 0 size. Fine Morocco leather, black. Each
No. 94T12. 3/0 size. Black leather. Each
No. 94T13. 0 size. Black leather. Each

An advertisement in the 1934 A. C. Becken catalog. Surprisingly enough, even in the 1930s there was still some demand for the old-fashioned leather "wristlets" that permitted small pocket watches to be worn on the wrist.

Magazine advertisements and jobbers' catalogs from the mid-1920s on through the early 1930s indicate that the majority of ladies' wristwatch models with wire-lug cases came with ribbon watchbands. A few models, however, came with simple black cord bands or metal bracelets fitted with endpieces that clipped onto the lugs of the watch (not hooks like those on the bands for transitional watches), and even a few ribbon bands occasionally had these types of metal endpieces. But most ribbon watchbands were sewn onto the watch.

Although the new-style ribbon watchbands rarely had metal endpieces (and the few that did had ones of a different style from those for transitional watches), they did continue to have clasps of the same type that the earlier ones had. More and more designs of these appeared, ranging from austere to intricate, and some of them employed fanciful figural motifs.

An array of yellow gold and yellow gold-filled clasps surrounding an Illinois "Glencoe" on its original ribbon watchband. *Top to bottom, Column 1:* Sturdy GF; Haywood GF; unidentified 14K; Hadley 14K; Hadley GF; unidentified 14K. *Column 2:* Sturdy 14K, on ribbon; Hadley GF (below ribbon). *Column 3:* Bugbee & Niles 14K (above watch); Hadley 14K (on Glencoe's watchband). *Column 4:* Hadley GF; Hadley 14K; Hadley GF; Hadley GF; Hadley GF

White gold and white gold-filled ribbon watchband clasps. Top to bottom, *Column 1*: Sturdy 14K; Hadley 18K, on ribbon fragment; Hadley Premier GF. *Column 2*: Hadley 14K, on ribbon fragment; Bugbee & Niles (Egyptian motif) GF; unidentified GF; Sturdy GF (marked Gruen); unidentified GF. *Column 3:* unidentified GF; D & C 18K, on ribbon fragment; Bugbee & Niles 14K (marked Gruen), on ribbon fragment

Egyptian-motif ribbon bracelet clasp by Bugbee & Niles. Egyptian Revival style, long a favorite in American decorative arts, became wildly popular after the discovery of King Tutankhamen's tomb in 1922.

Many of these clasps are exquisite examples of metalwork. Some are gold-filled, but others are solid 14K and 18K gold, and there are also attractive inexpensive ones made of base metal, often plated in chromium. Many catalogs offered ribbon watchbands with the metal clasps already stitched in, so all that had to be done was to sew the ends around the wire lugs of ladies' watches, but they also offered ribbon and findings if a lady chose to make her own or needed to replace a ribbon or clasp on a ribbon bracelet she already had.

CHOOSING A WATCHBAND

Often you may find an Illinois ladies' wristwatch for sale without a band. To put one on it, you have basically four choices, and the look is a matter of personal preference. Probably the easiest thing to do is to procure a vintage metal watch bracelet that is detachable, with endpieces that clip right onto the lugs. (There are others with endpieces that need to be put into place around the lugs by a jeweler.) Another possibility is to find an open-end leather watchband of the proper width to go over the lugs. Yet another possibility is to have a jeweler install a cord band with endpieces that go around the lugs. (Although it is possible to fit a modern expansion watchband on one of these watches, this is not recommended because the spring-loaded ends of such a watchband will tend to wear the lugs of the watch.)

If you're a purist, you may wish to make your own ribbon watchband for your wire-lug watch. To do so, you must first obtain some suitable ribbon and a period-correct clasp. The watchband that came on such a watch was usually made of black silk grosgrain (vertically ribbed) ribbon and had a clasp of metal content and color that matched the case (solid gold watches would thus have come with solid gold clasps). Since it can be difficult to find a source for silk grosgrain ribbon, you can substitute grosgrain made of a modern synthetic. As for antique watch clasps, you can sometimes find them on eBay and elsewhere.

For both ribbon and clasp, however, the width is crucial. Ribbon must be of a width that will go through not only the lugs of the watch case but also the clasp you provide. Most modern ribbon comes in 3/8 inch and 1/2 inch width rather than the popular 7/16 width of yesteryear, so you may have to choose between something slightly too narrow for the lugs and something slightly too wide. You just have to decide which width of ribbon will look better with your particular watch and then find a clasp of the proper width for the ribbon to go through. *—Bettie Mason*

Advertisements mentioning and sometimes even showing the clasps of ribbon watchbands on watches usually indicate that the clasps were made of metal that matched the metal of the watch cases; some of the clasps were even decorated with enamel to go with cases having enameled bezels.

Sturdy's enamel clasps for Elgin watches, listed in the 1929 Otto Young catalog. With a diagonally striped pattern of green, red, or black enamel, these clasps were obviously designed to be used with some of the models in Elgin's Parisienne line that came with enameled bezels having those colors and similar patterns (e.g., Agnes, Jenny, Premet, Molyneux).

Two Elgins with ribbon watchbands, each sporting a matching clasp by Hadley. *Left:* Model 177, designed by Lucien Lelong. *Right:* Model 111, with clasp in matching green enamel; the scene on the clasp shows two athletes and the Olympic flame, which was inaugurated at the 1928 Summer Games in Amsterdam.

Few ribbon bands on wire-lug watches have survived the test of time; by today, most have been replaced with leather straps or metal bracelets. But since clasps can occasionally be found, it is possible to fabricate ribbon watchbands if they are desired.

Many different styles of metal watch bracelets were available, and it is easy to figure out why these became popular. Although an advertisement for Elgin's Parisienne line in the May 1929 issue of *Hearst's International-Cosmopolitan* proclaimed that "it's so simple to have extra ribbons to match the colors of your evening gowns," changing the ribbon on one of these watches meant disassembling the band that was on it, removing the two pieces of the clasp, and then stitching the replacement ribbon into place. Many ladies no doubt found it much simpler to swap the original ribbon band for a coordinating metal one, as that would likely go with whatever color of garments they chose to wear. (Elgin itself was offering metal bands of fine, delicate, ribbon-like mesh as optional upgrades for some of its higher-end models.)

Since some metal watch bracelets came with endpieces that were easy to put on and take off, ladies could have several in different styles to swap in and out if they so desired. Some presentation boxes for watches had linings with one or more additional compartments for holding other watch bracelets, or simply to be used for storing other small items of jewelry.

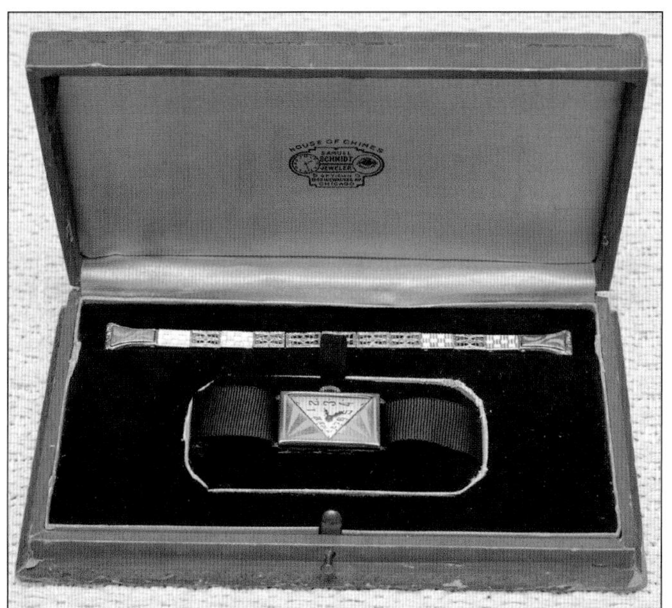

One of Elgin's Parisienne line, the "Captain Molyneux" model, in its original jeweler's box, which has an indentation for an alternate watch bracelet. The jeweler's logo on the satin lining of the box lid is a reminder that many jewelers of this period and earlier times also sold optical goods.

Many of these early watch bracelets were indeed bracelet-like, with delicate filigree work, and were offered not only in gold-filled but also in 14K or 18K solid gold, or even platinum; some had inset gemstones (or imitation ones). Although green gold and yellow gold watch cases could be found, particularly among the generic models, white gold was by far the most popular choice during the 1920s, and this was reflected in the vast numbers of watch bracelets available in that silvery color. Some actually were sterling silver, which was relatively inexpensive at the time. There were also inexpensive watch bracelets in base metal, such as stainless steel, sometimes with a chromium finish.

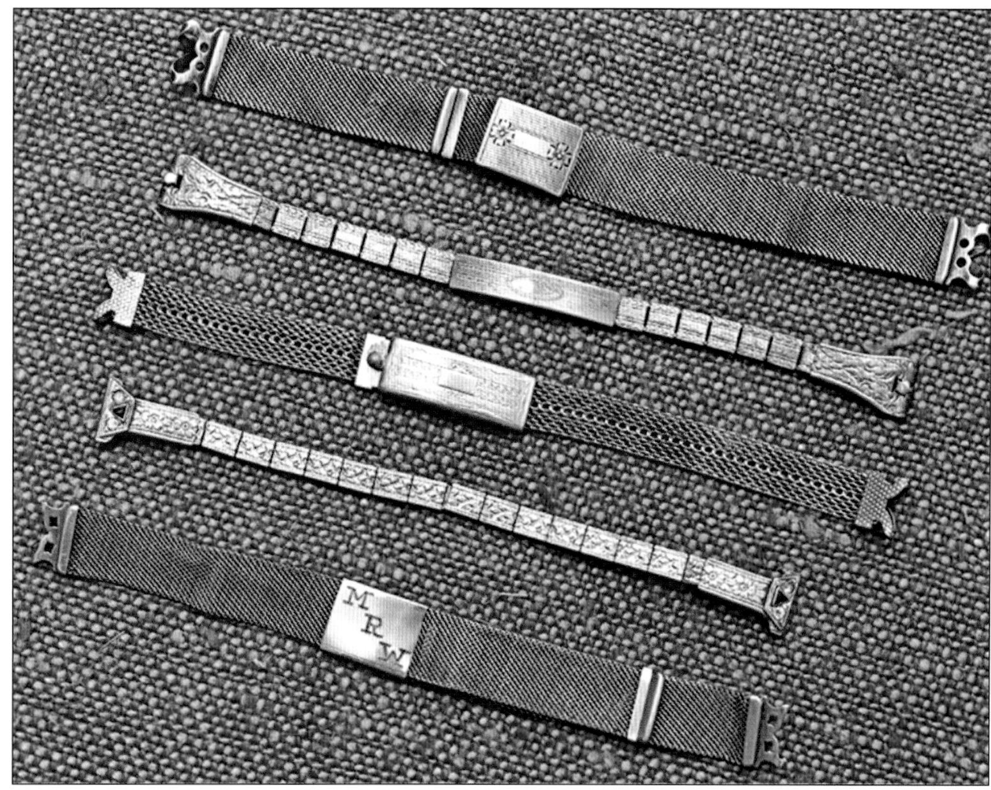

A group of watchbands, all sterling except the middle one. In addition to link bracelets, mesh bands were a popular choice, perhaps because fine mesh behaved much like ribbon on the wrist.

Watch bracelets came in many different styles (expansion links, regular links, or mesh, for example) and a bewildering number of designs, some even involving enameling.

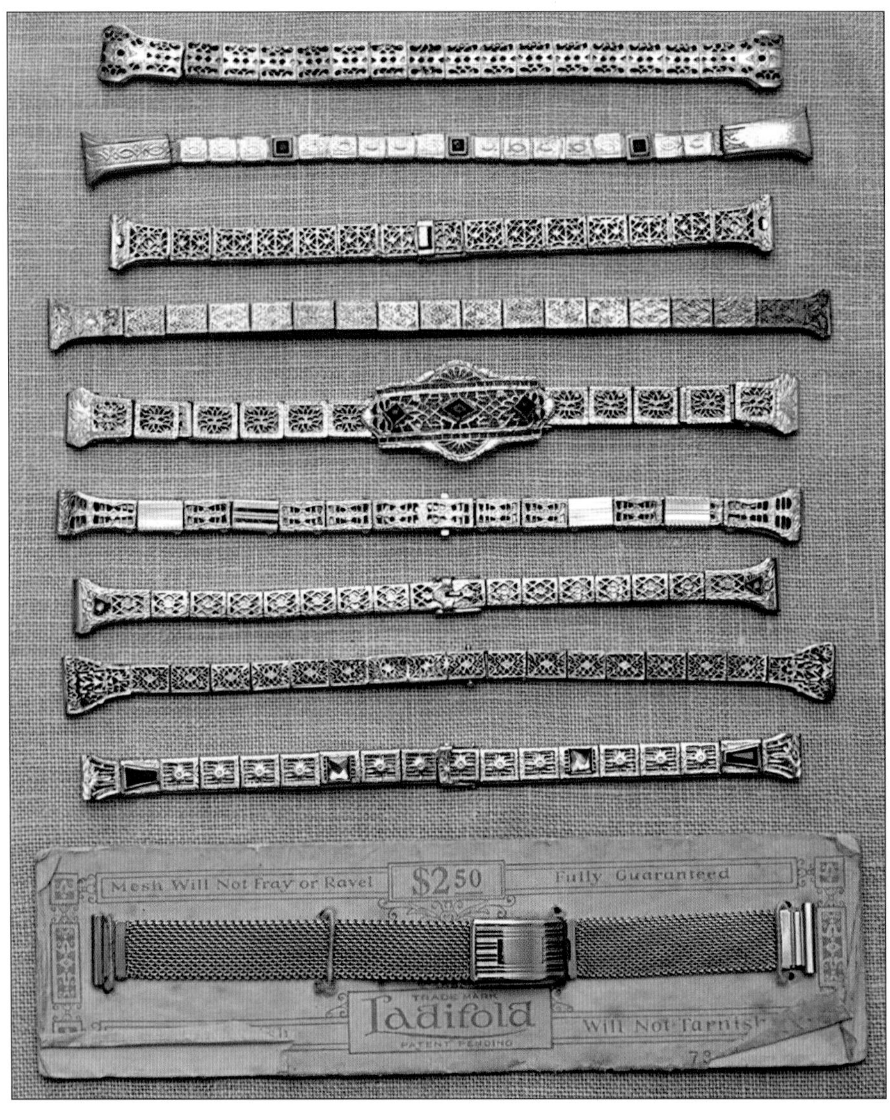

A group of ladies' watch bracelets. ***Top to bottom*****: Hayward, Claspet (Bates & Bacon), Flexe d'Or (Rosenheim), Gemex, Bates & Bacon, Betty Lou (Smith & Crosby), unmarked filigree with imitation emeralds, Lustern (Louis Stern), Nuflex, Ladifold mesh on original card. Information about most of these companies is included in the "Attachments" section of Chapter 8.**

Some manufacturers, such as Wadsworth and Sturdy, also offered metal watch straps that resembled cuff bracelets. (For information about these manufacturers, see the "Watch Attachments" section of Chapter 8.) Because ladies' wristwatches of various brands and models had lugs of different widths, and some were curved rather than straight, there were different widths of watch bracelets and types of endpieces available for the cuff-bracelet style as well as other styles.

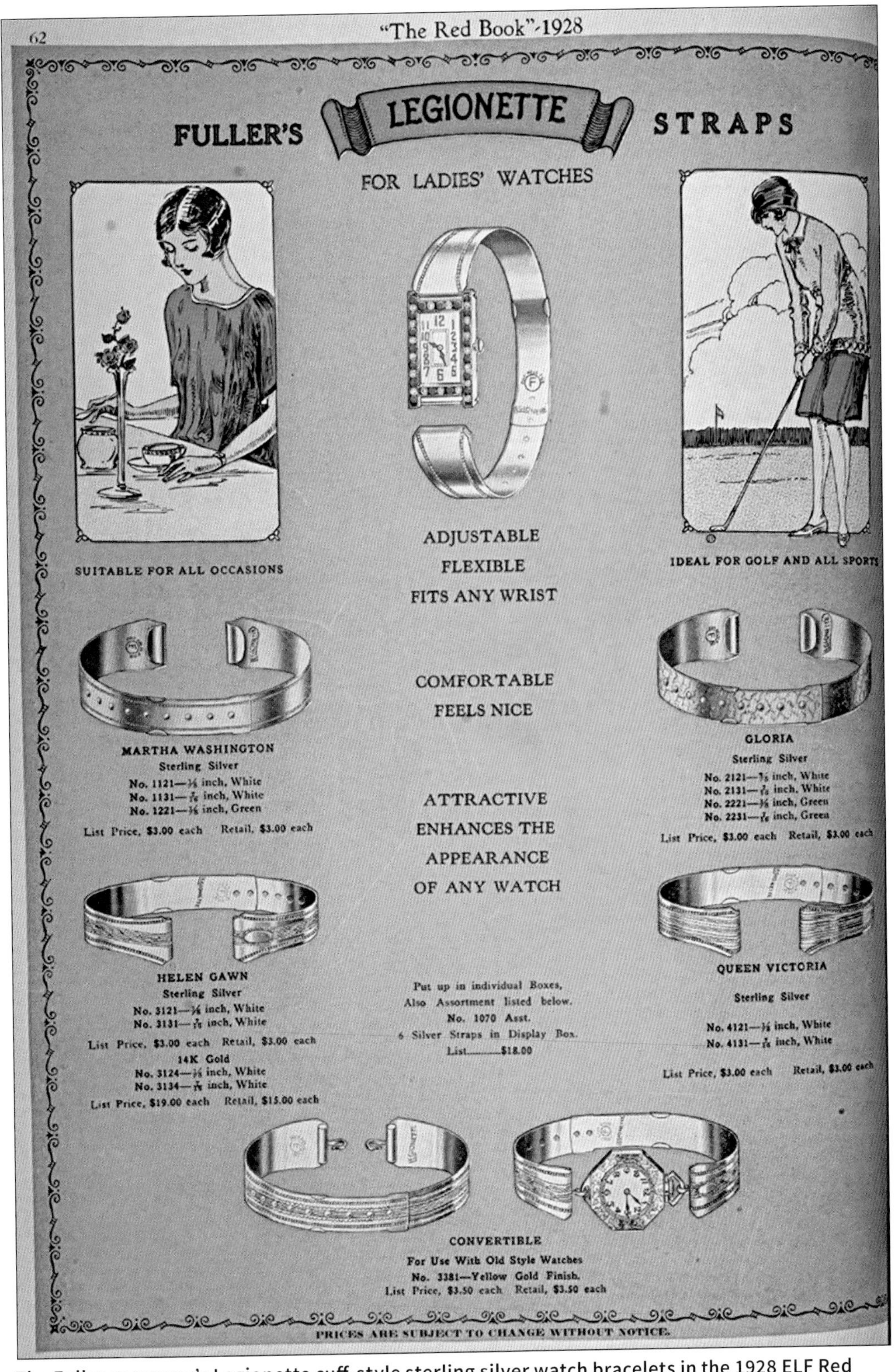

62 "The Red Book"-1928

FULLER'S LEGIONETTE STRAPS

FOR LADIES' WATCHES

SUITABLE FOR ALL OCCASIONS

ADJUSTABLE
FLEXIBLE
FITS ANY WRIST

IDEAL FOR GOLF AND ALL SPORTS

MARTHA WASHINGTON
Sterling Silver
No. 1121—3/8 inch, White
No. 1131—7/16 inch, White
No. 1221—3/8 inch, Green
List Price, $3.00 each Retail, $3.00 each

COMFORTABLE
FEELS NICE

GLORIA
Sterling Silver
No. 2121—3/8 inch, White
No. 2131—7/16 inch, White
No. 2221—3/8 inch, Green
No. 2231—7/16 inch, Green
List Price, $3.00 each Retail, $3.00 each

ATTRACTIVE
ENHANCES THE
APPEARANCE
OF ANY WATCH

HELEN GAWN
Sterling Silver
No. 3121—3/8 inch, White
No. 3131—7/16 inch, White
List Price, $3.00 each Retail, $3.00 each
14K Gold
No. 3124—3/8 inch, White
No. 3134—7/16 inch, White
List Price, $19.00 each Retail, $15.00 each

Put up in individual Boxes,
Also Assortment listed below.
No. 1070 Asst.
6 Silver Straps in Display Box.
List..........$18.00

QUEEN VICTORIA
Sterling Silver
No. 4121—3/8 inch, White
No. 4131—7/16 inch, White
List Price, $3.00 each Retail, $3.00 each

CONVERTIBLE
For Use With Old Style Watches
No. 3381—Yellow Gold Finish.
List Price, $3.50 each Retail, $3.50 each

PRICES ARE SUBJECT TO CHANGE WITHOUT NOTICE.

The Fuller company's Legionette cuff-style sterling silver watch bracelets in the 1928 ELF Red Book catalog, Notice the two convertible models, which have a yellow gold finish and special hooks on the ends to go with these "old style watches."

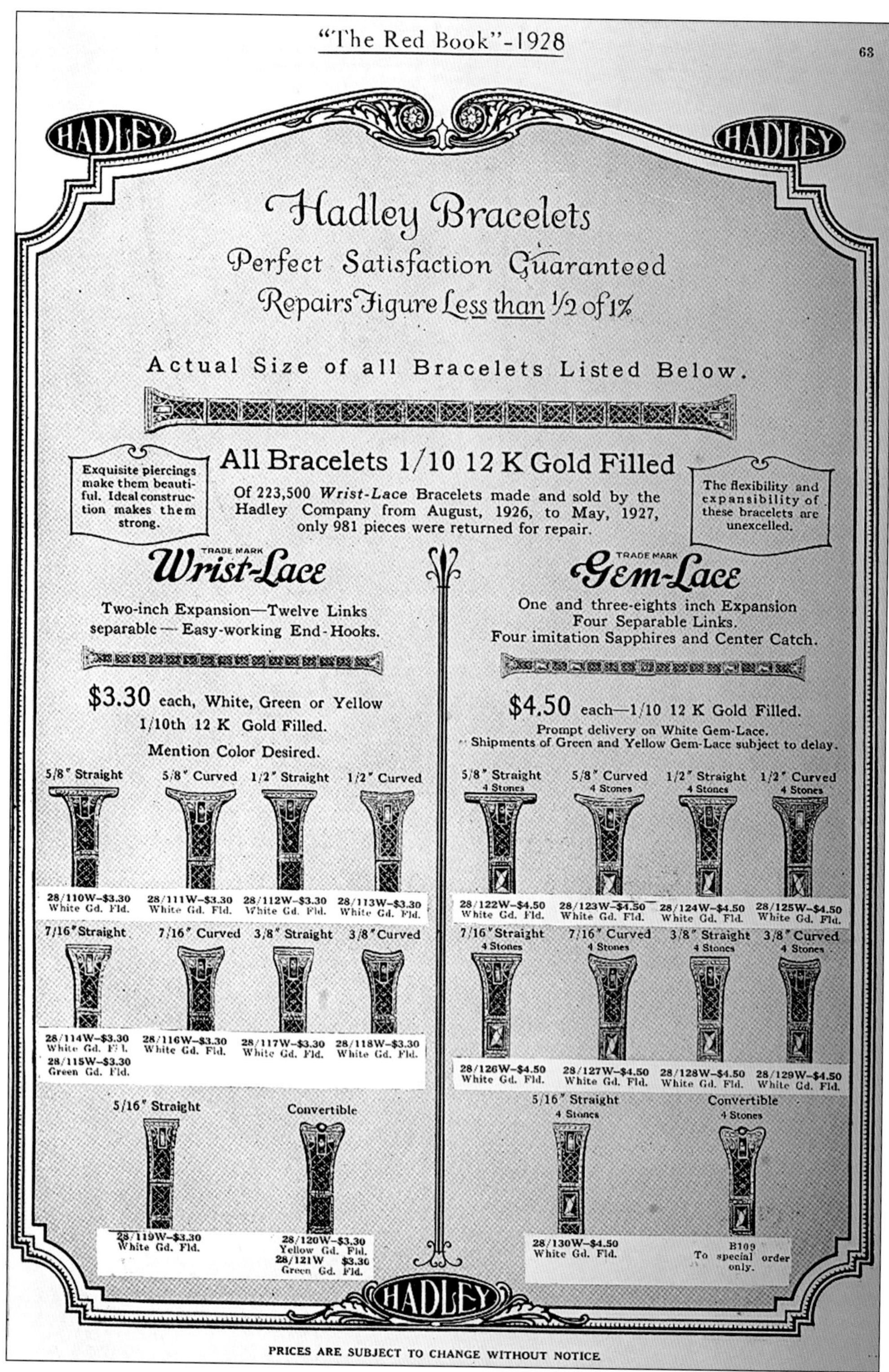

Hadley filigree ("pierced") watch bracelets in the 1928 ELF Red Book catalog. The Gem-Lace line was Wrist-Lace with imitation sapphires added; the filigree pattern was the same. Both lines were available in yellow and green gold-filled as well as white, with straight or curved endpieces in various sizes, and there was also a version for convertible watches.

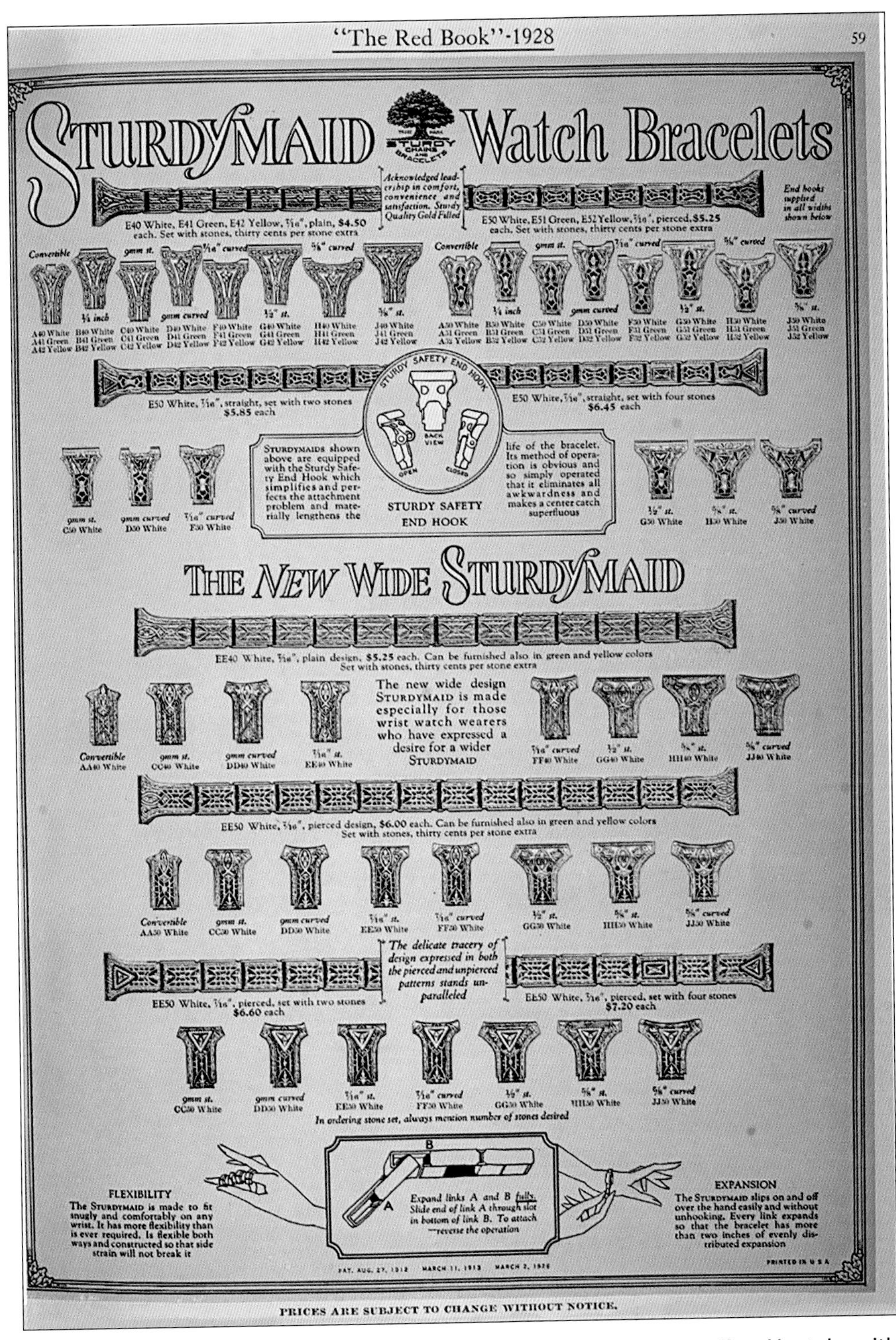

"The Red Book"-1928 59

Sturdymaid Watch Bracelets

Acknowledged leadership in comfort, convenience and satisfaction. Sturdy Quality Gold Filled

End hooks supplied in all widths shown below

E40 White, E41 Green, E42 Yellow, 7/16", plain, $4.50 each. Set with stones, thirty cents per stone extra

E50 White, E51 Green, E52 Yellow, 7/16", pierced, $5.25 each. Set with stones, thirty cents per stone extra

Convertible A40 White A41 Green A42 Yellow; *1/4 inch* B40 White B41 Green B42 Yellow; *9mm st.* C40 White C41 Green C42 Yellow; *9mm curved* D40 White D41 Green D42 Yellow; *7/16" curved* F40 White F41 Green F42 Yellow; *1/2" st.* G40 White G41 Green G42 Yellow; *5/8" curved* H40 White H41 Green H42 Yellow; *5/8" st.* J40 White J41 Green J42 Yellow

Convertible A50 White A51 Green A52 Yellow; *1/4 inch* B50 White B51 Green B52 Yellow; *9mm st.* C50 White C51 Green C52 Yellow; *9mm curved* D50 White D51 Green D52 Yellow; *7/16" curved* F50 White F51 Green F52 Yellow; *1/2" st.* G50 White G51 Green G52 Yellow; *5/8" curved* H50 White H51 Green H52 Yellow; *5/8" st.* J50 White J51 Green J52 Yellow

E50 White, 7/16", straight, set with two stones $5.85 each

E50 White, 7/16", straight, set with four stones $6.45 each

Sturdy Safety End Hook — Back View — Open — Closed

Sturdymaids shown above are equipped with the Sturdy Safety End Hook which simplifies and perfects the attachment problem and materially lengthens the life of the bracelet. Its method of operation is obvious and so simply operated that it eliminates all awkwardness and makes a center catch superfluous

STURDY SAFETY END HOOK

9mm st. C50 White; *9mm curved* D50 White; *7/16" curved* F50 White; *1/2" st.* G50 White; *5/8" st.* H50 White; *5/8" curved* J50 White

The New Wide Sturdymaid

EE40 White, 7/16", plain design, $5.25 each. Can be furnished also in green and yellow colors. Set with stones, thirty cents per stone extra

The new wide design Sturdymaid is made especially for those wrist watch wearers who have expressed a desire for a wider Sturdymaid

Convertible AA40 White; *9mm st.* CC40 White; *9mm curved* DD40 White; *7/16" st.* EE40 White; *7/16" curved* FF40 White; *1/2" st.* GG40 White; *5/8" st.* HH40 White; *5/8" curved* JJ40 White

EE50 White, 7/16", pierced design, $6.00 each. Can be furnished also in green and yellow colors. Set with stones, thirty cents per stone extra

Convertible AA50 White; *9mm st.* CC50 White; *9mm curved* DD50 White; *7/16" st.* EE50 White; *7/16" curved* FF50 White; *1/2" st.* GG50 White; *5/8" st.* HH50 White; *5/8" curved* JJ50 White

The delicate tracery of design expressed in both the pierced and unpierced patterns stands unparalleled

EE50 White, 7/16", pierced, set with two stones $6.60 each

EE50 White, 7/16", pierced, set with four stones $7.20 each

9mm st. CC50 White; *9mm curved* DD50 White; *7/16" st.* EE50 White; *7/16" curved* FF50 White; *1/2" st.* GG50 White; *5/8" st.* HH50 White; *5/8" curved* JJ50 White

In ordering stone set, always mention number of stones desired

FLEXIBILITY
The Sturdymaid is made to fit snugly and comfortably on any wrist. It has more flexibility than is ever required. Is flexible both ways and constructed so that side strain will not break it

Expand links A and B fully. Slide end of link A through slot in bottom of link B. To attach—reverse the operation

EXPANSION
The Sturdymaid slips on and off over the hand easily and without unhooking. Every link expands so that the bracelet has more than two inches of evenly distributed expansion

PAT. AUG. 27, 1912 MARCH 11, 1913 MARCH 2, 1926

PRINTED IN U S A

PRICES ARE SUBJECT TO CHANGE WITHOUT NOTICE.

Sturdymaid watch bracelets in the 1928 ELF Red Book catalog. These were offered in styles with either "pierced" (filigree) or "plain" (engraved) links and either straight or curved endpieces in various widths. Although there were yellow and green gold filled versions available, it is obvious that white GF was by far the most popular. Links with "stones" (probably imitation sapphires) could be added at an extra charge per stone. The diagram shows how to remove or add a link.

At some point during the Transitional Period, narrow leather watchbands for ladies' wristwatches had been introduced. Some of these early leather straps were actually sewn into place around the wire lugs.

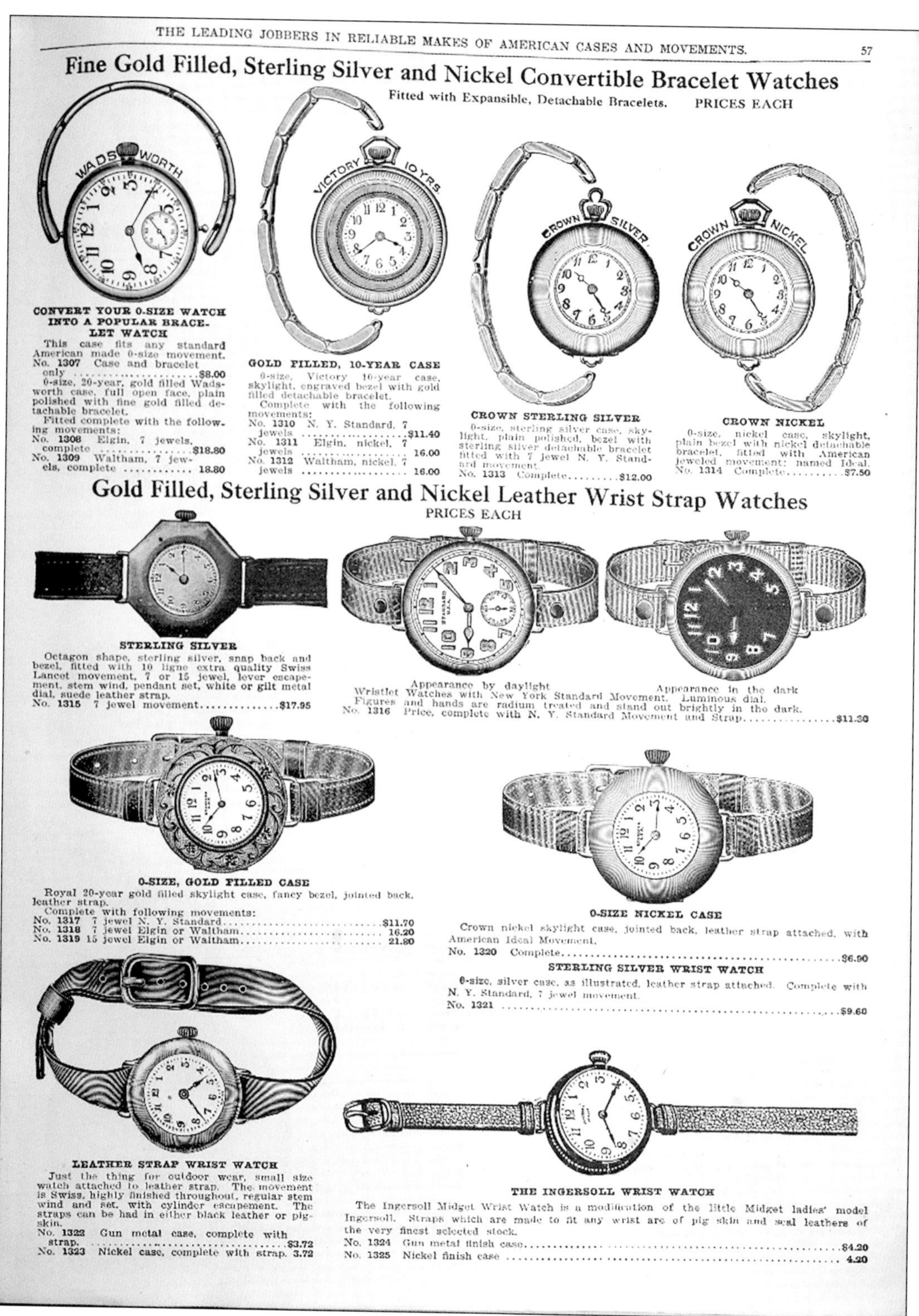

THE LEADING JOBBERS IN RELIABLE MAKES OF AMERICAN CASES AND MOVEMENTS. 57

Fine Gold Filled, Sterling Silver and Nickel Convertible Bracelet Watches

Fitted with Expansible, Detachable Bracelets. PRICES EACH

CONVERT YOUR 0-SIZE WATCH INTO A POPULAR BRACELET WATCH

This case fits any standard American made 0-size movement.
No. 1307 Case and bracelet only $8.00
0-size, 20-year, gold filled Wadsworth case, full open face, plain polished with fine gold filled detachable bracelet.
Fitted complete with the following movements:
No. 1308 Elgin, 7 jewels, complete $18.80
No. 1309 Waltham, 7 jewels, complete 18.80

GOLD FILLED, 10-YEAR CASE

0-size, Victory 10-year case, skylight, engraved bezel with gold filled detachable bracelet.
Complete with the following movements:
No. 1310 N. Y. Standard, 7 jewels $11.40
No. 1311 Elgin, nickel, 7 jewels 16.00
No. 1312 Waltham, nickel, 7 jewels 16.00

CROWN STERLING SILVER

0-size, sterling silver case, skylight, plain polished, bezel with sterling silver detachable bracelet fitted with 7 jewel N. Y. Standard movement.
No. 1313 Complete....................$12.00

CROWN NICKEL

0-size, nickel case, skylight, plain bezel with nickel detachable bracelet, fitted with American jeweled movement; named Ideal.
No. 1314 Complete....................$7.50

Gold Filled, Sterling Silver and Nickel Leather Wrist Strap Watches

PRICES EACH

STERLING SILVER

Octagon shape, sterling silver, snap back and bezel, fitted with 10 ligne extra quality Swiss Lancet movement, 7 or 15 jewel, lever escapement, stem wind, pendant set, white or gilt metal dial, suede leather strap.
No. 1315 7 jewel movement....................$17.95

Appearance by daylight — Appearance in the dark

Wristlet Watches with New York Standard Movement. Luminous dial. Figures and hands are radium treated and stand out brightly in the dark.
No. 1316 Price, complete with N. Y. Standard Movement and Strap....................$11.30

0-SIZE, GOLD FILLED CASE

Royal 20-year gold filled skylight case, fancy bezel, jointed back, leather strap.
Complete with following movements:
No. 1317 7 jewel N. Y. Standard....................$11.70
No. 1318 7 jewel Elgin or Waltham.................... 16.20
No. 1319 15 jewel Elgin or Waltham.................... 21.80

0-SIZE NICKEL CASE

Crown nickel skylight case, jointed back, leather strap attached, with American Ideal Movement.
No. 1320 Complete....................$6.90

STERLING SILVER WRIST WATCH

0-size, silver case, as illustrated, leather strap attached. Complete with N. Y. Standard, 7 jewel movement.
No. 1321 ....$9.60

LEATHER STRAP WRIST WATCH

Just the thing for outdoor wear, small size watch attached to leather strap. The movement is Swiss, highly finished throughout, regular stem wind and set, with cylinder escapement. The straps can be had in either black leather or pigskin.
No. 1322 Gun metal case, complete with strap. $3.72
No. 1323 Nickel case, complete with strap. 3.72

THE INGERSOLL WRIST WATCH

The Ingersoll Midget Wrist Watch is a modification of the little Midget ladies' model Ingersoll. Straps which are made to fit any wrist are of pig skin and seal leathers of the very finest selected stock.
No. 1324 Gun metal finish case....................$4.20
No. 1325 Nickel finish case 4.20

Group of early strap watches, A. C. Becken 1917 catalog

Other types of leather watchbands could also be found; as with today's leather straps, these were in two pieces, with a conventional buckle assembly. The model chosen depended upon whether the endpieces needed to fit on a wire-lug watch or one of the earlier transitional ones.

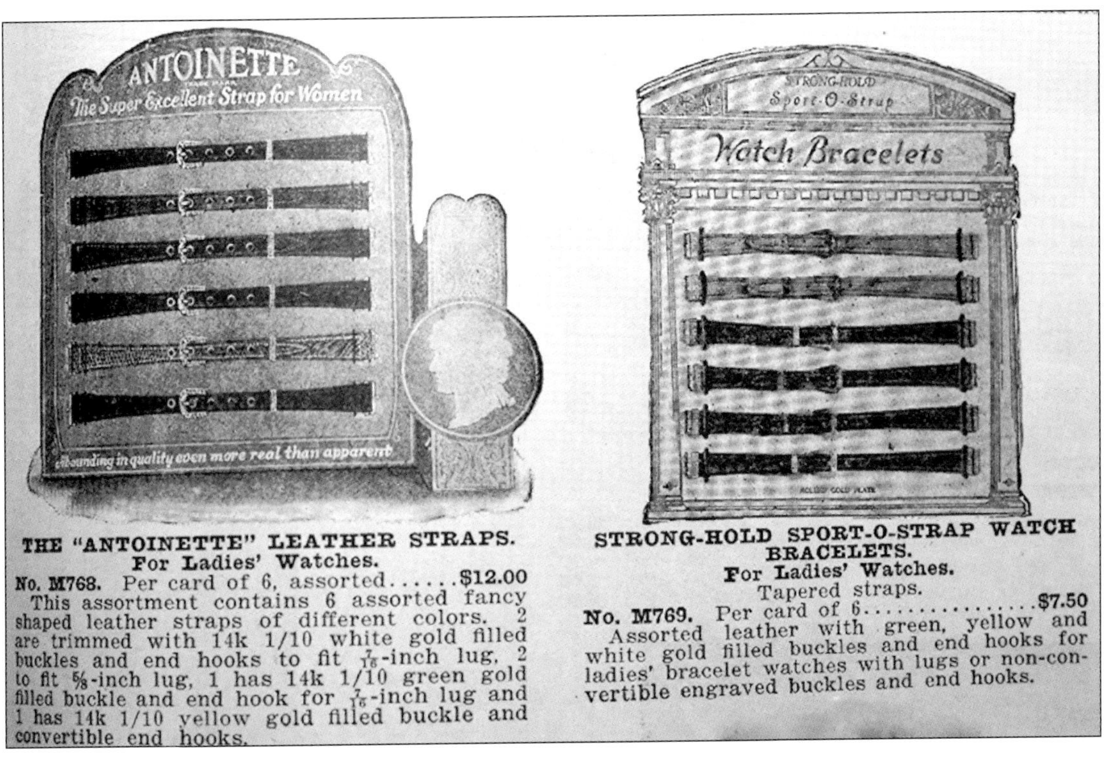

THE "ANTOINETTE" LEATHER STRAPS.
For Ladies' Watches.

No. M768. Per card of 6, assorted......**$12.00**
This assortment contains 6 assorted fancy shaped leather straps of different colors. 2 are trimmed with 14k 1/10 white gold filled buckles and end hooks to fit $\frac{7}{16}$-inch lug, 2 to fit ⅝-inch lug, 1 has 14k 1/10 green gold filled buckle and end hook for $\frac{7}{16}$-inch lug and 1 has 14k 1/10 yellow gold filled buckle and convertible end hooks.

STRONG-HOLD SPORT-O-STRAP WATCH BRACELETS.
For Ladies' Watches.
Tapered straps.

No. M769. Per card of 6................**$7.50**
Assorted leather with green, yellow and white gold filled buckles and end hooks for ladies' bracelet watches with lugs or non-convertible engraved buckles and end hooks.

Leather straps for ladies' wristwatches, Otto Young 1929 catalog

Cord bands reached their height of popularity later, but some watch manufacturers in the 1920s and early 1930s were already offering some models with that type of band. At least five Illinois models (the Barbara, Marionette, Muzette, Patricia and Vardon) came with silk cord bands that went into the unusual lug openings of those models. Most cord bands of the period, however, had metal endpieces that fit onto the full width of conventional wire-lug watch cases.

For catalog listings and magazine advertisements, the watch companies generally had their watches pictured with black ribbon bands (or, for certain models, cord bands). There were likely marketing reasons for doing so, as these plain bands showed the designs of the watch cases to advantage rather than competing with them.

For information about manufacturers of watch attachments, and more examples of ladies' watchbands, see Chapter 8.

Cases and Casemakers
Model Numbers and Names

Most Illinois Factory-Cased wristwatch cases that were designed for and sold to the Illinois Watch Company contain inside their case back a case model number: e.g., Model No. 169, for a lady's Coronado watch. (An updated list of the case model numbers is set forth in Chapter 8.)

The famous Mary Todd model, introduced in 1926, is known to have been Factory-Cased, but it has no case Model Number. It appears that Illinois did not begin assigning case Model Numbers to its ladies' models until a bit later, beginning with the group released in 1928. Occasionally, the case Model Number was not indicated on some of the models that would normally have the number. (Specimens of these that have been collected are noted in the individual identification listings later in this chapter.)

For the purposes of this chapter, I have relied greatly on the research of Farrell Gay, along with reviewing all available jobbers' catalogs as well as all obtainable published material from the Illinois Watch Company and the contemporary advertisements that were usually placed in the popular magazines of the time and trade publications for the jewelry industry. The magazines most utilized by the Illinois Watch Company for advertisements were the *Saturday Evening Post, Liberty, Collier's,* the *American Magazine* and the *National Geographic*; accordingly, I have examined many of those, as well as the two major jewelry industry trade publications, the *Keystone* and the *Jewelers' Circular*. The ladies' models featured were almost always included with a selection of men's wristwatches. Illinois watches were also featured in huge annual jewelry catalogues of that era produced by such companies as A. C. Becken, L. & C. Mayers, May & Malone, and Wallenstein Mayer, to name but a few.

Cases of Confusion

The case Model Numbers are particularly confusing for the ladies' watches because model numbers are the same for several different model names. For example, case Model Numbers 153, 154 and 155 all contain watches with the name Daytona. Thus, the Daytona model can be found in four different cases (case Model Numbers 153, 154, 155 and a case with no model number), and it can have at least five different bezel designs. Some Daytonas are in white gold-filled cases and some in solid white gold ones. The cases all feature a six-sided dial opening.

To further compound this confusion, case Model No. 153 also contains watches for the Long Beach, Redonda 153 and Saratoga models; case Model No. 154 for the Berkeley 154 and Redonda 154; and case Model No. 155 for the Del Monte 155, Miami 155 and Joan models as well as one Edgewater variant. The names themselves can be confusing when the same name is used for more than one model—not just Daytona, but Redonda, Berkeley and Edgewater as well.

For a serious collector of Illinois ladies' wristwatches, dealing with names of models and case Model Numbers can be a somewhat frustrating experience; as soon as you think you have pinned down a solid rule of thumb, an exception or new discovery pops up. But it is just this variety and surprise that adds to the fascination of collecting Illinois.

Economy was the reason for this "case confusion." Illinois, to save costs, could keep the case back and movement size the same for all these models but could easily differentiate them for marketing, sales purposes and consumer preference by changing the designs of the bezels and dials. For this reason, one might claim that the case Model Numbers for the ladies' models are not nearly as important as the case Model Numbers for the men's models because so many of the case backs are simply and easily interchangeable. In fact, many of the ladies' Illinois wristwatch models used the identical case back.

This interchangeability should be of no concern to a collector, however, because the critical distinguishing features of these ladies' models are their bezel designs and whether they had enamel bezels or solid gold cases.

Keystone Watch Case Company

The Keystone Watch Case Company was the primary manufacturer utilized by the Illinois Watch Company for the cases of its ladies' models. At least forty-seven different Factory-Cased models were in Keystone cases. Of these, at least sixteen were in solid gold, and at least five had enameled bezels. There were also some that were adorned with diamonds. (See discussion of Diamond-Set Cases, below, and the listing for **Diamond-Set Models** in the identification section of this chapter.)

Illinois Ladies' Factory-Cased Wristwatches in Keystone Cases

Model Name	Case Model Number
Narragansett	168
Princess	168
Countess	168
Coronado	169
Newport 174	174
Edgewater 175	175
Beverly 185	185
Lenox	185
Biloxi	186
Glenna 186	186
Berkshire	199
Fairport	200
Brighton	201
Mary Todd 203	203
Mary Todd 204	204
Avalon	205
Edgewater 208	208
Edgewater 222	222
Newport 223	223
No. 224 (Unknown)	224
Glencoe	238
Lakewood	238
Glenna 239	239
Roslyn	239
No. 241 (Unknown)	241
Minuette	701
Rosette	701
Coquette	702
Annette	703
Antoinette	703, No Number
Charmette	703
Florette	703
Alouette	704
Babette I	704
Lynette	710
Janette	711
Marilyn	830
Elissa	830
Irene	830
Sylvia	830
Hollywood	831
Rita	831
Patricia	833
Fairfax	834
Florentine	834
Beverly	852
Mary Todd	No Number
Mary Todd GG	No Number

808 THE JEWELERS' CIRCULAR-WEEKLY February 4, 1914.

1914 Keystone Watch Case Company advertisement for ladies' wristwatches

Illinois Ladies' Factory-Cased Wristwatches in Wadsworth Cases

Model Name	Case Model Number
Berkeley 153	153
Daytona 153	153
Long Beach	153
Redonda 153	153
Saratoga Leaf	153
Saratoga Notched Leaf	153
Daytona 154	154
Redonda 154	154
Berkeley 154A	154A
Daytona 155	155
Daytona 155A	155
Daytona 155B	155
Del Monte 155	155
Edgewater 155	155
Joan	155
Miami 155	155
Bar Harbor 156	156
Del Monte 157	157
Miami 157	157
Miami 157A	157
Bar Harbor 158	158
Vardon	240
Claudette	242
Vogue	242
Argyle	807-5
Arlene	807-5
Greta	807-5
Debutante	807-6
Vanity Fair	807-6
Gloria	828
Barbara	829
Constance	829
Lady Mary	807-5
Queen Anne	807-5
Wadsworth Special Model	No Number

Wadsworth Watch Case Company

The Wadsworth Watch Case Company was the second most utilized watch case manufacturer for the Illinois Watch Company's ladies' models. At least thirty-two different Factory-Cased models were in Wadsworth cases. Of these, at least ten were in solid gold, at least nine had enameled bezels, and two were in sterling silver.

Star Watch Case Company

Five ladies' Illinois wristwatch models were factory cased by Hamilton in Lancaster in Star Watch Case Company cases about 1934.

Illinois Ladies' Wristwatches Factory-Cased in Star Cases

Model Name	Case Model Number
Babette II	714
Juliette*	No Number
Juliette*	706
Muzette*	707
Sherwood	No Number
Suzette*	707
Suzette (14K)*	No Number

*Cased by Hamilton in Lancaster

Fahys Watch Case Company

Fahys Watch Case Company supplied at least one Illinois ladies' wristwatch model. Inside the case back is a standard Illinois Watch Company notation reading "Illinois Watch Special Model" and "Fahys 14K Gold Filled."

Patterns of Engraving on Case Backs and Sides

In the individual listings of Illinois ladies' models in the identification section later in this chapter, it is noted whether an individual model had an engraved case back or a plain one. Many models had plain backs. If there was engraving on case backs, however, a given manufacturer seems to have had a pattern, exclusive to itself, that it reserved for the backs of its Illinois ladies' watch cases. Wadsworth's characteristic pattern was a ribbon-like foliate and floral border with a tiny heart at the center of the long sides and at the center of the top and bottom sides. Keystone's engraving pattern for its case backs was similar to Wadsworth's, but with subtle geometric touches instead of hearts.

For the sides of cases, each casemaker also had one or more characteristic engraving patterns for its Illinois ladies' watch cases. It is fascinating to examine the intricate detailing of these patterns. The one known ladies' Illinois model from Fahys had repeated panels of flowers bracketed with stylized leaves.

Engraving of flowers and leaves on sides of Fahys case for Illinois ladies' Special Model

An examination of a sampling of cases by Wadsworth and Keystone suggests that the particular patterns each of them used appear to be tied to Illinois cases with particular case Model Numbers. For example, on the sides of case Model Nos. 153–156, Wadsworth used a repeated pattern of a simple figure resembling an integral sign.

One of Wadsworth's characteristic engravings for Illinois ladies' case sides, resembling an integral sign in mathematics, here on a Daytona 155

Other patterns are more complex, combining floral and geometric motifs (e.g., case Model Nos. 240 and 807-5, for example) or combining a ribbon loop with geometric motifs (e.g., case Model Nos. 242 and 807-6).

A Wadsworth engraving pattern for Illinois ladies' case sides, combining floral motifs with geometric ones, here on a Vardon

Ribbon loops and geometric motifs in a Wadsworth engraving pattern for Illinois ladies' case sides, here on a Claudette

Keystone's most frequently used engraving pattern for the sides of its Illinois ladies' models was a repeated leaflike form (e.g., case Model Nos. 169, 175 and 200, among others).

Leaflike forms, one of Keystone's characteristic patterns for case sides of ladies' Illinois models, here on a Brighton

For case Model Nos. 199 and 205, Keystone used something more austere: a pattern of graduated ovals.

Graduated ovals, another of Keystone's patterns for Illinois ladies' models, here on a Berkshire

And some of the later Keystone cases, such as case Model Nos. 830 and 831, had merely straight-line engraving around their sides.

Simple lines of engraving, used by Keystone on the case sides of some Illinois ladies' Moderne models, such as the Marilyn

Although the tiny 21/0 size baguette models all seem to have had plain backs, most had engraving on their sides. The patterns included geometric motifs, such as rectangles or diamonds, or simple dots and vertical bars.

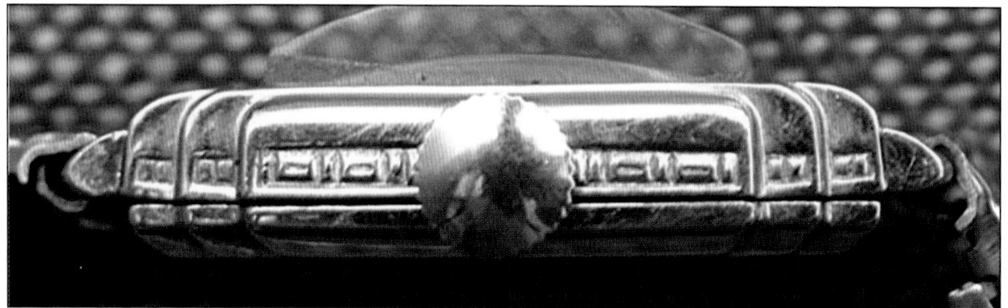

Geometric pattern of rectangles used by Keystone on case sides of the Minuette, a baguette model

Star's engraving pattern with geometric shapes such as diamonds for case sides of an Illinois baguette, the Juliette

Geometric pattern of dots and lines used by Keystone for case sides of another baguette model, the Lynette

14K WGF or 14K YGF Ladies' Illinois Wristwatch Models		
Annette	Fairport	Minuette
Berkeley 153	Florette	Muzette
Berkeley 154	Florentine	Newport 174
Berkshire	Glenna 186	Newport 223
Biloxi	Glenna 239	No. 241
Charmette	Gloria	Patricia
Claudette	Hollywood	Redonda
Coquette	Irene	Redonda 154
Daytona 153	Janette	Rita
Debutante	Joan	Roslyn
Del Monte 155	Juliette	Rosette
Del Monte 157	Lynette	Saratoga Leaf
Edgewater 155	Long Beach	Saratoga Notched Leaf
Edgewater 175	Mariette	Sylvia
Edgewater 208	Marilyn	Suzette
Edgewater 222	Marlette	Vanity Fair
Elissa	Marionette	Vogue
Fahys Special Model	Miami 155	
Fairfax	Miami 157	

Two-Tone Ladies' Models
Constance/ Barbara (14K GF)
Vardon (14K solid gold)

10K White or Yellow Gold-Filled Ladies' Models
Antoinette
Beverly 852
Janette
Lynette*
*Also came in 14K white gold-filled

Sterling Silver Ladies' Models
Lady Mary
Queen Anne

Illinois Factory-Cased Models

It appears that the Illinois and Hamilton factories cased at least eighty-six different models of Illinois ladies' wristwatches. This total does not include any ladies' watches of the Transitional or Generic Period, nor does it include any of the Diamond-Set Models other than the Glenna 186, Minuette/Rosette and No. 241. Surprisingly, at least thirty out of the total Factory-Cased models were made in solid gold, and of these, five were in 18K solid gold. Two models were made in sterling silver, three in 10K gold-filled cases and the remainder in 14K gold-filled cases. To add to this variety, at least sixteen models had some sort of inlaid enamel on their bezels.

The wide variety of the Illinois Watch Company's offerings over such a short time span is quite fascinating and makes collecting ladies' Illinois challenging but fun. To add to the challenge, there are at least eight Illinois ladies' models that remain unidentified.

Solid Gold Cases

In wristwatches, Illinois produced very few men's models in solid gold; as a result, they are today among the most desirable, collectible and valuable of the men's models. Illinois produced many more ladies' models in solid gold, releasing at least thirty different Factory-Cased solid gold ladies' models. Of these, one was in green gold, two were in yellow gold, at least twenty-six were in white gold (not counting the Diamond-Set Models), and one was two-tone. All of these solid gold models were in 14K or 18K.

The paucity of solid gold Illinois men's wristwatch models, discussed in Chapter 4, seems possibly the result of pressure from Hamilton not to challenge Hamilton's own high-end market. As for the relatively large number of Illinois' solid gold ladies' watches, an examination of catalogs of the period suggests that Hamilton at the time was much less interested in the ladies' market than the men's, and therefore let Illinois continue to do as it pleased with its own ladies' offerings

As was mentioned earlier, some of the known Factory-Cased solid gold Illinois ladies' models have no case Model Number: for example, the famous Mary Todd, introduced in 1926, which had a Keystone case of 18K solid white gold. Illinois apparently did not begin assigning case Model Numbers until somewhat later (the ladies' models released in 1928).

Keystone also produced other 18K white gold cases, which had bezels ornamented with diamonds and sometimes blue stones as well; these too had no case Model Numbers. Recent findings indicate that these watches were also part of Illinois' Mary Todd line. (For details, see the discussion under the listing for Diamond-Set Models in the identification section of this chapter.)

There are Wadsworth solid gold cases without case Model Numbers as well as Keystone ones. Gay has pointed out that there were Illinois movements cased in both Wadsworth's 19.2K solid white gold cases and its 18K solid white gold ones prior to the assignment of case Model Numbers. (Some of the 18K Wadsworth cases were decorated with inlaid black enamel and diamonds.) Given the recent discovery about the Mary Todd models, it seems plausible to hypothesize that the Illinois models in 19.2K and 18K Wadsworth cases were also likely to have been Factory Cased.

Solid Gold Illinois Factory-Cased Ladies' Wristwatches*			
Model Name	**Case Model Number**	**Karat**	**Casemaker**
Alouette	704	14K WG	Keystone
Argyle	807-5	14K WG	Wadsworth
Arlene	807-5	14K WG	Wadsworth
Avalon	205	14K WG	Keystone
Babette I	704	14K WG	Keystone
Babette II	714	14K WG, YG	Star
Bar Harbor 156	156	14K WG	Wadsworth
Bar Harbor 158	158	14K WG	Wadsworth
Berkeley 154A**	154	14K YG, WG	Wadsworth
Beverly 185	185	14K WG	Keystone
Brighton**	201	14K WG	Keystone
Coronado**	169	14K-WG	Keystone
Countess	168	14K WG	Keystone
Daytona 154	154	14K WG	Wadsworth
Daytona 155	155	14K WG	Wadsworth
Daytona 155A	155	14K WG	Wadsworth
Daytona 155B	155	14K WG	Wadsworth
Glencoe	238	14K WG YG	Keystone
Greta	807-5	14K WG	Wadsworth
Lakewood	238	14K WG, YG	Keystone
Lenox	185	14K WG, YG	Keystone
Mary Todd**	No Number	18K WG	Keystone
Mary Todd 203**	203	18K WG	Keystone
Mary Todd 204	204	18K WG	Keystone
Mary Todd GG	No Number	18K GG	Keystone
Miami 157A**	157	14K YG, WG	Wadsworth
Narragansett	168	14K WG	Keystone
Princess	168	14K WG	Keystone
Sherwood	No Number	14K WG, YG	Star
Suzette	No Number (normally 707)	14K WG, YG	Star
Vardon	240	14K WG/YG	Wadsworth
Victoria**	Unknown	18K WG	Unknown
Wadsworth Special Models	No Number	18K WG, 19.2 WG	Wadsworth

*This list does not include any Diamond-Set Models.
**Inlaid enamel

Diamond-Set Models

From time to time, Illinois watches were marketed with diamonds on the bezels. Some of these watches also had blue cut stones (probably synthetic sapphires). It was earlier thought unlikely that most of these models were cased in the Illinois Watch Company Factory, as no advertisements from the company had been found for these watches; instead, it was thought that they were most likely cased by jewelers in their stores. However, evidence has recently come to light that at least some of these watches were indeed Factory-Cased, and some were even special Mary Todd models. (For the details, see the entries for both the Diamond-Set Models and Mary Todd in the identification section later in this chapter.)

It is possible that jewelers, casemakers or even Illinois itself may have occasionally added diamonds to existing cases to meet customer demands. It was already known that at least two Illinois ladies' watches in 14K white gold-filled cases with diamonds on the bezels had been found in cases with Illinois case Model Numbers: the Minuette/Rosette (case Model No. 701) and the Glenna 186. These variants, likely custom orders, were ornamented with just two modest, almost understated diamonds, one on the top of the bezel and one on the bottom. In addition, a very rare variant of a very rare model, the Antoinette (case Model No. 703) has been found in a 10K white gold-filled case with six diamonds on its bezel; this too was likely a custom order.

The Illinois ladies' model No. 241 came in a Keystone case with both diamonds and sapphires ornamenting its bezel. Although it has recently been discovered that there were apparently other Illinois ladies' Factory-Cased watches having bezels ornamented with both kinds of jewels, this is the only known model of that sort bearing a case Model Number. To date, only two of these rare beauties have been found.

Enameled Bezels

Among the greatest attractions of the Illinois ladies' models are their unusual inlaid enamel designs. These rival even the terrific deco designs executed by Elgin under the direction of world-renowned French designer Lucien Lelong, whose studio was commissioned by the Elgin National Watch Company to design the spectacular "Parisienne" series of ladies' watches in the 1920s.

116 THE SATURDAY EVENING POST July 21, 1928

ELGIN PARISIENNE WATCH $35

MADE BY ELGIN

STYLED BY AGNÈS, PREMET, JENNY

GREAT COUTURIERS OF THE RUE DE LA PAIX

Entrez les Parisiennes . . . brilliantly modern, radiantly smart, vividly, unmistakably French.

For ELGIN turned to Paris for designs in *l'art moderne* . . . and now the miraculously precise, time-truthful ELGIN movements are exquisitely sheathed in *chic*.

So today your ELGIN PARISIENNE begs prettily (in a most intriguing French accent) for a place upon your wrist . . . to point the time to you and your timeliness to everyone.

And begs to join your hat and your handbag, frock and flower, shoes and shingle, in composing the perfect *ensemble*. The PARISIENNE is the final French and fashionable touch that emphasizes your entire smartness as an exclamation point accents a sentence.

Made by ELGIN...dressed by the Rue de la Paix!

Presented at a price born of ELGIN'S great efficiency, great volume and rich experience.

MADAME AGNÈS

The Madame Agnès . . . Moderniste Extraordinaire . . . artiste . . . a leader in brilliant Parisian circles . . . and the designer of this exquisite ELGIN. The case is fashioned with enamel . . . and originality. Jade, black, or ruby enamel, but the originality scoffs at mere description. $35

© *Elgin, 1928*

(Prices slightly higher in Canada)

MADAME CHARLOTTE

Directrice of the House of Premet

The Premet . . . "Costume by Premet" has ever been the hall-mark of distinction in the smartest places of the world. "Watch by Premet". . . what *chic*, what charm is conjured in the phrase, and borne out in this lovely oblong of jade, black, or ruby enamel $35

MADAME JENNY

The Madame Jenny . . . This notable member of the Haute Couture has gone straight to the heart of modern art, captured a lovely motif, and placed it upon your wrist. Brilliant as one of her famous frocks . . . and just as exclusive. In jade, black, or ruby enamel. $35

Advertisement for Elgin's new Parisienne line, *Saturday Evening Post*, July 21, 1928

The Illinois Watch Company provided at least seventeen different ladies' models that sported dazzling deco-styled enameled bezels.

Ladies' Illinois Factory-Cased Wristwatches with Enameled Bezels

Name	Case Model #	Casemaker	Material
Argyle	807-5	Wadsworth	14K WG
Berkeley 153	153	Wadsworth	14K WGF
Berkeley 154	154	Wadsworth	14K WGF
Berkeley 154A	154	Wadsworth	14K YG, WG
Brighton	201	Keystone	14K WG
Coronado	169	Keystone	14K WG
Del Monte 155	155	Wadsworth	14K WGF
Del Monte 157	157	Wadsworth	14K WGF
Mary Todd	203	Keystone	18K WG
Mary Todd	No Number	Keystone	18K WG
Miami 155	155	Wadsworth	14K WGF
Miami 157	157	Wadsworth	14K WGF
Miami 157A	157	Wadsworth	14K YG
Redonda 153	153	Wadsworth	14K WGF
Redonda 154	154	Wadsworth	14K WGF
Roslyn	239	Keystone	14K WGF
Victoria	Unknown	Unknown	18K WG

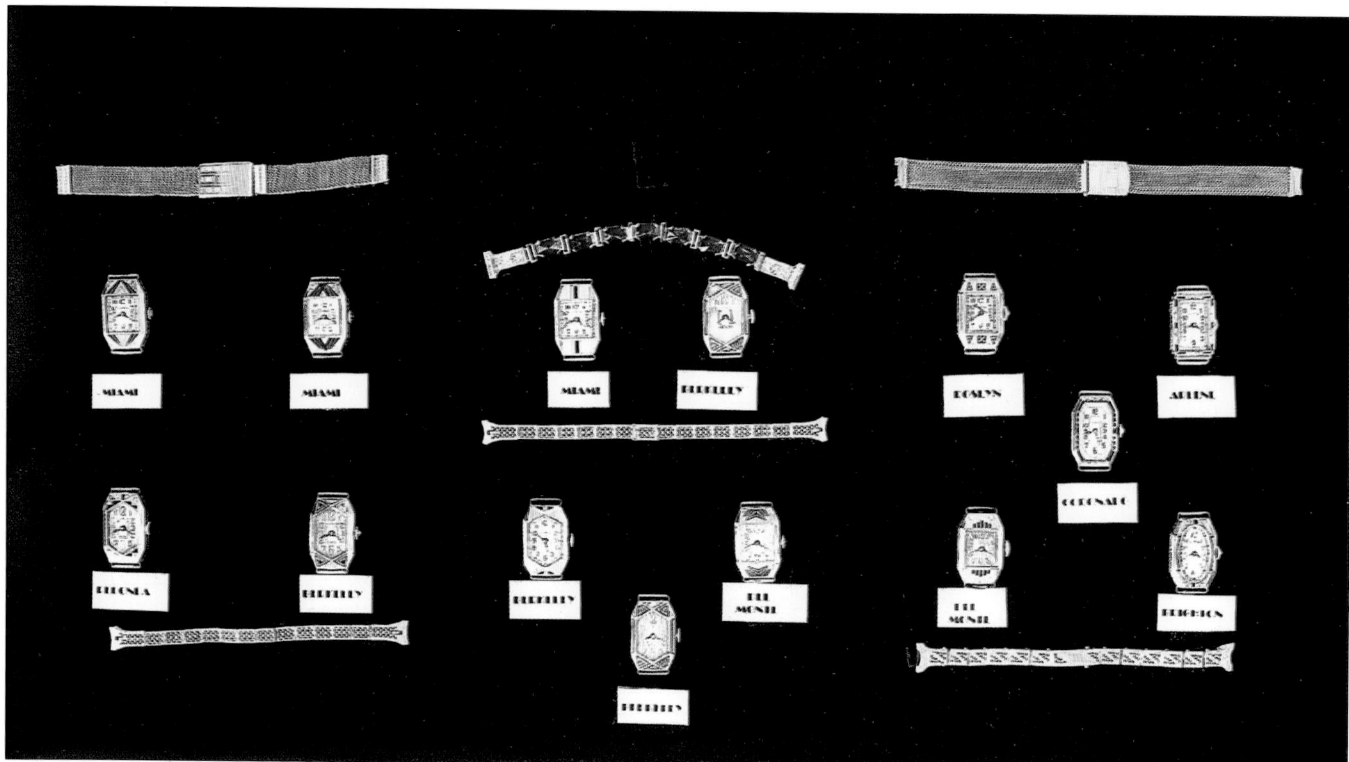

Group shot of enamel Illinois ladies' wristwatches and Deco bands

Iconic Art Deco design features that were utilized for the ladies' Illinois models included strong verticals and diagonals as well as Southwestern motifs. A classic deco color combination was black and silver, and a number of the ladies' watch cases thus feature black enamel touches on white gold cases. The creative use of colorful enameling (red and black, sea green and black, black and white, or two tones of blue) on their bezels also greatly enhances the appeal of many of the ladies' models.

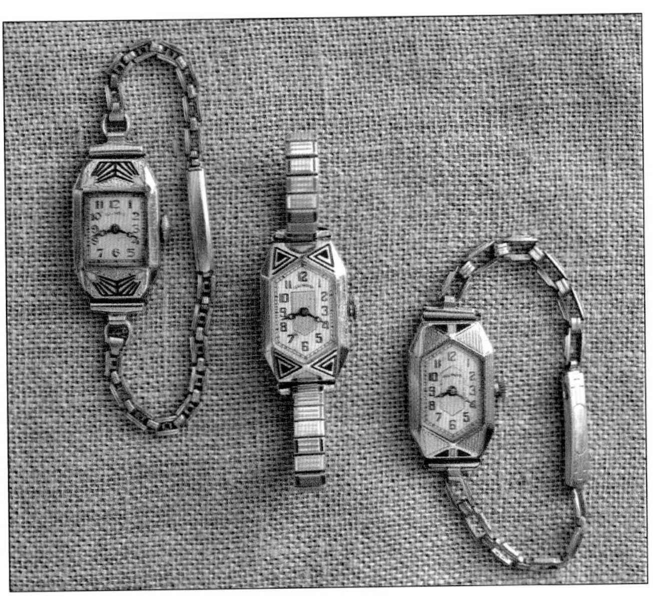

Illinois ladies' models featuring green enameling. *Left to right:* Del Monte 157, Redonda 154, Berkeley 153

A group of Illinois ladies' models with black inlaid enameling, listed in vertical rows from top to bottom. *Column 1*: Brighton, with modern suede band. *Column 2*: Mary Todd, with WGF Bugbee & Niles mesh bracelet; and Roslyn, with Kestenmade bracelet. *Column 3*: Wadsworth Special Model, with 4 diamonds, modern leather band. *Column 4*: Del Monte 155; and Coronado, with Hadley WGF mesh bracelet

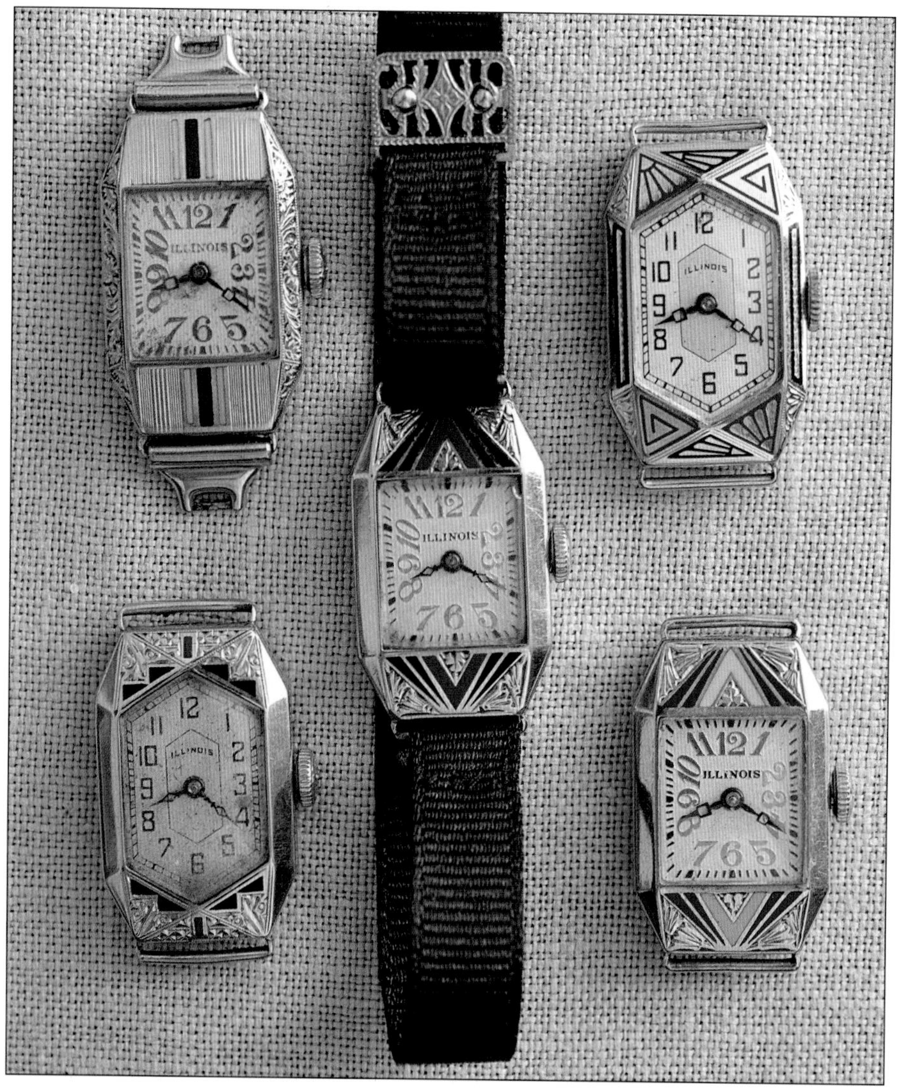

Illinois ladies' models featuring red or blue enameling. Top to bottom, *Column 1*: Miami 155 (two-tone blue) and Redonda 153 (red and black). *Column 2*: Miami 157 (red and black). *Column 3*: Berkeley 154 (red and black) and Miami 157 (two-tone blue)

Few if any watch companies have ever equaled, much less surpassed, the complex enamel designs of the Illinois Watch Company. These ladies' Illinois, along with the wonderful men's designs, clearly show that Illinois was one of the top manufacturers of deco-styled watches for its era.

Lugs

Without known exception, all of the ladies' Illinois' wristwatches came with fixed lugs. The lug sizes for these watches ranged from 8mm to 16mm, with the vast majority being 11mm.

Dials

As was noted earlier, the Illinois Watch Company used the same case back for different ladies' wristwatch models in order to control costs. A similar cost-saving measure was implemented in regard to dials, with several models sharing the same dial.

A particular watch model could also be provided with several other different styles of dial, though of course limited by the shape of the case and the shape of the dial opening of the bezel. (More dial options for given models are noted in the individual listings in the identification section later in this chapter.)

Some Dials in Common

Model Name	Dial Number	Model Name	Dial Number
Brighton	8090	Mary Todd GG	8174
Debutante	8090	Newport 174	8174
Fairport	8090	Newport 223	8174
Vanity Fair	8090	Patricia	8174
Alouette	8122	Berkshire	8191, 8192
Babette	8122	Avalon	8191, 8192
Marlette	8122	Vardon	8195
Débette	8122	Argyle	8195
Daytona153	8147	Arlene	8195
Daytona 154	8147	Gloria	8195
Daytona 155A	8147	Princess	8195
Long Beach	8147	Claudette	8282
Redonda 153	8147	Avalon	8282
Redonda 154	8147	Glencoe	8282
Edgewater 155	8169, 8170	Beverly 185	8394
Joan	8169, 8170, 8171	Beverly 852	8394
Edgewater 175	8169, 8170, 8171, 8364	Charmette	8732
Edgewater 208	8169. 8170, 8171, 8364	Annette	8732
Edgewater 222	8169, 8170, 8171, 8364	Antoinette	8732
Mary Todd	8174	Florette	8732
Mary Todd 203	8174		

Movements

The Illinois ladies' wristwatches utilized five different movement sizes: 0, 3/0, 6/0, 18/0 and 21/0. However, it appears that except for the 6/0 size Octagon and Tonneau models (listed in the identification section of this chapter), only the 18/0 and 21/0 movement sizes were Factory-Cased in Springfield or later in Lancaster. The 0, 3/0 and 6/0 size movements were used in cases of the Transitional and Generic Periods that were common to all manufacturers of the time. The 18/0 and 21/0 size movements were generally called "ladies' movements" and had no subsidiary seconds.

Many of these movements that came in 18/0 size could be interchangeable with 18/0 size movements in different jewel counts. As a result, it is quite possible that a given model came with a movement having either 15, 16 or 17 jewels.

Although ladies' Illinois wristwatches came in jewel counts of 15, 16 and 17, it should be noted that many of the ladies' Illinois wristwatches contained in this chapter have 18/0 size movements with 17 jewels. These movements were manufactured from 1926 to 1932. However, according to Meggers and Erhardt and Dr. Russell W. Snyder's electronic Illinois movement database, in 1948 the Hamilton Watch Company in its factory produced 18/0 size, grades 805 and 805A, 15-jewel movements. This information was apparently a rare error of the usually very reliable team of Meggers and Erhardt. (This matter is discussed in Chapter 6.)

NEW 18/0 SIZE MOVEMENT

Illinois issued a Supplementary Catalogue of Material and Prices effective January 1, 1926. On the first page, Illinois made the following statement "To the Trade":

"Due to the Manufacture of two new movements, the 16 size 14th model and the 18/0 size, we have published the supplement to the catalogue of December, 1923."

From this statement, it is thus clear that Illinois first started using its new 18/0 size movement in ladies' wristwatches in 1926 for its Mary Todd solid gold model.

Production Numbers

As with the Illinois men's wristwatches, there are no known existing production records for ladies' wristwatches. However, in total, there were 163,330 movements of 18/0 size manufactured by the Illinois Watch Company and 23,600 movements of 21/0 size. These movements, totaling 186,930, were used almost exclusively for eighty-four different models of ladies' watches over a span of eight years (excluding the Transitional, Generic and Diamond-Set Models and not counting the eight models that are so far unidentified).

A few Illinois men's or unisex watches also used the 18/0 size movement: the Biltmore 18/0, Sangamon, Tuxedo and Urbana models, and (later) the version of the Rockliffe 18/0 issued by Hamilton in 1935.

But rather than being cased in the Illinois Factory, in cases stipulated for specific models, many of the 18/0 size movements were instead used in other cases utilized by jewelers throughout the United States.

21/0 Size Movement Mysteries

The Illinois Watch Company in 1932 commenced the sale of very small ladies' wristwatches known in the trade as baguettes (or semi-baguettes) because of their long, narrow shape resembling the French bread of that name. After the Illinois Factory closed, Hamilton released more of these ladies' models under the Illinois name in 1934. All of these watches contained 21/0 size movements of 15 or 17 jewels.

No records pertaining to the production of these 21/0 size movements in the Illinois Factory have been located. However, there were at least nineteen models released in this size, many of which were released in 1932. These 21/0 size movements had to have been assembled in the Illinois Factory on or before early 1932. It is possible that these movements were mislabeled in the Illinois production records.

AMERICAN BEAUTY SERIES 17 JEWEL, 21/0 SIZE, 14K FILLED GOLD CASES

A page in the Illinois 1931–32 sales catalog featured the new American Beauty Series with this statement: "Dainty timepieces of American excellence for those who insist upon dependability, as well as perfected design, superb and delicately smart refinements. These exquisite watches are produced with the characteristic exacting craftsmanship that has made the Illinois Watch a favored timepiece for more than sixty years. They are a splendid contribution to American achievement and greater value."

In 1931, there was also a special sales brochure promoting this new series of 21/0 size watches as follows: "Exquisitely dainty timepieces, quite the newest, smartest vogue. The most distinctive feature of any lady's ensemble. Yet, for all their size refinement, each one is produced with the same fine craftsmanship in watchmaking which has made Illinois Watch famous for its accurate timekeeping for more than sixty years. At $52.50, a truly amazing value."

Evidently, the small, rather plain, low-priced ladies' offerings in 21/0 size were well-received in the market. According to a letter of November 10, 1931, from Jack L. Keenan, the Illinois Watch Company Sales Manager, during the past few weeks there had been "a decided pickup in the demand for our Greater Value ribbon and strap watches in $32.50, $35.00 and $37.50 range, to say nothing of the over demand on the 21/0 size American Beauty Series."

~~LETTER TO 3%~~ DISCOUNT ~~JOBBERS~~
Letter to jobbers when not earned
November 10th, 1931.

Dear Mr.

For several years now it has been necessary to advise those few customers of ours whose volume of purchases during the year became reduced below a minimum that the ~~3%~~ cash discount was not being earned and could not be applied to their accounts until yearly volume was reached.

You can readily appreciate the fact that the cost of affording service and providing you with assistance in the handling of our franchise; truly represents an expense and a loss in the small amount billed to you this year.

We have no desire to discontinue franchise and therefore advise you in advance that because of situation in general business volume, we have this year set a minimum of $5,000 volume on an accont that could be serviced to advantage for the year; this compares with $10,000 minimum used in 1929.

Your account for the year through October 25th shows purchases in the amount of $3,980; to reach our minimum requirement further purchases in November and December of $1,020 is necessary.

There has been during past fewweeks a decided pickup in the demand for our Greater Value ribbon and strap watches in $32.50, $35.00 and $37.50 range, to say nothing of the over demand on the 21/0 size American Beauty Series.

In bringing this matter to your attention now it seems reasonable that you can easily reach the volume of $5,000 for this year, therefore earn the 3% discount and enjoy taking 3% cash discont in 1932.

Should this $5,000 volume not be reached this year and you wish to retain our franchise the watches you buy in 1932 would be billed at cost price, net, until volume set for that year is reached.

We are confident you can and will meet the goal required during these next two months.

Very truly yours,

THE ILLINOIS WATCH

JLK:ET

Sales Manager.

Letter from Jack Keenan, dated November 10, 1931, noting the success of the 21/0 size "American Beauty Series" ladies' ribbon and strap watches

Baguette Style

Baguette watches seem to have already begun appearing in the 1920s, but they were most popular in the United States during the early 1930s. Although they were most frequently produced in 21/0 size, some companies made even smaller ones (for example, Elgin's 26/0 size models).

Illinois began introducing 21/0 size watches in its 1931–32 Sales Catalog and also offered them in the 1933 Pioneers of Greater Values Catalog, but in those catalogs the term "baguette" was not applied to them. (Hamilton also began offering 21/0 size models in 1932 and likewise did not call them baguettes.)

Finally, in the 1934 Illinois Pioneers of Greater Values Catalog, Illinois (via Hamilton) introduced a new line of eight ladies' wristwatches that it actually termed "Baguette Style." All came equipped with an Elinvar hairspring. The advertisement stated: "Accuracy, style and value distinguish these fine 21/0 size Semi-Baguette watches. They have 15 and 17-jewel movements and are available in filled or 14 Karat solid gold cases." (It seems odd, and somewhat confusing, for Illinois/Hamilton to have used the terms "Baguette" and "Semi-Baguette" simultaneously.)

Baguette Models

Year Introduced	Name
1931	Charmette
1931	Coquette
1931	Minuette
1932	Alouette
1932	Annette
1933	Babette I
1933	Florette
1933	Janette
1933	Juliette
1933	Lynette
1933	Muzette
1933	Rosette
1933	Suzette
1934	Antoinette
1934	Babette II
1934	Débette
1934	Janette
1934	Lynette
1934	Mariette
1934	Marionette
1934	Marlette

21/0 size dials for Baguette models from the Illinois catalog, 1936

ILLINOIS WATCHES

PIONEERS OF GREATER VALUE

BUY AMERICAN.

The "Buy American" campaign has been started. It will have a tremendous impression upon the buying public. America appreciates quality and will demand it this year. Get your clerks to "Sell American" as quality appeal with patriotism secondary.

Joan Crawford, one of the many popular motion picture stars, who have chosen the Illinois Watch as their selected timepiece. (Courtesy Metro-Goldwyn-Mayer.)

AMERICAN VALUE.

Illinois Watches are known as "The Great American Value in Watches." Lower price with improved quality, style and dependability. Upon this page are shown diminutively small wrist watches for the women, who demand dependability in a timepiece.

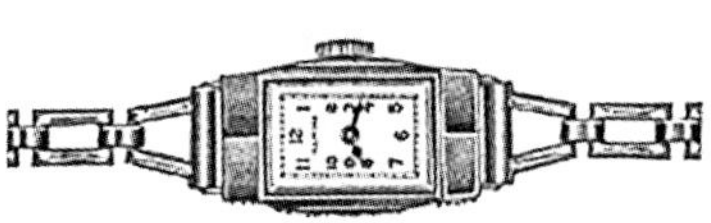

JANETTE.

No. 64W1. 15 jewels.................. **$50.50**
Consumer $47.50
Beautifully designed case of white filled gold with bracelet to match. Conservative, yet smart and tastefully appointed.

ANNETTE.

No. 64W2. 17 jewels.................. **$66.00**
Consumer $66.00
Gracefully engraved case of 14 karat white filled gold with bracelet of the same quality. Very attractive ensemble.

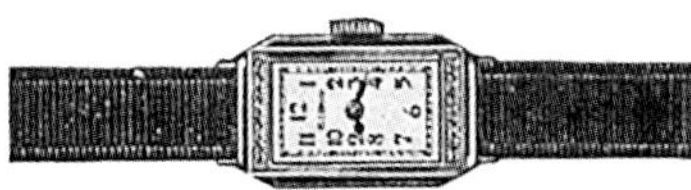

JULIETTE.

No. 64W3. 17 jewels.................. **$57.30**
Consumer $52.50
One of the latest creations by Illinois. Case is of 14 karat white or natural filled gold.

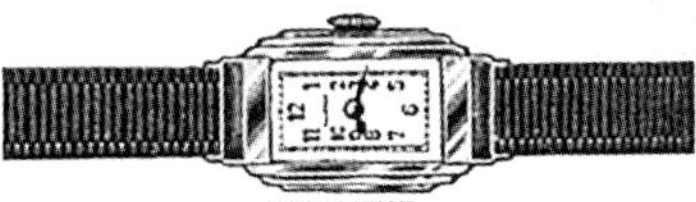

SUZETTE.

No. 64W4. 17 jewels.................. **$53.20**
Consumer $47.50
This 14 karat white filled gold model case is of original design and daintily small.

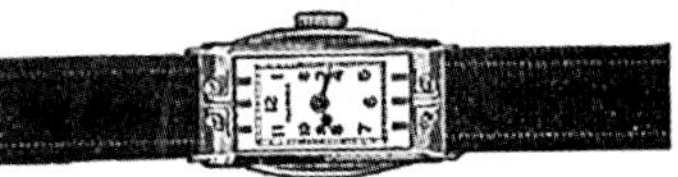

COQUETTE.

No. 64W5. 17 jewels.................. **$57.30**
Consumer $52.50
Model that has tremendous acceptance. The case is 14 karat white filled gold.

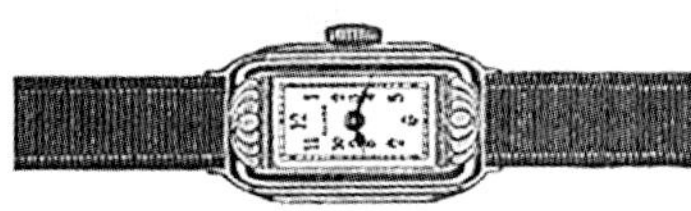

LYNETTE.

No. 64W6. 15 jewels.................. **$46.00**
Consumer $40.00
New low price for a quality watch such as the Illinois. 14 karat white filled gold.

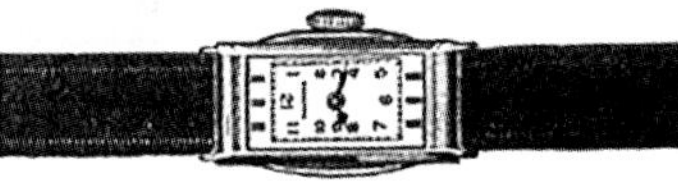

FLORETTE.

No. 64W7. 15 jewels.................. **$47.60**
Consumer $42.50
Conservatively neat and chic is this model available in 14k white or natural filled gold.

BABETTE.

No. 64W8. 15 jewels.................. **$51.90**
Consumer $50.00
14 karat solid white gold case of exquisite beauty. A watch of value and character.

MUZETTE.

No. 64W9. 17 jewels.................. **$58.50**
Consumer $55.00
14 karat white filled gold case with silk cord bracelet. Refinements of good artistry.

GREAT AMERICAN WATCHES.

The Illinois Watches shown on this page are 21/0 size (less than 5½ ligne). The movements are daintily small and constructed in such proportion to assure dependable timekeeping.

ROSETTE.

No. 64W10. 17 jewels.................. **$58.50**
Consumer $55.00
14 karat white filled gold case, with like quality bracelet giving pleasing ensemble.

64

Some Baguette Illinois watches advertised by Joan Crawford in 1933

Unisex Models

Not covered in the ladies' Illinois Identification Guide are the watches that Illinois at some point marketed to both sexes. (These may be some of the first unisex commercial products ever offered in the United States market.) These models are the Biltmore 18/0, Sangamon, Tuxedo and Urbana strap watches and the Caprice purse or desk watch. See Chapter 9, the men's Illinois Identification Guide, for information on them.

Two of the 18/0 size unisex wristwatches, the Sangamon and the Urbana, were also advertised for sale in conjunction with the eight baguette models issued in 1934.

The Rarest Ladies' Illinois

Name	Known to Exist
Argyle/Arlene with enameled bezel	1
Daytona 155A	1
Glenna 186	1
Miami 157A	1
Babette II	1
Saratoga Leaf	1
Antoinette	2
Daytona 155B	2
No. 241	2
Berkeley 154A	2
Sherwood	2
Mary Todd GG	3
Mary Todd 204	4
Daytona 155	4
Lenox	4

The Most Popular Ladies' Illinois

Ranking	Name
1	Coronado
2	Berkeley 154
3	Del Monte 157
4	Berkeley 153
5	Miami 157
6	Del Monte 155
7	Brighton
8	Mary Todd 203
9	Redonda 153
10	Redonda 154

Identity Remaining Unknown

Identity Remaining Unknown
Co-Ed*
Graduate*
Latonia*
Mayflower*
Pearl*
Priscilla*
Rhea**
Rose**
Ruth**

*18/0 Size
**21/0 Size

Caveat Emptor: Advice for the Buyer

Do not confuse the Illinois Watch Case Company (IWCCo) with the Illinois Watch Company. An Illinois Watch Case Company case does not make it an Illinois wristwatch. These were two different companies; the IWCCo made cases for watches, not the watches themselves.

If you are planning to buy an Illinois ladies' wristwatch, you also need to keep in mind that for its ladies' models the Illinois Watch Company:

- Did not use cabochon crowns.
- Did not use stainless steel backs for the cases.*
- Did not use base metal cases.*
- Did not use rolled-gold plate cases.
- Did not offer cases in rose gold.

*The Hamilton-Illinois line of the mid-1950s included a number of ladies' models with stainless steel backs and one model in an all-stainless case.

Ladies' Identification Guide

The guide that follows identifies all recognized ladies' Illinois wrist watch models and provides an entry for each, in alphabetical order. For models that may have been given more than one name, entries are provided for all of them, with a cross-reference to the primary model, where you will find full information.

At the beginning of each full entry is a list of the principal details to consider regarding that particular model. For interpreting the list, please refer to the key provided in "Introduction to the Guides," which appears at the beginning of Volume 3. That introduction also includes other information of interest to the collector.

Since Illinois had a rich and varied selection of ladies' models, there are many way to approach beginning a collection.

Alouette / Babette I / Babette II

Names = Alouette, Babette I, Babette II
Time Period = Moderne
Karat/Material = 14K WG (Alouette, Babette I), 14K WG, YG (Babette II)
Bezel = Engraved (Alouette, Babette I), Partially Engraved (Babette II)
Sides = Engraved
Lug Size = 8mm
Spring Bar = Fixed Lugs
Casemaker = Keystone (Alouette and Babette I); Star (Babette II)
Case Pieces = 2
Case Number = 704 (Alouette and Babette I), 714 (Babette II)
Case Back = Plain
Dimensions = 14 x 23mm
Durability = 🕓🕓🕓🕓
Movement Size = 21/0
Movement Grade/Jewels = 107/17, 105/15
Dial Number = 8122
Dial = Silver Finish
Dial Opening = Rectangular
Numerals = Painted
Hands = Steel
Seconds at = None
Cased in Factory = Yes

Alouette, white gold

Babette I, white gold

Collectibility = ◷◷◷◷ Alouette
◷◷◷◷◷◷◷ Babette I, Babette II
Rarity = ◷◷◷◷
Retail Price New = Alouette, $65.00 (17J); Babette I, $50.00 (15J); Babette II, $50.00 (17J)
Introduction Date = 1932 (Alouette); 1933 (Babette I); 1934 (Babette II)
Unique Case Design = No (Alouette, Babette I); Yes (Babette II)
Unique Dial Design = No
Advertisement = Yes
Marketing Themes = "Exquisite beauty" (Alouette)
"A watch of value and character"(Alouette)
"Chic engraving" (Babette I)
"Attractively engraved" (Babette II)

The Alouette, shown in the Spring 1932 Illinois Sales Catalog, is one of the tiny wristwatches known as baguettes or semi-baguettes that were in vogue during the 1930s. Its dainty case, Model No. 704, is solid gold and features delicate engraving along the top edge of the stepped sides of its bezel and an elegant engraved motif ornamenting the center of the bezel surfaces at the top and bottom of the dial. The Illinois Century of Progress Spring 1932 Sales Catalog advertised this model as one of "Exquisite beauty. A watch of value and character."

Babette II, yellow gold

BABETTE

"BABETTE" $50.00 SERIES

Pictured at left

21/0 Size Semi-Baguette
14K Solid White or Natural Yellow Gold Case

17-Jewel ILLINOIS MOVEMENT with "Elinvar" Hairspring

A most exquisite dainty size and style, enriched with artistically hand engraved ends. Embodied in construction is the finest of skilled workmanship, to insure the utmost of service and personal satisfaction.

Case and clasp are 14K solid gold, with choice of White or the ever increasing popular Natural yellow color. Highest quality silk ribbon.

Fitted with a 17-Jewel ILLINOIS movement, featured with "Elinvar" hairspring. Cased and timed at factory and encased in a lovely gift box, as shown above.

No. 9001 14K Solid White Gold, Each $57.60

No. 9002 14K Solid Natural Yellow Gold, Each...........$57.60

Babette II, Fort Dearborn 1935 catalog

Although the Alouette shares this case model with its sister, the Babette I, the Alouette was equipped with a 17-jewel movement, whereas the Babette I (introduced a year later, in 1933) had a 15-jewel one. Both came with ribbon bands. The Alouette and Babette I share not only the same case but also the same dial.

In the 1934 catalog, there is a Babette listed along with seven other "Baguette Style" models (the Antoinette, Débette, Janette, Lynette, Mariette, Marionette and Marlette), all with Elinvar hairsprings in their movements. However, this model, though called a Babette, differs in many respects from the 1933 model. Accordingly, we are here designating them Babette I and Babette II to distinguish them. Until very recently, the differences between the two Babettes had not been noted.

Only now has a specimen of the Babette II been found; it is 14K yellow gold and still has its original ribbon band with 14K Hadley clasp. Moreover, it has a sparkle dial.

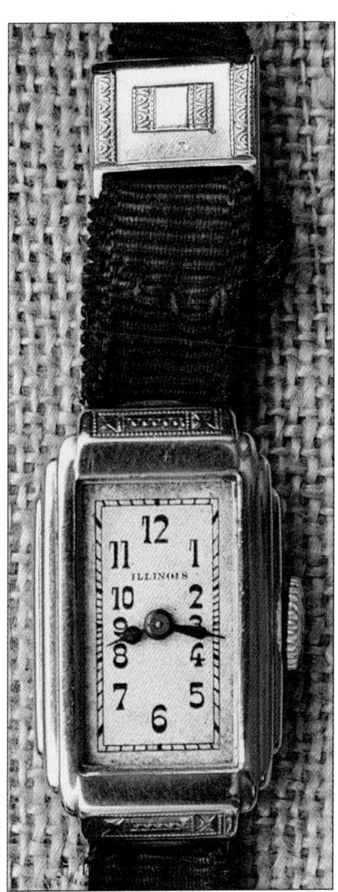

Babette II with original ribbon band and 14K Hadley clasp

Babette II case back

Babette II inside case back

The Babette I had a 15-jewel movement, but the Babette II came with a 17-jewel movement equipped with an Elinvar hair-spring. The case of the Babette II had a mostly plain bezel, with only a small band of engraving above the lugs, none down the sides, and much more pronounced steps. Moreover, the case of the Babette II was offered in 14K natural gold as well as white gold, whereas the Babette I was offered only in white gold. Both Babettes came with a ribbon band.

BABETTE

14 Karat solid white gold case with chic engraving. 15 jewels. (21/0 size.)

$50.00

Babette I, Illinois 1933 Sales Catalog

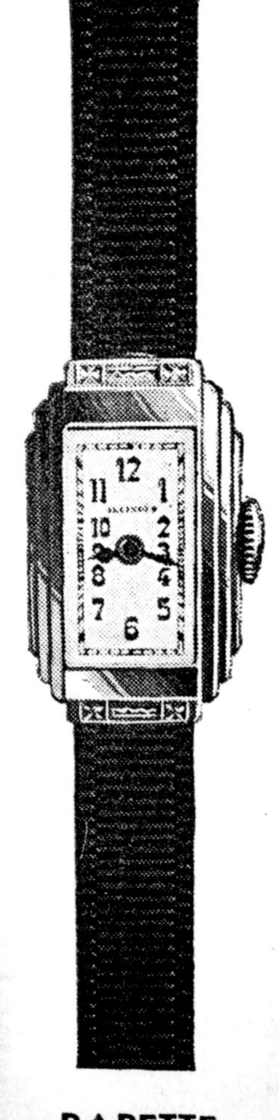

BABETTE

14K solid gold; white or natural. Attractively engraved. 17 jewels. Consumer, **$50.00.** Keystone list, **$50.00.**

Babette II, Illinois 1934 Sales Catalog

Illinois Sales Catalog, 1933

Baguette Style

WRIST WATCHES OF CHARM AND PRECISION

with Elinvar hairsprings

Accuracy, style and value distinguish these fine 21/o size Semi-Baguette watches. They have 15 and 17-jewel movements and are available in filled or 14 Karat solid gold cases.

Shown above in display box: JANETTE. Brilliantly modern wrist model in 10K filled gold; white or natural. Specially designed filled gold bracelet. 15 jewels. Consumer, **$40.00.**

BABETTE
14K solid gold; white or natural. Attractively engraved. 17 jewels. Consumer, **$50.00.**

DÉBETTE
14K filled gold; white or natural. Richly engraved. With bracelet to match. 17 jewels. Consumer, **$47.50.**

MARLETTE
14K filled gold; white or natural. Smartly engraved. 17 jewels. Consumer, **$42.50.**

MARIETTE
14K filled gold; white or natural. Modern design. 17 jewels. Consumer, **$42.50.**

LYNETTE
10K filled gold; white or natural. With new filled gold bracelet. 15 jewels. Consumer, **$40.00.**

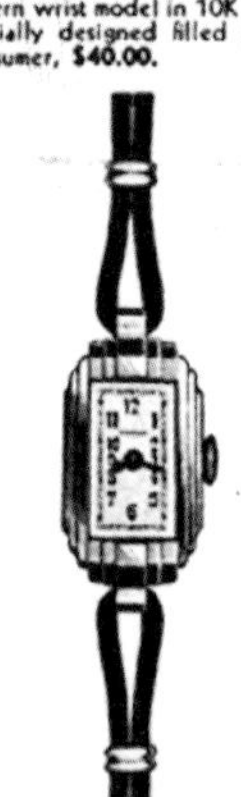

MARIONETTE
14K filled gold; white **only.** With silk cord and filled gold attachments. 15 jewels. Consumer, **$35.00.**

ANTOINETTE
Attractive new model in 10K filled gold; white or natural. 15 jewels. Consumer, **$32.50.**

ELINVAR

is a rustless nickel-steel alloy which is now used in the hairsprings of Illinois watches. Its use reduces the effect of magnetism and temperature changes to a minimum—thus assuring a constant rate under all conditions.

SANGAMON. Modish new sport leather strap model. In white **only,** with case of Sangamo metal—which is practically indestructible. Raised figure dial. 18/o size. 15 jewels. Consumer, **$25.00.**

MODERNE WRIST WATCHES

Sturdily constructed 18/o size timepieces for men or women. 15 jewels only. Elinvar equipped. These models meet the demand for a stylish wrist watch with clearly visible dials.

URBANA. Plain, modern design in brightly polished 10K filled gold; natural **only,** with leather strap; this watch particularly adapted to the use of leather cord attachment. Raised figure dial. 15 jewels. Consumer, **$32.50.**

PIONEERS OF GREATER VALUES

Illinois Sales Catalog, 1934

LOUETTE?

The name Louette for a model appears on one official Illinois list and is on one Hamilton list. Both lists contain some errors. It is possible the name is a typographical error for the Alouette's name, as no further documentation has been found for the Louette.

Annette

See listing for **Charmette/ Annette/Florette**

Antoinette

Name = Antoinette
Time Period = Moderne
Karat/Material = 10K WGF, 10K YGF
Bezel = Plain
Sides = Engraved
Lug Size = 8mm
Spring Bar = Fixed Lugs
Casemaker = Keystone
Case Pieces = 2
Case Number = 703, No Number
Case Back = Plain
Dimensions = 14 x 26mm
Durability = 🕒🕒🕒
Movement Size = 21/0
Movement Grade/Jewels = 105/15
Dial Number = 8500, 8732 (both by Hamilton)
Dial = Silver Finish
Dial Opening = Rectangular
Numerals = Flush Gold
Hands = Steel
Seconds at = None
Cased in Factory = Yes, by Hamilton in Lancaster
Collectibility = 🕒🕒🕒🕒
Rarity = 🕒🕒🕒🕒🕒🕒🕒

Antoinette, 10K white gold-filled

Antoinette, 10K white gold-filled custom watch

Retail Price New = $32.50 (15J); unknown, diamond variant
Introduction Date = 1934
Unique Case Design = Yes
Unique Dial Design = Yes
Advertisement = Yes
Marketing Theme = "Attractive new model"

The Antoinette has proved to be one of Illinois' most elusive models. For years, no specimen of the watch could be located, and its existence was documented only by catalogs, dial drawings and an outer cardboard box. Accordingly, we are excited that an Antoinette has recently been found. As yet, this is the only known example of the model as originally issued. (To add to the excitement: A diamond-set watch earlier thought to be a variant of another Illinois model has been identified as a rare, apparently custom order of the Antoinette.)

Antoinette case back

Antoinette inside case back

The Antoinette was shown along with seven other 21/0 size models (the Babette II, Débette, Janette, Lynette, Mariette, Marionette and Marlette) on a page in the 1934 Illinois Sales Catalog advertising these "Baguette Style" models as "wrist watches of charm and precision."

That catalog, the last ever issued for Illinois, was the company's only one in which the Antoinette appeared. Illinois made at least seventeen ladies' wristwatches that came in a yellow gold-filled case, and it was first thought that the Antoinette was one of these. However, the 1934 catalog indicates that it was actually available in a 10K gold-filled case of either white or yellow. The 15-jewel 21/0 size movement was equipped with an Elinvar hairspring.

The listing there does not mention the type of band, but the 1934 May & Malone catalog says it was a ribbon band. Moreover, images of the watch there and in the H. M. Manheim 1934 catalog actually show the ribbed pattern of grosgrain ribbon.

ILLINOIS "ANTOINETTE"

No. E416 Ladies, 21/0 Size, 10K White or Yellow Gold Filled, Plain Case, 15 Jewel Illinois Movement.

List Price
$45.50

Retail Price
$32.50

H. M. Manheim catalog, 1934

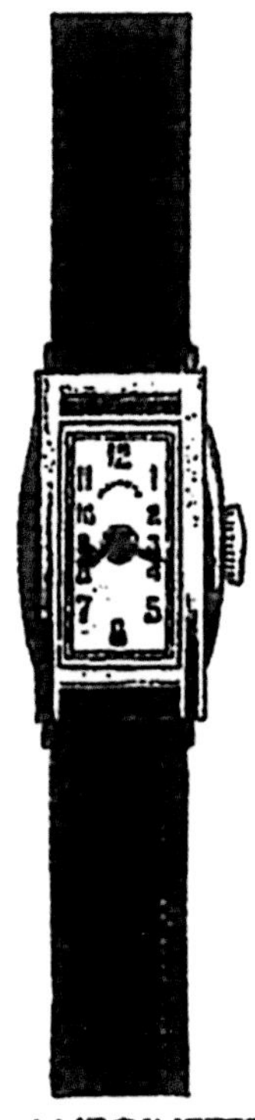

ANTOINETTE

"ANTOINETTE" $32.50 SERIES

Pictured at left

21/0 Size Semi-Baguette
10K White or Natural Yellow
Gold Filled Case

15-Jewel ILLINOIS Movement
with "Elinvar" Hairspring

If you are seeking a quality wat at a very low price, consider th charming number. It is of fine manufacture, accurate in its tim keeping performance, and is pric unusually low in this important se ing.

Perfectly plain design case, fi nished with choice of 10K White Natural Yellow Gold Filled, wi clasp to match. Highest quality ribbon.

Fitted with 15-Jewel ILLINO movement, featured with "Elinva hairspring. Cased and timed at fa tory and prepared in a lovely g case.

No. 9010 White Gold Filled. Each .... $43.

No. 9011 Natural Yellow Gold Filled. Each .... $43.

Fort Dearborn catalog, 1935

Most of the 21/0 size models apparently had dials with black painted numerals, but the Antoinette was issued a special dial with flush gold numerals.

Antoinette's dial with flush gold numerals

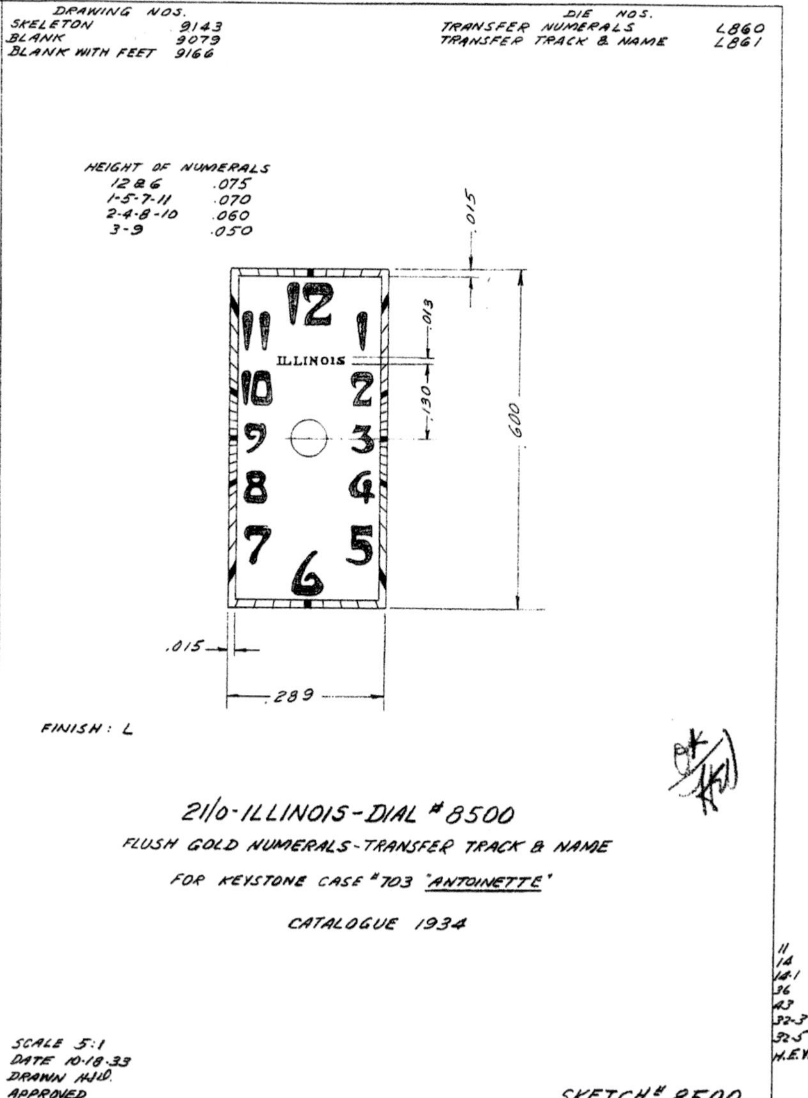

Hamilton dial drawing for an Illinois Antoinette, October 18, 1933

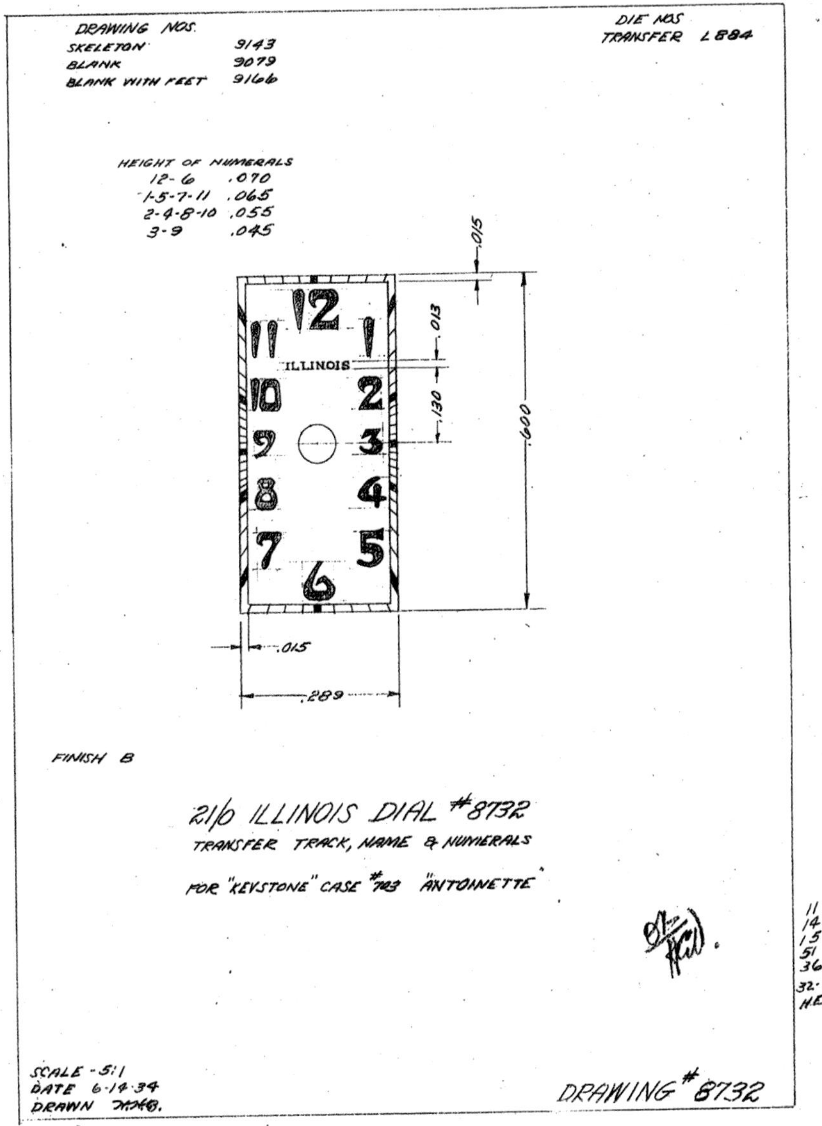

Hamilton dial drawing for an Illinois Antoinette, June 14, 1934

It was the case metal that allowed us finally to identify the rare diamond-set variant of the Antoinette. It was earlier thought to be a rare variant of a Florette, but that model came only in 14K GF, and this watch was in a 10K WGF case. Embellished with six diamonds, its Keystone case has no case Model No. We think it was likely a custom order. The movement is 15 jewels, as was advertised for the basic Antoinette model, but the custom version has a different dial.

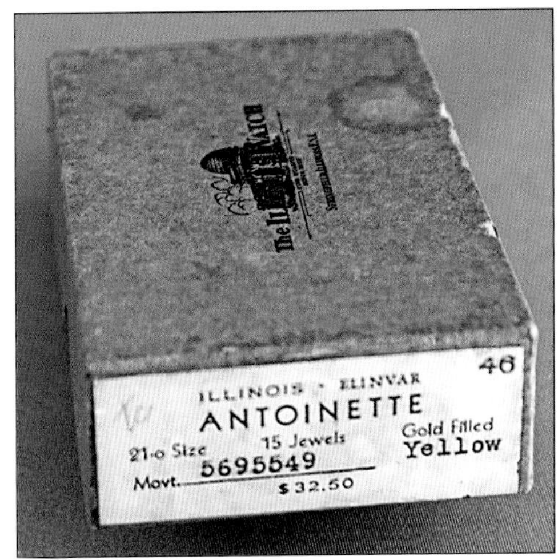

Antoinette's original outer cardboard box

Since a number of the 21/0 models are quite similar in appearance, they can be easily confused. See, for example, the listings for the 14K GF Charmette/Annette/Florette trio, (case Model No. 703), and the 14K GF Coquette (case Model No. 702). From the outside, the Antoinette looks just like some of these. Looking inside its case, however, reveals that although the Antoinette is in case Model No. 703, the case metal is 10K gold-filled rather than 14K gold-filled.

Argyle, white gold

Arlene, white gold

Argyle / Arlene

Names = Argyle/Arlene
Time Period = Moderne
Karat/Material = 14K WG, Black Inlaid Enamel (rare variant only)
Bezel = Plain, Engraved, Engraved/Enamel
Sides = Engraved
Lug Size = 11mm
Spring Bar = Fixed Lugs
Casemaker = Wadsworth
Case Pieces = 3
Case Number = 807-5
Case Back = Plain
Dimensions = 17 x 30mm
Durability = 🕒🕒🕒🕒
Movement Size = 18/0
Movement Grades/Jewels = 807/17, 805/15
Dial Numbers = 8195, 8346
Dial = Silver Finish, Butler Center
Dial Opening = Rectangular
Numerals = Painted
Hands = Steel
Seconds at = None
Cased in Factory = Yes
Collectibility = 🕒🕒🕒🕒
Rarity = 🕒🕒🕒🕒
🕒🕒🕒🕒🕒🕒🕒 with Black Enamel
Retail Price New = Argyle, $60.00 (17J); Arlene, $42.50 (15J)
Introduction Date = 1930 (Argyle); 1933 (Arlene)
Unique Case Design = No (Plain); Yes (Engraved)
Unique Dial Design = No
Advertisement = Yes
Marketing Themes = "Exquisite simplicity"
"Timely in the spirit of its design"
"Exquisite modernism, beautifully interpreted"
"Beautiful lap-finished case" (Arlene)

The Argyle and the Arlene, two of Illinois' ladies' watches in solid gold, are easily confused because they share one of the case options. The Argyle was offered with a case having either a plain bezel or an engraved one. (The Argyle pictured with the inlaid black enamel accents around the bezel is the only one known to exist.) The Arlene, however, came only with a plain bezel.

The Argyle shared the same dials with the Gloria and Vardon models. The Arlene had a similar dial, but with a butler center (though it is sometimes found with one of the Argyle's dials). Another difference between the two models was that the Argyle's movement was 17 jewels and the Arlene's 15 jewels. Both models, however, came with ribbon bands.

The Argyle appeared in the 1930–31 Illinois Sales Catalog and was shown along with the Caprice, Fairport, Glencoe, Roslyn, and Vanity Fair models in the December 6, 1930 issue of the *Saturday Evening Post*.

The 1930–31 Illinois Sales Catalog pictured the version of the Argyle with the plain bezel. The 1932 Illinois Spring Catalog, however, showed it with the engraved bezel, perhaps because the Arlene, which had only a plain bezel option, was to be introduced the very next year in the 1933 Illinois Pioneers of Greater Values catalog.

Argyle, white gold and black inlaid enamel; only one known to exist

FORM

September 12, 1932.

Gentlemen:

Today we are making shipment to you of one each complete watch of the following models:-

Pimlico	Wentworth
Rosette	Arlene
Lynette	Suzette
Irene	Florette

These watches are all new items going into the line, and you will find them illustrated in the proofs of catalog pages which you received from us a few days ago. Also, they appear on our new price list effective September 10th.

In view of the fact that you have not provided yourself with our Standard Sample Line, we feel that our supplying at this time samples of the complete watchesof the new models to be used in soliciting business from your customers would be of advantage.

We feel sure that you will be well pleased with these new numbers which go to make up the Illinois Watch Fall showing, and we shall greatly appreciate having your order for a quantity of these new models that you will require for stock.

With best wishes for a considerably increased business during the remainder of 1932, we are

Very truly yours,

THE ILLINOIS WATCH

AGS:ALD

By -

Sent to: E. H. Saxton.
A. Walker - exception Pimlico, Irene, Rosette.
I. Michaels.
H. Freund
M. Rosenbloom
King & Eisele
M. Sickles
Kolb
Sproehnle
Barnstone-Osgood.
L. Sickles.

Illinois Sales Department letter dated September 12, 1932, introducing the Arlene, among other models

Argyle's outer cardboard box and original price card

End of Argyle's outer cardboard box

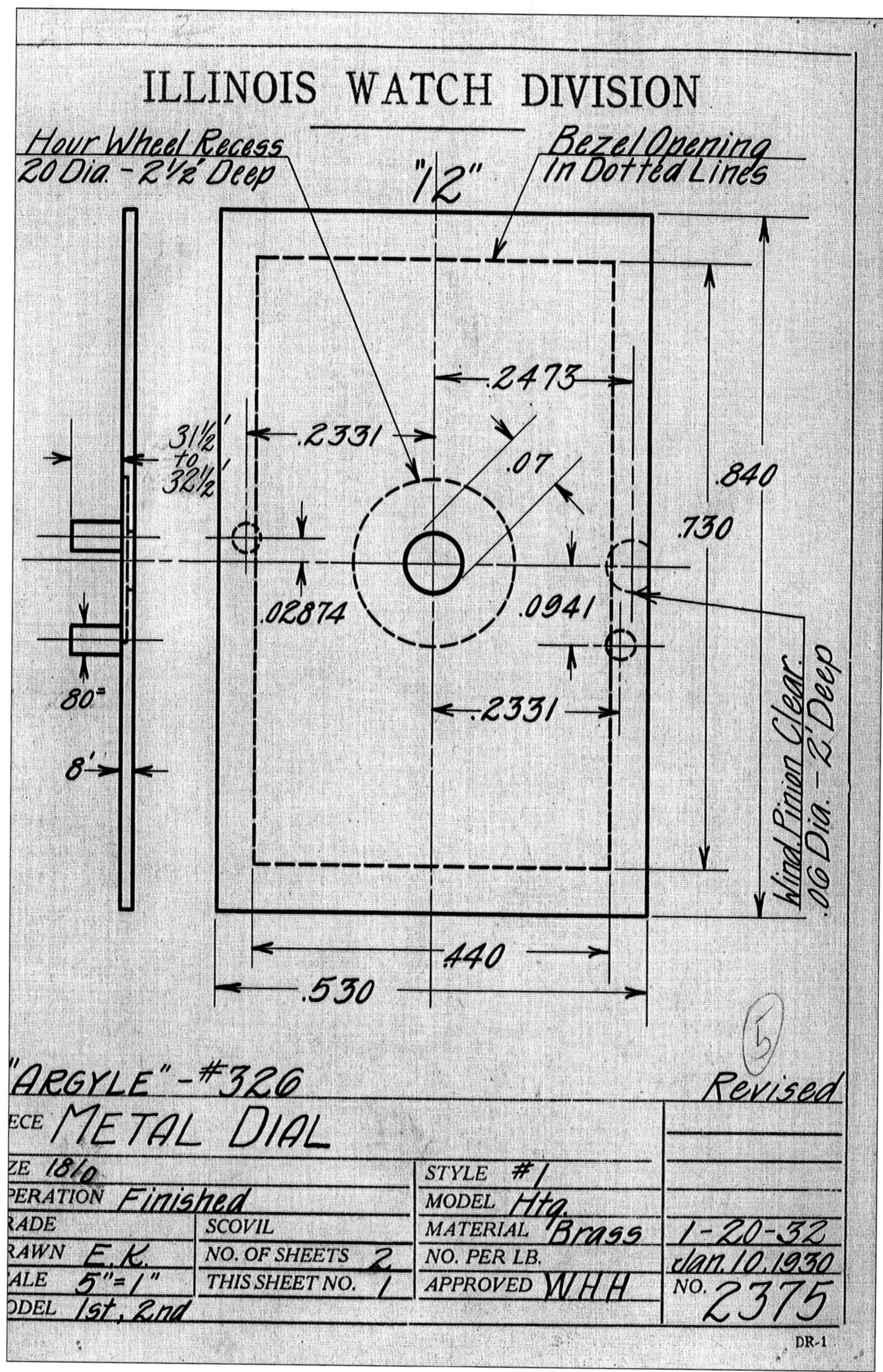

Blueprint for Argyle's dial blank

Avalon

Avalon, white gold; sterling silver Flückiger dial

Name = Avalon
Time Period = Deco
Karat/Material = 14K WG
Bezel = Plain
Sides = Engraved
Lug Size = 16mm
Spring Bar = Fixed Lugs
Casemaker = Keystone
Case Pieces = 3
Case Number = 205
Case Back = Plain
Dimensions = 17 x 31mm
Durability = 🕒🕒🕒🕒
Movement Size = 18/0
Movement Grade/Jewels = 807/17
Dial Numbers = 8191, 8192
Dial = Silver Finish, Butler Center; Silver Finish; Sterling Silver
Dial Opening = Rectangular
Numerals = Painted, Etched
Hands = Steel
Seconds at = None
Cased in Factory = Yes
Collectibility = 🕒🕒🕒🕒
Rarity = 🕒🕒🕒🕒🕒
Retail Price New = $65.00
Introduction Date = 1930
Unique Case Design = Yes
Unique Dial Design = No
Advertisement = Yes
Marketing Themes = "Refinement and beauty"
"Rectangular watch of simplicity"

We Sell Standard Quality Merchandise Only 41

THE ILLINOIS WATCH

Solid Gold Illinois Ribbon Watches

Correctly Styled » » 17 Jewels

Encased in 14K solid gold and constructed by master metal craftsmen, these 18/0 size watches are more than timepieces — they are articles of personal adornment.

The ARGYLE
Timely in the spirit of its design this dainty ribbon watch is proving exceedingly popular.
Suggested consumer price, $60.

The BRIGHTON
Delightful refinements are represented in this oval watch. The engraved case is inlaid with black enamel.
Suggested consumer price, $65.

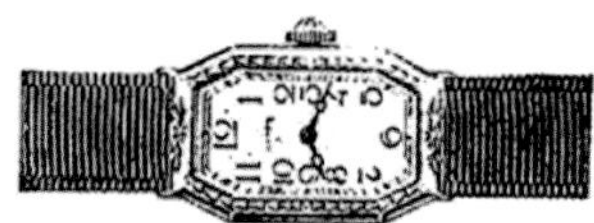

The NARRAGANSETT
Simplicity in design creates wide acceptance for this watch.
Suggested consumer price, $65.

The MARY TODD
A watch of rare beauty, cased in 18K solid gold. Offered in plain, engraved or inlaid enamel cases.
Suggested consumer price, $75.

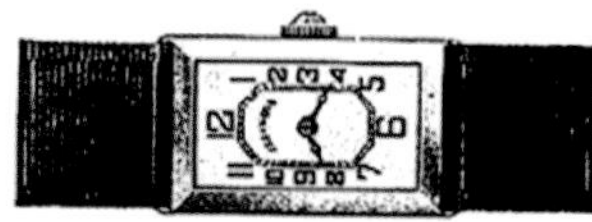

The AVALON
There is refinement and beauty in this rectangular watch of simplicity.
Suggested consumer price, $65.

The BAR HARBOR
Richly engraved and in excellent good taste.
Suggested consumer price, $65.

The GLENCOE
The gracefully engraved design of this watch gives it a lovely individuality. 14K natural solid gold and also available in a beautifully plain case.
Suggested consumer price, $60.

The CORONADO
A beautiful blend of white gold and inlaid jet black enamel.
Suggested consumer price, $65.

The LENOX—The BILOXI
Of conservative design, yet pleasingly attractive. The Lenox is 14K white or natural gold. The Biloxi is 14K filled white gold.
Suggested consumer prices, Lenox $65, Biloxi $50.

Ribbon Watches in 14K Filled Gold

Each of these 18/0 size ribbon watches have 17 jewels. All are beautifully designed and form a complete line for the customer's selection.

The MIAMI
A pleasing combination of inlaid blue enamel and lined white gold surface.
Suggested consumer price, $55.
Additional enamel watches available for your selection.

The BERKSHIRE
Perfect harmony of case and dial design make this a very feminine watch.
Suggested consumer price, $50.

The NEWPORT
Delicately engraved in a striking manner.
Suggested consumer price, $50.

The FAIRPORT
This watch is entirely feminine in appearance. The oval dial adds a charming touch.
Suggested consumer price, $50.

The ROSLYN
A new Illinois with gay touches of black inlaid enamel. This dainty timepiece will have a definite appeal to those who appreciate style correctness.
Suggested consumer price, $55.

The EDGEWATER
A pleasing design of bright polished surfaces and fine engraving.
Suggested consumer price, $50.

A GREAT AMERICAN WATCH SINCE 1870

Consumers' prices only on this page—for list prices see page 42

A. C. Becken catalog, 1931

The Avalon is another of the at least thirty Factory-Cased solid gold Illinois ladies' models that the company issued (not counting the Diamond-Set Models), significantly more than they offered for sale on the men's side. Larger and more solid-looking than the other Illinois ladies' wristwatches, the Avalon has a remarkably plain case, but elegant in its simplicity. It came with a ribbon band. Gay reports that the Avalon is a difficult model to find.

The striking dials used with the Avalon are beautifully set off by the austere design of the case. Most of these dials are shared with the Berkshire model. One features a butler center and an oval ring containing the dial numbers. Another has Roman numerals arranged radially (No. 8192). Yet another has a silver finish with a butler center and etched numerals (No. 8191). In addition, there is a dial with interesting black numerals and the celebrated Illinois sparkle finish. There is also a dial with attractive deco-style numerals that could be used with the Biltmore 18/0 model as well. Very unusual is the design of the sterling silver Flückiger dial, which has pinstriping and a delicate engraved ornament along with a butler center (dial number unknown, but this is the rectangular version of the octagonal dial No. 8154). A rarity: One gold butler center Avalon dial with etched gold numerals, as shown here.

Avalon, deco-style numerals

Avalon, gold butler center dial

The Avalon, along with the Fairport and Miami 155, was advertised by Illinois in the January 11, 1930 issue of *Collier's*. In that advertisement the Avalon is sporting the attractive pinstriped Flückiger dial.

See listing for **Constance/Barbara**

Bar Harbor 156, white gold

Bar Harbor 156

Name = Bar Harbor 156
Time Period = Deco
Karat/Material = 14K WG
Bezel = Engraved
Sides = Engraved
Lug Size = 11mm
Spring Bar = Fixed Lugs
Casemaker = Wadsworth
Case Pieces = 3
Case Number = 156
Case Back = Engraved
Dimensions = 17 x 31mm
Durability = 🕒🕒🕒🕒
Movement Size = 18/0
Movement Grade/Jewels = 807/17
Dial Numbers = 8169, 8170, 8364
Dial = Silver Finish, White Sparkle Finish, Silver Finish
Dial Opening = Short Rectangular
Numerals = Painted
Hands = Steel
Seconds at = None
Cased in Factory = Yes
Collectibility = 🕒🕒🕒🕒
Rarity = 🕒🕒🕒🕒
Retail Price New = $65.00 (17J)
Introduction Date = 1929
Unique Case Design = Yes
Unique Dial Design = No
Advertisement = Yes
Marketing Themes: "The good taste of its design"
"Richly engraved and in excellent good taste"

BAR HARBOR

17-jewel Illinois, 18/0 size 14k solid white gold case.
No. 380 White....................$70.00
Consumer price, $65.00.

A. C. Becken catalog, 1931

The Bar Harbor 156 was one of the at least thirty solid gold ladies' Illinois Factory-Cased wristwatches, not counting the Diamond-Set Models. It was listed with its picture in the 1929–30 Illinois sales catalog. This model came only in white gold and was equipped with a 17-jewel movement. It was issued with a ribbon band.

The advertisement for the Bar Harbor 156 called it "a richly engraved model notable for the good taste of its design and the high standard of its accuracy." The elaborately engraved bezel of the Bar Harbor 156 is indeed very attractive: fan-like patterns decorate the top and bottom of the bezel, and centered between each pair of "fans" is an ornament extending into an area of plain surface.

In addition to the dials noted above, the Bar Harbor 156 came with an interesting dial with exploding numerals, similar to dial No. 86 in the Illinois Dial and Hand Circular, May 1927, but without the embellishment at the center.

Gay notes that the Bar Harbor 156 is easier to find than the more elusive Bar Harbor 158.

Bar Harbor 156 in its display case, with its original price card

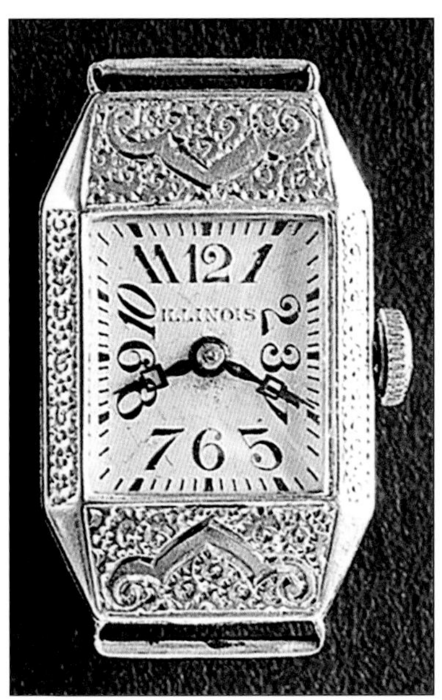

Bar Harbor 158, white gold

Bar Harbor 158

Name = Bar Harbor 158
Time Period = Deco
Karat/Material = 14K WG
Bezel = Engraved
Sides = Engraved
Lug Size = 11mm
Spring Bar = Fixed Lugs
Casemaker = Wadsworth
Case Pieces = 3
Case Number = 158
Case Back = Engraved
Dimensions = 17 x 31mm
Durability = Excellent
Movement Size = 18/0
Movement Grade/Jewels = 807/17
Dial Numbers = 8169, 8170, 8364
Dial = Silver Finish, Sparkle Finish
Dial Opening = Short Rectangular
Numerals = Painted
Hands = Steel
Seconds at = None
Cased in Factory = Yes
Collectibility = 🕒🕒🕒🕒
Rarity = 🕒🕒🕒🕒🕒
Retail Price New = $65.00 (17J)
Introduction Date = 1930
Unique Case Design = Yes
Unique Dial Design = No
Advertisement = Yes
Marketing Theme: "A richly engraved model"

The Bar Harbor 158 is yet another of the at least thirty solid gold ladies' Factory-Cased Illinois wristwatches (not counting the Diamond-Set Models). Its case came only in white gold, it was equipped with a 17-jewel movement and it was issued with a ribbon band.

The intricately engraved bezel of the Bar Harbor 158 is even more elaborate and eye-catching than that of the Bar Harbor 156. Except for the narrow triangular areas at the four corners and a delicate ribbon-like motif in the midst of the engraving at the top and bottom of the bezel, there is little that is unornamented.

In addition to the dials noted above, the Bar Harbor 158 as well as the Bar Harbor 156 came with an interesting dial with exploding numerals, similar to dial No. 86 in the Illinois Dial and Hand Circular, May 1927, but without the embellishment at the center.

In the September 28, 1930 issue of *Saturday Evening Post*, the Bar Harbor 158 was called "a richly engraved model notable alike for the good taste of its design and the high standard of its accuracy. A beautiful 14K, white solid gold case fitted with a 17-jeweled Illinois quality movement, $65.00."

The bezels of the two models have quite different engraving patterns, but strangely enough, Illinois advertisements described them exactly the same way, as Gay notes. He says that the Bar Harbor 158 is far more difficult to locate than the Bar Harbor 156.

Page 168 — The KEYSTONE — November, 1928

Creations for Milady—By Illinois

TO meet the demand for a high-grade ladies' watch, to sell from fifty to seventy-five dollars, Illinois has produced a complete line of rare and beautiful models. The cases are inlaid with enamel in a dainty and refreshing variety of colors, and are especially artistic in appearance, beauty and refinement. In planning a model for the wrist of Miss America, the Illinois Watch called in the best artists in case design, the results are shown by the illustrations on this page. The fine 17 jewel movement is a further tribute to the name Illinois and insures Milady of dependable time.

The NEWPORT. Delicately engraved 14K white gold filled case with full opening. $50.

The EDGEWATER. The delicate grace of its engraving gives this 14K white gold filled model a charm of its own. $50.

The BERKELEY. A delicate tracery of design in dark red and black hard enamel inlaid in a 14K white gold filled case. $55.

The REDONDA. Inlaid in its beautiful 14K gold filled case is a design in jet black and soft light green enamel. $55.

The MIAMI. The happy combination of warm red and black enamel inlaid in its 14K white gold filled case makes this model a favorite. $55.

The DEL MONTE. Soft, light green and jet black inlaid enamel form a charming tracery of design against its rich 14K white gold filled case. $55.

The BAR HARBOR. A richly engraved model notable alike for the good taste of its design and the high standard of its accuracy. $65.

The LONG BEACH. A charming watch rich in design, delicately engraved 14K gold filled case with octagonal opening. $50. Also in 14K solid gold. $65.

Men's Exclusive Straps

FOR THE MAN WHO CARES

The Marquis-Strap

This beautiful new and attractive model possesses an individuality characteristic of the Illinois Marquis-Autocrat pocket watch, a watch of comfort, as the 14K gold-filled case conforms to the arc of the wrist.

The Mate

The Illinois Mate centers the family of Illinois factory cased watches to supply a definite demand for a high grade, dependable, durable strap model at a moderate price. It is a watch for the man of action who demands accuracy under all conditions no matter what vocation or occupation.

The Consul

6/0 Size—19 Jewels

The Consul takes its place in the Illinois line as a watch for the man of affairs. The graceful contour of the case, the conservative engraving, the simplicity of which adds to the quiet dignity of the model makes the Consul all that the name implies. The dial is of new and special design, the figures are inlaid luminous over a soft mat background the center of which is sun rayed, a feature that adds to the charm of the complete watch.

H. A. OSGOOD & SON

15 MAIDEN LANE : : NEW YORK CITY

Keystone, November 1928

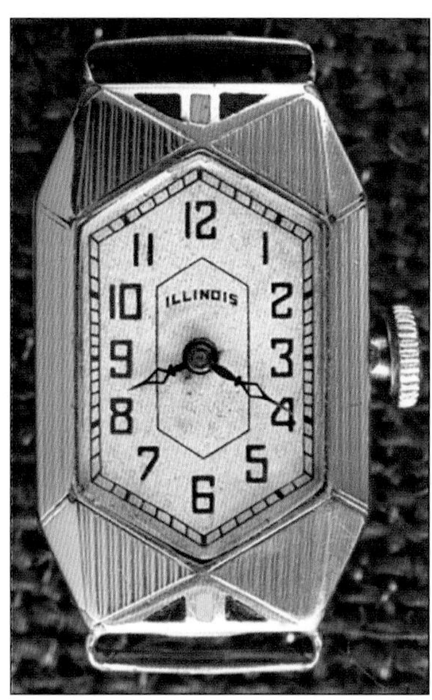

Berkeley 153, white gold-filled, green-and-black enamel

Berkeley 153

Name = Berkeley 153
Time Period = Deco
Karat/Material = 14K WGF, Green and Black Inlaid Enamel
Bezel = Engraved, with Enamel
Sides = Engraved
Lug Size = 11mm
Spring Bar = Fixed Lugs
Casemaker = Wadsworth
Case Pieces = 3
Case Number = 153
Case Back = Engraved
Dimensions = 17 x 31mm
Durability = ◷◷◷◷
Movement Size = 18/0
Movement Grade/Jewels = 807/17
Dial Number = 8147
Dial = Silver Finish, Butler Center; Sparkle Finish
Dial Opening = Hexagonal
Numerals = Painted
Hands = Steel
Seconds at = None
Cased in Factory = Yes
Collectibility = ◷◷◷◷
Rarity = ◷◷◷◷
Retail Price New = $55.00 (17J)
Introduction Date = 1929
Unique Case Design = Yes
Unique Dial Design = Yes
Advertisement = Yes
Marketing Theme = "A delicate tracery of design"

BERKELEY

17-jewel Illinois, 18/0 size 14k white gol filled case, enameled bezel.
No. 399 White.......................$55.0
Consumer price, $55.00.

A. C. Becken catalog, 1931

The Berkeley 153, with its striking inlaid green and black polished enamel, has a highly stylized deco design. Its 1929 advertisement adds emphasis to some of its other attributes: "A delicate tracery of design in green and black hard enamel inlaid in its 14K white gold-filled case and a six-sided opening for its beautiful dial are features of this charming model."

This is one of the highly collectible and sought-after enamel deco Illinois. Although this model is prone to minor corner wear, it can sometimes be located in excellent condition. The overall detailed design of the Berkeley 153 is fascinating. The butler center dial not only makes a pleasing contrast with the grooves on the bezel but also helps to bring out the highlights of the polished enamel. There was also a dial available with the unique Illinois white sparkle finish.

The Berkeley 153 was advertised in the July 27, 1929 issue of *Liberty,* along with the Edgewater 155, Mary Todd and Narragansett ladies' Illinois wristwatches. The men's watches in the advertisement were the Beau Brummell, Jolly Roger, Mate and Piccadilly.

July 27, 1929 — Liberty — 5

It's SMART to be RIGHT

AS YOU ALWAYS ARE WITH AN ILLINOIS WATCH

THE pulse of modern American life sets a rapid pace for smartness. It requires being right and looking right at all times.

This difficult standard is beautifully achieved in an Illinois Watch. Correct time and correct style—the beauty of accuracy, the charm of fashion—make Illinois the great American Watch it is today.

And now you can have this ideal smartness in some models for as little as $40.

Ask your jeweler to show you the new models in his line of Illinois Watches and ask his opinion of them. It's his business to know watches and he's known Illinois ever since he's been in business.

Let us send you, without obligation, our interesting illustrated booklet, "The Thrilling Beauty That Lies Within." Address The Illinois Watch, 1220 North Ninth St., Springfield, Ill.

The ILLINOIS WATCH

Established 1870

SPRINGFIELD, ILLINOIS

BEAUTY that is a timepiece

THE ILLINOIS BEAU BRUMMEL. *17 jewels, 14k gold-filled case, $50.*

THE ILLINOIS EDGEWATER. *17 jewels, engraved 14k gold-filled case, $50.*

THE ILLINOIS NARRAGANSETT. *17 jewels, 14k solid gold case, diamond engraving, $65.*

THE ILLINOIS MATE, *17 jewels, 14k gold-filled case, $42.50.*

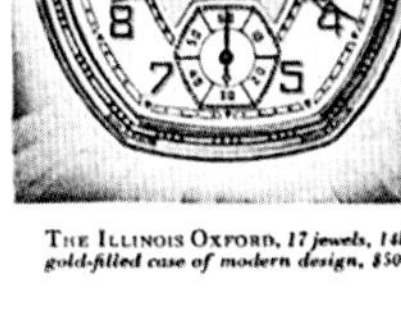

THE ILLINOIS PICCADILLY, *17 jewels, 14k gold-filled case, $45.*

THE ILLINOIS BERKELEY, *17 jewels, 14k gold-filled case, inlaid enamel, $55.*

THE ILLINOIS OXFORD, *17 jewels, 14k gold-filled case of modern design, $50.*

THE ILLINOIS MARY TODD, *17 jewels, 18k solid white gold case, $75.*

THE ILLINOIS JOLLY ROGER, *17 jewels, 14k gold-filled case, $42.50.*

MAKERS OF THE FAMOUS ILLINOIS BUNN SPECIAL RAILROAD WATCHES

Liberty, July 27, 1929

Berkeley 154, white gold-filled, red and black enamel

Berkeley 154A, yellow gold, red and black enamel

Berkeley 154 / Berkeley 154A

Name = Berkeley 154/Berkeley 154A
Time Period = Deco
Karat/Material = 14K WGF, 14K WG, 14K YG; Red and Black Inlaid Enamel
Bezel = Engraved, with Enamel
Sides = Engraved
Lug Size = 11mm
Spring Bar = Fixed Lugs
Casemaker = Wadsworth
Case Pieces = 3
Case Number = 154, No Number
Case Back = Engraved
Dimensions = 17 x 31mm
Durability = 🕒🕒🕒🕒
Movement Size = 18/0
Movement Grade/Jewels = 807/17
Dial Number = 8147
Dial = Embossed; Silver Finish, Butler Center; Sparkle Finish
Dial Opening = Hexagonal
Numerals = Painted, Embossed
Hands = Steel
Seconds at = None
Cased in Factory = Yes
Collectibility = 🕒🕒🕒🕒
Rarity = 🕒🕒🕒🕒🕒 in WGF
🕒🕒🕒🕒🕒🕒 in YG
🕒🕒🕒🕒🕒🕒🕒 in WG
Retail Price Now = $55.00 (WGF); $70.00 (WG); YG (unknown)
Introduction Date = 1928
Unique Case Design = Yes
Unique Dial Design = No
Advertisement = Yes
Marketing Theme = "A delicate tracery of design"

The awesome design of this model, with its striking black and red geometrically patterned enamel, makes it a very special and collectible watch, rivaling in style and deco appeal any of its contemporary competitors. The Berkeley 154 and the two versions each of the Del Monte and the Miami make up a spectacular series of Illinois colored enamel Art Deco wristwatches.

This Berkeley 154 model most commonly came in a 14K white gold-filled case. The model also came in solid 14K gold, here designated Berkeley 154A. At least two are known to exist in ultra-rare 14K yellow gold; these were probably custom orders. The Berkeley 154A in solid yellow gold also came in a case with no case Model Number.

The Berkeley 154 came with a beautiful embossed dial of unknown dial number (sometimes seen on various Daytona models as well) but is also found with a butler-center silver dial. In addition there was a white sparkle dial available.

It was earlier thought that no catalog listings of the Berkeley 154A existed, since it was assumed to be a custom model. However, it was recently discovered that not only the 1930 A. C. Becken catalog but also the 1931 and 1932 Oskamp Nolting catalogs pictured the Berkeley 154A model, noting it as being in solid white gold, but not mentioning the enameling and labeling the model a Daytona. Perhaps the Illinois advertising department and/or the jobbers slipped up and called the model a Daytona because the shape of the bezel and dial opening are the same as those of the Daytona. As yet, no specimens of the Berkeley 154A in solid white gold have been found.

THE DAYTONA

18/0Size, 14k Solid White Gold Case, Fancy Engraved, Octagonal Opening, Silk Ribbon Bracelet, 17 Jewel Movement, Silver Dial.
No. 11897—17 Jewel Illinois Movement $98.50

Oskamp Nolting 1931 catalog, with Berkeley 154A mislabeled as a Daytona model

Outer cardboard box for the Berkeley 154

The Berkeley 154 was advertised in the *Saturday Evening Post* on November 10, 1928, and again on December 1, 1928, and in the *American Magazine* in December 1928. The *Saturday Evening Post* advertisement read: "The Berkeley. The charming watch has a delicate tracery of design in dark red and black hard enamel inlaid in its 14K white gold-filled case." The Berkeley 154A has not been found to have been advertised with the Berkeley 154.

The Berkeley. This charming watch has a delicate tracery of design in dark red and black hard enamel inlaid in its 14k white gold-filled case. A 17-jewel watch of Illinois craftsmanship, which insures dependable timekeeping. $55.

The Beau Brummell is style plus! Tailored to the wrist, the eye and the heart. It is one of those watches that improve with the wearing, creating new pride of possession each day. Illinois tradition underwrites its fine 17-jewel movement in beautiful 14k gold-filled case. $50.

The Marquis-Autocrat. An unusual watch in both performance and appearance. A rare combination of the dignity of a pocket piece with the attractive influence of unconventional design. In 14k gold-filled cushion-shaped case, this 17-jewel watch deserves its popularity. $55.

'202

The Joy of Living

Bells, holly, packages, memories, smiles and joys—this is Christmas!

Good friends and kin are all at once a part of joyful life. It is good to live and give!

This for Brother and that for Mother with all the tingling satisfaction of selecting well and knowing that the Christmas seal hides a host of pleasures.

The pleasure of giving and receiving an Illinois Watch will not be momentary, but will last and grow with increasing pride in its sheer beauty and faithful service as a precious timepiece.

Behind such a gift are more than 50 years of Illinois painstaking craftsmanship and science—a half century of building more than a fine watch, a great American watch.

The
ILLINOIS WATCH
Established 1870
SPRINGFIELD, ILLINOIS

MAKERS OF THE FAMOUS ILLINOIS BUNN SPECIAL RAILROAD WATCHES

Saturday Evening Post, November 10, 1928. The watch labeled Berkeley has the correct caption description but the wrong image (for details, see the listing for the **Redonda 154**).

Berkshire

Name = Berkshire
Time Period = Deco
Karat/Material = 14K WGF
Bezel = Engraved
Sides = Engraved
Lug Size = 16mm
Spring Bar = Fixed Lugs
Casemaker = Keystone
Case Pieces = 3
Case Number = 199
Case Back = Plain
Dimensions = 17 x 31mm
Durability = 🕒🕒🕒🕒
Movement Size = 18/0
Movement Grade/Jewels = 807/17
Dial Numbers = 8191, 8192
Dial = Silver Finish, Butler Center; Silver Finish
Dial Opening = Rectangular
Numerals = Painted, Embossed
Hands = Steel
Seconds at = None
Cased in Factory = Yes
Collectibility = 🕒🕒🕒🕒
Rarity = 🕒🕒🕒🕒
Retail Price New = $50.00
Introduction Date = 1930
Unique Case Design = Yes
Unique Dial Design = No
Advertisement = Yes
Marketing Themes = "Cased with rare charm and individuality"
"Perfect harmony of case and dial design makes this a very feminine watch."

Berkshire, white gold-filled

Berkshire, white gold-filled

The Berkshire is one of the more robust-looking ladies' Illinois models, notwithstanding its marketing theme. Both it and the Avalon have 16mm lugs, unusual for the ladies' watches. Since its case was very durable as well, it is often found today in excellent condition. The Berkshire came with a 17-jewel movement and a ribbon band.

The Berkshire is greatly enhanced by its very interesting dial, No. 8191, which has exploding Roman numerals. Although the Berkshire and Avalon share that dial and several others, the visual effect of each dial on the two models is quite different, since the Berkshire has an engraved bezel and the Avalon a plain one.

The only two known advertisements for the Berkshire appeared in the January 1930 issue of the *Keystone* and the May 10, 1930 issue of *Collier's*; in the latter, it was featured along with the Coronado ladies' model.

Fine Watches Since 1870

When you buy an Illinois you have a watch that, during nearly three-quarters of a century, has steadily earned the increasing confidence of all good jewelers. And, after all, what other kind of watch is worth owning? . . . Illinois puts everything into a watch that makes it a perfected timepiece—that creates the *Beauty that Lies Within.* Nothing in the way of workmanship or material, testing or inspection, that could possibly contribute to accuracy and durability is left out . . . Cased with rare charm and individuality, it sells mostly at from $40 to $60 . . . Modernized prices. A new standard of value for fine watches has been established . . . Select a good jeweler and have him show you the complete new line of Illinois Watches for men and women. You will approve their beauty. He will testify to their reliability, for he has known Illinois ever since he's been in business.

Send for interesting story of Illinois, "The Thrilling Beauty that Lies Within." . . . Address The Illinois Watch, North Ninth Street, Springfield, Illinois.

AS ILLUSTRATED

ILLINOIS MEN'S POCKET WATCHES (*left to right*)

THE DORIAN with Rotor-second dial—17 jewels, 14k gold-filled case $55.00

THE BOURSE—19 jewels, 14k gold-filled case 75.00

ILLINOIS MEN'S STRAP WATCHES (*top row*)

THE TOWNSMAN—17 jewels, 14k gold-filled case $47.50

(*bottom row, left to right*)

THE NEW YORKER—17 jewels, 14k gold-filled case $50.00

THE FUTURA—17 jewels, 14k gold-filled case 55.00

ILLINOIS LADIES' RIBBON WATCHES (*left to right*)

THE BERKSHIRE—17 jewels, 14k gold-filled case $50.00

THE CORONADO—17 jewels, 14k solid gold case, inlaid enamel 65.00

One unalterable purpose expressed in beauty . . . the beauty of performance.

The ILLINOIS WATCH

Fine Watches since 1870

MAKERS OF THE FAMOUS ILLINOIS (*BUNN SPECIAL*) RAILROAD WATCHES

Collier's, May 10, 1930

An Illinois Watch
The Berkshire
$50.00
17 Jewel Movement 14K Gold Filled Case

Original Berkshire price card

Beverly 185

Beverly 185, white gold

Name = Beverly 185
Time Period = Deco
Karat/Material = 14K WG
Bezel = Plain
Sides = Engraved
Lug Size = 11mm
Spring Bar = Fixed Lugs
Casemaker = Keystone
Case Pieces = 2
Case Number = 185
Case Back = Plain
Dimensions = 17 x 30mm
Durability = Excellent
Movement Size = 18/0
Movement Grade/Jewels = 807/17
Dial Number = 8394
Dial = Silver Finish
Dial Opening = Octagonal
Numerals = Painted
Hands = Steel
Seconds at = None
Cased in Factory = Yes
Collectibility = 🕒🕒🕒🕒
Rarity = 🕒🕒🕒🕒
Retail Price New = $66.00
Introduction Date = 1929
Unique Case Design = No

Unique Dial Design = No
Advertisement = Yes
Marketing Themes = "Conservative adornment"
"Rich simplicity"

The Beverly 185 model is cleverly enhanced by the special deco design features on the top and bottom of its dial. It makes it unnecessary to have an engraved bezel as the dial makes the watch appear engraved.

The Beverly 185 is one of at least thirty solid gold Factory-Cased Illinois ladies' wristwatch models (not counting the Diamond-Set Models). Its case is nearly identical to the Biloxi case except the Biloxi is white gold-filled. However, both models share the same attractive dial. Both were listed in the 1929–30 Illinois sales catalog. A third sibling is the later-issued solid gold Lenox, a variant of the Beverly 185 that was issued with a different dial and offered in yellow gold as well as white.

An image representing the Beverly and the Biloxi (both unnamed), appears on the page of Illinois watches in the 1930 L. & C. Mayers catalog, where they are described as being "thin model cases of simple and dignified appearance" and are pictured with an "inlaid enamel dial," which is the interesting one mentioned above.

Illinois had another ladies' model named Beverly, but it is cased in the 10K white gold-filled case Model No. 852.

Beverly 185 inside caseback

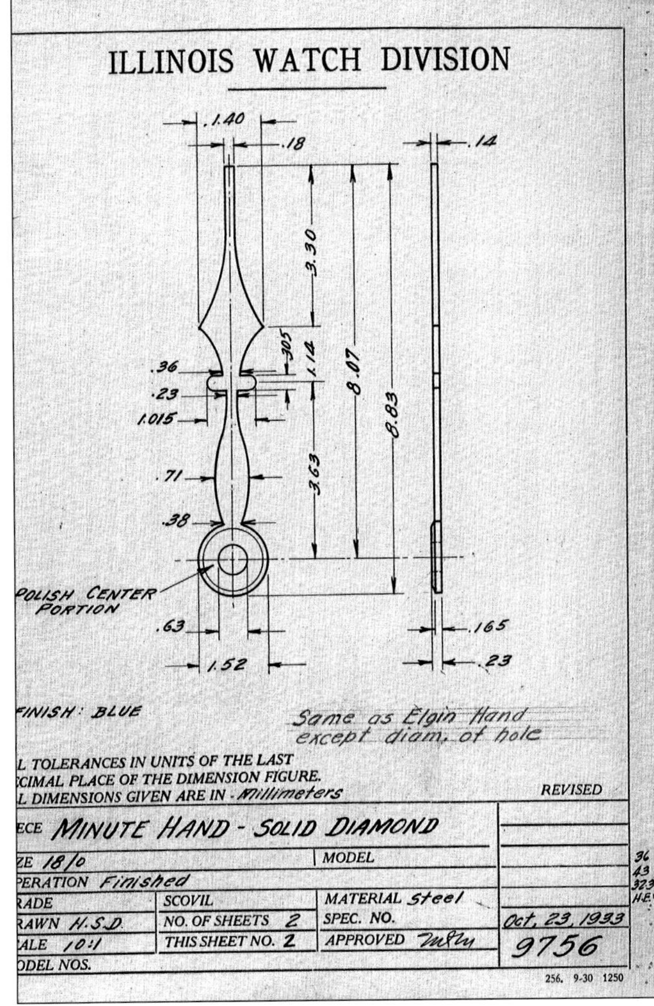

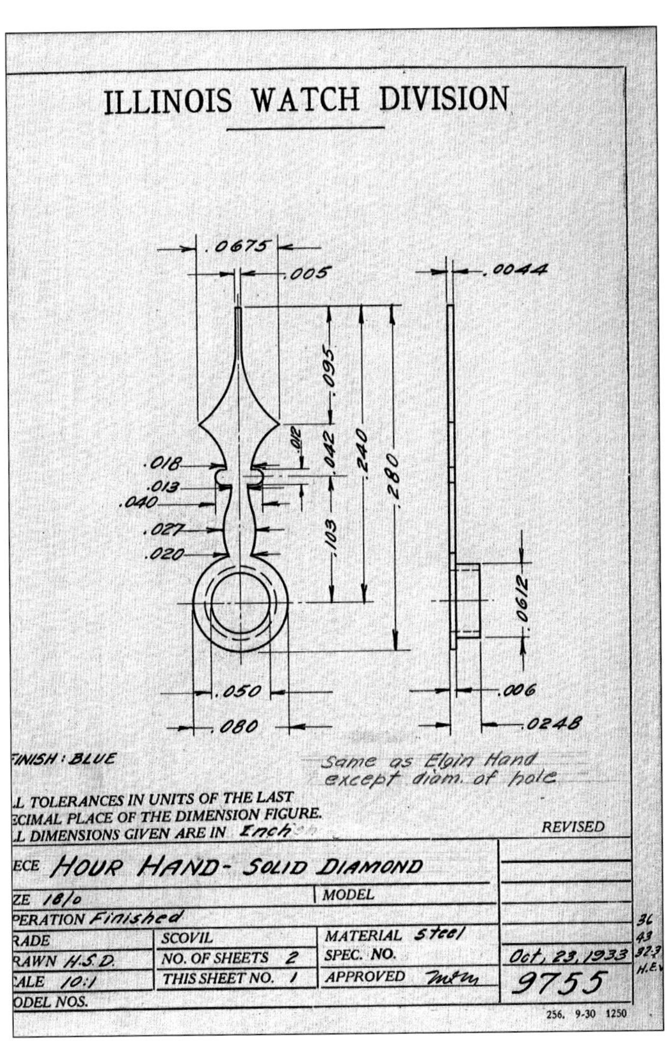

Hour and minute hand (solid diamond) drawings, October 23, 1933

Beverly 852, white gold-filled

Beverly 852, yellow gold-filled

Beverly 852

Name = Beverly 852
Time Period = Moderne
Karat/Material = 10K WGF, 10K YGF
Bezel = Engraved (partially)
Sides = Engraved
Lug Size = 11mm
Spring Bar = Fixed Lugs
Casemaker = Keystone
Case Pieces = 2
Case Number = 852
Case Back = Plain
Dimensions = 16 x 26mm
Durability = 🕒🕒🕒
Movement Size = 18/0
Movement Grade/Jewels = 807/17
Dial Number = 8394
Dial = Silver Finish
Dial Opening = Rectangular
Numerals = Painted
Hands = Steel
Seconds at = None
Cased in Factory = Yes
Collectibility = 🕒🕒🕒🕒
Rarity = 🕒🕒🕒🕒
Retail Price New = $37.50 (15J)
Introduction Date = 1932
Unique Case Design = Yes
Unique Dial Design = No
Advertisement = Yes
Marketing Themes = "Custom built"
"A charming pattern engraved"

Although the Beverly 852 shares a name with the 14K solid gold Beverly 185, it is instead a 10K gold-filled watch whose case not only has a different shape from that of the Beverly 185, but also has a partially engraved bezel rather than an unengraved one. The dial of the Beverly 852 (identical to that of the Patricia model) is very plain, without the deco decoration of the dial for the Beverly 185.

The Beverly 852 was offered in either a white or a yellow gold-filled case and came equipped with a ribbon band.

The Beverly 852 was listed in the Illinois Century of Progress sales catalog in 1932 and in the Illinois Greater Value Watches in 1933. It was pictured along with the 21/0 size Janette model in the November 1932 issue of the *Keystone*.

SPRINGFIELD, ILLINOIS, U.S.A.

October 28, 1932.

The buying season is well under way and we wish to take this opportunity to thank you and your representatives for the splendid effort you are giving our compact line of ILLINOIS WATCHES, announced in August 1932.

Practically all models are moving with favorable regularity. The condition of our case stock of a few of these models necessitates withdrawal of the particular dummy samples from your sample lines.

Will you, therefore, kindly return at once the dummy samples of the IRENE, WENTWORTH, GALLAHAD, and CHESTERFIELD? We need these cases for fulfillment of orders and we ask you to give the matter your earliest attention. At the same time, we trust you will send us your order to offset credit for samples withdrawn.

We are sending you dummy samples of the BEVERLY and CHICAGOAN. You have prices and complete information concerning these attractive watches. Orders previously placed for these two new watches will be filled immediately. Enclosed with the dummy samples mentioned will be corrected price tags for the JULIETTE samples.

Wishing you the greatest success, we are

Yours very truly,

THE ILLINOIS WATCH

J. L. Keenan

Sales Manager.

JLK-myl.

Letter from Jack Keenan, dated October 28, 1932, concerning dummy samples for the Beverly model, among other subjects

Biloxi, white gold-filled

BILOXI

Name = Biloxi
Time Period = Deco
Karat/Material = 14K WGF
Bezel = Plain
Sides = Engraved
Lug Size = 11mm
Spring Bar = Fixed Lugs
Casemaker = Keystone
Case Pieces = 3
Case Number = 186
Case Back = Plain
Dimensions = 17 x 30mm
Durability = ◷◷◷◷
Movement Size = 18/0
Movement Grade/Jewels = 807/17
Dial Numbers = Unknown
Dial = Silver Finish
Dial Opening = Octagonal
Numerals = Painted
Hands = Steel
Seconds at = None
Cased in Factory = Yes
Collectibility = ◷◷◷◷
Rarity = ◷◷◷◷
Retail Price New = $50.00
Introduction Date = 1929
Unique Case Design = No
Unique Dial Design = No
Advertisement = Yes
Marketing Themes = "Rich simplicity"
"Conservative adornment"

Except for being gold-filled rather than solid gold, the Biloxi model is virtually identical to the Beverly 185, including the very strikingly decorated dial.

The Biloxi and Beverly 185 models were advertised together in the 1929–30 Illinois sales catalog under one image and shared this oxymoronic caption: "For conservative adornment the rich simplicity of the Biloxi and Beverly plain cases is unexcelled." The Biloxi was advertised in the August 1930 issue of the *American Magazine*.

The BILOXI
14K Gold Filled Case
Consumer price, $50.00

The BEVERLY
14K Solid Gold Case
Consumer price, $65.00

For conservative adornment the rich simplicity of the Biloxi and Beverly plain cases is unexcelled. The 17 jeweled movement is unparalled for accuracy

A. G. Schwab catalog, 1930

W1830 14 Kt. white solid gold....**$88.80**
W1831 14 Kt. white gold filled.... **67.20**
18-0 size thin model cases of simple and dignified appearance. 17 Jewel rectangular movement; inlaid enamel dial.

L. & C. Mayers catalog, 1930 Biloxi unnamed

Gay has discovered that there may be a very subtle difference between the bezels of the two models: the Biloxi seems to have a slight frame-like ridge around its crystal, while the Beverly 185 bezel is slightly concaved on the top and bottom and has no frame-like ridge by its crystal.

To add to the confusion, the Biloxi has the same shape of case back and bezel as the Lenox. The Lenox model, however, was in 14K solid gold and came in either white or yellow, whereas the Biloxi came only in white gold-filled.

Brighton, white gold, black enamel

Brighton

Name = Brighton
Time Period = Deco
Karat/Material = 14K WG, Black Inlaid Enamel
Bezel = Engraved, with Enamel
Sides = Engraved
Lug Size = 11mm
Spring Bar = Fixed Lugs
Casemaker = Keystone
Case Pieces = 3
Case Number = 201
Case Back = Engraved
Dimensions = 17 x 31mm
Durability = 🕓🕓🕓🕓
Movement Size = 18/0
Movement Grade/Jewels = 807/17
Dial Number = 8090
Dial = Silver Finish, Sparkle Finish
Dial Opening = Oval
Numerals = Painted
Hands = Steel
Seconds at = None
Cased in Factory = Yes
Collectibility = 🕓🕓🕓🕓
Rarity = 🕓🕓🕓🕓🕓🕓
Retail Price New = $65.00
Introduction Date = 1930
Unique Case Design = Yes
Unique Dial Design = No
Advertisement = Yes
Marketing Theme = "Delightful refinements are represented in this oval watch."

The Brighton is a very rare and highly collectible model with a unique bezel design. It, the Coronado, and some of the Mary Todd models are all very special timepieces, unusual in that they were not only solid gold but were also ornamented with inlaid black enamel.

The oval dial of the Brighton is shared with the Debutante, Fairport and Vanity Fair models. Although the Fairport model is very similar to the Brighton, it is not in solid gold and lacks the enameling.

The Brighton was advertised in the May 24, 1930 issue of *Collier's* magazine as "The gift that keeps on giving. AN ILLINOIS WATCH. A watch is so intimate a possession. To trifle with the selection of such a life companion for the graduate you delight to honor is to miss all the precious significance of its purpose—enduring accuracy and endearing charm."

The Brighton was also advertised in the May 24 and May 30, 1930 issues of *Liberty* magazine. The Newport model was featured along with the Brighton in a January 11, 1930 *Collier's* advertisement and in a *Liberty* advertisement.

2 The American Magazine for June 1930

The gift that keeps on giving ❖
AN ILLINOIS WATCH

A watch is so intimate a possession. To trifle with the selection of such a life companion for the graduate you delight to honor is to miss all the precious significance of its purpose—enduring accuracy and endearing charm.

An Illinois is all you can ask in a watch. Encased in every one of these new, exclusive, attractive designs is that golden perfection of watch-making which has made Illinois renowned for accurate time-keeping for sixty years. So modestly priced, too, for what they will give in return—eloquent, abiding beauty and long, dependable, faithful service.

Select a good jeweler. He will be glad to show you his complete presentation of the latest Illinois Watches for men and women. Their beauty speaks for itself. He will vouch for their worth, for he knows the name Illinois has marked fine watches since 1870.

❖ ❖

AS ILLUSTRATED

ILLINOIS MEN'S STRAP WATCHES (*top row—left to right*)
THE ENSIGN – 17 jewels, 14k gold-filled case $15.00
THE FINALIST – 17 jewels, 14k gold-filled case 55.00
(*bottom row*)
THE BEAU BRUMMEL – 17 jewels, 14k gold-filled case $50.00
ILLINOIS LADIES' RIBBON WATCHES (*left to right*)
THE BRIGHTON – 17 jewels, 14k solid gold inlaid enamel case $65.00
THE NEWPORT – 17 jewels, 14k gold-filled case 50.00
ILLINOIS MEN'S POCKET WATCH
THE RIALTO – 17 jewels, 14k gold-filled case $50.00

The Birthright of every Illinois . . . the beauty of marvelous precision.

The ILLINOIS WATCH

Fine Watches since 1870

MAKERS OF THE FAMOUS ILLINOIS (*BUNN SPECIAL*) RAILROAD WATCHES

American Magazine, June 1930

WHY I COLLECT ILLINOIS

I got into collecting Illinois wristwatches by a very circuitous route. It all started with my husband's interest in railroad-grade pocket watches. Learning from him that Illinois pocket watches had particularly fine movements, I decided to be on the lookout for a ladies' model, and before long I found a lovely one, quite inexpensively. Later I turned up a couple of very nice Transitional models, again at very reasonable prices.

My collecting started getting serious after a friend let me borrow his copy of the April 2011 issue of the NAWCC *Watch & Clock Bulletin* to read. The cover showed a group of gorgeous Illinois ladies' wristwatches, and inside was the source of what has proved to be an ongoing obsession: a wonderful article by Farrell Gay, with an introduction by Fred Friedberg, on Illinois ladies' wristwatches. With pictures! Temptation upon temptation!

Soon thereafter, I found a beautiful Mary Todd with one of those wonderful "slinky" watchbands of fine mesh. And the watch even came with its original box and card, so I couldn't resist! Then things accelerated: a Redonda, a Miami 155, a Roslyn and . . . (just couldn't stop!). It's never a problem finding an Illinois watch to want. The problem is having the funds to keep adding to the collection!

Meanwhile, since my husband had started collecting Illinois wristwatches as well as pocket watches, an appropriate Christmas present for him was a copy of Fred's first book *(The Illinois Watch: The Life and Times of a Great American Watch Company).* The first Illinois watch I bought for him, a stunning white Chieftain, of course came from Fred.

Although I like a lot of Art Deco watches by other makers too, I especially admire the Illinois because of their excellent movements as well as their elegant and innovative case designs. Of the watches I've acquired, I've found that the Illinois movements have generally held up better than most others.

But as much as I value my Illinois watches and enjoy wearing them (both ladies' and men's models), I think I've gotten every bit as much pleasure from trying to find new information about them, accumulating a huge collection of jobbers' catalogs in the process. I'm delighted that "The Catalog Queen," as Fred calls me, was thus able to identify some of the hitherto unknown Illinois models. Thank you, Fred, for undertaking this monumental new book set and allowing me on board!

—Bettie Mason

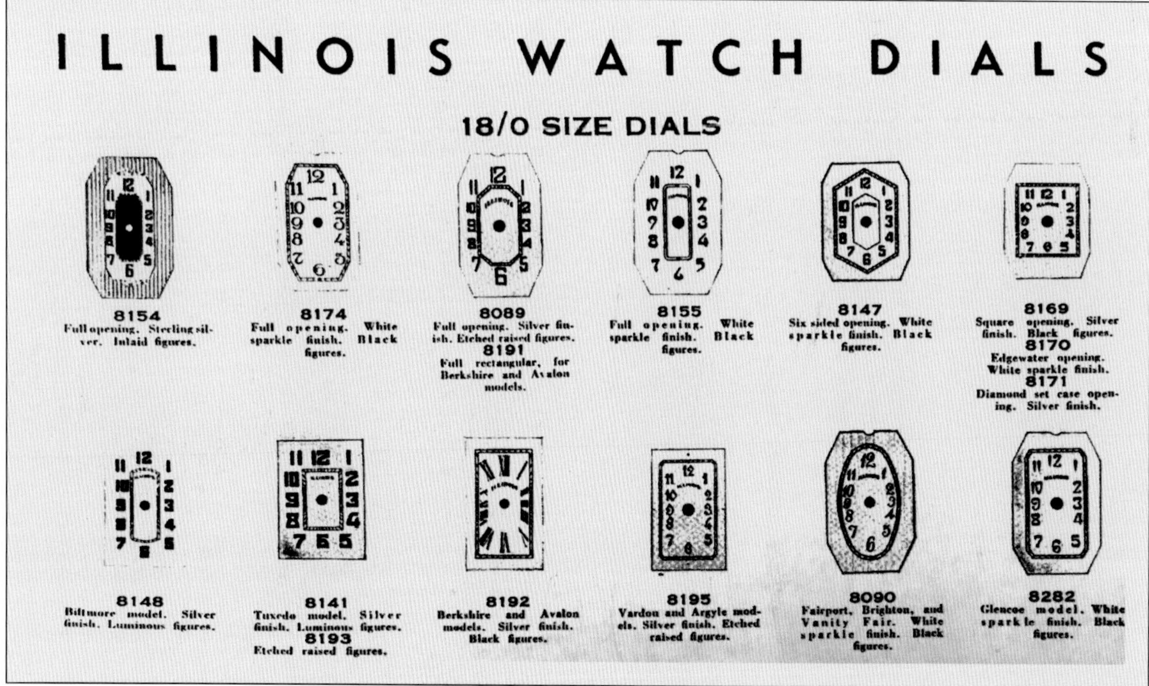

ILLINOIS WATCH DIALS

18/0 SIZE DIALS

8154
Full opening. Sterling silver. Inlaid figures.

8174
Full opening. White sparkle finish. Black figures.

8089
Full opening. Silver finish. Etched raised figures.
8191
Full rectangular, for Berkshire and Avalon models.

8155
Full opening. White sparkle finish. Black figures.

8147
Six sided opening. White sparkle finish. Black figures.

8169
Square opening. Silver finish. Black figures.
8170
Edgewater opening. White sparkle finish.
8171
Diamond set case opening. Silver finish.

8148
Biltmore model. Silver finish. Luminous figures.

8141
Tuxedo model. Silver finish. Luminous figures.
8193
Etched raised figures.

8192
Berkshire and Avalon models. Silver finish. Black figures.

8195
Vardon and Argyle models. Silver finish. Etched raised figures.

8090
Fairport, Brighton, and Vanity Fair. White sparkle finish. Black figures.

8282
Glencoe model. White sparkle finish. Black figures.

Illinois Dial and Hand catalog, December 26, 1930

Charmette / Annette / Florette

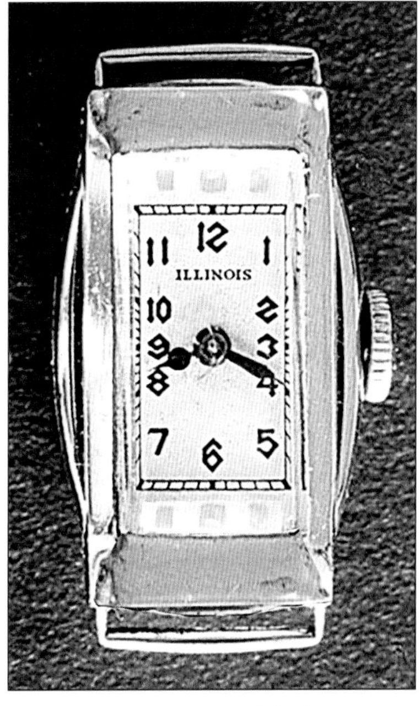

Florette, yellow gold-filled

Names = Charmette/Annette/Florette

Time Period = Moderne

Karat/Material = 14K WGF, 14K YGF (Florette only)

Bezel = Plain

Sides = Engraved

Lug Size = 8mm

Spring Bar = Fixed Lugs

Casemaker = Keystone

Case Pieces = 2

Case Number = 703

Case Back = Plain

Dimensions = 14 x 26mm

Durability = ◷◷◷◷

Movement Size = 21/0

Movement Grade/Jewels = 107/1, 105/15 (Florette only)

Dial Number = 8732

Dial = Silver Finish, Pinstripe

Dial Opening = Rectangular

Numerals= Painted

Hands = Steel

Seconds at = None

Cased in Factory = Yes

Collectibility = ◷◷◷◷

Rarity = ◷◷◷◷

Retail Price New = Charmette, $52.50 (17J); Annette, $60.00 (17J); Florette $42.50 (15J)

Introduction Date = 1931 (Charmette); 1932 (Annette); 1933 (Florette)

Unique Case Design = No

Unique Dial Design = No

Advertisement = Yes

Marketing Themes = "Gracefully engraved case" (Annette)
"Conservatively neat and chic" (Florette)
"Smart and slender" (Florette)
"Selective simplicity and distinction" (Charmette)

The Charmette is one of the small watches called baguettes or semi-baguettes that were popular in the early 1930s. It is easily confused with its sister models, the Annette and Florette, because all three are basically variants of case Model No. 703. All three had 14K gold-filled cases, but the Annette and Charmette came only in white gold-filled, while the Florette was available in either white or yellow.

Describing the Annette, the Illinois 1932 Spring sales catalog stated: "Gracefully engraved case of 14 karat white filled gold with bracelet of same quality. Very attractive ensemble." The Annette had a 17-jewel movement and came with a metal bracelet; the Charmette was 17 jewels also, but it was issued with a ribbon band. The Florette was like the Charmette except for having a 15-jewel movement.

To add to the confusion of the Charmette/Annette/Florette trio, there is another baguette model, the Coquette, which is housed in the similar but slightly different case Model No. 702. This case has a small engraving on the top and bottom of the bezel, whereas case Model No. 703, for the Charmette, Annette and Florette, has a plain bezel.

These and other baguettes were part of the Illinois Watch Company's participation in the "Buy American" campaign, beginning in 1932, that was sponsored jointly by the American Legion, American Federation of Labor and the Association of National Advertisers as a "War Against Depression" campaign by United Action for Employment.

SAMPLES

October 27th, 1932.

Gentlemen:

Included with the Beverly and Chicagoan samples we are sending you there are enough samples of the Florette model in natural color for your lines.

Please return the white samples of the Florette you have for credit in exchange.

This arrangement we feel sure you will find of advantage as the Florette model is particularly active in the natural color at this time. Also, a natural gold 21/0 size number will permit of a more balanced selection considering that your samples of these models are now all white.

We shall appreciate your making this exchange of samples as quickly as possible.

Very truly yours,

THE ILLINOIS WATCH

JLK:AD

Sales Manager.

Letter from Jack Keenan, dated October 27, 1932, indicating the Florette in yellow gold-filled "is particularly active"

Claudette / Vogue

Names = Claudette/Vogue
Time Period = Moderne
Karat/Material = 14K WGF, 14K YGF
Bezel = Plain
Sides = Engraved
Lug Size = 11mm
Spring Bar = Fixed Lugs
Casemaker = Wadsworth
Case Pieces = 3
Case Number = 242
Case Back = Plain
Dimensions = 17 x 30mm
Durability = ◷◷◷◷
Movement Size = 18/0
Movement Grade/Jewels = 805/15 (Claudette), 807/17 (Vogue)
Dial Number = 8282
Dial = Silver Finish
Dial Opening = Rectangular
Numerals= Painted
Hands = Steel
Seconds at = None
Cased in Factory = Yes
Collectibility = ◷◷◷◷
Rarity = ◷◷◷◷
Retail Price New = $32.50 (15J), $50.00 (17J)
Introduction Date = 1931 (Claudette); (1932) Vogue
Unique Case Design = No
Unique Dial Design = No
Advertisement = Yes
Marketing Themes = "An even greater bargain than the modern automobile" (Claudette)
"A charming ribbon watch" (Claudette)

Claudette, white gold-filled

Claudette, yellow gold-filled

The Claudette appeared in the 1931–32 Illinois sales catalog and was advertised in the December 12, 1931 issue of the *Saturday Evening Post* for the Christmas season. In that advertisement it appeared along with the Coquette, Constance, Debutante, Florentine, Glenna and Hollywood ladies' Illinois models and the Arlington, Beau Royale, Bostonian, Derby and Larchmont men's models, plus the Rialto model pocket watch.

"$32.50 to $60.00 will buy a finer watch than you've ever been able to get for the money," the advertisement began, in large type. "This advertisement is published to help you simplify your Christmas giving problem and save you money. . . . Never was there such an opportunity to give the most cherished of all Christmas gifts—a fine watch."

The Claudette was featured as the Illinois "Watch of the Month" in the October 1931 issue of the *Saturday Evening Post*.

Saturday Evening Post, October 1931 advertisement

The Claudette had a 15-jewel movement and was apparently targeted as a lower-priced watch, but it was offered with the choice of white gold-filled or yellow gold-filled case, and either a dial with very stylized numerals or one with plain numerals. It came equipped with a ribbon band.

It has recently been discovered that the hitherto unknown Vogue model was a Claudette supplied with a 17-jewel movement. It was listed in the Oskamp Nolting 1932 catalog and also in the Holsman 1932–33 one; the latter was obviously giving a deep discount to wholesalers and/or clearing out stock, as the price was listed as only $18.00.

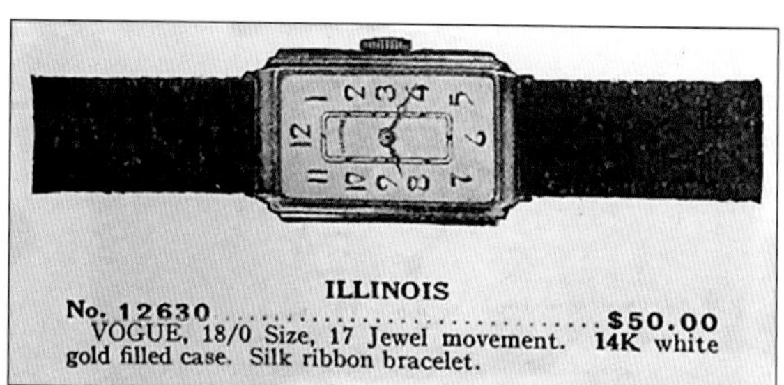

ILLINOIS

No. 12630 ....$50.00
VOGUE, 18/0 Size, 17 Jewel movement. 14K white gold filled case. Silk ribbon bracelet.

Oskamp Nolting catalog, 1932

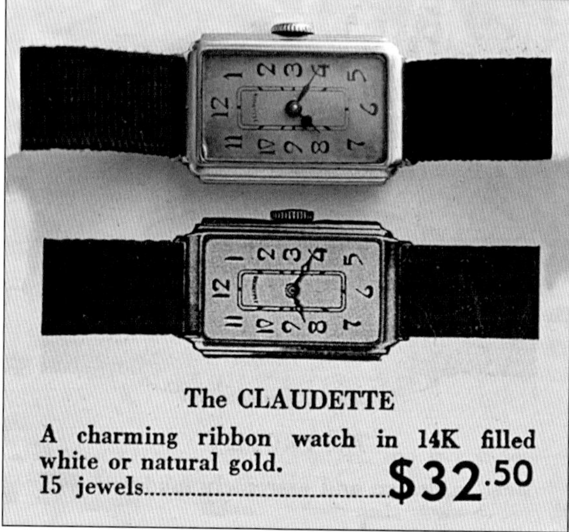

The CLAUDETTE

A charming ribbon watch in 14K filled white or natural gold.
15 jewels.......................................$32.50

J. Engel 1932 catalog, with superimposed Claudette

Constance / Barbara

Names = Constance/Barbara
Time Period = Moderne
Karat/Material = 14K WGF and 14K YGF (Two-Tone)
Bezel = Grooves
Sides = Engraved
Lug Size = 11mm, and for cord band
Spring Bar = Fixed Lugs, Silk Cord (Barbara)
Casemaker = Wadsworth
Case Pieces = 2
Case Number = 829
Case Back = Plain
Dimensions = 17 x 31mm
Durability = 🕒🕒🕒
Movement Size = 18/0
Movement Grades/Jewels = 805/15, 807/17
Dial Numerals = Unknown (Constance); 8169 (Barbara)
Dial = Silver Finish, Partial Pinstripe (Constance); Silver Finish (Barbara)
Dial Opening = Square
Numerals = Painted
Hands = Steel
Seconds at = None
Cased in Factory = Yes
Collectibility = 🕒🕒🕒🕒
Rarity = 🕒🕒🕒🕒
Retail Price New = Constance, $50.00 (15J), Barbara, $42.50 (15J)
Introduction Date = 1931 (Constance); 1932 (Barbara)
Unique Case Design = Yes
Unique Dial Design = Yes (Constance); No (Barbara)
Advertisement = Yes
Marketing Themes = "Authentically modern, smart and stylish"
"Extremely attractive in combination
14K filled white and natural gold"

Constance, two-tone gold-filled

Barbara, two-tone gold-filled

The Constance and Barbara are notable for being two of only three ladies' Illinois wristwatch models having two-tone cases. The Constance and its later-issued sister, the Barbara, shared the same two-tone gold-filled case, Model No. 829. (The third two-tone model is the Vardon, which has a solid gold case. It is technically a two-tone model because the lugs of one variant are white gold but the case is yellow gold.)

The Constance was fitted with a ribbon band and the Barbara with a silk cord band. The Constance had a nicely designed square dial featuring a center circle with pinstripes on the outside of the circle; the Barbara's dial was a plain square.

The Constance came with a 17-jewel movement; the Barbara, issued later, had one with 15 jewels. The number of jewels explains the price differences between these models.

The Constance was advertised along with the Claudette, Coquette, Debutante, Florentine, Glenna and Hollywood ladies' models in the 1931–32 Illinois sales catalog. These models also appeared together in an advertisement in the December 12, 1931 issue of the *Saturday Evening Post*, where they were featured as being "priced lower than ever before for such quality," as the impact of the Great Depression started to hit the watch industry head-on by mid-1931.

The Barbara, which was introduced a year later than the Constance, appeared in the Illinois Spring 1932 catalog on a page also advertising the Sylvia, Rita, Florentine, Greta, Glenna 239, Lakewood, Elissa, Princess and Argyle ladies' models. Although we have not located any magazine advertisement for the Barbara, we have found a newspaper advertisement that appeared in the *San Bernardino County Sun*, May 20, 1932, shown below.

San Bernardino County Sun (San Bernardino, CA), May 20, 1932; image from *newspapers.com*

Note: The 1932 Oskamp Nolting catalog lists a Constance as white gold-filled, not two-toned, thus indicating that there might have been a white gold-filled variant.

Convertible, yellow gold, without its bracelet

CONVERTIBLE

Name = Convertible (derived from Illinois advertisements that explained the convertible nature of these models as described below)
Time Period = Transitional
Karat/Material = 14K YGF; 14K YG
Bezel = Plain, Engraved
Sides = Plain
Lugs = N/A
Lug Size = None
Spring Bar = None
Casemakers = Various
Case Number = None
Case Shape = Round
Case Back = Plain, Engraved
Case Variations/Rarity = ◷ YGF/P
◷◷ YG/P
Case Closure = 3-Part Snap-On Bezel and Back, Hinged
Dimensions = Various
Durability = ◷◷◷◷
Movement Sizes = 0, 3/0, 6/0
Movement Grades/Jewels = Various
Dial Number = 8210
Dials = Enamel, Silver Finish, Gold Finish
Dial Opening = Round
Numerals = Painted
Hands = Steel
Seconds at = 6, None
Cased in Factory = Yes
Collectibility = ◷◷◷
Rarity = ◷ Silver Finish. Gold Finish
◷◷◷◷ Enamel 0, 3/0
◷◷◷◷◷◷ Enamel 6/0
Retail Price New = $42.50 in yellow gold.
Introduction Date = 1910
Unique Case Design = No
Unique Dial Design = No
Advertisements = Yes
Marketing Themes = "You can always rely on an Illinois."
"A convertible bracelet watch"

In 1910, the Convertible became the first "wristwatch" advertised by the Illinois Watch Company. The first Illinois advertisements were for a private-label "Ariste" model for the Marshall Field Department Store.

The Illinois advertisement for the convertible stated: "Bracelet Watches. You can always rely on an Illinois-Springfield bracelet watch for women." The advertisement continued, "These reliable timepieces are made in two grades, having 15 and 19 jewels respectively, and are cased in both solid gold and gold-filled cases with corresponding bracelets." The Illinois Factory advertised the Convertible "as a convertible bracelet watch."

6-0 Size Illinois Convertible Style Bracelet Watches

6/0 size. 10k gold filled jointed back case, three-quarter opening, plain polished. Fine 1/10 stock gold filled snap end. detachable bracelet.
No. **1983** Illinois, 15 jewel. Complete **$36.20**

6/0 size. 10k gold filled jointed back case, three-quarter opening, engraved bezel. Fine 1/10 stock gold filled snap end detachable bracelet.
No. **1984** Illinois, 15 jewel. Complete **$37.50**

6/0 size. 10k gold filled octagon plain polished case, three-quarter opening. Fine 1/10 stock. Detachable bracelet.
No. **1985** Illinois, 15 jewel. Complete **$36.20**

6/0 size. 10k gold filled octagon engraved case, three-quarter opening. Fine 1/10 stock. Detachable bracelet.
No. **1986** Illinois, 15 jewel. Complete **$37.50**

A selection of Illinois Convertibles in the 1925 G. W. Huntley & Co. catalog

This model was probably the first "wristwatch" that was cased and timed in the Illinois Factory. The watch was a "convertible" because it could be worn around the wrist, as a pendant or used as a pocket watch. This model was, in effect, a pendant watch with an attached bracelet. The Convertible was available in 0, 3/0 or 6/0 sizes. The first Convertibles issued were mostly 0 size and 3/0 size; later ones were mostly 6/0 size. This model is a ladies' watch but it is listed in the Men's as well as the Ladies' Identification Guides in this book owing to its historical importance.

C5853

15 Jewels 14K Solid Gold Price $42.50

ILLINOIS-SPRINGFIELD

BRACELET WATCH

15 jewel movement No. 3163731 has a double roller escapement, steel escape wheel and is guaranteed to be an exceptionally accurate and durable time piece. Case and bracelet are 14K solid gold.

ILLINOIS WATCH COMPANY

Convertible original price card

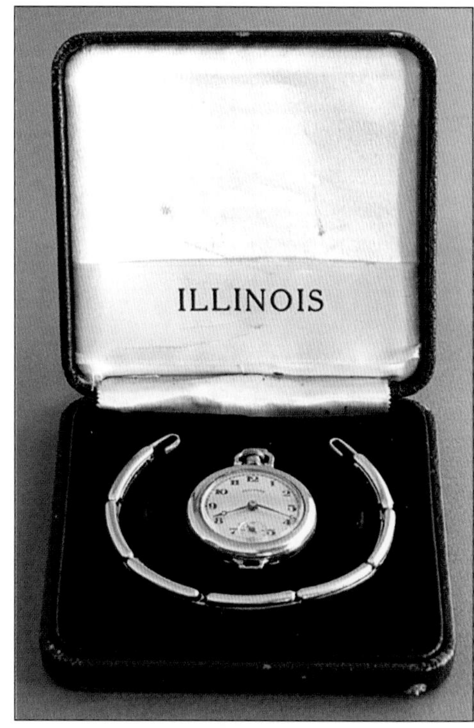

Convertible in its original display case

December 16, 1914. THE JEWELERS' CIRCULAR-WEEKLY 19

SEVEN WATCHES IN ONE

Always in Style for All Occasions

DEPOLLIER'S CONVERTIBLE WATCH

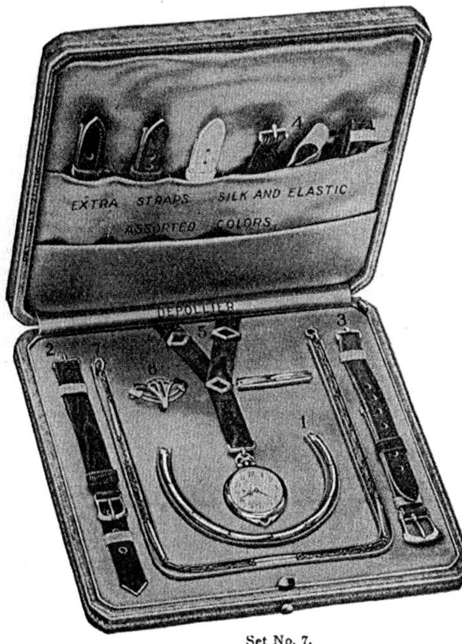

Set No. 7.

Waltham Patented Convertible Bracelet Watch

Set No. 8.

DEPOLLIER'S CREATION

Seven Watches in One

All parts interchangeable.
No. 1, Expansion Bracelet Watch.
No. 2, Moire Ribbon Wristlet Watch.
No. 3, Leather Wristlet Watch.
No. 4, Elastic Wristlet Watch.
No. 5, Silk Sautoir Watch, convertible into a drop watch.
No. 6, Chatelaine Watch.
No. 7, Chain Sautoir Watch.

Bracelets can be worn separately from the watch.

Made up in various combinations, one to seven.

Write for Illustrated Booklet

INSURANCE AGAINST LOSS

One of the many merits of the

"DD" Excess Expansion Bracelet

The unique construction of the safety locking device of our bracelet is a guarantee against loss.

Our "DD" Excess Expansion Bracelet is fool-proof, no open hooks or catches to interfere with garment or become accidentally detached.

The only detachable Bracelet that can be applied to the wrist by the wearer, without assistance of a second person.

ABSOLUTE SAFETY

Pat. Oct. 13, 1914.

Dubois Watch Case Co. has applied for Patent on hook in the United States and Canada.

Made in Platinum, 18, 14 and 10K. Gold
WRITE FOR SAMPLE.

Patent applied for in foreign countries. Brevet déposé dans tous pays. Auslands-Patente angemeldet.

We guarantee all our Bracelets to be *hard soldered, and have solid gold springs,* manufactured under License Pat. No. 1,034,471. The strongest Bracelet made, giving perfect service to the wearer.

JACQUES DEPOLLIER & SON

DUBOIS WATCH CASE CO.

Manufacturers of High Class Specialties

Established 1887

Platinum, Gold and Enamel Watch Cases, Chains, Lockets, etc.
Complete American and Swiss Watches,
Odd and Regular Shapes.

Main Office and Factory:
316 Herkimer St., Brooklyn, N. Y.

Salesroom:
15 Maiden Lane, N. Y.

Jewelers' Circular Weekly, December 16, 1914

Coquette

Name = Coquette
Time Period = Moderne
Karat/Material = 14K WGF, 14K YGF
Bezel = Plain, Engraved
Sides = Engraved
Lug Size = 10mm
Spring Bar = Fixed Lugs
Casemaker = Keystone
Case Pieces = 2
Case Number = 702
Case Back = Plain
Dimensions = 14 x 26mm
Durability = ◷◷◷◷
Movement Size = 21/0
Movement Grade/Jewels = 107/17
Dial Number = Unknown
Dial = Silver Finish, Ribbon Stripe
Dial Opening = Rectangular
Numerals= Painted
Hands = Steel
Seconds at = None
Cased in Factory = Yes
Collectibility = ◷◷◷◷
Rarity = ◷◷◷◷
Retail Price New = $52.50 (17J)
Introduction Date = 1931
Unique Case Design = Yes
Unique Dial Design = No
Advertisement = Yes
Marketing Theme = "Diminutively small and graceful"

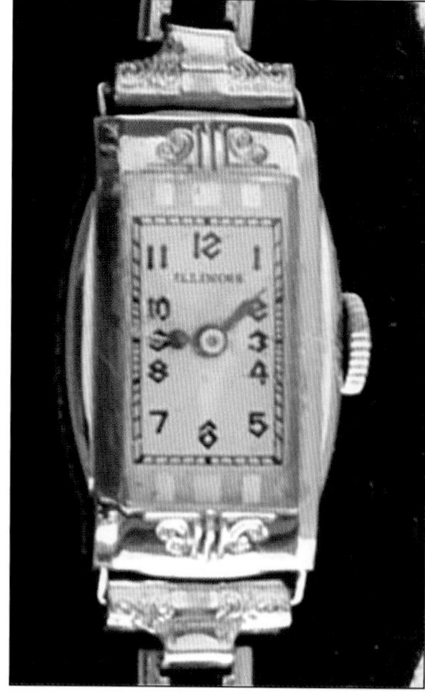

Coquette, white gold-filled

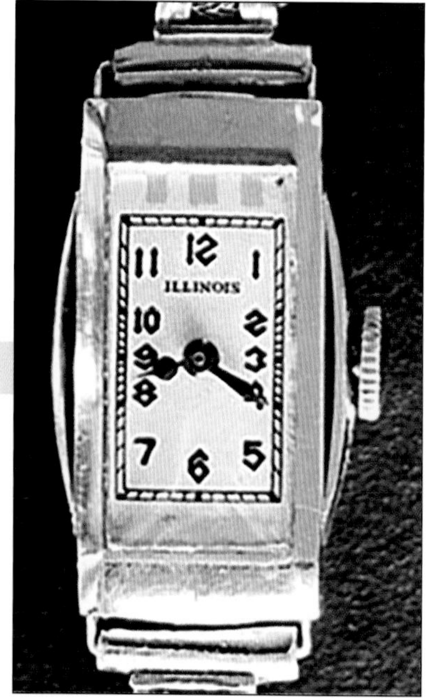

Coquette, white gold-filled

Coquette, yellow gold-filled

The Coquette was featured in an advertisement appearing in the December 12, 1931 issue of the *Saturday Evening Post* along with six other Illinois ladies' models (Constance, Claudette, Debutante, Florentine, Glenna and Hollywood) and a number of men's.

In this advertisement, both the illustration and the text give special attention to the Coquette: "Look at these few latest Illinois designs. Note especially the diminutively small and graceful Coquette. All these new models are beautiful. They are authentically modern, smart and stylish. They are sturdy, accurate timekeepers. And priced lower than ever before for such quality."

The Coquette was equipped with a 21/0 size, 17-jewel movement and ribbon band. Its dial has a very interesting design feature: bold silver racing (ribbon) stripes at the top and bottom of the dial, framing the rectangular minute track.

According to Gay, case Model No. 702, in which the Coquette is housed, is like the cases of the Annette, Charmette and Florette models (all No. 703), except the Coquette has engraving on its bezel and the bezels of the other three are plain.

Coquette in its original display box

The Coquette was featured in the 1931–32 Illinois sales catalog as part of the "American Beauty Series." The catalog noted that this model would not be available until October 26, 1931.

American Beauty Series

Exquisitely dainty timepieces. Quite the newest, smartest vogue. The most distinctive feature of my lady's ensemble today. Yet, for all their size refinement, each one produced with that same fine craftsmanship in watchmaking which has made the Illinois Watch famous for its accurate timekeeping for more than sixty years. At $52.50, a truly amazing value.

COQUETTE—Diminutively small and graceful case of 14k filled white gold with delicately engraved bezel. 17 jewels.. $52.50

MINUETTE—There is a mode of modern expression in this artistically engraved case of 14k filled white gold. 17 jewels... $52.50

CHARMETTE—Selective simplicity and distinction expressed in this 14k filled white gold case. 17 jewels...... $52.50

From Illinois American Beauty Series brochure, 1931

Coronado

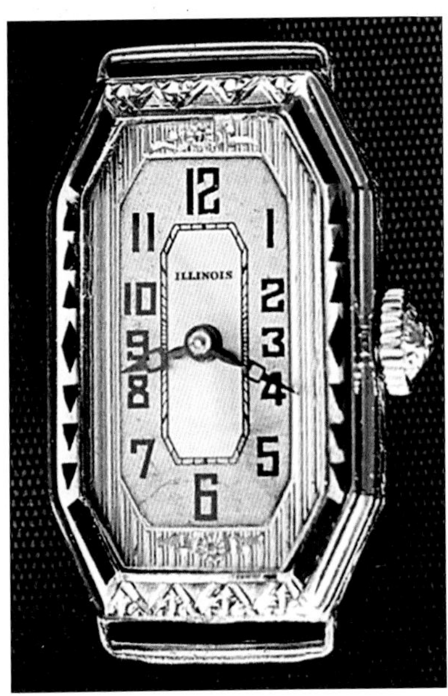

Coronado, white gold, black enamel

Name = Coronado
Time Period = Deco
Karat/Material = 14K WG, Black Inlaid Enamel
Bezel = Engraved, with Enamel
Sides = Engraved
Lug Size = 11mm
Spring Bar = Fixed Lugs
Casemaker = Keystone
Case Pieces = 3
Case Number = 169
Case Back = Engraved
Dimensions = 17 x 30mm
Durability = ◷◷◷◷
Movement Size = 18/0
Movement Grade/Jewels = 807/17
Dial Numbers = 8154, 8174, 8089
Dial = Sterling Silver; Sparkle Finish; Silver Finish, Butler Center
Dial Opening = Octagonal
Numerals= Painted
Hands = Steel
Seconds at = None
Cased in Factory = Yes
Collectibility = ◷◷◷◷
Rarity = ◷◷◷◷◷
Retail Price New = $65.00
Introduction Date = 1929
Unique Case Design = Yes
Unique Dial Design = No
Advertisement = Yes
Marketing Themes = "Precise, sturdy, enduring"
"A beautiful blend of white gold and inlaid jet black enamel"

One of the most popular Illinois ladies' wristwatch models, and one of the most well known, is the 14K white gold Coronado. Its daring, deco, arrow-like black enamel design around the bezel has a Southwestern flavor, reflected in its name. The Coronado had a 17-jewel movement and came with a ribbon band.

The dials used on the Coronado are also particularly interesting. One of them is No. 8154, a beautiful sterling silver Flückiger manufactured dial. Another one, No. 8174, which has particularly distinctive numerals, originally was issued with the famous Illinois white sparkle finish (1930 Illinois Dial and Hand Catalog) but later came only with a silver finish (1936 Illinois Materials Catalog). Yet another, No. 8089 from the 1930 Illinois Dial and Hand Catalog, has a butler center.

The Coronado was listed in the 1929–30 Illinois sales catalog and advertised in the August 1929 issue of the *American Magazine*, the October 19, 1929 issue of *Liberty* and the May 10, 1930 issue of *Collier's*. This model, the Newport and the various variations of the Mary Todd were the most advertised of the Illinois ladies' wristwatches.

October 19, 1929 Liberty 5

MODERN STYLE ILLINOIS ACCURACY

Above, reading down
The Mary Todd, 17 jewels, 18k solid gold, inlaid enamel $75
The Coronado, 17 jewels, 14k solid gold, inlaid enamel $65

Below, reading down
The Daytona, 17 jewels, 14k solid gold $65
The Tuxedo, 17 jewels, 14k solid gold $75

The Beauty of Truth lies in the golden perfection of Illinois workmanship.

Below, reading down
The Redonda, 17 jewels, 14k gold-filled, inlaid enamel $55
The Del Monte, 17 jewels, 14k gold-filled, inlaid enamel $55

.....SUSTAINED BY 59 YEARS OF FINE WATCHMAKING.....

Too frequently, watches of quite irreproachable appearance turn out to be no better than elegant perjurers...fair, but frail. For the truth is not in them.

Never has that soft impeachment been laid against an Illinois Watch. However delicately beautiful, these new ribbon watches... matchless in charm... exquisite in style... their beauty is more than case deep. Their's is the beauty that lies within... the beauty of inner perfection which alone makes a watch an accurate, dependable, truth-telling timepiece.

Your jeweler is showing these new Illinois models...all exclusive Illinois designs... cased and timed at the factory. In attractiveness and solid worth wholly typical of the entire line of Illinois Watches for men and women. And you can learn a lot more about how good they are by sending for our interesting, illustrated booklet, "The Thrilling Beauty that Lies Within." Address, The Illinois Watch, 1224 North Ninth St., Springfield, Ill.

Below, reading down
The Miami, 17 jewels, 14k gold-filled, inlaid enamel $55
The Long Beach, 17 jewels, 14k gold-filled $50
The Edgewater, 17 jewels, 14k gold-filled $50

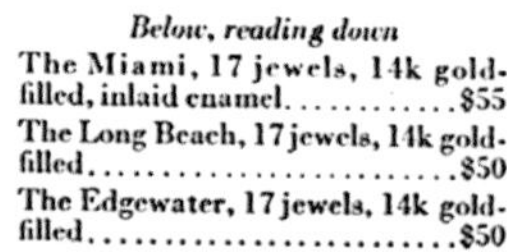

The ILLINOIS WATCH
Established 1870
SPRINGFIELD, ILLINOIS

MORE THAN A FINE WATCH — A GREAT AMERICAN WATCH

Liberty, October 19, 1929

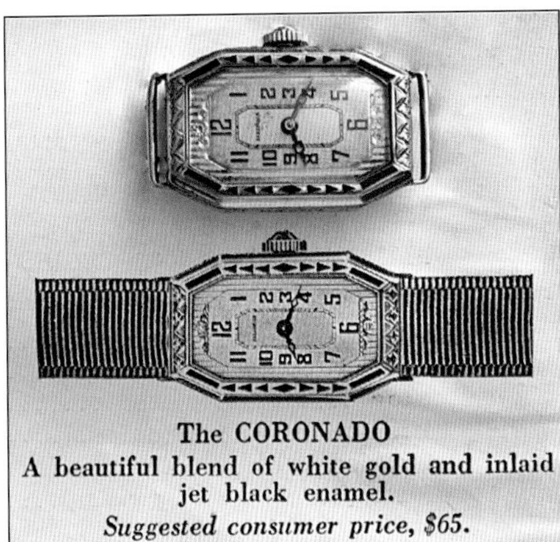

A. I. Hall 1930–31 catalog, with superimposed Coronado

Sometimes confused with the Coronado is the Mary Todd 203, which also has a very daring pattern of black enamel. (See its listing later in this chapter.)

Since the Mary Todd 203 was in 18K solid white gold rather than 14K, it was priced at $75.00, $10.00 more than the Coronado.

Page 30 — *The KEYSTONE* — September, 1929

We Present the New Models of American Watches

In addition to the styles pictured here, we have in stock, at all times, available for prompt delivery, all other models of

ELGIN, HAMILTON, HOWARD, ILLINOIS WATCHES AND WALTHAM WATCHES AND CLOCKS.

In addition, we have complete assortments of

HADLEY ATTACHMENTS, SMITH & CROSBY BRACELETS, HARVEY CLAP ANNE ELAINE BANDS, STURDY AND VIKING ATTACHMENTS.

We direct your attention especially to our fine diamond mounted ribbon watches.

Description of Articles in Panel

ILLINOIS CORONADO - Retail *$65.00*
HAMILTON PINEHURST - Retail *$90.00*
WALTHAM SPORTSTRAP Retail *$21.50*
HOWARD NORMAN - Retail *$75.00*
ELGIN - New leather folding clock 8-day. Ready for distribution in October.

"Specialists in American Watches and Attachments to the Retail Jeweler"

Louis Sickles
WHOLESALE WATCH SERVICE
1015 CHESTNUT STREET
Philadelphia, Pa.

Keystone, September 1929, Coronado on top

Countess

See listing for **Princess/Countess**

DAYTONA 153

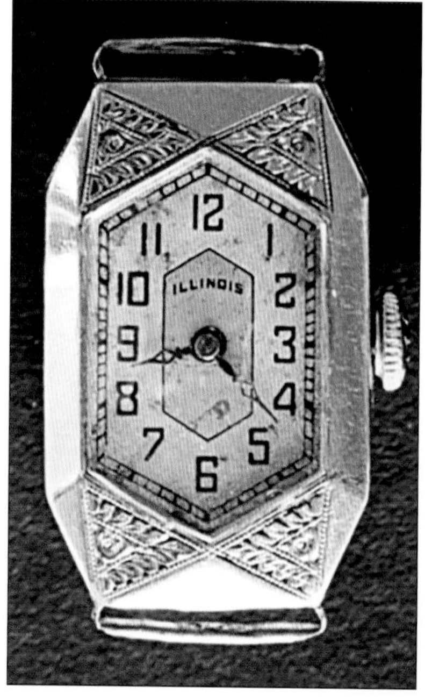

Daytona 153, white gold-filled

Name = Daytona 153
Time Period = Deco
Karat/Material = 14K WGF
Bezel = Engraved (partially)
Sides = Engraved
Lug Size = 11mm
Spring Bar = Fixed Lugs
Casemaker = Wadsworth
Case Pieces = 3
Case Number = 153
Case Back = Engraved
Dimensions = 17 x 31mm
Durability = 🕒🕒🕒🕒
Movement Size = 18/0
Movement Grade/Jewels = 807/17
Dial Number = 8147
Dial = Silver Finish, Butler Center; Sparkle Finish
Dial Opening = Hexagonal
Numerals= Painted
Hands = Steel
Seconds at = None
Cased in Factory = Yes
Collectibility = 🕒🕒🕒🕒
Rarity = 🕒🕒🕒
Retail Price New = $50.00
Introduction Date = 1929
Unique Case Design = Yes
Unique Dial Design = Yes
Advertisement = Yes
Marketing Theme = "Great beauty"

The various ladies' Illinois Daytona models represent Illinois at its most confusing best. There are at least four different case models that are named Daytona. To help clarify this confusion, we have renamed them as the Daytona 153, Daytona 154, Daytona 155, Daytona 155A and Daytona 155B. All of the Daytona models have 17-jewel movements and came with ribbon bands.

All of the Daytonas have octagonal cases. In addition, all also have hexagonal dial openings. Illinois adds to the confusion by using the same basic case designs on a number of other models, but with differences such as engraving, inlaid enamel and square-shaped dial openings. Unfortunately, many of these models share the same case Model No., and the case backs are interchangeable. For example, case Model No. 153 is used not just for the Daytona 153 but also for the Long Beach, the Saratoga Leaf, the Saratoga Notched Leaf, the Redonda 153 and the Berkeley 153.

The Daytona 153 is like the Daytona 155 except for being in a white gold-filled case rather than in solid white gold. The top and bottom of both bezels are embellished with leaf-like engravings, while the bezel area around the crystal has a smooth polished surface. Unidentified by name but pictured in the 1930 L. & C. Mayers catalog are these "thin model cases of great beauty." The solid gold model cost $15.00 more than the gold-filled one. Advertised in similar fashion, with one image to cover the pair, were the 14K white gold-filled Biloxi and the 14K solid white gold Beverly, which were likewise essentially the same model, just in different case metals.

The fancy dial pictured on the Daytona 153/Daytona 155 in the 1930 L. & C. Mayers catalog is one that is frequently seen on these models but is not shown in the extant Illinois materials catalogs. It has decoration in the center, there are larger numerals for 12 and 6, and the numbers and decoration are etched raised figures in gilt.

Daytona 154, white gold

Daytona 154

Name = Daytona 154
Time Period = Deco
Karat/Material = 14K WG
Bezel = Engraved (mostly)
Sides = Engraved
Lug Size = 11mm
Spring Bar = Fixed Lugs
Casemaker = Wadsworth
Case Pieces = 3
Case Number = 154
Case Back = Engraved
Dimensions = 17 x 31mm
Durability = ◷◷◷◷
Movement Size = 18/0
Movement Grade/Jewels = 807/17
Dial Number = 8147
Dial = Silver Finish, Butler Center; Sparkle Finish
Dial Opening = Hexagonal
Numerals= Embossed

Hands = Steel
Seconds at = None
Cased in Factory = Yes
Collectibility = ◷◷◷◷
Rarity = ◷◷◷◷◷
Retail Price New = $65.00
Introduction Date = 1929
Unique Case Design = Yes
Unique Dial Design = No
Advertisement = Yes
Marketing Theme = "A charming model harmoniously decorated"

Basically, the Daytona 154, Daytona 155, Daytona 155A, and Daytona 155B all differ from the Daytona 153 in that they are solid white gold and the other one is white gold-filled. But all have 17-jewel movements, and all were equipped with ribbon bands.

However, the Daytona 154 is packed with unique and eye-catching design features. It has a much more elaborate case than the Daytona 153 or 155. The bezel of the Daytona 154 is covered with intricate engravings of flowers and leaves except for the smooth, polished chevron-shaped areas at the top and bottom of the dial opening.

The Daytona 154 appeared in the 1929–30 Illinois Sales Catalog. The dial shown on it in the image there is the silver finish one with a butler center, but a special embossed dial with decoration in its center adds extra pizzazz to this already very interesting design. However, since this dial does not appear in any Illinois materials catalog that has yet been found, the model number is not known.

The DAYTONA

A charming model harmoniously decorated with polished surfaces and engraving. The case is 14K solid gold, the movement Illinois 17 jewels.

Consumer price, $65.00

Illinois Sales Catalog, 1929–30

Daytona 155

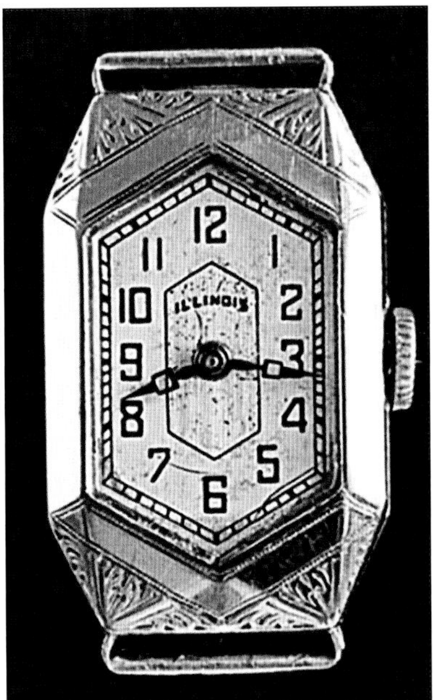

Daytona 155, white gold

Name = Daytona 155
Time Period = Deco
Karat/Material = 14K WG
Bezel = Engraved (partially)
Sides = Engraved
Lug Size = 11mm
Spring Bar = Fixed Lugs
Casemaker = Wadsworth
Case Pieces = 3
Case Number = 155
Case Back = Engraved
Dimensions = 17 x 27mm
Durability = 🕒🕒🕒🕒
Movement Size = 18/0
Movement Grade/Jewels = 807/17
Dial Number = 8147
Dial = Silver Finish, Butler Center; Sparkle Finish
Dial Opening = Hexagonal
Numerals= Painted
Hands = Steel
Seconds at = None
Cased in Factory = Yes
Collectibility = 🕒🕒🕒🕒
Rarity = 🕒🕒🕒🕒🕒🕒
Retail Price New = $65.00
Introduction Date = 1929
Unique Case Design = Yes
Unique Dial Design = No
Advertisement = Yes
Marketing Theme = "Beauty of performance"

The Daytona 155 is similar to the Daytona 154 in that both models are in 14K white gold cases and both have bezels that are partially engraved. The major difference between them is that the Daytona 154 is engraved down the sides of its bezel, whereas the sides of the bezel on the Daytona 155 are plain (they are part of a continuous smooth, polished band around the bezel, while the Daytona 154 has only smooth, polished chevron-shaped areas at the top and bottom of its bezel). In addition, the engraving of the Daytona 154 incorporates flowers as well as leaves in its design, whereas the Daytona 155 features only leaves. (The bezels of the solid gold Daytona 155A and Daytona 155B exhibit further differences,)

The Daytona 155 apparently came with a special embossed dial (noted also in the listings for the **Daytona 153** and **Daytona 154**), but other dials with suitable hexagonal openings could also be used with it, such as the one in silver finish with a silver butler center.

The Daytona 155 was advertised in the August 1929 issue of the *American Magazine* along with the two other 14K gold Illinois ladies' models, the Narragansett and the Coronado. It was also advertised in the October 19, 1929 issue of *Liberty*, along with the Coronado, Del Monte 155, Edgewater 155, Long Beach, Mary Todd, Miami 155, Redonda and Tuxedo.

According to Gay, the Daytona 155 is a very difficult watch to locate.

DAYTONA

The engraving of 14K solid gold in a delicate design offers in the DAYTONA an unusual appeal to milady, who prefers simplicity in adornment. Fitted with a 17 jeweled movement.
Retail, $65 ***List, $74***

W. J. Johnson Company advertisement, *Keystone*, June 1929

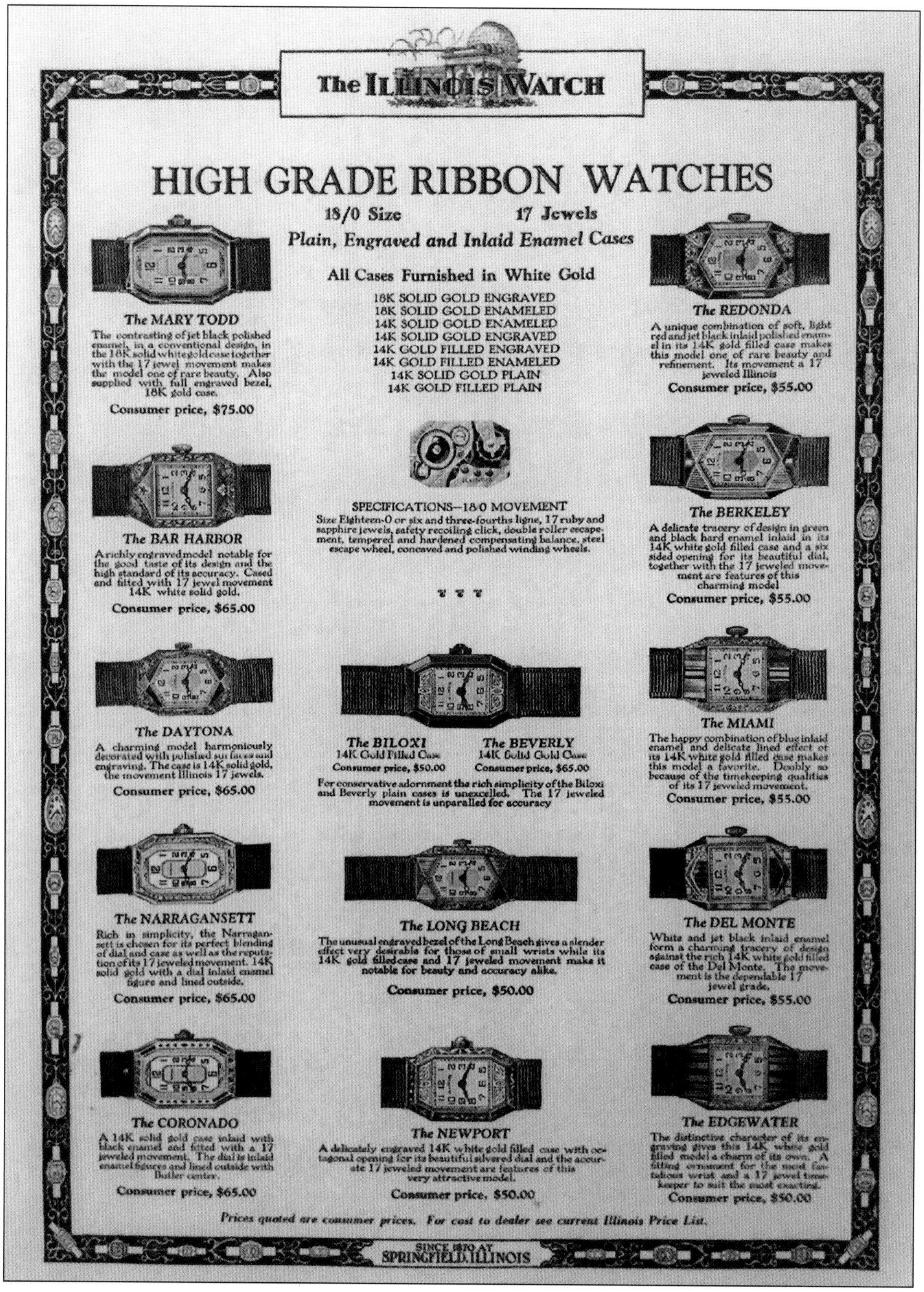

The ILLINOIS WATCH

HIGH GRADE RIBBON WATCHES

18/0 Size **17 Jewels**

Plain, Engraved and Inlaid Enamel Cases

All Cases Furnished in White Gold

18K SOLID GOLD ENGRAVED
18K SOLID GOLD ENAMELED
14K SOLID GOLD ENAMELED
14K SOLID GOLD ENGRAVED
14K GOLD FILLED ENGRAVED
14K GOLD FILLED ENAMELED
14K SOLID GOLD PLAIN
14K GOLD FILLED PLAIN

***The* MARY TODD**
The contrasting of jet black polished enamel, in a conventional design, in the 18K solid white gold case together with the 17 jewel movement makes the model one of rare beauty. Also supplied with full engraved bezel, 18K gold case.
Consumer price, $75.00

***The* REDONDA**
A unique combination of soft, light red and jet black inlaid polished enamel in its 14K gold filled case makes this model one of rare beauty and refinement. Its movement a 17 jeweled Illinois
Consumer price, $55.00

SPECIFICATIONS—18/0 MOVEMENT
Size Eighteen-0 or six and three-fourths ligne, 17 ruby and sapphire jewels, safety recoiling click, double roller escapement, tempered and hardened compensating balance, steel escape wheel, concaved and polished winding wheels.

***The* BAR HARBOR**
A richly engraved model notable for the good taste of its design and the high standard of its accuracy. Cased and fitted with 17 jewel movement 14K white solid gold.
Consumer price, $65.00

***The* BERKELEY**
A delicate tracery of design in green and black hard enamel inlaid in its 14K white gold filled case and a six sided opening for its beautiful dial, together with the 17 jeweled movement are features of this charming model
Consumer price, $55.00

***The* DAYTONA**
A charming model harmoniously decorated with polished surfaces and engraving. The case is 14K solid gold, the movement Illinois 17 jewels.
Consumer price, $65.00

***The* BILOXI**
14K Gold Filled Case
Consumer price, $50.00

***The* BEVERLY**
14K Solid Gold Case
Consumer price, $65.00

For conservative adornment the rich simplicity of the Biloxi and Beverly plain cases is unexcelled. The 17 jeweled movement is unparalled for accuracy

***The* MIAMI**
The happy combination of blue inlaid enamel and delicate lined effect of its 14K white gold filled case makes this model a favorite. Doubly so because of the timekeeping qualities of its 17 jeweled movement.
Consumer price, $55.00

***The* NARRAGANSETT**
Rich in simplicity, the Narragansett is chosen for its perfect blending of dial and case as well as the reputation of its 17 jeweled movement. 14K solid gold with a dial inlaid enamel figure and lined outside.
Consumer price, $65.00

***The* LONG BEACH**
The unusual engraved bezel of the Long Beach gives a slender effect very desirable for those of small wrists while its 14K gold filled case and 17 jeweled movement make it notable for beauty and accuracy alike.
Consumer price, $50.00

***The* DEL MONTE**
White and jet black inlaid enamel form a charming tracery of design against the rich 14K white gold filled case of the Del Monte. The movement is the dependable 17 jewel grade.
Consumer price, $55.00

***The* CORONADO**
A 14K solid gold case inlaid with black enamel and fitted with a 17 jeweled movement. The dial is inlaid enamel figures and lined outside with Butler center.
Consumer price, $65.00

***The* NEWPORT**
A delicately engraved 14K white gold filled case with octagonal opening for its beautiful silvered dial and the accurate 17 jeweled movement are features of this very attractive model.
Consumer price, $50.00

***The* EDGEWATER**
The distinctive character of its engraving gives this 14K white gold filled model a charm of its own. A fitting ornament for the most fastidious wrist and a 17 jewel timekeeper to suit the most exacting.
Consumer price, $50.00

Prices quoted are consumer prices. For cost to dealer see current Illinois Price List.

SINCE 1870 AT
SPRINGFIELD, ILLINOIS

Illinois Sales Catalog, 1929–30

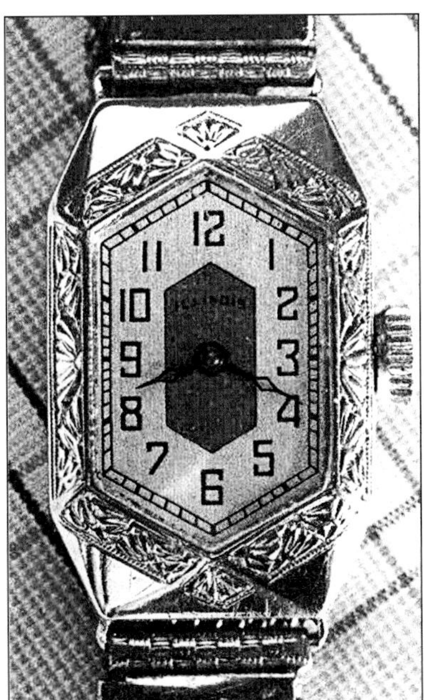

Daytona 155A, white gold

Daytona 155A

Name = Daytona 155A
Time Period = Deco
Karat/Material = 14K WG
Bezel = Engraved (partially)
Sides = Engraved
Lug Size = 11mm
Spring Bar = Fixed Lugs
Casemaker = Wadsworth
Case Pieces = 3
Case Number = 155
Case Back = Engraved
Dimensions = 17 x 31mm
Durability = 🕒🕒🕒🕒
Movement Size = 18/0
Movement Grade/Jewels = 807/17
Dial Number = 8147
Dial = Silver Finish
Dial Opening = Hexagonal
Numerals = Embossed
Hands = Steel
Seconds at = None
Cased in Factory = Yes
Collectibility = 🕒🕒🕒🕒
Rarity = 🕒🕒🕒🕒🕒🕒🕒
Retail Price New = Unknown
Introduction Date = 1929
Unique Case Design = Yes
Unique Dial Design = No
Advertisement = No
Marketing Theme = Unknown

Two variants of the Daytona 155 have recently been found. Each has a pattern of bezel engraving that is decidedly different from what is on the Daytona 153, Daytona 154, or Daytona 155. This model will be called the Daytona 155A.

The Daytona 155A features a band of exquisitely engraved leafy and floral forms around the dial opening. The band is not continuous at the top and bottom of the bezel; one motif, a single leaf, is set off by the narrow area of smooth surface on either side of it. Since other parts of the bezel are plan, the engraving stands out all the more.

The Daytona 155A shown here has dial No. 8147 with a silver finish and butler center rather than the special embossed dial of unknown number often found on the descriptions of other Daytona-family models, including the Daytona 155B. But of course the other dial would certainly be appropriate for this model also. This is as yet the only known specimen of the Daytona 155A. It seems likely that this model, as well as the Daytona 155B, was a custom-ordered watch. Whatever its provenance, it is a rare watch, very collectible and valuable.

DAYTONA 155B

Name = Daytona 155B
Time Period = Deco
Karat/Material = 14K WG
Bezel = Engraved (mostly)
Sides = Engraved
Lug Size = 11mm
Spring Bar = Fixed Lugs
Casemaker = Wadsworth
Case Pieces = 3
Case Number = 155
Case Back = Engraved
Dimensions = 17 x 31mm
Durability = ◷◷◷◷
Movement Size = 18/0
Movement Grade/Jewels = 807/17
Dial Number = Unknown
Dial = Silver Finish
Dial Opening = Hexagonal
Numerals = Painted
Hands = Steel
Seconds at = None
Cased in Factory = Yes
Collectibility = Excellent
Rarity = ◷◷◷◷◷◷
Retail Price New = Unknown
Introduction Date = 1929
Unique Case Design = Yes
Unique Dial Design = No
Advertisement = Yes
Marketing Theme = Unknown

Daytona 155B, white gold

Another recently discovered Daytona variant, designated Daytona 155B, has a special engraved bezel that clearly distinguishes it from the other three solid gold Daytona models. (Interestingly, a Wadsworth advertisement in the June 1, 1929 issue of the *Literary Digest* includes an image of this very model.)

The Daytona 155B shown here is sporting the unusual embossed dial mentioned earlier. Its number is unknown because it does not appear in any Illinois dial catalog that has been found thus far.

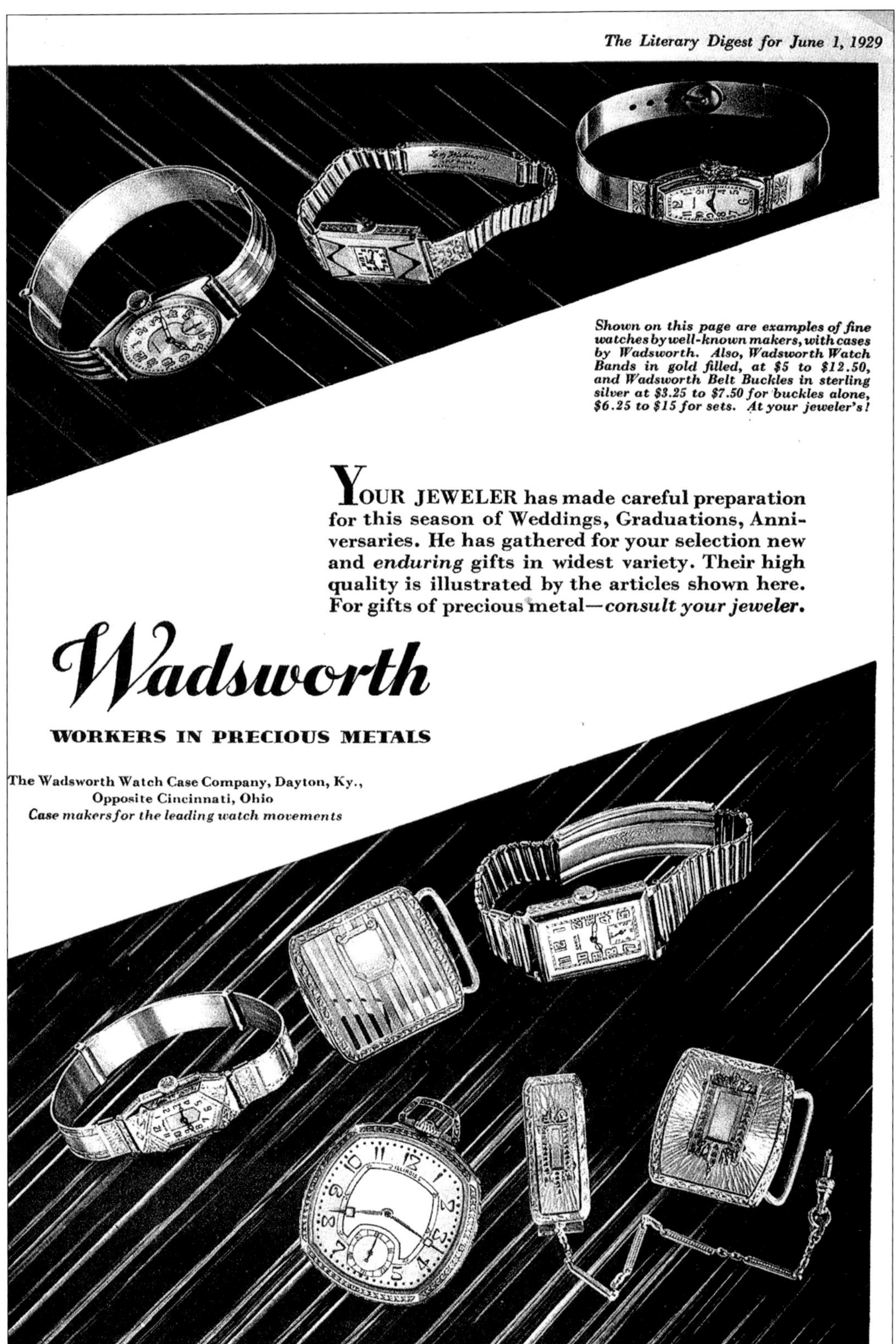

The Daytona 155B, as shown in a Wadsworth advertisement (*bottom, far left*) in the *Literary Digest*, June 1, 1929. The watch bracelet is Wadsworth's "Athena" model.

Literary Digest, **June 1, 1929 close up of Daytona 155B**

There are leaves and there are flowers in the engraving on the Daytona 155B, but they are in different combinations and positions from what is on either the Daytona 154 or the Daytona 155. There are other differences as well. The dial opening of the Daytona 155B is surrounded by a band of engraving, but the bezel of the Daytona 154 has a smooth chevron-shaped area at the top and bottom, and the band around the dial opening of the Daytona 155 is smooth.

Although the engraving pattern on the band around the dial opening of the Daytona 155B is identical to that of the Daytona 155A, the four corners of its bezel have additional decoration, a dainty flower. In contrast, the corners of the Daytona 155A have smooth surfaces.

The Daytona 155B shown on page 1133 is sporting the special embossed dial noted in the descriptions of the Daytona 153, Daytona 154 and Daytona 155.

As yet, there are only two specimens of the Daytona 155B known to exist. It is quite possible that this model, as well as the Daytona 155A, was a custom-ordered watch and is thus very collectible and valuable.

Daytona 155B inside case back and movement

Daytona 155B case

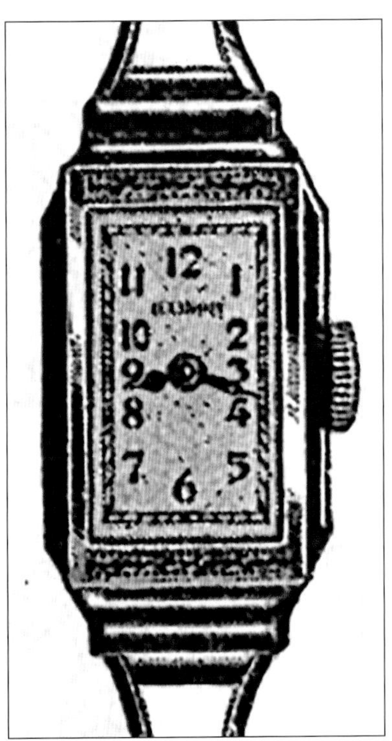
Débette

Débette

Name = Débette
Time Period = Moderne
Karat/Material = 14K WGF, 14K YGF
Bezel = Engraved (partially)
Sides = Unknown
Lug Size = 8mm
Spring Bar = Fixed Lugs
Casemaker = Unknown
Case Pieces = 2
Case Number = Unknown
Case Back = Plain
Dimensions = Unknown
Durability = Unknown
Movement Size = 21/0
Movement Grade/Jewels = 107/17
Dial Number = 8122
Dial = Silver Finish
Dial Opening = Rectangular
Numerals = Painted
Hands = Steel
Seconds at = None
Cased in Factory = Yes, by Hamilton in Lancaster
Collectibility = ◷◷◷◷
Rarity = ◷◷◷◷◷◷◷
Retail Price New = $47.50
Introduction Date = 1934
Unique Case Design = Unknown
Unique Dial Design = Unknown
Advertisement = Yes
Marketing Themes = "Richly engraved"
"With bracelet to match"

The Débette, called a "Semi-Baguette" watch, was equipped with a 17-jewel movement and came with a metal bracelet. It was one of the eight 21/0 size models advertised in the Illinois 1934 catalog as "Baguette Style Wrist Watches of Charm and Precision." The others were the Antoinette, Babette, Janette, Lynette, Mariette, Marionette and Marlette. All had Elinvar hairsprings.

The Illinois catalog advertisement, which showed those models plus the 18/0 size Sangamon and Urbana, appeared in the 1934 catalogs of such jobbers as A. C. Becken and Moore & Evans, among others. In addition, the Débette and Mariette models were advertised together in the 1934 Union and Hardware Metal Co. catalog; this firm was located at 411 E. First Street, Los Angeles, California.

The Hardware catalog listed the Débette at $60.00. The advertisement stated that Illinois ladies' wristwatches "are dependable and accurate. Illinois, since 1870, has made high-grade watches. It's as modern as the minute—incorporating all of the horological advances which have occurred in the past years."

ILLINOIS WATCHES

LADIES' WRIST WATCHES

Are dependable and accurate. Illinois, since 1870, has made high-grade watches. It's as modern as the minute —incorporating all of the horological advance which have occurred in the past years.

6½ Ligne, 14-karat white or natural gold filled. Richly engraved with bracelet to match, 17-jewel movement.

NO.	Size	Jewel	Finish	Cat. List EACH
Debette-N	6½	17	Natural	$60.00
Debette-W	6½	17	White	60.00

6½ Ligne, 14-karat white or natural gold filled. Smartly engraved, ribbon band, 17-jewel movement.

NO.	Size	Jewel	Finish	Cat. List EACH
Mariette-N	6½	17	Natural	$55.00
Mariette-W	6½	17	White	55.00

An attractive gift box with each watch.

1930 catalog, Union & Hardware Metal Company, 411 E. First St., Los Angeles, CA

To date, no specimen of the Débette model has been found. Although the casemaker is thus unknown, it is likely to have been Keystone. The Débette came with a matching metal bracelet.

The Débette was on the Illinois May 1, 1934 price list.

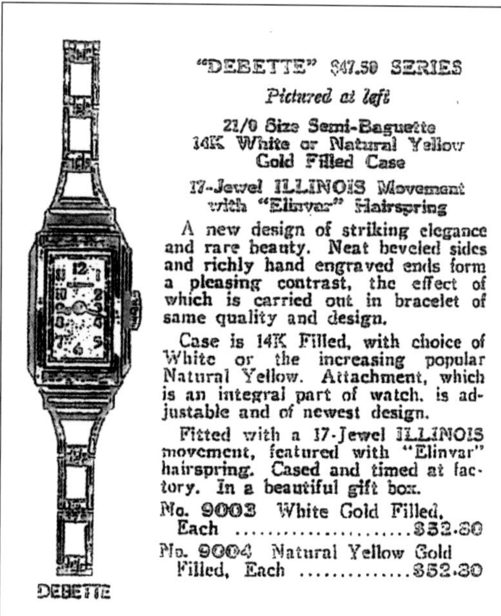

"DEBETTE" $47.50 SERIES

Pictured at left

21/0 Size Semi-Baguette
14K White or Natural Yellow
Gold Filled Case

17-Jewel ILLINOIS Movement
with "Elinvar" Hairspring

A new design of striking elegance and rare beauty. Neat beveled sides and richly hand engraved ends form a pleasing contrast, the effect of which is carried out in bracelet of same quality and design.

Case is 14K Filled, with choice of White or the increasing popular Natural Yellow. Attachment, which is an integral part of watch, is adjustable and of newest design.

Fitted with a 17-Jewel ILLINOIS movement, featured with "Elinvar" hairspring. Cased and timed at factory. In a beautiful gift box.

No. 9003 White Gold Filled, Each $52.80

No. 9004 Natural Yellow Gold Filled, Each $52.80

DEBETTE

Fort Dearborn catalog, 1935

Miss Toby Wing, budding star with Paramount.

NATURAL GOLD

Many of the watches in this JOHN PLAIN BOOK are offered in your choice of White Gold or Natural Yellow Gold. The beauty of natural gold is once again the height of good style. Whether you prefer White or Natural Gold, you will find a wide selection, America's most famous makes. Every watch comes with attractive gift box.

ILLINOIS "DEBETTE" FOR 1935

Movement: Illinois 17 jewel, 21/0 size. Case: White 14K gold filled, very fine quality. Fitted with flexible open link bracelet to match. Cased, timed and boxed at the Illinois factory.

2B23522 PRICE.. **$63.30**

NEW ILLINOIS "BABETTE"

White or Natural Gold

Movement: Illinois 17 jewel. 21/0 size. Case: Your choice of White or natural Yellow 14K solid gold, substantially heavy weight, fashionably small size. Fitted with adjustable silk ribbon. Cased, timed and boxed at the Illinois factory.

2B23523 White 14K Solid Gold. PRICE..................... **$66.70**

2B23524 Natural Yellow 14K Solid Gold. PRICE......... **66.70**

John Plain Book catalog, 1934

Debutante

See listing for **Vanity Fair/Debutante**

Del Monte 155

Del Monte 155, white gold-filled, black and white enamel

Name = Del Monte 155
Time Period = Deco
Karat/Material = 14K WGF, Black and White Inlaid Enamel
Bezel = Engraved, with Enamel
Sides = Engraved
Lug Size = 11mm
Spring Bar = Fixed Lugs
Casemaker = Wadsworth
Case Pieces = 3
Case Number = 155
Case Back = Engraved
Dimensions = 17 x 31mm
Durability = 🕒🕒🕒
Movement Size = 18/0
Movement Grade/Jewels = 807/17
Dial Number = 8169
Dial = Silver Finish
Dial Opening = Short Rectangular
Numerals = Painted, Embossed
Hands = Steel
Seconds at = None
Cased in Factory = Yes
Collectibility = 🕒🕒🕒🕒
Rarity = 🕒🕒🕒🕒🕒
Retail Price New = $55.00
Introduction Date = 1929
Unique Case Design = Yes
Unique Dial Design = No
Advertisement = Yes
Marketing Theme = "A charming tracery of design"

Del Monte 155, white gold-filled, black and white enamel

The two Del Monte models are among the most highly sought-after ladies' Illinois watches with deco-designed, enamel bezels.

The unique use of the inlaid black and white enamel on the Del Monte 155 makes it one of the finest deco-designed ladies' wristwatches ever produced. This watch is architectural in its design, perhaps inspired by the construction of the skyscrapers in major cities in the late 1920s. Its geometric simplicity is stunning.

The Del Monte 155 came equipped with a 17-jewel movement and a ribbon band. It was advertised in the 1929–30 Illinois Sales Catalog and in the October 19, 1929 issue of *Liberty*. An image of it was also included in a Wadsworth advertisement in a July 1930 issue of the *Keystone*, although the name of the model was not listed.

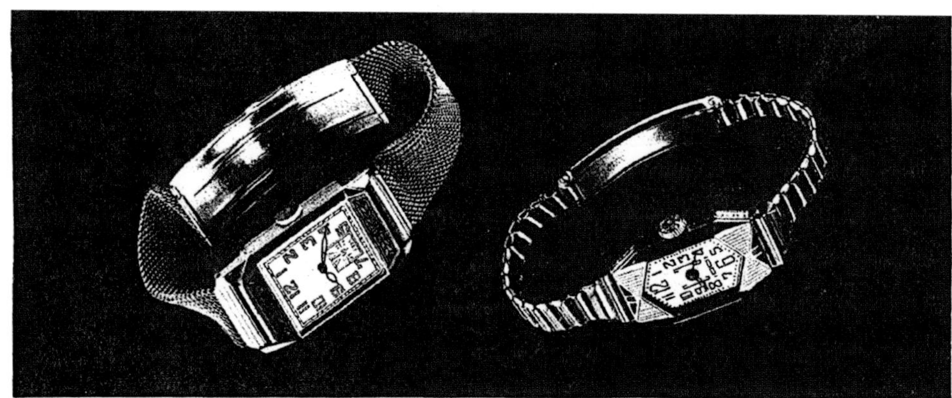

Completing the circle of quality

. . . a *Wadsworth Band!*

A PERSON takes pride in his watch. And if it happens to be a wrist watch, he doesn't want his pride to stop where the band begins. The band is an integral part of the ensemble—and he wants to be proud of that, too!

Any fine watch and a Wadsworth Band makes an endless circle of quality. The colors, the style, and the workmanship are the same. For Wadsworth Bands are made of precious metal—by the same skilled craftsmen who make Wadsworth Cases for the world's leading watch manufacturers.

Ask your wholesaler to show you these smart, nationally advertised bands. We're sure you'll agree that this is the band a fine watch deserves. The Wadsworth Watch Case Company, Dayton, Kentucky. Offices: New York, 20 W. 47th Street; San Francisco, 150 Post Street; Chicago, 35 E. Wacker Drive.

On the Air!

Every Wednesday evening, the powerful Blue Network Stations of the National Broadcasting Company listed below carry the Wadsworth message—*your* message—to a vast audience of radio listeners. Listen in!—and let us have your comments and suggestions.

City	Station	Time
Chicago	WLS	CDT—8:00 PM
Boston	WBZA	EDT—9:00 PM
Springfield	WBZ	EDT—9:00 PM
Detroit	WJR	EST—8:00 PM
Kansas City	WREN	CST—7:00 PM
St. Louis	KWK	CST—7:00 PM
New York	WJZ	EDT—9:00 PM
Rochester	WHAM	EDT—9:00 PM
Cincinnati	WCKY	EST—8:00 PM
Pittsburgh	KDKA	EDT—9:00 PM

CDT—Central Daylight Time
EDT—Eastern Daylight Time
EST—Eastern Standard Time
CST—Central Standard Time

The new Wadsworth Model B (upper left)—a flexible mesh band for men. Easily adjusted! Extremely comfortable! Not affected by perspiration. Locking device always remains in exact center of the wrist. Priced to the consumer at $10.

The "Lady Wadsworth" band for women, (upper right) like the "Lord Wadsworth" for men, is made in white or green gold filled. Advertised prices to consumer—$10 to $12.50.

The Wadsworth "Model A" bracelet (lower left) has links fastened together with pin bars, and is easily fitted without special tools. Priced to the consumer at $6.50.

WORKERS IN PRECIOUS METALS

Wadsworth Watch Case advertisement, *Keystone* July 1930. All three of the watches are Illinois, though not identified as such (Del Monte 155 is bottom, left).

Del Monte 157, white gold-filled

Del Monte 157

Name = Del Monte 157
Time Period = Deco
Karat/Material = 14K WGF, Green and Black Inlaid Enamel
Bezel = Engraved, with Enamel
Sides = Engraved
Lug Size = 11mm
Spring Bar = Fixed Lugs
Casemaker = Wadsworth
Case Pieces = 3
Case Number = 157
Case Back = Engraved
Dimensions = 17 x 31mm
Durability = ◷◷◷
Movement Size = 18/0
Movement Grade/Jewels = 807/17
Dial Number = 8169
Dial = Silver Finish
Dial Opening = Short Rectangular
Numerals = Painted
Hands = Steel
Seconds at = None
Cased in Factory = Yes
Collectibility = ◷◷◷◷
Rarity = ◷◷◷◷◷
Retail Price New = $55.00
Introduction Date = 1928
Unique Case Design = Yes
Unique Dial Design = Yes
Advertisement = Yes
Marketing Theme = "A charming tracery of design"

This model was adver-vertised by Illinois in the October 1928 issue of the *National Geographic* and the September 29, 1928 issue of the *Saturday Evening Post.*

The Del Monte 157 is one of the finest and most col-lectible deco-styled ladies' wristwatches with enamel bezels. The delicate design of black enamel radiating out of the sea-green inlaid enamel of the stylized floral figure in the corners of the bezel is highly unusual and very beautiful.

It seems strange that the Illinois advertising depart-ment used the same phras-ing to describe both Del Monte models (though, in the context of advertisements, noting the different colors of enameling). "Tracery of design" is quite appropriate for the Del Monte 157 but not for the strong architectural elements of the enameling pattern on the Del Monte 155.

The Del Monte. Soft, light green and jet black inlaid enamel form a charming tracery of design against its rich 14k. white gold-filled case. Fitted with fine Illinois 17-jeweled movement of high accuracy. $55.

A watch indeed!

An exceptionally small, fine watch movement—a jewel of a watch in a setting of enduring beauty and color—that is Illinois' brilliant new creation for the women of America.

Strikingly modern in its variety of color combinations in true enamel inlaid in charming designs, you will find it adorning the wrists of good taste. Yet, true to the Illinois tradition, it is first of all a timepiece—more than a fine watch, a great American watch.

That is a high honor. For here in America are made watches which for accuracy, service and value cannot be surpassed in the markets of the world. And for more than 50 years Illinois Watches have been recognized as outstanding examples of the best American workmanship.

See the new Illinois, in all its variety of selection, at your jeweler's. Only a few designs can be shown here. Put it on your wrist and recognize for yourself its beauty and style. Then ask the jeweler how good a watch it is. He has known Illinois Watches ever since he has been in business—and he knows.

The Miami. The happy combination of warm red and black enamel inlaid in its 14k. white gold-filled case, makes this model a favorite. Doubly so because of the timekeeping qualities of its fine Illinois 17-jeweled movement. $55.

The Newport. A delicately engraved 14k. white gold-filled case with octagonal opening for its beautiful silvered dial, features this attractive model. And its fine Illinois 17-jeweled movement insures dependable timekeeping. $50.

The watches on this page are reproduced in actual size.

The

ILLINOIS WATCH

Established 1870

SPRINGFIELD, ILLINOIS

MAKERS OF THE FAMOUS ILLINOIS BUNN SPECIAL RAILROAD WATCHES

National Geographic, October 1928

In the *Saturday Evening Post* advertisement, the Del Monte 157 was highlighted among the Bar Harbor 158, Edgewater 222 and the Newport 174. The advertisement for these ladies' models proclaimed:

> **A watch indeed!**
>
> An exceptionally small, fine watch movement—a jewel of a watch in a setting of enduring beauty and color—that is Illinois' brilliant new creation for the women of America.
>
> Strikingly modern in its variety of color combinations in true enamel inlaid in charming designs, you will find it adorning the wrists of good taste. Yet, true to the Illinois tradition, it is first of all a timepiece—more than a fine watch, a great American watch.
>
> That is a high honor. For here in America are made watches which for accuracy, service and value cannot be surpassed in the markets of the world. And for more than 50 years Illinois Watches have been recognized as outstanding examples of the best American workmanship.

The Del Monte 157 was also pictured in a Wadsworth Watch Case Company advertisement in the August 1929 issue of the *Keystone*, although the name of the watch was not noted.

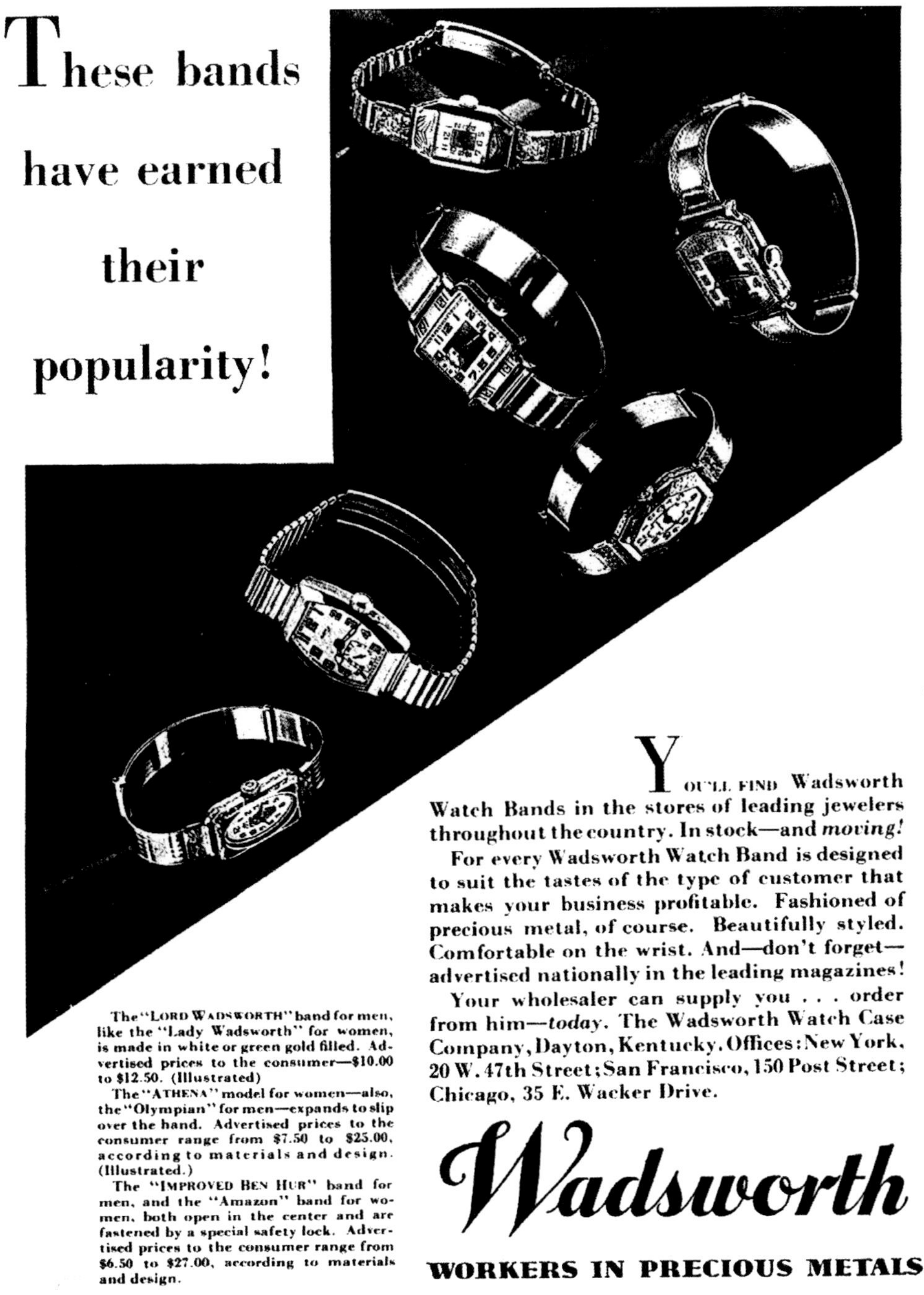

Wadsworth advertisement, *Keystone*, August 1929. Among various manufacturers' watches (all unnamed) are an Illinois Del Monte 157 (top, left) and New Yorker (below Del Monte)

Diamond-Set Models

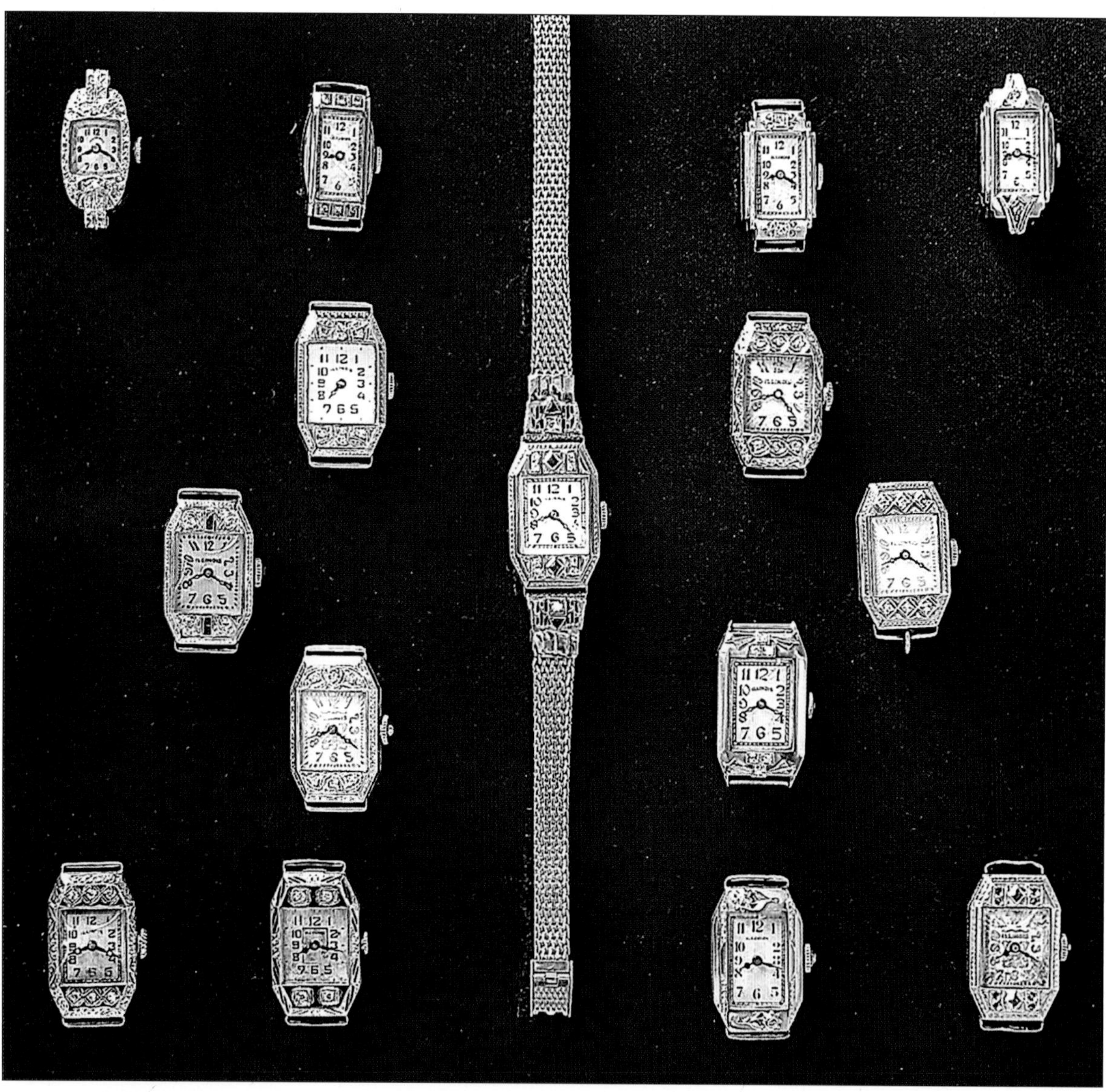

An array of Illinois diamond watches. Except for the four 21/0 size watches in the top row, all are 18/0 size. Some of the latter are among the individual Diamond-Set Models discussed in this section; others are among the named models included elsewhere in this chapter, such as the Mary Todds. (The 21/0 watches shown above are not treated in this section, as it deals only with 18/0 models. The four 21/0 watches are, *left to right:* custom 14K case with 40 diamonds; rare variant of Illinois' Antoinette model; rare variant of Illinois' Minuette model; and 14K custom-order Avon case.)

Name = Diamond-Set Models
Time Period = Deco
Karat/Material = 14K WG, 18K WG, 18K WG; diamonds
Bezel = Engraved, with Diamonds

Sides = Plain, Engraved
Lug Size = 11mm
Spring Bar = Fixed Lugs
Casemakers = Keystone, Wadsworth, Others
Case Pieces = 2, 3
Case Number = None
Case Back = Plain, Engraved
Dimensions = 17 x 31mm
Durability = 🕒🕒🕒🕒
Movement Size = 18/0
Movement Grade/Jewels = Unknown/16, 807/17
Dial Numbers = Various
Dial = Silver Finish, Embossed
Dial Openings = Short Rectangular, Rectangular
Numerals = Painted, Gilt Embossed
Hands = Steel
Seconds at = None
Cased in Factory = Yes
Collectibility = 🕒🕒🕒🕒
Rarity = 🕒🕒🕒🕒🕒
Retail Price New = Unknown
Introduction Date = 1928
Unique Case Design = Yes
Unique Dial Design = No
Advertisement = No

Two Diamond-Set Models in 18K white gold Keystone cases. *Left*, case with 8 diamonds; *right*, case with 6 diamonds and a 14K solid white gold bracelet with 4 diamonds and 2 sapphires

It was earlier thought that almost all of the various Illinois watches found with diamond bezels and without case Model Numbers were unlikely to have been Factory-Cased by Illinois and that more likely these cases were supplied by upscale jewelers for special clientele.

However, the Illinois Consumer and Keystone List Prices in the 1931 S. H. Clausin catalog as well as the A. C. Becken catalog show in "Uncased Watches" a listing for "Grade 807, Diamond Set, cased at Factory." Moreover, on another Illinois page in the Clausin catalog is this statement: "The Illinois 18/0 movement is available for use in diamond set cases only. It must be cased at the Illinois factory." It is plausible to surmise that this had been Illinois' practice for several years before that. In jobbers' catalogs from 1932 on, however, there are no uncased 18/0 size movements listed for sale.

UNCASED WATCHES

Grade 169, 19 Jewels, L.S. or P.S.	32.50	33.00
Grade 167, 17 Jewels, L.S. or P.S.	24.00	25.20
Grade 127	25.00	25.80
Grade 129	32.50	33.80
Grade 121	40.00	41.00
Grade 307 Hunting	30.00	30.00
Grade 807, Diamond Set, cased at Factory		48.50

Illinois Sales Catalog, 1931

There are several possible reasons for the stricture that diamond-set watches had to be cased at the factory. First of all, Illinois was insistent about quality and may have wanted to ensure that its movements did not appear in inferior cases. Furthermore, inserting diamonds into a bezel generally intrudes into the interior, and Illinois may have wanted to be certain that there was no interference with the movements. In addition, Illinois under Hamilton direction likely did not want to carry expensive inventory of diamond-encrusted solid gold watches and thus assembled diamond-set ones only when the appropriate cases were supplied by jobbers or jewelers on an order by order basis.

Wholesalers' catalogs as early as 1928 have now been found with Illinois diamond-set watches listed as Mary Todd models. (These are discussed in the **Mary Todd** listing in this chapter.)

The Illinois diamond-set watches are not gaudy watches covered with diamonds. Instead, they typically have only a few diamonds (usually 2, 4, 6 or 8) to highlight the elegant design of their cases. All of them found thus far have been solid white gold, usually 18K.

Most of the specimens found have had Keystone cases, though a few have been in cases by Wadsworth, Illinois' other primary casemaker for its ladies' models. There are some extraordinary Wadsworth cases in 18K white gold with black enameling decoration as well as four or six diamonds. (These are discussed in the listing for **Wadsworth Special Models** at the end of this chapter.)

One Wadsworth case, recently found, is 14K with an elaborately engraved bezel ornamented with six diamonds; the watch has a 17-jewel movement. The inside case back has no model number, but the watch is clearly a Daytona variant, as the bezel engraving is similar in style to that of the Daytona 154 and 155A. Moreover, we found that the case back will fit on those models.

Diamond-set 14K white gold Wadsworth

Diamond-set 14K white gold Wadsworth, case back

On a page headed "Illinois Wrist and Strap Watches," the 1930 L. & C. Mayers catalog lists among the eight ladies' models pictured two heavy-weight 18K solid white gold diamond-set models: the "Newport" and the "Ostend," the former with six diamonds, the latter with two. Both watches were 18/0 size, and came with 17-jewel movements.

W1936 2 fine diamonds, 17 Jewels.....**$120.00**
The Ostend. Illinois 7¾ ligne, 17 Jewel rectangular movement; 18 Kt. solid white gold case, set with 2 fine diamonds. Silk cord adjustable to wrist size.

L. & C. Mayers catalog, 1930

Ostend, white gold

Newport, white gold

W1937 6 fine diamonds, 17 Jewels....**$138.00**
The Newport. Illinois 7¾ ligne, 17 Jewel rectangular movement; 18 Kt. solid white gold case, set with 6 fine diamonds. Attractive dial.

L. & C. Mayers catalog, 1930

Although the catalog listing does not mention this detail, both of these watches have hinged cases rather than snap-on backs, which we know because at least one specimen of each has been found. These cases were atypical for Illinois ladies' models of the period, which normally had snap-on backs. However, the text at the top of the page, applying to all watches on that page, includes this statement: "All watches are cased, timed and regulated at the factory." Thus we can probably assume that both the Newport and the Ostend were Illinois Factory-Cased.

The "Newport" in the Mayers catalog bears no physical resemblance to either of the Illinois models of that name (the Newport 174 and Newport 223), though it has a case made by Keystone, as those also do, and came with a 17-jewel movement. The hinged case back of the "Ostend" has no casemaker's mark, only a serial number and the 18K mark. The specimen found is equipped with an Illinois 807 movement.

Given that we have not found these two watches advertised anywhere except in the L. & C. Mayers catalog, we think it is possible that both were custom models offered only by that wholesaler, and that Mayers had the Newport's case made by Keystone and the Ostend's by another casemaker, and then had both models cased at the Illinois factory.

A similar explanation seems plausible for not only the Illinois watches with Wadsworth 18K cases ornamented with black enamel and diamonds but also the 14K one with six diamonds. Since no advertisement or catalog listing has yet been found for any of them, we do not know what wholesaler or jeweler might have been responsible for having these beautiful watches made, but we feel that they were likely custom models.

Note: The Ostend model offered by L. & C. Mayers appears to be an anomaly. It is the only Illinois diamond-bezel watch with a hinged case and by an unknown casemaker (rather than by Keystone or Wadsworth) for which we have found any documentation as having been cased and timed by the Illinois Watch Company. Accordingly, the collector should be extremely cautious about acquiring any supposedly authentic Illinois diamond watch with a hinged case, or in a case made by a company other than Keystone or Wadsworth.

An 18K white gold Diamond-Set Model in an unsigned case, probably assembled by an Illinois jobber or jeweler

Edgewater 155, white gold-filled

Edgewater 155

Name = Edgewater 155
Time Period = Deco
Karat/Material = 14K WGF
Bezel = Engraved
Sides = Engraved
Lug Size = 11mm
Spring Bar = Fixed Lugs
Casemaker = Wadsworth
Case Pieces = 3
Case Number = 155
Case Back = Engraved
Dimensions = 17 x 31mm
Durability = 🕒🕒🕒🕒
Movement Size = 18/0
Movement Grade/Jewels = 807/17
Dial Numbers = 8170, 8364
Dial = Silver Finish, Sparkle Finish
Dial Opening = Short Rectangular
Numerals = Painted, Embossed Exploding Gold
Hands = Steel
Seconds at = None
Cased in Factory = Yes
Collectibility = 🕒🕒🕒🕒
Rarity = 🕒🕒🕒🕒
Retail Price New = $50.00
Introduction Date = 1929
Unique Case Design = Yes
Unique Dial Design = No
Advertisement = Yes
Marketing Themes = "The distinctive character of its engraving gives this 14K white gold filled model a charm of its own."
"A fitting ornament for the most fastidious wrist"

There are four known Illinois ladies' models with the name Edgewater, all of them different. It is amazing that the marketing department within the Illinois Watch Company did not try to clarify this confusion in model names. One of the cases is by Wadsworth (Edgewater 155) and three are by Keystone (Edgewaters 175, 208 and 222).

The Edgewater 155 has a very attractive Art Deco bezel with a vertical ribbon-like pattern of engraving at the top and bottom, and a narrow band of foliate engraving on the sides. The watch was equipped with a 17-jewel movement and a ribbon band.

In addition to the dials noted above, the Edgewater 155 came with an interesting dial with exploding numerals, similar to dial No. 86 in the Illinois Dial and Hand Circular, May 1927, but without the embellishment at the center. This dial (number unknown) also appears on the Bar Harbor 156 and Bar Harbor 158 as well as on the Edgewater 208 and Edgewater 222, and occasionally on the Edgewater 175 as well.

The Edgewater 155 appeared in the 1929–30 Illinois Sales Catalog. It also appeared in a July 27, 1929 *Liberty* advertisement along with the Berkeley 153, Narragansett and Mary Todd 204.

Collier's for September 7, 1929 — 55

The ILLINOIS MEDALIST 17 jewels, 14k gold-filled case . . . $60

THE NEWEST IN STRAP WATCHES—WITH ILLINOIS ACCURACY

The Illinois Medalist . . . with rectangular movement . . . . latest, neatest, smartest thing in strap watches . . . above all, a timepiece. Another demonstration of Illinois leadership in fine watchmaking . . . of that one unalterable purpose expressed in beauty.

The rectangular movement assures greater accuracy by permitting larger parts to be assembled in a thinner, narrower case . . . and in the Medalist, accuracy has been carried to an exceptional standard.

All the new Illinois models have surpassing beauty, charm and distinction. And, always, the beauty that lies within . . . that golden perfection of workmanship which makes an Illinois Watch so dependable.

Ask your jeweler. He knows Illinois Watches will give you unequalled dollar for dollar value. And you can learn a lot more about them from our interesting, illustrated booklet, "*The Beauty that Lies Within.*" Address, The Illinois Watch, 1212 North Ninth St., Springfield, Ill.

Left, reading down
The Edgewater, 17 jewels, 14k gold-filled . . . $50
The Miami, 17 jewels, 14k gold-filled, inlaid enamel . . . $55
The Mary Todd, 17 jewels, 14k solid gold, inlaid enamel . . . $75
The New Yorker, 17 jewels, 14k gold-filled $50
The Beau Brummel, 17 jewels, 14k gold-filled . . . $50
The A. Lincoln, 19 jewels, 14k solid gold $110

Below, reading down
The Ensign, 15 jewels, 14k gold-filled . . . $40
The Oxford, 17 jewels, 14k gold filled . . . $50

The ILLINOIS WATCH
MORE THAN A FINE WATCH—A GREAT AMERICAN WATCH
Established 1870
SPRINGFIELD, ILLINOIS

Collier's, September 7, 1929

In the November 2, 1929 issue of *Collier's* magazine, the Edgewater 155 was featured along with the Redonda and Narragansett in an advertisement headed "More than a Fine Watch. The Illinois. A Great American Watch":

> Illinois watches have been worn by gentlefolk since 1870. In many families the old Illinois is a treasured heirloom . . . still capable of ticking off the minutes (18,000 ticks an hour) as accurately and dependably as its youngest descendant, fresh from the factory. It is this long history of honorable service that has made Illinois the Great American Watch it is today.
>
> To the old standard of integrity in watchmaking . . . the beauty that is a time-piece . . . the new Illinois Watches add enchanting beauty and style. Never before has so much been given in a watch for the modest price of an Illinois.

Edgewater 175, white gold-filled

Edgewater 175

Name = Edgewater 175
Time Period = Deco
Karat/Material = 14K WGF, 14K YGF
Bezel = Engraved
Sides = Engraved
Lug Size = 11mm
Spring Bar = Fixed Lugs
Casemaker = Keystone
Case Pieces = 3
Case Number = 175, No Number
Case Back = Engraved
Dimensions = 17 x 31mm
Durability = 🕒🕒🕒🕒
Movement Size = 18/0
Movement Grades/Jewels = 807/17
Dial Numbers = 8170, 8364
Dial = Silver Finish, Sparkle Finish
Dial Opening = Short Rectangular
Numerals = Painted
Hands = Steel
Seconds at = None
Cased in Factory = Yes
Collectibility = 🕒🕒🕒🕒
Rarity = 🕒🕒🕒
Retail Price New = $50.00
Introduction Date = 1928
Unique Case Design = Yes
Unique Dial Design = No
Advertisement = Yes
Marketing Theme = "A fitting ornament for the most fastidious wrist"

The Edgewater 175 is notable for its beautiful, very ornate bezel. At the top and bottom of the bezel, the engraving features a distinctive fan-like motif flanked by curlicues. There is a narrow band of foliate engraving along the sides of the bezel. Of the four Edgewater models, the Model No. 175 seems to be the easiest to find.

Illinois "Book of Watches," 1928

Oskamp-Nolting catalog, 1932

Edgewater 175, yellow gold-filled

The watch came with a 17-jewel movement and is usually found in a white gold-filled case stamped with its Model No. 175, and sporting, a ribbon band. However, the Edgewater 175 can also sometimes be found with a case having no Model No. The yellow gold-filled version of the Edgewater 175 (pictured) is believed to be a custom one, according to Gay, as no other specimen like this one has been spotted; this watch came with a yellow gold-filled bracelet.

A dial with embossed exploding numerals, shown above on the Edgewater 175 in the Illinois "Book of Watches," is also shown on the same watch in the 1932 Oskamp-Nolting catalog. Some other jobbers' catalogs that we have examined show a plain dial with black numerals.

The Edgewater 175 model was well advertised in at least four different magazines in 1928 and 1929: the *Saturday Evening Post, Liberty,* the *American Magazine* and *Collier's*. The Illinois advertisement in the September 29, 1928 issue of the *Saturday Evening Post* described it as follows: "The delicate grace of its engraving gives this 14K white gold-filled model a charm all its own. A fitting ornament for the most fastidious wrist, and a timekeeper to suit the most exacting. Illinois quality 17-jeweled movement. $50." (It is surprising that Illinois used exactly the same description for the Edgewater 155, which has an entirely different type of design.)

Edgewater 208

Edgewater 208, white gold-filled

Name = Edgewater 208
Time Period = Deco
Karat/Material = 14K WGF
Bezel = Engraved
Sides = Engraved
Lug Size = 11mm
Spring Bar = Fixed Lugs
Casemaker = Keystone
Case Pieces = 3
Case Number = 208
Case Back = Engraved
Dimensions = 17 x 31mm
Durability = 🕒🕒🕒🕒
Movement Size = 18/0
Movement Grade/Jewels = 807/17
Dial Numbers = 8170, 8364, Unknown
Dial = Silver Finish, Sparkle Finish
Dial Opening = Short Rectangular
Numerals = Painted, Exploding Embossed Gold
Hands = Steel
Seconds at = None
Cased in Factory = Yes
Collectibility = 🕒🕒🕒🕒
Rarity = 🕒🕒🕒🕒
Retail Price New = $50.00
Introduction Date = 1930
Unique Case Design = Yes
Unique Dial Design = No
Advertisement = Yes
Marketing Themes = "Reflecting an unerring sense of what is smart"
"A pleasing design of bright polished surfaces and fine engraving"

The attractive Edgewater 208, introduced in 1930, is less ornate than the Edgewater 175. Its beautiful bezel, instead of being almost completely engraved, features the contrast between intricate engraving and smooth surfaces. A pattern of foliate curlicues at the top and bottom of the bezel is set off by unembellished curved areas extending down from the dial opening. The sides of the bezel are decorated only with a delicate rope-like pattern.

Like the other Edgewaters, the Model No. 208 had a 17-jewel movement and was equipped with a ribbon band. It often came with an interesting exploding numeral dial with gold embossed numerals, which heightens the effect of the case design.

The Edgewater 208 was advertised in the March 22, 1930 issue of *Collier's* magazine and in the April 1930 issue of the *American Magazine*. In the *Collier's* advertisement, it is featured along with the Mary Todd and Biltmore 18/0 models. The advertisement makes this pronouncement: "There is lasting satisfaction in the ownership of an Illinois watch. Timing the seconds for you with accurate, even pulse. Reflecting unerring sense of what is smart. Modern as tomorrow in their authentic interpretation of style and vogue in design and decoration. And, moreover, every Illinois deserves an owner who knows the importance of time and of such a timepiece."

34 **Collier's** *for March 22, 1930*

KEEPING TIME ◆ ***with beauty and enduring accuracy***

There is lasting satisfaction in the ownership of an Illinois watch. Timing the seconds for you with accurate, even pulse. Reflecting an unerring sense of what is smart. Modern as tomorrow in their authentic interpretation of style and vogue in design and decoration. And moreover, every Illinois deserves an owner who knows the importance of time and of such a timepiece . . . Illinois have been fine watches since 1870. Ever true, also, to that higher standard of beauty within—the beauty of perfection in workmanship which is the birthright of every Illinois and the secret of its enduring accuracy . . . Select a good jeweler. He can show you the full Illinois line — strap, pocket and ribbon watches, for men and women. Many of them at surprisingly low prices, considering their true value . . . And ask him to explain what the name Illinois stands for in fine watchmaking. He has known Illinois Watches ever since he's been in business.

Interesting booklet, "The Thrilling Beauty that Lies Within"—gladly sent on request. Address The Illinois Watch, 1222 North Ninth Street, Springfield, Illinois.

◆ ◆

AS ILLUSTRATED

ILLINOIS MEN'S POCKET WATCHES *(left to right)*

THE DEAN (Front and Side View) — 19 jewels, 14k white and natural solid gold case, gold figured dial $110.00

THE CUSHION — 17 jewels, 14k white gold-filled case 55.00

ILLINOIS LADIES' STRAP WATCH *(center)*

THE BILTMORE — 17 jewels, 14k gold-filled case .... $ 50.00

ILLINOIS LADIES' RIBBON WATCHES *(left to right)*

THE EDGEWATER — 17 jewels, 14k white gold-filled case .... $ 50.00

THE MARY TODD — 17 jewels, 18k solid white gold case, inlaid enamel 75.00

ILLINOIS MEN'S STRAP WATCHES *(left to right)*

THE CAVALIER — 17 jewels, 14k white or natural gold-filled case .... $ 45.00

THE TROPHY — 17 jewels, 14k white gold-filled case 55.00

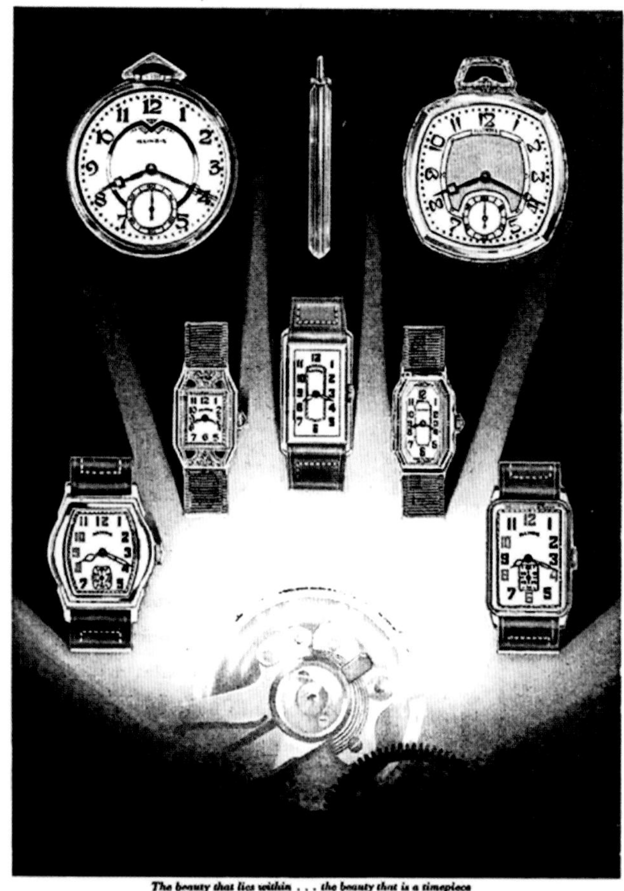

The beauty that lies within . . . the beauty that is a timepiece

The ILLINOIS WATCH

Established 1870

SPRINGFIELD, ILLINOIS

MAKERS OF THE FAMOUS ILLINOIS *(BUNN SPECIAL)* RAILROAD WATCHES

Collier's, March 22, 1930, showing Edgewater 208 (second from left)

Edgewater 222

Name = Edgewater 222
Time Period = Deco
Karat/Material = 14K WGF
Bezel = Engraved
Sides = Engraved
Lug Size = 11mm
Spring Bar = Fixed Lugs
Casemaker = Keystone
Case Pieces = 3
Case Number = 222
Case Back = Engraved
Dimensions = 17 x 31mm
Durability = ◷◷◷◷
Movement Size = 18/0
Movement Grade/Jewels = 807/17
Dial Numbers = 8170, 8364
Dial = Silver Finish, Sparkle Finish
Dial Opening = Short Rectangular
Numerals= Embossed Exploding Gold
Hands = Steel
Seconds at = None
Cased in Factory = Yes
Collectibility = ◷◷◷◷
Rarity = ◷◷◷◷◷
Retail Price New = Unknown
Introduction Date = 1930
Unique Case Design = Yes
Unique Dial Design = No
Advertisement = No
Marketing Theme = Unknown

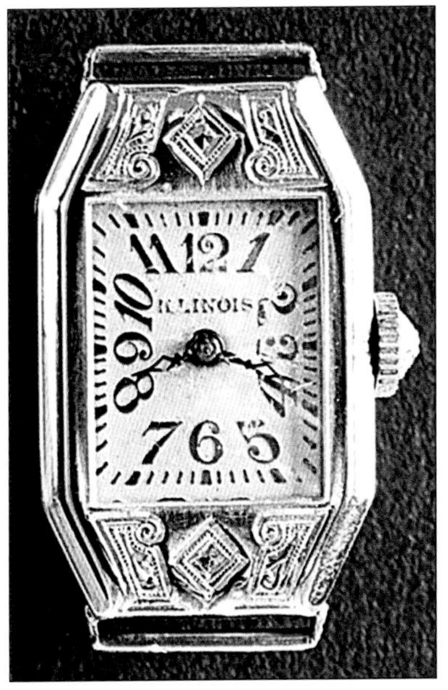

Edgewater 222, white gold-filled

The very architectural bezel design of the Edgewater 222 differs markedly from the patterns of other models in the Edgewater series. On the smooth surface at the top and bottom of the bezel is a diamond-shaped engraving in the center, bracketed by what looks like the two halves of an Ionic capital that has been split.

An exploding numeral dial of unknown number, also sometimes found with the other Edgewater models, produces a very striking effect in the small dial opening of the bezel.

Like the others in the series, the Edgewater 222 had a 17-jewel movement and was equipped with a ribbon band. No advertisement or other documentation for this Edgewater variant has yet been located. It is a very hard model to find.

Group of Edgewaters. ***Top, left to right:*** **Edgewater 175, Edgewater 175;** ***bottom, left to right:*** **Edgewater 208, Edgewater 155**

Elissa

See listing for **Marilyn/Elissa/Sylvia/Irene**

Fahys Special Model, white gold-filled

Fahys Special Model

Name = Fahys Special Model
Time Period = Deco
Karat/Material = 14K WGF
Bezel = Molded
Sides = Engraved
Lug Size = 11mm
Spring Bar = Fixed Lugs
Casemaker = Fahys
Case Pieces = 3
Case Number = No Number, signed "Special Model"
Case Back = Plain
Dimensions = 17 x 31mm
Durability = 🕒🕒🕒🕒
Movement Size = 18/0
Movement Grade/Jewels = 807/17
Dial Number = 8174
Dial = Silver Finish
Dial Opening = Octagonal
Numerals = Painted
Hands = Steel
Seconds at = None
Cased in Factory = Yes
Collectibility = 🕒🕒🕒🕒
Rarity = 🕒🕒🕒🕒🕒
Retail Price New = Unknown
Introduction Date = Unknown
Unique Case Design = Yes
Unique Dial Design = No
Advertisement = Unknown
Marketing Theme = Unknown

Although Fahys supplied cases for some of the Illinois men's wristwatch models, it was earlier thought that none of the ladies' models had cases by Fahys. However, Gay has found two specimens of an Illinois 18/0 size ladies' model with a standard Illinois Watch Company notation inside the back case: "Illinois Watch Special Model" and "Fahys 14K Gold Filled." Another collector has found two additional specimens of this model.

The white gold-filled case of the Fahys Special Model, octagonal in shape, might at first glance be mistaken for the Biloxi model, which has a Keystone case (case Model No. 186). But a closer look at the case reveals that instead of the plain, smooth surfaces on the Biloxi's bezel, there is a subtle decorative molding on the bezel of the Fahys Special Model. Running lengthwise on the sides of the bezel is a narrow indentation, and at each of the four corners there is a wider indentation that goes between the inside and outside edges of the bezel.

Fahys Special Model, white gold-filled, Deco dial

Fahys Special Model movement and inside case back

As Gay notes, Fahys used decorative molding on cases for two Illinois men's wristwatches, the Viking and the Beau Brummell/Viking, and the corner molding on the ladies' Special Model is similar to what is on the corners of those men's models. There also appears to be a relationship between the narrow indentation on the sides of the ladies' Special Model and the molding that Fahys used on the bezel of another Illinois model, the men's Medalist/Wembley.

The Fahys Special Model ladies' watch has engraving on the sides of the case (see the discussion of case engraving patterns in the introduction to this chapter), but the back of the case is plain.

The Fahys Special Model ladies' wristwatch was equipped with a 17-jewel movement and likely had a ribbon band. As yet, we have found no listings for the model in any jobbers' catalogs, nor have we found any magazine advertisements for it.

Fairfax

See listing for **Florentine/Fairfax**

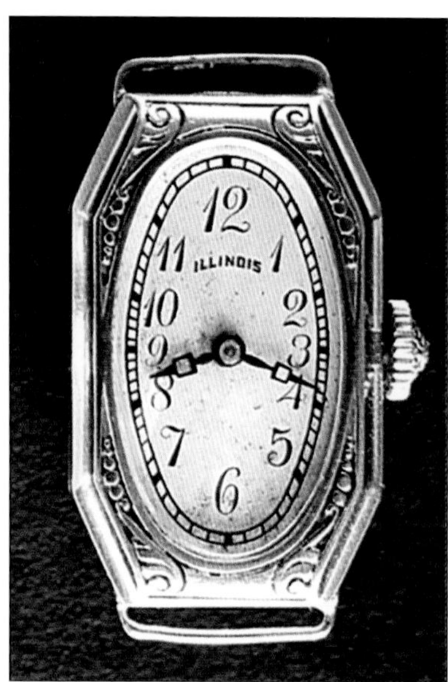

Fairport, white gold-filled

Fairport

Name =	Fairport
Time Period =	Deco
Karat/Material =	14K WGF
Bezel =	Engraved (partially)
Sides =	Engraved
Lug Size =	11mm
Spring Bar =	Fixed Lugs
Casemaker =	Keystone
Case Pieces =	3
Case Number =	200
Case Back =	Engraved
Dimensions =	17 x 30mm
Durability =	🕒🕒🕒🕒
Movement Size =	18/0
Movement Grade/Jewels =	807/17
Dial Number =	8090
Dial =	Silver Finish, Sparkle Finish
Dial Opening =	Oval
Numerals =	Painted
Hands =	Steel
Seconds at =	None
Cased in Factory =	Yes
Collectibility =	🕒🕒🕒🕒
Rarity =	🕒🕒🕒🕒🕒
Retail Price New =	$50.00
Introduction Date =	1930
Unique Case Design =	Yes
Unique Dial Design =	No
Advertisement =	Yes
Marketing Theme =	"This watch is entirely feminine in appearance."

The Fairport, which came only in a white gold-filled case and with a ribbon band, is notable for the oval dial opening of its delicately engraved bezel. The Brighton is very similar, but its case is 14K white gold and has black enamel accents. The Fairport can be a little difficult to find, but the Brighton is much more so.

The Fairport had dial commonality with the Vanity Fair and Debutante models as well as with the Brighton. From time to time, Illinois employed this methodology to keep costs down and to reduce design efforts.

In the January 11, 1930 issue of *Collier's*, the Fairport was featured along with the Avalon and Miami 155 ladies' models in an advertisement mentioning that "the [Fairport's] oval dial adds a charming touch." In addition, the Fairport was advertised in the January 1930 issue of the *American Magazine*. It also appeared in an Illinois advertisement in the December 6, 1930 issue of the *Saturday Evening Post* for the holiday shopping season.

The Fairport was advertised as being priced "modestly," since Hamilton was starting to position Illinois as its low-priced brand offering, but it was nonetheless equipped with a 17-jewel movement.

Now—*the watch you should have had for Christmas*

An ILLINOIS—that Gift of Gifts. Maybe there was a check in your Christmas stocking that will make it easy for you to give yourself the watch you hoped for—the watch somehow unthought of or forgotten by those who did their loving best to make you happy.

. . . Don't wait, then, these eleven long months 'til next Christmas comes around. Satisfy your desire to own one of these smart, beautiful watches to regulate your time through 1930 and the years to come, and give you constant joy in its possession . . . Among the attractive showing of the latest Illinois designs at any good jeweler's, you can find just the watch you'd be proud to wear. Each one an example of fine watchmaking—eloquent of that inner beauty which makes every Illinois so accurate and dependable a timepiece . . . Men's strap and pocket and ladies' ribbon watches, priced so modestly you need no longer deny yourself the pleasure and the profit of owning this fine watch —Illinois—a Great American Watch. Send for interesting, illustrated booklet, "The Thrilling Beauty that Lies Within." It tells why Illinois Watches are as good as they are beautiful . . . Address The Illinois Watch, 1211 North Ninth St., Springfield, Illinois.

AS ILLUSTRATED

ILLINOIS MAN'S POCKET WATCH

THE TRUSTEE — 17 jewels, 14k gold-filled....$55.00

ILLINOIS LADIES' RIBBON WATCHES (*left to right*)

THE FAIRPORT — 17 jewels, 14k filled, white gold....$50.00

THE AVALON — 17 jewels, 14k solid white gold.... 65.00

THE MIAMI — 17 jewels, 14k gold-filled, inlaid enamel.... 55.00

ILLINOIS MEN'S STRAP WATCHES (*left to right*)

THE NEW YORKER — 17 jewels, 14k gold-filled....$50.00

THE MEDALIST — 17 jewels, rectangular movement, 14k gold-filled.... 60.00

Where Illinois Beauty lives and endures . . . the beauty of performance.

The ILLINOIS WATCH

Established 1870

SPRINGFIELD, ILLINOIS

MAKERS OF THE FAMOUS ILLINOIS (*BUNN SPECIAL*) RAILROAD WATCHES

Collier's, January 11, 1930, with Fairport (top, left)

Fairfax, white gold-filled

Florentine / Fairfax

Names = Florentine/Fairfax
Time Period = Moderne
Karat/Material = 14K WGF
Bezel = Engraved
Sides = Engraved
Lug Size = 11mm
Spring Bar = Fixed Lugs
Casemaker = Keystone
Case Pieces = 2
Case Number = 834
Case Back = Plain
Dimensions = 17 x 31mm
Durability = 🕒🕒🕒🕒
Movement Size = 18/0
Movement Grades/Jewels = 805/15, 807/17
Dial Number = Unknown
Dial = Silver Finish, Racing (Ribbon) Stripe
Dial Opening = Rectangular Small Cut Corners
Numerals = Painted
Hands = Steel
Seconds at = None
Cased in Factory = Yes
Collectibility = 🕒🕒🕒🕒
Rarity = 🕒🕒🕒🕒🕒
Retail Price New = Florentine, $37.50 (15J), Fairfax, $50.00 (17J)
Introduction Date = 1931 (Florentine); 1932 (Fairfax)
Unique Case Design = No
Unique Dial Design = No
Advertisement = Yes (Florentine)
Marketing Theme = "Smartly styled in the modern trend" (Florentine)

Case Model No. 834 served two differently named Illinois ladies' wristwatches with few differences between them: the 15-jewel Florentine and its 17-jewel sister, the Fairfax. They are particularly notable for the unusual dial they share, which has interesting silver racing (ribbon) stripes at the top and bottom. Unfortunately, the catalog number of the dial is as yet unknown, as it does not appear in any Illinois materials catalogs that have been found thus far.

The Florentine was listed in both the 1931–32 Illinois Sales Catalog and the Illinois Spring 1932 sales catalog. It was also one of the watches featured in the Illinois advertisement in the December 12, 1931 issue of the *Saturday Evening Post* for the holiday season.

ILLINOIS WATCHES

PIONEERS OF GREATER VALUE

QUALITY WATCHES. 15 jewels, Illinois ribbon and bracelet watches in precious metal cases that are dependable. Watches featured on this page are of the 18/0 size.

HONORED ACCEPTANCE. Beautifully proportioned, exquisitely engraved and plain patterns, with harmonious dial, case and attachments are these fine watches.

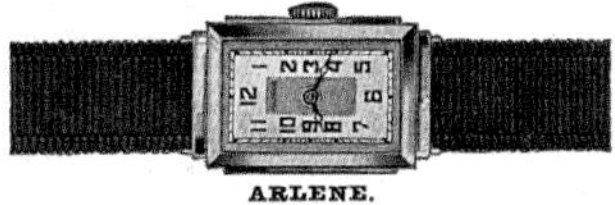

ARLENE.
No. 65W1. 15 jewels....................**$46.40**
Consumer $42.50
14 karat solid white gold case of exquisite simplicity.

THE Illinois Watch craftsmen are noted for their exacting workmanship. Every delicate timepiece must meet rigid time requirements before it is placed on the market. The small watches illustrated on this page are what might be termed custom built. Each and every part is so constructed to meet the most severe inspection insuring splendid performance and general satisfaction.

ELISSA.
No. 65W2. 15 jewels....................**$44.80**
Consumer $41.25
Handsomely engraved case of 14k natural or white filled gold.

IRENE.
No. 65W3. 15 jewels....................**$44.80**
Consumer $40.00
Attractive case of 14 karat filled white or natural gold.

FLORENTINE.
No. 65W4. 15 jewels....................**$44.00**
Consumer $41.25
Neatly engraved case of 14 karat filled white gold.

GLENNA.
No. 65W5. 15 jewels....................**$48.40**
Consumer $46.75
14 karat white filled gold with bracelet attached.

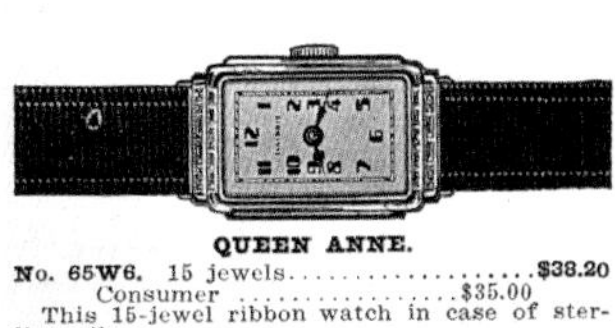

QUEEN ANNE.
No. 65W6. 15 jewels....................**$38.20**
Consumer $35.00
This 15-jewel ribbon watch in case of sterling silver.

BEVERLY.
No. 65W7. 15 jewels....................**$39.90**
Consumer $37.50
Available in either natural or white filled gold.

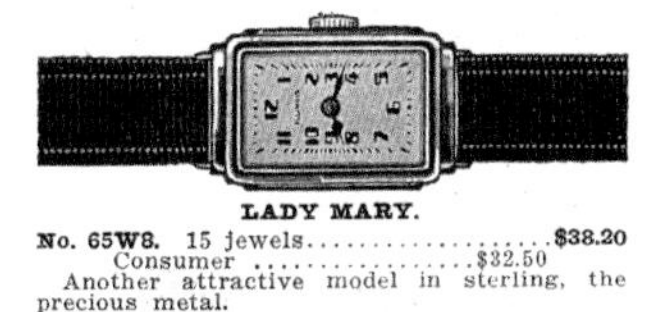

LADY MARY.
No. 65W8. 15 jewels....................**$38.20**
Consumer $32.50
Another attractive model in sterling, the precious metal.

65

Illinois Pioneers of Greater Value catalog, 1931–32

There are some mysteries involving the Fairfax. Because neither an Illinois catalog listing of the model nor a magazine advertisement of it has been found, it is not known exactly what year it was introduced. When issuing two versions of essentially the same watch but with movements of different grades, Illinois' usual pattern seems to have been to release the 17-jewel version a year or more before the 15-jewel one. Two jobbers' catalogs showing the watch have been found. However, since one of them is for 1932–33 and the other for 1933, it appears that Fairfax was likely introduced sometime in 1932, about a year after the Florentine.

Yet another mystery involves the watchbands for this model. The Fairfax apparently came with a ribbon band. However, the 1933 John Plain catalog shows the Fairfax with a 17-jewel movement and a metal bracelet, noting that it was "completely cased, timed and boxed at the factory."

The Holsman Company's catalog No. 180 (1932–33), which likewise pictures this model, lists it as a 17-jewel "Fairfax DeLuxe" with a Hadley gold-filled bracelet. Given Illinois' practice with some other models, it is possible that the "Fairfax" was reissued with a metal bracelet and given a slight name change. But if so, why did the John Plain listing omit "DeLuxe" from the name? Or was the "DeLuxe" simply Holsman's designation for it?

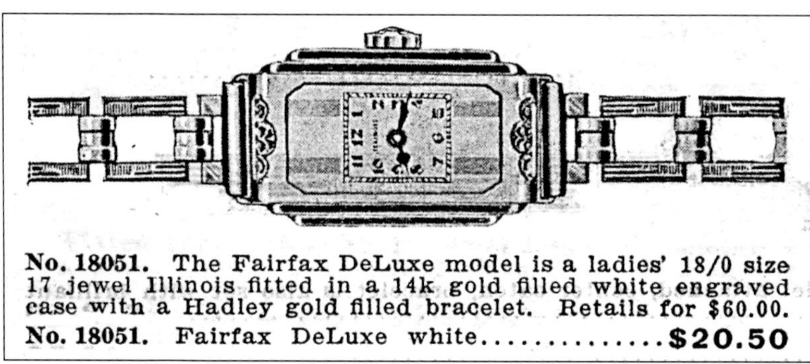

No. 18051. The Fairfax DeLuxe model is a ladies' 18/0 size 17 jewel Illinois fitted in a 14k gold filled white engraved case with a Hadley gold filled bracelet. Retails for $60.00.
No. 18051. Fairfax DeLuxe white..............**$20.50**

Holsman catalog, 1932–33

Fairfax original price card

Florette

See listing for **Charmette/Annette/Florette**

Generic Watches

Generic Watches, white gold-filled

Name = Generic Watches
Time Period = Generic
Karat/Material = Various
Bezel = Plain, Engraved
Sides = Plain, Engraved
Lug Size = Various
Spring Bar = Fixed Lugs
Casemaker = Fahys, Star, Philadelphia, Wadsworth, B & B, Others
Case Pieces = 2, 3
Case Number = None
Case Back = Plain, Engraved
Dimensions = Various
Durability = ◷◷◷
Movement Sizes = 3/0, 6/0
Movement Grades/Jewels = Various
Dial Numbers = Various
Dial = Silver Finish, Green or Yellow Gold Finish

Dial Openings = Round, Tonneau
Numerals = Painted
Hands = Steel
Seconds at = None, 6, 9 (both 6 and 9 are rare)
Cased in Factory = No
Collectibility = 🕐🕐🕐
Rarity = 🕐 to 🕐🕐🕐🕐🕐🕐
Retail Price New = Various
Introduction Date = Early 1920s
Unique Case Design = No
Unique Dial Design = No
Advertisement = No
Marketing Theme = Various

During the Generic Period, jewelers and jobbers purchased and sold the same basic cases containing movements and dials manufactured most usually by the three principal watch manufacturers of that era: Elgin, Illinois and Waltham. Examples of men's Illinois wristwatches of this period are shown in Chapter 9.

Likewise, Illinois ladies' wristwatch models of the Generic Period were provided with cases that could also be fitted with Elgin or Waltham dials and movements. Examples of such models are shown here. The A. C. Becken and other catalogs show ladies' Generic wristwatches with fixed lugs and ribbon bracelets already being offered by various other manufacturers in 1917, though these watches did not reach their height of popularity until later.

For ladies' Generic models, the most usual case shapes were round, octagonal or decagonal. Given that so many different casemakers offered cases in these shapes, it is not surprising that there were a bewildering number of different engraving patterns for the bezels of the cases. The case backs were commonly plain, though some had borders of delicate engraving. The most popular case colors during this period were white gold and green (either solid gold or gold filled for both); yellow gold, popular for the earlier Transitional watches, was not favored. Green gold was initially very popular during the Generic Period, but later it was white gold that was seen most frequently.

Generic, green gold-filled

To our knowledge, no Illinois ladies' Generic watches were Factory-Cased except for two particular models, each with a 6/0 movement and a special moiré dial: the Octagon and the Tonneau (see the listing for each later in this chapter). Other Illinois ladies' watches found in octagonal or tonneau cases are not to be considered Factory-Cased.

Glencoe / Lakewood

Glencoe in yellow gold (left), and two Lakewoods in white gold

Name = Glencoe
Time Period = Deco
Karat/Material = 14K WG, 14K YG
Bezel = Plain, Engraved
Sides = Engraved
Lug Size = 11mm
Spring Bar = Fixed Lugs
Casemaker = Keystone
Case Pieces = 3
Case Number = 238
Case Back = Plain
Dimensions = 17 x 30mm
Durability = ◷◷◷◷
Movement Size = 18/0
Movement Grades/Jewels = 807/17, 805/15
Dial Number = 8282
Dial = Silver Finish
Dial Opening = Octagonal
Numerals= Painted
Hands = Steel
Seconds at = None
Cased in Factory = Yes
Collectibility = ◷◷◷◷
Rarity = ◷◷◷◷
Retail Price New = $60.00 (Glencoe,17J); $47.50 (Lakewood,15J)
Introduction Date = 1930 (Glencoe), 1932 (Lakewood)

Unique Case Design = No
Unique Dial Design = No
Advertisement = Yes
Marketing Theme = "The gracefully engraved design of this watch gives it a lovely individuality."

The 17-jewel Glencoe and its 15-jewel sister, the Lakewood, are two more models of the many solid gold ladies' Illinois wristwatch offerings. However, these two are unusual in being offered not only in solid white gold but also in a very rare yellow gold version. At that time there were very few ladies' models in any brand offered in yellow gold.

The purchasers could also select a model with an engraved or plain bezel in addition to a white gold or a yellow gold case. The Glencoe and Lakewood are two of the very few ladies' models that offered such variety, whereas with the Illinois men's wristwatches, it was more the rule than the exception.

The Glencoe appeared in the 1931–32 Illinois Sales Catalog. It was also advertised in the December 6, 1930 issue of the *Saturday Evening Post*. The Lakewood appeared in the Spring 1932 Illinois Sales Catalog.

The GLENCOE

The gracefully engraved design of this watch gives it a lovely individuality. 14K natural solid gold and also available in a beautifully plain case.

Suggested consumer price, $60.

A. I. Hall catalog, 1930–31

Glencoe, plain bezel, yellow gold

Glenna 186

Glenna 186, white gold-filled

Name = Glenna 186
Time Period = Moderne
Karat/Material = 14K WGF
Bezel = Sculpted/Diamonds/Engraved
Sides = Engraved
Lug Size = 11mm
Spring Bar = Fixed Lugs
Casemaker = Keystone
Case Pieces = 3
Case Number = 186
Case Back = Plain
Dimensions = 17 x 31mm
Durability = ◷◷◷◷
Movement Size = 18/0
Movement Grade/Jewels = 805/15
Dial Number = Unknown
Dial = Silver Finish
Dial Opening = Rectangular
Numerals= Painted
Hands = Steel
Seconds at = None
Cased in Factory = Yes
Collectibility = ◷◷◷◷
Rarity = ◷◷◷◷◷◷◷
Retail Price New = Unknown
Introduction Date = Unknown
Unique Case Design = Yes
Unique Dial Design = No
Advertisement = No
Marketing Theme = Unknown

The Glenna 186 is an ultra-rare model, and there is no known advertisement for it. Although its case Model No. is 186, the bezel appears to be that of the Glenna 239, but with a custom modification. At the top and bottom of the bezel is a sculpted flower, each with a diamond at its center.

Since only one of these very rare models is known to exist, it is highly likely that the Glenna 186 was a custom-order watch.

Glenna 239, white gold-filled

GLENNA 239

Name =	Glenna 239
Time Period =	Moderne
Karat/Material =	14K WGF
Bezel =	Plain (Partially Engraved)
Sides =	Engraved
Lug Size =	11mm
Spring Bar =	Fixed Lugs
Casemaker =	Keystone
Case Pieces =	2
Case Number =	239
Case Back =	Plain
Dimensions =	17 x 31mm
Durability =	◷◷◷◷
Movement Size =	18/0
Movement Grade/Jewels =	805/15
Dial Number =	Unknown
Dial =	Silver Finish
Dial Opening =	Rectangular
Numerals=	Painted
Hands =	Steel
Seconds at =	None
Cased in Factory =	Yes
Collectibility =	◷◷◷◷
Rarity =	◷◷◷◷
Retail Price New =	$42.50
Introduction Date =	1931
Unique Case Design =	Yes
Unique Dial Design =	No
Advertisement =	Yes
Marketing Themes =	"Chic, smart, modern, sturdy, refreshingly styled" "A delightful ensemble"

The Glenna 239 is unusual in that it came with a matching metal bracelet, whereas most other Illinois ladies' models were offered with only a ribbon band. A 1931 Illinois brochure describes the Glenna 239 as "a delightful ensemble of 14K filled white gold case and perfectly matched bracelet," as do the 1932 A. C. Becken and J. Engel catalogs. Unfortunately, very few of the original ribbon and metal bracelets on Illinois ladies' wristwatches have withstood the test of time, and it is extremely rare to find one with its original band intact.

The understated but nonetheless very distinctive case of the Glenna 239 has a stepped bezel, the top and bottom of which have a smooth surface. Along each side of the bezel, next to the dial opening, there is an unusual design touch: a small smooth area shaped like a segment of a circle at the midpoint of a narrow vertical row of delicate engraving.

According to Gay (who has studied hundreds of specimens of Illinois ladies' models), the Edgewater 222, Newport 223, Lenox, Roslyn and Glenna 239 have interchangeable case backs and the Glenna 239 and Roslyn share the same case Model No. 239. This was a practice of Illinois to achieve economies of scale and lower production costs for case parts.

The Glenna 239 was listed in the 1931–32 Illinois Sales Catalog as well as in the Spring 1932 one. It was advertised in the December 12, 1931 and October 3, 1932 issues of the *Saturday Evening Post.* This model came equipped with a 15-jewel movement.

From the Illinois American Beauty Series brochure, 1931

Gloria, white gold-filled

GLORIA

Name = Gloria
Time Period = Moderne
Karat/Material = 14K WGF, 14K YGF
Bezel = Grooved
Sides = Engraved
Lug Size = 11mm
Spring Bar = Fixed Lugs
Casemaker = Wadsworth
Case Pieces = 2
Case Number = 828
Case Back = Engraved
Dimensions = 17 x 30mm
Durability = ◷◷◷◷
Movement Size = 18/0
Movement Grade/Jewels = 807/17
Dial Number = 8346
Dial = Silver Finish
Dial Opening = Rectangular
Numerals= Painted
Hands = Steel
Seconds at = None
Cased in Factory = Yes
Collectibility = ◷◷◷◷
Rarity = ◷◷◷◷
Retail Price New = $45.00
Introduction Date = 1931
Unique Case Design = Yes
Unique Dial Design = No
Advertisement = Yes
Marketing Theme = "Beautifully modern lined case"

Gloria, yellow gold-filled

With a bezel that is grooved and stepped, the Gloria is quite distinctive in appearance; Its case design is unmistakable. This model is a nice example of Moderne style to have in a collection.

The Gloria came with a 17-jewel movement in either a white gold-filled or yellow gold-filled case that was fitted with a ribbon band. It shared the same dial with the Vardon and Argyle models.

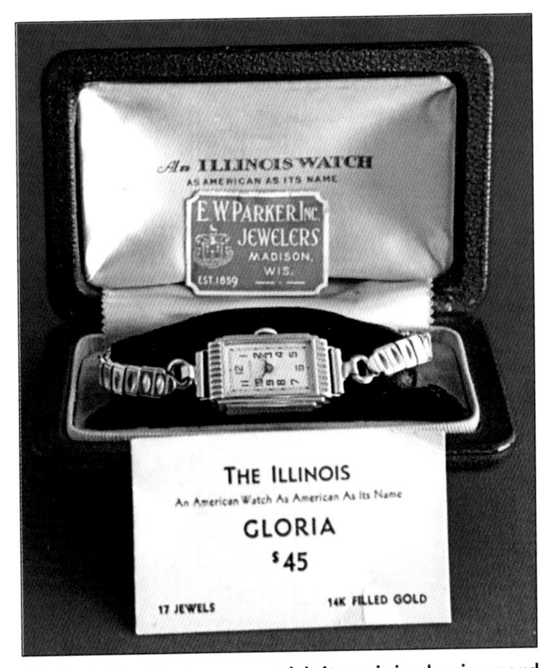

Gloria in its display case with its original price card

Greta

Name = Greta
Time Period = Moderne
Karat/Material = 14K WG
Bezel = Plain
Sides = Engraved
Lug Size = 11mm
Spring Bar = Fixed Lugs
Casemaker = Wadsworth
Case Pieces = 2
Case Number = 807-5
Case Back = Plain
Dimensions = 17 x 29mm
Durability = ◷◷◷◷
Movement Size = 18/0
Movement Grade/Jewels = 805/15
Dial Number = 8346
Dial = Silver Finish
Dial Opening = Rectangular
Numerals= Painted
Hands = Steel
Seconds at = None
Cased in Factory = Yes
Collectibility = ◷◷◷◷

Greta, white gold

Rarity = ◷◷◷◷
Retail Price New = $50.00
Introduction Date = 1932
Unique Case Design = No
Unique Dial Design = No
Advertisement = Yes
Marketing Theme = "Exquisite simplicity"

The Greta, a fairly plain watch with a 15-jewel movement, came in a solid white gold case, surprisingly. It also came with a matching solid white gold bracelet.

The Greta has the same case Model No. 807-5 as the Argyle and Arlene models but has no engraving on its bezel; thus its case is like the plain-bezel option of those models. Its case style is also somewhat similar to the Lady Mary and Queen Anne models. However, both of those are in sterling silver cases.

The Greta was listed in the 1931–32 Illinois Sales Catalog.

John Plain 1933 catalog, with superimposed Greta

Hollywood / Rita

Names = Hollywood/Rita
Time Period = Moderne
Karat/Material = 14K WGF, 14K YGF
Bezel = Engraved
Sides = Engraved
Lug Size = 11mm
Spring Bar = Fixed Lugs
Casemaker = Keystone
Case Pieces = 2
Case Number = 831
Case Back = Plain
Dimensions = 17 x 31mm
Durability = 🕒🕒🕒
Movement Size = 18/0
Movement Grades/Jewels = 807/17, 805/15
Dial Number = 8344
Dial = Silver Finish
Dial Opening = Tonneau
Numerals= Painted
Hands = Steel
Seconds at = None
Cased in Factory = Yes
Collectibility = 🕒🕒🕒🕒
Rarity = 🕒🕒🕒 in YGF
🕒🕒🕒🕒🕒 in WGF
Retail Price New = $40.00 (17J), $35.00 (15J)
Introduction Date = 1931 (Hollywood); 1932 (Rita)
Unique Case Design = No
Unique Dial Design = No
Advertisement = Yes
Marketing Themes = "Smart, beautiful"
"Pleasantly designed with a touch of engraving"

Hollywood, white gold-filled

Hollywood, yellow gold-filled

The Hollywood, listed in the 1931–32 Illinois Sales Catalog, was featured in an advertisement in the April 25, 1931 issue of the *Saturday Evening Post.* as "The Watch of the Month." With an appealing tonneau-shaped dial area and a delicate floral motif engraved at the top and bottom of the bezel, it is a very attractive model.

The Hollywood was equipped with a ribbon band and came with a 17-jewel movement in case Model No. 831. The Hollywood's later-issued sister, the Rita, shared the same case but had a 15-jewel movement. Both came with ribbon bands. Although these watches were available in yellow gold-filled cases as well as white gold-filled, the yellow gold-filled ones are much more difficult to find.

In the December 12, 1931 issue of the *Saturday Evening Post*, the Hollywood was featured along with the Coquette, Claudette, Constance, Debutante, Florentine and Glenna ladies' models in an advertisement proclaiming that "$32.50 to $60.00 will buy a finer watch than you've ever been able to get for the money," and that "this advertisement is published to help you simplify your Christmas giving problem and save you money."

The Rita was listed in the 1932 Illinois Spring sales catalog along with nine other ladies' models. It is interesting that with one exception, the 17-jewel Argyle, all came with 15-jewel movements. Five models (the Sylvia, Florentine, Barbara, Glenna and Elissa) came in 14K gold-filled cases, as did the Rita. The other four (the Greta, Lakewood, Princess and Argyle) had cases of solid gold.

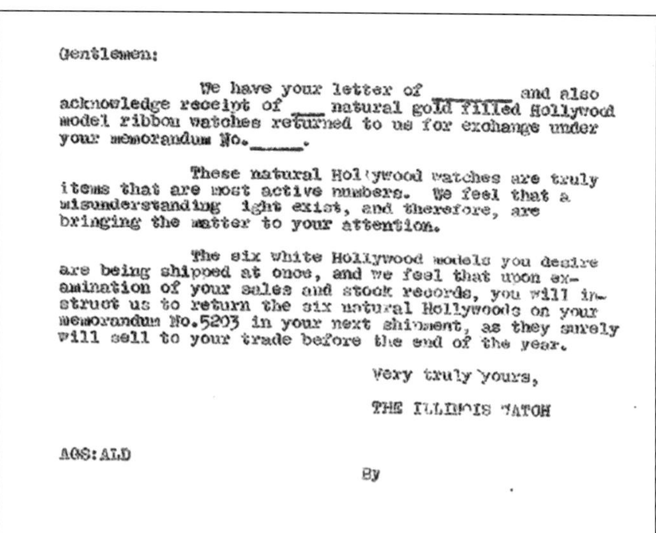

Gentlemen:

We have your letter of ________ and also acknowledge receipt of ___ natural gold filled Hollywood model ribbon watches returned to us for exchange under your memorandum No.______.

These natural Hollywood watches are truly items that are most active numbers. We feel that a misunderstanding ight exist, and therefore, are bringing the matter to your attention.

The six white Hollywood models you desire are being shipped at once, and we feel that upon examination of your sales and stock records, you will instruct us to return the six natural Hollywoods on your memorandum No.5203 in your next shipment, as they surely will sell to your trade before the end of the year.

Very truly yours,

THE ILLINOIS WATCH

AGS:ALD

By

Illinois considered the yellow gold-filled Hollywoods to be "most active numbers."

Hollywood in its display case with its original price card

See listing for **Marilyn/Elissa/Sylvia/Irene**

JANETTE

Name = Janette
Time Period = Moderne
Karat/Material = 10K WGF, 10K YGF
Bezel = Sculpted
Sides = Plain, Engraved
Lug Size = 10mm
Spring Bar = Fixed Lugs
Casemaker = Keystone
Case Pieces = 2
Case Number = 711
Case Back = Plain
Dimensions = 14 x 27mm
Durability = ◷◷◷
Movement Size = 21/0
Movement Grades/Jewels = 105/15, 107/17
Dial Number = 8385
Dial = Silver Finish
Dial Opening = Rectangular
Numerals= Painted
Hands = Steel
Seconds at = None
Cased in Factory = Yes, by Hamilton in Lancaster
Collectibility = ◷◷◷◷
Rarity = ◷◷◷◷
Retail Price New = $47.50 (15J)
Introduction Date = 1933
Unique Case Design = Yes
Unique Dial Design = No
Advertisement = Yes
Marketing Themes = "Brilliantly modern wrist model"
"Of brilliantly faceted white filled gold"

Janette, white gold-filled

Janette, yellow gold-filled

The Janette, which came in a choice of 10K white or yellow gold-filled, was one of only five Illinois ladies' watches ever offered in a 10K gold-filled case. It had a 15-jewel movement and came with a metal bracelet.

The 1933 Illinois Pioneers of Greater Values sales catalog described the Janette as being "of brilliantly faceted white filled gold . . . with bracelet to match." In this catalog the Janette and seven other Illinois baguettes were shown on a page featuring not only those 21/0 size models, but also some 18/0 size ladies' models.

In the Pioneers of Greater Value catalog of 1934, the only ladies' watches shown were 21/0 size, and the Janette was the featured model. The picture of the Janette in its box, which showed the "specially designed filled gold bracelet" mentioned in its listing, took up about as much space as all seven of the other baguettes on the page. The main heading on the page called them "Baguette Style" but later described them as "Semi-Baguette" watches. There is special emphasis on the fact that all eight of the baguettes were equipped with Elinvar hairsprings.

It is interesting that of the eight baguette models listed in the 1933 catalog, only the Janette and Lynette were included again in 1934. (The Babette of 1934 has a different case from the 1933 one; only the name is repeated.)

In the 1934 catalog, there are five entirely new baguette models (the Antoinette, Débette, Mariette, Marlette and Marionette). Listed along with these 21/0 size models are two 18/0 "Moderne Wrist Watches" that were unisex/men's models (the Sangamon and Urbana).

All of these models were offered as part of the Illinois "Buy American" campaign.

ELINVAR

Elinvar is a corrosion-resistant nickel-steel-chromium alloy that is elasticity invariant with respect to temperature. Its use was to reduce the effect of magnetism and temperature changes to a minimum—to assure a constant rate under all conditions.

Page 74 *The KEYSTONE* November, 1932

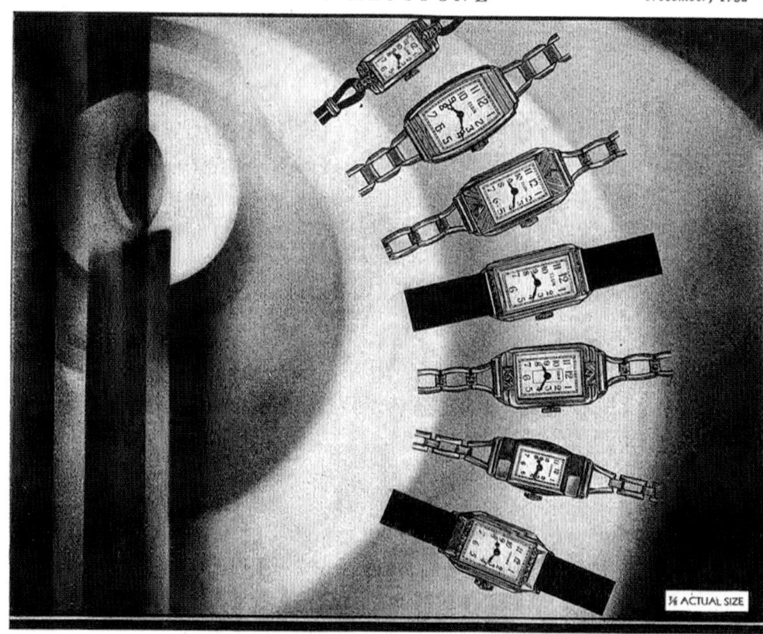

KEYSTONE'S CONTRIBUTION TO A SUCCESSFUL HOLIDAY SEASON

The models shown are featured for the holiday season by the Illinois Division of the Hamilton Watch Company and the Elgin National Watch Company. That these cases bear Keystone trade-marks is due to the trade's recognition of this well-known principle: Cases in which inherent quality, beauty of design and fine workmanship are effectively combined, increase the selling value of the finest watch. This principle applied to the selection of watch cases is responsible for the fact that, for more than three-quarters of a century, Keystone Cases have been the preferred choice of the country's leading movement manufacturers.

KEYSTONE WATCH CASE CORPORATION
Established 1853
RIVERSIDE, NEW JERSEY
NEW YORK · CHICAGO · CINCINNATI · SAN FRANCISCO

Keystone, November 1932. Janette is the next-to-bottom watch.

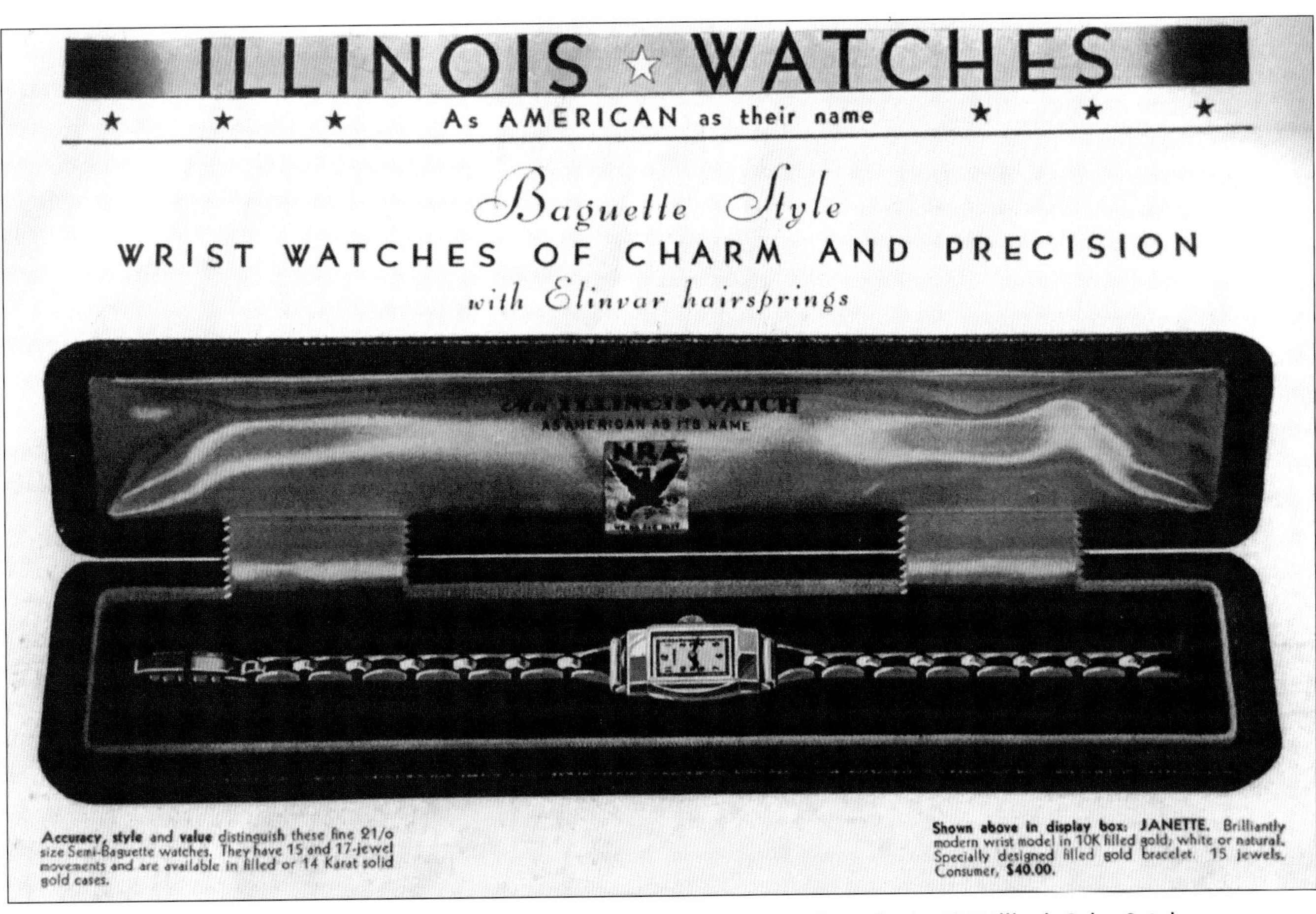

Illinois Pioneers of Greater Values catalog, 1933. The same advertisement was shown in the 1934 Illinois Sales Catalog.

PIONEERS OF GREATER VALUES

ILLINOIS WATCHES

— ««« MADE IN SPRINGFIELD, ILLINOIS »»» —

CONSUMER AND KEYSTONE PRICE LIST

(INCLUDING FEDERAL EXCISE TAX)

LADIES' WATCHES

	Keystone List	Consumer
Grade 805, 18/0 Size, 15 Jewels.		
Lady Mary, Sterling Silver	$38.20	$32.50
Queen Anne, Sterling Silver	38.20	35.00
Beverly, 10K white or natural gold filled	39.90	37.50
Irene, 14K white or natural gold filled, bracelet attachment	44.80	40.00
Arlene, 14K solid white gold	46.40	42.50
Grade 105, 21/0 Size, 15 Jewels.		
Lynette, 14K white gold filled	46.00	40.00
Florette, 14K white or natural gold filled	47.60	42.50
Janette, 10K white gold filled, bracelet attachment	50.50	47.50
Babette, 14K solid white gold	51.90	50.00
Grade 107, 21/0 Size, 17 Jewels.		
Suzette, 14K white gold filled	53.20	47.50
Juliette, 14K white or natural gold filled	57.30	52.50
Rosette, 14K white gold filled, bracelet attachment	58.50	55.00
Muzette, 14K white gold filled, silk cord attachment	58.50	55.00

Illinois Pioneers of Greater Values Catalog, 1933 ladies' models' prices

Joan

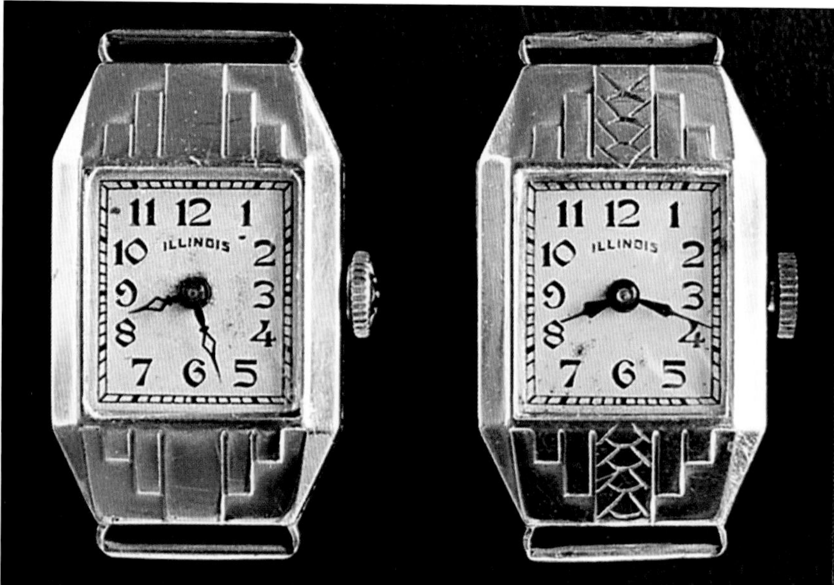

Joans, white gold-filled, with three different bezels

Name = Joan
Time Period = Moderne
Karat/Material = 14K WGF
Bezel = Sculpted, Sculpted and Engraved
Sides = Engraved
Lug Size = 11mm
Spring Bar = Fixed Lugs
Casemaker = Wadsworth
Case Pieces = 2
Case Number = 155
Case Back = Engraved
Dimensions = 17 x 31mm
Durability = 🕓🕓🕓🕓
Movement Size = 18/0
Movement Grade/Jewels = 807/17
Dial Numbers = 8169, 8170, 8171
Dial = Silver Finish
Dial Opening = Short Rectangular
Numerals = Painted
Hands = Steel
Seconds at = None
Cased in Factory = Yes
Collectibility = 🕓🕓🕓🕓
Rarity = 🕓🕓🕓🕓

Retail Price New = $44.00 (17J)
Introduction Date = 1931
Unique Case Design = Yes
Unique Dial Design = No
Advertisement = Yes
Marketing Themes = "Very distinctive"
"Trim and good looking"

The Joan came in a choice of three highly Art Deco/ Moderne bezels. The stepped imprint on the top and bottom of the bezel is very reminiscent of the skyscrapers that appeared in major United States cities in the late 1920s and early 1930s. It is difficult for one to look at these watches and not think of the Empire State and Chrysler buildings in New York City.

Another version of the Joan has an added engraving on the center panel of the imprint at the top and bottom. A third version comes with more elaborate Deco-style engraving, appearing on all panels of its bezel. As yet there is only one model known to exist with the more extensive engraving. All versions of this model came equipped with 17-jewel movements and had ribbon bands.

Given the striking case design, it is surprising that all three versions of the Joan seem thus far to have been largely unappreciated by collectors.

The Joan was listed in the 1931–32 Illinois Sales Catalog and in a special Illinois sales brochure.

Montgomery Ward 1932 catalog, showing Hollywood (*left*) and Joan (*right*)

Juliette, white gold-filled

Juliette, yellow gold-filled

Juliette

Name =	Juliette
Time Period =	Moderne
Karat/Material =	14K WGF, 14K YGF
Bezel =	Engraved
Sides =	Engraved
Lug Size =	9mm
Spring Bar =	Fixed Lugs
Casemaker =	Star
Case Pieces =	2
Case Number =	706, No Number
Case Back =	Plain
Dimensions =	14 x 26mm
Durability =	◷◷◷◷
Movement Size =	21/0
Movement Grade/Jewels =	107/17
Dial Number =	8122
Dial =	Silver Finish
Dial Opening =	Rectangular
Numerals=	Painted
Hands =	Steel
Seconds at =	None
Cased in Factory =	Yes, by Hamilton in Lancaster
Collectibility =	◷◷◷◷
Rarity =	◷◷◷◷
Retail Price New =	$52.50 (17J)
Introduction Date =	1933
Unique Case Design =	Yes
Unique Dial Design =	No
Advertisement =	Yes
Marketing Theme =	"Neatly engraved case"

The Juliette was listed as one of the Pioneers of Greater Value watches in the 1933 Illinois Sales catalog. It was offered in either a white gold-filled or yellow gold-filled Star Watch Case and was cased by Hamilton in Lancaster, Pennsylvania.

By mid-1933, the Illinois Factory had been shuttered. Some of its workers and some of the production equipment necessary to finish certain works-in-progress were in the process of being transferred to Lancaster.

Illinois had never offered a Factory-Cased watch in a Star case until this model. Hamilton was designing dials for Illinois watches in Star cases starting in 1933 (see Chapter 5).

Other 21/0 size models appearing in the 1933 Illinois Sales catalog were the Babette I, Florette, Janette, Lynette, Muzette, Rosette and Suzette. All of these were part of the Illinois "Buy American" campaign. Several 18/0 size models were also listed in the catalog: the Arlene, Beverly 852, Irene, Lady Mary and Queen Anne.

BUY AMERICAN

The Illinois Pioneers of Greater Values 1933 catalog promoted "Buy American," stating:

"The 'Buy American' campaign has been started. It will have a tremendous impression upon the buying public. America appreciates quality and will demand it this year. Get your clerks to 'Sell American' as quality appeal with patriotism secondary."

Lady Mary/Queen Anne

Names = Lady Mary/Queen Anne
Time Period = Moderne
Karat/Material = Sterling Silver
Bezel = Engraved
Sides = Plain
Lug Size = 11mm
Spring Bar = Fixed Lugs
Casemaker = Wadsworth
Case Pieces = 2
Case Number = 807-5
Case Back = Plain
Dimensions = 17 x 29mm
Durability = 🕒🕒🕒🕒
Movement Size = 18/0
Movement Grade/Jewels = 807/17
Dial Number = 8364
Dial = Silver Finish
Dial Opening = Short Rectangular
Numerals= Painted
Hands = Steel
Seconds at = None
Cased in Factory = Yes
Collectibility = 🕒🕒🕒🕒
Rarity = 🕒🕒🕒🕒🕒
Retail Price New = $32.50 (15J)
Introduction Date = 1932
Unique Case Design = No (Lady Mary); Yes (Queen Anne)
Unique Dial Design = No

Lady Mary, sterling silver

Queen Anne, sterling silver

Advertisement = Yes
Marketing Themes = "Conservative plain design in brightly polished sterling silver" (Lady Mary)
"Finely engraved in scintillating style in sterling silver" (Queen Anne)

The Lady Mary and its sister, the Queen Anne, are the only sterling silver Factory-Cased Illinois wristwatches and for that reason are highly collectible. The backs of their case Model No. 807-5 are interchangeable in size and shape with those of the Argyle, Arlene, and Greta, though the case metal of those three is 14K solid white gold rather than sterling silver.

The case design of the Lady Mary is similar but not identical to that of the Argyle (plain-bezel version), Arlene, and Greta. The Queen Anne has light engraving along the top and bottom of its bezel, whereas the Lady Mary, the plain-bezel Argyle and the Arlene do not; and the engraved-bezel Argyle has engraving on the sides of the bezel as well as the top and bottom.

The Lady Mary and Queen Anne were released mid-year in 1932 and thus did not appear in the Illinois Sales Catalog until their listings among the Pioneers of Greater Values catalog in 1933. Promotional cards announcing these new releases as "Two Business Builders" were apparently sent in advance to Illinois' jobbers, such as J. Engel of Baltimore.

These watches were introduced during the Great Depression to meet Hamilton's needs for low-price offerings. It is somewhat surprising that the sterling models sold for significantly less than their gold-filled contemporaries.

NEW ILLINOIS WATCHES

18/0 Size • 15 Jewels • Sterling Silver Cases

LADY MARY		QUEEN ANNE	
CONSUMER	$29.75	CONSUMER	$32.50
KEYSTONE LIST	$34.50	KEYSTONE LIST	$34.50

TWO 1932 BUSINESS BUILDERS

ILLINOIS GREATER VALUE WATCHES

LADY MARY

QUEEN ANNE

Promotional card for the Lady Mary and Queen Anne, found inside a J. Engel 1932 catalog

In the June 1932 issue of the *Jewelers' Circular*, the Lady Mary and Queen Anne were featured in an advertisement proclaiming that "Sterling points the way to increased profits" because "Sterling Silver is one of those few standards of quality which Merchants and Public alike can always accept with confidence." For sellers, each of these new watches, "in precious metal tarnish-resisting case to compete with watches of lower jewel content and cases of nondescript metals—chromium, nickel and what not" represented "a new low priced quality product."

STERLING SILVER WATCHES

The following articles from *Jewelers' Circular* and *Keystone* announced the two new sterling silver ladies' wristwatches for Illinois in June 1932.

Illinois Watch Co. Offers New Watch in Sterling Silver Case

The Illinois Watch Co. recently announced a new low consumer price in a quality watch. The new watches introduced to the trade during the early part of May are the quality 15-jewel Illinois movements in an attractive case of sterling silver. The Wadsworth Watch Case Co. manufactured the cases and will guarantee them against loss of color and tarnish. Arthur Wadsworth is especially enthusiastic concerning the perfection of these precious metal cases. It is understood he has taken steps to patent the alloy used, which gives the sterling silver case permanency and stability. J. L. Keenan, sales manager of the Illinois Watch Co., states that jewelers now have a quality watch in a precious metal case which competes in price with those watches that have been encased" in nondescript cases. The lower consumer price will interest the retail jeweler.

Jewelers' Circular, June 1932

FOR *the* BUYER

New Line Illinois Watches

THE ILLINOIS WATCH COMPANY, Springfield, Ill., has just placed on the market a new line of Illinois watches, cased in sterling silver, to retail at $29.75. The movement is 15-jewel and of standard Illinois quality.

The company has been featuring "Greater Value" watches for more than a year without sacrificing quality in the famous Illinois movement.

Cases for the new watches are made by the Wadsworth Watch Case Company, Dayton, Ky., from a special alloy. Arthur Wadsworth is especially enthusiastic concerning the perfection of these precious metal cases. It is understood that he has taken steps to patent the alloy used, which gives the sterling case permanency and stability.

There is no question of the consumer appeal of sterling silver. Women desire to possess sterling, knowing it has intrinsic value as a precious metal.

The new watches are meeting with favorable acceptance among the trade.

Keystone, June 1932

FOR *the* BUYER

Illinois Sterling Silver Watch Cases Proving Successful

THE ILLINOIS WATCH some time ago announced an innovation in the adoption of sterling silver watch cases. Sterling is one of the few standards of quality which merchants and public can always accept with confidence. Watches with sterling silver cases point the way to greater value and greater profits.

Retail jewelers can merchandise these new Illinois Watches with utmost confidence. The particular cases used by the Illinois Watch and manufactured by the Wadsworth Watch Case Co. resist tarnish and are of the finest quality. According to the manufacturer of the case, they will not tarnish in the jeweler's stock.

This is because the cases are plated with rhodium. The alloy will not tarnish as long as this plate remains. There is little danger of the plate being disturbed, because of the unusual hardness. The only portion of the case where rhodium might be worn is on the back. Owing to the constant rubbing of the back of case on the wrist of the owner, there is very little chance of tarnish on this part of case.

The manufacturer of the case in recent experiment found it necessary to use lea buff to remove the rhodium. This type of buff is charged with emery and normally used for polishing steel.

The alloy used in the manufacture of these cases has as much, if not more, resiliency than the hardest material found for gold filled cases, according to the case manufacturer.

Illinois has something which is most acceptable to the public in Sterling Silver cases. Progressive jewelers are pushing the sale of these watches. They realize they now have a quality watch in a precious metal case that competes in price with watches of lower jewel content or watches with nondescript cases.

It is reported that other watch companies are adopting sterling silver cases.

Keystone, February 1933

LAKEWOOD

See listing for **Glencoe/Lakewood**

Lenox, yellow gold

LENOX

Name =	Lenox
Time Period =	Deco
Karat/Material =	14K WG, 14K YG
Bezel =	Plain
Sides =	Engraved
Lug Size =	11mm
Spring Bar =	Fixed Lugs
Casemaker =	Keystone
Case Pieces =	3
Case Number =	185
Case Back =	Plain
Dimensions =	17 x 30mm
Durability =	◷◷◷◷
Movement Size =	18/0
Movement Grade/Jewels =	807/17
Dial Number =	8174
Dial =	Silver Finish, Sparkle Finish
Dial Opening =	Octagonal
Numerals=	Painted
Hands =	Steel
Seconds at =	None
Cased in Factory =	Yes
Collectibility =	◷◷◷◷
Rarity =	◷◷◷◷◷◷
Retail Price New =	$65.00 (17J)
Introduction Date =	1930
Unique Case Design =	No
Unique Dial Design =	No
Advertisement =	Yes
Marketing Theme =	"Of conservative design, yet pleasingly attractive"

The Lenox appeared in the 1930–31 Illinois Sales Catalog with a number of other solid gold ladies' Illinois watches. In this advertisement, Illinois paired the Lenox with its gold-filled sister, the Biloxi, just as it had done earlier with another sister, the solid gold Beverly 185. All three of these models were equipped with 17-jewel movements and came with ribbon bands.

The Lenox is a solid gold variation of the Biloxi, as is the Beverly 185; however, the Biloxi came only in white gold-filled. Another difference among the sisters is that the Lenox came in either white gold or yellow gold, whereas the Beverly 185 was available only in white gold.

In addition, the Lenox came with a relatively plain dial, but both the Biloxi and Beverly 185 had a very interesting dial with an Art Deco design in enameling. The dial of the Lenox is nonetheless well designed, with interesting numerals.

The Lenox is rated "extremely rare" by Gay.

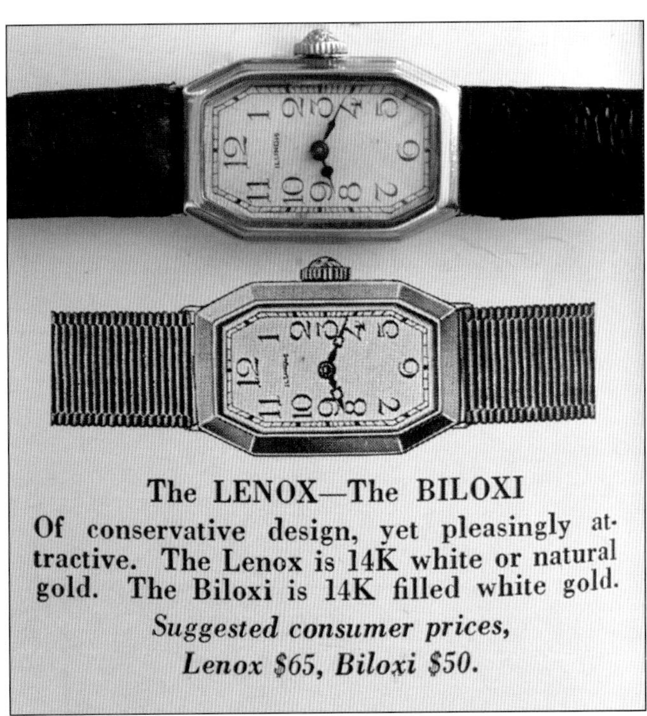
The LENOX—The BILOXI
Of conservative design, yet pleasingly attractive. The Lenox is 14K white or natural gold. The Biloxi is 14K filled white gold.
Suggested consumer prices,
Lenox $65, Biloxi $50.

A. I. Hall 1930–31 catalog, with Lenox superimposed.
As Gay has noted, the bezel of the Biloxi is slightly different from that of the Beverly; the difference is therefore also apparent when the Beverly's twin, the Lenox, is here paired with the Biloxi.

Lenox inside case back and movement

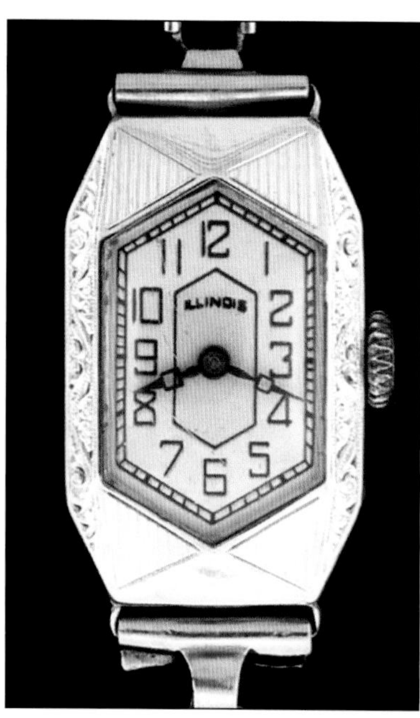

Long Beach, white gold-filled

Long Beach

Name = Long Beach
Time Period = Deco
Karat/Material = 14K WGF, 14K WG
Bezel = Engraved (partially)
Sides = Engraved
Lug Size = 11mm
Spring Bar = Fixed Lugs
Casemaker = Wadsworth
Case Pieces = 3
Case Number = 153
Case Back = Engraved
Dimensions = 17 x 31mm
Durability = ◷◷◷◷
Movement Size = 18/0
Movement Grade/Jewels = 807/17
Dial Number = 8147
Dial = Silver Finish, Butler Center
Dial Opening = Hexagonal
Numerals= Painted
Hands = Steel
Seconds at = None
Cased in Factory = Yes
Collectibility = ◷◷◷◷
Rarity = ◷◷◷
Retail Price New = $50.00
Introduction Date = 1929
Unique Case Design = Yes
Unique Dial Design = No
Advertisement = Yes
Marketing Themes = "Matchless in charm"
"The unusual engraved bezel . . . gives a slender effect very desirable for those of small wrists."

The Long Beach shares the same case Model No. 153 with the Daytona 153, but its bezel has interesting pinstriped engraving rather than the leaf-like engraving of the Daytona 153. Both models feature an attractive dial with a butler center.

Case Model No. 153 was used with the Redonda and Berkeley models in addition to the Long Beach and Daytona 153. This was an effort by the Illinois Factory to keep costs down.

The Long Beach was listed in the 1929–30 Illinois Sales Catalog. An advertisement for it in the October 19, 1929 issue of *Liberty* also included the Coronado, Daytona 153, Del Monte 155, Edgewater 155, Miami 155, Mary Todd 203 and Redonda. Each had a 17-jewel movement and was offered for sale with a ribbon band.

Illinois "Book of Watches," 1928. Interestingly, what is pictured is not a Long Beach but a Daytona 153 (WGF)/ Daytona 155 (WG). Further Illinois confusion of nomenclature!

Lynette

Name = Lynette
Time Period = Moderne
Karat/Material = 14K WGF (1933); 10K WGF, YGF (1934)
Bezel = Engraved
Sides = Engraved
Lug Size = 9mm
Spring Bar = Fixed Lugs
Casemaker = Keystone
Case Pieces = 2
Case Number = 710
Case Back = Plain
Dimensions = 14 x 26mm
Durability = ◷◷◷◷
Movement Size = 21/0
Movement Grade/Jewels = 105/15
Dial Number = 8372
Dial = Silver Finish
Dial Opening = Rectangular
Numerals= Painted
Hands = Steel
Seconds at = None
Cased in Factory = Yes, by Hamilton in Lancaster

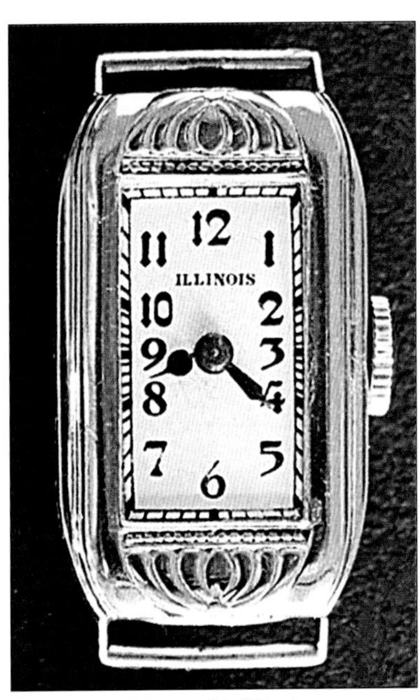

Lynette, white gold-filled

Lynette, yellow gold-filled

Collectibility =	◷◷◷◷
Rarity =	◷◷◷◷
Retail Price New =	$40.00 (15J)
Introduction Date =	1933
Unique Case Design =	Yes
Unique Dial Design =	No
Advertisement =	Yes
Marketing Themes =	"Beautifully carved case" (1933) "New filled gold bracelet" (1934)

The Lynette was advertised in the Illinois 1933 sales catalog and in the April 1933 issue of the *Keystone*. The advertisement in the latter featured the Lynette, along with the Lady Mary, with the headline "Price Is Never Too High When Compared With Something Worth While."

Introduced in 1933, the Lynette appeared again among the Greater Value Elinvar Watches in the 1934 Illinois Sales Catalog. It is interesting that although the case design remained the same, there were several changes made to this model. In 1933 the Lynette had a 14K white gold-filled case and a ribbon band. In 1934 the case had become 10K gold-filled but was offered in yellow as well as white, and a new metal bracelet was offered instead of the ribbon band. In addition, the 15-jewel movement was offered with an Elinvar hairspring in 1934. Changes notwithstanding, Illinois' price of $40.00 for the Lynette remained constant.

"LYNETTE" $40.00 SERIES

Pictured at left

21/0 Size Semi-Baguette
10K White or Natural Yellow
Gold Filled Case and Bracelet
15-Jewel ILLINOIS Movement
with "Elinvar" Hairspring

Rectangular opening, rounded corners, and artistically engraved ends. A distinctive model, of finest workmanship and finish, accurate in its timekeeping qualities.

Case and bracelet to match, are furnished with choice of 10K White or Natural Yellow Gold Filled. Attachment is of the new close-link design.

Fitted complete with 15-Jewel ILLINOIS movement, featured with "Elinvar" hairspring. Encased in an exquisite gift box for presentation.

No. 9006 White Gold Filled, Each $46.90

No. 9007 Natural Yellow Gold Filled, Each $46.90

Fort Dearborn catalog, 1935

The 1934 version of the Lynette, which also had a Keystone case, was cased by Hamilton in its Lancaster watch factory and came with a ribbon band. The price of $46.90 shown in the Fort Dearborn catalog listing is likely the "Keystone Price," upon which the typical wholesale discount of 50% would have been applied. The suggested "Consumer Price" (retail) would still have been $40.00, as shown in the Illinois 1934 Sales Catalog.

The Lynette was included along with the Illinois men's Potomac model in the March 1933 issue of the *Keystone*, in an Illinois advertisement listing "Popular American Watch Models."

In April 1933 the Lynette again appeared in an Illinois advertisement in the *Keystone*, this time with the Lady Mary.

The Lynette was also advertised with the Florette and Pimlico watches in the April 1933 issue of the *Jewelers' Circular.*

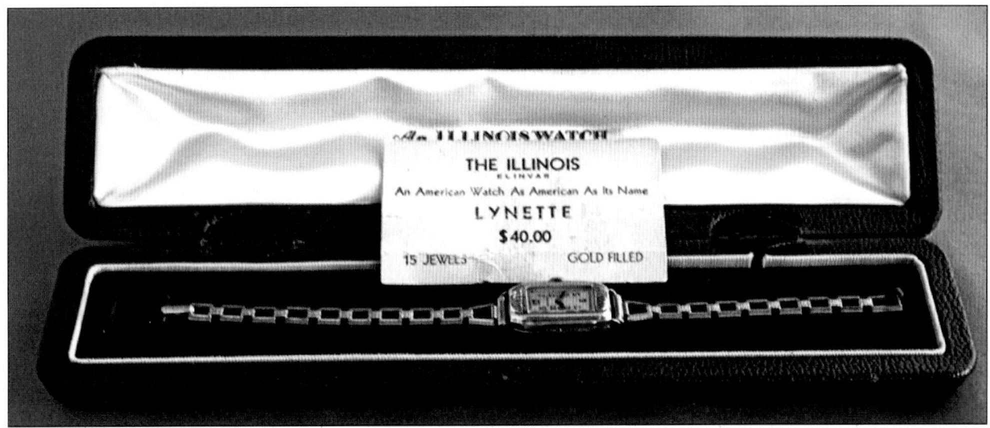

Lynette in its display box with its original price card

AS AMERICAN AS ITS NAME

In the 1933 Illinois Pioneers of Greater Values catalog, the company's "Exquisite Wrist Watches 21/0 Size" were touted as "Great achievement in the perfection of a diminutively small timepiece of dependability."

See listing for **Suzette**

Marilyn, white gold-filled

Marilyn, yellow gold-filled

Marilyn / Elissa / Sylvia / Irene

Names = Marilyn, Elissa, Sylvia, Irene
Time Period = Moderne
Karat/Material = 14K WGF, 14K YGF
Bezel = Plain, Engraved (Elissa only)
Sides = Engraved
Lug Size = 11mm
Spring Bar = Fixed Lugs
Casemaker = Keystone
Case Pieces = 2
Case Number = 830
Case Back = Plain
Dimensions = 17 x 31mm
Durability = ◷◷◷◷
Movement Size = 18/0
Movement Grades/Jewels = 805/15, 807/17
Dial Number = Unknown
Dial = Silver Finish
Dial Opening = Rectangular with Cut Corners
Numerals = Painted
Hands = Steel
Seconds at = None
Cased in Factory = Yes
Collectibility = ◷◷◷◷
Rarity = ◷◷◷ WGF
◷◷◷◷◷ YGF
Retail Price New = Marilyn, $40.00 (17J); Elissa, $37.50 (15J);
Sylvia, $32.50 (15J); Irene, $40.00 (15J)
Introduction Date = 1931 (Marilyn), 1932 (Elissa, Sylvia), 1933 (Irene)
Unique Case Design = No /Yes (Elissa only)
Unique Dial Design = No
Advertisement = Yes
Marketing Themes = "With like quality bracelet attached" (Irene)
"Unusually attractive" (Marilyn)

The Marilyn, Elissa, Sylvia and Irene are four Illinois ladies' models that came in case Model No. 830. All were offered in white gold-filled or yellow gold-filled cases, but yellow gold-filled specimens are more difficult to find than white gold-filled and therefore far more collectible.

The Marilyn was equipped with a 17-jewel movement and the Elissa, Irene and Sylvia with 15-jewel ones. The Irene, advertised among the Pioneers of Greater Values in the Illinois 1933 sales catalog, was fitted with a bracelet and the others with ribbon bands.

ELISSA—15 jewels, 18/0 size, 14 filled white or natural engraved gold. . $37.50

Elissa, in Spring 1932 Illinois Sales Catalog

IRENE
14 Karat white or natural gold filled with like quality bracelet attached. 15 jewels. (18/0 size)
$40.00

Irene, shown in Benj. Allen 1933 catalog

SYLVIA—15 jewels, 18/0 size, 14k filled white or natural gold $32.50

Sylvia, in Spring 1932 Illinois Sales Catalog

The Elissa is notable for being the only one of the four that has any engraving on its bezel. Both the Elissa and its sister Sylvia were listed on the same page in the Spring 1932 Illinois Sales Catalog. It might seem odd to have two so closely related in the same advertisement; however, from the pictures one would not have guessed that they were siblings, since the former had an engraved bezel and the latter a plain one.

Some of these models were advertised in the August 25, 1931 issue of the *Saturday Evening Post* and in the 1932 and 1933 Illinois Century of Progress sales catalogs.

The Marilyn was featured as "The WATCH of the MONTH" in the March 28, 1931 issue of the *Saturday Evening Post*. The advertisement noted: "The spotlight below features the MARILYN. Latest, loveliest creation among those exclusive designs that bring such winsome beauty and the unmistakable stamp of style to every Illinois Watch."

Saturday Evening Post, March 28, 1931

Notwithstanding the advertising copy, the Marilyn and its sisters are very plain, basic-looking watches. But that was the latest trend in fashion of the times; sleek lines were part of the Streamlined/Moderne era's "un-mistakable strong style." Accordingly, the Marilyn has the distinction of being featured along with the men's Rockliffe and Ritz men's wristwatches in one of Illinois' most stunning advertisements, which uses an image of the Chrysler building to help convey that message.

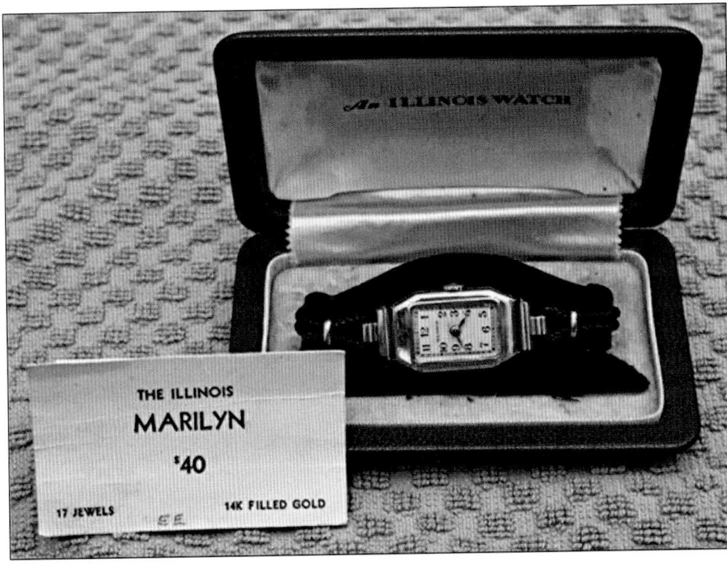

Marilyn in its display case, with original price card

Elissa's original outer cardboard box

Marionette

See listing for **Muzette/Marionette**

Marlette

See listing for **Minuette/Rosette**

Mary Todd, white gold

Mary Todd, white gold with enamel

Mary Todd

Name = Mary Todd
Time Period = Deco
Karat/Material = 18K WG, 18K GG
Bezel = Hand Engraved (with or without Inlaid Enamel); Diamond-Set
Sides = Engraved
Lug Size = 11mm
Spring Bar = Fixed Lugs
Casemaker = Keystone
Case Pieces = 3, Hinged
Case Number = No Number
Case Back = Engraved
Dimensions = 17 x 31mm
Durability = 🕓🕓🕓🕓
Movement Size = 18/0
Movement Grade/Jewels = Unknown/16, 807/17
Dial Numbers = 85, 86, 87, 89 (Octagonal); 8169, 8170 (Short Rectangular)
Dials = Silver Finish, Sparkle Finish, Embossed
Dial Openings = Octagonal, Short Rectangular
Numerals= Painted, Embossed
Hands = Steel
Seconds at = None
Cased in Factory = Yes
Collectibility = 🕓🕓🕓🕓
Rarity = 🕓🕓🕓🕓 in WG, with or without Enamel
🕓🕓🕓🕓🕓 in WG Diamond-Set
🕓🕓🕓🕓🕓🕓 in GG
Retail Price New = $75.00
Introduction Date = 1926
Unique Case Design = Yes
Unique Dial Design = No
Advertisements = Yes
Marketing Themes = "Extremely small and smart"
"Especially artistic appearance"
"Beauty and refinement"

The Mary Todd, named for Abraham Lincoln's wife, was to the ladies' Illinois wristwatches as the Consul was to the men's: the top of the line. The Consul, however, came in solid 14K gold, the Mary Todd solid 18K. At $75.00, the Mary Todds were the highest-priced ladies' Illinois watch, costing the same as a 19-jewel Consul on the men's side. Both of these high-end solid gold models were released before the Great Depression hit the watch industry. As with the Consul, there are a few ultra-rare all-green gold versions of the Mary Todd; however, the Consul also came in a two-tone green and white case, but the Mary Todd did not.

Mary Todd, green gold

The ILLINOIS WATCH
SINCE 1870 AT
SPRINGFIELD, ILLINOIS

18/0 or 6 3/4 Ligne Rectangular

The Mary Todd

17 Ruby and Sapphire Jewels

THE Eighteen-O rectangular watch was produced by Illinois to meet the approval of the most fastidious women who desire a timepiece of rare beauty and refinement in a small, thin rectangular shape, one accurate and dependable that is not a mere ornament. ¶The fine 17 jewel movement has been the pride of Illinois craftsmen, whose privilege it has been to produce it. To these people it is more than just a watch movement, it is an accomplishment they are proud of. ¶The beautiful 18K solid gold cases, used on the Mary Todd model, were designed by the best artists in the industry. They are especially artistic in appearance and worthy to become a part of Illinois. Some are hand engraved while others are hand engraved and delicately inlaid with enamel. The models illustrated on this page give an idea of the various case designs. The attractive dials illustrated are etched and finished with white silvered back ground, the numerals etched raised and gold finished.

Engraved Full Opening
18K Solid White Gold
Retail $75.00 List $86.00

Engraved Full Opening
18K Solid White Gold
Retail $75.00 List $86.00

SPECIFICATIONS

Size Eighteen-0 or six and three-fourths ligne, 17 ruby and sapphire jewels, safety recoiling click, double roller escapement, tempered and hardened compensating balance, steel escape wheel, concaved and polished winding wheels.

Enamel Case Full Opening
18K Solid White Gold
Retail $75.00 List $86.00

Engraved Square Opening
18K Solid White Gold
Retail $75.00 List $86.00

Prices Subject to Change Without Notice

Otto Young catalog, 1929

American Magazine, May 1928

Illinois offered many different dial and bezel variations for the Mary Todd. Such variety makes collecting this model very challenging, but also very enjoyable and rewarding. These are all very captivating pieces and belong in any collection of deco ladies' wristwatches.

Illinois apparently introduced the Mary Todd in 1926, and advertisements in various catalogs began appearing the next year. One Mary Todd style appeared in the 1927 catalog of the Memphis jeweler Geo. T. Brodnax and another one in the 1927 catalog of the Chicago department store Carson Pirie Scott & Co. Three styles of the Mary Todd were shown in the 1928 Carson Pirie Scott catalog.

Geo. T. Brodnax catalog, 1927

ILLINOIS MARY TODD

R10197 18/0 size 18k solid white gold case, hand carved bezel. 16J Illinois rectangular movement. Plain or raised figured dial. Each $100.00

Carson Pirie Scott catalog, 1927

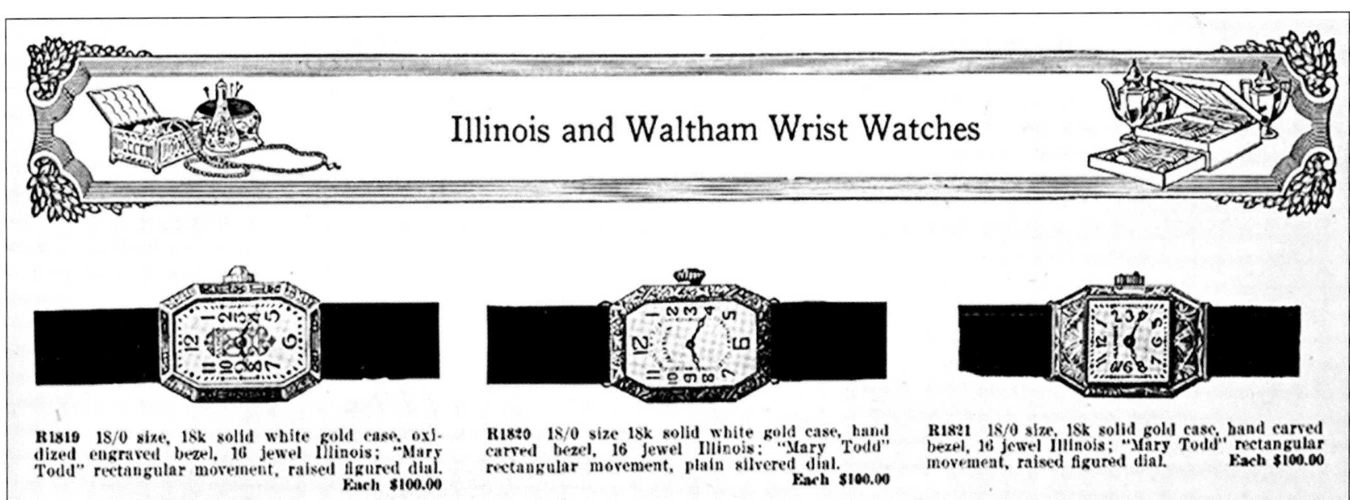

Carson Pirie Scott catalog, 1928

In terms of magazine advertisements, the Mary Todd was the most advertised Illinois ladies' wristwatch, appearing multiple times in various periodicals. It was advertised in both the April and May 1928 issues of the *National Geographic*, though not identified by name. This caption accompanied the image of one of the enameled models: "Extremely small and smartly rectangular wrist watch with fine 17-jeweled movement in 18K solid white gold case, hand engraved or inlaid enamel. $75.00." The Marquis-Autocrat pocket watch and "new" Marquis Strap wristwatch were also featured in this same advertisement. The Mary Todd appeared as early as June 1928 in the *American Magazine*.

Some people just seem to have the gift of giving. Their gifts are always useful and, above all, appropriate.

The secret lies in giving what the recipient would choose for himself. And what could delight any Noble more than the beautiful Shriners' Special? For husband, father, brother—for any member of the Mystic Shrine—this watch, specially designed by request for Nobles, is the perfect gift they would be proud to own.

Give him a Shriners' Special. It will be a joy to him for a lifetime. Distinctive, individual, it will be an enduring symbol of his affiliation, a treasured possession as well as a superior timepiece, backed by the Illinois guarantee.

The Shriners' Special has a 17-jeweled movement, guaranteed for accuracy, durability and service. It is fitted in a thin-model case of 14K filled white gold, full chased. The beautiful Shrine Emblem dial is the work of a real artist. The dial is of satin-finish sterling silver with raised numerals in gold. The center of the dial, beneath the emblem, is highly polished so that the enameled gold, blue and red of the emblem are strikingly effective.

At all leading jewelers, $43.50.

Give other members of the family an Illinois wrist watch. The model illustrated here is the Mary Todd, an extremely fine watch of excellent timekeeping quality in addition to its artistic appearance. A 17-jeweled movement in solid 18K white gold, hand engraved or inlaid enamel cases, $75.00.

Illinois Watches

ILLINOIS WATCH COMPANY, Springfield, Illinois

MAKERS OF HIGH-GRADE WATCHES EXCLUSIVELY

American Magazine, December 1927

The Mary Todd was earlier thought to be the first Factory-Cased Illinois ladies' wristwatch to leave the Springfield Plant. However, it now appears that there may have been some even earlier high-karat solid gold models with 18/0 size movements that were likely Factory-Cased. (See the listing for Wadsworth Special Models later in this chapter.) The design for the new Illinois 18/0 movement was apparently finished in 1922, with production beginning in 1923 (see Chapter 6).

Models with Engraved and Enameled Bezels

There are so many Mary Todd variations that it amounts to a watch line rather than being just a model. Not counting the Mary Todd 203 and Mary Todd 204, which have case Model Numbers, and an indeterminate number of diamond-set models (discussed below), the Mary Todd line without case Model Numbers comprised at least seven different bezel styles, four of which included delicate geometric patterns in inlaid black enamel. These enameled models, each with a different pattern of enameling, were also embellished with an understated pattern of repeated X's on the corners of the bezels.

A group of Mary Todds. The lower far right model is a Mary Todd 203.

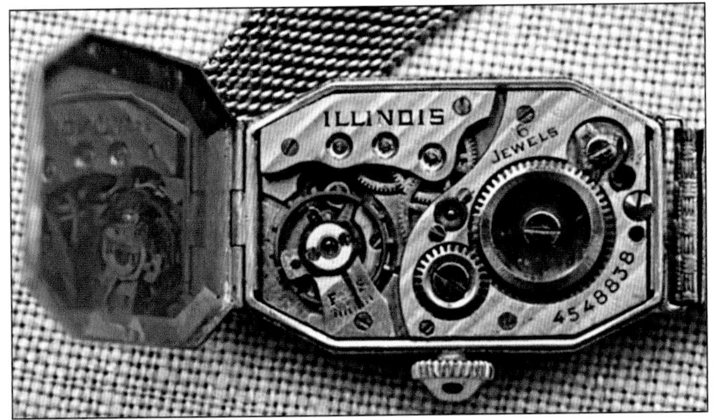

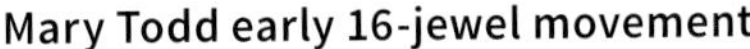

Mary Todd early 16-jewel movement

There were also at least three different patterns of bezel engraving for unenameled models. Two of these were for models with octagonal dial openings: one pattern featured a floral pattern with small flowers and leaves; the other had different foliate forms. A third model had a short rectangular dial opening and an ornate fan-like motif at the top and bottom of the bezel (perhaps foreshadowing the design of the Edge-water 175).

Interestingly, the early Mary Todd models have a different engraving pattern on the sides of their cases from those that Keystone uses for later 18/0 size Illinois models (including the Mary Todd 203 and Mary Todd 204). Nonetheless, the pattern on the case backs is the same for both the earlier and the later Keystone cases. (A discussion of case engraving appears in the introduction to this chapter.)

Side engraving of an early Mary Todd model

There were also a number of different dials used with these early Mary Todd models, at least three of which are pictured in the 1927 Illinois Dial and Hand Circular (see Chapter 7). For the models with octagonal dial openings there were several choices. The one with the floral-engraved bezel was frequently shown with a butler-center dial having exploded numerals at 12 and 6 (dial No. 89). Another dial was a very ornate one with exploding numerals and an embossed pattern not only in the center of the dial but also in the area above and below the numeral area, which gives the dial a square effect, even though the whole area is octagonal. This dial (No. 86) is what is shown on the engraved and enameled model shown in the

1927 Brodnax catalog and the 1928 *National Geographic* advertisements mentioned above. Yet another dial, shown on the enameled model in the 1928 Illinois "Book of Watches" as well as in the 1928 Carson Pirie Scott catalog, has an elongated embossed motif in the center of the dial (No. 87). The model with foliate engraving on its bezel is shown in the 1929 Otto Young catalog with an elaborately embossed dial (No. 85) whose radial numerals are arranged in an oval pattern.

Illinois "Book of Watches," 1928

The Mary Todd with the short rectangular dial opening used the embossed dial No. 86, mentioned above, just in a different way. The bezel on this model simply covered up the decoration at the top and bottom of the dial area, leaving only the embossed decoration at the center visible. This model could also have been found with a plain dial, such as No. 8169 or 8170 in the 1930 Illinois Dial and Hand catalog (see Chapter 7).

The Rare Green Gold Model

It was earlier thought that the Mary Todd was offered only in 18K white gold because an Illinois Watch Company brochure/price list of August 1927 states that "the Mary Todd is supplied only in solid 18K white gold cases with either hand engraved or inlaid enamel bezels." However, a few specimens in solid 18K green gold have been found.

The green gold Mary Todd specimens we have examined have an octagonal dial opening, and the bezel appears to have the same pattern of foliate engraving as the white gold Mary Todd of that sort, mentioned above. The beautiful, ornate embossed gilt dial (No. 85) came with either gilt or black painted numerals.

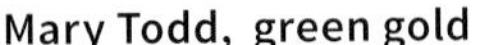
Mary Todd, green gold

Mary Todd green gold case back

Our theory is that these Mary Todds may have been made in green gold rather than white gold as special orders. This seems to be supported by the following statement in the 1928 ELF (Edwards-Ludwig-Fuller) Red Book catalog: "The Mary Todd is *regularly* [emphasis added] supplied only in Solid 18K White Gold, Hand Engraved or Inlaid Enamel cases."

> **The Mary Todd is regularly supplied only in Solid 18k White Gold, Hand Engraved or Inlaid Enamel Cases. The Mary Todd is one of the smallest watches made in America and is made throughout of the finest material obtainable. It is a watch that any jeweler can conscientiously recommend. Furnished in an attractive velvet-lined Jewel Case. Suggested retail price, $80.00.**

ELF Red Book catalog, 1928

Diamond-Set Models

For a number of years, Illinois watches have been found in 18K white gold Keystone cases set with four, six, or eight diamonds, and a few set with sapphires as well. Since jobbers' catalogs have been found listing some of these specifically as Mary Todd models, we believe that many others in 18K Keystone cases of similar styles are also Mary Todds because they tend to have cases of the characteristic Mary Todd shape. These are not gaudy, diamond-encrusted watches; the modest number of diamonds (and sapphires, when present) complement the elegant engraving patterns of the bezels.

Quite a few different styles of these diamond-set 18K Keystone cases have been found. We think that the case styles were possibly custom designs for particular jobbers and jewelers, and likely unique to each company. The diamond-set models listed as Mary Todds in the 1928 Wallenstein Mayer catalog are somewhat different in style from those in the 1928 A. C. Becken catalog, one of which has sapphires as well as diamonds. And two specimens of an Illinois in an 18K white gold diamond-set Keystone case have been found that appear to match the image of a diamond-set 18K Illinois in a 1930 John Plain catalog.

A Mary Todd Diamond-Set Model, 18K white gold Keystone case

No. 808709, $176.00
18/0 Size. 18K White Solid Gold Rectangular Shape Case Set with 8 Diamonds. Fit with 16 Jewel Illinois Movement. Black Ribbon Bracelet. The Mary Todd Bracelet Watch.
No. 808710, $160.00
Same as Above, Set with 6 Diamonds.

Wallenstein-Mayer catalog, 1928

Mary Todd Diamond-Set model, 18K white gold, diamonds and sapphires

ILLINOIS
18/0 size, 16-jewel Illinois; Mary Todd rectangular 18k solid white gold case. 8 fine diamonds, 2 sapphires. 18k gold buckle.
No. 2117...........$164.50

A. C. Becken catalog, 1928; watch at right

Mary Todd Diamond-Set model, 18K white gold, diamonds and sapphires

ILLINOIS
18/0 size, 16-jewel Illinois; Mary Todd rectangular 18k solid gold case. 6 fine diamonds. 18k solid gold buckle.
No. **2118**...........**$152.50**

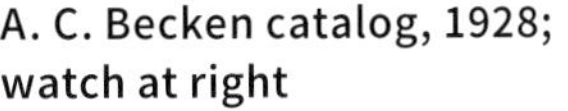

A. C. Becken catalog, 1928; watch at right

Mary Todd Diamond-Set model, 18K white gold, diamonds

No diamond-set watches appear ever to have been issued as Mary Todd models by Illinois itself. The Mary Todd models in Illinois Factory catalog listings have engraving and/or enameling, but no diamonds (or sapphires). Thus our theory is that Illinois allowed certain of its regular jobbers and jewelers to market particular diamond-set 18K models, cased at the Illinois Factory, as Mary Todd offerings of their own.

No. 808711, $144.00
18/0 Size. 18K White Solid Gold **Rectangular** Shape Case Set with 4 Diamonds. Fit with 16 Jewel Illinois Movement. Black Ribbon Bracelet. The Mary Todd Bracelet Watch.

Wallenstein-Mayer catalog, 1928; image matches watch at right. (Although the catalog caption says "4 diamonds," six are shown in the image.)

Mary Todd Diamond-Set model, 18K white gold, six diamonds.

Mary Todd Diamond-Set side view

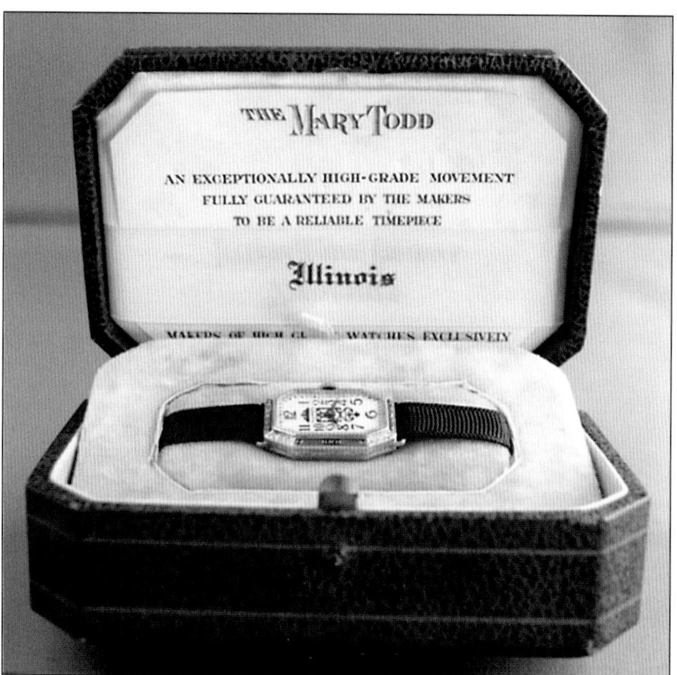

Mary Todd in its display box

Mary Todd display box

Mary Todd 203

Mary Todd 203, white gold

Name = Mary Todd 203
Time Period = Deco
Karat/Material = 18K WG, Black Inlaid Enamel
Bezel = Engraved, with Enamel
Sides = Engraved
Lug Size = 11mm
Spring Bar = Fixed Lugs
Casemaker = Keystone
Case Pieces = 3
Case Number = 203
Case Back = Engraved
Dimensions = 17 x 31mm
Durability = 🕒🕒🕒🕒
Movement Size = 18/0
Movement Grade/Jewels = 807/17
Dial Numbers = 8154, 8174
Dial = Sterling Silver; Sparkle Finish, Silver Finish
Dial Opening = Octagonal
Numerals = Painted
Hands = Steel
Seconds at = None
Cased in Factory = Yes
Collectibility = 🕒🕒🕒🕒
Rarity = 🕒🕒🕒🕒🕒
Retail Price New = $75.00
Introduction Date = 1929
Unique Case Design = Yes
Unique Dial Design = No
Advertisement = Yes
Marketing Themes = "Surpassing beauty, charm and distinction"
"A watch of rare beauty"

By 1929, the early Mary Todd styles were perhaps beginning to seem a bit old-fashioned, so Illinois introduced two new 18K solid white gold models for its flagship ladies' line, this time with case Model Numbers. One of the two was the Mary Todd 203, whose striking Deco slashes of black enamel on the white gold bezel made the model particularly stylish and unusual. (The other model, the unenameled Mary Todd 204, is discussed below in a separate listing.)

Because of the interesting use of deco-style enameling on its solid gold case, the Mary Todd 203 is highly sought-after and collectible. It was one of seven Illinois ladies' wristwatches with solid gold cases and inlaid enamel. The Mary Todd 203 came equipped with a 17-jewel movement; it had a silk ribbon band with a clasp also of solid gold, but few of those delicate bands have survived.

The Mary Todd 203 is often found with the special Flückiger dial (No. 8154; see Chapter 7), and this is the one with which it was usually pictured in advertisements. Another dial that was used with it is plain, but with interesting numerals (No. 8174).

The Mary Todd 203 was introduced in the 1929–30 Illinois catalog, the cover of which had a picture of an Illinois watch movement and the motto "The Thrilling Beauty that Lies Within." This became the theme of Illinois' advertising campaign for those years.

Advertisements for the Mary Todd 203 appeared in the August 2, September 7 and October 5, 1929 issues of *Collier's* magazine and, for the holiday trade, in the December 1929 issue of the *American Magazine*. Headed "A watch to grace the years . . . an Illinois," this advertisement provided holiday shoppers with many fine choices. Shown along with the Mary Todd 203 were the Newport, New Yorker, Ensign, Futura, Medalist, Consul and Jolly Roger wristwatches, plus two pocket watches, the Trustee and the Dean. The advertisement offered this assurance:

> When you give or receive an Illinois Watch, you have done doubly well—for in "the thrilling beauty that lies within" you have the surpassing performance that alone makes a watch worth having; and in the beautiful new Illinois models for both men and women, you have just that charm, that smartness and style, to delight the most fastidious owner.
>
> Let your gift watch be eloquent of thoughtfulness and regard. Let it be a significant token of love and esteem that will grace the years to come. Let it be an Illinois!

This new version of the Mary Todd was advertised in many jobbers' catalogs, including the 1930 A. C. Becken and the 1930 one of A. G. Schwab and Sons. These, like many others using Illinois factory pages directly, had this description for the Mary Todd 203: "The contrasting of jet-black polished enamel, in a conventional design, in the 18K solid white gold case together with the 17 jewel movement makes the model one of rare beauty. Also supplied with full engraved bezel, 18K gold case." (The latter seems to be a reference to the Mary Todd 204, which has an engraved but unenameled bezel.)

It is strange to find the very bold deco enameling of the Mary Todd 203 described as "a conventional design." The explanation is that the Illinois advertising department used exactly the same verbiage they had earlier applied to the old-style Mary Todd with very delicate black enameling that was shown in the little 1928 "Book of Watches" rather than taking the trouble to create appropriate copy for the new Mary Todd 203. This tendency is sometimes apparent in advertising copy for other Illinois models as well.

Mary Todd 204

Two specimens of the Mary Todd 204, white gold

Name = Mary Todd 204
Time Period = Deco
Karat/Material = 18K WG
Bezel = Engraved
Sides = Engraved
Lug Size = 11mm
Spring Bar = Fixed Lugs
Casemaker = Keystone
Case Pieces = 3
Case Number = 204
Case Back = Engraved
Dimensions = 17 x 31mm
Durability = 🕒🕒🕒🕒
Movement Size = 18/0
Movement Grade/Jewels = 807/17

Dial Numbers = 88, 8154, 8174
Dial = Sterling Silver; Sparkle Finish; Embossed
Dial Opening = Octagonal
Numerals= Painted, Gilt Etched
Hands = Steel
Seconds at = None
Cased in Factory = Yes
Collectibility = 🕓🕓🕓🕓
Rarity = 🕓🕓🕓🕓🕓🕓
Retail Price New = $75.00
Introduction Date = 1929
Unique Case Design = Yes
Unique Dial Design = No
Advertisement = Unknown
Marketing Theme = Unknown

The Mary Todd 204 has only recently been documented. For a number of years, collectors have been wondering what this beautiful Illinois model was, though from the shape and size of its 18K white gold Keystone case it appeared to be another case variation of the already identified models in the Mary Todd series.

Documentation for the Mary Todd 204 has been found in the 1931 and 1932 Oskamp Nolting catalogs, which show an image of the watch, with its name and the following caption: "18/0 Size, 18K Solid White Gold Case, Fancy Engraved, Silk Ribbon Bracelet, 17 Jewel Illinois Movement, Silver Dial." In addition, one collector also has a specimen of the watch that came with its original display box and price card.

Oskamp Nolting 1932 catalog, with superimposed Mary Todd 204

The engraving on the bezel is most unusual. The top and bottom of the bezel are dominated by outlines of a segment of a circle, enclosing a pair of loose curlicues facing each other. (These interior motifs are repeated at the corners of the bezel.) The curved outlines of the engraving serve to soften the basic angularity of what is an octagonal case. Even more unusual is that there are actually two levels of engraving on the sides of the bezel: the narrow front surface has delicate, elongated foliate patterns; the second level, which includes the engraved bezel corners, has a compact foliate motif centered between them.

The dial shown on the Mary Todd 204 in the Oskamp Nolting catalogs is the beautiful sterling silver one by Flückiger (No. 8154). However, specimens of this watch have also been found with other dials: an ornate embossed dial (No. 88, from the 1927 Dial and Hand Circular) and a very attractive plain dial with interesting numerals (No. 8174).

Strangely enough, on one page in a 1930 A. C. Becken catalog, the Mary Todd 204 is labeled as a Coronado—doubly strange, because elsewhere in the catalog an actual Illinois factory page has an image of the real Coronado!

The Mary Todd 204 is a rare model, according to Gay. As yet, no magazine advertisements for it have been found.

A MARY TODD MYSTERY

When the new Mary Todd models (case Models No. 203 and No. 204) were introduced in 1929, the Mary Todd 203 was assigned descriptive verbiage about its enameling that was the same as what had been used in the 1928 Book of Watches for an earlier model, even though the new model had an entirely different style of enameling. (There was also a "full engraved version" offered in 1929; this was the Mary Todd 204.)

At some point, however, Illinois changed the catalog description. The 1930–31 catalogs of A. I. Hall and S. H. Clausin, as well as the 1931 A. C. Becken one, all show the same Illinois factory advertisement with the following caption for the new-style Mary Todds: "A watch of rare beauty, cased in 18K solid gold. Offered in plain, engraved or inlaid enamel cases."

The MARY TODD

A watch of rare beauty, cased in 18K solid gold. Offered in plain, engraved or inlaid enamel cases.

Suggested consumer price, $75.

A. I. Hall catalog, 1930–31

The inlaid enamel case must be the Mary Todd 203 and the engraved case the Mary Todd 204, but what model was the plain case? The catalog image itself shows what appears to be a plain case with neither engraving nor enameling (and a similarly plain dial, No. 8174), but to our knowledge no 18K solid white gold Illinois in a plain Keystone case of Mary Todd shape has yet been found.

Mary Todd 204 in its display box with its original price card

Miami 155, white gold-filled, two-tone blue enamel

Miami 155

Name =	Miami 155
Time Period =	Deco
Karat/Material =	14K WGF, Light and Dark Blue Inlaid Enamel
Bezel =	Engraved, with Enamel
Sides =	Engraved
Lug Size =	11mm
Spring Bar =	Fixed Lugs
Casemaker =	Wadsworth
Case Pieces =	3
Case Number =	155
Case Back =	Engraved
Dimensions =	17 x 31mm
Durability =	◷◷
Movement Size =	18/0
Movement Grade/Jewels =	807/17
Dial Numbers =	8169, 8170
Dial =	Silver Finish, Sparkle Finish
Dial Opening =	Short Rectangular
Numerals=	Painted, Embossed
Hands =	Steel
Seconds at =	None
Cased in Factory =	Yes
Collectibility =	◷◷◷◷
Rarity =	◷◷◷◷
Retail Price New =	$55.00
Introduction Date =	1929
Unique Case Design =	Yes
Unique Dial Design =	No
Advertisement =	Yes
Marketing Theme =	"A pleasing combination of inlaid blue enamel and lined white gold surface"

The Miami 155, another of Illinois' fabulous Art Deco enameled-bezel ladies' models, has a strong pattern of vertical stripes on a smooth-surfaced panel at the top and bottom of the bezel. At the center is the dominant stripe, of cobalt blue, which is flanked by a stripe of polished surface and then a narrow stripe of light blue. The pattern of enameling is subtly echoed by the lined pattern of engraving on either side of the enameled area, with wider engraved lines flanked by narrower ones.

The Miami 155 was listed in the 1929–1930 Illinois Sales Catalog, with this description: "The happy combination of blue inlaid enamel and delicately lined effect of the 14K white gold filled case makes this model a favorite." It was equipped with a 17-jewel movement and came with a ribbon band.

A. I. Hall 1930–31 catalog, with superimposed Miami 155

As with the cases of other Illinois enameled ladies' models, the enameling on the bezels is only part of the attraction, though it is what immediately seizes the eye. The bezels have exquisite engraving as well. On the Miami 155, for example, the sides of the bezel are decorated with a delicate foliate pattern.

The Miami 155 appeared in at least four magazine advertisements. It was shown in the September 7, 1929 issue of *Collier's*, which also introduced the Medalist, a men's model using the first Illinois 12/0 size, 207 grade rectangular movement. It appeared again in *Collier's* in January 11, 1930.

That advertisement, headed "NOW—the watch you should have had for Christmas," points out that the watch in question was, of course, "An Illinois—that gift of gifts." But even if an Illinois wasn't among your presents, it might still be possible to have one:

> Maybe there was a check in your Christmas stocking that will make it easy for you to give yourself the watch you hoped for—the watch somehow unthought of or forgotten by those who did their loving best to make you happy... Don't wait, then, these eleven long months 'til next Christmas comes around. Satisfy your desire to own one of these smart, beautiful watches to regulate your time through 1930 and the years to come, and give you constant joy in its possession . . .

Shown in that advertisement was a wide range of choices: for the gentlemen, the New Yorker and Medalist wristwatches and the Trustee pocket watch; for the ladies, not only the Miami 155 but also the Fairport and Avalon.

The Miami 155 was also advertised in the October 19, 1929 and May 31, 1930 issues of *Liberty*. In the former (shown here), its companions were the Long Beach and the Edgewater 155.

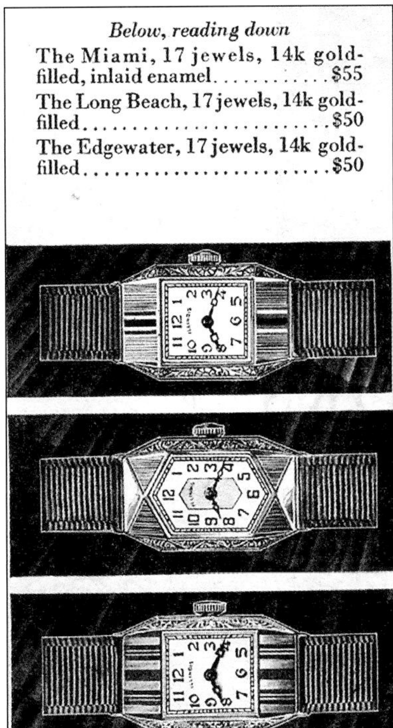

***Liberty*, October 19, 1929**

In addition to the Miami 155, there is a Miami 157 that also has two-tone blue enameling, but in a very striking chevron pattern rather than vertical striping. The Miami 155, however, is more easily found than the earlier Miami 157, though it is often prone to some case wear and enamel chipping. Nonetheless, it makes a wonderful addition to a collection.

The Miami 155, often seen with a plain silver finish or white sparkle finish dial with plain black numerals, sometimes has a more elaborate dial with exploding gilt numerals.

At least five other Illinois ladies' wristwatches shared case Model No. 155.

Miami 157, white gold-filled red and black enamel

Miami 157 / Miami 157A

Name = Miami 157, Miami 157A (Solid Gold)
Time Period = Deco
Karat/Material = 14K WGF, Two-Tone Blue Enamel or Red and Black Enamel; 14K YG, Red and Black Enamel
Bezel = Engraved, with Enamel
Sides = Engraved
Lug Size = 11mm
Spring Bar = Fixed Lugs
Casemaker = Wadsworth
Case Pieces = 3
Case Number = 155
Case Back = Engraved
Dimensions = 17 x 31mm
Durability = 🕒🕒🕒
Movement Size = 18/0
Movement Grade/Jewels = 807/17
Dial Numbers = 8169, 8170
Dial = Silver Finish, Sparkle Finish
Dial Opening = Short Rectangular
Numerals= Black, Gilt
Hands = Steel
Seconds at = None
Cased in Factory = Yes
Collectibility = 🕒🕒🕒🕒
Rarity = 🕒🕒🕒🕒🕒 in WGF
🕒🕒🕒🕒🕒🕒🕒 in YG
Retail Price New = $55.00 in WGF, $75.00 in Solid Gold
Introduction Date = 1928
Unique Case Design = Yes
Unique Dial Design = No
Advertisement = Yes
Marketing Themes = "A watch in a setting of enduring beauty and color"
"Strikingly modern in its variety of color combinations"
"Happy combination of warm red and black enamel"

The Miami

The happy combination of warm red and black enamel inlaid in its 14 karat white gold filled case, makes this model a favorite.

60W05. Price.. **$74.40**

May & Malone 1930 catalog, with superimposed Miami 157

Miami 157, white gold-filled, two-tone blue enamel

The Miami 157 is one of the most highly sought-after Illinois deco watches with enamel bezels. The case with red and black enamel in a dramatic chevron pattern is extremely difficult to find, and the two-tone blue version may be even more elusive. Both are highly collectible.

There is one very rare version of the red and black enamel Miami 157A that has a solid yellow gold case. This is probably either a custom model or a special watch for the exclusive use of the Kay Jewelry Company, as Kay advertised this model in solid gold of unspecified color in 1930. Since only one complete model is known to exist, it is therefore probably the rarest and most desirable ladies' Illinois wristwatch. (As yet, no Miami 157A has been found in solid white gold, or in either color of solid gold with two-tone blue enamel.)

A 1930 Kay Jewelry Company advertisement, including a solid gold Miami 157A, also shows Kay's clever promotion campaign "Who owns the oldest watch?" with the new "Vanity Fair" as the prize. *Oakland Tribune* (Oakland, CA), August 8, 1930; image from *newspapers.com*

Illinois was very proud of its stunning new line of enameled ladies' watches. and the Miami 157 appeared in various versions of the advertisement "A watch indeed!" The text of this advertisement actually addressed not just the Miami but Illinois' whole line of enameled beauties, whose color combinations and designs no doubt were introduced to compete head-to-head with Elgin's Parisienne line:

> An exceptionally small, fine watch movement—a jewel of a watch in a setting of enduring beauty and color—that is Illinois' brilliant new creation for the women of America.
>
> Strikingly modern in its variety of color combinations in true enamel inlaid in charming designs, you will find it adorning the wrists of good taste.

The Miami 157 was introduced in 1928 in the little Illinois "Book of Watches," and the description used there was what appeared in advertisements for it: "The happy combination of warm red and black hard enamel inlaid in its 14K white gold-filled case makes this model a favorite. Doubly so because of the timekeeping qualities of its fine Illinois 17-jeweled movement." The watch came with a ribbon band.

The Miami

THE happy combination of warm red and black enamel inlaid in its 14k white gold filled case makes this model a favorite. Doubly so because of the timekeeping qualities of its fine Illinois 17 jeweled movement.

$55

Illinois "Book of Watches," 1928

The striking pattern of enameling made the Miami 157 an ideal candidate to picture in Illinois advertisements, even without color added. The red and black version was advertised many times, including the September 29, 1928 and October 20, 1928 issues of the *Saturday Evening Post* and the October and November 1928 issues of the *National Geographic*. The two-tone blue version appeared shortly thereafter in the November 10, 1928 issue of the *Saturday Evening Post*, where the description of the watch remained the same except for the colors of the enamel: "two tones of beautiful blue" instead of "warm red and black."

The bezel of the Miami 157 is beautifully engraved as well as beautifully enameled. The delicate foliate patterns engraved on the corners of the bezel and the motif in the center of the enameled chevron bear a resemblance to some of the patterns used on some of the Daytona models. The sides of the bezel are not engraved.

Although the Miami 157 is often seen with a silver finish or white sparkle finish dial with plain black numerals, it sometimes comes with a more elaborate dial that has gilt numerals in an exploding pattern (this is what seems to be pictured in many advertisements of the model).

An Illinois Watch
The Miami
$55.00
17 Jewel Movement
14K Gold Filled Case
Inlaid Enamel

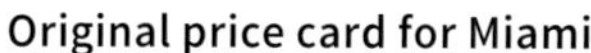

Original price card for Miami

End of Miami's outer cardboard box

WHY I COLLECT ILLINOIS

My introduction to the watch collector's world began with a chance meeting. I met a fascinating man in town on business, while dining with a friend. We talked about the world and compared notes on many things. We continued to communicate even though we lived on opposite ends of the East Coast. I learned that he was an avid collector of vintage watches, Illinois watches in particular. One evening he said to me, "You really should read *The Illinois Watch: The Life and Times of a Great American Watch Company* by Fred Friedberg." I ordered the book promptly and devoured it when it arrived. While I have always been drawn to the Art Deco period from the perspective of art, architecture and fashion, this was an entirely new avenue for me. From that day on I was hooked and I found my new friend fascinating in his knowledge! Our evening phone calls became great lessons in these magnificent works of art. He took me page by page through "The Book" as we referred to it. Every time he acquired a new treasure he would call excitedly and tell me which page to turn to. Another lesson would ensue!

I got the chance to visit with my new friend and I knew we would get the chance to talk watches. He picked me up at the airport and surprised with a pouch; inside was my first ladies' Illinois watch! I recognized it instantly from Fred's book! I was taken aback by the elegance, the enamel detail and the overall beauty. My heart was pounding! My very own Illinois wristwatch! I felt like I was transported to the era where these fine pieces of art were born as he placed it on my wrist. Over time, as my collection grew, each piece also came with a sentimental meaning for me.

The next day we spent hours sitting on the floor of his home as he presented one by one, his collection. Fred's book in front of us, he gave me a history lesson on each of his prized possessions. I was totally in awe! I was so envious of the depth of his knowledge and felt so privileged that he shared his collection with me.

From that day on, I was hooked! I scoured every city in my travels for the next great find . . . from antique shops, to vintage stores and neighborhood watchmakers.

My ultimate quest became to acquire the Miami and for several years the hunt was on. I even got the opportunity to meet Mr. Friedberg and his lovely wife over dinner. I peppered Fred with questions and spoke of the quest for my holy grail . . . the Miami! Shortly after that evening I was able to track down a nearly perfect enameled Miami, complete with the original box. To this day, it is one of my most prized possessions.

(Continued on next page)

I continue to hunt the ladies' versions from the Illinois Watch Company. The ladies' selection is much smaller and much more difficult to uncover. As I am currently in the accessory business, I am most appreciative of the quality of these watches. I have visited modern-day factories where similar production occurs such as the hand enameling. It is truly an art form. Those who created these originally were artisans and craftsmen; the fine detail, the enamel and the precision are stellar. Any time I am wearing one, I receive multiple compliments.

When I put one of these on my wrist I am transported back to that time, where I am certain my soul resided at some point! Each one is a treasure. I look forward to uncovering more as time goes on. I thank Mr. Friedberg for the time and passion he has put into researching this brand and bringing it to so many others. It is a piece of history and a form of art that could very easily been lost.

—Leslie Feltinton

Minuette / Rosette / Marlette

Names = Minuette/Rosette/Marlette
Time Period = Moderne
Karat/Material = 14k WGF (Minuette, Rosette); 14K WGF or YGF (Marlette)
Bezel = Plain, Engraved (Partially); Diamonds
Sides = Engraved
Lug Size = 9mm
Spring Bar = Fixed Lugs
Casemaker = Keystone
Case Pieces = 2
Case Number = 701
Case Back = Plain
Dimensions = 14 x 28mm
Durability = 🕒🕒🕒🕒
Movement Size = 21/0
Movement Grade/Jewels = 107/17
Dial Number = 8122
Dial = Silver Finish, Sparkle Finish
Dial Opening = Rectangular
Numerals= Painted
Hands = Steel
Seconds at = None
Cased in Factory = Yes
Collectibility = 🕒🕒🕒🕒
Rarity = 🕒🕒🕒🕒🕒 in WGF or YGF
🕒🕒🕒🕒🕒🕒 with Diamonds
Retail Price New = $52.50 (Minuette), $55.00 (Rosette), $42.50 (Marlette)
Introduction Date = 1932 (Minuette), 1933 (Rosette), 1934 (Marlette)
Unique Case Design = No
Unique Dial Design = No
Advertisement = Yes

Minuette, white gold-filled

Marketing Themes = "There is a mode of modern expression in this artistically engraved case." (Minuette)
"Designed and engraved in baguette style" (Rosette)
"Smartly engraved" (Marlette)

The Minuette, one of the Illinois American Beauty Series, was listed in the 1931–32 Illinois Sales Catalog, the Rosette in the Illinois Pioneers of Greater Values 1933 catalog and the Marlette in the 1934 Illinois Sales Catalog, which was Illinois' last catalog.

These three models show a familiar pattern for Illinois under Hamilton ownership, particularly in the last few years that Illinois existed. They are all basically the same watch, simply reissued with new names and minor changes of presentation to justify the renaming.

The Minuette, Rosette and Marlette all came with 17-jewel movements; the Marlette's movement had the newly introduced Elinvar hairspring. The Minuette came with a ribbon band, the Rosette with a metal bracelet, which increased the price by $2.50; the Marlette returned to the ribbon band. All three came in white gold-filled cases; the Marlette, however, was also offered in yellow gold-filled. The price of the Marlette was $10 less than what the Minuette, the earliest issued of the trio, had been.

A rare variant of the Minuette/Rosette/Marlette has been found with diamonds on its bezel; this is likely a custom model.

Another interesting discovery is that dials with sparkle finish have recently been found on two specimens of the Minuette. Earlier it was thought that this model came only with a silver finish dial.

Minuette custom diamond model

The Minuette appeared in a November 1931 advertisement in the Keystone, which stated, "In the new Illinois American Beauty Series are the smallest American made watches of this price. This is but a step in the style evolution of Illinois' beautiful timekeepers. Look at the Greater Value Watches. Have you seen comparable watches? Illinois' Styling Department is an institution—watch its progress."

An Illinois Minuette case model was included among the cases featured in the Keystone Watch Case Company's advertisement in the March 1932 issue of the Keystone. The advertising copy commented, "Whether or not the customer has already decided to purchase a certain movement is immaterial. In the final analysis, it's the case that sells the watch." (This statement is certainly accurate but reflects only the case company's perspective; the dial was also an important selling feature.)

Page 82 The KEYSTONE March, 1932

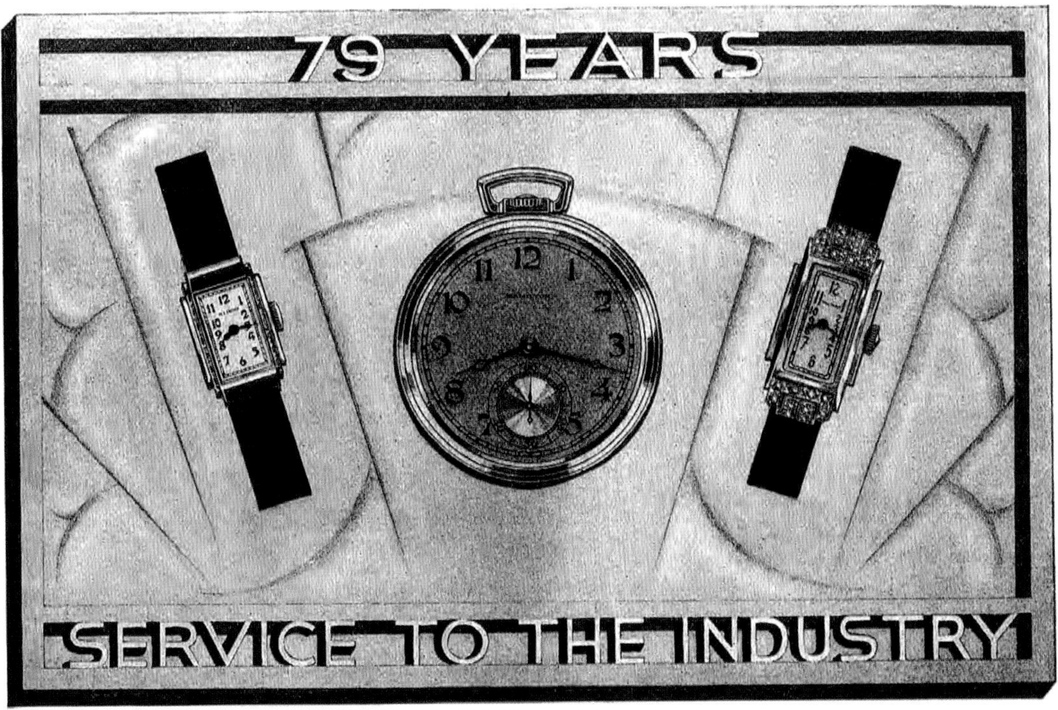

"Interrupting" Designs

Whether or not the customer has already decided to purchase a certain movement is immaterial. In the final analysis, it's the case that sells the watch. Hence, a case which *interrupts* the customer's mental process of selection by prompting him to buy a watch is a good case. If it gives the wearer excellent service it is a still better case.

That Keystone Cases, by virtue of their beautiful design and inherent quality, increase the selling value of the finest watch is amply confirmed by the fact that cases bearing Keystone trade-marks are the preferred choice of leading movement manufacturers everywhere.

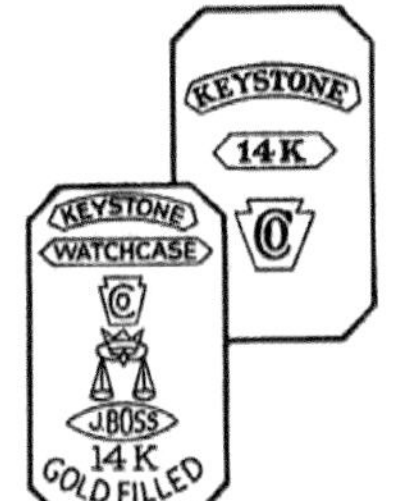

KEYSTONE WATCH CASE CORPORATION
Established 1853
RIVERSIDE, NEW JERSEY
NEW YORK · CHICAGO · CINCINNATI · SAN FRANCISCO

Keystone Case Company advertisement, showing a Minuette on the left; *Keystone*, March 1932

Meet Hollywood's new No. 1 Comedienne—none other than Jean Harlow, who has been the No. 1 Siren of the silver screen since her very first picture. In her latest production, "The Girl from Missouri," she gives a splendid performance that wins for her fresh praise from movie critics and fans. "Some girls have just everything!" Miss Harlow just sent us this lovely new portrait—it's one of her favorites.

ILLINOIS "LYNETTE" 15 JEWEL

Movement: Illinois 15 jewel 21/0 size. Case: White 10K Gold filled, beautifully hand engraved, with flexible link bracelet to match. Cased, timed and boxed at the Illinois factory.

2B23565 PRICE.. **$53.30**

ILLINOIS "MARLETTE"

Movement: Illinois 17 jewel, 21/0 size. Case: Your choice of White or natural Yellow 14K gold filled, very fine quality. Fitted with adjustable silk ribbon. Cased, timed and boxed at the Illinois factory.

2B23566 White 14K Gold Filled, PRICE................ **$56.65**
2B23567 Natural Yellow 14K Gold Filled, PRICE.. **56.65**

Montgomery Ward catalog, 1934

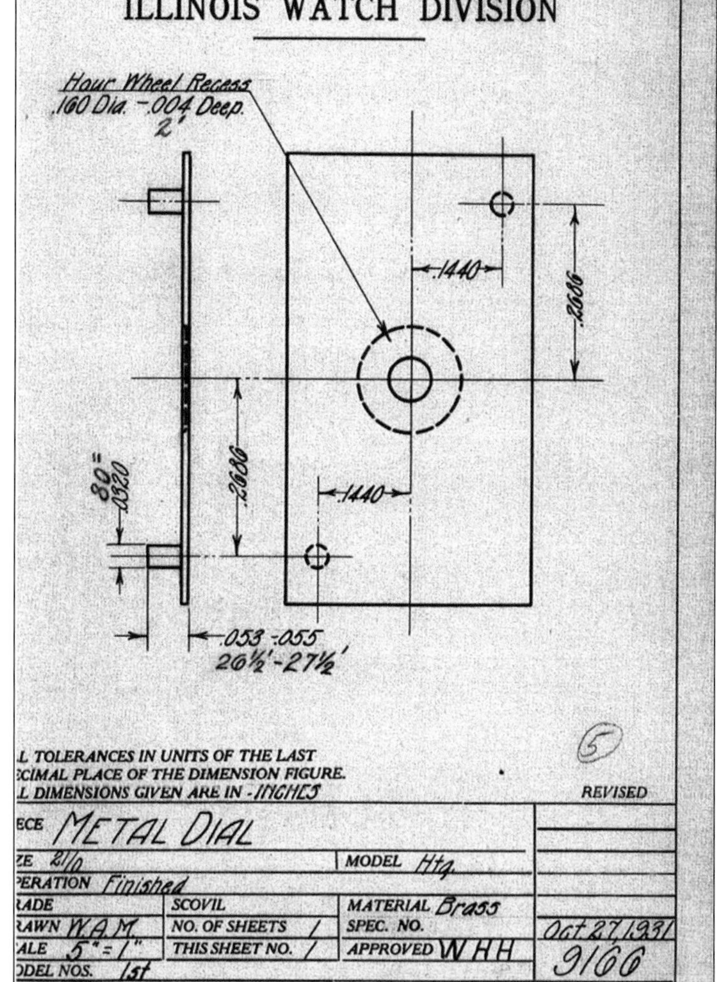

Illinois drawing for 21/0 size dial blank, dated October 27, 1931

Muzette / Marionette

Muzette, white gold-filled

Names = Muzette/Marionette
Time Period = Moderne
Karat/Material = 14K WGF, 10K WGF
Bezel = Sculpted
Sides = Engraved
Lug Size = For Cord Band
Spring Bar = For Cord Band
Casemaker = Star
Case Pieces = 2
Case Number = 707, No Number
Case Back = Plain
Dimensions = 14 x 29mm
Durability = ◷◷◷
Movement Size = 21/0
Movement Grade/Jewels = 107/17 (Muzette), 105/15 (Marionette)
Dial Number = 8374
Dial = Silver Finish
Dial Opening = Rectangular
Numerals= Painted
Hands = Steel
Seconds at = None
Cased in Factory = Yes, by Hamilton in Lancaster
Collectibility = ◷◷◷◷
Rarity = ◷◷◷◷
Retail Price New = $55.00 (Muzette, 17J), $35.00 (Marionette, 15J)
Introduction Date = 1933 (Muzette), 1934 (Marionette)
Unique Case Design = No
Unique Dial Design = No
Advertisement = Yes
Marketing Themes = "Exquisite ensemble" (Muzette)
"With silk cord and filled gold attachments" (Marionette)

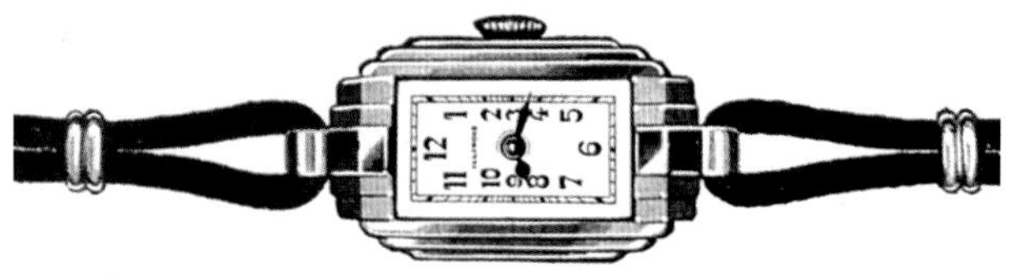

MUZETTE
Exquisite ensemble of 14 Karat white filled gold and silk cord bracelet. 17 jewels. (21/0 size.)
No. F23W15 Each $58.50

N. Shure catalog, 1933

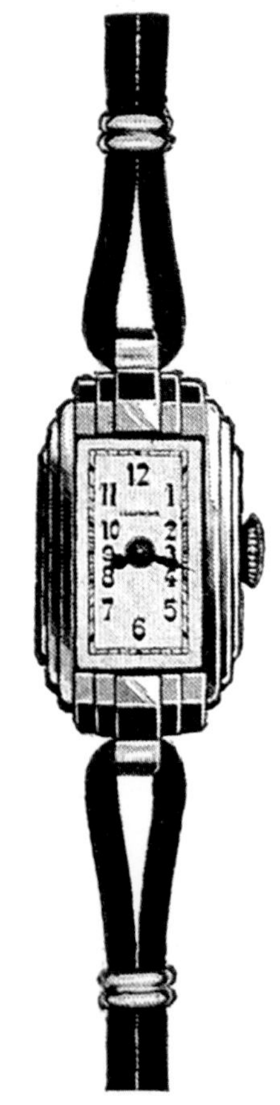

MARIONETTE
14K filled gold; white **only.** With silk cord and filled gold attachments. 15 jewels. Consumer, **$35.00.** Keystone list, **$40.00.**

A. C. Becken catalog, 1934

The Muzette and the Marionette provide another example of Hamilton's pattern of handling some Illinois ladies' models toward the end of Illinois' existence. These two models are essentially the same watch, and they were introduced only one year apart. The Muzette appeared in the 1933 Illinois Sales Catalog and the Marionette in the 1934 Illinois Sales Catalog. The latter, issued by Hamilton from Lancaster, was the final sales catalog for the Illinois Watch Company.

Both of these 21/0 size watches came in identical cases, offered only in white gold-filled, and were equipped with cord bands. The Muzette and the Marionette are two of only five ladies' Illinois wristwatches that were offered with a cord band; the others are the Barbara, Patricia and Vardon.

The one difference between them was the movement; the Muzette's was 17 jewels and the Marionette's 15 jewels (though with the new Elinvar hairspring). This difference was reflected in the price: $20 less for the Marionette, which had the lower grade movement.

The Muzette and Marionette shared the same case back (case Model No. 707) with another 21/0 size model, the Suzette, but had a much nicer stepped sculpted bezel. (The Suzette had the same stepped sides as the other two, but a plain bezel and a ribbon band.)

Very recently discovered was a Marionette in a 10K WGF case (marked thus on both the inside and outside of the case back). The case is Keystone, but instead of 707 it has no Model Number. The movement is the expected 15 jewels.

Marionette, 10K white gold-filled

Marionette, 10K white gold-filled, inside case back

Narragansett

Name = Narragansett
Time Period = Deco
Karat/Material = 14K WG
Bezel = Engraved
Sides = Engraved
Lug Size = 11mm
Spring Bar = Fixed Lugs
Casemaker = Keystone
Case Pieces = 3
Case Number = 168
Case Back = Engraved
Dimensions = 17 x 31mm
Durability = ◷◷◷◷
Movement Size = 18/0
Movement Grade/Jewels = 807/17
Dial Numbers = 8154, 8174
Dial = Silver Finish, Butler Center
Dial Opening = Octagonal
Numerals = Painted
Hands = Steel
Seconds at = None

Narragansett, white gold

Cased in Factory = Yes
Collectibility = 🕓🕓🕓🕓
Rarity = 🕓🕓🕓🕓🕓
Retail Price New = $65.00
Introduction Date = 1929
Unique Case Design = Yes
Unique Dial Design = No
Advertisement = Yes
Marketing Themes = "Rich in simplicity"
"Perfect blending of dial and case"

The Narragansett, another of the solid gold ladies' Illinois offerings, is fairly difficult to find. Sporting the beautiful sterling silver Flückiger dial (No. 8154), this model was featured in advertisements in *Liberty*, *Collier's* and the *American Magazine* in 1929 as well as in the 1929–30 Illinois Sales Catalog.

The long center of the Flückiger dial and its "lining outside" the center, mentioned in the advertising copy, helped to emphasize the length of the case design, and the delicate ornament at the top and bottom of the dial goes beautifully with the engraving of the bezel. That engraving was called "diamond engraving" by Illinois in its magazine advertisements, such as the one in the June 1, 1929 issue of *Collier's*.

The Narragansett was issued in 1929 with a ribbon band. Several years later, however, the 1933 John Plain catalog showed the Narragansett with a white gold-filled bracelet. At this point, the model was likely being discontinued by Illinois since it was advertised as having a "greatly reduced price" ($59.50). The watch was nonetheless still "cased, timed and boxed at the factory." The dial pictured on it was not the Flückiger dial but instead dial No. 8174 (plain but with interesting numerals), which was also sometimes used on other solid gold Illinois ladies' models.

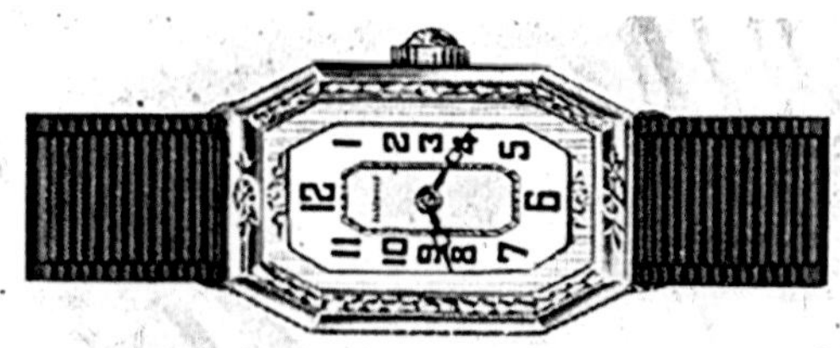

***American Magazine*, August 1929**

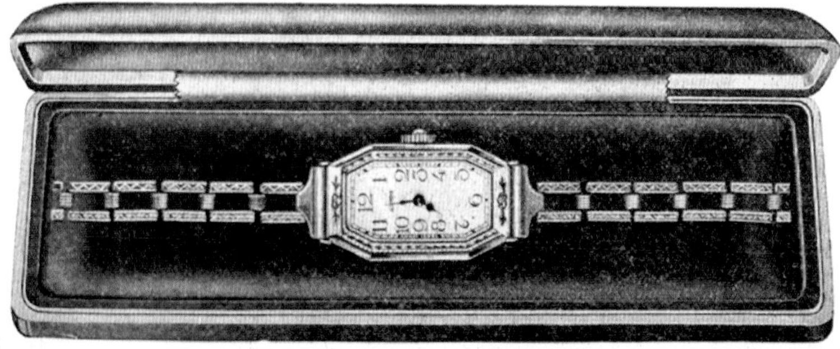

THE ILLINOIS "NARRAGANSETT"—17 JEWEL SOLID GOLD

Movement: Illinois, 18/0 size, 17 jewel. **Case:** 14K solid white gold, popular rectangular style; easy reading dial. **Bracelet:** Engraved open link, adjustable, gold filled. Completely cased, timed, and boxed at the factory. Greatly reduced price.

2R23290 PRICE **$59.50**

95

John Plain catalog, 1933

The Narragansett was advertised in the July 27, 1929 issue of *Liberty*, together with the Berkeley 153, the Edgewater 155 and an 18K white gold Mary Todd (one of the early styles with no case Model No.). It was also featured in an advertisement in the August 1929 issue of the *American Magazine*.

The 1929–30 Illinois Sales Catalog had on its cover the motto "The Thrilling Beauty That Lies Within" beneath an image of an Illinois movement. This image and theme are used for a number of Illinois magazine advertisements in those years, such as the one with the heading "One unalterable purposed Expressed in Beauty" that appeared in the August 1929 issue of the *American Magazine* mentioned above. Shown there along with the Narragansett were the Coronado, Daytona 155, Tuxedo, Piccadilly, Consul, Chieftain and Beau Brummell wristwatches, plus two pocket watches, an A. Lincoln and a Marquis-Autocrat.

In that advertisement, the image of a movement appears with the caption "The pulsing heart of an Illinois watch reveals the beauty of accuracy," and the text of the advertisement reads:

To be above all a timepiece—precise, sturdy, enduring—that is the unalterable purpose which has made Illinois more than a fine watch—a great American Watch.

Such beauty of performance within demands a fitting setting, and Illinois provides cases exquisitely designed to reflect it.

You can have this Illinois accuracy and charm in some models for as little as $40.00. Ask your jeweler. He knows watches. And he has known Illinois ever since he has been in business.

Narragansett original price card

Newport 174, white gold-filled

Newport 174

Name =	Newport 174
Time Period =	Deco
Karat/Material =	14K WGF, 14K WG (rare)
Bezel =	Engraved
Sides =	Engraved
Lug Size =	11mm
Spring Bar =	Fixed Lugs
Casemaker =	Keystone
Case Pieces =	3
Case Numbers =	174, No Number
Case Back =	Plain, Engraved
Dimensions =	17 x 31mm
Durability =	◷◷◷◷
Movement Size =	18/0
Movement Grade/Jewels =	807/17
Dial Numbers =	85, 86, 8089, 8154, 8174
Dials =	Silver Finish, Butler Center; Sterling Silver; Sparkle Finish; Silver Finish
Dial Opening =	Octagonal
Numerals =	Painted, Gilt Etched
Hands =	Steel
Seconds at =	None
Cased in Factory =	Yes
Collectibility =	◷◷◷◷
Rarity =	◷◷◷ WGF ◷◷◷◷◷◷ WG
Retail Price New =	$50.00
Introduction Date =	1929
Unique Case Design =	Yes
Unique Dial Design =	No
Advertisement =	Yes
Marketing Themes =	"Delicately engraved in a striking manner" "Beautifully silvered dial"

The NEWPORT
Delicately engraved in a striking manner.
Suggested consumer price, $50.

A. I. Hall 1930–31 catalog, with superimposed Newport 174

The Newport 174, for some reason, was one of the most advertised of the Illinois ladies' models, second only to the top-of-the-line Mary Todd. One collector thinks it might have been because it had an engraved case of the same shape as the more expensive solid gold Mary Todd and thus produced the same sort of effect on the wrist of the wearer but without costing as much. In fact, the Newport 174 is occasionally found sporting a very fancy dial often used on some early Mary Todd models; it has an elaborate etched design at the top and bottom of the dial as well as at the center, plus radially arranged gilt or black figures (this is dial No. 86 from the Illinois Dial and Hand Circular, May 1927).

The Newport 174 also sometimes appeared in magazine advertisements and catalogs with another very special dial: the lovely sterling silver Flückiger one that Illinois seems generally to have reserved for its solid gold models.

A number of other very interesting dials were used with the Newport 174. One is the very attractive dial No. 85, whose oval shape inside the octagonal bezel opening, coupled with exploding numerals, produces a great deco effect (advertising copy for the Newport states, quite accurately, that "the oval dial adds a charming touch"). The Newport is also frequently found with a dial having a silver finish and butler center and etched raised gilt numerals (No. 8089).

In 1929 and later, when the Mary Todd 203 had generally replaced the early Mary Todds, the Newport still had a prominent place in Illinois catalog and magazine advertisements. The dials shown on it in these later advertisements are modern-looking ones that brought the model up to date. For example, in the December 1929 issue of the *American Magazine*, where it was pictured just below the Mary Todd 203, the Newport has dial No. 8174, a plain dial but with very interesting numerals. (Later, in 1936, the Hamilton-issued Illinois Materials catalog referred to this dial as the Newport Model.) In the A. C. Becken 1930 catalog, the Newport is sporting the same interestingly decorated Art Deco dial (of unknown catalog number) as the Biloxi and Beverly models.

The Newport (right). A delicately engraved 14k. white gold-filled case with octagonal opening for its beautiful silvered dial features this attractive model. And its fine Illinois 17-jeweled movement insures dependable timekeeping. $50.

Newport from a Sept. 29, 1928 Illinois advertisement in the *Saturday Evening Post*

The Newport 174 came in a Keystone case with case Model No. 174 as well as in the same case with no case Model Number. According to Gay, this case held up well and can still be found today in excellent condition. The watch was equipped with a 17-jewel movement and came with a ribbon band.

An advertisement in the 1930 John Plain catalog showed the Newport 174 not only in white gold-filled but also in 14K solid white gold. For the former, the catalog listed a price of $70.80; for the latter, $92.00.

The Newport 174 was listed in the 1929–30 Illinois Sales Catalog and appeared in many Illinois advertisements placed in national magazines. These included the September 29, 1928 issue of the *Saturday Evening Post*; the October 1928 issue of the *National Geographic*; the May 31, 1929, December 18, 1929, and May 31, 1930 issues of *Liberty*; the April 1929 and June 1930 issues of the *American Magazine* as well as the December 1929 issue noted above; and the May 24, 1930 issue of *Collier's*.

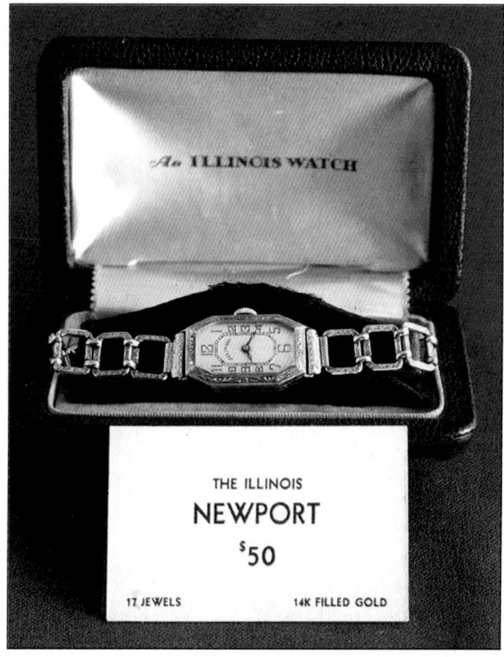

Newport 174 in its display box with its original price card

Newport 223

Newport 223, white gold-filled

Name = Newport 223
Time Period = Deco
Karat/Material = 14K WGF
Bezel = Engraved
Sides = Engraved
Lug Size = 11mm
Spring Bar = Fixed Lugs
Casemaker = Keystone
Case Pieces = 3
Case Number = 223
Case Back = Engraved
Dimensions = 17 x 31mm
Durability = ◷◷◷◷
Movement Size = 18/0
Movement Grade/Jewels = 807/17
Dial Numbers = 8089, 8154, 8174
Dial = Silver Finish, Butler Center; Sterling Silver; Sparkle Finish; Silver Finish
Dial Opening = Octagonal
Numerals = Painted
Hands = Steel
Seconds at = None
Cased in Factory = Yes
Collectibility = ◷◷◷◷
Rarity = ◷◷◷◷
Retail Price New = Unknown
Introduction Date = 1930
Unique Case Design = Yes
Unique Dial Design = No
Advertisement = No
Marketing Theme = Unknown

There is no documentation to confirm the name of this model. However, since it is nearly identical to the Newport 174 model, we consider this watch to be a Newport variant, likely released a year after the Newport 174.

The Newport 223 has a slightly different engraving pattern on its bezel than the Newport 174. Both have understated foliate engraving along the sides, as well as at the top and bottom of the bezel, with a geometric motif at the center of each of these straight sides as well as in the four angled sides. Although both models have a tiny embellishment at the center of the geometric motif, this ornament is more fully developed on the Newport 223, appearing to be part of a flower. Furthermore, the engraving on the Newport 223 is better executed, with cleaner lines and smoother curves.

Case engraving of the Newport 174 and Newport 223, as well as the engraving of other Illinois cases, appears to have been done by hand, since there are minute differences between case details on even a given model; however, the engravers would have been using templates for the patterns. Perhaps it could have been improvements in the Newport bezel template that made the engraving of the Model 223 more refined than that of the Model 174?

The Newport 223 has been found with some of the same dials as the Newport 174, including the very nice elongated butler center dial as well as the beautiful sterling silver Flückiger dial.

Newport 174 Newport 223

Newport display box and its original paperwork

No. 224

Name = No. 224
Time Period = Deco
Karat/Material = 14K WGF
Bezel = Plain
Sides = Engraved
Lug Size = 11mm
Spring Bar = Fixed Lugs
Casemaker = Keystone
Case Pieces = 3
Case Number = 224
Case Back = Plain
Dimensions = 17 x 30mm
Durability = 🕒🕒🕒🕒
Movement Size = 18/0
Movement Grade/Jewels = 807A/17
Dial Numbers = Unknown
Dial = Silver Finish
Dial Opening = Octagonal
Numerals= Painted
Hands = Steel
Seconds at = None
Cased in Factory = Yes
Collectibility = 🕒🕒🕒🕒
Rarity = 🕒🕒🕒🕒🕒
Retail Price New = Unknown
Introduction Date = Unknown
Unique Case Design = No
Unique Dial Design = No
Advertisement = No
Marketing Theme = Unknown

No. 224, white gold-filled

Since we do not know the name of this Illinois ladies' wristwatch, we are calling it No. 224, after its case Model No. It has an elegantly plain octagonal white gold-filled case whose design is similar if not identical to that of the Biloxi (case Model No. 186). Both cases were made by Keystone.

Like the Biloxi, No. 224 has a 17-jewel movement. Its serial number of 5416334 indicates that it is an 807A movement manufactured in 1931.

The dial of No. 224 is very plain, unlike the Biloxi's very striking Art Deco one. Although the basic design of the dial bears some resemblance to dial No. 8414 in the Hamilton-issued 1936 Illinois Materials Catalog, there are noticeable differences in the style and placement of the numerals and the name "Illinois." Accordingly, the dial on the particular specimen found of this Illinois model may be an aftermarket or refinished one.

To judge from the pattern we have observed with some other Illinois models, it is likely that this unknown model is one of the earlier models that was given a new name and case Model Number and issued as a new model. The Biloxi was issued in 1929, and No. 224 seems a plausible candidate for the 1931–32 timeframe. (Perhaps it might be a watch on the list of as yet unidentified Illinois ladies' models?)

No. 241, white gold-filled, diamonds and sapphires

No. 241

Name = No. 241
Time Period = Moderne
Karat/Material = 14K WGF
Bezel = Diamonds and Sapphires
Sides = Engraved
Lug Size = 14mm
Spring Bar = Fixed Lugs
Casemaker = Keystone
Case Pieces = 3
Case Number = 241
Case Back = Plain
Dimensions = 17 x 26mm
Durability = 🕒🕒🕒🕒
Movement Size = 18/0
Movement Grade/Jewels = 807/17
Dial Numbers = 8169, 8170
Dial = Silver Finish
Dial Opening = Short Rectangular
Numerals = Painted
Hands = Steel
Seconds at = None
Cased in Factory = Yes
Collectibility = 🕒🕒🕒🕒
Rarity = 🕒🕒🕒🕒🕒🕒
Retail Price New = Unknown
Introduction Date = Unknown
Unique Case Design = Yes
Unique Dial Design = No
Advertisement = No
Marketing Theme = Unknown

Only two specimens of this very beautiful watch have been found to date. Because its case is marked with a specific Model Number, No. 241, it is deemed to be Illinois Factory-Cased.

It is the only known ladies' Illinois wristwatch with a case Model Number that has both diamonds and sapphires on its bezel. It is also unusual in having a gold-filled case; most diamond-set Illinois models are in solid gold cases. The movement is 17 jewels.

Most diamond-set cases with Illinois movements have no case model numbers. Documentation has been found to indicate that some of these watches were indeed Factory-Cased models (see the **Diamond-Set Models** listing earlier). However, many other diamond-set cases were likely just provided with Illinois movements by jewelers and jobbers, who then supplied the watches directly to consumers.

Octagon

Name = Octagon
Time Period = Generic
Karat/Material = 14K WGF, 14K WG
Bezel = Engraved
Sides = Engraved
Lug Size = Various
Spring Bar = Fixed Lugs
Casemaker = Philadelphia, Star, Others
Case Pieces = 2, Hinged
Case Number = None
Case Back = Engraved
Dimensions = Various
Durability = 🕒🕒🕒 WGF
🕒🕒🕒🕒 WG
Movement Size = 6/0
Movement Grade/Jewels = 903/15, 905/17, 907/19
Dial Numbers = 99, 100
Dial = Silver Finish with Moiré Center
Dial Opening = Round
Numerals= Painted
Hands = Steel
Seconds at = 9, None
Cased in Factory = Yes
Collectibility = 🕒🕒🕒
Rarity = 🕒🕒🕒🕒
Retail Price New = Unknown
Introduction Date = 1926
Unique Case Design = No
Unique Dial Design = No
Advertisements = Yes
Marketing Theme = "Unusually attractive"
"The dials with their fancy moiré centers add greatly to the beauty of the watch."

Octagon, white gold-filled

The Illinois Octagon and the Illinois Tonneau (listed later) were earlier thought to be simply Illinois movements in Generic Period cases, such as those advertised in the 1925 Illinois sales catalog. A page that showed "Wrist Watch Movements" in that catalog stated: "Illinois Wrist Watch Movements are high-grade and made for timekeeping purposes—not merely as ornaments. Attractive cases may be selected from stock at your retail jewelers." So in 1925 these were watches put together by jewelers, not ones that were cased and timed at the Illinois factory.

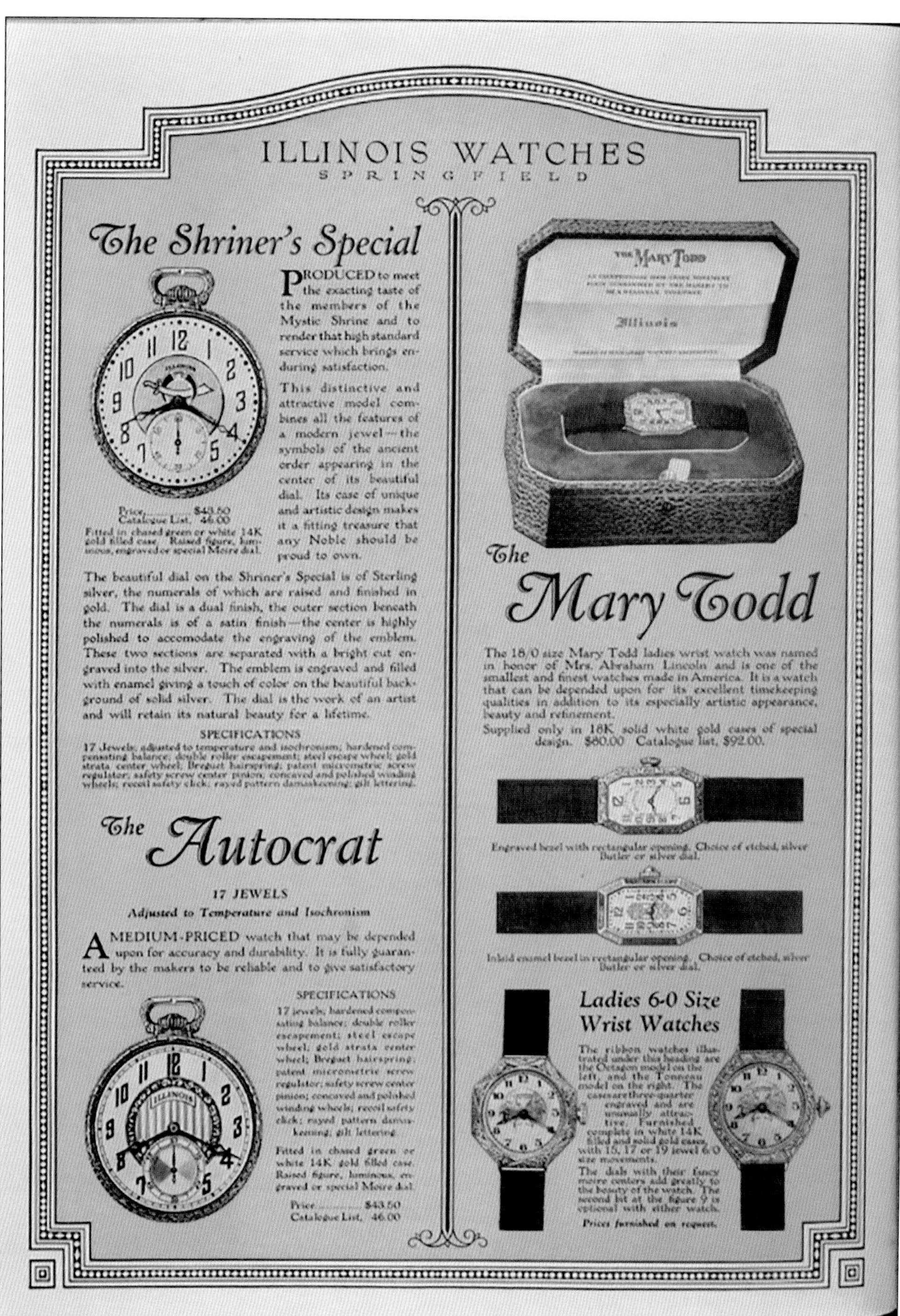

Illinois Watch Company advertisement, showing the Octagon and Tonneau models (*bottom, right*). This is part of an elegant multi-page Illinois insert that was placed in various jobbers' catalogs in 1928.

However, later advertisements indicate that a specific Octagon and a specific Tonneau were actually Factory-Cased models. Both of these had 6/0 movements and very special dials whose centers had decorative designs with a moiré finish, and they apparently came only in 14K white gold-filled or 14K solid white gold cases.

Octagon's moiré dial

The Octagon and the Tonneau were apparently introduced in 1926, about the same time as the Mary Todd. (Since neither was listed as a model in the 1925 catalog mentioned above, it is reasonable to surmise that they were introduced later.) The earliest advertisement that has thus far come to light for the Octagon and Tonneau is a page in the Illinois Watch Company insert printed in the 1928 catalogs of jobbers, such as A. C. Becken and Edwards-Ludwig-Fuller (ELF), and these catalogs likely went into production in 1927. This advertisement also shows several Mary Todd models as well as two Illinois pocket watches, the Shriner's Special and the Autocrat.

It is interesting to compare the Becken and ELF pages. They are exactly the same except for a neatly printed "Price Correction" card that had been affixed to the ELF page. There were price changes noted for almost every page in this Illinois insert. The 1928 Wallenstein Mayer catalog shows exactly the same price changes, but has them stamped in rather than by using a card. It is unclear why the Becken catalog does not show the various price changes; perhaps that catalog had gone into production earlier than the others, before Illinois had notified the jobbers about the changes. But we do not know why Illinois was changing the prices.

The only watch affected on the page shown here was the Mary Todd. The Octagon and Tonneau would not have been affected anyway; their listing had the notation "Prices furnished on request."

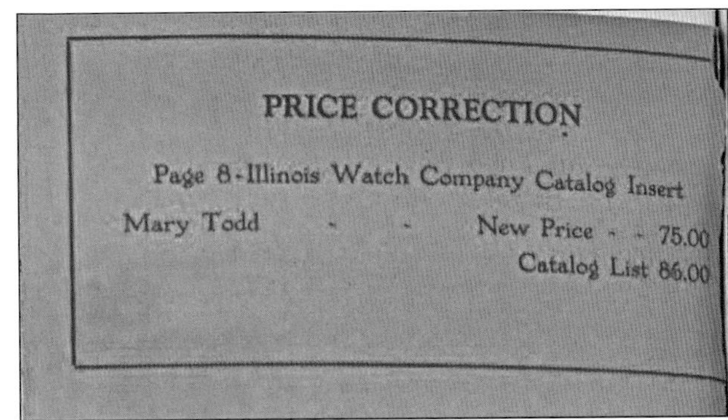

PRICE CORRECTION

Page 8-Illinois Watch Company Catalog Insert

Mary Todd - - New Price - - 75.00
Catalog List 86.00

Price correction in ELF Red Book 1928 catalog

Both the Octagon and Tonneau were available with movements of 15, 17 or 19 jewels and came equipped with ribbon bands. The notation "Furnished complete in white gold filled or solid gold cases" indicated that they were cased and timed at the Illinois factory.

To judge from two moiré-center dials shown in the 1927 Illinois Dial and Hand Circular (dial Nos. 99 and 100) as well as the ones present on specimens of the Octagon and Tonneau that have been examined, there were apparently two patterns for these attractive moiré-center dials, one with a floral motif and the other with a star-shaped pattern. The listing noted that the dials were available with an optional "second bit at 9," and this detail is included in the 1928 advertisement mentioned above.

A. C. Becken catalog, 1928

Although the Dial and Hand Circular shows that the dial with the floral motif (No. 100) was available in green finish as well as silver finish, the Illinois advertisement for the Octagon does not list green gold or gold-filled as an option. Instead, the dial with green finish was likely provided for use on a Generic watch, such as the round one shown on the page in the 1925 catalog.

Since there were many Generic Period octagon and tonneau wristwatch cases, the collector should be aware that an Illinois movement in a case of one of those shapes does not necessarily mean that the Illinois watch in question is a Tonneau or Octagon model. To be considered one of those Factory-Cased Illinois models, the watch must meet certain criteria: it must have a 6/0 size Illinois movement, a case that is either 14K solid white gold or 14K white gold-filled, and one of the special moiré dials.

Patricia

Name = Patricia
Time Period = Moderne
Karat/Material = 14K WGF, 14K YGF
Bezel = Engraved
Sides = Plain
Lug Size = 11mm
Spring Bar = Fixed Lugs, Cord Band
Casemaker = Keystone
Case Pieces = 2
Case Number = 833
Case Back = Plain
Dimensions = 17 x 31mm
Durability = 🕒🕒🕒
Movement Size = 18/0
Movement Grade/Jewels = 807/17
Dial Number = 8174
Dial = Silver Finish
Dial Opening = Rectangular, Slightly Cut Corners
Numerals= Painted
Hands = Steel
Seconds at = None
Cased in Factory = Yes
Collectibility = 🕒🕒🕒🕒
Rarity = 🕒🕒🕒🕒
Retail Price New = $47.50
Introduction Date = 1931
Unique Case Design = Yes
Unique Dial Design = No
Advertisement = Yes
Marketing Theme = "A most acceptable engraved case"

Patricia, white gold-filled

Patricia, yellow gold-filled

The Patricia was listed in the 1931–32 Illinois Sales Catalog but appeared in no other known advertisement.

The Patricia was offered in both white gold-filled and yellow gold-filled cases, and it was one of five Illinois ladies' wristwatches that came with a silk cord band. The catalog illustration shows that although the case had fixed lugs, there was an added fitting through which the cord was threaded. Today one is more likely to find the Patricia equipped with a metal watch bracelet.

Although the shape of the Patricia's case is somewhat similar to that of the Marilyn and the Beverly 852, it can easily be distinguished from those. The delicate engraving of paired curlicues at the top and bottom of the Patricia's bezel is centered on the smooth surface. The bezel of the Beverly 852 has a much smaller area of engraving, and it runs just along the edges near the dial, leaving much of the smooth surface plain. The Marilyn has a completely plain bezel.

The Patricia's dial was very similar if not identical to that of the Beverly 852 and the Marilyn.

The PATRICIA

A most acceptable engraved case in 14K filled white or natural gold. Cord to match. 17 jewels....... $47.50

A. I. Hall 1930–31 catalog

Princess / Countess

Princess, white gold

Name = Princess
Time Period = Moderne
Karat/Material = 14K WG
Bezel = Plain and Engraved (partially)
Sides = Engraved
Lug Size = 11mm
Spring Bar = Fixed Lugs
Casemaker = Keystone
Case Pieces = 3
Case Number = 168
Case Back = Engraved
Dimensions = 17 x 31mm
Durability = ◷◷◷◷
Movement Size = 18/0
Movement Grade/Jewels = 805/15 (Princess), 807/17 (Countess)
Dial Number = 8195
Dial = Silver Finish

Dial Opening = Rectangular
Numerals= Painted
Hands = Steel
Seconds at = None
Cased in Factory = Yes
Collectibility = 🕐🕐🕐🕐
Rarity = 🕐🕐🕐🕐🕐
Retail Price New = $50.00
Introduction Date = 1932
Unique Case Design = No
Unique Dial Design = No
Advertisement = Yes
Marketing Theme = "Beautifully cased"

The Princess, listed in the 1932 Illinois Spring sales catalog, is another of the solid gold Illinois ladies' wristwatches. This model was available only in white gold and came with a ribbon band.

The case is very attractive, if somewhat plain, having only a row of delicate engraving on the sides of the bezel. The shape of the case and the design bear a resemblance to that of the Glenna 239.

The PRINCESS
Beautifully cased in 14K solid white gold. 15 jewels.................................... **$50**

J. Engel catalog, 1932

The Princess was apparently available only with a 15-jewel movement. It may seem surprising to find a solid gold wristwatch with a 15-jewel movement, but this combination reflects the impact of the Great Depression on the Illinois Watch Company. Nonetheless, in the very next year, the Princess was reincarnated as the Countess, partnered with a 17-jewel movement and a gold-filled bracelet to match.

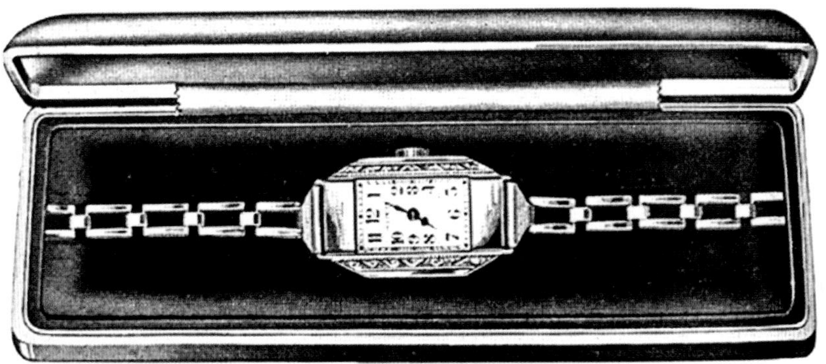

A NEW AND BEAUTIFUL ILLINOIS—THE "COUNTESS"
Exceedingly popular wrist watch offered at a greatly reduced price. The "Countess" is cased, timed and boxed complete at the Illinois factory. The movement is 17 jewels, 18/0 size, and the case is 14K solid white gold. The case is engraved on sides and perfectly plain on either end. It is very beautiful and very popular. Comes complete with a gold filled adjustable bracelet to match.
2R23248 PRICE **$60.00**

John Plain catalog, 1933

QUEEN ANNE

See listing for **Lady Mary/Queen Anne**

Redonda 153, white gold-filled, red and black enamel

Redonda 153

Name =	Redonda 153
Time Period =	Deco
Karat/Material =	14K WGF, Red and Black Inlaid Enamel
Bezel =	Engraved, with Enamel
Sides =	Engraved
Lug Size =	11mm
Spring Bar =	Fixed Lugs
Casemaker =	Wadsworth
Case Pieces =	3
Case Number =	153
Case Back =	Engraved
Dimensions =	17 x 31mm
Durability =	◷◷
Movement Size =	18/0
Movement Grade/Jewels =	807/17
Dial Number =	8147
Dial =	Silver Finish, Butler Center; Embossed
Dial Opening =	Hexagonal
Numerals=	Painted, Embossed
Hands =	Steel
Seconds at =	None
Cased in Factory =	Yes
Collectibility =	◷◷◷◷
Rarity =	◷◷◷◷
Retail Price New =	$55.00
Introduction Date =	1929
Unique Case Design =	Yes
Unique Dial Design =	No
Advertisement =	Yes
Marketing Theme =	"Rare beauty and refinement"

The Redonda 153 is one in a stunning series of colored enamel, deco-styled Illinois wristwatches, all of which are very sought-after by watch collectors and decophiles. The combination of the black and red enamel inlaid in the engraved bezel, along with an embossed deco dial, makes for a very striking piece.

The design of the Redonda's bezel is one of the most fascinating that Illinois produced for its ladies' watches. At the top and bottom of the bezel is an interesting pattern of engraving: in each corner is a swirl much like a motif at the top of an Ionic capital, and in between there is crosshatching. Because the sides of the bezel are unengraved, with a smooth, polished surface, the engraving stands out all the more. The architectural pattern of the black enameling leads the eye to the vertical bars of red enamel, suggesting a skyscraper.

The Redonda 153 was equipped with a 17-jewel movement and came with a ribbon band. It was listed in the 1929–30 Illinois Sales Catalog and advertised in the October 5, 1929 issue of *Collier's*, the October 19, 1929 issue of *Liberty*, and again in the November 2, 1929 issue of *Collier's*.

The Illinois catalog showed the Redonda with a silver-finish dial (No. 8147), whose butler center produced a very pleasing effect on the watch. Even more striking, however, was an embossed dial with exploded numerals at 12 and 6 and a geometric ornament in the center, so it is not surprising that many specimens of the Redonda are found with this dial rather than the other one. This beautiful dial is also frequently found on the Daytona 153, which of course has the same case Model Number as the Redonda 153. Unfortunately, its number is unknown because there is no image of it in any of the extant dial catalogs.

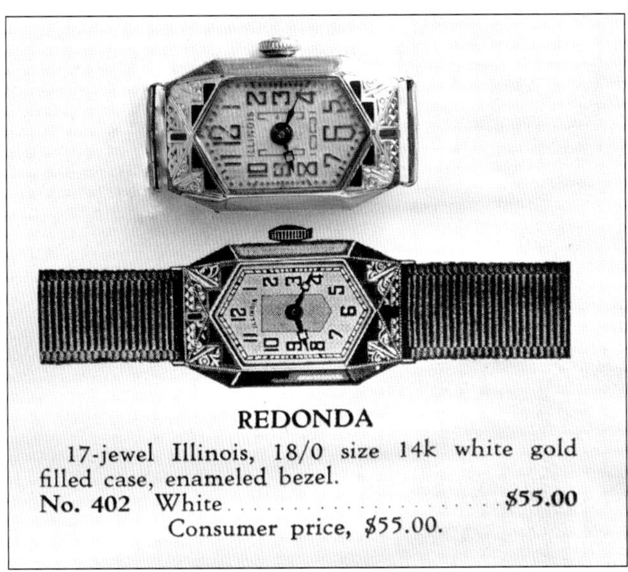

A. C. Becken 1931 catalog, with superimposed Redonda 153

The 1929–30 Illinois Sales Catalog described the Redonda 153 this way: "A unique combination of soft, light red and jet black inlaid polished enamel in its 14K gold filled case makes this model one of rare beauty and refinement." The Redonda case was very prone to corner wear, however.

Redonda in its display case with its original paperwork

Redonda 154, white gold-filled, green and black enamel

Redonda 154

Name = Redonda 154
Time Period = Deco
Karat/Material = 14K WGF, Green and Black Inlaid Enamel
Bezel = Engraved, with Enamel
Sides = Engraved
Lug Size = 11mm
Spring Bar = Fixed Lugs
Casemaker = Wadsworth
Case Pieces = 3
Case Number = 154
Case Back = Engraved
Dimensions = 17 x 31mm
Durability = ◷◷◷◷
Movement Size = 18/0
Movement Grade/Jewels = 807/17
Dial Number = 8147
Dial = Silver Finish, Butler Center; Embossed
Dial Opening = Hexagonal
Numerals= Painted; Embossed
Hands = Steel
Seconds at = None
Cased in Factory = Yes
Collectibility = ◷◷◷◷
Rarity = ◷◷◷◷◷
Retail Price New = $55.00
Introduction Date = 1928
Unique Case Design = Yes
Unique Dial Design = No
Advertisement = Yes
Marketing Theme = "A unique combination of soft, light green and jet black enameling"

The Redonda 154, with the bold green and black enameling on the triangular surfaces of its bezel, is one of the most eye-catching ladies' enameled watches of the deco era—every bit the equal of its beautifully designed enameled Elgin and Gruen contemporaries. The sides of the bezel, like those of the Redonda 153, are plain, the better to maximize the effect of the dramatic enameling at the top and bottom of the bezel.

The Redonda and Berkeley models are all greatly enhanced by the creative Illinois deco embossed dial with its exploded numerals 12 and 6. This is the dial shown with the Redonda 154 in both the little 1928 Illinois "Book of Watches" and in the 1930 John Plain catalog. As with the Redonda 153, an attractive silver finish dial with a butler center was also sometimes used with the Redonda 154.

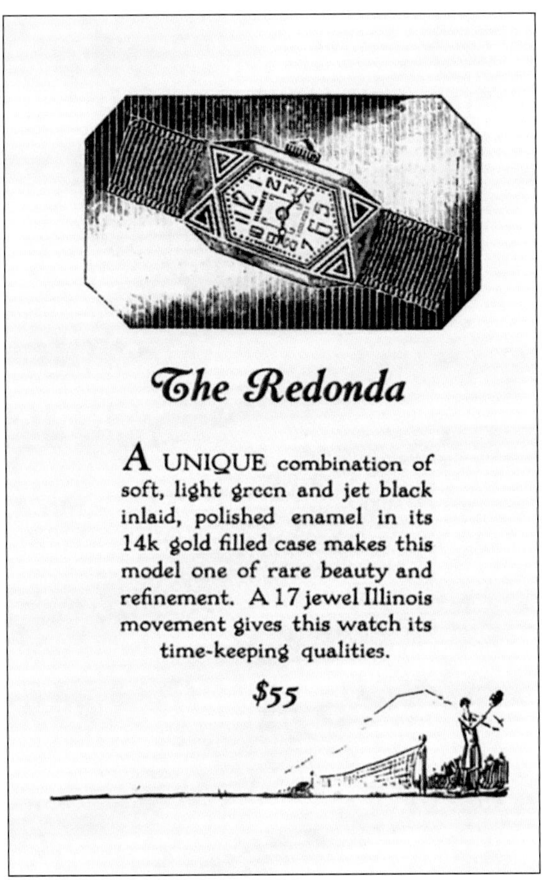

Illinois "Book of Watches," 1928

The dial and the very stylized deco enameling of the Redonda 154 show the Illinois Watch Company at its innovative designing best.

Although the Illinois 1928 "Book of Watches" calls this model the Redonda and says specifically that it has "a unique combination of soft, light green and jet black enamel," some magazine advertisements have it listed as a Berkeley and say the enameling is red and black. In the Illinois advertisement appearing in the December 1928 issue of the *National Geographic*, for example, there is an image of the Redonda 154 with the following in its caption: "The Berkeley. This charming watch has a delicate tracery of design in dark red and black hard enamel inlaid in its 14K white gold-filled case." Since this description is accurate for the Berkeley 154 but not the Redonda 154, it would seem that someone must have accidentally mismatched text and image. Over the years, it has caused great confusion for the collector.

Rita

See listing for **Hollywood/Rita**

Rosette

See listing for **Minuette/Rosette/Marlette**

Roslyn, white gold-filled, black enamel

Roslyn

Name = Roslyn
Time Period = Deco
Karat/Material = 14K WGF, Black Inlaid Enamel
Bezel = Engraved, with Enamel
Sides = Engraved
Lug Size = 11mm
Spring Bar = Fixed Lugs
Casemaker = Keystone
Case Pieces = 3
Case Number = 239
Case Back = Plain
Dimensions = 17 x 30mm
Durability = 🕐🕐🕐🕐
Movement Size = 18/0
Movement Grade/Jewels = 807/17
Dial Numbers = 8169, 8170
Dial = Silver Finish, Sparkle Finish
Dial Opening = Short Rectangular
Numerals = Painted
Hands = Steel
Seconds at = None
Cased in Factory = Yes
Collectibility = 🕐🕐🕐🕐
Rarity = 🕐🕐🕐🕐🕐
Retail Price New = $55.00
Introduction Date = 1930
Unique Case Design = Yes
Unique Dial Design = No
Advertisement = Yes
Marketing Theme – "A new Illinois with gay touches of black inlaid enamel"

The Roslyn is one of the very deco Illinois ladies' wristwatches with creatively designed enamel bezels. These are all very collectible and usually highly sought-after, not only by watch collectors but also by deco fanciers. The Roslyn is a model that is fairly difficult to locate.

The design of the Roslyn's bezel is one of Illinois' most unusual. Illinois often drew inspiration for case designs from architecture, and skyscraper motifs were a favorite. For the Roslyn, however, the design elements come from architecture of a much earlier time: Gothic cathedrals. The outlines in the bezel engraving are Gothic arches and partial arches, within which the black enameling is in patterns suggesting the tracery in stained glass windows.

The Keystone Watch Case Company included the Roslyn case in a 1931 advertisement.

A. I. Hall 1930–31 catalog, with superimposed Roslyn

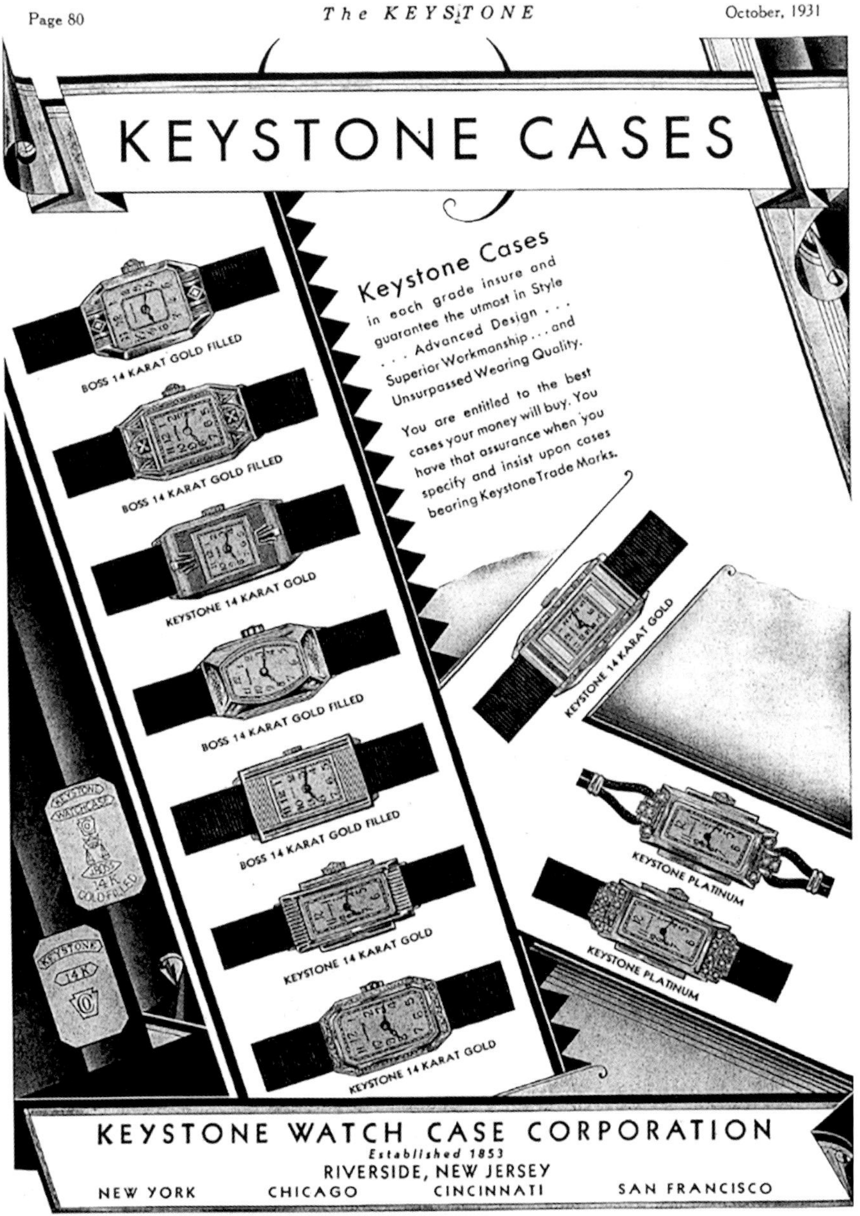

***Keystone*, October 1931. Roslyn is second from top, Hollywood is fourth from top.**

Advertising copy from Illinois used in the 1930–31 A. I. Hall catalog and others noted that "this dainty timepiece will have a definite appeal to those who appreciate style and correctness." The Roslyn came equipped with a 17-jewel movement and had a ribbon band.

For the holiday season, the Roslyn appeared in the December 6, 1930 issue of the *Saturday Evening Post* in an advertisement offering "Good Tidings of Greater Values. Richer Beauty . . . Finer Quality . . . Lower Prices . . . $37.50 to $60.00." The Fairport, Vanity Fair, Glencoe and Argyle ladies' models were also included in the advertisement.

Santa Fe

Santa Fe

Name = Santa Fe (derived from a Santa Fe Watch Company advertisement in *Popular Mechanics*, November 1926)
Time Period = Generic
Karat/Material = Unknown
Bezel = Engraved
Sides = Unknown
Lug Size = Unknown
Spring Bar = Fixed Lugs
Casemaker = Unknown
Case Pieces = Unknown
Case Number = No Number
Case Back = Unknown
Dimensions = Unknown
Durability = Unknown
Movement Size = 6/0
Movement Grade/Jewels = Various
Dial Number = No Number
Dial = No Number
Dial Opening = Rectangular Cut Corners
Numerals= Painted
Hands = Steel
Seconds at = None
Cased in Factory = Unknown
Collectibility = 🕒🕒🕒
Rarity = 🕒🕒🕒🕒🕒🕒🕒
Retail Price New = Unknown
Introduction Date = 1926
Unique Case Design = No
Unique Dial Design = No
Advertisement = Yes
Marketing Theme = "Newest watch case designs"

The Santa Fe ladies' model is very similar to the Illinois ladies' Generic model shown below but for the shape of the bezel opening. The Illinois is in a Fahys, white gold-filled case and contains a 15-jewel, 6/0 size movement.

It is possible the Santa Fe is an elusive model for the Santa Fe Watch Company. However, the dial appears to be signed "Illinois," so Santa Fe likely purchased the cases for this model and cased and timed it. (This was Santa Fe's practice with its private-label movements and dials that it ordered from the Illinois Watch Company, as is discussed in Chapter 6.) It is not known if there currently exists a Santa Fe ladies' model as advertised in *Popular Mechanics* since one has not been seen.

Generic, white gold-filled

POPULAR MECHANICS ADVERTISING SECTION 129

Mail Coupon for FREE Watch Book→

Clip the coupon, fill out and receive the FREE WATCH BOOK. All the newest watch case designs in white or green gold, fancy shapes and thin models, are shown. Read our easy payment offer. Select the watch you would like to see; we will send it to you on approval, express prepaid. Wear the watch 30 days FREE. Return at our expense if not fully satisfied.

SANTA FE WATCH COMPANY
Dept. B 6 Thomas Building Topeka, Kansas
The Home of the Great Santa Fe Railway

SANTA FE WATCH CO.
Dept. B 6, Thomas Building
Topeka, Kansas

Please send prepaid and without obligation your Watch Book Free, explaining your "No Money Down" Offer on the Santa Fe Special Watch.

Name..

Address..

Popular Mechanics, November 1926

Saratoga Leaf, white gold-filled

SARATOGA LEAF

Name = Saratoga Leaf
Time Period = Deco
Karat/Material = 14K WGF
Bezel = Engraved
Sides = Engraved
Lug Size = 11mm
Spring Bar = Fixed Lugs
Casemaker = Wadsworth
Case Pieces = 3
Case Number = No Number
Case Back = Engraved
Dimensions = 17 x 31mm
Durability = 🕒🕒🕒🕒
Movement Size = 18/0
Movement Grade/Jewels = 807/17
Dial Number = 8147
Dial = Silver Finish, Butler Center
Dial Opening = Hexagonal
Numerals= Painted
Hands = Steel
Seconds at = None
Cased in Factory = Yes
Collectibility = 🕒🕒🕒🕒
Rarity = 🕒🕒🕒🕒🕒🕒🕒
Retail Price New = Unknown
Introduction Date = 1930
Unique Case Design = Yes
Unique Dial Design = No
Advertisement = No
Marketing Theme = Unknown

The Saratoga Leaf is one of two different Illinois ladies' models named Saratoga, both of which feature leaf engravings on the bezel. There are noticeable differences between the two models. This version has beautiful full-leaf engravings in all of the three triangles on the top and bottom of the bezel rather than in just two of them. In addition, the leaves themselves are a different pattern from those of the Saratoga Notched Leaf model, and the sides of the bezel are engraved rather than plain.

Gay says that the watch pictured here is the only known example of this extremely rare full-leaf bezel. As a result, it is highly collectible when and if it can be found. The Saratoga Leaf apparently came with a 17-jewel movement, which is what this specimen has. Unfortunately, there are no known catalog listings or advertisements for this model.

Saratoga Notched Leaf

Name = Saratoga Notched Leaf
Time Period = Deco
Karat/Material = 14K WGF
Bezel = Engraved (partially)
Sides = Engraved
Lug Size = 11mm
Spring Bar = Fixed Lugs
Casemaker = Wadsworth
Case Pieces = 3
Case Number = 153
Case Back = Engraved
Dimensions = 17 x 31mm
Durability = ◷◷◷◷
Movement Size = 18/0
Movement Grade/Jewels = 807/17
Dial Number = 8147
Dial = Silver Finish, Butler Center
Dial Opening = Hexagonal
Numerals= Painted
Hands = Steel
Seconds at = None
Cased in Factory = Yes
Collectibility = ◷◷◷◷
Rarity = ◷◷◷◷
Retail Price New = $55.00
Introduction Date = 1930
Unique Case Design = Yes
Unique Dial Design = No
Advertisement = Yes
Marketing Themes = "Forms an ensemble of beauty with its matched bracelet"
"A dainty timepiece"

Saratoga Notched Leaf, white gold-filled

The Saratoga Notched Leaf differs from the Saratoga Leaf in having a bezel with only part of the top and bottom areas engraved with leaf patterns, whereas the Saratoga Leaf has the entire top and bottom engraved with them. In addition, the leaf patterns themselves are different. Gay calls this model "Notched Leaf" because the design of leaves is only in the corners of the bezel, not in the middle (the "notch"); it also helps distinguish this model from the Saratoga Leaf model. Another difference is that the sides of the bezel on the Saratoga Notched Leaf have smooth, polished surfaces, while those on the Saratoga Leaf are engraved.

Both the Saratoga Notched Leaf and the Saratoga Leaf are members of the Daytona "family," and the case of the Saratoga Notched Leaf can at first glance be confused with that of the Daytona 153. However, the bezel engravings are different. A quick distinguishing mark is that the bezel of the Daytona 153 has a smooth, polished band all the way around the dial opening, whereas the Saratoga Notched Leaf has this banding only on the bezel sides, not the top and bottom.

Daytona 153 **Saratoga Notched Leaf**

The SARATOGA

A dainty timepiece with metal bracelet attached. Both are constructed of 14K filled white gold and form an exceedingly harmonious unit.

Suggested consumer price, $55.

A. I. Hall 1930–31 catalog, with superimposed Saratoga Notched Leaf

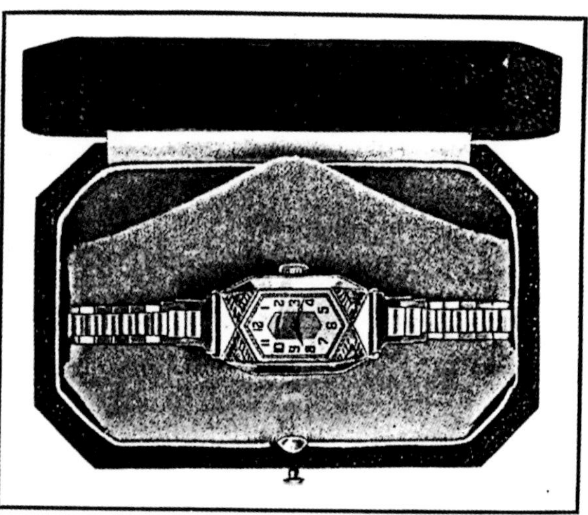

THE SARATOGA

A new creation—link bracelet model. Case is 14 karat white gold filled with modern design of engraving. Bracelet is fine quality gold filled, dainty and flexible with fold-over buckle. Can be adjusted to fit any wrist. Illinois, 18/0 size, 17 jewel rectangular movement. Retails for $55.00.

A58W05. Price...$66.00

Complete in presentation box as illustrated.

May & Malone catalog, 1931

April, 1930 *The KEYSTONE* Page 53

Louis Sickles Service Satisfies

NEW WINGS

for your

HAMILTON and ILLINOIS Watch Sales

This squadron of new Hamiltons and Illinois — models of beauty and distinction — ushers in the Spring season . . . with a rush!

You will want to display them in your store . . . in your windows . . . for national advertising is already creating enthusiastic consumer demand for them.

As always, you can depend on us to supply you with the best service possible. Write or wire us your orders *early* to insure prompt delivery.

The Saratoga, with a dainty bracelet to match, is the newest 17-jewel Illinois ladies' watch — List price $59.50. The Floyd Bennett is a new Hamilton — a 19-jewel strap watch in 14K yellow or white gold—List Price $170.00.

The Skyway, specially designed for aviators and meeting with Government specifications, with 17-jewel movement, opens a profitable new field for the wide awake jeweler—List Price $46.00.

Exceedingly smart is the Monticello, a popular, new 17-jewel Hamilton, in 14K filled green or white gold. Consumer, $50.00; list $60.60. Extra charge dial as shown, consumer, $3.00; list $3.60.

MONTICELLO
Consumer, $53.00

THE SARATOGA
Consumer, $55.00

THE SKYWAY
Con sumer, $45.00

FLOYD BENNETT
Consumer, $150.00

LOUIS SICKLES

Wholesale Watch Service

1015 Chest'nut Street

PHILADELPHIA, PA.

Keystone, April 1930

SHERWOOD

Sherwood, white gold (*left*), Sherwood, yellow gold (*right*)

Name = Sherwood
Time Period = Moderne
Karat/Material = 14K WG, 14K YG
Bezel = Stepped
Sides = Unengraved Stepped
Lug Size = 10mm
Spring Bar = Fixed Lugs
Casemaker = Star
Case Pieces = 2
Case Number = No Number
Case Back = Plain
Dimensions = 17 x 26mm
Durability = 🕒🕒
Movement Size = 18/0
Movement Grade/Jewels = 805/15
Dial Number = Unknown
Dial = Silver Finish, Deco Decoration
Dial Opening = Rectangular
Numerals = Painted

Hands = Steel
Seconds at = None
Cased in Factory = Yes
Collectibility = ◷◷◷◷
Rarity = ◷◷◷◷◷◷
Retail Price New = $52.50
Introduction Date = Unknown (likely 1933)
Unique Case Design = Yes
Unique Dial Design = Yes
Advertisement = Unknown
Marketing Theme = Unknown

Not long before the final manuscript of these books was sent to the publisher, there was an exciting discovery: the original display box, original price card, and outer cardboard box for an unidentified Illinois model called the Sherwood. To add to the excitement, this discovery subsequently enabled the identification of two specimens of what had been an Illinois "mystery model."

One original price card for this model had earlier been found. The card showed that the Sherwood, priced $52.50, had a 15-jewel movement and a 14K solid gold case. At the time, the information on the card, sparse as it was, seemed to suggest that the Sherwood might be the name for the men's model with a 14K solid yellow gold case and 15-jewel movement that had heretofore been known simply as No. 650, after its case model number. Later, however, the No. 650 was conclusively identified as the Varsity model (see its listing in Chapter 9 for the details).

Even if the identity of the No. 650 had not already been determined, this new discovery would have completely upended the theory that Sherwood was its name. The two Sherwood boxes show conclusively that the watch was a ladies' model rather than a men's. The inner box and its insert are of a size and style used for ladies' models and would not accommodate a men's model, or even a unisex one.

Sherwood in its display case with its original price card

Moreover, the outer box shows that the Sherwood was an 18/0 size watch; the No. 650 is 6/0 size. And although the box is imprinted "14K Solid Gold," the stamping "White" indicates that the watch that had been in it was white gold, not yellow gold; all known specimens of the No. 650 are yellow gold. (The stamping is on an area of the box that had been covered by the jewelry store's label. However, the label was loose and fell off, revealing what was beneath.)

End of the outer cardboard Sherwood box with its jewelers sticker in place (*top*) before it fell off and without its sticker (*bottom*)

The fact that the case color is stamped on the box indicates that the Sherwood came in more than one color, as shown by the stamping on two recently found boxes for Illinois models known to have been offered in both yellow and white gold or gold-filled cases.

Elissa outer cardboard box

Antoinette outer cardboard box

Although it was clear from the outer box that the Sherwood was an 18/0 size ladies' model in a case of white or yellow 14K solid gold, what the case design looked like was initially unknown because an image in an advertisement had not been found, nor were there at first any Illinois watches that appeared to be likely candidates. Then a collector remembered acquiring two unknown Illinois ladies' models, identical except for the case color. They checked out: 18/0 size case in 14K gold, one white and one yellow, and 15-jewel movements.

In addition, the case design and construction provided important clues about how this pair of watches might have fitted into the Illinois story. The case, by Star, is essentially a scaled-up 18/0 version of the case for a 21/0 size model, the Suzette, which was also made by Star.

The Suzette, one of the models in the December 1, 1932 "List of Names of Cased Illinois Watches by Sizes," was introduced in the 1933 Illinois sales catalog. Since neither the Sherwood nor the Varsity name was on that list of cased Illinois models, it is likely that both models were produced sometime during 1933.

As with the Varsity, the genesis of the Sherwood is shrouded in mystery. Perhaps, it too, might have been produced at the request of an important Illinois customer, such as a large jobber, wanting to be supplied with some new solid gold Illinois models. (See the listing about the **Varsity** in Chapter 9.)

The Sherwood, like its "little sister" the Suzette, has an elegant case with a stepped bezel and stepped sides. (The steps on the sides of the Suzette are engraved, while those on the Sherwood are plain.) And like the rare solid gold specimens of the Suzette, the two Sherwoods that have been found lack a case Model Number.

(*Left to right*) Sherwood, yellow gold; Suzette, yellow gold; and Sherwood, white gold

Each of these two Sherwoods sports an unusual dial decorated with an interesting deco-style geometric pattern, similar but not identical to that of a dial often appearing on the earlier Beverly 185 and Biloxi models.

Although solid gold, the case of the Sherwood is of a much lighter weight than earlier solid gold Illinois models. It is thus likely to be prone to case damage, a problem observed with the Varsity. However, the Sherwood specimens found thus far fortunately show nothing more than a ding or two.

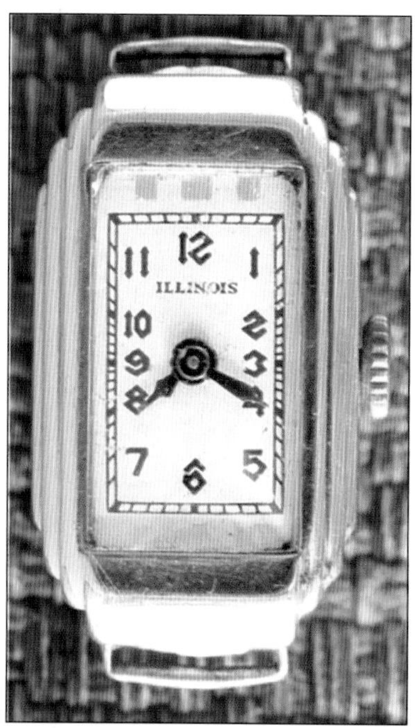

Suzette, white gold-filled

Suzette, yellow gold

Suzette / Mariette

Names = Suzette/Mariette
Time Period = Moderne
Karat/Material = 14K WGF, 14K YGF (Mariette only), 14K WG, 14K YG
Bezel = Stepped
Sides = Engraved Stepped
Lug Size = 7mm
Spring Bar = Fixed Lugs
Casemaker = Star
Case Pieces = 2
Case Numbers = 707, No Number
Case Back = Plain
Dimensions = 14 x 27mm
Durability = ⌚⌚⌚
Movement Size = 21/0
Movement Grade/Jewels = 107/17
Dial Number = 8374
Dial = Silver Finish
Dial Opening = Rectangular
Numerals = Painted
Hands = Steel
Seconds at = None
Cased in Factory = Yes, by Hamilton in Lancaster
Collectibility = ⌚⌚⌚⌚
Rarity = ⌚⌚⌚⌚ in WGF, YGF
⌚⌚⌚⌚⌚⌚ in WG, YG
Retail Price New = $47.50 (Suzette, 17J), $42.50 (Mariette)
Introduction Date = 1933 (Suzette), 1934 (Mariette)
Unique Case Design = No
Unique Dial Design = No
Advertisement = Yes
Marketing Themes = "Of original design and daintily small"
"Handsomely designed case"

The Suzette is for all practical purposes the same model as the Mariette. The Suzette appeared in the Illinois Pioneers of Greater Values sales catalog in 1933, was renamed the Mariette and appeared the next year in the 1934 Illinois sales catalog along with seven other 21/0 size "Baguette Style" watches. Both the Suzette and the Mariette came with 17-jewel movements; the Mariette's was equipped with the new Elinvar hairspring. The only other difference between the two models was that the Suzette came only in a white gold-filled case, whereas the Mariette was offered in either white or yellow gold-filled.

The Suzette was also listed in the 1933 Illinois Century of Progress sales catalog.

SUZETTE

Handsomely designed case of 14 Karat white filled gold. 17 jewels. (21/0 size.)

No. F23W17 Each $53.20

1933 Chicago World's Fair Edition of the Shure Winners Catalog

The Suzette shares the case Model No. 707 with another 21/0 size model, the Muzette, which was also introduced in 1933. The Muzette was equipped with a 17-jewel movement, offered only in a white gold-filled case and came with a ribbon band. Although the Suzette has a plain bezel and the Muzette a stepped, sculpted one, both have interesting stepped sides.

At least one Suzette has been located by Gay in a solid white gold case with no case Model Number indicated. Another collector has recently acquired a Suzette in a solid yellow gold case, likewise by Star and with no case Model Number.

Suzette yellow gold inside case back

AMERICAN VALUE

The Pioneers of Greater Values catalog stated: "Illinois watches are known as 'The Great American Value' in Watches: Lower price with improved quality, style and dependability. Upon this page are shown diminutively small wrist watches for the women who demand dependability in a timepiece."

The Suzette has recently been found to have two "big sisters" in 18/0 size cases of the same basic design, just larger. These are twins in solid gold cases of identical design by Star, one white and the other yellow, and neither has a case Model Number. Both have 15-jewel movements. These watches have been identified as being the Sherwood model (see its listing in this chapter).

ILLINOIS
1933
WATCHES

We've Struck the Keynote

A SMALL LINE PLUS POPULAR PRICES GIVE RAPID TURNOVER AND ADEQUATE NET PROFITS

You can offer your public **something more** than "just another watch" if you take 13 models in ladies' wrist watches—nine models in men's wrist watches. That's the ILLINOIS line for 1933. With prices ranging from $32.50 to $75.00 (including tax) here are twenty-two quality watches, all dependably accurate and smartly styled. Every jeweler who stocks this line of quick-turnover items will net a SPLENDID profit. These sound business fundamentals are the backbone of ILLINOIS WATCH policy, already a proven success.

And in the popular price range are beautiful, new sterling silver, gold filled and solid gold cases, yet these quality watches are priced as low as $32.50. None have less than 15 jewels. Show a complete line of Illinois Watches this Christmas. Greater optimism indicates good Holiday Business.

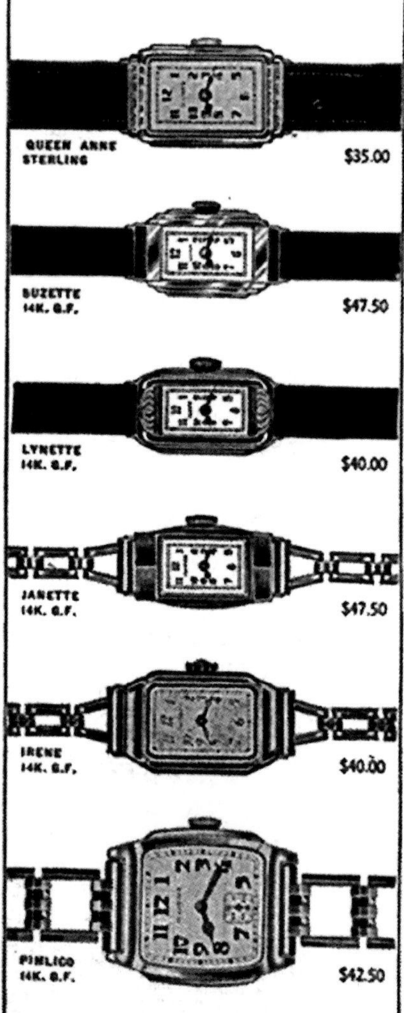

Jewelers' Circular, November 1932. *Top left*, Lady Mary; *top right*, Queen Anne; then Suzette, Lynette, Janette, Irene, and a Pimlico, a men's model

See listing for **Marilyn/Elissa/Sylvia/Irene**

Tonneau

Tonneau, white gold-filled

Name = Tonneau
Time Period = Generic
Karat/Material = 14K WGF, 14K WG
Bezel = Engraved
Sides = Engraved
Lug Size = Various
Spring Bar = Fixed Lugs, Hinged Lugs
Casemaker = Star, Philadelphia, Others
Case Pieces = 2, Hinged
Case Number = None
Case Back = Engraved
Dimensions = Various
Durability = 🕒🕒🕒 WGF
🕒🕒🕒🕒 WG
Movement Size = 6/0
Movement Grades/Jewels = 903/15, 905/17, 907/19
Dial Numbers = 99, 100
Dial = Silver Finish with Moiré Center
Dial Openings = Round
Numerals = Painted
Hands = Steel
Seconds at = 9, None
Cased in Factory = Yes
Collectibility = 🕒🕒🕒
Rarity = 🕒🕒🕒🕒
Retail Price New = Unknown
Introduction Date = c 1926
Unique Case Design = No
Unique Dial Design = No
Advertisements = Yes
Marketing Themes = "Unusually attractive"
"The dials with their fancy moiré centers add greatly to the beauty of the watch."

Although the Illinois Tonneau as well as the Illinois Octagon were originally thought to be simply Illinois movements in Generic Period cases, we have found that both are specific Illinois models, cased and timed at the Illinois factory.

These two models have 6/0 movements and very special dials with a decorative design and moiré finish in the center. (For detailed discussion, see the listing for Octagon above.)

There are many Generic Period watches that have octagon- or tonneau-shaped cases and Illinois movements. However, to be considered a Factory-Cased Illinois Octagon or Illinois Tonneau model, the watch must have a 6/0 size Illinois movement, a case of either 14K solid white gold or 14K white gold-filled, and a special moiré dial.

Tonneau moiré dial

Tonneau case back

Tonneau inside case back

Tonneau hinged case

Transitional Watches

Name = Transitional Watches
Time Period = Transitional
Karat/Material = Various
Bezel = Plain, Engraved
Sides = Plain, Engraved
Lug Size = Various
Spring Bar = Fixed Lugs
Casemaker = Various
Case Pieces = 2, 3
Case Number = None
Case Back = Plain
Dimensions = Various
Durability = 🕒🕒🕒
Movement Size = Various
Movement Grades/Jewels = Various
Dial Numbers = Various
Dial = Silver Finish, Gold Finish, Embossed, Others
Dial Openings = Round
Numerals = Painted, Embossed, Others
Hands = Steel
Seconds at = 6, None
Cased in Factory = No, except for the Illinois Convertible (named model)
Collectibility = 🕒
Rarity = 🕒
Retail Price New = Various
Introduction Date = Pre–World War I to the early 1920s.
Unique Case Design = No
Unique Dial Design = No
Advertisement = Yes
Marketing Theme = Various

Transitional, yellow gold-filled

Transitional, yellow gold-filled

During the Transitional Period, ladies' wristwatches mostly started out as pendant or pocket watches and were modified to fit on a wrist or to be worn as a pendant or pocket watch; thus, the pendant or pocket watch "transitioned" to the wrist.

The first such watches were called "convertibles" because they could be worn many different ways. As time progressed, they evolved from being just converted pocket watches to being more wristwatch-like in design.

Of these transitional watches with Illinois movements, apparently the only model that was Factory-Cased was the specifically named Illinois "Convertible" model, which a 1915 Illinois Factory advertisement listed as a "complete watch." This terminology was usually an indication that the watch was cased and timed at the Illinois factory. (See the Introduction of this chapter for further explanation about convertibles in general and Illinois' "Convertible" model in particular.)

These transitional watches are easy to find and can be fun to collect since they come in different shapes of cases and styles, some plain and others ornate, as well has having various types of dials. Some of these watches can even be found with their little metal bracelets or ribbon watchbands still intact; it is also possible to find such watchbands for them separately. Since these watches are usually 6/0 or 3/0 size, the dials are a size that is very easy to read. Accordingly, they are nice to have as timepieces, whether worn as wristwatches or attached to chains or watch pins.

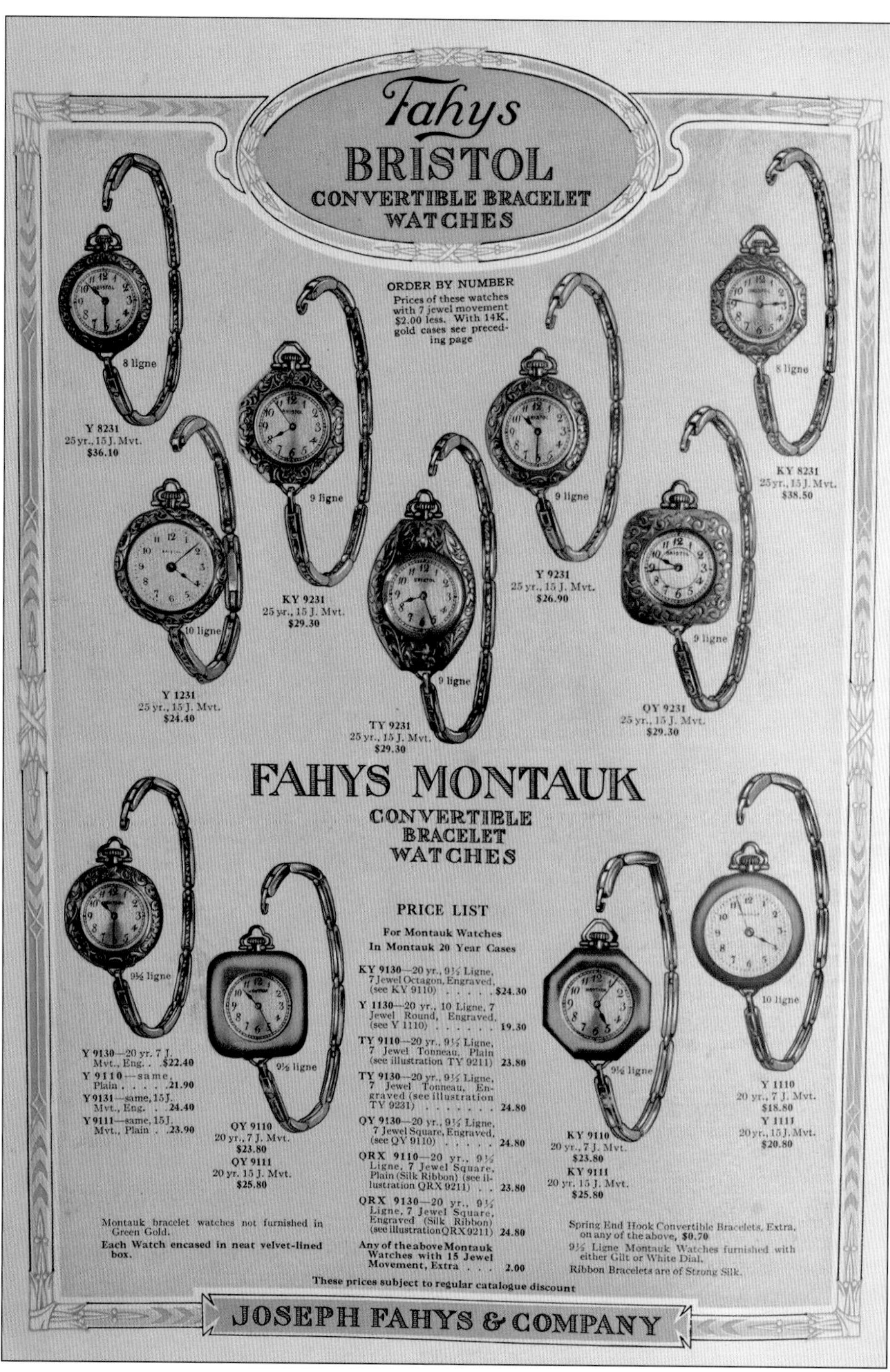

A page of Transitionals (Convertibles), A. C. Becken catalog, 1917

Vanity Fair / Debutante

Names = Vanity Fair/Debutante
Time Period = Deco
Karat/Material = 14K WGF, 14K YGF
Bezel = Engraved
Sides = Engraved
Lug Size = 11mm
Spring Bar = Fixed Lugs
Casemaker = Wadsworth
Case Pieces = 2
Case Number = 807-6
Case Back = Plain
Dimensions = 17 x 31mm
Durability = ◷◷◷◷
Movement Size = 18/0
Movement Grade/Jewels = 807/17, 805/15
Dial Numbers = 8090
Dial = Silver Finish, Pinstripe
Dial Opening = Rectangular with Rounded Corners
Numerals = Painted, Embossed Gilt
Hands = Steel
Seconds at = None
Cased in Factory = Yes
Collectibility = ◷◷◷◷
Rarity = ◷◷◷◷
Retail Price New = Vanity Fair, $45.00; Debutante, $35.00
Introduction Date = 1930 (Vanity Fair), 1931 (Debutante)
Unique Case Design = No
Unique Dial Design = No
Advertisement = Yes
Marketing Themes = "America's smallest full jeweled watch"
"Delicately engraved case"

Vanity Fair, white gold-filled

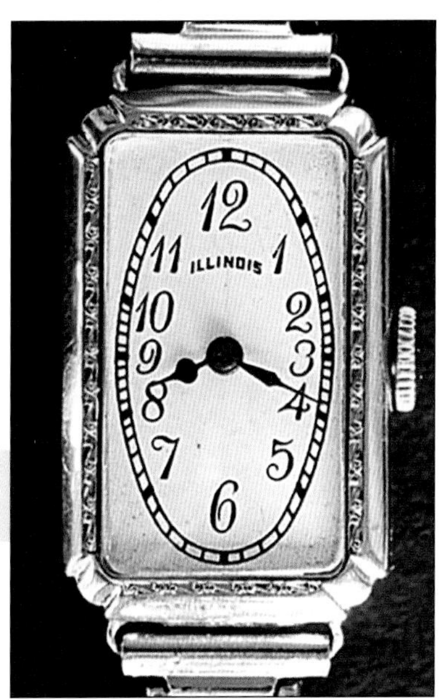

Vanity Fair, yellow gold-filled

The Vanity Fair and the Debutante, two beautiful and very feminine Illinois wristwatches, shared the same case Model No. 807-6. Both came in either white gold-filled or yellow gold-filled, and both were fitted with ribbon bands, but they had different movements. The Debutante, with a 15-jewel movement, was produced a year later than its sister, the Vanity Fair, which was 17 jewels.

The Debutante had an attractive oval-centered dial, that it shared with the Fairport and the Brighton. The Vanity Fair used a variant of this dial with pinstripes added.

It is interesting to see that with different shapes of bezels, the oval-centered dial produces two different visual effects. With the bezel of the Fairport or the Brighton, the dial area becomes oval; with the bezel of the Debutante and the Vanity Fair, however, the dial area is rectangular, with just an oval center.

The Vanity Fair was listed in the 1930–31 Illinois Sales Catalog, and an advertisement featuring it appeared in the October 1930 issue of the *American Magazine*. (Also shown were the Vardon and Ritz wristwatches and the Rialto pocket watch.) The advertising copy proclaimed:

> Here's the happiest answer to your desire for a smart, reliable ribbon watch at a moderate price—Illinois Vanity Fair—the smallest 17-jewel American ribbon watch under $50.00 in case of highest quality next to solid gold.
>
> Women, today, must have a watch that is more than an ornament. They need a dependable timepiece, and Vanity Fair fulfills both requirements. Exquisitely beautiful, ultra stylish, modern to the last jewel—and, being Illinois, it will give you accurate time for many years. For beauty of appearance it is matched by that beauty of inner perfection which alone makes a watch a reliable timepiece.

2 The American Magazine for October 1930

BEAUTIFUL . . .
STYLISH . . . AND
ACCURATE
$45.00

17 JEWELS — 14K FILLED GOLD

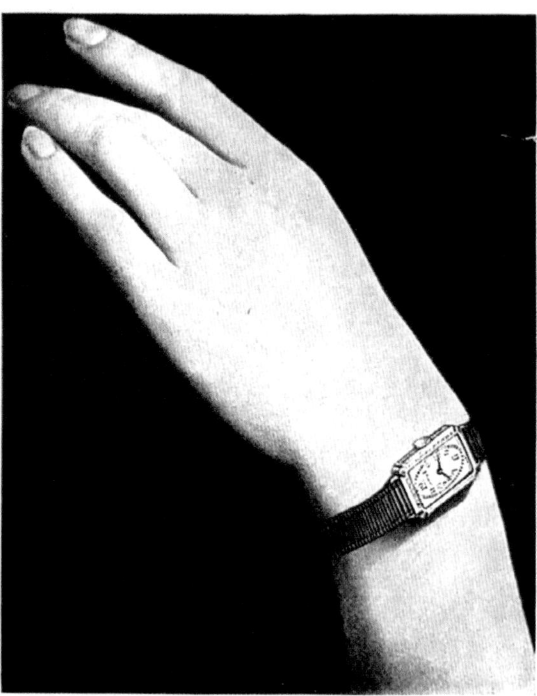

THE VARDON, $75.00 THE RIALTO, $50.00 THE RITZ, $42.50

ILLINOIS

A GREAT AMERICAN
WATCH SINCE 1870
THE ILLINOIS WATCH
SPRINGFIELD, ILLINOIS

Here's the happiest answer to your desire for a smart, reliable ribbon watch at a moderate price—Illinois Vanity Fair—the smallest 17-jewel American ribbon watch under $50.00 in case of highest quality next to solid gold.

Women, today, must have a watch that is more than an ornament. They need a dependable timepiece, and Vanity Fair fulfills both requirements. Exquisitely beautiful, ultra stylish, modern to the last jewel—and, being Illinois, it will give you accurate time for many years. For beauty of appearance is matched by that beauty of inner perfection which alone makes a watch a reliable timepiece.

Ask any good jeweler to show you the Vanity Fair and his complete line of Illinois watches for men and women. Priced mostly from $40.00 to $60.00—setting a new standard of value for fine watches.

American Magazine, October 1930

For the holiday season, the Vanity Fair was featured in an Illinois advertisement in the *Saturday Evening Post* on December 6, 1930, along with the Argyle, Fairport, Glencoe and Roslyn ladies' Illinois models. The Caprice purse or desk watch also appeared in this advertisement.

The Debutante was listed in the 1931–32 Illinois Sales Catalog and was advertised in the December 12, 1931 issue of the *Saturday Evening Post* along with the Coquette, Claudette, Constance, Florentine, Glenna and Hollywood ladies' models.

THE VANITY FAIR

The new Illinois popular priced ladies' watch. 18/0 size, 17 jewel, 14 karat white gold filled. Top bezel neatly engraved—side bezel plain, bright polished. Dial is white with black figures. Retails for $45.00.
A58W06. Price $60.50
Complete in box like A58W01. The lug size is 7/16 inches.

May & Malone catalog, 1930

Vardon

Vardon, white gold

Name = Vardon
Time Period = Deco
Karat/Material = 14K WG, 14K YG/TT
Bezel = Plain
Sides = Engraved
Lug Size = For Cord Band
Spring Bar = Cord Band
Casemaker = Wadsworth
Case Pieces = 3
Case Number = 240
Case Back = Plain
Dimensions = 17 x 32mm
Durability = 🕓🕓🕓🕓
Movement Size = 18/0
Movement Grade/Jewels = 807/17
Dial Numbers = 8195, 8346
Dial = Silver Finish
Dial Opening = Rectangular with Rounded Corners
Numerals = Painted
Hands = Steel
Seconds at = None
Cased in Factory = Yes
Collectibility = 🕓🕓🕓🕓 in YG
🕓🕓🕓🕓 in WG
Rarity = 🕓🕓🕓🕓🕓 in WG
🕓🕓🕓🕓🕓🕓🕓 in YG/TT

Vardon, yellow gold

Retail Price New = $75.00
Introduction Date = 1930
Unique Case Design = Yes
Unique Dial Design = No
Advertisement = Yes
Marketing Themes = "Nothing more beautiful and correctly styled"
"An exquisite 18/0 size Illinois"
"Chic modernism in keeping with style trends"

The Vardon, a stunning new model, appeared on the cover of the 1930–31 Illinois Sales Catalog in which it was introduced. Its description: "An exquisite 18/0 size Illinois with newest in cord attachment. 14K solid white or natural gold. Cord catch also solid gold."

The Beauty that Lies Within . . . the Beauty that is a Timepiece

A Great American Watch

There is nothing more beautiful and correctly styled in watches today than these new Illinois. Moreover, when you buy an Illinois you have a watch that, during nearly three-quarters of a century, has steadily earned the increasing confidence of all good jewelers—and what other kind of watch is worth owning? . . . Illinois puts everything into a watch that makes it a perfected timepiece—that creates *The Beauty that Lies Within*—and cases this accuracy and durability with rare charm and individuality . . . Priced mostly from $40 to $60—setting a new standard of value for fine watches. At all good jewelers.

The ILLINOIS WATCH
SPRINGFIELD, ILLINOIS
A great American watch since 1870

AS ILLUSTRATED
Only a few of the many exquisite models

ILLINOIS MEN'S POCKET WATCH
(*top center*)
THE TRUSTEE—17 jewels, 14k filled natural or white gold $55.00

ILLINOIS MEN'S STRAP WATCHES
(*left to right*)
THE ARDSLEY—17 jewels, rectangular, 14k filled natural or white gold $60.00
THE NEW YORKER—17 jewels, 14k filled natural or white gold, plain or engraved case $50.00
With 21 jewels 75.00

ILLINOIS LADIES' RIBBON WATCH
(*lower left*)
THE BILOXI—17 jewels, 14k filled white gold $50.00

ILLINOIS LADIES' WATCH (*lower right*)
With fashionable cord bracelet
THE VARDON—17 jewels, 14k solid natural or white gold $75.00

American Magazine, **August 1930**

The Vardon was one of only five Illinois ladies' wristwatch models that came equipped with a cord band, and its very striking double-lug configuration was different from any of the others.

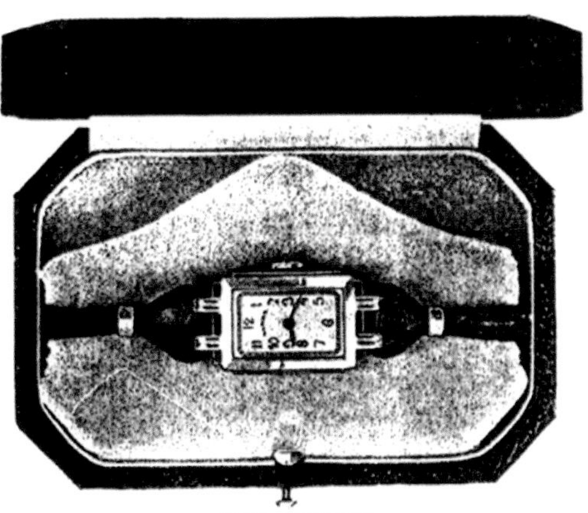

THE VARDON

Dainty—Smart is this new Vardon Cord watch by Illinois. 18/0 size, 17 jewel, 14 karat solid white or Natural gold case of rich, plain design. Dial is white with embossed gold etched numerals. Attachments are of plain solid gold to match case. Retails for $75.00.
A58W01. White Gold. Price $95.80
A58W02. Natural. Price 95.80
Comes in presentation box as illustrated.

May & Malone catalog, 1930

The VARDON

Chic modernism in keeping with style trends. 14K solid white gold with perfectly matched cord. 17 jewels.................... $75

J. Engel catalog, 1932

It was also one of the few models that were offered in a choice of white or yellow solid gold. According to Gay, the white gold Vardon is much easier to find than the very rare yellow gold version, but it is still a difficult model to locate. Gay further reports that the yellow gold Vardon has white gold lugs, which, in effect, makes it a two-tone watch.

The Vardon had a 17-jewel movement.

For economy of scale, Illinois usually had the same dial serve on several different models. That was again the case with the Vardon, which shared dial No. 8195 (silver finish, etched raised figures) with the Argyle, and dial No. 8346 (silver finish, black figures) with the Gloria as well as the Argyle. (Since the Arlene, the Argyle's sister model, came with a beautiful butler-center silver-finish dial of unknown number, it is possible that this dial might sometimes be seen on the Vardon as well.)

Courtesy Metro-Goldwyn-Mayer

JOAN CRAWFORD wears an ILLINOIS WATCH

"What could be more appropriate for my picture 'This Modern Age' than this lovely modern ILLINOIS watch"

Joan Crawford

1930 Joan Crawford advertising poster for an Illinois Vardon model

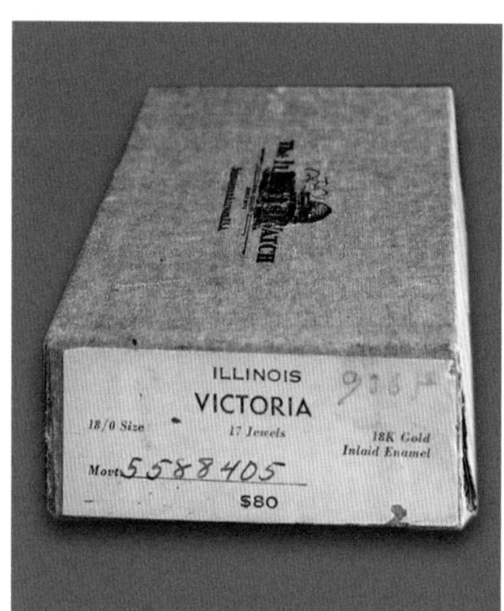

Victoria outer cardboard box

Victoria

Name = Victoria
Time Period = Deco
Karat/Material = 18K WG, Black Inlaid Enamel
Bezel = Unknown
Sides = Unknown
Lug Size = Unknown
Spring Bar = Fixed Lugs
Casemaker = Unknown
Case Pieces = 2
Case Number = Unknown
Case Back = Unknown
Dimensions = Unknown
Durability = 🕒🕒🕒🕒
Movement Size = 18/0
Movement Grade/Jewels = 807/17
Dial Number = Unknown
Dial = Unknown
Dial Opening = Unknown
Numerals = Unknown
Hands = Unknown
Seconds at = None
Cased in Factory = Yes
Collectibility = 🕒🕒🕒🕒
Rarity = 🕒🕒🕒🕒🕒🕒🕒🕒
Retail Price New = $80.00
Introduction Date = Unknown
Unique Case Design = Unknown
Unique Dial Design = Unknown
Advertisement = Unknown
Marketing Theme = Unknown

There is no known documentation for this model other than its outer cardboard box pictured above. Most of the information noted here has been gleaned from that box.

At a sales price of $80.00, the Victoria was the most expensive Illinois ladies' wristwatch offering, surpassing even the Mary Todd in price.

During the years it was owned by Hamilton, Illinois had a pattern of making certain changes, such as the type of dial and/or the type of watchband, and reissuing certain models under new names. Accordingly, it is more than likely that the Victoria is a renamed earlier model rather than a new design.

One theory is that since the outer box indicates that the Victoria came in an 18K white gold and black enamel case, perhaps this model was a Mary Todd 203 that was equipped with a metal bracelet and renamed. That might explain the higher price, since the pattern with other Illinois models seemed to be that a metal bracelet increased the price of a given model.

VOGUE

See listing for **Claudette/Vogue**

WADSWORTH SPECIAL MODELS

Wadsworth Special Model, 18K white gold

Name = Wadsworth Special Models
Time Period = Deco
Karat/Material = 18K WG, 19.2K WG; 8K WG, Black Inlaid Enamel, Diamonds
Bezel = Engraved
Sides = Engraved
Lug Size = 11mm
Spring Bar = Fixed Lugs
Casemaker = Wadsworth
Case Pieces = 3
Case Number = None
Case Back = Engraved
Dimensions = 17 x 31mm
Durability = 🕒🕒🕒🕒
Movement Size = 18/0
Movement Grade/Jewels = Unknown/16J, Unknown/17J
Dial Number = 86
Dial = Embossed
Dial Opening = Octagonal
Numerals = Painted, Embossed
Hands = Steel
Seconds at = None
Cased in Factory = Likely
Collectibility = 🕒🕒🕒🕒
Rarity = 🕒🕒🕒🕒🕒
Retail Price New = Unknown
Introduction Date = 1926
Unique Case Design = Yes
Unique Dial Design = No
Advertisement = Unknown
Marketing Theme = Unknown

Illinois advertisements indicate that the early Mary Todd models were cased and timed at the Illinois factory at a time before Illinois began to assign wristwatch case Model Numbers. The Mary Todds all appear to have been housed in 18K Keystone cases. However, it is likely that there were early Factory-Cased ladies' Illinois models in high-karat cases by Wadsworth as well.

Both Gay and other collectors have found other 18/0 size Illinois watches in solid 18K white gold Wadsworth cases of styles resembling some that Keystone used later for Mary Todds. These, too, have movements of either 16 or 17 jewels, most dating from 1926.

Interestingly, the cases for these 18K Wadsworth cases have exactly the same engraving patterns for the sides and the backs that are on some later 14K Wadsworth models, such as the Bar Harbor 156. These early 18K Wadsworth models typically came with ornate embossed dials, such as the beautiful No. 86 (listed in the May 1927 Illinois Dial and Hand Circular), which was offered with exploding numerals of either gilt or black finish.

Gay notes that he has also found a number of 18/0 size Illinois ladies' wristwatches with movements from 1923 and 1924 that were cased in Wadsworth 19.2K solid white gold cases. Most of the movements were 16 jewels, though a few were 17 jewels.

Side view of a Wadsworth Special Model, showing engraving pattern

Wadsworth Special Model inside case back and movement

Neither the 19.2K nor the 18K Wadsworth-cased early 18/0 models are common. However, Gay reports that enough of them have been found to suggest that they were likely part of Illinois' high-end ladies' offerings before case model numbers were introduced.

Wadsworth Special Diamond-Set Models

Among the most stunning of the Illinois ladies' wristwatches are two Wadsworth models with cases in 18K white gold with black inlaid enamel and either four or six diamonds. These models are extremely rare, much rarer than even the Mary Todd diamond-set models, and only a few specimens have been found.

The few that we have examined tended to have 16-jewel movements. Gay has noted that serial numbers for the movements ranged from 4627xxx to 4752xxx and the case numbers for them were all 1268xxx.

As yet, no advertisements for these elegant watches have been found. We suspect that they may have been custom orders for a prestigious jeweler.

Wadsworth 18K white gold case with black enamel and 4 diamonds

Wadsworth 18K white gold case with black enamel and 4 diamonds

Wadsworth 18K white gold case with black enamel and 6 diamonds

ILLINOIS

CHAPTER 11

Hamilton-Illinois Wristwatches: History and Identification Guide

The labor-intensive nature of watchmaking made manufacturing extremely sensitive to wage changes. Wage increases experienced in the United States during and after World War II diminished Hamilton's ability to produce reliable, accurate timepieces at affordable prices. Accordingly, Hamilton explored several paths for producing a more affordable product.

One possible alternative lay in following Bulova, Benrus and Gruen by purchasing or manufacturing movements built with cheaper labor in Switzerland. Another possibility was simply to engineer a cheaper watch, making parts less expensively and streamlining manufacturing processes, following the example of the United States Time Corporation's product line, rebranded as Timex in 1950.

On Tuesday, May 31, 1949, the local Lancaster newspaper, the *Intelligencer Journal*, reported that certain Hamilton executives had returned from an extended trip to Europe (actually Switzerland in particular).[1]

SDAY, MAY 31, 1949

HAMILTON OFFICIALS RETURN FROM EUROPE

Further information revealed that Hamilton officials visited ten different Swiss watchmaking factories. Although Hamilton executives did not reveal the purpose of the trip at the time, the fact-finding mission may have served two goals: first, to identify new techniques to improve watch production efficiency and low costs; and second, perhaps, to scope out prospects for using imported movements. It is known that during this same period, Hamilton also had a team working in the Research Laboratory to see if an in-house, inexpensive movement might be a viable option.

Hamilton debated the move to Swiss movements for several years, then opted to offer a new line of wristwatches using Swiss movements as a trial balloon. Hamilton resurrected the Illinois brand for its moderately priced line of men's and ladies' wristwatches. When these movements turned out to be acceptable to Hamilton jewelers, and to consumers, the company started to introduce some Swiss movements into Hamilton-branded products as well.

Starting a Lower-Priced Line

On May 23, 1952, almost exactly three years after the trip to Switzerland, Hamilton publicly announced, via a letter to its stockholders, that it was planning "to launch a line of lower-priced 17-jewel, imported wristwatches early the next year."[2] The letter, from George P. Luckey, Hamilton's president, informed the stockholders that the Hamilton board felt this move would "broaden the base of the Company's sales, and will put us in a better competitive position with greater opportunity for increased profits."[3] It did require additional working capital, however.

Luckey was quick to emphasize that "the move will in no way affect the production of the world-famous Hamilton watch. . . . The new line will be marketed under a brand name other than 'Hamilton'."[4] The vagueness of the wording suggests that it is possible that at the time of this announcement, the company had not yet decided to name its new low-priced imported watch line "Illinois."

In order to maintain profitability, Hamilton had concluded that it needed to lower its production costs and price points. After years of study, the firm thus decided to take the plunge with low-cost imported Swiss movements and mostly low-end rolled gold plate cases with stainless steel casebacks. So as not to harm the Hamilton brand, these models

Hamilton To Launch Lower Priced Line Of Imported Watches

Intelligencer Journal (Lancaster, PA), May 23, 1952

Hamilton Firm Plans To Import Cheaper Watches

Berkshire Eagle, (Pittsfield, MA), May 26, 1952; image from *newspapers.com*

June 16, 1952

Hamilton Adds New Line Of Timepieces

Lower-Cost Swiss Watch To Be Sold; Alter Distribution

The Hamilton Watch Co. has announced the addition of an imported lower-cost line to its regular manufacture of fine watches.

In addition, the company is switching from its wholesaler system to marketing direct through retailers. Here are some excerpts from president George C. Luckey's letter to stockholders explaining the changes:

"During the past sixty years, the Hamilton Watch Company has earned an enviable reputation with both the buying public and the jewelry trade, and has secured each year a highly desirable portion of the fine watch business. . . .

"First, the importation of increasing quantities of low cost Swiss watches has greatly complicated marketing problems. Slightly more than eight million watches were imported from Switzerland in 1950. In 1951 there were over eleven million watches imported. There is now pending before the United States Tariff Commission a proceeding seeking an increase in duties on these imports, but to date there has been no tariff relief. While it is hoped that some relief will be granted, there is little likelihood that it can be great enough to completely offset the labor cost advantage enjoyed by imported watches.

New Line Added

"Accordingly, in addition to continuing to manufacture Hamilton watches domestically, your Company is completing final arrangements for the importation of a line of 17 jewel watches to be released to the trade early in 1953 under a brand name other than "Hamilton," and in a lower price range. This will broaden the base of our Company's sales, and will put us in a better competitive position with greater opportunity for increased profits. It will, however, require additional working capital.

"Second, a decision from the Supreme Court in May, 1951, has curtailed the protection previously afforded by the Fair Trade laws which has been so important to the successful distribution of Hamilton watches. This decision has resulted in an increase of cut-price sales and other "deal" promotions which make it difficult for a watch manufacturer to compete profitably through wholesale distribution in today's watch market.

Effective August 1

"After thorough studies of Hamilton's market position and careful consideration of the problems involved, your Company has decided that effective August 1, 1952, it will discontinue selling through wholesale distributors and will start selling its product directly to retail jewelers. This program involves the problem of financing sales to a large number of retailers instead of to a small group of wholesalers. It will require a substantial increase in working capital. It will also involve a program of increased advertising which has been developed and readied for activation. . ."

Unidentified trade journal report, June 16, 1952

were at first branded Illinois, but they, in fact, had nothing in common with that great American watch company of times past.

Why the Illinois Name?

More information about the venture came at the end of fiscal year 1952, when Luckey notified shareholders that in early 1953, Hamilton would introduce its new line of watches under the "Illinois" name and that they would be "styled and priced in the $35 to $60 price range to compete in the volume watch market."[5]

It has long been thought that the Hamilton Watch Company offered the Hamilton-Illinois wristwatches to renew, preserve, and extend the "Illinois" trade name and brand. This may have been a minor reason for the existence of these watches with "Illinois" signed on their dials and cases, and in most instances marked the "Illinois Watch Company" on their Swiss-manufactured movements. To preserve its trademark rights, however, Hamilton could have branded any of its men's and ladies' wristwatches models as an Illinois. The reason for the resurrection of the Illinois name, therefore, must be found elsewhere.

It is far more likely, however, that Hamilton had a threefold purpose in mind with the introduction of the Hamilton-Illinois wristwatches. Besides its desire to renew and protect the "Illinois" brand name for its exclusive use on watches, a second goal would have been to enable the Hamilton Watch Company to introduce a "budget brand" of wristwatches that would not dilute the value and reputation of its Hamilton brand. Lastly, Hamilton, concerned about production and labor costs in the United States, probably wanted for competitive reasons to try out cheaper Swiss-produced movements without risking damage to its Hamilton brand name. In the post–World War II era, known as the "Atomic Age," Hamilton needed suitable products at the right prices to compete with low-cost foreign and domestic watch manufacturers because the company could not lower its development and production costs enough to compete effectively otherwise.

Union Reaction

On May 22, 1952, Walter W. Cenerazzo, president of the American Watch Workers Union, had strongly criticized Hamilton's plan to market a line of watches utilizing Swiss-made movements. Cenerazzo stated: "Of necessity, we must criticize harshly this decision of the Hamilton board of directors to import a secondary line of Swiss watches subordinate to the Hamilton line.[6]

Apparently, Cenerazzo tacitly accepted Hamilton's decision to sacrifice the once-valuable Illinois trade name, as he added, "We do think it a wise decision, however, not to place the Hamilton name on Swiss movements as Waltham is now doing."

It is interesting that Cenerazzo was reacting to Hamilton's plan before it was announced publicly on May 23. Possibly Hamilton discussed the plan in advance with the union head to avoid taking the union by surprise and also to gauge the degree of its predictable negative reaction.

Cenerazzo Voices Criticism Of Acti

BOSTON, May 22—Walter W. Cenerazzo, president of the American Watch Workers Union, said here tonight that "of necessity we must criticize harshly" the action taken today by the board of directors of the Hamilton Watch Company.

The Hamilton Watch Workers Union is affiliated with the American Watch Workers Union.

Text of Cenerazzo's statement ollows:

"It is with great sadness that we heard about the decision of the Hamilton Watch board of directors in becoming Swiss watch importers.

"The American jewel watch industry has been dealt body blow after body blow by the failure of the Truman administration to act against the flood of Swiss watch imports. The employes of Elgin, Waltham and now Hamilton are the sufferers in the long range because of this flood of imports.

"We cannot understand this decision being made prior to Aug. 15, before the Tariff Commission and the President of the United States act on the question of raising watch tariffs.

CRITICIZES ACTION

"We have criticized Waltham and Elgin for jumping the gun and becoming Swiss watch importers prematurely. Of necessity, we must criticize harshly this decision of the Hamilton board of directors to import a secondary line of Swiss watches subordinated to the Hamilton line.

"We do think it a wise decision, however, on their part not to place the Hamilton name on Swiss movements as Waltham is doing.

"We will have to await the impact of this decision before we can properly estimate what it will do to future employment of Hamilton employes.

"To me as national president of the American Watch Workers Union it is a body blow against 10 long unfruitful years of effort."

Intelligencer Journal (Lancaster, PA), May 23, 1952

Walter W. Cenerazzo, 1947

WALTER W. CENERAZZO (1913–1968)

Walter William Cenerazzo was the president of the independent American Watch Workers Union. An article in *Fortune* magazine described him as a "fluent, belligerent, stocky" man who was "a printer by trade, a politician by nature, an organizer by profession."*

He first established a union at Waltham, then one at Elgin, and in May 1944 one at Hamilton. Within three years he won wage increases at Hamilton of about fifty percent, seniority guarantees, and six paid holidays per year.

Cenerazzo joined the battle for watch import protection, routinely "browbeating government officials into turning a more sympathetic ear toward the competitive problems of the domestic industry." He strongly argued for limiting imports of foreign-made watch movements.

He continued in his union leadership role until at least the late 1950s.

*"Hamilton Watch," *Fortune* (January 1947), p. 198. Quotations are from this article.

Hamilton-Illinois Official Introduction

Hamilton was not only presenting a new line of watches but also instituting a new distribution system, as Luckey noted in his May 23, 1952 letter to the Hamilton stockholders. One of the reasons that the company needed additional working capital at the time, he said, was that the new system "involves financing sales to the many small jewelers who sell Hamilton watches, instead of financing a small group of wholesalers."[7]

On May 5, 1953, Hamilton announced the release of its new watch line in a letter to the Hamilton Watch Jewelers.

Manufacturers of the Watch of Railroad Accuracy

Hamilton Watch Company

Lancaster, Penna., U. S. A.

May 5, 1953

To Hamilton Watch Jewelers:

Hamilton's long-awaited companion watch line is here!

NOW - - you can get Hamilton quality, Hamilton profit, Hamilton protection, Hamilton prestige....on watches starting as low as $33.95.

We invite your serious consideration of this new line... we invite your orders and your sales efforts. For the new ILLINOIS - - like the new HAMILTON - - is more than ever the jeweler's watch - - your watch! It's the only line of fine watches that gives you everything you need for a satisfactory, profitable watch volume.

Please read the enclosed presentation carefully. Note that the new ILLINOIS has promotion behind it, too....promotion that builds sales that will help you.

Note the illustrations of the first seventeen ILLINOIS watches to be released and their prices. And your cost!

And note the order form. If your Hamilton representative has not as yet contacted you - - here's enough information to write your initial order. Remember, until July 1st, an initial order of ten or more brings you FREE the beautiful new ILLINOIS motion display as well as the complete promotion kit. (After July 1st, it will take fifteen watches!) This display sells for $10.00 with a smaller order. Jewelers ordering six or more automatically receive the promotion kit.

Everybody is talking about the new ILLINOIS. Soon everybody will be selling it! Meanwhile, you can be among the first to feature the finest watch in its price range...made to Hamilton specifications, sold as only Hamilton watches are sold. Priced for profit - - and guaranteed by Hamilton - - most trusted name in watches.

Cordially,

E. B. Silvius

Director of Sales

EBSilvius/tth

The May 5, 1953 letter was accompanied by a four-page color brochure proclaiming that "the new Illinois is here!" This 1953 brochure is shown below.

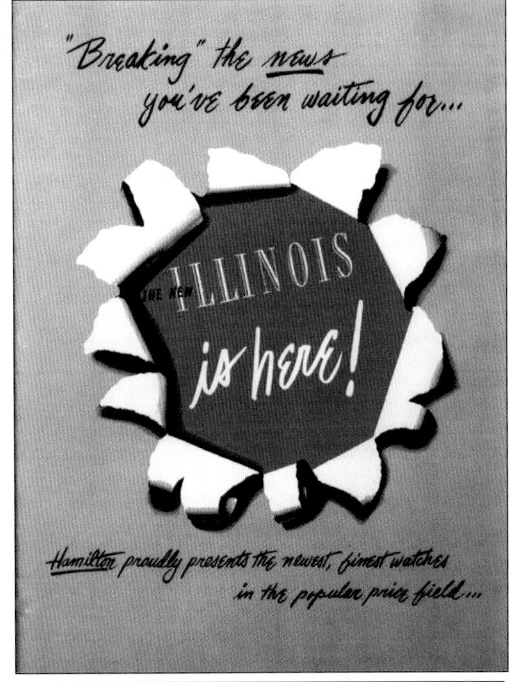

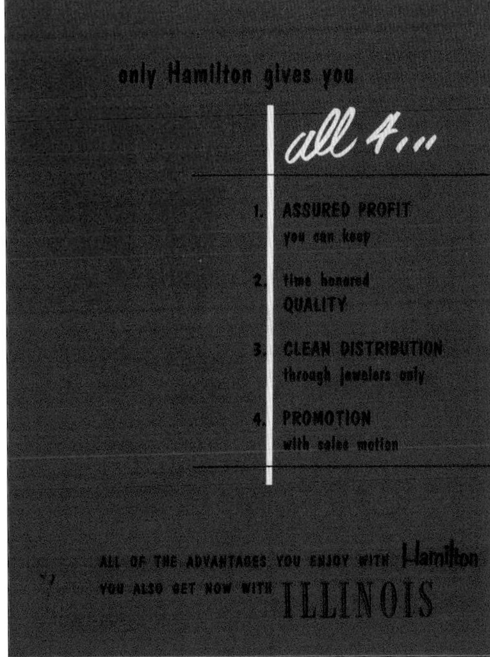

Letter of May 5, 1953, from Hamilton to the Hamilton Watch Jewelers

cash in on this sensational
INTRODUCTORY
DEAL!
FREE! with your order of only
15 WATCHES
10 until July 1st
deliveries will start May 1st
LOOK at all you get in the Promotion Kit
with the Big Deal!
ILLINOIS PROMOTION KIT
Identification sign
Envelope & package enclosures (100 free) more @ $10 M
Book Matches
Radio-TV Copy
Sales Letter Copy
Newspaper mats (individual watches & signatures)
Newspaper mats (complete advertisement)
Movie Theatre Playlets (available on request)
Action Packed, That's It!
Striking design with motion that means business . . . a smart, permanent display of top-quality materials throughout. Not a cardboard display, but a solid three-dimensional unit with motion that will sell. Size: 12" wide, 7" deep and 16" high with space for display of five Illinois Watches.
THE ILLINOIS

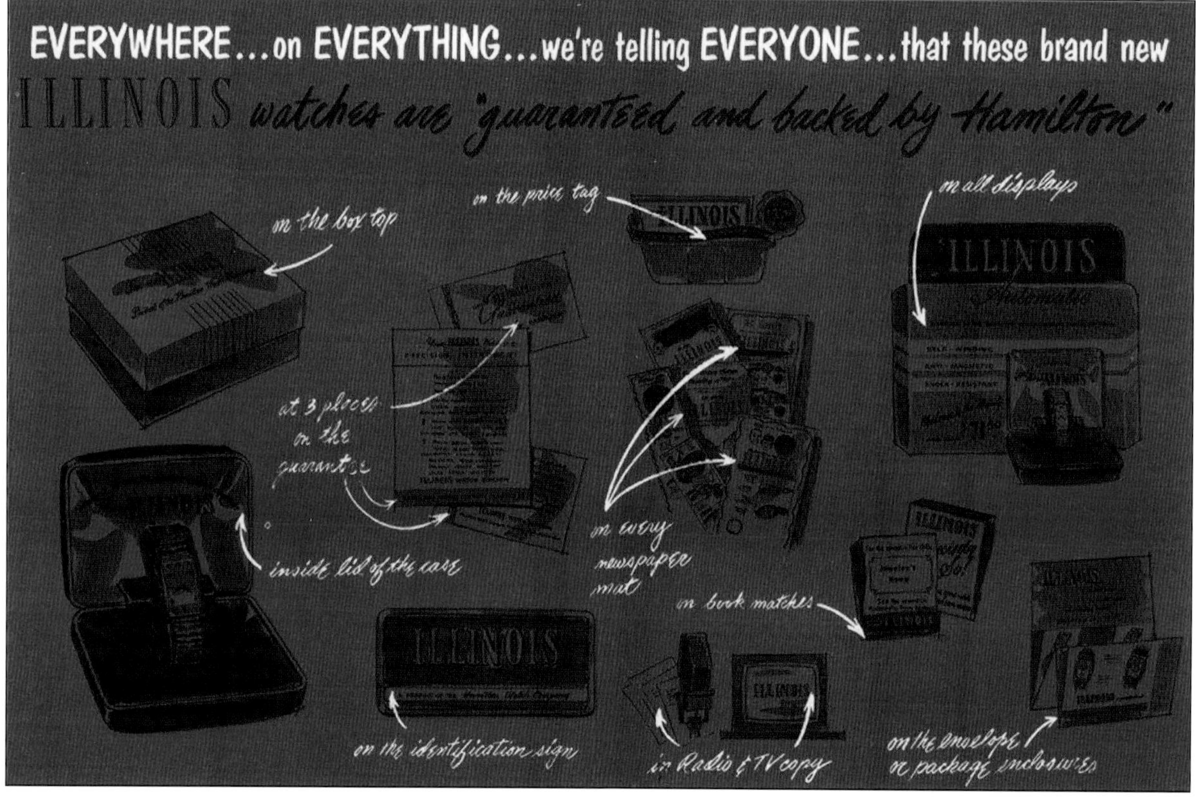
EVERYWHERE...on EVERYTHING...we're telling EVERYONE...that these brand new
ILLINOIS watches are "guaranteed and backed by Hamilton"
on the box top
on the price tag
on all displays
ILLINOIS
at 3 places on the guarantee
inside lid of the case
on every newspaper mat
on book matches
ILLINOIS
on the identification sign
in Radio & TV copy
on the envelope or package enclosures

HAMILTON WATCH COMPANY

M E M O R A N D U M

Copies to: From: Process Develop. Dept. Engr. Services Sec. Date: June 1, 1953

*J. Basso
*F. Boulton
*R. Braner
*J. Burkhart
*W. Carey
*B. Dulaney
*L. Erb
*C. Erisman
R. Foultz
*S. Gast
*W. Geisler
*S. Griffith
*E. Hendrix
*R. Hoxworth
*J. Huber
*F. Huehnergarth
*J. Leaman
*J. Marion
*F. Orr
A. Peiffer
M. Sabinash
*F. Stegner
*H. Vermot
*R. Welk
*R. Wilson
*R. Frey

Subject: New "Illinois" Product Specifications

This memorandum announces the issuance of new permanent specifications for Illinois models recently released by the Styling and Product Development Division.

The new specifications are as follows:

Specification	Model	Grade
90050	9005 (GOLDEN TREASURE "A")-W	601
90060	9006 (GOLDEN TREASURE "A")-Y	601
90100	9010 (COQUETTE "A")-W	601
90110	9011 (COQUETTE "A")-Y	601
90140	9014 (LADY GAY "A")-Y	600
90150	9015 (LADY GAY "B")-Y	600
90180	9018 (COQUETTE "B")-Y	600
90190	9019 (COQUETTE "C")-W	600
90200	9020 (COQUETTE "C")-Y	600
90210	9021 (CAREER GIRL "A")-SS	602
90220	9022 (CAREER GIRL "B")-Y	602
95070	9507 (DEBONAIR "B")-Y	655
95080	9508 (DEBONAIR "F")-Y	656
95090	9509 (TOPPER "A")-Y	655
95100	9510 (TOPPER "B")-Y	655
95110	9511 (DEBONAIR "C")-Y	657

-2-

Specification	Model	Grade
95120	9512 (DEBONAIR "D")-Y	653
95130	9513 (DEBONAIR "E")-Y	654
95150	9515 (AUTOMATIC "B")-SS	651
95160	9516 (SIGNAMATIC)-SS	652

The temproary specifications previously issued for these models are to be destroyed or marked "DISCONTINUED".

The new specifications are issued with this memorandum to the persons designated (*).

MS

C.A. Yecker

C.C.M. File
Part No.

90050	90220
90060	95070
90100	95080
90110	95090
90140	95100
90150	95110
90180	95120
90190	95130
90200	95150
90210	95160

Internal memorandum, dated June 1, 1953, introducing new "Illinois" product specifications and movement grades

Early Hamilton-Illinois jewelry store promotional sign

Budget-Focused View

Hamilton's frugality was exhibited in its design and production of the Illinois line. Coupled with the cheaper movements were low-end cases. On most models embossed chapter markers and numerals were used rather than gold ones—a move that further reduced material costs as well as the labor to install them. Following are some of the advertising themes used by Hamilton for its Hamilton-Illinois line in both advertisements and sales catalogs:

- "Fine Watches at Modest Prices"
- "Watches in the Popular Price Range"
- "For the budget conscious man . . ."
- "Outstanding values"
- ". . . made to the most exacting specifications ever established for watches in the popular-price field . . ."
- ". . . some of the best buys in fine watches for men"
- "Fine watch luxury at a most modest price"
- "Best popular-priced fine watch value!"
- "Best buy in new large size with sweep-seconds for accurate timing"
- "A handsome, practical timepiece"
- "Outstanding watch value"
- "Embossed numerals and markers like expensive watches"
- "Illinois first choice among popular-priced watches"
- "Hamilton presents the newest name in fine watches at modest prices."

Clearly, these Hamilton-Illinois watches were aimed at the budget-conscious consumer. The men's Hamilton-branded watches in 1953 ranged from a low price of $57.75 to a high price of $225.00, and the women's Hamilton models extended from $57.75 to $275.00. During the same time period, however, the Hamilton-Illinois wristwatches for men were priced from a low of $33.95 to a high of $71.50 and the Hamilton-Illinois ladies' watches from $33.95 to $95.00.

1953 cover of the first Hamilton-Illinois sales catalog

1953
HISTORICAL NOTES

- President Truman announces the development of the hydrogen bomb.
- Marshal Tito becomes president of Yugoslavia.
- John Foster Dulles is appointed Secretary of State.
- *You Are There* premieres on CBS-TV with Walter Cronkite.
- F. Crick and J. Watson discover the structure of the DNA molecule.
- Nikita Khrushchev becomes secretary of the Communist Party.
- The United States performs a nuclear test at the Nevada Test Site.
- Dr. Jonas Salk's polio vaccine is announced.
- The first West-to-East jet transatlantic non-stop flight takes place.
- Coronation of Queen Elizabeth II takes place.
- California adopts a sales tax.
- The USSR performs nuclear tests.
- The New York Yankees win their fifth consecutive World Series.
- Swanson sells its first "TV dinner."

In some of its Hamilton-Illinois announcements, Hamilton somewhat disingenuously advertised that "Illinois was a new name in watches," notwithstanding the fact that the Illinois name was first used for watches in 1870. However, in its first catalogs containing the Hamilton-Illinois models, it did explain the history and tradition behind the "Illinois" name.

For instance, the 1953 Hamilton and Illinois Watch Catalog reintroduced "Illinois" to jewelers and its customers stating:

> *"What ILLINOIS is"*: Remarking on the "proud old name," Hamilton announced watches in a "popular price range" that had the full backing of the company.
>
> *"What ILLINOIS means to the Jeweler"*: Hamilton assured the jeweler that it not only backed the product but also would support service and marketing.
>
> *"What ILLINOIS means to the Customer"*: Hamilton stressed value and styling, "plus the backing and guarantee of Hamilton . . . the most trusted name in fine watches."

As was now the case with its primary line, Hamilton intended to work directly with the jewelers, not employing jobbers to supply the product.

What ILLINOIS is

ILLINOIS is a proud old name in American watch history now used exclusively to identify a *new* line of fine seventeen jewel watches in the popular-price range. ILLINOIS watches are manufactured to exacting specifications under constant inspection of the Hamilton Watch Company. Thus the quality is so fine that *all* ILLINOIS *Watches are guaranteed by the Hamilton Watch Company*.

What ILLINOIS means to the Jeweler

ILLINOIS Watches are styled, guaranteed and *distributed* by the Hamilton Watch Company, assuring the Jeweler of complete support and every assistance in selling and servicing ILLINOIS Watches.

What ILLINOIS means to the Customer

ILLINOIS Watches give the customer one hundred cents worth of fine watch value for every dollar, *plus* beautiful advanced styling and all the dependable service expected of a fine watch, *plus* the backing and guarantee of Hamilton . . . the most trusted name in fine watches.

ALL PRICES SHOWN IN THIS CATALOG INCLUDE FEDERAL TAX AND ARE SUBJECT TO CHANGE WITHOUT NOTICE

Second page of the first Hamilton-Illinois sale catalog, 1953

The name "Hamilton-Illinois" was a registered trademark of the Hamilton Watch Company. The first assembly of a Swiss movement into a watch in the Lancaster facility occurred when Hamilton introduced the Hamilton-Illinois line in 1953. These Swiss movements were both manual and automatic. Starting with the 1954 model year, Hamilton also introduced Swiss movements in its own branded automatics. With the demise of the Hamilton-Illinois line at the end of 1955, Hamilton rebranded some Hamilton-Illinois watches as Hamiltons, keeping the Swiss manual and automatic movements. Then, by 1956, Hamilton extended the practice by placing Swiss manual movements in its own branded watches in place of its Lancaster-manufactured ones.

1954
HISTORICAL NOTES

- The first shopping mall opens in Southfield, Michigan.
- RCA manufactures the first color TV set (12.5 inch screen for $1,000).
- The first Burger King is opened in Miami, Florida.
- Linus Pauling wins the Nobel Prize in Chemistry.

Low-Cost Features

The Hamilton Watch Company adopted several apparently new marketing features and practices with the release of the Hamilton-Illinois watch brand to enable Hamilton to offer a low priced alternative watch. Some of these features were:

- Inexpensive stainless steel case backs.
- 10K rolled gold plate bezels. Although Hamilton used the low-grade rolled gold plate wristwatches in its Hamilton-Illinois wristwatch line, it also introduced this case material in some of their own pocket watches at least as early as 1951.
- Cases described in Hamilton sales materials merely as yellow or white without a clear indication of their material content in advertisements and catalogs
- Swiss movements imported at a cost lower than comparable movements could have been made in Lancaster

ROLLED GOLD PLATE

The Federal Trade Commission ordered the Diel Watch Case Co., Inc., New York, to discontinue selling watch cases which are stamped with the phrase "Rolled Gold Plate" or words of like import, and from using that phrase in advertising watch cases unless the cases contain not less than three one-thousandths of an inch in thickness of gold on the outside thereof, and not less than one one-thousandth of an inch in thickness of gold on the inside.

The Commission issued its complaint April 28, 1932, and the company refrained from contesting the proceeding, and consented that the commission serve upon it an order to cease and desist.

The Illinois Springfield Factory, in its entire history, never produced any model in rolled gold plate or stainless steel.[8] In addition, it never Factory-Cased a single watch with a stainless back and a bezel of a different material. On a few occasions, Illinois produced wristwatch models with 10K gold-filled cases, but only one such model was offered pre-acquisition. In most instances, Illinois offered its watches in 14k gold or 14K gold-filled.

An Illinois purist could plausibly argue that the Hamilton executive management sacrificed the good brand name "Illinois" by pushing all of Hamilton's low-end, cost-reduced, inexpensive, dollar-saving features onto a non-Hamilton branded item. On the other hand, a Hamilton purist could certainly counter that this was a wise strategy by upper management at Hamilton to preserve the good-will and good name of the long-standing and surviving Hamilton brand. In any event, Hamilton offered no new Illinois-branded watch model after 1934 other than a very limited offering of the "Illinois Whitman" model introduced in 1942 and/or 1946 to help preserve the company's "Illinois" brand name (see this model in Chapter 9).

Many Illinois collectors enjoyed the fact that Hamilton reached into its heritage to revive the Illinois brand for use in the 1953–55 time period, regardless of the reasons Hamilton had for doing so. The Mid-Century Modern designs of these models are of course completely different from the Illinois models released from 1928 through 1934.

MID-CENTURY MODERN

"Mid-Century Modern is an architectural, interior, product and graphic design that generally describes mid-20th century developments in modern design, architecture, and urban development from roughly 1933 to 1965."*

Many consider Frank Lloyd Wright's principal movement of organic architecture, combined with Arts and Crafts, as a jumping-off point for the aesthetic of Mid-Century Modern design in America.

Examples of Mid-Century Modern design

*https://en.wikipedia.org/wiki/Mid-century_modern

Simplified Naming Conventions

Perhaps indicative of the low value Hamilton assigned to the Hamilton-Illinois wristwatch line is Hamilton's complete lack of originality in naming these wristwatches. Although most of the models differed significantly in case and dial design from one another, they did not apparently warrant the marketing capital of the Hamilton Watch Company to accord them proper individual names. For example, the Debonair series goes from Debonair Model A through to Debonair Model L, although all were different in appearance. The same can be said for the Automatic Model A through Automatic Model D, and again for the Lady Gay Model A through Lady Gay Model H. Other examples of this lack of originality include the Signamatic, Topper, Career Girl, Coquette, Golden Treasure and Kimberly series. However, once Hamilton started to slide down this slope, it continued the pattern of uninspired sequencing, particularly for the models with Swiss movements, such as the Accumatic.

Hamilton's experience in making railroad watches

RAILWAY SPECIAL #15, $71.50 RAILWAY SPECIAL "A", $89.50

means greater accuracy in all other **Hamiltons**

CELESTE with bracelet, $65.00 KENMORE with matching band, $71.50 SHARON with cord, $79.50

and means extra value in **ILLINOIS** watches by Hamilton

Prices include Federal Tax. © HWC, Lancaster, Pa.

Life, 1954. A Hamilton advertisement that, astoundingly enough, mentions Illinois without showing any Hamilton-Illinois watch!

A Separate Brand

Hamilton expert René Rondeau summarizes Hamilton's foray into the Illinois line as follows: "1950s series was originally kept separate from Hamilton and meant to compete with Bulova, Timex and others. Hamilton tried making a 7-jewel version of its 987A to cheapen the cost but apparently found that they would be better off buying 17J Swiss movements than producing a low-quality movement in-house. The goal was to find a way to make a low-cost watch. This was pretty much standard operating procedure in the Hamilton R&D lab. Management almost always had different experiments running concurrently, aiming toward the same goal but from another angle. It happened with battery research, the battle between permanent magnet versus moving magnet electrics, and so on."

Rondeau adds about Hamilton-Illinois that "over twenty different styles were cataloged, using exclusively imported Swiss movements and stainless steel, gold-filled, or rolled gold plate (RGP) cases with stainless backs. However, there are some known in 14K gold. I've seen pictures of one complete with box and label so it's obviously legit, but it's very odd since it goes against everything the brand was designed for: lower quality and lower cost.

"Although the idea was to keep the brand separate from Hamilton, the watches sold so poorly that in 1954 Hamilton hyphenated the name and sold the watches as 'Hamilton-Illinois.' Unfortunately this was also unsuccessful and the line was closed out at the end of 1955."[9]

A Short-Lived Experiment

The resurrection of the "Illinois" name via the Hamilton-Illinois brand lasted only from 1953 through 1955. One can only speculate as to the reasons for its demise. Perhaps the "Illinois" name had lost its appeal to contemporary jewelers and customers by the mid-1950s. Possibly the budget-targeted audience was not receptive to Hamilton's sales pitches. Maybe the Hamilton-Illinois line was too similar in design, style and mechanics to other Hamilton models, causing the budget offering to cannibalize the sale of Hamilton's primary lines of watches. Also, according to Hamilton collector Bob Ayer, Hamilton appeared to have a three-year design cycle for its moderately successful watches. Many of the Hamilton-Illinois models came out in 1953; therefore, 1955 would have been the end of their Hamilton life cycle.

The only prototype known to exist of Hamilton's attempt to make a 7-jewel low-cost wristwatch movement. Note that Hamilton again chose to use the Illinois brand name for this low-end item.

Prototype Hamilton with the 7-jewel Hamilton movement signed "*Illinois*"; only one known to exist

Whatever the reason, Hamilton eliminated the Illinois brand entirely from the Hamilton catalogs after 1955, although some of the Hamilton-Illinois watches lived on as stand-alone Hamilton models, usually with the same dial but signed only Hamilton, and the same case and the same Swiss movement still signed Illinois.

The Hamilton-Illinois brand suffered its demise at the end of 1955. The elimination of the line sparked a fire sale of these models as jewelers rushed to unload their inventory. They did so by reducing prices by 50% and offering "E.Z. Credit" terms of one dollar per week. Luckey's predecessors as president of Hamilton, who for so long had protested low prices, cost cutters, discounters and E.Z. Credit jewelers in the late 1920s and early 1930s, would have viewed this situation as their worst nightmare.

A full-page advertisement for a Christmas credit, half-price sale on at least eighteen different Hamilton-Illinois models, *El Paso Herald-Post*, December 14, 1955; image from *newspapers.com*

1955 HISTORICAL NOTES

- The first atomic submarine, the USS *Nautilus*, is officially launched at Groton, Connecticut, for Navy service.
- Columbia University scientists develop an atomic clock, accurate to within one second in 300 years.
- Dr. Jonas Salk successfully tests the polio vaccine.
- Ray Kroc starts McDonald's fast food restaurants.

After the Experiment

What Hamilton had begun with the Hamilton-Illinois experiment did not end with the discontinuation of that brand name. Features, and indeed whole watch designs introduced in the experiment, continued in Hamilton's product line for the rest of the company's existence as an American watch producer.

A Case by Another Name

Notwithstanding the demise of the Hamilton-Illinois watch brand by 1955, some of the models lived on as Hamiltons, requiring only a dial and name change. All appear in the Hamilton 1956 Sales Catalog. Since 1955 was the end of the road for "Hamilton-Illinois," Hamilton wasted no time getting more mileage out of the movements and case designs. The degree to which they wished to integrate these watches in their product line is reflected in the practice of actually marking some inside casebacks with their new Hamilton names. Examples of this phenomenon follow.[10]

- The Hamilton-Illinois Debonair Model C morphed into the Hamilton Clive.
- The Hamilton-Illinois Debonair Model D morphed into the Hamilton Drew.
- The Hamilton-Illinois Debonair Model E morphed into the Hamilton Essex.
- The Hamilton-Illinois Debonair G morphed into the Hamilton Gallant B.
- The Hamilton-Illinois Debonair Model J morphed into the Hamilton Jarvis.
- The Hamilton-Illinois Debonair Model L morphed into the Hamilton Laird.

Hamilton Jarvis

Hamilton Essex

Hamilton also recycled the dials and movements of the Datomatic in their Automatic K575 and K576. The movement (with power-reserve indicator) from the Signamatic series appeared in the Accumatic II "B" and possibly other models.

On the ladies side, there are the following cognates:

- The Hamilton-Illinois Coquette Model D became the Hamilton Dinah.
- The Hamilton-Illinois Coquette Model E became the Hamilton Elise.
- The Hamilton-Illinois Lady Gay E became the Hamilton Enid.
- The Hamilton-Illinois Lady Gay Model F became the Hamilton Flora.
- The Hamilton-Illinois Lady Gay Model G became the Hamilton Gwen.
- The Hamilton-Illinois Lady Gay Model H became the Hamilton Hedy.
- The Hamilton-Illinois Lady Gay Model K became the Hamilton Kaye.

HAMILTON CROSS COUNTRY

The Cross Country issued by the Hamilton Watch Company in 1956 was one of several watches that used leftover Hamilton-Illinois Swiss movements after Hamilton shut down the Hamilton-Illinois wristwatch line. According to Hamilton expert and historian René Rondeau, the Cross Country proved to be popular enough that once all of the Illinois-signed Swiss movements were used up, Hamilton redesigned the inside of the case back to accept a Hamilton movement and sold it at a higher price as the Cross Country II model.

SIGNAMATIC MOVEMENT USE BY HAMILTON

Hamilton Accumatic II "B"

In another instance (according to Rondeau), the Hamilton-Illinois Signamatic movement was used by Hamilton in a Hamilton watch that was never catalogued by it. Although the movement was used in the Hamilton-Illinois series, this model had a completely different dial and case setup. Rondeau speculates that "Hamilton did not have enough up/down movements left to warrant cataloging it, but there were enough to warrant putting some watches together for sale under the Hamilton name. It is only speculation, but most likely they were only sold to one or two major accounts, probably at a favorable price just to clear out the dead movement inventory. It is the only Hamilton up/down watch, so it's a very interesting piece."

None of Hamilton models experimented with the low-cost features prior to their "trial" use in the Hamilton-Illinois models. According to Bob Ayer, the first rolled gold plate Hamilton models appeared in 1956, and the first Hamiltons with Swiss movements appeared in 1954.

Listed here are the rolled gold plate cases offered on Hamilton watches from 1956 to 1960. Several are former Hamilton-Illinois models.

Rolled Gold Plate Hamilton Models 1956–1960

Year	Model
1956	Clive
1953	Colby B
1956	Drew B
1956	Essex
1956	Gallant B
1956	Jarvis
1956	Laird
1956	Landon B
1956	Nautilus IIB
1956	Paxton
1956	Accumatic II
1957	Cadet
1957	Arnold
1957	Colby
1957	Drew
1957	Grant
1957	Kinematic I
1957	Landon
1957	Nautilus II
1957	Seabrook
1957	Viking
1958	Boatswain
1958	Carlyle
1958	Coburn
1958	Deauville
1958	Farrell
1958	Harrow
1958	Keane
1958	Lowell
1958	Prentice
1958	Seabeach
1958	Accumatic III
1959	Accumatic VI
1959	Accumatic VII
1959	Automatic K650
1959	Dexter
1959	Gardner
1959	Sea Mate
1959	Sea Scape
1959	Thinomatic T650
1959	Trevo
1960	Carson
1960	First Mate
1960	Kinematic II
1960	Romanesque T
1960	Sea Breeze

The Experiment in Perspective

Don Sauers explained in *Time for America* that Hamilton entered into the 1950s with high hopes but "the later '50s were years of stress, upheaval and finally, failure in the American jeweled watch industry. The decade had begun with a period of strong sales stimulated by fears of shortages during the Korean War, but the boom turned out to be a bust as shortages never developed and huge inventories of unsold watches led to price cutting, production cutbacks and worker layoffs."[11]

In 1950, Hamilton's total dollars in watch sales were $18,719,000; in 1951 it dropped to approximately $16,000,000 and in 1952 it dropped to $14,000,000.[12] It was partially because of these disappointing results that Luckey at the end of May 1952 announced the plans to import cheaper Swiss-made watches. Although Hamilton sought in this way to increase its profits and improve its competitive position, Luckey assured its shareholders and employees that these imports would not impact Hamilton's domestic production.

Luckey explained that this move was necessary owing to two factors: (1) Swiss watch imports went from $8 million in 1950 to $11 million in 1951; and (2) President Truman rejected any tariff relief to increase duties on imported watches.[13]

In a simultaneous action, effective August 1, 1952, Hamilton eliminated distribution through wholesalers as it moved to sell directly to over 12,000 retail jewelers throughout the country, via a newly recruited staff of salesmen. Further reflecting Hamilton's financial concerns was that it omitted its quarterly dividend on its common stock.[14]

Added to Hamilton's woes during 1952 was the threat of a takeover by the Benrus Watch Company. Benrus, by the early 1950s, had overtaken Hamilton and become the third largest watch company in the United States, behind Bulova and Elgin. Benrus watches ranged in retail price from $24.75 up; Hamilton's from $49.50 up. In 1952, Hamilton began to import Swiss movements for sale in the United States under the name of "Illinois"; this line of watches was to retail from about $30.00. Beginning in 1952, Benrus had quietly begun purchasing Hamilton stock on the open market. By mid-1952 it owned 10%, and by early 1953 owned over 24% of Hamilton's outstanding stock. This percentage of ownership would have allowed Benrus to appoint one new member to the board of directors per year and thus potentially have access to Hamilton's confidential information. While fighting these threats, Hamilton suffered a loss of over $670,746.00 in the first quarter of 1952. An additional difficulty for Hamilton was that since 1950 the Hamilton management had been reorganized, two successive presidents and a vice president in charge of sales having died.[15]

ILLINOIS

Fine Watches at Modest Prices

. . . for WOMEN **. . . for MEN**

ILLINOIS DIVISION

HAMILTON WATCH COMPANY

LANCASTER, PENNSYLVANIA

1954 Price List

1952 QUARTERLY LOSS

Hamilton's president, George P. Luckey, blamed the company's 1952 first-quarter loss of $670,746.00 on the U.S. Government, complaining of "the indecisive policies of government procurement agencies, burdensome income and other taxes which have drained off consumer purchasing power and imports of foreign watches which have glutted the United States market." (He reiterated these points, among others, in the announcement he made a few weeks later about Hamilton's new line of watches.)

Hamilton Watch Losses Blamed On Government

LANCASTER, April 28 –(INS) The Hamilton Watch company's loss of $670,746 in 1952 first quarter earnings today prompted President Charles P. Luckey to blame government taxes and defense procurement policies plus foreign importations.

Luckey contrasted what he called "the unprecedented first quarter loss" with a profit of $130,177 in the corresponding period last year.

He credited the loss to "the indecisive policies of government procurement agencies, burdensome income and other taxes which have drained off consumer purchasing power and imports of foreign watches which have glutted the United States market."

He expressed the hope that the loss can be offset by increased sale and the untangling procurement policies which have snarled Hamilton's production.

"Hamilton's defense production," said Luckey, "has been delayed over many months by repeated changes in specifications and poor deliveries of certain components.

"It is expected that this situation will clear up and our deliveries will improve."

Higher income tax and other taxes in the first quarter of 1952, he added, "aggravated normal seasonal sales problems" which reflect importations of the jeweled watches made by "cheap foreign labor" and distress liquidation of such merchandise.

Somerset Daily American (Somerset, PA), April 29, 1952; image from *newspapers.com*. Luckey's first name is given there as "Charles," which is incorrect.

BENRUS WATCH COMPANY SUED BY HAMILTON

HAMILTON INJUNCTION IS SUSTAINED

Intelligencer Journal (Lancaster, PA), July 2, 1953

Hamilton, to counter Benrus's aggressive posture, filed an antitrust action in Federal Court under the Clayton Act, alleging that the action by Benrus would serve to substantially lessen interstate commerce in the watch industry. Hamilton also sought an injunction to prevent Benrus from voting its stock. The request for the injunction was granted by the court. As a result, Benrus divested its Hamilton shares and dropped its plans for taking over Hamilton. However, Hamilton's actions provided little respite; by the middle of 1954, employment in the watch industry of the United States had dropped to four thousand from a postwar high of over ten thousand in 1948.[16]

Although Hamilton introduced weekly closures in certain months to cut costs and preserve employment, it also laid off employees in response to the decreased demand. Some of Hamilton's layoffs were temporary; others were permanent. According to Sauers, most of the layoffs at Elgin and Waltham were permanent. Waltham "filed for bankruptcy in 1949, then reorganized, struggled for a few more years, and finally folded in 1957."[17]

Elgin's fall took even longer. It paid its last dividend in 1957. Then, to cut labor costs, it opened an assembly plant in South Carolina in 1963. The main plant in Elgin, Illinois, was declared obsolete and sold in 1965. The South Carolina facility was shut down by 1967. "Under new ownership the company assembled some watches in New York using imported movements but, in the early '70's, ended all domestic watch production."[18]

Hamilton, notwithstanding its treatment of Illinois following the acquisition, always was striving to do what it deemed best for the Hamilton shareholders and its employees. This was only natural, and it is unfair to be unreasonably harsh towards Hamilton about the ultimate fate of Illinois under its control; with better planning by Hamilton and less panic in the 1930s, Illinois could likely have survived as well. However, partly because of those actions, the Hamilton company was able to last in the fiercely competitive watch market as long as any of its domestic competitors; that, in and of itself, was a fine achievement.

Hamilton-Illinois Ébauches (Movements)

Hamilton's records show a lot about what movements it selected for the Hamilton-Illinois project, what suppliers it used, and how it kept track of the results. Most of the Swiss Hamilton-Illinois watch movements were manufactured for Hamilton by ETA SA Manufacture Horlogère Suisse (ETA SA, Swiss Horological Manufactory). Some were made by the A. Schild Company and at least one by Kurth Frères. ETA provided both manual- and automatic-winding mechanical movements for this special line of watches for Hamilton.

ETA

ETA was founded by Eterna in 1856, but some parts of its production line can be traced to the 1793 founding of Fabriques d'Horlogerie de Fontainemelon (FHF). Currently, after a series of mergers (including Valjoux, Peseux and Lemania), ETA has become the largest manufacturer of Swiss watch movements and now controls a virtual monopoly over movement production and supply. Owing to its market dominance, ETA has been subject to several Swiss government investigations. As a result, ETA's business practices are governed to a certain extent by an agreement with the Swiss government and its regulators.

Today, ETA is located in Grenchen, Switzerland, and is now a wholly-owned subsidiary of the Swatch Group, Ltd. Currently, ETA supplies an overwhelming majority of movements found in Swiss watches. These movements are considered the workhorses of this industry.[19]

ETA IN THE SWISS WATCH INDUSTRY

According to wristwatch expert and author Bruce Shawkey, "ETA was an offshoot of Eterna. Eterna was making its own watches, but also selling ébauches to other companies. So eventually, they formed this subsidiary for the express purpose of making ébauches to supply other companies. Eventually, they became part of Ébauches SA in the late 1920s/early 1930s to control the manufacture and distribution of ébauches across the industry. Eventually, 17 companies would comprise Ébauches SA, including ETA.

"There have been a whole series of consolidations in the Swiss watchmaking industry over the years. Now, it is as if the child has become the parent because there is no more Ébauches SA. All the companies that made up Ébauches SA have either gone out of business, or were absorbed by ETA. So now, ETA SA holds a virtual monopoly on the manufacture of mechanical movements. But, paradoxically enough, the company is itself a wholly owned subsidiary of Swatch Group Ltd., which of course is the mother of all watch companies. They own Breguet, Blancpain, Glashütte Original, Jaquet Droz, Léon Hatot, Omega, Longines, Rado, Union Glashütte, Tissot, Calvin Klein Watches + Jewelry, Balmain, Certina, Mido, Hamilton, Swatch, Flik Flak, Endura, and Tourbillon. And with a few exceptions, most of the companies obtain their mechanical ébauches from ETA SA. But back in the day when ETA was supplying ébauches for Hamilton-Illinois watches (and Hamilton watches) they were a completely different (and obviously smaller) company."*

*Bruce Shawkey, email exchanges with the author, October 18, 2012

A. Schild Company

In addition to purchasing its first Swiss movements from ETA, Hamilton also purchased Swiss-made movements from A. Schild Company. It appears that the A. Schild movements were used in the Hamilton-Illinois ladies' models.

Anthony Young provides the following information about the company:

> Adolph Schild-Hugi opened his ébauche and movement manufacture in Grenchen, within the canton of Solothurn, in the late 1890s. He offered his manual-wind calibers in all sizes and quickly became one of the largest movement makers in Switzerland, eventually employing more than 2,000 people. During the course of the company's history, it manufactured several hundred different calibers.
>
> In 1926, A. Schild, along with AD Michel SA in Grenchen and FHF in Fontainmelon, formed Ēbauches SA. Each company kept its identity and manufacturing base and among the three factories produced about 75 percent of all the ébauches in Switzerland. The A. Schild movements were identified starting in 1939 by an ébauche stamp under the balance wheel consisting of a shield outline with the capital letters AS inside.
>
> A. Schild did not venture into the popular chronograph segment as that form of complication would have added dramatically to manufacturing cost and warranty servicing, so it was left to other makers like Valjoux and Lémania to fill that niche. Instead, the company focused on affordable, reliable three-hand and date movements. It survived the economic depression of the 1930s, the commercial lull during World War II and experienced dramatic growth in the 1950s and 1960s.
>
> The crisis for A. Schild came in the late 1970s with the advent of quartz development and a severe recession. Between 1978 and 1979 the company merged with ETA (also in Grenchen) and reduced its caliber production by two-thirds.[20]

Kurth Frères

Hamilton also purchased at least one automatic movement from Kurth Frères of Grenchen, Switzerland, for its grade 658 (as explained in the following internal Hamilton memorandum, dated October 20, 1953).

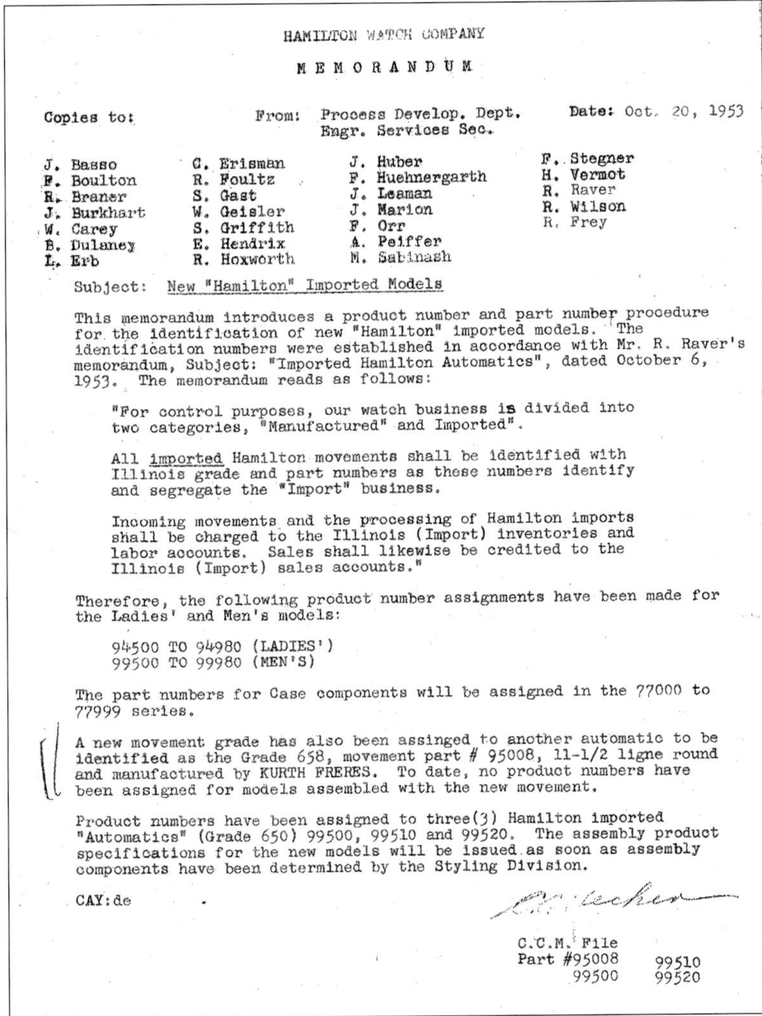

HAMILTON WATCH COMPANY

M E M O R A N D U M

Copies to: From: Process Develop. Dept. Engr. Services Sec. Date: Oct. 20, 1953

J. Basso	C. Erisman	J. Huber	F. Stegner
F. Boulton	R. Foultz	F. Huehnergarth	H. Vermot
R. Braner	S. Gast	J. Leaman	R. Raver
J. Burkhart	W. Geisler	J. Marion	R. Wilson
W. Carey	S. Griffith	F. Orr	R. Frey
B. Dulaney	E. Hendrix	A. Peiffer	
L. Erb	R. Hoxworth	M. Sabinash	

Subject: New "Hamilton" Imported Models

This memorandum introduces a product number and part number procedure for the identification of new "Hamilton" imported models. The identification numbers were established in accordance with Mr. R. Raver's memorandum, Subject: "Imported Hamilton Automatics", dated October 6, 1953. The memorandum reads as follows:

"For control purposes, our watch business is divided into two categories, "Manufactured" and Imported".

All imported Hamilton movements shall be identified with Illinois grade and part numbers as these numbers identify and segregate the "Import" business.

Incoming movements and the processing of Hamilton imports shall be charged to the Illinois (Import) inventories and labor accounts. Sales shall likewise be credited to the Illinois (Import) sales accounts."

Therefore, the following product number assignments have been made for the Ladies' and Men's models:

94500 TO 94980 (LADIES')
99500 TO 99980 (MEN'S)

The part numbers for Case components will be assigned in the 77000 to 77999 series.

A new movement grade has also been assinged to another automatic to be identified as the Grade 658, movement part # 95008, 11-1/2 ligne round and manufactured by KURTH FRERES. To date, no product numbers have been assigned for models assembled with the new movement.

Product numbers have been assigned to three(3) Hamilton imported "Automatics" (Grade 650) 99500, 99510 and 99520. The assembly product specifications for the new models will be issued as soon as assembly components have been determined by the Styling Division.

CAY:de

C.C.M. File
Part #95008 99510
99500 99520

Hamilton internal memorandum, October 20, 1953

Certina Kurth Frères is a Swiss luxury watchmaker company founded in Grenchen in 1888 by Adolph and Alfred Kurth. Not surprisingly, they are now owned by the ubiquitous SWATCH group.

Incabloc, S.A.

In addition to ébauche makers ETA, A. Schild, and Kurth, another Swiss company was involved in the fabrication of the Hamilton-Illinois models.

Certain of these models were shockproof: the ones that were almost always labeled INCABLOC on the dial. As a result, many of these dials were signed Hamilton, Illinois and Incabloc.

The Incabloc shock protection system was invented in 1934 by Swiss engineers Georges Braunschweig and Fritz Marti at Universal Escapement, Ltd., of La Chaux-de-Fonds, Switzerland. It is manufactured by Incabloc, S.A. The majority of the watches made in Switzerland today use this system to protect their balance-staff pivots from shocks.[21]

The common Incabloc spring, illustration from Mike Gorlewski's *"Shock Absorbers: A Magical Part,"* NAWCC *Bulletin* (Sept./Oct. 2014), p. 490

An "Incabloc" Mystery. On the Hamilton list of "Illinois Finished Movements" there is another fascinating discovery. It appears, as indicated in Chapter 6 (Movements), that Hamilton at some point requested Illinois in the 1930s to develop a "25/0 size Illinois Incabloc Shock Absorbing Device." There is a notation on Hamilton's internal records that it was an "Unfinished Model." This project was described by Halligan in the 1940s in his sales research, so he probably called this "Shock Absorbing Device" project "Incabloc" after the fact, as Incabloc itself was the first to produce one. Therefore, it is likely that Hamilton attempted to develop its own shock-absorbing movement via its Illinois Watch Division in the early 1930s, well before purchasing it from the Swiss manufacturer ETA. By 1956, the "make or buy" decision for Hamilton became much easier as its then president Luckey made the extremely difficult major decision to pull the plug on the manufacturing of movements in Lancaster in favor of importing Swiss-manufactured movements for all of Hamilton's watches.

HAMILTON'S VIEW OF INCABLOC

In an internal Hamilton "Trip to Switzerland" report from April 17 to May 9, 1955, J. C. Brooks notes from his factory visits that "INCABLOC produces the shockproofing unit used on our men's wrist watches.

"Bolts are produced on a Progressive Roll-Fed Die. Blocks are produced on a 9 station-merry-go-round machine that has 7 processing stations, one unloading station and a loading station, all finished operations are completed in 3½ seconds.

"Retaining springs are assembled to the block by hand."

This report also noted VIBAGRAM was part of Incabloc and manufactured timing machines. It had one machine that tests all different beat watches.

Finally, Brooks noted that Kurth Frères (Certina), a watch assembly and parts house, made "all the parts except the hairspring, mainspring, and the balance wheel and produces the Hamilton Automatic."*

**Source*: HRC:NAWCC.

Swiss Movement Grades and Production Quantities

Hamilton apparently converted the Swiss movement grades to its own movement nomenclature. Some of these conversions are in the table below.

Swiss movements used by Hamilton*

Swiss Model	Hamilton Grade	Production Quantities
AS 1406	600	156,747
AS 976	601	33,397
AS 1240	602	10,132
ETA 1248T (Eternamatic)	650	12,055
Eterna (ETA)	650-659	
ETA 1256 (Etarotor)	651	26,011
ETA 1256 (Indimatic)	652	24,443
AS 1201	653	11,346
ETA 1081	654	21,290
ETA 1220	655	
ETA 1190	656	10,421
AS 1200	657	19,841
ETA 1258	660	6,011
ETA 1257	Unknown	
Kurth 25-55	658**	16,123
ETA 1248T	659**	8,440
Kurth 25-45	661**	104,269
Kurth 25-45	662**	3,600
	664**	1
	671**	1,916
	672**	2,310

*After 1995, many of the above movements were then used in the Hamilton cognates of the Hamilton-Illinois models
**Only for Hamilton Models

The performance of the first ETA movements was tracked by Hamilton's head watchmaker, R. W. Slaugh, who issued the table of "Ratio of Free Service to Previous Year's Sales by Grades." This table also shows at the bottom the 1953 sales numbers and returns for that year for the ETA 1256 (grades 651 and 652), ETA 1258 and Eterna (grades 650–659) movements. See Appendix 7 for the Hamilton-Illinois watches' partial factory specification sheets and Appendix 8 for the ETA factory specifications for the ETA 1256 movement.

TABLE V

RATIO OF FREE SERVICE TO PREVIOUS YEAR'S SALES BY GRADES

DOMESTIC

GRADE		SIZE	REMARKS	1953 SALES	1954 RETURNS	PERCENT
750		21/0	17J	216,957	5,839	2.70%
751		21/0	17J	20,215	662	3.22
TOTAL LADIES				237,172	6,501	2.75
752		12/0	17J	25,307	144	.57%
753		12/0	19J	40,080	273	.67
754		12/0	19J	19,756	173	.88
747		8/0	17J	34,540	645	1.86
748		8/0	Center Sec.	42,038	1,174	2.80
TOTAL MEN'S STRAP				161,721	2,409	1.49
917		10	17J	5,168	45	.88%
921		10	21J	2,000	30	1.50
923		10	23J	67	0	0
TOTAL POCKET				7,235	75	1.04
992B		16	21J	26,873	228	.85%
950B		16	23J	2,769	57	2.05
TOTAL RAILROAD				29,642	285	.96
IMPORTED						
	SWISS CAL.					
600	FHF 60	6-3/4x8		10,310	73	.71%
601	AS 976	5		1,693	25	1.47
602	AS 1240	8	Center Sec.	1,602	21	1.30
TOTAL LADIES				13,605	129	.95
653	AS 1201	11-1/2		1,618	26	1.61%
654	ETA 1081	11-1/2	Center Sec.	3,869	78	2.02
655	ETA 1220	8 x 9		2,148	24	1.12
656	ETA 1190	8 x 9	Center Sec.	381	8	2.10
657	AS 1200	10-1/2		1,414	7	.50
TOTAL MEN'S STRAP MANUAL WIND				9,430	143	1.52
650-659	ETERNA	11-1/2	Ill. & Ham.	4,769	272	5.70%
651	ETA 1256	11-1/2	Ill. Auto.	2,612	141	5.40
652	ETA 1256	11-1/2	Ill. Signamatic	2,368	103	4.35
660	ETA 1258	11-1/2	Ill. Datomatic	0*	5	-
658	Kurth 25-55	11-1/2	Ham. Screw Rotor	0*	279	-
661	Kurth 25-45	11-1/2	Ham. Bolt Rotor	0*	16	-
662	Kurth 25-45	11-1/2	Ham. Calendar	0*	0	-
TOTAL MEN'S AUTOMATIC				9,749	816	-

* Not sold in 1953.

Hamilton product performance study November 16, 1954, by R. W. Slaugh, Head Watchmaker; HRC:NAWCC

Hamilton-Illinois Casemakers

For most of its Hamilton-Illinois models, Hamilton turned to the American casemakers who supplied cases for its primary business. The most frequently used company for these new lines was Schwab and Wuischpard, followed by Star. A couple of cases were made by Pioneer. (More about these companies can be found in Chapter 8.) For some special models with elaborate diamond bezels, Hamilton turned to the Major Watch Case Company, which was already in use by the customer that may have commissioned these watches, Zale's Jewelers. Cases for the Hamilton-Illinois models in stainless steel were made by the Swiss manufacturer Huguenin.

Hamilton used the Pioneer Watch Case Company for only two Hamilton-Illinois models, the Debonair Model K and the Lady Gay Model E. These cases are marked only by a "P" in an inverted triangle, and the identity of the symbol was for a long time unknown. (The inside case back of Hamilton's Lamar model was marked the same way.) Fortunately, we learned from Jack Wood, a Gruen specialist, that he had a Gruen wristwatch with the Pioneer name inside the case back and the mystery symbol outside, which confirms that the mark is for Pioneer. He has kindly provided the accompanying photographs for documentation.

Wood's photographs are of the case back of a Gruen waterproof watch likely from the early 1940s; the patent marked on the case dates from 1941. Like the cases Pioneer later made for Hamilton, this Gruen has a gold-filled bezel and stainless steel back. The patent itself is for a "water tight watchcase."

Inside case back of Debonair Model K, showing Pioneer symbol

Inside case back of Gruen case by Pioneer

Outside of Gruen case, showing Pioneer symbol

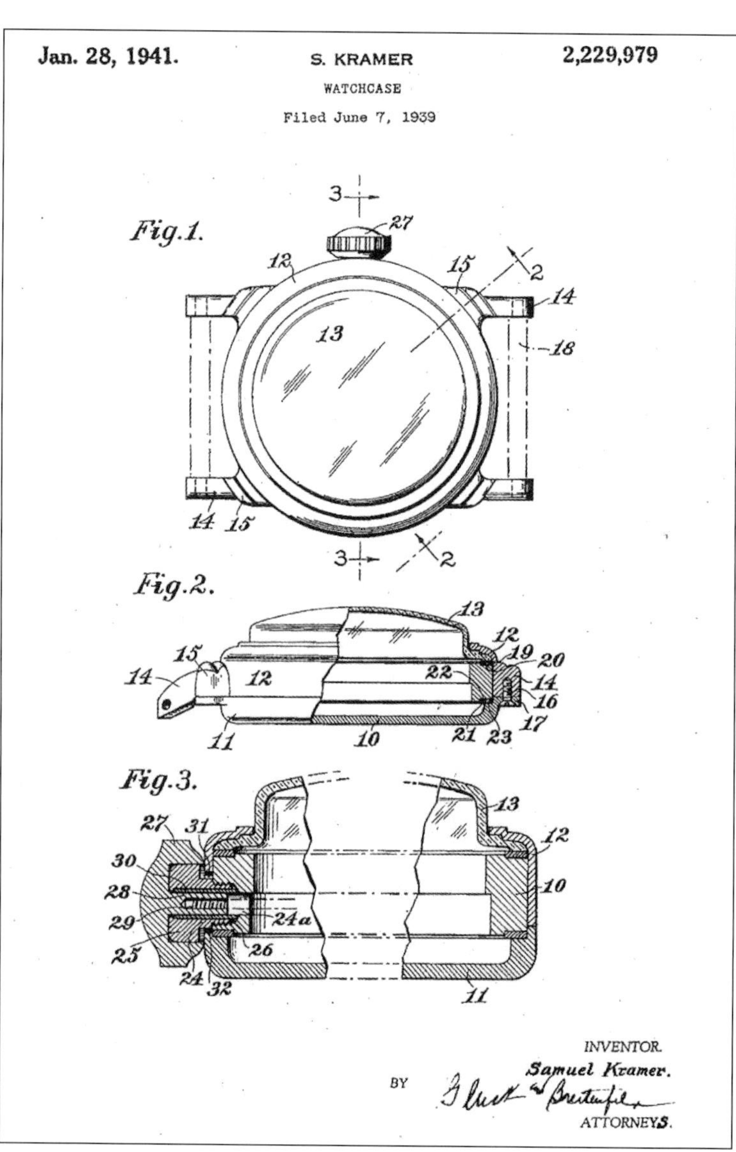

Pioneer Patent

Complete Watches

All but five of the Swiss movements purchased by Hamilton were assembled into cases at the Hamilton factory in Lancaster. The models that were purchased as complete watches were the Career Girl Model A, the Automatic Model B, the Nautilus Model A, the Signamatic Model A, and the Signamatic Model B. The stainless steel cases for all of these models were manufactured by Huguenin Frères.

HUGUENIN FRÈRES

Huguenin was an old maker of medallions, founded in 1868, which had supplemented its income during the Depression by making watch cases. Their logo was originally an artist's palette with the letters "HF" and the word "Niel", for the niello process used to decorate their medallions. For the watch cases, this logo was simplified to show just the initials.

Huguenin Frères logo from 1888

Huguenin Frères logo from the case of a Signamatic Model B

Hamilton must have liked the work done by Huguenin Frères: in 1955 they bought the watch-case business from them. The company still exists as Faude & Huguenin SA, makers of medals, trophies, jewelry and commemorative coins in Le Locle, Switzerland.

Replacement Parts

Hamilton instructed jewelers and watchmakers to order replacement parts for Hamilton-Illinois watches from their regular Material Supply House, or from Eterna Watch Co. of America, Inc. on Fifth Avenue in New York City. This notification appears in the early Hamilton-Illinois sales catalogs.

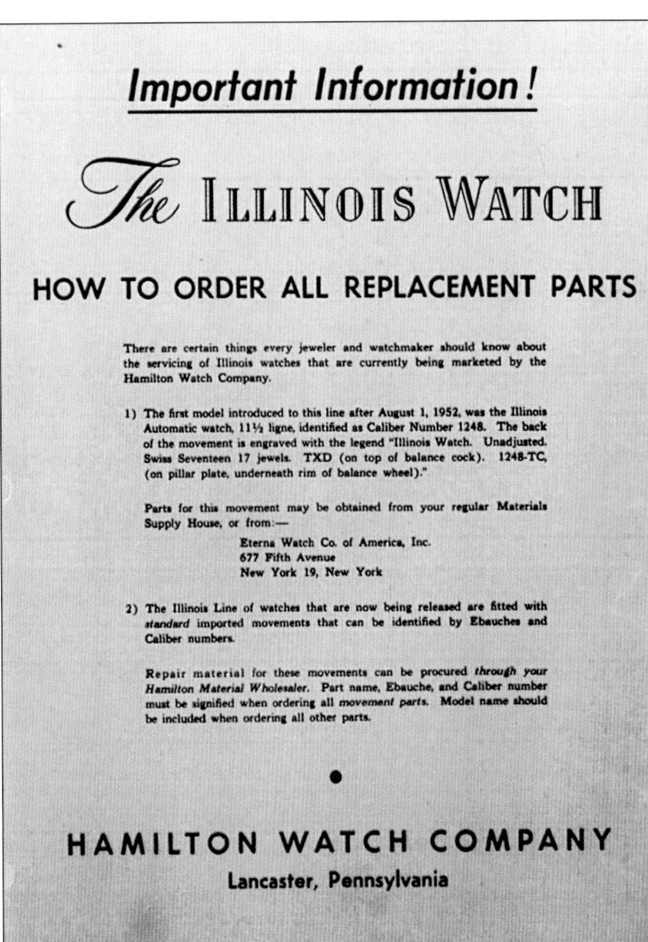

Important Information!

The ILLINOIS WATCH

HOW TO ORDER ALL REPLACEMENT PARTS

There are certain things every jeweler and watchmaker should know about the servicing of Illinois watches that are currently being marketed by the Hamilton Watch Company.

1) The first model introduced to this line after August 1, 1952, was the Illinois Automatic watch, 11½ ligne, identified as Caliber Number 1248. The back of the movement is engraved with the legend "Illinois Watch. Unadjusted. Swiss Seventeen 17 jewels. TXD (on top of balance cock). 1248-TC, (on pillar plate, underneath rim of balance wheel)."

   Parts for this movement may be obtained from your regular Materials Supply House, or from:—

   Eterna Watch Co. of America, Inc.
   677 Fifth Avenue
   New York 19, New York

2) The Illinois Line of watches that are now being released are fitted with *standard* imported movements that can be identified by Ebauches and Caliber numbers.

   Repair material for these movements can be procured *through your Hamilton Material Wholesaler.* Part name, Ebauche, and Caliber number must be signified when ordering all *movement parts.* Model name should be included when ordering all other parts.

•

HAMILTON WATCH COMPANY
Lancaster, Pennsylvania

Instructions for ordering Hamilton-Illinois replacement parts

The Uncollected Watches: Hidden Gems?

Strangely enough, the collector world has yet to discover or embrace the retro appeal and Mid-Century Modern design of the Hamilton-Illinois wristwatches. For that reason, it has been difficult to find photographs for the Hamilton-Illinois Identification Guide. One pair of collectors, however, have accumulated a significant number of Hamilton-Illinois watches, and their collection has been the source for many of the photographs in this section. In an effort to be consistent in appearance, many of the illustrations of the watches depicted here have been taken from Hamilton sales catalogs for 1953, 1954 and 1955. Finally, there are instances in which we know the name of the watch and perhaps some of its specifications, but do not have an image of the watch. A determined effort has been made to uncover all of the details of these hidden gems but this effort still remains somewhat a work-in-progress. Therefore the Identification Guide for some models is not complete.

One might ask whether the Hamilton-Illinois experiment was a failure. At first glance, it might seem so: this line of watches appeared, lasted three years, and then abruptly disappeared from Hamilton's product line. The watches themselves are what Hamilton intended them to be, inexpensive watches of competent design and manufacture. There is little to distinguish them from other watches of similar types that were being sold on the American market in the same era. Neither the cases nor the movements are representative of the finest horological work that was being done in either Switzerland or America. Nonetheless, these watches have turned out to be durable and are still affordable for collectors. The ETA movements, in particular, have turned out to be quite durable, perhaps because of the Incabloc shock protectors.

So far as the Illinois name was concerned, and for those who might still remember Illinois wristwatches of the 1920s and early 1930s, the experiment might be deemed a disappointment. But from the perspective of the Hamilton Watch Company, it might be considered a success. The number of watches from the Hamilton-Illinois line that continued into the Hamilton line is a partial indication of what the company thought. But Hamilton also learned from the experiment that Swiss movements were durable enough for American buyers and that it could sell watches with such movements without destroying the Hamilton brand. And that is perhaps the most significant outcome of the experiment because it helped Hamilton outlast the other American manufacturers that were older and had been much larger than it was. And for the collector, the Hamilton-Illinois line may become another significant area of interest.

14K SOLID GOLD

René Rondeau thinks that collecting Hamilton-Illinois would be both fascinating and challenging. He believes that there are some uncataloged Hamilton-Illinois men's models in addition to those listed in this chapter. He once saw a photograph of one with its original box and label noting that it was "14K solid gold." As Rondeau points out, this flies in the face of the line being a bargain-priced one.

Very recently a watch has come to light that might be the very sort of thing Rondeau saw; it has been positively identified as the Golden Male "A," and it is included in the alphabetic listings of men's models in the identification guide in this chapter. Since then, two more specimens of this model have been found. Now it appears likely that this was not an isolated model, but instead part of a series: other 14K models, different from each other as well as from the Golden Male "A," surfaced right before this work was going to press! (For details, see the **Golden Male "A"** listing in the identification guide.)

There are also at least two Hamilton-Illinois ladies' models in 14K white gold with diamonds that are also apparently uncataloged. Until they are identified, they will be called Model No. 5312 and Model No. 5557 after their case model numbers. A third solid gold ladies' watch, in two-tone 14K, with diamonds, has also been found; it has no case model number. These watches appear in the listings of ladies' models in the identification guide.

Search Process

In an attempt to learn the details of the Hamilton-Illinois wristwatches, the following research steps were undertaken:

- Searched all available Hamilton archives
- Consulted with Hamilton and Illinois experts and collectors
- Reviewed all Hamilton watch catalogs for 1953, 1954 and 1955
- Reviewed all Hamilton advertisements for 1953, 1954 and 1955
- Reviewed Hamilton Watch Company partial factory specification records for these models. Much of this material is shown in the Identification Guide for Hamilton-Illinois wristwatches and in Appendix 7, which contains various Hamilton factory specification sheets for many of these models.
- Reviewed all Hamilton documents and records in the Hamilton—Ravel Collection, NAWCC [National Association of Watch and Clock Collectors] Library and Research Center.

The Product Lines

In its 1954 catalog, Hamilton advertised that the Hamilton/Illinois men's watches were:

> For the budget-conscious man who demands reliable performance, his choice should be Hamilton-Illinois. These watches are carefully checked at the Hamilton factory to be sure that they conform to the high technical standards set by Hamilton engineers. And remember, every Hamilton/Illinois watch is:
>
> FULLY JEWELED
> DUST PROOF
> LIFETIME MAINSPRING
> SHOCK RESISTANT
> ANTI-MAGNETIC

Many are also WATERPROOF.

The ladies' watches were introduced in similar fashion:

> With moderate price and dependable performance, Hamilton-Illinois ladies' watches are the finest in the low price field. Timed and tested at the Hamilton factory, these outstanding watches meet all the rigid standards prescribed by Hamilton engineers.
>
> FULLY JEWELED
> DUST PROOF
> LIFETIME MAINSPRING
> ANTI-MAGNETIC

Those descriptions are a good summary for the whole product line. Even though 1955 was the last year Hamilton offered these watches under the Hamilton-Illinois name, the company remained consistent in its goals for the line and its marketing. Hamilton was inconsistent in some of its terminology, however. In the 1953 catalog, it used "waterproof" and "shockproof" for the relevant models. In the 1954 catalog, Hamilton used the terms "water resistant" and "shock resistant" for both the Hamilton-Illinois line and for the earliest automatic watches introduced under the Hamilton name. In 1955 the original terminology returned for both lines, and descriptive blocks like those for Hamilton-Illinois also appeared for Hamilton.

One of the most significant aspects of the Hamilton-Illinois project was that it was how self-winding watches were introduced to Hamilton's product line. Self-winding, or "automatic" watches had been available in the American market since before the war, as Swiss imports. Elgin had already experimented with bumper automatics and would go on to introduce its remarkably advanced 760 and 761 self-winding watches with free-sprung balances only a few years after Hamilton's succumbing to Swiss movements. But Hamilton's R&D resources were already concentrating on the company's project for an electric watch and it probably could not afford to create yet another new kind of movement. So it turned to Eterna and the proven ETA 1248 and 1256/1257 movements.

The 1953 Hamilton and Illinois Watch Catalogue emphasized that its Automatic Series were: "AUTOMATIC . . . SELF WINDING . . . WATERPROOF" adding that "These Automatics are superb examples of expert watchmakers' ingenuity and skill. Normal wearing keeps them powered to tell accurate time day after day; just set them and forget them! The waterproof cases do more than seal out water and harmful dust. They seal in extra years of fine performance." This description set the stage for the Hamilton automatics that continue in production more than half a century later.

The automatic models in the Hamilton-Illinois line included Models A, B, and D, the Datomatic A, and the Signamatics A and B. (There was no cataloged Automatic C.) The A and D were in gold-filled cases; all the others were in stainless steel cases imported with the movements.

The other series models were the Debonair A, B, C, D, E, F, G, J, K, and L; and the Topper A and B. The Debonair series all had 10K rolled gold plate bezels and stainless steel backs. The Topper watches had 10K gold-filled cases, both bezel and back.

There was one other men's model: the Nautilus A. Like some of the automatics, it was in a Swiss stainless steel case. Although the Nautilus never grew into a series watch, the name appealed to Hamilton and it was later used repeatedly in Hamilton's own highly prized electric watch line.

The ladies' watches were similarly divided into series. Career Girl was two watches with sweep seconds hands, probably targeted at nurses. Lady Gay had rolled gold plate bezels and stainless steel backs. Coquette had gold-filled cases. Moving somewhat upscale, the Golden Treasure series had solid gold cases and the Kimberly models had diamonds on gold-filled cases. As with the men's watches, there were some uncataloged models with solid gold cases; some of these had diamond-set bezels.

A significant difference between the ladies' models and the men's is that dial designs were shared across several ladies' models. The men's models had unique dial designs, and several models had more than one dial option. Of course, the ladies' watches were much smaller than the men's and so offered a smaller palette for design.

Hamilton-Illinois Display Boxes

Most of the Hamilton-Illinois models came in interesting green leatherette–covered display boxes. When the lid of the box was opened, the watch inside, attached around a curved support arm, rotated from lying on its side to standing straight up and down. This box is shown below, closed and open.

Hamilton-Illinois display box

Open display box with Automatic Model B and papers

Hamilton-Illinois Models

Hamilton-Illinois Wristwatches Identified Models

Model Number	Model Name	Case Material
Unknown	Golden Male "A"	14K YG
Unknown	Golden Male "B"	14K YG
Unknown	Golden Male "C"	14K YG
Unknown	Unknown	14K WG/YG/Diamonds
5312	Unknown	14K WG/Diamonds
5557	Unknown	14K WG/Diamonds
9005	Golden Treasure Model A	10K WG
9006	Golden Treasure Model A	10K YG
9007	Golden Treasure Model B	10K WG
9008	Golden Treasure Model B	10K YG
9009	Kimberly Model A	WGF
9010	Coquette Model A	WGF
9011	Coquette Model A	YGF
9012	Kimberly Model B	WGF
9013	Kimberly Model B	YGF
9014	Lady Gay Model A	YRGP/SSB
9015	Lady Gay Model B	YRGP/SSB
9016	Lady Gay Model C	YRGP/SSB
9017	Lady Gay Model D	YRGP/SSB
9018	Coquette Model B	YGF
9019	Coquette Model C	WGF
9020	Coquette Model C	YGF
9021	Career Girl Model A	SS
9022	Career Girl Model B	RYGP/SSB
9023	Kimberly Model C	WGF
9024	Kimberly Model C	YGF
9025	Lady Gay Model F	YRGP/SSB
9036	Lady Gay Model G	WRGP/SSB
9027	Lady Gay Model H	YRGP/SSB
9028		
9029		
9030	Coquette Model E	YGF
9031	Coquette Model D	YGF
9032	Lady Gay Model K	YRGP/SSB
9033	Lady Gay Model K	WRGP/SSB
9034		
9035	Lady Gay Model F	WRGP/SSB
9036	Lady Gay Model G	YRGP/SSB
9037	Lady Gay Model H	WRGP/SSB
9038		
9039		
9040	Coquette Model E	WGF
9041	Coquette Model D	WGF
9042		
9045	Lady Gay Model E	YRGP/SSB
9046	Lady Gay Model E	WRGP/SSB
9505	Automatic Model A	YGF
9506	Debonair Model A	YRGP/SSB
9507	Debonair Model B	YRGP/SSB
9508	Debonair Model F	YRGP/SSB
9509	Topper Model A	YGF
9510	Topper Model B	YGF
9511	Debonair Model C	YRGP/SSB
9512	Debonair Model D	YRGP/SSB
9513	Debonair Model E	YRGP/SSB
9514	Nautilus Model A	SS
9515	Automatic Model B	SS
9516	Signamatic Model A	SS
9517	Automatic Model D	YGF
9518	Debonair Model J	YRGP/SSB
9519	Debonair Model K	YRGP/SSB
9520	Debonair Model L	YRGP/SSB
9521	Signamatic Model B	SS
9522	Datomatic Model A	SS
9523	Debonair Model G	YRGP/SSB

Red =Ladies
Black =Men's

Hamilton-Illinois Men's Models Identification Guide

Hamilton-Illinois sales catalog, 1953

AUTOMATICS

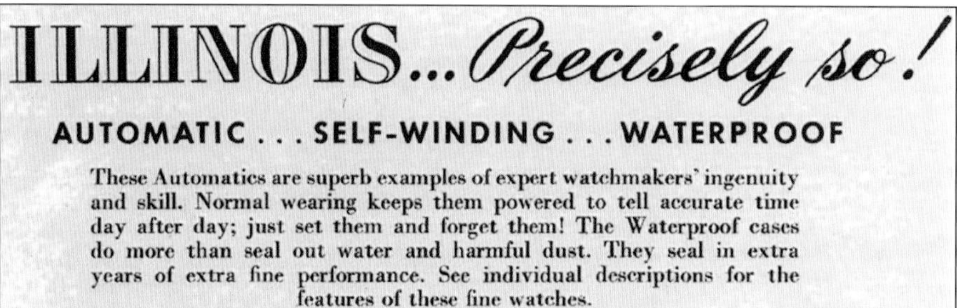

ILLINOIS... Precisely so!

AUTOMATIC . . . SELF-WINDING . . . WATERPROOF

These Automatics are superb examples of expert watchmakers' ingenuity and skill. Normal wearing keeps them powered to tell accurate time day after day; just set them and forget them! The Waterproof cases do more than seal out water and harmful dust. They seal in extra years of extra fine performance. See individual descriptions for the features of these fine watches.

The first statement about a Hamilton-Illinois self-winding watch, from the first Hamilton-Illinois catalog, 1953

Automatic Model A

AUTOMATIC MODEL A

The original Illinois Automatic and still a great favorite. Beautifully finished gold-filled case. Embossed numerals and markers. Sweep-seconds. 17 jewels, shock-proof, anti-magnetic.

Leather strap....950511.....$71.50

Name = Automatic Model A
Time Period = Mid-Century Modern
Karat/Material = 10K YGF
Bezel = Plain
Sides = Plain
Lug Size = 5/8
Spring Bar = Male
Model No. = 95050
Casemaker = Schwab and Wuischpard
Case Pieces = 2
Case Number = 95050
Dimensions = 32 x 41mm
Movement Grade/Jewels = Eternamatic, ETA 1248-T, 650/17 (11 ½ Ligne)
Dial Signed = Illinois Automatic
Dial Number = 9505/58000
Dial Shape = Round
Numbers = Embossed
Markers = Embossed
Hands = Brass
Seconds at = Sweep seconds
Anti-Magnetic = Yes
Shockproof = Yes
Waterproof = No
Dustproof = Yes
Automatic = Yes
Power Indicator = No
Cased in Factory = Yes
Retail Price New = $71.50, leather strap (1953)
Production Date = 1953
Unique Case Design = Yes
Unique Dial Design = Yes
Advertisement = Yes

The Automatic Model A was described in the 1953 Hamilton and Illinois Watch Catalog as "The original Illinois Automatic and still a great favorite. Beautifully finished gold-filled case. Embossed numerals and markers. Sweep seconds, 17 jewels, shockproof, anti-magnetic."

According to internal Hamilton records, 12,055 grade 650 Eternamatic movements were produced for its Hamilton-Illinois models.

Automatic Model A

ETA 1248-T movement

The Automatic A is still reasonably easy to find. The bezel holds up well, but the 10K case has a tendency to wear through on the back where a finger will rub when winding the watch by hand. The ETA 1248 movement, which was used only on this model, is quite durable.

Automatic Model A advertisement in the *Winona Republican-Herald* (Winona, MN), March 26, 1953; image from *newspapers.com*

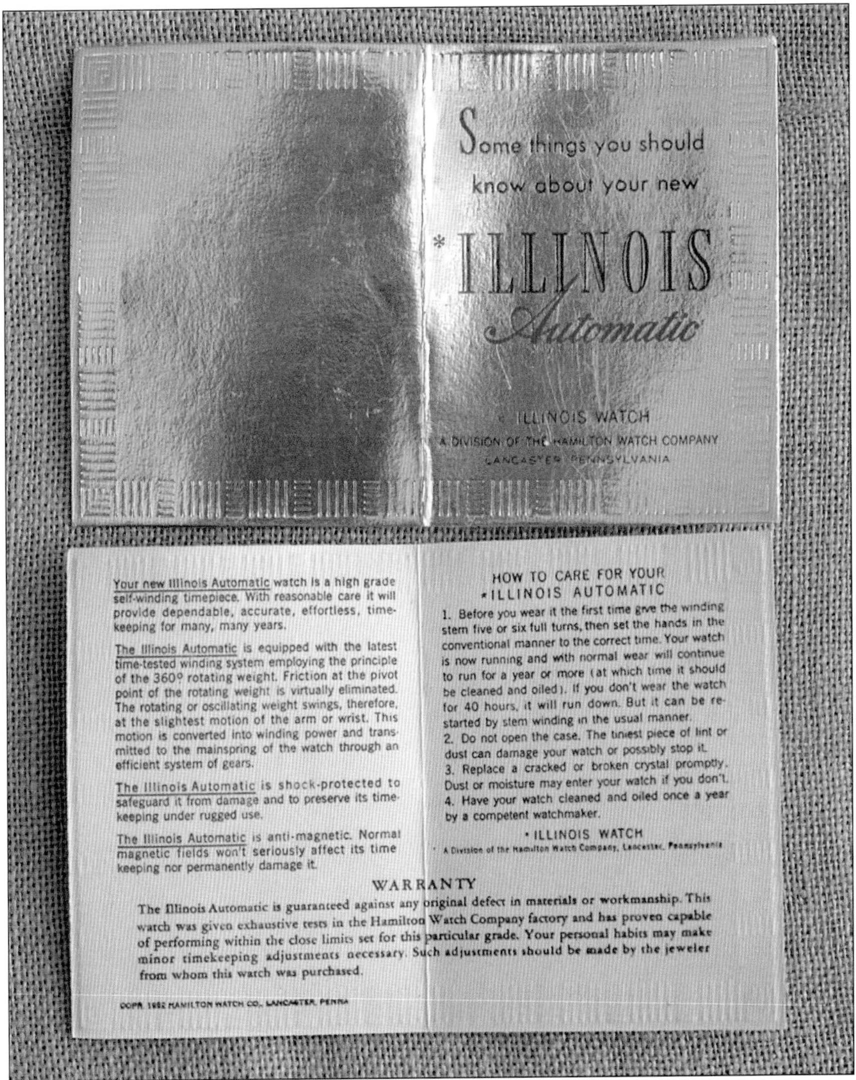

Some things you should know about your new

*ILLINOIS *Automatic*

• ILLINOIS WATCH
A DIVISION OF THE HAMILTON WATCH COMPANY
LANCASTER PENNSYLVANIA

Your new Illinois Automatic watch is a high grade self-winding timepiece. With reasonable care it will provide dependable, accurate, effortless, time-keeping for many, many years.

The Illinois Automatic is equipped with the latest time-tested winding system employing the principle of the 360° rotating weight. Friction at the pivot point of the rotating weight is virtually eliminated. The rotating or oscillating weight swings, therefore, at the slightest motion of the arm or wrist. This motion is converted into winding power and transmitted to the mainspring of the watch through an efficient system of gears.

The Illinois Automatic is shock-protected to safeguard it from damage and to preserve its time-keeping under rugged use.

The Illinois Automatic is anti-magnetic. Normal magnetic fields won't seriously affect its time keeping nor permanently damage it.

HOW TO CARE FOR YOUR
*ILLINOIS AUTOMATIC

1. Before you wear it the first time give the winding stem five or six full turns, then set the hands in the conventional manner to the correct time. Your watch is now running and with normal wear will continue to run for a year or more (at which time it should be cleaned and oiled). If you don't wear the watch for 40 hours, it will run down. But it can be re-started by stem winding in the usual manner.
2. Do not open the case. The tiniest piece of lint or dust can damage your watch or possibly stop it.
3. Replace a cracked or broken crystal promptly. Dust or moisture may enter your watch if you don't.
4. Have your watch cleaned and oiled once a year by a competent watchmaker.

• ILLINOIS WATCH
* A Division of the Hamilton Watch Company, Lancaster, Pennsylvania

WARRANTY

The Illinois Automatic is guaranteed against any original defect in materials or workmanship. This watch was given exhaustive tests in the Hamilton Watch Company factory and has proven capable of performing within the close limits set for this particular grade. Your personal habits may make minor timekeeping adjustments necessary. Such adjustments should be made by the jeweler from whom this watch was purchased.

COPR. 1952 HAMILTON WATCH CO., LANCASTER, PENNA

Original paperwork and warranty for an Automatic Model A

Hamilton-Illinois outer cardboard box and closed display case

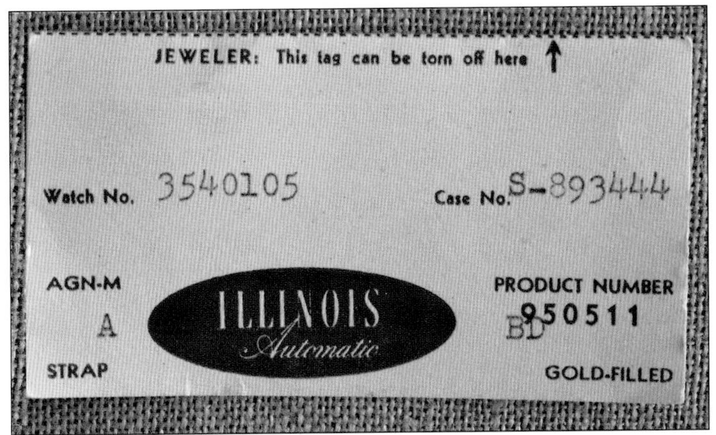

JEWELER: This tag can be torn off here ↑

Watch No. 3540105 Case No. S-893444

AGN-M
A
STRAP

ILLINOIS *Automatic*

PRODUCT NUMBER
BD 950511
GOLD-FILLED

A factory tag for the Automatic Model A, with serial numbers

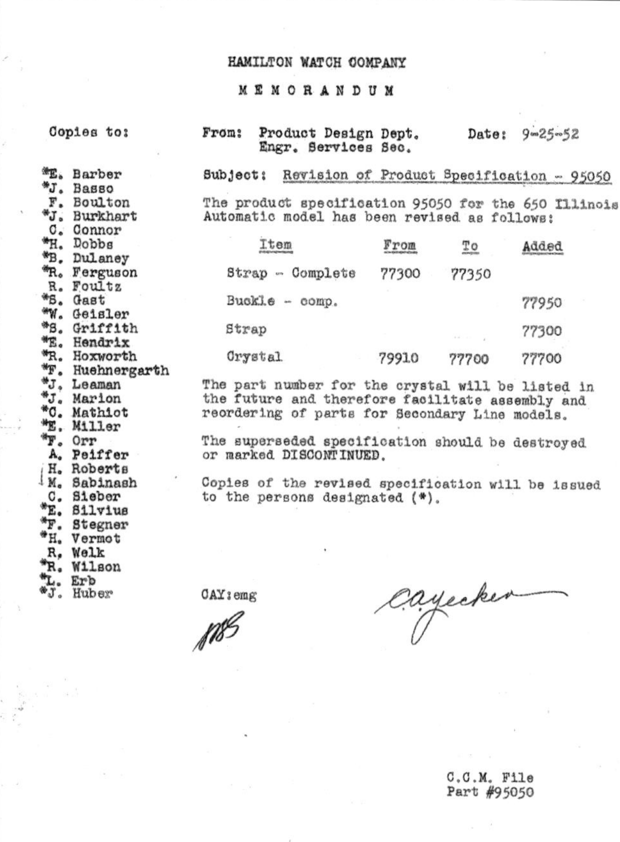

HAMILTON WATCH COMPANY

M E M O R A N D U M

Copies to:

*E. Barber
*J. Basso
F. Boulton
*J. Burkhart
C. Connor
*H. Dobbs
*B. Dulaney
*R. Ferguson
R. Foultz
*S. Gast
*W. Geisler
*S. Griffith
*E. Hendrix
*R. Hoxworth
*F. Huehnergarth
*J. Leaman
*J. Marion
*C. Mathiot
*E. Miller
*F. Orr
A. Peiffer
H. Roberts
M. Sabinash
C. Sieber
*E. Silvius
*F. Stegner
*H. Vermot
R. Welk
*R. Wilson
*L. Erb
*J. Huber

From: Product Design Dept.
Engr. Services Sec.

Date: 9-25-52

Subject: Revision of Product Specification - 95050

The product specification 95050 for the 650 Illinois Automatic model has been revised as follows:

Item	From	To	Added
Strap - Complete	77300	77350	
Buckle - comp.			77950
Strap			77300
Crystal	79910	77700	77700

The part number for the crystal will be listed in the future and therefore facilitate assembly and reordering of parts for Secondary Line models.

The superseded specification should be destroyed or marked DISCONTINUED.

Copies of the revised specification will be issued to the persons designated (*).

CAY:emg

C.C.M. File
Part #95050

Internal memorandum, dated September 25, 1952, advising of product specification changes for the Automatic Model A

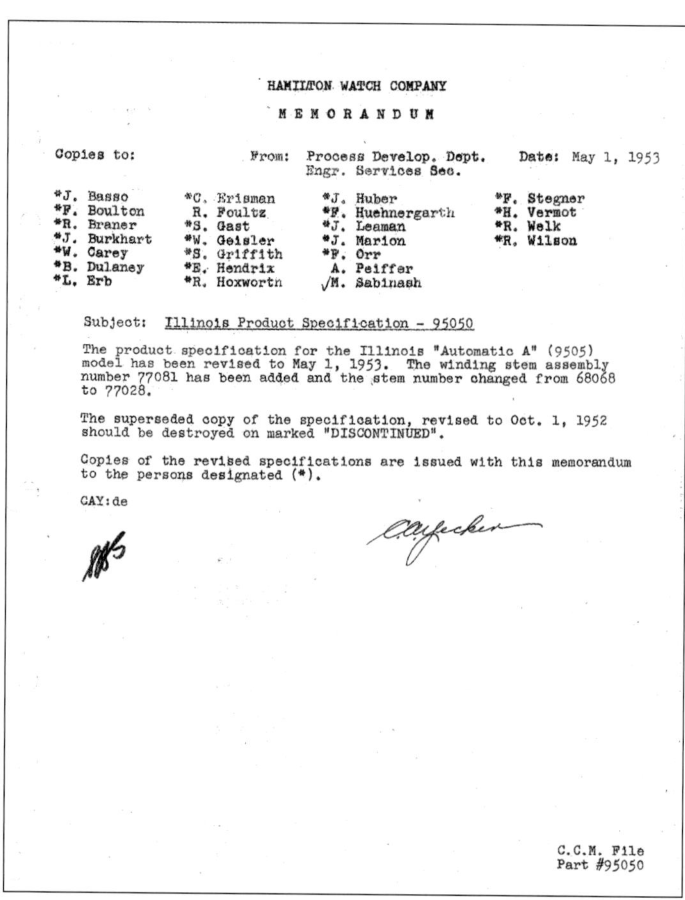

HAMILTON WATCH COMPANY

M E M O R A N D U M

Copies to:

From: Process Develop. Dept.
Engr. Services Sec.

Date: May 1, 1953

*J. Basso
*F. Boulton
*R. Braner
*J. Burkhart
*W. Carey
*B. Dulaney
*L. Erb
*C. Erisman
R. Foultz
*S. Gast
*W. Geisler
*S. Griffith
*E. Hendrix
*R. Hoxworth
*J. Huber
*F. Huehnergarth
*J. Leaman
*J. Marion
*F. Orr
A. Peiffer
√M. Sabinash
*F. Stegner
*H. Vermot
*R. Welk
*R. Wilson

Subject: Illinois Product Specification - 95050

The product specification for the Illinois "Automatic A" (9505) model has been revised to May 1, 1953. The winding stem assembly number 77081 has been added and the stem number changed from 68068 to 77028.

The superseded copy of the specification, revised to Oct. 1, 1952 should be destroyed on marked "DISCONTINUED".

Copies of the revised specifications are issued with this memorandum to the persons designated (*).

CAY:de

C.C.M. File
Part #95050

Internal memorandum, dated May 1, 1953, advising of a revision to the winding stem assembly

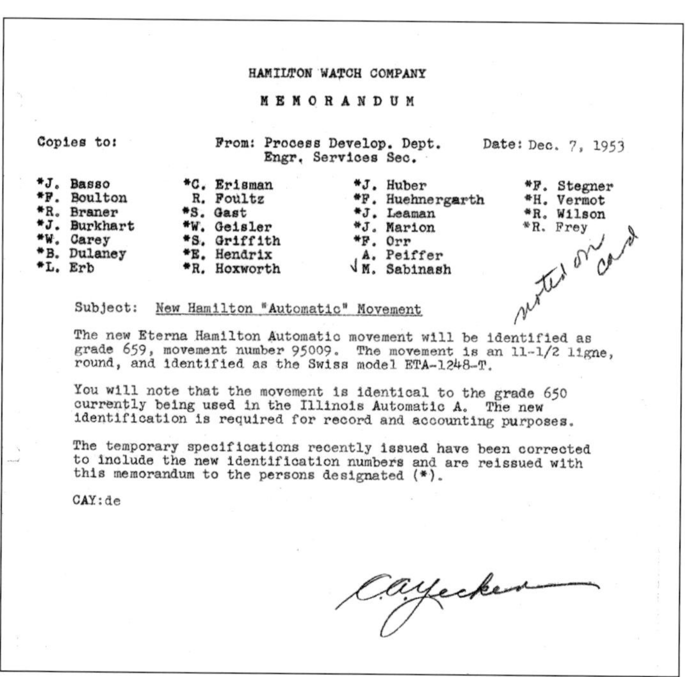

HAMILTON WATCH COMPANY

M E M O R A N D U M

Copies to:

From: Process Develop. Dept.
Engr. Services Sec.

Date: Dec. 7, 1953

*J. Basso
*F. Boulton
*R. Braner
*J. Burkhart
*W. Carey
*B. Dulaney
*L. Erb
*C. Erisman
R. Foultz
*S. Gast
*W. Geisler
*S. Griffith
*E. Hendrix
*R. Hoxworth
*J. Huber
*F. Huehnergarth
*J. Leaman
*J. Marion
*F. Orr
A. Peiffer
√M. Sabinash
*F. Stegner
*H. Vermot
*R. Wilson
*R. Frey

noted on card

Subject: New Hamilton "Automatic" Movement

The new Eterna Hamilton Automatic movement will be identified as grade 659, movement number 95009. The movement is an 11-1/2 ligne, round, and identified as the Swiss model ETA-1248-T.

You will note that the movement is identical to the grade 650 currently being used in the Illinois Automatic A. The new identification is required for record and accounting purposes.

The temporary specifications recently issued have been corrected to include the new identification numbers and are reissued with this memorandum to the persons designated (*).

CAY:de

Internal memorandum, dated December 7, 1953, advising that the new Eterna Hamilton Automatic movement would be called grade 659. It was a Swiss model ETA-1248T. This movement was identical to the grade 650 used in the Illinois Automatic A. Grade 658 was also designated solely for Hamilton use. But the grade 658 was manufactured by Kurth Frères, a third Swiss ébauche maker used by Hamilton. Grades 658 and 659 were only for use in Hamilton models.

Automatic Model A Case

According to René Rondeau, "Hamilton used the Automatic Model A case for all of the earliest Hamilton Electric prototypes, including the Kohler EM-1, all of the PM-1 prototypes, and 21 Model 2 wear-test watches. There was no special reason for the choice beyond the fact that the case was suitably sized. For the PM-2 and Model 2 dials, they used the same Illinois dial but with a Hamilton name and lightning bolt logo."

The "Mark I" photograph below is in a factory photograph. The original watch is now in the Smithsonian Institute in Washington, D.C.

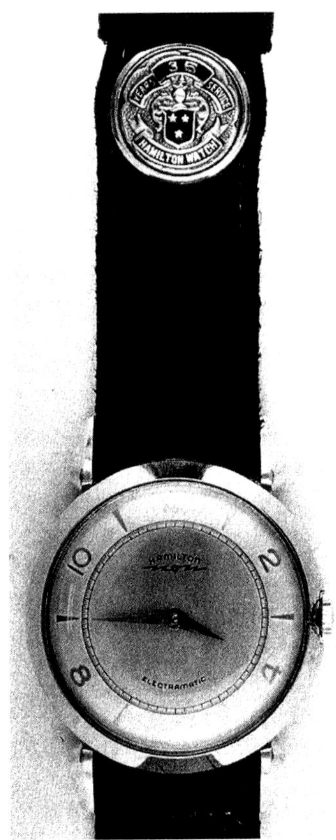

The battery would not fit in the case, so it was hidden in the strap by the Hamilton award medallion.

The Hamilton Electric Model EM-1, which was the first cased prototype Hamilton electric watch, had a unique dial. The photograph below is of the actual watch. The picture of the back is a 1952 factory one. The image shows that the Automatic Model A case was not deep enough to accommodate the battery, so Hamilton cut a hole into the back of the case for the battery to fit, and made a plate to screw on over the top.

The Electric Model 2 was a significant step past the earliest prototypes but was still very early and crude in 1954. This model, however, did allow for the battery to fit inside the case without alteration.

From the earliest electric prototypes, all had dials based on the Hamilton-Illinois patterns with the exception of the addition of the Hamilton electric bolt logo.

AUTOMATIC MODEL B

A rugged waterproof Automatic in gleaming stainless steel. Embossed numerals. Luminous markers, dots and hands. Sweep-seconds. 17 jewels, shockproof, anti-magnetic.

Gray pigskin strap. . 951521. . $59.95
Flexible band. . . . . . . 951522. . 65.00

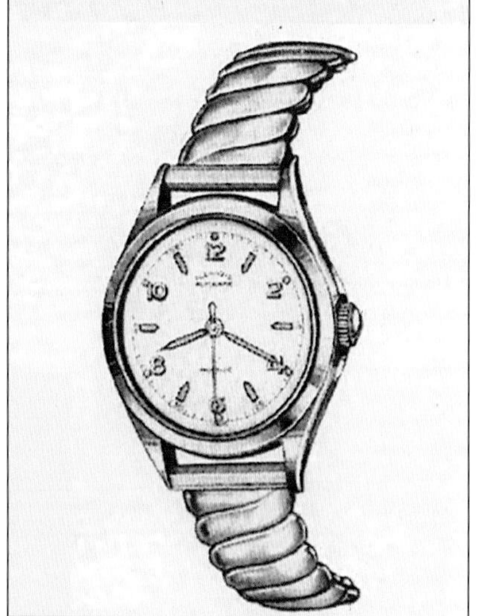

Automatic Model B

Name = Automatic Model B
Time Period = Mid-Century Modern
Karat/Material = SS
Bezel = Plain
Sides = Plain
Lug Size = 5/8
Spring Bar = Male
Model No. = 9515
Casemaker = Huguenin
Case Pieces = 2
Case Number = 9515
Dimensions = 32 x 40mm
Movement Grade/Jewels = ETA Etamatic 1256, 652/17
Dial Signed = Hamilton-Illinois Automatic or Illinois Automatic Incabloc
Dial Number = 9515/58100
Dial Shape = Round, three choices
Numbers = Embossed
Markers = Luminous
Dots = Luminous
Hands = Luminous
Seconds at = Sweep seconds
Anti-Magnetic = Yes
Shockproof = Yes
Waterproof = Yes
Dustproof = Yes
Automatic = Yes
Power Indicator = No
Cased in Factory = Yes

Retail Price New = $65.00, flexible band; $59.95, grey pigskin strap (1954–1955)
Production Date = 1954
Unique Case Design = Yes
Unique Dial Design = Yes
Advertisement = Yes

The Automatic Model B was advertised in the *Saturday Evening Post* issues dated November 21, 1953, and May 8, 1954, as well as in the 1955 Hamilton Watch Catalog.

This model came with the choice of four dials: (1) yellow embossed numerals, (2) embossed numerals and luminous markers, (3) embossed numerals and luminous markers and dots, or (4) a black dial with embossed numerals and luminous markers. Hamilton purchased this model as a complete watch from Switzerland.

Because of its stainless case, the Automatic B has turned out to be a very durable watch. The ETA 1256 movement used on the Automatic B was shared with most other Hamilton-Illinois watches and some of the early Hamilton automatics. For some reason, Hamilton never issued an Automatic C; the next model in the series was called Automatic D.

Automatic Model B

Automatic Model B, alternate dial

Automatic Model B case back

Automatic Model B black dial

Automatic Model B ETA1256 movement

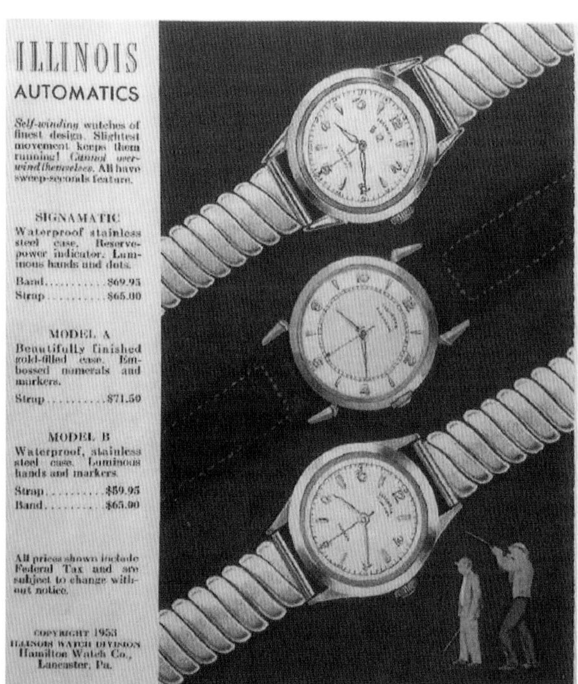

ILLINOIS
AUTOMATICS

Self-winding watches of finest design. Slightest movement keeps them running! *Cannot overwind themselves.* All have sweep-seconds feature.

SIGNAMATIC
Waterproof stainless steel case. Reserve-power indicator. Luminous hands and dots.
Band $69.95
Strap $65.00

MODEL A
Beautifully finished gold-filled case. Embossed numerals and markers.
Strap $71.50

MODEL B
Waterproof, stainless steel case. Luminous hands and markers.
Strap $59.95
Band $65.00

All prices shown include Federal Tax and are subject to change without notice.

COPYRIGHT 1953
ILLINOIS WATCH DIVISION
Hamilton Watch Co.,
Lancaster, Pa.

Hamilton-Illinois sales catalog, 1953

Advertisement for an Automatic Model B, *Corpus Christi Caller-Times*, April 29, 1955; image from *newspapers.com*

Automatic Model D

AUTOMATIC D

17 Jewels. Yellow Gold-filled Case. Luminous Dial. Water resistant,* Shock resistant and Anti-magnetic. Sweep Seconds.

Bracelet.........951722...........$79.50
Strap...........951721........... 71.50

Name = Automatic Model D
Time Period = Mid-Century Modern
Karat/Material = 10K YGF
Bezel = Plain
Sides = Plain
Lug Size = 5/8
Spring Bar = Male
Model No. = 9517
Casemaker = Schwab and Wuischpard
Case Pieces = 2
Case Number = 95170
Dimensions = 32 x 41 mm
Movement Grade/Jewels = ETA1256, 651/17
Dial Signed = Hamilton-Illinois Automatic
Dial Number = 9517/58101
Dial Shape = Round
Numbers = Embossed
Markers = Embossed
Hands = Brass
Seconds at = Sweep seconds
Anti-Magnetic = Yes
Shockproof = Yes
Waterproof = Yes
Dustproof = Yes
Automatic = Yes
Power Indicator = No
Cased in Factory = Yes
Retail Price New = $71.50, strap; $79.50, bracelet
Production Date = 1954
Unique Case Design = Yes
Unique Dial Design = Yes
Advertisement = Yes

The Automatic D is the only model in the Hamilton-Illinois line to claim to be waterproof without having a stainless steel case with a screw-on back. The Automatic D has a snap-on back with a rubber O-ring gasket. As is the case with the Automatic A, the 10K back has a tendency to wear through. According to internal Hamilton records, 26,011 grade Etarotor 651 movements were produced for its Hamilton-Illinois models.

Automatic Model D

Automatic Model D dial

Automatic Model D case back

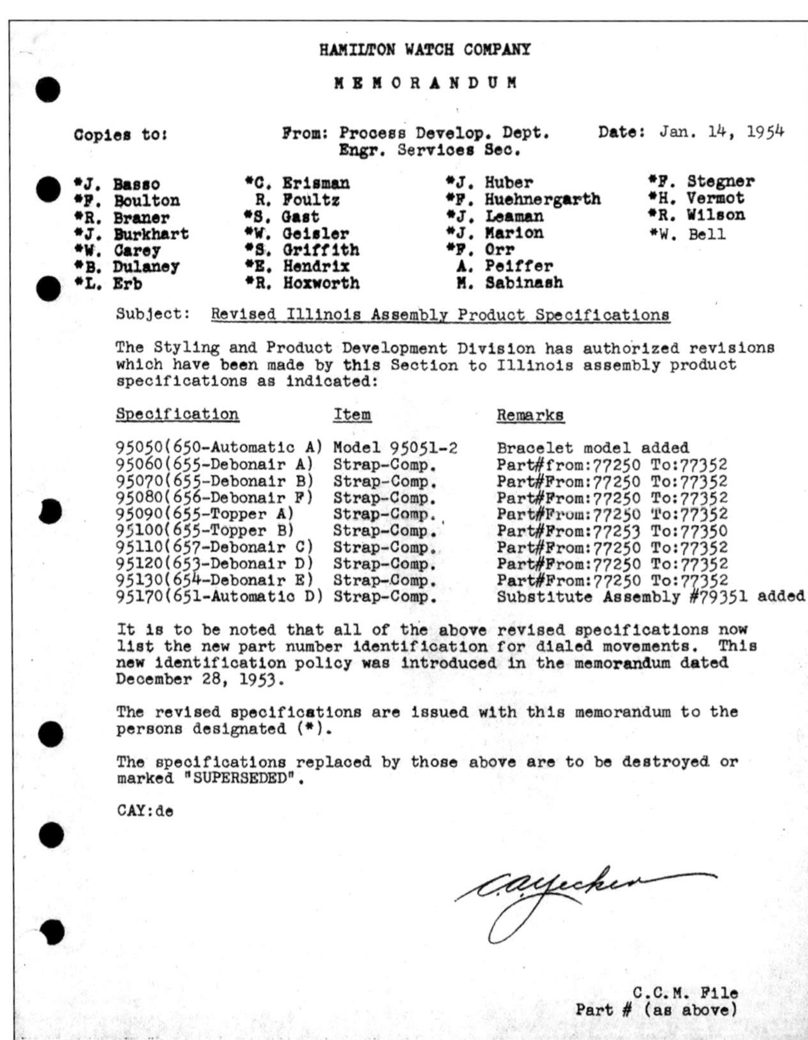

HAMILTON WATCH COMPANY

M E M O R A N D U M

Copies to: From: Process Develop. Dept. Engr. Services Sec. Date: Jan. 14, 1954

*J. Basso
*F. Boulton
*R. Braner
*J. Burkhart
*W. Carey
*B. Dulaney
*L. Erb
*C. Erisman
R. Foultz
*S. Gast
*W. Geisler
*S. Griffith
*E. Hendrix
*R. Hoxworth
*J. Huber
*F. Huehnergarth
*J. Leaman
*J. Marion
*F. Orr
A. Peiffer
M. Sabinash
*F. Stegner
*H. Vermot
*R. Wilson
*W. Bell

Subject: Revised Illinois Assembly Product Specifications

The Styling and Product Development Division has authorized revisions which have been made by this Section to Illinois assembly product specifications as indicated:

Specification	Item	Remarks
95050(650-Automatic A)	Model 95051-2	Bracelet model added
95060(655-Debonair A)	Strap-Comp.	Part#from:77250 To:77352
95070(655-Debonair B)	Strap-Comp.	Part#From:77250 To:77352
95080(656-Debonair F)	Strap-Comp.	Part#From:77250 To:77352
95090(655-Topper A)	Strap-Comp.	Part#From:77250 To:77352
95100(655-Topper B)	Strap-Comp.	Part#From:77253 To:77350
95110(657-Debonair C)	Strap-Comp.	Part#From:77250 To:77352
95120(653-Debonair D)	Strap-Comp.	Part#From:77250 To:77352
95130(654-Debonair E)	Strap-Comp.	Part#From:77250 To:77352
95170(651-Automatic D)	Strap-Comp.	Substitute Assembly #79351 added

It is to be noted that all of the above revised specifications now list the new part number identification for dialed movements. This new identification policy was introduced in the memorandum dated December 28, 1953.

The revised specifications are issued with this memorandum to the persons designated (*).

The specifications replaced by those above are to be destroyed or marked "SUPERSEDED".

CAY:de

C. A. Yecker

C.C.M. File
Part # (as above)

Internal memorandum, dated January 14, 1954, for changing specifications on Illinois models

Datomatic Model A

Name = Datomatic Model A (Calendar)
Time Period = Mid-Century Modern
Karat/Material = SS
Bezel = Plain
Sides = Plain
Lug Size = 5/8
Spring Bar = Male
Model No. = 9522
Casemaker = Huguenin
Case Pieces = 2
Case Number = 95220
Dimensions = 33 x 44 mm
Movement Grade/Jewels = ETA 1257/17
Dial Signed = Hamilton-Illinois Automatic
Dial Number = 95221
Dial Shape = Embossed, Round, two choices
Numbers = Embossed, Luminous
Markers = Embossed, Luminous
Dots = Luminous
Hands = Luminous
Seconds at = Sweep seconds
Anti-Magnetic = Yes
Shockproof = Yes
Waterproof = Yes
Dustproof = Yes
Automatic = Yes
Power Indicator = No
Cased in Factory = No
Retail Price New = $69.95, bracelet; $65.00, strap (1954/1955)
Production Date = 1954
Unique Case Design = Yes
Unique Dial Design = Yes
Advertisement = Yes

DATOMATIC A (Calendar)

17 Jewels. Stainless Steel Case. Embossed Numerals and Markers or Embossed Numerals and Luminous Markers and Dots. Water resistant,* Shock resistant and Anti-magnetic.

	Numerals and Markers	Numerals, Luminous Markers and Dots	
Bracelet	952212	952242	$69.95
Strap	952211	952241	65.00

"AUTOMATIC" SERIES

MODEL A	Yel.		Strap	950511	$ 65.00	$ 71.50
	Yel.		Brac.	950512	65.00	79.50
MODEL B	SS	Lum.	Strap	951521	54.50	59.95
	SS	Lum.	Brac.	951522	56.30	65.00
	SS	Lum.	Strap	951541	54.50	59.95
	SS	Lum.	Brac.	951542	56.30	65.00
MODEL D	Yel.	Lum.	Strap	951721	65.00	71.50
DATOMATIC	SS		Strap	952211	56.30	65.00
	SS		Brac.	952212	60.60	69.95
	SS		Strap	952241	56.30	65.00
	SS		Brac.	952242	60.60	69.95
SIGNAMATIC A	SS	Lum.	Strap	951621	59.10	65.00
	SS	Lum.	Brac.	951622	60.60	69.95
SIGNAMATIC B	SS	Lum.	Strap	952141	59.10	65.00
	SS	Lum.	Brac.	952142	60.60	69.95
	SS	Lum.	Strap	952161	59.10	65.00
	SS	Lum.	Brac.	952162	60.60	69.95

1954 Price List

The Datomatic Model A was shown in the Hamilton-Illinois Watch Catalog for 1954 and in the 1955 Hamilton Watch Catalog. This model also appeared in the *Saturday Evening Post* on May 8, 1954, in an advertisement that read, in part: ". . . It's shock and water resistant. You don't have to baby it while you fish, hike, shoot, knock around camp. And forget about winding it—it'll always be ready with accurate time."

The Datomatic must have been a very successful model for Hamilton. The stainless steel case has proved to be very durable, and the watch is easy to find on the used market. It was Hamilton's first watch with a date indicator; and after the Hamilton-Illinois line was discontinued, the company reused the movement and dial in several Hamilton Automatic models, including the K575 and K576.

Saturday Evening Post, May 8, 1954

The Datomatic A came with a red date track with the numerals centered in white in the red background. This model was available with a choice of two dials—one with embossed numerals and arrow markers and one with embossed numerals and luminous markers (this version also had light blue luminous dots inside the hour numerals).

Datomatic Model A with brass markers

Datomatic Model A with luminous dots

Datomatic Model A

Datomatic Model A case back

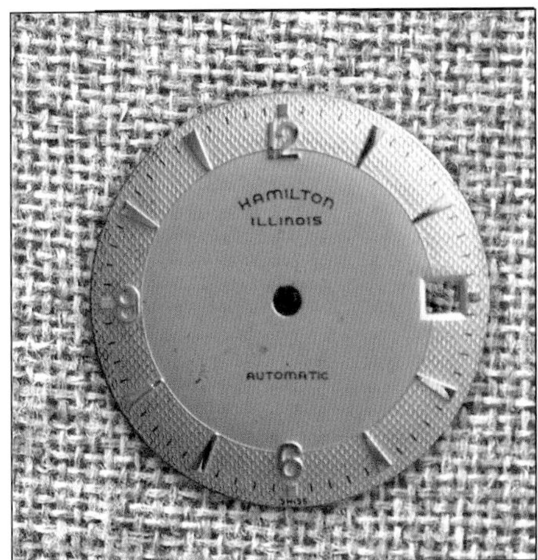

Datomatic Model A dial

Datomatic Model A movement front, with date ring

ETA 1257 movement

A Hamilton advertisement for its two calendar watches in the *Saturday Evening Post*, 1954. This is one of the rare times that Hamilton offered its own branded watch with an Illinois-branded one

DEBONAIR SERIES

The Debonair series was Hamilton's budget-priced line of Hamilton-Illinois watches, with rolled gold plate bezels and stainless steel backs. Perhaps because of the steel backs, these watches have proved to be durable, so most of them are readily found today.

The Illinois "Debonair" series was advertised as "a group name for a series of models which include some of the best buys in fine watches for men. All of these models have 17 jewels, shockproof, anti-magnetic movements."

The 1953 Illinois Catalog by Hamilton stated: "Hamilton presents the newest name in fine watches at modest prices. ILLINOIS made to the most exacting specifications ever established for watches in the popular-price field and **guaranteed by Hamilton**, the most trusted name in watches."

In 1953, the prices for the Debonair Series ranged from $33.95 to $47.50.

Debonair Model A

Name = Debonair Model A
Time Period = Mid-Century Modern
Karat/Material = 10K YRGP/SSB
Bezel = Sculpted
Sides = Sculpted
Lug Size = 5/8
Spring Bar = Male
Model No. = 9506
Casemaker = Schwab and Wuischpard
Case Pieces = 2
Case Number = 95060
Dimensions = 37 x 24mm
Movement Grade/Jewels = ETA 1220, 655/17
Dial Signed = Hamilton-Illinois Incabloc
Dial Number = 9505/58000
Dial Shape = Rectangular (with rounded corners)
Numbers = Embossed
Markers = None
Hands = Brass
Seconds at = 6
Anti-Magnetic = Yes
Shockproof = Yes
Waterproof = No
Dustproof = No
Automatic = No
Power Indicator = No
Cased in Factory = Yes

Advertisement = Yes
Retail Price New = $39.95, pigskin strap; $47.50, matching band (1953–1955)
Production Date = 1953
Unique Case Design = Yes
Unique Dial Design = Yes

The Debonair Model A was advertised in the 1953 Illinois Watch Catalog, the 1953 Hamilton and Illinois Watch Company Catalog, in the 1954 Hamilton-Illinois Catalog and in the 1955 Hamilton Watch Catalog.

In the 1953 Hamilton catalog it was described as "Fine watch luxury at a most modest price."

Debonair Model A

Debonair Model A dial

ETA1220 movement

Debonair Model A inside case back (The S&W is for Schwab & Wuischpard.)

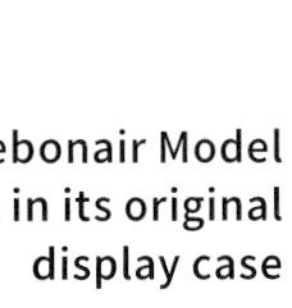
Debonair Model A in its original display case

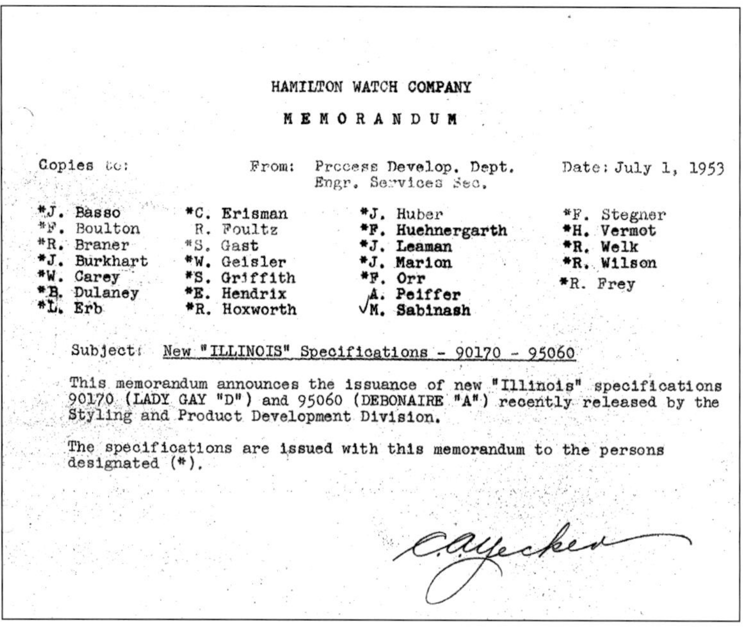

HAMILTON WATCH COMPANY

MEMORANDUM

Copies to: From: Process Develop. Dept. Engr. Services Sec. Date: July 1, 1953

*J. Basso *C. Erisman *J. Huber *F. Stegner
*F. Boulton R. Foultz *F. Huehnergarth *H. Vermot
*R. Braner *S. Gast *J. Leaman *R. Welk
*J. Burkhart *W. Geisler *J. Marion *R. Wilson
*W. Carey *S. Griffith *F. Orr *R. Frey
*B. Dulaney *E. Hendrix A. Peiffer
*L. Erb *R. Hoxworth √M. Sabinash

Subject: New "ILLINOIS" Specifications - 90170 - 95060

This memorandum announces the issuance of new "Illinois" specifications 90170 (LADY GAY "D") and 95060 (DEBONAIRE "A") recently released by the Styling and Product Development Division.

The specifications are issued with this memorandum to the persons designated (*).

Hamilton's July 1, 1953 internal introduction of the Lady Gay Model D and Debonair Model A. Note "Debonair" is misspelled.

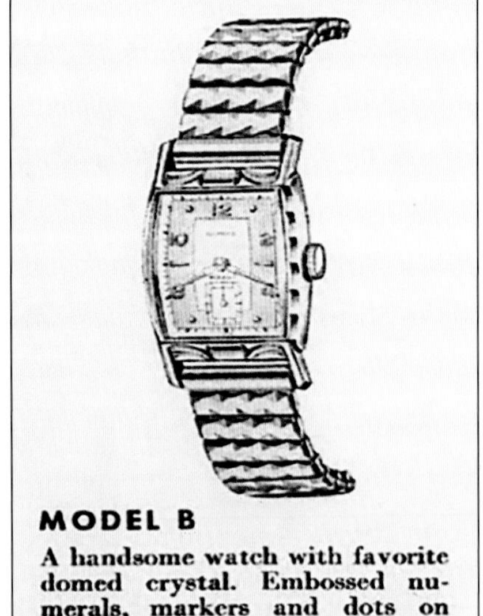

Debonair Model B

Name = Debonair Model B
Time Period = Mid-Century Modern
Karat/Material = 10K YRGP/SSB
Bezel = Sculpted
Sides = Sculpted
Lug Size = 5/8
Spring Bar = Male
Model No. = 9507
Casemaker = Schwab and Wuischpard
Case Pieces = 2
Case Number = 95070
Dimensions = 37 x 23mm
Movement Grade/Jewels = ETA1220, 655/17
Dial Signed = Illinois Incabloc
Dial Number = 9507/58501
Dial Shape = Two-tone Rectangular
Numbers = Embossed
Markers = Embossed
Dots = Embossed
Hands = Brass
Seconds at = 6
Anti-Magnetic = Yes
Shockproof = Yes

Waterproof = Yes
Dustproof = No
Automatic = No
Power Indicator = No
Cased in Factory = Yes
Retail Price New = $39.95, pigskin strap; $47.50, matching band (1954)
Production Date = 1953
Unique Case Design = Yes
Unique Dial Design = Yes
Advertisement = Yes

The 1954 Illinois Catalog stated that the Debonair Model B was "A handsome watch with favorite domed crystal. Embossed numerals, markers and dots on modern two-tone dial."

The Debonair B was advertised in the 1953 Illinois by Hamilton Watch Catalog and in the 1955 Hamilton Watch Catalog.

Debonair Model B

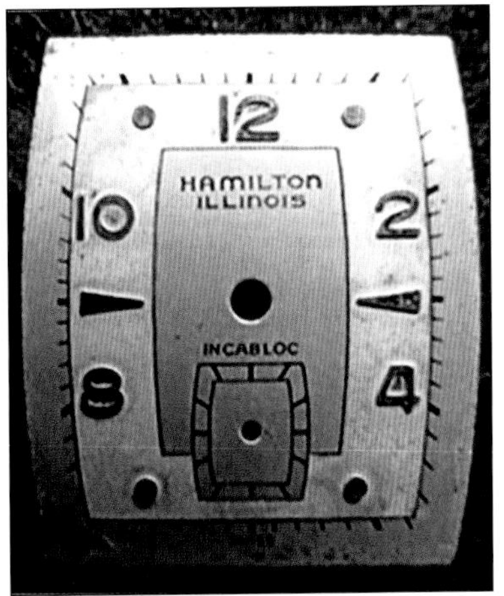

Debonair Model B dial

Debonair Model B case back

Debonair Model B inside case back

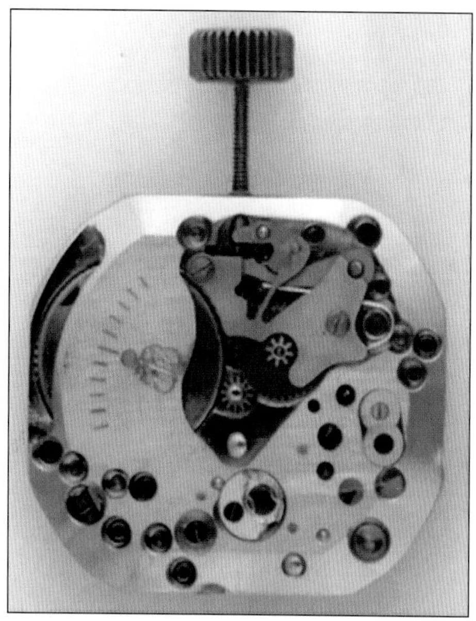

Front and back of an ETA 1220 movement, Hamilton factory photographs

DEBONAIR C

Yellow Case. Stainless Steel Back. Shock resistant.

Bracelet.........951112......$47.50
Strap...........951111...... 39.95

Debonair Model C

Name = Debonair Model C
Time Period = Mid-Century Modern
Karat/Material = 10K YGRP/SSB
Bezel = Plain and Sculpted
Sides = Plain
Lug Size = 5/8
Spring Bar = Male
Model No. = 9511
Casemaker = Schwab and Wuischpard
Case Pieces = 2
Case Number = 95110
Dimensions = 37 x 26mm
Movement Grade/Jewels = AS1200, 657/17
Dial Signed = Illinois Incabloc
Dial Number = 9511/58700
Dial Shape = Square
Numbers = Embossed
Markers = Embossed
Dots = Embossed
Hands = Brass
Seconds at = 6, Recessed
Anti-Magnetic = Yes
Shockproof = Yes

Waterproof = No
Dustproof = No
Automatic = No
Power Indicator = No
Cased in Factory = Yes
Advertisement = Yes
Retail Price New = $39.95, pigskin strap; $47.50, matching band (1953–1955)
Production Date = 1953
Unique Case Design = Yes
Unique Dial Design = Yes

The Debonair C was advertised in the 1953 Hamilton catalog as an "Outstanding value with better watch styling like domed crystal and recessed seconds. Embossed numerals, markers and dots. Shockproof, anti-magnetic 17 jewel movement."

Debonair Model C

Debonair Model C dial

AS 1200 movement

Debonair Model C inside case back

Advertisement for the Debonair Model C and two other Hamilton-Illinois models in the *Plain Speaker* (Hazleton, PA), December 3, 1954; image from *newspapers.com*

The Debonair Model C was advertised in the November 16, 1953 issue of *Life* magazine and in another *Life* advertisement in 1954 as well as being listed in the 1953 and 1954 Hamilton-Illinois Catalogs, and in the 1955 Hamilton Watch Catalog.

According to internal Hamilton records, 19,841 grade 657 movements were produced for Hamilton-Illinois models.

Front (*top*) and back of an AS 1200 movement, Hamilton factory photographs

Debonair Model D

Name = Debonair Model D
Time Period = Mid-Century Modern
Karat/Material = 10K YRGP/SSB
Bezel = Plain
Sides = Plain
Lug Size = 5/8
Spring Bar = Male
Model No. = 9512
Casemaker = Star
Case Pieces = 2
Case Number = 95120
Dimensions = 40 x 32mm
Movement Grades/Jewel = AS1200, 657/17
Dial Signed = Hamilton-Illinois Incabloc
Dial Number = Unknown
Dial Shape = Round
Numbers = Etched
Markers = None
Hands = Brass
Seconds at = 6
Anti-Magnetic = Yes
Shockproof = Yes
Waterproof = No
Dustproof = No
Automatic = No
Power Indicator = No
Cased in Factory = Yes
Advertisement = Yes
Retail Price New = $33.95, strap; $39.95, bracelet (1953–1955)
Production Date = 1953
Unique Case Design = Yes
Unique Dial Design = Yes

DEBONAIR D

Yellow Case. Stainless Steel Back. Shock resistant.

Bracelet.........951212......$39.95
Strap...........951211......33.95

The Debonair Model D was advertised in the May 8, 1954 issue of the *Saturday Evening Post* and in *Life* magazine in 1954. It was listed in the 1953 and 1954 Hamilton-Illinois Watch Catalogs and in the 1955 Hamilton Watch Catalog.

Cover of the 1953 holiday catalog

Debonair Model D

Debonair Model D dial

Debonair Model D case back

Debonair Model D inside case back

AS 1200 movement

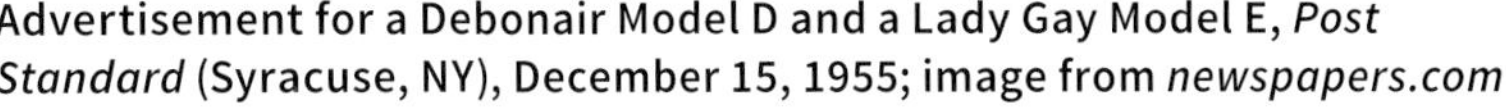
Advertisement for a Debonair Model D and a Lady Gay Model E, *Post Standard* (Syracuse, NY), December 15, 1955; image from *newspapers.com*

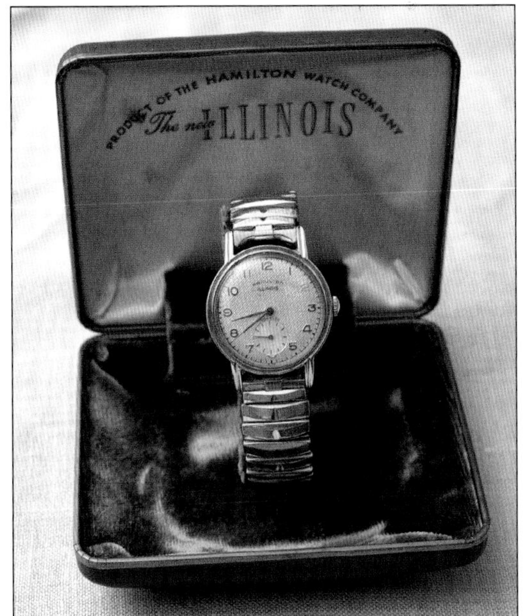

Debonair Model D in its display box

THE SATURDAY EVENING POST

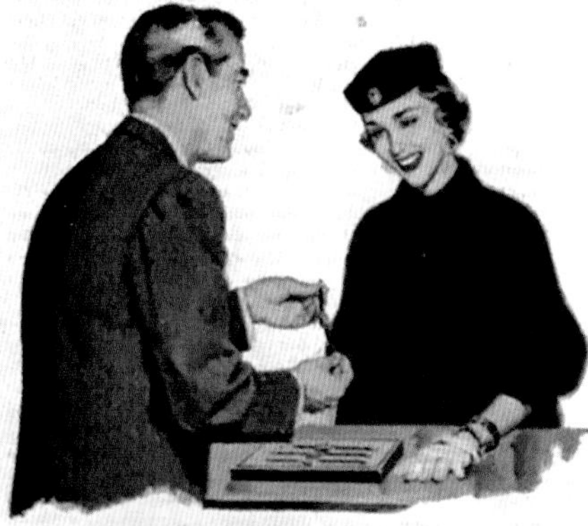

Styled by HAMILTON
Guaranteed by HAMILTON

Dollar for dollar we sincerely feel these are the most beautifully designed, dependable, accurate—*and modern*—watches you can buy. Hamilton, the most trusted name in watches, presents them proudly.

ILLINOIS

A completely new line of fine watches from $33.95!

What marvelous gifts these Illinois watches make! There are shockproof, waterproof, anti-magnetic watches. There are self-winding watches. There are watches with sweep second hands. When you're looking for a fine watch, see these beautiful new Illinois watches at your jeweler's. He'll be proud to show them to you.

Guarantee

Your Illinois watch is guaranteed by the Hamilton Watch Company against all original defects in material or workmanship. Cased and timed in the Hamilton Watch factory, it has passed exhaustive tests proving it capable of giving accurate time within the close limits set for it.

HAMILTON WATCH COMPANY
ILLINOIS WATCH DIVISION
LANCASTER, PA.

1. DEBONAIR "D"—17 jewels, shockproof, anti-magnetic, leather strap, $33.95. 2. TOPPER "A"—17 jewels, shockproof, anti-magnetic, gold-filled case, leather strap, $44.95. 3. AUTOMATIC "B"—17 jewels, self-winding, sweep second luminous hands, waterproof, shockproof, anti-magnetic, stainless steel, leather strap, $59.95. 4. COQUETTE "C"—17 jewels, anti-magnetic, yellow or white gold-filled case, silk cord, $44.95. 5. COQUETTE "B"—17 jewels, anti-magnetic, yellow gold-filled case, silk cord, $44.95. 6. LADY GAY "A"—17 jewels, anti-magnetic, embossed numerals, silk cord, $37.50. 7. DEBONAIR "F"—17 jewels, shockproof, anti-magnetic, sweep second, expansion band, $49.95; leather strap, $42.50.

PRICES INCLUDE FEDERAL TAX. ©HWC

Saturday Evening Post, May 8, 1953

Debonair Model E

Name = Debonair Model E
Time Period = Mid-Century Modern
Karat/Material = 10K YRGP/SSB
Bezel = Plain
Sides = Plain
Lug Size = 5/8
Spring Bar = Male
Model No. = 9513
Casemaker = Schwab and Wuischpard
Case Pieces = 2
Case Number = 95130
Dimensions = 40 x 31mm
Movement Grade/Jewels = ETA1081, 654/17
Dial Signed = Illinois Incabloc
Dial Number = 9513/58400
Dial Shape = Round
Numbers = Embossed
Markers = Embossed
Hands = Brass
Seconds at = Sweep seconds
Anti-Magnetic = Yes
Shockproof = Yes
Waterproof = No
Dustproof = No
Automatic = No
Power Indicator = No
Cased in Factory = Yes
Advertisement = Yes
Retail Price New = $39.95, strap; $47.50, matching band (1953–1955)
Production Date = 1953
Unique Case Design = Yes
Unique Dial Design = Yes

DEBONAIR E

Yellow Case. Stainless Steel Back. Shock resistant. Sweep Seconds.

Bracelet.........951312......$47.50
Strap...........951311...... 39.95

In the 1953 Illinois Catalog, the Debonair Model E was called the "Best buy in new larger size with sweep-seconds for accurate timing."

This watch was advertised in the 1953 Illinois Watch Catalog, the 1953 Hamilton and Illinois Watch Catalog, the November 16, 1953 issue of *Life* magazine, the 1954 Hamilton-Illinois Catalog, the May 8, 1954 issue of the *Saturday Evening Post* and the 1955 Hamilton Watch Catalog.

Debonair Model E

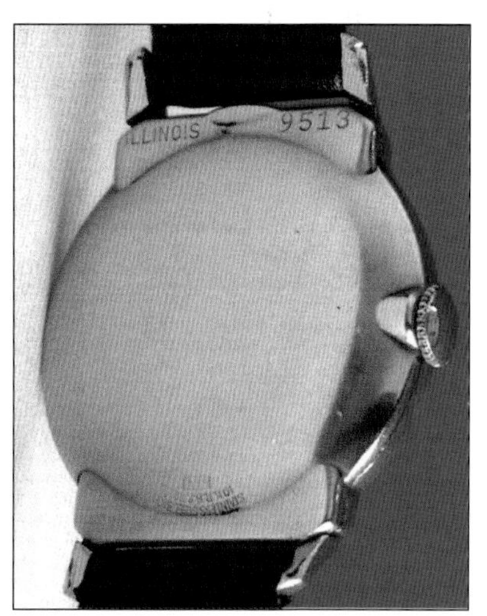

Debonair Model E case back

Debonair Model E inside case back

From $33.95 . . . and guaranteed by Hamilton

Save your shopping steps. See lovely Illinois watches at your Hamilton jeweler's. Nowhere else will you find such beautiful watches so modestly priced! Illinois watches include shock-resistant, water-resistant* models . . . even self-winding models. Dollar for dollar, Illinois watches are the most accurate and dependable you can buy.

ILLINOIS Watches
by Hamilton

DEBONAIR "E," $39.95 LADY GAY "D," $39.95 Prices include Federal tax.

FREE: *Color folder of 1954 watch styles. Send name and address to Dept. L-11, Hamilton Watch Company, Lancaster, Pa.*
**Provided original seal is restored if opened for servicing.* ©HWC.

Debonair E and Lady Gay D, *Life*; November 16, 1953

ETA1081 movement front (*top*) and back, Hamilton factory photographs

Debonair Model F

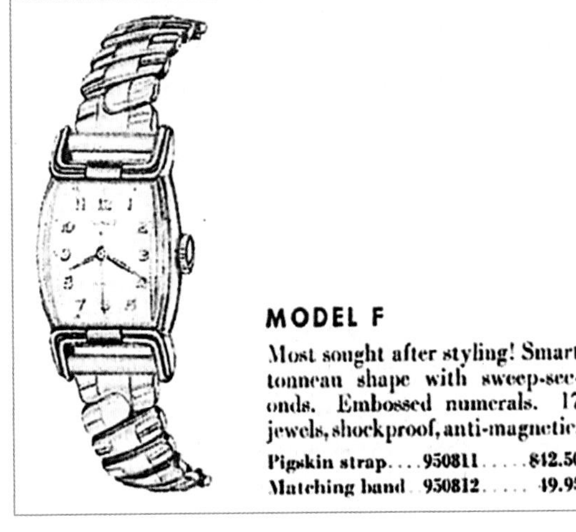
MODEL F
Most sought after styling! Smart tonneau shape with sweep-seconds. Embossed numerals. 17 jewels, shockproof, anti-magnetic.
Pigskin strap....950811.....$42.50
Matching band. 950812..... 49.95

Name = Debonair Model F
Time Period = Mid-Century Modern
Karat/Material = 10K YRGP/SSB
Bezel = Plain
Sides = Plain
Lug Size = 5/8
Spring Bar = Female
Model No. = 9508
Casemaker = Schwab and Wuischpard
Case Pieces = 2
Case Number = 95080
Movement Grade/Jewels = ETA1190, 656/17 (8 x 9 ligne)
Dial Signed = Illinois Incabloc
Dial Number = 9508/586000
Dial Shape = Tonneau
Numbers = Embossed
Markers = None
Hands = Brass
Seconds at = Sweep seconds
Anti-Magnetic = Yes
Shockproof = Yes
Waterproof = No
Dustproof = No
Automatic = No
Power Indicator = No
Cased in Factory = Yes
Advertisement = Yes
Retail Price New = $42.50, pigskin strap; $49.95, matching band (1954)
Production Date = 1953
Unique Case Design = Yes
Unique Dial Design = Yes

The 1953 and 1954 Catalogs described the Model F as having the "Most sought after styling! Smart Tonneau shape with sweep-seconds." The Model F seems to be the rarest of all the catalogued men's Hamilton-Illinois models. The design is unusual, having a sweep second hand in a case that is not circular. The lugs, extending out from a central boss, are reminiscent of some Hamilton designs, such as the Brandon.

Debonair Model F

Debonair Model F dial

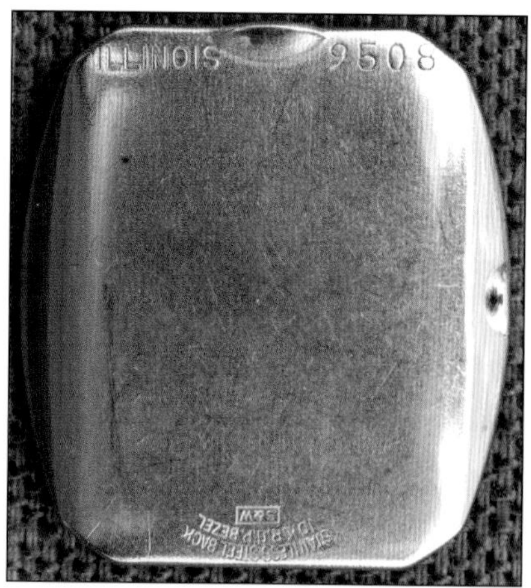

Debonair Model F case back

The Debonair Model F was also advertised in the November 21, 1953 issue of the *Saturday Evening Post* and appeared in the 1955 Hamilton Watch Catalog.

Debonair Model F inside case back

Page from 1953 Hamilton-Illinois holiday sales brochure

ETA 1190 movement

According to internal Hamilton records, 10,421 grade 656 movements were produced for Hamilton-Illinois models.

Debonair Model G

Name = Debonair Model G
Time Period = Mid-Century Modern
Karat/Material = 10K YRGP/SSB
Bezel = Plain
Sides = Plain
Lug Size = 5/8
Spring Bar = Male
Model No. = 9523
Casemaker = Star
Case Pieces = 2
Case Number = 95230
Dimensions = 40 x 32 mm
Movement Grade/Jewels = AS 1200, 653/17
Dial Signed = Hamilton-Illinois Incabloc Swiss
Dial Number = Unknown
Dial Shape = Round
Numbers = Embossed
Markers = Etched
Hands = Brass
Seconds at = 6
Anti-Magnetic = Yes
Shockproof = Yes
Waterproof = No
Dustproof = No
Automatic = No
Power Indicator = No
Cased in Factory = Yes
Retail Price New = $33.95, strap; $39.95, bracelet (1954–1955)
Production Date = 1954
Unique Case Design = Yes
Unique Dial Design = Yes
Advertisement = Yes

The Debonair Model G was listed in the 1954 Hamilton-Illinois Watch Catalog and in the 1955 Hamilton Watch Catalog. Hamilton issued no Debonair Model H or Debonair Model I.

Debonair Model G

Debonair Model G dial

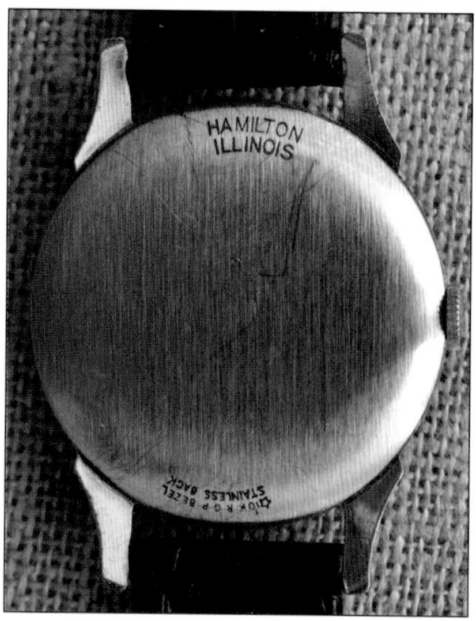

Debonair Model G case back

Debonair Model G inside case back

DEBONAIR J

17 Jewels. Yellow Case. Stainless Steel Back. Anti-magnetic.

Bracelet.........951812...........$44.95

Debonair Model J

Name = Debonair Model J
Time Period = Mid-Century Modern
Karat/Material = 10K YRGP/SSB
Bezel = Plain
Sides = Plain
Lug Size = 5/8
Spring Bar = Male
Model No. = 9518
Casemaker = Star
Case Pieces = 2
Case Number = 95180
Dimensions = 38 x 22 mm
Movement Grade/Jewels = ETA 1220, 655/17
Dial Signed = Hamilton-Illinois Incabloc Swiss
Dial Number = Unknown

Dial Shape = Rectangular
Numbers = Embossed
Markers = Embossed
Hands = Brass
Seconds at = 6
Anti-Magnetic = Yes
Shockproof = Yes
Waterproof = No
Dustproof = No
Automatic = No
Power Indicator = No
Cased in Factory = Yes
Retail Price New = $44.95, bracelet
Production Date = 1954
Unique Case Design = Yes
Unique Dial Design = Yes

Debonair Model J

Debonair Model J dial

Hamilton Jarvis

Debonair Model J case back

Debonair J inside case back

The Debonair Model J was listed in the 1954 Hamilton-Illinois Watch Catalog. It was reincarnated in 1956 as a Hamilton named Jarvis. The Jarvis differed from the Debonair J in having round markers, rather than pointed, and only the word Hamilton on the dial. However, the Jarvis case retained its original Hamilton-Illinois markings.

ILLINOIS

guaranteed by the Hamilton Watch Company

Debonair

"Debonair" is a group name for a series of models which includes some of the best buys in fine watches for men. All of these models have 17 jewel, shockproof, anti-magnetic movements.

MODEL B
A handsome watch with favorite domed crystal. Embossed numerals and markers on modern two-tone dial.
Pigskin strap. . . .950711. . $44.95
Matching band. . .950712. . $52.50

MODEL C
Outstanding value with better watch styling like domed crystal and recessed seconds.
Pigskin strap. . . .951111. . $39.95
Matching band. . .951112. . $47.50

MODEL E
Best buy in new larger size with sweep-seconds for accurate timing.
Pigskin strap. . . .951311. . $39.95
Matching band. . .951312. . $47.50

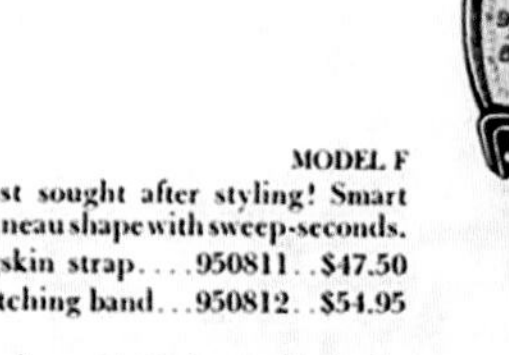

MODEL F
Most sought after styling! Smart tonneau shape with sweep-seconds.
Pigskin strap. . . .950811. . $47.50
Matching band. . .950812. . $54.95

All prices include Federal tax and are subject to change without notice.

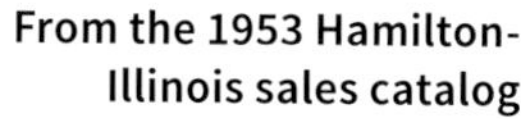

From the 1953 Hamilton-Illinois sales catalog

Debonair Model K

Name = Debonair Model K
Time Period = Mid-Century Modern
Karat/Material = 10K YRGP/SSB
Bezel = Plain
Sides = Plain
Lug Size = 11/16
Spring Bar = Male
Model No. = 9519
Casemaker = Pioneer
Case Pieces = 2
Case Number = 95190
Dimensions = 37 x 22mm
Movement Grade/Jewels = ETA1220, 655/17
Dial Signed = Hamilton-Illinois Incabloc Swiss
Dial Number = 9519
Dial Shape = Rectangular two-tone
Numbers = Etched
Markers = Etched
Hands = Brass
Seconds at = 6
Anti-Magnetic = Yes
Shockproof = Yes
Waterproof = No
Dustproof = No
Automatic = No
Power Indicator = No
Cased in Factory = Yes
Advertisement = Yes
Retail Price New = $39.95, strap; $44.95, bracelet (1954–1955)
Production Date = 1954
Unique Case Design = Yes
Unique Dial Design = Yes

The Debonair Model K was listed in the 1954 Hamilton-Illinois Watch Catalog and in the 1955 Hamilton Watch Catalog. The most striking feature of the Debonair K is its two-tone dial, divided into quadrants along the diagonals. The effect is achieved by fine brushing, with one pair of opposite quadrants lined vertically and the other pair horizontally. Which quadrants appear light and which dark appears to change as the angle of view changes. Hamilton later used the same effect on a number of dials in its primary line.

Debonair Model K

Debonair Model K dial

Debonair Model K inside case back

Debonair Model K case back

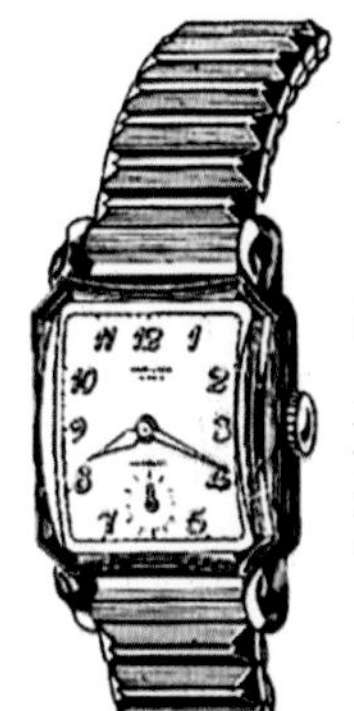

DEBONAIR L

17 Jewels. Yellow Case. Stainless Steel Back.

Bracelet.........**952012**..........**$44.95**
Strap..........**952011**.......... **39.95**

DEBONAIR MODEL L

Name = Debonair Model L
Time Period = Mid-Century Modern
Karat/Material = 10K YRGP/SB
Bezel = Plain
Sides = Plain
Lug Size = 5/8
Spring Bar = Male
Model No.= 9520
Casemaker = Schwab and Wuischpard
Case Pieces = 2
Case Number = 95200
Dimensions = 26 x 37 mm
Movement Grade/Jewels = ETA1220, 655/17
Dial Signed = Hamilton-Illinois Incabloc
Dial Number = 9519

Dial Shape = Square
Numbers = Etched
Markers = None
Hands = Brass
Seconds at = 6
Anti-Magnetic = Yes
Shockproof = Yes
Waterproof = No
Dustproof = No
Automatic = No
Power Indicator = No
Cased in Factory = Yes
Advertisement = Yes
Retail Price New = $39.95, strap; $44.95, bracelet (1955)
Production Date = 1954
Unique Case Design = Yes
Unique Dial Design = Yes

The Debonair Model L apparently first appeared in the 1955 Hamilton Watch Catalog. This model came with the choice of a white or black dial. Being a new model, the Debonair L would have come to an early end the next year had Hamilton not instead chosen to reissue it as the Hamilton Laird.

Debonair Model L, numeral dial

Debonair Model L, numeral and marker dial

Debonair Model L, black dial

Debonair Model L dial, numerals and markers

Debonair Model L inside case back

You Can Buy With Confidence at COMMUNITY JEWELERS SILVERSMITHS

FAMOUS NAMES

You Can Trust . . . All On Easy Credit !

Bulova • Benrus • Hamilton • Gruen • Elgin • Longine-Wittnauer • Sunbeam • Speidel • Ronson • Sheaffer Toastmaster • Parker • Swank • General Electric • Wm. Rogers • Holmes & Edwards • and many others!

OUR GUARANTEE TO YOU:

★ Your moneys worth or your money back.

★ If you can buy it for less—we'll refund the difference.

★ Nobody but nobody—under-sells Community's

COMMUNITY

SAVE ½ - - SPEIDEL

JEWELRY

½ OFF

COMMUNITY IMPORTS DIAMONDS

Direct from Antwerp

The Diamond Center of the World

½ CARAT

$99

$50

12 DIAMOND

$166

6 x 30 BINOCULARS

$24.88

$49.95

Just Arrived

1955 STYLES

RHINESTONE PINS

88¢

BUY THEM FOR XMAS

$2.44

$2.88

$29.95

$12.95

$39.95

$79

STORY BOOK WATCHES

We're Out To Make All The Kiddies Happy!

•HOWDY-DOODY

•ROY ROGERS

•DALE EVANS

•SUPERMAN

$3.99

Nationally Famous Make

23 JEWELS

SWANK - ANSON & FLEX-LET

MEN'S JEWELRY

$2.50

Famous "Fashion Queen"

$6.66

WALES & BUXTON WALLETS

$2.50

FAMOUS MEDANA-SHOCK-PROOF WATCHES

10 Piece DRESSER SET

$12.95

$14.88

$33.88

Parker — Sheaffer & Waterman

$5.00

One Carat ZIRCONS

$9

$12

TRAVEL ALARMS

$4.99

LAY AWAY NOW FOR XMAS

THE LODGE-ICAL CHOICE FRATERNAL RINGS

$19.95

HAMILTON Illinois Watches

33.95

No Money Down

Absolutely New . . .

17-JEWEL BENRUS WATCHES

Your Choice

$24.75

Lay Them Away For Christmas Now!

NO MONEY DOWN

Smith-Corona-Underwood & Royal

$1.00 Weekly

COMMUNITY

JEWELERS SILVERSMITHS

Advertisement for a Debonair Model L and a ladies' Hamilton-Illinois, *Daily Record* (Stroudsburg, PA), November 26, 1954; image from *newspapers.com*

ILLINOIS ORDER FORM

The attached order form spells out the cost retailers paid for the Hamilton-Illinois models and their consumer prices. The prices to consumers were to be marked up over 100%.

ILLINOIS WATCH ORDER FORM

DATE______ NO.______

SHIP TO______ CHARGE TO______

CODE______ CODE______

SHIP BY______ CUSTOMER'S ORDER NO.______

TO BE FILLED IN BY MAIN OFFICE — CREDIT DEPT.

SALESMAN'S CODE NO.______

SHIP BY—CODE______

TERMS—CODE______ TERMS: 2% 10TH OF FOLLOWING MONTH—NET 60 DAYS THEREAFTER

CONSUMER PTI	QUANTITY	PRODUCT NUMBER	WATCH NAME		COLOR	ATTACH-MENT	RETAILER COST	TOTAL
$39.95		901411	LADY GAY	Model A	Yel.	Cord	$18.15	
44.95		901412			Yel.	Brac.	20.45	
33.95		901511		Model B	Yel.	Cord	15.45	
39.95		901512			Yel.	Brac.	18.15	
54.95		901011	COQUETTE	Model A	Wh.	Cord	25.00	
62.50		901012			Wh.	Brac.	27.05	
54.95		901111			Yel.	Cord	25.00	
62.50		901112			Yel.	Brac.	27.05	
49.95		901811		Model B	Yel.	Cord	22.70	
57.50		901812			Yel.	Brac.	24.90	
49.95		901911		Model C	Wh.	Cord	22.70	
54.95		901912			Wh.	Brac.	23.80	
49.95		902011			Yel.	Cord	22.70	
54.95		902012			Yel.	Brac.	23.80	
59.95		900511	GOLDEN TREASURE	Model A	Wh.	Cord	27.25	
59.95		900611			Yel.	Cord	27.25	
49.95		902121	CAREER GIRL	Model A	Wh.	Strap	22.70	
54.95		902122			Wh.	Brac.	23.80	
49.95		902211		Model B	Yel.	Cord	22.70	
54.95		902212			Yel.	Brac.	23.80	
44.95		950711	DEBONAIR	Model B	Yel.	Strap	20.45	
52.50		950712			Yel.	Brac.	22.70	
39.95		951111		Model C	Yel.	Strap	18.15	
47.50		951112			Yel.	Brac.	20.55	
33.95		951211		Model D	Yel.	Strap	17.25	
39.95		951212			Yel.	Brac.	20.30	
39.95		951311		Model E	Yel.	Strap	18.15	
47.50		951312			Yel.	Brac.	20.55	
47.50		950811		Model F	Yel.	Strap	21.60	
54.95		950812			Yel.	Brac.	23.80	
49.95		950911	TOPPER	Model A	Yel.	Strap	22.70	
59.95		950912			Yel.	Brac.	25.95	
49.95		951011		Model B	Yel.	Strap	22.70	
57.50		951012			Yel.	Brac.	24.90	
71.50		950511	AUTOMATIC	Model A	Yel.	Strap	32.50	
59.95		951521		Model B	Wh.	Strap	27.25	
65.00		951522			Wh.	Brac.	28.15	
65.00		951621		Signamatic	Wh.	Strap	29.55	
69.95		951622			Wh.	Brac.	30.30	
		← TOTALS →						

PRICES SUBJECT TO CHANGE WITHOUT NOTICE

ORDERS BECOME EFFECTIVE ONLY ON ACCEPTANCE BY THE OFFICE AT LANCASTER, PENNSYLVANIA

Hamilton-Illinois watch order form. Note the retailer cost.

"DEBONAIR" SERIES

MODEL A	Yel.	Strap	950611	$ 36.30	$ 39.95
	Yel.	Brac.	950612	41.10	47.50
MODEL B	Yel.	Strap	950711	36.30	39.95
	Yel.	Brac.	950712	41.10	47.50
MODEL C	Yel.	Strap	951111	36.30	39.95
	Yel.	Brac.	951112	41.10	47.50
MODEL D	Yel.	Strap	951211	34.50	33.95
	Yel.	Brac.	951212	36.30	39.95
MODEL E	Yel.	Strap	951311	36.30	39.95
	Yel.	Brac.	951312	41.10	47.50
MODEL F	Yel.	Strap	950811	38.60	42.50
	Yel.	Brac.	950812	43.20	49.95
MODEL J	Yel.	Brac.	951812	40.90	44.95
MODEL K	Yel.	Strap	951911	36.30	39.95
	Yel.	Brac.	951912	40.80	44.95
MODEL L	Yel.	Strap	952011	36.30	39.95
	Yel.	Brac.	952012	40.80	44.95

1954 Price List

Golden Male "A"

Golden Male Model "A", yellow gold

Name =	Golden Male "A"
Time Period =	Mid-Century Modern
Karat/Material =	14K YG
Bezel =	Plain, ornate lugs
Sides =	Plain
Lug Size =	5/8
Spring Bar =	Male
Model No. =	Unknown
Casemaker =	Unknown
Case Pieces =	2
Case Number =	Unknown
Dimensions =	40 x 32mm
Movement Grades/Jewel =	ETA1081, 653/17
Dial Signed =	Hamilton-Illinois Incabloc
Dial Number =	Unknown
Dial Shape =	Round
Numbers =	Etched
Markers =	None
Hands =	Brass
Seconds at =	6
Anti-Magnetic =	Yes
Shockproof =	Yes
Waterproof =	No
Dustproof =	No
Automatic =	No
Power Indicator =	No
Cased in Factory =	Yes
Advertisement =	No
Retail Price New =	$110.00
Production Date =	Unknown
Unique Case Design =	Yes
Unique Dial Design =	No (uses dial from Debonair Model D)

This very unusual watch confirms René Rondeau's recollection of having seen a solid gold Hamilton-Illinois. The case is very plain, except for the lugs, which have little spirals with forked ends. The outside of the case is marked only "Illinois" and "14K," without a model number. Inside, for a maker's mark, there is a script capital "A" with decorative marks on either side, along with "14K" and a serial number. The dial, hands, and movement are identical to those used by the Debonair Model D.

When this watch was found, we had no idea what this model had been called. Luckily, we discovered that Jeff Hess had found another one of these watches several years ago, complete with its inner and outer boxes and paperwork. Although he no longer had the watch in his possession, he still had the pictures he had made of it and its boxes. From the latter we learned its name: Golden Male "A." I am grateful to Jeff for sharing his pictures and permitting their use in this book.

Three specimens of the Golden Male "A" have been found thus far. That the case serial numbers are almost 500 apart for the two that have been examined suggests that Hamilton probably produced more than just a few of this model. The designs of the inner and outer boxes is different from those used for other Hamilton-Illinois watches and features the Hamilton crest, which did not appear on the papers or boxes of the other watches. Perhaps these watches were produced for some major customer that could demand special treatment.

14K Golden Male "A" inside case back

14K Golden Male "A" outer cardboard box

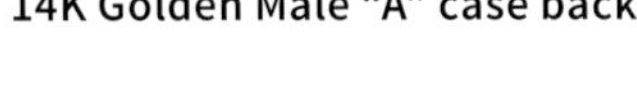

14K Golden Male "A" case back

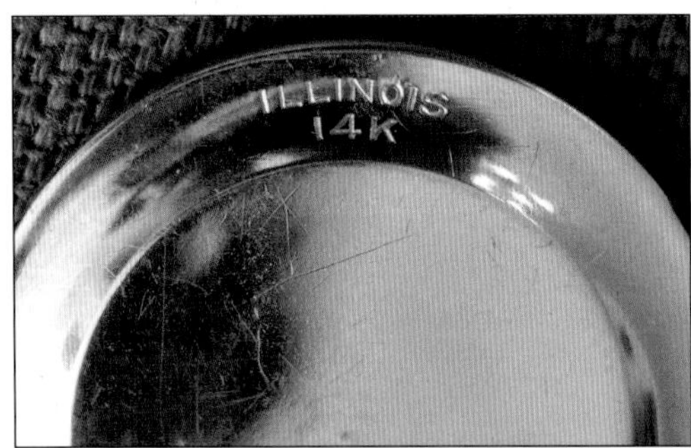

14K Golden Male "A" case back marking

14K Golden Male "A", side of its outer cardboard box

14K Golden Male "A" in its display box

14K Golden Male "A" inner and outer boxes

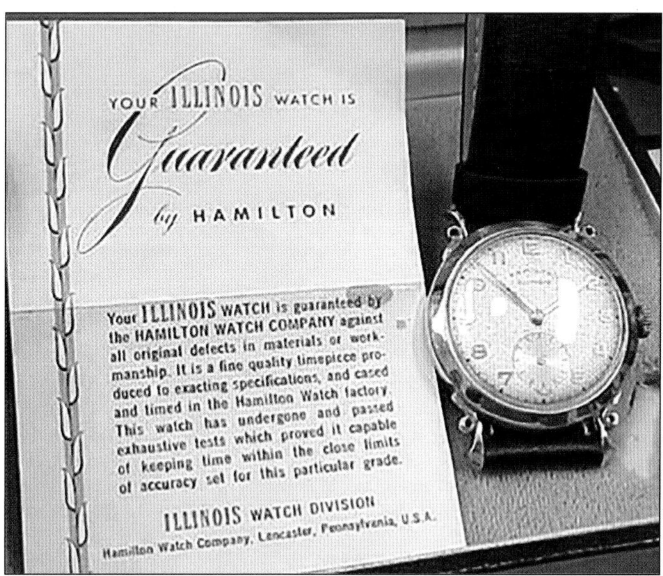

14K Golden Male "A" with its guarantee

New Solid Gold Models Discovered

Until recently, many issues remained open about the Golden Male "A", such as whether there were additional models in the series. However, after this work was submitted to the publisher, two more solid gold models appeared. Both have inner and outer case markings like the model "A". These we are calling Golden Male "B" and Golden Male "C" until further knowledge is gained.

The single example of the Golden Male "B" reuses the dial and movement of the Debonair Model J. One example of the Golden Male "C", like all instances of the Golden Male "A" observed so far, uses the dial and movement of the Debonair Model D. The other, however, uses the dial and movement of the Debonair Model E. This is possible because the AS 1200 movement in the Debonair D and the ETA 1081 in the Debonair E are the same shape and size. It is unusual for the same case to be used with both sweep and subsidiary seconds, but Hamilton may simply have been trying to use up stocks of movements or they may actually have considered these separate models.

When the work was about to go to press, a third additional solid gold model surfaced. Like the previously discovered models, it has the name "Illinois" and "14K" inscribed on its case back, but it has no case model or serial numbers and no maker's mark. It also uses the dial and movement of the Debonair Model D. We are inclined to consider this to be an authentic Hamilton-Illinois watch, but because of design and manufacturing differences and the absence of the casemaker's mark, we hesitate at this time to include it in the Golden Male series.

We may never know why Hamilton developed these models. There may have been requests from one or more influential customers, as seems to have been the case with the solid gold, diamond-set ladies' models. And then Hamilton, having seen it could sell budget watches with Swiss movements, may have decided to experiment also with luxury models. Whatever their origins, however, these uncataloged solid gold watches are an interesting and attractive extension to Hamilton-Illinois collecting and add new challenges for the watch aficionado.

Golden Male "B", yellow gold

Golden Male "B" case back

Golden Male " B" inside case back

Golden Male "C", yellow gold, subsidiary seconds

Golden Male “C”, yellow gold, sweep seconds

Unidentified solid gold model, only one known to exist

Nautilus Model A

NAUTILUS A

17 Jewels. Stainless Steel Case. White Embossed Numerals and Markers or Yellow Embossed Numerals with Luminous Markers or White Embossed Numerals and Luminous Markers on Black Dial. Water resistant,* Shock resistant, Anti-magnetic, Sweep Seconds.

	Numerals and Markers Silver Dial	Numerals, Luminous Markers Silver Dial	Numerals Luminous Markers Black Dial	
Bracelet	951412	951442	951432	$49.95
Strap	951411	951441	951431	44.95

Name = Nautilus Model A
Time Period = Mid-Century Modern
Karat/Material = SS
Bezel = Plain
Sides = Plain
Lug Size = 11/16
Spring Bar = Male
Model No. = 9514
Casemaker = Huguenin
Case Pieces = 2
Case Number = 95140
Dimensions = 41 x 33mm
Movement Grade/Jewels = ETA 1257/17
Dial Signed = Hamilton-Illinois Incabloc Swiss
Dial Number = 9514/58401/58401/58402/58403
Dial Shape = Round
Numbers = White or Yellow Embossed, Luminous
Markers = Embossed, Luminous
Hands = Brass, Luminous
Seconds at = Sweep seconds
Anti-Magnetic = Yes
Shockproof = Yes
Waterproof = Yes
Dustproof = Yes
Automatic = No
Power Indicator = No
Cased in Factory = No
Advertisement = Yes
Retail Price New = $44.95, gray pigskin strap; $49.95, flexible band (1953 –1955)
Production Date = 1953
Unique Case Design = Yes
Unique Dial Design = At least 3

The Nautilus Model A was advertised in the November 16, 1953 issue of *Life* magazine; it was listed in the 1954 Hamilton-Illinois Watch Catalog and in the 1955 Hamilton Watch Catalog. Hamilton purchased this model from Switzerland as a complete watch.

In naming its new waterproof watch, Hamilton made a canny choice: Nautilus. This was a name long associated with submarines, beginning with Robert Fulton's experimental boat of 1800 and made famous by Captain Nemo's vessel, named for Fulton's, in Jules Verne's 1870 novel, *20,000 Leagues Under the Sea*. The name Nautilus was much on the public mind in 1953, when the new watch was introduced, because it was well known that the U.S. Navy had started building the world's first nuclear submarine and that it was to be given that name.

Disney's release in 1954 of a movie of Verne's novel served to further increase popularity of the name. Hamilton registered the name as a trademark for watches, and it continued to use the name for about two dozen further electric models after the end of the Hamilton-Illinois line.

The Nautilus was available with more variants of dials and hands than most other Hamilton-Illinois models. The listings in the Hamilton catalog for 1955 showed three different dials. The models with luminous hands and markers had an early version of what Hamilton later called "Silhouette Hands" when used on its own line of watches. These hands have an inverted "V" cross section, and the back was filled with the luminescent paint. The intent was to have a soft glow bounced off the dial surrounding the hands. On the Nautilus, the hands also had a narrow slit down the apex of the "V" so that some light also appeared on the front.

THE USS *NAUTILUS*

The keel of the USS *Nautilus* (SSN-571) was formally laid on June 14, 1952, making it the sixth Navy ship to bear that name. Though the submarine was not launched until January 21, 1954 to undergo fitting out and tests before being formally commissioned on January 17, 1955, the press was following the progress of its construction.

The *Nautilus* went on to greater fame in the years after the end of the Hamilton-Illinois project, most notably becoming the first ship to reach the North Pole, on August 3, 1958. The continued fame of the *Nautilus*, which remained in service until March 3, 1980, allowed Hamilton to profit from the name with further watches throughout the 1950s.

In retirement, *Nautilus* has returned to its old home base at Groton, Connecticut, as part of the Submarine Force Museum.

LAKEWOOD'S $5,500 float to be entered in next New Year's Day's Tournament of Roses Parade will be the first "double decker" in the history of the Pasadena event, reports Fred SanChez, president of the Lakewood group. Lakewood's float will depict the epic voyage of the Nautilus submarine under the polar ice-cap, with the ice-cap forming a "second story" to the float.

* * * *

Independent (Long Beach, CA), October 16, 1958; image from *newspapers.com*

"NAUTILUS" SERIES
WATERPROOF • STAINLESS STEEL CASE

MODEL A	SS		Strap	951411	$ 40.90	$ 44.95
	SS		Brac	951412	43.20	49.95
	SS	Lum	Strap	951441	40.90	44.95
	SS	Lum	Brac	951442	43.20	49.95
	SS	Lum	Strap	951431	40.90	44.95
	SS	Lum	Brac	951432	43.20	49.95

1954 Price List

Nautilus Model A

Nautilus Model A with a different dial

Nautilus Model A with a two-tone dial

Nautilus Model A with a black dial

Nautilus black dial, showing radiation burn from its silhouette hands at 2:00

Nautilus Model A case back

Silhouette hands on a Hamilton Automatic K-352, from the 1956 catalog

Three versions of the Nautilus

Three Nautilus dials

The 1953 Hamilton and Illinois Watch Catalog described this watch as "An exceptionally fine 17-jewel, waterproof watch at a remarkably low price. Shockproof and anti-magnetic-. Embossed numerals and markers. Brilliant, polished stainless steel case."

National Geographic, May 1954. The Nautilus and the Lady Gay H are the last two watches in the row.

Signamatic / Signamatic Model A

Name = Signamatic, Signamatic Model A
Time Period = Mid-Century Modern
Karat/Material = SS
Bezel = Plain
Sides = Plain
Lug Size = 5/8
Spring Bar = Plain
Model No. = 9516
Casemaker = Huguenin
Case Pieces = 2
Case Number = 95160
Dimensions = 31.5 x 41mm
Movement Grade/Jewels = ETA Indimatic 1256, 652/17 (11 ½ ligne)
Dial Signed = Illinois Automatic Incabloc - Swiss
Dial Number = 9516/58200, 9505
Dial Shape = Round
Numbers = Embossed
Markers = Embossed
Dots = Luminous
Hands = Luminous
Seconds at = Sweep seconds
Anti-Magnetic = Yes
Shockproof = Yes
Waterproof = Yes
Dustproof = No
Automatic = Yes
Power Indicator = Yes
Cased in Factory = No
Advertisement = Yes
Retail Price New = $69.95, flexible band; $65.00, gray pigskin band (1953)
Production Date = 1953
Unique Case Design = Yes
Unique Dial Design = Yes

SIGNAMATIC

The Automatic which tells you how many hours it will continue to run when not worn! Waterproof, shockproof, anti-magnetic. Sweep-seconds. 17 jewels. Embossed numerals and markers with luminous dots and hands.

Gray pigskin strap . . . 951621 . . . . . . $65.00

SIGNAMATIC A

17 Jewels. Stainless Steel Case. Luminous Dial. Water resistant,* Shock resistant and Anti-magnetic, Self-winding, Signamatic Wind Indicator. Sweep Seconds.

Bracelet . . . . 951622 . . . . $69.95
Strap . . . . 951621 . . . . 65.00

The Signamatic Model A first appeared in the 1953 Illinois Catalog just as the Signamatic. At that point, there was no Model B. With the 1954 catalog and the appearance of the B, the name gained the A identifier.

The 1953 Illinois Catalog for this model states: "Window in dial shows how many hours watch will continue to run when not worn!"

The "Automatic" models were advertised as "Self-winding watches with time proven movements. Just set and wear . . . that's your full share of attention for accurate time always with an Illinois Automatic. All are shockproof, anti-magnetic, 17 jewels, sweep-seconds."

An Illinois by Hamilton 1953 catalog proclaimed that the automatics were "*Self-winding* watches of finest design. Slightest movement keeps them running! *Cannot overwind themselves*. All have sweep-seconds feature."

The Signamatic Model A was also advertised in the May 8, 1954 issue of the *Saturday Evening Post* and in the 1953 Hamilton and Illinois Watch Catalog. Hamilton purchased this model from Switzerland as a complete watch.

A page from the 1953 Hamilton-Illinois holiday brochure. Top to bottom: Signamatic, Automatic Model A, and Automatic Model B

Signamatic

Signamatic case back

Signamatic inside case back

Signamatic movement

Signamatic dial

Signamatic black dial

According to internal Hamilton records, 24,443 grade 652 movements were produced for Hamilton-Illinois models; and, 26,011 grade 651 movements were made for Hamilton's use.

The movement (with power-reserve indicator) from the Signamatic series appeared in the Hamilton Accumatic II "B" and possibly other models. In the Accumatic II, the usual Accumatic II dial design is modified with a window for the indicator (and there is also a cutout in the back to clear the indicator disk). Hamilton also stamped some inside case backs with "B" (quotation marks theirs) as though this might have been intended to be a cataloged model. The dial and movement from the Accumatic II "B" have also been spotted in the case for the Automatic K-455 (which usually has a different dial from the Accumatic II).

Hamilton Accumatic II "B"

Hamilton Accumatic II "B" case back

This movement was popular with other watchmakers as well. Ball sold a watch using it as the Indimatic (ETA's name for this version of the movement) in their Garland line, using a gold filled case that looks similar to the Signamatic A.

Hamilton Accumatic II "B" inside case back markings

Hamilton Accumatic II "B" movement

Hamilton K-455 with Accumatic II "B" dial

Signamatic Model B

SIGNAMATIC B

17 Jewels. Stainless Steel Case. Luminous Dial.

	Luminous Dots	Luminous Markers	
Bracelet	952142	952162	$69.95
Strap	952141	952161	65.00

Name = Signamatic Model B
Time Period = Mid-Century Modern
Karat/Material = SS
Bezel = Plain
Sides = Plain
Lug Size = 5/8
Spring Bar = Male
Model No. = 9521
Casemaker = Huguenin
Case Pieces = 2
Case Number = 95210
Dimensions = 32 x 39 mm
Movement Grade/Jewels = ETA Indimatic1256/17, 652/17
Dial Signed = Hamilton-Illinois Automatic Incabloc Swiss
Dial Number = 9515
Dial Shape = Round

Numbers = Embossed
Markers = Embossed
Dots = Luminous
Hands = Luminous
Seconds at = Red Sweep Seconds
Anti-Magnetic = Yes
Shockproof = Yes
Waterproof = Yes
Dustproof = Yes
Automatic = Yes
Power Indicator = Yes
Cased in Factory = No
Retail Price New = $59.95, Strap; $65.00, Flexible Band (1953); $65.00, Strap; $69.95, Bracelet (1954–1955)
Production Date = 1953
Unique Case Design = Yes
Unique Dial Design = Yes
Advertisement = Yes

The Signamatic Model B was advertised as "A rugged waterproof Automatic in gleaming stainless steel." Hamilton also pointed out that a "Dial Window Shows Hours of Reserve Running Power."

This model was advertised in the 1953 Illinois Watch Catalog and in the 1954 and 1955 Hamilton-Illinois Watch Catalog.

The watch was offered with a choice of dials, one with numbers and luminous dots and one with markers and luminous dots, which is why two pictures are featured in the 1955 Hamilton Watch Catalog.

Signamatic Model B, numeral dial

Signamatic Model B, numeral and marker dial

Signamatic B case back

Signamatic Model B inside case back

ETA 1256 movement with power reserve indicator, referred to as an "Indimatic"

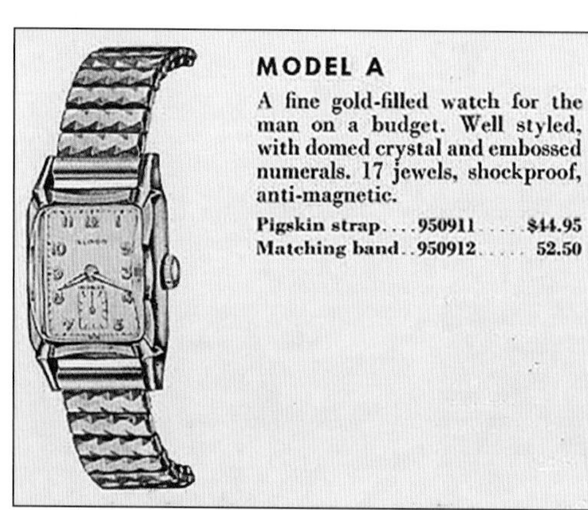

Topper Model A

Name = Topper Model A
Time Period = Mid-Century Modern
Karat/Material – 10K YGF
Bezel = Plain, curved
Sides = Plain
Lug Size = 5/8
Spring Bar = Male
Model No. = 9509
Casemaker = Schwab & Wuischpard
Case Pieces = 2
Case Number = 95090
Dimensions = 38 x 24 mm
Movement Grade/Jewels = ETA1220, 655/17 (8 x 9 ligne)
Dial Signed = Hamilton-Illinois Incabloc
Dial Number = 9509/58502
Dial Shape = Rectangular
Numbers = Embossed
Markers = None
Hands = Brass

Seconds at = 6
Anti-Magnetic = Yes
Shockproof = Yes
Waterproof = No
Dustproof = No
Automatic = No
Power Indicator = No
Cased in Factory = Yes
Advertisement = Yes
Retail Price New = $47.50, matching band; $44.95, pigskin strap band (1953); $52.50, matching band; $49.95, pigskin strap band (1954); $52.50, bracelet; $44.95, strap (1955)
Production Date = 1953
Unique Case Design = Yes
Unique Dial Design = Yes

The Topper Series was Hamilton's higher-end line of Illinois models, using cases with gold-filled backs as well as bezels. The Topper watches are more difficult to find than the Debonair models. At this point, it is hard to know whether this is because fewer were sold because of the higher prices or because the 10K gold-filled backs held up less well than stainless steel ones.

Hamilton advertised that "These Illinois watches have fine shockproof, anti-magnetic, 17 jewel movements in smart, sturdy gold-filled cases."

The 1953 Hamilton Catalog had slightly different advertising copy: "A fine gold-filled watch for the man on a budget. Well styled, with domed crystal and embossed numerals. 17 jewels, shockproof, anti-magnetic."

The Topper Series in 1953 ranged in price from $39.95 to $52.50. The prices of these models apparently increased by $5.00 from 1953 to 1954 but dropped again in 1955 (for the strap option).

The Topper Model A was advertised in the 1953 Illinois Division of Hamilton Watch Catalog, in the November 21, 1953 issue of the *Saturday Evening Post*, in the 1954 Hamilton-Illinois Watch Catalog and in the May 8, 1954 issue of the *Saturday Evening Post*.

According to internal Hamilton records, 59,653 grade 655 movements were produced for Hamilton-Illinois models.

Topper Model A

Topper Model A dial

Topper Model A case back

Topper Model A inside case back

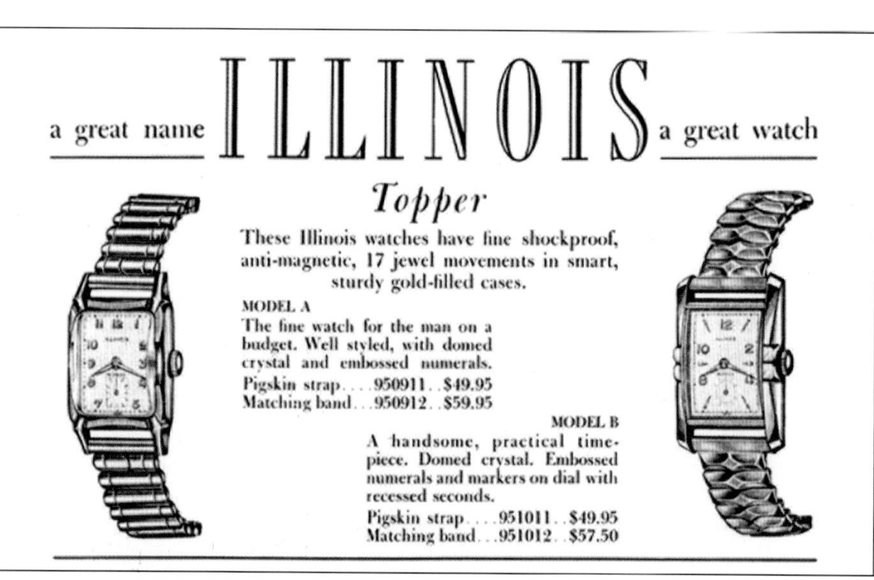

From the 1954 Hamilton-Illinois sales catalog

Topper Model B

Name = Topper Model B
Time Period = Mid-Century Modern
Karat/Material = 10K YGF
Bezel = Plain, Notched
Sides = Plain
Lug Size = 11/16
Spring Bar = Female
Model No. = 9510
Casemaker = Schwab & Wuischpard
Case Pieces = 2
Case Number = 95100
Dimensions = 22.5 x 40mm
Movement Grade/Jewels = ETA1220, 655/17 (8 x 9 ligne)
Dial Signed = Illinois Incabloc
Dial Number = 9510/58503
Dial Shape = Rectangular
Numbers = Embossed
Markers = Embossed
Hands = Brass
Seconds at = 6, Recessed
Anti-Magnetic = Yes
Shockproof = Yes
Waterproof = No
Dustproof = No
Automatic = No
Power Indicator = No
Cased in Factory = Yes
Retail Price New = $44.95, pigskin strap; $52.50, matching band (1953), $44.95, pigskin strap; $59.50, matching band (1954).
Production Date = 1953
Unique Case Design = Yes
Unique Dial Design = Yes
Advertisement = Yes

TOPPER B

17 Jewels. Yellow Gold-filled Case. Anti-magnetic, Shock resistant. Recessed Seconds.

Bracelet.........951012...........$52.50
Strap...........951011........... 44.95

"TOPPER" SERIES

MODEL A	Yel.	Strap	950911	$ 40.90	$ 44.95
	Yel.	Brac.	950912	45.50	52.50
MODEL B	Yel.	Strap	951011	40.90	44.95
	Yel.	Brac.	951012	45.50	52.50

1954 Price List

Advertised as "A handsome, practical timepiece. Domed crystal. Embossed numerals and markers on dial with recessed seconds. 17 jewels, shockproof, anti-magnetic movement."

Topper Model B

Topper Model B in its display case

The Topper Model B was advertised in the November 16, 1953 issue of *Life* magazine, in the 1954 Hamilton-Illinois Watch Catalog, in *Life* magazine in 1954, in the May 8, 1954 issue of the *Saturday Evening Post* and in the 1955 Hamilton Watch Catalog.

Hamilton advertisement for the Illinois line at Christmas, *Life*, 1953

Hamilton-Illinois Ladies' Models Identification Guide

Career Girl SERIES

The Career Girl models were advertised as "a series of fine Illinois watches featuring 17 jewel, anti-magnetic movements and sweep-seconds to keep nurses and technicians, business and sports women precisely on time through their busy careers." The Career Girls were the only watches in the Hamilton-Illinois ladies' line to have sweep seconds—in fact, the only ones with any second hands, since such things were unusual on ladies' watches of the period. The Career Girl Model A was the only waterproof watch in the line.

Career Girl Model A

MODEL A

Waterproof, powderproof stainless steel case. Embossed numerals and luminous markers. *Sweep-seconds* for extra accurate timing. 17 jewels, anti-magnetic.

Gray pigskin strap 902121 $49.95
Bracelet.......... 902122 54.95

Name = Career Girl Model A
Time Period = Mid-Century Modern
Karat/Material = SS
Bezel = Plain
Sides = Plain
Lug Size = 7/16
Spring Bar = Male
Model No. = 9021
Casemaker = Huguenin
Case Pieces = 2
Case Number = 90210
Dimensions = 31 x 24 mm
Movement Grade/Jewels = AS1240, 602/17 (x ¾ ligne)
Dial Signed = Hamilton-Illinois Incabloc
Dial Number = 9021/54400
Dial Shape = Round
Numbers = Embossed
Markers = Luminous
Hands = Luminous
Seconds at = Sweep seconds
Anti-Magnetic = Yes
Shockproof = No
Powderproof = Yes
Waterproof = Yes
Automatic = No
Power Indicator = No
Cased in Factory = No
Retail Price New = $49.95, pigskin strap; $54.95, bracelet

Production Date = 1953
Unique Case Design = Yes
Unique Dial Design = No (two versions, one shared with Career Girl B)
Advertisement = Yes

The 1953 Illinois Catalog described the Career Girl Model A as having a "Waterproof, powderproof case of brilliant stainless steel. Embossed numerals. Luminous markers and hands. Ideal for an active Career Girl!" (It is a sign of the times when these watches were marketed that an advertiser could get away with saying "powder-proof" rather than the more usual "dust proof.")

The Career Girl Model A was advertised in the 1953 Illinois Watch Catalog, the 1953 Hamilton and Illinois Catalog, the 1954 and 1955 Hamilton Catalog and in *Life* magazine on November 16, 1953 and again in *Life* in 1954.

According to internal Hamilton records, 10,132 grade 602 movements were produced for Hamilton-Illinois models. This model was purchased as a complete watch by Hamilton.

The Career Girl Model A is a nice size, and both versions of the dial are easy to read. (The black dial is especially striking.)

Career Girl A, two dial variants

Career Girl A case back

Career Girl A inside case back

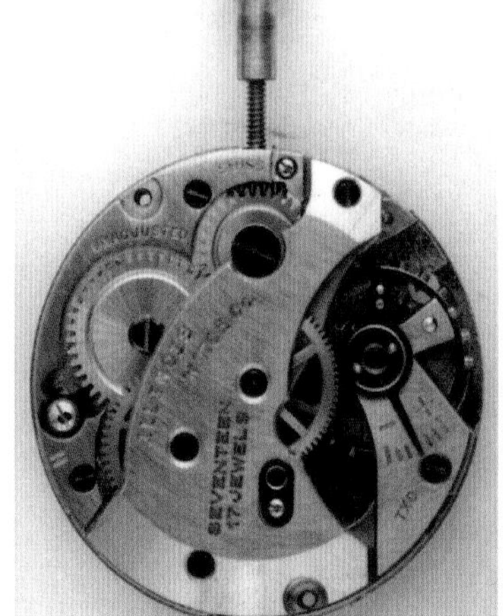

AS 1240 movement, front (*top*) and back; Hamilton factory photographs

Career Girl Model B

Name = Career Girl Model B
Time Period = Mid-Century Modern
Karat/Material = YRGF/SSB
Bezel = Plain and sculpted
Sides = Plain
Model No. = 9022
Casemaker = Schwab & Wuischpard
Case Pieces = 2
Case Number = 90220
Movement Grade/Jewels = AS1240, 602/17
Dial Signed = Hamilton-Illinois
Dial Number = 9021/54400
Dial Shape = Round
Numbers = Embossed
Markers = Embossed
Hands = Steel
Seconds at = Sweep seconds
Anti-Magnetic = Yes
Shockproof = No
Waterproof = No
Dustproof = No
Power Indicator = No
Cased in Factory = Yes
Advertisement = Yes
Retail Price New = $52.50, bracelet; $44.95, coordinating band (1953); $54.95, matching bracelet; $49.95, silk cord (1954); $47.50, yellow or white bracelet (1955)
Production Date = 1953
Unique Case Design = Yes
Unique Dial Design = No (shared with Career Girl A)

MODEL B

Sweep-seconds and easy to read embossed numerals and markers. Ideal for Nurse, Technician or Business Woman!

Silk cord . . . 902211 . . . . $44.95
Bracelet . . . . 902212 . . . . 52.50

The Career Girl Model B was described by Hamilton as follows: "Compact, smartly styled case. Easy to read embossed numerals and markers." It shared its dial and movement with the Career Girl A. However, the Career Girl B's case design and types of bracelet attachments made it a dressier watch than its sibling. Its dimensions are unusually generous for a ladies' dress watch of the period, and the dial is indeed easy to read.

"CAREER GIRL" SERIES

MODEL A	SS	Lum.	Strap	902121	$ 45.40	$ 49.95
	SS	Lum.	Brac.	902122	46.00	54.95
MODEL B	Yel.		Cord	902211	40.90	44.95
	Yel.		Brac.	902212	45.50	52.50

1954 Price List

This model appeared in the 1954 Illinois Watch Catalog, in the 1954 and 1955 Hamilton Watch Catalogs and in the May 8, 1954 issue of the *Saturday Evening Post*.

Career Girl Model B

Career Girl Model B dial

Career Girl Model B case back

AS 1240 movement

Career Girl Model B inside case back

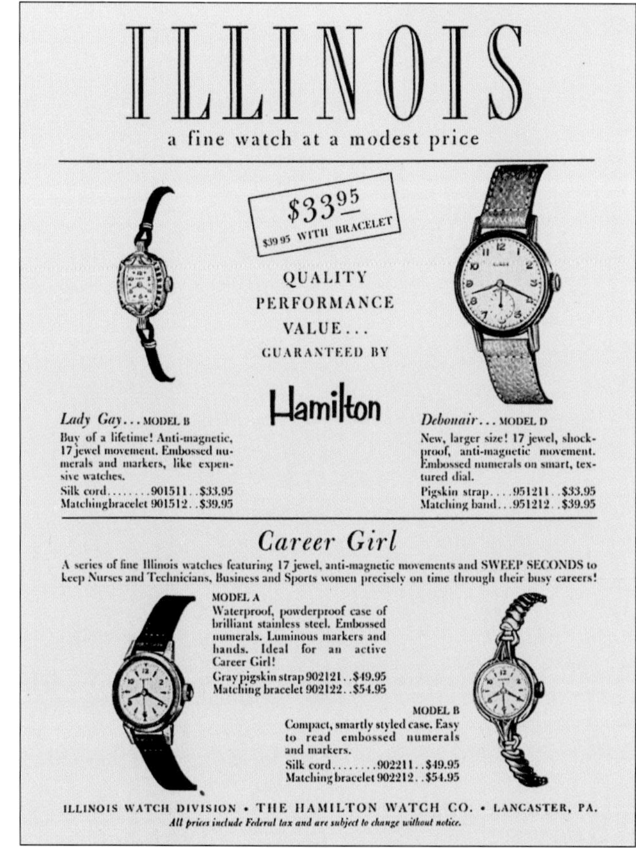

1954 Hamilton-Illinois sales catalog

The Coquette models were the more expensive of the two main lines of Hamilton-Illinois ladies' watches (the other main line was the Lady Gay series). As with the Topper series of men's watches, the Coquettes, with one exception (Model D), had full gold-filled cases rather than being rolled gold plate with stainless backs.

The Coquette line was provided with the following advertising copy: "This group of fine Illinois watches has beautifully styled white or yellow gold-filled cases. All have 17 jewel, anti-magnetic movements."

Coquette Model A

Name = Coquette Model A
Time Period = Mid-Century Modern
Karat/Material = 10K YGF or 10K WGF
Bezel = Sculpted
Sides = Plain
Model No. = 9011/9010
Casemaker = Schwab & Wuischpard
Case Pieces = 2
Case Number = 90100 WGF, 90110 YGF
Dimensions = 27 x 16mm
Movement Grade/Jewels = AS976, 601/17 (5 ligne)
Dial Signed = Hamilton-Illinois
Dial Number = 9021/54400
Dial Shape = Rectangular
Numbers = Embossed
Markers = None
Hands = Brass
Seconds at = None
Anti-Magnetic = Yes
Shockproof = No
Waterproof = No
Dustproof = No
Cased in Factory = Yes
Retail Price New = $54.95, WGF or YGF, silk cord; $62.50, WGF or YGF, matching bracelet (1953), $62.50, WGF or YGF, silk cord; $49.95, WGF or YGF, bracelet (1954).
Production Date = 1953
Unique Case Design = Yes
Unique Dial Design = No
Advertisement = Yes

MODEL A

Tiny gem in white or yellow gold-filled, made to grace a slender wrist. Embossed numerals and 17 jewel movement.

Silk Cord, White . 901011 . $49.95
Silk Cord, Yellow . 901111 . 49.95
Bracelet, White . . 901012 . . $57.50
Bracelet, Yellow . 901112 . 57.50

The Coquette Model A was noted as being "Tiny . . . to grace a slender wrist. Silk cord."

The 1953 Hamilton Catalog called the Coquette A as a "Tiny gem in yellow or white gold-filled." In addition, this model appeared in the 1953 Hamilton and Illinois Watch Catalog and in the 1954 and 1955 Hamilton Watch Catalogs.

According to Hamilton internal records, 33,397 grade 601 movements were produced for Hamilton-Illinois models.

Coquette Model A

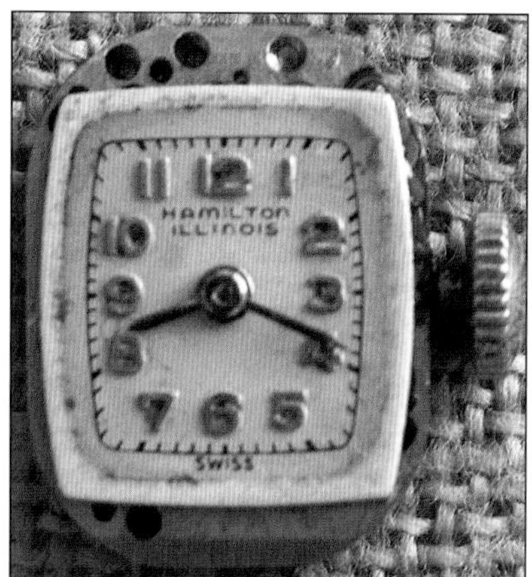

Coquette Model A dial

Coquette Model A case back

AS 976 movement

Coquette Model A inside case back

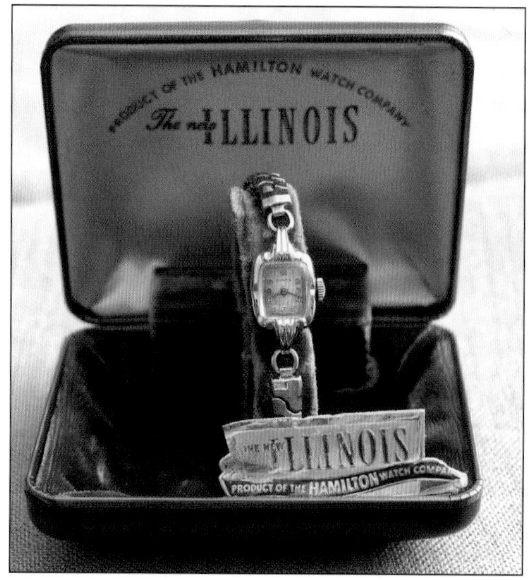

Coquette Model A in its display box

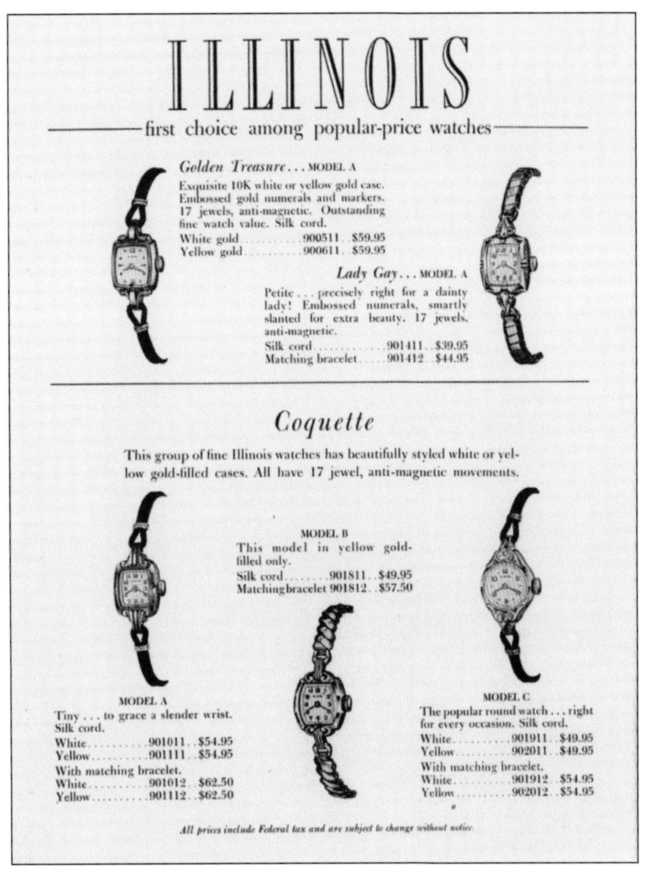

ILLINOIS

—first choice among popular-price watches—

Golden Treasure... MODEL A

Exquisite 10K white or yellow gold case. Embossed gold numerals and markers. 17 jewels, anti-magnetic. Outstanding fine watch value. Silk cord.

White gold..........900511..$59.95
Yellow gold..........900611..$59.95

Lady Gay... MODEL A

Petite... precisely right for a dainty lady! Embossed numerals, smartly slanted for extra beauty. 17 jewels, anti-magnetic.

Silk cord..........901411..$39.95
Matching bracelet.....901412..$44.95

Coquette

This group of fine Illinois watches has beautifully styled white or yellow gold-filled cases. All have 17 jewel, anti-magnetic movements.

MODEL B

This model in yellow gold-filled only.

Silk cord.......901811..$49.95
Matchingbracelet 901812..$57.50

MODEL A

Tiny... to grace a slender wrist. Silk cord.

White..........901011..$54.95
Yellow..........901111..$54.95

With matching bracelet.

White..........901012..$62.50
Yellow..........901112..$62.50

MODEL C

The popular round watch... right for every occasion. Silk cord.

White..........901911..$49.95
Yellow..........902011..$49.95

With matching bracelet.

White..........901912..$54.95
Yellow..........902012..$54.95

All prices include Federal tax and are subject to change without notice.

A page from the 1953 Hamilton-Illinois sales catalog

Coquette Model B

Name = Coquette Model B
Time Period = Mid-Century Modern
Karat/Material = 10K YGF
Bezel = Sculpted
Sides = Plain
Model No. = 9018
Casemaker = Schwab & Wuischpard
Case Pieces = 2
Case Number = 90180
Movement Grade/Jewels = AS1406, 600/17
Dial Signed = Hamilton-Illinois
Dial Number = 9018/54006
Dial Shape = Tonneau
Numbers = Embossed
Markers = None
Hands = Brass

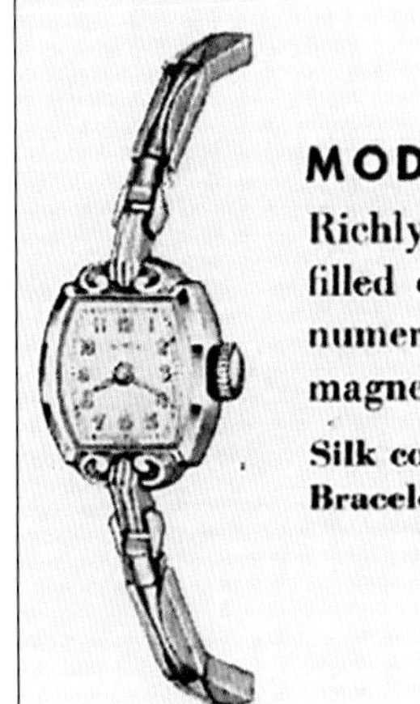

MODEL B

Richly designed yellow gold-filled case and full, embossed numeral dial. 17 jewels, anti-magnetic.

Silk cord...901811.......$44.95
Bracelet....901812....... 52.50

Seconds at = None
Anti-Magnetic = Yes
Shockproof = No
Waterproof = No
Dustproof = No
Cased in Factory = Yes
Advertisement = Yes
Retail Price New = $44.95, cord; $52,50, bracelet (1953); $57.50, matching bracelet; $49.95, silk cord (1954); $52.50, bracelet; $44.95, silk cord (1955)
Production Date = 1953
Unique Case Design = Yes
Unique Dial Design = No

The Coquette Model B appeared in the first Hamilton and Illinois Watch Catalog in 1953 and again in the 1954 and 1955 Hamilton Watch Catalogs. The 1953 catalog had this description for it: "Richly designed yellow gold-filled case and full, embossed numeral dial. 17 jewels, anti-magnetic." The 1954 catalog noted that this model came "in yellow gold-filled only."

The Coquette B was also advertised in the *Saturday Evening Post* issues of November 21, 1953 and May 8, 1954.

According to internal Hamilton records, 156,747 grade 600 movements were produced for Hamilton-Illinois models.

Coquette Model B

Coquette Model B dial

Coquette Model B case back

Coquette Model B inside case back

Coquette Model C

Name = Coquette Model C
Time Period = Mid-Century Modern
Karat/Material = 10K YGF or 10K WGF
Bezel = Plain and sculpted
Sides = Plain
Model No. = 9019 in WGF, 9020 in YGF
Casemaker = Schwab & Wuischpard
Case Pieces = 2
Case Number = 9019 WGF; 90191 YGF
Movement Grade/Jewels = AS1406, 600/17
Dial Signed = Hamilton-Illinois
Dial Number = 9019/54007 WGF; 9020/54008 YGF
Dial Shape = Round
Numbers = Embossed
Markers = Embossed
Hands = Brass
Seconds at = None
Anti-Magnetic = Yes
Shockproof = No
Waterproof = No
Dustproof = No
Cased in Factory = Yes

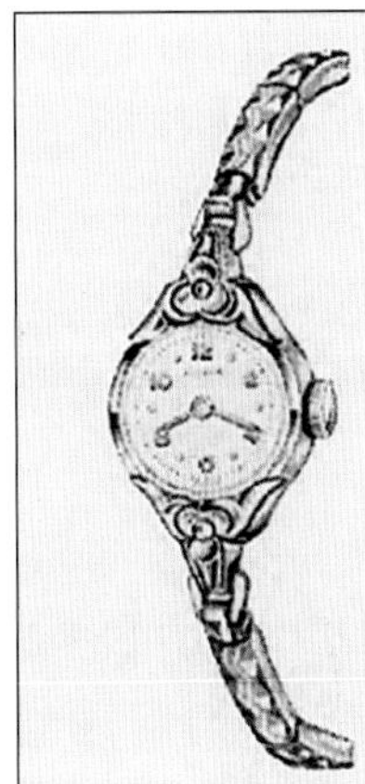

MODEL C

The ever popular round watch . . . right for every occasion. Embossed numerals and dots, 17 jewels, anti-magnetic. White or yellow gold-filled case.

Silk Cord, White . 901911 . $44.95
Silk Cord, Yellow . 902011 . 44.95

Bracelet, White . . 901912 . . $52.50
Bracelet, Yellow . 902012 . 52.50

Retail Price New = $44.95, WGF/YGF, cord (1953); $44.95, WGF/YGF, silk cord; $52.50, WGF/YGF, matching bracelet (1954); $52.50, WGF/YGF, bracelet; $44.95, WGF/YGF, cord (1955)
Production Date = 1953
Unique Case Design = Yes
Unique Dial Design = No
Advertisement = Yes

The Coquette Model C was described in the 1953 and 1954 Illinois Catalogs as "The ever popular round watch . . . right for every occasion." This model was also advertised in the November 21, 1953 issue of the *Saturday Evening Post* and in the 1954 and 1955 Hamilton Watch Catalogs.

Coquette Model C

Coquette Model C dial

Coquette Model C case back

Coquette Model C inside case back

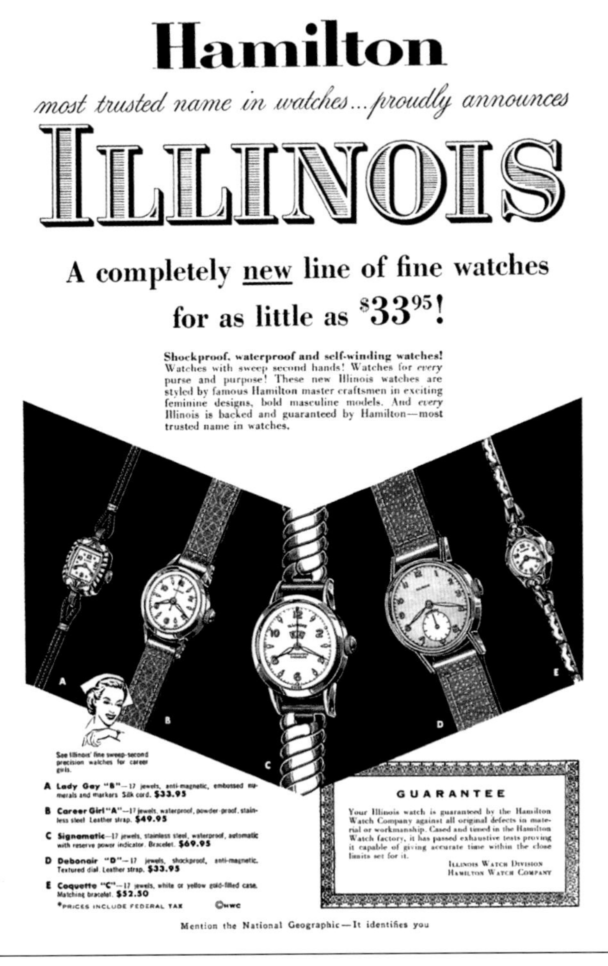

In its 1954 Watch Catalog, Hamilton described its ladies' Illinois models this way: "Maximum jeweled for finest performance, anti-magnetic, and twice tested for accuracy, fine Hamilton-Illinois ladies' watches are designed in fashionable up-to-the-minute styles. For the budget conscious buyer these fine timepieces offer performance value well in excess of their modest prices."

***National Geographic*, October 1953. *Left to right*: Lady Gay Model B, Career Girl Model A, Signamatic, Debonair Model D and Coquette Model C**

Coquette Model D

Name = Coquette Model D
Time Period = Mid-Century Modern
Karat/Material = 10K YRGP/SSB or 10K WRGP/SSB; 10K YRGP/SSB or 10K WRGP/SSB
Bezel = Plain and sculpted
Sides = Plain
Model No. = 9031, YGRP; 9041 WRGP
Casemaker = Schwab & Wuischpard
Case Pieces = 2
Case Number = 90310, YRGP; 90410, WRGP
Movement Grade/Jewels = AS1406, 600/17
Dial Signed = Hamilton-Illinois
Dial Number = Unknown

COQUETTE D
Yellow or White Case. Stainless Steel Back.
Yellow White
Bracelet..903112...904112....$47.50

Dial Shape = Rectangular
Numbers = Embossed
Markers = Embossed
Hands = Brass
Seconds at = None
Anti-Magnetic = Yes
Shockproof = No
Waterproof = No
Dustproof = No
Cased in Factory = Yes
Advertisement = Yes
Retail Price New = $47.50, YGF or WGF, bracelet (1955)
Production Date = 1955
Unique Case Design = Yes
Unique Dial Design = No

The Coquette Model D was given only a brief listing in the 1955 Hamilton Watch Catalog: "Yellow or White Case, Stainless Steel Back."

This was the only model in the Coquette series that had a rolled gold plate case with a stainless steel back; all the others were in 10K gold-filled cases (both bezel and back).

The Coquette D was renamed the Dinah as a Hamilton model. It was listed in the 1956 Hamilton catalog but appears to have been discontinued after that.

Coquette Model D

Coquette Model D case back

Coquette Model D inside case back

Coquette Model E

COQUETTE E

17 Jewels. Yellow or White Gold-filled Case.

	Yellow	White	
Bracelet....	903012.....	904012.....	$49.95

Name = Coquette Model E
Time Period = Mid-Century Modern
Karat/Material = 10K YGF or 10K WGF
Bezel = Plain and sculpted
Sides = Plain
Model No. = 9030, YGF; 9040, WGF
Casemaker = Schwab & Wuischpard
Case Pieces = 2
Case Number = 90300, YGF; 90400, WGF
Movement Grades/Jewels = AS 976, 600/17
Dial Signed = Hamilton-Illinois
Dial Number = Unknown
Dial Shape = Rectangular
Numbers = Embossed
Markers = Embossed
Hands = Brass
Seconds at = None
Anti-Magnetic = Yes
Shockproof = No
Waterproof = No
Dustproof = No
Cased in Factory = Yes
Advertisement = Yes
Retail Price New = $47.95, cord; $49.50, bracelet (1954, 1955)
Production Date = 1954
Unique Case Design = Yes
Unique Dial Design = No

The Coquette Model E was advertised in *Life* magazine in 1954 and was listed in the 1954 and 1955 Hamilton Watch Catalogs. Renamed Elise as a Hamilton model, It was listed in the 1956 Hamilton catalog but appears to have been discontinued after that.

"COQUETTE" SERIES

MODEL A	Yel.	Cord	901111	$ 45.40	$ 49.95
	Yel.	Brac.	901112	49.80	57.50
	Wh.	Cord	901011	45.40	49.95
	Wh.	Brac.	901012	49.80	57.50
MODEL B	Yel.	Cord	901811	40.90	44.95
	Yel.	Brac.	901812	45.50	52.50
MODEL C	Yel.	Cord	902011	40.90	44.95
	Yel.	Brac.	902012	45.50	52.50
	Wh.	Cord	901911	40.90	44.95
	Wh.	Brac.	901912	45.50	52.50
MODEL E	Yel.	Brac.	904012	45.50	49.95
	Wh.	Brac.	903012	45.50	49.95

1954 Price List

Coquette Model E

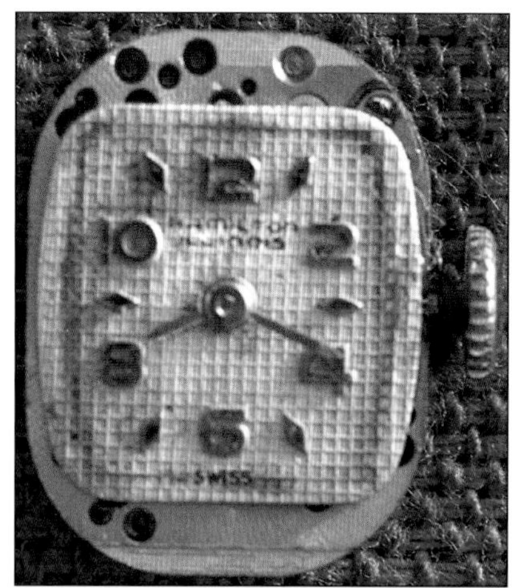

Coquette Model E dial

Coquette Model E case back

Coquette Model E inside case back

Life magazine, 1954

The Golden Treasure series were at the high end of the cataloged ladies' Hamilton-Illinois models. Unlike the other watches, they were cased in solid gold, though in keeping with the budget emphasis, it was only 10K gold. The original watches were equipped with cord bands made by Hadley.

Golden Treasure Model A

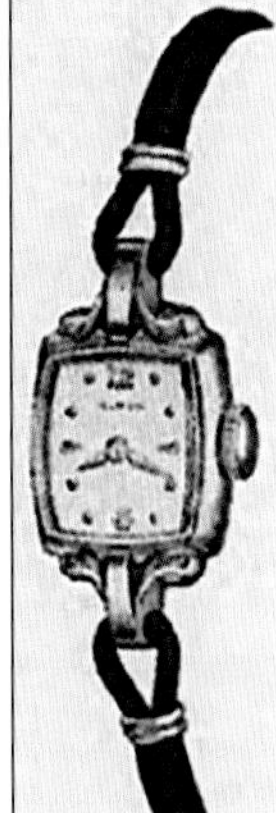

MODEL A

Exquisite 10K white or yellow gold case. Embossed numerals, markers and dots. 17 jewels, anti-magnetic. Outstanding fine watch value. Silk cord.

White......900511.......$54.95
Yellow......900611.......54.95

Name = Golden Treasure Model A
Time Period = Mid-Century Modern
Karat/Material = 10K YG or 10K WG
Bezel = Plain and sculpted
Sides = Plain
Model No. = 9005, WG; 9006, YG
Casemaker = Schwab & Wuischpard
Case Pieces = 2
Case Number = 90050, WG; 90060, YG
Movement Grades/Jewels = AS976, 601/17 (5 ligne)
Dial Signed = Hamilton-Illinois
Dial Number = 9005/54200, WG; 9006/54201, YG
Dial Shape = Rectangular
Numbers = Embossed
Markers = Embossed
Hands = Brass
Seconds at = None
Anti-Magnetic = Yes
Shockproof = No
Waterproof = No
Dustproof = No
Cased in Factory = Yes
Advertisement = Yes
Retail Price New = $54.95, WG or YG, cord; $59.95, bracelet, 1953–1955
Production Date = 1953
Unique Case Design = Yes
Unique Dial Design = No

The Golden Treasure Model A was given this description by Hamilton: "Exquisite 10K white or yellow gold case. Embossed gold numerals, markers and dots. 17 jewels, anti-magnetic. Outstanding watch value. Silk cord."

This solid gold model was advertised in the 1953 Hamilton and Illinois Watch Catalog and in the November 16, 1953 issue of *Life* magazine; in the 1954 Illinois Watch Catalog; in the 1954 and 1955 Hamilton Watch Catalogs; in the May 8, 1954 issue of the *Saturday Evening Post* and in *Life* magazine again in 1954.

Golden Treasure Model A

Golden Treasure Model A dial

Golden Treasure Model A case back

Golden Treasure Model A with its original Hadley band

Golden Treasure Model A inside case back

Golden Treasure Model A original band with Hadley mark

Saturday Evening Post, May 8, 1954

Golden Treasure Model B

Name = Golden Treasure Model B
Time Period = Mid-Century Modern
Karat/Material = 10K YG or 10K WG
Bezel = Plain and sculpted
Sides = Plain
Model No. = 9007, WG; 9008, YG
Casemaker = Schwab & Wuischpard
Case Pieces = 2
Case Number = 90070, WG; 90080, YG
Movement Grade/Jewels = AS976, 601/17 (5 ligne)
Dial Signed = Hamilton-Illinois
Dial Number = 9007/54202, WG; 9006/54203, YG
Dial Shape = Rectangular
Numbers = Embossed
Markers = Embossed

MODEL B

Styled to wear on every dress-up occasion! 10K white or yellow gold case. Embossed numerals and dots. 17 jewels, anti-magnetic. Silk cord.

White. . . . . 900711. . . . . . . $54.95
Yellow. . . . . 900811. . . . . . . 54.95

Dots = Embossed
Hands = Brass
Seconds at = None
Anti-Magnetic = Yes
Shockproof = No
Waterproof = No
Dustproof = No
Cased in Factory = Yes
Advertisement = Yes
Retail Price New = $54.95, WG or YG, cord; $59.95, bracelet, (1953–1955)
Production Date = 1953
Unique Case Design = Yes
Unique Dial Design = No

The 1953 Hamilton and Illinois Watch Catalog proclaimed that the Golden Treasure Model B was "Styled to wear on every dress-up occasion! 10K white or yellow gold case. Embossed numerals and dots. 17 jewels, anti-magnetic. Silk cord."

This model also appeared in the 1954 and 1955 Hamilton Watch Catalogs.

Golden Treasure Model B

Golden Treasure Model B dial

Golden Treasure Model B case back

"GOLDEN TREASURE" SERIES

MODEL A	Yel.	Cord	900611	$ 50.00	$ 54.95
	Wh.	Cord	900511	50.00	54.95
MODEL B	Yel.	Cord	900811	50.00	54.95
	Wh.	Cord	900711	50.00	54.95

1954 Price List

Golden Treasure Model B inside case back

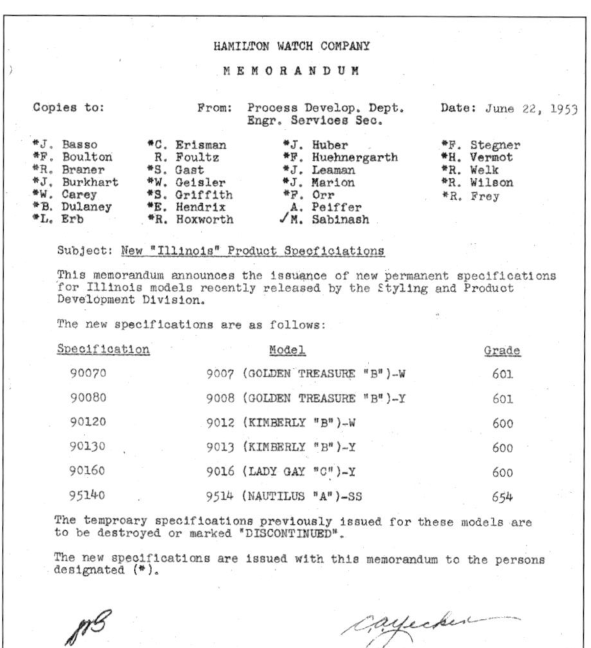

HAMILTON WATCH COMPANY

MEMORANDUM

Copies to: From: Process Develop. Dept. Engr. Services Sec. Date: June 22, 1953

*J. Basso	*C. Erisman	*J. Huber	*F. Stegner
*F. Boulton	R. Foultz	*F. Huehnergarth	*H. Vermot
*R. Braner	*S. Gast	*J. Leaman	*R. Welk
*J. Burkhart	*W. Geisler	*J. Marion	*R. Wilson
*W. Carey	*S. Griffith	*F. Orr	*R. Frey
*B. Dulaney	*E. Hendrix	A. Peiffer	
*L. Erb	*R. Hoxworth	✓M. Sabinash	

Subject: New "Illinois" Product Specficiations

This memorandum announces the issuance of new permanent specifications for Illinois models recently released by the Styling and Product Development Division.

The new specifications are as follows:

Specification	Model	Grade
90070	9007 (GOLDEN TREASURE "B")-W	601
90080	9008 (GOLDEN TREASURE "B")-Y	601
90120	9012 (KIMBERLY "B")-W	600
90130	9013 (KIMBERLY "B")-Y	600
90160	9016 (LADY GAY "C")-Y	600
95140	9514 (NAUTILUS "A")-SS	654

The temproary specifications previously issued for these models are to be destroyed or marked "DISCONTINUED".

The new specifications are issued with this memorandum to the persons designated (*).

Internal memorandum, dated June 22, 1953, introducing the Golden Treasure Model B and five other Hamilton-Illinois watches

The Kimberly series takes its name from the Kimberly mine in South Africa, one of the most famous sources of diamonds. Like the Golden Treasure series, the Kimberly series is at the high end of the cataloged ladies' Hamilton-Illinois models. Although the Golden Treasure models were solid 10K gold, the Kimberly cases were only 10K gold-filled; however, they had diamond-set bezels. In 1953 the Kimberly Series watches ranged in price from $49.95 to $95.00.

It is interesting that after discontinuing the Hamilton-Illinois line, Hamilton took the Kimberly name for one series of diamond watches of its own, which it introduced in 1957. (There were 12 models, all in 10K solid gold instead of the 10K GF of the Hamilton-Illinois Kimberlys, and they had 4 to 24 diamonds, depending on the particular model. A few of these were offered in either white or yellow gold, but the vast majority were the former.)

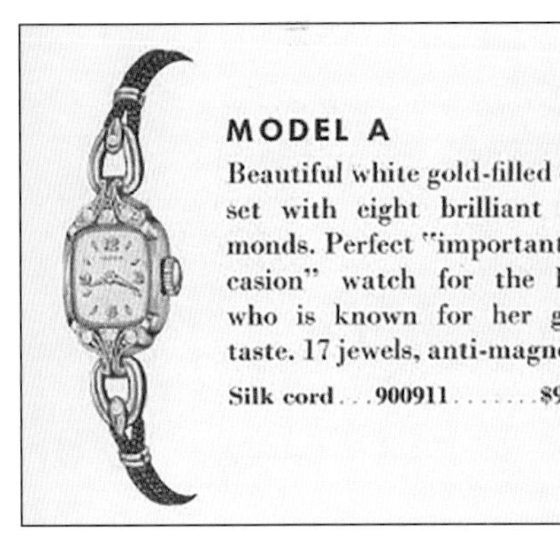

Kimberly Model A

Name = Kimberly Model A
Time Period = Mid-Century Modern
Karat/Material = 10K WGF
Bezel = Sculpted and plain, eight diamonds
Sides = Plain
Model No. = 9009
Casemaker = Schwab & Wuischpard
Case Pieces = 2
Case Number = 90090
Movement Grade/Jewels = AS 976, 600/17
Dial Signed = Hamilton-Illinois
Dial Number = 9009/54204
Dial Shape = Rectangular
Numbers = Embossed
Markers = Embossed
Hands = Brass
Seconds at = None
Anti-Magnetic = Yes
Shockproof = No
Waterproof = No
Dustproof = No
Cased in Factory = Yes
Advertisement = Yes
Retail Price New = $95.00, silk cord (1953); $85.00, cord or bracelet (1954–1955)
Production Date = 1953
Unique Case Design = Yes
Unique Dial Design = No

The Kimberly Model A debuted in the 1953 Hamilton and Illinois Watch Catalog, where it was called a "Beautiful white gold-filled case set with eight brilliant diamonds. Perfect 'important occasion' watch for the lady who is known for her good taste. 17 jewels, anti-magnetic."

The 1954 Hamilton Watch Catalog pointed out that "Hamilton-Illinois is the extension of the Hamilton line into the moderate price range. These imported watches are engineered and processed to exacting Hamilton specifications. They have been exhaustively tested here and abroad and pronounced worthy members of the Hamilton family of dependable watches."

This model also appeared in the 1955 Hamilton Watch Catalog.

Kimberly Model A dial

Kimberly Model A

Kimberly Model A case back

Kimberly Model A inside case back

MODEL B

Two genuine diamonds highlight this sparkling gold-filled beauty. A fine diamond-set watch at an unbelievably low price! 17 jewel, anti-magnetic movement. Silk cord.

White......901211.......$49.95
Yellow......901311....... 49.95

Kimberly Model B

Name = Kimberly Model B
Time Period = Mid-Century Modern
Karat/Material = 10K WGF or 10 YGF
Bezel = Engraved and sculpted, two diamonds
Sides = Plain
Model No. = 9012, WGF; 9013, YGF
Casemaker = Schwab & Wuischpard
Case Pieces = 2
Case Number = 90120, WGF; 90130, YGF
Movement Grade/Jewels = AS1406, 600/17
Dial Signed = Hamilton-Illinois
Dial Number = 9012/54000, WGF; 9013/54001, YGF
Dial Shape = Rectangular
Numbers = Embossed
Markers = Embossed
Hands = Brass
Seconds at = None
Anti-Magnetic = Yes
Shockproof = No
Waterproof = No
Dustproof = No
Cased in Factory = Yes
Advertisement = Yes
Retail Price New = $49.95, WGF or YGF (1953–1954); $54.95, YGF, bracelet (1955)
Production Date = 1953
Unique Case Design = Yes
Unique Dial Design = No

The 1953 Hamilton and Illinois Watch Catalog noted: "Two genuine diamonds highlight this sparkling gold-filled beauty. A fine diamond-set watch at an unbelievable low price! 17 jewels, anti-magnetic. Silk cord."

The Kimberly Model B also appeared in the 1955 Hamilton Watch Catalog, where it was listed with a gold-filled expansion band. This was by Speidel and had a delicate engraving pattern matching that on the watch.

Kimberly Model B

Kimberly Model B dial

Kimberly Model B case back

Kimberly Model B inside case back

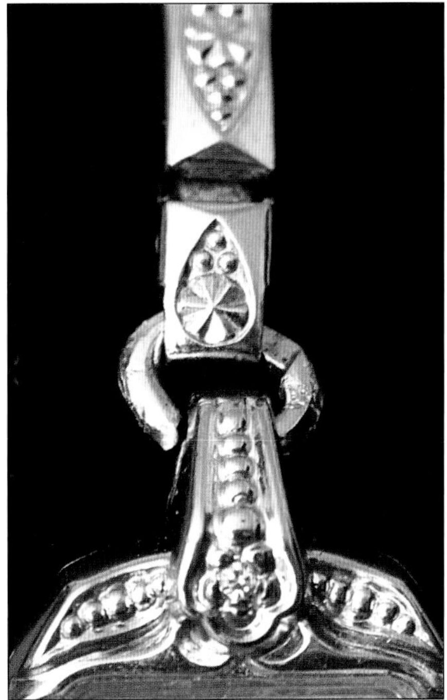

Detail of original Speidel band made to match the Kimberly Model B case

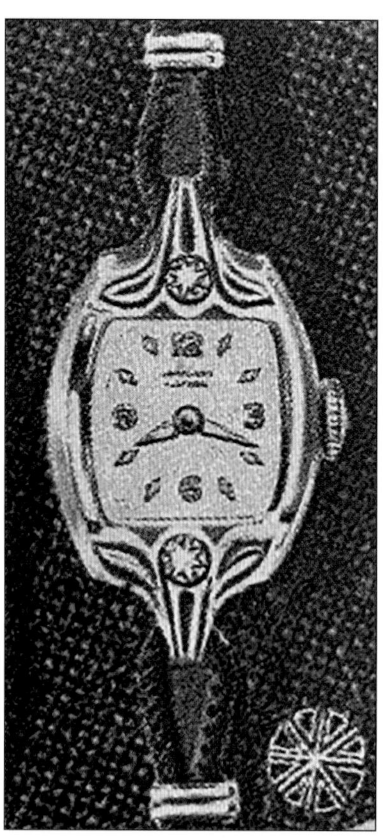

Kimberly Model C

Kimberly Model C

Name =	Kimberly Model C
Time Period =	Mid-Century Modern
Karat/Material =	10K WGF or 10 YGF
Bezel =	Engraved and sculpted, two diamonds
Sides =	Plain
Model No. =	9023, WGF; 9024, YGF
Casemaker =	Schwab & Wuischpard
Case Pieces =	2
Case Number =	90230, WGF; 90240, YGF
Movement Grade/Jewels =	AS1406, 600/17
Dial Signed =	Hamilton-Illinois
Dial Number =	9023/54009, WGF; 9024/54010, YGF
Dial Shape =	Rectangular
Numbers =	Embossed
Markers =	Embossed
Hands =	Brass
Seconds at =	None
Anti-Magnetic =	Yes
Shockproof =	No
Waterproof =	No
Dustproof =	No
Cased in Factory =	Yes
Advertisement =	Yes
Retail Price New =	$49.95, WGF or YGF (1953); $49.95, WGF or YGF (1954); $54.95, YGF, bracelet (1955)
Production Date =	1953
Unique Case Design =	Yes
Unique Dial Design =	No

The Kimberly C, advertised in a Hamilton holiday brochure that appeared in the December 1954 issue of *Coronet*, was described as having "Two sparkling diamonds exquisitely set in a dainty yellow or white gold-filled case."

In the 1955 Hamilton Watch Catalog, the "Hamilton-Illinois Watches for Women" were described as follows: "With moderate prices, superb beauty and dependable performance, Hamilton-Illinois ladies' watches are the finest in the low price field. Timed and tested at the Hamilton factory, these outstanding watches meet all the rigid standards prescribed by Hamilton engineers."

"KIMBERLY" SERIES

MODEL A	Wh.	Cord	900911	$ 75.40	$ 85.00
MODEL B	Yel.	Cord	901311	45.40	49.95
	Wh.	Cord	901211	45.40	49.95

1954 Price List

Cover page to a fifteen-page advertisement in the December, 1954 *Coronet*, containing two pages displaying sixteen Hamilton/Illinois models

Lady Gay SERIES

The Lady Gay series was the least expensive line in the Hamilton-Illinois catalog. Like the Debonair series of men's watches, they had rolled gold plate bezels but stainless-steel backs. And like the Debonairs, they are more common today than the watches with full gold-filled cases.

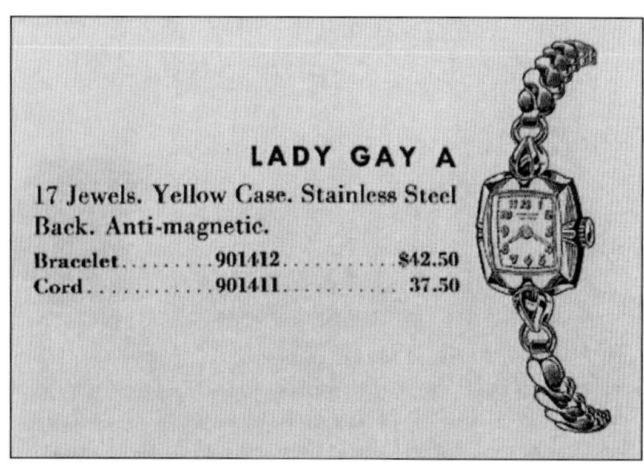
LADY GAY A

17 Jewels. Yellow Case. Stainless Steel Back. Anti-magnetic.

Bracelet	901412	$42.50
Cord	901411	37.50

LADY GAY MODEL A

Name = Lady Gay Model A
Time Period = Mid-Century Modern
Karat/Material = 10K YRGP/SSB
Bezel = Sculpted
Sides = Plain
Model No. = 9014
Casemaker = Star
Case Pieces = 2
Case Number = 90140
Movement Grade/Jewels = AS1406, 600/17
Dial Signed = Hamilton-Illinois
Dial Number = 9014/54002
Dial Shape = Square
Numbers = Embossed and "Smartly Slanted"
Markers = Embossed
Hands = Brass
Seconds at = None
Anti-Magnetic = Yes
Shockproof = No
Waterproof = No
Dustproof = No
Cased in Factory = Yes
Advertisement = Yes
Retail Price New = $37.50, silk cord; $42.50, bracelet (1954)
Production Date = 1953
Unique Case Design = Yes
Unique Dial Design = No

In its 1954 watch catalog, Hamilton described the Lady Gay Model A as "Petite . . . precisely right for a dainty lady! Embossed numerals, smartly slanted for extra beauty. 17 jewels, anti-magnetic." This watch also appeared in the November 21, 1953 issue of the *Saturday Evening Post*, in the 1953 Hamilton and Illinois Watch Catalog, in the 1954 and 1955 Hamilton Watch Catalogs, in the 1954 Illinois Watch Catalog and in the May 8, 1954 issue of the *Saturday Evening Post*.

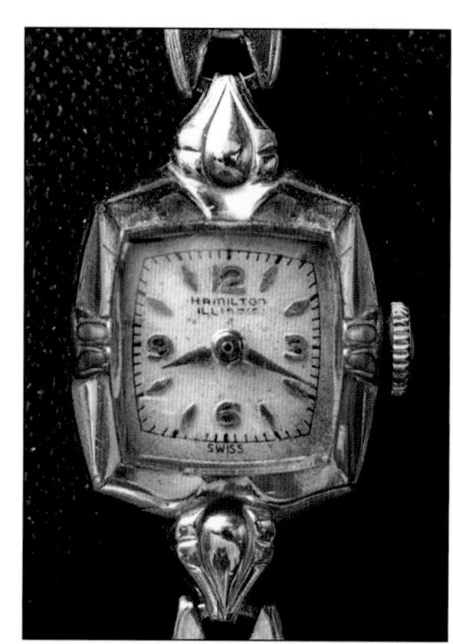

Lady Gay Model A dial

Lady Gay Model A dial

Lady Gay Model A case back

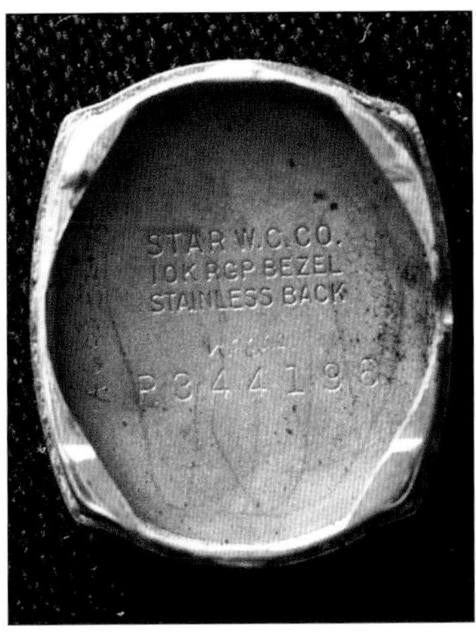

Lady Gay Model A inside case back

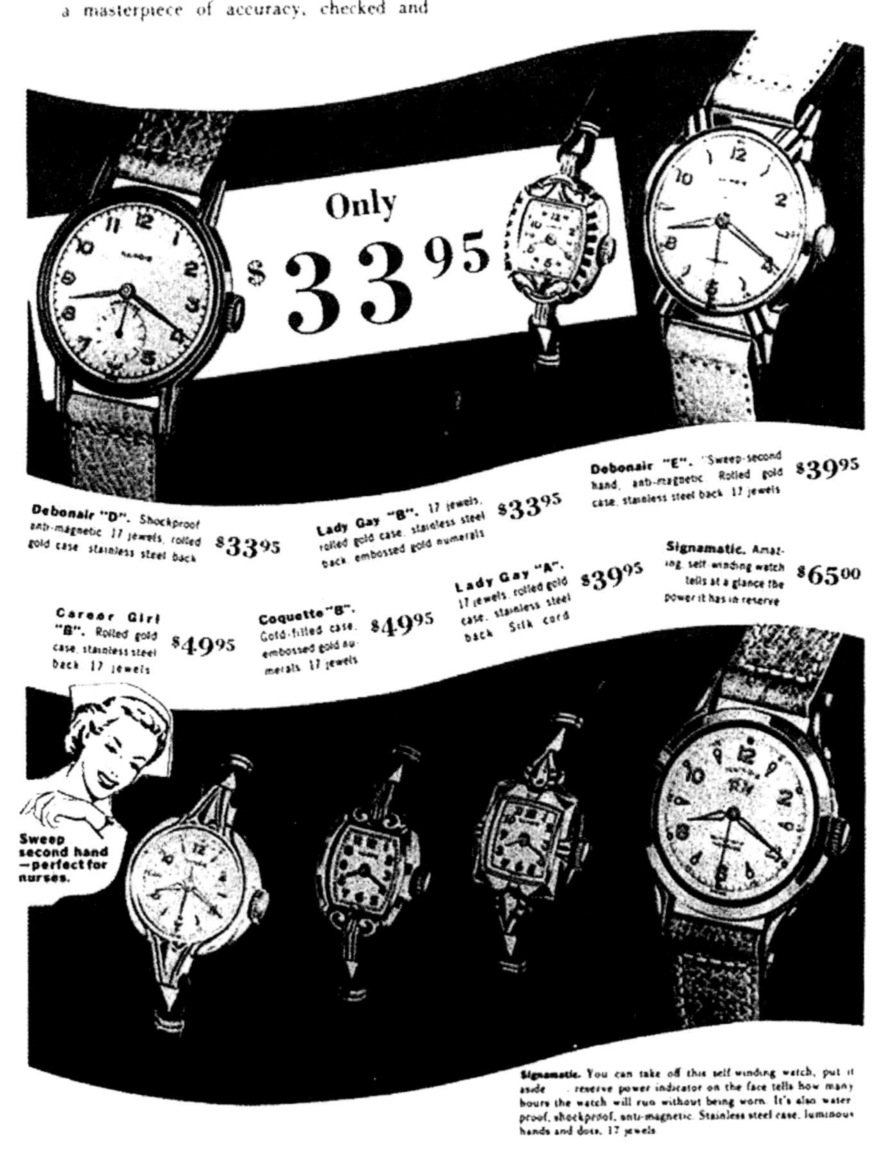

Saturday Evening Post, November 21, 1953

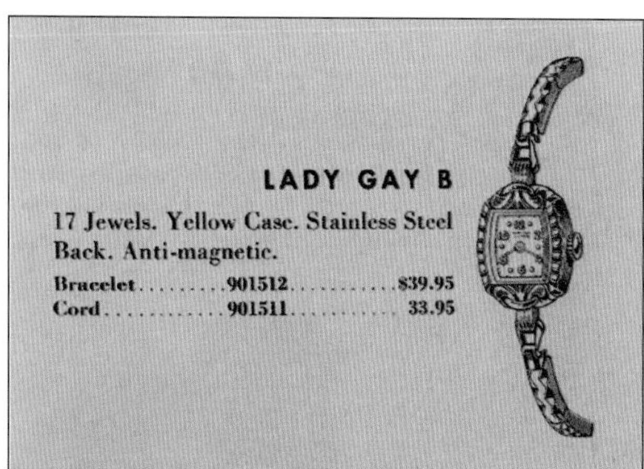
LADY GAY B

17 Jewels. Yellow Case. Stainless Steel Back. Anti-magnetic.

Bracelet	901512	$39.95
Cord	901511	33.95

Lady Gay Model B

Name = Lady Gay Model B
Time Period = Mid-Century Modern
Karat/Material = 10K YRGP/SSB
Bezel = Sculpted
Sides = Plain
Model No. = 9015
Casemaker = Star
Case Pieces = 2
Case Number = 90150
Dimensions = 27 x 14 mm
Movement Grade/Jewels = AS1406, 600/17
Dial Signed = Hamilton-Illinois
Dial Number = 90151/54003
Dial Shape = Tonneau
Numbers = Embossed
Markers = Embossed
Hands = Brass
Seconds at = None
Anti-Magnetic = Yes
Shockproof = No
Waterproof = No
Dustproof = No
Cased in Factory = Yes
Advertisement = Yes
Retail Price New = $33.95, cord; $39.95, bracelet (1954)
Production Date = 1953
Unique Case Design = Yes
Unique Dial Design = No

The 1953 Illinois Catalog called the Lady Gay Model B the "Buy of a lifetime! Anti-magnetic, 17 jewel movement. Embossed numerals and markers, like expensive watches." In addition, this model was advertised in the November 1, 1953 issue of *Life* magazine, in the 1953 Hamilton and Illinois Watch Catalog, in the 1954 Hamilton Watch Catalog and again in 1954 in *Life* magazine.

Lady Gay Model B

Lady Gay Model B case back

Advertisement for a Debonair Model D and a Lady Gay Model B, *Troy Record* (Troy, NY), October 7, 1954; image from *newspapers.com*

Nautilus and Lady Gay Model B in Illinois by Hamilton advertisement, *Life*, 1954

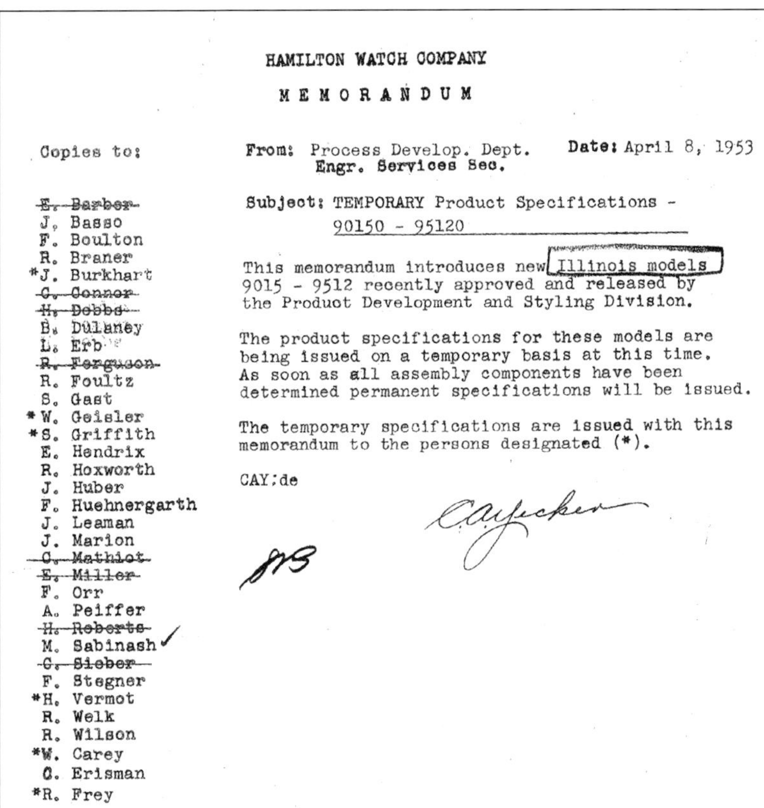

HAMILTON WATCH COMPANY

M E M O R A N D U M

Copies to:

~~E. Barber~~
J. Basso
F. Boulton
R. Braner
*J. Burkhart
~~C. Connor~~
~~H. Dobbs~~
B. Dulaney
L. Erb
~~R. Ferguson~~
R. Foultz
S. Gast
*W. Geisler
*S. Griffith
E. Hendrix
R. Hoxworth
J. Huber
F. Huehnergarth
J. Leaman
J. Marion
~~C. Mathiot~~
~~E. Miller~~
F. Orr
A. Peiffer
~~H. Roberts~~
M. Sabinash ✓
~~C. Sieber~~
F. Stegner
*H. Vermot
R. Welk
R. Wilson
*W. Carey
C. Erisman
*R. Frey

From: Process Develop. Dept.
Engr. Services Sec.

Date: April 8, 1953

Subject: TEMPORARY Product Specifications -
90150 - 95120

This memorandum introduces new Illinois models 9015 - 9512 recently approved and released by the Product Development and Styling Division.

The product specifications for these models are being issued on a temporary basis at this time. As soon as all assembly components have been determined permanent specifications will be issued.

The temporary specifications are issued with this memorandum to the persons designated (*).

CAY:de

Internal memorandum, dated April 8, 1953, introducing the new Lady Gay Model B, Lady Gay Model A and Kimberly Model B

A Lady Gay Model B in its display case

LADY GAY MODEL C

Name = Lady Gay Model C
Time Period = Mid-Century Modern
Karat/Material = 10K YRGP/SSB
Bezel = Plain and Sculpted
Sides = Plain
Model No. = 9016
Casemaker = Schwab & Wuischpard
Case Pieces = 2
Case Number = 90160
Movement Grade/Jewels = AS1406, 600/17
Dial Signed = Hamilton-Illinois
Dial Number = 9016/54004
Dial Shape = Square
Numbers = Embossed
Markers = Embossed
Hands = Brass
Seconds At = None
Anti-Magnetic = Yes
Shockproof = No
Waterproof = No
Dustproof = No
Cased in Factory = Yes
Advertisement = Yes
Retail Price New = $44.95, bracelet; $37.50, cord (1954)
Production Date = 1953
Unique Case Design = Yes
Unique Dial Design = No

The Lady Gay Model C appeared in the 1953 Illinois Watch Catalog, in a *Life* magazine advertisement in 1954 and in the 1954 and 1955 Hamilton Watch Catalogs.

In the 1953 Hamilton and Illinois Watch Catalog, the Lady Gay Model C was described as "Styled for today . . . and many tomorrows, too. Numerals and markers are embossed. 17 jewels, anti-magnetic."

Lady Gay Model C

Lady Gay Model C dial

Lady Gay Model C case back

Lady Gay Model C inside case back

A page from the 1953 Hamilton-Illinois holiday brochure

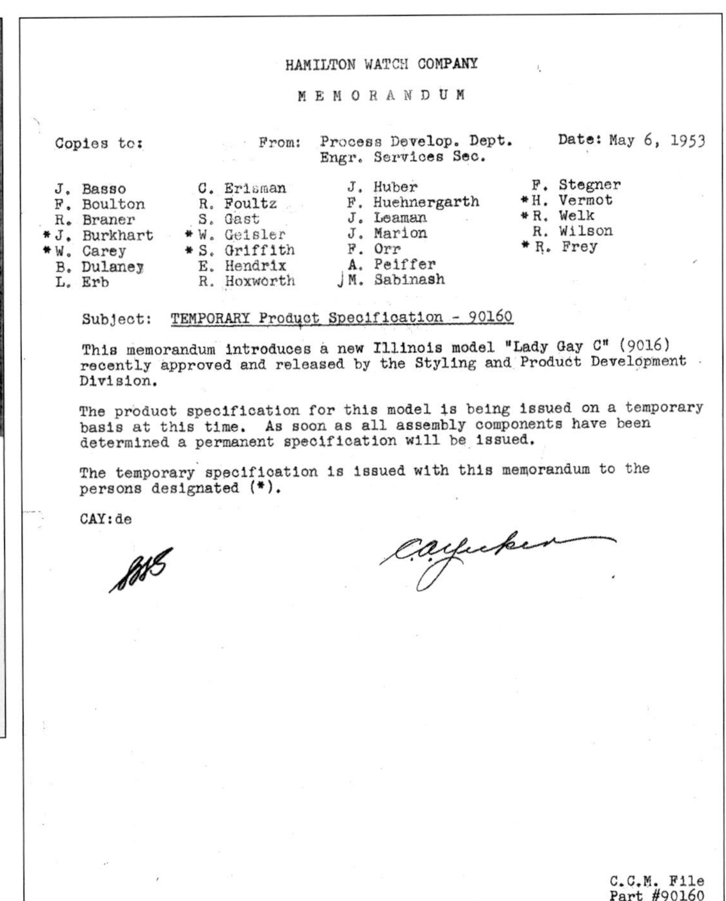

HAMILTON WATCH COMPANY

M E M O R A N D U M

Copies to: From: Process Develop. Dept. Engr. Services Sec. Date: May 6, 1953

J. Basso	C. Erisman	J. Huber	F. Stegner
F. Boulton	R. Foultz	F. Huehnergarth	*H. Vermot
R. Braner	S. Gast	J. Leaman	*R. Welk
*J. Burkhart	*W. Geisler	J. Marion	R. Wilson
*W. Carey	*S. Griffith	F. Orr	*R. Frey
B. Dulaney	E. Hendrix	A. Peiffer	
L. Erb	R. Hoxworth	M. Sabinash	

Subject: TEMPORARY Product Specification - 90160

This memorandum introduces a new Illinois model "Lady Gay C" (9016) recently approved and released by the Styling and Product Development Division.

The product specification for this model is being issued on a temporary basis at this time. As soon as all assembly components have been determined a permanent specification will be issued.

The temporary specification is issued with this memorandum to the persons designated (*).

CAY:de

C.C.M. File
Part #90160

Internal Hamilton memorandum dated May 6, 1953 introducing the Lady Gay Model C

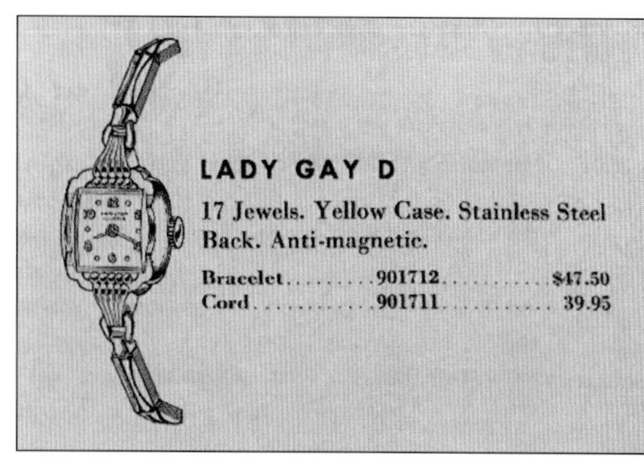
LADY GAY D

17 Jewels. Yellow Case. Stainless Steel Back. Anti-magnetic.

Bracelet.........901712...........$47.50
Cord...........901711........... 39.95

Lady Gay Model D

Name = Lady Gay Model D
Time Period = Mid-Century Modern
Karat/Material = 10K YRGP/SSB
Bezel = Engraved and sculpted
Sides = Plain
Model No. = 9017
Casemaker = Schwab & Wuischpard
Case Pieces = 2
Case Number = 90170
Movement Grade/Jewels = AS1406, 600/17
Dial Signed = Hamilton-Illinois Swiss
Dial Number = 9017/54005
Dial Shape = Square
Numbers = Embossed
Markers = Embossed
Dots = Embossed
Hands = Brass
Seconds At = None
Anti-Magnetic = Yes
Shockproof = No
Waterproof = No
Dustproof = No
Cased in Factory = Yes
Advertisement = Yes
Retail Price New = $39.95, silk cord; $47.50, bracelet (1954–1955)
Production Date = 1953
Unique Case Design = Yes
Unique Dial Design = No

The Lady Gay Model D was featured in the 1953 Hamilton and Illinois Catalog, where it was described as having "charm and grace in every line of beauty. 17 jewels, anti-magnetic embossed numerals and dots."

This watch was also listed in the 1954 and 1955 Hamilton Watch Catalogs.

Lady Gay Model D

Lady Gay Model D dial

Lady Gay Model D case back

Lady Gay Model D inside case back

HAMILTON WATCH COMPANY

M E M O R A N D U M

Copies: From: Process Develop. Dept.
Engr. Services Sec. Date: Feb. 23, 1954

*J. Basso	*L. Erb	*S. Griffith	M. Sabinash
W. Bell	*C. Erisman	*E. Hendrix	*F. Stegner
*F. Boulton	*S. Fedor	*R. Hoxworth	*H. Vermot
*R. Braner	R. Foultz	*J. Huber	*R. Wilson
*J. Burkhart	*R. Frey	*F. Huehnergarth	
*W. Carey	*S. Gast	*J. Leaman	
*B. Dulaney	*W. Geisler	*F. Orr	

Subject: Record of Part Number Applications for Hamilton-Illinois Case Supplies

This memorandum announces the issuance of a Record of Part Number Applications for Hamilton-Illinois Case Supplies. Previously there had been two(2) separate lists for case supplies. The consolidation was accomplished by the elimination of all existing Illinois part numbers, 77000 to 77999, and by the reassignment of those numbers in the Hamilton Case Supply category. The purpose of the consolidation was twofold, first, it eliminated the need of carrying two part numbers for one item (instances where Hamilton supplies are substituted) and secondly, it simplified procedure both in the transfer and the accounting of Illinois Case components. The sections directly concerned with the change over have been furnished a cross reference list of the part numbers effected. The changeover is to become effective March 1, 1954.

The Illinois assembly product specifications will be revised to contain the new part number assignments and will be reissued in the near future.

The Record of Part Number Applications for Hamilton Case Supplies, revised to 11-9-53, is to be destroyed or marked "SUPERSEDED". The R.P.A. for Illinois Case Supplies, revised to 11-6-53, is to be destroyed or marked "OBSOLETE".

The R.P.A. for Hamilton-Illinois Case Supplies is issued with this Memorandum to the persons designated (*).

CAY:de

C.A.Yecker

C.C.M. File
R.P.A. File

Internal memorandum dated February 23, 1954 eliminating separate case numbers for Hamilton cases and Illinois cases

Lady Gay Model E

Name = Lady Gay Model E
Time Period = Mid-Century Modern
Karat/Material = 10K YRGP/SSB, 10K WRGP/SSB
Bezel = Notched
Sides = Plain
Model No. = 9045, YRGP/SSB; 9046, WRGP/SSB
Casemaker = Pioneer
Case Pieces = 2
Case Number = 904500 YRGF/SSB, 90460, WRGF/SSB
Dimensions = 27 x 16 mm
Movement Grade/Jewels = AS1406, 600/17
Dial Signed = Hamilton-Illinois Swiss
Dial Number = 9017/54005
Dial Shape = Square
Numbers = Embossed
Markers = None
Hands = Brass
Seconds at = None
Anti-Magnetic = Yes
Shockproof = No
Waterproof = No
Dustproof = No
Cased in Factory = Yes
Advertisement = Yes
Retail Price New = $39.95, silk cord; $39.95, bracelet (1954–1955)
Production Date = 1953
Unique Case Design = Yes
Unique Dial Design = Yes

The Lady Gay Model E appears in the 1954 Hamilton Watch Catalog with this brief listing: "17 jewels, yellow or white case. Stainless steel back." Although it is among the most commonly found models today, the Lady Gay Model E is particularly interesting for its unique dial, which has a textured surface in an expanding pattern similar to that of the florets of a sunflower.

The Lady Gay E was renamed Enid in 1956 as a Hamilton model. It continued to be offered by Hamilton in 1957 and 1958.

Lady Gay Model E

Lady Gay Model E dial

Lady Gay Model E case back

Lady Gay Model E inside case back

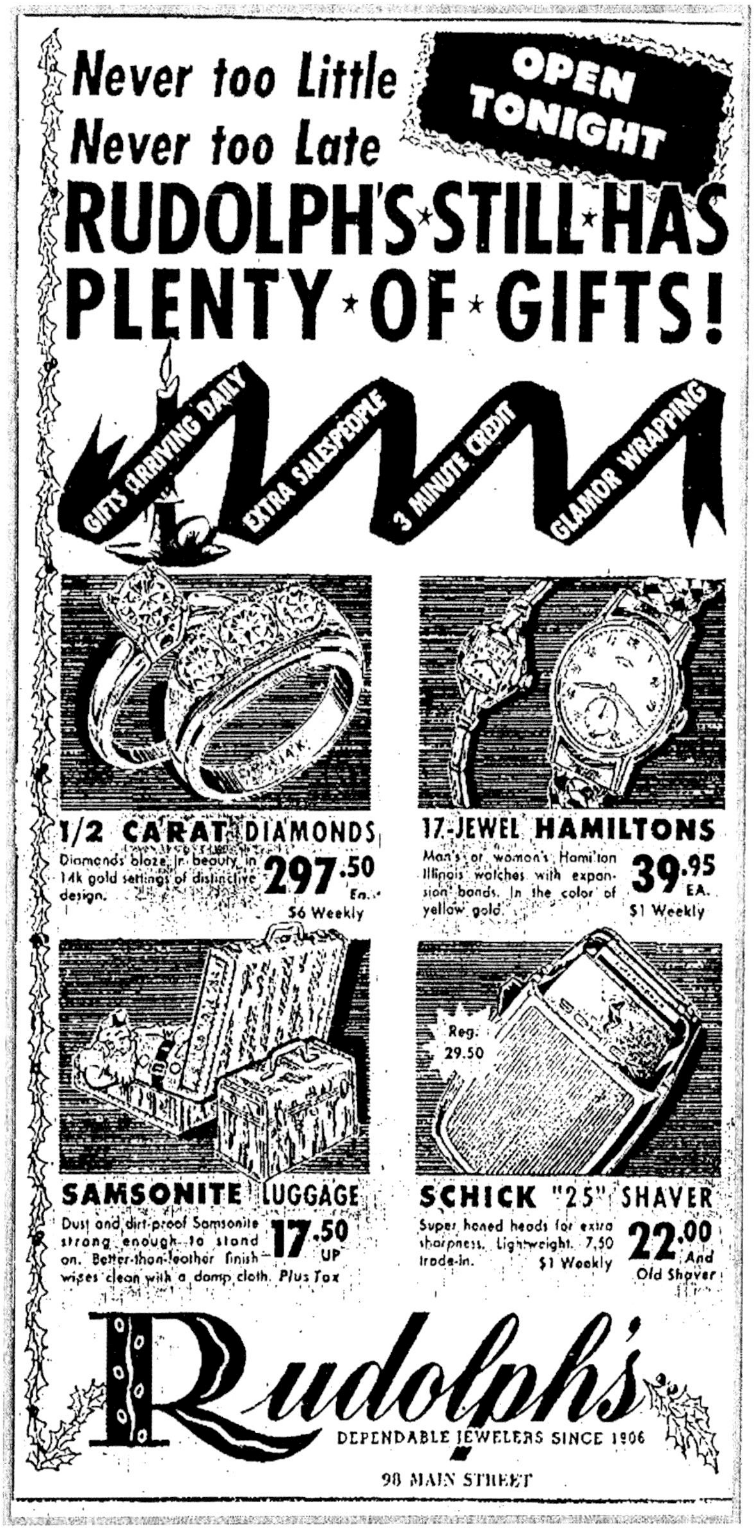

Never too Little
Never too Late

OPEN TONIGHT

RUDOLPH'S★STILL★HAS PLENTY★OF★GIFTS!

GIFTS ARRIVING DAILY · EXTRA SALESPEOPLE · 3 MINUTE CREDIT · GLAMOR WRAPPING

1/2 CARAT DIAMONDS
Diamonds blaze in beauty in 14k gold settings of distinctive design. 297.50 Ea. $6 Weekly

17-JEWEL HAMILTONS
Man's or woman's Hamilton Illinois watches with expansion bands. In the color of yellow gold. 39.95 EA. $1 Weekly

SAMSONITE LUGGAGE
Dust and dirt-proof Samsonite strong enough to stand on. Better-than-leather finish wipes clean with a damp cloth. Plus Tax 17.50 UP

SCHICK "25" SHAVER
Reg. 29.50
Super honed heads for extra sharpness. Lightweight. 7.50 trade-in. $1 Weekly 22.00 And Old Shaver

Rudolph's
DEPENDABLE JEWELERS SINCE 1906
98 MAIN STREET

Advertisement for a Lady Gay Model E and a Debonair Model D, *North Adams Transcript* (North Adams, MA), December 22, 1955; image from *newspapers.com*

Lady Gay Model F

Name = Lady Gay Model F
Time Period = Mid-Century Modern
Karat/Material = 10K YRGP/SSB, 10K WRGP/SSB
Bezel = Sculpted
Sides = Plain
Model No. = 9025, YRGP; 9035, WRGP
Casemaker = Star
Case Pieces = 2
Case Number = 90250, YRGP; 90350, WRGP
Movement Grade/Jewels = AS1406, 600/17
Dial Signed = Hamilton-Illinois Swiss
Dial Number = Unknown
Dial Shape = Rectangular
Numbers = Embossed
Markers = None
Hands = Brass
Seconds at = None
Anti-Magnetic = Yes
Shockproof = No
Waterproof = No
Dustproof = No
Cased in Factory = Yes
Advertisement = Yes
Retail Price New = $44.95, white or yellow with bracelet; $39.95, silk cord (1955)
Production Date = 1953
Unique Case Design = Yes
Unique Dial Design = Yes

The Lady Gay Model F appeared in the 1955 Hamilton Watch Catalog with this listing: "Yellow or White Case. Stainless Steel Back." The dial has a geometric pattern similar to the engine-turned dials on some Illinois men's models.

This model became the Hamilton Flora in 1956 and continued to be offered in 1957 and 1958. As with the men's Hamilton-Illinois watches that reappeared as Hamiltons, the movement retained the Illinois markings, though the dial and case were modified to say Hamilton.

Lady Gay Model F

Hamilton Flora

Lady Gay Model F dial

Hamilton Flora dial

Lady Gay Model F case back

Hamilton Flora case back

Lady Gay Model F inside case back

Hamilton Flora inside case back

Lady G Model F movement

Hamilton Flora movement

LADY GAY G

17 Jewels. Yellow or White Case. Stainless Steel Back.

	Yellow	White	
Bracelet	902622	903622	$39.95

LADY GAY MODEL G

Name = Lady Gay Model G
Time Period = Mid-Century Modern
Karat/Material = 10K YRGP/SSB, 10K WRGP/SSB
Bezel = Plain and sculpted
Sides = Plain
Model No. = 9026, WRGP; 9036, YRGP
Casemaker = Schwab & Wuischpard
Case Pieces = 2
Case Number = 90260, WRGP; 90360, YRGP
Movement Grade/Jewels = AS1406, 600/17
Dial Signed = Hamilton-Illinois
Dial Number = Unknown
Dial Shape = Square
Numbers = Brass
Markers = Brass
Hands = Brass
Seconds at = None
Anti-Magnetic = Yes
Shockproof = No
Waterproof = No
Dustproof = No
Cased in Factory = Yes
Advertisement = Yes
Retail Price New = $39.95, cord band (1954–1955)
Production Date = 1954
Unique Case Design = Yes
Unique Dial Design = No

The Lady Gay Model G was advertised in the May 8, 1954 issue of the *Saturday Evening Post* and also was in the 1954 and 1955 Hamilton Watch Catalogs. In 1956, it became the Hamilton model named Gwen, which continued to be offered in 1957 and 1958.

Lady Gay Model G

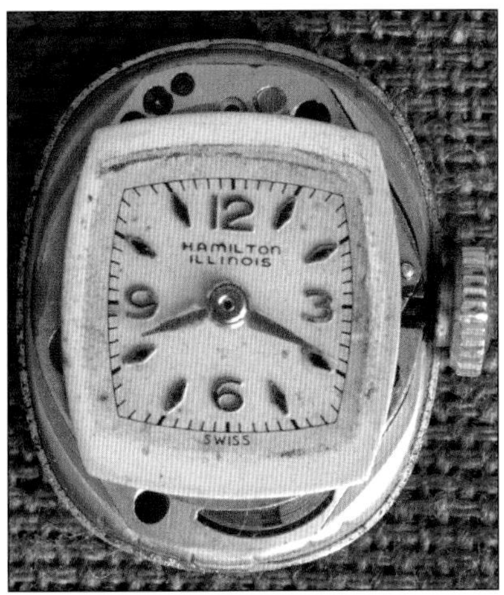

HAMILTON
ILLINOIS
SWISS
Lady Gay Model G dial

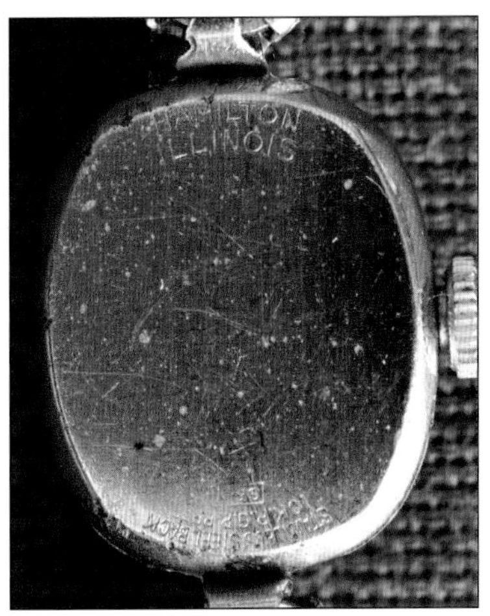

HAMILTON
ILLINOIS
Lady Gay Model G case back

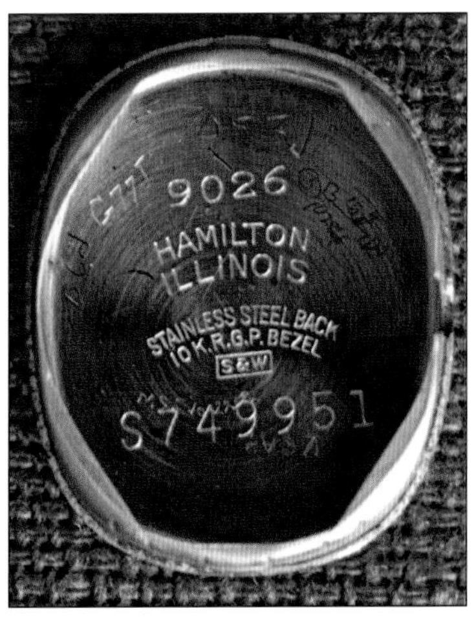

9026
HAMILTON
ILLINOIS
STAINLESS STEEL BACK
10 K.R.G.P. BEZEL
S&W
S749951
Lady Gay Model G inside case back

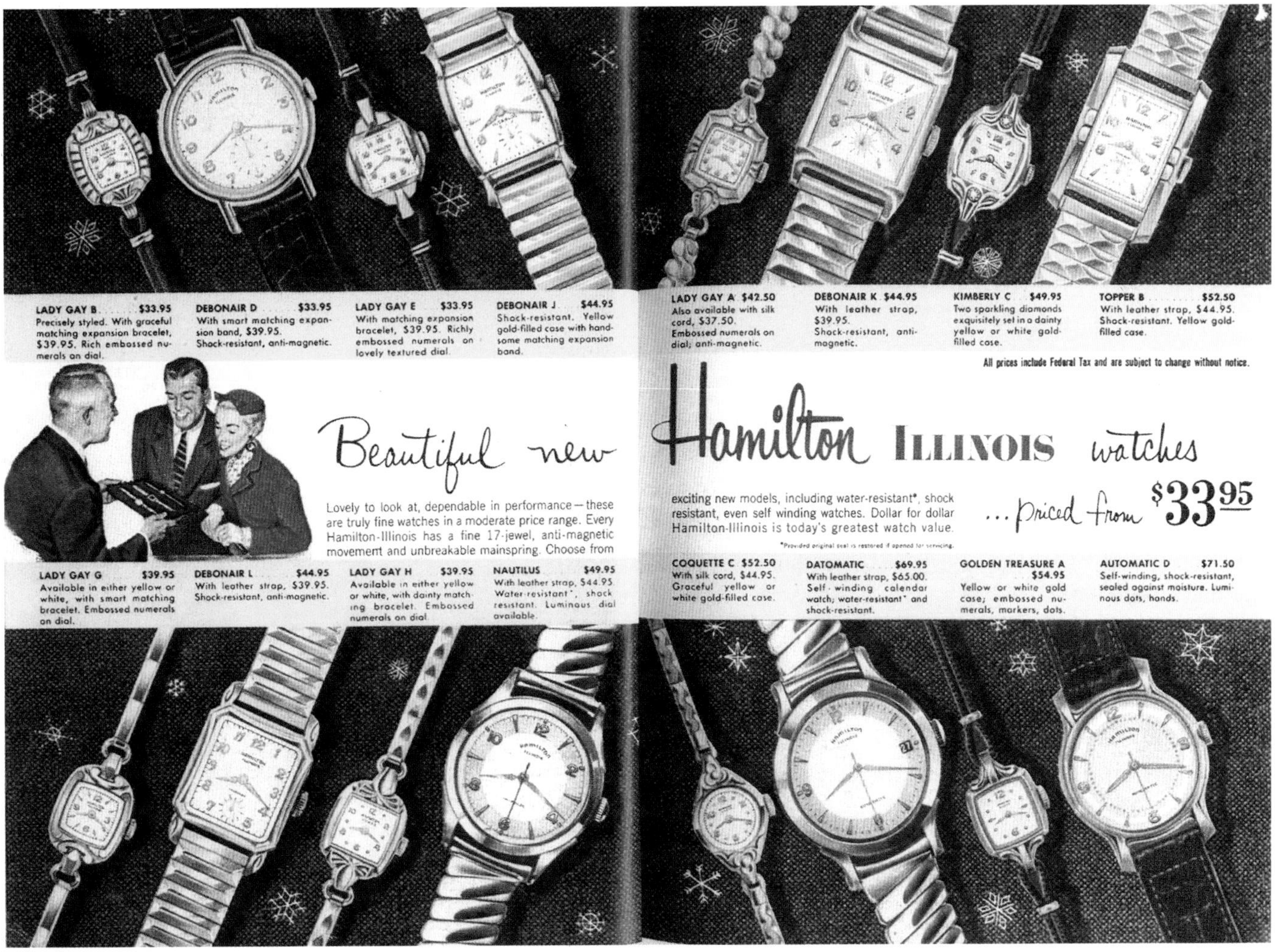

LADY GAY B $33.95
Precisely styled. With graceful matching expansion bracelet, $39.95. Rich embossed numerals on dial.
DEBONAIR D $33.95
With smart matching expansion band, $39.95.
Shock-resistant, anti-magnetic.
LADY GAY E $33.95
With matching expansion bracelet, $39.95. Richly embossed numerals on lovely textured dial.
DEBONAIR J $44.95
Shock-resistant. Yellow gold-filled case with handsome matching expansion band.
LADY GAY A $42.50
Also available with silk cord, $37.50.
Embossed numerals on dial; anti-magnetic.
DEBONAIR K $44.95
With leather strap, $39.95.
Shock-resistant, anti-magnetic.
KIMBERLY C $49.95
Two sparkling diamonds exquisitely set in a dainty yellow or white gold-filled case.
TOPPER B $52.50
With leather strap, $44.95.
Shock-resistant. Yellow gold-filled case.
All prices include Federal Tax and are subject to change without notice.
Beautiful new Hamilton ILLINOIS watches
Lovely to look at, dependable in performance—these are truly fine watches in a moderate price range. Every Hamilton-Illinois has a fine 17-jewel, anti-magnetic movement and unbreakable mainspring. Choose from exciting new models, including water-resistant*, shock resistant, even self winding watches. Dollar for dollar Hamilton-Illinois is today's greatest watch value.
...priced from $33.95
*Provided original seal is restored if opened for servicing.
LADY GAY G $39.95
Available in either yellow or white, with smart matching bracelet. Embossed numerals on dial.
DEBONAIR L $44.95
With leather strap, $39.95.
Shock-resistant, anti-magnetic.
LADY GAY H $39.95
Available in either yellow or white, with dainty matching bracelet. Embossed numerals on dial.
NAUTILUS $49.95
With leather strap, $44.95.
Water-resistant*, shock resistant. Luminous dial available.
COQUETTE C $52.50
With silk cord, $44.95.
Graceful yellow or white gold-filled case.
DATOMATIC $69.95
With leather strap, $65.00.
Self-winding calendar watch; water-resistant* and shock-resistant.
GOLDEN TREASURE A $54.95
Yellow or white gold case; embossed numerals, markers, dots.
AUTOMATIC D $71.50
Self-winding, shock-resistant, sealed against moisture. Luminous dots, hands.
Advertisement of Lady Gay G and fifteen other Hamilton-Illinois models, *Coronet*, December 1954

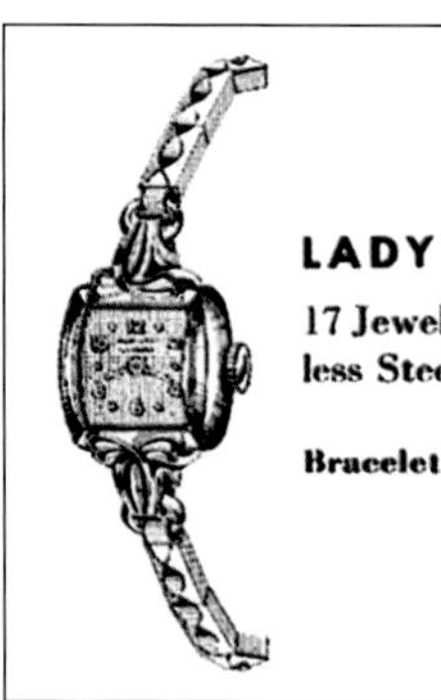

LADY GAY H

17 Jewels. Yellow or White Case. Stainless Steel Back.

	Yellow	White	
Bracelet	902722	903722	$39.95

Lady Gay Model H

Name = Lady Gay Model H
Time Period = Mid-Century Modern
Karat/Material = 10K YRGP/SSB, 10K WRGP/SSB
Bezel = Plain, Sculpted
Sides = Plain
Lug Size = None
Spring Bar = None
Model No. = 9027, YRGP; 9037, YRGP
Casemaker = Schwab & Wuischpard
Case Pieces = 2
Case Number = 90270, YRGP; 90370, WRGP
Movement Grade/Jewels = AS976, 600/17
Dial Signed = Hamilton-Illinois
Dial Number = Unknown
Dial Shape = Square
Numbers = Embossed
Markers = Brass
Hands = Brass
Seconds at = None
Anti-Magnetic = Yes
Shockproof = No
Waterproof = No
Dustproof = No
Cased in Factory = Yes
Advertisement = Yes
Retail Price New = $39.95, white or yellow, bracelet (1954–1955)
Production Date = 1954
Unique Case Design = Yes
Uniquc Dial Design = No

The Lady Gay Model H was advertised in the November 16, 1953 issue of the *Saturday Evening Post*, in a 1954 *Life* magazine advertisement and in the 1954 and 1955 Hamilton Watch Catalogs. In 1956 it became the Hamilton model called Hedy; Hamilton also offered the model again in 1957 but appears to have discontinued it after that.

Lady Gay Model H

Lady Gay Model H dial

Lady Gay Model H case back

Lady Gay Model H inside case back

Lady Gay Model K

Name = Lady Gay Model K
Time Period = Mid-Century Modern
Karat/Material = 10K YRGP/SSB, 10K WRGP/SSB
Bezel = Sculpted
Sides = Plain
Model No. = 9032, YRGP, 9033, YRGP
Casemaker = Schwab & Wuischpard
Case Pieces = 2
Case Number = 9032, YRGP, 9033, WRGP
Movement Grade/Jewels = AS1406, 600/17
Dial Signed = Hamilton-Illinois
Dial Number = Unknown
Dial Shape = Rectangular
Numbers = Embossed
Markers = Embossed
Hands = Brass
Seconds at = None
Anti-Magnetic = Yes
Shockproof = No
Waterproof = No
Dustproof = No
Cased in Factory = Yes
Advertisement = Yes
Retail Price New = $39.95, white or yellow, cord; $44.95, white or yellow, bracelet (1955)

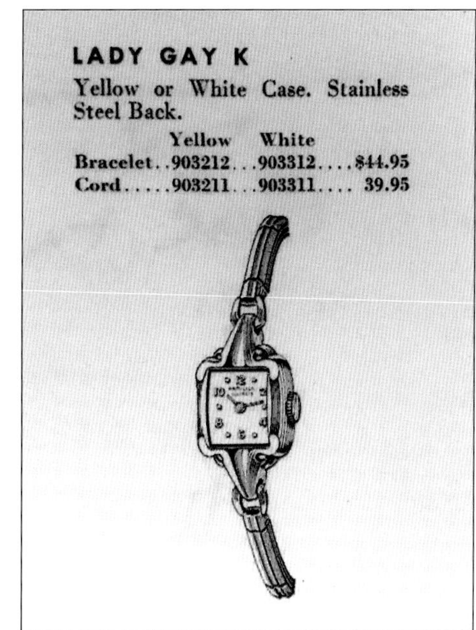
LADY GAY K

Yellow or White Case. Stainless Steel Back.

	Yellow	White	
Bracelet	903212	903312	$44.95
Cord	903211	903311	39.95

The last of the Lady Gay series was the Lady Gay Model K, which appeared in the 1955 Hamilton Watch Catalog with this brief notation: "Yellow or White Case. Stainless Steel Back." The watch had a very attractive textured dial.

In 1956 the Hamilton-Illinois Lady Gay Model K became the Hamilton Kaye; it was offered again in 1957 and 1958.

Lady Gay Model K

Lady Gay Model K dial

Lady Gay Model K case back

Lady Gay Model K inside case back

"LADY GAY" SERIES

MODEL A	Yel.	Cord	901411	$ 35.90	$ 37.50
	Yel.	Brac.	901412	38.60	42.50
MODEL B	Yel.	Cord	901511	34.50	33.95
	Yel.	Brac.	901512	36.30	39.95
MODEL C	Yel.	Cord	901611	35.90	37.50
	Yel.	Brac.	901612	38.90	44.95
MODEL D	Yel.	Cord	901711	36.30	39.95
	Yel.	Brac.	901712	41.10	47.50
MODEL G	Yel.	Brac.	902622	36.30	39.95
	Wh.	Brac.	903622	36.30	39.95
MODEL H	Yel.	Brac.	902722	36.30	39.95
	Wh.	Brac.	903722	36.30	39.95

1954 Price List

UNCATALOGED 14K DIAMOND-SET MODELS

Three uncataloged ladies' Hamilton-Illinois models have recently come to light, each in a 14K solid gold case with a diamond-set bezel. The cases of all three were made by the Major Watch Case Company of Brooklyn, a manufacturer that seems to have specialized in manufacturing diamond-decorated cases in the mid-1950s. We wondered what the connection might be; Perhaps all were special orders for a large department store or jewelry store chain? After studying the information available, we have come to the conclusion that these watches were likely to have been models produced by Hamilton for the Zale's Jewelry Company.

A LITTLE ZALE'S HISTORY

In 1924 the Zale Jewelry Company was founded in Wichita, Texas, by Morris B. Zale, William Zale and Ben Lipshy, who had "a revolutionary marketing strategy with a credit plan of 'a penny down and a dollar a week,' making jewelry and other merchandise affordable to the average working American."*

The strategy was a resounding success and led to the business becoming a chain, with 12 stores in Texas and Oklahoma by 1941. After World War II, the company moved its headquarters from Wichita Falls to Dallas in 1946.

Zale's continued to expand, eventually becoming the largest jewelry company in the United States. In 2014, Zale's was acquired by Signet Jewelers Ltd., which also owns Sterling Jewelers, the company that absorbed Kay's.

*http://www.zales.com/corp

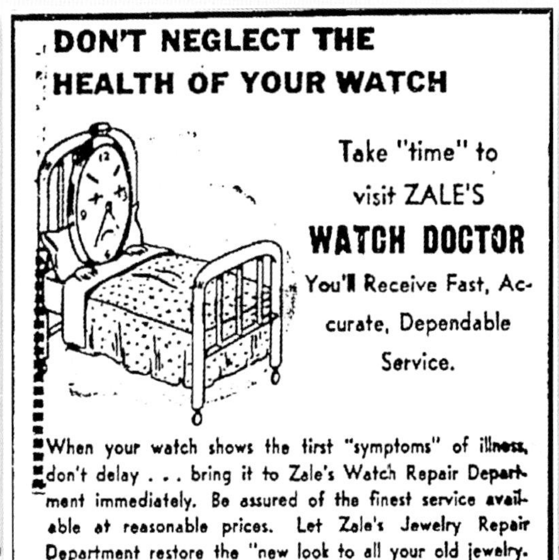

Lubbock Avalanche-Journal (Lubbock, TX), September 17, 1950; image from *newspapers.com*

Zale's began in 1924 with just one store in Texas, but by the 1950s, it had become a large national chain with 63 stores in 10 states. Some of its stores, such as Corrigan's in Houston, were prestigious independent jewelers that the chain had acquired but continued to operate under the original names.

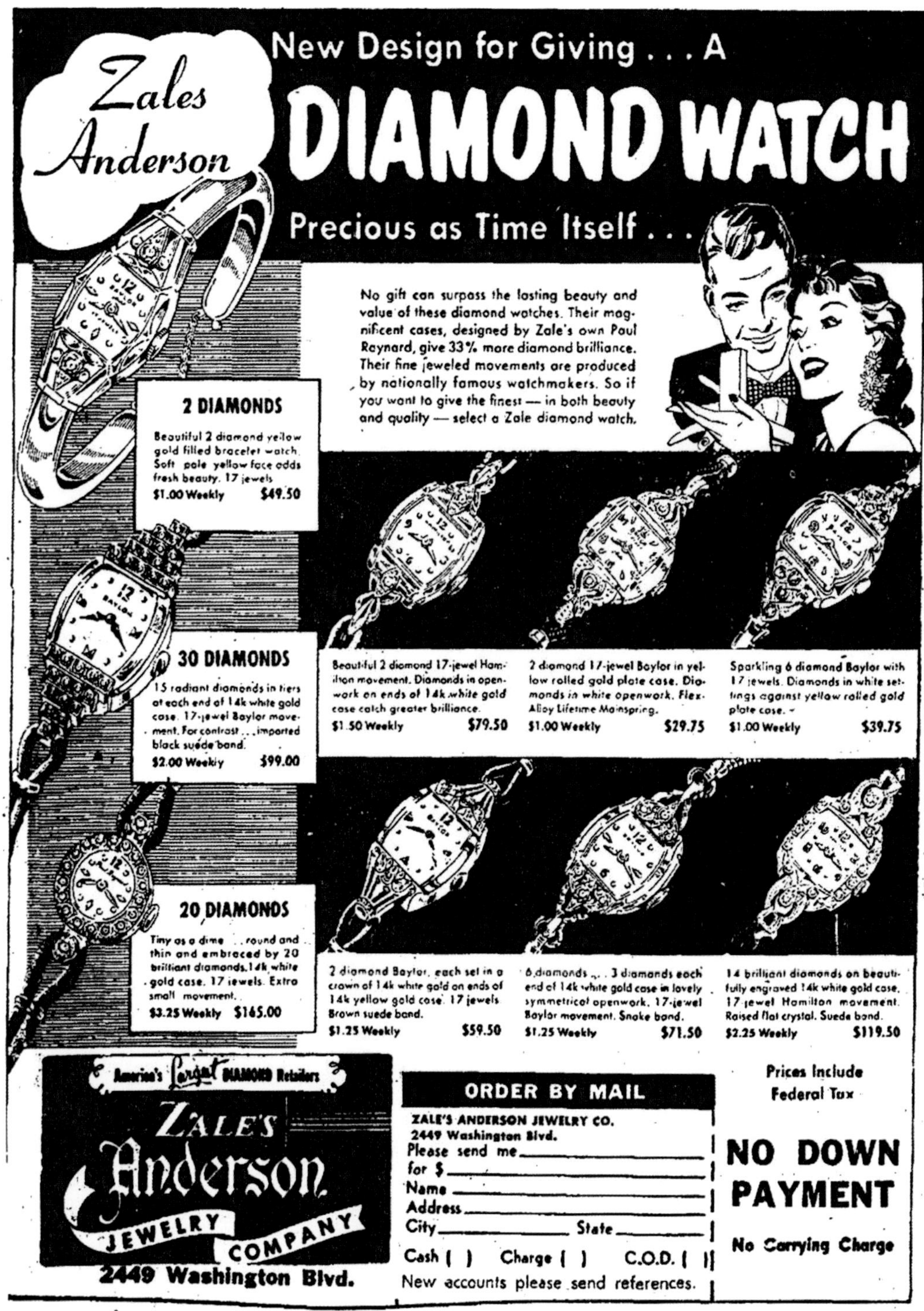

Zale's Anderson Jewelry Company advertisement, *Ogden Standard-Examiner* (Ogden, UT), June 17, 1956; image from *newspapers.com.* Anderson & Co., one of Zale's acquisitions, had been founded in 1927. It had been a sales agent for the Illinois Watch Company as well as other major watch manufacturers.

Of the watches on the two horizontal rows in the advertisement, two are Hamiltons (*1st watch, row 1; and last watch, row 2*); the other four are Zale's house brand, Baylor. In the vertical row, the middle watch is a Baylor and the others are unidentified.

Since Zale's was based in Texas, it is not surprising that many Zale's advertisements of the 1950s are to be found in Texas newspapers. From these we learned that Zale's carried Hamilton wristwatches and Hamilton-Illinois as well during the period the line existed.

A Hamilton-Illinois ladies' Kimberly Model B, advertised by Zale's in the *El Paso Herald-Post*, March 16, 1955; image from *newspapers.com*. Pictured with the watch is its matching Speidel band. Notice that Zale's is emphasizing only the "Hamilton" in the name of the line.

In addition to Hamilton, Zale's carried lines of other major manufacturers, including Bulova, Elgin, Gruen and Longines. The company prided itself on being able to provide not only its own guarantee for those watches, but the manufacturers' guarantees as well, and offering servicing by watchmakers trained at the factories.

★ **ZALE WATCHES ARE "FACTORY FRESH."** Watchmakers, like chemists, are constantly searching for ways to improve their watches, technically and mechanically. Each model has greatly improved features. At Zale's, you're assured of the newest and best of these mechanical improvements. This is made possible by RAPID TURN-OVER of merchandise through our 39 store distribution.

★ **ZALE WATCHES ARE NEWEST IN STYLING . . .** every day watch craftsmen are creating new and different modes of design. Smarter cases, ultra-modern dials, crystals, and bracelets. Your watch can date you. Be fashionable with a "FRESH" Zale watch.

★ **ZALE WATCHES ARE EXPERTLY SERVICED . . .** from time to time watches need oiling and dependable service. Zale's expert watchmakers are FACTORY-TRAINED. In their capable hands the watch you buy from us will prove an accurate timekeeper and preserve its loveliness for years to come.

★ **ZALE WATCHES CARRY A FACTORY-BACKED GUARANTEE.** Only authorized dealers can give you this manufacturer's protection. Zale's is a FACTORY-AUTHORIZED dealer, appointed by world famous watchmakers. When you buy a watch at Zale's you get a factory guarantee PLUS our own guarantee. And it's so easy to buy on our low credit terms. Choose your watch from Zale's complete selection today . . . because 151,087 people can't be wrong!

Portion of text from Zale's advertisement, *Pampa Daily News* (Pampa, TX), March 5, 1952; image from *newspapers.com*

No. 5312, white gold

No. 5312

Name = Model No. 5312
Time Period = Mid-Century Modern
Karat/Material = 14K WG
Bezel = Sculpted and engraved; diamonds
Sides = Plain
Casemaker = Major Watch Case Company
Case Pieces = 2
Case Number = 5312
Dimensions = 19 x 14.20mm (with crown)
Movement Grade/Jewels = AS1406, 600/17
Dial Signed = Hamilton-Illinois
Dial Number = Unknown
Dial Shape = Extended ornate
Numbers = Embossed
Markers = Dots
Hands = Brass
Seconds at = None
Anti-Magnetic = No
Shockproof = No
Waterproof = No
Dustproof = No
Cased in Factory = Likely, but unknown
Advertisement = No
Retail Price New = Unknown
Production Date = Unknown
Unique Case Design = Yes
Unique Dial Design = No

There is no known advertisement for this watch, which appears to be a very high-end model. As there is no known name for it, it will here be called model No. 5312 after its case Model Number.

This watch is quite spectacular looking. The bezel is covered with diamonds, which ornament the sides of the bezel as well as the elaborate elongated extensions at the top and bottom.

We feel it is likely that this watch, as well as the other two uncataloged 14K gold diamond-set Hamilton-Illinois models we have found, was a special order for Zale's. The solid gold and diamond cases for all three of these models were made by the Major Watch Case Company.

No. 5312 case back

No. 5557

Name = Model No. 5557
Time Period = Mid-Century Modern
Karat/Material = 14K WG
Bezel = Engraved and sculpted; 14 Diamonds
Sides = Plain
Casemaker = Major Watch Case Company
Case Pieces = 2
Case Number = 5557
Dimensions = 39 x 15 mm
Movement Grade/Jewels = AS1406, 600/17
Dial Signed = Hamilton-Illinois
Dial Number = Unknown
Dial Shape = Extended ornate
Numbers = Embossed
Markers = Dots and Arrows
Hands = Brass
Seconds At = None
Anti-Magnetic = No
Shockproof = No
Waterproof = No
Dustproof = No
Cased in Factory = Likely, but unknown
Advertisement = No
Retail Price New = Unknown
Production Date = Unknown
Unique Case Design = Yes
Unique Dial Design = No

No. 5557, white gold

As with model No. 5312, this upscale watch has not been found in any advertisement, so here it will be called No. 5557 after its case model number. Its exquisite diamond-encrusted 14K white gold case was also manufactured by the Major Watch Case Company.

We feel that this watch, too, was likely a special-order model for Zale's, possibly for one of the high-end stores the chain had acquired.

Its case design is similar to that of No. 5312 in having diamonds along the sides of the bezel as well as the elongated extensions at the top and bottom. Those extensions are markedly different in pattern, however.

The two models appear to share the same dial. Since we did not have No. 5312 in hand to study, we could not examine its movement, but No. 5557 is equipped with an AS 1406.

No. 5557 dial

No. 5557 case back

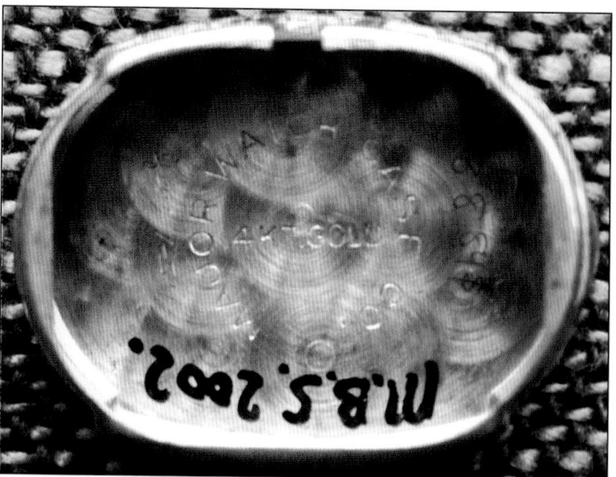

No. 5557 inside case back

Diamond two-tone, white and yellow gold

Diamond Two-Tone Case

Name = Unknown
Time Period = Mid-Century Modern
Karat/Material = 14K WG/YG
Bezel = Engraved and sculpted; 2 Diamonds
Sides = Plain
Casemaker = Major Watch Case Company
Case Pieces = 2
Case Number = None
Dimensions = 39 x 15 mm
Movement Grade/Jewels = AS1406, 600/17
Dial Signed = Hamilton-Illinois
Dial Number = Unknown
Dial Shape = Tonneau with Contrasting Extensions
Numbers = Embossed
Markers = Dots and Arrows
Hands = Brass
Seconds At = None
Anti-Magnetic = No
Shockproof = No
Waterproof = No

Dustproof = No
Cased in Factory = Likely, but unknown
Advertisement = No
Retail Price New = Unknown
Production Date = Unknown
Unique Case Design = Yes
Unique Dial Design = No

This attractive Hamilton-Illinois two-tone 14K diamond-set ladies' watch without model number has the same casemaker as Nos. 5312 and 5557: the Major Watch Case Company. Like them, it has not been found in any advertisement.

Diamond two-tone dial

Diamond two-tone case back

Diamond two-tone inside case back

Although this watch, too, has elaborate extensions at the top and bottom of its bezel, both the shape of the case and the pattern of decoration are different from those of model Nos. 5312 and 5557. Moreover, the case is two-tone 14K yellow and white gold rather than all white, and its bezel is set with only two diamonds.

The basic design of its case is closer to that of an unknown Hamilton-Illinois solid white gold watch with four diamonds that appeared in a 1954 Zale's advertisement.

An uncataloged Hamilton-Illinois ladies' model in 14K solid gold, with four diamonds, advertised by Zale's in the *Lubbock Evening Journal* (Lubbock, TX), October 28, 1954; image from *newspapers.com*. (Notice that the name "Hamilton" is very prominent and the "Illinois" barely visible.) It is not known if this case had Hamilton-Illinois model numbers on the back of its case, as we have never seen this model in person.

It is interesting that in its house-brand Baylor line, Zale's offered some inexpensive diamond watches, also with cases by Major, but of rolled gold plate with stainless steel backs, though with ornate extensions at the top and bottom of the bezel in patterns related to those for the 14K Hamilton-Illinois models. (Some of Zale's elaborate 14K diamond-set Baylor watches pictured in advertisements of the 1950s also probably had cases by Major, but we have not been able to locate and examine any of those.)

Two Zale's Baylor diamond-set models with rolled gold watch plate cases and stainless steel backs

Stainless steel case back of a Baylor watch

Baylor watch inside case back and AS 1406 movement

As with the 14K Hamilton-Illinois watches, the cases of these Baylor watches are by the Major Watch Case Company. The watches are equipped with exactly the same movement as the Hamilton-Illinois diamond models (the AS 1406), and the cases speak the same design language.

A question to ponder: The 1956 advertisement for the Zale's Anderson Company, pictured earlier, mentions that Zale's own designer Paul Raynard was responsible for the designs of some of the company's diamond watches. A few years earlier, might he have designed the cases of the mystery Hamilton-Illinois diamond-set 14K gold models?

No gift can surpass the lasting beauty and value of these diamond watches. Their magnificent cases, designed by Zale's own Paul Raynard, give 33% more diamond brilliance. Their fine jeweled movements are produced by nationally famous watchmakers. So if you want to give the finest — in both beauty and quality — select a Zale diamond watch.

Portion of text from Zale's Anderson Jewelry Company advertisement, *Ogden Standard-Examiner* (Ogden, UT), June 17, 1956. This mentions Zale's own designer.

12
3
9
ILLINOIS
60
10
50
20
40
30

ILLINOIS

Illinois Watch Company

SPRINGFIELD.
U.S.A.

THE ILLINOIS WATCH & ITS HAMILTON YEARS

VOL 5

THE FINALE OF A GREAT AMERICAN WATCH COMPANY

Collecting Illinois

BY
FREDRIC J. FRIEDBERG

4880 Lower Valley Road • Atglen, PA 19310

Library of Congress Control Number: 2017933341

Designed by Chris Cornforth, www.chrisworx.com
Cover designs by Fred, Joy, Zach Friedberg and Chris Cornforth

ISBN:978-0-7643-5371-0
Printed in China
Published by Schiffer Publishing, Ltd.
4880 Lower Valley Road
Atglen, PA 19310
Phone: (610) 593-1777; Fax: (610) 593-2002
E-mail: Info@schifferbooks.com
Web: www.schifferbooks.com

Chapter 12

Ephemera, Memorabilia and Miscellany Expanded

This chapter contains items of interest concerning marketing, advertising, advertisements, brochures, drawings, display boxes, tools, correspondence, related material, and ephemera involving Illinois, plus a selection of items pertaining to Hamilton at the time of its acquisition of Illinois.

Early Illinois advertising sign for jewelry stores

Illinois Watch Company

An extremely early, if not the first, Springfield Watch Company promotional sign, c. 1870. It has a gesso frame and is a chromolithograph. There are only two such signs known still to exist.

The Treasurer of the Springfield Watch Company
Will pay the bearer TWENTY-FIVE DOLLARS
on the first day of May, 1877,
bein[illegible] interest on [illegible] No. 101
for $500.
Pres't.

Bearer coupon issued by the Springfield Watch Company on May 1, 1877, promising to pay $25.00 interest

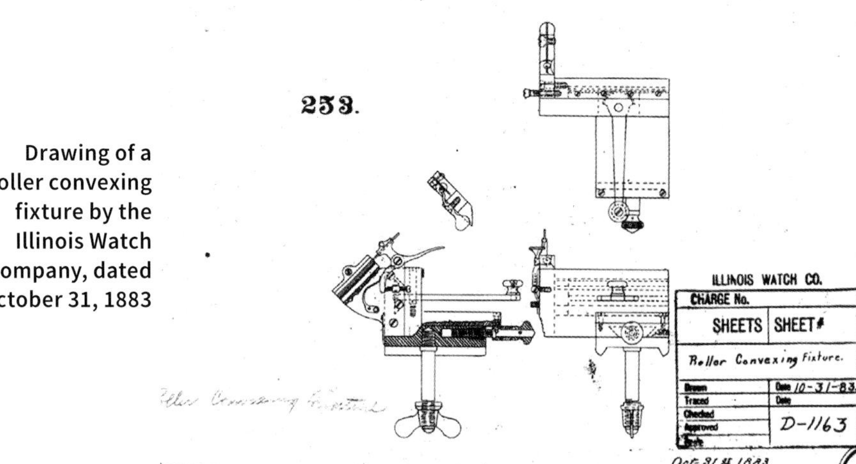

Drawing of a roller convexing fixture by the Illinois Watch Company, dated October 31, 1883

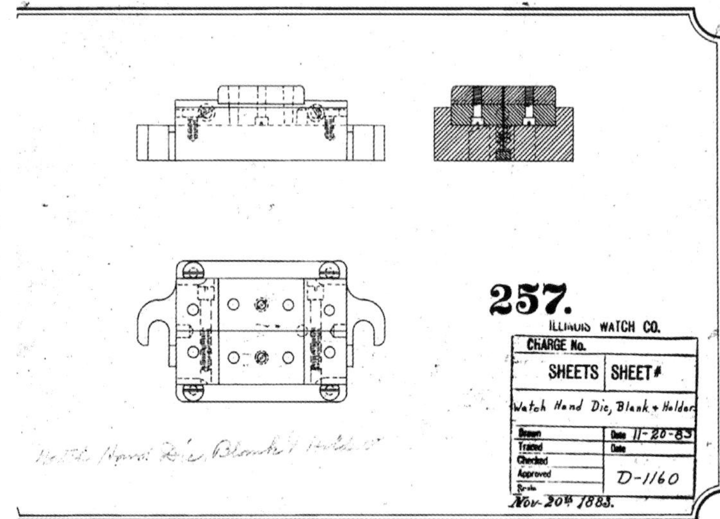

Drawing of a watch hand die, blank and holder by the Illinois Watch Company, dated November 20, 1883

308

ILLINOIS WATCH CO.
CHARGE No.
SHEETS
SHEET #
Balance Inside Finishing Chuck
1-13-85
D-1157

Drawing of a balance inside finishing chuck by the Illinois Watch Company, dated January 13, 1885

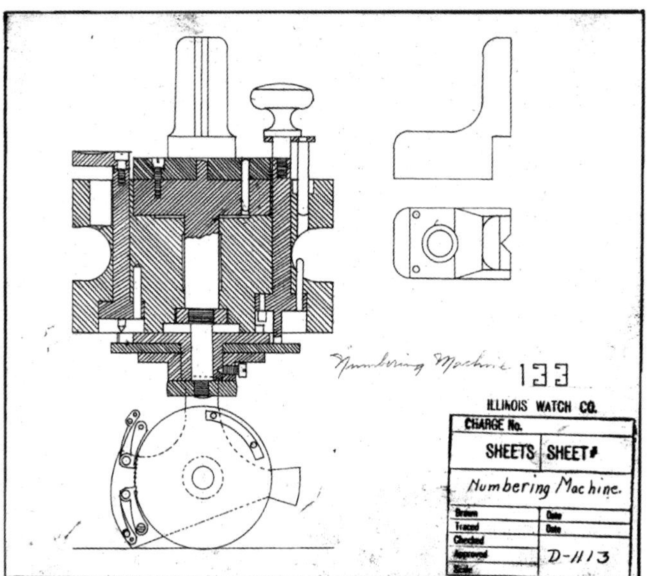

Numbering machine drawing by the Illinois Watch Company undated, c. 1880s

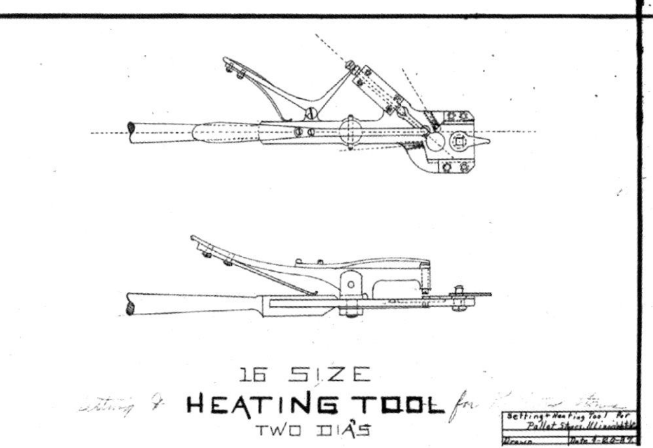

16-size setting and heating tool for pallet stones, drawing by the Illinois Watch Company dated April 20, 1887

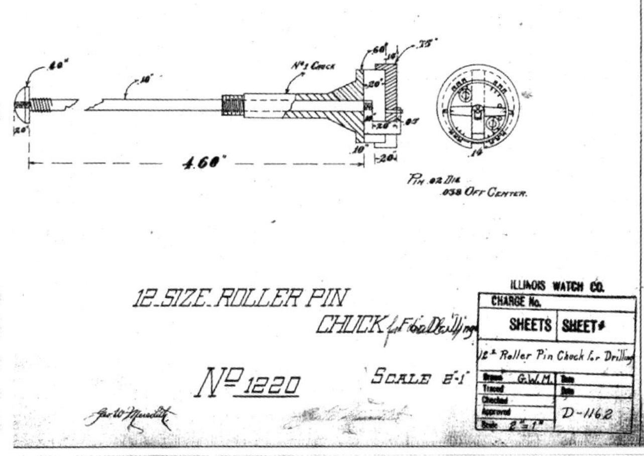

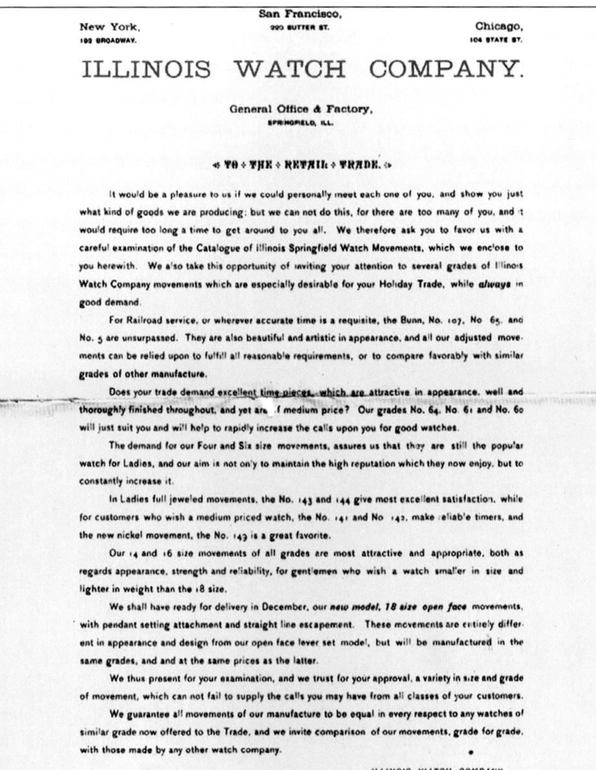

New York, 192 BROADWAY. San Francisco, 220 SUTTER ST. Chicago, 104 STATE ST.

ILLINOIS WATCH COMPANY.

General Office & Factory, SPRINGFIELD, ILL.

TO THE RETAIL TRADE.

It would be a pleasure to us if we could personally meet each one of you, and show you just what kind of goods we are producing; but we can not do this, for there are too many of you, and it would require too long a time to get around to you all. We therefore ask you to favor us with a careful examination of the Catalogue of Illinois Springfield Watch Movements, which we enclose to you herewith. We also take this opportunity of inviting your attention to several grades of Illinois Watch Company movements which are especially desirable for your Holiday Trade, while *always* in good demand.

For Railroad service, or wherever accurate time is a requisite, the Bunn, No. 107, No 65, and No. 5 are unsurpassed. They are also beautiful and artistic in appearance, and all our adjusted movements can be relied upon to fulfill all reasonable requirements, or to compare favorably with similar grades of other manufacture.

Does your trade demand excellent time-pieces, which are attractive in appearance, well and thoroughly finished throughout, and yet are [o]f medium price? Our grades No. 64, No. 61 and No. 60 will just suit you and will help to rapidly increase the calls upon you for good watches.

The demand for our Four and Six size movements, assures us that they are still the popular watch for Ladies, and our aim is not only to maintain the high reputation which they now enjoy, but to constantly increase it.

In Ladies full jeweled movements, the No. 143 and 144 give most excellent satisfaction, while for customers who wish a medium priced watch, the No. 141 and No 142, make reliable timers, and the new nickel movement, the No. 149 is a great favorite.

Our 14 and 16 size movements of all grades are most attractive and appropriate, both as regards appearance, strength and reliability, for gentlemen who wish a watch smaller in size and lighter in weight than the 18 size.

We shall have ready for delivery in December, our ***new model, 18 size open face*** movements, with pendant setting attachment and straight line escapement. These movements are entirely different in appearance and design from our open face lever set model, but will be manufactured in the same grades, and and at the same prices as the latter.

We thus present for your examination, and we trust for your approval, a variety in size and grade of movement, which can not fail to supply the calls you may have from all classes of your customers.

We guarantee all movements of our manufacture to be equal in every respect to any watches of similar grade now offered to the Trade, and we invite comparison of our movements, grade for grade, with those made by any other watch company.

ILLINOIS WATCH COMPANY.

Springfield, Nov. 16th, '89.

Illinois Watch Company 1889 letter to the retail trade (dated November 16, 1889), advising of its movement grades available for upcoming holiday business

Left: Drawing of a chuck for drilling the hole for the roller pin on a balance by the Illinois Watch Company, undated (probably late 1880s)

Photograph of an Illinois Factory department, c. 1900s. Of the people pictured, more than one-third were women.

Illinois Watch movement sales catalog, March 1, 1899 (3" x 5.5")

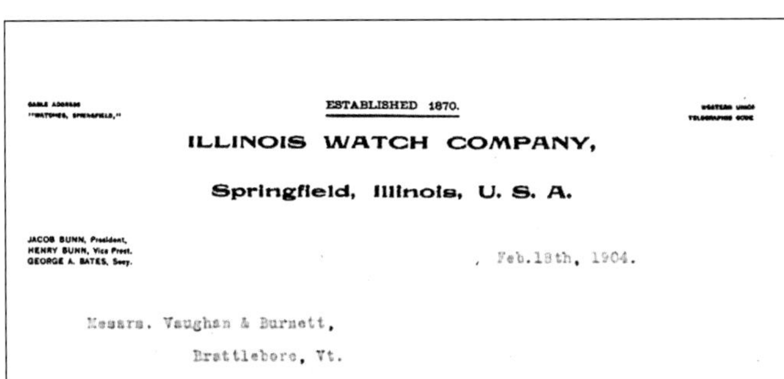

CABLE ADDRESS "WATCHES, SPRINGFIELD." ESTABLISHED 1870. WESTERN UNION TELEGRAPHIC CODE

ILLINOIS WATCH COMPANY,

Springfield, Illinois, U. S. A.

JACOB BUNN, President,
HENRY BUNN, Vice Prest.
GEORGE A. BATES, Secy.

, Feb.18th, 1904.

Messrs. Vaughan & Burnett,
Brattleboro, Vt.

Gentlemen:-

We are sending you some signs which we would be glad to have you use in your store. We also enclose herewith price list with circular in reference to retail selling prices which we have established on Rail Road grade movements of our manufacture, and which are being maintained. In the few instances we have learned of prices being cut, we immediately took steps to avoid same being repeated.

If you are not familiar with the quality of our Rail Road watches, we are very sure it would be to your interest to investigate same. We are making every effort to make the best Rail Road watch possible, which we believe is equal, if not superior , to the best of any other make. We allow a discount of 15 & 6% ten days from enclosed list, making the net price to the jeweler less than that for corresponding grades of other makes.

In addition to supplying our goods direct, you can also obtain same from the following jobbers:

D. C. Percival & Co., Boston, Mass.
W. J. Johnston Co., Pittsburgh, Pa.
J. W. Forsinger, #2 Maiden Lane, New York City.
J. W. Forsinger, #103 State St., Chicago, Ill.
A. C. Becken, #156 Wabash Ave. " "
Sproehnle & Co., #92 State St. " "
Otto Young & Co., #149 State St. "
Eisenstadt Manfg. Co., St.Louis, Mo.

Very truly yours,

Illinois letter dated February 18, 1904, notifying jewelers that it was sending them Illinois promotional signs to display in their stores

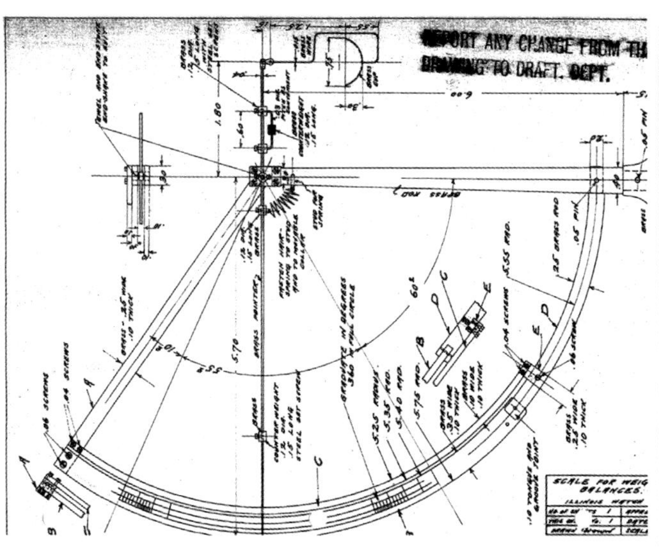

Illinois Watch Company drawing of a scale to weigh balances, c. 1907

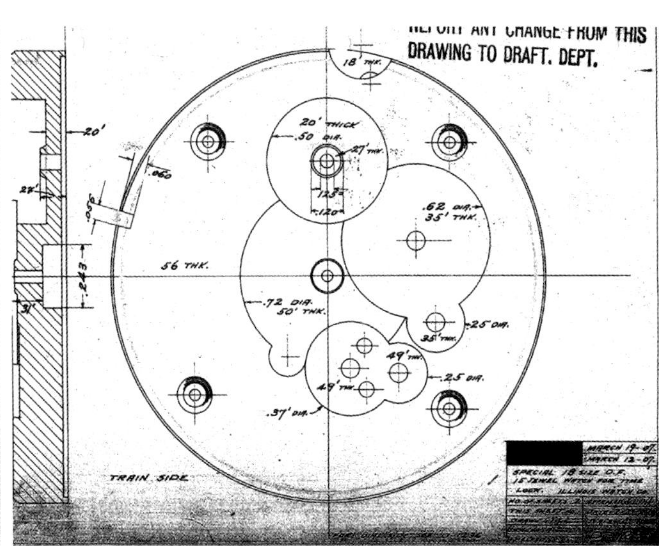

Illinois Watch Company drawing of a special 18-size, 15-jewel watch for a safe time lock, dated February 21, 1907

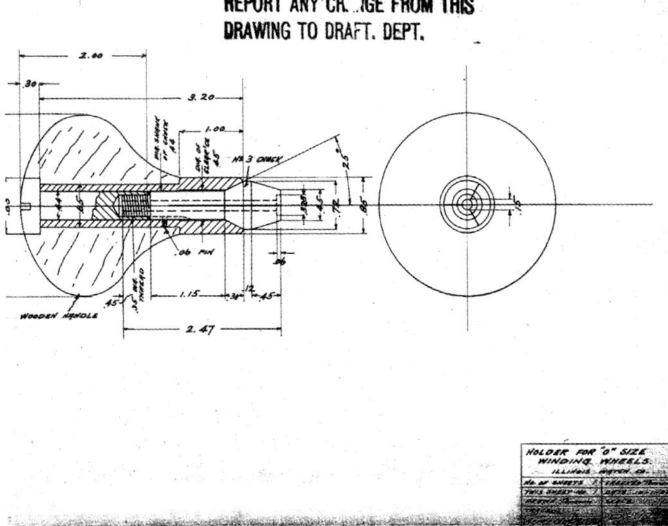

Illinois Watch Company drawing of a holder for 0-size winding wheels, dated October 1, 1906

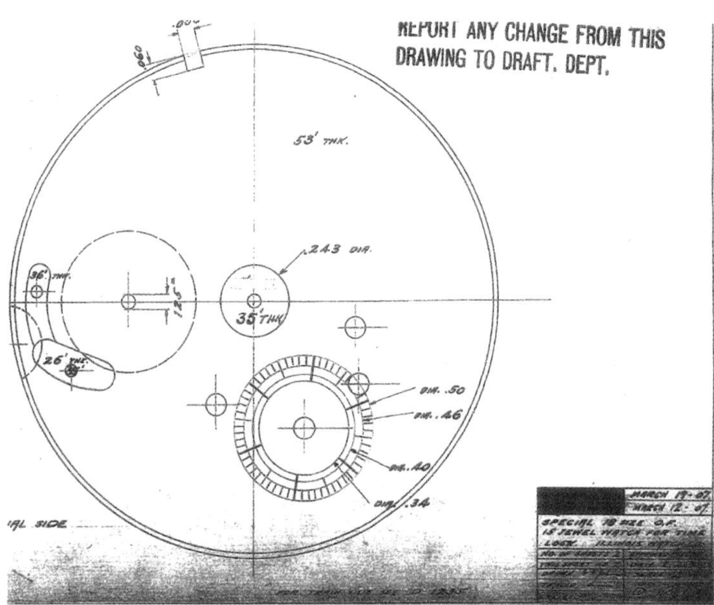

Illinois drawing for a special 18-size open face, 15-jewel watch for a safe time lock dated, March 19, 1907

Safe Time Lock produced by the Illinois Watch Company

SAFE TIME LOCK

Banks demanded more protection, and safe makers responded by designing larger, heavier safes. Safes with a key lock were still vulnerable through the key hole, and bank robbers soon learned to blast off the door by pouring explosives in this opening. In 1861, inventor Linus Yale, Jr. introduced the modern combination lock. Bankers quickly adopted Yale's lock for their safes, but bank robbers came up with several ways to get past the new invention. It was possible to use force to punch the combination lock through the door. Other experienced burglars learned to drill holes into the lock case and use mirrors to view the slots in the combination wheels inside the mechanism.

A more direct approach was to simply kidnap the bank manager and force him to reveal the combination.

After the invention of the combination lock, James Sargent, an employee of Yale's, developed the "theft proof lock." This was a combination lock that worked on a timer. The vault or safe door could be opened only after a set number of hours had passed, thus a kidnapped bank employee could not open the lock in the middle of the night even under force.

Time locks became widespread at banks in the 1870s. This reduced the kidnappings, but set bank robbers to work again at prying or blasting open vaults.

—Greg Hart

Safe Time Lock close-up

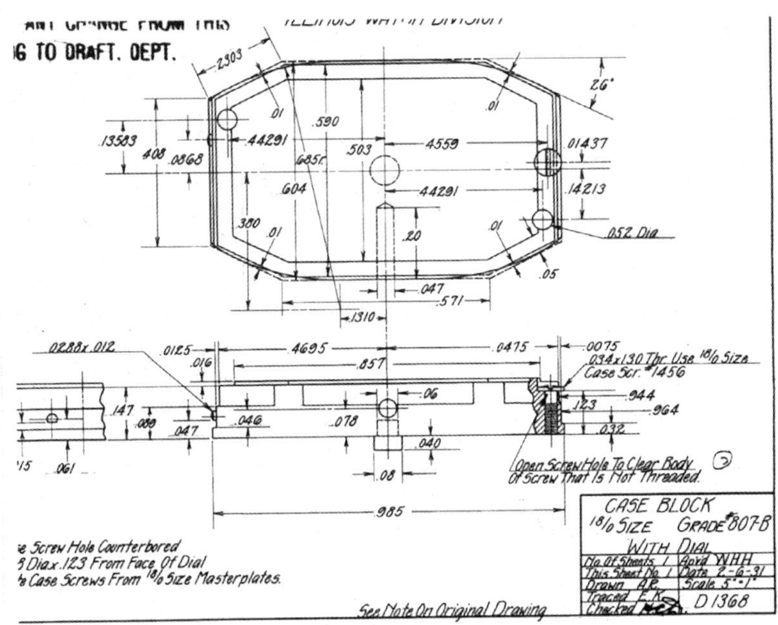

Illinois case block drawing with dial for an 18/0 size, grade 807B Illinois movement, dated February 6, 1931

Lithographed tin sign used as a promotional item in jewelry stores that sold and repaired Illinois pocket watches

A very heavy cast iron Illinois pocket watch sign designed to hang outside a jewelry store that sold Illinois watches. This is the only such sign known still to be in existence.

The actual glass transom from the doorway of the Engraving Department at the Illinois Watch Factory

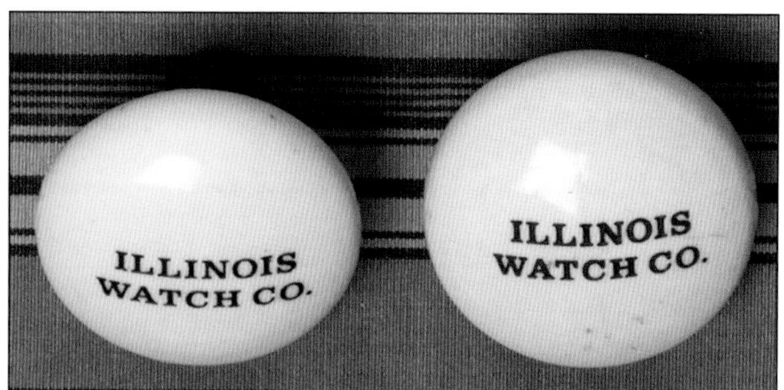

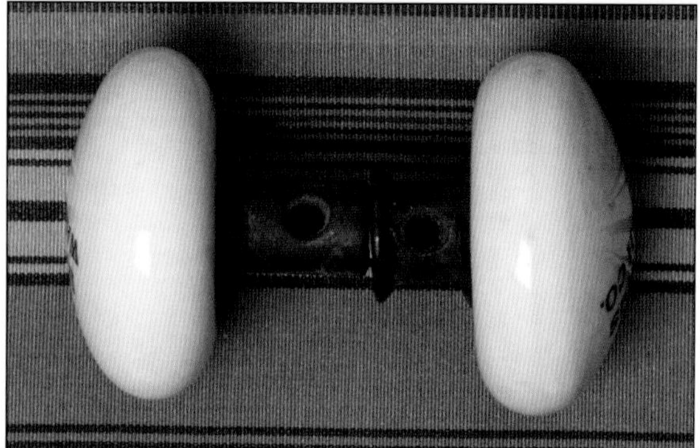

Enamel doorknobs signed Illinois Watch Co. from the Watch Factory

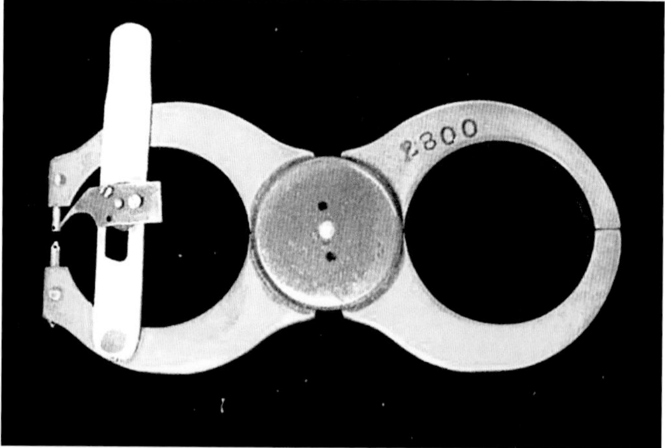

Illinois Watch Company brass truing caliper poising tool

Image of printer's block for a 16-size Illinois pocket watch movement

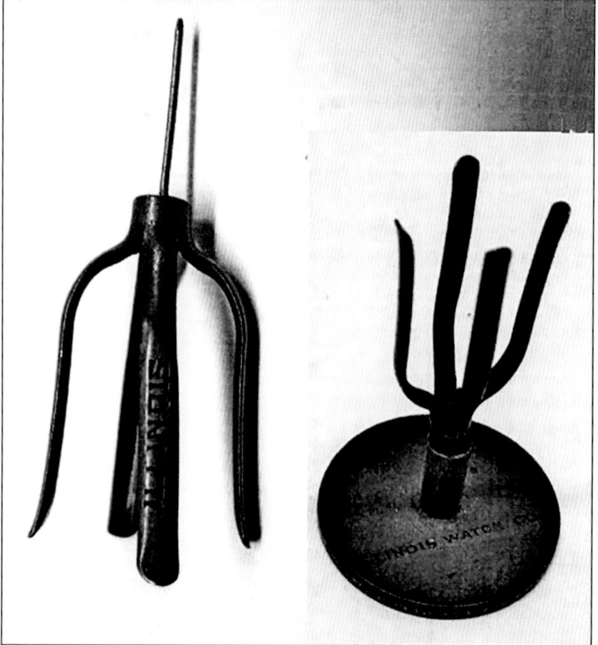

Illinois Watch mainspring let-down tool with its stand. Using this tool with the spring legs over a fingertip, the user could release the click while holding a watch movement with one hand and then let down the mainspring with a bench key in the other hand. Both parts of the tool shown here are signed Illinois.

A rare paper decal advertising sign, c. 1911, for Illinois Springfield watches. On the back is printed "Meyercord Genuine Decalomania Window Signs," along with directions for applying the sign to the inside surface of a window. The decal measures about 8.75 x 5.25 inches; the date 14-5.11 is stamped on the back. The Meyercord Co., founded in Chicago in 1896, became one of the world's leading producers of lithographic transfers for branding consumer products.

The Watch Factory band was actively giving community concerts in 1916, as indicated by the public announcements shown here.

Popular Mechanics, January 1913

Meet Your Friends at

Litchfield, Saturday, Oct. 7

Dairy Day and Exposition

Big Free Barbecue,
Monster Parade,
Ten Bands, Floats, Drills,
Free Vaudeville,
$3,000 in Premiums,

Aeroplane Flights,
Bull Fights,
Carl Vrooman, Ass't, Sec. of Agriculture, and other prominent speakers.

Illinois Watch Factory Band, donated by Illinois Traction System, will play during the day.

FREQUENT ELECTRIC RAILWAY SERVICE
VIA

Illinois Traction System
(McKinley Lines)

Edwardsville Intelligencer (Edwardsville, IL), October 6, 1916; image from *newspapers.com*

Popular Mechanics, January 1913

Join the Decatur Trades Labor men in their joint celebration in the Capitol City

MONDAY, SEPT. 4

Here Is The Program

10:30 a. m.—Monster Parade, four military bands.
1:30 p. m.—Speaking and music in Court House square, with following speakers: John F. Doyle, Mt. Vernon, secretary Farmers' Co-operative Association; A. W. Kerr, chief counsel U. M. W. of A.; Thos. J. Condon, attorney for Railroad Brotherhood Association; N. H. Prescott, Bloomington, member Order Railroad Conductors.
8:30 p. m.—Concert by Illinois Watch Factory Band in State Armory.
9:30 p. m.—Grand Ball, State Armory.

Illinois Traction System

OFFICIAL ROUTE

75c ROUND TRIP FROM DECATUR 75c.

Above rate good going and returning on all trains.

Daily Review (Decatur, IL), August 30, 1916; image from *newspapers.com*

Boston Post (Boston,MA), April 11, 1917; image from *newspapers.com*

The Illinois "Peerless" was apparently a private-label watch for Treco Bros. of Boston, MA. It was cased and timed at the Watch Factory.

Pith Supplies

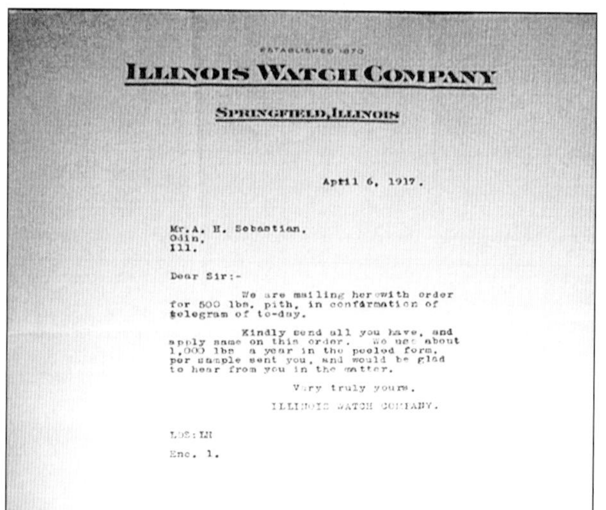

ESTABLISHED 1870

ILLINOIS WATCH COMPANY

SPRINGFIELD, ILLINOIS

April 6, 1917.

Mr. A. H. Sebastian,
Odin,
Ill.

Dear Sir:-

We are mailing herewith order for 500 lbs. pith, in confirmation of telegram of to-day.

Kindly send all you have, and apply same on this order. We use about 1,000 lbs a year in the peeled form, per sample sent you, and would be glad to hear from you in the matter.

Very truly yours,

ILLINOIS WATCH COMPANY.

LDS:LH

Enc. 1.

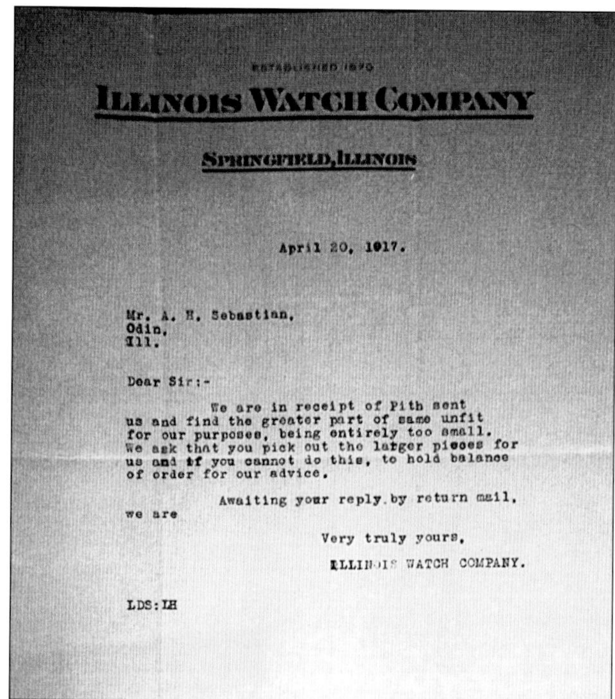

ESTABLISHED 1870

ILLINOIS WATCH COMPANY

SPRINGFIELD, ILLINOIS

April 20, 1917.

Mr. A. H. Sebastian,
Odin,
Ill.

Dear Sir:-

We are in receipt of Pith sent us and find the greater part of same unfit for our purposes, being entirely too small. We ask that you pick out the larger pieces for us and if you cannot do this, to hold balance of order for our advice.

Awaiting your reply by return mail, we are

Very truly yours,

ILLINOIS WATCH COMPANY.

LDS:LH

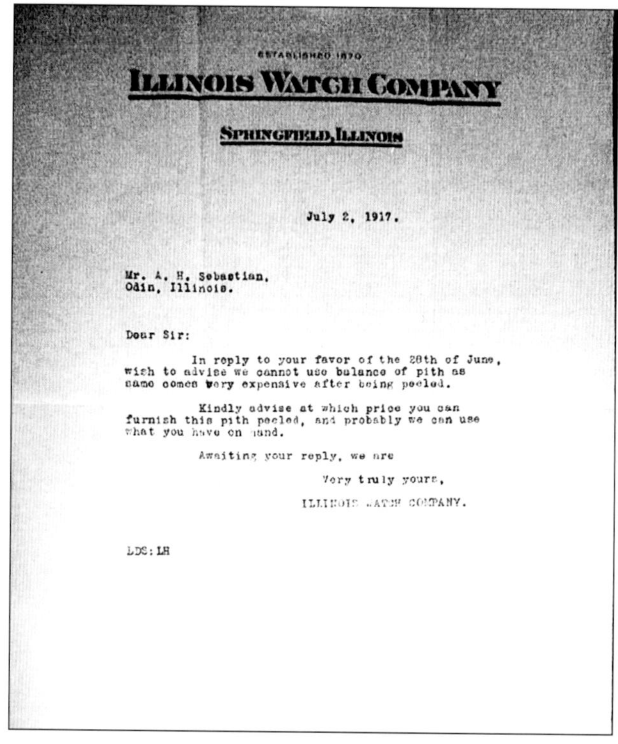

ESTABLISHED 1870

ILLINOIS WATCH COMPANY

SPRINGFIELD, ILLINOIS

July 2, 1917.

Mr. A. H. Sebastian,
Odin, Illinois.

Dear Sir:

In reply to your favor of the 28th of June, wish to advise we cannot use balance of pith as same comes very expensive after being peeled.

Kindly advise at which price you can furnish this pith peeled, and probably we can use what you have on hand.

Awaiting your reply, we are

Very truly yours,

ILLINOIS WATCH COMPANY.

LDS:LH

Three Illinois letters from 1917 dealing with issues Illinois had with pith it had purchased

KITCHENER TRENCH WATCH
For the Soldier's Gift

If he hasn't a military watch, now is the time to get one for him. It is an ideal Christmas Gift—and he may need it in a foreign land soon.

We have a small supply of these dependable watches now on hand. We can supply a limited number of our friends with Kitcheners for the boys. Only two more days to make him happy.

The Kitchener is absolutely guaranteed to give entire satisfaction and keep accurate time. At our low wholesale price it is the best military watch value on the market.

Signet Locket Rings, $12.50—See them—Something new.

Plain Signet Rings—$3.50 up

Identification Tag Lockets—Arranged for regular official tag and photo—U. S. Gov. Model, $3.00

Topeka Daily Capitol (Topeka, KS), December 15, 1917; image from *newspapers.com*

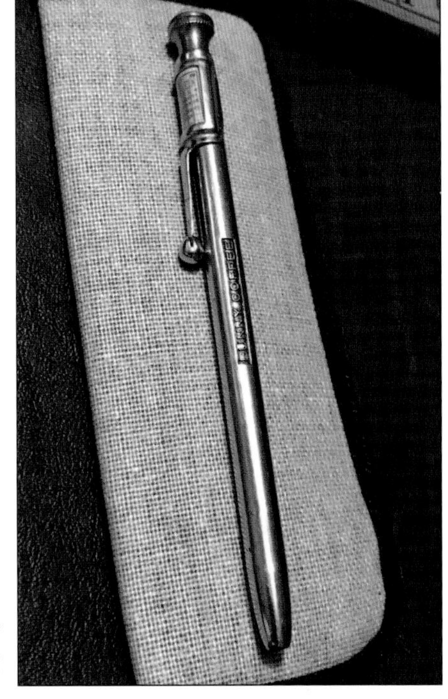

John W. Bunn & Co. promotional calendar pen, 1919, signed "Bunny Coffee"

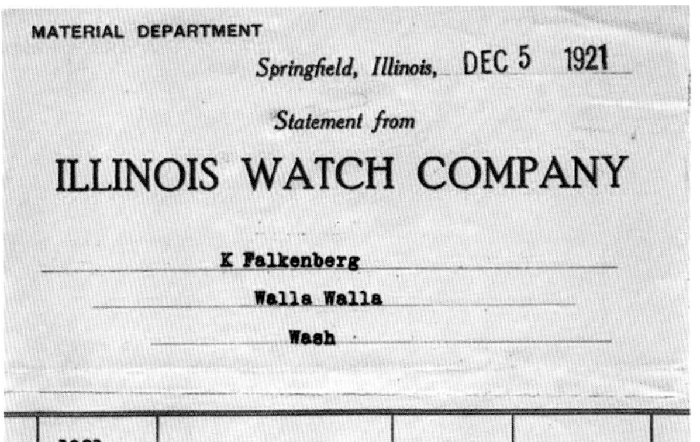

MATERIAL DEPARTMENT

Springfield, Illinois, DEC 5 1921

Statement from

ILLINOIS WATCH COMPANY

K Falkenberg
Walla Walla
Wash

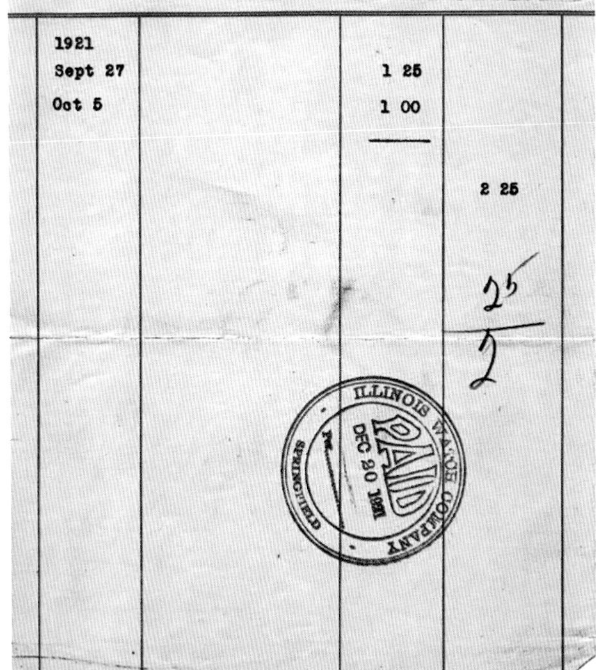

1921			
Sept 27		1 25	
Oct 5		1 00	
			2 25
			25
			2

ILLINOIS WATCH COMPANY PAID DEC 20 1921 Per SPRINGFIELD

MATERIAL DEPARTMENT

Springfield, Illinois, MAR 1 - 1923

Statement from

ILLINOIS WATCH COMPANY

K FALKENBERG
WALLA WALLA WASH

FEB 2	3 43
	43
	3

ILLINOIS WATCH COMPANY PAID MAR 9 1923 Per

Two Illinois Material Department invoices from 1921 and 1923, respectively, both stamped "PAID"

The 23 Jewel, 60 Hour
Bunn Special
Is Now On Display

WE are now displaying the new 23 Jewel Bunn Special and we can readily recommend this accurate, dependable railroad watch. ¶Illinois Watches are exclusively high grade and are entirely satisfactory. They not only carry our guarantee but the guarantee of the makers, The Illinois Watch of Springfield, Illinois. ¶It is part of our store policy to sell only high quality merchandise that we can guarantee and the new Bunn Special is an excellent example of the policy maintained by us.

OTTO YOUNG & CO.
29 E. Madison St.
Chicago, Illinois

6

Brochure, c. 1928 (outside surface), advertising the 23-jewel version of the Illinois 60-hour Bunn Special. Illinois prepared such advertisements for their jobbers, who could then add their name to the outside, as this example shows. The same graphic of a locomotive also appears in the pages advertising the Bunn Special that Illinois sent to the jobbers for their 1929 catalogs, which would have been prepared in 1928.

The Last Word in Timing the Trains

Illinois 23 Jewel Bunn Special

THE new 23 Jewel Bunn Special is the watch that will always be standard for railroad time service. The 17 jewel and 19 jewel watches have passed into the discard in favor of better timepieces. But the new 23 jewel Bunn Special so far exceeds railroad requirements that it will meet any demands this service can ever impose. Its Superior Motor Barrel permits the use of a longer, thinner mainspring which drives the watch 60 hours from one winding — a tremendous factor of safety, since the watch will maintain its even, accurate rate for more than 48 hours. But its most important function is to create through regular 24 hour winding a reserve tension which is the most fundamental kind of compensation yet devised for the variation in tension of the usual mainspring. The adjustment to six positions, instead of the usual five, insures the highest accuracy and uniformity of time in all positions.

The new 23 jewel Bunn Special is for the railroad man who takes real pride in his equipment. Its case is just about the handsomest and most serviceable ever designed for railroad use. Be a leader in watch equipment. Come in and let us show you one of these beautiful 60 hour, 6 position, 23 jewel Illinois watches.

In 14k white or green gold filled case $75.00

In 10k yellow gold filled case, ... $70.00

Sixty Hours - Six Positions

The ILLINOIS WATCH
Established 1870
SPRINGFIELD, ILLINOIS
ILLINOIS WATCHES ARE BETTER THAN THEY HAVE TO BE

Bunn Special brochure, c. 1928 (inside surface). The 60-hour Bunn Special may have been one of Illinois' products that attracted Hamilton to purchase the company

Lindbergh Flies Air Mail from Springfield

On April 15, 1926, United States Air Mail service began in Springfield on a route from St. Louis to Springfield to Peoria to Chicago. The two pilots on the first trip were Charles A. Lindbergh and Phil R. Love. They are pictured here.

Photo courtesy Esther B. Mueller, St. Louis, Mo.

PILOTS WHO FLEW AIR MAIL FROM SPRINGFIELD

Charles A. Lindbergh, left, and Phil R. Love, when they flew the first air mail over the St. Louis-Springfield-Peoria-Chicago route on April 15, 1926.

After they arrived in Springfield, "Lindbergh and Love were presented with commemorative medallions through the courtesy of the Illinois Watch Company. Fred Morgan, representing the company (see Chapter 2), made the presentation to the fliers, and turned over a third medallion to Post-master Conkling to be presented to another of the air mail pilots at a later date. These souvenir medallions were about two and one-half inches in diameter, with an embossed picture of Lincoln and the dates 1809–1865 on one side, and on the reverse the inscription 'Inaugurating Air Mail Service, Springfield, Illinois, April 15, 1926' and the name of the pilot" (William A Steiger, Lindbergh Flies Air Mail from Springfield, dig.lib.edu ISHS 1954 Summer).

To my knowledge, none of these rare commemorative medallions has ever been found.

Illinois Jobbers 1923 List

JOBBERS OF ILLINOIS WATCH MATERIAL

Illinois Watch Company
Springfield

DECEMBER 1923

ALABAMA

F. T. Skelton.................Birmingham
213½ N. 20th St.

CALIFORNIA

Armer & Brown Co............Los Angeles
503 Title Guarantee Bldg.

E. W. Reynolds Co............Los Angeles
3rd Floor Metropolitan Bldg.

C. F. Sischo & Sons...........Los Angeles
747 S. Hill St.

Morgan & Allen Co.........San Francisco
150 Post St.

R. & L. Myers Co...........San Francisco
717 Market St.

Nordman & Aurich...........San Francisco
150 Post St.

COLORADO

The Edward Lehman Jewelry Co.. .Denver
A. C. Foster Bldg.

CONNECTICUT

M. S. Levenson..................Hartford
943 Main St.

DELAWARE

B. Kleitz & Brother Co..........Wilmington
6th & Market Sts.

DISTRICT OF COLUMBIA

Alpher-Kur-Greenberg Co.......Washington
417 Seventh St., N. W.

A. Miller & Son................Washington
802 F. St., N. W.

FLORIDA

F. L. Reames.......................Tampa
311½ Zack St.

GEORGIA

Ewing Brothers.....................Atlanta
11 Whitehall St.

Timms Jewelry Co.................Atlanta
37 S. Broad St.

ILLINOIS

Benj. Allen & Co..................Chicago
10 S. Wabash Ave.

Emil Braude & Sons, Inc...........Chicago
Heyworth Bldg.

The C. & E. Marshall Co............Chicago
5 S. Wabash Ave.

Henry Paulson & Co...............Chicago
37 S. Wabash Ave.

F. W. H. Schmidt..................Chicago
1108 Heyworth Bldg.

Swartchild & Co..................Chicago
29 E. Madison St.

Victoria Watch Co.................Chicago
159 N. State St.

Otto Young & Co..................Chicago
Heyworth Bldg.

Peoria Jewelry Co..................Peoria
321 Main St.

A. S. Wormood.................Springfield
Ferguson Bldg.

INDIANA

Hoffman & Co................Indianapolis
905 State Life Bldg.

IOWA

M. A. Lumbard Co.............Des Moines
415 Locust St.

E. E. Robinson Co..............Des Moines
Fifth & Grand Ave.

T. R. J. Ayres & Sons.............Keokuk
511 Main St.

KENTUCKY

George Katzman Co..............Louisville
508 S. 3rd St.

LOUISIANA

W. E. Taylor Co...............New Orleans
115 Exchange Place

MAINE

The Skillin Co....................Portland
235½ Middle St.

MARYLAND

Max Kohner ....Baltimore
104 W. Fayette St.

John A. Tschantre...............Baltimore
28 E. Baltimore St.

MASSACHUSETTS

I. Alberts' Sons, Inc.................Boston
Jewelers Bldg.

Harkins, Kirby, Murphy Co..........Boston
373 Washington St.

J. M. Kirby Co......................Boston
373 Washington St.

M. & V. Co., Inc......................Boston
373 Washington St.

Charles May & Son Co..............Boston
373 Washington St.

A. Paul & Co........................Boston
373 Washington St.

D. C. Percival & Co.................Boston
373 Washington St.

Travis, Farber Co...................Boston
373 Washington St.

MICHIGAN

Cutler Jewelers' Supply Co..........Detroit
506 Liggett Bldg.

Detroit Jewelers' Supply Co.........Detroit
407 Liggett Bldg.

MICHIGAN (Continued)

H. W. Himelhoch Co.................Detroit
402 Liggett Bldg.

The C. & E. Marshall Co............Detroit
15 John R. St.

Noack & Gorenflo..................Detroit
22-28 E. Jefferson Ave.

Henry Staats ....Detroit
1111 Griswold St.

MINNESOTA

Duluth Jewelers' Supply Co.........Duluth
Armstead Bldg.

J. M. Bennett Co.............. Minneapolis
First Ave. N. at Seventh St.

S. H. Clausin & Co............Minneapolis
17 Sixth St. S.

C. M. Thomsen Co.............Minneapolis
413 Lumber Exchange

Josten Mfg. Co..................Owatonna
105 Main St.

Esslinger & Schaeppi Co...........St. Paul
505 Ryan Bldg.

Irvin & Beard Co.................St. Paul
Ryan Bldg.

MISSOURI

Clark Tool & Material Co......Kansas City
1010 Walnut St.

Edwards, Ludwig, Fuller Jlry. Co..Kas. City
1113 Walnut St.

Lange & Wetteroth Mat. Co....Kansas City
921 Walnut St.

Meyer Jewelry Co............Kansas City
Boley Bldg.

C B. Norton Jewelry Co..... Kansas City
1016 Walnut St.

Bauman-Massa Jewelry Co. ...... St. Louis
214 N. Sixth St.

Ilch & Radecke....................St. Louis
632-634 Arcade Bldg.

W. F. Kemper Co.................St. Louis
307 Equitable Bldg.

NEBRASKA

The Bergman-Koppel Co............Omaha
City National Bank Bldg.

L. E. Griffith.......................Omaha
1514 Howard St.

NEW YORK

Eliassof Brothers & Co.............Albany
100 State St.

King & Eisele Co..................Buffalo
Franklin & Huron Sts.

Queen City Material Co............Buffalo
403 Main St.

John D. Lewis......................Elmira
323 Carroll St.

F. J. Boesse & Co...............New York
68 Nassau St.

Conover & Quayle...............New York
2 Maiden Lane

Cross & Beguelin...............New York
23 Maiden Lane

George J. Doehrmann...........New York
51-53 Maiden Lane

A. A. Goldfuss & Co.............New York
21 Maiden Lane

W. Green & Co..................New York
81 Nassau St.

Hammel, Riglander & Co........New York
209-211 W. 14th St.

L. H. Keller & Co...............New York
110 Fulton St.

Korones Bros ....New York
37 Maiden Lane

Henry S. Kramer................New York
176 Fulton St.

M. J. Lampert & Sons, Inc........New York
119 Fulton St.

Lieberman Brothers ....New York
64 Nassau St.

Pennant Watch & Supply House..New York
466 Broome St.

NEW YORK (Continued)

Peltock & Seeler Co....... ....New York
15 Maiden Lane

Philip Sloves....................New York
37 Maiden Lane

S. Stanley Solomon.............New York
21 Maiden Lane

Sussfeld, Lorsch & Schimmel....New York
153 W. 23rd St.

Weber-Lisson Co., Inc...........New York
75 Maiden Lane

Henry Zimmern & Co...........New York
45 John St.

Glazer Jewelry Co................Rochester
207 Chamber of Commerce Bldg.

Morris Rosenbloom & Co....... ..Rochester
156 E. Main St.

Geo. A. Fleischman...............Syracuse
314 Cahill Bldg.

W. P. Hitchcock Co...............Syracuse
Elks' Temple

A. H. Pond Co., Inc...............Syracuse
214-216 S. Warren St.

Gould & Gould.................Watertown
101 Charlebois Bldg.

NORTH CAROLINA

C. M. Waldorf..................Wilmington
511 Southern Bldg.

OHIO

J. F. Mabry..........................Akron
10 S. Main St.

Lindner & Co...................Cincinnati
125 E. Third St.

Chas. Swigart ....Cincinnati
Seventh & Vine St.

E. & J. Swigart Co..............Cincinnati
Sixth & College St.

Cleveland Jewelers' Supply Co....Cleveland
308 C. A. C. Bldg.

OHIO (Continued)

The Merit Co....................Cleveland
647 Euclid Ave.

The Sigler Brothers Co...........Cleveland
1017 Euclid Ave.

Earl Sculler.....................Columbus
401 Citizens Bank Bldg.

Wm. S. McCaw Co.................Toledo
315 Superior St.

Youngstown Jewelers' Supply Co......
34 Commercial St., W......Youngstown

OREGON

Bernard Italie Co.................Portland
211 Gerlinger Bldg.

Butterfield Brothers...............Portland
164 Third St.

PENNSYLVANIA

H. S. Meiskey Co.................Lancaster
Duke & Chestnut Sts.

Saul L. Solomon.................Lancaster
209 N. Queen St.

Aisenstein & Gordon...........Philadelphia
712 Sansom St.

Jos. Bechtel & Co.............Philadelphia
729 Sansom St.

R. M. Cooper & Son...........Philadelphia
713 Sansom St.

Chas. H. O'Bryon.............Philadelphia
735 Sansom St.

Rothman & Meyer.............Philadelphia
136 S. 8th St.

M Sickles & Sons.............Philadelphia
900 Chestnut St.

Martin Gluck & Son.............Pittsburgh
718 Penn Ave.

Heeren Brothers Co.............Pittsburgh
Penn Ave. & 8th St.

J. M. Kurtz Co.................Pittsburgh
214 Bessemer Bldg.

PENNSYLVANIA (Continued)

Landaw Brothers Co.............Pittsburgh
214 Pittsburgh Life Bldg.

A. J. Wagner.....................Scranton
318 Traders Bank Bldg.

Watchmaker's Supply House..Wilkes Barre
20-24 Laning Bldg.

RHODE ISLAND

Geo. H. Taylor & Co............Providence
204 Westminster St.

TENNESSEE

J. H. Mednikow & Co.............Memphis
117 Monroe Ave.

Young-Neal Co...................Nashville
215 6th Ave. North

TEXAS

H. H. Hawley Co....................Dallas
1521-23 Commerce St.

Houghton-Reardon Co................Dallas
1103½ Main St.

John H. Clary Co..................El Paso
Mills Bldg.

C. U. Spawn & Co.................Houston
413½ Fannin St.

B. M. Hammond & Co..........San Antonio
227 W. Commerce St.

UTAH

Primrose-Jolliffe Corp...... ..Salt Lake City
Clift Bldg.

VERMONT

Bogle Brothers........White River Junction

VIRGINIA

J. H. Lesser.......................Norfolk
115 College Place

Southern Jewelers' Supply Co., Inc........
408½ E. Broad St..............Richmond

WASHINGTON

I. Lachaman & Sons Co............Seattle
1404 Second Ave.

Mayer Brothers ....Seattle
359 Colman Bldg.

S. H. Clausin & Co................Spokane
305 Hyde Bldg.

Petersen Brothers Co..............Spokane
414 Mohawk Bldg.

WISCONSIN

O. H. Bingenheimer Co..........Milwaukee
Enterprise Bldg.

Boszhardt-Possin Co.............Milwaukee
209 Grand Ave.

—

CANADA

ALBERTA

McGeachie & Holdsworth..........Calgary
Leeson & Lineham Block

NOVA SCOTIA

Arthur W. Thomas.................Halifax
P. O. Box 393.

ONTARIO

E. & A. Gunther Co................Toronto
316 Spadina Ave.

P. W. Ellis & Co., Ltd.............Toronto
33 Wellington St.

Klein & Burrows..................Toronto
40 Colborne St.

Rixon, Lacy & McCarroll, Ltd......Toronto
26 King St., W.

QUEBEC

H. R. Millard....................Montreal
146 St. James St.

Watch Factory watercolor, c. 1920s

The Factory Behind The Watch

Plant of the Illinois Watch Company, Springfield, Illinois, also showing America's highest grade railroad watch, the "SANGAMO SPECIAL."

This Factory is Devoted Exclusively to the Manufacture of High-Grade Watches

Established in 1870

For more than 50 years, high-grade watches have been produced in this factory. The reputation established in these years for high-quality products is in itself a guarantee.

Every Illinois-Springfield Watch is fully guaranteed to be perfect in construction and to be a satisfactory timekeeper.

ILLINOIS WATCH COMPANY
SPRINGFIELD, ILLINOIS

Pere Marquette Magazine, January 1923, back page of the issue

Early promotional case openers

Tablespoon and teaspoon in sterling silver from the Illinois Factory lunchroom, c. 1920s

Early Illinois materials tin

Small Illinois materials tin (1" diameter)

Parts tin from a Springfield watchmaker

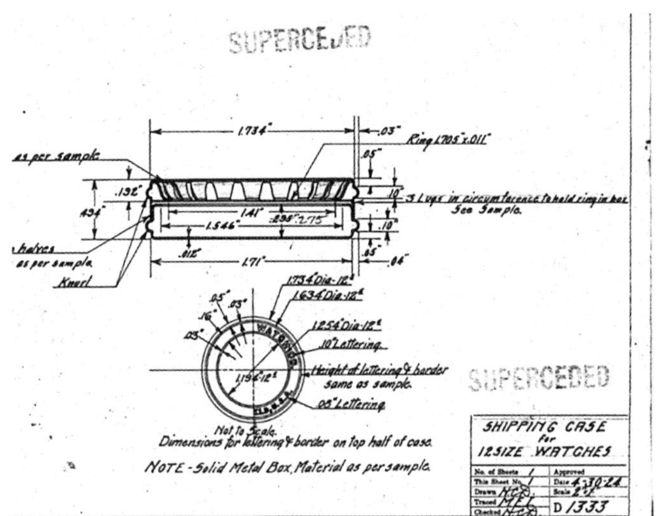

Illinois drawing for a solid metal movement shipping container for a 12-size watch, dated April 30, 1924

Examples of the actual movement tins

April 9th, 1930.

A. H. Varnes,
Ritzville, Washington.

Dear Sir:

We are in receipt of your favor of the 3rd instant, regarding the shipping cases from movements of our manufacture, which you desire to return to us for credit.

On January 1st, 1928, we advised the trade we discontinued the purchase of empty movement boxes with the exception of the glass front and back display cases in which we cased some of our railroad grades. Due to the fact that the bulk of our product today is cased in gold cases and sold from our factory as complete watches, on June 1st, 1928 we also discontinued the purchase of empty movement cases and under the circumstances are not in a position to make you any allowance for these boxes.

We thank you for inquiring about this matter before forwarding these shipping cases to us and with the information as stated, trust that you will appreciate our position in the matter,

Very truly yours,

ILLINOIS WATCH

Repair Department

WW:RD

Illinois ultimately stopped the repurchase of empty movement containers unless they had front and back glass for movement display.

Examples of the actual movement tins

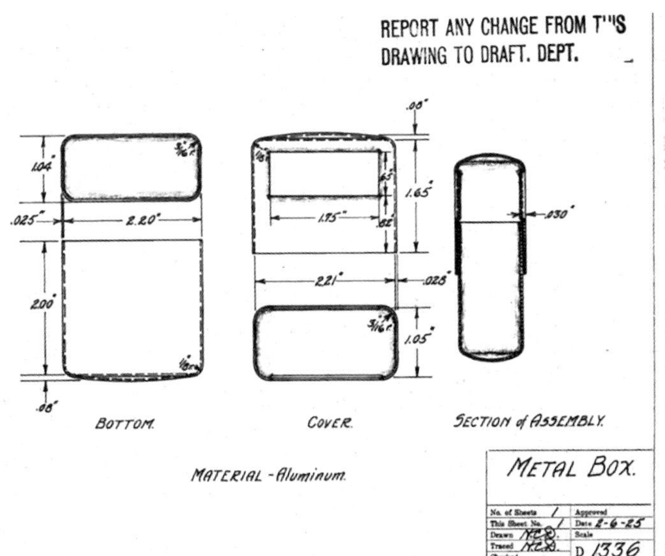

Illinois drawing of the Bunn Special aluminum shipping container, dated February 6, 1925. Note that the drawing was prepared by H.C. Dobbs, who ultimately relocated to Lancaster when Springfield was shuttered. *Right:* Actual Bunn Special Container.

The original reverse image used to produce the Illinois Observatory promotional colored painting on tin

Illinois display case that appears to have been constructed out of an Illinois advertising frame, c. 1920

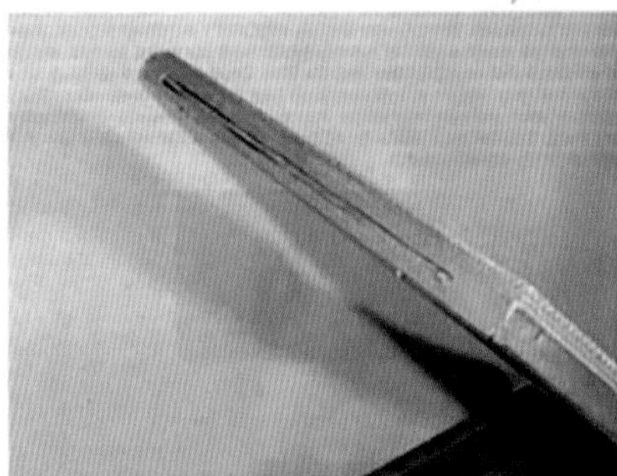

Glass display cabinet supplied by the Illinois Watch Company to jewelers for the display and promotion of Illinois watches, c. 1920s

Display Cases and Outer Box

An early Illinois sales catalog from the late 1920s indicates that each Factory-Cased model "is boxed at the factory in an attractive leatherette covered, silk and plush lined display case. Our price and description card is inserted in the lid of each box." Today, some of these price cards can still be found; many are shown throughout this book.

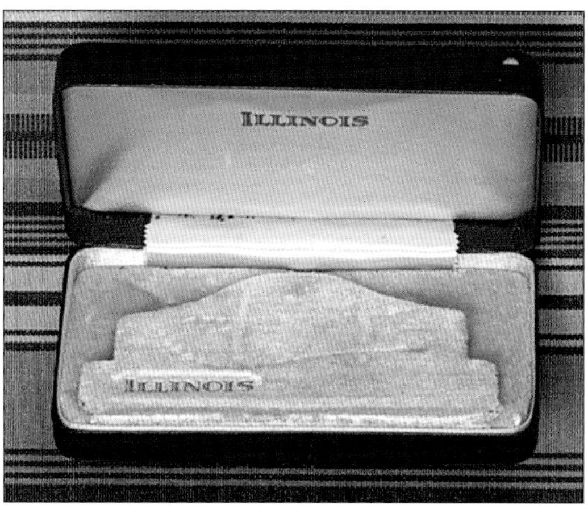

Illinois display box

Top of outer box

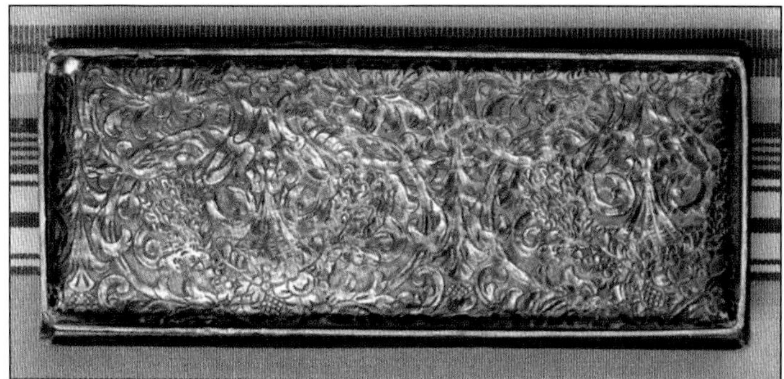

Top of dark blue Illinois display box

Illinois display box with sticker for John W. Fee, Jeweler, 218 South Sixth Street, Springfield, Illinois

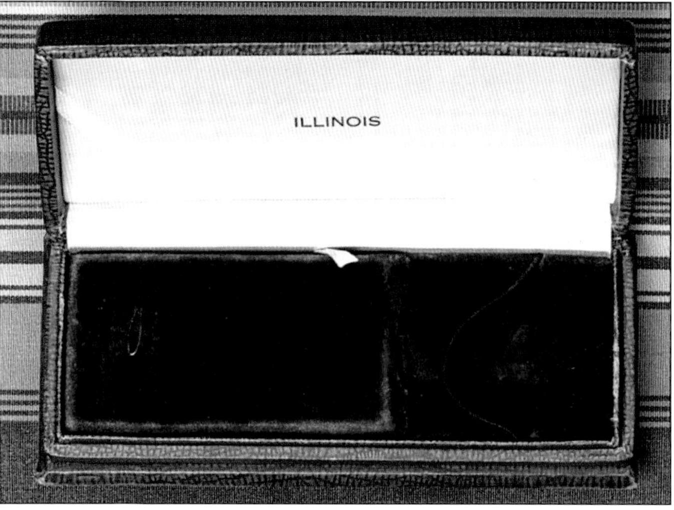

An unusual dark blue Illinois display box

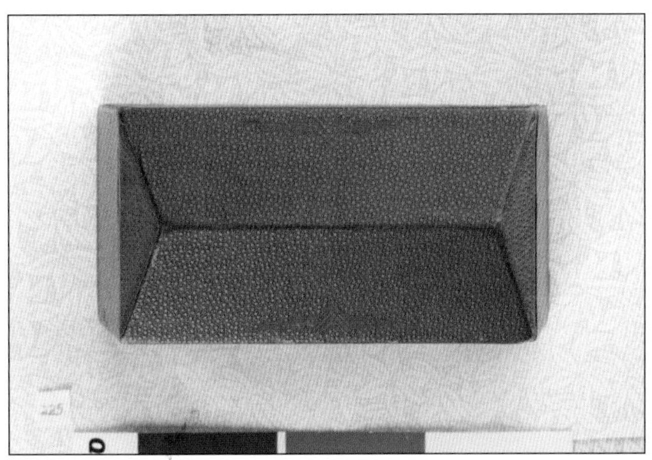

A special Illinois display box for an Illinois Chieftain model that flips open from the front with the watch attached to the black material

Aftermarket mainsprings

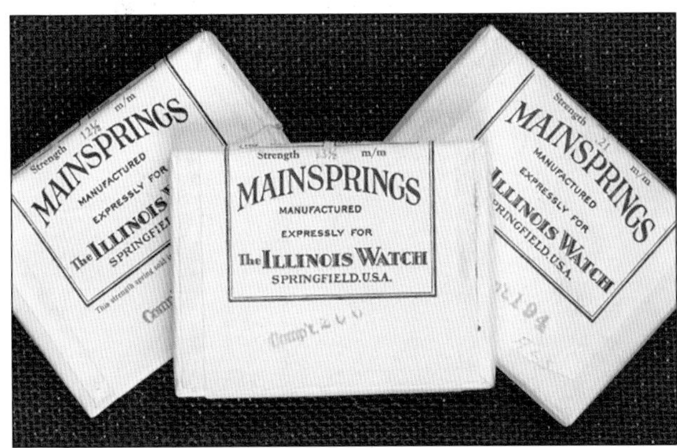

Other aftermarket mainsprings

Aftermarket mainsprings

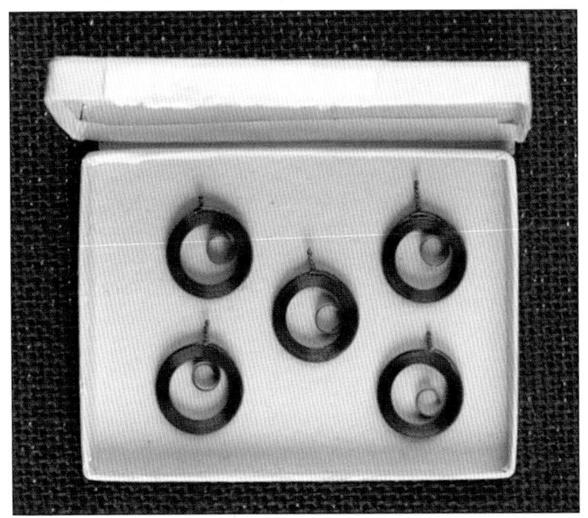
Aftermarket mainsprings

Aftermarket mainsprings

President Lincoln in Illinois Advertising

The Illinois Watch Company, with its home in Springfield and early ties to Abraham Lincoln, used his name to help promote the company. The Watch Company issued one pocket watch in his name. It also provided a Springfield and Lincoln Souvenir printed portfolio of different photographs and views of Springfield, including the Illinois Watch Company and various Lincoln landmarks, compliments of the Watch Company. This 1885 booklet for its day was very elaborate and polished in appearance. Illinois also produced and sold Lincoln pocket watch fobs, sponsored the Lincoln High School Essay Contest with its Lincoln medallion prize and sold a Lincoln lithograph portrait. Additionally, Lincoln historian John Hoffmann points out that "Publications of the company routinely noted its proximity to the Lincoln tomb."[1]

Front and back cover of the Springfield and Lincoln Souvenir book (2.5" x 5")

Pictures inside the souvenir book

The A. Lincoln Fob

Hoffman notes that to augment the A. Lincoln pocket watch, the Illinois Watch Company distributed "a medalet and chain, to serve as a watch fob for the Lincoln watch. On the front was a profile of the president, with his name and dates on the circumference. On the back, between an eagle and a Roman fasces—or bundle of rods—was written in capital letters, *Illinois / Watch Company / Springfield / Makers of the / A. Lincoln / Watch.*

"B. L. (Bela Lyon) Pratt, a leading Boston sculptor, designed the medalet, which was only about one and a quarter inches in diameter. The piece, although too small to be precisely rendered, was exceedingly popular. The watch company distributed hundreds of medalets both with and without its A. Lincoln watches." They frequently are offered for sale on eBay.

A. Lincoln watch fob front

A. Lincoln watch fob back

A. Lincoln Lithographic Portrait

Hoffman further notes: "Beginning in 1913, the company also distributed a lithographic portrait of Lincoln on canvas. This print included an embossed, circular stamp in the lower right corner, with the words *Illinois Watch Co. Springfield* on the circumference and *The Lincoln Watch* in the middle, all in capital letters. Placed in a gesso-and gilt-covered wood frame (about 11-by-14 inches), the print (about 7-by-10 inches) was produced by a lithographic process that made it appear as if it were an oil painting. The Illinois Watch Company sent its lithograph of Lincoln to dealers for one dollar each for display next to Illinois watches, a promotional effort that reinforced the company's use of Lincoln."

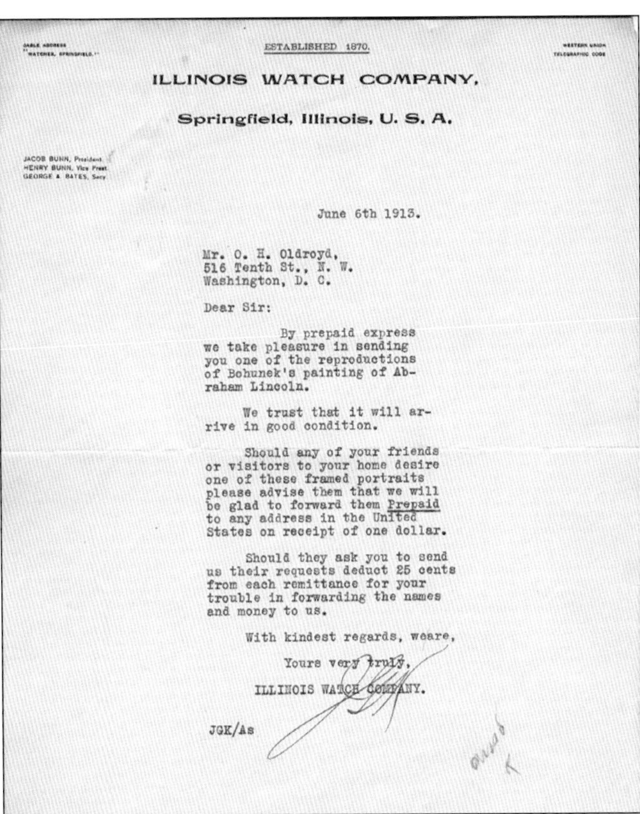

CABLE ADDRESS "WATCHES, SPRINGFIELD."

ESTABLISHED 1870.

WESTERN UNION TELEGRAPHIC CODE

ILLINOIS WATCH COMPANY,

Springfield, Illinois, U. S. A.

JACOB BUNN, President
HENRY BUNN, Vice Prest.
GEORGE A. BATES, Secy.

June 6th 1913.

Mr. O. H. Oldroyd,
516 Tenth St., N. W.
Washington, D. C.

Dear Sir:

By prepaid express we take pleasure in sending you one of the reproductions of Bohunek's painting of Abraham Lincoln.

We trust that it will arrive in good condition.

Should any of your friends or visitors to your home desire one of these framed portraits please advise them that we will be glad to forward them Prepaid to any address in the United States on receipt of one dollar.

Should they ask you to send us their requests deduct 25 cents from each remittance for your trouble in forwarding the names and money to us.

With kindest regards, weare,

Yours very truly,
ILLINOIS WATCH COMPANY.

JGK/As

Letter regarding the Lincoln "painting"

Hoffman points out that "hundreds of the prints survive and have become a staple of online auctions, where they are inaccurately or incompletely described. Even when the picture is recognized as a print, not a painting, the piece is sold without identifying Rudolf Bohunek as the artist whose portrait of Lincoln was the basis of the print. 'R. Bohunek' was indistinctly stamped on the back of the canvas, and part of his last name was folded under the frame."

Lincoln Essay Contest and Medal

In 1924, Illinois, then under the leadership of Jacob Bunn, Jr., launched a nationwide high school essay contest on A. Lincoln.

According to historian Hoffmann (and perhaps unfairly asserted), "It was but a small step from Lincoln paraphernalia that advertised the A. Lincoln watch to an essay contest that would associate the Lincoln name and image with the company's entire stock. By implication, each watch was as reliable and as steadfast as the Savior of the Union, each timepiece as honest as Honest Abe. Moreover, the essay contest was a popular vehicle of civic education in the Progressive era, and no president more fully embodied the American creed than Lincoln."

Lincoln essay medals

As Hoffman notes: "Jacob Bunn . . . reflected this perspective in sending the following announcement to the high schools of the nation: 'In view of this city being the former home and burial place of our martyred president, Abraham Lincoln, and desiring to encourage the study of his life and character, this company without selfish motives have [sic] been considering for some time the advisability of presenting annually, to a student in the senior class of each High School in the United States, a very handsome medal of Abraham Lincoln. The idea in mind', Bunn continued, 'is to present the medal on Lincoln's birthday" to the student at each high school who is deemed by a panel of at least three teachers to have written 'the best short essay' on Lincoln."

Lincoln Essay booklet

Some of Douglas Volk's Lincoln portraitures are now in the National Gallery of Art and on various postage stamps. However, Volk protested using the Illinois Watch Company name on the medal, so it was finally eliminated by Bunn.

"The booklet announcing the contest was sent to twenty-three thousand American high schools . . . Although the medals first struck for the contest were dated on the anniversary of Lincoln's birthday in 1924, the booklet concluded with a letter of March 4, written by Francis G. Blair, the Illinois Superintendent of Public Instruction, which referred to 'unavoidable delays' in starting the contest—delays occasioned at least partly by Volk's stand against commercializing Lincoln. When Volk opened the shipping carton containing the finished product, however, he must have been surprised to see that the medallion itself rested in a velvet-lined display case, on the lid of which was printed, in capital letters, the words Presented by / *Illinois Watch Co. / Springfield.*"

MEDALS ARE AWARDED IN LINCOLN CONTEST

The Illinois Watch Company, of Springfield, has undertaken to create interest and increase knowledge and admiration of Lincoln among school children in the United States. As a civic duty and part of the Lincoln program this company offered a beautiful bronze medal to a pupil in each High School in the United States for writing the best short essay on the life of Lincoln.

A number of High Schools in Venango county took part in the contest this year and awards of the medal were made on Lincoln's birthday in the Polk and Rocky Grove schools. The medal for the Polk winner was on display at the W. O. McDivitt store and for Miss Elsie Noel, of Reno, the winner at Rocky Grove, the award was displayed at the E. D. Jordan jewelery store in this city.

The medal is three inches in diameter. The head of Lincoln is a reproduction of Douglas Volk's famous painting, "Abraham Lincoln." The sculpturing is the work of Charles Louis Hinton, an artist of note. Both artists are Americans. A space is provided on the back of the medal for the name of the winner. No advertising of any kind is found on the medal.

The first medal was presented to Lloyd George, on the occasion of his visit to the tomb of Lincoln in the Fall of 1923. Others have been placed in Lincoln collections and libraries throughout the country, but none has been sold or none will be sold; they are not for sale at any price.

Springfield, Illinois, was the home of Abraham Lincoln. His body was interred in that city. A magnificent monument, erected largely by the pennies and small coins of the children of the nation, shelters his body.

A local Pennsylvania article announcing the Lincoln essay winners, *News-Herald* (Franklin, PA), February 13, 1924; image from *newspapers.com*

A Lincoln Medal in its display case

Outer shipping box to a winner of a Lincoln medal

Volk undoubtedly would have been upset if he had read about this giveaway of Lincoln booklets and two thousand medals from the Illinois Watch Company via the Springfield Chamber of Commerce booth at the 1924 Travel Exposition at the Sherman Hotel in Chicago.

Seven thousand pieces of literature on Springfield, including Lincoln book lets, and two thousand medals given by the Illinois Watch company of this city, were distributed from the Spring field Chamber of Commerce booth at the International Travel Exposition held at the Sherman hotel in Chicago recently. Springfield was the only city in the Middle West, with the exception of Chicago and Hot Springs, having a booth at the exposition. England, Germany, France, Switzerland, Norway, Denmark and other European countries, Mexico, Canada, and many cities and states in the United States had booths and exhibits.

Springfield's booth was wholly a Lincoln booth, the chamber of commerce also representing the Lincoln Centennial association. A large bust of Lincoln was the centerpiece of the local exhibit. Twelve thousand visitors attended the show on Thanksgiving day.

The Pioneer (Riverdale, IL), December 9, 1927; image from *newspapers.com*

Illinois sent an announcement (shown below) directly to the retail jewelers to seek their support for the contest.

ESTABLISHED 1870

ILLINOIS WATCH COMPANY

SPRINGFIELD, ILLINOIS

IMPORTANT

To the Retail Jeweler:

On Lincoln's Birthday, February 12th, 1924, this company will present a very handsome medal to the student in your high school writing the best short essay on the life of Abraham Lincoln.

We are anxious to have this medal displayed prior to its presentation, in order that the greatest interest may be worked up among the students, and in view of the fact that your name has been suggested to us by the school officials, we will appreciate it very much if you will kindly advise us on the enclosed postal card whether it will be agreeable to you to display the medal.

As there will be considerable advertising value attached to the displaying of this medal, we would ask that in return, you have the name of the student winning the medal engraved on the reverse side of same, as it would be an almost endless task for us to attempt to do this here, as the medals are being presented to a majority of the high schools in the United States.

We will greatly appreciate your immediate reply, as we will be prepared to forward the medals within the next few weeks.

Very truly yours,

ILLINOIS WATCH COMPANY.

The essay contest ended on February 12, 1928, shortly after the Hamilton Watch Company acquisition of Illinois. Hoffman observes that the Hamilton Watch Company "discontinued" the competition, as it was pointed out that Hamilton's attention to business may "leave little room for ventures used as this" one. It was further noted that the venture was "pure philanthropy, since the company's name had not appeared in any manner (at least not on the medal itself)."

Keystone, April 1928, perhaps the first Illinois Watch advertisement following the January 1, 1928 acquisition

Keystone, August 1928. Illinois would was claiming "that it advertised its Bunn Special "In Twenty-One of the Leading Railroad Publications."

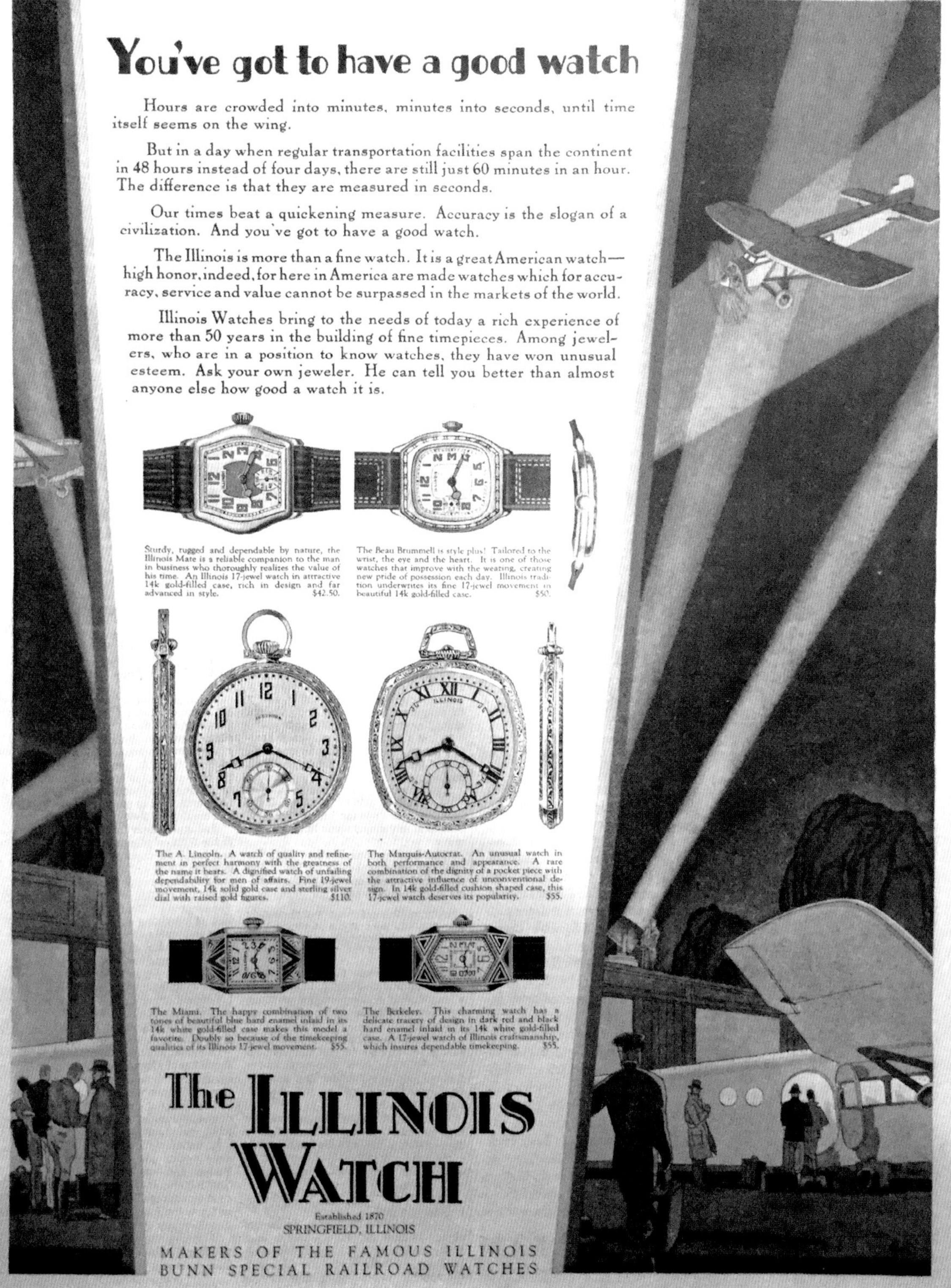

Saturday Evening Post, November 10, 1928

The American Magazine for November 1928 101

18,000 ticks an hour

Every second an Illinois Watch ticks five times—18,000 ticks an hour. And the loss or gain of just one tick out of each 18,000 would mean a variation in accuracy of more than 33 seconds a week.

Illinois Watches have brought the almost magic touch of accuracy to a point unsurpassed in watchmaking. It is significant of their perfection in design and construction that the famous Illinois Bunn Special railroad watches, for instance, are made to run 60 hours and more from one winding—an Illinois achievement never yet successfully duplicated, providing not only an important feature of safety, but also a vital factor in increased accuracy.

It is that kind of devotion to the ideals of fine watchmaking which has become an Illinois tradition. It is that kind of craftsmanship which endows every Illinois watch with added value for the price you pay.

See them at your jeweler's. Your taste will recognize their beauty and charm. Then ask the jeweler how good they are. He knows watches. And he knows that for more than 50 years Illinois Watches have been made with all the care worthy of such a fine art.

The Miami. The happy combination of warm red and black hard enamel inlaid in its 14k white gold-filled case, makes this model a favorite. Doubly so because of the time-keeping qualities of its fine Illinois 17-jeweled movement. $55.

The Marquis-Strap. One of the most popular strap models made, because of its unusually attractive 14k gold-filled case, curved to the arc of the wrist, and its fine 17-jeweled movement of very high quality. $50.

The A. Lincoln. Very thin, beautiful in design and performance alike, it is truly a watch worthy of its name. In 14k green or white solid gold case, fitted with exceptionally accurate 19-jeweled adjusted, motor-barrel movement. $100.

The Illini. An unusually beautiful watch, unequaled in quality of workmanship, with exceptionally fine 21-jeweled adjusted, motor-barrel movement. It is the highest grade thin model made by Illinois and is furnished in 14k solid gold case at $160, and in 18k solid gold case at $200.

The Marquis-Autocrat. Cushion Model. A thin model watch of great popularity because of its unusual beauty and dependability as a timepiece. Its fine 17-jeweled adjusted movement, motor-barrel equipped, is fitted in 14k gold-filled case, plain or engraved oxidized. $55.

The ILLINOIS WATCH

Established 1870

National Geographic, November 1928

2 *The American Magazine for June 1929*

"The Better Half of Beauty ~ **THE BEAUTY THAT LIES WITHIN"**

It keeps time *Beautifully*

THIS GREAT AMERICAN WATCH

THE NEW THIN ILLINOIS A. LINCOLN, *19 jewels, solid gold, $110. Other men's pocket watches from $40 to $120 and more.*

THE ILLINOIS EDGEWATER, *17 jewels, 14k gold-filled, $50. Other ladies' ribbon watches from $50 to $75 and more.*

THE NEW ILLINOIS PICCADILLY, *17 jewels, 14k gold-filled case, raised figure dial with luminous dots, $45. Other men's strap watches from $40 to $75.*

The beauty of an Illinois Watch is more than case-deep. It only begins there. Inside is a marvelous beauty of precision which alone makes a watch worth having.

That is why an Illinois watch keeps time—beautifully. And you can own one—a truly beautiful watch—in some models that cost as little as forty dollars.

It takes from eight months to a year to make an Illinois Watch. Many long hours to attain its almost unbelievably fine adjustments; weeks and months of timing, testing, proving at every step, so that when an Illinois Watch reaches the jeweler who sells it to you, it is a timepiece in every sense—good for years to come.

And because such workmanship deserves a setting of comparable beauty, you will find the Illinois Watch encased in many exquisite designs which express the decorative trend of today's styles with most authority and charm.

All this you buy in an Illinois Watch. That is why the watches shown on this page represent such unusual values. And that is why, for over fifty years, the Illinois has been recognized as more than a fine watch—a great American watch.

Ask your jeweler to show you his Illinois Watches—the new models for men and women. He will tell you how good they are. For it's his business to know watches.... and he has known Illinois ever since he's been in business.

Let us send you, without obligation, the Illinois Book of Watches. It illustrates a wide choice of models, with the price of each. Simply address Dept. A, The Illinois Watch, Springfield, Illinois.

MAKERS OF THE FAMOUS ILLINOIS BUNN SPECIAL RAILROAD WATCHES

The ILLINOIS WATCH

American Magazine, June 1929

Collier's, June 1, 1929

Collier's *for November 2, 1929* 43

MORE THAN A FINE WATCH

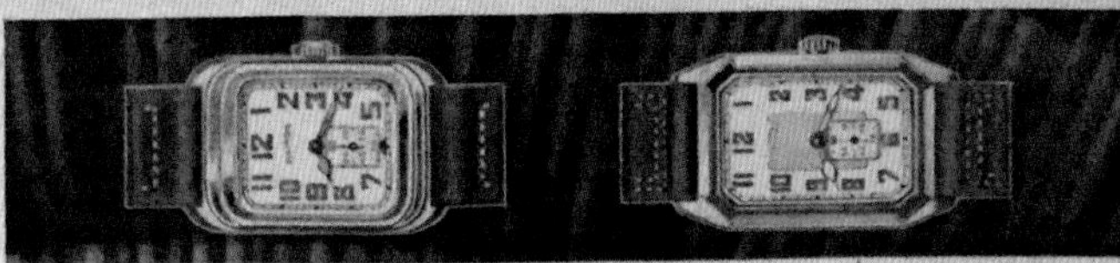

The ILLINOIS

A GREAT AMERICAN WATCH

Illinois Watches have been worn by American gentlefolk since 1870. In many families the old Illinois is a treasured heirloom . . . still capable of ticking off the minutes (18,000 ticks an hour) as accurately and dependably as its youngest descendant, fresh from the factory. It is this long history of honorable service that has made Illinois the Great American Watch it is today.

To the old standard of integrity in watchmaking . . . the beauty that is a timepiece . . . the new Illinois Watches add enchanting beauty and style. Never before has so much been given in a watch for the modest price of an Illinois.

Your jeweler has a wonderful presentation of the latest Illinois models for men and women. And write for our interesting, illustrated booklet, "The Beauty that Lies Within." It tells all you'd like to know about Illinois. Address, The Illinois Watch, 1216 North Ninth Street, Springfield, Ill.

One unalterable purpose expressed in beauty... the beauty of performance

Top of page, left to right—
The FUTURA, 17 jewels, rectangular movement, 14k gold-filled $60
The MEDALIST, 17 jewels, rectangular movement, 14k gold-filled $60

Above, reading down—
The DORIAN, 19 jewels, 14k gold-filled, new "Rotor-second" dial $55
The TRUSTEE, 17 jewels, 14k gold-filled $55

Above at right, reading down—
The NARRAGANSETT, 17 jewels, 14k solid gold $65
The REDONDA, 17 jewels, 14k gold-filled, inlaid enamel, ... $55
The EDGEWATER, 17 jewels, 14k gold-filled $50

At right—
The PICCADILLY, 17 jewels, 14k gold-filled $45

At extreme right, reading down—
The NEW YORKER, 17 jewels, 14k gold-filled $50
The BEAU BRUMMEL, 17 jewels, 14k gold-filled $50

MAKERS OF THE FAMOUS ILLINOIS BUNN SPECIAL RAILROAD WATCHES

Collier's, November 2, 1929

Saturday Evening Post, December 12, 1931

RETAIL PRICE LIST
The ILLINOIS WATCH
SEPTEMBER 1, 1929

	Retailer	Consumer
18/0 SIZE, 17 Jewel, STRAP WATCH		
TUXEDO, 14K white or green, plain or eng. or comb. solid gold case, luminous dial	$43.00	$75.00
Sterling Silver, applied 14K gold fig. dial	5.50	10.00
FACTORY CASED RIBBON WATCHES		
18/0 SIZE, 17 Jewels.		
BILOXI, 14K white gold filled, plain bezel	28.00	50.00
NEWPORT, 14K white gold filled, engraved	28.00	50.00
EDGEWATER, 14K white gold filled	28.00	50.00
LONG BEACH, 14K white gold filled	28.00	50.00
BERKELEY, 14K white gold filled, enameled	31.00	55.00
REDONDA, 14K white gold filled, enameled	31.00	55.00
MIAMI, 14K white gold filled, enameled	31.00	55.00
DEL MONTE, 14K white filled, enameled	31.00	55.00
BEVERLY, 14K white solid gold, plain bezel	37.00	65.00
NARRAGANSETT, 14K white solid gold, eng	37.00	65.00
BAR HARBOR, 14K white solid gold	37.00	65.00
DAYTONA, 14K white solid gold	37.00	65.00
CORONADO, 14K white solid gold, enameled	37.00	65.00
MARY TODD, 18K white solid gold, eng	43.00	75.00
MARY TODD, 18K white inlaid enamel	43.00	75.00

16 size supplied with either white enamel or silvered dials.

12 size supplied with silver Butler center or three different styles of fancy raised figure etched dial, no extra charge.

	Retailer	Consumer
12 size sterling silver with 18K applied figures, extra	5.50	10.00
All shapes of full luminous dials for 6-0 size uncased watches supplied for cases of standard make, extra	2.00	3.50
Price of No. 307 uncased watch includes all shapes luminous raised figures or plain dial.		
Montgomery numerical dials can be had on all railroad grades without extra charge; extra when fitted to other grades, 16 and 12 size	.50	------

Prices to retailer subject to a cash discount of 6 per cent if paid within ten days.

RETAIL PRICE LIST
The ILLINOIS WATCH
SEPTEMBER 1, 1929

	Retailer	Consumer
FACTORY CASED RAILROAD GRADES		
Sangamo Special, 23 Jewels. 60 Hour, 6 Position, Motor Barrel, 16 Size		
14K white, green or natural solid gold hinged case, with inside cap	$92.50	$150.00
14K white, green or natural gold filled case, hinged inside cap, also screw bezel and back, plain or eng. back	50.00	90.00
Bunn Special, 23 Jewels. 60 Hour, 6 Position, Motor Barrel, 16 Size		
Model 28, 14K white, green or comb. gold filled case	40.75	75.00
Model 28, 10K natural gold filled case	37.25	70.00
Cases with Engraved backs, extra	.75	2.00
Bunn Special, 21 Jewels. 60 Hour, 6 Position, Motor Barrel, 16 Size		
First Model, 14K white or green gold filled case	36.00	65.00
First Model, 10K natural gold filled case	32.50	60.00
Model 29, 14K white or green gold filled case	36.00	65.00
Model 29, 10K natural gold filled case	32.50	60.00
Model 181, 14K white gold filled	36.00	65.00
Model 181, 10K natural gold filled	32.50	60.00
Cases with Engraved backs, extra	.75	2.00
DISPATCHER, 16 Size, 19 Jewels, Adj. Temp. & 3 Pos. Pend. or Lever Set.		
14K white gold filled case	21.35	45.00
10K natural gold filled case	19.85	40.00
Cases with Engraved back, extra	.50	......
16 SIZE UNCASED WATCHES, Open Face Lever or Pendant Setting		
No. 167, (old No. 305) 17 J., Adj., S. S. Dial	12.60	24.00
No. 169, (old No. 707) Special, 19 J. Adj., 3 pos	16.50	32.50
12 SIZE UNCASED WATCHES, Open Face		
No. 127, (old No. 405) 17 Jewels, Adj	12.25	24.00
No. 129, (old No. 407) 19 J., Adj. 3 pos	16.90	32.50
No. 121, (old No. 279) 21 J., Adj. 3 pos	20.50	40.00
3/0 SIZE UNCASED WATCH.		
No. 307, (old No. 24) 17 Jewels Pat. Reg. luminous or printed dial	15.00	30.00
6/0 SIZE UNCASED WATCH.		
No. 605, (old No. 903) 15 J., steel escape	14.50	25.00

Illinois Retail Price List, dated September 1, 1929 (outside surface). The card, folded, was found tucked inside a 1930 Benj. Allen catalog. The discovery was made as this book set was going to press.

RETAIL PRICE LIST

The ILLINOIS WATCH

SEPTEMBER 1, 1929

FACTORY CASED POCKET WATCHES	Retailer	Consumer
A. Lincoln, 19 Jewels, 12 Size.		
Thin Model, Adjusted 5 Positions		
Pioneer Model, 14K white or green gold filled	$43.00	$75.00
Cushion Model, 14K white gold filled	43.00	75.00
Acorn Model, 14K green gold filled, inside cap. plain Bassine	43.00	75.00
Trustee, 14K white or natural gold filled	43.00	75.00
Barrister Model (A) 14K white or green solid gold, etched Roman figure dial	60.00	100.00
Barrister Model (B) 14K white or green solid gold, Sterling silver, 18K gold applied figure dial	67.50	110.00
Director, 14K white solid gold with 18K gold applied figure dial	67.50	110.00
Marquis-Autocrat, 17 J., 12 Size.		
Thin Model, Adjusted 3 Positions.		
Rialto, 14K white, green or natural gold filled	28.00	50.00
Eton Model, 14K white or green gold filled	28.00	50.00
Oxford, 14K white or green gold filled case	28.00	50.00
Cushion Model, 14K white gold filled, plain or engraved bezel	30.50	55.00
Trustee, 14K white or natural gold filled	30.50	55.00
Bourse, 14K white, green or comb. gold filled	43.00	75.00
Cambridge Model (A) 14K green or white solid gold Queen case, raised figure dial	43.00	75.00
Cambridge Model (B) 14K green or white solid gold Queen case, Sterling silver, 18K applied figure dial	50.50	85.00
Autocrat, 17 J., Adj., 12 Size.		
14K white or green gold filled case, raised figure, Butler center dial	23.00	43.50
Dorian 19 J., Adj. 3 Pos., 12 Size.		
14K white or natural gold filled case, special etched dial	25.75	50.00
Dorian with "Rotor-Second" dial	27.00	55.00

RETAIL PRICE LIST

The ILLINOIS WATCH

SEPTEMBER 1, 1929

FACTORY CASED STRAP WATCHES	Retailer	Consumer
3/0 SIZE. 17 J. Pat. Regulator.		
MAJOR, 17 Jewels, 14K white or green, plain or engraved, comb. gold filled case	$21.75	$42.50
MATE, 17 Jewels, 14K white or natural, plain or eng. or comb. gold filled case	21.75	42.50
JOLLY ROGER, 17J, 14K white or green gold filled case, plain or engraved	21.75	42.50
SPEEDWAY, 17 J., 14K white filled eng. case	21.75	42.50
6/0 SIZE.		
CONSUL, 21 Jewels, 14K white, green or comb. solid gold case, luminous dial	51.75	90.00
CONSUL, 19 Jewels, 14K white, green or comb. solid gold case, luminous dial	43.00	75.00
Consul supplied with silver dial with 14K gold applied figures, extra	5.50	10.00
NEW YORKER, 21 Jewels, 14K white or natural gold filled plain or engraved case	40.50	75.00
NEW YORKER, 17 Jewels, 14K white or natural gold filled plain or engraved case	28.50	50.00
MARQUIS-STRAP, 19 J., 14K white or green, plain or eng. or comb. gold filled case	31.75	60.00
MARQUIS-STRAP, 17 J., 14K white or green, plain or eng. or comb. gold filled case	29.00	50.00
BEAU BRUMMELL, 19 J., 14K white or green, plain or eng. or nat. gold filled case	31.75	60.00
BEAU BRUMMELL, 17 J., 14K white or green, plain or eng. or nat. gold filled case	29.00	50.00
PICCADILLY, 17 Jewels, 14K white or green plain gold filled case	25.00	45.00
CHIEFTAIN, 15 Jewels, 14K white or natural gold filled case	21.60	40.00
ENSIGN, 15 Jewels, 14K white, green or natural gold filled, plain or engraved case	21.60	40.00
12/0 SIZE, 17 J., Rectangular Movement.		
MEDALIST, 14K white gold filled, plain case	33.50	60.00
FUTURA, 14K white or natural gold filled, plain case	33.50	60.00

Illinois Retail Price List, dated September 1, 1929 (inside surface). This card contains the only Illinois listing found thus far for the Consul wristwatch model in solid green gold.

The "Big Watch"

The Illinois Watch *Motor Barrel*

The "Big Watch" Is More Than a Display

Jewelers Everywhere Praise it as A Real Salesman for "ILLINOIS WATCHES"

EVERY day—throughout the country—the ILLINOIS "Big Watch" display is attracting thousands of prospective customers to jewelers' windows. Some stop and merely look on, but in many instances they stop and buy.

We receive a steady flow of letters of actual sales the "Big Watch" has made for the jeweler who has displayed it. Here are a few of the comments we receive: "The 'Big Watch' is doing its bit, we sold a strap watch *this morning*"—"an excellent sales promotion idea"—"*we have had many inquiries* for ILLINOIS Watches since the display was in our window"—"the 'Big Watch' increased our watch sales"—and other similar comments too numerous to print.

The "Big Watch" is an accurate timekeeper because of the Hamilton-Sangamo electric clock movement it contains. This adds to the value of the display, and jewelers tell us that many onlookers set their watches by it.

The display is loaned by the ILLINOIS Watch for a period of ten days to two weeks. There is no cost to the jeweler, and no obligation other than that of making the window an exclusive ILLINOIS watch display while the "Big Watch" is being shown. If you are interested in obtaining the Beau Brummel for your store, write to the Sales Promotion Department, ILLINOIS WATCH, Springfield, Ill., stating whether your current is alternating or direct. You will be listed for the display in the order your request is received.

"What a wrist watch!" says Irving Mitchell, actor, to Max Strasburg, Hollywood jeweler, as he compares the "Big Watch" with the ILLINOIS Beau Brummel he is wearing. This unusual idea proved valuable to Mr. Strasburg and received some excellent publicity in the Hollywood papers. This is an outstanding example of the possibilities connected with using the "Big Watch" display.

Upper left: Regner, jewelers of Kenosha, Wisconsin, used the Beau Brummel Display to advantage in their large, well arranged show window.

Upper right: LeRoy's, jewelers of Fairbury, Nebraska, displayed the "Big Watch" in a very attractive manner. They were very well satisfied with the publicity this display gained for them during its stay in their window.

Page EIGHT

Announcement of the availability of "The Big Watch," Illinois Watch *Motor Barrel*, Vol. 2, #8, December 1929. Unfortunately, this is the only issue of this publication that has been found.

[*Author's note*: Illinois apparently had dozens of the Beau Brummell clocks made to accommodate the many nationwide requests expected. I own one labeled No. 52, so there must have been at least that many. The labeling was done by means of a metal plate stamped with the numbering and affixed to the back of the clock. When Hamilton later converted the clocks for its own use, the numbered plates were removed.]

The "Big Watch" seems to have made its debut at the 4th Annual Jewelry and Allied Trade Show in Chicago, August 5–9, 1929 (see Chapter 4). Newspaper advertisements for jewelers who borrowed the display for their windows began appearing soon thereafter. (Perhaps Illinois let those who were interested sign up right there at the convention.)

The "Big Watch" proved to be a real winner for Illinois' Sales Promotion Department. Jewelers all over the United States took advantage of the company's offer to loan the display for their windows, as newspaper advertisements attest. Among the states we have found represented were Arkansas, California, Delaware, Florida, Illinois, Indiana, Iowa, Louisiana, Michigan, Mississippi, Missouri, Montana, Nevada, New Jersey, New York, Ohio, Pennsylvania, South Dakota, Texas, Virginia, Washington and Wisconsin.

The jewelers were apparently supplied with a stock advertisement which they could then personalize by adding the name of their firm and its address. Practically all of the participating jewelers seem to have done little more than that, as most of the advertisements we have located are virtually identical. A few showed some creativity in adapting the material they had been given.

The World's Largest Strap Watch

now on display at

GOULDING'S

THE GIFT STORE—111 WEST THIRD ST.

A greatly enlarged replica of this fine Illinois strap watch, the Beau Brummell model, is now on display at our store. It keeps accurate time—just as all ILLINOIS WATCHES have done for sixty years. Stop and see it.

Get correct time from the world's largest strap watch

This is the earliest example of the stock advertisement for the "Big Watch" that we have found. It appeared a mere three weeks after the trade show at which Illinois apparently introduced the display. *Alton Evening Telegraph* (Alton, IL), August 28, 1929; image from *newspapers.com*

The World's Largest Strap Watch

now on display at

South Dakota's Most Beautiful Jewelry Store

***Ben's** of course*

The Home of American Watches

A greatly enlarged replica of this fine Illinois strap watch, the Beau Brummell model, is now on display at our store. It keeps accurate time—just as all ILLINOIS WATCHES have done for sixty years. Stop and see it.

Get correct time from the world's largest strap watch

FREE All Makes of WATCH CRYSTALS

Regardless whether watch purchased here or not.

Phone 4069 ~ ~ ~ 120 S. Phillips Ave.

The jeweler's normal advertising slogans and graphics are in play here to customize the stock advertisement. *Argus-Leader* (Sioux Falls, SD), November 10, 1929; image from *newspapers.com*

No image of the "Big Watch" appears here, but the ornate picture-frame border for the text is a nice touch, and the Hamilton-Sangamo clock movement gets a little publicity. *Evening News* (Wilkes-Barre, PA), November 12, 1929; image from *newspapers.com*

This firm graced their advertisement with appropriate touches for something named Beau Brummell: a little graphic of top hat, cane, and gloves, and also some fancy script. Illinois usually used the spelling of the last name shown there, correct for the English dandy George Bryan ("Beau") Brummell. But sometimes the spelling "Brummel" slips in (as can be seen in the Illinois Watch *Motor Barrel* article included earlier). *Orlando Evening Star* (Orlando, FL), January 19, 1930; image from *newspapers.com*

* * *

World's Largest Wrist Watch Attracts Crowd

WICHITA, KAN.—The world's largest wrist watch on display in the window of the Southwestern Jewelry Co., attracted many people to the window of the company to witness this marvel of wrist timepieces. The watch is more than a foot across the face and keeps time accurately by means of an electrical movement. Around the watch were grouped watches offered during a special sale conducted by the company.

* * *

The large Illinois display clock, released in 1929, got an enthusiastic response in Wichita, Kansas, as was reported in the *Jewelers' Circular* in January 1930.

Holding the giant Beau Brummell clock is Dorothy Standley, showing the comparative size of her own watch on her wrist. This glossy print is dated January 23, 1930, but the exact date of the original photo is unknown, as is the identity of the jewelry store where it was made. (We have found nothing to identify exactly who Ms. Standley was.)

By 1934, Hamilton had appropriated the Illinois "Big Watch" for its own use. (See Chapter 1.) The engraved bezel was filled in, making it plain, and the dial was changed to read "Hamilton". The Hamilton clock-watch then appeared at trade shows all over the country.

Hollywood celebrity Mel Blanc, known as "The Man of a Thousand Voices," once owned one of the Hamilton-converted Beau Brummell clocks.

Illinois Watch Promotion by Plane

A photograph of a biplane with "Illinois Watch" painted on the fuselage has been discovered, and the pilot pictured with the plane is no less than Lee Gehlbach, a celebrated ace of the early 1930s. Born in 1902, near Lincoln, Illinois, he graduated from the University of Illinois in 1924. After serving in the U.S. Army, he became a test pilot with various companies. In air races of the period, Gehlbach was famous for winning the 1930 All-American Air Derby.

Unfortunately, there is nothing on the back of the photograph to indicate the location, the date or the context. However, we think it is likely that the picture was taken sometime around 1930 or 1931. The lettering on the plane suggests that the Illinois Watch Company may have sponsored Gehlbach during one of the air races or perhaps engaged him for some special event.

GEHLBACH WINS AIR DERBY

Lee Gehlbach of Detroit Friday won the $15,000 first prize offered in the all-American air derby of 5,500 miles when he landed in Detroit approximately four hours ahead of his nearest rival. His average speed was 127.1 miles an hour for the entire distance.

Detroit Aviator Wins $15,000 All-American Derby Prize; His Plane Makes 127 Miles an Hour

Roars Across Finish Line Far in Advance of Competitors After 5,500-Mile Jaunt; Springfield, Mass., Man Second

Gehlbach as winner of 1930 All-American Air Derby. *Great Falls Tribune* (Great Falls, MT), August 2, 1930; image from *newspapers.com*

LEE GEHLBACH

Pilot Lee Gehlbach signed the Davis-Monthan Register on August 24, 1931. He was solo flying Waco INF NC11452 (S/N 3450 manufactured in 1930). Based in Detroit, MI, he did not indicate his itinerary. His airplane was registered to the Michigan Aeronautical Corp., Ypsilanti, MI, so he may have been on company business.

Gehlbach was born October 6, 1902 near Lincoln, IL. He graduated as an engineer (aeronautical) from the University of Illinois (Go Illini!) in 1924. He enlisted as a flying cadet in the U.S. Army on September 14, 1924 and graduated from the primary flying and advanced pursuit schools. He was commissioned September 8, 1926 and spent three years with the First Pursuit Group, Selfridge Field until September 30, 1929.

He left the Army and entered test work, including engineering, with various companies (Michigan Aeronautical among them). From 1933-35 he was chief test pilot for Great Lakes Aircraft Corp. His racing experience included the All American Air Derby of 1930 (winner, see left sidebar), the 1931 National Air Tour, the Wedell-Williams Team, 1933 (several 1st, 2nd and 3rd places flying the W-W racer NR536V), and Granville Team during the National Air Races (NAR), 1934.

Below, a signed U.S. postal cachet from July 4,1933 that commemorates the NAR that year. This cachet comes to us courtesy of site visitor Joe Kranz. Mr. Kranz has shared numerous cachets with us that are distributed across the site. See, for example, Ruth Nichols, Eddie Bellande and Amelia Earhart.

Lt. Lee Gehlbach (Source: NASM)

U.S. Postal Cachet, July 4, 1933 (Source: Kranz)

Below, shared with us by site visitor Jeff Staines, is a U.S. postal cachet commemorating the 1934 NAR. It was signed by Gehlbach on the first day of the NAR. Mr. Staines says about his cachet, "This cover is signed by Lee Gehlbach when he was flying at the 1934 National Air Race.... Lee Gehlbach (# 77) finished third place in the Bendix Trophy Race after experiencing engine cowl trouble flying the Granville Brother's R6H Q.E.D."

U.S. Postal Cachet, August 31, 1934 (Source: Staines)

Lee Gehlbach's GeeBee #77, "Q.E.D." (Source: Staines)

Page with Gehlbach memorabilia, c. 1930s. *Source:* National Air and Space Museum, Washington, DC

Gehlbach also appeared in a Camel cigarettes advertisement in November 1936 indicating that "Smoking Camels helps to keep my digestion tuned up and running smooth."

November, 1936 129

LEE GEHLBACH

America's No. 1 Test Pilot

stands terrific strain in his meteoric power-dives and blinding pull-outs, as planes disintegrate in mid-sky!

STRAIGHT DOWN from 4 miles up—Gehlbach tears earthward at 400 to 600 m.p.h. At the bottom of the dive—a sharp pull-out wrenches plane and pilot to the limit. Such tests make planes safer. Just a tiny flaw—and the plane can fly to pieces. But Gehlbach eats heartily and *enjoys* his food. Note the Camel in his hand—one of many Camels Lee enjoys at meals.

"SMOKING CAMELS HELPS TO KEEP MY DIGESTION TUNED UP AND RUNNING SMOOTH"——SAYS LEE

"CAMELS set me right!" Gehlbach says. "You know, chance is only 10% of my business. Keeping alert and in the finest possible condition is the other 90%. I smoke Camels with my meals and afterward—for digestion's sake. And when I say Camels don't get on my nerves, it means a lot."

Good digestion and healthy nerves are important assets for every man and woman in this wide-awake, swift, and busy era. So make Camel *your* cigarette. Enjoying Camels at mealtime and after speeds up the flow of digestive fluids—increases alkalinity—helps bring a sense of ease and digestive well-being. Smoke Camels—for digestion's sake—for their pleasing, invigorating "lift"—and for their matchless mildness and fine taste. Camels set you right!

Costlier Tobaccos

Camels are made from finer, MORE EXPENSIVE TOBACCOS ...Turkish and Domestic... than any other popular brand.

For Digestion's Sake... Smoke Camels

Life, November 1930

Illinois billfolds in red leather. Most were in black.

A special jewelry store advertising sign most likely to promote the Illinois Skyway wristwatch, which was released in 1930. The sign was manufactured by the Meyercord Co., which also made the decal shown on page 1420. Only three of these signs are known to exist.

A small Illinois Watch advertising penknife, closed

Small knife, open

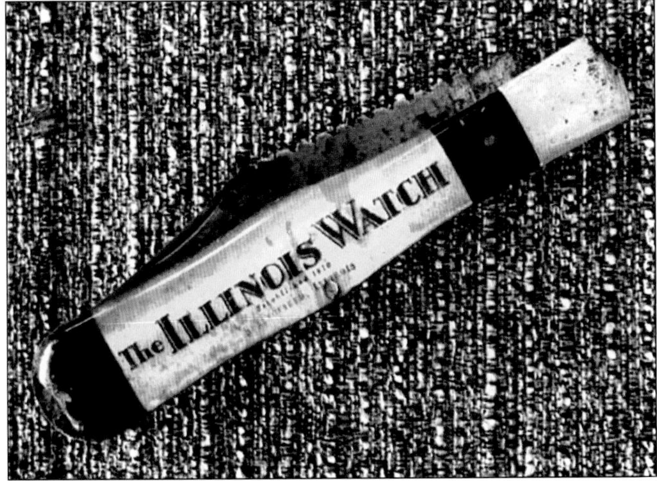

Large Illinois Watch promotional knife

EXPORT

February 19, 1930.

Mr. Byron Beans,
280-382 George St. So.,
Sydney, Australia.

Dear Mr. Beans:

Supplementing Illinois Watch Company's letter of January 28th, with reference to your handling the representation of Illinois watches, in addition to the Hamilton line, we are very glad indeed to advise you that we will give you the Illinois line on exactly the same basis as the Hamilton line, as outlined in our letter of December 19th.

We will furnish you with samples on a consignment basis. The first lot of samples which we will send you will consist of three or four solid yellow gold strap models, which will be shipped to you within a short time.

Orders you send in to us are to be shipped direct to the dealer in Australia, accompanied by sight draft through whatever bank may be selected, which information will be specified on your order.

The Illinois line is to be sold by you at wholesale list prices, which appear on the price list submitted to you by Mr. Port in his letter of January 28th. These Illinois prices are F.O.B. Lancaster, Penna, and postage and insurance charges extra.

Your remuneration for selling Illinois watches is to be at the same rate as for Hamilton; that is, 10% of the wholesaler's list prices - this commission to be payable twice a year, the first of July and the first of January respectively.

Illinois material will be furnished at the same discount of 40% and the suggestions as contained in our letter of December 19th, regarding Hamilton material are also made in connection with Illinois material.

In connection with the Illinois line, there is possibly a little more latitude with which you can work. For example, the Illinois 6/0 size, 15 and 17 jewel movementx are of the same size as the Elgin 6/0 size, and the movements may be fitted in cases that are made up for Elgin. I believe the Keystone has a number of models which could possibly be used. The Illinois also has 12 and 16 size standard movements in 17, 19 and 21 jewel, and it is very possible that there may be an opportunity to do some business along these lines. They also have a 3/0 size

EXPORT

Mr. Byron Beans - #2.

movement, which the writer knows is a very popular size in Australia, and by using English made cases, there might be a combination worked up which would prove of interest to the Australian trade.

The samples mentioned in the first part of this letter will be prepared and shipped to you just as promptly as possible.

We wish to call your attention to the fact that all export business of both Illinois and Hamilton is handled from this office, and that all orders and correspondence in connection with both Illinois and Hamilton should be addressed to the Export Department, Hamilton Watch Company, Lancaster, Pa.

I sincerely trust that your return voyage to Australia was a very pleasant one, and that you are enjoying the very best of health.

Looking forward to hearing from you at an early date, and with best wishes, we are

Very truly yours,

THE HAMILTON WATCH CO.

Export Manager.

F.J.Boulton.

A Hamilton February 19, 1930 letter to an Australian jobber, explaining the export guidelines and the added latitude that the Illinois line provides to this Hamilton distributor

Combined Research Departments

NOTICE

To All Foremen

Under date of June 3rd, 1930 the Hamilton Division at Lancaster announced the establishment of a Research Department.

The Hamilton Company long ago adopted the policy of building the utmost obtainable accuracy in timekeeping into the watches it produced and because it felt that its responsibility has continued even after the watch has been sold, has built up a reputation which is second to none in the American watchmaking industry. To continue to hold this position of high esteem in the future, it is necessary to continuously improve the accuracy, durability, reliability and appearance of their product.

There used to be a time when research work could be done in different departments of the factory, but it seemed far more economical to work out all of the problems that come up in the development and production of the product in one department and that department is now called the Research Department.

The Research Department will be responsible for the study of the fundamental problems in connection with timekeeping, and will also study means of obtaining economic solutions of those problems arising in connection with watch production, which cannot be readily solved by other departments without interfering with production. The Research Department will eventually be able to relieve production departments of the necessity of interrupting production schedules to do development work and will aid them to the best of its facilities in their efforts to construct a better watch at less cost.

The Research Department will welcome suggestions for the improvement of the product. Such suggestions should be coordinated with the Mechanical and the Technical Superintendents to avoid any duplication of work, and the sending in of such suggestions should come to the Superintendent's Office.

This Department established at Lancaster is established for the benefit of both Divisions of the Company. In fact for all three Divisions of the Company, that is, Hamilton Watch, Illinois Watch and Hamilton-Sangamo Corporation, and it is done with the idea of guaranteeing the perpetuity of the present success of the Company and lifting it to an even higher position than it holds at present in the timekeeping field of America.

Robert E. Miller's memorandum dated June 3, 1930, announcing the formation of one centralized Research Department for Hamilton, Illinois and Hamilton-Sangamo. This memorandum merely mirrored the one his father had issued at Hamilton at that time.

-2-

As Mr. Charles F. Miller, President, said in his announcement, it is his feeling that the evolution of the world will not end with the manufacture of the best watches made in America, but that other things will come, and may come before long, that will make it necessary to completely change our present plans. There is nothing surer in this world than changes. They have been coming and will come, and in order that we may be prepared from now on for anything that might come, and at the same time develop anything that might seem wise for us to take up, the Research Department has been established, and we hope to obtain from it over a period of years a very definitely helpful result.

The Research Department is under the charge of Mr. George P. Luckey, who before joining the Hamilton organization had many years of experience in commercial research development and has held important positions in that field.

We are bringing this all to your attention in the Illinois Division because we believe you are interested in what has been done, in what is being done and because we believe, as we have often said, that the combined thought of all of us on the many problems with which we are faced in industry today will best bring about the solution of our problem - the building of a stronger, better business.

General Manager

6-17-30

Hoover Will Be Given Watch Made In City

When President Hoover goes fishing again he will carry with him a souvenir of his visit to Springfield.

Through a special committee of the Chamber of Commerce the citizens of Springfield will today present the president with a fisherman's special watch, a Springfield product, made by the Illinois Watch company.

The presentation will be made at the governor's mansion just before lunch is served to the presidential party. The committee will present the watch to Governor Emmerson, who will in turn make the gift speech to President Hoover. In the committee will be Donald S. Funk, president of the Springfield Chamber of Commerce; A. W. Hillier, former president of the Chamber of Commerce; A. D. Mackie, general manager of the Illinois Power company; W. C. Hurst, senior vice president of the Chicago & Illinois Midland railway; Robert E Miller, general manager of the Illinois Watch company and H. L. Williamson, chairman of the publicity committee of the Illinois Chamber of Commerce.

Inside the white gold, waterproof case, designed to be carried in the trousers pocket of the fisherman are engraved these words: "President of the United States, Herbert Hoover from the citizens of Springfield, June 17, 1931.

Report of an Illinois pocket watch given to President Hoover during his visit to Springfield, *Illinois State Journal*, June 17, 1931

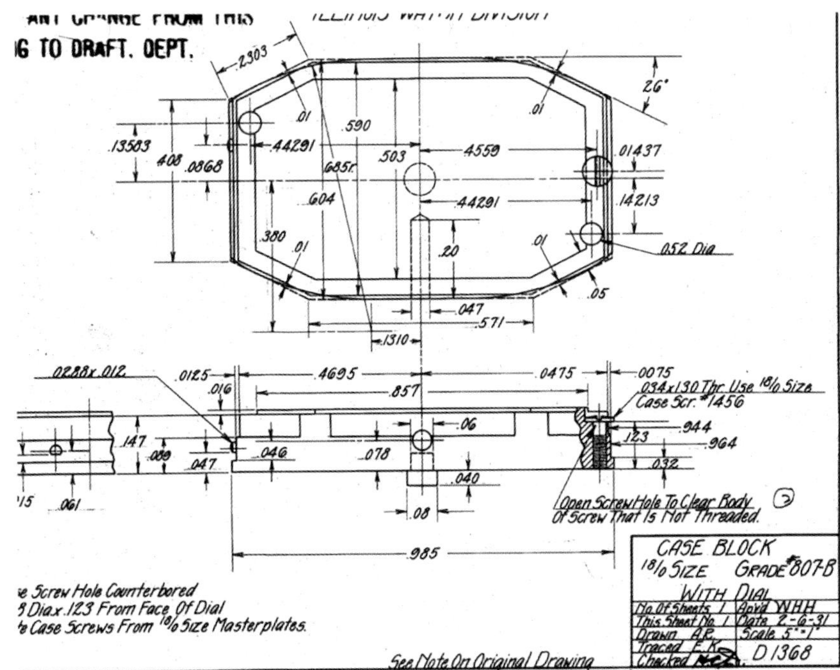

Illinois case block drawing with dial for an 18/0 size, grade 807B Illinois movement, dated February 6, 1931

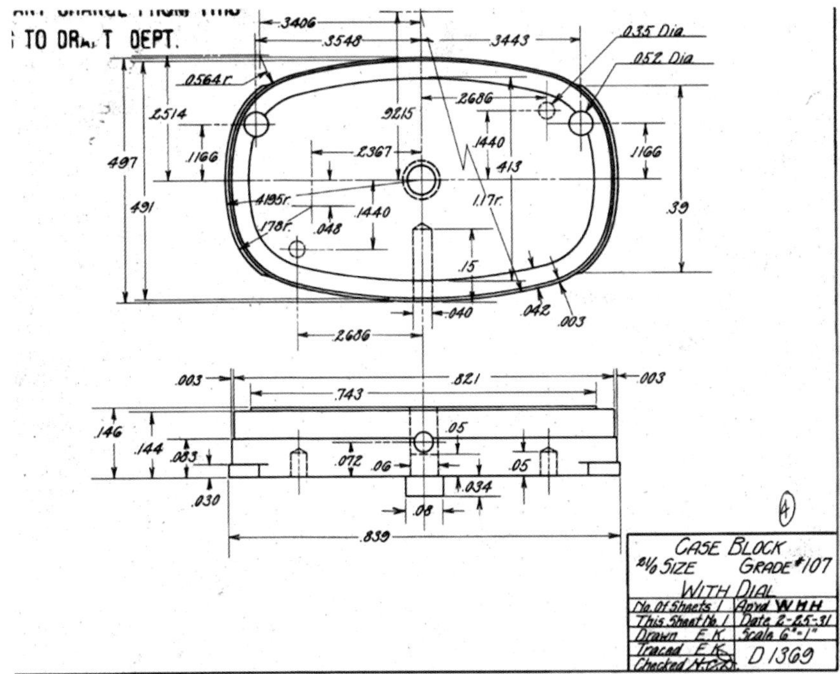

Illinois case block drawing with dial for a 21/0 size, grade 107 Illinois movement, dated February 25, 1931

ILLINOIS WATCH ORDER

Send to

I. Ollendorff Co., Inc., 20 W. 47th, New York—717 Liberty Ave., Pittsburgh, Pa.

Gentlemen:

Enter our order for the following ILLINOIS watches for shipment ____________

Quantity		Quantity	
____	**Finalist**	____	**Skyway**
____	**Futura**		
____	**Chieftain**		
____	**Jolly Roger**		

Your Name ____________

Address ____________

The » »
Dark Horse
Of 1930

Helps You
To Greater
« « Profits

A two-page 1930 Illinois sales flyer *(outside)*

FULL RECTANGULAR ILLINOIS WATCHES

You cannot afford to pass up the opportunity to merchandise Illinois watches. They are smart—chic, if you please—and dependable. Characteristic excellent Illinois workmanship has so constructed this watch to permit a larger barrel, resulting in longer run. The even rate, freedom of performance, and more compact casing, give this watch its popularity.

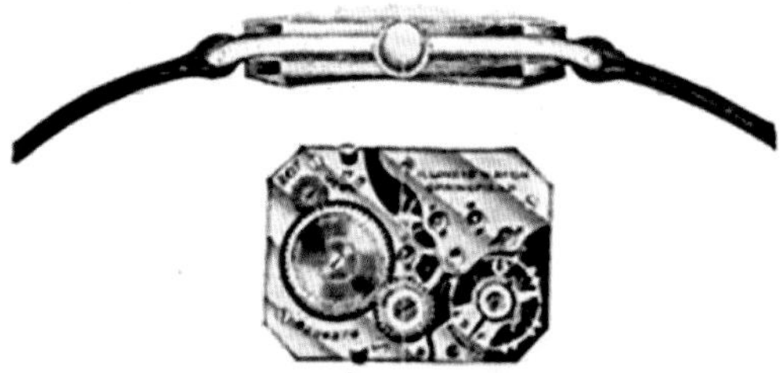

The Finalist. Supplied in 14 karat natural and white gold filled — plain or engraved — 17 jewels—luminous dial. Retailer price, $31.00. Consumer price, $55.00.

The Futura. 17 jeweled 12/0 size Illinois with case of 14 karat natural and white gold filled. Retailer price, $31.00 Consumer price, $55.00.

REAL VALUE IN STRAP MODELS

The Chieftain. 15 jewels, 6/0 size — natural or white gold filled. Retailer price. $21.60. Consumer price. $40.00.

The Skyway. America is rapidly becoming airminded and here is the watch that is in keeping with this progress. 17 jewels. 3/0 size Illinois. Designed to meet government aeronautical standards. The case is absolutely dust-proof—screw back and bezel — extra heavy crystal — 14 karat white gold filled case. Policemen, firemen, and traction company employees are also good prospects for this particular model. Retailer price, $23.00. Consumer price, $45.00.

The Jolly Roger. 17 jewels, 3/0 size Illinois in 14 karat filled white or green gold. Retailer price, $21.75. Consumer, $42.50.

A two-page 1930 Illinois sales flyer *(inside)*

Saturday Evening Post, c. October 1930

Replacement Parts

SPRINGFIELD, ILLINOIS, U.S.A.

December 16, 1931

TO OUR MATERIAL DISTRIBUTORS:

We are enclosing two condensed Retail Price Lists covering the Refill Material and Mainsprings for the $25.00 and $50.00 Material Cabinets. These prices are in accordance with the new Retail Material Price List of October 26, 1931, but we believe you will find this list more convenient when billing Refill or Compartment numbers.

A similar list is being sent to all the jewelers of whom we have a record as owners of $25.00 Material Cabinets. The letter, accompanying the list, advised them to mark all prices on the charts received with these cabinets - "Void." This was done in order to prevent any confusion.

As there are approximately 1,000 Material Cabinets on the market at the present time, we suggest that you carefully check over your stock of Refill and Compartment Material, and place a stock order so as to be in a position to promptly fill all orders for this material.

Very truly yours,

THE ILLINOIS WATCH

RFF:EGP
Encls.

R. F. Fulkerson
Material Sales Department

December 16, 1931 letter to Illinois material distributors concerning the price lists for replacement parts for the approximately 1,000 Illinois Material Cabinets then in use throughout the United States

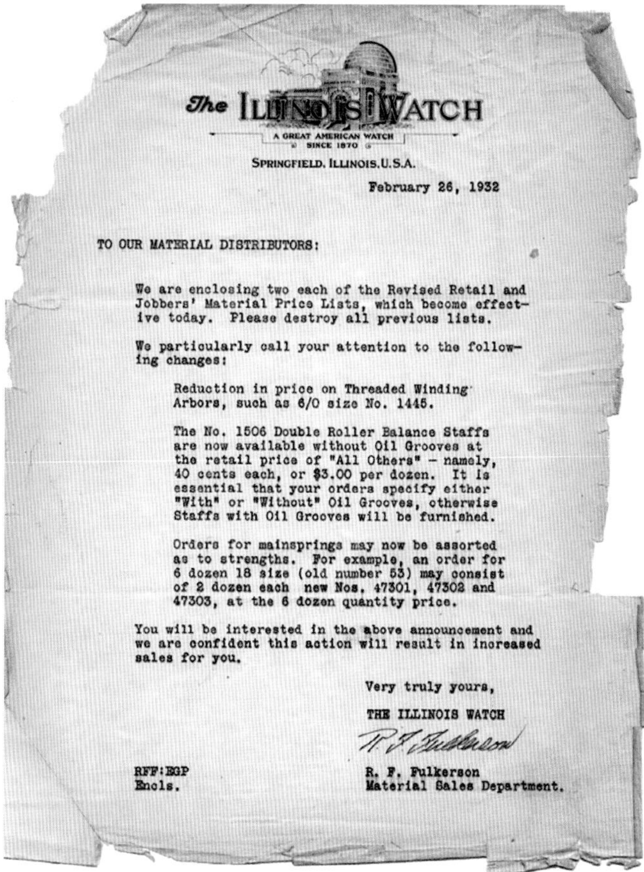

The ILLINOIS WATCH
A GREAT AMERICAN WATCH
SINCE 1870
SPRINGFIELD, ILLINOIS, U.S.A.

February 26, 1932

TO OUR MATERIAL DISTRIBUTORS:

We are enclosing two each of the Revised Retail and Jobbers' Material Price Lists, which become effective today. Please destroy all previous lists.

We particularly call your attention to the following changes:

Reduction in price on Threaded Winding Arbors, such as 6/0 size No. 1445.

The No. 1506 Double Roller Balance Staffs are now available without Oil Grooves at the retail price of "All Others" - namely, 40 cents each, or $3.00 per dozen. It is essential that your orders specify either "With" or "Without" Oil Grooves, otherwise Staffs with Oil Grooves will be furnished.

Orders for mainsprings may now be assorted as to strengths. For example, an order for 6 dozen 18 size (old number 53) may consist of 2 dozen each new Nos. 47301, 47302 and 47303, at the 6 dozen quantity price.

You will be interested in the above announcement and we are confident this action will result in increased sales for you.

Very truly yours,

THE ILLINOIS WATCH

R. F. Fulkerson

RFF:EGP
Encls.

R. F. Fulkerson
Material Sales Department.

February 26, 1932 letter to Illinois Material Distributors, enclosing Revised Retail and Jobbers' Material Price Lists

Robert E. Miller's April 1, 1932 Memorandum

April 1, 1932

To: Progressive Retail Jewelers

Subject: Illinois Watch Program for 1932

Gentlemen:

We believe you are interested in knowing our program for the remainder of 1932, as it affects your line of Illinois Watches, their style, price range and the marketability of that line. In other words, we are endeavoring to give you the answer to the possible question in your mind "How can I make my Illinois Watch franchise more profit producing in 1932?"

Four years ago, in January 1928, we adopted certain clearly definded policies and plans for this business.

1. To improve the quality of Illinois Watches wherever possible.

2. To bring Illinois Watches into what we have termed "the middle price range to the consumer."

3. To afford a variety of size and style appeal in Illinois Watches, for men and women, in sprit with the modern tempo.

4. To limit the franchise for Illinois Watches to those wholesalers whose volume warranted a wholesale franchise; and who sell to and merchandise their lines with the better class of retail jewelers.

5. To support the sale of Illinois Watches with a vigorous and well sustained National advertising program, thereby building consumer acceptance and affording greater sales turnover on the line for you.

6. To plan the line with a three years' "look-ahead", and recognizing the desirability of the smallest line, consistent with maximum variety demand, as a means of keeping your inventories to a minimum. Recognizing a definite downward trend in commodity prices for the consumer.

7. And last, but not least, a well sustained and constantly expanding program of dealer education on the line through our own sales force, realizing that the strength and permanence of any producer must be measured in terms of the strength of his retailing organization.

-2-

As we look back over the past four years, and view our condition today, we feel we have achieved the purposes outlined.

This is the period of the bicentennial of Washington's birth, and valuable lessons have been drawn by orators and editors from Washington's experience. We think of Washington and his comrades in arms at Valley Forge, holding fast to their faith that the dark clouds would break and that their particular perplexities would vanish eventually. With far less to suffer from, we of the present day are much given to doubt and to bearish imaginings. Prosperous eras have made us weak and our sense of perspective is lost when the prosperity prop is taken away. But I believe we have learned a lot in this period of adversity and that we are gaining strength constantly. Let us emulate the sprit which Washington and his men showed during that bleak Winter at Valley Forge.

During 1931 we had a program of liquidating certain small groups of merchandise, representing items to be taken out of our line, the manufacture of which was completed in the previous year. We pursued the same plan during January and February of this year in the same orderly manner, and without any unpleasant reaction to our current program of regular line sales.

By reducing the number of grades of watches and styles of cases, we have eliminated those numbers which were slow movers, and by doing this have made our line extremely compact and more entirely attractive and popular.

That brings us to the announcement of the balanced Illinois Watch line. The enclosed illustrated catalogue and price list are for your convenience. An examination of these enclosures will indicate the splendid range of prices and show very clearly the wonderful values offered in the current and continuing line of Illinois Watches.

We know we can count on your wholehearted cooperation in making this plan effective, and thereby insuring a stabilization within the industry and valorization for 1932 of your Illinois Watch franchise.

With all best wishes to this end,

Sincerely yours,

R E Miller

General Manager

REM:RH

"Illinois Watch Program for 1932" sent from Robert E. Miller directly to "progressive" retail jewelers. It contains at least some revisionist history, in my view (FJF).

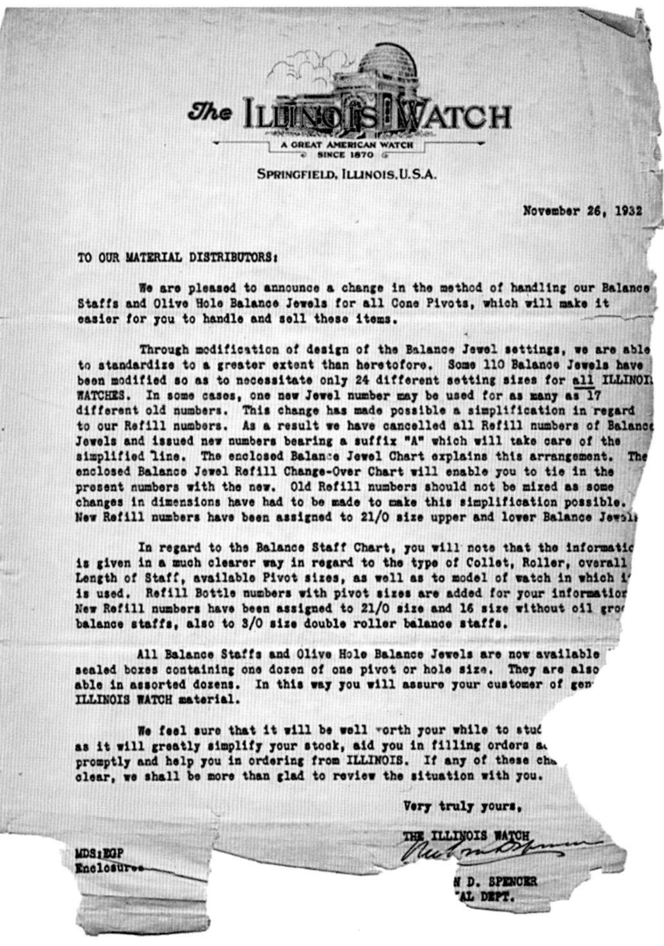

The ILLINOIS WATCH
A GREAT AMERICAN WATCH
SINCE 1870
SPRINGFIELD, ILLINOIS, U.S.A.

November 26, 1932

TO OUR MATERIAL DISTRIBUTORS:

We are pleased to announce a change in the method of handling our Balance Staffs and Olive Hole Balance Jewels for all Cone Pivots, which will make it easier for you to handle and sell these items.

Through modification of design of the Balance Jewel settings, we are able to standardize to a greater extent than heretofore. Some 110 Balance Jewels have been modified so as to necessitate only 24 different setting sizes for all ILLINOI WATCHES. In some cases, one new Jewel number may be used for as many as 17 different old numbers. This change has made possible a simplification in regard to our Refill numbers. As a result we have cancelled all Refill numbers of Balance Jewels and issued new numbers bearing a suffix "A" which will take care of the simplified line. The enclosed Balance Jewel Chart explains this arrangement. The enclosed Balance Jewel Refill Change-Over Chart will enable you to tie in the present numbers with the new. Old Refill numbers should not be mixed as some changes in dimensions have had to be made to make this simplification possible. New Refill numbers have been assigned to 21/0 size upper and lower Balance Jewel

In regard to the Balance Staff Chart, you will note that the informatic is given in a much clearer way in regard to the type of Collet, Roller, overall Length of Staff, available Pivot sizes, as well as to model of watch in which i is used. Refill Bottle numbers with pivot sizes are added for your informatior New Refill numbers have been assigned to 21/0 size and 16 size without oil gro balance staffs, also to 3/0 size double roller balance staffs.

All Balance Staffs and Olive Hole Balance Jewels are now available sealed boxes containing one dozen of one pivot or hole size. They are also able in assorted dozens. In this way you will assure your customer of gen ILLINOIS WATCH material.

We feel sure that it will be well worth your while to stu as it will greatly simplify your stock, aid you in filling orders a promptly and help you in ordering from ILLINOIS. If any of these ch clear, we shall be more than glad to review the situation with you.

Very truly yours,

THE ILLINOIS WATCH

N D. SPENCER
AL DEPT.

MDS:EGP
Enclosures

November 26, 1932 letter to Illinois Material Distributors, announcing a change in the method of handling Illinois Balance Staffs and Olive Hole Balance Jewels for all Cone Pivots

May 17, 1930 memorandum from Jack Keenan advising his sales team how to handle any questions that may arise from retailers concerning "desirable and required mark-up" on Illinois products.

" MARK-UP "

May 17th, '30.

From time to time you will find it necessary to discuss very thoroughly with your retail friends, the matter pertaining to desirable and required mark-up.

Mark-up is figured on the amount obtained between list price plus cash discount, and the consumer price. The percentage is the amount of profit divided by the net cost.

Merely as an opportunity for conversation, we would let you have some information that has come to our attention recently.

There is no subject as close to the heart of jewelry business man as that item covering profit, and it is interesting, - the different opinions that will develop in discussion of the matter.

One is that as a group, jewelers do not make as much of a success of their business as they should. Granting that this is true, there must be reasons why such a condition exists. The average jeweler, we do not believe, realizes the importance of his watch department, as compared to other departments in his store, such as silverware and diamonds, on which the turnover is considerably less than that on watches.

In the application of cost of operating, watches must bear an equal burden with other items instead of this expense being divided according to the space required.

Take silver for example - - the mark-up is small compared to watches, - - the turnover very considerably slower and the space required really tremendous, as compared with that for a watch department. On the other hand, the sale of watches, and especially, American watches - - make more real friends for the jeweler than does the sale of silverware. The sale of a good watch brings back many customers for the purchase of other merchandise, and most always provides the opportunity for additional business through returns for usual service.

When the retail jeweler recognizes the fact that good domestic watches are easier to service than foreign watches, that one and all, they are a far better made products, they will see that real money is to be made in the sale of American watches.

Another angle in connection with what has already been said is taken from the thought of a very excellently operated installment jewelry store. Only a broad consideration can be given to applying of mark-ups on the basis of cost of operating a store, because so much depends on proper management and the volume obtained.

- 2 -

The storekeeper without ability, who does only a small business with the expectation that it must pay a large and unreasonable mark-up, makes it difficult to consider fairly the merchant who is a good manager.

The buying public are continuously becoming more intelligent. Truthful advertising statements must be made. People formerly knew they were being charged for credit extension, but they now expect to be permitted to have credit at cash prices, and they cannot be fooled on values. It has been proven that the only way to operate a business successfully, is by being fair to yourself, as a merchant, and truly fair to your customers in the matter of proper mark-up. The installment business is no different than the cash business, aside from the cost of collections, and bookkeeping. It has advantages through the forcing of sales to obtain greater volume, by means of the operation of extension of credit. This is not quite as possible where an absolute full payment by cash is required.

The so called cash business also, has its problems of bookkeeping and collections, but only on small percentage of accounts.

All undue mark-ups are really detrimental to any retail business, whether cash or installment, and no business can survive where unreasonable profits are charged on staple merchandise. There are times when seasonable merchandise must carry the expense of being had at the time desired, but on staple merchandise reasonable mark-ups must be offered.

Yours very truly,

ILLINOIS WATCH

Sales Manager.

J. L. Keenan.

A Stock Control System

Slow-Moving Items Are Reduced 10% Every Six Months in This Store

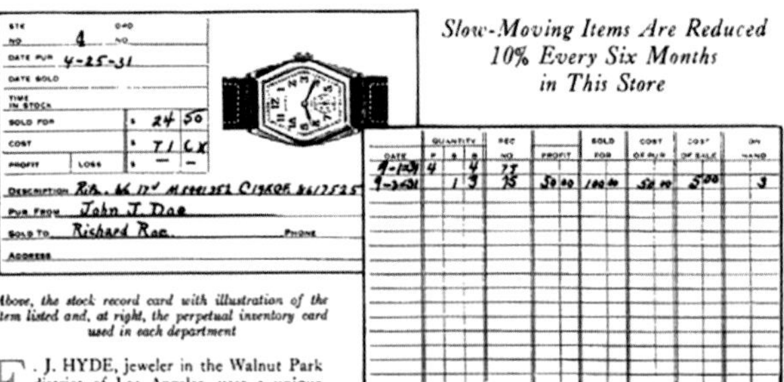

Above, the stock record card with illustration of the item listed and, at right, the perpetual inventory card used in each department

"When an article has been in stock six months," says Mr. Hyde, "it is time to do something about it." And here is what he does and how he does it, with a system that any jeweler can afford to adopt

F. J. HYDE, jeweler in the Walnut Park district of Los Angeles, uses a unique stock control system of his own devising. This enables him to tell at a glance what he has purchased, how long it has been in stock, how fast each item moves, and when the price should be reduced in order to move it quickly.

The system consists of a number of three by five filing cards in two drawers. One drawer contains cards for merchandise on hand, and the other for merchandise sold. There is a card for each item in stock, this containing a written description of the article, date of purchase, cost, selling price, from whom purchased and other similar information. This card also has a small picture of the article, cut from the manufacturer's catalog or advertising material, or a rough sketch if nothing better is available. Thus Mr. Hyde knows exactly how long an item has been in stock and he also has an accurate means of reference in case he is considering a reorder of the same merchandise.

When an item is sold, its card is removed from one drawer and the concluding information regarding profit or loss, time in stock, name of purchaser and so forth is filled in. These cards are then allowed to accumulate until the end of the week. Then Mr. Hyde runs through them and determines which items are moving fast enough to warrant stocking them again. Following this, the cards are filed in the second drawer, which is just like the first one except that it is a record of goods sold rather than stock on hand.

At the top of each card in the first drawer is placed a colored tab representing a date six months after the item was stocked. When a certain article has been in stock for six months, as shown by the colored tab on the card, it is automatically reduced 10% in price. If twelve months go by and the item is still unsold, the discount is raised to 20%, and so on, adding 10% for each six months the goods remain in stock.

"The longer an article remains in the store," says Mr. Hyde, "the harder it is to sell. Changing styles in jewelry make the public demand up-to-the-minute merchandise. I feel that sales demoralize a jewelry business and instead of holding them take this means of giving my customers the benefit of price reductions."

The reduction is not marked on the price ticket in figures. A little dot is merely placed beside the price for each six months period. In other words, one dot means a 10% reduction, and two dots mean 20% off the marked price. If a prospect questions the modernity of an item, Mr. Hyde has only to show him the card.

Since the store has a number of departments, the cards are grouped according to these various divisions. At the head of each classification is a yellow card bearing the perpetual inventory of that department. This card shows the number of items on hand, quantity purchased and when, number sold, cost of sales and other information of a similar nature. These inventory cards enable the jeweler to ascertain quickly which of his several departments are the most active.

The name of the person to whom an article is sold, especially in the case of watches, is recorded on the appropriate card, which in effect makes the stock record system a customers' file as well. In case the customer loses the watch, the store has all necessary information.

The outstanding feature of this system is the fact that it gives at all times, and with very little trouble, a full record of the items that sell readily and those that don't. It takes away the necessity for relying on memory as to the date a certain article was stocked, and substitutes for this a black and white record of the actual facts. By using the date on the cards, the manager or buyer is enabled to pick his merchandise with a clear understanding of what has sold well in the past and what has not. In this way, his buying is rendered more efficient and turnover is quickened.

THE KEYSTONE Page 21

A stock control system featured in the *Keystone* in 1931 interestingly pictures an Illinois Ritz model.

LETTER SENT TO ALL DISTRIBUTORS ON MARCH 22nd, 23rd and 24th.

Should send out in march and September each year to Keep our list of wholesalers Salesmen up-to-date.

Gentlemen:

From time to time we have various interesting points concerning Illinois watches as well as advertising copy which we would like to have the opportunity of placing at the disposal of your various representatives as an assistance to them in discussing our product more intelligently with their customers.

We realize that during the last few years there have been perhaps many changes made in the personnel of your sales organization much in the same manner that we have been obliged to restrict our activities in this department.

However, with the return of confidence of the American people and an increase in buying we expect as soon as conditions permit to expand our selling force and other businesses, including our distributors, will no doubt do likewise.

In preparation for the return to normal we shall appreciate your sending us a list of the traveling salesmen whom you employ at present as well as those individuals closely connected with sales at your office, together with their home addresses. It has been some time since this information with which you have provided us has been revised and it is badly out of date.

We shall be very glad to have this list at your convenience, and it would also be very helpful if you could let us know the name and addresses of any new salesmen as they are employed.

Thanking you, and with best wishes

Very truly yours,

THE ILLINOIS WATCH

AGS:D By -

A letter that was to be sent to Illinois jobbers twice a year to keep the Illinois Sales Department list of jobbers' salesmen current.

Various Keenan Memoranda

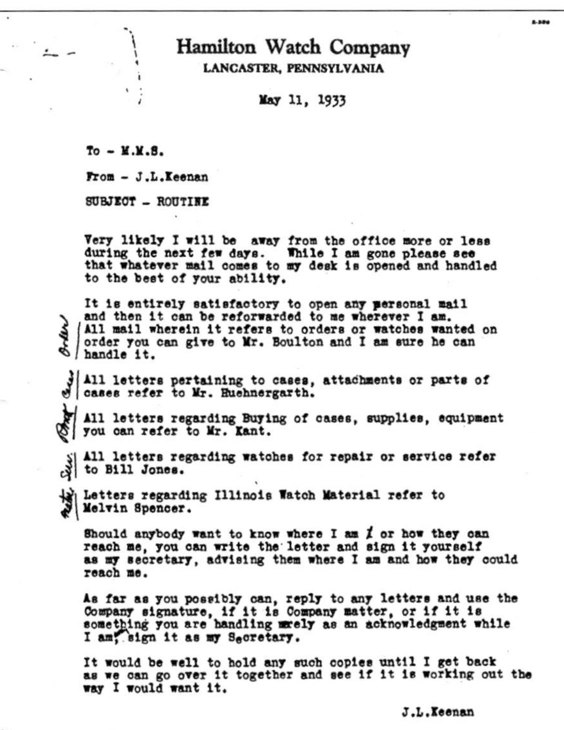

Hamilton Watch Company
LANCASTER, PENNSYLVANIA

May 11, 1933

To - M.M.S.

From - J.L.Keenan

SUBJECT - ROUTINE

Very likely I will be away from the office more or less during the next few days. While I am gone please see that whatever mail comes to my desk is opened and handled to the best of your ability.

It is entirely satisfactory to open any personal mail and then it can be reforwarded to me wherever I am. All mail wherein it refers to orders or watches wanted on order you can give to Mr. Boulton and I am sure he can handle it.

All letters pertaining to cases, attachments or parts of cases refer to Mr. Huehnergarth.

All letters regarding Buying of cases, supplies, equipment you can refer to Mr. Kant.

All letters regarding watches for repair or service refer to Bill Jones.

Letters regarding Illinois Watch Material refer to Melvin Spencer.

Should anybody want to know where I am or how they can reach me, you can write the letter and sign it yourself as my secretary, advising them where I am and how they could reach me.

As far as you possibly can, reply to any letters and use the Company signature, if it is Company matter, or if it is something you are handling merely as an acknowledgment while I am, sign it as my Secretary.

It would be well to hold any such copies until I get back as we can go over it together and see if it is working out the way I would want it.

J.L.Keenan

A memorandum dated May 11, 1933, from Jack Keenan, advising Hamilton administrative personnel how to direct matters while is he out of the office. MMS was Miss M. Sabinash, an Administrative Assistant to Keenan.

April 30, 1934

Memorandum to - Mr. C. S. Reese
Copies to Mr. W. R. Atkinson
Mr. F. J. Boulton
Miss M. Sabinash

From - J. L. Keenan

Illinois Information

As practically all of the equipment in J.L.K.'s office will be sent to Chicago for use out there, I have asked Miss Sabinash to maintain here the large book covering breakdown of retail sales on Illinois, such as she has been doing, which means possibly several hours work each month when the Statistical Department make up their report.

Also, there is a book which I term the Illinois Production Records and she maintains in that the file copies of weekly and monthly reports.

In addition to that, there are ten or a dozen old record books covering the Illinois transactions from 1930 on.

The idea of this memorandum is that possibly in connection with the stenographers' office, a table can be set aside to be known as 'Illinois Record Table' and on it Miss Sabinash could be detailed to take care of the record books, such as I mentioned above, or any similar reports, such as Illinois Watch Daily Sales Reports thru the year 1934.

From time to time J.L.K. of course, will be in Lancaster and would possibly use that table on his visits covering any Illinois detail matters.

Miss Sabinash understands most of the replies to general Illinois inquiry letters and, of course, all sales matters that come up are and have been very well handled by Mr. Boulton.

Whenever any definite thing comes up that cannot be readily handled, of course, it can be referred to J.L.K. who can from his experience, without doubt, give the assistance needed.

J.L.K. will have, in Chicago, the general file that he has maintained on Illinois history and things of that charact

#2-

and with the establishment of an Illinois table, and the files kept upon it, I am quite sure that there would be a good clearan providing, of course, Miss Sabinash were permitted to have some time each day or during the month to keep the matter up-to-date.

J.L. KEENAN

Memorandum dated April 30, 1934, from Jack Keenan, describing how office operations for Illinois are to be managed once he relocated to Chicago.

Illinois Chronometer

An Illinois Chronometer supposedly made for the United States Merchant Marine, one of a very few known to exist. Ten or fewer of these were rumored to have been made by the Illinois Watch Company. These were to be used on merchant ships. The movement is signed “Hardey Fritz, Oil City, PA”, probably a jeweler. The movement dates to c. 1900.

Save the Tower Story

An article by Chris Dettro in the July 11, 2012 issue of the Springfield *State Journal-Register* delineated a potential threat to the last surviving part of the Illinois Watch Factory complex, the clock tower and part of the 1918 administration building built in front of the original building. Consolidation and rerouting of railroad rights of way through the city would send tracks through the space occupied by the Illinois Environmental Protection Agency, whose buildings surround not only the Illinois clock tower but also the last remaining part of the Sangamo Electric facility.

A *Record of Decision* on the project shows a preference for the route through the former factory site, but funding has not been obtained, and no work appears imminent. The maps in the *Record of Decision* show the proposed right of way well clear of both the remaining Illinois and Sangamo buildings but passing directly through part of the main Illinois EPA building.

As this book goes to press, the status of the project would appear to be in limbo. However, who knows what the future may hold?

The most relevant part of Dettro's article follows:

Local preservationists are keeping an eye on the possible effects of Springfield rail consolidation on a surviving monument to the city's industrial history. The 10th Street rail plan would cause the removal of several properties, including the clock tower erected by the Illinois Watch Co. in 1918 at 11th Street and North Grand Avenue.

Illinois Department of Transportation is recommending that passenger and freight rail traffic through Springfield be rerouted along the 10th Street corridor, a move that under the current, preliminary plan would result in almost 150 properties being acquired to connect new 10th Street tracks to the existing Union Pacific rail alignment.

One of those properties is the 14-acre, four-square-block Illinois Environmental Protection Agency offices at 11th Street and North Grand Avenue. And on that property is the clock tower erected by the Illinois Watch Co. in 1918.

"It is the most visible symbol of a 63-year history of watch-making here that made the company nationally prominent and internationally recognized," said Jerry Jacobson, spokesman for Save Old Springfield, a local preservation group.

The Illinois Department of Transportation endorsed the $315 million rail-consolidation project in a draft environmental impact statement posted last month on the city of Springfield website.

However, it appears from the overhead map accompanying the draft that the clock tower and some other buildings would be spared if there are no changes to the current plan, which has a long way to go before final approval.

IDOT spokesman Josh Kauffman called the draft "very preliminary and subject to change."

"It's very early in the process," he said.

A series of public outreach meetings will be scheduled and comments accepted before a final draft is approved.

"We're just beginning to become aware of the situation," Jacobson said, adding there currently is no organized effort to help ensure the clock tower is preserved.

"Hopefully, there will be," he said.

Steve Myers, who is on the board of Downtown Springfield Inc. and a member of the Springfield Historic Sites Commission, said the tower's age and role in Springfield history make it worth saving.

"I'm sure it would be brought up before the commission to look at it," he said.

"There are positives and negatives to any plan," Myers said. He cited the removal of the divided Ninth Street underpass just north of Converse Avenue as a positive.

"There will be ample opportunities to bring up important things," he said. "These are 150-year decisions. That's the impact of what's going to go on here."

Sangamo Electric Company

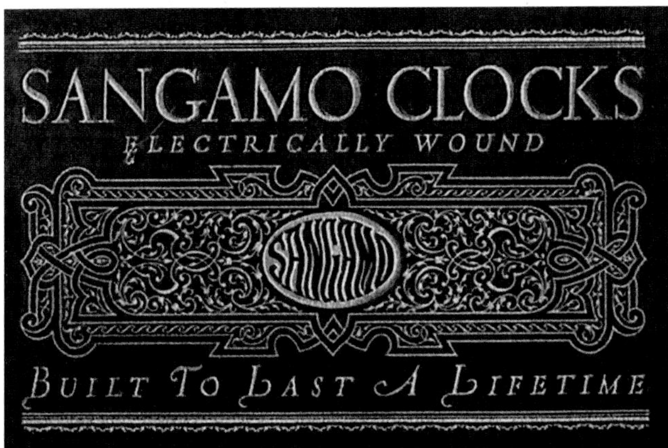

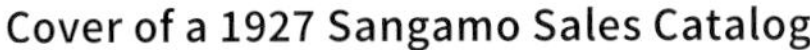
Cover of a 1927 Sangamo Sales Catalog

Sangamo Sales Catalog, 1927

Sangamo Experimental Clock

This is one of fewer than fifty first original experimental test clocks Sangamo produced. The movements were installed into third-party cases so that they could be used and tested. This particular clock is in a Waltham case and was the personal clock of Robert Carr Lanphier, a founder of Sangamo along with Jacob Bunn, Jr. The Illinois Watch Company custom made these platforms to Sangamo specifications, and they utilize 16-size, 11-jewel, Illinois movements.

Sangamo Promotional Items

Sangamo 50th anniversary promotional cocktail glass, decorated with a pun on the company's product, a tipsy Sangamo electrolytic capacitor, which asks, "How's your capacity?"

A real Sangamo capacitor, in a Heathkit amplifier from the early 1950s

Sangamo promotional match book

Sangamo employee anniversary pins and Sangamo 50th anniversary pin

Sangamo promotional key

Hamilton Watch Company

Hamilton Announcement

In the April 1928 issue of the *Hamilton Watch Word*, an internal Hamilton publication, the following appointments were announced:

SOME RECENT APPOINTMENTS

Mr. Robert E. Miller, Vice-President, who has given so much of his time and thought in coordinating the work of the Hamilton and Illinois Plants, has been appointed General Manager of the Illinois Watch Division.

Mr. J. W. Armbruster, of Springfield, Illinois, who has been building good will for Illinois Watches a great many years, has been appointed Sales Manager of that plant.

Mr. W. R. Atkinson, formerly Assistant Sales Manager of the Hamilton Watch Company has been elevated to the position of Sales Manager.

Mr. Harry Ruthhart, Material Sales Manager of the Hamilton Watch Company, has been given the added responsibility of the Material Sales Managership of the Illinois Watch Division in Springfield, Illinois.

Mr. Robert Waddell, of the Advertising Department, has been appointed Assistant Director of Sales Promotion for Hamilton Watches.

This good-looking trio is none other than the Manby family— Mr. Milton F. and his attractive wife and little daughter. We desire to publicly thank Mr. Manby for his valuable monthly contributions to the Technical Page in "Watch Words", the object of the page being to give the employees a working knowledge of the various parts of a watch in everyday factory terms. Mr. Manby and his father, who is Technical Supt. of the Hamilton Plant, have contributed in no small way to the

This picture of the Milton F. Manby family appeared in the April 1928 issue of the *Hamilton Watch Word*.

AMBASSADORS OF GOOD WILL

Under the leadership of Mr. F. C. Beckwith, Vice-President, these men shoulder the responsibility of advertising and selling our high class product. Judging from their good humor and smiling faces, they are enthusiastic about the prospects for 1928.

Back row, left to right: C. W. DREPPERD, Advertising Manager; F. C. BECKWITH, Vice-President; ROBERT WADDELL, Asst. Sales Promotion Manager. Second row, left to right: HARRY RUTHHART, Material Sales Manager; W. M. RUDOLPH, Western Sales District; R. M. KANT, Eastern Sales District. First row, left to right: A. WEIDMAN, New England Sales District; W. R. ATKINSON, Sales Manager; CHARLES S. GAUSE, Southern Sales District and J. R. PHILIP, Southwestern Sales District.

Our district representatives spent the entire week of March 12th at the factory and the 15th and 16th in conference with MR. C. F. MILLER, MR. F. C. BECKWITH, MR. W. R. ATKINSON and MR. C. W. DREPPERD. The Friday, March 12th meeting was addressed by Mr. S. H. BUSSER of the George Batten Company.

On Friday evening the men were entertained at a theater party which they greatly enjoyed. They got quite a kick out of some of the remarks and jokes of the Fulton players with reference to Hamilton Watches.

The Hamilton 1928 sales team

HAMILTON ~ ILLINOIS

WITH HARMONY AND GOOD WILL PREVAILING ON BOTH SIDES, ALL CAN PROSPER.

This new slogan appeared in the May-June 1928 issue of the *Hamilton Watch Word*.

SPRINGFIELD BUSINESS MEN GREET R. E. MILLER

RECEPTION HELD AT SANGAMO CLUB

Since early January Springfield, the community, has extended to the new management through Mr. Robert E. Miller unstinted courtesies and friendliness. The spirit has been so evidently sincere that one could not but feel its force.

On April 20, Springfield once more displayed a fineness of soul in what might be termed an official reception. It was held at the Sangamo Club.

A list of those present would be a futile gesture. Springfield was present—more than that, Springfield's national and international personages were present. Possibly all of the leaders did not drop in, but memory serves the many rather than the few.

The reception was as the meeting of friends, rather than the introduction of another business man.

Mr. Holbrook, President of the Sangamo Club, introduced Mr. Miller and in his introductory comments he outlined the history of the acquisition of the Illinois Watch Company assets by the Hamilton Watch Company.

Mr. Miller's talk was brief and cleared up some questions which may have been lurking in the minds of his auditors. He outlined the plans which have been laid for a very brilliant future for Illinois Watches. The plans embrace a generous National advertising campaign, the maintenance of the Illinois Watch Company master workmanship and economical operations through the reduction of waste.

An article in the May-June 1928 issue of the *Hamilton Watch Word* about Springfield businessmen welcoming Robert E. Miller to Springfield at the Sangamo Club. Interestingly, it mentions that, "Mr. Miller's talk was brief and cleared up some questions which may have been lurking in the minds of his auditors."

MR. WILLIAM E. PORT

Appointed Assistant General Manager of Illinois Watch Division

Mr. Port, appointed Assistant General Manager of the Illinois Watch Division effective April 27th, has had a long and varied experience in business. He has held executive positions and has been interested in the cost and analytical end of many different businesses. He comes to our joint family highly qualified for the responsibilities placed upon him.

Watch Words voices the best wishes of the management of the two plants and of his business associates.

This announcement appeared in the May-June 1928 issue of the *Hamilton Watch Word.*

Congratulations to the Illinois 30-Year Club

Watch Words is proud to have this picture grace its pages—proud to know that we are affiliated with such a splendid group of men and women. And we are setting down the names of each one, thinking that some of our Hamilton veterans will probably recognize old friends and associates in the watch making business. You will note that Mr. Julius Armbruster, Sales Manager for Illinois, who has visited us here in Lancaster, is the second one on the list:

Employee	*Employee*	*Employee*
Amundsen, Louis H.	Freidinger, William	Morgan, Fredrick N.
Armbruster, Julius	Furrow, George	Nichols, Charles
Brane, Mollie	Goetsch, Herman	Nielson, David
Barbier, Henry	Gordon, Samuel	O'Brien, John
Beck, Charles	Gough, Frank	O'Brien, M. F.
Bergman, Fred	Haendle, George	Page, A. M.
Bergman, John	Haendle, John	Pfarrer, Anna
Billington, Thomas	Hahn, Herman	Phillips, William
Birt, William	Haller, Matthew	Radcliffe, Charles
Brennan, John	Hamel, George	Reinhart, Margaret
Brown, Emil	Hansen, Paul	Scharf, George
Buckley, Fred	Hatfield, Mentor	Scharf, Louis
Burkhart, Herman	Hickox, James	Scharf, Phillip
Bunn, Jacob	Hoff, Carl	Schlipf, John
Carpenter, Chester	Hoge, Louise	Schultz, Herbert
Casdorf, Fred	Hood, Ed. H.	Sherlow, Sarah
Chapin, Walter	Hood, Samuel	Shinkle, Cyrus
Christiansen, C.	Jones, David	Shouldis, Agnes
Clarke, Fred	Jones, Richard	Sleven, Mary
Clarke, William	Keene, William	Smith, Axel
Craft, Joseph	Keithley, James	Smurr, John
Dee, Margaret	Kindred, Granville	Somdal, T. A.
Delaney, Frank	Larsen, Karl	Sower, William
Doerfler, Barbara	Larsen, Peter	Steinhauser, Alex
Doocy, Margaret	Lawrence, Oliver	Swenson, Hans
DeSilva, Joseph	Loeb, Emma	Vandervort, Frank
Early, Clint	Louiseau, Rene	Watkins, John
Edwards, John	Maisenbacher, Joseph	Wilson, Percy
Eifert, Fred	Maisenbacher, Phillip	Wendling, George
Fernandes, Joseph	McCoubrey, Agnes	Woodward, Charles
Finnegan, Robert	Maurer, Charles	
Fountain, Herbert	Maurer, William	

Hamilton's congratulations to the Illinois 30-Year Club members in the May-June issue of the *Hamilton Watch Word*

FIRST "LONG DISTANCE" BOWLING MATCH IS A "WIN" FOR HAMILTON!

The first long-distance bowling match ever played was staged on May 22d between a picked team of Illinois and Hamilton crack bowlers. The Hamilton boys were lucky enough to slip through with a margin of 35 pins—but we have not yet been able to measure their heads to see if they are wearing larger hats since it all happened.

Watch Words hopes to see a return match played some day—and a third one if necessary. This thing has got to be decided one way or another. But be that as it may, the scores show . . .

Read 'em and Weep!!!

HAMILTON Name	Score	*ILLINOIS* Name	Score
Harry Duke, Capt.		J. G. Moore, Capt.	
Ralph McLane	626	E. Bahlow	510
Frank Foose	579	H. Busch	549
Clayton Kreider	545	F. Metze	579
Herbert Bauer	587	F. Larsen	567
Samuel Evans	525	J. Moore	622
Total	2862	Total	2827

JEWELING DEPARTMENT WINS ILLINOIS BOWLS CROWN

The Illinois Watch Division Bowling League has been declared by all those interested in bowling as one of the best in Springfield, not only for the high scores turned in but for the interest that was shown. The Jeweling Department won the championship of the League by six games over the Escape Department, which finished in second place. Jake Moore, of the Escape Department, led all the bowlers for the season with the grand average of 192 for 87 games. F. Larsen, of the Finishing Department No. 1 Team, was second, with the average of 182, while Frank Metze, of the Escape Department, was third was 179.

FINAL STANDING

Team—	W.	L.	Pct.	HG.	H3G.	Av.
Jeweling	65	34	.657	977	2655	824
Escape	59	40	.596	981	2730	839
Hospital	56	43	.566	961	2751	759
Plate	51	48	.515	918	2560	764
Finish No. 1	51	48	.515	931	2604	803
Flat Steel	51	48	.515	958	2637	782
Finish No. 2	51	48	.515	912	2626	722
Machine	47	52	.475	910	2656	758
Auto Screw	46	53	.465	939	2630	724
Office-Print	45	54	.455	943	2664	727
Timing	42	57	.424	943	2542	751
Train	30	69	.303	974	2597	706

An article in the May-June 1928 issue of the *Hamilton Watch Word* describing the first "long distance" bowling match designed to build goodwill between the two Hamilton Watch Divisions. Also listed are the Illinois bowling results.

PRESIDENT MILLER ENTERTAINS THE MANAGEMENT AND FOREMEN AT THE LANCASTER COUNTRY CLUB.

It has been President Miller's habit for a number of years past to entertain the management and foremen. This year as the warm breath of spring was turning every barren twig and tree into leaf and flower, we received our invitations to attend Mr. Miller's dinner at the Country Club. And then the fellows got busy—'steen 'teen photographs were taken, a little testimonial prepared and a surprise tendered our genial President. Following the "eats," Mr. Burkhart presented Mr. Miller with a framed picture—with a fitting personal testimonial from the entire management and foreman group. Watch Words is favored in being permitted to reproduce the re-grouped photograph, and has added Mr. Miller's picture in order that it may be complete. Read the testimonial on the following page.

GROUP PHOTOGRAPH

Top row Left to Right: H. A. Ruthart, Robert Waddell, C. W. Dreppard, R. E. Miller, C. F. Miller, F. C. Beckwith, C. M. Kendig, W. R. Atkinson, C. S. Reece.

2d row: George P. Luckey, E. F. Carlstrom, F. Hauer, W. H. Manby, J. Willis, W. E. Broome, M. Manby, H. S. Shaub.

3d row: J. H. Koch, J. C. Weise, A. B. Burkhart, R. W. Cunningham, A. T. Buch, C. E. Wilson, H. L. Coho, W. S. Welchans, G. J. Ganse.

4th row: A. Hammersley, J. Rushton, H. Ziplinsky, G. McCauley, P. S. Lindsey, C. Hostetter, A. Fenstermacher, R. Metzger, H. E. Duttenhofer.

5th row: W. G. Martin, W. I. Everett, W. Breen, W. Hoffert, J. H. Leonard, J. Graf, H. Lawrence, E. J. Hodgen, E. M. Eshelman, J. J. Hergenrother.

A group portrait of the Hamilton executive team and all of its foremen that appeared in the May-June 1928 issue of *Hamilton Watch Word*

MESSRS. KENDIG *and* ATKINSON
Ready to "FLY" *for* TROUT---

Mr. C. M. Kendig, Secretary and Assistant Treasurer, and Mr. W. R. Atkinson, Sales Manager of the Hamilton Watch Company, report having a great time of it in Pike County over a recent week-end. Mr. Atkinson was Mr. Kendig's guest at the Saw Creek Club where fishing for brook trout is unexcelled. They had an excellent catch according to their story, but we wish we had the space here to make a drawing of the "whale of a one" Mr. Atkinson let get away. For further particulars, get in touch with W. R. A.

With the acquisition only a few months old, Calvin Kendig (apparently not in Springfield) was free to take Ross Atkinson to Kendig's Fishing Club, as was reported in the May-June 1928 issue of the *Hamilton Watch Word.*

Hamilton and Illinois Personnel Are to be Congratulated on Their Fine Response to Welfare Work

[*The employees of the two plants contributed a total of $5,806.30 to the Lancaster and Springfield Campaigns*]

It is with a great deal of pride and satisfaction in the splendid spirit manifested by the personnel of the Hamilton Watch Company—in both the Hamilton and Illinois plants—that these few paragraphs are written.

In the successful city campaign last month in which $283,850 was raised for the fifteen participating agencies of the Lancaster Welfare Federation, 969 of the 1,056 employees of the Hamilton Watch plant contributed a total of $3,216.15—an average contribution per person of $3.31. This is exclusive of the contribution by the Company and its officials who were solicited by the Big Gifts Committee.

In the Community Chest Campaign in Springfield, Illinois, held during November, the following splendid showing was made by our fellow workers in the Illinois plant out in the prairie country. 740 of the 876 employees of the Illinois plant subscribed a total of $2,590.15—or an average of $3.50 per employee.

At the final workers' meeting during the Lancaster campaign the City Industrial Division received a fine round of applause when it announced the returns from the Hamilton Watch Company.

And with the successful conclusion of the campaigns, many of the slanderous and ridiculous misstatements of fact faded out, as such statements usually do in hotly waged campaigns, be they political or welfare.

The sober, sound good judgment of our people lets them know in the calm of the aftermath that the Welfare Federation idea is the most economical and intelligent method of administering charity and welfare yet devised. Everyone realizes that the unselfish and public-spirited citizens who jealously watch and foster the activities of welfare federations are self-consecrated to our common responsibility in making our community a better place to live, and in assuring immunity to coming generations from blights that are constantly being checked in the bud by the various splendid, specialized charitable and welfare agencies included in the Federation.

The *Hamilton Watch Word*, in its May–June 1928 issue, reported on the employees' welfare contributions to the respective community chests in Springfield and Lancaster.

Now—All Together!

(To the tune of Mr. Gallagher and Mr. Shean)

HOW DO YOU DO, ILLINOIS,
HOW DO YOU DO?
HOW DO YOU DO, ILLINOIS,
HOW DO YOU DO?
WE ARE PROUD TO WELCOME YOU,
FOR WE KNOW WHAT YOU CAN DO,
HOW DO YOU DO, ILLINOIS,
HOW DO YOU DO?

The *Hamilton Watch Word*, May–June 1928. Five months after the acquisition, Hamilton came up with this cheerful ditty.

Chapter 13

Collecting Illinois

I have found hunting for and collecting Illinois wristwatches to be an avocation that has provided me with years of challenges and my fair share of "Fantastic Finds." More importantly, though, it has provided me with the opportunity to meet people with similar interests. Many have become friends for life. A number of these friends have generously provided their comments and more in various contributions to this book.

When asked by potential collectors about the best ways to start collecting Illinois watches, I advise them first to learn as much as they can about the subject. Reading my books, *The Illinois Watch: The Life and Times of a Great American Watch Company* and this five-volume set should help. Then I recommend that the novice collector set goals and concentrate on fulfilling them; otherwise, collecting wristwatches can be an overwhelming and expensive undertaking.

For example, collecting every possible combination of Illinois case, dial, movement and jewel variation of each watch listed in Chapter 9 of the Men's Identification Guide would entail trying to amass over 18,000 individual watches. Even with sufficient resources and the contacts, it would be impossible to reach this goal. Collecting every possible combination of each Illinois Factory-Cased men's wristwatches would reduce this goal by half. Even this goal would mean finding almost 10,000 different watches, still a daunting target.

My goal was only slightly more reasonable. In 1988, I set out to collect every case variation of every Factory-Cased men's Illinois wristwatch. Even this modest goal meant searching for about two hundred different Illinois watches. After a quarter of a century, I have not achieved my objective, but I have loved every minute of the fascinating quest to do so.

Complete Collecting

The collector defines the collection. The lists and advice in this chapter present various ways the collector might approach completing his or her collection.

For instance, the collector might set a goal of collecting every combination of the Factory-Cased ladies' wristwatches. This would mean locating and procuring at least 109 different watches, a more manageable but still challenging target.

A complete collection based only on catalogued Hamilton-Illinois models offered by Hamilton in the early 1950s would require locating only about thirty men's models and about thirty-five ladies' models if all the major variants were desired. This goal could be made even more manageable if it included only one example of each model. This would reduce the size of the quest to twenty men's and twenty-one ladies' models.

As the above numbers indicate, the ability of completing a collection depends upon the goal set. Hopefully, the lists below and the advice of collectors contained in this chapter show that collecting Illinois watches can be a very reasonable hobby if approached properly.

Subset Collecting

The following subset lists of Illinois watch models give some idea of how to approach Illinois without losing one's house or one's mind. For the most part, the lists represent manageable and affordable collections while achieving a complete subset of Illinois models. The following lists represent most of the possible subset collecting targets. (Men's models are in black, ladies' in red, and unisex in blue.)

Another approach to subset collecting is to focus on only one particular model, but in every possible combination. Among the men's models, one might concentrate on the Marquis Strap, the Consul or the New Yorker, for example; or, among the ladies' models, the Mary Todds, the Daytonas, the Edgewaters or the Berkeleys.

At the end of this chapter, a great friend and perhaps one of the consummate Illinois collectors explains how to go about locating in today's market the Illinois you seek.

Solid Gold Models		
Men's	**Ladies'**	
Ace[1]	Alouette	Greta
Admiral Evans	Argyle	Lakewood
Baronet	Arlene	Lenox
Chrysanthemum	Avalon	Mary Todd
Canby[2]	Babette I	Mary Todd 203
Consul	Babette II	Mary Todd 204
Convertible[3]	Bar Harbor 156	Mary Todd GG
"D-D" Utility[4]	Bar Harbor 158	Miami 157A
Decagon	Berkeley 154A	Narragansett
Devon[5]	Beverly 185	Princess
Eagle[1]	Brighton	Sherwood
Finalist Deco[6]	Coronado	Suzette
No. 250/Schmukler	Countess	Vardon
Notched Lug[7]	Daytona 154	Victoria
Rockliffe	Daytona 155	
Rockliffe 18/0	Daytona 155A	
Special Cushions[8]	Daytona 155B	
Tuxedo	Diamond-Set	
Varsity	Glencoe	

[1]There is one known solid gold Ace, and one Eagle.
[2]Certain Canbys were solid gold.
[3]Some Convertibles were solid gold. The Convertible was a ladies' model but is included with the men's models in this and other subsets because it was the very first Illinois wristwatch.
[4]Advertisements listed the "D-D" Utility as available in solid gold, but as yet none has been found.
[5]Solidarity made a white or green gold Cushion-Cushion engraved model that was Factory-Cased.
[6]A Finalist Deco has been found in solid yellow gold, likely a special order.
[7]Also came in sterling silver.
[8]Made by Fahys or Solidarity.

White Gold Models		
Men's	**Ladies'**	
Baronet	Alouette	Daytona 155A
Canby	Argyle	Daytona 155B
Chrysanthemum	Arlene	Diamond-Set
Consul	Avalon	Glencoe
Devon	Babette I	Greta
Rockliffe	Babette II	Lakewood
Rockliffe 18/0	Bar Harbor 156	Lenox
Special Cushion Solidarity	Bar Harbor 158	Mary Todd
Tuxedo	Berkeley 154A	Mary Todd 203
	Beverly 185	Mary Todd 204
	Brighton	Narragansett
	Coronado	Princess
	Countess	Sherwood
	Daytona 154	Victoria
	Daytona 155	

Yellow Gold Models	
Men's	**Ladies'**
Ace*	Babette II
Baronet	Berkeley 154A
Chrysanthemum	Glencoe
Convertible	Lakewood
Eagle*	Lenox
No. 250/Schmukler	Miami 157A*
Rockliffe	Sherwood
Rockliffe 18/0	
Varsity	
Finalist Deco**	

*Only one known to exist
**Special order watch

Green Gold Models	
Men's	**Ladies'**
Canby	Mary Todd GG
Consul	
Devon	
Special Cushion Solidarity	

Two-Tone Solid Gold Models	
Men's	**Ladies'**
Consul	Vardon
Tuxedo	

14K Gold-Filled Models		
Men's		
Ardsley	Finalist	Off-Duty
Arlington	Futura	Paul Revere
Atlantic	Gallahad	Piccadilly
Atlantic Enamel	Greystone	Pimlico
Beau Brummell	Greyhound	Puritan
Beau Brummell/Viking	Guardian	Rectangular
Beau Geste	Guardsman	Richmond 12/0
Beau Monde	Haddon Hall	Riley
Beau Royale	Hawthorne	Ritz
Belmont	Hudson	Skyway
Biltmore 18/0	Jolly Roger	Speedway
Biltmore 6/0	Kenilworth	Speedway 178
Blackstone	Kingston	Sportsman
Cadet	Larchmont	Townsman
Canby	LaSalle	Trophy
Chesterfield	Major	Valedictorian
Chesterfield Stepped Bezel	Manhattan	Vernon
Chieftain	Marquis Strap	Viking
Convertible	Mate	Wayne
Derby	Maxine	Wembley
Devon	Medalist	Wentworth
Ensign	Motor Coach	Westchester
Exeter	New Yorker	Yankee Clipper
Fifth Avenue	New Yorker Enamel	Yorktown
Ladies'		
Annette	Fairfax	Minuette
Berkeley 153	Fairport	Muzette
Berkeley 154	Florette	Newport 174
Berkshire	Florentine	Newport 223
Biloxi	Glenna 186	No. 241
Charmette	Glenna 239	Patricia
Claudette	Gloria	Redonda 153
Coquette	Hollywood	Redonda 154
Daytona 153	Irene	Rita
Debutante	Joan	Roslyn
Del Monte 155	Juliette	Rosette
Del Monte 157	Long Beach	Saratoga Leaf
Edgewater 155	Mariette	Saratoga Notched Leaf
Edgewater 175	Marilyn	Sylvia
Edgewater 208	Marlette	Suzette
Edgewater 222	Marionette	Vanity Fair
Elissa	Miami 155	Vogue
Fahys Special Model	Miami 157	

18K Gold Models, Ladies'	
Diamond-Set	Mary Todd GG
Mary Todd	Victoria
Mary Todd 203	Wadsworth Special*
Mary Todd 204	
*Some early ones have also been found in 19.2K white gold cases.	

10K Gold-Filled Models		
Men's		Ladies'
Andover	Potomac	Antoinette
Chatham	Rockingham	Beverly 852
Exeter	Standish	Janette
Illinois Whitman	Urbana	Lynette

Models in White Gold-Filled Only		
Men's	Ladies'	
Caprice	Berkeley 153	Joan
Chesterfield Stepped Bezel	Berkshire	Marionette
Greyhound	Biloxi	Miami 155
Motor Coach	Daytona 153	Miami 157
Off-Duty	Del Monte 155	Model No. 241
Skyway	Del Monte 157	Muzette
Speedway	Edgewater 155	Newport 174
Speedway 178	Edgewater 208	Newport 223
	Edgewater 222	Redonda 153
	Fairfax	Redonda 154
	Fairport	Roslyn
	Florentine	Saratoga Leaf
	Glenna	Saratoga Notched Leaf

Models in Yellow Gold-Filled Only, Unisex
Urbana

WHY I COLLECT ILLINOIS

Well, it kinda goes like this: I met Mike Fultz in the early 1980s when we were friendly competitors for fountain pens. We would run into each other at antique shows and flea markets and frequently meet for coffee or a sandwich and show each other what great treasures we had unearthed. Eventually we became friends and worked closely together to buy and split entire collections. We never had a dispute or argument over a pen and it was really a great thing. In those days, Mike was more of a historian than I was, but he had a bit more time than me.

In the 1980s Mike was a big pocket watch collector and had little interest in wristwatches. Most of his pocket watches were American manufacture: Walthams, Elgins, Hamiltons and a few Illinois. However, he started researching the Illinois Watch Company and found out that as compared to the other well-known domestic manufacturers Illinois made many fewer wristwatches (only about one million), that they had great deco designs and that the standard Illinois movement was 15 or 17 jewels as compared to say Elgin which only had 7 jewels. Even better, Illinois wristwatches hadn't really been "discovered" and so we weren't competing with a lot of other collectors.

We met a fellow, Bernie Pygan, who dealt in Illinois wristwatches and he gave us a basic education in some of the more interesting models. (Bernie was selling a lot of his Illinois wristwatches to then Illinois Governor, Jim Thompson).

One day Mike called me up and told me to meet him and to bring what for me was a significant amount of cash. I didn't question him but we met a tree surgeon by the name of Bob Coonfield at a coffee shop and forked over a pretty hefty amount for his entire Illinois wristwatch collection (about two hundred or so). Well, that was the start. Mike and I divided the Coonfield collection and then bought and split a couple more collections along the way. We both started to study the Illinois Watch Company and to accumulate what scant literature such as catalogs and advertising that we could find. Eventually we both put together a nice collection of Illinois wristwatches although as you know, his collection was substantially larger than mine. *— Daniel A. Zazove*

Green Gold-Filled Models, Men's		
Ace	Ensign	Special
Atlantic	Guardsman	Sportsman
Atlantic Enamel	Jolly Roger	Square
Beau Brummell	Kingston	Square Cut Corner
Beau Brummell/Viking	Marquis Strap	Tank
Beau Royale	Mate	Wayne
Biltmore 18/0	Maxine	Whippet
Cadet	Piccadilly	Yankee Clipper
Canby	Riley	
Devon	Southampton	

Two-Tone Gold-Filled Models		
Men's		Ladies'
Ace	Major	Barbara
Beau Brummell	Marquis Strap	Constance
Beau Brummell/Viking*	Mate	
Beau Royale	Metropolitan	
Biltmore 18/0	Piccadilly**	
Blackstone*	Puritan	
Chesterfield	Ritz	
Ensign	Square Cut Corner*	
Guardian	Townsman	
Guardsman	Valedictorian	
Kingston	Whippet	

* Only one known to exist

** One claimed to exist, but unconfirmed

Sterling Silver Models		
Men's		Ladies'
Admiral Benson	General Joffre	Lady Mary
Admiral Benson, Jr.	Guardsman Military	Queen Anne
Admiral Evans	Integrated Guard	
Admiral Evans, Jr.	Notched Lug	
Ariston	Off-Set Crowns	
Armored Case	Ongard	
Aviator	Ongard Off-Set	
Burlington	Police Special	
Cut Bezel	Special Cushion Fahys	
"D-D" Utility Watch	Telephone Dial	
General Funston	Washington Watch Co.	

Base Metal Model , Men's		
Blackhawk	Osgood	Senator
Brandt Rock	Sangamon	Seneca

WHY I COLLECT ILLINOIS

I'm born and raised in Illinois so it was an easy decision for me. But the real reason was when I was little and my father would come home from work and we'd sit down to dinner, I was seated on his left and I'd always notice his watch when he passed food, etc. This gave me a strange comforting feeling just knowing he was home and we were sharing a meal together.

We fast forward to 1991. I always told my father he needed to take better care of his watch as it was a classic. He just beat it up daily as a truck driver. At Christmas 1991 he gave it to me in a box—without a strap as he went through every strap imaginable. I told him I'd get it back in tip-top shape. It looked terrible from a daily beating it took with the rigors of being a truck driver. I took it to my watch guy to have it serviced, refinished and cleaned up. He put a great leather band on it. When I presented it back to my father, he said it looked great but "now it's your watch". He wouldn't take it back but it always gave me great joy knowing it was his and what he went through every day taking care of his family. *— Mike Hughes*

Engraved Bezel Models		
Men's		
Ace	Finalist	Special
Atlantic	Finalist Deco	Special Cushions
Atlantic Enamel	Guardian	Speedway
Beau Brummell	Guardsman	Speedway 178
Beau Geste	Jolly Roger	Square
Beau Monde	Kingston	Square Cut Corner
Beau Royale	Locke	Square Cut Corner Large
Cadet	Major	Sterling
Canby	Manhattan	Tank
Chesterfield Stepped Bezel	Marquis Strap	Townsman
Chieftain	Mate	Tuxedo
Chrysanthemum	Maxine	Urbana
Consul	New Yorker	Wayne
Cushion	Piccadilly	Whippet
Devon	Riley	Yankee Clipper
Ensign	Senator	Yorktown
Fifth Avenue	Southampton	
Ladies'		
Babette I	Edgewater 155	Mary Todd GG
Babette II	Edgewater 175	Miami 155
Bar Harbor 156	Edgewater 208	Miami 157
Bar Harbor 158	Edgewater 222	Miami 157A
Berkeley 153	Elissa	Minuette
Berkshire	Fairfax	Narragansett
Beverly 852	Fairport	Newport 174
Brighton	Florentine	Newport 223
Coquette	Glencoe	Patricia
Coronado	Glenna	Princess
Countess	Hollywood	Queen Anne
Daytona 153	Joan	Redonda 153
Daytona 154	Juliette	Rita
Daytona 155	Lakewood	Rosette
Daytona 155A	Long Beach	Roslyn
Daytona 155B	Lynette	Saratoga Leaf
Débette	Marlette	Saratoga Notched Leaf
Debutante	Mary Todd	Vanity Fair
Del Monte 155	Mary Todd 203	
Del Monte 157	Mary Todd 204	

Plain Bezel Models

Men's		
Ace	Ensign	New Yorker
Admiral Evans	Finalist	No. 250/Schmukler
Akron (Aluminum Prototype)	Finalist Deco	Notched Lug
Ardsley	Frontenac	Paul Revere
Arlington	Futura	Piccadilly
Baronet	Gallahad	Pimlico
Beau Brummell	Greystone	Potomac
Beau Royale	Guardian	Richmond 12/0
Belmont	Haddon Hall	Ritz
Biltmore 18/0	Hawthorne	Rockliffe
Biltmore 6/0	Hudson	Rockliffe 18/0
Blackhawk	Illinois Whitman	Rockingham
Blackstone	Jolly Roger	Seneca
Bostonian	Kenilworth	Sportsman
Chatham	LaSalle	Standish
Commander	Larchmont	Tuxedo
Commodore	Major	Valedictorian
Consul	Manhattan	Varsity
Convertible	Marquis Strap	Vernon
Derby	Mate	Wembley
Devon	Medalist	Wentworth
Ladies'		
Annette	Claudette	Lenox
Antoinette	Convertible	Marilyn
Argyle	Coquette	Suzette
Arlene	Florette	Sylvia
Avalon	Glencoe	Vardon
Beverly 185	Greta	Vogue
Biloxi	Irene	
Charmette	Lady Mary	

Enameled Bezel Models

Men's	Ladies'	
Atlantic Enamel	Argyle	Mary Todd*
Atlantic, Jr.	Berkeley 153	Mary Todd 203
Brandt Rock	Berkeley 154	Miami 155
Chevalier	Berkeley 154A	Miami 157
New Yorker Enamel	Brighton	Miami 157A
Osgood	Coronado	Redonda 153
Southampton*	Del Monte 155	Redonda 154
Square Enamel	Del Monte 157	Roslyn
	Diamond-Set**	Victoria

*Also came without enamel
**A few Wadsworth 18K cases also have black enamel.

Molded Bezel Models

Men's	Ladies'
Beau Brummell/Viking	Fahys Special Model
Eagle	Gloria
Greyhound	Janette
Motor Coach	Joan
Off-Duty	Lynette
Sangamon	Marionette
Skyway	Muzette
Viking	Sherwood

Stars on Bezel Models, Men's

Eagle	Motor Coach	Skyway
Greyhound	Off-Duty	Whippet

Black Dial Models, Men's

"D-D" Utility Watch	Off-Duty	United States Army
Kitchener	Skyway	

Butler Center Dial Models

Men's		
Ace	Major	Rockingham
Atlantic	Manhattan	Southampton
Beau Brummell	Marquis Strap	Speedway
Beau Brummell/Viking	Mate	Speedway 178
Beau Royale	Maxine	Square
Canby	Medalist	Square Cut Corner
Chieftain	New Yorker	Varsity
Ensign	New Yorker Enamel	Wayne
Fifth Avenue	Potomac	Wembley
Jolly Roger	Rectangular	Whippet
Kingston	Riley	Yankee Clipper
Ladies'		
Avalon	Daytona 155	Narragansett
Berkeley 153	Del Monte 157	Newport 223
Coronado	Long Beach	Saratoga Leaf
Daytona 153	Miami 157	Saratoga Notched Leaf

WHY I COLLECT ILLINOIS

I started collecting Illinois wristwatches in May of 2001. It all began when a friend gave me an Illinois pocket watch for Christmas. It was so beautiful and unusual at the same time. And, it was about eighty years old. I liked the Art Deco look and it was in perfect condition. And, since my grandfather left me a pocket watch when he died, I decided to try to find some others to possibly collect.

This led me to a website that actually listed pocket watches and wristwatches. As soon as I saw the collection of wristwatches, I was totally sold on collecting wristwatches rather than pocket watches. They all had different dials, bezels, second hands, metals and designs. I couldn't believe the beauty of them and they all looked different. I chose to collect them immediately.

For the first few years I bought most of them online at miscellaneous auctions and at antique shows. As my wife saw how excited I was with each new purchase, she gave me a watch collecting book authored by Fred Friedberg. That gift really opened my eyes to what this hobby was about. Pages and pages of beautiful watches, rated by rarity, estimated values and collectibility. It contained information on the history of the Illinois Watch Company and Illinois watches, with each watch listed in the book, accompanied by color pictures. I contacted Fred via e-mail and continued growing my collection through purchases from him.

Today I have about seventy-five watches. My collection is varied in price, condition and appearance. I have some of the rarest watches, some of the most common, some expensive and some very affordable. I have them all in a jewelry showcase in my office and look at them every day. I enjoy winding them, as it gives me time to re-familiarize myself with their beauty and assure they are in working order. This has been a hobby that has involved education, fun and commitment. I enjoy it immensely.

Today I am focusing on finding the "rarest of the rare," a task that has led me in a lot of different directions. But even if I do not end up with all the watches on my wish list, I continue to check at every flea market and antique show for that "pearl in the oyster" watch that might be found in some jeweler's case. *—John Whalen*

Exploding Numeral Dial Models

Men's		Ladies'
Cushion	Speedway	Edgewater 155
Devon	Speedway 178	Edgewater 208
Jolly Roger	Whippet	Edgewater 222
Major		Newport 174

Egyptian Numeral Models Only, Men's

Gallahad	Ritz
Kenilworth	Valedictorian

WHY I COLLECT ILLINOIS

In the early 1990s a friend bought a pocket watch lot at a local auction, the watches all European models with the exception of one American watch. Seeing my interest, he asked me if I would like to have the watch. It turned out to be a size 12 Illinois Watch Company extra thin grade 525 "The Marquis" model, and that's how my collection and research into size 12 watches began.

As I came from Scotland, you may find my fascination with Illinois watches strange. Buying watch books and joining watch forums, I was able to get help from the Illinois watch experts. I joined the NAWCC in 2003, and I have managed to visit the museum and the research library in Columbia, PA. And I went to a NAWCC National Convention a few years back. This was a great experience for me. The great variety of named and private-label watches with so many damaskeening patterns and jewel configurations makes Illinois watches ideal for collecting and researching. *—Jim Carroll*

Sparkle Finish Dial Models		
Men's		
Andover	Finalist	Paul Revere
Ardsley	Finalist Deco	Richmond 12/0
Arlington	Futura	Ritz
Baronet	Gallahad	Rockliffe
Beau Geste	Hawthorne	Valedictorian
Beau Monde	Hudson	Vernon
Caprice	Kenilworth	Wembley
Chesterfield	Larchmont	Wentworth
Chesterfield Stepped Bezel	Medalist	
Commander	Metropolitan	
Exeter	No. 250/Schmukler	
Ladies'		
Babette II	Miami 157	Roslyn
Miami 155	Minuette	

Enamel Dial Models, Men's		
Admiral Benson	Chevalier	Integrated Guard
Admiral Benson, Jr.	Chrysanthemum	Major
Admiral Evans	Convertible	Motor Coach
Admiral Evans, Jr.	Cut Bezel	Off-Set Crowns
Ariston	"D-D" Utility Watch	Speedway
Armored Case	General Funston	Speedway 178
Aviator	General Joffre	Telephone Dial
Burlington	Greyhound	Washington Watch Company

Sunburst Dial Models, Men's
Consul

Pinstripe or Racing Stripes Dials		
Men's	**Ladies'**	
Bryce	Annette	Fairfax
Canby	Avalon*	Florette
Consul	Barbara	Florentine
	Charmette	Mary Todd 203*
	Constance	Mary Todd 204*
	Coquette	Narragansett*
	Coronado*	Vanity Fair
	Debutante	

*Dial #1854 (Flückiger sterling silver)

Collier's, December 7, 1929

Rotor-Subsidiary Seconds Models, Men's		
Akron (Aluminum Prototype)	Guardian	Seneca
	Guardsman	Sterling
Blackhawk	Military Guardsman	

21-Jewel Models, Men's		
Baronet	Consul	New Yorker
Beau Brummell	Fifth Avenue	New Yorker Enamel
Beau Brummell/Viking	Kingston	
Beau Monde	Manhattan	

Rectangular Case Models, Men's		
Andover	Frontenac	Rectangular
Ardsley	Futura	Richmond 12/0
Arlington	Gallahad	Rockliffe
Baronet	Hawthorne	Rockliffe 18/0
Biltmore	Hudson	Sangamon
Biltmore 18/0	Illinois Whitman	Sterling
Bryce	Kenilworth	Tank
Canby	Larchmont	Trophy
Chatham	Locke	Tuxedo
Chesterfield	Manhattan	Urbana
Chesterfield Stepped Bezel	Medalist	Varsity
Commander	New Yorker	Vernon
Derby	New Yorker Enamel	Viking
Exeter	No. 250/Schmukler	Wembley
Fifth Avenue	Paul Revere	Wentworth
Finalist	Pimlico	Westchester
Finalist Deco	Potomac	Yorktown

Round Case Models, Men's		
Ariston	Guardian	Ongard
Armored Case	Guardsman	Ongard Off-Set
Convertible	Guardsman Military	Police Special
Cut Bezel	Integrated Guard	Skyway
"D-D" Utility Watch	Kitchener	Special
Depollier Water/Dust Proof	Major	Telephone Dial
General Funston	Motor Coach	United States Army
General Joffre	Off-Duty	Washington Watch Company
Greyhound	Off-Set Crowns	

Square Case Models, Men's		
Burlington	Caprice (When Closed)	Square

Tonneau Case Models		
Men's		
Akron (Aluminum Prototype)	Beau Royale	Mate
	Blackhawk	Riley
Atlantic	Burlington	Ritz
Atlantic Enamel	Chieftain	Seneca
Atlantic Enamel, Jr.	Cadet	Standish
Beau Brummell	Consul	Sterling
Beau Brummell/Viking	Ensign	Whippet
Beau Geste	Kingston	Yankee Clipper
Beau Monde	Marquis Strap	
Ladies'		
Tonneau		

Cut-Corner Case Models, Men's		
Bryce	Rectangular	Square Cut Corner
Canby	Senator	Square Cut Corner Large

Cushion Case Models, Men's		
Admiral Benson	Cushion	Notched Lug
Admiral Benson, Jr.	Cut Bezel	Puritan
Ariston	Devon	Special Cushions
Armored Case	Eagle	Speedway
Aviator	Integrated Guard	Speedway 178
Burlington	Jolly Roger	Sportsman
Chevalier	Masonic Dial	Townsman
Chrysanthemum	Metropolitan	

Oval Case Models, Men's
Piccadilly

Octagon Case Models		
Men's		
Ace	Admiral Evans, Jr.	Wayne
Admiral Evans	Riley	
Ladies'		
Octagon		

Off-Set Crown Models, Men's		
Admiral Evans Off-Set	Decagon, Jr. Off-Set	Notched Lug
Admiral Evans Jr. Off-Set	Integrated Guard Off-Set	Off-Set Crown
Armored Case Off-Set	Military Off-Set	Ongard Off-Set

Military Models, Men's		
Admiral Benson	Burlington	Integrated Guard
Admiral Benson, Jr.	Cut Bezel	Off-Set Crown
Admiral Evans	"D-D" Utility Watch	Ongard
Admiral Evans, Jr.	Depollier Water/Dust Proof	Ongard Off-Set
Armored Case	General Funston	United States Army
Aviator	General Joffre	
Bullet Dial	Guardsman Military	

Subsidiary Seconds at 9 Models, Men's		
Ace[1]	Devon[2]	Southampton
Beau Brummell[1]	Ensign[1]	Square
Beau Brummell/Viking[1]	Fifth Avenue[1]	Special Cushion
Beau Royale[1]	Kingston[2]	Special[2]
Bryce[1]	Locke[2]	Square Cut Corner
Cadet[2]	Manhattan[1]	Standish[1]
Canby	Marquis Strap[2,3]	Tank[3]
Chieftain	New Yorker[1]	Telephone Dial[1]
Chrysanthemum	New Yorker Enamel[1]	Whippet[1]
Consul[2]	Piccadilly	
Cushion[1]	Rectangular[1]	
Ladies'		
Octagon	Tonneau	

[1]Also has seconds at 6
[2]Also has seconds at 6 or no seconds
[3]Also has no seconds

Subsidiary Seconds at 6 Models, Men's		
Ace[1]	Finalist Deco	Ongard
Admiral Evans	Frontenac	Ongard Off-Set
Admiral Evans, Jr.	Futura	Paul Revere
Andover	Gallahad	Pimlico
Ardsley	General Funston	Police Special
Ariston	General Joffre	Potomac
Arlington	Gift Series	Puritan
Armored Case	Greyhound	Richmond 12/0
Atlantic	Haddon Hall	Riley
Atlantic Enamel	Hawthorne	Ritz
Atlantic Enamel, Jr.	Hudson	Rockliffe
Aviator	Illinois Whitman	Rockingham
Baronet	Integrated Guard	Skyway
Beau Brummell[1]	Jolly Roger	Special[2]
Beau Brummell/ Viking[1]	Kenilworth	Speedway
Beau Geste	Kensington	Speedway 178
Beau Monde	Kingston	Sportsman
Beau Royale[1]	LaSalle	Standish[2]
Belmont	Larchmont	Telephone Dial[1]
Cadet	Locke[1]	Townsman
Chatham	Major	Trophy
Chesterfield	Manhattan	United States Army
Chesterfield Stepped Bezel	Marquis Strap[2]	Valedictorian
Chevalier	Masonic Dial	Varsity
Commander	Mate	Vernon
Consul[2]	Maxine	Viking
Convertible	Medalist	Washington Watch Co.
"D-D" Utility Watch	Metropolitan	Wayne
Depollier Water/Dust Proof	Motor Coach	Wembley
Derby	New Yorker[1]	Wentworth
Devon	New Yorker Enamel[1]	Westchester
Ensign	No. 250/Schmukler	Yankee Clipper
Exeter	Notched Lug	Yorktown
Finalist	Off-Duty	
	Off-Set Crowns	

[1]Also had subs at 9 or no subs
[2]Also had subs at 9

No Subsidiary Second Models		
Men's		
Brandt Rock	Eagle	Sangamon
Bryce[1]	Marquis Strap[1]	Tuxedo
Cadet[1]	Osgood	Urbana
Caprice	Rectangular[1]	
Consul[1]	Rockliffe 18/0	
Ladies'		
All ladies' models, except for certain specimens of the Octagon and Tonneau, and certain Generic specimens		
[1]Also has subs at 6 or 9		

3/0 Size Models, Men's		
Ace	Greyhound	Senator
Akron	Guardian	Seneca
(Aluminum Prototype)	Guardsman	Skyway
Atlantic	Guardsman Military	Special
Atlantic Enamel	Jolly Roger	Special Cushion
Aviator	Major	Speedway
Blackhawk	Marquis Strap	Speedway 178
Burlington	Masonic Dial	Sportsman
Caprice	Mate	Telephone Dial
Chevalier	Maxine	United States Army
Convertible	Motor Coach	Viking
"D-D" Utility Watch	Off-Duty	Washington Watch Co.
Depollier Water/Dust Proof	Osgood	Wayne
Devon	Police Special	Whippet
	Riley	

6/0 Size Models		
Men's		
Arlington	Ensign	Rockingham
Baronet	Fifth Avenue	Southampton
Beau Brummell	Gift Series	Special
Beau Brummell/Viking	Hawthorne	Special Cushion
Beau Geste	Kingston	Square
Beau Monde	Manhattan	Square Cut Corner
Beau Royale	Metropolitan	Standish
Burlington	New Yorker	Tank
Canby	New Yorker Enamel	Townsman
Chatham	Notched Lug	Valedictorian
Chieftain	Piccadilly	Varsity
Chrysanthemum	Potomac	Whippet
Consul	Puritan	Yankee Clipper
Convertible	Rectangular	Yorktown
Devon	Richmond 6/0	
Eagle	Ritz	
Ladies'		
Octagon	Tonneau	

12/0 Size Models, Men's		
Andover	Futura	Richmond 12/0
Ardsley	Gallahad	Rockliffe
Chesterfield	Hudson	Trophy
Chesterfield Stepped Bezel	Kenilworth	Vernon
Commander	Kensington	Wembley
Exeter	Larchmont	Wentworth
Finalist	Medalist	Westchester
Finalist Deco	No. 250/Schmukler	
Frontenac	Paul Revere	

14/0 Size Models, Men's
Illinois Whitman

18/0 Size Models, Men's		
Biltmore 18/0	Sangamon	Urbana
Rockliffe 18/0	Tuxedo	

WHY I COLLECT ILLINOIS

PLACE… Springfield, Illinois. TIME… 1979

My small second-floor, three-room office, in an old remodeled early 1900s house was getting a little cramped, so I called a realtor friend of mine and asked him to find me something a little bit larger. A day or two later, he picked me up and drove me out to the north end of town, and we pulled up to a huge TWO-SQUARE-BLOCK industrial site formally known as the ILLINOIS WATCH/SANGAMO ELECTRIC COMPLEX. The Watch Company had vacated the site in 1932. Sangamo Electric purchased the property from Hamilton Watch Company around 1933 and vacated the site around 1972. The place had been unoccupied for seven years.

My realtor friend said, "PICK A BUILDING." We both had a good laugh at the time, but within months my two St. Louis partners and I bought the two-square-block complex (except for one building which we acquired a few months later).

Having grown up as a poor kid in Iowa, I never had a watch until graduation in the early '50s. Some twenty-plus years later, I took an interest in old wristwatches and started picking up a few, mostly from the '40s and '50s era. It wasn't until the mid to late 1980s that it dawned on me to start collecting ILLINOIS wristwatches. I figured, why not? I owned the old factory.

Most of my early Illinois finds were from around town. Somewhere along the way, I had picked up a couple of Illinois mailing lists, including one from Mike Fultz out of Chicago, from whom I bought quite a number of Illinois pieces. Mike became a good friend and tutor. At about the same time period, Fred Friedberg and I became good friends (and still are) and did a lot of trading together. We would meet at watch shows, have dinner and talk "ILLINOIS." At Mike Fultz's invitation we attended the "ILLINOIS SUMMIT" at his Wisconsin home, where Mike tried to talk each of the four attendees into writing the *ILLINOIS WRISTWATCH* book. He got no takers. We all ganged up on Fred, and though it took a while (several months before he agreed) it was well worth our waiting. His book has brought light to thousands of wristwatch collectors across the country thanks to his remarkable research and depth of knowledge on ILLINOIS.

P.S. From my perspective, there was one other eventful occurrence at the SUMMIT. I had the opportunity to see several ILLINOIS ladies' watches, and after viewing them, especially the enamel pieces, I was hooked. Thanks to my friends, Fred and Mike, my men's collection was mostly complete by then, and I took on the challenge of going after the Illinois ladies' pieces. The result of my research was published in the NAWCC *Watch and Clock Bulletin* in April 2011.

The introduction to my article was written by Fred Friedberg.

—Farrell Gay

18/0 Size Models, Ladies'		
Argyle	Del Monte 155	Mary Todd 204
Arlene	Del Monte 157	Mary Todd GG
Avalon	Edgewater 155	Miami 155
Bar Harbor 156	Edgewater 175	Miami 157
Bar Harbor 158	Edgewater 208	Miami 157A
Barbara	Edgewater 222	Narragansett
Berkeley 153	Elissa	Newport 174
Berkeley 154	Fahys Special Model	Newport 223
Berkeley 154A	Fairfax	No. 241
Berkshire	Fairport	Patricia
Beverly 185	Florentine	Princess
Beverly 852	Glencoe	Queen Anne
Biloxi	Glenna	Redonda 153
Biltmore 18/0	Gloria	Redonda 154
Brighton	Greta	Rita
Claudette	Hollywood	Roslyn
Constance	Irene	Saratoga Leaf
Coronado	Joan	Saratoga Notched Leaf
Countess	Lady Mary	Sherwood
Daytona 153	Lakewood	Sylvia
Daytona 154	Lenox	Vanity Fair
Daytona 155	Long Beach	Vardon
Daytona 155A	Marilyn	Vogue
Daytona 155B	Mary Todd	
Debutante	Mary Todd 203	

21/0 Size Models, Ladies'		
Alouette	Débette	Marionette
Annette	Florette	Marlette
Antoinette	Janette	Minuette
Babette I	Juliette	Muzette
Babette II	Louette	Rosette
Charmette	Lynette	Suzette
Coquette	Mariette	

Transitional Period Models, Men's		
Admiral Benson	Convertible	Masonic Dial
Admiral Benson, Jr.	Cut Bezel	Notched Lug
Admiral Evans	"D-D" Utility Watch	Off-Set Crowns
Admiral Evans, Jr.	Depollier Water/ Dust Proof	Ongard
Ariston	General Funston	Ongard Off-Set
Armored Case	General Joffre	Police Special
Aviator	Guardsman Military	Telephone Dial
Bullet Dial	Integrated Guard	United States Army
Burlington	Kitchener	Washington Watch Co.

Generic Period Models		
Men's		
Ace	Devon	Special Cushion
Atlantic	Gift Series	Sportsman
Atlantic Enamel	Locke	Square
Atlantic Enamel, Jr.	Maxine	Square Cut Corner
Bryce	Rectangular	Square Cut Corner Large
Canby	Riley	Tank
Cushion	Southampton	Wayne
Cushion Form	Special	Whippet
Ladies'		
Octagon	Tonneau	

Deco Period Models		
Men's		
Akron	Eagle	Off-Duty
Aluminum Prototype	Ensign	Osgood
Beau Brummell	Fifth Avenue	Piccadilly
Beau Brummell/Viking	Greyhound	Richmond 6/0
Beau Geste	Guardian	Ritz
Beau Monde	Guardsman	Seneca
Beau Royale	Jolly Roger	Skyway
Blackhawk	Kingston	Special
Brandt Rock	Major	Speedway
Cadet	Manhattan	Speedway 178
Caprice	Marquis Strap	Sportsman
Chevalier	Mate	Sterling
Chieftain	Motor Coach	Viking
Chrysanthemum	New Yorker	Yankee Clipper
Consul	New Yorker Enamel	Yorktown
Ladies'		
Avalon	Del Monte 155	Miami 155
Bar Harbor 156	Del Monte 157	Miami 157
Bar Harbor 158	Diamond-Set Models	Miami 157A
Berkeley 153	Edgewater 155	Narragansett
Berkeley 154	Edgewater 175	Newport 174
Berkeley 154A	Edgewater 208	Newport 223
Berkshire	Edgewater 222	No. 244
Beverly 185	Fahys Special Model	Redonda 153
Biloxi	Fairpoint	Redonda 154
Brighton	Glencoe	Roslyn
Coronado	Lakewood	Saratoga Leaf
Daytona 153	Lenox	Saratoga Notched Leaf
Daytona 154	Long Beach	Vanity Fair
Daytona 155	Mary Todd	Vardon
Daytona 155A	Mary Todd 203	Victoria
Daytona 155B	Mary Todd 204	Wadsworth Special Models
Debutante	Mary Todd GG	

Moderne Period Models		
Men's		
Andover	Gallahad	Rockingham
Ardsley	Hawthorne	Sangamon
Arlington	Hudson	Senator
Baronet	Illinois Whitman	Standish
Biltmore 18/0	Kenilworth	Townsman
Chatham	Kensington	Trophy
Chesterfield	Larchmont	Tuxedo
Chesterfield Stepped Bezel	Medalist	Urbana
Connerics	Metropolitan	Varsity
Derby	No. 250/Schmukler	Vernon
Exeter	Pimlico	Wembley
Finalist	Potomac	Wentworth
Finalist Deco	Richmond 12/0	Westchester
Frontenac	Rockliffe	
Futura	Rockliffe 18/0	
Ladies'		
Alouette	Elissa	Queen Anne
Babette I	Fairfax	Mariette
Babette II	Florentine	Marilyn
Annette	Florette	Marionette
Antoinette	Glenna 186	Marlette
Argyle	Glenna 239	Minuette
Arlene	Gloria	Muzette
Barbara	Greta	Patricia
Beverly 852	Hollywood	Princess
Charmette	Irene	Rita
Claudette	Janette	Rosette
Constance	Joan	Sherwood
Coquette	Juliette	Sylvia
Countess	Lady Mary	Suzette
Débette	Lynette	Vogue

Models Advertised with Curved Case Backs, Men's		
Ardsley	Cadet	Medalist
Beau Brummell	Gallahad	Rockliffe
Beau Brummell/Viking	Hudson	Rockliffe 18/0
Beau Geste	Kenilworth	Wembley
Beau Monde	Marquis Strap	Yankee Clipper
Beau Royale	Mate	

Unisex Models		
Biltmore 18/0	Sangamon	Urbana
Caprice	Tuxedo	

Cross Pattern Dials		
Ace	Canby	Riley
Atlantic	Locke	Square Cut Corner, Large
Atlantic Enamel	Maxine	Tank
Bryce	Rectangular	Wayne

Drop Shadow Dials		
Derby	Kenilworth	No. 250/Schmukler
Gallahad	Metropolitan	Pimlico

Recessed Crown Models		
Biltmore	Rockliffe	Tuxedo
Biltmore 18/0	Rockliffe 18/0	
No. 250/Schmukler		

Advice from an Expert Illinois Collector

Greg Hart, perhaps currently the world's most enthusiastic and dedicated Illinois collector, volunteered to write this section to share his passion for Illinois wristwatches and his up-to-date techniques for collecting Illinois wristwatches. Greg explains, as follows:

The Hunt:

Collecting is in your blood, like a hunter on a deer post waiting for that 20-point buck . . . the feeling of the hunt or chase is many times more rewarding than the actual capture.

In the case of a rare group of watches that started off in Springfield, Illinois, almost one hundred years ago and got released into the wild, finding them and getting them all together is a daunting task the size of Mt. Everest.

In 2008 I remember my dad coming up to me and handing me an article he found in *HR Magazine* (Watches and Lifestyles). He said "Hey, Illinois made wristwatches, too!" (My great-grandfather passed down to my dad an Illinois pocket watch and he was always intrigued with the company.) The article showed a beautiful "Jolly Roger," and the author said, "So while the rest of you are showing off your $3,000 to $10,000 2008 stainless steel creation, I will dazzle the crowd with my under $1,500 Illinois Jolly Roger." I remember staring at the shape of this watch with the beautiful engraving and font on the dial . . . and I was determined to find one of these watches if it killed me . . . The hunt was on.

Game On!

So how does a super collector really think and what makes someone cross the line from casual collector to obsessed hunter? Believe me, once you get one, you are going to want another one. What I have learned to do is pace myself; this "sport" is a marathon, not a sprint.

The first thing a rookie will do is drool and get all excited ready to hit the "Buy It Now" button (on eBay). Experience tells me to wait, take a deep breath and assess the auction very quickly. Where is the product? Who is the seller? How much do I really need this? What condition is the watch really in? A photo speaks one thousand words and good clear photos can be your best friend. I look at the dial first; are the minute tracks right? Is it a re-dial? The bezel; I go right to the corners. So many people miss this easy trick. A worn bezel is so easy to miss and so is the fine wear on the edges of the case back. If all seems good, what is the movement like? Does it run? How many jewels? Was it recently serviced? (Do I care?) Is it rare? I can do all this in about one minute.

Persistence

So many people ask me: "How did you find that?!" Luck, maybe; persistence, for sure. If you really want to be good at this, you must know your hunting grounds. There are dozens of sites I check on a daily, yes, daily basis. Things pop up randomly and if you cast the net wide, you are more likely to grab the bigger fish. From small jewelry stores, to other collectors, to forum sales to every possible watch-related site I can find; they are in my "favorites" and many times checked late at night or an early strike in the morning. I have scored many rarities by this very methodical and consistent process of looking.

This game is one of records; I know every watch I bought, from whom, what price I paid and when; this comes in very handy when dealing with a seller. Repeat customers almost always get first priority when two people are interested in a watch. If I find someone with one Illinois, the first thing I ask is: "Do you have any others that I don't know about?" This simple question has yielded some super scores!

I recently tracked down a very rare movement that a collector refused to sell. The person didn't have the proper case for it, but I did. When I explained that I was a collector and not a dealer, the person warmed up to the idea of putting an original piece of horology back together. I must have had a dozen emails and calls back and forth with the seller. After six months, the deal was made. Many folks fear that what they own will be flipped for a quick buck and the preservation of the brand is something that most people are happy to do. I shared photos of the final product with the seller and he was thrilled that he was a part of Illinois history for future generations to enjoy. I try to look at all this as saving a true piece of Americana, a very rewarding experience.

Think Outside of the Box

This is something most people never do; they look at the same places and never venture outside of their comfort zone. I have found amazing finds by simply looking in places I never checked out before. Almost every city has a large jewelry store or antique district. The bigger ones have websites and a call to see if they have any Illinois watches lying around never can hurt. On a recent trip to Florida, I decided to hit all the gold buying/ pawn shop type stores I passed by. I left my name and number with the manager telling them I would almost always pay more for an Illinois watch than its gold melt value, call me first!

I scour the Internet for hours sometimes looking in different places I normally don't look at. Just remember, not everything is always posted on someone's website, and a simple call to ask if they have anything Illinois that is not on the site has also yielded some treats.

Know Your Competition and Make Friends with Other Collectors

I have made friends with just about all the major collectors of all the major vintage brands out there; I know what they need and they keep an eye out for Illinois for me. I get calls all the time from other collectors who have spotted something good for me and grabbed it knowing I will return the favor someday. I have, on occasion, checked with a friend to see if they were bidding on an item so we didn't fight over the same watch; no need to drive up a price for a friend!

Know Everything About Your Brand

I have learned so much from reading Fred's first book; I have worn the pages down from reading it so many times. I have studied and memorized every model, movement and possible known combination in case something pops up in the wild. Know your brand well and it will pay off down the road. This especially comes in handy with dials. Over the years dials have been switched and swapped, winding up on the wrong case. The dial is one of the most important things on the watch and to find them in great condition will increase the value of the watch for sure. I have bought many entire watches just for the dial.

Study Shapes and Sizes

A great photo can be nice but a fuzzy photo can be your best friend. I have studied the shapes and sizes of all the known watches to memory. In my travels, I have seen horrible photos but could make out a clear shape that I used to figure out what the watch actually was. Many sellers will throw a bunch of watches in a pile, take a photo, and sell it as a "Lot." Among the pile, knowing the shape of a watch can yield a nice score.

Look At It Like a Second Job

This is a second job, period. We all have a dream that an engraved "Piccadilly" will pop up on eBay with a "Buy It Now" for $50 bucks, but the chances are slim; and most likely, the more you keep your eyes open and put in the extra time, the more you will get the big scores. Look all over the web early in the morning and late at night; you never know when or where a "find" will pop up.

Not just on the web either. NAWCC events still have lots of things pop up. If you can't attend, have a friend keep an eye out for you and text a photo of a potential purchase. I recently had a good friend find a solid yellow gold Illinois "Ace" this way. Good friends are essential in this game.

Look at Rarity Versus Cost to Fix

Here is a constant dilemma. You see a great watch at a good price but it doesn't work. If the watch is not worth much in the first place, you have to calculate and factor in your repair costs. I love watches that are sold as broken or not working or for parts only. This scares off most people who have no way of getting these watches fixed or fear the cost to repair is not worth it. A great watchmaker is the first thing you should get, but we will get to that later.

Start From Hard to Easier

If watches are easy to get, then don't worry about them now; start off on the more difficult ones and work your way down to the easier later. There are always guys looking to sell the easier-to-find examples. Get a few entry-level ones to get a feel for the brand, but when you get serious, think rarity.

Get a Really Good Watchmaker

This is the most important thing you need to do. When I first started collecting, I had a wonderful watchmaker who did great work. He also charged me an arm and a leg as I learned later. Ask your friends, go onto forums, check around the web; whatever you do, have someone you can trust that has access to original parts and you will never fear that broken watch for sale again.

Get another good watchmaker. Have a few guys that are good at different watch related things. There are case restorers, dial guys, movement masters and crystal folks. Know all the players you can in the watch business; you never know who you will need for what.

Hunt Down Parts and Save Them For a Rainy Day

I am always on the lookout for parts, any and all parts: spare movements, dials, cases, hands, crystals, crowns, whatever. These were made in abundance back in the day and to have a supply of NOS or solid replacement parts is a huge help down the line. That spare part will come in handy someday, believe me!

Dials, Dials, Dials!

Fred and I both came to the realization that sometimes we have both bought watches just for the dials. Many folks have come to understand that the dial is one of the most important features of the watch. There are many examples where the dial is very hard to come by and hunting for the right one can be a daunting task. Over the years, many watchmakers swapped dials, cases and other parts into different watches. There is nothing more exciting than finding a NOS rare Illinois "Chatham" "broken line" dial in the wrong case. This happened to me and I just happened to have an extra case looking for that dial.

I am very against a redial as is Fred. Many folks out there want to have their dials clean and looking like new, so they get a poor dial refinished. A true collector will take a poor original over a redial any day.

No Exact Science

To this day, there are new and exciting things being discovered about the Illinois brand. Just when I think I have seen it all, I will pop off the back of a watch and discover something that I haven't seen before. Almost one hundred years later this brand is still bringing enjoyment, wonderment and excitement. The folks in Springfield really knew what they were doing. How many things bought off the shelf today will be cool, collected and still working next century? Most of it will wind up in a landfill, I am sure.

—Greg Hart

WHY I COLLECT ILLINOIS

What can be said about the excitement of a new book on Illinois Watches by Fred Friedberg?

Fred is perhaps the closest we will become to H. G. Wells' *Time Traveler.* But here, these amazing *"time machines"* themselves are the story. With Fred's works, we are transported to a time, to an iconic era, descriptions evoked with just one word: deco, prohibition, Gatsby. Whisked away to a place and time, where American ingenuity and craftsmanship meant simply the best and unparalleled technology; where we learn of amazing designs with such descriptive names, from the Jolly Roger to the Ritz.

Fred delivers to us a glimpse of these marvels of the era. Now we know each model's rarity and original cost, what metals it came in and how rare they are, the development of the Illinois Watch Company itself, and the Bunn family.

Collecting these amazing "time machines" is the equivalent of wanting a first edition printing of a Fitzgerald novel, a vintage car, or even as simple as a special coin or stamp. Why? In its purest form, it is a direct connection; a link for the collector to experience that earlier moment; the joy of collecting . . . studying . . . appreciating. Collecting watches is the perfect blend of reaching that direct connection with a past time, and rational functionality. Cars take space. Books gather dust. But a vintage Illinois watch that can be appreciated and worn, combining artistry with the simplicity of the function of telling the time. Don't look at the ubiquitous cell phone for the time; appreciate the beauty on your wrist. Recall a simpler time when the wristwatch was a marvel of new fashion and technology. Fred's books tell the story displayed on your wrist of these amazing engineers, craftsmen, artisans. From the precision watchmakers to the dial painters, unknowingly damaging their health and life for their art.

Unfortunately, the Illinois Watch Company did not survive into the 21st Century. But the craft of these engineers and artists did, for us to study, understand and appreciate. Now, over eight decades after the company's demise, Fred has done an amazing job preserving the history of the company, and is now certainly the unofficial "Company Historian." Thanks to Fred, the memory and history of this amazing company, its technology and art will be preserved for at least another 100 years. The Bunn family would be proud of this appreciation and preservation of their accomplishments.

—Hank Greenblatt

ILLINOIS' VIEW OF WATCH COLLECTING

In March 1931, a jeweler contacted the Illinois Watch Company and asked if it had any interest in buying back an old Illinois watch belonging to a customer. The Illinois Sales Department replied, in part:

"We regret, however, that we would have no use whatever in this old Illinois watch. We are in possession of the first and second, third and fourth watches ever manufactured by the Illinois Watch Company, together with one of each of the models we have made, and as we have no desire to increase this collection, the watch in question would be of no value to us.

"The only suggestion we could offer would be that you get in touch with some watch collector who would be interested in the purchase of this old timepiece. We do not know where you could reach anyone making the collection of old watches a hobby. . ." If they only knew then what we know now!

INDIVIDUAL

F. E. Sackett,
Stone Mountain, Ga.

Dear Sir:

We are pleased to acknowledge receipt of your letter of March 4th, regarding an old Illinois watch which is owned by one of your customers who desires to dispose of it.

We regret, however, that we would have no use whatever for this old Illinois watch, We are in possession of the first and second, third and fourth watches ever manufactured by the Illinois Watch Company, together with one of each of the models we have made, and as we have no desire to increase this collection the watch in question would be of no value to us.

The only suggestion we could offer would be that you get in touch with some watch collector who could be interested in the purchase of this old timepiece. We do not know where you could reach anyone making the collection of old watches a hobby, unless this information could be supplied through the Commerce Department, Washington, D. C. or from Mr. Frederick J. Haskins, Washington, D. C.

Thanking you for your inquiry and trusting what we have been able to tell you will be helpful, we are

Very truly yours,

THE ILLINOIS WATCH

AGS:ALD By-

Illinois letter regarding watch collecting

Collector Interviews

To help explain the allure of collecting Illinois watches, I interviewed four collectors located in four different regions of the United States. The questions were asked by me (FJF) and the replies were from Farrell Gay (FG), Greg Hart (GH), Jim Mason (JM) and Rick Vess (RV). The interview follows:

1. **FJF: What is your favorite Illinois wristwatch case design feature?**

GH: I have always been fascinated with the "Skyway" case and its screw-on caseback and bezel features. The fact that so few of these cases survived without being pried apart and ruined is amazing. You would think that the Watch Company would have made some note to alert owners that this was not your normal pop-off case. Imagine the frustration of an unknowing watchmaker going nuts trying to figure this out. I love that there are stars on the back of the caseback just like the front. The fact that there are 5 different dial variations of this watch is a testament to the "cool factor" of this incredible case.

JM: Art Deco design that was pushed further than among their competitors at the time. (This isn't a single feature: if I had to pick one, it would be interplay of the straight lines on the bezel of the Ritz with the steps on the midcase.)

RV: I'm a big fan of two-tone wristwatches, and Illinois likely offered more two-tone models than any other early watchmaker. (I also collect Hamilton wristwatches, and although there was a time when most collectors thought that Hamilton had offered two-tones in all of their early solid gold Geometric models, now it's known that they might have only made them in the Square and Square B for maybe one year; the rest are just tarnished yellow.) The fact that two-tone Illinois models came in both solid gold models and gold-filled models means examples are available at all prices for all levels of collectors. I should also say that I'm not a big fan of most round watches, so I tend to focus on rectangular-shaped cases.

FG: My favorites are any Deco cases with interesting engraving and/or inlaid enamel.

WHY I COLLECT ILLINOIS

I'm not sure I can tell you much in a rational way why I collect Illinois (in as limited a way as I do, given that I collect a few other brands also, as you know). I think it has much to do with the aesthetics of their designs, perhaps also with the evocative nature of the model names. I have been interested in the '20s and '30s period for a long time; Art Deco and Art Moderne styles, aesthetics, music culture. I also collect original recordings of this period, *inter alia*, and vintage phonographs. I first began collecting Hamiltons in the late '90s. It took quite a while before I felt I knew something about this hobby—a lot of trial and error. The Internet's wealth of information certainly helped. (Obsessively, I accumulated jpegs and gifs of various watches.) Illinois came soon after. And then there was your book to inspire me. I'm not nearly as obsessive about all of it as some other collectors we both know, but I think I have a nice core Illinois collection (but still no Piccadilly!)

—*Adam Dubin*

2. **FJF: What is your favorite Illinois wristwatch dial design feature?**

   GH: The dial is the most important part of the watch, in my opinion, next to case wear. I am a sucker for almost any sparkle finish dial. I also go nuts for an authentic black dial variation of a normal white dial. And I love a drop-shadow numeral dial as well. I think that putting a butler center on the sub 6 area is also fascinating.

   JM: Today it's the moiré dials on some pocket watches and ladies' watches. Tomorrow it might be sparkle finish or something else.

   RV: The Consul sunburst dial and Consul pinstripe dial are my favorite Illinois dials. Both are terrific!

   FG: I love the dials with the special sparkle finish.

3. **FJF: What is your favorite Illinois wristwatch movement feature, if any?**

   GH: When I open a watch and see damaskeen on a 307, it just makes my heart pound. I have two aluminum movements and they are simply incredible to look at, true works of art.

   JM: General high quality of design and construction. Some special features: micrometric regulators on 3/0 size, motor barrels on 6/0. I tend to think of Illinois movements as being just good, solid movements, at least as good as anything made in America. In the time when Illinois was making watches, there wasn't the urge to add expensive complications for the sake of showing technical prowess (like modern tourbillions). I supposed the Illinois Motor Barrel was pushing wristwatch design pretty far for the time.

   RV: While I tend to focus on cases and dials more than movements, nice 21 jewel, 6/0 movements (601 and 909) are terrific runners. I also like the damaskeening on the 607A and 307 movements.

   FG: None. They are all good.

4. **FJF: What do you find most appealing about Illinois wristwatches?**

   GH: The incredible variety of shapes and designs just boggles the mind. The more you collect these things, the more you realize just how special they are and the amount of effort and thought went into them. The products that came out of the Factory still turn heads generations later.

   JM: General Art Deco design, much more extreme than the contemporary competition.

   RV: I'm a contrarian by nature, so I like the fact that they are neither common nor well known by non-collectors.

   FG: Appealing? More likely a dedication! I lived in Springfield for 15 years before I knew anything about the Illinois Watch Company. My first introduction to the Watch Factory was in 1979 when my two partners and I purchased the two square blocks that was the home of the Illinois Watch Company and the Sangamo Electric Company. It took me a while, but when I did learn about these two incredible companies and their impact on Springfield, Illinois, it was then I decided I would do my best to keep them both "alive," at least in Springfield. I began to collect Illinois wristwatches and, to a smaller extent, Sangamo electric clocks. That passion with Illinois wristwatches was more than appealing, it was a dedication. The collection is well known in the city and has often been displayed in the

Elijah Iles House – Museum of Springfield History (1837).

5. **FJF: What are your top five favorite Illinois wristwatches?**

GH: Jolly Roger
Skyway
Varsity
Chevalier
Admiral Evans

JM: (I'm taking this to be watches in my collection.) In no particular order: Ritz, Jolly Roger, Chieftain, Consul, New Yorker Enamel YGF.

RV: Consul green gold engraved, Consul two-tone engraved, Jolly Roger white engraved, Marquis two-tone engraved, Ritz.

FG: Men's in no special order: Akron, Piccadilly fully-engraved bezel, Decagon, Jr. 14KYG (personal engraving on back and dated 9-24-18, St. Louis, MO), Police Special, Major w/ custom dial, shows sunset, lagoon, palm tree.

6. **FJF: Do you also collect Illinois pocket watches?**

GH: I only have a few. It was, in fact, an Illinois pocket watch passed down from my great-grandfather that got me into collecting Illinois wristwatches. My dad and I both collect them now.

JM: I started my Illinois watch collection with a 60-hour 23J Sangamo Special and I still collect pocket watches. I have more wristwatches than pocket watches because railroad-grade pocket watches are more expensive than a lot of wristwatches.

RV: No, I can't figure out how to attach an alligator wrist strap to one.

FG: Only a select few.

7. **FJF: Do you also collect other brands of wristwatches?**

GH: Before I started seriously concentrating on Illinois, I dabbled in many different brands, mostly American and a few Swiss, all vintage. Once I found Illinois, it was all over.

JM: Hamilton (I have almost as many as Illinois), Elgin, Bulova, plus a scattering of Gruen, Omega, and Waltham. With Illinois, it's now the result of a deliberate effort to find more watches; with the others it's the occasional purchase of something that catches my eye.
RV: Yes, the focus of my collection is early Art Deco models from Illinois, Hamilton, Elgin, and Gruen, but I have a few other makers also. I also like later asymmetrical watches from Hamilton and 1930s–1950s Pierce chronographs.

FG: No, have always stayed with Illinois.

8. **FJF: Would you encourage others to collect Illinois wristwatches?**

GH: Here is what I have to say about this. Illinois watches are like a Lay's potato chip; you can't have just one. Do your homework before buying and you will have a blast. If you don't have Fred's books, you are wasting your time and will not be an informed collector, I see it all the time with the rookies. The last thing you want to do is needlessly waste time and money, and that happens when someone buys something they "think" is a good deal instead of "knowing" it is a good deal. Just have fun collecting them!

WHY I COLLECT ILLINOIS

I became enamored with the beauty of Illinois watches as a child. Every week or so, my paternal grandfather would hit the pawn shops and bring home an old pocket watch or two. Over time, he had quite a collection, and I can well remember that whenever he would get an Illinois, I would go with my father to see exactly what model he had acquired. They were all different, with different dials and cases, and I can remember specifically the intrigue I had looking over my father's shoulders as he sat with his father discussing the merits and condition of those beautiful, ticking, time machines from the past. I knew little of what I was looking at or of what jargon they were speaking but only that I was mesmerized by those beautiful movements and their rhythmic ticking. Their mysterious past was also fascinating for me to contemplate at such a young and innocent age . . . but I would learn much in the coming years.

Fast forward a dozen years or so and I became a pilot, traveling the country for a major airline and suddenly had the time, desire, means and hopes to acquire a collection of my own. The problem was, while I greatly enjoyed and appreciated them, I still knew so little of what I was buying in regard to rarity or correct components, at first. I would buy one and, with great anticipation, take it over to show my dad; and, without fail, every time he would find something wrong with it. Even though it was running fine, he would find some component that was either wrong, missing, or slightly damaged, and it would greatly disappoint me. He would gently laugh and encourage me to pay more attention to details next time and remind me that problems are the reason most watches are for sale.

I was intensely determined to remedy my ignorance and began reading Bill Meggers' book on Illinois, from 1985; numerous times . . . and then several more. The trouble with that was it still did not answer or satisfy all my hundreds of questions, but it did fuel my lust for becoming an expert on Illinois watches. So I began doing my own intense research, recording numbers, details and making hundreds of notes on all details of the many different models and variants. I also began to acquaint myself with the best collectors in the country at various shows and began attending auctions and frequented many large metropolitan shops on my travels. It was tons of fun, and the years went much too fast. I didn't realize it at the time, but because it was before the Internet, I had the ability to find some really great watches, at reasonable prices, before the "market" caught up. My research and information served me well in those years and in conjunction with doing my homework to develop some great contacts, I was also blessed with a little luck and some great timing, all of which gave me an advantage to build a great collection, over time.

After a couple of decades and well over ten thousand hours of research, I could hold my own with about any one of the Illinois gurus and usually give them a pointer or two regarding a detail they had missed or never known. While that level of experience is satisfying, I find, more importantly, that I'm still learning and occasionally something new will turn up, which will re-spark my interest and fire me back up like I was in my younger years. As a good friend of mine always says, "You know, we still haven't seen it all . . . yet."

Yet, if I could give just one reason why I still enjoy Illinois watches and still maintain a very small collection of my favorite, rare variants, I would be compelled to say that I still find them amazing. There are so many styles and variants to enjoy, with different dials and cases of various fashions, all of which are still like eye candy to me, even today. Much the same reason I loved them as a child, they truly have a fit and finish that is still astounding to me. I know, too, that left undamaged and with a little oil and servicing, their soft, smooth ticking can last a thousand years or more, and their sound gives me such a feeling of relaxation. From time to time, I still fantasize about the stories they might tell, if they could only talk! Basically, the watches take me back to my childhood, and there I am again, out in the yard on a lazy summer afternoon with my father and grandfather looking at a quality timepiece; made in a slower period of time, when America was at its industrial peak and pride in one's work and integrity stood for something. Something special . . . and that's what Illinois watches represent to me and why I collect them. They do indeed have a special quality and beauty that I have enjoyed most all my life.
Happy Hunting!

—Mike Chamelin

JM: Yes, except I hate to encourage the competition!

RV: Yes, but I secretly hope they ignore me.

FG: Yes, all the time.

9. **FJF: What are your Illinois collecting objectives?**

GH: When I first started out, all I wanted was to get all the watches on the front cover of Fred's first book. Then the back cover, then every known model in almost every combination. At this point, I want to have the greatest and rarest collection of Illinois ever put together. I am getting there . . . The quest never ends.

JM: I keep asking myself this. I guess it's to get some cool watches to wear.

RV: I focus on watches large enough for me to wear, so unlike my friend Greg H., I have no interest in owning every model. That said, I am a sucker for the models I do like . . . so while I have allowed some to wander off, I have more than a dozen Marquis and quite a few Consuls, Jolly Rogers, and Ritz models.

FG: To have the best and most complete collection of wristwatches and Illinois Watch Co. ephemera ever assembled.

10. **FJF: What is your favorite series of Illinois wristwatches?**

GH: I think case Model Number 196 fascinates me the most. Think of all the cool variations of this that came out from the Chesterfield, Stepped Bezel, Finalist and Finalist Deco. A very sleek and clean design that just works.

JM: In theory, watches with 207 movements; in practice, judging by how many I have, the Beau series, followed by the Marquis series.

RV: Marquis and Consul.

FG: New Yorker, Manhattan, Fifth Avenue, Yorktown, Richmond 6/0 and the New Yorker Enamel series is my favorite.

11. **FJF: What is your most prized Illinois wristwatch acquisition?**

GH: I have to tell you, there are quite a few. Anytime I find something that is the only known example, I get nuts. I have to say, I have quite a few of these. I get really excited when I put on the Akron. It is so light, and I really prize this watch, because it never really went into production and I wish it had.

JM: That I bought for myself, the Varsity; that I was given, the New Yorker Enamel.

RV: While I have located a few rare examples (the second sub-6 Marquis and the only known two-tone plain bezel Marquis), my favorite watch is my green gold Consul. If I lost it somehow, my two-tone plain Marquis would be my most prized Illinois. I would have a hard time replacing my green Consul as there are very few, and no collector who has one would sell theirs to me or likely anyone else.

FG: Akron.

NOT JUST MERE DOLLARS AND CENTS

The Illinois Watch Company in 1931 had no knowledge of or interest in collecting old Illinois watches, but did opine that such a watch may "have a greater sentimental value attached to it than just mere dollars and cents, and would mean much more to you as a keepsake."

INDIVIDUAL

March 7th, 1931.

Gentlemen:

We are pleased to acknowledge receipt of your letter of February 16th, regarding an old Illinois watch which you have in your possession, given you by a jeweler some twenty years ago.

It is gratifying to us to know that it is still giving satisfactory service. However, we regret to advise that we would have no use for this watch of yours, as we have never called in old timepieces, and the only old watches which we keep here are the first and second watches ever manufactured by the Illinois Watch Company, together with one of each of the models we have made.

The value of the watch you have would depend upon how much you would be able to get for it. No doubt, some jeweler would be willing to make you a fair allowance for your old Illinois watch to apply upon the purchase price of a new one. The allowance he could make would depend upon the quality and price of the new model that you would purchase. On the other hand, it may have a greater sentimental value attached to it, than just mere dollars and cents, and would mean much more to you as a keepsake.

Thanking you for your inquiry and assuring you of our appreciation of your interest in Illinois watches, we are

Very truly yours,

THE ILLINOIS WATCH

AGS:ALD By

"Keepsake" letter

12. FJF: What Illinois wristwatch do you desire the most that you do not currently own?

GH: Do I need to answer this?

JM: Radial dial green Jolly Roger and plain Consul with pinstriped dial. (My wife jokes that she really wants the Eagle but would accept a Skyway; she doesn't have an Illinois "bird" wristwatch, just pocket watches.)

RV: The Eagle, I guess, or maybe a few of the uber-rare Consul variations.

FG: A Greyhound.

13. FJF: What watch is the rarest Illinois wristwatch in your view?

GH: What is it like to own the only known example of an Illinois watch? It is great until some guy comes into the room and says, "Hey I have one of those!" I must have a dozen or more one-off examples and they are all very special.

JM: Probably some one-off custom beast like the Eagle; other than that, I don't have enough firsthand data to have an informed opinion. (Maybe the Akron?)

RV: I guess any watch, like my two-tone plain Marquis, where only one is known. That said, if I could acquire any, it would likely be the Eagle. Although I have always doubted if the case was truly made for an Illinois, it is still a strikingly amazing watch.

FG: Akron.

14. FJF: Do you repair your own wristwatches?

GH: I can take the movements out, change dials, and do light cleaning of dials and change bands. Other than that, I have the best Illinois repair guy on the planet.

JM: Yes, when it's within my skill set.

RV: I am happy to do my own dial cleaning. I can also swap hands, dials, stems, crowns, but I am unable to do serious work on movements . . . I wish I could!

FG: No, I do not.

15. FJF: Have you found excellent Illinois repairpersons?

GH: My guy took years to find, and the first thing I bought him was your first book. The second thing I bought him was a big storage cabinet, and I continue to send him parts, parts, and more parts to fix, repair and maintain my collection.

JM: The guy who sold me my first Illinois and has been my primary mentor in watch repair.

RV: Thankfully, I am friends with Ed Kulha, so he does most of the work on my watches. I have tried others, but Ed is amazingly honest and also very capable for the vast majority of the work I need done.

FG: Yes, I have always been fortunate in that regard.

16. FJF: Is finding parts ever a problem?

GH: I spend just as much time looking for parts as I do watches these days. You can never have enough spare parts!

JM: Certainly, but I buy parts movements whenever possible.

RV: Sometimes—I have now been collecting watches for almost 15 years and Illinois for about 12 years. Over the years, I have bought extra movements and plenty of mainsprings, stems, crowns, etc. for all of the watches I have. Normally, the hardest part is sorting through thousands of old stock cases to find the proper crown I need for the watch I'm working on.

FG: They are getting more and more scarce.

17. **FJF: How do you prefer to purchase Illinois wristwatches?**

GH: Through trusted friends and the web. I have dozens of sites I check on a regular basis.

JM: I have a few that came from individual collectors, but most of mine came off eBay. That's about the only way to get them around here; I've never been to a show or to any store other than my mentor's.

RV: It depends on the model. If it is a very rare example, I will buy whatever condition I can find. However, since I focus on watches large enough to wear, I also focus on wrist-worthy examples. While I won't buy junk, I am more than happy to buy watches or parts that need service or repair.

FG: From trusted friends like Fred, and eBay and NAWCC Shows.

18. **FJF: Does the great scarcity of some of the Illinois models diminish your enthusiasm for collecting Illinois wristwatches?**

GH: Not at all. Just when I think I have seen it all, a super-rare Illinois pops up on the market and it is fun to watch all the collectors go crazy.

JM: Not at all. The challenge makes collecting more interesting.

RV: Not really—there are more nice examples out there still undiscovered.

FG: Not in the least.

19. **FJF: What is the best part of collecting Illinois wristwatches?**

GH: The community of collectors is amazing and the friendships I have developed over the years is something I could have never expected. Collectors are generally happy to share knowledge and resources when they can. A super bunch of great guys for the most part.

JM: 1. Getting cool watches to wear.
2. Meeting other crazy people who are obsessed with Illinois.

RV: I just love the smell of bubble wrap in the morning! Seriously, unwrapping an incoming USPS shipment is exciting when I know a new Illinois is inside.

FG: Finding a rare specimen.

20. **FJF: What is the worst part of collecting Illinois wristwatches?**

GH: It is very addicting. I need an AA program for Illinois watches. The tough part is keeping track of the collection when it gets really big and just when you think you have them all, another rarity pops up and you go crazy trying to get it. Start with a few and take it slow, as I have come to learn, there are so many cool combinations of these watches. Enjoy the hunt.

JM: That I'll probably never be able to afford some I'd like.

RV: Knowing that the prices will continue to increase into the future. I have already seen prices on the Consul double in the last 10 years, and I have a feeling that this trend will continue.

FG: Not buying a watch when you had the opportunity.

21. FJF: Do you also collect Illinois ladies' wristwatches?

GH: I stick to men's. My girl has a few ladies.

JM: That's my wife's territory, though I help her maintain them.

RV: Not really, but with a daughter and wife, over the years I have acquired a few of them . . . I guess I should give the watches to them one day.

FG: Yes, very often.

22. FJF: Do you have a favorite Illinois ladies' wristwatch?

GH: Miami with blue or red enamel . . . An incredible watch.

JM: Hard to choose: almost any of the ones with enamel bezels.

RV: I prefer those with enamel bezels and 6-sided bezel openings. Favorites include the Berkeley, Redonda, Roslyn, Del Monte, and the Miami.

FG: Several, but I'll mention two. (1) Berkeley 14K yellow gold, with red and black inlaid enamel; (2) 18K green gold Mary Todd.

23. FJF: Do you wear your Illinois wristwatches daily?

GH: Yes, I mix and match, depending on the mood.

JM: I buy watches to wear, even the Varsity. I wear a lot of the Illinois, but many of them can't be worn during the week because I can't take radium dials where I work.

RV: Yes, I have a dozen or so I rotate among most often.

FG: Usually, but not on days when I playing golf.

24. FJF: How often do you change the Illinois wristwatch that you wear?

GH: I hardly wear the same one for more than a day or two.

JM: I change watches almost every day. Sometimes I mix brands, but sometimes I do a week of Illinois or Hamilton or Elgin.

RV: Daily.

FG: Runs in spurts. I will pick out 5 or 6 pieces and rotate them for a couple of weeks and then repeat the same process with 5 or 6 more.

25. FJF: Do you have a least favorite Illinois wristwatch?

GH: Interesting, the Chatham and Standish are some of the rarest and most valuable Illinois there are, due to their rarity, but they are not very exciting in shape and design compared to some earlier models. I still like them though.

JM: No. I sometimes take a contrarian view that I couldn't see myself wearing a Piccadilly, but there isn't an Illinois that I really don't like.

RV: I'm not a big fan of the early 1930s Hamilton-like tank watches—like the Varsity, No. 250/Schmukler, and others of the like.

FG: No, like them all.

26. FJF: From a condition point of view, what is the most important thing to consider when buying an Illinois wristwatch?

GH: Dial first, is it in good shape or not? I love dials. Case condition next, is there too much case wear for the rarity of the model? If it is a common model, wait for one to come up in better condition.

JM: 1. Case. 2. Dial.

RV: When looking at gold-filled cases, I pay close attention to bezel, lug, and back wear. I hate seeing this wear when I'm wearing a watch. Obviously, a clean aged (original) dial is preferred also.

FG: I prefer no case wear.

27. FJF: Would you buy an Illinois wristwatch that is not running?

GH: I prefer them not running. Chances are they will sell for less and hopefully they have less wear and abuse because someone didn't bother to get it fixed and left it sitting in a drawer. I once bought a super-rare Piccadilly that had been sitting in a watchmaker's drawer for decades. My watchmaker got it running in a day. It was in incredible shape.

JM: Have done it many times; I'm not afraid to get into the movement.

RV: Every day!

FG: Yes, I often do. This is not a problem.

28. FJF: Would you buy an Illinois wristwatch that has case wear?

GH: Rarer the watch the more case wear I will tolerate. Always trade up.

JM: I have to; pristine ones are too rare and too expensive.

RV: Yes, but not on a common model.

FG: Only if it would fill a gap in the collection until I find a better example.

29. FJF: Would you buy an Illinois wristwatch that has a poor original dial?

GH: Poor original trumps redial any day for value. Just my opinion, but a great redial can change my mind for wearing it around.

JM: Sure, though it's hard to get replacements for some.

RV: Yes, I am not adverse to a well redone dial, but I obviously prefer nice original dials. That said, I think many to most dials that collectors think of as original are actually aged redone dials . . . likely from a servicing in the 1930s or 1940s when redoing the dial was just a standard part of every service.

FG: Yes, I often do. This is not a problem.

30. FJF: Do you ever get your dials refinished?

GH: Only sent one dial to ID (International Dial), it came out great. Found an original and swapped it out.

JM: On a Hamilton or Elgin, occasionally; on an Illinois, never yet.

RV: Yes, International Dial does a nice job on most. Eagle Dial does nice work also if they have the proper plate/die.

FG: Yes, but only to give to friends, non-collectors, and charity groups for auctions.

31. FJF: Would you buy an Illinois that has a redone dial?

GH: Sure, would just go on the hunt for an original someday.

JM: Yes, if it's a good job and it's on a case I want: I look at the whole package.

RV: Yes, gladly. Thankfully I have collected quite a few old dials, so I am sometimes able to locate a proper aged or original dial to replace for a poor redone dial.

FG: Yes, can always replace it.

32. FJF: Would you ever get a worn case replated?

GH: Have done it only once. It has to be done right using real gold. I was a rookie.

JM: Not on an Illinois. I've had it done once on a rare Hamilton that needed major surgery.

RV: Only if I was having a broken lug repaired. I know a great goldsmith who does nice spot work on cases. That said, I hate poorly replated cases, as they do not hold up to wear.

FG: No.

33. FJF: Have you ever regretted the purchase of an Illinois watch?

GH: I bought a Skyway dial in a generic case and it turned out to be a redial. Again, I was a rookie.

JM: No.

RV: Sure, but I have regretted more that I have not bought and even more that I have sold or traded.

FG: Yes, we all make mistakes.

34. FJF: Do you also collect Illinois ephemera?

GH: I love this stuff! I think one of my favorites is my solid gold "30 Year Club" pin given to workers at the Factory who put in 30 years of service. So cool!

JM: Yes, particularly advertising and catalogs.

RV: Not really, but I do collect old original boxes, cases, and the Illinois Lincoln medals.

FG: Yes! All I can find.

35. FJF: What advice, in twenty-five words or less, would you give to a new Illinois collector?

GH: Simple: buy Fred's books first so you can do your homework and make educated decisions before buying anything. Then, make friends with other collectors!

JM: Keep looking.

RV: When you see a watch you want, don't delay as someone else will want it too!

FG: Get copies of Fred's books and read them thoroughly. Have an idea what you would like (and can afford), and get your feet wet.

36. FJF: What do you most look forward to reading about in this new box set?

GH: I have always been fascinated as to why this incredible company, at the height of success and innovation, was acquired by Hamilton and basically erased from the planet. A collector can only dream what would have happened if Hamilton had just run Illinois as a totally separate company and let it "do its thing." I am also so excited to see all the new discoveries and names of watches you have discovered since the last book. It will be hard to top your first book, but I bet you will!

JM: Finding out what's been learned since the first book.

RV: I want to know more about the purchase by Hamilton—both before and after the move to Lancaster. I know that Fred's research will be gold!

FG: Finding out new discoveries previously unknown.

These are just four of the incredible and wonderful friends that I have made collecting Illinois wristwatches. Many others have helped tremendously in the preparation of these books, as described in the acknowledgments. Most Illinois collectors are this bright, engaging, and interesting, and the value of these friendships far exceeds that of my Illinois collection.

Chapter 14

Test Your Knowledge

Purely for fun, take the following rather lengthy quiz. The answers to all the questions are contained in this book, although some answers may not be readily obvious. This is meant to be an open-book quiz with no time limit, so please enjoy it at your own pace. Each correct answer is worth 2 points; thus a perfect score is 1,500 points. Eventually I will place the answers on my website **illinoiswatches.com.** In the meantime, if you get stuck on any question or have a question concerning a query, please contact me at **fred@illinoiswatches.com** or **fredric777@gmail.com.** Have fun, and good luck!

1. Name six Factory-Cased unidentified Illinois men's wristwatch models.

2. How many original Consul dials with subsidiary seconds at 6 are known to exist?

3. How many employees did Waltham have at the end of January 1932?

4. Name an 18k solid gold Factory-Cased Illinois wristwatch.

5. Who was Ross Atkinson?

6. Name the Illinois wristwatch model H. A. Osgood sold.

7. Name three Illinois men's models that share the same dial.

8. Name the watch company that was located on Lexington Avenue in Brooklyn, New York.

9. Which Illinois model that Illinois sold in a yellow gold-filled case shared its case design with a white gold-filled Waltham case and a yellow rolled gold plate Elgin case?

10. What was Richter & Phillips?

11. Name the watch company promoter who was the mayor of Chicago twice.

12. What was the name of the first Illinois wristwatch offered for sale?

13. Name the publisher of the *Keystone* in the late 1920s.

14. What was advertised as "a quick-acting stimulator of sales"?

15. What country was the largest manufacturer of clocks and watches in 1925?

16. Name the Illinois men's wristwatch model that came in 14K and 10K gold-filled cases?

17. How many jewels are in a size 3/0, grade 25 movement?

18. What was referred to as "a promiscuous affair"?

19. Name the watch company started by John C. Adams in Lancaster.

20. Name three men that served as the president of the Hamilton Watch Company.

21. What were Hamilton sales in 1935?

22. Name an Illinois model that came with two different lug sizes?

23. What casemaker manufactured watches signed "E. Howard Watch Co."?

24. What lawmakers drafted national price maintenance legislation?

25. Who was Edward B. Duncuff?

26. Name two Illinois sales managers.

27. Who was considered Beckwith's protégé?

28. Name the jobber that wanted to return thirty-two watches to Illinois in early 1932.

29. What made the dollar famous?

30. Name the person that maintained the Illinois Price List "Bible."

31. What model was dial #8745 used for?

32. Did Burlington Watch Company sell wristwatches?

33. Name four Illinois models that came with 21 jewels.

34. What is another name for a Westchester?

35. Who bought the Bay State Watch Case Company?

36. Name the union that the Hamilton Watch Workers Union was affiliated with.

37. Which Illinois model was advertised as "a clever design"?

38. Name an inventor that sold his inventions to at least two different watch bracelet makers.

39. Who purchased the Queen City Watch Case Company?

40. Why is it difficult to locate dials for the Chatham, Sangamon and Urbana models?

41. What were Hamilton's profits in 1929?

42. Name two Illinois men's wristwatches that have female spring bars.

43. The trademark "The Empire Watch" was owned by which company?

44. What size is the Penn Charter model?

45. What was special about Hamilton's release of its new Grant model?

46. Name a watch case company that was located in Ohio.

47. When did Illinois close down and "throw" one thousand employees out of work?

48. What watch executive was arrested for industrial espionage?

49. Who sold a "sweat proof" watch band?

50. What did Frederick S. Miller do?

51. Name the watch company that had a sales office virtually next door to the Illinois Watch Company's New York City sales location.

52. Name the person that followed E. N. Bates as the president of Illinois.

53. What is a Cadet model?

54. Why would the NRA have failed?

55. Name the watch company that was ordered to stop stamping its watch cases Rolled Gold Plate.

56. How many 7-jewel movements did Hamilton produce?

57. Which Illinois model was advertised as "quite popular with both sexes"?

58. Name four 18K solid gold Illinois ladies' wristwatches.

59. What did the United Electric Railway Co. request?

60. Name the inventor of the Depollier with its crown at 12.

61. What was a blackfish used for?

62. Which United States watch company was hurt most by the Smoot-Hawley Act?

63. How many Illinois jobbers were selling Illinois watches in 1935?

64. True or false? Hamilton was still selling Illinois parts as late as 1947.

65. Name an Illinois men's model that only came in yellow gold-filled.

66. What two major adverse events occurred in 1931 for Hamilton?

67. True or False? Illinois was unionized.

68. Name the watch model that had a double-thick crystal.

69. Who was Hamilton's hand-picked historian?

70. Name six Baguette style Illinois ladies' wristwatches.

71. What event brought watches from the "well heeled" to the "common man"?

72. How much equity did John Adams have in the Illinois Watch Company?

73. Name the watch employee who committed suicide shortly after Illinois was shut down.

74. What Illinois model was announced as a 1934 model but already could not be delivered near the end of 1933?

75. Name the Hamilton cognate for the Lady Gay Model K.

76. Who said "It's an error to let it die"?

77. Who told jewelers not to sell junk?

78. Name a large department store Illinois sold to in Los Angeles.

79. Who was put in charge of the Illinois materials department by Hamilton?

80. How many 12/0 size, grade 207 movements did Illinois produce?

81. Name the Illinois model "built to withstand the severe shock and strains of work or play."

82. Who was Reed Smoot?

83. Name three Swiss companies that made ébauches for Hamilton in the mid-1950s.

84. What was created to discourage ruinous price cutting?

85. Which Illinois model was for a man of small stature?

86. Name two low-cost features of the Hamilton-Illinois wristwatch line.

87. Who owned the "Victory" trademark?

88. In what year did Illinois produce its first 18/0 size movement?

89. Name a large department store Illinois sold to in San Francisco.

90. How many American jewelers sold Elgin watches?

91. What is the difference between a LaSalle and a Belmont?

92. Name two Illinois models that had two different case model numbers and no model number.

93. What month and year did John L. Keenan move to Chicago from Lancaster?

94. Name three Illinois men's models that did not have subsidiary seconds.

95. Who invented the time microscope?

96. When was Illinois first shut down by Hamilton?

97. Name two watch-related companies based in Providence, Rhode Island.

98. What model was formerly known as an "Aviator"?

99. What is a "Cursive" dial?

100. Name the ladies' Illinois wristwatch with black and white inlaid enamel.

101. What model came with a gunmetal finish?

102. Name the company that offered the Anne Louise model for sale.

103. What model was named after its band?

104. Did Illinois make movements with 7 jewels?

105. Who said in 1931 "Let's . . . go to the Cathedral and pray"?

106. Name the buyer at S. H. Clausin.

107. What is the difference between a Beau Geste and a Beau Monde?

108. Did the Santa Fe Watch Company sell wristwatches?

109. Name the movement considered the workhorse of the industry.

110. What does a movement stamped "AS" mean?

111. Who invented the Incabloc system?

112. Name the metal bracelet made in "1/10th 12K gold filled."

113. On what model did Wadsworth hit the trifecta?

114. What Illinois model was advertised as "expressing a new thought in watch design"?

115. What spurred the development of watchmaking in the West?

116. Name the founder of the Illinois Watch Company.

117. What did the *Jewelers' Circular* announce in October 1930?

118. What is a "jobber"?

119. Name the company that supplied replacement parts for Hamilton-Illinois wristwatches.

120. Who funded the formation of Elgin?

121. Which Illinois Factory-Cased men's model was claimed to be "shock-proof"?

122. What movement is claimed to be the father of all ETA self-winding movements?

123. Name Hamilton's head watchmaker in 1954.

124. Name four models that Hamilton-Illinois purchased as complete watches from the Swiss.

125. Which of the following companies did not sell wristwatches: Burlington, Washington, Santa Fe or NAWCo.?

126. Name the Hamilton director of sales in 1953.

127. Why were so few solid gold men's Illinois models made?

128. Name the watch-related company that made pencils, knives and lockets in addition to watch bracelets.

129. The Illinois Baronet resembles what Hamilton watch?

130. How many 18-jewel, 18/0 size movements did Illinois produce?

131. Name two trade names R. H. Macy and Company used on its watches.

132. Name two Illinois models that had subsidiary seconds at 6, 9 or no subsidiaries.

133. What movement did Kurth Frères make for Hamilton?

134. Who was Alfred Wilm?

135. How many pinstripe Consul dials are known to exist?

136. Where did Jacob Bunn emigrate from?

137. What company owned the "Sportsman" trademark?

138. Name the Illinois wristwatch model that came in either a two- or three-piece case.

139. What Illinois model has covered lugs?

140. What did Otis T. Hoyt do at the Illinois Watch Company?

141. Why did Hamilton introduce the Hamilton-Illinois watch line?

142. Who owned Jacques Depollier & Son company?

143. What Hamilton-Illinois had a sweep second hand with a red arrow?

144. Name a large department store Illinois sold to in New York City.

145. What was S&W?

146. What Illinois model took its name from a racetrack where the ten top drivers were wearing those wristwatches?

147. Name the company that used the trade name "Viking."

148. What watch at times had a horseshoe engraved on its caseback?

149. When was an aluminum watch first advertised?

150. Who was Jack Samuels?

151. Name the person who was the Republican Party's first corporate supporter.

152. Why was the Illinois Watch Company reincorporated in 1929?

153. Who made the watch case for the "Moon Watch"?

154. Name the Illinois men's model that used nickel spacers.

155. What was the name of the Bunn Bank?

156. Who advertised an "Egyptian" model?

157. Why is the Chesterfield an unusual two-tone model?

158. When did Beckwith announce that "the worst of the depression is past"?

159. What is the difference between a Beau Brummell and a Beau Royale?

160. Name two watch-related companies located in Attleboro, Massachusetts.

161. How many Factory-Cased ladies' Illinois wristwatches were made in solid gold (not counting Diamond-Set models)?

162. In what year was the *Jewelers' Circular* started?

163. Name the person who almost severed the thumb of John Stuart.

164. Which case manufacturer made the most ladies' cases for Illinois?

165. How many jobbers did Hamilton have at the end of May 1934?

166. Name the model that at times had gold center movement spacers.

167. What was the "American Beauty Series"?

168. Did Illinois make movements with 15 jewels?

169. What American city featured 60¢ watch repairing?

170. Name a large department store Illinois sold to in Brooklyn.

171. What Illinois watch can be found in a Brooklyn Watch Case Company case?

172. What was the most common wristwatch dial finish used by Illinois in the late 1920s and early 1930s?

173. Name three Illinois men's wristwatches with rotor subsidiary seconds.

174. What model is a John Alden?

175. Name a two-tone Illinois ladies' wristwatch.

176. What is a frequent cause of cracks in enamel dials besides dropping your watch?

177. Name three very early Factory-Cased Illinois ladies' wristwatches.

178. Did the Plymouth Watch Company also sell wristwatches?

179. Are there Illinois 3/0 size, grade 307 movements signed Hamilton?

180. Name the Hamilton-Illinois calendar watch.

181. How many Illinois wristwatch movements did Hamilton produce in 1948?

182. In 1820 what was the main business of Springfield?

183. Name the Illinois dials that look identical but do not fit properly in each other's cases.

184. How many direct sales personnel did Illinois have in 1929?

185. Name six watchmakers that were once located in Illinois.

186. Where was the Wadsworth Watch Case Company located?

187. What Illinois men's watch was advertised the most?

188. What watch case company was robbed by a gang of bandits and some of the missing gold later found in a creekbed?

189. What men's model was advertised as a "double duty strap watch"?

190. Name the Illinois president who graduated from Williams College.

191. What company did the Star Watch Case Company merge with in 1948?

192. Why was the Rockingham introduced?

193. Name the Illinois model that was in a 15K gold case.

194. Who is the author of *Time and Timekeepers?*

195. Name the ladies' Illinois wristwatch that was advertised with "gay touches of black inlaid enamel."

196. Did Illinois have a design department?

197. What watch case company was once located in Carlstadt, New Jersey?

198. What are the names of two as yet unidentified 12/0 size men's Illinois watch models?

199. True or False? The Admiral Evans was a Factory-Cased Illinois model.

200. When did Keenan write his "True Situation" memorandum to the Hamilton's salesmen?

201. Name the watch bracelet company based in Washington, D.C.

202. Who was Everit B. Terhune?

203. Name the way in which Lord Kitchener died.

204. Who once was in charge of the Hamilton Tachometer Division?

205. What Hamilton model resembles a Rockliffe?

206. Name a large department store Illinois sold to in Detroit.

207. What was Waltham's percentage of wristwatch sales in 1930?

208. Name the buyer at A. C. Becken.

209. Who was Beulah Paulson?

210. True or False? Illinois made a nurse's watch.

211. What is another name for a Seneca?

212. Who was once the general agent of the Cornell Watch Company?

213. Who was Max C. Eppenstein?

214. Who started the Columbus Watch Manufacturing Company?

215. Name the company that filed a patent infringement lawsuit to protect its "expansible securing device for watch bracelets."

216. Who claimed to have a plant with a personality?

217. What happened to the NRA?

218. Name four Illinois men's models that only came with 15 jewels.

219. Name the most important watch industry entrepreneur in the 19th century?

220. How many employees did Illinois have at the date of the acquisition?

221. Who encouraged Illinois to build an 18/0 size movement?

222. How many jobbers did Illinois have in 1928?

223. Name the evil faced by the metal watch attachment industry.

224. What makes a sparkle dial sparkle?

225. Who was John L. Keenan?

226. Name the factory freelance at Illinois.

227. Where was the New York Standard Watch Company located?

228. What case model was used for the first Hamilton electric watches?

229. Name the year the first Illinois Convertible model was advertised.

230. Which Illinois was advertised as "Gay, unconventional design"?

231. Who replaced Keenan when he left Lancaster for Chicago?

232. What two prominent Chicago department stores sold Illinois watches?

233. Who was Franz Baumgartner?

234. Name three inventors who assigned patents to the Depollier & Dubois companies.

235. Name the three major Chicago jobbers that merged in early 1929.

236. Name the United States president who received an Illinois Watch in Springfield.

237. Name two Hamilton-Illinois watches that came with a domed crystal.

238. In what area of Springfield did the Bunn family reside?

239. Who advertised "an exclusive model of our own creation"?

240. Name an Illinois model that has an engine-turned case.

241. Who owned the Washington Watch Company?

242. How many American watchmakers went to Russia for a year to teach the Russians how to make watches?

243. What is another name for a Potomac?

244. Why did the Bunn Bank fail?

245. Which model was "as sturdy in construction as the average 12 size pocket model"'?

246. Name the lowest-priced Illinois men's wristwatch.

247. What did Hamilton call its rotor-subsidiary second feature?

248. Name a movie star who advertised Illinois watches.

249. When did Illinois announce that it could no longer accept any more orders?

250. What men's wristwatch was advertised in *Outing* magazine?

251. Name a large department store Illinois sold to in Boston.

252. Name two Illinois models that can be found in Keystone "Victory" cases.

253. Name three positions Frank C. Beckwith served in at Hamilton.

254. Name three Illinois men's wristwatches that only came in yellow cases.

255. Name the watch company that had its factory on Ravenswood Avenue in Chicago.

256. Who purchased Dueber-Hampden in 1925?

257. Name four Illinois men's wristwatches that only came in white cases.

258. Who authored *Elgin Time*?

259. Name two Illinois models that had molded bezels.

260. What Illinois model has an integrated watch band?

261. What company was known for its enamel deco mesh purses?

262. Name the Hamilton-Illinois that was called the "Best buy in new larger size with sweep seconds."

263. How many 21-jewel, 6/0 size movements did Illinois produce?

264. Who accused Hamilton of engaging in a monopoly by acquiring Illinois?

265. How many Swiss watchmakers were unemployed in 1928?

266. What does "s.a.w." stand for?

267. Why did the Depollier Waterproof/Dustproof model come with a solid gold disc on its case back?

268. Name three Illinois men's watches with recessed crowns.

269. What is the main difference between an Illinois 207 movement and a Hamilton 401 movement?

270. What major event happened August 21, 1928 at the Illinois Watch Company?

271. What Illinois watch model came in a NAWCo case?

272. Was cyanide ever recommended for cleaning watch dials?

273. Who was the largest producer of watches in the United States in the 1920s?

274. Name the watch company that used the word "Ateliers" in its advertisement.

275. What is considered the signature Illinois wristwatch model?

276. Name two casemakers used for Conneric cases.

277. Name the author of *The History of the American Watch Case*.

278. Name the person who wrote the book Sangamo.

279. Which Illinois men's model had the most durable case?

280. Name the rarest Daytona model.

281. Name two famous watchmakers that immigrated to the United States from England.

282. Who perfected the first waterproof watch?

283. How many parts are in a normal Illinois movement?

284. What did Hamilton do with the Illinois grade 528 movement?

285. What was the first Illinois department consolidated with the Hamilton Watch Company?

286. Why did Hamilton lay off Illinois workers in 1928?

287. Name three case shapes used by Burlington for its wristwatches.

288. What aircraft record did the Depollier Waterproof/Dustproof set?

289. Who sold the "Bull Dog" watch?

290. What Illinois model was considered "an active seller"?

291. Name three things that a Sangamon, Urbana and Tuxedo have in common.

292. Name three Illinois models that were offered with black dials.

293. Which model was called "the Great American Strap Watch"?

294. What watch-related company was located in Dayton, Kentucky?

295. Name three Illinois men's watches that had 21/0 size movements.

296. What is another name for the Valedictorian model?

297. Name the Hamilton president before Charles F. Miller.

298. Which Illinois wristwatch was advertised as the "Watch of the Month" in April 1931?

299. What watch-related company was located in Ludington, Michigan?

300. Did any of the men's Hamilton-Illinois men's watches come in solid gold?

301. Who painted the Illinois portrait advertisement of Abraham Lincoln?

302. Name the year that "Standard Time" was adopted in the United States.

303. Who at Hamilton announced the launch of the Hamilton-Illinois line of wristwatches?

304. How many workers were employed at Illinois in September 1932?

305. Name two Hamilton-Illinois models that could come with black dials.

306. Which Illinois model has two different watch casemakers?

307. Who was Calvin Kendig?

308. What is another name for a Commander?

309. What are the differences between a Potomac and Rockingham?

310. How many solid green gold Consuls are known to exist?

311. Name the watch company that first offered exclusive franchises.

312. How many aluminum movements total did Illinois produce?

313. Name the president that signed the Smoot-Hawley Tariff Bill.

314. Who wrote in November 1932 "I am an American"?

315. What was the date of the last Illinois sales catalog?

316. Who bought the rights to the "Hampden" name?

317. What Hamilton's executive style "irritated almost everyone"?

318. In what year did Waltham go out of business?

319. Which Illinois was advertised as "conservative in design"?

320. Whose motto was "because we make so many?"

321. Name the Hamilton-Illinois model that was "powderproof."

322. What did Hamilton announce on May 1, 1934?

323. Who was Dr. Charles Edouard Guillaume?

324. Who owned the "Tivoli" trade name?

325. What does "JDLR" stand for?

326. Who was upset with Hamilton's inventory liquidation practices for Illinois?

327. What Illinois watch was inspired by "America's First people"?

328. Name the watch-related company located in Rochester, New York.

329. Which of the following models are not solid gold: Lakewood, Princess, Greta and Argyle?

330. What did the Blue Eagle logo symbolize?

331. Did Hamilton ever try to make its own "incabloc" shock absorbing movement?

332. How many vials are contained in the Illinois two-drawer material cabinet?

333. Name three Illinois men's wristwatches that only came in two-tone.

334. Name the ladies' Illinois wristwatch advertised as "a richly engraved model".

335. President Roosevelt rolled back the tariff on Swiss watch movements by what percentage?

336. When was the National Association of Credit Jewelers formed?

337. At the date of the acquisition, who owned all of the Illinois stock?

338. Name the model described as "Tiny . . . to grace a slender wrist."

339. Who advertised Hamilton-Illinois diamond-set models?

340. What company made the Rolex Skyrocket case?

341. True or False? Illinois produced enamel dials.

342. What was named the "Illinois Motor Barrel"?

343. Name the Illinois wristwatch models made exclusively for the Richter-Phillips Company.

344. What model has case Model Number 170?

345. What are the most desired Illinois men's wristwatch dials?

346. What is a dial "tell"?

347. Name the year the silent film of the Illinois Watch Company was introduced.

348. Who made the "Warrior" watchband?

349. Name the cities where Illinois had regional sales offices.

350. What size movement was grade 206?

351. What movement had a double roller?

352. Which Illinois was advertised as "masculine smartness"?

353. Who designed the Illinois men's wristwatch cases?

354. Name an Illinois ladies' wristwatch made out of 18K gold.

355. Name the three key people who developed the Hamilton Zone Distribution Plan.

356. List three Depression-inspired Illinois wristwatch offerings.

357. What company made the "Heavy Duty" case?

358. Name five solid gold Illinois men's wristwatches.

359. What does the "Stellar" indication mean?

360. Name the only "nationally advertised watch crystal."

361. Name two persons with a major impact on Illinois Watch Company history who first worked at case companies.

362. True or False? The Telephone dial came with radium numerals.

363. Who was the second president of the Illinois Watch Company?

364. What was the minimum wage per hour under the 1933 NRA?

365. Name three solid gold Illinois ladies' wristwatches with inlaid enamel.

366. What case company made the most Illinois Conneric models?

367. What Illinois model can be found in a Regal case?

368. Name the first three presidents of the Illinois Watch Company.

369. Who formed the New York Standard Watch Company?

370. How many Hamilton grade 400 watches were produced?

371. What does "Conneric" stand for?

372. Name the company that patented the wristlet.

373. Who made the "Marquis" watchband?

374. What jobber sued Hamilton?

375. In what year did Illinois employment peak?

376. What company imported diamonds and made platinum jewelry?

377. Which company considered itself the "Railroad timekeeper of the world"?

378. Where are the seconds on an open-face movement?

379. What is a Rockliffe 18/0?

380. What company made the Norden Bomb-Sight?

381. Name three Illinois models that came in case model No. 830.

382. What were Hamilton's losses in 1932?

383. How many aluminum pocket watch movements were made by Illinois?

384. Name the war in which the U.S. soldiers first used wristlets.

385. What is the heart of a watch?

386. Where are the seconds on a hunting-configured movement?

387. What is the rarest Illinois Consul dial?

388. What did Hamilton consider to be the two most important features of a watch?

389. What is another name for a Wembley?

390. How many jobbers did Illinois usually use?

391. Name six Illinois watches that also came with 19 jewels.

392. Name three men's wristwatches that Illinois had in limited supply in 1933.

393. What models used case Model No. 211?

394. What was the Capper-Kelly Bill?

395. What casemaker was the largest manufacturer of silverware in the United States in the 20th century?

396. What model was formerly known as a "Prince"?

397. Name the Illinois model A. C. Becken advertised in white only.

398. What is the "Diplomat" series?

399. What color is the enamel on a yellow gold-filled New Yorker Enamel model?"

400. Did Illinois make movements with 18 jewels?

401. What is Michael Harold's view of watchmaking in the United States?

402. What Illinois models resemble a Hamilton Turner?

403. What watch was named for a person who fought in the Civil War?

404. What watch company was rumored to be moving to Springfield in the 1930s?

405. Name the watch case made both by Fahys and by the Brooklyn Watch Case Company.

406. True or False? Hamilton produced over 250,000 12/0 size movements.

407. Who owned the "Scepter" trade name?

408. What do the Hindenburg airship and the Akron model have in common?

409. How many employees did Waltham have working full-time at the end of 1934?

410. What is the major difference between an Illinois "Special" and an Illinois "Sportsman" model?

411. Name two watch attachment firms from which Illinois definitely purchased watchbands.

412. What campaign was started by the American Legion and the American Federation of Labor in 1932?

413. What two Illinois pocket watch models were in good supply in June 1934?

414. Name the Hamilton movement that was modified via a "conversion kit" to become an Illinois.

415. Name the president of the Solidarity Watch Case Company.

416. What were the November 1935 sales results of Illinois watches?

417. Name the owners of the Fredonia Watch Company.

418. What does the term "short time" mean?

419. In what year did Hamilton introduce the Elinvar mainspring?

420. Who designed the Elgin Parisienne watches?

421. What casemakers patented a special pantograph machine?

422. What was the "*Manheimer Watchman*"?

423. Did Hamilton maintain separate financial records for its Illinois Watch Division?

424. How many departments did Illinois have in 1932?

425. What watch company did the Babson Brothers own?

426. Who was president of Gruen during the Depression?

427. Why did Illinois advertise in the *Jewelers' Circular* and the *Keystone*?

428. What is a cliché used for?

429. What were Hamilton's sales in 1929?

430. What Hamilton executive was known as a very unhappy man?

431. Who bought the Hamilton-Sangamo Company?

432. "Elinvar" is made up of what two words?

433. Who turned out to be the major player for Illinois following the acquisition?

434. Why isn't the Illinois Chatham model on the Illinois list of Factory-Cased watches?

435. Name the two most sought-after features of Illinois dials.

436. Which historian did not like the Illinois Watch Company's "commercialization of Lincoln"?

437. Name two politicians who ran for office against Stephen Douglas.

438. Name three Illinois models that were Factory-Cased in Star Watch Case Company cases.

439. Name the watch executive who ran for governor of New Jersey.

440. Who was president of the Illinois Watch Company in 1927?

441. Name three famous people who served in the Blackhawk War.

442. Which three Illinois models have stars on the back of their cases?

443. Why are there four-digit numbers scratched on the back of a refinished dial?

444. Name three Illinois jobbers that were based in Chicago.

445. How many Illinois men's wristwatches were made of 18K gold?

446. Who invented the "safety barrel" for Illinois?

447. Name three Illinois models that have screw-on bezels and case backs.

448. Which Illinois model has two different two-tone cases?

449. What watch was advertised as "style comes into the case"?

450. What company owned the Hallmark trade name?

451. Name the company that developed "rembordedfinish."

452. Who told Keenan that Waltham was having labor problems?

453. What was significant about July 31, 1933?

454. How many yellow Frontenacs are known to exist?

455. Name five of the unidentified ladies' Illinois models.

456. Name two Illinois men's wristwatches that also came with a Braille case configuration.

457. Why did Hamilton use the Illinois name on the Hamilton-Illinois line of watches?

458. Name an Illinois ladies' wristwatch that comes with red and black inlaid enamel.

459. Why did former Illinois employees sue Hamilton?

460. Did Illinois make movements with 16 jewels?

461. Where was the Boston Watch Company located?

462. Name the cities Fahys had offices in.

463. True or False? The Telephone dial never had subsidiary seconds at 9.

464. Name four ladies' model that came with cord bands.

465. Who started at Illinois as an errand boy?

466. True or False? Illinois made a doctor's watch.

467. How long did John W. Bunn serve as president of Illinois Watch Company?

468. Name four pocket watch chain companies that started making metal watch bracelets.

469. How do you tighten the mainspring on a wristwatch?

470. What watch company heavily advertised that a quality watch should have more than 15 jewels?

471. Name the first Illinois men's wristwatch advertised after the company was acquired by Hamilton.

472. Where was the J. Selinger Jewelry Store located?

473. How many manufacturing operations did an Illinois movement undergo?

474. What watch component started as a rough pebble?

475. Which case manufacturer made the most men's cases for Illinois?

476. Name the metal bracelet company that started out in business making watch cases.

477. Why did E. Howard, Dueber-Hampden and South Bend go out of business?

478. What was the Hamilton "Service Honor Roll"?

479. Did Illinois use cushioned pivots?

480. What major event took place for Waltham in 1923?

481. In what year did Hamilton sell the Springfield property?

482. What two new Hamilton wristwatches were introduced along with the Dixon model?

483. Name the attorney for the Bunn grocery store.

484. What watch case models did J. Milhening make for Illinois?

485. Name the company that made the first solderless expansion bracelet.

486. What is a master plate?

487. Did some of the 18/0 size movements come with 15 jewels?

488. What is the significance of an "Avon" watch movement?

489. Name the most famous French maker of clocks and watches.

490. Name five ladies models that had Elinvar hairsprings.

491. Why didn't Hamilton sell more 3/0 size movements?

492. Explain what the "Convict Consul" is.

493. Who authored *Timing a Century?*

494. What watchmaker produced more private-label movements than Illinois?

495. What is an "Etarotor"?

496. Name the two most popular Illinois men's transitional models.

497. Who was Roland Rohlfs?

498. Name an Illinois model that was offered for sale with a "rock crystal."

499. What company had a trademark with a hand and the letters "ROY" on the hand?

500. Name two watch casemakers that also sold completed watches.

501. What is an Illinois "Penn Charter" model?

502. Name the Bunn business that survived for over 170 years.

503. How many grade 401 movements did Illinois produce for Hamilton?

504. The Hamilton Barrel B model resembles what Illinois watch?

505. Name the metal band company that wanted to "rigidly uphold" its resale prices.

506. What was the worst year for watchmakers during the Great Depression?

507. Who wrote the biography of Jacob Bunn?

508. Name the first Hamilton men's wristwatch to use a Star Case.

509. For what did Hamilton use the Illinois grade 528 movement?

510. Name the four cities where Illinois had the most jobbers selling its product.

511. Why did Keenan start to doubt the viability of Illinois?

512. In what year was the *American Horological Review* started?

513. Name the person who said that "Camels" aided his digestion.

514. Who was president of the Pioneer Watch Case Company?

515. What watch company was the first one to announce a complete line of American watches equipped with Elinvar hairsprings and monometallic balance wheels?

516. What model contained the first grade 207, 12/0 size movement?

517. Name the Illinois model deemed the most valuable.

518. What inspired the design of the Ritz model?

519. Who discovered the Illinois 6/0 size movement "stamped" Hamilton?

520. Name the Hamilton executive who served as the president of the Lancaster Chamber of Commerce.

521. Who was once in charge of sales research at Hamilton?

522. What United States watch company went out of business in 1957?

523. Name the company that was an outgrowth of Jacques Kreisler & Co.

524. True or False? Dr. Guillaume won the Nobel Prize for the Elinvar hairspring.

525. What role did Armand Hammer play in the watch business?

526. What is another name for a Devon?

527. Name the watch person who had the nickname "Soapy".

528. What watch company was based in Woodside, New York?

529. What model has case Model No. 171?

530. Name the company that for years produced gold and platinum watch attachments.

531. Who won fame in the Battle of Omdurman?

532. What men's model was advertised as having a "17 jewel military movement"?

533. When was the Philadelphia Centennial Exposition?

534. Name the company that pioneered the manufacture of open-link watch attachments.

535. What model was once known as a "Bennett"?

536. In what territory did Illinois have the most jobbers?

537. What is the highest jewel count an Illinois wristwatch movement contained?

538. How many Illinois aluminum grade 525 movements are known to exist?

539. Which Illinois was advertised as "for the air-minded America"?

540. Who bought the E. Howard Watch Company's goodwill and trademarks?

541. What association promoted two watches for every man?

542. Name two Illinois wristwatches that came with moiré dials.

543. What was Mappin & Webb?

544. Name two Factory-Cased ladies' models with diamonds on their bezels.

545. Whom or what did Illinois target in its advertisements at the end of the 19th century?

546. Name the buyer at Albert Wacker.

547. Who first produced the "Dollar Watch"?

548. How many two-toned gold Illinois Consul models are known to exist?

549. Who invented radium dial paint?

550. What two companies merged to form the American Waltham Watch Company?

551. What was the Non-Retailing Company?

552. Who was a Chief of Staff during the Second Boer War?

553. How many unprofitable years did Waltham experience during the Depression?

554. Who sold the "Royal Order" watch?

555. What Illinois pocket watch and wristwatch models shared the same name?

556. What Illinois model is nearly identical to the Biloxi model?

557. What is another name for an Ardsley?

558. What was a magnifier projector used for in the Illinois factory?

559. Name the watchbands that had solid gold and platinum tops.

560. What kind of worker installed the winding and setting mechanism and the main wheels in an Illinois watch?

561. What Illinois wristwatches were advertised in *Popular Mechanics* magazine?

562. What watch company tried to blanket the market?

563. What did Illinois use a pantograph machine for?

564. What company advertised the General Joffre model?

565. Why were Hamilton watches on sale in barber shops?

566. What is an Illinois "Motor Coach" model?

567. True or False? Illinois produced its own metal dials.

568. Which Illinois wristwatch model could come with Egyptian numerals?

569. Name the person commissioned to build a watch for Marie-Antoinette.

570. Name four Illinois unisex watches.

571. Name the jobber that sold the "Brandt Rock" model.

572. Which watch company wanted to use interchangeable parts?

573. Name two racetracks in Illinois that two Illinois men's models were named after.

574. What operation required the highest skill in watchmaking in the Illinois Factory?

575. How did damaskeening the movement help its performance?

576. Name the company that succeeded the Louis Manheimer & Son Co.

577. What Illinois Factory-Cased model shares a case design with models by Elgin, Gruen and Longines?

578. Who was L. Michael Fultz?

579. What model did the Rosenberg Brothers sell?

580. Why did Hamilton acquire Illinois?

581. What was the purpose of the Gift Series watches?

582. Name the Illinois military watch that sold for $11.75.

583. What helped with "eye appeal" when selling an Illinois watch?

584. What was a flat-plate rose engine used for?

585. How many watch casemakers in the United States were still in business in 1934?

586. Name three men who served as the president of Elgin.

587. Name the Factory-Cased Illinois ladies' wristwatch with diamonds and sapphires on its bezel that has a case Model No. but an unknown name.

588. How many employees did Illinois have in 1929?

589. Name two positions in which George Luckey served at Hamilton.

590. What ladies' Illinois wristwatch comes with an exploding Roman numeral dial?

591. What Illinois men's models came at times in three-piece double-hinge cases?

592. Which of the following names was not an Illinois private label: The Time King, Special Time King, Time-Pilot, True-Time.

593. In what year did Waltham produce its first sub-0–sized movement?

594. Name the first U.S. Chief of Naval Operations.

595. What Illinois watch was for the "handbag, pocket or desk"?

596. Name two watchband makers that invented some of their own bands.

597. In what year did Illinois offer its first 0-size movement?

598. In what year did Illinois offer its first 19-jewel 3/0 size movement?

599. What Illinois men's model also had a case with diamonds on its bezel?

600. What Illinois model came in a wood display case?

601. Name the watch firm that had offices in New York, Chicago, San Francisco, Cincinnati, London and Toronto.

602. Who claimed to have the trademark rights to the name "KHAKI"?

603. What is the key difference between the 6/0 size, 21-jewel, grade 601 and grade 909 movements?

604. Name the Illinois executive who served as a director at the Lancaster YMCA.

605. Which Illinois Factory-Cased men's model was advertised as "shock-proof, weather-proof, dust-proof and moisture-proof"?

606. Who made the watch case for the Pulsar watch?

607. Name the watch firm that had an office at 704 Market Street in San Francisco.

608. What is another name for the Hawley-Smoot Tariff Act?

609. Who said that 1931 was "a year that has tried men's souls"?

610. Who helped establish the Amtorg Watch Company?

611. What was Waltham's percentage of U.S. wristwatch sales in 1926?

612. What war did John Stuart, Jefferson Davis, Zachary Taylor and Abraham Lincoln fight in?

613. What Illinois wristwatch model has a red twelve?

614. Name two Hamilton presidents who first served as head of sales.

615. What two companies made solid gold Special Cushion models for Illinois?

616. Name an Illinois Factory-Cased model made in base metal.

617. What two items did the Illinois jobbers travelers use to help make sales?

618. How many Illinois aluminum grade 307 movements are known to exist?

619. What metal band "hugs every wrist without binding"?

620. Name the Illinois ladies' wristwatch that had light and dark blue inlaid enamel.

621. What Illinois jobber was located on Wacker Drive in Chicago?

622. Name the Illinois president who was twice a POW.

623. Whom did Illinois send to Europe to study how the Swiss and other countries were making watches?

624. Name three watch case companies that also made metal bands.

625. Which watch case company made the aluminum wristwatch case for Illinois?

626. Name the watch person who started in the rubber stamp business.

627. How many Illinois movements in total may have been "stamped Hamilton"?

628. Who was appointed foreman of the Hamilton Escape Department in 1933?

629. What did Hamilton do as a "temporary and economic expediency"?

630. Name the Bunn who was an initial Illinois board member.

631. What watch model is the No. 650 now known as?

632. Name the most significant feature of a 6/0 size Motor Barrel movement.

633. What Illinois movement had 16 jewels?

634. What material is made up of copper, magnesium and manganese?

635. Who invented the "lug-less" watch?

636. Name the watch company that had an office in the Heyworth Building in Chicago.

637. What motorcycle brand was used in World War I by the U.S. Army?

638. Name seven Illinois ladies' models with enamel bezels.

639. What is another name for a Richmond 12/0?

640. Name the company that sold metal bands "in every modish color."

641. What is the difference between a New Yorker and a Manhattan?

642. Name the company that made the "Legionette."

643. What watch case company was started in 1857?

644. In what year did the first Illinois private-label movement appear?

645. What did the Scheufele family invent?

646. What watch company positioned itself as the "Trust Busting" company?

647. Who was George F. Johnson?

648. Did any of the Hamilton-Illinois ladies' watches come in solid gold?

649. What watch company was located on Lincoln Highway?

650. What Gruen brother served as its treasurer?

651. What was the second Illinois department to be consolidated with the Hamilton Watch Company?

652. Name three Illinois men's chrome watches.

653. Who advertised "Be On Time"?

654. What Illinois wristwatch once appeared on the cover of an NAWCC *Bulletin*?

655. What watch company did Sears, Roebuck and Company own?

656. What Illinois model is at times called the "Locks" model?

657. Name three 10K gold-filled ladies' Illinois wristwatches.

658. What is a Biltmore 6/0?

659. Which Illinois was advertised as "for the man of action"?

660. Which company's motto was "Give the lady what she wants"?

661. Name the general manager of Waltham in May 1934.

662. Who co-founded the Sangamo Electric Company?

663. Which case manufacturer made the most Hamilton-Illinois models?

664. What Illinois ladies' watch was advertised the most?

665. Name three pre-1935 Hamilton acquisitions.

666. Name two ladies' Illinois wristwatches made in sterling silver.

667. Why do some Illinois watch models have hinged bezels?

668. How did Hamilton fund the acquisition of Illinois?

669. How many 12-jewel, 3/0 size Illinois movements were produced?

670. Name the two Illinois models advertised by the Union and Hardware Metal Company.

671. What does "OSCO" stand for?

672. What does H.I.A. stand for?

673. Who commanded the Great White Fleet?

674. What does ANRJA stand for?

675. Name the buyer at Smith-Patterson.

676. What was the major cause for the decline in pocket watch sales?

677. Who said that "Illinois watches are a technology time capsule"?

678. Name the company that made the "Adonis" metal band.

679. What Bunn worked as a bank teller?

680. Name the future executive who started at Hamilton as an "errand boy."

681. What is a "Lord Wadsworth?"

682. What watch company did the Soviet government buy?

683. How did the enactment of the NRA codes end up hurting Illinois?

684. Name the person who invented the Sangamo Electric Meter.

685. What watch company was located in Sag Harbor, New York?

686. Name an Illinois ladies' wristwatch that did not have fixed lugs.

687. What program was instituted "to place fine watch merchandising above the ruinous practices of price competition"?

688. Name two watch companies that were based in Topeka, Kansas.

689. How did the Great Depression impact the *Jewelers' Circular*?

690. Name the watch company that started a war conservation request because enough watches could not be produced.

691. Who was Milton H. Manby?

692. Who owned the "Herald Square" trade name?

693. Name the watch company that sold a model called "The West Pointer."

694. Name two Illinois jobbers based in Cincinnati.

695. Name two companies that offered a "Ben Hur" model.

696. What is the most sought-after Illinois men's wristwatch model?

697. In what year was the *Keystone* started?

698. Name two Illinois General Funston models.

699. Name the doctor who would visit the Illinois infirmary.

700. What is the "Undertaker's Consul"?

701. Who was William E. Port?

702. What year did Hamilton introduce its 18/0 size movement?

703. Name the Illinois ladies' model that has sculpted flowers on its bezel.

704. Name two mail-order watch companies.

705. What is considered a "full-jeweled" movement?

706. Who called the Hamilton acquisition of Illinois "ace high"?

707. Which Illinois model was advertised as the "Watch of the Month" in March 1931?

708. What was Ingersoll known for?

709. Name John Stuart's protégé.

710. Name the watch company that had an office at 20 W. 47th Street in New York City.

711. What jobber was located in the Temple Bar Building?

712. For whom did Charles Tost invent watch bands?

713. What sizes of movements did Illinois wristwatches come in? List them all.

714. What watch case company at one time sold Waltham movements and dials exclusively with its models?

715. Who holds the patent for the Standish case?

716. Name two different models that have rope-like engraving on their sides.

717. What two things does a Wentworth have in common with a Finalist?

718. What watch line was described "as modern as the minute"?

719. Name the Illinois model advertised in twenty-one leading railroad publications.

720. What Illinois model was called the "latest thing in novelty watches"?

721. What was "Black Tuesday"?

722. Name two Illinois models where the numeral 6 is replaced with a half-moon radium shape.

723. What model was considered "a departure from the usual"?

724. Who imported watch parts made in Madre-Biel Switzerland?

725. Name the company that used the "Pera-agon" trade name.

726. Who was Judge Stanley Struble?

727. When did the first ladies' wristwatch appear?

728. What Illinois jobber was located in Philadelphia?

729. Name a Hamilton Export Manager.

730. Who owned the Elgin Giant trade name?

731. How many sides does a Southhampton have?

732. Name three "special accounts" for Illinois.

733. What legislation was passed to increase the tariff on imports?

734. Name the sales manager at Elgin in May 1934.

735. Name an Illinois men's watch that is engraved only on the sides of its bezel.

736. What model was considered "far above the novelty watch class"?

737. How many direct sales personnel did Illinois have in 1924?

738. Name the Illinois Watch Company jobber that also made its own watch straps.

739. Name two Illinois wristwatches that came in solid green gold.

740. What model "***glows*** time brightly" according to its advertisement?

741. Name four Illinois men's watches that had curved case backs.

742. Name the model sold with a "form-fitting" back.

743. Who claimed to sell watches at "rock bottom prices"?

744. Name the jobber that stated "the Illinois line is becoming more popular each year."

745. Name three Hamilton historians.

746. Who said their strap watches "are no longer considered effeminate"?

747. Name the Hamilton model that came with an integrated metal band.

748. When did the first Illinois private-label movement appear?

749. Name the company that sold watches under the Lexington name.

750. Name the author of the Illinois watch book published in 2004.

APPENDIX 1

The DeLong Escapement

In watchmaking, mechanical efficiency is justly valued. Although there is considerable torque available from the mainspring, by the time it has passed through four stages of step-up gearing, it has been divided by 3,600 in a typical watch. As a consequence, very little power can be supplied by the escapement to drive the balance wheel. Much of the innovation of horological developers has been concentrated on getting the best performance at the escapement. Charles DeLong was responsible for one of the most interesting American advances in escapement design.

Noted horology expert Michael C. Harrold described the DeLong Escapement as follows:

> In essence: DeLong found that semicircular pallets had a theoretical advantage of obtaining effectively large draw with little recoil of the escape wheel. Draw angle kept the lever held against its banking pins so that it could not shake loose, but this was accomplished at the expense of recoil. This meant that as the escapement unlocked, the escape wheel was forced to recoil backward against the mainspring. By reducing recoil DeLong's escapement had higher mechanical efficiency, and a brisk balance motion was obtained with a 3/4-strength mainspring. In addition, the weaker mainspring reduced forces through the geartrain, which also reduced wear. These escapements were interchangeable with conventional lever escapements in Abe Lincoln model watches where they were tried, so that when they failed to reach production some of the 100 may have been switched. Technical problems were reported as the reason for rejection, but the greatest difficulty was most likely the fact that DeLong escapements were different.[1]

In the *American Jeweler,* in 1915, Chamberlain provided the first published description of the "DeLong escapement." He pointed out that at first sight, it gave an impression of similarity to the pin escapement or to the Brocot escapement often *seen* in front of the dial in French clocks; and he also discussed the entirely new feature of securing a stronger lock with a diminished recoil of escape wheel in unlocking.

The illustration shown here compares an ordinary lever escapement with the DeLong, and the DeLong structural plan is shown in Figure 3 of the illustration. Chamberlain wrote: "The pallets are slightly over half-cylinders staked into a steel anchor having holes with spring action and requiring no cement. The specifications were 1-1/2 degree lift on the escape wheel tooth, 7 degree lift on pallets, 27 degree draw and a five percent increase in escape wheel diameter. And the most surprising and apparently contradictory requirement, considering the increased draw, was that of using with it a mainspring of approximately three-quarters the strength of that used in watches in which this escapement had displaced the usual form. The structural advantages claimed were decreased manufacturing costs and permanent location of pallets."[2]

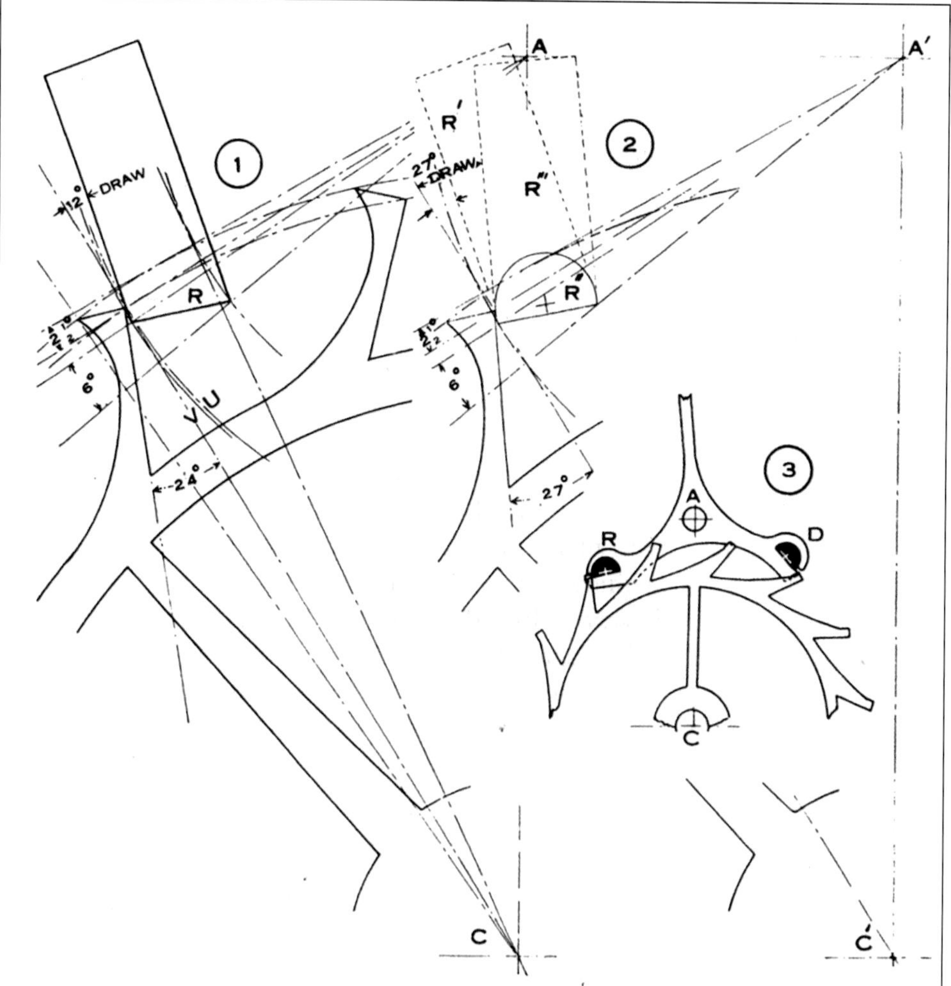

COMPARISON OF THE ORDINARY LEVER ESCAPEMENT AND THE DELONG ESCAPEMENT

Fig. 1.—Receiving pallet action in ordinary lever escapement. The distance between arcs V and U show the distance the escape wheel must be turned back by stored energy in the balance during unlocking.

Fig. 2.—With same center distances and same lift and lock the arrangement of the DeLong partly cylindrical pallet giving 27 degree lock instead of 12 degree as in Fig. 1. The pallet R‴ with rounded locking corner is a possible substitution of R″.

Fig. 3.—The DeLong escapement in which the R and D pallets are staked into spring friction holes in the anchor.

For purposes of comparison, Chamberlain showed in Fig. 1 of the illustration the common form of escapement with the usual pallet and in Fig. 2 the DeLong with the same center distances, the same lift of pallet and of teeth. In Fig. 1, the arcs V and U represent by the distance between them the amount that the escape wheel must be turned backward against the force of the mainspring by energy stored in the balance. In Fig. 2 the tooth has been given a slightly increased angle. It will be *seen* that in the position of deepest lock the angle of draw has been increased from 12 degrees (shown in Fig. 1) to 27 degrees but that the amount of recoil of the escape wheel would be considerably less due to the curvature of the pallet R'' as used in the DeLong escapement. It will also be *seen* that the angle of draw during the unlocking will be constantly decreased. It is obvious that in action the draw angle at the moment of drop lock will be very much less. It might be feared that the drop lock or beginning of lock might not have enough draw to complete the slide to banking or final lock. There is, however, the considerable stored energy in the mass of the fork and pallets which tends to carry the pallets to the final lock.[3]

Reviewing the escapement after more than twenty years, Chamberlain claimed with reasonable assurance that the DeLong escapement in several hundred watches of such makers as Ball, Hamilton and Illinois proved all the claims of safety of lock and decreased spring power. It also showed a better position rate.[4]

1. Michael C. Harrold, *American Watchmaking: A Technical History of the American Watch Industry, 1850–1930*, NAWCC *Bulletin*, Supplement No. 14 (Spring 1984), p. 111.

2. Paul M. Chamberlain, *It's About Time* (London, UK: Holland Press, 1964), pp 101–102.

3. Ibid., pp. 102–103.

4. Ibid.

APPENDIX 2

Antitrust Fallout from the Hamilton Zone Distribution Plan

On May 1, 1934, with great fanfare, Hamilton launched its Zone Distribution Plan, which was to prove highly successful. It eliminated dozens of distributors/jobbers and provided exclusive sales territories for its hand-picked remaining distributors. Emboldened by its increased sales at comfortable price points, Hamilton commenced a series of practices to help maintain and enforce this plan. When others in the watch and jewelry industries began to mirror Hamilton's controlled Zone Distribution practices, these added enforcement techniques attracted the attention of the United States Department of Justice.

As a result, by November 1941, the Department of Justice sought and won criminal antitrust grand jury indictments against Hamilton, Waltham, Elgin and many of their jobbers, including the watch companies' key management employees. In addition to the Hamilton company itself and its then-president Kendig, its vice presidents Atkinson, Halligan, Luckey, Kant, Smith and two district sales managers, Hall and Keenan, were sued and personally named as defendants in the litigation. (Waltham and Elgin were similarly sued.) Hamilton and its employees were always represented by the same legal counsel, the employees undoubtedly at the company's expense.

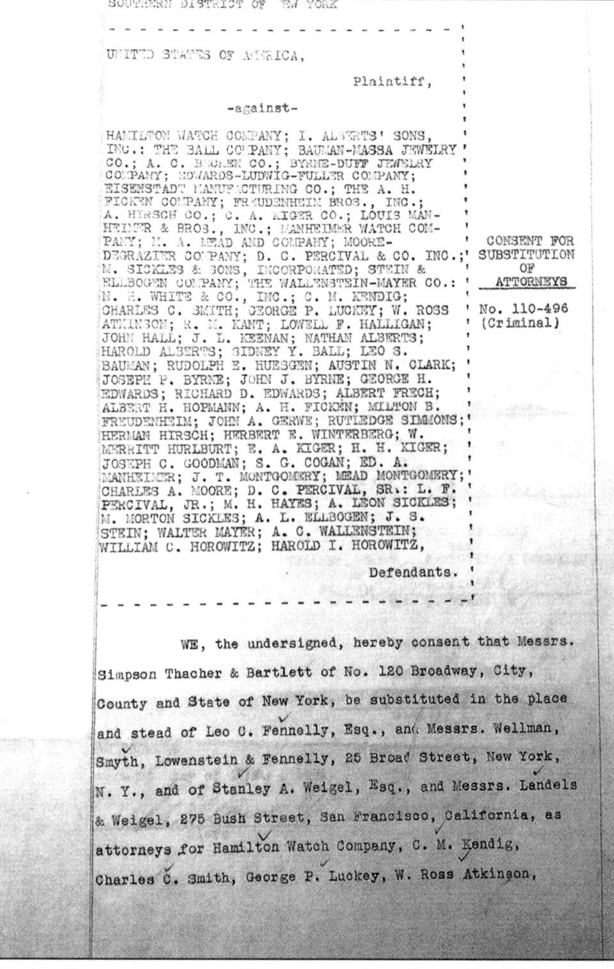

SOUTHERN DISTRICT OF NEW YORK

UNITED STATES OF AMERICA,

Plaintiff,

-against-

HAMILTON WATCH COMPANY; I. ALBERTS' SONS, INC.: THE BALL COMPANY; BAUMAN-MASSA JEWELRY CO.; A. C. BECKEN CO.; BYRNE-DUFF JEWELRY COMPANY; EDWARDS-LUDWIG-FULLER COMPANY; EISENSTADT MANUFACTURING CO.; THE A. H. FICKEN COMPANY; FREUDENHEIM BROS., INC.; A. HIRSCH CO.; C. A. KIGER CO.; LOUIS MANHEIMER & BROS., INC.; MANHEIMER WATCH COMPANY; M. A. MEAD AND COMPANY; MOORE-DEGRAZIER COMPANY; D. C. PERCIVAL & CO. INC.; M. SICKLES & SONS, INCORPORATED; STEIN & ELLBOGEN COMPANY; THE WALLENSTEIN-MAYER CO.: N. H. WHITE & CO., INC.; C. M. KENDIG; CHARLES C. SMITH; GEORGE P. LUCKEY; W. ROSS ATKINSON; R. M. KANT; LOWELL F. HALLIGAN; JOHN HALL; J. L. KEENAN; NATHAN ALBERTS; HAROLD ALBERTS; SIDNEY Y. BALL; LEO S. BAUMAN; RUDOLPH E. HUESGEN; AUSTIN N. CLARK; JOSEPH P. BYRNE; JOHN J. BYRNE; GEORGE H. EDWARDS; RICHARD D. EDWARDS; ALBERT FRECH; ALBERT H. HOPMANN; A. H. FICKEN; MILTON B. FREUDENHEIM; JOHN A. GERWE; RUTLEDGE SIMMONS; HERMAN HIRSCH; HERBERT E. WINTERBERG; W. MERRITT HURLBURT; E. A. KIGER; H. H. KIGER; JOSEPH C. GOODMAN; S. G. COGAN; ED. A. MANHEIMER; J. T. MONTGOMERY; MEAD MONTGOMERY; CHARLES A. MOORE; D. C. PERCIVAL, SR.: L. F. PERCIVAL, JR.; M. H. HAYES; A. LEON SICKLES; M. MORTON SICKLES; A. L. ELLBOGEN; J. S. STEIN; WALTER MAYER; A. C. WALLENSTEIN; WILLIAM C. HOROWITZ; HAROLD I. HOROWITZ,

Defendants.

CONSENT FOR SUBSTITUTION OF ATTORNEYS

No. 110-496 (Criminal)

WE, the undersigned, hereby consent that Messrs. Simpson Thacher & Bartlett of No. 120 Broadway, City, County and State of New York, be substituted in the place and stead of Leo C. Fennelly, Esq., and Messrs. Wellman, Smyth, Lowenstein & Fennelly, 25 Broad Street, New York, N. Y., and of Stanley A. Weigel, Esq., and Messrs. Landels & Weigel, 275 Bush Street, San Francisco, California, as attorneys for Hamilton Watch Company, C. M. Kendig, Charles C. Smith, George P. Luckey, W. Ross Atkinson,

An April 23, 1946, court document signed by all of the Hamilton defendants, consenting to a change of attorneys (page 1)

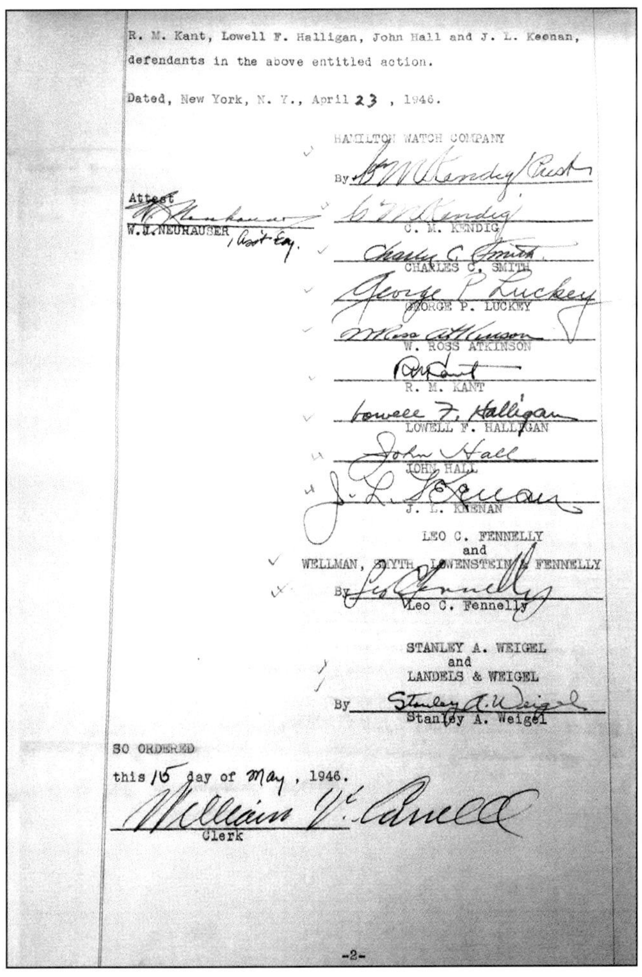
R. M. Kant, Lowell F. Halligan, John Hall and J. L. Keenan, defendants in the above entitled action.

Dated, New York, N. Y., April 23, 1946.

HAMILTON WATCH COMPANY

By [signature] Prest

Attest [signature]
W. J. NEUHAUSER, Asst. Secy.

C. M. KENDIG

CHARLES C. SMITH

GEORGE P. LUCKEY

W. ROSS ATKINSON

R. M. KANT

LOWELL F. HALLIGAN

JOHN HALL

J. L. KEENAN

LEO C. FENNELLY
and
WELLMAN, SMYTH, LOWENSTEIN & FENNELLY
By [signature]
Leo C. Fennelly

STANLEY A. WEIGEL
and
LANDELS & WEIGEL
By [signature]
Stanley A. Weigel

SO ORDERED
this 15 day of May, 1946.

[signature]
Clerk

-2-

(page 2)

The Hamilton case was aimed at its alleged violations of the Sherman Antitrust Law, commencing in 1934. The U.S. Government asserted that since 1934, Hamilton engaged in a wrongful and unlawful combination and conspiracy to restrain and restrict the sale of its watches, and to discriminate against certain "catalog houses" (persons engaged in the sale of watches to retail dealers, watch repairers, general storekeepers, large industrial concerns, manufacturing firms, banking houses, ships' posts, commissaries and other retail outlets), "upstair houses" (firms not maintaining a store on the street level but on a floor above the street level); "sub-jobbers" (firms not purchasing directly from Hamilton but from a Hamilton–approved jobber); "wholesalers" (selling to other than consumers) and "retailers" (selling directly to consumers) in violation of Section 1 of the Sherman Act, which was enacted to protect trade and commerce against unlawful restraints and monopolies.

The Government went on to allege that Hamilton instituted a series of practices to enforce its restraint of trade. Some of the Hamilton enforcement methods were alleged to be:

1. Meeting with its co-defendants to arbitrarily determine the "proper outlets" for the sale of Hamilton products;

2. Conspiring to prevent jobbers, sub-jobbers, upstair houses and retailers from selecting their outlets, customers and accounts;

3. Using threats and fear of being excluded ("blacklisted") as an approved Hamilton seller to enforce its conspiracy;

4. Holding regular in-person and telephonic meetings with other defendants to:

   a. Eliminate certain retailers;

   b. Maintain a "blacklist" of certain catalog houses, upstair houses, sub-jobbers and retailers that were not to be sold to;

   c. Conduct a "tracing" practice to determine where its watches were being sold so it could take action against those that violated its distribution rules;

   d. Employ "shoppers" to find out which entities were violating its policies so it could take disciplinary actions and engage in further blacklisting;

e. Establish a policy of daily and weekly reports on all sales of its products for the enforcement of rigid resale restrictions upon wholesalers and retailers; and

f. Install a policy of "zoning distribution" by allocating territories to certain approved distributors who were then precluded from selling outside of their defined territories.

The Government maintained that these practices resulted in a combination and conspiracy to prevent numerous catalog houses, sub-jobbers, upstairs houses, wholesalers and retailers from buying, selling, distributing or dealing in Hamilton products.

Hamilton and all of the individually named defendants pled not guilty on December 3, 1941. The handwritten recordation of their not-guilty pleas by the court is shown below (John L. Keenan is on the first page).

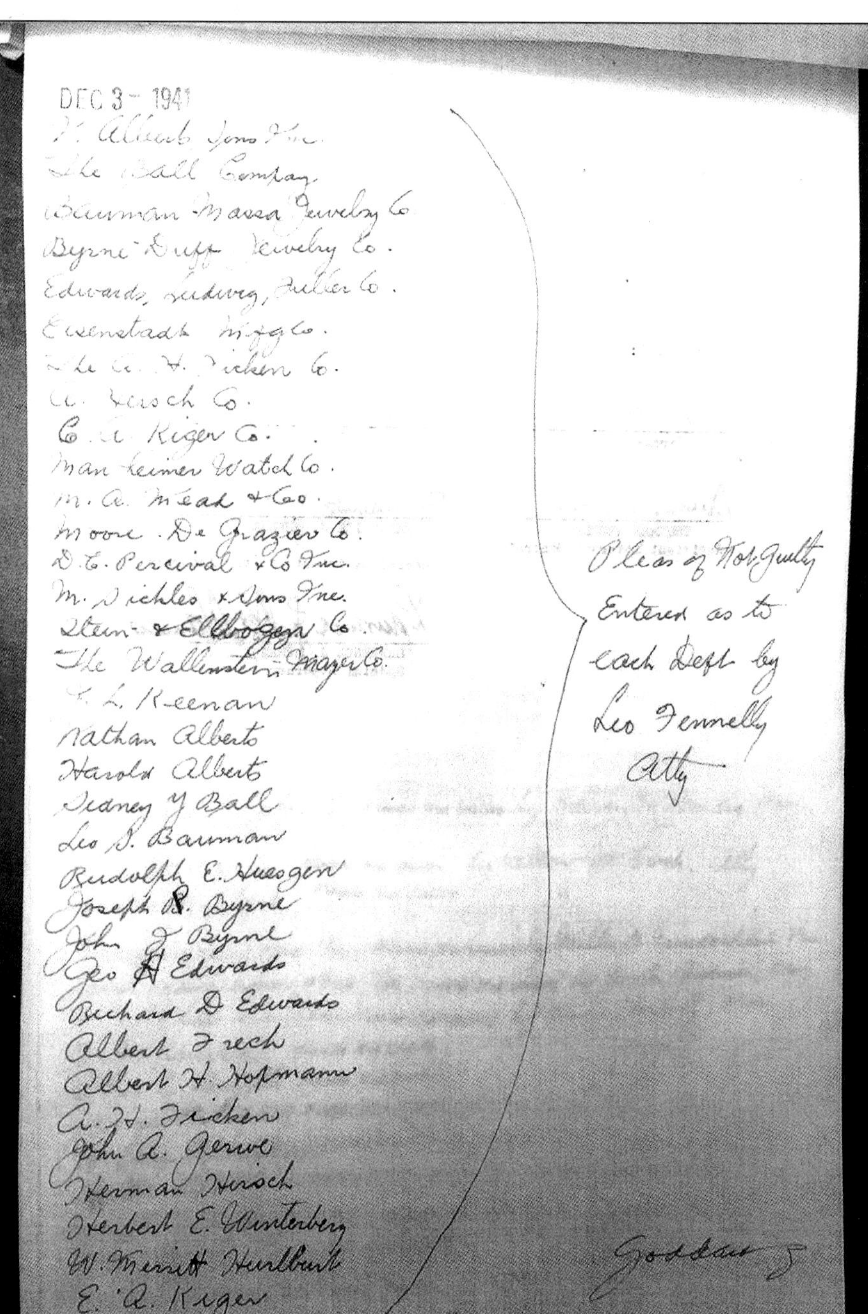

DEC 3 - 1941

Albert Sons Inc.
The Ball Company.
Bauman Massa Jewelry Co
Byrne-Duff Jewelry Co.
Edwards, Ludwig, Fuller Co.
Eisenstadt Mfg Co.
The A. H. Ficken Co.
A. Hirsch Co.
E. A. Kiger Co.
Manheimer Watch Co.
M. A. Mead & Co.
Moore-De Grazier Co.
D. C. Percival & Co Inc.
M. Sickles & Sons Inc.
Stein & Ellbogen Co.
The Wallenstein Mayer Co.
J. L. Keenan
Nathan Alberts
Harold Albert
Sidney Y Ball
Leo S. Bauman
Rudolph E. Huesgen
Joseph R. Byrne
John J Byrne
Geo H Edwards
Richard D Edwards
Albert Frech
Albert H. Hofmann
A. H. Ficken
John A. Gerwe
Herman Hirsch
Herbert E. Winterberg
W. Merritt Hurlburt
E. A. Kiger

Pleas of Not Guilty Entered as to each Deft by Leo Fennelly Atty

Goddard J

The court's handwritten recordation of the not guilty pleas of the defendants in the Hamilton case, dated Dec. 3, 1941 (page 1)

This litigation lasted until November 1946, although the record is not complete. The litigation may have been suspended during the height of World War II, upon motion by Hamilton, once it was engaged wholly in the production of vital instruments of war and was no longer manufacturing watches that were the subject matter of this lawsuit. This litigation practice was common during the war.

Finally, on November 27, 1946, Hamilton, on motion to the court, changed its pleas from not guilty to *nolo contendere*, basically a plea of no contest in a criminal case such as this, where the defendants neither admits nor disputes a charge. A no contest plea, while not technically a guilty plea, has the same immediate effect as a guilty plea. The court accepted this plea with the imposition of a monetary fine and the case was dismissed.

The court's handwritten recordation of the not guilty pleas of the defendants in the Hamilton case, dated Dec. 3, 1941 (page 2)

District Court of the United States

FOR THE

DISTRICT OF

DIVISION

United States of America

v.

HAMILTON WATCH CO

No. C110/496

On this 27th day of November, 1946 came the attorney for the government and the defendant appeared by Whitney Seymour, Atty

IT IS ADJUDGED that the defendant has been convicted upon its plea of [2] Nolo Contendre

of the offense of Sherman Anti Trust Act Sec 1 Title 15 USC

as charged [3]

and the court having asked the defendant whether it has anything to say why judgment should not be pronounced, and no sufficient cause to the contrary being shown or appearing to the Court,

IT IS ADJUDGED that the defendant is guilty as charged and convicted.

IT IS ADJUDGED that the defendant is

fined $5000.

IT IS ORDERED that the Clerk deliver a certified copy of this judgment and commitment to the United States Marshal or other qualified officer and that the copy serve as the commitment of the defendant.

United States District Judge.

[1] Insert "by counsel" or "without counsel; the court advised the defendant of his right to counsel and asked him whether he desired to have counsel appointed by the court, and the defendant thereupon stated that he waived the right to the assistance of counsel." [2] Insert (1) "guilty," (2) "not guilty, and a verdict of guilty," (3) "not guilty, and a finding of guilty," or (4) "nolo contendere," as the case may be. [3] Insert "in count(s) number " if required. [4] Enter (1) sentence or sentences, specifying counts if any; (2) whether sentences are to run concurrently or consecutively and, if consecutively, when each term is to begin with reference to termination of preceding term or to any other outstanding or unserved sentence; (3) whether defendant is to be further imprisoned until payment of fine or fine and costs, or until he is otherwise discharged as provided by law. [5] Enter any order with respect to suspension and probation. [6] For use of Court wishing to recommend a particular institution.

Court paper showing Hamilton "guilty as charged and convicted"; *United States of America v: Hamilton Watch Co.*, USDL, Southern District of New York, 1946.

A Postscript

After the antitrust case was dismissed, Hamilton presumably modified its conduct going forward to avoid further litigation and financial penalties with the United States Government concerning the allegations in this case. However, by 1955, Hamilton, Waltham and Elgin (among others) were again subject to an antitrust action filed by the United States Department of Justice concerning an alleged conspiracy to unreasonably restrain trade and commerce in watchmaking machinery. These violations were in connection with an alleged "Collective Convention" entered into in 1931 by a number of Swiss watch organizations and co-conspirators. This case, *inter alia*, alleged that the convention required all the signatories to deal only with each other in the purchase and sale of certain watch parts and forbade them to establish manufacturing facilities outside Switzerland or to give assistance in the form of machinery or advice to any watch firm outside Switzerland.*

**United States of America v: Hamilton Watch Co.*, USDL, Southern District of New York, 1955.

APPENDIX 3

Illinois Movements Intended for Wristwatches by Dates, Serial Numbers & Production Quantities

3/0 Size, 11-Jewel Movements, Grade 21			
Year	Model	Serial Numbers	Quantity
1915	3	2,793,901–2,793,940	40
1915	3	2,793,961–2,793,970	10
1915	3	2,793,981–2,794,000	20
1915	4	2,806,104–2,806,230	130
1915	4	2,806,241–2,806,280	40
1915	3	2,816,201–2,816,320	120
1915	3	2,816,341–2,816,510	170
1915	3	2,816,521–2,816,550	30
1915	4	2,816,561–2,816,600	40
1915	4	2,817,001–2,817,270	270
1915	4	2,817,281–2,817,500	220
1915	4	2,827,101–2,827,200	100
1915	4	2,827,211–2,827,300	90
1915	4	2,827,311–2,827,320	10
1915	4	2,827,331–2,827,750	420
1915	4	2,887,761–2,827,770	10
1915	4	2,827,781–2,827,790	10
1915	4	2,827,801–2,827,850	80
1915	4	2,827,871–2,827,890	20
1915	4	2,827,901–2,827,910	10
1915	4	2,827,921–2,827,940	20
1915	4	2,827,951–2,827,970	20
1915	4	2,827,981–2,827,990	10
1915	4	2,844,001–2,864,100	100
1915	4	2,844,301–2,844,900	600
1915	3	2,861,501–2,862,000	500
1915	3	2,863,001–2,863,100	100
1915	4	2,863,701–2,864,000	300
1915	4	2,871,001–2,871,300	300
1915	4	2,871,901–2,872,100	100
1915	4	2,884,101–2,884,700	600
1915	4	2,891,301–2,891,700	400
		Total	**4,890**

3/0 Size, 11-Jewel Movements, Grade 32			
Year	Model	Serial Numbers	Quantity
1915	3	2,799,901–2,840,100	100
		Total	**100**
1916	3	2,903,001–2,903,040	40
1916	4	2,903,161–2,903,310	150
1916	4	2,903,451–2,903,510	60
1916	4	2,940,101–2,940,200	100
1916	3	2,940,451–2,940,500	50
1916	3	3,036,001–3,036,100	100
1916	4	3,036,701–3,036,860	160
		Total	**660**
1917	3	3,103,901–3,104,000	100
1917	4	3,120,901–3,120,960	60
1917	?	3,170,781–3,170,800	20
1917	?	3,233,801–3,233,900	100
1917	?	3,235,501–3,235,600	100
		Total	**380**
1918	?	3,301,701–3,301,900	200
1918	4	3,374,151–3,374,200	50
1918	4	3,374,901–3,375,000	100
		Total	**350**
1919	3	3,429,551–3,429,600	50
		Total	**50**

3/0 Size, 11-Jewel Movements, Grade 21			
Year	Model	Serial Numbers	Quantity
1916	4	2,879,001–2,879,500	500
1916	3	2,884,101–2,884,700	600
1916	3	2,891,301–2,891,700	400
1916	4	2,902,301–2,902,700	400
1916	3	2,909,101–2,909,700	600
1916	3	2,913,301–2,913,900	600
1916	3	2,922,501–2,923,000	500
1916	3	2,930,001–2,930,100	100
1916	4	2,930,701–2,930,800	100
1916	4	2,938,001–2,938,500	500
1916	3	2,938,701–2,939,000	300
1916	4	2,943,001–2,943,300	300
1916	3	2,943,301–2,943,900	600
1916	3	2,949,501–2,950,000	500
1916	3	2,962,001–2,963,000	1,000
1916	3	2,964,701–2,964,900	200
1916	3	2,984,001–2,985,000	1,000
1916	4	2,992,001–2,992,200	200
1916	3	2,992,201–2,993,000	800
1916	3	3,034,001–3,035,000	1,000
		Total	**10,200**
1917	3	3,102,001–3,103,900	1,900
1917	3	3,160,001–3,161,000	1,000
1917	3	3,209,001–3,209,900	900
1917	4	3,233,001–3,233,300	300
1917	4	3,233,301–3,233,500	200
1917	4	3,233,501–3,233,700	200
1917	4	3,233,701–3,233,800	100
1917	4	3,233,901–3,234,000	100
		Total	**4,700**
1918	3	3,279,001–3,279,800	800
1918	4	3,279,801–3,279,900	100
1918	4	3,279,901–3,280,000	100
1918	3	3,312,471–3,312,490	20
1918	3	3,314,001–3,314,600	600
1918	3	3,314,901–3,315,000	100
1918	3	3,316,901–3,317,000	100
1918	4	3,322,001–3,322,500	500
		Total	**2,320**

3/0 Size, 12-Jewel Movements, Grade 21			
Year	Model	Serial Numbers	Quantity
1916	3	2,964,901–2,965,000	100
1916	3	3,042,901–3,043,000	100
1917	3	3,161,401–3,161,700	300
1918	3	3,314,601–3,314,900	300
		Total	**800**

3/0 Size, 15-Jewel Movements, Grade 23			
Year	Model	Serial Numbers	Quantity
1915	3	2,817,841–2,817,900	10
1915	4	2,844,901–2,845,000	100
1915	4	2,861,001–2,861,200	200
1915	3	2,863,101–2,863,400	300
1915	4	2,871,301–2,871,600	300
		Total	**910**
1916	4	2,879,501–2,879,900	400
1916	3	2,884,701–2,885,000	300
1916	3	2,891,701–2,892,000	300
1916	4	2,902,701–2,903,000	300
1916	3	2,909,701–2,910,000	300
1916	3	2,913,001–2,913,100	100
1916	3	2,913,901–2,914,000	100
1916	3	2,922,001–2,922,300	300
1916	3	2,930,101–2,930,500	400
1916	4	2,930,801–2,930,900	100
1916	4	2,938,501–2,938,700	200
1916	3	2,943,901–2,944,000	100
1916	3	2,949,001–2,949,300	300
1916	3	2,963,001–2,964,000	1,000
1916	3	2,985,001–2,986,000	1,000
1916	4	2,994,001–2,995,000	1,000
1916	3	3,035,001–3,036,000	1,000
		Total	**7,200**

3/0 Size, 15-Jewel Movements, Grade 23 (pt 2)			
Year	Model	Serial Numbers	Quantity
1917	4	3,120,701–3,120,900	200
1917	3	3,161,001–3,161,400	400
1917	3	3,161,701–3,162,000	300
1917	3	3,209,901–3,211,000	1,100
1917	4	3,234,001–3,234,200	200
1917	4	3,234,201–3,234,500	300
1917	4	3,234,501–3,234,700	200
1917	4	3,234,701–3,235,000	300
		Total	**3,000**
1918	?	3,263,001–3,263,500	500
1918	4	3,263,501–3,263,600	100
1918	4	3,263,601–3,264,000	400
1918	4	3,280,801–3,281,000	200
1918	4	3,302,001–3,303,000	1,000
1918	3	3,312,491–3,312,500	10
1918	3	3,312,501–3,312,510	10
1918	3	3,315,001–3,315,800	800
1918	4	3,322,501–3,324,000	1,500
1918	3	3,329,001–3,330,000	1,000
1918	3	3,333,001–3,334,000	1,000
1918	4	3,356,001–3,357,000	1,000
1918	4	3,364,001–3,364,600	600
1918	4	3,364,601–3,365,000	400
1918	3	3,375,301–3,376,000	700
1918	3	3,393,801–3,394,000	200
1918	4	3,396,001–3,397,000	1,000
1918	4	3,415,001–3,417,000	2,000
1918	4	3,419,001–3,420,000	1,000
		Total	**13,420**
1919	4	3,426,001–3,427,000	1,000
1919	4	3,437,001–3,438,000	1,000
1919	4	3,443,001–3,444,000	1,000
1919	4	3,452,001–3,453,400	1,400
1919	3	3,470,001–3,471,000	1,000
		Total	**5,400**
1920	3	3,658,001–3,660,000	2,000
1920	?	3,670,001–3,671,000	1,000
1920	3	3,692,001–3,693,000	1,000
		Total	**4,000**

3/0 Size, 15-Jewel Movements, Grade 34			
Year	Model	Serial Numbers	Quantity
1915	3	2,699,711–2,644,750	40
1915	3	2,799,801–2,799,900	100
		Total	**140**
1916	3	2,903,041–2,903,080	40
1916	4	2,903,311–2,903,410	100
1916	4	2,903,511–2,903,570	60
1916	4	2,904,201–2,904,300	100
1916	4	3,036,901–3,037,000	100
		Total	**400**
1917	4	3,120,961–3,120,900	30
1917	4	3,170,951–3,171,000	50
1917	?	3,235,601–3,235,700	100
		Total	**180**
1918	?	3,301,901–3,302,000	100
1918	4	3,309,101–3,309,200	100
1918	4	3,375,001–3,375,300	300
		Total	500
1919	3	3,453,401–3,453,600	200
		Total	**200**

3/0 Size, 17-Jewel Movements, Grade 24			
Year	Model	Serial Numbers	Quantity
1915	3	2,827,041–2,827,050	10
1915	4	2,844,101–2,844,200	100
1915	4	2,844,211–2,844,240	30
1915	4	2,844,251–2,844,200	10
1915	4	2,861,201–2,861,500	300
1915	3	2,863,401–2,863,700	300
1915	4	2,871,601–2,871,900	300
		Total	**1,050**
1916	4	2,879,901–2,880,000	100
1916	4	2,884,001–2,884,100	100
1916	3	2,891,001–2,891,300	300
1916	3	2,902,001–2,902,150	150
1916	4	2,909,001–2,909,100	100
1916	4	2,913,101–2,913,300	200
1916	3	2,922,301–2,922,500	200
1916	3	2,930,501–2,930,200	200

3/0 Size, 17-Jewel Movements, Grade 24 (pt 2)			
Year	Model	Serial Numbers	Quantity
1916	4	2,930,901–2,931,000	100
1916	3	2,949,301–2,949,500	200
1916	3	2,964,001–2,964,700	700
1916	4	2,996,001–2,996,200	200
1916	3	2,996,201–2,996,900	700
		Total	**3,250**
1917	3	3,211,001–3,211,200	200
1917	3	3,211,301–3,211,400	100
1917	4	3,237,001–3,238,000	1,000
		Total	**1,300**
1918	4	3,248,001–3,249,000	1,000
1918	4	3,256,001–3,256,300	300
1918	4	3,256,301–3,257,000	700
1918	?	3,280,601–3,280,800	200
1918	4	3,308,001–3,309,000	1,000
1918	3	3,312,511–3,312,530	20
1918	?	3,312,801–3,313,000	200
1918	3	3,316,001–3,316,500	500
1918	4	3,316,501–3,316,900	400
1918	4	3,365,001–3,365,200	200
1918	4	3,365,601–3,366,000	400
		Total	**4,920**
1919	4		0
1920	4		0
1921	4		0
1922	4		0
1923	4		0
1924	4		0
1925	4		0
		Total	**0**
1926	4	4,794,001–4,796,000	1,000
1926	3	4,811,001–4,812,000	1,000
1926	4	4,835,001–4,836,000	1,000
		Total	3,000
1927	4	4,851,001–4,853,000	2,000
1927	4	4,908,271–4,908,500	230
1927	4	4,909,001–4,910,000	1,000
1927	4	4,938,001–4,940,000	2,000
1927	4	4,949,001–4,949,000	2,000
1927	4	4,969,001–4,970,000	1,000

3/0 Size, 17-Jewel Movements, Grade 24 (pt 3)			
Year	Model	Serial Numbers	Quantity
1927	4	4,971,001–4,972,000	1,000
1927	4	4,981,001–4,982,000	1,000
1927	4	4,991,001–4,992,000	1,000
1927	4	4,993,001–4,994,000	1,000
		Total	**12,230**
1928	4	5,012,001–5,014,000	2,000
1928	4	5,025,001–5,027,000	2,000
1928	4	5,032,001–5,033,000	1,000
1928	4	5,041,001–5,042,000	1,400
1928	4	5,042,401–5,042,700	300
1928	4	5,042,701–5,043,000	300
1928	4	5,047,001–5,048,600	1,600
1928	4	5,048,601–5,049,000	400
1928	4	5,055,001–5,057,000	2,000
1928	4	5,065,001–5,066,050	1,050
1928	4	5,066,051–5,066,200	150
1928	4	5,066,201–5,067,000	800
1928	4	5,085,001–5,086,000	1,000
1928	4	5,090,001–5,092,000	2,000
1928	4	5,104,001–5,105,550	1,550
1928	4	5,105,551–5,105,600	50
1928	4	5,105,601–5,106,000	400
1928	4	5,112,001–5,114,000	2,000
1928	4	5,126,001–5,123,000	2,000
1928	4	5,135,001–5,136,000	1,000
1928	4	5,142,001–5,144,000	2,000
		Total	**25,000**
1929	4	5,149,001–5,151,000	2,000
1929	4	5,153,001–5,155,000	2,000
1929	4	5,159,001–5,161,000	2,000
1929	4	5,165,001–5,166,000	1,000
1929	4	5,167,001–5,168,000	1,000
1929	4	5,169,001–5,170,000	1,000
1929	4	5,173,001–5,175,000	2,000
1929	4	5,177,001–5,179,000	2,000
1929	4	5,183,001–5,188,000	5,000
1929	4	5,189,001–5,191,000	2,000
1929	4	5,194,001–5,196,000	2,000
1929	4	5,197,001–5,199,000	2,000
1929	4	5,202,001–5,203,000	1,000
1929	4	5,205,001–5,206,400	1,400
1929	4	5,206,401–5,206,800	400

3/0 Size, 17-Jewel Movements, Grade 24 (pt 4)			
Year	Model	Serial Numbers	Quantity
1929	4	5,206,801–5,207,000	200
1929	4	5,209,001–5,210,200	1,200
1929	4	5,210,201–5,210,600	400
1929	4	5,210,601–5,211,000	400
1929	4	5,213,001–5,214,000	1,000
1929	4	5,214,001–5,214,400	400
1929	4	5,214,401–5,215,000	600
1929	4	5,219,001–5,219,800	800
1929	4	5,219,801–5,220,200	400
1929	4	5,220,201–5,221,000	800
1929	4	5,226,001–5,226,600	600
1929	4	5,226,601–5,227,000	400
1929	4	5,231,001–5,237,000	6,000
1929	4	5,243,001–5,245,000	2,000
1929	4	5,249,001–5,250,000	1,000
1929	4	5,259,001–5,201,000	2,000
1929	4	5,204,001–5,266,000	2,000
1929	4	5,267,001–5,269,000	2,000
1929	4	5,270,001–5,272,000	2,000
1929	4	5,285,001–5,286,000	1,000
1929	4	5,294,001–5,295,000	1,000
1929	4	5,298,001–5,299,000	1,000
		Total	**54,000**
1930	4	5,302,001–5,302,500	500
1930	4	5,302,501–5,303,000	500
1930	4	5,306,001–5,308,000	2,000
1930	4	5,310,001–5,313,000	3,000
		Total	**6,000**
1931	4		0
1932	4		0
		Total	**0**

3/0 Size, 17-Jewel Movements, Grade 36			
Year	Model	Serial Numbers	Quantity
1915	3	2,845,001–2,845,200	200
1915	4	2,845,201–2,846,000	1,000
		Total	**1,200**
1916	4	2,903,571–2,903,600	30
1916	3	2,942,901–2,943,000	100
1916	3	2,945,001–2,945,650	650
1916	4	2,947,001–2,947,400	400
1916	3	3,036,381–3,036,400	20
1916	4	3,045,701–3,046,000	300
		Total	**1,500**
1917	4	3,057,501–3,057,950	450
1917	3	3,077,201–3,077,350	150
1917	4	3,120,991–3,121,000	10
1917	3	3,170,801–3,170,950	150
1917	?	3,188,301–3,188,800	500
1917	3	3,211,201–3,211,300	100
1917	?	3,235,001–3,235,500	500
1917	?	3,235,701–3,235,750	50
		Total	**1,910**
1918	4	3,301,001–3,301,700	700
1918	3	3,312,781–3,312,800	20
1918	4	3,365,201–3,365,600	400
1918	4	3,376,001–3,376,600	600
1918	3	3,376,601–3,376,700	100
1918	3	3,384,991–3,385,000	10
		Total	**1,830**
1919	4	3,486,001–3,487,000	1,000
		Total	**1,000**
1920			0
		Total	**0**
1921	4	3,802,001–3,802,450	450
		Total	**450**

3/0 Size, 17-Jewel Movements, Grade 36 (pt 2)			
Year	Model	Serial Numbers	Quantity
1922			0
1923			0
1924			0
1925			0
1926			0
1927			0
1928			0
1929			0
1930			0
1931			0
1932			0
		Total	**0**

3/0 Size, 17-Jewel Movements, Grade 307			
Year	Model	Serial Numbers	Quantity
1930	4	5,319,001–5,320,000	1,000
1930	4	5,322,001–5,324,000	2,000
1930	4	5,325,001–5,326,000	1,000
1930	4	5,327,001–5,329,000	2,000
1930	4	5,331,001–5,332,000	1,000
1930	4	5,336,001–5,338,000	2,000
1930	4	5,339,001–5,341,000	2,000
1930	4	5,343,001–5,344,000	1,000
1930	4	5,346,001–5,347,000	1,000
1930	4	5,348,001–5,349,000	1,000
1930	4	5,350,001–5,351,000	1,000
1930	4	5,352,001–5,353,000	1,000
1930	4	5,354,001–5,355,000	1,000
1930	4	5,357,001–5,358,000	1,000
1930	4	5,359,001–5,361,000	2,000
1930	4	5,365,001–5,367,000	2,000
1930	4	5,367,001–5,367,500	500
1930	4	5,367,501–5,368,000	500
1930	4	5,371,001–5,374,000	3,000
1930	4	5,378,001–5,380,000	2,000
1930	4	5,382,001–5,384,000	2,000
		Total	**30,000**

3/0 Size, 17-Jewel Movements, Grade 307 (pt 2)

Year	Model	Serial Numbers	Quantity
1931			0
		Total	**0**
1932	4	5,489,001–5,490,000	1,000
1932	4	5,499,001–5,501,000	2,000
1932	4	5,512,001–5,514,000	2,000
1932	4	5,516,001–5,517,000	1,000
1932	4	5,531,001–5,533,000	2,000
1932	4	5,536,001–5,538,000	2,000
1932	4	5,542,801–5,543,000	200*
1932	4	5,559,001–5,560,900	1,900
1932	4	5,566,001–5,567,000	1,000
1932	4	5,574,001–5,576,000	2,000
1932	4	5,586,001–5,588,000	2,000
1932	4	5,598,001–5,599,000	1,000
		Total	**18,100**
1932	4	5,622,001–5,624,000	2,000
1932	4	5,681,001–5,683,700	2,700
		Total	**4,700**

*This run of 200 was of the 307 S.A.W (Special Aluminum Watch) movements with aluminum plates.

3/0 Size, Unknown Jewel Movements, Grade 30

Year	Model	Serial Numbers	Quantity
1915	3	2,799,731–2,799,800	70
		Total	**70**

3/0 Size, Unknown Jewel Movements, Grade 25

Year	Model	Serial Numbers	Quantity
1918	?	3,280,001–3,280,600	600
		Total	**600**

6/0 Size, 15-Jewel Movements, Grade 903 (pt 1)

Year	Model	Serial Numbers	Quantity
1915	1	2,689,101–2,690,000	900
1915	1	2,782,601–2,783,000	400
		Total	**1,300**
1916	1	2,918,001–2,918,800	800
1916	1	2,940,601–2,940,650	50
1916	1	3,003,501–3,003,650	150
1916	1	3,003,701–3,004,000	300
1916	1	3,005,001–3,006,000	1,000
1916	1	3,025,001–3,026,000	1,000
1916	1	3,037,001–3,038,000	1,000
1916	1	3,050,001–3,051,000	1,000
		Total	**5,300**
1917	1	3,090,001–3,091,000	1,000
1917	1	3,101,801–3,102,000	200
1917	1	3,108,001–3,108,800	800
1917	1	3,135,001–3,136,000	1,000
1917	1	3,158,001–3,159,000	1,000
1917	1	3,168,911–3,168,960	50
1917	1	3,181,001–3,181,500	500
1917	1	3,181,501–3,182,000	500
1917	1	3,192,001–3,192,400	400
1917	1	3,192,901–3,193,000	100
1917	1	3,202,001–3,203,000	1,000
1917	1	3,228,001–3,229,000	1,000
		Total	**7,550**
1918	1	3,254,001–3,254,100	100
1918	1	3,254,501–3,255,000	500
1918	1	3,271,001–3,271,650	650
1918	1	3,271,701–3,272,000	300
1918	1	3,286,001–3,287,000	1,000
1918	1	3,295,001–3,296,000	1,000
1918	1	3,297,001–3,297,400	400
1918	1	3,297,501–3,297,700	200
1918	1	3,318,501–3,318,900	400
1918	1	3,339,501–3,340,000	500
1918	1	3,340,101–3,341,000	900
1918	1	3,355,201–3,355,800	600
1918	1	3,376,701–3,377,000	300
1918	1	3,392,911–3,392,930	20
1918	1	3,408,001–3,409,000	1,000
		Total	**7,870**

6/0 Size, 15-Jewel Movements, Grade 903 (pt 2)			
Year	Model	Serial Numbers	Quantity
1919	1	3,472,001–3,472,700	700
1919	1	3,492,001–3,493,000	1,000
1919	1	3,504,001–3,505,600	1,600
1919	1	3,520,101–3,521,000	900
1919	1	3,526,001–,3,526,100	100
1919	1	2,526,501–3,527,000	500
1919	1	3,536,001–3,537,000	1,000
1919	1	3,547,001–3,547,700	700
1919	1	3,547,901–3,548,000	100
1919	1	3,575,001–3,575,600	600
1919	1	3,576,101–3,577,000	900
1919	1	3,548,001–3,585,000	1,000
1919	1	3,589,501–3,590,000	500
1919	1	3,599,001–3,600,000	1,000
		Total	**10,600**
1920	1	3,615,001–3,616,000	1,000
1920	1	3,623,001–3,623,600	600
1920	1	3,625,101–3,625,800	700
1920	1	3,637,301–3,638,000	700
1920	1	3,653,001–3,654,000	1,000
1920	1	3,662,001–3,663,000	1,000
1920	1	3,667,001–3,678,000	1,000
1920	1	3,678,801–3,679,000	200
1920	1	3,684,001–3,684,900	900
1920	1	3,700,301–3,701,000	700
1920	1	3,727,001–3,728,000	1,000
1920	1	3,740,001–3,740,300	300
1920	1	3,740,701–3,741,000	300
1920	1	3,764,001–3,765,000	1,000
		Total	**10,400**
1921	1	3,805,001–3,807,000	2,000
1921	1	3,848,001–3,849,000	1,000
1921	1	3,886,001–3,888,000	2,000
1921	1	3,942,001–3,943,000	1,000
		Total	**6,000**
1922	1	3,981,001–3,983,000	2,000
1922	1	4,023,001–4,025,000	2,000
1922	1	4,087,001–4,088,000	1,000
1922	1	4,096,001–4,098,000	2,000
1922	1	4,110,001–4,111,000	1,000
1922	1	4,123,001–4,125,000	2,000

6/0 Size, 15-Jewel Movements, Grade 903 (pt 3)			
Year	Model	Serial Numbers	Quantity
1922	1	4,127,001–4,133,000	1,000
1922	1	4,133,001–4,134,000	1,000
1922	1	4,143,001–4,144,000	1,000
1922	1	4,161,001–4,162,000	1,000
		Total	**16,000**
1923	1	4,170,001–4,172,000	2,000
1923	1	4,190,001–4,192,000	2,000
1923	1	4,202,001–4,203,000	1,000
1923	1	4,217,001–4,219,000	2,000
1923	1	4,230,001–4,231,000	1,000
1923	1	4,256,001–4,258,000	2,000
1923	1	4,268,001–4,269,000	1,000
1923	1	4,283,001–4,284,000	1,000
1923	1	4,285,001–4,286,000	1,000
1923	1	4,297,001–4,298,000	1,000
1923	1	4,311,001–4,313,000	2,000
1923	1	4,367,001–4,368,000	1,000
1923	1	4,369,001–4,370,000	1,000
1923	1	4,409,001–4,410,000	1,000
1923	1	4,435,001–4,437,000	2,000
1923	1	4,457,001–4,458,000	1,000
		Total	**22,000**
1924	1	4,496,001–4,498,000	2,000
1924	1	4,544,001–4,546,000	2,000
		Total	**4,000**
1925	1	4,624,001–4,625,000	1,000
1925	1	4,641,001–4,642,000	1,000
1925	1	4,643,001–4,644,000	1,000
		Total	**3,000**
1926	1	4,715,001–4,716,000	1,000
1926	1	4,729,001–,4,730,000	1,000
1926	1	4,731,001–4,732,000	1,000
1926	1	4,749,001–4,751,000	2,000
1926	1	4,790,001–4,791,000	1,000
1926	1	4,802,001–4,804,000	2,000
1926	1	4,816,001–4,818,000	2,000
1926	1	4,831,001–4,832,000	1,000
1926	1	4,843,001–4,845,000	2,000
		Total	**13,000**

6/0 Size, 15-Jewel Movements, Grade 903 (pt4)			
Year	Model	Serial Numbers	Quantity
1927	1	4,860,001–4,861,000	1,000
1927	1	4,876,001–4,878,000	2,000
1927	1	4,889,001–4,890,000	1,000
1927	1	4,898,001–4,900,000	2,000
1927	1	4,907,001–4,908,000	1,000
1927	1	4,917,001–4,919,000	2,000
1927	1	4,930,001–4,931,000	1,000
1927	1	4,941,001–4,942,000	1,000
1927	1	4,943,001–4,944,000	1,000
1927	1	4,953,001–4,955,000	2,000
1927	1	4,963,001–4,965,000	2,000
1927	1	4,975,001–4,976,000	1,000
1927	1	4,982,001–4,984,000	2,000
1927	1	4,994,001–4,995,000	1,000
		Total	**20,000**
1928	1	5,002,001–5,004,000	2,000
1928	1	5,007,001–5,008,000	1,000
1928	1	5,011,001–5,012,000	1,000
1928	1	5,023,001–5,024,000	1,000
1928	1	5,029,001–5,030,000	1,000
1928	1	5,035,001–5,035,600	600
1928	1	5,035,601–5,036,000	400
1928	1	5,034,001–5,039,100	100
1928	1	5,039,101–5,039,300	200
1928	1	5,039,301–5,039,400	600
1928	1	5,039,401–5,040,000	100
1928	1	5,043,401–5,044,000	600
1928	1	5,045,001–5,045,400	400
1928	1	5,045,001–5,045,700	300
1928	1	5,045,701–5,045,800	100
1928	1	5,045,801–5,046,000	200
1928	1	5,049,001–5,049,300	300
1928	1	5,049,301–5,050,000	700
1928	1	5,053,001–5,054,000	1,000
1928	1	5,061,001–5,062,000	1,000
1928	1	5,080,001–5,081,000	1,000
1928	1	5,088,001–5,088,600	600
1928	1	5,088,601–5,089,000	400
1928	1	5,093,001–5,093,200	200
1928	1	5,093,201–5,093,250	50
1928	1	5,093,251–5,094,000	750
1928	1	5,118,001–5,119,000	1,000
		Total	**16,600**

6/0 Size, 15-Jewel Movements, Grade 903 (pt 5)			
Year	Model	Serial Numbers	Quantity
1929	1	5,175,001–5,176,000	1,000
1929	1	5,191,001–5,192,000	1,000
1929	1	5,196,001–5,197,000	1,000
1929	1	5,199,001–5,200,000	1,000
1929	1	5,203,001–5,204,000	1,000
1929	1	5,207,001–5,208,000	1,000
1929	1	5,211,001–5,213,000	2,000
1929	1	5,223,001–5,224,000	1,000
1929	1	5,225,001–5,226,000	1,000
1929	1	5,227,001–5,228,000	1,000
1929	1	5,229,901–5,230,000	100
1929	1	5,237,001–5,238,000	1,000
1929	1	5,247,001–5,249,000	2,000
1929	1	5,250,001–5,252,000	2,000
1929	1	5,253,001–5,254,000	1,000
1929	1	5,255,001–5,256,000	1,000
1929	1	5,258,001–5,259,000	1,000
1929	1	5,262,001–5,264,000	2,000
1929	1	5,275,001–5,276,000	1,000
1929	1	5,279,001–5,280,000	1,000
1929	1	5,286,001–5,287,000	1,000
		Total	**24,100**
1930			0
1931			0
1932			0
1948			0
		Total	**0**

6/0 Size, 15-Jewel Movements, Grade 605 & 605A			
Year	**Model**	**Serial Numbers**	**Quantity**
1932–1933	6	5,613,001–5,616,000	3,000
1932–1933	6	5,628,001–5,630,000	2,000
1932–1933	6	5,632,001–5,634,000	2,000
1932–1933	6	5,635,001–5,637,000	2,000
1932–1933	6	5,639,001–5,639,900	900
1932–1933	6	5,642,001–5,644,000	2,000
1932–1933	6	5,646,001–5,649,000	3,000
1932–1933	6	5,659,001–5,660,000	1,000
1932–1933	6	5,660,001–5,660,600	600
1932–1933	7	5,692,501–5,694,500	2,000
		Total	**18,500**

6/0 Size, 15-Jewel Movements, Grade 585			
Year	**Model**	**Serial Numbers**	**Quantity**
1931	3	5,423,001–5,424,000	1,000
		Total	**1,000**
1932	3	5,503,001–5,504,000	1,000
		Total	**1,000**

6/0 Size, 17-Jewel Movements, Grade 904			
Year	**Model**	**Serial Numbers**	**Quantity**
1915			0
1916	1	3,049,001–3,050,000	1,000
1917	1	3,071,001–3,072,000	1,000
1917	1	3,192,401–3,192,900	500
1917	1	3,211,601–3,212,000	400
		Total	**1,900**
1918	1	3,297,401–3,297,500	100
1918	1	3,318,001–3,318,500	500
1918	1	3,339,001–3,339,500	500
1918	1	3,383,201–3,383,700	500
		Total	**1,600**
1919	1	3,451,301–3,451,500	200
1919	1	3,472,701–3,473,000	300
1919	1	3,505,601–3,506,000	400
1919	1	3,520,001–3,520,100	100
1919	1	3,526,901–3,526,500	400
1919	1	3,575,601–3,576,100	500
1919	1	3,589,001–3,589,500	500
		Total	**2,400**
1920	1	3,625,801–3,626,000	200
1920	1	3,637,001–3,637,300	300
1920	1	3,678,001–3,678,800	800
1920	1	3,684,901–3,685,000	100
1920	1	3,700,001–3,700,300	300
1920	1	3,740,301–3,740,700	400
		Total	**2,100**
1921			0
1922			0
1923			0
1924			0
1925			0
1926			0
1927			0
		Total	**0**

6/0 Size, 17-Jewel Movements, Grade 905			
Year	Model	Serial Numbers	Quantity
1928	2	5,015,001–5,017,000	2,000
1928	2	5,024,001–5,025,000	1,000
1928	2	5,037,001–5,038,000	1,000
1928	2	5,043,401–5,044,000	400
1928	2	5,046,001–5,046,500	500
1928	2	5,046,501–5,047,000	500
1928	2	5,050,001–5,050,100	100
1928	2	5,050,101–5,050,200	100
1928	2	5,050,201–5,052,000	1,800
1928	2	5,057,001–5,058,000	1,000
1928	2	5,063,000–5,065,000	2,000
1928	2	5,078,001–5,079,000	1,000
1928	2	5,081,001–5,082,000	1,000
1928	2	5,083,001–5,084,000	1,000
1928	2	5,089,001–5,089,700	700
1928	2	5,089,701–5,090,000	300
1928	2	5,098,001–5,098,900	900
1928	2	5,098,901–5,098,950	50
1928	2	5,098,951–5,100,000	1,050
1928	2	5,101,001–5,102,000	1,000
1928	2	5,106,001–5,107,000	1,000
1928	2	5,111,001–5,112,000	1,000
1928	2	5,117,001–5,118,000	1,000
1928	2	5,119,001–5,120,000	1,000
1928	2	5,123,001–5,125000	2,000
1928	2	5,127,001–5,128,000	1,000
1928	2	5,136,001–5,138,000	2,000
1928	2	5,145,001–5,146,000	1,000
1928	2	5,147,001–5,148,000	1,000
		Total	**28,400**
1929	2	5,151,001–5,152,000	1,000
1929	2	5,155,001–5,156,000	1,000
1929	2	5,157,001–5,158,000	1,000
1929	2	5,171,001–5,172,000	1,000
1929	2	5,179,001–5,180,000	1,000
1929	2	5,192,001–5,193,000	1,000
1929	2	5,200,001–5,201,000	1,000
1929	2	5,274,001–5,275,000	1,000
1929	2	5,277,001–5,278,000	1,000
1929	2	5,280,001–5,282,000	2,000
1929	2	5,290,001–5,291,000	1,000
1929	2	5,296,001–5,297,000	1,000
		Total	**13,000**

6/0 Size, 17-Jewel Movements, Grade 905 (pt 2)			
Year	Model	Serial Numbers	Quantity
1930	2	5,314,001–5,315,000	1,000
1930	2	5,316,001–5,317,000	1,000
1930	2	5,324,001–5,325,000	1,000
		Total	**3,000**

6/0 Size, 17-Jewel Movements, Grade 607			
Year	Model	Serial Numbers	Quantity
1930	4	5,364,001–5,365,000	1,000
1930	4	5,387,001–5,388,000	1,000
1930	4	5,394,001–5,396,000	2,000
1930	4	5,398,001–5,400,000	2,000
		Total	**6,000**
1931	4	5,408,001–5,409,000	1,000
1931	4	5,418,001–5,420,000	2,000
1931	4	5,427,001–5,428,000	1,000
1931	4	5,434,001–5,436,000	2,000
1931	4	5,442,001–5,443,000	1,000
1931	4	5,449,001–5,451,000	2,000
1931	4	5,454,001–5,455,000	1,000
1931	4	5,462,001–5,464,000	2,000
1931	4	5,467,001–5,468,000	1,000
1931	4	5,475,001–5,477,000	2,000
1931	4	5,482,001–5,483,000	1,000
		Total	**16,000**
1932	4	5,490,001–5,493,000	3,000
1932	4	5,498,001–5,499,000	1,000
1932	4	5,506,001–5,508,000	2,000
1932	4	5,514,001–5,516,000	2,000
1932	4	5,519,001–5,520,000	1,000
1932	4	5,538,001–5,542,800	4,800
1932	6	5,551,001–5,553,000	2,000
1932	6	5,590,001–5,590,000	2,000
1932	6	5,595,001–5,597,000	2,000
1932	6	5,599,001–5,601,000	2,000
1932	6	5,605,001–5,607,000	2,000
		Total	**23,800**
1932–1933	6	5,660,601–5,661,000	400
1932–1933	6	5,663,001–5,664,200	1,200
		Total	**1,600**

6/0 Size, 19-Jewel Movements, Grade 907			
Year	**Model**	**Serial Numbers**	**Quantity**
1915	1	2,782,001–2,782,000	600
		Total	**600**
1916	1	2,918,801–2,919,000	200
1916	1	2,940,651–2,940,700	50
1916	1	3,003,001–3,003,500	500
1916	1	3,003,651–3,003,700	1,000
		Total	**1,750**
1917	1	3,211,401–3,211,600	200
		Total	**200**
1918	1	3,254,101–3,254,500	400
1918	1	3,271,651–3,271,700	50
1918	1	3,297,701–3,298,000	300
1918	1	3,318,901–3,319,000	100
1918	1	3,340,001–3,340,100	100
1918	1	3,355,001–3,355,200	200
1918	1	3,355,801–3,356,000	200
1918	1	3,383,701–3,383,900	200
		Total	**1,550**
1919	1	3,547,701–3,547,900	200
		Total	**200**
1920	1	3,623,601–3,624,000	400
1920	1	3,625,001–3,625,100	100
		Total	**500**
1921			0
		Total	**0**
1922			0
		Total	**0**
1923	2	4,231,001–4,232,000	1,000
		Total	**1,000**
1924			0
		Total	**0**
1925			0
		Total	**0**

6/0 Size, 19-Jewel Movements, Grade 907 (pt 2)			
Year	**Model**	**Serial Numbers**	**Quantity**
1926	1	4,716,001–4,717,000	1,000
1926	1	4,832,001–4,833,000	1,000
		Total	**2,000**
1927	1	4,878,001–4,879,000	1,000
1927	1	4,919,001–4,920,000	1,000
1927	1	4,984,001–4,985,000	1,000
		Total	**3,000**
1928	2	5,058,001–5,058,050	50
1928	2	5,058,051–5,059,000	950
1928	2	5,109,001–5,109,850	850
1928	2	5,109,851–5,109,000	50
1928	2	5,109,901–5,110,000	100
1928	2	5,125,001–5,126,000	1,000
1928	1	5,133,001–5,134,000	1,000
		Total	**4,000**
1929	1	5,161,001–5,161,250	250
1929	1	5,161,251–5,161,300	50
1929	1	5,161,301–5,162,000	700
1929	1	5,193,001–5,194,000	1,000
1929	1	5,204,001–5,204,700	700
1929	1	5,204,761–5,204,850	150
1929	1	5,204,851–5,204,900	50
1929	1	5,204,901–5,205,006	100
1929	2	5,292,001–5,293,000	1,000
1929	2	5,299,001–5,300,000	1,000
		Total	**5,000**
1930	2	5,303,001–5,304,000	1,000
		Total	**1,000**

6/0 Size, 21-Jewel Movements, Grade 909			
Year	Model	Serial Numbers	Quantity
1923	3	4,241,161–4,241,190	30
		Total	**30**
1924			0
1925			0
1926			0
1927			0
1928			0
		Total	**0**
1929	3	5,229,001–5,229,900	900
1929	3	5,239,001–5,240,000	1,000
1929	3	5,266,001–5,267,000	1,000
		Total	**2,900**
1930	3	5,304,001–5,305,000	1,000
		Total	**1,000**

6/0 Size, 21-Jewel Movements, Grade 601			
Year	Model	Serial Numbers	Quantity
1931	5	5,461,001–5,462,000	1,000
		Total	**1,000**
1932	5	5,488,001–5,489,000	1,000
1932	5	5,524,001–5,525,000	1,000
1932	5	5,526,001–5,527,000	1,000
1932	5	5,564,001–5,565,000	1,000
		Total	**4,000**

12/0 Size, 17-Jewel Movements, Grade 207			
Year	Model	Serial Numbers	Quantity
1930	1	5,308,001–5,309,000	1,000
1930	1	5,320,001–5,321,000	1,000
1930	1	5,333,001–5,334,000	1,000
1930	1	5,338,001–5,339,000	1,000
1930	1	5,344,001–5,345,000	1,000
1930	1	5,349,001–5,350,000	1,000
1930	1	5,358,001–5,359,000	1,000
1930	1	5,361,001–5,362,000	1,000
1930	1	5,376,001–5,378,000	2,000
1930	1	5,384,001–5,386,000	2,000

12/0 Size, 17-Jewel Movements, Grade 207 (pt 2)			
Year	Model	Serial Numbers	Quantity
1930	1	5,392,001–5,394,000	2,000
1930	1	5,396,001–5,398,000	2,000
		Total	**16,000**
1931	1	5,402,001–5,406,000	4,000
1931	1	5,409,001–5,413,000	4,000
1931	1	5,422,001–5,423,000	1,000
1931	1	5,430,001–5,432,000	2,000
1931	1	5,438,001–5,440,000	2,000
1931	1	5,447,001–5,448,000	1,000
1931	1	5,452,001–5,454,000	2,000
1931	1	5,459,001–5,461,000	2,000
1931	1	5,471,001–5,473,000	2,000
1931	1	5,479,001–5,480,000	1,000
		Total	**21,000**
1932	1	5,504,001–5,506,000	2,000
1932	1	5,522,001–5,524,000	2,000
1932	1	5,543,001–5,545,000	2,000
		Total	**6,000**

18/0 Size, Unknown Jewel Movements, Grade 6-3/4			
Year	Model	Serial Numbers	Quantity
1923	1	4,241,141–4,241,160	20
1923	1	4,241,191–4,241,200	10
		Total	**30**

18/0 Size, 16-Jewel Movements, Grade 18			
Year	**Model**	**Serial Numbers**	**Quantity**
1923	1	4,484,001–4,485,000	1,000
		Total	**1,000**
1924			0
		Total	**0**
1925	1	4,548,001–4,549,000	1,000
1925	1	4,627,001–4,628,000	1,000
1925	1	4,687,001–,4,688,000	1,000
		Total	**3.000**
1926	1	4,753,001–4,754,000	1,000
		Total	**1,000**
1927	1	4,870,001–4,870,500	500
		Total	**500**

18/0 Size, 17-Jewel Movements, Grade 181			
Year	**Model**	**Serial Numbers**	**Quantity**
1927	1	4,870,501–4,871,000	500
		Total	**500**

18/0 Size, 17-Jewel Movements, Grade 206			
Year	**Model**	**Serial Numbers**	**Quantity**
1927	1	4,937,001–4,938,000	1,000
1927	1	4,985,001–4,986,000	1,000
1927	1	4,992,001–4,993,000	1,000
		Total	**3,000**
1928	1	5,014,001–5,015,000	1,000
1928	1	5,019,001–5,020,000	1,000
1928	1	5,031,001–5,032,000	1,000
1928	1	5,033,001–5,034,000	1,000
1928	1	5,059,001–5,060,000	1,000
1928	1	5,079,001–5,080,000	1,000
1928	1	5,087,001–5,088,000	1,000
1928	1	5,103,001–5,104,000	1,000
1928	1	5,115,001–5,116,000	1,000
1928	1	5,131,001–5,132,000	1,000
1928	1	5,148,001–5,149,000	1,000
		Total	**11,000**

18/0 Size, 17-Jewel Movements, Grade 206 (pt 2)			
Year	**Model**	**Serial Numbers**	**Quantity**
1929	1	5,283,001–5,284,000	1,000
1929	1	5,291,001–5,292,000	1,000
1929	1	5,295,001–5,296,000	1,000
		Total	**3,000**
1930	1	5,309,001–5,310,000	1,000
1930	1	5,318,001–5,318,600	600
1930	1	5,318,701–5,319,000	300
		Total	**1,900**

18/0 Size, 17-Jewel Movements, Grade 807				
Year	**Grade**	**Model**	**Serial Numbers**	**Quantity**
1930	807	2	5,318,601–5,318,700	100
1930	807	2	5,326,001–5,327,000	1,000
1930	807	2	5,332,001–5,333,000	1,000
1930	807	2	5,335,001–5,336,000	1,000
1930	807	2	5,342,001–5,343,000	1,000
1930	807A	3	5,345,001–5,346,000	1,000
1930	807	2	5,347,001–5,348,000	1,000
1930	807	2	5,353,001–5,354,000	1,000
1930	807	2	5,355,001–5,356,000	1,000
1930	807	2	5,363,001–5,364,000	1,000
1930	807	2	5,368,001–5,369,000	1,000
1930	807	2	5,380,001–5,382,000	2,000
1930	807	2	5,388,001–5,390,000	2,000
			Total	**14,100**
1931	807	2	5,400,001–5,402,000	2,000
1931	807	2	5,406,001–5,408,000	2,000
1931	807A	3	5,415,001–5,417,000	2,000
1931	807	2	5,425,001–5,427,000	2,000
1931	807A	3	5,432,001–5,434,000	2,000
1931	807	2	5,443,001–5,445,000	2,000
1931	807	2	5,451,001–5,452,000	1,000
1931	807	2	5,455,001–5,456,000	1,000
1931	807A	3	5,458,001–5,459,000	1,000
1931	807	2	5,465,001–5,467,000	2,000
1931	807	2	5,470,001–5,471,000	1,000
1931	807A	3	5,478,001–5,479,000	1,000
1931	807A	3	5,485,001–5,488,000	3,000
			Total	**22,000**

18/0 Size, 17-Jewel Movements, Grade 807 (pt 2)

Year	Grade	Model	Serial Numbers	Quantity
1932	807A	3	5,495,001–5,496,000	1,000
1932	807A	3	5,501,001–5,503,000	2,000
1932	807A	3	5,517,001–5,519,000	2,000
1932	807A	3	5,528,001–5,531,000	3,000
1932	807A	3	5,535,001–5,536,001	1,000
1932	807A	3	5,546,001–5,548,000	2,000
1932	807A	3	5,555,001–5,557,000	2,000
1932	807A	3	5,567,001–5,568,000	1,000
1932	807A	3	5,572,001–5,574,000	2,000
1932	807A	3	5,578,001–5,580,000	2,000
1932	807A	3	5,583,001–5,586,000	3,000
1932	807A	3	5,588,001–5,590,000	2,000
1932	807A	3	5,593,001–5,595,000	2,000
1932	807A	3	5,597,001–5,598,000	1,000
1932	807A	3	5,601,001–5,604,600	3,600
1932	807B	4	5,604,601–5,605,000	400
1932	807B	4	5,607,001–5,609,000	2,000
			Total	**32,000**
1932–1933	807B	4	5,611,001–5,612,200	1,200
1932–1933	807B	4	5,612,701–5,613,000	300
1932–1933	807B	4	5,619,401–5,619,600	200
1932–1933	807B	4	5,672,001–5,673,400	1,400
			Total	**3,100**

18/0 Size, 15-Jewel Movements, Grade 805/805A

Year	Grade	Model	Serial Numbers	Quantity
1932–1933	805	3	5,616,001–5,618,000	2,000
1932–1933	805A	5	5,619,601–5,620,000	400
1932–1933	805	3	5,620,001–5,622,000	2,000
1932–1933	805	3	5,626,001–5,628,000	2,000
1932–1933	805	3	5,630,001–5,632,000	2,000
1932–1933	805	3	5,634,001–5,635,000	1,000
1932–1933	805	3	5,637,001–5,639,000	2,000
1932–1933	805A	5	5,639,901–5,640,000	100
1932–1933	805	3	5,640,001–5,642,000	2,000
1932–1933	805	3	5,644,001–5,646,000	2,000
1932–1933	805	3	5,653,001–5,655,000	2,000
1932–1933	805	3	5,657\,001–5,659,000	2,000
1932–1933	805	3	5,661,001–5,663,000	2,000
1932–1933	805A	5	5,664,201–5,665,000	800
1932–1933	805	3	5,667,001–5,669,000	2,000
1932–1933	805	3	5,671,001–5,671,400	400

18/0 Size, 15-Jewel Movements, Grade 805/805A (pt 2)

Year	Grade	Model	Serial Numbers	Quantity
1932–1933	805A	5	5,671,401–5,672,000	600
1932–1933	805B	4	5,672,001–5,673,400	1,400
1932–1933	805A	5	5,673,401–5,675,000	1,600
1932–1933	805A	5	5,677,001–5,678,400	1,400
			Total	**29,700**

21/0 Size, 17-Jewel Movements, Grade 107

Year	Model	Serial Numbers	Quantity
1932–1933	1	5,624,001–5,626,000	2,000
1932–1933	1	5,649,001–5,650,000	1,000
1932–1933	1	5,650,001–5,653,000	3,000
1932–1933	1	5,655,001–5,657,000	2,000
1932–1933	1	5,669,001–5,671,000	2,000
1932–1933	1	5,675,001–5,677,000	2,000
1932–1933	1	5,679,001–5,680,800	1,800
		Total	**13,800**

21/0 Size, 15-Jewel Movements, Grade 105

Year	Model	Serial Numbers	Quantity
1932–1933	1	5,680,801–5,681,000	200
1932–1933	1	5,685,001–5,687,000	2,000
1932–1933	1	5,689,001–5,691,000	2,000
1932–1933	1	5,695,001–5,698,800	3,800
		Total	**8,000**

APPENDIX 4

ILLINOIS WATCH COMPANY INTELLECTUAL PROPERTY: PARTIAL LIST

Inventor	Invention	Patent Number	Date Issued
Daniel G. Currier	Improvement in Construction of Watches	108332	1870
John. K. and J. K. Bigelow*	Improvement in Reversible Pinion	131208	1872
J.K. Bigelow*	Watch	169512	1875
Otis Hoyt	Improvement in Stem Winding and Setting	206674	1878
Ryland L. Taft	Stem Winding and Setting Watch	330273	1885
Ryland L. Taft	Stem Winding and Setting Mechanism	345193	1886
Ryland L. Taft	Device for Letting Down the Mainspring	340386	1886
Ryland Lee Taft	Machine for Ruling Dial	312227	1895
Charles T. Higginbotham*	Improvement in Pendant-Set Watches	706656	1902
George F. Johnson	Watch Barrel	804728	1905
George F. Johnson	Safety Barrel	804727	1905
John E. Johnson	Design for a Pendant Stem	41782	1911
Charles E. DeLong	Improved Means for Avoiding Objections Due to Holding of the Mainspring at the Extreme Limit of Its Winding	1283476	1918
Charles E. DeLong	Improved Construction of the Gearing Mechanism of a Stem-Winding Watch	1292269	1919

*Both Bigelow and Higginbotham served as Superintendent of the Illinois Watch Factory at one point.

Charles T. Higgenbotham, the superintendent of the Illinois Factory, was appointed as juror of awards for a machinery exposition in 1901.

Charles T. Higgenbotham Appointed.

SPRINGFIELD, Ill., July 20.—Charles T. Higgenbotham, superintendent of the Illinois Watch company, has been appointed juror of awards in machinery at the Pan-American exposition, Buffalo, and will leave for there tomorrow.

InterOcean, (Chicago, Illinois), Sunday, July 21, 1901; image from *newspapers.com*

Appendix 5

Illinois Private Labels

This list is a compilation of names from Meggers and Ehrhardt's *American Pocket Watches, Vol. 2: Illinois Watch Co.*, supplemented with additional names, images and advertisements that have since been found. The ongoing thread "Illinois private-labels" (http://mb.nawcc.org/showthread.php?3302-Illinois-private-labels), started in 2004 by Fred Hansen on the NAWCC website, has been of help.

Abbott & Co. (matching dial), c. 1894
Accurate Timer, Cosmopolitan Watch Co., U.S.A.
Ace (on subseconds dial; Illinois in normal position on dial), 12 size, 21 jewels, grade 279
Ackerman, V., Nyack, NY, c. 1895
Acme (*see* Standard Watch Co.)
Acton, R.C., & Son, Alexandria, VA, c. 1896
Acton's Special, Alexandria, VA, c. 1894
Adams Street (matching dial), c. 1900 (*see also* Field, Marshall, & Co.)
Adams Street Special (matching dial), c. 1900
Addison, c. 1883
Admiral, The (*see* Becken, A.C., & Co.)
Adonis, c. 1923
Aetna, c. 1884
Ahlstrom, John A., Freehold, NJ (dial), c. 1895
Aicher, Simon, Philadelphia (dial: Simon Aicher), c. 1882
AJH Special, c. 1912 [A.J. Heeson]
Ak-Sar-Ben ["Nebraska" spelled backwards], c. 1917
Alleghany, c. 1883
Allen, John S., & Co., Minneapolis, MN, c. 1892
Ambassador, Illinois Watch Co., Springfield, c. 1920
American Star, The, c. 1914 (*see also* Gamse, N)
Anderson, A.N., Minneapolis (matching dial), c. 1898
Anderson, Carl W., Manchester, NH, c. 1896
Andrews, J.W., & Co., St. Louis, c. 1882
Ankeny, C.H., Lafayette, IN, c. 1886–1905
Anners, Wm., Chicago, IL, c. 1881

Anshutz, Frank, Shenadoah, IA, c. 1911
Anson, Steward N., ME, c. 1873–1883
Ansonia, Adjusted, c. 1894
Anthony, C.F. & Co., Lafayette, IN, c. 1886
Anthracite, c. 1880
Arell Special, The, Milwaukee, WI, c. 1894
Aristocrat, Made for The Kay Co. by Illinois Watch Co. (dial: Illinois Aristocrat), c. 1918
Ariston, Ariston, Jr., Ariste, and/or MF Co. (in monogram, for Marshall Field & Co.), Chicago, IL (*see also* Field, Marshall, & Co.)
Arkema (dial: Archie K. May, York, PA), c. 1915 (*see also* May, Archie K.)
Arlington Special, Springfield, Ill., c. 1901
Armbruster, A. & Co., Springfield, IL
Armbruster, O.J., Springfield, IL, c. 1903
Armer, D.P., Richmond, KY, c. 1882
Armstrong the Jeweler, Galesburg, IL, c. 1885
Army & Navy (*see* Washington Watch Co.)
Arongon Bros., Expressly Made for, Dunkirk, KY, c. 1919
Arrow Watch Co. (matching dial), c. 1910

Arrow Watch Co.

Arrow Watch Co.

Arsenal Special (dial: A.P. Co.), c. 1909
Artes, Chas. E., Evansville, IN, c. 1891
Atlantic, Philadelphia (dial: Mc.C. & H.), c. 1882. [initials likely for McCarty & Hurlburt, a Philadelphia firm in business from 1876 to 1888; succeeded by H.O. Hurlburt & Sons]
Atlantic Coast Line, Special (dial: Geo. W. Huggins, Wilmington, NC), c. 1893
Austin, St. Louis, KL & Co. (monogram), c. 1882
Austin (dial: L&B monogram), c. 1881 [initials likely for Louis Bauman & Co., of St. Louis]
Avery, A.W., Plymouth, ND, c. 1895
B. & M. Special
B. & O. R.R. Special (Baltimore & Ohio Railroad Special), c. 1898
B. & O. Standard, H.A. Kingsbury's (matching dial), c. 1896
B. & O. Standard, Little's (dial: S.T. Little & Sons, Cumberland, MD), c. 1897
B.C. & Co. (Monogram), Springfield, IL, c. 1883
B.F.N. & Co. (matching dial), c. 1880
Badger, c. 1885
Baer Bros. Co., NY (sold private-label Illinois watches listed under "The Fifth Avenue")
Baier, Frank W., St. Louis, Mo. (matching dial), c. 1894
Baier's Special (matching dial), c. 1882–1894
Bailey, O.W., Calais, ME (dial: *see* Chapter 7)
Baker, S., Medina, NY (dial: S. Baker), c. 1887
Ball Co., Webb C., c. 1895 (*see also* The Garland)
Ball Watch Co., Cleveland, OH (RRWI); bought watches from Illinois Watch Co. between 1927 and 1935. Movements were made to Ball's specifications and are not identifiable in the regular Illinois Factory serial number listing.
Balliett & Weld Special, Waterloo, IA, c. 1895
Baltimore (dial, in script), c. 1907
Bank Vault Time Lock Movement marked "Made Special by Illinois Watch Co., Springfield," c. 1920–1930
Banker, The, c. 1924

Bankers, St. Louis, USA, c. 1911
Banner, Springfield, IL (dial: monogram), c. 1883
Barborka, Iowa City, IA, c. 1882
Bard, H.D., Brazil, IN, c. 1896

H.D. Bard

Barker & Freisens, Cincinnati, OH, c. 1896
Barnard, John S., c. 1888
Barnes, C.P., Louisville, KY, c. 1887
Barnes, C.P., & Bro., Louisville, KY, c. 1877
Barnes, L. M., North Adams, MA (dial: L. M. Barnes), c. 1880
Barnes, Merritt, Avoca, IA (matching dial), c. 1882
Barnes Special, Avoca, IA, c. 1913
Bartens & Rice, 20 John St., NY (matching dial), c. 1891
Barthman, Wm., New York, c. 1896
Bartholmee, J.J., Baltimore, MD (matching dial), c. 1911

J.J. Bartholmee

Bartlett, J.F., Clinton, MA (Boston & Maine RR), c. 1896
Basch & Co., c. 1918 (had stores in Detroit,Toledo and Cleveland)

Basch & Co.

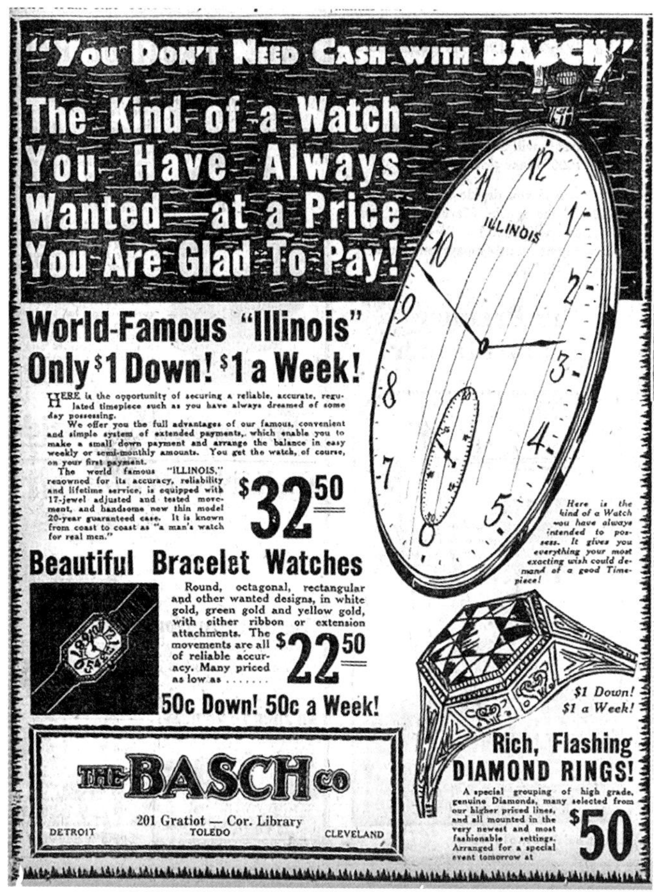

Detroit News, March 22, 1923

YOU DON'T NEED CASH WITH BASCH

VACATION SPECIALS

Handsome Genuine

DIAMOND RINGS

You'll find here a splendid assortment of handsome full cut genuine Diamonds. The mountings of 18 kt. white gold and 14 kt. green gold come in a wide variety of the new and rarely beautiful designs that will be sure to please. Select one Friday or Saturday. Wear it on your vacation and pay us a little each week.

$27.50 — 50c a Week
$45 — $1 a Week
$75 — $1.50 a Week
$95 — $2 a Week

14-Karat White Gold

WRIST WATCH

These handsome Wrist Watches have high grade 15-jewel movement and are guaranteed accurate timekeepers. The cases are of 14 kt. solid white gold in beautifully engraved designs.

$37.50

$1 a Week

20-year gold filled high grade 15-jewel Wrist Watches as low as

$22.50

50c a Week

$1 DOWN

17-Jewel

Illinois Watch

A handsome thin model Watch of the famous Illinois make. The 17-jewel adjusted movement with steel escape wheel and double roller assures accurate timekeeping. The hand engraved gold filled cases are guaranteed for 20 years.

$32.50

$1.00 a Week

Men's Fine

DIAMOND RINGS

A beautiful sparkling genuine Diamond, set in a handsomely engraved 18 kt. white gold or 14 kt. fancy green gold with white gold tip mountings that any man would be proud to own. We have a wide range of designs for you to choose from. Select one Friday or Saturday and have it to wear on your vacation.

$75 $1.50 a Week

Others at $45—$1 a Week

THE BASCH CO

201 Gratiot Ave., Cor. Library

***Detroit News*, July 12, 1923**

Bassett, M.W., Hartford, CT, c. 1906

M.W. Bassett

Baude, R., Louisville, KY (matching dial), c. 1896

Bay State, c. 1883 [likely referring to Massachusetts]

Bean, O.A., c. 1883 (jeweler in Garland, ME)

Beard, W.E., Reading, MA (dial: W.E. Beard), c. 1882

Beardsley, B.C., Litchfield, IL, c. 1878

Beattie, Robt,, Detroit, MI, c. 1923

Beck, John A., Portland, OR (matching dial), c. 1877

Beck's Special (dial: John Becks, Michigan City, IN), c. 1895

Becken, A.C. & Co., Chicago, c. 1900–1915 (sold private-label Illinois watches listed under their grade names, such as Admiral, Grant, Lady Martha, Lincoln, Lincoln Park, Logan, Tecumseh, Warrington and Washington)

Beitel, J.C., & Son, Catasauqua, PA, c. 1901–1920

Belknap & Crist, Newburgh, NY, c. 1885
Belmont, c. 1909–1920
Bement, Geo., Brodhead, WI, c. 1901–1920
Ben Franklin, Springfield, IL, c. 1882
Bendix, Julius, 792 Third Ave., c. 1892
Benedict Brothers, NY, c. 1895
Benicia, c. 1883
Benoit, N. E., Rockford, IL (matching dial), c. 1878
Berg, Hyman & Co., Chicago, IL (matching dial: *see* Chapter 7), c. 1903

Hyman Berg & Co.

Bergguist, C., & Co, Minneapolis (dial), c. 1907
Berry, Leon W., Carthage, IL, c. 1884
Best, The, Adjusted (dial: John S. Allen & Co., Minneapolis), c. 1884
Bethel, J. H., Lewiston, ID, c. 1902
Billings, F. E., Special (matching dial), Fort Fairfield, ME
Bills , J.A., & Son, Hinton, IA, c. 1894
Birdsey, Arthur J., Fairport, NY, c. 1889
Birkenbusch, Henry, Pekin, IL (matching dial), c. 1894
Birmingham Special, c. 1928
Bisanar, Geo E., Hickory, NY, c. 1914
Black, August, Clintonville, WI, c. 1894
Black, T.W., Huntington, PA, c. 1878–1885
Blair, W.V., Meriden, CT, c. 1894
Blake, Charles R., Marion, IN, c. 1894
Bleich, J.J., Paducah, KY, c. 1882
Blethen, H.A., Dexter, ME, c. 1878
Bloedel, A., Milwaukee (dial), c. 1907
Bloedel, A., Milwaukee, WI (dial: A. Bloedel), c. 1910

A. Bloedel

Blossom, E.W., Woodstock, IL (matching dial), c. 1882
Bockstruck, Henry, St. Paul, Minn. (matching dial),
Bode, F.C., Jr, Philadelphia PA, c. 1893
Bodwell, H.F., Lynn, MA (matching dial), c. 1882
Boediger Bros. & Co., Belleville, IL, c. 1893
Boettinger and Walter, Baltimore, MD, c. 1894
Bohm, Henry, Denver, CO (matching dial), c. 1890
Bohm-Allen Co., Denver, c. 1906
Bolender, Adam H., Scientific Watchmaker, c. 1897 (company located in Rockford, IL)
Bonar, B.J., Richland Center, WI, c. 1923
Bonnet, F.F., Col. [Columbus], OH, c. 1896
Booth, John H., Alton, IL
Born, E.J., & Co., Ashland, WI
Bornstein, H. P., Boston, MA (dial: H. P. Bornstein), c. 1890
Boss, The, W.W. True, Flint, MI, c. 1880
Boutelle, J.G., East Pepperell, MA, c. 1905

Bovard, M.M., & Son, Manayunk, Philadelphia (matching dial: *see* Chapter 7), c. 1896

M.M. Bovard

Bowdoin, c. 1885
Bowen, W.A., Kewanee, IL
Bowl, Claring, Hamilton, Ont. (dial), c. 1905
Bowyer, E. G., Algona, IA (matching dial), c. 1891
Boyd, I.T., Fall River, MA, c. 1894
Boynton, A.P., State & 12th St., Chicago, IL, c. 1872
Bradbury's Railroad King, c. 1896
Bradford, C., c. 1885
Bradley & Co., C.C., Batavia, NY, c. 1896
Bradshaw, W.H., Paris, IL (matching dial), c. 1891
Braun, J., Standard, Two Rivers, WI, c. 1894
Braun, Leo, Springfield, OH, c. 1882
Bremen, F.M. & Co., Atlantic, IA, c. 1895
Bridges, W.W., Marine City, MI, c. 1890
Brighton, c. 1881
Brilleman, I., Albany, NY, c. 1895
Brisson, J.N., Montreal, c. 1906
Broer, B.H., Toledo, OH., c. 1878 [Miller grade]
Broer, B.H., Toledo, OH (matching dial), c. 1893
Broer, Wm H., Toledo, OH (dial), c. 1899
Bronson, A.M., Susquehanna, PA, c. 1888
Brooke, The Jeweler, Coshocton, OH, c. 1918
Brown, Chas. H., Howell, MI, c. 1883
Brown, Geo. A., & Co., Los Angeles, CA (matching dial); c. 1909
Brown's Jewelry Store, Hannibal, MO, c. 1899
Brown's Special, Hannibal, MO (dial: Brown's Jewelry Store, Hannibal, MO), c. 1897
Broyles & Champion, Gainsville, TX (dial); Time King (movement), 1921

Broyles & Champion

Buckeye, c. 1880
Buder, E. A., Cairo, IL (dial)
Bullard Bros., St. Paul, MN (dial: Bullard Brothers, Saint Paul), c. 1900
Burbank, A.L., & Co., Worcester, MA (matching dial), c. 1887
Burkitt, J.W., Arlington Heights, IL, c. 1895
Burkitt's Special, Arlington Heights, IL, c. 1895
Burlington Watch Co., Chicago, IL (The proper dial is marked "Burlington" or includes the name "Burlington." All Burlington watches were sold originally cased in Burlington Watch Co.-marked cases, c. 1907–1930.)
Burlington Watch Co., U.S.A.
Burns Watch Co., Coshocton, OH, c. 1896
Burritt, L.D., Rochester, NY, c. 1904

Busch, Geo. J., Newark, NJ (matching dial), c. 1896

Butler Bros., Chicago, IL (sold private-label watches made by Illinois, listed under their Grade names: Butler, Knapp, Scott and Stillwell), c. 1897–1908

Butler, Edward B., The Special, c. 1905 (*see also* Butler Bros)

Butterwick, N. L., Allentown, PA, c. 1887

B.W.Co., Chicago (scarce dial for Burlington Watch Company)

C. & A. Special, E.K. Crothers, Bloomington, IL

C. & O. Favorite (special dial: Chas. F. Lentz, Covington & Clifton Forge, VA), c. 1900

C. & O. Special, c. 1898 (21J), c. 1922 (17J)

C.B. & Co., (monogram) Springfield, IL, c. 1882

Cadillac, The, c. 1897

Cady & Olmstead, Kansas City, MO, c. 1880–920

Camm, E.I., Monmouth, IL, c. 1897

Campbell & Co., South Chicago (matching dial), c. 1895

Campbell, A. R., Morrisville, VT (dial), c. 1895

Campbell Bros., Henry, IL (dial), c. 1888

Canargua Valley, c. 1893

Capitol, c. 1917 (a private label of Sterling Jewelry Co.)

Capitol

Cincinnati Enquirer, May 25, 1919; image from *newspapers.com*

Cincinnati Enquirer, November 16, 1919; image from newspapers.com

Capitol Watch Company (dial: Capitol image), c. 1888
Captain (*see* Landis Watch Co., Chicago, IL)
Carle, Wm. G., Philadelphia, PA, c. 1904
Carlson, C.J., Escanaba, MI (dial: C.J. Carlson), c. 1883
Carlson & Anderson, Jamestown, NY (matching dial), c. 1893
Carpenter, C.H., Middleboro, MA (matching dial)

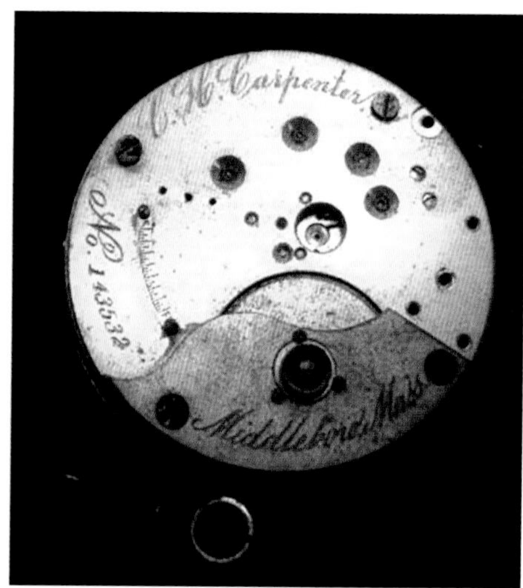

C. H. Carpenter

Carpenter, G.A., c. 1880
Carson Pirie Scott & Co., Chicago, IL. (sold Private Label watches made by Illinois, listed under their grade names. *See* Graham and Moulton listings below).
Carter, O.G., Jr., New London, OH, c. 1887
Carthage Electric Railway (dial: Deal Bros., Carthage, MO), c. 1895
Case, G.G., Jackson, MI (dial), c. 1882
Castelberg's, Washington DC, c. 1898
Central (was a private label of the Enggass Jewelry Store, Detroit, Michigan; *see* Chapter 6)
Central Park, c. 1881
Central Trunk Railroad
Chalmers, R.E. & Co., Chicago (dial)
Chapman & Armstrong, Galesburg, IL (matching dial), c. 1895
Chatelain & Golden, Va. & Carson (matching dial), c. 1890

Chatteron, Crife, c. 1883
Chatterton, Springfield, IL, c. 1890
Chesapeake & Ohio Favorite, c. 1896
Chesapeake & Ohio Special, c. 1897
Chesapeake & Ohio Special Favorite (dial: R.H. Smith, Hinton, WV)
Chesapeake & Ohio Standard, c. 1896
Chicago Watch Co. The, Chicago, IL (matching dial), c. 1885
Chieftain, c. 1884
Child, S.J., Clyde, NY (dial: S.J. Child), c. 1882
Chipman Jewelry Co., Provo, UT, c. 1889
Choende, B.T., Chicago, IL, c. 1894
Chopard, J.A., Kansas City, MO (matching dial)
Christophersen & Holth, Illinois Watch Co. (dial: roman numerals, images of logs), c. 1912
Chronometer, Springfield, IL, c. 1893
Chronos (matching dial), c. 1911

Chronos

Churchill, Geo. H., Amsterdam, NY (matching dial), c. 1903
Clarke, E.M., Lowell, MA, c. 1881
Clarke, Russell, Cleveland, OH (matching dial), c. 1902
Clarkson, S.N., Chicago, IL, The Rail Roader, c. 1894
Claus, A., Springfield, IL (matching dial), c. 1892
Clement, C.A., Springfield, MO (matching dial)
Clement Special, c. 1909
Cleveland, S.B. or B.S. (monogram), c. 1882
Cleveland, S.L. & M. Co. (monogram), c. 1882
Clinton Watch Co., c. 1911
Clipper (*see* Standard Watch Co.)
Coats, Robert W., Clinton, Ontario (matching dial), c. 1887
Coatsworth, J. W., & Co., Galena, IL (matching dial), c. 1895
Cole, C.A., Winterset, IA (dial: C.A. Cole, Winterset, Iowa), c. 1898
College City, Springfield, IL, c. 1892
College Park, Springfield, IL, c. 1884
Colonel, The (*see* Landis Watch Co., Chicago, IL)
Colonel, The, c. 1896

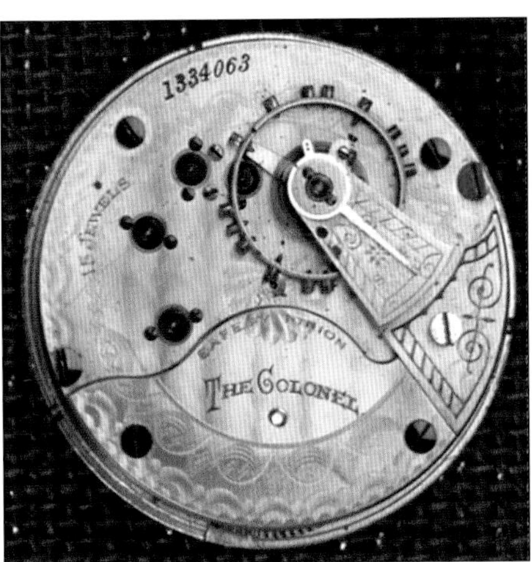

The Colonel, c. 1896

Columbia, Springfield, IL, c. 1889 (name originally applied to an 18-size, 11-jewel model but used again in the 1920s, perhaps as a private label, for a 16-size, 19-jewel Illinois model advertised by the California jewelry chain Gensler-Lee)

$37.75

"Columbia" Illinois
19-Jewel Movement
Standard 16 Size
Gold Filled Case

SPLENDID timekeeper is this 19-jewel Illinois watch, adjusted to three positions, temperature and isochronism. Gold center wheel. Breguet hairspring, etc., real quality! Heavy gold filled, dust and waterproof Railroad case, screw back and bezel! Unusual value! $37.75 on terms of $1.00 DOWN, $1.00 a week.

Oakland Tribune (Oakland, CA), November 6, 1925; image from *newspapers.com*

Columbia Special

Columbus Time, Springfield, IL, c. 1884

Comet, Springfield, IL, c. 1882 (*see also* Knights, C.H., & Co.)

Commodore, The, adjusted, c. 1898

Commodore, The, c. 1924

Commodore Perry, Special (O. Cohen, Erie, PA)

Commonwealth, c. 1898

Conard's Special, c. 1899

Conductor, c. 1883

Congressional, The, c. 1928

Conklin's Special, c. 1906

Conqueror (dial: Iowa Watch. Co), c. 1881 (*see also* Iowa Watch Co.)

Constant, St. Louis, U.S.A., c. 1907

Constant

Cooley, George W., Sidney, NY (dial), c. 1910
Cooley, S.M. Mayville & North Branch, MI (matching dial), c. 1900
Corkhart, R.S., Jackson, MI, c. 1883
Cornelius, A.W., Asbury Park, NJ, c. 1902

A.W. Cornelius

Ogden Standard Examiner (Ogden, UT), December 9, 1927; image from *newspapers.com*

Cosmopolitan Watch Co., c. 1900
Councillor, The (sold by R.H. Macy Co., Chicago, IL), c. 1924
Cowell & Hubbard Co., The (dial), c. 1913 (jewelers in Cleveland, OH)
Cox, W.H., Medina, NY, c. 1921
Crane & Rouse; Mt. Pleasant, IA (dial), c. 1895
Crawford, R.E., Amsterdam, NY (matching dial)
Crescent (*see* Standard Watch Co.)
Crescent City, c. 1882
Criterion, c. 1882 (11-jewel movement; Illinois resurrected the name for a private-label 21-jewel pocket watch and 17-jewel wristwatch in the 1920s)

Ogden Standard Examiner (Ogden, UT), January 20, 1928; image from *newspapers.com*

Critz-Hazerodt Co., The, Elyria, OH, c. 1900
Crosman, W.C., Auburn, NY, c. 1894
Cross, A. Jay, c. 1878
Crothers, E.K., For Rail Road Service, made especially for, Bloomington, IL, c. 1896
Crown Jewel, Springfield, IL, c. 1878
Cruttenden, A.A., & Co., Des Moines, IA (dial: A.A. Cruttenden & Co.), c. 1884
Curtis, Frank, Decatur, IL, c. 1895
Cushing & Polley, Waltham, MA, c. 1882
D. & R. G. Special [Denver & Rio Grande], c. 1917
Dale Special, Illinois Watch, Springfield, IL, c. 1926
Dana, L.D., Antigo, WI, c. 1892
Daniels, J.D., Albion, NY, c. 1902
Darlington Special, c. 1917
Dauntless, c. 1884
Davenport, C.O., Gardiner, ME, c. 1895
Davidson, G.D., Jersey City, NJ (matching dial: *see* Chapter 7), c. 1905

G.D. Davidson

Davis, Brunswick, ME, c. 1887
Defiance, R.W. Sears Watch Co., Chicago IL, c. 1882
Delaware, c. 1886
Deluxe, The, c. 1923
Dependon, John V. Farwell Co., Chicago, c. 1916

Dependon, John V. Farwell Co.

Des Moines Watch Co., Des Moines, IA (matching dial), c. 1882–1886
Despatch, c. 1882
Dettling, Paul, Buffalo, NY (dial), c. 1898
Devlin, John, Providence, RI (dial), c. 1893
Dewey, C.A., c. 1882
Dexter, c. 1882
Diamond, c. 1911–1919
Diamond Palace (dial: A. Andrews, San Francisco, CA), c. 1888
Diamond Watch Co.

Dickinson Co., T. & E., Buffalo, NY (dial: T. & E. Dickinson Co.), c. 1894
Dillon, Harry A., Gloversville, NY (adjusted), c. 1900
Diplomat (matching dial), c. 1918

Diplomat

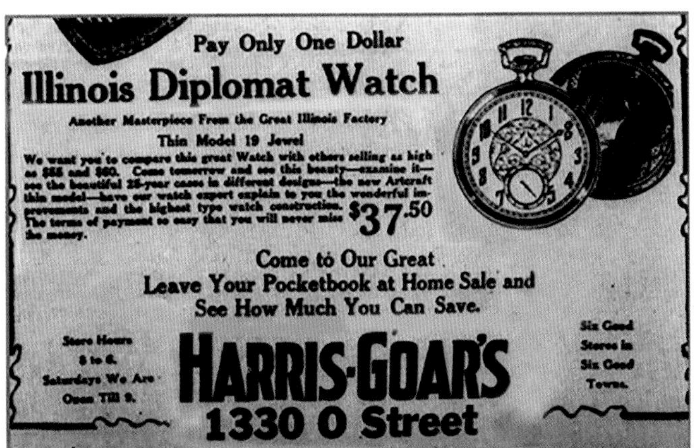

Lincoln Star (Lincoln, NE), October 17, 1924; image from *newspapers.com*

Dispatcher, c. 1893
Doerflinger, Wm. F., Brunswick GA, c. 1882
Donald, R.B., Made Expressly For, Washington DC (dial: Castelberg's National Jewelry Company, Washington, DC), c. 1895
Drabnick, C.F., Louisville, KY, c. 1878
DuBois, Calvin, Walton, NY (dial)

Calvin Du Bois

Dubois, Myron, Little Falls, NY (matching dial), c. 1895
Duetz, R.J., & Co., Trenton, NJ, c. 1894
Duke, Linn, Fayetteville, AR, c. 1882
Dunbar, G.J., and Co., Princeton, IL (matching dial), c. 1896
Duncan, I., Syracuse, NY, c. 1895
Durant & Rogers, Lowell, MA, c. 1892
Earle, Wm. G., Philadelphia, PA (dial: Wm. G. Earle, Philadelphia), c. 1902
Eastern Watch Co., Belmont, c. 1883
Eastlake, c. 1883
Eaton, Colo. (dial: W.H. Scheer), c. 1900
Eberhart, J.B., South Chicago, IL (dial: J.B. Eberhart, South Chicago), c. 1895
Echo, c. 1882
Eckert, Henry E., West Troy, NY, c. 1889

Eclipse (*see* Standard Watch Co.)

Eclipse (with monogram W & R or R & W), c. 1884

Eddystone, c. 1882

Edgewood, c. 1917

Ehmann, Wm., & Son, Buffalo, NY (dial)

Wm. Ehmann & Son

Ehrlich, J.H., Expressly made for, by Illinois Watch Co., c. 1921 (a private label for the J.H. Ehrlich Jewelry Store at 227 Gratiot Avenue, Detroit, MI)

J.H. Ehrlich

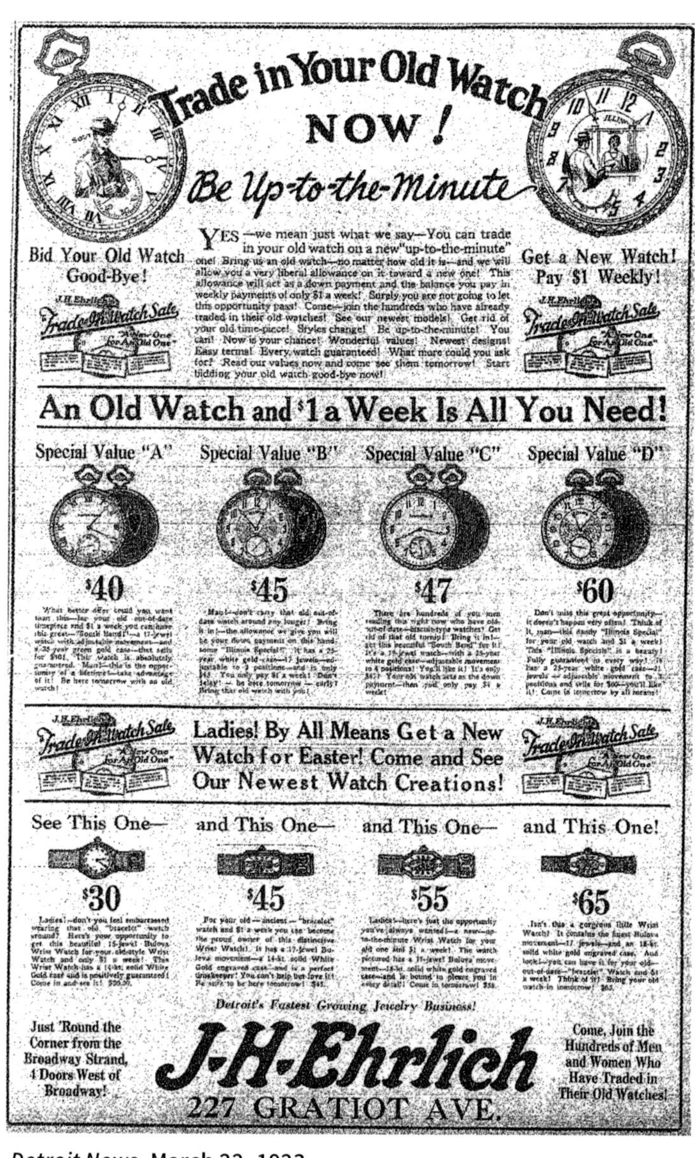

Trade in Your Old Watch NOW!

Be Up-to-the-Minute

Bid Your Old Watch Good-Bye!

YES—we mean just what we say—You can trade in your old watch on a new "up-to-the-minute" one! Bring us an old watch—no matter how old it is—and we will allow you a very liberal allowance on it toward a new one! This allowance will act as a down payment and the balance you pay in weekly payments of only $1 a week! Surely you are not going to let this opportunity pass! Come—join the hundreds who have already traded in their old watches! See our newest models! Get rid of your old time-piece! Styles change! Be up-to-the-minute! You can! Now is your chance! Wonderful values! Newest designs! Easy terms! Every watch guaranteed! What more could you ask for? Read our values now and come see them tomorrow! Start bidding your old watch good-bye now!

Get a New Watch! Pay $1 Weekly!

J.H. Ehrlich Trade-In Watch Sale

An Old Watch and $1 a Week Is All You Need!

Special Value "A"	Special Value "B"	Special Value "C"	Special Value "D"
$40	$45	$47	$60

Ladies! By All Means Get a New Watch for Easter! Come and See Our Newest Watch Creations!

See This One—	and This One—	and This One—	and This One!
$30	$45	$55	$65

Detroit's Fastest Growing Jewelry Business!

Just 'Round the Corner from the Broadway Strand, 4 Doors West of Broadway!

J-H-Ehrlich

227 GRATIOT AVE.

Come, Join the Hundreds of Men and Women Who Have Traded in Their Old Watches!

Detroit News, March 22, 1923

Elbridge, P., c. 1881

P. Elbridge

Elbros, c. 1923

Eldridge, R.C., Milford, MA, c. 1877

Electric Railroad Special, c. 1914

Electric Railroad Standard, c. 1907

Elite, c. 1919

Elite

Elliott, C.A., Marshalltown, IA, c. 1892

Elson, M.V.B., Freeport's Leading Jeweler, Freeport, IL (dial: M.V.B. Elson, Freeport, IL), c. 1891

Emperor, c. 1908 (name originally applied to this 18-size 21-jewel model but resurrected for a new 12-size 21-jewel thin model advertised by Gensler-Lee in 1925, perhaps as a private label)

$47.75

"Emperor" Illinois
21-Jewel Movement
Small, Thin 12 Size.
Extraordinary Value!

HERE is a masterpiece! Small, thin 12 size 21-jewel Illinois Watch! And just look at the price—for a 21-jewel watch! Adjusted to three positions, temperature, etc. Gold settings, patent regulator, exceptional quality! Newest design Green Gold Filled Polygon case with fancy dial. $1.00 DOWN, $1.25 a week.

Oakland Tribune (Oakland, CA), November 6, 1925; image from *newspapers.com*

Empire, c. 1881 (name was used again for a new 19-jewel thin model offered in 1917 by Klivans Bros., likely as a private label; the dial image and the advertisement text suggest that the watch was named only "Empire," with "Special" as an adjective indicating simply that it was a "Special Model" for Klivans)

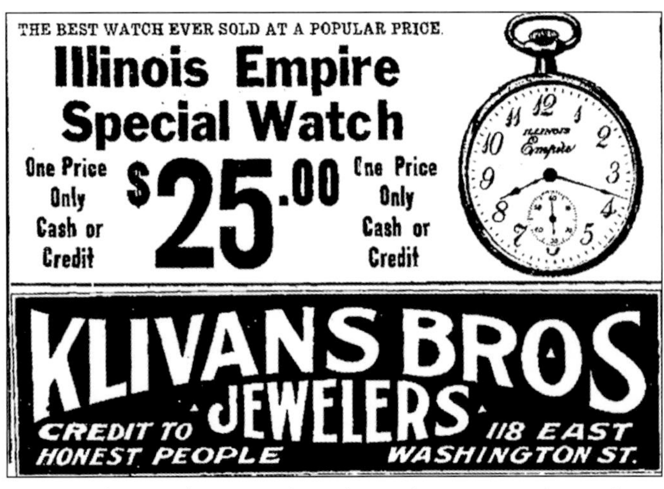

New Castle News **(New Castle, PA), October 12, 1917; image from** ***newspapers.com***

Engel Natl. Watch Co., Chicago, IL (matching dial), c. 1894

Engelskind, R. (matching dial), c. 1905 (jeweler in St. Louis, MO)

Engle, Sylvester, Hazleton, PA, c. 1877

Enterprise, Chicago (dial: C.H.K. & Co.), c. 1882 (*see also* Knights, C.H., & Co.)

Ephraim, Canton, OH, c. 1888

Epstein, E., Jeweler, Oshkosh, WI (matching dial), c. 1897

Ethan Allen, F.W. Sim & Co., Troy, NY (dial: F.W. Sim & Co.). c. 1893

Ettinger, Charles, Cleveland (dial only), c. 1902

Eureka, c. 1879

Eustis Bros., Minneapolis (dial: Eustis Brothers, Minneapolis), c. 1897

Euteneuer, J., Jr., Havana, IL (matching dial), c. 1893

Evans, G. R., Kendall, WI (matching dial), 1895

Evans Special, c. 1894

Eversole, H.C., Logansport, IN (dial: H.C. Eversole), c. 1883

Excelsior (matching dial), c. 1881 (*see also* Standard Watch Co.)

Excelsior

Executive, c. 1925

Executive

Express, c. 1882
F & L or F.L. (in monogram): *see* L & F
Fairchild, E., & Co., Johnstown, NY, c. 1889
Faraway, W.F., Glenwood, WA, c. 1900
Farrell & Lohmiller, Escanaba, MI (dial), c. 1911
Farringdon, The (matching dial), c. 1888
Fausel, C.F., Manchester, MI (matching dial), c. 1890
Favorite, c. 1884
Favro, F.J., Providence, RI, c. 1891
Fawcett, W.S., Xenia, OH, c. 1882
Feddersen, A.E., Belle Plaine, IA
Federal, Illinois Watch Co. (dial: "Supreme" above "Illinois"), c. 1922
Federal Watch Co., Chicago, IL, U.S.A., c. 1911

Federal Watch Co.

Federal Watch Co., Philadelphia, PA, c. 1911
Fehrs, G.A., Manitowoc, WI, c. 1898
Feldman, B.J., Franklin, PA, c. 1883
Feldman's Sons, B.J., Franklin, PA (matching dial), c. 1901
Fenderson & Mitchell, Saco, ME, c. 1896

Fenderson & Mitchell

Ferguson, R.T., Philadelphia, PA

R.T. Ferguson

Ferris, G.H., Bath, NY (matching dial), c. 1898

Fey Brothers, c. 1893

Field, Marshall, & Co., Chicago, IL (Known as "The Tiffany of Chicago," Marshall Field's sold private-label watches made by Illinois and listed under such names as: Adams Street, Ariston, Quincy Street, Fifth Avenue, Franklin Street), c. 1900–1912

Fifth Avenue, c. 1900 (*see also* Field, Marshall, & Co.)

Fifth Avenue, The (Baer Bros. Co.), c. 1922

The Fifth Avenue

Filson & Van Antwerp, Huntington, IN, c. 1888

Fisher, Elmira, & Lorain, D., c. 1891

Fisk, F.P., Epping, NH, c. 1897

Fisk, R.C., Big Rapids, MI (matching dial), c. 1873

Fiske Bros., Minneapolis, MN

Fiske Bros.

Flenning, V.Z., St. Mary's, OH, c. 1906

Flower City Watch Co., Rochester, NY, c. 1891

Folsom & Faunce, Great Falls, NH, c. 1877

Folsom, H.D., Rock Island, IL (matching dial), c. 1898

Folson, L.W., Sumpter, SC, c. 1891

Foltz & Frank, Akron, OH, c. 1883

Forchheimer, Max, Cleveland, OH, c. 1881

Forest City, c. 1882

Forrest, Cincinnati, OH, c. 1888

Forsyth & Hoffman, Philadelphia, PA, c. 1895

Fort & Goodwin Special, Trenton, N.J. (dial: Fort & Goodwin), c. 1913
Fortier, U.D. (dial only: reads "U.D. Fortier's Special"), c. 1886 (Fortier was in St. Anne, IL)
Forum, c. 1922

Forum

Forum (dial: Klee & Groh), c. 1922. Forum was apparently the private label of Klee & Groh, Gold & Silversmiths, Rochester, NY
Foss, J.P., & Co., Oconomowoc, WI (dial: J.P. Foss & Co), c. 1893
Fox & Fulmer, Easton, PA (matching dial), c. 1896
Fraiberg, H., & Son, Cleveland, OH, c. 1916
Franklin. c. 1918
Franklin Street, c. 1900 (*see also* Field, Marshall, & Co.)
Fraphagen, James, Newark, NJ
Fredeking, Will L., Hinton, WV, c. 1915
French, H.E., c. 1889
Frenzer, Joseph P., Omaaha, NE, c. 1897
Freuberg, L.A., Washington, DC, c. 1915
Freund, M.M., Brooklyn, NY
Fried, C.C., Springfield, OH, c. 1882
Frisch Bros, Buffalo, NY
Fritz, Harvey, Oil City, PA (matching dial), c. 1902
Froeb, A.F., & Co., Terre Haute, IN (dial only), c. 1892
Frost, R. Chester, Chicago (matching dial), c. 1899
Fruend, M.M., Brooklyn (dial)
Fuchs, John A., Berlin, Ont., c. 1883
Fuller, J.W., Los Angeles, CA, c. 1888
Fulton, c. 1920
Funke, Fred, Kansas City, MO. c. 1882
Furbish, Oakes & Quimbly, Rangeley, ME (matching dial), c. 1896
Gagnon, E.S., Escanaba, MI, c. 1882
Gale, Jos. H., Baltimore MD, c. 1877
Gale, Jos. H., Baltimore MD (dial: Larmour & Co., Baltimore MD), c. 1877
Gale-Ford Co., Norfolk, VA, c. 1911

Gale-Ford Co.

Galt & Brother, Washington, DC (dial), c. 1900
Gamse, N., NY, The American Star, c. 1914
Gamse, N., NY, U.S.A., The Manhattan, c. 1917
Gamse, N., NY, U.S.A., The Queen Extra (matching dial), c. 1917
Gamsey, A.E., Sanford, ME (matching dial), c. 1906
Ganargua Valley, c. 1893
Garden City, monogram (dial: monogram), c. 1883
Gardner, C.D., c. 1886 (Gardner was in Manistee, MI)
Garfield, James A., Illinois Watch Co., Springfield, c. 1919
Garland, The, Illinois Watch Co. (Sold by Webb C. Ball), c. 1925

Garman, Geo. J., Williamsport, PA
Garnsey, A.E., Sanford, ME
Garnsey's Special (matching dial), c. 1906
Garretson, W.E., The Dalles. OR (matching dial), c. 1885
Garwood, Champaign, IL, c. 1885
Gaudette, Charles A., Arctic Center, RI, c. 1896
Gaudette, Chas. A., Fall River, MA, c. 1896–1905
General (*see* Landis Watch Co.)
General, The, c. 1901 (a private label for the Landis Watch Co., Chicago, IL)
General Grant, c. 1882
General Lee, The
General Reno, Cambridge, MA, c. 1876
Gibbons, William, Philadelphia, PA, c. 1896
Giering, Chas. J., Middletown, NY, c. 1901

Charles J. Giering

Gies, A.C., Pittsburgh, PA (matching dial), c. 1895
Gieselmann, F.W., Malon City, MO, c. 1899
Gifford, C.E., Fall River, MA, c. 1879
Gigon, Jos. C., Philadelphia, PA, c. 1882
Gilbert, A.M., Springfield, IL, c. 1892
Gilbert, Will, c. 1881
Gillet, Leon A., Lake Linden, MI, c. 1882
Gilmore, Chas., Kenton, OH (dial: Gilmore's), c. 1901
Girzi, Ed, Ishpeming, MI, c. 1882
Gladstone, Springfield, IL, c. 1886
Globe, The, c. 1882
Glover, Wm., Jr., Hazleton, PA. (matching dial), c. 1895
Goddard & Moses, Springfield, IL (Adjusted), c. 1886
Gold Bond, c. 1922
Gold Medal. c. 1926
Goldberg's Special, E. (dial: E. Goldberg), c. 1893
Golden Age (dial: C.H. Knights & Co. monogram), c. 1897
Goldine, Springfield, IL, c. 1889
Goldman, D., Milwaukee, WI, c. 1907
Goodnough, P.A., Erie, PA, c. 1909
Goodwin, A.W., Tunnton, MA, c. 1878
Goodwin, S.F., Amesburg, MA, c. 1892
Gordon & Burgin, Boston, MA (dial), c. 1896
Gorham (dial: O.A. Bean), c. 1887
Gottdiner & Wicht Special, Cleveland (dial: Gottdiner & Wicht), c. 1901
Gould, Jay,1882
Governor, Boston (dial: D.C.P. & Co.), c. 1879 [possibly D.C. Percival & Co., of Boston.]
Graham, c. 1903
Graham, David, c. 1903
Grant, USA (*see* Becken, A.C., & Co.)
Graves, A., Co., Memphis TN, c. 1895
Graves, A., Special, c. 1920
Graves, D.F., Warren, MA, c. 1888
Gray, J.C., Cortland, NY (matching dial), c. 1890
Gray, J.C., Portland, NY, c. 1894
Great Falls Special (dial: Huseth & Wiethoff), c. 1899
Great Northern Special, Illinois Watch Co., Springfield, c. 1922
Green, Edw. S., Roanoke, VA (dial: N & W Special), c. 1896
Green, R. C., & Son, Pottsville, PA, c. 1882
Greenwich (dial: Washington Watch Co.), c. 1914–1919 (*see also* Washington Watch Co.)
Gregory, A.L., Lapeer, MI, c. 1888
Greiger, John, Port Henry, NY, c. 1922
Gustafson, Carl A., Petersburg, IL, c. 1896
Gutter, B. & Sons, NY, specially made for (dial: B. Gutter & Sons, NY), c. 1919
H & B Co. (monogram), Chicago, IL, c. 1905

H.F.H. & Co., Chicago, c. 1880
HMJ&S (monogram for H.M. Jacobsen & Son); *see* Pennsylvania Special, Adjusted
H.R.S., Cincinnati, OH, c. 1897
HTK (monogram), Illinois Watch Co., Springfield, IL, c. 1883
Haines, Wm., Philadelphia, PA, c. 1895
Halbkat, Chas. F., Watertown, SD
Hall, J.S., Morristown, NJ, c. 1895
Hall Special (dial: J. Herbert Hall, Pasadena), c. 1903
Hallmark (matching dial), c. 1917–1921 (*see also* Macy, R.H., Co.)

Hallmark dial

Hallmark movement

Hamilton, U.S.A., c. 1931
Hammer, Chas. H., Phildelphia, PA, c. 1902
Hanna, J.C., & Son, New Castle, PA, c. 1887
Hanna & Eroe, New Castle, PA (matching dial), c. 1895
Hannberg, O., McPherson, KS, c. 1882
Harding, G. L., Cleveland, OH (matching dial), 1901
Harmon, Harry, Afton, IA (matching dial), c. 1894
Harrington, Chas M., Kirksville, MO, c. 1897
Harrington & Freeman, Boston, MA

Harrington & Freeman

Harris, I.P., Plymouth, PA, c. 1884
Harris, R., & Co., Washington, DC, c. 1897
Harris & Esterly, Duluth, MN (matching dial), c. 1904
Harrison, B., c. 1884
Hartdegen, Chas., & Co., Newark, NJ, c. 1894
Hartman, L., & Co., Tiffin, OH (matching dial), c. 1894
Haug, E.P., Paris, IL (matching dial)
Hawkins, O.D., NY, c. 1895
Haymarket Watch Co., Chicago, IL, c. 1888
Heath, W.D., Lakeport, NY, c. 1889

Heckart, H.M., c. 1884

Heesen, A.J., Toledo, OH (matching dial)

A.J. Heesen dial

A.J. Heesen movement

Heesen, A.J., AJH Special, c. 1912

Heineman, Otto E., Allegheny, PA, c. 1894

Henn & Hanes, Chillicothe, OH, c. 1896

Hennegan, Bates Co., Baltimore, MD, c. 1914

Hensley, Decatur, IN, c. 1906

Herald Square, c. 1902–1912 (*see also* Macy, R.H., Co.)

Hero, Chicago (dial: Imperial Watch Co.), c. 1883 (*see also* Knights, C.H., & Co.)

Herzberg, J. & Bro., Philadelphia, PA (matching dial), c. 1890

Hess, Geo. W., Bloomsburg, PA, c. 1895

Hess, John P. Co., Fond du Lac, WI (matching dial), c. 1916

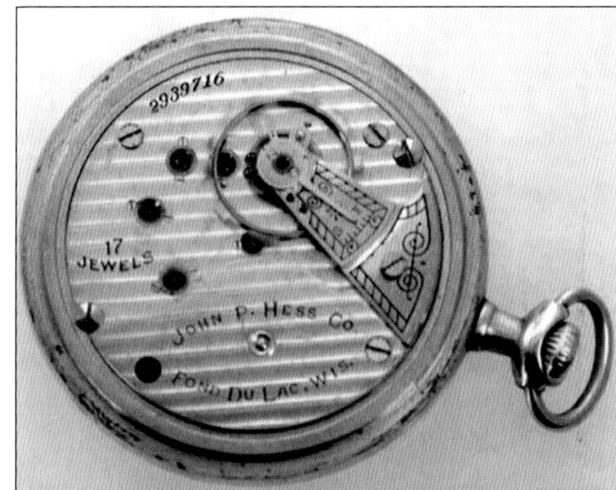

John P. Hess Co.

Hess & Culbertson (dial: *see* Chapter 7)

Hesselbom, J.A., Chicago, IL (matching dial), 1896

Hewett & Co., Herman S., Brockton, MA, c. 1891
Heynhold, G., Chicago, IL (dial: monogram GH), c. 1881
Hill, A.M., New Orleans, LA, c. 1886
Hill, C.C. & Co., Pittsburgh, PA, c. 1895
Hill City, The, c. 1885
Hillman, H.E., & Co., Wheeling, WV (dial: H.E. Hillman & Co.), c. 1889
Hinman, W.J., Oneida, NY (dial: W.J. Hinman), c. 1894
Hinrichs, August, Clinton, IA, c. 1899
Hobbs, H.P., Des Moines, IA, c. 1883
Hoenninger, Ch., New York, c. 1897
Hoffer, J.M., Kane, PA. c. 1907
Hofman, J.H. & R.E., Bucyrus, OH, c. 1877 [coin silver case marked for the Hofmans]
Hoffman & Robinson, Newark, NY, c. 1886
Hohrfeldt, Paul, Escanaba, MI, c. 1902
Hollis, Chas. R., Bryan, OH, c. 1877
Holmes, George R., St. Paul, MN

George R. Holmes. St. Paul, MN

Holtz & Frank, Akron, OH, c. 1889
Homer, Springfield, IL, c. 1882
Homer (dial: E.J. Martel, Somersworth, NH)
Homuth, Will H., Bloomington, IL, c. 1899
Hopkins, E.H., Penn Yan, NY, c. 1897
Hopkins, F.H., Special, c. 1893
Horn, The B.B., Co., Boston, MA (matching dial)

The B.B. Horn Co.

Hotfilter, H.C., Sacramento, CA (matching dial), c. 1890
How Bros., La Porte, IN (matching dial), c. 1906
Howard, c. 1882
Howard & Anderson, Chatfield, MN (matching dial), c. 1893
Howard & Rice, c. 1878
Howard Bros., Independent, Fredonia, NY (proper dial marked Howard Bros., Fredonia, NY), c. 1879–1880; *see also* Independent
Howe, George & Co., Lynn, MA, c. 1880
Howes Bros., Clinton, IA, c. 1896
Hoyler, A.H., Buffalo, NY (dial), c. 1909

Hubash, Larson & Wilson, Cal. Watch & Jewelry Co., San Francisco (dial: Hubash, Larson & Wilson), c. 1881
Hudson, also marked "M.B." (in a monogram), c. 1882 (*See* Meister & Bierbaum)
Hulse Bros., Middletown, NY, c. 1917
Hunn Watch Co., Detroit (dial: Hunn Special), c. 1914
Hunnicutt, Charley, Rockville, IN, c. 1887
Hunt, William, Uniontown, PA, c. 1893
Huntley, Clyde O. (matching dial), c. 1888
Huntley, F.H., Cadillac, MI, c. 1882
Huntley, Frank, Cadillac, MI, c. 1883
Hurlbut, Mack A., Fort Dodge, IA (matching dial), c. 1900
Hutchinson, F.J., Hornellsville, NY, c. 1882
Hyde, P.S., Piedmont, WV, c. 1873
Hyman Berg & Co., Chicago, IL
Hyole, H.L., Martinsburg, WV, c. 1876
Ide, Fred F., c. 1882 (Fred F. Ide was an employee of the Illinois Watch Co. and made or had made this custom watch. The plates are completely hand-engraved all over with flowers and decorations.)
Illinois Central, c. 1919. Illinois Central was a private label for the Enggass Jewelry Store in Detroit, MI. (*see* Chapter 6)
Illinois Electric Railroad Standard (dial), c. 1907

Illinois Electric Railroad Standard

Illinois Watch Case Co. (matching dial and movement), Chicago, IL, c. 1889–1920 (*see* Chapter 8)
Imperial, c. 1882
Imperial Special, c. 1902
Imperial Watch Co., Chicago, c. 1891
Independence, c. 1882
Independent Watch Co., Fredonia, NY, c. 1894
Independent, Fredonia, NY, c. 1880
Inspector's Special (dial: Will I. Fredeking, Hinton, WV), c. 1909–1915
Interior, Springfield, IL, c. 1876
Interprise, Chicago (dial: CRR & Co.), c. 1889
Interstate Chronometer (a private label sold by Sears, Roebuck & Co. only in 1911; proper dial is marked "InterState Chronometer." All watches were originally sold cased in John C. Dueber, 20 Year Yellow Gold Filled cases, according to the advertisement in the 1911 Sears Roebuck catalog.)

Interstate Chronometer

Interurban Special, Made for the Kay Co. by Illinois Watch Co. (dial: Electric Railroad Standard), c. 1921

Invincible, c. 1917

Iowa (dial: Great Western Watch Co.), c. 1878

Iowa (dial: Iowa Watch Co.) *See also* Iowa Watch Co.

Iowa Watch Co., c. 1849–1882 (sold Illinois Watches under various labels, including Conqueror, Iowa, Lincoln, Seneca, and Star of the West; dials are marked "Iowa Watch Co." and movements marked with that as well as the label name)

Irmen, I.M., & Co., Atlantic, IA, c. 1892

Iron City, c. 1881

JMR monogram (John M. Roberts Co., Pittsburgh) has shown up on several dials and movements. The movements on some are marked "Railroad Dispatch" and may have been one of his private-label marks. (*See also* Roberts, John M.)

J.M.S. Co., Chicago (dial: J.M.S.Co.) [John M. Smyth Co.], c. 1909

Jaccard, Eugene, & Co., St. Louis, MO (dial: E.J. & Co. monogram), c. 1881

Jaccard, Eugene, & Co., St. Louis, MO, c. 1883

Jaccard, Standard, Kansas City, MO, c. 1890

Jaccard's Railway Watch, c. 1885

Jacob Special, A.C. Ca., Wapakoneta, OH (dial: A.C. Ca. Jacob, Wapakoneta, OH), c. 1908

A.C. Jacob Special

Jacobs, August, Quincy, IL, c. 1908

Jacobs, S., & Co., Minneapolis (dial: Jacobs & Co.), c. 1901

Jacobson, H.M., & Son, Philadelphia, PA (matching dial), c. 1904

Jahnke, Richmond, VA (matching dial), c. 1905 [Albert F. Jahnke]

James, J.S., Inc. (dial: *see* Chapter 7)

James, T.A., Petersburg, VA, c. 1921

Jefferson, L.B. & Co. (dial: L.B. & Co.), c. 1908

Jefferson, St. Louis (dial: L. B. & Co.), c. 1881

Jefferson Special, c. 1902

Jenks, M.P., Meadeville, PA, c. 1882

Jepson, N.H., Washington, IN (dial)

N.H. Jepson

Jewett, A.M., Cortland, NY (Star of David on dial and movement), c. 1901

Jobe, A.K., Jackson, TN & Water Valley, MS (matching dial), c. 1891–1910

Johnson, W.E., Cannonsburgh, PA (matching dial), c. 1895

Jones, W.L. & Co., Martinsburg, WV, c. 1900

Joseph, H., Mattoon, IL (dial), c. 1907

Joseph, S., Des Moines, IA, c. 1894
Joseph, S., Special, Des Moines, IA, c. 1897 [Solomon, Joseph founded S. Josephs & Sons in 1871. The store still exists in Des Moines as Josephs.]
Josephson, C.G., & Son, Moline, IL, c. 1893
Josephson, C.G., Moline, IL, c. 1894
Joy, Walter, Springfield, IL, c. 1873
Judd, Anderson, IN (matching dial), c. 1894
Judd, M., Co., Toledo, OH (dial), c. 1905
Judson & Robie, Rochester, NY, c. 1887
K & S (monogram), Illinois Watch Co, Springfield, IL, c. 1881
Kaempfer, A., Chicago, IL, c. 1895
Kaiser, A.B., Walkerton, Ont., c. 1887
Kalish, B.S., Bangor, ME (matching dial), c. 1881
Kansas, L.B. & Co., St. Louis, c. 1881 [initials likely for Louis Bauman & Co., of St. Louis]
Kapp, J.G.; Toledo, OH (dial), c. 1907
Karsch, Bernard, NY (matching dial), c. 1890
Karthaus, E., Sons, Huntsville, AL (matching dial), c. 1906
Katz, Geo. S., 1943 Germantown Ave., Philadelphia, PA, c. 1896
Kauffman, S., Syracuse, NY, c. 1903
Kay Jewelry Co., Made for, by Illinois Watch Co., c. 1921
Kelley, W.L., Helena, AR, c. 1893
Kemper, G. Heit, Co. Portland, OR, c. 1880
Kemper, William F., St. Louis, MO, c. 1891
Kent, Frank V., Grand Forks, ND (matching dial), c. 1882
Kent Bros., Toronto, Ont., c. 1884
Kern, Joseph, Wilmington, DE (matching dial), c. 1912
Kerr, Wm., & Son, Boston, MA (dial: William Kerr & Son), c. 1897
Kesselmeier & Bechtol, Galion, OH
Keystone (matching dial), c. 1887
Keystone Watch Case Co., Philadelphia, PA, c. 1889
King, J. S. Townsend, Chicago (dial: monogram with CW or WC), c. 1881
King Henry (with monogram) B.B.C. & Co., c. 1882
King Landis (a private label for the Landis Watch Co., Chicago, IL)
King of the Road (*see* Wilson Brothers)
King Phillip, c. 1897
King Special (matching dial), 1899
Kingsbury (*see* B & O Standard)
Kircher, T., Davenport, IA, c. 1896
Klaholt, J.C., Springfield, IL, c. 1883–1890
Kleiner & Hein, Chicago, IL, c. 1900
Klivans Bros. c. 1918 (firm was located in New Castle, PA; *see also* Empire)

Klivans Bros.

Knapp, H.P., The Special, c. 1900 (*see also* Butler Bros.)
Kness, D.E., c. 1876
Kness, D.K., Altona, IL, c. 1877
Knickerbocker Jewelry Co., NY, "R.R. Employees" (dial: K.J. Co., New York), c. 1899
Knights, C.H. & Co., Chicago (sold Illinois-made watches under various private labels. such as Comet, Enterprise, Hero, and Queen), c. 1879–1883
Koch, C.H., Milwaukee, WI, c. 1894
Kornberger, J.F., Lawrenceburg, IN, c. 1887
Korp, Henry, Cincinnati, OH (dial), c. 1906
Kranich, Chas., Philadelphia, PA, c. 1916
Kremer, T.C., Phoenixville, PA (matching dial), c. 1895
Krezdorn, H., & Son, Seguin, TX (matching dial), c. 1912
Krumrich-Konrad, Oshkosh, WI, c. 1908

Kuesel & Puls, Milwaukee, WI (dial: Kuesel & Puls, Milwaukee), c. 1896

Kuster, C.A., Buffalo, NY, c. 1896

L. & F., Chicago, IL, c. 1881

L. & F. or R. & L. (monogram) Illinois Watch Co., Springfield, IL, c. 1882

L. & F. or F. & L. (monogram) Stuart, Springfield, IL, c. 1880

Lackritz, Paul N., Chicago (dial), c. 1900

Laclede, Illinois Watch Co., Springfield, IL, c. 1881

Lady Martha, Illinois Watch Co., Springfield, IL (*see* Becken, A.C., & Co.)

Lady Perry, O. Cohen, Erie, PA, c. 1916

Lady Perry

Lady Stewart, c. 1917 (*see also* Stewart)

Lady Stewart

Lady Washington, c. 1886

Lafayette, c. 1883 (*see also* Washington Watch Co.)

Lafee, P. A., Dayton, OH (dial: Springfield Watch Co.), c. 1873

Lake Erie, c. 1881

Lake Shore, c. 1879

Lake & Strobel, Waterbury, CT (dial), c. 1903

Lakeshore, Adjusted (matching dial), c. 1906

Lakeside, c. 1881

Lambert Bros., NY, 59th & 3rd Ave. (dial: Lambert Bros., New York), c. 1898–1903

Lambert Bros.

Landas, G. L., Titusville, PA, c. 1887

Landis Watch Co., Chicago, c. 1905–1910 (usually marked "Landis Watch Co., Chicago" on the movement and "Landis" on the dial; sometimes found in "Landis Watch Co." signed cases. Some movements are given military names: Captain, Colonel, General, Lieutenant, Major)

Laneis & Pugh, Jackson, OH (matching dial), c. 1877

Lanz, G., Norristown, PA, c. 1896

Lanz, Gustave, Norristown, PA (dial: Gustave Lanz), c. 1905

Laraway, W.F., Glenwood, IA (matching dial)

Lark, c. 1923

Lark

Larmour & Co., Baltimore, MD, c. 1872

LaRue, H.A., Oskaloosa IA, c. 1891

Lawrence, The R. W. Sears Watch Co., Chicago, IL, c. 1883 [perhaps named for Arthur Lawrence, bookkeeper of the original Sears company, who is mentioned by Meggers in "Richard Warren Sears and His Watch Companies," NAWCC *Bulletin,* October 1990, p. 428]

Le Rette, H.W., Morris, IL (dial: Le Rette, Morris, IL), c. 1910

Leader, c. 1923

Leader, The, c. 1926

LeBolt & Co., New York and Chicago, c. 1909

Lee Bros.

LeBron, Galena, IL, c. 1896

Richard Lee

Lee Bros. Special, Rail Road Service, c. 1897

Lee, Richard, Waterloo, IA (matching dial), c. 1909

Leeland, O.S., Manistee, MI, c. 1894

Legault & Co., Lowell, MA (Adjusted) 17 Jewels, c. 1911

Legg, H.M., Syracuse, NY (matching dial), c. 1889

Leibenow, J., Green Bay, WI

Leith, John, Bay City, c. 1882

Lemon, Francis, Ashland, NB, c. 1893

Leppert, John C., Chicago. IL (dial: John C. Leppert, Chicago), c. 1892

John C. Leppert

Lewis, D.R., Special, c. 1909
Lewis & Dimmick Railway Special (dial: Lewis & Dimmick), c. 1911 [firm was located in Norwich, NY]
Lewis Jewelry Co., Cleveland, OH (dial: L.J. Co.), c. 1906
Lewkowitz, F., New York (matching dial), c. 1901
Lexington Watch Co., Providence, RI, c. 1916 (private label of the Baird-North Co.)
Liberty Bell (*see* Washington Watch Co.)

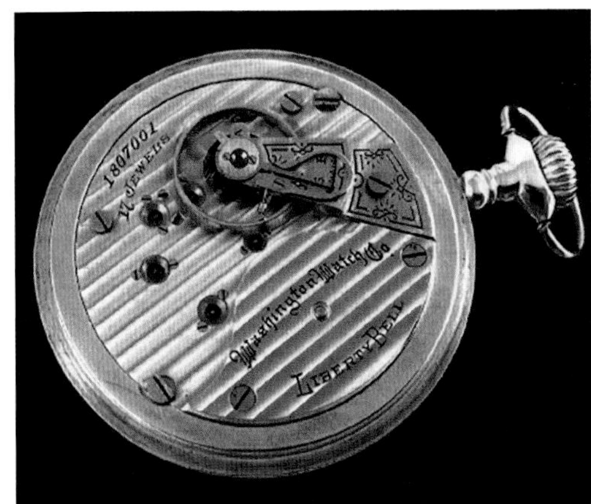

Liberty Bell

Liebenow, J., Green Bay, WI (dial: J. Liebenow), c. 1905 [Julius Liebenow, Jeweler and Optometrist]
Liebenow, C., & Sons, Manitowoc, WI (matching dial), c. 1891
Lieutenant (*see* Landis Watch Co.)
Lifetime Series, The, c. 1926
Lightning Express, Springfield, Il, c. 1882
Lincoln (*see* Iowa Watch Co.)
Lincoln, U.S.A. (*see* Becken, A.C., & Co.)
Lincoln Park, Springfield, IL (*see* Becken, A.C., & Co.)
Lincoln Park, U.S.A. or Illinois Watch Co., Springfield (*see* Becken, A.C., & Co.)
Link, Oscar, St. Louis, c. 1882
Linnenbrink, J., Rochester, PA, c. 1897
Little, S. T., & Sons, Cumberland, MD (dial: Railway Engineer), c. 1895 (*see also* B. & O. Standard)
Loch, August, Pittsburgh (dial), c. 1907
Lockhart, K.S., Dearborn, MI, c. 1889
Logan, U.S.A. (*see* Becken, A.C., & Co.)
Lorch, Vic, Louisville, KY, c. 1901
Lovett & Joyce, Larned, KS (dial: Sigma Special), c. 1899
Low, Daniel, & Co., Salem, MA (matching dial), c. 1915
Lucke, Hermann, Worcester, MA, c. 1891
Lundborg, A.P., Worcester, MA, c. 1894
Lundy, T., San Francisco, c. 1914
Lurie, Robt., Special, 121 Madison St., Chicago, IL, c. 1894
Lurchin & Lurchin, St. Johnsbury, VT (dial: Lurchin & Lurchin), c. 1911
Lushbaugh, H.F., Mt. Pulask, IL, c. 1893
Luyten & Co., Pontiac, IL (matching dial), c. 1887
Lynch, Charles B., Philadelphia, PA (matching dial), c. 1891
Lynch, T., 1 & 3 Union Square, NY (matching dial), c. 1895
Lyons, S.J., Philadelphia, PA, c. 1912
M.&B., St. Louis, MO (matching dial), c. 1887 (*see* Meister & Bierbaum)
MC (monogram), Illinois Watch Co., Springfield, IL, c. 1882
M.J. Co., Toledo, OH (dial), c. 1906
M.Z. (monogram), Springfield, IL, c. 1883
MacDonald, J. L., Baltimore, MD (matching dial), c. 1894
Mace, J. H., Illinois Loaner
[dial, "Illinois/J.H.Mace/Loaner" on very rare 1926 60-hour 19J Bunn model, in case marked "J H Mace Company/Union Station, KC,MO/139" Mace was a major inspector of railroad watches, based in the terminal at Kansas City. Loaners were sent out with railwaymen who had brought their own watches in for servicing; Mace did enough business to contract for special dials with both Illinois and Elgin, as well as their own numbered cases.]
Macy, R.H., Co. (sold Illinois-made watches under various private labels, such as Hallmark and Herald Square), c. 1917–1921
Madison, Springfield, IL, c. 1882
Maiden America, Goodman Bros. (dial: Maiden America), c. 1916
Maiden Lane, c. 1884
Maier, F., Bowling Green, KY, c. 1886

Maier, Joseph, Brooklyn, NY (matching dial), c. 1894
Maier Jewelry Co., Aberdeen, MS, c. 1907

Maier Jewelry Co.

Maier & Berkele, Atlanta, GA (matching dial), c. 1891
Majestic Special, 1902
Major (*see* Landis Watch Co.)
Major, J.W., Co. (monogram), c. 1880
Mallove's (dial only, with "Illinois" below jeweler's name), c. 1927 [firm located in Middletown, CT, and still in existence]
Manhattan, The, c. 1919 (*see also* Gamse, N.)
Manhattan, W. & M. (monogram), c. 1882
Manis Hyams Diamond & Watch Co., Union Square, New York (dial: Diamond & Watch Co., New York), c. 1891
Marine Special (matching dial), c. 1925

Marine Special

Lincoln Star (Lincoln, NE), October 17, 1924; image from *newspapers.com*

Maritime, Illinois Watch Co., Springfield, c. 1924
Market St. Special, Illinois Watch Co., Springfield, U.S.A., c. 1923
Marks, E., Troy, NY, c. 1899
Marquardt, G.W., Iowa City, IA, c, 1879
Marshall. R.L., Elizabethtown, KY (matching dial), c. 1881
Marston & Seaman, Albany, NY (dial), c. 1923
Martin, J.H., Blackstone, VA (matching dial), c. 1911
Marvel, Illinois Watch Co., Springfield, c. 1923
Master, The, Illinois Watch Co., Springfield, c. 1924

The Master

Masterpiece, c. 1918
Mauch, Herman (dial only), St. Louis, MO, 1906
Mauch & Adams, Marshall, MO, c. 1897
May, Archie K., York, PA (dial: Arkema Special), c. 1917
Maynard, F.C., Saratoga Springs, NY, c. 1896
Mayo, Benj. J., Newark, NJ, c. 1891
McDougall, Wm. G., 927 Eighth Ave, New York (dial: Wm. G. McDougall), c. 1908
McDougall's Special (dial: Wm. M. McDougall, Brooklyn, New York City), c. 1896
McGee, J.M., Cherokee, IA, c. 1891
McKee, D.C., Corning, NY, c. 1886
McNamara & Kinsey, Eureka, CA, c. 1882
Mead Special, The, c. 1924
Mechanic, c. 1881
Meister & Bierbaum, St. Louis, MO (dial: monogram), c. 1881 [firm was known to have used several different monogram styles on their dials and movements]
Menger Bro. & Wagner, Baltimore, MD, c. 1895
Mercereau & Connell (dial only), c. 1896 [Jewelers and Silversmiths, Scranton, PA; movement, unmarked, is Grade 181, ser. no. 1304917]
Meritime, Illinois Watch, Springfield, c. 1923 (a private label of the Gensler-Lee Jewelry Co.)
Mermod Jaccard Standard

Meritime

$39
17 Jewel Illinois
MERITIME
$1.00 DOWN

17-JEWEL Illinois MeriTime, adjusted movement. Bridge model, patent michrometric regulator and other advanced features. Finest quality double-stock 14K Green or White Gold-filled case. Fancy Platinum finish dial. Complete with silver Gift box at $39. $1.00 DOWN, then $1.00 a week.

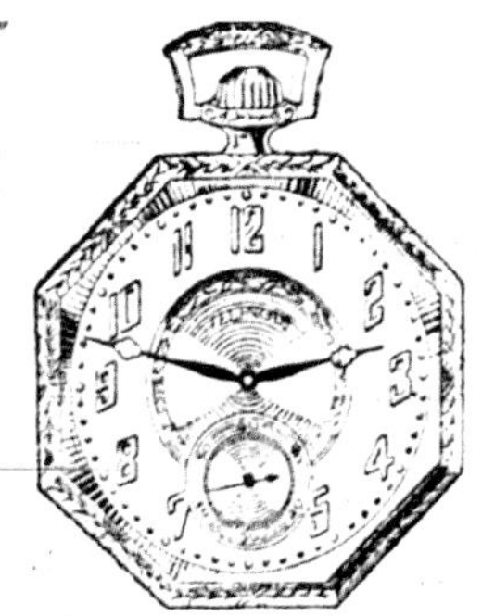

19 Jewel Solid Gold
Illinois MeriTime $75
$1.00 DOWN!

19-JEWEL Illinois MeriTime, adjusted to three positions, temperature, etc. Solid gold center wheel, screws and regulator also of solid gold; double roller, Breguet hairspring. The case is a beauty—octagon design in 14K White or Green Solid Gold, richly engraved. The dial is platinum finish with raised solid gold numerals and dots! $75. $1.00 DOWN, $2.25 a week.

GENSLER-LEE. "LEADING CREDIT JEWELE

Two Illinois Meritime models, *Oakland Tribune* (Oakland, CA), December 12, 1924; image from *newspapers.com*

$60
"MERITIME" Illinois
14K Solid Gold, Cushion
17 Jewel Movement

$1.00 DOWN

HERE'S a 17 jewel Illinois MeriTime, adjusted to position, etc. Latest Cushion design case, 14K. Green or White SOLID GOLD. Fancy damaskeene dial. A most artistic watch! $60, on terms of $1.00 DOWN, then $2.00 a week. Open an account now—same price cash or credit. Call in now!

Knife and Chain Free!

Illinois Meritime Cushion model, *Oakland Tribune* (Oakland, CA), February 5, 1926; image from *newspapers.com*

Merrill, Fred L., & Co., Portland, ME, c. 1895
Merry, C.L., Norwalk, OH, c. 1876
Metcalfe & Hacker, Baltimore, MD (matching dial), c. 1898
Michael, Adolf, Made expressly for (dial: Adolf Michael, Green Bay, WI), c. 1896
Milkey, G.F., Turners Falls, MA, c. 1891
Miller, H.S., Milwaukee, WI, c. 1891
Miller, J., Cleveland, c. 1882
Miller, John A., Cairo, IL, c. 1897
Miller, Wm. B., Sacramento, CA (matching dial), c. 1887
Miller, Wm. J., Baltimore, MD, c. 1902
Miller Special, Marshalltown, IA, c. 1898
Millikan & Hickle, Athens, OH (matching dial), c. 1907
Miner's Watch, The (dial: S.W. Manning, Virginia, NV), c. 1877
Minneapolis, c. 1882
Mitchell, E.H., Saco, ME (dial), c. 1911
Monarch Watch Co. USA, Made by Rogers, Thurman & Co., Chicago, IL, c. 1912 (Date is from a 1912 advertisement. Monarch Watch Co. watches are very scarce and only a few have been *seen*,)
Monitor, c. 1882
Monroe (*see* Washington Watch Co.)
Moor, Herbert L. (dial: *see* Chapter 7)
Moore, Law. L., Co., Seattle (matching dial), c. 1911
Morch, Jacob, Made Expressly for, Brooklyn E.D. [East District], c. 1882
Morck Bros, Warren, PA (dial: Morck Bros.), c. 1893
Morck & Kirberger, Made for, c. 1903
Morley, C.E., Jordan, NY, c. 1908
Morris Jewelry Co., Chicago, U.S.A. (matching dial), c. 1905
Morse, W.F., Special, Danvers, MA (matching dial), c. 1903
Moser, Wapakoneta, OH, c. 1902

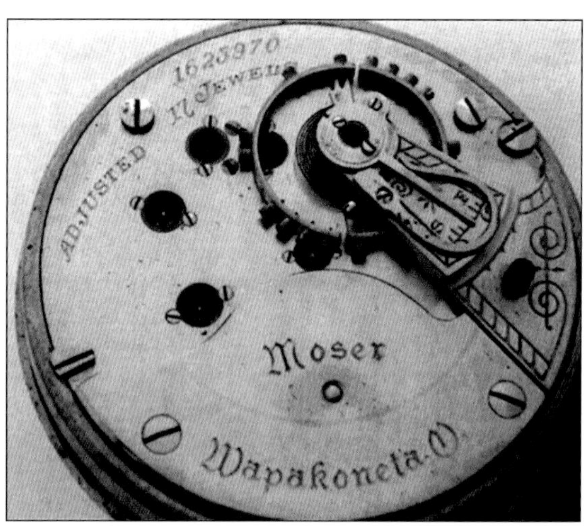

Moser

Motsinger, M.J., Rector, AR (dial: Motsinger's Cotton Belt), c. 1907
Moulton, R.H. (sold by Carson Pirie Scott, Chicago), c. 1903
Mount, C.V., Shenandoah, IA (matching dial), c. 1891
Mt. Vernon (*see* Washington Watch Co.)
Muller & Son, Brooklyn, NY (matching dial), c. 1898
Mulloy, William, Great Falls, NH, c. 1880
Murphy, A.H., Erie, PA, c. 1889
Muscatine Watch Co., Muscatine, IA, c. 1891–1894
Muscatine Watch Co., Muscatine, IA (dial with "F.W. Swan, Manager")
NBF & Co. (monogram), c. 1880
Nabob, c. 1882
Nabstedt, M.E., & Sons, Davenport, IA (matching dial), c. 1895
Naegele Watch & Jewelry Co. (dial), c. 1891
Nassagaweya, The, c. 1888
Nation, Springfield, IL, c. 1889 (*see also* Standard Watch Co.)

National, The, Chicago (matching dial), c. 1894

The National

Navigator Special, c. 1912
Neasham, J.W., Ottumwa, IA (matching dial), c. 1906
Neenah Special (dial: Wm. C. Nelson), c. 1896
Negley Watch Co., Chicago, IL, c. 1890–1892
Nelson, L.M., Special, c. 1908
Nelson's Special (dial: J.E. Nelson), c. 1907
Nesler, Ferd. A., Dubuque, IA (matching dial), c. 1896

Ferd. A. Nesler

Neusaner, E.A. & Co., Iron Mt., MI, c. 1896
New Railroad King, Springfield, IL, c. 1894
Newhall, S.C., Lyman, MA, c. 1882
Newton, W.C., Southern Special, c. 1895
Niagara (dial: B.F.N. & Co.), c. 1880
Nichaus, F.H., St, Louis, MO, c. 1882
Nichols, Samuel P., Palmyra, NY, c. 1887
Nickel, c. 1881

Noack, Chas. J., Sacramento, CA, c. 1880
Non-Magnetic Watch Co. (*see* Paillard Non-Magnetic Watch Co.)
Norton, A. (matching dial), c. 1881
Norton, A., 21 Special, Illinois Watch Co., Springfield, IL, c. 1912
No. 5, c. 1879
No. 13, Cincinnati, OH, c. 1880
No. 22, E. Jaccard Jewelry Co., St. Louis, Mo, c. 1882
No. 65, Illinois Watch Co., Springfield; Illinois (dial), c. 1913
No. 80, Cincinnati, OH, c. 1879
No. 333, c. 1898
No. 444, c 1900–1906
No. 500, c. 1921
No. 523, c. 1898
No. 555, c. 1899
No. 777, c. 1899
No. 805, Illinois Watch Co., Springfield, c. 1922
No. 850, Illinois Watch Co., Springfield, c. 1921
No. 900, Illinois Watch Co., Springfield, c. 1921
No. 989 Special, Illinois Watch Co., Springfield, c. 1909
No. 999 Special; *Note:* according to Meggers and Ehrhardt, the number appears on an 18S DS Bunn dial. [Note: 999 was the number for a famous New York Central locomotive.]
No. 1901, Illinois Watch Co., Springfield, c. 1898
No. 1905 Special, Illinois Watch Co., Springfield, c. 1904
No. 1908 Special, Illinois Watch Co., Springfield, c. 1904
O. and E. Special (matching dial), c. 1916
O B & V, NY (dial: O B & V), c. 1879 (Oppenheimer Bros. & Veith)
O.K., Springfield, IL, c. 1879

O.K.

O'Connell, W.H., Audubon, IA (matching dial), c. 1897
Oesterle, C., Joliet, IL (matching dial), c. 1882 [Carl Oesterle]
Offenhaeuser, O., Schenectady, NY (dial: O. Offenhaeuser), c. 1890
Oklahoman, The, c. 1911
Olympia (dial: customized), c. 1896 [elaborate colored dial with flower center and letters of the name "Reuben Ellis", or possibly "Ellis Reuben", encircling the dial)
Olympia, Springfield, c. 1898
Opequon (dial: W.L. Jones & Co., Martinsburg, WV), c. 1896 (Opequon is a river)
Oppenstein Bros., Kansas City, MO, c. 1910
Oregon, c. 1881
Oriental, c. 1891
Orleans Watch Co., Orleans, NE, c. 1907
Our No. 1, c. 1895
Overland Special, Illinois Watch Co., Springfield, IL, c. 1917
Paegel Jewelry Mfg. Co., Minneapolis, c. 1904
Paillard Non-Magnetic Watch Co. or Paillard Watch Co., Chicago, IL, U.S.A. (dial: Paillard Non-Magnetic Watch Co., Chicago, U.S.A.), c. 1895–1910
Paine & Chickering, Suncook, NH, c. 1877
Pape, C.F.T., & Bro., Butler, PA, c. 1888
Paramount, c. 1922
Park Side, c. 1881
Parker, Jos. M., Jr., Philadelphia, PA (matching dial: *see* Chapter 7), c. 1910

Jos. M. Parker, Jr.

Parlin, C.A., Oroville, CA, c. 1882
PDL (monogram), Illinois Watch Co., Springfield, c. 1893
Peacock, C.D., c. 1906 (renowned Chicago jewelry company)
Pecaut, A., DeSoto, MO, c. 1888
Peck's Special, Michigan City, IN, c. 1896
Peckham, Lee & Co., Branford, CT, c. 1894
Peerless, Springfield, IL, c. 1893 (*see* Chapter 12) [The c. 1893 watch was 18 size. An advertisement in 1917 for a "Peerless" in 16 size suggests that at least this later model was a private label for Treco Bros., a Boston jeweler, and was cased and timed at the Illinois Factory.]
Penfold, C.C., Buffalo, NY (matching dial), c. 1894
Penn Special, Illinois Watch Co., Springfield, c. 1920–1927
Pennsylvania Special, Adjusted (matching dial); the Pennsylvania Special was a Private Label of H.M. Jacobsen & Son, Philadelphia, PA, c. 1903 (Ehrhardt & Meggers note that the dials for 18-size, 17-jewel watches have the company's HMJ&S monogram.)
Pepper & Horner, Cleveland, TN, c. 1883
Perkins, E., Springfield, IL, c. 1883
Perry, c. 1991
Person, Frank A., Baltimore, MD, c. 1895
Peters, H.L., Brooklyn (matching dial), c. 1905
Peterson, Chas., Honesdale, PA, c. 1893
Pettit, F.E., Belvidere, IL, c. 1886
Pfenning, V.S., & Co, St. Marys, OH
Phelps & Perry, NY (dial), c. 1911
Pierik, John C., & Son, Springfield, IL, c. 1909
Pitman, A.B., Trenton, NJ (dial only), c. 1886
Place Co., F.F., Boston, MA, c. 1898
Plank, N.S., Iowa City, IA, c. c. 1893
Planter, c. 1881
Plymouth Watch Co., U.S.A. (private label of Sears Roebuck & Co., sold after approximately 1904; proper dial is marked Plymouth Watch Co.)
Poole, A.A. & Son, Washington, PA (matching dial), c. 1896
Porte & Markle, Winnipeg

Potomac, c. 1909 (*see* Washington Watch Co.)
Potter & Gray, Providence, RI (dial: Potter & Gray, Special for Railway Service), c. 1896
Potthoff, H.B., Latrobe, PA (matching dial), c. 1890
Powers, Frank M., Youngstown, OH (dial intricate monogram FMP), c. 1898
Pratt, H.H., Fremont, NE, c. 1890
Precise, Illinois Watch Co., Springfield, IL, c. 1926–1928 [likely a private label for Rogers & Co., as a 1928 advertisement suggests]
Present, c. 1885
President, New York (dial: "W. P. & H."), c. 1882
President, The, mid-1890s
Preston, H.W., Albion, NY, c. 1882
Price, Frank, Kansas City, MO, c. 1892
Price & Landers, Titusville, PA, c. 1910
Prince Charlie, BBG & Co. (monogram), c. 1882
Princess (*see* Standard Watch Co.)
Prochaska, John, Toledo, OH, Made for (dial: Toledo Special), c. 1894
Proctor Bros., Iowa Falls, IA (dial), c. 1890
Proudman, J.C., New York (dial: J.C. Proudman, 307 Eighth Ave., New York), c. 1896
Putney, C.F., Independence, IA, c. 1882
Quaker City, c. 1883
Queen, Springfield, IL, c. 1879 (*see also* Knights, C.H., & Co.)
Queen City Special, John Farrior's, c. 1894
Queen Extra, The (dial: The Queen, N. Gamse, New York, U.S.A.), c. 1917 (*see also* Gamse, N)
Quincy Street, c. 1900 (*see also* Field, Marshall, & Co.)
R. T. & Co., Monarch, Chicago, IL, c. 1909 (monogram is for Rogers, Thurman & Co.)
Rack & Learman Co., Milwaukee WI (matching dial), c. 1893
Raddant Special (dial: C.G. Raddant, Shawano, WI), c. 1896
Rae, Wm. T., & Co., Newark, NJ (dial: hunting scene), c. 1901
Rail Road King (dial: Illinois Watch Co., Special for Railway Service), c. 1883
Rail Road King Special
Rail Road King Standard
Rail Road Standard, c. 1887
Rail Roader, The, Adjusted (matching dial), c. 1892–1897
Rail Roader, The, S.N. Clarkson, Chicago, IL, c. 1894
Rail Roader, The (matching dial), c. 1894
Railroad Construction (dial: Frank Anshutz, Shenandoah, IA), c. 1916
Railroad Dispatcher (dial: JMR monogram for John M. Roberts Co.), c. 1900–1916
Railroad Dispatcher Extra, I.W.Co. or Illinois Watch Co, c. 1904–1912
Railroad Employee's Special (dial: "Chas. Spanday, Pittsburgh, Pa."), c. 1896 (Meggers and Ehrhardt note that the dial so marked may or may not be correct.)
Railroad Inspector's Special, c. 1910
Railroad King
Railroad Official, c. 1903
Railroad Special (dial: Will L. Fredeking, Hinton, WV), c. 1918
Railroader, The, c. 1897 [model apparently acquired the name "The Railroader" because an engraving of a locomotive appears on the movement; the name itself does not appear on the dial or on the movement.]
Railway, Springfield, IL, c. 1880
Railway Engineer (on 18-size Roman dial)
Railway Queen, c. 1894
Railway Regulator, c. 1879–1881
Rajah, The, Illinois Watch Co., Springfield, c. 1926

Ramser, J., Rock Island, IL (dial: Rock Island Special; *see* Chapter 7), c. 1898

J. Ramser

Randolph, E. F., Willaimson, WV (matching dial), c. 1901
Rankin, A.J., & Co. Roanoke, VA., c. 1901
Raynes, Harry, Lowell, MA (dial: Harry Raynes), c. 1895
Reed, J.H. Paris, IL (matching dial), c. 1896
Reed, J.R., Pittsburgh, PA, c. 1874
Reed & Co., J.R., Pittsburgh, PA, c. 1897
Reeves, Truman, San Bernardino, CA (matching dial), c. 1882
Regulator, Chicago, IL (dial: G.B. & Co., Chicago), c. 1881 [possibly Giles Brothers and Co., of Chicago]
Regulator No. 44, The (dial: Strow Bros., Ft. Dodge, Iowa), c. 1894
Reiche, F.M., Los Angeles, CA (dial: F.M. Reiche), c. 1888
Reineman Bros., Allegheny, PA (dial), c. 1895
Reinhardt & MIttendorff, Lincoln, IL (matching dial), c. 1894
Reliable, Chicago, IL, c. 1882
Relgis, Illinois Watch Co., Springfield, c. 1922
Remington Watch Co., Cincinnati, U.S.A., Guaranteed (dial: The Remington Watch Co.). Made by Illinois and sold through the American Watch Club (operated by the Walker Edmund Co., Cincinnnati, OH) with cases supplied by the Bell Watch Case Co., Mansfield OH), c. 1900–1910.
Republic, c. 1881
Retsloff, O.C., Winnebago City, MN
Revere, Paul, c. 1888
Rhein, Henry, Chicago (dial), c. 1901
Ricard, Frank, Lowell & Lawrence, MA (matching dial), c. 1904
Richards, F.I., Rochester, NH, c. 1895
Richmond, W., Mt. Morris, NY (dial: W. Richmond), c. 1882
Riggs & Bros., c. 1913
Riley, Zi, Special, Champaign, IL, c. 1891
Rinkenback, E.L., Harrisburg, PA, c. 1902

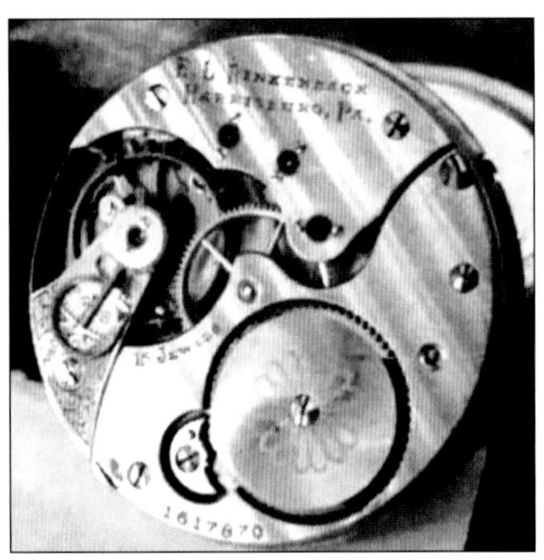

E.L. Rinkenback

Ritter, J., New York (dial only), c. 1892
Rivinius, Carl, Ebensburg, PA (dial), c. 1907
Roberts, E.P, & Sons, Pittsburgh, PA

E.P. Roberts & Sons

Roberts, H.A., & Son, Veedersburg, IN, c. 1910

Roberts, John M., Pittsburgh, c. 1880–1897

Roberts, No. 5, Pittsburgh, c. 1876

Roberts Special, The T.M., Minneapolis (dial: The T.M. Roberts), 1896

Robinson Bros., Council Bluffs, IA, c. 1891

Rockland, c. 1923 (apparently a private label of the Lenox Jewelry Co., Boston, MA)

Greatest Watch Value
IN THE WORLD
19-JEWEL
Illinois
Rockland
Adjusted to
Temperature and
Positions
20-YEAR GOLD-FILLED CASE
$38.75
For Men

Knife and Chain Free

Gold filled. Same knife that we have been selling regularly for $5. This is a Christmas gift to each purchaser of this watch before Xmas.

This watch has gold centre wheel, steel escape wheel, concaved winding wheels, double roller and double sunk dial and all the important features of a $60 watch. We guarantee this watch to be the finest quality American-made at anywhere near this price. It takes six months from the time the Illinois Watch Co. start to make a watch until it is finished. Every piece of material, every adjustment is thoroughly inspected as it goes from department to department, and when it is O.K.'d on the final inspection they know and we know that the watch is a masterpiece of construction and will run within a variation of 30 seconds a month. A watch at double this price will not do any better. We absolutely guarantee this movement and 20-year gold-filled case—gold filled, understand, with a strata of solid gold, not washed or electroplated—the makers of movement and case also guarantee them. Money refunded within 10 days if you can buy this watch elsewhere for less than double our price. Mail orders filled.

LENOX JEWELRY Co.
·16 Bromfield St. Boston

Boston Post (Boston, MA), December 9, 1920; image from *newspapers.com*

Roddin, E.V., & Co., Chicago, IL (matching dial), c. 1891

Rogers, A.E., Scranton, PA, c. 1894

Roosevelt, c. 1923

Rose, Emil, LaCrosse, WI, c. 1882

Rose, John, Bay City, MI (dial: "C.T.S." for Central Trunk System), c. 1877

Rose Special (matching dial), c. 1915; a rose is engraved on the movement plate as well as on the inside of the case cuvette, the latter also showing the name Rose Watch Company, New York. The rose mark belonged to the New york jeweler Henry Freund & Bro.

Rosencrans, O.L. & Thatcher Co., Milwaukee, WI (dial:

Rose Special (front)

Rose Special, close-up of movement showing rose engraving

OLR&T Co.), c. 1882
Rotzler, H.A., Freeport, IL, c. 1908

O.L. Rosencrans & Thatcher Co.

Roulet & Armstrong, Toledo, OH, c. 1895
Rowe Bros., Chicago, c. 1897

Rowe Bros.

Royal Blue Special, Springfield, IL, c. 1895
Rubiyat, Goodnough, Erie, PA, c. 1909
Ruby, Jacob T., Coffeyville, KS (dial), c. 1891
Rudd, O.D., Ilion, NY (matching dial), c. 1896
Rudert, Max, Duquesne, PA; matching dial, c. 1894
Rudisill Bros., Altoona, PA (matching dial), c. 1896
Ruger, M.A., Emira, NY, c. 1885
Runkel, E.E., & Co., Telluride, CO (matching dial), c. 1891
Runyeon, Irwin, Reading, PA, c. 1893
Russell, C.E., Kansas City, MO (matching dial), c. 1882
S.R & Co. Special, Chicago, U.S.A., c. 1904
St. Julien, Springfield, IL, c. 1884
St. Lawrence, c. 1889
St. Louis, with monogram L. B. & Co., c. 1881
[initials likely for Louis Bauman & Co., of St. Louis.]
St. Maurice, c. 1882
Salco (Sallen Jewelry Co., Detroit), c. 1919
San Juan, c. 1881
Sanders, D.T., & Son, Greenville, ME (dial), c. 1892
Santa Fe Special (dial: Santa Fe Special, Illinois), c. 1913–1931 (All Santa Fe Special watches were sold originally cased in Santa Fe Watch Co.-marked cases.)
Saup, Frank, Dayton, OH, c. 1886
Schaefer & Addison, Baltimore, MD (dial)

Schaefer & Addison

Schario, F. & L.E. Danville, IL (matching dial), c. 1901
Schaub, Albert, Detroit MI, c. 1895
Schearer & McCollum, Webb City, MO (dial only), c. 1891
Scheele, Theo., Milwaukee, WI (matching dial), c. 1896
Scheer, W.H. (dial: Eaton, CO), c. 1912
Scheller, George A., Newark, NJ, c. 1895
Schimpff, E., Scranton, PA, c. 1896
Schmedtie Bros., Washington, DC (matching dial), c. 1891

Schmedtie Bros.

Schmedtie Bros.

Schmidt, E.W., Co., Milwaukee, WI, c. 1914
Schmidt & Feinstein, Lebanon, PA, c. 1890
Schmidt, P.P., San Francisco, CA (matching dial), c. 1895
Schneider, Ben, Jewelry Co., Cincinnati, OH

Ben Schneider Jewelry Co.

Schoenfeld, Jerry, Red Bluff, CA (dial: Jerry Schoenfeld), c. 1883
Schuetz, Herman, Olean, NY (matching dial), c. 1890
Scott, G., Springfield, IL, c. 1880
Scott, Geo. E., Hibbing, MN (matching dial), c. 1899
Scott, J. W. & Son, Cadiz, OH, c. 1896
Scott, Walter, The Special, c. 1905 (*see also* Butler Bros.)
Scribner & Loehr Co., The (dial), c. 1915 (company was located in Cleveland, OH)
Sears, Roebuck & Co., Chicago (sold watches under various private labels, such as Plymouth Watch Co., Interstate Chronometer, and Sears, Roebuck & Co. Special)
Sears, Roebuck & Co., Chicago, U.S.A. (matching dial), c. 1895–1904
Seewald, L., Springfield, IL, c. 1876
Seewald, L., Tiffin, OH, c. 1877
Segerstrom, J., Watch Maker, Rhinelander, WI (dial: J. Segerstrom, Rhinelander, WI), c. 1893
Segerstrom's Illinois Special, Rhinelander, WI, c. 1894–1918

Seidel, R., Milwaukee, WI, c. 1896
Selts, H. W., Clay Center, KS (dial: H. W. Selts Special), c. 1902
Senate, c. 1902 (*see also* Washington Watch Co.)
Seneca (*see* Iowa Watch Co.)
Senter, Wm. & Co., Portland, ME (matching dial), c. 1900
Shaffer Bros., Carlyle, IL (matching dial), c. 1881
Sheridan, L., St. Charles, MN, (matching dial), c. 1894
Sherman, L., & Co., Taunton, MA, c. 1880
Sherwood, C.S., Portsmouth VA (dial: S.A.L. Special), c. 1895
Shourds, Storey, & Kasper, Chicago, IL (dial: Shourds, Storey, & Kasper), c. 1885
Sieghold, C., Salinas City, CA, c. 1880
Sigler Bros. Co., The, Cleveland, OH, c. 1904
Silver Star, Springfield, IL, c. 1882
Simmons, Wm. A., Frederick, MD (matching dial), c. 1901
Simson & Lowery, Victor, PA, c. 1886
Sloan & Feinberg, Ironwood, MI, c. 1886
Smedul, R.W., Made expressly for (dial: R.W. Smedul, Gleason, WI), c. 1888
Smith, C.R. & Son, Philadelphia, PA, c. 1899
Smith, J. Kendall, Newark, NJ, c. 1882–1889
Smith, R.H., Hinton, WV
Smith Sturgent & Co, Detroit, MI, c. 1894
Smyth, John M., Co., Special, Chicago, c. 1909
Smythe, J.H., Ft. Smith, AR, c. 1891
Snyder, C.F., Pittsburgh, PA (matching dial), c. 1895
Sommer & Pierik, Bunn Special, Springfield, IL, c. 1896
Sommer & Pierik, Springfield, IL, c. 1888–1896
Soo Special, H. B. Shellito & Co. (dial: H. B. Shellito & Co., Sault Ste. Marie, MI), c. 1899
Sorenson Co., S.F., CA. "Special" (dial: Sorenson Co., S.F., CA) [S.F. is abbreviation for San Francisco]
Southern Railroad Special (dial: Castelberg's National Jewelry Company, Washington, DC), c. 1895
Southern Railroad Special, c. 1897
Southern Special, M.C. Newton, c. 1895
South Park, c. 1881 [likely referring to that Colorado area; and the Denver, South Park, and Pacific Railroad in particular]
Special, c. 1882
Special Railroader, C.A. Schlechter, Reading, PA (dial: Special Railroader), c. 1894
Special Time King, c. 1912
Spencer, John, & Daughter, Edgerton, WI (matching dial), c. 1909
Spoesser, W.D., Watertown, WI, c. 1896
Springer, W.S.H., c. 1889
Standard Watch Co., Pittsburgh, PA, c. 1883–1889 (sold private-label watches made by Illinois; all or some of these same grade names also were made by Lancaster W. Co., Hampden W. Co., Swiss and possibly Elgin Nat'l W. Co.: Acme, Excelsior, Crescent, Triumph, Eclipse, Clipper, Nation, Princess)
Standard, St. Louis, MO, U.S.A., c. 1908
Standard, St. Louis, U.S.A. (matching dial), Mermod, Jaccard & King Co., St. Louis, c. 1912
Stanley, c. 1925

Stanley

Stanners, A.C., Toronto, c. 1912
Star of David Picture (on movement and dial), Illinois Watch Co., Springfield, IL, c. 1916
Star of the West (*see* Iowa Watch Co.)

Star Light, c. 1883
Stark, Charles, Toronto (matching dial), c. 1888
Statz, O.H., & Bro., Terre Haute, IN (dial), c. 1896
Staudt & Co., Columbus, OH (dial), c. 1882
Staufenbeil, A.R., Dubuque, IA (matching dial), c. 1895
Steadley Bros., Carthage, MO (matching dial), c. 1893
Stebbins, Ashtabula, OH, c. 1902
Stebbins, F.H., Jacksonville, IL (dial)

F.H. Stebbins

Steffeck, Jos., Chicago, IL, c. 1896
Stein, Fred, Genesco, IL, c. 1895
Steinmann, J.P., Alleghany, PA (dial: J.P. Steinmann), c. 1894
Stentzel, C. Wm., & Son, c. 1915 [Firm was in Brooklyn, NY]
Stephenson, Thos., Columbus, OH, c. 1873

Sterling, Illinois, Springfield or Illinois Watch Co., Springfield, c. 1923–1936 (Sterling was a private label for the Kay Jewelry Co.)

Sterling dial

Reading Times (Reading, PA), April 21, 1917; image from *newspapers.com*

Sterling movement

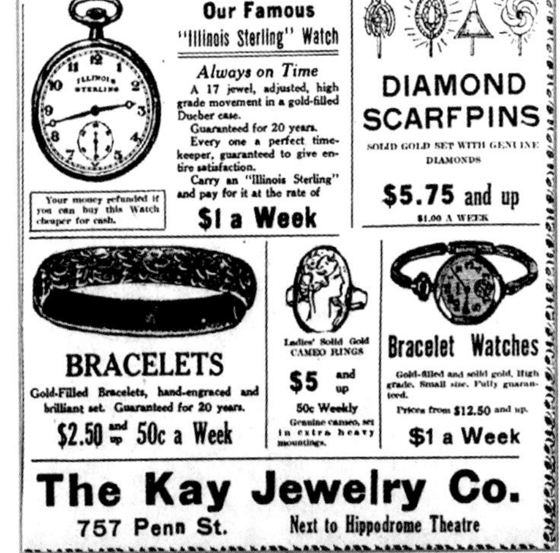

Reading Times (Reading, PA), December 18, 1917; image from *newspapers.com*

Stevens, J.P. & Bros., Atlanta, GA, c. 1885
Stewart Special, Chicago, U.S.A., c. 1897–1923 ("Stewart" was a private label of Sproehnle & Co., Chicago)

Sproehnle & Co. promotional paperweight. Sproehnle, an Illinois jobber, had Stewart as a private label.

Stief, B.H., Jewelry Co., Nashville, TN, c. 1892
Stillwell, H.A., The Special, c. 1905 (*see also* Butler Bros.)
Stoecker, John, Syracuse, NY, c. 1914

John Stoecker

Stone, L.L., Canton, PA (matching dial), c. 1897
Stone, W.M., Minneapolis, MN (dial)
Stonewall, c. 1881
Stonich, Jacob, Chicago, IL, 17 Jewels, Adjusted, c. 1895
Stoops, J.F., Leechburg, PA, c. 1899
Story W.H., Hillsboro Bridge, NH (dial: W.H. Story), c. 1892
Strang, George, St. Louis, 1904 (dial)
Strathearn, Geo., Midland, Ont. (dial: Strathearn's Special), c. 1906
Stratton, E.E., Hinsdale, NH, c. 1894
Straus, M., c. 1905
Strauss, M., Brooklyn, NY
Strouse, Charles, Shenandoah, PA (matching dial), c. 1894
Sturdy, c. 1925
Sturmer, Simon, Sacramento, CA, c. 1888
Sumner, Charles, Boston (dial: Charles Sumner), c. 1881
Sumner's Special, London, Ont., c. 1908
Sun-Dial (dial), c. 1894
Sunderlin (dial), Rochester, NY, c. 1906 [L. Sunderlinn & Co.]
Sunny South, c. 1880
Sunny South, A. M. Hill, New Orleans, c. 1892
Sunrise, Springfield, IL (dial: L.B. & Co). c. 1880 [initials likely for Louis Bauman & Co., of St. Louis]
Superior, Springfield, IL, c. 1882
Supreme, c. 1920
Sutor, Fred G., Philadlphia, c. 1898
Sutton, Harry, Lancaster, PA, c. 1882
Swan, F.W. (*see also* Muscatine Watch Co.), c. 1886
T.H.K. (monogram), Illinois Watch Co., Springfield, IL), c. 1882
Taintor & McAlpine, Easthampton, MA, c. 1891
Talbott, Edwin H., Brooklyn, IA (dial only), c. 1893
Talcott Brothers, Olympia, WA (matching dial), c. 1908
Tanke, T.G., Buffalo, NY, c. 1898
Tappins, Troy, NY (dial: Tappins), c. 1898
Tarlton, G.H., Watertown, MA (matching dial), c. 1885

Tasco Perfex, 1916 [a private label for the Albert S. Samuels Co., San Francisco. "Tasco" is a catchy abbreviation for "**T**he **A**lbert **S**amuels **Co**mpany."

Taylor, H. V., Special, Waterloo, IA (dial), c. 1897

H. V. Taylor Special

Tecumseh, The, c. 1900 (*see also* Becken, A.C., & Co.)

Tegtmeyer, Archie, Milwaukee, WI (dial: Archie Tegtmeyer, Milwaukee), c. 1898

Telegram, c. 1882

Texan, The, Illinois Watch Co., Springfield, c. 1918

Texas, St. Louis (dial: LB & Co. monogram), c. 1879

Texas Special, Illinois Watch Co., Springfield, IL, c. 1918

Texas Special

Thoendel, H.I., Chicago, IL, c. 1893

Thoma, 1838, c. 1914

Thomas & Brand, Findley, OH (dial: Thomas & Brand), c. 1890

Thompson, D.S., Livermore Falls, ME, c. 1895

Thompson, S.W., and Co., Salem, OR (matching dial)

Thorn Bros., Pennsylvania, c. 1902

Thorp, W.H., Beaver Dam, WI, c. 1883

Thorpe & Hoberg, Sioux City, IA (dial), c. 1907

Thurley, H.H., Creston, IA, c. 1899

Tiffany Watch, The (matching dial), c. 1894

Tilden, T.H., Boston, MA (dial: Old Colony), c. 1897

Time King, c. 1898–1926. The Time King name was used by S&N Katz in Baltimore, Maryland, on Hamilton as well as Illinois dials and movements. Hamilton would fill orders for a minimum quantity of 10 between 1925 and 1930

Time King

Time King tin movement shipping container

Timpane & Jackson, Troy, NY (dial), c. 1896
Tinsley Bros., Harlan, IA (matching dial), c. 1887
Tobie, E.L., Keithsburg, IL, c. 1888
Tobie's Special, Keithsburg, IL (dial: E.L. Tobie, Keithsburg, IL), c. 1895
Tomlinson & Coxeter, Bridgeport, CN (dial: Tomlinson & Coxeter), c. 1890
Topeka, marked L.B. & Co., St. Louis (dial: L.B. & Co.), c. 1881 [initials likely for Louis Bauman & Co., of St. Louis.]
Topelius the Grant, Illinois Watch Co. (matching dial), c. 1914
Tower Grove (dial: marked M.E. & Co.), c. 1882
Tower Grove, Springfield, IL, c. 1886
Transit, c. 1920
Traphagen, James, Newark, NJ, c. 1892
Trask, R.H., Ottawa, IL, c. 1882
Triumph, c. 1882 (*see* Standard Watch Co.)
Truckenbrod, H.H., Mendota, IL (matching dial), c. 1896
Tucker, J.W. & Co., San Francisco (dial: Tucker's Granger Watch), c. 1884
Tunehorst's Special, c. 1911
Turner, W.L., Newman, GA, c. 1910

W.L. Turner (matching dial: see Chapter 7)

Twin City (dial: Wm. O. Nelson), c. 1884
Union Pacific, The, N. Gamse, NY (matching dial), c. 1918
U.S. Signal Corps, c. 1907

U.S. Signal Corps (dial only)

Van Doren, J. W., Special, Minonk, IL, c. 1901
Vanderbilt (dial: Frank Curtis), c. 1888
Vendome, 17 Jewels, c. 1901
Viau & Co., Chas. G., Fall River, MA, c. 1895
Victor (matching dial: *see* Chapter 7), c. 1922–1924
Victoria, Springfield, IL, c. 1883
Vim, c. 1924
Viorol, Frank J., Ft. Wayne, IN (matching dial), c. 1894
Vognild, E.L., Chicago (matching dial), c. 1897
Vogt, Anthony, Wilkes Barre, PA, c. 1892
Von der Heydt, J., Chicago, IL, c. 1898
Voorhees & Van Wickle, New Brunswick, NJ, c. 1882
Wagner, H.G. & J.E., 1894 (jewelers in Washington, DC)
Wait, Dewey & Co., Ravenna, OH, c. 1877
Waldin, Chas., Burlington, IA, c. 1898
Wall Bros., Buffalo, NY (dial), c. 1890
Wallace & Simmons, Providence, RI (dial: Wallace & Simmons), c. 1893

Wallenhorst, O.O., Baltimore, MD, c. 1894
Walter, A., & Son, Jersey City, NJ (matching dial), c. 1896
Wanamaker Accuratus Series, c. 1910 (Wanamaker's was the first department store in Philadelphia and one of the first in the United States.)

Wanamaker Accuratus Series

Wanamaker, John (matching dial), c. 1905

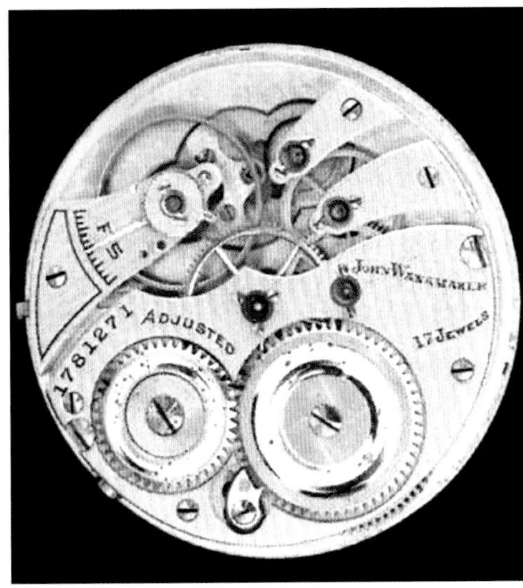

John Wanamaker

Ward, Chas. P., Yonkers, NY (matching dial)

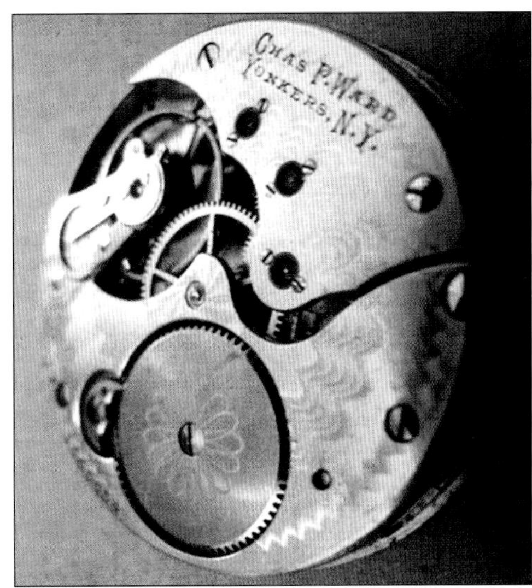

Chas P. Ward

Ward, Montgomery, & Co., Extra Railroad Timer (dial: Montgomery Ward & Co.), c. 1895
Ward, Montgomery, & Co., Railroad Timer, c. 1895-1901
Ward, Montgomery, & Co., Train Dispatchers Special, 21 Ruby Jewels-Adjusted (Tu-Tone) (marked dial), c. 1896
Warren, Geo O., Scaymore, IL, c. 1893
Warrington, U.S.A. or Illinois Watch Co., Springfield, IL (*see also* Becken, A.C, & Co.)
Washburn, H.E., Plymouth, MA (matching dial), c. 1897
Washington, c. 1899 (*see also* Becken, A.C., & Co.)
Washington, Geo. (with flowers), c. 1881
Washington, Geo., P & K., c. 1879
Washington, Springfield, IL, c. 1881
Washington Watch Co. (private label of Montgomery Ward; sold watches made by Illinois, listed under their grade names: Army and Navy, Greenwich, Lafayette, Liberty Bell, Monroe, Mt. Vernon, Potomac, Senate, Martha Washington)
Wathier's Quick Train Watch, Chicago, IL, c. 1895

Wathier's Railroad Challenger, Chicago (matching dial), c. 1898
Wathier's Railway Watch, Chicago, IL (dial: Walthier), c. 1891
Wathier's Watch, Extra Jeweled (dial: Walthier)
Watts, J.R., Ashland, NB (dial: Platt Valley Watch), c. 1880
Weaver, Henry, Minneapolis, MN, c. 1892
Webb Special, Corbin, KY (dial: Webb Special), c. 1883
Webers Warranted Watch (dial: Weber), 1879
Webster, A.A. & Co., Brooklyn, NY, c. 1896
Wehmanen & Co., Made expressly for, c. 1916
Wehrle, E.N., Punxsutawney, PA (dial)
Weiler, Jason, & Son, Boston, c. 1911
Weindieck, H.H., Red Bluff, CA, c. 1888
Weiss, Julius A., Montgomery, AL, c. 1884
Welf, Joseph (dial: Joseph Welf, Cleveland, OH), c. 1904
Wellstein, Jos., & Co., Milwaukee, WI, c. 1896
Wellstein, Jos., & Co., Milwaukee (dial: Wellstein's Special), c. 1897
Welsh & Bro., Baltimore, MD (matching dial), c. 1894
Wentworth, E.O., Sandbornville, NH (matching dial), c. 1896
Western, St. Louis (dial: L.B. & Co.), c. 1880
Wettstein, Springfield, IL, c. 1882
Wheaton, C. (K. & S. monogram), c. 1879
Wheeler & Son, Salem, NJ, c. 1893
Wheeler's Jewelry Store, Rutland, VT, c. 1880
White, Albert, Buffalo, NY (matching dial), c. 1893
White, Chas W., Buffalo, NY, c. 1894
White, J.R., & Co., Rochester, NY (matching dial), c. 1906
Whitman, C.A., Adams, MA, c. 1891
Wickens, Charles B., Syracuse, NY, c. 1893
Wilbur & Peterson, Galesburg, IL (matching dial), c. 1890
Wilbur, Lanphear, c. 1895
Wilbur, Lanphear & Tryner, Galesburg, IL (matching dial), c. 1894
Will & Co., C.C., Pittsburgh, PA, c. 1896
Willard, c. 1882
Williams, F.J., Adams, NY (dial: *see* Chapter 7)
Williams, Jos. A., Boston, MA (matching dial), c. 1893
Wilson, John D., Fort Edward, NY, c. 1882
Wilson Brothers, Boston, MA, King of the Road, c. 1895
Wilson & Bequillard, Mexico, NY (matching dial), c. 1887
Wilson & Kennedy, Hoopeston, IL (dial), c. 1892
Winnipeg, c. 1883
Winthrop, c. 1882
Winzenried, R., Cleveland, OH, c. 1896
Wisconsin (with flower spray), c. 1882
Wise, Wm., & Son (dial only), c. 1920
Wiss, J., & Sons, Newark, NJ (dial), c. 1899
Witzel & Pafenbach, Pittsburgh, PA (matching dial), c. 1891
Woelfe, J.C., Peoria, IL, c. 1890–1894
Wolf, C.A., Topeka, KS, c. 1901
Wollman, M., Council Bluffs, IA, c. 1900
Wolverine, c. 1881
Wonder, c. 1928
Woodward, H.R.
Woodward, J.J., Great Falls, NH, c. 1877
World, The, c. 1881
Wormood, W.W., Dubuque, IA; matching dial, c. 1887
Wright, A.N., Charlton, IA, c. 1885
Wuesteman, Albert E., Champaign, IL, c. 1904
Yale & Dillion, Gloversville, NY
Ye Jewelry Shop, Independence, KS, c. 1907
Yo Semite, The, Stockton, CA (dial: W.H. Keeler, Stockton, Cal.), c. 1880
Young, S.E., & Co., Laconia, NH, c. 1877
Zack, S.R., Philadelphia (dial: Illinois), c. 1908
Zeitler, J.F., St. Louis, MO, c. 1886
Zeitler, John F., St. Louis, MO (matching dial), c. 1894
Zerby, L.W., Huntingdon, PA, c. 1897
Zodiac, Illinois, c. 1911
Zoellner, Otto, & Bro. (dial), c. 1885 (firm in Portsmouth, OH)
Zufall, Louis, Newtown, Long Island, c. 1887

APPENDIX 6

When I first started collecting vintage wristwatches in 1988, many collectors and watch experts advised me not to purchase watches with engravings or inscriptions on the case back. They thought that such inscriptions diminished the value of the watches. Frequently, watches bear inscriptions that commemorate an important event, such as recognition of a military career, an anniversary, birthday, or a graduation. Early wristwatch inscriptions are mostly on transition-period military watches that contain a person's name, rank, and/or hometown engraved on their case backs. Others advised that inscriptions on watch backs were meaningful because it helps establish the historical provenance of the watch and adds character and personal interest to the piece, "bringing it to life," so to speak. As a collector, I am never reluctant to buy watches with inscriptions or former owners' names or initials engraved on their case backs. It is an interesting historical connection to have knowledge of the former owner and the basis for the gift, for example, as with a presentation piece to an employee for 25 years of dedicated and loyal service to a company.

Two wristwatches in my collection serve to reinforce the view that inscriptions help preserve the history of the watch and in so doing add interest and value to the watch. This article briefly elaborates on this theme.

Figure 1. Advertisement from December 1929.

The Consul

At the end of 1928 the Illinois Watch Company released the most expensive watch in its history—a solid-gold model named "The Consul." It sold in 1928-1929 with 19 jewels for $75 and with 21 jewels for the then sky-high price, for the Illinois Watch Company, of $90. By 1930 the Illinois Factory Catalog listed the Consul for as high as $137 at retail. This was clearly the high-end, solid-gold centerpiece of the Illinois Watch Company's wristwatch offerings. In today's dollars a $90 watch in 1928 would sell for $1,149.43 in 2010.

The Consul's style was clearly deco, and the case was made by the well-known and highly respected Solidarity Watch Case Company. Solidarity commenced operations in New York City in 1885, in the then-thriving jewelry hub on Maiden Lane in Manhattan, with a staff of eight men. For a long time it made exclusively solid-gold watch cases for pocket and wristwatches. In four years its staff grew substantially to 94 employees.[1]

The Consul case came in four solid gold varieties: white gold with an engraved bezel; two-tone white and green solid gold with an engraved bezel; white gold with a plain (un-engraved) bezel; and green gold with an engraved bezel.

Figure 2. Consuls: **Left,** solid green gold; **center**, solid white gold (with subdial at 6); **right**, two-tone solid green and white gold (with starburst dial).

There were also several Consul dial variations: sunbursts; pinstripes; plain; and custom. All are highly thought of; the Consul has become one of the most valuable and sought-after Illinois watches.

The prices of the watches that were offered for sale in 1928 were from $75 to $90 per model, and can now fetch (depending on its configuration) over $4,000 today.

The "Convict Consul"

Returning to the fascination of watch inscriptions, on June 30, 1929, a very expensive and one-of-a-kind Consul wristwatch was engraved in cursive as follows:

Presented
To Dr. R. L. Finch.
June 30-1929
By Inmates.
S.H. of C. & B.P.
Marquette. Mich.

After some research, it was determined that "Dr. R. L. Finch" was in fact Dr. Russell L. Finch, the prison doctor at the then S.H. of C., B.P. (State House of Corrections, Bureau Prisons). He must have been a wonderful doctor and person for the prisoners to present him with such an expensive gift at the cusp of the Great Depression.

Dr. Finch was born in 1893 and died in 1965. Upon graduating from the University of Michigan in the class of 1917, he entered medical school and ultimately became the first full-time medical director of the "Hard Labor" Marquette State Prison.

In 1985 Professor Robert W. Barrington wrote in the Foreward for *One Hundred Years at Hard Labor: A History of Marquette State Prison*:

"Throughout the second half of its history, Marquette Branch Prison has been understood by career criminals who notice such things as a place to avoid...Marquette has been a name with an Alcatraz connotation...Even today, despite decades of reform and a massive increase in legalisms, being transferred to Marquette has a special meaning throughout the huge and still growing corrections system in Michigan. It still signifies an end to official tolerance of recalcitrant attitudes, immaturity and juvenile rebellion... ."[2]

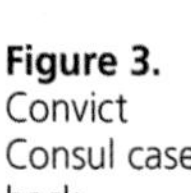

Figure 3. Convict Consul case back.

In 1922 Alton Roberts, a Michigan prison commissioner, "wrote a blistering letter to [then] Prison Commissioner Charles Blaney...[regarding the] hiring [of] a full-time physician for Marquette Prison and raising the salary to $3,500.00." He said:

"Dear Blaney – I haven't anymore to say about a full-time physician than I have already said. If the warden and I can be shown that such a position could render us additional services we would agree to the appointment. This matter was brought up when the governor...(was)...here last. At that time, the warden reported he couldn't see what further services the doctor could render, and the service provided was most satisfactory. It was then left to the warden and me to handle the matter, and we were authorized to pay Dr. Markham $2,000.00 more a year if we could dig up some additional work for him such as sanitary inspection of the kitchen, the food, sewer system, etc. I talked with Markham and he said that he was already taking care of these details almost daily, and it would be foolish for the state to pay any more when it already was being taken care of. I understand the intention is to pay a full-time physician $3,500.00 a year. If this is done, Warden Corgan and I want it distinctly understood it is being done over our positive objection, and this is $2,000.00 for which the prison commission and the administration can be criticized for spending foolishly. I am through talking about the matter and I want this protest on record."[3]

Notwithstanding this protest, after a decent interval, Dr. Markham was approached regarding coming to the prison as its full-time physician. The doctor remarked that he would have to leave his practice and his patients in Marquette and he didn't wish to do so. He advised the committee to look elsewhere for a physician who would be interested in the job. Shortly thereafter, Dr. Russell L. Finch, freshly out of medical school, accepted the job and remained at Marquette Prison for six and a half years, starting at the enhanced annual salary of $3,500.

During this time the inmate population was suffering from almost 60 percent over-capacity, with at least 150 inmates "sleeping in the corridors on bunks no more than two feet apart."[4] The prison, with an original capacity of 312, had over 487 prisoners in 1925.[5] Finally, the prison was expanded in the 1924-25 time period to house 714 inmates.[6] Although the new "F" block was to house 48 prisoners suffering from communicable diseases, this cell block was quickly converted for use by "maximum security prisoners."[7]

Convict Doctor

During Dr. Finch's tenure at Marquette he contended with numerous jailbreaks, shootings, and influenza outbreaks. In fact, Prison Commissioner "Roberts conceded that escapes had been discussed at the recent prison board meeting in Lansing but only as to the possibility of making some improvements on the 20-foot wall at Marquette. An electrified fence to top the wall was suggested but voted down. A better alternative was to top the wall with a ten-foot heavy link hurricane fence capped with six strands of barbed wire. Anyone gaining the top of the thirty-foot barrier would still have the barbed wire to contend with. This was approved, and the banker's association financed the project since many of the recent escapes involved bank robbers and safe artists. After the fence was installed both the bankers and the citizens of Marquette slept better."[8]

"In addition to the jail breaks and shootings, Dr. Finch had to handle a severe flu epidemic during the holidays [1928] that hit the institution, laying low a goodly percentage of the staff and inmate body, from the warden on down. Many of the prisoners were too sick to go to the dining room, but their Christmas dinners were brought to them in the cell block."[9]

In the fall of 1925 a new 40-bed infirmary was opened for Dr. Finch's use. "The all-new facility had a modern and fully-equipped lab, a new x-ray unit and secure medical and drug storage area."[10]

During the early summer of 1929, Dr. Finch resigned as prison physician to go into private practice in Lansing. He left the prison after six and a half years and was "credited by the state health department for having brought prison health standards to an unusually high mark."[11]

The Purple Gang

Dr. Finch's tenure at the State Prison encompassed the time period of the reign of terror of the "Purple Gang," a mob of bootleggers and hijackers in the 1920s. The Purple Gang was made up of mostly, but not exclusively, young Jewish immigrants. The gang operated out of Detroit, their base of operations to run illegal alcohol over the Canadian border during Prohibition. They controlled Detroit like Al Capone and his mob-controlled Chicago. However, the Purple Gang were perhaps the most ruthless bootleggers of their time; they killed over 500 members of rival bootlegging gangs during Detroit's bootleg wars. It is interesting that they did not feud with the Capone mob, as they successfully thwarted Capone's plans to expand into Detroit. The Purple Gang and Capone ultimately established a détente over their respective territories.

The gang supposedly got its name during a conversation between two Detroit merchants, each Purple Gang victims. One remarked: "They're rotten, purple like the color of bad meat."

It is reported that bootlegging netted the Purple Gang millions of dollars, but the mob was also involved in extortion, hijacking, armed robbery, gambling, murder, and jewelry thefts. The "Purples" ruled the Detroit underworld with blazing guns for approximately five years, from 1927 to 1932.

Several of the gang members, when captured and sentenced, end-

Figure 4. Purple Gang members hide their faces from the camera at their arrest in 1929 on charge of providing protection to Detroit narcotics dealers.

ed up under the medical care of Dr. Finch in the State Prison of Southern Michigan. It is amazing that these prisoners (along with other hardened felons) would contribute to the purchase of a solid gold watch to present to their prison doctor upon his resignation.

If it were not for the inscription engraved on the back of the watch case given to Dr. Finch, this bit of history would not have survived to be recounted here—50 years after the death of Dr. Finch and over 80 years after the date of its presentation.

Special Convict Dial

The Convict Consul is a very rare watch because it has a pinstripe dial; only ten or so of these dials probably exist today. However, this dial also has an ultrarare and possibly exclusive feature: subseconds at 9. This is the only pinstripe dial with subs at 9 known to exist and it is the only Consul ever found with subseconds at 9, thus making this watch especially rare, valuable, and collectible.

Moreover, this Consul came with a 14K gold center section spacer that held the movement in place, which is more valuable than other Consuls that came with center spacer sections made of nickel. At first it was speculated that because the Consul was released right before the Great Depression, Illinois opted to sell the watch with the center section spacer to hold the movement made out of nickel instead of solid gold, to reduce its cost to manufacture. However, paradoxically, Illinois collector Rick Vess's research does not necessarily support this hypothesis; his analysis of almost three dozen Consuls demonstrates that by mid-1929, entering the teeth of the Depression, the center spacer sections were offered only in solid gold, not nickel. Of course, the outer center section of the case was always solid gold.

Figure 5. The Convict Consul (ultrarare pinstripe dial with subdial at 9).

All in all, this is probably the most expensive configured Illinois wristwatch ever produced, and it is surprising and interesting that it was obtained by a group of imprisoned felons, crooks, murderers, and gang thugs as a farewell gift for their prison doctor.

The "Undertaker Consul"

Thanks to another fascinating case back inscription, we learn that six months after Dr. Finch received a solid gold Consul from the inmates of a Michigan prison, the employees of a funeral parlor in St. Louis, MO, presented a similar gold watch to their boss. This Consul model watch was also special because it contained a custom dial that spelled out the employer's name in lieu of numerals around the dial.

It also has a beautifully engraved case back inscription that reads:

Geo L. Pleitsch
From Your
Employees
Dec 25 1929

The funeral parlor owner was George L. Pleitsch, who operated a funeral home in the Wellston Business District of St. Louis at 5966-68 Easton Avenue) (changed to Martin Luther King Drive in 1972). Other nearby Easton Avenue businesses during this time were a local business college, a motor supply store, a furniture store, a J. C. Penney store, a record shop, a hat store, a shoe store, and a post office.

Figure 6.
Undertaker Consul (factory-made custom dial).

Figure 7.
Undertaker Consul case back inscription.

Mr. Pleitsch was born July 16, 1878, and died on August 4, 1951, at age 72. His funeral home was first opened in 1915 on Easton Avenue. He lived with his wife, 16 years his junior, the former Mary C. Decker, at 6943 Pershing Avenue, University City, MO. They had been married for 20 years prior to his death. He left a stepdaughter, two granddaughters, and two sisters. Thus, George L. Pleitsch was 52 when he married Mary C. Decker on January 7, 1931, at the Gronis Baptist Church in St. Louis. Mary was 36 years old at the time. She had a daughter at their marriage, so she was either divorced or more likely widowed at the time. Pleitsch's entire estate was valued at $272,852.23. In 2010 dollars, that would equate to $2,287,876.44.

According to records at the St. Louis Genealogy Society, he was a member of the Local Undertaker's Association as early as 1906 and performed 300 burials that year.[12] Pleitsch was also a member of Wellston Lodge No. 613, St. Aldemar Commandery No. 18, Moolah Temple, Drum Corps Alhambra Grotto, Rob Morris Chapter No. 328 O.E.S., Wellston Chapter No. 138 R.A.M., and McArthur High 12 Club. Pleitsch probably belonged to these Shriners, Elks, Masons, and Knights Templar organizations to meet future patrons for his funeral business.[13]

According to the Saint Louis Public Library, most of our ancestors belonged to fraternal societies of one type or another, the Masons being the most popular, and many groups patterned themselves after the Masons. A number of the fraternal orders were open to everyone and some were limited to certain special groups. Many of these organizations are Insurance and Death Benefit Societies that were developed after the Civil War as a means of leaving something behind for families or as a means of paying for a funeral and/or headstone. Dues were collected regularly to pay these costs, but this was by no means the only activity of these societies. Many held regular social gatherings, had musical subgroups, and a few had paramilitary-type subgroups.[14]

Pleitsch Funeral Home was incorporated as Geo. L. Pleitsch, Inc., exactly as his name appears on the custom dial. His vice-president and treasurer was Philip Leim and L. W. Kraeger was the corporation's secretary. Their funeral parlor's service mark was "Our Telephone Makes Us Neighbors."

St. Louis–Thriving Business

In 1929, when undertaker Pleitsch received his beautiful and thoughtful gift from his employees, his funeral parlor was one of over 300 in operation in St. Louis from 1870 to 1929. At least seven of these were dedicat-

Figure 8. Yellow Page Directory ad, 1918.

ed for use by "colored" people only during the era of racial discrimination. According to the 1930 Census, St. Louis City proper had an overall population of 821,960, and the total number of "colored" people living in St. Louis in 1930 was 4,729.

Then Versus Now

Horological issues aside, in addition to the inscriptions helping us discover some of the key biographical details of their owners, they also tell us a bit of the sociological differences between our society then and now.

One wonders if a group of prison inmates or employees of an undertaker would, in this day and age, make similar gifts to their prison doctor or employer. To answer this question, each of us has to determine if people of today have the same sense of loyalty, respect, values, character, and appreciation for others that existed in the late 1920s. I suspect that most of us would say that in most cases contemporary society's possession of these traits is not nearly as strong as those of our forefathers.

These presentations were made to Dr. Finch and Mr. Pleitsch at the beginning of and near the heart of the Great Depression; nevertheless, these expensive, solid gold watches were presented as gifts. Today, we are still feeling the effects of the worst depression in the United States since the Great Depression, and it seems highly unlikely that many (if any) of us would consider similar gifts to our doctor or employer as we all struggle to get by with less.

It is unfair to draw hard and fast conclusions based on these observations because there are always exceptions. But, hopefully, it will point to the need to be more appreciative and respectful of those around us who help us routinely in our daily lives.

Acknowledgments

I thank NAWCC member and friend Rick Vess for taking the pictures of the watches featured in this article and for the email dialogue we exchanged on this subject over a period of many months. I also thank Philip Welsh, noted dealer and horologist, for coining the "Convict Consul" sobriquet, and Cynthia Ballard, a relative of Dr. Finch, for bringing the Convict Consul and the Purple Gang to my attention.

Technical Details

For the technical details on these watches and the history of the Illinois Watch Company, please see the author's book, *The Illinois Watch: The Life and Times of a Great American Watch Company.*

Notes

1. Fredric J. Friedberg, *The Illinois Watch: The Life and Times of a Great American Watch Company* (Atglen, PA: Schiffer Publishing Limited, 2004): 72.
2. Ike Wood, *One Hundred Years at Hard Labor"* (KA-ED Publishing Co., 1985): Foreward.
3. Ibid., 121-123.
4. Ibid., 114 and 147.
5. Ibid., 14.
6. Ibid., 147.
7. Ibid., 147-148.
8. Ibid., 166.
9. Ibid., 185.
10. Ibid., 166.
11. Ibid., 186.
12. St. Louis Genealogical Society. 314-647-8549.
13. www.saintlouispubliclibrary.com.
14. St. Louis Public Library, revised July 2001.

About the Author

Fred Friedberg is senior vice-president and chief legal officer of Toshiba America Medical Systems, Inc., in Tustin, CA. He is also president of two Toshiba research & development companies, one located in Chicago and the other in Edinburgh, Scotland. Fred has written other articles for the *NAWCC Bulletin* and is the author of three books: *The Illinois Watch,* noted in Technical Details above; *Surviving Your Deposition* and *Turning 18 and the Law.* Fred lives in Irvine, CA, Chicago, and Edinburgh.

Appendix 7

The Hamilton-Illinois Watches: Some Factory Specification Sheets

Hamilton's records, in the form of handwritten specification lists, show what parts they selected for the Hamilton-Illinois project, what suppliers they used, and how they kept track of the results. (The extant copies are testimony to the primitive state of copying technology in the 1950s.)

MOV'T SIZE	MOV'T DESCRIPTION	MODEL DESIGNATION	NAME AND PROD. NO.	CASE SHAPE	CASE AND QUALITY	COLOR
8 × 9	CONV. SEC.	1 S-W. #197	9506	ODD	RGP	S.S.
8 × 9	CONV. SEC.	1 S-W #199	9507	ODD	RGP	S.S.
8 × 9	CENT. SEC.	1 S-W #202	9508	ODD	RGP	S.S.
8 × 9	CONV. SEC.	1 S-W. #195	9509	ODD	10KGF	YEL.
8 × 9	CONV. SEC.	1 S-W #200	9510	ODD	10KGF	YEL.
10½	CONV. SEC.	1 S-W. # 203	9511	ODD	RGP	S.S.
11½	CONV. SEC.	1 S-W #207	9512	ROUND	RGP	S.S.
11½	CENT. SEC.	1 #226 S-W NOT WATER PROOF	9513	ROUND	RGP	S.S.
11½	CENT. SEC.	1 IMPORTED	9514	ROUND	WATER PROOF	S.S.
ETAMATIC	CENT. SEC.	1 IMPORTED	9515	ROUND	WATER PROOF	S.S.
INDIMATIC	CENT. SEC.	1 IMPORTED	9516	ROUND	WATER PROOF	S.S.
ETERNAMATIC	CENT. SEC.	1 #111 S-W. IN PROD.	9505	ROUND	10KGF	YEL.

HRC: NAWCC

MEN'S

ILLINOIS MODELS DATA

MODEL	COLOR	HAMILTON PART NUMBER						
		DIAL	HOUR HAND	MIN. HAND	SEC. HAND	CENT. SEC. HAND	CROWN	CRYSTAL
9505	Y	55500	75000	75100		75300	77050	77700
9506	Y	55501	75013	75113	75213		77051	77701
9507	Y	55502	75014	75114	75214		77051	77702
9508	Y	55503	75015	75115		75315	77051	77703
9509	Y	55504	75016	75116	75216		77051	77704
9510	Y	55505	75017	75117	75217		77051	77705
9511	Y	55506	75018	75118	75218		77051	77706
9512	Y	55507	75019	75119	75219		77051	77707
9513	Y	55508	75020	75120		75320	77051	77708
* 9514	SS	55509	75021	75121		75321	77053	77709
* 9515	SS	55510	75022	75122		75322	77053	77710
* 9516	SS	55511	75023	75123		75323	77053	77711
9517	Y	55512	75024	75124		75324	77052	77712

HRC: NAWCC

CASE & DIAL DATA

ILLINOIS & HAMILTON IMPORTED MEN'S MODELS

	CASE #	MODEL #	NAME		DIALED MOV'T OLD	DIALED MOV'T NEW	DIAL DESCRIPTION
	95050	95051-1	AUTO. A	Y	9505	58000	YENM TRSF TRACK
	95060	95061-1	DEBONAIR A	Y	9506	58500	YEN TRSF TRACK
	95070	95071-1	" B	Y	9507	58501	YENM-DOTS TRS TRACK
	95080	95081-1	" F	Y	9508	58600	YEN TRSF TRACK 5"
	95090	95091-1	TOPPER A	Y	9509	58502	YEN TRS TRACK
	95100	95101-1	" B	Y	9510	58503	YENM TRS TRACK
	95110	95111-1	DEBONAIR C	Y	9511	58700	YENM-DOTS TRS TRACK
	95120	95121-1	" D	Y	9512	58300	YEN TRS TRACK
	95130	95131-1	" E	Y	9513	58400	YENM TRS TRACK [illegible]
*	95140	95141-1 95194-1 95193-1	NAUTILUS A	SS	9514	58401 58402 58403	WENM "6174 TSF TRACK ENAME YENM-LUM WENM-CO-LUM
*	95150	95152-1	AUTO. B	SS	9515	58100	YENM LUM TRS [illegible] YENM N [illegible]
*	95160	95162-1	SIGNAMATIC	SS	9516	58200	WENM LUM TRS TRACK [illegible]
	95170	95172-1	AUTO. D	YEL	9517	58101	YENM LUM [illegible] TRACK
	95180						[illegible]
	95190						YENM TRS TRACK
	95200						YEN TRS TRACK
	95210						YENM LUM TRS [illegible] YENM LUM TRS [illegible]

* PURCHASED COMPLETE

HRC: NAWCC

LADIES'

ILLINOIS MODELS DATA

MODEL	COLOR	HAMILTON PART NUMBER						
		DIAL	HOUR HAND	MIN. HAND	SEC. HAND	CENT. SEC. HAND	CROWN	CRYSTAL
9005	W	55000	75001	75101			77000	77500
9006	Y	55001	75002	75102			77001	77500
9007	W	55002	75003	75103			77000	77501
9008	Y	55003	75004	75104			77001	77501
9009	W	55004	75001	75101			77000	77502
9010	W	55005	75003	75103			77000	77503
9011	Y	55006	75004	75104			77001	77503
9012	W	55007	75005	75105			77000	77504
9013	Y	55008	75006	75106			77001	77504
9014	Y	55009	75007	75107			77001	77505
9015	Y	55010	75007	75107			77001	77506
9016	Y	55011	75006	75106			77001	77507
9017	Y	55012	75007	75107			77001	77508
9018	Y	55013	75008	75108			77001	77509
9019	W	55014	75009	75109			77000	77510
9020	Y	55015	75010	75110			77001	77510
9021	SS	55016	75011	75111		75311	77002	77511
[illegible]	Y	55017	75012	75112		75312	77001	77512

IMPORTED complete

HRC: NAWCC

CASE & DIAL DATA

ILLINOIS LADIES' MODELS

CASE #	MODEL #	NAME		DIALED MCVT. OLD	DIALED MCVT. NEW	DIAL DESCRIPTION
90050	90051-1	GOLD. TREA. A	W	9005	54200	WENM · DOTS NO TRACK
90060	90061-1	GOLD. TREA. A	Y	9006	54201	YENM · DOTS NO TRACK
90070	90071-1	GOLD TREA B	W	9007	54202	WEN DOTS TRS TRACK
90080	90081-1	GOLD. TREA. B	Y	9008	54203	YEN DOTS TRS TRACK
90090	90091-1	KIMBERLY A	W	9009	54204	WENM NO TRACK
90100	90101-1	CROQUETTE A	W	9010	54205	WEN TRS TRACK
90110	90111-1	"	Y	9011	54206	YEN TRS TRACK
90120	90121-1	KIMBERLY B	W	9012	54000	WENM NO TRACK
90130	90131-1	"	Y	9013	54001	YENM NO TRACK
90140	90141-1	LADY GAY A	Y	9014	54002	YEN TRS TRACK
90150	90151-1	" B	Y	9015	54003	YEN TRS TRACK
90160	90161-1	" C	Y	9016	54004	YENM TRS TRACK
90170	90171-1	" D	Y	9017	54005	YEN DOTS NO TRACK
90180	90181-1	CROQUETTE B	Y	9018	54006	YEN TRS TRACK
90190	90191-1	" C	W	9019	54007	WEN [illegible]
90200	90201-1	" C	Y	9020	54008	YEN DOTS TRS TRACK
* 90210	90212-1	CAREER GIRL A	SS	9021	54400	YENM [illegible]

HRC: NAWCC

Appendix 8

Specification Sheet from Ebauches S. A. for ETA 1256 Movement

B18F1

EBAUCHES S.A.
NEUCHATEL
SWITZERLAND

Edited and published by Ebauches S. A. (French, English, German, Italian, Spanish) Copyright 1952 by Ebauches S. A.

FABRIQUE D'EBAUCHES
ETA S. A., GRENCHEN

11½''' 1256
25.6 mm

Lever movement, self-winding, with sweep second

Enlarged movement

TECHNICAL AND PRACTICAL COMMUNICATION FOR THE GUIDANCE OF WATCH REPAIRERS

6

2nd edition

March 1953

Printed in Switzerland

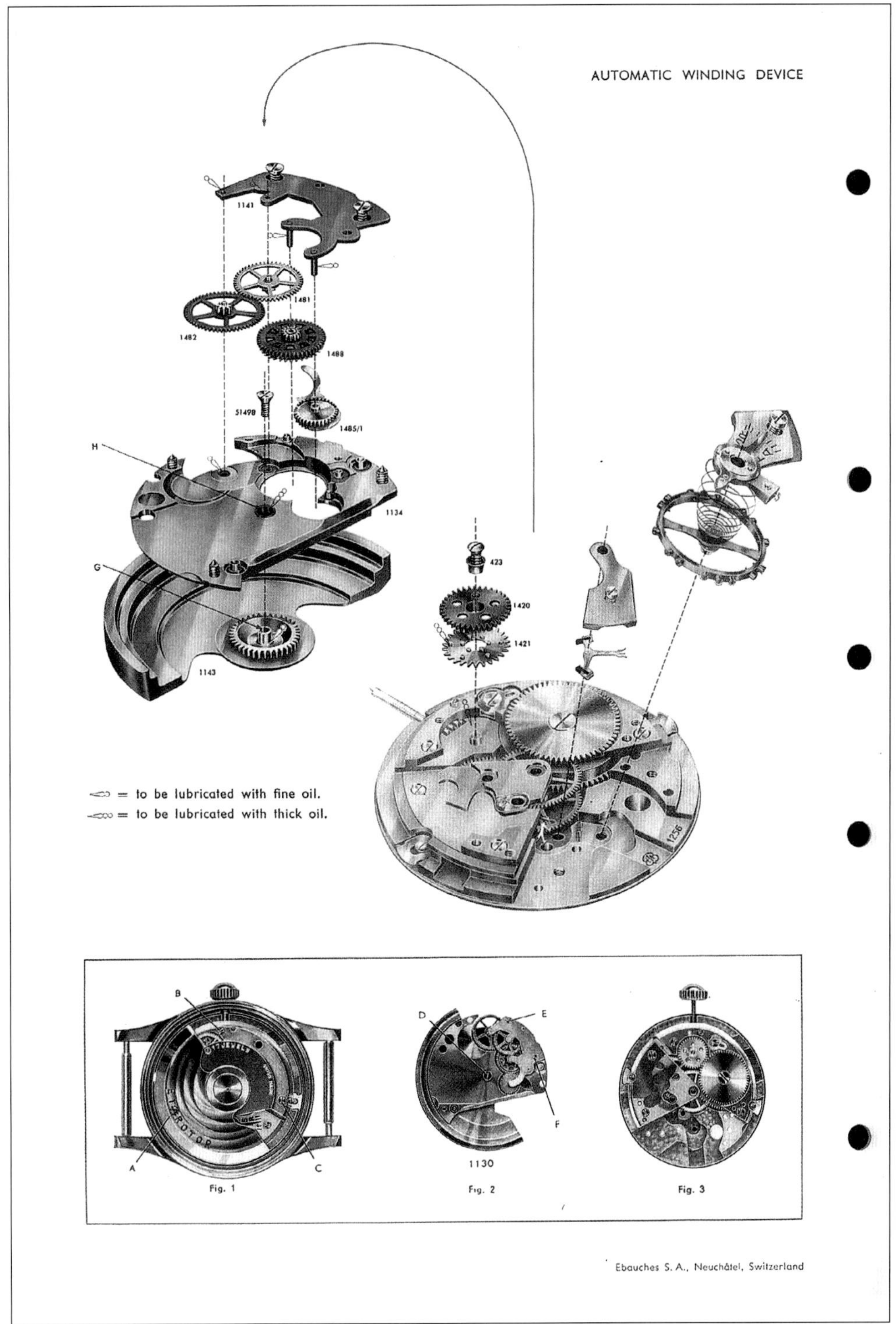
AUTOMATIC WINDING DEVICE
1141
1481
1482
1488
51498
1485/1
H
1134
G
1143
423
1420
1421
= to be lubricated with fine oil.
= to be lubricated with thick oil.
B
A
C
Fig. 1
D
E
F
1130
Fig. 2
Fig. 3
Ebauches S. A., Neuchâtel, Switzerland

THE REPAIR OF THIS MOVEMENT IS SIMPLIFIED BY THE FACT THAT THE AUTOMATIC WINDING DEVICE IS ENTIRELY INDEPENDENT OF THE WATCH MOVEMENT PROPER

DISASSEMBLING AND ASSEMBLING THE WATCH MOVEMENT PROPER:

1. Open case (see under CASING).
2. Remove mounted automatic device 1130 from the watch movement by unscrewing the 3 screws A, B and C of framework 1134 (fig. 1 and 2).
3. Remove winding stem ; then, if the proposed repair makes it necessary, take the movement out of the case ; remove hands and dial, then replace winding stem.
4. If it is necessary to disassemble the movement completely, remove balance wheel and pallet fork, then disassemble the watch movement and clean all its parts in the ordinary way; check cleanness and wear of parts, oil all pivot holes and friction points, then reassemble the movement, including pallet fork and balance wheel. The mainspring may be replaced without disassembling the movement proper (fig. 3).

Mainspring : If the mainspring and brake spring are working normally, **they should not be removed from the barrel** (the brake spring should not slip until the mainspring has been wound 5-6 turns). On the other hand, if the mainspring or brake spring is damaged, it should be replaced by a spring of good quality and of the prescribed dimensions, viz.

Mainspring: breadth 1.48 mm. - thickness 0.10 mm. - length 260 mm.
Brake spring: breadth 1.34 mm. - thickness 0.165 mm. - length 30.8 mm.

Grease the entire inner circumference of the barrel. Fit brake spring, bending it as little as possible, then fit mainspring, oiling it in the ordinary way (remember to check the slipping of the brake spring).

Crown wheel : The crown wheel consists of 2 distinct wheels: lower crown wheel 1421 (to be fitted first, with its lever pins upwards) and upper crown wheel 1420 (to be fitted on top of lower crown wheel, with the click between its rows of lever pins). Then fit crown wheel core 423 and its screw (left-hand thread). The 2 wheels should turn freely and independently of each other: when turned in the direction of winding, however, the lower wheel will drive the upper wheel through the action of the click. The friction surfaces, the click and the lower surface of the lower crown wheel should be lubricated with thick oil.

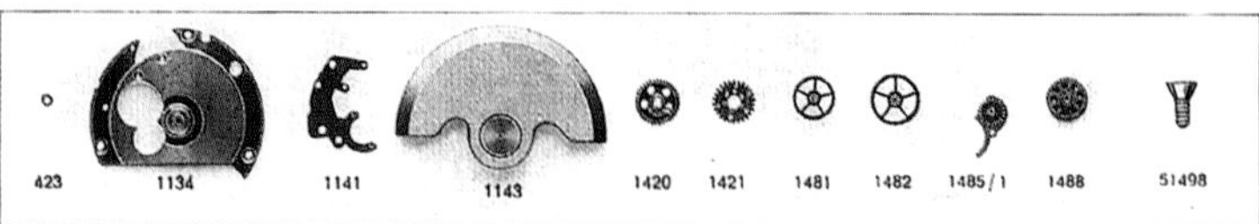

DISASSEMBLING THE AUTOMATIC DEVICE:

1. Remove oscillating weight 1143 (fig. 2) from mounted framework 1134/1, by taking out screw D (screw 51498 for bearing wheel of oscillating weight). The bearing wheel should only be removed from the oscillating weight if it has to be replaced.
2. Remove : lower bridge 1141 of automatic device (by unscrewing the 2 screws E and F, fig. 2), reduction gear 1481, driving gear 1482 of crown wheel, and then, simultaneously, mounted pawl winding wheel 1488 and mounted reverser 1485/1. Check cleanness and wear of all these parts.

ASSEMBLING THE AUTOMATIC DEVICE:

1. Place framework 1134 of automatic device on a holder, with its inner side upwards; then fit mounted reverser 1485/1 into its countersink, the arm being located by a pin.
2. Fit complete pawl winding wheel 1488, with its pinion upwards, from the side, so that the arm of mounted reverser 1485/1 lies between the 2 wheels; then fit driving gear 1482 of crown wheel (large), with its pinion upwards, and reduction gear 1481 (small), with its pinion downwards.
3. Place in position lower bridge 1141 of automatic device by fitting its 2 pins into the holes in mounted reverser 1485/1 and pawl winding wheel 1488, then tighten the 2 screws E and F.

Lubrication : Use fine oil to lubricate upper and lower pivot holes of reduction gear 1481 and driving gear 1482 of crown wheel, as well as the 2 pins on lower bridge 1141 of automatic device, which act as pivots for mounted reverser 1485/1 and complete pawl winding wheel 1488.

4. Place mounted framework 1134/1 on oscillating weight 1143 fitted with its bearing wheel 1498 (fig. 2); then tighten screw 51498 (conical head) of bearing wheel of oscillating weight.

To correct end-shake of oscillating weight, proceed as follows: to reduce end-shake, adjust inner cone of hub of bearing wheel 1498 (see arrow G on colored plate opposite). To increase end-shake, adjust inner cone of tube of framework 1134 (see arrow H on colored plate opposite). To fraise the cones, use a 60° conical fraise held in an ordinary chuck. When end-shake has been corrected, the 2 cones should be lubricated with good-quality fine oil, and bearing wheel screw 51498 should be screwed home.

5. Fit dial and hands, and place movement in case. Fit mounted automatic device 1130 on to the watch movement by means of the 3 screws A, B and C. Before tightening the screws, slightly turn the winding stem to cause driving gear 1482 of crown wheel to mesh with upper crown wheel 1420; then drive the 3 screws home.

Ebauches S. A., Neuchâtel, Switzerland

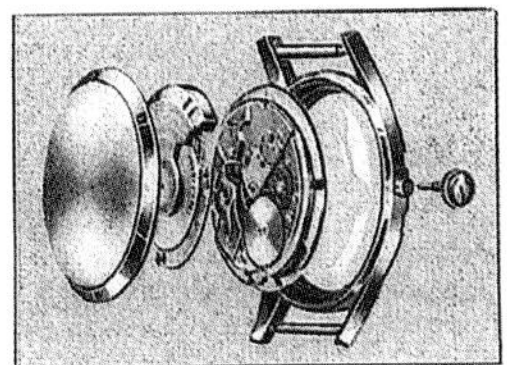

Fig. 4

Casing : **Ordinary 3-piece cases** give no trouble, but there are many different kinds of **waterproof cases,** of which those illustrated are among the most popular.

Fig. 4 shows a type of waterproof case of which the back opens to enable the movement to be taken out.

Fig. 5 shows a type of which the bezel is snapped on and is opened by a knife-blade inserted at the point indicated by the arrow; when the crown (with 2-piece winding stem) has been removed, the movement is taken out from the dial side.

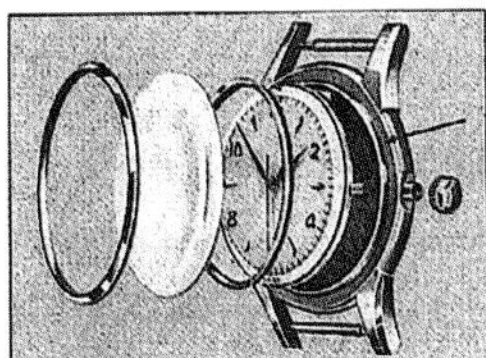

Fig. 5

This movement may be fitted with special casing clamps; the positions of these are shown in the diagram below.

Position for ordinary case.

Position for waterproof case.

When fitting a movement into a waterproof case, it is essential, in order to avoid excessive friction, to center the winding stem correctly in the tube.

Description and numbering of spare parts according to the " Technological Dictionary of Watch Parts ", 2nd edition.

100 Plate
105 Barrel bridge
110 Train wheel bridge
121 Balance cock for flat hairspring
125 Pallet cock
126 Center wheel cock
166 Casing clamp
182 Barrel and cover (without arbor)
195 Barrel arbor
206 Center wheel and pinion (without cannon pinion)
210 Third wheel and pinion
227 Sweep second wheel and pinion
245 Cannon pinion with clam notch
255 Hour wheel
260 Minute wheel
301 Regulator for flat hairspring
311 Upper cap jewel, with end-piece, for balance
330 Lower cap jewel, with end-piece, for balance
336 Upper cap jewel, with end-piece, for escape wheel
342 Bearing plate for sweep second wheel
346 Lower cap jewel, with end-piece, for escape wheel
401 Winding stem
407 Clutch wheel
410 Winding pinion
415 Ratchet wheel
423 Crown wheel core
425 Click
430 Click spring
435 Yoke (clutch lever)
440 Yoke spring (set spring)
443 Setting lever (detent)
445 Setting lever spring (set bridge)
450 Setting wheel
462 Minute work cock
702 Escape wheel and pinion, pivoted, for 2 end-pieces
710 Jewelled pallet fork and staff
714 Pallet staff
721 Balance with flat hairspring, regulated
723 Balance staff, pivoted
730 Roller
770 Mainspring
775 Brake spring
1134 Framework for automatic device
1141 Lower bridge for automatic device
1143 Oscillating weight
1420 Upper crown wheel
1421 Lower crown wheel
1481 Reduction gear
1482 Driving gear for crown wheel
1485/1 Reverser, mounted
1488 Pawl winding wheel, complete
1650 Bushing for automatic device
1663 Bushing for oscillating weight, lower

5105 Barrel bridge screw - 5110 Train wheel bridge screw, low head - 5110' Train wheel bridge screw, high head - 5121 Balance cock screw - 5125 Pallet cock screw - 5126 Center wheel cock screw - 5166 Casing clamp screw - 5311 Screw for upper end-piece of balance - 5330 Screw for lower end-piece of balance - 5336 Screw for upper end-piece of escape wheel - 5342 Screw for bearing plate of sweep second wheel - 5346 Screw for lower end-piece of escape wheel - 5415 Ratchet wheel screw - 5423 Crown wheel core screw - 5425 Click screw - 5443 Setting lever screw - 5445 Screw for setting lever spring - 5462 Minute work cock screw - 5738 Hairspring stud screw - 5750 Dial screw - 51134 Screw for framework of automatic device - 51141 Screw for lower bridge of automatic device - 51498 Screw for bearing wheel of oscillating weight.

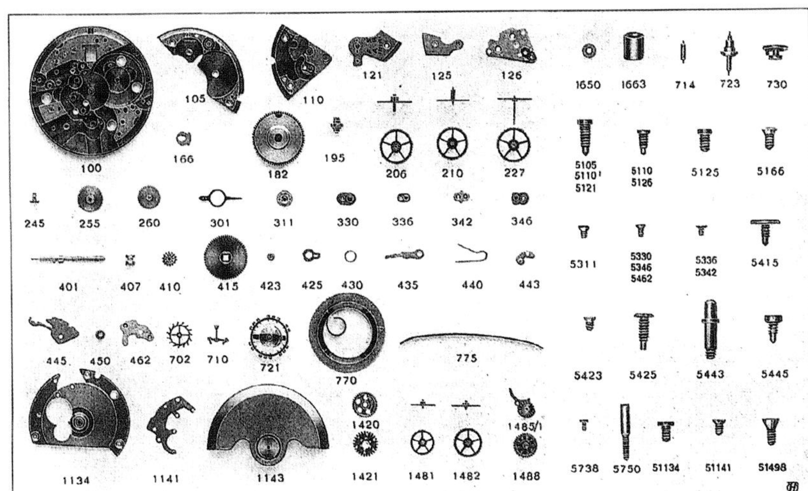

When ordering parts for a shock-protecting device, make certain to specify its exact type. For further details of the description and numbering of spare parts, see the " Technological Dictionary of Watch Parts ", 2nd edition, published by Ebauches S. A.

Order repair parts through your jobber, giving the numbers and designations, thus insuring prompt and efficient deliveries.

P. Attinger S. A., Neuchâtel

NOTES

Chapter 1

1. Parts of this description are based on L. Michael Fultz, "John C. Adams: Watch Entrepreneur," *InSync Magazine* (Feb. 2009), pp. 132–35; and Henry G. Abbott, *The Watch Factories of America* (Chicago: Hazlitt, 1888).
2. Abbott, pp. 67, 68.
3. Fultz, p. 134.
4. Andrew Taylor Call, *Jacob Bunn: Legacy of an Illinois Industrial Pioneer* (Bath, ME: Brunswick Publishing Co., 2005), p. 5.
5. William H. Herndon and Jesse W. Weik, *Herndon's Life of Abraham Lincoln* (New York: A. & C. Boni, 1930), p. 287.
6. Benjamin P. Thomas, *Abraham Lincoln: A Biography* (New York: Knopf, 1952), pp. 41–42.
7. Edward J. Kemp, *Abraham Lincoln's Philosophy of Common Sense: An Analytical Biography of a Great Mind* (New York: New York Academy of Sciences, 1965), vol. 1, p. 171.
8. Herndon and Weik, p. 147.
9. Gerald M. Capers, *Stephen A. Douglas: Defender of the Union* (Boston: Little Brown. 1959), p. 14.
10. William E. Barton, *The Life of Abraham Lincoln* (Indianapolis: Bobbs-Merrill, c. 1925), p. 232.
11. Albert A. Woldman, *Lawyer Lincoln* (Boston and New York: Houghton Mifflin, 1936), p. 26.
12 Harry E. Pratt, "The Republication of Lincoln's War Policy in 1862: Stuart-Swett Congressional Campaign," *Journal of the Illinois State Historical Society* (April 1931), pp. 10–11.
13. William "Bill" Meggers and Roy Ehrhardt, *American Pocket Watches, Vol. 2: Illinois Watch Co.* (Heart of America Press, 1985).
14. Fredric J. Friedberg, *The Illinois Watch: The Life and Times of a Great American Watch Company* (Atglen, PA: Schiffer, 2004), p. 9. Ten acres of the land were donated by Converse and the other four purchased from him.
15. Meggers and Ehrhardt, p. 23.
16. Meggers and Ehrhardt, p. 32.
17. Ibid.
18 Ibid.
19. Information about the life of Bates was drawn from Joseph Wallace, *Past and Present of the City of Springfield and Sangamon County, Illinois* (Chicago: S. J. Clarke, 1904), p. 644.
20. Much of the description of the life and accomplishments of Jacob Bunn and John Whitfield Bunn are drawn from Call's excellent study, cited in n. 4, above.
21. Call, pp. 27–28.
22. Call, pp. 73–74.
23. John H. White, *The American Railroad Passenger Car* (Baltimore: Johns Hopkins Univ. Press, 1978), p. 248–49.
24. Call, p. 189.
25. Call, p. 192.
26. Call, p. 76.
27. The Panic of 1873 and the failure of the Bunn bank are discussed in Friedberg, pp. 10, 12.
28. Many of the details about the life of John W. Bunn are taken from the *Wikipedia* article on the lives of John Whitfield Bunn and Jacob Bunn, http://en.wikipedia.org/wiki/John_Whitfield_Bunn_and_Jacob_Bunn.
29. James Alfred Ellis, *History of the Bunn Family in America* (Chicago: Romanzo Norton Bunn, 1928), p. 210.
30. George H. Drury, *The Historical Guide to North American Railroads* (Waukesha, WI: Kalmbach, 1991), p. 325.
31. While this may *seem* like a very large number, it does not mean that all the railroads existed at once. Many companies were chartered but failed to raise capital and so never laid any track. Even among companies that did build lines, there was a constant churning of charters and names as companies were reorganized, recapitalized, and merged or renegotiated agreements. *See* http://en.wikipedia.org/wiki/List_of_Illinois_railroads.
32. For much of the information about the friendship of DeLong and McIntyre, as well as their working relationship, I am indebted to Tom McIntyre's website about the McIntyre Watch Company: http://www.awco.org/mwco/
33. Paul M. Chamberlain, *It's About Time* (London, UK: Holland Press, 1964), pp. 467–70.

34. Chamberlain, p. 417.
35 McIntyre website.
36. Chamberlain, p. 472.
37. McIntyre website.
38. Chamberlain, p. 472.
39. For information about the charter and incorporation of the company, *see* the McIntyre website.
40. McIntyre website.
41. Chamberlain, p. 470.
42. Ibid.
43. A point made by Doug Pokorski, *Heartland Magazine*, May 17, 2002.
44. Wallace, p. 184.
45. Ibid.
46. Pokorski.
47. Robert C. Lanphier and Benjamin P. Thomas, *Sangamo: A History of Fifty Years* (Chicago: Privately printed, 1949). The volume consists of Lanphier's *Forty years of Sangamo* and Thomas's *Sangamo in Peace and War.*
48. Lanphier remained president of Sangamo until his death on January 29, 1930, after a long illness. His obituary in the *New York Times* the next day detailed his career but also mentioned his activity "in philanthropic and civic affairs of Springfield." Bob Cavanaugh, in "Robert Lanphier Lights Up Springfield" (*Illinois Times,* June 10, 2004), noted: "Lamphier's death . . . was "front-page banner-headline news in Springfield. Because of his generosity, civic involvement, and concern for the welfare of his employees and the citizens of Springfield, he is honored in our memory by the attachment of his name to the high school and adjacent park."
49. Bunn obituary, *Illinois State Register* (Springfield), May 11, 1926.
50. Ibid.
51. As the "SangamonLink" (sangamoncountyhistory.org) notes, "A Bunn family 'who's-who' is complicated by a family tradition of passing names down through generations."
52. Call, p. 198.
53. Bunn obituary.
54. Call, p. 199.
55. Bunn obituary.
56. Donald J. Sauers, *Time for America: Hamilton Watch, 1892–1992* (Lititz, PA: Sutter House, 1992), p.59.
57. Ibid.
58. Ibid.
59. Ibid.
60. Willard ("Bunch") Bunn (1913–2002), interview by John Bucari, 1973. "Springfield Marine Bank Project," tape and typed transcription, Archives/Special Collections, Library of the University of Illinois at Springfield. http://library.uis.edu/archives/collections/oral/oralb.html

Chapter 2

1. This and other quotations in the paragraph are from E. C. Alft and William H. Briska, *Elgin Time: A History of the Elgin National Watch Company, 1864–1964* (Elgin, IL: Elgin Historical Society, 2003), p. 32.
2. I am indebted to Bill Briska, on behalf of the authors of *Elgin Time,* for graciously permitting the use of the material in that book concerning working conditions and related matters.
3. Alft and Briska, p. 31.
4. *Salem Daily News* (Salem, OH), Feb. 5, 1889. Her injury apparently received wide attention nationally, with notices of it appearing not only in other newspapers in the Midwest but also in those as far east as New York, as far north as South Dakota, and as far south as North Carolina and Texas.
5. Alft and Briska, p. 47.
6. Alft and Briska, p. 47.
7. Alft and Briska, p. 35.
8. The film itself can be viewed online: http://www.youtube.com/watch?v=vTQT6PwgJTA
9. Quotations from Jo Anna Lynn Harner and the people she interviewed come from a feature article by Doug Pokorski, "Remembering the Illinois Watch Company," that appeared in the "Lifestyle" section of the *Springfield State Journal-Register* on August 11, 1985. I am grateful to her for what her research has contributed to the history of the Illinois Watch Company. (Unfortunately, because of tragic personal circumstances, Ms. Harner was unable to complete what seemed to be a very promising thesis.)
10. Fredric J. Friedberg, *The Illinois Watch: The Life and Times of a Great American Watch Company* (Atglen, PA: Schiffer, 2004), Chapter 3.
11. Quotations from interviews with Illinois EPA employees come from "Another Day, Another Dollar . . . And Another Generation," an article in the Fall 1998 issue of the agency's quarterly publication, *Environmental Progress.*
12. Alft and Briska, p. 35.
13. Friedberg, p. 9.
14. Friedberg, p. 26.
15. Friedberg, p. 25.
16. *Republican-Northwestern* (Belvidere, IL), Feb. 19, 1926.
17. Friedberg, p. 24.
18. Friedberg, pp. 30–31.
19. A mention of Lehmann's successor, Hartlieb, appeared in the *Jacksonville Daily Journal* (Jacksonville, IL), May 4, 1924 (his name was misspelled "Hartleb"); one of his compositions was to be included in the Watch Factory Band's concert that was being announced.

20. In the *Edwardsville Intelligencer* (Edwardsville, IL), Aug. 28, 1924, was an article about the virtuoso cornetist Lorch, "a former Edwardsville boy," who had just been heard with the Watch Factory Band in a radio broadcast from St. Louis. His appointment as conductor of the Illinois Watch Factory Band, previously announced in the *Springfield Register*, was written up in the *Decatur Review* (Decatur, IL), April 22, 1927, which laid claim to him as a "former Decatur boy."
21. Many articles about the band appeared in newspapers of the time. It was not only Springfield's de facto municipal band but was also used at ceremonial functions for the state as well, Springfield being the state capital. The band apparently had professional status, as there are mentions of its having been "hired" or "engaged" on a contract basis by others.
22. http://www.springfield.il.us/Commissions/Band/index.htm
23. Friedberg, p. 30; a photograph of Weineke appears on p. 31.
24. *Daily Review* (Decatur, IL), Sept. 17, 1912.
25. The extended quotations from E. C. Alft are from his book *Elgin: An American History* (ElginHistory.com, 2000), chap. 5 ("Boom and Panic"), sec. 3 ("Unions"). The book was published in 1984 to celebrate the City of Elgin's sesquicentennial, 1835–1985. I am grateful to the author for permission to quote.
26. Friedberg, pp. 28–29.
27. Friedberg, pp. 25–28.

Chapter 3

1. Bruce Shawkey, "Wristwatches: Gruen," NAWCC *Bulletin*, No. 331 (April 2001), p. 243.
2. For the Bulova, *see* http://www.watchophilia.com/general-information/bulova-lone-eagle-series; and for the Longines, Ken Kessler, "Modern Classics: Longines, Weems and Lindbergh," www.qpmagazine.com/media/38585/Modern_Classics.pdf.
3. Pierre-Yves Donzé, *History of the Swiss Watch Industry from Jacques David to Nicholas Hayek*, trans. Pierre-Yves Donzé and Richard Watkins (Bern, Switzerland: Peter Lang AG, 2011), p 20.
4. Willis I. Milham, *Time & Timekeepers* (New York: Macmillan, 1944), p 403.
5. Vincent Carosso, "The Waltham Watch Company: A Case History," *Business History Review*, Vol. 23, No. 4 (Dec. 1949), p. 176.
6. Ibid.
7. http://en.wikipedia.org/wiki/E._Howard_%26_Co.
8. Milham, p. 403.
9. http://en.wikipedia.org/wiki/Elgin_National_Watch_Company
10. E. C. Alft and William H. Briska, *Elgin Time: A History of the Elgin National Watch Company, 1864–1964* (Elgin, IL: Elgin Historical Society, 2003), p. 23.
11. Hulburd was quoted in the *Jewelers' Circular,* March 20, 1928, p. 61.
12. Alft and Briska, p. 23.
13. Ibid.
14. For much of the information on Dueber-Hampden, I am indebted to Alan Garratt's excellent and extensive blog, "Beyond Springfield & Moscow: The Remarkable Story of Hampden Watches," http://hampdenwatches.blogspot.com.
15. Robert I. McCollough, "Hamilton Watch Company, Lancaster, Penna., U.S.A.: Some Notes on Its Founding and History, Part III," NAWCC *Bulletin*, No. 124 (Oct. 1966), p. 485.
16. Bryan Girouard and Will Roseman, "The 0-Size Wristwatch: Hamilton's First Wristwatch for Men," NAWCC *Bulletin,* No. 361 (April 2006), pp. 167–68.
17. Hamilton—Ravel Collection, NAWCC [National Association of Watch and Clock Collectors] Library and Research Center, Columbia, Pennsylvania. Unless otherwise identified in the text, all archival Illinois and Hamilton material is from this collection.
18. Milham, pp. 407–8.
20. http://www.pocketwatchrepair.com/histories/nys.html.
21. See Clay-Hanson patent for the "worm escapement": http://www.google.com/patents/US356189.
22. O. B. Frye, "Jesse Elwood Coleman and the South Bend Story," NAWCC Bulletin, No. 252 (Feb. 1988), pp. 17–18.
23. O. B. Frye, "South Bend Watches," NAWCC Bulletin, No. 239 (Dec. 1985), p. 644.
24. Paul Berg, "The Studebakers and the South Bend Watch Co.," NAWCC Bulletin, No. 153 (Aug. 1971), p. 1185.
25. Berg, pp. 1189–90.
26. Berg, p. 1192.
27. Ibid.
28. The data are derived from Figure 6.1, "Swiss watchmaking exports (volume) as percentage of movements, 1890–1935," in Pierre-Yves Donzé's article "The Swiss Cartel and the Control of Technology Flows," in Organizing Global Technology Flows: Institutions, Actors, and Processes, ed. Pierre-Yves Donzé and Shigehiro Nishimura (London: Routledge, 2013).
29. The data are derived from Table 6.1, "Main destinations of movement exports for Swiss watches, 1900–1930," in Donzé, "The Swiss Cartel and the Control of Technology Flows."
30. Donzé, "The Swiss Cartel and the Control of Technology Flows," p. 127.
31. For much of the Gruen history, I am indebted to Paul Schliesser's fine website, "Gruen: The Art & Mystery of Watchmaking, 1874–1958": http://www.pixelp.com/gruen/.

32. Ibid.
33. I am grateful for the valuable information about Bulova's history at http://www.watchophilia.com/general-information/early-bulova-wristwatches/.
34. http://en.wikipedia.org/wiki/Wittnauer.
35. Much of the information on Benrus comes from Kevin James's very helpful history of the company at http://thewatchguy.homestead.com/pages/BENRUS.html.
36. Donzé, "The Swiss Cartel and the Control of Technology Flows," p. 127.
37. Donald J. Sauers, Time for America: Hamilton Watch, 1892–1992 (Lititz, PA: Sutter House, 1992), p. 71.
38. Ibid.
39. Sauers, p. 57.
40. Sauers, p. 74.
41. Sauers, p 75.
42. Ibid.
43. Ibid.
44. Ibid.
45. Sauers, p. 80.
46. Bruce Shawkey, "Wristwatches: The Hamilton Explorer Series," NAWCC *Bulletin*, no. 368 (June 2007), p. 353.
47. Shawkey. n. 1, pp. 354–55.
48. McCullough, p. 485.
49. Jerry Treiman, interview with author, Pasadena, CA, Jan. 31, 2014.
50. Fred A. Hansen explains: "Hamilton did build 10 Prototype 992 movements with 60 hour mainsprings shortly after the purchase of the Illinois Watch Company. Nine were left in the grey, and one was fully finished and engraved. The 992B was a completely new design of almost 10 years later. The mainsprings used in the 992B were the 534B (steel) 3.00 mm wide x .015 - 015-1/2 – .016 thick x 23-1/2 inches long and #35433-34-35 Dynavar (alloy) 3.00 mm wide x min. - stand. - max. x 29-1/2 inches long. The Illinois 60 hour mainspring was 3.00 mm x .015-1/2 thick x 27 inches long. So the Hamilton mainsprings for the 992B, except for small difference in length and end brace, are almost identical to the Illinois 60 hour" (email message to author, June 2, 2014).
51. Michael Chamelin, email exchanges with author, Nov. 2013 through March 2014; and interview with author, Orlando, FL, Feb. 14, 2014.
52. E. C. Alft, *Elgin: An American History* (ElginHistory.com, 2000), chap. 7 ("Whirling Twenties"), sec. 3 ("Industrial Leadership"), par. 1. The book was written in 1984 to celebrate the City of Elgin's sesquicentennial, 1835–1985.

Chapter 4

1. *Illinois State Journal,* April 28, 1928.
2. Hamilton—Ravel Collection, NAWCC [National Association of Watch and Clock Collectors] Library and Research Center, Columbia, Pennsylvania. Unless otherwise identified in the text, all archival Illinois and Hamilton material is from this collection.
3. Earlier, in the *Jewelers' Circular* on May 3, 1928, Levy had called price-cutting "an evil of the first magnitude."
4. Elgin data from *Jewelers' Circular,* July 26, 1928.
5. Elgin data from *Jewelers' Circular,* Jan. 10, 1929.
6. Elgin data from *Jewelers' Circular,* July 26, 1928.
7. Bulova data from the cover of "Bulova Convertible Preferred Stock Prospectus," *Jewelers' Circular,* Feb. 28, 1929.
8. Hulburd's remarks were reported in the *Jewelers' Circular,* March 14, 1929.
9. Quoted in the *Jewelers' Circular,* July 18, 1929.
10. The table is from http://www.gregsteer.net/IWC/Cresarrow/The%201930's%20and%20tariff%20increases.html.
11. Pierre-Yves Donzé, *History of the Swiss Watch Industry from Jacques David to Nicholas Hayek,* trans. Pierre-Yves Donzé and Richard Watkins (Bern, Switzerland: Peter Lang AG, 2011), p. 79.
12. http://www.gregsteer.net/IWC/Cresarrow/The%20 1930's%20and%20tariff%20increases.html.
13. Eugene T. Fuller, *The Priceless Possession of a Few,* Supplement No. 10, NAWCC *Bulletin,* 1974, p. 56.
14. E. C. Alft and William H. Briska, *Elgin Time: A History of the Elgin National Watch Company, 1864–1964* (Elgin, IL: Elgin Historical Society, 2003), p. 74.

Chapter 5

1. Charles W. Moore, *Timing a Century: History of the Waltham Watch Company,* Harvard Studies in Business History, no. 11. (Cambridge, MA: Harvard Univ. Press, 1945), p. 333.
2. E. C. Alft and William H. Briska, *Elgin Time: A History of the Elgin National Watch Company, 1864–1964* (Elgin, IL.: Elgin Historical Society, 2003). Profit number, p. 108; employee numbers, p. 74.
3. Alft and Briska, p. 74. Elgin's financial results added by the present author.
4. Ibid. Comment from the General Manager of Manufacturing added by the present author.
5. Moore, p. 207.
6. Ibid.
7. Gruen data and quotation, *Jewelers' Circular,* Nov. 1931.
8. Ibid.

9. *Jewelers' Circular,* Oct. 1931.
10. *Keystone,* Oct. 1931.
11. Hamilton—Ravel Collection, NAWCC [National Association of Watch and Clock Collectors] Library and Research Center, Columbia, Pennsylvania. Unless otherwise identified in the text, all archival Illinois and Hamilton material is from this collection.
12. René Rondeau, personal communications.
13. Michael Chamelin, *The 16 Size Illinois Bunn Special, 1913–1948* (Privately printed, 2013), p. 300.
14. *Jeweler's Circular,* Feb. 1932.
15. Moore, p. 208.
16. Moore, p. 209.
17. *Jewelers' Circular,* Feb. 1932.
18. Ibid.
19. Moore, p. 210.
20. Ibid.
21. Ibid.
22. Percentages derived from table in Moore, p. 218.
23. Moore, p. 212.
24. Chamelin, p. 213.
25. Alft and Briska, p. 75.
26. *Jewelers' Circular,* April 1933.
27. Eugene T. Fuller, *The Priceless Possession of a Few,* Supplement No. 10, NAWCC *Bulletin,* 1974, p. 65.
28. Moore, p. 218.
29. Moore, p. 221.
30. Donald J. Sauers, *Time for America: Hamilton Watch, 1892–1992* (Lititz, PA: Sutter House, 1992), p. 82.
31. *Jewelers' Circular,* May 1934.
32. Chamelin, p. 300, and interview by author, Daytona Beach, FL, Feb. 14, 2014.
33. Sauers, p. 79. Elgin data from Alft and Briska, p. 108.
34. Robert Irving McCollough, "Hamilton Watch Company, Lancaster, Penna., U.S.A.: Some Notes on Its Founding and History, Part III," NAWCC *Bulletin*, no. 124 (Oct. 1966), pp. 489–90.
35. McCollough, p. 490.
36. Moore, p. 221.
37. Number of employees from Alft and Briska, p. 75. Data on profits added by the present author.
38. *Keystone,* April 1935.
39. Alft and Briska, p. 75.

Chapter 6

1. Further details about how the movement progressed through the various Illinois Watch Company production departments are discussed in Chapter 4 of Fredric J. Friedberg, *The Illinois Watch: The Life and Times of A Great American Watch Company* (Atglen, PA: Schiffer, 2004).
2. Ibid. The chapter includes still shots from the film, showing many of the operations being performed. The film itself can be viewed online: http://www.youtube.com/watch?v=vTQT6PwgJTA
3. Greg Frauenhoff, Tom McIntyre and Russ Snyder, "The Illinois Watch Company's Grades 104 and 105," NAWCC *Bulletin,* Vol. 44 (Aug. 2002), pp. 419–28.
4. Frauenhoff, McIntyre and Snyder, p. 424.
5. W. F. Meggers, Jr., "The Jeweling of Illinois Watch Company Movements," NAWCC *Bulletin,* whole No. 210 (Feb. 1981), pp. 36–49.
6. For additional details about these fine wristwatch movements, *see* Friedberg, p. 51.
7. William "Bill" Meggers and Roy Ehrhardt, *American Pocket Watches, Vol. 2: Illinois Watch Co.* (Heart of America Press, 1985), p. 230.
8. Meggers and Ehrhardt, p. 231.

Chapter 7

1. For a further discussion of the "radium girls," *see* Fredric J. Friedberg, *The Illinois Watch: The Life and Times of a Great American Watch Company* (Atglen, PA: Schiffer, 2004), pp. 58–59.
2. Adam Harris, email message to Jim Mason, June 5, 2015.
3. The analysis of the two types of sparkle dials was carried out by the Materials Engineering and Testing Corp., Oak Ridge, TN, under the direction of its president, Patrick Werner. I am indebted to Jim Mason for making this important discovery and for facilitating the analysis of the dials.
4. Friedberg, p. 158.
5. Stan Czubernat, email exchange with the author, September 2013.

Chapter 8

1. Warren H. Niebling, *History of the American Watch Case* (Philadelphia, PA: Whitmore Publishing, 1971), p. 49. Niebling is a valuable source for the basic histories of the various companies.
2. John H. Wilterding, Jr., "Fahys of Sag Harbor, New York, Part I," NAWCC *Bulletin,* No. 332 (June 2001), 316–24. A later article by Wilterding, coauthored with is also helpful: "Early Industrial Watchcases, Part II," NAWCC *Bulletin,* No. 355 (April 2005), pp. 147-64.
3. Wilterding, "Fahys of Sag Harbor," p. 319, quoting Helen Gerard, *Needles and Thread: Jewish Life in Suffolk County* (Stony Brook, NY: Long Island Studies Council, 1986).
4. "Pioneer Watch Company Grew From Small Partnership," *Daily Argus* (Mount Vernon, NY), April 1, 1942.
5. *Daily Argus,* April 1, 1942. There was a brief obituary for Herbert Kolberg in the *New York Times* (Feb. 2, 1942),

noting that he was president and founder of the company and also a Mount Vernon civic leader; he had died "after an illness of a few days."

6. *Daily Argus,* April 1, 1942.
7. Charles W. Moore, *Timing a Century: History of the Waltham Watch Company,* Harvard Studies in Business History, no. 11. (Cambridge, MA: Harvard Univ. Press, 1945), pp. 326–27.
8. L. Michael Fultz, "The Story of the Depollier & Gruen Waterproof Wristwatches," *InSync Magazine,* April/May 1998, p. 42.
9. Ibid.
10. Ibid.
11. Jack Linahan, "Star Watch Case Company, 1897–1982," NAWCC *Bulletin,* No. 360 (Feb. 2006), p. 4.
12. Ibid.
13. Ibid.
14. *Ludington Daily News,* March 20, 1995, pp. 10–11.
15. Linahan, p. 6.
16. *New York Times,* March 30, 1926.
17. Linahan, p. 6.
18. https://en.wikipedia.org/wiki/Star_Watch_Case_Company
19. *Ludington Daily News,* April 16, 1994, p. 1.
20. Linahan, p. 6.
21. Ibid.
22. Linahan, pp. 6–7.
23. Linahan, p. 7.
24. René Rondeau, *The Watch of the Future: The Story of the Hamilton Electric Watch,* 4th rev. ed. (Corte Madera, CA: René Rondeau, 2006), pp. 53–58.
25. Warren Niebling, interviews by the author, June 5, 12 and 17, 2001.
26. Genevieve Cummins, *How the Watch Was Worn: A Fashion for 500 Years* (Woodbridge, Suffolk, UK: Antique Collectors' Club, 2010), pp. 233–37.
27. "History of the Watch Attachment Industry: The Origin and Growth of leading Concerns," an article that appeared in the October 1932 issue of the *Keystone,* is an invaluable resource. It is cited hereafter as *Keystone,* "Watch Attachment Industry."
28. Orra L. Stone, *History of Massachusetts Industries: Their Inception, Growth and Success,* 4 vols. (Chicago and Boston: S. J. Clarke Publishing Co, 1930). Although I have been unable to locate the books themselves, I have found two very useful segments online: "Attleboro: Center of Jewelry Production in the East" (http://www.rmlonline.org/sites/rmlonline.org/files/attachments/Stone%20chapter%20xiv.pdf) and "North Attleboro: Center of Jewelry Production" (http://www.rmlonline.org/sites/rmlonline.org/files/attachments/Stone%20North%20Attleboro.pdf). These will be cited hereafter as Stone, "Attleboro" and Stone, "North Attleboro," respectively; unfortunately, I cannot ascertain exact page numbers.
29. Stone, "Attleboro."
30. Obituary of Frederick Sturdy, *Jewelers' Circular,* June 28, 1922.
31. *Keystone,* "Watch Attachment Industry."
32. Ibid.
33. https://en.wikipedia.org/wiki/Speidel
34. "Alien Enemy Property Sale," *Jewelers' Circular-Weekly,* Dec. 11, 1918.
35. *Alien Enemy Custodian Report: A Detailed Report by the Alien Property Custodian of All Proceedings Had by Him under the Trading with the Enemy Act during the Calendar Year 1918 and to the Close of Business on February 15, 1919* (Washington: Government Printing Office, 1919), Appendix, Schedule 2—"List of enemy-owned patents in connection with corporations sold by Alien Property Custodian, Washington, D.C.," p. 453.
36. *Keystone,* "Watch Attachment Industry."
37. http://www.watch-band-center.com/watchstrap-h795-Hirsch.html
38. *Keystone,* "Watch Attachment Industry." (The company's location and date of founding are confirmed by Stone, "Attleboro.")
39. Suzanne G. Beyer and John S. Pfarr, *The Inventor's Fortune Up for Grabs: The Legacy of the Expansion Bracelet* (Bothell, WA: Book Publishers Network, 2011), pp. xxiii–xxiv. Arthur Hadley's fortune was left in two trusts without clear instructions as to how the assets were to be distributed if his children died without having biological children, and the book details the very complicated court case that resulted. Suzanne Beyer is the great-niece of Art Hadley, and John Pfarr is the attorney who represented her and one group of Hadley's descendants, who were pitted against other descendants. *Note:* She owns the original expansion bracelet that was Hadley's invention, patented February 11, 1913.
40. *Keystone,* "Watch Attachment Industry."
41. Ibid.
42. Ibid.
43. Ibid.
44. http://www.zoominfo.com/p/Jacques-Kreisler/43539869
45. http://www.trufauxjewels.com/Jewelry-Makers.html#Kreisler
46. *Keystone,* "Watch Attachment Industry."
47. Ibid.

48. *Jewelers' Circular,* Jan. 31, 1923.
49. *Keystone,* "Watch Attachment Industry."
50. Stone, "Attleboro."
51. *Keystone,* "Watch Attachment Industry."
52. Ibid.
53. Ibid.
54. Ibid.
55. Ibid.
56. Ibid.
57. Ibid.
58. Ibid.
59. "For the Buyer," *Keystone,* April 1929.
60. Stone, "Attleboro."
61. Stone, "North Attleboro."
62. Lynell K. Schwartz, *Vintage Purses at their Best*, rev. 2nd ed. (Atglen, PA: Schiffer, 2004), p. 97.
63. Schwartz, pp. 97–98.
64. Schwartz, p. 98.

Chapter 9

1. Stan Czubernat, email exchanges with the author, May 15, 2014.
2. Although some collectors have in the past called the color of the enamel "turquoise" (as did *The Illinois Watch: The Life and Times of a Great American Watch Company*), it has recently been determined that the enamel is actually the same sea-green color that Illinois used on several of the ladies' white gold-filled models (e.g., the Redonda 154, Berkeley 153 and Del Monte 157). Our guess is that since there is the slightest bit of blue in the green (it is not a grass green), it may perhaps appear turquoise to some eyes when it is used in conjunction with a yellow gold-filled case rather than a white one.
3. This detail was provided by Czubernat.
4. The directory is in the collection of the Androscoggin Historical Society (Auburn ME), which kindly supplied the information. (Lewiston is in Androscoggin County, and Auburn is the county seat.)
5. It is interesting that in the catalog advertisement (which comes directly from the 1934 Illinois Sales Catalog) the name "Illinois" on the Urbana is positioned differently from the way it is in the dial drawing. The former has it curved, the latter in a straight line (the 1936 materials catalog also shows it that way). Was a mistake made in the catalog drawing, or was that a dial variant that was perhaps actually produced? (For the Sangamon, however, the dial shown in the catalog matches the one in the dial drawing.)
6. Other watch manufacturers also used the name "Senator." Most notable, perhaps, was Bulova, which gave the name to many different models, beginning in 1926 and continuing through the decades until 1973.
7. The Illinois advertisement appearing in the 1930 John Plain catalog offered more details about the race but unfortunately misidentified the model of the watch: "In the record-breaking automobile races held at Indianapolis on May 30th last, ten Illinois Major watches were worn by Ray Keech, Louis Myers, Louis Chiron, Jimmie Gleason, and other drivers of international fame. Watch experts were thunderstruck that Illinois should make such a test. Ten Illinois Majors went into the race and came out accurate to the second—a race that shattered nerves and twisted steel."
8. Among Seaver-Williams's imports were binoculars, "French and German make!" These were described as "Ideal for hunting, motoring, vacations, camping auto races, boxing bouts, mountain climbing, observation, bird and nature study, football, baseball games, etc. We sell thousands to Army and Navy Officers, Commanders, Explorers, Big Game Hunters, Globe-Trotters, Naturalists."
9. An advertisement for the Emerson Watch Case Co., Inc. in the July 26, 1922 issue of the *Jewelers' Circular* lists the company's New York City office as being at 47–49 Maiden Lane and its factory at 178–180 Emmett St., Newark, NJ. The advertising copywriter indulged in an extended pun, beginning with the heading: "Judging 'Cases' on their Merits!" and continuing, "That's what the trade has been doing with Emerson Watch Cases. The verdict, rendered after years of constant use, is: Perfection in Design and Workmanship [and] Quality Unexcelled. In short, cases of character and distinction, backed by a reputable concern whose success has been won solely on the merits of its products. Justice to Yourself demands a fair trial of Emerson Watch Cases."
10. We have also discovered that the Kay Jewelry Company marketed Illinois pocket watches under another of its private labels, the Aristocrat. In addition, Kay's was known to advertise Illinois wristwatches; at least one of these, the solid gold version of the ladies' Miami 157, appears to have been a custom order (*see* Chapter 10).
11. Stan Czubernat, *Elgin Trench Watches of the Great War* (Atglen, PA: Schiffer, 2015), pp. 16–17.

Chapter 10

1. Fredric J. Friedberg, *The Illinois Watch: The Life and Times of a Great American Watch Company* (Atglen, PA: Schiffer, 2004), p. 226.
2. Much of the detailed identification information used in this chapter is drawn from Farrell Gay's article "An Illinois Watch Company Ladies' Wristwatch Collection," NAWCC *Bulletin,* No. 391 (April 2011), pp. 161–76.
3. Dominique Fléchon, "Origins of the Wristwatch before 1900," *HH Magazine,* July 18, 2007. http://journal.hautehorlogerie.org/en/article/origins-of-the-wristwatch-before-1900/

4. Not mentioned by Fléchon is the famous advertisement by the Gruen Guild that featured a scene depicting Dudley's presentation of his gift to Queen Elizabeth. It appeared in 1926 in a number of magazines, including the *Literary Digest* and the *Saturday Evening Post*.
5. Genevieve Cummins's beautiful book *How the Watch Was Worn: A Fashion for 500 Years* (Woodbridge, Suffolk, UK: Antique Collectors' Club, 2010) has much interesting information and many pictures of ladies' convertible and transitional watches (pp. 232–236). An 1889 advertisement by the London jeweler Le Roy et Fils shows its "registered combination bracelet-watch, chatelaine, & brooch"; the firm claimed to be "originators of the bracelet watch," according to an advertisement from 1893 (p. 233).
6. Iris Wimmer-Olbort, *Karl Scheufele, 1904–2004: A Family Business Around the Clock* (Geneva: Le Petit-Fils de L.U. Chopard, 2004), p. 29.
7. Wimmer-Olbort, p. 30.

Chapter 11

1. *Intelligencer Journal*, Lancaster, PA, May 31, 1949. Hamilton–Ravel Collection, NAWCC [National Association of Watch and Clock Collectors] Library and research Center, Columbia, PA; hereafter cited as HRC:NAWCC in both notes and text.
2. Clipping from *Intelligencer Journal*, Lancaster, PA, May 23, 1952, with handwritten notation "May 23, 1952"; HRC:NAWCC. Hamilton's announcement was national news, and various passages from Luckey's letter were quoted in the media. Someone from the Associated Press filed a report the day of the announcement; the article, datelined "Lancaster, Pa., May 23," was published the next day in the *New York Times*. The *Somerset Daily American* ran essentially the same article as the *NYT,* but not until May 26.
3. Ibid.
4. Unidentified trade journal report, June 16, 1952; HRC:NAWCC.
5. *Intelligencer Journal*, Lancaster, PA, Feb. 20, 1953.
6. Clipping datelined "Boston, May 22," from *Intelligencer Journal*, Lancaster, PA, May 23, 1952. HRC:NAWCC.
7. The Sangamon's case was made of "Sangamo metal," a base metal, but not stainless steel. Although some Larchmont, Standish and Chatham models have been found in rose-gold rolled gold plate cases, these were not likely cased at the Illinois Factory. For more details about these two models, *see* the listings for them in Chapter 9.
8. "May 23, 1952" clipping, HRC:NAWCC.
9. René Rondeau, email exchanges with the author, July 5, 2014.
10. The cognates were provided by Bob Ayer and by Jim and Bettie Mason.
11. Donald J. Sauers, *Time for America: Hamilton Watch, 1892–1992* (Lititz, PA: Sutter House, 1992), p. 177.
12. Cited in "Findings of Fact" in Hamilton Watch Co. v. Benrus Watch Co., Inc., 114 F. Supp. 307 (D. Conn. 1953), https://www.courtlistener.com/opinion/2254210/hamilton-watch-co-v-benrus-watch-co/
13. "May 23, 1952" clipping, HRC:NAWCC.
14. Ibid; also cited in the lawsuit.
15. All this information appears in "Findings of Fact" in the lawsuit mentioned in n. 11.
16. Sauers, p. 177.
17. Ibid.
18. Ibid.
19. https://en.wikipedia.org/wiki/ETA_SA
20. Anthony Young, "Five Vintage Hearts," *IW Magazine,* Dec. 2, 2011.
21. http://www.incabloc.ch/en/incabloc_sa.php

Chapter 12

1. John Hoffmann, "Lincoln Essay Contests, Lincoln Medals, and the Commercialization of Lincoln," *Journal of the Abraham Lincoln Association*, Vol. 24, Issue 2 (Summer 2003), pp. 36–62. Material in this section of the chapter is drawn from Hoffman's article. As I have been able to access it only online, I cannot provide page citations. The article can be found at http://quod.lib.umich.edu/j/jala/2629860.0024.205?view=text;rgn=main

Bibliography

Abbott, Henry G. *The Watch Factories of America.* Chicago: Hazlitt, 1888.

Alft, E. C. *Elgin: An American History.* ElginHistory.com, 2000.

Alft, E. C., and William H. Briska. *Elgin Time: A History of the Elgin National Watch Company.* Elgin, IL: Elgin Historical Society, 2003.

Call, Andrew Taylor. *Jacob Bunn: Legacy of an Illinois Industrial Pioneer.* Bath, ME: Brunswick Publishing Co., 2005.

Carosso, Vincent. "The Waltham Watch Company: A Case History." *Business History Review*, Vol. 23, No. 4 (Dec. 1949), pp. 165–87.

Chamberlain, Paul M. *It's About Time*. London, UK: Holland House, 1964.

Chamelin, Michael. *The 16 Size Illinois Bunn Special, 1913–1948.* Privately printed, 2013.

Cummins, Genevieve. *How the Watch Was Worn: A Fashion for 500 Years.* Woodbridge, Suffolk, UK: Antique Collectors' Club, 2010.

Czubernat, Stan. *Elgin Trench Watches of the Great War.* Atglen, PA: Schiffer, 2015.

Donzé, Pierre-Yves. *History of the Swiss Watch Industry from Jacques David to Nicholas Hayek*, trans. Pierre-Yves Donzé and Richard Watkins. Bern, Switzerland: Peter Lang AG, 2011.

Frauenhoff, Greg, Tom McIntyre and Russ Snyder. "The Illinois Watch Company's Grades 104 and 105." *NAWCC Bulletin,* Vol. 44 (Aug. 2002), pp. 419–28.

Friedberg, Fredric J. *The Illinois Watch: The Life and Times of a Great American Watch Company.* Atglen, PA: Schiffer, 2004.

Fuller, Eugene T. *The Priceless Possession of a Few,* Supplement No. 10, *NAWCC Bulletin,* 1974.

Fultz, L. Michael. "John C. Adams: Watch Entrepreneur." *InSync Magazine,* Feb. 2009, pp. 132–35.

Fultz, L. Michael. "The Story of the Depollier & Gruen Waterproof Wristwatches." *InSync Magazine,* April/May 1998, p. 42.

Garratt, Alan. "Beyond Springfield & Moscow: The Remarkable Story of Hampden Watches." http://hampdenwatches.blogspot.com.

Gay, Farrell. "An Illinois Watch Company Ladies' Wristwatch Collection." *NAWCC Bulletin,* No. 391 (April 2011), pp. 161–76.

Girouard, Bryan, and Will Roseman. "The 0-Size Wristwatch: Hamilton's First Wristwatch for Men." *NAWCC Bulletin,* No. 361 (April 2006), pp. 167–73.

Hoffmann, John. "Lincoln Essay Contests, Lincoln Medals, and the Commercialization of Lincoln." *Journal of the Abraham Lincoln Association*, Vol. 24, Issue 2 (Summer 2003), pp. 36–62. Accessed online: http://quod.lib.umich.edu/j/jala/2629860.0024.205/--lincoln-essay-contests-lincoln-medals?rgn=main;view=fulltext

Lanphier, Robert C., and Benjamin P. Thomas. *Sangamo: A History of Fifty Years.* [The volume consists of Lanphier's *Forty Years of Sangamo* and Thomas's *Sangamo in Peace and War.*] Chicago: Privately printed, 1949.

Linahan, Jack. "Star Watch Case Company, 1897–1982." *NAWCC Bulletin,* No. 360 (Feb. 2006), pp. 4–9.

McCollough, Robert Irving. "Hamilton Watch Company, Lancaster, Penna., U.S.A.: Some Notes on Its Founding and History, Part III," *NAWCC Bulletin*, No. 124 (Oct. 1966), pp. 484–93, p. 518.

McIntyre, Tom. "McIntyre Watch Company." http://www.awco.org/MWCo/

Meggers, W. F., Jr. "The Jeweling of Illinois Watch Company Movements." *NAWCC Bulletin,* No. 210 (Feb. 1981), pp. 36–49.

Meggers, William "Bill," and Roy Ehrhardt. *American Pocket Watches, Vol. 2: Illinois Watch Co.* Heart of America Press, 1985.

Milham, Willis I. *Time & Timekeepers.* New York: Macmillan, 1944.

Moore, Charles W. *Timing a Century: History of the Waltham Watch Company.* Harvard Studies in Business History, no. 11. Cambridge, MA: Harvard Univ. Press, 1945.

Niebling, Warren H. *History of the American Watch Case.* Philadelphia, PA: Whitmore Publishing, 1971.

Rondeau, René. *The Watch of the Future: The Story of the Hamilton Electric Watch,* 4th rev. ed. Corte Madera, CA: René Rondeau, 2006.

Sauers, Donald J. *Time for America: Hamilton Watch, 1892–1992.* Lititz, PA: Sutter House, 1992.

Shawkey, Bruce. "Wristwatches: Gruen." *NAWCC Bulletin*, No. 331 (April 2001), pp. 243–45.

Shawkey, Bruce. "Wristwatches: The Hamilton Explorer Series." *NAWCC Bulletin,* No. 368 (June 2007), pp. 352–55.

Wilterding, John H., Jr. "Fahys of Sag Harbor, New York, Part I." *NAWCC Bulletin,* No. 332 (June 2001), pp. 316–24.

Wilterding, John H., Jr. and Mike Harrold. "Early Industrial Watchcases, Part II." *NAWCC Bulletin,* No. 355 (April 2005), pp. 147–64.

INDEX

Illinois Watch Company

SPRINGFIELD.

U. S. A.